KEY TO TITLE CODES
FOR USE IN LOCATING SOURCES

Detailed bibliographical information about the sources
listed below appears on page ix.

AmSCAP	The ASCAP Biographical Dictionary of Composers, Authors and Publishers
BiDFlm	A Biographical Dictionary of Film
BiE&WWA	The Biographical Encyclopaedia & Who's Who of the American Theatre
CelR	Celebrity Register
CmMov	A Companion to the Movies: From 1903 to the Present Day
CnMD	The Concise Encyclopedia of Modern Drama
CnThe	A Concise Encyclopedia of the Theatre
ConDr	Contemporary Dramatists
CroCD	Crowell's Handbook of Contemporary Drama
DcFM	Dictionary of Film Makers
EncMT	Encyclopaedia of the Musical Theatre
FamA&A	Famous Actors and Actresses on the American Stage
Film	Filmarama
FilmgC	Filmgoer's Companion
HolP	Hollywood Players
IntMPA	International Motion Picture Almanac
MGM	The MGM Stock Company
McGWD	McGraw-Hill Encyclopedia of World Drama
ModWD	Modern World Drama
MotPP	Motion Picture Performers
MovMk	The Movie Makers
NatPD	National Playwrights Directory
NewMT	New Complete Book of the American Musical Theater
NewYTET	The New York Times Encyclopedia of Television
NotNAT	Notable Names in the American Theatre
OxFilm	The Oxford Companion to Film
OxThe	The Oxford Companion to the Theatre
PlP&P	Plays, Players, & Playwrights
REnWD	The Reader's Encyclopedia of World Drama
ThFT	They Had Faces Then
TwYS	Twenty Years of Silents
Vers	The Versatiles
WhScrn	Who Was Who on Screen
WhThe	Who Was Who in the Theatre
WhoHol	Who's Who in Hollywood
WhoStg	Who's Who on the Stage
WhoThe	Who's Who in the Theatre
WomWMM	Women Who Make Movies
WorEnF	The World Encyclopedia of Film

THEATRE, FILM AND TELEVISION BIOGRAPHIES MASTER INDEX

THEATRE, FILM AND TELEVISION BIOGRAPHIES MASTER INDEX

A consolidated guide to over 100,000 biographical sketches of persons living and dead, as they appear in over 40 of the principal biographical dictionaries devoted to the theatre, film and television.

Edited by Dennis La Beau

FIRST EDITION

Gale Biographical Index Series No. 5

Gale Research Company   Book Tower   Detroit, Michigan 48226

Editor: Dennis La Beau

Assistant Editors: Miranda Herbert, Barbara McNeil

Editorial Assistants: Doris Goulart, Ann Blake, Dorothy Cotter, Terry Lafaro, Sue Lynch, Paula Morgan, Midge Piccini, Jean Portfolio, Joyce M. Stone, Sharon Wagner

Proofreaders: Barbara Brandenburg, Toni Grow

Production Manager: Michaeline Nowinski

Cover Design: Art Chartow

Computerized photocomposition by
Computer Composition Corporation, Madison Heights, Michigan

Library of Congress Cataloging in Publication Data

La Beau, Dennis.
    Theatre, film and television biographies master
index.

    (Gale biographical index series ; no. 5)
    Bibliography: p. ix
    1. Performing arts--Biography--Dictionaries--
Indexes. I. Title.
PN1583.L3   016.791'092'2 [B]   77-2470
ISBN 0-8103-1081-3

Introduction

Theatre, Film and Television Biographies Master Index enables the researcher to locate, without tedious searching, biographical information on a single person from more than 100,000 entries in over 40 biographical dictionaries and directories devoted to the theatre, film or television. In function, but not content, it is a counterpart to Gale's *Biographical Dictionaries Master Index,* published in 1975-76, Gale's *Author Biographies Master Index,* 1978, *Journalist Biographies Master Index,* 1979, and several similar publications now in preparation.

TF&T tells the user which edition of which publication to consult or, almost equally as helpful, it reveals that there is no listing for a given individual in any of the publications indexed. In cases where *TF&T* has multiple listings for the same person, the searcher is able to choose the source which is most convenient to him, or to locate multiple sketches to compare with one another.

All names in an indexed work are listed in *TF&T,* whether living or deceased. There is no need to consult the work itself if the desired name is not shown by *TF&T* to be in the work, since it has been the editorial policy to index every name found in a particular book.

How to Read a Citation

Each citation gives the person's name, followed by the years of birth and/or death. If there is no year of birth, the death date is preceded by a lower case *d*. The codes for the books indexed follow after the dates:

Sweatman, Wilbur C 1882-1961 *AmSCAP 1966*

A list of the works indexed in *TF&T,* and the codes used to refer to them, is printed on the endsheets, as well as in the *Bibliographic Key* that follows this introduction.

TF&T is a Unique Reference Work

TF&T is the first attempt in recent times to offer an index to biographical material on these popular performing arts. While the works covered are of several distinct types (biographical dictionaries, directories, filmographies, etc.), all have one common characteristic: each includes at least a moderate amount of biographical, critical, or career-related information on individuals connected with the theatre, film or television, and most include a substantial amount of information.

The books cited in *TF&T* are readily available and widely held in most reference collections. These books include, for example, *The New York Times Encyclopedia of Television,* St. Martin's *Contemporary Dramatists,* Oxford University Press' *The Oxford Companion to the Theatre,* Bowker's *Famous Actors and Actresses on the American Stage,* Leslie Halliwell's *The Filmgoer's Companion,* and many more.

Two filmographies and one index to the periodic press have been included even though they do not provide biographical information, other than dates. They do, however, give extensive credits, or refer to articles that contain valuable information.

Editorial Practices

TF&T follows standard alphabetizing rules used by the Library of Congress, with the exception of *Mac* and *Mc,* which are filed strictly letter by letter. Not all source books use this method of alphabetizing. Some names, therefore, may have an alphabetic position in a source book different from this book.

To simplify the listings, and to help the user, some standardization of names has been instituted when it appeared certain that the same person was referred to by the variant spellings. Years of birth and death are repeated as found in the source works. If a source has indicated that the dates may not be accurate, the questionable date(s) are followed by a question mark: 1950? If a given individual's name has spellings that differ substantially from publication to publication, or if there is any other reason to believe that more than one person is referred to by the various spellings or dates, the citations have retained those discrepancies:

> **Swanson,** Gloria *MotPP, WomWMM*
> **Swanson,** Gloria 1897 *FilmgC, ThFT*
> **Swanson,** Gloria 1898 *BiDFlm, Film 1,*
> *Film 2, MovMk, OxFilm, TwYS, WorEnF*
> **Swanson,** Gloria 1899 *BiE&WWA, CelR 3,*
> *IntMPA 1977, WhoHol A, WhoThe 16*

All the above citations refer to the same person, but, because of variations in the year of birth the editors were not able to determine which is the actual date, or what should be supplied for the missing date. Such information can be of importance to anyone attempting to establish biographical details about various personalities.

Users should be careful in searching for some citations. An individual could have more than one listing if the source books differ greatly in how that person's name appears:

Archainbaud, George *and* **Archinbaud**, George

Searchers may need to look under all possible listings for a name, especially in the case of names with prefixes or suffixes, Spanish names which may be listed in sources under either part of the surname, Chinese names which may be entered in sources in direct or inverted order, transliterated names from non-Roman alphabets, etc.:

Chekhov, Anton *and* **Tchekov**, Anton

Cross references appearing in the publications indexed have been retained in *TF&T*.

Suggestions are Welcome

Future editions of *TF&T* are planned. Additional sources will be added to these new editions as their availability and usefulness become known. The editors will welcome suggestions from users for additional works which could be indexed, or any other comments and suggestions.

Bibliographic Key to Publication Codes
for Use in Locating Sources

Unless otherwise noted, the books indexed by *Theatre, Film and Television Biographies Master Index* provide biographical information.

CODE	BOOK INDEXED

CODE   *BOOK INDEXED*

AmSCAP 1966   The *ASCAP Biographical Dictionary of Composers, Authors and Publishers.* 1966 edition. Compiled and edited by The Lynn Farnol Group, Inc. New York: The American Society of Composers, Authors and Publishers, 1966.

BiDFlm   A *Biographical Dictionary of Film.* By David Thomson. New York: William Morrow and Company, Inc., 1976.

BiE&WWA   The *Biographical Encyclopaedia & Who's Who of the American Theatre.* Edited by Walter Rigdon. New York: James H. Heineman, Inc., 1966.

Biographical section begins on page 227.

CelR 3   *Celebrity Register.* Third edition. Edited by Earl Blackwell. New York: Simon and Schuster, 1973.

CmMov   A *Companion to the Movies: From 1903 to the Present Day.* By Roy Pickard. New York: Hippocrene Books, Inc., 1972.

Use the index in the back of the book to locate biographies.

CnMD   The *Concise Encyclopedia of Modern Drama.* By Siegfried Melchinger. Translated by George Wellwarth. Edited by Henry Popkin. New York: Horizon Press, 1964.

Biographies begin on page 159. A supplemental list of 21 playwrights with short biographical notices begins on page 287, and is cited in this index by the code Sup.

CnThe   A *Concise Encyclopedia of the Theatre.* By Robin May. Reading, Berkshire, England: Osprey Publishing Limited, 1974.

Use the index in the back of the book to locate biographies.

ConDr 1973   *Contemporary Dramatists.* Edited by James Vinson. London: St. James Press; New York: St. Martin's Press, 1973.

Biographies are given in the following sections: Contemporary Dramatists, *page 7;* Screen Writers, *page 847;* Radio Writers, *page 857;* Television Writers, *page 867;* Musical Librettists, *page 875;* The Theatre of Mixed Means, *page 889. Biographies in this edition are not cited if they also appear in the later edition (see below).*

ConDr 1977   *Contemporary Dramatists.* Second Edition. Edited by James Vinson. London: St. James Press; New York: St. Martin's Press, 1977.

Biographies are given in the following sections: Contemporary Dramatists, *page 9;* Screen Writers, *indicated in this index by the code* A, *page 893;* Radio Writers, *indicated by the code* B, *page 903;* Television Writers, *indicated by the code* C, *page 915;* Musical Librettists, *indicated by the code* D, *page 925;* The Theatre of Mixed Means, *indicated by the code* E, *page 941;* Appendix, *indicated by the code* F, *page 969.*

CroCD *Crowell's Handbook of Contemporary Drama.* By Michael Anderson, Jacques Guicharnaud, Kristin Morrison, Jack D. Zipes, and others. New York: Thomas Y. Crowell Company, 1971.

DcFM *Dictionary of Film Makers.* By Georges Sadoul. Translated, edited, and updated by Peter Morris. Berkeley and Los Angeles: University of California Press, 1972.

Originally published as Dictionnaire des Cineastes, *1965.*

EncMT *Encyclopaedia of the Musical Theatre.* By Stanley Green. New York: Dodd, Mead & Company, 1976.

FamA&A *Famous Actors and Actresses on the American Stage: Documents of American Theater History.* 2 volumes. By William C. Young. New York: R.R. Bowker, 1975.

Film 1 *Filmarama, Volume I: The Formidable Years, 1893-1919.* Compiled by John Stewart. Metuchen, New Jersey: Scarecrow Press, 1975.

An index to actors and their films.

Film 2 *Filmarama, Volume II: The Flaming Years, 1920-1929.* Compiled by John Stewart. Metuchen, New Jersey: Scarecrow Press, 1977.

An index to actors and their films.

FilmgC *The Filmgoer's Companion.* Fourth edition. By Leslie Halliwell. New York: Hill and Wang, 1974.

HolP 30 *Hollywood Players: The Thirties.* By James Robert Parish and William T. Leonard. New Rochelle, New York: Arlington House Publishers, 1976.

HolP 40 *Hollywood Players: The Forties.* By James Robert Parish and Lennard DeCarl. New Rochelle, New York: Arlington House Publishers, 1976.

IntMPA 1977 *International Motion Picture Almanac.* Edited by Richard Gertner. New York: Quigley Publishing Company, Inc., 1977.

See the Who's Who in Motion Pictures and Television *section. The listings are identical with those in the* International Television Almanac.

MGM *The MGM Stock Company; The Golden Era.* By James Robert Parish and Ronald L. Bowers. New Rochelle, New York: Arlington House, 1973.

Appendix, indicated in this index by the code A, *begins on page 796.*

McGWD *McGraw-Hill Encyclopedia of World Drama;* An international reference work in four volumes. New York: McGraw-Hill Book Company, 1972.

ModWD *Modern World Drama: An Encyclopedia.* By Myron Matlaw. New York: E.P. Dutton & Co., Inc., 1972.

MotPP *Motion Picture Performers: A Bibliography of Magazine and Periodical Articles, 1900-1969.* Compiled by Mel Schuster. Metuchen, New Jersey: Scarecrow Press, Inc., 1971.

MovMk *The Movie Makers.* By Sol Chaneles and Albert Wolsky. Secaucus, New Jersey: Derbibooks Inc., 1974.

NatPD *National Playwrights Directory.* Edited by Phyllis Johnson Kaye. Waterford, Connecticut: O'Neill Theater Center, 1977. Distributed by Gale Research Company, Detroit, Michigan.

NewMT *New Complete Book of the American Musical Theater.* By David Ewen. New York: Holt, Rinehart and Winston, 1970.

Biographies begin on page 607.

NewYTET   *The New York Times Encyclopedia of Television.* By Les Brown. New York: New York Times Book Company, Inc., 1977.

NotNAT   *Notable Names in the American Theatre.* Clifton, New Jersey: James T. White & Company, 1976. Previous edition published as *The Biographical Encyclopaedia & Who's Who of the American Theatre.* New York: James H. Heineman, Inc., 1966.

> *The* Biographical Bibliography, *indicated by the code* A, *begins on page 309. The* Necrology, *indicated by the code* B, *begins on page 343. The* Main Biographical Section *begins on page 489. NOTE: This book often alphabetizes on titles of address, i.e.: Dr., Mrs., and Sir.*

OxFilm   *The Oxford Companion to Film.* Edited by Liz-Anne Bawden. New York: Oxford University Press, 1976.

OxThe   *The Oxford Companion to the Theatre.* Third edition. Edited by Phyllis Hartnoll. London: Oxford University Press, 1967.

PlP&P   *Plays, Players, & Playwrights.* By Marion Geisinger. Updated by Peggy Marks. New York: Hart Publishing Company, Inc., 1975.

> *The main index to articles and biographies begins on page 575. A supplemental index to* The Theatre of the Seventies *starts on page 797, and is indicated in this publication by the addition of the code* A.

REnWD   *The Reader's Encyclopedia of World Drama.* Edited by John Gassner and Edward Quinn. New York: Thomas Y. Crowell Company, 1969.

ThFT   *They Had Faces Then: Super Stars, Stars and Starlets of the 1930's.* By John Springer and Jack Hamilton. Secaucus, New Jersey: Citadel Press, 1974.

TwYS   *Twenty Years of Silents, 1908-1928.* Compiled by John T. Weaver. Metuchen, New Jersey: Scarecrow Press, Inc., 1971.

> *Screen credits. Citations are found in three sections:* The Players *begins on page 27;* Directors, *indicated in this index by the code* A, *begins on page 407;* Producers, *indicated by the code* B, *begins on page 502.*

Vers   *The Versatiles: A Study of Supporting Character Actors and Actresses in the American Motion Picture, 1930-1955.* By Alfred E. Twomey and Arthur F. McClure. South Brunswick and New York: A.S. Barnes and Company, 1969.

> *This book is divided into two sections. The biographical section, indicated by the code* A, *begins on page 27. The non-biographical section, indicated by the code* B, *begins on page 251.*

WhScrn 1   *Who Was Who on Screen.* By Evelyn Mack Truitt. New York: R.R. Bowker Company, 1974.

WhScrn 2   *Who Was Who on Screen.* Second edition. By Evelyn Mack Truitt. New York: R.R. Bowker Company, 1977.

WhThe   *Who Was Who in the Theatre: 1912-1976;* A biographical dictionary of actors, actresses, directors, playwrights, and producers of the English-speaking theatre. 4 Volumes. Gale Composite Biographical Dictionary Series Number 3. Detroit: Gale Research Company, 1978.

> *Compiled from* Who's Who in the Theatre, *Volumes 1-15 (1912-1972).*

WhoHol   *Who's Who in Hollywood, 1900-1976.* By David Ragan. New Rochelle, New York: Arlington House Publishers, 1976.

> *This dictionary is divided into three sections. The section on* Living Players, *indicated in this index by the code* A, *begins on page 11. The*

section on Late Players, *indicated by the code* B, *begins on page 539.* Necrologies, *indicated by the code* C, *begin on page 845.*

WhoStg 1906 — *Who's Who on the Stage.* New York: Walter Browne & F.A. Austin, 1906.

Some entries are not in strict alphabetical sequence.

WhoStg 1908 — *Who's Who on the Stage, 1908.* Edited by Walter Browne and E. De Roy Koch. New York: B.W. Dodge & Company, 1908.

Some entries are not in strict alphabetical sequence.

WhoThe 16 — *Who's Who in the Theatre: A Biographical Record of the Contemporary Stage.* Sixteenth Edition. Edited by Ian Herbert. London: Pitman Publishing Ltd.; Detroit: Gale Research Company, 1977.

Biographies begin on page 333.

WomWMM — *Women Who Make Movies.* By Sharon Smith. New York: Hopkinson and Blake, 1975.

Names in part one can be located through the index beginning on page 299. Part two, The New Filmakers, *indicated by the code* A, *begins on page 145.* The Directory, *part three, indicated by the code* B, *starts on page 223.*

WorEnF — *The World Encyclopedia of the Film.* Edited by John M. Smith and Tim Cawkwell. (New York): A & W Visual Library, 1972.

A

A E 1867-1935 *PIP&P*
A E *see also* A E
Aabel, Hauk d1961 *NotNAT B*
Aadland, Beverly *WhoHol A*
Aaes, Erik 1899- *DcFM*
Aanrud, Hans 1864-1953 *NotNAT B*
Aaron, Chloe *NewYTET*
Aaron, Hank 1934- *CelR 3*
Aaron, John A d1972 *NewYTET*
Aaron, Paul *NotNAT*
Aarons, Alex *PIP&P*
Aarons, Alexander A 1891-1943 *NotNAT B,*
  WhThe
Aarons, Alfred E 1865-1936 *NotNAT B, WhThe,*
  WhoStg 1906, WhoStg 1908
Aaronson, Irving 1895-1963 *AmSCAP 1966,*
  NotNAT B
Aaronson, Max *Film 1*
Aasen, John 1887-1938 *Film 2, NotNAT B,*
  WhScrn 2, WhoHol B
Abag *McGWD*
Abarbanel, Sam X 1914- *IntMPA 1977*
Abarbanell, Lena 1880-1963 *WhoStg 1908*
Abarbanell, Lina 1880-1963 *NotNAT B, WhThe*
Abba, Marta 1907- *WhThe*
Abbas, Hector 1884-1942 *Film 2, WhThe*
Abbas, Khwaga Ahmad 1914- *WorEnF*
Abbas, Khwaja Ahmad 1914- *DcFM*
Abbe, Charles S d1932 *Film 1, WhoHol B*
Abbe, Charles S 1859-1932 *NotNAT B*
Abbe, Charles S 1860-1932 *WhScrn 1, WhScrn 2*
Abbe, Jack *Film 2*
Abbey, Henry Edwin 1846-1896 *NotNAT B*
Abbey, Henry Eugene 1846-1896 *OxThe*
Abbey, May *Film 1*
Abbey, May Evers 1872-1952 *NotNAT B*
Abbott, Al 1884-1962 *NotNAT B, WhScrn 1,*
  WhScrn 2
Abbott, Bessie 1877-1919 *NotNAT B*
Abbott, Bessie 1878- *WhoStg 1908*
Abbott, Bessie *see also* Abott, Bessie
Abbott, Bud d1974 *MotPP, WhoHol B*
Abbott, Bud 1895-1974 *CmMov, FilmgC, OxFilm,*
  WorEnF
Abbott, Bud 1896-1974 *WhScrn 2*
Abbott, Bud 1898-1974 *MovMk, NotNAT B*
Abbott, C 1726-1817 *NotNAT B*
Abbott, Charlie 1903- *AmSCAP 1966*
Abbott, Clara Barnes 1874-1956 *NotNAT B*
Abbott, Dolly 1887-1955 *NotNAT B*
Abbott, Dorothy d1968 *WhScrn 2, WhoHol B*
Abbott, Dorothy L 1886-1937 *NotNAT B*
Abbott, Edward B 1882-1932 *NotNAT B*
Abbott, Edward S 1914-1936 *NotNAT B*
Abbott, Emma 1850-1891 *NotNAT B*
Abbott, Frank 1879-1957 *WhScrn 1, WhScrn 2,*

  WhoHol B
Abbott, George 1887- *BiE&WWA, CelR 3,*
  CnThe, ConDr 1977, EncMT, FilmgC,
  McGWD, ModWD, NewMT, NotNAT,
  NotNAT A, OxThe, PIP&P, WhoThe 16,
  WorEnF
Abbott, George 1889- *CnMD*
Abbott, Harry 1861-1942 *NotNAT B*
Abbott, James Francis 1873-1954 *WhScrn 1,*
  WhScrn 2
Abbott, John 1905- *BiE&WWA, FilmgC,*
  MovMk, NotNAT, Vers B, WhThe,
  WhoHol A
Abbott, Judith *BiE&WWA, NotNAT*
Abbott, Marion *Film 2*
Abbott, Marion 1866-1937 *NotNAT B,*
  WhoHol B
Abbott, Nancy Ann 1901-1964 *NotNAT B*
Abbott, Paul d1872 *NotNAT B*
Abbott, Philip 1923- *FilmgC*
Abbott, Philip 1924- *BiE&WWA, NotNAT,*
  WhoHol A
Abbott, Richard 1899- *BiE&WWA, NotNAT,*
  WhoHol A
Abbott, William 1789-1843 *NotNAT B, OxThe*
Abbott, Yarnell 1871-1938 *NotNAT B*
Abbott And Costello *MotPP*
Abbound, Phyllis *WomWMM B*
Abdul-Jabbar, Kareem 1947- *CelR 3*
Abdulhak Hamit 1852-1937 *REnWD*
Abdushelli, Zurab 1913-1957 *NotNAT B*
Abe, Utake *Film 1*
Abegglen, Homer N 1901- *BiE&WWA, NotNAT*
Abel, Albert 1865-1937 *WhScrn 1*
Abel, Alfred 1865-1937 *NotNAT B, WhoHol B*
Abel, Alfred 1880-1937 *FilmgC, WhScrn 2*
Abel, Alfred 1880-1939 *Film 2*
Abel, Jeanne *WomWMM*
Abel, Lionel 1910- *CnMD, ModWD, NotNAT*
Abel, Neal 1882-1952 *NotNAT B*
Abel, Robert *Film 2*
Abel, Walter 1898- *BiE&WWA, FilmgC,*
  IntMPA 1977, MotPP, MovMk, NotNAT,
  Vers B, WhoHol A, WhoThe 16
Abeles, Arthur 1914- *IntMPA 1977*
Abeles, Edward 1870-1919 *Film 1, WhScrn 2*
  WhoHol B
Abeles, Edward S 1869-1919 *NotNAT B, WhThe,*
  WhoStg 1908
Abeles, Joseph 1911- *BiE&WWA, NotNAT*
Abell, Kjeld 1901-1961 *CnMD, CnThe, McGWD,*
  ModWD, OxThe, REnWD
Abelson, Hope 1919- *BiE&WWA, NotNAT*
Abend, Sheldon 1929- *BiE&WWA,*
  IntMPA 1977, NotNAT
Aber, Johnny *Film 2*

Abercrombie, Lascelles 1881-1938 WhThe
Aberg, Sivi WhoHol A
Abernathy, Ralph 1926- CelR 3
Abeson, Marion 1914- AmSCAP 1966
Abingdon, W B Film 1
Abingdon, William 1888-1959 WhThe
Abingdon, William L 1859-1918 NotNAT B,
    WhScrn 2, WhThe, WhoHol B
Abingdon, William L 1862-1918 WhoStg 1906,
    WhoStg 1908
Abington, Frances 1731-1815 NotNAT A,
    NotNAT B
Abington, Frances 1737-1815 CnThe, OxThe
Able, Will B 1923- BiE&WWA, NotNAT
Ableman, Paul 1927- ConDr 1977
Ables, Richard Louis 1911- AmSCAP 1966
Aborn, Louis H 1912- BiE&WWA, NotNAT
Aborn, Milton 1864-1933 NotNAT B, WhThe
Aborn, Sargent d1956 NotNAT B
Abott, Bessie 1878- WhoStg 1906
Abott, Bessie see also Abbott, Bessie
Abouchar, Joan 1937- BiE&WWA
Abraham, Paul d1960 WhThe
Abrahamian, Arousiak 1890-1973 WhScrn 2
Abrahams, A E 1873-1966 WhThe
Abrahams, Doris Cole 1925- WhoThe 16
Abrahams, Ian John 1921- IntMPA 1977
Abrahams, Maurice 1883-1931 AmSCAP 1966
Abrahams, Mort 1916- IntMPA 1977, NewYTET
Abramovitz, Max BiE&WWA
Abrams, Creighton 1914- CelR 3
Abrams, Dolores 1927- NotNAT
Abramson, Charles H 1902- BiE&WWA,
    NotNAT
Abranches, Aura d1962 NotNAT B
Abrash, Merritt 1930- NatPD
Abravanel, Maurice 1903- BiE&WWA, NotNAT
Abse, Dannie 1923- ConDr 1977
Abthorpe, Thomas PIP&P
Abu Saif, Salah 1915- DcFM
Abudu, Mungu Kimya 1948- NatPD
Abuladze, Tenghis 1924- DcFM
Aburto, Armando 1910-1955 WhScrn 1,
    WhScrn 2
Abzug, Bella 1920- CelR 3
Accius, Lucius 170?BC-086BC NotNAT B,
    OxThe
Accord, Art 1890-1931 WhScrn 1
Ace, Goodman 1899- CelR 3, NewYTET
Ace, Jane 1900-1974 WhScrn 2
Achard, Marcel Film 2, WhThe
Achard, Marcel 1899-1974 CnMD, FilmgC,
    McGWD, ModWD, WorEnF
Achard, Marcel 1900-1974 BiE&WWA, DcFM,
    NotNAT B
Acharekar, M R 1905- DcFM
Achron, Isidor 1892-1948 AmSCAP 1966
Achron, Joseph 1886-1943 AmSCAP 1966
Achterberg, Fritz Film 2
Achurch, Janet 1864-1916 CnThe, NotNAT B,
    OxThe, WhThe
Acker, Eugene Film 2
Acker, Jean Film 1, Film 2, TwYS
Acker, Sharon WhoHol A
Ackerman, Bettye 1928- FilmgC, IntMPA 1977,
    WhoHol A
Ackerman, Chantal WomWMM
Ackerman, Floyd F 1927- BiE&WWA
Ackerman, Harry S 1912- IntMPA 1977,
    NewYTET
Ackerman, Irene d1916 NotNAT B,
    WhoStg 1908
Ackerman, P Dodd, Sr. d1963 NotNAT B
Ackerman, Walter Film 1

Ackerman, Walter 1881-1938 WhScrn 1,
    WhScrn 2, WhoHol B
Ackermann, Charlotte 1757-1774 NotNAT B,
    OxThe
Ackermann, Dorothea 1752-1821 NotNAT B,
    OxThe
Ackermann, Konrad Ernst 1710-1771 NotNAT B
Ackermann, Konrad Ernst 1712-1771 OxThe
Ackermann, Sophia Carlotta Schroder 1714-1792
    OxThe
Ackermans, The CnThe
Ackers, Andrew Acquarulo 1919- AmSCAP 1966
Ackland, Joss 1928- FilmgC, WhoThe 16
Ackland, Rodney 1908- BiE&WWA, ConDr 1977,
    FilmgC, NotNAT, NotNAT A, WhThe
Ackley, Alfred Henry 1887-1960 AmSCAP 1966
Ackley, Bentley D 1872-1958 AmSCAP 1966
Ackman, Herman 1904- AmSCAP 1966
Ackroyd, Jack Film 2
Acord, Art 1890-1931 Film 1, Film 2, TwYS,
    WhScrn 2, WhoHol B
Acord, Art 1891-1931 FilmgC
Acosta, Enrique Film 2
Acosta, Rodolfo 1920-1974 FilmgC, WhScrn 2
Acosta, Rudolfo 1920-1974 WhoHol B
Acquanetta 1920- FilmgC, WhoHol A
Acquaviva, Nicholas 1927- AmSCAP 1966
Acres, Birt 1854-1918 FilmgC
Acrobats Of The Folies Bergere Film 1
Actman, Irving 1907-1967 AmSCAP 1966,
    NotNAT B
Acton-Bond, Acton WhThe
Acuff, Eddie 1902-1956 FilmgC, MovMk
Acuff, Eddie 1908-1956 Vers B, WhScrn 1,
    WhScrn 2, WhoHol B
Acuna, Judith Shaw WomWMM B
Ada-May WhThe
Adair, Alice Film 2
Adair, Jack 1894-1940 WhScrn 1, WhScrn 2,
    WhoHol B
Adair, Jean d1953 NotNAT B, WhThe
Adair, Jean d1963 WhoHol B
Adair, Jean 1872-1953 FilmgC
Adair, Jean 1873-1953 WhScrn 1, WhScrn 2
Adair, John 1885-1952 WhScrn 1, WhScrn 2,
    WhoHol B
Adair, Josephine Film 2
Adair, Robert 1900-1954 WhScrn 1, WhScrn 2,
    WhoHol B
Adair, Robyn Film 1
Adair, Thomas M 1913- AmSCAP 1966
Adair, Tim Film 2
Adair, Yvonne 1925- BiE&WWA, NotNAT
Adalbert, Max 1874-1933 Film 2, WhScrn 2
Adam De La Halle 1240?-1286? McGWD, OxThe
Adam, Alfred 1909- FilmgC
Adam, Ken 1921- DcFM, FilmgC, IntMPA 1977,
    WorEnF
Adam, Noelle 1933- BiE&WWA
Adam, Ronald 1896- FilmgC, WhoThe 16
Adam, Ronald 1897- IntMPA 1977
Adamov, Arthur 1908-1970 CnMD, CnThe,
    CroCD, McGWD, ModWD, NotNAT B,
    OxThe, PIP&P, REnWD
Adamowska, Helenka Film 2
Adams, Abigail d1955 NotNAT B
Adams, Alice Baldwin d1936 NotNAT B
Adams, Audri 1925- AmSCAP 1966
Adams, Beverley 1945- FilmgC
Adams, Beverly WhoHol A
Adams, Bret 1930- BiE&WWA, NotNAT
Adams, Casey 1917- FilmgC, WhoHol A
Adams, Claire Film 1, Film 2, TwYS
Adams, Constance 1893-1960 WhScrn 2

Adams, David C *IntMPA 1977, NewYTET*
Adams, Dick 1889- *WhThe*
Adams, Dorothy 1915?- *FilmgC, WhoHol A*
Adams, Edie *BiE&WWA, MotPP, NewYTET,*
NotNAT, WhoHol A, WhoThe 16
Adams, Edie 1929- *FilmgC, MovMk*
Adams, Edie 1931- *IntMPA 1977*
Adams, Edith 1879-1957 *WhScrn 1, WhScrn 2*
Adams, Edwin 1834-1877 *FamA&A, NotNAT B,*
OxThe
Adams, Ernest Harry 1886-1959 *AmSCAP 1966*
Adams, Ernest S 1885-1947 *WhScrn 1, WhScrn 2*
Adams, Ernie S 1885-1947 *Film 2, WhoHol B*
Adams, Frances Sale d1969 *WhoHol B*
Adams, Frank R 1883-1963 *AmSCAP 1966,*
NotNAT B
Adams, Frank Steward d1964 *NotNAT B*
Adams, Franklin Pierce 1881-1960 *NotNAT B*
Adams, George 1904- *AmSCAP 1966*
Adams, Gerald Drayson 1904?- *FilmgC,*
IntMPA 1977
Adams, Harry *Film 2*
Adams, Howard 1909-1936 *WhScrn 1, WhScrn 2,*
WhoHol B
Adams, Ida d1960 *NotNAT B, WhThe*
Adams, Isabel 1856-1936 *WhScrn 2*
Adams, Jeff 1936-1967 *WhScrn 2*
Adams, Jill d1964 *NotNAT B*
Adams, Jill 1931- *FilmgC, WhoHol A*
Adams, Jimmie *Film 2*
Adams, Joey 1911- *BiE&WWA, CelR 3,*
NotNAT A, WhoHol A
Adams, John Cranford 1903- *BiE&WWA*
Adams, John Wolcott 1874-1925 *WhScrn 2*
Adams, Joseph Quincy 1881-1946 *NotNAT B*
Adams, Julie *MotPP, WhoHol A*
Adams, Julie 1926- *FilmgC*
Adams, Julie 1928- *IntMPA 1977*
Adams, Kathryn 1894-1959 *Film 1, Film 2,*
MotPP, NotNAT B, WhScrn 1, WhScrn 2,
WhoHol B
Adams, Lee 1924- *AmSCAP 1966, BiE&WWA,*
EncMT, NewMT, NotNAT
Adams, Leslie d1934 *WhoHol B*
Adams, Leslie 1887-1936 *NotNAT B, WhScrn 2*
Adams, Lionel d1952 *Film 2, NotNAT B,*
WhoHol B
Adams, Margie 1881-1937 *NotNAT B*
Adams, Marla *WhoHol A*
Adams, Mary d1973 *WhScrn 2, WhoHol B*
Adams, Maud *WhoHol A*
Adams, Maude 1872-1953 *CnThe, FamA&A,*
NotNAT A, NotNAT B, OxThe, PIP&P,
WhThe, WhoStg 1906, WhoStg 1908
Adams, Mildred *Film 1*
Adams, Miriam 1907- *WhThe*
Adams, Neile *WhoHol A*
Adams, Nicholas d1935 *NotNAT B*
Adams, Nick d1968 *MotPP, WhoHol B*
Adams, Nick 1931-1968 *FilmgC, MovMk*
Adams, Nick 1932-1968 *WhScrn 1, WhScrn 2*
Adams, Nick 1935-1968 *NotNAT B*
Adams, Paul E 1922- *AmSCAP 1966*
Adams, Peggy *Film 1*
Adams, Peter *WhoHol A*
Adams, Robert 1906- *FilmgC, WhThe*
Adams, Robert K 1909- *BiE&WWA, NotNAT*
Adams, Roger 1917- *BiE&WWA, NotNAT*
Adams, Samuel Hopkins 1871-1958 *NotNAT B*
Adams, Stanley *WhoHol A*
Adams, Stanley 1907- *AmSCAP 1966,*
BiE&WWA, NotNAT
Adams, Stella d1961 *Film 1, Film 2, WhScrn 2*
Adams, Suzanne 1872-1953 *NotNAT B,*

WhoStg 1906, WhoStg 1908
Adams, Tom 1938- *FilmgC*
Adams, Tommye d1955 *WhScrn 2*
Adams, W Bridges *WhThe*
Adams, W Davenport d1904 *NotNAT B*
Adams, William Perry 1887-1972 *WhScrn 2,*
WhoHol B
Adamson, Harold 1906- *AmSCAP 1966, NewMT*
Adamson, James 1896-1956 *WhScrn 2*
Adato, Perry Miller *WomWMM A,*
WomWMM B
Addams, Augustus A d1851 *FamA&A*
Addams, Charles 1912- *CelR 3*
Addams, Dawn 1930- *FilmgC, IntMPA 1977,*
MotPP, OxFilm, WhoHol A, WhoThe 16
Adderley, Julian Cannonball 1928- *CelR 3*
Addinsell, Richard 1904- *BiE&WWA, FilmgC,*
IntMPA 1977, NotNAT, OxFilm,
WhoThe 16
Addison, Carlotta 1849-1914 *WhThe*
Addison, John 1920- *BiE&WWA, CmMov,*
FilmgC, IntMPA 1977, NotNAT, OxFilm
Addison, Joseph 1672-1719 *McGWD, NotNAT B,*
OxThe, PIP&P
Addy, Wesley 1912- *FilmgC*
Addy, Wesley 1913- *BiE&WWA, NotNAT,*
WhoHol A, WhoThe 16
Ade, George 1866-1944 *McGWD, ModWD,*
NewMT, NotNAT A, NotNAT B, OxThe,
WhThe, WhoStg 1906, WhoStg 1908
Adelman, Louis C *NatPD*
Adeney, Eric *Film 1*
Aderer, Adolphe 1855- *WhThe*
Adickes, Frances Wood 1889- *AmSCAP 1966*
Adix, Vern 1912- *BiE&WWA, NotNAT*
Adjani, Isabelle *WhoHol A*
Adkinson, Harvey E 1934- *AmSCAP 1966*
Adlam, Basil G *AmSCAP 1966*
Adler, Adolph J d1961 *NotNAT B*
Adler, Allen A d1964 *NotNAT B*
Adler, Bob 1906- *IntMPA 1977*
Adler, Buddy d1960 *NotNAT B*
Adler, Buddy 1906-1960 *DcFM*
Adler, Buddy 1908-1960 *FilmgC*
Adler, Buddy 1909-1960 *WorEnF*
Adler, Felix d1963 *NotNAT B*
Adler, Frances 1891-1964 *BiE&WWA,*
NotNAT B
Adler, Hyman d1945 *NotNAT B*
Adler, Jacob P 1855-1926 *Film 1, NotNAT B,*
WhScrn 2, WhThe, WhoHol B
Adler, Jay 1907?- *FilmgC, WhoHol A*
Adler, Jerry *NotNAT*
Adler, Larry 1914- *BiE&WWA, FilmgC,*
NotNAT, WhoHol A
Adler, Luther 1903- *BiE&WWA, FilmgC,*
IntMPA 1977, MotPP, MovMk, NotNAT,
PIP&P, Vers B, WhoHol A, WhoThe 16
Adler, Maurice E 1909-1960 *WorEnF*
Adler, Richard 1921- *AmSCAP 1966,*
BiE&WWA, EncMT, NotNAT, WhoThe 16
Adler, Richard 1923- *NewMT*
Adler, Samuel 1928- *AmSCAP 1966*
Adler, Sarah d1953 *NotNAT B*
Adler, Stella *BiE&WWA, NotNAT, PIP&P,*
WhoHol A
Adler, Stella 1895- *FilmgC*
Adler, Stella 1902- *WhoThe 16*
Adlon, Louis d1947 *WhScrn 1, WhScrn 2,*
WhoHol B
Adolfi, John 1888- *TwYS A*
Adolfi, John G *Film 1*
Adolfi, John G 1888-1933 *WhScrn 2*
Adolfo 1933- *CelR 3*

Adolph, Johann Baptist 1657-1708 *OxThe*
Adoree, Renee d1933 *MotPP, WhoHol B*
Adoree, Renee 1898-1933 *BiDFlm, Film 2,*
  FilmgC, MovMk, TwYS, WhScrn 1,
  WhScrn 2, WorEnF
Adoree, Renee 1902-1933 *NotNAT B*
Adorian, Paul *IntMPA 1977*
Adrian 1903-1959 *DcFM, FilmgC*
Adrian, Diane *AmSCAP 1966*
Adrian, Gilbert d1959 *NotNAT B*
Adrian, Iris 1913- *FilmgC, IntMPA 1977,*
  MovMk, WhoHol A
Adrian, Iris 1915- *Vers A*
Adrian, Max 1902-1973 *FilmgC*
Adrian, Max 1903-1973 *BiE&WWA, EncMT,*
  NotNAT B, WhScrn 2, WhThe, WhoHol B
Adrian, Rhys *ConDr 1977B*
Adrienne, Jean 1905- *WhThe*
Adye, Oscar d1914 *WhThe*
AE 1867-1935 *OxThe*
AE *see also* A E
Aeschylus 524?BC-456?BC *CnThe, McGWD,*
  REnWD
Aeschylus 525BC-456BC *NotNAT B, OxThe,*
  PIP&P
Aesopus, Claudius *OxThe*
Aess, Eric *DcFM*
Afinogenov, Aleksander Nikolayevich 1904-1941
  CnMD, McGWD, ModWD
Afinogenov, Alexander Mikolaevich 1904-1941
  NotNAT B
Afinogenov, Alexander Nikolaevich 1904-1941
  OxThe
Afranius, Lucius *OxThe*
African Roscius *OxThe*
Afrique 1907-1961 *NotNAT B, WhScrn 1,*
  WhScrn 2, WhoHol B
Afton, Richard Lord *IntMPA 1977*
Agaoglu, Adalet 1929- *CnThe, REnWD*
Agar, Dan 1881- *WhThe*
Agar, Florence Leonide Charvin 1836-1891
  NotNAT B
Agar, Grace Hale d1963 *NotNAT B*
Agar, Jane 1889-1948 *WhScrn 1, WhScrn 2,*
  WhoHol B
Agar, John 1921- *FilmgC, IntMPA 1977,*
  MotPP, WhoHol A
Agar-Lyons, Harry *Film 2*
Agate, James Evershed 1877-1947 *NotNAT A,*
  NotNAT B, OxThe, WhThe
Agate, May 1892-1960 *OxThe, WhThe*
Agathon *OxThe*
Agay, Denes 1911- *AmSCAP 1966*
Agee, James 1909-1955 *FilmgC, OxFilm,*
  WorEnF
Ager, Milton 1893- *AmSCAP 1966*
Aggas, Robert 1619?-1679 *OxThe*
Aghayan, Ray *NotNAT*
Agnew, Robert 1899- *Film 2, TwYS*
Agnew, Spiro 1918- *CelR 3*
Agostini, Philippe 1910- *DcFM, FilmgC, OxFilm,*
  WorEnF
Agradoot *DcFM*
Agragami, Nishith Bannerjee 1924- *DcFM*
Agrell, Alfhild 1849-1923 *OxThe*
Agronsky, Martin *NewYTET*
Aguglia, Mimi 1885-1970 *WhScrn 1, WhScrn 2,*
  WhoHol B
Aguilar, Tony *WhoHol A*
Aguirre, Manuel B 1907-1957 *WhScrn 1,*
  WhScrn 2
Agutter, Jenny 1952- *FilmgC*
Ahbez, Eden 1908- *AmSCAP 1966*
Ahearn, Lillian M 1886- *AmSCAP 1966*

Ahearne, Thomas 1906-1969 *WhoHol B*
Ahearne, Tom 1906-1969 *WhScrn 1, WhScrn 2*
Ahern, George *Film 1*
Ahern, James *McGWD*
Aherne, Brian 1902- *BiE&WWA, Film 2,*
  FilmgC, IntMPA 1977, MotPP, MovMk,
  NotNAT, NotNAT A, OxFilm, WhThe,
  WhoHol A
Aherne, Lassie Lou *Film 2*
Aherne, Pat 1901-1970 *WhoHol B*
Aherne, Patrick 1901-1970 *Film 2, WhScrn 1,*
  WhScrn 2
Ahlander, Thecla Ottilia 1855- *WhThe*
Ahlberg, Harry 1912- *AmSCAP 1966*
Ahlers, Anny 1906-1933 *NotNAT B, WhScrn 2,*
  WhThe, WhoHol B
Ahlert, Fred E 1892-1953 *AmSCAP 1966,*
  NotNAT B
Ahlm, Philip E 1905-1954 *WhScrn 1, WhScrn 2*
Ahlschlager, Walter W, Sr. 1887-1965 *NotNAT B*
Ahlsen, Leopold 1927- *CnMD, CroCD, McGWD,*
  ModWD
Ahn, Philip 1911- *FilmgC, IntMPA 1977,*
  MovMk, Vers B, WhoHol A
Ahrendt, Carl Frederick William 1842-1909
  NotNAT B
Aicken, Elinor *Film 1*
Aidman, Charles 1925- *AmSCAP 1966,*
  BiE&WWA, NotNAT, WhoHol A
Aidman, Charles 1929- *FilmgC*
Aidoo, Ama Ata 1942- *ConDr 1977*
Aiken, Conrad Potter 1889-1973 *CnMD, ModWD*
Aiken, Frank Eugene 1840-1910 *NotNAT B,*
  WhoStg 1908
Aiken, George 1892- *CelR 3*
Aiken, George L 1830-1876 *McGWD, NotNAT B,*
  OxThe, PIP&P, REnWD
Aiken, Kenneth 1885- *AmSCAP 1966*
Aiken, Mary *Film 2*
Ailes, Roger *NewYTET*
Ailey, Alvin 1931- *BiE&WWA, CelR 3,*
  NotNAT, WhoHol A
Aimee, Anouk 1932- *BiDFlm, FilmgC, MovMk,*
  OxFilm, WhoHol A, WorEnF
Aimee, Anouk 1934- *IntMPA 1977*
Ainge, Susan M *WomWMM B*
Ainley, Henry *PIP&P*
Ainley, Henry Hinchliffe 1879-1945 *CnThe,*
  Film 1, Film 2, FilmgC, NotNAT B,
  OxThe, WhScrn 1, WhScrn 2, WhThe,
  WhoHol B
Ainley, Richard 1910-1967 *FilmgC, NotNAT B,*
  WhScrn 1, WhScrn 2, WhThe, WhoHol B
Ainslee, Adra d1963 *NotNAT B*
Ainsley, Charles *Film 1*
Ainsley, Norman 1881-1948 *WhScrn 1,*
  WhScrn 2, WhoHol B
Ainsworth, Cupid *Film 2*
Ainsworth, Helen Shumate d1961 *NotNAT B*
Ainsworth, Phil *Film 2*
Ainsworth, Sidney 1872-1922 *Film 2, WhScrn 1,*
  WhScrn 2, WhoHol B
Ainsworth, Sydney 1872-1922 *Film 1, Film 2,*
  NotNAT B
Ainsworth, Virginia *Film 2*
Aiston, Arthur C 1868-1924 *NotNAT B*
Aitken, Frank Spottiswoode 1869-1933 *WhScrn 2*
Aitken, Frank Spottsworth 1869-1933 *WhScrn 1*
Aitken, Hugh 1924- *AmSCAP 1966*
Aitken, Maria 1945- *WhoThe 16*
Aitken, Spottiswoode 1869-1933 *Film 1, Film 2,*
  TwYS, WhoHol B
Akar, John J d1975 *WhoHol C*
Akat, Lutfu 1916- *DcFM*

Aked, Muriel 1887-1955 *FilmgC, NotNAT B, WhScrn 1, WhScrn 2, WhThe, WhoHol B*
Akers, Henry Carl Hank 1908-1967 *WhScrn 1, WhScrn 2*
Akers, Howard E 1913- *AmSCAP 1966*
Akimou, Nikolai 1901-1968 *NotNAT B*
Akimov, Nikolai Pavlovich 1901-1968 *CnThe, OxThe*
Akin, Mary *Film 2*
Akins, Claude *IntMPA 1977, WhoHol A*
Akins, Claude 1918- *FilmgC*
Akins, Claude 1926- *Vers A*
Akins, Zoe 1886-1958 *CnMD, FilmgC, McGWD, ModWD, NotNAT B, OxThe, WhThe, WomWMM*
Akiyoshi, Toshiko 1929- *AmSCAP 1966*
Aksal, Sabahattin Kudret 1920- *REnWD*
Akst, Harry 1894-1963 *AmSCAP 1966, NotNAT B, PlP&P*
Aktasheva, Irina *WomWMM*
Alabaster, William *PlP&P*
Aladdin 1913-1970 *WhScrn 1, WhScrn 2*
Alagna, Matthew 1920-1965 *AmSCAP 1966*
Alaimo, Louise *WomWMM B*
Alarcon, Juan Ruiz De 1581?-1639 *CnThe, OxThe*
Alarcon Y Mendoza, Juan Ruiz Di 1588-1639 *NotNAT B*
Alarie, Amanda 1889-1965 *WhScrn 2*
Alazraki, Benito 1923- *OxFilm, WorEnF*
Albanesi, Margharita 1899-1923 *NotNAT A*
Albanesi, Meggie 1899-1923 *Film 2, WhThe*
Albani, Madame 1852- *WhoStg 1908*
Albani, Emma 1847-1930 *NotNAT B*
Albaugh, John W, Jr. 1867-1910 *NotNAT B, WhoStg 1906, WhoStg 1908*
Albaugh, John W, Sr. 1837-1909 *NotNAT B, WhoStg 1906, WhoStg 1908*
Albee, Edward 1927- *CnMD*
Albee, Edward 1928- *BiE&WWA, CelR 3, CnThe, ConDr 1977, CroCD, FilmgC, McGWD, ModWD, NatPD, NotNAT, NotNAT A, OxThe, PlP&P, PlP&P A, REnWD, WhoThe 16*
Albee, Edward Franklin 1857-1930 *NotNAT B, OxThe*
Albee, Edward Franklin 1860-1930 *WhoStg 1908*
Alberg, Mildred Freed 1920- *BiE&WWA, NewYTET, NotNAT*
Alberghetti, Anna Maria 1936- *BiE&WWA, FilmgC, IntMPA 1977, MotPP, MovMk, NotNAT, WhoHol A*
Alberghetti, Carla 1939- *BiE&WWA*
Alberni, Luis 1887-1962 *Film 2, FilmgC, MotPP, MovMk, NotNAT B, Vers B, WhScrn 1, WhScrn 2, WhoHol B*
Alberoni, Sherri *WhoHol A*
Albers, Hans 1892-1960 *Film 2, FilmgC, MotPP, NotNAT B, WhScrn 1, WhScrn 2, WhoHol B*
Albers, John Kenneth 1924- *AmSCAP 1966*
Albert, Allan 1945- *NotNAT*
Albert, Ben 1876- *WhThe*
Albert, Carl 1908- *CelR 3*
Albert, Dan 1890-1919 *WhScrn 2*
Albert, Eddie 1908- *BiE&WWA, CelR 3, EncMT, FilmgC, HolP 30, IntMPA 1977, MotPP, MovMk, NotNAT, PlP&P, WhoHol A, WhoThe 16*
Albert, Edward 1951- *CelR 3, IntMPA 1977, WhoHol A*
Albert, William 1863- *WhThe*
Albert-Lambert, Raphael 1865- *WhThe*
Albertano, Linda *WomWMM B*
Alberti, Fritz *Film 2*

Alberti, Rafael 1902- *CnMD, McGWD, ModWD*
Alberti, Solon 1889- *AmSCAP 1966*
Alberts, Al 1922- *AmSCAP 1966*
Albertson, Arthur W 1891-1926 *WhScrn 2*
Albertson, Coit *Film 1, Film 2*
Albertson, Frank 1909-1964 *Film 2, FilmgC, MotPP, MovMk, NotNAT B, Vers A, WhScrn 1, WhScrn 2, WhoHol B*
Albertson, Grace *WhoHol A*
Albertson, Jack 1910- *FilmgC, IntMPA 1977, MovMk, NotNAT, WhoHol A, WhoThe 16*
Albertson, Lillian d1962 *NotNAT B, WhoHol B*
Albertson, Mabel 1900?- *FilmgC, MotPP, WhoHol A*
Albery, Sir Bronson James 1881-1971 *CnThe, OxThe, WhThe*
Albery, Donald Arthur Rolleston 1914- *BiE&WWA, CnThe, EncMT, NotNAT, OxThe, WhoThe 16*
Albery, James 1838-1889 *NotNAT B, OxThe*
Albicocco, Jean-Gabriel 1930- *FilmgC*
Albrecht, Elmer 1901-1959 *AmSCAP 1966*
Albright, Bob Oklahoma 1884-1971 *WhScrn 1, WhScrn 2*
Albright, H Darkes 1907- *BiE&WWA, NotNAT*
Albright, Hardie 1903-1975 *FilmgC, HolP 30, MotPP, MovMk, WhScrn 2, WhThe, WhoHol C*
Albright, Lola 1924- *MotPP*
Albright, Lola 1925- *FilmgC, IntMPA 1977, MovMk, WhoHol A*
Albright, Wally, Jr. *Film 2, WhoHol A*
Alcaide, Chris *WhoHol A*
Alcaide, Mario 1927-1971 *WhoHol B*
Alcalde, Mario 1927-1971 *WhScrn 2*
Alcendor, Ralph R 1926- *AmSCAP 1966*
Alcock, Douglas 1908-1970 *WhScrn 2, WhoHol B*
Alcoriza, Luis 1920- *WorEnF*
Alcorn, Olive Ann *Film 2*
Alcott, John *FilmgC*
Alcott, Louisa M 1832-1888 *FilmgC*
Alda, Alan 1936- *BiE&WWA, FilmgC, IntMPA 1977, MotPP, MovMk, NewYTET, NotNAT, WhoHol A, WhoThe 16*
Alda, Robert 1914- *BiE&WWA, FilmgC, HolP 40, IntMPA 1977, MotPP, MovMk, NotNAT, PlP&P, WhoHol A, WhoThe 16*
Aldan, Daisy *WomWMM B*
Aldea, Mercedes d1954 *WhScrn 1, WhScrn 2*
Alden, Betty 1898-1948 *WhScrn 1, WhScrn 2, WhoHol B*
Alden, Hortense 1903- *BiE&WWA, NotNAT, WhThe*
Alden, Joan d1968 *WhoHol B*
Alden, John d1962 *NotNAT B*
Alden, John W 1895- *AmSCAP 1966*
Alden, Joseph Reed 1886-1951 *AmSCAP 1966*
Alden, Mary 1883-1946 *Film 1, Film 2, MotPP, NotNAT B, TwYS, WhScrn 1, WhScrn 2, WhoHol B*
Alden, Norman *WhoHol A*
Alderham, Joseph 1925- *AmSCAP 1966*
Alderson, Clifton 1864-1930 *NotNAT B, WhThe*
Alderson, Erville 1883-1957 *Film 2, Vers B, WhScrn 1, WhScrn 2, WhoHol B*
Alderson, John *WhoHol A*
Alderson, John 1896- *IntMPA 1977*
Alderton, John 1940- *FilmgC, WhoThe 16*
Aldin, Arthur 1872- *WhThe*
Aldo, G R 1902-1953 *DcFM, FilmgC, OxFilm*
Aldo, G R 1905-1953 *WorEnF*
Aldon, Mari *IntMPA 1977*
Aldon, Mari 1929- *WhoHol A*

5

Aldon, Mari 1930- *FilmgC*
Aldredge, Theoni V *BiE&WWA, NotNAT, WhoThe 16*
Aldredge, Thomas 1928- *BiE&WWA, NotNAT*
Aldredge, Tom 1928- *WhoHol A, WhoThe 16*
Aldrich, Charles T 1872- *WhThe*
Aldrich, Louis 1843-1901 *NotNAT B, OxThe*
Aldrich, Mariska 1881-1965 *WhScrn 2*
Aldrich, Richard 1863-1937 *NotNAT B*
Aldrich, Richard S 1902- *BiE&WWA, WhThe*
Aldrich, Robert 1918- *BiDFlm, CmMov, DcFM, FilmgC, IntMPA 1977, MovMk, OxFilm, WorEnF*
Aldrich, Thomas Bailey 1836-1907 *NotNAT B*
Aldridge, Alfred 1876-1934 *WhScrn 1, WhScrn 2, WhoHol B*
Aldridge, Ira Frederick 1804-1867 *CnThe, OxThe, PIP&P*
Aldridge, Ira Frederick 1807-1867 *NotNAT A, NotNAT B*
Aldridge, Michael 1920- *WhoThe 16*
Aldrin, Edwin Buzz 1930- *CelR 3*
Alea, Tomas Gutierrez 1928- *OxFilm*
Alea, Tomas Guttierrez 1928- *DcFM*
Alecsandri, Vasile 1821-1890 *McGWD*
Alee *Film 2*
Aleichem, Sholem 1859-1916 *PIP&P*
Aleichem, Sholem *see also* Sholem Aleichem
Aleichem, Sholom 1859-1916 *NotNAT B, OxThe*
Alejandro, Miguel *WhoHol A*
Alekan, Henri 1909- *DcFM, FilmgC, OxFilm, WorEnF*
Alemann, Claudia *WomWMM*
Alemann, Johanna *WomWMM B*
Alencar, Jose Mariniano De 1829-1877 *OxThe*
Alenikoff, Frances *WomWMM B*
Aleotti, Giovanni Battista 1546-1636 *OxThe*
Aletter, Frank *WhoHol A*
Alexander The Great 356BC-323BC *FilmgC*
Alexander, A L 1906-1967 *WhScrn 2*
Alexander, Ben 1911-1969 *Film 1, Film 2, FilmgC, MotPP, MovMk, TwYS, WhScrn 1, WhScrn 2, WhoHol B*
Alexander, C K 1923- *BiE&WWA, NotNAT*
Alexander, Chris 1920- *WhoHol A*
Alexander, Claire 1898-1927 *WhScrn 1, WhScrn 2, WhoHol B*
Alexander, Cris 1920- *BiE&WWA, NotNAT*
Alexander, David *NewYTET*
Alexander, Dick *Film 2*
Alexander, Edward 1888-1964 *Film 1, WhScrn 1, WhScrn 2, WhoHol B*
Alexander, Frank Fatty 1879-1937 *WhScrn 1, WhScrn 2, WhoHol B*
Alexander, Georg 1889?-1945 *Film 2, WhScrn 2*
Alexander, Sir George 1858-1918 *CnThe, NotNAT A, NotNAT B, OxThe, PIP&P, WhThe, WhoStg 1908*
Alexander, George 1918- *AmSCAP 1966*
Alexander, Gus *Film 1*
Alexander, James 1902-1961 *WhScrn 2*
Alexander, Jamie *WhoHol A*
Alexander, Jane 1939- *NotNAT, PIP&P A, WhoHol A, WhoThe 16*
Alexander, Jane 1943- *FilmgC*
Alexander, Janet d1961 *WhThe*
Alexander, Jeff 1910- *AmSCAP 1966*
Alexander, John 1865-1951 *WhScrn 1, WhScrn 2*
Alexander, John 1897- *BiE&WWA, FilmgC, IntMPA 1977, NotNAT, Vers B, WhoHol B, WhoThe 16*
Alexander, Josef *AmSCAP 1966*
Alexander, Katherine 1901- *BiE&WWA, FilmgC, MovMk, NotNAT, PIP&P, ThFT, WhThe*

Alexander, Larry 1939- *AmSCAP 1966*
Alexander, Lois A 1891-1962 *WhScrn 2*
Alexander, Mara 1914-1965 *WhScrn 2*
Alexander, Muriel 1898-1975 *Film 2, WhThe, WhoHol C*
Alexander, Perry 1895- *AmSCAP 1966*
Alexander, Queen *Film 1*
Alexander, Rene d1914 *WhScrn 2*
Alexander, Richard *Film 2*
Alexander, Robert *NotNAT*
Alexander, Rod 1919- *BiE&WWA, NotNAT*
Alexander, Rod 1920- *BiE&WWA, WhoHol A*
Alexander, Ronald 1917- *BiE&WWA, NotNAT*
Alexander, Ross 1907-1937 *FilmgC, NotNAT B, WhScrn 1, WhScrn 2, WhoHol B*
Alexander, Ross 1934- *NatPD*
Alexander, Sara 1839-1926 *WhScrn 1, WhScrn 2, WhoHol B*
Alexander, Suzanne d1975 *WhScrn 2, WhoHol C*
Alexander, Terence 1923- *FilmgC, WhoHol A, WhoThe 16*
Alexander, Van 1915- *AmSCAP 1966*
Alexander The Great d1933 *WhScrn 2*
Alexanderson, Ernst F W d1975 *NewYTET*
Alexandre, Rene 1885-1946 *Film 1, NotNAT B, WhThe*
Alexandresco *Film 2*
Alexandrov, Grigori 1903- *DcFM, Film 2, FilmgC, OxFilm, WorEnF*
Alexeieff, Alexander 1901- *WorEnF*
Alexeieff, Alexandre 1901- *DcFM, OxFilm*
Alexieff, Alexandre 1901- *FilmgC*
Alexis *OxThe*
Alfaro, Keiva *WhoHol A*
Alfaro, Rhonda *WhoHol A*
Alfidi, Joseph 1961- *AmSCAP 1966*
Alfieri, Count Vittorio Amedeo 1749-1803 *CnThe, McGWD, NotNAT B, OxThe, REnWD*
Alfonso, Don 1899- *AmSCAP 1966*
Alford, Walter 1912- *BiE&WWA, NotNAT*
Alfred, Roy 1916- *AmSCAP 1966*
Alfred, William 1922- *ConDr 1977, CroCD, McGWD, NotNAT*
Algar, James 1912- *IntMPA 1977*
Algar, James 1914- *DcFM, FilmgC*
Algaro, Gabriel 1888-1951 *WhScrn 1, WhScrn 2*
Algier, Sidney H 1889-1945 *WhScrn 1, WhScrn 2, WhoHol B*
Algren, Nelson 1909- *FilmgC*
Ali, George 1866-1947 *Film 2, WhScrn 2*
Alin, Morris 1905- *AmSCAP 1966, IntMPA 1977*
Alippi, Elias d1942 *WhScrn 1, WhScrn 2*
Alison, Dorothy 1925- *FilmgC*
Alison, George d1936 *NotNAT B*
Alizon *OxThe*
Allan, Elizabeth 1908- *FilmgC, ThFT, WhoHol A*
Allan, Hugh 1903- *Film 2, TwYS*
Allan, Jed *WhoHol A*
Allan, Lewis *AmSCAP 1966*
Allan, Louise Rosalie 1810-1856 *NotNAT B, OxThe*
Allan, Marguerite *Film 2*
Allan, Maud 1883-1956 *NotNAT A, NotNAT B, WhThe*
Allan, Ted *IntMPA 1977*
Allan, Ted 1916- *ConDr 1977*
Alland, William 1916- *FilmgC, IntMPA 1977*
Allandale, Fred 1872- *WhThe*
Allardt, Arthur *Film 1*
Allasio, Marisa *MotPP*
Allbeury, Daisy 1885-1961 *WhScrn 1, WhScrn 2*
Allbritton, Joe L *NewYTET*

Allbritton, Louise 1920- *FilmgC, HolP 40, MotPP, WhoHol A*
Alleborn, Al 1892-1968 *WhScrn 1, WhScrn 2*
Allegret, Catherine *WhoHol A*
Allegret, Marc 1900-1973 *BiDFlm, DcFM, FilmgC, MovMk, OxFilm, WhScrn 2, WorEnF*
Allegret, Yves 1907- *BiDFlm, DcFM, FilmgC, MovMk, OxFilm, WorEnF*
Allegro, Anita d1964 *NotNAT B*
Allen, A Hylton 1879- *WhThe*
Allen, Adrianne 1907- *BiE&WWA, FilmgC, NotNAT, WhoHol A*
Allen, Alfred 1866-1947 *Film 1, Film 2, WhScrn 2*
Allen, Arthur B 1881-1947 *WhScrn 1, WhScrn 2, WhoHol B*
Allen, Bambi d1973 *WhScrn 2*
Allen, Barbara Jo 1904?-1974 *FilmgC, WhoHol B*
Allen, Barclay 1918- *AmSCAP 1966*
Allen, C J *Film 2*
Allen, Charles Leslie 1830-1917 *NotNAT B, WhThe, WhoStg 1906, WhoStg 1908*
Allen, Chesney 1894- *FilmgC*
Allen, Chesney 1896- *WhThe*
Allen, Corey 1934- *FilmgC, WhoHol A*
Allen, Creighton 1900- *AmSCAP 1966*
Allen, Dayton 1919- *IntMPA 1977*
Allen, Deborah *PIP&P A*
Allen, Dede 1924- *IntMPA 1977, WomWMM*
Allen, Diana *Film 2*
Allen, Dick 1942- *CelR 3*
Allen, Dorothy 1896-1970 *Film 2, WhScrn 1, WhScrn 2, WhoHol B*
Allen, Edith *Film 2*
Allen, Elizabeth 1916- *MovMk*
Allen, Elizabeth 1934- *BiE&WWA, FilmgC, NotNAT, WhoHol A, WhoThe 16*
Allen, Ethan 1882-1940 *WhScrn 1, WhScrn 2, WhoHol B*
Allen, Florence *Film 2*
Allen, Frank 1851- *WhThe*
Allen, Fred 1894-1956 *EncMT, FilmgC, NewYTET, NotNAT A, NotNAT B, OxFilm, WhScrn 1, WhScrn 2, WhoHol B*
Allen, G Everett 1899- *AmSCAP 1966*
Allen, George 1922- *CelR 3*
Allen, Gloria *WomWMM B*
Allen, Gracie 1899-1964 *ThFT*
Allen, Gracie 1902-1964 *Film 2, FilmgC, MotPP, MovMk, WhoHol B*
Allen, Gracie 1906-1964 *NotNAT A, NotNAT B, WhScrn 1, WhScrn 2*
Allen, Harry *Film 2*
Allen, Henry, Jr. 1900- *AmSCAP 1966*
Allen, Herb 1913- *IntMPA 1977*
Allen, Herbert 1927- *AmSCAP 1966*
Allen, Hugh 1886-1966 *Film 2, WhScrn 2*
Allen, Inglis d1943 *NotNAT B*
Allen, Irving 1905- *FilmgC, IntMPA 1977*
Allen, Irwin 1916- *CmMov, FilmgC, IntMPA 1977, NewYTET*
Allen, Ivan, Jr. 1911- *CelR 3*
Allen, Jack 1907- *WhoThe 16*
Allen, Jack Major *Film 1*
Allen, Jane Marie 1916-1970 *WhScrn 2, WhoHol B*
Allen, Jay Presson 1922- *McGWD, NotNAT, WomWMM*
Allen, Jim *ConDr 1977C*
Allen, Joe 1888-1955 *WhScrn 1, WhScrn 2, WhoHol B*
Allen, John Piers 1912- *WhoThe 16*
Allen, Jonelle *WhoHol A*

Allen, Joseph 1840-1917 *NotNAT B*
Allen, Joseph, Jr. 1918-1962 *MotPP, WhScrn 1, WhScrn 2, WhoHol B*
Allen, Joseph, Jr. 1918-1963 *NotNAT B*
Allen, Joseph, Sr. 1872-1952 *Film 1, Film 2, NotNAT B, WhScrn 1, WhScrn 2, WhoHol B*
Allen, Judith 1913- *ThFT, WhoHol A*
Allen, Kelcey 1875-1951 *NotNAT B, WhThe*
Allen, Lester 1891-1949 *Film 2, NotNAT B, WhScrn 1, WhScrn 2, WhoHol B*
Allen, Lewis 1905- *FilmgC, IntMPA 1977*
Allen, Lewis M 1922- *BiE&WWA, FilmgC, NotNAT*
Allen, Louise d1909 *NotNAT B, WhoStg 1908*
Allen, Marguerite *Film 2*
Allen, Maude d1956 *WhScrn 1, WhScrn 2, WhoHol B*
Allen, Mel 1913- *IntMPA 1977, NewYTET*
Allen, Norma *WomWMM B*
Allen, Patrick 1927- *FilmgC, WhoHol A, WhoThe 16*
Allen, Penny *WhoHol A*
Allen, Percy d1959 *NotNAT B*
Allen, Phyllis 1861-1938 *Film 1, Film 2, TwYS, WhScrn 1, WhScrn 2, WhoHol B*
Allen, Rae 1926- *BiE&WWA, NotNAT, WhoHol A, WhoThe 16*
Allen, Reginald 1905- *BiE&WWA, NotNAT*
Allen, Rex 1922- *FilmgC, IntMPA 1977, WhoHol A*
Allen, Ricca *Film 1, Film 2*
Allen, Richard Gould 1924- *AmSCAP 1966*
Allen, Rita d1968 *BiE&WWA, NotNAT B*
Allen, Robert 1906- *IntMPA 1977, WhoHol A*
Allen, Robert E 1920- *AmSCAP 1966*
Allen, Robert F 1928- *AmSCAP 1966*
Allen, Sam 1861-1934 *Film 2, WhScrn 1, WhScrn 2, WhoHol B*
Allen, Seth *WhoHol A*
Allen, Sheila 1932- *WhoThe 16*
Allen, Sian Barbara *WhoHol A*
Allen, Steve 1921- *AmSCAP 1966, BiE&WWA, CelR 3, FilmgC, IntMPA 1977, NewYTET, WhoHol A*
Allen, Susan Westford d1944 *NotNAT B*
Allen, Tex *Film 1*
Allen, Vera 1897- *BiE&WWA, NotNAT, PIP&P, WhThe*
Allen, Viola 1867-1948 *FamA&A, NotNAT B*
Allen, Viola 1869-1948 *Film 1, OxThe, WhScrn 2, WhThe, WhoHol B, WhoStg 1906, WhoStg 1908*
Allen, Vivian Beaumont d1962 *NotNAT B, PIP&P*
Allen, Willi *Film 2*
Allen, William d1647 *OxThe*
Allen, Woody 1935- *CelR 3, FilmgC, IntMPA 1977, MovMk, NotNAT, NotNAT A, WhoHol A, WhoThe 16*
Allenby, Frank 1898-1953 *WhThe*
Allenby, Peggy 1905-1967 *WhThe*
Allenby, Thomas 1861-1933 *WhScrn 1, WhScrn 2, WhoHol B*
Allentuck, Max 1911- *BiE&WWA*
Allers, Franz 1905- *BiE&WWA, CelR 3, NotNAT*
Allerton, Helen 1888-1959 *WhoHol B*
Allerton, Little Helen 1888-1959 *WhScrn 1, WhScrn 2*
Alley, Ben d1970 *WhoHol B*
Alleyn, Edward 1566-1626 *CnThe, NotNAT A, NotNAT B, OxThe, PIP&P*
Allgeier, Sepp 1890-1968 *FilmgC*

Allgood, Maire O'Neill 1887-1952 OxThe
Allgood, Sara 1883-1950 CnThe, Film 2, FilmgC,
   MotPP, OxThe, PIP&P, Vers A, WhScrn 1,
   WhScrn 2, WhThe, WhoHol B
Allgood, Sara 1893-1950 MovMk
Allgood, Sarah 1883-1950 NotNAT B
Alliluyeva, Svetlana 1926- CelR 3
Allinson, Michael BiE&WWA, NotNAT,
   WhoThe 16
Allio, Rene 1924- BiDFlm, FilmgC, OxFilm,
   WorEnF
Allison, Fran IntMPA 1977, NewYTET
Allison, John A 1914- AmSCAP 1966
Allison, May 1895- Film 1, Film 2, MotPP,
   TwYS, WhoHol A
Allison, Steve 1916-1969 WhScrn 1, WhScrn 2,
   WhoHol B
Allister, Claud 1891-1967 WhThe
Allister, Claud 1891-1970 FilmgC
Allister, Claud 1893-1970 WhScrn 1, WhScrn 2
Allister, Claud 1894-1970 WhoHol B
Allister, Claude 1891-1970 MovMk
Allister, Claude 1894-1970 Film 2
Allman, Elvia WhoHol A
Allman, Michael L 1911- AmSCAP 1966
Allton, Minette 1916- AmSCAP 1966
Allworth, Frank Film 2
Allwyn, Astrid 1909- FilmgC, ThFT, WhoHol A
Allyn, Alyce d1976 WhoHol C
Allyn, Lilly 1866-1944 WhScrn 1, WhScrn 2
Allyson, June 1917- BiDFlm, FilmgC,
   IntMPA 1977, MGM, MotPP, MovMk,
   WhoHol A, WorEnF
Allyson, June 1926- OxFilm
Alma-Tadema, Sir Lawrence 1836-1912
   NotNAT B, OxThe, PIP&P
Almar The Clown WhScrn 1, WhScrn 2
Almeida, Laurindo 1917- AmSCAP 1966
Almendros, Nestor 1930- OxFilm
Almond, Paul 1931- FilmgC, IntMPA 1977
Almqist, Carl Jonas Love 1793-1866 OxThe
Almroth, Grete Film 1
Aloma, Harold David 1908- AmSCAP 1966
Aloni, Nissim 1926- CnThe, REnWD
Alonso, Julio 1906-1955 WhScrn 1, WhScrn 2,
   WhoHol B
Alonso Millan, Juan Jose 1936- CroCD
Alonzo, John A FilmgC
Alov, Alexander 1923- DcFM
Alpar, Gitta 1900- WhThe
Alper, Murray 1904- Vers B
Alperson, Edward L 1896-1969 FilmgC
Alperson, Edward Lee, Jr. 1925- AmSCAP 1966
Alpert, Herb 1937- CelR 3, WhoHol A
Alpert, Mickey 1904-1965 NotNAT B
Alpert, Milton I 1904-1965 AmSCAP 1966
Alpert, Pauline AmSCAP 1966
Alphonsine 1829-1883 NotNAT B, OxThe
Alsen, Elsa 1881-1975 Film 2, WhScrn 2,
   WhoHol C
Alsop, Joseph 1910- CelR 3
Alsop, Stewart 1914- CelR 3
Alston, Walter 1911- CelR 3
Alstrup, Carl 1877-1942 WhScrn 2
Alswang, Ralph 1916- BiE&WWA, NotNAT,
   PIP&P, WhoThe 16
Alt, Natalie WhThe
Altem, Mademoiselle Film 2
Altendorf, Wolfgang 1921- CnMD, CroCD
Alter, Lottie WhoStg 1906, WhoStg 1908
Alter, Louis 1902- AmSCAP 1966
Alterman, Joseph George 1919- IntMPA 1977
Alterman, Nathan 1910-1970 REnWD
Althoff, Charles R 1890-1962 NotNAT B,

WhScrn 1, WhScrn 2, WhoHol B
Althouse, Earl F 1893-1971 WhScrn 1, WhScrn 2,
   WhoHol B
Altman, Arthur AmSCAP 1966
Altman, Charles BiE&WWA
Altman, Frieda 1904- BiE&WWA, NotNAT,
   WhoHol A
Altman, Richard 1932- BiE&WWA, NotNAT
Altman, Robert 1922- FilmgC
Altman, Robert 1925- BiDFlm, CelR 3,
   IntMPA 1977, MovMk, OxFilm
Altman, Ruth BiE&WWA, WhThe
Alton, John 1901- FilmgC, IntMPA 1977,
   WorEnF
Alton, Robert 1897-1957 EncMT
Alton, Robert 1903-1957 CmMov, FilmgC,
   NotNAT B
Alton, Robert 1906-1957 WorEnF
Alvarado, Don 1900-1967 FilmgC, WhScrn 1,
   WhScrn 2
Alvarado, Don 1904-1967 Film 2, TwYS,
   WhoHol B
Alvardo, Don 1900-1967 MotPP, MovMk
Alvarez, Signor WhoStg 1908
Alvarez, Albert Raymond 1861-1933 NotNAT B
Alvarez, Alejandro Rodriguez McGWD
Alvarez, Carmen BiE&WWA, NotNAT
Alvarez, Luis 1911- CelR 3
Alvarez, Santiago OxFilm
Alvarez Quintero, Joaquin 1873-1944 McGWD,
   ModWD, OxThe
Alvarez Quintero, Serafin 1871-1938 McGWD,
   ModWD, OxThe
Alvin, John 1917- IntMPA 1977, WhoHol A
Alwyn, William 1905- FilmgC, IntMPA 1977,
   OxFilm, WorEnF
Alyn, Kirk 1910- WhoHol A
Alyoshin, Samuil 1913- CnMD, ModWD
Amado, Jorge 1912- CelR 3
Amadori, Luis Cesar 1902- DcFM
Amaral, Nestor 1913-1962 AmSCAP 1966
Amarante, Estevao 1890-1952 WhScrn 1,
   WhScrn 2
Amateau, Rod NewYTET
Amateau, Rod 1923- FilmgC
Amateau, Rod 1927- IntMPA 1977
Amatniek, Kathie WomWMM B
Amato, Giuseppe 1899-1964 FilmgC, WhScrn 2
Amato, Pasquale d1942 WhoHol B
Amaya, Carmen 1913-1963 NotNAT B,
   WhScrn 1, WhScrn 2, WhoHol B
Amber, Mabel d1945 NotNAT B
Amber, Maude d1938 NotNAT B
Amberg, Gustave 1844-1921 NotNAT B
Ambesser, Axel Von 1910- CnMD
Ambient, Mark 1860-1937 NotNAT B, WhThe
Ambler, Eric 1909- FilmgC, OxFilm
Ambler, Joss 1900-1959 FilmgC, WhScrn 1,
   WhScrn 2, WhoHol B
Ambrogini, Angelo McGWD
Ambrosi, Marietta NotNAT A
Ambrosio, Arturo 1869-1960 DcFM, OxFilm
Ameche, Don 1908- BiE&WWA, CmMov,
   EncMT, FilmgC, IntMPA 1977, MotPP,
   MovMk, WhoHol A, WhoThe 16
Ameche, Don 1910- OxFilm
Ameipsias OxThe
Ames, Adrienne d1947 MotPP, NotNAT B,
   WhoHol B
Ames, Adrienne 1907-1947 ThFT
Ames, Adrienne 1909-1947 WhScrn 1, WhScrn 2
Ames, Florenz 1884- WhThe
Ames, Gerald 1881-1933 Film 1, Film 2,
   NotNAT B, WhScrn 1, WhScrn 2, WhThe,

Anderson, Judith 1898- *BiE&WWA, CelR 3,*
  CnThe, FamA&A, FilmgC, IntMPA 1977,
  MotPP, MovMk, NotNAT, OxFilm, OxThe,
  WhoHol A, WhoThe 16
Anderson, Julia 1864-1950 *NotNAT B*
Anderson, Lawrence 1893-1939 *WhScrn 2,*
  WhThe
Anderson, Leroy 1908- *AmSCAP 1966,*
  BiE&WWA, NotNAT
Anderson, Lillian 1881-1962 *WhScrn 2*
Anderson, Lindsay 1923- *BiDFlm, DcFM,*
  FilmgC, IntMPA 1977, MovMk, NotNAT,
  OxFilm, WhoThe 16, WorEnF
Anderson, Madeline *WomWMM A,*
  WomWMM B
Anderson, Marian 1902- *CelR 3*
Anderson, Mary 1859-1940 *FamA&A, Film 1,*
  Film 2, MotPP, NotNAT A, NotNAT B,
  OxThe, WhThe, WhoStg 1906,
  WhoStg 1908
Anderson, Mary 1920- *FilmgC, WhoHol A*
Anderson, Max 1914-1959 *FilmgC*
Anderson, Maxwell 1888-1959 *AmSCAP 1966,*
  CnMD, CnThe, CroCD, EncMT, FilmgC,
  McGWD, ModWD, NewMT, NotNAT A,
  NotNAT B, OxThe, PIP&P, REnWD,
  WhThe, WorEnF
Anderson, Michael 1920- *BiDFlm, CmMov,*
  FilmgC, IntMPA 1977, MovMk, WorEnF
Anderson, Michael, Jr. 1943- *FilmgC,*
  IntMPA 1977, WhoHol A
Anderson, Mignon *Film 1, MotPP*
Anderson, Nellie *Film 1*
Anderson, Percy d1928 *NotNAT B*
Anderson, Phyllis Stohl d1956 *NotNAT B*
Anderson, R Alex 1894- *AmSCAP 1966*
Anderson, Richard 1926- *BiE&WWA, FilmgC,*
  MovMk, NotNAT, WhoHol A
Anderson, Robert *Film 1, Film 2*
Anderson, Robert 1917- *BiE&WWA, CelR 3,*
  CnMD, ConDr 1977, CroCD, McGWD,
  ModWD, NatPD, NotNAT, WhoThe 16
Anderson, Roland *IntMPA 1977*
Anderson, Rona 1926- *FilmgC*
Anderson, Rona 1928- *WhoThe 16*
Anderson, Sherwood 1876-1941 *NotNAT B*
Anderson, Sylvia *IntMPA 1977, WomWMM*
Anderson, Thomas *WhoHol A*
Anderson, Warner 1911- *FilmgC, IntMPA 1977,*
  MotPP, MovMk, WhoHol A
Anderson, William 1916- *AmSCAP 1966*
Anderson, William H 1911- *IntMPA 1977*
Andersson, Bibi 1935- *BiDFlm, CelR 3, FilmgC,*
  MotPP, OxFilm, WhoHol A, WorEnF
Andersson, Bibi 1936- *MovMk*
Andersson, Bibi *see also* Anderson, Bibi
Andersson, Harriet 1932- *BiDFlm, FilmgC,*
  OxFilm, WhoHol A, WorEnF
Andes, Keith 1920- *BiE&WWA, FilmgC,*
  IntMPA 1977, MotPP, NotNAT, WhoHol A
Andjaparidze, Marija *WomWMM*
Andor, Paul *WhoHol A*
Andra, Anny *Film 2*
Andra, Fern 1893-1974 *WhScrn 2, WhoHol B*
Andrade, Jorge 1922- *REnWD*
Andre, Fabian 1910-1960 *AmSCAP 1966*
Andre, Gaby d1972 *WhScrn 2, WhoHol B*
Andre, Gwili 1908-1959 *MotPP, NotNAT B,*
  WhScrn 1, WhScrn 2, WhoHol B
Andre, John 1751-1780 *NotNAT B, PIP&P*
Andre, Lona *WhoHol A*
Andre, Lona 1915- *ThFT*
Andre, Victor *Film 1*
Andreev, Leonid Nikolayevich 1871-1919 *ModWD*

Andreeva-Babakhan, Anna Misaakovna 1923-
  WhThe
Andreini, Francesco 1548-1624 *OxThe, PIP&P*
Andreini, Giovanni Battista 1578?-1654 *OxThe*
Andreini, Isabella Canali 1562-1604 *OxThe,*
  PIP&P
Andreini, Virginia Ramponi 1583?-1627? *OxThe*
Andreini, Virginia Rotari *OxThe*
Andres, Stefan 1906-1970 *CnMD, CroCD*
Andress, Ursula 1936- *BiDFlm, CelR 3, FilmgC,*
  IntMPA 1977, MotPP, MovMk, OxFilm,
  WhoHol A, WorEnF
Andretti, Mario 1940- *CelR 3*
Andreva, Stella *WhThe*
Andrew, M *Film 2*
Andrews, Adora d1956 *NotNAT B, WhoHol B*
Andrews, Albert Gracia d1950 *NotNAT B*
Andrews, Ann 1895- *BiE&WWA, NotNAT,*
  WhThe, WhoHol A
Andrews, Bart d1969 *WhScrn 2*
Andrews, Charles *NewYTET*
Andrews, Dana *MotPP, WhoHol A*
Andrews, Dana 1909- *BiDFlm, FilmgC, MovMk,*
  OxFilm
Andrews, Dana 1912- *BiE&WWA, CmMov,*
  IntMPA 1977, WhoThe 16, WorEnF
Andrews, Del 1903?- *TwYS A*
Andrews, Eamonn 1922- *IntMPA 1977,*
  NewYTET
Andrews, Edward *IntMPA 1977, MotPP,*
  WhoHol A
Andrews, Edward 1914- *NotNAT*
Andrews, Edward 1915- *FilmgC*
Andrews, Elizabeth 1821-1910 *NotNAT B*
Andrews, Frank *Film 2*
Andrews, Harry 1911- *CmMov, CnThe, FilmgC,*
  IntMPA 1977, MotPP, MovMk, WhoHol A,
  WhoThe 16
Andrews, Julie *MotPP, PIP&P, WhoHol A*
Andrews, Julie 1934- *CmMov, FilmgC*
Andrews, Julie 1935- *BiDFlm, BiE&WWA,*
  CelR 3, EncMT, FamA&A, IntMPA 1977,
  MovMk, NotNAT, NotNAT A, OxFilm,
  WhThe, WorEnF
Andrews, LaVerne 1913-1967 *FilmgC*
Andrews, LaVerne 1915-1967 *MotPP, WhScrn 1,*
  WhScrn 2, WhoHol B
Andrews, Lois 1924-1968 *FilmgC, MotPP,*
  NotNAT B, WhScrn 1, WhScrn 2,
  WhoHol B
Andrews, Louise d1950 *NotNAT B*
Andrews, Lyle D d1950 *NotNAT B*
Andrews, Maidie *WhThe*
Andrews, Mark 1875-1939 *AmSCAP 1966*
Andrews, Maxene 1916- *MotPP, WhoHol A*
Andrews, Maxine 1916- *FilmgC*
Andrews, Nancy 1924- *BiE&WWA, NotNAT,*
  WhoThe 16
Andrews, Orville d1968 *WhScrn 1, WhScrn 2*
Andrews, Patti 1918- *WhoHol A*
Andrews, Patty 1918- *FilmgC, MotPP*
Andrews, Robert 1895- *WhThe*
Andrews, Robert Hardy *IntMPA 1977*
Andrews, Stanley 1892-1969 *Vers B, WhScrn 1,*
  WhScrn 2, WhoHol B
Andrews, Tige 1923?- *FilmgC, WhoHol A*
Andrews, Tod 1920-1972 *BiE&WWA,*
  NotNAT B, WhScrn 2, WhThe, WhoHol B
Andrews Sisters, The *FilmgC, HolP 40, MotPP,*
  MovMk, PIP&P A
Andreyev, Leonid Nikolaievitch 1871-1919
  NotNAT B
Andreyev, Leonid Nikolaivich 1871-1919 *OxThe*
Andreyev, Leonid Nikolayevich 1871-1919 *CnMD,*

Anzarut, Raymond 1912- *IntMPA 1977*
Anzengruber, Ludwig 1839-1889 *McGWD,*
    NotNAT B, OxThe, REnWD
Aoki, Tsura d1961 *WhoHol B*
Aoki, Tsuru d1961 *MotPP*
Aoki, Tsuru 1892-1962 *Film 1, Film 2, TwYS*
Aoki, Tsuru 1893-1961 *WhScrn 1, WhScrn 2*
Apfel, Edwin R 1934- *IntMPA 1977*
Apfel, Oscar C d1938 *Film 1, Film 2, TwYS,*
    TwYS A, WhScrn 1, WhScrn 2, WhoHol B
Aplon, Boris *WhoHol A*
Apollinaire, Guillaume 1880-1918 *CnMD,*
    McGWD, ModWD, NotNAT B, REnWD
Apollodorus *OxThe*
Apollon, Dave d1972 *WhoHol B*
Apolon, Uni *Film 2*
Appareti, Luigi 1924- *AmSCAP 1966*
Appel, Anna 1888-1963 *NotNAT B, WhScrn 1,*
    WhScrn 2, WhoHol B
Appel, Wendy *WomWMM*
Appelbaum, Gertrude 1918- *BiE&WWA,*
    NotNAT
Appell, David 1922- *AmSCAP 1966*
Appell, Don *BiE&WWA, ConDr 1977D,*
    NewYTET
Appia, Adolph 1862-1928 *CnThe*
Appia, Adolphe 1862-1928 *NotNAT A,*
    NotNAT B, OxThe, PIP&P
Applebaum, Stanley 1922- *AmSCAP 1966*
Appleby, Dorothy 1908- *WhThe, WhoHol A*
Applegarth, Jonas 1920-1965 *WhScrn 1,*
    WhScrn 2
Applegate, Eddie *WhoHol A*
Applegate, Hazel 1886-1959 *WhScrn 1,*
    WhScrn 2, WhoHol B
Applegate, Roy *Film 2*
Appleman, Herbert 1933- *NatPD*
Appleton, George J d1926 *NotNAT B*
Applewhite, Eric Leon 1897-1973 *WhoHol B*
Applewhite, Ric 1897-1973 *WhScrn 2*
Applin, George d1949 *NotNAT B*
Appling, Bert *Film 1*
Apstein, Theodore 1918- *BiE&WWA, NotNAT*
Aquanetta *FilmgC*
Aquistapace, Jean 1882-1952 *WhScrn 1,*
    WhScrn 2
Aragon, Louis 1897- *ModWD*
Arakelian, Hagop 1894- *DcFM*
Aranha, Ray *NatPD*
Arbeid, Ben 1924- *FilmgC, IntMPA 1977*
Arbenina, Stella 1887- *WhThe*
Arbenz, Arabella 1945-1965 *WhScrn 1,*
    WhScrn 2
Arbuckle, Andrew *Film 1, Film 2*
Arbuckle, Dorothy Fry 1910- *AmSCAP 1966*
Arbuckle, Fatty 1887-1933 *WorEnF*
Arbuckle, Macklyn 1866-1931 *Film 1, TwYS,*
    WhScrn 1, WhScrn 2
Arbuckle, Mrs. Maclyn *Film 2*
Arbuckle, Maclyn 1863-1931 *NotNAT B*
Arbuckle, Maclyn 1866-1931 *Film 2, WhThe,*
    WhoHol B
Arbuckle, Maclyn 1867-1931 *WhoStg 1906,*
    WhoStg 1908
Arbuckle, Roscoe 1881-1932 *OxFilm*
Arbuckle, Roscoe 1887-1933 *BiDFlm, NotNAT B,*
    WorEnF
Arbuckle, Roscoe Fatty 1887-1933 *Film 1, Film 2,*
    FilmgC, MotPP, MovMk, TwYS, TwYS A,
    WhScrn 1, WhScrn 2, WhoHol B
Arbury, Guy 1907-1972 *WhScrn 2*
Arbusov, Alexey Nikolayevitch 1908- *CnMD*
Arbuzov, Aleksei Nikolayevich 1908- *OxThe*
Arbuzov, Alexey Nikolayevich 1908- *CnThe,*

McGWD, ModWD
Arcady, Jean 1912- *DcFM*
Arcaro, Eddie 1916- *CelR 3*
Arcaro, Flavia 1876-1937 *NotNAT B*
Archainbaud, George *IntMPA 1977*
Archainbaud, George 1890-1959 *FilmgC, TwYS A,*
    WhScrn 2, WhoHol B
Archainbaud, George *see also* Archinbaud, George
Archard, Bernard 1922- *FilmgC*
Archdall, Mabel *Film 2*
Archer, Anne *WhoHol A*
Archer, Anne 1912-1959 *WhScrn 1, WhScrn 2*
Archer, Belle 1858-1900 *NotNAT B*
Archer, Fred R d1963 *NotNAT B*
Archer, Harry *Film 1*
Archer, Harry 1888-1960 *AmSCAP 1966,*
    NewMT, NotNAT B
Archer, Joe *WhThe*
Archer, John 1915- *BiE&WWA, FilmgC,*
    IntMPA 1977, Vers A, WhThe, WhoHol A
Archer, Nicholas *NewYTET*
Archer, Osceola 1890- *NotNAT*
Archer, Thomas d1848 *NotNAT B*
Archer, William 1856-1924 *CnMD, ModWD,*
    NotNAT A, NotNAT B, OxThe, PIP&P,
    WhThe
Archerd, Army *IntMPA 1977, WhoHol A*
Archibald, Douglas 1919- *ConDr 1977*
Archibald, James 1920- *IntMPA 1977*
Archibald, Nancy *WomWMM*
Archibald, Nate 1948- *CelR 3*
Archibald, William 1924-1970 *BiE&WWA,*
    McGWD, NotNAT B
Archinbaud, George 1890-1959 *WhScrn 1*
Archinbaud, George *see also* Archainbaud, George
Ardell, John E 1881-1949 *WhScrn 1, WhScrn 2*
Arden, Eddie 1908-1952 *WhScrn 1, WhScrn 2*
Arden, Edwin Hunter Pendleton 1864-1918 *Film 1,*
    NotNAT B, WhScrn 2, WhThe, WhoHol B,
    WhoStg 1906, WhoStg 1908
Arden, Eve 1912- *BiE&WWA, CmMov, EncMT,*
    FilmgC, IntMPA 1977, MotPP, MovMk,
    NotNAT, ThFT, WhoHol A, WhoThe 16
Arden, Jane *ConDr 1977*
Arden, John 1930- *CnMD, CnThe, ConDr 1977,*
    CroCD, McGWD, ModWD, NotNAT,
    OxThe, PIP&P, REnWD, WhoThe 16
Arden, Mary 1910- *IntMPA 1977*
Arden, Mildred *Film 2*
Arden, Robert 1921- *FilmgC, WhoHol A*
Arden, Victor 1893-1962 *NotNAT B, WhScrn 1,*
    WhScrn 2
Ardrey, Robert 1908- *BiE&WWA, CelR 3,*
    CnMD, ConDr 1977, ModWD, NotNAT,
    PIP&P, WhThe, WorEnF
Arellano, George I 1923- *AmSCAP 1966*
Arenas, Miguel 1902-1965 *WhScrn 1, WhScrn 2*
Arendt, Hannah 1906- *CelR 3*
Arens, Ruth *WomWMM B*
Arent, Arthur 1904-1972 *BiE&WWA, CnMD,*
    McGWD, ModWD, NotNAT B
Aretino, Pietro 1492-1556 *CnThe, McGWD,*
    NotNAT B, OxThe, PIP&P, REnWD
Arey, Wayne *Film 1*
Argentina d1936 *NotNAT B, WhThe*
Argentina, Sareno S 1917- *AmSCAP 1966*
Argentinita 1905-1945 *NotNAT B*
Argento, Dario 1943- *FilmgC*
Argento, Dominick 1927- *AmSCAP 1966*
Argus, Edwin *Film 2*
Argyle, Pearl 1910-1949 *WhScrn 2, WhThe*
Arinbasarova, Natalia *WhoHol A*
Arion, Of Lesbos 625?BC-585BC *OxThe*
Ariosto, Lodovico 1474-1533 *CnThe, OxThe,*

REnWD
Ariosto, Ludovico 1474-1533 McGWD,
    NotNAT B, PIP&P
Aristophanes 448?BC-385?BC CnThe, McGWD,
    OxThe, PIP&P, REnWD
Aristophanes 448?BC-388?BC NotNAT B
Aristotle 384BC-322BC CnThe, NotNAT B,
    OxThe, PIP&P, REnWD
Arkell, Elizabeth WhThe
Arkell, Reginald 1882-1959 NotNAT B, WhThe
Arkin, Alan 1934- AmSCAP 1966, BiE&WWA,
    CelR 3, FilmgC, IntMPA 1977, MotPP,
    MovMk, NotNAT, WhoThe A, WhoThe 16
Arkin, David 1906- AmSCAP 1966
Arkin, Robert B 1923- AmSCAP 1966
Arkoff, Samuel Z 1918- FilmgC, IntMPA 1977,
    WorEnF
Arlecchino OxThe
Arledge, John 1906-1947 WhScrn 1, WhScrn 2,
    WhoHol B
Arledge, Roone NewYTET
Arlega, Sophie Film 2
Arlen, Betty 1904-1966 WhScrn 2, WhoHol B
Arlen, Harold 1905- AmSCAP 1966, BiE&WWA,
    CelR 3, EncMT, FilmgC, IntMPA 1977,
    NewMT, NotNAT, OxFilm, WhoThe 16
Arlen, Harold 1906- PIP&P
Arlen, Jeanne Burns 1917- AmSCAP 1966
Arlen, Jerry BiE&WWA
Arlen, Judith 1914-1968 WhScrn 2, WhoHol B
Arlen, Michael 1895-1956 NotNAT B, WhThe
Arlen, Richard d1976 WhoHol C
Arlen, Richard 1898-1976 FilmgC
Arlen, Richard 1899-1976 MotPP, MovMk,
    TwYS
Arlen, Richard 1900-1976 Film 2
Arlen, Stephen 1913- WhThe
Arletty 1898- BiDFlm, FilmgC, MovMk,
    OxFilm, WhoHol A, WorEnF
Arley, Cecil Film 1
Arley, Cecile WhScrn 2
Arling, Arthur E 1906- FilmgC, IntMPA 1977,
    WorEnF
Arling, Charles Film 1
Arling, Joyce 1911- BiE&WWA, WhThe,
    WhoHol A
Arlington, Billy 1873- WhThe
Arliss, Florence d1950 Film 2, NotNAT B,
    WhScrn 1, WhScrn 2, WhoHol B
Arliss, George 1868-1946 FamA&A, Film 2,
    FilmgC, MotPP, MovMk, NotNAT A,
    NotNAT B, OxFilm, OxThe, PIP&P, TwYS,
    WhScrn 1, WhScrn 2, WhThe, WhoHol B,
    WhoStg 1908, WorEnF
Arliss, Leslie 1901- FilmgC, WorEnF
Armand, Margot Film 2
Armand, Teddy V 1874-1947 WhScrn 1,
    WhScrn 2
Armand-Bernard, Monsieur Film 2
Armat, Thomas 1866-1948 NotNAT B
Armbruster, Robert AmSCAP 1966
Armen, Kay AmSCAP 1966
Armendariz, Pedro 1912-1963 FilmgC, MotPP,
    MovMk, NotNAT B, WhScrn 1, WhScrn 2,
    WhoHol B, WorEnF
Armentrout, Lee 1909- AmSCAP 1966
Armetta, Henry 1888-1945 Film 2, FilmgC,
    MovMk, NotNAT B, TwYS, Vers A,
    WhScrn 1, WhScrn 2, WhoHol B
Armida 1913- Film 2
Armin, Robert 1568?-1611? NotNAT B, OxThe
Armitage, Buford 1898- BiE&WWA
Armitage, Merle 1893- NotNAT A
Armitage, Walter W 1907-1953 NotNAT B,

WhScrn 1, WhScrn 2, WhoHol B
Armocida, William Francis 1922- AmSCAP 1966
Armour, Reginald 1905- IntMPA 1977
Arms, Russell WhoHol A
Armstrong, Anne 1927- CelR 3
Armstrong, Anthony 1897- WhThe
Armstrong, Barney 1870- WhThe
Armstrong, Billy Film 1
Armstrong, Clyde 1879-1937 WhScrn 1,
    WhScrn 2
Armstrong, Edwin H 1890-1954 NotNAT B
Armstrong, Gordon 1937- IntMPA 1977
Armstrong, Harry 1879-1951 AmSCAP 1966,
    NotNAT B
Armstrong, Sir Harry Gloster d1938 NotNAT B
Armstrong, John NatPD
Armstrong, Lillian Hardin 1902- AmSCAP 1966
Armstrong, Louis 1900-1971 AmSCAP 1966,
    FilmgC, MovMk, WhoHol B
Armstrong, Louis Satchmo 1900-1971 WhScrn 1,
    WhScrn 2
Armstrong, Margot Film 2
Armstrong, Marguerite Film 1, Film 2
Armstrong, Ned d1961 NotNAT B
Armstrong, Neil 1930- CelR 3
Armstrong, Paul 1869-1915 NotNAT B, OxThe,
    WhThe, WhoStg 1908
Armstrong, R G 1920?- FilmgC, WhoHol A
Armstrong, Robert 1890-1973 FilmgC, HolP 30,
    WhoHol B
Armstrong, Robert 1896-1973 Film 2, MovMk,
    TwYS, Vers B, WhScrn 2, WhThe
Armstrong, Sinclair 1912- AmSCAP 1966
Armstrong, Suzanne WomWMM B
Armstrong, Sydney WhoStg 1906, WhoStg 1908
Armstrong, Todd 1939- FilmgC
Armstrong, Will H 1869-1943 NotNAT B,
    WhScrn 1, WhScrn 2, WhoHol B
Armstrong, Will Steven 1930-1969 BiE&WWA,
    NotNAT B, WhThe
Armstrong, William NotNAT B
Armstrong, William 1882-1952 NotNAT B,
    OxThe, WhThe
Arna, Lissi d1964 WhoHol B
Arna, Lissy d1964 NotNAT B, WhScrn 1,
    WhScrn 2
Arnaboldi, Joseph P 1920- AmSCAP 1966
Arnall, Ellis Gibbs 1907- IntMPA 1977
Arnall, Julia 1931- FilmgC
Arnatt, John 1917- FilmgC, WhoThe 16
Arnatt, Ronald 1930- AmSCAP 1966
Arnaud, Georges 1917- McGWD
Arnaud, Leo 1904- IntMPA 1977
Arnaud, Yvonne 1892-1958 FilmgC, NotNAT A,
    NotNAT B, OxThe, PIP&P, WhScrn 1,
    WhScrn 2, WhThe, WhoHol B
Arnaz, Desi NewYTET, WhoHol A
Arnaz, Desi 1915- FilmgC
Arnaz, Desi 1917- IntMPA 1977
Arnaz, Desi, Jr. 1953- IntMPA 1977, WhoHol A
Arndt, Felix 1889-1918 AmSCAP 1966,
    NotNAT B
Arndt, Nola AmSCAP 1966
Arne, Peter MotPP
Arne, Peter 1922- FilmgC, IntMPA 1977
Arne, Thomas Augustine d1778 NotNAT B
Arnell, Peter IntMPA 1977
Arness, James 1923- CelR 3, FilmgC,
    IntMPA 1977, MotPP, MovMk, NewYTET,
    WhoHol A
Arngrin, Stevan WhoHol A
Arnheim, Gus 1897-1955 AmSCAP 1966
Arnheim, Gus 1899-1955 WhScrn 1, WhScrn 2,
    WhoHol B

Arnheim, Rudolf *OxFilm*
Arnhein, Gus 1897-1955 *Film 2*
Arniches, Carlos 1866-1943 *CnMD*
Arniches Y Barrera, Carlos 1866-1943 *McGWD*
Arno, Siegfried 1895-1975 *Film 2*
Arno, Sig 1895-1975 *BiE&WWA, FilmgC, MovMk, NotNAT B, Vers A, WhScrn 2, WhoHol C*
Arnold, Bernard 1915- *AmSCAP 1966*
Arnold, Cecile d1931 *Film 1, WhScrn 2, WhoHol B*
Arnold, Danny *NewYTET*
Arnold, Danny 1925- *IntMPA 1977*
Arnold, Dorothy *WhoHol A*
Arnold, Eddie *WhoHol A*
Arnold, Eddie d1962 *NotNAT B*
Arnold, Eddy 1918- *CelR 3, IntMPA 1977*
Arnold, Edward d1966 *WhoHol B*
Arnold, Edward 1890-1956 *Film 1, FilmgC, MGM, MotPP, MovMk, NotNAT A, NotNAT B, Vers A, WhScrn 1, WhScrn 2*
Arnold, Edward 1890-1957 *OxFilm*
Arnold, Eve *WomWMM A, WomWMM B*
Arnold, Franz 1878-1960 *NotNAT B*
Arnold, Gertrude *Film 2*
Arnold, Helen *Film 1*
Arnold, Jack d1962 *NotNAT B*
Arnold, Jack 1912- *DcFM*
Arnold, Jack 1916- *CmMov, FilmgC, IntMPA 1977, MovMk, WorEnF*
Arnold, Jeanne *WhoHol A*
Arnold, Jessie 1877-1971 *Film 2, WhScrn 2*
Arnold, Laura d1962 *NotNAT B*
Arnold, Lilian d1974 *BiE&WWA, NotNAT B*
Arnold, Mabel 1889-1964 *WhScrn 1, WhScrn 2*
Arnold, Malcolm 1921- *CmMov, FilmgC, OxFilm, WorEnF*
Arnold, Marcella 1911-1937 *WhScrn 2*
Arnold, Matthew 1822-1888 *NotNAT B, OxThe*
Arnold, Phil 1909-1968 *MotPP, Vers A, WhScrn 1, WhScrn 2, WhoHol B*
Arnold, Reggie d1963 *NotNAT B*
Arnold, Samuel James d1852 *NotNAT B*
Arnold, Seth 1885-1955 *NotNAT B, WhScrn 1, WhScrn 2, WhoHol B*
Arnold, Tom d1969 *WhThe*
Arnold, William R 1883-1940 *WhScrn 1, WhScrn 2, WhoHol B*
Arnot, Louise d1919 *NotNAT B*
Arnott, Peter 1931- *BiE&WWA, NotNAT*
Arnoul, Francoise 1931- *BiDFlm, FilmgC, IntMPA 1977, WhoHol A, WorEnF*
Arnould, Sophie 1740-1802 *NotNAT A, NotNAT B*
Arnoux, Alexandre 1884-1973 *McGWD*
Arnoux, Robert 1900-1964 *WhScrn 2*
Arnow, Maxwell *IntMPA 1977*
Arnst, Bobbe *Film 2*
Arnstam, Leo 1905- *DcFM*
Arnt, Charles 1908- *FilmgC, MovMk, Vers A, WhoHol A*
Aromando, Joseph S 1912- *AmSCAP 1966*
Aronson, Boris 1900- *BiE&WWA, CelR 3, CnThe, NotNAT, OxThe, PIP&P, WhoThe 16*
Aronson, Gustaf *Film 1*
Aronson, Rudolph 1856-1919 *NotNAT A, NotNAT B, WhoStg 1906, WhoStg 1908*
Aronstein, Martin 1936- *NotNAT, WhoThe 16*
Arouet, Francois Marie *McGWD, REnWD*
Arquette, Cliff 1905-1974 *AmSCAP 1966, WhScrn 2, WhoHol B*
Arrabal, F *PIP&P*
Arrabal, Fernando 1932- *CnMD, CroCD,*

McGWD, ModWD, WhoThe 16
Arrabal, Fernando 1933- *CnThe, REnWD*
Arras, Harry 1882-1942 *WhScrn 1, WhScrn 2, WhoHol B*
Arrato, Ubaldo 1897-1947 *DcFM*
Arrau *PIP&P*
Arrau, Claudio 1903- *CelR 3*
Arrick, Lawrence 1928- *NotNAT*
Arrowsmith, William 1924- *BiE&WWA, NotNAT*
Arruza, Carlos El Ciclon 1920-1966 *WhScrn 2*
Artaud, Antonin 1896?-1948 *CnThe, CroCD, FilmgC, McGWD, ModWD, NotNAT A, NotNAT B, OxFilm, OxThe, REnWD, WhScrn 2, WorEnF*
Artauld, Antonin *Film 2*
Artega, Sophia *Film 2*
Artemal, Talat 1902-1957 *WhScrn 1, WhScrn 2*
Arthur, Art 1911- *IntMPA 1977*
Arthur, Bea *WhoHol A*
Arthur, Beatrice *BiE&WWA, EncMT, IntMPA 1977, NotNAT*
Arthur, Beatrice 1920?- *CelR 3*
Arthur, Beatrice 1924- *FilmgC*
Arthur, Beatrice 1926- *WhoThe 16*
Arthur, Carol 1935- *BiE&WWA, NotNAT, WhoHol A*
Arthur, Daphne 1925- *WhThe*
Arthur, Edward B 1915- *IntMPA 1977*
Arthur, George K *MotPP*
Arthur, George K 1884-1952 *Film 2*
Arthur, George K 1899- *FilmgC, TwYS, WhoHol A*
Arthur, George K 1900- *MovMk*
Arthur, Hartney J 1917- *BiE&WWA*
Arthur, Helen d1939 *NotNAT B*
Arthur, Jean 1905- *BiDFlm, BiE&WWA, CmMov, FilmgC, MotPP, NotNAT, OxFilm, ThFT, TwYS, WhThe, WhoHol A*
Arthur, Jean 1908- *Film 2, IntMPA 1977, MovMk, WorEnF*
Arthur, Johnny 1883-1951 *Film 2, TwYS, WhScrn 1, WhScrn 2, WhoHol B*
Arthur, Johnny 1884-1952 *Vers A*
Arthur, Joseph 1848-1906 *NotNAT B*
Arthur, Julia 1869-1950 *Film 1, NotNAT B, PIP&P, TwYS, WhScrn 1, WhScrn 2, WhThe, WhoHol B, WhoStg 1906, WhoStg 1908*
Arthur, Karen *WomWMM B*
Arthur, Maureen *WhoHol A*
Arthur, Paul *Film 1*
Arthur, Paul 1859-1928 *NotNAT B, WhThe, WhoStg 1908*
Arthur, Robert d1929 *WhThe*
Arthur, Robert 1909- *FilmgC, IntMPA 1977*
Arthur, Robert 1925- *FilmgC, IntMPA 1977, WhoHol A*
Arthur, Robert 1928- *AmSCAP 1966*
Arthurs, George 1875-1944 *NotNAT B, WhThe*
Artois, Armand D' *NotNAT B*
Artsybashev, Mikhail Petrovich 1878-1927 *CnMD, ModWD*
Artus, Louis 1870- *WhThe*
Artzybashev, Mikhail Petrovitch 1878-1927 *NotNAT B*
Arundale, Grace *WhThe*
Arundale, Sybil 1882-1965 *WhThe*
Arundell, Denis 1898- *FilmgC*
Arundell, Dennis 1898- *WhThe*
Arvan, Jan *WhoHol A*
Arvele, Ritva *WomWMM*
Arvey, Verna 1910- *AmSCAP 1966*
Arvidson, Linda 1884-1949 *Film 1, TwYS,*

WhScrn 1, WhScrn 2, WhoHol B
Arvold, Alfred G 1882-1957 *NotNAT A,*
NotNAT B
Arzner, Dorothy 1900- *DcFM, FilmgC,*
IntMPA 1977, OxFilm, TwYS A,
WomWMM
Asbaje Y Ramirez DeCantillana, Juana I 1651-1695
NotNAT B
Asch, Sholem 1880-1957 *CnMD, CnThe,*
McGWD, ModWD, NotNAT B, REnWD
Asch, Sholom 1880-1957 *OxThe*
Asche, Lily Brayton 1876-1953 *OxThe*
Asche, Oscar d1936 *WhoHol B*
Asche, Oscar 1871-1936 *EncMT, OxThe,*
WhScrn 2, WhThe
Asche, Oscar 1872-1936 *NotNAT A, NotNAT B*
Ascher, Emil 1859-1922 *AmSCAP 1966*
Asena, Orhan 1922- *REnWD*
Ash, Arty d1954 *NotNAT B*
Ash, Gordon d1929 *NotNAT B, WhThe*
Ash, Jerry *Film 1*
Ash, Maie 1888- *WhThe*
Ash, Paul 1891-1958 *AmSCAP 1966*
Ash, Rene 1939- *IntMPA 1977*
Ash, Roy L 1918- *CelR 3*
Ash, Russell 1910-1974 *WhScrn 2, WhoHol B*
Ash, Sam 1884-1951 *WhoHol B*
Ash, Samuel Howard 1884-1951 *WhScrn 1,*
WhScrn 2
Ashby, Hal 1936- *FilmgC, IntMPA 1977*
Ashby, Johnnie *Film 2*
Ashby, Ruth *Film 2*
Ashcroft, Peggy 1907- *BiE&WWA, CnThe,*
FilmgC, NotNAT, NotNAT A, OxThe,
PIP&P, WhoHol A, WhoThe 16
Ashe, Arthur, Jr. 1943- *CelR 3*
Ashe, Warren d1944 *WhoHol B*
Ashe, Warren d1947 *NotNAT B, WhScrn 1,*
WhScrn 2
Asher, Irving 1903- *IntMPA 1977*
Asher, Jack 1916- *CmMov, FilmgC,*
IntMPA 1977
Asher, Jane 1946- *FilmgC, WhoHol A,*
WhoThe 16
Asher, Max 1880-1957 *Film 1, Film 2, MotPP,*
NotNAT B, WhScrn 1, WhScrn 2,
WhoHol B
Asher, Robert 1917?- *FilmgC, IntMPA 1977*
Asher, William 1919?- *FilmgC, NewYTET*
Asherman, Edward M 1913- *AmSCAP 1966*
Asherman, Nat 1909- *AmSCAP 1966*
Ashermann, Otto 1903- *BiE&WWA*
Asherson, Renee 1920- *FilmgC, IntMPA 1977,*
WhoHol A, WhoThe 16
Ashford, Harry d1926 *NotNAT B*
Ashley, Annie d1947 *NotNAT B*
Ashley, Arthur *Film 1*
Ashley, Barbara *BiE&WWA*
Ashley, Beaulah d1965 *WhScrn 2*
Ashley, Beulah d1965 *WhScrn 1*
Ashley, Celeste 1930- *BiE&WWA, NotNAT*
Ashley, Edward 1904- *FilmgC, WhoHol A*
Ashley, Elizabeth 1939- *BiE&WWA, FilmgC,*
IntMPA 1977, MovMk, NotNAT,
WhoHol A, WhoThe 16
Ashley, Helen d1954 *NotNAT B*
Ashley, Iris 1909- *WhThe*
Ashley, John 1934- *IntMPA 1977, WhoHol A*
Ashley, Marta *WomWMM*
Ashley, Minnie 1875-1945 *NotNAT B,*
WhoStg 1906, WhoStg 1908
Ashley, Ted 1922- *BiE&WWA, IntMPA 1977,*
NewYTET, NotNAT
Ashmore, Basil 1915- *WhoThe 16*

Ashmore, Peter 1916- *BiE&WWA, WhThe*
Ashton, Charles *Film 2*
Ashton, Dorrit 1873-1936 *WhScrn 1, WhScrn 2,*
WhoHol B
Ashton, Frederick 1906- *NotNAT A, WhThe*
Ashton, Herbert *Film 2*
Ashton, Sylvia 1880-1940 *Film 1, Film 2,*
NotNAT B, TwYS, WhScrn 1, WhScrn 2,
WhoHol B
Ashton, Vera d1965 *WhScrn 1, WhScrn 2*
Ashton, Winifred *McGWD*
Ashur, Geri *WomWMM B*
Ashwell, Lena 1872-1957 *NotNAT A,*
NotNAT B, OxThe, WhThe, WhoStg 1906,
WhoStg 1908
Asimov, Isaac 1920- *CelR 3*
Askam, Earl 1899-1940 *WhScrn 1, WhScrn 2,*
WhoHol B
Askam, Perry 1898-1961 *NotNAT B, WhScrn 2*
Askan, Perry 1898-1961 *WhoHol B*
Askew, Luke *WhoHol A*
Askey, Arthur Bowden 1900- *FilmgC,*
IntMPA 1977, WhoThe 16
Askin, Harry d1934 *NotNAT B*
Askin, Leon 1920?- *FilmgC, WhoHol A*
Aslan, Gregoire 1908- *FilmgC*
Asmodi, Herbert 1923- *CnMD, CroCD*
Asner, Edward 1925?- *FilmgC, IntMPA 1977,*
WhoHol A
Aspenstrom, Werner 1918- *CnThe, CroCD,*
McGWD, REnWD
Asper, Frank W 1892- *AmSCAP 1966*
Asquith, Anthony 1902-1968 *BiDFlm, CmMov,*
DcFM, FilmgC, MovMk, OxFilm,
WhScrn 1, WhScrn 2, WhThe, WorEnF
Asquith, Elizabeth *Film 1*
Asquith, Mary d1942 *NotNAT B*
Asseyev, Tamara *WomWMM*
Assis *WomWMM*
Astaire, Adele 1898- *BiE&WWA, EncMT,*
Film 1, NotNAT, PIP&P, WhThe
Astaire, Fred 1899- *AmSCAP 1966, BiDFlm,*
BiE&WWA, CelR 3, CmMov, EncMT,
Film 1, FilmgC, MGM, MotPP, MovMk,
NewYTET, NotNAT, NotNAT A, OxFilm,
PIP&P, WhoHol A, WorEnF
Astaire, Fred 1900- *IntMPA 1977, WhThe*
Astangov, Mikhail 1901-1965 *WhScrn 1,*
WhScrn 2, WhoHol B
Astar, Ben *WhoHol A*
Astell, Betty 1912- *Film 2*
Asther, Nils *MotPP*
Asther, Nils 1897- *FilmgC, WhoHol A*
Asther, Nils 1901- *Film 2, TwYS*
Asther, Nils 1902- *MovMk*
Astin, John 1930- *FilmgC, IntMPA 1977,*
WhoHol A
Astley, John *WhThe*
Astley, John d1821 *NotNAT B*
Astley, Philip 1742-1814 *NotNAT B*
Aston, Anthony *OxThe, PIP&P*
Aston, Tony *NotNAT A, NotNAT B*
Astor, Adelaide d1951 *NotNAT B*
Astor, Camille *Film 1, Film 2*
Astor, Gertrude 1889- *WhoHol A*
Astor, Gertrude 1906- *Film 1, Film 2, TwYS*
Astor, Junie 1918-1967 *WhScrn 1, WhScrn 2,*
WhoHol B
Astor, Mary 1906- *BiDFlm, BiE&WWA,*
CelR 3, Film 2, FilmgC, IntMPA 1977,
MGM, MotPP, MovMk, NotNAT A,
OxFilm, ThFT, TwYS, WhoHol A, WorEnF
Astor, Richard 1927- *BiE&WWA, NotNAT*
Astredo, Humbert Allen *WhoHol A*

Astrin, Neal 1906- *AmSCAP 1966*
Astruc, Alexandre 1923- *BiDFlm, DcFM,*
  FilmgC, OxFilm, WorEnF
Asvaghosa *OxThe*
Atay, Cahit 1925- *CnThe, REnWD*
Atchley, Hooper 1887-1943 *NotNAT B,*
  WhScrn 1, WhScrn 2, WhoHol B
Ates, Roscoe *MotPP*
Ates, Roscoe 1892-1962 *Film 2, FilmgC, MovMk,*
  WhScrn 1, WhScrn 2
Ates, Roscoe 1895-1962 *NotNAT B, Vers A,*
  WhoHol B
Atherton, Alice 1860-1899 *NotNAT B*
Atherton, Daisy d1961 *NotNAT B*
Atherton, Ella *Film 2*
Atherton, William 1949- *IntMPA 1977,*
  WhoHol A
Athis, Alfred 1873- *WhThe*
Atienza, Edward 1924- *BiE&WWA, NotNAT,*
  WhoThe 16
Atkerson, Paul 1921- *AmSCAP 1966*
Atkin, Charles 1910- *BiE&WWA*
Atkin, Nancy 1904- *WhThe*
Atkins, Alfred 1900-1941 *NotNAT B, WhScrn 1,*
  WhScrn 2
Atkins, Chet 1924- *CelR 3*
Atkins, Eileen 1934- *FilmgC, NotNAT,*
  WhoHol A, WhoThe 16
Atkins, Robert *Film 1*
Atkins, Robert 1886-1972 *CnThe, OxThe, PIP&P,*
  WhScrn 2, WhThe
Atkinson, Brooks 1894- *BiE&WWA, CelR 3,*
  NotNAT, OxThe
Atkinson, Charles H d1909 *NotNAT B*
Atkinson, David 1921- *BiE&WWA, NotNAT*
Atkinson, Evelyn 1900-1954 *WhScrn 1,*
  WhScrn 2, WhoHol B
Atkinson, Frank 1893-1963 *NotNAT B,*
  WhScrn 1, WhScrn 2, WhoHol B
Atkinson, George A 1877-1968 *Film 2, WhScrn 2*
Atkinson, George H d1955 *NotNAT B*
Atkinson, Harry 1866- *WhThe*
Atkinson, Ione *Film 2*
Atkinson, J Brooks 1894- *WhoThe 16*
Atkinson, Josephine *Film 1*
Atkinson, Rosalind 1900- *BiE&WWA, PIP&P,*
  WhoThe 16
Atlas 1864- *WhThe*
Atlas, Leopold 1907-1954 *NotNAT B*
Atlass, H Leslie d1960 *NewYTET*
Atlee, Howard 1926- *BiE&WWA, NotNAT*
Atmar, Ann 1939-1966 *WhScrn 2*
Atta *OxThe*
Attaway, Ruth *BiE&WWA, NotNAT,*
  WhoHol A
Attenborough, David 1926- *IntMPA 1977*
Attenborough, Richard 1923- *BiDFlm, CelR 3,*
  CmMov, FilmgC, IntMPA 1977, MotPP,
  MovMk, OxFilm, WhoHol A, WhoThe 16,
  WorEnF
Atterbom, Daniel Amadeus 1790-1835 *OxThe*
Atterbury, Malcolm 1907- *IntMPA 1977,*
  WhoHol A
Atteridge, Harold Richard 1886-1938
  AmSCAP 1966, NewMT, NotNAT B,
  WhThe
Attles, Joseph 1903- *NotNAT*
Attwell, Hugh d1621 *OxThe*
Attwooll, Hugh 1914- *IntMPA 1977*
Atwater, Barry *WhoHol A*
Atwater, Edith 1911- *BiE&WWA, NotNAT,*
  WhThe, WhoHol A
Atwater, Gladys *IntMPA 1977*
Atwell, Ben H d1951 *NotNAT B*

Atwell, Roy d1962 *NotNAT B*
Atwell, Roy 1878-1962 *AmSCAP 1966*
Atwell, Roy 1880-1962 *Film 2, WhScrn 1,*
  WhScrn 2, WhoHol B
Atwill, Lionel 1885-1946 *CmMov, Film 1,*
  Film 2, FilmgC, MotPP, MovMk,
  NotNAT B, Vers A, WhScrn 1, WhScrn 2,
  WhThe, WhoHol B
Atwood, Lorena E d1947 *NotNAT B,*
  WhoStg 1908
Auberjonois, Rene 1940- *FilmgC, NotNAT,*
  WhoHol A, WhoThe 16
Aubert, Jeanne 1906- *WhThe*
Aubert, Lenore 1918?- *FilmgC*
Aubert, Louis 1879-1944 *DcFM*
Aubignac, Francois Hedeli, Abbe D' 1604-1676
  NotNAT B
Aubignac, Francois Hedelin, Abbe D' 1604-1676
  OxThe
Aubrey, Anne 1937- *FilmgC*
Aubrey, Georges 1928-1975 *WhScrn 2,*
  WhoHol C
Aubrey, James T, Jr. 1918- *CelR 3,*
  IntMPA 1977, NewYTET
Aubrey, Jimmy *Film 1, Film 2, TwYS*
Aubrey, Madge 1902-1970 *WhThe*
Aubrey, Skye 1945- *FilmgC, WhoHol A*
Aubrey, Will 1894-1958 *WhScrn 1, WhScrn 2*
Aubry, Cecile 1929- *FilmgC*
Aubuchon, Jacques 1924- *NotNAT*
Auburn, Jane *Film 2*
Auburn, Joy *Film 2, WhScrn 1, WhScrn 2*
Auchincloss, Louis 1917- *CelR 3*
Auclair, Michel 1922- *FilmgC*
Aude, Joseph 1755-1841 *NotNAT B, OxThe*
Auden, W H 1907-1973 *AmSCAP 1966,*
  BiE&WWA, CelR 3, CnMD, ConDr 1973,
  McGWD, ModWD, PIP&P, WhThe
Auden, Wystan Hugh 1907-1973 *OxThe*
Audiard, Michel 1920- *DcFM, FilmgC, WorEnF*
Audiberti, Jacques 1899-1965 *CnMD, CnThe,*
  CroCD, McGWD, ModWD, OxThe
Audley, Eleanor *WhoHol A*
Audley, Maxine 1923- *FilmgC, WhoHol A,*
  WhoThe 16
Audran, Edmond 1840-1901 *NotNAT B*
Audran, Edmond 1919-1951 *WhScrn 1,*
  WhScrn 2, WhoHol B
Audran, Stephane *OxFilm, WhoHol A*
Audran, Stephane 1933- *BiDFlm*
Audran, Stephane 1938- *FilmgC*
Audre *BiE&WWA, NotNAT*
Audry, Jacqueline 1908- *DcFM, FilmgC, OxFilm,*
  WomWMM
Auen, Signe d1966 *Film 1, WhoHol B*
Auer, Anna *WhScrn 1, WhScrn 2*
Auer, Florence 1880-1962 *Film 1, Film 2, TwYS,*
  WhScrn 2, WhoHol B
Auer, John H d1975 *NewYTET*
Auer, John H 1909- *FilmgC*
Auer, Leopold 1845-1930 *AmSCAP 1966*
Auer, Mischa 1905-1967 *Film 2, FilmgC, MotPP,*
  MovMk, NotNAT B, TwYS, Vers A,
  WhScrn 1, WhScrn 2, WhoHol B
Auerbach, Arnold 1917- *CelR 3*
Auerbach, Arthur 1903-1957 *WhScrn 1,*
  WhScrn 2
Auerbach, Artie d1957 *NotNAT B*
Auerbach, Henry L d1916 *WhScrn 2*
Auerbach, Leonard *BiE&WWA, NotNAT*
Auerbach-Levy, William d1961 *NotNAT B*
Aug, Edna 1878-1938 *NotNAT B*
Augarde, Adrienne d1913 *NotNAT B, WhThe,*
  WhoStg 1908

Ayme, Marcel 1902-1967 *BiE&WWA, CnMD,*
  CnThe, McGWD, ModWD, NotNAT B
Aynesworth, Allan 1864-1959 *NotNAT B*
Aynesworth, Allan 1865-1959 *WhThe*
Ayrenhoff, Cornelius Von 1733-1819 *OxThe*
Ayrer, Jacob 1543-1605 *REnWD*
Ayrer, Jakob 1543?-1605 *OxThe*
Ayres, Agnes d1940 *MotPP, TwYS, WhoHol B*
Ayres, Agnes 1896-1940 *Film 1, Film 2, FilmgC,*
  MovMk
Ayres, Agnes 1898-1940 *WhScrn 1, WhScrn 2*
Ayres, Gerald *IntMPA 1977*
Ayres, Gordon *WhoHol A*
Ayres, Lemuel *PIP&P*
Ayres, Lew 1908- *BiDFlm, Film 2, FilmgC,*
  IntMPA 1977, MGM, MotPP, MovMk,
  OxFilm, WhoHol A, WorEnF
Ayres, Mitchell 1910-1969 *AmSCAP 1966*
Ayres, Mitchell 1911-1969 *WhScrn 2, WhoHol B*
Ayres, Robert 1914-1968 *FilmgC, WhScrn 1,*
  WhScrn 2, WhoHol B
Ayres, Sydney d1916 *WhScrn 2*
Ayres, Warren Joyce 1908- *AmSCAP 1966*
Ayrton, Louise *Film 2*
Ayrton, Norman 1924- *WhoThe 16*
Ayrton, Randle 1869-1940 *Film 2, WhThe*
Ayrton, Robert d1924 *NotNAT B*
Azcarraga, Emilio d1973 *NewYTET*
Azevedo, Artur 1855-1908 *REnWD*
Aznavour, Charles 1924- *CelR 3, FilmgC,*
  MovMk, OxFilm, WhoHol A, WorEnF
Azzara, Candy *WhoHol A*
Azzato, Anthony *IntMPA 1977*

B

Babanova, Maria Ivanovna 1900- *OxThe*
Babb, Kroger 1906- *IntMPA 1977*
Babbin, Jacqueline *NewYTET*, *WomWMM B*
Babbitt, Harry *WhoHol A*
Babcock, Dwight V 1909- *IntMPA 1977*
Babcock, Theron C 1925- *AmSCAP 1966*
Babe, Angelus *Film 2*
Babe, Thomas 1941- *NatPD*
Babel, Isaak Emanuilovich 1894-1941? *CnMD,
    McGWD, ModWD*
Babin, Victor 1908- *AmSCAP 1966*
Babits, Linda 1940- *AmSCAP 1966*
Baburao Painter 1892- *DcFM*
Baby Laurence 1921-1974 *WhScrn 2*
Baby LeRoy 1932- *MotPP, WhoHol A*
Baby LeRoy *see also* LeRoy, Baby
Baby Marie *WhoHol A*
Baby Marie *see also* Osborne, Baby Marie
Baby Peggy 1918- *Film 2, WhoHol A*
Baby Peggy *see also* Peggy, Baby
Baby Sandy 1938- *WhoHol A*
Bac, Andre 1905- *DcFM*
Bacal, Harvey 1915- *AmSCAP 1966*
Bacal, Melanie Ella 1948- *AmSCAP 1966*
Bacall, Lauren 1924- *BiDFlm, BiE&WWA,
    CelR 3, CmMov, EncMT, FilmgC,
    IntMPA 1977, MotPP, MovMk, NotNAT,
    OxFilm, WhoHol A, WhoThe 16, WorEnF*
Baccaloni, Salvatore 1900-1969 *WhScrn 1,
    WhScrn 2, WhoHol B*
Baccaloni, Salvatore 1900-1970 *FilmgC*
Bacchelli, Riccardo 1891- *CnMD*
Bacevicius, Vytautas 1905- *AmSCAP 1966*
Bach *WhScrn 1, WhScrn 2*
Bach, Fernand d1953 *NotNAT B*
Bach, Margaret Lesser *WomWMM B*
Bach, Reginald 1886-1941 *NotNAT B, WhThe*
Bach, Mrs. Rudi d1960 *WhScrn 1, WhScrn 2*
Bachand, Treva *WomWMM B*
Bacharach, Bert 1898- *CelR 3*
Bacharach, Burt *NewMT*
Bacharach, Burt 1928- *AmSCAP 1966, EncMT*
Bacharach, Burt 1929- *CelR 3, FilmgC,
    NotNAT*
Bachauer, Gina 1913- *CelR 3*
Bachelet, Jean 1894- *DcFM, WorEnF*
Bachelin, Franz *IntMPA 1977*
Bachelor, Stephanie *WhoHol A*
Bachner, Annette *WomWMM A, WomWMM B*
Bachrach, Doro *WomWMM, WomWMM B*
Bachvarova, Radka *WomWMM*
Back *Film 2*
Back, Leon B 1912- *IntMPA 1977*
Backe, John D *NewYTET*
Backes, Alice *WhoHol A*
Backner, Arthur *Film 1*

Backner, Constance *Film 1*
Backus, E Y d1914 *NotNAT B*
Backus, George 1858-1939 *Film 2, NotNAT B,
    WhScrn 1, WhScrn 2, WhoHol B*
Backus, Henny *WhoHol A*
Backus, Jim 1913- *CelR 3, FilmgC,
    IntMPA 1977, MotPP, MovMk, WhoHol A*
Backus, Richard 1945- *WhoThe 16*
Baclanova, Olga d1974 *MotPP, WhoHol B*
Baclanova, Olga 1896-1974 *TwYS*
Baclanova, Olga 1899-1974 *FilmgC, ThFT,
    WhScrn 2, WhThe*
Baclanova, Olga 1900-1974 *Film 2*
Bacon, Bessie 1886-1952 *WhScrn 1, WhScrn 2*
Bacon, David 1914-1942 *NotNAT B*
Bacon, David 1914-1943 *WhScrn 1, WhScrn 2,
    WhoHol B*
Bacon, Ernst 1898- *AmSCAP 1966*
Bacon, Faith 1909-1956 *NotNAT B, WhScrn 1,
    WhScrn 2, WhoHol B*
Bacon, Francis, Viscount St. Albans 1561-1626
    NotNAT B, PIP&P
Bacon, Frank 1864-1922 *Film 1, ModWD,
    NotNAT B, OxThe, WhScrn 1, WhScrn 2,
    WhThe, WhoHol B*
Bacon, Irving 1892-1965 *FilmgC*
Bacon, Irving 1893-1965 *Film 2, MovMk, TwYS,
    WhScrn 1, WhScrn 2, WhoHol B*
Bacon, Irving 1904-1965 *Vers A*
Bacon, Irwin *Film 2*
Bacon, Jane d1956 *NotNAT B*
Bacon, Jane 1895- *PIP&P, WhThe*
Bacon, Lloyd 1889-1955 *CmMov, DcFM,
    MovMk, WorEnF*
Bacon, Lloyd 1890-1955 *BiDFlm, Film 1,
    FilmgC, OxFilm, TwYS A, WhScrn 1,
    WhScrn 2, WhoHol B*
Bacon, Mai 1898- *WhThe*
Bacon, Phannel d1783 *NotNAT B*
Bacon, Walter Scott 1891-1973 *WhScrn 2*
Bacus, Lucia *WhScrn 1, WhScrn 2*
Badal, Janos 1927- *WorEnF*
Badal, Jean 1927- *WorEnF*
Baddeley, Angela d1976 *PIP&P, WhoHol C*
Baddeley, Angela 1900-1976 *FilmgC*
Baddeley, Angela 1904-1976 *WhoThe 16*
Baddeley, Hermione *BiE&WWA, MotPP,
    WhoHol A*
Baddeley, Hermione 1906- *EncMT, FilmgC,
    MovMk, WhoThe 16*
Baddeley, Hermione 1908- *Film 2, IntMPA 1977*
Baddeley, Robert 1732-1794 *OxThe*
Baddeley, Robert 1733-1794 *NotNAT B*
Baddeley, Sophia Snow 1745-1786 *NotNAT A,
    NotNAT B, OxThe*
Badel, Alan 1923- *FilmgC, WhoHol A,*

WhoThe 16
Badel, Allan 1923- *BiE&WWA, NotNAT*
Badel, Sarah 1943- *WhoThe 16*
Badgely, Helen *Film 1*
Badger, Clarence 1880-1964 *FilmgC, NotNAT B, TwYS A, WorEnF*
Badham, Mary 1952- *FilmgC, MotPP, WhoHol A*
Badillo, Herman 1929- *CelR 3*
Badiole, Charles *Film 2*
Badrakhan, Ahmed 1909- *DcFM*
Badzian, Teresa *WomWMM B*
Baer, Abel 1893- *AmSCAP 1966*
Baer, Arthur Bugs 1886-1969 *WhScrn 2*
Baer, Buddy 1915- *FilmgC, WhoHol A*
Baer, Bugs d1969 *WhoHol B*
Baer, Charles E 1870-1962 *AmSCAP 1966*
Baer, John *WhoHol A*
Baer, Max 1909-1959 *FilmgC, NotNAT B, WhScrn 1, WhScrn 2, WhoHol B*
Baer, Max, Jr. *WhoHol A*
Baer, Parley *WhoHol A*
Baer, Thais 1929-1930 *WhScrn 1, WhScrn 2*
Baeraud, George *Film 2*
Baez, Joan 1941- *CelR 3*
Baffico, Giuseppe 1852-1927 *McGWD*
Bagdad, William d1975 *WhScrn 2, WhoHol C*
Bagdasarian, Ross d1972 *WhoHol B*
Bagdasarian, Ross 1919-1972 *AmSCAP 1966*
Bagdasarian, Ross 1920-1972 *WhScrn 2*
Baggett, Lynne 1928-1960 *WhScrn 1, WhScrn 2, WhoHol B*
Baggot, King d1948 *MotPP*
Baggot, King 1874-1948 *WhScrn 1, WhScrn 2*
Baggot, King 1880-1948 *Film 1, NotNAT B*
Baggott, King d1948 *WhoHol B*
Baggott, King 1879-1948 *FilmgC*
Baggott, King 1880-1948 *Film 2, TwYS, TwYS A*
Bagley, Ben 1933- *BiE&WWA, EncMT, NotNAT*
Bagley, Eugenie *WomWMM B*
Bagley, Sam 1903-1968 *WhScrn 1, WhScrn 2, WhoHol B*
Bagnall, George L 1896- *IntMPA 1977*
Bagni, John 1911-1954 *WhScrn 1, WhScrn 2, WhoHol B*
Bagnold, Enid 1889- *BiE&WWA, CnMD, ConDr 1977, ModWD, NotNAT, NotNAT A, PIP&P, WhoThe 16*
Bahati, Amirh *NatPD*
Bahn, Chester B 1962 *NotNAT B*
Bahr, Hermann 1863-1934 *CnMD, McGWD, ModWD, NotNAT B, OxThe*
Baierl, Helmut 1926- *CroCD*
Bailey, Albert 1891-1952 *WhScrn 1, WhScrn 2, WhoHol B*
Bailey, Bryan 1922-1960 *NotNAT B, OxThe*
Bailey, David *WhoHol A*
Bailey, Edward Lorenz 1883-1951 *WhScrn 1, WhScrn 2*
Bailey, Edwin B 1873-1950 *WhScrn 1, WhScrn 2*
Bailey, Elizabeth *WomWMM B*
Bailey, F Lee 1933- *CelR 3*
Bailey, Frankie 1859-1953 *NotNAT B, WhScrn 1, WhScrn 2, WhoHol B*
Bailey, Gordon 1875- *Film 1, WhThe*
Bailey, H C 1878-1961 *WhThe*
Bailey, Harry P 1912- *AmSCAP 1966*
Bailey, Jack *NewYTET*
Bailey, James A 1847-1906 *NotNAT B*
Bailey, Joseph W 1910- *IntMPA 1977*
Bailey, Margery 1891-1963 *NotNAT B*
Bailey, Mildred d1951 *NotNAT B*

Bailey, Mollie 1841-1918 *NotNAT A*
Bailey, Norton *Film 2*
Bailey, Pearl 1918- *AmSCAP 1966, BiE&WWA, CelR 3, EncMT, FilmgC, IntMPA 1977, MotPP, MovMk, NotNAT, NotNAT A, WhoHol A, WhoThe 16*
Bailey, Raymond 1904- *FilmgC, WhoHol A*
Bailey, Robin 1919- *BiE&WWA, FilmgC, IntMPA 1977, NotNAT, WhoHol A, WhoThe 16*
Bailey, Ruth *BiE&WWA, NotNAT*
Bailey, William Norton 1886-1962 *Film 1, NotNAT B, WhScrn 1, WhScrn 2, WhoHol B*
Bailin, Harriett 1923- *AmSCAP 1966*
Baillie, Joanna 1762-1851 *NotNAT B*
Baim, Harold *IntMPA 1977*
Bain, Conrad 1923- *BiE&WWA, NotNAT, WhoHol A, WhoThe 16*
Bainbridge, Katharine 1863- *AmSCAP 1966*
Baines, Beulah 1905-1930 *WhScrn 1, WhScrn 2, WhoHol B*
Baines, Florence 1877-1918 *NotNAT B, WhThe*
Bainter, Fay d1968 *MotPP, WhoHol B*
Bainter, Fay 1891-1968 *WhScrn 1, WhScrn 2, WhThe*
Bainter, Fay 1892-1968 *FilmgC, MGM, MovMk, NotNAT B, ThFT*
Bainter, Fay 1893-1968 *BiE&WWA*
Baird, Bil 1904- *BiE&WWA, CelR 3, NotNAT*
Baird, Claribel 1904- *BiE&WWA*
Baird, Cora 1912-1967 *BiE&WWA, NotNAT B*
Baird, Cora 1913-1967 *WhScrn 1, WhScrn 2*
Baird, Dorothea 1875-1933 *NotNAT B, OxThe, WhThe, WhoStg 1906, WhoStg 1908*
Baird, Dorothy *WhScrn 2*
Baird, Ethel *WhThe*
Baird, Hugh *Film 2*
Baird, Jeanne *WhoHol A*
Baird, John Logie d1946 *NewYTET*
Baird, Leah d1971 *MotPP, WhoHol B*
Baird, Leah 1887-1971 *Film 1, Film 2, TwYS*
Baird, Leah 1891-1971 *WhScrn 1, WhScrn 2*
Baird, Stuart d1947 *NotNAT B*
Baird, Teddy 1900?- *FilmgC*
Bairnsfather, Bruce 1887-1959 *NotNAT A, NotNAT B*
Baise, Paul 1922- *IntMPA 1977*
Bajor, Gisi d1951 *NotNAT B*
Bajor, Gizi d1951 *WhoHol B*
Bakaleinikoff, Constantin 1898-1966 *FilmgC*
Bakaleinikoff, Mischa d1960 *NotNAT B*
Bakalinsky, Adah *WomWMM B*
Baker, Anna Willis 1860-1944 *WhScrn 1, WhScrn 2*
Baker, Art 1898-1966 *WhScrn 1, WhScrn 2, WhoHol B*
Baker, Belle 1895-1957 *Film 2, NotNAT B, WhScrn 1, WhScrn 2, WhoHol B*
Baker, Benjamin A 1818-1890 *NotNAT B, OxThe*
Baker, Benny 1907- *Vers B, WhThe, WhoHol A*
Baker, Betty Bly *Film 2*
Baker, Bob 1901-1975 *WhScrn 2, WhoHol C*
Baker, Carroll *IntMPA 1977, MotPP, WhoHol A*
Baker, Carroll 1931- *FilmgC, MovMk, WorEnF*
Baker, Carroll 1932- *BiDFlm, OxFilm*
Baker, Carroll 1935- *BiE&WWA*
Baker, Charles Adams 1920- *BiE&WWA*
Baker, Daniel E d1939 *NotNAT B*
Baker, David 1926- *BiE&WWA, NotNAT*
Baker, David Erskine d1767 *NotNAT B*
Baker, Diane 1938- *FilmgC, MotPP, MovMk, WhoHol A*

Baker, Don 1903- *AmSCAP 1966*
Baker, Don 1931- *IntMPA 1977*
Baker, Doris *Film 2*
Baker, Dorothy 1907-1968 *BiE&WWA, NotNAT B*
Baker, Eddie 1897-1968 *TwYS A, WhScrn 1, WhScrn 2, WhoHol B*
Baker, Elizabeth d1962 *WhThe*
Baker, Elsie 1893-1971 *WhScrn 1, WhScrn 2*
Baker, Fay *WhoHol A*
Baker, Floyd 1906-1943 *WhScrn 1, WhScrn 2*
Baker, Gene *Film 1*
Baker, George 1885- *WhThe*
Baker, George 1929- *FilmgC*
Baker, George 1931- *IntMPA 1977, WhoHol A, WhoThe 16*
Baker, George D *TwYS A*
Baker, George Pierce 1866-1935 *McGWD, NotNAT A, NotNAT B, OxThe, PIP&P, WhThe*
Baker, Harold 1914- *AmSCAP 1966*
Baker, Henrietta 1837-1909 *OxThe*
Baker, Herbert G 1920- *AmSCAP 1966*
Baker, Howard 1905- *BiE&WWA, NotNAT*
Baker, Hylda 1909- *FilmgC*
Baker, Iris 1901- *WhThe*
Baker, Jane *WomWMM*
Baker, Joby *WhoHol A*
Baker, Joe Don *IntMPA 1977, WhoHol A*
Baker, Josephine 1906-1975 *BiE&WWA, CelR 3, OxFilm, WhScrn 2, WhoHol C, WhoThe 16*
Baker, Kenny 1912- *BiE&WWA, FilmgC, WhoHol A*
Baker, Lauretta *WomWMM B*
Baker, Lee 1876-1948 *Film 2, NotNAT B, WhScrn 1, WhScrn 2, WhThe, WhoHol B*
Baker, Lenny *NotNAT*
Baker, Leslie F 1903- *IntMPA 1977*
Baker, Lewis J d1962 *NotNAT B*
Baker, Mark d1972 *WhoHol B*
Baker, Mark 1946- *NotNAT*
Baker, Nellie Bly *Film 2*
Baker, Paul 1911- *BiE&WWA, NotNAT*
Baker, Phil 1896-1963 *AmSCAP 1966, NotNAT B, WhoHol B*
Baker, Phil 1898-1963 *WhScrn 1, WhScrn 2*
Baker, Reginald P 1896- *IntMPA 1977*
Baker, Richard E 1916- *AmSCAP 1966*
Baker, Robert S 1916- *FilmgC, IntMPA 1977*
Baker, Roy Ward 1916- *FilmgC, IntMPA 1977, WorEnF*
Baker, Russell 1925- *CelR 3*
Baker, Sam *Film 2*
Baker, Sarah 1736?-1816 *OxThe*
Baker, Stanley *MotPP, WhoHol A*
Baker, Stanley 1927- *BiDFlm, CmMov, FilmgC, OxFilm*
Baker, Stanley 1928- *MovMk, WorEnF*
Baker, Tarkington d1924 *NotNAT B*
Baker, Tom 1941- *FilmgC*
Baker, William d1916 *WhScrn 2*
Baker, William S 1925- *AmSCAP 1966*
Baker, Word 1923- *BiE&WWA, NotNAT*
Bakewell, William 1908- *Film 2, MovMk, TwYS, WhoHol A*
Bakkar, Selma *WomWMM*
Bakst, Leon 1868-1924 *NotNAT A, NotNAT B*
Baky, Josef Von 1902-1966 *DcFM*
Balaban, A J 1889-1962 *IntMPA 1977, NotNAT A, NotNAT B*
Balaban, Barney 1887-1971 *WorEnF*
Balaban, Barney 1888-1971 *FilmgC*
Balaban, Burt 1922-1965 *FilmgC*
Balaban, Elmer *IntMPA 1977*

Balaban, Harry 1903- *IntMPA 1977*
Balanchine, George 1904- *BiE&WWA, CelR 3, EncMT, NotNAT A, PIP&P, WhoThe 16*
Balasz, Bela 1884-1949 *FilmgC*
Balasz, Bela 1885-1949 *WorEnF*
Balazs, Bela 1884-1949 *OxFilm*
Balch, Marston 1901- *BiE&WWA, NotNAT*
Balch, Slim d1967 *WhoHol B*
Balchin, Nigel 1908-1970 *FilmgC*
Balcon, Jill 1925- *FilmgC*
Balcon, Sir Michael 1896- *BiDFlm, DcFM, FilmgC, IntMPA 1977, OxFilm, WorEnF*
Balderston, John L 1889-1954 *CnMD, FilmgC, McGWD, ModWD, NotNAT B, WhThe*
Balderstone, John L 1889-1954 *CmMov*
Baldi, Gian Vittorio 1930- *DcFM, WorEnF*
Baldra, Charles M 1899-1949 *WhScrn 1, WhScrn 2*
Baldra, Chuck 1899-1949 *WhoHol B*
Baldwin, Bill *WhoHol A*
Baldwin, Billy 1903- *CelR 3*
Baldwin, Dick *WhoHol A*
Baldwin, George d1923 *WhScrn 1, WhScrn 2*
Baldwin, James 1924- *CelR 3, ConDr 1977, CroCD, McGWD, ModWD, NotNAT, NotNAT A*
Baldwin, Joseph B 1918- *BiE&WWA*
Baldwin, Kitty 1853-1934 *WhScrn 1, WhScrn 2*
Baldwin, Peter *WhoHol A*
Baldwin, Roger 1884- *CelR 3*
Baldwin, Ruth Ann *WomWMM*
Baldwin, Walter *Vers B, WhoHol A*
Bale, John, Bishop Of Ossary 1495-1563 *NotNAT B*
Bale, John, Bishop Of Ossory 1495-1563 *McGWD, OxThe*
Bales, Richard 1915- *AmSCAP 1966*
Balfe, Michael William 1808-1870 *NotNAT B*
Balfour, Augustus *Film 2*
Balfour, Betty 1903- *Film 2, FilmgC, WhoHol A*
Balfour, Eva *Film 2*
Balfour, Katharine *WhoHol A*
Balfour, Lorna 1913-1932 *WhScrn 1, WhScrn 2, WhoHol B*
Balfour, Michael 1918- *FilmgC, WhoHol A*
Balfour, Sue *Film 1*
Balfour, William d1964 *NotNAT B*
Balfour-Frazer, Anne *WomWMM B*
Balieff, Nikita 1877-1936 *NotNAT B, OxThe, WhScrn 2, WhoHol B*
Balin, Ina 1937- *BiE&WWA, FilmgC, IntMPA 1977, MotPP, WhoHol A*
Balin, Mireille 1909-1968 *FilmgC, WhoHol B*
Balin, Mireille 1911-1968 *WhScrn 1, WhScrn 2*
Ball, Ernest R 1878-1927 *AmSCAP 1966, NotNAT B*
Ball, F C *ConDr 1977B*
Ball, J Meredith d1915 *NotNAT B*
Ball, Jane *WhoHol A*
Ball, Lewis d1905 *NotNAT B*
Ball, Lucille *IntMPA 1977, MotPP, NewYTET, WhoHol A*
Ball, Lucille 1910- *CmMov, EncMT, FilmgC, MovMk, OxFilm*
Ball, Lucille 1911- *BiDFlm, BiE&WWA, CelR 3, Film 2, MGM, ThFT, WorEnF*
Ball, Robert Hamilton 1902- *BiE&WWA, NotNAT*
Ball, Susan *MotPP*
Ball, Suzan 1933-1955 *FilmgC, NotNAT B, WhScrn 1, WhScrn 2, WhoHol B*
Ball, William 1931- *BiE&WWA, NotNAT, WhoThe 16*

Ballantine, Carl *WhoHol A*
Ballantine, E J 1888-1968 *WhScrn 1, WhScrn 2, WhoHol B*
Ballantine, Edward D 1907- *AmSCAP 1966*
Ballantyne, Nell d1959 *WhScrn 1, WhScrn 2, WhoHol B*
Ballantyne, Paul 1909- *BiE&WWA, NotNAT, WhoThe 16*
Ballantyne, Tanya *WomWMM*
Ballard, Elmer *Film 2*
Ballard, Francis Drake 1899-1960 *AmSCAP 1966*
Ballard, Frederick 1884-1957 *NotNAT B*
Ballard, Kaye 1926- *BiE&WWA, CelR 3, EncMT, FilmgC, NotNAT, WhoHol A, WhoThe 16*
Ballard, Lucien 1908- *CmMov, DcFM, FilmgC, IntMPA 1977, OxFilm, WorEnF*
Ballard, Lucinda 1906- *NotNAT*
Ballard, Lucinda 1908- *BiE&WWA*
Ballard, Robert H 1913- *AmSCAP 1966*
Ballaseyus, Virginia 1893- *AmSCAP 1966*
Ballet, Arthur H *NotNAT*
Ballew, Leighton M 1916- *BiE&WWA, NotNAT*
Ballew, Smith 1902- *WhoHol A*
Ballin, Hugo d1956 *NotNAT B*
Ballin, Mabel 1885-1958 *Film 1, Film 2, MotPP, NotNAT B, TwYS, WhScrn 1, WhScrn 2, WhoHol B*
Ballou, Marion 1871-1939 *WhScrn 1, WhScrn 2, WhoHol B*
Balmain, Pierre 1914- *CelR 3*
Balmain, Rollo d1920 *NotNAT B*
Balogh, Erno 1897- *AmSCAP 1966*
Balsam, Martin 1919- *BiE&WWA, CelR 3, FilmgC, IntMPA 1977, MotPP, MovMk, NotNAT, WhoHol A, WhoThe 16*
Balter, Allan 1925- *IntMPA 1977*
Balter, Diane Robb *WomWMM B*
Baltor, Harold 1915- *AmSCAP 1966*
Balucki, Michael 1837-1901 *ModWD*
Balzac, Honore De 1799-1850 *McGWD, NotNAT B, OxThe*
Bamattre, Martha 1892-1970 *WhScrn 1, WhScrn 2, WhoHol B*
Bamberger, Theron d1953 *NotNAT B*
Bamboschek, Giuseppe 1890- *AmSCAP 1966*
Bamester, Katherine d1919 *WhScrn 2*
Ban, Frigyes 1902- *DcFM*
Banbury, Frith 1912- *WhoThe 16*
Bances Y Lopez-Candamo, Francisco A 1662-1704 *McGWD*
Bancroft, Lady 1839-1921 *NotNAT B, WhThe*
Bancroft, Lady *see also* Bancroft, Marie Effie Wilton
Bancroft, Anne 1931- *BiDFlm, BiE&WWA, CelR 3, CnThe, FilmgC, IntMPA 1977, MotPP, MovMk, NotNAT, OxFilm, WhoHol A, WhoThe 16, WorEnF*
Bancroft, Charles 1911-1969 *WhScrn 1, WhScrn 2, WhoHol B*
Bancroft, George 1882-1956 *CmMov, Film 2, FilmgC, MotPP, MovMk, NotNAT B, TwYS, Vers A, WhScrn 1, WhScrn 2, WhoHol B, WorEnF*
Bancroft, George Pleydell 1868-1956 *NotNAT A, NotNAT B, WhThe*
Bancroft, Marie Effie Wilton 1839-1921 *CnThe, NotNAT A, OxThe, PIP&P*
Bancroft, Marie Effie Wilton *see also* Bancroft, Lady
Bancroft, Sir Squire 1841-1926 *CnThe, NotNAT A, NotNAT B, OxThe, PIP&P, WhThe*
Band, Albert 1924- *FilmgC, IntMPA 1977*
Bandini, Albert Jacovino 1916- *AmSCAP 1966*
Bandmann, Daniel Edward 1840-1905 *NotNAT A,*

NotNAT B
Bandmann-Palmer, Mrs. d1926 *NotNAT B*
Bando, Mitsugoro d1975 *WhScrn 2*
Bando, Tsumasaburo 1898-1953 *WhScrn 1, WhScrn 2*
Bane, Martin J 1900- *AmSCAP 1966*
Bang, Herman Joachim 1857-1912 *NotNAT B*
Bang, Joy *WhoHol A*
Bangs, Frank C 1833-1908 *NotNAT B, OxThe*
Bangs, John Kendrick 1862-1922 *NotNAT B, WhThe, WhoStg 1906, WhoStg 1908*
Banim, John d1842 *NotNAT B*
Banjamin, Gladys d1948 *WhScrn 2*
Bank, Mirra *WomWMM A, WomWMM B*
Bankhead, Tallulah d1968 *MotPP, PIP&P, WhoHol B*
Bankhead, Tallulah 1902-1965 *OxFilm*
Bankhead, Tallulah 1902-1968 *BiDFlm, Film 1, Film 2, FilmgC, ThFT, WhScrn 1, WhScrn 2*
Bankhead, Tallulah 1903-1968 *BiE&WWA, CnThe, FamA&A, MovMk, NotNAT A, NotNAT B, WhThe, WorEnF*
Banks, Charles O 1899-1944 *AmSCAP 1966*
Banks, Estar *Film 2*
Banks, John 1650?-1706 *NotNAT B, OxThe*
Banks, Leslie 1890-1952 *FilmgC, MovMk, NotNAT B, OxThe, WhScrn 1, WhScrn 2, WhThe, WhoHol B*
Banks, Monty 1897-1950 *Film 2, FilmgC, NotNAT B, TwYS, WhScrn 1, WhScrn 2, WhoHol B*
Bankson, Budd 1916- *NotNAT A*
Banky, Vilma *MotPP*
Banky, Vilma 1898- *ThFT*
Banky, Vilma 1902- *FilmgC*
Banky, Vilma 1903- *Film 2, MovMk, TwYS, WhoHol A, WorEnF*
Bannard, Robert *WhoHol A*
Bannen, Ian 1928- *FilmgC, IntMPA 1977, MotPP, MovMk, WhoHol A, WhoThe 16*
Banner, Bob 1921- *IntMPA 1977, NewYTET*
Banner, John 1910-1973 *FilmgC, WhScrn 2, WhoHol B*
Bannerman, Celia 1946- *WhoThe 16*
Bannerman, Kay 1919- *WhoThe 16*
Bannerman, Margaret 1896-1976 *BiE&WWA, NotNAT B, WhThe*
Bannister, Charles 1738-1804 *NotNAT B*
Bannister, Charles 1741-1804 *OxThe*
Bannister, Harry d1961 *Film 2, WhoHol B*
Bannister, Harry 1889-1961 *WhScrn 1, WhScrn 2*
Bannister, Harry 1893-1961 *NotNAT B, WhThe*
Bannister, John 1760-1836 *NotNAT A, NotNAT B, OxThe*
Bannister, Nathaniel Harrington 1813-1847 *NotNAT B, OxThe*
Bannon, Jim 1911- *FilmgC, WhoHol A*
Banos, Ricardo De 1882-1939 *DcFM*
Bantau, J W 1904- *IntMPA 1977*
Banthim, Larry *Film 2*
Bantock, Leedham d1928 *NotNAT B*
Banton, Travis 1894- *DcFM*
Banville, Theodore Faullain De 1823-1891 *McGWD, NotNAT B, OxThe*
Banyai, George 1905- *BiE&WWA*
Banzet, Janet d1970? *WhScrn 2*
Banzhaf, Max 1915- *IntMPA 1977*
Bao, Miguel Gomez d1961 *WhScrn 2*
Baptista, Carlos 1900-1950 *WhScrn 2*
Bar, Jacques Jean Louis 1921- *FilmgC, IntMPA 1977*
Bara, Theda 1890-1955 *BiDFlm, Film 1, Film 2, FilmgC, MotPP, MovMk, NotNAT B,*

OxFilm, TwYS, WhScrn 1, WhScrn 2,
  WhoHol B, WorEnF
Barab, Seymour 1921- AmSCAP 1966
Baragrey, John d1975 WhoHol C
Baragrey, John 1918-1975 BiE&WWA, NotNAT,
  NotNAT B
Baragrey, John 1919-1975 IntMPA 1977,
  WhScrn 2
Baraka, Imamu Amiri 1934- CelR 3,
  ConDr 1977, McGWD, NotNAT,
  WhoThe 16
Baral, Robert 1910- BiE&WWA, NotNAT
Baranovskaya, Vera Film 2
Barasch, Norman 1922- BiE&WWA, NotNAT
Barash, Olivia WhoHol A
Baratier, Jacques 1918- DcFM, FilmgC,
  WorEnF
Barban, Harvey Film 2
Barbanell, Fred 1931-1959 WhScrn 1, WhScrn 2
Barbaro, Umberto 1902-1959 OxFilm, WorEnF
Barbat, Percy 1883-1965 Film 2, WhScrn 2
Barbee, Richard 1887- WhThe
Barber, Arnold IntMPA 1977
Barber, Benjamin R NatPD
Barber, Red NewYTET
Barber, Samuel 1910- AmSCAP 1966, CelR 3
Barbera, Joe 1911- FilmgC
Barbera, Joseph 1911- OxFilm, WorEnF
Barbette 1906-1973 WhScrn 2, WhoHol B
Barbier, George W 1865-1945 FilmgC, MovMk,
  NotNAT B, Vers A, WhScrn 1, WhScrn 2,
  WhoHol B
Barbier, Jules d1901 NotNAT B
Barbieri, Niccolo d1640? OxThe
Barbor, H R 1893-1933 NotNAT B, WhThe
Barbour, Alan G 1933- IntMPA 1977
Barbour, Dave 1912-1965 WhScrn 2
Barbour, David 1912-1965 AmSCAP 1966
Barbour, Edwin Wilbour d1914 WhScrn 2
Barbour, Joyce 1901- WhThe
Barbour, Malcolm 1934- IntMPA 1977
Barbour, Ross 1928- AmSCAP 1966
Barcelo, Randy 1946- NotNAT
Barclay, Adela Film 1
Barclay, Delancey d1917 WhScrn 2
Barclay, Don 1892-1975 Film 1, WhScrn 2,
  WhoHol C
Barclay, John WhoHol A
Barclay, Lola Film 1
Barclift, Nelson 1917- AmSCAP 1966
Barcroft, Roy 1902-1969 FilmgC, MotPP,
  Vers A, WhScrn 2, WhoHol B
Bard, Ben Film 2, TwYS
Bard, Katharine WhoHol A
Bard, Maria 1901-1944 WhScrn 1, WhScrn 2
Bard, Wilkie 1870-1944 NotNAT B, OxThe
Bard, Wilkie 1874- WhThe
Barda, Antonio Film 2
Bardem, Juan Antonio 1922- BiDFlm, DcFM,
  FilmgC, OxFilm, WorEnF
Bardette, Trevor 1902- Vers A, WhoHol A
Bardon, Henry 1923- WhoThe 16
Bardot, Brigitte MotPP, WhoHol A
Bardot, Brigitte 1933- FilmgC
Bardot, Brigitte 1934- BiDFlm, CelR 3,
  IntMPA 1977, MovMk, OxFilm, WorEnF
Bare, Richard L 1909?- FilmgC, IntMPA 1977
Baren, Harvey M 1931- IntMPA 1977
Barenboim, Daniel 1942- CelR 3
Barer, Marshall L 1923- AmSCAP 1966,
  BiE&WWA, EncMT, NotNAT
Barey, Pat WomWMM B
Bargagli, Girolamo 1537-1586 McGWD
Barge, Gillian 1940- WhoThe 16

Bari, Gwen 1927- AmSCAP 1966
Bari, Lynn MotPP
Bari, Lynn 1913- HolP 30, ThFT
Bari, Lynn 1915- FilmgC, WhoHol A
Bari, Lynn 1916- MovMk
Bari, Lynn 1917- IntMPA 1977
Barillet, Pierre 1923- McGWD
Baring, Aubrey 1912- IntMPA 1977
Baring, Maurice 1874-1945 NotNAT B, WhThe
Baring, Norah 1907- Film 2
Barish, Sherlee NewYTET
Barkan, Stanley Howard 1936- AmSCAP 1966
Barker, Bradley 1883-1951 Film 1, Film 2,
  WhScrn 1, WhScrn 2, WhoHol B
Barker, Cecil NewYTET
Barker, Clive 1931- WhoThe 16
Barker, Corrine Film 2
Barker, Dale 1920- AmSCAP 1966
Barker, Eric Film 1
Barker, Eric 1912- FilmgC, IntMPA 1977
Barker, Florence 1891-1913 Film 1, WhScrn 2
Barker, Harley Granville- 1877-1946 CnThe,
  NotNAT A, OxThe, WhThe, WhoStg 1908
Barker, Helen Granville- WhThe
Barker, Howard 1946- ConDr 1977, WhoThe 16
Barker, Jack d1950 NotNAT B
Barker, Jack 1922- AmSCAP 1966
Barker, James Nelson 1784-1858 McGWD,
  NotNAT B, OxThe, REnWD
Barker, Jess MotPP
Barker, Jess 1914- FilmgC
Barker, Jess 1915- WhoHol A
Barker, Lex 1919-1973 FilmgC, MotPP, MovMk,
  WhScrn 2, WhoHol B
Barker, Norman IntMPA 1977
Barker, Reginald 1886-1936 TwYS A
Barker, Reginald 1886-1937 DcFM
Barker, Reginald 1886-1945 NotNAT B,
  WhScrn 1, WhScrn 2
Barker, Richard d1903 NotNAT B
Barker, Robert William IntMPA 1977
Barker, Ronnie 1929- FilmgC, WhoThe 16
Barker, Will G 1867-1951 FilmgC, OxFilm
Barker, William George 1867-1951 DcFM
Barkhausen, Hans WomWMM
Barkley, Deanne WomWMM
Barkworth, Peter 1929- FilmgC, WhoThe 16
Barlach, Ernst Heinrich 1870-1938 CnMD,
  McGWD, ModWD, NotNAT B
Barleon, Amelia Film 1
Barlog, Boleslaw 1906- WhThe
Barlow, Anna Marie NatPD
Barlow, Billie 1862-1937 NotNAT B, WhThe
Barlow, H J 1892-1970 WhThe
Barlow, Harold 1915- AmSCAP 1966
Barlow, Howard 1892- AmSCAP 1966
Barlow, Jeff Film 2
Barlow, Kitty Film 2
Barlow, Reginald 1867-1943 Film 2, NotNAT B,
  WhScrn 1, WhScrn 2, WhoHol B
Barlow, Wayne 1912- AmSCAP 1966
Barlow, William Film 2
Barnabe, Bruno 1905- WhoThe 16
Barnabee, Henry Clay 1833-1917 NotNAT A,
  NotNAT B, WhoStg 1906, WhoStg 1908
Barnard, Annie d1941 NotNAT B
Barnard, Charles d1920 NotNAT B
Barnard, Christiaan 1922- CelR 3
Barnard, Ivor 1887-1953 Film 2, FilmgC,
  NotNAT B, WhThe, WhoHol B
Barnathan, Julius NewYTET
Barnell, Nora Ely 1882-1933 WhScrn 1,
  WhScrn 2, WhoHol B
Barnelle, Mary Beth Film 2

Barnes, Al G 1862-1931 *NotNAT A*
Barnes, Barnabe 1569?-1609 *CnThe, REnWD*
Barnes, Barnabee 1569?-1609 *NotNAT B*
Barnes, Barry K 1906-1965 *FilmgC, WhScrn 1,*
  WhScrn 2, WhThe, WhoHol B
Barnes, Bianca *WomWMM*
Barnes, Billy 1927- *BiE&WWA, NotNAT*
Barnes, Billy *see also* Barnes, William
Barnes, Binnie 1905- *FilmgC, HolP 30, MotPP,*
  ThFT, WhThe, WhoHol A
Barnes, Binnie 1906- *Film 2, MovMk*
Barnes, Charlotte Mary Sanford 1818-1863
  NotNAT B, OxThe
Barnes, Christina *WomWMM B*
Barnes, Clifford P 1897- *AmSCAP 1966*
Barnes, Clive Alexander 1927- *CelR 3, NotNAT,*
  WhoThe 16
Barnes, Djuna 1892- *CnMD, ConDr 1977*
Barnes, Edna Reming 1883-1935 *WhScrn 1,*
  WhScrn 2
Barnes, Edward Shippen 1887-1958
  AmSCAP 1966
Barnes, Florence d1975 *WhoHol C*
Barnes, Florence Pancho 1902-1975 *WhScrn 2*
Barnes, Frank d1940 *Film 2, WhScrn 1,*
  WhScrn 2, WhoHol B
Barnes, Fred 1884- *WhThe*
Barnes, George 1890-1949 *Film 1, WhScrn 1,*
  WhScrn 2, WhoHol B
Barnes, George 1893-1953 *FilmgC, WorEnF*
Barnes, Hellen 1908- *AmSCAP 1966*
Barnes, Howard 1904-1968 *NotNAT B, WhThe*
Barnes, J H *Film 1, WhoStg 1906*
Barnes, J H 1850-1925 *NotNAT A, NotNAT B,*
  WhThe
Barnes, J H 1852- *WhoStg 1908*
Barnes, Joanna 1934- *FilmgC, MotPP,*
  WhoHol A
Barnes, Joe d1964 *NotNAT B*
Barnes, John 1761-1841 *NotNAT B*
Barnes, Justice D *Film 1*
Barnes, Justus D 1862-1946 *WhScrn 1, WhScrn 2,*
  WhoHol B
Barnes, Sir Kenneth Ralph 1878-1957 *NotNAT A,*
  NotNAT B, OxThe, WhThe
Barnes, Mabel Thomas d1962 *NotNAT B*
Barnes, Mac M *Film 2*
Barnes, Mae 1907- *BiE&WWA, NotNAT,*
  WhoHol A
Barnes, Peter 1931- *ConDr 1977, WhoThe 16*
Barnes, Ray *Film 2*
Barnes, Roy T d1937 *WhoHol B*
Barnes, T Roy 1880-1936 *Film 2, TwYS*
Barnes, T Roy 1880-1937 *NotNAT B, WhScrn 1,*
  WhScrn 2
Barnes, Thomas 1785-1841 *OxThe*
Barnes, V L 1870-1949 *Film 2, WhScrn 1,*
  WhScrn 2, WhoHol B
Barnes, Wade 1917- *AmSCAP 1966*
Barnes, William 1927- *AmSCAP 1966*
Barnes, William *see also* Barnes, Billy
Barnes, William E 1936- *IntMPA 1977*
Barnes, Winifred 1894-1935 *WhThe*
Barnet, Boris 1902-1965 *DcFM, Film 2, OxFilm,*
  WorEnF
Barnet, Robert Ayers 1853-1933 *NotNAT B*
Barnett, Alan 1926- *IntMPA 1977*
Barnett, Alice 1886- *AmSCAP 1966*
Barnett, Battling *Film 1*
Barnett, C Z d1890 *NotNAT B*
Barnett, Charles *Film 1*
Barnett, Chester A 1885-1947 *Film 1, NotNAT B,*
  WhScrn 1, WhScrn 2, WhoHol B
Barnett, Griff 1885-1958 *WhScrn 1, WhScrn 2,*

WhoHol B
Barnett, Jack 1920- *AmSCAP 1966*
Barnett, Morris d1856 *NotNAT B*
Barnett, Vince 1902- *FilmgC, MovMk, Vers A*
Barnett, Vince 1903- *WhoHol A*
Barney, Jay *BiE&WWA, NotNAT, WhoHol A*
Barnhill, James 1922- *BiE&WWA, NotNAT*
Barnouw, Erik *NewYTET*
Barnum, George *Film 2*
Barnum, George William d1937 *NotNAT B*
Barnum, Phineas Taylor 1810-1891 *CnThe,*
  NotNAT A, NotNAT B, OxThe
Baron, Andre 1602?-1655 *OxThe*
Baron, Auguste 1853-1938 *DcFM*
Baron, Etienne 1676-1711 *OxThe*
Baron, Jeanne Ausoult 1625-1662 *OxThe*
Baron, Jonny 1925- *AmSCAP 1966*
Baron, Lewis d1920 *NotNAT B*
Baron, Lita *WhoHol A*
Baron, Maurice 1889-1964 *AmSCAP 1966,*
  NotNAT B
Baron, Michael 1653?-1729 *NotNAT B*
Baron, Michel 1653-1729 *OxThe*
Baron, Robert Alex 1920- *BiE&WWA, NotNAT*
Baron, Vic 1910- *AmSCAP 1966*
Baroncelli, Jacques De 1881-1951 *DcFM, OxFilm*
Baronova, Irina 1919- *WhThe*
Baronova, Irina 1922- *WhoHol A*
Baross, Jan 1943- *WomWMM B*
Baroux, Lucien 1889-1968 *WhScrn 1, WhScrn 2*
Barovick, Fred *AmSCAP 1966*
Barr, Albert E 1931- *AmSCAP 1966*
Barr, Anthony 1921- *AmSCAP 1966,*
  IntMPA 1977
Barr, Byron 1917-1966 *WhScrn 2, WhoHol B*
Barr, Geoffrey 1924- *BiE&WWA*
Barr, Jeanne 1932-1967 *WhScrn 1, WhScrn 2,*
  WhoHol B
Barr, Michael 1927- *AmSCAP 1966*
Barr, Patrick 1908- *FilmgC, IntMPA 1977,*
  WhoHol A, WhoThe 16
Barr, Richard 1917- *BiE&WWA, NotNAT,*
  WhoThe 16
Barraclough, Sydney d1930 *NotNAT B*
Barranger, M S 1937- *NotNAT*
Barras, Charles M 1826-1873 *NotNAT B, PIP&P*
Barrat, Robert 1891-1970 *FilmgC, MovMk,*
  Vers B, WhScrn 1, WhScrn 2, WhoHol B
Barratt, Augustus *WhThe*
Barratt, Walter Augustus d1947 *NotNAT B*
Barratt, Watson 1884-1962 *NotNAT B, WhThe*
Barraud, George 1894- *Film 2*
Barrault, Jean-Louis 1910- *BiE&WWA, CnThe,*
  FilmgC, MovMk, NotNAT A, OxFilm,
  OxThe, WhThe, WhoHol A, WorEnF
Barre, Albert d1910 *NotNAT B*
Barre, Nigel 1889- *Film 2*
Barrere, Jean 1918- *BiE&WWA*
Barreto, Lima 1905- *FilmgC, OxFilm*
Barreto, Victor Lima 1905- *WorEnF*
Barreto, Vitor De Lima 1905- *DcFM*
Barrett, Charles C 1871-1929 *WhScrn 1,*
  WhScrn 2
Barrett, Edith 1906- *WhThe*
Barrett, George 1869-1935 *NotNAT B, WhThe*
Barrett, George Edward 1849-1894 *NotNAT B,*
  OxThe
Barrett, Mrs. George H d1857 *NotNAT B*
Barrett, George Horton 1794-1860 *NotNAT B,*
  OxThe
Barrett, Henry Michael d1872 *NotNAT B*
Barrett, Ivy Rice 1898-1962 *NotNAT B,*
  WhScrn 1, WhScrn 2, WhoHol B
Barrett, James Lee 1929- *CmMov, FilmgC,*

IntMPA 1977
Barrett, Jane 1923-1969 *FilmgC, WhScrn 1,*
WhScrn 2, WhoHol B
Barrett, Jimmie d1964 *NotNAT B*
Barrett, Judith *WhoHol A*
Barrett, Laurinda *WhoHol A*
Barrett, Lawrence 1838-1891 *FamA&A,*
NotNAT A, NotNAT B, OxThe
Barrett, Leslie *WhoHol A*
Barrett, Lester *WhThe*
Barrett, Majel *WhoHol A*
Barrett, Nathan Noble *NatPD*
Barrett, Oscar, Jr. 1875-1941 *WhThe*
Barrett, Oscar, Jr. 1875-1943 *NotNAT B*
Barrett, Oscar, Sr. d1941 *NotNAT B*
Barrett, Pat 1889-1959 *WhScrn 2, WhoHol B*
Barrett, Ray 1926- *FilmgC*
Barrett, Rona *NewYTET*
Barrett, Tony 1916-1974 *WhScrn 2, WhoHol B*
Barrett, Wilson 1846-1904 *NotNAT B, OxThe*
Barrett, Wilson 1900- *WhThe*
Barri, Mario d1963 *WhScrn 1, WhScrn 2,*
WhoHol B
Barri, Odoardo d1920 *NotNAT B*
Barrie, Amanda 1939- *FilmgC, WhoThe 16*
Barrie, Barbara 1931- *NotNAT, WhoHol A,*
WhoThe 16
Barrie, Eddie *Film 1*
Barrie, Elaine *WhoHol A*
Barrie, Sir James Matthew 1860-1937 *CnMD,*
CnThe, FilmgC, McGWD, ModWD,
NotNAT A, NotNAT B, OxThe, PIP&P,
REnWD, WhScrn 2, WhThe, WhoStg 1906,
WhoStg 1908
Barrie, Mona 1909- *FilmgC, IntMPA 1977,*
MovMk
Barrie, Nigel 1889- *Film 1, Film 2, TwYS*
Barrie, Wendy 1912- *FilmgC, MotPP, MovMk,*
ThFT
Barrie, Wendy 1913- *IntMPA 1977, WhoHol A*
Barrier, Edgar 1902-1964 *WhScrn 1*
Barrier, Edgar 1906-1964 *FilmgC, MovMk*
Barrier, Edgar 1907-1964 *WhScrn 2, WhoHol B*
Barriere, Theodore 1823-1877 *NotNAT B, OxThe*
Barringer, Barry 1888-1938 *WhScrn 2*
Barringer, Ned d1976 *WhoHol C*
Barrington, Herbert 1872-1933 *Film 1, WhScrn 1,*
WhScrn 2
Barrington, Rutland 1853-1922 *NotNAT A,*
NotNAT B, WhThe
Barris, Chuck *NewYTET*
Barris, Harry 1905-1962 *AmSCAP 1966,*
NotNAT B, WhScrn 2, WhoHol B
Barriscale, Bessie 1884-1965 *Film 1, Film 2,*
MotPP, TwYS, WhScrn 1, WhScrn 2,
WhoHol B, WomWMM
Barrois, Charles *Film 2*
Barron, Arthur *ConDr 1977C, NewYTET*
Barron, Arthur Ray 1934- *IntMPA 1977*
Barron, Billy Malloy 1925- *AmSCAP 1966*
Barron, Evelyn *WomWMM*
Barron, Frederick C 1888-1955 *WhScrn 1,*
WhScrn 2
Barron, Keith 1934- *FilmgC*
Barron, Marcus d1944 *NotNAT B, WhThe,*
WhoHol B
Barron, Mark d1960 *NotNAT B*
Barron, Muriel 1906- *WhThe*
Barron, Ted 1879-1943 *AmSCAP 1966*
Barron, Winston *IntMPA 1977*
Barros, Jose Leitao De 1896- *DcFM*
Barroso, Ary d1964 *NotNAT B*
Barroux, Lucien d1968 *WhoHol B*
Barrow, Bernard 1927- *BiE&WWA, NotNAT*

Barrows, Henry A 1875?-1945 *Film 1, Film 2,*
WhScrn 2
Barrows, James C 1853-1925 *NotNAT B*
Barrows, James O 1853-1925 *Film 2, WhScrn 1,*
WhScrn 2, WhoHol B, WhoStg 1908
Barry, A *Film 2*
Barry, Al 1903- *AmSCAP 1966*
Barry, Ann Spranger d1801 *NotNAT B*
Barry, Bob 1930- *NatPD*
Barry, Bobby d1964 *NotNAT B*
Barry, Cecil *Film 2*
Barry, Christine 1911- *WhThe*
Barry, Dave 1918- *AmSCAP 1966*
Barry, Diane *WomWMM B*
Barry, Don Red 1912- *FilmgC, MotPP,*
WhoHol A
Barry, Donald *IntMPA 1977*
Barry, Doris *Film 2*
Barry, Elaine d1948 *NotNAT B*
Barry, Elizabeth 1653-1713 *PIP&P*
Barry, Elizabeth 1658-1713 *NotNAT B, OxThe*
Barry, Fred d1964 *NotNAT B*
Barry, Gene 1921- *FilmgC, IntMPA 1977,*
MotPP, WhoHol A
Barry, Gerald *Film 2*
Barry, Gerry 1913- *AmSCAP 1966*
Barry, Helen d1904 *NotNAT B*
Barry, Iris 1895-1969 *FilmgC*
Barry, Iris 1896-1969 *OxFilm*
Barry, Jack 1918- *IntMPA 1977, NewYTET*
Barry, Joan 1901- *WhThe*
Barry, Joan 1903- *Film 2*
Barry, Joe d1974 *WhScrn 2, WhoHol B*
Barry, John 1933- *CmMov, EncMT, FilmgC,*
IntMPA 1977, OxFilm, WorEnF
Barry, Kevin M 1932- *AmSCAP 1966*
Barry, Leon *Film 2*
Barry, Lydia d1932 *NotNAT B*
Barry, Michael 1910- *IntMPA 1977*
Barry, Patricia *WhoHol A*
Barry, Paul *NotNAT, WhoHol A*
Barry, Pauline *Film 1*
Barry, Philip 1896-1949 *CnMD, CnThe, FilmgC,*
McGWD, ModWD, NotNAT A, NotNAT B,
OxThe, PIP&P, REnWD, WhThe
Barry, Philip, Jr. *NewYTET*
Barry, Rick 1944- *CelR 3*
Barry, Robert 1901-1931 *WhScrn 1, WhScrn 2*
Barry, Sheil 1882-1897 *NotNAT B*
Barry, Shiel 1882-1897 *WhThe*
Barry, Spranger 1719-1777 *NotNAT B, OxThe*
Barry, Thomas 1798-1876 *NotNAT B*
Barry, Tom 1884-1931 *NotNAT B, WhScrn 1,*
WhScrn 2, WhoHol B
Barry, Viola 1894-1964 *Film 1, NotNAT B,*
WhScrn 1, WhScrn 2, WhoHol B
Barry, Wesley 1906- *WhoHol A*
Barry, Wesley 1907- *Film 1, Film 2, TwYS*
Barry, William 1911- *AmSCAP 1966*
Barrye, Emily 1896-1957 *Film 2, WhScrn 1,*
WhScrn 2, WhoHol B
Barrymore, Diana 1921-1960 *FilmgC, HolP 40,*
MotPP, NotNAT A, NotNAT B, WhScrn 1,
WhScrn 2, WhThe, WhoHol B
Barrymore, Elaine *NotNAT A*
Barrymore, Ethel 1878-1959 *WhoStg 1908*
Barrymore, Ethel 1879-1959 *CnThe, FamA&A,*
Film 1, FilmgC, MGM, MotPP, MovMk,
NotNAT A, NotNAT B, OxFilm, OxThe,
PIP&P, ThFT, TwYS, WhScrn 1,
WhScrn 2, WhThe, WhoHol B,
WhoStg 1906, WorEnF
Barrymore, Georgiana Drew 1856-1893 *OxThe,*
PIP&P

Barrymore, Georgie Drew 1856-1893 *NotNAT B*
Barrymore, John 1882-1942 *BiDFlm, CmMov,*
  CnThe, FamA&A, Film 1, Film 2, FilmgC,
  MGM, MotPP, MovMk, NotNAT A,
  NotNAT B, OxFilm, OxThe, PIP&P, TwYS,
  WhScrn 1, WhScrn 2, WhThe, WhoHol B,
  WorEnF
Barrymore, John, Jr. 1932- *FilmgC, WhoHol A*
Barrymore, John Blyth, Jr. 1932- *IntMPA 1977*
Barrymore, John Drew 1932- *MotPP, WhoHol A*
Barrymore, Lionel 1878-1954 *AmSCAP 1966,*
  BiDFlm, FamA&A, Film 1, Film 2, FilmgC,
  MGM, MotPP, MovMk, NotNAT A,
  NotNAT B, OxFilm, OxThe, PIP&P, TwYS,
  WhScrn 1, WhScrn 2, WhThe, WhoHol B,
  WorEnF
Barrymore, Maurice 1847-1905 *FamA&A,*
  NotNAT B, OxThe, PIP&P
Barrymore, Richard Barry, Earl Of 1769-1793
  OxThe
Barrymore, William d1845 *OxThe*
Barrymore, Mrs. William d1862 *NotNAT B*
Barrymore, William 1758-1830 *NotNAT B,*
  OxThe, PIP&P
Barrymore, William Henry d1845 *NotNAT B*
Barrymore Family *MotPP, NotNAT A*
Barsac, Madame *Film 2*
Barsacq, Leon 1906-1969 *DcFM*
Barskaya, Margarita *WomWMM*
Barsky, Philip 1914- *AmSCAP 1966*
Barsky, Vladimir *Film 2*
Bart, Jan 1919- *AmSCAP 1966*
Bart, Lionel 1930- *BiE&WWA, ConDr 1977D,*
  EncMT, FilmgC, NotNAT, WhoThe 16
Bart, Peter *IntMPA 1977*
Bart, Teddy 1936- *AmSCAP 1966*
Bartel, Jean *WhoHol A*
Bartell, Richard 1898-1967 *WhScrn 1, WhScrn 2,*
  WhoHol B
Bartels, Louis John 1895-1932 *Film 2,*
  NotNAT B, WhScrn 1, WhScrn 2,
  WhoHol B
Bartenieff, George 1933- *NotNAT*
Barter, Teddy 1889-1939 *WhScrn 1, WhScrn 2*
Bartet, Jeanne Julia 1854- *WhThe*
Bartet, Julia d1941 *Film 1, NotNAT B*
Barth, Belle d1971 *WhoHol B*
Barth, Cecil d1949 *NotNAT B, WhThe*
Barth, Hans 1897-1956 *AmSCAP 1966*
Barthelme, Donald 1931- *CelR 3*
Barthelmess, Richard d1963 *MotPP, WhoHol B*
Barthelmess, Richard 1895-1963 *BiDFlm, Film 2,*
  FilmgC, MovMk, NotNAT B, OxFilm,
  TwYS, WorEnF
Barthelmess, Richard 1897-1963 *WhScrn 1,*
  WhScrn 2
Barthlemess, Richard 1895-1963 *Film 1*
Bartholdi, Fred d1961 *NotNAT B*
Bartholemew, Freddie 1924- *FilmgC*
Bartholomae, Philip H d1947 *NotNAT B*
Bartholomae, Phillip H d1947 *WhThe*
Bartholomew, Agnes d1955 *WhScrn 1, WhScrn 2,*
  WhoHol B
Bartholomew, Ann d1862 *NotNAT B*
Bartholomew, Freddie 1924- *BiDFlm,*
  IntMPA 1977, MGM, MotPP, MovMk,
  OxFilm, WhoHol A, WorEnF
Bartholomew, Marshall Moore 1885-
  AmSCAP 1966
Bartles, Alfred H 1930- *AmSCAP 1966*
Bartlett, Basil 1905- *WhThe*
Bartlett, Clifford 1903-1936 *NotNAT B,*
  WhScrn 1, WhScrn 2, WhThe, WhoHol B
Bartlett, Elise *WhThe*

Bartlett, Elsie *Film 2*
Bartlett, Floyd A 1893- *AmSCAP 1966*
Bartlett, Freude *WomWMM B*
Bartlett, Hall 1922- *FilmgC, IntMPA 1977*
Bartlett, Hetta *Film 2*
Bartlett, Josephine d1910 *NotNAT B*
Bartlett, Martine *BiE&WWA, WhoHol A*
Bartlett, Michael 1901- *WhThe*
Bartlett, Sy 1909- *CmMov, FilmgC,*
  IntMPA 1977
Bartley, Mrs. George d1850 *NotNAT B*
Bartley, George 1782-1858 *NotNAT B*
Bartley, Robert T *NewYTET*
Bartok, Bela 1881-1945 *AmSCAP 1966*
Bartok, Eva 1926- *FilmgC*
Bartok, Eva 1929- *WhoHol A*
Bartolozzi, Josephine d1848 *NotNAT B*
Bartolozzi, Lucia Elizabeth *PIP&P*
Barton, Buzz 1914- *Film 2, TwYS*
Barton, Charles 1902- *FilmgC, IntMPA 1977*
Barton, Dora d1966 *WhThe*
Barton, Grace *WhoStg 1908*
Barton, James d1962 *MotPP, WhoHol B*
Barton, James 1890-1962 *EncMT, MovMk,*
  NotNAT B, Vers B, WhScrn 1, WhScrn 2,
  WhThe
Barton, James 1902-1962 *FilmgC*
Barton, Joe 1883-1937 *WhScrn 1, WhScrn 2,*
  WhoHol B
Barton, John 1872-1946, *NotNAT B, WhScrn 2*
Barton, John 1928- *WhoThe 16*
Barton, Lucy 1891- *BiE&WWA, NotNAT*
Barton, Margaret 1926- *WhThe, WhoHol A*
Barton, Mary d1970 *WhThe*
Barton, Robert Buzz *WhoHol A*
Barton, Sam d1941 *NotNAT B*
Barton, Ward J d1963 *NotNAT B*
Bartosch, Berthold 1883-1968 *WorEnF*
Bartosch, Berthold 1893-1968 *DcFM, FilmgC,*
  OxFilm
Bartosch, Chester 1899-1967 *WhScrn 1,*
  WhScrn 2
Bartsch, Hans d1952 *NotNAT B*
Barty, Billy *WhoHol A*
Barty, Jack d1943 *WhoHol B*
Barty, Jack 1888-1942 *NotNAT B, WhThe*
Barty, Jack 1889-1942 *WhScrn 2*
Barty, Jack 1889-1943 *WhScrn 1*
Barua, Pramathesh Chandra 1900-1951 *DcFM*
Baruch, Andre *IntMPA 1977*
Baruch, Ralph M 1923- *IntMPA 1977*
Barwick, Edwin d1928 *NotNAT B*
Barwyn, Max *Film 2*
Bary, Jean *Film 2*
Bary, Leon *Film 1*
Barzell, Wolfe 1897-1969 *WhScrn 1, WhScrn 2,*
  WhoHol B
Barzman, Ben 1910- *DcFM*
Barzman, Ben 1911- *FilmgC, WorEnF*
Barzman, Ben 1912- *OxFilm*
Barzun, Jacques 1907- *CelR 3*
Basaglia, Maria *WomWMM*
Basch, Buddy 1922- *IntMPA 1977*
Basch, Felix 1889-1944 *WhScrn 1, WhScrn 2,*
  WhoHol B
Bascomb, A W 1880-1939 *NotNAT B*
Basehart, Richard *WhoHol A*
Basehart, Richard 1914- *IntMPA 1977, MovMk,*
  WhoThe 16
Basehart, Richard 1915- *FilmgC*
Basehart, Richard 1919- *BiE&WWA, NotNAT,*
  OxFilm
Baseheart, Richard *MotPP*
Basford, Madaline Lee d1974 *WhoHol B*

Bashor, Wilma d1964 *NotNAT B*
Basie, Count 1904- *CelR 3*
Basie, William 1906- *AmSCAP 1966*
Basile, Joe 1889-1961 *AmSCAP 1966*
Baskcomb, A W 1880-1939 *WhThe*
Baskcomb, Lawrence 1883-1962 *WhThe*
Baskerville, David 1919- *AmSCAP 1966*
Baskett, James 1904-1948 *WhScrn 1, WhScrn 2, WhoHol B*
Baskette, Billy 1884-1949 *AmSCAP 1966*
Baskut, Cevat Fehmi 1905- *REnWD*
Basquette, Lina 1907- *Film 1, Film 2, TwYS, WhoHol A*
Bass, Alfie 1920- *FilmgC, WhoHol A*
Bass, Alfred 1921- *WhoThe 16*
Bass, Barbara DeJong 1946- *WomWMM B*
Bass, Elaine *WomWMM B*
Bass, George Houston 1938- *NotNAT*
Bass, Jules 1935- *AmSCAP 1966*
Bass, Roger 1925- *AmSCAP 1966*
Bass, Saul 1920- *DcFM, FilmgC, IntMPA 1977, OxFilm, WorEnF*
Bass, Sid 1913- *AmSCAP 1966*
Bassano, Enrico 1899- *McGWD*
Basserman, Albert 1867-1952 *CnThe, Film 2, FilmgC, MotPP, MovMk, NotNAT B, Vers B, WhoHol B*
Basserman, Else 1878-1961 *NotNAT B, WhoHol B*
Bassermann, Albert 1865-1952 *WhScrn 1, WhScrn 2*
Bassermann, Albert 1867-1952 *OxThe*
Bassermann, August 1848-1931 *NotNAT B, OxThe*
Bassermann-Schiff, Else 1878-1961 *WhScrn 1, WhScrn 2*
Basset, Serge d1917 *NotNAT B*
Bassett, Alfred Leon 1870- *WhThe*
Bassett, Karolyn Wells 1892-1931 *AmSCAP 1966*
Bassett, Russell 1846-1918 *Film 1, NotNAT B, WhScrn 2, WhoHol B*
Bassett, Tony 1885-1955 *WhScrn 1, WhScrn 2*
Bassey, Shirley 1937- *CelR 3*
Basshe, Emjo d1939 *NotNAT B*
Bassler, Robert 1903- *FilmgC*
Bassman, George 1914- *AmSCAP 1966, BiE&WWA*
Bastedo, Alexandra 1946- *FilmgC*
Bastian, Jack *Film 2*
Baston, J Thornton *Film 2*
Baston, Jack *Film 2*
Baston, John *Film 2*
Bataille, Henri 1872-1922 *McGWD*
Bataille, Henry 1872-1922 *CnMD, ModWD, NotNAT B, WhThe*
Bataille, Sylvie 1912- *OxFilm*
Batalof, M *Film 2*
Batalov, Alexei 1924- *WhoHol A*
Batalov, Alexei 1928- *WorEnF*
Batalov, Nikolai Petrovich 1899-1937 *Film 2, OxThe*
Batchelder, William H 1937- *NotNAT*
Batcheller, Joseph D 1915- *BiE&WWA, NotNAT*
Batchelor, Reverend Doctor *Film 2*
Batchelor, Joy 1914- *DcFM, FilmgC, IntMPA 1977, OxFilm, WomWMM, WomWMM B, WorEnF*
Bateman, Miss 1842-1917 *WhThe*
Bateman, Ellen Douglas 1844-1936 *NotNAT B, OxThe*
Bateman, Mrs. H L 1823-1881 *NotNAT B*
Bateman, Hezekiah Linthicum 1812-1875 *NotNAT B, OxThe*
Bateman, Isabel Emilie 1854-1934 *NotNAT A,*

NotNAT B, OxThe
Bateman, Jessie 1877-1940 *NotNAT B, WhThe*
Bateman, Kate Josephine 1842-1917 *NotNAT B*
Bateman, Kate Josephine 1843-1917 *FamA&A, OxThe*
Bateman, Leah 1892- *WhThe*
Bateman, Sidney Frances 1823-1881 *OxThe*
Bateman, Victory 1866-1926 *Film 1, Film 2, WhScrn 1, WhScrn 2, WhoHol B, WhoStg 1906, WhoStg 1908*
Bateman, Virginia Frances 1853-1940 *NotNAT B, OxThe, WhThe*
Bateman, Zillah 1900-1970 *WhThe*
Bates, Alan *MotPP, PIP&P, PIP&P A, WhoHol A*
Bates, Alan 1930- *FilmgC, OxFilm*
Bates, Alan 1934- *BiE&WWA, CelR 3, CnThe, IntMPA 1977, MovMk, NotNAT, WhoThe 16*
Bates, Barbara 1925-1969 *FilmgC, MotPP, WhScrn 1, WhScrn 2, WhoHol B*
Bates, Blanche 1873-1941 *FamA&A, Film 1, NotNAT B, OxThe, PIP&P, WhScrn 1, WhScrn 2, WhThe, WhoHol B, WhoStg 1906, WhoStg 1908*
Bates, Florence d1954 *MotPP, WhoHol B*
Bates, Florence 1888-1954 *FilmgC, MovMk, NotNAT B, WhScrn 1, WhScrn 2*
Bates, Florence 1890-1954 *Vers A*
Bates, Granville d1939 *WhoHol B*
Bates, Granville 1882-1940 *WhScrn 1, WhScrn 2*
Bates, Jeanne *WhoHol A*
Bates, Lawson d1975 *WhoHol C*
Bates, Les 1877-1930 *Film 2, WhoHol B*
Bates, Leslie A 1877-1930 *WhScrn 1, WhScrn 2*
Bates, Lulu *BiE&WWA, NotNAT*
Bates, Marie d1923 *NotNAT B*
Bates, Michael 1920- *WhoThe 16*
Bates, Michael 1929- *FilmgC*
Bates, Ralph 1940- *FilmgC*
Bates, Sally 1907- *WhThe*
Bates, Thorpe 1883-1958 *NotNAT B, WhThe*
Bates, Tom *Film 2*
Bates, William *NotNAT B*
Bateson, Timothy 1926- *PIP&P, WhoThe 16*
Bath, Albert J d1964 *NotNAT B*
Bath, Hubert 1883- *WhThe*
Bathyllus *OxThe*
Batie, Frank 1880-1949 *NotNAT B*
Batie, Franklin A 1880-1949 *WhoHol B*
Batie, Franklyn A 1880-1949 *WhScrn 2*
Batley, Dorothy 1902- *Film 1, WhThe*
Batley, Ernest G 1879-1917 *Film 1, WhScrn 2*
Batson, George 1918- *BiE&WWA, NotNAT*
Batten, John *Film 2*
Batten, Tom *WhoHol A*
Battier, Robert 1887-1946 *WhScrn 1, WhScrn 2, WhoHol B*
Battista, Miriam 1914- *Film 1, Film 2, TwYS*
Battle, Edgar William 1907- *AmSCAP 1966*
Battles, John 1921- *BiE&WWA, WhThe*
Batty, Archibald 1887-1961 *NotNAT B, WhScrn 1, WhScrn 2, WhThe, WhoHol B*
Batu, Selahattin 1905- *REnWD*
Baty, Gaston 1885-1952 *NotNAT B, OxThe, WhThe*
Bauchens, Anne 1882-1967 *CmMov, WomWMM*
Baudet, Louise *Film 2*
Baudin, Ginette 1921-1971 *WhScrn 2*
Baudin, Henri *Film 2*
Bauduc, Ray 1909- *AmSCAP 1966*
Bauer, David 1918-1973 *WhScrn 2*
Bauer, Friedhold 1934- *CroCD*
Bauer, Harold 1873-1951 *AmSCAP 1966*

Bauer, Harry 1881-1941 *Film 1, Film 2*
Bauer, William 1915- *AmSCAP 1966*
Bauer, Wolfgang 1941- *CroCD*
Bauer, Yevgeni 188-1917 *DcFM*
Bauer-Adamara *WomWMM*
Bauerle, Adolf 1786-1859 *OxThe*
Bauernfeld, Eduard 1802-1890 *OxThe*
Bauersfeld, Marjorie Mirandy 1890-1974
  WhScrn 2
Bauersmith, Paula 1909- *BiE&WWA, NotNAT,*
  WhoThe 16
Baughan, Edward Algernon 1865-1938 *NotNAT B,*
  WhThe
Baum, Bernie 1928- *AmSCAP 1966*
Baum, Claude 1928- *AmSCAP 1966*
Baum, Mrs. H William 1882-1970 *WhScrn 1,*
  WhScrn 2
Baum, Harry 1916-1974 *WhScrn 2, WhoHol B*
Baum, Lyman Frank 1856-1919 *FilmgC,*
  NotNAT B, PIP&P A, WhoStg 1906,
  WhoStg 1908
Baum, Martin 1924- *BiE&WWA, IntMPA 1977*
Baum, Maurice 1912- *IntMPA 1977*
Baum, Morton 1905-1968 *NotNAT B*
Baum, Vicki 1888-1960 *NotNAT A, NotNAT B*
Bauman, Suzanne *WomWMM B*
Baumbach, Jo Ann *WomWMM B*
Baumstone, Harold 1911- *IntMPA 1977*
Baur, Elizabeth *WhoHol A*
Baur, Franklyn d1950 *NotNAT B*
Baur, Harry 1881-1941 *Film 2, FilmgC*
Baur, Harry 1881-1943 *NotNAT B, WhScrn 1,*
  WhScrn 2, WhoHol B
Bava, Mario 1914- *BiDFlm, FilmgC, WorEnF*
Bavicchi, John 1922- *AmSCAP 1966*
Bavier, Frances *WhoHol A*
Bawn, Harry 1872- *WhThe*
Bax, Clifford 1886-1962 *McGWD, NotNAT B,*
  OxThe, WhThe
Baxley, Barbara *MotPP, WhoHol A*
Baxley, Barbara 1925- *NotNAT*
Baxley, Barbara 1927- *BiE&WWA, WhoThe 16*
Baxter, Alan 1908-1976 *BiE&WWA, FilmgC,*
  MovMk, NotNAT B, WhThe
Baxter, Alan 1911-1976 *Vers B*
Baxter, Anne 1923- *BiDFlm, BiE&WWA,*
  CelR 3, FilmgC, IntMPA 1977, MotPP,
  MovMk, NotNAT, WhoHol A, WhoThe 16,
  WorEnF
Baxter, Barry 1894-1922 *NotNAT B, WhThe*
Baxter, Beryl 1926- *FilmgC, WhThe*
Baxter, Sir Beverley 1891-1964 *NotNAT B,*
  WhThe
Baxter, Billy 1926- *IntMPA 1977*
Baxter, George *Film 2*
Baxter, Glenn E 1926- *AmSCAP 1966*
Baxter, James 1913-1964 *AmSCAP 1966*
Baxter, James C 1923-1969 *WhScrn 1, WhScrn 2*
Baxter, James Keir 1926-1972 *ConDr 1973*
Baxter, Jane 1909- *FilmgC, WhoHol A,*
  WhoThe 16
Baxter, Jimmy d1969 *WhoHol B*
Baxter, John 1896- *FilmgC*
Baxter, Keith *WhoHol A*
Baxter, Keith 1933- *IntMPA 1977, WhoThe 16*
Baxter, Keith 1935- *BiE&WWA, NotNAT*
Baxter, Larry 1924- *AmSCAP 1966*
Baxter, Les 1922- *AmSCAP 1966*
Baxter, Lora 1908-1955 *NotNAT B, WhScrn 1,*
  WhScrn 2, WhoHol B
Baxter, Phil 1896- *AmSCAP 1966*
Baxter, Richard 1593-1666? *OxThe*
Baxter, Richard 1618- *OxThe*
Baxter, Stanley 1926- *WhoThe 16*

Baxter, Stanley 1928- *FilmgC, IntMPA 1977*
Baxter, Warner d1951 *MotPP, NotNAT B,*
  WhoHol B
Baxter, Warner 1889-1951 *FilmgC*
Baxter, Warner 1891-1951 *WhScrn 1, WhScrn 2*
Baxter, Warner 1892-1951 *BiDFlm, CmMov*
Baxter, Warner 1893-1951 *Film 1, Film 2,*
  MovMk, TwYS, WorEnF
Baxter, Warner 1893-1952 *OxFilm*
Bay, Howard 1912- *BiE&WWA, NotNAT,*
  WhoThe 16
Bay, Susan *WhoHol A*
Bay, Tom 1901-1933 *WhScrn 1, WhScrn 2,*
  WhoHol B
Bayer, Charles W 1893-1953 *WhScrn 1,*
  WhScrn 2
Bayer, Konrad 1932-1964 *CroCD*
Bayes, Nora 1880-1928 *EncMT, FilmgC,*
  NotNAT B, WhThe
Bayfield, Peggy *Film 2*
Bayh, Birch 1928- *CelR 3*
Bayha, Charles A 1891-1957 *AmSCAP 1966*
Bayldon, Geoffrey 1924- *FilmgC*
Bayley, Caroline 1890- *WhThe*
Bayley, Eva *Film 1*
Bayley, Hilda d1971 *Film 2, WhThe*
Baylies, Edmund 1904- *BiE&WWA, NotNAT*
Baylis, Lilian 1874-1937 *CnThe, NotNAT A,*
  OxThe, WhThe
Baylis, Lillian 1874-1937 *NotNAT B*
Bayliss, Blanche *Film 1*
Bayliss, Lillian 1874-1937 *PIP&P*
Bayliss, Peter *WhoThe 16*
Bayly, Caroline *WhThe*
Bayly, Thomas Haynes d1839 *NotNAT B*
Bayne, Beverly 1895- *WhoHol A*
Bayne, Beverly 1896- *Film 1, Film 2, MotPP,*
  TwYS
Bayne, Donald S 1949- *NotNAT*
Baynton, Henry 1892-1951 *NotNAT B, WhThe*
Bayr, Rudolf 1919- *CnMD, CroCD*
Bazelon, David L *NewYTET*
Bazelon, Irwin A 1922- *AmSCAP 1966*
Bazin, Andre 1918-1958 *FilmgC, WorEnF*
Bazin, Andre 1919-1958 *OxFilm*
Bazzini, Allen B 1939- *IntMPA 1977*
Bazzini, Rosily 1941- *IntMPA 1977*
Beach, Ann 1938- *WhoThe 16*
Beach, Bruce C 1903- *AmSCAP 1966*
Beach, Floyd Orion 1898- *AmSCAP 1966*
Beach, Mrs. H H A 1867-1944 *AmSCAP 1966*
Beach, Rex 1877- *TwYS A*
Beach, William d1926 *NotNAT B*
Beacham, Stephanie 1949- *FilmgC*
Beaird, Barbara *WhoHol A*
Beal, Frank 1864-1934 *Film 2, WhScrn 1,*
  WhScrn 2, WhoHol B
Beal, John 1909- *BiE&WWA, FilmgC, HolP 30,*
  IntMPA 1977, MovMk, NotNAT,
  WhoHol A, WhoThe 16
Beal, Joseph Carleton 1900- *AmSCAP 1966*
Beal, Royal d1969 *WhoHol B*
Beal, Royal 1899-1969 *BiE&WWA, NotNAT B*
Beal, Royal 1900-1969 *WhScrn 1, WhScrn 2*
Beal, Scott 1890-1973 *WhScrn 2*
Bealby, George 1877-1931 *NotNAT B, WhThe*
Beale, Betty 1910?- *CelR 3*
Beamish, Frank 1881-1921 *WhScrn 1, WhScrn 2,*
  WhoHol B
Beams, Mary *WomWMM B*
Bean, Judge Roy 1823-1902 *FilmgC*
Bean, Orson 1928- *BiE&WWA, MotPP,*
  NotNAT, WhoHol A, WhoThe 16
Bear, Mary d1972 *WhScrn 2*

Beard, James 1903- *CelR 3*
Beard, John 1716?-1791 *NotNAT B, OxThe*
Beard, Matthew Stymie 1925- *WhoHol A*
Beard, Ray *Film 2*
Bearde, Chris *see* Blye, Allan
Bearden, Romare H 1914- *AmSCAP 1966*
Beardsley, Alice *WhoHol A*
Bearse, Richard Stuart 1939- *AmSCAP 1966*
Beasley, Byron d1927 *NotNAT B*
Beatles, The *FilmgC, MotPP, MovMk, OxFilm, WorEnF*
Beaton, Cecil 1902- *FilmgC*
Beaton, Cecil 1904- *BiE&WWA, CelR 3, CnThe, NotNAT, NotNAT A, OxFilm, WhoThe 16, WorEnF*
Beaton, Mary d1962 *WhScrn 2*
Beatty, Clyde R 1903-1965 *WhScrn 1, WhScrn 2, WhoHol B*
Beatty, George 1895-1971 *WhScrn 1, WhScrn 2, WhoHol B*
Beatty, Harcourt *WhThe*
Beatty, May 1881-1945 *NotNAT B, WhScrn 1, WhScrn 2, WhThe, WhoHol B*
Beatty, Morgan d1975 *NewYTET*
Beatty, Ned *WhoHol A*
Beatty, Norman 1924- *AmSCAP 1966*
Beatty, Robert 1909- *FilmgC, IntMPA 1977, MovMk, WhoHol A, WhoThe 16*
Beatty, Roberta 1891- *WhThe*
Beatty, Warren *BiE&WWA, MotPP, WhoHol A*
Beatty, Warren 1937- *BiDFlm, CelR 3, FilmgC, MovMk, OxFilm, WorEnF*
Beatty, Warren 1938- *IntMPA 1977*
Beau, Henry J 1911- *AmSCAP 1966*
Beaubien, Julien 1896-1947 *WhScrn 1, WhScrn 2, WhoHol B*
Beaubour, Louise Pitel 1665?-1740 *OxThe*
Beaubour, Pierre Trochon De 1662-1725 *OxThe*
Beauchamp, John d1921 *NotNAT B, WhThe*
Beauchateau *OxThe*
Beauchateau, Madeleine DePouget 1615-1683 *OxThe*
Beaudet, Louise 1861-1947 *NotNAT B, WhoHol B*
Beaudet, Louise 1861-1948 *Film 1, Film 2, TwYS*
Beaudet, Louise 1862-1947 *WhScrn 2*
Beaudine, William, Jr. d1970 *NewYTET*
Beaudine, William, Sr. 1892-1970 *FilmgC, MovMk, TwYS A, WhScrn 2*
Beaufort, John 1912- *NotNAT, WhoThe 16*
Beaumar, Constance *Film 1*
Beaumarchais, Pierre-Augustin Caron De 1732-1799 *CnThe, McGWD, NotNAT A, NotNAT B, OxThe, REnWD*
Beaumenard, Rose-Perrine LeRoy 1730-1799 *OxThe*
Beaumont, Charles 1929-1967 *FilmgC, WhScrn 2*
Beaumont, Cyril William 1891- *WhThe*
Beaumont, Diana Muriel 1909-1964 *NotNAT B, WhScrn 1, WhScrn 2, WhThe, WhoHol B*
Beaumont, Francis 1584-1616 *CnThe, McGWD, NotNAT A, NotNAT B, OxThe, PIP&P, REnWD*
Beaumont, Grace *Film 2*
Beaumont, Harry d1966 *Film 1, WhoHol B*
Beaumont, Harry 1888-1966 *TwYS A, WhScrn 1, WhScrn 2*
Beaumont, Harry 1893-1966 *CmMov, FilmgC, MovMk*
Beaumont, Hugh 1908-1973 *CnThe, EncMT, WhThe*
Beaumont, Hugh 1909- *FilmgC, IntMPA 1977,*

WhoHol A
Beaumont, James L 1940- *AmSCAP 1966*
Beaumont, John 1902- *WhThe*
Beaumont, Lucy 1873-1937 *Film 2, TwYS, WhScrn 1, WhScrn 2, WhoHol B*
Beaumont, Muriel 1881-1957 *NotNAT B, WhThe*
Beaumont, Nellie d1938 *NotNAT B*
Beaumont, Ralph 1926- *BiE&WWA, NotNAT*
Beaumont, Roma 1914- *WhThe*
Beaumont, Rose d1938 *NotNAT B*
Beaumont, Susan 1936- *FilmgC, WhoHol A*
Beaumont, Tom *Film 2*
Beaumont, Vertee 1889-1934 *WhScrn 1, WhScrn 2*
Beauplan, Marsha *Film 2*
Beaupre *OxThe*
Beaupre, Madeleine Lemoine *OxThe*
Beaupre, Marotte *OxThe*
Beauval 1635?-1709 *OxThe*
Beauval, Jeanne Olivier DeBourguignon 1648?-1720 *OxThe*
Beauval, Louise 1665?-1740 *OxThe*
Beauvoir, Simone De 1908- *CelR 3*
Beavers, Louise d1962 *MotPP, NotNAT B, WhoHol B*
Beavers, Louise 1889-1962 *Film 2*
Beavers, Louise 1898-1962 *Vers A, WhScrn 1, WhScrn 2*
Beavers, Louise 1902-1962 *FilmgC, HolP 30, MovMk, ThFT*
Beazley, Samuel 1786-1851 *NotNAT B, OxThe*
Beban, George 1873-1928 *Film 1, Film 2, MotPP, NotNAT B, TwYS, WhScrn 1, WhScrn 2, WhoHol B*
Bebderskaya, N *WomWMM*
Beberus, Virginia 1893-1964 *AmSCAP 1966*
Becaud, Gilbert *WhoHol A*
Beccari, Agostino d1598 *OxThe*
Bech, Lili 1885-1939 *OxFilm, WhScrn 2*
Becher, Lady *OxThe*
Becher, Johannes Robert 1891-1958 *CnMD, ModWD*
Becher, John C 1915- *BiE&WWA, NotNAT, WhoHol A*
Becher, Thomas *BiE&WWA*
Becher, Ulrich 1910- *CnMD, CroCD, McGWD*
Bechtal, William 1867-1930 *Film 2*
Bechtel, William 1867-1930 *Film 1, Film 2, WhScrn 1, WhScrn 2, WhoHol B*
Beck, Alexander J 1922- *IntMPA 1977*
Beck, Billy *WhoHol A*
Beck, Cornish *Film 1*
Beck, Danny 1904-1959 *WhScrn 1, WhScrn 2, WhoHol B*
Beck, Gordon 1929- *BiE&WWA, NotNAT*
Beck, Heinrich 1760-1803 *OxThe*
Beck, J Emmett *Film 2*
Beck, Jackson *IntMPA 1977*
Beck, James 1932-1973 *WhScrn 2, WhoHol B*
Beck, John *Film 2, WhoHol A*
Beck, Julian 1925- *BiE&WWA, CelR 3, NotNAT, NotNAT A, PIP&P, WhoThe 16*
Beck, Kimberly *WhoHol A*
Beck, Mabel *Film 2*
Beck, Martha *AmSCAP 1966*
Beck, Martin 1869?-1940 *NotNAT B*
Beck, Mrs. Martin 1889- *BiE&WWA*
Beck, Myer P *IntMPA 1977*
Beck, Nelson C 1887-1952 *WhScrn 1, WhScrn 2*
Beck, Vincent *WhoHol A*
Becker, Bruce 1925- *BiE&WWA*
Becker, F G *Film 2*
Becker, Fred *Film 2*
Becker, Jacques 1906-1960 *BiDFlm, DcFM,*

FilmgC, OxFilm, WhScrn 2, WorEnF
Becker, Jean 1933- *FilmgC*
Becker, John C d1963 *NotNAT B*
Becker, Terry *WhoHol A*
Becker, Theodor *Film 2*
Becker, Viola S *IntMPA 1977*
Becker, William 1927- *BiE&WWA, NotNAT*
Becker-Theodore, Lee 1933- *BiE&WWA*
Beckerman, Bernard 1921- *BiE&WWA, NotNAT*
Beckersache, Carl *Film 2*
Beckett, Gilbert A d1856 *NotNAT B*
Beckett, Samuel 1906- *BiE&WWA, CelR 3,*
  CnMD, CnThe, ConDr 1977, CroCD,
  McGWD, ModWD, NotNAT, NotNAT A,
  OxThe, PIP&P, REnWD
Beckett, Scotty 1929-1968 *FilmgC, MotPP,*
  MovMk, NotNAT B, WhScrn 1, WhScrn 2,
  WhoHol B
Beckett, Wheeler 1898- *AmSCAP 1966*
Beckhard, Arthur J *WhThe*
Beckhelm, Paul 1906- *AmSCAP 1966*
Beckingham, Charles d1731 *NotNAT B*
Beckley, Beatrice Mary 1885- *Film 1, WhThe*
Beckley, Tony *FilmgC, WhoHol A*
Beckman, Henry *WhoHol A*
Beckmann, Karl *Film 2*
Beckwith, Aaron 1914- *IntMPA 1977*
Beckwith, Bainard *Film 2*
Beckwith, Reginald 1908-1965 *FilmgC, MovMk,*
  WhScrn 1, WhScrn 2, WhThe, WhoHol B
Beckwith, Roger *WhScrn 1, WhScrn 2*
Becque, Henri Francois 1837-1899 *CnThe,*
  NotNAT B
Becque, Henry Francois 1837-1899 *CnMD,*
  McGWD, ModWD, OxThe, REnWD
Becwar, George 1917-1970 *WhScrn 2*
Beddoe, Don 1888- *WhoHol A*
Beddoe, Don 1891- *FilmgC, MovMk*
Beddoe, Don 1903- *Vers A*
Beddoes, Thomas Lovell 1803-1849 *NotNAT B*
Bedelia, Bonnie *WhoHol A*
Bedelia, Bonnie 1946- *FilmgC*
Bedelia, Bonnie 1948- *NotNAT*
Bedell, Robert Leech 1909- *AmSCAP 1966*
Bedells, Phyllis 1893- *WhThe*
Bedford, Barbara *Film 2, TwYS*
Bedford, Brian 1935- *BiE&WWA, CelR 3,*
  FilmgC, MotPP, NotNAT, PIP&P,
  WhoHol A, WhoThe 16
Bedford, Harry d1939 *NotNAT B*
Bedford, Henry d1923 *NotNAT B*
Bedford, Paul 1792?-1871 *NotNAT A,*
  NotNAT B, OxThe
Bedini, Jean d1956 *NotNAT B*
Bedoya, Alfonso 1904-1957 *FilmgC, MovMk,*
  Vers A, WhScrn 1, WhScrn 2, WhoHol B
Bee, Molly *WhoHol A*
Beebe, Ford 1888- *FilmgC*
Beebe, Marjorie 1909- *Film 2*
Beech, Frances *Film 1*
Beecham, Sir Joseph d1916 *NotNAT B*
Beecham, Sir Thomas d1961 *NotNAT B*
Beecher, Ada 1862-1935 *WhScrn 1, WhScrn 2*
Beecher, Janet 1884-1955 *FilmgC, MotPP,*
  MovMk, NotNAT B, ThFT, WhScrn 1,
  WhScrn 2, WhThe, WhoHol B
Beecher, Johannes R 1891-1958 *CroCD*
Beecher, Sylvia *Film 2*
Beecher, William Gordon, Jr. 1904-
  AmSCAP 1966
Beecroft, Victor R 1887-1958 *WhScrn 1,*
  WhScrn 2
Beekman, Bernadette *WomWMM B*
Beelby, Malcolm 1907- *AmSCAP 1966*

Beene, Geoffrey 1927- *CelR 3*
Beer-Hofmann, Richard 1866-1945 *CnMD,*
  McGWD, ModWD, OxThe
Beerbohm, Clarence Evelyn d1917 *WhThe*
Beerbohm, Claude *Film 2*
Beerbohm, Sir Max 1872-1956 *CnMD, ModWD,*
  NotNAT A, NotNAT B, OxThe, WhThe
Beerbohn, Elizabeth *Film 2*
Beere, Mrs. Bernard 1856- *WhThe*
Beers, Francine *WhoHol A*
Beers, Jack *WhoHol A*
Beery, Noah 1884-1946 *CmMov, Film 1, Film 2,*
  FilmgC, MotPP, MovMk, OxFilm, TwYS,
  Vers B, WhScrn 1, WhScrn 2, WhoHol B
Beery, Noah, Jr. *MotPP, WhoHol A*
Beery, Noah, Jr. 1913- *Film 2, FilmgC*
Beery, Noah, Jr. 1915- *Vers B*
Beery, Noah, Jr. 1916- *IntMPA 1977, MovMk*
Beery, Noah, Sr. 1883-1946 *NotNAT B*
Beery, Wallace 1880?-1949 *FilmgC, WhoHol B*
Beery, Wallace 1881-1949 *NotNAT B*
Beery, Wallace 1885-1949 *WhScrn 1, WhScrn 2,*
  WorEnF
Beery, Wallace 1886-1949 *BiDFlm, Film 1,*
  Film 2, MGM, MotPP, MovMk, OxFilm
Beery, Wallace 1889-1949 *CmMov, TwYS*
Beery, William *Film 1*
Beeson, Coni Irene 1930- *WomWMM A,*
  WomWMM B
Beeson, Jack 1921- *AmSCAP 1966*
Beeston, Christopher 1570?-1638 *NotNAT B,*
  OxThe
Beeston, William 1606?-1682 *NotNAT B, OxThe,*
  PIP&P
Beet, Alice d1931 *NotNAT B, WhThe*
Begelman, David *IntMPA 1977*
Begg, Gordon *Film 2*
Beggs, Lee 1871-1943 *Film 2, WhScrn 2*
Beggs, Malcolm Lee 1907-1956 *WhScrn 1,*
  WhScrn 2, WhoHol B
Begley, Ed 1901-1970 *BiE&WWA, FilmgC,*
  MotPP, MovMk, NotNAT B, Vers A,
  WhScrn 1, WhScrn 2, WhThe, WhoHol B
Begley, Ed, Jr. *WhoHol A*
Beh, Siew Hwa *WomWMM B*
Behan, Brendan 1923-1964 *BiE&WWA, CnMD,*
  CnThe, ConDr 1977F, CroCD, McGWD,
  ModWD, NotNAT A, NotNAT B, PIP&P,
  REnWD, WhThe
Behn, Aphra 1640-1689 *McGWD, NotNAT A,*
  NotNAT B, OxThe, PIP&P
Behn, Noel 1928- *BiE&WWA, NotNAT*
Behr, Hans-Georg 1937- *CroCD*
Behrens, Frederick 1854-1938 *WhScrn 1,*
  WhScrn 2
Behrens, Jack 1935- *AmSCAP 1966*
Behrens, William *Film 1*
Behrle, Fred 1891-1941 *Film 2, WhScrn 1,*
  WhScrn 2, WhoHol B
Behrman, S N 1893-1973 *BiE&WWA, CmMov,*
  CnMD, CnThe, ConDr 1973, CroCD,
  FilmgC, McGWD, ModWD, NotNAT A,
  NotNAT B, REnWD
Behrman, Samuel Nathan 1893-1973 *PIP&P*
Behrman, Samuel Nathaniel 1893-1973 *OxThe,*
  WhThe
Behymer, L E d1947 *NotNAT B*
Behymer, Minetta S d1958 *NotNAT B*
Beich, Albert 1919- *FilmgC, IntMPA 1977*
Beil, Johann David 1754-1794 *OxThe*
Beim, Norman *NatPD*
Bein, Albert 1902- *BiE&WWA, CnMD,*
  ModWD, NotNAT
Beith, Sir John Hay 1876-1952 *NotNAT B*

Bejart, Armande-Gresinde-Claire-E 1641-1700 *OxThe*
Bejart, Armande-Gresinde-Claire-E 1642-1700 *NotNAT B*
Bejart, Genevieve 1624-1675 *OxThe*
Bejart, Joseph 1616-1659 *OxThe*
Bejart, Louis 1630-1678 *OxThe*
Bejart, Madeleine 1618-1672 *NotNAT B, OxThe*
Bejart Family *CnThe*
Bek-Nazarov, Amo 1892- *DcFM*
Bekassy, Stephen 1915?- *FilmgC*
Bel Geddes, Barbara 1922- *BiE&WWA, CelR 3, CnThe, FilmgC, IntMPA 1977, MotPP, MovMk, NotNAT, PIP&P, WhoHol A, WhoThe 16*
Bel Geddes, Edith Lutyens 1916- *BiE&WWA*
Bel Geddes, Edith Lutyens 1917- *NotNAT*
Bel Geddes, Norman 1893-1958 *CnThe, PIP&P*
Bel Geddes, Norman *see also* Geddes, Norman Bel
Bela, Nicholas d1963 *Film 2, NotNAT B, WhoHol B*
Belafonte, Harold George, Jr. 1927- *AmSCAP 1966*
Belafonte, Harry 1927- *BiE&WWA, CelR 3, FilmgC, IntMPA 1977, MotPP, MovMk, OxFilm, WhoHol A*
Belajeff, Olga *Film 2*
Belan, Cliff 1921- *AmSCAP 1966*
Belanger, Juliette *Film 2*
Belasco, David 1853-1931 *CnThe, McGWD, OxThe, REnWD, WhThe*
Belasco, David 1854-1931 *Film 1*
Belasco, David 1859-1931 *ModWD, NotNAT A, NotNAT B, PIP&P, WhoStg 1906, WhoStg 1908*
Belasco, Edward d1937 *NotNAT B*
Belasco, Frederick d1920 *NotNAT B*
Belasco, Genevieve 1871-1956 *NotNAT B, WhScrn 1, WhScrn 2, WhoHol B*
Belasco, Jay *Film 1*
Belasco, Leon 1902- *BiE&WWA, Film 2, FilmgC, Vers B, WhoHol A*
Belcari, Feo 1410-1484 *McGWD, OxThe*
Belcham, Henry d1917 *NotNAT B*
Belcher, Alice 1880-1939 *WhScrn 1, WhScrn 2, WhoHol B*
Belcher, Charles *Film 2*
Belcher, Ernest *Film 2*
Belcher, Frank H 1869-1947 *Film 1, WhScrn 2*
Beldon, Edwin *WhoStg 1908*
Beldon, Eileen 1901- *WhoThe 16*
Belfer, Hal B *IntMPA 1977*
Belfield, Frederick H 1901- *BiE&WWA*
Belford, Christine *WhoHol A*
Belford, Hazel *Film 1*
Belfrage, Bruce 1901- *WhThe*
Belgado, Maria 1906-1969 *WhScrn 1*
Belgrave, Cynthia *WhoHol A*
Belita 1924- *FilmgC, WhoHol A*
Belkin, Bestruce *Film 2*
Belkin, Jeanna 1924- *NotNAT*
Bell, Lady 1851-1930 *NotNAT B*
Bell, Ann 1939- *WhoThe 16*
Bell, Archie d1943 *NotNAT B*
Bell, Arnold *WhoHol A*
Bell, Campton d1963 *NotNAT B*
Bell, Charles *Film 2*
Bell, Clarence F d1963 *NotNAT B*
Bell, Colin *Film 2*
Bell, Daniel W 1891- *BiE&WWA*
Bell, Diana d1965 *WhScrn 1, WhScrn 2*
Bell, Digby Valentine 1849-1917 *WhoStg 1906, WhoStg 1908*
Bell, Digby Valentine 1851-1917 *Film 1,*

NotNAT B, WhThe, WhoHol B
Bell, Dita 1915- *AmSCAP 1966*
Bell, Enid 1888- *WhThe*
Bell, Gaston 1877-1963 *Film 1, NotNAT B, WhScrn 1, WhScrn 2, WhoHol B, WhoStg 1908*
Bell, Genevieve d1951 *WhScrn 1, WhScrn 2, WhoHol B*
Bell, George O d1969 *WhScrn 2, WhoHol B*
Bell, Hank 1892-1950 *WhScrn 1, WhScrn 2, WhoHol B*
Bell, James 1891-1973 *BiE&WWA, FilmgC, MovMk, WhScrn 2, WhThe, WhoHol B*
Bell, John 1745-1831 *NotNAT B, OxThe*
Bell, John Jay 1871-1938 *NotNAT B*
Bell, John Joy 1871-1934 *OxThe*
Bell, Karina *Film 2*
Bell, Laura Joyce d1904 *NotNAT B*
Bell, Leslie R d1962 *NotNAT B*
Bell, Lola d1967 *WhScrn 2*
Bell, Lucile Anderson *AmSCAP 1966*
Bell, Marie 1900- *CnThe, Film 2, FilmgC, OxFilm, WhoHol A*
Bell, Mary *WhoHol A*
Bell, Mary Hayley 1914- *BiE&WWA, NotNAT, NotNAT A, WhThe*
Bell, Monta 1891-1958 *FilmgC, TwYS A, WhScrn 1, WhScrn 2, WhoHol B*
Bell, Montana 1891-1958 *Film 1, Film 2*
Bell, Ralph W 1883-1936 *WhScrn 1, WhScrn 2, WhoHol B*
Bell, Rex 1905-1962 *Film 2, FilmgC, NotNAT B, WhScrn 1, WhScrn 2, WhoHol B*
Bell, Rex 1907-1962 *TwYS*
Bell, Richard d1672 *NotNAT B*
Bell, Robert d1867 *NotNAT B*
Bell, Rodney 1916-1968 *WhScrn 2*
Bell, Ruth 1907-1933 *WhScrn 1, WhScrn 2*
Bell, Spencer *Film 2*
Bell, Stanley 1881-1952 *NotNAT B, WhThe*
Bell, Tom 1932- *IntMPA 1977*
Bell, Tom 1933- *FilmgC*
Bell, Tula *Film 1*
Bell, William J *NewYTET*
Bella, Joseph F 1940- *NotNAT*
Bellah, James Warner *CmMov*
Bellamy, Anne 1727?-1788 *CnThe*
Bellamy, Daniel d1788 *NotNAT B*
Bellamy, Earl 1917- *FilmgC, IntMPA 1977*
Bellamy, Franklyn 1886- *WhThe*
Bellamy, George d1944 *NotNAT B, WhoHol B*
Bellamy, George Anne 1727?-1788 *NotNAT A, NotNAT B, OxThe*
Bellamy, Henry Ernest d1932 *NotNAT B*
Bellamy, Madge *MotPP*
Bellamy, Madge 1900- *ThFT, WhoHol A*
Bellamy, Madge 1903- *Film 2, MovMk, TwYS*
Bellamy, Ralph 1904- *BiE&WWA, CelR 3, Film 2, FilmgC, HolP 30, MotPP, MovMk, NotNAT, WhThe, WhoHol A*
Bellamy, Ralph 1905- *IntMPA 1977*
Bellamy, Somers *Film 2*
Bellamy, Thomas d1800 *NotNAT B*
Bellamy, Thomas Ludford d1843 *NotNAT B*
Bellaver, Harry 1905- *BiE&WWA, FilmgC, NotNAT, WhoHol A*
Belle, Anne *WomWMM B*
Belle, Barbara 1922- *AmSCAP 1966*
Belle, Fannie *Film 2*
Bellecourt 1725-1778 *OxThe*
Beller, Alex 1915- *AmSCAP 1966*
Beller, Jackie 1916- *AmSCAP 1966*
Bellerose 1600?-1670? *NotNAT B, OxThe*
Belleville *OxThe*

Belleville, Frederic De 1857- *WhThe*
Bellew, Cosmo Kyrle 1886-1948 *Film 2,*
  NotNAT B, TwYS, WhScrn 1, WhScrn 2,
  WhoHol B
Bellew, Dorothy 1891- *Film 1, Film 2*
Bellew, H Kyrle 1855-1911 *NotNAT B,*
  WhoHol B
Bellew, Harold Kyrle 1855-1911 *OxThe*
Bellew, Kryle 1855-1911 *Film 1*
Bellew, Kyrle 1855-1911 *WhoStg 1908*
Bellew, Kyrle 1857-1911 *FamA&A, WhScrn 2*
Bellew, Kyrle 1887- *WhThe*
Bellfort, Joseph *IntMPA 1977*
Belli, Melvin 1907- *CelR 3*
Bellido, Jose Maria 1922- *ModWD*
Bellin, Lewis Paul 1905- *AmSCAP 1966*
Bellin, Olga 1935- *BiE&WWA, NotNAT*
Bellino, Vito 1922- *AmSCAP 1966*
Belloc, Dan 1924- *AmSCAP 1966*
Bellocchio, Marco 1939- *BiDFlm, OxFilm,*
  WorEnF
Bellocchio, Marco 1940- *DcFM*
Bellochio, Marco 1940- *FilmgC*
Bellon, Yannick 1924- *DcFM, WomWMM*
Bellonini, Edna 1903- *WhThe*
Bellow, Alexander 1912- *AmSCAP 1966*
Bellow, Saul 1915- *CelR 3, ConDr 1977, CroCD,*
  NotNAT
Bellows, Phyllis 1934- *BiE&WWA*
Belloy, Pierre-Laurent Buirette De 1727-1775
  OxThe
Bellson, Louis P 1924- *AmSCAP 1966*
Bellwood, Bessie 1847-1896 *NotNAT B, OxThe*
Belmar, Henry 1849-1931 *WhScrn 1, WhScrn 2,*
  WhoHol B
Belmondo, Jean-Paul 1933- *BiDFlm, CelR 3,*
  FilmgC, IntMPA 1977, MotPP, MovMk,
  OxFilm, WhoHol A, WorEnF
Belmont, Baldy *Film 2*
Belmont, Eleanor *NotNAT A*
Belmont, Gladys *Film 2*
Belmont, Joe A 1860-1930 *WhScrn 1, WhScrn 2*
Belmont, Joseph *Film 1*
Belmont, Michael 1915-1941 *WhScrn 1,*
  WhScrn 2
Belmont, Mrs. Morgan *Film 2*
Belmont, Ralf 1892-1964 *WhScrn 2*
Belmont, Terry *WhoHol A*
Belmont, Vera *WomWMM*
Belmonte, Herman 1891-1975 *WhScrn 2,*
  WhoHol C
Belmonte Bermudez, Luis De 1587?-1650 *McGWD*
Belmore, Alice d1943 *NotNAT B*
Belmore, Bertha 1882-1953 *FilmgC, NotNAT B,*
  WhScrn 1, WhScrn 2, WhThe, WhoHol B
Belmore, Daisy 1874-1954 *Film 2, NotNAT B,*
  WhScrn 1, WhScrn 2, WhoHol B
Belmore, George d1956 *NotNAT B*
Belmore, Herbert d1952 *NotNAT B*
Belmore, Lionel 1867-1953 *Film 1, Film 2,*
  NotNAT B, TwYS, WhScrn 1, WhScrn 2,
  WhoHol B
Belmore, Lionel 1875-1940 *FilmgC*
Belniak, Susan Louise *WomWMM B*
Beloin, Edmund 1910- *FilmgC*
Belokurov, Vladimir V 1904-1973 *WhScrn 2*
Belot, Adolphe d1890 *NotNAT B*
Belot, Marthe *Film 2*
Belson, Edward 1898-1975 *WhScrn 2*
Belson, Hortense Gold 1915- *AmSCAP 1966*
Belson, Jane *WomWMM B*
Belson, Jerry *NewYTET*
Belt, Elmer 1893- *BiE&WWA, NotNAT*
Beltrame *OxThe*

Beltran, Raymond 1892-1967 *WhScrn 2*
Beltri, Ricardo 1899-1962 *WhScrn 1, WhScrn 2*
Belwin, Alma 1894?-1924 *NotNAT B, WhScrn 2*
Bemis, Connie *AmSCAP 1966*
Ben-Ami, Jacob 1890- *BiE&WWA, NotNAT,*
  WhThe
Ben-Ari, Raikin 1904-1968 *WhScrn 1, WhScrn 2,*
  WhoHol B
Ben-Veniste, Lorriane *WomWMM B*
Benaceraf, Margot 1926- *WomWMM*
Benacerraf, Margot 1926- *DcFM*
Benaderet, Bea 1906-1968 *NotNAT B, WhScrn 1,*
  WhScrn 2, WhoHol B
Benassi, Memo 1886-1957 *WhScrn 1, WhScrn 2,*
  WhoHol B
Benatzky, Ralph 1884-1957 *NotNAT B*
Benatzky, Ralph 1894-1957 *AmSCAP 1966*
Benaventa, Jacinto 1866-1954 *WhThe*
Benavente, Jacinto 1866-1954 *CnMD, McGWD,*
  ModWD, OxThe, PIP&P, REnWD
Benavente, Jacinto *see also* Benevente, Jacinto
Benavente Y Martinez, Jacinto 1866-1954
  NotNAT B
Bench, Johnny 1948- *CelR 3*
Benchley, Nathaniel 1915- *BiE&WWA, CelR 3,*
  NotNAT
Benchley, Robert 1889-1945 *Film 2, FilmgC,*
  MovMk, NotNAT A, NotNAT B, OxFilm,
  OxThe, PIP&P, WhScrn 1, WhScrn 2,
  WhThe, WhoHol B, WorEnF
Benda, W T d1948 *Film 2*
Benda, Wladyslaw Theodor d1948 *NotNAT B*
Bendall, Ernest Alfred 1846-1924 *WhThe*
Bender, Chief 1883-1954 *WhScrn 2*
Bender, Harry *Film 2*
Bender, Jack E 1918- *BiE&WWA, NotNAT*
Bender, Joan *AmSCAP 1966*
Bender, Milton d1964 *NotNAT B*
Bender, Russell 1910-1969 *WhScrn 1, WhScrn 2,*
  WhoHol B
Bendheim, Sam, III 1935- *IntMPA 1977*
Bendick, Robert 1917- *IntMPA 1977, NewYTET*
Bendinelli, Giacinto d1668 *OxThe*
Bendix, Doreen d1931 *NotNAT B*
Bendix, Lissen *Film 2*
Bendix, William d1964 *MotPP, NewYTET,*
  WhoHol B
Bendix, William 1906-1964 *BiE&WWA, CmMov,*
  FilmgC, HolP 40, MovMk, NotNAT B,
  OxFilm, WhScrn 1, WhScrn 2, WorEnF
Bendix, William 1907-1964 *CmMov*
Bendon, Bert d1964 *NotNAT B*
Bendow, Wilhelm *Film 2*
Benedek, Laslo 1907- *BiDFlm, DcFM, FilmgC,*
  IntMPA 1977, MovMk, WorEnF
Benedek, Laszlo 1907- *OxFilm*
Benedict, Billy 1906- *WhoHol A*
Benedict, Billy 1917- *FilmgC*
Benedict, Brooks d1968 *Film 2, WhScrn 2,*
  WhoHol B
Benedict, Dirk *IntMPA 1977, WhoHol A*
Benedict, Jean 1876-1943 *WhScrn 2*
Benedict, Kingsley *Film 1, Film 2*
Benedict, Lew d1920 *NotNAT B*
Benedict, Paul 1938- *NotNAT*
Benedict, Richard 1916- *FilmgC*
Benedict, William 1917- *Vers A*
Benedictus, David 1938- *WhoThe 16*
Benell, John Thomas 1915-1940 *WhScrn 1,*
  WhScrn 2
Benelli, Sem 1875-1949 *NotNAT B, OxThe,*
  PIP&P
Benelli, Sem 1877-1949 *CnMD, McGWD,*
  ModWD, REnWD, WhThe

Benesch, Kurt 1926- *CroCD*
Benet, Brenda *WhoHol A*
Benet, Harry d1948 *NotNAT B*
Benet, Stephen Vincent 1898-1943 *NotNAT B*
Benevente, Jacinto 1866-1954 *CnThe*
Benevente, Jacinto *see also* Benavente, Jacinto
Benfante, Ignazio 1914- *AmSCAP 1966*
Benfield, Robert d1649 *OxThe*
Bengal, Richard *WhoHol A*
Benge, Wilson 1875-1955 *Film 2, WhScrn 1,*
WhScrn 2, WhoHol B
Benger, Sir Thomas *OxThe*
Benham, Arthur d1895 *NotNAT B*
Benham, Dorothy 1910-1956 *Film 1, WhScrn 2*
Benham, Ethyle *Film 1*
Benham, Harry 1886-1969 *Film 1, Film 2,*
WhScrn 2
Benham, Leland *Film 1*
Benini, Ferruccio 1854-1925 *NotNAT B, OxThe,*
WhThe
Benjamin, Arthur 1893- *FilmgC*
Benjamin, Bennie 1907- *AmSCAP 1966*
Benjamin, Burton *NewYTET*
Benjamin, C B d1951 *NotNAT B*
Benjamin, Morris Edgar 1881- *WhThe*
Benjamin, Richard *WhoHol A*
Benjamin, Richard 1938- *CelR 3, FilmgC,*
MovMk
Benjamin, Richard 1939- *IntMPA 1977*
Benjamin, Robert S 1909- *NewYTET*
Benjamin, S Robert 1909- *IntMPA 1977*
Benline, Arthur J 1902- *BiE&WWA, NotNAT*
Bennard, George 1873-1958 *AmSCAP 1966*
Benner, Priscilla *Film 2*
Bennet, Spencer Gordon 1893- *FilmgC,*
IntMPA 1977, TwYS A
Bennett, Alan 1934- *BiE&WWA, CnThe,*
ConDr 1977, NotNAT, WhoThe 16
Bennett, Alma 1904-1958 *Film 2, TwYS,*
WhScrn 2, WhoHol B
Bennett, Arnold 1867-1931 *CnMD, FilmgC,*
McGWD, ModWD, OxThe, WhThe
Bennett, Barbara d1958 *NotNAT B, WhoHol B*
Bennett, Barbara 1902-1958 *Film 2, FilmgC*
Bennett, Barbara 1911-1958 *WhScrn 1,*
WhScrn 2
Bennett, Belle 1891-1932 *Film 1, Film 2, FilmgC,*
NotNAT B, TwYS, WhScrn 1, WhScrn 2,
WhoHol B
Bennett, Bernard 1915- *AmSCAP 1966*
Bennett, Billie *Film 1, Film 2*
Bennett, Bruce *IntMPA 1977*
Bennett, Bruce 1906- *WhoHol A*
Bennett, Bruce 1909- *FilmgC*
Bennett, Charles d1925 *WhScrn 1, WhScrn 2*
Bennett, Charles d1943 *WhoHol B*
Bennett, Charles 1891-1943 *Film 1, Film 2,*
WhScrn 1, WhScrn 2
Bennett, Charles 1899- *FilmgC, IntMPA 1977,*
WhThe, WorEnF
Bennett, Compton 1900- *FilmgC, WorEnF*
Bennett, Constance d1964 *BiE&WWA, MotPP*
Bennett, Constance d1965 *WhoHol B,*
WomWMM
Bennett, Constance 1904-1965 *FilmgC,*
NotNAT B, ThFT
Bennett, Constance 1905-1965 *BiDFlm, MovMk,*
NotNAT A, OxFilm, TwYS, WhScrn 1,
WhScrn 2, WorEnF
Bennett, Constance 1906-1965 *Film 2*
Bennett, David 1897- *AmSCAP 1966*
Bennett, Elsie M 1919- *AmSCAP 1966*
Bennett, Enid d1969 *MotPP, WhoHol B*
Bennett, Enid 1894-1969 *Film 1, Film 2, TwYS*

Bennett, Enid 1895-1969 *WhScrn 1, WhScrn 2*
Bennett, Enoch Arnold 1867-1931 *NotNAT B*
Bennett, Faith *WhThe*
Bennett, Fran *WhoHol A*
Bennett, Frank 1891-1957 *Film 1, WhScrn 2,*
WhoHol B
Bennett, George J 1897- *AmSCAP 1966*
Bennett, George John d1879 *NotNAT B*
Bennett, Gertrude *Film 2*
Bennett, Harve 1930- *IntMPA 1977, NewYTET*
Bennett, Hugh *Film 1*
Bennett, Hywel 1944- *FilmgC, WhoHol A,*
WhoThe 16
Bennett, J Moy *Film 2*
Bennett, Jill *WhoHol A*
Bennett, Jill 1930- *FilmgC*
Bennett, Jill 1931- *CnThe, IntMPA 1977,*
WhoThe 16
Bennett, Joan *BiE&WWA, MotPP*
Bennett, Joan 1910- *BiDFlm, CelR 3, CmMov,*
FilmgC, IntMPA 1977, MovMk, NotNAT A,
OxFilm, ThFT, WhoHol A, WhoThe 16,
WorEnF
Bennett, Joan 1911- *Film 2*
Bennett, Joe 1889-1967 *WhScrn 1, WhScrn 2*
Bennett, Johnstone 1870-1906 *NotNAT B*
Bennett, Mrs. Joseph d1943 *NotNAT B*
Bennett, Joseph 1869-1931 *Film 1, Film 2,*
TwYS, WhoHol B
Bennett, Joseph 1896-1931 *WhScrn 1, WhScrn 2*
Bennett, Joyce W 1923- *AmSCAP 1966*
Bennett, Julia d1903 *NotNAT B*
Bennett, Kathryn *Film 2*
Bennett, Lee 1911-1954 *WhScrn 1, WhScrn 2,*
WhoHol B
Bennett, Leila *ThFT, WhThe*
Bennett, Marjorie *WhoHol A*
Bennett, May *Film 2*
Bennett, Michael 1943- *ConDr 1977D, EncMT,*
NotNAT, WhoThe 16
Bennett, Mickey 1915-1950 *Film 2, WhScrn 1,*
WhScrn 2, WhoHol B
Bennett, Peter 1917- *WhoThe 16*
Bennett, Phil 1913- *AmSCAP 1966*
Bennett, Ray 1895-1957 *WhScrn 1, WhScrn 2,*
WhoHol B
Bennett, Red 1873-1941 *WhScrn 1, WhScrn 2*
Bennett, Richard *WhoStg 1908*
Bennett, Richard 1872-1944 *FamA&A*
Bennett, Richard 1873-1944 *Film 1, Film 2,*
FilmgC, NotNAT B, TwYS, Vers A,
WhScrn 1, WhScrn 2, WhThe, WhoHol B
Bennett, Richard Rodney 1936- *FilmgC*
Bennett, Robert Russell 1894- *AmSCAP 1966,*
BiE&WWA, CelR 3, NotNAT
Bennett, Roy C 1918- *AmSCAP 1966*
Bennett, Sam 1887-1937 *WhScrn 1, WhScrn 2*
Bennett, Tommy d1943 *WhScrn 2*
Bennett, Tony 1926- *CelR 3, WhoHol A*
Bennett, Vivienne 1905- *WhoThe 16*
Bennett, Wilda 1894-1967 *EncMT, WhScrn 1,*
WhScrn 2, WhThe, WhoHol B
Bennett, Wilda 1899- *Film 1*
Bennison, Andrew 1887-1942 *WhScrn 1,*
WhScrn 2
Bennison, Louis 1884-1929 *NotNAT B,*
WhScrn 1, WhScrn 2, WhoHol B
Benny, Jack 1894-1974 *BiDFlm, CelR 3, Film 2,*
FilmgC, MotPP, MovMk, NewYTET,
OxFilm, PIP&P, WhScrn 2, WhoHol B,
WorEnF
Benois, Alexander Nikolayevich 1870-1960
NotNAT A, NotNAT B
Benois, Alexandre 1870-1960 *OxThe*

Benoit, Victor *Film 1*
Benoit-Levy, Jean 1883-1959 *FilmgC*
Benoit-Levy, Jean 1888-1959 *DcFM,*
  IntMPA 1977, MovMk, OxFilm, WorEnF
Benrimo, J Harry 1874-1942 *WhThe*
Benrimo, Joseph Harry 1874-1942 *NotNAT B*
Benserade, Isaac De 1613-1691 *OxThe*
Benskin, Samuel 1922- *AmSCAP 1966*
Bensley, Robert 1742-1817 *OxThe*
Bensley, Russ *NewYTET*
Benson, Lady d1946 *NotNAT B, WhThe*
Benson, Annette *Film 2*
Benson, Arthur H 1919- *AmSCAP 1966*
Benson, Carol *WomWMM B*
Benson, Mrs. Frank Robert *Film 1*
Benson, Sir Frank Robert 1858-1939 *CnThe,*
  Film 1, NotNAT A, NotNAT B, OxThe,
  PIP&P, WhThe
Benson, George 1911- *BiE&WWA, FilmgC,*
  NotNAT, WhoHol A, WhoThe 16
Benson, Hugh 1917- *IntMPA 1977*
Benson, John *WhoHol A*
Benson, John J 1915- *AmSCAP 1966*
Benson, John William 1862-1926 *WhScrn 1,*
  WhScrn 2
Benson, Juliette V P 1875-1962 *WhScrn 1,*
  WhScrn 2
Benson, Leon *IntMPA 1977*
Benson, Lillian *WomWMM B*
Benson, Lucille *WhoHol A*
Benson, Martin 1918- *FilmgC, WhoHol A*
Benson, May d1916 *WhScrn 2*
Benson, Robby *WhoHol A*
Benson, Robin *WhoHol A*
Benson, Ruth 1873-1948 *NotNAT B, WhThe*
Benson, Sally 1897-1972 *BiE&WWA, NotNAT B,*
  WomWMM
Benson, Sandford 1914-1935 *WhScrn 1,*
  WhScrn 2
Benson, Warren Frank 1924- *AmSCAP 1966*
Bent, Buena d1957 *NotNAT B, WhThe*
Bent, Marion 1879-1940 *NotNAT B, WhScrn 2*
Bent, Philip 1941-1966 *WhScrn 2*
Bent, Rosetta Case 1918- *AmSCAP 1966*
Benter, Charles 1887-1964 *AmSCAP 1966*
Benthall, Michael 1919-1974 *BiE&WWA, CnThe,*
  NotNAT B, PIP&P, WhThe
Bentham, Frederick 1911- *WhoThe 16*
Bentham, Frederick 1916- *WhoThe 16*
Bentham, Josephine *BiE&WWA*
Bentine, Michael 1922- *FilmgC*
Bentley, Beatrice *Film 2*
Bentley, D B *Film 1*
Bentley, Doris d1944 *NotNAT B*
Bentley, Eric 1916- *AmSCAP 1966, BiE&WWA,*
  CelR 3, ConDr 1977, NotNAT
Bentley, Grendon 1877-1956 *Film 1, NotNAT B,*
  WhThe
Bentley, Irene d1940 *NotNAT B, WhThe,*
  WhoHol B, WhoStg 1906, WhoStg 1908
Bentley, Irene 1904-1965 *WhScrn 2*
Bentley, John 1916- *FilmgC, IntMPA 1977,*
  WhoHol A
Bentley, Richard d1782 *NotNAT B*
Bentley, Robert 1895-1958 *WhScrn 1, WhScrn 2,*
  WhoHol B
Bentley, Spencer d1963 *NotNAT B*
Bentley, Thomas 1880?- *FilmgC*
Bentley, Walter d1927 *NotNAT B*
Bentley, Will 1873- *WhThe*
Benton, Bessie d1917 *WhScrn 2*
Benton, Robert 1933- *ConDr 1977A,*
  IntMPA 1977
Benton, Thomas Hart 1889- *CelR 3*

Benzell, Mimi 1924- *BiE&WWA*
Benzon, Otto 1856-1927 *NotNAT B, OxThe*
Beolco, Angelo 1502-1542 *CnThe, OxThe,*
  REnWD
Beradino, John *WhoHol A*
Berain, Jean 1637-1711 *NotNAT B, OxThe*
Berain, Jean 1678-1726 *OxThe*
Beranger, Andre 1895-1973 *Film 1, Film 2,*
  TwYS, WhoHol B
Beranger, Annie *Film 2*
Beranger, Clara d1956 *NotNAT B, WomWMM*
Beranger, George 1895-1973 *Film 1, TwYS A,*
  WhScrn 2
Berangere, Madame d1928 *WhScrn 1, WhScrn 2*
Berard, Christian d1949 *NotNAT B*
Berard, Christian 1902-1949 *DcFM, OxFilm,*
  OxThe, WorEnF
Berard, Christian 1903-1949 *CnThe*
Berch, Jack 1907- *AmSCAP 1966*
Bercutt, Max 1910- *IntMPA 1977*
Berczy, Gezo *Film 2*
Beregi, Oscar, Sr. 1875-1965 *Film 2, WhScrn 1,*
  WhScrn 2, WhoHol B
Berendt, Rachel d1957 *NotNAT B, WhThe,*
  WhoHol B
Berenson, Marisa 1947- *MovMk, WhoHol A*
Beresford, Miss *Film 2*
Beresford, Harry 1864-1944 *WhScrn 1,*
  WhScrn 2, WhoHol B
Beresford, Harry 1867-1944 *Film 2, NotNAT B,*
  WhThe
Berezowsky, Nicolai T 1900-1953 *AmSCAP 1966*
Berg, Barry 1942- *NatPD*
Berg, David 1892-1944 *AmSCAP 1966*
Berg, Dick *NewYTET*
Berg, Ellen d1906 *NotNAT B*
Berg, Gertrude d1966 *NewYTET, WhoHol B*
Berg, Gertrude 1899-1966 *BiE&WWA, FilmgC,*
  NotNAT A, NotNAT B, WhThe
Berg, Gertrude 1900-1966 *WhScrn 1, WhScrn 2*
Berg, Gretchen *WomWMM*
Berg, Harold C 1900- *AmSCAP 1966*
Berg, Michael C d1964 *NotNAT B*
Berg, Nancy 1931- *BiE&WWA*
Berg, Stina 1869-1930 *WhScrn 2*
Bergantine, Borney 1909-1954 *AmSCAP 1966*
Bergel, John Graham 1902-1941 *NotNAT B,*
  WhThe
Bergelson, David 1884-1952 *OxThe*
Bergen, Arthur *Film 2*
Bergen, Candice 1946- *CelR 3, FilmgC,*
  IntMPA 1977, MotPP, MovMk, WhoHol A
Bergen, Edgar 1903- *FilmgC, MotPP, NewYTET,*
  WhoHol A
Bergen, Jerry *WhoHol A*
Bergen, Nella 1873-1919 *NotNAT B, WhThe,*
  WhoStg 1906, WhoStg 1908
Bergen, Polly *MotPP, WhoHol A*
Bergen, Polly 1919- *MovMk*
Bergen, Polly 1929- *FilmgC*
Bergen, Polly 1930- *BiE&WWA, CelR 3,*
  IntMPA 1977, NotNAT
Berger, Benjamin N 1896- *IntMPA 1977*
Berger, Bill 1928- *BiE&WWA*
Berger, Bror *Film 1*
Berger, Charly *Film 2*
Berger, Grete *Film 1*
Berger, Helmut 1942?- *FilmgC, IntMPA 1977,*
  WhoHol A
Berger, Henning 1872- *WhThe*
Berger, Jean 1909- *AmSCAP 1966*
Berger, Ludwig 1892-1969 *FilmgC, TwYS A*
Berger, Nicole 1934-1967 *FilmgC, WhScrn 1,*
  WhScrn 2, WhoHol B

Berger, Raimund 1917-1954 *CroCD*
Berger, Senta 1941- *FilmgC, MotPP, WhoHol A*
Berger, Sidney L 1936- *NotNAT*
Bergerac, Jacques 1927- *FilmgC, IntMPA 1977, MotPP, WhoHol A*
Bergerac, Savinien DeCyrano De 1619-1655 *NotNAT B, OxThe*
Bergerat, Emile 1845- *WhThe*
Bergere, Ouida d1974 *WhoHol B, WomWMM*
Bergere, Ouida 1866-1974 *Film 2*
Bergere, Ramona 1902-1941 *WhScrn 1, WhScrn 2*
Bergere, Roy 1899- *AmSCAP 1966*
Bergere, Valerie d1938 *WhoHol B, WhoStg 1906, WhoStg 1908*
Bergere, Valerie 1867-1938 *NotNAT B*
Bergere, Valerie 1872-1938 *WhThe*
Bergere, Valerie 1875-1938 *WhScrn 1, WhScrn 2*
Bergersen, Baldwin 1914- *AmSCAP 1966, BiE&WWA, NotNAT*
Berggren, Thommy 1937- *FilmgC, OxFilm*
Bergh, Arthur 1882-1962 *AmSCAP 1966*
Berghof, Herbert 1909- *BiE&WWA, FilmgC, NotNAT, WhoHol A, WhoThe 16*
Bergholm, Eija-Elina *WomWMM*
Berglund, Sven 1881-1937 *DcFM*
Bergman, Alan 1925- *AmSCAP 1966*
Bergman, Dewey 1900- *AmSCAP 1966*
Bergman, Henry 1870-1946 *Film 1, Film 2, FilmgC, WhScrn 1, WhScrn 2, WhoHol B*
Bergman, Henry 1870-1962 *NotNAT B*
Bergman, Hjalmar Frederik 1883-1931 *CnMD, CnThe, McGWD, ModWD, NotNAT B, OxThe, REnWD*
Bergman, Ingmar 1918- *BiDFlm, CelR 3, CnThe, DcFM, FilmgC, IntMPA 1977, MovMk, OxFilm, PIP&P A, WorEnF*
Bergman, Ingmar 1919- *OxThe*
Bergman, Ingrid *MotPP, PIP&P, WhoHol A*
Bergman, Ingrid 1915- *BiDFlm, BiE&WWA, CelR 3, CmMov, FilmgC, MovMk, NotNAT, OxFilm, ThFT, WhoThe 16, WorEnF*
Bergman, Ingrid 1916- *NotNAT A*
Bergman, Ingrid 1917- *IntMPA 1977*
Bergman, Joel *WhoHol A*
Bergman, Jules *NewYTET*
Bergman, Marilyn Keith 1929- *AmSCAP 1966*
Bergman, Maurice A *IntMPA 1977*
Bergmann, Ted 1920- *IntMPA 1977, NewYTET*
Bergner, Elisabeth 1898- *FilmgC*
Bergner, Elisabeth 1900- *BiE&WWA, MovMk, NotNAT, OxFilm, ThFT, WhoHol A, WhoThe 16, WorEnF*
Bergner, Elizabeth *MotPP*
Bergner, Elizabeth 1900- *Film 2*
Bergopzoomer, Johann Baptist 1742-1804 *OxThe*
Bergsma, William Laurence 1921- *AmSCAP 1966*
Bergstrom, Hilda *WhThe*
Bergstrom, Hjalmar 1868-1914 *NotNAT B, OxThe*
Berhard, Raymond *Film 2*
Beri, Ben d1963 *NotNAT B*
Beringer, Esme 1875-1972 *OxThe, WhThe*
Beringer, Mrs. Oscar 1856-1936 *NotNAT B, WhThe*
Beringer, Vera 1879-1964 *NotNAT B, OxThe, WhThe*
Beristain, Leopoldo 1883-1948 *WhScrn 1, WhScrn 2, WhoHol B*
Beristain, Luis 1918-1962 *WhScrn 1, WhScrn 2, WhoHol B*
Berk, Lew 1888- *AmSCAP 1966*
Berk, Morty 1900-1955 *AmSCAP 1966*

Berk, Sara 1898-1975 *WhScrn 2, WhoHol C*
Berke, William 1904-1958 *FilmgC*
Berkeley, Arthur 1896-1962 *NotNAT B, WhScrn 1, WhScrn 2, WhoHol B*
Berkeley, Ballard 1904- *FilmgC, WhThe, WhoHol A*
Berkeley, Busby 1895-1976 *BiDFlm, BiE&WWA, CmMov, DcFM, EncMT, FilmgC, MovMk, NotNAT A, OxFilm, WhoHol C, WhoThe 16, WorEnF*
Berkeley, Gertrude d1946 *Film 1, NotNAT B, WhoHol B, WhoStg 1908*
Berkeley, Reginald 1882-1936 *WhScrn 1, WhScrn 2*
Berkeley, Reginald Cheyne 1890-1935 *NotNAT B, WhThe*
Berkeley, Wilma *WhThe*
Berkes, John Patrick 1897-1951 *WhScrn 1, WhScrn 2, WhoHol B*
Berkey, Ralph 1912- *BiE&WWA*
Berkowitz, Sol 1922- *AmSCAP 1966, BiE&WWA, NotNAT*
Berkowsky, Paul B 1932- *BiE&WWA*
Berlanga, Luis Garcia 1921- *DcFM, FilmgC, OxFilm, WorEnF*
Berle, Milton 1908- *AmSCAP 1966, BiE&WWA, CelR 3, EncMT, Film 1, Film 2, FilmgC, IntMPA 1977, MovMk, NewYTET, NotNAT, NotNAT A, PIP&P, TwYS, WhoHol A, WhoThe 16*
Berle, Sandra 1877-1954 *WhScrn 1, WhScrn 2*
Berlein, Annie Mack d1935 *NotNAT B*
Berley, Andre *Film 2*
Berlin, Irving 1888- *AmSCAP 1966, BiE&WWA, CelR 3, CmMov, DcFM, EncMT, FilmgC, IntMPA 1977, McGWD, NewMT, NotNAT, NotNAT A, OxFilm, PIP&P, WhoThe 16*
Berlin, Jeannie *WhoHol A, WomWMM*
Berlin, Joyce *NatPD*
Berlin, Richard E 1894- *CelR 3*
Berliner, Martin 1896-1966 *WhScrn 1, WhScrn 2, WhoHol B*
Berlinger, Warren 1937- *BiE&WWA, FilmgC, IntMPA 1977, MotPP, NotNAT, WhoHol A, WhoThe 16*
Berlinski, Herman 1910- *AmSCAP 1966*
Berlyn, Alfred 1860-1936 *NotNAT B, WhThe*
Berlyn, Ivan d1934 *Film 2, NotNAT B*
Berman, A L 1890- *BiE&WWA*
Berman, Art Harry 1902-1959 *AmSCAP 1966*
Berman, Charles *IntMPA 1977*
Berman, Edward 1911- *AmSCAP 1966*
Berman, Mark *NatPD*
Berman, Monty 1913- *FilmgC, IntMPA 1977*
Berman, Monty M 1912- *IntMPA 1977*
Berman, Pandro S 1905- *FilmgC, IntMPA 1977, WorEnF*
Berman, Shelley 1926- *BiE&WWA, FilmgC, WhoHol A*
Berman, Shelly 1926- *NotNAT*
Bermange, Barry 1933- *ConDr 1977*
Bermel, Albert 1927- *NatPD*
Bermont, Georges 1901- *AmSCAP 1966*
Bern, Paul 1889-1932 *FilmgC, WhScrn 1, WhScrn 2*
Bern, Paul 1889-1939 *TwYS A*
Berna, Elsa *Film 1*
Bernanos, Georges 1888-1948 *CnMD, ModWD*
Bernard, Al 1888-1949 *AmSCAP 1966, WhScrn 1, WhScrn 2*
Bernard, Armand *Film 2*
Bernard, Barney 1877-1924 *Film 1, Film 2, NotNAT B, WhScrn 1, WhScrn 2, WhThe, WhoHol B*

Bernard, Barry *WhoHol A*
Bernard, Charles 1921- *IntMPA 1977*
Bernard, Dick d1925 *NotNAT B, WhoHol B*
Bernard, Dorothy 1890-1955 *Film 1, Film 2,
MotPP, NotNAT B, TwYS, WhScrn 1,
WhScrn 2, WhoHol B*
Bernard, Felix 1897-1944 *AmSCAP 1966*
Bernard, Guy 1907- *DcFM*
Bernard, Harry 1878-1940 *Film 1, Film 2,
WhScrn 1, WhScrn 2, WhoHol B*
Bernard, Ivor 1887-1953 *WhScrn 1, WhScrn 2*
Bernard, James 1925- *FilmgC*
Bernard, Jean-Jacques 1888-1972 *CnMD, CnThe,
McGWD, ModWD, OxThe, WhThe*
Bernard, John 1756-1828 *FamA&A, OxThe*
Bernard, Josephine *Film 2*
Bernard, Judd 1927- *IntMPA 1977*
Bernard, Kenneth 1930- *ConDr 1977, NatPD,
NotNAT*
Bernard, Kitty d1962 *NotNAT B*
Bernard, Leon d1935 *NotNAT B*
Bernard, Lester *Film 2*
Bernard, Lois 1898-1945 *WhScrn 1, WhScrn 2*
Bernard, Marvin A 1934- *IntMPA 1977*
Bernard, Paul d1958 *WhScrn 1, WhScrn 2,
WhoHol B*
Bernard, Peter 1888-1960 *WhScrn 1, WhScrn 2*
Bernard, Raymond 1891- *DcFM*
Bernard, Sam 1863-1927 *Film 1, NotNAT B,
WhScrn 1, WhScrn 2, WhThe, WhoHol B,
WhoStg 1906, WhoStg 1908*
Bernard, Sam 1889-1950 *NotNAT B, WhScrn 1,
WhScrn 2, WhoHol B*
Bernard, Sylvia *Film 2*
Bernard, Tristan 1866-1947 *CnMD, McGWD,
ModWD, NotNAT B, OxThe, WhThe*
Bernard, W Bayle d1875 *NotNAT B*
Bernard-Aubert, Claude 1930- *DcFM, WorEnF*
Bernard-Deschamps, Dominique 1892- *DcFM*
Bernard-Luc, Jean 1909- *McGWD*
Bernardi, Berel 1872?-1932 *NotNAT A*
Bernardi, Herschel 1923- *CelR 3, FilmgC,
NotNAT, WhoHol A*
Bernardi, Nerio 1899-1971 *Film 2, WhScrn 2*
Bernauer, Rudolph d1953 *NotNAT B*
Bernds, Edward *FilmgC*
Berndt, Julia Helen *AmSCAP 1966*
Bernede, Arthur *WhThe*
Bernes, Mark 1912-1969 *WhScrn 1, WhScrn 2,
WhoHol B*
Berney, Beryl *AmSCAP 1966*
Berney, William d1961 *NotNAT B*
Bernhagen, Roland F 1933- *NotNAT*
Bernhard, Thomas 1931- *CroCD*
Bernhardt, Curtis 1899- *BiDFlm, CmMov,
DcFM, Film 2, FilmgC, IntMPA 1977,
MovMk, WorEnF*
Bernhardt, Maurice d1928 *NotNAT B*
Bernhardt, Melvin *WhoThe 16*
Bernhardt, Sarah 1844-1923 *FamA&A, FilmgC,
NotNAT A, NotNAT B, OxFilm, PIP&P,
TwYS, WhScrn 1, WhScrn 2, WhoStg 1906,
WhoStg 1908, WorEnF*
Bernhardt, Sarah 1845-1923 *CnThe, Film 1,
Film 2, OxThe, WhThe, WhoHol B*
Bernie, Ben 1891-1943 *AmSCAP 1966,
NotNAT B, WhScrn 1, WhScrn 2,
WhoHol B*
Bernie, Dick d1971 *WhoHol B*
Bernier, Buddy 1910- *AmSCAP 1966*
Bernini, Giovanni Lorenzo 1598-1680 *OxThe*
Bernis, Blanche *Film 2*
Bernivici, Count 1884-1966 *WhScrn 1, WhScrn 2*
Berns, Larry 1908- *AmSCAP 1966*

Berns, Samuel D *IntMPA 1977*
Berns, Seymour *IntMPA 1977*
Bernstein, Baron 1899- *IntMPA 1977*
Bernstein, Lord 1899- *FilmgC*
Bernstein, Lord *see also* Bernstein, Sidney Lewis
Bernstein, Aline 1881-1955 *NotNAT B*
Bernstein, Aline 1882-1955 *OxThe, PIP&P,
WhThe*
Bernstein, Cecil *IntMPA 1977*
Bernstein, Elmer 1922- *AmSCAP 1966, CelR 3,
CmMov, DcFM, FilmgC, IntMPA 1977,
OxFilm, WorEnF*
Bernstein, Henry 1875-1953 *WhThe*
Bernstein, Henry 1876-1953 *CnMD, McGWD,
ModWD, NotNAT B, OxThe*
Bernstein, Herman d1963 *NotNAT B*
Bernstein, Karl *BiE&WWA, NotNAT*
Bernstein, Leonard 1918- *AmSCAP 1966,
BiE&WWA, CelR 3, EncMT, FilmgC,
McGWD, NewMT, NewYTET, NotNAT,
OxFilm, PIP&P, PIP&P A, WhoThe 16,
WorEnF*
Bernstein, Morris 1916- *AmSCAP 1966*
Bernstein, Richard 1922- *IntMPA 1977*
Bernstein, Sidney Lewis 1899- *OxFilm*
Bernstein, Sidney Lewis *see also* Bernstein, Baron
Bernstein, Sylvia 1924- *AmSCAP 1966*
Berolzheimer, Hobart F 1921- *BiE&WWA,
NotNAT*
Berquist, Bernard H 1903-1962 *AmSCAP 1966*
Berr, Georges 1867-1942 *McGWD, NotNAT B,
WhThe*
Berr DeTurique, Julien 1863-1923 *WhThe*
Berr DuTurique, Julien 1863-1923 *NotNAT B*
Berra, Yogi 1925- *CelR 3*
Berrell, George 1849-1933 *Film 2, WhScrn 2*
Berri, Claude 1934- *FilmgC*
Berrigan, Daniel 1921- *CelR 3*
Berrigan, Philip 1923- *CelR 3*
Berry, Aileen *Film 2*
Berry, Aline 1905-1967 *WhScrn 1, WhScrn 2,
WhoHol B*
Berry, Arthur Nelson 1887-1945 *WhScrn 1,
WhScrn 2*
Berry, David 1943- *NatPD*
Berry, Eric 1913- *BiE&WWA, NotNAT,
WhoHol A, WhoThe 16*
Berry, James 1883- *Film 1, WhThe*
Berry, John 1917- *BiDFlm, FilmgC, WorEnF*
Berry, Jules 1883-1951 *FilmgC, OxFilm,
WhScrn 1, WhScrn 2, WhoHol B*
Berry, Jules 1889-1951 *WorEnF*
Berry, Ken *FilmgC, WhoHol A*
Berry, Nyas d1951 *WhScrn 2*
Berry, William Henry 1870-1951 *WhThe,
WhoHol B*
Berry, William Henry 1872-1951 *NotNAT A,
NotNAT B*
Bersell, Michael *WhoHol A*
Bersell, Sean *WhoHol A*
Bersenev, Ivan Nikolayevich 1889-1951 *OxThe*
Berte, Charles d1908 *NotNAT B*
Berte, Heinrich 1858-1924 *NotNAT B*
Bertholdi, Madame *Film 1*
Berthomieu, Andre 1903-1960 *DcFM*
Berti, Marina *WhoHol A*
Bertin, Charles 1919- *CnMD, ModWD*
Bertinazzi, Carlin *PIP&P*
Bertinazzi, Carlo 1710-1783 *OxThe*
Bertini, Francesca *Film 1*
Bertini, Francesca 1888- *OxFilm*
Bertolazzi, Carlo 1870-1916 *McGWD, REnWD,
WhThe*
Bertolucci, Bernardo 1940- *BiDFlm, DcFM,*

FilmgC, OxFilm, WorEnF
Bertolucci, Bernardo 1941- *CelR 3, MovMk*
Berton, Pierre d1912 *NotNAT B*
Bertone, Alfredo *Film 2*
Bertozzi, Patricia *WomWMM B*
Bertram, Arthur 1860-1955 *NotNAT B, WhThe*
Bertram, Bert *WhoHol A*
Bertram, Eugene 1872-1941 *NotNAT B, WhThe*
Bertram, Frank d1941 *NotNAT B, WhoHol B*
Bertram, Helen 1869- *WhoStg 1906,*
WhoStg 1908
Bertram, Robert F 1916- *AmSCAP 1966*
Bertram, Vedah 1891-1912 *WhScrn 2, WhoHol B*
Bertram, William 1880-1933 *Film 2, WhScrn 2*
Bertram, William 1889- *TwYS A*
Bertrand, Mary d1955 *WhScrn 1, WhScrn 2*
Bertrand, Paul 1915- *DcFM*
Beruh, Joseph 1924- *BiE&WWA, NotNAT,*
WhoThe 16
Berwald, William 1864-1948 *AmSCAP 1966*
Berwin, Isabel *Film 1*
Beryl, Edwin *Film 1*
Besch, Lutz 1918- *CnMD*
Besci, Kurt 1920- *CroCD, McGWD*
Besier, Rudolf 1878-1942 *ModWD, NotNAT B,*
PIP&P, WhThe
Besier, Rudolph 1878-1942 *McGWD*
Beskow, Bernhard Von 1796-1868 *OxThe*
Besnard, Lucien 1872- *McGWD*
Besoyan, Rick 1924-1970 *BiE&WWA, EncMT,*
NotNAT B
Besozzi, Nino d1971 *WhScrn 2*
Besse, Robert 1920- *AmSCAP 1966*
Bessell, Ted *WhoHol A*
Bessent, Marie 1898-1947 *WhScrn 1, WhScrn 2*
Bessenyei, Gyorgy 1747-1811 *OxThe*
Besser, Joe d1972 *WhoHol B*
Besserer, Eugenie 1870-1934 *Film 1, Film 2,*
TwYS, WhScrn 1, WhScrn 2, WhoHol B
Bessie, Alvah *FilmgC, PIP&P*
Best, Barbara 1921- *IntMPA 1977*
Best, Dolly 1899-1968 *WhScrn 1, WhScrn 2*
Best, Edna 1900-1974 *BiE&WWA, Film 2,*
FilmgC, NotNAT B, ThFT, WhScrn 2,
WhThe, WhoHol B
Best, James 1926- *FilmgC, IntMPA 1977,*
WhoHol A
Best, Martyn *Film 2*
Best, Willie 1916-1962 *FilmgC, NotNAT B,*
Vers B, WhScrn 1, WhScrn 2, WhoHol B
Bestor, Don 1889- *AmSCAP 1966*
Beswick, Martine 1941- *FilmgC*
Betchel, William *Film 1*
Bethencourt, Francis 1926- *BiE&WWA, NotNAT,*
WhoHol A
Bethune, Zina 1945- *IntMPA 1977, WhoHol A*
Bettamy, F G d1942 *NotNAT B*
Bettelheim, Bruno 1903- *CelR 3*
Bettelheim, Edwin Sumner 1865-1938 *NotNAT B,*
WhThe
Betterton, Mary Sanderson d1712 *OxThe, PIP&P*
Betterton, Thomas 1635?-1710 *CnThe,*
NotNAT A, NotNAT B, OxThe, PIP&P
Betterton, Mrs. Thomas 1647?-1712 *NotNAT B*
Bettger, Lyle 1915- *FilmgC, IntMPA 1977,*
WhoHol A
Betti, Ugo 1892-1953 *CnMD, CnThe, McGWD,*
ModWD, NotNAT B, OxThe, REnWD
Bettinson, Ralph 1908- *IntMPA 1977*
Bettis, Valerie *BiE&WWA, NotNAT,*
WhoHol A, WhoThe 16
Bettmann, Otto L 1903- *BiE&WWA, NotNAT*
Betton, George d1969 *WhoHol B*
Betts, Edward William 1881- *WhThe*

Betts, William E 1856-1929 *Film 2, WhScrn 1,*
WhScrn 2, WhoHol B
Betty, William Henry West 1791-1874 *CnThe,*
NotNAT A, NotNAT B, OxThe, PIP&P
Betz, Carl 1920- *FilmgC, IntMPA 1977,*
WhoHol A
Betz, Mathew 1881-1938 *TwYS*
Betz, Matthew 1881-1938 *Film 2, WhScrn 1,*
WhScrn 2, WhoHol B
Betzner, John F 1908- *AmSCAP 1966*
Beugen, Joan *WomWMM B*
Beutel, Jack 1917- *WhoHol A*
Bevan, Billy 1887-1957 *Film 1, Film 2, FilmgC,*
MotPP, NotNAT B, OxFilm, TwYS,
Vers B, WhoHol B
Bevan, Billy 1897-1957 *WhScrn 1, WhScrn 2*
Bevan, Donald 1920- *BiE&WWA, NotNAT*
Bevan, Faith 1896- *WhThe*
Bevan, Frank 1903- *BiE&WWA*
Bevan, Isla 1910- *WhThe*
Bevani, Alexander *Film 2*
Bevans, Clem 1880-1963 *FilmgC, WhScrn 1,*
WhScrn 2, WhoHol B
Bevans, Clem 1897-1963 *Vers A*
Bevans, Lionel 1884-1965 *WhScrn 1, WhScrn 2*
Bevans, Philippa 1913-1968 *WhScrn 1, WhScrn 2,*
WhoHol B
Bevans, Philippa 1917-1968 *BiE&WWA*
Bevans, Phillippa 1913-1968 *NotNAT B*
Beveridge, Hortense *WomWMM A,*
WomWMM B
Beveridge, J D 1844-1926 *NotNAT B, WhThe,*
WhoStg 1906, WhoStg 1908
Beveridge, Thomas G 1938- *AmSCAP 1966*
Beverley, Helen *WhoHol A*
Beverley, Henry Roxby d1863 *NotNAT B*
Beverley, Hilda d1942 *NotNAT B*
Beverley, Mrs. W R d1851 *NotNAT B*
Beverley, William Roxby d1842 *NotNAT B*
Beverley, William Roxby 1814?-1889 *NotNAT B,*
OxThe
Beville, Hugh M, Jr. 1908- *IntMPA 1977*
Bewes, Rodney 1937- *FilmgC, WhoThe 16*
Bey, Turhan 1920- *FilmgC, HolP 40,*
IntMPA 1977, MotPP, MovMk, WhoHol A
Beyer, Charles *Film 2*
Beyer, Howard 1929- *AmSCAP 1966*
Beyers, Clara *Film 1*
Beymer, Richard 1939- *FilmgC, IntMPA 1977,*
MotPP, WhoHol A
Bezaire, Sara *WomWMM*
Bezzerides, A I *FilmgC*
Bharata *OxThe, REnWD*
Bhasa *OxThe, REnWD*
Bhaskar 1930- *BiE&WWA, NotNAT,*
WhoHol A
Bhatta Narayana *OxThe*
Bhavabhuti 750?- *CnThe, OxThe, REnWD*
Bianchetti, Suzanne 1894-1936 *Film 2, WhScrn 2*
Bianchi, Daniela 1942- *FilmgC, WhoHol A*
Bianchi, Georgio 1904-1968 *WhScrn 1, WhScrn 2*
Bianchi, Mario *Film 1*
Biancini, Ferrucio *Film 2*
Bianco, Robert 1934- *AmSCAP 1966*
Biancolelli, Caterina 1665-1716 *OxThe*
Biancolelli, Francesca Maria Apolline 1664-1747
OxThe
Biancolelli, Giuseppe Domenico 1637?-1688 *OxThe,*
PIP&P
Biancolelli, Isabella Franchini *OxThe*
Biancolelli, Orsola Cortesi 1636?-1718 *OxThe*
Biancolelli, Pietro Francesco 1680-1734 *OxThe*
Biancolelli Family *CnThe*
Bias, Albert *Film 2*

Bias, Chester 1917-1954 *WhScrn 1, WhScrn 2*
Bibas, Frank Percy 1917- *IntMPA 1977*
Bibbiena, Bernardo Dovizi Da 1470-1520 *OxThe, REnWD*
Bibbiena, Bernardo Dovizio Da 1470-1520 *McGWD*
Bibby, Charles 1878-1917 *WhThe*
Biberman, Abner 1909- *FilmgC, IntMPA 1977, Vers A, WhoHol A*
Biberman, Herbert J 1900-1971 *DcFM, FilmgC, OxFilm, WorEnF*
Bibiena, Alessandro 1687-1769? *NotNAT B, OxThe*
Bibiena, Antonio 1700-1774 *NotNAT B, OxThe*
Bibiena, Carlo 1728-1787 *NotNAT B, OxThe*
Bibiena, Ferdinando 1657-1743 *NotNAT B, OxThe*
Bibiena, Francesco 1659-1739 *NotNAT B, OxThe*
Bibiena, Giovanni Maria 1704?-1769 *NotNAT B, OxThe*
Bibiena, Giuseppe 1696-1757 *NotNAT B, OxThe*
Bibiena Family *NotNAT A*
Bibienas Family *CnThe*
Bibo, Irving 1889-1962 *AmSCAP 1966, NotNAT B*
Biby, Edward 1885-1952 *WhScrn 1, WhScrn 2, WhoHol B*
Bice, Robert d1968 *WhoHol B*
Bick, Jerry *IntMPA 1977*
Bickel, George L 1863-1941 *Film 2, NotNAT B, WhScrn 1, WhScrn 2, WhoHol B*
Bickerstaffe, Isaac 1735?-1812? *McGWD, NotNAT B, OxThe*
Bickford, Charles d1967 *MotPP, WhoHol B*
Bickford, Charles 1889-1967 *Film 2, FilmgC, HolP 30, MovMk, NotNAT B, OxFilm, WhScrn 1, WhScrn 2*
Bickford, Charles 1891-1967 *BiDFlm, BiE&WWA, WhThe, WorEnF*
Biddle, Baldy *Film 2*
Biddle, Craig *Film 2*
Bidermann, Jakob 1578-1639 *OxThe*
Bideu, Lou 1919- *AmSCAP 1966*
Bidou, Henri d1943 *NotNAT B*
Bidwell, Barnaby *PIP&P*
Bieber, Margarete 1879- *BiE&WWA, NotNAT*
Biedermann, Joseph 1800- *OxThe*
Biegel, Erwin 1896-1954 *WhScrn 1, WhScrn 2*
Bielek, Pal'o 1910- *DcFM*
Bielinska, Helina *WomWMM*
Bien, Walter H 1923- *IntMPA 1977*
Bienert, Gerhard *Film 2*
Biensfeldt, Paul *Film 2*
Bierling, Lore *WomWMM*
Bierman, Bernard 1908- *AmSCAP 1966*
Big Maybelle 1924-1972 *WhScrn 2*
Big Tree, Chief *Film 2*
Bigard, Leon Albany 1906- *AmSCAP 1966*
Bigelow, Charles A 1862-1912 *NotNAT B, WhoStg 1908*
Bigelow, Robert Wilcox 1890-1965 *AmSCAP 1966*
Biggers, Earl Derr 1884-1933 *FilmgC, NotNAT B, WhThe*
Biggs, Lottie Lovell 1913- *AmSCAP 1966*
Biggs, Richard Keys 1886-1962 *AmSCAP 1966*
Bigley, Isabel 1928- *BiE&WWA*
Bigot, Sieur De *McGWD*
Bigwood, G B d1913 *NotNAT B*
Bikel, Theodore 1924- *BiE&WWA, FilmgC, MotPP, MovMk, NotNAT, PIP&P, WhoHol A, WhoThe 16*
Bilbrooke, Lydia 1888- *WhThe*
Bilby, Kenneth W 1918- *IntMPA 1977, NewYTET*
Bilder, Robert M 1913-1961 *AmSCAP 1966*

Bilderback, Carolyn *WomWMM B*
Bildt, Paul 1885-1957 *Film 2, WhScrn 1, WhScrn 2, WhoHol B*
Bilgrey, Felix J 1924- *IntMPA 1977*
Bilhaud, Paul 1854-1933 *NotNAT B, WhThe*
Bilik, Jerry H 1933- *AmSCAP 1966*
Bilimoria, N M 1922- *IntMPA 1977*
Bill, Buffalo, Jr. 1902- *Film 2*
Bill, Buffalo, Jr. *see also* Buffalo Bill, Jr.
Bill, Maude *Film 2*
Bill, Teddy *Film 2*
Bill, Tony 1940- *FilmgC, IntMPA 1977, WhoHol A*
Bill-Belotserkovsky, Vladimir Naumovich 1884-1959 *ModWD*
Bill-Belotserkovsky, Vladimir Naumovich 1885-1959 *OxThe*
Bill-Bjelozerkowski, Vladimir 1884- *CnMD*
Billbrew, A C H *Film 2*
Billetdoux, Francois 1927- *CnMD, CnThe, CroCD, McGWD, ModWD, REnWD*
Billing, H Chiswell 1881-1934 *WhThe*
Billinger, Richard 1893-1965 *CnMD, CroCD, McGWD, ModWD*
Billings, Billie *Film 1*
Billings, Elmo 1913-1964 *Film 2, WhScrn 1, WhScrn 2, WhoHol B*
Billings, Florence *Film 1, Film 2*
Billings, George A 1871-1934 *Film 2, WhScrn 1, WhScrn 2, WhoHol B*
Billings, William 1746-1800 *NotNAT B*
Billingsley, Barbara *WhoHol A*
Billingsley, Jennifer *WhoHol A*
Billington, Adeline 1825- *WhThe*
Billington, Elizabeth d1818 *NotNAT B*
Billington, Francelia *Film 1, MotPP*
Billington, Fred d1917 *NotNAT B*
Billington, John d1904 *NotNAT B*
Billington, Mrs. John d1917 *NotNAT B*
Billington, Kevin 1933- *FilmgC*
Billington, Michael 1939- *WhoThe 16*
Billitteri, Salvatore 1921- *IntMPA 1977*
Billoups, Robert *Film 2*
Billsbury, John H d1964 *NotNAT B*
Billy The Kid 1859-1881 *OxFilm*
Bilotti, Anton 1906-1963 *AmSCAP 1966*
Bilotti, John J 1916- *AmSCAP 1966*
Bilowit, Ira J 1925- *BiE&WWA, NatPD, NotNAT*
Bilson, George *IntMPA 1977*
Bilton, Belle d1908 *NotNAT B*
Bimboni, Alberto 1882-1960 *AmSCAP 1966*
Binder, Abraham Wolfe 1895- *AmSCAP 1966*
Binder, Fred d1963 *NotNAT B*
Binder, Maurice 1925- *FilmgC*
Binder, Steve *NewYTET*
Binder, Sybille d1962 *NotNAT B, WhoHol B*
Binford, Mira *WomWMM B*
Bing, Gus 1893-1967 *WhScrn 1, WhScrn 2, WhoHol B*
Bing, Herman 1889-1946 *Vers A*
Bing, Herman 1889-1947 *Film 2, FilmgC, NotNAT B, WhScrn 1, WhScrn 2, WhoHol B*
Bing, Herman 1899-1947 *MovMk*
Bing, Rudolf 1902- *CelR 3*
Bingham, Amelia 1869-1927 *NotNAT B, WhThe, WhoStg 1906, WhoStg 1908*
Bingham, George *WhScrn 1, WhScrn 2*
Bingham, J Clarke d1962 *NotNAT B*
Bingham, Leslie d1945 *NotNAT B*
Bingham, Seth 1882- *AmSCAP 1966*
Bingley, Ward 1757-1818 *OxThe*
Binner, Margery 1908- *WhThe*

Binney, Constance 1900- *Film 1, Film 2, MotPP, TwYS, WhThe, WhoHol A*
Binney, Fair *TwYS*
Binney, Faire *Film 1, Film 2*
Binns, Edward *IntMPA 1977, MotPP, WhoHol A*
Binns, George H 1886-1918 *Film 1, WhScrn 2*
Binyon, Claude 1905- *FilmgC, IntMPA 1977*
Binyon, Laurence 1869-1946 *OxThe, WhThe*
Binyon, Lawrence 1869-1946 *PIP&P*
Binyon, Robert Laurence 1869-1943 *NotNAT B*
Biondi, Guy *IntMPA 1977*
Birabeau, André 1890- *CnMD, McGWD, ModWD*
Biran, Tova *WomWMM*
Birch, Frank 1889-1956 *NotNAT B, WhThe*
Birch, Patricia 1934?- *EncMT, NotNAT, WhoThe 16*
Birch, Paul *FilmgC*
Birch, Paul d1964 *WhoHol B*
Birch, Paul d1969 *WhScrn 2*
Birch, Robert Fairfax *AmSCAP 1966*
Birch, Samuel d1841 *NotNAT B*
Birch, William 1918- *IntMPA 1977*
Bird, Betty *Film 2*
Bird, Billie *WhoHol A*
Bird, Charles *Film 2*
Bird, Charles A d1925 *NotNAT B*
Bird, Charlotte *Film 2*
Bird, David 1907- *WhoThe 16*
Bird, George T 1900- *AmSCAP 1966*
Bird, Getty *Film 2*
Bird, John 1936- *WhoThe 16*
Bird, Montgomery *PIP&P*
Bird, Norman 1920?- *FilmgC, WhoHol A*
Bird, Richard 1894- *FilmgC, WhThe*
Bird, Robert Montgomery 1806-1854 *CnThe, McGWD, NotNAT B, OxThe, REnWD*
Bird, Theophilus 1608-1664 *NotNAT B, OxThe*
Bird, William d1624 *NotNAT B, OxThe*
Birdt, Robert 1935- *AmSCAP 1966*
Birell, Tala 1908-1959 *FilmgC, WhoHol B*
Birimisa, George 1924- *ConDr 1977*
Birkett, Michael 1929- *FilmgC*
Birkett, Viva 1887-1934 *Film 2, NotNAT B, WhScrn 2, WhThe, WhoHol B*
Birkin, Jane *WhoHol A*
Birman, Serafima Germanovna 1890- *OxThe*
Birmingham, George A 1865-1950 *NotNAT B, WhThe*
Birmingham, Paul A 1937- *IntMPA 1977*
Birmingham, Stephen 1931- *CelR 3*
Birney, David *NotNAT, WhoHol A*
Biro, Lajos 1880-1948 *FilmgC, NotNAT B, OxThe, WorEnF*
Biroc, Joseph F 1903- *FilmgC, IntMPA 1977, WorEnF*
Birrell, Francis d1935 *NotNAT B*
Birri, Fernando 1925- *DcFM*
Birt, Daniel 1907-1955 *FilmgC*
Bischoff, Samuel 1890- *FilmgC*
Bishop, Detective Sergeant *Film 2*
Bishop, Alfred 1848-1928 *NotNAT B, WhThe*
Bishop, Chester 1858-1937 *WhScrn 1, WhScrn 2, WhoHol B*
Bishop, David 1931- *NotNAT*
Bishop, Elizabeth 1911- *CelR 3*
Bishop, George Walter 1886-1965 *OxThe, WhThe*
Bishop, Jim 1907- *CelR 3*
Bishop, Joe 1907- *AmSCAP 1966*
Bishop, Joey 1918- *CelR 3, FilmgC, WhoHol A*
Bishop, Julie *MotPP*
Bishop, Julie 1914- *WhoHol A*
Bishop, Julie 1917- *FilmgC, IntMPA 1977,*

MovMk
Bishop, Kate 1847-1923 *NotNAT B, WhThe*
Bishop, Richard 1898-1956 *NotNAT B, WhScrn 1, WhScrn 2, WhoHol B*
Bishop, Robert H, III 1916- *BiE&WWA*
Bishop, Stark, Jr. 1932-1945 *WhScrn 1, WhScrn 2*
Bishop, Terry 1912- *FilmgC*
Bishop, Walter 1905- *AmSCAP 1966*
Bishop, Will 1867-1944 *NotNAT B, WhThe*
Bishop, William d1959 *MotPP, WhoHol B*
Bishop, William 1917-1959 *WhScrn 1, WhScrn 2*
Bishop, William 1918-1959 *FilmgC, NotNAT B*
Biskar, John L 1918- *AmSCAP 1966*
Bispham, David S 1857-1921 *NotNAT B, WhoStg 1906*
Bissell, Richard 1913- *BiE&WWA, NotNAT*
Bissell, Whit 1914?- *FilmgC, WhoHol A*
Bisset, Jacqueline 1944- *CelR 3, FilmgC, IntMPA 1977, WhoHol A*
Bisset, Jacqueline 1945- *MovMk*
Bissett, Donald J 1930- *BiE&WWA*
Bissett, Jacqueline *MotPP*
Bisson, Alexandre d1912 *NotNAT B*
Biswanger, Erwin *Film 2*
Bitgood, Roberta 1908- *AmSCAP 1966*
Bitner, W W *Film 1*
Bittner, Jack 1917- *NotNAT*
Bittner, William W 1866-1918 *WhScrn 2*
Bitzer, Billy 1870-1944 *WorEnF*
Bitzer, Billy 1874-1944 *DcFM, FilmgC, OxFilm*
Bivens, Burke 1903- *AmSCAP 1966*
Bivona, Gus 1917- *AmSCAP 1966*
Bivona, S Richard 1911-1964 *AmSCAP 1966*
Bixby, Bill 1934- *FilmgC, IntMPA 1977, WhoHol A*
Bizet, Georges 1838-1875 *NotNAT B*
Bjerregaard, Henrik 1792-1842 *OxThe*
Bjork, Anita 1923- *FilmgC, MotPP, OxFilm, WhoHol A, WorEnF*
Bjork, Jewel *WomWMM B*
Bjorkman, Edwin August 1866-1951 *NotNAT B*
Bjorne, Hugh d1966 *WhoHol B*
Bjorne, Hugo 1886-1966 *WhScrn 1, WhScrn 2*
Bjorneboe, Jens Ingvald 1920- *CroCD*
Bjornson, Bjorn 1859-1942 *NotNAT B, OxThe*
Bjornson, Bjornstjerne 1832-1910 *CnMD, CnThe, McGWD, ModWD, NotNAT B, OxThe, REnWD*
Bjornstrand, Gunnar 1909- *FilmgC, MovMk, OxFilm, WhoHol A, WorEnF*
Blache, Alice Guy 1873-1965 *DcFM*
Blache, Alice Guy 1873-1968 *WomWMM*
Blache, Alice Guy 1878- *TwYS A*
Blache, Herbert *TwYS A, WomWMM*
Blache, Simone *WomWMM*
Black, Alexander F 1918- *IntMPA 1977*
Black, Alfred 1913- *WhThe*
Black, Ben 1889-1950 *AmSCAP 1966*
Black, Bill *Film 1*
Black, Bill 1927-1965 *WhScrn 2*
Black, Buck *Film 2*
Black, Buddy 1918- *AmSCAP 1966*
Black, Charles 1903- *AmSCAP 1966*
Black, Cilla *WhoHol A*
Black, David 1931- *BiE&WWA, NotNAT, WhoThe 16*
Black, Dorothy 1899- *WhThe*
Black, Eugene R 1898- *BiE&WWA, NotNAT*
Black, Frank J 1896- *AmSCAP 1966*
Black, G Howe *Film 2*
Black, George 1890-1945 *EncMT, NotNAT B, OxThe, WhThe*
Black, George 1911-1970 *WhThe*

Black, Jennie Prince 1868-1945 *AmSCAP 1966*
Black, Karen *WhoHol A*
Black, Karen 1942- *CelR 3*
Black, Karen 1943- *IntMPA 1977, MovMk*
Black, Karen 1948- *FilmgC*
Black, Kitty 1914- *WhoThe 16*
Black, Malcolm 1928- *BiE&WWA, NotNAT*
Black, Maurice d1938 *Film 2, WhScrn 1, WhScrn 2, WhoHol B*
Black, Neal *NatPD*
Black, Noel 1937- *FilmgC*
Black, Shirley Temple 1928- *CelR 3*
Black, Shirley Temple *see also* Temple, Shirley
Black, Stanley 1913- *FilmgC, IntMPA 1977*
Black, Theodore R 1906- *IntMPA 1977*
Black, William *Film 2*
Blackburn, Clarice *WhoHol A*
Blackburn, Dorothy *BiE&WWA, NotNAT*
Blackburn, John M 1914- *AmSCAP 1966*
Blackburn, Maurice 1914- *DcFM*
Blackburn Twins, The *WhoHol A*
Blackford, Lottie *Film 2*
Blackford, Mary 1914-1937 *WhScrn 1, WhScrn 2, WhoHol B*
Blackino, Yvette *WomWMM B*
Blackler, Betty 1929- *WhThe*
Blackman, Don *WhoHol A*
Blackman, Eugene J 1922- *BiE&WWA, NotNAT*
Blackman, Fred J d1951 *NotNAT B*
Blackman, Fred J 1879- *WhThe*
Blackman, Honor 1926- *FilmgC, IntMPA 1977, MotPP, WhoHol A, WhoThe 16*
Blackman, Joan *FilmgC, WhoHol A*
Blackmer, Sidney 1895-1973 *BiE&WWA, Film 2, FilmgC, NotNAT B, WhThe, WhoHol B*
Blackmer, Sidney 1896-1973 *WhScrn 2*
Blackmer, Sidney 1898-1973 *MovMk, Vers A*
Blackmore, Carl 1904-1965 *AmSCAP 1966*
Blackmore, E Willard 1870-1949 *WhScrn 1, WhScrn 2*
Blackmore, Peter 1909- *WhThe*
Blackmun, Harry A 1908- *CelR 3*
Blackstone, Vivian *WomWMM B*
Blackton, Charles Stuart 1914- *Film 2*
Blackton, Greg *Film 2*
Blackton, J Stewart 1875-1941 *WorEnF*
Blackton, J Stuart 1868-1941 *FilmgC*
Blackton, J Stuart 1875-1941 *WhScrn 2*
Blackton, J Stuart 1875-1946 *TwYS A*
Blackton, James Stuart 1875-1941 *DcFM, OxFilm*
Blackton, Jay 1909- *AmSCAP 1966, BiE&WWA, NotNAT*
Blackton, Marian *Film 2*
Blackton, Violet Virginia *Film 2*
Blackwell, Carlyle d1955 *MotPP, NotNAT B, WhoHol B*
Blackwell, Carlyle 1880-1955 *Film 2*
Blackwell, Carlyle 1884-1955 *TwYS*
Blackwell, Carlyle 1888-1955 *Film 1, FilmgC, WhScrn 1, WhScrn 2*
Blackwell, Carlyle, Jr. 1913-1974 *WhScrn 2, WhoHol B*
Blackwell, Earl 1913- *CelR 3*
Blackwell, Earl 1914- *BiE&WWA, NotNAT*
Blackwell, Jim *Film 2*
Blackwood, Bonnie 1909-1949 *WhScrn 1, WhScrn 2*
Blackwood, Diana d1961 *WhScrn 1, WhScrn 2*
Blade, James P 1907- *AmSCAP 1966*
Blaga, Lucian 1895-1961 *CnMD*
Blagoi, George 1898-1971 *WhScrn 1, WhScrn 2, WhoHol B*
Blagrove, Thomas *OxThe*
Blain, Gerard 1930- *FilmgC, WhoHol A*

Blaine, Joan d1949 *WhScrn 2*
Blaine, Martin *WhoHol A*
Blaine, Rose d1974 *WhoHol B*
Blaine, Ruby *Film 2*
Blaine, Vivian *MotPP*
Blaine, Vivian 1921- *EncMT, FilmgC, HolP 40, WhoThe 16*
Blaine, Vivian 1923- *BiE&WWA, NotNAT*
Blaine, Vivian 1924- *IntMPA 1977, WhoHol A*
Blair, Betsy 1923- *BiE&WWA, FilmgC, IntMPA 1977, MotPP, OxFilm, WhoHol A*
Blair, David d1976 *WhoHol C*
Blair, Ella S 1895-1917 *WhScrn 2*
Blair, Eugenie d1922 *NotNAT B*
Blair, Frank 1915- *CelR 3, NewYTET*
Blair, George 1906-1970 *FilmgC*
Blair, Hal 1915- *AmSCAP 1966*
Blair, Isla 1944- *WhoThe 16*
Blair, Janet 1921- *BiE&WWA, FilmgC, HolP 40, IntMPA 1977, MotPP, MovMk, WhoHol A*
Blair, Joan *WhoHol A*
Blair, Joyce 1932- *WhoThe 16*
Blair, June *WhoHol A*
Blair, Larry 1935- *IntMPA 1977*
Blair, Linda *WhoHol A*
Blair, Lionel 1931- *WhoThe 16*
Blair, Mary *PIP&P*
Blair, Mary d1947 *NotNAT B*
Blair, Nicky *WhoHol A*
Blair, William 1896- *BiE&WWA, NotNAT*
Blair, William McCormick, Jr. 1916- *CelR 3*
Blaisdell, Charles d1930 *WhoHol B*
Blaisdell, William *Film 2*
Blaise, Pierre 1951-1975 *WhScrn 2, WhoHol C*
Blaisell, Charles Big Bill 1874-1930 *WhScrn 1, WhScrn 2*
Blake, A D *Film 1*
Blake, Al 1877-1966 *WhScrn 2*
Blake, Amanda 1929- *CelR 3, FilmgC, IntMPA 1977, WhoHol A*
Blake, Anne d1973 *WhScrn 2, WhoHol B*
Blake, Bebe 1925- *AmSCAP 1966*
Blake, Betty 1920- *BiE&WWA, NotNAT*
Blake, Charles *NotNAT*
Blake, David M 1948- *IntMPA 1977*
Blake, Eubie 1883- *AmSCAP 1966, EncMT*
Blake, Eugene Carson 1906- *CelR 3*
Blake, George 1917-1955 *AmSCAP 1966*
Blake, George M 1912- *AmSCAP 1966*
Blake, Harry 1866- *WhThe*
Blake, James W 1862-1935 *AmSCAP 1966*
Blake, Katherine 1928- *FilmgC*
Blake, Larry *WhoHol A*
Blake, Loretta *Film 1*
Blake, Lucius *Film 2*
Blake, Madge 1900-1969 *MotPP, WhScrn 1, WhScrn 2, WhoHol B*
Blake, Marie 1896- *MGM, ThFT, WhoHol A*
Blake, Myrtle Ann 1906- *AmSCAP 1966*
Blake, Oliver 1905- *Vers B*
Blake, Paul d1960 *WhScrn 1, WhScrn 2, WhoHol B*
Blake, Robert *WhoHol A*
Blake, Robert 1934- *FilmgC, MovMk*
Blake, Robert 1938- *IntMPA 1977*
Blake, Tom *Film 1, Film 2*
Blake, Whitney *WhoHol A*
Blakeclock, Alban d1966 *WhScrn 1, WhScrn 2, WhoHol A*
Blakeley, James 1873-1915 *NotNAT B, WhThe, WhoStg 1908*
Blakeley, John E 1889-1958 *FilmgC*
Blakeley, Tom 1918- *FilmgC*

Blakelock, Denys 1901-1970 *WhThe*
Blakely, Colin 1930- *CnThe, FilmgC, PIP&P, WhoHol A, WhoThe 16*
Blakely, Gene 1922- *BiE&WWA*
Blakely, James *WhoHol A*
Blakely, Susan *IntMPA 1977, WhoHol A*
Blakemore, Erik F 1926- *IntMPA 1977*
Blakemore, Michael 1928- *NotNAT, WhoThe 16*
Blakeney, Olive 1903-1959 *WhScrn 1, WhScrn 2, WhoHol B*
Blakiston, Clarence 1864-1943 *NotNAT B, WhThe*
Blakley, Ronee *WhoHol A*
Blalock, Richard *IntMPA 1977*
Blanc, Mel 1908- *AmSCAP 1966, FilmgC, IntMPA 1977, WhoHol A*
Blanc, Sally *Film 2*
Blanc-Maeterlinck, Georgette *Film 2*
Blancard, Rene 1897-1965 *WhScrn 2*
Blanchar, Pierre 1892-1963 *Film 2, FilmgC, OxFilm*
Blanchar, Pierre 1893-1963 *WhScrn 1, WhScrn 2*
Blanchar, Pierre 1896-1963 *NotNAT B, OxThe, WhoHol B*
Blanchard, Doc 1925- *WhoHol A*
Blanchard, Edward Leman 1820-1889 *NotNAT B, OxThe*
Blanchard, Eleanor *Film 1*
Blanchard, Mari 1927-1970 *FilmgC, WhScrn 1, WhScrn 2, WhoHol B*
Blanchard, William 1769-1835 *NotNAT B, OxThe*
Blanchard, William G 1905- *AmSCAP 1966*
Blanche, Ada 1862-1953 *NotNAT B, WhThe*
Blanche, August Theodore 1811-1868 *OxThe*
Blanche, Belle 1891-1963 *NotNAT B, WhoStg 1908*
Blanche, Francis d1974 *WhoHol B*
Blanche, Francis 1921-1974 *WorEnF*
Blanche, Francis 1922-1974 *WhScrn 2*
Blanche, Kate *Film 2*
Blanche, Marie 1893- *WhThe*
Blanco, Richard M *IntMPA 1977*
Bland, Alan 1897-1946 *WhThe*
Bland, George d1807 *NotNAT B, OxThe*
Bland, Harcourt d1875 *NotNAT B*
Bland, James 1798-1861 *NotNAT B, OxThe*
Bland, James A 1854-1911 *NotNAT B*
Bland, John d1788 *NotNAT B*
Bland, Joyce 1906-1963 *WhScrn 1, WhScrn 2, WhThe, WhoHol B*
Bland, Maria Theresa Romanzini 1769-1838 *OxThe*
Bland, R Henderson d1941 *Film 1, NotNAT B, WhoHol B*
Blande, Edith d1923 *NotNAT B*
Blandick, Clara 1880-1962 *ThFT*
Blandick, Clara 1881-1962 *Film 2, FilmgC, MotPP, MovMk, NotNAT B, Vers A, WhScrn 1, WhScrn 2, WhoHol B*
Blane, Ralph 1914- *AmSCAP 1966, BiE&WWA, EncMT, IntMPA 1977, NotNAT*
Blane, Sally 1910- *Film 2, FilmgC, MovMk, ThFT, TwYS, WhoHol A*
Blaney, Charles Edward d1944 *NotNAT B, WhThe*
Blaney, H Clay 1908-1964 *BiE&WWA*
Blaney, Harry Clay 1874- *WhoStg 1906, WhoStg 1908*
Blaney, Henry Clay 1908-1964 *NotNAT B*
Blaney, May 1874-1953 *WhScrn 2*
Blaney, Norah *WhThe*
Blank, Edward L *IntMPA 1977*
Blank, Myron 1911- *IntMPA 1977*
Blanke, Henry 1901- *FilmgC, IntMPA 1977,*

WorEnF
Blanke, Kate *Film 1, Film 2*
Blanke, Tom *Film 2*
Blankfort, Michael 1907- *BiE&WWA, IntMPA 1977, NatPD, NotNAT*
Blankman, George 1877-1925 *WhScrn 1, WhScrn 2, WhoHol B*
Blankman, Howard Milford 1925- *AmSCAP 1966*
Blankner, Frederika *NatPD*
Blasetti, Alessandro 1900- *DcFM, FilmgC, OxFilm, WorEnF*
Blass, Bill 1922- *CelR 3*
Blatcher, William *Film 2*
Blatchford, William 1886-1936 *WhScrn 1, WhScrn 2, WhoHol B*
Blatt, Edward A 1905- *BiE&WWA, FilmgC*
Blattner, Gerry 1913- *IntMPA 1977*
Blatty, William Peter *FilmgC, IntMPA 1977*
Blau, Bela d1940 *NotNAT B*
Blau, Herbert 1926- *BiE&WWA, NotNAT, PIP&P*
Blau, Martin 1924- *IntMPA 1977*
Blaufuss, Walter 1883-1945 *AmSCAP 1966*
Blaustein, Julian 1913- *FilmgC, IntMPA 1977, WorEnF*
Blauvelt, Lillian Evans 1873- *WhoStg 1906, WhoStg 1908*
Blavet, Emile 1838- *WhThe*
Blaydon, Richard *Film 2*
Blayney, May 1875-1953 *NotNAT B, WhThe*
Bleckner, Jeff *WhoThe 16*
Bledsoe, Earl d1962 *NotNAT B*
Bledsoe, George 1921- *AmSCAP 1966*
Bledsoe, Jules d1943 *WhoHol B*
Bledsoe, Jules 1898-1943 *NotNAT B*
Bledsoe, Jules 1899-1943 *WhScrn 1, WhScrn 2*
Blees, Robert *IntMPA 1977*
Bleibtreau, Hedwig 1868-1958 *WhScrn 1, WhScrn 2*
Bleibtreu, Hedwig 1868-1958 *WhoHol B*
Bleier, Edward 1929- *IntMPA 1977, NewYTET*
Bleifer, John *Film 2, WhoHol A*
Bleiman, Mikhail 1904- *DcFM*
Blender, Leon Philip 1920- *IntMPA 1977*
Blensfeld, Paul *Film 2*
Bletcher, Billy 1894- *Film 2, WhoHol A*
Bley, Maurice 1910- *BiE&WWA, NotNAT*
Blick, Newton 1899-1965 *WhScrn 1, WhScrn 2, WhThe, WhoHol B*
Blier, Bernard 1916- *FilmgC*
Blin, Roger 1907- *CnThe*
Blinn, Benjamin F 1872-1941 *WhScrn 1, WhScrn 2, WhoHol B*
Blinn, Edward 1938- *AmSCAP 1966*
Blinn, Genevieve d1956 *Film 1, Film 2, WhScrn 1, WhScrn 2, WhoHol B*
Blinn, Holbrook 1872-1928 *Film 1, Film 2, MotPP, NotNAT B, TwYS, WhScrn 1, WhScrn 2, WhThe, WhoHol B, WhoStg 1906, WhoStg 1908*
Blinn, Nellie Holbrook d1909 *NotNAT B*
Blinn, William *NewYTET*
Bliokh, Yakov 1895-1957 *DcFM*
Bliss, Anthony A 1913- *BiE&WWA*
Bliss, Sir Arthur 1891- *FilmgC* \
Bliss, Hebe d1956 *NotNAT B*
Bliss, Helena 1917- *BiE&WWA, NotNAT, WhoThe 16*
Blissett, Francis d1824 *NotNAT B*
Blitzstein, Marc 1905-1964 *AmSCAP 1966, BiE&WWA, CnMD, EncMT, McGWD, ModWD, NewMT, NotNAT B, PIP&P*
Bloch, Bertram 1892- *BiE&WWA, NotNAT*
Bloch, Ernest 1880-1959 *AmSCAP 1966*

Bloch, Raymond A 1902- *AmSCAP 1966*
Bloch, Robert 1917- *FilmgC, IntMPA 1977*
Block, Anita Cahn 1882-1967 *NotNAT B*
Block, Dorothy *Film 2*
Block, Richard C *NewYTET*
Block, Sheridan *Film 1, WhoStg 1906, WhoStg 1908*
Block, Steven 1928- *BiE&WWA*
Block, Will J *WhoStg 1908*
Block, Willard 1930- *IntMPA 1977*
Block, William J d1932 *NotNAT B*
Blocker, Dan 1928-1972 *FilmgC*
Blocker, Dan 1929-1972 *WhScrn 2, WhoHol B*
Blodget, Alden S d1964 *NotNAT B*
Blofson, Richard 1933- *BiE&WWA, NotNAT*
Blok, Aleksandr Aleksandrovich 1880-1921 *McGWD, ModWD*
Blok, Alexander 1880-1921 *CnMD*
Blom, August 1869-1942 *WorEnF*
Blom, August 1869-1947 *DcFM*
Blomberg, Erik 1913- *DcFM*
Blomfield, Derek 1920-1964 *FilmgC, NotNAT B, WhScrn 2, WhThe, WhoHol B*
Blomquist, Allen 1928- *BiE&WWA, NotNAT*
Blomstedt, George *Film 2*
Blondell, Gloria *WhoHol A*
Blondell, Joan *MotPP, WhoHol A*
Blondell, Joan 1909- *BiDFlm, CelR 3, FilmgC, MovMk, OxFilm, ThFT, WhoThe 16, WorEnF*
Blondell, Joan 1912- *BiE&WWA, IntMPA 1977, NotNAT*
Blood, Adele d1936 *NotNAT B*
Bloodgood, Clara 1870-1907 *NotNAT B*
Bloom, Claire *BiE&WWA, MotPP, WhoHol A*
Bloom, Claire 1928- *OxFilm*
Bloom, Claire 1931- *BiDFlm, CelR 3, CnThe, FilmgC, IntMPA 1977, MovMk, NotNAT, WhoThe 16, WorEnF*
Bloom, Harold Jack *NewYTET*
Bloom, Larry 1914- *AmSCAP 1966*
Bloom, Milton 1906- *AmSCAP 1966*
Bloom, Murray 1889- *AmSCAP 1966*
Bloom, Murray Teigh *NatPD*
Bloom, Philip 1918- *BiE&WWA*
Bloom, Rube 1902- *AmSCAP 1966*
Bloom, Seymour L 1911- *AmSCAP 1966*
Bloom, Vera 1898-1959 *AmSCAP 1966*
Bloom, Verna *IntMPA 1977, WhoHol A*
Bloom, William 1915- *IntMPA 1977*
Bloomer, Raymond *Film 2*
Bloomer, Raymond J *Film 1*
Bloomfield, Derek 1920-1964 *WhScrn 1*
Bloomgarden, Kermit 1904-1976 *BiE&WWA, NotNAT B, PIP&P, WhoThe 16*
Bloomingdale, Alfred 1916- *CelR 3*
Blore, Eric d1959 *MotPP, WhoHol B*
Blore, Eric 1887-1959 *FilmgC, MovMk, NotNAT B, WhScrn 1, WhScrn 2, WhThe*
Blore, Eric 1888-1959 *Film 2, Vers A*
Bloss, Schmid *Film 2*
Blossom, Henry Martyn, Jr. 1866-1919 *AmSCAP 1966, EncMT, NewMT, NotNAT B, WhThe, WhoStg 1906, WhoStg 1908*
Blossom, Rose *Film 2*
Blossom, Winter *Film 2*
Blount, Helon 1929- *WhoThe 16*
Blow, Mark d1921 *NotNAT B*
Blow, Sydney 1878-1961 *NotNAT A, NotNAT B, WhThe*
Blowitz, John S *IntMPA 1977*
Blowitz, William F d1964 *NotNAT B*
Blue, Ben d1975 *WhoHol C*

Blue, Ben 1900-1975 *FilmgC, MovMk*
Blue, Ben 1901-1975 *Film 2, WhScrn 2*
Blue, James 1930- *WorEnF*
Blue, Monte 1890-1963 *Film 1, Film 2, FilmgC, MotPP, MovMk, NotNAT B, TwYS, Vers A, WhScrn 1, WhScrn 2, WhoHol B*
Blue, Vida 1949- *CelR 3*
Bluette, Isa 1898-1939 *WhScrn 2*
Bluhdorn, Charles G *IntMPA 1977*
Blum, Daniel 1899-1965 *NotNAT B*
Blum, Daniel 1900-1965 *BiE&WWA, FilmgC*
Blum, Edward 1928- *BiE&WWA, NotNAT*
Blum, Ernest d1907 *NotNAT B*
Blum, Harry 1926- *AmSCAP 1966*
Blum, Max 1874-1944 *WhScrn 1, WhScrn 2*
Blum, Sam d1945 *Film 2, WhoHol B*
Blum, Sammy 1889-1945 *WhScrn 1, WhScrn 2*
Blum, William 1901- *BiE&WWA*
Blumberg, Harold D 1922- *BiE&WWA*
Blume, Bernhard 1901- *CnMD, ModWD*
Blumenfeld, Joseph 1901- *IntMPA 1977*
Blumenstock, Sid *IntMPA 1977*
Blumenthal, Ann E *WomWMM B*
Blumenthal, George 1862-1943 *NotNAT A*
Blumenthal, Oscar 1852-1917 *NotNAT B*
Blumenthal, Richard M d1962 *NotNAT B*
Blumenthal-Tamarina, Maria d1938 *NotNAT B, WhoHol B*
Blumofe, Robert F *IntMPA 1977*
Bly, Albert E 1892- *AmSCAP 1966*
Bly, Nellie *Film 2*
Blyden, Larry 1925-1975 *BiE&WWA, FilmgC, NotNAT, NotNAT B, WhScrn 2, WhoHol C, WhoThe 16*
Blye, Allan And Chris Bearde *NewYTET*
Blye, Maggie *WhoHol A*
Blystone, John G 1892-1938 *FilmgC, TwYS A*
Blystone, Stanley 1894-1956 *Film 2, WhScrn 2, WhoHol B*
Blyth, Ann 1928- *FilmgC, HolP 40, IntMPA 1977, MGM, MotPP, MovMk, WhoHol A, WomWMM, WorEnF*
Blyth, Henry 1910- *IntMPA 1977*
Blyth-Pratt, Charles Edward 1869- *WhThe*
Blyth-Pratt, Violet *WhThe*
Blythe, Betty 1893-1972 *Film 1, Film 2, FilmgC, MotPP, MovMk, TwYS, WhScrn 2, WhoHol B*
Blythe, Bobby 1894- *WhThe*
Blythe, Coralie 1880-1928 *NotNAT B, WhThe*
Blythe, Erik *WhoHol A*
Blythe, John *WhoHol A*
Blythe, John 1921- *FilmgC, WhoThe 16*
Blythe, Violet *WhThe*
Boaden, James 1762-1839 *NotNAT B, OxThe*
Boag, William d1939 *NotNAT B*
Boardman, Eleanor 1898- *Film 2, FilmgC, MotPP, MovMk, ThFT, TwYS, WhoHol A*
Boardman, Lillian d1953 *NotNAT B*
Boardman, True 1882-1918 *Film 1, WhScrn 2, WhoHol B*
Boardman, Virginia True 1889-1971 *Film 2, WhScrn 1, WhScrn 2, WhoHol B*
Boasberg, Charles 1906- *IntMPA 1977*
Boatner, Edward H 1898- *AmSCAP 1966*
Boatwright, Howard 1918- *AmSCAP 1966*
Boaz, Chuck *WhoHol A*
Bobadilla, Pepita *WhThe*
Bobards, James *Film 2*
Bobczynski, Michele 1946- *WomWMM B*
Bobeche 1791-1840? *OxThe*
Bobrick, Sam 1932- *AmSCAP 1966*
Bobs, The Two *WhThe*
Bocage 1797-1863 *NotNAT B, OxThe*

Bocage, Paul 1824-1887 *OxThe*
Bocage, Pierre Francois 1797-1863 *CnThe*
Bocci, Gildo *Film 2*
Bochco, Steven *NewYTET*
Bochner, Lloyd 1924- *FilmgC, WhoHol A*
Bock, Fred 1939- *AmSCAP 1966*
Bock, Jerry 1928- *BiE&WWA, CelR 3, EncMT, NewMT, NotNAT, PIP&P, WhoThe 16*
Bock, Lothar *NewYTET*
Bocquet, Florence *WomWMM*
Bodard, Mag 1927- *FilmgC, WomWMM*
Bodart, Madame *Film 2*
Boddey, Martin *WhoHol A*
Bode, Lenore *WomWMM B*
Bode, Milton 1860-1938 *NotNAT B, WhThe*
Bodeen, DeWitt 1908- *CmMov, FilmgC*
Bodel, Burman 1911-1969 *WhScrn 2, WhoHol B*
Bodel, Jean d1210? *McGWD, OxThe*
Bodenheim, Maxwell 1893-1954 *NotNAT B*
Bodie, Walford 1870- *WhThe*
Bodner, Phil 1919- *AmSCAP 1966*
Boeck, Johann A 1917- *CroCD*
Boeck, Johann Michael 1743-1793 *OxThe*
Boehm, Karl 1928- *FilmgC, WhoHol A*
Boehm, Sidney 1908- *FilmgC*
Boehm, Sydney 1908- *IntMPA 1977, WorEnF*
Boese, Joachim 1933-1971 *WhScrn 2*
Boesen, William 1924-1972 *WhScrn 2*
Boetiger, Julia 1852-1938 *WhScrn 1, WhScrn 2*
Boetler, Wade *Film 2*
Boettcher, Henry F 1903- *BiE&WWA*
Boettcher, Budd 1916- *BiDFlm, CmMov, DcFM, FilmgC, MovMk, OxFilm, WorEnF*
Boetticher, Budd 1918- *IntMPA 1977*
Boetticher, Oscar 1916- *WorEnF*
Boffety, Jean *IntMPA 1977*
Boganny, Joe 1874- *WhThe*
Bogard, Travis 1918- *BiE&WWA, NotNAT*
Bogarde, Dirk *MotPP, WhoHol A*
Bogarde, Dirk 1920- *CmMov, FilmgC, MovMk, WhThe, WorEnF*
Bogarde, Dirk 1921- *BiDFlm, CelR 3, IntMPA 1977, OxFilm*
Bogart, Andrew 1874- *WhoStg 1908*
Bogart, David d1964 *NotNAT B*
Bogart, Humphrey 1899-1957 *BiDFlm, CmMov, FilmgC, MotPP, MovMk, OxFilm, PIP&P, WhScrn 1, WhScrn 2, WhThe, WhoHol B, WorEnF*
Bogart, Humphrey 1900-1957 *NotNAT B*
Bogart, Paul 1919- *FilmgC, IntMPA 1977, NewYTET*
Bogdanoff, Rose d1957 *NotNAT B*
Bogdanovich, Peter 1939- *BiDFlm, CelR 3, IntMPA 1977, MovMk*
Bogdanovich, Peter 1940- *OxFilm*
Bogdanovitch, Peter 1939- *FilmgC*
Bogeaus, Benedict E 1904-1968 *FilmgC, WorEnF*
Boggetti, Victor 1895- *WhThe*
Bogie, Duane *NewYTET*
Bogin, Abba 1925- *NotNAT*
Bogusch, Ronald A 1931- *AmSCAP 1966*
Boguslawski, Wojciech 1757-1829 *NotNAT B*
Bohan, Marc 1926- *CelR 3*
Bohannon, E J Bo 1896-1966 *WhScrn 2*
Bohdiewicz, Antoni 1906-1970 *OxFilm*
Bohem, Endre *IntMPA 1977*
Bohler, Fred *Film 2*
Bohm, Karl 1894- *CelR 3*
Bohm, Karlheinz *MotPP*
Bohme, David M 1916- *AmSCAP 1966*
Bohn, Jack Lionel *Film 2*
Bohnen, Michael 1887-1965 *Film 2, WhScrn 2*
Bohnen, Roman 1894-1949 *FilmgC, NotNAT B,*

PIP&P, WhScrn 1, WhScrn 2, WhThe, WhoHol B
Bohnen, Roman 1899-1949 *Vers A*
Boileau, Nicolas 1633?-1711 *NotNAT B*
Boileau-Despreaux, Nicolas 1636-1711 *OxThe*
Boindin, Nicolas 1676-1751 *OxThe*
Bois, Curt 1900- *FilmgC, WhoHol A*
Bois, Ilse *Film 2*
Boisrobert, Francois LeMetel De 1592-1662 *OxThe*
Boisrobert, Francois LeNutel DeAbbe 1592-1662 *NotNAT B*
Boisrond, Michel 1921- *DcFM*
Boisset, Yves 1939- *FilmgC*
Boito, Arrigo 1842-1918 *NotNAT B, OxThe*
Bok, Derek Curtis 1930- *CelR 3*
Boker, George Henry 1823-1890 *CnThe, McGWD, NotNAT A, NotNAT B, OxThe, REnWD*
Bolam, James 1938- *WhoThe 16*
Boland, Bridget *WomWMM*
Boland, Bridget 1904- *FilmgC*
Boland, Bridget 1913- *ConDr 1977*
Boland, Clay A 1903-1963 *AmSCAP 1966*
Boland, Clay A, Jr. 1931- *AmSCAP 1966*
Boland, Eddie 1883-1935 *WhScrn 1, WhScrn 2*
Boland, Eddie 1885-1935 *Film 1, Film 2, TwYS*
Boland, Mary 1880-1965 *EncMT, Film 1, FilmgC, ThFT, WhScrn 1, WhScrn 2*
Boland, Mary 1882-1965 *MotPP, MovMk, TwYS, Vers A, WhoHol B*
Boland, Mary 1885-1965 *BiE&WWA, NotNAT B, WhThe*
Bolasni, Saul 1923- *BiE&WWA, NotNAT*
Bolder, Robert 1859-1937 *Film 1, Film 2, WhScrn 1, WhScrn 2, WhoHol B*
Boldt, Deborah *WomWMM*
Bolen, Lin *NewYTET*
Boles, Jim *WhoHol A*
Boles, John d1969 *BiE&WWA, MotPP, WhoHol B*
Boles, John 1890-1969 *TwYS*
Boles, John 1895-1969 *EncMT, Film 2, FilmgC, HolP 30, MovMk, WhScrn 1, WhScrn 2*
Boles, John 1896-1969 *NotNAT B*
Boles, John 1900-1969 *WhThe*
Boleslavski, Richard 1889-1937 *PIP&P*
Boleslavsky, Richard 1889-1937 *BiDFlm, WorEnF*
Boleslawski, Richard 1889-1937 *FilmgC, NotNAT A, NotNAT B, WhThe, WorEnF*
Boley, May 1882-1963 *Film 2, NotNAT B, WhScrn 1, WhScrn 2, WhoHol B*
Bolger, Ray *WhoHol A*
Bolger, Ray 1903- *CmMov*
Bolger, Ray 1904- *BiE&WWA, EncMT, FilmgC, MovMk, NotNAT, WhoThe 16*
Bolger, Ray 1906- *IntMPA 1977*
Bolger, Robert Bo 1937-1969 *WhScrn 2*
Bolin, Nicolai P 1908- *AmSCAP 1966*
Bolin, Shannon 1917- *BiE&WWA, NotNAT*
Bolkan, Florinda *FilmgC, WhoHol A*
Boll, Heinrich 1917- *CelR 3*
Boller, Robert O, Sr. d1962 *NotNAT B*
Bolling, Tiffany *WhoHol A*
Bollinger, Anne d1962 *NotNAT B*
Bollow, Ludmilla *NatPD*
Bolm, Adolph 1887-1951 *NotNAT B, WhThe*
Bologna, Joseph *IntMPA 1977, NotNAT, WhoHol A, WomWMM*
Bolognini, Mauro 1923- *BiDFlm, DcFM, WorEnF*
Bolt, Carol 1941- *ConDr 1977*
Bolt, Robert 1924- *BiE&WWA, CelR 3, CnThe, ConDr 1977, CroCD, FilmgC, IntMPA 1977, McGWD, ModWD, NotNAT, OxThe, REnWD, WhoThe 16, WorEnF*

Bolte, Carl E, Jr. 1929- *AmSCAP 1966*
Bolton, Betty *Film 2*
Bolton, Guy *ConDr 1977D, PIP&P*
Bolton, Guy 1884- *AmSCAP 1966, ConDr 1973, EncMT, ModWD, WhoThe 16*
Bolton, Guy 1885- *FilmgC*
Bolton, Guy 1886- *BiE&WWA, NewMT, NotNAT, NotNAT A*
Bolton, Helen *Film 2*
Bolton, Jack d1962 *NotNAT B*
Bolton, Whitney 1900-1969 *BiE&WWA, NotNAT B*
Bolvary, Geza Von 1897- *DcFM*
Bombard, Lottie Gertrude 1908-1913 *WhScrn 2*
Bomberger, Edward C 1933- *IntMPA 1977*
Bomer, Marjorie *Film 2*
Bompiani, Valentino 1898- *CnMD, McGWD*
Bon, Francesco Augusto 1788-1858 *McGWD*
Bonacio, Bennie 1903- *AmSCAP 1966*
Bonafe, Pepa *Film 1*
Bonano, Joseph 1904- *AmSCAP 1966*
Bonanova, Fortunio 1893-1969 *WhScrn 1, WhScrn 2*
Bonanova, Fortunio 1896-1969 *FilmgC, WhoHol B*
Bonanova, Fortunio 1905-1969 *Vers B*
Bonaparte, Napoleon *Film 2*
Bonarelli DellaRovere, Guidobaldo 1563-1608 *OxThe*
Bonbrest, Joseph B 1895- *AmSCAP 1966*
Bond, Acton d1941 *NotNAT B, WhThe*
Bond, Anson 1914- *IntMPA 1977*
Bond, Bert d1964 *NotNAT B*
Bond, Brenda *Film 2*
Bond, C G 1945- *ConDr 1977*
Bond, Carrie Jacobs 1862-1946 *AmSCAP 1966, NotNAT B*
Bond, David *WhoHol A*
Bond, Derek *WhoHol A*
Bond, Derek 1919- *FilmgC*
Bond, Derek 1920- *IntMPA 1977*
Bond, Edward 1934- *ConDr 1977*
Bond, Edward 1935- *CnThe, CroCD, NotNAT, PIP&P A, WhoThe 16*
Bond, Frank *Film 2*
Bond, Frederic 1861-1914 *WhThe*
Bond, Frederick 1861-1914 *Film 1, NotNAT B, WhoStg 1906, WhoStg 1908*
Bond, Gary 1940- *FilmgC, WhoThe 16*
Bond, Jack 1899-1952 *WhScrn 1, WhScrn 2*
Bond, Jessie 1853-1942 *NotNAT B, WhThe*
Bond, Julian 1940- *CelR 3*
Bond, Lilian 1910- *ThFT, WhThe*
Bond, Lillian 1910- *FilmgC, WhoHol A*
Bond, Lyle 1917-1972 *WhScrn 2*
Bond, Ralph 1906- *IntMPA 1977*
Bond, Rudy 1913- *BiE&WWA, NotNAT, WhoHol A*
Bond, Sheila 1928- *BiE&WWA, NotNAT, WhThe, WhoHol A*
Bond, Shelly 1910- *AmSCAP 1966*
Bond, Sudie 1928- *BiE&WWA, NotNAT, WhoHol A, WhoThe 16*
Bond, Thomas d1635 *OxThe*
Bond, Tommy Butch *WhoHol A*
Bond, Ward d1960 *MotPP, NotNAT B, WhoHol B*
Bond, Ward 1903-1960 *FilmgC, OxFilm, WhScrn 1, WhScrn 2*
Bond, Ward 1904-1960 *MovMk*
Bond, Ward 1905-1960 *CmMov, Film 2*
Bondarchuk, Serge 1920- *MovMk*
Bondarchuk, Sergei 1920- *DcFM, OxFilm, WhoHol A, WorEnF*

Bondartchuk, Sergei 1920- *FilmgC*
Bondhill, Gertrude 1880-1960 *WhScrn 1, WhScrn 2, WhoHol B*
Bondi, Alex *Film 2*
Bondi, Beulah 1892- *BiE&WWA, FilmgC, IntMPA 1977, MotPP, MovMk, NotNAT, ThFT, Vers A, WhThe, WhoHol A*
Bondire *Film 2*
Bonds, Margaret 1913- *AmSCAP 1966*
Bondwin, Billy *Film 2*
Bondy, Ed 1932- *BiE&WWA*
Bone, Gene 1948- *AmSCAP 1966*
Bonelli, Mona Modini 1903- *AmSCAP 1966*
Bonerz, Peter *WhoHol A*
Boness, Clarence M 1931- *AmSCAP 1966*
Bonfils, Helen 1889-1972 *BiE&WWA, NotNAT B, WhThe*
Bongini, Rafael *Film 2*
Bonham, Kathy *WomWMM B*
Boni, Carmen *Film 2*
Boniface, Mrs. George C d1883 *NotNAT B*
Boniface, George C, Jr. d1912 *NotNAT B*
Boniface, Symona 1894-1950 *WhScrn 1, WhScrn 2, WhoHol B*
Bonifant, Carmen 1890-1957 *WhScrn 1, WhScrn 2*
Bonillas, Myrna 1890-1959 *WhScrn 1, WhScrn 2, WhoHol B*
Bonillas, Myrta *Film 2*
Bonime, Josef 1891-1959 *AmSCAP 1966*
Bonita 1886- *WhoStg 1908*
Bonn, Ferdinand *Film 2*
Bonn, Frank 1873-1944 *WhScrn 1, WhScrn 2, WhoHol B*
Bonn, Walter 1889-1953 *WhScrn 1, WhScrn 2, WhoHol B*
Bonnaire, Henri 1869- *WhThe*
Bonnard, Mario 1889-1965 *WhScrn 1, WhScrn 2*
Bonnardot, Jean-Claude 1923- *DcFM*
Bonnell, Jay *WhoHol A*
Bonnell, Lee *WhoHol A*
Bonner, Isabel 1908-1955 *NotNAT B, WhScrn 1, WhScrn 2, WhoHol B*
Bonner, Joe 1882-1959 *WhScrn 2, WhoHol B*
Bonner, Marjorie *Film 2*
Bonner, Priscella *Film 2*
Bonner, Priscilla *TwYS*
Bonner, Ronnie 1920- *AmSCAP 1966*
Bonney, William H *OxFilm*
Bono, Sonny *IntMPA 1977, WhoHol A*
Bonomo, Joe 1898- *Film 2, WhoHol A*
Bonsall, Bessie d1963 *NotNAT B*
Bonstelle, Jessie 1872-1932 *NotNAT B, OxThe*
Bontempelli, Massimo 1878-1960 *CnMD, McGWD, ModWD*
Bontsema, Peter H 1897- *AmSCAP 1966*
Bonucci, Alberto 1919-1969 *WhScrn 1, WhScrn 2*
Bonus, Ben *WhoThe 16*
Bonx, Nathan J 1900-1950 *AmSCAP 1966*
Bonynge, Leta *WhoHol A*
Bonzo *FilmgC*
Book-Asta, George *Film 2*
Booke, Sorrell *WhoHol A*
Booke, Sorrell 1926- *FilmgC*
Booke, Sorrell 1930- *NotNAT, WhoThe 16*
Booker, Beulah *Film 2*
Booker, Harry 1850-1924 *Film 1, WhScrn 1, WhScrn 2, WhoHol B*
Booker, Sue 1946- *WomWMM A, WomWMM B*
Bookman, Leo 1932- *BiE&WWA, NotNAT*
Boon, Robert *WhoHol A*
Boone, Daniel 1734-1820 *FilmgC*
Boone, Pat 1934- *AmSCAP 1966, CelR 3,*

FilmgC, IntMPA 1977, MotPP, MovMk,
WhoHol A
Boone, Randy *WhoHol A*
Boone, Richard *MotPP, WhoHol A*
Boone, Richard 1915- *CmMov*
Boone, Richard 1917- *BiE&WWA, CelR 3,*
FilmgC, IntMPA 1977, MovMk
Boor, Frank d1938 *NotNAT B, WhThe*
Boorman, John 1933- *DcFM, FilmgC,*
IntMPA 1977, OxFilm, WorEnF
Boorman, John 1934- *BiDFlm*
Boosey, William d1933 *NotNAT B*
Boot, Gladys 1890-1964 *WhScrn 1, WhScrn 2,*
WhThe, WhoHol B
Boote, Rosie 1878-1958 *OxThe*
Booth, Adrian 1924- *WhoHol A*
Booth, Agnes 1847-1910 *NotNAT B*
Booth, Anthony 1937- *FilmgC*
Booth, Barton 1681-1733 *NotNAT A,*
NotNAT B, OxThe, PIP&P
Booth, Blanche DeBar d1930 *NotNAT B*
Booth, Edwin Thomas 1833-1893 *CnThe,*
FamA&A, NotNAT A, NotNAT B, OxThe,
PIP&P
Booth, Edwina 1909- *Film 2, FilmgC,*
WhoHol A
Booth, Elmer 1882-1915 *Film 1, WhScrn 2*
Booth, Helen d1971 *WhScrn 1, WhScrn 2,*
WhoHol B
Booth, Hope 1872-1933 *NotNAT B,*
WhoStg 1908
Booth, James 1930- *FilmgC*
Booth, James 1931- *IntMPA 1977*
Booth, James 1933- *WhoThe 16*
Booth, John Erlanger 1919- *BiE&WWA,*
NotNAT
Booth, John Wilkes 1838-1865 *FamA&A*
Booth, John Wilkes 1839-1865 *NotNAT A,*
NotNAT B, OxThe, PIP&P
Booth, Junius Brutus 1796-1852 *FamA&A,*
NotNAT A, NotNAT B, OxThe, PIP&P
Booth, Junius Brutus, III d1912 *NotNAT B*
Booth, Junius Brutus, Jr. 1821-1883 *NotNAT B,*
OxThe, PIP&P
Booth, Karen *MotPP*
Booth, Karin 1923- *FilmgC*
Booth, Margaret *WomWMM*
Booth, Marie *Film 1*
Booth, Nesdon d1964 *NotNAT B, WhoHol B*
Booth, Nesdon 1918-1964 *WhScrn 2*
Booth, Nesdon 1919-1964 *WhScrn 1*
Booth, Richard *PIP&P*
Booth, Sallie d1902 *NotNAT B*
Booth, Sarah 1794-1867 *NotNAT B*
Booth, Sheila *WomWMM A, WomWMM B*
Booth, Shirley 1907- *BiE&WWA, CelR 3,*
EncMT, FilmgC, IntMPA 1977, MotPP,
MovMk, NotNAT, PIP&P, WhoHol A,
WhoThe 16, WorEnF
Booth, Sydney Barton 1873-1937 *NotNAT B,*
OxThe
Booth, Walter *Film 2*
Booth, Webster 1902- *WhThe*
Booth Family *NotNAT A*
Boothe, Clare 1903- *BiE&WWA, McGWD,*
ModWD, WhThe
Boothe, James R 1917- *AmSCAP 1966*
Borberg, Svend 1888-1947 *CnMD*
Borchers, Cornell 1925- *FilmgC, IntMPA 1977,*
WhoHol A
Borchers, Gladys 1891- *BiE&WWA, NotNAT*
Borchert, Brigette *Film 2*
Borchert, Wolfgang 1921-1947 *CnMD, CnThe,*
CroCD, McGWD, ModWD, REnWD

Bordas, Emilia F 1874-1958 *WhScrn 1, WhScrn 2*
Bordeaux, Joe 1894-1950 *Film 1, WhScrn 2*
Borden, Eddie 1888-1955 *Film 2, WhScrn 1,*
WhScrn 2, WhoHol B
Borden, Eugene 1897-1972 *Film 2, WhScrn 2*
Borden, Martin *Film 2*
Borden, Olive d1947 *MotPP, WhoHol B*
Borden, Olive 1906-1947 *Film 2, ThFT, TwYS*
Borden, Olive 1907-1947 *NotNAT B, WhScrn 1,*
WhScrn 2
Borden, Olive 1908?-1947 *MovMk*
Bordon, Eugene 1897-1972 *WhoHol B*
Bordoni, Irene 1894-1953 *Film 2*
Bordoni, Irene 1895-1953 *EncMT, NotNAT B,*
WhScrn 1, WhScrn 2, WhThe, WhoHol B
Borell, Louis 1906-1973 *WhScrn 2, WhThe,*
WhoHol B
Borelli, Lyda 1888-1958 *WhScrn 1, WhScrn 2*
Borello, Marco 1899-1966 *WhScrn 2*
Boren, Charles 1907- *IntMPA 1977*
Boreo, Emil 1885-1951 *WhScrn 1, WhScrn 2,*
WhoHol B
Boreo, Emile 1885-1951 *NotNAT B*
Boretz, Allen 1900- *AmSCAP 1966, BiE&WWA,*
NatPD, NotNAT
Boretz, Alvin 1919- *AmSCAP 1966*
Borg, Sven Hugo *Film 2, WhoHol A*
Borg, Veda Ann 1915-1973 *FilmgC, MotPP,*
MovMk, ThFT, Vers A, WhScrn 2,
WhoHol B
Borgato, Agostino 1871-1939 *Film 2, WhScrn 1,*
WhScrn 2, WhoHol B
Borgato, Augustino *Film 2*
Borgato, Emilo *Film 2*
Borge, Victor *IntMPA 1977, WhoHol A*
Borge, Victor 1908- *CelR 3*
Borge, Victor 1909- *AmSCAP 1966, BiE&WWA,*
NotNAT
Borgen, Johan 1902- *CnMD*
Borges, Jorge Luis 1899- *CelR 3*
Borgia, Cesare 1476-1507 *FilmgC*
Borgia, Lucretia 1480-1519 *FilmgC*
Borgnine, Ernest *MotPP, WhoHol A*
Borgnine, Ernest 1915- *CelR 3, FilmgC*
Borgnine, Ernest 1917- *MovMk, OxFilm*
Borgnine, Ernest 1918- *BiDFlm, IntMPA 1977,*
WorEnF
Borgstrom, Hilda 1871-1953 *Film 1, Film 2,*
WhScrn 1, WhScrn 2
Boring, Edwin *Film 1*
Borio, Josephine *Film 2*
Borisoff, S *Film 2*
Borisova, Yulia Konstantinovna 1925- *OxThe*
Borjessen, Johan 1790-1866 *OxThe*
Borland, Barlowe *Film 2*
Borlaug, Norman 1914- *CelR 3*
Borlin, Jean *Film 2, WhThe*
Borne, Hal 1911- *AmSCAP 1966*
Bornet, Francois 1915- *AmSCAP 1966*
Bornschein, Franz 1879-1948 *AmSCAP 1966*
Bornstein, Allen *IntMPA 1977*
Boro, Susan *WomWMM B*
Borodin, Aleksandr 1833-1887 *NotNAT B*
Borodin, Elfriede *Film 2*
Borodkin, Abram E 1906- *AmSCAP 1966*
Boros, Ferike 1880-1951 *WhScrn 1, WhScrn 2,*
WhoHol B
Borowczyk, Walerian 1923- *BiDFlm, DcFM,*
FilmgC, OxFilm, WorEnF
Borowski, Felix 1872-1956 *AmSCAP 1966*
Borowsky, Marvin S 1907-1969 *BiE&WWA,*
NotNAT B
Borradaile, Osmond 1892?- *FilmgC*
Borrodaile, Osmond 1892- *CmMov*

Borst, Stephen 1944- NotNAT
Borstwick, Edith Film 2
Borthwick, A T d1943 NotNAT B
Boruff, John 1910- BiE&WWA, NotNAT
Borzage, Dan d1975 WhoHol C
Borzage, Daniel d1975 WhScrn 2
Borzage, Frank 1893-1961 DcFM, OxFilm
Borzage, Frank 1893-1962 BiDFlm, CmMov,
   Film 1, FilmgC, MovMk, TwYS A,
   WhScrn 1, WhScrn 2, WhoHol B, WorEnF
Borzage, Rena d1966 WhoHol B
Bos, Annie 1887-1975 WhScrn 2
Bosakowski, Philip A 1946- NatPD
Bosc, Henri Film 2
Bosco, Philip 1930- BiE&WWA, NotNAT,
   WhoThe 16
Bosco, Wallace Film 2
Bose, Debaki Kumar 1898- DcFM
Bose, Lucia 1931- FilmgC, WorEnF
Bose, Nitin 1901- DcFM
Bosillo, Nick d1964 NotNAT B
Bosky, Marquisette Film 2
Bosley, Tom 1927- BiE&WWA, FilmgC,
   NotNAT, WhoHol A, WhoThe 16
Bosocki, Madam Film 2
Bosper, Albert 1913- CnMD
Boss, Yale Film 1
Bossak, Jerzy 1910- DcFM, OxFilm
Bosse-Vingard, Harriet Sofie 1878- WhThe
Bossick, Bernard B 1918-1975 WhScrn 2
Bossone, Frank 1924- AmSCAP 1966
Bossu D'Arras, Le OxThe
Bost, Pierre 1901- DcFM, FilmgC, WorEnF
Bostan, Elizabeth WomWMM
Bostick, Calvin T 1928- AmSCAP 1966
Bostick, Robert L 1909- IntMPA 1977
Bostock, Claude W 1891- IntMPA 1977
Bostock, Edward H 1858-1940 NotNAT A
Bostock, Thomas H 1899- WhThe
Boston, Nelroy Buck 1911-1962 NotNAT B,
   WhScrn 1, WhScrn 2
Bostwick, E F Film 2
Bostwick, Edith Film 2
Bosustow, Nick 1940- IntMPA 1977
Bosustow, Stephen 1911- DcFM, FilmgC,
   IntMPA 1977, NewYTET, OxFilm
Bosustow, Stephen 1912- WorEnF
Bosustow, Tee 1938- IntMPA 1977
Boswell, Connee AmSCAP 1966, WhoHol A
Boswell, Martha 1905-1958 WhScrn 1, WhScrn 2,
   WhoHol B
Boswell, Vet WhoHol A
Boswell Sisters, The ThFT
Bosworth, Hobart 1867-1943 Film 1, Film 2,
   FilmgC, MotPP, MovMk, NotNAT B,
   TwYS, WhScrn 1, WhoHol B
Bosworth, Hobart 1876-1943 WhScrn 2
Boteler, Wade d1945 Film 2, TwYS
Boteler, Wade 1891-1943 Film 1, Vers B,
   WhScrn 1, WhScrn 2, WhoHol B
Bothwell, John F 1921-1967 WhScrn 1, WhScrn 2,
   WhoHol B
Botkin, Perry 1907-1973 AmSCAP 1966,
   WhScrn 2, WhoHol B
Botley, Betty WomWMM
Botsford, George 1874-1949 AmSCAP 1966
Botsford, Richard Film 2
Botsford, Talitha 1901- AmSCAP 1966
Bott, Alan 1894- WhThe
Bottcher, Herman Film 2
Bottner, Barbara WomWMM B
Bottomley, Gordon 1874-1948 OxThe, PIP&P,
   WhThe
Bottomley, Roland 1880-1947 Film 1, Film 2,

WhScrn 2, WhoHol B
Bottomly, Gordon 1874-1948 NotNAT B
Bottomly, Roland d1947 NotNAT B
Bottoms, Joseph 1954- IntMPA 1977, WhoHol A
Bottoms, Sam WhoHol A
Bottoms, Timothy WhoHol A
Bottoms, Timothy 1949- FilmgC
Bottoms, Timothy 1950- MovMk
Bottoms, Timothy 1951- IntMPA 1977
Bouber, Herman 1880- CnMD
Boucher, Francois 1703-1770 NotNAT B, OxThe
Boucher, Robert 1919- AmSCAP 1966
Boucher, Victor 1879-1942 NotNAT B,
   WhScrn 1, WhScrn 2, WhThe
Boucher, Vivian E 1915- AmSCAP 1966
Bouchet, Barbara 1943- FilmgC
Bouchey, Willis 1900- FilmgC, WhoHol A
Bouchier, Chili 1909- FilmgC, WhoHol A,
   WhoThe 16
Bouchier, Chili 1910- Film 2
Boucicault, Agnes Kelly Robertson 1833-1916
   OxThe
Boucicault, Aubrey 1868- WhoStg 1906,
   WhoStg 1908
Boucicault, Aubrey 1869-1913 NotNAT B,
   WhThe
Boucicault, Dion 1820?-1890 McGWD, REnWD
Boucicault, Dion 1822-1890 CnThe, NotNAT A,
   NotNAT B, PIP&P
Boucicault, Mrs. Dion 1833-1916 NotNAT B,
   WhThe
Boucicault, Dion G 1859-1929 NotNAT B,
   WhScrn 2, WhThe
Boucicault, Dionysius George 1859-1929 OxThe
Boucicault, Dionysius Lardner 1822-1890 OxThe
Boucicault, Nina 1867-1950 Film 2, NotNAT B,
   OxThe, WhScrn 2, WhThe, WhoHol B
Boucot d1949 WhoHol B
Boucot, Louis 1889-1949 WhScrn 1, WhScrn 2
Boudouris, A 1918- IntMPA 1977
Boudreau, John T 1901- AmSCAP 1966
Boudreaux, Joseph WhoHol A
Boudwin, Jimmy Film 2
Boughner, Ruth WomWMM
Boughton, Rutland 1878-1960 NotNAT B,
   WhThe
Boughton, Walter 1918- BiE&WWA, NotNAT
Boulanger, Robert F 1940- AmSCAP 1966
Boularan, Jacques 1894?-1972 McGWD
Bould, Beckett 1880- WhThe
Boulden, Edward Film 1
Boulder, Robert Film 2
Bouley, Frank WhoHol A
Boulez, Pierre 1925- CelR 3
Boulos, Joseph T 1935- AmSCAP 1966
Boulter, Rosalyn 1916- WhThe
Boulting, Ingrid WhoHol A
Boulting, John 1913- BiDFlm, CmMov, DcFM,
   FilmgC, IntMPA 1977, OxFilm, WorEnF
Boulting, John 1914- MovMk
Boulting, Roy 1913- BiDFlm, CmMov, DcFM,
   FilmgC, IntMPA 1977, OxFilm, WorEnF
Boulting, Roy 1914- MovMk
Boulton, David FilmgC
Boulton, Guy Pelham 1890- WhThe
Boulton, Matthew 1893-1962 WhScrn 2,
   WhoHol B
Bouquet, Michel OxFilm
Bourchier, Arthur 1863-1927 Film 1, NotNAT B,
   OxThe, WhThe, WhoHol B
Bourdelle, Thomy Film 2
Bourdet, Edouard 1877-1945 OxThe
Bourdet, Edouard 1887-1945 CnMD, McGWD,
   ModWD, NotNAT B

Bourdon, Rosario 1889-1961 *AmSCAP 1966*
Bourgeois, Gerard 1874-1944 *DcFM*
Bourget, Paul 1852-1935 *NotNAT B, WhThe*
Bourgholtzer, Frank *NewYTET*
Bourgignon, Serge 1928- *FilmgC*
Bourgoin, Jean 1913- *DcFM, WorEnF*
Bourgoin, Yves 1913- *WorEnF*
Bourguignon, Serge 1928- *DcFM*
Bourguignon, Serge 1929- *WorEnF*
Bourke, Fan 1886-1959 *WhScrn 1, WhScrn 2, WhoHol B*
Bourne, Adeline *Film 1, WhThe*
Bourne, William Payne 1936-1972 *WhScrn 2*
Bourneuf, Philip 1912- *BiE&WWA, NotNAT, WhoHol A, WhoThe 16*
Boursault, Edme 1638-1701 *McGWD, OxThe*
Bourvil d1976 *NotNAT B*
Bourvil 1913-1970 *WhScrn 1, WhScrn 2, WhoHol B*
Bourvil 1917-1970 *FilmgC, OxFilm, WorEnF*
Bouschet, Jan *OxThe*
Boutelje, Phil 1895- *AmSCAP 1966*
Boutnikoff, Ivan 1893- *AmSCAP 1966*
Bouton, Betty *Film 2*
Bouton, Jim *WhoHol A*
Bouton, Jim 1939- *CelR 3*
Bouwmeester, Louis 1842- *WhThe*
Bova, Basil 1919- *AmSCAP 1966*
Bova, Joseph 1924- *BiE&WWA, NotNAT, WhoHol A, WhoThe 16*
Bovasso, Julie 1930- *BiE&WWA, ConDr 1977, NotNAT, WhoHol A, WhoThe 16*
Bovill, C H 1878-1918 *WhThe*
Bovy, Berthe 1887- *WhThe*
Bow, Clara d1965 *MotPP, WhoHol B, WomWMM*
Bow, Clara 1904-1965 *Film 2, ThFT, TwYS*
Bow, Clara 1905-1965 *BiDFlm, FilmgC, MovMk, OxFilm, WhScrn 1, WhScrn 2, WorEnF*
Bowden, Charles 1913- *BiE&WWA, NotNAT, WhoThe 16*
Bowden, Christine M 1908- *AmSCAP 1966*
Bowden, Dorris 1915- *ThFT*
Bowdler, Thomas 1754-1825 *NotNAT B*
Bowdon, Dorris *WhoHol A*
Bowe, Rosemarie *WhoHol A*
Bowen, Frances C 1905- *BiE&WWA*
Bowen, John 1924- *CnThe, ConDr 1977, CroCD, WhoThe 16*
Bowen, John G 1896- *AmSCAP 1966*
Bowen, Roger *WhoHol A*
Bower, Dallas 1907- *FilmgC, IntMPA 1977*
Bower, Marian d1945 *NotNAT B, WhThe*
Bower, Maurice L 1922- *AmSCAP 1966*
Bower, Robert *Film 1*
Bower, Roger 1908- *IntMPA 1977*
Bowers, D P d1857 *NotNAT B*
Bowers, Mrs. D P d1895 *NotNAT B*
Bowers, Faubion 1917- *BiE&WWA, NotNAT*
Bowers, Frederick V 1874-1961 *AmSCAP 1966*
Bowers, John 1891-1936 *Film 1, Film 2, TwYS*
Bowers, John 1899-1936 *WhScrn 1, WhScrn 2, WhoHol B*
Bowers, Lally 1917- *WhoThe 16*
Bowers, Lyle 1896-1943 *WhScrn 1, WhScrn 2*
Bowers, Robert Hood 1877-1941 *AmSCAP 1966, NotNAT B, WhThe*
Bowers, Viola d1962 *NotNAT B*
Bowers, William 1916- *FilmgC, IntMPA 1977*
Bowery Boys, The *FilmgC*
Bowes, Alice d1969 *WhThe*
Bowes, Cliff *Film 1*
Bowes, Lawrence A *Film 1*
Bowes, Major Edward 1874-1946 *NotNAT B,*

WhScrn 1, WhScrn 2, WhoHol B
Bowie, David *WhoHol A*
Bowie, Jim 1796-1836 *FilmgC*
Bowkett, Sidney d1937 *NotNAT B*
Bowles, Chester 1901- *CelR 3*
Bowles, Frank *Film 2*
Bowles, Jane 1917- *BiE&WWA*
Bowles, Paul 1910- *AmSCAP 1966, BiE&WWA, NotNAT*
Bowles, Richard W 1918- *AmSCAP 1966*
Bowley, Flora Juliet *WhoStg 1906, WhoStg 1908*
Bowman, Brooks 1913-1937 *AmSCAP 1966*
Bowman, Euday L 1887-1949 *AmSCAP 1966*
Bowman, Laura 1881-1957 *NotNAT A, NotNAT B, WhScrn 2*
Bowman, Lee *MotPP*
Bowman, Lee 1910- *FilmgC*
Bowman, Lee 1914- *BiE&WWA, IntMPA 1977, MovMk, WhoHol A*
Bowman, Lewis Edward 1886-1961 *WhScrn 2*
Bowman, Nellie 1878- *WhThe*
Bowman, Palmer 1883-1933 *WhScrn 1, WhScrn 2, WhoHol B*
Bowman, Patricia *Film 2*
Bowman, Ross 1926- *BiE&WWA*
Bowman, Walter P 1910- *BiE&WWA, NotNAT*
Bowman, Wayne 1914- *BiE&WWA, NotNAT*
Bowman, William J *Film 1*
Bowmer, Angus L 1904- *BiE&WWA, NotNAT*
Bowne, Owen O d1963 *NotNAT B*
Bowyer, Frederick d1936 *NotNAT B*
Bowyer, Michael d1645 *OxThe*
Box, Betty 1920- *FilmgC, IntMPA 1977, WomWMM*
Box, John 1920- *FilmgC*
Box, Joy *WomWMM*
Box, Muriel 1905- *FilmgC, WomWMM*
Box, Sydney 1907- *FilmgC*
Boxer, John *WhoHol A*
Boxer, John 1909- *WhoThe 16*
Boyadgieva, Lada *WomWMM*
Boyajian, Aram *NewYTET*
Boyar, Ben A 1895-1964 *BiE&WWA*
Boyar, Benjamin A 1895-1964 *NotNAT B*
Boyar, Monica *BiE&WWA*
Boyar, Sully *WhoHol A*
Boyars, Albert 1924- *IntMPA 1977*
Boyce, Jack 1885-1923 *WhScrn 1, WhScrn 2*
Boyd, Betty *Film 2, WhoHol A*
Boyd, Blanche Deedee 1889-1959 *WhScrn 1, WhScrn 2*
Boyd, Dorothy 1907- *Film 2*
Boyd, Elisse *AmSCAP 1966, BiE&WWA*
Boyd, Elsie Thompson 1904- *AmSCAP 1966*
Boyd, Frank M 1863- *WhThe*
Boyd, Jimmy *WhoHol A*
Boyd, Malcolm 1923- *CelR 3*
Boyd, Marilynn *Film 2*
Boyd, Mildred *Film 2*
Boyd, Richard 1937- *BiE&WWA*
Boyd, Sam, Jr. 1915- *BiE&WWA, NotNAT*
Boyd, Stephen 1928- *CmMov, FilmgC, IntMPA 1977, MotPP, MovMk, WhoHol A, WorEnF*
Boyd, William d1972 *MotPP, NewYTET, WhoHol B*
Boyd, William 1895-1972 *FilmgC, WhScrn 2*
Boyd, William 1898-1972 *CmMov, Film 1, Film 2, MovMk, OxFilm*
Boyd, William Bill 1898-1972 *TwYS*
Boyd, William Henry 1890-1935 *NotNAT B*
Boyd, William Stage 1890-1935 *FilmgC, WhScrn 1, WhScrn 2, WhoHol B*
Boyd, Wynn Leo 1902- *AmSCAP 1966*

Boyer, Charles 1897- *MovMk, OxFilm, WorEnF*
Boyer, Charles 1899- *BiDFlm, BiE&WWA,*
CelR 3, CmMov, Film 2, FilmgC,
IntMPA 1977, MotPP, WhThe, WhoHol A
Boyer, Eleanor Anderson *WomWMM B*
Boyer, Francois 1920- *DcFM*
Boyer, Phil *IntMPA 1977*
Boyer, Rachel d1935 *NotNAT B*
Boylan, Mary *WhoHol A*
Boyle, Billy 1945- *WhoThe 16*
Boyle, Catherine 1929- *FilmgC*
Boyle, Charles P *CmMov*
Boyle, E Roger 1907- *BiE&WWA, NotNAT*
Boyle, George F 1886-1948 *AmSCAP 1966*
Boyle, Harry J *NewYTET*
Boyle, John *Film 1*
Boyle, Joseph C 1890- *TwYS A*
Boyle, Peter *IntMPA 1977, WhoHol A*
Boyle, Peter 1933- *FilmgC*
Boyle, Peter 1936- *MovMk*
Boyle, Ray 1925- *BiE&WWA*
Boyle, Robert *FilmgC, WorEnF*
Boyle, Roger 1621-1679 *NotNAT B, OxThe*
Boyle, William 1853-1923 *McGWD, NotNAT B,*
OxThe, WhThe
Boyle, William Neal *IntMPA 1977*
Boyne, Clifton 1874-1945 *WhThe*
Boyne, Leonard 1853-1920 *NotNAT B, WhThe*
Boyne, Sunny 1883-1966 *WhScrn 1, WhScrn 2,*
WhoHol B
Boynton, Charles Ted 1921-1968 *WhScrn 2*
Boyt, John 1921- *BiE&WWA, NotNAT*
Boytler, Arcady 1895- *DcFM*
Boyton, Betty *Film 2*
Bozo, Little *WhScrn 1, WhScrn 2*
Bozyk, Max 1899-1970 *WhScrn 2, WhoHol B*
Braban, Harvey 1883- *Film 2, WhThe*
Brabin, Charles 1883-1957 *FilmgC*
Brabin, Charles J 1882-1957 *WhScrn 2*
Brabin, Charles J 1883-1959 *TwYS A*
Brabourne, Lord 1924- *IntMPA 1977*
Brabourne, John 1924- *FilmgC*
Bracco, Roberto d1943 *NotNAT B*
Bracco, Roberto 1861-1943 *CnThe, McGWD,*
ModWD, REnWD
Bracco, Roberto 1862-1943 *OxThe*
Bracco, Roberto 1863-1943 *WhThe*
Brace, Norman C 1892-1954 *WhScrn 1,*
WhoHol B
Bracegirdle, Anne 1663?-1748 *CnThe, NotNAT B,*
PIP&P
Bracegirdle, Anne 1673?-1748 *OxThe*
Bracey, Clara T 1847-1941 *WhScrn 2, WhoHol B*
Bracey, Sidney 1877-1942 *WhScrn 1, WhScrn 2,*
WhoHol B
Bracho, Julio 190-?- *DcFM*
Bracken, Bertram *TwYS A*
Bracken, Eddie 1920- *BiE&WWA, FilmgC,*
HolP 40, IntMPA 1977, MotPP, MovMk,
NotNAT, WhoHol A, WhoThe 16
Brackenridge, Hugh Henry 1748-1816 *NotNAT B,*
OxThe
Brackett, Charles 1892-1969 *CmMov, FilmgC,*
NotNAT B, WorEnF
Brackett, Leigh *CmMov, FilmgC, WomWMM*
Brackman, Marie L d1963 *NotNAT B*
Bracy, Clara T 1847-1941 *Film 1, WhScrn 1*
Bracy, Sidney 1882-1941 *Film 1, Film 2, TwYS*
Bradbury, Allan *WhoHol A*
Bradbury, James, Jr. 1894- *Film 2, TwYS*
Bradbury, James, Sr. 1857-1940 *Film 2,*
NotNAT B, TwYS, WhScrn 1, WhScrn 2,
WhThe, WhoHol B
Bradbury, Kitty *Film 2*

Bradbury, Ray 1920- *CelR 3, CmMov, FilmgC*
Bradbury, Ray 1922- *WorEnF*
Bradbury, Robert North *TwYS A*
Braddell, Maurice *Film 2*
Bradel, John F d1962 *NotNAT B*
Braden, Bernard 1916- *FilmgC, WhThe*
Braden, Edward Allen 1863- *WhoStg 1906*
Braden, Frank d1962 *NotNAT B*
Braden, Waldo W 1911- *BiE&WWA, NotNAT*
Bradfield, W Louis 1866-1919 *WhThe*
Bradford, Benjamin 1925- *NatPD*
Bradford, Charles Avery 1873-1926 *WhScrn 1,*
WhScrn 2
Bradford, James C 1885-1941 *AmSCAP 1966*
Bradford, James M d1933 *NotNAT B*
Bradford, Lane 1923-1973 *WhScrn 2, WhoHol B*
Bradford, Marshall 1896-1971 *WhScrn 1,*
WhScrn 2, WhoHol B
Bradford, Perry 1893- *AmSCAP 1966*
Bradford, Peter 1919- *IntMPA 1977*
Bradford, Richard *WhoHol A*
Bradford, Roark 1896-1948 *AmSCAP 1966,*
PIP&P
Bradford, Sylvester 1937- *AmSCAP 1966*
Bradford, Virginia *Film 2*
Bradin, Jean *Film 2*
Bradley, Amanda d1916 *WhScrn 2*
Bradley, Benjamin R 1898-1950 *WhScrn 1,*
WhScrn 2
Bradley, Betty d1973 *WhoHol B*
Bradley, Bill 1921- *IntMPA 1977*
Bradley, Bill 1943- *CelR 3*
Bradley, Buddy 1908- *WhThe*
Bradley, Buddy 1913- *BiE&WWA*
Bradley, Claire *WomWMM B*
Bradley, David 1920?- *OxFilm, WorEnF*
Bradley, Edson P 1907- *AmSCAP 1966*
Bradley, Estelle *Film 2*
Bradley, Grace 1913- *ThFT, WhoHol A*
Bradley, H Dennis d1934 *NotNAT B*
Bradley, Harry C 1869-1947 *WhScrn 1,*
WhScrn 2, WhoHol B
Bradley, Leonora d1935 *NotNAT B*
Bradley, Leslie *WhoHol A*
Bradley, Lilian Trimble 1875- *WhThe*
Bradley, Lovyss 1906-1969 *WhScrn 1, WhScrn 2,*
WhoHol B
Bradley, Malcolm *Film 2*
Bradley, Omar 1893- *CelR 3*
Bradley, Oscar d1948 *NotNAT B*
Bradley, Sandra Wentworth *WomWMM B*
Bradley, Truman 1905-1974 *NewYTET,*
WhScrn 2, WhoHol B
Bradna, Olympe 1920- *FilmgC, MotPP, ThFT,*
WhoHol A
Bradnum, Frederick *ConDr 1977B*
Bradshaw, Eunice 1893-1973 *WhScrn 2,*
WhoHol B
Bradshaw, Fanny 1897-1973 *NotNAT B*
Bradshaw, Fanny 1900- *BiE&WWA*
Bradshaw, Lionel M 1892-1918 *WhScrn 2*
Bradshaw, Terry 1948- *CelR 3*
Bradt, Clifton E d1961 *NotNAT B*
Brady, Alice d1939 *MotPP, WhoHol B*
Brady, Alice 1892-1939 *MovMk, NotNAT B,*
OxThe, ThFT, TwYS, Vers A, WhScrn 1,
WhScrn 2, WhThe
Brady, Alice 1893-1939 *Film 1, Film 2, FilmgC*
Brady, Ed 1889-1942 *TwYS*
Brady, Edward 1889-1942 *Film 2, WhoHol B*
Brady, Edward J 1888-1942 *WhScrn 1, WhScrn 2*
Brady, Edwin J 1889-1942 *Film 1, Film 2*
Brady, Frank L 1914- *IntMPA 1977*
Brady, Fred 1912-1961 *WhScrn 2*

Brady, Grace George 1879-1961 *OxThe*
Brady, Hugh d1921 *NotNAT B*
Brady, James 1928- *CelR 3*
Brady, Leo B 1917- *BiE&WWA, NotNAT*
Brady, Pat 1914-1972 *WhScrn 2, WhoHol B*
Brady, Philip *Film 2*
Brady, Scott 1924- *FilmgC, HolP 40,*
   IntMPA 1977, MotPP, WhoHol A
Brady, Terence 1939- *WhoThe 16*
Brady, Veronica 1890-1964 *NotNAT B, WhThe*
Brady, W A 1865-1950 *WhoStg 1906,*
   WhoStg 1908
Brady, William A 1863-1950 *NotNAT A,*
   NotNAT B, OxThe, WhThe
Brady, William A, Jr. 1900-1935 *NotNAT B,*
   WhThe
Brae, June 1918- *WhThe*
Braeden, Eric *WhoHol A*
Braga, Eurico 1894-1962 *NotNAT B, WhScrn 1,*
   WhScrn 2
Bragaglia, Carlo Ludovico 1894- *WorEnF*
Bragaglia, Marinella *WhThe*
Bragdon, Claude Fayette 1866-1946 *NotNAT A,*
   NotNAT B
Bragg, Bernard 1928- *NotNAT A*
Braggiotti, Francesca *WhoHol A*
Braggiotti, Mario 1909- *AmSCAP 1966*
Braham, David 1838-1905 *NewMT, NotNAT B*
Braham, Harry 1874-1923 *NotNAT B, WhScrn 1,*
   WhScrn 2, WhoHol B
Braham, Horace 1893-1955 *NotNAT B,*
   WhScrn 1, WhScrn 2, WhThe, WhoHol B
Braham, Leonora 1853-1931 *WhThe*
Braham, Lionel 1879-1947 *Film 1, Film 2,*
   NotNAT B, WhScrn 1, WhScrn 2, WhThe,
   WhoHol B
Braham, Philip 1881-1934 *NotNAT B, WhThe*
Brahm, John 1893- *FilmgC, IntMPA 1977,*
   WorEnF
Brahm, John 1898- *BiDFlm*
Brahm, Otto 1856-1912 *NotNAT A, NotNAT B,*
   OxThe
Brahms, Caryl *ConDr 1977D, WhoThe 16*
Braidon, Thomas *Film 2*
Braidwood, Frank *Film 2*
Brainin, Jerome 1916- *AmSCAP 1966*
Braithwaite, Lilian 1871-1948 *WhScrn 1,*
   WhoHol B
Braithwaite, Lilian 1873-1948 *CnThe, OxThe,*
   WhScrn 2, WhThe
Braithwaite, Lillian 1873-1948 *Film 2,*
   NotNAT B, PIP&P
Brakhage, Stan 1933- *DcFM, OxFilm, WorEnF*
Brambell, Wilfrid 1912- *FilmgC, IntMPA 1977,*
   WhoThe 16
Bramble, A V 1880?-1963 *FilmgC*
Brambrick, Gertrude *Film 1*
Bramley, Flora *Film 2, WhoHol A*
Bramley, Raymond 1891- *BiE&WWA, NotNAT,*
   WhoHol A
Bramley, William *WhoHol A*
Bramson, Karen d1936 *NotNAT B*
Bramson, Sam d1962 *NotNAT B*
Brancati, Vitaliano 1907-1954 *McGWD*
Branch, Eileen 1911- *WhThe*
Branch, Sarah 1938- *FilmgC*
Brand, Barbarina d1854 *NotNAT B*
Brand, Hannah d1821 *NotNAT B*
Brand, Max 1892-1944 *FilmgC*
Brand, Neville *MotPP, WhoHol A*
Brand, Neville 1920- *FilmgC*
Brand, Neville 1921- *IntMPA 1977*
Brand, Oscar 1920- *NatPD, NotNAT*
Brand, Oswald d1909 *NotNAT B*

Brand, Phoebe 1907- *BiE&WWA, NotNAT,*
   PIP&P
Brandane, John 1869-1947 *OxThe*
Brandeis, Ruth *WhoHol A*
Brander, Allen *Film 2*
Brandes, Edvard 1847-1931 *OxThe*
Brandes, Esther Charlotte Henrietta 1746-1784
   OxThe
Brandes, Georg Morris Cohen 1842-1927
   NotNAT B, OxThe
Brandes, Johann Christian 1735-1799 *OxThe*
Brandes, Marthe 1862-1930 *NotNAT B, WhThe*
Brandes, Minna 1765-1788 *OxThe*
Brando, Jocelyn 1919- *FilmgC, IntMPA 1977,*
   MotPP, WhoHol A
Brando, Marlon 1924- *BiDFlm, BiE&WWA,*
   CelR 3, FilmgC, IntMPA 1977, MotPP,
   MovMk, NotNAT A, OxFilm, PIP&P,
   WhoHol A, WorEnF
Brandon, Arthur F 1925-1975 *WhScrn 2*
Brandon, Dickie *Film 2*
Brandon, Dolores 1917-1959 *WhScrn 1,*
   WhScrn 2
Brandon, Dorothy *WhThe*
Brandon, Florence 1879-1961 *WhScrn 1,*
   WhScrn 2
Brandon, Francis 1886-1924 *WhScrn 2*
Brandon, Henry 1910- *FilmgC, WhoHol A*
Brandon, Jocelyn d1948 *NotNAT B*
Brandon, Johnny *NatPD*
Brandon, Liane 1939- *WomWMM A,*
   WomWMM B
Brandon, Mary *Film 2*
Brandon, Michael *WhoHol A*
Brandon, Peter 1926- *BiE&WWA, NotNAT*
Brandon-Thomas, Amy d1974 *WhoHol B*
Brandon-Thomas, Amy Marguerite 1890- *WhThe*
Brandon-Thomas, Jevan 1898- *WhThe*
Brands, X *WhoHol A*
Brandstaetter, Roman 1906- *ModWD*
Brandstatter, Roman 1906- *CnMD*
Brandt, Alvin 1922- *BiE&WWA, NotNAT*
Brandt, Charles 1864-1924 *Film 1, WhScrn 2*
Brandt, Eddie 1924- *AmSCAP 1966*
Brandt, George 1916-1963 *NotNAT B*
Brandt, Ivan 1903- *WhThe*
Brandt, Louise 1877-1959 *WhScrn 1, WhScrn 2,*
   WhoHol B
Brandt, Mathile *Film 2*
Brandt, Richard Paul 1927- *IntMPA 1977*
Brandt, Walter *Film 2*
Brandt, Willy 1913- *CelR 3*
Brandwynne, Nat 1910- *AmSCAP 1966*
Brandy, Howard 1929- *IntMPA 1977*
Branen, Jeff T 1872-1927 *AmSCAP 1966*
Branion, Antonio *Film 2*
Branner, Hans Christian 1903-1966 *CnMD*
Brannigan, Owen 1909-1973 *WhScrn 2*
Brannum, Hugh 1910- *IntMPA 1977*
Bransby Williams *OxThe*
Branscombe, Arthur d1924 *NotNAT B*
Branscombe, Gina 1881- *AmSCAP 1966*
Branscome, Lilly *Film 1*
Branson, Walter E *IntMPA 1977*
Brant, Ira 1921- *AmSCAP 1966*
Brantford, Albert *Film 2*
Brantford, Mickey 1912- *Film 2*
Brascia, John *WhoHol A*
Brasfield, Rod d1958 *WhScrn 2*
Brasloff, Stanley H 1930- *IntMPA 1977*
Brasmer, William 1921- *BiE&WWA, NotNAT*
Brass, Tinto 1933- *WorEnF*
Brasselle, Keefe 1923- *AmSCAP 1966, FilmgC,*
   IntMPA 1977, MotPP, NewYTET,

WhoHol A

Brasseur, Albert Jules 1862-1932 *NotNAT B,
WhThe*

Brasseur, Jules d1890 *NotNAT B*

Brasseur, Pierre 1903-1972 *Film 2, FilmgC,
MovMk, WhScrn 2, WorEnF*

Brasseur, Pierre 1905-1972 *BiDFlm, CnThe,
OxFilm, WhoHol B*

Braswell, Charles 1925-1974 *WhScrn 2,
WhoHol B*

Bratanov, Ivan 1920-1968 *WhScrn 2*

Brathwayt, Raymond *Film 2*

Bratton, John Walter 1867-1947 *AmSCAP 1966,
NotNAT B, WhoStg 1906, WhoStg 1908*

Brau, Alexis 1921- *AmSCAP 1966*

Brauer, LeRoy 1902- *IntMPA 1977*

Brault, Michel 1928- *OxFilm, WorEnF*

Braun, Felix 1885-1973 *CnMD, CroCD*

Braun, Mattias 1933- *CnMD*

Braun, Volker 1939- *CroCD*

Braunagel, Jack D 1912- *IntMPA 1977*

Braunberger, Pierre 1905- *DcFM, OxFilm*

Brausewetter, Hans *Film 2*

Brautigan, Richard 1935- *CelR 3*

Braverman, Charles 1944- *IntMPA 1977*

Braverman, Chuck *NewYTET*

Braverman, Millicent *IntMPA 1977*

Bravo, Jaime 1932-1970 *WhoHol B*

Bravo, Jamie 1932-1970 *WhScrn 1, WhScrn 2*

Brawn, John P *Film 1*

Brawn, John P 1869-1943 *WhScrn 1, WhScrn 2*

Bray, Helen *Film 1*

Bray, John F 1906-1955 *WhScrn 1, WhScrn 2,
WhoHol B*

Bray, John Randolph 1879- *IntMPA 1977,
WorEnF*

Bray, Lew 1907- *IntMPA 1977*

Bray, Paul, Jr. *IntMPA 1977*

Bray, Robert 1917- *FilmgC, WhoHol A*

Bray, Yvonne De 1889- *WhThe*

Brayfield, George d1968 *WhScrn 2, WhoHol B*

Brayton, Lily 1876-1953 *NotNAT B, OxThe,
WhScrn 2, WhThe*

Brazzi, Lidia *WhoHol A*

Brazzi, Rossano 1916- *CmMov, FilmgC,
IntMPA 1977, MotPP, MovMk, WhoHol A*

Brdecka, Jiri 1917- *DcFM, WorEnF*

Breacher, Harold 1910- *IntMPA 1977*

Breakston, George 1920-1973 *WhScrn 2,
WhoHol B*

Breakston, George 1922-1973 *FilmgC*

Breamer, Sylvia 1896-1943 *Film 1, Film 2,
TwYS*

Breamer, Sylvia 1903-1943 *MotPP, WhScrn 1,
WhScrn 2, WhoHol B*

Breau, Louis 1893-1928 *AmSCAP 1966*

Breaux, Marc *BiE&WWA, NotNAT*

Brecher, Egon 1885-1946 *Film 2, NotNAT B,
WhScrn 1, WhScrn 2, WhThe, WhoHol B*

Brecher, Irving 1914- *FilmgC, IntMPA 1977*

Brecher, Leo *IntMPA 1977*

Brecht, Bertold 1898-1956 *PIP&P*

Brecht, Bertolt 1898-1956 *CnMD, CnThe,
CroCD, DcFM, FilmgC, McGWD, ModWD,
NotNAT A, NotNAT B, OxFilm, OxThe,
REnWD, WorEnF*

Brecht, George *ConDr 1977E*

Breck, Carrie Ellis 1855-1934 *AmSCAP 1966*

Breck, Peter *WhoHol A*

Brecker, Fred *Film 2*

Breckner, Gary 1896-1945 *WhScrn 2*

Brecourt 1638-1685 *OxThe*

Bredero, Gerbrand A 1585-1618 *CnThe, OxThe,
REnWD*

Breeden, John *Film 2*

Breen, Bobby 1927- *FilmgC, WhoHol A*

Breen, Harry *Film 1*

Breen, Helen 1902- *WhThe*

Breen, Hurley Red 1913-1963 *WhScrn 1,
WhScrn 2*

Breen, Joseph 1890-1965 *FilmgC*

Breen, Margaret d1960 *WhScrn 1, WhScrn 2,
WhoHol B*

Breen, Mary *WhoHol A*

Breen, May Singhi *AmSCAP 1966*

Breen, Richard L 1919-1967 *FilmgC, WorEnF*

Breen, Robert 1914- *BiE&WWA, NotNAT*

Breer, Robert 1926- *WorEnF*

Brees, Bud 1921- *AmSCAP 1966*

Breese, Edmond 1871-1936 *MovMk*

Breese, Edmund 1870-1936 *WhoStg 1908*

Breese, Edmund 1871-1935 *Film 1, Film 2,
TwYS*

Breese, Edmund 1871-1936 *NotNAT B,
WhScrn 1, WhScrn 2, WhThe, WhoHol B,
WhoStg 1906*

Breeskin, Barnee 1910- *AmSCAP 1966*

Breeze, Lou d1969 *WhoHol B*

Bregman, Martin *IntMPA 1977*

Bregmer, Sylvia *Film 2*

Breit, Harvey 1909-1968 *NotNAT B*

Breit, Harvey 1913- *BiE&WWA*

Breitenstrater, Hans *Film 2*

Brel, Jacques 1929- *CelR 3, WhoHol A*

Bremen, Leonard *WhoHol A*

Bremer, Lucille 1922- *FilmgC*

Bremer, Lucille 1923- *MGM, WhoHol A*

Bren, Robert J *IntMPA 1977*

Brendel, El d1964 *NotNAT B*

Brendel, El 1890-1964 *WhScrn 1, WhScrn 2*

Brendel, El 1891-1964 *FilmgC, Vers A,
WhoHol B*

Brendel, El 1896-1964 *MovMk*

Brendel, El 1898-1964 *Film 2, TwYS*

Brendlin, Andre 1911-1934 *WhScrn 1, WhScrn 2*

Breneman, Tom 1902-1948 *WhScrn 1, WhScrn 2,
WhoHol B*

Brennan, Dennis *Film 2*

Brennan, Eileen 1935- *BiE&WWA,
IntMPA 1977, NotNAT, WhoHol A*

Brennan, Frederick Hazlitt d1962 *NotNAT B*

Brennan, J Keirn 1873-1948 *AmSCAP 1966,
NotNAT B*

Brennan, James Alexander 1885-1956
AmSCAP 1966

Brennan, Jay d1961 *NotNAT B*

Brennan, John E 1865-1940 *WhScrn 2*

Brennan, Johnny *Film 1*

Brennan, Joseph *Film 2*

Brennan, Michael 1912- *FilmgC, WhoHol A*

Brennan, Peter J 1918- *CelR 3*

Brennan, Robert 1892-1940 *WhScrn 1, WhScrn 2*

Brennan, Teri *WhoHol A*

Brennan, Walter 1894-1974 *BiDFlm, CelR 3,
CmMov, Film 2, FilmgC, MotPP, MovMk,
OxFilm, TwYS, Vers A, WhScrn 2,
WhoHol B, WorEnF*

Brennan, William J, Jr. 1906- *CelR 3*

Brenner, Joseph 1918- *IntMPA 1977*

Brenner, Raymond 1927- *AmSCAP 1966*

Brenner, Selma Hautzik 1912- *AmSCAP 1966*

Brenner, Walter 1906- *AmSCAP 1966*

Brenon, Herbert 1880-1958 *DcFM, Film 1,
FilmgC, TwYS A, WhScrn 1, WhScrn 2,
WhoHol B, WorEnF*

Brenon, Juliet *Film 2*

Brent, Earl Karl 1914- *AmSCAP 1966*

Brent, Eve 1930- *FilmgC, WhoHol A*

Brent, Evelyn 1899-1975 *Film 1, Film 2, FilmgC, MotPP, MovMk, ThFT, TwYS, WhScrn 2, WhoHol C*
Brent, George 1904- *CmMov, FilmgC, IntMPA 1977, MotPP, MovMk, WhoHol A*
Brent, Harry 1904- *AmSCAP 1966*
Brent, Romney 1902- *BiE&WWA, FilmgC, NotNAT, PIP&P, WhThe, WhoHol A*
Brentano, Felix d1961 *NotNAT B*
Brentano, Lowell d1950 *NotNAT B*
Brenton, Howard 1942- *ConDr 1977, WhoThe 16*
Breon, Edmond 1882-1951 *WhThe*
Breon, Edmund 1882-1951 *FilmgC, WhScrn 1, WhScrn 2, WhoHol B*
Brereton, Austin 1862-1922 *NotNAT B, WhThe*
Brereton, Thomas d1722 *NotNAT B*
Brerton, Tyrone 1894-1939 *WhScrn 1, WhScrn 2, WhoHol B*
Bresil, Marguerite 1880-1923 *WhThe*
Bresler, Jerry 1912- *AmSCAP 1966, FilmgC, IntMPA 1977, WorEnF*
Breslin, Jimmy 1930- *CelR 3*
Bresnan, William J *NewYTET*
Bressart, Felix 1880-1949 *WhScrn 1, WhScrn 2*
Bressart, Felix 1890-1949 *FilmgC*
Bressart, Felix 1892-1949 *Vers A, WhoHol B*
Bresslaw, Bernard 1933- *FilmgC*
Bresson, Robert 1907- *BiDFlm, DcFM, FilmgC, MovMk, OxFilm, WorEnF*
Bretherton, Howard 1896-1969 *FilmgC, TwYS A*
Breton, Andre 1896-1966 *ModWD, REnWD*
Breton DeLosHerreros, Manuel 1796-1873 *McGWD, NotNAT B, OxThe*
Brett, Angela *Film 2*
Brett, Arabella d1803 *NotNAT B*
Brett, Jeremy 1935- *FilmgC, WhoHol A, WhoThe 16*
Brett, Stanley 1879-1923 *NotNAT B, WhThe*
Brettel, Colette *Film 2*
Breuder, W Edward 1911- *AmSCAP 1966*
Breuer, Ernest 1886- *AmSCAP 1966*
Breuer, Marcel 1902- *CelR 3, PIP&P*
Brewer, George E, Jr. 1899-1968 *BiE&WWA, NotNAT B*
Brewer, Monte 1934-1942 *WhScrn 1, WhScrn 2, WhoHol B*
Brewer, Roy M 1909- *IntMPA 1977*
Brewer, Teresa 1931- *AmSCAP 1966, WhoHol A*
Brewster, Kingman 1919- *CelR 3*
Brewster, Margaret *WhoHol A*
Brewster, Townsend 1924- *NatPD*
Brialy, Claude 1933- *WorEnF*
Brialy, Jean-Claude 1933- *FilmgC, MovMk, WhoHol A*
Brian, David 1914- *FilmgC, IntMPA 1977, MotPP, WhoHol A*
Brian, Donald 1871-1948 *WhScrn 1, WhScrn 2*
Brian, Donald 1875-1948 *Film 1*
Brian, Donald 1877-1948 *EncMT, NotNAT B, WhThe, WhoHol B, WhoStg 1908*
Brian, Mary 1908- *Film 2, FilmgC, HolP 30, MovMk, ThFT, TwYS, WhoHol A*
Briant, George Hamilton 1922-1946 *WhScrn 1, WhScrn 2*
Briccetti, Thomas B 1936- *AmSCAP 1966*
Brice, Betty 1892-1935 *WhScrn 2*
Brice, Betty 1896-1935 *Film 2, WhScrn 1, WhoHol B*
Brice, Carol 1918- *NotNAT*
Brice, Carol 1920- *BiE&WWA*
Brice, Fanny 1891-1951 *EncMT, FamA&A, Film 2, FilmgC, MovMk, NotNAT A, NotNAT B, OxFilm, PIP&P, ThFT,*

Brice, Monte d1962 *NotNAT B*
Brice, Monte 1895- *TwYS A*
Brice, Rosetta *Film 1, MotPP*
Brickell, Beth *WhoHol A*
Bricker, Betty 1890-1954 *WhScrn 1, WhScrn 2, WhoHol B*
Bricker, Herschel 1905- *NotNAT*
Bricker, Hershel 1905- *BiE&WWA*
Brickert, Carlton 1891-1943 *WhScrn 1, WhScrn 2, WhoHol B*
Brickley, Charles E 1891-1949 *WhScrn 2*
Brickner, Roy 1904- *IntMPA 1977*
Bricusse, Leslie 1931- *EncMT, FilmgC, NotNAT*
Bridge, Al 1891-1957 *Vers B*
Bridge, Alan 1891-1957 *WhScrn 2*
Bridge, Loie 1890-1974 *WhScrn 2*
Bridge, Peter 1925- *WhoThe 16*
Bridges, Alan 1927- *FilmgC*
Bridges, Beau *WhoHol A*
Bridges, Beau 1941- *CelR 3, FilmgC, IntMPA 1977*
Bridges, Beau 1942- *MovMk*
Bridges, Ethel 1897- *AmSCAP 1966*
Bridges, Harry 1901- *CelR 3*
Bridges, James *IntMPA 1977*
Bridges, Jeff 1950- *FilmgC, MovMk, WhoHol A*
Bridges, Jeff 1951- *IntMPA 1977*
Bridges, John *OxThe*
Bridges, Lloyd 1913- *CelR 3, FilmgC, IntMPA 1977, MotPP, MovMk, WhoHol A*
Bridges, Lou 1917- *AmSCAP 1966*
Bridges, Otis C 1916- *AmSCAP 1966*
Bridges-Adams, William 1889-1965 *BiE&WWA, WhThe*
Bridgewater, Leslie 1893- *WhThe*
Bridie, James 1888-1951 *CnMD, CnThe, CroCD, McGWD, ModWD, NotNAT A, NotNAT B, OxThe, PIP&P, REnWD, WhThe, WorEnF*
Briegel, George F 1890- *AmSCAP 1966*
Brien, Alan 1925- *WhoThe 16*
Brien, Anja *WomWMM*
Brien, Lige *IntMPA 1977*
Briercliffe, Nellie d1966 *WhThe*
Brierley, David 1936- *WhoThe 16*
Briers, Richard 1934- *FilmgC, WhoThe 16*
Briesc, Gerd *Film 2*
Brieux, Eugene 1858-1932 *CnMD, CnThe, McGWD, ModWD, NotNAT B, OxThe, REnWD, WhThe*
Briggs, Donald *WhoHol A*
Briggs, G Wright 1916- *AmSCAP 1966*
Briggs, Hal 1881-1925 *WhScrn 2*
Briggs, Harlan 1880-1952 *NotNAT B, Vers A, WhScrn 1, WhScrn 2, WhoHol B*
Briggs, Hedley 1907-1968 *WhThe*
Briggs, Matt 1883-1962 *NotNAT B, WhScrn 1, WhScrn 2, WhoHol B*
Briggs, Norma *WomWMM B*
Briggs, Oscar 1877-1928 *WhScrn 1, WhScrn 2, WhoHol B*
Briggs, Wallace Neal 1914- *BiE&WWA, NotNAT*
Briggs, William A 1915- *BiE&WWA, NotNAT*
Brigham, William Stanhope 1938- *BiE&WWA*
Brighouse, Harold 1882-1958 *CnMD, CnThe, McGWD, ModWD, NotNAT B, OxThe, WhThe*
Bright, Houston 1916- *AmSCAP 1966*
Bright, Richard *WhoHol A*
Bright, Robert *WhoHol A*
Bright, Ronnell L 1930- *AmSCAP 1966*
Bright, Sol Kekipi 1919- *AmSCAP 1966*
Brightman, Homer H *IntMPA 1977*

Brightman, Stanley 1888-1961 *WhThe*
Brighton, Albert 1876-1911 *WhScrn 2*
Brignone, Mercedes *Film 1*
Brill, Marty *WhoHol A*
Brill, Patti 1923-1963 *WhScrn 2*
Brimhall, John 1928- *AmSCAP 1966*
Brinckerhoff, Burt 1936- *BiE&WWA, NotNAT*
Brind, Tessa *WhoHol A*
Brindeau, Jeanne *Film 2*
Brindley, Charles *Film 1*
Brindley, Madge d1968 *WhScrn 2*
Brindmour, George 1870-1941 *WhScrn 1, WhScrn 2*
Brinegar, Paul *WhoHol A*
Brink, Elga *Film 2*
Brinkley, David 1920- *CelR 3, IntMPA 1977, NewYTET*
Brinkley, Neil *Film 2*
Brinkman, Dolores *Film 2*
Brinkman, Ernest 1872-1938 *WhScrn 1, WhScrn 2*
Brinson, Rosemary Greene 1917- *AmSCAP 1966*
Brioni *CelR 3*
Briquet, Jean 1864-1936 *NotNAT B*
Brisbane, Arthur *Film 2*
Briscoe, Chesley 1900- *AmSCAP 1966*
Briscoe, Lottie d1950 *NotNAT B, WhoHol B*
Briscoe, Lottie 1881-1950 *WhScrn 1, WhScrn 2*
Briscoe, Lottie 1883-1950 *Film 1*
Briskin, Barney 1893- *IntMPA 1977*
Briskin, Irving 1903- *IntMPA 1977*
Briskin, Mort *IntMPA 1977*
Brissac, Virginia *WhoHol A*
Brisson, Carl d1958 *WhoHol B*
Brisson, Carl 1893-1958 *WhScrn 1, WhScrn 2*
Brisson, Carl 1895-1958 *EncMT, FilmgC, NotNAT B, WhThe*
Brisson, Carl 1897-1958 *Film 2*
Brisson, Cleo 1894-1975 *WhScrn 2*
Brisson, Frederick 1913- *BiE&WWA, IntMPA 1977, NotNAT, WhoThe 16*
Brisson, Frederick 1915?- *FilmgC*
Brisson, Frederick 1917- *CelR 3*
Brister, Robert S 1889-1945 *WhScrn 1, WhScrn 2, WhoHol B*
Bristol, Margaret *AmSCAP 1966*
Bristow, Charles 1928- *WhoThe 16*
Britain, Radie 1904- *AmSCAP 1966*
Brito, Phil 1915- *AmSCAP 1966*
Britt, Addy 1891-1938 *AmSCAP 1966*
Britt, Elton 1912-1972 *WhScrn 2*
Britt, Elton 1913- *AmSCAP 1966*
Britt, May 1933- *FilmgC, MotPP, WhoHol A*
Britten, Benjamin 1913- *CelR 3, OxFilm*
Britton, Barbara *IntMPA 1977, MotPP*
Britton, Barbara 1919- *HolP 40*
Britton, Barbara 1920- *FilmgC, WhoHol A*
Britton, Barbara 1923- *MovMk*
Britton, Clifton d1963 *NotNAT B*
Britton, Edna *Film 1*
Britton, Ethel 1915-1972 *WhScrn 2, WhoHol B*
Britton, Hutin 1876-1965 *Film 1, Film 2, OxThe, WhThe*
Britton, Keith 1919-1970 *WhScrn 2*
Britton, Lilian *WhoStg 1908*
Britton, Milt 1894-1948 *WhScrn 1, WhScrn 2, WhoHol B*
Britton, Pamela 1923-1974 *MotPP, WhScrn 2, WhoHol B*
Britton, Tony 1924- *IntMPA 1977, WhoHol A, WhoThe 16*
Britton, Tony 1925- *FilmgC*
Brix, Herman *WhoHol A*
Brizard, Jean-Baptiste 1721-1791 *OxThe*

Broad, Kid *Film 2*
Broadhurst, Cecil 1908- *AmSCAP 1966*
Broadhurst, George Howells 1866-1952 *ModWD, NotNAT B, OxThe, WhThe*
Broadhurst, Thomas W d1936 *NotNAT B*
Broadley, Edward d1947 *WhScrn 2*
Broca, Philippe De 1935- *DcFM*
Brocco, Peter *WhoHol A*
Broccoli, Albert R 1909- *FilmgC, IntMPA 1977*
Brochet, Henri 1898-1952 *OxThe*
Brock, Baby Dorothy *Film 2*
Brock, Blanche Kerr 1888-1958 *AmSCAP 1966*
Brock, Dorothy *Film 2*
Brock, Tony d1924 *WhScrn 2*
Brock, Virgil P 1887- *AmSCAP 1966*
Brockband, Harrison d1947 *NotNAT B*
Brockett, O G 1923- *BiE&WWA, NotNAT*
Brockett, Timothy C 1922- *AmSCAP 1966*
Brockington, John 1948- *CelR 3*
Brockman, James 1886- *AmSCAP 1966*
Brockman, Susan *WomWMM B*
Brockmann *Film 2*
Brockmann, Johann Franz Hieronymus 1745-1812 *OxThe*
Brockway, Jennie M 1886- *AmSCAP 1966*
Brockwell, Billie *Film 1*
Brockwell, Gladys d1929 *MotPP, WhoHol B*
Brockwell, Gladys 1893-1930 *Film 1, Film 2, TwYS*
Brockwell, Gladys 1894-1929 *WhScrn 1, WhScrn 2*
Brod, Max 1884-1968 *McGWD*
Broder, Jane *BiE&WWA*
Broderick, Helen d1959 *MotPP, WhoHol B*
Broderick, Helen 1890-1959 *FilmgC*
Broderick, Helen 1891-1959 *EncMT, Film 2, MovMk, NotNAT B, ThFT, Vers A, WhScrn 1, WhScrn 2, WhThe*
Broderick, James 1929- *NotNAT, WhoHol A*
Broderick, Johnny 1901- *AmSCAP 1966*
Brodie, Buster 1886-1948 *Film 2, WhScrn 1, WhScrn 2, WhoHol B*
Brodie, Steve 1919- *FilmgC, WhoHol A*
Brodine, Norbert 1895?-1970 *FilmgC*
Brodine, Norbert 1897- *WorEnF*
Brodkin, Herbert 1912- *IntMPA 1977, NewYTET*
Brodney, Oscar 1905- *FilmgC, IntMPA 1977*
Brodshaug, Melvin 1900- *IntMPA 1977*
Brodsky, Jack *IntMPA 1977*
Brodszky, Nicholas 1905- *FilmgC*
Brody, Ann 1884-1944 *WhScrn 1, WhScrn 2*
Brody, Ann 1894-1944 *Film 2, WhoHol B*
Brody, Anna 1894-1944 *Film 1, TwYS*
Brody, Estelle 1904- *Film 2*
Brody, Murray Lee 1909- *AmSCAP 1966*
Brody Singers *OxThe*
Broeder, Ray 1898- *BiE&WWA, NotNAT*
Broekman, David Hendrines 1902-1958 *AmSCAP 1966*
Brogden, Gwendoline 1891- *WhThe*
Broidy, Steve 1905- *IntMPA 1977*
Brokaw, Charles 1898-1975 *WhScrn 2, WhoHol C*
Brokaw, Norman R 1927- *IntMPA 1977*
Brokaw, Tom *NewYTET*
Broke, Charles Frederick Tucker 1883-1946 *NotNAT B*
Brolin, James *IntMPA 1977, WhoHol A*
Brolin, James 1940- *MovMk*
Brolin, James 1941- *FilmgC*
Bromberg, Edward J *MotPP*
Bromberg, J Edward 1903-1951 *FilmgC, MovMk, NotNAT B, PIP&P, WhScrn 1, WhScrn 2,*

WhoHol B

Bromberg, J Edward 1904-1951 *Vers A, WhThe*

Bromberger, Herve 1918- *FilmgC*

Brome, Alexander d1666 *NotNAT B*

Brome, Richard 1590?-1652? *CnThe, McGWD, REnWD*

Brome, Richard 1590?-1653 *NotNAT B, OxThe*

Bromfield, John 1922- *FilmgC, IntMPA 1977, MotPP, WhoHol A*

Bromfield, Louis 1896-1956 *NotNAT B*

Bromhead, Michael 1924- *IntMPA 1977*

Bromhead, Ralph S 1906- *IntMPA 1977*

Bromiley, Dorothy 1935- *FilmgC*

Bromilow, Peter *WhoHol A*

Bromley, Nellie d1939 *NotNAT B*

Bromley, Sheila 1911- *ThFT, WhoHol A*

Bromley-Davenport, Arthur 1867-1946 *NotNAT B, WhThe*

Bron, Eleanor 1934- *FilmgC, IntMPA 1977, WhoHol A, WhoThe 16*

Broncho Billy *MotPP, OxFilm*

Brondfield, Jerome 1913- *IntMPA 1977*

Broneau, Helen *Film 2*

Bronnen, Arnolt 1895-1959 *CnMD, CroCD, McGWD, ModWD*

Bronner, Edwin 1926- *BiE&WWA, NotNAT*

Bronner, Robert *WorEnF*

Bronson, Benjamin 1896- *AmSCAP 1966*

Bronson, Betty 1906-1971 *Film 2, FilmgC, MotPP, MovMk, ThFT, TwYS, WhScrn 1, WhoHol B*

Bronson, Betty 1907-1971 *WhScrn 2*

Bronson, Charles *WhoHol A*

Bronson, Charles 1920- *IntMPA 1977, MovMk*

Bronson, Charles 1922- *CelR 3, FilmgC*

Bronson, Lillian 1902- *Vers A, WhoHol A*

Bronston, Samuel 1909- *WorEnF*

Bronston, Samuel 1910- *CmMov, DcFM, FilmgC, IntMPA 1977*

Bronte, Charlotte 1816-1855 *FilmgC, NotNAT B*

Bronte, Emily 1818-1848 *FilmgC*

Bronte, Jean *Film 2*

Brook, Barry S 1918- *AmSCAP 1966*

Brook, Clive 1887-1974 *FilmgC, MotPP, MovMk, WhScrn 2, WhThe, WhoHol B, WorEnF*

Brook, Clive 1891-1974 *BiDFlm, Film 2, TwYS*

Brook, Faith 1922- *FilmgC, WhoThe 16*

Brook, Helen *Film 2*

Brook, Hugh *Film 2*

Brook, Lesley 1916- *FilmgC*

Brook, Lesley 1917- *WhThe*

Brook, Lyndon 1926- *FilmgC*

Brook, Olive *Film 2*

Brook, Peter 1925- *BiDFlm, BiE&WWA, CelR 3, CnThe, CroCD, DcFM, FilmgC, MovMk, NotNAT, NotNAT A, OxFilm, OxThe, PIP&P, WhoThe 16, WorEnF*

Brook, Sara *WhoThe 16*

Brook-Jones, Elwyn 1911-1962 *FilmgC, NotNAT B, WhScrn 1, WhScrn 2, WhThe, WhoHol B*

Brooke, Claude 1853-1933 *Film 2, WhScrn 1, WhScrn 2, WhoHol B*

Brooke, Clifford 1872-1951 *WhScrn 1, WhScrn 2, WhoHol B*

Brooke, Cynthia 1875-1949 *NotNAT B, WhThe*

Brooke, Mrs. E H d1915 *WhThe*

Brooke, Edward 1919- *CelR 3*

Brooke, Emily d1953 *NotNAT B, WhThe*

Brooke, Frances d1789 *NotNAT B*

Brooke, Gustavus Vaughan 1818-1860 *NotNAT A, NotNAT B*

Brooke, Gustavus Vaughan 1818-1866 *OxThe*

Brooke, H Sullivan d1923 *NotNAT B*

Brooke, Harold 1910- *WhoThe 16*

Brooke, Henry 1703-1783 *NotNAT B*

Brooke, Hillary 1914- *WhoHol A*

Brooke, Hillary 1916- *FilmgC, MovMk*

Brooke, Iris 1908- *BiE&WWA, NotNAT*

Brooke, Myra 1865-1944 *WhScrn 1, WhScrn 2*

Brooke, Peter R 1921- *IntMPA 1977*

Brooke, Ralph 1920-1963 *WhScrn 2*

Brooke, Sarah *WhThe*

Brooke, Tyler 1891-1943 *Film 2, TwYS, WhScrn 1, WhScrn 2, WhoHol B*

Brooke, VanDyke d1921 *Film 1, Film 2, TwYS, WhScrn 2*

Brooke, Walter *WhoHol A*

Brookes, Charles *Film 1*

Brookes, Jacqueline 1930- *BiE&WWA, NotNAT, WhoThe 16*

Brookfield, Charles Hallam Elton 1857-1913 *NotNAT B, WhThe*

Brookfield, Sydney F d1916 *NotNAT B*

Brooking, Dorothea 1916- *IntMPA 1977*

Brooks, Alan 1888-1936 *Film 2, WhScrn 1, WhScrn 2, WhoHol B*

Brooks, Anne Sooy 1911- *AmSCAP 1966*

Brooks, David 1920- *BiE&WWA, NotNAT*

Brooks, Dick *IntMPA 1977*

Brooks, Donald 1928- *BiE&WWA, CelR 3, NotNAT*

Brooks, Geraldine 1925- *BiE&WWA, FilmgC, HolP 40, IntMPA 1977, NotNAT A, WhoHol A*

Brooks, Gwendolyn 1917- *CelR 3*

Brooks, Hank d1925 *WhScrn 1, WhScrn 2, WhoHol B*

Brooks, Harry 1895- *AmSCAP 1966*

Brooks, Harvey Oliver 1899- *AmSCAP 1966*

Brooks, Hazel *WhoHol A*

Brooks, Iris *WhoHol A*

Brooks, Jack 1912- *AmSCAP 1966*

Brooks, James L And Allan Burns *NewYTET*

Brooks, Jean 1921- *FilmgC*

Brooks, Jess Lee 1894-1944 *WhScrn 1, WhScrn 2, WhoHol B*

Brooks, John Benson 1917- *AmSCAP 1966*

Brooks, Lawrence 1912- *BiE&WWA, NotNAT*

Brooks, Leslie 1922- *FilmgC, WhoHol A*

Brooks, Louise *MotPP*

Brooks, Louise 1900- *Film 2, FilmgC, MovMk, WorEnF*

Brooks, Louise 1905- *WhoHol A*

Brooks, Louise 1906- *BiDFlm, OxFilm, ThFT, TwYS*

Brooks, Marion *Film 1*

Brooks, Mary *WhoHol A*

Brooks, May K d1963 *NotNAT B*

Brooks, Mel *BiE&WWA, NewYTET*

Brooks, Mel 1926- *IntMPA 1977, MovMk*

Brooks, Mel 1928- *FilmgC*

Brooks, Pauline 1913-1967 *WhScrn 1, WhScrn 2, WhoHol B*

Brooks, Phyllis 1914- *FilmgC, ThFT, WhoHol A*

Brooks, Rand 1918- *FilmgC, WhoHol A*

Brooks, Randy 1918-1967 *WhScrn 1, WhScrn 2, WhoHol B*

Brooks, Ray 1939- *FilmgC*

Brooks, Richard 1912- *BiDFlm, CelR 3, ConDr 1977A, DcFM, FilmgC, IntMPA 1977, MovMk, OxFilm, WorEnF*

Brooks, Roy *Film 2*

Brooks, Shelton 1886- *AmSCAP 1966*

Brooks, Shirley d1874 *NotNAT B*

Brooks, Thor L *IntMPA 1977*

Brooks, Virginia *WomWMM B*

Brooks, Virginia Fox *WhThe*

Brooks, Wilson d1967 *WhoHol B*
Broones, Martin 1892- *AmSCAP 1966, WhThe*
Brophy, Brigid 1929- *ConDr 1977*
Brophy, Ed 1895-1960 *WhoHol B*
Brophy, Edward 1895-1960 *Film 2, FilmgC, MotPP, NotNAT B, WhScrn 1, WhScrn 2*
Brophy, Edward 1900-1960 *MovMk, Vers A*
Brosig, Egon 1890-1961 *WhScrn 1, WhScrn 2*
Broske, Octavia *Film 2*
Broszkiewicz, Jerzy 1922- *CroCD, ModWD*
Brother Bones *WhScrn 2*
Brotherhood, William *Film 1*
Brothers, Cassandra F *WhoHol A*
Brothers, Joyce 1928- *CelR 3, NewYTET*
Brotherson, Eric 1911- *WhoThe 16*
Brouett, Albert *WhThe*
Brough, Fanny Whiteside 1854-1914 *NotNAT B, OxThe, WhThe*
Brough, Lionel 1836-1900 *NotNAT B, OxThe*
Brough, Mary 1863-1934 *Film 2, FilmgC, NotNAT B, OxThe, WhScrn 1, WhScrn 2, WhThe, WhoHol B*
Brough, Robert d1906 *NotNAT B*
Brough, Mrs. Robert d1932 *NotNAT B, WhThe*
Brough, Robert Barnabas 1828-1860 *NotNAT B, OxThe*
Brough, Sydney 1868-1911 *NotNAT B, OxThe*
Brough, William 1826-1870 *NotNAT B, OxThe*
Brougham, John 1810-1880 *FamA&A, NotNAT B, OxThe, PIP&P*
Broughton, James *WorEnF*
Broughton, Jessie 1885- *WhThe*
Broughton, Philip F 1893- *AmSCAP 1966*
Broughton, Phyllis d1926 *WhThe*
Broughton, Simon J d1964 *NotNAT B*
Broumas, John G 1917- *IntMPA 1977*
Broun, Heywood 1888-1939 *NotNAT B, WhThe*
Broun, Heywood Hale 1918- *BiE&WWA, NotNAT, NotNAT A, PIP&P*
Browder, Robert *Film 2*
Brower, David 1912- *CelR 3*
Brower, Otto 1895-1946 *Film 2, TwYS A, WhScrn 1, WhScrn 2, WhoHol B*
Brower, Robert 1850-1934 *Film 2, TwYS, WhScrn 2*
Brown, A Seymour 1885-1947 *AmSCAP 1966*
Brown, Adeline E *AmSCAP 1966*
Brown, Al W 1884-1924 *AmSCAP 1966*
Brown, Albert O d1945 *NotNAT B*
Brown, Anne *PIP&P*
Brown, Arvin 1940- *NotNAT*
Brown, Athaleen 1908- *AmSCAP 1966*
Brown, Barbara *WomWMM B*
Brown, Barbara d1975 *WhScrn 2, WhoHol C*
Brown, Barnetta 1859-1938 *AmSCAP 1966*
Brown, Barry *IntMPA 1977, WhoHol A*
Brown, Bertrand 1888-1964 *AmSCAP 1966, NotNAT B*
Brown, Beth *AmSCAP 1966*
Brown, Bly 1898-1950 *WhScrn 1, WhScrn 2*
Brown, Carrie Clarke Ward d1926 *NotNAT B*
Brown, Chamberlain d1955 *NotNAT B*
Brown, Charles D d1948 *Film 2, NotNAT B, WhoHol B*
Brown, Charles D 1887-1948 *Film 1, FilmgC, WhScrn 1, WhScrn 2*
Brown, Charles D 1888-1948 *Vers B*
Brown, Clarence 1890- *BiDFlm, CmMov, DcFM, FilmgC, IntMPA 1977, MovMk, OxFilm, TwYS A, WorEnF*
Brown, Clark d1943 *NotNAT B*
Brown, David 1916- *IntMPA 1977*
Brown, David Paul 1795-1875 *NotNAT B*
Brown, DeMarcus 1900- *BiE&WWA, NotNAT*

Brown, Dorothy *Film 2, WhoHol A*
Brown, Edward *Film 1*
Brown, Edwin *Film 2*
Brown, Firman H, Jr. 1926- *BiE&WWA*
Brown, Ford Madox *PIP&P*
Brown, Forman 1901- *AmSCAP 1966*
Brown, Fred *Film 1*
Brown, Gene 1928- *AmSCAP 1966*
Brown, Georg Stanford *WhoHol A*
Brown, George Anderson d1920 *NotNAT B*
Brown, George H 1913- *FilmgC, IntMPA 1977*
Brown, George Murray 1880-1960 *AmSCAP 1966*
Brown, George R 1910- *AmSCAP 1966*
Brown, Georgia 1933- *BiE&WWA, FilmgC, NotNAT, WhoHol A, WhoThe 16*
Brown, Gilmor d1960 *NotNAT A, PIP&P*
Brown, Gilmorn d1960 *NotNAT B*
Brown, Glenn J 1900-1960 *AmSCAP 1966*
Brown, Gwen *WomWMM B*
Brown, Hal *Film 1*
Brown, Halbert *Film 2*
Brown, Harry d1966 *WhoHol B*
Brown, Harry 1917- *CmMov, FilmgC, IntMPA 1977*
Brown, Harry Joe 1890-1972 *TwYS A*
Brown, Harry Joe 1892-1972 *FilmgC*
Brown, Harry Joe 1893-1972 *WorEnF*
Brown, Harry W 1918-1966 *WhScrn 2*
Brown, Helen 1902- *BiE&WWA*
Brown, Helen Gurley 1922- *CelR 3*
Brown, Helen Mina 1916-1974 *WhScrn 2*
Brown, Helen W d1974 *WhoHol B*
Brown, Henry 1899- *IntMPA 1977*
Brown, Himan 1910- *IntMPA 1977*
Brown, Howard C 1901- *IntMPA 1977*
Brown, Irving 1922- *BiE&WWA, NotNAT*
Brown, Ivor 1891- *BiE&WWA, OxThe, WhThe*
Brown, James 1920- *FilmgC, MotPP, WhoHol A*
Brown, James 1934- *CelR 3*
Brown, Jean Patricia *WomWMM B*
Brown, Jim *MotPP, WhoHol A*
Brown, Jim 1935- *CelR 3*
Brown, Jim 1936- *FilmgC, IntMPA 1977, MovMk*
Brown, Joe *Film 2*
Brown, Joe 1941- *FilmgC*
Brown, Joe, Jr. *WhoHol A*
Brown, Joe E 1891-1973 *FilmgC*
Brown, Joe E 1892-1973 *BiE&WWA, EncMT, Film 2, MotPP, MovMk, NotNAT A, OxFilm, WhScrn 2, WhThe, WhoHol B*
Brown, John d1957 *WhScrn 2*
Brown, John Edwin 1892- *Film 2, TwYS*
Brown, John Mack 1904-1974 *FilmgC, MotPP, MovMk*
Brown, John Mason 1900-1969 *BiE&WWA, NotNAT A, NotNAT B, OxThe, PIP&P*
Brown, John Moulder 1951- *FilmgC*
Brown, John Russell 1923- *WhoThe 16*
Brown, Johnny *WhoHol A*
Brown, Johnny Mack 1904-1974 *CmMov, Film 2, TwYS, WhoHol B*
Brown, Johnny Mack 1904-1975 *WhScrn 2*
Brown, Josephine *Film 2*
Brown, Julia *Film 2*
Brown, Kay 1902- *BiE&WWA*
Brown, Keith Crosby 1885-1948 *AmSCAP 1966*
Brown, Kelly 1928- *BiE&WWA, NotNAT*
Brown, Kenneth H 1936- *ConDr 1977*
Brown, Kenneth H 1937?- *NatPD, NotNAT, PIP&P*
Brown, L Slade 1922- *BiE&WWA, NotNAT*
Brown, Larry 1947- *CelR 3*
Brown, Lennox *NatPD*

Brown, Les 1912- *AmSCAP 1966*
Brown, Lew *WhoHol A*
Brown, Lew 1893-1958 *AmSCAP 1966, EncMT, NewMT, NotNAT B*
Brown, Lionel d1964 *NotNAT B*
Brown, Lucille *Film 1*
Brown, Lyman C d1961 *NotNAT B*
Brown, Marcia *WomWMM B*
Brown, Margaret Wise 1910-1952 *AmSCAP 1966*
Brown, Marshall R 1920- *AmSCAP 1966*
Brown, Martin 1885-1936 *NotNAT B*
Brown, Maurice John Edwin 1906?- *AmSCAP 1966*
Brown, Maxine Velena 1897-1956 *WhScrn 2*
Brown, Melville 1888-1938 *TwYS A, WhScrn 1, WhScrn 2*
Brown, Milton *Film 1*
Brown, Nacio, Jr. 1921- *AmSCAP 1966*
Brown, Nacio Herb 1896-1964 *AmSCAP 1966, Film 2, FilmgC, NotNAT B*
Brown, Pamela 1917-1975 *BiE&WWA, FilmgC, NotNAT B, OxFilm, PIP&P, WhScrn 2, WhoHol C*
Brown, Paul 1908- *CelR 3*
Brown, Peggy *Film 2*
Brown, Peter *WhoHol A*
Brown, Phil 1916?-1973 *FilmgC, WhScrn 2, WhoHol B*
Brown, Philip *WhoHol A*
Brown, Raymond 1880-1939 *WhScrn 1, WhScrn 2, WhoHol B*
Brown, Reed, Jr. d1962 *NotNAT B*
Brown, Richard Peyron 1936- *NotNAT*
Brown, Robert 1918?- *FilmgC*
Brown, Ronald C 1911-1962 *WhScrn 1, WhScrn 2*
Brown, Rowland 1901-1963 *FilmgC*
Brown, Russ 1892-1964 *WhScrn 1, WhScrn 2, WhoHol B*
Brown, Sedley d1928 *NotNAT B*
Brown, T Allston d1918 *NotNAT B*
Brown, Tom 1913- *Film 2, FilmgC, IntMPA 1977, MovMk, TwYS, Vers B, WhoHol A*
Brown, Troy, Jr. d1944 *WhScrn 2*
Brown, Vanessa 1928- *FilmgC, MotPP, WhoHol A*
Brown, Virginia *Film 2*
Brown, W H *Film 1, Film 2*
Brown, Wally d1961 *NotNAT B*
Brown, Wally 1898-1961 *FilmgC*
Brown, Wally 1904-1961 *Vers B, WhScrn 1, WhScrn 2, WhoHol B*
Brown, Walter Earl 1928- *AmSCAP 1966*
Brown, Willet Henry *IntMPA 1977*
Brown, William *Film 1*
Brown, William F 1928- *AmSCAP 1966, ConDr 1977D, NatPD*
Brown, William H, Jr. *IntMPA 1977*
Brown, Winnie *MotPP*
Brown-Potter, Mrs. James 1859-1936 *NotNAT B, OxThe*
Browne, Bradford *AmSCAP 1966*
Browne, Coral 1913- *BiE&WWA, FilmgC, MotPP, MovMk, NotNAT, WhoHol A, WhoThe 16*
Browne, E Martin 1900- *BiE&WWA, NotNAT, OxThe, WhoThe 16*
Browne, Earle 1872-1944 *WhScrn 1, WhScrn 2, WhoHol B*
Browne, Ernest D 1900- *AmSCAP 1966*
Browne, Harry C *Film 2*
Browne, Irene 1891-1965 *BiE&WWA, FilmgC, WhoHol B*

Browne, Irene 1893-1965 *Film 2, ThFT, WhScrn 1, WhScrn 2*
Browne, J Edwin *Film 2*
Browne, John Lewis 1866-1933 *AmSCAP 1966*
Browne, Kathie *WhoHol A*
Browne, Kathryn *Film 1*
Browne, Maurice 1881-1955 *ModWD, NotNAT A, NotNAT B, OxThe*
Browne, Porter Emerson 1879-1934 *NotNAT B*
Browne, Raymond A 1871-1922 *AmSCAP 1966*
Browne, Robert *OxThe*
Browne, Roscoe Lee 1925- *BiE&WWA, FilmgC, IntMPA 1977, NotNAT, WhoHol A, WhoThe 16*
Browne, W Graham 1870-1937 *Film 1, NotNAT B, WhScrn 2, WhoHol B*
Browne, Walter 1856-1911 *NotNAT B, WhoStg 1908*
Browne, Wynyard Barry d1964 *NotNAT B*
Brownell, Barbara *WhoHol A*
Browning, Edith d1926 *NotNAT B*
Browning, John 1933- *CelR 3*
Browning, Kirk 1921- *IntMPA 1977, NewYTET*
Browning, Mortimer 1891-1953 *AmSCAP 1966*
Browning, Ricou 1930- *FilmgC, NewYTET*
Browning, Robert 1812-1889 *CnThe, McGWD, OxThe, PIP&P, REnWD*
Browning, Susan 1941- *WhoThe 16*
Browning, Tod 1880-1962 *TwYS A*
Browning, Tod 1882-1962 *BiDFlm, CmMov, DcFM, Film 1, FilmgC, MovMk, OxFilm, WhScrn 2, WorEnF*
Browning, William E d1930 *WhScrn 1, WhScrn 2, WhoHol B*
Brownlee, Frank 1874-1948 *Film 1, Film 2, WhScrn 2*
Brownlee, John 1901- *BiE&WWA*
Brownlow, Kevin 1938- *FilmgC, OxFilm*
Brownstone, Joseph 1920- *BiE&WWA*
Brox Sisters, The *Film 2*
Broyde, Ruth *WomWMM*
Brubaker, Robert *WhoHol A*
Brubeck, Dave 1920- *CelR 3*
Bruce, Angela *WomWMM*
Bruce, Belle d1960 *Film 1, WhScrn 2, WhoHol B*
Bruce, Betty 1920-1974 *WhScrn 2, WhoHol B*
Bruce, Betty 1925-1974 *BiE&WWA, NotNAT B*
Bruce, Beverly d1925 *WhScrn 1, WhScrn 2, WhoHol B*
Bruce, Billy *Film 2*
Bruce, Brenda *WhoHol A, WhoThe 16*
Bruce, Brenda 1918- *FilmgC*
Bruce, Brenda 1922- *IntMPA 1977*
Bruce, Carol 1919- *BiE&WWA, EncMT, NotNAT, WhoHol A, WhoThe 16*
Bruce, Clifford 1885-1919 *Film 1, Film 2, WhScrn 2*
Bruce, David 1914- *FilmgC, MotPP*
Bruce, George 1898- *IntMPA 1977*
Bruce, Geraldine d1953 *NotNAT B*
Bruce, Kate 1858-1946 *Film 1, Film 2, TwYS, WhScrn 2*
Bruce, Lenny 1926-1966 *WhScrn 2*
Bruce, Michael *Film 2*
Bruce, Nigel 1895-1953 *Film 2, FilmgC, MotPP, MovMk, NotNAT B, Vers A, WhScrn 1, WhScrn 2, WhoHol B*
Bruce, Nigel 1895-1954 *CmMov*
Bruce, Paul d1971 *WhScrn 1, WhScrn 2, WhoHol B*
Bruce, Raymon R 1934- *NatPD*
Bruce, Robert 1915- *AmSCAP 1966*
Bruce, Shelley *WhoHol A*

Bruce, Tonie Edgar WhScrn 1, WhScrn 2
Bruce, Tony d1937 NotNAT B, WhoHol B
Bruce, Virginia 1910- Film 2, FilmgC, MGM,
    MotPP, MovMk, ThFT, WhoHol A
Bruckman, Clyde 1894-1955 WorEnF
Bruckman, Clyde 1895-1955 FilmgC
Bruckner, Ferdinand 1891-1958 CnMD, McGWD,
    ModWD, NotNAT B, OxThe
Bruckner, Friedrich 1891-1958 CroCD
Bruckner, Johannes 1730-1786 OxThe
Bruckner, Sidney Thomas 1914- IntMPA 1977
Brues, Otto 1897-1967 CnMD, ModWD
Brueys, David-Augustin De 1640-1723 McGWD,
    OxThe
Bruford, Rose Elizabeth 1904- WhoThe 16
Bruggeman, George 1904-1967 WhScrn 2
Bruggerman, George d1967 WhoHol B
Bruhn, Erik 1928- CelR 3
Bruhns, George Frederick William 1874-1963
    AmSCAP 1966
Brule, Andre Film 1
Brumberg, Valentina 1899- DcFM, WomWMM
Brumberg, Zenajeda 1900- WomWMM
Brumberg, Zinaida 1900- DcFM
Brummell, Beau 1778-1840 FilmgC
Brun, Joseph WorEnF
Brun, Nordahl 1745-1816 OxThe
Brundage, Avery 1887- CelR 3
Brundage, Bertha 1860-1939 WhScrn 1,
    WhScrn 2, WhoHol B
Brundage, Mathilde 1871-1939 Film 1, WhScrn 2
Brundage, Matilde Film 2
Brunel, Adrian 1892-1958 Film 2, FilmgC
Brunelleschi, Filippo 1377-1446 OxThe
Brunelli, Louis Jean 1925- AmSCAP 1966
Bruner, Richard W 1926- NatPD
Brunette, Fritzi 1890-1943 WhScrn 1, WhScrn 2,
    WhoHol B
Brunette, Fritzi 1894-1943 Film 1, Film 2,
    TwYS
Brunetti, Argentina WhoHol A
Brunetti, Miro 1908-1966 WhScrn 2
Bruning, Albert d1929 NotNAT B
Bruning, Francesca 1907- BiE&WWA, NotNAT
Brunius, Jacques 1906-1967 FilmgC, OxFilm,
    WhScrn 2
Brunius, John W 1884-1937 DcFM, WhScrn 2
Brunius, Pauline WomWMM
Brunner, Robert F 1938- AmSCAP 1966
Brunns, Julia d1927 WhoHol B
Bruno, Giordano 1548-1600 McGWD, OxThe,
    REnWD
Bruno, James 1917- AmSCAP 1966
Bruno, Jennie Film 2
Bruno-Ruby, Jane WomWMM
Brunot, Andre 1880-1973 WhScrn 2, WhoHol B
Bruns, Edna d1960 NotNAT B
Bruns, Julia 1895-1927 NotNAT B
Brunton, Ann 1768-1808 NotNAT B
Brunton, Anne 1769-1808 OxThe
Brunton, Garland Lewis d1975 WhoHol C
Brunton, John 1741-1822 NotNAT B, OxThe
Brunton, John 1775-1848 OxThe
Brunton, John 1775-1849 NotNAT B
Brunton, Louisa 1779-1860 NotNAT B, OxThe
Brunton, William Film 1
Bruscambille OxThe
Brush, Mrs. Clinton E 1911- BiE&WWA
Brush, Clinton E, III 1911- BiE&WWA
Brush, Ruth J 1910- AmSCAP 1966
Bruski, Natalio 1906- IntMPA 1977
Bruskin, Perry 1916- BiE&WWA
Brusseau, William E 1926- IntMPA 1977
Brust, Alfred 1891-1934 ModWD

Brustein, Robert 1927- BiE&WWA, CelR 3,
    NotNAT, WhoThe 16
Bruun Olsen, Ernst 1923- CroCD
Bryan, Alfred 1871-1958 AmSCAP 1966
Bryan, Arthur Q 1899-1959 WhScrn 1, WhScrn 2,
    WhoHol B
Bryan, Charles Faulkner 1911-1955
    AmSCAP 1966
Bryan, Dora IntMPA 1977, WhoHol A
Bryan, Dora 1923- FilmgC
Bryan, Dora 1924- EncMT, WhoThe 16
Bryan, George 1910-1969 WhScrn 2, WhoHol B
Bryan, Hal 1891-1948 NotNAT B
Bryan, Herbert George d1948 NotNAT B
Bryan, Jackson Lee 1909-1964 WhScrn 1,
    WhScrn 2
Bryan, Jane 1918- FilmgC, MotPP, ThFT,
    WhoHol A
Bryan, John 1911-1969 DcFM, FilmgC
Bryan, Ruth Film 1
Bryan, Ruth Jennings WomWMM
Bryant, Billy NotNAT A
Bryant, Charles 1879-1948 NotNAT B,
    WhScrn 1, WhScrn 2, WhoHol B,
    WomWMM
Bryant, Charles 1887-1948 Film 1, Film 2,
    TwYS
Bryant, Dan 1833-1875 NotNAT B
Bryant, J V 1889-1924 NotNAT B
Bryant, James Film 1
Bryant, John WhoHol A
Bryant, Kay Film 2
Bryant, Margaret C 1908- BiE&WWA
Bryant, Mary 1936- BiE&WWA, NotNAT
Bryant, Michael 1928- FilmgC, WhoThe 16
Bryant, Nana 1888-1955 FilmgC, MovMk,
    NotNAT B, Vers A, WhScrn 1, WhScrn 2,
    WhoHol B
Bryant, Paul 1913- CelR 3
Bryant, Robin d1976 WhoHol C
Bryant, Willie 1908-1964 AmSCAP 1966,
    NotNAT B
Bryar, Claudia WhoHol A
Bryar, Paul 1910- Vers B, WhoHol A
Bryden, Bill 1942- WhoThe 16
Bryden, Ronald 1927- WhoThe 16
Brydon, Wilson P 1918- AmSCAP 1966
Brydone, Alfred Film 1
Brymn, J Tim 1881-1946 AmSCAP 1966
Brynner, Yul BiE&WWA, IntMPA 1977,
    MotPP, PIP&P, WhoHol A
Brynner, Yul 1915- BiDFlm, CelR 3, CmMov,
    EncMT, FilmgC, MovMk, WorEnF
Brynner, Yul 1916- CmMov, OxFilm
Bryson, Arthur Film 2
Bryson, Betty WhoHol A
Bryson, E J 1915- IntMPA 1977
Bryson, Winifred Film 2, TwYS
Brzozowska, Natalia WomWMM
Bua, Gene WhoHol A
Bubbles, John W PIP&P
Bucalossi, Brigata d1924 NotNAT B
Bucalossi, Ernest d1933 NotNAT B
Bucalossi, Procida d1918 NotNAT B
Buccola, Guy Film 2
Buchan, Annabelle Whitford d1961 NotNAT B
Buchan, John 1875-1940 FilmgC
Buchanan, Annabel Morris 1888- AmSCAP 1966
Buchanan, Charles L d1962 NotNAT B
Buchanan, Claud Film 2
Buchanan, Cynthia NatPD
Buchanan, Edgar 1902- CmMov, FilmgC,
    IntMPA 1977, MotPP, MovMk, WhoHol A
Buchanan, Jack 1890-1957 CnThe

Buchanan, Jack 1891-1957 *EncMT, Film 1,*
 Film 2, FilmgC, MotPP, NotNAT B,
 OxFilm, WhScrn 1, WhScrn 2, WhoHol B
Buchanan, Meg d1970 *WhScrn 2*
Buchanan, Patrick J *NewYTET*
Buchanan, Robert d1901 *NotNAT B*
Buchanan, Stuart 1894-1974 *WhScrn 2*
Buchanan, Thompson 1877-1937 *NotNAT B*
Buchanan, Virginia d1931 *NotNAT B*
Buchannan, Patricia *WomWMM B*
Bucharoff, Simon 1881-1955 *AmSCAP 1966*
Buchholz, Horst 1933- *BiE&WWA, FilmgC,*
 IntMPA 1977, MotPP, MovMk, WhoHol A,
 WorEnF
Buchma, Ambrose *Film 2*
Buchman, Sidney 1902- *FilmgC, WorEnF*
Buchner, Georg 1813-1837 *CnThe, McGWD,*
 NotNAT B, OxThe, PIP&P, REnWD
Buchowetzki, Dimitri 1895-1932 *DcFM*
Buchowetzki, Dmitri 1895-1932 *BiDFlm*
Buchowetzski, Dimitri 1895-1932 *TwYS A*
Buchtel, Forrest L 1899- *AmSCAP 1966*
Buchwald, Art 1925- *CelR 3*
Buck, Carlton C 1907- *AmSCAP 1966*
Buck, Charles Stary 1928- *AmSCAP 1966*
Buck, David 1936- *WhoThe 16*
Buck, Elizabeth 1912-1934 *WhScrn 1, WhScrn 2*
Buck, Ford d1955 *WhScrn 1, WhScrn 2,*
 WhoHol B
Buck, Frank 1888-1950 *FilmgC, WhScrn 1,*
 WhScrn 2, WhoHol B
Buck, Gene 1885-1957 *AmSCAP 1966, EncMT,*
 NewMT, NotNAT B
Buck, Sir George *OxThe*
Buck, Inez 1890-1957 *NotNAT B, WhScrn 1,*
 WhScrn 2, WhoHol B
Buck, Jack *NewYTET*
Buck, Jules 1917- *FilmgC, IntMPA 1977*
Buck, Nell Roy *Film 2*
Buck, Pearl S 1892-1973 *BiE&WWA, FilmgC*
Buck, Richard Henry 1870?-1956 *AmSCAP 1966*
Buckham, Bernard d1963 *NotNAT B*
Buckham, Hazel *Film 1*
Buckingham, George Villiers, Duke Of 1628-1687
 OxThe
Buckingham, Lillian *Film 1*
Buckingham, Robert *WhoHol A*
Buckler, Hugh 1870-1936 *NotNAT B, WhScrn 2,*
 WhoHol B
Buckler, John 1896-1936 *NotNAT B, WhScrn 2,*
 WhoHol B
Buckley, Annie d1916 *NotNAT B, WhoStg 1908*
Buckley, Charles T d1920 *NotNAT B*
Buckley, F Rauson d1943 *NotNAT B*
Buckley, Floyd 1874-1956 *Film 1, NotNAT B,*
 WhScrn 1, WhScrn 2, WhoHol B
Buckley, Hal *WhoHol A*
Buckley, James 1923- *CelR 3*
Buckley, Joseph 1875-1930 *WhScrn 1, WhScrn 2*
Buckley, May 1880- *WhoStg 1906, WhoStg 1908*
Buckley, William *Film 2*
Buckley, William F, Jr. 1925- *CelR 3*
Buckner, Barbara *WomWMM*
Buckner, Robert H 1906- *FilmgC, IntMPA 1977*
Buckstone, J C 1858-1924 *NotNAT B*
Buckstone, John Baldwin 1802-1879 *NotNAT B,*
 OxThe
Buckstone, Roland 1862-1922 *Film 1*
Buckstone, Rowland 1860-1922 *NotNAT B*
Buckstone, Rowland 1861-1922 *WhoStg 1906,*
 WhoStg 1908
Buckton, Florence *PIP&P*
Bucky, Frida Sarsen *AmSCAP 1966*
Bucquet, Harold S 1891-1946 *FilmgC, WhScrn 1,*

 WhScrn 2
Buczkowski, Leonard 1900-1966 *OxFilm*
Budd, John W 1923- *AmSCAP 1966*
Budka, Harry H 1913- *AmSCAP 1966*
Budka, Mildred Livesay 1912- *AmSCAP 1966*
Bueche, Gregory A 1903- *AmSCAP 1966*
Buehler, Arthur d1962 *NotNAT B*
Buerkle, Russell C 1915- *AmSCAP 1966*
Buero Vallejo, Antonio 1916- *CnMD, CroCD,*
 McGWD, ModWD
Buetel, Jack 1917- *FilmgC*
Bufano, Remo d1948 *NotNAT B*
Buffalo Bill 1846-1917 *OxFilm, OxThe*
Buffalo Bill, Jr. d1961 *TwYS, WhoHol B*
Buffalo Bill, Jr. *see also* Bill, Buffalo, Jr.
Buffington, Don 1907- *AmSCAP 1966*
Buffington, Sam d1960 *WhScrn 2*
Bufman, Zev 1930- *BiE&WWA, WhoThe 16*
Bugatch, Samuel 1898- *AmSCAP 1966*
Bughardt, George *Film 2*
Buhler, Richard 1876-1925 *Film 1, NotNAT B,*
 WhScrn 2, WhoHol B
Buhler, William *Film 1*
Buhrman, Albert John, Jr. 1915- *AmSCAP 1966*
Bujold, Genevieve 1942- *CelR 3, FilmgC,*
 IntMPA 1977, WhoHol A
Buka, Donald 1921- *WhoHol A*
Bulajic, Velko 1928- *DcFM*
Bulandra, Lucia Sturdza 1873-1961 *OxThe*
Bulfinch, Charles 1763-1844 *NotNAT B*
Bulgakov, Barbara *BiE&WWA, NotNAT*
Bulgakov, Leo 1889-1948 *NotNAT B, PIP&P,*
 WhScrn 1, WhScrn 2, WhoHol B
Bulgakov, Michael Afanasyev 1891-1940 *OxThe*
Bulgakov, Mikhail 1891-1940 *CnMD, CnThe,*
 ModWD
Bulgakov, Mikhail Afanasyev 1891-1940
 NotNAT B
Bulgakov, Mikhail Afanasyevich 1891-1940
 McGWD, REnWD
Bulger, Harry d1926 *NotNAT B*
Bulifant, Joyce *WhoHol A*
Bull, Charles Edward *Film 2*
Bull, Ole Borneman 1810-1880 *OxThe*
Bull, Peter 1912- *BiE&WWA, FilmgC, MotPP,*
 NotNAT, NotNAT A, PIP&P, WhoHol A
Bullerjahn, Curt *Film 2*
Bullins, Ed *CroCD*
Bullins, Ed 1934- *NotNAT*
Bullins, Ed 1935- *ConDr 1977, PIP&P A,*
 WhoThe 16
Bullock, Boris *Film 2*
Bullock, Christopher d1724 *NotNAT B, PIP&P*
Bullock, Dick d1971 *WhScrn 2*   •
Bullock, John Malcolm 1867-1938 *NotNAT B*
Bullock, Walter 1907-1953 *AmSCAP 1966*
Buloff, Joseph 1907- *BiE&WWA, NotNAT,*
 WhoHol A, WhoThe 16
Bulwer-Lytton, Edward George E Lytton 1803-1873
 McGWD, NotNAT A, NotNAT B, OxThe,
 PIP&P
Bumbry, Grace 1937- *CelR 3*
Bump, Edmond 1877-1938 *WhScrn 1, WhScrn 2*
Bumpas, Bob 1911-1959 *WhoHol B*
Bumpas, H W Bob 1911-1959 *WhScrn 1,*
 WhScrn 2
Bunce, Alan 1903-1965 *BiE&WWA, WhScrn 1,*
 WhScrn 2, WhoHol B
Bunce, Oliver Bell 1828-1890 *NotNAT B*
Bunch, Boyd 1889- *AmSCAP 1966*
Bundel, Raymond *Film 1*
Bundy, Brooke *WhoHol A*
Bundy, Eve M 1910- *AmSCAP 1966*
Bundy, Frank 1908- *IntMPA 1977*

Bundy, McGeorge 1919- *CelR 3*
Bundy, William 1917- *CelR 3*
Bunke, Ralph *Film 2*
Bunker, Ralph 1889-1966 *WhScrn 1, WhScrn 2, WhoHol B*
Bunn, Alfred 1798-1860 *CnThe, NotNAT B, OxThe*
Bunn, Margaret Agnes Somerville 1799-1883 *OxThe*
Bunnage, Avis *WhoThe 16*
Bunny, George 1870-1952 *Film 2, WhScrn 1, WhScrn 2, WhoHol B*
Bunny, John 1863-1915 *Film 1, FilmgC, MotPP, NotNAT B, TwYS, WhScrn 2, WhoHol B*
Bunston, Herbert 1874-1935 *Film 2, WhScrn 1, WhScrn 2, WhoHol B*
Bunuel, Luis 1900- *BiDFlm, CelR 3, DcFM, FilmgC, IntMPA 1977, MovMk, OxFilm, WorEnF*
Buonarotti, Michelangelo 1568-1642 *McGWD*
Buono, Victor *MotPP, WhoHol A*
Buono, Victor 1938- *FilmgC, MovMk*
Buono, Victor 1939- *IntMPA 1977*
Buontalenti, Bernardo 1536-1608 *OxThe*
Buquor, Robert 1935-1966 *WhScrn 2*
Burani, Michelette 1882-1957 *Film 2, NotNAT B, WhScrn 1, WhScrn 2, WhoHol B*
Burbadge, Cuthbert 1566?-1636 *NotNAT B*
Burbadge, James 1530?-1597 *NotNAT B*
Burbage, Cuthbert 1566?-1636 *OxThe, PIP&P*
Burbage, James 1530?-1597 *OxThe, PIP&P*
Burbage, Richard 1567?-1619 *CnThe, NotNAT A, NotNAT B, OxThe, PIP&P*
Burbank, Goldie 1880-1954 *WhScrn 1, WhScrn 2*
Burbeck, Frank d1930 *NotNAT B*
Burbridge, Edward *WhoThe 16*
Burch, Betty Evans 1888-1956 *WhScrn 1, WhScrn 2*
Burch, Dean 1927- *CelR 3, NewYTET*
Burch, Helen *Film 2*
Burch, John 1896-1969 *WhScrn 1, WhScrn 2, WhoHol B*
Burchardt, Elsa *Film 2*
Burden, Carter 1941- *CelR 3*
Burden, Hugh 1913- *FilmgC, WhoHol A, WhoThe 16*
Burdette, Eugene 1900- *AmSCAP 1966*
Burdette, Jack *Film 2*
Burdette, Winston *NewYTET*
Burdge, Gordon 1906- *AmSCAP 1966*
Burdick, Rose *Film 2*
Burel, Leonce-Henri 1892- *WorEnF*
Burel, Leonce-Henry 1892- *DcFM*
Burg, Eugen *Film 2*
Burge, Stuart 1918- *FilmgC, WhoThe 16*
Burger, Henry 1915- *IntMPA 1977*
Burger, Jack 1925- *AmSCAP 1966*
Burger, Warren E 1907- *CelR 3*
Burgess, Anthony 1917- *CelR 3*
Burgess, Dorothy 1907-1961 *Film 2, ThFT, WhScrn 2, WhoHol B*
Burgess, Hazel 1910-1973 *WhScrn 2*
Burgess, Helen 1918-1937 *WhScrn 1, WhScrn 2, WhoHol B*
Burgess, Neil 1846-1910 *NotNAT B, WhoStg 1908*
Burgess, William 1867-1948 *WhScrn 2*
Burggraf, Waldfried *McGWD*
Burgher, Fairfax 1897-1965 *WhScrn 2*
Burghoff, Gary *WhoHol A*
Burgie, Irving 1924- *AmSCAP 1966*
Burgoyne, John 1722-1792 *NotNAT B, PIP&P*
Burgund, Ann *WomWMM B*
Burian, Emil Frantisek 1904-1959 *OxThe*

Burian, Jarka M 1927- *BiE&WWA, NotNAT*
Burian, Vlasta 1891-1962 *WhScrn 1, WhScrn 2*
Burk, John Daly d1808 *NotNAT B*
Burk, Robert 1908-1940 *AmSCAP 1966*
Burke, Alfred 1918- *FilmgC, IntMPA 1977, WhoThe 16*
Burke, Billie d1970 *MotPP, WhoHol B*
Burke, Billie 1884-1970 *BiE&WWA, OxFilm*
Burke, Billie 1885-1970 *FilmgC, MGM, MovMk, NotNAT A, ThFT, TwYS, Vers B, WhScrn 1, WhScrn 2*
Burke, Billie 1886-1970 *Film 1, Film 2, NotNAT B, WhoStg 1906, WhoStg 1908*
Burke, Charles 1822-1854 *NotNAT B, OxThe*
Burke, David 1934- *WhoThe 16*
Burke, Georgia 1906- *BiE&WWA, NotNAT*
Burke, J Francis 1914- *AmSCAP 1966*
Burke, J Frank 1867-1918 *Film 1, WhScrn 2*
Burke, James d1968 *MotPP, Vers B, WhScrn 1, WhoHol B*
Burke, James 1886-1968 *WhScrn 2*
Burke, James 1898-1968 *FilmgC*
Burke, Joanne *WomWMM*
Burke, Joe *Film 2*
Burke, Johnny 1908-1964 *AmSCAP 1966, BiE&WWA, Film 2, FilmgC, NotNAT B*
Burke, Joseph *Film 1, Film 2*
Burke, Joseph 1884-1942 *WhScrn 2*
Burke, Joseph A 1884-1950 *AmSCAP 1966*
Burke, Kathleen 1913- *ThFT*
Burke, Marie 1894- *FilmgC*
Burke, Marie R *Film 2*
Burke, Michael 1918- *CelR 3*
Burke, Myra d1944 *NotNAT B*
Burke, Patricia 1917- *FilmgC, IntMPA 1977, WhoThe 16*
Burke, Paul 1926- *FilmgC, IntMPA 1977, WhoHol A*
Burke, Thomas F d1941 *WhScrn 1, WhScrn 2*
Burke, Walter *WhoHol A*
Burkhard, Charles d1927 *WhScrn 2*
Burkhard, Leonard A 1911- *AmSCAP 1966*
Burks, J Cooper 1919- *IntMPA 1977*
Burks, Robert 1910-1968 *CmMov, FilmgC, WorEnF*
Burlando, Claude 1918-1938 *WhScrn 1, WhScrn 2*
Burleigh, Bertram *Film 2*
Burleigh, Cecil 1885- *AmSCAP 1966*
Burleigh, Harry T 1886-1949 *AmSCAP 1966*
Burlingame, Lloyd *WhoThe 16*
Burlinson, John J, Jr. 1930- *IntMPA 1977*
Burlo, Josephine *Film 2*
Burmaster, Augusta 1860-1934 *Film 1, WhScrn 2*
Burmeister, Augusta *Film 2*
Burnaby, Anne 1922- *IntMPA 1977*
Burnaby, Dave 1881-1949 *WhScrn 2*
Burnaby, Davy 1881-1949 *Film 2, FilmgC, WhScrn 1, WhoHol B*
Burnaby, G Davy 1881-1949 *NotNAT B*
Burnacini, Giovanni d1656 *OxThe*
Burnacini, Lodovico Ottavio 1636-1707 *NotNAT B, OxThe*
Burnand, Sir Francis Cowley 1836-1917 *NotNAT B, OxThe*
Burne, Nancy 1913-1954 *WhScrn 1, WhScrn 2, WhoHol B*
Burne-Hones, Sir Edward *PIP&P*
Burnell, Buster d1964 *NotNAT B*
Burness, Pete 1910- *FilmgC*
Burness, Peter 1910- *DcFM*
Burnet, Dana d1962 *NotNAT B*
Burnett, Al 1906-1973 *WhScrn 2*
Burnett, Carol 1933- *CelR 3, EncMT,*

WhoHol A, WhoThe 16
Burnett, Carol 1934- *FilmgC*
Burnett, Carol 1935- *BiE&WWA*
Burnett, Carol 1936- *IntMPA 1977*
Burnett, Ernie 1884-1959 *AmSCAP 1966*
Burnett, Frances Hodgson 1849-1924 *NotNAT B,*
PIP&P, WhoStg 1906, WhoStg 1908
Burnett, June 1914- *AmSCAP 1966*
Burnett, W R 1899- *CmMov, FilmgC,*
IntMPA 1977, WorEnF
Burnette, Lester Alvin Smiley 1911-1967 *MovMk*
Burnette, Lester Alvin Smiley 1912-1967 *Vers A*
Burnette, Smiley 1911-1967 *FilmgC, MotPP,*
WhScrn 1, WhScrn 2, WhoHo! B
Burney, Hal 1900-1933 *WhScrn 1, WhScrn 2*
Burnham, Beatrice *Film 2*
Burnham, Charles C d1938 *NotNAT B*
Burnham, Nicholas 1860-1925 *Film 2, WhScrn 2*
Burnim, Kalman A 1928- *NotNAT*
Burns, Allan *see* Brooks, James L And Allan Burns
Burns, Anne K d1968 *NotNAT B*
Burns, Annelu 1889-1942 *AmSCAP 1966*
Burns, Arthur F 1904- *CelR 3*
Burns, Bart *WhoHol A*
Burns, Bob 1893-1956 *FilmgC, WhoHol B*
Burns, Bob Bazooka 1893-1956 *WhScrn 1,*
WhScrn 2
Burns, Bobby *Film 2*
Burns, Carol *WomWMM B*
Burns, Catherine *WhoHol A*
Burns, David 1901-1971 *WhScrn 1, WhScrn 2,*
WhoHol B
Burns, David 1902-1970 *FilmgC*
Burns, David 1902-1971 *BiE&WWA, EncMT,*
NotNAT B
Burns, Dorothy *WhScrn 2*
Burns, Eddie d1957 *WhScrn 2*
Burns, Eddie 1892- *Film 2*
Burns, Edmund 1892- *Film 1, Film 2, TwYS,*
WhoHol A
Burns, Edward 1892- *Film 2*
Burns, Eileen *WhoHol A*
Burns, Fred *Film 1, Film 2*
Burns, Fred d1955 *WhoHol B*
Burns, George 1896- *CelR 3, Film 2, FilmgC,*
IntMPA 1977, MotPP, MovMk, NotNAT A,
WhoHol A
Burns, Harry 1884-1939 *WhScrn 1, WhScrn 2,*
WhoHol B
Burns, Harry 1885-1948 *WhScrn 1, WhScrn 2,*
WhoHol B
Burns, Irving 1914-1968 *WhScrn 1, WhScrn 2,*
WhoHol B
Burns, James d1975 *WhScrn 2, WhoHol C*
Burns, James F 1898-1960 *AmSCAP 1966*
Burns, James MacGregor 1918- *CelR 3*
Burns, Jerry d1962 *NotNAT B*
Burns, Lulu *WhScrn 1, WhScrn 2*
Burns, Mark 1937- *FilmgC*
Burns, Michael *WhoHol A*
Burns, Nat 1887-1962 *NotNAT B, WhScrn 1,*
WhScrn 2, WhoHol B
Burns, Neal 1892-1962 *Film 1, Film 2, TwYS*
Burns, Paul *Film 2*
Burns, Paul E 1881-1967 *WhScrn 1, WhScrn 2*
Burns, Paul E 1889-1967 *Vers B, WhoHol B*
Burns, Ralph 1922- *AmSCAP 1966, BiE&WWA*
Burns, Robert *Film 1, Film 2*
Burns, Robert d1947 *WhScrn 2*
Burns, Robert Bobby *TwYS*
Burns, Robert E 1885-1957 *WhScrn 2, WhoHol B*
Burns, Robert Patrick 1929-1955 *WhScrn 1,*
WhScrn 2
Burns, Ronnie *WhoHol A*

Burns, William John 1861-1932 *WhScrn 2*
Burns And Allen *MotPP*
Burnside, R H 1870-1952 *AmSCAP 1966, EncMT,*
NotNAT B
Burnside, William W, Jr. d1976 *WhoHol C*
Burnup, Peter d1964 *NotNAT B*
Burr, Courtney d1961 *NotNAT B*
Burr, Donald 1907- *BiE&WWA, NotNAT*
Burr, Edmund d1975 *WhoHol C*
Burr, Eugene d1940 *Film 2, WhScrn 2*
Burr, Raymond 1917- *BiDFlm, CelR 3, FilmgC,*
IntMPA 1977, MotPP, MovMk, NewYTET,
WhoHol A, WorEnF
Burr, Robert *WhoThe 16*
Burrell, George *Film 1, Film 2*
Burrell, Kenny 1931- *AmSCAP 1966*
Burrell, Sheila 1922- *WhoThe 16*
Burrell-Davis, D 1918- *IntMPA 1977*
Burress, William *Film 1*
Burrill, Chris *WomWMM A, WomWMM B*
Burrill, Timothy 1931- *IntMPA 1977*
Burris-Meyer, Harold 1902- *BiE&WWA,*
NotNAT
Burrough, Tom 1869-1929 *WhScrn 2*
Burroughs, Bob 1937- *AmSCAP 1966*
Burroughs, Edgar Rice 1875-1950 *FilmgC*
Burroughs, Eric d1960 *WhScrn 1, WhScrn 2,*
WhoHol B
Burroughs, James *Film 2*
Burroughs, Marie 1866- *WhoStg 1906,*
WhoStg 1908
Burroughs, Robert C 1923- *BiE&WWA, NotNAT*
Burroughs, William 1914- *CelR 3*
Burrowes, James d1926 *NotNAT B*
Burrows, Abe 1910- *AmSCAP 1966, BiE&WWA,*
CelR 3, ConDr 1977, EncMT, FilmgC,
ModWD, NewMT, NotNAT, WhoThe 16
Burrows, John 1945- *ConDr 1977*
Burrows, John H 1924- *IntMPA 1977*
Burrud, Bill 1924- *NewYTET*
Burrud, Bill 1925- *IntMPA 1977, WhoHol A*
Burry, Solen d1953 *NotNAT B*
Burstyn, Ellen 1932- *IntMPA 1977, MovMk,*
WhoHol A, WomWMM
Burstyn, Neil *WhoHol A*
Burt, Benjamin Hapgood 1882-1950
AmSCAP 1966
Burt, Frank A d1964 *NotNAT A, NotNAT B*
Burt, Frederic 1876-1943 *WhScrn 1, WhScrn 2*
Burt, Frederick 1876-1943 *NotNAT B,*
WhoHol B
Burt, Harriet 1885-1935 *NotNAT B,*
WhoStg 1908
Burt, Laura 1872-1952 *NotNAT B, WhScrn 2*
Burt, Laura 1882- *WhoStg 1906, WhoStg 1908*
Burt, Margaret *Film 2*
Burt, Nellie *Film 1*
Burt, William P 1873-1955 *Film 2, NotNAT B,*
WhScrn 1, WhScrn 2, WhoHol B
Burte, Hermann 1879-1960 *ModWD*
Burtis, James 1893-1939 *WhScrn 2*
Burtnett, Earl 1896-1936 *AmSCAP 1966*
Burton, Bernard *IntMPA 1977*
Burton, Charlotte 1882-1942 *Film 1, MotPP,*
WhScrn 1, WhScrn 2, WhoHol B
Burton, Clarence 1882-1933 *Film 1, Film 2,*
TwYS, WhScrn 1, WhScrn 2, WhoHol B
Burton, Edward J 1926- *NatPD*
Burton, Eldin 1913- *AmSCAP 1966*
Burton, Ethel *Film 1*
Burton, Frances *WomWMM B*
Burton, Frederick 1871-1957 *Film 1, Film 2,*
WhScrn 1, WhScrn 2
Burton, George H 1900-1955 *WhScrn 1,*

WhScrn 2, WhoHol B
Burton, John Film 1
Burton, Julian WhoHol A
Burton, Langhorne 1872-1949 Film 1, Film 2,
  NotNAT B
Burton, Margaret WhoHol A
Burton, Margaret 1924- IntMPA 1977
Burton, Nat 1901-1945 AmSCAP 1966
Burton, Ned 1850?-1922 Film 2, WhScrn 1,
  WhScrn 2, WhoHol B
Burton, Percy 1878-1948 NotNAT A, NotNAT B
Burton, Philip 1904- BiE&WWA, NotNAT,
  NotNAT A
Burton, Richard 1925- BiDFlm, BiE&WWA,
  CelR 3, CmMov, CnThe, EncMT, FilmgC,
  IntMPA 1977, MotPP, MovMk, NotNAT,
  NotNAT A, OxFilm, WhoHol A,
  WhoThe 16, WorEnF
Burton, Robert d1955 NotNAT B
Burton, Robert d1962 WhoHol B
Burton, Robert 1895-1964 WhScrn 2
Burton, Val 1899- AmSCAP 1966
Burton, William Evans 1804-1860 FamA&A,
  NotNAT A, NotNAT B, OxThe
Burton, William H Film 1
Burton, William H 1845-1926 NotNAT B,
  WhScrn 1, WhScrn 2, WhoHol B
Burtwell, Frederick d1948 NotNAT B
Burwell, Clifford R 1898- AmSCAP 1966
Bury, John 1925- CnThe, NotNAT, WhoThe 16
Busby, Amy 1872-1957 NotNAT B, WhScrn 2
Buscaglione, Fred 1921-1960 WhScrn 1,
  WhScrn 2
Busch, August, Jr. 1899- CelR 3
Busch, Mae d1946 MotPP
Busch, Mae 1891-1946 WhScrn 1, WhScrn 2,
  WhoHol B
Busch, Mae 1895-1944 TwYS
Busch, Mae 1895-1946 ThFT
Busch, Mae 1897-1946 Film 1, Film 2, FilmgC,
  MovMk
Busch, Mae 1902-1946 NotNAT B
Busch, Niven 1903- CmMov, FilmgC,
  IntMPA 1977, WorEnF
Busey, Bernice Bland 1918- AmSCAP 1966
Bush, Anita d1974 NotNAT B, WhScrn 2
Bush, Billy Green WhoHol A
Bush, Frances Cleveland d1967 WhoHol B
Bush, Frank d1927 NotNAT B
Bush, George 1858-1937 WhScrn 1, WhScrn 2,
  WhoHol B
Bush, George 1924- CelR 3
Bush, Grace E 1884- AmSCAP 1966
Bush, Kenneth R Film 2
Bush, Louis F 1910- AmSCAP 1966
Bush, Pauline 1886-1969 Film 1, Film 2, MotPP,
  WhScrn 2
Bush, Renee Film 2
Bush, Vannevar 1890- CelR 3
Bush-Fekete, Ladislas 1898- CnMD
Bush-Fekete, Leslie 1896- BiE&WWA
Bushell, Anthony 1904- Film 2, FilmgC,
  WhoHol A
Bushkin, Joseph 1916- AmSCAP 1966
Bushman, Francis X 1883-1966 Film 2, FilmgC,
  MotPP, MovMk, OxFilm, TwYS, WhScrn 1,
  WhScrn 2, WhoHol B
Bushman, Francis X 1885-1966 Film 1
Bushman, Francis X, Jr. 1903- Film 2, TwYS
Bushman, Ralph E Film 2
Buskirk, Bessie Film 1
Busley, Jessie 1869-1950 NotNAT B, WhScrn 1,
  WhScrn 2, WhoHol B
Busnach, William d1907 NotNAT B

Busquets, Joaquin 1875-1942 WhScrn 1,
  WhScrn 2
Busse, Henry 1894-1955 AmSCAP 1966
Bussey, Hank 1891-1971 WhScrn 1, WhScrn 2
Bussi, Solange WomWMM
Bussieres, Raymond 1907- FilmgC
Buster, Budd 1891-1965 WhScrn 2, WhoHol B
Butcher, Dwight 1911- AmSCAP 1966
Butcher, Ernest 1885-1965 FilmgC, WhScrn 1,
  WhScrn 2, WhoHol B
Bute, Mary Ellen WomWMM
Buti, Carlo 1902-1963 NotNAT B, WhScrn 1,
  WhScrn 2
Butkus, Dick 1942- CelR 3
Butland, William Film 2
Butler, Alice Augarde 1868-1919 NotNAT B,
  WhoStg 1908
Butler, Charles d1920 NotNAT B, WhoHol B
Butler, David 1894- BiDFlm, CmMov, Film 1,
  Film 2, FilmgC, IntMPA 1977, MovMk,
  TwYS, WhoHol A, WorEnF
Butler, David 1895- TwYS A
Butler, Daws 1916- IntMPA 1977
Butler, Eddie 1888-1944 WhScrn 1, WhScrn 2
Butler, Frank 1890-1967 Film 2, FilmgC,
  WhScrn 1, WhScrn 2, WhoHol B
Butler, Frank R Film 2
Butler, Fred J Film 1, Film 2, TwYS
Butler, Fred J 1867- WhoStg 1908
Butler, George Film 2
Butler, Hugo 1914-1968 WorEnF
Butler, Jack 1924- AmSCAP 1966
Butler, James 1921-1945 WhScrn 1, WhScrn 2
Butler, James H 1908- BiE&WWA, NotNAT
Butler, Jimmie d1945 WhoHol B
Butler, John 1920- BiE&WWA
Butler, John A 1884-1967 WhScrn 2, WhoHol B
Butler, Louise d1958 WhScrn 1, WhScrn 2
Butler, Michael 1926- CelR 3
Butler, Rachel Barton d1920 NotNAT B
Butler, Richard William 1844-1928 NotNAT B
Butler, Roy d1973 WhoHol B
Butler, Royal 1895-1973 WhScrn 2
Butler, Samuel d1945 NotNAT B
Butler, William J Daddy 1860-1927 Film 1,
  WhScrn 1, WhScrn 2, WhoHol B
Butlin, Jan 1940- WhoThe 16
Butova PIP&P
Butt, Alfred 1878-1962 EncMT
Butt, Johnny Film 2
Butt, Lawson Film 2
Butt, Thelma AmSCAP 1966
Butt, W Lawson Film 1
Butterfield, Elizabeth IntMPA 1977
Butterfield, Everett d1925 NotNAT B
Butterfield, Herb 1896-1957 WhoHol B
Butterfield, Herbert 1896-1957 WhScrn 1,
  WhScrn 2
Butterworth, Charles d1946 MotPP, WhoHol B
Butterworth, Charles 1896-1946 FilmgC,
  NotNAT B, WhScrn 1, WhScrn 2
Butterworth, Charles 1897-1946 Film 2, MovMk,
  Vers A
Butterworth, Donna 1956- FilmgC
Butterworth, Ernest Film 2
Butterworth, F Film 1
Butterworth, Joe Film 2
Butterworth, Peter 1923?- FilmgC
Butterworth, Walter T 1893-1962 NotNAT B,
  WhScrn 1, WhScrn 2, WhoHol B
Butti, Enrico Annibale 1868-1912 McGWD
Buttolph, David 1902- AmSCAP 1966, CmMov,
  IntMPA 1977
Button, Dick 1929- BiE&WWA, CelR 3,

WhoHol A
Buttons, Red *MotPP, NewYTET, WhoHol A*
Buttons, Red 1918- *FilmgC*
Buttons, Red 1919- *AmSCAP 1966,*
  IntMPA 1977, MovMk
Buttram, Pat *NewYTET, WhoHol A*
Butts, Billy *Film 2*
Butts, R Dale 1910- *AmSCAP 1966,*
  IntMPA 1977
Butumkin, Gregory *Film 2*
Buxbaum, James M *IntMPA 1977*
Buxton, Frank *NewYTET*
Buys, Peter 1881-1964 *AmSCAP 1966*
Buysse, Cyriel 1859-1932 *ModWD*
Buyukas, George 1898- *AmSCAP 1966*
Buzario, Antonio *OxThe*
Buzo, Alexander 1944- *ConDr 1977, WhoThe 16*
Buzzati, Dino 1906-1972 *CnMD, CroCD*
Buzzatti, Dino 1907- *CnThe*
Buzzell, Eddie 1897- *Film 2, WhoHol A*
Buzzell, Edward 1897- *FilmgC, MovMk*
Buzzell, Edward 1900- *AmSCAP 1966*
Buzzell, Edward 1907- *IntMPA 1977*
Buzzi, Pietro d1921 *WhScrn 1, WhScrn 2*
Buzzi, Ruth 1936- *CelR 3*
Buzzi-Peccia, Arturo 1854-1943 *AmSCAP 1966*
Byer, Charles *Film 2*
Byerley, Vivienne *WhoThe 16*
Byford, Roy 1873-1939 *Film 2, NotNAT B,*
  WhScrn 1, WhScrn 2, WhoHol B
Bygraves, Max 1922- *FilmgC, IntMPA 1977,*
  WhoHol A
Byington, Spring 1893-1971 *BiE&WWA, FilmgC,*
  MGM, MotPP, MovMk, NewYTET, ThFT,
  WhScrn 1, WhScrn 2, WhoHol B
Byington, Spring 1898-1971 *Vers A*
Byles, Bobby 1931-1969 *WhScrn 1, WhScrn 2,*
  WhoHol B
Byng, Douglas 1893- *EncMT, WhoThe 16*
Bynner, Witter 1881-1968 *NotNAT B*
Byram, John 1901- *BiE&WWA, NotNAT*
Byram, Marian 1904- *BiE&WWA, NotNAT*
Byram, Ronald d1919 *Film 1, WhScrn 2*
Byrd, Caruth C 1942- *IntMPA 1977*
Byrd, Harry F, Jr. 1914- *CelR 3*
Byrd, John *IntMPA 1977*
Byrd, Ralph 1909-1952 *FilmgC, WhScrn 1,*
  WhScrn 2, WhoHol B
Byrd, Sam 1908-1955 *NotNAT B*
Byrens, Myer 1840-1933 *WhScrn 1, WhScrn 2*
Byrne, Betsy *Film 2*
Byrne, Bridget *WomWMM*
Byrne, Eddie 1911- *FilmgC, IntMPA 1977,*
  WhoHol A
Byrne, Francis M 1875-1923 *NotNAT B,*
  WhoStg 1908
Byrne, James A d1927 *NotNAT B*
Byrne, Patsy 1933- *WhoThe 16*
Byrne, Peter 1928- *WhoThe 16*
Byrne, Rosalind *Film 2*
Byrnes, Edd 1933- *FilmgC, WhoHol A*
Byrnes, Edward 1933- *IntMPA 1977, MotPP*
Byrnes, Nancy Rosenbluth 1915-1962 *WhScrn 1,*
  WhScrn 2
Byroade, George 1883-1975 *WhScrn 2*
Byron, Al 1932- *AmSCAP 1966*
Byron, Arthur William 1872-1943 *NotNAT B,*
  PIP&P, WhScrn 1, WhScrn 2, WhoHol B,
  WhoStg 1906, WhoStg 1908
Byron, Charles Anthony 1919- *IntMPA 1977*
Byron, Eva *Film 2*
Byron, Lord George Gordon 1788-1824 *CnThe,*
  McGWD, NotNAT B, OxThe, REnWD
Byron, Henrietta d1924 *NotNAT B*

Byron, Henry James 1834-1884 *NotNAT B,*
  OxThe, PIP&P
Byron, Jack *Film 2*
Byron, Jean *WhoHol A*
Byron, Kate d1920 *NotNAT B*
Byron, Kathleen 1922- *FilmgC, IntMPA 1977,*
  WhoHol A
Byron, Katy 1918-1970 *WhScrn 2*
Byron, Marion 1910- *ThFT*
Byron, Marion 1911- *Film 2*
Byron, Oliver Doud 1842-1920 *NotNAT B,*
  WhoStg 1906, WhoStg 1908
Byron, Paul 1891-1959 *WhScrn 1, WhScrn 2,*
  WhoHol B
Byron, Peanut *Film 2*
Byron, Richard 1908- *AmSCAP 1966*
Byron, Roy d1943 *Film 2, WhoHol B*
Byron, Royal James 1887-1943 *WhScrn 1,*
  WhScrn 2
Byron, Walter 1901-1972 *Film 2, FilmgC,*
  WhoHol B
Byron, Ward 1910- *IntMPA 1977*
Byrum, John 1947- *IntMPA 1977*
Bystrom, Walter E 1894-1969 *WhScrn 1,*
  WhScrn 2
Bytell, Walter *Film 1*

C

Caan, James *WhoHol A*
Caan, James 1938- *FilmgC*
Caan, James 1939- *IntMPA 1977, MovMk*
Caan, James 1940- *CelR 3*
Cabal, Robert *WhoHol A*
Cabanne, Christy William 1888-1950 *DcFM, FilmgC, WhoHol B*
Cabanne, William Christy 1888-1950 *TwYS A, WhScrn 1, WhScrn 2*
Cabbane, Christy W 1888-1950 *Film 1*
Cabo, Louise *Film 2*
Cabot, Bruce 1904-1972 *FilmgC, HolP 30, MotPP, WhScrn 2, WhoHol B*
Cabot, Bruce 1905-1972 *MovMk*
Cabot, Eliot 1899-1938 *NotNAT B, WhThe*
Cabot, Elliott *Film 2*
Cabot, Sebastian 1918- *CelR 3, FilmgC, MotPP, MovMk, WhoHol A*
Cabot, Susan 1927- *FilmgC, WhoHol A*
Cacavas, John 1930- *AmSCAP 1966*
Cacoyannis, Michael 1922- *BiDFlm, CelR 3, DcFM, FilmgC, IntMPA 1977, MovMk, NotNAT, OxFilm, WorEnF*
Caddigan, Jack J 1879-1952 *AmSCAP 1966*
Cade, Rose *Film 2*
Cadell, Jean 1884-1967 *Film 2, FilmgC, IntMPA 1977, PIP&P, WhScrn 1, WhScrn 2, WhThe, WhoHol B*
Cadman, Charles Wakefield 1881-1946 *AmSCAP 1966*
Cadman, Ethel 1886- *WhThe*
Cadmus, Paul 1904- *CelR 3*
Cady, Frank *WhoHol A*
Caecilius Statius 219?BC-168BC *CnThe, OxThe, REnWD*
Caen, Herb 1916- *CelR 3*
Caesar, Irving 1895- *AmSCAP 1966, BiE&WWA, EncMT, IntMPA 1977, NewMT, NotNAT, WhoThe 16*
Caesar, Sid 1922- *AmSCAP 1966, BiE&WWA, CelR 3, EncMT, FilmgC, IntMPA 1977, MovMk, NewYTET, WhoHol A, WhoThe 16*
Cagan, Sermet 1929- *CnThe, REnWD*
Cage, John 1912- *AmSCAP 1966, CelR 3, ConDr 1977E*
Cage, Ruth 1923- *BiE&WWA, NotNAT*
Cagney, James *MotPP, PIP&P*
Cagney, James 1899- *FilmgC, WhoHol A, WorEnF*
Cagney, James 1904- *BiDFlm, BiE&WWA, CelR 3, CmMov, Film 2, IntMPA 1977, MovMk, OxFilm*
Cagney, Jeanne 1919- *BiE&WWA, FilmgC, IntMPA 1977, MotPP, NotNAT, WhThe, WhoHol A*

Cagney, William J 1902- *FilmgC, IntMPA 1977*
Cahill, Frank E, III 1932- *IntMPA 1977*
Cahill, Frank E, Jr. *IntMPA 1977*
Cahill, Lilly 1886-1955 *WhScrn 1, WhScrn 2*
Cahill, Lily 1886-1955 *Film 1, NotNAT B, WhThe, WhoHol B*
Cahill, Marie d1933 *WhThe, WhoHol B, WhoStg 1906, WhoStg 1908*
Cahill, Marie 1870-1933 *EncMT, NotNAT B*
Cahill, Marie 1871-1933 *Film 1*
Cahill, Marie 1874-1933 *WhScrn 1, WhScrn 2*
Cahill, Thomas M 1889-1953 *WhScrn 1, WhScrn 2*
Cahlman, Robert 1924- *BiE&WWA, NotNAT*
Cahn, Dana d1973 *WhoHol B*
Cahn, Edward L 1899-1963 *FilmgC*
Cahn, Julius d1921 *NotNAT B*
Cahn, Sammy 1913- *AmSCAP 1966, CelR 3, EncMT, FilmgC, IntMPA 1977, NewMT, NotNAT, NotNAT A, WhoThe 16*
Cahoon, Millian Benedict 1860-1951 *WhScrn 1, WhScrn 2*
Caiani, Joe 1929- *AmSCAP 1966*
Cail, Harold L d1968 *NotNAT B*
Caillavet, Gaston Arman De 1869-1915 *McGWD, NotNAT B*
Cailliet, Lucien 1897- *AmSCAP 1966*
Caillou, Alan *WhoHol A*
Cain, Andrew *OxThe*
Cain, Henri 1857- *WhThe*
Cain, James M 1892- *BiE&WWA, CelR 3, FilmgC, NotNAT*
Cain, Noble 1896- *AmSCAP 1966*
Cain, Patrick J d1949 *NotNAT B*
Cain, Robert 1887-1954 *Film 1, Film 2, MotPP, NotNAT B, WhScrn 1, WhScrn 2, WhoHol B*
Cain, Sugar *IntMPA 1977, WomWMM B*
Caine, Derwent Hall 1892- *Film 1, WhThe*
Caine, Georgia 1876-1964 *NotNAT B, WhScrn 1, WhScrn 2, WhoHol B*
Caine, Sir Hall 1853-1931 *NotNAT B, WhThe, WhoStg 1908*
Caine, Henry 1888-1962 *WhThe*
Caine, Howard *WhoHol A*
Caine, Lily Hall d1914 *WhThe*
Caine, Michael 1933- *BiDFlm, CelR 3, CmMov, FilmgC, IntMPA 1977, MotPP, MovMk, OxFilm, WhoHol A, WorEnF*
Caiola, Al 1920- *AmSCAP 1966*
Cairnes, Sally 1920-1965 *WhScrn 1, WhScrn 2*
Cairns, Angus d1975 *WhoHol C*
Cairns, Dallas *Film 2*
Caits, Joe 1889-1957 *WhoHol B*
Caits, Joseph 1889-1957 *WhScrn 1, WhScrn 2*
Cajati, Mario 1902- *AmSCAP 1966*

Calabrese, Anthony 1938- *NatPD*
Calabresi, Oreste 1857- *WhThe*
Calabro, Louis 1926- *AmSCAP 1966*
Calagni, Ann Curtis *WomWMM B*
Calamai, Clara 1915- *OxFilm*
Calamity Jane 1852?-1903 *OxFilm*
Caldara, Orme d1925 *Film 1, NotNAT B, WhoHol B*
Calder, Alexander 1898- *CelR 3*
Calder, King 1900-1964 *NotNAT B, WhScrn 1, WhScrn 2, WhoHol B*
Calder-Marshall, Anna 1947- *WhoThe 16*
Calder-Marshall, Anna 1949- *FilmgC*
Calderisi, David 1940- *WhoThe 16*
Calderon, George 1868- *WhThe*
Calderon, Ian 1948- *NotNAT*
Calderon DeLaBarca, Pedro 1600-1681 *CnThe, McGWD, NotNAT B, OxThe, REnWD*
Caldicot, Richard 1908- *WhoThe 16*
Caldwell, Anne 1867-1936 *AmSCAP 1966, EncMT, NewMT, NotNAT B, WhThe*
Caldwell, Betty *Film 2*
Caldwell, Erskine 1903- *CelR 3, FilmgC, PIP&P*
Caldwell, Henry d1961 *NotNAT B*
Caldwell, Jack d1944 *WhScrn 2*
Caldwell, Marianne d1933 *WhThe*
Caldwell, Mary Elizabeth 1909- *AmSCAP 1966*
Caldwell, Minna d1969 *WhoHol B*
Caldwell, Orville 1896-1967 *BiE&WWA, Film 1, Film 2, TwYS, WhScrn 1, WhScrn 2, WhoHol B*
Caldwell, Taylor 1900- *CelR 3*
Caldwell, Virginia *Film 1*
Caldwell, Zoe *PIP&P, PIP&P A*
Caldwell, Zoe 1933- *CelR 3, NotNAT*
Caldwell, Zoe 1934- *WhoThe 16*
Cale, Johnny 1909- *AmSCAP 1966*
Calhern, Louis 1895-1956 *BiDFlm, FamA&A, Film 2, FilmgC, MGM, MotPP, MovMk, NotNAT B, OxFilm, PIP&P, Vers A, WhScrn 1, WhScrn 2, WhThe, WhoHol B*
Calhoun, Barbara *WomWMM B*
Calhoun, Alice 1903-1966 *Film 1, Film 2, TwYS*
Calhoun, Alice 1904-1966 *WhScrn 1, WhScrn 2, WhoHol B*
Calhoun, Eleanor d1957 *NotNAT B*
Calhoun, Jeanne *Film 2*
Calhoun, Kathleen *Film 2*
Calhoun, Pat *Film 2*
Calhoun, Robert 1930- *BiE&WWA, NotNAT*
Calhoun, Rory *MotPP*
Calhoun, Rory 1922- *FilmgC, MovMk, WhoHol A*
Calhoun, Rory 1923- *IntMPA 1977*
Caligan, Woodrow W 1913- *AmSCAP 1966*
Calisher, Hortense 1911- *CelR 3*
Calker, Darrell W 1905-1964 *AmSCAP 1966*
Call, Charles W *IntMPA 1977*
Call, John 1907-1973 *WhScrn 2, WhoHol B*
Callaci, Gloria *WomWMM B*
Callahan, Andrew J *Film 2*
Callahan, Billy 1911-1964 *NotNAT B, WhScrn 1, WhScrn 2*
Callahan, Bobby d1938 *WhoHol B*
Callahan, Charles S 1891-1964 *WhScrn 1, WhScrn 2*
Callahan, Chuck d1964 *WhoHol B*
Callahan, J Will 1874-1946 *AmSCAP 1966*
Callahan, James *WhoHol A*
Callahan, Joseph *Film 1*
Callahan, Marie J *AmSCAP 1966*
Callahan, Robert 1896-1938 *WhScrn 1, WhScrn 2*
Callam, D *Film 1*

Callan, Michael 1935- *FilmgC, IntMPA 1977, MotPP, WhoHol A*
Callas, Charlie *WhoHol A*
Callas, Maria 1923- *CelR 3, WhoHol A*
Callaway, Paul 1909- *BiE&WWA, NotNAT*
Calleia, Joseph 1897-1975 *BiE&WWA, FilmgC, MovMk, WhScrn 2, WhThe, WhoHol C*
Calleia, Joseph 1898- *Vers A*
Callender, George 1918- *AmSCAP 1966*
Calley, John 1930- *IntMPA 1977*
Calliga, George *Film 2*
Calligan, Edward O d1962 *NotNAT B*
Callinicos, Constantine 1913- *AmSCAP 1966*
Callipides *OxThe*
Callis, Clifford *Film 1*
Callis, David 1888-1934 *Film 2, WhScrn 1, WhScrn 2, WhoHol B*
Callot, Jacques 1592-1635 *NotNAT B*
Callow, Everett C *IntMPA 1977*
Calloway, Cab 1907- *AmSCAP 1966, CelR 3, FilmgC, WhoHol A, WhoThe 16*
Calloway, Cab 1908- *MovMk*
Calmettes, Andre 1861-1942 *DcFM*
Calmo, Andrea 1509?-1561? *OxThe*
Calmour, Alfred C *WhThe*
Calthorp, Donald 1888-1940 *Film 1*
Calthrop, David d1940 *WhoHol B*
Calthrop, Dion Clayton 1878-1937 *NotNAT B, WhThe*
Calthrop, Donald 1888-1940 *Film 2, FilmgC, NotNAT B, WhScrn 1, WhScrn 2, WhThe*
Calthrop, Gladys E *WhThe*
Calve, Emma 1864- *WhoStg 1906, WhoStg 1908*
Calvert, Adelaide Helen 1837-1921 *NotNAT A, NotNAT B, OxThe*
Calvert, Catherine d1971 *Film 1, Film 2, MotPP, TwYS, WhoHol B*
Calvert, Catherine 1890-1971 *WhThe*
Calvert, Catherine 1891-1971 *WhScrn 1, WhScrn 2*
Calvert, Cecil G 1871- *WhThe*
Calvert, Charles 1828-1879 *NotNAT B, OxThe*
Calvert, Mrs. Charles 1837-1921 *Film 1, WhThe*
Calvert, E H 1873-1941 *WhoHol B*
Calvert, E H 1890- *Film 1, Film 2, TwYS*
Calvert, Elisha H 1873-1941 *WhScrn 1, WhScrn 2*
Calvert, Louis 1859-1923 *Film 1, NotNAT B, OxThe, WhScrn 2, WhThe*
Calvert, Patricia 1908- *WhThe*
Calvert, Phyllis *MotPP*
Calvert, Phyllis 1915- *CmMov, FilmgC, MovMk, OxFilm, WhoHol A, WhoThe 16*
Calvert, Phyllis 1917- *IntMPA 1977*
Calvet, Corinne *IntMPA 1977, MotPP*
Calvet, Corinne 1925- *FilmgC, WhoHol A*
Calvet, Corinne 1926- *MovMk*
Calvin, Henry 1918-1975 *WhScrn 2, WhoHol C*
Calvo Sotelo, Joaquin 1905- *CroCD, McGWD, ModWD*
Calzabigi, Ranieri Da 1714-1795 *OxThe*
Camarata, Salvador 1913- *AmSCAP 1966*
Camargo, Marie Anne DeCupis De 1710-1770 *NotNAT B*
Cambern, May Hogan *AmSCAP 1966*
Cambridge, Godfrey *MotPP, WhoHol A*
Cambridge, Godfrey 1929- *OxFilm*
Cambridge, Godfrey 1933- *CelR 3, FilmgC, IntMPA 1977, MovMk, NotNAT*
Camden, Dorothea *Film 1*
Camelia, Muriel 1913-1925 *WhScrn 1, WhScrn 2, WhoHol B*
Camere, Manuel *Film 2*
Camerini, Mario 1895- *DcFM, FilmgC, OxFilm,*

WorEnF
Cameron, Alan 1900- *AmSCAP 1966*
Cameron, Beatrice 1868-1940 *NotNAT B, OxThe*
Cameron, Bruce 1910-1959 *WhScrn 1, WhScrn 2*
Cameron, Donald 1889-1955 *Film 1, MotPP,*
	NotNAT B, WhScrn 1, WhScrn 2, WhThe,
	WhoHol B
Cameron, Earl 1925- *FilmgC*
Cameron, Gene d1928 *Film 2, WhScrn 1,*
	WhScrn 2, WhoHol B
Cameron, Hugh 1879-1941 *Film 2, NotNAT B,*
	WhScrn 2, WhoHol B
Cameron, Jack *Film 2*
Cameron, Kathryn d1954 *NotNAT B*
Cameron, Kenneth Neill 1908- *NatPD*
Cameron, Rod *MotPP*
Cameron, Rod 1910- *FilmgC*
Cameron, Rod 1912- *CmMov, HolP 40,*
	IntMPA 1977, WhoHol A
Cameron, Rudolph 1894-1958 *Film 1, Film 2,*
	WhScrn 2
Cameron, Violet 1862-1919 *WhThe*
Camillo, Marvin Felix *PIP&P A*
Caminelli, Antonio 1436-1502 *OxThe*
Camoes, Luis De *OxThe, REnWD*
Camp, Hamilton *WhoHol A*
Camp, Shep 1882-1929 *WhoHol B*
Camp, Sheppard 1882-1929 *WhScrn 1, WhScrn 2*
Campanari, Giuseppe *Film 1*
Campanella, Frank *WhoHol A*
Campanella, Joseph 1927- *BiE&WWA, FilmgC,*
	NotNAT, WhoHol A
Campanella, Roy 1921- *CelR 3*
Campanini, Cleofonte d1919 *NotNAT B*
Campbell, Alan 1905-1963 *WhScrn 1, WhScrn 2*
Campbell, Bartley 1843-1888 *NotNAT B, OxThe*
Campbell, Beatrice 1923- *FilmgC, WhoHol A*
Campbell, Betty *Film 2*
Campbell, Charles d1964 *NotNAT B*
Campbell, Colin d1966 *Film 1, Film 2,*
	WhoHol B
Campbell, Colin 1883-1966 *WhScrn 1, WhScrn 2*
Campbell, Colin 1888-1966 *TwYS A*
Campbell, Daisy *Film 2*
Campbell, Douglas 1922- *BiE&WWA, CnThe,*
	NotNAT, WhoThe 16
Campbell, Eric d1917 *TwYS, WhoHol B*
Campbell, Eric 1870-1917 *Film 1*
Campbell, Eric 1878-1917 *FilmgC*
Campbell, Eric 1879-1917 *WhScrn 2*
Campbell, Eva *Film 1*
Campbell, Frances d1948 *NotNAT B*
Campbell, Frank 1847-1934 *WhScrn 1, WhScrn 2,*
	WhoHol B
Campbell, Glen *IntMPA 1977, WhoHol A*
Campbell, Glen 1935- *FilmgC*
Campbell, Glen 1938- *CelR 3*
Campbell, Henry C 1926- *AmSCAP 1966*
Campbell, Herbert 1844-1904 *NotNAT B, OxThe,*
	PIP&P
Campbell, Jim *WhoHol A*
Campbell, Judy 1916- *FilmgC, WhoHol A,*
	WhoThe 16
Campbell, Lily Bess 1883- *BiE&WWA*
Campbell, Louise *WhoHol A*
Campbell, Margaret 1873-1939 *Film 2, WhScrn 1,*
	WhScrn 2
Campbell, Margaret 1894- *WhThe*
Campbell, Norman *NewYTET*
Campbell, Mrs. Patrick 1865-1940 *CnThe,*
	FamA&A, FilmgC, NotNAT A, NotNAT B,
	OxFilm, OxThe, PIP&P, ThFT, WhScrn 1,
	WhScrn 2, WhThe, WhoHol B
Campbell, Mrs. Patrick 1867-1940 *WhoStg 1906,*

WhoStg 1908
Campbell, Mrs. Patrick 1886-1940 *WhThe*
Campbell, Patrick 1907- *FilmgC*
Campbell, Patton 1926- *BiE&WWA, NotNAT,*
	WhoThe 16
Campbell, Robert Maurice 1922- *IntMPA 1977*
Campbell, Shawn *WhoHol A*
Campbell, Violet d1970 *WhoHol B*
Campbell, Violet 1892-1970 *WhThe*
Campbell, Violet 1893-1970 *WhScrn 1, WhScrn 2*
Campbell, Webster 1893-1972 *Film 1, Film 2,*
	WhScrn 2, WhoHol B
Campbell, William 1926- *FilmgC, IntMPA 1977,*
	MotPP, WhoHol A
Campbell-Watson, Frank 1898- *AmSCAP 1966*
Campeau, Frank 1864-1943 *Film 1, Film 2,*
	NotNAT B, TwYS, WhScrn 1, WhScrn 2,
	WhoHol B
Campeau, George *WhoHol A*
Campen, Jacob Van *OxThe*
Campion, Cyril 1894-1961 *WhThe*
Campion, Thomas 1567-1620 *OxThe*
Campistron, Jean Galbert De 1656-1723 *CnThe,*
	OxThe, REnWD
Camplin, R S *IntMPA 1977*
Campos, Rafael *WhoHol A*
Campos, Victor *WhoHol A*
Campton, David 1924- *ConDr 1977, CroCD,*
	McGWD
Camus, Albert 1913-1960 *CnMD, CnThe, CroCD,*
	McGWD, ModWD, NotNAT A, NotNAT B,
	OxThe, REnWD
Camus, Marcel 1912- *DcFM, FilmgC, OxFilm,*
	WorEnF
Canaday, John 1907- *CelR 3*
Canale, Gianna Maria 1927- *FilmgC,*
	IntMPA 1977, WhoHol A
Canary, David *WhoHol A*
Canby, Vincent 1924- *IntMPA 1977*
Cancelmo, Joe 1897- *AmSCAP 1966*
Candler, Peter 1926- *BiE&WWA, NotNAT*
Candlyn, T Frederick H 1892-1964 *AmSCAP 1966*
Cane, Andrew *OxThe*
Cane, Charles 1899-1973 *WhScrn 2, WhoHol B*
Canetti, Elias 1905- *CnMD, CroCD*
Canfield, Alyce *IntMPA 1977*
Canfield, Cass 1897- *BiE&WWA*
Canfield, Curtis 1903- *BiE&WWA, NotNAT*
Canfield, Mary Grace *WhoHol A*
Canfield, William F d1925 *NotNAT B,*
	WhScrn 2
Canham, Erwin D 1904- *CelR 3*
Caniff, Milton 1907- *CelR 3*
Canizares, Jose De 1676-1750 *McGWD*
Cankar, Ivan 1876-1918 *CnMD*
Cannan, Denis 1919- *ConDr 1977, CroCD,*
	WhoThe 16
Cannan, Gilbert 1884-1955 *NotNAT B, WhThe*
Cannon, Dyan *WhoHol A*
Cannon, Dyan 1937- *IntMPA 1977, MovMk*
Cannon, Dyan 1938- *FilmgC*
Cannon, J D 1922- *BiE&WWA, FilmgC,*
	NotNAT, WhoHol A
Cannon, Judy 1938- *IntMPA 1977*
Cannon, Maurice *Film 2*
Cannon, Norman *Film 2*
Cannon, Pomeray *Film 2*
Cannon, Raymond *Film 1, Film 2*
Cannon, Robert 1901-1964 *DcFM, FilmgC*
Cannon, Robert 1910-1964 *WorEnF*
Cannon, William 1937- *IntMPA 1977*
Cano, Edward, Jr. 1927- *AmSCAP 1966*
Canosa, Michael Raymond 1920- *AmSCAP 1966*
Canova, Judy 1916- *FilmgC, IntMPA 1977,*

MotPP, MovMk, WhoHol A
Canova, Zeke *WhoHol A*
Cansino, Eduardo 1895-1968 *WhScrn 2*
Cansino, Eduardo, Jr. 1920-1974 *WhScrn 2, WhoHol B*
Cansino, Gabriel d1963 *NotNAT B*
Cantagrel, Marc 1879-1960 *DcFM*
Canter, Lynn *WhScrn 2*
Cantinflas *MotPP, WhoHol A*
Cantinflas 1911- *FilmgC, OxFilm*
Cantinflas 1917- *MovMk*
Canton, Arthur H *IntMPA 1977*
Canton, Don 1915- *AmSCAP 1966*
Cantor, Arthur 1920- *BiE&WWA, NotNAT, WhoThe 16*
Cantor, Charles 1898-1966 *WhScrn 1, WhScrn 2, WhoHol B*
Cantor, Eddie d1964 *MotPP, NewYTET, PIP&P, WhoHol B*
Cantor, Eddie 1892-1964 *AmSCAP 1966, BiE&WWA, EncMT, Film 2, FilmgC, MovMk, NotNAT B, TwYS, WhScrn 1, WhScrn 2, WhThe*
Cantor, Eddie 1893-1964 *NotNAT A, OxFilm, WorEnF*
Cantor, Herman 1896-1953 *WhScrn 1, WhScrn 2*
Cantor, Ida 1892-1962 *WhScrn 2*
Cantor, Nat 1897-1956 *NotNAT B, WhScrn 1, WhScrn 2*
Cantow, Roberta *WomWMM B*
Cantrell, Lana 1944- *CelR 3*
Cantway, Fred R 1883-1939 *WhScrn 1, WhScrn 2*
Canty, Marietta *Vers B*
Canutt, Yakima 1895- *CmMov, Film 2, FilmgC, IntMPA 1977, OxFilm, TwYS, WhoHol A, WorEnF*
Canzoneri, Tony d1959 *WhScrn 2*
Capalbo, Carmen 1925- *BiE&WWA, NotNAT*
Capano, Frank 1899-1956 *AmSCAP 1966*
Capek *PIP&P*
Capek, Josef 1887-1927 *NotNAT B*
Capek, Josef 1887-1945 *CnThe, REnWD*
Capek, Karel 1890-1938 *CnMD, CnThe, McGWD, ModWD, NotNAT B, OxThe, REnWD, WhThe*
Capellani, Albert 1870-1931 *DcFM, FilmgC*
Capellani, James 1874-1931 *TwYS A*
Capellani, Paul *Film 1*
Capelli, Dante *Film 1*
Capers, Virginia 1925- *NotNAT, PIP&P A, WhoHol A*
Caplan, Harry 1908- *IntMPA 1977*
Capli, Erdogan 1926- *AmSCAP 1966*
Caplin, Gertrude 1921- *BiE&WWA, NotNAT*
Capon, William 1757-1827 *NotNAT B, OxThe, PIP&P*
Capone, Al 1899-1947 *FilmgC, OxFilm*
Capote, Truman *ConDr 1977D, WhoHol A*
Capote, Truman 1924- *AmSCAP 1966, BiE&WWA, CelR 3, CnMD, ModWD, NotNAT*
Capote, Truman 1925- *FilmgC, OxFilm*
Capozzi, Alberto *Film 1*
Capp, Al 1909- *CelR 3*
Cappelli, Amy Spencer 1904- *AmSCAP 1966*
Cappy, Ted *BiE&WWA, NotNAT*
Capra, Frank 1897- *BiDFlm, CelR 3, CmMov, DcFM, FilmgC, IntMPA 1977, MovMk, OxFilm, TwYS A, WorEnF*
Capri, Ahna *WhoHol A*
Caprice, June 1899-1936 *Film 1, Film 2, MotPP, NotNAT B, TwYS, WhScrn 1, WhScrn 2, WhoHol B*

Caprioli, Vittorio 1921- *WorEnF*
Capuana, Luigi 1839-1915 *McGWD*
Capucine 1933- *FilmgC, IntMPA 1977, MotPP, MovMk, WhoHol A*
Capus, Alfred 1858-1922 *CnMD, McGWD, ModWD, NotNAT B, WhThe*
Caputo, George 1916- *IntMPA 1977*
Carabetta, Frank 1944- *AmSCAP 1966*
Caragiale, Ion Luca 1852-1912 *CnMD, McGWD*
Caranda, Michael J 1918- *AmSCAP 1966*
Carazo, Castro 1895- *AmSCAP 1966*
Carballido, Emilio 1925- *CroCD*
Carbasse, Louise *Film 1*
Carberry, Joe *PIP&P A*
Carbine, Patricia 1931- *CelR 3*
Carbonara, Gerard 1886-1959 *AmSCAP 1966*
Carbone, Antony *WhoHol A*
Carbonnaux, Norbert 1918- *DcFM*
Carbrey, John d1962 *NotNAT B*
Card, Kathryn 1893-1964 *NotNAT B, WhScrn 1, WhScrn 2, WhoHol B*
Card, Virginia 1918- *AmSCAP 1966*
Carder, Emmeline d1961 *NotNAT B*
Cardi, Pat *WhoHol A*
Cardiff, Jack 1914- *BiDFlm, CmMov, DcFM, FilmgC, IntMPA 1977, OxFilm, WorEnF*
Cardin, Pierre *CelR 3*
Cardinale, Claudia 1939- *BiDFlm, FilmgC, IntMPA 1977, MotPP, MovMk, OxFilm, WhoHol A, WorEnF*
Cardini, George 1913- *AmSCAP 1966*
Cardoni, Frank 1940- *AmSCAP 1966*
Cardoni, Mary 1938- *AmSCAP 1966*
Cardwell, Albert C 1921-1954 *WhScrn 1*
Cardwell, James 1921-1954 *WhScrn 2, WhoHol B*
Carell, Annette d1967 *WhScrn 1, WhScrn 2, WhoHol B*
Carelsen, Fie 1890-1975 *WhScrn 2*
Carere, Christine 1930- *FilmgC, WhoHol A*
Carette 1897-1966 *FilmgC, WhScrn 1, WhScrn 2, WhoHol B*
Carette, Julien 1897-1966 *BiDFlm, OxFilm, WorEnF*
Carette, Louis *McGWD*
Carew, Arthur Edmund 1894-1937 *Film 1, TwYS, WhScrn 1, WhScrn 2, WhoHol B*
Carew, Helen *BiE&WWA, NotNAT*
Carew, James 1876-1938 *Film 1, Film 2, NotNAT B, WhScrn 1, WhScrn 2, WhThe, WhoHol B, WhoStg 1908*
Carew, Ora 1893-1955 *Film 1, Film 2, MotPP, NotNAT B, TwYS, WhScrn 1, WhScrn 2, WhoHol B*
Carewe, Andrew *Film 2*
Carewe, Arthur Edmund 1894-1937 *Film 2*
Carewe, Edwin 1883-1940 *Film 1, Film 2, FilmgC, TwYS, TwYS A, WhScrn 1, WhScrn 2, WhoHol B*
Carewe, Millicent *Film 2*
Carewe, Rita 1908-1955 *Film 2, TwYS, WhScrn 1, WhoHol B*
Carey, Bill 1916- *AmSCAP 1966*
Carey, David 1926- *AmSCAP 1966*
Carey, Denis 1909- *BiE&WWA, NotNAT, WhoThe 16*
Carey, Eleanor 1852- *WhoStg 1908*
Carey, George Saville d1807 *NotNAT B*
Carey, Harry 1875-1947 *Film 1, Film 2*
Carey, Harry 1878-1947 *FilmgC, MotPP, MovMk, NotNAT B, TwYS, Vers A, WhScrn 1, WhScrn 2, WhoHol B, WorEnF*
Carey, Harry 1880-1947 *CmMov*
Carey, Harry, Jr. 1921- *CmMov, FilmgC, IntMPA 1977, MovMk, WhoHol A*

Carey, Henry 1690-1743 *NotNAT B*
Carey, Joseph A d1964 *NotNAT B*
Carey, Josie 1930- *AmSCAP 1966*
Carey, Joyce *IntMPA 1977, WhoHol A*
Carey, Joyce 1898- *FilmgC, MovMk, OxFilm, WhoThe 16*
Carey, Joyce 1905- *BiE&WWA, NotNAT*
Carey, Leonard 1893- *FilmgC*
Carey, Macdonald 1913- *BiE&WWA, FilmgC, HolP 40, IntMPA 1977, MotPP, MovMk, WhoHol A*
Carey, Michele *WhoHol A*
Carey, Olive *WhoHol A*
Carey, Patrick 1916- *OxFilm*
Carey, Phil 1925- *FilmgC, IntMPA 1977, MotPP*
Carey, Philip 1925- *WhoHol A*
Carey, Thomas 1904-1972 *BiE&WWA, NotNAT B*
Carey, Timothy 1925?- *FilmgC*
Carfax, Bruce 1905-1970 *WhThe*
Cargill, Patrick 1918- *FilmgC, WhoHol A, WhoThe 16*
Carhart, James L 1843-1937 *NotNAT B, WhoStg 1908*
Carillo, Mario *Film 2*
Cariou, Len 1939- *NotNAT, WhoThe 16*
Carl, Karl 1789-1854 *OxThe*
Carl, M Roger *Film 2*
Carl, Renee *Film 2, WomWMM*
Carl, Roger *Film 2*
Carlberg, Hilbur *Film 2*
Carle, C E 1899- *IntMPA 1977*
Carle, Frankie 1903- *AmSCAP 1966, WhoHol A*
Carle, Richard 1871-1941 *Film 2, FilmgC, NotNAT B, TwYS, Vers A, WhScrn 1, WhScrn 2, WhThe, WhoHol B, WhoStg 1906, WhoStg 1908*
Carle, Richard 1876-1941 *MovMk*
Carles, Romeo 1896-1971 *WhScrn 2*
Carleton, Claire 1913- *WhThe, WhoHol A*
Carleton, George 1885-1950 *WhScrn 1, WhScrn 2, WhoHol B*
Carleton, Henry *Film 1*
Carleton, Henry Guy 1851-1910 *WhoStg 1906, WhoStg 1908*
Carleton, Henry Guy 1856-1910 *NotNAT B*
Carleton, Lloyd B 1872-1933 *Film 1, WhScrn 1, WhScrn 2, WhoHol B*
Carleton, Marjorie d1964 *NotNAT B*
Carleton, Robert Louis 1896-1956 *AmSCAP 1966*
Carleton, Will C 1871-1941 *WhScrn 1, WhScrn 2*
Carleton, William P 1873-1947 *Film 2, WhScrn 1, WhScrn 2, WhoHol B*
Carleton, William T 1859-1930 *Film 1, Film 2, WhScrn 2*
Carley, Karleen *AmSCAP 1966*
Carlidge, William 1910- *IntMPA 1977*
Carlie, Edward 1878-1938 *WhScrn 1, WhScrn 2, WhoHol B*
Carlier, Madeleine *WhThe*
Carlile, James d1691 *NotNAT B*
Carlin *OxThe*
Carlin, George *WhoHol A*
Carlin, Lynn 1930- *FilmgC, WhoHol A*
Carlin, Steve *NewYTET*
Carliner, Mark *NewYTET*
Carling, Foster G 1898- *AmSCAP 1966*
Carlino, Lewis John 1932- *ConDr 1977, IntMPA 1977, NewYTET, NotNAT*
Carlisle, Alexandra 1886-1936 *NotNAT B, WhScrn 1, WhScrn 2, WhThe, WhoHol B*
Carlisle, Jack *Film 2*
Carlisle, Kitty *WhoHol A*

Carlisle, Kitty 1914- *EncMT, ThFT, WhoThe 16*
Carlisle, Kitty 1915- *BiE&WWA, CelR 3, FilmgC, NotNAT*
Carlisle, Margaret 1905- *WhThe*
Carlisle, Mary 1912- *FilmgC, MotPP, MovMk, ThFT, WhoHol A*
Carlisle, Peggy *Film 2*
Carlisle, Rita *Film 2*
Carlisle, Robert 1906- *IntMPA 1977*
Carlisle, Sybil 1871- *WhThe*
Carlisle, William *NewYTET*
Carlo, Monte 1883- *AmSCAP 1966, BiE&WWA*
Carlo-Rim 1905- *DcFM, FilmgC*
Carlsen, Henning 1927- *OxFilm, WorEnF*
Carlsen, John A 1915- *WhThe*
Carlson, Harry A 1904- *AmSCAP 1966*
Carlson, Karen *WhoHol A*
Carlson, Richard *IntMPA 1977, MotPP*
Carlson, Richard 1912- *FilmgC, MovMk*
Carlson, Richard 1914- *WhoHol A*
Carlson, Steve *WhoHol A*
Carlson, Veronica 1945- *FilmgC, WhoHol A*
Carlton 1880- *WhThe*
Carlton, Barbara *Film 1*
Carlton, Kathleen d1964 *NotNAT B*
Carlton, Richard 1919- *IntMPA 1977*
Carlton, Steve 1944- *CelR 3*
Carlton, William Probert *Film 1*
Carlye, Grace *Film 2*
Carlyle, Aileen *AmSCAP 1966*
Carlyle, Francis *Film 1*
Carlyle, Helen 1893-1933 *WhScrn 1, WhScrn 2, WhoHol B*
Carlyle, Richard *WhoHol A*
Carlyle, Richard 1879-1942 *Film 1, Film 2, TwYS, WhScrn 1, WhScrn 2, WhoHol B*
Carlyle, Russ 1914- *AmSCAP 1966*
Carlyle, Sidney *Film 2*
Carmagnole Dancers, The *Film 2*
Carme, Pamela 1902- *WhThe*
Carmel, Roger C 1929- *FilmgC, WhoHol A*
Carmen, Jean *WhoHol A*
Carmen, Jewel *Film 1, Film 2, TwYS*
Carmi, Maria 1880-1957 *Film 1, WhScrn 1, WhScrn 2*
Carmichael, Hoagey 1899- *WorEnF*
Carmichael, Hoagy 1899- *AmSCAP 1966, CelR 3, FilmgC, IntMPA 1977, MotPP, MovMk, OxFilm, WhoHol A*
Carmichael, Ian 1920- *CmMov, EncMT, FilmgC, IntMPA 1977, WhoHol A, WhoThe 16*
Carmichael, Myra d1974 *WhScrn 2, WhoHol B*
Carminati, Tulio 1894-1971 *TwYS*
Carminati, Tullio 1894-1971 *Film 2, FilmgC, MovMk, WhScrn 1, WhScrn 2, WhThe, WhoHol B*
Carmines, Al 1936- *ConDr 1977D, NotNAT, WhoThe 16*
Carmody, Jay *BiE&WWA*
Carnahan, Suzanne d1952 *WhoHol B*
Carne, Judy 1939- *FilmgC, WhoHol A*
Carne, Marcel 1903- *FilmgC*
Carne, Marcel 1909- *BiDFlm, DcFM, MovMk, OxFilm, WorEnF*
Carnera, Primo 1906-1967 *WhScrn 2, WhoHol B*
Carnes, Josef R 1903- *AmSCAP 1966*
Carney, Alan 1911-1973 *FilmgC, Vers A, WhScrn 2, WhoHol B*
Carney, Art 1918- *BiE&WWA, CelR 3, FilmgC, IntMPA 1977, NewYTET, NotNAT, WhoHol A, WhoThe 16*
Carney, Augustus *Film 1*
Carney, Daniel *Film 2*
Carney, Don 1897-1954 *WhScrn 1, WhScrn 2*

Carney, Frank 1904- *BiE&WWA, NotNAT*
Carney, Fred 1914- *IntMPA 1977*
Carney, George d1948 *WhoHol B*
Carney, George 1887-1947 *FilmgC, WhScrn 1, WhScrn 2, WhThe*
Carney, Harry 1910-1974 *WhScrn 2*
Carney, Kate 1868-1950 *OxThe*
Carney, Kate 1869-1950 *NotNAT B*
Carney, Kate 1870- *WhThe*
Carney, Richard E 1923- *AmSCAP 1966*
Carnovsky, Morris *MotPP, PIP&P, WhoHol A*
Carnovsky, Morris 1897- *BiE&WWA, FamA&A, MovMk, NotNAT, WhoThe 16*
Carnovsky, Morris 1898- *CnThe, FilmgC, IntMPA 1977*
Carnow, Howard N 1912- *IntMPA 1977*
Carns, Roscoe *Film 2*
Caro, Annibale 1507-1566 *McGWD*
Caro, Warren 1907- *BiE&WWA, NotNAT, WhoThe 16*
Carol, Cindy *WhoHol A*
Carol, Diane 1940-1966 *WhScrn 2*
Carol, John 1910-1968 *WhScrn 2*
Carol, Martine d1967 *MotPP, WhoHol B*
Carol, Martine 1921-1967 *MovMk, WhScrn 1, WhScrn 2*
Carol, Martine 1922-1967 *BiDFlm, FilmgC, OxFilm, WorEnF*
Carol, Sue 1907- *FilmgC, MotPP, ThFT*
Carol, Sue 1908- *Film 2, MovMk, TwYS, WhoHol A*
Caroll, Evelyn *AmSCAP 1966*
Caron, Cecile *WhThe*
Caron, Irma *Film 2*
Caron, Leslie 1931- *BiDFlm, CelR 3, CmMov, FilmgC, IntMPA 1977, MGM, MotPP, MovMk, OxFilm, WhThe, WhoHol A, WorEnF*
Caron, Marguerite *WhThe*
Caron, Patricia *Film 2*
Caron, Pierre Augustin 1875-1952 *McGWD*
Carpenter, Betty *Film 2*
Carpenter, Billy *Film 1*
Carpenter, Carleton 1926- *AmSCAP 1966, BiE&WWA, FilmgC, IntMPA 1977, MotPP, NotNAT, WhoHol A, WhoThe 16*
Carpenter, Charles E 1912- *AmSCAP 1966*
Carpenter, Constance 1906- *BiE&WWA, NotNAT, WhoHol A, WhoThe 16*
Carpenter, Edward Childs 1872-1950 *NotNAT B, WhThe*
Carpenter, Elliot J 1894- *AmSCAP 1966*
Carpenter, Francis *Film 1*
Carpenter, Freddie 1908- *WhoThe 16*
Carpenter, Gloria 1927-1958 *WhScrn 1, WhScrn 2*
Carpenter, Horace B 1875-1945 *Film 1, WhScrn 1, WhScrn 2, WhoHol B*
Carpenter, Imogen 1919- *AmSCAP 1966*
Carpenter, Jean *Film 2*
Carpenter, Jeanne *Film 2*
Carpenter, John *WhoHol A*
Carpenter, John Alden 1876-1951 *AmSCAP 1966*
Carpenter, M Scott 1925- *CelR 3*
Carpenter, Maud d1967 *WhThe*
Carpenter, Merta *Film 1*
Carpenter, Paul 1921-1964 *FilmgC, NotNAT B, WhScrn 1, WhScrn 2, WhoHol B*
Carpenter, Peter *Film 2*
Carpenter, Thelma 1922- *BiE&WWA, NotNAT*
Carpenter, William *Film 1*
Carpentier, Georges 1894-1975 *Film 2, WhScrn 2, WhoHol B*
Carr, Alexander 1878-1946 *Film 2, NotNAT B,*

WhScrn 1, WhScrn 2, WhThe, WhoHol B
Carr, Alexander 1880- *WhoStg 1908*
Carr, Arnold 1931- *IntMPA 1977*
Carr, Cameron *Film 1, Film 2*
Carr, Darleen *WhoHol A*
Carr, F Osmond 1858-1916 *WhThe*
Carr, Fatty *Film 2*
Carr, George d1962 *WhThe*
Carr, Georgia 1925-1971 *WhScrn 1, WhScrn 2, WhoHol B*
Carr, Geraldine 1917-1954 *WhScrn 1, WhScrn 2, WhoHol B*
Carr, Gertrude d1969 *WhoHol B*
Carr, Ginna 1937-1972 *WhScrn 2*
Carr, Howard 1880-1960 *WhThe*
Carr, Jack d1951 *WhScrn 2*
Carr, Jack d1967 *WhoHol B*
Carr, Jack 1899-1968 *WhScrn 2*
Carr, Jane 1909-1957 *FilmgC, NotNAT B, WhScrn 1, WhScrn 2, WhThe, WhoHol B*
Carr, Jimmie *Film 2*
Carr, Joseph William Comyns 1849-1916 *NotNAT B, WhThe*
Carr, Lawrence 1916-1969 *BiE&WWA, WhThe, WhoHol B*
Carr, Leon 1910- *AmSCAP 1966*
Carr, Louella *Film 2*
Carr, Margie 1900- *AmSCAP 1966*
Carr, Martin 1932- *IntMPA 1977, NewYTET*
Carr, Mary 1874-1973 *Film 1, Film 2, FilmgC, MovMk, TwYS, WhScrn 2, WhoHol B*
Carr, May Beth *Film 2*
Carr, Michael 1900-1968 *WhScrn 2*
Carr, Nat 1886-1944 *Film 2, WhScrn 1, WhScrn 2, WhoHol B*
Carr, Paul *WhoHol A*
Carr, Percy 1865-1926 *Film 2, WhScrn 1, WhScrn 2, WhoHol B*
Carr, Philip d1969 *WhoHol B*
Carr, Philip 1874-1957 *NotNAT B, WhThe*
Carr, Rosemary *Film 2*
Carr, Sade 1889-1940 *WhScrn 1, WhScrn 2, WhoHol B*
Carr, Stephen *Film 2*
Carr, Thomas 1907- *FilmgC, IntMPA 1977*
Carr, William 1867-1937 *Film 2, WhScrn 1, WhScrn 2, WhoHol B*
Carr-Cook, Madge 1856-1933 *NotNAT B, WhThe*
Carra, Lawrence 1909- *BiE&WWA, NotNAT*
Carradine, David 1940- *FilmgC, IntMPA 1977, MotPP, WhoHol A*
Carradine, John 1906- *BiE&WWA, CmMov, FilmgC, MotPP, MovMk, OxFilm, Vers A, WhoHol A, WhoThe 16, WorEnF*
Carradine, John 1908- *IntMPA 1977*
Carradine, Keith *IntMPA 1977, WhoHol A*
Carradine, Robert *WhoHol A*
Carrado, Gino *Film 2*
Carras, Nicholas S 1922- *AmSCAP 1966*
Carre, Albert 1852-1938 *NotNAT B, WhThe*
Carre, Bartlett A 1897-1971 *WhScrn 1, WhScrn 2, WhoHol B*
Carre, Fabrice 1855- *WhThe*
Carre, Michel d1872 *NotNAT B*
Carre, Michel 1865- *WhThe*
Carreau, Margaret 1899- *AmSCAP 1966*
Carrera, Barbara *WhoHol A*
Carreras, Sir James 1910- *FilmgC, IntMPA 1977*
Carreras, Michael 1927- *FilmgC, IntMPA 1977*
Carretta, Jerry 1915- *AmSCAP 1966*
Carretto, Galeotto Del *OxThe*
Carricart, Robert *WhoHol A*
Carrick, Edward 1905- *FilmgC, WhThe*

Carrick, Hartley 1881-1929 *NotNAT B*, *WhThe*
Carrickson, S B *Film 2*
Carrico, Charles 1888-1967 *WhScrn 1*, *WhScrn 2*
Carrier, Albert *WhoHol A*
Carriere, Jean-Claude 1931- *OxFilm*
Carrigan, Thomas J 1886-1941 *Film 1*, *Film 2*,
    NotNAT B, *WhScrn 1*, *WhScrn 2*,
    WhoHol B
Carril, Hugo Del 1912- *DcFM*
Carrillo, Cely *WhoHol A*
Carrillo, Leo d1961 *MotPP*, *WhThe*, *WhoHol B*
Carrillo, Leo 1880-1961 *FilmgC*, *MovMk*
Carrillo, Leo 1881-1961 *Film 2*, *NotNAT B*,
    WhScrn 2
Carrilo, Leo 1881-1961 *WhScrn 1*
Carrington, Ethel 1889-1962 *WhThe*
Carrington, Evelyn 1876-1942 *Film 2*, *NotNAT B*,
    WhScrn 1, *WhScrn 2*, *WhoHol B*
Carrington, Frank d1975 *WhoHol C*
Carrington, Frank 1901-1975 *BiE&WWA*,
    NotNAT B
Carrington, Frank 1902-1975 *WhScrn 2*
Carrington, Helen 1895-1963 *WhScrn 1*,
    WhScrn 2, *WhoHol B*
Carrington, Katherine d1953 *NotNAT B*
Carrington, Murray 1885-1941 *Film 1*,
    NotNAT B, *WhThe*
Carroll, Adam 1897- *AmSCAP 1966*
Carroll, Albert d1956 *NotNAT B*
Carroll, Barbara 1925- *AmSCAP 1966*
Carroll, Carroll 1902- *AmSCAP 1966*,
    ·*IntMPA 1977*
Carroll, Diahann 1935- *BiE&WWA*, *CelR 3*,
    EncMT, *FilmgC*, *MotPP*, *NotNAT*,
    WhoHol A, *WomWMM*
Carroll, Earl 1892-1948 *NotNAT B*
Carroll, Earl 1893-1948 *AmSCAP 1966*, *EncMT*,
    OxThe, *PIP&P*, *WhScrn 2*, *WhThe*
Carroll, Garnet H d1964 *NotNAT B*
Carroll, Gene 1898- *AmSCAP 1966*
Carroll, Georgia *WhoHol A*
Carroll, Georgia Lillian 1914- *AmSCAP 1966*
Carroll, Gordon 1928- *IntMPA 1977*
Carroll, Harry 1892-1962 *AmSCAP 1966*,
    NotNAT B
Carroll, Helena *BiE&WWA*, *NotNAT*
Carroll, Irv 1907- *AmSCAP 1966*
Carroll, Janice *WhoHol A*
Carroll, Jimmy 1913- *AmSCAP 1966*
Carroll, John *MotPP*
Carroll, John 1907- *Film 2*
Carroll, John 1908- *FilmgC*, *MovMk*,
    WhoHol A
Carroll, John 1913- *MGM*
Carroll, June *AmSCAP 1966*, *BiE&WWA*,
    NotNAT, *WhoHol A*
Carroll, Laurie 1935- *IntMPA 1977*
Carroll, Lawrence W d1963 *NotNAT B*
Carroll, Leo G 1892-1972 *BiE&WWA*, *CmMov*,
    FilmgC, *MotPP*, *MovMk*, *NotNAT B*,
    Vers A, *WhScrn 2*, *WhThe*, *WhoHol B*
Carroll, Lewis 1832-1898 *FilmgC*
Carroll, Madeleine 1906- *BiDFlm*, *BiE&WWA*,
    Film 2, *FilmgC*, *IntMPA 1977*, *MotPP*,
    MovMk, *OxFilm*, *ThFT*, *WhThe*,
    WhoHol A, *WorEnF*
Carroll, Moon *Film 2*
Carroll, Nancy d1965 *MotPP*, *WhoHol B*,
    WomWMM
Carroll, Nancy 1904-1965 *ThFT*
Carroll, Nancy 1905-1965 *Film 2*, *FilmgC*,
    TwYS
Carroll, Nancy 1906-1965 *MovMk*, *WhScrn 1*,
    WhScrn 2, *WhThe*

Carroll, Nancy 1909-1965 *BiE&WWA*,
    NotNAT B
Carroll, Pat *WhoHol A*
Carroll, Pat 1927- *BiE&WWA*, *IntMPA 1977*,
    NotNAT
Carroll, Patrick Francis 1902-1965 *BiE&WWA*,
    NotNAT B
Carroll, Paul Vincent 1900-1968 *BiE&WWA*,
    CnMD, *CnThe*, *McGWD*, *ModWD*,
    NotNAT B, *OxThe*, *PIP&P*, *REnWD*,
    WhThe
Carroll, Richard Field 1865-1925 *NotNAT B*,
    WhoStg 1908
Carroll, Sidney *NewYTET*
Carroll, Sydney W 1877-1958 *NotNAT B*, *OxThe*,
    WhThe
Carroll, Taylor *Film 2*
Carroll, Vinnette 1922- *BiE&WWA*, *NotNAT*,
    WhoThe 16
Carroll, William A 1876-1928 *Film 1*, *Film 2*,
    WhScrn 1, *WhScrn 2*, *WhoHol B*
Carron, George 1930-1970 *WhScrn 1*, *WhScrn 2*
Carruthers, Bill *NewYTET*
Carruthers, Bruce C 1901-1954 *WhScrn 1*,
    WhScrn 2
Carsey, Mary 1938-1973 *WhScrn 2*, *WhoHol B*
Carson, Charles 1885- *FilmgC*, *WhoHol A*,
    WhoThe 16
Carson, Charles L d1901 *NotNAT B*
Carson, Mrs. Charles L d1919 *WhThe*
Carson, Doris 1910- *WhThe*
Carson, Frances 1895- *BiE&WWA*, *WhThe*
Carson, Jack 1910-1963 *FilmgC*, *HolP 40*,
    MotPP, *MovMk*, *NotNAT B*, *OxFilm*,
    WhScrn 1, *WhScrn 2*, *WhoHol B*
Carson, James B 1885-1958 *WhScrn 1*, *WhScrn 2*,
    WhoHol B
Carson, Jeannie *IntMPA 1977*, *MotPP*,
    WhoHol A
Carson, Jeannie 1928- *FilmgC*
Carson, Jeannie 1929- *BiE&WWA*, *WhoThe 16*
Carson, John David *WhoHol A*
Carson, Johnny 1925- *CelR 3*, *IntMPA 1977*,
    NewYTET
Carson, Kit 1809-1868 *FilmgC*, *OxFilm*
Carson, Lionel 1873-1937 *WhThe*
Carson, Lionel 1875-1937 *NotNAT B*
Carson, Mindy 1926- *BiE&WWA*
Carson, Murray 1865-1917 *WhThe*, *WhoStg 1906*,
    WhoStg 1908
Carson, Robert *IntMPA 1977*, *WhoHol A*
Carson, S Murray 1865-1917 *NotNAT B*
Carson, Sunset 1922- *MotPP*, *WhoHol A*
Carson, William G B 1891- *BiE&WWA*,
    NotNAT
Carstairs, John Paddy 1910-1970 *OxFilm*
Carstairs, John Paddy 1912-1971 *FilmgC*
Carstensen, Vern 1914- *IntMPA 1977*
Carte, Mrs. D'Oyly d1948 *WhThe*
Carte, Rupert D'Oyly *WhThe*
Cartellieri, Carmen *Film 2*
Carten, Audrey 1900- *WhThe*
Carter, Ben 1911-1947 *Vers A*, *WhoHol B*
Carter, Ben F 1911-1946 *WhScrn 2*
Carter, Bennett Lester 1907- *AmSCAP 1966*
Carter, Boake d1944 *WhScrn 2*
Carter, Calvert 1859-1932 *Film 2*, *WhoHol B*
Carter, Calvin *Film 1*
Carter, Captain *Film 2*
Carter, Charles Calvert 1859-1932 *WhScrn 1*,
    WhScrn 2
Carter, Desmond d1939 *EncMT*, *NotNAT B*,
    WhThe
Carter, Dixie *WomWMM B*

Carter, Elizabeth *WomWMM*
Carter, Frank d1920 *WhScrn 1, WhScrn 2,*
  WhoHol B
Carter, Frederick 1900-1970 *WhThe*
Carter, H Everett 1919- *AmSCAP 1966*
Carter, Harry *Film 1, Film 2*
Carter, Helena *MotPP*
Carter, Helena 1923- *FilmgC*
Carter, Hubert *Film 2*
Carter, Hubert d1934 *WhThe*
Carter, Jack 1923- *IntMPA 1977, WhoHol A*
Carter, Janis 1921- *FilmgC, MotPP, WhoHol A*
Carter, June *WhoHol A*
Carter, Leslie d1921 *NotNAT B*
Carter, Mrs. Leslie 1862-1937 *FamA&A, Film 1,*
  FilmgC, NotNAT B, OxThe, PIP&P, TwYS,
  WhScrn 1, WhScrn 2, WhThe, WhoHol B,
  WhoStg 1906, WhoStg 1908
Carter, Lincoln J d1926 *NotNAT B*
Carter, Lonnie 1942- *ConDr 1977, NatPD*
Carter, Louise 1875-1957 *WhScrn 1, WhScrn 2,*
  WhoHol B
Carter, Lynne *WhoHol A*
Carter, Margaret *WhThe*
Carter, Maurice 1913- *IntMPA 1977*
Carter, Monte 1886-1950 *WhScrn 1, WhScrn 2,*
  WhoHol B
Carter, Nan *Film 1*
Carter, Nell 1894-1965 *WhThe*
Carter, Ray 1908- *AmSCAP 1966*
Carter, Richard *AmSCAP 1966, Film 2*
Carter, Richard C 1919- *IntMPA 1977*
Carter, Steve 1929- *NatPD*
Carter, Terry *WhoHol A*
Carter, Tracy 1940- *IntMPA 1977*
Carter, William R 1908- *AmSCAP 1966*
Carter-Edwards, James 1840-1930 *WhThe*
Carteret, Anna 1942- *WhoThe 16*
Cartier, Inez Gibson 1918-1970 *WhScrn 1,*
  WhScrn 2
Cartier, Rudolph 1908- *IntMPA 1977*
Cartier-Bresson, Henri 1908- *DcFM, OxFilm,*
  WorEnF
Carton, Gwen *Film 2*
Carton, Harold *Film 2*
Carton, Katherine Mackenzie Compton 1853-1928
  OxThe
Carton, Pauline d1974 *Film 2, WhoHol B*
Carton, Pauline 1885-1974 *WhScrn 2*
Carton, Pauline 1888-1974 *OxFilm*
Carton, R C 1853-1928 *WhThe*
Carton, R Claude 1854-1928 *WhoStg 1906,*
  WhoStg 1908
Carton, Richard Claude 1853-1928 *NotNAT B*
Carton, Richard Claude 1856-1928 *OxThe*
Cartwright, Angela *WhoHol A*
Cartwright, Charles 1855-1916 *NotNAT B,*
  WhThe, WhoStg 1908
Cartwright, Peggy 1912- *WhThe*
Cartwright, Peggy 1915- *Film 2*
Cartwright, Veronica *WhoHol A*
Cartwright, William *OxThe*
Cartwright, William 1611-1643 *REnWD*
Carus, Emma 1879-1927 *NotNAT B, WhThe,*
  WhoStg 1906, WhoStg 1908
Caruso, Anthony 1913?- *FilmgC, MovMk,*
  Vers A, WhoHol A
Caruso, Enrico 1873-1921 *Film 1, FilmgC,*
  TwYS, WhScrn 1, WhScrn 2, WhoHol B
Carver, Miss *Film 1*
Carver, James 1932- *NotNAT*
Carver, Kathryn 1906-1947 *Film 2, NotNAT B,*
  TwYS, WhScrn 1, WhScrn 2, WhoHol B
Carver, Louise d1956 *MotPP, NotNAT B,*

  WhoHol B
Carver, Louise 1868-1956 *FilmgC*
Carver, Louise 1869-1956 *WhScrn 1, WhScrn 2*
Carver, Louise 1875-1956 *Film 1, Film 2, TwYS*
Carver, Lynn 1909-1955 *WhScrn 1, WhScrn 2*
Carver, Lynne 1909-1955 *MotPP, NotNAT B,*
  WhoHol B
Carver, Mary *PIP&P*
Carver, Norman 1899- *BiE&WWA, NotNAT*
Carvil, Bert Forrest 1880- *WhoStg 1908*
Carvil, Harry 1880- *WhoStg 1908*
Carvill, Henry d1941 *Film 2, NotNAT B,*
  WhoHol B
Cary, Christopher *WhoHol A*
Cary, Falkland L 1897- *WhoThe 16*
Cary, Jim *Film 2*
Cary, Richard Durant 1916- *AmSCAP 1966*
Cary, W Sterling 1927- *CelR 3*
Caryll, Ivan d1921 *WhThe*
Caryll, Ivan 1860-1921 *EncMT, NewMT*
Caryll, Ivan 1861-1921 *NotNAT B*
Casadesus, Mathilde 1921-1965 *WhScrn 1,*
  WhScrn 2, WhoHol B
Casajuana, Maria *Film 2*
Casale, Michael 1949- *NatPD*
Casaleggio, Giovanni 1880-1955 *WhScrn 1,*
  WhScrn 2
Casalini, Angelo *BiE&WWA*
Casals, Pablo 1876-1973 *AmSCAP 1966, CelR 3,*
  WhScrn 2
Casanave, Chester F 1919- *IntMPA 1977*
Casanova, Felipe 1898- *AmSCAP 1966*
Casanova, Jimmy 1920- *AmSCAP 1966*
Casares, Maria 1922- *CnThe, FilmgC, MotPP,*
  OxFilm, WhoHol A, WorEnF
Casartelli, Gabrielle 1910- *WhThe*
Cascarino, Romeo 1922- *AmSCAP 1966*
Case, Anna 1889- *Film 1, WhoHol A*
Case, Frank 1877-1946 *NotNAT A*
Case, Helen *Film 1*
Case, Nelson *IntMPA 1977*
Case, Paul 1895-1933 *WhScrn 1, WhScrn 2*
Case, Russell D 1912-1964 *AmSCAP 1966*
Casella, Albert 1891- *McGWD*
Caselli, Ernest *Film 1*
Caselli, Lamar 1921- *IntMPA 1977*
Caserini, Mario 1874-1920 *DcFM, OxFilm*
Caserio, Jesse 1918- *AmSCAP 1966*
Casey, Bernie *WhoHol A*
Casey, Claude 1912- *AmSCAP 1966*
Casey, Dolores 1917-1945 *WhScrn 1, WhScrn 2,*
  WhoHol B
Casey, John *McGWD*
Casey, Kenneth 1899-1965 *AmSCAP 1966,*
  Film 1, WhScrn 1, WhScrn 2, WhoHol B
Casey, Lawrence *WhoHol A*
Casey, Michael *ConDr 1977D*
Casey, Pat d1962 *NotNAT B*
Casey, Rosemary 1904- *BiE&WWA, NotNAT*
Casey, Stuart F 1896-1948 *WhScrn 1, WhScrn 2,*
  WhoHol B
Casey, Sue *WhoHol A*
Casey, Wesley Eugene 1933- *AmSCAP 1966*
Cash, Johnny 1932- *CelR 3, FilmgC, WhoHol A*
Cash, June *WomWMM*
Cash, Morny *WhThe*
Cash, Rosalind *WhoHol A*
Cash, Rosalind 1938- *WhoThe 16*
Cash, Rosalind 1945- *FilmgC*
Cash, William F 1880?-1963 *NotNAT B,*
  WhScrn 1, WhScrn 2, WhoHol B
Cashel, Oliver d1747 *NotNAT B*
Casher, Izadore 1887-1948 *WhScrn 2*
Cashier, Isidore *Film 2*

Cashman, Betty *BiE&WWA, NotNAT*
Cashman, Harry *Film 1*
Cashman, Harry d1912 *WhScrn 2*
Casler, Herman *Film 1*
Casolaro, Hugo A 1914- *IntMPA 1977*
Cason, Barbara *WhoHol A*
Cason, John d1961 *WhScrn 2*
Casona, Alejandro 1903-1965 *CnMD, CroCD,
    McGWD, ModWD*
Caspary, Vera 1904- *BiE&WWA, FilmgC,
    NotNAT, WorEnF*
Casper, Billy 1931- *CelR 3*
Caspersen, Karen *Film 2*
Cass, Guy 1921-1959 *WhScrn 1, WhScrn 2*
Cass, Henry 1902- *FilmgC, PIP&P, WhoThe 16*
Cass, Maurice 1884-1954 *FilmgC, Vers B,
    WhScrn 1, WhScrn 2, WhoHol B*
Cass, Peggy *MotPP, WhoHol A*
Cass, Peggy 1924- *WhoThe 16*
Cass, Peggy 1925- *CelR 3*
Cass, Peggy 1926- *BiE&WWA, NotNAT*
Cass, Ray *WhoHol A*
Cass, Ronald 1923- *WhoThe 16*
Cassady, James 1869-1928 *Film 1, WhScrn 2*
Cassavant, Nina *Film 2*
Cassavetes, John 1929- *BiDFlm, CelR 3,
    ConDr 1977A, DcFM, FilmgC,
    IntMPA 1977, MotPP, MovMk, OxFilm,
    WhoHol A, WorEnF*
Cassel, Irwin M 1886- *AmSCAP 1966*
Cassel, Jean-Pierre 1932- *FilmgC, IntMPA 1977,
    MovMk, OxFilm, WhoHol A, WorEnF*
Cassel, Seymour *WhoHol A*
Cassel, Sid 1897-1960 *WhScrn 1, WhScrn 2,
    WhoHol B*
Cassell, Wally *WhoHol A*
Cassey, Charles R 1933- *AmSCAP 1966*
Cassidy, Bill 1876-1943 *WhScrn 1, WhScrn 2,
    WhoHol B*
Cassidy, Claudia 1905?- *BiE&WWA, CelR 3,
    NotNAT*
Cassidy, David 1950- *CelR 3*
Cassidy, Ed 1893-1968 *WhScrn 1, WhScrn 2,
    WhoHol B*
Cassidy, Ellen *Film 1, Film 2*
Cassidy, J Rice d1927 *NotNAT B*
Cassidy, Jack *WhoHol A*
Cassidy, Jack 1925- *EncMT*
Cassidy, Jack 1926- *FilmgC*
Cassidy, Jack 1927- *BiE&WWA, NotNAT,
    WhoThe 16*
Cassidy, Joanna *WhoHol A*
Cassinari, John 1920- *AmSCAP 1966*
Cassinelli, Dolores *Film 1, Film 2, TwYS*
Cassini, Oleg 1913- *CelR 3*
Cassity, Ellen *Film 2*
Cassjuana, Maria *Film 2*
Casson, Ann 1915- *CnThe, WhThe*
Casson, Christopher 1912- *WhThe*
Casson, John 1909- *WhThe*
Casson, Sir Lewis 1875-1969 *BiE&WWA,
    NotNAT A, NotNAT B, OxThe, PIP&P,
    WhThe, WhoHol B*
Casson, Sir Lewis 1875-1970 *CnThe*
Casson, Sir Lewis 1876-1969 *WhScrn 1,
    WhScrn 2*
Casson, Louis d1950 *NotNAT B*
Casson, Mary 1914- *WhThe*
Castagna, Joe 1934-1970 *WhScrn 2*
Castaldo, Joseph F 1927- *AmSCAP 1966*
Castell, Antonio 1911- *IntMPA 1977*
Castellani, Brute *Film 2*
Castellani, Renato 1913- *DcFM, FilmgC, OxFilm,
    WorEnF*

Castellano, Richard *WhoHol A*
Castellano, Richard 1931- *FilmgC*
Castellano, Richard 1934- *CelR 3*
Castellano, Richard S 1933- *IntMPA 1977*
Castelnuovo, Nino 1937- *FilmgC, WhoHol A*
Castelnuovo-Tedesco, Mario 1895- *AmSCAP 1966*
Castiglioni, Iphigene 1901-1963 *WhScrn 1,
    WhScrn 2*
Castiglioni, Iphigenia d1963 *WhoHol B*
Castile, Lynn 1898-1975 *WhScrn 2*
Castle, Betty d1962 *NotNAT B*
Castle, Don 1917-1966 *WhScrn 1, WhScrn 2*
Castle, Don 1919-1966 *FilmgC, WhoHol B*
Castle, Egerton 1858-1920 *NotNAT B*
Castle, Harry *Film 2*
Castle, Irene 1892-1969 *NotNAT B*
Castle, Irene 1893-1968 *Film 2, OxFilm*
Castle, Irene 1893-1969 *EncMT, Film 1, FilmgC,
    PIP&P, TwYS, WhScrn 1, WhScrn 2,
    WhoHol B*
Castle, John 1940- *WhoThe 16*
Castle, Lillian 1865-1959 *WhScrn 1, WhScrn 2,
    WhoHol B*
Castle, Mary 1931- *FilmgC, WhoHol A*
Castle, Nicholas 1910- *AmSCAP 1966*
Castle, Nick 1910-1968 *FilmgC, WhScrn 1,
    WhScrn 2, WhoHol B*
Castle, Peggie 1927- *FilmgC*
Castle, Peggy 1926-1973 *WhScrn 2, WhoHol B*
Castle, Robert *Film 2*
Castle, Vernon d1918 *PIP&P, WhoHol B*
Castle, Vernon 1885-1918 *Film 1, FilmgC,
    OxFilm*
Castle, Vernon 1887-1918 *EncMT, NotNAT B,
    WhScrn 2*
Castle, Walter H 1905- *IntMPA 1977*
Castle, William 1914- *FilmgC, IntMPA 1977,
    NewYTET, WorEnF*
Castleton, Barbara 1896- *Film 1, Film 2, TwYS*
Castro, Armando 1904-1961 *AmSCAP 1966*
Castro, Fidel *WhoHol A*
Castro, Steven 1864-1952 *WhScrn 1, WhScrn 2*
Castro Y Bellvis, Guillen De 1569-1631 *McGWD,
    OxThe*
Castro Y Bellvis, Guillende 1569-1631 *NotNAT B*
Caswell, Oscar Charles 1913- *AmSCAP 1966*
Catalano, Thomas J 1933- *AmSCAP 1966*
Catelain, Jacques *Film 2*
Cates, George 1911- *AmSCAP 1966*
Cates, Gilbert 1934- *BiE&WWA, IntMPA 1977,
    NewYTET, NotNAT*
Cates, Joseph 1924- *BiE&WWA, NewYTET,
    NotNAT*
Cates, Madlyn *WhoHol A*
Catizone, Joseph 1902- *AmSCAP 1966*
Catlett, Walter 1889-1960 *EncMT, Film 2,
    FilmgC, MotPP, MovMk, NotNAT B,
    Vers A, WhScrn 1, WhScrn 2, WhThe,
    WhoHol B*
Catling, Thomas 1838-1920 *WhThe*
Cator, Peter *ConDr 1977B*
Catron, John H 1916- *AmSCAP 1966*
Cattle, Harry *Film 2*
Cattley, Cyril 1876-1937 *WhThe*
Catto, Max 1907- *FilmgC, WhThe*
Catton, Bruce 1899- *CelR 3*
Cau, Jean 1925- *CnMD*
Caubisens, Henri *BiE&WWA*
Caufield, Marie Celene *WomWMM B*
Caulfield, Joan 1922- *FilmgC, IntMPA 1977,
    MotPP, WhoHol A*
Caulkins, Rufus d1935 *WhScrn 1, WhScrn 2*
Caulson, Roy *Film 2*
Caussin, Nicolas 1580-1651 *OxThe*

Caute, David 1936- *ConDr 1977*
Cauvin, Andre 1907- *DcFM*
Cavacchioli, Enrico 1885-1954 *McGWD*
Cavalcanti, Alberto 1897- *BiDFlm, DcFM, FilmgC, IntMPA 1977, MovMk, OxFilm, WorEnF*
Cavalier, Alain 1931- *WorEnF*
Cavalieri, Lina 1874-1944 *Film 1, Film 2, TwYS, WhScrn 2, WhoHol B*
Cavallaro, Carmen 1913- *AmSCAP 1966*
Cavallaro, Jeanne Fisher *WomWMM B*
Cavan, Allan *Film 2*
Cavanagh, Lilian d1932 *WhThe*
Cavanagh, Paul 1895- *Vers A, WhThe*
Cavanagh, Paul 1895-1959 *Film 2, WhoHol B*
Cavanagh, Paul 1895-1960 *MovMk*
Cavanagh, Paul 1895-1964 *FilmgC, WhScrn 2*
Cavanaugh, Bob 1902- *AmSCAP 1966*
Cavanaugh, Helene *Film 2*
Cavanaugh, Hobart d1950 *Film 2, NotNAT B, WhoHol B*
Cavanaugh, Hobart 1886-1950 *FilmgC, Vers A*
Cavanaugh, Hobart 1887-1950 *MovMk, WhScrn 1, WhScrn 2*
Cavanaugh, James *AmSCAP 1966*
Cavanaugh, Page 1922- *AmSCAP 1966*
Cavanaugh, William *Film 1, Film 2*
Cavani, Liliana *WomWMM*
Cavanna, Elise 1902-1963 *NotNAT B, WhScrn 1, WhScrn 2, WhoHol B*
Cavanna, Elsie *Film 2*
Cave, Joe Arnold 1823-1912 *OxThe*
Caven, Allan 1880-1941 *WhScrn 1, WhScrn 2, WhoHol B*
Cavender, Glen W 1884-1962 *Film 1, WhScrn 1, WhScrn 2, WhoHol B*
Cavender, Glenn W 1884-1962 *Film 2, NotNAT B*
Cavendish, Ada 1847-1895 *NotNAT B*
Cavendish, David 1891-1960 *WhScrn 1, WhScrn 2, WhoHol B*
Cavens, Fred 1882-1962 *CmMov, Film 2, WhScrn 2*
Cavett, Dick *NewYTET*
Cavett, Dick 1936- *CelR 3*
Cavett, Dick 1937- *IntMPA 1977*
Cavin, Jess *Film 2*
Cawarden, Sir Thomas *OxThe*
Cawthorn, Joseph 1867-1949 *EncMT, Film 2, NotNAT B, TwYS, WhThe, WhoHol B*
Cawthorn, Joseph 1868-1949 *WhScrn 1, WhScrn 2, WhoStg 1906, WhoStg 1908*
Cawthorne, Ann *WomWMM*
Cawthorne, Peter *Film 2*
Cawthron, Janie M 1888- *AmSCAP 1966*
Cayatte, Andre 1909- *BiDFlm, DcFM, FilmgC, OxFilm, WorEnF*
Cayrol, Jean 1911- *DcFM, OxFilm, WorEnF*
Cayvan, Georgia 1857-1906 *FamA&A*
Cayvan, Georgia 1858-1906 *NotNAT B*
Cazale, John *PIP&P, WhoHol A*
Cazenuve, Paul d1925 *Film 2, WhScrn 1, WhScrn 2, WhoHol B*
Ceccarelli, Vincenzo 1889-1969 *WhScrn 1, WhScrn 2*
Cecchetti, Enrico 1847-1928 *WhThe*
Cecchetti, Enrico 1850-1928 *NotNAT B*
Cecchi, Emilio 1884-1966 *DcFM*
Cecchi, Giovan Maria 1518-1587 *McGWD*
Cecchi, Giovanni Maria 1518-1587 *OxThe*
Cecchi D'Amico, Suso 1914- *DcFM, OxFilm, WomWMM, WorEnF*
Cecchini, Orsola *OxThe*
Cecchini, Pier Maria 1575-1645 *OxThe*

Cecil, Edward 1888-1940 *Film 1, Film 2, WhScrn 1, WhScrn 2, WhoHol B*
Cecil, Henry 1902- *WhoThe 16*
Cecil, Mary 1885-1940 *WhScrn 1, WhScrn 2, WhoHol B*
Cecil, Nora 1879- *Film 1, Film 2, TwYS, Vers B*
Cecil, Sylvia 1906- *WhThe*
Cedar, Dayna d1974 *WhScrn 2*
Cedar, Ivan d1937 *WhScrn 2*
Cederborg, Gucken *Film 2*
Cederstrom, Ellen *Film 2*
Cekalski, Eugeniusz *WomWMM*
Celeste, Celine 1814-1882 *NotNAT B, OxThe*
Celeste, Olga 1887-1969 *WhScrn 1, WhScrn 2*
Celestin, Jack 1894- *WhThe*
Celi, Adolfo 1922- *FilmgC, WhoHol A*
Celler, Emanuel 1888- *CelR 3*
Celli, Faith 1888-1942 *NotNAT B, WhThe*
Cellier, Alfred 1844-1891 *NotNAT B*
Cellier, Antoinette 1913- *WhThe*
Cellier, Frank 1884-1948 *FilmgC, NotNAT B, WhScrn 1, WhScrn 2, WhThe, WhoHol B*
Cendrars, Blaise 1887-1961 *OxFilm*
Centlivre, Susannah 1667?-1723 *McGWD, NotNAT B, OxThe*
Cerbus, Paul 1919- *AmSCAP 1966*
Cere, Mindie A 1910- *AmSCAP 1966*
Cerf, Bennett 1898- *BiE&WWA, PIP&P*
Cerito, Ada *WhThe*
Cerny, Berthe *WhThe*
Cerrito, Fanny 1821-1899 *NotNAT B*
Cervantes, Miguel De 1547-1616 *CnThe, McGWD, REnWD*
Cervantes Saavedra, Miguel De 1547-1616 *NotNAT B, OxThe*
Cervenkova, Thea *WomWMM*
Cervi, Gino 1901-1974 *FilmgC, MovMk, OxFilm, WhScrn 2, WhoHol B*
Cesaire, Aime 1913- *CnMD, CroCD, REnWD*
Cesana, Otto 1905- *AmSCAP 1966*
Cesana, Renzo 1907-1970 *WhScrn 1, WhScrn 2, WhoHol B*
Cesana, Renzo 1917- *AmSCAP 1966*
Cesar, M d1921 *WhScrn 1, WhScrn 2*
Chabrier, Marcel 1888-1946 *WhScrn 1, WhScrn 2*
Chabrol, Claude 1930- *BiDFlm, CelR 3, DcFM, FilmgC, IntMPA 1977, MovMk, OxFilm, WorEnF*
Chadbon, Tom 1946- *WhoThe 16*
Chadwick, Clive *Film 2*
Chadwick, Cyril *Film 2, TwYS*
Chadwick, Helene 1897-1940 *Film 1, Film 2, MotPP, TwYS, WhScrn 1, WhScrn 2, WhoHol B*
Chaffee, Joan *WomWMM B*
Chaffey, Don 1917- *FilmgC, IntMPA 1977*
Chagall, Marc 1887- *CelR 3*
Chagnon, Jack *Film 1*
Chagrin, Francis 1905- *FilmgC*
Chagrin, Julian 1940- *WhoThe 16*
Chaikin, Joseph 1935- *NotNAT, WhoThe 16*
Chaikin, William E 1919- *IntMPA 1977*
Chaine, Pierre *WhThe*
Chaires, Nestor d1971 *WhoHol B*
Chajes, Julius 1910- *AmSCAP 1966*
Chakeres, Michael H *IntMPA 1977*
Chakiris, George *MotPP, WhoHol A*
Chakiris, George 1933- *FilmgC*
Chakiris, George 1934- *IntMPA 1977, MovMk*
Chakolouny *Film 2*
Chaliapin, Fedor, Jr. *Film 2*
Chaliapin, Feodor 1873-1938 *FilmgC, OxFilm,*

WhScrn 1, WhScrn 2, WhoHol B
Challee, William 1912- *Vers A, WhoHol A*
Challenger, Percy *Film 1, Film 2*
Challenor, Bromley 1884-1935 *WhThe*
Challis, Christopher 1919- *FilmgC, WorEnF*
Chalmers, Thomas 1884-1966 *BiE&WWA, NotNAT B*
Chalmers, Thomas 1890-1966 *Film 2, WhScrn 1, WhScrn 2, WhoHol B*
Chalzel, Leo 1901-1953 *NotNAT B, WhScrn 1, WhScrn 2, WhThe, WhoHol B*
Chamberlain, Cyril 1909- *FilmgC*
Chamberlain, George 1891- *WhThe*
Chamberlain, Howland *WhoHol A*
Chamberlain, Richard 1935- *CelR 3, FilmgC, IntMPA 1977, MotPP, MovMk, WhoHol A, WhoThe 16*
Chamberlain, Roy S 1907- *AmSCAP 1966*
Chamberlain, Wilt 1936- *CelR 3*
Chamberlin, Frank 1870-1935 *WhScrn 1, WhScrn 2*
Chamberlin, Ione 1880- *WhoStg 1908*
Chamberlin, Riley C 1854-1917 *WhScrn 2, WhoHol B*
Chamberlin, Ward B, Jr. *NewYTET*
Chambers, C Haddon 1860-1921 *WhoStg 1908*
Chambers, Charles Haddon 1860-1921 *NotNAT B, WhThe*
Chambers, Emma *WhThe*
Chambers, Ernest *see* Ilson, Paul And Ernest Chambers
Chambers, Ernest A 1928- *AmSCAP 1966*
Chambers, Everett 1926- *IntMPA 1977, NewYTET*
Chambers, H Kellett 1867-1935 *WhThe*
Chambers, Haddon 1861- *WhoStg 1906*
Chambers, Henry Kellett 1867-1935 *NotNAT B*
Chambers, J Wheaton 1888-1958 *WhScrn 1, WhScrn 2*
Chambers, J Wheaton *see also* Chambers, Wheaton
Chambers, Jane *NatPD*
Chambers, Kathleen *Film 2*
Chambers, Kellett 1867-1935 *WhoStg 1906, WhoStg 1908*
Chambers, Lyster d1947 *NotNAT B*
Chambers, Margaret d1965 *Film 2, WhScrn 1, WhScrn 2, WhoHol B*
Chambers, Marie 1889-1933 *Film 1, Film 2, WhScrn 1, WhScrn 2, WhoHol B*
Chambers, Marilyn *WhoHol A*
Chambers, Norma d1953 *NotNAT B*
Chambers, Ralph 1892-1968 *NotNAT B, WhScrn 2, WhoHol B*
Chambers, Wheaton 1888-1958 *WhoHol B*
Chambers, Wheaton *see also* Chambers, J Wheaton
Chambers, William 1910- *BiE&WWA, NotNAT*
Chamier, Francis *Film 1*
Champagne Charlie *OxThe*
Champion, George *Film 1*
Champion, Gower *MotPP*
Champion, Gower 1920- *EncMT, WhoThe 16*
Champion, Gower 1921- *BiE&WWA, CelR 3, CmMov, FilmgC, IntMPA 1977, MGM, MovMk, NotNAT, WhoHol A, WorEnF*
Champion, Harry 1866-1942 *NotNAT B, OxThe, WhThe*
Champion, John C 1923- *IntMPA 1977*
Champion, Marge *IntMPA 1977, MotPP*
Champion, Marge 1919- *WhoHol A*
Champion, Marge 1923- *CmMov, FilmgC, MGM, MovMk*
Champion, Marge 1925- *BiE&WWA, NotNAT*
Champions *MotPP*
Champlin, Charles D 1926- *IntMPA 1977*

Champmesle, Charles Chevillet 1642-1701 *NotNAT B, OxThe*
Champmesle, Marie Desmares 1642-1698 *NotNAT B, OxThe*
Chan, Oie d1967 *WhoHol B*
Chan, Mrs. Pon Y 1870-1958 *WhScrn 1, WhScrn 2*
Chance, Anna 1884-1943 *WhScrn 1, WhScrn 2, WhoHol B*
Chance, Frank 1879-1924 *WhScrn 2*
Chance, Naomi 1930-1964 *FilmgC, WhoHol B*
Chancellor, Betty *WhThe*
Chancellor, John 1927- *CelR 3, IntMPA 1977, NewYTET*
Chancellor, Joyce 1906- *WhThe*
Chancerel, Leon 1886-1965 *OxThe*
Chandler, Anna 1887-1957 *WhScrn 1, WhScrn 2, WhoHol B*
Chandler, Chick 1905- *FilmgC, IntMPA 1977, MovMk, WhoHol A*
Chandler, Edward *Film 2*
Chandler, George *MotPP*
Chandler, George 1902- *Film 2, FilmgC, TwYS, Vers A, WhoHol A*
Chandler, George 1905- *MovMk*
Chandler, Helen 1906-1965 *HolP 30, ThFT, WhScrn 1, WhScrn 2, WhoHol B*
Chandler, Helen 1909-1965 *BiE&WWA, Film 2, NotNAT B, WhThe*
Chandler, Helen 1909-1968 *FilmgC, MovMk*
Chandler, James *WhoHol A*
Chandler, James Robert 1860-1950 *WhScrn 1, WhScrn 2, WhoHol B*
Chandler, Jeff 1918-1961 *AmSCAP 1966, BiDFlm, CmMov, FilmgC, MotPP, MovMk, NotNAT B, OxFilm, WhScrn 1, WhScrn 2, WhoHol B, WorEnF*
Chandler, John Davis 1937- *FilmgC, WhoHol A*
Chandler, Lane 1899-1972 *Film 2, TwYS, WhoHol B*
Chandler, Mimi *WhoHol A*
Chandler, Mrs. Norman 1901- *CelR 3*
Chandler, Otis 1927- *CelR 3*
Chandler, Pat 1922- *AmSCAP 1966*
Chandler, Raymond 1888-1959 *DcFM, FilmgC, OxFilm, WorEnF*
Chandler, Raymond 1889-1962 *CmMov*
Chandos, John *WhoHol A*
Chaney, Chubby 1918-1936 *WhoHol B*
Chaney, Chubby *see also* Chaney, Norman Chubby
Chaney, Frances *WhoHol A*
Chaney, Frances 1889-1967 *WhScrn 2*
Chaney, Lon 1883-1930 *CmMov, Film 1, Film 2, FilmgC, MotPP, MovMk, NotNAT B, TwYS, WhScrn 1, WhScrn 2, WhoHol B, WorEnF*
Chaney, Lon 1886-1930 *BiDFlm, OxFilm*
Chaney, Lon, Jr. 1900-1973 *WhoHol B*
Chaney, Lon, Jr. 1905-1973 *WhScrn 2*
Chaney, Lon, Jr. 1906-1973 *FilmgC, Vers A*
Chaney, Lon, Jr. 1907-1973 *MovMk*
Chaney, Lon, Jr. 1912-1973 *CmMov*
Chaney, Lon, Jr. 1915-1973 *OxFilm*
Chaney, Norman Chubby 1918-1936 *Film 2, WhScrn 1, WhScrn 2*
Chaney, Norman Chubby *see also* Chaney, Chubby
Chaney, Stewart 1910-1969 *BiE&WWA, NotNAT B, PlP&P, WhThe*
Chanfrau, Mrs. F S 1837-1909 *NotNAT B*
Chanfrau, Francis S 1824-1884 *FamA&A, NotNAT B*
Chanfrau, Frank S 1824-1884 *OxThe*
Chanfrau, Henrietta Baker 1837-1909 *OxThe*
Chang, King Hoo *Film 2*

Chang, Tisa *WhoHol A*
Changar, Myra *WomWMM*
Changar, Myrna Harrison *WomWMM B*
Changas, Estelle *WomWMM B*
Channing, Carol 1921- *BiE&WWA, CelR 3,
   EncMT, FamA&A, FilmgC, MotPP,
   NotNAT, WhoHol A, WhoThe 16*
Channing, Stockard *IntMPA 1977, WhoHol A*
Chanslor, Roy d1964 *NotNAT B*
Chapel, Eugenia d1964 *NotNAT B*
Chapelle, Pola *WomWMM B*
Chapin, Alice 1858-1934 *Film 2, NotNAT B,
   WhScrn 2, WhoHol B*
Chapin, Benjamin 1875-1918 *Film 1, WhScrn 2*
Chapin, Harold 1886-1915 *CnMD, ModWD,
   NotNAT A, NotNAT B, WhThe*
Chapin, Jacques *Film 2*
Chapin, Louis LeBourgeois 1918- *WhoThe 16*
Chapin, Slocum 1913- *IntMPA 1977*
Chaplin, Alice *Film 2*
Chaplin, Charles 1889- *BiDFlm, CmMov, DcFM,
   FilmgC, IntMPA 1977, MotPP, MovMk,
   OxFilm, WhThe, WhoHol A, WorEnF*
Chaplin, Charles, Jr. 1925-1968 *WhScrn 1,
   WhScrn 2, WhoHol B*
Chaplin, Charles S 1911- *IntMPA 1977*
Chaplin, Charlie 1889- *CelR 3, ConDr 1977A,
   Film 1, Film 2, TwYS, TwYS A*
Chaplin, Geraldine 1944- *FilmgC, MotPP,
   WhoHol A*
Chaplin, Marian Wood 1914- *AmSCAP 1966*
Chaplin, Mildred Harris *Film 2*
Chaplin, Saul 1912- *AmSCAP 1966, CmMov,
   FilmgC, IntMPA 1977, OxFilm*
Chaplin, Sidney 1885-1965 *Film 2*
Chaplin, Syd 1885-1965 *Film 1, Film 2, FilmgC*
Chaplin, Sydney 1885-1965 *Film 2, MotPP,
   TwYS, WhScrn 1, WhScrn 2, WhoHol B*
Chaplin, Sydney 1926- *BiE&WWA, EncMT,
   FilmgC, MotPP, NotNAT, WhoHol A*
Chapman, Blanche 1851-1941 *NotNAT B,
   WhScrn 1, WhScrn 2, WhoHol B*
Chapman, Charles *Film 1*
Chapman, Constance 1912- *WhoThe 16*
Chapman, Edward 1901- *FilmgC, MovMk,
   WhThe*
Chapman, Edythe 1863-1948 *Film 1, Film 2,
   NotNAT B, TwYS, WhScrn 1, WhScrn 2,
   WhoHol B*
Chapman, George 1559?-1634 *CnThe, NotNAT B,
   REnWD*
Chapman, George 1560?-1634 *McGWD, OxThe,
   PIP&P*
Chapman, Gilbert W 1902- *BiE&WWA*
Chapman, Henry 1822-1865 *NotNAT B*
Chapman, John 1900-1972 *BiE&WWA,
   NotNAT B*
Chapman, John R 1927- *WhoThe 16*
Chapman, Leonard *Film 2*
Chapman, Lonny 1920- *BiE&WWA, NotNAT,
   WhoHol A*
Chapman, Marcia *Film 2*
Chapman, Marguerite *MotPP*
Chapman, Marguerite 1916- *FilmgC*
Chapman, Marguerite 1920- *WhoHol A*
Chapman, Marguerite 1921- *HolP 40*
Chapman, Ned *Film 1*
Chapman, Richard *WhoHol A*
Chapman, Robert H 1919- *BiE&WWA, NotNAT*
Chapman, Tedwell 1917- *IntMPA 1977*
Chapman, Thomas H 1896-1969 *WhScrn 1,
   WhScrn 2*
Chapman, Walter Lynn 1913- *AmSCAP 1966*
Chapman, William *Film 2*

Chapman, William 1764-1839 *NotNAT B, OxThe*
Chappell, Dorothy *Film 2*
Chappell, William 1908- *EncMT, WhoThe 16*
Chappelle, Frederick W 1895- *WhThe*
Chapple, Wendy Wood *WomWMM A,
   WomWMM B*
Chappuzeau, Samuel 1625-1701 *OxThe*
Charbeneau, Oscar d1915 *WhScrn 2*
Charell, Erik 1895- *DcFM, WhThe*
Charell, Erik *see also* Charrell, Erik
Chari, V K N 1913- *IntMPA 1977*
Charig, Phil 1902-1960 *AmSCAP 1966,
   NotNAT B*
Charig, Philip 1902-1960 *EncMT*
Charisse, Cyd *MotPP, WhoHol A*
Charisse, Cyd 1921- *BiDFlm, FilmgC, MGM*
Charisse, Cyd 1922- *WorEnF*
Charisse, Cyd 1923- *CmMov, IntMPA 1977,
   MovMk*
Charisse, Cyd 1924- *OxFilm*
Charkovsky, Willis 1918- *AmSCAP 1966*
Charland, Ainse *Film 2*
Charland, Alme *Film 2*
Charlap, Mark *BiE&WWA*
Charlap, Morris 1928- *AmSCAP 1966*
Charle, Gustav *Film 2*
Charles, Dick 1919- *AmSCAP 1966*
Charles, Ernest 1895- *AmSCAP 1966*
Charles, Fred d1904 *NotNAT B*
Charles, John *Film 1*
Charles, Lewis *WhoHol A*
Charles, Maria 1929- *IntMPA 1977*
Charles, Michael d1967 *WhoHol B*
Charles, Pamela 1932- *WhoThe 16*
Charles, Ray 1918- *AmSCAP 1966*
Charles, Ray 1932- *CelR 3*
Charles, Rosalind *Film 2*
Charleson, Leslie *WhoHol A*
Charleson, Mary 1885-1968 *Film 1, Film 2,
   TwYS*
Charleson, Mary 1893-1961 *MotPP, NotNAT B,
   WhScrn 2*
Charlesworth, Florence M 1885- *AmSCAP 1966*
Charlesworth, John 1935-1960 *FilmgC, WhScrn 1,
   WhScrn 2, WhoHol B*
Charley, John *Film 1*
Charlia, Georges *Film 2*
Charlier, Monsieur *Film 2*
Charlita *WhoHol A*
Charlot, Andre 1882-1956 *CnThe, EncMT,
   NotNAT B, WhScrn 2, WhThe*
Charlton, Harold C d1954 *NotNAT B*
Charlton, Maryette *WomWMM B*
Charmoli, Tony *NewYTET*
Charnin, Martin 1934- *AmSCAP 1966,
   BiE&WWA, NewYTET, NotNAT,
   WhoThe 16*
Charny, Suzanne *WhoHol A*
Charon, Jacques 1920-1975 *PIP&P, WhScrn 2,
   WhoHol C*
Charpentier, Gaston L G 1912- *IntMPA 1977*
Charpentier, Gustave 1860-1956 *NotNAT B*
Charpin, Fernand 1887-1944 *OxFilm*
Charrell, Erik 1895- *WorEnF*
Charrell, Erik *see also* Charell, Erik
Charren, Peggy *NewYTET*
Charrier, Jacques *WhoHol A*
Charriere, Henri 1907-1973 *WhScrn 2*
Charsky, Boris 1893-1956 *Film 2, WhScrn 1,
   WhScrn 2, WhoHol B*
Chart, Henry Nye 1868-1934 *WhThe*
Charteris, Leslie 1907- *FilmgC, IntMPA 1977*
Charters, Spencer 1875-1943 *NotNAT B, Vers B,
   WhScrn 1, WhScrn 2, WhoHol B*

Charters, Spencer 1878-1943 *Film 2, FilmgC, MovMk*
Chartoff, Robert *IntMPA 1977*
Charvay, Robert 1858- *WhThe*
Charvein, Denise *WomWMM*
Chase, Albert *Film 2*
Chase, Arline 1900-1926 *WhScrn 1, WhScrn 2, WhoHol B*
Chase, Barrie *WhoHol A*
Chase, Borden *CmMov*
Chase, Borden 1899?-1971 *FilmgC*
Chase, Borden 1900-1971 *WorEnF*
Chase, Brandon *IntMPA 1977*
Chase, Bud *Film 1*
Chase, Charley 1893-1940 *MotPP, OxFilm, TwYS, WhScrn 1, WhScrn 2, WhoHol B, WorEnF*
Chase, Charlie 1893-1940 *Film 1, Film 2, FilmgC*
Chase, Chevy *NewYTET*
Chase, Colin 1886-1937 *Film 2, WhScrn 1, WhScrn 2, WhoHol B*
Chase, Doris Totten 1923- *WomWMM B*
Chase, Edna 1888- *WhoStg 1906, WhoStg 1908*
Chase, George Washington 1890-1918 *WhScrn 2*
Chase, Hal 1883-1947 *WhScrn 2*
Chase, Ilka *BiE&WWA, MotPP, NotNAT*
Chase, Ilka 1900- *FamA&A, FilmgC*
Chase, Ilka 1903- *ThFT*
Chase, Ilka 1905- *CelR 3, Film 2, IntMPA 1977, MovMk, NotNAT A, WhoHol A, WhoThe 16*
Chase, J Newell 1904-1955 *AmSCAP 1966*
Chase, Lucia 1907- *CelR 3*
Chase, Mary 1907- *BiE&WWA, CnMD, ConDr 1977, McGWD, ModWD, NotNAT, PIP&P, WhoThe 16*
Chase, Pauline 1885-1962 *NotNAT B, WhThe, WhoStg 1908*
Chase, Stanley 1928- *BiE&WWA, NotNAT*
Chase, Stephen *WhoHol A*
Chase, William B d1948 *NotNAT B*
Chaseman, Joel *NewYTET*
Chasen, Dave 1899-1973 *WhScrn 2*
Chasen, Heather 1927- *WhoThe 16*
Chasins, Abram 1903- *AmSCAP 1966*
Chasman, David 1925- *IntMPA 1977*
Chastain, Don *WhoHol A*
Chater, Geoffrey 1921- *WhoThe 16*
Chatham, Pitt d1923 *NotNAT B*
Chatrian, Louis Gratien C Alexandre 1826-1890 *NotNAT B*
Chattaway, Thurland 1872-1947 *AmSCAP 1966*
Chatterton, Ruth 1893-1961 *BiDFlm, CmMov, Film 2, FilmgC, MotPP, MovMk, NotNAT B, ThFT, WhScrn 1, WhScrn 2, WhThe, WhoHol B, WomWMM*
Chatterton, Thomas 1881-1952 *Film 1, WhScrn 1, WhScrn 2, WhoHol B*
Chatton, Sydney 1918-1966 *WhScrn 1, WhScrn 2, WhoHol B*
Chatwin, Margaret d1937 *WhThe*
Chaudet, Louis 1884- *TwYS A*
Chaudet, Mary 1920- *AmSCAP 1966*
Chaudhri, Amin Qamar 1938- *IntMPA 1977*
Chaumont, Celine d1926 *NotNAT B*
Chautard, Emile 1881-1934 *DcFM, Film 1, Film 2, TwYS, WhScrn 1, WhScrn 2, WhoHol B*
Chautard, Emile 1892-1964 *TwYS A*
Chauvel, Charles E 1897-1959 *FilmgC, OxFilm, WhScrn 1, WhScrn 2*
Chauvenet, Virginia d1949 *NotNAT B*
Chauvin, Lilyan *WhoHol A*

Chavez, Carlos 1899- *AmSCAP 1966*
Chavez, Cesar 1927- *CelR 3*
Chavez, Edmund M 1926- *NotNAT*
Chayefsky, Paddy 1923- *AmSCAP 1966, BiE&WWA, CelR 3, CnMD, CnThe, ConDr 1977, CroCD, DcFM, IntMPA 1977, McGWD, ModWD, NotNAT, OxFilm, PIP&P, WhoThe 16, WorEnF*
Chayevsky, Paddy 1923- *FilmgC, NewYTET*
Cheatham, Jack 1894-1971 *WhScrn 2*
Cheatham, Kitty d1946 *NotNAT B, WhoStg 1906, WhoStg 1908*
Chebat, Georges *Film 2*
Checchi, Andrea 1916-1974 *WhScrn 2, WhoHol B*
Checco, Al *WhoHol A*
Checker, Chubby 1941- *AmSCAP 1966, FilmgC, WhoHol A*
Cheeseman, Peter 1932- *WhoThe 16*
Cheever, John 1912- *CelR 3*
Chef Milani 1892-1965 *WhScrn 2*
Chefe, Jack 1894-1975 *WhoHol C*
Chefee, Jack 1894-1975 *Film 2, TwYS, WhScrn 2*
Cheiffetz, Hyman 1901- *AmSCAP 1966*
Cheirel, Jeanne 1868-1934 *WhScrn 1*
Cheirel, Jeanne 1869-1934 *WhScrn 2*
Cheirel, Micheline *WhoHol A*
Chekhov, Anton Pavlovich 1860-1904 *CnMD, CnThe, McGWD, ModWD, NotNAT A, NotNAT B, OxThe, PIP&P, PIP&P A, REnWD*
Chekhov, Michael 1891-1955 *FilmgC, MotPP, NotNAT B, OxThe, WhScrn 1, WhScrn 2, WhThe, WhoHol B*
Chekhov, Olga Knipper 1869-1959 *OxThe*
Chekhova, Olga 1869-1959 *WomWMM*
Chekova, Olga 1869-1959 *Film 2*
Chelton, Nick 1946- *WhoThe 16*
Chen, Betty *WomWMM B*
Chenal, Pierre 1903- *DcFM, FilmgC*
Chene, Dixie *Film 1*
Chene, Ethel d1972 *WhoHol B*
Chenette, Edward Stephen 1895-1963 *AmSCAP 1966*
Cheney, Sheldon 1886- *BiE&WWA, NotNAT, WhThe*
Chenier, Louise *WomWMM*
Chenier, Marie-Joseph 1764-1811 *NotNAT B, OxThe*
Chenis, Patti-Lee *WomWMM B*
Chenoweth, Wilbur 1899- *AmSCAP 1966*
Cher 1946- *IntMPA 1977, NewYTET, WhoHol A*
Cherdak, Jeanne 1915- *AmSCAP 1966*
Cheri, Rose 1824-1861 *OxThe*
Cherin, Robert 1936- *BiE&WWA*
Cherkasov, Nikolai 1903-1966 *OxFilm, WhThe, WorEnF*
Cherkassov, Nicolai 1903-1966 *FilmgC*
Cherkassov, Nikolai 1903-1966 *WhScrn 1, WhScrn 2, WhoHol B*
Chermak, Cy *NewYTET*
Cherne, Leo 1912- *CelR 3*
Cherney, Boris E 1921- *AmSCAP 1966*
Cherniavsky, Josef 1895-1959 *AmSCAP 1966*
Chernis, Jay 1906- *AmSCAP 1966*
Chernuck, Dorothy *BiE&WWA, NotNAT*
Cheron, Andre *Film 2*
Cherrell, Gwen 1926- *WhoThe 16*
Cherrill, Virginia 1908- *FilmgC, MotPP, MovMk, ThFT, TwYS, WhoHol A*
Cherrington, Ruth *Film 2*
Cherry, Addie d1942 *NotNAT B*

Cherry, Andrew 1762-1812 *NotNAT B*
Cherry, Charles 1872-1931 *NotNAT B, WhThe, WhoHol B, WhoStg 1906, WhoStg 1908*
Cherry, Effie d1944 *NotNAT B*
Cherry, Ellen d1934 *NotNAT B*
Cherry, Helen 1915- *FilmgC, WhThe, WhoHol A*
Cherry, Jessie d1903 *NotNAT B*
Cherry, Kate *Film 2*
Cherry, Lizzie d1936 *NotNAT B*
Cherry, Malcolm 1878-1925 *NotNAT B*
Cherry, Wal 1932- *WhoThe 16*
Cherryman, Rex 1898-1928 *Film 2, NotNAT B, WhScrn 1, WhScrn 2, WhoHol B*
Chertok, Harvey 1932- *IntMPA 1977*
Chertok, Jack *IntMPA 1977, NewYTET*
Chesebro, George 1888-1959 *Film 1, WhScrn 2, WhoHol B*
Chesebro, George 1890-1959 *Film 2*
Cheshire, Harry V Pappy 1892-1968 *WhScrn 2, WhoHol B*
Cheshire, Maxine 1930- *CelR 3*
Cheskin, Irving W 1915- *BiE&WWA, NotNAT, WhoThe 16*
Chesney, Arthur 1882-1949 *Film 2, NotNAT B, WhScrn 1, WhScrn 2, WhThe, WhoHol B*
Chessler, Deborah *AmSCAP 1966*
Chester, Alma 1871-1953 *WhScrn 1, WhScrn 2, WhoHol B*
Chester, Betty 1895-1943 *WhThe*
Chester, Brock 1947-1971 *WhScrn 1, WhScrn 2*
Chester, Mrs. George Randolph *WomWMM*
Chester, Giraud *NewYTET*
Chester, Hal E 1921- *FilmgC, IntMPA 1977*
Chester, Robert T 1908- *AmSCAP 1966*
Chester, Samuel K d1921 *NotNAT B*
Chester, Virginia *Film 1*
Chesterton, Gilbert Keith 1874-1936 *NotNAT B*
Chetham-Strode, Warren 1897- *WhThe*
Chetkin, Leonard 1928- *AmSCAP 1966*
Chettle, Henry 1560?-1607? *CnThe, NotNAT B, OxThe, REnWD*
Chetwood, William Rufus d1766 *NotNAT B*
Chetwyn, Robert 1933- *WhoThe 16*
Chetwynd, Lionel 1940- *IntMPA 1977*
Cheung, Louie *Film 2*
Chevalier, Albert 1861-1923 *NotNAT A, NotNAT B, OxThe, PIP&P, WhScrn 2, WhThe, WhoStg 1908*
Chevalier, Gus d1947 *NotNAT B*
Chevalier, Marcelle *WhThe*
Chevalier, Maurice 1887-1972 *CmMov*
Chevalier, Maurice 1888-1972 *BiDFlm, BiE&WWA, Film 1, Film 2, FilmgC, MotPP, MovMk, NotNAT B, OxFilm, OxThe, WhScrn 2, WhThe, WhoHol B, WorEnF*
Chevalier, Maurice 1889-1972 *NotNAT A*
Chevalier, May d1940 *NotNAT B*
Chevallay, Annie *WomWMM*
Chew, Frank *Film 2*
Chew, Virgilia *WhoHol A*
Cheyney, Peter 1896-1951 *FilmgC*
Chi, Greta *WhoHol A*
Chiaffarelli, Alberte 1884-1945 *AmSCAP 1966*
Chiang, Ching *WomWMM*
Chiarelli, Luigi 1880-1947 *McGWD, ModWD*
Chiarelli, Luigi 1884-1947 *OxThe, REnWD*
Chiarelli, Luigi 1886-1947 *CnMD*
Chiari, Mario 1909- *FilmgC, WorEnF*
Chiari, Walter 1924- *FilmgC, WhoHol A*
Chiarini, Luigi 1900- *DcFM, OxFilm*
Chiasson, Warren 1934- *AmSCAP 1966*
Chiaureli, Mikhail 1894- *DcFM*

Chicago, Judy 1939- *WomWMM B*
Chichester, Emily *Film 1, Film 2*
Chichkova, Ludmilla *WomWMM*
Chidester, L W 1906- *AmSCAP 1966*
Chief Black Hawk d1975 *WhScrn 2, WhoHol C*
Chief Jack 1877-1943 *WhScrn 1, WhScrn 2, WhoHol B*
Chief John Big Tree 1865-1967 *WhScrn 1, WhScrn 2, WhoHol B*
Chief Many Treaties 1875-1948 *WhScrn 1, WhScrn 2, WhoHol B*
Chief Nipo Strongheart 1891-1966 *WhScrn 1, WhScrn 2*
Chief Standing Bear d1939 *WhScrn 2*
Chief Thundercloud 1889-1955 *WhScrn 1, WhScrn 2, WhoHol B*
Chief Thundercloud 1898-1967 *WhScrn 1, WhScrn 2, WhoHol B*
Chief Thundercloud *see also* Thundercloud, Chief
Chief Yowlachie 1891-1966 *WhScrn 2, WhoHol B*
Chikada, Tadashi 1919- *IntMPA 1977*
Chikamatsu, Monzayemon 1653?-1724 *NotNAT B*
Chikamatsu Monzaemon 1653-1725 *CnThe, McGWD, REnWD*
Child, Abigail *WomWMM A, WomWMM B*
Child, Harold Hannyngton 1869-1945 *NotNAT B, WhThe*
Child, Julia 1912- *CelR 3*
Childers, Naomi d1964 *MotPP, NotNAT B, WhoHol B*
Childers, Naomi 1892-1964 *Film 1, Film 2, TwYS*
Childers, Naomi 1893-1964 *WhScrn 1, WhScrn 2*
Childress, Alice 1920- *ConDr 1977, NotNAT, PIP&P A*
Childress, Alvin *NotNAT*
Childs, Gilbert d1931 *NotNAT B, WhThe, WhoHol B*
Childs, Marquis 1903- *CelR 3*
Childs, Monroe 1891-1963 *WhScrn 1, WhScrn 2*
Chiles, Linden *WhoHol A*
Chiles, Lois *WhoHol A*
Chilton, T E 1929- *IntMPA 1977*
Chin, Frank *NatPD*
Chin, Tsai 1938?- *FilmgC*
Ching, William *WhoHol A*
Ching, William 1912- *FilmgC*
Ching, William 1913- *IntMPA 1977, Vers B*
Chinich, Jesse 1921- *IntMPA 1977*
Chinlund, Jennifer *WomWMM B*
Chinlund, Phyllis *WomWMM A, WomWMM B*
Chinnappa, P U d1951 *WhScrn 2*
Chinoy, Helen Krich 1922- *BiE&WWA, NotNAT*
Chionides *OxThe*
Chirello, George Shorty 1897-1963 *WhScrn 1, WhScrn 2, WhoHol B*
Chirgwin, George H 1854-1922 *OxThe, WhThe*
Chirskov, Boris 1904- *DcFM*
Chisholm, Robert 1898-1960 *NotNAT B, WhThe, WhoHol B*
Chisholm, Shirley 1924- *CelR 3*
Chissell, Noble 1910- *IntMPA 1977, WhoHol A*
Chistyakov, A *Film 2*
Chittison, Herman d1967 *WhScrn 1, WhScrn 2*
Chivers, Alan 1918- *IntMPA 1977*
Chivot, Henri d1897 *NotNAT B*
Chivvis, Chic 1884-1963 *WhScrn 1, WhScrn 2, WhoHol B*
Chkeidze, Revas 1926- *DcFM*
Chlumberg, Hans 1897-1930 *CnMD, McGWD, ModWD*
Chmara, Grigory *Film 2*
Choate, Edward 1908-1975 *BiE&WWA, NotNAT, NotNAT B*

Choate, Robert B, Jr. *NewYTET*
Chocolate-Coloured Coon *OxThe*
Chodorov, Edward *WhThe*
Chodorov, Edward 1904- *CnMD, FilmgC, ModWD*
Chodorov, Edward 1914- *BiE&WWA, IntMPA 1977, NotNAT*
Chodorov, Jerome 1911- *BiE&WWA, ConDr 1977D, FilmgC, McGWD, ModWD, NatPD, NewMT, NotNAT, WhoThe 16*
Choerilus *OxThe*
Chomette, Henri 1891-1941 *OxFilm*
Chomon, Segundo De 1871-1929 *DcFM, OxFilm*
Chomsky, Marvin J *IntMPA 1977, NewYTET*
Chomsky, Noam 1928- *CelR 3*
Chooluck, Leon 1920- *IntMPA 1977*
Chopin, Frederic 1810-1849 *NotNAT B*
Chopra, Joyce *WomWMM A, WomWMM B*
Chorell, Walentin 1912- *CroCD, REnWD*
Chorpenning, Ruth 1905- *WhThe*
Chotzinoff, Samuel d1964 *NotNAT B*
Chou En-Lai, Madame *WomWMM*
Choureau, Etchika 1923- *FilmgC, WhoHol A*
Chow, David *WhoHol A*
Chretien, Henri 1879-1956 *DcFM, FilmgC, OxFilm, WorEnF*
Chris, Marilyn *WhoHol A*
Chrisman, H Ed 1914- *IntMPA 1977*
Chrisman, Pat *Film 1, Film 2*
Christensen, Benjamin 1879-1959 *BiDFlm, DcFM, Film 2, FilmgC, OxFilm, WhScrn 2, WorEnF*
Christensen, Benjamin *see also* Christiansen, Benjamin
Christensen, Lew 1906- *BiE&WWA*
Christensen, Mary *Film 2*
Christensen, William F 1902- *BiE&WWA*
Christiakov, A P *Film 2*
Christian, Bobby 1911- *AmSCAP 1966*
Christian, John 1884-1950 *WhScrn 1, WhScrn 2*
Christian, Linda *MotPP, WhoHol A*
Christian, Linda 1923- *FilmgC*
Christian, Linda 1924- *IntMPA 1977*
Christian, Mary *Film 2*
Christian, Michael *WhoHol A*
Christian, Paul *WhoHol A*
Christian-Jaque 1904- *BiDFlm, DcFM, FilmgC, OxFilm, WorEnF*
Christiano, Eleanor Irene 1912-1932 *WhScrn 2*
Christians, George 1869-1921 *Film 2, WhoHol B*
Christians, Mady 1900-1951 *FilmgC, MotPP, MovMk, NotNAT B, ThFT, WhScrn 1, WhScrn 2, WhThe, WhoHol B*
Christians, Mady 1900-1959 *Film 2*
Christians, Margarete *Film 1*
Christians, Rudolph 1869-1921 *Film 2, WhScrn 1, WhScrn 2*
Christiansen, Benjamin 1879-1959 *TwYS A*
Christiansen, Benjamin *see also* Christensen, Benjamin
Christiansen, Rasmus *Film 2*
Christiansen, Robert W & Rick Rosenberg *NewYTET*
Christie, Agatha 1890-1976 *BiE&WWA, CelR 3, CnThe, ConDr 1977, PIP&P, WhoThe 16*
Christie, Agatha 1891-1976 *FilmgC*
Christie, Al 1886-1951 *DcFM, FilmgC, NotNAT B, TwYS B*
Christie, Audrey 1912- *BiE&WWA, NotNAT, WhoHol A, WhoThe 16*
Christie, Campbell 1893-1963 *WhThe*
Christie, Charles H d1955 *NotNAT B*
Christie, Dorothy *Film 2*
Christie, Dorothy 1896- *WhThe*

Christie, George 1873-1949 *NotNAT B, WhScrn 2, WhThe*
Christie, Howard J 1912- *FilmgC, IntMPA 1977*
Christie, Ivan *Film 2*
Christie, John d1962 *NotNAT B*
Christie, Julie *MotPP, WhoHol A*
Christie, Julie 1940- *FilmgC, MovMk, OxFilm*
Christie, Julie 1941- *BiDFlm, CelR 3, IntMPA 1977, WorEnF*
Christine, Lillian *Film 2*
Christine, Virginia *IntMPA 1977*
Christine, Virginia 1917- *FilmgC*
Christine, Virginia 1920- *WhoHol A*
Christman, Marion H 1902- *AmSCAP 1966*
Christo 1935- *CelR 3*
Christopher, Jordan 1941- *IntMPA 1977, MotPP, WhoHol A*
Christopher, May 1912- *AmSCAP 1966*
Christy, Ann *MotPP*
Christy, Ann 1905- *WhoHol A*
Christy, Ann 1909- *Film 2, TwYS*
Christy, Bill 1925-1946 *WhScrn 1, WhScrn 2, WhoHol B*
Christy, Edwin P d1862 *NotNAT B*
Christy, Floyd d1962 *NotNAT B*
Christy, Ivan 1888-1949 *WhScrn 1, WhScrn 2, WhoHol B*
Christy, Ken 1895-1962 *NotNAT B, WhScrn 1, WhScrn 2, WhoHol B*
Christy, Lya *Film 2*
Christy Minstrels *OxThe*
Chronegk, Ludwig 1837-1891 *OxThe*
Chu, Shih-Ling *DcFM*
Chudleigh, Arthur 1858-1932 *WhThe*
Chukhrai, Grigori 1921- *WorEnF*
Chukrai, Grigori 1920- *FilmgC*
Chukrai, Grigori 1921- *DcFM, OxFilm*
Chung, Ling Soo *WhThe*
Church, Esme 1893-1972 *WhScrn 2, WhThe*
Church, Frank 1924- *CelR 3*
Church, Frederick *Film 1*
Church, Sandra *BiE&WWA, NotNAT, WhoHol A*
Church, Stanley *WhoHol A*
Church, Tony 1930- *WhoThe 16*
Churchill, Allen 1911- *BiE&WWA*
Churchill, Berton 1876-1940 *Film 2, FilmgC, NotNAT B, Vers A, WhScrn 1, WhScrn 2, WhThe, WhoHol B*
Churchill, Berton 1876-1946 *MovMk*
Churchill, Caryl 1938- *ConDr 1977*
Churchill, Charles d1764 *NotNAT B*
Churchill, Diana 1913- *FilmgC, WhThe, WhoHol A*
Churchill, Donald 1930- *ConDr 1977C, FilmgC*
Churchill, Frank E 1901-1942 *AmSCAP 1966*
Churchill, Joan *WomWMM B*
Churchill, Marguerite 1909- *ThFT, WhoHol A*
Churchill, Marguerite 1910- *Film 2, FilmgC, WhThe*
Churchill, Ruth *Film 1*
Churchill, Sarah *WhoHol A*
Churchill, Sarah 1914- *FilmgC, WhoThe 16*
Churchill, Sarah 1916- *IntMPA 1977*
Churchill, Winston 1871-1947 *NotNAT B, WhThe*
Churchill, Sir Winston Spencer 1874-1965 *FilmgC, OxFilm*
Chute, Marchette 1909- *BiE&WWA, NotNAT*
Chuvelyov, Ivan *Film 2*
Chytilova, Vera 1929- *OxFilm, WomWMM, WorEnF*
Ciampi, Yves 1921- *DcFM, WorEnF*
Cianelli, Alma 1892-1968 *WhScrn 1,. WhScrn 2*

Cianelli, Eduardo 1887-1969 *MotPP, WhScrn 1, WhScrn 2*
Ciannelli, Alma d1968 *WhoHol B*
Ciannelli, Eduardo 1884-1969 *MovMk*
Ciannelli, Eduardo 1887-1969 *FilmgC, WhoHol B*
Ciannelli, Eduardo 1891-1969 *Vers A*
Ciannelli, Lewis E 1923- *IntMPA 1977*
Ciarcia, John 1940- *AmSCAP 1966*
Ciardi, John 1916- *CelR 3*
Cibber, Charlotte 1713-1760? *NotNAT A, NotNAT B, OxThe*
Cibber, Colley 1671-1757 *CnThe, McGWD, NotNAT A, NotNAT B, OxThe, PIP&P, REnWD*
Cibber, Susanna Maria Arne 1714-1766 *NotNAT B, OxThe*
Cibber, Susannah Maria Arne 1714-1766 *NotNAT A, PIP&P*
Cibber, Theophilus 1703-1758 *NotNAT B, OxThe*
Cicalello, Joseph 1908- *AmSCAP 1966*
Ciceri, Charles *PIP&P*
Cicero *PIP&P*
Cichy, Theodora *WomWMM B*
Cicogna, Countess Marina *WomWMM*
Cicognini, Alessandro 1906- *DcFM, FilmgC*
Cicognini, Giacinto Andrea 1606-1660 *OxThe*
Cidoni, Jomar *WhoHol A*
Cilento, Diane *MotPP, WhoHol A, WhoThe 16*
Cilento, Diane 1933- *BiE&WWA, FilmgC, MovMk, NotNAT*
Cilento, Diane 1934- *IntMPA 1977*
Cimber, Matt 1936- *BiE&WWA, NotNAT*
Cimino, Michael 1943- *IntMPA 1977*
Cina, Albert I 1896- *AmSCAP 1966*
Cinader, Robert A *NewYTET*
Cini, Giovanni Battista d1586 *McGWD*
Cino, Joe 1931-1967 *NotNAT B*
Cinquevalli, Paul 1859-1918 *NotNAT B, OxThe, WhThe*
Cinthio, Il *OxThe*
Cinthio, Giambattista Giraldi *McGWD*
Cioffi, Charles *WhoHol A*
Ciolli, Augusta 1901-1967 *WhScrn 2*
Cirillo, Michael 1903-1968 *WhScrn 2*
Cirillo, Tony 1910-1968 *WhScrn 2*
Cirker, Mitchell d1953 *NotNAT B*
Cisney, Marcella *BiE&WWA, NotNAT*
Citron, Michele *WomWMM B*
Ciulei, Liviu 1923- *DcFM*
Clagett, Manning 1913- *IntMPA 1977*
Clair, Ethlyne 1908- *TwYS, WhoHol A*
Clair, Mavis 1916- *WhThe*
Clair, Rene 1898- *BiDFlm, DcFM, Film 2, FilmgC, IntMPA 1977, MovMk, OxFilm, WorEnF*
Claire, Bernice 1907- *Film 2, ThFT*
Claire, Ethlyne 1908- *Film 2*
Claire, Gertrude 1852-1928 *Film 1, Film 2, TwYS, WhScrn 1, WhScrn 2, WhoHol B*
Claire, Helen 1906-1974 *WhScrn 2, WhoHol B*
Claire, Helen 1911-1974 *BiE&WWA, NotNAT B, WhThe*
Claire, Ina *MotPP*
Claire, Ina 1892- *EncMT, Film 1, Film 2, FilmgC, ThFT, WhoHol A*
Claire, Ina 1895- *BiE&WWA, FamA&A, NotNAT, WhThe*
Claire, Ludi 1922- *BiE&WWA, NotNAT*
Clairon, Claire-Josephe-H L DeLaTude 1723-1803 *OxThe*
Clairon, Hyppolite 1723-1803 *NotNAT A*
Clairon, Hyppolyte 1723-1803 *NotNAT B*
Clampett, Bob *NewYTET*
Clancy, Deirdre 1943- *WhoThe 16*

Clancy, George *Film 1*
Clancy, James 1912- *BiE&WWA, NotNAT*
Clanton, Ralph 1914- *WhoThe 16*
Clapham, Charlie d1959 *NotNAT B*
Clapham, Leonard d1963 *Film 1, Film 2, WhoHol B*
Clapp, Charles 1899-1962 *AmSCAP 1966, NotNAT B*
Clapp, Charles Edwin, Jr. d1957 *NotNAT B*
Clapp, Henry Austin 1841-1904 *NotNAT A*
Clapton, Eric 1945- *CelR 3*
Clar, Arden 1915- *AmSCAP 1966*
Clarance, Arthur 1883-1956 *WhScrn 1, WhScrn 2*
Clare, Madelyn 1894-1975 *WhScrn 2, WhoHol C*
Clare, Mary 1894-1970 *Film 2, FilmgC, WhScrn 1, WhScrn 2, WhThe, WhoHol B*
Clare, Phyllis 1908-1947 *NotNAT B, WhScrn 2, WhoHol B*
Clare, Sidney 1892- *AmSCAP 1966*
Clare, Thomas Truitt 1924- *AmSCAP 1966*
Clare, Tom 1876- *WhThe*
Clarence 1960-1969 *WhScrn 2*
Clarence, O B 1870-1955 *FilmgC, NotNAT A, NotNAT B, WhScrn 1, WhScrn 2, WhThe, WhoHol B*
Clarendon, Hal *Film 2*
Clarendon, J Hayden 1879- *WhoStg 1908*
Clarens, Henry F 1860-1928 *WhScrn 1, WhScrn 2*
Claretie, Jules 1840-1913 *NotNAT B*
Clarges, Berner *Film 1*
Clarges, Verner 1848-1911 *WhScrn 2, WhoHol B*
Clarida, Orville Clifton 1910- *AmSCAP 1966*
Claridge, Norman 1903- *WhoThe 16*
Clariond, Aime 1894-1960 *WhScrn 2*
Clark, Mr. *Film 2*
Clark, Alexander 1901- *BiE&WWA, NotNAT, WhoHol A*
Clark, Alfred *WhThe*
Clark, Allan 1907- *AmSCAP 1966*
Clark, Amy Ashmore 1882-1954 *AmSCAP 1966*
Clark, Andrew *Film 2*
Clark, Andrew J 1903-1960 *WhScrn 1, WhScrn 2*
Clark, Andy 1903-1960 *Film 1, Film 2, WhoHol B*
Clark, Barrett H 1890-1953 *NotNAT B, WhThe*
Clark, Bill d1973 *WhScrn 2*
Clark, Bobby 1888-1960 *EncMT, Film 2, FilmgC, NotNAT A, NotNAT B, WhScrn 1, WhScrn 2, WhThe, WhoHol B*
Clark, Brian *ConDr 1977C*
Clark, Bridgetta *Film 2*
Clark, Buddy 1911-1949 *NotNAT B, WhScrn 2, WhoHol B*
Clark, Candy *IntMPA 1977, WhoHol A*
Clark, Charles Dow 1870-1959 *Film 2, NotNAT B, WhScrn 1, WhScrn 2, WhoHol B*
Clark, China *NatPD*
Clark, Cliff 1893-1953 *FilmgC, Vers B, WhScrn 1, WhScrn 2, WhoHol B*
Clark, Cuthbert 1869-1953 *NotNAT B*
Clark, Dane 1913- *FilmgC, MotPP, MovMk, WhoHol A*
Clark, Dane 1915- *HolP 40, IntMPA 1977*
Clark, Dian Manners *AmSCAP 1966*
Clark, Dick 1929- *IntMPA 1977, NewYTET, WhoHol A*
Clark, Dowling *Film 2*
Clark, E Holman 1864-1925 *NotNAT B, WhThe*
Clark, Ed d1954 *WhoHol B*
Clark, Eddie 1879-1954 *WhScrn 1, WhScrn 2*
Clark, Edward 1878-1954 *AmSCAP 1966*

Clark, Edwin A 1871- *Film 1, WhoStg 1908*
Clark, Ernest 1912- *FilmgC, WhoThe 16*
Clark, Estelle *Film 2*
Clark, Ethel 1916-1964 *NotNAT B, WhScrn 1, WhScrn 2, WhoHol B*
Clark, F Donald 1913- *BiE&WWA, NotNAT*
Clark, Frank *Film 1*
Clark, Frank d1945 *WhScrn 2*
Clark, Frank J 1922- *AmSCAP 1966*
Clark, Fred 1914-1968 *BiE&WWA, FilmgC, MotPP, MovMk, NotNAT B, Vers A, WhScrn 1, WhScrn 2, WhThe, WhoHol B*
Clark, Gene Emmet 1910- *AmSCAP 1966*
Clark, Harry *Film 2*
Clark, Harry 1911-1956 *NotNAT B, WhScrn 2, WhoHol B*
Clark, Harvey 1886-1938 *Film 2, WhScrn 1, WhScrn 2, WhoHol B*
Clark, Helen 1895-1974 *WhScrn 2*
Clark, Herbert *Film 2*
Clark, Hugh d1653 *OxThe*
Clark, Ivan-John d1967 *WhScrn 2*
Clark, Jack *Film 1*
Clark, Jack J 1887-1947 *WhoHol B*
Clark, Jackie *AmSCAP 1966*
Clark, James B *FilmgC*
Clark, Jim 1931- *FilmgC*
Clark, Jimmy d1972 *WhoHol B*
Clark, John J 1877-1947 *Film 2, WhScrn 1, WhScrn 2*
Clark, John L 1907- *IntMPA 1977*
Clark, John Pepper 1935- *ConDr 1977, ModWD, REnWD*
Clark, John R, Jr. 1915- *IntMPA 1977*
Clark, John Richard 1932- *WhoThe 16*
Clark, Johnny 1916-1967 *AmSCAP 1966, WhScrn 1, WhScrn 2, WhoHol B*
Clark, Ken *WhoHol A*
Clark, Kendall 1912- *BiE&WWA, NotNAT*
Clark, Kenneth 1899- *IntMPA 1977*
Clark, Kenneth B 1914- *CelR 3*
Clark, Kenneth Sherman 1882-1943 *AmSCAP 1966*
Clark, Les 1907-1959 *WhScrn 1, WhScrn 2, WhoHol B*
Clark, Lon *WhoHol A*
Clark, Marguerite d1940 *MotPP, WhoHol B, WhoStg 1906, WhoStg 1908*
Clark, Marguerite 1882-1940 *TwYS*
Clark, Marguerite 1883-1940 *Film 1, Film 2, FilmgC*
Clark, Marguerite 1887-1940 *NotNAT B, WhScrn 1, WhScrn 2, WhThe*
Clark, Marilyn *WhoHol A*
Clark, Marjory 1900- *WhThe*
Clark, Mark 1896- *CelR 3*
Clark, Michele d1972 *NewYTET*
Clark, Norman 1887- *BiE&WWA*
Clark, Paul 1927-1960 *WhScrn 1, WhScrn 2, WhoHol B*
Clark, Peggy 1915- *BiE&WWA, NotNAT*
Clark, Perceval *WhThe*
Clark, Petula 1932- *CelR 3, FilmgC, IntMPA 1977, MotPP, MovMk, WhoHol A*
Clark, Ramsey 1927- *CelR 3*
Clark, Robert 1905- *FilmgC, IntMPA 1977*
Clark, Rogie 1917- *AmSCAP 1966*
Clark, Ronald 1933- *AmSCAP 1966*
Clark, Rose Francis Langdon d1962 *NotNAT B*
Clark, Samuel H 1914- *IntMPA 1977*
Clark, Susan 1940- *FilmgC, IntMPA 1977, WhoHol A*
Clark, Susan Hansen *WomWMM B*
Clark, T Sealey d1909 *NotNAT B*

Clark, Trilby *Film 2*
Clark, Wallis d1961 *WhoHol B*
Clark, Wallis 1888-1961 *NotNAT B, WhThe*
Clark, Wallis 1889-1961 *Vers B, WhScrn 1, WhScrn 2*
Clark, Walter E, Jr. *NatPD*
Clark, Westcott *Film 2*
Clark, William T d1925 *NotNAT B*
Clarke, Angela *WhoHol A*
Clarke, Arthur C 1917- *CelR 3*
Clarke, Austin 1896-1974 *CnMD Sup*
Clarke, Betty Ross *Film 2, WhScrn 2*
Clarke, C Downing *Film 2*
Clarke, Charles G 1899- *IntMPA 1977, WorEnF*
Clarke, Creston 1865-1910 *NotNAT B, WhoStg 1906, WhoStg 1908*
Clarke, Cuthbert 1869-1953 *WhThe*
Clarke, David 1908- *BiE&WWA, NatPD, NotNAT, WhoHol A*
Clarke, Downing George d1930 *WhScrn 1, WhScrn 2, WhoHol B*
Clarke, Gage 1900-1964 *WhScrn 2*
Clarke, George *Film 1*
Clarke, George 1840-1900 *NotNAT B*
Clarke, George 1840-1906 *WhoStg 1906, WhoStg 1908*
Clarke, George 1886-1946 *NotNAT B, WhThe*
Clarke, Gordon B 1907-1972 *WhScrn 2, WhoHol B*
Clarke, Grant 1891-1931 *AmSCAP 1966*
Clarke, H Saville d1893 *NotNAT B*
Clarke, Harry Corson d1923 *NotNAT B, WhoStg 1906, WhoStg 1908*
Clarke, Harvey *Film 2*
Clarke, Herbert Lincoln 1867-1945 *AmSCAP 1966*
Clarke, J I C 1846-1925 *NotNAT A, NotNAT B*
Clarke, John *WhoHol A*
Clarke, John Sleeper 1833-1899 *NotNAT B, OxThe*
Clarke, Mae *MotPP*
Clarke, Mae 1907- *HolP 30, ThFT, WhThe*
Clarke, Mae 1910- *Film 2, FilmgC, WhoHol A*
Clarke, Mae 1916- *MovMk*
Clarke, Nigel 1895- *WhThe*
Clarke, Rebecca 1886- *AmSCAP 1966*
Clarke, Redfield *Film 2*
Clarke, Richard *WhoHol A*
Clarke, Robert *WhoHol A*
Clarke, Sir Rupert 1865-1926 *WhThe*
Clarke, Shirley 1925- *DcFM, FilmgC, OxFilm, WomWMM, WorEnF*
Clarke, T E B 1907- *CmMov, ConDr 1977A, DcFM, FilmgC, OxFilm, WorEnF*
Clarke, Tom *ConDr 1977C*
Clarke, Wescott B *Film 2*
Clarke, Wilfred d1945 *NotNAT B*
Clarke, William Hutchinson 1865- *WhoStg 1908*
Clarke-Smith, D A 1888-1959 *FilmgC, WhScrn 1, WhScrn 2, WhoHol B*
Clarke-Smith, Douglas A 1888-1959 *WhThe*
Clarkson, Geoffrey 1914- *AmSCAP 1966*
Clarkson, Harry F 1882-1959 *AmSCAP 1966*
Clarkson, Joan 1903- *WhThe*
Clarkson, Willie *Film 1*
Clarkson, Willie 1861-1934 *WhThe*
Clary, Charles 1873-1931 *Film 1, Film 2, WhScrn 2*
Clary, Robert 1926- *BiE&WWA, WhoHol A*
Claty, Charles *Film 2*
Claude, Toby *Film 2*
Claudel, Paul 1868-1955 *CnMD, CnThe, McGWD, ModWD, NotNAT A, NotNAT B, OxThe, PIP&P, REnWD, WhThe*
Claudius, Dane 1874-1946 *WhScrn 1, WhScrn 2,*

WhoHol B
Claughton, Susan *WhThe*
Claus, Hugo 1929- *CnMD, ModWD*
Clausen, Svend 1893-1961 *CnMD*
Claussen, Joy 1938- *BiE&WWA*
Clavel, Maurice 1918- *CnMD*
Clavell, James 1922- *FilmgC*
Clavell, James 1924- *WorEnF*
Claver, Bob *NewYTET*
Claver, Robert E 1928- *AmSCAP 1966*
Claxton, Kate 1848-1924 *FamA&A, OxThe*
Claxton, Kate 1850-1924 *NotNAT B*
Claxton, William F *NewYTET*
Clay, Cecil d1920 *NotNAT B*
Clayburgh, Jill *WhoHol A*
Claypoole, Edward B 1883-1952 *AmSCAP 1966*
Clayton, Arthur *Film 2*
Clayton, Bessie d1948 *NotNAT B*
Clayton, Buck 1912- *AmSCAP 1966*
Clayton, Dick *WhoHol A*
Clayton, Donald 1890-1964 *WhScrn 2*
Clayton, Eddie *Film 2*
Clayton, Edward *Film 2*
Clayton, Ethel 1884-1966 *Film 1, Film 2, MotPP,*
   TwYS, WhScrn 1, WhScrn 2, WhoHol B
Clayton, Gilbert 1860-1950 *Film 2, WhScrn 2*
Clayton, Hazel 1886-1963 *NotNAT B, WhScrn 1,*
   WhScrn 2, WhoHol B
Clayton, Herbert 1876-1931 *NotNAT B, WhThe*
Clayton, Jack 1921- *BiDFlm, DcFM, FilmgC,*
   IntMPA 1977, MovMk, OxFilm, WorEnF
Clayton, Jan 1917- *BiE&WWA, EncMT,*
   IntMPA 1977, NotNAT, WhoHol A
Clayton, Jane *WhoHol A*
Clayton, Lou 1887-1950 *NotNAT B, WhScrn 1,*
   WhScrn 2, WhoHol B
Clayton, Marguerite *MotPP*
Clayton, Marguerite 1894?-1968 *WhScrn 2*
Clayton, Marguerite 1896- *Film 1, Film 2,*
   TwYS
Clayton, Una *WhoStg 1908*
Clayworth, June *WhoHol A*
Cleander *OxThe*
Cleary, Chip 1910- *IntMPA 1977*
Cleary, Leo Thomas 1895-1955 *WhScrn 1,*
   WhScrn 2, WhoHol B
Cleary, Michael *Film 2*
Cleary, Michael H 1902-1954 *AmSCAP 1966*
Cleary, Peggy 1892-1972 *WhScrn 2, WhoHol B*
Cleary, Ruth *AmSCAP 1966*
Cleather, Gordon 1872- *WhThe*
Cleave, Arthur *Film 1*
Cleave, Arthur 1884- *WhThe*
Cleaver, Eldridge 1935- *CelR 3*
Clebanoff, Herman 1917- *AmSCAP 1966*
Cleese, John 1939- *FilmgC*
Clegg, Cy *Film 2*
Clegg, Valce V 1888-1947 *WhScrn 1, WhScrn 2,*
   WhoHol B
Cleghorn, John H 1909- *IntMPA 1977*
Cleman, Majel *Film 2*
Clemens, Brian 1931- *FilmgC, IntMPA 1977*
Clemens, LeRoy 1889- *Film 2, WhThe*
Clemens, William 1905- *FilmgC*
Clement, Clay 1888-1956 *NotNAT B, WhScrn 1,*
   WhScrn 2, WhThe, WhoHol B
Clement, Dick 1937- *FilmgC*
Clement, Donald 1941-1970 *WhScrn 1, WhScrn 2,*
   WhoHol B
Clement, Elfrida *WhThe*
Clement, Eloise *Film 1*
Clement, Frank d1937 *NotNAT B*
Clement, Rene 1913- *BiDFlm, DcFM, FilmgC,*
   MovMk, OxFilm, WorEnF

Clement-Scott, Joan 1907-1969 *WhThe*
Clement-Scott, Margaret *WhThe*
Clemente, Steve *Film 1, Film 2*
Clemento, Steve *Film 2*
Clements, Colin d1948 *NotNAT B*
Clements, Dudley 1889-1947 *NotNAT B,*
   WhScrn 2, WhoHol B
Clements, Sir John 1910- *CnThe, FilmgC, PlP&P,*
   WhoHol A, WhoThe 16
Clements, Miriam *WhThe*
Clements, Otis G, Jr. 1926- *AmSCAP 1966*
Clements, Stanley 1926- *FilmgC, Vers B,*
   WhoHol A
Clemons, James K 1883-1950 *WhScrn 1,*
   WhScrn 2, WhoHol B
Clerget, Paul 1867-1935 *Film 1, Film 2,*
   WhScrn 1, WhScrn 2, WhoHol B
Cleveland, Anna 1880-1954 *WhScrn 2*
Cleveland, George d1957 *MotPP, NotNAT B,*
   WhoHol B
Cleveland, George 1883-1957 *WhScrn 1,*
   WhScrn 2
Cleveland, George 1886-1957 *FilmgC, Vers A*
Cleveland, George 1886-1965 *MovMk*
Clewing, Carl *Film 1, Film 2*
Clewlow, F D d1957 *NotNAT B*
Cliburn, Van 1934- *CelR 3*
Cliff, Charles Joseph 1912- *AmSCAP 1966*
Cliff, Laddie 1891-1937 *EncMT, NotNAT B,*
   WhScrn 1, WhScrn 2, WhThe, WhoHol B
Cliffe, H Cooper 1862-1939 *Film 1, Film 2,*
   NotNAT B, WhScrn 1, WhScrn 2, WhThe,
   WhoHol B, WhoStg 1908
Clifford, Camille *WhThe*
Clifford, Charles d1943 *NotNAT B*
Clifford, Clark 1906- *CelR 3*
Clifford, Gordon 1902-1968 *AmSCAP 1966,*
   NotNAT B
Clifford, Jack 1880-1956 *NotNAT B, WhScrn 1,*
   WhScrn 2, WhoHol B
Clifford, Kathleen *Film 1, Film 2*
Clifford, Kathleen d1963 *NotNAT B*
Clifford, Kathleen 1887-1962 *WhScrn 1,*
   WhScrn 2, WhThe, WhoHol B
Clifford, Larry d1955 *WhScrn 2*
Clifford, Margaret Ellen 1908- *BiE&WWA*
Clifford, Ruth 1900- *Film 1, Film 2, TwYS,*
   WhoHol A
Clifford, Mrs. W K d1929 *NotNAT B, WhThe*
Clifford, William d1941 *Film 1, Film 2,*
   WhoHol B
Clifford, William 1878-1941 *WhScrn 2*
Clifforn, William 1877-1941 *WhScrn 1*
Clift, Denison 1893- *IntMPA 1977*
Clift, Ernest Paul 1881-1963 *WhThe*
Clift, Montgomery 1920-1966 *BiDFlm,*
   BiE&WWA, CmMov, FilmgC, MotPP,
   MovMk, NotNAT B, OxFilm, WhScrn 1,
   WhScrn 2, WhThe, WhoHol B, WorEnF
Clifton, Bernard 1902-1970 *WhThe*
Clifton, Elmer d1949 *NotNAT B, WhoHol B,*
   WomWMM
Clifton, Elmer 1890-1947 *Film 2*
Clifton, Elmer 1890-1949 *Film 1, FilmgC,*
   TwYS A
Clifton, Elmer 1893-1949 *WhScrn 1, WhScrn 2*
Clifton, Elmer 1895-1947 *TwYS*
Clifton, Emma *Film 1*
Clifton, Harry 1832-1872 *OxThe*
Clifton, Herbert 1884-1947 *WhScrn 1, WhScrn 2,*
   WhoHol B
Clifton, Josephine d1847 *NotNAT B*
Clifton, Michelle Gamm 1944- *WomWMM B*
Clifton-James, M E 1898-1963 *WhScrn 2*

Climenhaga, Joel Ray 1922- *BiE&WWA,*
NotNAT
Cline, Brady *Film 2*
Cline, Eddie 1892-1948 *WorEnF*
Cline, Eddie 1892-1961 *TwYS A, WhScrn 1,*
WhScrn 2, WhoHol B
Cline, Edward 1892-1961 *DcFM, Film 1, Film 2,*
FilmgC, MovMk
Cline, George *Film 2*
Cline, Maggie 1857-1934 *NotNAT B*
Cline, Robert *Film 2*
Clint, H O'Reilly 1900-1961 *AmSCAP 1966*
Clinton, Edward J 1948- *NatPD*
Clinton, Geoffrey *Film 2*
Clinton, Kate d1935 *NotNAT B*
Clinton, Larry 1909- *AmSCAP 1966*
Clisbee, Ethel *Film 1*
Clitheroe, Jimmy 1923-1973 *WhScrn 2*
Cliutmas, Harry F d1964 *NotNAT B*
Clive, Colin 1898-1937 *CmMov, FilmgC, MovMk,*
PIP&P, WhScrn 1, WhScrn 2, WhoHol B
Clive, Colin 1900-1937 *NotNAT B, WhThe*
Clive, David J 1923- *BiE&WWA*
Clive, E E 1879-1940 *FilmgC, MovMk*
Clive, E E 1880-1940 *Vers A, WhoHol B*
Clive, E E 1898-1940 *WhScrn 1, WhScrn 2*
Clive, Edward E d1940 *NotNAT B*
Clive, Henry 1883-1960 *Film 1, WhScrn 1,*
WhScrn 2, WhoHol B
Clive, Kitty 1711-1785 *CnThe, NotNAT A,*
NotNAT B, OxThe, PIP&P
Clive, Vincent d1943 *WhThe*
Cloche, Maurice 1907- *DcFM, FilmgC*
Cloerec, Rene 1911- *DcFM*
Clokey, Joseph Waddel 1890-1961 *AmSCAP 1966*
Clonbough, G Butler *Film 1*
Clonebaugh, G Butler d1943 *WhoHol B*
Cloninger, Ralph *Film 2*
Clooney, Rosemary 1928- *FilmgC, WhoHol A*
Cloquet, Ghislain 1924- *WorEnF*
Clore, Leon *IntMPA 1977*
Clork, Harry *IntMPA 1977*
Close, Iva *Film 2*
Close, Ivy 1890-1968 *WhScrn 1, WhScrn 2*
Close, Ivy 1893- *Film 1, Film 2*
Close, John d1964 *WhScrn 2*
Closser, Louise 1872- *WhThe*
Closson, Herman 1901- *ModWD*
Clothier, William H 1903- *CmMov, FilmgC,*
WorEnF
Cloutier, Maurice E 1933- *AmSCAP 1966*
Cloutier, Suzanne 1927- *FilmgC, WhoHol A*
Clouzot, Henri-Georges 1907- *BiDFlm, DcFM,*
FilmgC, IntMPA 1977, MovMk, OxFilm,
WorEnF
Clouzot, Vera 1921-1960 *FilmgC, WhScrn 1,*
WhoHol B
Clouzout, Vera d1960 *WhScrn 2*
Clovelly, Cecil 1891-1965 *Film 2, WhScrn 1,*
WhScrn 2, WhoHol B
Cloward, Robert Louis 1934- *AmSCAP 1966*
Clowes, Richard 1900- *WhThe*
Clubley, John Sherwood d1964 *NotNAT B*
Cluchey, Rick 1933- *ConDr 1977*
Clugston, H M *Film 2*
Clunes, Alec S 1912-1970 *FilmgC, NotNAT A,*
NotNAT B, WhScrn 2, WhThe, WhoHol B
Clunes, Alex 1913-1970 *WhScrn 1*
Clurman, Harold 1901- *BiE&WWA, CnThe,*
FilmgC, NotNAT, NotNAT A, OxThe,
PIP&P, WhoThe 16, WorEnF
Clute, Chester 1891-1956 *FilmgC, Vers B,*
WhScrn 1, WhScrn 2, WhoHol B
Clute, Sidney *WhoHol A*

Clyde, Andy 1892-1967 *Film 2, FilmgC, MotPP,*
TwYS, Vers A, WhScrn 1, WhScrn 2,
WhoHol B
Clyde, David 1855-1945 *WhScrn 1, WhScrn 2,*
WhoHol B
Clyde, Jean 1889-1962 *NotNAT B, WhScrn 1,*
WhScrn 2, WhoHol B
Clyde, June 1909- *Film 2, ThFT, WhoHol A*
Clyde, Thomas *IntMPA 1977*
Clymer, Beth 1887-1952 *WhScrn 1, WhScrn 2*
Clyne, Lionel 1908- *IntMPA 1977*
Coad, Joyce Marie *Film 2*
Coad, Oral Sumner 1887- *NotNAT*
Coakley, Marion *Film 2, WhThe*
Coakley, Patty *Film 2*
Coalter, Frazer *Film 2*
Coan, Nonee Edward 1910- *AmSCAP 1966*
Coates, Anne V *WomWMM*
Coates, Carolyn 1930- *WhoHol A, WhoThe 16*
Coates, Franklin *Film 2*
Coates, Paul 1921-1968 *WhScrn 2*
Coates, Phyllis *WhoHol A*
Coates, Robert 1772-1848 *OxThe*
Coates, William David D 1916- *IntMPA 1977*
Coats, R Roy 1898- *AmSCAP 1966*
Cobb, Clifford *Film 2*
Cobb, Edmund 1892-1974 *Film 1, Film 2, TwYS,*
Vers A, WhScrn 2, WhoHol B
Cobb, George L 1886-1942 *AmSCAP 1966*
Cobb, Grover C d1975 *NewYTET*
Cobb, Irvin S 1876-1944 *Film 1, NotNAT B,*
WhScrn 1, WhScrn 2, WhoHol B
Cobb, Joe Fat 1917- *Film 2*
Cobb, Joe Wheezer *WhoHol A*
Cobb, Joey 1917- *TwYS*
Cobb, Lee J 1911-1976 *BiDFlm, BiE&WWA,*
CelR 3, CmMov, FamA&A, FilmgC,
MotPP, MovMk, NotNAT B, OxFilm,
PIP&P, WhThe, WhoHol C, WorEnF
Cobb, Ty 1886-1961 *WhScrn 2*
Cobb, Will D 1876-1930 *AmSCAP 1966*
Coben, Cy 1919- *AmSCAP 1966*
Cobey, Louis 1897- *AmSCAP 1966*
Cobey, Philip Sheridan 1910- *IntMPA 1977*
Coborn, Charles 1852-1945 *FilmgC, WhScrn 2,*
WhThe
Coborn, Charlie 1852-1945 *NotNAT B, OxThe*
Coburn, Charles 1877-1961 *BiDFlm, FilmgC,*
MotPP, MovMk, NotNAT B, OxFilm,
OxThe, Vers A, WhScrn 1, WhScrn 2,
WhThe, WhoHol B, WorEnF
Coburn, Dorothy *Film 2*
Coburn, Gladys *Film 2*
Coburn, Ivah Wills 1882-1937 *NotNAT B, OxThe*
Coburn, James 1928- *BiDFlm, CelR 3, FilmgC,*
IntMPA 1977, MotPP, MovMk, OxFilm,
WhoHol A, WorEnF
Coburn, Richard 1886-1952 *AmSCAP 1966*
Coca, Imogene *IntMPA 1977, NewYTET,*
WhoHol A
Coca, Imogene 1908- *EncMT, WhoThe 16*
Coca, Imogene 1909- *BiE&WWA, FilmgC,*
NotNAT
Cocaine d1973? *WhScrn 2*
Cocchi, John 1939- *IntMPA 1977*
Coccia, Aurelio *Film 2*
Cocea, Alice 1899- *WhThe*
Cochran, C B 1872-1951 *NotNAT A*
Cochran, Sir Charles Blake 1872-1951 *EncMT,*
NotNAT B, OxThe, WhThe
Cochran, Sir Charles Blake 1873-1951 *CnThe*
Cochran, Eddie 1929-1960 *WhScrn 2*
Cochran, Ron 1912- *IntMPA 1977*
Cochran, Steve 1917-1965 *BiE&WWA, FilmgC,*

HolP 40, MotPP, MovMk, WhScrn 1,
WhScrn 2, WhoHol B, WorEnF
Cochrane, Frank 1882-1962 *NotNAT B,*
WhScrn 1, WhScrn 2, WhThe, WhoHol B
Cockburn, Catherine d1749 *NotNAT B*
Cockburn, John M d1964 *NotNAT B*
Cockelberg, Louis J 1880-1962 *WhScrn 1,*
WhScrn 2
Coco, James *PIP&P, WhoHol A*
Coco, James 1928- *FilmgC*
Coco, James 1929- *CelR 3, IntMPA 1977,*
WhoThe 16
Coco, James 1930- *NotNAT*
Cocteau, Jean 1889-1963 *BiDFlm, CnMD, CnThe,*
DcFM, FilmgC, McGWD, ModWD,
MovMk, NotNAT B, OxFilm, OxThe,
REnWD, WhScrn 2, WhThe, WorEnF
Cocteau, Jean 1891-1963 *NotNAT A*
Code, Grant Hyde 1896-1974 *WhScrn 2,*
WhoHol B
Codee, Ann 1890-1961 *FilmgC, MovMk,*
WhScrn 1, WhScrn 2, WhoHol B
Codian, Michael 1915- *AmSCAP 1966*
Codrington, Ann 1895- *WhThe*
Codron, Michael 1930- *WhoThe 16*
Cody, Albert *Film 2*
Cody, Bill, Sr. 1891-1948 *NotNAT B, WhScrn 1,*
WhScrn 2, WhoHol B
Cody, Buffalo Bill 1846-1917 *WhoHol B*
Cody, Emmett F 1920-1960 *WhoHol B*
Cody, Ethel d1957 *NotNAT B, WhoHol B*
Cody, Harry 1896-1956 *WhScrn 1, WhScrn 2,*
WhoHol B
Cody, Iron Eyes *MotPP, WhoHol A*
Cody, Kathleen *WhoHol A*
Cody, Lew d1934 *MotPP, WhoHol B*
Cody, Lew 1884-1934 *Film 1, Film 2, FilmgC,*
MovMk, TwYS
Cody, Lew 1887-1934 *NotNAT B, WhScrn 1,*
WhScrn 2
Cody, William Buffalo Bill 1891-1948 *Film 1,*
Film 2
Cody, William Frederick 1846-1917 *FilmgC,*
NotNAT B, OxFilm, OxThe, WhScrn 2
Coe, Barry *FilmgC, WhoHol A*
Coe, Donald G 1914- *IntMPA 1977*
Coe, Fred 1914- *BiE&WWA, FilmgC,*
IntMPA 1977, NewYTET, NotNAT,
WhoThe 16
Coe, Peter 1929- *BiE&WWA, FilmgC, NotNAT,*
WhoHol A, WhoThe 16
Coe, Richard L 1916- *BiE&WWA, IntMPA 1977,*
NotNAT
Coe, Rose *Film 2*
Coe, Vivian *WhoHol A*
Coedel, Lucien 1905-1947 *WhScrn 1, WhScrn 2,*
WhoHol B
Coello Y Ochoa, Antonio 1611-1652 *McGWD*
Coen, Guido *IntMPA 1977*
Coffee, Lenore *Film 2, WomWMM*
Coffel, Clarence M 1900- *AmSCAP 1966*
Coffer, Jack 1939-1967 *WhScrn 1, WhScrn 2*
Coffey, Clark *Film 2*
Coffey, Denise 1936- *WhoThe 16*
Coffey, John 1909-1944 *WhScrn 1, WhScrn 2*
Coffin, C Hayden 1862-1935 *NotNAT A,*
NotNAT B, WhThe
Coffin, Hank 1904-1966 *WhScrn 1, WhScrn 2,*
WhoHol B
Coffin, Tristram *WhoHol A*
Coffyn, Frank *Film 2*
Coffyn, Pauline *Film 2*
Cogan, Alma 1933-1966 *WhScrn 2*
Cogan, David J 1923- *BiE&WWA, NotNAT*

Cogan, Fanny Hay 1866-1929 *WhScrn 1,*
WhScrn 2, WhoHol B
Cogane, Nelson 1902- *AmSCAP 1966*
Cogdell, Josephine 1901-1969 *WhScrn 1,*
WhScrn 2, WhoHol B
Cogert, Jed d1961 *NotNAT B*
Coghill, Nevill 1899- *ConDr 1977D, WhoThe 16*
Coghlan, Charles F d1972 *WhScrn 2*
Coghlan, Charles F 1841-1899 *NotNAT B*
Coghlan, Charles F 1842-1899 *OxThe, PIP&P*
Coghlan, Gertrude 1879-1952 *WhThe*
Coghlan, Gertrude Evelyn 1876-1952 *NotNAT B,*
WhoStg 1906, WhoStg 1908
Coghlan, Junior 1916- *FilmgC*
Coghlan, Junior 1917- *Film 2, TwYS,*
WhoHol A
Coghlan, Katherine 1889-1965 *WhScrn 1,*
WhScrn 2, WhoHol B
Coghlan, Rosalind d1937 *NotNAT B*
Coghlan, Rose d1932 *PIP&P, WhoHol B*
Coghlan, Rose 1850-1932 *WhScrn 1, WhScrn 2,*
WhThe
Coghlan, Rose 1851-1932 *FamA&A, NotNAT B,*
OxThe
Coghlan, Rose 1853-1932 *Film 1, Film 2,*
WhoStg 1906, WhoStg 1908
Cogley, Nicholas 1869-1936 *WhScrn 1,*
WhScrn 2
Cogley, Nick 1869-1936 *Film 1, Film 2, TwYS,*
WhoHol B
Cohan, Agnes Merrill d1972 *WhoHol B*
Cohan, Charles 1886- *WhThe*
Cohan, George M 1878-1942 *AmSCAP 1966,*
CnMD, EncMT, FamA&A, Film 1, FilmgC,
McGWD, ModWD, NewMT, NotNAT A,
NotNAT B, OxThe, PIP&P, TwYS,
WhScrn 1, WhScrn 2, WhThe, WhoHol B,
WhoStg 1906, WhoStg 1908
Cohan, George M 1879-1942 *CnThe*
Cohan, Georgette 1900- *WhThe*
Cohan, Helen *WhoHol A*
Cohan, Helen Frances Costigan 1854-1928
NotNAT B
Cohan, Jere J 1848-1917 *NotNAT B*
Cohan, Josephine 1876-1916 *NotNAT B*
Cohen, Alexander H 1920- *BiE&WWA, CelR 3,*
EncMT, NotNAT, WhoThe 16
Cohen, Allen Laurence *NatPD*
Cohen, Av Shalom 1928- *AmSCAP 1966*
Cohen, Charles 1912- *IntMPA 1977*
Cohen, David 1927- *AmSCAP 1966*
Cohen, Edward M *NatPD*
Cohen, Ellis A 1945- *IntMPA 1977*
Cohen, Fred 1939- *AmSCAP 1966*
Cohen, Frederick 1904-1967 *BiE&WWA,*
NotNAT B
Cohen, Gustave 1879-1958 *OxThe*
Cohen, Harry L 1891- *WhThe*
Cohen, Herman 1928?- *FilmgC, IntMPA 1977*
Cohen, Janelle *WomWMM*
Cohen, Joseph 1918- *AmSCAP 1966*
Cohen, Joseph M 1917- *AmSCAP 1966*
Cohen, Katie d1946 *NotNAT B*
Cohen, Kip 1940- *BiE&WWA*
Cohen, Leonard 1934- *CelR 3*
Cohen, Martin B 1923- *BiE&WWA, NotNAT*
Cohen, Maxi M *WomWMM B*
Cohen, Milton E *IntMPA 1977*
Cohen, Nathan 1905- *IntMPA 1977*
Cohen, Nathan 1923- *BiE&WWA*
Cohen, Norman 1936- *FilmgC*
Cohen, Octavus Roy 1891-1959 *NotNAT B*
Cohen, Sammy *Film 2*
Cohen, Sara B d1963 *NotNAT B*

Cohen, Selma Jeanne 1920- *BiE&WWA,*
NotNAT
Cohen, Sheldon 1933- *AmSCAP 1966*
Cohen, Sol B 1891- *AmSCAP 1966*
Cohill, William *Film 1*
Cohl, Emile 1857-1938 *DcFM, Film 1, FilmgC,*
OxFilm, WorEnF
Cohn, Al 1925- *AmSCAP 1966*
Cohn, Arthur 1910- *AmSCAP 1966*
Cohn, Arthur 1928- *FilmgC*
Cohn, Bennett 1894- *TwYS A*
Cohn, Gregory P 1919- *AmSCAP 1966*
Cohn, Harry 1891-1958 *FilmgC, NotNAT A,*
NotNAT B, OxFilm, TwYS B, WorEnF
Cohn, James 1928- *AmSCAP 1966*
Cohn, Janet *BiE&WWA*
Cohn, Judith *WomWMM B*
Cohn, Julia 1902-1975 *WhScrn 2, WhoHol C*
Cohn, Robert 1920- *IntMPA 1977*
Cohn, Sidra Gay 1937- *NatPD*
Cohn, Stewart 1921- *AmSCAP 1966*
Cokayne, Sir Aston d1684 *NotNAT B*
Coke, Peter 1913- *WhThe*
Coke, Richard d1955 *NotNAT B*
Coker, Wilson 1928- *AmSCAP 1966*
Colamosca, Frank 1910- *AmSCAP 1966*
Colanzi, Richard P 1929- *AmSCAP 1966*
Colas, Monsieur *Film 2*
Colbert, Claudette *MotPP, PIP&P, WomWMM*
Colbert, Claudette 1905- *BiDFlm, BiE&WWA,*
Film 2, FilmgC, OxFilm, ThFT, WhoHol A,
WhoThe 16, WorEnF
Colbert, Claudette 1907- *CelR 3, IntMPA 1977,*
MovMk
Colbert, Robert *WhoHol A*
Colbin, Rod 1923- *BiE&WWA, NotNAT*
Colbourne, Maurice 1894-1965 *WhThe*
Colbron, Grace Isabel d1943 *NotNAT B, WhThe*
Colburn, Carrie 1859-1932 *WhScrn 1, WhScrn 2,*
WhoHol B
Colby, Anita 1914- *MotPP, WhoHol A*
Colby, Barbara 1940-1975 *WhScrn 2, WhoHol C*
Colby, Ethel 1908- *BiE&WWA, IntMPA 1977,*
NotNAT
Colby, Herbert 1839-1911 *WhScrn 2*
Colby, Robert *AmSCAP 1966*
Colcock, Erroll Hay *AmSCAP 1966*
Colcord, Mabel 1872-1952 *WhScrn 1, WhScrn 2,*
WhoHol B
Coldwell, Goldie *Film 1*
Cole, Alonzo Deen d1971 *WhoHol B*
Cole, Bob 1869-1912 *NotNAT B*
Cole, Brian 1944-1972 *WhScrn 2*
Cole, Buddy 1916-1964 *WhScrn 2*
Cole, Corinne *WhoHol A*
Cole, Dennis *WhoHol A*
Cole, Edith 1870-1927 *WhThe*
Cole, Edward C 1904- *BiE&WWA, NotNAT*
Cole, Edward N 1909- *CelR 3*
Cole, Franklin 1909- *AmSCAP 1966*
Cole, Fred 1901-1964 *WhScrn 1, WhScrn 2,*
WhoHol B
Cole, George 1925- *FilmgC, IntMPA 1977,*
WhoHol A, WhoThe 16
Cole, Jack 1914-1974 *BiE&WWA, CmMov,*
EncMT, FilmgC, NotNAT B, WhScrn 2,
WhoHol B, WorEnF
Cole, James *Film 1*
Cole, Johnny d1974 *WhScrn 2*
Cole, Lester 1900-1962 *WhScrn 1, WhScrn 2,*
WhoHol B
Cole, Marie Keith 1914-1975 *WhoHol C*
Cole, Mary Keith 1914-1975 *WhScrn 2*
Cole, Michael *WhoHol A*

Cole, Nat King 1919-1965 *AmSCAP 1966,*
FilmgC, MovMk, NewYTET, WhScrn 1,
WhScrn 2, WhoHol B
Cole, Robert L 1915- *AmSCAP 1966*
Cole, Sidney 1908- *IntMPA 1977*
Cole, Slim *Film 1, Film 2*
Cole, Tina *WhoHol A*
Cole, Toby 1916- *BiE&WWA, NotNAT*
Cole, Ulric 1905- *AmSCAP 1966*
Cole, Wendell 1914- *BiE&WWA, NotNAT*
Colean, Chuck 1908-1971 *WhScrn 1, WhScrn 2*
Coleburn, Catherine *Film 2*
Coleby, Wilfred T 1865- *WhThe*
Colee, Forest R 1893-1962 *WhScrn 2*
Coleman, Mrs. *PIP&P*
Coleman, Carole d1964 *NotNAT B*
Coleman, Charles 1885-1951 *Film 2, FilmgC,*
MovMk, Vers A, WhScrn 1, WhScrn 2,
WhoHol B
Coleman, Cherrie *Film 1*
Coleman, Claudia 1889-1938 *WhScrn 1,*
WhScrn 2, WhoHol B
Coleman, Cy 1929- *AmSCAP 1966, BiE&WWA,*
CelR 3, EncMT, NewMT, NotNAT
Coleman, Dabney *WhoHol A*
Coleman, Deborah 1919- *BiE&WWA*
Coleman, Delle *WomWMM*
Coleman, Don *Film 2*
Coleman, Emil 1893-1965 *WhScrn 1, WhScrn 2,*
WhoHol B
Coleman, Fanny 1840-1919 *WhThe*
Coleman, Fay R 1918- *BiE&WWA, NotNAT*
Coleman, Frank J *Film 1*
Coleman, Jim *Film 2*
Coleman, John 1831-1904 *NotNAT A,*
NotNAT B
Coleman, Lonnie 1920- *BiE&WWA, NotNAT*
Coleman, Mabel *Film 2*
Coleman, Majel *Film 2*
Coleman, Major *Film 2*
Coleman, Margret *WhoHol A*
Coleman, Nancy *IntMPA 1977, MotPP*
Coleman, Nancy 1914- *BiE&WWA, WhoHol A*
Coleman, Nancy 1917- *FilmgC, NotNAT*
Coleman, Ornette 1930- *AmSCAP 1966*
Coleman, Richard E 1933- *AmSCAP 1966*
Coleman, Robert, Jr. 1900- *BiE&WWA, WhThe*
Coleman, Shepard 1924- *BiE&WWA, NotNAT*
Coleman, Thomas 1897-1959 *WhScrn 1,*
WhScrn 2
Coleman, Vincent *Film 2*
Coleman, Warren R 1901-1968 *NotNAT B,*
WhScrn 1, WhScrn 2, WhoHol B
Coleman, Willette *WomWMM B*
Coleman, William S E 1926- *NotNAT*
Coleridge, Amy d1951 *NotNAT B*
Coleridge, Ethel 1883- *WhThe*
Coleridge, Samuel Taylor 1772-1834 *NotNAT B,*
OxThe
Coleridge, Sylvia 1909- *WhoThe 16*
Coles, Robert 1929- *CelR 3*
Coles, Russell 1909-1960 *WhScrn 1, WhScrn 2*
Colette 1873-1954 *FilmgC, NotNAT B, OxFilm*
Coley, Thomas *WhoHol A*
Colfach, Elsa *WomWMM*
Colicchio, Ralph 1896- *AmSCAP 1966*
Colicos, John 1928- *FilmgC, NotNAT,*
WhoThe 16
Colin, Georges *WhThe*
Colin, Jean 1905- *FilmgC, WhThe, WhoHol A*
Colin, Lotte *WomWMM*
Colin, Ralph *NewYTET*
Coll, Owen G 1879-1960 *WhScrn 1, WhScrn 2*
Colla, Richard J *FilmgC*

Collazo, Bobby 1916- *AmSCAP 1966*
Colle, Charles 1709-1783 *OxThe*
Colleano, Bonar 1923-1958 *NotNAT B, WhThe*
Colleano, Bonar 1924-1958 *FilmgC, MotPP, WhScrn 1, WhScrn 2, WhoHol B*
Colleano, Bonar, Sr. d1957 *NotNAT B*
Colleran, Bill *IntMPA 1977*
Colleran, William A *NewYTET*
Collet, Richard 1885-1946 *WhThe*
Collette, Charles 1842-1924 *WhThe*
Collette, William M 1921- *AmSCAP 1966*
Collier, Buster 1900- *Film 2*
Collier, Constance d1955 *MotPP, PIP&P, WhoHol B*
Collier, Constance 1875-1955 *ThFT*
Collier, Constance 1878-1955 *Film 1, Film 2, FilmgC, MovMk, NotNAT A, NotNAT B, OxThe, TwYS, WhScrn 1, WhScrn 2, WhThe*
Collier, Constance 1880-1955 *Vers A*
Collier, Gaylan Jane 1924- *BiE&WWA, NotNAT*
Collier, J Walter d1920 *NotNAT B*
Collier, Jeremy 1650-1726 *NotNAT B*
Collier, Jeremy 1656-1726 *OxThe*
Collier, John 1901- *FilmgC*
Collier, John Payne 1789-1883 *NotNAT B, OxThe*
Collier, Lizzie Hudson d1924 *NotNAT B*
Collier, Lois *WhoHol A*
Collier, Patience 1910- *WhoThe 16*
Collier, Sherlee d1972 *WhoHol B*
Collier, William, Jr. 1900- *Film 2, TwYS*
Collier, William, Jr. 1903- *Film 1*
Collier, William, Sr. 1866-1944 *Film 1, Film 2, FilmgC, MovMk, NotNAT B, WhScrn 1, WhScrn 2, WhThe*
Collier, William, Sr. 1868-1944 *WhoHol B, WhoStg 1906, WhoStg 1908*
Collier, William E 1924- *AmSCAP 1966*
Collin, John 1931- *FilmgC*
Collin-Barbie DuBocage, Louis *McGWD*
Collinge, Patricia 1894-1974 *BiE&WWA, FilmgC, NotNAT B, OxFilm, Vers B, WhScrn 2, WhThe, WhoHol B*
Collingham, G G d1923 *NotNAT B*
Collings, Ann *WhoHol A*
Collings, Blanche d1968 *WhoHol B*
Collingwood, Charles 1917- *CelR 3, NewYTET*
Collingwood, Monica *WomWMM*
Collins, A Greville 1896- *WhThe*
Collins, Alfred *DcFM*
Collins, Allen Frederick 1915- *BiE&WWA, NotNAT*
Collins, Arthur 1863- *WhThe*
Collins, Barry 1941- *ConDr 1977*
Collins, Bert d1962 *NotNAT B*
Collins, Blanche M 1910-1968 *WhScrn 2*
Collins, C E 1873-1951 *WhScrn 2*
Collins, C Pat *Film 2*
Collins, Charles d1964 *NotNAT B*
Collins, Charles 1904- *WhThe*
Collins, Cora Sue 1927- *ThFT*
Collins, Daniel d1964 *NotNAT B*
Collins, Dorothy *PIP&P A*
Collins, Eddie 1884-1940 *FilmgC, Vers B, WhScrn 1, WhScrn 2, WhoHol B*
Collins, Eddy 1866-1916 *WhScrn 2*
Collins, Frank 1878-1957 *NotNAT B, WhThe*
Collins, G Pat 1895-1959 *WhScrn 1, WhScrn 2*
Collins, Gary *WhoHol A*
Collins, George Pat 1895-1959 *WhoHol B*
Collins, Hal 1920- *IntMPA 1977, NewYTET*
Collins, Horace 1875-1964 *WhThe*
Collins, Jack *WhoHol A*

Collins, Jackie *WhoHol A*
Collins, Joan 1933- *FilmgC, IntMPA 1977, MotPP, MovMk, WhoHol A*
Collins, John d1808 *NotNAT B*
Collins, Jose 1887-1958 *EncMT, Film 1, NotNAT B, OxThe, WhScrn 1, WhScrn 2, WhThe, WhoHol B*
Collins, Judy 1939- *CelR 3*
Collins, Kathleen *Film 2*
Collins, Larry 1929- *CelR 3*
Collins, LeRoy *NewYTET*
Collins, Lottie 1866-1910 *NotNAT B, OxThe*
Collins, Mae *Film 2*
Collins, Mary Sharacio *WomWMM B*
Collins, May d1955 *NotNAT B, WhoHol B*
Collins, Michael 1931- *CelR 3*
Collins, Monte, Sr. *Film 2*
Collins, Monte F, Jr. 1898-1951 *Film 2, WhScrn 1, WhScrn 2, WhoHol B*
Collins, Norman 1907- *IntMPA 1977*
Collins, Pamela 1948-1974 *WhScrn 2*
Collins, Pat 1935- *IntMPA 1977*
Collins, Pauline 1940- *WhoThe 16*
Collins, Ray d1965 *MotPP, WhoHol B*
Collins, Ray 1889-1965 *NotNAT B*
Collins, Ray 1890-1965 *FilmgC, MovMk, Vers A, WhScrn 1, WhScrn 2*
Collins, Russell 1897-1965 *BiE&WWA, FilmgC, NotNAT B, PIP&P, WhScrn 1, WhScrn 2, WhThe, WhoHol B*
Collins, S D J 1907-1947 *WhScrn 1, WhScrn 2, WhoHol B*
Collins, Sam 1826-1865 *NotNAT B, OxThe*
Collins, Sewell 1876-1934 *NotNAT B, WhThe*
Collins, Susan Trieste *WomWMM B*
Collins, Ted d1964 *NotNAT B*
Collins, Tom d1973 *WhScrn 2, WhoHol B*
Collins, Una d1964 *NotNAT B*
Collins, Wilkie 1824-1889 *NotNAT B, PIP&P*
Collins, Will 1893- *AmSCAP 1966*
Collins, Winnie 1896- *WhThe*
Collinson, Laurence 1925- *ConDr 1977*
Collinson, Peter 1936- *IntMPA 1977*
Collinson, Peter 1938- *FilmgC*
Collison, Wilson 1892-1941 *WhThe*
Collison, Wilson 1893-1941 *NotNAT B*
Collum, John 1926-1962 *NotNAT B, WhScrn 1, WhScrn 2, WhoHol B*
Collyer, Bud *NewYTET*
Collyer, Dan d1918 *NotNAT B*
Collyer, June 1907-1968 *Film 2, FilmgC, NotNAT B, ThFT, TwYS, WhScrn 1, WhScrn 2, WhoHol B*
Colman, Booth *WhoHol A*
Colman, George 1732-1794 *McGWD, NotNAT A, NotNAT B, OxThe, PIP&P*
Colman, George, Jr. 1762-1836 *NotNAT A, NotNAT B, OxThe*
Colman, Irene 1915-1975 *WhScrn 2*
Colman, Maria Logan 1770-1844 *OxThe*
Colman, Ronald 1891-1958 *BiDFlm, Film 1, Film 2, FilmgC, MotPP, MovMk, NotNAT B, OxThe, TwYS, WhScrn 1, WhScrn 2, WhThe, WhoHol B, WorEnF*
Colman, Ronald 1891-1959 *CmMov*
Colmans, Edward *WhoHol A*
Colombier, Marie 1842?-1910 *NotNAT B, OxThe*
Colombo, Russ 1908-1934 *Film 2*
Colombo, Russ *see also* Columbo, Russ
Colon, Jenny 1808-1842 *OxThe*
Colon, Miriam 1945- *NotNAT, WhoHol A, WhoThe 16*
Colonna, Jerry 1903- *FilmgC*
Colonna, Jerry 1904- *AmSCAP 1966, MovMk,*

WhoHol A
Colony, Alfred T d1964 *NotNAT B*
Colosse, M *Film 2*
Colpi, Henri 1912- *DcFM*
Colpi, Henri 1921- *FilmgC, OxFilm, WorEnF*
Colson-Malleville, Marie *WomWMM*
Colt, Alvin 1915- *BiE&WWA, NotNAT,*
WhoThe 16
Colt, Ethel Barrymore 1912- *NotNAT*
Colton, John B 1889-1946 *McGWD, NotNAT B,*
WhThe
Coltrane, John 1926-1967 *NotNAT B*
Colum, Padraic 1881-1972 *AmSCAP 1966,*
CnMD, McGWD, ModWD, NotNAT A,
OxThe, PIP&P, REnWD
Columbo, Russ 1908-1934 *FilmgC, WhScrn 1,*
WhScrn 2, WhoHol B
Columbo, Russ *see also* Colombo, Russ
Colvig, Vance 1892-1967 *FilmgC, WhoHol B*
Colvig, Vance D Pinto 1892-1967 *WhScrn 1,*
WhScrn 2
Colville, John *IntMPA 1977*
Colvin, Gilly *Film 2*
Colvin, Marion *Film 2*
Colvin, William *Film 2*
Comanche, Laurence Tex 1908-1932 *WhScrn 1,*
WhScrn 2
Comandini, Adele *WomWMM*
Comant, Mathilda 1888-1938 *WhScrn 1,*
WhScrn 2
Combe, Boyce *Film 1, Film 2*
Comber, Bobbie 1886-1942 *WhThe*
Comber, Bobbie 1890-1942 *WhScrn 1, WhScrn 2*
Combermere, Edward 1888- *WhThe*
Comberousse, Alexis De 1793-1862 *OxThe*
Combs, Jackie *Film 2*
Comden, Betty *AmSCAP 1966, BiE&WWA,*
ConDr 1977D, IntMPA 1977, WomWMM
Comden, Betty 1915- *EncMT, NewMT*
Comden, Betty 1916- *CmMov, OxFilm, WorEnF*
Comden, Betty 1918- *FilmgC*
Comden, Betty 1919- *CelR 3, NotNAT,*
WhoThe 16
Comegys, Kathleen 1895- *BiE&WWA, NotNAT,*
WhoHol A
Comella, Luciano Francisco 1751-1812 *OxThe*
Comelli, Attilio d1925 *NotNAT B*
Comencini, Luigi 1916- *DcFM, FilmgC, WorEnF*
Comer, Anjanette 1942- *FilmgC, MotPP,*
WhoHol A
Comerford, Maurice d1903 *NotNAT B*
Comfort, Lance 1908-1966 *FilmgC*
Comi, Paul *WhoHol A*
Comingore, Dorothy 1913-1971 *FilmgC*
Comingore, Dorothy 1918-1971 *WhScrn 1,*
WhScrn 2, WhoHol B
Comini, Raiberto 1907- *AmSCAP 1966*
Commandon, Jean 1877- *DcFM, OxFilm*
Comment, Constance *WomWMM B*
Commerford, Thomas 1855-1920 *Film 1,*
WhScrn 2
Commire, Anne *NatPD*
Commoner, Barry 1917- *CelR 3*
Como, Perry 1912- *CelR 3, FilmgC,*
IntMPA 1977, NewYTET, WhoHol A
Comont, M *Film 2*
Comont, Mathilde d1938 *Film 2, WhoHol B*
Comont, Nattie *Film 2*
Companeez, Nina *WomWMM*
Compson, Betty 1897-1974 *Film 1, Film 2,*
FilmgC, MotPP, MovMk, ThFT, TwYS,
WhScrn 2, WhoHol B
Compson, John d1913 *Film 1, WhoHol B*
Compton, Betty 1907-1944 *NotNAT B,*

WhScrn 1, WhScrn 2, WhoHol B
Compton, Mrs. Edward 1853-1940 *NotNAT B,*
WhThe
Compton, Edward 1854-1918 *NotNAT B, OxThe,*
WhThe
Compton, Mrs. Edward *see also* Bateman, Virginia
Frances
Compton, Mrs. Edward *see also* Compton, Virginia
Frances Bateman
Compton, Fay 1894- *BiE&WWA, Film 1,*
Film 2, FilmgC, NotNAT, NotNAT A,
OxThe, PIP&P, WhThe, WhoHol A
Compton, Fay 1895- *CnThe*
Compton, Forrest *WhoHol A*
Compton, Francis 1885-1964 *BiE&WWA,*
NotNAT B, WhScrn 1, WhScrn 2,
WhoHol B
Compton, Henry 1805-1877 *NotNAT A,*
NotNAT B, OxThe
Compton, Joyce *IntMPA 1977, MotPP,*
WhoHol A
Compton, Joyce 1907- *Film 2, FilmgC, MovMk*
Compton, Joyce 1908- *ThFT*
Compton, Juleen *WomWMM A, WomWMM B*
Compton, Juliette *Film 2*
Compton, Katherine Mackenzie 1853-1928
NotNAT B, WhThe
Compton, Madge d1970 *WhThe*
Compton, Sydney d1938 *NotNAT B*
Compton, Viola 1886-1971 *WhScrn 2, WhThe,*
WhoHol B
Compton, Virginia Frances Bateman 1853-1940
OxThe
Compton, Virginia Frances Bateman *see also*
Compton, Mrs. Edward
Comstock, Anthony B 1844-1915 *NotNAT B*
Comstock, F Ray 1880-1949 *EncMT, NotNAT B,*
WhThe
Comstock, Frank 1922- *AmSCAP 1966*
Comstock, Nanette 1873-1942 *NotNAT B,*
WhThe, WhoStg 1908
Comstock, William Collins 1924- *AmSCAP 1966*
Conaway, Donald F *BiE&WWA*
Conchita d1940 *NotNAT B*
Conde, Johnny 1895-1960 *WhScrn 1, WhScrn 2*
Conde, Rita *WhoHol A*
Condell, Henry d1627 *NotNAT B, OxThe*
Condon, Albert Edwin 1905-1973 *AmSCAP 1966*
Condon, Jackie *Film 1*
Condon, Jackie 1913- *Film 2*
Condon, Jackie 1923- *TwYS*
Condos, Steve *WhoHol A*
Cone, Fairfax M d1977 *NewYTET*
Cone, Mike Zets 1910-1969 *WhScrn 1, WhScrn 2,*
WhoHol B
Cones, Nancy Ford *WomWMM*
Conesa, Marie *Film 1*
Confer, Robert 1931- *AmSCAP 1966*
Confrey, Edward E 1895- *AmSCAP 1966*
Congdon, James *WhoHol A*
Congreve, William 1670-1729 *CnThe, McGWD,*
NotNAT A, NotNAT B, OxThe, PIP&P,
REnWD
Conkey, Thomas d1927 *NotNAT B*
Conkle, E P 1899- *BiE&WWA, CnMD, ModWD,*
NotNAT
Conklin, Charles Heinie 1880-1959 *Film 1, Film 2,*
TwYS, WhScrn 1, WhScrn 2
Conklin, Chester 1886-1971 *OxFilm, TwYS*
Conklin, Chester 1888-1971 *Film 1, Film 2,*
FilmgC, MotPP, MovMk, WhScrn 1,
WhScrn 2, WhoHol B
Conklin, Heinie 1880-1959 *WhoHol B*
Conklin, Peggy 1910- *ThFT*

Constantine, Michael 1927- *BiE&WWA, FilmgC,*
  WhoHol A
Constantini, Nino *Film 2*
Consuella, Senorita *Film 2*
Contat, Louise 1760-1813 *OxThe*
Conte, Donald J 1941- *IntMPA 1977*
Conte, John 1915- *BiE&WWA, IntMPA 1977,*
  WhThe
Conte, Richard *MotPP*
Conte, Richard d1975 *WhoHol C*
Conte, Richard 1914-1975 *FilmgC, HolP 40,*
  WhScrn 2, WorEnF
Conte, Richard 1915-1975 *MovMk*
Conte, Richard 1919-1975 *CmMov*
Conti, Albert 1887-1967 *Film 2, TwYS,*
  WhScrn 1, WhScrn 2, WhoHol B
Conti, Italia 1874-1946 *NotNAT A, NotNAT B,*
  OxThe, WhThe
Conti, Louise *Film 2*
Contino, Dick *WhoHol A*
Converse, Frank 1938- *IntMPA 1977, WhoHol A*
Converse, Frederick Shepherd 1871-1940
  AmSCAP 1966
Converse, Peggy *WhoHol A*
Converse, Thelma *Film 2*
Conville, David 1929- *WhoThe 16*
Conville, Robert *Film 1*
Convy, Bert *WhoHol A*
Convy, Bert 1934- *WhoThe 16*
Convy, Bert 1936- *BiE&WWA, NotNAT*
Conway, Booth *Film 2*
Conway, Curt 1915-1974 *BiE&WWA,*
  NotNAT B, WhScrn 2, WhoHol B
Conway, Frederick Bartlett 1819-1874 *NotNAT B,*
  OxThe
Conway, Gary 1938- *FilmgC, WhoHol A*
Conway, Harold 1906- *WhThe*
Conway, Hugh d1885 *NotNAT B*
Conway, Jack d1951 *WhScrn 1, WhScrn 2,*
  WhoHol A
Conway, Jack 1887-1952 *CmMov, DcFM, Film 1,*
  FilmgC, MovMk, NotNAT B, TwYS A,
  WhScrn 1, WhScrn 2, WhoHol B, WorEnF
Conway, John Ashby 1905- *BiE&WWA,*
  NotNAT
Conway, Joseph 1889?-1959 *WhScrn 1,*
  WhScrn 2
Conway, Martin *Film 2*
Conway, Minnie 1854-1896 *NotNAT B, OxThe*
Conway, Morgan *WhoHol A*
Conway, Pat *WhoHol A*
Conway, Russ *WhoHol A*
Conway, Sarah Crocker 1834-1875 *NotNAT B,*
  OxThe
Conway, Shirl 1916- *BiE&WWA, IntMPA 1977,*
  NotNAT, WhoHol A
Conway, Tim 1933- *IntMPA 1977, NewYTET,*
  WhoHol A
Conway, Tom 1904-1967 *FilmgC, HolP 40,*
  MotPP, MovMk, WhScrn 1, WhScrn 2,
  WhoHol B
Conway, William Augustus 1789-1828 *NotNAT B,*
  OxThe
Conwell, Carolyn *WhoHol A*
Conyers, Darcy 1919-1973 *FilmgC*
Conyers, Joseph d1920 *NotNAT B*
Conyngham, Fred 1909- *WhThe*
Coogan, Gene B d1972 *WhScrn 2*
Coogan, Jack, Sr. 1880-1935 *Film 2, WhScrn 2*
Coogan, Jackie *MotPP*
Coogan, Jackie 1914- *FilmgC, IntMPA 1977,*
  MovMk, OxFilm, TwYS, WhoHol A
Coogan, Jackie 1915- *Film 1, Film 2*
Coogan, Robert *WhoHol A*

Cook, Al 1882-1935 *WhScrn 1, WhScrn 2,*
  WhoHol B
Cook, Barbara 1927- *BiE&WWA, EncMT,*
  NotNAT, WhoThe 16
Cook, Carole *WhoHol A*
Cook, Caroline Frances *Film 2*
Cook, Charles Emerson d1941 *NotNAT B*
Cook, Clyde 1891- *Film 1, Film 2, TwYS*
Cook, Donald 1900-1961 *FilmgC*
Cook, Donald 1900-1967 *MovMk*
Cook, Donald 1901-1961 *HolP 30, MotPP,*
  NotNAT B, WhScrn 1, WhScrn 2, WhThe,
  WhoHol B
Cook, Douglas 1929- *NotNAT*
Cook, Edward Dutton 1829-1883 *NotNAT B,*
  OxThe
Cook, Elisha, Jr. *WhoHol A*
Cook, Elisha, Jr. 1902- *CmMov, FilmgC,*
  MovMk, WhThe
Cook, Elisha, Jr. 1906- *BiE&WWA, NotNAT,*
  WorEnF
Cook, Elisha, Jr. 1907- *CmMov, IntMPA 1977,*
  OxFilm, Vers B
Cook, Ethyle 1880-1949 *WhScrn 2*
Cook, Fielder 1923- *FilmgC, IntMPA 1977,*
  NewYTET
Cook, Fred *WhoHol A*
Cook, George Cram 1873-1924 *CnMD, ModWD,*
  NotNAT B
Cook, Ira 1916- *AmSCAP 1966*
Cook, Joe 1890-1959 *EncMT, NotNAT B,*
  WhScrn 2, WhThe, WhoHol B
Cook, John *Film 1*
Cook, John Russell 1911-1964 *NotNAT B*
Cook, Ken 1914-1963 *NotNAT B, WhScrn 1,*
  WhScrn 2
Cook, Kwenam David 1922- *IntMPA 1977*
Cook, Lillian 1898-1918 *WhScrn 2*
Cook, Lucius 1891-1952 *WhScrn 2*
Cook, Madge Carr 1856-1933 *NotNAT B*
Cook, Mary d1944 *WhScrn 1, WhScrn 2*
Cook, Mary Lou d1944 *WhoHol B*
Cook, Michael 1933- *ConDr 1977*
Cook, Peter 1937- *BiE&WWA, FilmgC,*
  NotNAT, WhoHol A, WhoThe 16
Cook, Ross 1898-1930 *WhScrn 1, WhScrn 2*
Cook, Tommy *WhoHol A*
Cook, W Mercer 1903- *AmSCAP 1966*
Cook, Warren 1879-1939 *Film 1, Film 2,*
  WhScrn 1, WhScrn 2
Cook, Will Marion 1869-1944 *AmSCAP 1966,*
  NotNAT B
Cooke, Al *Film 2, TwYS*
Cooke, Alexander d1614 *NotNAT B*
Cooke, Alistair 1908- *CelR 3, IntMPA 1977,*
  NewYTET
Cooke, Baldwin *Film 2*
Cooke, Beach 1898-1948 *Film 2, WhoHol B*
Cooke, Beach *see also* Cooke, Stephen Beach
Cooke, Charles L 1891-1958 *AmSCAP 1966*
Cooke, Eddie d1942 *NotNAT B*
Cooke, Frank *Film 2*
Cooke, George Frederick 1756-1811 *CnThe*
Cooke, George Frederick 1756-1812 *FamA&A,*
  NotNAT A, NotNAT B, OxThe, PIP&P
Cooke, Harry d1958 *NotNAT B*
Cooke, Jack Kent *NewYTET*
Cooke, James Francis 1875-1960 *AmSCAP 1966*
Cooke, Marjorie Benton d1920 *NotNAT B*
Cooke, Ray *Film 2*
Cooke, Richard P 1904- *BiE&WWA, NotNAT*
Cooke, Sam d1964 *WhoHol B*
Cooke, Stanley 1868-1931 *Film 2, WhThe*
Cooke, Stephen Beach 1898-1948 *WhScrn 1,*

WhScrn 2
Cooke, Stephen Beach see also Cooke, Beach
Cooke, Cardinal Terence 1921- CelR 3
Cooke, Thomas d1756 NotNAT B
Cooke, Thomas Coffin d1939 NotNAT B
Cooke, Thomas Potter 1786-1864 NotNAT B,
   OxThe
Cooke, Warren 1897-1939 WhoHol B
Cooke, Warren see also Cook, Warren
Cookman, Anthony Victor 1894-1962 NotNAT B,
   OxThe, WhThe
Cooksey, Curtis 1892-1962 Film 2, NotNAT B,
   WhScrn 1, WhScrn 2, WhoHol B
Cookson, Georgina WhThe
Cookson, Peter WhoHol A
Cookson, Peter 1913- BiE&WWA, NotNAT
Cookson, S A d1947 Film 1, NotNAT B
Cool, Harold 1890-1949 AmSCAP 1966
Cooley, Charles 1903-1960 WhScrn 1, WhScrn 2,
   WhoHol B
Cooley, Denton 1920- CelR 3
Cooley, Frank L 1870-1941 Film 2, WhScrn 1,
   WhScrn 2, WhoHol B
Cooley, Hallam 1888- Film 1, Film 2, TwYS
Cooley, James R 1880-1948 Film 1, Film 2,
   WhScrn 1, WhScrn 2, WhoHol B
Cooley, Spade 1910-1969 WhScrn 1, WhScrn 2,
   WhoHol B
Cooley, Willard Film 1, Film 2
Coolidge, Martha WomWMM, WomWMM A,
   WomWMM B
Coolidge, Peggy Stuart AmSCAP 1966
Coolidge, Philip 1908-1967 BiE&WWA,
   NotNAT B, WhScrn 1, WhScrn 2,
   WhoHol B
Coolus, Romain 1868-1952 McGWD, WhThe
Coombe, Carol 1911-1966 WhScrn 2, WhThe,
   WhoHol B
Coombs, Charles Whitney 1859-1940
   AmSCAP 1966
Coombs, Guy Film 1
Coombs, Jack 1883-1957 WhScrn 2
Coombs, Jackie Film 2
Coonan, Dorothy WhoHol A
Cooney, Joan Ganz 1929- CelR 3, NewYTET
Cooney, Ray 1932- WhoThe 16
Coons, Johnny 1917-1975 WhScrn 2
Coop, Colin d1937 NotNAT B
Coop, Denys 1920- FilmgC
Cooper, Alice 1948- CelR 3
Cooper, Anthony Kemble 1908- BiE&WWA,
   NotNAT, WhThe
Cooper, Ashley 1882-1952 NotNAT B, WhScrn 1,
   WhScrn 2, WhoHol B
Cooper, Ben 1930- FilmgC, IntMPA 1977,
   MotPP, WhoHol A
Cooper, Bigelow Film 1, Film 2
Cooper, Bud 1899- AmSCAP 1966
Cooper, Budge WomWMM
Cooper, Charles Kemble d1923 NotNAT B
Cooper, Cheryl AmSCAP 1966
Cooper, Clancy d1975 WhScrn 2, WhoHol C
Cooper, Claude 1881-1932 Film 1, WhScrn 1,
   WhScrn 2, WhoHol B
Cooper, Clifford d1895 NotNAT B
Cooper, Mrs. Clifford 1823-1895 NotNAT B
Cooper, Daley 1872- WhThe
Cooper, Diana 1892- NotNAT A
Cooper, Earl Film 1
Cooper, Edna Mae Film 1, Film 2
Cooper, Edward d1956 NotNAT B, WhScrn 2,
   WhoHol B
Cooper, Edward 1903- IntMPA 1977
Cooper, Edward 1925- AmSCAP 1966

Cooper, Edwin WhoHol A
Cooper, Enid 1902- WhThe
Cooper, Evelyne Love AmSCAP 1966
Cooper, F B Film 1
Cooper, Frances d1872 NotNAT B
Cooper, Frank BiE&WWA
Cooper, Frank Kemble 1857-1918 NotNAT B,
   WhThe
Cooper, Frederick Film 2
Cooper, Frederick 1890-1945 NotNAT B, WhThe,
   WhoHol B
Cooper, G Melville 1896- WhThe
Cooper, Gary 1901-1961 BiDFlm, CmMov,
   Film 2, FilmgC, MotPP, MovMk,
   NotNAT B, OxFilm, TwYS, WhScrn 1,
   WhScrn 2, WhoHol B, WorEnF
Cooper, George 1891- Film 1, Film 2, TwYS
Cooper, George 1892-1943 WhScrn 2
Cooper, George A WhoHol A
Cooper, George A 1913- MovMk
Cooper, George A 1916- FilmgC
Cooper, Georgia 1882-1968 WhScrn 1, WhScrn 2
Cooper, Georgie 1882-1968 WhoHol B
Cooper, Giles 1918-1966 ConDr 1977F, CroCD,
   NotNAT B, WhThe
Cooper, Gladys 1888-1971 BiE&WWA, CnThe,
   Film 1, Film 2, FilmgC, MGM, MotPP,
   MovMk, Vers A, WhScrn 1, WhScrn 2,
   WhThe, WhoHol B
Cooper, Gladys 1889-1971 NotNAT A,
   NotNAT B
Cooper, Greta Kemble WhThe
Cooper, Hal 1923- IntMPA 1977
Cooper, Harry 1882-1957 WhScrn 1, WhScrn 2
Cooper, Herman E BiE&WWA
Cooper, Jack Film 2
Cooper, Jackie MotPP, NewYTET, WhoHol A
Cooper, Jackie 1921- FilmgC
Cooper, Jackie 1922- BiE&WWA, Film 2,
   IntMPA 1977, MGM, MovMk
Cooper, James Fenimore 1789-1851 FilmgC
Cooper, Jeanne WhoHol A
Cooper, John Craig 1925- AmSCAP 1966
Cooper, Kent 1880-1965 AmSCAP 1966
Cooper, Lillian Kemble 1891- WhThe
Cooper, Margaret d1922 NotNAT B
Cooper, Margaret Gernon WhThe
Cooper, Marilyn 1935- BiE&WWA
Cooper, Melville 1896-1973 BiE&WWA, FilmgC,
   MovMk, NotNAT B, Vers A, WhScrn 2,
   WhoHol B
Cooper, Meriam C 1893-1973 TwYS A
Cooper, Merian C 1893-1973 BiDFlm, DcFM,
   FilmgC, WhScrn 2, WorEnF
Cooper, Merian C 1894-1973 OxFilm
Cooper, Miriam 1893-1976 WhoHol A
Cooper, Miriam 1894-1976 Film 1, Film 2,
   TwYS
Cooper, Richard 1893-1947 NotNAT B, WhThe,
   WhoHol B
Cooper, Robert W 1925- AmSCAP 1966
Cooper, Rose Marie 1937- AmSCAP 1966
Cooper, Rosemary Film 2
Cooper, Sidney 1918- AmSCAP 1966
Cooper, Terence WhoHol A
Cooper, Tex 1877-1951 WhScrn 1, WhScrn 2,
   WhoHol B
Cooper, Theodore Gleston 1939- NotNAT
Cooper, Thomas Abthorpe 1776-1849 FamA&A,
   NotNAT B, OxThe, PIP&P
Cooper, Tommy 1921- IntMPA 1977
Cooper, Violet Kemble 1886-1961 FilmgC
Cooper, Violet Kemble 1889-1961 NotNAT B,
   WhThe

Cooper, Wilkie 1911- *FilmgC*
Cooperman, Alvin 1923- *IntMPA 1977,*
    NewYTET
Coopersmith, Harry 1902?- *AmSCAP 1966*
Coopersmith, Jacob Maurice 1903- *AmSCAP 1966*
Coors, Joseph *NewYTET*
Coote, Bernard *IntMPA 1977*
Coote, Bert 1867-1938 *NotNAT B*
Coote, Bert 1868-1938 *WhScrn 1, WhScrn 2,*
    WhThe
Coote, Robert 1909- *BiE&WWA, FilmgC,*
    MotPP, MovMk, NotNAT, Vers B,
    WhoHol A, WhoThe 16
Coots, J Fred 1897- *AmSCAP 1966, BiE&WWA,*
    EncMT, NewMT, NotNAT
Copani, Peter 1942- *NatPD*
Copas, Cowboy 1914-1963 *WhScrn 2*
Cope, Kenneth 1931- *FilmgC*
Copeau, Jacques 1878-1949 *CnThe, NotNAT B,*
    WhThe
Copeau, Jacques 1879-1949 *CnMD, McGWD,*
    ModWD, OxThe, PIP&P, WhScrn 2
Copeland, Allan 1926- *AmSCAP 1966*
Copeland, Isabella d1912 *NotNAT B*
Copeland, Joan 1922- *BiE&WWA, NotNAT,*
    WhoHol A, WhoThe 16
Copeland, Julia Viola 1916- *AmSCAP 1966*
Copeland, Mary Dowell d1963 *NotNAT B*
Copeland, Nicholas W 1895-1940 *WhScrn 1,*
    WhScrn 2
Copeland, Nick d1940 *WhoHol B*
Copland, Aaron 1900- *AmSCAP 1966, CelR 3,*
    FilmgC, OxFilm, WorEnF
Copley, Peter 1915- *FilmgC, WhoHol A,*
    WhoThe 16
Coppa, Joe *Film 2*
Coppee, Francois Edouard Joachim 1842-1908
    CnMD, McGWD, ModWD, NotNAT B
Coppel, Alec 1910-1972 *BiE&WWA, FilmgC,*
    WhThe
Coppen, Hazel 1925-1975 *WhScrn 2*
Coppola, Anton 1918- *BiE&WWA, NotNAT*
Coppola, Carmine 1910- *AmSCAP 1966*
Coppola, Francis Ford 1933- *OxFilm*
Coppola, Francis Ford 1939- *BiDFlm, FilmgC,*
    IntMPA 1977, MovMk, WorEnF
Coppola, Francis Ford 1940- *CelR 3*
Coppola, Talia *WhoHol A*
Coquelin *PIP&P*
Coquelin, Benoit Constant 1841-1909 *NotNAT B,*
    WhoHol B
Coquelin, Constant-Benoit 1841-1909 *CnThe,*
    OxThe
Coquelin, Ernest-Alexandre-Honore 1848-1909
    NotNAT B, OxThe
Coquelin, Jean 1865-1944 *NotNAT B, OxThe,*
    WhThe, WhoHol B
Coquillon, John *FilmgC*
Coram 1883- *WhThe*
Corb, Morty 1917- *AmSCAP 1966*
Corbe, Eduardo 1878-1967 *WhScrn 2*
Corbet, Ben *Film 2*
Corbett, Ben 1892-1961 *Film 1, WhScrn 1,*
    WhScrn 2
Corbett, Benny 1892-1961 *WhoHol B*
Corbett, Glenn 1929- *FilmgC, WhoHol A*
Corbett, Gretchen 1947- *WhoThe 16*
Corbett, Harry H 1925- *FilmgC, IntMPA 1977,*
    WhoThe 16
Corbett, James J 1866-1933 *NotNAT B,*
    WhoStg 1906, WhoStg 1908
Corbett, James J 1867-1933 *Film 1, Film 2,*
    WhScrn 1, WhScrn 2, WhoHol B
Corbett, Leonora d1960 *WhoHol B*

Corbett, Leonora 1907-1960 *FilmgC*
Corbett, Leonora 1908-1960 *NotNAT B,*
    WhScrn 1, WhScrn 2, WhThe
Corbett, Mary 1926-1974 *WhScrn 2*
Corbett, Ronnie 1933- *FilmgC*
Corbett, Thalberg 1864- *WhThe*
Corbett, William D *Film 2*
Corbin, Gladys *MotPP*
Corbin, John 1870-1959 *NotNAT B, WhThe*
Corbin, Virginia Lee 1910-1942 *Film 1, Film 2,*
    WhScrn 1, WhScrn 2, WhoHol B
Corbin, Virginia Lee 1912- *TwYS*
Corbucci, Sergio *FilmgC*
Corby, Ellen 1913- *FilmgC, MovMk, Vers A,*
    WhoHol A
Corcoran, Brian 1951- *WhoHol A*
Corcoran, Donna 1942- *WhoHol A*
Corcoran, Hugh *WhoHol A*
Corcoran, Jane *WhThe*
Corcoran, Katharine 1857-1943 *OxThe*
Corcoran, Katherine 1857-1943 *NotNAT B,*
    PIP&P
Corcoran, Kelly 1958- *WhoHol A*
Corcoran, Kevin 1949- *WhoHol A*
Corcoran, Noreen 1943- *WhoHol A*
Cord, Alex 1931- *CelR 3, FilmgC,*
    IntMPA 1977, MotPP, WhoHol A
Corda, Maria *Film 2*
Corda, Michael 1921- *AmSCAP 1966*
Corday, Leo 1902- *AmSCAP 1966*
Corday, Mara 1932- *FilmgC, WhoHol A*
Corday, Marcelle *Film 2, TwYS*
Corday, Paula 1924- *FilmgC, WhoHol A*
Corday, Raymond d1956 *Film 2*
Cordell, Cathleen *WhoHol A*
Cordell, Cathleen 1916- *WhThe*
Cordell, Cathleen 1917- *BiE&WWA*
Corden, Henry *WhoHol A*
Corder, Bruce *BiE&WWA*
Corder, Leeta 1890-1956 *WhScrn 1, WhScrn 2*
Cordier, Charles 1911- *CnMD*
Cording, Harry 1891-1954 *WhScrn 2*
Cording, Harry 1894-1954 *Film 2, Vers B,*
    WhScrn 1, WhoHol B
Cordoba, Pedro De 1881-1950 *Vers A*
Cordy, Henry 1908-1965 *WhScrn 1, WhScrn 2,*
    WhoHol B
Cordy, Raymond 1898-1956 *FilmgC, WhScrn 1,*
    WhScrn 2, WhoHol B
Corelli, Franco 1923- *CelR 3*
Corey, Eugene *Film 2*
Corey, Irwin *WhoHol A*
Corey, Jeff 1914- *FilmgC, IntMPA 1977,*
    Vers B, WhoHol A
Corey, Joseph 1927-1972 *WhScrn 2, WhoHol B*
Corey, Wendell 1914-1968 *BiE&WWA,*
    FilmgC, HolP 40, MotPP, MovMk,
    NotNAT B, WhScrn 1, WhScrn 2, WhThe,
    WhoHol B, WorEnF
Corfield, John 1893- *FilmgC*
Corigliano, John 1938- *AmSCAP 1966*
Corinne 1873-1937 *NotNAT B, WhoStg 1908*
Corinne 1875-1937 *WhoStg 1906*
Corio, Ann *CelR 3, WhoHol A*
Corley, Robert d1971 *WhScrn 2*
Corman, Gene *IntMPA 1977*
Corman, Roger 1926- *BiDFlm, CmMov, DcFM,*
    FilmgC, IntMPA 1977, MovMk, OxFilm,
    WorEnF
Cormon, Nelly *Film 2*
Corneille, Pierre 1606-1684 *CnThe, McGWD,*
    NotNAT A, NotNAT B, OxThe, PIP&P,
    REnWD
Corneille, Thomas 1625-1709 *McGWD,*

NotNAT B, OxThe, REnWD
Cornelius, Henry 1913-1958 CmMov, DcFM, FilmgC, MovMk, OxFilm
Cornelius, O Henry 1913-1958 WorEnF
Cornell, John 1913- BiE&WWA
Cornell, Jonas 1938- WorEnF
Cornell, Katharine 1893-1974 FamA&A, PIP&P, WhScrn 2, WhoHol B
Cornell, Katharine 1898-1974 BiE&WWA, CelR 3, CnThe, NotNAT A, NotNAT B, OxThe, WhThe
Cornell, Melva Film 2
Corner, James W 1919-1944 WhScrn 1, WhScrn 2, WhoHol B
Corner, Sally 1894-1959 WhScrn 1, WhScrn 2, WhoHol B
Cornett, Alice 1911- AmSCAP 1966
Cornfield, Hubert 1929- FilmgC, WorEnF
Cornish, Roger N NatPD
Cornsweet, Harold 1918- IntMPA 1977
Cornthwaite, Robert WhoHol A
Cornwall, Anne 1897- Film 1, Film 2, TwYS, WhoHol A
Cornwell, Judy 1942- WhoThe 16
Cornyn, Stan 1933- AmSCAP 1966
Coronado, Elida WomWMM B
Corradine, Tom J 1924- IntMPA 1977
Corrado, Gino Film 1, Film 2, TwYS
Correa, Julio OxThe
Correl, Gladis d1962 NotNAT B
Correll, Charles J 1890-1972 WhScrn 2, WhoHol B
Corri, Adrienne WhoHol A
Corri, Adrienne 1930- FilmgC
Corri, Adrienne 1933- IntMPA 1977
Corri, Charles Montague 1861- PIP&P, WhThe
Corrie, Joe 1894-1968 OxThe
Corrigan, Charles 1894-1966 WhScrn 1, WhScrn 2
Corrigan, D'Arcy Film 2
Corrigan, Douglas Wrong Way 1907- WhoHol A
Corrigan, E Film 2
Corrigan, Emmett d1932 Film 2, WhoHol B
Corrigan, Emmett 1867-1932 WhScrn 1, WhScrn 2
Corrigan, Emmett 1868-1932 NotNAT B, WhoStg 1908
Corrigan, Emmett 1871-1932 WhThe
Corrigan, James 1871-1929 Film 2, TwYS, WhScrn 1, WhScrn 2, WhoHol B
Corrigan, Lloyd 1900-1969 Film 2, FilmgC, MovMk, Vers B, WhScrn 1, WhScrn 2, WhoHol B
Corrigan, Ray Crash 1907- FilmgC, WhoHol A
Corrigan, Robert W 1927- BiE&WWA, NotNAT
Corrigan, Thomas J Film 1, WhScrn 2
Corrigan, Tom Film 2
Corrington, Joyce WomWMM
Corsari, Franco WhoHol A
Corsaro, Frank 1924- BiE&WWA, NotNAT, WhoThe 16
Corsaut, Aneta WhoHol A
'Corson, Richard BiE&WWA, NotNAT
Cort, Bud 1950- FilmgC, MovMk, WhoHol A
Cort, Harry Linsley d1937 NotNAT B
Cort, John d1929 NotNAT B
Cort, Robert W IntMPA 1977
Cortes, Armand 1880-1948 Film 1, Film 2, WhScrn 2
Cortesa, Valentina 1924- FilmgC
Cortesa, Valentina 1925- IntMPA 1977, MovMk
Cortese, Valentina 1925- WhoHol A, WorEnF
Cortesi, Giulio Film 2
Cortesi, Mrs. Giulio Film 2

Cortez, Armand Film 2
Cortez, Leon 1898-1970 WhScrn 1, WhScrn 2, WhoHol B
Cortez, Ricardo 1899- Film 2, FilmgC, MotPP, MovMk, WhoHol A
Cortez, Richard 1899- TwYS
Cortez, Stanley 1908- FilmgC, IntMPA 1977, OxFilm, WorEnF
Corthell, Herbert 1875-1947 Film 2, NotNAT B, WhScrn 1, WhScrn 2, WhoHol B, WhoStg 1908
Corwin, Betty L 1920- AmSCAP 1966
Corwin, Bruce Conrad 1940- IntMPA 1977
Corwin, Norman 1910- AmSCAP 1966, BiE&WWA, IntMPA 1977, NewYTET, NotNAT
Corwin, Sherrill C IntMPA 1977
Cory, George 1920- AmSCAP 1966
Cory, Robert 1883-1955 WhScrn 1, WhScrn 2
Cos, Joachim DcFM
Cosby, Bill NewYTET, WhoHol A
Cosby, Bill 1937- CelR 3
Cosby, Bill 1938- FilmgC, IntMPA 1977
Coscia, Silvio 1899- AmSCAP 1966
Cosell, Howard 1920- CelR 3, NewYTET
Cosgrave, Jack Film 1, Film 2
Cosgrave, Luke 1862-1949 Film 2, NotNAT A, WhScrn 1, WhScrn 2, WhoHol B
Cosgrove, John Film 2
Cosgrove, Robert 1900-1960 WhScrn 1, WhScrn 2
Cosima, Renee WomWMM
Coslow, Sam 1902- AmSCAP 1966
Coslow, Sam 1905- IntMPA 1977
Cossa, Pietro 1830-1881 McGWD, NotNAT B, OxThe
Cossaeus, Sophie 1893-1965 WhScrn 1, WhScrn 2
Cossar, John Hay 1865-1935 Film 2, WhScrn 1, WhScrn 2, WhoHol B
Cossart, Ernest 1876-1951 Film 1, FilmgC, NotNAT B, PIP&P, WhScrn 1, WhScrn 2, WhThe, WhoHol B
Cossart, Valerie 1910- WhThe
Cossins, James 1932- FilmgC
Costa, Miss Film 2
Costa, Lucile WomWMM
Costa, Mary WhoHol A
Costa, Sebastiano 1876-1935 WhScrn 1, WhScrn 2
Costa, Sylvia Bess 1937- WomWMM B
Costa, William F 1920- AmSCAP 1966
Costa-Gavras 1933- CelR 3, FilmgC
Costa-Gavras, Costi 1933- OxFilm, WorEnF
Costa-Gavras, Henri 1933- IntMPA 1977, MovMk
Costantini, Angelo 1655?-1729 OxThe
Costantini, Costantino OxThe
Costantini, Domenica OxThe
Costantini, Giovan Battista d1720 OxThe
Costanzo, Jack AmSCAP 1966
Coste, Maurice R 1875-1963 WhScrn 1, WhScrn 2
Costello, Anthony WhoHol A
Costello, Bartley C 1871-1941 AmSCAP 1966
Costello, Carmen Film 2
Costello, Delmar 1906-1961 WhScrn 2
Costello, Diosa WhoHol A
Costello, Dolores 1904- ThFT
Costello, Dolores 1905- Film 1, Film 2, FilmgC, MotPP, MovMk, TwYS, WhoHol A
Costello, Don 1901-1945 WhScrn 1, WhScrn 2, WhoHol B
Costello, Helene d1957 MotPP, NotNAT B,

WhoHol B
Costello, Helene 1903-1957 *Film 1, Film 2, TwYS, WhScrn 1, WhScrn 2*
Costello, Helene 1904-1957 *FilmgC*
Costello, Helene 1905-1957 *ThFT*
Costello, John *Film 2*
Costello, Lou 1906-1959 *CmMov, FilmgC, MotPP, MovMk, NotNAT B, OxFilm, WhScrn 1, WhScrn 2, WhoHol B, WorEnF*
Costello, Maurice 1877-1950 *Film 1, Film 2, FilmgC, MotPP, NotNAT B, TwYS, WhScrn 1, WhScrn 2, WhoHol B*
Costello, Mildred *Film 2*
Costello, Tom 1863- *WhThe*
Costello, Tom 1863-1943 *NotNAT B*
Costello, Tom 1863-1945 *OxThe*
Costello, Ward *WhoHol A*
Costello, William A 1898-1971 *Film 2, WhScrn 1, WhScrn 2, WhoHol B*
Coster, Nicolas *WhoHol A*
Costigan, James 1928- *BiE&WWA, NewYTET, NotNAT*
Costillo, Carmen *Film 2*
Cotes, Peter 1912- *IntMPA 1977, WhoThe 16*
Cotopouli, Marika d1954 *NotNAT B*
Cotsworth, Staats 1908- *BiE&WWA, IntMPA 1977, NotNAT, WhoHol A, WhoThe 16*
Cott, Ted d1973 *NewYTET*
Cottafavi, Vittorio 1914- *BiDFlm, DcFM, FilmgC, OxFilm, WorEnF*
Cotten, Joseph 1905- *BiDFlm, BiE&WWA, CmMov, FilmgC, IntMPA 1977, MotPP, MovMk, NotNAT, OxFilm, PIP&P, WhoHol A, WhoThe 16, WorEnF*
Cottens, Victor De 1862- *WhThe*
Cotto DelValle, Luis 1913-1971 *WhScrn 1, WhScrn 2*
Cotton, Billy 1900-1969 *Film 2, WhScrn 1, WhScrn 2, WhoHol B*
Cotton, Charles d1687 *NotNAT B*
Cotton, Fred d1964 *WhoHol B*
Cotton, Fred Ayers 1907-1964 *NotNAT B*
Cotton, Fred Ayres 1907-1964 *WhScrn 1, WhScrn 2*
Cotton, George 1903-1975 *WhScrn 2*
Cotton, Lucy 1891-1948 *Film 1, Film 2, NotNAT B, TwYS, WhScrn 1, WhScrn 2, WhoHol B*
Cotton, Richardson d1916 *WhScrn 2*
Cotton, Robert F *NotNAT B*
Cotton, Wilfred 1873- *WhThe*
Cottrell, Cherry 1909- *WhThe*
Cottrell, Richard 1936- *WhoThe 16*
Cottrelly, Mathilde 1851-1933 *NotNAT B*
Cotts, Campbell 1903-1964 *NotNAT B, WhScrn 2*
Coty, Anny *Film 2*
Coty, Henri Roland 1922- *IntMPA 1977*
Coubier, Heinz 1905- *CnMD*
Couch, Robert *Film 2*
Couffer, Jack 1922- *FilmgC*
Coughlin, Kevin d1976 *WhoHol C*
Couldock, Charles Walter 1815-1898 *NotNAT B, OxThe*
Couloris, George *MotPP*
Coulouris, George 1903- *BiE&WWA, FilmgC, MovMk, NotNAT, Vers A, WhoHol A, WhoThe 16*
Coulson, Roy *Film 2*
Coulter, Frazer 1848-1937 *Film 1, NotNAT B, WhoStg 1906, WhoStg 1908*
Coulter, Frazer 1849-1937 *WhScrn 2*
Coulter, Frazier *Film 2*

Counsell, John 1905- *OxThe, WhoThe 16*
Countess Ducella d1921 *WhScrn 1, WhScrn 2*
Countiss, Cathrine *WhoStg 1908*
Couper, Barbara 1903- *WhThe*
Courant, Curt 1895?- *DcFM, FilmgC, OxFilm, WorEnF*
Courant, Curtis *WorEnF*
Courcel, Nicole 1930- *FilmgC, WhoHol A*
Court, Alfred C 1886-1953 *WhScrn 1, WhScrn 2*
Court, Dorothy *WhThe*
Court, Hazel 1926- *FilmgC, WhoHol A*
Court, Margaret Smith 1942- *CelR 3*
Courteline, Georges 1858-1929 *CnMD, CnThe, McGWD, ModWD, OxThe, PIP&P, REnWD*
Courteline, Georges 1860-1929 *WhThe*
Courteline, Georges 1861-1929 *NotNAT B*
Courtenay, Tom 1937- *CelR 3, FilmgC, IntMPA 1977, MotPP, MovMk, OxFilm, WhoHol A, WhoThe 16, WorEnF*
Courtenay, William 1875-1933 *Film 2, NotNAT B, WhScrn 1, WhScrn 2, WhThe, WhoHol B, WhoStg 1908*
Courteney, Fay d1943 *NotNAT B*
Courteney, Shelia *Film 2*
Courtice, Michael 1888-1962 *WorEnF*
Courtland, Jerome 1926- *FilmgC, IntMPA 1977, MotPP, WhoHol A*
Courtleigh, Edna d1962 *NotNAT B*
Courtleigh, Stephen d1968 *WhScrn 2*
Courtleigh, William 1867-1930 *NotNAT B*
Courtleigh, William 1876-1930 *WhoStg 1906, WhoStg 1908*
Courtleigh, William, Jr. 1869-1930 *Film 1, Film 2, WhScrn 1, WhScrn 2, WhThe, WhoHol B*
Courtleigh, William, Sr. 1892-1918 *WhScrn 2*
Courtneay, Peter *Film 1*
Courtneay, William F 1875-1933 *Film 1*
Courtneidge, Charles d1935 *NotNAT B*
Courtneidge, Cicely 1893- *EncMT, FilmgC, NotNAT A, WhoHol A, WhoThe 16*
Courtneidge, Mrs. Robert d1914 *NotNAT B*
Courtneidge, Robert 1859-1939 *EncMT, NotNAT A, NotNAT B, WhThe*
Courtneidge, Rosaline 1903-1926 *NotNAT B, WhThe*
Courtney, Alan 1912- *AmSCAP 1966*
Courtney, C C *ConDr 1977D*
Courtney, Dan *WhoHol A*
Courtney, Fay d1941 *NotNAT B*
Courtney, Gordon 1895-1964 *WhThe*
Courtney, Inez 1908-1975 *ThFT, WhScrn 2, WhoHol C*
Courtney, John d1865 *NotNAT B*
Courtney, Maud 1884- *WhThe*
Courtney, Oscar W d1963 *NotNAT B*
Courtney, Oscar W 1877-1962 *WhScrn 1, WhScrn 2*
Courtney, Pat *Film 2*
Courtney, William Leonard 1850-1928 *NotNAT B, WhThe*
Courtois, Leon *Film 2*
Courtot, Juliette *Film 2*
Courtot, Marguerite 1897- *Film 1, Film 2, MotPP, TwYS*
Courtright, Clyde 1885-1967 *WhScrn 1, WhScrn 2*
Courtright, Jennie Lee *Film 1*
Courtright, William 1848-1933 *WhScrn 1, WhScrn 2*
Courtwright, William 1848-1933 *Film 2, WhoHol B*
Courville, Albert Pierre De 1887-1960 *OxThe*
Cousin Jody d1975 *WhoHol C*

Cousins, M Thomas 1914- *AmSCAP 1966*
Cousins, Norman 1915- *CelR 3*
Cousteau, Jacques-Yves 1910- *CelR 3, DcFM, FilmgC, OxFilm, WorEnF*
Cousy, Bob 1928- *CelR 3*
Coutard, Raoul 1924- *DcFM, FilmgC, OxFilm, WorEnF*
Couzin, Sharon *WomWMM A, WomWMM B*
Covans, The Four *Film 2*
Coventry, Tom *Film 2*
Covington, Bruce *Film 2*
Covington, Warren 1921- *AmSCAP 1966*
Covington, Z Wall *Film 2*
Cowan, Jerome 1897-1972 *BiE&WWA, FilmgC, MovMk, NotNAT B, Vers A, WhScrn 2, WhoHol B*
Cowan, Lester 1905?- *FilmgC*
Cowan, Louis G d1976 *NewYTET*
Cowan, Lynn F 1888-1973 *AmSCAP 1966, Film 2, WhScrn 2*
Cowan, Maurice A 1891- *FilmgC, WhThe*
Cowan, Michael 1944- *AmSCAP 1966*
Cowan, Rubey 1891-1957 *AmSCAP 1966*
Cowan, Stanley Earl 1918- *AmSCAP 1966*
Cowan, Theodore *IntMPA 1977*
Cowan, Warren J *IntMPA 1977*
Coward, Noel 1899-1973 *BiE&WWA, CnMD, CnThe, ConDr 1973, CroCD, DcFM, EncMT, FamA&A, Film 1, FilmgC, McGWD, ModWD, MovMk, NotNAT A, NotNAT B, OxFilm, OxThe, PIP&P, REnWD, WhScrn 2, WhThe, WhoHol B, WorEnF*
Cowden, Irene d1961 *NotNAT B*
Cowden, John P *NewYTET*
Cowell, Florence 1852-1926 *OxThe*
Cowell, Joe 1792-1863 *FamA&A*
Cowell, Joseph Leathley 1792-1863 *NotNAT A, NotNAT B, OxThe*
Cowell, Samuel Houghton 1820-1864 *NotNAT A, NotNAT B, OxThe*
Cowell, Sydney 1846-1925 *NotNAT B, OxThe*
Cowell, Sydney 1872-1941 *OxThe*
Cowen, Laurence 1865-1942 *NotNAT B, WhThe*
Cowen, Louis d1925 *NotNAT B*
Cowen, Ron 1944- *ConDr 1977, NatPD*
Cowen, William Joyce d1964 *NotNAT B*
Cowger, Roger R 1938- *AmSCAP 1966*
Cowgill, Bryan *NewYTET*
Cowie, Laura 1892-1969 *PIP&P, WhThe*
Cowie, Laure *Film 1*
Cowl, George *Film 2*
Cowl, Jane d1950 *PIP&P, WhoHol B*
Cowl, Jane 1884-1950 *FamA&A, NotNAT B*
Cowl, Jane 1887-1950 *WhScrn 1, WhScrn 2*
Cowl, Jane 1890-1950 *Film 1, FilmgC, WhThe*
Cowles, Cecil *AmSCAP 1966*
Cowles, Chandler 1917- *BiE&WWA, NotNAT*
Cowles, Eugene d1948 *NotNAT B, WhoStg 1906, WhoStg 1908*
Cowles, Gardner 1901- *CelR 3*
Cowles, Jules 1878-1943 *Film 2, WhScrn 1, WhScrn 2, WhoHol B*
Cowles, Mathew *WhoHol A*
Cowles, Matthew *PIP&P*
Cowley, Abraham 1618-1667 *NotNAT B, OxThe*
Cowley, Eric 1886-1948 *NotNAT B, WhThe, WhoHol B*
Cowley, Hannah 1743-1809 *NotNAT B, OxThe*
Cowley, Hilda *Film 2*
Cowley, Malcolm 1898- *CelR 3*
Cowley, Richard d1619 *NotNAT B, OxThe*
Cowper, Clara d1917 *NotNAT B*
Cowper, William C 1853-1918 *WhScrn 2*

Cox, Brian 1946- *WhoThe 16*
Cox, Constance 1915- *WhoThe 16*
Cox, Freddie *Film 2*
Cox, Harold 1905- *IntMPA 1977*
Cox, James M, Jr. d1974 *NewYTET*
Cox, Kenneth A *NewYTET*
Cox, Larry 1942- *AmSCAP 1966*
Cox, Lester Morgan 1910- *AmSCAP 1966*
Cox, Nell *WomWMM A, WomWMM B*
Cox, Olive *Film 1*
Cox, Ralph 1884-1941 *AmSCAP 1966*
Cox, Robert d1655 *OxThe*
Cox, Robert 1895-1974 *WhScrn 2, WhoHol B*
Cox, Ronny *WhoHol A*
Cox, Tom 1892-1914 *WhScrn 2*
Cox, Vivian 1915- *FilmgC*
Cox, Wally 1924-1973 *FilmgC, NewYTET, NotNAT A, NotNAT B, WhScrn 2, WhoHol B*
Coxe, Louis O 1918- *BiE&WWA, McGWD, NotNAT*
Coxen, Ed 1884-1954 *WhoHol B*
Coxen, Edward Albert 1884-1954 *Film 2, WhScrn 1, WhScrn 2*
Coy, A Wayne d1957 *NewYTET*
Coy, Johnnie 1921-1973 *WhScrn 2*
Coy, Johnny d1973 *MotPP, WhoHol B*
Coy, Walter 1906-1974 *WhScrn 2, WhoHol B*
Coyan, Betty 1901-1935 *WhScrn 1, WhScrn 2*
Coyle, J J 1928- *NatPD*
Coyle, John E d1964 *NotNAT B*
Coyle, Walter V 1888-1948 *WhScrn 1, WhScrn 2*
Coyne, Jeanne 1923-1973 *WhScrn 2*
Coyne, Joseph 1867-1941 *EncMT, NotNAT B, WhThe*
Coyne, Joseph 1870- *WhoStg 1908*
Coyne, Joseph Stirling d1868 *NotNAT B*
Cozeneuve, Paul *Film 2*
Crabbe, Buster 1907- *FilmgC, IntMPA 1977, MotPP, WhoHol A*
Crabbe, Larry Buster 1907- *MovMk*
Crabbe, Larry Buster 1908- *HolP 30*
Crabtree, Arthur 1900- *CmMov, FilmgC*
Crabtree, Charlotte 1847-1924 *NotNAT B, OxThe, WhoStg 1906, WhoStg 1908*
Crabtree, Lotta 1847-1924 *FamA&A, NotNAT A*
Crabtree, Paul 1918- *AmSCAP 1966, BiE&WWA, NotNAT*
Craddock, Claudia 1889-1945 *WhScrn 1, WhScrn 2, WhoHol B*
Craft, Lynne d1975 *WhScrn 2*
Craft, Virginia *Film 1*
Craft, William J 1886- *TwYS A*
Crafts, Griffin 1900-1973 *WhScrn 2, WhoHol A*
Craggs, The *WhThe*
Craig, Alec 1878-1945 *FilmgC*
Craig, Alec 1885-1945 *Vers A, WhScrn 1, WhScrn 2, WhoHol B*
Craig, Blanche 1878- *Film 1, Film 2, TwYS*
Craig, Bob *Film 2*
Craig, Burton *Film 2*
Craig, Carolyn d1970 *WhScrn 2*
Craig, Catherine *WhoHol A*
Craig, Charles *Film 1, Film 2*
Craig, Mrs. Charles *Film 2*
Craig, Mrs. Charles G *Film 2*
Craig, David 1923- *BiE&WWA, NotNAT*
Craig, Edith 1869-1947 *NotNAT A, NotNAT B, OxThe, WhThe, WhoHol B, WhoStg 1908*
Craig, Edward Gordon 1872-1966 *BiE&WWA, CnThe, NotNAT A, NotNAT B, OxFilm, WhThe*
Craig, Frances B 1869?-1925 *WhScrn 1, WhScrn 2*

Craig, Francis 1900- *AmSCAP 1966*
Craig, Godfrey 1915-1941 *WhScrn 1, WhScrn 2, WhoHol B*
Craig, Gordon *Film 2*
Craig, Gordon d1973 *WhoHol B*
Craig, Gordon 1872-1966 *OxThe, PIP&P*
Craig, Hal *Film 2*
Craig, Hardin 1875-1968 *BiE&WWA, NotNAT B*
Craig, Helen 1912- *BiE&WWA, MotPP, NotNAT, WhoHol A, WhoThe 16*
Craig, James 1912- *FilmgC, MGM, MotPP, MovMk, WhoHol A*
Craig, John *WhoHol A*
Craig, John d1932 *NotNAT B, WhoHol B*
Craig, Marjorie 1912?- *CelR 3*
Craig, May 1889-1972 *WhScrn 2, WhoHol B*
Craig, Michael *WhoHol A*
Craig, Michael 1928- *FilmgC, WhoThe 16*
Craig, Michael 1929- *IntMPA 1977*
Craig, Nell 1891-1965 *Film 1, Film 2, TwYS, WhScrn 1, WhScrn 2, WhoHol B*
Craig, R Gordon *Film 2*
Craig, Richy, Jr. 1902-1933 *WhScrn 1, WhScrn 2, WhoHol B*
Craig, Robert *Film 2*
Craig, Robert W *Film 2*
Craig, Stanley Herbert *IntMPA 1977*
Craig, Wendy 1934- *FilmgC, WhoHol A, WhoThe 16*
Craig, William C 1908- *BiE&WWA*
Craig, Yvonne 1941- *FilmgC, WhoHol A*
Craigie, Jill 1914- *FilmgC, WomWMM*
Crain, Harold 1911- *BiE&WWA, NotNAT*
Crain, Jeanne 1925- *BiDFlm, FilmgC, IntMPA 1977, MotPP, MovMk, WhoHol A, WorEnF*
Cram, James D 1931- *AmSCAP 1966*
Cram, Mildred *WomWMM*
Cramer, Dick 1889- *Film 2*
Cramer, Douglas S 1931- *IntMPA 1977, NewYTET*
Cramer, Edd 1924-1963 *NotNAT B, WhScrn 1, WhScrn 2, WhoHol B*
Cramer, Marguerite *Film 2*
Cramer, Richard 1889-1960 *Film 2, WhScrn 2, WhoHol B*
Cramer, Susanne 1938-1969 *WhScrn 1, WhScrn 2, WhoHol B*
Crampton, Howard *Film 1, Film 2*
Crandall, Edward *Film 2*
Crandell, David Miller 1914- *BiE&WWA*
Crandell, L Lee *WomWMM B*
Crane, Bob 1928- *IntMPA 1977, WhoHol A*
Crane, Dagne *WhoHol A*
Crane, Dean 1932- *BiE&WWA*
Crane, Dixie 1888-1936 *WhScrn 1, WhScrn 2*
Crane, Doc *Film 1*
Crane, Earl *Film 2*
Crane, Edith 1865-1912 *NotNAT B, WhoStg 1908*
Crane, Ethel G d1930 *WhScrn 1, WhScrn 2*
Crane, Frank *Film 1, Film 2*
Crane, Harry F *Film 1*
Crane, Helen *Film 2*
Crane, James *Film 1, Film 2*
Crane, Jimmie 1910- *AmSCAP 1966*
Crane, Les *NewYTET*
Crane, Mae 1925-1969 *WhScrn 1, WhScrn 2, WhoHol B*
Crane, Norma 1931-1973 *WhScrn 2, WhoHol B*
Crane, Philip Miller 1930- *AmSCAP 1966*
Crane, Phyllis *Film 2*
Crane, Ralph 1550?-1621? *OxThe*

Crane, Richard *MotPP*
Crane, Richard 1944- *WhoThe 16*
Crane, Richard O 1918-1969 *WhScrn 1, WhScrn 2, WhoHol B*
Crane, Shirley *WomWMM B*
Crane, Steve *WhoHol A*
Crane, Violet *Film 2*
Crane, W H 1845-1928 *WhThe*
Crane, Ward 1891-1928 *Film 1, Film 2, TwYS, WhScrn 1, WhScrn 2, WhoHol B*
Crane, William H 1845-1928 *FamA&A, Film 1, Film 2, NotNAT A, NotNAT B, OxThe, PIP&P, WhScrn 1, WhScrn 2, WhoHol B, WhoStg 1906, WhoStg 1908*
Crane, William H 1892-1957 *WhScrn 1, WhScrn 2*
Cranston, Mary *Film 1*
Crater, Allene d1957 *NotNAT B*
Crates *OxThe*
Cratinus 520?BC-423?BC *OxThe*
Crauford, J R 1847-1930 *WhThe*
Crauford, Kent *Film 2*
Cravat, Nick 1911- *FilmgC, WhoHol A*
Cravat, Noel 1910-1960 *WhScrn 1, WhScrn 2, WhoHol B*
Craven, Arthur Scott d1917 *NotNAT B, WhThe*
Craven, Elise 1898- *WhThe*
Craven, Frank d1945 *MotPP, WhoHol B*
Craven, Frank 1875-1945 *FilmgC, MovMk, NotNAT B, WhScrn 1, WhScrn 2*
Craven, Frank 1878-1945 *Film 2, Vers A*
Craven, Frank 1880-1945 *OxThe, WhThe*
Craven, Gemma 1950- *WhoThe 16*
Craven, Hawes 1837-1910 *NotNAT B, OxThe*
Craven, Henry Thornton 1818-1905 *NotNAT B*
Craven, Robin 1906- *BiE&WWA, NotNAT*
Craven, Ruby d1964 *NotNAT B*
Craven, T A M *NewYTET*
Craven, Tom 1868-1919 *NotNAT B, WhThe*
Craven, Walter S *Film 1*
Crawford, Alice 1882- *Film 2, WhThe*
Crawford, Andrew 1917- *FilmgC, WhoHol A*
Crawford, Anne 1920-1956 *FilmgC, NotNAT B, WhScrn 1, WhScrn 2, WhThe, WhoHol B*
Crawford, Bessie 1882-1943 *WhScrn 1, WhScrn 2*
Crawford, Broderick *MotPP, WhoHol A*
Crawford, Broderick 1910- *BiDFlm, FilmgC, MovMk, OxFilm*
Crawford, Broderick 1911- *BiE&WWA, CelR 3, IntMPA 1977, WorEnF*
Crawford, Cheryl 1902- *BiE&WWA, EncMT, NotNAT, PIP&P, WhoThe 16*
Crawford, Christina *WhoHol A*
Crawford, Clifton 1875-1920 *NotNAT B, WhScrn 2*
Crawford, Dorothy Maude 1885- *BiE&WWA*
Crawford, Florence *Film 2*
Crawford, Francis Marion 1854-1909 *NotNAT B*
Crawford, Howard Marion 1914-1969 *WhScrn 1, WhScrn 2*
Crawford, Jack 1847-1917 *WhScrn 2*
Crawford, Jack Randall 1878-1968 *BiE&WWA, NotNAT B*
Crawford, Jesse 1895-1962 *AmSCAP 1966, NotNAT B*
Crawford, Joan *MotPP, WhoHol A, WomWMM*
Crawford, Joan 1904- *CmMov, WorEnF*
Crawford, Joan 1906- *BiDFlm, FilmgC*
Crawford, Joan 1908- *CelR 3, Film 2, IntMPA 1977, MGM, MovMk, OxFilm, ThFT, TwYS*
Crawford, Joanna *WomWMM*
Crawford, John *WhoHol A*

Crawford, Johnny *WhoHol A*
Crawford, Michael 1942- *FilmgC, IntMPA 1977,
  MotPP, WhoHol A, WhoThe 16*
Crawford, Mimi d1966 *WhThe*
Crawford, Nan 1893-1975 *WhScrn 2, WhoHol C*
Crawford, Richard *Film 2*
Crawford, Robert M 1899-1961 *AmSCAP 1966*
Crawford, Sam *Film 2*
Crawford, Tad 1946- *NatPD*
Crawley, Constance 1879-1919 *Film 1, WhScrn 2*
Crawley, Hazel L 1921- *NatPD*
Crawley, J Sayre d1948 *NotNAT B*
Crawley, Sayre d1948 *WhScrn 2*
Creamer, Charles 1894-1971 *WhScrn 1,
  WhScrn 2*
Creamer, Henry 1879-1930 *AmSCAP 1966*
Creamer, John *WhoHol A*
Crean, Robert d1974 *NewYTET*
Creatore, Luigi 1920- *AmSCAP 1966*
Crebillon, Prosper Jolyot De 1674-1762 *CnThe,
  McGWD, NotNAT B, OxThe, REnWD*
Credan, Simone *Film 2*
Creedon, Dennis 1880- *WhThe*
Creel, Frances d1957 *NotNAT B*
Cregan, David 1931- *ConDr 1977, WhoThe 16*
Cregar, Laird d1944 *WhoHol B*
Cregar, Laird 1913-1944 *WhScrn 2*
Cregar, Laird 1916-1944 *CmMov, FilmgC,
  HolP 40, MovMk, NotNAT B*
Cregar, Laird 1916-1945 *BiDFlm*
Cregar, Laird 1917-1944 *WhScrn 1*
Creham, Joseph d1966 *Film 1*
Crehan, Joseph d1966 *MotPP, WhoHol B*
Crehan, Joseph 1884-1966 *FilmgC, MovMk*
Crehan, Joseph 1886-1966 *Vers A, WhScrn 1,
  WhScrn 2*
Crehan, Thomas J 1912- *IntMPA 1977*
Crehore, Tom Oliver *NatPD*
Creighton, Cleva *WhScrn 2*
Creighton, Walter R *Film 1*
Crenna, Richard *MotPP, WhoHol A*
Crenna, Richard 1926- *FilmgC*
Crenna, Richard 1927- *IntMPA 1977, MovMk*
Cresap, Sally Williss *WomWMM B*
Crespi, Todd *WhoHol A*
Crespo, Jose *Film 2*
Cressall, Maud 1886-1962 *WhThe*
Cressy, Will M 1863-1930 *NotNAT A,
  WhoStg 1908*
Cressy, William 1863-1930 *NotNAT B*
Creston, Paul 1906- *AmSCAP 1966*
Creswell, Helen d1949 *NotNAT B*
Cretinetti *OxFilm*
Crevena, Alfredo *DcFM*
Crewe, Bertie d1937 *NotNAT B*
Crews, Kay C 1901-1959 *WhScrn 1, WhScrn 2,
  WhoHol B*
Crews, Laura Hope 1879-1942 *ThFT*
Crews, Laura Hope 1880-1942 *Film 1, Film 2,
  FilmgC, MotPP, MovMk, NotNAT B,
  Vers A, WhScrn 1, WhScrn 2, WhThe,
  WhoHol B, WhoStg 1908*
Cribari, Joe 1920- *AmSCAP 1966*
Cribbins, Bernard 1928- *FilmgC, WhoThe 16*
Crichton, Charles 1910- *CmMov, DcFM, FilmgC,
  IntMPA 1977, MovMk, OxFilm, WorEnF*
Crichton, Kyle S 1896-1960 *NotNAT B*
Crichton, Madge 1881- *WhThe, WhoStg 1908*
Crichton, Michael 1942- *CelR 3, FilmgC,
  IntMPA 1977*
Crick, Francis 1916- *CelR 3*
Crick, Monte d1969 *WhoHol B*
Crimmins, Dan *Film 2*
Crimmins, Daniel 1863-1945 *WhScrn 2*

Crinley, William A d1927 *WhScrn 1, WhScrn 2,
  WhoHol B*
Cripanuk, Michael *WhoHol A*
Cripps, Kernan 1886-1953 *Film 2, WhScrn 2*
Crisham, Walter *WhThe*
Crisman, Arline C d1956 *WhScrn 1, WhScrn 2*
Crisp, Donald d1974 *MotPP, WhoHol B*
Crisp, Donald 1880-1974 *BiDFlm, FilmgC,
  MovMk, OxFilm, TwYS, TwYS A,
  WhScrn 2, WorEnF*
Crisp, Donald 1882-1974 *CmMov, Film 1,
  Film 2, Vers A*
Crisp, Marie *Film 2*
Crisp, Samuel d1783 *NotNAT B*
Crispi, Ida *WhThe, WhoStg 1908*
Criss, Louis 1925- *NotNAT*
Crist, Bainbridge 1883- *AmSCAP 1966*
Crist, Judith 1922- *CelR 3, IntMPA 1977*
Cristal, Linda 1936- *FilmgC, MotPP, WhoHol A*
Cristaldi, Franco 1924- *IntMPA 1977*
Cristina, Ines 1875- *WhThe*
Critchfield, Edward 1919- *IntMPA 1977*
Crittenden, Dwight *Film 1, Film 2*
Crittenden, T D *Film 1*
Crocker, Harry 1893-1958 *Film 2, WhScrn 2*
Crocker, Henry d1937 *NotNAT B*
Crocker-King, C H 1873-1951 *Film 2*
Crocker-King, C H see also Croker-King, C H
Crockett, Charles B 1872-1934 *Film 2, WhScrn 1,
  WhScrn 2*
Crockett, Davy 1786-1836 *FilmgC, OxFilm*
Croft, Anne 1896-1959 *NotNAT B, WhThe*
Croft, Esther *WomWMM*
Croft, Mary Jane *WhoHol A*
Croft, Michael 1922- *WhoThe 16*
Croft, Nita 1902- *WhThe*
Croft, Paddy *WhoThe 16*
Croisset, Francis De 1877-1937 *McGWD, WhThe*
Croke, Wentworth 1871-1930 *WhThe*
Croker, T F Dillon 1831-1912 *NotNAT B, WhThe*
Croker-King, C H 1873-1951 *WhThe, WhoHol B*
Croker-King, C H see also Crocker-King, C H
Croker-King, Charles H 1873-1951 *NotNAT B*
Croly, George 1780-1860 *NotNAT B*
Crommelynck, Fernand 1885-1970 *CnMD,
  McGWD, ModWD, REnWD, WhThe*
Crommie, Liege *Film 1, Film 2*
Crompton, Richmal 1890-1970 *FilmgC*
Crompton, William H 1843-1909 *NotNAT B*
Cromwell, John *Film 2, NatPD*
Cromwell, John 1887- *BiE&WWA, NotNAT,
  WhoHol A, WhoThe 16*
Cromwell, John 1888- *BiDFlm, CmMov, DcFM,
  FilmgC, MovMk, OxFilm, WorEnF*
Cromwell, Oliver *PIP&P*
Cromwell, Richard 1910-1960 *FilmgC, HolP 30,
  MovMk, NotNAT B, WhScrn 1, WhScrn 2,
  WhoHol B*
Cron, John B 1923- *IntMPA 1977*
Crone, Adeline Leipnik d1962 *NotNAT B*
Cronin, A J 1896- *FilmgC*
Cronjager, Edward 1904-1960 *CmMov, FilmgC,
  WorEnF*
Cronkite, Kathy *WhoHol A*
Cronkite, Walter 1916- *CelR 3, IntMPA 1977,
  NewYTET*
Cronyn, Hume 1911- *BiE&WWA, CelR 3,
  FilmgC, IntMPA 1977, MGM, MotPP,
  MovMk, NotNAT, PIP&P, WhoHol A,
  WhoThe 16*
Crook, John d1922 *NotNAT B, WhThe*
Crooker, Earle T 1899- *AmSCAP 1966*
Cropper, Roy 1898-1954 *NotNAT B, WhThe*
Crosby, Bing *MotPP, NewYTET*

Crosby, Bing 1901- *BiDFlm, CmMov, FilmgC, OxFilm*

Crosby, Bing 1904- *AmSCAP 1966, CelR 3, IntMPA 1977, MovMk, WhoHol A, WorEnF*

Crosby, Bob 1913- *AmSCAP 1966, FilmgC, IntMPA 1977, WhoHol A*

Crosby, Cathy *WhoHol A*

Crosby, Cathy Lee *WhoHol A*

Crosby, Dennis *WhoHol A*

Crosby, Edward Harold d1934 *NotNAT B*

Crosby, Floyd 1899- *FilmgC, WorEnF*

Crosby, Floyd 1900- *CmMov, OxFilm*

Crosby, Gary *MotPP, WhoHol A*

Crosby, Hazel d1964 *NotNAT B*

Crosby, Jack *Film 2*

Crosby, Juliette *Film 2*

Crosby, Kathryn 1933- *IntMPA 1977*

Crosby, Lindsay *WhoHol A*

Crosby, Marshal 1883-1954 *WhScrn 1, WhScrn 2*

Crosby, Phillip *WhoHol A*

Crosby, Wade 1905-1975 *WhScrn 2, WhoHol C*

Croset, Paule *FilmgC, WhoHol A*

Crosland, Alan 1891-1936 *TwYS A*

Crosland, Alan 1894-1936 *BiDFlm, DcFM, FilmgC, MovMk, WorEnF*

Crosland, Alan, Jr. *Film 2*

Crosman, Henrietta d1944 *PIP&P, WhoHol B*

Crosman, Henrietta 1861-1944 *FamA&A, NotNAT B, ThFT, WhScrn 1, WhScrn 2*

Crosman, Henrietta 1865-1944 *Film 1, WhThe*

Crosman, Henrietta 1871-1944 *WhoStg 1906, WhoStg 1908*

Crosman, Henriette 1865-1944 *Film 2*

Cross, Alfred Francis 1891-1938 *WhScrn 1, WhScrn 2, WhoHol B*

Cross, Beverley 1931- *ConDr 1977, WhoThe 16*

Cross, Dennis *WhoHol A*

Cross, Douglass 1920- *AmSCAP 1966*

Cross, Eric 1902- *FilmgC*

Cross, Jimmie *AmSCAP 1966*

Cross, Jimmy *WhoHol A*

Cross, John S d1976 *NewYTET*

Cross, Julian 1851-1925 *WhThe*

Cross, Milton J 1897-1975 *CelR 3, WhScrn 2*

Cross, Perry *IntMPA 1977*

Cross, Rhoda M *Film 2*

Cross, Wellington *PIP&P*

Crosse, Rupert 1928-1973 *WhScrn 2, WhoHol B*

Crossley, Sid 1885-1960 *WhScrn 1, WhScrn 2, WhoHol B*

Crossley, Syd *Film 2*

Crossley-Taylor, E W d1963 *NotNAT B*

Crosswell, Anne Pearson *AmSCAP 1966*

Crosthwaite, Ivy 1898-1962 *Film 1, WhScrn 2, WhoHol B*

Croswell, Anna *NotNAT*

Croswell, Anne *BiE&WWA*

Crothers, Rachel 1878-1958 *CnMD, CnThe, FilmgC, McGWD, ModWD, NotNAT B, OxThe, REnWD, WhThe, WomWMM*

Crothers, Scatman *WhoHol A*

Crothers, Sherman 1910- *AmSCAP 1966*

Crouch, Jack H 1918- *BiE&WWA, NotNAT*

Crouch, Worth 1917-1943 *WhScrn 1, WhScrn 2*

Crouse, Russel 1893-1966 *BiE&WWA, CnThe, EncMT, McGWD, ModWD, NewMT, NotNAT B, WhThe*

Crowden, Graham 1922- *PIP&P, WhoThe 16*

Crowe, Gillian 1934- *BiE&WWA*

Crowell, Arthur *Film 2*

Crowell, Bubbles *Film 2*

Crowell, Burt 1873-1946 *WhScrn 1, WhScrn 2*

Crowell, Joseph *Film 2*

Crowell, Josephine d1929 *Film 1, Film 2, TwYS*

Crowley, Alice Lewisohn *BiE&WWA*

Crowley, Kathleen *WhoHol A*

Crowley, Mart *WhoThe 16*

Crowley, Mart 1935- *ConDr 1977, McGWD, NatPD, NotNAT*

Crowley, Mart 1936- *CelR 3*

Crowley, Matt *WhoHol A*

Crowley, Pat 1929- *FilmgC, MotPP*

Crowley, Patricia *WhoHol A*

Crown, Alfred W 1913- *IntMPA 1977*

Crowne, John 1640?-1703? *McGWD, OxThe*

Crowne, John 1640?-1710? *NotNAT B*

Crowther, Bosley *IntMPA 1977*

Crowther, Leslie 1933- *WhoThe 16*

Croxton, Arthur 1868- *WhThe*

Croy, Homer 1883-1965 *WhScrn 2*

Croydon, John 1907- *IntMPA 1977*

Crozet, Simone *WomWMM*

Cruickshank, Andrew 1907- *FilmgC, PIP&P, WhoHol A, WhoThe 16*

Cruickshank, Gladys 1902- *WhThe*

Cruikshank, A Stewart 1877-1949 *WhThe*

Cruikshank, Sally *WomWMM B*

Cruikshank, Stewart 1908-1966 *WhThe*

Cruikshanks, Charles 1844-1928 *WhThe*

Crume, Camilla 1874-1952 *WhScrn 1, WhScrn 2*

Crumit, Frank 1888-1943 *NotNAT B*

Crumit, Frank 1889-1943 *AmSCAP 1966, EncMT*

Crummles, Vincent *OxThe*

Cruster, Aud 1889-1938 *WhScrn 1, WhScrn 2, WhoHol B*

Crutchley, Rosalie 1921- *FilmgC, WhThe, WhoHol A*

Crute, Sally 1886-1971 *Film 1, Film 2, WhScrn 1, WhScrn 2, WhoHol B*

Cruttwell, Hugh 1918- *WhoThe 16*

Cruz, Ramon DeLa 1731-1794 *McGWD*

Cruz, Sor Juana Ines DeLa 1648?-1695 *CnThe, REnWD*

Cruz, Sor Juana Ines DeLa 1651-1695 *OxThe*

Cruz Cano Y Olmedilla, Ramon F DeLa 1731-1794 *OxThe*

Cruze, James d1942 *WhoHol B, WomWMM*

Cruze, James 1884-1942 *BiDFlm, CmMov, DcFM, Film 1, FilmgC, MovMk, NotNAT B, OxFilm, TwYS A, WorEnF*

Cruze, James 1894-1942 *WhScrn 1, WhScrn 2*

Cruze, Mae 1891-1965 *WhScrn 1, WhScrn 2, WhoHol B*

Cruzon, Virginia *WhoHol A*

Cryer, David 1936- *NotNAT, WhoThe 16*

Cryer, Gretchen *ConDr 1977D*

Crystal, Lester *NewYTET*

Csiky, Gergely 1842-1891 *McGWD, OxThe*

Csokor, Franz Theodor 1885-1969 *CnMD, CroCD, McGWD, ModWD*

Csokor, Franz Theodor 1891-1969 *OxThe*

Csonka, Larry 1946- *CelR 3*

Cubillo DeAragon, Alvaro 1596?-1661 *McGWD*

Cucciolla, Ricardo 1932- *FilmgC*

Cuenca, Pedro Fernandez d1940 *NotNAT B*

Cueva, Juan DeLa 1550?-1610? *McGWD, OxThe*

Cueva, Juan DeLa 1550?-1615? *NotNAT B*

Cugat, Carmen d1967 *WhoHol B*

Cugat, Xavier 1900- *CelR 3, FilmgC, WhoHol A*

Cuka, Frances 1936- *WhoThe 16*

Cukor, George 1899- *BiDFlm, BiE&WWA, CelR 3, CmMov, DcFM, FilmgC, IntMPA 1977, MovMk, NewYTET, OxFilm, WorEnF*

Culbertson, Earl 1897- *AmSCAP 1966*

Culder, Mary *Film 2*

Culkin, John *NewYTET*
Cull, Howard *Film 2*
Cullen, Arthur *Film 2*
Cullen, Bill 1920- *IntMPA 1977, NewYTET*
Cullen, Edward 1899- *BiE&WWA*
Cullen, Edward L d1964 *NotNAT B*
Cullen, James F *Film 2*
Cullen, James V 1938- *IntMPA 1977*
Culley, Frederick 1879-1942 *NotNAT B, WhThe, WhoHol B*
Cullinan, Ralph d1950 *NotNAT B*
Cullington, Margaret 1891-1925 *Film 2, WhScrn 1, WhScrn 2, WhoHol B*
Cullman, Howard S 1891-1972 *BiE&WWA, NotNAT B*
Cullman, Marguerite *BiE&WWA, NotNAT*
Cullum, John 1930- *EncMT, NotNAT, WhoHol A, WhoThe 16*
Culp, Robert 1930- *CelR 3, FilmgC, IntMPA 1977, MotPP, WhoHol A*
Culpepper, Edward J 1903- *AmSCAP 1966*
Culver, D Jay 1902- *BiE&WWA*
Culver, David Jay 1902-1968 *NotNAT B*
Culver, Roland 1900- *BiE&WWA, FilmgC, IntMPA 1977, MovMk, NotNAT, WhoHol A, WhoThe 16*
Cumali, Necati 1921- *REnWD*
Cumberland, Gerald 1879-1926 *NotNAT B, WhThe*
Cumberland, John d1866 *NotNAT B*
Cumberland, John 1880- *Film 1, WhThe*
Cumberland, Richard 1732-1811 *McGWD, NotNAT B, OxThe, PIP&P*
Cummerford, Tom *Film 1*
Cumming, Dorothy *Film 2*
Cumming, Richard 1928- *AmSCAP 1966*
Cumming, Ruth 1904-1967 *WhScrn 1, WhScrn 2*
Cummings, Bob 1910- *BiE&WWA, CelR 3, IntMPA 1977, WorEnF*
Cummings, Bob see also Cummings, Robert
Cummings, Constance 1910- *BiE&WWA, CnThe, FilmgC, HolP 30, IntMPA 1977, MotPP, MovMk, NotNAT, ThFT, WhoHol A, WhoThe 16*
Cummings, Dorothy *Film 2, TwYS*
Cummings, E E 1894-1962 *CnMD, McGWD, ModWD*
Cummings, Edward Estlin 1894-1962 *NotNAT B*
Cummings, Frances d1923 *WhScrn 1, WhScrn 2*
Cummings, Irving 1888-1959 *CmMov, Film 1, Film 2, FilmgC, MovMk, TwYS, TwYS A, WhScrn 1, WhScrn 2, WhoHol B*
Cummings, Irving, Jr. *IntMPA 1977*
Cummings, Jack *IntMPA 1977*
Cummings, Jack 1900- *CmMov, FilmgC*
Cummings, Jack 1906- *WorEnF*
Cummings, Nathan 1896- *CelR 3*
Cummings, Patricia Hager 1924- *AmSCAP 1966*
Cummings, Richard 1858-1938 *Film 1, Film 2, WhScrn 1, WhScrn 2, WhoHol B*
Cummings, Robert 1867-1949 *Film 1, WhScrn 2*
Cummings, Robert 1908- *FilmgC, MovMk*
Cummings, Robert 1910- *MotPP, WhoHol A, WorEnF*
Cummings, Robert see also Cummings, Bob
Cummings, Sandy 1913- *IntMPA 1977*
Cummings, Vicki d1969 *BiE&WWA, WhoHol B*
Cummings, Vicki 1913-1969 *NotNAT B, WhThe*
Cummings, Vicki 1919-1969 *WhScrn 1, WhScrn 2*
Cummins, Dwight W 1901- *IntMPA 1977*
Cummins, Peggy *MotPP*
Cummins, Peggy 1925- *FilmgC, WhThe, WhoHol A*

Cummins, Peggy 1926- *IntMPA 1977*
Cumpson, John R *Film 1*
Cumpson, John R 1868-1913 *WhScrn 2*
Cunard, Grace d1967 *MotPP, WhoHol B, WomWMM*
Cunard, Grace 1893-1967 *Film 1, Film 2, FilmgC, TwYS, WhScrn 2*
Cunard, Grace 1894-1967 *WhScrn 1*
Cunard, Mina *Film 1*
Cundall, C W *Film 2*
Cuneo, Lester 1888-1925 *Film 1, Film 2, TwYS, WhScrn 2, WhoHol B*
Cuningham, Philip 1865- *WhThe*
Cunliffe, Richard R 1906- *AmSCAP 1966*
Cunliffe, Whit *WhThe*
Cunning, Patrick *Film 2*
Cunningham, Aloysius d1936 *WhScrn 1, WhScrn 2*
Cunningham, Arthur d1955 *NotNAT B*
Cunningham, Arthur 1928- *AmSCAP 1966*
Cunningham, Cecil 1888-1959 *Film 2, ThFT, WhScrn 2, WhoHol B*
Cunningham, George 1904-1962 *NotNAT B, WhScrn 1, WhScrn 2, WhoHol B*
Cunningham, Joe 1890-1943 *WhScrn 2*
Cunningham, John d1773 *NotNAT B*
Cunningham, Merce *ConDr 1977E*
Cunningham, Paul 1890-1960 *AmSCAP 1966*
Cunningham, Phyllis Fenn *WomWMM B*
Cunningham, Robert *Film 2*
Cunningham, Robert 1866- *WhThe*
Cunningham, Mrs. Rudolph 1907- *AmSCAP 1966*
Cunningham, Sarah *WhoHol A*
Cunningham, Vera *Film 1*
Cunningham, Zamah 1893-1967 *WhScrn 1, WhScrn 2, WhoHol B*
Cunnington, Phillis *BiE&WWA*
Cunny, Joe *Film 2*
Cuny, Alain 1908- *FilmgC, OxFilm, WhoHol A*
Cuny, Joe *Film 1*
Cuomo, Edward A 1925- *AmSCAP 1966*
Cuppett, Charles Harold 1894- *AmSCAP 1966*
Curbelo, Fausto 1911- *AmSCAP 1966*
Curci, Gennaro 1888-1955 *WhScrn 2*
Curel, Francois De 1854-1928 *CnMD, McGWD, ModWD, NotNAT B, WhThe*
Curel, Francois De 1854-1929 *OxThe*
Curley, Miss *Film 1*
Curley, James *Film 1*
Curley, Leo 1878-1960 *WhScrn 2*
Curley, Pauline *Film 1, Film 2*
Curll, Edmund d1747 *NotNAT B*
Curnow, Allen 1911- *ConDr 1977*
Currah, Brian Mason 1929- *WhoThe 16*
Curran, Sir Charles *NewYTET*
Curran, Homer F d1952 *NotNAT B*
Curran, Pearl Gildersleeve 1875-1941 *AmSCAP 1966*
Curran, Thomas A 1880-1941 *WhScrn 1, WhScrn 2, WhoHol B*
Currie, Clive 1877-1935 *NotNAT B, WhThe, WhoHol B*
Currie, Finlay 1878-1968 *CmMov, FilmgC, MotPP, MovMk, NotNAT B, Vers A, WhScrn 1, WhScrn 2, WhThe, WhoHol B*
Currie, George *Film 2*
Currie, Louise *WhoHol A*
Currie, Thomas A 1929- *BiE&WWA*
Currier, Art *Film 2*
Currier, Frank 1857-1928 *Film 1, Film 2, MotPP, NotNAT B, TwYS, WhScrn 1, WhScrn 2, WhoHol B*
Curris, Irwin *AmSCAP 1966*
Currlin, Lee *NewYTET*

Curry, Dora Dean 1911-1931 WhScrn 2
Curry, Jack A 1902- AmSCAP 1966
Curry, John Film 2
Curry, Richard Orr 1931- AmSCAP 1966
Curry, W Lawrence 1906-1966 AmSCAP 1966
Curtin, John P 1915- IntMPA 1977
Curtis, Alan 1909-1953 FilmgC, MotPP,
    NotNAT B, WhScrn 1, WhScrn 2,
    WhoHol B
Curtis, Allen d1961 NotNAT B, WhoHol B
Curtis, Beatrice 1901-1963 WhScrn 1, WhScrn 2,
    WhoHol B
Curtis, Billy WhoHol A
Curtis, Billy 1885-1954 AmSCAP 1966
Curtis, Charlotte 1928- CelR 3
Curtis, Dan IntMPA 1977, NewYTET
Curtis, Dick 1902-1952 Vers B, WhScrn 1,
    WhScrn 2, WhoHol B
Curtis, Eddie 1927- AmSCAP 1966
Curtis, Jack 1880-1956 Film 1, Film 2, TwYS,
    WhScrn 1, WhScrn 2, WhoHol B
Curtis, Jack B 1926-1970 WhScrn 2
Curtis, Jackie 1947- ConDr 1977
Curtis, Keene 1923- BiE&WWA, NotNAT,
    WhoHol A, WhoThe 16
Curtis, Ken 1916- IntMPA 1977, WhoHol A
Curtis, King d1971 WhoHol B
Curtis, Loyal 1877-1947 AmSCAP 1966
Curtis, Mann 1911- AmSCAP 1966
Curtis, Marie Film 1
Curtis, Paul J 1927- NotNAT
Curtis, Spencer M 1856-1921 WhScrn 1,
    WhScrn 2
Curtis, Thomas B NewYTET
Curtis, Tony 1925- BiDFlm, CelR 3, CmMov,
    FilmgC, IntMPA 1977, MotPP, MovMk,
    OxFilm, WhoHol A, WorEnF
Curtis, Willa Pearl 1896-1970 WhScrn 2
Curtiz, David d1962 NotNAT B
Curtiz, Michael 1888-1962 BiDFlm, CmMov,
    DcFM, FilmgC, MovMk, OxFilm,
    WhScrn 1, WhScrn 2, WorEnF
Curtiz, Michael 1889-1962 TwYS A
Curto, Ramada d1961 NotNAT B
Curtwright, Jorja WhoHol A
Curvin, Jonathan W 1911- BiE&WWA, NotNAT
Curwen, Patric 1884-1949 NotNAT B, WhThe,
    WhoHol B
Curwood, Bob Film 2
Curzon, Frank 1868-1927 NotNAT B, WhThe
Curzon, George 1896- FilmgC
Curzon, George 1898- WhThe
Cusack, Cyril 1910- BiE&WWA, Film 1,
    FilmgC, IntMPA 1977, MovMk, NotNAT,
    WhoHol A, WhoThe 16
Cusack, Dymphna WomWMM
Cusack, Sinead 1949- FilmgC
Cuscaden, Sarah D 1873-1954 WhScrn 1,
    WhScrn 2
Cusenza, Frank Jerome 1899- AmSCAP 1966
Cushing, Catherine Chisholm 1874-1952
    AmSCAP 1966, NotNAT B, WhThe
Cushing, Peter 1913- CmMov, FilmgC,
    IntMPA 1977, MotPP, WhoHol A,
    WhoThe 16
Cushing, Sidney Film 1
Cushing, Tom 1879-1941 NotNAT B, WhThe
Cushman, Charlotte Saunders 1816-1876 CnThe,
    FamA&A, NotNAT A, NotNAT B, OxThe,
    PIP&P
Cushman, Nancy 1913- BiE&WWA, NotNAT
Cushman, Susan 1822-1859 NotNAT B, OxThe
Cusmich, Mario Film 2
Custer, Bob 1898-1974 Film 2, TwYS,

WhScrn 2, WhoHol B
Custer, George Armstrong 1839-1876 OxFilm
Custis, George Washington Parke 1781-1857
    NotNAT B
Cutelli, Count Gaetano d1944 WhScrn 1,
    WhScrn 2
Cuthbert, Neil 1951- NatPD
Cuthbertson, Allan 1921?- FilmgC
Cuthbertson, Iain 1930- WhoThe 16
Cutler, Kate 1870-1955 NotNAT B, WhThe,
    WhoHol B
Cutler, Peggy d1945 NotNAT B
Cutter, Murray 1902- AmSCAP 1966
Cutting, Richard H 1912-1972 WhScrn 2,
    WhoHol B
Cutts, Graham 1885-1958 FilmgC
Cutts, Patricia 1926-1974 FilmgC, WhScrn 2,
    WhoHol B
Cutts, Patricia 1931-1974 BiE&WWA,
    NotNAT B
Cuvillier, Charles 1879- WhThe
Cwojdzinski, Antoni 1896- ModWD
Cybulski, Zbigniew d1967 MotPP, WhoHol B
Cybulski, Zbigniew 1927-1967 FilmgC, MovMk,
    OxFilm, WhScrn 1, WhScrn 2
Cybulski, Zbygniew 1928-1967 WorEnF
Czerwonky, Richard Rudolph 1886-1949
    AmSCAP 1966
Czettel, Ladislas Philip d1949 NotNAT B
Czinner, Paul 1890-1972 BiDFlm, DcFM, FilmgC,
    OxFilm, WorEnF

D

Dabbs, H R d1913 *NotNAT B*
Dable, Frances *Film 2*
Dabney, Augusta *WhoHol A*
Dabney, Ford T 1883-1958 *AmSCAP 1966*
Daborne, Robert d1628 *NotNAT B*
Dace, Wallace *NatPD*
Dacia, Mademoiselle *Film 2*
DaCosta, Morton 1914- *BiE&WWA, FilmgC,
   NotNAT, WhoThe 16, WorEnF*
DaCunha, Jose 1889-1956 *WhScrn 1, WhScrn 2*
Dade, Frances 1910-1968 *WhScrn 1, WhScrn 2,
   WhoHol B*
Dade, Stephen 1909- *FilmgC*
Dadswell, Pearl d1963 *NotNAT B*
Daff, Alfred Edward 1902- *IntMPA 1977*
Dagerman, Stig 1923-1954 *CnMD, CnThe,
   CroCD, McGWD, ModWD, REnWD*
Daget, Robert True d1975 *WhScrn 2, WhoHol C*
Daghofer, Lillitts *Film 2*
Dagmar *NewYTET*
Dagmar, Florence *Film 1*
Dagmar, Marie d1925 *NotNAT B*
Dagna, Jeanette *Film 2*
Dagnall, Ells 1868-1935 *WhThe*
Dagnall, Thomas C d1926 *WhThe*
D'Agostino, Albert S 1893-1970 *CmMov, FilmgC*
D'Agostino, Joseph D 1929- *AmSCAP 1966*
Dagover, Lil *Film 2*
Dagover, Lil 1894- *TwYS*
Dagover, Lil 1897- *Film 1, FilmgC, MovMk,
   OxFilm, WhoHol A, WorEnF*
Daguerre, Louis 1787-1851 *FilmgC*
Daguerre, Mande 1789-1851 *DcFM*
Dahl, Arlene *MotPP, WhoHol A*
Dahl, Arlene 1924- *FilmgC, MGM, MovMk*
Dahl, Arlene 1925- *IntMPA 1977*
Dahl, Arlene 1928- *CelR 3*
Dahl, Ingolf 1912- *AmSCAP 1966*
Dahl, Tessa *WhoHol A*
Dahlbeck, Eva *WhoHol A*
Dahlbeck, Eva 1920- *OxFilm, WorEnF*
Dahlbeck, Eva 1921- *FilmgC*
Dahlberg, Edward 1900- *CelR 3*
Dahlgren, Fredrik August 1816-1895 *OxThe*
Dai, Alima *WomWMM*
Dai, Lin 1931-1964 *NotNAT B, WhScrn 1,
   WhScrn 2, WhoHol B*
Dai, Yona *WomWMM*
Dailey, Dan *MotPP, WhoHol A*
Dailey, Dan 1914- *FilmgC*
Dailey, Dan 1915- *BiDFlm, CmMov,
   WhoThe 16*
Dailey, Dan 1917- *MovMk, WorEnF*
Dailey, Irene 1920- *BiE&WWA, WhoHol A,
   WhoThe 16*
Dailey, Irene 1930- *NotNAT*

Dailey, Joseph *Film 1*
Dailey, Peter F 1868-1908 *NotNAT B,
   WhoStg 1906, WhoStg 1908*
Daily, Bill *WhoHol A*
Dainton, Marie 1881-1938 *NotNAT B, WhThe*
Dainton, Patricia 1930- *FilmgC*
Daisne, Johan 1912- *ModWD*
Daix, Daisy 1930-1950 *WhScrn 1, WhScrn 2*
Dalberg, Baron Wolfgang Heribert Von 1750-1806
   NotNAT B, OxThe
D'Albert, George d1949 *NotNAT B*
D'Albert, George 1870- *WhThe*
Dalbert, Suzanne d1971 *WhoHol B*
Dalbert, Suzanne 1927-1970 *WhScrn 2*
Dalbrook, Sidney *Film 1*
D'Albrook, Sidney 1886-1948 *Film 2, TwYS,
   WhScrn 2*
D'Albrook, Sydney *Film 2*
Dalby, Amy 1888?-1969 *FilmgC, WhScrn 1,
   WhScrn 2, WhoHol B*
Dale, Alan 1861-1928 *NotNAT B, WhThe*
Dale, Anne *Film 2*
Dale, Charles 1881-1971 *WhScrn 1, WhScrn 2,
   WhoHol B*
Dale, Charlie 1881-1971 *Film 2*
Dale, Dana *WhoHol A*
Dale, Dorothy 1883-1957 *WhScrn 1, WhScrn 2,
   WhoHol B*
Dale, Dorothy 1925-1937 *WhScrn 1, WhScrn 2,
   WhoHol B*
Dale, Esther d1961 *MotPP, NotNAT B,
   WhoHol B*
Dale, Esther 1885-1961 *ThFT*
Dale, Esther 1886-1961 *FilmgC, Vers A,
   WhScrn 1, WhScrn 2*
Dale, Frank Q 1911- *AmSCAP 1966*
Dale, Gretchen 1886- *WhoStg 1906,
   WhoStg 1908*
Dale, Grover 1936- *BiE&WWA, NotNAT*
Dale, James Littlewood 1886- *WhThe*
Dale, Jean 1904- *AmSCAP 1966*
Dale, Jim 1935- *FilmgC, PIP&P A, WhoHol A,
   WhoThe 16*
Dale, Jimmie 1917- *AmSCAP 1966*
Dale, Jimmy 1901- *AmSCAP 1966*
Dale, Margaret 1880-1972 *Film 2, WhScrn 2,
   WhThe, WhoHol B, WhoStg 1908*
Dale, Margaret 1922- *WhThe*
Dale, Margie d1962 *NotNAT B*
Dale, Peggy 1903-1967 *WhScrn 1, WhScrn 2,
   WhoHol B*
Dale, Rube L *WomWMM B*
Dale, Vikki 1931- *AmSCAP 1966*
Dales, John L 1907- *BiE&WWA, NotNAT*
Dales, L John 1907- *IntMPA 1977*
Daley, Cass 1915-1975 *FilmgC, HolP 40, MotPP,*

WhScrn 2, WhoHol C
Daley, Guilbert A 1923- *BiE&WWA, NotNAT*
Daley, Jack 1882-1967 *WhScrn 2, WhoHol B*
Daley, Mary Patricia 1932- *BiE&WWA*
Daley, Richard J 1902- *CelR 3*
Daley, Robert *IntMPA 1977*
Daley, Sandy *WomWMM B*
D'Algy, Antonio *Film 2*
D'Algy, Helena *Film 2*
D'Algy, Tony *Film 2*
Dali, Salvador 1904- *CelR 3, FilmgC, OxFilm, WorEnF*
Dalin, Olaf 1708-1763 *NotNAT B*
Dalin, Olof 1708-1763 *OxThe*
Dalio, Marcel 1900- *BiDFlm, FilmgC, MovMk, OxFilm, WhoHol A, WorEnF*
Dall, Evelyn 1914?- *FilmgC*
Dall, John 1918-1971 *FilmgC, MotPP, MovMk, WhScrn 1, WhScrn 2, WhoHol B*
Dallam, Helen *AmSCAP 1966*
Dallas, Charlene *WhoHol A*
Dallas, J J 1853-1915 *WhThe*
Dallas, Meredith 1916- *BiE&WWA, NotNAT*
Dallas, Mitzi 1928- *AmSCAP 1966*
Dallesandro, Joe 1948- *CelR 3, WhoHol A*
Dalleui, Monsieur *Film 2*
Dallimore, Maurice 1912-1973 *WhScrn 2, WhoHol B*
Dallin, Leon 1918- *AmSCAP 1966*
Dalmatoff, B 1862- *WhThe*
Dalmores, Charles 1871-1939 *NotNAT B, WhoStg 1908*
D'Alroy, Evelyn d1915 *WhThe*
Dalroy, Harry Rube 1879-1954 *WhScrn 1, WhScrn 2, WhoHol B*
Dalrymple, Ian 1903- *FilmgC*
Dalrymple, Jean 1910- *BiE&WWA, EncMT, NotNAT, NotNAT A, WhoThe 16*
Dalton, Abby *WhoHol A*
Dalton, Audrey 1934- *FilmgC, MotPP, WhoHol A*
Dalton, Charles d1942 *WhoHol B*
Dalton, Charles 1864-1942 *NotNAT B, WhThe*
Dalton, Charles 1866-1942 *WhoStg 1908*
Dalton, Doris 1910- *WhThe*
Dalton, Dorothy d1972 *MotPP, WhoHol B*
Dalton, Dorothy 1893-1972 *TwYS, WhScrn 2, WhThe*
Dalton, Dorothy 1894-1972 *Film 1, Film 2, FilmgC*
Dalton, Emmet d1937 *WhScrn 2*
Dalton, Irene 1901-1934 *Film 2, WhScrn 1, WhScrn 2, WhoHol B*
Dalton, Timothy 1944- *FilmgC, WhoHol A*
Daltrey, Roger *WhoHol A*
Daly, Arnold 1875-1927 *Film 1, NotNAT A, NotNAT B, OxThe, PIP&P, WhScrn 1, WhScrn 2, WhThe, WhoHol B, WhoStg 1906, WhoStg 1908*
Daly, Augustin 1838-1899 *CnThe, McGWD, ModWD, NotNAT A, NotNAT B, REnWD*
Daly, Augustin 1839-1899 *OxThe, PIP&P*
Daly, Blyth 1902- *WhThe*
Daly, Bob *Film 1*
Daly, Dan 1858-1904 *NotNAT B*
Daly, Dixie d1963 *NotNAT B*
Daly, Dutch 1848- *WhThe*
Daly, Hazel *Film 1, Film 2, TwYS*
Daly, Herbert 1902-1940 *WhScrn 2*
Daly, Jack d1968 *WhScrn 2*
Daly, James 1918- *BiE&WWA, FilmgC, IntMPA 1977, NotNAT, WhoHol A, WhoThe 16*
Daly, James L 1852-1933 *WhScrn 1, WhScrn 2,*

WhoHol B
Daly, John 1937- *IntMPA 1977*
Daly, John Charles *NewYTET*
Daly, Jonathan *WhoHol A*
Daly, Joseph 1891- *AmSCAP 1966*
Daly, Lawrence d1900 *NotNAT B*
Daly, Mae d1962 *NotNAT B*
Daly, Marcella *Film 2*
Daly, Mark 1887-1957 *FilmgC, NotNAT B, WhScrn 1, WhScrn 2, WhThe, WhoHol B*
Daly, Pat 1891-1947 *WhScrn 1, WhScrn 2, WhoHol B*
Daly, Robert *Film 2*
Daly, Robert A *NewYTET*
Daly, Tyne *WhoHol A*
Dalya, Jacqueline *WhoHol A*
Dalzell, Allan C 1896- *BiE&WWA*
Dalzell, Lyda St. Clair d1974 *WhoHol B*
Dam, H J W d1906 *NotNAT B*
Damala, Jacques d1889 *NotNAT B*
Damato, Anthony 1927- *NatPD*
D'Amboise, Jacques 1934- *CelR 3, WhoHol A*
D'Ambricourt, Adrienne d1946 *Film 2*
D'Ambricourt, Adrienne 1888-1957 *WhScrn 1, WhScrn 2, WhoHol B*
Dameral, George d1936 *NotNAT B*
Damerel, Donna 1913-1941 *WhScrn 2, WhoHol B*
Dameron, Tadley 1917-1965 *AmSCAP 1966*
Damiani, Damiano 1922- *WorEnF*
D'Amico, Silvio 1887-1955 *OxThe*
D'Amico, Suso Cecchi *DcFM*
Damita, Lili *Film 2, MotPP*
Damita, Lili 1901- *FilmgC, ThFT*
Damita, Lili 1904- *WhoHol A*
Damita, Lili 1906- *MovMk*
Damm, Walter J d1962 *NewYTET*
Damon, Les 1909-1962 *NotNAT B, WhScrn 2, WhoHol B*
Damon, Mark 1935- *FilmgC, MotPP, WhoHol A*
Damon, Stuart 1937- *BiE&WWA, FilmgC, NotNAT, WhoThe 16*
Damone, Vic 1929- *FilmgC, IntMPA 1977, WhoHol A*
Dampier, Claude 1879-1955 *WhScrn 2*
Dampier, Claude 1885-1955 *FilmgC, WhScrn 1, WhoHol B*
Damrosch, Walter Johannes 1862-1950 *AmSCAP 1966, NotNAT B, WhScrn 2*
Dana, Barbara *WhoHol A*
Dana, Bill 1924- *AmSCAP 1966, WhoHol A*
Dana, Henry 1855-1921 *NotNAT B, WhThe*
Dana, Leora 1923- *BiE&WWA, FilmgC, NotNAT, WhoHol A, WhoThe 16*
Dana, Mark *WhoHol A*
Dana, Mary Louise d1946 *NotNAT B*
Dana, Viola *MotPP*
Dana, Viola 1891- *TwYS*
Dana, Viola 1897- *Film 1, Film 2, FilmgC, WhoHol A*
Danby, Charles d1906 *NotNAT B*
Dance, Sir George 1858-1932 *NotNAT B, OxThe*
Dance, Sir George 1865-1932 *WhThe*
Dancer, Stanley 1927- *CelR 3*
Danchenko, Vladimir Nemirovich- 1859-1943 *NotNAT B, OxThe, PIP&P*
Dancoff, Judy *WomWMM B*
Dancourt, Florent Carton 1661-1725 *CnThe, McGWD, NotNAT B, OxThe, REnWD*
Dancourt, Marie-Anne-Armande 1684-1745 *OxThe*
Dancourt, Marie-Anne-Michelle 1685-1780 *OxThe*
Dancourt, Marie Therese Lenoir 1663-1725 *OxThe*
Dancy, Jeanette *Film 2*

Dando, W P d1944 *NotNAT B*
D'Andrea, Tom *MotPP, WhoHol A*
Dandridge, Dorothy d1965 *MotPP, WhoHol B*
Dandridge, Dorothy 1923-1965 *FilmgC, MovMk,*
 WhScrn 1, WhScrn 2
Dandridge, Dorothy 1924-1965 *NotNAT A*
Dandridge, Ruby 1902- *WhoHol A*
Dandy, Jess 1871-1923 *NotNAT B, WhScrn 1,*
 WhScrn 2, WhoHol B
Dane, Clemence 1888-1965 *BiE&WWA, CnMD,*
 McGWD, ModWD, NotNAT B, OxThe,
 WhThe
Dane, Dorothy *Film 1*
Dane, Essex d1962 *NotNAT B, WhoStg 1908*
Dane, Ethel *WhThe*
Dane, Frank *Film 2*
Dane, Karl 1886-1934 *Film 1, Film 2, FilmgC,*
 MovMk, TwYS, WhScrn 1, WhScrn 2,
 WhoHol B
Dane, Karl 1887-1934 *NotNAT B*
Dane, Marjorie 1898- *WhThe*
Daneel, Sylvia 1931- *BiE&WWA, NotNAT*
Danegger, Theodor 1891-1959 *WhScrn 1,*
 WhScrn 2, WhoHol B
Daneman, Paul 1925- *PIP&P, WhoThe 16*
Daneman, Paul 1930- *FilmgC*
Daneri, Julie 1914-1957 *WhScrn 1, WhScrn 2*
Danforth, William 1867-1941 *NotNAT B, WhThe,*
 WhoHol B
Dangcil, Linda *WhoHol A*
D'Angelo, Bill *NewYTET*
D'Angelo, Carlo 1919-1973 *WhScrn 2*
Dangerfield, Rodney *WhoHol A*
Dangeville, Marie-Anne Botot 1714-1796
 NotNAT B, OxThe
Dangman, William *Film 1*
Daniel, Billy 1912-1962 *NotNAT B, WhScrn 2*
Daniel, George d1864 *NotNAT B*
Daniel, Rita d1951 *NotNAT B*
Daniel, Samuel 1562?-1619 *NotNAT B*
Daniel, Samuel 1563?-1619 *OxThe, PIP&P,*
 REnWD
Daniel, T 1945- *NotNAT*
Daniel, Tamara *WhoHol A*
Daniel, Viora *Film 2*
Danielewski, Tad 1921- *BiE&WWA,*
 IntMPA 1977
Daniell, Henry 1894-1963 *CmMov, Film 2,*
 FilmgC, MotPP, MovMk, NotNAT B,
 PIP&P, Vers A, WhScrn 1, WhScrn 2,
 WhThe, WhoHol B
Daniels, Bebe 1901-1971 *BiDFlm, Film 2,*
 FilmgC, MotPP, MovMk, NotNAT B,
 OxFilm, ThFT, TwYS, WhScrn 1,
 WhScrn 2, WhThe, WhoHol B, WomWMM
Daniels, Bebe 1909-1971 *Film 1*
Daniels, Billy *WhoHol A*
Daniels, Danny 1924- *BiE&WWA, NotNAT*
Daniels, David 1927- *BiE&WWA, NotNAT*
Daniels, Frank 1860-1935 *Film 1, NotNAT B,*
 PIP&P, WhScrn 1, WhScrn 2, WhThe,
 WhoHol B, WhoStg 1906, WhoStg 1908
Daniels, Frank Albert 1856-1935 *OxThe*
Daniels, Hank, Jr. 1919-1973 *WhScrn 2,*
 WhoHol B
Daniels, Harold *IntMPA 1977*
Daniels, Harold 1903-1971 *WhScrn 2*
Daniels, Lisa *WhoHol A*
Daniels, Mabel Wheeler 1879- *AmSCAP 1966*
Daniels, Marc 1912?- *NotNAT*
Daniels, Mark *WhoHol A*
Daniels, Mickey 1914- *Film 2, WhoHol A*
Daniels, Richard *Film 2*
Daniels, Thelma *Film 2*

Daniels, Victor *WhScrn 1, WhScrn 2*
Daniels, Violet *Film 2*
Daniels, Walter 1875-1928 *Film 2, WhScrn 1,*
 WhScrn 2, WhoHol B
Daniels, William 1895-1970 *CmMov, DcFM,*
 FilmgC, OxFilm, WorEnF
Daniels, William 1927- *BiE&WWA, NotNAT,*
 PIP&P, WhoHol A
Danielson, Dale H *IntMPA 1977*
Daniely, Lisa 1930- *FilmgC, WhoHol A*
Danilo, Don *WhScrn 1, WhScrn 2*
Danilova, Alexandra 1906- *BiE&WWA*
Danilova, Alexandra 1907- *WhThe*
Danis, Aimee *WomWMM*
Danis, Ida d1921 *WhScrn 1, WhScrn 2*
Danischewsky, Monja 1911- *FilmgC*
Danjuro, Ichikawa d1903 *NotNAT B*
Dank, David 1895- *BiE&WWA*
Danks, Hart Pease 1834-1903 *NotNAT B*
Dankworth, John 1927- *OxFilm*
Dankworth, Johnny 1927- *FilmgC*
Dann, Michael H *NewYTET*
Danner, Blythe *IntMPA 1977, WhoHol A,*
 WhoThe 16
D'Annunzio, Gabriele 1863-1938 *CnMD, CnThe,*
 McGWD, ModWD, OxThe, PIP&P,
 REnWD, WorEnF
D'Annunzio, Gabriele *see also* Annunzio, Gabriele D'
D'Annunzio, Lola d1956 *NotNAT B, WhoHol B*
Dano, Royal *WhoHol A*
Danoff, Sid 1920- *AmSCAP 1966*
Danova, Cesare 1926- *FilmgC, WhoHol A*
Dansereau, Mireille *WomWMM*
Dansey, Herbert 1870-1917 *WhScrn 2, WhThe*
Danson, Harold L 1905- *IntMPA 1977*
Danson, Linda d1975 *WhScrn 2, WhoHol C*
Dante 1884-1955 *WhScrn 1, WhScrn 2*
Dante The Magician 1884-1955 *WhoHol B*
Dante, Ethel d1954 *NotNAT B*
Dante, Lionel 1907-1974 *WhScrn 2, WhoHol B*
Dante, Michael 1931- *FilmgC, WhoHol A*
Dantine, Helmut *IntMPA 1977, MotPP*
Dantine, Helmut 1917- *WhoHol A*
Dantine, Helmut 1918- *FilmgC, MovMk*
Dantis, Suzanne *Film 2*
Danton, Ray 1931- *FilmgC, IntMPA 1977,*
 WhoHol A, WorEnF
D'Antoni, Philip 1929- *IntMPA 1977, NewYTET*
D'Antonio, Carmen *WhoHol A*
Danvers, Billy d1964 *NotNAT B*
Danvers, Johnnie 1860-1939 *OxThe*
Danvers, Johnny 1870-1939 *NotNAT B, WhThe*
Danvers-Walker, Bob *IntMPA 1977*
Danz, Fredric A 1918- *IntMPA 1977*
Danzig, Evelyn 1902- *AmSCAP 1966*
Danziger Brothers, The *FilmgC*
DaPonte, Lorenzo 1749-1838 *REnWD*
Daquin, Louis 1908- *DcFM, OxFilm, WorEnF*
D'Aragon, Lionel *Film 2*
Darbaud, Monique 1924-1971 *WhScrn 2*
Darby, Ken 1909- *CmMov*
Darby, Kenneth Lorin 1909- *AmSCAP 1966*
Darby, Kim *WhoHol A*
Darby, Kim 1937- *FilmgC*
Darby, Kim 1948- *IntMPA 1977*
Darby, Nettie Bell *Film 2*
Darby, Ray 1912- *AmSCAP 1966*
Darby, Rhy *Film 1*
Darbyshire, Iris 1905- *WhThe*
Darc, Mireille *WhoHol A*
Darc, Mireille 1939- *WorEnF*
Darc, Mireille 1940- *FilmgC*
Darcel, Denise 1925- *FilmgC, WhoHol A*
Darcey-Roche, Clara *Film 2*

Darciea, Edy *Film 2*
D'Arcy, Alex 1908- *Film 2, FilmgC, WhoHol A*
D'Arcy, Belle d1936 *NotNAT B, WhoStg 1908*
D'Arcy, Camille 1879-1916 *Film 1, WhScrn 2*
D'Arcy, Colin 1912- *AmSCAP 1966*
Darcy, Georgine *WhoHol A*
D'Arcy, Hugh Antoine d1925 *NotNAT B*
D'Arcy, Roy 1894-1969 *Film 1, Film 2, TwYS, WhScrn 1, WhScrn 2, WhoHol B*
Darcy, Sheila *WhoHol A*
Darcy, Thomas F, Jr. 1895- *AmSCAP 1966*
Darden, Severn 1937- *FilmgC, NotNAT, WhoHol A*
Dare, Daphne *WhoThe 16*
Dare, Doris *Film 1*
Dare, Dorris 1899-1927 *WhScrn 1, WhScrn 2, WhoHol B*
Dare, Eva d1931 *NotNAT B*
Dare, Phyllis 1890-1975 *EncMT, Film 2, WhScrn 2, WhThe, WhoHol C*
Dare, Richard d1964 *NotNAT B, WhoHol B*
Dare, Virginia d1962 *NotNAT B, WhScrn 1, WhScrn 2, WhoHol B*
Dare, Zena 1887-1975 *Film 2, WhScrn 2, WhThe, WhoHol C*
Darewski, Herman 1883-1947 *NotNAT B, WhThe*
Darewski, Max 1894-1929 *NotNAT B, WhThe*
Dargan, Olive Tilford d1968 *NotNAT B*
Darian, Fred 1927- *AmSCAP 1966*
Darien, Frank, Jr. d1955 *Vers B, WhScrn 1, WhScrn 2, WhoHol B*
Darin, Bobby 1936-1973 *FilmgC, MotPP, MovMk, WhScrn 2, WhoHol B*
Darion, Joe 1917- *EncMT, NewMT*
Darion, Joseph 1917- *AmSCAP 1966*
Dark, Christopher d1971 *WhScrn 1, WhScrn 2, WhoHol B*
Dark, Michael *Film 2*
Dark, Sidney 1874-1947 *NotNAT B, WhThe*
Dark, Stanley 1874- *WhoStg 1906, WhoStg 1908*
Dark Cloud *Film 1*
Dark Cloud, Beulah d1946 *WhoHol B*
Darkcloud, Beulah d1946 *WhScrn 1, WhScrn 2*
Darkfeather, Mona *Film 1*
Darley, Brian *Film 2*
Darley, Dick *IntMPA 1977*
Darling, Candy 1948-1974 *WhScrn 2, WhoHol B*
Darling, Denver 1909- *AmSCAP 1966*
Darling, Grace 1896- *Film 1, Film 2, TwYS*
Darling, Helen *Film 2*
Darling, Ida 1875-1936 *Film 1, Film 2, WhScrn 1, WhScrn 2, WhoHol B*
Darling, Jean 1922- *Film 2, TwYS*
Darling, Jean 1925- *BiE&WWA, NotNAT, WhoHol A*
Darling, Joan 1935- *BiE&WWA, WhoHol A*
Darling, Ruth *Film 1, Film 2*
Darling, Ruth d1918 *WhScrn 2*
Darlington, William Aubrey 1890- *BiE&WWA, NotNAT, OxThe, WhoThe 16*
Darmatow, Ossip *Film 2*
Darmond, Grace 1898-1963 *Film 2, MotPP, TwYS, WhScrn 1, WhScrn 2, WhoHol B*
Darmond, Grace 1898-1964 *Film 1*
Darmont, Albert d1909 *NotNAT B*
Darnay, Toni *WhoHol A*
Darnborough, Anthony 1913- *FilmgC*
Darnborough, Antony *IntMPA 1977*
Darnell, Jean 1889-1961 *Film 1, WhScrn 2, WhoHol B*
Darnell, Linda d1965 *MotPP, WhoHol B*
Darnell, Linda 1921-1965 *FilmgC, ThFT, WhScrn 1, WhScrn 2*

Darnell, Linda 1923-1965 *BiDFlm, MovMk, WorEnF*
Darnley, Herbert d1947 *NotNAT B, WhThe*
Darnley, J H d1938 *NotNAT B*
Darnold, Blaine A 1886-1926 *WhScrn 1, WhScrn 2*
Darnton, Charles d1950 *NotNAT B*
Darnton, Fred *Film 1*
Darr, Kathryn *Film 2*
Darr, Vondell *Film 2*
Darragh, Miss d1917 *NotNAT B, WhThe*
D'Arrast, Harry D'Abbadie 1893-1968 *FilmgC*
D'Arrast, Harry D'Abbadie 1893-1968 *BiDFlm, WorEnF*
Darrell, Charles d1932 *NotNAT B*
Darrell, J Stevan 1905-1970 *WhScrn 1, WhScrn 2*
Darrell, Maisie 1901- *WhThe*
Darrell, Steve d1970 *WhoHol B*
Darren, James 1936- *FilmgC, IntMPA 1977, MotPP, MovMk, WhoHol A*
Darrid, William 1923- *BiE&WWA*
Darrieux, Danielle 1917- *BiDFlm, FilmgC, IntMPA 1977, MotPP, MovMk, OxFilm, ThFT, WhoHol A, WorEnF*
Darrin, Diana *WhoHol A*
Darro, Frankie 1917- *Film 2, FilmgC, MovMk, WhoHol A*
Darro, Frankie 1918- *Vers B*
Darrow, Barbara *WhoHol A*
Darrow, Frankie 1917- *TwYS*
Darrow, Henry *WhoHol A*
Darrow, John *Film 2*
Darrow, Johnny *WhoHol A*
Darst, W Glen 1896- *AmSCAP 1966*
D'Artega, Alfonso 1907- *AmSCAP 1966*
Darthy, Gilda *WhThe*
Dartigue, John 1940- *IntMPA 1977*
Dartnall, Gary 1937- *IntMPA 1977*
Darvas, Charles *Film 2*
Darvas, Jozsef 1912- *CroCD*
Darvas, Lili 1902-1974 *NotNAT, WhScrn 2, WhoHol B*
Darvas, Lili 1906- *BiE&WWA, WhThe*
Darvi, Bella d1971 *WhoHol B*
Darvi, Bella 1927-1971 *FilmgC*
Darvi, Bella 1928-1971 *WhScrn 1, WhScrn 2*
D'Arvil, Yola *Film 2*
D'Arville, Camille 1863-1932 *NotNAT B, WhThe, WhoStg 1906, WhoStg 1908*
Darwell, Jane d1967 *MotPP, WhoHol B*
Darwell, Jane 1879-1967 *ThFT, Vers A*
Darwell, Jane 1880-1967 *BiDFlm, Film 1, Film 2, FilmgC, MovMk, OxFilm, TwYS, WhScrn 1, WhScrn 2, WorEnF*
Dash, Julian 1916- *AmSCAP 1966*
Dash, Pauly 1918-1974 *WhScrn 2, WhoHol B*
Dashiell, Willard 1867-1943 *WhScrn 1, WhScrn 2, WhoHol B*
Dashington, James J d1962 *NotNAT B*
DaSilva, Henry 1881-1947 *WhScrn 1, WhScrn 2*
DaSilva, Howard 1909- *BiE&WWA, EncMT, FilmgC, IntMPA 1977, MovMk, NotNAT, PIP&P, WhoHol A, WhoThe 16*
Dassin, Jules *ConDr 1977A, IntMPA 1977, WhoHol A*
Dassin, Jules 1911- *BiDFlm, BiE&WWA, CmMov, FilmgC, OxFilm, WorEnF*
Dassin, Jules 1912- *DcFM, MovMk*
Dastagir, Sabu *WhScrn 1, WhScrn 2*
Daste, Jean 1904- *OxFilm*
Dastree, Anne *WomWMM*
Datas 1876- *WhThe*
Date, Keshavrao 1939-1971 *WhScrn 1, WhScrn 2*
D'Attino, Giacomo *Film 2*

D'Auban, Ernest d1941 *NotNAT B*
Daube, Harda 1888-1959 *WhScrn 1, WhScrn 2, WhoHol B*
Daubeny, Peter 1921- *CnThe, OxThe, WhThe*
Daudet, Alphonse 1840-1897 *McGWD, NotNAT B*
Daudet, Ernest 1837-1921 *NotNAT B*
Daudet, Jeanette *Film 2*
Daufel, Andre 1919-1975 *WhScrn 2*
Daugherty, Herschel *FilmgC*
Daugherty, Jack d1938 *Film 2, WhoHol B*
Daumerey, Carey *Film 2*
D'Aumery, Carrie *Film 2*
Daumery, Carry *Film 2*
Dauncey, Sylvanus d1912 *NotNAT B*
Daunch, Virginia Obenchain 1919- *AmSCAP 1966*
Daunt, William 1893-1938 *NotNAT B, WhThe*
Dauphin, Claude *IntMPA 1977, MotPP, WhoHol A*
Dauphin, Claude 1903- *FilmgC, WhoThe 16*
Dauphin, Claude 1904- *BiE&WWA, MovMk, NotNAT*
D'Auray, Jacques *Film 2*
D'Auril, Yola *Film 2*
Dauvilliers, Nicolas Dorne d1690 *OxThe*
Dauvilliers, Victoire-Francoise 1657?-1733 *OxThe*
Dauvray, Marise *Film 2*
Davalos, Richard *MotPP, WhoHol A*
Davee, Lawrence W 1900- *IntMPA 1977*
Daven, Andre *Film 2*
Davenant, Lady *PIP&P*
Davenant, Charles *PIP&P*
Davenant, Sir William 1606-1668 *CnThe, McGWD, NotNAT A, NotNAT B, OxThe, PIP&P, REnWD*
Davenport, A Bromley *Film 2*
Davenport, Alice 1853?-1936 *WhScrn 2*
Davenport, Alice 1864- *Film 1, TwYS*
Davenport, Alice Shepard *WhoHol B*
Davenport, Ann d1968 *WhScrn 1, WhScrn 2, WhoHol B*
Davenport, Blanch *Film 2*
Davenport, Butler 1871-1958 *NotNAT B*
Davenport, Charles 1895-1955 *AmSCAP 1966*
Davenport, David N 1925- *AmSCAP 1966*
Davenport, Doris *WhoHol A*
Davenport, Dorothy 1895- *Film 1, Film 2, TwYS, WhoHol A*
Davenport, Edgar Longfellow 1862-1918 *NotNAT B, OxThe*
Davenport, Edward Loomis 1815-1877 *FamA&A, NotNAT A, NotNAT B, OxThe*
Davenport, Eva d1932 *NotNAT B, WhoStg 1906, WhoStg 1908*
Davenport, Fanny 1860-1898 *PIP&P*
Davenport, Fanny Elizabeth Vining 1829-1891 *NotNAT B, OxThe*
Davenport, Fanny Lily Gypsy 1850-1898 *FamA&A, NotNAT B, OxThe*
Davenport, George Gosling d1814 *NotNAT B*
Davenport, Harry 1866-1949 *Film 1, Film 2, FilmgC, MotPP, MovMk, NotNAT B, OxThe, Vers A, WhScrn 1, WhScrn 2, WhThe, WhoHol B, WhoStg 1906, WhoStg 1908*
Davenport, Harry J 1858-1929 *WhScrn 2*
Davenport, Harry J 1858-1949 *WhScrn 1*
Davenport, Havis 1933-1975 *WhScrn 2, WhoHol C*
Davenport, Jean Margaret 1829-1903 *NotNAT B, OxThe*
Davenport, Kate 1896-1954 *WhScrn 1, WhScrn 2, WhoHol B*
Davenport, Kenneth 1879-1941 *WhScrn 1,*

WhScrn 2, WhoHol B
Davenport, Mary d1916 *NotNAT B*
Davenport, May 1856-1927 *NotNAT B, OxThe*
Davenport, Milla 1871-1936 *Film 1, Film 2, TwYS, WhScrn 1, WhScrn 2, WhoHol B*
Davenport, Millia 1895- *BiE&WWA, NotNAT*
Davenport, Millie *Film 2*
Davenport, Nigel 1928- *FilmgC, WhoHol A, WhoThe 16*
Davenport, Pembroke M 1911- *AmSCAP 1966, BiE&WWA, NotNAT*
Davenport, Rebecca *WomWMM B*
Davenport, Suzanne *WomWMM B*
Davenport, T D *OxThe*
Daves, Delmer 1904- *BiDFlm, CmMov, DcFM, Film 2, FilmgC, IntMPA 1977, MovMk, OxFilm, WorEnF*
Davesnes, Edouard *Film 1*
Davey, Florence *WomWMM B*
Davey, Nuna 1902- *WhThe*
Davey, Peter 1857-1946 *NotNAT B, WhThe*
David, Benjamin 1896- *AmSCAP 1966*
David, Clifford 1933- *BiE&WWA, NotNAT*
David, Hal 1921- *AmSCAP 1966, CelR 3, EncMT, NotNAT*
David, Lee 1891- *AmSCAP 1966*
David, Mack 1912- *AmSCAP 1966, BiE&WWA, NotNAT*
David, Madeline Bloom *NewYTET*
David, Meridith Bar *WomWMM B*
David, Michael *PIP&P A*
David, Saul 1921- *IntMPA 1977*
David, Thayer 1927- *NotNAT, WhoHol A*
David, Vincent 1924- *AmSCAP 1966*
David, William 1882-1965 *WhScrn 1, WhScrn 2, WhoHol B*
David, Worton d1940 *NotNAT B, WhThe*
Davidoff, Serafin d1975 *WhScrn 2*
Davids, Heintje 1888-1975 *WhScrn 2*
Davidson, Bill 1918- *BiE&WWA*
Davidson, Bing 1939-1965 *WhScrn 1, WhScrn 2*
Davidson, Charles 1929- *AmSCAP 1966*
Davidson, Cliff *Film 2*
Davidson, Dore 1850-1930 *Film 1, Film 2, NotNAT B, WhScrn 1, WhScrn 2, WhoHol B*
Davidson, Gordon 1933- *WhoThe 16*
Davidson, Gordon 1934?- *NotNAT*
Davidson, Harold P 1909- *AmSCAP 1966*
Davidson, J B *WhScrn 1*
Davidson, James *WhoHol A*
Davidson, James B *WhScrn 2*
Davidson, John 1886-1968 *Film 1, Film 2, TwYS, WhScrn 2, WhoHol B*
Davidson, John 1941- *IntMPA 1977, MotPP, WhoHol A*
Davidson, Lawford *Film 2*
Davidson, Maitland d1936 *NotNAT B*
Davidson, Max 1875-1946 *TwYS*
Davidson, Max 1875-1950 *Film 1, Film 2, WhScrn 1, WhScrn 2, WhoHol B*
Davidson, Milton *BiE&WWA*
Davidson, Morrey 1899- *AmSCAP 1966*
Davidson, Richard 1918- *BiE&WWA, NotNAT*
Davidson, William B 1888-1947 *Film 1, Film 2, TwYS, WhScrn 1, WhScrn 2, WhoHol B*
Davidt, Michael 1877-1944 *WhScrn 1, WhScrn 2*
Davies, Acton 1870-1916 *NotNAT B, WhThe*
Davies, Betty Ann 1910-1955 *FilmgC, NotNAT B, WhScrn 1, WhScrn 2, WhThe, WhoHol B*
Davies, Brian 1912- *BiE&WWA*
Davies, Brian 1938- *BiE&WWA*
Davies, David d1920 *WhScrn 1, WhScrn 2*

Davies, David Ivor *McGWD*
Davies, Edna 1905- *WhThe*
Davies, George 1891-1960 *WhScrn 1, WhScrn 2*
Davies, Harry Parr 1914-1955 *NotNAT B, WhThe*
Davies, Howard *Film 1*
Davies, Hubert Henry 1869-1917 *NotNAT B, WhThe*
Davies, Jack 1913- *FilmgC, IntMPA 1977*
Davies, John Howard 1939- *FilmgC, WhoHol A*
Davies, John W 1908- *IntMPA 1977*
Davies, Lewis A 1911- *AmSCAP 1966*
Davies, Lilian 1895-1932 *NotNAT B, WhThe*
Davies, Marion d1961 *MotPP, WhoHol B*
Davies, Marion 1897-1961 *BiDFlm, Film 1, Film 2, FilmgC, MGM, MovMk, NotNAT B, ThFT, WhThe, WorEnF*
Davies, Marion 1898-1961 *OxFilm, WhScrn 1, WhScrn 2*
Davies, Marion 1900-1961 *TwYS*
Davies, Marion Hall *Film 2*
Davies, Mary Carolyn *AmSCAP 1966*
Davies, Phoebe *WhoStg 1906, WhoStg 1908*
Davies, Reine *Film 1*
Davies, Robertson 1913- *CnThe, ConDr 1977, McGWD, REnWD*
Davies, Rupert 1916- *FilmgC, IntMPA 1977, WhoHol A*
Davies, Thomas d1785 *NotNAT B*
Davies, William C 1932- *IntMPA 1977*
Davion, Alexander 1929- *FilmgC, WhoHol A*
Daviot, Gordon d1952 *NotNAT B, WhThe*
Davis, Adelle 1904- *CelR 3*
Davis, Alfred 1899- *IntMPA 1977*
Davis, Allan 1913- *WhoThe 16*
Davis, Allan 1913-1943 *WhScrn 2*
Davis, Allan 1922- *AmSCAP 1966*
Davis, Allen, III *NatPD*
Davis, Angela 1944- *CelR 3*
Davis, Ann d1961 *NotNAT B*
Davis, Ann B *WhoHol A*
Davis, Anna 1890-1945 *WhScrn 1, WhScrn 2*
Davis, Annette *WhoHol A*
Davis, Ariel Rual 1912- *NotNAT*
Davis, Arthur 1917- *IntMPA 1977*
Davis, Barbara *WomWMM*
Davis, Bea *WomWMM*
Davis, Benny 1895- *AmSCAP 1966*
Davis, Bette 1908- *BiDFlm, BiE&WWA, CelR 3, CmMov, EncMT, FilmgC, IntMPA 1977, MotPP, MovMk, NotNAT, NotNAT A, OxFilm, ThFT, WhoHol A, WhoThe 16, WorEnF*
Davis, Bill *NewYTET*
Davis, Blevins 1903-1971 *BiE&WWA, NotNAT B*
Davis, Bob 1909- *AmSCAP 1966*
Davis, Bob Alabam 1910-1971 *WhScrn 1, WhScrn 2*
Davis, Boyd 1885-1963 *NotNAT B, WhScrn 1, WhScrn 2, WhThe, WhoHol B*
Davis, Buster 1920- *AmSCAP 1966, BiE&WWA, NotNAT*
Davis, Carl 1936- *WhoThe 16*
Davis, Charles *WhoHol A*
Davis, Charles Belmont d1926 *NotNAT B*
Davis, Clifton *WhoHol A*
Davis, Conrad d1969 *WhoHol B*
Davis, Danny 1929-1970 *WhScrn 1, WhScrn 2*
Davis, Danny 1930- *AmSCAP 1966*
Davis, David And Lorenzo Music *NewYTET*
Davis, Desmond 1927- *FilmgC*
Davis, Desmond 1928- *WorEnF*
Davis, Dolly *Film 2*

Davis, Donald 1928- *BiE&WWA, NotNAT, WhoHol A*
Davis, Eddie d1958 *NotNAT B*
Davis, Edward d1936 *Film 1, Film 2, WhoHol B*
Davis, Edwards 1871-1936 *WhScrn 1, WhScrn 2*
Davis, Elias And David Pollock *NewYTET*
Davis, Elmer d1958 *NewYTET*
Davis, Fay 1872-1945 *NotNAT B, WhThe, WhoStg 1906, WhoStg 1908*
Davis, Fitzroy 1912- *BiE&WWA, NotNAT*
Davis, Frank 1894- *AmSCAP 1966*
Davis, Frank I 1919- *IntMPA 1977*
Davis, Frederick 1909- *AmSCAP 1966*
Davis, Freeman 1903-1974 *WhScrn 2, WhoHol B*
Davis, Gail *WhoHol A*
Davis, Gary 1896-1972 *WhScrn 2*
Davis, Genevieve 1889-1950 *AmSCAP 1966*
Davis, George 1889-1965 *Film 2, Vers B, WhScrn 1, WhScrn 2, WhoHol B*
Davis, George Collin 1867-1929 *AmSCAP 1966*
Davis, George W 1914- *IntMPA 1977*
Davis, Gilbert 1899- *WhThe*
Davis, Glenn *WhoHol A*
Davis, H O d1964 *NotNAT B*
Davis, Hallie Flanagan 1890- *BiE&WWA*
Davis, Harry 1874-1929 *WhScrn 1, WhScrn 2, WhoHol B*
Davis, Harry E 1905-1968 *BiE&WWA, NotNAT B*
Davis, Hazel 1907- *AmSCAP 1966*
Davis, J Edward *Film 2*
Davis, J Gunnis 1874-1937 *Film 2, WhoHol B*
Davis, Jack *WhoHol A*
Davis, Jack d1968 *WhScrn 2*
Davis, Jackie *Film 2*
Davis, Jackson 1920- *AmSCAP 1966*
Davis, James 1915- *FilmgC*
Davis, James Gunnis 1874-1937 *WhScrn 1, WhScrn 2*
Davis, Jean Reynolds 1927- *AmSCAP 1966*
Davis, Jed H 1921- *BiE&WWA, NotNAT*
Davis, Jeff 1884-1968 *WhScrn 2*
Davis, Jerry *NewYTET*
Davis, Jessie Bartlett 1861-1905 *NotNAT B*
Davis, Jim *MotPP*
Davis, Jim 1915- *WhoHol A*
Davis, Joan d1961 *MotPP, WhoHol B*
Davis, Joan 1906-1961 *WhThe*
Davis, Joan 1907-1961 *ThFT, WhScrn 1, WhScrn 2*
Davis, Joan 1908-1961 *FilmgC, MovMk*
Davis, Joan 1913?-1961 *NotNAT B*
Davis, Joe 1912- *WhoThe 16*
Davis, Sir John 1906- *FilmgC, IntMPA 1977*
Davis, John Carlyle 1878-1948 *AmSCAP 1966*
Davis, Jordan P 1933- *IntMPA 1977*
Davis, Joseph M 1896- *AmSCAP 1966*
Davis, Katherine K 1892- *AmSCAP 1966*
Davis, Keith *BiE&WWA*
Davis, Lemuel A 1914- *AmSCAP 1966*
Davis, Lou 1881-1961 *AmSCAP 1966*
Davis, Luther 1916- *BiE&WWA, NotNAT*
Davis, Luther 1921- *IntMPA 1977*
Davis, Luther 1938- *NatPD*
Davis, Mack 1898-1947 *AmSCAP 1966*
Davis, Martin S *IntMPA 1977*
Davis, Mary *PIP&P*
Davis, Meyer 1893- *CelR 3*
Davis, Meyer 1896- *BiE&WWA*
Davis, Mildred 1900-1969 *WhScrn 1, WhScrn 2, WhoHol B*
Davis, Mildred 1903-1969 *Film 1, Film 2, TwYS*
Davis, Miles 1926- *CelR 3*

Davis, Nancy 1924- *FilmgC, MotPP, WhoHol A*
Davis, Newnham- *WhThe*
Davis, Ossie 1917- *BiE&WWA, CelR 3,*
   ConDr 1977, FilmgC, IntMPA 1977, MotPP,
   MovMk, NotNAT, PIP&P A, WhoHol A,
   WhoThe 16
Davis, Owen 1874-1956 *CnMD, McGWD,*
   ModWD, NotNAT A, NotNAT B, OxThe,
   WhThe
Davis, Owen, Jr. 1907-1949 *Film 2, NotNAT B,*
   WhScrn 1, WhScrn 2, WhThe, WhoHol B
Davis, Paul 1925- *IntMPA 1977*
Davis, Peter *NewYTET*
Davis, Philip L 1911- *AmSCAP 1966*
Davis, Phoebe 1865- *WhThe*
Davis, Ray C *WhoThe 16*
Davis, Rex *Film 2*
Davis, Richard Harding 1864-1916 *NotNAT B,*
   WhThe, WhoStg 1906, WhoStg 1908
Davis, Robert *WhoHol A*
Davis, Roger *Film 2*
Davis, Roger H 1923- *IntMPA 1977*
Davis, Rufe 1908-1974 *Vers A, WhScrn 2,*
   WhoHol B
Davis, Ryrrell *Film 2*
Davis, Sammy, Jr. 1925- *BiE&WWA, CelR 3,*
   EncMT, FilmgC, IntMPA 1977, MotPP,
   MovMk, NotNAT, NotNAT A, OxFilm,
   WhoHol A, WhoThe 16
Davis, Sheila 1927- *AmSCAP 1966*
Davis, Stringer 1896- *FilmgC, WhoHol A*
Davis, Sylvia *WhoHol A*
Davis, Tom Buffen 1867-1931 *NotNAT B,*
   WhThe
Davis, Will J *WhoStg 1908*
Davis, William *Film 2*
Davis, William A *NewYTET*
Davis, William Boyd 1885- *WhThe*
Davis, Willis J d1963 *NotNAT B*
Davison, Bruce 1948- *FilmgC, IntMPA 1977,*
   WhoHol A
Davison, Davey *WhoHol A*
Davison, Lesley *AmSCAP 1966*
Davison, Maria d1858 *NotNAT B*
Davison, Wayne Marshall 1916- *AmSCAP 1966*
D'Avril, Yola 1907- *Film 2, TwYS*
Daw, Evelyn 1912-1970 *FilmgC, WhScrn 1,*
   WhScrn 2, WhoHol B
Daw, Marjorie 1902- *Film 1, Film 2, MotPP,*
   TwYS
Dawe, Carlton d1935 *NotNAT B*
Dawe, Thomas F 1881-1928 *WhThe*
Dawley, J Searle *TwYS A*
Dawn, Allan *Film 1*
Dawn, Dolly *AmSCAP 1966*
Dawn, Doris *Film 1*
Dawn, Dorothy *Film 2*
Dawn, Hazel *MotPP*
Dawn, Hazel 1891- *EncMT, Film 1, Film 2,*
   TwYS, WhThe
Dawn, Hazel 1894- *BiE&WWA, NotNAT,*
   WhoHol A
Dawn, Hazel, Jr. *WhoHol A*
Dawn, Isabel 1905-1966 *WhScrn 1, WhScrn 2,*
   WomWMM
Dawn, Janet *Film 2*
Dawn, Marpessa *MotPP*
Dawn, Norman 1887- *TwYS A*
Dawson, Anna *WhoThe 16*
Dawson, Anthony 1916- *FilmgC, IntMPA 1977,*
   WhoHol A
Dawson, Beatrice 1908-1976 *WhoThe 16*
Dawson, Dorice 1909-1950 *WhScrn 1*
Dawson, Doris 1909- *Film 2, TwYS, WhoHol A*

Dawson, Eli 1880-1960 *AmSCAP 1966*
Dawson, Forbes 1860- *WhThe*
Dawson, Frank 1870-1953 *WhScrn 1, WhScrn 2,*
   WhoHol B
Dawson, Hal K *Vers B, WhoHol A*
Dawson, Ivo d1934 *Film 2, NotNAT B,*
   WhoHol B
Dawson, Jenny d1936 *NotNAT B*
Dawson, Mark 1920- *BiE&WWA, NotNAT*
Dawson, Nancy Juno *WhoHol A*
Dawson, Ralph d1962 *NotNAT B*
Dawson, Richard *WhoHol A*
Dawson, Thomas H *NewYTET*
Dax, Jean *Film 2*
Day, Alice 1905- *Film 2, TwYS, WhoHol A*
Day, Anna 1884- *WhoStg 1906, WhoStg 1908*
Day, Cyrus L 1900-1968 *NotNAT B*
Day, Dennis *MotPP*
Day, Dennis 1917- *WhoHol A*
Day, Dennis 1921- *FilmgC*
Day, Doris 1924- *BiDFlm, CelR 3, CmMov,*
   FilmgC, IntMPA 1977, MotPP, MovMk,
   OxFilm, WhoHol A, WorEnF
Day, Dorothy 1897- *CelR 3*
Day, Dorothy 1898- *BiE&WWA*
Day, Dulcie 1911-1954 *WhScrn 1, WhScrn 2*
Day, Edith 1896-1971 *EncMT, Film 1,*
   NotNAT B, WhScrn 1, WhScrn 2, WhThe,
   WhoHol B
Day, Frances 1908- *EncMT, Film 2, FilmgC,*
   WhThe, WhoHol A
Day, Gordon M 1918- *IntMPA 1977*
Day, James *NewYTET*
Day, James F 1917- *AmSCAP 1966*
Day, Jill 1932- *FilmgC*
Day, John d1584 *NotNAT B*
Day, John 1574-1640? *CnThe, NotNAT B,*
   OxThe, REnWD
Day, Josette 1914- *FilmgC, WhoHol A*
Day, Juliette d1957 *NotNAT B, WhoHol A*
Day, Laraine *MotPP*
Day, Laraine 1917- *FilmgC, ThFT*
Day, Laraine 1919- *MGM, MovMk, WhoHol A*
Day, Laraine 1920- *IntMPA 1977*
Day, Lynda *WhoHol A*
Day, Marceline 1907- *Film 2, TwYS*
Day, Marceline 1908- *WhoHol A*
Day, Marie L 1855-1939 *WhScrn 1, WhScrn 2,*
   WhoHol B
Day, Marjorie *Film 2*
Day, Marjorie 1889- *WhThe*
Day, Olga *Film 2*
Day, Ralph W 1895- *AmSCAP 1966*
Day, Richard d1973 *WhoHol B*
Day, Richard 1894-1972 *FilmgC*
Day, Richard 1896- *WorEnF*
Day, Richard Digby 1940- *WhoThe 16*
Day, Robert 1922- *FilmgC, IntMPA 1977*
Day, Roy d1963 *NotNAT B*
Day, Shannon *Film 2, WhoHol A*
Day, Stanley A 1894- *AmSCAP 1966*
Day, Tom *Film 2*
Day, Yvonne 1920- *Film 2*
Dayan, Assaf *WhoHol A*
Dayan, Moshe 1915- *CelR 3*
Daykarhanova, Tamara 1892- *BiE&WWA,*
   NotNAT
Dayman, Bain, Sr. d1964 *NotNAT B*
Dayne, Blanche d1944 *NotNAT B*
Dayton, Frank 1865-1924 *Film 1, WhScrn 2*
Dayton, Lewis *Film 1, Film 2*
Dayton, Lyman D 1941- *IntMPA 1977*
Daze, Mercedes 1892-1945 *WhScrn 1, WhScrn 2,*
   WhoHol B

Dazey, Charles Turner 1853-1938 NotNAT B,
  WhThe, WhoStg 1906, WhoStg 1908
Dazie, Mademoiselle 1882-1952 WhThe
Dazie, Mademoiselle 1884-1952 NotNAT B,
  WhoStg 1906, WhoStg 1908
Deacon, Mary Connor 1907- AmSCAP 1966
Deacon, Richard 1923- FilmgC, MotPP,
  WhoHol A
Deacy, Jane BiE&WWA
Deagan, Charles 1880-1932 WhScrn 1, WhScrn 2
Deagon, Arthur d1927 NotNAT B
Deagon, Arthur 1873- WhoStg 1908
DeAlba, Carlos 1925-1960 WhScrn 1, WhScrn 2
Dean, Alexander PIP&P
Dean, Alexander d1939 NotNAT B
Dean, Barbara Film 2
Dean, Barney 1904-1954 WhScrn 1, WhScrn 2,
  WhoHol B
Dean, Basil 1888- Film 2, FilmgC, ModWD,
  OxThe, WhThe
Dean, Dacia Film 2
Dean, Dinky Film 2, WhoHol A
Dean, Dorris Film 2
Dean, Eddie 1908?- FilmgC, IntMPA 1977,
  WhoHol A
Dean, Fabian 1930-1971 WhScrn 1, WhScrn 2,
  WhoHol B
Dean, Hector Film 1
Dean, Isabel 1918- FilmgC, WhoHol A,
  WhoThe 16
Dean, Ivor d1964 WhoHol B
Dean, Ivor 1917-1974 WhScrn 2
Dean, Jack 1875-1950 Film 1, WhScrn 2,
  WhoHol B
Dean, James 1931-1955 BiDFlm, FilmgC, MotPP,
  MovMk, NotNAT B, OxFilm, WhScrn 1,
  WhScrn 2, WhoHol B, WorEnF
Dean, Jimmy 1928- IntMPA 1977, WhoHol A
Dean, John W d1950 NotNAT B
Dean, Julia 1830-1868 NotNAT B, OxThe
Dean, Julia 1830-1869 FamA&A
Dean, Julia 1878-1952 Film 1, FilmgC, Vers B,
  WhScrn 1, WhScrn 2, WhoHol B
Dean, Julia 1878-1953 TwYS
Dean, Julia 1880-1952 NotNAT B, WhThe
Dean, Julie MotPP
Dean, Louis Film 1
Dean, Man Mountain 1890-1953 WhScrn 1,
  WhScrn 2, WhoHol B
Dean, Margia WhoHol A
Dean, May d1937 WhScrn 1, WhScrn 2,
  WhoHol B
Dean, Nelson 1882-1923 WhScrn 1, WhScrn 2
Dean, Philip Hayes PIP&P A
Dean, Priscilla 1896- Film 1, Film 2, MotPP,
  TwYS, WhoHol A
Dean, Ralph 1868-1923 WhScrn 1, WhScrn 2
Dean, Rose 1892-1952 WhScrn 1, WhScrn 2
Dean, Ruby 1887-1935 WhScrn 1, WhScrn 2
Dean, Sherry WhoHol A
DeAnda, Agustin 1935-1960 WhScrn 1,
  WhScrn 2
Deane, Barbara 1886- WhThe
Deane, Doris 1901-1974 WhScrn 2, WhoHol B
Deane, Eddie V 1929- AmSCAP 1966
Deane, Hazel Film 1, Film 2, TwYS
Deane, Martha 1909- CelR 3
Deane, Sidney Film 2
Deane, Sydney Film 1
Deane, Tessa WhThe
Deane, Verna Film 2
DeAngelis, Jefferson 1859-1933 NotNAT A,
  NotNAT B, WhScrn 2, WhThe,
  WhoStg 1906, WhoStg 1908

DeAngelis, Peter 1929- AmSCAP 1966
DeAngelis, Thomas Jefferson 1859-1933 OxThe
DeAngelo, Carlo d1962 NotNAT B
Deans, F Harris 1886-1961 NotNAT B, WhThe
Deans, Marjorie WomWMM
Dearden, Basil 1911-1971 BiDFlm, CmMov,
  DcFM, FilmgC, MovMk, OxFilm, WorEnF
Dearden, Harold 1882- WhThe
Dearholt, Ashton Film 1, Film 2
Dearing, Edgar 1893-1974 Film 2, Vers B,
  WhScrn 2, WhoHol B
Dearing, Peter 1912- WhThe
Dearly, Max 1874-1943 NotNAT B, WhScrn 1,
  WhScrn 2, WhoHol B
Dearly, Max 1875-1943 WhThe
Dearner, Mrs. Percy d1915 NotNAT B
Dearth, Harry 1876-1933 NotNAT B, WhThe
Dease, Bobby 1899-1958 WhScrn 1, WhScrn 2,
  WhoHol B
D'Eaubonne, Jean 1903-1971 DcFM, WorEnF
DeAubry, Diane 1890-1969 WhScrn 1, WhScrn 2,
  WhoHol B
Deaves, Ada d1920 NotNAT B
Debain, Henri Film 2
DeBakey, Michael 1908- CelR 3
DeBalzac, Jeanne d1930 WhScrn 2
DeBanzie, Brenda 1915- BiE&WWA, FilmgC,
  IntMPA 1977, NotNAT, WhThe,
  WhoHol A
DeBanzie, Lois WhoHol A
DeBaroncelli, Jacques 1881-1951 DcFM, WorEnF
DeBasil, Wassily d1951 WhThe
DeBear, Archibald 1889-1970 WhThe
DeBeaumarchais, Pierre-Augustin Caron PIP&P
DeBeck, Billy Film 2
DeBecker, Harold 1889-1947 WhScrn 1,
  WhScrn 2, WhoHol B
DeBecker, Marie 1881-1946 WhScrn 1,
  WhScrn 2, WhoHol B
DeBelleville, Frederic 1857-1923 NotNAT B,
  WhThe, WhoStg 1906, WhoStg 1908
Debenham, Cicely 1891-1955 NotNAT B, WhThe
DeBeranger, Andre Film 2
DeBergerac, Cyrano OxThe
Debi, Arundhati WomWMM
Debin, Nat 1911- BiE&WWA
DeBlasio, Gene 1940-1971 WhScrn 2
DeBlasis, James 1931- BiE&WWA
DeBodamere, Madame Film 2
DeBoer VanRijk, Esther d1937 NotNAT B
DeBord, Sharon WhoHol A
DeBornier, Henri d1901 NotNAT B
DeBosio, Gianfranco 1924- WorEnF
DeBourbon, Princess Marie Film 2
DeBozoky, Barbara 1871-1937 WhScrn 2
DeBray, Harold 1874-1932 WhScrn 1, WhScrn 2
DeBray, Henri 1889-1965 WhScrn 1, WhScrn 2
DeBray, Henry 1889-1965 WhThe
DeBray, Yvonne 1889-1954 FilmgC, WhScrn 1,
  WhScrn 2, WhoHol B
DeBrey, Claire Film 1
DeBriac, Jean Film 2
DeBriac Twins Film 2
Debrie, Andre 1880-1967 OxFilm
DeBrie, Catherine Leclerc DuRozet 1630?-1706
  OxThe
DeBrie, Edme Villequin 1607-1676 OxThe
DeBroca, Philippe 1920- OxFilm
DeBroca, Philippe 1933- BiDFlm, FilmgC,
  IntMPA 1977, WorEnF
DeBroca, Philippe 1935- DcFM, MovMk
DeBroyer, Lisette WomWMM
DeBrulier, Nigel 1878-1948 Film 1, Film 2,
  FilmgC, TwYS, WhScrn 1, WhScrn 2,

WhoHol B
Debucourt, Jean 1894-1958 *Film 2, FilmgC, WhScrn 1, WhScrn 2, WhoHol B*
Deburau, Charles 1829-1873 *NotNAT B, OxThe*
Deburau, Jean-Baptiste Gaspard 1796-1846 *NotNAT A, NotNAT B*
Deburau, Jean-Gaspard 1796-1846 *CnThe, OxThe*
DeBurgh, Aimee d1946 *NotNAT B, WhThe*
Debuskey, Merle 1923- *BiE&WWA, NotNAT*
DeBusschere, Dave 1940- *Ce!R 3*
Decae, Henri 1915- *FilmgC, OxFilm, WorEnF*
Decae, Henry 1915- *DcFM*
DeCaesar, Gabriel 1928- *IntMPA 1977*
DeCamp, Dot *NatPD*
DeCamp, Rosemary *MotPP, WhoHol A*
DeCamp, Rosemary 1913- *FilmgC, IntMPA 1977, MovMk*
DeCamp, Rosemary 1914- *Vers B*
DeCampo, Guiseppe *Film 2*
DeCanonge, Maurice *Film 2*
DeCaprio, Al *IntMPA 1977*
DeCarlo, Yvonne *MotPP, PIP&P A, WhoHol A*
DeCarlo, Yvonne 1922- *BiDFlm, CmMov, FilmgC, MovMk, WorEnF*
DeCarlo, Yvonne 1924- *CelR 3, CmMov, IntMPA 1977*
DeCarlos, Perla Granda 1903-1973 *WhScrn 2*
DeCarlton, George *Film 1, Film 2*
DeCarmo, Pussy d1964 *NotNAT B*
DeCasalis, Jeanne d1966 *WhoHol B*
DeCasalis, Jeanne 1896-1966 *FilmgC*
DeCasalis, Jeanne 1897-1966 *WhScrn 1, WhScrn 2, WhThe*
DeCastrejon, Blanca 1916-1969 *WhScrn 2*
DeCastrejon, Blance 1916-1969 *WhScrn 1*
DeCastro, Dolores *WomWMM B*
DeCevee, Alice 1904- *AmSCAP 1966*
DeCicco, Pat *WhoHol A*
DeCimber, Joseph V 1898- *AmSCAP 1966*
DeCisneros, Eleonora 1878-1934 *NotNAT B*
Decker, Diana 1926- *FilmgC*
Decker, John 1895-1947 *WhScrn 1, WhScrn 2*
Decker, Kathryn Browne d1919 *WhScrn 2*
Deckers, Eugene 1917- *FilmgC, WhoHol A*
DeCoeur, A *Film 2*
Decoeur, M Albert *Film 1*
Decoin, Henri 1896-1969 *DcFM, FilmgC, WorEnF*
DeCola, Felix 1910- *AmSCAP 1966*
Decombie, Guy d1964 *WhScrn 2*
DeConde, Syn *WhoHol A*
DeCoppett, Theodosia *WhScrn 1, WhScrn 2*
DeCordoba, Pedro 1881-1950 *Film 1, Film 2, FilmgC, MotPP, MovMk, NotNAT B, TwYS, WhScrn 1, WhScrn 2, WhThe, WhoHol B*
DeCordova, Arturo d1973 *MotPP, WhoHol B*
DeCordova, Arturo 1907-1973 *WhScrn 2*
DeCordova, Arturo 1908-1973 *FilmgC*
DeCordova, Fred 1910- *NewYTET*
DeCordova, Frederick 1910- *FilmgC, IntMPA 1977*
DeCordova, Leander 1878-1936 *WhScrn 2*
DeCordova, Rudolf *Film 2*
DeCordova, Rudolph 1860-1941 *NotNAT B, WhThe*
DeCormier, Robert 1922- *AmSCAP 1966*
DeCorsia, Ted 1904-1973 *WhScrn 2, WhoHol B*
DeCorsia, Ted 1906- *FilmgC*
DeCosta, Harry 1885-1964 *AmSCAP 1966*
DeCosta, Morris 1890-1957 *WhScrn 1, WhScrn 2*
Decourcelle, Adrien d1892 *NotNAT B*
Decourcelle, Pierre 1856-1926 *NotNAT B, WhThe*

DeCourcy, Nanette *Film 2*
DeCourelle, Rose Marie *Film 2*
Decoursey, Nettie d1964 *NotNAT B*
DeCourville, Albert P 1887-1960 *FilmgC, NotNAT A, NotNAT B, WhThe*
DeCoy, Robert d1975 *WhScrn 2*
DeCrescenzo, Vincenzo 1875-1964 *AmSCAP 1966*
DeCroisset, Francis d1937 *NotNAT B*
Dectreaux, Evelyn 1902-1952 *WhScrn 1, WhScrn 2*
DeCuir, John 1918- *FilmgC, IntMPA 1977*
DeCurel, Francois Viscomte d1928 *NotNAT B*
DeCyr, Zel *IntMPA 1977*
Dedinstev, A *Film 2*
Dee, Frances *MotPP, WhoHol A, WomWMM*
Dee, Frances 1907- *FilmgC, HolP 30, ThFT*
Dee, Frances 1908- *MovMk*
Dee, Freddie 1924-1958 *WhScrn 1, WhScrn 2, WhoHol B*
Dee, Ruby *BiE&WWA, MotPP, NotNAT, WhoHol A, WomWMM*
Dee, Ruby 1923- *WhoThe 16*
Dee, Ruby 1924- *CelR 3, FilmgC, MovMk*
Dee, Sandra 1942- *FilmgC, IntMPA 1977, MotPP, MovMk, WhoHol A*
Dee, Sylvia 1914- *AmSCAP 1966*
Deed, Andre 1884- *OxFilm, WhScrn 2*
Deeflos, Huguette *Film 2*
Deel, Sandra *WhoHol A*
Deeley, Ben 1878-1924 *Film 1, Film 2, WhoHol B*
Deeley, J Bernard Ben 1878-1924 *WhScrn 1, WhScrn 2*
Deeley, Michael 1931- *FilmgC*
Deeley, Michael 1932- *IntMPA 1977*
Deems, Mickey 1925- *BiE&WWA, NotNAT*
Deen, Nedra d1975 *WhScrn 2, WhoHol C, WomWMM B*
Deer, Alma *Film 2*
Deer, Louis *Film 2*
Deering, John d1955 *WhoHol B*
Deering, John 1905-1959 *WhScrn 1, WhScrn 2*
Deering, Marda d1961 *WhoHol B*
Deering, Olive *NotNAT, WhoHol A, WhoThe 16*
Deering, Patricia *Film 2*
Deering, Tommy 1938- *AmSCAP 1966*
Deery, Jack *Film 2*
Dees, Sylvia *WomWMM B*
Deeter, Jasper 1893-1972 *BiE&WWA, NotNAT B*
Deeter, Jasper 1895-1972 *WhScrn 2*
Deevy, Teresa d1963 *NotNAT B*
DeFas, Boris *Film 2*
DeFast, Boris *Film 2*
DeFelice, Alfredo *Film 2*
DeFeraudy, Maurice *Film 2*
DeFeraudy, Maurice d1873 *NotNAT B*
DeFeraudy, Maurice 1859-1932 *WhScrn 2*
DeFilippi, Amedeo 1900- *AmSCAP 1966*
DeFilippo, Eduardo 1900- *CnMD, CnThe, CroCD, McGWD, ModWD, OxThe, REnWD, WorEnF*
DeFilippo, Peppino 1903- *OxThe*
DeFilippo, Titina 1898-1963 *OxThe*
DeFillippo, Eduardo 1900- *FilmgC*
DeFlers, Robert d1927 *NotNAT B*
DeFoe, Annette 1889-1960 *Film 2, WhScrn 2, WhoHol B*
Defoe, Daniel 1660?-1731 *FilmgC*
DeFoe, Louis Vincent 1869-1922 *NotNAT B, WhThe*
DeFontenoy, Diane 1878- *WhThe*
DeFoor, John W 1929- *AmSCAP 1966*

DeFore, Don *MotPP, WhoHol A*
DeFore, Don 1916- *BiE&WWA, NotNAT*
Defore, Don 1917- *FilmgC, MovMk*
DeForest, Charles 1928- *AmSCAP 1966*
DeForest, Hal 1862-1938 *WhScrn 1, WhScrn 2, WhoHol B*
DeForest, Lee 1873-1961 *FilmgC, NewYTET, WorEnF*
DeForest, Marian d1935 *NotNAT B*
DeFrancesco, Louis E 1888- *AmSCAP 1966*
DeFranco, Boniface 1923- *AmSCAP 1966*
DeFrece, Lady 1864-1952 *NotNAT A*
DeFrece, Lauri 1880-1921 *WhThe*
DeFrece, Walter 1870- *WhThe*
Defresne, August 1893- *CnMD*
DeFunes, Louis 1908- *FilmgC*
DeFunes, Louis 1914- *WorEnF*
DeGaetani, Thomas 1929- *BiE&WWA*
DeGaetano, Michael A 1939- *IntMPA 1977*
DeGarde, Adele *Film 1, TwYS*
DeGastyne, Serge 1930- *AmSCAP 1966*
Degelin, Emile 1926- *DcFM*
Degener, Claire S 1928- *BiE&WWA*
DeGeorge, Carleton *Film 2*
Degermark, Pia *WhoHol A*
DeGivray, Claude 1933- *WorEnF*
DeGraff, Robert 1909- *AmSCAP 1966*
DeGraft, Joe *ConDr 1977*
DeGrasse, Joseph 1873-1940 *TwYS A, WhScrn 1, WhScrn 2, WhoHol B, WomWMM*
DeGrasse, Robert 1900-1971 *FilmgC*
DeGrasse, Sam 1875-1953 *Film 1, Film 2, MotPP, NotNAT B, TwYS, WhScrn 1, WhScrn 2, WhoHol B*
DeGravonne, Gabriel *Film 2*
DeGray, Sidney *Film 1*
DeGray, Sydney *Film 2*
DeGresac, Fred d1943 *NotNAT B*
DeGroff, Etta *Film 1*
DeGroot, Walter 1896- *WhThe*
DeGrunwald, Anatole 1910-1967 *FilmgC, WorEnF*
DeGrunwald, Dimitri *IntMPA 1977*
DeGrunwald, Dmitri 1913?- *FilmgC*
DeGuingand, Pierre d1964 *Film 2, WhScrn 2*
DeHaas, Max 1903- *DcFM*
DeHartog, Jan 1914- *BiE&WWA, CnMD, NotNAT*
DeHaven, Carter *Film 1, Film 2, IntMPA 1977, TwYS*
DeHaven, Mrs. Carter 1883-1950 *Film 1, Film 2, TwYS, WhScrn 2, WhoHol B*
DeHaven, Flora 1883-1950 *WhScrn 2*
DeHaven, Gloria *MotPP, WhoHol A*
DeHaven, Gloria 1924- *MGM, MovMk*
DeHaven, Gloria 1925- *BiE&WWA, FilmgC*
DeHavilland, Olivia 1916- *BiDFlm, BiE&WWA, CelR 3, CmMov, FilmgC, IntMPA 1977, MotPP, MovMk, OxFilm, ThFT, WhoHol A, WorEnF*
DeHedemann, Baroness *Film 2*
Dehelly, Emile 1871- *WhThe*
DeHirsch, Storm *WomWMM A, WomWMM B*
Dehn, Dorothy *Film 2*
Dehn, Paul 1912-1976 *FilmgC, IntMPA 1977, OxFilm, WhoThe 16*
Dehner, John 1915- *CmMov, FilmgC*
Dehni, Salah 1929- *DcFM*
Deighton, Len 1929- *IntMPA 1977*
Deighton, Marga Ann d1971 *WhScrn 2*
Dein, Edward *IntMPA 1977*
Deitch, Donna *WomWMM B*
Deitch, Hyman 1914- *AmSCAP 1966*
Deitrich, Angela *WomWMM B*
DeJardins, Silvoin *Film 1*

Dejazet, Pauline-Virginie 1798-1875 *NotNAT B, OxThe*
DeKeczer, Irma *Film 2*
DeKerekjarto, Duci 1901-1962 *WhScrn 1, WhScrn 2, WhoHol B*
Dekeukeleire, Charles 1905- *DcFM*
DeKirby, Annette *Film 2*
DeKirby, Ivar *Film 2*
Dekker, Albert d1968 *MotPP, WhoHol B*
Dekker, Albert 1900-1968 *Vers B*
Dekker, Albert 1904-1968 *WhScrn 1, WhScrn 2*
Dekker, Albert 1905-1968 *BiE&WWA, FilmgC, MovMk, NotNAT B, WhThe*
Dekker, Maurits Rudolph Joell 1896-1962 *CnMD*
Dekker, Thomas 1570-1632? *NotNAT A*
Dekker, Thomas 1570?-1641? *NotNAT B*
Dekker, Thomas 1572?-1632? *CnThe, McGWD, OxThe, PIP&P, REnWD*
DeKnight, Fannie Belle *Film 2*
DeKnight, Jimmy *AmSCAP 1966*
DeKock, Hubert 1863-1941 *WhScrn 1, WhScrn 2*
DeKooning, Willem 1904- *CelR 3*
DeKova, Frank *WhoHol A*
DeKoven, Henry Louis Reginald 1859-1920 *NotNAT B*
DeKoven, Reginald 1859-1920 *AmSCAP 1966, NewMT, PIP&P, WhThe, WhoStg 1906, WhoStg 1908*
DeKoven, Reginald 1861-1920 *EncMT*
DeKoven, Roger 1907- *BiE&WWA, NotNAT*
DeKowa, Viktor 1904-1973 *WhScrn 2*
DeKruif, Paul 1890- *BiE&WWA*
DeLacey, Jack *Film 2*
DeLacey, Philippe 1917- *WhoHol A*
DeLacey, Phillipe 1917- *TwYS*
DeLacey, Robert *TwYS A*
Delacorte, George 1894- *CelR 3*
DeLaCruz, Joe 1892-1961 *WhScrn 2*
DeLaCruze, Jimmy *Film 2*
DeLacy, Philippe 1917- *Film 2, MotPP*
DeLacy, Phillipe 1917- *Film 2*
Delafield, E M 1890-1943 *NotNAT B, WhThe*
DeLaHaye, Ina 1906- *WhThe*
Delair, Paul d1894 *NotNAT B*
Delair, Suzy 1916- *FilmgC, WhoHol A*
Delamare, Gil d1966 *WhScrn 1, WhScrn 2*
DeLamarter, Eric 1880-1953 *AmSCAP 1966*
DeLaMothe, Leon 1880-1943 *Film 1, WhScrn 1, WhScrn 2*
DeLaMotte, Marguerite d1950 *MotPP, WhoHol B*
DeLaMotte, Marguerite 1902-1950 *NotNAT B, TwYS*
DeLaMotte, Marguerite 1903-1950 *Film 1, Film 2, FilmgC*
DeLaMotte, Marguriete 1902-1950 *WhScrn 1, WhScrn 2*
Delancy, Henriette *Film 2*
DeLanda, Juan 1894-1968 *WhScrn 1, WhScrn 2, WhoHol B*
Delane *PIP&P*
DeLane Lea, Jacques 1931- *IntMPA 1977*
DeLane Lea, William 1900-1964 *FilmgC*
Delaney, Charles 1892-1959 *Film 2, NotNAT B, TwYS, WhScrn 1, WhScrn 2, WhoHol B*
Delaney, Charles 1925- *AmSCAP 1966*
Delaney, Iria *Film 2*
Delaney, Jere A 1888-1954 *Film 2, WhScrn 1, WhScrn 2, WhoHol B*
Delaney, Jerry *Film 1*
Delaney, Leo 1885-1920 *Film 1, WhScrn 2*
Delaney, Maureen 1888-1961 *NotNAT B, WhScrn 1, WhScrn 2, WhoHol B*
Delaney, Shelagh 1939- *BiE&WWA, CnMD,*

ConDr 1977, CroCD, McGWD, ModWD,
NotNAT, PIP&P, WhoThe 16
DeLange, Eddie 1904-1949 WhScrn 1, WhScrn 2
DeLange, Edgar 1904-1949 AmSCAP 1966
DeLange, Herman 1851-1929 NotNAT B, WhThe
Delannoy, Henriette Film 2
Delannoy, Jean 1908- DcFM, FilmgC,
IntMPA 1977, WorEnF
Delano, Clothilde Film 2
Delano, Gwen 1882-1954 WhScrn 1, WhScrn 2
Delano, James Film 1
Delanoy, Edmond d1888 NotNAT B
DeLanti, Stella Film 2
DeLaParelle, Marion Film 1
DeLaPasture, Mrs. Henry 1866-1945 NotNAT B,
WhThe
DeLaPatelliere, Denys 1921- FilmgC, WorEnF
Delaplane, Stan 1907- CelR 3
DeLappe, Gemze 1922- BiE&WWA, NotNAT
DeLaRenta, Oscar 1932- CelR 3
Delaro, Hattie Film 1, Film 2
DeLaRoche, Mazo 1879-1961 NotNAT B
DeLaroux, Hugues d1925 NotNAT B
Delarue, Allison NotNAT
DeLaTour, Frances 1944- WhoThe 16
Delaunay, Louis 1854- WhThe
Delaunay, Louis-Arsene 1826-1903 OxThe
Delauney, Louis-Arsene 1826-1903 NotNAT B
DeLaurentiis, Dino 1919- BiDFlm, CmMov,
DcFM, FilmgC, IntMPA 1977, OxFilm,
WorEnF
DeLavallade, Carmen 1931- BiE&WWA,
NotNAT
DeLaVarre, Andre, Jr. 1934- IntMPA 1977
DeLaVega, Alfredo Gomez 1897-1958 WhScrn 1,
WhScrn 2
Delavigne, Casimir 1793-1843 McGWD
Delavigne, Germain d1868 NotNAT B
Delavigne, Jean Francois Casimir 1793-1843
NotNAT B
Delavrancea, Barbu 1858-1918 McGWD
DeLay, Mel 1900-1947 WhScrn 1, WhScrn 2
DeLay, Peggy WomWMM B
DelCampo, Santiago d1963 NotNAT B
Delderfield, R F 1912- WhThe
DeLeath, Vaughn 1896-1943 AmSCAP 1966
DeLegh, Kitty 1887- WhThe
DeLeon, Aristides 1904-1954 WhScrn 1,
WhScrn 2
DeLeon, Don Pedro Film 2
DeLeon, Jack 1897-1956 NotNAT B, WhThe
DeLeon, Millie d1922 NotNAT B
DeLeon, Raoul 1905-1972 WhScrn 2, WhoHol B
DeLeon, Robert 1904-1961 AmSCAP 1966
DeLeone, Francesco Bartolomeo 1887-1948
AmSCAP 1966
Delerue, Georges 1924- FilmgC, IntMPA 1977,
OxFilm
Delerue, Georges 1925- DcFM, WorEnF
DeLetraz, Jean d1954 NotNAT B
Delevanti, Cyril 1887-1975 FilmgC, WhScrn 2,
WhoHol C
Delevines, The WhThe
Delf, Harry 1892-1964 AmSCAP 1966,
NotNAT B
Delfont, Bernard 1909- BiE&WWA, EncMT,
IntMPA 1977, WhoThe 16
Delgado, Maria 1906-1969 WhScrn 2, WhoHol B
Delgado, Ramon 1937- NatPD
Delgado, Roger 1920-1973 WhScrn 2
DelGiudice, Filippo 1892-1961 FilmgC, OxFilm,
WorEnF
DeLiagre, Alfred, Jr. 1904- BiE&WWA,
NotNAT, WhoThe 16

Deliane, Helen Film 1
Delight, June 1898-1975 WhScrn 2, WhoHol C
DeLiguoro, Countess Eugenio Film 2
DeLiguoro, Rina 1893-1966 Film 2, WhScrn 1,
WhScrn 2, WhoHol B
DeLimur, Jean Film 2
Delinsky, Victor A 1883-1951 WhScrn 1,
WhScrn 2
Dell, Claudia 1910- ThFT
Dell, Dorothy 1915-1934 ThFT, WhScrn 1,
WhScrn 2, WhoHol B
Dell, Floyd 1887-1969 NotNAT B, PIP&P,
WhThe
Dell, Gabriel 1919- NotNAT
Dell, Gabriel 1921- WhoHol A
Dell, Gabriel 1923- WhoThe 16
Dell, Jeffrey 1899- WhThe
Dell, Jeffrey 1904- FilmgC
Dell, Myrna WhoHol A
Della-Chiesa, Vivienne IntMPA 1977
Della-Cioppa, Guy NewYTET
Della Femina, Jerry 1936- CelR 3
DellaPorta, Giambattista 1535-1615 McGWD
DellaPorta, Giambattista 1538-1613 OxThe
Dellaripa, Dominic J 1921- AmSCAP 1966
DellaValle, Federico 1560?-1628 McGWD
Dello Joio, Norman 1913- CelR 3
Dell'olio, Anselma WomWMM B
Delluc, Louis 1890-1924 DcFM, OxFilm,
WorEnF
Delluc, Louis 1892-1924 FilmgC
Delmaine, Barry IntMPA 1977
DelMar, Claire 1901-1959 WhScrn 1, WhScrn 2,
WhoHol B
Delmar, Dezso 1891- AmSCAP 1966
Delmar, Eddie 1886-1944 WhScrn 1, WhScrn 2
Delmar, Herbert Film 1
Delmar, Kenny WhoHol A
Delmar, Thomas Film 2
Delmar, Vina WomWMM
Delmas, Suzanne Film 2
Delmonte, Jack 1889-1973 WhScrn 2
DelMonte, Louis J 1912- AmSCAP 1966
Delmore, Ralph d1923 NotNAT B, WhoStg 1908
Delon, Alain 1935- BiDFlm, CelR 3, FilmgC,
IntMPA 1977, MotPP, MovMk, OxFilm,
WhoHol A, WorEnF
Delon, Nathalie WhoHol A
Delores, Jean Film 2
DeLorez, Claire Film 2
Delorme, Daniele 1926- FilmgC, OxFilm,
WhoHol A
Delorme, Hugues WhThe
DeLory, Alfred V 1930- AmSCAP 1966
DeLoutherbourg, Philip James 1740-1812 OxThe,
PIP&P
DeLoutherbourg, Philippe Jacques 1740-1812
NotNAT B
Delphin 1882-1938 OxFilm, WhScrn 2
Delpini OxThe
Delpini, Carlo d1828 NotNAT B
DelRey, Pilar WhoHol A
DelRio, Dolores Film 2, MotPP
DelRio, Dolores 1904- ThFT
DelRio, Dolores 1905- BiDFlm, CelR 3, Film 1,
FilmgC, IntMPA 1977, MovMk, OxFilm,
TwYS, WhoHol A, WorEnF
Delroy, Irene 1898- EncMT, WhThe
DelRuth, Hampton 1888- TwYS A
DelRuth, Roy 1895-1961 BiDFlm, CmMov,
FilmgC, MovMk, TwYS A, WorEnF
Delsarte, Francois 1811-1871 NotNAT A, PIP&P
Delschaft, Mady Film 2
Delsol, Paule WomWMM

Delson, Sue *WomWMM B*
Deluc, Germaine *WomWMM B*
DeLuce, Virginia 1921- *BiE&WWA, NotNAT, WhoHol A*
Delugg, Anne Renfer 1922- *AmSCAP 1966*
Delugg, Milton 1918- *AmSCAP 1966*
DeLuise, Dom *IntMPA 1977, WhoHol A*
DeLungo, Tony 1892- *Film 2, WhThe*
DeLussan, Zelie d1949 *NotNAT B, WhoStg 1908*
Delvair, Jeanne *Film 1*
DelVal, Jean 1892-1975 *Film 2, WhScrn 2, WhoHol C*
DelValle, Jaime 1910- *IntMPA 1977*
DelValle, John 1904- *IntMPA 1977*
DelValle, Luis Cotto *WhScrn 1, WhScrn 2*
Delvaux, Andre 1926- *BiDFlm, FilmgC, WorEnF*
DelVicario, Silvio P 1921- *AmSCAP 1966*
Delysia, Alice 1888- *EncMT*
Delysia, Alice 1889- *CnThe, OxThe, WhThe*
DeMadina, Francisco 1907- *AmSCAP 1966*
DeMain, Gordon 1897-1967 *Film 2, WhScrn 2*
DeMar, Carrie d1963 *NotNAT B*
DeMarco, Norman 1910- *BiE&WWA*
DeMarco, Tony 1898-1965 *WhScrn 1, WhScrn 2, WhoHol B*
Demare, Lucas 1910- *DcFM*
DeMare, Rolf *Film 2*
Demarest, Drew *Film 2*
Demarest, Rube 1886-1962 *WhoHol B*
Demarest, Rubin 1886-1962 *NotNAT B, WhScrn 1, WhScrn 2*
Demarest, William 1892- *Film 2, FilmgC, IntMPA 1977, MotPP, MovMk, TwYS, Vers A, WhoHol A*
DeMarney, Derrick 1906- *FilmgC, IntMPA 1977, WhThe, WhoHol A*
DeMarney, Terence 1909-1971 *FilmgC, WhThe, WhoHol B*
DeMarney, Terrence 1909-1971 *WhScrn 1, WhScrn 2*
DeMarthold, Jules d1927 *NotNAT B*
DeMartin, Imelda 1936- *BiE&WWA*
DeMasi, Joseph 1904- *AmSCAP 1966*
DeMasi, Joseph Anthony 1935- *AmSCAP 1966*
DeMatteo, Donna 1941- *NatPD*
DeMaupassant, Guy 1850-1893 *FilmgC*
DeMave, Jack *WhoHol A*
DeMax, Edouard d1924 *Film 2, NotNAT B*
Dembo, Joseph T *NewYTET*
Demby, Emanuel H 1919- *IntMPA 1977*
Demby, Jill *WomWMM B*
DeMendoza, Carlo *Film 2*
DeMendoza, Fernando Diaz d1930 *NotNAT B*
Demeny, Georges 1850-1917 *OxFilm*
Demetrakas, Johanna *WomWMM A, WomWMM B*
Demick, Irina 1937- *FilmgC, WhoHol A*
Demidoff, Madame *Film 1*
DeMille, Agnes *BiE&WWA, NotNAT*
DeMille, Agnes 1905- *CelR 3, EncMT, WhoThe 16*
DeMille, Agnes 1908- *NotNAT A*
DeMille, Beatrice M d1923 *NotNAT B*
DeMille, Cecelia *Film 1*
DeMille, Mrs. Cecil d1960 *NotNAT B*
DeMille, Cecil B 1881-1959 *BiDFlm, CmMov, DcFM, FilmgC, MovMk, NotNAT B, OxFilm, TwYS A, WhScrn 1, WhScrn 2, WhThe, WhoHol B, WomWMM, WorEnF*
DeMille, Henry C 1850-1893 *NotNAT B, PIP&P*
DeMille, Katherine 1911- *FilmgC, ThFT, WhoHol A*
DeMille, William C 1878-1955 *DcFM, FilmgC,*

NotNAT B, TwYS A, WhScrn 1, WhScrn 2, WhThe, WhoHol B
Deming, Walter *Film 2*
Deming, Will d1926 *NotNAT B*
DeMinil, Renee d1941 *NotNAT B*
Demming, Lanson F 1902- *AmSCAP 1966*
DeMol, Francoise *WomWMM*
Demongeot, Mylene 1936- *FilmgC, MotPP, WhoHol A*
DeMontherlant, Henry 1896- *WhThe*
DeMoore, Harry *Film 1*
Demoss, Lyle *IntMPA 1977*
DeMott, John A 1912-1975 *WhScrn 2, WhoHol C*
Dempsey, Clifford 1865-1938 *Film 2, NotNAT B, WhScrn 1, WhScrn 2, WhoHol B*
Dempsey, Jack 1895- *CelR 3, Film 2, WhoHol A*
Dempsey, James E 1876-1918 *AmSCAP 1966*
Dempsey, Thomas 1862-1947 *WhScrn 1, WhScrn 2, WhoHol B*
Dempster, Austin *FilmgC*
Dempster, Carol *MotPP*
Dempster, Carol 1901- *FilmgC*
Dempster, Carol 1902- *Film 1, Film 2, TwYS, WhoHol A*
Dempster, Hugh 1900- *WhThe, WhoHol A*
Demy, Jacques 1931- *BiDFlm, DcFM, FilmgC, MovMk, OxFilm, WorEnF*
DeNaut, George Matthews 1915- *AmSCAP 1966*
Dench, Judi 1934- *FilmgC, IntMPA 1977, WhoThe 16*
Dench, Judi 1935- *CnThe*
Deneau, Sidney G *IntMPA 1977*
DeNeergaard, Beatrice 1908- *BiE&WWA*
DeNeergaard, Virginia *AmSCAP 1966*
Denenholz, Reginald 1913- *BiE&WWA*
Denes, Oscar 1893- *WhThe*
Deneuve, Catherine *MotPP, WhoHol A*
Deneuve, Catherine 1943- *BiDFlm, CelR 3, FilmgC, MovMk, OxFilm, WorEnF*
Deneuve, Catherine 1945- *IntMPA 1977*
Denham, Isolde 1920- *WhThe*
Denham, Maurice 1909- *FilmgC, IntMPA 1977, WhoHol A, WhoThe 16*
Denham, Reginald 1894- *BiE&WWA, NotNAT, WhoThe 16*
Denim, Kate d1907 *NotNAT B*
DeNiro, Robert *WhoHol A*
DeNiro, Robert 1943- *MovMk*
DeNiro, Robert 1945- *IntMPA 1977*
Denis, Michaela *WomWMM*
Denison, Merrill 1893- *McGWD, REnWD*
Denison, Michael 1915- *FilmgC, IntMPA 1977, WhoHol A, WhoThe 16*
Denker, Henry 1912- *BiE&WWA, CnMD Sup, NotNAT*
Denmark, L Kirk 1916- *BiE&WWA, NotNAT*
Denner, Charles 1933?- *FilmgC*
D'Ennery, Adolphe Eugene Philippe 1811-1899 *NotNAT B*
D'Ennery, Guy *Film 2*
Dennes, Eileen *Film 2*
Denni, Gwynne 1882-1949 *AmSCAP 1966*
Denni, Lucien 1886-1947 *AmSCAP 1966*
Denniker, Paul 1897- *AmSCAP 1966*
Denning, Frank 1909- *AmSCAP 1966*
Denning, Richard 1914- *FilmgC, MotPP, MovMk, WhoHol A*
Denning, Wade F, Jr. 1922- *AmSCAP 1966*
Denning, Will H d1926 *NotNAT B*
Dennis, Crystal 1893-1973 *WhScrn 2, WhoHol B*
Dennis, Danny *WhoHol A*
Dennis, Eddie *Film 2*

Dennis, Ginny Maxey 1923- *AmSCAP 1966*
Dennis, John *WhoHol A*
Dennis, John 1657-1734 *NotNAT B*
Dennis, Matt 1914- *AmSCAP 1966*
Dennis, Nick *WhoHol A*
Dennis, Nigel 1912- *CnMD, CnThe, ConDr 1977, CroCD, ModWD*
Dennis, Russell 1916-1964 *NotNAT B, WhScrn 1, WhScrn 2, WhoHol B*
Dennis, Ruth *Film 1*
Dennis, Sandy 1937- *BiE&WWA, CelR 3, FilmgC, IntMPA 1977, MotPP, MovMk, NotNAT, WhoHol A, WhoThe 16*
Dennis, Will d1914 *NotNAT B*
Dennison, Eva *Film 2*
Dennison, Frank d1964 *NotNAT B*
Denniston, Reynolds 1881-1943 *NotNAT B, WhScrn 2*
Denny, Charles R, Jr. *NewYTET*
Denny, Ernest 1869-1943 *NotNAT B, WhThe*
Denny, Ike *WhoHol A*
Denny, Malcolm *Film 2*
Denny, Martin 1911- *AmSCAP 1966*
Denny, Reginald 1891-1967 *BiE&WWA, Film 1, Film 2, FilmgC, MotPP, MovMk, NotNAT B, TwYS, Vers A, WhScrn 1, WhScrn 2, WhThe, WhoHol B*
Denny, William Henry Leigh 1853-1915 *NotNAT B, WhThe, WhoStg 1906, WhoStg 1908*
Denoff, Samuel 1928- *AmSCAP 1966*
Denola, Georges 1880?-1950 *DcFM*
DeNoon, David 1928- *AmSCAP 1966*
DeNormand, George *IntMPA 1977*
Densmore, John H 1880-1943 *AmSCAP 1966*
Dent, Alan 1905- *WhoThe 16*
Dent, Frederick B 1922- *CelR 3*
Dent, Vernon d1963 *Film 2, TwYS, WhoHol B*
Dent, Vernon 1894-1963 *FilmgC*
Dent, Vernon 1900-1963 *WhScrn 1, WhScrn 2*
Denton, Crahan 1914-1966 *BiE&WWA, NotNAT, WhScrn 1, WhScrn 2, WhoHol B*
Denton, Frank 1878-1945 *NotNAT B, WhThe*
Denton, George 1865-1918 *WhScrn 2*
Denver, Bob 1935- *FilmgC, WhoHol A*
Denville, Alfred 1876-1955 *NotNAT B, WhThe*
DePackh, Maurice 1896-1960 *AmSCAP 1966*
DePalma, Brian 1940- *IntMPA 1977*
DePalma, Brian 1944- *FilmgC*
DePalowski, Gaston *NotNAT B*
Depardieu, Gerard *WhoHol A*
DeParis, Wilbur 1901-1973 *WhScrn 2*
DePasquali, Bernice d1925 *NotNAT B*
DePasse, Suzanne *WomWMM*
DePaul, Gene 1919- *AmSCAP 1966, BiE&WWA*
DePaur, Leonard *AmSCAP 1966*
Depew, Joe *Film 2*
Depew, Joseph *Film 2*
Depew, Richard H 1925- *IntMPA 1977*
DePirro, Nicola 1898- *IntMPA 1977*
Depp, Harry 1886-1957 *Film 2, WhScrn 1, WhScrn 2, WhoHol B*
Deppe, Hans 1898-1969 *WhScrn 1, WhScrn 2*
Deppen, Jessie L 1881-1956 *AmSCAP 1966*
Depre, Ernest 1854- *WhThe*
DePue, Wallace Earl 1932- *AmSCAP 1966*
DePutti, Lya d1932 *WhoHol B*
DePutti, Lya 1901-1931 *FilmgC, WhScrn 1, WhScrn 2*
DePutti, Lya 1904-1931 *Film 2, TwYS*
DerAbrahamian, Arousiak *WhScrn 2*
Derain, Lucy *WomWMM*
DeRamey, Pierre *Film 2*
DeRavenne, Caroline Marie 1883-1962 *WhScrn 2,*

WhoHol B
DeRavenne, Charles *Film 2*
DeRavenne, Raymond 1904-1950 *WhScrn 1, WhScrn 2*
Deray, Jacques 1929- *FilmgC, WorEnF*
Derba, Mimi 1894-1953 *WhScrn 1, WhScrn 2*
DeReeder, Pierre 1887-1966 *AmSCAP 1966*
Derek, John 1926- *CmMov, FilmgC, MotPP, MovMk, WhoHol A, WorEnF*
DeRemer, Ruby *Film 1, Film 2, TwYS*
Deren, Maya 1908-1961 *DcFM, OxFilm, WhScrn 2, WomWMM, WorEnF*
DeReyes, Consuelo 1893-1948 *NotNAT B, WhThe*
DeRienzo, Silvio 1909- *AmSCAP 1966*
Derigney, Louise *Film 2*
DeRiso, Camillo *Film 2*
DeRita, Joe *MotPP, WhoHol A*
Dern, Bruce *WhoHol A*
Dern, Bruce 1936- *FilmgC*
Dern, Bruce 1937- *IntMPA 1977*
DeRobertis, Francesco 1902-1959 *DcFM, OxFilm*
DeRobertis, Francesco 1903-1959 *WorEnF*
DeRoche, Charles 1880-1952 *Film 1, Film 2, MotPP, TwYS, WhScrn 1, WhScrn 2, WhoHol B*
DeRochemont, Louis 1899- *DcFM, FilmgC, IntMPA 1977, OxFilm, WorEnF*
DeRochemont, Richard *IntMPA 1977*
DeRocher, L E 1912- *BiE&WWA*
DeRosa, A *Film 2*
DeRosa, Carmella Millie 1914- *AmSCAP 1966*
DeRosas, Enrique d1948 *WhScrn 1, WhScrn 2*
DeRose, Peter 1896-1953 *NotNAT B*
DeRose, Peter 1900-1953 *AmSCAP 1966*
DeRoy, Harry *Film 1*
Derr, Richard 1917- *BiE&WWA, FilmgC, NotNAT, WhThe, WhoHol A*
Derrick, Samuel d1769 *NotNAT B*
DeRue, Baby *Film 1*
DeRuiz, Nick F *Film 2*
Dervis, Charles *Film 2*
Derwent, Clarence 1884-1959 *NotNAT A, NotNAT B, OxThe, WhScrn 1, WhScrn 2, WhThe, WhoHol B*
Derwent, Elfrida d1958 *NotNAT B*
Dery, Tibor 1894- *CroCD*
DeSai, V H d1950? *WhScrn 2*
Desailly, Jean 1920- *FilmgC, WorEnF*
DeSales, Francis *WhoHol A*
DeSanctis, Alfredo *WhThe*
DeSantis, Emidio 1893- *AmSCAP 1966*
DeSantis, Giuseppe 1917- *DcFM, FilmgC, IntMPA 1977, OxFilm, WorEnF*
DeSantis, Joe 1909- *FilmgC, NotNAT, Vers A, WhoHol A*
DeSarigny, Peter 1911- *FilmgC*
DesAutels, Van 1911-1968 *WhScrn 1, WhScrn 2, WhoHol B*
Desbiens, Francine *WomWMM*
Desborough, Philip 1883- *WhThe*
Descaves, Lucien 1861-1949 *McGWD, WhThe*
DeSchaap, Philip 1911- *IntMPA 1977*
Desclee, Aimee-Olympe 1836-1874 *NotNAT B, OxThe*
Desclos, Jeanne *Film 2*
DeSegurola, Andre 1875-1953 *Film 2*
DeSegurola, Andreas 1875-1953 *WhScrn 1, WhScrn 2*
DeSegurola, Andres 1875-1953 *TwYS, WhoHol B*
Deseine, Mademoiselle d1759 *NotNAT B, OxThe*
DeSelincourt, Hugh 1878-1951 *NotNAT B, WhThe*
Deses, Greta *WomWMM*

DeSeta, Vittorio 1923- *DcFM, FilmgC, OxFilm, WorEnF*
Desfis, Angelo 1888-1950 *WhScrn 1, WhScrn 2*
Desfontaines, Henri 1876- *WhThe*
Deshayes, Paul d1891 *NotNAT B*
Deshon, Florence *Film 2*
Deshon, Florence 1894-1922 *WhScrn 2*
Deshon, Florence 1898?- *WhoHol B*
DeSica, Vittorio 1901-1974 *OxFilm, WhScrn 2*
DeSica, Vittorio 1902-1974 *BiDFlm, CelR 3, DcFM, FilmgC, MovMk, WhoHol B, WorEnF*
DeSilva, David 1936- *BiE&WWA*
DeSilva, Frank 1890-1968 *NotNAT B, WhScrn 1, WhScrn 2*
DeSilva, Fred *Film 2*
DeSilva, N 1868-1949 *WhThe*
DeSilva, Nina 1868-1949 *NotNAT B*
Desjardins, Marie-Catherine-Hortense 1632-1683 *NotNAT B, OxThe*
Desjardins, Maxime *WhThe*
Desjardins, Maxine *Film 2*
Deslaw, Eugene 1900- *DcFM*
Deslys, Gaby 1884-1920 *Film 1, NotNAT B, OxThe, WhScrn 1, WhScrn 2, WhThe, WhoHol B*
Deslys, Kay *Film 2*
Desmares, Charlotte 1682-1753 *OxThe*
Desmares, Nicolas 1645?-1714 *OxThe*
Desmarets DeSaint-Sorlin, Jean 1595-1676 *CnThe, REnWD*
Desmaretz DeSaint-Sorlin, Jean 1595-1676 *McGWD, OxThe*
Desmond, Dagmar *Film 2*
Desmond, Eric *Film 1*
Desmond, Ethel 1874-1949 *WhScrn 1, WhScrn 2*
Desmond, Florence *WhoHol A*
Desmond, Florence 1905- *FilmgC, NotNAT A, WhThe*
Desmond, Florence 1907- *EncMT*
Desmond, Johnny *WhoHol A*
Desmond, Johnny 1923- *IntMPA 1977*
Desmond, Johnny 1925- *AmSCAP 1966*
Desmond, Lucille 1894-1936 *WhScrn 1, WhScrn 2*
Desmond, William 1878-1949 *Film 1, Film 2, FilmgC, MotPP, NotNAT B, TwYS, WhScrn 1, WhScrn 2, WhoHol B*
Desmonde, Jerry 1908-1967 *FilmgC, WhScrn 1, WhScrn 2, WhoHol B*
Desni, Tamara 1913- *FilmgC, WhoHol A*
Desni, Xenia *Film 2*
Desny, Ivan 1922- *FilmgC, WhoHol A*
Desoeillets, Mademoiselle 1621-1670 *OxThe*
DeSolla, Rachel d1920 *NotNAT B*
DeSoto, Henry 1888-1963 *WhScrn 2*
DeSousa, May 1882-1948 *NotNAT B*
DeSousa, May 1887-1948 *WhThe*
DeSouza, Edward 1933- *FilmgC*
Despo *WhoHol A*
Despres, Suzanne 1875-1951 *NotNAT B, WhThe, WhoHol B*
Desprez, Frank 1853-1916 *NotNAT B, WhThe*
DeStafini, Helen 1880-1938 *WhScrn 1, WhScrn 2*
Deste, Luli 1902-1951 *WhScrn 1, WhScrn 2, WhoHol B*
D'Esterre, Madame *Film 2*
Destinn, Emmy 1878-1930 *WhScrn 2*
Destouches 1680-1754 *REnWD*
Destouches, Philippe Nericault 1680-1754 *CnThe, McGWD, NotNAT B, OxThe*
DesUrlis *OxThe*
Desvallieres, Maurice 1857-1926 *NotNAT B, WhThe*

DeSylva, B G 1895-1950 *AmSCAP 1966, EncMT, WhThe*
DeSylva, B G 1896-1950 *NotNAT B*
DeSylva, Brown, And Henderson *NewMT*
DeTellier, Mariette 1891-1957 *WhScrn 1, WhScrn 2, WhoHol B*
DeTitta, Arthur A 1904- *IntMPA 1977*
DeTolly, Deena d1976 *WhoHol C*
DeToth, Andre *IntMPA 1977*
DeToth, Andre 1900- *CmMov, MovMk*
DeToth, Andre 1910- *WorEnF*
DeToth, Andre 1912- *FilmgC*
DeToth, Andre 1913- *BiDFlm*
Detoy, Charles 1897- *BiE&WWA*
Dett, Robert Nathaniel 1882-1943 *AmSCAP 1966*
Dettmer, Roger 1927- *BiE&WWA, NotNAT*
Deutsch, Adolph 1890- *IntMPA 1977*
Deutsch, Adolph 1897- *AmSCAP 1966*
Deutsch, Armand S 1913- *BiE&WWA, IntMPA 1977*
Deutsch, Benoit-Leon 1892- *WhThe*
Deutsch, David 1926- *FilmgC, IntMPA 1977*
Deutsch, Emery 1907- *AmSCAP 1966*
Deutsch, Ernest 1891-1969 *WhoHol B*
Deutsch, Ernst 1891-1969 *Film 2, WhScrn 1, WhScrn 2*
Deutsch, Gregory Paul 1952- *AmSCAP 1966*
Deutsch, Helen *AmSCAP 1966, IntMPA 1977, WomWMM*
Deutsch, Lou 1898-1968 *WhScrn 2, WhoHol B*
DeVahl, Anders 1869- *WhThe*
Deval, Jacques d1972 *PlP&P*
Deval, Jacques 1890-1972 *BiE&WWA, ModWD, NotNAT B*
Deval, Jacques 1893-1972 *CnMD*
Deval, Jacques 1894-1972 *McGWD*
Deval, Jacques 1895-1972 *WhThe*
DeValasco, Mercedes *Film 2*
DeValdez, Carlos J 1894-1939 *WhScrn 1, WhScrn 2, WhoHol B*
DeValois, Ninette 1898- *PlP&P, WhThe*
Devane, William *WhoHol A*
Devant, David 1863- *WhThe*
DeVarney, Emil *Film 1*
DeVaull, Billie *Film 2*
DeVaull, William P 1871-1945 *Film 1, WhScrn 1, WhScrn 2, WhoHol B*
DeVeaux, Alexis 1948- *NatPD*
Dever, Joseph X 1919- *CelR 3*
DeVera, Cris 1925-1974 *WhScrn 2*
DeVerdier, Anton *Film 2*
Devere, Arthur 1883-1961 *WhScrn 1, WhScrn 2*
DeVere, Daisy *Film 1*
Devere, Francesca 1891-1952 *NotNAT B, WhoHol B*
Devere, Francesca Frisco 1891-1952 *WhScrn 1, WhScrn 2*
DeVere, George F d1910 *NotNAT B*
Devere, Harry *Film 2*
Devere, Margaret 1889-1918 *WhScrn 2*
Devereaux, Jack 1882-1958 *NotNAT B, WhScrn 1, WhScrn 2, WhoHol B*
Devereaux, Louise Drew d1954 *NotNAT B*
Deverell, John W 1880-1965 *WhScrn 2, WhThe*
Devereux, William d1945 *NotNAT B, WhThe*
DeVernon, Frank 1845-1923 *WhScrn 1, WhScrn 2, WhoHol B*
DeVesa, Leonardo *Film 2*
DeVestel, Guy d1973 *WhScrn 2*
Devhrys, Rachel *Film 2*
Devi, Kamala *WhoHol A*
Devi, Prova d1952 *WhScrn 2*
Devi, Seeta *Film 2*
DeVilbiss, Robert *Film 2*

Deville, Michel 1931- *BiDFlm, DcFM, FilmgC, WorEnF*
DeVilliers *OxThe*
Devine, Andy 1905- *CmMov, Film 2, FilmgC, IntMPA 1977, MotPP, MovMk, OxFilm, TwYS, WhoHol A*
Devine, George 1901-1966 *CnThe*
Devine, George 1910-1965 *OxThe, PIP&P*
Devine, George 1910-1966 *BiE&WWA, CroCD, NotNAT B, WhScrn 2, WhThe*
Devine, Jerry *Film 2*
Devine, John *Film 2*
DeVine, Lawrence 1935- *NotNAT*
DeVinna, Clyde 1892-1953 *FilmgC*
DeVito, Albert 1919- *AmSCAP 1966*
Devlin, Bernadette 1947- *CelR 3*
Devlin, Joe A 1899-1973 *WhScrn 2, WhoHol B*
Devlin, William 1911- *WhThe*
Devoe, Bert 1884-1930 *WhScrn 1, WhScrn 2, WhoHol B*
DeVoght, Carl *Film 2*
DeVogt, Carl *Film 1*
DeVol, Frank 1911- *AmSCAP 1966*
DeVoll, Calvin Joseph 1886- *AmSCAP 1966*
Devon, Laura 1940- *FilmgC*
Devon, Richard *WhoHol A*
Devore, Dorothy 1901- *Film 1, Film 2, TwYS, WhoHol A*
Devore, Gaston 1859- *WhThe*
Devoyod, Suzanne *WomWMM*
Devrient, Eduard 1801-1877 *NotNAT B, OxThe*
Devrient, Emil 1803-1872 *NotNAT B, OxThe*
Devrient, Hans 1878-1927 *OxThe*
Devrient, Karl 1797-1872 *NotNAT B, OxThe*
Devrient, Ludwig 1784-1832 *CnThe, NotNAT B, OxThe*
Devrient, Max 1857-1929 *NotNAT B, OxThe*
Devrient, Otto 1838-1894 *NotNAT B, OxThe*
DeVries, Henri *Film 1*
DeVries, Henry *WhThe*
DeVries, John 1915- *AmSCAP 1966*
DeVries, Peter 1910- *BiE&WWA, CelR 3, NotNAT*
DeVry, William C 1908- *IntMPA 1977*
DeWarfaz, George 1889-1966 *WhThe*
Dewell, Michael 1931- *BiE&WWA, NotNAT, WhoThe 16*
Dewever, Jean 1927- *WorEnF*
Dewey, Arthur *Film 2*
Dewey, Earl S 1881-1950 *WhScrn 1, WhScrn 2, WhoHol B*
Dewey, Elmer 1884-1954 *WhScrn 1, WhScrn 2, WhoHol B*
Dewey, Priscilla B *NatPD*
Dewhurst, Coleen 1926- *CnThe*
Dewhurst, Colleen 1926- *BiE&WWA, CelR 3, MovMk, NotNAT, PIP&P A, WhoHol A, WhoThe 16*
Dewhurst, George *Film 1, Film 2*
Dewhurst, Jonathan d1913 *NotNAT B*
Dewhurst, Keith 1931- *ConDr 1977*
Dewhurst, William 1888-1937 *WhScrn 1, WhScrn 2, WhoHol B*
DeWild, Gene 1929- *BiE&WWA*
DeWilde, Brandon 1942-1972 *BiE&WWA, FilmgC, MotPP, MovMk, NotNAT B, OxFilm, WhScrn 2, WhoHol B*
DeWilde, Frederic 1914- *BiE&WWA*
DeWinton, Albert *Film 2*
DeWinton, Alice *WhThe*
DeWit, Jacqueline *WhoHol A*
DeWitt, Elizabeth *Film 1*
DeWitt, Fay 1935- *BiE&WWA, NotNAT*
DeWitt, Jennings *Film 2*

DeWitt, Johann *PIP&P*
DeWolfe, Billy d1974 *BiE&WWA, MotPP, WhoHol B*
DeWolfe, Billy 1905-1974 *Vers B*
DeWolfe, Billy 1907-1974 *FilmgC, HolP 40, MovMk, NotNAT B, WhScrn 2, WhThe*
DeWolfe, Elsie Anderson 1865-1950 *Film 2, NotNAT A, NotNAT B, WhThe, WhoStg 1906, WhoStg 1908*
Dews, Peter 1929- *NotNAT, WhoThe 16*
DeXandoval, Guerrero *Film 2*
Dexter, Alan *WhoHol A*
Dexter, Anthony 1919- *FilmgC, MotPP*
Dexter, Aubrey 1898-1958 *NotNAT B, WhThe, WhoHol B*
Dexter, Brad 1917- *WhoHol A*
Dexter, Brad 1922- *FilmgC*
Dexter, Elliot 1870-1941 *Film 1, NotNAT B*
Dexter, Elliott 1870-1941 *Film 2, TwYS, WhScrn 1, WhScrn 2, WhoHol B*
Dexter, John *PIP&P A, WhoThe 16*
Dexter, John 1925- *CnThe, NotNAT*
Dexter, John 1935- *FilmgC*
Dexter, Maury 1927- *FilmgC*
Dey, Larry 1910- *AmSCAP 1966*
Dey, Manju *WomWMM*
Dey, Susan *WhoHol A*
Deyers, Lien *Film 2*
DeYzarduy, Madame *Film 2*
Dezel, Albert 1900- *IntMPA 1977*
Dhelia, France d1964 *WhScrn 2*
Dhepley, Ruth *Film 2*
Dhery, Robert 1921- *BiE&WWA, FilmgC, NotNAT*
Dhiegh, Khigh *WhoHol A*
Dia, Dick 1917- *AmSCAP 1966*
Diaghileff, Serge 1872-1929 *WhThe*
Diaghilev, Serge 1872-1929 *OxThe*
Dial, Patterson *Film 2*
Diamant, Lincoln 1923- *IntMPA 1977*
Diamant-Berger, Henri 1895- *DcFM*
Diamante, Juan Bautista 1625-1687 *McGWD*
Diamond, Bernard 1918- *IntMPA 1977*
Diamond, David Leo 1915- *AmSCAP 1966*
Diamond, Don *WhoHol A*
Diamond, I A L *CmMov*
Diamond, I A L 1915- *FilmgC*
Diamond, I A L 1920- *IntMPA 1977, OxFilm, WorEnF*
Diamond, Leo *AmSCAP 1966*
Diamond, Leo G 1907- *AmSCAP 1966*
Diamond, Lillian d1962 *NotNAT B*
Diamond, Margaret 1916- *WhoThe 16*
Diamond, Neil 1941- *CelR 3*
Diamond, William d1812 *NotNAT B*
Diaz, Jorge 1930- *CroCD*
Diaz, Rudy *WhoHol A*
Dibdin, Charles 1745-1814 *NotNAT A, NotNAT B, OxThe*
Dibdin, Charles Isaac Mungo Pitt 1768-1833 *NotNAT A, NotNAT B, OxThe*
Dibdin, Thomas John Pitt 1771-1841 *NotNAT A, NotNAT B, OxThe, PIP&P*
DiBenedetta, Marie *Film 2*
Dibley, Mary *Film 2*
DiBonaventura, Sam 1923- *AmSCAP 1966*
Dicenta, Joaquin 1860- *WhThe*
Dicenta, Manuel 1904-1974 *WhScrn 2, WhoHol B*
Dicenta Y Benedicto, Joaquin 1863-1917 *McGWD*
Dichter, Ernest 1907- *CelR 3*
Dick, C S Cotsford d1911 *NotNAT B*
Dick, Dorothy 1900- *AmSCAP 1966*
Dick, Douglas 1920- *FilmgC, WhoHol A*

Dick, Marcel 1898- *AmSCAP 1966*
Dickens, C Stafford 1896-1967 *WhThe*
Dickens, Charles 1812-1870 *FilmgC, NotNAT B,*
  OxFilm, OxThe, PIP&P
Dickenson, Jennie *Film 1*
Dickenson, Margaret *WomWMM B*
Dickerson, Dudley d1968 *WhoHol B*
Dickerson, Henry 1906-1968 *WhScrn 2*
Dickerson, Milton *Film 2*
Dickey, James 1923- *CelR 3*
Dickey, Paul d1933 *Film 2, WhoHol B*
Dickey, Paul 1884-1933 *WhThe*
Dickey, Paul 1885-1933 *NotNAT B, WhScrn 1,*
  WhScrn 2
Dickinson, Angie *MotPP, WhoHol A*
Dickinson, Angie 1931- *BiDFlm, FilmgC,*
  WorEnF
Dickinson, Angie 1932- *CelR 3*
Dickinson, Angie 1936- *IntMPA 1977, MovMk*
Dickinson, Clarence 1873- *AmSCAP 1966*
Dickinson, Desmond 1902- *FilmgC,*
  IntMPA 1977
Dickinson, Genevieve 1909- *BiE&WWA,*
  NotNAT
Dickinson, Glen, Jr. 1914- *IntMPA 1977*
Dickinson, Hal 1914-1970 *WhScrn 2, WhoHol B*
Dickinson, Harold H, Jr. 1913- *AmSCAP 1966*
Dickinson, Helen Adell 1875-1957 *AmSCAP 1966*
Dickinson, Homer 1890-1959 *WhScrn 1,*
  WhScrn 2
Dickinson, June McWade 1924- *AmSCAP 1966*
Dickinson, Maggie d1949 *NotNAT B*
Dickinson, Milton *Film 2*
Dickinson, Robert Preston 1924- *IntMPA 1977*
Dickinson, Thorold 1903- *BiDFlm, DcFM,*
  FilmgC, IntMPA 1977, OxFilm, WorEnF
Dickison, Maria Bobrowska 1902- *AmSCAP 1966*
Dickson, Deborah *WomWMM B*
Dickson, Donald 1911-1972 *WhScrn 2*
Dickson, Dorothy 1896- *EncMT, WhThe*
Dickson, Dorothy 1900- *BiE&WWA, NotNAT*
Dickson, Dorothy 1902- *Film 1, Film 2, FilmgC,*
  WhoHol A
Dickson, Gloria d1945 *MotPP, NotNAT B,*
  WhoHol B
Dickson, Gloria 1916-1945 *WhScrn 1, WhScrn 2*
Dickson, Gloria 1917-1945 *ThFT*
Dickson, Lamont d1944 *NotNAT B, WhoHol B*
Dickson, LaRue 1901- *AmSCAP 1966*
Dickson, Lydia 1878-1928 *Film 2, NotNAT B,*
  WhScrn 1, WhScrn 2, WhoHol B
Dickson, Paul 1920- *FilmgC*
Dickson, William Kennedy Laurie 1860-1935
  Film 1, OxFilm, WorEnF
Dickson, William Kennedy Laurie 1860-1937
  DcFM
Diderot, Denis 1713-1784 *CnThe, McGWD,*
  NotNAT B, OxThe, REnWD
Didion, Joan *WomWMM*
Didrickson, Babe 1914-1956 *WhScrn 2*
Didring, Ernst 1868-1931 *NotNAT B, OxThe,*
  WhThe
Didway, Ernest 1872-1939 *WhScrn 1, WhScrn 2*
Die Asta *WhScrn 2*
Diebold, Jerome C 1909- *IntMPA 1977*
Diegelmann, Wilhelm *Film 1, Film 2*
Diehl, Karl Ludwig 1897-1958 *WhScrn 1,*
  WhScrn 2
Diemer, Emma Lou 1927- *AmSCAP 1966*
Diener, Joan 1934- *BiE&WWA, EncMT,*
  IntMPA 1977, NotNAT, WhoThe 16
Dieni, John 1924- *AmSCAP 1966*
Dieni, Joseph 1923- *AmSCAP 1966*
Dierkes, John 1908-1975 *FilmgC, WhScrn 2,*

WhoHol C
Dierkop, Charles *WhoHol A*
Dierlam, Robert J 1917- *BiE&WWA, NotNAT*
Diers, Hank 1931- *BiE&WWA, NotNAT*
Diesel, Gustav 1900-1948 *Film 2, WhScrn 1,*
  WhScrn 2
Diesel, Leota *BiE&WWA, NotNAT*
Diessl, Gustav 1900-1948 *WhoHol B*
Diestal, Edith *Film 1*
Dieterle, Eugene *Film 2*
Dieterle, Til *AmSCAP 1966*
Dieterle, Wilhelm 1893-1973 *BiDFlm*
Dieterle, William 1893- *DcFM, MovMk,*
  WorEnF
Dieterle, William 1893-1972 *CmMov, FilmgC,*
  OxFilm, WhScrn 2
Dieterle, William 1893-1973 *BiDFlm*
Dieterle, William 1894-1973 *Film 2*
Dietrich, Antonia *Film 2*
Dietrich, Daniel P 1944- *NotNAT*
Dietrich, John E 1913- *BiE&WWA, NotNAT*
Dietrich, Marlene *MotPP, WhoHol A*
Dietrich, Marlene 1900- *Film 2, WhoThe 16*
Dietrich, Marlene 1901- *BiDFlm, MovMk, ThFT,*
  WorEnF
Dietrich, Marlene 1902- *CmMov, FilmgC,*
  OxFilm, TwYS
Dietrich, Marlene 1904- *CelR 3, CmMov,*
  IntMPA 1977
Dietrich, Tina *Film 2*
Dietz, Howard 1896- *AmSCAP 1966,*
  BiE&WWA, CelR 3, ConDr 1977D, EncMT,
  FilmgC, ModWD, NewMT, NotNAT,
  NotNAT A, PIP&P, WhoThe 16
Dietz, Linda d1920 *NotNAT B*
Dietzenschmidt, Anton 1893-1955 *CnMD*
Dieu Donne, Albert *Film 1*
Dieudonne, M d1922 *NotNAT B*
Diffen, Ray 1922- *BiE&WWA, NotNAT*
Diffring, Anton 1918- *FilmgC, IntMPA 1977,*
  WhoHol A
DiGaetano, Adam 1907-1966 *WhScrn 2*
Digges, Dudley d1947 *PIP&P, WhoHol B*
Digges, Dudley 1879-1947 *Film 2, FilmgC,*
  MovMk, NotNAT B, OxThe, WhScrn 1,
  WhScrn 2, WhThe
Digges, Dudley 1880-1947 *FamA&A*
Digges, Dudley West 1720-1786 *NotNAT A,*
  NotNAT B, OxThe
Diggins, Peggy *WhoHol B*
Diggle, Roland 1887-1954 *AmSCAP 1966*
Diggs, John *WhoHol A*
Dighton, John 1909- *FilmgC, WhoThe 16*
DiGiacomo, Salvatore 1860-1934 *McGWD*
Dignam, Basil 1905- *FilmgC, WhoHol A*
Dignam, Mark 1909- *FilmgC, WhoHol A,*
  WhoThe 16
Dignon, Edmond *Film 2*
DiGolconda, Ligia 1884-1942 *WhScrn 1,*
  WhScrn 2
DiJulio, Max 1919- *AmSCAP 1966*
Dikie, Alexei Denisovich 1889-1955 *OxThe*
DiLanti, Stella *Film 2*
Dilday, William H, Jr. *NewYTET*
DiLeva, Anthony *WhoHol A*
Dill, Max M 1878-1949 *WhScrn 2*
Dill, William L 1913- *AmSCAP 1966*
Dillard, Burt 1909-1960 *WhScrn 1, WhScrn 2*
Dillard, Douglas F 1937- *AmSCAP 1966*
Dille, John F, Jr. *NewYTET*
Diller, Barry *IntMPA 1977, NewYTET*
Diller, Marie *Film 2*
Diller, Phyllis 1917- *CelR 3, Film 2, FilmgC,*
  IntMPA 1977, MotPP, WhoHol A

Dilligil, Avni 1909-1971 *WhScrn 1*, *WhScrn 2*
Dillinger, John 1903-1934 *OxFilm*
Dillingham, Charles Bancroft 1868-1934 *EncMT*,
    NotNAT B, *OxThe*, *WhThe*
Dillion, John Webb *Film 2*
Dillman, Bradford 1930- *BiE&WWA*, *FilmgC*,
    IntMPA 1977, *MotPP*, *MovMk*, *NotNAT*,
    WhoHol A
Dillon, Andrew *Film 2*
Dillon, Charles d1881 *NotNAT B*
Dillon, Charles E d1964 *NotNAT B*
Dillon, Clara d1898 *NotNAT B*
Dillon, Dick 1896-1961 *WhScrn 1*, *WhScrn 2*,
    WhoHol B
Dillon, Douglas 1909- *CelR 3*
Dillon, Eddie *Film 2*, *TwYS*
Dillon, Edward 1880-1933 *Film 1*, *Film 2*,
    TwYS A, *WhScrn 1*, *WhScrn 2*, *WhoHol B*
Dillon, Fannie Charles 1881-1947 *AmSCAP 1966*
Dillon, Frances d1947 *NotNAT B*, *WhThe*
Dillon, George 1888-1965 *WhoHol B*
Dillon, George Tim 1888-1965 *WhScrn 1*,
    WhScrn 2
Dillon, George Tim *see also* Dillon, Tim
Dillon, Jack 1887-1934 *Film 1*, *TwYS A*,
    WhoHol B
Dillon, John 1876-1937 *WhScrn 1*, *WhoHol B*
Dillon, John Francis 1884-1934 *WhScrn 2*
Dillon, John Francis 1887-1934 *WhScrn 1*
Dillon, John T 1866-1937 *Film 2*, *WhScrn 2*
Dillon, John Webb 1877-1949 *Film 1*, *Film 2*,
    WhScrn 1, *WhScrn 2*, *WhoHol B*
Dillon, Josephine 1884-1971 *WhScrn 2*,
    WhoHol B
Dillon, Melinda 1939- *BiE&WWA*, *NotNAT*
Dillon, Paul *Film 1*
Dillon, Stella 1878-1934 *WhScrn 1*, *WhScrn 2*
Dillon, Thomas Patrick 1896-1962 *NotNAT B*,
    WhScrn 1, *WhScrn 2*
Dillon, Tim 1888-1965 *WhScrn 2*
Dillon, Tim *see also* Dillon, George
Dillon, Tom d1962 *WhoHol B*
Dillon, Tom d1965 *WhoHol B*
Dillon, William A 1877-1966 *AmSCAP 1966*
Dillow, Jean Carmen *IntMPA 1977*, *WomWMM*
Dills, Barbara *WomWMM B*
Dills, William *Film 2*
Dillson, Clyde 1900-1957 *WhScrn 2*
Dilmen, Gungor 1930- *REnWD*
DiLorenzo, Tina d1930 *NotNAT B*
Dilsner, Laurence *AmSCAP 1966*
Dilson, John H 1893-1944 *WhScrn 1*, *WhScrn 2*,
    WhoHol B
Dilworth, Gordon 1913- *BiE&WWA*, *NotNAT*
DiMaggio, Joe 1914- *CelR 3*, *WhoHol A*
DiMarzio, Matilde *Film 1*
Dimbleby, Richard 1913-1965 *NewYTET*,
    WhScrn 2
Dime, James *Film 2*
DiMinno, Daniel 1911- *AmSCAP 1966*
Dimitri, Michele *WomWMM*
Dimmock, Peter 1920- *IntMPA 1977*, *NewYTET*
Dimon, Florence Irene *WhScrn 1*, *WhScrn 2*
DiNapoli, Mario 1914- *AmSCAP 1966*
DiNapoli, Raffele *Film 1*
DiNardo, Nicholas 1906- *AmSCAP 1966*
DiNardo, Thomas C 1905- *AmSCAP 1966*
Dine, Jim *ConDr 1977E*
Dine, Jim 1935- *CelR 3*
Dinehart, Alan 1886-1944 *FilmgC*, *MovMk*
Dinehart, Alan 1889-1944 *NotNAT B*, *WhScrn 1*,
    WhScrn 2
Dinehart, Alan 1890-1944 *WhThe*, *WhoHol B*
Dinensen, Marie *Film 2*

Dinensen, Robert *Film 2*
Dinesen, Isak 1885-1962 *WomWMM*
Dinesen, Robert 1874?-1940 *DcFM*
Dingelstedt, Franz 1814-1881 *OxThe*
Dingle, Charles 1887-1956 *FilmgC*, *MotPP*,
    NotNAT B, *Vers A*, *WhScrn 1*, *WhScrn 2*,
    WhoHol B
Dingle, Charles 1888-1956 *MovMk*
Dingle, Tom d1925 *NotNAT B*
Dingwall, Alexander W d1918 *NotNAT B*
DiNovi, Eugene 1928- *AmSCAP 1966*
Dinu, Robert A 1928- *AmSCAP 1966*
Dion, Carmen *AmSCAP 1966*
Dion, Hector *Film 1*, *Film 2*
Dione, Rose *Film 1*, *Film 2*, *TwYS*
Dionne, Emelie 1934-1954 *WhScrn 1*, *WhScrn 2*
Dionne, Emilie 1934-1954 *WhoHol B*
Dionne, Marie 1934-1970 *WhScrn 1*, *WhScrn 2*,
    WhoHol B
Dior, Christian 1905-1957 *NotNAT B*
DiPalma, Carlo 1925- *WorEnF*
Diphilus d290BC *OxThe*
DiPirani, Eugenio 1852-1939 *AmSCAP 1966*
Dippel, Johann Andreas 1866-1932 *NotNAT B*
Dipson, William D 1916- *IntMPA 1977*
Dirksen, Everett 1896-1969 *WhScrn 2*
DiSangro, Elena *Film 2*
Discant, Mack 1916-1961 *AmSCAP 1966*
Disher, Maurice Willson 1893-1969 *WhThe*
Dishy, Bob *NotNAT*, *WhoThe 16*
Diskant, George E 1907-1965 *FilmgC*
Disney, Roy E 1930- *IntMPA 1977*
Disney, Walt 1901-1966 *DcFM*, *FilmgC*,
    NewYTET, *OxFilm*, *WhoHol B*, *WorEnF*
Disney, Walt 1901-1968 *TwYS B*
Disraeli, Benjamin 1804-1881 *FilmgC*
Distler, P Antonie 1937- *NotNAT*
Dithmar, Edward A 1854-1917 *NotNAT B*
Ditrichstein, Leo James 1865-1928 *NotNAT B*,
    WhThe, *WhoStg 1906*, *WhoStg 1908*
Ditt, Josephine 1868-1939 *WhScrn 2*
Dittenhaver, Sarah L 1901- *AmSCAP 1966*
DiTursi, Mary *WomWMM*
DiVenanzo, Gianni 1920-1966 *DcFM*, *FilmgC*,
    OxFilm, *WorEnF*
Dix, Beulah Marie 1876- *WhThe*, *WhoStg 1908*,
    WomWMM
Dix, Billy 1911-1973 *WhScrn 2*
Dix, Dorothy 1892-1970 *WhThe*
Dix, Lillian d1922 *NotNAT B*
Dix, Mae 1895-1958 *WhScrn 1*, *WhScrn 2*
Dix, Richard 1894-1949 *BiDFlm*, *CmMov*,
    Film 1, *Film 2*, *FilmgC*, *NotNAT B*, *TwYS*,
    WhScrn 1, *WhScrn 2*
Dix, Richard 1895-1945 *MovMk*
Dix, Richard 1898-1949 *MotPP*, *WhoHol B*
Dix, Robert *WhoHol A*
Dix, William 1956- *FilmgC*
Dixey, Henry E 1859-1943 *EncMT*, *Film 1*,
    NotNAT B, *WhScrn 1*, *WhScrn 2*, *WhThe*,
    WhoHol B, *WhoStg 1906*, *WhoStg 1908*
Dixey, Phyllis d1964 *NotNAT B*
Dixie Jubilee Singers, The *Film 2*
Dixit d1949 *WhScrn 2*
Dixon, Adele 1908- *WhThe*
Dixon, Alfred d1964 *NotNAT B*
Dixon, Campbell 1895-1960 *NotNAT B*, *WhThe*
Dixon, Charles *Film 1*
Dixon, Charlotte L d1970 *WhScrn 1*, *WhScrn 2*
Dixon, Cliff 1889- *AmSCAP 1966*
Dixon, Conway 1874-1943 *NotNAT B*, *WhScrn 2*
Dixon, Denver 1890-1972 *WhScrn 2*, *WhoHol B*
Dixon, Florence *Film 1*, *Film 2*
Dixon, Glenn *WhoHol A*

Dixon, Gloria d1945 *WhScrn 2*
Dixon, Harland d1969 *WhoHol B*
Dixon, Henry 1871-1943 *WhScrn 1, WhScrn 2*
Dixon, Ivan 1931- *MovMk, WhoHol A*
Dixon, James 1949-1974 *WhScrn 2*
Dixon, Jean *Film 2*
Dixon, Jean 1894- *NotNAT*
Dixon, Jean 1896- *BiE&WWA, ThFT, WhThe,*
  WhoHol A
Dixon, Jeane 1918- *CelR 3*
Dixon, Lee 1911-1953 *NotNAT B, WhoHol B*
Dixon, Lee 1914-1953 *WhScrn 1, WhScrn 2*
Dixon, Lillian B d1962 *NotNAT B*
Dixon, Marcia *WhoHol A*
Dixon, Marion *Film 2*
Dixon, Mort 1892-1956 *AmSCAP 1966*
Dixon, Paul d1975 *NewYTET*
Dixon, Paul 1918-1974 *WhScrn 2*
Dixon, Thomas, Jr. 1864-1946 *FilmgC,*
  NotNAT B, WhoStg 1906, WhoStg 1908
Dizenzo, Charles 1938- *ConDr 1977*
D'Joseph, Jac 1919- *AmSCAP 1966*
D'Lower, I Del 1912- *AmSCAP 1966*
D'Lugoff, Burton C 1928- *AmSCAP 1966*
Dmitrevsky, Ivan Afanasyevich 1733-1821
  NotNAT B, OxThe
Dmitri Of Rostov, Saint 1651-1709 *OxThe*
Dmytryk, Edward 1908- *BiDFlm, CmMov,*
  DcFM, FilmgC, IntMPA 1977, MovMk,
  OxFilm, WorEnF
Doane, Dorothy *AmSCAP 1966*
Dobbelin, Karl Theophilus 1727-1793 *OxThe*
Dobbins, Earl E 1911-1949 *WhScrn 1, WhScrn 2*
Dobie, Alan 1932- *FilmgC, PIP&P, WhoThe 16*
Dobkin, Larry *WhoHol A*
Doble, Budd d1919 *WhScrn 2*
Doble, Frances 1902-1969 *Film 2, WhScrn 2,*
  WhThe
Dobson, Edward d1925 *WhScrn 2*
Dobson, James *WhoHol A*
Dobson, Jane *WomWMM B*
Dobson, Tamara *WhoHol A*
Dobujinsky, Mstislav 1875-1957 *OxThe*
Dockson, Evelyn 1888-1952 *WhScrn 1, WhScrn 2,*
  WhoHol B
Dockstader, Lew 1856-1924 *OxThe, PIP&P*
Doczy, Lajos 1845-1919 *OxThe*
Dodd, Claire d1973 *MotPP, WhoHol B*
Dodd, Claire 1908-1973 *MovMk, ThFT*
Dodd, Claire 1909?-1973 *WhScrn 2*
Dodd, Elan E 1868-1935 *WhScrn 1, WhScrn 2*
Dodd, Emily d1944 *NotNAT B*
Dodd, James William 1734-1796 *NotNAT B,*
  OxThe
Dodd, Jimmie 1910-1964 *AmSCAP 1966,*
  WhScrn 1, WhScrn 2
Dodd, Jimmy 1910-1964 *WhoHol B*
Dodd, Joseph A *Film 2*
Dodd, Ken 1929- *WhoThe 16*
Dodd, Lee Wilson 1879-1933 *NotNAT B, OxThe,*
  WhThe
Dodd, Neal 1878-1966 *Film 2, WhScrn 1,*
  WhScrn 2
Dodd, Neal 1878-1969 *WhoHol B*
Dodd, Ruth Carrell *AmSCAP 1966*
Dodd, Thomas J d1971 *NewYTET*
Dodd, Wilfrid E 1923- *IntMPA 1977*
Dodds, Chuck 1936-1967 *WhScrn 1, WhScrn 2*
Dodds, Jack 1927-1962 *NotNAT B, WhScrn 1,*
  WhScrn 2
Dodds, Jamieson 1884-1942 *NotNAT B, WhThe*
Dodds, William *BiE&WWA, NotNAT*
Dodge, Anna *Film 2*
Dodge, Henry Irving 1861-1934 *WhThe*

Dodge, Roger 1898-1974 *WhScrn 2*
Dodge, Shirlee *BiE&WWA, NotNAT*
Dodimead, David 1919- *WhoThe 16*
Dodsley, James d1797 *NotNAT B*
Dodsley, Robert 1703-1764 *NotNAT B, OxThe*
Dodson, Edgar *AmSCAP 1966*
Dodson, John E 1857-1931 *NotNAT B, WhThe,*
  WhoStg 1906, WhoStg 1908
Dodson, Owen 1914- *BiE&WWA, NotNAT*
Dodsworth, Charles d1920 *NotNAT B*
Dodsworth, John 1910-1964 *WhScrn 2*
Doerfel, Herbert 1924- *AmSCAP 1966*
Doerfer, John C *NewYTET*
Doggett, Thomas 1670?-1721 *NotNAT A,*
  NotNAT B, OxThe, PIP&P
D'Oisley, Maurice d1949 *NotNAT B*
Dolan, Anton *Film 2*
Dolan, Joann *WhoHol A*
Dolan, John 1929- *AmSCAP 1966*
Dolan, Lida 1912- *AmSCAP 1966*
Dolan, Mary 1919- *BiE&WWA*
Dolan, Michael J d1954 *NotNAT B*
Dolan, Robert Emmett 1906-1972 *AmSCAP 1966,*
  FilmgC
Dolan, Robert Emmett 1908-1972 *BiE&WWA,*
  NotNAT B
Dolaro, Hattie d1941 *NotNAT B*
Dolce, Lodovico 1508-1568 *McGWD, OxThe*
Dole, Robert Joseph 1923- *CelR 3*
Doleman, Guy 1923- *FilmgC*
Dolenz, George 1908-1963 *FilmgC, NotNAT B,*
  WhScrn 1, WhScrn 2, WhoHol B
Dolenz, Mickey *WhoHol A*
Dolin, Anton 1904- *WhThe*
Dolin, Boris 1903- *DcFM*
Doll, Bill 1910- *BiE&WWA, NotNAT*
Doll, Dora *WhoHol A*
Dollinger, Irving 1905- *IntMPA 1977*
Dolly, Jennie 1892-1941 *WhThe*
Dolly, Jenny 1892-1941 *NotNAT B, WhScrn 1,*
  WhScrn 2, WhoHol B
Dolly, Lady 1876-1953 *WhScrn 1, WhScrn 2*
Dolly, Rosie 1892-1970 *WhScrn 1, WhScrn 2,*
  WhThe, WhoHol B
Dolly, Roziska 1892- *Film 1*
Dolly, Yancsi 1892-1941 *Film 1*
Dolly Sisters *EncMT*
Dolman, Richard 1895- *WhThe*
Dolorez, Mademoiselle *Film 2*
Dolph, John M 1895-1962 *AmSCAP 1966*
Dombre, Barbara 1950-1973 *WhScrn 2*
Domergue, Faith 1925- *FilmgC, MotPP,*
  WhoHol A
Domingo, Placido 1941- *CelR 3*
Dominguez, Beatrice d1921 *Film 2, WhScrn 1,*
  WhScrn 2, WhoHol B
Dominguez, Joe 1894-1970 *WhScrn 2, WhoHol B*
Dominici, Mario *Film 2*
Dominicus, Evelyn *Film 1*
Dominique *OxThe*
Dominique, Ivan 1928-1973 *WhScrn 2*
Don, Carl *WhoHol A*
Don, David L 1867-1949 *WhScrn 2*
Donaghey, Frederick 1870-1937 *NotNAT B,*
  WhoStg 1906, WhoStg 1908
Donahue, Bonnie *WomWMM B*
Donahue, Elinor *WhoHol A*
Donahue, Jack 1892-1930 *EncMT, NotNAT A,*
  NotNAT B, WhScrn 1, WhScrn 2, WhThe
Donahue, Phil *NewYTET*
Donahue, Troy *MotPP, WhoHol A*
Donahue, Troy 1936- *FilmgC*
Donahue, Troy 1937- *IntMPA 1977, MovMk*
Donahue, Vincent J d1976 *WhoHol C*

Donald, James 1917- *FilmgC, IntMPA 1977, WhThe, WhoHol A*
Donaldson, Arthur *Film 2*
Donaldson, Arthur 1869-1955 *NotNAT B, WhoStg 1908*
Donaldson, Herbert 1918- *AmSCAP 1966*
Donaldson, Jack 1910-1975 *WhScrn 2, WhoHol C*
Donaldson, Sam *NewYTET*
Donaldson, Ted 1933- *FilmgC*
Donaldson, Walter 1793?-1877 *NotNAT A, NotNAT B*
Donaldson, Walter 1893-1947 *AmSCAP 1966, EncMT, NotNAT B*
Donaldson, Will 1891-1954 *AmSCAP 1966*
Donat, Peter 1928- *BiE&WWA, NotNAT, WhoHol A*
Donat, Robert 1905-1958 *BiDFlm, FilmgC, MotPP, MovMk, NotNAT B, OxFilm, OxThe, PIP&P, WhScrn 1, WhScrn 2, WhThe, WhoHol B, WorEnF*
Donath, Ludwig 1900-1967 *FilmgC, MotPP, WhScrn 1, WhScrn 2, WhoHol B*
Donath, Ludwig 1905-1967 *Vers A*
Donath, Ludwig 1907-1967 *BiE&WWA, MovMk, NotNAT B, WhThe*
Donati, Maria 1902-1966 *WhScrn 2*
Donato, Anthony 1909- *AmSCAP 1966*
Doncaster, Caryl 1923- *IntMPA 1977*
Dondoni, Cesare *Film 1*
Donehue, Vincent J 1916-1966 *FilmgC*
Donehue, Vincent J 1920-1966 *BiE&WWA, WhThe*
Donehue, Vincent Julian 1915-1966 *NotNAT B*
Donelly, Henry V d1910 *NotNAT B*
Donen, Stanley 1924- *BiDFlm, CmMov, DcFM, FilmgC, IntMPA 1977, MovMk, OxFilm, WorEnF*
Donenfeld, James 1917- *AmSCAP 1966*
Doner, Maurice 1905-1971 *WhScrn 1, WhScrn 2*
Doner, Rose 1905-1926 *WhScrn 1, WhScrn 2*
Donez, Ian 1891- *AmSCAP 1966*
Doniger, Walter 1917- *FilmgC, IntMPA 1977*
Doniol-Valcroze, Jacques 1920- *BiDFlm, DcFM, OxFilm, WorEnF*
Donisthorpe, G Sheila 1898-1946 *NotNAT A, NotNAT B, WhThe*
Donlan, James 1889-1938 *Film 2, WhScrn 1, WhScrn 2, WhoHol B*
Donlan, Mike *Film 2*
Donlan, Yolande 1920- *FilmgC, IntMPA 1977, WhoHol A, WhoThe 16*
Donleavy, J P 1926- *CnMD, ConDr 1977, ModWD, WhoThe 16*
Donlevy, Brian d1972 *BiE&WWA, MotPP, WhoHol B*
Donlevy, Brian 1899-1972 *BiDFlm, FilmgC, OxFilm, WhScrn 2*
Donlevy, Brian 1901-1972 *Film 2, HolP 30*
Donlevy, Brian 1903-1972 *MovMk, NotNAT B, WhThe*
Donlin, Mike 1877-1933 *Film 2, WhScrn 1, WhScrn 2, WhoHol B*
Donnay, Charles Maurice 1859-1945 *NotNAT B*
Donnay, Maurice 1859-1945 *CnMD, McGWD, ModWD, WhThe*
Donnell, Jeff 1921- *FilmgC, IntMPA 1977, MotPP, WhoHol A*
Donnell, Patrick 1916- *WhoThe 16*
Donnelly, Andrew 1893-1955 *AmSCAP 1966*
Donnelly, Donal 1931- *WhoThe 16*
Donnelly, Donal 1932- *FilmgC*
Donnelly, Donald *Film 2*
Donnelly, Dorothy 1880-1928 *AmSCAP 1966,*

EncMT, Film 1, NewMT, NotNAT B, WhThe, WhoStg 1908
Donnelly, James 1865-1937 *Film 1, WhScrn 1, WhScrn 2, WhoHol B*
Donnelly, Leo 1878-1935 *WhScrn 1, WhScrn 2, WhoHol B*
Donnelly, Ruth 1896- *BiE&WWA, Film 2, FilmgC, MovMk, NotNAT, ThFT, Vers A, WhoHol A*
Donnenfeld, Bernard 1926- *IntMPA 1977*
Donner, Clive *IntMPA 1977*
Donner, Clive 1920- *FilmgC*
Donner, Clive 1926- *BiDFlm, OxFilm, WhoThe 16, WorEnF*
Donner, Jorn 1933- *BiDFlm, FilmgC, OxFilm, WorEnF*
Donner, Maurice d1971 *WhoHol B*
Donner, Richard *FilmgC*
Donner, Robert *WhoHol A*
Donner, Vyvyan *WomWMM*
Donnet, Jacques 1917- *AmSCAP 1966*
Donnie *Film 2*
Donohue, Jack 1908- *WhoThe 16*
Donohue, Jack 1912- *BiE&WWA, FilmgC, NotNAT*
Donohue, Jack 1914- *IntMPA 1977*
Donohue, Joe d1921 *Film 1, WhoHol B*
Donohue, Joseph 1884-1921 *Film 2, WhScrn 1, WhScrn 2*
Donovan *WhoHol A*
Donovan, Carrie *CelR 3*
Donovan, Henry B 1914- *IntMPA 1977*
Donovan, Jack *Film 2*
Donovan, King 1919?- *FilmgC, WhoHol A*
Donovan, Michael *Film 2*
Donovan, Walter 1888-1964 *AmSCAP 1966, NotNAT B*
Donovan, Wilfred *Film 2*
Donovan, William *Film 2*
Donskoi, Marc 1901- *WorEnF*
Donskoi, Mark 1897- *FilmgC*
Donskoi, Mark 1901- *BiDFlm, DcFM, MovMk, OxFilm*
Donskoy, Mark 1901- *DcFM*
Dontchos, Patricia Ann 1946- *NotNAT*
Doohan, James *WhoHol A*
Dooley, Billy 1893-1938 *Film 1, Film 2, TwYS, WhScrn 1, WhScrn 2, WhoHol B*
Dooley, Edna Mohr 1907- *AmSCAP 1966*
Dooley, Gordon *Film 2*
Dooley, James d1949 *NotNAT B*
Dooley, John Anthony *NatPD*
Dooley, Johnny 1887-1928 *Film 1, Film 2, TwYS, WhScrn 1, WhScrn 2, WhoHol B*
Dooley, Rae *BiE&WWA, NotNAT, WhoHol A*
Dooley, Ray 1896- *EncMT, WhThe*
Doolittle, James 1896- *CelR 3*
Doolittle, James 1914- *BiE&WWA, NotNAT*
Doonan, George 1897-1973 *WhScrn 2*
Doonan, Patric 1927-1958 *FilmgC, WhScrn 1, WhoHol B*
Doonan, Patrick 1927-1958 *WhScrn 2*
Doph, Josephine *Film 2*
DoQui, Robert *WhoHol A*
D'Ora, Daisy *Film 2*
Dora, Josefine *Film 2*
Doraiswamy, V 1912- *IntMPA 1977*
Doraldina 1888-1936 *WhScrn 1, WhScrn 2*
Doraldina, Mademoiselle 1888-1936 *TwYS*
Doralinda 1888-1936 *WhoHol B*
Doralinda, Mademoiselle 1888-1936 *Film 1, Film 2*
Doran, Ann *MotPP, WhoHol A*
Doran, Ann 1913- *MovMk*

Doran, Ann 1914- *FilmgC*
Doran, Charles 1877-1964 *NotNAT B, WhThe*
Doran, Elsa 1915- *AmSCAP 1966*
Doran, John 1807-1878 *NotNAT B*
Doran, Mary 1907- *Film 2, ThFT*
Dore, Adrienne *Film 2*
Dore, Alexander 1923- *WhoThe 16*
Dore, Gustave *PIP&P*
Doretto, Roberta *Film 1*
Dorety, Charles R 1898-1957 *WhScrn 1, WhScrn 2, WhoHol B*
Dorety, Charley *Film 2*
Dorfman, Irvin S 1924- *BiE&WWA, IntMPA 1977*
Dorfman, Nat 1895- *BiE&WWA, NotNAT*
Dorfman, Robert S 1930- *IntMPA 1977*
Dorfmann, Robert *FilmgC*
Dorfsman, Louis *NewYTET*
D'Orgemont d1665? *OxThe*
Dorgere, Arlette *WhThe*
Dorham, Kenny 1924-1972 *WhScrn 2*
Doria, Vera *Film 1*
Dorian, Charles 1893-1942 *Film 1, WhScrn 1, WhScrn 2*
Dorimond 1628?-1664? *OxThe*
Dorival, Georges d1939 *NotNAT B*
Dorlag, Arthur H 1922- *BiE&WWA, NotNAT*
Dorleac, Francoise 1941-1967 *FilmgC, MotPP, OxFilm, WhScrn 1, WhScrn 2, WhoHol B*
Dorman, Shirley *Film 2*
D'Orme, Aileen 1877-1939 *NotNAT B, WhThe*
Dormer, Charles *Film 2*
Dormer, Daisy 1889- *WhThe*
Dorn, Dolores 1935- *BiE&WWA, FilmgC, NotNAT, WhoHol A*
Dorn, Philip d1975 *MotPP, WhoHol C*
Dorn, Philip 1902-1975 *WhScrn 2*
Dorn, Philip 1905-1975 *FilmgC*
Dorn, William 1893- *AmSCAP 1966*
Dornay, Jules *WhThe*
Dorne, Mary *Film 2*
Dorne, Sandra 1925- *FilmgC, WhoHol A*
Dorney, Richard d1921 *NotNAT B*
Dornton, Charles d1900 *NotNAT B*
Doro, Marie d1956 *MotPP, WhoHol B, WhoStg 1908*
Doro, Marie 1881-1956 *Film 1*
Doro, Marie 1882-1956 *Film 2, FilmgC, NotNAT B, WhScrn 1, WhScrn 2, WhThe*
Dorr, Dorothy 1867- *WhThe, WhoStg 1908*
Dorr, Lester *WhoHol A*
Dorraine, Lucy *Film 2*
Dorree, Babette Bobbie 1906-1974 *WhScrn 2*
Dors, Diana 1931- *FilmgC, IntMPA 1977, MotPP, MovMk, WhoHol A*
Dorsay, Edmund 1897-1959 *WhScrn 1, WhScrn 2*
D'Orsay, Fifi *MotPP, WhoHol A*
D'Orsay, Fifi 1904- *ThFT*
D'Orsay, Fifi 1907- *Film 2, FilmgC, MovMk*
D'Orsay, Lawrance 1853-1931 *WhThe, WhoStg 1906, WhoStg 1908*
D'Orsay, Lawrence d1931 *Film 1, Film 2, WhoHol B*
D'Orsay, Lawrence 1853-1931 *NotNAT B*
D'Orsay, Lawrence 1860-1931 *WhScrn 1, WhScrn 2*
Dorsch, Kaethe 1889-1957 *WhScrn 1, WhScrn 2*
Dorset, Earl Of *McGWD*
Dorsey, Edmund d1959 *WhoHol B*
Dorsey, Jimmy 1904-1957 *AmSCAP 1966, FilmgC, NotNAT B, WhScrn 1, WhScrn 2, WhoHol B*
Dorsey, John *NewYTET*

Dorsey, Tommy 1905-1956 *NotNAT B, WhScrn 1, WhScrn 2, WhoHol B*
Dorso, Dick *NewYTET*
Dorst, Tankred 1925- *CnMD Sup, CroCD, McGWD, ModWD*
Dortort, David 1916- *IntMPA 1977, NewYTET*
Dorval 1798-1849 *NotNAT B*
Dorval, Mareal *Film 2*
Dorval, Marie-Thomase-Amelie 1798-1849 *OxThe*
Dorvigny 1742-1812 *NotNAT B, OxThe*
Dorziat, Gabrielle 1880- *FilmgC, MovMk, WhThe*
Doscher, Doris 1882-1970 *Film 1, WhoHol B*
DosPassos, John 1896-1970 *BiE&WWA, CnMD, ModWD*
DosSantos, Nelson Pereira *DcFM*
Dossett, Chappell *Film 2*
Dossick, Jane *WomWMM*
Dostoievsky, Feodor Mikhailovich 1821-1881 *NotNAT B, OxThe*
Dostoievsky, Fyodor 1821-1881 *FilmgC*
Dotrice, Karen 1955- *FilmgC, WhoHol A*
Dotrice, Michele *WhoHol A*
Dotrice, Roy *WhoHol A*
Dotrice, Roy 1923- *FilmgC*
Dotrice, Roy 1925- *WhoThe 16*
Doty, Weston 1915-1934 *WhScrn 1, WhScrn 2, WhoHol B*
Doty, Winston 1915-1934 *WhScrn 1, WhScrn 2, WhoHol B*
Doucet, Catharine 1875-1958 *NotNAT B, ThFT, WhoHol B*
Doucet, Catherine 1875-1958 *WhScrn 2, WhThe*
Doucet, H Paul 1886-1928 *Film 2*
Doucet, M Paul 1886-1928 *WhScrn 1, WhScrn 2*
Doucet, Paul 1886-1928 *Film 1, WhoHol B*
Doucette, John *WhoHol A*
Dougall, Ian *ConDr 1977B*
Dougherty, Anne Helena 1908- *AmSCAP 1966*
Dougherty, Ariel *WomWMM B*
Dougherty, Celius 1902- *AmSCAP 1966*
Dougherty, Dan 1897-1955 *AmSCAP 1966*
Dougherty, Frances Ann *BiE&WWA, NotNAT*
Dougherty, Jack 1895-1938 *Film 2*
Dougherty, Jennie 1888- *AmSCAP 1966*
Dougherty, Virgil Jack 1895-1938 *WhScrn 1, WhScrn 2*
Douglas, Al 1907- *AmSCAP 1966*
Douglas, Bert 1900-1958 *AmSCAP 1966*
Douglas, Byron 1865-1935 *Film 2, NotNAT B, WhScrn 1, WhScrn 2, WhoHol B*
Douglas, Diana *WhoHol A*
Douglas, Don 1905-1945 *WhScrn 1, WhScrn 2, WhoHol B*
Douglas, Donald 1905-1945 *FilmgC*
Douglas, Donald 1905-1947 *Film 2*
Douglas, Donna *MotPP, WhoHol A*
Douglas, Doris 1918-1970 *WhScrn 2, WhoHol B*
Douglas, Dorothea d1962 *NotNAT B*
Douglas, Felicity 1910- *WhoThe 16*
Douglas, Gordon 1909- *BiDFlm, CmMov, FilmgC, IntMPA 1977, MovMk, WhoHol A, WorEnF*
Douglas, Helen Gahagan *BiE&WWA*
Douglas, James *WhoHol A*
Douglas, Josephine *WhoHol A*
Douglas, Keith d1973 *WhoHol B*
Douglas, Kenneth d1923 *WhThe*
Douglas, Kent d1966 *WhScrn 1, WhScrn 2, WhoHol B*
Douglas, Kirk *MotPP, WhoHol A*
Douglas, Kirk 1916- *BiDFlm, CelR 3, CmMov, FilmgC, MovMk, OxFilm, WorEnF*
Douglas, Kirk 1918- *IntMPA 1977*

Douglas, Kirk 1920- *BiE&WWA*, *NotNAT*
Douglas, Larry 1914- *BiE&WWA*, *NotNAT*
Douglas, Larry 1917- *AmSCAP 1966*
Douglas, Leal *Film 1*, *Film 2*
Douglas, Lewis W 1894- *BiE&WWA*
Douglas, Lillian *Film 2*
Douglas, Lloyd C 1877-1951 *FilmgC*
Douglas, Marian *WhoHol A*
Douglas, Marie Booth d1932 *NotNAT B*
Douglas, Melvin 1901- *BiE&WWA*, *NotNAT*
Douglas, Melvyn 1901- *BiDFlm*, *CelR 3*,
    FamA&A, *FilmgC*, *IntMPA 1977*, *MGM*,
    MotPP, *MovMk*, *OxFilm*, *WhoHol A*,
    WhoThe 16, *WorEnF*
Douglas, Michael 1945- *FilmgC*, *IntMPA 1977*,
    WhoHol A
Douglas, Mike 1925- *CelR 3*, *NewYTET*,
    WhoHol A
Douglas, Milton 1906-1970 *WhScrn 2*, *WhoHol B*
Douglas, Pamela *WomWMM*
Douglas, Paul 1899-1959 *OxFilm*
Douglas, Paul 1907-1959 *BiDFlm*, *FilmgC*,
    MotPP, *MovMk*, *NotNAT B*, *WhScrn 1*,
    WhScrn 2, *WhoHol B*, *WorEnF*
Douglas, R H d1935 *NotNAT B*
Douglas, Richard d1911 *NotNAT B*
Douglas, Robert 1909- *CmMov*, *FilmgC*, *Vers A*,
    WhThe
Douglas, Robert 1910- *BiE&WWA*, *NotNAT*,
    WhoHol A
Douglas, Sharon *WhoHol A*
Douglas, Tom 1903- *Film 2*, *WhThe*
Douglas, Torrington *WhoThe 16*
Douglas, Valerie 1938-1969 *WhScrn 2*,
    WhoHol B
Douglas, Wallace d1958 *WhoHol B*
Douglas, Wallace 1911- *WhoThe 16*
Douglas, Wally *WhScrn 1*, *WhScrn 2*
Douglas, William O 1898- *CelR 3*
Douglass, Albert 1864-1940 *WhThe*
Douglass, Mrs. David d1773 *PIP&P*
Douglass, David d1786 *NotNAT B*, *OxThe*,
    PIP&P
Douglass, John d1874 *NotNAT B*
Douglass, John d1917 *NotNAT B*
Douglass, Margaret d1949 *NotNAT B*
Douglass, R H *WhThe*
Douglass, Stephen 1921- *BiE&WWA*, *NotNAT*,
    WhoThe 16
Douglass, Vincent 1900-1926 *NotNAT B*, *WhThe*
Dourif, Brad *WhoHol A*
Douvan-Torzow, J N *Film 2*
Douy, Max 1914- *DcFM*
Dove, Billie *MotPP*
Dove, Billie 1900- *FilmgC*, *MovMk*, *ThFT*
Dove, Billie 1904- *Film 2*, *TwYS*, *WhoHol A*
Dove, Lewis U, Jr. 1925-1965 *AmSCAP 1966*
Dover, Nancy *Film 2*
Dovey, Alice 1885-1969 *Film 1*, *WhScrn 1*,
    WhScrn 2, *WhThe*, *WhoHol B*
Dovorsko, Jess *Film 2*
DoVries, Harry *Film 2*
Dovzhenko, Alexander 1894-1956 *BiDFlm*, *DcFM*,
    FilmgC, *MovMk*, *OxFilm*, *WhScrn 1*,
    WhScrn 2, *WomWMM*, *WorEnF*
Dow, Ada d1926 *NotNAT B*
Dow, Alexander d1779 *NotNAT B*
Dow, Clara 1883-1969 *WhThe*
Dow, Maree *WhoHol A*
Dow, Mary E *Film 2*
Dow, Peggy 1928- *FilmgC*, *MotPP*, *WhoHol A*
Dowd, Harrison 1897-1964 *BiE&WWA*,
    NotNAT B, *WhoHol A*
Dowd, Kaye *WhoHol A*

Dowd, M'el *BiE&WWA*, *NotNAT*, *WhoHol A*,
    WhoThe 16
Dowd, Nancy Ellen *WomWMM B*
Dowell, Horace Kirby 1904- *AmSCAP 1966*
Dowlan, William C *Film 1*
Dowling, Allan 1903- *AmSCAP 1966*
Dowling, Constance 1923-1969 *FilmgC*,
    WhoHol B
Dowling, Doris 1921- *FilmgC*, *WhoHol A*
Dowling, Eddie d1976 *Film 2*, *WhoHol C*
Dowling, Eddie 1894-1976 *BiE&WWA*, *EncMT*,
    NotNAT B, *PIP&P*, *WhThe*
Dowling, Eddie 1895-1976 *AmSCAP 1966*
Dowling, Joan 1928-1954 *NotNAT B*, *WhScrn 1*,
    WhScrn 2, *WhThe*, *WhoHol B*
Dowling, Joan 1929-1954 *FilmgC*
Dowling, Joseph 1848-1928 *WhoHol B*
Dowling, Joseph 1850-1928 *Film 2*, *TwYS*
Dowling, Joseph J 1848-1928 *WhScrn 1*,
    WhScrn 2
Dowling, Joseph S 1850-1928 *Film 1*
Dowling, Robert W 1895-1973 *BiE&WWA*,
    NotNAT B
Dowlining, Constance 1920-1969 *WhScrn 1*,
    WhScrn 2
Down, John *Film 2*
Downer, Alan 1912- *BiE&WWA*
Downes, John *OxThe*
Downes, Olin 1886-1955 *WhScrn 1*, *WhScrn 2*
Downey, Fairfax Davis 1893- *AmSCAP 1966*
Downey, Morton *WhoHol A*
Downey, Morton 1901- *AmSCAP 1966*
Downey, Morton 1902-1961 *Film 2*
Downey, Raymond Joseph 1914- *AmSCAP 1966*
Downey, Sean Morton 1933- *AmSCAP 1966*
Downing, Harry 1894-1972 *WhScrn 2*, *WhoHol B*
Downing, Joseph 1903-1975 *WhScrn 2*,
    WhoHol C
Downing, Robert d1975 *WhoHol C*
Downing, Robert 1914-1975 *BiE&WWA*,
    NotNAT, *NotNAT B*
Downing, Robert 1915-1975 *WhScrn 2*
Downing, Robert L 1857-1944 *NotNAT B*,
    WhoStg 1906, *WhoStg 1908*
Downing, Walter 1874-1937 *WhScrn 1*,
    WhScrn 2, *WhoHol B*
Downs, Cathy 1924- *FilmgC*, *MotPP*
Downs, Hugh 1921- *CelR 3*, *IntMPA 1977*,
    NewYTET
Downs, Jane *WhoThe 16*
Downs, Johnny 1913- *Film 2*, *FilmgC*,
    WhoHol A
Downs, William Andrew 1890- *AmSCAP 1966*
Dowsey, Rose Walker *WhScrn 1*, *WhScrn 2*
Dowson, Graham R 1923- *IntMPA 1977*
Dowton, Emily d1924 *NotNAT B*
Dowton, William 1764-1851 *NotNAT B*, *OxThe*
Doyle, Sir Arthur Conan 1859-1930 *FilmgC*,
    NotNAT B, *PIP&P*, *WhThe*
Doyle, Bobby *Film 2*
Doyle, Buddy 1901-1939 *WhScrn 1*, *WhScrn 2*,
    WhoHol B
Doyle, David *WhoHol A*
Doyle, Gene 1909- *BiE&WWA*
Doyle, James d1927 *NotNAT B*
Doyle, James S *Film 2*
Doyle, John T 1873-1935 *Film 2*, *NotNAT B*,
    WhScrn 2, *WhoHol B*
Doyle, Kevin 1933- *IntMPA 1977*
Doyle, Len 1893-1959 *NotNAT B*, *WhScrn 1*,
    WhScrn 2
Doyle, Mariam d1962 *NotNAT B*
Doyle, Maxine 1915-1973 *WhScrn 2*, *WhoHol B*
Doyle, Mimi *WhoHol A*

Doyle, Patricia 1915-1975 *WhScrn 2, WhoHol C*
Doyle, Regina 1907-1931 *Film 2, TwYS,*
   WhScrn 1, WhScrn 2
Doyle, Walter 1899-1945 *AmSCAP 1966*
D'Öyly Carte, Richard 1844-1901 *NotNAT B,*
   OxThe
D'Öyly Carte, Rupert 1876-1948 *NotNAT B,*
   WhThe
Dozier, William 1908- *FilmgC, NewYTET*
Drabble, Margaret *WomWMM*
Drachmann, Holger Henrik Herholdt 1846-1908
   NotNAT B, OxThe
Drago, Cathleen d1938 *NotNAT B*
Dragon, Carmen 1914- *AmSCAP 1966*
Dragonette, Jessica *PIP&P*
Dragun, Osvaldo 1929- *CroCD*
Drain, Emile *Film 2*
Drainie, John 1916-1966 *WhScrn 1, WhScrn 2,*
   WhoHol B
Drake, Alfred 1914- *BiE&WWA, CelR 3,*
   CnThe, EncMT, FamA&A, FilmgC,
   NotNAT, WhoHol A, WhoThe 16
Drake, Betsy 1923- *FilmgC, MotPP, WhoHol A*
Drake, Charles 1914- *FilmgC, IntMPA 1977,*
   WhoHol A
Drake, Charlie 1925- *FilmgC, IntMPA 1977*
Drake, Dona 1920- *FilmgC, IntMPA 1977,*
   WhoHol A
Drake, Donna *MotPP*
Drake, Dorothy *Film 1, WhoHol A*
Drake, Ervin M *AmSCAP 1966, NewMT*
Drake, Fabia 1904- *FilmgC, WhThe, WhoHol A*
Drake, Frances 1908- *ThFT, WhoHol A*
Drake, Frances Ann Denny d1875 *NotNAT B*
Drake, Jim 1935- *AmSCAP 1966*
Drake, Josephine S d1929 *Film 2, WhScrn 1,*
   WhScrn 2, WhoHol B
Drake, Milton 1916- *AmSCAP 1966*
Drake, Pauline *WhoHol A*
Drake, Ronald 1928- *BiE&WWA*
Drake, Samuel, Sr. 1768-1854 *FamA&A*
Drake, Steve 1923-1948 *WhScrn 1, WhScrn 2*
Drake, Tom *IntMPA 1977, MotPP*
Drake, Tom 1918- *MGM, WhoHol A*
Drake, Tom 1919- *FilmgC, MovMk*
Drake, William A 1899-1965 *WhThe*
Drane, Sam Dade d1916 *WhScrn 2*
Dranem 1869-1935 *WhScrn 1, WhScrn 2,*
   WhoHol B
Drange, Emily d1961 *NotNAT B*
Draper, Anne 1938- *BiE&WWA, NotNAT*
Draper, Joseph d1962 *NotNAT B*
Draper, Old Colonel 1855?-1915 *WhScrn 2*
Draper, Paul 1909- *WhoHol A*
Draper, Paul 1913- *BiE&WWA, NotNAT*
Draper, Peter 1925- *FilmgC*
Draper, Ruth 1884-1956 *NotNAT A, NotNAT B,*
   OxThe
Draper, Ruth 1889-1956 *WhThe*
Draper, Stephen 1906- *BiE&WWA, NotNAT*
Drasnin, Irv *NewYTET*
Drawbaugh, Jacob W, Jr. 1928- *AmSCAP 1966*
Draycott, Wilfred 1848- *WhThe*
Draylin, Paul d1970 *WhoHol B*
Drayson, Edith d1926 *NotNAT B*
Drayton, Alfred 1881-1949 *Film 2, FilmgC,*
   NotNAT B, WhScrn 1, WhScrn 2, WhThe,
   WhoHol B
Drayton, Michael 1563-1631 *McGWD, PIP&P*
Dreher, Walter Arthur d1962 *NotNAT B*
Dreier, Hans 1884-1966 *FilmgC*
Dreier, Hans 1885- *WorEnF*
Dreier, John T 1913- *BiE&WWA*
Dreifuss, Arthur 1908- *FilmgC, IntMPA 1977*

Dreiser, Edward M d1958 *NotNAT B*
Dreiser, Theodore 1871-1945 *CnMD, FilmgC,*
   ModWD, NotNAT B, WhThe
Dresdel, Sonia 1909-1976 *FilmgC, WhoHol A,*
   WhoHol C, WhoThe 16
Dresden, Albert Curley *Film 2*
Dresser, Louise d1965 *MotPP, WhoHol B*
Dresser, Louise 1878-1965 *ThFT*
Dresser, Louise 1879-1965 *Film 2, MovMk,*
   TwYS
Dresser, Louise 1881-1965 *FilmgC*
Dresser, Louise 1882-1965 *WhScrn 1, WhScrn 2,*
   WhThe
Dresser, Paul 1857-1906 *AmSCAP 1966,*
   NotNAT B
Dressler, Eric 1896- *BiE&WWA, NotNAT*
Dressler, Eric 1900- *WhThe*
Dressler, Marie d1934 *MotPP, WhoHol B,*
   WhoStg 1906, WhoStg 1908
Dressler, Marie 1868-1934 *ThFT*
Dressler, Marie 1869-1934 *BiDFlm, EncMT,*
   Film 1, Film 2, FilmgC, MGM, MovMk,
   NotNAT B, OxFilm, TwYS, WhScrn 1,
   WhScrn 2, WhThe, WorEnF
Dressler, Marie 1871-1934 *OxThe*
Drever, Constance d1948 *NotNAT B, WhThe*
Dreville, Jean 1906- *DcFM, FilmgC*
Drew, Ann 1891-1974 *Film 2, WhScrn 2,*
   WhoHol B
Drew, David *WhoHol A*
Drew, Ellen 1915- *FilmgC, IntMPA 1977,*
   MotPP, MovMk, ThFT, WhoHol A
Drew, Gene *WhoHol A*
Drew, Georgiana *PIP&P*
Drew, Gladys Rankin d1914 *WhScrn 2*
Drew, Jerry *Film 2*
Drew, Mrs. John 1818-1897 *FamA&A*
Drew, Mrs. John 1820-1897 *PIP&P*
Drew, John 1827-1862 *FamA&A, NotNAT B,*
   OxThe
Drew, John 1853-1927 *CnThe, FamA&A, Film 1,*
   NotNAT A, NotNAT B, OxThe, PIP&P,
   WhThe, WhoStg 1906, WhoStg 1908
Drew, Lillian *Film 1*
Drew, Louisa d1954 *NotNAT B*
Drew, Louisa Lane 1820-1897 *NotNAT A,*
   NotNAT B, OxThe
Drew, Lowell *Film 2*
Drew, Lucille McVey d1925 *NotNAT B*
Drew, Philip Yale *Film 2*
Drew, Polly *WomWMM*
Drew, Robert J *WhoHol A*
Drew, Roland 1903- *Film 2, TwYS*
Drew, S Rankin 1892-1918 *Film 1, WhScrn 2*
Drew, Sidney 1864-1919 *TwYS, WhScrn 2,*
   WhoHol B, WomWMM
Drew, Sidney 1864-1920 *Film 1, FilmgC*
Drew, Sidney 1868-1919 *OxThe*
Drew, Mrs. Sidney 1868-1925 *FilmgC*
Drew, Mrs. Sidney 1890-1925 *WhScrn 1,*
   WhScrn 2, WhoHol B
Drew, Mrs. Sidney 1895-1925 *TwYS*
Drewitt, Stanley 1878- *WhThe*
Drexel, Nancy 1910- *Film 2, TwYS*
Drexler, Elias J 1911- *IntMPA 1977*
Drexler, Rosalyn 1926- *ConDr 1977, NotNAT*
Dreyer, Carl Theodor 1889-1968 *BiDFlm, DcFM,*
   FilmgC, MovMk, OxFilm, WorEnF
Dreyer, Dave 1894- *AmSCAP 1966*
Dreyer, Max 1862-1946 *ModWD*
Dreyfus, Alfred 1859-1935 *FilmgC, OxFilm*
Dreyfuss, Henry 1904- *WhThe*
Dreyfuss, Jane 1924- *BiE&WWA*
Dreyfuss, Michael 1928-1960 *NotNAT B,*

WhScrn 1, WhScrn 2, WhoHol B
Dreyfuss, Richard 1949- *IntMPA 1977, WhoHol A*
Driggers, Donald Clayton 1893-1972 *WhScrn 2, WhoHol B*
Driggs, Collins H 1911- *AmSCAP 1966*
Drinkwater, Albert Edwin d1923 *NotNAT B, WhThe*
Drinkwater, John 1882-1937 *CnMD, CnThe, McGWD, ModWD, NotNAT A, NotNAT B, OxThe, PIP&P, WhThe*
Driscoll, Bobby 1936-1968 *FilmgC*
Driscoll, Bobby 1937-1968 *HolP 40, WhScrn 1, WhScrn 2, WhoHol B*
Driscoll, Patricia *WhoHol A*
Driscoll, Sam W 1868-1956 *WhScrn 1, WhScrn 2*
Driscoll, Tex *Film 1*
Drivas, Robert 1938- *BiE&WWA, MotPP, NotNAT, PIP&P, WhoHol A, WhoThe 16*
Driver, Donald 1952- *ConDr 1977D, WhoThe 16*
Driver, Tom F 1925- *BiE&WWA, NotNAT*
Droeshout, Adrian 1897-1965 *WhScrn 2*
Drollet, David *Film 2*
Dromgold, George *Film 2*
Dromgoole, Patrick 1930- *WhoThe 16*
Drouet, Robert 1870-1914 *NotNAT B, WhScrn 2, WhThe, WhoStg 1906, WhoStg 1908*
Dru, Joanne 1923- *BiDFlm, CmMov, FilmgC, IntMPA 1977, MotPP, WhoHol A, WorEnF*
Druce, Herbert 1870-1931 *NotNAT B*
Druce, Hubert 1870-1931 *Film 2, WhScrn 2, WhThe*
Druks, Renate *WomWMM B*
Drulie, Sylvia 1928- *BiE&WWA, NotNAT*
Drumier, Jack *Film 2*
Drumier, Jack d1939 *WhoHol B*
Drumier, Jack 1869-1929 *WhScrn 1, WhScrn 2*
Drumm, George 1874-1959 *AmSCAP 1966*
Drummond, Alexander M 1884-1956 *NotNAT B*
Drummond, Alice *WhoHol A*
Drummond, Dolores 1834-1926 *NotNAT B, WhThe*
Druriolanus, Augustus *OxThe*
Drury, Allen 1918- *CelR 3*
Drury, Charles 1890- *AmSCAP 1966*
Drury, James 1934- *FilmgC, IntMPA 1977, MotPP, WhoHol A*
Drury, Weston, Jr. 1916- *IntMPA 1977*
Drury, William Price 1861-1949 *NotNAT B, WhThe*
Druten, John Van *OxThe, PIP&P*
Drutman, Irving 1910- *AmSCAP 1966*
Druxman, Michael B 1941- *IntMPA 1977*
Dryden, John 1631-1700 *CnThe, McGWD, NotNAT A, NotNAT B, OxThe, PIP&P, REnWD*
Dryden, Vaughan 1875- *WhThe*
Drye, John W, Jr. 1900- *BiE&WWA, NotNAT*
Dryhurst, Edward 1904- *FilmgC*
Duane, Frank 1926- *BiE&WWA*
Duane, Jack *Film 2, WhScrn 2*
Duane, L Ray 1897- *AmSCAP 1966*
Duarte, Anselmo 1920- *DcFM, WorEnF*
Duarte, Maria Eva Evita 1919-1952 *WhScrn 2*
Dubbins, Don 1929- *FilmgC, IntMPA 1977, WhoHol A*
Dube, Marcel 1930- *CnThe, McGWD, REnWD*
Dubencourt, Jean *Film 2*
Dubens, Stanley 1920- *IntMPA 1977*
Dubensky, Arcady 1890- *AmSCAP 1966*
Dubensky, Leo 1914- *AmSCAP 1966*
Duberman, Martin 1930- *ConDr 1977, CroCD, NatPD*
Duberstein, Helen 1926- *NatPD*

Dubey, Matt 1928- *AmSCAP 1966, BiE&WWA, NotNAT*
Dubillard, Roland 1923- *CnMD Sup, CroCD, ModWD, REnWD*
Dubin, Al 1891-1945 *AmSCAP 1966, NotNAT B*
Dubin, Charles S *NewYTET*
Dubin, Joseph S *IntMPA 1977*
Duboff, Al 1909- *AmSCAP 1966*
Dubois, Gene d1962 *NotNAT B*
DuBois, Gladys *Film 2*
DuBois, Helen *Film 2*
DuBois, Jean 1888-1957 *WhScrn 1, WhScrn 2*
DuBois, Raoul Pene 1914- *WhoThe 16*
Dubos, Rene 1901- *CelR 3*
Dubosc, Gaston d1941 *NotNAT B*
Dubourg, A W d1910 *NotNAT B*
DuBray, Claire 1893- *Film 2*
DuBrey, Clair 1893- *Film 2*
DuBrey, Claire 1893- *Film 1, TwYS*
DuCello, Countess *Film 1*
Ducey, Lillian *WomWMM*
Duchamp, Marcel *Film 2*
Duchamps, Marcel 1887-1968 *WhScrn 2*
Duchess Olga 1899-1953 *WhScrn 1, WhScrn 2*
Duchin, Eddy 1909-1951 *WhScrn 1, WhScrn 2, WhoHol B*
Duchin, Peter 1937- *CelR 3, WhoHol A*
Ducis, Jean-Francois 1733-1816 *NotNAT B, OxThe*
Duckworth, Willie Lee 1924- *AmSCAP 1966*
Duclos 1668-1748 *OxThe*
Duclos 1688?-1748 *NotNAT B*
Ducloux, Walter 1913- *AmSCAP 1966*
Duclow, Geraldine 1946- *NotNAT*
DuCroisy 1626-1695 *OxThe*
DuCroisy, Philibert Gassot 1626-1695 *NotNAT B*
DuCrow, Tate *Film 2*
Duddy, John H 1904- *AmSCAP 1966*
Duddy, Lyn *AmSCAP 1966*
Dudelson, Stanley E 1924- *IntMPA 1977*
Dudgeon, Elspeth 1871-1955 *WhScrn 2*
Dudlah, David 1892-1947 *WhScrn 1, WhScrn 2*
Dudlay, Adeline d1934 *NotNAT B*
Dudley, Bernard *Film 2*
Dudley, Bide 1877-1944 *WhThe*
Dudley, Charles *Film 1, Film 2*
Dudley, Doris *WhoHol A*
Dudley, Florence *Film 2*
Dudley, John 1894-1966 *WhScrn 2*
Dudley, Robert Y 1875-1955 *Film 2, WhScrn 1, WhScrn 2, WhoHol B*
Dudley, Walter Bronson 1877-1944 *AmSCAP 1966, NotNAT B*
Dudley, William 1947- *WhoThe 16*
Dudley-Ward, Penelope *WhoHol A*
Dudow, Slatan 1903-1963 *DcFM, OxFilm, WorEnF*
Duel, Pete 1940-1971 *FilmgC*
Duel, Peter d1972 *WhoHol B*
Duel, Peter 1940-1971 *WhScrn 1, WhScrn 2*
Duering, Carl *WhoHol A*
Duerr, Edwin 1906- *BiE&WWA, NotNAT*
Duerrenmatt, Friedrich 1921- *BiE&WWA, NotNAT*
Duey, Philip Alexander 1901- *AmSCAP 1966*
Duff, Howard *MotPP, WhoHol A*
Duff, Howard 1913- *MovMk*
Duff, Howard 1917- *FilmgC, IntMPA 1977*
Duff, John 1787-1831 *NotNAT B*
Duff, Mary Ann 1794-1857 *NotNAT A, NotNAT B, OxThe*
Duff, Warren 1904-1973 *WhScrn 2*
Duffell, Peter 1939?- *FilmgC*
Duffield, Harry *Film 2*

Duffield, Kenneth 1885- *WhThe*
Duffy, Albert 1903- *IntMPA 1977*
Duffy, Henry 1890-1961 *NotNAT B, WhScrn 1, WhScrn 2*
Duffy, Herbert d1952 *NotNAT B*
Duffy, Jack 1879-1939 *Film 2, TwYS*
Duffy, Jack 1882-1939 *WhScrn 1, WhScrn 2, WhoHol B*
Duffy, James *Film 2*
Duffy, James E *IntMPA 1977, NewYTET*
Duffy, John *Film 1*
Duffy, Maureen 1933- *ConDr 1977*
Dufkin, Sam 1891-1952 *WhScrn 1*
Duflos, Huguette *Film 2*
Duflos, Raphael d1946 *NotNAT B, WhThe*
Dufort, Alphonse *Film 1*
Dufraine, Rosa 1901-1935 *WhScrn 1, WhScrn 2*
Dufresne 1693-1767 *NotNAT B, OxThe*
Dufresne, Catherine-Marie-Jeanne Dupre d1759 *OxThe*
Dufresne, Charles 1611?-1684? *NotNAT B, OxThe*
Dufresny, Charles-Riviere 1654-1724 *McGWD, NotNAT B, OxThe*
Duga, Irene Verbitsky *WomWMM B*
Dugan, James *Film 2*
Dugan, Marie *WhScrn 1, WhScrn 2*
Dugan, Mary *Film 2*
Dugan, Tom 1889-1955 *FilmgC, Vers B, WhScrn 1, WhScrn 2, WhoHol B*
Dugan, Tom 1889-1958 *Film 2, TwYS*
Dugan, Tommy 1889-1958 *Film 2*
Dugan, Walter *Film 2*
Dugan, William Francis *Film 2*
Dugas, Emma L N *AmSCAP 1966*
Dugazon, Jean-Baptiste-Henri Gourgaud 1746-1809 *NotNAT B, OxThe*
Dugazon, Louise Rosalie d1821 *NotNAT B*
Dugazon, Marie-Marguerite Gourbaud 1742-1799 *NotNAT B*
Dugazon, Marie-Marguerite Gourgaud 1742-1799 *OxThe*
Duggan, Andrew 1923- *BiE&WWA, FilmgC, MotPP, WhoHol A*
Duggan, Edmund d1938 *NotNAT B*
Duggan, Maggie d1919 *NotNAT B*
Duggan, Pat 1910- *FilmgC*
Duggan, Tom 1915-1969 *WhScrn 1, WhScrn 2, WhoHol B*
Duhamel, Georges 1884-1966 *ModWD*
Dukakis, Olympia *NotNAT, WhoHol A*
Dukas, James *WhoHol A*
Duke, Angier Biddle 1915- *CelR 3*
Duke, Billy 1927- *AmSCAP 1966*
Duke, Doris 1912- *CelR 3*
Duke, Ivy 1895- *Film 1, Film 2, FilmgC*
Duke, Ivy 1896- *WhThe*
Duke, John 1899- *AmSCAP 1966*
Duke, Patty *MotPP, WhoHol A*
Duke, Patty 1946- *BiE&WWA, CelR 3, FilmgC, MovMk, NotNAT*
Duke, Patty 1947- *IntMPA 1977*
Duke, Robert 1917- *BiE&WWA, NotNAT*
Duke, Vernon 1903- *AmSCAP 1966, BiE&WWA*
Duke, Vernon 1903-1968 *NewMT*
Duke, Vernon 1903-1969 *EncMT, NotNAT A, NotNAT B, WhThe*
Duke Of Buckingham *PIP&P*
Dukes, Ashley 1885-1959 *CnThe, NotNAT A, NotNAT B, OxThe, WhThe*
Dulac, Arthur 1910-1962 *NotNAT B, WhScrn 1, WhScrn 2, WhoHol B*
Dulac, Germaine 1882-1942 *BiDFlm, DcFM, FilmgC, OxFilm, WomWMM, WorEnF*

Dulien, Tobe 1893-1969 *WhScrn 2*
Dullea, Keir *MotPP, WhoHol A*
Dullea, Keir 1936- *CelR 3, FilmgC, IntMPA 1977, NotNAT, WhoThe 16*
Dullea, Keir 1939- *MovMk*
Dullin, Charles 1885-1949 *CnThe, Film 2, NotNAT B, OxThe, WhScrn 2, WhThe, WhoHol B*
Dullzell, Paul 1879-1961 *NotNAT B, WhThe*
Dulmage, Will E 1883-1953 *AmSCAP 1966*
DuLuart, Yolanda *WomWMM B*
DuLuart, Yolande *WomWMM*
Duma, Evelyn *Film 2*
Dumar, Luis *Film 2*
Dumas, Alexandre *PIP&P*
Dumas, Alexandre, Fils 1824-1895 *CnThe, FilmgC, McGWD, NotNAT A, NotNAT B, OxThe, REnWD*
Dumas, Alexandre, Pere 1802-1870 *CnThe, FilmgC, McGWD, NotNAT A, NotNAT B, REnWD*
Dumas, Alexandre, Pere 1803-1870 *OxThe*
Dumas, Jean *Film 2*
DuMaurier, Daphne 1907- *BiE&WWA, FilmgC, NotNAT, OxThe, WhThe*
DuMaurier, George Louis Palmella Busson 1834-1896 *NotNAT B, OxThe*
DuMaurier, Sir Gerald Hubert Edward 1873-1934 *CnThe, Film 1, NotNAT A, NotNAT B, OxThe, WhScrn 2, WhThe, WhoHol B*
DuMaurier, Guy 1865-1916 *NotNAT B, OxThe*
DuMaurier, Muriel Beaumont 1881-1957 *OxThe*
Dumbar, Helen *Film 2*
Dumbrille, Douglas 1890-1974 *FilmgC, MovMk*
Dumbrille, Douglass 1890-1974 *Vers A, WhScrn 2, WhoHol B*
Dumeny, Camille d1920 *NotNAT B*
Dumercier, Jean *Film 1*
Dumesnil, Marie-Francoise 1713-1803 *NotNAT B, OxThe*
Dumke, Ralph 1900-1964 *FilmgC, NotNAT B, WhScrn 1, WhScrn 2, WhoHol B*
Dumo, Evelyn *Film 2*
DuMond, Joseph H 1898- *AmSCAP 1966*
DuMont, Allen B d1965 *NewYTET*
Dumont, Gene *Film 2*
DuMont, Gordon 1894-1965 *WhoHol B*
DuMont, Gordon 1894-1966 *WhScrn 2*
Dumont, J M *Film 1, Film 2*
Dumont, Louise d1932 *NotNAT B*
Dumont, Margaret 1889-1965 *BiDFlm, Film 2, MotPP, OxFilm, ThFT, WhScrn 1, WhScrn 2, WhoHol B, WorEnF*
Dumont, Margaret 1890-1965 *FilmgC, MovMk, Vers A*
Dumont, Montague *Film 1*
Dumont, Paul *WhoHol A*
Duna, Steffi 1913- *FilmgC, ThFT, WhoHol A*
Dunaway, Faye 1941- *BiDFlm, CelR 3, FilmgC, IntMPA 1977, MotPP, MovMk, OxFilm, WhoHol A, WhoThe 16, WorEnF*
Dunayevsky, Isaac 1900-1955 *DcFM*
Dunbar, Dave *Film 2*
Dunbar, David 1893-1953 *WhScrn 1, WhScrn 2, WhoHol B*
Dunbar, Dixie 1919- *ThFT, WhoHol A*
Dunbar, Dorothy *Film 2*
Dunbar, Erroll *WhoStg 1908*
Dunbar, Helen 1868-1933 *Film 1, Film 2, TwYS, WhScrn 1, WhScrn 2, WhoHol B*
Duncan, A E *Film 1*
Duncan, Albert Bud 1886-1961 *Film 2, TwYS*
Duncan, Alma *WomWMM*
Duncan, Andrew *WhoHol A*

Duncan, Angus 1912- *BiE&WWA, NotNAT,*
　WhoHol A, WhoThe 16
Duncan, Archie 1914- *FilmgC, WhoHol A,*
　WhoThe 16
Duncan, Augustin 1873-1954 *NotNAT B, WhThe*
Duncan, Beverly *WomWMM B*
Duncan, Bob 1904-1967 *WhScrn 1, WhScrn 2,*
　WhoHol B
Duncan, Bud 1883-1960 *WhScrn 2, WhoHol B*
Duncan, Dell *Film 1*
Duncan, Edith Johnson *WhScrn 1, WhScrn 2*
Duncan, Evelyn 1893-1972 *WhScrn 2, WhoHol B*
Duncan, F Martin *DcFM*
Duncan, Isadora 1878-1927 *NotNAT B*
Duncan, Isadora 1880-1927 *WhThe*
Duncan, Jimmy 1935- *AmSCAP 1966*
Duncan, Keene 1902-1972 *WhScrn 2*
Duncan, Kenne 1902-1972 *WhoHol B*
Duncan, Malcolm 1878-1942 *NotNAT B,*
　WhoStg 1908
Duncan, Malcolm 1881-1942 *WhThe*
Duncan, Mary 1903- *MotPP, ThFT, WhThe,*
　WhoHol A
Duncan, Mary 1905- *Film 2*
Duncan, Ronald 1914- *CnMD, CnThe,*
　ConDr 1977, CroCD, ModWD, WhoThe 16
Duncan, Rosetta d1959 *WhThe, WhoHol B*
Duncan, Rosetta 1900-1959 *AmSCAP 1966,*
　WhScrn 1, WhScrn 2
Duncan, Rosetta 1902-1959 *NotNAT B*
Duncan, Sandy 1946- *EncMT, FilmgC,*
　IntMPA 1977, WhoHol A, WhoThe 16
Duncan, Taylor *Film 2*
Duncan, Ted *Film 1, Film 2*
Duncan, Todd 1900- *EncMT, WhThe*
Duncan, Todd 1903- *BiE&WWA, NotNAT,*
　PIP&P, WhoHol A
Duncan, Virginia Bauer 1929- *WomWMM B*
Duncan, Vivian *WhThe*
Duncan, Vivian 1899- *WhoHol A*
Duncan, Vivian 1902- *AmSCAP 1966*
Duncan, William 1878-1961 *Film 1, Film 2*
Duncan, William 1880-1961 *MotPP, NotNAT B,*
　TwYS, TwYS A, WhScrn 1, WhScrn 2,
　WhoHol B
Duncan, William Cary 1874-1945 *AmSCAP 1966,*
　NotNAT B, WhScrn 1, WhScrn 2, WhThe,
　WhoHol B
Duncan Sisters, The *EncMT, Film 2, ThFT*
Dundee, Jimmy 1901-1953 *WhScrn 1, WhScrn 2,*
　WhoHol B
Dundreary *OxThe*
Dunfee, Jack 1901- *WhThe*
Dungan, Olive 1903- *AmSCAP 1966*
Dunham, Corydon B, Jr. *NewYTET*
Dunham, Joanna 1936- *WhoThe 16*
Dunham, Katherine 1910- *AmSCAP 1966,*
　BiE&WWA, NotNAT, NotNAT A,
　WhoHol A, WhoThe 16
Dunham, Phil 1885-1974 *WhoHol B*
Dunham, Phillip 1885-1972 *Film 2, WhScrn 2*
Dunham, William D 1910- *AmSCAP 1966*
Duning, George 1908- *AmSCAP 1966, CmMov,*
　FilmgC, IntMPA 1977, WorEnF
Dunkels, Dorothy 1907- *WhThe*
Dunkels, Marjorie 1916- *WhThe*
Dunkinson, Harry *Film 1, Film 2*
Dunkley, Ferdinand Luis 1869-1956
　AmSCAP 1966
Dunlap, Ethel Margaret d1968 *WhoHol B*
Dunlap, Florence *WhoHol A*
Dunlap, Louis M 1911- *AmSCAP 1966*
Dunlap, Richard D 1923- *IntMPA 1977*
Dunlap, Scott 1892- *TwYS A*

Dunlap, William 1766-1839 *CnThe, McGWD,*
　NotNAT A, NotNAT B, OxThe, PIP&P,
　REnWD
Dunlevy, Brian *Film 2*
Dunlop, Frank 1927- *PIP&P A, WhoThe 16*
Dunlop, Ian 1927- *OxFilm*
Dunmar, David *Film 2*
Dunn, Arthur d1932 *NotNAT B*
Dunn, Bobby d1939 *Film 1, Film 2, WhoHol B*
Dunn, Bonnie 1920- *AmSCAP 1966*
Dunn, Eddie 1896-1951 *Film 2, Vers B,*
　WhoHol B
Dunn, Edward F 1896-1951 *WhScrn 1, WhScrn 2*
Dunn, Edwin Wallace d1931 *NotNAT B*
Dunn, Emma 1875-1966 *Film 2, FilmgC, Vers A,*
　WhScrn 1, WhScrn 2, WhThe, WhoHol B
Dunn, Geoffrey 1903- *WhoThe 16*
Dunn, Gregg d1964 *NotNAT B*
Dunn, Harvey B 1894-1968 *WhScrn 2, WhoHol B*
Dunn, J E *Film 1*
Dunn, J Malcolm d1946 *NotNAT B, WhScrn 1,*
　WhScrn 2, WhoHol B
Dunn, Jack 1917-1938 *WhScrn 1, WhScrn 2*
Dunn, James d1967 *MotPP, WhoHol B*
Dunn, James 1901-1967 *HolP 30*
Dunn, James 1905-1967 *FilmgC, MovMk,*
　WhScrn 1, WhScrn 2
Dunn, James 1906-1967 *BiE&WWA, NotNAT B*
Dunn, James Philip 1884-1936 *AmSCAP 1966*
Dunn, John J 1906-1938 *Film 1, WhScrn 1,*
　WhScrn 2
Dunn, John P 1908- *NatPD*
Dunn, Johnny 1906-1938 *WhoHol B*
Dunn, Joseph Barrington d1920 *NotNAT B*
Dunn, Josephine 1906- *Film 2, MovMk, ThFT,*
　TwYS, WhoHol A
Dunn, Malcolm d1946 *Film 2*
Dunn, Marion *WomWMM*
Dunn, Michael d1973 *MotPP, WhoHol B*
Dunn, Michael 1918- *AmSCAP 1966*
Dunn, Michael 1934-1973 *BiE&WWA,*
　NotNAT B, WhScrn 2
Dunn, Michael 1935-1973 *FilmgC, MovMk*
Dunn, Ralph 1900-1968 *BiE&WWA, NotNAT*
Dunn, Ralph 1902-1968 *Vers B, WhScrn 2,*
　WhoHol A, WhoHol B
Dunn, Rebecca Welty 1890- *AmSCAP 1966*
Dunn, Robert 1891-1939 *WhScrn 1, WhScrn 2*
Dunn, Robert H 1896-1960 *WhScrn 1, WhScrn 2,*
　WhoHol B
Dunn, Violet *WhoHol A*
Dunn, William *Film 2*
Dunn, William R *Film 1*
Dunne, Charles d1951 *WhScrn 1, WhScrn 2*
Dunne, Dominick *IntMPA 1977*
Dunne, Irene *IntMPA 1977, MotPP, WhoHol A,*
　WomWMM
Dunne, Irene 1901- *EncMT, FilmgC, ThFT*
Dunne, Irene 1904- *BiDFlm, BiE&WWA,*
　CelR 3, CmMov, MovMk, OxFilm, WhThe,
　WorEnF
Dunne, J W *PIP&P*
Dunne, Philip 1908- *BiDFlm, DcFM, FilmgC,*
　IntMPA 1977, WorEnF
Dunne, Steve *WhoHol A*
Dunning, George 1920- *DcFM, OxFilm, WorEnF*
Dunning, John 1916- *IntMPA 1977*
Dunning, Philip Hart 1890- *CnMD, WhThe*
Dunning, Philip Hart 1890-1968 *ModWD*
Dunning, Philip Hart 1891- *BiE&WWA,*
　NotNAT
Dunning, Philip Hart 1891-1957 *McGWD*
Dunning, Philip Hart 1891-1968 *NotNAT B*
Dunning, Ruth 1911- *WhoHol A, WhoThe 16*

Dunnock, Mildred *BiE&WWA, CnThe,*
   IntMPA 1977, MotPP, NotNAT, PIP&P,
   WhoHol A
Dunnock, Mildred 1900- *Vers A, WhoThe 16*
Dunnock, Mildred 1904- *FilmgC*
Dunnock, Mildred 1906- *CelR 3, MovMk*
Dunphie, Charles J d1908 *NotNAT B*
Dunrobin, Lionel Claude 1875-1950 *WhScrn 1,*
   WhScrn 2
Dunsany, Alfred, Lord 1878-1957 *NotNAT A,*
   NotNAT B
Dunsany, Lord Edward John M D Plunkett
   1878-1957 *CnMD, CnThe, McGWD, ModWD,*
   OxThe, PIP&P, REnWD, WhThe
Dunskus, Erich 1890-1967 *WhScrn 1, WhScrn 2*
Dunsmuir, Alexander 1877-1938 *WhScrn 1,*
   WhScrn 2
Dunstedter, Eddie 1897- *AmSCAP 1966*
Dunton, Helen d1920 *WhScrn 1, WhScrn 2*
Dunton, John *Film 2*
Dunville, T E 1870?-1924 *NotNAT B, OxThe*
DuPage, Florence *AmSCAP 1966*
DuPage, Richard 1908- *AmSCAP 1966*
DuParc 1630?-1664 *OxThe*
DuParc, Marquise-Therese DeGorla 1633-1668
   NotNAT B, OxThe
DuParc, Rene Berthelot d1664 *NotNAT B*
DuPea, Tatzumbie 1849-1970 *WhScrn 2*
Duperey, Anny *WhoHol A*
DuPont, Miss 1894-1973 *Film 2, TwYS,*
   WhoHol B
Dupont, Adley 1946- *IntMPA 1977*
Dupont, E A 1891-1956 *BiDFlm, FilmgC*
Dupont, Ewald Andre 1891-1956 *DcFM, OxFilm,*
   WorEnF
DuPont, Patricia 1894-1973 *WhScrn 2*
DuPont, Paul d1957 *NotNAT B*
Dupre, Jimmy R 1906- *AmSCAP 1966*
Dupree, Harry 1911- *AmSCAP 1966*
Dupree, Minnie d1947 *WhoHol B, WhoStg 1908*
Dupree, Minnie 1873-1947 *Film 2, FilmgC,*
   NotNAT B, WhScrn 1, WhScrn 2
Dupree, Minnie 1875-1945 *ThFT*
Dupree, Minnie 1875-1947 *WhThe*
Duprez, Fred 1884-1938 *NotNAT B, WhScrn 2,*
   WhThe, WhoHol B
Duprez, June 1918- *FilmgC, MotPP, WhThe,*
   WhoHol A
Duprez, May Moore d1946 *NotNAT B*
Dupuis, Adolphe d1891 *NotNAT B*
DuPuis, Arthur 1901-1952 *WhScrn 2*
Dupuis, Paul 1916- *FilmgC, WhoHol A*
Duquesne, Edmond 1855- *WhThe*
Duquette, Tony 1918- *BiE&WWA, NotNAT*
Duran, Val 1896-1937 *WhScrn 1, WhScrn 2,*
   WhoHol B
Durand, Charles 1912- *BiE&WWA, NotNAT*
Durand, David *Film 2*
Durand, Edouard 1871-1926 *NotNAT B,*
   WhScrn 1, WhScrn 2, WhoHol B
Durand, Edward *Film 2*
Durand, Jean 1882-1946 *DcFM, WhScrn 2*
Durand, Wade Hampton 1887-1964
   AmSCAP 1966
Durang, Charles 1796-1870 *NotNAT B*
Durang, John 1768-1822 *NotNAT A*
Durant, Ariel 1898- *CelR 3*
Durant, Edouard *Film 2*
Durant, M *Film 2*
Durant, Thomas *Film 2*
Durant, Will 1885- *CelR 3*
Durante, Jimmy 1893- *AmSCAP 1966,*
   BiE&WWA, CelR 3, EncMT, Film 2,
   FilmgC, IntMPA 1977, MGM, MotPP,

MovMk, NewYTET, NotNAT, NotNAT A,
   WhThe, WhoHol A
Duras, Marguerite 1914- *CnMD Sup, CnThe,*
   CroCD, FilmgC, McGWD, ModWD,
   OxFilm, REnWD, WhoThe 16, WomWMM,
   WorEnF
Durbin, Deanna 1921- *CmMov, FilmgC, MotPP,*
   MovMk, ThFT, WhoHol A, WorEnF
Durbin, Deanna 1922- *BiDFlm, OxFilm*
Durbin, Maud d1936 *NotNAT B*
Durbridge, Francis 1912- *IntMPA 1977*
Duret, Marie d1881 *NotNAT B*
Durfee, Minta d1975 *MotPP, WhoHol C*
Durfee, Minta 1889-1975 *TwYS*
Durfee, Minta 1890-1975 *WhScrn 2*
Durfee, Minta 1897-1975 *Film 1, FilmgC*
D'Urfey, Thomas 1653-1723 *NotNAT B, OxThe*
Durgin, Cyrus W 1907-1962 *NotNAT B*
Durgin, Don 1924- *IntMPA 1977, NewYTET*
Durham, Eddie 1909- *AmSCAP 1966*
Durham, Thomas J, Sr. 1924- *AmSCAP 1966*
Durieux, Tilla 1881-1971 *Film 2, WhScrn 1,*
   WhScrn 2, WhoHol B
Durkin, Eleanor *WhScrn 1, WhScrn 2,*
   WhoHol B
Durkin, James Peter 1879-1934 *NotNAT B,*
   WhScrn 1, WhScrn 2, WhoHol B
Durkin, Junior 1915-1935 *FilmgC, WhScrn 1,*
   WhScrn 2, WhoHol B
Durland, Edward *Film 2*
Durning, Bernard *Film 1, Film 2*
Durning, Bernard J 1893-1923 *WhScrn 1,*
   WhScrn 2, WhoHol B
Durning, Charles 1923- *NotNAT, PIP&P A,*
   WhoHol A
Durocher, Leo 1906- *CelR 3*
Durr, Clifford J d1975 *NewYTET*
Durrell, Lawrence 1912- *CnMD, ConDr 1977,*
   ModWD
Durrenmatt, Friedrich 1921- *CnMD, CnThe,*
   CroCD, McGWD, ModWD, OxThe, PIP&P,
   REnWD, WhoThe 16
Durst, Edward 1917-1945 *WhScrn 1, WhScrn 2,*
   WhoHol B
Durston, David E 1925- *IntMPA 1977*
Duru, Alfred d1889 *NotNAT B*
Durwood, Stanley H 1920- *IntMPA 1977*
Duryea, Dan 1907-1968 *BiDFlm, CmMov,*
   FilmgC, HolP 40, MotPP, MovMk,
   NotNAT B, OxFilm, WhScrn 1, WhScrn 2,
   WhoHol B, WorEnF
Duryea, George 1904-1963 *Film 2, TwYS,*
   WhScrn 1, WhScrn 2, WhoHol B
Duryea, Mary d1949 *NotNAT B*
DuRyer, Pierre 1606-1658 *McGWD*
Dusbury, Elspeth 1912-1967 *WhScrn 1*
Duse, Carl *Film 2*
Duse, Eleanora 1858-1924 *Film 2, NotNAT A,*
   NotNAT B, WhScrn 1, WhScrn 2,
   WhoHol B, WorEnF
Duse, Eleanora 1859-1924 *WhoStg 1908*
Duse, Elenora 1859-1924 *Film 1*
Duse, Eleonora 1858-1924 *FamA&A, FilmgC,*
   OxFilm, OxThe, PIP&P
Duse, Eleonora 1859-1924 *CnThe, WhThe*
DuSouchet, Henry A 1852-1922 *NotNAT B,*
   WhThe
Dussault, Nancy 1936- *BiE&WWA, EncMT,*
   WhoThe 16
Dussault, Nancy 1938- *NotNAT*
D'Usseau, Arnaud 1916- *BiE&WWA, NotNAT,*
   WhThe
DuTerreaux, Louis Henry d1878 *NotNAT B*
Dutertre, Armand *Film 2*

Dutfield, Ray *IntMPA 1977*
Dutourd, Jean 1920- *McGWD*
Duval, Georges 1847-1919 *NotNAT B, WhThe*
Duval, Georgette *Film 2*
DuVal, Joe 1907-1966 *WhScrn 2, WhoHol B*
Duval, Juan d1954 *WhScrn 2*
Duval, Paulette *Film 2*
Duvall, Robert 1931- *FilmgC, IntMPA 1977,*
 MovMk, WhoHol A
Duvall, Shelley *WhoHol A*
Duvalle, William *Film 1*
Duvalles 1895-1971 *WhScrn 2*
Duveen, Lorna *Film 2*
Duvernois, Henri 1875-1937 *McGWD,*
 NotNAT B
Duvivier, Julien 1896-1967 *BiDFlm, DcFM,*
 FilmgC, MovMk, OxFilm, WorEnF
Duvoisin, Yvette *Film 1*
Dux, Emilienne 1874- *WhThe*
Duxbury, Elspeth 1909-1967 *WhThe*
Duxbury, Elspeth 1912-1967 *WhScrn 2,*
 WhoHol B
Dvonch, Frederick 1914- *BiE&WWA, NotNAT*
Dvorak, Ann 1912- *Film 2, FilmgC, HolP 30,*
 MotPP, MovMk, ThFT, WhoHol A
Dwan, Alan 1885- *MovMk*
Dwan, Allan 1885- *BiDFlm, DcFM, FilmgC,*
 IntMPA 1977, OxFilm, TwYS A, WorEnF
Dwan, Dorothy *Film 2, TwYS*
Dwiggens, Jay d1919 *Film 1*
Dwiggins, Jay d1919 *WhScrn 2*
Dwire, Earl 1884-1940 *WhScrn 2, WhoHol B*
Dworkin, Susan *NatPD*
Dwyer, Ada d1952 *NotNAT B, WhThe,*
 WhoStg 1908
Dwyer, Hilary *WhoHol A*
Dwyer, John T 1877-1936 *Film 2, WhScrn 2*
Dwyer, Leslie 1906- *Film 2, FilmgC,*
 IntMPA 1977, WhThe, WhoHol A
Dwyer, Ruth *Film 1, Film 2*
Dyal, Susan *WomWMM B*
Dyall, Franklin 1874-1950 *Film 2, FilmgC,*
 NotNAT B, WhScrn 1, WhScrn 2, WhThe,
 WhoHol B
Dyall, Valentine 1908- *FilmgC, WhoHol A,*
 WhoThe 16
Dyananana *Film 2*
Dybwad, Johanne 1867-1950 *OxThe*
Dycke, Marjorie L 1916- *BiE&WWA, NotNAT*
D'Yd, Jean d1964 *Film 2, WhScrn 2*
Dye, Carol Finch d1962 *NotNAT B*
Dye, Lyle, Jr. 1930- *BiE&WWA, NotNAT*
Dyer, Anson *FilmgC*
Dyer, Bob 1900-1965 *WhScrn 1, WhScrn 2*
Dyer, Charles 1928- *BiE&WWA, ConDr 1977,*
 CroCD, NotNAT, WhoHol A, WhoThe 16
Dyer, John E 1884-1951 *WhScrn 1, WhScrn 2*
Dyer, Madge *Film 1*
Dyer, William *Film 2*
Dyer, William J *Film 1*
Dyers, Lien *Film 2*
Dyess, Tony R Q 1910- *AmSCAP 1966*
Dyett, Walter Fairman 1873- *WhoStg 1906,*
 WhoStg 1908
Dylan, Bob 1941- *AmSCAP 1966, CelR 3*
Dylan, Robert 1941- *AmSCAP 1966*
Dymov, Ossip 1878-1959 *CnMD, ModWD,*
 OxThe
Dyne, Michael *NotNAT*
Dyneley, Peter 1921- *FilmgC, WhoHol A*
Dyott, George M *Film 2*
Dyrenforth, James *WhThe*
Dyrese, Jacqueline *Film 2*
Dysart, Richard A 1929?- *NotNAT, PIP&P A,*

WhoHol A, WhoThe 16
Dyson, Hal 1884- *AmSCAP 1966*
Dyson, Laura d1950 *NotNAT B*
Dzigan, Yefim 1898- *DcFM*

E

Eades, Wilfrid 1920- *IntMPA 1977*
Eadie, Dennis 1869-1928 *WhThe*
Eadie, Dennis 1875-1928 *NotNAT B*
Eady, David 1924- *FilmgC*
Eagan, Evelyn 1908-1946 *WhScrn 1, WhScrn 2*
Eagan, Jack *Film 2*
Eagels, Jeanne 1890-1929 *FamA&A, ThFT*
Eagels, Jeanne 1894-1929 *Film 2, FilmgC,
    NotNAT A, NotNAT B, TwYS, WhScrn 1,
    WhScrn 2, WhThe, WhoHol B*
Eager, Edward 1911-1964 *AmSCAP 1966*
Eager, Johnney 1930-1963 *WhScrn 1, WhScrn 2*
Eager, Johnny 1930-1963 *WhoHol B*
Eager, Mary Ann *AmSCAP 1966*
Eagle, Chief Black *Film 1*
Eagle, Dan Red *Film 2*
Eagle, Frances Red *Film 2*
Eagle, James 1907-1959 *Film 2, WhScrn 2*
Eagle Eye *Film 2*
Eagle Eye, William *Film 2*
Eagle Wing, Chief *Film 2*
Eagles, Jeanne 1894-1929 *Film 1*
Eagleshirt, William *Film 1*
Eagleton, Thomas 1929- *CelR 3*
Eaker, Ira 1922- *BiE&WWA, NotNAT*
Eakin, Vera 1900- *AmSCAP 1966*
Eames, Charles 1907- *WorEnF*
Eames, Clare 1896-1930 *Film 2, NotNAT B,
    WhScrn 1, WhScrn 2, WhThe, WhoHol B*
Eames, Juanita *AmSCAP 1966*
Eames, Ray *WorEnF*
Eames, Virginia d1971 *WhoHol B*
Earhart, Amelia 1898-1937 *WomWMM*
Earhart, Will 1871-1960 *AmSCAP 1966*
Earl, Catherine V 1886-1946 *WhScrn 1,
    WhScrn 2*
Earl, Kathleen 1913-1954 *WhScrn 1, WhScrn 2*
Earl, Virginia 1875-1937 *WhoStg 1906,
    WhoStg 1908*
Earl, Virginia *see also* Earle, Virginia
Earl Of Rochester *PIP&P*
Earlcott, Gladys d1939 *WhScrn 1, WhScrn 2*
Earle, Arthur *Film 1, Film 2*
Earle, Blanche 1883-1952 *WhScrn 1, WhScrn 2,
    WhoHol B*
Earle, Dorothy d1958 *Film 2, WhScrn 1,
    WhScrn 2, WhoHol B*
Earle, Edna *Film 2, TwYS*
Earle, Edward *MotPP*
Earle, Edward 1882-1972 *WhScrn 2*
Earle, Edward 1884-1972 *Film 1, Film 2, TwYS*
Earle, Jack 1906-1952 *Film 2, WhScrn 2*
Earle, Josephine *Film 1, Film 2*
Earle, Lilias d1935 *NotNAT B*
Earle, Virginia 1875-1937 *NotNAT B, WhThe*
Earle, Virginia *see also* Earl, Virginia

Earles, Harry *Film 2*
Early, Margot 1915-1936 *WhScrn 1, WhScrn 2,
    WhoHol B*
Early, Pearl M 1879-1960 *WhScrn 1, WhScrn 2,
    WhoHol B*
Earnfred, Thomas 1894- *NotNAT*
Earnfred, Thomas 1915- *BiE&WWA*
Earnhart, Myron L 1913- *AmSCAP 1966*
Earp, Wyatt 1848-1929 *OxFilm*
Easdale, Brian 1909- *FilmgC*
Easmon, R Sarif *ConDr 1977*
Eason, B Reeves 1886-1956 *FilmgC, OxFilm*
Eason, Breezy 1913-1921 *WhoHol B*
Eason, Lorraine *Film 2*
Eason, Myles 1915- *WhoThe 16*
Eason, Reeves 1866-1956 *Film 2, TwYS*
Eason, Reeves 1891-1956 *TwYS A*
Eason, Reeves B Breezy 1886-1956 *WhScrn 2*
Eason, Reeves Breezy, Jr. 1913-1921 *WhScrn 2*
East, Ed 1894-1952 *AmSCAP 1966*
East, Ed 1896-1952 *WhScrn 1, WhScrn 2,
    WhoHol B*
East, John M 1866-1924 *NotNAT A, WhoHol B*
Eastes, Helen M 1892- *AmSCAP 1966*
Eastham, Richard *WhoHol A*
Eastlake, Mary d1911 *NotNAT B*
Eastland, James O 1904- *CelR 3*
Eastman, Andrea *WomWMM*
Eastman, Carole *WomWMM*
Eastman, Charles *NatPD*
Eastman, Frederick 1859-1920 *NotNAT B,
    WhThe*
Eastman, George 1854-1932 *DcFM, FilmgC,
    OxFilm, WorEnF*
Eastman, Peter *WhoHol A*
Easton, Jay *Film 2*
Easton, Joyce *WhoHol A*
Easton, Lorraine *Film 2*
Easton, Richard 1933- *BiE&WWA, NotNAT,
    WhoThe 16*
Easton, Robert 1930- *Vers A, WhoHol A*
Easton, Sidney 1896- *AmSCAP 1966*
Eastwood, Clint 1930- *BiDFlm, CelR 3, FilmgC,
    IntMPA 1977, MotPP, MovMk, OxFilm,
    WhoHol A, WorEnF*
Eaton, Charles *Film 2*
Eaton, Cyrus 1883- *CelR 3*
Eaton, Doris *Film 2*
Eaton, Elwin *Film 1*
Eaton, Evelyn 1924-1964 *WhScrn 2*
Eaton, James 1934-1964 *WhScrn 2*
Eaton, Jay 1900-1970 *Film 2, WhScrn 1,
    WhScrn 2, WhoHol B*
Eaton, Jimmy 1906- *AmSCAP 1966*
Eaton, John C 1935- *AmSCAP 1966*
Eaton, Mabel d1916 *WhScrn 2*

Eaton, Malcolm 1914- *AmSCAP 1966*
Eaton, Mary d1948 *NotNAT B, WhThe, WhoHol B*
Eaton, Mary 1901-1948 *WhScrn 1, WhScrn 2*
Eaton, Mary 1902-1948 *EncMT, Film 2*
Eaton, Shirley 1936- *FilmgC, MotPP, WhoHol A*
Eaton, Wallas 1917- *WhoThe 16*
Eaton, Walter Prichard 1878-1957 *NotNAT B, PIP&P, WhThe*
Eaubonne, Jean D' 1903-1971 *DcFM*
Eaves, Hilary 1914- *WhThe*
Ebb, Fred 1932- *ConDr 1977D, EncMT, NewMT, NotNAT*
Ebb, Fred 1933- *WhoThe 16*
Ebbins, Milton Keith 1914- *AmSCAP 1966*
Eben, Al *WhoHol A*
Eberg, Victor 1925-1972 *WhScrn 2*
Eberhart, Constance *BiE&WWA*
Eberhart, Nelle Richmond 1871-1944 *AmSCAP 1966*
Eberhart, Richard 1904- *BiE&WWA, NotNAT*
Eberle, Bob *WhoHol A*
Eberle, Eugene A 1840-1917 *NotNAT B, WhoStg 1906, WhoStg 1908*
Eberson, Drew 1904- *IntMPA 1977*
Ebert, Bernie 1915-1969 *WhScrn 1, WhScrn 2*
Ebert, Carl *Film 1, Film 2*
Ebert, Joyce 1933- *BiE&WWA, NotNAT, WhoThe 16*
Ebi, Earl 1903-1973 *WhScrn 2*
Ebinger, Blandine *Film 2*
Ebsen, Buddy 1908- *AmSCAP 1966, EncMT, FilmgC, IntMPA 1977, MotPP, MovMk, NewYTET, WhoHol A*
Ebsen, Vilma *WhoHol A*
Ebsworth, Joseph d1868 *NotNAT B*
Ebsworth, Mary Emma d1881 *NotNAT B*
Eburne, Maude 1875-1960 *FilmgC, MotPP, MovMk, NotNAT B, ThFT, WhScrn 1, WhScrn 2, WhoHol B*
Eby, George W 1914- *IntMPA 1977*
Eby-Rock, Helen *WhoHol A*
Eccles, Aimee *WhoHol A*
Eccles, Donald 1908- *WhoThe 16*
Eccles, Jane 1896-1966 *WhScrn 1, WhScrn 2, WhoHol B*
Eccles, Janet 1895-1966 *WhThe*
Eccles, Ted *WhoHol A*
Eccleston, William d1625? *OxThe*
Echegaray, Jose d1832 *NotNAT B*
Echegaray, Jose 1832-1916 *CnMD, McGWD, ModWD, OxThe*
Echegaray, Miguel *WhThe*
Eckart, Jean 1921- *BiE&WWA, NotNAT, PIP&P, WhoThe 16*
Eckart, William Joseph 1920- *BiE&WWA, NotNAT, PIP&P, WhoThe 16*
Eckenberg, Johann Carl 1685-1748 *OxThe*
Ecker, Judith K 1933- *AmSCAP 1966*
Ecker, Thomas R 1935- *AmSCAP 1966*
Eckerlein, John E 1884-1926 *WhScrn 1, WhScrn 2, WhoHol B*
Eckert, George 1927- *BiE&WWA, NotNAT*
Eckhardt, Oliver J 1873-1952 *Film 2, WhScrn 1, WhScrn 2, WhoHol B*
Eckles, Lewis C 1888-1950 *WhScrn 2*
Eckles, Robert d1975 *WhoHol C*
Ecklund, Carol 1934-1939 *WhScrn 1, WhScrn 2*
Eckstein, George *NewYTET*
Eckstein, Maxwell 1905- *AmSCAP 1966*
Eckstine, Billy *WhoHol A*
Eddinger, Lawrence *Film 2*
Eddinger, Wallace 1881-1929 *NotNAT B, WhThe*

Eddington, John P *Film 2*
Eddington, Paul 1927- *WhoThe 16*
Eddison, Robert 1908- *WhoThe 16*
Eddy, Arthur W *IntMPA 1977*
Eddy, Augusta Rossner 1860-1925 *WhScrn 1, WhScrn 2*
Eddy, David Manton 1928- *AmSCAP 1966*
Eddy, Dorothy 1907-1959 *WhScrn 1, WhScrn 2, WhoHol B*
Eddy, Edward 1822-1875 *NotNAT B, OxThe*
Eddy, Helen Jerome 1897- *Film 1, Film 2, MotPP, ThFT, TwYS*
Eddy, Lorraine *Film 2*
Eddy, Nelson 1901-1967 *CmMov, FilmgC, MGM, MotPP, MovMk, NotNAT B, OxThe, WhScrn 1, WhScrn 2, WhThe, WhoHol B*
Eddy, Ted 1904- *AmSCAP 1966*
Edele, Durand J *IntMPA 1977*
Edelheit, Harry 1891-1955 *AmSCAP 1966*
Edelheit, Martha *WomWMM B*
Edell, Nancy *WomWMM B*
Edelman, Herb 1930- *FilmgC, WhoHol A*
Edelman, Louis F d1976 *NewYTET*
Edelson, Edward 1929- *AmSCAP 1966*
Eden, Barbara 1934- *FilmgC, MovMk, WhoHol A*
Edens, Roger 1905-1970 *AmSCAP 1966, CmMov, FilmgC, WorEnF*
Ederle, Gertrude 1907?- *WhoHol A*
Edeson, Arthur 1891-1970 *CmMov, DcFM, FilmgC, WorEnF*
Edeson, Robert 1868-1930 *MovMk*
Edeson, Robert 1868-1931 *Film 1, Film 2, NotNAT B, OxThe, TwYS, WhScrn 1, WhScrn 2, WhThe, WhoHol B, WhoStg 1906, WhoStg 1908*
Edgar, David 1948- *ConDr 1977*
Edgar, Marriott 1880-1951 *FilmgC, NotNAT B, WhThe*
Edgar, Mrs. Richard d1937 *NotNAT B*
Edgar, Tripp d1927 *NotNAT B*
Edgar-Bruce, Toni 1892-1966 *WhScrn 1, WhScrn 2, WhoHol B*
Edgar-Bruce, Tonie *WhThe*
Edgett, Edwin Francis 1867-1946 *NotNAT B, WhThe*
Edgeworth, Jane 1922- *WhoThe 16*
Edginton, May d1957 *WhThe*
Edington, John P *Film 2*
Edington, May d1957 *NotNAT B*
Edison, Harry 1915- *AmSCAP 1966*
Edison, Thomas Alva 1847-1931 *DcFM, FilmgC, NotNAT B, OxFilm, WorEnF*
Ediss, Connie 1871-1934 *NotNAT B, WhThe*
Ediss, Connie 1877- *WhoStg 1908*
Edler, Charles 1877-1942 *WhScrn 1, WhScrn 2, WhoHol B*
Edlin, Tubby 1882- *Film 2, WhThe*
Edman, Goesta 1887-1938 *WhScrn 1*
Edmonds, Shepard N 1876-1957 *AmSCAP 1966*
Edmund, Lada, Jr. *WhoHol A*
Edmunds, John 1913- *AmSCAP 1966*
Edmundsen, Al 1896-1954 *Film 2, WhScrn 2*
Edmundson, Garth 1900- *AmSCAP 1966*
Edmundson, Harry *Film 1*
Edney, Florence 1879-1950 *NotNAT B, WhThe*
Edouarde, Carl *Film 2*
Edouart, Farciot *FilmgC*
Edouin, May d1944 *NotNAT B*
Edouin, Rose 1844-1925 *NotNAT B, WhThe*
Edouin, Willie 1846-1908 *NotNAT B, OxThe*
Edstrom, Katherine 1901-1973 *WhScrn 2*
Edthofer, Anton *Film 2*
Edward, Nils *Film 2*

Edwardes, Conway d1880 *NotNAT B*
Edwardes, Felix d1954 *NotNAT B, WhThe*
Edwardes, George 1852-1915 *CnThe, NotNAT A, NotNAT B, OxThe, PIP&P, WhThe, WhoStg 1906, WhoStg 1908*
Edwardes, George 1855-1915 *EncMT*
Edwardes, Olga 1917- *WhThe*
Edwardes, Paula *WhThe, WhoStg 1906, WhoStg 1908*
Edwards, A C 1909- *BiE&WWA, NotNAT*
Edwards, Alan d1954 *MotPP, NotNAT B, WhoHol B*
Edwards, Alan 1893-1954 *Film 2*
Edwards, Alan 1900-1954 *WhScrn 1, WhScrn 2*
Edwards, Ben 1916- *BiE&WWA, NotNAT, WhoThe 16*
Edwards, Bill 1918- *WhoHol A*
Edwards, Blake 1922- *BiDFlm, CmMov, FilmgC, IntMPA 1977, MovMk, NewYTET, OxFilm, WorEnF*
Edwards, Bruce d1927 *NotNAT B*
Edwards, Clara *AmSCAP 1966*
Edwards, Cliff 1895-1971 *Film 2, FilmgC, MotPP, MovMk, Vers B, WhScrn 1, WhScrn 2, WhoHol B*
Edwards, Douglas 1917- *IntMPA 1977, NewYTET*
Edwards, Edith *Film 2*
Edwards, Edna Park 1895-1967 *WhScrn 1, WhScrn 2, WhoHol B*
Edwards, Edwin B 1891-1963 *AmSCAP 1966*
Edwards, Eleanor 1883-1968 *WhScrn 1, WhScrn 2, WhoHol B*
Edwards, Fred 1860- *WhoStg 1908*
Edwards, G Spencer d1916 *WhThe*
Edwards, Gus d1945 *WhoHol B*
Edwards, Gus 1879-1945 *AmSCAP 1966, Film 2, NotNAT B*
Edwards, Gus 1881-1945 *WhScrn 1, WhScrn 2*
Edwards, Harry *Film 1, Film 2*
Edwards, Henry 1882-1952 *FilmgC, WhScrn 1, WhScrn 2*
Edwards, Henry 1883-1952 *Film 1, Film 2, NotNAT B, WhThe*
Edwards, Hilton 1903- *OxThe, PIP&P, WhoThe 16*
Edwards, J Gordon d1925 *TwYS A*
Edwards, J Gordon, Jr. *Film 2*
Edwards, Jack *Film 2*
Edwards, Jack 1922- *AmSCAP 1966*
Edwards, James 1912-1970 *WhScrn 1, WhScrn 2*
Edwards, James 1922-1970 *FilmgC, MovMk, WhoHol B*
Edwards, Jennifer *WhoHol A*
Edwards, Jimmy 1920- *FilmgC, WhoHol A*
Edwards, Joan 1920- *AmSCAP 1966*
Edwards, Julian 1855-1910 *NotNAT B, WhoStg 1906, WhoStg 1908*
Edwards, Karen *WomWMM*
Edwards, Leo 1886- *AmSCAP 1966*
Edwards, Mattie 1886-1944 *WhScrn 1, WhScrn 2, WhoHol B*
Edwards, Meredith 1917- *FilmgC, WhoHol A*
Edwards, Michael 1893-1962 *AmSCAP 1966*
Edwards, Nate 1902-1972 *WhScrn 2*
Edwards, Neely 1889-1965 *Film 1, TwYS, WhScrn 1, WhScrn 2, WhoHol B*
Edwards, Neely 1889-1975 *Film 2*
Edwards, Osman 1864-1936 *NotNAT B, WhThe*
Edwards, Penny 1919- *FilmgC*
Edwards, Penny 1928- *WhoHol A*
Edwards, Ralph 1913- *CelR 3, NewYTET*
Edwards, Richard d1566 *NotNAT B*
Edwards, Richard d1604 *NotNAT B*

Edwards, Sam *WhoHol A*
Edwards, Sarah 1883-1955 *Film 2, Vers B, WhoHol B*
Edwards, Sarah 1883-1965 *WhScrn 1, WhScrn 2*
Edwards, Sherman 1919- *AmSCAP 1966, EncMT, WhoThe 16*
Edwards, Snitz d1960 *Film 2, TwYS*
Edwards, Snitz 1862-1937 *WhScrn 1, WhScrn 2, WhoHol B*
Edwards, Susie d1963 *NotNAT B*
Edwards, Ted 1883-1945 *WhScrn 1, WhScrn 2, WhoHol B*
Edwards, Thornton *Film 1*
Edwards, Tom 1880- *WhThe*
Edwards, Vince 1928- *FilmgC, IntMPA 1977, MotPP, MovMk, WhoHol A*
Edwards, Virginia d1964 *NotNAT B, WhScrn 1, WhScrn 2, WhoHol B*
Edwards, Vivian *Film 1*
Edwards, Walter *TwYS A*
Edwin, Elizabeth Rebecca Richards 1771?-1854 *OxThe*
Edwin, John 1749-1790 *OxThe*
Edwin, John 1768-1803 *OxThe*
Edwin, T Emery d1951 *NotNAT B*
Effendy, Basuki 192-?- *DcFM*
Effinger, Cecil 1914- *AmSCAP 1966*
Effrat, John 1908-1965 *BiE&WWA, NotNAT B*
Effros, Robert 1900- *AmSCAP 1966*
Egan, Frank C d1927 *NotNAT B*
Egan, Gladys *Film 1*
Egan, Jack *Film 2, TwYS*
Egan, Jefferson *WhoStg 1908*
Egan, Jenny *NotNAT, PIP&P, WhoHol A*
Egan, John C 1892-1940 *AmSCAP 1966*
Egan, Michael 1895-1956 *NotNAT B, WhThe*
Egan, Mishka 1891-1964 *WhScrn 1, WhScrn 2*
Egan, Mishska 1891-1964 *NotNAT B*
Egan, Pierce 1772-1849 *NotNAT A, NotNAT B, OxThe*
Egan, Raymond B 1890-1952 *AmSCAP 1966*
Egan, Richard *MotPP*
Egan, Richard 1921- *FilmgC, MovMk, WhoHol A*
Egan, Richard 1923- *IntMPA 1977*
Egbert, Brothers *WhThe*
Egbuna, Obi 1938- *ConDr 1977*
Ege, Julie 1947?- *FilmgC, WhoHol A*
Eger, John *NewYTET*
Egerton, George d1945 *NotNAT B, WhThe*
Eggan, Carel Rowe *WomWMM B*
Eggar, Jack 1904- *WhThe*
Eggar, Samantha *MotPP, WhoHol A*
Eggar, Samantha 1939- *CelR 3, FilmgC, MovMk*
Eggar, Samantha 1940- *IntMPA 1977*
Egge, Peter 1869-1959 *CnMD*
Eggeling, Viking 1880-1925 *DcFM, OxFilm, WorEnF*
Eggenton, Joseph 1870-1946 *WhScrn 1, WhScrn 2, WhoHol B*
Eggert, E W *Film 2*
Eggerth, Marta *WhoHol A*
Eggerth, Marta 1916- *WhThe*
Eggerth, Marta 1919- *BiE&WWA, NotNAT*
Eggerton, Beryl *Film 2*
Egli, Joseph E 1900-1974 *WhScrn 2*
Eglington, J *WomWMM*
Egnatzik, Joseph 1920- *AmSCAP 1966*
Egner, Philip 1870-1956 *AmSCAP 1966*
Egressy, Gabor 1808-1866 *OxThe*
Egri, Lajos 1888-1967 *BiE&WWA, NotNAT B*
Ehfe, William 1887-1940 *WhScrn 2*
Ehlers, Christl *Film 2*

Ehrensperger, Harold A 1897-1973 *BiE&WWA,*
  NotNAT B
Ehret, Walter 1918- *AmSCAP 1966*
Ehrhart, Barbara *WhoHol A*
Ehrie, Kurt *Film 2*
Ehrlich, Gretal 1946- *WomWMM B*
Ehrlich, Sam 1872-1927 *AmSCAP 1966*
Eibenschutz, Lia *Film 2*
Eichberg, Richard 1888-1952 *WhScrn 2*
Eichelbaum, Samuel 1894-1967 *ModWD, OxThe*
Eichelbaum, Stanley 1926- *BiE&WWA, NotNAT*
Eichendorff, Baron Joseph Von 1788-1857 *McGWD*
Eichhorn, Hermene Warlick 1906- *AmSCAP 1966*
Eichler, Julian 1910- *AmSCAP 1966*
Eichman, Mark 1949- *NatPD*
Eichnor, Edna *Film 2*
Eigsti, Karl 1938- *WhoThe 16*
Eilers, Sally 1908- *Film 2, FilmgC, HolP 30,*
  MotPP, MovMk, ThFT, TwYS, WhoHol A
Einstein, Harry 1904-1958 *NotNAT B, WhScrn 1,*
  WhScrn 2
Eisele, Robert H 1948- *NatPD*
Eiseley, Loren 1907- *CelR 3*
Eisen, Max *BiE&WWA*
Eisenhauer, William G 1925- *AmSCAP 1966*
Eisenhower, Mamie 1896- *CelR 3*
Eisenhower, Milton 1899- *CelR 3*
Eisenstein, Alfred *AmSCAP 1966*
Eisenstein, Sam A 1932- *NatPD*
Eisenstein, Sergei 1898-1948 *BiDFlm, DcFM,*
  FilmgC, MovMk, OxFilm, WorEnF
Eisenstein, Sergei 1898-1949 *WomWMM*
Eisinger, Irene 1906- *WhThe*
Eisinger, Jo *FilmgC*
Eisler, Hanns 1898-1962 *DcFM, OxFilm,*
  WorEnF
Eisler, Hanns 1898-1963 *FilmgC*
Eisley, Anthony *WhoHol A*
Eisman, Mark 1948- *NatPD*
Eisner, Lotte *OxFilm*
Eisner, Michael D *NewYTET*
Ekberg, Anita 1931- *FilmgC, IntMPA 1977,*
  MotPP, MovMk, WhoHol A, WorEnF
Ekborg, Lars 1926-1969 *WhScrn 2*
Ekhof, Konrad 1720-1778 *CnThe, NotNAT B,*
  OxThe
Ekk, Nikolai 1898- *DcFM, WorEnF*
Ekk, Nikolai 1902- *OxFilm*
Ekland, Britt 1942- *FilmgC, IntMPA 1977,*
  WhoHol A
Eklund, Alice *WomWMM*
Ekman, Goesta 1887-1938 *WhScrn 2, WhoHol B*
Ekman, Gosta 1887-1937 *Film 2, FilmgC*
Ekman, Gosta 1890-1938 *OxFilm*
Ekman, Hasse 1915- *OxFilm, WorEnF*
Ekman, John 1880-1949 *Film 1, Film 2,*
  WhScrn 2
Ekstrand, Ray 1917- *AmSCAP 1966*
Ekstrom, Marta 1899-1952 *WhScrn 1, WhScrn 2*
El Nahhas, Hashim *WomWMM*
El Sheikh, Kamel 1918- *DcFM*
Elaine *CelR 3*
Elam, Jack *MotPP, WhoHol A*
Elam, Jack 1916- *FilmgC, MovMk*
Elam, Jack 1917- *CmMov*
Elba, Marta 1920-1954 *WhScrn 1, WhScrn 2*
Elcar, Dana 1927- *BiE&WWA, NotNAT,*
  WhoHol A
Elder, Dottie 1929-1965 *WhScrn 1, WhScrn 2*
Elder, Eldon 1924- *BiE&WWA, NotNAT,*
  WhoThe 16
Elder, Lonne, III *NatPD, NewYTET, PIP&P A*
Elder, Lonne, III 1931- *ConDr 1977, WhoThe 16*
Elder, Lonne, III 1933- *NotNAT*

Elder, Richard 1911-1963 *WhScrn 1, WhScrn 2*
Elder, Ruth *Film 2*
Elder, Sarah *WomWMM B*
Eldred, Arthur d1942 *NotNAT B, WhThe*
Eldredge, John 1904-1960 *MovMk*
Eldredge, John 1904-1961 *FilmgC, WhoHol B*
Eldredge, John 1905-1961 *Vers A*
Eldridge, Anna Mae 1894-1950 *WhScrn 1,*
  WhScrn 2
Eldridge, Charles 1854-1922 *Film 1, Film 2,*
  WhScrn 1, WhScrn 2, WhoHol B
Eldridge, Florence 1901- *BiE&WWA, CnThe,*
  Film 2, FilmgC, MotPP, MovMk, NotNAT,
  ThFT, WhThe, WhoHol A
Eldridge, John 1904-1961 *WhScrn 1, WhScrn 2*
Eldridge, John 1917- *FilmgC*
Eldridge, Louisa d1905 *NotNAT B*
Elek, Judit 1937- *OxFilm, WomWMM*
Elen, Gus 1862-1940 *NotNAT B, OxThe, PIP&P,*
  WhThe, WhoStg 1908
Eles, Sandor 1946- *FilmgC*
Elfand, Martin *IntMPA 1977*
Elg, Taina 1931- *FilmgC, IntMPA 1977, MotPP,*
  WhoHol A
Elg-Lundberg, Otto *Film 2*
Elgar, Avril 1932- *WhoThe 16*
Elias, Hal *IntMPA 1977*
Elias, Hector *WhoThe 16*
Elias, Michael 1918- *AmSCAP 1966*
Elias, Miriam *Film 2*
Elias, Rosalind 1931- *CelR 3*
Eliasberg, Jay *NewYTET*
Elie, Justin 1883-1931 *AmSCAP 1966*
Eline, Marie *Film 1*
Elinor, Carli D 1890-1958 *WhScrn 1, WhScrn 2*
Elinor, Peggy *Film 2*
Elinore, Kate d1924 *NotNAT B*
Eliot, Arthur d1936 *NotNAT B*
Eliot, Max d1911 *NotNAT B*
Eliot, T S 1888-1965 *BiE&WWA, CnThe,*
  CroCD, McGWD, ModWD, NotNAT A,
  PIP&P, REnWD, WhThe
Eliot, Thomas Stearns 1888-1965 *CnMD,*
  NotNAT B, OxThe
Eliscu, Edward *AmSCAP 1966*
Eliscu, Fernanda 1882-1968 *WhScrn 2, WhThe*
Elitch, Mary d1936 *NotNAT A*
Elizaroff, E *Film 2*
Elizondo, Hector 1936- *IntMPA 1977,*
  WhoHol A, WhoThe 16
Elizondo, Joaquin 1896-1952 *WhScrn 1,*
  WhScrn 2
Elkas, Edward *Film 2*
Elkin, Saul 1932- *NotNAT*
Elkins, Hillard 1929- *CelR 3, NotNAT A,*
  WhoThe 16
Elkins, Marie Louise d1961 *NotNAT B*
Elkins, Saul 1907- *IntMPA 1977*
Elkus, Albert 1884-1946 *AmSCAP 1966*
Elkus, Edward *Film 1*
Elkus, Jonathan 1931- *AmSCAP 1966*
Ellenstein, Robert *WhoHol A*
Ellerbe, Harry *BiE&WWA, NotNAT,*
  WhoHol A
Elliman, Yvonne *WhoHol A*
Ellinger, Desíree 1893-1951 *NotNAT B, WhThe*
Ellingford, William 1863-1936 *Film 1, Film 2,*
  WhScrn 1, WhScrn 2, WhoHol B
Ellington, Duke 1899-1974 *AmSCAP 1966,*
  BiE&WWA, CelR 3, FilmgC, NotNAT A,
  NotNAT B, WhScrn 2, WhoHol B
Ellington, Mercer 1919- *AmSCAP 1966*
Ellingwood, Helmert 1907-1971 *WhScrn 2,*
  WhoHol B

Elliot, Arthur d1936 *NotNAT B*
Elliot, Biff *WhoHol A*
Elliot, Cass 1943-1974 *CelR 3, WhoHol B*
Elliot, Cass *see also* Elliott, Cassandra
Elliot, George 1899- *WhThe*
Elliot, Grace *WomWMM*
Elliot, Laura 1929- *FilmgC*
Elliot, William d1931 *NotNAT B*
Elliott, Alonzo 1891-1964 *AmSCAP 1966, NotNAT B*
Elliott, Bert 1929-1972 *WhScrn 2*
Elliott, Bob 1923- *CelR 3*
Elliott, Cassandra 1941-1974 *WhScrn 2*
Elliott, Cassandra *see also* Elliot, Cass
Elliott, David *WhoHol A*
Elliott, Del *Film 2*
Elliott, Denholm 1922- *BiE&WWA, CnThe, FilmgC, IntMPA 1977, NotNAT, WhoHol A, WhoThe 16*
Elliott, Dick 1886-1961 *NotNAT B, Vers A, WhScrn 1, WhScrn 2, WhoHol B*
Elliott, Don 1926- *BiE&WWA, NotNAT*
Elliott, Frank *Film 2*
Elliott, George Henry 1884-1962 *NotNAT B, OxThe, WhThe*
Elliott, Gertrude 1874-1950 *Film 1, NotNAT B, WhScrn 1, WhScrn 2, WhThe, WhoHol B, WhoStg 1908*
Elliott, Gertrude *see also* Elliott, May Gertrude
Elliott, Gordon 1904-1965 *WhScrn 1, WhScrn 2, WhoHol B*
Elliott, Gordon William 1906-1965 *Film 2*
Elliott, John B 1907- *AmSCAP 1966*
Elliott, John H 1876-1956 *Film 2, WhScrn 2*
Elliott, John M 1914- *AmSCAP 1966*
Elliott, John Tiffany d1963 *NotNAT B*
Elliott, Leonard *WhoHol A*
Elliott, Lester 1888-1954 *WhScrn 1, WhScrn 2*
Elliott, Lewis 1921- *AmSCAP 1966*
Elliott, Lillian 1875-1959 *Film 2, WhScrn 1, WhScrn 2, WhoHol B*
Elliott, Madge 1898-1955 *NotNAT B, WhThe*
Elliott, Maxine 1868-1940 *FamA&A, NotNAT A, NotNAT B, OxThe*
Elliott, Maxine 1871-1940 *Film 1, Film 2, TwYS, WhThe*
Elliott, Maxine 1873-1940 *WhScrn 1, WhScrn 2, WhoHol B, WhoStg 1906, WhoStg 1908*
Elliott, May Gertrude 1872-1950 *OxThe*
Elliott, May Gertrude *see also* Elliott, Gertrude
Elliott, Michael 1931- *WhoThe 16*
Elliott, Milton Skeets 1896-1920 *WhScrn 2*
Elliott, Patricia 1942- *NotNAT, WhoThe 16*
Elliott, Paul 1941- *WhoThe 16*
Elliott, Peggy *WomWMM*
Elliott, Robert d1963 *WhoHol B*
Elliott, Robert 1879-1951 *Film 1, Film 2, TwYS, WhScrn 1, WhScrn 2, WhoHol B*
Elliott, Ross *WhoHol A*
Elliott, Sam *WhoHol A*
Elliott, Stephen 1945- *NotNAT, WhoHol A, WhoThe 16*
Elliott, Sue *WomWMM B*
Elliott, Sumner Locke 1917- *BiE&WWA, NotNAT*
Elliott, Wild Bill d1965 *MotPP, WhoHol B*
Elliott, Wild Bill 1903-1965 *HolP 40*
Elliott, Wild Bill 1906-1965 *CmMov, FilmgC*
Elliott, William *WhoHol A*
Elliott, William 1880-1932 *WhScrn 2*
Elliott, William 1885-1932 *Film 1, NotNAT B, WhThe, WhoHol B*
Elliott, William Wild Bill 1904-1965 *WhScrn 1, WhScrn 2*

Ellis, Anita 1926- *BiE&WWA, NotNAT*
Ellis, Anthony L d1944 *NotNAT B, WhThe*
Ellis, Brandon d1916 *NotNAT B*
Ellis, Diane 1909-1930 *Film 2, WhScrn 1, WhScrn 2, WhoHol B*
Ellis, Edith d1960 *NotNAT B, WhThe*
Ellis, Edward 1871-1952 *Vers A, WhScrn 1, WhScrn 2, WhoHol B*
Ellis, Edward 1872-1952 *FilmgC, NotNAT B, WhThe*
Ellis, Elaine *Film 2*
Ellis, Evelyn 1894-1958 *NotNAT B, WhScrn 1, WhScrn 2, WhoHol B*
Ellis, Frank *Film 2*
Ellis, Frank B d1969 *WhScrn 2, WhoHol B*
Ellis, Jack 1908- *AmSCAP 1966*
Ellis, Lillian *Film 2*
Ellis, Mary *BiE&WWA, NotNAT*
Ellis, Mary 1899- *ThFT, WhoHol A*
Ellis, Mary 1900- *EncMT, FilmgC, WhoThe 16*
Ellis, Max d1964 *NotNAT B*
Ellis, Michael 1917- *BiE&WWA, NotNAT*
Ellis, Patricia 1916-1970 *FilmgC, ThFT, WhScrn 1, WhScrn 2, WhoHol B*
Ellis, Paul *Film 2*
Ellis, Raymond *Film 2*
Ellis, Robert 1892-1935 *Film 1, Film 2, TwYS, WhScrn 1, WhScrn 2, WhoHol B*
Ellis, Robert 1933-1973 *WhScrn 2, WhoHol B*
Ellis, Seger 1904- *AmSCAP 1966*
Ellis, Vivian 1904- *EncMT, WhoThe 16*
Ellis, Walter 1874-1956 *NotNAT B, WhThe*
Ellis-Fermor, Una Mary 1894-1958 *NotNAT B*
Ellison, James 1910- *FilmgC, MovMk, WhoHol A*
Ellison, Margorie *Film 1*
Ellison, Sydney d1930 *NotNAT B*
Elliston, Daisy 1894- *WhThe*
Elliston, Grace 1881-1950 *NotNAT B, WhThe, WhoStg 1906, WhoStg 1908*
Elliston, Robert William 1774-1831 *NotNAT A, NotNAT B, OxThe, PIP&P*
Ellman, Stephen A 1935- *IntMPA 1977*
Ellrod, John G 1924- *NatPD*
Ellsasser, Richard 1926- *AmSCAP 1966*
Ellsler, Effie 1823-1918 *NotNAT B*
Ellsler, Effie 1855-1942 *Film 2, NotNAT B, WhScrn 1, WhScrn 2, WhoHol B*
Ellsler, John Adam 1822-1900 *NotNAT A*
Ellstein, Abraham 1907-1963 *AmSCAP 1966, NotNAT B*
Ellsworth, Jack Herschel 1911-1949 *WhScrn 1, WhScrn 2*
Ellsworth, James 1927- *IntMPA 1977*
Ellsworth, Robert *Film 2*
Ellsworth, Robert H 1895- *AmSCAP 1966*
Elman, Harry Ziggy 1914-1968 *AmSCAP 1966, WhScrn 1, WhScrn 2*
Elman, Irving 1922- *AmSCAP 1966*
Elman, Mischa 1891- *AmSCAP 1966, Film 2*
Elman, Ziggy 1914-1968 *WhoHol B*
Elmer, Billy 1870-1945 *Film 1, WhScrn 1, WhScrn 2, WhoHol B*
Elmer, Cedric Nagel 1939- *AmSCAP 1966*
Elmer, Clarence Jay *Film 1, Film 2*
Elmer, Rita *WomWMM*
Elmer, William *Film 2*
Elmes, Guy 1920- *FilmgC, IntMPA 1977*
Elmore, Bruce 1885-1940 *WhScrn 2*
Elmore, Pearl *Film 1*
Elmore, Robert 1913- *AmSCAP 1966*
Elmslie, Kenward 1929- *AmSCAP 1966*
Elnecave, Viviane *WomWMM*
Elow, Lawrence 1927- *AmSCAP 1966*

Elphistone, Emma d1888 *NotNAT B*
Elser, Frank B d1935 *NotNAT B*, *PIP&P*
Elsie, Lily 1886-1962 *EncMT*, *NotNAT B*, *WhThe*
Elsmo, Ralph Norman 1919- *AmSCAP 1966*
Elsmo, Sverre S 1910- *AmSCAP 1966*
Elsom, Isobel 1893- *Film 1*, *Film 2*, *FilmgC*, *MovMk*, *WhThe*
Elsom, Isobel 1894- *Vers A*, *WhoHol A*
Elsom, Isobel 1896- *BiE&WWA*, *NotNAT*
Elson, Anita 1898- *WhThe*
Elson, Charles 1909- *NotNAT*
Elson, Norman 1907- *IntMPA 1977*
Elssler, Fanny 1810-1884 *NotNAT B*
Elston, Robert 1934- *BiE&WWA*, *NotNAT*
Elter, Amielka *Film 2*
Eltinge, Julian 1882-1940 *WhoHol B*
Eltinge, Julian 1882-1941 *Film 1*, *Film 2*, *FilmgC*
Eltinge, Julian 1883-1941 *NotNAT B*, *OxThe*, *TwYS*, *WhScrn 1*, *WhScrn 2*, *WhThe*
Elton, Sir Arthur 1906-1973 *FilmgC*, *OxFilm*, *WorEnF*
Elton, Edmund *Film 1*
Elton, Edward William 1794-1843 *NotNAT B*, *OxThe*
Elton, Frank d1954 *NotNAT B*
Elton, George 1875-1942 *NotNAT B*, *WhThe*
Elvey, Maurice 1887-1967 *Film 1*, *FilmgC*, *OxFilm*, *WhThe*, *WorEnF*
Elvidge, June 1893-1965 *Film 1*, *Film 2*, *TwYS*, *WhScrn 1*, *WhScrn 2*, *WhoHol B*
Elvin, Joe 1862-1935 *NotNAT B*, *OxThe*, *WhThe*
Elvin, Violetta 1925- *WhThe*
Elward, James *NatPD*
Elwell, George 1896-1916 *WhScrn 2*
Elwell, Herbert 1898- *AmSCAP 1966*
Ely, G A *Film 1*
Ely, Harry R 1883-1951 *WhScrn 1*, *WhScrn 2*
Ely, Lyn *BiE&WWA*, *NotNAT*
Ely, Ron *MotPP*, *WhoHol A*
Elzer, Karl *Film 2*
Eman, Dawn *WhoHol A*
Eman, Tracey *WhoHol A*
Emanuel, David 1910- *IntMPA 1977*
Embree, Charles B, Jr. 1919- *AmSCAP 1966*
Emden, Henry d1930 *NotNAT B*
Emden, Margaret d1946 *NotNAT B*
Emerald, Charles *Film 2*
Emerald, Connie d1959 *NotNAT B*, *WhThe*, *WomWMM*
Emerick, Besse 1875-1939 *WhScrn 1*, *WhScrn 2*, *WhoHol B*
Emerick, Robert 1916-1973 *WhScrn 2*
Emerson, Edward 1910-1975 *WhScrn 2*, *WhoHol C*
Emerson, Eric 1945-1975 *WhScrn 2*
Emerson, Faye 1917- *BiE&WWA*, *FilmgC*, *HolP 40*, *MotPP*, *MovMk*, *NewYTET*, *WhThe*, *WhoHol A*
Emerson, Hope d1960 *MotPP*, *NotNAT B*, *WhoHol B*
Emerson, Hope 1897-1960 *FilmgC*, *WhScrn 1*, *WhScrn 2*
Emerson, Hope 1898-1960 *MovMk*, *Vers A*
Emerson, John 1874-1956 *Film 1*, *NotNAT B*, *TwYS A*, *WhScrn 1*, *WhScrn 2*, *WhThe*, *WhoHol B*, *WorEnF*
Emerson, John 1878-1946 *DcFM*
Emerson, Mary d1921 *NotNAT B*
Emerson, Ralph *Film 2*
Emerton, Roy 1892-1944 *FilmgC*, *NotNAT B*, *WhScrn 1*, *WhScrn 2*, *WhThe*, *WhoHol B*

Emery, Dick 1919- *FilmgC*
Emery, Mrs. Edward *WhScrn 1*, *WhScrn 2*
Emery, Edward 1861-1938 *NotNAT B*, *WhoStg 1906*, *WhoStg 1908*
Emery, Edwin T d1951 *NotNAT B*
Emery, Frederick d1930 *NotNAT B*
Emery, Gilbert *MotPP*
Emery, Gilbert 1875-1945 *FilmgC*, *NotNAT B*, *Vers B*, *WhScrn 1*, *WhScrn 2*, *WhThe*, *WhoHol B*
Emery, Gilbert 1882-1934 *WhScrn 1*, *WhScrn 2*
Emery, Gilbert 1889-1945 *Film 2*, *MovMk*
Emery, John 1777-1822 *OxThe*
Emery, John 1822-1965 *NotNAT B*
Emery, John 1905-1964 *BiE&WWA*, *FilmgC*, *MotPP*, *MovMk*, *Vers A*, *WhScrn 1*, *WhScrn 2*, *WhThe*, *WhoHol B*
Emery, Katherine 1908- *BiE&WWA*, *NotNAT*, *PIP&P*, *WhThe*
Emery, Louise d1943 *NotNAT B*
Emery, Pollie 1875-1958 *NotNAT B*, *WhThe*
Emery, Polly 1875-1958 *WhoHol B*
Emery, Rose d1934 *NotNAT B*
Emery, Samuel Anderson 1817-1881 *NotNAT B*, *OxThe*
Emery, Winifred 1862-1924 *NotNAT B*, *OxThe*, *WhThe*
Emhardt, Robert 1901.?- *BiE&WWA*, *FilmgC*, *NotNAT*, *WhThe*, *WhoHol A*
Emil-Behnke, Kate d1957 *NotNAT B*
Emlyn, Fairy *Film 2*
Emmer, Luciano 1918- *DcFM*, *FilmgC*, *OxFilm*, *WorEnF*
Emmerich, Robert D 1904- *AmSCAP 1966*
Emmes, David 1939- *NotNAT*
Emmet, Alfred 1908- *WhoThe 16*
Emmet, Katherine d1960 *NotNAT B*, *WhScrn 1*, *WhScrn 2*
Emmett, Catherine d1960 *Film 2*, *WhoHol B*
Emmett, Dan 1815-1904 *NotNAT B*
Emmett, Daniel *PIP&P*
Emmett, E V H 1902- *FilmgC*
Emmett, Fern 1896-1946 *WhScrn 1*, *WhScrn 2*, *WhoHol B*
Emmett, J K d1891 *NotNAT B*
Emmons, Louise 1852-1935 *WhScrn 1*, *WhScrn 2*, *WhoHol B*
Emmons, M *Film 1*
Emney, Fred 1865-1917 *OxThe*, *WhThe*
Emney, Fred 1900- *FilmgC*, *OxThe*, *WhoThe 16*
Emney, Joan Fred *WhThe*
Emny, Fred 1865-1917 *NotNAT B*
Emory, Gilbert *Film 2*
Emory, Maude *Film 1*, *Film 2*
Emory, May *Film 1*
Empey, Arthur Guy 1883-1963 *TwYS A*
Empey, Arthur Guy 1884-1963 *WhScrn 1*, *WhScrn 2*
Empey, Guy d1963 *Film 1*, *WhoHol B*
Empress, Marie *Film 1*
Empy, Guy d1963 *NotNAT B*
Emshwiller, Ed 1925- *OxFilm*
Emurian, Ernest K 1912- *AmSCAP 1966*
Ena, Rose *Film 2*
Encina, Juan Del 1468?-1537? *NotNAT B*, *OxThe*
Encina, Juan Del 1469?-1529? *McGWD*
Enders, Harvey 1892-1947 *AmSCAP 1966*
Enders, Robert *IntMPA 1977*
Endfield, C Raker 1914- *WorEnF*
Endfield, Cy 1914- *BiDFlm*, *FilmgC*, *WorEnF*
Endore, Guy 1901-1970 *NotNAT B*
Endrey, Eugene *NotNAT A*
Enei, Yevgeni 1890- *DcFM*

Enfield, Cy 1914- *IntMPA 1977*
Enfield, Cyril Raker 1914- *DcFM*
Enfield, Hugh *WhScrn 1, WhScrn 2*
Engblom, Verne A 1919- *AmSCAP 1966*
Engel, Alexander 1902-1968 *WhScrn 1, WhScrn 2, WhoHol B*
Engel, Billie *Film 2*
Engel, Carl 1883-1944 *AmSCAP 1966*
Engel, Erich 1891- *OxFilm*
Engel, Lehman 1910- *BiE&WWA, NotNAT, NotNAT A*
Engel, Marie d1971 *WhoHol B*
Engel, Morris 1918- *DcFM, FilmgC, IntMPA 1977, OxFilm, WomWMM, WorEnF*
Engel, Olga *Film 2*
Engel, Roy *WhoHol A*
Engel, Samuel 1904- *FilmgC*
Engel, Susan 1935- *WhoHol A, WhoThe 16*
Engels, Georg d1907 *NotNAT B*
England, Barry 1934- *ConDr 1977*
England, Daisy d1943 *NotNAT B*
England, Paul 1893-1968 *WhScrn 2, WhThe*
England, Sue *WhoHol A*
Englander, Ludwig d1914 *WhThe, WhoStg 1906, WhoStg 1908*
Englander, Ludwig 1853-1914 *EncMT*
Englander, Ludwig 1859-1914 *NewMT, NotNAT B*
Englander, Roger *NewYTET*
Engle, Billy 1889-1966 *WhScrn 1, WhScrn 2, WhoHol B*
Engle, Marie 1902-1971 *WhScrn 1, WhScrn 2*
Englefield, Violet 1886-1946 *NotNAT B*
Engleman, Andrews *Film 2*
Englisch, Lucie 1897-1956 *WhoHol B*
Englisch, Lucie 1897-1965 *WhScrn 1, WhScrn 2*
English, Colonel *Film 2*
English, Deidre *WomWMM B*
English, Granville 1900- *AmSCAP 1966*
English, James *Film 2*
English, Robert *Film 2*
English Aristophanes, The *OxThe*
Englund, George H 1926- *FilmgC, IntMPA 1977*
Englund, Ken 1914- *FilmgC, IntMPA 1977*
Englund, Maude Beatrice Galbraith 1891-1962 *NotNAT B*
Englund, Patricia *WhoHol A*
Ennery, Adolphe D' 1812-1899 *NotNAT B*
Ennis, Charles 1917- *BiE&WWA*
Ennis, Patrick *Film 1*
Ennis, Skinnay 1907-1963 *WhScrn 1, WhScrn 2, WhoHol B*
Ennius, Quintus 239BC-169BC *NotNAT B, OxThe*
Enrico, Robert 1931- *FilmgC, OxFilm, WorEnF*
Enright, Florence d1961 *WhScrn 1, WhScrn 2, WhoHol B*
Enright, Josephine d1976 *WhoHol C*
Enright, Ray 1896-1965 *BiDFlm, FilmgC, TwYS A*
Enright, Raymond 1896-1965 *WorEnF*
Enright, Sara 1888-1963 *NotNAT B*
Enstedt, Howard *Film 2*
Enters, Angna 1907- *BiE&WWA, NotNAT, NotNAT A, OxThe*
Enters, Warren 1927- *BiE&WWA, NotNAT*
Enthoven, Gabrielle 1868-1950 *NotNAT B, OxThe, WhThe*
Entratter, Jack 1913-1971 *WhScrn 2*
Entwistle, Harold 1865-1944 *WhScrn 1, WhScrn 2, WhoHol B*
Entwistle, Lillian Millicent d1932 *NotNAT B*
Entwistle, Peg 1908-1932 *WhScrn 1, WhScrn 2,*

WhoHol B
Eorsi, Istvan 1931- *CroCD*
Ephraim, Lee 1877-1953 *WhThe*
Ephriam, Lee 1877-1953 *NotNAT B*
Ephron, Henry 1912- *BiE&WWA, FilmgC, NotNAT, WomWMM*
Ephron, Phoebe 1916-1971 *BiE&WWA, NotNAT B, WomWMM*
Ephros, Gershon 1890- *AmSCAP 1966*
Epicharmus 550?BC-460BC *NotNAT B, OxThe, PIP&P*
Epperson, Don 1938-1973 *WhScrn 2*
Eppert, Carl 1882-1961 *AmSCAP 1966*
Epstein, Alvin 1925- *BiE&WWA, NotNAT, PIP&P, WhoThe 16*
Epstein, David M 1930- *AmSCAP 1966*
Epstein, Donald K 1933- *AmSCAP 1966*
Epstein, Jean 1897-1953 *BiDFlm, DcFM, FilmgC, OxFilm, WorEnF*
Epstein, Julius J 1909- *BiE&WWA, FilmgC, NotNAT, WorEnF*
Epstein, Marie *WomWMM*
Epstein, Mel 1910- *IntMPA 1977*
Epstein, Philip G 1909-1952 *FilmgC, NotNAT B*
Erastoff, Edith 1887-1945 *Film 1, WhScrn 2*
Erbacher, Shirley *WomWMM B*
Erckmann, Emile 1822-1899 *NotNAT B*
Erckmann-Chatrian *OxThe, PIP&P*
Erdman, Ernie 1879-1946 *AmSCAP 1966*
Erdman, Jean *NotNAT*
Erdman, Nikolai Robertovich 1902-1970 *ModWD*
Erdman, Richard 1925- *FilmgC, IntMPA 1977, MotPP, Vers B, WhoHol A*
Erdman, Theodore John 1930- *AmSCAP 1966*
Erdmann, Nikolai 1902-1936 *CnMD*
Erdody, Leo 1888-1949 *AmSCAP 1966*
Erduran, Refik 1928- *REnWD*
Erenberg, Elena *WomWMM B*
Erhardt, Thomas 1928- *BiE&WWA*
Eric, Fred 1874-1935 *NotNAT B, WhThe*
Erickson, Chris 1945-1971 *WhScrn 2*
Erickson, Corydon 1944- *IntMPA 1977*
Erickson, Eddy G 1925- *IntMPA 1977*
Erickson, Frank 1923- *AmSCAP 1966*
Erickson, Jack 1898- *AmSCAP 1966*
Erickson, Knute 1871-1946 *Film 2, WhScrn 1, WhScrn 2, WhoHol B*
Erickson, Launcelot 1949- *IntMPA 1977*
Erickson, Leif 1911- *BiE&WWA, FilmgC, IntMPA 1977, MotPP, MovMk, WhoHol A*
Ericson, John *BiE&WWA, WhoHol A*
Ericson, John 1926- *IntMPA 1977, NotNAT*
Ericson, John 1927- *FilmgC, MGM*
Ericson, Leif 1911- *PIP&P*
Erikson, Erik 1902- *CelR 3*
Erlanger, Abraham L 1860-1930 *EncMT, NotNAT B, WhThe*
Ermelli, Claudio 1892-1964 *WhScrn 1, WhScrn 2, WhoHol B*
Ermler, Friedrich 1898-1967 *DcFM, WorEnF*
Ermler, Friedrich 1908-1967 *OxFilm*
Ermolieff, Joseph N 1890-1962 *NotNAT B*
Erne, Vincent 1884- *WhThe*
Ernst, Earle 1911- *BiE&WWA, NotNAT*
Ernst, Max 1891- *CelR 3*
Ernst, Otto 1862-1926 *ModWD*
Ernst, Paul 1866-1933 *CnMD, McGWD, ModWD, NotNAT B, OxThe*
Errol, Leon 1881-1951 *EncMT, Film 2, FilmgC, MotPP, MovMk, NotNAT B, PIP&P, WhScrn 1, WhScrn 2, WhThe, WhoHol B*
Errol, Leon 1881-1952 *Vers B*
Erskin, Chester 1903- *WhThe*
Erskine, Chester 1905- *FilmgC*

Erskine, Sir David d1837 *NotNAT B*
Erskine, Howard 1926- *BiE&WWA, NotNAT, WhoThe 16*
Erskine, John 1879-1951 *NotNAT B*
Erskine, Marilyn *WhoHol A*
Erskine, Wallace *WhoStg 1908*
Erskine, Wallace 1862-1943 *NotNAT B, WhScrn 1, WhScrn 2, WhoHol B*
Ertegun, Ahmet 1923- *CelR 3*
Ertugrul, Mushin 1888- *DcFM*
Ervin, Sam 1896- *CelR 3*
Ervine, John St. John Greer 1883-1971 *OxThe*
Ervine, St. John 1883-1971 *CnMD, CnThe, McGWD, ModWD, NotNAT B, PIP&P, REnWD, WhThe*
Erwin, Barbara *WhoHol A*
Erwin, George 1913- *AmSCAP 1966*
Erwin, June 1918-1965 *WhScrn 1, WhScrn 2, WhoHol B*
Erwin, Lee 1908- *AmSCAP 1966*
Erwin, Madge d1967 *WhoHol B*
Erwin, Roy 1925-1958 *WhScrn 1, WhScrn 2*
Erwin, Stu 1903-1967 *BiE&WWA, NotNAT B*
Erwin, Stuart d1967 *MotPP, WhoHol B*
Erwin, Stuart 1902-1967 *WhScrn 1, WhScrn 2*
Erwin, Stuart 1903-1967 *Film 2, FilmgC, MovMk*
Escande, Maurice 1893-1973 *WhScrn 2*
Escoffier, Marcel 1910- *DcFM*
Esdale, Charles 1873-1937 *Film 2, WhScrn 2*
Eskilson, Richard E 1923- *AmSCAP 1966*
Eslava, Fernan Gonzalez De *OxThe*
Esler, Lemist 1888-1960 *NotNAT B*
Esmelton, Fred *Film 1*
Esmelton, Frederick *Film 2*
Esmond, Annie 1873-1945 *Film 2, NotNAT B, WhThe, WhoHol B*
Esmond, Carl 1905- *FilmgC, WhThe*
Esmond, Carl 1906- *IntMPA 1977, Vers A, WhoHol A*
Esmond, Georgette *Film 2*
Esmond, Henry V 1869-1922 *NotNAT B, OxThe, WhThe, WhoStg 1908*
Esmond, Jill 1908- *FilmgC, WhThe, WhoHol A*
Espar, Sheri Gillette *WomWMM B*
Espinosa, Edouard 1872-1950 *NotNAT A, WhThe*
Espinosa, Julio Garcia 193-?- *DcFM*
Esposito, Giancarlo *WhoHol A*
Esposito, Robert *NatPD*
Esposito, Vincent *WhoHol A*
Espy, L' *OxThe*
Espy, William Gray *WhoHol A*
Essen, Viola *WhoHol B*
Essenfeld, Barry 1936- *IntMPA 1977*
Esser, Peter 1896-1970 *WhScrn 1, WhScrn 2*
Essex, David 1947- *IntMPA 1977, WhoHol A*
Essex, Francis 1929- *IntMPA 1977*
Essex, Harry J 1910- *FilmgC, IntMPA 1977*
Essig, Hermann 1878-1918 *CnMD, ModWD*
Esslair, Ferdinand 1772-1840 *OxThe*
Essler, Fred 1896-1973 *WhScrn 2, WhoHol B*
Esslin, Martin 1918- *BiE&WWA, NotNAT, WhoThe 16*
Esson, Louis 1879-1943 *ModWD*
Estabrook, Howard 1884- *TwYS A, WhThe*
Estabrook, Howard 1894- *Film 1, FilmgC*
Estcourt, Dick 1668-1712 *OxThe*
Estcourt, Richard 1668-1712 *NotNAT B*
Estee, Adelyn 1871-1941 *WhScrn 1, WhScrn 2*
Estelita d1966 *WhoHol B*
Esten, Mrs. 1763-1865 *NotNAT B*
Esterhazy, Countess Agnes *Film 2*
Estrada, Arthur *IntMPA 1977*

Estrella, Joseph C 1908- *AmSCAP 1966*
Estridge, Robin 1920- *FilmgC*
Estudillo, Leo B 1900-1957 *WhScrn 1, WhScrn 2*
Etaix, Pierre 1928- *BiDFlm, DcFM, FilmgC, OxFilm, WorEnF*
Ethel, Agnes 1852-1903 *FamA&A*
Ethel, Agnes 1853-1903 *NotNAT B*
Etherege, Sir George 1634?-1691? *CnThe, OxThe, REnWD*
Etherege, Sir George 1635?-1691 *McGWD, NotNAT A, NotNAT B, PIP&P*
Etherington, James 1902-1948 *NotNAT B, WhThe*
Ethier, Alphonse 1875-1943 *Film 1, Film 2, WhScrn 1, WhScrn 2, WhoHol B*
Ethier, Alphonz *TwYS*
Etkes, Nadine *WomWMM B*
Etting, Ruth 1897- *WhoHol A*
Etting, Ruth 1907- *EncMT, WhThe*
Ettinger, Edwin D 1921- *IntMPA 1977*
Ettinger, Solomon 1800?-1856 *McGWD*
Ettlinger, John A 1924- *IntMPA 1977*
Ettlinger, Karl *Film 2*
Ettore, Eugene 1921- *AmSCAP 1966*
Eugene, Billy *Film 2*
Eugene, William *Film 2*
Eulenberg, Herbert 1876-1949 *CnMD, ModWD, NotNAT B*
Eulo, Ken 1939- *NatPD*
Eunson, Dale 1904- *BiE&WWA, NotNAT*
Euphorion *OxThe*
Eupolis 446?BC-411?BC *OxThe*
Euripedes 480BC-406BC *REnWD*
Euripedes 484BC-406BC *CnThe*
Euripedes 485?BC-406?BC *McGWD*
Euripides 484BC-406?BC *OxThe*
Euripides 484BC-407BC *PIP&P*
Euripides 486?BC-407BC *NotNAT A, NotNAT B*
Eustace, Fred *Film 1*
Eustace, Jennie A 1865-1936 *NotNAT B, WhoStg 1908*
Eustrel, Antony 1904- *WhThe*
Eva, Evi *Film 2*
Evald, Johanna *Film 2*
Evangelisti, Victor *Film 2*
Evans, Albert *NatPD*
Evans, Alison Ridley 1929- *BiE&WWA*
Evans, Barry 1943- *IntMPA 1977*
Evans, Barry 1945- *FilmgC*
Evans, Bergen 1904- *CelR 3, NewYTET*
Evans, Bob 1904-1961 *WhScrn 2*
Evans, Brandon d1958 *WhoHol B*
Evans, Bruce *WhoHol A*
Evans, Caradoc d1945 *NotNAT B, WhThe*
Evans, Cecile *Film 2*
Evans, Cecilia 1902-1960 *WhScrn 1, WhScrn 2, WhoHol B*
Evans, Charles E 1856-1945 *NotNAT B, WhoStg 1906, WhoStg 1908*
Evans, Charles E 1857-1945 *Film 2, WhScrn 1, WhScrn 2, WhoHol B*
Evans, Clifford 1912- *FilmgC, IntMPA 1977, WhThe, WhoHol A*
Evans, Dale 1912- *AmSCAP 1966, FilmgC, HolP 40, MotPP, MovMk, WhoHol A*
Evans, Don *NatPD*
Evans, Douglas 1904-1968 *WhScrn 1, WhScrn 2, WhoHol B*
Evans, Edith 1888- *CelR 3, CnThe, Film 1, FilmgC, IntMPA 1977, MotPP, MovMk, NotNAT A, OxFilm, OxThe, PIP&P, WhoHol A, WhoThe 16, WorEnF*
Evans, Edith 1894-1962 *WhScrn 1, WhScrn 2,*

WhoHol B

Evans, Edwin d1945 *NotNAT B*

Evans, Evan 1901-1954 *WhScrn 1, WhScrn 2, WhoHol B*

Evans, Evan E 1875-1962 *NotNAT B*

Evans, Evans *WhoHol A*

Evans, Frank *Film 1, Film 2*

Evans, Fred 1889-1951 *Film 1, Film 2*

Evans, Gene *WhoHol A*

Evans, Gene 1922- *FilmgC*

Evans, Gene 1924- *IntMPA 1977*

Evans, Helena Phillips 1875-1955 *WhScrn 1, WhScrn 2, WhoHol B*

Evans, Herbert 1883-1952 *Vers B, WhScrn 1, WhScrn 2, WhoHol B*

Evans, Jack 1893-1950 *Film 2, WhScrn 1, WhScrn 2, WhoHol B*

Evans, Jerome M 1923- *IntMPA 1977*

Evans, Jessie 1918- *WhoThe 16*

Evans, Joan 1934- *FilmgC, MotPP, WhoHol A*

Evans, Joe 1891-1967 *Film 1, Film 2*

Evans, Joe 1916-1973 *WhScrn 2*

Evans, Julius *IntMPA 1977*

Evans, Karin *Film 2*

Evans, Leo L 1927- *AmSCAP 1966*

Evans, Linda *WhoHol A*

Evans, Lyle *PIP&P*

Evans, Madge 1909- *BiE&WWA, Film 1, Film 2, FilmgC, MGM, MotPP, MovMk, ThFT, TwYS, WhThe, WhoHol A*

Evans, Marguerite *Film 2*

Evans, Marion 1926- *AmSCAP 1966*

Evans, Mark *WomWMM*

Evans, Mary Jane 1923- *BiE&WWA, NotNAT*

Evans, Maurice 1901- *BiE&WWA, CnThe, EncMT, FamA&A, FilmgC, IntMPA 1977, MotPP, MovMk, NewYTET, NotNAT, OxThe, PIP&P, WhoHol A, WhoThe 16*

Evans, Michael 1922- *WhThe*

Evans, Michael 1926- *BiE&WWA, NotNAT*

Evans, Mike *WhoHol A*

Evans, Myddleton *Film 2*

Evans, Nancy d1963 *WhScrn 1, WhScrn 2, WhoHol B*

Evans, Nancy 1915- *WhThe*

Evans, Norman d1962 *NotNAT B*

Evans, Pat *WomWMM B*

Evans, Paul 1938- *AmSCAP 1966*

Evans, Pauline 1917-1952 *WhScrn 1, WhScrn 2*

Evans, Ray 1915- *BiE&WWA, FilmgC, IntMPA 1977, NotNAT*

Evans, Raymond B 1915- *AmSCAP 1966*

Evans, Redd 1912- *AmSCAP 1966*

Evans, Renee 1908-1971 *WhScrn 1, WhScrn 2*

Evans, Rex 1903-1969 *FilmgC, Vers A, WhScrn 1, WhScrn 2, WhoHol B*

Evans, Richard *WhoHol A*

Evans, Robert 1930- *CelR 3, FilmgC, IntMPA 1977, MotPP, WhoHol A*

Evans, Rothbury d1944 *NotNAT B*

Evans, Rowland, Jr. 1921- *CelR 3*

Evans, Sy *IntMPA 1977*

Evans, Tenniel 1926- *WhoThe 16*

Evans, Wilbur 1908- *BiE&WWA, NotNAT, WhoHol A*

Evans, Will 1873-1931 *NotNAT B, WhThe*

Evans, Will 1875-1931 *OxThe*

Evans, Winifred 1890- *WhThe*

Evanson, Edith *WhoHol A*

Evarts, William H d1940 *NotNAT B*

Evein, Bernard 1929- *DcFM, FilmgC, WorEnF*

Eveling, Stanley 1925- *ConDr 1977, WhoThe 16*

Evelyn, Baby *Film 2*

Evelyn, Clara 1886- *WhThe*

Evelyn, Judith 1913-1967 *BiE&WWA, FilmgC, MotPP, NotNAT B, WhScrn 1, WhScrn 2, WhThe, WhoHol B*

Evelyn, Mildred *Film 2*

Evelynne, May 1856-1943 *WhScrn 1, WhScrn 2*

Evennett, Wallace 1888- *WhThe*

Everard, Walter d1924 *NotNAT B*

Everest, Barbara d1968 *MotPP, WhoHol B*

Everest, Barbara 1890-1968 *NotNAT B, WhScrn 1, WhScrn 2, WhThe*

Everest, Barbara 1891-1968 *FilmgC*

Everett, Chad *WhoHol A*

Everett, Chad 1936- *CelR 3, IntMPA 1977*

Everett, Chad 1937- *FilmgC*

Everett, Chad 1939- *MovMk*

Everett, Sophie d1963 *NotNAT B*

Everett, Tim 1938- *NotNAT*

Everett, Timmy 1938- *BiE&WWA*

Everhart, Rex 1920- *BiE&WWA, NotNAT, WhoThe 16*

Everitt, Richard M 1935- *AmSCAP 1966*

Everleigh, Kate d1926 *NotNAT B*

Evers, Ann *WhoHol A*

Evers, Arthur *Film 1*

Evers, Charles 1922- *CelR 3*

Evers, Ernest P 1874-1945 *WhScrn 1, WhScrn 2*

Evers, Jason *WhoHol A*

Evers, King *Film 2*

Evershed-Martin, Leslie *PIP&P*

Everson, William K 1929- *IntMPA 1977*

Evert, Chris 1954- *CelR 3*

Everth, Francis *Film 2*

Everton, Paul 1868-1948 *NotNAT B, WhoStg 1908*

Everton, Paul 1869-1948 *Film 1, Film 2, Vers A, WhScrn 1, WhScrn 2, WhoHol B*

Evesson, Isabelle d1914 *NotNAT B*

Evesson, Isabelle 1870- *WhoStg 1906, WhoStg 1908*

Evett, Robert 1874-1949 *NotNAT B, WhThe*

Eville, William *Film 1, Film 2*

Evreinoff *PIP&P*

Evreinov, Nikolai Nikolaivich 1879-1953 *CnMD, CnThe, OxThe*

Ewald, Johannes 1743-1781 *CnThe, NotNAT B, OxThe, REnWD*

Ewart, Stephen T 1869- *WhThe*

Ewbank, Weeb 1907- *CelR 3*

Ewell, Caroline d1909 *NotNAT B*

Ewell, Tom 1909- *BiE&WWA, FilmgC, IntMPA 1977, MotPP, MovMk, NotNAT, WhoHol A, WhoThe 16, WorEnF*

Ewen, David 1907- *BiE&WWA*

Ewing, Roger *WhoHol A*

Exter, Alexander *PIP&P*

Exton, Clive *ConDr 1977C*

Eyen, Tom 1941- *ConDr 1977, NatPD, WhoThe 16*

Eyre, Gerald d1885 *NotNAT B*

Eyre, John Edmund d1816 *NotNAT B*

Eyre, Laurence 1881-1959 *NotNAT B, WhThe*

Eyre, Peter 1942- *WhoHol A, WhoThe 16*

Eyre, Richard 1943- *WhoThe 16*

Eyre, Ronald 1929- *WhoThe 16*

Eysoldt, Gertrud 1870-1955 *OxThe*

Eysoldt, Gertrud 1871-1955 *WhScrn 1, WhScrn 2*

Eysselinck, Walter 1931- *WhoThe 16*

Eythe, William 1918-1947 *FilmgC*

Eythe, William 1918-1957 *HolP 40, MotPP, NotNAT B, WhScrn 1, WhScrn 2, WhThe, WhoHol B*

Eytinge, Rose 1835-1911 *FamA&A, NotNAT A, NotNAT B, WhoStg 1906, WhoStg 1908*

Eyton, Bessie 1890- *Film 1, Film 2, TwYS*

Eyton, Frank 1894- *WhThe*
Ezell, Helen Ingle 1903- *AmSCAP 1966*

F

Fabares, Shelley 1942- *FilmgC, WhoHol A*
Fabbri, Diego 1911- *CnMD, CnThe, McGWD, ModWD, OxThe*
Fabbrichesi, Salvatore 1760-1827 *OxThe*
Faber, Beryl d1912 *WhThe*
Faber, Erwin *Film 2*
Faber, Leslie 1879-1929 *NotNAT B, WhThe, WhoHol B*
Faber, Mrs. Leslie 1880- *WhThe*
Faber, William E 1902- *AmSCAP 1966*
Fabian 1942- *FilmgC, MotPP, WhoHol A*
Fabian *see also* Forte, Fabian
Fabian, Francoise 1935- *CelR 3, WhoHol A*
Fabian, Madge 1880- *WhThe*
Fabray, Nanette *MotPP, NotNAT, WhoHol A*
Fabray, Nanette 1920- *BiE&WWA, Film 2, FilmgC, IntMPA 1977, WhoThe 16*
Fabray, Nanette 1922- *EncMT*
Fabre, Emile 1869-1955 *McGWD, NotNAT B*
Fabre, Emile 1870- *WhThe*
Fabre, Fernand *Film 2*
Fabre, Saturnin 1884-1961 *WhScrn 1, WhScrn 2, WhoHol B*
Fabre D'Eglantine, Philippe-Francois N 1755-1794 *OxThe*
Fabregas, Virginia 1870-1950 *WhScrn 1, WhScrn 2*
Fabri, Zoltan 1917- *DcFM, FilmgC, OxFilm, WorEnF*
Fabrizi, Aldo 1905- *FilmgC, IntMPA 1977, MovMk, WhoHol A*
Fabrizi, Mario 1925-1963 *NotNAT B, WhScrn 1, WhScrn 2, WhoHol B*
Fabrizzi, Aldo 1905- *OxFilm*
Factor, Alan Jay 1925- *IntMPA 1977*
Fadden, Genevieve d1959 *WhScrn 1, WhScrn 2, WhoHol B*
Fadden, Tom 1895- *Vers A, WhoHol A*
Fadiman, Clifton 1904- *CelR 3, IntMPA 1977*
Faesi, Robert 1883-1972 *CnMD*
Fagan, Barney 1850-1937 *NotNAT B*
Fagan, James Bernard 1873-1933 *CnThe, NotNAT B, OxThe, WhThe*
Fagan, Joan 1934- *BiE&WWA, NotNAT*
Fagan, Myron C *WhThe*
Fagas, Jimmie 1924- *AmSCAP 1966*
Fagella, Anthony 1899- *AmSCAP 1966*
Fahey, Myrna 1939-1973 *WhScrn 2, WhoHol B*
Fahrney, Madcap Merry d1974 *WhoHol B*
Fahrney, Milton H 1871-1941 *WhScrn 1, WhScrn 2, WhoHol B*
Faichney, James B *IntMPA 1977*
Faiko, Alexei Mikhailovich 1893- *OxThe*
Fain, John 1915-1970 *WhScrn 1, WhScrn 2, WhoHol B*
Fain, Sammy 1902- *AmSCAP 1966, BiE&WWA,*

EncMT, IntMPA 1977, NewMT, NotNAT
Faine, Hy 1910- *BiE&WWA*
Fair, Adrah 1897- *WhThe*
Fair, Charles B 1921- *AmSCAP 1966*
Fair, Elinor 1902-1957 *Film 1, Film 2, TwYS, WhoHol B*
Fair, Elinor 1903-1957 *WhScrn 2*
Fair, Florence *Film 2*
Fair, William B 1851-1909 *OxThe*
Fairbanks, Douglas 1883-1939 *BiDFlm, CmMov, Film 1, Film 2, FilmgC, MotPP, MovMk, NotNAT B, OxFilm, WhScrn 1, WhScrn 2, WhThe, WhoHol B, WorEnF*
Fairbanks, Douglas 1884-1939 *TwYS*
Fairbanks, Douglas, Jr. *MotPP, WhoHol A*
Fairbanks, Douglas, Jr. 1907- *FilmgC*
Fairbanks, Douglas, Jr. 1908- *OxFilm*
Fairbanks, Douglas, Jr. 1909- *BiDFlm, CelR 3, CmMov, Film 2, IntMPA 1977, MovMk, TwYS, WhoThe 16, WorEnF*
Fairbanks, Flobelle *Film 2*
Fairbanks, Gladys *Film 1*
Fairbanks, Jerry *IntMPA 1977*
Fairbanks, Madeleine *Film 1*
Fairbanks, Marion *Film 1*
Fairbanks, William 1894-1945 *Film 2, TwYS, WhScrn 2*
Fairbanks Twins *Film 2*
Fairbrother, Sidney d1941 *WhoHol B*
Fairbrother, Sydney 1872-1941 *NotNAT A, NotNAT B, OxThe, WhScrn 1, WhScrn 2, WhThe*
Fairbrother, Sydney 1873-1941 *Film 1, Film 2, FilmgC*
Fairchild, Edgar 1898- *AmSCAP 1966*
Fairchild, John 1927- *CelR 3*
Fairchild, William 1918- *CmMov, FilmgC, IntMPA 1977*
Fairclough, Thomas H 1905- *AmSCAP 1966*
Faire, Betty *Film 2*
Faire, Virginia Brown 1899-1948 *WhScrn 1, WhoHol B*
Faire, Virginia Brown 1904-1948 *Film 2, TwYS*
Fairfax, James 1897-1961 *WhScrn 1, WhScrn 2, WhoHol B*
Fairfax, Lance 1899- *WhThe*
Fairfax, Lettice 1876-1948 *NotNAT B, WhThe*
Fairfax, Marion 1879- *WhThe, WomWMM*
Fairfax, Thurman *Film 2*
Fairhurst, Lyn 1920- *FilmgC*
Fairman, Austin 1892-1964 *NotNAT B, WhScrn 1, WhScrn 2, WhThe, WhoHol B*
Fairman, George 1881-1962 *AmSCAP 1966*
Fairweather, David Carnegy 1899- *WhoThe 16*
Fairweather, Helen *Film 2*
Fairweather, Virginia 1922- *WhoThe 16*

Faison, George *PlP&P A*
Fait, A *Film 2*
Faith, Adam 1940- *FilmgC*
Faith, Percy 1908- *AmSCAP 1966*
Faith, Russell 1929- *AmSCAP 1966*
Faithfull, Geoffrey 1894- *FilmgC, IntMPA 1977*
Faithfull, Marianne *WhoHol A*
Faithfull, Marianne 1946- *WhoThe 16*
Faithfull, Marianne 1947- *FilmgC*
Falana, Lola *WhoHol A*
Falciglia, Patrick 1942- *AmSCAP 1966*
Falck, Karin *WomWMM*
Falck, Lionel 1889-1971 *WhThe*
Falco, Anthony M 1923- *AmSCAP 1966*
Falconer, Edmund 1815-1879 *NotNAT B*
Falconetti 1901-1946 *FilmgC, WhoHol B*
Falconetti, Maria 1902-1946 *Film 2*
Falconetti, Marie *MotPP*
Falconetti, Renee 1893-1946 *WorEnF*
Falconetti, Renee 1901-1946 *OxFilm, WhScrn 1, WhScrn 2*
Falconi, Armando *WhThe*
Falconi, Arturo d1934 *NotNAT B, WhoHol B*
Faleron, Jean *Film 2*
Fales, Victoria Nancy *NatPD*
Falk, Lee *NatPD*
Falk, Peter 1927- *BiE&WWA, CelR 3, FilmgC, IntMPA 1977, MotPP, MovMk, NotNAT, WhoHol A*
Falk, Richard 1912- *BiE&WWA, NotNAT*
Falk, Sawyer 1898-1961 *NotNAT B*
Falkenburg, Jinx 1919- *FilmgC, WhoHol A*
Falkenhain, Patricia 1926- *BiE&WWA, NotNAT*
Falkenstein, Julius *Film 1, Film 2*
Fall, Leo 1873-1925 *NotNAT B*
Fallon, Charles 1885-1936 *WhScrn 1, WhScrn 2, WhoHol B*
Fallon, Richard 1923- *BiE&WWA, NotNAT*
Falls, Gregory A 1922- *BiE&WWA, NotNAT*
Fanck, Arnold 1889-1974 *DcFM, OxFilm, WorEnF*
Fancourt, Darrell 1888-1953 *NotNAT B, WhThe*
Fane, Dorothy *Film 2*
Fang, Charles *Film 1, Film 2*
Fanning, Frank B 1880-1934 *WhScrn 1, WhScrn 2, WhoHol B*
Fanning, Win 1918- *BiE&WWA*
Fantoni, Sergio 1930- *FilmgC, WhoHol A*
Fantozzi, Tony 1933- *IntMPA 1977*
Fapp, Daniel *FilmgC, WorEnF*
Faraday, Philip Michael 1875-1944 *NotNAT B, WhThe*
Farago, Ladislas 1906- *CelR 3*
Farber, Burton A 1913- *AmSCAP 1966*
Farber, Nathaniel C 1918- *AmSCAP 1966*
Farberman, Harold 1930- *AmSCAP 1966*
Farebrother, Violet 1888-1969 *Film 2, WhScrn 2, WhThe, WhoHol B*
Farentino, James 1938- *FilmgC, IntMPA 1977, MotPP, WhoHol A*
Farfan, Marian 1913-1965 *WhScrn 1, WhScrn 2*
Farfariello 1881-1946 *WhScrn 1, WhScrn 2*
Farina *Film 2*
Farina, Richard 1937-1966 *WhScrn 2*
Farine, Jean *OxThe*
Farjeon, Benjamin Leopold d1903 *NotNAT B*
Farjeon, Herbert 1887-1945 *EncMT, NotNAT B, OxThe, WhThe*
Farjeon, Joseph Jefferson 1883-1955 *NotNAT B, WhThe*
Farkoa, Maurice 1864- *WhoStg 1908*
Farkoa, Maurice 1867-1916 *WhThe*
Farleigh, Lynn 1942- *WhoThe 16*
Farley, Charles d1859 *NotNAT B*

Farley, Dot 1881-1971 *WhScrn 2*
Farley, Dot 1894-1971 *Film 1, Film 2, MotPP, TwYS*
Farley, Edward J 1904- *AmSCAP 1966*
Farley, James 1882-1947 *Film 1, Film 2, TwYS, WhScrn 1, WhScrn 2, WhoHol B*
Farley, James 1888- *CelR 3*
Farley, Morgan 1898- *BiE&WWA, Film 2, NotNAT, WhoHol A*
Farley, Morgan 1901- *WhThe*
Farley, Roland 1892-1932 *AmSCAP 1966*
Farmer, Frances d1970 *MotPP, PlP&P, WhoHol B*
Farmer, Frances 1913-1970 *ThFT*
Farmer, Frances 1914-1970 *FilmgC, HolP 30, NotNAT A, WhScrn 1, WhScrn 2*
Farmer, Frances 1915-1970 *MovMk*
Farmer, Mimsy 1945- *FilmgC, WhoHol A*
Farney, Billy *Film 2*
Farney, Milton *Film 2*
Farnie, H B d1889 *NotNAT B*
Farnol, Lynn d1963 *NotNAT B*
Farnon, Robert 1917- *FilmgC*
Farnsworth, Philo T d1971 *NewYTET*
Farnum, Dorothy *WomWMM*
Farnum, Dustin d1929 *MotPP, WhoHol B*
Farnum, Dustin 1870-1929 *FilmgC*
Farnum, Dustin 1874-1929 *Film 1, Film 2, NotNAT B, TwYS, WhScrn 1, WhScrn 2, WhThe*
Farnum, Dustin 1876-1929 *WhoStg 1906, WhoStg 1908*
Farnum, Franklyn d1961 *NotNAT B, WhoHol B*
Farnum, Franklyn 1876-1961 *Film 1, FilmgC, WhScrn 1, WhScrn 2*
Farnum, Franklyn 1883-1961 *Film 2, TwYS*
Farnum, G Dustin d1912 *NotNAT B*
Farnum, Helen *Film 2*
Farnum, William 1872-1953 *TwYS*
Farnum, William 1876-1953 *Film 1, Film 2, FilmgC, MotPP, MovMk, NotNAT B, WhScrn 1, WhScrn 2, WhThe, WhoHol B*
Farquhar, George 1678-1707 *CnThe, McGWD, NotNAT B, OxThe, PlP&P, REnWD*
Farquhar, Malcolm 1924- *WhoThe 16*
Farquhar, Robroy 1916- *BiE&WWA, NotNAT*
Farquharson, Robert d1966 *WhoHol B*
Farquharson, Robert 1877-1966 *WhThe*
Farquharson, Robert 1878-1966 *WhScrn 1, WhScrn 2*
Farr, Derek 1912- *FilmgC, IntMPA 1977, WhoHol A, WhoThe 16*
Farr, Felicia 1932- *FilmgC, IntMPA 1977, MotPP, WhoHol A*
Farr, Florence 1860-1917 *NotNAT B, OxThe, WhThe*
Farr, Frankie 1903-1953 *WhScrn 1, WhScrn 2*
Farr, Jamie *WhoHol A*
Farr, Karl d1961 *WhScrn 2*
Farr, Patricia 1915-1948 *WhScrn 1, WhScrn 2, WhoHol B*
Farrah, Abd' Elkader 1926- *WhoThe 16*
Farrar, David 1908- *FilmgC, IntMPA 1977, WhoHol A*
Farrar, Geraldine 1882-1967 *AmSCAP 1966, Film 1, Film 2, FilmgC, TwYS, WhScrn 1, WhScrn 2, WhoHol B*
Farrar, Gwen 1899-1944 *WhThe, WhoHol B*
Farrar, Margaret 1901-1925 *WhScrn 1, WhScrn 2*
Farrar, Stanley 1911-1974 *WhScrn 2*
Farrar, Walton T 1918- *AmSCAP 1966*
Farrell, Anthony B 1899- *BiE&WWA*
Farrell, Catherine F d1964 *NotNAT B*

Farrell, Charles *MotPP*
Farrell, Charles 1901- *Film 2, FilmgC,*
   IntMPA 1977, MovMk
Farrell, Charles 1902- *Film 2, TwYS,*
   WhoHol. A
Farrell, Charles 1906- *IntMPA 1977,*
   WhoThe 16
Farrell, Charles Skip 1919-1962 *WhScrn 1,*
   WhScrn 2
Farrell, Eileen 1920- *CelR 3*
Farrell, Glenda 1904-1971 *BiE&WWA, Film 2,*
   FilmgC, HolP 30, MotPP, MovMk,
   NotNAT B, OxFilm, ThFT, WhScrn 1,
   WhScrn 2, WhThe, WhoHol B
Farrell, Henry *IntMPA 1977*
Farrell, John J *WhoStg 1908*
Farrell, John W 1885-1953 *WhScrn 1, WhScrn 2,*
   WhoHol B
Farrell, M J 1905- *WhThe*
Farrell, Marguerite d1951 *NotNAT B*
Farrell, Mary *BiE&WWA, NotNAT*
Farrell, Mike *WhoHol A*
Farrell, Paul 1893- *WhThe*
Farrell, Sharon *WhoHol A*
Farrell, Skip 1919-1962 *WhoHol B*
Farrell, Skip *see also* Farrell, Charles Skip
Farrell, Tommy *WhoHol A*
Farrell, Vessie 1890-1935 *WhScrn 1, WhScrn 2,*
   WhoHol B
Farren, Babs 1904- *WhThe*
Farren, Elizabeth 1759-1829 *NotNAT A,*
   NotNAT B, OxThe
Farren, Ellen 1848-1904 *OxThe*
Farren, Fred d1956 *NotNAT B, WhThe*
Farren, George Francis d1935 *NotNAT B*
Farren, George Percy d1861 *NotNAT B*
Farren, Henry 1826-1860 *NotNAT B, OxThe*
Farren, Jack *IntMPA 1977*
Farren, Nellie 1848-1904 *NotNAT B*
Farren, Percival 1784-1843 *NotNAT B, OxThe*
Farren, William 1725-1795 *NotNAT B, OxThe*
Farren, William 1786-1861 *NotNAT B, OxThe*
Farren, William 1825-1908 *NotNAT B, OxThe*
Farren, William Percival 1853-1937 *NotNAT B,*
   OxThe, WhThe
Farrer, Ann 1916- *WhThe*
Farrington, Adele 1867-1936 *Film 1, Film 2,*
   WhScrn 1, WhScrn 2, WhoHol B
Farrington, Betty d1968 *Film 2, WhScrn 2*
Farrington, Frank 1874-1924 *Film 1, Film 2,*
   WhScrn 1, WhScrn 2, WhoHol B
Farrow, John 1904-1963 *BiDFlm, CmMov,*
   FilmgC, MovMk, NotNAT B, WorEnF
Farrow, Johnny 1912- *AmSCAP 1966*
Farrow, Mia *IntMPA 1977, MotPP, WhoHol A*
Farrow, Mia 1945- *BiDFlm, CelR 3, FilmgC,*
   OxFilm, WorEnF
Farrow, Mia 1946- *MovMk, WhoThe 16*
Farrow, Tisa *WhoHol A*
Farwell, Arthur 1872-1952 *AmSCAP 1966*
Fascinato, Jack 1915- *AmSCAP 1966*
Fáss, M Monroe 1901- *IntMPA 1977*
Fassbinder, Rainer Werner 1946- *BiDFlm,*
   OxFilm
Fassett, Jay 1889- *BiE&WWA, NotNAT,*
   WhoHol A
Fates, Gil *NewYTET*
Father Of The Halls *OxThe*
Fatima 1880-1921 *Film 1*
Fatima, LaBelle 1880-1921 *WhScrn 2*
Fauche, Miriam *Film 2*
Fauchois, Rene 1882-1962 *McGWD, ModWD,*
   WhThe
Faucit, Harriet 1789-1857 *NotNAT B*

Faucit, Helen 1817-1898 *NotNAT A, NotNAT B,*
   OxThe
Faulds, Andrew 1923- *FilmgC*
Faulk, John Henry *NewYTET, WhoHol A*
Faulkner, Edward *WhoHol A*
Faulkner, Fred 1941- *AmSCAP 1966*
Faulkner, Jack 1918- *AmSCAP 1966*
Faulkner, James *WhoHol A*
Faulkner, Ralph 1891- *WhoHol A*
Faulkner, Seldon 1929- *BiE&WWA, NotNAT*
Faulkner, William 1897-1962 *CnMD, CroCD,*
   DcFM, FilmgC, ModWD, NotNAT B,
   OxFilm, WorEnF
Faure, Elie 1873-1937 *OxFilm, WorEnF*
Faussett, Hudson 1917- *IntMPA 1977*
Faust, Edward *Film 2*
Faust, Hazel Lee 1910-1973 *WhScrn 2,*
   WhoHol B
Faust, Johann 1488-1541 *FilmgC*
Faust, Lotta 1880- *WhoStg 1908*
Faust, Lotta 1881-1910 *NotNAT B*
Faust, Martin 1886-1943 *Film 1, Film 2,*
   WhScrn 1, WhScrn 2, WhoHol B
Faustman, Erik Hampe 1919-1961 *WhScrn 2*
Faustmann, Erik 1919-1961 *DcFM*
Favart, Madame 1727-1772 *NotNAT B*
Favart, Charles-Simon 1710-1792 *NotNAT B,*
   OxThe
Favart, Edmee d1941 *NotNAT B, WhThe*
Favart, Maria 1833-1908 *NotNAT B*
Favart, Marie-Justine-Benoiste D 1727-1772 *OxThe*
Faversham, Edith Campbell d1945 *NotNAT B*
Faversham, Julie Opp 1871-1921 *NotNAT B*
Faversham, Philip *WhoHol A*
Faversham, William 1868-1940 *FamA&A, Film 1,*
   Film 2, NotNAT B, OxThe, PIP&P, TwYS,
   WhScrn 1, WhScrn 2, WhThe, WhoHol B,
   WhoStg 1906, WhoStg 1908
Favieres, Henry *Film 2*
Favre, Gina *WhThe*
Favreau, Michele *WomWMM*
Fawcett, Charles S 1855-1922 *NotNAT B,*
   WhThe
Fawcett, Eric 1904- *WhThe*
Fawcett, Farrah *WhoHol A*
Fawcett, Mrs. George d1945 *Film 2, WhoHol B*
Fawcett, George 1860-1939 *Film 1, Film 2,*
   MotPP, NotNAT B, TwYS, WhScrn 1,
   WhScrn 2, WhThe, WhoHol B
Fawcett, George 1861-1939 *MovMk*
Fawcett, James 1905-1942 *WhScrn 1, WhScrn 2*
Fawcett, John *PIP&P*
Fawcett, L'Estrange *WhThe*
Fawcett, Marion 1886-1957 *NotNAT B, WhThe*
Fawcett, Owen 1839-1904 *NotNAT B*
Fawcett, William d1974 *WhScrn 2, WhoHol B*
Fawn, James 1850-1923 *WhThe*
Fax, Jesslyn d1975 *WhoHol C*
Fay, Brendan 1921-1975 *WhScrn 2, WhoHol A,*
   WhoHol C
Fay, Dorothy *WhoHol A*
Fay, Eddy *WhoHol A*
Fay, Edward M d1964 *NotNAT B*
Fay, Frank 1894-1961 *WhScrn 1, WhScrn 2*
Fay, Frank 1897-1961 *EncMT, Film 2,*
   NotNAT A, NotNAT B, WhThe,
   WhoHol B
Fay, Frank G 1870-1931 *NotNAT B*
Fay, Frank J 1870-1931 *OxThe*
Fay, Gaby *WhScrn 2*
Fay, Hugh *Film 1, Film 2*
Fay, Jack 1903-1928 *WhScrn 1, WhScrn 2*
Fay, Patrick J *IntMPA 1977*
Fay, Terry *BiE&WWA*

Fay, W G 1872-1947 *WhoHol B*
Fay, William George 1872-1947 *NotNAT B,*
   OxThe, WhScrn 1, WhScrn 2
Fay, William George 1872-1949 *WhThe*
Faye, Alice *MotPP, WhoHol A*
Faye, Alice 1912- *BiDFlm, CmMov, FilmgC,*
   MovMk, ThFT, WorEnF
Faye, Alice 1915- *CelR 3, OxFilm*
Faye, Herbie *WhoHol A*
Faye, Joey 1910- *BiE&WWA, NotNAT,*
   WhoHol A, WhoThe 16
Faye, Julia d1966 *MotPP, WhoHol B*
Faye, Julia 1894-1966 *Film 1, Film 2, TwYS*
Faye, Julia 1896-1966 *WhScrn 1, WhScrn 2*
Faylauer, Adolph 1884-1961 *WhScrn 1,*
   WhScrn 2, WhoHol B
Faylen, Frank *IntMPA 1977, MotPP*
Faylen, Frank 1907- *FilmgC, MovMk,*
   WhoHol A
Faylen, Frank 1909- *Vers A*
Fayman, Lynn *WomWMM B*
Fayne, Greta *WhThe*
Fayolle, Berthe d1934 *NotNAT B*
Fayre, Eleanor 1910- *WhThe*
Fazalbhoy, M A 1902- *IntMPA 1977*
Fazan, Adrienne *WomWMM*
Fazan, Eleanor 1930- *WhoThe 16*
Fazenda, Louis d1962 *NotNAT B*
Fazenda, Louise d1962 *MotPP, WhoHol B*
Fazenda, Louise 1889-1962 *WhScrn 1, WhScrn 2*
Fazenda, Louise 1895-1962 *Film 1, Film 2,*
   FilmgC, MovMk, ThFT, TwYS, WorEnF
Fazioli, Bernardo 1897-1942 *AmSCAP 1966*
Fazioli, Billy 1898-1924 *AmSCAP 1966*
Fealy, Margaret *Film 2*
Fealy, Maude 1881-1971 *MotPP, WhScrn 1,*
   WhScrn 2, WhoHol B
Fealy, Maude 1883- *WhThe*
Fealy, Maude 1886- *WhoStg 1906, WhoStg 1908*
Fearnley, Jane *Film 1*
Fearnley, John 1914- *BiE&WWA, NotNAT*
Fearon, George Edward 1901- *WhThe*
Fears, Peggy *WhoHol A*
Feather, Leonard G 1914- *AmSCAP 1966*
Featherston, Eddie *Film 2*
Featherston, Vane 1864-1948 *NotNAT B, WhThe*
Featherstone, John *Film 1*
Fechter, Charles Albert 1824-1879 *FamA&A,*
   NotNAT A, NotNAT B, OxThe, PIP&P
Fedderson, Don *NewYTET*
Feder, A H 1909- *WhoThe 16*
Feder, Abe 1909- *BiE&WWA, NotNAT*
Feder, I *Film 1*
Federlein, Gottfried Harrison 1883-1952
   AmSCAP 1966
Fedorovitch, Sophie 1893-1953 *OxThe*
Feducha, Bertha *Film 2*
Fee, Vickie 1947-1975 *WhScrn 2, WhoHol C*
Feely, Terence John 1928- *WhoThe 16*
Feeney, Francis *Film 2*
Feferman, Linda *WomWMM B*
Fegte, Ernst 1900- *FilmgC*
Feher, Friedrich *Film 1*
Feher, Friedrich 1889-1945 *DcFM*
Feher, Friedrich 1895- *OxFilm*
Feher, Imre 1926- *OxFilm, WorEnF*
Fehmiu, Bekim 1932- *FilmgC, WhoHol A*
Fehr, Rudi *IntMPA 1977*
Feibel, Frederick 1906- *AmSCAP 1966*
Feiffer, Judy *WomWMM*
Feiffer, Jules 1929- *CelR 3, CnThe,*
   ConDr 1977, CroCD, FilmgC, McGWD,
   NotNAT, WhoThe 16
Feigay, Paul 1920- *BiE&WWA, NotNAT*

Feiler, Herta 1916-1970 *WhScrn 1, WhScrn 2,*
   WhoHol B
Feiler, Max Christian 1904- *CnMD*
Fein, Irving A 1911- *IntMPA 1977, NewYTET*
Fein, Pearl *AmSCAP 1966*
Feinberg, Abe I d1962 *NotNAT B*
Feinberg, Milton *IntMPA 1977*
Feinman, Sigmund d1909 *NotNAT B*
Feinstein, Harry 1906- *IntMPA 1977*
Feirstein, Frederick *NatPD*
Feist, Felix E 1910-1965 *FilmgC*
Feist, Gene 1930- *NotNAT, WhoThe 16*
Fejos, Paul 1893-1963 *FilmgC*
Fejos, Paul 1897-1963 *WorEnF*
Fejos, Paul 1898-1963 *DcFM*
Feld, Fritz 1900- *Film 2, FilmgC, IntMPA 1977,*
   MovMk, TwYS, Vers A, WhoHol A
Feld, Irvin 1919- *CelR 3*
Feld, Norman *IntMPA 1977*
Feldary, Eric 1920-1968 *WhScrn 1, WhScrn 2,*
   WhoHol B
Feldhaus-Weber, Mary *NatPD, WomWMM B*
Feldkamp, Fred 1914- *IntMPA 1977*
Feldman, Andrea d1972 *WhScrn 2, WhoHol B*
Feldman, Charles K 1904-1968 *FilmgC, WorEnF*
Feldman, Charles K 1905-1968 *NotNAT B*
Feldman, Edward H *NewYTET*
Feldman, Edward S 1929- *IntMPA 1977*
Feldman, Edythe A 1913-1971 *WhScrn 1,*
   WhScrn 2, WhoHol B
Feldman, Gladys d1974 *Film 2, WhoHol B*
Feldman, Gladys 1892-1974 *WhScrn 2*
Feldman, Gladys 1899-1974 *BiE&WWA*
Feldman, Laurence 1926- *BiE&WWA*
Feldman, Marty 1933- *FilmgC, WhoHol A*
Feldman, Phil 1922- *IntMPA 1977*
Feldon, Barbara *WhoHol A*
Feldstein, Saul 1940- *AmSCAP 1966*
Felgate, Peter 1919- *WhThe*
Feliciano, Jose 1945- *CelR 3*
Felipe, Alfredo 1931-1958 *WhScrn 1, WhScrn 2*
Felix, George 1866-1949 *Film 1, WhScrn 1,*
   WhScrn 2, WhoHol B
Felix, Hugo 1866-1934 *NotNAT B, WhThe*
Felix, Maria *WhoHol A*
Felix, Maria 1915- *FilmgC*
Felix, Maria 1916?- *OxFilm*
Felix, Sarah d1877 *NotNAT B*
Felix, Seymour 1892-1961 *CmMov, FilmgC*
Felker, Clay S 1928- *CelR 3*
Fell, Norman *WhoHol A*
Feller, Sherman 1918- *AmSCAP 1966*
Fellerman, Max 1899- *IntMPA 1977*
Fellini, Federico 1920- *BiDFlm, CelR 3, DcFM,*
   FilmgC, IntMPA 1977, MovMk,
   WomWMM, WorEnF
Fellini, Federico 1921- *OxFilm*
Fellman, Daniel R 1943- *IntMPA 1977*
Fellman, Nat D 1910- *IntMPA 1977*
Fellowes, Amy *OxThe*
Fellowes, Rockcliffe 1885-1950 *MotPP,*
   NotNAT B
Fellowes, Rockcliffe 1885-1950 *Film 1, Film 2,*
   FilmgC, TwYS, WhScrn 1, WhScrn 2,
   WhoHol B
Fellowes-Robinson, Dora d1946 *NotNAT B,*
   WhThe
Fellows, Dexter William 1871-1937 *NotNAT A,*
   NotNAT B
Fellows, Edith 1923- *Film 2, FilmgC, ThFT,*
   WhoHol A
Fellows, Harold E d1960 *NewYTET*
Fellows, Robert 1903-1969 *FilmgC*
Fells, George 1902-1960 *WhScrn 1, WhScrn 2*

Felsenfeld, Herb 1940- NotNAT
Felt, Irving Mitchell 1910- CelR 3
Felter, Susan WomWMM B
Felton, Happy 1908-1964 WhScrn 1, WhScrn 2,
  WhoHol B
Felton, Norman NewYTET
Felton, Verna 1890-1966 FilmgC, Vers B,
  WhScrn 1, WhScrn 2, WhoHol B
Felumb, Mathilde Film 2
Felyne, Renee 1884-1910 NotNAT B
Fenady, Andrew J 1928- IntMPA 1977
Fendall, Percy d1917 NotNAT B
Fendler, Edvard AmSCAP 1966
Fenemore, Hilda WhoHol A
Fenimore, Ford d1941 WhScrn 1, WhScrn 2
Fenn, Ezekiel 1620- OxThe
Fenn, Frederick 1868-1924 NotNAT B, WhThe
Fenn, George Manville 1831-1909 NotNAT B
Fenn, Peggy BiE&WWA
Fennell, James 1766-1816 FamA&A, NotNAT A,
  NotNAT B, OxThe
Fennelly, Parker WhoHol A
Fennelly, Vincent M 1920- IntMPA 1977,
  NewYTET
Fenneman, George IntMPA 1977
Fenner, Beatrice 1904- AmSCAP 1966
Fenner, Walter S 1882-1947 WhScrn 2
Fenno, Dick 1927- AmSCAP 1966
Fenoux, Jacques d1930 NotNAT B
Fenster, Harry 1919- AmSCAP 1966
Fenstock, Belle AmSCAP 1966
Fenton, Frank 1906-1957 FilmgC, NotNAT B,
  PIP&P, Vers A, WhScrn 1, WhScrn 2,
  WhoHol B
Fenton, Howard AmSCAP 1966
Fenton, Lavinia 1708-1760 NotNAT A,
  NotNAT B, OxThe
Fenton, Leslie MotPP
Fenton, Leslie 1902- Film 2, FilmgC, TwYS
Fenton, Leslie 1903- MovMk
Fenton, Lucile 1916?-1966 WhoHol B
Fenton, Lucille 1916?-1966 WhScrn 1, WhScrn 2
Fenton, Mabel 1868-1931 NotNAT B, WhScrn 1,
  WhScrn 2, WhoHol B
Fenton, Mabel 1872- WhoStg 1908
Fenton, Marc Film 1, Film 2
Fenton, Mark 1870-1925 WhScrn 1, WhScrn 2,
  WhoHol B
Fenwick, Irene 1887-1936 Film 1, NotNAT B,
  WhScrn 1, WhScrn 2, WhThe, WhoHol B
Feodoroff, Leo 1867-1949 Film 2, WhScrn 1,
  WhScrn 2, WhoHol B
Feodorovna, Vera d1910 NotNAT B
Feraudy, Jacques De Film 2, WhThe
Feraudy, Maurice De 1859- WhThe
Ferber, Edna 1887-1968 BiE&WWA, CnMD,
  CnThe, FilmgC, McGWD, ModWD,
  NotNAT A, NotNAT B, OxThe, PIP&P,
  WhThe
Ferber, Mel NewYTET
Ferchiou, Sofia WomWMM
Ferdin, Pamelyn WhoHol A
Ferdinand, Roger 1898- CnMD, McGWD
Ferguson, Al 1888-1971 Film 2, TwYS,
  WhScrn 2
Ferguson, Allyn 1924- AmSCAP 1966
Ferguson, Barney d1924 NotNAT B
Ferguson, Betty June 1933- WomWMM B
Ferguson, Casson 1891-1929 Film 1, Film 2,
  TwYS, WhoHol B
Ferguson, Casson 1894-1929 WhScrn 1,
  WhScrn 2
Ferguson, Catherine 1895- WhThe
Ferguson, Elsie d1961 MotPP, WhoHol B

Ferguson, Elsie 1883-1961 Film 1, Film 2,
  FilmgC, MovMk, NotNAT B, TwYS,
  WhScrn 1, WhScrn 2
Ferguson, Elsie 1885-1961 WhThe
Ferguson, Frank d1937 NotNAT B
Ferguson, Frank 1899- FilmgC, MovMk,
  WhoHol A
Ferguson, George S 1884-1944 WhScrn 1,
  WhScrn 2, WhoHol B
Ferguson, Helen 1901- Film 1, Film 2,
  IntMPA 1977, MotPP, TwYS, WhoHol A
Ferguson, Hilda 1903-1933 WhScrn 1, WhScrn 2,
  WhoHol B
Ferguson, Mattie Film 1
Ferguson, Myrtle Film 2
Ferguson, Robert S 1915- IntMPA 1977
Ferguson, Robert V WhoStg 1908
Ferguson, W J 1845-1930 WhoHol B
Ferguson, William d1961 NotNAT B
Ferguson, William J 1845-1930 Film 2,
  NotNAT B, WhScrn 1, WhScrn 2,
  WhoStg 1908
Fergusson, Francis 1904- BiE&WWA, NotNAT
Ferkauf, Betty Film 2
Ferlinghetti, Lawrence 1919- CelR 3,
  ConDr 1977, CroCD
Fern, Fritzie 1901-1932 WhScrn 1, WhScrn 2,
  WhoHol B
Fern, Sable 1876- WhThe
Fernald, Chester Bailey 1869-1938 NotNAT B,
  WhThe
Fernald, John Bailey 1905- OxThe, WhoThe 16
Fernandel 1903-1971 FilmgC, MotPP, MovMk,
  OxFilm, WhScrn 1, WhScrn 2, WhoHol B,
  WorEnF
Fernandes, Berta Luisa 1935-1954 WhScrn 1,
  WhScrn 2
Fernandes, Nascimento 1880?-1955? WhScrn 1,
  WhScrn 2
Fernandez, Bijou 1877-1961 Film 2, NotNAT B,
  WhScrn 1, WhScrn 2, WhThe, WhoHol B,
  WhoStg 1906, WhoStg 1908
Fernandez, E L Film 1
Fernandez, Emilio 1904- DcFM, FilmgC, OxFilm,
  WhoHol A, WorEnF
Fernandez, Esther WhoHol A
Fernandez, James 1835-1915 WhThe
Fernandez, Lucas 1474-1542 McGWD
Fernandez, Peter WhoHol A
Fernandez, Ramon S 1922-1962 WhScrn 1,
  WhScrn 2
Fernandez, Severo d1961 WhScrn 2
Fernandez Ardavin, Luis 1892- McGWD
Fernandez DeMoratin, Leandro 1760-1828
  McGWD, OxThe
Fernandez DeMoratin, Nicolas 1737-1780 McGWD,
  OxThe
Fernett, Gene IntMPA 1977
Ferraday, Lisa WhoHol A
Ferrand, Eula Pearl d1970 WhScrn 1, WhScrn 2
Ferrante, Arthur 1921- AmSCAP 1966
Ferrar, Ada d1951 NotNAT B
Ferrar, Beatrice d1958 NotNAT B, WhThe
Ferrar, Gwen 1899-1944 NotNAT B
Ferrare, Cristina WhoHol A
Ferrari, Angelo Film 2
Ferrari, Paolo 1822-1889 McGWD, NotNAT B,
  OxThe
Ferrari, William d1962 NotNAT B
Ferraris, Richard 1922- AmSCAP 1966
Ferraro, Joseph 1895- AmSCAP 1966
Ferravilla, Edoardo 1846-1915 NotNAT B, OxThe
Ferre, Clifford F 1920- AmSCAP 1966
Ferreira, Antonio OxThe, REnWD

Ferreira, Djalma 1913- *AmSCAP 1966*
Ferreira, Procopio *OxThe*
Ferreol, Marcel Auguste 1899-1974 *McGWD*
Ferrer, Jose *MotPP, WhoHol A*
Ferrer, Jose 1909- *FilmgC, WorEnF*
Ferrer, Jose 1912- *BiDFlm, BiE&WWA, CelR 3, CnThe, EncMT, IntMPA 1977, MovMk, NotNAT, OxFilm, WhoThe 16*
Ferrer, Mel 1917- *BiDFlm, BiE&WWA, FilmgC, IntMPA 1977, MGM, MotPP, MovMk, NotNAT, OxFilm, WhoHol A, WorEnF*
Ferreri, Marco 1928- *BiDFlm, DcFM, FilmgC, WorEnF*
Ferrero, Leo 1903-1933 *CnMD, McGWD*
Ferrers, George d1579 *NotNAT B*
Ferrers, Helen d1943 *NotNAT B, WhThe*
Ferreyra, Jose A 1889-1943 *DcFM*
Ferri, Roger *IntMPA 1977*
Ferridr, Paul 1843-1920 *NotNAT B*
Ferris, Audrey 1909- *Film 2, WhoHol A*
Ferris, Barbara *WhoHol A, WhoThe 16*
Ferris, Barbara 1940- *FilmgC*
Ferris, Barbara 1943- *NotNAT*
Ferris, Dillon J 1914-1951 *WhScrn 1, WhScrn 2*
Ferris, Don A 1919- *AmSCAP 1966*
Ferry, Felix d1953 *NotNAT B*
Ferry, Jean 1906- *DcFM*
Ferry, Minna *Film 2*
Ferzetti, Gabriele 1925- *FilmgC, OxFilm, WorEnF*
Fescourt, Herni 1880-1966 *DcFM*
Festa Campanile, Pasquale 1927- *WorEnF*
Fetchit, Stepin *MotPP*
Fetchit, Stepin 1892- *WhoHol A*
Fetchit, Stepin 1898- *FilmgC*
Fetchit, Stepin 1902- *Film 2, HolP 30, MovMk*
Fetchit, Stepin *see also* Stepin Fetchit
Fetherston, Eddie d1965 *WhScrn 1, WhScrn 2*
Fetherstone, Eddie d1965 *WhoHol B*
Fetter, Ted 1910- *AmSCAP 1966*
Fetzer, John E 1901- *IntMPA 1977*
Feuchtwanger, Lion 1884-1958 *CnMD, McGWD, ModWD*
Feuchtwanger, Lion 1884-1959 *NotNAT B*
Feuer, Cy 1911- *BiE&WWA, CelR 3, EncMT, NotNAT, WhThe 16*
Feuillade, Louis 1873-1925 *BiDFlm, DcFM, FilmgC, OxFilm, WorEnF*
Feuillere, Edwige 1907- *CnThe, FilmgC, MovMk, OxFilm, OxThe, WhThe, WhoHol A, WorEnF*
Feuillet, Octave 1821-1890 *NotNAT B*
Feusier, Norman 1885-1945 *WhScrn 1, WhScrn 2, WhoHol B*
Feval, Paolo d1887 *NotNAT B*
Feydeau, Georges 1862-1921 *CnMD, CnThe, FilmgC, McGWD, ModWD, NotNAT A, NotNAT B, OxThe, PIP&P, REnWD*
Feyder, Jacques 1885-1948 *DcFM*
Feyder, Jacques 1887-1948 *BiDFlm, OxFilm, WorEnF*
Feyder, Jacques 1888-1948 *FilmgC, MovMk*
Feyder, Jacques 1894-1948 *TwYS A*
Feyne, Buddy 1912- *AmSCAP 1966*
Ffolkes, David 1912- *WhThe*
Ffolliott, Gladys d1928 *NotNAT B, WhThe*
Ffrangcon-Davies, Gwen 1896- *CnThe, PIP&P, WhoThe 16*
Fialka, Ladislav *CroCD*
Fichandler, William 1886- *AmSCAP 1966*
Fichandler, Zelda 1924- *BiE&WWA, NotNAT, PIP&P, WhoThe 16*
Fichthorn, Claude L 1885- *AmSCAP 1966*
Fickett, Mary *BiE&WWA, NotNAT,*

WhoHol A
Fickovskaya, Lena *Film 2*
Fiddes, Josephine d1923 *NotNAT B*
Fidler, Ben 1867-1932 *WhScrn 1, WhScrn 2*
Fidler, Jimmie 1900- *WhoHol A*
Fiedel, Sam S 1916- *AmSCAP 1966*
Fiedler, Arthur 1894- *CelR 3*
Fiedler, John 1925- *BiE&WWA, FilmgC, NotNAT, WhoHol A*
Fiedler, Leslie 1917- *CelR 3*
Field, Al G 1852-1921 *NotNAT A, NotNAT B*
Field, Alexander 1892- *WhThe*
Field, Barbara *NatPD*
Field, Ben d1939 *Film 2, NotNAT B, WhThe, WhoHol B*
Field, Betty 1918-1973 *BiE&WWA, FilmgC, HolP 40, MotPP, MovMk, NotNAT B, PIP&P, ThFT, WhScrn 2, WhoHol B, WhoThe 16*
Field, Chester *Film 2*
Field, Crystal *NotNAT*
Field, Edward Salisbury d1936 *NotNAT B, WhThe*
Field, Elinor *Film 2*
Field, Eugene 1850-1895 *AmSCAP 1966*
Field, George 1878-1925 *Film 1, Film 2, WhScrn 2*
Field, Gladys d1920 *Film 2, WhScrn 1, WhScrn 2*
Field, Grace *Film 1*
Field, Jonathan 1912- *WhThe*
Field, Joseph M d1856 *NotNAT B*
Field, Kate d1896 *NotNAT B*
Field, Leonard S 1908- *BiE&WWA, NotNAT*
Field, Lila d1954 *NotNAT B*
Field, Madalynne *Film 2*
Field, Margaret *WhoHol A*
Field, Marshall, V 1941- *CelR 3*
Field, Mary *WhoHol A*
Field, Mary 1896-1968 *FilmgC, WomWMM*
Field, Nat 1587-1620 *PIP&P*
Field, Nathan 1587-1620 *CnThe, NotNAT A, NotNAT B, OxThe, REnWD*
Field, Nathaniel d1633 *NotNAT B*
Field, Norman 1879-1956 *WhScrn 1, WhScrn 2, WhoHol B*
Field, Percy *Film 2*
Field, Rachel 1894-1942 *FilmgC, NotNAT B*
Field, Robert *WhScrn 2*
Field, Ron *WhoThe 16*
Field, Ron 1932?- *NotNAT*
Field, Ron 1934- *EncMT*
Field, Sally 1946- *FilmgC, WhoHol A*
Field, Shirley Ann 1938- *FilmgC, MotPP, WhoHol A*
Field, Shirley Anne 1938- *IntMPA 1977*
Field, Sid 1904-1950 *FilmgC, NotNAT A, NotNAT B, WhScrn 1, WhScrn 2, WhThe, WhoHol B*
Field, Sylvia *Film 2, WhoHol A*
Field, Sylvia 1901- *BiE&WWA, NotNAT*
Field, Sylvia 1902- *WhThe*
Field, Virginia 1917- *FilmgC, IntMPA 1977, MovMk, ThFT, WhThe, WhoHol A*
Fielder, Charles N 1900- *AmSCAP 1966*
Fielder, Margaret *WomWMM*
Fielding, Clarissa *Film 2*
Fielding, Claude *Film 2*
Fielding, Edward 1880-1945 *NotNAT B, WhScrn 2, WhoHol B*
Fielding, Edward 1885-1945 *WhScrn 1*
Fielding, Fenella *WhoHol A*
Fielding, Fenella 1930?- *FilmgC*
Fielding, Fenella 1934- *WhoThe 16*

Fielding, Gerald *Film 2*
Fielding, Harold *EncMT, WhoThe 16*
Fielding, Henry 1707-1754 *CnThe, McGWD,*
  NotNAT B, OxThe, PlP&P, REnWD
Fielding, Jerry 1922- *AmSCAP 1966, FilmgC,*
  IntMPA 1977
Fielding, Lee 1888-1963 *AmSCAP 1966*
Fielding, Margaret *Film 2*
Fielding, Marjorie 1892-1956 *FilmgC, NotNAT B,*
  WhScrn 1, WhScrn 2, WhThe, WhoHol B
Fielding, Minnie 1871-1936 *WhScrn 1, WhScrn 2*
Fielding, Romaine d1927 *Film 1, TwYS A,*
  WhoHol B
Fielding, Romaine 1877-1927 *Film 2, TwYS*
Fielding, Romaine 1882-1927 *WhScrn 1,*
  WhScrn 2
Fielding, Temple 1913- *CelR 3*
Fielding, Timothy d1738 *OxThe*
Fields, Arthur 1888-1953 *AmSCAP 1966,*
  NotNAT B
Fields, Arthur B 1889-1965 *NotNAT B*
Fields, Benny 1894-1959 *NotNAT B, WhScrn 1,*
  WhScrn 2, WhoHol B
Fields, Buddy 1889-1965 *AmSCAP 1966*
Fields, Dorothy d1974 *WhoHol B*
Fields, Dorothy 1904-1974 *EncMT, WhScrn 2*
Fields, Dorothy 1905-1974 *AmSCAP 1966,*
  BiE&WWA, CelR 3, ConDr 1973, NewMT,
  NotNAT B, WhThe
Fields, Freddie 1923- *IntMPA 1977*
Fields, Gracie 1898- *FilmgC, MotPP, MovMk,*
  NotNAT A, OxFilm, OxThe, ThFT, WhThe,
  WhoHol A
Fields, Harry D d1961 *NotNAT B*
Fields, Herbert 1897-1958 *EncMT, NewMT,*
  NotNAT B, WhThe
Fields, Irving 1915- *AmSCAP 1966*
Fields, John 1876-1938 *WhScrn 1, WhScrn 2*
Fields, Joseph 1885- *NewMT*
Fields, Joseph 1895-1966 *BiE&WWA, CnMD,*
  EncMT, McGWD, ModWD, NotNAT B,
  WhThe
Fields, Kathy *WhoHol A*
Fields, Lew 1867-1941 *EncMT, FamA&A,*
  Film 1, Film 2, NotNAT A, NotNAT B,
  TwYS, WhScrn 1, WhScrn 2, WhThe,
  WhoHol B, WhoStg 1908
Fields, Lewis Maurice 1867-1941 *WhoStg 1906*
Fields, Phyllis *WomWMM B*
Fields, Robert *WhoHol A*
Fields, Shep *WhoHol A*
Fields, Sid 1898-1975 *WhScrn 2*
Fields, Sidney 1898-1975 *WhoHol C*
Fields, Stanley 1880-1941 *MovMk, WhScrn 1,*
  WhScrn 2, WhoHol B
Fields, Stanley 1884-1941 *FilmgC*
Fields, Sylvia *Film 2*
Fields, Verna *WomWMM*
Fields, W C 1869-1946 *FamA&A*
Fields, W C 1879-1946 *BiDFlm, CmMov, EncMT,*
  Film 1, Film 2, FilmgC, MotPP, MovMk,
  NotNAT A, NotNAT B, OxFilm, PlP&P,
  TwYS, WhScrn 1, WhScrn 2, WhThe,
  WhoHol B, WorEnF
Fields, William d1961 *NotNAT B*
Fields, William Claude 1879-1946 *OxThe*
Fien, Lupin 1908- *AmSCAP 1966*
Fierro, Paul *WhoHol A*
Fifield, Elaine 1930- *WhThe*
Fifth Dimension, The *CelR 3*
Figman, Max d1952 *Film 1, Film 2, NotNAT B,*
  WhoHol B
Figman, Max 1867-1952 *WhScrn 2*
Figman, Max 1868-1952 *WhThe, WhoStg 1906,*

WhoStg 1908
Figman, Oscar Brimberton 1882-1930 *Film 2,*
  NotNAT B, WhScrn 2, WhoHol B
Figueiredo, Guilherme 1915- *CnThe, REnWD*
Figueroa, Gabriel 1907- *DcFM, FilmgC, OxFilm,*
  WorEnF
Figueroa, Ruben *WhoHol A*
Filandre 1616-1691 *OxThe*
Filas, Thomas J 1908- *AmSCAP 1966*
Filauri, Antonio 1889-1964 *WhScrn 2*
Fildes, Audrey 1922- *WhThe*
Filippi, Rosina 1866-1930 *NotNAT B, WhThe*
Filkins, Grace d1962 *NotNAT B, WhThe,*
  WhoStg 1906, WhoStg 1908
Filler, Harry 1908- *AmSCAP 1966*
Fillmore, Clyde 1874-1946 *WhScrn 2*
Fillmore, Clyde 1876-1948 *Film 1, Film 2,*
  TwYS, WhoHol B
Fillmore, Henry 1881-1956 *AmSCAP 1966*
Fillmore, Nellie 1864-1942 *WhScrn 1, WhScrn 2*
Filmer, A E *WhThe*
Filoi *Film 2*
Fils, Baron *Film 2*
Filson, Al W *Film 1, Film 2*
Filson, Mrs. Al W *Film 1*
Fimberg, Harold Alfred 1907- *AmSCAP 1966*
Fina, Jack 1913-1968 *AmSCAP 1966, WhScrn 2*
Finberg, Jack Gerald *IntMPA 1977*
Finch, Dick 1898-1955 *AmSCAP 1966*
Finch, Flora 1869-1940 *Film 1, Film 2, FilmgC,*
  NotNAT B, TwYS, WhScrn 1, WhScrn 2,
  WhoHol B
Finch, John *ConDr 1977C*
Finch, John 1911- *NatPD*
Finch, Jon 1941- *FilmgC, WhoHol A*
Finch, Kaye *WomWMM A, WomWMM B*
Finch, Peter 1916- *BiDFlm, CmMov, FilmgC,*
  IntMPA 1977, MotPP, MovMk, OxFilm,
  WhThe, WhoHol A, WorEnF
Finch, Ruth Goddard 1906- *AmSCAP 1966*
Finck, Herman 1872- *WhThe*
Finck, Joan *WomWMM B*
Finckel, Edwin A 1917- *AmSCAP 1966*
Findlater, John *WhoHol A*
Findlay, Roberta *WomWMM*
Findlay, Ruth 1904-1949 *NotNAT B, WhScrn 1,*
  WhScrn 2, WhoHol B
Findlay, Thomas Bruce 1874-1941 *Film 2,*
  NotNAT B, WhoHol B
Findley, Thomas Bruce 1874-1941 *WhScrn 1,*
  WhScrn 2
Findon, B W 1859-1943 *NotNAT B, WhThe*
Fine, Aaron d1963 *NotNAT B*
Fine, Bud *Film 2*
Fine, Harry *IntMPA 1977*
Fine, Irving 1914-1962 *AmSCAP 1966*
Fine, Jack Wolf 1922- *AmSCAP 1966*
Fine, Larry 1911-1975 *MotPP, WhScrn 2,*
  WhoHol C
Fine, Sidney 1904- *AmSCAP 1966*
Fine, Sylvia *AmSCAP 1966*
Fine, William 1926- *CelR 3*
Finegan, William J 1917- *AmSCAP 1966*
Fineshriber, William H, Jr. 1909- *IntMPA 1977*
Fink, Emma 1910-1966 *WhScrn 1, WhScrn 2*
Fink, Henry 1893-1963 *AmSCAP 1966, Film 2*
Fink, John *WhoHol A*
Fink, Michael 1939- *AmSCAP 1966*
Finke, John, Jr. 1898-1965 *AmSCAP 1966*
Finkel, Bob *NewYTET*
Finkelstein, Herman 1903- *IntMPA 1977*
Finklehoffe, Fred F 1911- *BiE&WWA, FilmgC,*
  NotNAT
Finlay, Bob d1929 *Film 1, WhoHol B*

Finlay, Frank 1926- *CnThe, FilmgC, PIP&P, WhoHol A, WhoThe 16*
Finlay, Redmon *Film 2*
Finlay, Robert 1888-1929 *WhScrn 1, WhScrn 2*
Finlayson, Henderson 1887-1953 *WhScrn 1, WhScrn 2*
Finlayson, James 1877-1953 *FilmgC*
Finlayson, James 1887-1953 *Film 1, Film 2, WhoHol B*
Finlayson, Jimmy 1887-1953 *TwYS*
Finley, Charles O 1918- *CelR 3*
Finley, Lorraine Noel 1899- *AmSCAP 1966*
Finley, Ned d1920 *Film 1, WhScrn 2*
Finn, Arthur *WhThe*
Finn, Henry James 1790?-1840 *NotNAT B, OxThe*
Finn, Konstantin Yakovlevich 1904- *OxThe*
Finn, Sam 1893-1958 *WhScrn 1, WhScrn 2*
Finn, William J 1881-1961 *AmSCAP 1966*
Finnegan, Walter 1873-1943 *WhScrn 1, WhScrn 2*
Finnell, Carrie d1963 *NotNAT B*
Finnerty, Louis 1883-1937 *WhScrn 1, WhScrn 2, WhoHol B*
Finnerty, Walter d1974 *WhoHol B*
Finnerty, Warren 1934-1974 *WhScrn 2*
Finney, Albert 1936- *BiDFlm, BiE&WWA, CelR 3, CnThe, FilmgC, IntMPA 1977, MotPP, MovMk, NotNAT, PIP&P, WhoHol A, WhoThe 16, WorEnF*
Finney, Albert 1937- *OxFilm*
Finney, Benjamin F, Jr. *Film 2*
Finney, Edward *IntMPA 1977*
Finney, Jameson Lee 1863- *WhoStg 1908*
Finney, Mary 1906-1973 *BiE&WWA, NotNAT B*
Finney, Ross Lee 1906- *AmSCAP 1966*
Finston, Nat W *AmSCAP 1966*
Fio Rito, Ted 1900-1971 *WhScrn 1, WhScrn 2, WhoHol B*
Fio Rito, Ted *see also* Fiorito, Ted
Fiore, Joan *WomWMM*
Fiorentino, Imero *NewYTET*
Fiorenza, Alfredo 1868-1931 *WhScrn 1, WhScrn 2*
Fiorilli, Tiberio 1608-1694 *NotNAT B*
Fiorillo, Beatrice Vitelli *OxThe*
Fiorillo, Giovan Battista *OxThe*
Fiorillo, Silvio d1632? *OxThe*
Fiorillo, Tiberio 1608-1694 *OxThe*
Fiorillo, Tiborio 1608-1694 *PIP&P*
Fiorino, Vincent C 1899- *AmSCAP 1966*
Fiorito, Ernest 1907-1960 *AmSCAP 1966*
Fiorito, Ted 1900-1971 *AmSCAP 1966*
Fiorito, Ted *see also* Fio Rito, Ted
Firestone, Cinda *WomWMM A, WomWMM B*
Firestone, Eddie 1920- *BiE&WWA, WhoHol A*
Firestone, Elizabeth *WomWMM*
Firestone, Harvey S, Jr. 1898- *CelR 3*
Firestone, Idabelle 1874-1954 *AmSCAP 1966*
Firestone, Raymond 1908- *CelR 3*
Firpo, Luis Angel *Film 2*
Firth, Anne 1918- *WhThe*
Firth, Elizabeth 1884- *WhThe*
Firth, Mike *NatPD*
Firth, Peter *PIP&P A*
Firth, Tazeena 1935- *WhoThe 16*
Firth, Thomas Preston 1883-1945 *WhScrn 2*
Fischer, Alice 1869-1947 *NotNAT B, WhThe, WhoStg 1908*
Fischer, Bobby 1943- *CelR 3*
Fischer, Carl Theodore 1912-1954 *AmSCAP 1966*
Fischer, Clifford C d1951 *NotNAT B*
Fischer, Edna *AmSCAP 1966*
Fischer, Felix *Film 2*

Fischer, Gunnar 1910- *DcFM, OxFilm, WorEnF*
Fischer, Gunnar 1911- *FilmgC*
Fischer, Joseph A *IntMPA 1977*
Fischer, Leck 1904-1956 *CnMD*
Fischer, Lynn Connor 1935- *WomWMM A, WomWMM B*
Fischer, Margarita 1886-1975 *WhScrn 2*
Fischer, Margarita 1893- *Film 1*
Fischer, Max 1909-1974 *WhoHol A*
Fischer, Max *see also* Fisher, Max
Fischer, O W 1915- *FilmgC*
Fischer, Robert *Film 2*
Fischer, Robert E 1923- *BiE&WWA*
Fischer, Ruth 1895- *BiE&WWA*
Fischer, Ruth 1919- *BiE&WWA*
Fischer-Dieskau, Dietrich 1925- *CelR 3*
Fischer-Koppe, Hugo *Film 2*
Fischinger, Oskar 1900-1967 *DcFM, OxFilm, WorEnF*
Fischman, David 1910-1958 *WhScrn 1, WhScrn 2*
Fishbein, Frieda 1895- *NotNAT*
Fishbein, Lawrence 1904- *BiE&WWA*
Fisher, Al *IntMPA 1977*
Fisher, Alfred 1849-1933 *Film 2, WhScrn 1, WhScrn 2, WhoHol B*
Fisher, Anne *WomWMM B*
Fisher, Art *NewYTET*
Fisher, Carl 1909- *BiE&WWA*
Fisher, Carrie *WhoHol A*
Fisher, Clara 1811-1898 *FamA&A, NotNAT A, NotNAT B, OxThe*
Fisher, Dan 1920- *AmSCAP 1966*
Fisher, Doris 1915- *AmSCAP 1966*
Fisher, Eddie 1928- *FilmgC, IntMPA 1977, NewYTET, WhoHol A*
Fisher, Frank H 1907- *IntMPA 1977*
Fisher, Fred 1875-1942 *AmSCAP 1966, NotNAT B*
Fisher, Freddie Schnickelfritz 1904-1967 *WhScrn 2*
Fisher, Frederick Schnickelfritz 1904-1967 *WhoHol B*
Fisher, George 1894-1960 *Film 1, Film 2, WhScrn 1, WhScrn 2, WhoHol B*
Fisher, Gerry 1926- *FilmgC*
Fisher, Harry d1923 *NotNAT B, WhoHol B*
Fisher, Harry 1885-1917 *WhScrn 2*
Fisher, Holly *WomWMM B*
Fisher, Irving d1959 *NotNAT B*
Fisher, Jane d1869 *NotNAT B*
Fisher, Jessie 1909- *AmSCAP 1966*
Fisher, John C d1921 *NotNAT B*
Fisher, Jules 1937- *BiE&WWA, NotNAT, WhoThe 16*
Fisher, Larry *Film 2*
Fisher, Laurence *Film 2*
Fisher, Lewis T 1915- *BiE&WWA*
Fisher, Lois *WomWMM*
Fisher, Lola *BiE&WWA, NotNAT*
Fisher, Lola 1892-1926 *NotNAT B*
Fisher, Lola 1896-1926 *WhThe*
Fisher, Maggie 1854-1938 *WhScrn 1, WhScrn 2*
Fisher, Maisie *Film 2*
Fisher, Margarita 1893- *Film 2, TwYS*
Fisher, Margarite *WhScrn 2*
Fisher, Marjorie Williams 1916- *AmSCAP 1966*
Fisher, Mark 1895-1948 *AmSCAP 1966*
Fisher, Marve A 1907-1957 *AmSCAP 1966*
Fisher, Marvin 1916- *AmSCAP 1966*
Fisher, Max 1909-1974 *WhScrn 2*
Fisher, Max *see also* Fischer, Max
Fisher, Millicent *Film 2*
Fisher, Nelle 1914- *BiE&WWA, NotNAT*
Fisher, Nicholas E 1894-1961 *AmSCAP 1966*
Fisher, Nicola *WomWMM*

Fisher, Reuben 1923- AmSCAP 1966
Fisher, Sallie 1881-1950 NotNAT B, WhoHol B
Fisher, Sally 1881-1950 WhScrn 1, WhScrn 2
Fisher, Shug WhoHol A
Fisher, Terence 1904- BiDFlm, CmMov, DcFM,
    FilmgC, IntMPA 1977, WorEnF
Fisher, William 1868-1933 WhScrn 1, WhScrn 2,
    WhoHol B
Fisher, William Arms 1861-1948 AmSCAP 1966
Fisher, William G 1883-1949 WhScrn 1,
    WhScrn 2
Fishko, Sara WomWMM B
Fishman, Henry d1964 NotNAT B
Fisk, James PIP&P
Fiske, Mrs. 1865-1932 Film 1
Fiske, Harrison Grey 1861-1942 NotNAT B,
    WhThe, WhoStg 1906, WhoStg 1908
Fiske, Homer 1914- AmSCAP 1966
Fiske, Minnie Maddern 1865-1932 FamA&A,
    NotNAT A, NotNAT B, OxThe, PIP&P,
    WhScrn 2, WhThe, WhoHol B,
    WhoStg 1906, WhoStg 1908
Fiske, Richard 1915-1944 WhScrn 2
Fiske, Robert L 1889-1944 WhScrn 2
Fiske, Stephen 1840-1916 NotNAT B, WhThe
Fisz, Benjamin 1922- FilmgC, IntMPA 1977
Fitch, Clyde 1865-1909 CnMD, CnThe, McGWD,
    ModWD, NotNAT A, NotNAT B, PIP&P,
    REnWD
Fitch, Joseph 1921- BiE&WWA, NotNAT
Fitch, Theodore F 1900- AmSCAP 1966
Fitch, William Clyde 1865-1909 OxThe,
    WhoStg 1906, WhoStg 1908
Fitelson, H William 1905- IntMPA 1977
Fitts, Dudley 1903-1968 BiE&WWA, NotNAT B
Fitz, Charles E d1920 NotNAT B
Fitz-Gerald, S J Adair 1859-1925 WhThe
Fitz-Gerald, S J Adair see also Fitzgerald, S J Adair
Fitzball, Edward 1792-1873 NotNAT B, OxThe
Fitzgerald, Aubrey Film 2
Fitzgerald, Aubrey Whitestone 1876- WhThe
Fitzgerald, Barry 1888-1961 BiDFlm, FilmgC,
    HolP 40, MotPP, MovMk, NotNAT B,
    OxFilm, PIP&P, WhScrn 1, WhScrn 2,
    WhThe, WhoHol B
Fitzgerald, Cissy 1874-1941 Film 2, NotNAT B,
    WhScrn 1, WhScrn 2, WhoHol B
Fitzgerald, Cissy 1894-1941 Film 1, TwYS
Fitzgerald, Dallas M TwYS A
Fitzgerald, Deborah WomWMM B
Fitzgerald, Edward 1876- WhThe, WhoStg 1908
Fitzgerald, Edward P 1883-1942 WhScrn 1,
    WhScrn 2, WhoHol B
Fitzgerald, Ella 1918- AmSCAP 1966, CelR 3
Fitzgerald, F Scott 1896-1940 CnMD, FilmgC,
    NotNAT B, OxFilm
Fitzgerald, Florence Irene 1890-1962 NotNAT B,
    WhScrn 1, WhScrn 2, WhoHol B
Fitzgerald, Francis Scott Key 1896-1940 WorEnF
Fitzgerald, Geraldine MotPP, PIP&P A
Fitzgerald, Geraldine 1912- FilmgC
Fitzgerald, Geraldine 1914- BiE&WWA, HolP 40,
    IntMPA 1977, MovMk, NotNAT, ThFT,
    WhoHol A, WhoThe 16
Fitzgerald, James M 1897-1919 WhScrn 2
Fitzgerald, Lilian d1947 NotNAT B
Fitzgerald, Lillian d1947 WhScrn 2, WhoHol B
Fitzgerald, Neil WhoHol A
Fitzgerald, Neil 1898- WhoThe 16
Fitzgerald, Pegeen IntMPA 1977
Fitzgerald, Percy Hetherington 1834-1925
    NotNAT B, WhThe
Fitzgerald, Robert 1925- IntMPA 1977
Fitzgerald, S J Adair 1859-1925 NotNAT B

Fitzgerald, S J Adair see also Fitz-Gerald, S J Adair
Fitzgerald, Walter 1896- BiE&WWA, FilmgC,
    IntMPA 1977, WhThe, WhoHol A
Fitzgibbon, Louis A d1961 NotNAT B
Fitzgibbons, Esme Film 2
Fitzharris, Edward 1890-1974 WhScrn 2,
    WhoHol B
Fitzmaurice, George 1877-1963 CnThe, McGWD,
    ModWD, REnWD
Fitzmaurice, George 1885-1940 CmMov, FilmgC,
    WhoHol B
Fitzmaurice, George 1895-1940 TwYS A,
    WhScrn 1, WhScrn 2
Fitzmaurice, Michael T 1908-1967 WhScrn 1,
    WhScrn 2, WhoHol B
Fitzpatrick, Charlotte Film 1
Fitzpatrick, James A 1902- FilmgC,
    IntMPA 1977
Fitzpatrick, Michael J 1863-1950 AmSCAP 1966
Fitzpatrick, Pat WhoHol A
Fitzroy, Emily 1861-1954 Film 1, Film 2, TwYS,
    WhScrn 1, WhScrn 2, WhoHol B
Fitzroy, Louis Film 1
Fitzsimmons, Frank 1908- CelR 3
Fitzsimmons, Robert Film 1
Fix, Paul 1901- Film 2, TwYS
Fix, Paul 1902- FilmgC, IntMPA 1977, MovMk,
    Vers B, WhoHol A
Fix, Ress 1893-1975 WhScrn 2
Fjelde, Rolf NatPD
Fjord, Olaf Film 2
Flack, Luise WomWMM
Flagello, Nicholas 1928- AmSCAP 1966
Flagg, Fannie WhoHol A
Flagg, James Montgomery 1877-1960 Film 1,
    WhScrn 2
Flagler, Robert S 1890-1935 AmSCAP 1966
Flagstad, Kirsten 1895-1962 FilmgC, WhScrn 1,
    WhScrn 2, WhoHol B
Flaherty, Pat J, Sr. 1903-1970 WhScrn 1,
    WhScrn 2, WhoHol B
Flaherty, Robert 1884-1951 BiDFlm, DcFM,
    FilmgC, MovMk, OxFilm, WomWMM,
    WorEnF
Flaiano, Ennio 1910- OxFilm
Flamm, Donald 1899- BiE&WWA, NotNAT
Flamma, Luca Film 2
Flanagan, Bud WhScrn 1, WhScrn 2
Flanagan, Bud 1896-1968 EncMT, FilmgC,
    NotNAT B, WhScrn 1, WhScrn 2, WhThe,
    WhoHol B
Flanagan, Edward J 1880-1925 WhScrn 1,
    WhScrn 2, WhoHol B
Flanagan, Fionnuala WhoHol A
Flanagan, Hallie 1890-1969 BiE&WWA,
    NotNAT B, OxThe, PIP&P, WhThe
Flanagan, Kellie WhoHol A
Flanagan, Ralph 1919- AmSCAP 1966
Flanagan, Rebecca 1876-1938 WhScrn 1,
    WhScrn 2
Flanagan, Richard d1917 NotNAT B, WhThe
Flanders, Ed 1934- NotNAT
Flanders, Michael 1922-1975 BiE&WWA,
    NotNAT B, OxThe, WhScrn 2, WhThe,
    WhoHol C
Flanigan, Robert Lee 1926- AmSCAP 1966
Flanner, Janet 1892- CelR 3
Flannery, Susan WhoHol A
Flanz, Marta WomWMM
Flaster, Karl 1905-1965 AmSCAP 1966
Flateau, Georges 1882-1953 NotNAT B,
    WhScrn 1, WhScrn 2, WhoHol B
Flato, Ludwig 1911- AmSCAP 1966
Flatow, Leon 1889-1944 AmSCAP 1966

Flatt, Ernest O 1918- *NewYTET, NotNAT*
Flattery, Thomas L 1922- *IntMPA 1977*
Flaum, Thea *WomWMM B*
Flavin, James 1906- *FilmgC, MovMk, Vers B, WhoHol A*
Flavin, Martin 1883-1967 *BiE&WWA, CnMD, McGWD, ModWD, NotNAT B, WhThe*
Flavio *OxThe*
Flaxman, John P 1934- *IntMPA 1977*
Fleay, Frederick Gard d1909 *NotNAT B*
Fleck, Charles S 1916- *AmSCAP 1966*
Fleck, Johann Friedrich Ferdinand 1757-1801 *NotNAT B, OxThe*
Flecker, James Elroy 1884-1915 *CnThe, McGWD, NotNAT B, OxThe*
Fleeson, Neville 1887-1945 *AmSCAP 1966*
Fleetwood, Charles d1745? *NotNAT B, OxThe, PIP&P*
Fleetwood, Susan 1944- *WhoThe 16*
Fleigel, Gustaf *Film 2*
Fleischer, Dave 1894- *AmSCAP 1966, IntMPA 1977, OxFilm, WorEnF*
Fleischer, David 1894- *DcFM*
Fleischer, Max 1889- *DcFM, WorEnF*
Fleischer, Max 1889-1972 *OxFilm*
Fleischer, Max 1889-1973 *FilmgC*
Fleischer, Richard 1916- *BiDFlm, CmMov, DcFM, FilmgC, IntMPA 1977, OxFilm, WorEnF*
Fleischhacker, David 1933- *AmSCAP 1966*
Fleischman, David 1912- *AmSCAP 1966*
Fleischman, Maurice L d1963 *NotNAT B*
Fleischman, Stephen *NewYTET*
Fleischmann, Harry 1899-1943 *WhScrn 1, WhScrn 2, WhoHol B*
Fleischmann, Julius 1900-1968 *BiE&WWA, NotNAT B*
Fleisher, Bud *NatPD*
Fleisher, Mark 1907- *AmSCAP 1966*
Fleisher, Richard 1916- *MovMk*
Fleisser, Marieluise 1901-1974 *CnMD*
Fleming, Alice 1882-1952 *NotNAT B, WhScrn 1, WhScrn 2, WhoHol B*
Fleming, Art *WhoHol A*
Fleming, Bob 1878-1933 *WhScrn 2*
Fleming, Brandon 1889- *WhThe*
Fleming, Carroll *Film 2*
Fleming, Claude *Film 2*
Fleming, Conn 1941- *NatPD*
Fleming, Eric d1966 *WhoHol B*
Fleming, Eric 1924-1966 *FilmgC*
Fleming, Eric 1926-1966 *WhScrn 1, WhScrn 2*
Fleming, Erin *WhoHol A*
Fleming, George 1858-1938 *NotNAT B, WhThe*
Fleming, Ian 1888-1969 *FilmgC, WhScrn 1, WhScrn 2, WhThe, WhoHol B*
Fleming, Ian 1906-1964 *FilmgC*
Fleming, Louise *WomWMM B*
Fleming, Lucy 1947- *WhoThe 16*
Fleming, Noel d1950 *NotNAT B*
Fleming, Peggy 1948- *CelR 3*
Fleming, Philip B *Film 2*
Fleming, Rhonda *IntMPA 1977, MotPP, WhoHol A*
Fleming, Rhonda 1922- *FilmgC*
Fleming, Rhonda 1923- *BiDFlm, MovMk, WorEnF*
Fleming, Robert *Film 1*
Fleming, Susan 1909- *ThFT, WhoHol A*
Fleming, Tom 1927- *WhoThe 16*
Fleming, Victor 1883-1949 *BiDFlm, DcFM, FilmgC, MovMk, OxFilm, TwYS A, WorEnF*
Fleming, William d1921 *NotNAT B*

Flemming, Bill *NewYTET*
Flemming, Claude 1884-1952 *NotNAT B, WhThe*
Flemyng, Gordon 1934- *FilmgC*
Flemyng, Robert 1912- *BiE&WWA, FilmgC, IntMPA 1977, NotNAT, WhoHol A, WhoThe 16*
Flers, P L 1867-1932 *NotNAT B, WhThe*
Flers, Robert, Marquis De 1872-1927 *McGWD, ModWD, NotNAT B, WhThe*
Fleschelles *OxThe*
Fletcher, Allen 1922- *BiE&WWA, NotNAT, WhoThe 16*
Fletcher, Archie 1890- *AmSCAP 1966*
Fletcher, Bramwell 1904- *Film 2, WhoHol A, WhoThe 16*
Fletcher, Bramwell 1906- *BiE&WWA, NotNAT*
Fletcher, Branwell 1904- *FilmgC*
Fletcher, Cecil *Film 1*
Fletcher, Cyril 1913- *FilmgC*
Fletcher, Grant 1913- *AmSCAP 1966*
Fletcher, Jack *WhoHol A*
Fletcher, James Chipman 1919- *CelR 3*
Fletcher, John *ConDr 1977B*
Fletcher, John 1579-1625 *CnThe, McGWD, NotNAT A, NotNAT B, OxThe, PIP&P, REnWD*
Fletcher, Lawrence M 1902-1970 *WhScrn 1, WhScrn 2, WhoHol B*
Fletcher, Lester *WhoHol A*
Fletcher, Louise *IntMPA 1977, WhoHol A*
Fletcher, Percy 1879-1932 *NotNAT B, WhThe*
Fletcher, Robert 1923- *BiE&WWA, NotNAT, WhoThe 16*
Fletcher, Tex 1910- *AmSCAP 1966*
Fletcher, Tom 1873-1954 *NotNAT A*
Fletcher, Yvonne *WomWMM*
Fleu, Dorris Bell 1922-1955 *WhScrn 1, WhScrn 2, WhoHol B*
Fleury 1750-1822 *NotNAT A, NotNAT B, OxThe*
Flexer, David 1909- *IntMPA 1977*
Flexner, Anne Crawford 1874-1955 *NotNAT B, WhThe*
Flick, Pat C 1899-1955 *WhScrn 1, WhScrn 2, WhoHol B*
Flick-Flood, Dora *AmSCAP 1966*
Flicker, Theodore J 1929?- *FilmgC*
Flicker, Theodore J 1930- *BiE&WWA, NewYTET, NotNAT, OxFilm, WorEnF*
Fliegel, Mrs. Ernie d1966 *WhScrn 1, WhScrn 2, WhoHol B*
Flimm, Florence *Film 1*
Flinn, John C 1917- *IntMPA 1977*
Flint, Hazel 1893-1959 *WhScrn 1, WhScrn 2, WhoHol B*
Flint, Helen 1898-1967 *WhScrn 1, WhScrn 2, WhoHol B*
Flint, Joseph W 1893-1933 *WhScrn 1, WhScrn 2*
Flint, Sam 1882- *Vers B*
Flint-Shipman, Veronica 1931- *WhoThe 16*
Flippen, Jay C d1971 *MotPP, WhoHol B*
Flippen, Jay C 1898-1971 *FilmgC, MovMk, Vers B, WhScrn 1, WhScrn 2*
Flippen, Jay C 1899-1971 *CmMov*
Flipper d1971 *WhScrn 1, WhScrn 2*
Floersheimer, Albert, Jr. 1917- *IntMPA 1977*
Flohrs, Virginia *Film 2*
Flon, Suzanne *WhoHol A*
Flood, James 1895-1953 *TwYS A*
Flood, John d1924 *NotNAT B*
Florath, Albert 1888-1957 *WhScrn 2*
Florath, Albert 1889-1957 *WhScrn 1*
Florea, John 1916- *IntMPA 1977*
Florelle 1901-1974 *WhScrn 2*

Florelle, Odette *Film 2*
Floren, Myron 1919- *AmSCAP 1966*
Florence, Katherine *WhoStg 1908*
Florence, William Jermyn 1831-1891 *FamA&A,*
  NotNAT B, OxThe, PIP&P
Florence, Mrs. William Jermyn 1831-1906
  NotNAT B, PIP&P
Flores, Ignacio F 1934- *AmSCAP 1966*
Floresco, Michel d1925 *WhScrn 2*
Florey, Robert 1900- *BiDFlm, CmMov, DcFM,*
  Film 2, FilmgC, MovMk, OxFilm, TwYS A,
  WorEnF
Floridor 1608-1672 *OxThe*
Flory, Regine 1894-1926 *NotNAT B, WhThe*
Flouker, Mack *Film 2*
Flower, Alice *Film 2*
Flower, Sir Archibald d1950 *NotNAT B*
Flowers, Bess 1900- *Film 2, TwYS, WhoHol A*
Flowerton, Consuelo 1900-1965 *WhScrn 1,*
  WhScrn 2, WhoHol B
Flowler, Gene 1890-1960 *NotNAT B*
Floyd, Calvin James 1931- *AmSCAP 1966*
Floyd, Carlisle 1926- *AmSCAP 1966*
Floyd, Gwendolen d1950 *NotNAT B, WhThe*
Floyd, Henrietta *Film 2*
Fluellen, Joel *WhoHol A*
Flugrath, Edna *Film 1*
Fluker, Mack *Film 2*
Fly, James Lawrence d1966 *NewYTET*
Flynn, Allan 1894-1965 *AmSCAP 1966*
Flynn, Don *NatPD*
Flynn, Edward F 1913- *AmSCAP 1966*
Flynn, Edythe *Film 2*
Flynn, Elinor 1910-1938 *WhScrn 2*
Flynn, Emmett 1892-1937 *TwYS A*
Flynn, Errol 1909-1959 *BiDFlm, CmMov,*
  FilmgC, MotPP, MovMk, NotNAT B,
  OxFilm, WhScrn 1, WhScrn 2, WhoHol B,
  WorEnF
Flynn, Frank 1900-1964 *AmSCAP 1966*
Flynn, Hazel E 1899-1964 *NotNAT B, WhScrn 1,*
  WhScrn 2, WhoHol B
Flynn, Joe 1924-1974 *WhScrn 2, WhoHol B*
Flynn, John *IntMPA 1977*
Flynn, M B Lefty *Film 2*
Flynn, Maurice 1876-1959 *Film 2, TwYS*
Flynn, Maurice B Lefty 1893-1959 *WhScrn 2*
Flynn, Maurice Lefty d1959 *WhoHol B*
Flynn, Rita *Film 2*
Flynn, Sean *MotPP*
Fo, Dario 1926- *CroCD*
Foch, Nina 1924- *BiE&WWA, FilmgC, HolP 40,*
  IntMPA 1977, MotPP, MovMk, NotNAT,
  WhoHol A, WhoThe 16
Fodor, Ladislaus 1898- *CnMD, WhThe*
Fody, Ilona 1920- *AmSCAP 1966*
Fogarty, Frank d1925 *NotNAT B*
Fogarty, J Paul 1893- *AmSCAP 1966*
Fogarty, Jack V *IntMPA 1977*
Fogarty, Joseph R *NewYTET*
Fogazzaro, Antonio 1842-1911 *McGWD*
Fogel, V P *Film 2*
Fogel, Vladimir *Film 2*
Fogelson, Andrew 1942- *IntMPA 1977*
Fogelson, David 1903- *IntMPA 1977*
Fogerty, Elsie 1866-1945 *NotNAT A, NotNAT B,*
  OxThe, WhThe
Fokine, Michel 1880-1942 *NotNAT B, WhThe*
Foley, George *Film 1, Film 2*
Foley, George F 1919- *IntMPA 1977*
Foley, Joe d1955 *WhoHol B*
Foley, Joseph F 1910-1955 *WhScrn 1, WhScrn 2*
Foley, Paul A 1902- *NotNAT*
Foley, Paul A 1905- *BiE&WWA*

Foley, Red 1910-1968 *WhScrn 1, WhScrn 2,*
  WhoHol B
Foley, Syd 1909- *AmSCAP 1966*
Folger, Henry Clay 1857-1930 *NotNAT B, OxThe*
Folkenstein, Julius *Film 2*
Folkina, Vera d1958 *NotNAT B*
Follis, Dorothy 1802-1923 *NotNAT B*
Follmer, Patricia *WomWMM B*
Folsey, George *IntMPA 1977, WorEnF*
Folsey, George J 1898- *FilmgC*
Folsey, George J 1900- *CmMov*
Folsom, Frank M d1970 *NewYTET*
Folwell, Denis 1905-1971 *WhScrn 2, WhoHol B*
Folz, Hans *OxThe*
Fomeen, Basil 1902- *AmSCAP 1966*
Fonda, Henry 1905- *BiDFlm, BiE&WWA,*
  CelR 3, CmMov, FilmgC, IntMPA 1977,
  MotPP, MovMk, NotNAT, PIP&P,
  WhoHol A, WhoThe 16, WorEnF
Fonda, Jane 1937- *BiDFlm, BiE&WWA, CelR 3,*
  FilmgC, IntMPA 1977, MotPP, MovMk,
  NotNAT, NotNAT A, OxFilm, WhoHol A,
  WhoThe 16, WomWMM, WorEnF
Fonda, Peter *MotPP, WhoHol A*
Fonda, Peter 1939- *CelR 3, FilmgC,*
  IntMPA 1977, MovMk, OxFilm
Fonda, Peter 1940- *BiDFlm*
Fonda Family *NotNAT A*
Fong, Benson *WhoHol A*
Fong, Brian *WhoHol A*
Fong, Hiram 1907- *CelR 3*
Fong, Kam *WhoHol A*
Fonss, Olaf 1882-1949 *Film 1, WhScrn 1,*
  WhScrn 2
Fontaine, Eddie *WhoHol A*
Fontaine, Frank *IntMPA 1977, WhoHol A*
Fontaine, Joan 1917- *BiDFlm, BiE&WWA,*
  CelR 3, CmMov, FilmgC, IntMPA 1977,
  MotPP, MovMk, OxFilm, ThFT, WhoHol A,
  WomWMM, WorEnF
Fontaine, Lilian 1886-1975 *WhScrn 2, WhoHol C*
Fontaine, Tony 1927-1974 *WhScrn 2, WhoHol B*
Fontane, Tony *AmSCAP 1966*
Fontanne, Lynn *BiE&WWA, NotNAT, PIP&P,*
  WhoHol A
Fontanne, Lynn 1887- *CelR 3, CnThe,*
  FamA&A, Film 2, FilmgC, NotNAT A,
  OxThe, ThFT
Fontanne, Lynn 1892- *WhoThe 16*
Fontenelle, Bernard LeBovier De 1657-1757 *OxThe*
Fonteyn, Margot 1919- *CelR 3, WhThe*
Fonvizin, Denis 1745-1782 *CnThe, McGWD,*
  REnWD
Fonvizin, Denis Ivanovich 1744-1792 *NotNAT B,*
  OxThe
Foo, Lee Tung d1966 *WhScrn 2*
Foo, Wing 1910-1953 *WhScrn 1, WhScrn 2,*
  WhoHol B
Fook, Monte 1908-1933 *WhScrn 1, WhScrn 2*
Foote, Courtenay d1925 *Film 1, Film 2, MotPP,*
  TwYS
Foote, Courteney d1925 *WhScrn 2*
Foote, Horton *BiE&WWA, ConDr 1977C,*
  NotNAT, WhoThe 16
Foote, John Taintor d1950 *NotNAT B*
Foote, Lydia 1844-1892 *NotNAT B, OxThe*
Foote, Maria 1797?-1867 *OxThe*
Foote, Samuel 1720-1777 *McGWD, NotNAT A,*
  NotNAT B, OxThe
Foran, Arthur F 1912-1967 *WhScrn 1, WhScrn 2*
Foran, Dick 1910- *FilmgC, IntMPA 1977,*
  WhoHol A
Foran, Richard 1910- *MovMk*
Forbes, Athol d1917 *NotNAT B*

Forbes, Brenda 1909- *BiE&WWA, NotNAT, WhoHol A, WhoThe 16*
Forbes, Bryan 1926- *BiDFlm, CmMov, ConDr 1977A, FilmgC, IntMPA 1977, MovMk, OxFilm, WhoHol A, WorEnF*
Forbes, Freddie 1895-1952 *WhThe*
Forbes, James 1871-1938 *ModWD, NotNAT B, WhThe*
Forbes, Lou 1902- *AmSCAP 1966*
Forbes, Malcolm 1919- *CelR 3*
Forbes, Mary 1880-1974 *WhScrn 2, WhThe, WhoHol B*
Forbes, Mary Elizabeth 1880-1964 *Film 1, Film 2, FilmgC, MovMk, Vers A, WhScrn 1, WhScrn 2, WhoHol B*
Forbes, Meriel 1913- *BiE&WWA, FilmgC, NotNAT, WhoHol A, WhoThe 16*
Forbes, Norman *Film 1*
Forbes, Norman 1858-1932 *WhThe*
Forbes, Norman *see also* Forbes-Robertson, Norman
Forbes, Ralph d1951 *MotPP, WhoHol B*
Forbes, Ralph 1896-1951 *Film 1, TwYS, WhScrn 1, WhScrn 2*
Forbes, Ralph 1902-1951 *FilmgC, MovMk*
Forbes, Ralph 1905-1951 *NotNAT B, WhThe*
Forbes, Scott *WhoHol A*
Forbes-Robertson, Beatrice 1883-1967 *WhThe*
Forbes-Robertson, Eric 1865-1935 *NotNAT B, OxThe*
Forbes-Robertson, Frank 1885-1947 *NotNAT B, WhThe*
Forbes-Robertson, Lady Gertrude *PIP&P*
Forbes-Robertson, Ian 1858-1936 *OxThe*
Forbes-Robertson, Ian *see also* Robertson, Ian
Forbes-Robertson, Jean 1905-1962 *NotNAT B, OxThe, PIP&P, WhScrn 2, WhThe*
Forbes-Robertson, Sir Johnston 1853-1937 *CnThe, FamA&A, Film 1, NotNAT A, NotNAT B, OxThe, PIP&P, WhScrn 1, WhScrn 2, WhThe, WhoHol B, WhoStg 1906, WhoStg 1908*
Forbes-Robertson, Norman 1858-1932 *NotNAT B*
Forbes-Robertson, Norman 1859-1932 *OxThe*
Forbes-Robertson, Norman *see also* Forbes, Norman
Force, Floyd Charles 1876-1947 *WhScrn 1, WhScrn 2, WhoHol B*
Ford, Aleksander 1908- *DcFM, OxFilm, WorEnF*
Ford, Alexander 1908- *FilmgC*
Ford, Arthur *Film 1*
Ford, Audrey *WhThe*
Ford, Barry *WhoHol A*
Ford, Carl 1920- *AmSCAP 1966*
Ford, Cecil F 1911- *FilmgC, IntMPA 1977*
Ford, Charles 1908- *OxFilm*
Ford, Clarence *Film 2*
Ford, Constance *BiE&WWA, FilmgC, MotPP, NotNAT, WhoHol A*
Ford, Daisy 1906-1959 *WhScrn 1, WhScrn 2*
Ford, Ed E *WhThe*
Ford, Ernest B 1916- *AmSCAP 1966*
Ford, Ernest Jennings 1919- *AmSCAP 1966*
Ford, Eugenie 1898-1940 *Film 1, Film 2*
Ford, Eugenie *see also* Forde, Eugenie
Ford, Francis d1953 *MotPP, NotNAT B, WhoHol B, WomWMM*
Ford, Francis 1882-1953 *TwYS, TwYS A, Vers B, WhScrn 1, WhScrn 2*
Ford, Francis 1883-1953 *Film 1, Film 2, FilmgC*
Ford, Frank 1916- *BiE&WWA, NotNAT*
Ford, Frank B *NatPD*
Ford, Frederick W *NewYTET*
Ford, George 1879- *NotNAT*
Ford, Gerald 1913- *CelR 3*

Ford, Glenn 1916- *BiDFlm, CelR 3, CmMov, FilmgC, IntMPA 1977, MotPP, MovMk, OxFilm, WhoHol A, WorEnF*
Ford, Harriet d1949 *NotNAT B, WhThe*
Ford, Harrison *MotPP, WhoHol A*
Ford, Harrison 1884-1957 *NotNAT B, WhoHol B*
Ford, Harrison 1892-1959 *Film 1, Film 2, TwYS*
Ford, Harrison 1894-1957 *WhScrn 1, WhScrn 2*
Ford, Harry 1877- *WhThe*
Ford, Helen *BiE&WWA, EncMT, NotNAT, WhThe*
Ford, Henry, II 1917- *CelR 3*
Ford, Hugh *TwYS A*
Ford, James *Film 2*
Ford, Joan 1921- *AmSCAP 1966*
Ford, John d1963 *NotNAT B*
Ford, John 1586-1639? *CnThe, McGWD, NotNAT A, OxThe, PIP&P, REnWD*
Ford, John 1586-1640? *NotNAT B*
Ford, John 1895-1973 *BiDFlm, CmMov, DcFM, Film 1, Film 2, FilmgC, MovMk, OxFilm, TwYS A, WhScrn 2, WorEnF*
Ford, John Thomson 1829-1894 *NotNAT B, OxThe*
Ford, Lori 1928- *AmSCAP 1966*
Ford, Marty 1900-1954 *WhScrn 1, WhScrn 2*
Ford, Paul 1901-1976 *BiE&WWA, FilmgC, MotPP, NotNAT, NotNAT B, WhoThe 16*
Ford, Paul 1902- *MovMk*
Ford, Phil *Film 1*
Ford, Philip *Film 2*
Ford, Philip d1976 *WhoHol C*
Ford, Ross *WhoHol A*
Ford, Ruth 1920- *BiE&WWA, CelR 3, NotNAT, WhoHol A, WhoThe 16*
Ford, Sherman, Jr. 1929- *AmSCAP 1966*
Ford, Tennessee Ernie 1919- *IntMPA 1977, NewYTET*
Ford, Tony 1925- *IntMPA 1977*
Ford, Wallace d1966 *MotPP, WhoHol B*
Ford, Wallace 1897-1966 *FilmgC, MovMk*
Ford, Wallace 1898-1966 *BiE&WWA, NotNAT B, WhThe*
Ford, Wallace 1899-1966 *Vers B, WhScrn 1, WhScrn 2*
Forde, Eugene 1898- *Film 1, FilmgC*
Forde, Eugenie 1898-1940 *Film 2, TwYS, WhScrn 2*
Forde, Eugenie *see also* Ford, Eugenie
Forde, Florrie 1876-1940 *NotNAT B, OxThe, WhThe*
Forde, Hal d1955 *Film 1, Film 2, NotNAT B, WhoHol B*
Forde, Stanley H 1881-1929 *Film 2, WhScrn 2*
Forde, Stanley Hamilton 1878- *WhoStg 1908*
Forde, Victoria 1897-1964 *Film 1, WhScrn 2, WhoHol B*
Forde, Walter 1896- *FilmgC*
Forde, Walter 1897- *Film 2*
Fordin, Hugh G 1935- *BiE&WWA, NotNAT*
Fordred, Dorice 1902- *WhThe*
Foreman, Carl 1914- *BiDFlm, CmMov, ConDr 1977A, DcFM, FilmgC, IntMPA 1977, OxFilm, WorEnF*
Foreman, George 1949- *CelR 3*
Foreman, John *IntMPA 1977*
Foreman, Richard 1937- *ConDr 1977*
Forepaugh, Adam 1830-1890 *NotNAT B*
Forepaugh, John A d1895 *NotNAT B*
Forest, Alan *Film 1*
Forest, Ann *Film 2*
Forest, Frank 1896-1976 *WhScrn 2*
Forest, Jean *Film 2*

Forest, Karl *Film 2*
Forest, Mark 1933- *FilmgC, WhoHol A*
Forest, Michael *WhoHol A*
Forestelle, W H *Film 1*
Forester, C S 1899-1966 *FilmgC*
Forgay, Wenonnah *Film 2*
Forman, J Denis 1917- *IntMPA 1977*
Forman, Janet *WomWMM B*
Forman, Joel *WhoHol A*
Forman, Justice Miles d1915 *NotNAT B*
Forman, Milos 1932- *BiDFlm, DcFM, FilmgC,
    IntMPA 1977, MovMk, OxFilm, WorEnF*
Forman, Tom 1893-1926 *WhScrn 2*
Forman, Tom 1893-1938 *Film 1, Film 2, MotPP,
    TwYS, TwYS A, WhoHol B*
Forman, William R 1913- *IntMPA 1977*
Formby, George *WhThe*
Formby, George 1904-1961 *Film 1, OxFilm,
    WhScrn 1, WhScrn 2, WhoHol B*
Formby, George 1905-1961 *FilmgC, OxThe*
Formes, Carl, Jr. *Film 1*
Fornes, Maria Irene 1930- *ConDr 1977, NotNAT*
Fornia, Rita d1922 *NotNAT B*
Forquet, Philippe *WhoHol A*
Forrest, Alan 1889-1941 *Film 1, Film 2,
    WhScrn 1, WhScrn 2, WhoHol B*
Forrest, Allan 1889-1941 *MotPP, TwYS*
Forrest, Allen *Film 2*
Forrest, Ann 1897- *Film 1, Film 2, MotPP,
    TwYS*
Forrest, Anne 1897- *WhThe*
Forrest, Arthur 1859-1933 *Film 2, NewYTET,
    NotNAT B, WhoHol B*
Forrest, Belford 1878-1938 *WhScrn 1, WhScrn 2,
    WhoHol B*
Forrest, Ben 1907- *AmSCAP 1966*
Forrest, Edwin 1806-1872 *CnThe, FamA&A,
    NotNAT A, NotNAT B, OxThe, PIP&P*
Forrest, Mrs. Edwin 1817-1891 *NotNAT B*
Forrest, Frederic *IntMPA 1977*
Forrest, Fredric *WhoHol A*
Forrest, George 1915- *AmSCAP 1966,
    BiE&WWA, EncMT, NewMT, NotNAT*
Forrest, Helen *WhoHol A*
Forrest, John R *AmSCAP 1966*
Forrest, Sally 1928- *FilmgC, MotPP, WhoHol A,
    WomWMM*
Forrest, Sam 1870-1944 *NotNAT A, NotNAT B,
    WhThe*
Forrest, Steve 1924- *FilmgC, IntMPA 1977,
    WhoHol A*
Forrest, Thomas *PIP&P*
Forrest, William *WhoHol A*
Forrester, Frederick C d1952 *NotNAT B*
Forrester, Jack d1963 *NotNAT B*
Forrester, Larry 1924- *IntMPA 1977*
Forrester, Ross *PIP&P*
Forshay, Harold *Film 1*
Forssell, Lars 1928- *CnMD, CroCD, McGWD,
    REnWD*
Forst, Willi 1903- *DcFM, Film 2, OxFilm*
Forster, Dorothy 1884-1950 *AmSCAP 1966*
Forster, Friedrich 1895-1958 *CnMD, McGWD*
Forster, John 1812-1876 *NotNAT B, OxThe*
Forster, Ralph *Film 1*
Forster, Robert *WhoHol A*
Forster, Robert 1941- *IntMPA 1977*
Forster, Robert 1942- *FilmgC*
Forster, Rudolf 1884-1968 *NotNAT B, WhScrn 2,
    WhoHol B*
Forster, Rudolf 1885-1969 *Film 2*
Forster, Rudolph 1884-1968 *FilmgC*
Forster, Wilfred 1872-1924 *NotNAT B, WhThe*
Forster-Bovill, W B 1871- *WhThe*

Forsyth, Bertram d1927 *NotNAT B*
Forsyth, Bruce 1921- *FilmgC*
Forsyth, Bruce 1928- *WhoThe 16*
Forsyth, Cecil 1870-1941 *AmSCAP 1966*
Forsyth, James 1913- *BiE&WWA, CnMD,
    ConDr 1977, ModWD, NotNAT*
Forsyth, Matthew 1896-1954 *NotNAT B, WhThe*
Forsyth, Neil 1866-1915 *WhThe*
Forsyth, Rosemary 1944- *FilmgC, WhoHol A*
Forsythe, Charles 1928- *BiE&WWA, NotNAT*
Forsythe, Henderson 1917- *BiE&WWA, NotNAT,
    WhoThe 16*
Forsythe, John 1918- *BiE&WWA, CelR 3,
    FilmgC, IntMPA 1977, MotPP, MovMk,
    NotNAT, WhoHol A, WhoThe 16*
Forsythe, Mimí 1922-1952 *WhScrn 1, WhScrn 2,
    WhoHol B*
Fort, Eleanor H 1914- *AmSCAP 1966*
Forte, Chet *NewYTET*
Forte, Fabian 1940- *IntMPA 1977*
Forte, Fabian *see also* Fabian
Forte, Joe 1896-1967 *WhScrn 1, WhScrn 2,
    WhoHol B*
Forte, Rene *Film 2*
Fortescue, Miss 1862-1950 *WhThe*
Fortescue, Julia d1899 *NotNAT B*
Fortescue, Kenneth *MotPP*
Fortescue, May 1862-1950 *NotNAT B*
Fortescue, Viola d1953 *NotNAT B*
Fortier, Herbert 1867-1949 *WhScrn 1, WhScrn 2,
    WhoHol B*
Fortier, Monique *WomWMM*
Fortis, Johnny 1913- *AmSCAP 1966*
Fortune, Edmund 1863-1939 *WhScrn 2*
Fortune, Wallace 1884-1926 *WhScrn 1,
    WhScrn 2*
Fortuny, Mariano 1871-1949 *OxThe*
Forzano, Giovacchino 1884-1970 *CnMD, ModWD*
Fosco, Piero *OxFilm*
Foscolo, Ugo 1778-1827 *McGWD*
Foshay, Harold A 1884-1953 *WhScrn 1,
    WhScrn 2, WhoHol B*
Foss, Darrell *Film 1*
Foss, George R 1859-1938 *NotNAT B, WhThe*
Foss, Kenelm 1885-1963 *Film 1, Film 2*
Foss, Lukas 1922- *AmSCAP 1966*
Fosse, Bob *ConDr 1977D, WhoHol A*
Fosse, Bob 1925- *OxFilm, WorEnF*
Fosse, Bob 1927- *BiDFlm, BiE&WWA, CelR 3,
    CmMov, EncMT, FilmgC, IntMPA 1977,
    MovMk, NotNAT, WhoThe 16*
Fosse, Bunty 1916- *Film 2*
Fossey, Brigitte 1945- *FilmgC, WhoHol A*
Foster, Al 1924- *AmSCAP 1966*
Foster, Allan K *Film 2*
Foster, Barry 1931- *FilmgC, WhoHol A,
    WhoThe 16*
Foster, Basil S 1882-1959 *NotNAT B, WhThe*
Foster, Buddy *WhoHol A*
Foster, Claiborne 1896- *WhThe*
Foster, Darby *Film 2*
Foster, David H 1929- *IntMPA 1977, NewYTET*
Foster, Dianne 1928- *FilmgC, MotPP,
    WhoHol A*
Foster, Donald 1889-1969 *WhScrn 1, WhScrn 2,
    WhoHol B*
Foster, Dudley 1925-1973 *WhScrn 2, WhoHol B*
Foster, Edna *Film 1*
Foster, Edward 1876-1927 *WhThe*
Foster, Fay 1886-1960 *AmSCAP 1966*
Foster, Frances *WhoHol A*
Foster, Frank Benjamin 1928- *AmSCAP 1966*
Foster, Gloria 1936- *NotNAT, WhoHol A,
    WhoThe 16*

Foster, Helen 1907- *Film 2, TwYS, WhoHol A*
Foster, J Morris 1882-1966 *Film 1, WhScrn 2, WhoHol B*
Foster, Jodie *IntMPA 1977, WhoHol A*
Foster, Julia *WhoHol A*
Foster, Julia 1941- *FilmgC*
Foster, Julia 1942- *WhoThe 16*
Foster, Julia 1944- *IntMPA 1977*
Foster, Lawrence J 1909- *AmSCAP 1966*
Foster, Lewis 1900- *FilmgC*
Foster, Lewis R 1898- *AmSCAP 1966*
Foster, Lillian d1949 *NotNAT B*
Foster, Maurice David *IntMPA 1977*
Foster, May *Film 2*
Foster, Norman 1900- *BiDFlm, Film 2, FilmgC, MovMk, NewYTET, WhThe, WhoHol A, WorEnF*
Foster, Paul 1931- *ConDr 1977, NatPD, WhoThe 16*
Foster, Phil *WhoHol A*
Foster, Phoebe 1896- *WhThe*
Foster, Preston d1970 *MotPP, WhoHol B*
Foster, Preston 1900-1970 *AmSCAP 1966, WhScrn 1, WhScrn 2*
Foster, Preston 1901-1970 *FilmgC, HolP 30*
Foster, Preston 1902-1970 *MovMk*
Foster, Ron *WhoHol A*
Foster, Rudolph 1884-1968 *WhScrn 1*
Foster, Stephen 1826-1864 *FilmgC, NotNAT B, PIP&P*
Foster, Susanna 1924- *FilmgC, HolP 40, MotPP, MovMk, WhoHol A*
Foster, Warren 1904- *AmSCAP 1966*
Foster, Zena *WomWMM B*
Foster Kemp, Cecil R *IntMPA 1977*
Foti, Jacques 1924- *AmSCAP 1966*
Fotin, Larry 1911- *AmSCAP 1966*
Fou, Sen *DcFM*
Fougers, Pierre d1922 *WhScrn 1, WhScrn 2*
Fougez, Anna 1895-1966 *WhScrn 1, WhScrn 2*
Foulger, Byron d1970 *MotPP, WhoHol B*
Foulger, Byron 1899-1970 *Vers A*
Foulger, Byron 1900-1970 *FilmgC, WhScrn 1, WhScrn 2*
Foulk, Robert *WhoHol A*
Fountaine, William *Film 2*
Fouts, Tom C 1918- *AmSCAP 1966*
Fowler, Art 1902-1953 *WhScrn 1, WhScrn 2*
Fowler, Brenda 1883-1942 *WhScrn 1, WhScrn 2, WhoHol B*
Fowler, Gertrude d1935 *NotNAT B*
Fowler, Harry 1926- *FilmgC, IntMPA 1977, WhoHol A*
Fowler, J *Film 2*
Fowler, John C 1869-1952 *WhScrn 2*
Fowler, Keith 1939- *NotNAT*
Fowler, Marjorie *WomWMM*
Fowler, Richard d1643 *OxThe*
Fowler, William Randolph 1922- *AmSCAP 1966*
Fowles, John 1926- *CelR 3*
Fowley, Douglas 1911- *FilmgC, IntMPA 1977, MovMk, Vers A, WhoHol A*
Fowlie, Wallace 1908- *BiE&WWA, NotNAT*
Fox, Barbara B *WomWMM B*
Fox, Bernard *WhoHol A*
Fox, Beryl 1931- *WomWMM*
Fox, Charles Kemble 1833-1875 *OxThe*
Fox, Della May 1871-1913 *NotNAT B, WhThe*
Fox, Della May 1872-1913 *WhoStg 1906, WhoStg 1908*
Fox, Edward 1937- *FilmgC, MovMk, WhoHol A*
Fox, Franklyn 1894-1967 *WhScrn 1, WhScrn 2, WhoHol B*
Fox, Fred 1884-1949 *WhScrn 2*

Fox, Frederick 1910- *BiE&WWA, NotNAT, WhThe*
Fox, George Washington Lafayette 1825-1877 *NotNAT B, OxThe*
Fox, Glory M 1918- *AmSCAP 1966*
Fox, Harry 1882-1959 *Film 1, NotNAT B, WhScrn 1, WhScrn 2, WhoHol B*
Fox, Irwin *NewYTET*
Fox, J Bertram 1881-1946 *AmSCAP 1966*
Fox, James 1939- *FilmgC, IntMPA 1977, MovMk, WhoHol A*
Fox, Janet *WhoHol A*
Fox, John, Jr. *Film 2*
Fox, Josephine 1877-1953 *WhScrn 2*
Fox, Lucy *Film 2*
Fox, Mary *Film 2*
Fox, Matthew d1964 *NewYTET*
Fox, Maxine 1943- *NotNAT*
Fox, Oscar J 1879-1961 *AmSCAP 1966*
Fox, Ray Errol *NatPD*
Fox, Reginald *Film 2*
Fox, Robin 1913-1971 *WhThe*
Fox, Rose 1899-1966 *WhScrn 2, WhoHol B*
Fox, Sidney 1910-1942 *NotNAT B, ThFT, WhScrn 1, WhScrn 2, WhThe, WhoHol B*
Fox, Stuart d1951 *NotNAT B*
Fox, Virginia *Film 2*
Fox, Wallace 1895- *TwYS A*
Fox, Wilbur *Film 2*
Fox, Will H 1858- *WhThe*
Fox, William 1879-1952 *DcFM, FilmgC, OxFilm, WorEnF*
Fox, William 1911- *WhoThe 16*
Foxe, Earle *MotPP*
Foxe, Earle 1888- *TwYS*
Foxe, Earle 1891- *Film 1, Film 2*
Foxwell, Ivan 1914- *FilmgC, IntMPA 1977*
Foxworth, Robert *IntMPA 1977*
Foxx, Red 1922- *IntMPA 1977*
Foxx, Redd 1922- *CelR 3, WhoHol A*
Foy, Bryan 1900- *FilmgC, IntMPA 1977*
Foy, Charles *WhoHol A*
Foy, Eddie 1854-1928 *EncMT, Film 1, FilmgC, WhScrn 1, WhScrn 2, WhThe, WhoHol B, WhoStg 1906, WhoStg 1908*
Foy, Eddie 1856-1928 *NotNAT A, NotNAT B, OxThe*
Foy, Eddie, III *WhoHol A*
Foy, Eddie, Jr. 1905- *EncMT, FilmgC, WhoHol A, WhoThe 16*
Foy, Eddie, Jr. 1910- *BiE&WWA, Film 2, NotNAT*
Foy, Mary *Film 2, WhoHol A*
Foy, Richard d1947 *NotNAT B*
Foyer, Eddie 1883-1934 *WhScrn 1, WhScrn 2, WhoHol B*
Foys, Seven Little *Film 1*
Foyt, A J 1935- *CelR 3*
Frackenpohl, Arthur R 1924- *AmSCAP 1966*
Fradetal, Marcel 1908- *WorEnF*
Fraganza, Trixie *Film 2*
Fragson, Harry 1869-1913 *OxThe*
Fraker, William A 1923- *FilmgC, IntMPA 1977, WorEnF*
Fralick, Freddie 1888-1958 *WhScrn 1, WhScrn 2, WhoHol B*
Framer, Walt 1908- *IntMPA 1977, NewYTET*
Framer, Walter H 1908- *AmSCAP 1966*
Franca Junior, Joaquin Jose Da *OxThe*
France, Alexis 1906- *WhThe*
France, Anatole 1844- *PIP&P, WhThe*
France, C V 1868-1949 *FilmgC, WhoHol B*
France, Charles Vernon 1868-1949 *NotNAT B, WhScrn 1, WhScrn 2, WhThe*

France, Rachel 1936- *NotNAT*
France, Richard 1930- *BiE&WWA*, *NotNAT*
France, Richard 1938- *NatPD*
France-Ellys *WhThe*
Francen, Victor 1888- *Film 2*, *FilmgC*,
  IntMPA 1977, *MovMk*, *Vers B*, *WhoHol A*
Frances, Paula 1924- *AmSCAP 1966*
Franceschi, M *Film 2*
Francesci, Paul *Film 2*
Francey, Bill *Film 2*
Franchi, Sergio *WhoHol A*
Franchina, Sandra *WomWMM*
Franchini, Anthony J 1898- *AmSCAP 1966*
Francine, Anne 1917- *BiE&WWA*, *NotNAT*,
  WhoHol A
Franciolini, Gianni 1910-1960 *DcFM*
Franciosa, Anthony 1928- *BiE&WWA*, *FilmgC*,
  IntMPA 1977, *MotPP*, *MovMk*, *NotNAT*,
  WhoHol A
Francis *FilmgC*
Francis, Alec B 1857-1934 *Film 1*, *Film 2*,
  TwYS, *WhScrn 1*, *WhScrn 2*, *WhoHol B*
Francis, Alfred 1909- *WhoThe 16*
Francis, Alma *Film 2*
Francis, Anne *IntMPA 1977*, *MotPP*,
  WhoHol A
Francis, Anne 1930- *MGM*, *MovMk*
Francis, Anne 1932- *FilmgC*
Francis, Anne 1934- *WorEnF*
Francis, Annette 1928- *AmSCAP 1966*
Francis, Arlene *BiE&WWA*, *NewYTET*,
  NotNAT, *WhoHol A*
Francis, Arlene 1908- *FilmgC*, *IntMPA 1977*,
  WhoThe 16
Francis, Arlene 1912- *CelR 3*
Francis, Coleman 1919-1973 *WhScrn 2*
Francis, Connie 1938- *AmSCAP 1966*, *FilmgC*,
  IntMPA 1977, *MotPP*, *WhoHol A*
Francis, Doris 1903- *WhThe*
Francis, Eugene *WhoHol A*
Francis, Eva *Film 2*
Francis, Freddie 1917- *DcFM*, *FilmgC*,
  IntMPA 1977
Francis, Freddie 1918- *WorEnF*
Francis, Ivor *WhoHol A*
Francis, J O d1956 *NotNAT B*
Francis, Kay d1968 *MotPP*, *WhoHol B*
Francis, Kay 1899-1968 *FilmgC*, *OxFilm*
Francis, Kay 1903-1968 *CmMov*, *MovMk*, *ThFT*,
  WhScrn 1, *WhScrn 2*, *WorEnF*
Francis, Kay 1905-1968 *WhThe*
Francis, Kay 1906-1968 *BiDFlm*, *Film 2*
Francis, Kevin 1944- *IntMPA 1977*
Francis, M E d1930 *NotNAT B*, *WhThe*
Francis, Martha *Film 2*
Francis, Noel *ThFT*
Francis, Olin 1892-1952 *Film 2*, *WhScrn 1*,
  WhScrn 2
Francis, Paul P 1911- *AmSCAP 1966*
Francis, Robert 1930-1955 *FilmgC*, *MotPP*,
  NotNAT B, *WhScrn 1*, *WhScrn 2*,
  WhoHol B
Francis, Seseen 1937- *AmSCAP 1966*
Francis, Wilma *WhoHol A*
Francisco, Betty 1900-1950 *Film 2*, *TwYS*,
  WhScrn 1, *WhScrn 2*, *WhoHol B*
Franciscus, James 1934- *FilmgC*, *IntMPA 1977*,
  MotPP, *WhoHol A*
Franck, Hans d1964 *NotNAT B*
Franck, Hans 1879-1963? *ModWD*
Francks, Don 1932- *FilmgC*, *WhoHol A*
Franco, Debra *WomWMM B*
Francois, Charles *Film 2*
Franey, Agnes *Film 2*

Franey, Billy 1885-1940 *WhoHol B*
Franey, William 1885-1940 *Film 1*, *Film 2*,
  WhScrn 1, *WhScrn 2*
Frangkiser, Carl 1894- *AmSCAP 1966*
Franju, George 1912- *WorEnF*
Franju, Georges 1912- *BiDFlm*, *DcFM*, *FilmgC*,
  MovMk, *OxFilm*
Frank, Arlyne 1930- *BiE&WWA*
Frank, Barry *NewYTET*
Frank, Bernice *Film 2*
Frank, Bruno 1887-1945 *CnMD*, *McGWD*,
  ModWD, *NotNAT B*, *WhThe*
Frank, Bruno 1887-1946 *OxThe*
Frank, Camilla Mays 1899- *AmSCAP 1966*
Frank, Carl 1909-1972 *WhScrn 2*, *WhoHol B*
Frank, Charles 1910- *FilmgC*
Frank, Christian J 1890-1967 *Film 2*, *WhScrn 2*
Frank, Fredric M 1911- *CmMov*, *IntMPA 1977*
Frank, Harriet *FilmgC*, *WomWMM*
Frank, Herbert *Film 1*, *Film 2*
Frank, Jacob *Film 2*
Frank, Leonhard 1882-1961 *CnMD*, *McGWD*,
  ModWD
Frank, Marcel Gustave 1909- *AmSCAP 1966*
Frank, Mary K 1911- *BiE&WWA*, *NotNAT*
Frank, Melvin *IntMPA 1977*
Frank, Melvin 1913- *WorEnF*
Frank, Melvin 1917- *FilmgC*
Frank, Rene 1910-1965 *AmSCAP 1966*
Frank, Reuven *NewYTET*
Frank, Robert 1924- *WorEnF*
Frank, Ruth Verd 1899- *AmSCAP 1966*
Frank, Sandy *NewYTET*
Frank, T David 1944- *NotNAT*
Frank, Will 1880-1925 *Film 2*, *WhoHol B*
Frank, William 1880-1925 *WhScrn 1*, *WhScrn 2*
Frankau, Ronald 1894-1951 *FilmgC*, *NotNAT B*,
  WhScrn 1, *WhScrn 2*, *WhThe*, *WhoHol B*
Frankel, Benjamin 1906-1973 *FilmgC*, *OxFilm*
Frankel, Cyril 1921- *FilmgC*
Frankel, Daniel 1903- *IntMPA 1977*
Frankel, Franchon 1874-1937 *WhScrn 1*,
  WhScrn 2, *WhoHol B*
Frankel, Gene 1923- *NotNAT*, *WhoThe 16*
Frankel, Harry d1948 *WhScrn 2*
Franken, Mannus 189-?-1953 *DcFM*
Franken, Rose 1895- *WhThe*
Franken, Rose 1898- *BiE&WWA*, *CnMD*,
  ModWD, *NotNAT*
Franken, Steve *WhoHol A*
Frankenfield, Parke T 1929- *AmSCAP 1966*
Frankenheimer, John 1930- *BiDFlm*, *DcFM*,
  FilmgC, *IntMPA 1977*, *MovMk*, *NewYTET*,
  OxFilm, *WorEnF*
Frankenthaler, Helen 1928- *CelR 3*
Frankeur, Paul 1905-1974 *WhScrn 2*, *WhoHol B*
Frankham, David *WhoHol A*
Frankiss, Betty 1912- *WhThe*
Franklin, Alberta d1976 *WhoHol C*
Franklin, Aretha 1942- *CelR 3*
Franklin, Bonnie *WhoHol A*
Franklin, Chester M 1890- *TwYS A*
Franklin, Dave *AmSCAP 1966*
Franklin, Elsa *WomWMM*
Franklin, Harold B 1890-1941 *NotNAT B*,
  WhThe
Franklin, Hugh *WhoHol A*
Franklin, Irene d1941 *WhoHol B*
Franklin, Irene 1876-1941 *NotNAT B*, *WhThe*
Franklin, Irene 1884?-1941 *WhScrn 1*, *WhScrn 2*
Franklin, J E *NatPD*
Franklin, Jimmie 1909- *AmSCAP 1966*
Franklin, Joe *NewYTET*
Franklin, Malvin M 1889- *AmSCAP 1966*

Franklin, Marjorie *WomWMM B*
Franklin, Martha 1876-1929 *Film 2, WhScrn 2*
Franklin, Pamela *WhoHol A*
Franklin, Pamela 1949- *FilmgC*
Franklin, Pamela 1950- *IntMPA 1977*
Franklin, Rupert 1862-1939 *WhScrn 1, WhScrn 2, WhoHol B*
Franklin, Sidney 1870-1931 *Film 2, WhScrn 1, WhScrn 2, WhoHol B*
Franklin, Sidney 1893-1972 *BiDFlm, DcFM, FilmgC, MovMk, TwYS A, WorEnF*
Franklin, Sidney *see also* Franklyn, Sidney
Franklin, Wendell *Film 2*
Franklyn, Arthur R 1928- *IntMPA 1977*
Franklyn, Beth d1956 *NotNAT B*
Franklyn, Blanche 1895- *AmSCAP 1966*
Franklyn, Irwin 1904-1966 *WhScrn 2, WhoHol B*
Franklyn, Leo 1897-1975 *WhScrn 2, WhThe, WhoHol C*
Franklyn, Milt J 1897-1962 *AmSCAP 1966*
Franklyn, Sidney 1893-1972 *CmMov*
Franklyn, Sidney *see also* Franklin, Sidney
Franklyn, William 1926- *FilmgC*
Franklyn-Lynch, Grace *WhoStg 1908*
Frankman, Charles *Film 1*
Frankovich, M J 1910- *IntMPA 1977, WorEnF*
Frankovich, Mike 1910- *FilmgC, WhoHol A, WorEnF*
Franks, Dennis 1902-1967 *WhScrn 1, WhScrn 2*
Franks, Tillman B 1920- *AmSCAP 1966*
Frantz, Dalies 1908-1965 *WhScrn 2, WhoHol B*
Franz, Adele *BiE&WWA*
Franz, Arthur 1920- *FilmgC, IntMPA 1977, Vers B, WhoHol A*
Franz, Eduard 1902- *MotPP, WhoHol A, WhoThe 16*
Franz, Edward 1902- *FilmgC*
Franz, Ellen *OxThe*
Franz, Joseph J *Film 2*
Fraser, Agnes *WhThe*
Fraser, Alec 1884- *WhThe*
Fraser, Bill *WhoHol A*
Fraser, Bill 1907- *FilmgC*
Fraser, Bill 1908- *WhoThe 16*
Fraser, Bryant *WhoHol A*
Fraser, Claud Lovat 1890-1921 *NotNAT B*
Fraser, Claude Lovat 1890-1921 *OxThe*
Fraser, Constance 1910-1973 *WhScrn 2, WhoHol B*
Fraser, Elizabeth *WhoHol A*
Fraser, Harry 1889-1974 *Film 1, WhScrn 2*
Fraser, John 1931- *FilmgC, WhoHol A*
Fraser, Liz 1933- *FilmgC*
Fraser, Lovat 1908- *WhThe*
Fraser, Moyra 1923- *FilmgC, WhoHol A, WhoThe 16*
Fraser, Phyllis *WhoHol A*
Fraser, Richard 1913-1971 *FilmgC, WhoHol B*
Fraser, Robert 1891-1944 *Film 1, Film 2*
Fraser, Robert *see also* Frazer, Robert
Fraser, Sir Robert 1904- *IntMPA 1977*
Fraser, Ronald 1930- *FilmgC, IntMPA 1977, PIP&P, WhoHol A*
Fraser, Shelagh *WhoHol A, WhoThe 16*
Fraser, Stanley *WhoHol A*
Fraser, Tony *Film 2*
Fraser, Winifred 1872- *WhThe*
Fraser-Simpson, Harold 1878-1944 *NotNAT B*
Fraser-Simson, Harold 1878-1944 *WhThe*
Fratti, Mario 1927- *ConDr 1977, CroCD, ModWD, NatPD*
Frawley, T Daniel d1936 *NotNAT B*
Frawley, William 1887-1966 *Film 1, Film 2, FilmgC, MotPP, MovMk, Vers B,*

WhScrn 1, WhScrn 2, WhoHol B
Frayn, Michael 1933- *ConDr 1977, WhoThe 16*
Frazee, Harry Herbert 1880-1929 *NotNAT B, WhThe*
Frazee, Jane 1918- *FilmgC, WhoHol A*
Frazer, Alex 1900-1958 *WhScrn 1, WhScrn 2, WhoHol B*
Frazer, Austin *IntMPA 1977*
Frazer, Dan *WhoHol A*
Frazer, Robert 1891-1944 *Film 2, TwYS, WhScrn 1, WhScrn 2, WhoHol B*
Frazer, Robert *see also* Fraser, Robert
Frazier, Cliff 1934- *IntMPA 1977*
Frazier, Joe 1944- *CelR 3*
Frazier, Richard *Film 2*
Frazier, Robert *Film 2*
Frazier, Sheila E 1948- *WhoHol A*
Frazier, Shelia E 1948- *IntMPA 1977*
Frazier, Walt 1945- *CelR 3*
Frazin, Gladys 1901-1939 *Film 2, WhScrn 1, WhScrn 2, WhoHol B*
Frazzini, Al 1890-1963 *AmSCAP 1966*
Frear, Fred *WhoStg 1908*
Frears, Stephen 1931- *FilmgC*
Freberg, Stan 1926- *AmSCAP 1966, WhoHol A*
Frechette, Mark 1947-1975 *WhScrn 2, WhoHol C*
Freda, Riccardo 1909- *BiDFlm, DcFM, FilmgC, WorEnF*
Frede, Richard 1934- *NatPD*
Frederic, Marc 1916- *IntMPA 1977*
Frederic, William *Film 2*
Frederici, Blanche 1878-1933 *Film 2, NotNAT B, TwYS, WhScrn 2, WhoHol B*
Frederick 1800-1876 *OxThe*
Frederick, Freddie Burke *Film 2*
Frederick, Hal *WhoHol A*
Frederick, Pauline d1938 *CelR 3, MotPP, NewYTET, WhoHol B*
Frederick, Pauline 1881-1938 *TwYS*
Frederick, Pauline 1883-1938 *Film 1, Film 2, FilmgC, OxFilm, ThFT*
Frederick, Pauline 1884-1938 *WhScrn 1, WhScrn 2, WhoStg 1908*
Frederick, Pauline 1885-1938 *MovMk, NotNAT A, NotNAT B, WhThe*
Fredericks, Albert d1901 *NotNAT B*
Fredericks, Charles 1920-1970 *WhScrn 1, WhScrn 2, WhoHol B*
Fredericks, Ellsworth *FilmgC*
Fredericks, Fred d1939 *NotNAT B*
Fredericks, Marc 1927- *AmSCAP 1966*
Fredericks, Sam d1922 *NotNAT B*
Fredericks, William A 1924- *AmSCAP 1966*
Frederickson, H Gray, Jr. 1937- *IntMPA 1977*
Fredman, Alice d1950 *NotNAT B*
Fredrickson, Thomas 1928- *AmSCAP 1966*
Fredrik, Burry 1925- *BiE&WWA*
Fredro, Count Aleksander 1793-1876 *CnThe, McGWD, OxThe, REnWD*
Freear, Louie 1871-1939 *NotNAT B, WhThe*
Freeborn, Cassius d1954 *NotNAT B*
Freed, Alan 1922-1965 *WhScrn 2*
Freed, Arthur 1894-1973 *AmSCAP 1966, BiDFlm, CmMov, DcFM, FilmgC, OxFilm, WorEnF*
Freed, Bert *WhoHol A*
Freed, Fred d1974 *NewYTET*
Freed, Isadore 1900-1961 *AmSCAP 1966*
Freed, Lazar *Film 2*
Freed, Ralph 1907- *AmSCAP 1966*
Freed, Ruth *AmSCAP 1966*
Freed, Sam *PIP&P A*
Freed, Walter 1903- *AmSCAP 1966*

Freedley, George 1904-1967 *BiE&WWA,*
   NotNAT B, OxThe, WhThe
Freedley, Vinton 1891-1969 *BiE&WWA, EncMT,*
   NotNAT B, PIP&P, WhThe
Freedley, Vinton 1892-1969 *WhScrn 2*
Freedman, Bill 1929- *WhoThe 16*
Freedman, Gerald 1927- *AmSCAP 1966,*
   NotNAT, WhoThe 16
Freedman, Guy L 1916- *AmSCAP 1966*
Freedman, Harold *BiE&WWA*
Freedman, Herman W 1925- *IntMPA 1977*
Freedman, Irwin B 1924- *IntMPA 1977*
Freedman, Lenore d1964 *NotNAT B*
Freedman, Lewis *NewYTET*
Freedman, Max C 1893-1962 *AmSCAP 1966*
Freedman, Robert 1934- *AmSCAP 1966*
Freel, Aleta d1935 *NotNAT B*
Freeland, Thornton 1898- *FilmgC*
Freeman, Al 1884-1956 *WhScrn 1, WhScrn 2,*
   WhoHol B
Freeman, Al, Jr. 1934- *NotNAT, WhoHol A,*
   WhoThe 16
Freeman, Al, Jr. 1939- *FilmgC*
Freeman, Arnie *WhoHol A*
Freeman, Arny 1908- *WhoThe 16*
Freeman, Bud 1915- *AmSCAP 1966*
Freeman, Charles J d1964 *NotNAT B*
Freeman, Charles K 1900- *BiE&WWA, NotNAT*
Freeman, David 1945- *ConDr 1977, NatPD*
Freeman, Ernest 1922- *AmSCAP 1966*
Freeman, Everett 1911- *FilmgC, IntMPA 1977*
Freeman, Frank 1892-1962 *WhThe*
Freeman, Frank Y 1890- *FilmgC*
Freeman, George D 1937- *AmSCAP 1966*
Freeman, H A d1929 *NotNAT B*
Freeman, Harry *WhThe*
Freeman, Howard 1899-1967 *BiE&WWA, FilmgC,*
   MotPP, Vers B, WhScrn 1, WhScrn 2,
   WhoHol B
Freeman, Joan *WhoHol A*
Freeman, Kathleen 1919?- *FilmgC, WhoHol A*
Freeman, Lawrence 1906- *AmSCAP 1966*
Freeman, Leonard d1973 *NewYTET*
Freeman, Maurice 1872-1953 *WhScrn 1,*
   WhScrn 2, WhoHol B
Freeman, Max d1912 *NotNAT B, WhoStg 1906,*
   WhoStg 1908
Freeman, Mona 1926- *FilmgC, HolP 40, MotPP,*
   MovMk, WhoHol A
Freeman, Sir N Bernard 1896- *IntMPA 1977*
Freeman, Ned 1895- *AmSCAP 1966*
Freeman, Pam *WhoHol A*
Freeman, Raoul 1894-1971 *WhScrn 2*
Freeman, Robert 1935?- *FilmgC*
Freeman, Russell 1926- *AmSCAP 1966*
Freeman, Stan 1920- *AmSCAP 1966, NotNAT*
Freeman, Stella 1910-1936 *NotNAT B, WhThe*
Freeman, Ticker 1911- *AmSCAP 1966*
Freeman, William B d1932 *WhScrn 2*
Freeman-Mitford, Rupert 1895-1939 *WhScrn 1,*
   WhScrn 2, WhoHol B
Freemen, William *Film 1*
Frees, Paul 1920- *AmSCAP 1966, WhoHol A*
Freezer, Herbert J d1963 *NotNAT B*
Fregoli, Leopold d1936 *NotNAT B*
Fregonese, Hugo 1908- *BiDFlm, FilmgC,*
   IntMPA 1977, WorEnF
Freil, Edward 1878-1938 *WhScrn 1, WhScrn 2*
Freitag, Dorothea 1914- *BiE&WWA, NotNAT*
Freitas, Richard 1915- *AmSCAP 1966*
Freleng, Friz *WorEnF*
Fremault, Anita *Film 2*
Fremont, Alfred *Film 1, Film 2*
French, Arthur *WhoHol A*

French, Brandon *WomWMM B*
French, Charles K 1860-1952 *Film 1, Film 2,*
   TwYS, WhScrn 1, WhScrn 2, WhoHol B
French, David 1939- *ConDr 1977*
French, Dick *Film 2*
French, Elizabeth *WhThe*
French, Elsie *WhThe*
French, Evelyn *Film 2*
French, George B 1883-1961 *Film 1, Film 2,*
   TwYS, WhScrn 1, WhScrn 2, WhoHol B
French, Harold 1897- *Film 2, FilmgC*
French, Harold 1900- *IntMPA 1977, WhoThe 16*
French, Helen 1863-1917 *WhScrn 2*
French, Herbert C d1924 *NotNAT B*
French, Hermene 1924- *WhThe*
French, Hugh 1910- *WhThe*
French, Leigh *WhoHol A*
French, Leslie *WhoHol A*
French, Leslie 1899- *FilmgC*
French, Leslie 1904- *WhoThe 16*
French, Pauline *Film 2, WhoStg 1906,*
   WhoStg 1908
French, Samuel d1898 *NotNAT B*
French, Stanley J 1908-1964 *NotNAT B, WhThe*
French, Susan *WhoHol A*
French, T Henry d1902 *NotNAT B*
French, Valerie *WhoHol A*
French, Valerie 1931- *FilmgC*
French, Valerie 1932- *WhoThe 16*
French, Victor *NewYTET, WhoHol A*
French, William 1885- *TwYS A*
Frend, Charles 1909- *CmMov, DcFM, FilmgC,*
   IntMPA 1977, OxFilm, WorEnF
Frenke, Eugene *IntMPA 1977*
Frenyear, Mabel *Film 1*
Frerks, Geraldine *WomWMM B*
Fresco, Robert M 1928- *IntMPA 1977*
Freshman, William A 1905- *Film 2*
Fresnay, Pierre 1897- *BiE&WWA, CnThe,*
   Film 2, FilmgC, WhThe, WorEnF
Fresnay, Pierre 1897-1973 *MovMk*
Fresnay, Pierre 1897-1975 *OxFilm, WhScrn 2,*
   WhoHol C
Freud, Sigmund 1856-1939 *FilmgC*
Freudenthal, Josef 1903-1964 *AmSCAP 1966*
Freulich, Henry 1906- *IntMPA 1977*
Freund, Karl 1890-1969 *BiDFlm, CmMov, DcFM,*
   FilmgC, OxFilm, WorEnF
Frey, Arno 1900-1961 *WhScrn 2, WhoHol B*
Frey, Hugo 1873-1952 *AmSCAP 1966*
Frey, Leonard *WhoHol A*
Frey, Leonard 1938- *NotNAT*
Frey, Leonard 1939- *FilmgC*
Frey, Nathaniel 1913-1970 *WhScrn 1, WhScrn 2,*
   WhThe, WhoHol B
Frey, Nathaniel 1923-1970 *BiE&WWA,*
   NotNAT B
Frey, Sidney 1920- *AmSCAP 1966*
Freyer, Ellen *WomWMM B*
Freytag, Gustav 1816-1895 *McGWD, OxThe,*
   REnWD
Fric, Martin 1902-1968 *DcFM, OxFilm, WorEnF*
Frid, Jonathan *WhoHol A*
Friderici, Blanche *Film 2*
Fridolin *OxThe*
Friebus, Florida 1909- *BiE&WWA, NotNAT*
Friebus, Theodore 1879-1917 *Film 1, WhScrn 2*
Fried, Gerald 1928- *AmSCAP 1966*
Fried, Martin *AmSCAP 1966, NotNAT*
Fried, Walter 1910-1975 *BiE&WWA, NotNAT B,*
   PIP&P
Friedan, Betty 1921- *CelR 3*
Friederich, W J 1916- *BiE&WWA, NotNAT*
Friedgen, John Raymond 1893-1966 *WhScrn 2*

NotNAT, PlP&P A, WhoThe 16
Fujikawa, Jerry *WhoHol A*
Fujimoto, Sanezumi 1910- *IntMPA 1977*
Fujino, Hideo *Film 2*
Fujita, Toyo *Film 1, Film 2*
Fukuda, Tsuneari 1912- *CnMD, ModWD*
Fulbright, J William 1905- *CelR 3*
Fuld, Leo 1913- *AmSCAP 1966*
Fulda, Ludwig 1862-1939 *ModWD, NotNAT B*
Fuleihan, Anis 1900- *AmSCAP 1966*
Fuley, Elizabeth *Film 2*
Fulford, David 1925- *BiE&WWA, NotNAT*
Fulkerson, Tavi *WomWMM B*
Fuller, Barbra *WhoHol A*
Fuller, Sir Benjamin John 1875- *WhThe*
Fuller, Bobby 1942-1966 *WhScrn 2*
Fuller, Charles *Film 1, NatPD*
Fuller, Clem 1909-1961 *WhScrn 1, WhScrn 2, WhoHol B*
Fuller, Clement 1907- *CelR 3*
Fuller, Dale 1897- *Film 1, Film 2, TwYS*
Fuller, Dean 1922- *AmSCAP 1966, BiE&WWA, NotNAT*
Fuller, Esther Mary 1907- *AmSCAP 1966*
Fuller, Frances 1907- *BiE&WWA, NotNAT, ThFT, WhoHol A*
Fuller, Frances 1908- *WhThe*
Fuller, Haidee *Film 1*
Fuller, Irene *WhScrn 1, WhScrn 2*
Fuller, Irene 1898-1945 *WhScrn 1, WhScrn 2, WhoHol B*
Fuller, Isaac 1606-1672 *OxThe*
Fuller, Jack Dubose 1921- *IntMPA 1977*
Fuller, John G 1913- *BiE&WWA, NotNAT*
Fuller, Lance *WhoHol A*
Fuller, Leland F 1899-1962 *NotNAT B*
Fuller, Leslie 1889-1948 *FilmgC, WhScrn 1, WhScrn 2, WhoHol B*
Fuller, Loie d1928 *WhThe, WhoStg 1906, WhoStg 1908*
Fuller, Loie 1862-1928 *WomWMM*
Fuller, Loie 1863-1928 *NotNAT B*
Fuller, Margaret 1905-1952 *WhScrn 1, WhScrn 2, WhoHol B*
Fuller, Mary 1893- *Film 1, MotPP, TwYS*
Fuller, Mollie 1865-1933 *NotNAT B, WhoStg 1906*
Fuller, Olive Gordon 1896- *Film 1, Film 2, TwYS*
Fuller, R Buckminster 1895- *CelR 3*
Fuller, Robert 1934- *FilmgC, WhoHol A*
Fuller, Rosalinde 1901- *Film 2, OxThe, WhoThe 16*
Fuller, Samuel *IntMPA 1977*
Fuller, Samuel 1911- *DcFM, FilmgC, OxFilm, WorEnF*
Fuller, Samuel 1912- *BiDFlm*
Fuller, Samuel 1916- *CmMov*
Fullerton, Fiona 1955- *FilmgC*
Fulton, Charles J 1857-1938 *NotNAT B, WhThe*
Fulton, Eileen *BiE&WWA, WhoHol A*
Fulton, Jack 1903- *AmSCAP 1966*
Fulton, James F *Film 2*
Fulton, Joan *WhoHol A*
Fulton, John P 1902- *DcFM, FilmgC*
Fulton, Maude 1881-1950 *Film 2, NotNAT B, WhScrn 1, WhScrn 2, WhThe, WhoHol B*
Fulton, Reg 1924- *AmSCAP 1966*
Fung, Willie 1896-1945 *Film 2, WhScrn 2*
Fung, Willie 1900- *Vers B*
Funicello, Annette 1942- *FilmgC, MotPP, WhoHol A*
Funke, Lewis 1912- *BiE&WWA, NotNAT*
Funt, Allen 1914- *AmSCAP 1966, FilmgC,*

NewYTET
Fuqua, Charles 1911-1971 *WhScrn 1, WhScrn 2*
Fuqua, Charlie 1911-1971 *WhoHol B*
Furber, Douglas 1885-1961 *EncMT, NotNAT B, WhThe*
Furber, Percival E 1906- *IntMPA 1977*
Furbish, Ralph E 1914-1974 *WhScrn 2*
Furey, Barney 1888-1938 *WhScrn 2*
Furie, Sidney J 1933- *FilmgC, IntMPA 1977, MovMk, OxFilm, WorEnF*
Furley, Shelagh d1951 *NotNAT B*
Furman, Sam H 1918- *AmSCAP 1966*
Furnberg, Louis 1909-1957 *CnMD*
Furneaux, Yvonne 1928- *FilmgC, IntMPA 1977, WhoHol A*
Furness, Betty 1916- *CelR 3, NewYTET, ThFT, WhoHol A*
Furney, James A *Film 1*
Furniss, Grace Livingston d1938 *NotNAT B, WhThe*
Furniss, Harry 1854-1925 *WhScrn 2*
Furnival, F J 1825-1910 *NotNAT B*
Furnstman, Georgia *Film 1*
Furse, Jill d1944 *NotNAT A*
Furse, Judith 1912- *FilmgC, WhThe, WhoHol A*
Furse, Roger 1903-1972 *FilmgC, NotNAT B, WhThe, WorEnF*
Furse, Russell L 1908- *IntMPA 1977*
Furst, William Wallace 1852-1917 *NotNAT B*
Furstenberg, Diane Von 1946- *CelR 3*
Furstenberg, Egon Von 1946- *CelR 3*
Furstenberg, Ira *WhoHol A*
Furtado, Teresa 1845-1877 *NotNAT B*
Furtado, Thomas A 1928- *AmSCAP 1966*
Furtenbach, Josef 1591-1667 *OxThe*
Furth, George 1932- *ConDr 1977D, NatPD, PlP&P A, WhoHol A, WhoThe 16*
Furth, Jaro *Film 2*
Furthman, Jules 1888-1960 *OxFilm*
Furthman, Jules 1888-1966 *DcFM, FilmgC, WorEnF*
Fury, Barney *Film 2*
Fury, Ed *WhoHol A*
Fury, Loretta *WhoHol A*
Fusco, Giovanni 1906- *DcFM, FilmgC, OxFilm, WorEnF*
Fusier-Gir, Jeanne d1974 *WhoHol B*
Fuss, Kurt *Film 2*
Fuzelier, Louis 1672-1752 *OxThe*
Fyfe, H Hamilton 1869-1951 *NotNAT B, WhThe*
Fyffe, Will 1884-1947 *FilmgC, WhScrn 1, WhoHol B*
Fyffe, Will 1885-1947 *NotNAT B, OxThe*
Fyffe, Will 1911-1947 *WhScrn 2*
Fyles, Franklin d1911 *NotNAT B*

G

Gaal, Charles J 1893- *AmSCAP 1966*
Gaal, Franceska 1909- *FilmgC*
Gaal, Franciska 1904-1972 *ThFT, WhoHol B*
Gaal, Istvan 1933- *OxFilm*
Gabel, Martin 1912- *BiE&WWA, FilmgC, MovMk, NotNAT, WhoHol A, WhoThe 16*
Gabel, Scilla 1937- *FilmgC*
Gabin, Jean 1904- *BiDFlm, FilmgC, IntMPA 1977, MotPP, MovMk, OxFilm, WhoHol A, WorEnF*
Gable, Clark 1901-1960 *BiDFlm, CmMov, Film 2, FilmgC, MGM, MotPP, MovMk, NotNAT B, OxFilm, WhScrn 1, WhScrn 2, WhThe, WhoHol B, WorEnF*
Gable, June 1945- *NotNAT*
Gabler, Milton 1911- *AmSCAP 1966*
Gabor, Eva *MotPP, WhoHol A*
Gabor, Eva 1921- *FilmgC*
Gabor, Eva 1924- *MovMk*
Gabor, Eva 1926- *BiE&WWA, CelR 3*
Gabor, Pal 1932- *OxFilm*
Gabor, Zsa Zsa *MotPP, WhoHol A*
Gabor, Zsa Zsa 1919- *FilmgC*
Gabor, Zsa Zsa 1921?- *CelR 3*
Gabor, Zsa Zsa 1923- *IntMPA 1977, MovMk*
Gabriel, Charles H, Jr. 1892-1934 *AmSCAP 1966*
Gabriel, Charles Hutchinson 1856-1932 *AmSCAP 1966*
Gabriel, Gilbert W 1890-1952 *NotNAT B, WhThe*
Gabriel, John *WhoHol A*
Gabrielli, Francesco d1654 *OxThe*
Gabrielli, Giovanni 1588?-1635? *OxThe*
Gabrielli, Girolamo *OxThe*
Gabrielli, Giulia *OxThe*
Gabrio, Gabriel *Film 2*
Gaburo, Kenneth Louis 1926- *AmSCAP 1966*
Gaby, Frank 1896-1945 *WhScrn 1, WhScrn 2, WhoHol B*
Gachet, Alice d1960 *NotNAT B*
Gad, Peter Urban 1879-1947 *DcFM*
Gadd, Renee 1908- *WhThe, WhoHol A*
Gade, Jacob d1963 *NotNAT B*
Gade, Sven 1877-1952 *DcFM*
Gade, W *Film 2*
Gaden, Alexander *Film 1*
Gadson, Jacqueline *Film 2*
Gaffney, Floyd 1930- *NotNAT*
Gaffney, Liam 1911- *WhThe*
Gaffney, Marjorie *WomWMM*
Gaffney, Robert 1931- *IntMPA 1977*
Gafford, Charlotte *WomWMM A, WomWMM B*
Gage, Edwin 1915- *IntMPA 1977*
Gage, Erford 1913-1945 *WhScrn 2*
Gage, Richard N 1905- *BiE&WWA*
Gagliano, Frank 1931- *ConDr 1977, NatPD,*

WhoThe 16
Gahagan, Helen 1900- *BiE&WWA, NotNAT, WhThe, WhoHol A*
Gaidaroff, E *Film 2*
Gaidarov, Vladimir *Film 2*
Gaige, Crosby 1882-1949 *NotNAT A, NotNAT B, WhThe*
Gaige, Russell d1974 *WhScrn 2, WhoHol B*
Gaige, Truman *BiE&WWA, NotNAT*
Gail, Jane *Film 1*
Gail, Zoe *WhThe*
Gailing, Gretchen 1918-1961 *WhScrn 1, WhScrn 2*
Gaillard, Bulee 1916- *AmSCAP 1966*
Gaillard, Robert *Film 1*
Gaines, Ernestine *Film 2*
Gaines, James M 1911- *IntMPA 1977*
Gaines, Lee 1914- *AmSCAP 1966*
Gaines, Richard H 1904-1975 *WhScrn 2, WhoHol C*
Gaines, Samuel Richards 1869-1945 *AmSCAP 1966*
Gaines, William *Film 2*
Gainey, Celeste *WomWMM*
Gaisseau, Pierre-Dominique 1923- *DcFM*
Gaites, Joseph M d1940 *NotNAT B*
Gaither, Gant *IntMPA 1977*
Galanos, James 1924- *CelR 3*
Galante, M Christina 1942- *IntMPA 1977*
Galbraith, John Kenneth 1908- *CelR 3*
Galdos *OxThe*
Galdos, Benito Perez 1845-1920 *NotNAT B*
Gale, Alice *Film 1*
Gale, David *WhoHol A*
Gale, Eddra *WhoHol A*
Gale, George *IntMPA 1977*
Gale, Jean *WhoHol A*
Gale, John 1929- *WhoThe 16*
Gale, June *WhoHol A*
Gale, Kira *WomWMM B*
Gale, Margaret *Film 1*
Gale, Marguerite H 1885-1948 *WhScrn 1, WhScrn 2, WhoHol B*
Gale, Zona 1874-1938 *CnMD, McGWD, ModWD, NotNAT A, NotNAT B, WhThe*
Galeen, Henrik 1881-1949 *FilmgC*
Galeen, Henrik 1882-1949 *BiDFlm, DcFM, OxFilm, WhScrn 2, WorEnF*
Galento, Tony 1910- *WhoHol A*
Galeron, Jean *Film 2*
Galiani, Ferdinando 1728-1787 *McGWD*
Galimafre *OxThe*
Galindo, Alejandro 1911- *DcFM*
Galindo, Nacho d1973 *WhScrn 2, WhoHol B*
Galipaux, Felix 1860-1931 *NotNAT B, WhThe*
Gallacher, Tom 1934- *ConDr 1977*

Gallagher, Donald *Film 2*
Gallagher, Edward A 1928- *AmSCAP 1966*
Gallagher, Glen B 1909-1960 *WhScrn 1,
    WhScrn 2*
Gallagher, Helen 1926- *BiE&WWA, CelR 3,
    EncMT, NotNAT, PIP&P, WhoHol A,
    WhoThe 16*
Gallagher, James R 1943- *AmSCAP 1966*
Gallagher, Johnny *Film 2*
Gallagher, Ray 1889-1953 *Film 1, Film 2, TwYS*
Gallagher, Richard 1896-1955 *MovMk,
    NotNAT B*
Gallagher, Richard 1900-1955 *WhThe*
Gallagher, Richard Skeets 1891-1955 *Film 2,
    HolP 30, TwYS*
Gallagher, Skeets d1955 *MotPP, WhoHol B*
Gallagher, Skeets 1891-1955 *FilmgC, WhScrn 1,
    WhScrn 2*
Gallaher, Donald 1895- *Film 1, Film 2, WhThe*
Galland, Bertha 1876-1932 *NotNAT B, WhThe,
    WhoStg 1908*
Gallant, Ann d1973 *WhoHol B*
Gallardo, Luis Rojas d1957 *WhScrn 1, WhScrn 2*
Gallatin, Alberta d1948 *NotNAT B*
Gallaudet, John 1903- *Vers A*
Gallaway, Marian 1903- *BiE&WWA, NotNAT*
Gallegos, Charles B *AmSCAP 1966*
Gallegos, Dora Marie *AmSCAP 1966*
Gallery, Tom *Film 2, TwYS*
Galli, Rosina d1940 *NotNAT B, WhoHol B*
Galli-Bibbiena *OxThe*
Galli-Bibiena *OxThe*
Galli DaBibbiena *OxThe*
Gallian, Ketti 1913-1972 *ThFT, WhScrn 2,
    WhoHol B*
Galliari, Bernardino 1707-1794 *NotNAT B*
Galliari, Fabrizio 1709-1790 *NotNAT B*
Galliari, Gaspare 1761-1823 *NotNAT B*
Galliari, Giovanni 1746-1818 *NotNAT B*
Galliari, Giuseppino 1752-1817 *NotNAT B*
Galliari Family *OxThe*
Gallico, Grace Lane 1921- *AmSCAP 1966*
Gallico, Paul 1897- *FilmgC*
Gallienne, Eva Le *OxThe*
Gallimore, Catherine d1962 *NotNAT B*
Gallimore, Florrie 1867- *WhThe*
Gallo, Alberto d1964 *NotNAT B*
Gallo, Fortune 1878-1970 *NotNAT B*
Gallo, Lillian *NewYTET*
Gallo, Mario 1878-1945 *DcFM*
Gallon, Nellie Tom d1938 *NotNAT B*
Gallon, Tom d1914 *NotNAT B*
Gallone, Carmine 1886-1973 *DcFM, FilmgC,
    WorEnF*
Gallop, Sammy 1915- *AmSCAP 1966*
Galloway, Don *WhoHol A*
Galloway, Louise d1949 *NotNAT B*
Galloway, Morgan *WhoHol A*
Galloway, Tod B 1863-1935 *AmSCAP 1966*
Gallu, Samuel 1918- *FilmgC*
Gallup, George 1901- *CelR 3*
Galm, Tina d1962 *NotNAT B*
Galsworthy, John 1867-1933 *CnMD, CnThe,
    FilmgC, McGWD, ModWD, NotNAT A,
    NotNAT B, OxThe, PIP&P, REnWD,
    WhThe*
Galt, John d1839 *NotNAT B*
Galton, Ray 1930- *FilmgC*
Galvani, Dino 1890-1960 *Film 2, FilmgC,
    NotNAT B, WhScrn 1, WhScrn 2, WhThe,
    WhoHol B*
Galvin, Kathy *WhoHol A*
Galvin, Robby *WhoHol A*
Gam, Rita *MotPP, PIP&P, WhoHol A*

Gam, Rita 1928- *BiE&WWA, FilmgC, NotNAT*
Gam, Rita 1929- *MovMk*
Gambarelli, Maria *WhoHol A*
Gamble, Fred d1939 *Film 1, Film 2, WhoHol B*
Gamble, Fred 1868-1939 *WhScrn 2*
Gamble, Fred 1869-1939 *WhScrn 1*
Gamble, Jerry *Film 2*
Gamble, Ralph 1902-1966 *WhScrn 1, WhScrn 2,
    WhoHol B*
Gamble, Theodore Roosevelt d1960 *NotNAT B*
Gamble, Tom 1898- *WhThe*
Gamble, Warburton d1945 *Film 1, Film 2,
    NotNAT B, WhoHol B*
Gambold, Fred *Film 2*
Gambon, Michael 1940- *WhoThe 16*
Gamby-Hale Ballet Girls *Film 2*
Gamut, David *Film 2*
Gan, Chester 1909-1959 *WhScrn 1, WhScrn 2,
    WhoHol B*
Ganassa, Zan *OxThe*
Gance, Abel 1889- *BiDFlm, DcFM, FilmgC,
    OxFilm, WorEnF*
Gance, Marguerite *Film 2*
Gandillot, Leon d1912 *NotNAT B*
Gane, Nolan d1915 *WhScrn 2*
Ganis, Sidney M 1940- *IntMPA 1977*
Gannett, Kent 1887- *AmSCAP 1966*
Gannino, Ruth Lillian 1916- *AmSCAP 1966*
Gannon, John 1903-1969 *WhScrn 1, WhScrn 2*
Gannon, Kim 1900- *AmSCAP 1966*
Ganthony, Richard d1924 *NotNAT B*
Ganthony, Robert d1931 *NotNAT A, NotNAT B*
Gantillon, Simon 1887-1961 *McGWD*
Gantvoori, Carl *Film 2*
Gantvoort, Herman L 1887-1937 *WhScrn 1,
    WhScrn 2*
Ganz, Rudolph 1877- *AmSCAP 1966*
Ganzhern, Jack 1881-1956 *Film 2*
Ganzhorn, Jack 1881-1956 *WhoHol B*
Ganzhorn, John 1881-1956 *WhScrn 1, WhScrn 2*
Gaona, Ralph Raymond, Sr. 1925- *AmSCAP 1966*
Garagiola, Joe 1926- *CelR 3, NewYTET*
Garat, Monsieur *Film 2*
Garat, Henri 1902-1959 *MotPP, NotNAT B,
    WhScrn 1, WhScrn 2*
Garat, Henry 1902-1959 *WhoHol B*
Garber, Matthew 1956- *FilmgC, WhoHol A*
Garbini, Aristide *Film 2*
Garbo, Greta *MotPP, WhoHol A*
Garbo, Greta 1905- *BiDFlm, CelR 3, CmMov,
    Film 2, FilmgC, MGM, MovMk, OxFilm,
    ThFT, WorEnF*
Garbo, Greta 1906- *IntMPA 1977, TwYS*
Garborg, Arne 1851-1924 *CnMD*
Garcia, Al Ernest *Film 1*
Garcia, Albert Y 1938- *AmSCAP 1966*
Garcia, Allan *Film 2*
Garcia, Allen 1887-1938 *WhScrn 2*
Garcia, Felix 1906- *AmSCAP 1966*
Garcia, Henry 1904-1970 *WhScrn 1, WhScrn 2*
Garcia, Humberto Rodriguez 1915-1960 *WhScrn 1,
    WhScrn 2*
Garcia, Russell 1916- *AmSCAP 1966*
Garcia DeLaHuerta, Vicente 1734-1787 *McGWD,
    OxThe*
Garcia Gutierrez, Antonio 1813-1884 *McGWD,
    NotNAT B, OxThe*
Garcia Lorca, Federico 1898-1936 *McGWD,
    ModWD, OxThe, REnWD*
Garcia Lorca, Federico 1899-1936 *NotNAT A,
    NotNAT B*
Garcia Lorca, Federico *see also* Lorca, Federico
    Garcia
Gard, Alex d1948 *NotNAT B*

Gard, Robert E 1910- BiE&WWA, NotNAT
Garde, Betty 1905- BiE&WWA, Film 2,
   NotNAT, WhoHol A, WhoThe 16
Gardel, Carlos 1887?-1935 WhScrn 1, WhScrn 2
Gardella, Tess d1950 NotNAT B
Garden, E W 1845-1939 NotNAT B, WhThe
Garden, Faith Film 2
Garden, Mary 1874-1967 WhScrn 1, WhScrn 2
Garden, Mary 1875-1967 Film 1, TwYS,
   WhoHol B
Gardener, Buster Film 2
Gardenia, Vincent PIP&P A, WhoHol A
Gardenia, Vincent 1922- FilmgC, WhoThe 16
Gardenia, Vincent 1923- BiE&WWA,
   IntMPA 1977, NotNAT
Gardin, Vladimir 1877-1965 DcFM, OxFilm,
   WhScrn 2
Gardin, W R WomWMM
Gardiner, Cyril 1897- WhThe
Gardiner, Patrick 1926-1970 WhScrn 1,
   WhScrn 2
Gardiner, Reece Film 1
Gardiner, Reginald 1903- BiE&WWA, FilmgC,
   MotPP, MovMk, Vers A, WhThe,
   WhoHol A
Gardner, Amelia Film 1
Gardner, Arthur IntMPA 1977
Gardner, Ava 1922- BiDFlm, CelR 3, FilmgC,
   IntMPA 1977, MGM, MotPP, MovMk,
   OxFilm, WhoHol A, WorEnF
Gardner, Betty Film 2
Gardner, Charles A d1924 NotNAT B
Gardner, Cyril 1898-1942 WhScrn 1, WhScrn 2
Gardner, Don 1932-1958 WhScrn 2
Gardner, Donald Yetter 1912- AmSCAP 1966
Gardner, Ed 1901-1963 NotNAT B, WhScrn 1,
   WhScrn 2, WhoHol B
Gardner, Erle Stanley 1889-1970 FilmgC
Gardner, George 1868-1929 WhScrn 1, WhScrn 2
Gardner, Helen d1968 Film 1, Film 2, MotPP,
   WhScrn 1, WhScrn 2, WhoHol B
Gardner, Herb 1934- BiE&WWA, NotNAT
Gardner, Hunter 1899-1952 WhScrn 1, WhScrn 2,
   WhoHol B
Gardner, Jack d1950 NotNAT B
Gardner, Jack 1876-1929 Film 1, Film 2,
   WhScrn 1, WhScrn 2, WhoHol B
Gardner, Jack 1915-1955 WhScrn 1, WhScrn 2,
   WhoHol B
Gardner, James Film 2, TwYS
Gardner, Janet WomWMM B
Gardner, Joan 1914- FilmgC, WhoHol A
Gardner, Joan A WomWMM B
Gardner, John 1912- CelR 3
Gardner, Maurice 1909- AmSCAP 1966
Gardner, Michael 1920- AmSCAP 1966
Gardner, Peter 1898-1953 WhScrn 1, WhScrn 2
Gardner, Richard d1972 WhoHol B
Gardner, Rita BiE&WWA, NotNAT
Gardner, Samuel 1891- AmSCAP 1966
Gardner, Shayle 1890-1945 Film 2, NotNAT B,
   WhThe, WhoHol B
Gardner, Will 1879- WhThe
Gardner, William Henry 1865-1932 AmSCAP 1966
Garfein, Jack 1930- BiE&WWA, FilmgC,
   NotNAT, WorEnF
Garfield, Allen WhoHol A
Garfield, John 1913-1952 BiDFlm, CmMov,
   FilmgC, MotPP, MovMk, NotNAT A,
   NotNAT B, OxFilm, PIP&P, WhScrn 1,
   WhScrn 2, WhThe, WhoHol B, WorEnF
Garfield, John David WhoHol A
Garfield, Julie WhoHol A
Garfield, Warren 1936- IntMPA 1977

Garfinkle, Louis 1928- IntMPA 1977, NatPD
Garfunkel, Art 1941- CelR 3
Garfunkel, Arthur IntMPA 1977
Garfunkel, Arthur 1937- FilmgC
Gargan, Ed 1902-1964 FilmgC
Gargan, Edward d1964 NotNAT B, WhoHol B
Gargan, Edward 1901-1964 Vers A
Gargan, Edward 1902-1964 MovMk, WhScrn 1,
   WhScrn 2
Gargan, William 1905- FilmgC, HolP 30,
   IntMPA 1977, MotPP, MovMk, WhThe,
   WhoHol A
Garibay, Emilio 1927-1965 WhScrn 2
Garland, Beverly MotPP, WhoHol A
Garland, Beverly 1926- FilmgC, MovMk
Garland, Beverly 1930- IntMPA 1977
Garland, Hamlin 1860-1940 NotNAT B
Garland, Joseph C 1903- AmSCAP 1966
Garland, Judy 1922-1969 BiDFlm, CmMov,
   FilmgC, MGM, MotPP, MovMk,
   NewYTET, NotNAT A, OxFilm, ThFT,
   WhScrn 1, WhScrn 2, WhoHol B, WorEnF
Garland, P Harvey 1919- IntMPA 1977
Garland, Patrick WhoThe 16
Garland, Richard d1969 WhScrn 2, WhoHol B
Garland, Robert 1895-1955 NotNAT B, WhThe
Garlock, Thomas M 1929- AmSCAP 1966
Garly, Edward H d1938 WhScrn 1, WhScrn 2
Garmes, Lee IntMPA 1977
Garmes, Lee 1897- FilmgC
Garmes, Lee 1898- CmMov, DcFM, OxFilm,
   WorEnF
Garner, Adam 1898- AmSCAP 1966
Garner, Erroll 1921- CelR 3
Garner, Erroll 1923- AmSCAP 1966
Garner, James 1928- CelR 3, CmMov, FilmgC,
   IntMPA 1977, MotPP, MovMk, WhoHol A,
   WorEnF
Garner, Linton S 1915- AmSCAP 1966
Garner, Peggy Ann MotPP, WhoHol A
Garner, Peggy Ann 1931- FilmgC, MovMk
Garner, Peggy Ann 1932- HolP 40, IntMPA 1977
Garnett, Edward 1868-1937 NotNAT B, WhThe
Garnett, Tay IntMPA 1977, NewYTET
Garnett, Tay 1892- OxFilm
Garnett, Tay 1895- FilmgC
Garnett, Tay 1898- BiDFlm, DcFM, MovMk
Garnett, Tay 1905- WorEnF
Garnett, Tony 1936- FilmgC, OxFilm
Garnier, Robert 1535?-1600? OxThe
Garnier, Robert 1544-1590 McGWD
Garnier, Robert 1545?-1590 CnThe, REnWD
Garon, Norm 1934-1975 WhScrn 2
Garon, Norman 1934-1975 WhoHol C
Garon, Pauline 1901-1965 Film 2, MotPP, TwYS,
   WhScrn 1, WhScrn 2, WhoHol B
Garon, Pauline 1901-1967 Film 1
Garr, Eddie 1900-1956 WhScrn 1, WhScrn 2,
   WhoHol B
Garr, Teri WhoHol A
Garralagna, Martin WhoHol A
Garrel, S Film 2
Garrett, Almeida 1799-1854 CnThe, REnWD
Garrett, Arthur 1869-1941 WhThe
Garrett, Betty IntMPA 1977, MotPP
Garrett, Betty 1919- CmMov, FilmgC, MGM,
   MovMk, WhoHol A, WhoThe 16
Garrett, Betty 1920- BiE&WWA, NotNAT
Garrett, Hank WhoHol A
Garrett, Joao Baptista DaS L DeAlmeida OxThe
Garrett, Lloyd Fry 1886- AmSCAP 1966
Garrett, Oliver H P 1897-1952 FilmgC,
   NotNAT B
Garrick, David 1717-1779 CnThe, FilmgC,

McGWD, NotNAT A, NotNAT B, OxThe, PIP&P
Garrick, Mrs. David 1724-1822 NotNAT B
Garrick, Gus WhThe
Garrick, Helen Collier d1954 NotNAT B
Garrick, John 1902- Film 2, FilmgC, WhThe, WhoHol A
Garrick, Richard T 1879-1962 NotNAT B, WhScrn 1, WhScrn 2, WhoHol B
Garrison, Greg NewYTET
Garrison, Isabelle Film 2
Garrison, Michael 1923-1966 WhScrn 1, WhScrn 2
Garrison, Paul IntMPA 1977
Garrison, Robert Film 2
Garrison, Sean 1937- FilmgC, WhoHol A
Garrison, William Allen Slickem Film 2
Garron, Kurt Film 2
Garroway, Dave 1913- CelR 3, IntMPA 1977, NewYTET
Garry, Charles d1939 NotNAT B
Garry, Claude d1918 NotNAT B, WhoHol B
Garsia, Marston Film 2
Garside, John 1887-1958 NotNAT B, WhThe
Garson, Arline WomWMM, WomWMM B
Garson, Barbara 1941- NatPD
Garson, Greer IntMPA 1977, MotPP
Garson, Greer 1906- OxFilm, ThFT
Garson, Greer 1908- CmMov, FilmgC, MGM, MovMk, WhThe, WhoHol A, WorEnF
Garson, Greer 1914- BiDFlm
Garson, Harry TwYS A
Garson, John WhoHol A
Garson, Mort 1924- AmSCAP 1966
Garten, H F 1904- BiE&WWA, NotNAT
Garth, Otis 1901-1955 WhScrn 1, WhScrn 2, WhoHol B
Gartian, George H 1882-1963 AmSCAP 1966
Garutso, Stephen E d1964 NotNAT B
Garver, Kathy WhoHol A
Garvey, Ed 1865-1939 Film 2
Garvie, Ed 1865-1939 WhScrn 2
Garvie, Edward 1865-1939 NotNAT B
Garvin, Anita 1907- Film 1, Film 2, TwYS
Garvin, Lawrence W 1945- NotNAT
Garwood, John WhoHol A
Garwood, William 1884-1950 Film 1, WhScrn 2
Gary, Harold WhoHol A
Gary, John WhoHol A
Gary, John 1932- AmSCAP 1966
Gary, Lorraine WhoHol A
Gary, Romain 1914- WorEnF
Gary, Sid 1901-1973 WhScrn 2
Garyine, Anita Film 2
Garza, Eva 1917-1966 WhScrn 1, WhScrn 2
Gascoigne, Bamber 1935- WhoThe 16
Gascoigne, George 1535?-1577 McGWD, OxThe
Gascoigne, George 1542?-1577 CnThe, REnWD
Gascon, Jean 1921- WhoThe 16
Gaskell, Jane WomWMM
Gaskill, Clarence 1892-1947 AmSCAP 1966
Gaskill, William 1930- WhoThe 16
Gasnier, Louis d1963 NotNAT B
Gasnier, Louis 1880-1963 TwYS A
Gasnier, Louis 1882-1962 OxFilm
Gasnier, Louis J 1882- DcFM
Gaspar, Margit 1908- CroCD
Gassman, Josephine d1962 NotNAT B
Gassman, Vittorio MotPP, WhoHol A
Gassman, Vittorio 1922- BiDFlm, FilmgC, IntMPA 1977, MovMk, WorEnF
Gassmann, Vittorio 1912- OxThe
Gassner, John 1903-1967 BiE&WWA, NotNAT B, WhThe

Gasso, Bernard 1926- AmSCAP 1966
Gastelle, Stella d1936 NotNAT B
Gaston, George 1843-1937 NotNAT B
Gaston, Lyle R 1929- AmSCAP 1966
Gaston, Mae Film 1
Gastoni, Lisa 1935- FilmgC
Gastrock, Phail Film 1
Gates, B Cecil 1877-1941 AmSCAP 1966
Gates, Bert 1883-1952 WhScrn 1, WhScrn 2
Gates, Crawford 1921- AmSCAP 1966
Gates, Eleanor 1875-1951 NotNAT B, WhThe, WomWMM
Gates, Larry 1915- BiE&WWA, FilmgC, NotNAT, WhoHol A, WhoThe 16
Gates, Maxine WhoHol A
Gates, Nancy 1926- FilmgC, MotPP, WhoHol A
Gates, Ruth 1888-1966 BiE&WWA, NotNAT B
Gateson, Marjorie 1891- BiE&WWA, NotNAT, ThFT, WhoHol A
Gateson, Marjorie 1897- WhThe
Gateson, Marjorie 1900- MovMk
Gath, Joseph NatPD
Gatti, Armand 1924- CnMD Sup, CnThe, CroCD, DcFM, McGWD, ModWD, REnWD, WorEnF
Gatti, Sir John M 1872-1929 WhThe
Gatti-Casazza, Guilio d1940 NotNAT B
Gattie, A W d1925 NotNAT B
Gatty, Scott Film 2
Gaudard, Lucette WomWMM
Gaudio, Cheryl WomWMM B
Gaudio, Tony 1885-1951 DcFM, FilmgC, WorEnF
Gauge, Alexander 1914-1960 FilmgC, NotNAT B, WhScrn 1, WhScrn 2, WhoHol B
Gauguin, Lorraine 1924-1974 WhScrn 2
Gaul, George 1885-1939 NotNAT B, PIP&P, WhThe
Gaul, Harvey Bartlett 1881-1945 AmSCAP 1966
Gault, Mildred 1905-1938 WhScrn 1, WhScrn 2
Gaultier, Henry Film 2
Gaultier-Garguille 1573?-1633 NotNAT B, OxThe
Gaumont, Leon 1863-1946 DcFM, FilmgC, OxFilm, WomWMM, WorEnF
Gaunt, Percy 1852-1896 NotNAT B
Gauntier, Gene d1966 MotPP, WomWMM
Gauntier, Gene 1880?-1966 WhScrn 1, WhScrn 2
Gauntier, Gene 1891-1966 Film 1, TwYS
Gaussin, Jeanne-Catherine 1711-1767 OxThe
Gautier, Dick WhoHol A
Gautier, Dick 1931- AmSCAP 1966
Gautier, Dick 1939- FilmgC
Gautier, Gene d1966 WhoHol B
Gautier, Theophile 1811-1872 NotNAT B
Gavault, Paul 1867- WhThe
Gaver, Jack BiE&WWA, NotNAT
Gavin, John IntMPA 1977, MotPP, WhoHol A
Gavin, John 1928- FilmgC
Gavin, John 1934- MovMk
Gavras, Costa 1933- CelR 3
Gawthorne, Peter 1884-1962 Film 2, FilmgC, NotNAT B, WhScrn 1, WhScrn 2, WhThe, WhoHol B
Gaxton, William 1893-1963 EncMT, Film 2, FilmgC, NotNAT B, PIP&P, WhScrn 1, WhScrn 2, WhThe, WhoHol B
Gay, Byron 1886-1945 AmSCAP 1966
Gay, Dixie Film 2
Gay, Fred 1882-1955 WhScrn 1, WhScrn 2
Gay, Gregory Film 2, WhoHol A
Gay, Inez d1975 WhoHol C
Gay, John 1685-1732 CnThe, McGWD, NotNAT A, NotNAT B, OxThe, PIP&P, PIP&P A, REnWD

Gay, Maisie 1883-1945 *EncMT, NotNAT B, WhScrn 1, WhScrn 2, WhThe*
Gay, Maria d1943 *NotNAT B*
Gay, Marjorie 1917- *Film 2*
Gay, Noel 1898-1954 *EncMT, NotNAT B, WhThe*
Gay, Ramon 1917-1960 *WhScrn 1, WhScrn 2*
Gay, Walter d1936 *NotNAT B*
Gay, Ynex d1975 *WhScrn 2*
Gaye, Albie d1965 *WhScrn 1, WhScrn 2, WhoHol B*
Gaye, Freda 1907- *BiE&WWA, NotNAT, WhThe*
Gaye, Gregory 1900- *Film 2, Vers B*
Gaye, Howard *Film 1, Film 2, TwYS A*
Gaye, Lisa *WhoHol A*
Gayer, Echlin 1878-1926 *Film 2, NotNAT B, WhScrn 2, WhoHol B*
Gaylard, James W, III 1943- *IntMPA 1977*
Gaylard, James W, Jr. 1915- *IntMPA 1977*
Gayle, Peter 1944- *IntMPA 1977*
Gayler, Charles 1820-1892 *NotNAT B*
Gaynes, George 1917- *BiE&WWA, NotNAT, WhoHol A, WhoThe 16*
Gaynor, Charles 1909-1975 *AmSCAP 1966, BiE&WWA, EncMT, NotNAT B*
Gaynor, Janet 1906- *BiDFlm, Film 2, FilmgC, MotPP, MovMk, OxFilm, ThFT, TwYS, WhoHol A, WorEnF*
Gaynor, Janet 1907- *CmMov*
Gaynor, Mitzi 1930- *CmMov, FilmgC, IntMPA 1977, MotPP, MovMk, OxFilm, WhoHol A, WorEnF*
Gaynor, Ruth d1919 *WhScrn 2*
Gayson, Eunice 1931- *FilmgC*
Gaythorne, Pamela 1882- *WhThe*
Gaziadis, Dimitrios 1897-1961 *DcFM*
Gazzara, Ben 1930- *BiDFlm, BiE&WWA, CelR 3, FilmgC, IntMPA 1977, MotPP, MovMk, NotNAT, OxFilm, PIP&P A, WhoHol A, WhoThe 16*
Gazzo, Michael V 1923- *BiE&WWA, McGWD, NotNAT, PIP&P, WhoHol A*
Gear, Luella *Film 2, PIP&P, WhoHol A*
Gear, Luella 1897- *EncMT*
Gear, Luella 1899- *BiE&WWA, NotNAT, WhThe*
Gearhart, Livingston 1916- *AmSCAP 1966*
Geary, Bud 1899-1946 *WhScrn 1, WhScrn 2, WhoHol B*
Geary, Maine *Film 2*
Gebel, Bruno *DcFM*
Gebel-Williams, Gunther 1937- *CelR 3*
Gebert, Ernst d1961 *NotNAT B*
Gebest, Charles J 1872-1937 *AmSCAP 1966*
Gebhardt, Mrs. Frank *Film 1*
Gebhardt, Frank *Film 1*
Gebhardt, Fred 1925- *IntMPA 1977*
Gebhardt, George M 1879-1919 *WhScrn 2*
Gebuehr, Otto 1877-1954 *Film 2, WhScrn 1, WhScrn 2*
Gebuhr, Otto 1877-1954 *Film 2*
Geddes, Barbara Bel 1922- *MotPP, OxThe*
Geddes, Barbara Bel *see also* Bel Geddes, Barbara
Geddes, Henry 1912- *IntMPA 1977*
Geddes, Norman Bel 1893-1958 *NotNAT A, NotNAT B, OxThe, PIP&P, WhThe*
Geddes, Norman Bel *see also* Bel Geddes, Norman
Gee, George 1895-1959 *NotNAT B, WhScrn 1, WhScrn 2, WhThe, WhoHol B*
Gee, George D d1917 *WhScrn 2*
Gee, Shirley *ConDr 1977B*
Geer, Ellen 1941- *BiE&WWA, NotNAT, WhoHol A*

Geer, Lennie *WhoHol A*
Geer, Will 1902- *BiE&WWA, FilmgC, IntMPA 1977, MovMk, NotNAT, WhoHol A, WhoThe 16*
Geersh, Eafim 1899- *AmSCAP 1966*
Geesink, Joop 1913- *DcFM, FilmgC*
Geeson, Judy 1948- *FilmgC, IntMPA 1977, MovMk, WhoHol A*
Geeson, Sally 1950- *FilmgC*
Gehman, Richard 1921- *BiE&WWA*
Gehrig, Lou 1903-1941 *WhScrn 2*
Gehring, Viktor *Film 2*
Gehrman, Lucy d1954 *WhScrn 1, WhScrn 2*
Geibel, Adam 1855-1933 *AmSCAP 1966*
Geiger, George 1905- *AmSCAP 1966*
Geiger, Hermann 1913-1966 *WhScrn 1, WhScrn 2*
Geiringer, Jean d1962 *NotNAT B*
Geisel, Theodor Seuss 1904- *AmSCAP 1966, NewYTET*
Geizel, John *Film 2*
Gelabert, Fructuoso 1874-1955 *DcFM*
Gelb, Arthur 1924- *BiE&WWA, NotNAT*
Gelb, Barbara *NotNAT*
Gelb, James *BiE&WWA, NotNAT*
Gelbart, Larry *NewYTET*
Gelbart, Larry 1928- *AmSCAP 1966*
Gelbart, Larry S 1923- *BiE&WWA, NotNAT*
Gelber, Jack 1926- *CnMD*
Gelber, Jack 1932- *BiE&WWA, CnThe, ConDr 1977, CroCD, McGWD, ModWD, NotNAT, PIP&P, REnWD, WhoThe 16*
Gelber, Stanley Jay 1936- *AmSCAP 1966*
Gelckler, Robert *Film 2*
Geld, Gary 1935- *AmSCAP 1966*
Geldart, Clarence 1867-1935 *WhoHol B*
Geldart, Clarence 1867-1936 *Film 1*
Geldert, Clarence 1867-1935 *WhScrn 1, WhScrn 2*
Geldert, Clarence 1867-1936 *Film 2, TwYS*
Gelenbevi, Baha 1902- *DcFM*
Gelin, Daniel 1921- *BiDFlm, FilmgC, OxFilm, WhoHol A, WorEnF*
Gelinas, Gratien 1909- *McGWD, REnWD*
Gelinas, Gratien 1910- *CnThe*
Gell-Mann, Murray 1929- *CelR 3*
Geller, Bruce 1930- *AmSCAP 1966, IntMPA 1977, NewYTET*
Geller, Henry *NewYTET*
Geller, Joyce *WomWMM*
Gellert, Lawrence 1898- *AmSCAP 1966*
Gellner, Julius 1899- *WhoThe 16*
Gelman, Harold S 1912- *AmSCAP 1966*
Gelman, Larry *WhoHol A*
Gemier, Firmin d1933 *Film 2, WhoHol B*
Gemier, Firmin 1865-1933 *NotNAT B, OxThe, WhThe*
Gemier, Firmin 1886-1933 *WhScrn 2*
Gemmell, Don 1903- *WhoThe 16*
Gemora, Charlie 1903-1961 *WhScrn 1, WhScrn 2, WhoHol B*
Gendron, Pierre 1896-1956 *Film 2, MotPP, NotNAT B, WhScrn 1, WhScrn 2, WhoHol B*
Genee, Adeline 1878-1970 *WhThe, WhoStg 1908*
Genee, Alexander d1938 *NotNAT B*
Genella, Julian 1907- *AmSCAP 1966*
Genest, John d1839 *NotNAT B*
Genet, Jean 1909- *CnThe, REnWD*
Genet, Jean 1910- *BiE&WWA, CelR 3, CnMD, CroCD, McGWD, ModWD, NotNAT, NotNAT A, OxThe, PIP&P, PIP&P A, WhoThe 16*
Genevieve 1930- *BiE&WWA*

Gengenbach, Pamphilus OxThe
Genger, Roger AmSCAP 1966
Geniat, Marcelle d1959 NotNAT B, WhThe,
  WhoHol B
Genina, Augusto 1892-1947 FilmgC
Genina, Augusto 1892-1957 DcFM, WorEnF
Genn, Edward P d1947 NotNAT B
Genn, Leo 1905- BiE&WWA, FilmgC,
  IntMPA 1977, MotPP, MovMk, NotNAT,
  WhoHol A, WhoThe 16
Gennaro, Peter 1924- BiE&WWA, CelR 3,
  EncMT, NotNAT
Genock, Ted 1907- IntMPA 1977
Genovese, Gen 1917- AmSCAP 1966
Gensler, Lewis E 1896- AmSCAP 1966
Gentle, Alice 1889-1958 WhScrn 1, WhScrn 2,
  WhoHol B
Gentle, Lili WhoHol A
Gentleman, Francis 1728-1784 NotNAT B, OxThe
Gentry, Amelia d1963 NotNAT B
Gentry, Bob d1962 NotNAT B, WhoHol B
Genus, Karl NewYTET
Geoly, Andrew 1907- BiE&WWA, NotNAT
George, Mademoiselle 1787-1867 NotNAT B,
  OxThe
George II Of Saxe-Meiningen OxThe
George, A E 1869-1920 NotNAT B, WhThe
George, Anthony WhoHol A
George, Christopher 1929- FilmgC, WhoHol A
George, Colin 1929- WhoThe 16
George, Dan 1899- CelR 3, FilmgC, WhoHol A
George, Don 1909- AmSCAP 1966
George, Don R 1903- AmSCAP 1966
George, Earl 1924- AmSCAP 1966
George, George Louis 1907- IntMPA 1977
George, George W 1920- IntMPA 1977
George, Gladys d1954 MotPP, WhoHol B
George, Gladys 1900-1954 FilmgC, MovMk,
  WhScrn 1, WhScrn 2
George, Gladys 1902-1954 Film 1, Film 2
George, Gladys 1904-1954 NotNAT B, ThFT,
  TwYS, Vers A, WhThe
George, Grace 1879-1961 FamA&A, NotNAT B,
  OxThe, WhScrn 1, WhScrn 2, WhThe,
  WhoHol B
George, Grace 1880-1961 WhoStg 1906,
  WhoStg 1908
George, Heinrich 1893-1946 Film 2, WhScrn 1,
  WhScrn 2, WhoHol B
George, Isabel WhoHol A
George, John ConDr 1977B
George, John 1898-1968 Film 2, WhScrn 2
George, Lynda Day WhoHol A
George, Marie 1879-1955 NotNAT B, WhThe,
  WhoStg 1906, WhoStg 1908
George, Maud 1890- Film 1, Film 2, TwYS
George, Muriel 1883-1965 FilmgC, WhScrn 1,
  WhScrn 2, WhThe, WhoHol B
George, Paul Film 2
George, Peggy Film 1
George, Phyllis NewYTET
George, Susan 1950- FilmgC, IntMPA 1977,
  MovMk, WhoHol A
George, Voya 1895-1951 Film 2, WhScrn 1,
  WhScrn 2, WhoHol B
Georges, Katerine d1973 WhScrn 2
Georgi, Katja WomWMM
Geppert, Carl Film 2
Gerachty, Carmelita 1901-1966 Film 2
Geraghty, Carmelita 1901-1966 MotPP, TwYS,
  WhScrn 1, WhScrn 2, WhoHol B
Geraghty, Maurice 1908- IntMPA 1977
Gerald, Ara 1900-1957 NotNAT B, WhThe,
  WhoHol B

Gerald, Florence d1942 NotNAT B
Gerald, Frank 1855-1942 NotNAT B
Gerald, Helen IntMPA 1977
Gerald, Jim 1889-1958 Film 2, FilmgC,
  WhScrn 1, WhScrn 2, WhoHol B
Gerald, Peter Film 1
Geraldy, Paul 1885- CnMD, McGWD, ModWD,
  WhThe
Gerard, Ambassador Film 1
Gerard, Carl Film 1, Film 2
Gerard, Charles Film 1, Film 2
Gerard, Jenny WomWMM
Gerard, Joseph Film 2
Gerard, Joseph Smith 1871-1949 WhScrn 1,
  WhScrn 2
Gerard, Lillian IntMPA 1977
Gerard, Philip R 1913- IntMPA 1977
Gerard, Richard 1876-1948 AmSCAP 1966
Gerard, Rolf 1910?- NotNAT
Gerard, Teddie d1942 Film 2, WhoHol B
Gerard, Teddie 1890-1942 WhScrn 1, WhScrn 2
Gerard, Teddie 1892-1942 WhThe
Gerard, Teddie see also Gerrard, Teddie
Gerasch, Alfred Film 2
Gerasimov, Sergei 1906- BiDFlm, DcFM, Film 2,
  FilmgC, OxFilm, WorEnF
Geray, Steve 1904- FilmgC, MovMk, WhThe
Geray, Steven 1898-1973 WhScrn 2
Geray, Steven 1904-1973 IntMPA 1977, Vers B,
  WhoHol B
Gerber, Alex 1895- AmSCAP 1966
Gerber, Daisy WomWMM B
Gerber, David IntMPA 1977, NewYTET
Gerber, Ella 1916- BiE&WWA, NotNAT
Gerber, Michael H 1944- IntMPA 1977
Gerber, Neva Film 1, Film 2, TwYS
Gerdes, Emily Film 2
Gerhard, Karl d1964 NotNAT B
Gerich, Valentine 1898- AmSCAP 1966
Gering, Marion 1901- FilmgC
Gerlach, Arthur Von 1877-1925 DcFM
Gerlach-Jacobi Film 2
Germaine, Auguste d1915 NotNAT B
Germaine, Mary 1933- FilmgC, WhoHol A
German, Sir Edward 1862- WhThe, WhoStg 1908
Germanova, Maria Nikolaevna 1884-1940 OxThe,
  PIP&P
Germi, Pietro 1904-1974 FilmgC, WhScrn 2
Germi, Pietro 1914-1974 DcFM, MovMk, OxFilm,
  WhoHol B, WorEnF
Germon, Effie d1914 NotNAT B, WhoStg 1908
Germonprez, Valerie Film 1
Gernreich, Rudi 1922- CelR 3
Gerold, Arthur 1923- BiE&WWA, NotNAT
Geroule, Henri d1934 NotNAT B
Gerrard, Charles 1887- Film 1, Film 2, MotPP,
  TwYS
Gerrard, Douglas 1885-1950 TwYS A
Gerrard, Douglas 1888-1950 Film 1, Film 2,
  TwYS, WhScrn 2
Gerrard, Gene 1892-1971 FilmgC, WhScrn 1,
  WhScrn 2, WhThe, WhoHol B
Gerrard, Teddie 1892-1942 NotNAT B
Gerrard, Teddie see also Gerard, Teddie
Gerringer, Robert 1926- BiE&WWA, NotNAT
Gerritsen, Lisa WhoHol A
Gerron, Kurt Film 2
Gerron, Kurt d1943 WhoHol B
Gerron, Kurt d1944 WhScrn 2
Gerry, Alex 1908- Vers A, WhoHol A
Gershenson, Joseph 1904- FilmgC, IntMPA 1977
Gershwin, Arthur 1900- AmSCAP 1966
Gershwin, George 1898-1937 AmSCAP 1966,
  CmMov, EncMT, McGWD, NewMT,

NotNAT A, NotNAT B, OxFilm, PIP&P,
WhThe
Gershwin, George 1899-1937 *DcFM, FilmgC*
Gershwin, Ira 1896- *AmSCAP 1966, BiE&WWA,*
CelR 3, EncMT, FilmgC, IntMPA 1977,
NewMT, NotNAT, NotNAT A, PIP&P,
WhThe
Gershwins, The *PIP&P*
Gerson, Betty Lou *WhoHol A*
Gerson, Charles *Film 2*
Gerson, Eva 1903-1959 *WhScrn 1, WhScrn 2,*
WhoHol B
Gerson, Paul 1871-1957 *WhScrn 1, WhScrn 2,*
WhoHol B
Gerstad, John 1924- *BiE&WWA, NotNAT,*
WhoThe 16
Gerstad, Merritt B *CmMov*
Gerstein, Cassandra *WomWMM B*
Gersten, Bernard 1923- *BiE&WWA, NotNAT,*
WhoThe 16
Gersten, Berta 1894-1972 *WhScrn 2, WhoHol B*
Gerstenberg, Heinrich Wilhelm Von 1737-1823
McGWD
Gerstle, Frank 1915-1970 *WhScrn 2*
Gerstle, Frank 1917-1970 *WhScrn 1, WhoHol B*
Gerstman, Felix G d1967 *BiE&WWA, NotNAT,*
NotNAT B
Gert, Valeska 1900- *Film 2, OxFilm*
Gertner, Richard *IntMPA 1977*
Gertsman, Maury 1910?- *FilmgC*
Gertz, Irving 1915- *IntMPA 1977*
Gerussi, Bruno *WhThe*
Gervais-L'Heureux, Suzanne *WomWMM*
Gesek, Tadeusz 1925- *NotNAT*
Gesensway, Louis 1906- *AmSCAP 1966*
Gesner, Clark 1938- *AmSCAP 1966, EncMT,*
NatPD
Gesoff, Hilda I *AmSCAP 1966*
Gest, Inna 1922-1965 *WhScrn 1, WhScrn 2,*
WhoHol B
Gest, Morris 1881-1942 *NotNAT B, WhThe*
Getchell, Charles Munro 1909-1963 *NotNAT B*
Getchell, Summer *Film 2*
Gettinger, William d1966 *WhScrn 2, WhoHol B*
Gettman, Lorraine *WhoHol A*
Getty, J Paul *CelR 3*
Getty, J Ronald 1929- *IntMPA 1977*
Getz, Johnnie G d1964 *NotNAT B*
Getzov, Ramon M 1925- *AmSCAP 1966*
Geurin-Catelain, Raymond *Film 2*
Geva, Tamara 1907- *BiE&WWA, EncMT,*
Film 2, NotNAT, WhThe, WhoHol A
Geymond, Vital *Film 2*
Geyra, Ellida *WomWMM*
Ghaffary, Farrokh 1922- *DcFM*
Ghatak, Ritwik 1924- *DcFM*
Ghelderode, Michel De 1898-1962 *CnMD, CnThe,*
McGWD, ModWD, NotNAT B, OxThe,
REnWD
Ghent, Derek *Film 2*
Gheon, Henri 1875-1943 *OxThe*
Gheon, Henri 1875-1944 *CnMD, CnThe,*
McGWD, ModWD
Gherardi, Evaristo 1663-1700 *NotNAT B, OxThe*
Gherardi, Gherardo 1890-1949 *CnMD*
Gherardi, Gherardo 1891-1949 *McGWD*
Gherardi, Giovanni *OxThe*
Gherardi, Piero 1909-1971 *WorEnF*
Gheusi, Pierre B 1867- *WhThe*
Ghio, Nino 1887-1956 *WhScrn 1, WhScrn 2*
Ghione, Emile *Film 2*
Ghione, Emilio 1879-1930 *DcFM, WorEnF*
Ghione, Franco 1886-1964 *NotNAT B*
Gholson, Julie *WhoHol A*

Ghosal, Mrs. 1857-1932 *NotNAT B*
Ghosh, Girish Chandra *REnWD*
Ghostley, Alice 1926- *BiE&WWA, MotPP,*
NotNAT, WhoHol A, WhoThe 16
Giachetti, Fosco 1904-1974 *WhScrn 2, WhoHol B*
Giacometti, Paolo 1816-1882 *McGWD,*
NotNAT B, OxThe
Giacomino 1884-1956 *WhScrn 1, WhScrn 2*
Giacosa, Giuseppe 1847-1906 *CnThe, McGWD,*
ModWD, NotNAT B, OxThe, REnWD
Giallelis, Stathis 1939- *FilmgC, WhoHol A*
Giami, Guiliano *WhoHol A*
Giancarli, Gigio Artemio *McGWD*
Giandomenico, Emilio 1939- *AmSCAP 1966*
Giannini, Giancarlo 1942- *IntMPA 1977,*
WhoHol A
Giannini, Olga *WhThe*
Giannini, Vittorio 1903- *AmSCAP 1966*
Giannotti, Donato 1492-1573 *McGWD*
Giarratano, Tony 1907- *AmSCAP 1966*
Giasson, Paul E 1921- *AmSCAP 1966*
Gibb, Robert W 1893-1964 *AmSCAP 1966*
Gibberson, William 1919- *BiE&WWA*
Gibbons, Arthur 1871-1935 *NotNAT B, WhThe*
Gibbons, Cedric 1893-1956 *OxFilm*
Gibbons, Cedric 1893-1960 *DcFM, WorEnF*
Gibbons, Cedric 1895-1960 *FilmgC, NotNAT B*
Gibbons, Irene 1907-1962 *NotNAT B*
Gibbons, Rose 1886-1964 *NotNAT B, WhScrn 1,*
WhScrn 2, WhoHol B
Gibbs, Mrs. 1770-1844 *NotNAT B, OxThe*
Gibbs, Arthur H 1895-1956 *AmSCAP 1966*
Gibbs, Gerald 1910?- *FilmgC*
Gibbs, Nancy d1956 *NotNAT B, WhThe*
Gibbs, Raton *Film 1*
Gibbs, Robert Paton d1940 *NotNAT B*
Gibbs, Sheila Shand *WhoHol A*
Gibbs, Terry 1924- *AmSCAP 1966*
Gibbs, Wolcott 1902-1958 *NotNAT B, OxThe*
Giblyn, Charles d1933 *Film 2, TwYS A*
Gibney, Frank 1924- *BiE&WWA*
Gibson, Albert Andrew 1913-1961 *AmSCAP 1966*
Gibson, Brenda 1870- *WhThe*
Gibson, Charles Dana 1867-1944 *WhScrn 2*
Gibson, Chloe 1899- *WhThe*
Gibson, Edward Hoot 1892-1962 *WhScrn 2*
Gibson, Ethlyn *Film 2*
Gibson, Florence *Film 2*
Gibson, Helen 1892- *Film 1, Film 2, FilmgC,*
WhoHol A
Gibson, Helen 1893- *TwYS*
Gibson, Henry *WhoHol A*
Gibson, Hoot 1892-1962 *Film 1, Film 2, FilmgC,*
MotPP, MovMk, NotNAT B, OxFilm,
TwYS, WhoHol B
Gibson, Hoot Edward 1892-1962 *WhScrn 1*
Gibson, James 1866-1938 *Film 2, WhScrn 1,*
WhScrn 2, WhoHol B
Gibson, Kenneth *Film 2*
Gibson, Kenneth 1932- *CelR 3*
Gibson, Madeline 1909- *WhThe*
Gibson, Margaret *Film 1, WhScrn 2*
Gibson, Preston d1937 *NotNAT B*
Gibson, Virginia *WhoHol A*
Gibson, Vivian *Film 2*
Gibson, William 1914- *BiE&WWA, CnMD,*
ConDr 1977, McGWD, ModWD, NatPD,
NotNAT, NotNAT A, PIP&P, WhoThe 16
Gibson, Wynne *MotPP*
Gibson, Wynne 1899- *FilmgC, MovMk*
Gibson, Wynne 1903- *HolP 30*
Gibson, Wynne 1905- *BiE&WWA, ThFT,*
WhThe, WhoHol A
Gibson, Wynne 1907- *Film 2*

Giddens, George 1845-1920 *NotNAT B, WhThe*
Giddens, George 1855-1920 *WhoStg 1906,*
  WhoStg 1908
Gidding, Nelson 1915?- *FilmgC*
Giddings, Jack *Film 2*
Gide, Andre 1869-1951 *CnMD, ModWD,*
  NotNAT B, OxThe, REnWD
Gideon, Johnny d1901 *NotNAT B*
Gideon, Melville J 1884-1933 *NotNAT B, WhThe*
Giehse, Therese 1899-1975 *WhScrn 2, WhoHol C*
Gielgud, Sir John 1904- *BiDFlm, BiE&WWA,*
  CelR 3, CnThe, FamA&A, Film 2, FilmgC,
  IntMPA 1977, MotPP, MovMk, NotNAT,
  NotNAT A, OxFilm, OxThe, PIP&P,
  WhoHol A, WhoThe 16, WorEnF
Gielgud, Val 1900- *NotNAT A, WhThe*
Gierasch, Stefan 1926- *NotNAT, WhoHol A*
Giere, Helen *Film 2*
Gierlach, Chester 1919- *AmSCAP 1966*
Gierow, Karl Ragnar Kunt 1904- *CnMD, ModWD*
Giesler, Jerry d1962 *NotNAT B*
Giffard, Henry 1694?-1772 *NotNAT B, OxThe*
Giffen, Robert Lawrence d1946 *NotNAT B*
Gifford, Alan *WhoHol A*
Gifford, Alan 1905- *FilmgC*
Gifford, Alan 1911- *IntMPA 1977*
Gifford, Frances *MotPP*
Gifford, Frances 1920- *WhoHol A*
Gifford, Frances 1922- *FilmgC, MGM*
Gifford, Frank 1930- *CelR 3, NewYTET,*
  WhoHol A
Gifford, Gordon d1962 *NotNAT B*
Gifford, H Eugene 1908- *AmSCAP 1966*
Gifford, Henry *PIP&P*
Giftos, Elaine *WhoHol A*
Gigandet, Joseph H 1915- *AmSCAP 1966*
Gigli, Beniamino d1958 *WhoHol B*
Gigli, Beniamino 1890-1957 *FilmgC, WhScrn 1,*
  WhScrn 2
Giglio, A Gino *BiE&WWA, NotNAT*
Gignoux, Regis 1878- *WhThe*
Gil, David 1930- *IntMPA 1977*
Gil Y Zarate, Antonio 1793-1861 *McGWD*
Gil'ad, Nelly *WomWMM*
Gilardoni, Eugenio *Film 2*
Gilbert, Anne 1821-1904 *NotNAT A*
Gilbert, Arthur N 1920- *IntMPA 1977*
Gilbert, Benjamin A 1904- *BiE&WWA*
Gilbert, Billy *MotPP*
Gilbert, Billy 1891-1961 *WhScrn 1, WhScrn 2*
Gilbert, Billy 1893-1971 *FilmgC, WhoHol B*
Gilbert, Billy 1894-1971 *BiE&WWA, Film 1,*
  Film 2, MovMk, NotNAT B, TwYS,
  WhScrn 1, WhScrn 2
Gilbert, Billy 1896-1971 *Vers A*
Gilbert, Bob 1898-1973 *WhoHol B*
Gilbert, Bobby 1898-1973 *WhScrn 2*
Gilbert, Edwin J *Film 1*
Gilbert, Eugenia *TwYS*
Gilbert, Eugenie *Film 2*
Gilbert, Florence *Film 2*
Gilbert, Gabriel 1620?-1680? *OxThe*
Gilbert, Mrs. George H 1821-1904 *FamA&A,*
  NotNAT B, OxThe, PIP&P
Gilbert, George Henry d1866 *NotNAT B*
Gilbert, Jack *Film 1*
Gilbert, Jean 1879-1943 *NotNAT B, WhThe*
Gilbert, Joanne *WhoHol A*
Gilbert, Jody *WhoHol A*
Gilbert, Joe 1903-1959 *WhScrn 1, WhScrn 2*
Gilbert, John d1936 *MotPP, WhoHol B*
Gilbert, John 1810-1889 *FamA&A, NotNAT B,*
  OxThe, PIP&P
Gilbert, John 1895-1936 *CmMov, Film 1, Film 2,*

  FilmgC, TwYS
Gilbert, John 1897-1936 *BiDFlm, MovMk,*
  NotNAT B, OxFilm, WhScrn 1, WhScrn 2,
  WorEnF
Gilbert, L Wolfe 1886- *AmSCAP 1966*
Gilbert, Lauren *WhoHol A*
Gilbert, Leatrice Joy *WhoHol A*
Gilbert, Lewis 1920- *BiDFlm, CmMov, Film 2,*
  FilmgC, IntMPA 1977, MovMk, WorEnF
Gilbert, Lou 1909- *BiE&WWA, NotNAT,*
  WhoHol A, WhoThe 16
Gilbert, Maude d1953 *WhScrn 1, WhScrn 2*
Gilbert, Mercedes d1952 *NotNAT B*
Gilbert, Nicole *WomWMM*
Gilbert, Oh Gran *WhScrn 1*
Gilbert, Olive *WhoThe 16*
Gilbert, Paul 1924-1975 *FilmgC, WhoHol C*
Gilbert, Philip *WhoHol A*
Gilbert, Ray 1912- *AmSCAP 1966*
Gilbert, Richard E 1919- *AmSCAP 1966*
Gilbert, Ronnie *WhoHol A*
Gilbert, Ruth *WhoHol A*
Gilbert, Walter 1887-1947 *NotNAT B, WhScrn 2,*
  WhoHol B
Gilbert, Sir William Schwenck 1836-1911 *CnThe,*
  FilmgC, McGWD, ModWD, NotNAT A,
  NotNAT B, OxThe, REnWD, WhoStg 1908
Gilbert, Willie 1916- *BiE&WWA, NotNAT*
Gilbert And Sullivan *PIP&P*
Gilbertson, Virginia M 1914- *AmSCAP 1966*
Gilbride, Claire 1919- *AmSCAP 1966*
Gilchrist, Connie 1865-1946 *NotNAT B, OxThe*
Gilchrist, Connie 1901- *FilmgC, WhoHol A*
Gilchrist, Connie 1904- *MovMk*
Gilchrist, Connie 1906- *MGM, Vers A*
Gilchrist, Rubina d1956 *NotNAT B*
Gildea, Agnes d1964 *NotNAT B*
Gildea, Mary d1957 *NotNAT B*
Gilder, Jeanette d1916 *NotNAT B*
Gilder, Rosamond *BiE&WWA, NotNAT,*
  PIP&P
Gilder, Rosamond 1891- *WhoThe 16*
Gilder, Rosamond 1900- *OxThe*
Gildon, Charles d1724 *NotNAT B*
Giles, Anna 1874-1973 *WhScrn 2, WhoHol B*
Giles, Corliss *Film 2*
Giles, Johnny 1911- *AmSCAP 1966*
Giles, Paul Kirk 1895- *BiE&WWA, NotNAT*
Gilfether, Daniel 1854-1919 *Film 1, WhScrn 2*
Gilfond, Henry *NatPD*
Giford, Jack *BiE&WWA, IntMPA 1977,*
  NotNAT, PIP&P, WhoHol A, WhoThe 16
Giford, Jack 1907- *FilmgC*
Giford, Jack 1913- *EncMT*
Giford, Jack 1919- *MovMk*
Gilhooley, Jack *NatPD*
Gilkey, Stanley 1900- *BiE&WWA, NotNAT*
Gilkison, Anthony 1913- *IntMPA 1977*
Gill, Basil 1877-1955 *Film 1, Film 2,*
  NotNAT B, WhScrn 1, WhScrn 2, WhThe,
  WhoHol B
Gill, Brendan 1914- *BiE&WWA, NotNAT,*
  NotNAT A, WhoThe 16
Gill, Carolyn 1918- *AmSCAP 1966*
Gill, Elizabeth *WomWMM B*
Gill, Florence 1877-1965 *WhScrn 2*
Gill, Henry d1954 *NotNAT B*
Gill, Maud *Film 2*
Gill, Michael *NewYTET*
Gill, Paul d1934 *WhThe*
Gill, Paul d1953 *NotNAT B*
Gill, Peter 1939- *ConDr 1977, WhoThe 16*
Gill, Ralph 1919- *AmSCAP 1966*
Gill, Tom 1916-1971 *WhoHol A, WhoThe 16*

Gillam, David S 1915- *AmSCAP 1966*
Gillaspy, Richard M 1927- *IntMPA 1977,*
  NewYTET
Gillen, Ernest *Film 2*
Gilles, D B 1947- *NatPD*
Gilles, Eloise 1929- *AmSCAP 1966*
Gilles, Genevieve 1946- *FilmgC*
Gillespie, A Arnold 1899- *IntMPA 1977*
Gillespie, Albert T *Film 1*
Gillespie, Dizzy 1917- *AmSCAP 1966, CelR 3*
Gillespie, Haven 1888- *AmSCAP 1966*
Gillespie, Marian Evans 1889-1946 *AmSCAP 1966*
Gillespie, Richard Henry 1878-1952 *NotNAT B,*
  WhThe
Gillespie, William 1894- *Film 1, Film 2, TwYS*
Gillet, Florence *Film 1*
Gillett, Elma 1874-1941 *WhScrn 1, WhScrn 2*
Gillett, Eric 1893- *WhThe*
Gillette, A S 1904- *BiE&WWA, NotNAT*
Gillette, Anita 1936- *BiE&WWA, NotNAT,*
  WhoThe 16
Gillette, Leland J 1912- *AmSCAP 1966*
Gillette, Robert *Film 2*
Gillette, Ruth 1907- *BiE&WWA, NotNAT,*
  WhoHol A
Gillette, Viola *WhoStg 1908*
Gillette, William d1937 *NotNAT A*
Gillette, William 1853-1937 *TwYS, WhoStg 1906,*
  WhoStg 1908
Gillette, William 1855-1937 *FamA&A, Film 1,*
  FilmgC, McGWD, ModWD, NotNAT B,
  OxThe, PIP&P, WhThe
Gillette, William 1856-1937 *WhScrn 1, WhScrn 2,*
  WhoHol B
Gilliam, Stu *WhoHol A*
Gilliat, Leslie 1917- *FilmgC, IntMPA 1977*
Gilliat, Sidney 1908- *DcFM, FilmgC,*
  IntMPA 1977, OxFilm, WorEnF
Gilliatt, Penelope *FilmgC, WomWMM*
Gillie, Jean 1915-1949 *FilmgC, NotNAT B,*
  WhScrn 1, WhScrn 2, WhThe, WhoHol B
Gilligan, Sonja Carl 1936- *WomWMM B*
Gilliland, Helen 1897-1942 *NotNAT B, WhThe*
Gilliland, Thomas d1816? *NotNAT B*
Gillin, Donald T 1914- *IntMPA 1977*
Gilling, John 1912- *FilmgC, IntMPA 1977*
Gillingwater, Claude 1870-1939 *FilmgC,*
  WhScrn 1, WhScrn 2, WhoHol B
Gillingwater, Claude 1870-1940 *MovMk*
Gillingwater, Claude 1879-1939 *Film 2, TwYS*
Gillis, Ann 1927- *FilmgC, WhoHol A*
Gillis, Anne 1927- *IntMPA 1977*
Gillis, Don 1912- *AmSCAP 1966*
Gillis, Sylvester 1899- *AmSCAP 1966*
Gillis, William S d1946 *WhScrn 1, WhScrn 2,*
  WhoHol B
Gillman, Arita *Film 2*
Gillman, Mabelle 1880- *WhThe, WhoStg 1908*
Gillmore, Frank 1867-1943 *NotNAT B, WhThe,*
  WhoStg 1906, WhoStg 1908
Gillmore, Frank *see also* Gilmore, Frank
Gillmore, Margalo 1897- *BiE&WWA, FilmgC,*
  MotPP, NotNAT, NotNAT A, WhThe,
  WhoHol A
Gilman, Ada d1921 *NotNAT B*
Gilman, Fred *Film 2*
Gilman, Sam *WhoHol A*
Gilmore, Barney *Film 2*
Gilmore, Barney 1867- *WhoStg 1906,*
  WhoStg 1908
Gilmore, Douglas d1950 *Film 2, NotNAT B,*
  WhoHol B
Gilmore, Elizabeth McCabe 1874-1953
  AmSCAP 1966

Gilmore, Frank 1867-1943 *WhoHol B*
Gilmore, Frank *see also* Gilmore, Frank
Gilmore, Helen 1900-1947 *Film 2, WhScrn 2*
Gilmore, J H *Film 2*
Gilmore, Janette 1905- *WhThe*
Gilmore, Lillian *Film 2*
Gilmore, Lowell 1907-1960 *FilmgC, WhScrn 1,*
  WhScrn 2, WhoHol B
Gilmore, Peter 1931- *WhoHol A, WhoThe 16*
Gilmore, Virginia 1919- *BiE&WWA, FilmgC,*
  HolP 40, MotPP, MovMk, NotNAT,
  WhThe, WhoHol A
Gilmore, W H *WhThe*
Gilmour, Brian 1894-1954 *NotNAT B, WhThe*
Gilmour, Edith 1896- *AmSCAP 1966*
Gilmour, Gordon d1962 *NotNAT B*
Gilmour, J H *WhoStg 1908*
Gilmour, John *Film 1*
Gilmour, John H d1922 *NotNAT B*
Gilpin, Charles S 1878-1930 *FamA&A,*
  NotNAT B, OxThe, WhThe, WhoHol B
Gilpin, Charles S 1879-1930 *WhScrn 1, WhScrn 2*
Gilroy, Frank D 1925- *ConDr 1977, CroCD,*
  McGWD, ModWD, NotNAT, WhoThe 16
Gilroy, John 1872-1937 *AmSCAP 1966*
Gilson, Charles *Film 2*
Gilson, Lottie d1912 *NotNAT B*
Gilson, Tom 1934-1962 *WhScrn 2, WhoHol B*
Gim, H W 1908-1973 *WhScrn 2, WhoHol B*
Gimbel, Norman 1927- *BiE&WWA*
Gimbel, Peter 1928- *CelR 3*
Gimbel, Roger *IntMPA 1977*
Gimenez Arnau Y Gran, Jose Antonio 1912-
  McGWD
Gindhart, Thomas J 1908- *AmSCAP 1966*
Ging, Jack *WhoHol A*
Gingold, Dan *IntMPA 1977*
Gingold, Baroness Helene d1926 *NotNAT B*
Gingold, Hermione *MotPP, PIP&P, WhoHol A*
Gingold, Hermione 1897- *BiE&WWA, CelR 3,*
  EncMT, FilmgC, MovMk, WhoThe 16
Gingold, Hermione 1899- *NotNAT*
Gingrich, Arnold 1903- *CelR 3*
Ginisty, Paul d1932 *NotNAT B*
Ginisty, Paul 1858- *WhThe*
Giniva, John Alaska Jack 1868-1936 *WhScrn 1,*
  WhScrn 2
Ginn, Wells Watson 1891-1959 *WhScrn 1,*
  WhScrn 2
Ginna, Robert Emmett, Jr. 1925- *IntMPA 1977*
Ginner, Ruby 1886- *WhThe*
Ginnes, Abram S 1914- *BiE&WWA*
Ginsberg, Allen 1926- *CelR 3, PIP&P A*
Ginsberg, Harry *Film 2*
Ginsberg, Henry 1897- *IntMPA 1977*
Ginsberg, Sidney 1920- *IntMPA 1977*
Ginsberg, Sol 1885-1963 *AmSCAP 1966*
Ginsburg, Lewis S 1914- *IntMPA 1977*
Ginsbury, Norman 1902- *BiE&WWA, NotNAT*
Ginsbury, Norman 1903- *WhoThe 16*
Ginty, Elizabeth Beall d1949 *NotNAT B*
Gioi, Vivi 1917-1975 *WhScrn 2, WhoHol C*
Giono, Jean 1895- *CnMD, McGWD*
Giono, Jean 1895-1970 *ModWD*
Giono, Jean 1895-1971 *OxFilm*
Giovaninetti, Silvio 1901-1959 *McGWD*
Giovanni, Jose 1923- *WorEnF*
Giovanni, Nikki 1943- *CelR 3*
Giovannini, Caesar 1925- *AmSCAP 1966*
Giovannone, Anthony J 1923- *AmSCAP 1966*
Giracci, Mary *Film 1, Film 2*
Giraci, Mary *Film 2*
Giradot, Etienne 1856-1939 *WhScrn 1, WhScrn 2*
Giradot, Etienne *see also* Girardot, Etienne

Giraldi, Giambattista 1504-1573 *OxThe*
Giraldi, Giovanni Battista 1504-1573 *NotNAT B*
Giraldi Cinthio, Giambattista 1504-1573 *McGWD*
Girard, Bernard 1929?- *FilmgC*
Girard, Henri *McGWD*
Girard, Joe 1871-1949 *WhScrn 2*
Girard, Joseph 1871-1949 *Film 1, Film 2, TwYS,
    WhoHol B*
Girard, Kate d1885 *NotNAT B*
Girard, Pete *Film 1*
Girardin, Ray *WhoHol A*
Girardot, Annie 1931- *FilmgC, IntMPA 1977,
    OxFilm, WhoHol A, WorEnF*
Girardot, Etienne 1856-1939 *Film 1, FilmgC,
    MovMk, NotNAT B, Vers B, WhoHol B,
    WhoStg 1906, WhoStg 1908*
Girardot, Etienne *see also* Giradot, Etienne
Girardot, Isabelle *WhoStg 1906, WhoStg 1908*
Giraud, Giovanni 1776-1834 *McGWD,
    NotNAT B*
Giraudoux, Jean 1882-1944 *CnMD, CnThe,
    McGWD, ModWD, NotNAT A, NotNAT B,
    OxThe, PIP&P, REnWD, WhThe*
Giritlian, Virginia *WomWMM*
Girotti, Massimo 1918- *FilmgC, WhoHol A,
    WorEnF*
Giroud, Francoise *WomWMM*
Giroux, Lee 1911-1973 *WhScrn 2*
Gish, Dorothy 1898-1968 *BiE&WWA, FamA&A,
    Film 1, Film 2, FilmgC, MotPP, MovMk,
    NotNAT A, NotNAT B, OxFilm, TwYS,
    WhScrn 1, WhScrn 2, WhThe, WhoHol B,
    WomWMM, WorEnF*
Gish, Lillian *MotPP, PIP&P, WomWMM*
Gish, Lillian 1893- *FamA&A, ThFT,
    WhoThe 16*
Gish, Lillian 1896- *BiDFlm, CelR 3, CmMov,
    Film 1, Film 2, FilmgC, MovMk,
    NotNAT A, TwYS, WhoHol A, WorEnF*
Gish, Lillian 1899- *BiE&WWA, IntMPA 1977,
    NotNAT, OxFilm*
Gish, Mary *Film 1*
Gissey, Henri 1621-1673 *OxThe*
Gist, Robert 1924- *FilmgC*
Gitana, Gertie 1887-1957 *NotNAT B, WhThe*
Gitana, Gertie 1889-1957 *OxThe*
Githens, W French 1906- *IntMPA 1977*
Gitlin, Irving d1967 *NewYTET*
Giusti, Vincenzo 1532-1619 *McGWD*
Givens, Jimmie d1964 *NotNAT B*
Givler, Mary Louise d1964 *NotNAT B*
Givney, Kathryn *WhoHol A*
Givot, George 1903- *FilmgC, MovMk*
Gladden, James *TwYS*
Glade, Sven *TwYS A*
Gladman, Annabelle 1899-1948 *WhScrn 1,
    WhScrn 2*
Gladman, Florence d1956 *NotNAT B*
Glagolin, Boris 1879-1948 *NotNAT A*
Glagolin, Boris S 1878-1948 *WhScrn 1, WhScrn 2*
Glanville, Maxwell *NatPD*
Glarum, L Stanley 1908- *AmSCAP 1966*
Glasel, John 1930- *AmSCAP 1966*
Glaser, Darel *WhoHol A*
Glaser, Hy 1923- *AmSCAP 1966*
Glaser, Lillian d1969 *WhoHol B*
Glaser, Lulu 1874-1958 *NotNAT B, WhThe,
    WhoHol B, WhoStg 1906, WhoStg 1908*
Glaser, Michael *WhoHol A*
Glaser, Sam 1912- *AmSCAP 1966*
Glaser, Sidney 1912- *IntMPA 1977*
Glaser, Sioma 1919- *AmSCAP 1966*
Glaser, Vaughan 1872-1958 *WhScrn 1, WhScrn 2*
Glaser, Vaughn 1872-1958 *WhoHol B*

Glaser, Victoria 1918- *AmSCAP 1966*
Glason, Billy 1904- *AmSCAP 1966*
Glaspell, Susan 1882-1948 *CnMD, McGWD,
    ModWD, NotNAT B, OxThe, PIP&P,
    WhThe*
Glass, Dudley 1899- *WhThe*
Glass, Everett 1891-1966 *WhScrn 2, WhoHol B*
Glass, Gaston d1965 *MotPP, WhoHol B*
Glass, Gaston 1898-1965 *WhScrn 1, WhScrn 2*
Glass, Gaston 1899-1965 *Film 1, Film 2, TwYS*
Glass, George 1910- *IntMPA 1977*
Glass, Joanna M *NatPD*
Glass, Montague 1877-1934 *NotNAT B, WhThe*
Glass, Ned *WhoHol A*
Glass, Paul Eugene 1934- *AmSCAP 1966*
Glass, Seamon *WhoHol A*
Glassberg, Irving *WorEnF*
Glasser, Albert 1916- *AmSCAP 1966*
Glassford, David 1866-1935 *NotNAT B, WhThe*
Glassman, Judith M 1946- *WomWMM B*
Glassman, Seth 1947- *NatPD*
Glassmire, Augustin J Gus 1879-1946 *WhScrn 1,
    WhScrn 2*
Glassmire, Gus 1879-1946 *WhoHol B*
Glassner, Erika *Film 2*
Glaum, Louise d1970 *MotPP, WhoHol B*
Glaum, Louise 1894-1970 *Film 1, Film 2, TwYS*
Glaum, Louise 1900-1970 *WhScrn 1, WhScrn 2*
Glazer, Eve F 1903-1960 *WhScrn 1, WhScrn 2*
Glazer, Melvin 1931- *AmSCAP 1966*
Glazer, Tom 1914- *AmSCAP 1966*
Glazier, Sidney 1918- *IntMPA 1977*
Gleason, Ada *Film 1, Film 2*
Gleason, Fred 1854-1933 *WhScrn 1, WhScrn 2*
Gleason, Jackie 1916- *AmSCAP 1966,
    BiE&WWA, CelR 3, EncMT, FilmgC,
    IntMPA 1977, MovMk, NewYTET,
    WhoHol A*
Gleason, James 1886-1959 *Film 2, FilmgC,
    MotPP, MovMk, NotNAT B, TwYS,
    Vers A, WhScrn 1, WhScrn 2, WhThe,
    WhoHol B*
Gleason, John 1941- *WhoThe 16*
Gleason, Keogh *IntMPA 1977*
Gleason, Lucile Webster d1947 *NotNAT B*
Gleason, Lucille 1886-1947 *Film 2, FilmgC*
Gleason, Lucille 1888-1947 *WhScrn 1, WhScrn 2,
    WhoHol B*
Gleason, Mary M 1931- *AmSCAP 1966*
Gleason, Russell d1945 *NotNAT B, WhoHol B*
Gleason, Russell 1906-1945 *MovMk*
Gleason, Russell 1908-1945 *Film 2, FilmgC,
    WhScrn 1, WhScrn 2*
Glebov, Anatoli Glebovich 1899- *ModWD*
Gleckler, Gayle *WomWMM*
Gleckler, Robert P 1890-1939 *Film 2, WhScrn 1,
    WhScrn 2, WhoHol B*
Gleich, Joseph Alois 1772-1841 *OxThe*
Gleizer, Judith *Film 2*
Glen, Irma *AmSCAP 1966*
Glendenning, Ernest 1884-1936 *Film 2, TwYS*
Glendinning, Ernest 1884-1936 *NotNAT B,
    WhScrn 1, WhScrn 2, WhThe, WhoHol B*
Glendinning, Ethel 1910- *WhThe*
Glendinning, John 1857-1916 *NotNAT B, WhThe,
    WhoStg 1906, WhoStg 1908*
Glendon, Frank d1937 *WhoHol B*
Glendon, J Frank 1885-1937 *Film 1, Film 2,
    TwYS*
Glendon, Jonathan Frank 1887-1937 *WhScrn 1,
    WhScrn 2*
Glenister, Frank 1860-1945 *WhThe*
Glenn, Charles Owen 1938- *IntMPA 1977*
Glenn, John 1921- *CelR 3*

Glenn, Raymond d1974 *Film 2, WhScrn 2,*
WhoHol B
Glenn, Roy E, Sr. 1915-1971 *WhScrn 1,*
WhScrn 2, WhoHol B
Glenn, Tyree 1912- *AmSCAP 1966*
Glennie, Brian 1912- *WhThe*
Glennon, Bert 1893-1967 *FilmgC*
Glennon, Bert 1895-1967 *CmMov, WorEnF*
Glenny, Charles H 1857-1922 *NotNAT B, WhThe*
Glenville, Peter 1913- *BiE&WWA, CelR 3,*
CnThe, FilmgC, NotNAT, WhoThe 16,
WorEnF
Glenville, Shaun 1884-1968 *NotNAT B, WhThe*
Gless, Eleanor M 1908- *AmSCAP 1966*
Glick, Hyman J 1904- *IntMPA 1977*
Glick, Jesse G M 1874-1938 *AmSCAP 1966*
Glickman, Fred 1903- *AmSCAP 1966*
Glickman, Joel 1930- *IntMPA 1977*
Glickman, Will 1910- *BiE&WWA*
Glicksman, Frank *NewYTET*
Globus, Diane *WomWMM B*
Gloeckner-Kramer, Pepi 1874-1954 *WhScrn 1,*
WhScrn 2
Glogau, Jack 1886-1953 *AmSCAP 1966*
Glori, Enrico 1901-1966 *WhScrn 1, WhScrn 2*
Glory, Mary *Film 2*
Glossop, Joseph d1835 *NotNAT B*
Glossop, Mrs. Joseph d1853 *NotNAT B*
Glossop-Harris, Florence 1883-1931 *NotNAT B,*
WhThe
Glover, Bruce *WhoHol A*
Glover, Charles William d1863 *NotNAT B*
Glover, David Carr, Jr. 1925- *AmSCAP 1966*
Glover, Edmund 1813-1860 *NotNAT B, OxThe*
Glover, Halcott 1877-1949 *NotNAT B, WhThe*
Glover, James Mackey 1861- *WhThe*
Glover, Joe 1903- *AmSCAP 1966*
Glover, Julia 1779-1850 *OxThe*
Glover, Julia 1781-1850 *NotNAT B*
Glover, Julian 1935- *FilmgC, WhoHol A,*
WhoThe 16
Glover, William 1911- *BiE&WWA, NotNAT*
Gluck, John 1925- *AmSCAP 1966*
Gluck, Norman E 1914- *IntMPA 1977*
Gluckman, Bernard L 1909- *AmSCAP 1966*
Gluckman, Leon 1922- *WhoThe 16*
Glucksman, Ernest D *IntMPA 1977, NewYTET*
Glyn, Elinor 1864-1943 *Film 2, FilmgC, OxFilm,*
WomWMM
Glyn, Neva Carr d1975 *WhScrn 2, WhoHol C*
Glynne, Angela 1933- *WhThe*
Glynne, Derke *Film 2*
Glynne, Marg 1898-1954 *Film 1, Film 2*
Glynne, Mary 1898-1954 *FilmgC, NotNAT B,*
WhScrn 1, WhScrn 2, WhThe, WhoHol B
Gnass, Friedrich 1892-1958 *WhScrn 2*
Gnessin, Menahem 1882-1953 *OxThe*
Goatman, Alan H 1918- *IntMPA 1977*
Gobbi, Anna *WomWMM*
Gobble, Harry A Hank 1923-1961 *WhScrn 1,*
WhScrn 2
Gobeil, Charlotte *WomWMM*
Gobel, George 1919- *FilmgC, NewYTET,*
WhoHol A
Goberman, Max d1962 *NotNAT B*
Godard, Jean-Luc 1930- *BiDFlm, CelR 3, DcFM,*
FilmgC, MovMk, OxFilm, WomWMM,
WorEnF
Godbold, Geoff 1935- *IntMPA 1977*
Godd, Barbara d1944 *NotNAT B*
Goddard, Alf *Film 2*
Goddard, Charles W 1879-1951 *NotNAT B,*
WhThe
Goddard, Glendon Boyce 1899- *AmSCAP 1966*

Goddard, Mark *WhoHol A*
Goddard, Paulette 1911- *BiDFlm, CelR 3,*
CmMov, Film 2, FilmgC, IntMPA 1977,
MotPP, MovMk, OxFilm, ThFT, WhoHol A,
WorEnF
Goddard, Willoughby 1926- *WhoThe 16*
Goddard, Willoughby 1927- *FilmgC*
Godden, Jimmy 1879-1955 *NotNAT B, WhThe*
Godden, Rumer 1907- *FilmgC*
Godderis, Albert 1882-1971 *WhScrn 2*
Goderis, Albert 1882-1971 *WhoHol B*
Godfrey, Arthur 1903- *AmSCAP 1966, CelR 3,*
IntMPA 1977, NewYTET, WhoHol A
Godfrey, Bob 1921- *FilmgC*
Godfrey, Charles 1851-1900 *OxThe*
Godfrey, Derek 1924- *WhoThe 16*
Godfrey, G W d1897 *NotNAT B*
Godfrey, George *Film 2*
Godfrey, Keith d1976 *NewYTET*
Godfrey, Peter 1899-1970 *FilmgC, WhScrn 1,*
WhScrn 2, WhThe, WhoHol B
Godfrey, Renee Haal 1920-1964 *NotNAT B,*
WhScrn 1, WhScrn 2, WhoHol B
Godfrey, Robert H 1904- *IntMPA 1977*
Godfrey, Robert H 1905- *AmSCAP 1966*
Godfrey, Sam d1935 *WhoHol B*
Godfrey, Samuel T 1891-1935 *WhScrn 1,*
WhScrn 2
Godfrey, Thomas 1736-1763 *NotNAT B, OxThe,*
PIP&P
Godfrey-Turner, L *WhThe*
Godmilow, Jill *WomWMM A, WomWMM B*
Godowsky, Dagmar 1897-1975 *Film 2, MotPP,*
TwYS, WhScrn 2, WhoHol C
Godowsky, Dagmar *see also* Gowdowsky, Dagmar
Godowsky, Leopold 1870-1938 *AmSCAP 1966*
Godsell, Vanda 1919?- *FilmgC, WhoHol A*
Godwin, Edward William 1833-1886 *NotNAT B,*
OxThe
Godwin, Frank *IntMPA 1977*
Godwin, Harry E 1906- *AmSCAP 1966*
Goehring, George 1933- *AmSCAP 1966*
Goell, Kermit 1915- *AmSCAP 1966*
Goering, Al 1898-1963 *AmSCAP 1966*
Goering, Reinhard 1887-1936 *CnMD, McGWD,*
ModWD
Goethals, Stanley *Film 2*
Goethe, Johann Wolfgang Von 1749-1832 *CnThe,*
McGWD, NotNAT B, OxThe, REnWD
Goetschius, Marjorie 1915- *AmSCAP 1966*
Goetz, Augustus d1957 *NotNAT B*
Goetz, Ben 1891- *FilmgC*
Goetz, Carl *Film 2*
Goetz, Curt 1888-1960 *CnMD, CroCD, McGWD*
Goetz, E Ray 1886-1954 *AmSCAP 1966, EncMT,*
NewMT, NotNAT B
Goetz, Harry M 1888- *IntMPA 1977*
Goetz, Ruth Goodman 1912- *BiE&WWA,*
NotNAT, WhoThe 16
Goetz, William 1903-1968 *FilmgC, WorEnF*
Goetz, Wolfgang 1885-1955 *CnMD, ModWD*
Goetzke, Bernard *Film 2*
Goetzke, Bernhard 1884-1964 *WhScrn 2*
Goetzl, Anselm d1923 *NotNAT B*
Goff, Ivan 1910- *FilmgC, WorEnF*
Goff, Lewin 1919- *BiE&WWA, NotNAT*
Goff, Norris 1906- *WhoHol A*
Goffin, Cora 1902- *WhThe*
Goffin, Peter 1906- *WhThe*
Goforth, Frances *BiE&WWA, NotNAT*
Gofton, E Story d1939 *NotNAT B*
Gogoberidze, Lana *WomWMM*
Gogol, Nikolai Vasilievich 1809-1852 *CnThe,*
OxThe, PIP&P, REnWD

Gogol, Nikolai Vassilievitch 1809-1852 *NotNAT A,*
  NotNAT B
Gogol, Nikolay Vasilyevich 1809-1852 *McGWD*
Gohman, Donald 1927- *AmSCAP 1966*
Going, Frederica 1895-1959 *WhScrn 2*
Golan, Gila 1940?- *FilmgC, WhoHol A*
Golan, Menahem 1931- *FilmgC*
Gold, Anita 1932- *AmSCAP 1966*
Gold, Belle *WhoStg 1906, WhoStg 1908*
Gold, Bert 1917- *AmSCAP 1966*
Gold, Edward Louis 1947- *NatPD*
Gold, Ernest 1921- *AmSCAP 1966, FilmgC,*
  OxFilm, WorEnF
Gold, Jack 1930- *FilmgC*
Gold, Jacob 1921- *AmSCAP 1966*
Gold, Jimmy 1886-1967 *FilmgC, WhScrn 1,*
  WhScrn 2, WhoHol B
Gold, Joe 1894- *AmSCAP 1966*
Gold, Lloyd *NatPD*
Gold, Martin 1915- *AmSCAP 1966*
Gold, Melvin 1909- *IntMPA 1977*
Gold, Michael 1894-1967 *CnMD, ModWD*
Gold, Wally 1928- *AmSCAP 1966*
Goldbeck, Willis 1900- *FilmgC, WorEnF*
Goldberg, Arthur 1908- *CelR 3*
Goldberg, Fred 1921- *IntMPA 1977*
Goldberg, Harry 1912- *AmSCAP 1966*
Goldberg, Jenny *WomWMM B*
Goldberg, Leon 1900- *IntMPA 1977*
Goldberg, Leonard *IntMPA 1977*
Goldberg, Mark L 1927- *AmSCAP 1966*
Goldberg, Nathan d1961 *NotNAT B*
Goldberg, Reuben L 1883-1970 *AmSCAP 1966*
Goldberg, Rube 1883-1970 *WhScrn 2*
Goldberg, Sharon *WomWMM B*
Goldberger-Jacoby, Susan *WomWMM B*
Goldblatt, Harold M 1888- *AmSCAP 1966*
Golde, Walter H 1887-1963 *AmSCAP 1966*
Goldemberg, Rose Leiman *NatPD*
Golden, Bill d1959 *NewYTET*
Golden, Bob *WhoHol A*
Golden, Edward J, Jr. 1934- *BiE&WWA,*
  NotNAT
Golden, Ernie 1890- *AmSCAP 1966*
Golden, Harry 1902- *CelR 3*
Golden, Herbert L *IntMPA 1977*
Golden, Jerome B 1917- *IntMPA 1977*
Golden, John 1874-1955 *AmSCAP 1966,*
  NotNAT A, NotNAT B, WhThe
Golden, Joseph 1928- *BiE&WWA, NotNAT*
Golden, Marta *Film 1*
Golden, Michael *WhoHol A*
Golden, Michael 1913- *WhoThe 16*
Golden, Nathan D 1895- *IntMPA 1977*
Golden, Olive *Film 1*
Golden, Olive Fuller. *WhoHol A*
Golden, Richard 1854- *WhoStg 1906,*
  WhoStg 1908
Golden, Sylvia *AmSCAP 1966*
Goldenberg, Morris 1911- *AmSCAP 1966*
Goldenberg, Sam d1945 *WhoHol B*
Goldenberg, Samuel 1886-1945 *WhScrn 1,*
  WhScrn 2
Goldenberg, William Leon 1936- *AmSCAP 1966*
Goldenson, Leonard H 1905- *CelR 3,*
  IntMPA 1977, NewYTET
Golder, Jennie d1928 *NotNAT B*
Golder, Lew d1962 *NotNAT B*
Goldfaden, Abraham 1840-1908 *CnThe, McGWD,*
  ModWD, NotNAT B, OxThe, REnWD
Goldfaden, Wolf *Film 2*
Goldie, F Wyndham 1897-1957 *NotNAT B,*
  WhThe
Goldie, Hugh 1919- *WhoThe 16*

Goldie, Wyndham 1897-1957 *WhoHol B*
Goldin, Horace *WhThe*
Goldin, Pat 1902-1971 *WhScrn 2*
Goldina, Miriam 1898- *BiE&WWA, NotNAT,*
  WhoHol A
Golding, David *IntMPA 1977*
Golding, William 1911- *ModWD*
Goldini, Carlo 1707-1793 *CnThe*
Goldman, A E O 1947- *NatPD*
Goldman, Edmund 1906- *IntMPA 1977*
Goldman, Edwin Franko 1878-1956 *AmSCAP 1966,*
  NotNAT B
Goldman, Irving 1909- *BiE&WWA*
Goldman, James 1927- *BiE&WWA, ConDr 1977,*
  FilmgC, McGWD, NotNAT
Goldman, Les 1913- *IntMPA 1977*
Goldman, Maurice *AmSCAP 1966*
Goldman, Michael F 1939- *IntMPA 1977*
Goldman, Michal *WomWMM B*
Goldman, Milton 1914- *BiE&WWA*
Goldman, Richard Franko 1910- *AmSCAP 1966*
Goldman, Robert 1932- *AmSCAP 1966*
Goldman, William 1931- *BiE&WWA,*
  ConDr 1977A, FilmgC, NotNAT
Goldmark, Peter C *NewYTET*
Goldner, Charles 1900-1955 *FilmgC, NotNAT B,*
  WhScrn 1, WhScrn 2, WhThe, WhoHol B
Goldoni, Carlo 1707-1793 *McGWD, NotNAT A,*
  NotNAT B, OxThe, PIP&P, REnWD
Goldoni, Lelia 1938?- *FilmgC, WhoHol A*
Goldsboro, Bobby 1941- *CelR 3*
Goldsby, Robert 1926- *BiE&WWA, NotNAT*
Goldscholl, Mildred *WomWMM*
Goldscholl, Morton *WomWMM*
Goldsholl, Millie *WomWMM B*
Goldsmith, Frank *Film 1*
Goldsmith, George *BiE&WWA*
Goldsmith, Jerry 1930- *CmMov, FilmgC,*
  IntMPA 1977, WorEnF
Goldsmith, Lee 1923- *NatPD*
Goldsmith, Martin M 1913- *IntMPA 1977*
Goldsmith, Oliver 1728?-1774 *McGWD,*
  NotNAT A, NotNAT B
Goldsmith, Oliver 1730?-1774 *CnThe, OxThe,*
  PIP&P, REnWD
Goldsmith, Silvianna *WomWMM B*
Goldsmith, Ted 1909- *BiE&WWA*
Goldstein, Becky 1887-1971 *WhScrn 1, WhScrn 2*
Goldstein, David M 1937- *IntMPA 1977*
Goldstein, Jennie 1897-1960 *NotNAT B,*
  WhoHol B
Goldstein, Kay *WomWMM B*
Goldstein, Milton 1926- *IntMPA 1977*
Goldstein, Robert Gary 1938- *AmSCAP 1966*
Goldstein, William S 1926- *AmSCAP 1966*
Goldstone, James 1931- *FilmgC, IntMPA 1977*
Goldstone, Jules C 1900- *IntMPA 1977*
Goldstone, Richard 1912- *FilmgC, IntMPA 1977*
Goldsworthy, William Arthur 1878-
  AmSCAP 1966
Goldwater, Barry 1909- *CelR 3*
Goldwurm, Jean *IntMPA 1977*
Goldwyn, Sam 1884- *TwYS B*
Goldwyn, Samuel 1882-1974 *CelR 3, FilmgC,*
  OxFilm
Goldwyn, Samuel 1884-1974 *BiDFlm, DcFM,*
  WorEnF
Goldwyn, Samuel, Jr. 1926- *FilmgC,*
  IntMPA 1977
Golestan, Ebrahim 1923- *DcFM*
Golitzen, Alexander 1907- *WorEnF*
Golizin, Natalie *Film 2*
Goll, Yvan 1891-1950 *ModWD*
Gollahon, Gladys 1908- *AmSCAP 1966*

Gollings, Franklin *IntMPA 1977*
Golm, Ernest 1886-1962 *WhScrn 2*
Golm, Lisa d1964 *WhScrn 2*
Golonka, Arlene 1936- *BiE&WWA, NotNAT, WhoHol A*
Golovnya, Anatoli N 1900- *DcFM*
Golson, Benny 1929- *AmSCAP 1966*
Golubeff, Gregory d1958 *WhScrn 1, WhScrn 2, WhoHol B*
Golz, Rosemary 1880-1963 *WhScrn 2*
Gomarov, Mikhail *Film 2*
Gombauld, Jean 1570-1666 *OxThe*
Gombell, Minna 1892-1973 *MovMk, WhScrn 2, WhoHol B*
Gombell, Minna 1893-1973 *ThFT, WhThe*
Gombell, Minna 1900-1973 *Film 2, FilmgC*
Gombrowicz, Witold 1904-1969 *CnMD, CroCD, McGWD, ModWD*
Gomez, Augustine Augie Whitecloud 1891-1966 *WhScrn 1, WhScrn 2*
Gomez, Inez *Film 2*
Gomez, Ralph 1897-1954 *WhScrn 1, WhScrn 2*
Gomez, Thomas 1905-1971 *BiE&WWA, CmMov, FilmgC, MovMk, NotNAT B, Vers A, WhScrn 1, WhScrn 2, WhoHol B*
Gomez, Vicente 1911- *AmSCAP 1966*
Gomez DeAvellaneda, Gertrudis 1814-1873 *CnThe, REnWD*
Gomez-Quinones, Ronda *WomWMM*
Gomorov, G *Film 2*
Gomorov, Mikhail *Film 2*
Goncharova, Nathalie 1881-1962 *OxThe*
Goncourt, Edmond-Louis-Antoine Huot De 1822-1896 *NotNAT B, OxThe*
Goncourt, Jules-Alfred Huot De 1830-1870 *NotNAT B, OxThe*
Gonder, Bill *Film 2*
Gondi, Harry 1900-1968 *WhScrn 1, WhScrn 2*
Gonsalves, John P 1925- *AmSCAP 1966*
Gonzales, Gilberto d1954 *WhoHol B*
Gonzales, Jimmy d1971 *WhoHol B*
Gonzales, Mark *Film 2*
Gonzales, Myrtle *Film 1*
Gonzales, Pancho 1928- *CelR 3*
Gonzalez, Aaron 1908- *AmSCAP 1966*
Gonzalez, Gilberto 1906-1954 *WhScrn 1, WhScrn 2*
Gonzalez, Gloria *NatPD*
Gonzalez, Mario Tecero 1919-1957 *WhScrn 1, WhScrn 2*
Gonzalez, Myrtle 1891-1918 *WhScrn 2*
Gonzalez, Nilda 1929- *BiE&WWA*
Gonzalez-Gonzales, Pedro 1926- *WhoHol A*
Gonzalez-Gonzales, Pedro 1926- *IntMPA 1977*
Gonzalo, Maria Eduarda 1929-1955 *WhScrn 1, WhScrn 2*
Gooch, Steve 1945- *ConDr 1977*
Good, Kip 1919-1964 *NotNAT B, WhScrn 1, WhScrn 2, WhoHol B*
Goodale, Elois *Film 2*
Goodale, George P d1920 *NotNAT B*
Goodall, Charlotte d1830 *NotNAT B*
Goodall, Edyth 1886-1929 *NotNAT B, WhThe*
Goodall, Grace *Film 2*
Goode, Jack 1908-1971 *WhScrn 1, WhScrn 2, WhoHol B*
Goode, Richard L 1922- *IntMPA 1977*
Goodfried, Robert *IntMPA 1977*
Goodhart, Al 1905-1955 *AmSCAP 1966*
Goodhart, William *NotNAT*
Goodis, Jay 1931- *AmSCAP 1966*
Goodliffe, Michael 1914-1976 *FilmgC, WhoHol C, WhoThe 16*
Goodman, Abe I *IntMPA 1977*

Goodman, Alfred 1890- *AmSCAP 1966, BiE&WWA*
Goodman, Benny 1909- *AmSCAP 1966, CelR 3, FilmgC, WhoHol A*
Goodman, Cardell 1649?-1699 *OxThe*
Goodman, Cardell 1653-1713? *NotNAT A*
Goodman, Cardonnel 1649?-1699 *OxThe*
Goodman, Dody *BiE&WWA, NotNAT, WhoHol A, WhoThe 16*
Goodman, Edward d1962 *NotNAT B, PIP&P*
Goodman, Frank 1894-1958 *AmSCAP 1966*
Goodman, Frank 1916- *BiE&WWA*
Goodman, John B 1901- *CmMov, IntMPA 1977*
Goodman, Jules Eckert 1876-1962 *McGWD, NotNAT B, WhThe*
Goodman, Julian 1922- *IntMPA 1977, NewYTET*
Goodman, Lillian Rosedale 1887- *AmSCAP 1966*
Goodman, Linda *CelR 3*
Goodman, Mark D 1880- *AmSCAP 1966*
Goodman, Maurice, Jr. 1921- *AmSCAP 1966*
Goodman, Mort 1910- *IntMPA 1977*
Goodman, Murray 1911- *IntMPA 1977*
Goodman, Paul 1911-1972 *ConDr 1973*
Goodman, Pearlyn *WomWMM B*
Goodman, Philip d1940 *NotNAT B, WhThe*
Goodman, Randolph 1908- *BiE&WWA, NotNAT*
Goodman, Saul *AmSCAP 1966*
Goodner, Carol 1904- *BiE&WWA, NotNAT, WhThe, WhoHol A*
Goodpaster, Andrew J 1915- *CelR 3*
Goodrich, Amy 1889-1939 *WhScrn 1, WhScrn 2*
Goodrich, Arthur 1878-1941 *NotNAT B, WhThe*
Goodrich, Charles W 1861-1931 *WhScrn 1, WhScrn 2*
Goodrich, Diane *WomWMM B*
Goodrich, Edna 1883- *Film 1, WhThe, WhoStg 1906, WhoStg 1908*
Goodrich, Edna 1883-1971 *WhScrn 2*
Goodrich, Edna 1883-1974 *WhoHol B*
Goodrich, Frances *BiE&WWA, NotNAT, WomWMM*
Goodrich, Frances 1891?- *McGWD, WorEnF*
Goodrich, Frances 1896- *CmMov*
Goodrich, Frances 1901- *FilmgC*
Goodrich, G W d1931 *WhoHol B*
Goodrich, Jack *Film 2*
Goodrich, Katherine *Film 1*
Goodrich, Louis 1865-1945 *NotNAT B, WhScrn 1, WhScrn 2, WhThe, WhoHol B*
Goodsell, Alice *Film 2*
Goodsell, G Dean 1907- *BiE&WWA*
Goodson, Mark 1915- *IntMPA 1977*
Goodwin, Aline *Film 2*
Goodwin, Bernard 1907- *IntMPA 1977*
Goodwin, Bill d1959 *WhoHol B*
Goodwin, Bill 1910-1958 *FilmgC, MotPP, WhScrn 1, WhScrn 2*
Goodwin, Charles D 1929- *AmSCAP 1966*
Goodwin, Ewart 1907- *BiE&WWA*
Goodwin, Harold *WhoHol A*
Goodwin, Harold 1902- *Film 1, Film 2, TwYS, Vers B*
Goodwin, Harold 1917- *FilmgC*
Goodwin, J Cheever 1850- *WhThe, WhoStg 1906, WhoStg 1908*
Goodwin, Jim *WhoHol A*
Goodwin, Joe 1889-1943 *AmSCAP 1966*
Goodwin, John 1921- *WhoThe 16*
Goodwin, Nat C 1857-1919 *NotNAT A, NotNAT B, OxThe, WhScrn 2, WhThe*
Goodwin, Nat C 1857-1920 *WhScrn 1, WhoHol B*
Goodwin, Nat C 1859-1919 *Film 1*
Goodwin, Nathaniel Carl, Jr. 1857-1919 *FamA&A, WhoStg 1906, WhoStg 1908*

Goodwin, Rom *Film 1*
Goodwin, Ron *CmMov, FilmgC*
Goodwin, Ronald *IntMPA 1977*
Goodwin, Ruby Berkley d1961 *WhScrn 1,*
　WhScrn 2, WhoHol B
Goodwin, Tom *Film 2*
Goodwin, Walter 1889- *AmSCAP 1966*
Goodwins, Ercell Woods *WhScrn 1, WhScrn 2*
Goodwins, Fred *Film 1, Film 2*
Goodwins, Leslie 1899-1969 *FilmgC, WhScrn 1,*
　WhScrn 2, WhoHol B
Goolagong, Evonne 1951- *CelR 3*
Goold, Sam 1893-1931 *AmSCAP 1966*
Goolden, Richard 1891- *WhoThe 16*
Goolden, Richard 1895- *FilmgC*
Goossens, Sir Eugene d1962 *NotNAT B*
Gopal, Ram 1917- *WhThe*
Gopo, Ion Popescu *DcFM*
Goralski, Robert *NewYTET*
Gorcey, Bernard 1888-1955 *Film 2, FilmgC,*
　NotNAT B, Vers B, WhScrn 1, WhScrn 2,
　WhoHol B
Gorcey, Leo 1915-1969 *FilmgC, MotPP, MovMk,*
　WhScrn 1, WhScrn 2, WhoHol B
Gorchakov, Nicolai Mikhailovich 1899-1958 *OxThe*
Gordin, Jacob 1853-1909 *CnThe, McGWD,*
　ModWD, NotNAT B, OxThe, REnWD
Gordon, A George 1882-1953 *WhScrn 1,*
　WhScrn 2
Gordon, Alen 1932- *AmSCAP 1966*
Gordon, Alex 1922- *IntMPA 1977*
Gordon, Barbara *WomWMM B*
Gordon, Barry 1948- *BiE&WWA*
Gordon, Bert 1898-1974 *WhScrn 2, WhoHol B*
Gordon, Bert I 1922- *FilmgC, IntMPA 1977*
Gordon, Bette *WomWMM B*
Gordon, Betty *Film 2*
Gordon, Bobby 1904-1973 *WhScrn 2*
Gordon, Bobby 1913- *Film 2*
Gordon, Bruce *TwYS, WhoHol A*
Gordon, Bruce 1916- *BiE&WWA, NotNAT*
Gordon, Bruce 1919- *Film 2, FilmgC*
Gordon, C Henry d1940 *MotPP, WhoHol B*
Gordon, C Henry 1874-1940 *MovMk*
Gordon, C Henry 1883-1940 *WhScrn 1,*
　WhScrn 2
Gordon, C Henry 1884-1940 *FilmgC, Vers A*
Gordon, Charles *Film 2*
Gordon, Charles Kilbourn 1888- *WhThe*
Gordon, Clarke *WhoHol A*
Gordon, Colin 1911-1972 *FilmgC, WhScrn 2,*
　WhThe, WhoHol B
Gordon, Constance Kitty 1888-1974 *WhScrn 2*
Gordon, Constance Kitty *see also* Gordon, Kitty
Gordon, Daniel *WhoHol A*
Gordon, Don *WhoHol A*
Gordon, Dorothy *Film 2, WhoHol A*
Gordon, Douglas *WhoHol A*
Gordon, Douglas 1871-1935 *NotNAT B, WhThe*
Gordon, Edward R 1886-1938 *WhScrn 1,*
　WhScrn 2, WhoHol B
Gordon, Eva *Film 2*
Gordon, G Swayne 1880-1949 *NotNAT B,*
　WhScrn 1, WhScrn 2
Gordon, Gale 1906- *FilmgC, IntMPA 1977,*
　MovMk, WhoHol A
Gordon, Gavin 1901-1970 *Film 2, FilmgC,*
　NotNAT B, WhScrn 1, WhScrn 2, WhThe,
　WhoHol B
Gordon, George Lash d1895 *NotNAT B*
Gordon, Gloria d1962 *NotNAT B, WhScrn 1,*
　WhScrn 2, WhoHol B
Gordon, Grace *Film 2*
Gordon, Grant *WhoHol A*

Gordon, Hal 1894-1946 *FilmgC, WhoHol B*
Gordon, Hal 1910- *AmSCAP 1966*
Gordon, Harold 1919-1959 *WhScrn 1, WhScrn 2,*
　WhoHol B
Gordon, Harris 1887-1947 *Film 2, WhScrn 1,*
　WhScrn 2, WhoHol B
Gordon, Hayes 1920- *BiE&WWA, WhoThe 16*
Gordon, Huntley 1897-1956 *Film 1, MotPP,*
　MovMk, NotNAT B, TwYS, WhoHol B
Gordon, Huntly 1897-1956 *Film 2, WhScrn 1,*
　WhScrn 2
Gordon, Irving 1915- *AmSCAP 1966*
Gordon, James 1881-1941 *Film 2, WhScrn 1,*
　WhScrn 2, WhoHol B
Gordon, James M d1944 *NotNAT B*
Gordon, Joan *Film 2*
Gordon, Julia Swayne 1879-1933 *Film 1, Film 2,*
　TwYS, WhScrn 1, WhScrn 2, WhoHol B
Gordon, Kay *Film 2*
Gordon, Kitty 1870- *Film 1, TwYS*
Gordon, Kitty 1878-1974 *WhThe, WhoHol B*
Gordon, Kitty *see also* Gordon, Constance Kitty
Gordon, Leo 1922- *FilmgC, WhoHol A*
Gordon, Leon 1884-1960 *WhThe*
Gordon, Leon 1895-1960 *NotNAT B, WhoHol B*
Gordon, Mack 1904-1959 *AmSCAP 1966,*
　NotNAT B, WhoHol B
Gordon, Marjorie 1893- *WhThe*
Gordon, Mary d1963 *MotPP, WhoHol B*
Gordon, Mary 1881-1963 *Film 2*
Gordon, Mary 1882-1963 *FilmgC, MovMk, ThFT,*
　Vers B, WhScrn 1, WhScrn 2
Gordon, Maud Turner 1868-1940 *WhScrn 2*
Gordon, Maude Turner 1870- *Film 1, Film 2,*
　TwYS
Gordon, Max 1892- *BiE&WWA, EncMT,*
　NotNAT, NotNAT A, WhThe
Gordon, Michael 1909- *BiDFlm, BiE&WWA,*
　FilmgC, IntMPA 1977, MovMk, NotNAT,
　WorEnF
Gordon, Noele 1923- *WhThe*
Gordon, Nora 1894-1970 *WhScrn 1, WhScrn 2,*
　WhoHol B
Gordon, Paul 1886-1929 *NotNAT B, WhScrn 2*
Gordon, Pete *Film 2*
Gordon, Peter 1888-1943 *WhScrn 1, WhScrn 2*
Gordon, Philip 1894- *AmSCAP 1966*
Gordon, Richard 1925- *IntMPA 1977*
Gordon, Richard H 1893-1956 *WhScrn 1,*
　WhScrn 2, WhoHol B
Gordon, Robert *NatPD*
Gordon, Robert 1895-1971 *Film 1, Film 2,*
　TwYS, WhScrn 1, WhScrn 2, WhoHol B
Gordon, Robert C 1941- *AmSCAP 1966*
Gordon, Robert J 1911- *AmSCAP 1966*
Gordon, Roy Turner *Film 2*
Gordon, Ruth 1896- *BiE&WWA, CelR 3,*
　CnThe, Film 1, FilmgC, IntMPA 1977,
　MotPP, MovMk, NatPD, NotNAT,
　NotNAT A, OxFilm, PIP&P, WhoHol A,
　WhoThe 16, WomWMM, WorEnF
Gordon, Sadie *Film 2*
Gordon, Vera 1886-1948 *Film 2, MovMk,*
　NotNAT B, TwYS, WhScrn 1, WhScrn 2,
　WhoHol B
Gordon, Walter d1892 *NotNAT B*
Gordon-Lee, Kathleen *WhThe*
Gordon-Lennox, Cosmo 1869-1921 *NotNAT B,*
　WhThe
Gordone, Charles *PIP&P, WhoHol A*
Gordone, Charles 1925- *ConDr 1977, McGWD,*
　NotNAT
Gordone, Charles Edward 1927- *WhoThe 16*
Gordoni, Arthur *Film 2*

Gordy, Berry, Jr. *CelR 3, IntMPA 1977*
Gore, Catherine d1861 *NotNAT B*
Gore, Lesley , *WhoHol A*
Gore, Rosa 1867-1941 *Film 2, WhScrn 1,*
  WhScrn 2, WhoHol B
Gore-Browne, Robert 1893- *WhThe*
Gorelik, Mordecai 1899- *BiE&WWA, NotNAT,*
  PIP&P, WhoThe 16
Goren, Charles 1901- *CelR 3*
Gorgeous George 1915-1963 *NewYTET,*
  WhScrn 1, WhScrn 2, WhoHol B
Gorgey, Gabor 1929- *CroCD*
Gorham, Charles *Film 2*
Gorin, Igor 1908- *AmSCAP 1966*
Goring, Marius 1912- *CnThe, FilmgC,*
  IntMPA 1977, MotPP, MovMk, PIP&P,
  WhoHol A, WhoThe 16
Gorki, Maxim 1868-1936 *CnMD, NotNAT A,*
  NotNAT B, PIP&P, PIP&P A
Gorky, Maxim 1868-1936 *CnThe, FilmgC,*
  McGWD, ModWD, OxFilm, OxThe,
  REnWD
Gorley, Edward *Film 2*
Gorman, Bill *Film 2*
Gorman, Charles *Film 2*
Gorman, Cliff *WhoHol A, WhoThe 16*
Gorman, Cliff 1936- *NotNAT*
Gorman, Cliff 1937- *CelR 3*
Gorman, Eric 1886-1971 *WhScrn 1, WhScrn 2,*
  WhoHol B
Gorman, Patrick E 1892- *AmSCAP 1966*
Gorman, Stephanie 1949-1965 *WhScrn 2*
Gorman, Tom 1908-1971 *WhScrn 1, WhScrn 2,*
  WhoHol B
Gorme, Eydie 1932- *CelR 3*
Gorney, Jay 1896- *AmSCAP 1966, BiE&WWA,*
  NewMT, NotNAT
Gorney, Karen *WhoHol A*
Gorody, George 1914- *AmSCAP 1966*
Gorog, Laszlo 1903- *IntMPA 1977*
Gorshin, Frank 1935- *FilmgC, WhoHol A*
Gorss, Saul M 1908-1966 *WhScrn 1, WhScrn 2,*
  WhoHol B
Gorsse, Henry De 1868- *WhThe*
Gortner, Marjoe *WhoHol A*
Gosden, Freeman F 1896-1976 *NewYTET,*
  WhoHol A
Gosfield, Maurice 1913-1964 *WhScrn 1,*
  WhScrn 2, WhoHol B
Gosford, Alice Peckham 1886-1919 *WhScrn 2*
Gosho, Heinosuke 1901- *FilmgC*
Gosho, Heinosuke 1902- *BiDFlm, DcFM,*
  OxFilm, WorEnF
Gosling, Harold 1897- *WhThe*
Gosnell, Evelyn 1896-1947 *Film 2, WhScrn 2*
Goss, Helen *WhoHol A*
Goss, Walter *Film 2*
Gosse, Sir Edmund William 1849-1928 *NotNAT B*
Gossett, Lou 1936- *WhoHol A*
Gossett, Louis 1936- *BiE&WWA, NotNAT*
Gossman, Irving d1964 *NotNAT B*
Gosson, Stephen 1554-1642 *NotNAT B*
Gosting, Richard 1941- *AmSCAP 1966*
Got, Edmond-Francois-Jules 1822-1901 *NotNAT B,*
  OxThe
Gotham Quartette, The *Film 2*
Gothie, Robert *WhoHol A*
Gott, Barbara d1944 *Film 2, WhThe*
Gottel, Oscar *Film 2*
Gottel, Otto *Film 2*
Gottesfeld, Chone d1964 *NotNAT B*
Gottfried, Martin 1933- *BiE&WWA, NotNAT*
Gottler, Archie *Film 2*
Gottler, Archie 1896-1959 *AmSCAP 1966*

Gottler, Jerome 1915- *AmSCAP 1966*
Gottlieb, Alex 1906- *IntMPA 1977*
Gottlieb, Arthur d1962 *NotNAT B*
Gottlieb, David d1962 *NotNAT B*
Gottlieb, Ira 1916- *IntMPA 1977*
Gottlieb, Jack 1930- *AmSCAP 1966*
Gottlieb, Linda *WomWMM, WomWMM B*
Gottlieb, Louis E 1923- *AmSCAP 1966*
Gottlieb, Morton 1921- *BiE&WWA, NotNAT,*
  WhoThe 16
Gottlieb, Stan 1917- *IntMPA 1977*
Gottlober, Abraham Dov Ber 1811-1899 *McGWD*
Gottlober, Sigmund 1888-1967 *NotNAT B*
Gottowt, John *Film 2*
Gottschalk, Christian *Film 2*
Gottschalk, Ferdinand 1858-1944 *MovMk,*
  NotNAT B, WhThe
Gottschalk, Ferdinand 1869-1944 *Film 2,*
  WhScrn 1, WhScrn 2, WhoHol B
Gottschalk, Joachim 1904-1941 *WhScrn 2*
Gottschalk, Robert 1918- *IntMPA 1977*
Gottschall, Rudolf Von d1909 *NotNAT B*
Gottsched, Johann Christoph 1700-1766 *CnThe,*
  McGWD, NotNAT B, OxThe, REnWD
Gottuso, Tony 1916- *AmSCAP 1966*
Gotwals, John W, III 1938- *AmSCAP 1966*
Gotz, Carl *Film 2*
Gotz, Curt *Film 2*
Gotz, Karl *Film 2*
Gouch, John 1897- *Film 2*
Goudal, Jetta 1898- *Film 2, FilmgC, MotPP,*
  MovMk, TwYS, WhoHol A
Goudeau, Lee, Jr. 1936- *AmSCAP 1966*
Gough, Alexander 1614- *OxThe*
Gough, John 1897-1968 *TwYS, WhScrn 1,*
  WhScrn 2, WhoHol B
Gough, Lloyd *WhoHol A*
Gough, Michael 1917- *FilmgC, MovMk,*
  WhoHol A, WhoThe 16
Gough, Robert d1625 *OxThe*
Gough, Wilfred Captain *Film 2*
Gould, Bernard d1945 *NotNAT B*
Gould, Billy 1869-1950 *Film 2, NotNAT B,*
  WhScrn 2, WhoHol B
Gould, Chester 1931- *CelR 3*
Gould, Danny 1911- *AmSCAP 1966*
Gould, Diana *WomWMM A, WomWMM B*
Gould, Diana 1913- *WhThe*
Gould, Dorothy *WhoHol A*
Gould, Edith Kingdon d1921 *NotNAT B*
Gould, Edward E 1911- *AmSCAP 1966*
Gould, Elizabeth 1904- *AmSCAP 1966*
Gould, Elliott 1938- *BiE&WWA, CelR 3,*
  EncMT, FilmgC, IntMPA 1977, MovMk,
  WhoHol A, WhoThe 16
Gould, Fred d1917 *NotNAT B*
Gould, Harold *WhoHol A*
Gould, Harold d1952 *NotNAT B*
Gould, Harry 1898- *BiE&WWA*
Gould, Howard d1938 *NotNAT B, WhoStg 1908*
Gould, Jack 1917- *AmSCAP 1966, NewYTET*
Gould, James F 1908- *IntMPA 1977*
Gould, John 1940- *WhoThe 16*
Gould, Joseph 1915- *IntMPA 1977*
Gould, Julian 1915- *AmSCAP 1966*
Gould, Morton 1913- *AmSCAP 1966,*
  BiE&WWA, NewMT, NotNAT
Gould, Myrtle 1880-1941 *WhScrn 1, WhScrn 2*
Gould, Sandra *WhoHol A*
Gould, Shane *CelR 3*
Gould, Sid *WhoHol A*
Gould, Violet 1884-1962 *WhScrn 1, WhScrn 2*
Gould, William *Film 2*
Gould, William A 1915-1960 *WhScrn 2*

Goulding, Alf 1896-1972 *Film 2*
Goulding, Alfred 1896-1972 *FilmgC, TwYS A*
Goulding, Alfred Alf 1896-1972 *WhScrn 2*
Goulding, Edmund 1891-1951 *CmMov*
Goulding, Edmund 1891-1959 *AmSCAP 1966,*
  BiDFlm, DcFM, FilmgC, MovMk,
  NotNAT B, OxFilm, TwYS A, WhScrn 2,
  WhThe, WorEnF
Goulding, Ivis *WhScrn 2*
Goulding, Ray 1922- *CelR 3*
Goulet, Robert 1933- *BiE&WWA, CelR 3,*
  EncMT, FilmgC, IntMPA 1977, NotNAT,
  WhoHol A, WhoThe 16
Gounod, Charles Francois 1818-1893 *NotNAT B*
Gouse-Renal, Christine *WomWMM*
Govi, Gilberto 1885-1966 *WhScrn 1, WhScrn 2*
Govsky, John M 1921- *AmSCAP 1966*
Gow, James 1907-1952 *NotNAT B, WhThe*
Gow, Ronald 1897- *ConDr 1977, WhoThe 16*
Goward, Annie d1907 *NotNAT B*
Goward, Mary Ann 1806-1899 *NotNAT B*
Gowdowsky, Dagmar 1897-1975 *Film 1*
Gowdowsky, Dagmar *see also* Godowsky, Dagmar
Gowdy, Curt 1919- *CelR 3, IntMPA 1977,*
  NewYTET
Gowers, Sulky d1970 *WhScrn 1, WhScrn 2*
Gowing, Gene *Film 2*
Gowland, Gibson 1872-1951 *WhScrn 1, WhScrn 2,*
  WhoHol B
Gowland, Gibson 1882-1951 *Film 1, Film 2,*
  FilmgC, TwYS
Gowman, Milton J 1907-1952 *WhScrn 1,*
  WhScrn 2
Goya, Mona *WhoHol A*
Goya, Tito *PIP&P A*
Goyer, Echlen *Film 2*
Gozzi, Carlo 1720-1806 *CnThe, McGWD,*
  NotNAT A, NotNAT B, OxThe, REnWD
Gozzi, Patricia 1950- *FilmgC*
Grabbe, Christian Dietrich 1801-1836 *CnThe,*
  McGWD, NotNAT B, OxThe, REnWD
Grable, Betty 1913-1973 *ThFT*
Grable, Betty 1916-1973 *BiDFlm, CelR 3,*
  CmMov, Film 2, FilmgC, MotPP, MovMk,
  OxFilm, WhScrn 2, WhThe, WhoHol B,
  WorEnF
Graccia, Ugo *Film 2*
Grace, Princess Of Monaco 1929- *CelR 3*
Grace, Amy d1945 *NotNAT B*
Grace, Carol 1923- *BiE&WWA, NotNAT*
Grace, Charity 1879-1965 *WhScrn 1, WhScrn 2*
Grace, Dick 1915-1965 *WhScrn 2*
Grace, Dinah d1963 *WhScrn 1, WhScrn 2*
Grace, Frank Devaney 1891- *AmSCAP 1966*
Gracie, Charlie 1936- *AmSCAP 1966*
Gracie, Sally *BiE&WWA, NotNAT, WhoHol A*
Gracq, Julien 1910- *CnMD*
Grade, Lord Lew *IntMPA 1977, NewYTET*
Gradus, Ben 1918- *IntMPA 1977*
Grady, Billy d1973 *NotNAT A*
Grady, Billy, Jr. 1917- *IntMPA 1977*
Grady, Don *WhoHol A*
Graetz, Paul 1890-1937 *Film 2, WhScrn 1,*
  WhScrn 2, WhoHol B
Graetz, Paul 1899-1966 *WorEnF*
Graetz, Paul 1901-1966 *FilmgC*
Graf, Peter 1872-1951 *WhScrn 1, WhScrn 2*
Graf, Robert 1923-1966 *WhScrn 2*
Graff, E Jonny 1911- *AmSCAP 1966*
Graff, George 1886-1973 *AmSCAP 1966*
Graff, Richard 1924- *IntMPA 1977*
Graff, Robert D 1919- *IntMPA 1977*
Graff, Sigmund 1898- *ModWD*
Graff, Wilton 1903-1969 *BiE&WWA, WhScrn 1,*

WhScrn 2, WhoHol B
Graffenried-Villars, Baron Emmanuel De d1964
  NotNAT B
Grafton, Louise *Film 2*
Grafton, Sue *WomWMM*
Graham, Betty Jane *Film 2*
Graham, Billy 1918- *CelR 3*
Graham, Charles *Film 1, Film 2*
Graham, Charlie 1897-1943 *WhScrn 1, WhScrn 2,*
  WhoHol B
Graham, Diane T *WomWMM B*
Graham, Ernest d1945 *NotNAT B*
Graham, Frank 1915-1950 *WhScrn 1, WhScrn 2,*
  WhoHol B
Graham, Fred *WhoHol A*
Graham, Frederick H *Film 2*
Graham, George d1939 *NotNAT B*
Graham, Harold L 1897- *AmSCAP 1966*
Graham, Harry 1874-1936 *EncMT, NotNAT B,*
  WhThe
Graham, Irvin 1909- *AmSCAP 1966,*
  BiE&WWA, NotNAT
Graham, J F 1850-1932 *NotNAT B*
Graham, Joe F 1850-1933 *NotNAT A*
Graham, John *WhoHol A*
Graham, Johnny 1911- *AmSCAP 1966*
Graham, Julia Ann 1915-1935 *WhScrn 1,*
  WhScrn 2, WhoHol B
Graham, Katharine M 1917- *CelR 3, NewYTET*
Graham, Kenneth L 1915- *BiE&WWA, NotNAT*
Graham, Lewis 1900- *AmSCAP 1966*
Graham, Martha *Film 2*
Graham, Martha 1894- *CelR 3, NotNAT A*
Graham, Martha 1902- *BiE&WWA, WhThe*
Graham, Morland 1891-1949 *FilmgC, NotNAT B,*
  PIP&P, WhScrn 1, WhScrn 2, WhThe,
  WhoHol B
Graham, Robert Emmet 1858- *WhoStg 1906,*
  WhoStg 1908
Graham, Robert V 1912- *AmSCAP 1966*
Graham, Roger 1885-1938 *AmSCAP 1966*
Graham, Ronald 1912-1950 *NotNAT B,*
  WhScrn 1, WhScrn 2, WhoHol B
Graham, Ronny 1919- *AmSCAP 1966,*
  BiE&WWA, NotNAT, WhoHol A,
  WhoThe 16
Graham, Sheilah 1908?- *CelR 3*
Graham, Violet 1890-1967 *WhThe*
Graham, Virginia d1964 *NotNAT B*
Graham, Virginia 1912- *CelR 3*
Graham, William 1930?- *FilmgC*
Graham-Browne, W *WhThe*
Grahame, Bert 1892-1971 *WhScrn 1, WhScrn 2,*
  WhoHol B
Grahame, Gloria *MotPP*
Grahame, Gloria 1924- *FilmgC*
Grahame, Gloria 1925- *BiDFlm, MGM, MovMk,*
  WhoHol A, WorEnF
Grahame, Gloria 1929- *IntMPA 1977*
Grahame, Margot 1911- *FilmgC, ThFT, WhThe,*
  WhoHol A
Grahm, Ruth Lillian 1924- *AmSCAP 1966*
Grahn, Mary 1901- *BiE&WWA, NotNAT*
Grainer, Ron *IntMPA 1977*
Grainer, Ron 1922- *WhoThe 16*
Grainer, Ron 1925?- *FilmgC*
Grainger, Edmund 1906- *FilmgC*
Grainger, Gawn 1937- *WhoThe 16*
Grainger, James Edmund *IntMPA 1977*
Grainger, Jimmy, Jr. *Film 2*
Grainger, Percy Aldridge 1882-1961
  AmSCAP 1966, NotNAT B
Grainger, William F 1854-1938 *WhScrn 1,*
  WhScrn 2

Gralla, Dina *Film 2*
Gramatica, Emma d1965 *WhThe, WhoHol B*
Gramatica, Emma 1874-1965 *OxThe*
Gramatica, Emma 1875-1965 *WhScrn 1,*
 WhScrn 2
Gramatica, Irma 1873-1962 *OxThe, WhThe*
Gran, Albert 1862-1932 *Film 1, Film 2,*
 WhScrn 1, WhScrn 2, WhoHol B
Granach, Alexander 1879-1945 *NotNAT A,*
 NotNAT B
Granach, Alexander 1890-1945 *Film 2, FilmgC,*
 WhoHol B
Granach, Alexander 1891-1945 *WhScrn 1,*
 WhScrn 2
Granado, Manuel *Film 2*
Granath, Herbert A *NewYTET*
Granby, Cornelius W d1886 *NotNAT B*
Granby, Joseph 1885-1965 *Film 1, WhScrn 1,*
 WhScrn 2, WhoHol B
Grand, Georges d1921 *NotNAT B*
Grand, Murray 1919- *AmSCAP 1966*
Grand Funk Railroad *CelR 3*
Grandais, Susanne d1920 *WhScrn 1, WhScrn 2*
Grandee, George *Film 2*
Grandin, Elmer *Film 1*
Grandin, Elmer d1933 *NotNAT B*
Grandin, Ethel 1896- *Film 1, Film 2, MotPP,*
 TwYS
Grandin, Francis *Film 1*
Grandjany, Marcel 1891- *AmSCAP 1966*
Grandjean, Louise d1934 *NotNAT B*
Grandon, Frank *Film 1, TwYS A*
Grand'Ry, Genevieve *WomWMM*
Grandstedt, Greta *Film 2*
Grandval, Charles-Francois Racot De 1711-1784
 NotNAT B
Grandval, Charles-Francois Racot De 1714-1784
 OxThe
Graner, Gertrude *WhoHol A*
Granet, Bert 1910- *IntMPA 1977*
Grange, Red 1903- *Film 2, WhoHol A*
Granger, Dorothy *Film 2, MotPP, WhoHol A*
Granger, Elsa G 1904-1955 *WhScrn 1, WhScrn 2*
Granger, Farley 1925- *BiDFlm, BiE&WWA,*
 FilmgC, HolP 40, IntMPA 1977, MotPP,
 MovMk, NotNAT, WhoHol A, WorEnF
Granger, Stewart 1913- *BiDFlm, CmMov,*
 FilmgC, IntMPA 1977, MGM, MotPP,
 MovMk, OxFilm, WhThe, WhoHol A,
 WorEnF
Granger, William F 1854-1938 *WhScrn 2,*
 WhoHol B
Grangier, Gilles 1911- *DcFM, FilmgC, WorEnF*
Granick, Harry *NatPD*
Granier, Jeanne d1939 *NotNAT B, WhThe*
Granik, Theodore d1970 *NewYTET*
Granlund, Nils Thor 1882-1957 *NotNAT A,*
 NotNAT B
Granovsky, Alexander 1890-1937 *NotNAT B,*
 OxFilm, OxThe
Granstedt, Greta *TwYS*
Grant, Alfred J 1914- *AmSCAP 1966*
Grant, Allan 1892- *AmSCAP 1966*
Grant, Anne *WomWMM B*
Grant, Arthur 1915?-1972 *CmMov, FilmgC*
Grant, B Donald *NewYTET*
Grant, Barney d1962 *NotNAT B*
Grant, Bert 1878-1951 *AmSCAP 1966*
Grant, Bob 1932- *WhoThe 16*
Grant, Cary 1904- *BiDFlm, CelR 3, CmMov,*
 EncMT, FilmgC, IntMPA 1977, MotPP,
 MovMk, OxFilm, WhoHol A, WorEnF
Grant, Charles N 1887-1937 *AmSCAP 1966*
Grant, Corrine *Film 1*

Grant, Earl 1931-1970 *WhScrn 1, WhScrn 2,*
 WhoHol B
Grant, Frances Miller *Film 2*
Grant, Harry 1922- *AmSCAP 1966*
Grant, Harry Allen *Film 2*
Grant, James Edward 1902-1966 *CmMov, FilmgC*
Grant, James Edward 1904-1966 *WorEnF*
Grant, Jerry 1923- *AmSCAP 1966*
Grant, Katherine *Film 2*
Grant, Kathryn 1933- *FilmgC, MotPP,*
 WhoHol A
Grant, Kirby 1911- *WhoHol A*
Grant, Kirby 1914- *FilmgC*
Grant, Lawrence 1870-1952 *MovMk, WhScrn 1,*
 WhScrn 2, WhoHol B
Grant, Lawrence 1898-1952 *Film 1, Film 2,*
 TwYS
Grant, Lee 1929- *BiE&WWA, FilmgC,*
 IntMPA 1977, MotPP, MovMk, NotNAT,
 WhoHol A
Grant, M Arnold 1908- *IntMPA 1977*
Grant, Marshall 1926- *AmSCAP 1966*
Grant, Maxwell d1961 *NotNAT B*
Grant, Neil 1882- *WhThe*
Grant, Pauline 1915- *WhoThe 16*
Grant, Shelby *WhoHol A*
Grant, Sydney 1873-1953 *Film 1, NotNAT B,*
 WhScrn 1, WhScrn 2, WhoHol B
Grant, Valentine 1894-1948 *Film 1, TwYS,*
 WhScrn 2
Grant, W F d1923 *NotNAT B*
Grantham, Wilfrid 1898- *WhThe*
Granville, Audrey 1910-1972 *WhScrn 2,*
 WhoHol B
Granville, Bernard 1886-1936 *NotNAT B, WhThe*
Granville, Bonita 1923- *FilmgC, HolP 30, MotPP,*
 MovMk, ThFT, WhoHol A
Granville, Charlotte 1863-1942 *WhScrn 2, WhThe*
Granville, George d1735 *NotNAT B*
Granville, Louise 1896-1969 *WhScrn 1, WhScrn 2,*
 WhoHol B
Granville, Sydney d1959 *NotNAT B, WhThe*
Granville-Barker, Harley 1877-1946 *CnMD,*
 McGWD, ModWD, NotNAT A, NotNAT B,
 OxThe, PIP&P, REnWD, WhThe
Granville-Barker, Harley *see also* Barker, Harley
 Granville-
Granville-Barker, Helen d1950 *NotNAT B,*
 WhThe
Grapewin, Charles *MotPP*
Grapewin, Charles 1869-1956 *NotNAT B*
Grapewin, Charles 1875-1956 *MovMk, WhScrn 1,*
 WhScrn 2, WhoHol B
Grapewin, Charles 1896-1956 *Vers A*
Grapewin, Charley 1869-1956 *FilmgC*
Grapewin, Charley 1896-1956 *Film 2*
Gras, Enrico 1919- *DcFM*
Grasgreen, Martin 1925- *IntMPA 1977*
Grass, Gunter 1927- *CelR 3, CroCD, McGWD,*
 ModWD, REnWD
Grass, Gunter 1928- *CnMD*
Grass, Gunther 1927- *CnThe*
Grassby, Bertram 1880-1953 *Film 1, Film 2,*
 TwYS, WhScrn 2
Grassby, Mrs. Gerard A 1877-1962 *WhScrn 1,*
 WhScrn 2
Grasshoff, Alex *IntMPA 1977*
Grasso, Giovanni 1875-1930 *NotNAT B, OxThe,*
 WhThe
Grasso, Ralph 1934- *AmSCAP 1966*
Grateful Dead *CelR 3*
Grattan, H Plunkett d1889 *NotNAT B*
Grattan, Harry 1867-1951 *WhThe*
Grattan, Lawrence d1941 *NotNAT B*

Gratton, Fred 1894-1966 *WhThe*
Gratton, Harry 1867-1951 *NotNAT B*
Gratton, Stephen *Film 2*
Gratz, Paul *Film 2*
Grau, Jacinto 1877-1958 *ModWD*
Grau, Jorge 1930- *WorEnF*
Grau, Maurice 1851-1907 *NotNAT B*
Grau, Maurice 1857-1934 *NotNAT B*
Grau, Robert d1916 *NotNAT B*
Grau Delgado, Jacinto 1877-1958 *McGWD*
Grauer, Ben *Film 1*
Grauer, Ben 1908- *IntMPA 1977*
Grauer, Bunny *Film 2*
Grauman, Sid 1879-1950 *NotNAT B, WhoHol B*
Grauman, Walter 1922- *FilmgC*
Graumann, Karl *Film 2*
Gravel, Mike 1930- *CelR 3*
Gravenson, Anne W *WomWMM B*
Graves, Clo d1932 *NotNAT B*
Graves, Clotilde Inez Mary 1863-1932 *WhThe*
Graves, Ernest *WhoHol A*
Graves, George 1876-1949 *NotNAT A,
     NotNAT B, WhScrn 2, WhThe, WhoHol B*
Graves, Laura d1925 *NotNAT B*
Graves, Nancy *WomWMM B*
Graves, Peter 1911- *FilmgC, IntMPA 1977,
     WhoHol A, WhoThe 16*
Graves, Peter 1925- *FilmgC, MotPP, MovMk,
     WhoHol A*
Graves, Peter 1936- *CelR 3, IntMPA 1977*
Graves, Ralph 1900- *Film 1, Film 2, MotPP,
     MovMk, TwYS*
Graves, Ralph Seaman, Jr. 1923- *AmSCAP 1966*
Graves, Taylor *Film 2*
Graves, Teresa *WhoHol A*
Graves, William 1916- *AmSCAP 1966*
Gravet, Fernand 1904-1970 *FilmgC, MovMk,
     WhScrn 1, WhScrn 2, WhoHol B*
Gravina, Caesare 1858- *Film 1, Film 2*
Gravina, Cesare 1858- *TwYS*
Gray, Alexander 1902-1975 *Film 2, MotPP,
     WhScrn 2*
Gray, Allan 1904- *OxFilm*
Gray, Amlin 1946- *NatPD*
Gray, Arnold *Film 2*
Gray, Barry *IntMPA 1977*
Gray, Barry 1916- *CelR 3*
Gray, Betty d1919 *Film 1, WhScrn 2*
Gray, Billy *WhoHol A*
Gray, Billy Joe 1941-1966 *WhScrn 2*
Gray, Carole 1940- *FilmgC*
Gray, Charles D 1928- *BiE&WWA, FilmgC,
     NotNAT, WhoHol A, WhoThe 16*
Gray, Chauncey 1904- *AmSCAP 1966*
Gray, Clifford *Film 2*
Gray, Coleen 1922- *IntMPA 1977, MotPP,
     WhoHol A*
Gray, Colleen 1922- *FilmgC*
Gray, Dallas A 1898- *AmSCAP 1966*
Gray, Dolores *MotPP, WhoHol A*
Gray, Dolores 1924- *EncMT, FilmgC,
     WhoThe 16*
Gray, Dolores 1930- *BiE&WWA, NotNAT*
Gray, Don 1901-1966 *WhScrn 2*
Gray, Donald 1914- *FilmgC, WhoHol A*
Gray, Dulcie 1919- *FilmgC, IntMPA 1977,
     WhoHol A, WhoThe 16*
Gray, Eddie 1898-1969 *WhScrn 2, WhoHol B*
Gray, Eden *Film 2*
Gray, Elspet 1929- *WhoThe 16*
Gray, Elwood *Film 2*
Gray, Eve 1904- *Film 2, WhThe*
Gray, Gary 1936- *FilmgC*
Gray, Gene 1899-1950 *WhScrn 1, WhScrn 2,*

    WhoHol B
Gray, George *WhThe*
Gray, George Arthur *Film 2*
Gray, George G 1894-1967 *WhScrn 1, WhScrn 2,
     WhoHol B*
Gray, Gilda d1959 *MotPP, NotNAT B,
     WhoHol B*
Gray, Gilda 1899-1959 *Film 1, Film 2, TwYS*
Gray, Gilda 1901-1959 *FilmgC, WhScrn 1,
     WhScrn 2*
Gray, Glen 1900-1963 *WhScrn 1, WhScrn 2,
     WhoHol B*
Gray, Gordon 1905- *IntMPA 1977*
Gray, Harry *Film 2*
Gray, Ida M d1942 *NotNAT B*
Gray, Iris *Film 2*
Gray, Jack 1880-1956 *WhScrn 1, WhScrn 2,
     WhoHol B*
Gray, Jack 1927- *ConDr 1977*
Gray, Jean 1902-1953 *WhScrn 1, WhScrn 2*
Gray, Jennifer 1916-1962 *WhThe*
Gray, Jerry 1915- *AmSCAP 1966*
Gray, Joe d1971 *WhScrn 2*
Gray, Lawrence 1898-1970 *Film 2, TwYS,
     WhScrn 1, WhScrn 2, WhoHol B*
Gray, Leonard d1964 *NotNAT B*
Gray, Lilian *Film 2*
Gray, Linda 1910- *WhoThe 16*
Gray, Linda 1913-1963 *WhScrn 1, WhScrn 2,
     WhoHol B*
Gray, Madeline *Film 2*
Gray, Margery *BiE&WWA*
Gray, Nadia 1923- *Film 1, FilmgC, WhoHol A*
Gray, Nicholas Stuart 1919- *WhoThe 16*
Gray, Paul 1930- *BiE&WWA*
Gray, Richard 1896- *WhThe*
Gray, Robert S 1911- *BiE&WWA*
Gray, Sally 1916- *FilmgC, WhThe, WhoHol A*
Gray, Simon 1936- *CnThe, ConDr 1977,
     NotNAT, PIP&P A, WhoThe 16*
Gray, Stella *Film 1*
Gray, Stephen *Film 1*
Gray, Terence 1895- *OxThe, WhThe*
Gray, Thomas J 1888-1924 *AmSCAP 1966,
     NotNAT B*
Gray, Timothy *AmSCAP 1966, BiE&WWA,
     NotNAT*
Gray, Vernon *IntMPA 1977, WhoHol A*
Gray, William d1943 *NotNAT B*
Graybill, Joseph 1887-1913 *Film 1, WhScrn 2,
     WhoHol B*
Graydon, J L 1844- *WhThe*
Grayson, Alan 1930- *AmSCAP 1966*
Grayson, Bette d1954 *NotNAT B*
Grayson, Kathryn *MotPP, WhoHol A*
Grayson, Kathryn 1921- *MovMk*
Grayson, Kathryn 1922- *CmMov, FilmgC, MGM*
Grayson, Kathryn 1923- *IntMPA 1977*
Grayson, Richard 1925- *BiE&WWA, NotNAT*
Grazer, Wanda *Film 2*
Graziano, Ann 1928- *AmSCAP 1966*
Graziano, Caesar Frankie 1904- *AmSCAP 1966*
Graziano, Rocky 1922- *CelR 3, WhoHol A*
Grazzini, Anton Francesco 1503-1584 *McGWD*
Greanias, George 1948- *NatPD*
Greatheed, Bertie d1826 *NotNAT B*
Greatorex, Wilfred *ConDr 1977C*
Greaza, Walter N 1897-1973 *BiE&WWA,
     NotNAT B, WhScrn 2, WhoHol B*
Greaza, Walter N 1900-1973 *WhThe*
Grebanier, Bernard 1903- *BiE&WWA, NotNAT*
Greco, Armando 1926- *AmSCAP 1966*
Greco, Jose 1918- *CelR 3, WhoHol A*
Greco, Juliette 1927- *FilmgC, WhoHol A*

Grede, Kjell 1936- *OxFilm, WorEnF*
Gredy, Jean-Pierre 1920- *McGWD*
Greear, Geraine *Film 2*
Greeley, Evelyn *Film 1*
Greely, Evelyn *Film 2*
Green, Abel 1900-1973 *AmSCAP 1966,*
  BiE&WWA, CelR 3, NotNAT B,
  WhScrn 2, WhThe
Green, Adolph *BiE&WWA, CmMov,*
  ConDr 1977D, IntMPA 1977, NotNAT,
  OxFilm, WhoThe 16
Green, Adolph 1915- *AmSCAP 1966, EncMT,*
  FilmgC, NewMT, WorEnF
Green, Adolph 1918- *CelR 3*
Green, Alfred E 1889-1960 *FilmgC, MovMk*
Green, Alfred E 1890-1960 *TwYS A*
Green, Bernard 1908- *AmSCAP 1966*
Green, Bud 1897- *AmSCAP 1966*
Green, Calvin E *AmSCAP 1966*
Green, Carelton d1962 *NotNAT B*
Green, Carolyn *BiE&WWA, NotNAT*
Green, Charles *Film 2*
Green, Danny 1903- *FilmgC, WhoHol A*
Green, Denis 1905-1954 *WhScrn 1, WhScrn 2,*
  WhoHol B
Green, Dennis d1954 *NotNAT B*
Green, Dorothy *WhoHol A*
Green, Dorothy 1886-1961 *NotNAT B, WhThe*
Green, Dorothy 1892-1963 *Film 1, NotNAT B,*
  WhScrn 1, WhScrn 2, WhoHol B
Green, Eve *WomWMM*
Green, Fred E 1890-1940 *WhScrn 1, WhScrn 2,*
  WhoHol B
Green, Gilbert *WhoHol A*
Green, Guy 1913- *BiDFlm, FilmgC,*
  IntMPA 1977, WorEnF
Green, H Leland 1907- *AmSCAP 1966*
Green, Harold 1912- *AmSCAP 1966*
Green, Harry 1892-1958 *Film 2, FilmgC, MotPP,*
  WhScrn 1, WhScrn 2, WhThe, WhoHol B
Green, Helen *Film 1*
Green, Howard P, Sr. 1892- *AmSCAP 1966*
Green, Hughie 1920- *FilmgC, WhoHol A*
Green, Ingeborg *WomWMM*
Green, Isadore d1963 *NotNAT B*
Green, James Burton d1922 *NotNAT B*
Green, Jane *PIP&P*
Green, Janet 1914- *BiE&WWA, FilmgC,*
  IntMPA 1977, WhThe
Green, John *OxThe*
Green, John 1908- *AmSCAP 1966, IntMPA 1977*
Green, John H 1915- *BiE&WWA, NotNAT*
Green, Johnny 1908- *BiE&WWA, CmMov,*
  FilmgC
Green, Joseph 1905- *IntMPA 1977*
Green, Judd *Film 2*
Green, Julian 1900- *ModWD*
Green, Julien 1900- *CnMD, McGWD, REnWD*
Green, Kenneth 1908-1969 *WhScrn 1, WhScrn 2,*
  WhoHol B
Green, Lewis G 1909- *AmSCAP 1966*
Green, Mabel 1890- *WhThe*
Green, Marion 1890-1956 *NotNAT B, WhThe*
Green, Martyn 1899-1975 *BiE&WWA, FilmgC,*
  NotNAT A, NotNAT B, WhScrn 2,
  WhoHol C, WhoThe 16
Green, Michael L *IntMPA 1977*
Green, Mitzi 1920-1969 *Film 2, FilmgC,*
  HolP 30, MotPP, NotNAT B, ThFT,
  WhScrn 1, WhScrn 2, WhThe, WhoHol B
Green, Morris d1963 *NotNAT B*
Green, Morton J 1919- *AmSCAP 1966*
Green, Nathaniel Charles 1903- *IntMPA 1977*
Green, Nigel 1924-1972 *FilmgC, WhScrn 2,*

WhoHol B
Green, Paul 1894- *AmSCAP 1966, BiE&WWA,*
  CnMD, CnThe, ConDr 1977, McGWD,
  ModWD, NotNAT, NotNAT A, OxThe,
  PIP&P, REnWD, WhoThe 16
Green, Philip 1917?- *FilmgC, IntMPA 1977*
Green, Ray 1909- *AmSCAP 1966*
Green, Richard d1914 *NotNAT B*
Green, Robert 1940-1965 *WhScrn 2*
Green, Ruth *BiE&WWA*
Green, Sanford 1914- *AmSCAP 1966*
Green, Stanley 1923- *BiE&WWA, NotNAT*
Green, Sue 1902-1939 *WhScrn 1, WhScrn 2,*
  WhoHol B
Green, Urban Clifford 1926- *AmSCAP 1966*
Green, William 1913- *AmSCAP 1966*
Green, William 1926- *NotNAT*
Green, William M *NatPD*
Greenbank, Henry H d1899 *NotNAT B*
Greenbank, Percy 1878-1968 *EncMT, NotNAT B,*
  WhThe
Greenbaum, Hyam 1910- *WhThe*
Greenberg, Abner 1889-1959 *AmSCAP 1966*
Greenberg, Berry 1912- *IntMPA 1977*
Greenberg, Edward M 1924- *NotNAT*
Greenberg, Henry F 1912- *AmSCAP 1966*
Greene, Angela *WhoHol A*
Greene, Billy M 1897-1973 *WhScrn 2, WhoHol B*
Greene, Billy M 1927-1970 *WhoHol B*
Greene, Billy M *see also* Greene, William
Greene, Clarence 1918?- *FilmgC*
Greene, Clay Meredith 1850-1933 *NotNAT B,*
  WhThe, WhoStg 1908
Greene, David 1924- *BiDFlm, FilmgC,*
  IntMPA 1977
Greene, Eric 1876-1917 *NotNAT B*
Greene, Evie 1876-1917 *WhThe, WhoStg 1906,*
  WhoStg 1908
Greene, Graham 1904- *BiE&WWA, CelR 3,*
  CnMD, CnThe, ConDr 1977, CroCD,
  FilmgC, McGWD, ModWD, NotNAT,
  NotNAT A, OxFilm, OxThe, PIP&P,
  WhoThe 16, WorEnF
Greene, Harrison 1884-1945 *WhScrn 1,*
  WhScrn 2, WhoHol B
Greene, Harry 1928- *AmSCAP 1966*
Greene, Herbert 1921- *BiE&WWA, NotNAT*
Greene, Joe 1915- *AmSCAP 1966*
Greene, John L 1912- *AmSCAP 1966*
Greene, Kempton 1890- *Film 1, Film 2, TwYS*
Greene, Lorne 1915- *BiE&WWA, CelR 3,*
  FilmgC, IntMPA 1977, MotPP, MovMk,
  WhoHol A
Greene, Max 1896-1968 *FilmgC*
Greene, Milton L *AmSCAP 1966, BiE&WWA,*
  NotNAT
Greene, Mort 1912- *AmSCAP 1966*
Greene, Nancy Ellen *WomWMM B*
Greene, Norman d1945 *NotNAT B*
Greene, Norman 1930- *AmSCAP 1966*
Greene, Patterson 1899-1968 *BiE&WWA,*
  NotNAT B
Greene, Reuben *WhoHol A*
Greene, Richard *MotPP*
Greene, Richard 1914- *HolP 30*
Greene, Richard 1918- *FilmgC, MovMk,*
  WhoHol A
Greene, Robert 1558-1592 *CnThe, McGWD,*
  NotNAT B, PIP&P, REnWD
Greene, Robert 1560?-1592 *OxThe*
Greene, Schuyler 1880-1927 *AmSCAP 1966*
Greene, Shecky *WhoHol A*
Greene, Stanley *WhoHol A*
Greene, Walter d1963 *NotNAT B*

Greene, Will 1923- *BiE&WWA*
Greene, William 1927-1970 *WhScrn 1, WhScrn 2*
Greene, William *see also* Greene, Billy M
Greener, Dorothy 1917-1971 *BiE&WWA,*
  NotNAT B, WhThe
Greenfield, Amy *WomWMM A, WomWMM B*
Greenfield, Irving H 1902- *IntMPA 1977*
Greenfield, Leo 1916- *IntMPA 1977*
Greenfield, Lois *WomWMM B*
Greenhill, Mitch 1944- *AmSCAP 1966*
Greenholz, Martin 1904- *AmSCAP 1966*
Greenhouse, Martha *WhoHol A*
Greenlaw, Walter 1900- *AmSCAP 1966*
Greenleaf, Mace d1912 *WhScrn 2*
Greenleaf, Raymond 1892-1963 *FilmgC,*
  NotNAT B, WhScrn 1, WhScrn 2,
  WhoHol B
Greenlund, Alys 1902- *AmSCAP 1966*
Greenspan, Lou *IntMPA 1977*
Greenstreet, Sidney 1879-1954 *FilmgC, MovMk*
Greenstreet, Sydney 1879-1954 *BiDFlm, CmMov,*
  HolP 40, MotPP, NotNAT B, OxFilm,
  Vers A, WhScrn 1, WhScrn 2, WhThe,
  WhoHol B, WorEnF
Greenwald, Joel 1938- *AmSCAP 1966*
Greenwald, Joseph d1938 *NotNAT B, WhThe*
Greenway, Ann *Film 2*
Greenwood, Charlotte 1893- *BiE&WWA, EncMT,*
  Film 1, Film 2, FilmgC, IntMPA 1977,
  MotPP, MovMk, NotNAT, ThFT, Vers A,
  WhThe, WhoHol A
Greenwood, Ethel 1898-1970 *WhScrn 1,*
  WhScrn 2
Greenwood, Jack 1919- *FilmgC, IntMPA 1977*
Greenwood, Jane 1934- *NotNAT, WhoThe 16*
Greenwood, Joan 1921- *BiDFlm, BiE&WWA,*
  CnThe, FilmgC, IntMPA 1977, MotPP,
  MovMk, NotNAT, OxFilm, WhoHol A,
  WhoThe 16, WorEnF
Greenwood, John 1889- *FilmgC*
Greenwood, Walter 1903- *ConDr 1973, WhThe*
Greenwood, Winifred 1892-1961 *Film 1, Film 2,*
  TwYS, WhScrn 2
Greenwood, Winnifred 1892-1961 *WhoHol B*
Greer, Dabbs *WhoHol A*
Greer, Edward G 1920- *NotNAT*
Greer, Germaine 1939- *CelR 3*
Greer, Jane 1924- *FilmgC, IntMPA 1977,*
  MotPP, MovMk, WhoHol A
Greer, Jesse 1896- *AmSCAP 1966*
Greer, Julian 1871-1928 *WhScrn 1, WhScrn 2,*
  WhoHol B
Greer, Michael 1917- *CelR 3, WhoHol A*
Greet, Sir Ben 1857-1936 *OxThe, PIP&P,*
  WhoStg 1906, WhoStg 1908
Greet, Clare 1871-1939 *Film 2, NotNAT B,*
  WhScrn 1, WhScrn 2, WhThe, WhoHol B
Greet, Maurice d1951 *NotNAT B*
Greet, Mildred C d1964 *NotNAT B*
Greet, Sir Philip 1857-1936 *NotNAT A,*
  NotNAT B, WhThe
Grefe, William *IntMPA 1977*
Gregg, Arnold *Film 2*
Gregg, Everley 1903-1959 *NotNAT B, WhThe,*
  WhoHol B
Gregg, Everly d1959 *WhScrn 1, WhScrn 2*
Gregg, Hubert *WhoHol A*
Gregg, Hubert 1914- *FilmgC*
Gregg, Hubert 1916- *WhoThe 16*
Gregg, Mary Louise 1921- *AmSCAP 1966*
Gregg, Virginia *WhoHol A*
Gregor, Nora d1949 *NotNAT B, OxFilm,*
  WhScrn 1, WhScrn 2, WhoHol B
Gregoretti, Ugo 1930- *WorEnF*

Gregori, Mercia 1901- *WhThe*
Gregory, Lady 1852-1932 *ModWD, PIP&P*
Gregory, Lady 1859-1932 *WhThe*
Gregory, Lady *see also* Gregory, Lady Isabella
  Augusta
Gregory, Andre *NotNAT, WhoThe 16*
Gregory, Anne *WomWMM B*
Gregory, Lady Augusta 1852-1932 *CnThe,*
  McGWD, NotNAT B, OxThe
Gregory, Bobby 1900-1971 *AmSCAP 1966,*
  WhScrn 1, WhScrn 2
Gregory, David *IntMPA 1977*
Gregory, Dick 1932- *CelR 3, NotNAT A,*
  WhoHol A
Gregory, Dora 1872-1954 *NotNAT B, WhThe*
Gregory, Dora 1873-1954 *WhScrn 1, WhScrn 2,*
  WhoHol B
Gregory, Edna 1905-1965 *Film 2, TwYS,*
  WhScrn 1, WhScrn 2
Gregory, Ena *Film 2, TwYS, WhoHol A*
Gregory, Frank 1884- *WhThe*
Gregory, Lady Isabella Augusta 1852-1932 *REnWD*
Gregory, Lady Isabella Augusta *see also* Gregory,
  Lady
Gregory, James 1911- *BiE&WWA, FilmgC,*
  MotPP, MovMk, NotNAT, WhoHol A
Gregory, Johann Gottfried 1631-1675 *OxThe*
Gregory, John R 1918- *IntMPA 1977*
Gregory, Mollie 1940- *WomWMM A,*
  WomWMM B
Gregory, Paul 1905?- *FilmgC*
Gregory, Paul 1920- *BiE&WWA, NewYTET,*
  NotNAT
Gregory, Sara 1921- *WhThe*
Gregory, Thea *WhoHol A*
Gregory, W A 1923- *BiE&WWA*
Gregory, Will d1926 *Film 2, WhoHol B*
Gregory, William H d1926 *WhScrn 1, WhScrn 2*
Gregson, James R 1889- *WhThe*
Gregson, John 1919-1975 *CmMov, FilmgC,*
  WhScrn 2, WhoHol C
Greif, Andreas *McGWD*
Greig, Robert 1880-1958 *FilmgC, MovMk,*
  Vers B, WhScrn 1, WhScrn 2, WhoHol B
Grein, Mrs. J T *WhThe*
Grein, J T 1862-1935 *WhThe*
Grein, Jack Thomas 1862-1935 *OxThe, PIP&P*
Grein, Jacob Thomas 1862-1935 *NotNAT A,*
  NotNAT B
Greiner, Alvin G 1911- *AmSCAP 1966*
Greiner, Fritz *Film 2*
Greiner, Nancy *WomWMM B*
Greines, Edwin 1934- *AmSCAP 1966*
Greive, Thomas 1799-1882 *NotNAT B*
Greive, William 1800-1844 *NotNAT B*
Gremillon, Jean 1901-1959 *BiDFlm, FilmgC,*
  OxFilm, WorEnF
Gremillon, Jean 1902-1959 *DcFM*
Grene, David 1913- *BiE&WWA*
Greneker, Claude P d1949 *NotNAT B*
Grenet, Eliseo 1893-1950 *AmSCAP 1966*
Grenet-Dancourt, E d1913 *NotNAT B*
Grenfell, Joyce 1910- *BiE&WWA, EncMT,*
  FilmgC, MotPP, MovMk, NotNAT, OxThe,
  WhoHol A, WhoThe 16
Grennan, Jacqueline *CelR 3*
Grennan, Laurie *WomWMM*
Grennard, Elliott 1907- *AmSCAP 1966*
Gresac, Fred *WhThe*
Gresham, Herbert d1921 *NotNAT B*
Greshler, Abner J 1914- *IntMPA 1977*
Gresset, Jean-Baptiste-Louis 1709-1777 *McGWD,*
  OxThe
Gressieker, Hermann 1903- *CnMD*

Greth, Roma *NatPD*
Gretillat *Film 1*
Gretillat, Jacques *Film 2*
Gretler, Heinrich *Film 2*
Grevenius, Herbert 1901- *ModWD*
Grever, Maria 1894-1951 *AmSCAP 1966*
Greville, Edmond T 1906-1966 *FilmgC, WhScrn 2, WorEnF*
Greville, Sir Fulke 1554-1628 *REnWD*
Grevin, Jacques 1538?-1570? *OxThe*
Grew, Mary 1902-1971 *NotNAT B, WhThe*
Grey, Anne 1907- *Film 2, WhThe*
Grey, Beryl 1927- *WhThe*
Grey, Clifford 1887-1941 *AmSCAP 1966, EncMT, NewMT, NotNAT B, WhThe*
Grey, Ethel *Film 2*
Grey, Eve *WhThe*
Grey, Frank H 1883-1951 *AmSCAP 1966, NotNAT B*
Grey, Gloria 1909-1947 *Film 2, WhScrn 1, WhScrn 2, WhoHol B*
Grey, Jack *Film 2*
Grey, Jane 1883-1944 *Film 1, NotNAT B, WhScrn 1, WhScrn 2, WhThe, WhoHol B*
Grey, Jerry 1910-1954 *WhScrn 1, WhScrn 2*
Grey, Joel 1932- *CelR 3, EncMT, IntMPA 1977, NotNAT, WhoHol A, WhoThe 16*
Grey, Joseph W 1879-1956 *AmSCAP 1966*
Grey, Katherine 1873-1950 *NotNAT B, WhScrn 2, WhThe, WhoStg 1906, WhoStg 1908*
Grey, Lanny 1909- *AmSCAP 1966*
Grey, Leonard d1918 *WhScrn 2*
Grey, Lita *MotPP*
Grey, Lita 1908- *Film 2*
Grey, Lita 1909- *WhoHol A*
Grey, Lynda 1913-1963 *WhScrn 2*
Grey, Lytton d1931 *NotNAT B*
Grey, Madeline 1887-1950 *WhScrn 1, WhScrn 2, WhoHol B*
Grey, Marie De d1897 *NotNAT B*
Grey, Marion d1949 *NotNAT B*
Grey, Mary *WhThe*
Grey, Minna *Film 2*
Grey, Nan 1918- *FilmgC, MovMk, ThFT, WhoHol A*
Grey, Olga 1897-1973 *Film 1, WhScrn 2*
Grey, Ray *Film 1, Film 2*
Grey, Sylvia d1958 *NotNAT B*
Grey, Virginia 1917- *Film 2, FilmgC, MGM, ThFT, WhoHol A*
Grey, Virginia 1918- *MovMk*
Grey, Virginia 1923- *IntMPA 1977*
Grey, Zane 1875-1939 *FilmgC*
Gribble, George Dunning 1882-1956 *WhThe*
Gribble, Harry Wagstaff 1896- *BiE&WWA, NotNAT, WhThe*
Gribbon, Eddie 1890-1965 *Vers A, WhoHol B*
Gribbon, Eddie 1892-1965 *Film 1, Film 2, TwYS*
Gribbon, Edward T 1890-1965 *WhScrn 1, WhScrn 2*
Gribbon, Harry 1886-1961 *NotNAT B, WhScrn 1, WhScrn 2*
Gribbon, Harry 1888-1960 *Film 1, Film 2, TwYS, WhoHol B*
Gribov, Alexei Nikolaevich 1902- *WhThe*
Griboyedov, Aleksandr 1793-1829 *McGWD*
Griboyedov, Alexander 1793-1829 *CnThe, REnWD*
Griboyedov, Alexander 1795-1829 *NotNAT B, OxThe, PIP&P*
Gribunin, V F *PIP&P*
Grieb, Herbert C 1898- *AmSCAP 1966*
Grieg, Edvard Hagerup 1843-1907 *NotNAT B*

Grieg, Nordahl Brun 1902-1943 *CnMD, CnThe, McGWD, ModWD, NotNAT B, OxThe, REnWD*
Griem, Helmut 1940- *FilmgC, WhoHol A*
Grier, James W 1902-1959 *AmSCAP 1966*
Grier, Jimmy 1902-1959 *WhScrn 2*
Grier, Pam *WhoHol A*
Grier, Rosey *WhoHol A*
Grierson, John 1898-1972 *BiDFlm, DcFM, FilmgC, OxFilm, WorEnF*
Gries, Thomas S *IntMPA 1977*
Gries, Tom d1976 *NewYTET*
Gries, Tom 1922- *CmMov, FilmgC*
Griesbaum, Leonard 1932- *AmSCAP 1966*
Griese, Bob 1945- *CelR 3*
Griese, Friedrich 1890-1975 *CnMD, ModWD*
Grieve, John Henderson 1770-1845 *NotNAT B, OxThe*
Grieve, Thomas 1799-1882 *OxThe*
Grieve, Thomas Walford 1841-1882 *OxThe*
Grieve, William 1800-1844 *OxThe*
Griffell, Jose Martinez 1905-1955 *WhScrn 1, WhScrn 2*
Griffen, Benjamin d1740 *NotNAT B*
Griffes, Charles Tomlinson 1884-1920 *AmSCAP 1966*
Griffies, Ethel 1878-1975 *BiE&WWA, FilmgC, MotPP, MovMk, NotNAT, WhScrn 2, WhThe, WhoHol C*
Griffin, Arthur d1953 *NotNAT B*
Griffin, Basil *Film 2*
Griffin, Carlton Elliott 1893-1940 *Film 2, WhScrn 1, WhScrn 2, WhoHol B*
Griffin, Carlton Elliott *see also* Griffith, Carlton
Griffin, Charles 1888-1956 *WhScrn 1, WhScrn 2*
Griffin, Elsie *WhThe*
Griffin, Frank 1861- *TwYS A*
Griffin, Frank L 1889-1953 *WhScrn 1, WhScrn 2*
Griffin, Gerald d1840 *NotNAT B*
Griffin, Gerald d1962 *NotNAT B*
Griffin, Gerald 1854-1919 *Film 1, WhScrn 2*
Griffin, Gerald 1891-1962 *AmSCAP 1966*
Griffin, Gerald 1892-1962 *WhScrn 2*
Griffin, Hayden 1930- *BiE&WWA*
Griffin, Hayden 1943- *WhoThe 16*
Griffin, Josephine 1928- *FilmgC, WhoHol A*
Griffin, Margaret Fuller *WhScrn 1, WhScrn 2*
Griffin, Merv 1925- *CelR 3, IntMPA 1977, NewYTET, WhoHol A*
Griffin, Norman 1887- *WhThe*
Griffin, Russell Francis *Film 2*
Griffin, Susan 1943- *NatPD*
Griffin, Wally *AmSCAP 1966*
Griffin, William *NatPD*
Griffin, Z Wayne 1907- *IntMPA 1977*
Griffis, Elliot 1893- *AmSCAP 1966*
Griffith, Andy 1926- *BiE&WWA, CelR 3, FilmgC, IntMPA 1977, MotPP, WhoHol A*
Griffith, Carlton 1893-1940 *Film 2*
Griffith, Carlton *see also* Griffin, Carlton Elliott
Griffith, Corinne *AmSCAP 1966, MotPP*
Griffith, Corinne 1896?- *ThFT*
Griffith, Corinne 1898- *Film 1, Film 2, FilmgC, MovMk, TwYS*
Griffith, Corinne 1899?- *WhoHol A*
Griffith, D W d1948 *WhoHol B, WomWMM*
Griffith, D W 1874-1948 *FilmgC*
Griffith, D W 1875-1948 *BiDFlm*
Griffith, D W 1880-1948 *CmMov*
Griffith, David Wark 1875-1948 *DcFM, Film 1, MovMk, OxFilm, TwYS, TwYS A, WhScrn 1, WhScrn 2, WorEnF*
Griffith, David Wark 1880-1948 *WhThe*
Griffith, Edward H 1894- *FilmgC, TwYS A*

Griffith, Eleanor *Film 2*
Griffith, Gordon 1907-1958 *Film 1, Film 2,*
WhScrn 1, WhScrn 2, WhoHol B
Griffith, Hubert 1896-1953 *NotNAT B, OxThe,*
WhThe
Griffith, Hugh 1912- *BiE&WWA, FilmgC,*
IntMPA 1977, MotPP, MovMk, NotNAT,
WhoHol A, WhoThe 16
Griffith, James *WhoHol A*
Griffith, James 1916- *AmSCAP 1966, Vers A*
Griffith, James 1919- *FilmgC*
Griffith, Katherine 1858-1934 *Film 1, Film 2,*
WhoHol B
Griffith, Kenneth 1921- *FilmgC, WhoHol A*
Griffith, Linda 1884-1949 *NotNAT B, WhScrn 1,*
WhScrn 2
Griffith, Lydia Eliza 1832-1897 *NotNAT B*
Griffith, Melanie *WhoHol A*
Griffith, Raymond d1957 *MotPP, NotNAT B,*
WhoHol B
Griffith, Raymond 1890-1957 *TwYS, WhScrn 1,*
WhScrn 2
Griffith, Raymond 1894-1937 *FilmgC*
Griffith, Raymond 1896-1957 *Film 1, Film 2,*
MovMk
Griffith, Richard 1912-1969 *FilmgC*
Griffith, Robert 1907-1961 *EncMT, Film 2,*
NotNAT B, WhoHol B
Griffith, William M 1897-1960 *WhScrn 1,*
WhScrn 2, WhoHol B
Griffiths, Derek 1946- *WhoThe 16*
Griffiths, Jane *WhoHol A*
Griffiths, Jane 1929-1975 *WhScrn 2*
Griffiths, Jane 1930- *FilmgC, WhThe*
Griffiths, Trevor 1935- *ConDr 1977, WhoThe 16*
Griffo *Film 1*
Grigg, Ann *Film 2*
Griggs, John 1909-1967 *WhScrn 1, WhScrn 2,*
WhoHol B
Griggs, Loyal 1904- *FilmgC, WorEnF*
Grillo, Basil F 1910- *IntMPA 1977*
Grillo, John 1942- *ConDr 1977*
Grillparzer, Franz 1791-1872 *CnThe, McGWD,*
NotNAT B, OxThe, REnWD
Grimaldi, George H d1951 *NotNAT B*
Grimaldi, Joseph 1778-1837 *CnThe, OxThe,*
PIP&P
Grimaldi, Joseph 1779-1837 *NotNAT A*
Grimaldi, Marion 1926- *WhoThe 16*
Grimani, Julia d1806 *NotNAT B*
Grimault, Paul 1905- *DcFM, OxFilm, WorEnF*
Grimes, Gary 1955- *IntMPA 1977, WhoHol A*
Grimes, Tammy 1934- *BiE&WWA, CelR 3,*
CnThe, EncMT, MotPP, NotNAT,
WhoHol A, WhoThe 16
Grimes, Thomas 1887-1934 *WhScrn 2*
Grimm, Baron Friedrich Melchior Von 1723-1807
OxThe
Grimm, Jakob 1785-1863 *FilmgC*
Grimm, Wilhelm 1786-1859 *FilmgC*
Grimoin-Sanson, Raoul 1860-1941 *DcFM, OxFilm*
Grimston, Dorothy May *WhThe*
Grimwood, Herbert 1875-1929 *Film 1, Film 2,*
NotNAT B, WhThe, WhoHol B
Grinberg, Sherman 1927- *IntMPA 1977*
Grinde, Nicholas 1894- *TwYS A*
Grinde, Nick 1891- *FilmgC*
Griner, Barbara 1934- *BiE&WWA, NotNAT*
Gringoire, Pierre 1470?-1539? *McGWD*
Gringore, Pierre *OxThe*
Gringore, Pierre 1480-1539 *NotNAT B*
Gripp, Harry *Film 1, Film 2*
Grippo, Jan 1906- *IntMPA 1977*
Grisel, Louis R 1848-1928 *WhScrn 1, WhScrn 2,*

WhoHol B
Grisel, Louis Racine 1849-1928 *WhoStg 1906,*
WhoStg 1908
Griselle, Thomas 1891-1955 *AmSCAP 1966*
Grisi, Carlotta 1819-1899 *NotNAT B*
Grisier, Georges d1909 *NotNAT B*
Grisman, Sam H *WhThe*
Grismer, Joseph Rhode 1849-1922 *NotNAT B,*
WhThe, WhoStg 1906, WhoStg 1908
Griswold, Grace d1927 *Film 2, NotNAT B,*
WhThe, WhoHol B
Griswold, Herbert Spencer *Film 2*
Griswold, James *Film 1*
Gritsch, Willy *Film 2*
Grizzard, George *WhoHol A*
Grizzard, George 1928- *BiE&WWA, CnThe,*
NotNAT, PIP&P, WhoThe 16
Grizzard, George 1929- *FilmgC*
Grock 1880-1959 *FilmgC, NotNAT A, OxThe,*
WhScrn 2
Grodin, Charles 1935- *CelR 3, NotNAT,*
WhoHol A, WhoThe 16
Groeneveld, Ben 1899-1962 *WhScrn 2*
Groenveld, Ben d1962 *NotNAT B*
Groesse, Paul 1906- *IntMPA 1977*
Groetz, Carl *Film 2*
Grofe, Ferde 1892- *AmSCAP 1966*
Grogan, Phil 1909- *AmSCAP 1966*
Grogan, Reb *Film 2*
Groh, David *WhoHol A*
Gromon, Francis 1890- *AmSCAP 1966*
Gronau, Ernst *Film 2*
Gronberg, Ake 1914-1969 *WhScrn 2*
Gronroos, Georg *Film 1*
Groody, Louise 1897-1961 *EncMT, NotNAT B,*
WhThe
Grooms, Red *ConDr 1977E*
Grooney, Ernest G d1946 *WhScrn 1, WhScrn 2*
Gropper, Milton Herbert 1896-1955 *NotNAT B,*
WhThe
Gros-Guillaume *OxThe*
Gros-Guillaume 1600-1634 *NotNAT B*
Grosbard, Ulu 1929- *BiE&WWA, NotNAT,*
WhoThe 16
Grosklos, Betsy *WomWMM B*
Gross, Anthony 1905- *WorEnF*
Gross, Bethuel 1905- *AmSCAP 1966*
Gross, Charles 1934- *AmSCAP 1966*
Gross, Jerry *IntMPA 1977*
Gross, Jesse 1929- *BiE&WWA, NotNAT*
Gross, Kenneth H *IntMPA 1977*
Gross, Robert 1912- *IntMPA 1977*
Gross, Shelly 1921- *BiE&WWA, NotNAT,*
WhoThe 16
Gross, Walter 1909- *AmSCAP 1966*
Gross, William J 1837-1924 *WhScrn 1, WhScrn 2,*
WhoHol B
Grossberg, Jack 1927- *IntMPA 1977*
Grosskurth, Kurt 1909-1975 *WhScrn 2,*
WhoHol C
Grossman, Bernard 1885-1951 *AmSCAP 1966*
Grossman, Edward 1891- *AmSCAP 1966*
Grossman, Ernie 1924- *IntMPA 1977*
Grossman, Lawrence K *NewYTET*
Grossman, Reda *WomWMM B*
Grossmith, Ena 1896-1944 *NotNAT B, WhThe*
Grossmith, George 1847-1912 *NotNAT B, OxThe*
Grossmith, George 1874-1935 *EncMT,*
NotNAT A, NotNAT B, OxThe, WhThe,
WhoHol B
Grossmith, George 1875-1935 *WhScrn 1,*
WhScrn 2
Grossmith, George, Jr. *WhoStg 1906,*
WhoStg 1908

Grossmith, Lawrence 1877-1944 *NotNAT B,*
  OxThe, WhScrn 1, WhScrn 2, WhThe,
  WhoHol B, WhoStg 1906, WhoStg 1908
Grossmith, Walter Weedon 1852-1919 *NotNAT A,*
  NotNAT B, OxThe
Grossmith, Weedon 1852-1919 *WhThe,*
  WhoStg 1906, WhoStg 1908
Grossvogel, David 1925- *BiE&WWA,* *NotNAT*
Grosvenor, Melville Bell 1901- *CelR 3*
Grosvenor, Ralph L 1893- *AmSCAP 1966*
Grosz, Paul *IntMPA 1977*
Grot, Anton 1884- *FilmgC*
Groto, Luigi 1541-1585 *McGWD, OxThe*
Grotowski, Jerzy 1933- *NotNAT A*
Groulx, Gilles 1931- *WorEnF*
Grout, James 1927- *WhoThe 16*
Grout, Philip 1930- *WhoThe 16*
Grouya, Theodor J 1910- *AmSCAP 1966*
Grove, F C d1902 *NotNAT B*
Grove, Fred 1851-1927 *NotNAT B, WhThe*
Grove, Gerald *Film 2*
Grove, Richard D 1927- *AmSCAP 1966*
Grove, Sybil 1891- *Film 2, TwYS*
Grover, Arthur 1918- *AmSCAP 1966*
Grover, Leonard d1926 *NotNAT B*
Grover, Stanley 1926- *BiE&WWA, NotNAT*
Groves, Charles d1909 *NotNAT B*
Groves, Charles 1875-1955 *NotNAT B, WhThe*
Groves, Fred *Film 2*
Groves, Fred 1880-1955 *NotNAT B, WhThe*
Grower, Russell Gordon d1958 *WhScrn 1,*
  WhScrn 2
Grubcheva, Ivanka *WomWMM*
Grube, Max d1934 *NotNAT B*
Gruber, Frank 1904-1969 *FilmgC*
Gruber, Ludwig *McGWD*
Gruel, Henri 1923- *DcFM, WorEnF*
Gruelle, Johnny 1880?-1938 *AmSCAP 1966*
Gruen, Robert 1913- *IntMPA 1977*
Gruenberg, Axel 1902- *IntMPA 1977*
Gruenberg, Jerry 1927- *IntMPA 1977*
Gruenberg, Leonard S 1913- *IntMPA 1977*
Gruenberg, Louis 1884?-1964 *AmSCAP 1966,*
  NotNAT B
Gruendgens, Gustaf 1900-1963 *WhScrn 1,*
  WhScrn 2
Gruener, Allan *WhoHol A*
Gruenwald, Alfred 1886-1951 *AmSCAP 1966*
Gruise, Thomas S *Film 2*
Grun, Bernard 1901- *WhThe*
Grunberg, Jacques *AmSCAP 1966*
Grunberg, Karl 1891- *CnMD*
Grunberg, Max *Film 2*
Grundgens, Gustaf 1899-1963 *CroCD, NotNAT B,*
  OxThe
Grundgens, Gustav 1899-1963 *CnThe*
Grundman, Clare Ewing 1913- *AmSCAP 1966,*
  BiE&WWA, NotNAT
Grundy, Lily *WhThe*
Grundy, Sydney 1848-1914 *McGWD, NotNAT B,*
  OxThe, WhThe, WhoStg 1906,
  WhoStg 1908
Grune, Karl 1885-1962 *OxFilm*
Grune, Karl 1890-1962 *DcFM*
Gruning, Ilka *Film 2*
Grunn, Homer 1880-1944 *AmSCAP 1966*
Grunwald, Alfred d1951 *NotNAT B*
Grunwald, Harry *Film 2*
Gruver, Elbert A d1962 *NotNAT B*
Gruzinsky, D *Film 2*
Gryphius, Andreas 1616-1664 *CnThe, McGWD,*
  OxThe, REnWD
Grzanna, Donald E 1931- *AmSCAP 1966*
Gual, Adria 1872-1943 *OxThe*

Guard, Kit 1894-1961 *Film 2, NotNAT B,*
  TwYS, WhScrn 1, WhScrn 2, WhoHol B
Guard, Sully d1916 *WhScrn 2*
Guard, William J d1932 *NotNAT B*
Guardino, Harry 1925- *BiE&WWA, FilmgC,*
  IntMPA 1977, MovMk, WhoHol A
Guare, John 1938- *CelR 3, ConDr 1977, NatPD,*
  NotNAT, PIP&P A, WhoThe 16
Guareschi, Giovanni 1908-1968 *FilmgC*
Guarini, Alfredo 1901- *IntMPA 1977*
Guarini, Gian Battista 1538-1612 *McGWD*
Guarini, Giovan Battista 1538-1612 *REnWD*
Guarini, Giovanni Battista 1537-1612 *OxThe*
Guarnieri, John Albert 1917- *AmSCAP 1966*
Guazzoni, Enrico 1876-1949 *DcFM, WorEnF*
Guber, Lee 1920- *BiE&WWA, NotNAT,*
  WhoThe 16
Gubin, S *Film 2*
Gucci, Aldo 1909- *CelR 3*
Guccione, Bob 1930- *CelR 3*
Gude, John *NewYTET*
Gudegast, Hans *WhoHol A*
Gudgeon, Bertrand C d1948 *WhScrn 1,*
  WhScrn 2, WhoHol B
Gudrun, Ann *WhoHol A*
Guelstorff, Max 1882-1947 *Film 2, WhScrn 1,*
  WhScrn 2, WhoHol B
Guensteq, F F 1862-1936 *WhScrn 1, WhScrn 2*
Guenther, Johannes Von 1866- *McGWD*
Guenther, Ruth 1910-1974 *WhScrn 2, WhoHol B*
Guerin, Bruce *Film 2*
Guerin D'Etriche, Isaac Francois 1636?-1728 *OxThe*
Guernsey, Otis L, Jr. 1918- *NatPD*
Guerra, Armand *Film 2*
Guerra, Ruy 1931- *WorEnF*
Guerrero 1868-1928 *WhThe*
Guerrero, Maria 1868-1928 *NotNAT B*
Guertzman, Paul *Film 2*
Guest, Charlie *Film 2*
Guest, Jean H 1921- *BiE&WWA, NotNAT*
Guest, Val 1911- *FilmgC, IntMPA 1977*
Guetary, Georges *WhoHol A*
Guetary, Georges 1915- *FilmgC*
Guetary, Georges 1917- *WhThe*
Guette, Toto *Film 2*
Guettel, Henry 1928- *BiE&WWA, NotNAT*
Guffey, Burnett 1905- *CmMov, DcFM, FilmgC,*
  IntMPA 1977, WorEnF
Guggenheim, Peggy 1898- *CelR 3*
Guglielmi, Bernadine 1907- *AmSCAP 1966*
Guglielmi, Danny 1909- *AmSCAP 1966*
Guhl, George d1943 *WhScrn 1, WhScrn 2,*
  WhoHol B
Guiches, Gustave 1860- *WhThe*
Guide, Paul *Film 2*
Guilbert, Yvette d1944 *Film 2, WhoHol B,*
  WhoStg 1906, WhoStg 1908
Guilbert, Yvette 1865-1944 *NotNAT A,*
  NotNAT B
Guilbert, Yvette 1868-1944 *WhScrn 2, WhThe*
Guilbert, Yvette 1869-1944 *OxThe*
Guild, Nancy *MotPP*
Guild, Nancy 1925- *WhoHol A*
Guild, Nancy 1926- *FilmgC*
Guiler, William *Film 2*
Guilfoyle, James 1892-1964 *Film 2, WhScrn 2*
Guilfoyle, Paul 1902-1961 *FilmgC, MotPP,*
  MovMk, NotNAT B, Vers A, WhScrn 1,
  WhScrn 2, WhoHol B
Guilhene, Jacques *Film 1*
Guillemaud, Marcel 1867- *WhThe*
Guillemot, Agnes *WomWMM*
Guillermin, John 1923- *BiDFlm*
Guillermin, John 1925- *CmMov, FilmgC,*
  IntMPA 1977, WorEnF

Guillon, Madeleine *WomWMM*
Guillot-Gorju 1600-1648 *OxThe*
Guimard, La 1743-1816 *NotNAT B*
Guimera, Angel d1924 *WhThe*
Guimera, Angel 1845-1924 *NotNAT B*
Guimera, Angel 1847-1924 *McGWD, OxThe*
Guinan, Texas d1934 *WhoHol B*
Guinan, Texas 1891-1933 *Film 1, Film 2,*
   NotNAT B, TwYS, WhScrn 1, WhScrn 2
Guinness, Sir Alec 1914- *BiDFlm, BiE&WWA,*
   CelR 3, CmMov, CnThe, FamA&A,
   FilmgC, IntMPA 1977, MotPP, MovMk,
   NotNAT, NotNAT A, OxFilm, OxThe,
   PIP&P, WhoHol A, WhoThe 16, WorEnF
Guinon, Albert 1863- *WhThe*
Guiol, Fred 1898-1964 *FilmgC, NotNAT B*
Guion, David W 1892- *AmSCAP 1966*
Guise, Thomas *Film 1, Film 2*
Guise, Wyndham *Film 2*
Guitry, Jean d1920 *NotNAT B*
Guitry, Lucien-Germain 1860-1925 *NotNAT B,*
   OxThe, WhThe
Guitry, Sacha 1885-1957 *BiDFlm, CnMD, CnThe,*
   DcFM, FilmgC, McGWD, ModWD,
   MovMk, NotNAT A, NotNAT B, OxFilm,
   OxThe, PIP&P, WhScrn 1, WhScrn 2,
   WhThe, WhoHol B, WorEnF
Guitry, Yvonne Printemps 1895- *OxThe*
Guitty, Madeleine 1871-1936 *Film 2, WhScrn 1,*
   WhScrn 2, WhoHol B
Guizar, Tito *WhoHol A*
Gulager, Clu 1935- *FilmgC, WhoHol A*
Gulesian, Grace Warner *AmSCAP 1966*
Gullan, Campbell d1939 *Film 2, NotNAT B,*
   WhThe, WhoHol B
Gulliver, Charles 1882-1961 *WhThe*
Gulliver, Dorothy 1913- *Film 2, TwYS,*
   WhoHol A
Gulsdorff, Max *Film 2*
Gumble, Albert 1883-1946 *AmSCAP 1966*
Gumm, Suzanne d1964 *NotNAT B*
Gump, Richard 1906- *AmSCAP 1966*
Gunn, Charles E 1883-1918 *Film 1, WhScrn 2*
Gunn, Earl 1902-1963 *WhScrn 2*
Gunn, Franzi *Film 2*
Gunn, Gilbert 1912?- *FilmgC*
Gunn, Haidee 1882-1961 *WhThe*
Gunn, Hartford N, Jr. *NewYTET*
Gunn, Judy 1914- *WhThe*
Gunn, Moses 1929- *IntMPA 1977, WhoHol A,*
   WhoThe 16
Gunnell, John 1911- *BiE&WWA*
Gunnell, Richard d1634 *OxThe*
Gunning, Louise 1879-1960 *NotNAT B, WhThe*
Gunsberg, Sheldon 1920- *IntMPA 1977*
Gunsky, Maurice J 1888-1945 *AmSCAP 1966*
Guntekin, Resat Nuri 1889-1956 *REnWD*
Gunter, A C d1907 *NotNAT B*
Gunter, Edward C 1917- *AmSCAP 1966*
Gunter, Patricia *WomWMM B*
Gunther, Paul *Film 2*
Gunther, William 1924- *AmSCAP 1966*
Gunzburg, M L *IntMPA 1977*
Gurie, Sigrid 1911-1969 *FilmgC, ThFT,*
   WhScrn 1, WhScrn 2, WhoHol B
Gurievitch, Grania *WomWMM B*
Gurin, Ellen 1948-1972 *WhScrn 2, WhoHol B*
Gurit, Anna *WomWMM*
Gurnee, Hal *NewYTET*
Gurney, A R, Jr. 1930- *ConDr 1977, NatPD*
Gurney, Claud 1897-1946 *NotNAT B, WhThe*
Gurney, Dennis 1897- *BiE&WWA, NotNAT*
Gurney, Edmund 1852-1925 *Film 2, NotNAT B,*
   WhScrn 1, WhScrn 2, WhoHol B

Gurney, Rachel *WhoThe 16*
Gurnyak, K *Film 2*
Gurtler, Arnold B, Jr. *BiE&WWA*
Gusikoff, Michel 1895- *AmSCAP 1966*
Gusman, Meyer 1894-1960 *AmSCAP 1966*
Guss, Jack Raphael 1919- *NatPD*
Guss, Louis 1918- *BiE&WWA, NotNAT*
Gussin, David 1899- *AmSCAP 1966*
Gustafson, Carol 1925- *BiE&WWA, NotNAT*
Gustafson, Vera 1918- *AmSCAP 1966*
Gustav III 1746-1782 *OxThe*
Gustine, Paul 1893-1974 *WhScrn 2*
Gusyev, Victor Mikhailovich 1908-1944 *NotNAT B,*
   OxThe
Guterson, Vladimar d1964 *NotNAT B*
Guthrie, A B, Jr. *CmMov*
Guthrie, Arlo 1947- *CelR 3, WhoHol A*
Guthrie, Charles W 1871-1939 *WhScrn 1,*
   WhScrn 2
Guthrie, Sir Tyrone 1900-1971 *BiE&WWA,*
   CnThe, NotNAT A, NotNAT B, OxThe,
   PIP&P, WhThe, WhoHol B
Gutierrez, Alicia 1928-1967 *WhScrn 2*
Gutkelch, Walter 1901- *CnMD*
Gutman, D *Film 2*
Gutman, Karl *Film 2*
Gutowski, Eugene 1925- *IntMPA 1977*
Gutowski, Gene 1925- *FilmgC*
Gutzkow, Karl Ferdinand 1811-1878 *McGWD,*
   NotNAT B, OxThe
Guy, Alice *Film 1*
Guy, Eula d1960 *WhScrn 2*
Guy-Blache, Alice 1873-1965 *DcFM, FilmgC,*
   MovMk, OxFilm
Guyett, Harold P 1920- *IntMPA 1977*
Guynes, Charlsa Anne 1933- *AmSCAP 1966*
Guzmab, Robert E *Film 2*
Gwenn, Edmond d1959 *PIP&P*
Gwenn, Edmund 1875-1959 *Film 1, Film 2,*
   FilmgC, MotPP, MovMk, NotNAT B,
   OxFilm, WhScrn 1, WhScrn 2, WhThe,
   WhoHol B
Gwenn, Edmund 1876-1959 *Vers A*
Gwenn, Edmund 1877-1959 *BiDFlm*
Gwilym, Mike 1949- *WhoThe 16*
Gwinnett, Richard d1717 *NotNAT B*
Gwirtz, Irvin R 1903-1957 *AmSCAP 1966*
Gwyn, Nell 1650-1687 *NotNAT A, NotNAT B*
Gwynn, Michael 1916-1976 *FilmgC, WhoHol A,*
   WhoThe 16
Gwynn, Nell 1650-1687 *CnThe, OxThe*
Gwynne, Anne 1918- *FilmgC, IntMPA 1977,*
   MotPP, WhoHol A
Gwynne, Fred *WhoHol A*
Gwynne, Fred 1924?- *FilmgC*
Gwynne, Fred 1926- *NotNAT, WhoThe 16*
Gwynne, Julia d1934 *NotNAT B*
Gwynne, Michael C *WhoHol A*
Gwynne, Nell 1650-1687 *PIP&P*
Gwyther, Geoffrey Matheson 1890-1944
   NotNAT B, WhThe
Gyarfas, Laszlo *Film 2*
Gyarfas, Miklos 1915- *CroCD*
Gyllenborg, Carl 1679-1746 *OxThe*
Gynt, Greta 1916- *FilmgC, WhThe, WhoHol A*
Gypsy Gould *WhScrn 1, WhScrn 2*
Gyrmathy, Livia *WomWMM*

H

Ha Ha, Minnie *Film 1*
Haack, Bruce C 1932- *AmSCAP 1966*
Haack, Kaethe *Film 2*
Haade, William 1903-1966 *WhScrn 2, WhoHol B*
Haag, Jan *WomWMM B*
Haaga, Agnes 1916- *BiE&WWA*
Haagen, Al H 1871-1953 *WhScrn 1, WhScrn 2*
Haal, Renee d1964 *WhScrn 1, WhScrn 2, WhoHol B*
Haanstra, Bert 1916- *DcFM, FilmgC, OxFilm, WorEnF*
Haas, Charles F 1913- *FilmgC, WorEnF*
Haas, Dolly 1910- *BiE&WWA, NotNAT, WhoHol A*
Haas, Dolly 1911- *FilmgC*
Haas, Hugh d1968 *WhoHol B*
Haas, Hugo d1968 *MotPP*
Haas, Hugo 1901-1968 *FilmgC*
Haas, Hugo 1902-1968 *NotNAT B, WhScrn 1, WhScrn 2*
Haas, Robert M d1962 *NotNAT B*
Haas, Walter 1900- *IntMPA 1977*
Haase, Friedrich d1911 *NotNAT B*
Haavikko, Paavo 1931- *CroCD*
Habash, John 1926- *AmSCAP 1966*
Habay, Andree *Film 2*
Habeeb, Tony 1927- *IntMPA 1977*
Habeebullah, Shyama *WomWMM*
Haber, Joyce 1931?- *CelR 3*
Haber, Joyce 1932- *IntMPA 1977*
Haberfield, Graham 1941-1975 *WhScrn 2, WhoHol C*
Habington, William d1654 *NotNAT B*
Hack, Herman 1899-1967 *WhScrn 1, WhScrn 2*
Hack, Signe 1899-1973 *WhScrn 2, WhoHol B*
Hackady, Hal *NatPD*
Hackathorne, George 1896-1940 *Film 1, Film 2, MotPP, TwYS, WhScrn 1, WhScrn 2, WhoHol B*
Hacker, Charles R *IntMPA 1977*
Hacker, Maria 1904-1963 *NotNAT B, WhScrn 1, WhScrn 2*
Hacker, Samuel 1903- *IntMPA 1977*
Hackerman, Nancy *WomWMM B*
Hackett, Albert 1900- *BiE&WWA, CmMov, Film 1, Film 2, FilmgC, ModWD, NotNAT, TwYS, WorEnF*
Hackett, Alfred *Film 2*
Hackett, Buddy 1924- *AmSCAP 1966, BiE&WWA, CelR 3, FilmgC, IntMPA 1977, MotPP, MovMk, WhoHol A*
Hackett, Catharine Lee Sugg 1797-1845 *OxThe*
Hackett, Charles d1942 *NotNAT B*
Hackett, Florence 1882-1954 *Film 1, MotPP, NotNAT B, WhScrn 1, WhScrn 2, WhoHol B*

Hackett, Hal 1923-1967 *WhScrn 1, WhScrn 2, WhoHol B*
Hackett, Mrs. J H d1909 *NotNAT B*
Hackett, Mrs. J H 1797-1845 *NotNAT B*
Hackett, James Henry 1800-1871 *FamA&A, NotNAT B, OxThe, PIP&P*
Hackett, James K 1869-1926 *FamA&A, Film 1, NotNAT B, OxThe, PIP&P, WhScrn 1, WhScrn 2, WhThe, WhoHol B, WhoStg 1906, WhoStg 1908*
Hackett, Jeanette *Film 1*
Hackett, Joan *BiE&WWA, MotPP, NotNAT, WhoHol A*
Hackett, Joan 1933- *MovMk*
Hackett, Joan 1934- *FilmgC*
Hackett, Joan 1942- *IntMPA 1977*
Hackett, Karl 1893-1948 *WhScrn 1, WhScrn 2, WhoHol B*
Hackett, Lillian 1899-1973 *Film 2, WhScrn 2, WhoHol B*
Hackett, Norman Honore 1874- *WhThe*
Hackett, Raymond d1958 *MotPP, WhoHol B*
Hackett, Raymond 1902-1958 *FilmgC, NotNAT B, WhScrn 1, WhScrn 2, WhThe*
Hackett, Raymond 1903-1958 *Film 1, Film 2*
Hackett, Walter 1876-1944 *NotNAT B, WhThe*
Hackman, Gene *WhoHol A*
Hackman, Gene 1930- *BiDFlm, CmMov, FilmgC, IntMPA 1977*
Hackman, Gene 1931- *CelR 3, MovMk, OxFilm*
Hackney, Alan 1924- *FilmgC*
Hackney, Mabel d1914 *NotNAT B, WhThe*
Hacks, Peter 1928- *CnMD, CroCD, McGWD, ModWD*
Hadden, Frances Roots 1910- *AmSCAP 1966*
Hadden, Richard M 1910- *AmSCAP 1966*
Haddon, Archibald 1871-1942 *NotNAT B, WhThe*
Haddon, Peter 1898-1962 *Film 2, FilmgC, NotNAT B, WhScrn 1, WhScrn 2, WhThe, WhoHol B*
Haddrick, Ron 1929- *WhoThe 16*
Haden, Sara 1897-1973 *MGM, MovMk, WhoHol A*
Haden, Sara 1899- *FilmgC, Vers A*
Hadfield, Harry *Film 1*
Hading, Jane d1941 *NotNAT B*
Hading, Jane 1859-1933 *NotNAT B, WhThe*
Hadjidakis, Manos 1925- *OxFilm, WorEnF*
Hadley, Bert *Film 2*
Hadley, Henry 1871-1937 *AmSCAP 1966*
Hadley, R W, Jr. *IntMPA 1977*
Hadley, Reed 1911-1974 *FilmgC, Vers B, WhScrn 2, WhoHol B*
Hadlock, Channing M *IntMPA 1977*
Haecker, Hans Joachim 1910- *CnMD*

Haefeli, Charles Jockey 1889-1955 *WhScrn 1,*
  WhScrn 2, WhoHol B
Haenckels, Paul *Film 2*
Haenschen, Gustave *AmSCAP 1966*
Haeussler, Paul 1895- *AmSCAP 1966*
Hafez, Bahija *WomWMM*
Hafner, Philipp 1735-1764 *OxThe*
Hafter, Robert 1897-1955 *WhScrn 2*
Hagan, James B d1947 *NotNAT B*
Hagart, Dorothy *Film 1*
Hagel, Robert K 1940- *IntMPA 1977*
Hageman, Richard 1882-1966 *AmSCAP 1966,*
  CmMov, WhScrn 2
Hagen, Charles F 1872-1958 *WhScrn 1,*
  WhScrn 2, WhoHol B
Hagen, Chet *NewYTET*
Hagen, Edna *Film 2*
Hagen, Jean *IntMPA 1977, MotPP, WhoHol A*
Hagen, Jean 1924- *FilmgC, MGM*
Hagen, Jean 1925- *MovMk*
Hagen, John Milton 1902- *AmSCAP 1966*
Hagen, Kevin *WhoHol A*
Hagen, Margarethe 1890-1966 *WhScrn 1,*
  WhScrn 2
Hagen, Ross *WhoHol A*
Hagen, Uta 1919- *BiE&WWA, CnThe, NotNAT,*
  PIP&P, WhoHol A, WhoThe 16
Hager, Clyde d1944 *WhoHol B*
Hager, Clyde 1886-1944 *AmSCAP 1966*
Hager, Clyde 1887-1944 *WhScrn 1, WhScrn 2*
Hagerthy, Ron *WhoHol A*
Hagerty, James C *NewYTET*
Haggar, George A 1897- *AmSCAP 1966*
Haggar, William 1851-1924 *FilmgC*
Haggard, Sir H Rider 1856-1925 *FilmgC*
Haggard, Merle 1937- *CelR 3, WhoHol A*
Haggard, Piers 1939- *FilmgC*
Haggard, Stephen d1943 *WhoHol B*
Haggard, Stephen 1911-1943 *NotNAT A,*
  NotNAT B, WhThe
Haggard, Stephen 1912-1943 *WhScrn 1,*
  WhScrn 2
Haggart, Robert 1914- *AmSCAP 1966*
Haggerty, Charles *Film 1*
Haggerty, Don *WhoHol A*
Haggerty, H B *WhoHol A*
Haggin, James Ben Ali 1882-1951 *NotNAT B*
Haggott, John Cecil d1964 *NotNAT B*
Hagman, Larry 1930- *FilmgC, WhoHol A*
Hagmann, Stuart 1939- *FilmgC*
Hagney, Frank 1884-1973 *Film 2, TwYS,*
  WhScrn 2, WhoHol B
Hague, Albert 1920- *AmSCAP 1966,*
  BiE&WWA, EncMT, NewMT, NotNAT,
  WhoThe 16
Hahn, Carl 1874-1929 *AmSCAP 1966*
Hahn, Herbert R 1924- *IntMPA 1977*
Hahn, Jess *WhoHol A*
Hahn, Paul *WhoHol A*
Hahn, Sally 1908-1933 *WhScrn 1, WhScrn 2*
Haid, Grit *WhScrn 2*
Haid, Liane *Film 2*
Haid, William 1901- *AmSCAP 1966*
Haieff, Alexei 1914- *AmSCAP 1966*
Haig, Douglas *Film 2*
Haig, Emma 1898-1939 *NotNAT B, WhThe*
Haig, Raymond V 1917-1963 *WhScrn 1,*
  WhScrn 2
Haig, Sid *WhoHol A*
Haigh, Kenneth 1929- *BiE&WWA, CnThe,*
  FilmgC, NotNAT, PIP&P, WhoHol A,
  WhoThe 16
Haight, George 1905- *BiE&WWA, WhThe*
Hailey, Marian *NotNAT*

Hailey, Oliver 1932- *ConDr 1977, NatPD,*
  NotNAT, WhoThe 16
Haim, Harry *Film 2*
Hain, Nadine *WomWMM*
Haine, Horace J 1868-1940 *WhScrn 1, WhScrn 2,*
  WhoHol B
Haines, Connie *WhoHol A*
Haines, Donald d1942? *Film 2, WhScrn 2*
Haines, Edmund 1914- *AmSCAP 1966*
Haines, Ella *Film 1*
Haines, Herbert E 1880-1923 *NotNAT B, WhThe*
Haines, Horace J *Film 1*
Haines, J Talbot d1843 *NotNAT B*
Haines, James A 1925- *AmSCAP 1966*
Haines, Joseph d1701 *OxThe, PIP&P*
Haines, Louis *Film 2*
Haines, Rea *TwYS*
Haines, Rhea 1895-1964 *Film 2, NotNAT B,*
  WhScrn 1, WhScrn 2, WhoHol B
Haines, Robert Terrel 1870-1943 *Film 1, Film 2,*
  NotNAT B, TwYS, WhScrn 1, WhScrn 2,
  WhThe, WhoStg 1906, WhoStg 1908
Haines, William 1900-1973 *Film 2, FilmgC,*
  MotPP, MovMk, TwYS, WhScrn 2,
  WhoHol B
Haines, William Wister 1908- *BiE&WWA,*
  ModWD, NotNAT
Haire, Wilson John 1932- *ConDr 1977*
Hairston, Jester 1901- *AmSCAP 1966,*
  WhoHol A
Hairston, William *NatPD*
Haisman, Irene *Film 2*
Hajman, L *Film 2*
Hajos, Karl 1889-1950 *AmSCAP 1966*
Hajos, Mitzi 1891- *WhThe*
Hakansson, Julia Mathilda 1853- *WhThe*
Hakim, Andre 1915- *FilmgC*
Hakim, Raymond 1909- *FilmgC, OxFilm*
Hakim, Robert 1907- *FilmgC, OxFilm*
Halas, George 1895- *CelR 3*
Halas, John 1912- *DcFM, FilmgC,*
  IntMPA 1977, OxFilm, WorEnF
Halas, Joy Batchelor 1914- *FilmgC*
Halas, Susan *WomWMM B*
Halbe, Max 1865-1944 *CnMD, McGWD,*
  ModWD, NotNAT B
Halberstam, David 1934- *CelR 3*
Haldeman, Oakley 1909- *AmSCAP 1966*
Hale, Alan 1892-1950 *CmMov, Film 1, Film 2,*
  FilmgC, MotPP, MovMk, NotNAT B,
  TwYS, Vers A, WhScrn 1, WhScrn 2,
  WhoHol B
Hale, Alan, Jr. 1918- *FilmgC, IntMPA 1977,*
  WhoHol A
Hale, Barbara 1922- *FilmgC, IntMPA 1977,*
  MotPP, MovMk, WhoHol A
Hale, Barnaby 1927-1964 *WhScrn 1, WhScrn 2,*
  WhoHol B
Hale, Binnie 1899- *EncMT, FilmgC, WhThe,*
  WhoHol A
Hale, Chanin *WhoHol A*
Hale, Creighton 1882-1965 *Film 1, Film 2,*
  FilmgC, MotPP, MovMk, TwYS, WhScrn 1,
  WhScrn 2, WhoHol B
Hale, Dorothy 1905-1938 *NotNAT B, WhScrn 2,*
  WhoHol B
Hale, Edward Everett, III d1953 *NotNAT B*
Hale, Florence *Film 2*
Hale, George d1956 *NotNAT B*
Hale, Georgia *MotPP, WhoHol A*
Hale, Georgia 1905?- *MovMk*
Hale, Georgia 1906- *Film 2, TwYS*
Hale, Helen *WhoStg 1908*
Hale, J Robert 1874-1940 *NotNAT B, WhThe*

Hale, J Robert *see also* Hale, Robert
Hale, Jean *WhoHol A*
Hale, John d1947 *NotNAT B, WhoHol B*
Hale, John 1926- *ConDr 1977*
Hale, Jonathan d1966 *MotPP, WhoHol B*
Hale, Jonathan 1891-1966 *WhScrn 1, WhScrn 2*
Hale, Jonathan 1892-1966 *FilmgC, MovMk, Vers B*
Hale, Lionel 1909- *WhoThe 16*
Hale, Louise Closser 1872-1933 *Film 2, MotPP, MovMk, NotNAT B, OxThe, ThFT, WhScrn 1, WhScrn 2, WhThe, WhoHol B*
Hale, Monte 1919- *IntMPA 1977*
Hale, Monte 1921- *WhoHol A*
Hale, Philip d1934 *NotNAT B*
Hale, Prentis Cobb 1910- *CelR 3*
Hale, Richard *WhoHol A*
Hale, Robert 1874-1940 *WhScrn 1, WhScrn 2, WhoHol B*
Hale, Robert *see also* Hale, J Robert
Hale, Robertson 1891-1967 *WhScrn 1, WhScrn 2*
Hale, Ruth d1934 *NotNAT B*
Hale, S T 1899- *WhThe*
Hale, Sonnie 1902-1959 *EncMT, Film 2, FilmgC, NotNAT B, WhScrn 1, WhScrn 2, WhThe, WhoHol B*
Hale, William 1928- *FilmgC*
Haleff, Maxine *WomWMM B*
Hales, Jonathan 1937- *WhoThe 16*
Hales, Thomas 1740?-1780 *NotNAT B*
Halevy, Leon d1883 *NotNAT B*
Halevy, Ludovic 1834-1908 *McGWD, ModWD, NotNAT B, PIP&P*
Haley, Bill 1925- *AmSCAP 1966*
Haley, Jack *WhoHol A*
Haley, Jack 1899- *FilmgC, MovMk*
Haley, Jack 1901- *BiE&WWA*
Haley, Jack 1902- *EncMT, WhThe*
Haley, Jack, Jr. *IntMPA 1977, NewYTET*
Halfpenny, Tony 1913- *WhThe*
Hall, Adelaide 1895- *EncMT*
Hall, Adelaide 1910- *BiE&WWA, NotNAT*
Hall, Adrian 1928- *BiE&WWA, NotNAT*
Hall, Alexander 1894-1968 *FilmgC, MovMk, NotNAT B, WhScrn 1, WhScrn 2, WhoHol B*
Hall, Alfred Henry 1880-1943 *WhScrn 1, WhScrn 2*
Hall, Alice 1924- *AmSCAP 1966*
Hall, Anmer 1863-1953 *NotNAT B, WhThe*
Hall, Ben *Film 2*
Hall, Bettina 1906- *EncMT, WhThe*
Hall, Betty 1914- *Film 2*
Hall, Bob 1907- *BiE&WWA*
Hall, Charles D 1899-1959 *DcFM, Film 2, FilmgC, WhScrn 1, WhScrn 2*
Hall, Charlie d1959 *TwYS, WhoHol B*
Hall, Cliff d1972 *WhoHol B*
Hall, Conrad 1926- *FilmgC, OxFilm, WorEnF*
Hall, Conrad 1927- *CmMov, IntMPA 1977*
Hall, David 1929- *WhThe*
Hall, Donald 1878-1948 *Film 1, Film 2, WhScrn 2*
Hall, Dorothy 1906-1953 *Film 2, NotNAT B, WhScrn 1, WhScrn 2, WhThe, WhoHol B*
Hall, Dudley d1960 *WhoHol B*
Hall, Edmond 1901- *AmSCAP 1966*
Hall, Ella 1896- *Film 1, Film 2, TwYS, WhoHol A*
Hall, Ethel May d1967 *WhoHol B*
Hall, Ethel May *see also* Halls, Ethel May
Hall, Evelyn Walsh *Film 2, TwYS*
Hall, Fred 1898-1964 *AmSCAP 1966*
Hall, Gabrielle d1967 *WhScrn 1, WhScrn 2*

Hall, George M 1890-1930 *Film 1, WhScrn 1, WhScrn 2, WhoHol B*
Hall, Geraldine 1905-1970 *WhScrn 1, WhScrn 2, WhoHol B*
Hall, Gertrude 1912- *AmSCAP 1966*
Hall, Grayson *MotPP, NotNAT, WhoHol A, WhoThe 16*
Hall, Hallene d1966 *WhoHol B*
Hall, Helen *AmSCAP 1966*
Hall, Henry Leonard d1954 *Film 2, WhScrn 1, WhScrn 2, WhoHol B*
Hall, Huntz 1920- *FilmgC, IntMPA 1977, MovMk, WhoHol A*
Hall, J A *Film 1*
Hall, J Robinson *Film 1*
Hall, J W *WhThe*
Hall, James 1897-1940 *Film 2, TwYS*
Hall, James 1900-1940 *FilmgC, MovMk, NotNAT B, WhScrn 1, WhScrn 2, WhoHol B*
Hall, Jane 1880-1975 *WhScrn 2*
Hall, Jenni *WomWMM*
Hall, John 1878-1936 *WhScrn 1, WhScrn 2, WhoHol B*
Hall, John C, Jr. 1929- *BiE&WWA*
Hall, Jon 1913- *CmMov, FilmgC, IntMPA 1977, MovMk, WhoHol A*
Hall, Josephine *Film 2*
Hall, Josephine d1920 *NotNAT B*
Hall, Joyce 1891- *CelR 3*
Hall, Juanita d1968 *BiE&WWA, MotPP, WhoHol B*
Hall, Juanita 1901-1968 *EncMT, FilmgC, NotNAT B*
Hall, Juanita 1902-1968 *WhScrn 1, WhScrn 2*
Hall, Kathryn *WhScrn 1*
Hall, Ken G 1901- *IntMPA 1977*
Hall, Laura Nelson 1876- *WhThe*
Hall, Lillian *Film 1, Film 2*
Hall, Lois *WhoHol A*
Hall, Mark *WhoHol A*
Hall, Monty 1923- *CelR 3, NewYTET*
Hall, Natalie 1904- *EncMT, WhThe*
Hall, Nelson L 1881-1944 *WhScrn 1, WhScrn 2*
Hall, Newton *Film 2*
Hall, Owen 1853-1906 *WhoStg 1906, WhoStg 1908*
Hall, Owen 1853-1907 *EncMT, NotNAT B*
Hall, Pauline d1974 *WhoHol B*
Hall, Pauline 1860-1919 *NotNAT B, WhThe, WhoStg 1906, WhoStg 1908*
Hall, Peter 1930- *BiE&WWA, CnThe, CroCD, FilmgC, NotNAT, OxFilm, OxThe, PIP&P, WhoThe 16, WorEnF*
Hall, Porter d1953 *MotPP, WhoHol B*
Hall, Porter 1883-1963 *MovMk*
Hall, Porter 1888-1953 *FilmgC, NotNAT B, Vers B, WhScrn 1, WhScrn 2*
Hall, Ruth 1912- *WhoHol A*
Hall, Mrs. S C d1881 *NotNAT B*
Hall, Sharon *WomWMM B*
Hall, Thurston d1958 *MotPP, WhoHol B*
Hall, Thurston 1882-1958 *NotNAT B, WhThe, WhoStg 1906, WhoStg 1908*
Hall, Thurston 1883-1958 *FilmgC, MovMk, Vers B, WhScrn 1, WhScrn 2*
Hall, Thurston 1883-1959 *Film 1, Film 2, TwYS*
Hall, Wendell Woods 1896- *AmSCAP 1966*
Hall, Willard Lee *Film 2*
Hall, Willis 1929- *CnMD, CnThe, ConDr 1977, CroCD, FilmgC, ModWD, PIP&P, WhoThe 16*
Hall, Winter 1878-1947 *Film 1, Film 2, TwYS, WhScrn 2*

Hall, Zooey *WhoHol A*
Hall-Caine, Lily d1914 *NotNAT B*
Hall-Davies, Lillian 1901-1933 *WhoHol B*
Hall-Davis, Lillian 1901-1933 *Film 1, Film 2,*
  WhScrn 1, WhScrn 2
Hallagan, Robert H 1926- *AmSCAP 1966*
Hallam, Miss *PIP&P*
Hallam, Adam d1738 *NotNAT B, PIP&P*
Hallam, Ann d1740 *NotNAT B*
Hallam, Basil 1889-1916 *NotNAT B, WhThe*
Hallam, Harry *Film 2*
Hallam, Henry *Film 1*
Hallam, Isabella 1746-1826 *OxThe*
Hallam, John *WhoHol A*
Hallam, Mrs. Lewis d1773 *NotNAT B, PIP&P*
Hallam, Lewis 1714-1756 *NotNAT B, OxThe,*
  PIP&P
Hallam, Lewis, Jr. 1740?-1808 *FamA&A,*
  NotNAT B, OxThe, PIP&P
Hallam, Nancy 1759-1761 *NotNAT B*
Hallam, Sarah *NotNAT B*
Hallam, Thomas d1735 *NotNAT B*
Hallam, William d1758 *NotNAT B, PIP&P*
Hallard, C M 1866-1942 *WhScrn 1, WhScrn 2,*
  WhoHol B
Hallard, Charles Maitland 1865-1942 *NotNAT B,*
  WhThe
Hallatt, Henry 1888-1952 *NotNAT B, WhThe,*
  WhoHol B
Hallatt, Mary *WhoHol A*
Hallatt, May 1882- *FilmgC*
Hallatt, W H d1927 *NotNAT B*
Halldoff, Jan 1940- *WorEnF*
Halleck, Deedee *WomWMM A, WomWMM B*
Haller, Daniel *CmMov*
Haller, Daniel 1928- *FilmgC*
Haller, Daniel 1929- *WorEnF*
Haller, Ernest 1896-1970 *CmMov, DcFM,*
  FilmgC, OxFilm, WorEnF
Haller, Ray *Film 2*
Halleran, Edith *Film 1*
Hallet, Agnes 1880-1954 *WhScrn 1, WhScrn 2*
Hallet, Judith *WomWMM B*
Hallett, Albert 1870-1935 *WhScrn 1, WhScrn 2,*
  WhoHol B
Hallett, Jim *Film 2*
Hallett, John C *AmSCAP 1966*
Halliday, Andrew d1877 *NotNAT B*
Halliday, Gardner 1910-1966 *WhScrn 1,*
  WhScrn 2
Halliday, John 1880-1947 *Film 2, FilmgC,*
  MovMk, NotNAT B, WhScrn 1, WhScrn 2,
  WhThe, WhoHol B
Halliday, Lena d1937 *NotNAT B, WhThe*
Halliday, Richard 1905-1973 *BiE&WWA,*
  NotNAT B
Halliday, Robert 1893- *EncMT, WhThe*
Halligan, Lillian *Film 2*
Halligan, William 1884-1957 *WhScrn 1,*
  WhScrn 2, WhoHol B
Halliwell, David 1936- *ConDr 1977, WhoThe 16*
Halliwell, David 1937- *CroCD*
Halliwell-Phillips, James Orchard d1888
  NotNAT B
Hallor, Edith 1896-1971 *WhScrn 1, WhScrn 2,*
  WhoHol B
Hallor, Ray 1900-1944 *Film 1, Film 2, TwYS,*
  WhScrn 1, WhScrn 2, WhoHol B
Halloran, Edward G 1909- *AmSCAP 1966*
Hallowell, Russell F 1897-1965 *AmSCAP 1966*
Halls, Ethel May 1882-1967 *WhScrn 1,*
  WhScrn 2, WhoHol B
Hallstrom, Per 1866-1960 *ModWD, OxThe,*
  WhThe

Hallward, M *Film 1*
Halm, Friedrich 1806-1871 *OxThe*
Halm, Harry *Film 2*
Halop, Billy 1920- *FilmgC, IntMPA 1977*
Halop, Billy 1922- *WhoHol A*
Halop, Florence *WhoHol A*
Halperin, Nan d1963 *NotNAT B*
Halperin, Victor 1895- *FilmgC*
Halpern, Leivick *McGWD, REnWD*
Halpern, Leon 1908- *AmSCAP 1966*
Halpern, Martin 1929- *NotNAT*
Halpern, Morty *BiE&WWA*
Halpern, Nathan L 1914- *IntMPA 1977*
Halpin, Luke *WhoHol A*
Halprin, Ann *ConDr 1977E*
Halprin, Daria *WhoHol A*
Halsey, Betty *Film 2*
Halsey, Brett *MotPP, WhoHol A*
Halstan, Margaret 1879- *WhThe*
Halstead, William P 1906- *BiE&WWA, NotNAT*
Halston 1932- *CelR 3*
Halston, Howard *Film 2*
Halt, James *Film 2*
Haltiner, Fred 1936-1973 *WhScrn 2*
Halton, Charles *MotPP*
Halton, Charles 1876-1959 *FilmgC, MovMk,*
  Vers A, WhScrn 1, WhScrn 2, WhoHol B
Ham, Harry 1891-1943 *Film 1, Film 2, TwYS,*
  WhScrn 2
Hamar, Clifford E 1914- *BiE&WWA, NotNAT*
Hamblen, Bernard 1877-1962 *AmSCAP 1966*
Hamblen, Suzy *AmSCAP 1966*
Hambleton, Anne B C d1962 *NotNAT B*
Hambleton, T Edward 1911- *BiE&WWA,*
  NotNAT, PIP&P, WhoThe 16
Hamblin, Mrs. T S d1849 *NotNAT B*
Hamblin, Mrs. T S d1873 *NotNAT B*
Hamblin, Thomas Sowerby 1800-1853 *NotNAT B,*
  OxThe
Hambling, Arthur 1888- *WhThe*
Hamelin, Clement d1957 *NotNAT B*
Hamer, Fred B 1873-1953 *WhScrn 1, WhScrn 2*
Hamer, Gerald 1886-1972 *WhScrn 2, WhoHol B*
Hamer, Gerald 1886-1973 *FilmgC*
Hamer, Gladys *Film 2*
Hamer, Robert 1911-1963 *BiDFlm, CmMov,*
  DcFM, FilmgC, MovMk, NotNAT B,
  OxFilm, WorEnF
Hamer, Rusty *WhoHol A*
Hamerstein, Oscar *Film 2*
Hamid, Sweeney 1898?-1968 *WhScrn 1,*
  WhScrn 2
Hamil, Lucille *Film 1*
Hamill, Charlotte *Film 2*
Hamill, Pete 1935- *CelR 3, IntMPA 1977,*
  WomWMM
Hamilton, Arthur *AmSCAP 1966*
Hamilton, Bernie *WhoHol A*
Hamilton, Big John *WhoHol A*
Hamilton, Bob 1899- *AmSCAP 1966*
Hamilton, Charles *Film 2*
Hamilton, Cicely 1872-1952 *NotNAT B, WhThe*
Hamilton, Clayton 1881-1946 *NotNAT B, WhThe*
Hamilton, Cosmo 1879-1942 *NotNAT B, WhThe*
Hamilton, Diana 1898-1951 *NotNAT B, WhThe*
Hamilton, Dorothy 1897- *WhThe*
Hamilton, Dran *WhoHol A*
Hamilton, Foreststorn 1921- *AmSCAP 1966*
Hamilton, Frances *Film 2*
Hamilton, Frederick J 1895- *AmSCAP 1966*
Hamilton, George *MotPP, WhoHol A*
Hamilton, George 1939- *CelR 3, FilmgC,*
  IntMPA 1977
Hamilton, George 1940- *MovMk*

Hamilton, George W Spike 1901-1957
  AmSCAP 1966, WhScrn 1, WhScrn 2
Hamilton, Gladys *Film 2*
Hamilton, Gordon George d1939 *WhScrn 1,*
  WhScrn 2, WhoHol B
Hamilton, Guy 1922- *BiDFlm, CmMov, FilmgC,*
  IntMPA 1977, WorEnF
Hamilton, Hale 1880-1942 *MotPP, MovMk,*
  NotNAT B, TwYS, WhScrn 1, WhScrn 2,
  WhThe, WhoHol B
Hamilton, Hale 1883-1942 *Film 1, Film 2*
Hamilton, Henry d1918 *NotNAT B, WhThe*
Hamilton, Jack Shorty 1879?-1925 *Film 1, Film 2,*
  WhScrn 2
Hamilton, Joe *NewYTET*
Hamilton, John 1887-1958 *Vers B, WhScrn 1,*
  WhScrn 2, WhoHol B
Hamilton, John F 1893-1967 *BiE&WWA,*
  NotNAT B
Hamilton, John F 1894-1967 *WhScrn 1,*
  WhScrn 2
Hamilton, John Shorty d1967 *WhoHol B*
Hamilton, John T *Film 2*
Hamilton, Joseph H 1898-1965 *WhScrn 2*
Hamilton, Karen Sue 1946-1969 *WhScrn 1,*
  WhScrn 2
Hamilton, Kelly *NatPD*
Hamilton, Kim *WhoHol A*
Hamilton, Kipp *WhoHol A*
Hamilton, L Hill 1917- *AmSCAP 1966*
Hamilton, Lance *BiE&WWA*
Hamilton, Laurel L d1955 *WhScrn 1, WhScrn 2,*
  WhoHol B
Hamilton, Lindisfarne 1910- *WhThe*
Hamilton, Lloyd 1891-1935 *Film 1, Film 2,*
  TwYS, WhScrn 1, WhScrn 2, WhoHol B
Hamilton, Lloyd 1892-1935 *TwYS A*
Hamilton, Mahlon d1960 *MotPP, NotNAT B,*
  WhoHol B
Hamilton, Mahlon 1883-1960 *WhScrn 2*
Hamilton, Mahlon 1885-1960 *Film 1, Film 2,*
  TwYS
Hamilton, Margaret 1902- *BiE&WWA, FilmgC,*
  IntMPA 1977, MovMk, NotNAT, ThFT,
  Vers A, WhoHol A, WhoThe 16
Hamilton, Mark *Film 2*
Hamilton, Murray *BiE&WWA, NotNAT,*
  WhoHol A
Hamilton, Murray 1923- *FilmgC*
Hamilton, Murray 1925- *MovMk*
Hamilton, Nancy 1908- *AmSCAP 1966,*
  BiE&WWA, EncMT, NotNAT
Hamilton, Neil 1899- *BiE&WWA, Film 2,*
  FilmgC, MovMk, NotNAT, TwYS, WhThe,
  WhoHol A
Hamilton, Patrick 1904-1962 *CnMD, ModWD,*
  NotNAT B, WhThe
Hamilton, Rose 1874- *WhThe*
Hamilton, Theodore 1837- *WhoStg 1908*
Hamilton, Wallace *NatPD, PIP&P*
Hamler, John E 1891-1969 *WhScrn 1, WhScrn 2*
Hamlett, Dilys 1928- *WhoThe 16*
Hamley-Clifford, Molly d1956 *NotNAT B*
Hamlin, George 1920-1964 *BiE&WWA,*
  NotNAT B
Hamlin, William H 1885-1951 *WhScrn 1,*
  WhScrn 2
Hamlisch, Marvin 1944- *AmSCAP 1966*
Hamlish, Joseph *Film 1*
Hammack, Bobby 1922- *AmSCAP 1966*
Hammel, Claus 1932- *CroCD*
Hammer, Alvin *WhoHol A*
Hammer, Barbara *WomWMM B*
Hammer, Ben *WhoHol A*

Hammer, George *NatPD*
Hammer, Robert 1930- *AmSCAP 1966*
Hammer, Will 1887-1957 *FilmgC, NotNAT B*
Hammeren, Torsten *Film 2*
Hammerman, Herman 1912- *AmSCAP 1966*
Hammerstein, Alice 1921- *AmSCAP 1966*
Hammerstein, Arthur 1872-1955 *EncMT, PIP&P*
Hammerstein, Arthur 1873-1955 *NotNAT B*
Hammerstein, Arthur 1876-1955 *WhThe*
Hammerstein, Elaine 1897-1948 *Film 1, Film 2,*
  MotPP, TwYS, WhScrn 1, WhScrn 2,
  WhoHol B
Hammerstein, Elaine Allison 1898-1948 *NotNAT B*
Hammerstein, James 1931- *BiE&WWA, NotNAT,*
  WhoThe 16
Hammerstein, Oscar 1847-1919 *EncMT,*
  NotNAT A, NotNAT B, WhThe,
  WhoStg 1906, WhoStg 1908
Hammerstein, Oscar, II 1895-1960 *AmSCAP 1966,*
  EncMT, FilmgC, McGWD, ModWD,
  NewMT, NotNAT A, NotNAT B, OxThe,
  PIP&P, WhScrn 2, WhThe
Hammerton, Stephen *OxThe*
Hammett, Dashiell 1891-1961 *DcFM*
Hammett, Dashiell 1894-1961 *CmMov, FilmgC,*
  OxFilm, WorEnF
Hammid, Alexander 1910?- *FilmgC, WomWMM*
Hammitt, Orlin 1916- *AmSCAP 1966*
Hammon, William *Film 1*
Hammond, Aubrey 1893-1940 *NotNAT B,*
  WhThe
Hammond, Bert E 1880- *WhThe*
Hammond, C Norman *Film 2*
Hammond, Caleb 1915- *CelR 3*
Hammond, Charles *Film 2*
Hammond, Christopher *McGWD*
Hammond, Cleon E 1908- *AmSCAP 1966*
Hammond, Dorothy d1950 *NotNAT B,*
  WhScrn 2, WhThe
Hammond, Earl R 1886- *AmSCAP 1966*
Hammond, Gilmore *Film 1*
Hammond, Harriet *Film 2*
Hammond, Kay 1909- *CnThe, Film 2, FilmgC,*
  WhThe, WhoHol A
Hammond, Percy 1873-1936 *NotNAT A,*
  NotNAT B, OxThe, WhThe
Hammond, Peter 1923- *FilmgC, IntMPA 1977,*
  WhThe
Hammond, Virginia 1894-1972 *BiE&WWA,*
  Film 1, Film 2, NotNAT B, TwYS,
  WhScrn 2, WhoHol B
Hammond, William G 1874-1945 *AmSCAP 1966*
Hamner, Earl *NewYTET*
Hampden, Walter 1879-1955 *FamA&A, Film 1,*
  FilmgC, MotPP, MovMk, NotNAT B,
  Vers B, WhScrn 1, WhScrn 2, WhThe,
  WhoHol B, WhoStg 1908
Hampden, Walter 1879-1956 *OxThe*
Hamper, Genevieve 1889-1971 *Film 1, Film 2,*
  WhScrn 1, WhScrn 2, WhoHol B
Hample, Stuart 1926- *AmSCAP 1966*
Hampshire, Susan *WhoHol A*
Hampshire, Susan 1938- *FilmgC*
Hampshire, Susan 1941- *CelR 3, IntMPA 1977*
Hampshire, Susan 1942- *WhoThe 16*
Hampton, Christopher 1946- *CnThe, ConDr 1977,*
  WhoThe 16
Hampton, Christopher 1948- *CroCD*
Hampton, Faith 1909-1949 *WhScrn 1, WhScrn 2,*
  WhoHol B
Hampton, Gladys *Film 2*
Hampton, Grayce 1876-1963 *WhScrn 2*
Hampton, Hope 1901- *Film 2, MotPP, TwYS,*
  WhoHol A

Hampton, James *WhoHol A*
Hampton, Lionel 1913- *CelR 3, WhoHol A*
Hampton, Louise 1881-1954 *NotNAT B,*
  WhScrn 1, WhScrn 2, WhThe, WhoHol B
Hampton, Margaret *Film 2*
Hampton, Mary d1931 *NotNAT B*
Hampton, Myra 1901-1945 *Film 2, NotNAT B,*
  WhScrn 2, WhoHol B
Hampton, Paul *WhoHol A*
Hampton, Raphiel *WhoHol A*
Hamrick, Burwell F 1906-1970 *WhScrn 2,*
  WhoHol B
Hamsun, Knut 1859-1952 *CnMD, NotNAT B,*
  REnWD
Hamund, St. John d1929 *NotNAT B*
Hanako, Ohta 1882- *WhThe*
Hanalis, Blanche *WomWMM*
Hanauer, Walter W 1915- *AmSCAP 1966*
Hanaway, Frank *Film 1*
Hanbury, Lily d1908 *NotNAT B*
Hanbury, Maie *Film 2*
Hancock, Christopher 1928- *WhoThe 16*
Hancock, Eleanor *Film 2*
Hancock, John *PIP&P*
Hancock, John 1938- *MovMk*
Hancock, John 1939- *IntMPA 1977*
Hancock, Reba *WomWMM*
Hancock, Sheila 1933- *FilmgC, WhoThe 16*
Hancock, Tony 1924-1968 *FilmgC, NotNAT B,*
  WhScrn 1, WhScrn 2, WhoHol B
Hancox, Daisy 1898- *WhThe*
Hand, Bethlyn J *IntMPA 1977*
Hand, David 1900- *FilmgC*
Handa, Frank *Film 2*
Handel, Leo A *IntMPA 1977*
Handforth, Ruth *Film 1*
Handke, Peter 1942- *CroCD, McGWD,*
  PIP&P A
Handl, Irene *WhoHol A*
Handl, Irene 1901- *WhoThe 16*
Handl, Irene 1902- *FilmgC*
Handley, Tommy 1894-1949 *FilmgC*
Handley, Tommy 1902-1949 *WhScrn 1,*
  WhScrn 2, WhoHol B
Handman, Lou 1894-1956 *AmSCAP 1966*
Handman, Wynn 1922- *BiE&WWA, NotNAT,*
  WhoThe 16
Hands, Terry 1941- *WhoThe 16*
Handworth, Harry d1916 *WhScrn 2*
Handworth, Octavia *Film 1, MotPP*
Handy, William Christopher 1873-1958
  AmSCAP 1966, NotNAT B
Handyside, Clarence d1931 *Film 1, NotNAT B*
Handysides, Clarence d1931 *WhoHol B*
Haney, Carol 1924-1964 *EncMT, NotNAT B,*
  WhoHol B
Haney, Carol 1928-1964 *FilmgC*
Haney, Carol 1934-1964 *WhScrn 1, WhScrn 2*
Haney, J Francis d1964 *NotNAT B*
Haney, Ray 1921- *AmSCAP 1966*
Hanford, Charles B 1859-1926 *NotNAT B,*
  WhScrn 2
Hanford, Roy *Film 1*
Hangen, Welles *NewYTET*
Hani, Susumi *WomWMM B*
Hani, Susumu 1929- *WorEnF*
Hanighen, Bernard D *AmSCAP 1966*
Hanin, Roger *WhoHol A*
Hankin, Edward Charles St. John 1869-1909
  NotNAT B, OxThe
Hankin, St. John 1860-1909 *CnThe, REnWD*
Hankin, St. John 1869-1909 *CnMD, McGWD,*
  ModWD
Hanley, James 1901- *CnMD Sup, ConDr 1977*

Hanley, James Frederick 1892-1942
  AmSCAP 1966, EncMT
Hanley, Jimmy 1918-1970 *FilmgC, WhScrn 1,*
  WhScrn 2, WhoHol B
Hanley, Leo *Film 2*
Hanley, Linda *WomWMM B*
Hanley, Michael E 1858-1942 *WhScrn 1,*
  WhScrn 2
Hanley, William 1931- *BiE&WWA, CnMD Sup,*
  ConDr 1977, CroCD, ModWD, NotNAT,
  WhoThe 16
Hanley, William B, Jr. 1900-1959 *WhScrn 1,*
  WhScrn 2, WhoHol B
Hanlon, Alma *Film 1*
Hanlon, Bert 1895-1972 *AmSCAP 1966,*
  WhScrn 2, WhoHol B
Hanlon, Jack *Film 2*
Hanlon, Tom 1907-1970 *WhScrn 2*
Hanlon-Lees *OxThe*
Hann, Walter 1838-1922 *NotNAT B, WhThe*
Hanna, Franklyn *Film 1, Film 2*
Hanna, Lee *IntMPA 1977, NewYTET*
Hanna, R Philip 1910-1957 *AmSCAP 1966*
Hanna, William 1920- *FilmgC, OxFilm, WorEnF*
Hannan, Patricia *Film 1*
Hanne, Pat *Film 2*
Hanneford, Edwin Poodles 1892-1967 *WhScrn 1,*
  WhScrn 2
Hanneford, Poodles 1892-1967 *Film 2, WhoHol ·B*
Hannemann, Walter A *IntMPA 1977*
Hannemann, Yvonne *WomWMM B*
Hannen, Hermione 1913- *WhThe*
Hannen, Nicholas 1881-1972 *PIP&P, WhScrn 2,*
  WhThe
Hanofer, Frank 1897-1955 *WhScrn 1, WhScrn 2*
Hanoun, Marcel 1929- *WorEnF*
Hanray, Laurence 1874-1947 *WhoHol B*
Hanray, Lawrence 1874-1947 *NotNAT B, WhThe*
Hans Stockfisch *OxThe*
Hansberry, Lorraine 1930-1965 *BiE&WWA,*
  CnMD Sup, ConDr 1977F, CroCD,
  McGWD, ModWD, NotNAT B, PIP&P,
  PIP&P A
Hansen, Aksel H 1919- *AmSCAP 1966*
Hansen, Al *ConDr 1977E*
Hansen, Christiern d1545? *OxThe*
Hansen, Einar d1927 *TwYS, WhoHol B*
Hansen, Hans 1886-1962 *NotNAT B, WhScrn 1,*
  WhScrn 2, WhoHol B
Hansen, Harold I 1914- *BiE&WWA, NotNAT*
Hansen, Janis *WhoHol A*
Hansen, Juanita 1897-1961 *Film 1, Film 2,*
  MotPP, NotNAT B, TwYS, WhScrn 1,
  WhScrn 2, WhoHol B
Hansen, Karen *Film 2*
Hansen, Laura d1914 *NotNAT B*
Hansen, Lawrence William 1905- *AmSCAP 1966*
Hansen, Max *Film 2*
Hansen, Peter *WhoHol A*
Hansen, William 1911-1975 *WhScrn 2,*
  WhoHol C
Hanslip, Ann *WhoHol A*
Hanson, Einar 1899-1927 *Film 2*
Hanson, Einer 1899-1927 *WhScrn 1, WhScrn 2*
Hanson, Erling *Film 2*
Hanson, Ethwell *AmSCAP 1966*
Hanson, Gladys 1884-1973 *WhScrn 2, WhoHol B*
Hanson, Gladys 1887- *Film 1, WhThe*
Hanson, Harry 1895- *WhThe*
Hanson, Howard 1896- *AmSCAP 1966*
Hanson, John *IntMPA 1977*
Hanson, John 1922- *WhoThe 16*
Hanson, Kitty d1947 *NotNAT B*
Hanson, Lars d1965 *MotPP, WhoHol B*

Hanson, Lars 1886-1965 *OxFilm*
Hanson, Lars 1887-1965 *Film 1, Film, Film 2, FilmgC, TwYS, WhScrn 1, WhScrn 2*
Hanson, Peter *IntMPA 1977*
Hanson, Spook *Film 1*
Hansson, Sigrid Valborg 1874- *WhThe*
Hapgood, Elizabeth Reynolds 1894- *BiE&WWA, NotNAT*
Hapgood, Norman 1868-1937 *NotNAT B*
Haradon, Virginia 1913- *AmSCAP 1966*
Harareet, Haya 1934?- *FilmgC, MotPP*
Harari, Robert *IntMPA 1977*
Harbach, Otto 1873-1963 *AmSCAP 1966, EncMT, NewMT, NotNAT B, WhThe*
Harbach, William O 1919- *IntMPA 1977*
Harbacher, Karl *Film 2*
Harbage, Alfred 1901- *BiE&WWA, NotNAT*
Harbaugh, Carl 1886-1960 *Film 1, Film 2, WhScrn 1, WhScrn 2, WhoHol B*
Harben, Hubert 1878-1941 *Film 2, NotNAT B, WhScrn 1, WhScrn 2, WhThe, WhoHol B*
Harben, Joan 1909-1953 *NotNAT B, WhThe, WhoHol B*
Harbert, James K 1930- *AmSCAP 1966*
Harbord, Carl *Film 2, WhThe*
Harbord, Gordon 1901- *WhThe*
Harborough, William 1899-1924 *WhScrn 1, WhScrn 2*
Harbou, Thea Von 1888-1954 *DcFM, OxFilm*
Harburg, E Y 1898- *AmSCAP 1966, BiE&WWA, CelR 3, ConDr 1977D, EncMT, NewMT, NotNAT*
Harburg, Edgar Y 1898- *WhoThe 16*
Harburgh, Bert *Film 2*
Harbury, Charles d1928 *NotNAT B*
Harby, Isaac 1788-1828 *NotNAT B*
Harcourt, Cyril d1924 *NotNAT B, WhThe*
Harcourt, James 1873-1951 *NotNAT B, WhThe, WhoHol B*
Harcourt, Leslie 1890- *WhThe*
Harcourt, Peggie d1916 *WhScrn 2*
Hardacre, John Pitt 1855-1933 *NotNAT B, WhThe*
Harder, Emil, Jr. *Film 2*
Hardie, A C d1939 *NotNAT B*
Hardie, Russell 1904-1973 *BiE&WWA, MovMk, NotNAT B, WhScrn 2, WhoHol B*
Hardie, Russell 1906-1973 *WhThe*
Hardigan, Patrick *Film 2*
Hardiman, Terrence 1937- *WhoThe 16*
Hardin, Neil *Film 1*
Hardin, Ty 1930- *FilmgC, MotPP, WhoHol A*
Harding, Alfred d1945 *NotNAT B*
Harding, Ann *MotPP*
Harding, Ann 1901- *ThFT*
Harding, Ann 1902- *BiE&WWA, Film 2, FilmgC, MovMk, NotNAT, OxFilm, WhThe, WhoHol A*
Harding, Ann 1904- *IntMPA 1977*
Harding, Ben *Film 1*
Harding, D Lyn 1867-1952 *WhThe*
Harding, Gilbert 1907-1960 *WhScrn 1, WhScrn 2, WhoHol B*
Harding, J Rudge d1932 *NotNAT B*
Harding, John 1948- *ConDr 1977, PIP&P, WhoHol A, WhoThe 16*
Harding, June *WhoHol A*
Harding, Lyn 1867-1952 *Film 2, FilmgC, NotNAT B, WhScrn 1, WhScrn 2, WhoHol B*
Harding, Rudge *WhThe*
Harding, William H 1945- *IntMPA 1977*
Hardinge, H C M *WhThe*
Hardmuth, Paul 1889-1962 *NotNAT B*

Hards, Ira 1872-1938 *NotNAT B, WhThe*
Hardt, Eloise *WhoHol A*
Hardt, Ernst 1876-1947 *McGWD, ModWD*
Hardtmuth, Paul 1889-1962 *WhScrn 1, WhScrn 2, WhoHol B*
Hardwick, Archer 1918- *AmSCAP 1966*
Hardwick, Paul 1918- *WhoThe 16*
Hardwicke, Sir Cedric 1893-1964 *BiE&WWA, CnThe, Film 1, Film 2, FilmgC, MotPP, MovMk, NotNAT A, NotNAT B, OxFilm, OxThe, PIP&P, WhScrn 1, WhScrn 2, WhThe, WhoHol B*
Hardwicke, Sir Cedric 1896-1964 *BiDFlm*
Hardwicke, Clarice 1900- *WhThe*
Hardwicke, Edward 1932- *WhoThe 16*
Hardy, Alexandre 1570?-1632 *McGWD*
Hardy, Alexandre 1572?-1631 *NotNAT B*
Hardy, Alexandre 1575?-1631? *OxThe*
Hardy, Arthur *Film 2*
Hardy, Arthur F 1870- *WhThe*
Hardy, Ashton R *NewYTET*
Hardy, Betty 1904- *WhThe*
Hardy, Cherry d1963 *NotNAT B*
Hardy, Francoise *WhoHol A*
Hardy, Joseph *WhoHol A*
Hardy, Joseph 1918- *NotNAT*
Hardy, Joseph 1929- *WhoThe 16*
Hardy, Oliver 1892-1957 *CmMov, Film 1, Film 2, FilmgC, MGM, MotPP, MovMk, NotNAT B, OxFilm, TwYS, WhScrn 1, WhScrn 2, WhoHol B, WorEnF*
Hardy, Robert 1925- *CnThe, FilmgC, WhoHol A, WhoThe 16*
Hardy, Sam 1883-1935 *Film 1, Film 2, NotNAT B, TwYS, WhScrn 1, WhScrn 2, WhoHol B, WhoStg 1908*
Hardy, Sam 1905-1958 *WhScrn 2*
Hardy, Thomas 1840-1928 *FilmgC, ModWD*
Hardy, William *Film 2*
Hardy, William D 1913- *AmSCAP 1966*
Hare, Betty 1900- *WhThe*
Hare, David 1947- *CnThe, ConDr 1977, WhoThe 16*
Hare, Doris 1905- *WhoHol A, WhoThe 16*
Hare, Ernest Dudley 1900- *WhoThe 16*
Hare, F Lumsden 1874-1964 *WhScrn 1, WhScrn 2*
Hare, Gilbert 1869-1951 *NotNAT B, WhThe*
Hare, J Robertson 1891- *WhoThe 16*
Hare, Sir John 1844-1921 *NotNAT B, OxThe, PIP&P, WhScrn 2, WhThe, WhoStg 1908*
Hare, Kate d1957 *NotNAT B*
Hare, Lumsden d1964 *NotNAT B, WhoHol B*
Hare, Lumsden 1874-1964 *TwYS*
Hare, Lumsden 1875-1964 *BiE&WWA, Film 1, Film 2, FilmgC*
Hare, Lumsden 1895-1964 *MovMk*
Hare, Robertson 1891- *CnThe, FilmgC, WhoHol A*
Hare, Will 1919- *WhoThe 16*
Hare, Winifred 1875- *WhThe*
Harel-Lisztman, Colette *WomWMM*
Harens, Dean 1921- *WhoHol A*
Harford, W *WhThe*
Hargis, Billy James 1925- *CelR 3*
Hargitay, Mickey *WhoHol A*
Hargrave, Roy 1908- *WhThe*
Hargraves, William *Film 2*
Hargreaves, John *IntMPA 1977*
Hargrove, Dean *NewYTET*
Harian, Kenneth *Film 2*
Harien, Macey *Film 2*
Haring, Robert 1896- *AmSCAP 1966*
Harington, Joy 1914- *IntMPA 1977*

Harington, Joy see also Harrington, Joy
Harker, Frederick d1941 NotNAT B
Harker, Gordon 1885-1967 Film 2, FilmgC,
  WhScrn 1, WhScrn 2, WhThe, WhoHol B
Harker, Joseph 1892- WhThe
Harker, Joseph C 1855-1927 NotNAT A,
  NotNAT B, WhThe
Harkins, Dixie 1906-1963 WhScrn 1, WhScrn 2,
  WhoHol B
Harkins, Marion d1962 NotNAT B
Harkins, William S d1945 NotNAT B
Harkness, Carter B Film 1
Harkness, Rebekah 1915- AmSCAP 1966,
  CelR 3
Harlam, Macey d1923 Film 1, Film 2,
  WhoHol B
Harlan, Cris Film 2
Harlan, Kenneth 1895-1967 Film 1, Film 2,
  FilmgC, MotPP, MovMk, TwYS, WhScrn 1,
  WhScrn 2, WhoHol B
Harlan, Macey d1923 WhScrn 1, WhScrn 2
Harlan, Marion Film 2
Harlan, Otis 1865-1940 Film 1, Film 2, FilmgC,
  MotPP, NotNAT B, TwYS, WhScrn 1,
  WhScrn 2, WhThe, WhoHol B,
  WhoStg 1906, WhoStg 1908
Harlan, Richard Film 2
Harlan, Russell 1903-1974 CmMov, FilmgC,
  WhScrn 2, WorEnF
Harlan, Veidt 1899-1964 WorEnF
Harlan, Veit 1899-1964 BiDFlm, DcFM, FilmgC,
  OxFilm, WhScrn 2
Harlan, Viet 1899-1964 WhoHol B
Harlein, Lillian d1971 WhoHol B
Harleville, Collin D' 1755-1806 OxThe
Harley, Ed Film 1
Harley, Margot 1935- NotNAT
Harley, William G NewYTET
Harline, Leigh 1907-1969 AmSCAP 1966,
  FilmgC, OxFilm, WorEnF
Harling, W Franke 1887-1958 AmSCAP 1966
Harlow, Gertrude d1947 NotNAT B
Harlow, Jean 1911-1937 BiDFlm, Film 2,
  FilmgC, MGM, MotPP, MovMk,
  NotNAT B, OxFilm, ThFT, TwYS,
  WhScrn 1, WhScrn 2, WhoHol B, WorEnF
Harlow, John 1896- FilmgC
Harman, Hugh 1903- DcFM
Harmati, Sandor 1892-1936 AmSCAP 1966
Harmer, Jack P 1884-1962 AmSCAP 1966
Harmer, Lillian 1886-1946 WhScrn 1, WhScrn 2,
  WhoHol B
Harmon, Charlotte BiE&WWA, NotNAT
Harmon, Henry Film 1
Harmon, John Vers B, WhoHol A
Harmon, Lewis 1911- BiE&WWA, NotNAT
Harmon, Pat 1888-1958 WhScrn 1, WhScrn 2,
  WhoHol B
Harmon, Pat 1890- Film 1, Film 2, TwYS
Harmon, Tom 1919- IntMPA 1977, WhoHol A
Harmon Four Quartette Film 2
Harmony Emperor's Quartet Film 2
Harms, Valerie 1940- WomWMM B
Harnack, Curtis NatPD
Harned, Virginia 1868-1946 NotNAT B,
  WhoStg 1906, WhoStg 1908
Harned, Virginia 1872-1946 WhThe
Harnell, Joseph 1924- AmSCAP 1966
Harner, Dolly d1956 NotNAT B
Harnett, Sunny WhoHol A
Harney, Benjamin Robertson 1872?-1938
  NotNAT B
Harnick, Jay 1928- BiE&WWA, NotNAT
Harnick, Sheldon 1924- BiE&WWA, CelR 3,

EncMT, NewMT, NotNAT, PIP&P
Harolde, Ralf 1899-1974 FilmgC, WhScrn 2,
  WhoHol B
Harout, Yeghishe d1974 WhScrn 2
Harper PIP&P
Harper, Fred d1963 NotNAT B
Harper, Gerald 1929- WhoThe 16
Harper, James WhScrn 2
Harper, Joe 1941- IntMPA 1977
Harper, John D, Jr. 1943- IntMPA 1977
Harper, Kenneth IntMPA 1977
Harper, Marjorie AmSCAP 1966
Harper, Redd 1903- AmSCAP 1966
Harper, Richard A 1918- IntMPA 1977
Harper, Valerie IntMPA 1977, WhoHol A
Harper, William A 1915- IntMPA 1977
Harrigan, Edward 1843-1911 NotNAT A,
  WhoStg 1906, WhoStg 1908
Harrigan, Edward 1844-1911 EncMT
Harrigan, Edward 1845-1911 CnThe, FamA&A,
  McGWD, ModWD, NotNAT B, OxThe,
  PIP&P, REnWD
Harrigan, Nedda 1902- BiE&WWA, Film 2,
  WhThe, WhoHol A
Harrigan, William 1886-1966 NotNAT B
Harrigan, William 1887-1966 Film 2
Harrigan, William 1894-1966 BiE&WWA,
  FilmgC, WhScrn 1, WhScrn 2, WhThe,
  WhoHol B
Harriman, Averell 1891- CelR 3
Harring, Hildegard Film 2
Harrington, Countess Of OxThe
Harrington, Alice d1954 NotNAT B
Harrington, Buck d1971 WhScrn 2
Harrington, Curtis 1928- FilmgC, IntMPA 1977
Harrington, Donal 1905- BiE&WWA, NotNAT
Harrington, Florence d1942 NotNAT B
Harrington, J P 1865- WhThe
Harrington, Joe Film 2
Harrington, John Film 2
Harrington, John B, Jr. d1973 NewYTET
Harrington, Joy 1914- WomWMM
Harrington, Joy see also Harington, Joy
Harrington, Kate WhoHol A
Harrington, Michael 1928- CelR 3
Harrington, Pat, Jr. IntMPA 1977, WhoHol A
Harrington, Pat, Sr. 1900-1965 BiE&WWA,
  NotNAT B, WhoHol B
Harrington, Victor B 1915- AmSCAP 1966
Harrington, W Clark 1905- AmSCAP 1966
Harrington, William O 1918- AmSCAP 1966
Harris, Andrew B 1944- NatPD
Harris, Asa Ace 1910-1964 NotNAT B,
  WhScrn 2
Harris, Audrey Sophia 1901-1966 NotNAT B,
  WhThe
Harris, Sir Augustus 1851-1896 CnThe
Harris, Sir Augustus 1852-1896 NotNAT B,
  OxThe
Harris, Augustus Glossop 1825-1873 NotNAT B,
  OxThe
Harris, Averell d1966 WhScrn 1, WhScrn 2,
  WhoHol B
Harris, Barbara BiE&WWA, IntMPA 1977,
  MotPP, NotNAT, WhoHol A
Harris, Barbara 1935- CelR 3
Harris, Barbara 1937- EncMT, WhoThe 16
Harris, Barbara 1940- FilmgC
Harris, Belle 1926- AmSCAP 1966
Harris, Brad WhoHol A
Harris, Buddy Film 2
Harris, Caroline Film 1
Harris, Charles A d1962 NotNAT B
Harris, Charles Kassell 1865-1930 AmSCAP 1966,

Film 2, WhoStg 1908
Harris, Charles Kassell 1867-1930 *NotNAT B*
Harris, Clare d1949 *NotNAT B, WhThe*
Harris, Dave 1889- *AmSCAP 1966*
Harris, Edward C 1899- *AmSCAP 1966*
Harris, Edward M 1916- *IntMPA 1977*
Harris, Elmer Blaney 1878-1966 *BiE&WWA,*
Film 2, NotNAT B, WhThe
Harris, Elsie 1892-1953 *WhScrn 1, WhScrn 2*
Harris, Ethel Ramos *AmSCAP 1966*
Harris, Florence Glossop- 1883-1931 *WhThe*
Harris, Franco 1950- *CelR 3*
Harris, Frank 1856-1931 *CnMD, NotNAT B*
Harris, Fred Orin 1901- *BiE&WWA, NotNAT*
Harris, George *Film 2*
Harris, George W d1929 *NotNAT B*
Harris, Harry 1901- *AmSCAP 1966, NewYTET*
Harris, Helen *Film 2*
Harris, Henry 1634?-1704 *OxThe, PIP&P*
Harris, Henry B 1866-1912 *NotNAT B, WhThe,*
WhoStg 1908
Harris, Herbert H 1896?-1949 *NotNAT B*
Harris, Ivy *Film 2*
Harris, James B 1924- *FilmgC*
Harris, James B 1928- *IntMPA 1977*
Harris, Jay Morton 1928- *AmSCAP 1966*
Harris, Jed 1900- *BiE&WWA, NotNAT,*
NotNAT A, WhThe
Harris, Jenks *Film 2*
Harris, Jerry Weseley 1933- *AmSCAP 1966*
Harris, John H 1898- *IntMPA 1977*
Harris, Jonathan 1919?- *FilmgC, WhoHol A*
Harris, Joseph *BiE&WWA*
Harris, Joseph 1661-1699 *NotNAT B*
Harris, Joseph 1870-1953 *Film 1, WhScrn 1,*
WhScrn 2, WhoHol B
Harris, Judy *WhoHol A*
Harris, Julie 1925- *BiDFlm, BiE&WWA,*
CelR 3, CnThe, FilmgC, IntMPA 1977,
MovMk, NotNAT, OxFilm, PIP&P A,
WhoThe 16
Harris, Julius *WhoHol A*
Harris, Kay d1972 *WhoHol B*
Harris, Kay 1920-1971 *WhScrn 2*
Harris, Leland B 1912- *BiE&WWA*
Harris, Lenore 1879-1953 *Film 1, WhoHol B*
Harris, Leon A, Jr. 1926- *AmSCAP 1966*
Harris, Leonore 1879-1953 *NotNAT B,*
WhScrn 2
Harris, Louis 1906- *IntMPA 1977*
Harris, Louis 1921- *CelR 3*
Harris, Marcia *Film 1, Film 2*
Harris, Margaret F 1904- *WhoThe 16*
Harris, Maria *Film 2*
Harris, Marion *Film 2*
Harris, Mildred 1901-1944 *NotNAT B, TwYS,*
WhScrn 1, WhScrn 2, WhoHol B
Harris, Mildred 1905-1944 *Film 1, Film 2*
Harris, Mitchell 1883-1948 *NotNAT B,*
WhScrn 2, WhoHol B
Harris, Morris O d1974 *WhoHol B*
Harris, Myron 1922- *AmSCAP 1966*
Harris, Neil 1936- *NatPD*
Harris, Phil *MotPP, WhoHol A*
Harris, Phil 1901- *MovMk*
Harris, Phil 1906- *FilmgC, IntMPA 1977*
Harris, Remus Anthony 1916- *AmSCAP 1966*
Harris, Richard *MotPP, WhoHol A*
Harris, Richard 1930- *CelR 3, IntMPA 1977*
Harris, Richard 1932- *FilmgC, OxFilm*
Harris, Richard 1933- *BiDFlm, MovMk, WhThe,*
WorEnF
Harris, Robert 1900- *FilmgC, WhoHol A,*
WhoThe 16

Harris, Robert H 1909?- *FilmgC, WhoHol A*
Harris, Rosemary 1930- *BiE&WWA, CnThe,*
FilmgC, IntMPA 1977, MotPP, NotNAT,
WhoHol A, WhoThe 16
Harris, Sadie 1888- *WhoStg 1908*
Harris, Sam H 1872-1941 *EncMT, NotNAT B,*
WhThe, WhoStg 1906, WhoStg 1908
Harris, Stacy B 1918-1973 *WhScrn 2, WhoHol B*
Harris, Stan *NewYTET*
Harris, Susan K *WomWMM B*
Harris, Sylvia 1906-1966 *NotNAT B*
Harris, Theodore 1912- *AmSCAP 1966*
Harris, Vernon 1910?- *FilmgC*
Harris, Victor 1869-1943 *AmSCAP 1966*
Harris, Viola *WhoHol A*
Harris, Wadsworth 1865-1942 *Film 2, WhScrn 1,*
WhScrn 2, WhoHol B
Harris, Will J 1900-1967 *AmSCAP 1966,*
NotNAT B
Harris, William d1916 *NotNAT B*
Harris, William, Jr. 1884-1946 *NotNAT B,*
WhThe
Harris, Winifred *Film 1, Film 2*
Harris, Woody 1911- *AmSCAP 1966*
Harrison, Arthur 1902- *AmSCAP 1966*
Harrison, Austin 1873-1928 *NotNAT B, WhThe*
Harrison, Bob 1915- *AmSCAP 1966*
Harrison, Carey 1890-1957 *Film 2, WhScrn 1,*
WhScrn 2, WhoHol B
Harrison, Cass 1922- *AmSCAP 1966*
Harrison, Charles F 1883-1955 *AmSCAP 1966*
Harrison, Duncan d1934 *NotNAT B*
Harrison, Fanny d1909 *NotNAT B*
Harrison, Frederick d1926 *NotNAT B, WhThe*
Harrison, Gabriel d1902 *NotNAT B*
Harrison, George 1943- *CelR 3, MotPP,*
WhoHol A
Harrison, Irma *Film 2*
Harrison, Jeanne *WomWMM B*
Harrison, Jimmy *Film 1, Film 2, TwYS*
Harrison, Joan 1911- *FilmgC, IntMPA 1977,*
WomWMM
Harrison, John *ConDr 1977B*
Harrison, John 1922- *IntMPA 1977*
Harrison, John 1924- *WhoThe 16*
Harrison, June 1926-1974 *WhScrn 2, WhoHol B*
Harrison, Kathleen 1898- *FilmgC, IntMPA 1977,*
OxFilm, WhoHol A, WhoThe 16
Harrison, Lee d1916 *NotNAT B*
Harrison, Linda *WhoHol A*
Harrison, Louis d1936 *NotNAT B*
Harrison, Maud *WhoStg 1906, WhoStg 1908*
Harrison, Michael *WhoHol A*
Harrison, Mona d1957 *NotNAT B, WhThe*
Harrison, Noel *WhoHol A*
Harrison, Rex 1908- *BiDFlm, BiE&WWA,*
CelR 3, CnThe, EncMT, FamA&A, Film 2,
FilmgC, IntMPA 1977, MotPP, MovMk,
NotNAT, NotNAT A, OxFilm, PIP&P,
WhoHol A, WhoThe 16, WorEnF
Harrison, Richard Berry 1864-1935 *NotNAT B,*
OxThe, PIP&P
Harrison, Robert d1953 *NotNAT B*
Harriton, Maria *WomWMM A, WomWMM B*
Harrity, Richard 1907-1973 *BiE&WWA,*
NotNAT A, NotNAT B
Harrold, Orville d1933 *NotNAT B*
Harron, Mrs. *Film 1*
Harron, Bobby 1894-1920 *WhScrn 1, WhScrn 2*
Harron, Don 1924- *ConDr 1973*
Harron, Donald 1924- *BiE&WWA, NotNAT,*
WhoHol A
Harron, Jessie *Film 1*
Harron, John 1903-1939 *TwYS, WhScrn 1,*

WhScrn 2, WhoHol B
Harron, Johnny 1903-1939 Film 1, Film 2
Harron, Mary Film 1
Harron, Robert 1894-1920 Film 1, FilmgC,
    MotPP, NotNAT B, TwYS, WhoHol B
Harron, Robert Bobby 1894-1920 Film 2
Harron, Tessie d1920 WhScrn 1, WhoHol B
Harron, Tessie 1896-1918 WhScrn 2
Harryhausen, Ray 1920?- CmMov, FilmgC,
    IntMPA 1977
Harsa OxThe
Harsha, Sri 590?-647 CnThe, REnWD
Hart, Albert 1874-1940 Film 2, WhScrn 1,
    WhScrn 2, WhoHol B
Hart, Alex Film 2
Hart, Annie d1947 NotNAT B
Hart, Bernard 1911-1964 BiE&WWA,
    NotNAT B, WhThe
Hart, Billy 1864-1942 WhScrn 1, WhScrn 2
Hart, Bob Film 2
Hart, Bruce 1938- AmSCAP 1966
Hart, Charles d1683 OxThe, PIP&P
Hart, Diane 1926- WhoHol A, WhoThe 16
Hart, Dolores MotPP
Hart, Dolores 1938- FilmgC, WhoHol A
Hart, Dolores 1939- MovMk
Hart, Dorothy WhoHol A
Hart, Florence Film 2
Hart, Gypsy Film 1
Hart, Harvey 1928- FilmgC, IntMPA 1977
Hart, Helen Film 1
Hart, Indian Jack 1872-1974 WhoHol B
Hart, Isabella Film 1
Hart, Jack Indian Jack 1872-1974 WhScrn 2
Hart, James T 1868-1926 WhScrn 1, WhScrn 2
Hart, John WhoHol A
Hart, John d1937 NotNAT B
Hart, Joseph 1858-1921 NotNAT B,
    WhoStg 1906, WhoStg 1908
Hart, Joseph 1945- NatPD
Hart, Ken 1917- AmSCAP 1966
Hart, Lorenz 1895-1943 AmSCAP 1966, EncMT,
    McGWD, NewMT, NotNAT B, OxFilm,
    PIP&P, WhThe
Hart, M Blair 1907- BiE&WWA, NotNAT
Hart, Mabel 1886-1960 WhScrn 2
Hart, Mary WhoHol A
Hart, Maurice 1909- AmSCAP 1966
Hart, Moss 1904-1961 CnMD, CnThe, EncMT,
    FilmgC, McGWD, ModWD, NewMT,
    NotNAT A, NotNAT B, OxThe, PIP&P,
    REnWD, WhThe, WorEnF
Hart, Neal 1879-1949 Film 1, Film 2, TwYS,
    WhScrn 1, WhScrn 2, WhoHol B
Hart, Richard 1915-1951 FilmgC, MGM,
    NotNAT B
Hart, Richard 1916-1951 WhScrn 1, WhScrn 2,
    WhoHol B
Hart, Ruth Film 1
Hart, Sunshine 1886- Film 2, TwYS
Hart, Susan WhoHol A
Hart, Teddy 1897-1971 BiE&WWA, NotNAT B,
    WhScrn 1, WhScrn 2, WhThe, WhoHol B
Hart, Tony 1855-1891 EncMT, FamA&A,
    NotNAT A, NotNAT B, OxThe
Hart, Vivian WhThe
Hart, William S 1864-1946 MotPP
Hart, William S 1862-1946 WhScrn 1, WhScrn 2
Hart, William S 1864-1946 WhoHol B
Hart, William S 1870-1946 BiDFlm, CmMov,
    Film 1, Film 2, FilmgC, MovMk,
    NotNAT B, OxFilm, TwYS, WhThe,
    WorEnF
Hart, William V Pop 1867-1925 WhScrn 1,

WhScrn 2
Hartau, Ludwig Film 2
Harte, Betty 1883-1965 Film 1, WhScrn 1,
    WhScrn 2, WhoHol B
Harte, Francis Bret 1836-1902 NotNAT B
Hartford, David 1876-1932 Film 1, TwYS A,
    WhScrn 1, WhScrn 2, WhoHol B
Hartford, Dee 1927- WhoHol A
Hartford, Eden WhoHol A
Hartford, Huntington 1911- BiE&WWA, CelR 3
Hartford, K 1922- IntMPA 1977
Hartford-Davis, Robert 1923- FilmgC,
    IntMPA 1977
Hartig, Herbert 1930- AmSCAP 1966
Hartig, Michael Frank 1936- BiE&WWA,
    NotNAT
Hartigan, Pat 1881- Film 2, TwYS, TwYS A
Hartke, Gilbert 1907- BiE&WWA, NotNAT
Hartleben, Otto Erich 1864-1905 ModWD,
    NotNAT B
Hartley, Charles 1852-1930 WhScrn 1, WhScrn 2,
    WhoHol B
Hartley, Elda WomWMM A, WomWMM B
Hartley, Elizabeth 1751-1824 NotNAT B, OxThe
Hartley, Irving Film 2
Hartley, Mariette WhoHol A
Hartley, Neil 1919- BiE&WWA, NotNAT
Hartley, Pete Film 2
Hartley, Raymond Oswald 1929- AmSCAP 1966
Hartley, Ted WhoHol A
Hartley, Walter S 1927- AmSCAP 1966
Hartley-Milburn, Julie 1904-1949 Film 2, WhThe
Hartman, Agnes A 1860-1932 WhScrn 1,
    WhScrn 2
Hartman, David IntMPA 1977, NewYTET,
    WhoHol A
Hartman, Don 1900-1958 AmSCAP 1966
Hartman, Don 1901-1958 FilmgC, NotNAT B
Hartman, Elizabeth MotPP, WhoHol A
Hartman, Elizabeth 1941- FilmgC
Hartman, Elizabeth 1943- IntMPA 1977, MovMk
Hartman, Grace 1907-1955 NotNAT B,
    WhScrn 1, WhScrn 2, WhoHol B
Hartman, Gretchen 1897- Film 1, Film 2,
    MotPP, TwYS
Hartman, Jonathan William Pop 1872-1965
    WhScrn 1, WhScrn 2
Hartman, Margot WhoHol A
Hartman, Paul 1904-1973 Film 2, IntMPA 1977,
    MovMk, NotNAT B, WhScrn 2, WhoHol B
Hartman, Paul 1910- BiE&WWA
Hartmann, Arthur Martinus 1881-1956
    AmSCAP 1966
Hartmann, Sadakichi 1864?-1944 Film 2,
    WhScrn 2
Hartnell, William 1908-1975 FilmgC, WhScrn 2,
    WhThe, WhoHol C
Hartnoll, Phyllis 1906- BiE&WWA, NotNAT
Hartwig, Walter d1941 NotNAT B
Hartz, Jim 1940- IntMPA 1977, NewYTET
Hartzenbusch, Juan Eugenio 1806-1880 NotNAT B,
    OxThe
Hartzenbusch Y Martinez, Juan Eugenio 1806-1880
    McGWD
Hartzog, Tom 1937- NotNAT
Harve, M Film 1
Harvey, Anthony 1931- FilmgC, IntMPA 1977
Harvey, Don C d1963 NotNAT B, WhoHol B
Harvey, Don C 1911-1963 WhScrn 2
Harvey, Don C 1912-1963 WhScrn 1
Harvey, Edward 1893-1975 WhScrn 2,
    WhoHol C
Harvey, Fletcher Film 1
Harvey, Forrester 1880-1945 WhScrn 1,

WhScrn 2
Harvey, Forrester 1890-1945 *Film 2, FilmgC,
NotNAT. B, WhoHol B*
Harvey, Frank d1903 *NotNAT B*
Harvey, Frank 1885-1965 *WhThe*
Harvey, Frank 1912- *FilmgC, WhoThe 16*
Harvey, George Y *Film 2*
Harvey, Georgette d1952 *NotNAT B, WhoHol B*
Harvey, Georgia d1960 *NotNAT B*
Harvey, Hank d1929 *WhScrn 1, WhScrn 2*
Harvey, Harry *TwYS A*
Harvey, Harry, Sr. 1901- *Vers B, WhoHol A*
Harvey, Helen 1916- *BiE&WWA, NotNAT*
Harvey, Jack 1881-1954 *Film 1, WhoHol B*
Harvey, Jean 1900-1966 *WhScrn 2, WhoHol B*
Harvey, John 1881-1954 *WhScrn 1, WhScrn 2*
Harvey, John 1917-1970 *BiE&WWA, WhScrn 2,
WhoHol B*
Harvey, Sir John Martin- 1863-1944 *Film 2,
NotNAT B, OxThe, WhThe*
Harvey, Sir John Martin- *see also* Martin-Harvey,
Sir John
Harvey, Laurence d1973 *MotPP, WhoHol B*
Harvey, Laurence 1927-1973 *OxFilm*
Harvey, Laurence 1928-1973 *BiDFlm,
BiE&WWA, FilmgC, MovMk, NotNAT A,
NotNAT B, WhScrn 2, WhThe, WorEnF*
Harvey, Lew *Film 2*
Harvey, Lilian d1968 *WhoHol B*
Harvey, Lilian 1906-1968 *FilmgC, ThFT*
Harvey, Lilian 1907-1968 *Film 2, MovMk,
NotNAT B, OxFilm, TwYS, WhScrn 1,
WhScrn 2*
Harvey, Lillian d1968 *MotPP*
Harvey, Lillian 1907-1968 *WorEnF*
Harvey, Lottie 1890-1948 *WhScrn 1, WhScrn 2*
Harvey, Marilyn 1929-1973 *WhScrn 2*
Harvey, May d1930 *NotNAT B*
Harvey, Michael Martin *Film 2*
Harvey, Morris 1877-1944 *NotNAT B, WhThe,
WhoHol B*
Harvey, Paul 1884-1955 *Film 2, FilmgC, MovMk,
NotNAT B, Vers B, WhScrn 1, WhScrn 2,
WhoHol B*
Harvey, Paul 1918- *CelR 3, NewYTET*
Harvey, Peter 1933- *WhoThe 16*
Harvey, Rupert 1887-1954 *NotNAT B, WhThe*
Harvey, Stephanie *WomWMM B*
Harvey, Walter F W 1903- *IntMPA 1977*
Harvey, William *Film 2*
Harvis, Sidney *Film 2*
Harwood, Bobbie *Film 2*
Harwood, Harold Marsh 1874-1959 *NotNAT B,
OxThe, WhThe*
Harwood, Harry d1926 *NotNAT B*
Harwood, John 1876-1944 *NotNAT B, WhThe*
Harwood, John Edmund 1771-1809 *NotNAT B,
OxThe*
Harwood, Raven *WomWMM B*
Harwood, Ronald 1934- *IntMPA 1977*
Haryton, George *Film 2*
Has, Wojciech 1925- *BiDFlm, OxFilm, WorEnF*
Hasbrouck, Olive 1902- *Film 2*
Hasbrouck, Olive 1907- *TwYS*
Hasbrouck, Vera *Film 2*
Hascall, Lon d1932 *NotNAT B*
Hasegawa, Kazuo 1908- *OxFilm*
Hasenclever, Walter 1890-1940 *CnMD, McGWD,
ModWD*
Hasenhut, Anton 1766-1841 *OxThe*
Hash, Burl *PIP&P A*
Hashashian, Arousiak *WhScrn 2*
Hashim, Edmund 1932-1974 *WhScrn 2,
WhoHol B*

Hashr, Agha *REnWD*
Haskel, Leonhard *Film 2*
Haskell, Al d1969 *WhScrn 2, WhoHol B*
Haskell, Jean *Film 2*
Haskell, Molly *WomWMM*
Haskell, Peter *WhoHol A*
Haskin, Byron 1899- *BiDFlm, CmMov, FilmgC,
IntMPA 1977, MovMk, WorEnF*
Haskin, Charles W 1868-1927 *WhScrn 1,
WhScrn 2*
Haskins, Douglas 1928-1973 *WhScrn 2*
Haslam, Herbert 1928- *AmSCAP 1966*
Haslanger, Martha *WomWMM B*
Haslet, Jessie *Film 2*
Hassall, Christopher 1912-1963 *EncMT,
NotNAT B, WhThe*
Hassanein, Salah M *IntMPA 1977*
Hassell, George 1881-1937 *Film 1, Film 2,
NotNAT B, WhScrn 1, WhScrn 2,
WhoHol B*
Hasselquist, Jenny *Film 2, WhThe*
Hasselqvist, Jenny 1894- *OxFilm*
Hassen, Jamiel *Film 2*
Hassett, Marilyn *WhoHol A*
Hasso, Signe *MotPP, WhoHol A*
Hasso, Signe 1910- *FilmgC*
Hasso, Signe 1915- *MovMk*
Hasso, Signe 1918- *BiE&WWA, HolP 40,
NotNAT, WhoThe 16*
Hasti, Robert *WhThe*
Hastings, Basil Macdonald 1881-1928 *NotNAT B,
WhThe*
Hastings, Bob *WhoHol A*
Hastings, Carey L *Film 1*
Hastings, Don 1934- *IntMPA 1977*
Hastings, Fred *WhThe*
Hastings, Harold 1916- *AmSCAP 1966,
BiE&WWA*
Hastings, Hugh 1917- *WhoThe 16*
Hastings, Michael 1938- *ConDr 1977*
Hastings, Sir Patrick 1880-1952 *NotNAT B,
WhThe*
Hastings, Ross 1915- *AmSCAP 1966*
Hastings, Seymour *Film 1*
Hastings, Victoria d1934 *WhScrn 1, WhScrn 2*
Haswell, Percy 1871-1945 *NotNAT B, WhScrn 1,
WhScrn 2, WhThe, WhoHol B,
WhoStg 1906, WhoStg 1908*
Hatch, Frank d1938 *NotNAT B*
Hatch, Ike d1961 *NotNAT B, WhoHol B*
Hatch, James V 1928- *BiE&WWA, NotNAT*
Hatch, Riley 1865-1925 *WhScrn 2*
Hatch, William Riley *Film 1, Film 2*
Hatfield, Bobby 1940- *IntMPA 1977*
Hatfield, Hurd *IntMPA 1977, MotPP*
Hatfield, Hurd 1918- *BiDFlm, FilmgC, MovMk,
WhoHol A*
Hatfield, Hurd 1920- *BiE&WWA, NotNAT*
Hatfield, Mark 1922- *CelR 3*
Hatfield, Ted 1936- *IntMPA 1977*
Hathaway, Charles 1904-1966 *AmSCAP 1966*
Hathaway, Henry 1898- *BiDFlm, CmMov,
DcFM, FilmgC, IntMPA 1977, MovMk,
OxFilm, WorEnF*
Hathaway, Jean 1876-1938 *Film 1, WhScrn 1,
WhScrn 2, WhoHol B*
Hathaway, Lilian 1876-1954 *WhScrn 1,
WhScrn 2*
Hathaway, Lillian *Film 1*
Hathaway, Peggy *Film 2*
Hathaway, Red *Film 2*
Hathaway, Rhody 1869-1944 *WhScrn 1,
WhScrn 2*
Hathaway, Rod d1944 *WhoHol B*

Hatherton, Arthur d1924 *NotNAT B, WhThe*
Hatlen, Theodore 1911- *BiE&WWA*
Hatley, T Marvin 1905- *AmSCAP 1966*
Hatrak, Edward D 1920- *AmSCAP 1966*
Hatswell, Donald *Film 2*
Hatten, Charles *Film 2*
Hatton, Adele Bradford d1957 *NotNAT B*
Hatton, Alma W 1917- *AmSCAP 1966*
Hatton, Bradford 1906-1969 *WhScrn 2*
Hatton, Dick d1931 *WhoHol B*
Hatton, Fanny d1939 *NotNAT B, WhThe*
Hatton, Frances 1888-1971 *Film 2, WhScrn 1,
   WhScrn 2, WhoHol B*
Hatton, Frederick 1879-1946 *NotNAT B, WhThe*
Hatton, Joseph d1907 *NotNAT B*
Hatton, Mercy *Film 2*
Hatton, Raymond 1887-1971 *FilmgC, MotPP,
   WhoHol B*
Hatton, Raymond 1892-1971 *Film 1, Film 2,
   MovMk, TwYS, Vers B, WhScrn 1,
   WhScrn 2*
Hatton, Richard 1891-1931 *WhScrn 1, WhScrn 2*
Hatton, Rondo 1894-1946 *FilmgC, WhScrn 2,
   WhoHol B*
Hatton, Rondo 1895-1946 *WhScrn 1*
Hauber, Billy *Film 1, Film 2*
Haubiel, Charles 1892- *AmSCAP 1966*
Hauch, Johannes Carsten 1790-1872 *NotNAT B,
   OxThe*
Hauger, George 1921- *BiE&WWA*
Haughton, John Alan 1880-1951 *AmSCAP 1966*
Haupt, Ullrich 1887-1931 *WhScrn 1, WhScrn 2*
Haupt, Ulrich 1887-1931 *Film 2, TwYS,
   WhoHol B*
Hauptmann, Carl 1858-1921 *CnMD, McGWD,
   ModWD, NotNAT B*
Hauptmann, Gerhart 1862-1946 *CnMD, CnThe,
   McGWD, ModWD, NotNAT A, NotNAT B,
   OxThe, PIP&P, REnWD, WhThe*
Hause, Newton *Film 2*
Hauser, Frank 1922- *CnThe, WhoThe 16*
Hauser, Gaylord 1895- *CelR 3*
Hauser, Gustave M *NewYTET*
Hauser, Harald 1912- *CnMD, CroCD*
Hausman, Howard L 1914- *BiE&WWA,
   NotNAT*
Hausmann, Manfred 1898- *CnMD*
Hausner, Jerry *WhoHol A*
Haussermann, Reinhold *Film 2*
Hauteroche, Noel-Jacques LeBreton De 1616?-1707
   OxThe
Havard, William d1778 *NotNAT B*
Havel, Joe 1869-1932 *WhScrn 1, WhScrn 2,
   WhoHol B*
Havel, Vaclav 1936- *CnThe, CroCD, ModWD,
   REnWD*
Havelock-Allan, Anthony 1905- *FilmgC*
Havelock-Allen, Sir Anthony *IntMPA 1977*
Havemann, William G 1923- *AmSCAP 1966*
Haven, Charna 1925-1971 *WhScrn 2, WhoHol B*
Havens, John F 1912- *BiE&WWA*
Haver, June 1926- *CmMov, FilmgC, MotPP,
   MovMk, WhoHol A*
Haver, Phyllis 1899-1960 *Film 1, Film 2, FilmgC,
   MotPP, MovMk, NotNAT B, WhScrn 1,
   WhScrn 2*
Haver, Phyllis 1899-1961 *TwYS, WhoHol B*
Havergal, Giles 1938- *WhoThe 16*
Havez, Jean 1874-1925 *AmSCAP 1966*
Havez, Jean C *Film 2*
Havier, Alex J d1945 *WhoHol B*
Havier, Jose Alex 1909-1945 *WhScrn 1,
   WhScrn 2*
Haviland, Augusta d1925 *NotNAT B*

Haviland, Rena 1878-1954 *WhScrn 1, WhScrn 2*
Haviland, William 1860-1917 *NotNAT B, WhThe*
Havlin, John H d1924 *NotNAT B*
Havoc, June 1916- *BiE&WWA, FilmgC,
   HolP 40, IntMPA 1977, MotPP, MovMk,
   NotNAT, NotNAT A, WhoHol A,
   WhoThe 16*
Hawes, David S 1910- *NotNAT*
Hawes, David S 1919- *BiE&WWA*
Hawes, Mary *Film 2*
Hawk, Jeremy 1918- *WhoHol A, WhoThe 16*
Hawke, Rohn Olin 1924-1967 *WhScrn 1,
   WhScrn 2*
Hawkes, Jaquetta *PIP&P*
Hawkes, John 1925- *ConDr 1977, CroCD*
Hawkesworth, Walter d1606 *NotNAT B*
Hawkins, Anthony Hope d1933 *NotNAT B*
Hawkins, Charlotte *AmSCAP 1966*
Hawkins, Coleman Bean 1904-1969 *WhScrn 2*
Hawkins, Erskine 1914- *AmSCAP 1966*
Hawkins, Etta d1945 *NotNAT B*
Hawkins, Floyd W 1904- *AmSCAP 1966*
Hawkins, Iris 1893- *WhThe*
Hawkins, Jack 1910-1973 *BiDFlm, CmMov,
   FilmgC, MotPP, MovMk, NotNAT B,
   OxFilm, PIP&P, WhScrn 2, WhThe,
   WhoHol B, WorEnF*
Hawkins, Puny d1947 *WhScrn 1, WhScrn 2*
Hawkins, Stockwell 1874-1927 *NotNAT B,
   WhThe*
Hawks, Charles Monroe 1874-1951 *WhScrn 1,
   WhScrn 2*
Hawks, Howard 1896- *BiDFlm, CmMov, DcFM,
   FilmgC, IntMPA 1977, MovMk, OxFilm,
   TwYS A, WorEnF*
Hawks, Wells d1941 *NotNAT B*
Hawley, Allen Burton 1895-1925 *WhScrn 1,
   WhScrn 2, WhoHol B*
Hawley, Charles Beach 1858-1915 *AmSCAP 1966*
Hawley, Dudley 1879-1941 *Film 1, NotNAT B,
   WhScrn 1, WhScrn 2*
Hawley, Esther 1906-1968 *NotNAT B*
Hawley, H Dudley 1879-1941 *WhoHol B*
Hawley, Helen *Film 2*
Hawley, Ida *WhoStg 1908*
Hawley, Ormi 1890-1942 *Film 1, MotPP, TwYS,
   WhScrn 2*
Hawley, Wanda 1897- *Film 1, Film 2, MotPP,
   TwYS*
Hawn, Goldie 1945- *CelR 3, FilmgC,
   IntMPA 1977, MotPP, MovMk, WhoHol A*
Hawn, John Happy Jack 1883-1964 *WhScrn 2*
Haworth, Don *ConDr 1977B*
Haworth, Jill 1945- *FilmgC, MotPP, WhoHol A*
Haworth, Joseph 1855-1903 *NotNAT B*
Haworth, Martha d1966 *WhoHol B*
Hawrylo, Frank 1936- *AmSCAP 1966*
Hawthorne, David d1942 *Film 2, NotNAT B,
   WhThe, WhoHol B*
Hawthorne, Grace d1922 *NotNAT B*
Hawthorne, Lil *WhThe*
Hawthorne, Nathaniel 1804-1864 *FilmgC*
Hawthorne, Nigel 1929- *WhoThe 16*
Hawtrey, Anthony 1909-1954 *WhScrn 1,
   WhScrn 2, WhThe, WhoHol B*
Hawtrey, Charles 1855- *WhoStg 1906,
   WhoStg 1908*
Hawtrey, Charles 1914- *FilmgC, WhThe,
   WhoHol A*
Hawtrey, Sir Charles Henry 1858-1923 *CnThe,
   NotNAT A, NotNAT B, OxThe, WhScrn 2,
   WhThe*
Hawtrey, George P d1910 *NotNAT B*
Hawtrey, Marjory 1900- *WhThe*

Hawtrey, William P d1914 NotNAT B
Hawtry, Anthony 1909-1954 NotNAT B
Hay, Alexandra 1944?- FilmgC, WhoHol A
Hay, Austin WhoHol A
Hay, Charles Film 2
Hay, George D d1968 WhoHol B
Hay, Gyula 1900- CroCD, ModWD
Hay, Ian 1876-1952 NotNAT B, OxThe, WhThe
Hay, Joan 1894- WhThe
Hay, Julius 1900- CnMD
Hay, Mary 1901-1957 Film 1, Film 2,
    NotNAT B, WhScrn 1, WhScrn 2, WhThe,
    WhoHol B
Hay, Sara Henderson 1906- AmSCAP 1966
Hay, Valerie 1910- WhThe
Hay, Will 1888-1949 CmMov, FilmgC, OxFilm,
    WhoHol B, WorEnF
Hay, William 1888-1949 WhScrn 1, WhScrn 2
Hayakawa, S I 1908- CelR 3
Hayakawa, Sessue 1889-1973 Film 1, Film 2,
    FilmgC, MotPP, OxFilm, TwYS, WhScrn 2,
    WhoHol B
Hayakawa, Sessue 1890-1973 MovMk
Haydee, Marcia 1940- CelR 3
Haydel, Dorothy Film 1
Haydel, Richard 1927-1949 WhScrn 2
Hayden, Harry 1882-1955 WhScrn 1, WhScrn 2
Hayden, Harry 1884-1955 Vers B, WhoHol B
Hayden, Jeffrey NewYTET
Hayden, Linda 1951- FilmgC, WhoHol A
Hayden, Margaret WhScrn 1, WhScrn 2
Hayden, Mary WhoHol A
Hayden, Melissa WhoHol A
Hayden, Nora Film 2, WhoHol A
Hayden, Russell 1912- FilmgC, IntMPA 1977,
    WhoHol A
Hayden, Sterling IntMPA 1977, MotPP
Hayden, Sterling 1916- BiDFlm, FilmgC,
    HolP 40, WhoHol A, WorEnF
Hayden, Sterling 1917- MovMk, OxFilm
Hayden, Terese 1921- BiE&WWA, NotNAT,
    WhoThe 16
Hayden-Clarendon, J 1878- WhoStg 1906,
    WhoStg 1908
Hayden-Coffin, Adeline Film 2
Haydn, Richard IntMPA 1977
Haydn, Richard 1905- FilmgC, MovMk,
    WhoHol A, WorEnF
Haydn, Richard 1907- Vers B
Haydock, John d1918 WhScrn 2
Haydon, Ethel 1878-1954 WhThe
Haydon, Florence d1918 NotNAT B, WhThe
Haydon, John S d1907 NotNAT B
Haydon, Julie 1910- BiE&WWA, NotNAT,
    PIP&P, ThFT, WhThe, WhoHol A
Haye, Helen 1874-1957 Film 2, FilmgC,
    NotNAT B, OxThe, WhScrn 1, WhScrn 2,
    WhThe, WhoHol B
Hayer, Nicholas 1898- WorEnF
Hayer, Nicolas 1902- DcFM
Hayers, Sidney 1921- FilmgC
Hayes, Ada d1962 NotNAT B
Hayes, Alice Film 1
Hayes, Allison 1930- FilmgC, WhoHol A
Hayes, Bill 1925- BiE&WWA, NotNAT,
    WhoHol A
Hayes, Billie WhoHol A
Hayes, Billy AmSCAP 1966
Hayes, Carrie 1878-1954 WhScrn 1, WhScrn 2
Hayes, Catherine 1886-1941 WhScrn 1,
    WhScrn 2, WhoHol B
Hayes, Charles R 1914- AmSCAP 1966
Hayes, Daniel L Film 2
Hayes, Danny Film 2

Hayes, Edgar Junius 1905- AmSCAP 1966
Hayes, F W d1918 NotNAT B
Hayes, Frank d1924 Film 1, Film 2
Hayes, Frank 1875-1923 WhScrn 1, WhScrn 2,
    WhoHol B
Hayes, Gabby 1885-1969 OxFilm
Hayes, George 1888-1967 BiE&WWA, PIP&P,
    WhScrn 2, WhThe, WhoHol B
Hayes, George Gabby 1885-1969 CmMov, Film 2,
    FilmgC, MotPP, MovMk, Vers B,
    WhScrn 1, WhScrn 2, WhoHol B
Hayes, Hazel WhoHol A
Hayes, Helen MotPP, WhoHol A
Hayes, Helen 1900- BiE&WWA, CelR 3,
    CnThe, FamA&A, Film 1, Film 2, FilmgC,
    MGM, MovMk, NotNAT, NotNAT A,
    OxFilm, OxThe, PIP&P, ThFT, WhoThe 16,
    WorEnF
Hayes, Helen 1901- IntMPA 1977
Hayes, Hubert d1964 NotNAT B
Hayes, Isaac 1942- CelR 3, WhoHol A
Hayes, J Milton 1884-1940 WhThe
Hayes, Jimmy WhoHol A
Hayes, John Michael 1919- FilmgC,
    IntMPA 1977, WorEnF
Hayes, John S 1910- IntMPA 1977
Hayes, Joseph 1918- BiE&WWA, NotNAT
Hayes, Larry Ray 1940- AmSCAP 1966
Hayes, Laurence C 1903-1974 WhScrn 2,
    WhoHol B
Hayes, Maggie 1924- BiE&WWA
Hayes, Margaret 1924- WhoHol A
Hayes, Margaret 1925- IntMPA 1977
Hayes, Milton 1884-1940 NotNAT B
Hayes, Patricia 1909- WhThe
Hayes, Peter Lind 1915- AmSCAP 1966,
    BiE&WWA, IntMPA 1977, NotNAT,
    WhoHol A
Hayes, Rea AmSCAP 1966
Hayes, Reginald d1953 NotNAT B
Hayes, Richard IntMPA 1977
Hayes, Richard 1930- AmSCAP 1966
Hayes, Ron WhoHol A
Hayes, Sam 1905-1958 WhScrn 2
Hayes, Sidney 1865-1940 WhScrn 1, WhScrn 2
Hayes, William 1887-1937 Film 2, WhScrn 1,
    WhScrn 2
Hayes, Woody 1913- CelR 3
Hayle, Grace 1889-1963 WhScrn 1, WhScrn 2,
    WhoHol B
Hayman, Al d1917 NotNAT B, WhThe
Hayman, Alf 1865-1921 NotNAT B
Hayman, Leonard d1962 NotNAT B
Hayman, Lillian 1922- WhoHol A, WhoThe 16
Hayman, Richard 1920- AmSCAP 1966
Haymes, Dick 1916- FilmgC, HolP 40,
    IntMPA 1977, MotPP, WhoHol A
Haynes, Alfred W d1924 NotNAT B
Haynes, Arthur 1914-1966 WhScrn 1, WhScrn 2,
    WhoHol B
Haynes, Daniel L d1954 Film 2, WhScrn 1,
    WhScrn 2, WhoHol B
Haynes, Hilda WhoHol A
Haynes, Lloyd WhoHol A
Haynes, Roberta WhoHol A
Haynes, T P d1915 NotNAT B
Haynes, Tiger PIP&P A
Haynie, William S 1918- AmSCAP 1966
Hays, Bill 1938- WhoThe 16
Hays, Billy Silas 1898- AmSCAP 1966
Hays, David 1930- BiE&WWA, NotNAT,
    WhoThe 16
Hays, Guerney Film 2
Hays, Kathryn WhoHol A

Hays, Will d1937 *WhoHol B*
Hays, Will H 1879-1954 *DcFM, FilmgC, OxFilm,*
   TwYS B,. WorEnF
Hays, William Shakespeare 1837-1907 *NotNAT B*
Hayse, Emil *Film 2*
Hayter, James 1907- *FilmgC, IntMPA 1977,*
   WhoHol A, WhoThe 16
Haythorne, Joan 1915- *FilmgC, WhoHol A,*
   WhoThe 16
Hayton, Lennie *CmMov*
Hayton, Leonard George 1908- *AmSCAP 1966*
Hayward, Christopher R 1925- *AmSCAP 1966*
Hayward, Helen *Film 2*
Hayward, Leland 1902-1971 *BiE&WWA, EncMT,*
   FilmgC, NewYTET, NotNAT B, WhThe
Hayward, Lillie *WomWMM*
Hayward, Louis 1909- *CmMov, FilmgC,*
   IntMPA 1977, MotPP, MovMk, WhoHol A,
   WorEnF
Hayward, Susan 1918- *FilmgC, MotPP, OxFilm,*
   ThFT, WorEnF
Hayward, Susan 1918-1974 *CmMov*
Hayward, Susan 1918-1975 *BiDFlm, WhScrn 2*
Hayward, Susan 1919-1975 *MovMk, WhoHol C*
Haywell, Frederick d1889 *NotNAT B*
Haywood, Doris *Film 1*
Haywood, Eliza d1756 *NotNAT B*
Hayworth, Rita *MotPP, WhoHol A,*
   WomWMM
Hayworth, Rita 1918- *BiDFlm, CmMov, FilmgC,*
   MovMk, OxFilm, ThFT, WorEnF
Hayworth, Rita 1919- *CelR 3, IntMPA 1977*
Hayworth, Vinton J 1906-1970 *WhScrn 1,*
   WhScrn 2, WhoHol B
Hazam, Lou *NewYTET*
Hazel, Hy 1920-1970 *WhScrn 2*
Hazell, Hy 1920-1970 *FilmgC, WhScrn 1,*
   WhoHol B
Hazell, Hy 1922-1970 *EncMT, WhThe*
Hazeltin, George Cochrane, Jr. *WhoStg 1908*
Hazeltine, William 1866- *WhoStg 1908*
Hazelton, Joseph 1853-1936 *WhScrn 1,*
   WhScrn 2
Hazeltone, Miss *Film 1*
Hazen, Joseph H 1898- *IntMPA 1977*
Hazleton, George C d1921 *NotNAT B*
Hazleton, Joseph H *Film 2*
Hazlett, William *WhScrn 2*
Hazlewood, C H d1875 *NotNAT B*
Hazlewood, Lee 1929- *AmSCAP 1966*
Hazlitt, William 1778-1830 *NotNAT A,*
   NotNAT B, OxThe
Hazzard, John Edward 1881-1935 *AmSCAP 1966,*
   NotNAT B, WhThe
Head, Edith 1907- *CelR 3, FilmgC,*
   IntMPA 1977
Head, Murray *WhoHol A*
Headrick, Richard 1917- *Film 1, Film 2, TwYS*
Heagney, William H 1882-1955 *AmSCAP 1966*
Heal, Joan 1922- *WhoHol A, WhoThe 16*
Healey, Myron 1922- *IntMPA 1977, WhoHol A*
Healy, Dan 1889-1969 *Film 2, WhScrn 1,*
   WhScrn 2, WhoHol B
Healy, Gerald d1963 *NotNAT B*
Healy, John T *IntMPA 1977*
Healy, Mary 1918- *BiE&WWA, NotNAT,*
   WhoHol A
Healy, Ted 1886-1937 *FilmgC*
Healy, Ted 1896-1937 *WhScrn 1, WhScrn 2,*
   WhoHol B
Heard, Paul F 1913- *IntMPA 1977*
Heard, Richard 1936- *AmSCAP 1966*
Hearn, Edward 1888-1963 *Film 1, Film 2,*
   WhScrn 2, WhoHol B

Hearn, Fred *Film 1*
Hearn, George *Film 2*
Hearn, James d1913 *NotNAT B*
Hearn, Lew 1882- *Film 2, WhThe*
Hearn, Mary *Film 2*
Hearn, Sam 1889-1964 *WhScrn 1, WhScrn 2,*
   WhoHol B
Hearne, Edward 1888- *TwYS*
Hearne, James A *Film 2*
Hearne, Richard *WhoHol A*
Hearne, Richard 1908- *FilmgC*
Hearne, Richard 1909- *WhThe*
Hearst, William Randolph 1863-1950 *OxFilm*
Hearst, William Randolph 1863-1951 *DcFM,*
   FilmgC, WorEnF
Hearst, William Randolph, Jr. 1908- *CelR 3*
Heath, Arch B 1890- *TwYS A*
Heath, Bobby 1889-1952 *AmSCAP 1966*
Heath, Caroline d1887 *NotNAT B*
Heath, Dody *WhoHol A*
Heath, Eira 1940- *WhoThe 16*
Heath, George *WhoStg 1908*
Heath, Gordon 1918- *BiE&WWA, NotNAT*
Heath, Ida d1950 *NotNAT B*
Heath, Laurence *NewYTET*
Heath, Rosalie *Film 2*
Heath, Ted 1902-1969 *WhScrn 1, WhScrn 2,*
   WhoHol B
Heath, Walter Henry 1890-1965 *AmSCAP 1966*
Heathcote, A M d1934 *NotNAT B*
Heathcote, Thomas *WhoHol A*
Heatherley, Clifford 1888-1937 *WhScrn 1,*
   WhScrn 2, WhThe, WhoHol B
Heatherly, Clifford 1888-1937 *Film 2,*
   NotNAT B
Heatherton, Joey 1944- *FilmgC, MotPP,*
   WhoHol A
Heatherton, Ray 1910- *BiE&WWA, NotNAT*
Heaton, Wallace 1914- *AmSCAP 1966*
Heatter, Gabriel 1890-1972 *WhScrn 2*
Hebbel, Christian Friedrich 1813-1863 *NotNAT A,*
   NotNAT B
Hebbel, Friedrich 1813-1863 *CnThe, McGWD,*
   OxThe, REnWD
Hebert, Fred 1911-1972 *BiE&WWA, NotNAT B*
Hebert, Pierre 1944- *WorEnF*
Hecht, Ben 1893-1964 *CnMD, CnThe*
Hecht, Ben 1894-1964 *BiDFlm, CmMov, DcFM,*
   FilmgC, McGWD, ModWD, NotNAT A,
   NotNAT B, OxFilm, WhScrn 2, WhThe,
   WorEnF
Hecht, Harold 1907- *FilmgC, IntMPA 1977,*
   WorEnF
Hecht, Jenny 1943-1971 *WhScrn 2, WhoHol B*
Hecht, Ken *AmSCAP 1966*
Hecht, Paul 1941- *NotNAT*
Hecht, Ted 1908-1969 *WhScrn 1, WhScrn 2,*
   WhoHol B
Hechy, Alice *Film 2*
Heck, Stanton *Film 2*
Heckart, Eileen 1919- *BiE&WWA, CelR 3,*
   FilmgC, IntMPA 1977, MotPP, MovMk,
   NotNAT, PIP&P, WhoHol A, WhoThe 16
Heckroth, Hein 1897- *OxFilm*
Heckroth, Hein 1901-1970 *FilmgC*
Heckscher, August 1913- *BiE&WWA*
Hedberg, Tor 1862-1931 *CnMD, OxThe*
Hedburg, Franz 1828-1908 *NotNAT B*
Hedburg, Tor 1862-1931 *NotNAT B*
Hedin, June *WhoHol A*
Hedison, David 1928- *FilmgC, MotPP,*
   WhoHol A
Hedley, H B d1931 *NotNAT B, WhThe*
Hedley, Jack 1930- *FilmgC*

Hedlund, Guy 1884-1964 *Film 1*, *WhScrn 2*
Hedman, Martha 1888- *WhThe*
Hedmann, Trine *WomWMM*
Hedquist, Ivan *Film 2*
Hedren, Tippi 1935- *BiDFlm*, *FilmgC*, *MotPP*, *WhoHol A*
Hedrick, A Earl 1896- *IntMPA 1977*
Hedrick, Clarence d1969 *WhoHol B*
Hedwig, Gordon W 1913- *IntMPA 1977*
Heefner, David Kerry 1945- *NatPD*
Heeley, Desmond *WhoThe 16*
Heenan, James *Film 2*
Heerman, Victor 1893- *TwYS A*
Heestand, Diane *WomWMM B*
Heffernan, John 1934- *BiE&WWA*, *NotNAT*, *WhoHol A*, *WhoThe 16*
Heffley, Wayne *WhoHol A*
Heffner, Hubert 1901- *BiE&WWA*, *NotNAT*
Heffner, Richard D 1925- *IntMPA 1977*
Heffron, Richard T *IntMPA 1977*
Heffron, Thomas N 1872- *TwYS A*
Heflin, Frances *WhoHol A*
Heflin, Frances 1922- *BiE&WWA*, *NotNAT*
Heflin, Frances 1924- *WhThe*
Heflin, Kate *WhoHol A*
Heflin, Nora *WhoHol A*
Heflin, Van 1909-1971 *WhThe*
Heflin, Van 1910-1971 *BiDFlm*, *BiE&WWA*, *CmMov*, *FilmgC*, *MGM*, *MotPP*, *MovMk*, *NotNAT B*, *OxFilm*, *PIP&P*, *WhScrn 1*, *WhScrn 2*, *WhoHol B*, *WorEnF*
Hefner, Hugh 1926- *CelR 3*
Hefner, Keith 1929- *AmSCAP 1966*
Hefti, Neal 1922- *AmSCAP 1966*
Hegeman, Alice *Film 2*
Hegewald *Film 2*
Heggen, Thomas O 1919-1949 *McGWD*, *NotNAT B*
Heggie, O P 1879-1936 *Film 2*, *FilmgC*, *MovMk*, *NotNAT B*, *TwYS*, *WhScrn 1*, *WhScrn 2*, *WhThe*, *WhoHol B*
Hegira, Anne d1971? *WhScrn 2*, *WhoHol A*
Hegyi, Barnabas *DcFM*
Heiberg, Gunnar 1857-1929 *CnMD*, *CnThe*, *McGWD*, *ModWD*, *NotNAT B*, *OxThe*, *REnWD*
Heiberg, Johan Ludvig 1791-1860 *McGWD*, *NotNAT B*, *OxThe*, *REnWD*
Heiberg, Johanne Luise Patges 1812-1890 *OxThe*
Heiberg, Peder Andreas 1758-1841 *OxThe*
Heick, Susan *WomWMM B*
Heidemann, Paul 1886-1968 *Film 2*, *WhScrn 1*, *WhScrn 2*
Heider, Frederick 1917- *IntMPA 1977*
Heidt, Horace *WhoHol A*
Heidt, Joseph d1962 *NotNAT B*
Heifetz, Harold *NatPD*
Heifetz, Jascha 1901- *AmSCAP 1966*, *CelR 3*, *WhoHol A*
Heifetz, Vladimir 1893- *AmSCAP 1966*
Heifits, Joseph 1904- *FilmgC*
Heifits, Josif 1906- *OxFilm*
Heifitz, Joseph 1905- *WorEnF*
Heifitz, Josif 1905- *DcFM*
Heigh, Helene *WhoHol A*
Height, Jean d1967 *WhoHol B*
Heijermans, Herman 1864-1924 *CnMD*, *CnThe*, *McGWD*, *ModWD*, *OxThe*, *REnWD*, *WhThe*
Heijermans, Hermann 1864-1924 *NotNAT B*
Heilbronn, William 1879- *WhThe*
Heilweil, Samantha Lee *WomWMM B*
Heim, Emery 1906-1946 *AmSCAP 1966*
Heims, Jo *IntMPA 1977*

Hein, Albert d1949 *NotNAT B*
Hein, Beverly J 1920- *AmSCAP 1966*
Hein, Birgit *WomWMM*
Hein, Silvio 1879-1928 *AmSCAP 1966*, *NotNAT B*, *WhThe*
Hein, Wilhelm *WomWMM*
Heindorf, Ray 1910- *CmMov*, *FilmgC*, *IntMPA 1977*
Heindorf, Ray John 1908- *AmSCAP 1966*
Heinecke, Ruth C *IntMPA 1977*
Heinemann, Eda 1880- *BiE&WWA*, *NotNAT*
Heinemann, George *NewYTET*
Heink, Schuman *Film 2*
Heinlein, Mary Virginia d1961 *NotNAT B*
Heinrich Julius, Duke Of Brunswick 1564-1613 *OxThe*
Heinrich, George *Film 2*
Heins, Marjorie *WomWMM B*
Heinz, Gerard 1903-1972 *FilmgC*, *WhoHol B*
Heinz, Gerard 1904- *WhThe*
Heinz, H J, II 1908- *CelR 3*
Heinz, John F 1926- *AmSCAP 1966*
Heiremans, Luis Alberto 1928-1964 *CroCD*
Heiseler, Bernt Von 1907- *CnMD*, *ModWD*
Heiseler, Henry Von 1875-1928 *ModWD*
Heisler, Stuart 1894- *BiDFlm*, *FilmgC*, *IntMPA 1977*, *MovMk*, *WorEnF*
Heiss, Carol 1940- *FilmgC*
Helbert, Jack *Film 2*
Helbig, Otto H 1914- *AmSCAP 1966*
Helburn, Theresa 1887-1959 *EncMT*, *NotNAT A*, *NotNAT B*, *PIP&P*, *WhThe*
Held, Anna 1865-1918 *FamA&A*
Held, Anna 1873-1918 *EncMT*, *Film 1*, *NotNAT B*, *WhScrn 2*, *WhThe*, *WhoHol B*, *WhoStg 1906*, *WhoStg 1908*
Heldabrand, John *WhoHol A*
Helena, Edith 1876- *WhoStg 1908*
Helfer, Walter 1896-1959 *AmSCAP 1966*
Helfman, Max 1901-1963 *AmSCAP 1966*
Heller, Claire 1929- *BiE&WWA*, *NotNAT*
Heller, Frank *Film 2*
Heller, Franklin *IntMPA 1977*
Heller, Gloria *Film 2*
Heller, Hugh *IntMPA 1977*
Heller, Jeanne d1908 *NotNAT B*
Heller, John 1928- *AmSCAP 1966*
Heller, Joseph 1923- *ConDr 1977*, *NotNAT*
Heller, Lukas 1930- *FilmgC*
Heller, Otto 1896-1970 *FilmgC*, *OxFilm*, *WorEnF*
Heller, Paul M 1927- *IntMPA 1977*
Heller, Ray *Film 2*
Heller, Rosilyn *WomWMM*
Heller, Walter 1915- *CelR 3*
Heller, Wilson B 1893- *IntMPA 1977*
Hellerman, Fred 1927- *AmSCAP 1966*
Hellinger, Mark 1903-1947 *BiDFlm*, *CmMov*, *DcFM*, *FilmgC*, *NotNAT A*, *NotNAT B*, *OxFilm*, *WhScrn 2*, *WorEnF*
Hellman, Jerome *IntMPA 1977*
Hellman, Lillian *IntMPA 1977*, *WomWMM*
Hellman, Lillian 1905- *CelR 3*, *CnMD*, *CnThe*, *CroCD*, *DcFM*, *FilmgC*, *McGWD*, *ModWD*, *OxFilm*, *OxThe*, *PIP&P*, *REnWD*, *WhoThe 16*, *WorEnF*
Hellman, Lillian 1907- *BiE&WWA*, *ConDr 1977*, *NatPD*, *NotNAT*, *NotNAT A*
Hellman, Marcel 1898- *FilmgC*, *IntMPA 1977*
Hellman, Miriam *Film 2*
Hellman, Monte 1931- *FilmgC*
Hellman, Monte 1932- *BiDFlm*
Hellmer, Kurt 1909- *BiE&WWA*, *NotNAT*
Hellum, Barney *Film 2*

Helm, Anne *WhoHol A*
Helm, Brigette 1908- *Film 2*
Helm, Brigitta 1906- *OxFilm*
Helm, Brigitte 1906- *FilmgC, WhoHol A*
Helm, Brigitte 1907- *MovMk, WorEnF*
Helm, Fay *FilmgC*
Helm, Frances *BiE&WWA, NotNAT,*
  WhoHol A
Helmore, Arthur 1858-1941 *NotNAT B*
Helmore, Arthur 1859-1941 *WhThe*
Helmore, Tom 1916- *BiE&WWA, NotNAT,*
  WhoHol A
Helms, Richard 1913- *CelR 3*
Helms, Ruth *Film 2*
Helms, Ruth d1960 *WhScrn 2*
Helms, Ruth d1961 *WhoHol B*
Helmsley, Charles Thomas Hunt- 1865-1940
  NotNAT B, WhThe
Helpmann, Sir Robert 1909- *BiE&WWA, CnThe,*
  FilmgC, IntMPA 1977, MovMk, NotNAT,
  NotNAT A, OxThe, PIP&P, WhoHol A,
  WhoThe 16
Helprin, Morris 1904- *IntMPA 1977*
Heltai, Jeno 1871-1957 *OxThe*
Helton, Alf d1937 *NotNAT B*
Helton, Peggy *MotPP*
Helton, Percy 1894-1971 *Film 2, FilmgC, Vers A,*
  WhScrn 1, WhScrn 2, WhoHol B
Heming, John 1556-1630 *PIP&P*
Heming, Percy 1885- *WhThe*
Heming, Violet 1893- *Film 1, TwYS*
Heming, Violet 1895- *BiE&WWA, NotNAT,*
  WhThe, WhoHol A
Heming, Violet see also Hemming, Violet
Heminge, John 1556-1630 *NotNAT B, OxThe*
Hemingway, Ernest 1898-1961 *OxFilm*
Hemingway, Ernest 1899-1961 *CnMD, FilmgC,*
  ModWD, NotNAT B, WorEnF
Hemingway, Margaux *WhoHol A*
Hemingway, Marie 1893-1939 *NotNAT B,*
  WhThe, WhoHol B
Hemingway, Richard C *WhScrn 2*
Hemion, Dwight *NewYTET*
Hemion, Mac *NewYTET*
Hemment, Marguerite E 1908- *AmSCAP 1966*
Hemmer, Eugene 1929- *AmSCAP 1966*
Hemmerde, Edward George 1871-1948 *NotNAT B,*
  WhThe
Hemming, Alfred d1942 *NotNAT B*
Hemming, Violet 1893- *Film 2*
Hemming, Violet see also Heming, Violet
Hemmings, David 1941- *CelR 3, FilmgC,*
  IntMPA 1977, MotPP, MovMk, WhoHol A,
  WorEnF
Hemphill, F L *Film 1*
Hemsley, Estelle 1887-1968 *WhScrn 1, WhScrn 2,*
  WhoHol B
Hemsley, Estelle 1892-1968 *BiE&WWA,*
  NotNAT B
Hemsley, Harry May 1877-1951 *NotNAT B,*
  WhThe
Hemsley, W T 1850-1918 *NotNAT B, WhThe*
Henabery, Joseph 1888-1976 *Film 1*
Henabery, Joseph 1888-1976 *TwYS A,*
  WhoHol C
Henckels, Paul 1885-1967 *Film 2*
Henckles, Paul 1885-1967 *WhScrn 2*
Hendee, Harold F 1879-1966 *WhScrn 1,*
  WhScrn 2
Henderson, Alex F 1866-1933 *NotNAT B, WhThe*
Henderson, Bert *Film 2*
Henderson, Charles A 1907- *IntMPA 1977*
Henderson, Charles E 1907- *AmSCAP 1966*
Henderson, David 1853-1908 *NotNAT B,*

  WhoStg 1906, WhoStg 1908
Henderson, Del 1877-1956 *Film 1, Film 2,*
  NotNAT B
Henderson, Del 1883-1946 *TwYS A*
Henderson, Del 1883-1956 *TwYS, WhScrn 1,*
  WhScrn 2, WhoHol B
Henderson, Dickie 1922- *IntMPA 1977,*
  WhoThe 16
Henderson, Donald A 1903- *IntMPA 1977*
Henderson, Douglas *WhoHol A*
Henderson, Elvira 1903- *WhThe*
Henderson, Fletcher 1897-1952 *AmSCAP 1966*
Henderson, Florence 1934- *BiE&WWA, EncMT,*
  NotNAT, WhoHol A, WhoThe 16
Henderson, George A d1923 *WhScrn 1,*
  WhScrn 2, WhoHol B
Henderson, Grace 1860-1944 *Film 1, NotNAT B,*
  WhScrn 2, WhoHol B
Henderson, Gwen 1908- *AmSCAP 1966*
Henderson, Ivo d1968 *WhScrn 2, WhoHol B*
Henderson, J Raymond 1929- *AmSCAP 1966*
Henderson, Jack *Film 1*
Henderson, Jack d1957 *NotNAT B*
Henderson, John 1747-1785 *OxThe*
Henderson, John Raymond d1937 *NotNAT B*
Henderson, Joseph *Film 2*
Henderson, Laura d1944 *NotNAT B*
Henderson, Lucius 1848-1947 *Film 2, NotNAT B,*
  WhScrn 1, WhScrn 2, WhoHol B
Henderson, Luther 1919- *AmSCAP 1966,*
  BiE&WWA, NotNAT
Henderson, Marcia 1934- *IntMPA 1977*
Henderson, Marcia 1950- *FilmgC*
Henderson, Marie d1902 *NotNAT B*
Henderson, May 1884- *WhThe*
Henderson, Nancy *NatPD*
Henderson, Ray 1896-1970 *AmSCAP 1966,*
  BiE&WWA, EncMT, NewMT, NotNAT B,
  WhThe
Henderson, Robert 1904- *WhoThe 16*
Henderson, Robert Morton 1926- *NotNAT*
Henderson, Skitch 1918- *AmSCAP 1966, CelR 3,*
  IntMPA 1977
Henderson, Steffi d1967 *WhScrn 2*
Henderson, Talbot V 1879-1946 *WhScrn 1,*
  WhScrn 2, WhoHol B
Henderson, Ted d1962 *WhoHol B*
Henderson-Bland, Robert d1941 *WhScrn 1,*
  WhScrn 2, WhoHol B
Hendler, Herb 1918- *AmSCAP 1966*
Hendrick, Richard *Film 2*
Hendricks, Ben *Film 1*
Hendricks, Ben, Jr. 1893-1938 *Film 2, WhScrn 1,*
  WhScrn 2, WhoHol B
Hendricks, Ben, Sr. 1862-1930 *NotNAT B,*
  WhScrn 1, WhScrn 2, WhoHol B
Hendricks, Bill L *IntMPA 1977*
Hendricks, Cathy *WomWMM B*
Hendricks, Frederick Wilmoth 1901-
  AmSCAP 1966
Hendricks, Jon Carl 1921- *AmSCAP 1966*
Hendricks, Louis d1923 *Film 2, WhScrn 1,*
  WhScrn 2, WhoHol B
Hendrie, Ernest 1859-1929 *NotNAT B, WhThe*
Hendriks, Francis Milton 1883- *AmSCAP 1966*
Hendrikson, Anders 1896-1965 *WhScrn 2*
Hendrix, Jimi 1947-1970 *WhScrn 2, WhoHol B*
Hendrix, N E Shorty d1973 *WhScrn 2*
Hendrix, Wanda 1928- *FilmgC, HolP 40,*
  IntMPA 1977, MotPP, MovMk, WhoHol A
Hendry, Anita *Film 1*
Hendry, Gloria *WhoHol A*
Hendry, Ian 1931- *FilmgC, IntMPA 1977,*
  WhoHol A

Hendry, Thomas 1929- *ConDr 1977*
Heneker, David 1906- *EncMT, WhoThe 16*
Henie, Sonja d1969 *MotPP, WhoHol B*
Henie, Sonja 1910-1969 *FilmgC, ThFT*
Henie, Sonja 1912-1969 *Film 2, OxFilm, WhScrn 1, WhScrn 2*
Henie, Sonja 1913-1969 *CmMov, MovMk*
Henkel, George A 1903- *AmSCAP 1966*
Henkin, Howard H 1926- *IntMPA 1977*
Henley, E J d1898 *NotNAT B*
Henley, Herbert James 1882-1937 *NotNAT B, WhThe*
Henley, Hobart 1886-1964 *TwYS A*
Henley, Hobart 1891-1964 *Film 1, WhScrn 1, WhScrn 2, WhoHol B*
Henley, Joan 1904- *WhThe*
Henley, Rosina *Film 1*
Henley, William Ernest 1849-1903 *NotNAT B*
Henneberger, Barbara-Marie Barbi 1941-1964 *WhScrn 2*
Hennecke, Clarence R 1894-1969 *WhScrn 1, WhScrn 2, WhoHol B*
Hennequin, Alfred d1887 *NotNAT B*
Hennequin, Maurice d1926 *NotNAT B, WhThe*
Hennessey, David 1852-1926 *WhScrn 1, WhScrn 2*
Hennessey, Johnny *Film 2*
Hennessey, Sharon *WomWMM B*
Hennessy, Roland Burke 1870-1939 *NotNAT B, WhThe*
Henniger, Rolf 1925- *WhThe*
Henning, Linda Kaye 1944- *IntMPA 1977, WhoHol A*
Henning, Pat 1911-1973 *WhScrn 2, WhoHol B*
Henning, Paul 1911- *IntMPA 1977, NewYTET*
Henning, Uno *Film 2*
Henning-Jensen, Astrid 1914- *DcFM, WomWMM, WorEnF*
Henning-Jensen, Bjarne 1908- *DcFM, WorEnF*
Henninger, George R 1895-1953 *AmSCAP 1966*
Hennings, Betty 1850-1939 *NotNAT B, WhThe*
Hennings, John d1933 *WhScrn 1, WhScrn 2, WhoHol B*
Hennock, Frieda B d1960 *NewYTET*
Henreid, Monika *WhoHol A*
Henreid, Paul *MotPP*
Henreid, Paul 1907- *CmMov, FilmgC*
Henreid, Paul 1908- *BiDFlm, IntMPA 1977, MovMk, OxFilm, WhoHol A, WorEnF*
Henrey, Bobby 1939- *FilmgC, WhoHol A*
Henri, Louie d1947 *NotNAT B*
Henrickson, Richard 1948- *NatPD*
Henriques, Madeline d1929 *NotNAT B*
Henritze, Bette *NotNAT, WhoHol A, WhoThe 16*
Henry, Alexander Victor 1943- *WhThe*
Henry, Bill *WhoHol A*
Henry, Bob *NewYTET*
Henry, Buck 1930- *ConDr 1977A, FilmgC, IntMPA 1977, WhoHol A*
Henry, Charles 1890-1968 *NotNAT B, WhThe*
Henry, Charlotte 1913- *WhoHol A*
Henry, Charlotte 1914- *ThFT*
Henry, Charlotte 1916- *FilmgC*
Henry, Creagh d1946 *NotNAT B*
Henry, E William *NewYTET*
Henry, Francis 1905-1953 *AmSCAP 1966*
Henry, Frank Thomas Patrick 1894-1963 *WhScrn 1, WhScrn 2*
Henry, Fred *IntMPA 1977*
Henry, Gale 1893- *Film 1, Film 2, TwYS, WomWMM*
Henry, George H 1903- *BiE&WWA, NotNAT*
Henry, Gloria *WhoHol A*

Henry, Hank *WhoHol A*
Henry, Jay 1910-1951 *WhScrn 1, WhScrn 2, WhoHol B*
Henry, John 1738-1794 *NotNAT B, OxThe, PIP&P*
Henry, John 1882-1958 *WhScrn 1, WhScrn 2, WhoHol B*
Henry, John, Jr. d1974 *Film 2, WhScrn 2*
Henry, Maria *PIP&P*
Henry, Martha 1938- *NotNAT*
Henry, Martin 1872-1942 *NotNAT B, WhThe*
Henry, Mike 1939- *FilmgC, WhoHol A*
Henry, O 1862-1910 *FilmgC*
Henry, Patrick, II 1935- *BiE&WWA*
Henry, Robert Buzz 1931-1971 *WhScrn 2, WhoHol B*
Henry, William 1918- *Film 2, FilmgC, Vers A*
Hensel, Sophie Friederike 1738-1789 *NotNAT B, OxThe*
Hensen, Herwig 1917- *CnMD, ModWD*
Henshaw, James Ene 1924- *ConDr 1977, REnWD*
Henslowe, Philip d1616 *CnThe, NotNAT A, NotNAT B, OxThe, PIP&P*
Henson, Gladys 1897- *FilmgC, WhoHol A, WhoThe 16*
Henson, Jim *NewYTET*
Henson, Joan *WomWMM*
Henson, Leslie 1891-1957 *EncMT, FilmgC, NotNAT B, OxThe, WhScrn 1, WhScrn 2, WhThe, WhoHol B*
Henson, Leslie 1891-1958 *Film 1, Film 2*
Henson, Nicky 1945- *WhoThe 16*
Henson, Norris Christy 1918- *AmSCAP 1966*
Henson, Robert 1934- *AmSCAP 1966*
Hentschel, Carl d1930 *NotNAT B*
Hentschel, Irene 1891- *WhThe*
Henville, Sandra Lee *WhoHol A*
Hepburn, Audrey 1929- *BiDFlm, BiE&WWA, CelR 3, FilmgC, IntMPA 1977, MotPP, MovMk, NotNAT, OxFilm, WhoHol A, WorEnF*
Hepburn, Barton 1906-1955 *Film 2, WhScrn 1, WhScrn 2, WhoHol B*
Hepburn, Katharine *MotPP, PIP&P, WomWMM*
Hepburn, Katharine 1907- *FilmgC, MGM, ThFT, WhoHol A*
Hepburn, Katharine 1909- *BiDFlm, BiE&WWA, CelR 3, CmMov, EncMT, FamA&A, IntMPA 1977, MovMk, NotNAT, NotNAT A, OxFilm, WhoThe 16*
Hepburn, Katherine 1909- *CnThe, WorEnF*
Hepple, Jeanne 1936- *WhoThe 16*
Hepple, Peter 1927- *WhoThe 16*
Heppner, Rosa *WhoThe 16*
Hepworth, Baby *Film 1*
Hepworth, Mrs. Cecil *Film 1*
Hepworth, Cecil Milton 1874-1953 *DcFM, Film 1, FilmgC, OxFilm, WhScrn 1, WorEnF*
Herald, Douglas *Film 2*
Herald, Heinz d1964 *NotNAT B*
Herald, Peter 1920- *IntMPA 1977*
Heraud, John A 1799-1887 *NotNAT A, NotNAT B*
Herbert, A J *Film 2*
Herbert, Sir Alan Patrick 1870-1971 *EncMT*
Herbert, Sir Alan Patrick 1890-1971 *WhThe*
Herbert, Diana *WhoHol A*
Herbert, Don *BiE&WWA, NewYTET, NotNAT*
Herbert, Evelyn 1898- *EncMT, WhThe*
Herbert, F Hugh 1897-1957 *FilmgC*
Herbert, F Hugh 1897-1958 *McGWD, NotNAT B, WhThe*
Herbert, Gwynne *Film 1, Film 2*

Herbert, Hans 1875-1957 *WhScrn 1, WhScrn 2, WhoHol B*
Herbert, Helen 1873-1946 *WhScrn 1, WhScrn 2*
Herbert, Henry 1879-1947 *NotNAT B, WhThe, WhoHol B*
Herbert, Sir Henry 1596-1673 *NotNAT B, OxThe*
Herbert, Henry J 1879-1942 *Film 1, Film 2*
Herbert, Henry J 1879-1947 *WhScrn 1, WhScrn 2*
Herbert, Heyes *MotPP*
Herbert, Holmes 1882-1956 *Film 1, Film 2, FilmgC, IntMPA 1977, MotPP, MovMk, NotNAT B, TwYS, WhScrn 1, WhScrn 2, WhoHol B*
Herbert, Hugh 1887-1951 *Film 2, MovMk*
Herbert, Hugh 1887-1952 *FilmgC, MotPP, NotNAT B, Vers A, WhScrn 1, WhScrn 2, WhoHol B*
Herbert, Jack *Film 1, Film 2*
Herbert, Jean 1905- *AmSCAP 1966*
Herbert, Jocelyn 1917- *WhoThe 16*
Herbert, Jocelyn 1927- *NotNAT*
Herbert, Joe *Film 2*
Herbert, John 1926- *ConDr 1977*
Herbert, Joseph d1923 *NotNAT B*
Herbert, Lew 1903-1968 *WhScrn 1, WhScrn 2, WhoHol B*
Herbert, Louisa d1921 *NotNAT B*
Herbert, Percy 1925- *FilmgC, WhoHol A*
Herbert, Pitt *WhoHol A*
Herbert, Sidney *Film 2*
Herbert, Thomas F 1888-1946 *WhScrn 1, WhScrn 2*
Herbert, Tom d1946 *WhoHol B*
Herbert, Victor 1859-1924 *AmSCAP 1966, EncMT, McGWD, NewMT, NotNAT B, PIP&P, WhThe, WhoStg 1906, WhoStg 1908*
Herbert, Zbigniew 1924- *ModWD*
Herblock 1909- *CelR 3*
Herbst, Haring *Film 2*
Herbuveaux, Jules 1897- *IntMPA 1977, NewYTET*
Herczeg, Ferenc 1863-1950 *NotNAT B*
Herczeg, Ferenc 1863-1954 *OxThe*
Herczeg, Geza d1954 *NotNAT B*
Herd, Dick *WhoHol A*
Herdman, John *Film 2*
Hereford-Lambert, Johnny *AmSCAP 1966*
Heremans, Jean *CmMov*
Herendeen, Fred 1893-1962 *NotNAT B*
Herendeen, Frederick 1893-1962 *AmSCAP 1966*
Herfel, Chris 1927- *IntMPA 1977*
Herford, Beatrice d1952 *NotNAT B*
Herget, Bob 1924- *BiE&WWA, NotNAT*
Heriat, Philippe 1898-1971 *Film 2, WhScrn 2*
Heribell, Renee *Film 2*
Hering, Doris *BiE&WWA, NotNAT*
Herlein, Lillian 1895?-1971 *WhScrn 1, WhScrn 2, WhoHol B*
Herlie, Eileen *WhoHol A*
Herlie, Eileen 1919- *FilmgC, MovMk*
Herlie, Eileen 1920- *NotNAT, WhoThe 16*
Herlie, Eileen 1922- *BiE&WWA*
Herlihy, Ed *IntMPA 1977*
Herlihy, James Leo 1927- *BiE&WWA, CelR 3, ConDr 1977, NotNAT*
Herlinger, Carl *Film 2*
Herlth, Robert 1893-1962 *DcFM*
Herman, Al 1886-1967 *WhScrn 2, WhoHol B*
Herman, Helena *Film 2*
Herman, Henry d1894 *NotNAT B*
Herman, Jerry *AmSCAP 1966, NotNAT, PIP&P*

Herman, Jerry 1932- *EncMT*
Herman, Jerry 1933- *BiE&WWA, CelR 3, NewMT, WhoThe 16*
Herman, Jill Kraft 1931-1970 *WhScrn 1, WhScrn 2*
Herman, John *BiE&WWA*
Herman, Leonard Wood 1913- *IntMPA 1977*
Herman, Lewis 1905- *BiE&WWA*
Herman, Marguerite S 1914- *BiE&WWA*
Herman, Milton C 1896-1951 *WhScrn 1, WhScrn 2*
Herman, Norman *IntMPA 1977*
Herman, Pinky 1905- *AmSCAP 1966, IntMPA 1977*
Herman, Samuel 1891- *AmSCAP 1966*
Herman, Selma *WhoStg 1908*
Herman, Tom 1909-1972 *WhScrn 2*
Herman, Tommy d1972 *WhoHol B*
Herman, Wanda *WomWMM B*
Herman, Woodrow Wilson 1913- *AmSCAP 1966*
Herman, Woody 1913- *WhoHol A*
Hermann, David 1876-1930 *NotNAT B, OxThe*
Hermann, Ralph 1914- *AmSCAP 1966*
Hermant, Abel 1862-1950 *NotNAT B, WhThe*
Hermes, Alice *BiE&WWA*
Hermine, Hilda d1975 *WhScrn 2, WhoHol C*
Hern, Pepe *WhoHol A*
Hernandez, Albert 1899-1948 *WhScrn 1, WhScrn 2*
Hernandez, Alejandro Rene 1916- *AmSCAP 1966*
Hernandez, Anna 1867-1945 *Film 2, WhScrn 2*
Hernandez, Antonio Acevedo Y *OxThe*
Hernandez, George F 1863-1922 *Film 1, Film 2, WhScrn 2*
Hernandez, Juan G Juano 1896-1970 *WhScrn 1, WhScrn 2*
Hernandez, Juano d1970 *MotPP, WhoHol B*
Hernandez, Juano 1898-1970 *Vers A*
Hernandez, Juano 1900-1970 *FilmgC, MovMk*
Herndon, Agnes d1920 *NotNAT B*
Herndon, Anita *Film 1*
Herndon, Richard Gilbert d1958 *NotNAT B, WhThe*
Herndon, Venable 1927- *NatPD*
Herne, Chrystal 1883-1950 *NotNAT B, WhThe, WhoStg 1906, WhoStg 1908*
Herne, James A 1839-1901 *CnThe, FamA&A, McGWD, ModWD, NotNAT B, OxThe, PIP&P, REnWD*
Herne, Julie 1881-1955 *NotNAT B, WhoStg 1908*
Herne, Katharine Corcoran 1857-1943 *NotNAT B, PIP&P*
Hernon, Nan *WomWMM*
Herodas 300?BC-250BC *OxThe*
Herold, Douglas *Film 2*
Heron, Bijou d1937 *NotNAT B*
Heron, Dalziel d1911 *NotNAT B*
Heron, Joyce 1916- *WhoHol A, WhoThe 16*
Heron, Matilda Agnes 1830-1877 *FamA&A, NotNAT B, OxThe*
Heros, Eugene *WhThe*
Herr, Melvin 1916- *BiE&WWA, NotNAT*
Herraud, Marcel d1953 *NotNAT B*
Herren, Roger *WhoHol A*
Herrera, Ernesto 1886-1917 *ModWD*
Herrera, Ernesto 1887-1917 *OxThe*
Herrera, Humberto 1900- *AmSCAP 1966*
Herrick, Abbie *WomWMM B*
Herrick, Jack *Film 2*
Herrick, Joe *Film 2*
Herrick, Margaret *IntMPA 1977*
Herrick, Paul Young 1910-1958 *AmSCAP 1966*
Herridge, Frances *BiE&WWA, NotNAT*

Heywood, Thomas 1574?-1641 *CnThe, McGWD, REnWD*
Hiarne, Urban 1641-1724 *OxThe*
Hiatt, Ruth 1908- *Film 2, TwYS, WhoHol A*
Hibbard, Edna 1895-1942 *NotNAT B, WhScrn 1, WhScrn 2, WhThe, WhoHol B*
Hibberd, Jack 1940- *ConDr 1977*
Hibbert, Geoffrey 1922-1969 *FilmgC, WhScrn 1, WhScrn 2, WhoHol B*
Hibbert, Henry George 1862-1924 *NotNAT B, WhThe*
Hibbs, Jesse 1906- *FilmgC*
Hibler, Winston 1910- *AmSCAP 1966*
Hichens, Robert Smythe 1864-1950 *NotNAT B, WhThe*
Hickey, Howard L 1897-1942 *WhScrn 1, WhScrn 2*
Hickey, William 1928?- *BiE&WWA, NotNAT, WhoHol A*
Hicklin, Margery 1904- *WhThe*
Hickman, Alfred 1873-1931 *Film 1, Film 2, NotNAT B, WhScrn 1, WhScrn 2, WhoHol B*
Hickman, Art 1886-1930 *AmSCAP 1966*
Hickman, Charles 1905- *EncMT, WhoThe 16*
Hickman, Darryl 1931- *BiE&WWA, FilmgC, MovMk, WhoHol A*
Hickman, Darryl 1933- *IntMPA 1977*
Hickman, Dwayne 1934- *FilmgC, MotPP, MovMk, WhoHol A*
Hickman, Howard 1880-1949 *Film 1, Film 2, NotNAT B, TwYS, WhScrn 1, WhScrn 2, WhoHol B*
Hickman, J Hampton 1937- *BiE&WWA*
Hickman, Roger M 1888- *AmSCAP 1966*
Hickock, James Butler 1837-1876 *OxFilm*
Hickok, Rodney 1892-1942 *WhScrn 1, WhScrn 2, WhoHol B*
Hickox, Douglas 1929- *FilmgC*
Hickox, Harry *WhoHol A*
Hickox, Sidney 1895- *WorEnF*
Hicks, Bert 1920-1965 *WhScrn 1, WhScrn 2*
Hicks, Betty Seymour 1905- *WhThe*
Hicks, Brenda *WomWMM 2*
Hicks, Sir Edward Seymour 1871-1949 *NotNAT A, NotNAT B, WhThe, WhoStg 1908*
Hicks, Edwin 1914- *IntMPA 1977*
Hicks, Hilly *WhoHol A*
Hicks, Julian 1858-1941 *WhThe*
Hicks, Leonard M 1918-1971 *WhScrn 2*
Hicks, Maxine Elliott *Film 2, WhoHol A*
Hicks, Newton Treen d1873 *NotNAT B*
Hicks, Russell 1895-1957 *FilmgC, MotPP, MovMk, NotNAT B, Vers A, WhScrn 1, WhScrn 2, WhoHol B*
Hicks, Sir Seymour 1871-1949 *CnThe, EncMT, Film 1, Film 2, FilmgC, OxThe, WhScrn 1, WhScrn 2, WhoHol B*
Hickson, Joan 1906- *FilmgC, WhoHol A, WhoThe 16*
Hider, Robert T 1937- *AmSCAP 1966*
Hiers, Walter 1893-1933 *Film 1, Film 2, TwYS, WhScrn 1, WhScrn 2, WhoHol B*
Hift, Fred 1924- *IntMPA 1977*
Higby, Wilbur 1866-1934 *Film 1, Film 2, WhScrn 1, WhScrn 2, WhoHol B*
Higgie, T H d1893 *NotNAT B*
Higginbotham, Irene 1918- *AmSCAP 1966*
Higgins, David 1858-1936 *Film 2, NotNAT B, WhScrn 2, WhoHol B*
Higgins, Dick *ConDr 1977E*
Higgins, Joe *WhoHol A*
Higgins, Michael 1922- *BiE&WWA, NotNAT, WhoHol A*

Higgins, Norman 1898- *WhThe*
Higginson, Joseph Vincent 1896- *AmSCAP 1966*
High, Freeman 1897- *AmSCAP 1966*
Highet, Gilbert 1906- *CelR 3*
Highland, George A d1954 *NotNAT B*
Highley, Reginald 1884- *WhThe*
Hightower, Harold *Film 2*
Hightower, Marilyn 1923- *WhThe*
Highwater, Jamake 1942- *NatPD*
Hignell, Rose 1896- *WhThe*
Hignett, H R 1870-1959 *NotNAT B, WhThe, WhoHol B*
Hiken, Gerald 1927- *BiE&WWA, NotNAT, WhoHol A, WhoThe 16*
Hiken, Nat 1914-1968 *AmSCAP 1966, BiE&WWA, NewYTET, NotNAT B*
Hikmet, Nazim 1902-1963 *CnMD*
Hilary, Jennifer 1942- *WhoHol A, WhoThe 16*
Hilbert, Georg *Film 2*
Hildebrand, Lo 1894-1936 *WhoHol B*
Hildebrand, Rodney 1893-1962 *Film 2, WhScrn 2, WhoHol B*
Hildegarde 1906- *CelR 3*
Hilderbrand, Lo 1894-1936 *WhScrn 1, WhScrn 2*
Hildesheimer, Wolfgang 1916- *CnMD, CroCD, McGWD, ModWD*
Hildreth, Kathryn *Film 2*
Hildyard, Jack 1915- *FilmgC, WorEnF*
Hiler, Charlotte Ailene 1910-1958 *AmSCAP 1966*
Hilforde, Mary 1853-1927 *WhScrn 1, WhScrn 2*
Hill, Aaron 1685-1750 *NotNAT B, OxThe*
Hill, Al *Film 2*
Hill, Ann 1921- *BiE&WWA, NotNAT*
Hill, Annie d1943 *NotNAT B*
Hill, Arthur 1875-1932 *WhScrn 1, WhScrn 2*
Hill, Arthur 1922- *BiE&WWA, FilmgC, IntMPA 1977, MotPP, NotNAT, PIP&P, WhoHol A, WhoThe 16*
Hill, Ben A 1894-1969 *WhScrn 1, WhScrn 2, WhoHol B*
Hill, Benjamin 1925- *IntMPA 1977*
Hill, Benny 1925- *FilmgC, WhoHol A*
Hill, Benson Earle d1845 *NotNAT A, NotNAT B*
Hill, Billie *WhThe*
Hill, Billy 1899-1940 *NotNAT B*
Hill, Bonnie *Film 1*
Hill, Charles Lee 1910- *AmSCAP 1966*
Hill, Dedette Lee 1900-1950 *AmSCAP 1966*
Hill, Doris *Film 2, TwYS, WhoHol A*
Hill, Dudley S 1881-1960 *WhScrn 1, WhScrn 2*
Hill, Edward Burlingame 1872-1960 *AmSCAP 1966*
Hill, Emma *WomWMM*
Hill, Errol 1921- *ConDr 1977, NotNAT*
Hill, Frederic Stanhope d1851 *NotNAT B*
Hill, George d1934 *WhoHol B*
Hill, George 1872-1945 *WhScrn 1, WhScrn 2*
Hill, George 1888-1939 *FilmgC*
Hill, George Handel 1809-1849 *FamA&A, NotNAT A, NotNAT B*
Hill, George Roy *IntMPA 1977*
Hill, George Roy 1922- *BiDFlm, FilmgC, OxFilm, WhoThe 16, WorEnF*
Hill, George Roy 1923- *BiE&WWA, NotNAT*
Hill, George Roy 1926- *MovMk*
Hill, George William 1895-1934 *DcFM, TwYS A*
Hill, Gladys *WomWMM*
Hill, Hallene 1876-1966 *WhScrn 2*
Hill, Howard 1899-1975 *WhScrn 2, WhoHol C*
Hill, Jack *WhScrn 2*
Hill, James 1916- *FilmgC*
Hill, James 1919- *FilmgC, MovMk*
Hill, Jennie 1851-1896 *NotNAT B*

WhoThe 16
Hirsch, Louis Achille 1881-1924 *WhThe*
Hirsch, Louis Achille 1887-1924 *AmSCAP 1966,*
   EncMT, NewMT, NotNAT B
Hirsch, Max d1925 *NotNAT B*
Hirsch, Robert 1929- *FilmgC*
Hirsch, Samuel 1917- *BiE&WWA*
Hirsch, Walter 1891- *AmSCAP 1966*
Hirschbein, Peretz 1880-1948 *McGWD*
Hirschbein, Peretz 1880-1949 *NotNAT B, OxThe*
Hirschbein, Peretz *see also* Hirshbein, Peretz
Hirschfeld, Al 1903- *BiE&WWA, CelR 3,*
   NotNAT
Hirschfeld, Georg 1873-1942 *McGWD, ModWD*
Hirschfeld, Gerald *FilmgC*
Hirschfield, Alan J *IntMPA 1977*
Hirschman, Herbert *IntMPA 1977, NewYTET*
Hirschmann, Henri 1872- *WhThe*
Hirshan, Leonard 1927- *IntMPA 1977*
Hirshbein, Peretz 1880-1948 *CnThe, ModWD,*
   REnWD
Hirshbein, Peretz *see also* Hirschbein, Peretz
Hirshberg, Jack 1917- *IntMPA 1977*
Hirshhorn, Naomi Caryl *AmSCAP 1966*
Hirson, Roger O *NotNAT*
Hirst, Alan 1931-1937 *WhScrn 1, WhScrn 2*
Hirt, Al 1922- *IntMPA 1977*
Hiscott, Leslie 1894-1968 *FilmgC*
Hisle, Betsy Ann *Film 2*
Hislop, Joseph 1887- *WhThe*
Hitchcock, Alfred 1899- *BiDFlm, CelR 3,*
   CmMov, DcFM, Film 2, FilmgC,
   IntMPA 1977, MovMk, NewYTET, OxFilm,
   WorEnF
Hitchcock, Charles *Film 1*
Hitchcock, Keith d1966 *WhScrn 2, WhoHol B*
Hitchcock, Pat *WhoHol A*
Hitchcock, Raymond d1929 *MotPP, WhoHol B,*
   WhoStg 1906
Hitchcock, Raymond 1865-1929 *EncMT, Film 1,*
   Film 2, NotNAT B, TwYS, WhThe
Hitchcock, Raymond 1870-1929 *WhScrn 1,*
   WhScrn 2
Hitchcock, Raymond 1871-1929 *WhoStg 1908*
Hitchcock, Rex d1950 *WhoHol B*
Hitchcock, Robert d1809 *NotNAT B*
Hitchcock, Walter d1917 *WhScrn 2*
Hite, Les 1903-1962 *AmSCAP 1966*
Hite, Mabel 1885-1912 *NotNAT B,*
   WhoStg 1906, WhoStg 1908
Hitt, J T 1922- *IntMPA 1977*
Hively, Jack 1907?- *FilmgC*
Hivnor, Robert 1916- *ConDr 1977, CroCD*
Hix, Al 1918- *IntMPA 1977*
Hix, Don d1964 *WhScrn 1, WhScrn 2,*
   WhoHol B
Hjelde, Hakon *Film 2*
Hladnik, Bostjan 1929- *OxFilm*
Hmelev, Hmelyov *OxThe*
Ho, Chew *Film 2*
Ho, Laura *WomWMM B*
Ho-Chang, King *Film 2*
Hoadley, Bishop *PIP&P*
Hoadley, Benjamin d1757 *NotNAT B*
Hoadley, John d1776 *NotNAT B*
Hoadly, Benjamin 1706-1757 *OxThe*
Hoag, Mitzi *WhoHol A*
Hoagey, Catherine Y 1908- *AmSCAP 1966*
Hoagland, Harland 1896-1971 *WhScrn 1,*
   WhScrn 2
Hoare, Douglas 1875- *WhThe*
Hoare, Frank Alan 1894- *IntMPA 1977*
Hoare, Prince d1834 *NotNAT B*
Hoare, Victor J *IntMPA 1977*

Hoban, Agnes E d1962 *NotNAT B*
Hoban, Tana *WomWMM B*
Hobart, Doty d1958 *NotNAT B*
Hobart, George V 1867-1926 *AmSCAP 1966,*
   NotNAT B, WhThe, WhoStg 1908
Hobart, Rose 1906- *BiE&WWA, FilmgC,*
   MovMk, NotNAT, ThFT, WhThe,
   WhoHol A
Hobbes, Halliwell 1877-1962 *Film 2, FilmgC,*
   IntMPA 1977, MotPP, MovMk, NotNAT B,
   Vers A, WhScrn 1, WhScrn 2, WhoHol B
Hobbes, Herbert Halliwell 1877-1962 *WhThe*
Hobbes, John Oliver d1906 *NotNAT B*
Hobbes, Nancy Marsland d1968 *WhoHol B*
Hobbs, Carleton 1898- *WhThe*
Hobbs, Frederick 1880-1942 *NotNAT B, WhThe*
Hobbs, Hayford *Film 2*
Hobbs, J Kline 1938- *NatPD*
Hobbs, Jack 1893-1968 *Film 1, Film 2, FilmgC,*
   NotNAT B, WhScrn 2, WhThe
Hobbs, Peter *WhoHol A*
Hobbs, William 1939- *WhoThe 16*
Hobgood, Burnet 1922- *BiE&WWA, NotNAT*
Hobin, Bill 1923- *IntMPA 1977, NewYTET*
Hobley, McDonald *IntMPA 1977*
Hobson, Harold 1904- *BiE&WWA, CroCD,*
   NotNAT, WhoThe 16
Hobson, Maud d1913 *NotNAT B*
Hobson, May 1889- *WhThe*
Hobson, Valerie 1917- *FilmgC, MovMk, OxFilm,*
   ThFT, WhoHol A
Hoch, Emil H 1866-1944 *Film 2, WhScrn 2*
Hoch, Winton C 1908?- *CmMov, FilmgC,*
   IntMPA 1977, WorEnF
Hochberg, Victoria *WomWMM B*
Hochhuth, Rolf 1931- *CnMD, CnThe, CroCD,*
   McGWD, ModWD, NotNAT, REnWD,
   WhoThe 16
Hochman, Sandra *WomWMM B*
Hochuli, Paul d1964 *NotNAT B*
Hochwalder, Fritz 1911- *CnMD, CnThe, CroCD,*
   McGWD, ModWD, OxThe, REnWD
Hock, Mort 1929- *IntMPA 1977*
Hock, Richard 1933-1961 *WhScrn 1, WhScrn 2*
Hocker, David 1911- *BiE&WWA, NotNAT*
Hockridge, Edmund 1919- *WhThe*
Hoctor, Harriet 1907- *BiE&WWA, NotNAT,*
   WhThe
Hodas, Dorothy Gertrude 1912- *AmSCAP 1966*
Hodatyev, Nikolai *DcFM*
Hodd, Joseph B, Sr. 1896-1965 *WhScrn 1,*
   WhScrn 2
Hodder-Williams, Christopher 1927- *IntMPA 1977*
Hodes, Arthur W 1904- *AmSCAP 1966*
Hodes, Roberta *WomWMM A, WomWMM B*
Hodgdon, Samuel K d1922 *NotNAT B*
Hodge, Francis Richard 1915- *BiE&WWA,*
   NotNAT
Hodge, Merton 1904-1958 *NotNAT B, WhThe*
Hodge, Runa *Film 1*
Hodge, William Thomas 1874-1932 *NotNAT B,*
   OxThe, WhThe
Hodgeman, Thomas 1875-1931 *WhScrn 1,*
   WhScrn 2
Hodges, Eddie 1947- *BiE&WWA, MotPP,*
   WhoHol A
Hodges, Horace 1865-1951 *NotNAT B, WhThe,*
   WhoHol B
Hodges, James S 1885- *AmSCAP 1966*
Hodges, Johnny 1907- *AmSCAP 1966*
Hodges, Joy *WhoHol A*
Hodges, Ken 1922- *FilmgC*
Hodges, Mike 1932- *FilmgC*
Hodges, Russ d1971 *WhoHol B*

Hodges, William Cullen 1876-1961 *WhScrn 1,*
WhScrn 2, WhoHol B
Hodgins, Earl 1899-1964 *WhScrn 1, WhScrn 2,*
WhoHol B
Hodgins, Earle 1899-1964 *NotNAT B, Vers B*
Hodgins, Leslie 1885-1927 *WhScrn 1, WhScrn 2*
Hodgkinson, Mrs. John d1803 *NotNAT B,*
PIP&P
Hodgkinson, John 1765?-1805 *NotNAT B*
Hodgkinson, John 1767-1805 *FamA&A, OxThe,*
PIP&P
Hodgson, Leland d1949 *WhScrn 2*
Hodgson, Leyland 1893-1949 *Vers A, WhoHol B*
Hodiak, John 1914-1955 *CmMov, FilmgC,*
HolP 40, MGM, MotPP, MovMk,
NotNAT B, WhScrn 1, WhScrn 2,
WhoHol B
Hodowud, Edward Fred 1924- *AmSCAP 1966*
Hodson, Henrietta 1841-1910 *NotNAT B, OxThe*
Hodson, James Landsdale d1956 *NotNAT B*
Hodson, Kate d1917 *NotNAT B*
Hodson, Nellie d1940 *NotNAT B*
Hodson, Sylvia d1893 *NotNAT B*
Hodston, Leland d1949 *WhScrn 1*
Hoeflich, Lucie 1883-1956 *WhScrn 1, WhScrn 2*
Hoelcl, Gisela *WomWMM B*
Hoellering, George 1900- *FilmgC, OxFilm*
Hoelscher, Jean *WomWMM A, WomWMM B*
Hoey, Dennis d1961 *WhoHol B*
Hoey, Dennis 1893-1960 *FilmgC, NotNAT B,*
WhScrn 1, WhScrn 2, WhThe
Hoey, George J 1885-1955 *WhScrn 1, WhScrn 2*
Hoey, Iris 1885- *WhThe*
Hoey, William d1897 *NotNAT B*
Hofer, Chris 1920-1964 *NotNAT B, WhScrn 1,*
WhScrn 2
Hoff, J Robert 1909- *IntMPA 1977*
Hoff, Louise 1921- *BiE&WWA*
Hoff, Vivian Beaumont 1911- *AmSCAP 1966*
Hoffa, James 1913- *CelR 3*
Hoffe, Barbara *WhThe*
Hoffe, Monckton 1880-1951 *NotNAT B,*
WhScrn 1, WhScrn 2, WhThe, WhoHol B
Hoffer, Emil *Film 2*
Hoffer, Eric 1902- *CelR 3*
Hoffman, Aaron 1880-1924 *NotNAT B, WhThe*
Hoffman, Abbie 1936- *CelR 3*
Hoffman, Al 1902-1960 *AmSCAP 1966*
Hoffman, Bern *WhoHol A*
Hoffman, Bill d1962 *NotNAT B*
Hoffman, Dave A 1890-1958 *AmSCAP 1966*
Hoffman, David 1904-1961 *WhScrn 2*
Hoffman, Dustin 1937- *CelR 3, FilmgC,*
IntMPA 1977, MotPP, MovMk, OxFilm,
WhoHol A, WhoThe 16
Hoffman, Eberhard 1883-1957 *WhScrn 1,*
WhScrn 2, WhoHol B
Hoffman, Ferdi *WhoHol A*
Hoffman, Francois-Benoit 1760-1828 *OxThe*
Hoffman, Gertrude 1898-1955 *NotNAT B,*
WhScrn 1, WhScrn 2
Hoffman, Gertrude W 1871-1966 *WhScrn 1,*
WhScrn 2, WhoHol B
Hoffman, H F *Film 1*
Hoffman, Harold M 1908- *BiE&WWA*
Hoffman, Herman *IntMPA 1977*
Hoffman, Hermine H 1921-1971 *WhScrn 1,*
WhScrn 2
Hoffman, Howard R 1893-1969 *WhScrn 1,*
WhScrn 2, WhoHol B
Hoffman, Jack 1917- *AmSCAP 1966*
Hoffman, Jane *BiE&WWA, NotNAT,*
WhoHol A, WhoThe 16
Hoffman, Joseph *IntMPA 1977*

Hoffman, Maud *WhThe, WhoStg 1908*
Hoffman, Max d1963 *NotNAT B*
Hoffman, Max, Jr. 1902-1945 *NotNAT B,*
WhScrn 1, WhScrn 2, WhoHol B
Hoffman, Olivia Watson *AmSCAP 1966*
Hoffman, Otto 1879-1944 *Film 1, Film 2, TwYS,*
WhScrn 2
Hoffman, Renaud 1900- *TwYS A*
Hoffman, Roni *WomWMM B*
Hoffman, Ruby *Film 1, Film 2*
Hoffman, Stan *WhoHol A*
Hoffman, Stanley D 1926- *AmSCAP 1966*
Hoffman, Theodore 1922- *BiE&WWA, NotNAT*
Hoffman, William M 1939- *ConDr 1977,*
NotNAT
Hoffman-Uddgren, Anna *WomWMM*
Hoffmann, Adolf G 1890- *AmSCAP 1966*
Hoffmann, Max 1873-1963 *AmSCAP 1966*
Hofheinz, Roy 1912- *CelR 3*
Hoflich, Lucie d1956 *NotNAT B, WhoHol B*
Hofmannsthal, Hugo Von 1874-1929 *CnMD,*
CnThe, McGWD, ModWD, NotNAT B,
OxThe, REnWD
Hogan, Ben 1912- *CelR 3*
Hogan, Earl Hap d1944 *Film 2, WhScrn 2*
Hogan, Francis T 1916- *AmSCAP 1966*
Hogan, Frank *NatPD*
Hogan, J P *Film 2*
Hogan, Jack *WhoHol A*
Hogan, James P 1891-1943 *FilmgC, TwYS A*
Hogan, Michael 1898- *WhThe*
Hogan, Michael 1899- *IntMPA 1977*
Hogan, Pat 1931-1966 *WhScrn 1, WhScrn 2,*
WhoHol B
Hogan, Robert *WhoHol A*
Hogan, Society Kid 1899-1962 *WhScrn 1,*
WhScrn 2, WhoHol B
Hogarth, John M 1931- *IntMPA 1977*
Hogarth, Lionel 1874-1946 *NotNAT B*
Hogarth, William *PIP&P*
Hogg, Curly 1917-1974 *WhoHol B*
Hogg, Ian 1937- *WhoHol A, WhoThe 16*
Hogg, Jack Curly 1917-1974 *WhScrn 2*
Hohengarten, Carl 1902- *AmSCAP 1966*
Hohl, Arthur 1889-1964 *FilmgC, IntMPA 1977,*
Vers B, WhScrn 2
Hoiby, Lee 1926- *AmSCAP 1966*
Hoier, Esther W *Film 1*
Hoier, Thomas P d1951 *NotNAT B*
Hoijer, Bjorn-Erik 1907- *CnMD*
Hokanson, Margrethe 1893- *AmSCAP 1966*
Holberg, Ludvig 1684-1754 *CnThe, McGWD,*
OxThe, REnWD
Holberg, Ludwig Baron 1684-1754 *NotNAT B*
Holbrook, Ann Catherine d1837 *NotNAT B*
Holbrook, Hal 1925- *BiE&WWA, CelR 3,*
FilmgC, IntMPA 1977, MotPP, NotNAT,
WhoHol A, WhoThe 16
Holbrook, Louise *WhThe*
Holcomb, Helen *Film 2*
Holcombe, Harry *WhoHol A*
Holcombe, Ray Edward 1898- *BiE&WWA*
Holcroft, Thomas 1744-1809 *NotNAT B, OxThe*
Holden, Anne Stratton 1887- *AmSCAP 1966*
Holden, Fay d1973 *MotPP, WhoHol B*
Holden, Fay 1893-1973 *Vers A*
Holden, Fay 1894-1973 *FilmgC*
Holden, Fay 1895-1973 *MGM, MovMk, ThFT,*
WhScrn 2
Holden, Gloria 1908- *FilmgC*
Holden, Gloria 1911- *IntMPA 1977*
Holden, Harry Moore 1868-1944 *Film 1, Film 2,*
WhScrn 1, WhScrn 2, WhoHol B
Holden, Jan 1931- *WhoHol A, WhoThe 16*

Holden, Joyce *WhoHol A*
Holden, Libby 1923- *AmSCAP 1966*
Holden, Mary *Film 2*
Holden, Scott *WhoHol A*
Holden, Sidney 1900-1947 *AmSCAP 1966*
Holden, Viola d1967 *WhScrn 1, WhScrn 2, WhoHol B*
Holden, William 1872-1932 *Film 2, WhScrn 1, WhScrn 2, WhoHol B*
Holden, William 1918- *BiDFlm, CelR 3, CmMov, FilmgC, IntMPA 1977, MotPP, MovMk, OxFilm, WhoHol A, WorEnF*
Holder, Geoffrey 1930- *BiE&WWA, NotNAT, PIP&P A, WhoHol A, WhoThe 16*
Holder, Owen 1921- *WhoThe 16*
Holderlin, Friedrich 1770-1843 *McGWD*
Holderness, Fay *Film 1, Film 2*
Holding, Thomas 1880-1929 *Film 1, Film 2, TwYS, WhScrn 2*
Holdren, Judd 1915-1974 *WhScrn 2, WhoHol B*
Holdridge, Barbara 1929- *BiE&WWA*
Holdsworth, Gerard 1904- *IntMPA 1977*
Hole, Jonathan *WhoHol A*
Holger-Madsen 1878-1943 *DcFM*
Holiday, Billie d1959 *NotNAT B, WhoHol B*
Holiday, Billie *see also* Holliday, Billie
Holiday, Hope *WhoHol A*
Holiday, Leila *WhoHol A*
Holiner, Mann 1897-1958 *AmSCAP 1966*
Holinshed, Raphael d1580? *NotNAT B*
Hollaender, Frederich 1896- *WorEnF*
Holland, Anthony 1912- *WhoThe 16*
Holland, Anthony 1933- *BiE&WWA, NotNAT, WhoHol A*
Holland, Betty Lou 1931- *BiE&WWA, NotNAT, WhoHol A*
Holland, C Maurice d1974 *WhScrn 2*
Holland, Cecil *Film 2*
Holland, Charles d1796 *NotNAT B*
Holland, Charles d1849 *NotNAT B*
Holland, Clifford *Film 2*
Holland, Edmund Milton 1848-1913 *NotNAT B, OxThe, WhThe, WhoStg 1906, WhoStg 1908*
Holland, Edna *WhoHol A*
Holland, Edward *Film 1*
Holland, Edwin *Film 2*
Holland, Fanny d1931 *NotNAT B*
Holland, George d1910 *NotNAT B*
Holland, George 1791-1870 *FamA&A, NotNAT A, NotNAT B, OxThe*
Holland, Gladys *WhoHol A*
Holland, Joe *Film 2*
Holland, John *Film 2, WhoHol A*
Holland, Joseph Jefferson 1860-1926 *NotNAT B, OxThe*
Holland, Mildred 1869-1944 *NotNAT B, WhScrn 2, WhThe*
Holland, Miriam 1917-1948 *WhScrn 1, WhScrn 2*
Holland, R V 1916- *BiE&WWA, NotNAT*
Holland, Ralph 1888-1939 *WhScrn 1, WhScrn 2*
Hollander, Alice *WhThe*
Hollander, Frederick 1892- *FilmgC*
Hollander, Frederick 1896- *OxFilm*
Hollander, Ralph 1916- *AmSCAP 1966*
Hollenbeck, Don d1954 *NewYTET*
Hollender, Alfred L *IntMPA 1977*
Holler, John 1904- *AmSCAP 1966*
Holles, Antony 1901-1950 *FilmgC, NotNAT B, WhScrn 1, WhScrn 2, WhThe, WhoHol B*
Holles, Robert *ConDr 1977C*
Holles, William 1867-1947 *WhThe*
Holley, Ruth *Film 2*
Holliday, Billie 1915-1959 *WhScrn 2*

Holliday, Billie *see also* Holiday, Billie
Holliday, Frank, Jr. 1913-1948 *WhScrn 1, WhScrn 2*
Holliday, Fred *WhoHol A*
Holliday, John H 1850-1885 *OxFilm*
Holliday, Judy d1965 *BiE&WWA, MotPP, WhoHol B*
Holliday, Judy 1921-1965 *BiDFlm, EncMT, WorEnF*
Holliday, Judy 1922-1965 *FilmgC, MovMk, NotNAT B*
Holliday, Judy 1923-1965 *CmMov, OxFilm, WhScrn 1, WhScrn 2, WhThe*
Holliday, Marjorie 1920-1969 *WhScrn 1, WhScrn 2, WhoHol B*
Holliman, Earl 1928- *FilmgC, IntMPA 1977, MotPP, WhoHol A*
Hollinger, Hy *IntMPA 1977*
Hollingshead, Gordon 1892-1952 *WhScrn 1, WhScrn 2*
Hollingshead, John 1827-1904 *NotNAT A, NotNAT B, OxThe*
Hollingsworth, Alfred 1874-1926 *Film 1, WhScrn 1, WhScrn 2, WhoHol B*
Hollingsworth, Alfred 1875-1926 *NotNAT B*
Hollingsworth, Harry 1888-1947 *WhScrn 1, WhScrn 2, WhoHol B*
Hollingsworth, Thelka *AmSCAP 1966*
Hollins, Mabel 1887- *WhoStg 1906, WhoStg 1908*
Hollis, Alan *Film 2*
Hollis, Hylda *Film 1*
Hollis, William 1867-1947 *NotNAT B*
Hollister, Alice *MotPP*
Hollister, Alice 1886-1973 *WhScrn 2*
Hollister, Alice 1890- *Film 1, Film 2, TwYS*
Holloway, Baliol 1883-1967 *PIP&P, WhThe*
Holloway, Carol *Film 1, Film 2, TwYS*
Holloway, Stanley 1890- *BiE&WWA, EncMT, Film 2, FilmgC, IntMPA 1977, MovMk, NotNAT, NotNAT A, WhoHol A, WhoThe 16*
Holloway, Sterling 1905- *BiE&WWA, Film 2, FilmgC, IntMPA 1977, MotPP, MovMk, NotNAT, PIP&P, Vers B, WhoHol A*
Holloway, W J d1913 *NotNAT B*
Holloway, William Edwyn 1885-1952 *NotNAT B, WhThe*
Holly, Ellen 1931- *BiE&WWA, NotNAT, WhoHol A*
Hollywood, Daniel 1914- *BiE&WWA, NotNAT*
Hollywood, Edwin L *TwYS A*
Hollywood, Jimmy d1955 *WhScrn 2*
Holm, Astrid *Film 2*
Holm, Celeste 1919- *BiE&WWA, EncMT, FilmgC, HolP 40, IntMPA 1977, MotPP, MovMk, NotNAT, OxFilm, WhoHol A, WhoThe 16*
Holm, Darry *Film 2*
Holm, Eleanor 1914- *WhoHol A*
Holm, Hanya 1893- *BiE&WWA, EncMT, NotNAT, NotNAT A, WhoThe 16*
Holm, Ian *WhoHol A*
Holm, Ian 1931- *WhoThe 16*
Holm, Ian 1932- *FilmgC*
Holm, Jeanne 1921- *CelR 3*
Holm, John Cecil *WhoHol A*
Holm, John Cecil 1904- *BiE&WWA, ModWD, NotNAT, WhoThe 16*
Holm, John Cecil 1906- *CnMD*
Holm, Klaus 1920- *BiE&WWA, NotNAT*
Holm, Magda *Film 2*
Holm, Sonia 1922-1974 *WhScrn 2, WhoHol A*
Holman, Harry 1874-1947 *WhScrn 1, WhScrn 2,*

WhoHol B
Holman, Joseph G d1817 *NotNAT B*
Holman, Libby 1906-1971 *BiE&WWA, EncMT, NotNAT B, PIP&P, WhScrn 2, WhThe, WhoHol B*
Holman, Russell *IntMPA 1977*
Holme, Myra d1919 *NotNAT B*
Holme, Stanford 1904- *WhThe*
Holme, Thea 1907- *WhoThe 16*
Holmes, Ben 1890-1943 *Film 2, WhScrn 1, WhScrn 2, WhoHol B*
Holmes, Burton 1870-1958 *WhScrn 1, WhScrn 2, WhoHol B*
Holmes, Doloris *WomWMM B*
Holmes, G E 1873-1945 *AmSCAP 1966*
Holmes, Gerda *Film 1*
Holmes, Helen 1892-1950 *Film 1, Film 2, MotPP, NotNAT B, TwYS, WhScrn 1, WhScrn 2, WhThe, WhoHol B*
Holmes, Herbert *Film 2*
Holmes, Ione *Film 2*
Holmes, J Merrill 1889-1950 *WhScrn 2*
Holmes, Jack 1932- *BiE&WWA*
Holmes, Leon *Film 2*
Holmes, LeRoy 1913- *AmSCAP 1966*
Holmes, Lois *Film 1*
Holmes, Marian *WhoHol A*
Holmes, Marty 1925- *AmSCAP 1966*
Holmes, Milton *Film 2*
Holmes, Phillips d1942 *MotPP, WhoHol B*
Holmes, Phillips 1907-1942 *Film 2, HolP 30, MovMk, NotNAT B*
Holmes, Phillips 1909-1942 *FilmgC, WhScrn 1, WhScrn 2*
Holmes, Ralph 1889-1945 *NotNAT B, WhScrn 1, WhScrn 2, WhoHol B*
Holmes, Rapley 1868-1928 *WhScrn 2*
Holmes, Reed *Film 2*
Holmes, Richard G *WhoHol A*
Holmes, Robert 1899-1945 *Film 2, NotNAT B, WhThe, WhoHol B*
Holmes, Stuart 1887-1971 *Film 1, Film 2, TwYS, WhScrn 1, WhScrn 2, WhoHol B*
Holmes, Taylor d1959 *MotPP, WhoHol B*
Holmes, Taylor 1872-1959 *Film 1, Film 2, FilmgC, MovMk, TwYS, WhScrn 1, WhScrn 2*
Holmes, Taylor 1878-1959 *NotNAT B, Vers A, WhThe*
Holmes, Wendell 1915-1962 *NotNAT B, WhScrn 1, WhScrn 2, WhoHol B*
Holmes, William J 1877-1946 *WhScrn 1, WhScrn 2, WhoHol B*
Holmes-Gore, Dorothy 1896-1915 *WhThe*
Holmquist, Sigrid *Film 2*
Holmstrand, Jean Marie 1932- *AmSCAP 1966*
Holofcener, Lawrence 1926- *AmSCAP 1966*
Holt, Charlene 1939- *FilmgC, WhoHol A*
Holt, Clarence d1903 *NotNAT B*
Holt, Clarence d1920 *NotNAT B*
Holt, David Jack 1927- *AmSCAP 1966*
Holt, Denis *IntMPA 1977*
Holt, Edwart *Film 1*
Holt, Edwin *Film 1*
Holt, George *Film 1, Film 2, MotPP, TwYS A*
Holt, Gloria *Film 2*
Holt, Hans 1909- *CnMD*
Holt, Harold d1953 *NotNAT B*
Holt, Jack 1888-1951 *Film 1, Film 2, FilmgC, MotPP, MovMk, NotNAT B, TwYS, WhScrn 1, WhScrn 2, WhoHol B*
Holt, Jennifer *WhoHol A*
Holt, Nancy *WomWMM B*
Holt, Nat 1892-1971 *FilmgC*

Holt, Patrick 1912- *FilmgC, IntMPA 1977, WhoHol A*
Holt, Seth 1923-1971 *BiDFlm, DcFM, FilmgC, OxFilm, WorEnF*
Holt, Stella *BiE&WWA*
Holt, Tim d1973 *MotPP, WhoHol B*
Holt, Tim 1918-1973 *FilmgC, HolP 40, MovMk*
Holt, Tim 1919-1973 *WhScrn 2*
Holt, Will 1929- *AmSCAP 1966, PIP&P A*
Holton, Robert W 1922- *AmSCAP 1966*
Holtz, Lou 1898- *BiE&WWA, EncMT, NotNAT, WhThe*
Holtz, Tenen *Film 2*
Holtz, Tubea *Film 2*
Holtzman, David M 1908-1965 *NotNAT B*
Holtzmann, David Marshall 1908-1965 *BiE&WWA*
Holubar, Alan *Film 1*
Holubar, Allan 1889-1925? *TwYS A*
Holubar, Allen 1889-1925 *WhScrn 2*
Holz, Arno 1863-1929 *CnMD, ModWD, OxThe*
Holzer, Adela *WhoThe 16*
Holzer, Hans 1920- *AmSCAP 1966*
Holzer, Lou 1913- *AmSCAP 1966*
Holzman, Benjamin F d1963 *NotNAT B*
Holzmann, Abraham 1874-1939 *AmSCAP 1966*
Holzworth, Fred d1970 *WhScrn 1, WhScrn 2*
Homan, David 1907- *WhThe*
Homan, Gertrude d1951 *NotNAT B*
Homans, Robert E 1875-1947 *Film 2, TwYS, Vers B, WhScrn 1, WhScrn 2, WhoHol B*
Homberg, Hans 1903- *CnMD*
Home, John 1722-1808 *NotNAT B, OxThe*
Home, William Douglas 1912- *BiE&WWA, CnMD, CnThe, ConDr 1977, CroCD, ModWD, NotNAT, PIP&P, WhoThe 16*
Homeier, Skip 1929- *FilmgC*
Homeier, Skip 1930- *IntMPA 1977, WhoHol A*
Homer *PIP&P*
Homer, Benjamin 1917- *AmSCAP 1966*
Homer, Sidney 1864-1953 *AmSCAP 1966*
Homfrey, Gladys d1932 *NotNAT B, WhThe*
Homoki Nagy, Istvan 1914- *DcFM, FilmgC*
Homoky Nagy, Istvan 1914- *OxFilm*
Homolka, Oscar *MotPP*
Homolka, Oscar 1898- *WhThe, WhoHol A*
Homolka, Oscar 1899- *FilmgC, Vers A*
Homolka, Oscar 1900?- *MovMk*
Homolka, Oscar 1901- *BiDFlm, Film 2, OxFilm*
Homolka, Oscar 1903- *BiE&WWA, NotNAT*
Honda, Frank 1884-1924 *WhScrn 1, WhScrn 2, WhoHol B*
Hone, Mary 1904- *WhThe*
Honegger, Arthur 1892-1955 *DcFM, FilmgC, NotNAT B, OxFilm, WorEnF*
Honer, Mary 1914- *WhThe*
Honey, George Alfred 1823-1880 *NotNAT B*
Hong, James *WhoHol A*
Hong, Wilson S 1934- *IntMPA 1977*
Honig, Edwin 1919- *BiE&WWA, NotNAT*
Honn, Eldon 1890-1927 *WhScrn 1, WhScrn 2*
Honner, Robert d1852 *NotNAT B*
Honnett, Mickie *Film 2*
Honold, Rolf 1919- *CnMD*
Honore, Hal 1905- *IntMPA 1977*
Honri, Baynham *IntMPA 1977*
Honri, Percy 1874-1953 *NotNAT B, WhThe*
Honyman, John 1613-1636 *OxThe*
Honyman, Richard 1618- *OxThe*
Hood, Alan 1924- *AmSCAP 1966*
Hood, Basil 1864-1917 *EncMT, NotNAT B, WhThe*
Hood, Darla 1933- *WhoHol A*
Hood, Tom 1919-1950 *WhScrn 1, WhScrn 2*
Hook, Sidney 1902- *CelR 3*

Hook, Theodore d1842 *NotNAT B*
Hooker, Brian 1880-1946 *AmSCAP 1966, EncMT,
  NotNAT B*
Hooks, Benjamin L *NewYTET*
Hooks, David 1920- *BiE&WWA, NotNAT,
  WhoHol A*
Hooks, Kevin *WhoHol A*
Hooks, Robert 1937- *FilmgC, NotNAT,
  PIP&P A, WhoHol A, WhoThe 16*
Hoole, John d1803 *NotNAT B*
Hoope, Aaf Bouber-Ten d1974 *WhScrn 2*
Hooper, Edward d1865 *NotNAT B*
Hooper, Ewan 1935- *WhoThe 16*
Hooper, Frank *Film 2*
Hooper, Joyce *WomWMM*
Hoopes, Isabella *WhoHol A*
Hoopii, Sol 1905-1953 *WhScrn 1, WhScrn 2*
Hoops, Arthur 1870-1916 *Film 1, WhScrn 2*
Hoornik, Ed 1910-1970 *CnMD*
Hooser, William S *Film 2*
Hoosman, Al 1918-1968 *WhScrn 2*
Hooven, Joseph D *AmSCAP 1966*
Hooven, Marilyn 1924- *AmSCAP 1966*
Hoover, J Edgar 1895-1972 *WhScrn 2*
Hopcraft, Arthur *ConDr 1977C*
Hope, Adele Blood d1936 *NotNAT B*
Hope, Anthony 1863-1933 *FilmgC, NotNAT B,
  WhThe*
Hope, Bob *MotPP, NewYTET, WhoHol A*
Hope, Bob 1903- *BiE&WWA, CelR 3, EncMT,
  FilmgC, IntMPA 1977, MovMk, OxFilm,
  WhThe, WorEnF*
Hope, Bob 1904- *BiDFlm, CmMov*
Hope, Diana 1872-1942 *WhScrn 1, WhScrn 2,
  WhoHol B*
Hope, Evelyn d1966 *WhThe*
Hope, Gloria 1901- *Film 1, Film 2, MotPP,
  TwYS*
Hope, Harry *IntMPA 1977*
Hope, Mabel Ellams d1937 *NotNAT B*
Hope, Maidie 1881-1937 *NotNAT B, WhScrn 2,
  WhThe, WhoHol B*
Hope, Vida 1918-1962 *FilmgC, WhoHol B*
Hope, Vida 1918-1963 *NotNAT B, WhScrn 1,
  WhScrn 2, WhThe*
Hope-Wallace, Philip A 1911- *WhoThe 16*
Hopkins, Anthony *PIP&P, PIP&P A,
  WhoHol A*
Hopkins, Anthony 1937- *CnThe, WhoThe 16*
Hopkins, Anthony 1941- *FilmgC*
Hopkins, Arthur *PIP&P*
Hopkins, Arthur 1878-1950 *NotNAT A,
  NotNAT B, WhThe*
Hopkins, Bo *IntMPA 1977, WhoHol A*
Hopkins, Bob 1918-1962 *NotNAT B, WhScrn 1,
  WhScrn 2, WhoHol B*
Hopkins, Charles 1884-1953 *NotNAT B, WhThe*
Hopkins, Claude D 1906- *AmSCAP 1966*
Hopkins, Clyde *Film 1*
Hopkins, Joan 1915- *WhThe*
Hopkins, John 1931- *ConDr 1977, FilmgC,
  NotNAT*
Hopkins, Kenyon *WorEnF*
Hopkins, Linda *WhoHol A*
Hopkins, Mae *Film 1*
Hopkins, Maurice 1914- *Film 2*
Hopkins, Miriam 1902-1972 *BiDFlm, BiE&WWA,
  MotPP, MovMk, NotNAT B, OxFilm,
  ThFT, WhScrn 2, WhThe, WhoHol B,
  WorEnF*
Hopkins, Miriam 1902-1973 *FilmgC*
Hopkirk, Gordon *Film 2*
Hopper, Charles H d1916 *NotNAT B*
Hopper, Dennis *MotPP, WhoHol A*

Hopper, Dennis 1935- *FilmgC*
Hopper, Dennis 1936- *CelR 3, IntMPA 1977,
  MovMk*
Hopper, DeWolf 1858-1935 *EncMT, FamA&A,
  NotNAT A, NotNAT B, OxThe, TwYS,
  WhScrn 1, WhScrn 2, WhThe, WhoHol B*
Hopper, DeWolf *see also* Hopper, William DeWolf
Hopper, DeWolfe 1858-1935 *Film 1*
Hopper, DeWolfe, Jr. *Film 1*
Hopper, E Mason 1885-1966 *TwYS A*
Hopper, Edna Wallace *WhoStg 1906,
  WhoStg 1908*
Hopper, Edna Wallace 1864-1959 *NotNAT B,
  WhThe*
Hopper, Edna Wallace 1874-1959 *WhScrn 1,
  WhScrn 2*
Hopper, Frank *Film 2*
Hopper, Hal 1912-1970 *WhScrn 2*
Hopper, Harold S 1912- *AmSCAP 1966*
Hopper, Hedda 1885-1966 *ThFT*
Hopper, Hedda 1890-1966 *FilmgC, MovMk,
  NotNAT B, OxFilm, WhScrn 1, WhScrn 2,
  WorEnF*
Hopper, Hedda 1891-1966 *Film 1, Film 2,
  TwYS, WhoHol B*
Hopper, Jerry 1907- *FilmgC, IntMPA 1977*
Hopper, Rika d1963 *NotNAT B*
Hopper, Victoria 1909- *FilmgC, WhThe*
Hopper, William 1915-1969 *FilmgC*
Hopper, William 1915-1970 *WhScrn 1, WhScrn 2,
  WhoHol B*
Hopper, William DeWolf 1858-1935 *WhoStg 1906,
  WhoStg 1908*
Hopper, William DeWolf *see also* Hopper, DeWolf
Hopson, Violet *Film 1, Film 2*
Hopton, Russell 1900-1945 *WhScrn 1, WhScrn 2,
  WhoHol B*
Hopwood, Avery 1882-1928 *McGWD, ModWD,
  NotNAT B, WhThe*
Horan, Charles *TwYS A*
Horan, Edward 1898- *WhThe*
Horan, James 1908-1967 *WhScrn 1, WhScrn 2*
Horbiger, Paul *Film 2*
Hordern, Michael 1911- *CnThe, FilmgC,
  IntMPA 1977, MovMk, WhoHol A,
  WhoThe 16*
Horgan, Patrick *WhoHol A*
Horine, Charles 1912- *NatPD*
Horitz, Joseph F d1961 *NotNAT B*
Horkheimer, Herbert M d1962 *NotNAT B*
Horn, Camilla 1906- *Film 2, FilmgC, TwYS,
  WhoHol A*
Horn, Leonard 1926- *FilmgC*
Horn, Mary 1916- *WhThe*
Horn, Paul 1930- *AmSCAP 1966*
Hornbeck, William W 1901- *IntMPA 1977*
Hornblow, Arthur d1942 *NotNAT B*
Hornblow, Arthur, Jr. 1893- *FilmgC*
Hornbrook, Charles Gus 1874-1937 *WhScrn 1,
  WhScrn 2*
Horne *PIP&P*
Horne, A P *WhThe*
Horne, David 1898-1970 *FilmgC, IntMPA 1977,
  WhScrn 1, WhScrn 2, WhThe, WhoHol B*
Horne, Geoffrey 1933- *BiE&WWA, MotPP,
  NotNAT, WhoHol A*
Horne, James V 1880-1942 *CmMov, FilmgC*
Horne, James W 1880- *TwYS A*
Horne, James W 1881-1942 *WhScrn 2*
Horne, Kenneth 1900- *WhThe*
Horne, Lena 1917- *BiE&WWA, CelR 3,
  EncMT, FilmgC, IntMPA 1977, MGM,
  MotPP, MovMk, NotNAT, WhoHol A*
Horne, Marilyn 1934- *CelR 3*

Horne, Michael Jeffrey *WhoHol A*
Horne, Victoria 1920?- *FilmgC, WhoHol A*
Horne, W *Film 1*
Horner, Harry 1910- *FilmgC, IntMPA 1977,*
   WorEnF
Horner, Harry 1912- *BiE&WWA, NotNAT*
Horner, Jed 1922- *BiE&WWA, NotNAT*
Horner, Lottie d1964 *NotNAT B*
Horner, Peter P 1910- *IntMPA 1977*
Horner, Richard 1920- *BiE&WWA, NotNAT,*
   WhoThe 16
Horner, Violet *Film 1*
Horney, Brigitte *WhoHol A*
Horniman, Annie Elizabeth Fredericka 1860-1937
   CnThe, NotNAT A, NotNAT B, OxThe,
   WhThe
Horniman, Roy 1872-1930 *NotNAT B, WhThe*
Hornisher, Christina *WomWMM B*
Hornsby, Nancy 1910-1958 *NotNAT B, WhThe*
Horovitz, Israel 1939- *CelR 3, ConDr 1977,*
   CroCD, NatPD, NotNAT, PIP&P,
   WhoThe 16
Horowitz, Vladimir 1904- *CelR 3*
Horsbrugh, Walter *WhoHol A*
Horsley, John *WhoHol A*
Horsman, Charles d1886 *NotNAT B*
Horsnell, Horace 1883-1949 *NotNAT B, WhThe*
Horton, Benjamin 1872-1952 *WhScrn 1,*
   WhScrn 2
Horton, Clara 1904- *Film 1, Film 2, TwYS*
Horton, Clara Marie *MotPP*
Horton, Edward Everett d1970 *MotPP,*
   WhoHol B
Horton, Edward Everett 1866-1970 *TwYS*
Horton, Edward Everett 1886-1970 *BiE&WWA,*
   Film 2, FilmgC, OxFilm, WhScrn 1,
   WhScrn 2, WhThe
Horton, Edward Everett 1887-1970 *MovMk*
Horton, Edward Everett 1888-1970 *Vers A*
Horton, Edward Everett 1888-1971 *WorEnF*
Horton, Elizabeth 1902- *AmSCAP 1966*
Horton, Lewis Henry 1898- *AmSCAP 1966*
Horton, Louise *WhoHol A*
Horton, Philip 1912- *AmSCAP 1966*
Horton, Robert 1870- *WhThe*
Horton, Robert 1924- *FilmgC, IntMPA 1977,*
   MotPP, WhoHol A
Horton, Vaughn 1911- *AmSCAP 1966*
Horton, Walter *Film 2*
Horvath, Charles *WhoHol A*
Horvath, Joan *WomWMM A*
Horvath, Odon Von 1901-1938 *CnMD, CnThe,*
   McGWD, ModWD, REnWD
Horwich, Frances R *IntMPA 1977*
Horwin, C Jerome d1954 *NotNAT B*
Horwits, Al 1905- *IntMPA 1977*
Horwitt, Arnold B 1918- *AmSCAP 1966,*
   BiE&WWA, EncMT, NotNAT
Horwitz, Howie d1976 *NewYTET*
Horwitz, Joseph 1858-1922 *WhScrn 1, WhScrn 2*
Horwitz, Lewis M 1931- *IntMPA 1977*
Hoschna, Karl 1877-1911 *AmSCAP 1966,*
   EncMT, NewMT, NotNAT B
Hosey, Athena 1929- *AmSCAP 1966*
Hosford, Maud *Film 1*
Hoskin, Mai *WomWMM*
Hoskins, Allan Clayton Farina 1920- *Film 2*
Hoskins, Allen Clayton 1920- *WhoHol A*
Hoskins, Bob 1942- *WhoHol A, WhoThe 16*
Hoskins, Jannie *Film 2*
Hoskwith, Arnold K 1917- *BiE&WWA, NotNAT*
Hosmer, Lucius 1870-1935 *AmSCAP 1966*
Hossein, Robert 1927- *FilmgC, OxFilm,*
   WhoHol A, WorEnF

Hostetler, Paul 1921- *NotNAT*
Hostetter, Roy 1885-1951 *WhScrn 1, WhScrn 2*
Hostrup, Jens Christian 1818-1892 *OxThe*
Hot, Pierre *Film 2*
Hotaling, Arthur D 1872-1938 *WhScrn 1,*
   WhScrn 2, WhoHol B
Hotchkis, Joan *WhoHol A*
Hoteley, Mae *MotPP*
Hotely, Mae 1872-1954 *Film 1, WhScrn 2*
Hotton, Lucille *Film 2*
Hotvedt, Phyllis Shaw d1964 *NotNAT B*
Houck, Leo *Film 2*
Houdini, Harry 1873-1926 *FilmgC, TwYS,*
   WhThe
Houdini, Harry 1874-1926 *Film 1, Film 2,*
   OxFilm, WhScrn 1, WhScrn 2, WhoHol B
Hough, John *IntMPA 1977*
Hough, Will 1882-1962 *AmSCAP 1966,*
   NotNAT B
Houghton, Alice 1888-1944 *WhScrn 1, WhScrn 2*
Houghton, Belle d1964 *NotNAT B*
Houghton, Katharine 1945- *FilmgC, WhoHol A*
Houghton, Norris 1909- *BiE&WWA, NotNAT,*
   WhoThe 16
Houghton, Stanley 1881-1913 *CnMD, McGWD,*
   ModWD, NotNAT B, OxThe
Houk, Ralph 1919- *CelR 3*
House, Billy 1890-1961 *NotNAT B, Vers A,*
   WhScrn 1, WhScrn 2, WhoHol B
House, Eric *WhoThe 16*
House, Jack 1887-1963 *WhScrn 1, WhScrn 2,*
   WhoHol B
House, Marguerite *Film 1*
House, Newton *Film 2*
Houseman, Arthur 1890-1942 *WhScrn 1,*
   WhScrn 2
Houseman, John *NewYTET, WhoHol A*
Houseman, John 1902- *BiDFlm, BiE&WWA,*
   CelR 3, CnThe, FilmgC, IntMPA 1977,
   NotNAT, NotNAT A, PIP&P, WhoThe 16
Houseman, John 1903?- *WorEnF*
Houseman, Laurence 1865-1959 *CnThe*
Houser, Thomas J *NewYTET*
Housman, Arthur 1888-1942 *FilmgC, WhoHol B*
Housman, Arthur 1890-1937 *Film 1, Film 2,*
   TwYS
Housman, Laurence 1865-1959 *CnMD, McGWD,*
   ModWD, NotNAT A, NotNAT B, OxThe,
   WhThe
Houston, Cisco 1919-1961 *WhScrn 1, WhScrn 2,*
   WhoHol B
Houston, Donald 1923- *FilmgC, WhoHol A,*
   WhoThe 16
Houston, George d1945 *WhoHol B*
Houston, George 1900-1944 *NotNAT B,*
   WhScrn 1, WhScrn 2
Houston, Glyn 1926- *FilmgC, WhoHol A*
Houston, Jane *WhThe*
Houston, Jean d1965 *WhScrn 2*
Houston, Josephine 1911- *Film 2, WhThe*
Houston, Renee 1902- *FilmgC, WhoHol A,*
   WhoThe 16
Hovde, Ellen Giffard *WomWMM B*
Hovdesven, E A 1893- *AmSCAP 1966*
Hovey, Ann *WhoHol A*
Hovey, Tim 1945- *FilmgC, IntMPA 1977*
Hovick, Louise 1914-1970 *ThFT, WhoHol B*
Hovick, Rose Louise *WhScrn 1, WhScrn 2*
Hoving, Thomas P F 1931- *CelR 3*
Hoving, Walter 1897- *CelR 3*
Hovmand, Annelise *WomWMM*
Howard, Alan 1937- *WhoHol A, WhoThe 16*
Howard, Andree 1910-1968 *NotNAT B, WhThe*
Howard, Art 1892-1963 *NotNAT B, WhScrn 1,*

WhScrn 2
Howard, Arthur Film 1
Howard, Arthur 1910- FilmgC, WhoHol A
Howard, Bart 1915- AmSCAP 1966, BiE&WWA,
   NotNAT
Howard, Beatrice Thomas 1905- AmSCAP 1966
Howard, Bert 1873-1958 WhScrn 1, WhScrn 2
Howard, Booth 1889-1936 WhScrn 1, WhScrn 2
Howard, Boothe 1889-1936 WhoHol B
Howard, Bronson 1842-1908 CnThe, McGWD,
   ModWD, NotNAT A, NotNAT B, OxThe,
   PIP&P, REnWD, WhoStg 1906,
   WhoStg 1908
Howard, Cecil d1895 NotNAT B
Howard, Charles 1882-1947 WhScrn 2
Howard, Clint WhoHol A
Howard, Constance Film 2
Howard, Cordelia 1848-1941 NotNAT B
Howard, Curly 1906-1952 MotPP, WhoHol B
Howard, Curly see also Howard, Jerome Curly
Howard, Cy 1915- FilmgC, IntMPA 1977
Howard, Cyril IntMPA 1977
Howard, David H 1860-1944 WhScrn 1,
   WhScrn 2
Howard, Eddy 1909-1963 WhScrn 1, WhScrn 2,
   WhoHol B
Howard, Eddy 1914-1963 AmSCAP 1966
Howard, Ernest 1875-1940 WhScrn 1, WhScrn 2
Howard, Esther 1893-1965 FilmgC, WhScrn 1,
   WhScrn 2, WhoHol B
Howard, Eugene 1880-1965 WhThe
Howard, Eugene 1881-1965 BiE&WWA, Film 2,
   NotNAT B, WhScrn 1, WhScrn 2,
   WhoHol B
Howard, Florence 1879- WhoStg 1908
Howard, Florence 1888-1954 WhScrn 1,
   WhScrn 2
Howard, Frances Film 2
Howard, Frankie 1921- FilmgC
Howard, Fred 1896- AmSCAP 1966
Howard, Frederick Film 2
Howard, George d1921 NotNAT B
Howard, George Bronson d1922 NotNAT B
Howard, George Sallade 1903- AmSCAP 1966
Howard, George W Film 2
Howard, Gertrude 1892-1934 Film 2, WhScrn 1,
   WhScrn 2, WhoHol B
Howard, Harold 1875- WhoStg 1908
Howard, Helen 1899-1975 Film 1, Film 2,
   WhScrn 2
Howard, J B d1895 NotNAT B
Howard, J Bannister 1867-1946 NotNAT A,
   NotNAT B, WhThe
Howard, Jack Film 2
Howard, Jack 1910- CelR 3
Howard, Jason WhoHol A
Howard, Jean WhoHol A
Howard, Jerome Curly 1906-1952 WhScrn 1,
   WhScrn 2
Howard, Jerome Curly see also Howard, Curly
Howard, John 1913- FilmgC, MotPP, MovMk,
   WhoHol A
Howard, John Tasker 1890-1964 AmSCAP 1966,
   NotNAT B
Howard, Joseph A 1928- AmSCAP 1966
Howard, Joseph E 1867-1961 NotNAT B
Howard, Joseph Edgar 1878-1961 AmSCAP 1966
Howard, Joyce 1922- FilmgC, WhoHol A
Howard, Kathleen 1879-1956 FilmgC, WhScrn 1,
   WhScrn 2, WhoHol B
Howard, Keble 1875-1928 NotNAT B, WhThe
Howard, Ken 1944- NotNAT, WhoHol A,
   WhoThe 16
Howard, Leslie d1943 MotPP, PIP&P,

WhoHol B
Howard, Leslie 1890-1943 FilmgC
Howard, Leslie 1893-1943 BiDFlm, CmMov,
   FamA&A, Film 1, Film 2, MovMk,
   NotNAT A, NotNAT B, OxFilm, WhScrn 1,
   WhScrn 2, WhThe, WorEnF
Howard, Lewis d1956 WhoHol B
Howard, Lewis 1919-1951 WhScrn 2
Howard, Lisa K 1930-1963 WhScrn 2
Howard, Lisa K 1930-1965 WhoHol B
Howard, Mabel 1884- WhoStg 1908
Howard, Marjorie WhoHol A
Howard, Mary WhoHol A
Howard, May 1870-1935 WhScrn 1, WhScrn 2
Howard, Mel 1912- AmSCAP 1966
Howard, Michael WhoHol A
Howard, Moe 1897-1975 MotPP, WhScrn 2,
   WhoHol C
Howard, Norah 1901-1968 NotNAT B, WhThe
Howard, Paul Mason 1909- AmSCAP 1966
Howard, Peter 1878-1969 WhScrn 1, WhScrn 2
Howard, Peter 1908-1965 WhScrn 2
Howard, Peter 1927- BiE&WWA, NotNAT
Howard, Peter 1934-1968 WhScrn 2, WhoHol B
Howard, Rance WhoHol A
Howard, Ray Film 2
Howard, Richard Film 2
Howard, Richard 1890- AmSCAP 1966
Howard, Sir Robert d1698 NotNAT B, PIP&P
Howard, Robert T IntMPA 1977, NewYTET
Howard, Roger 1938- ConDr 1977
Howard, Ron WhoHol A
Howard, Ron 1954- IntMPA 1977
Howard, Ronald 1918- FilmgC, IntMPA 1977,
   WhoHol A
Howard, Ronny 1953- FilmgC
Howard, Ruth 1894-1944 WhScrn 1, WhScrn 2,
   WhoHol B
Howard, Sam d1964 NotNAT B
Howard, Samuel Shemp 1900-1955 WhScrn 1,
   WhScrn 2
Howard, Sandy 1927- IntMPA 1977
Howard, Shemp d1955 MotPP, WhoHol B
Howard, Shemp 1901-1955 FilmgC
Howard, Sidney Coe 1891-1939 CnMD, CnThe,
   FilmgC, McGWD, ModWD, NotNAT B,
   OxThe, PIP&P, REnWD, WhThe
Howard, Sydney 1884-1946 Film 2, FilmgC,
   WhoHol B
Howard, Sydney 1885-1946 EncMT, NotNAT B,
   WhScrn 1, WhScrn 2, WhThe
Howard, Tom 1886-1955 WhScrn 1, WhScrn 2,
   WhoHol B
Howard, Trevor 1916- BiDFlm, CelR 3, CmMov,
   FilmgC, IntMPA 1977, MotPP, MovMk,
   OxFilm, PIP&P, WhoHol A, WhoThe 16,
   WorEnF
Howard, Vince WhoHol A
Howard, Vincente Film 1
Howard, Walter 1866-1922 NotNAT B, WhThe
Howard, Wanda Film 1
Howard, Wendy 1925-1972 WhScrn 2,
   WhoHol B
Howard, William 1884-1944 WhScrn 1,
   WhScrn 2, WhoHol B
Howard, William J 1899-1954 TwYS A
Howard, William K 1899-1954 BiDFlm, FilmgC,
   MovMk, OxFilm, WorEnF
Howard, William W d1963 NotNAT B
Howard, Willie d1949 Film 2, WhoHol B
Howard, Willie 1883-1949 WhThe
Howard, Willie 1886-1949 EncMT, NotNAT B
Howard, Willie 1887-1949 WhScrn 1, WhScrn 2
Howarth, Donald 1931- ConDr 1977, WhoThe 16

Howat, Clark *WhoHol A*
Howatt, William *Film 2*
Howdy, Clyde 1920-1969 *WhScrn 2*
Howe, Betty *Film 1*
Howe, George 1900- *BiE&WWA, WhoThe 16*
Howe, George Warren 1909- *AmSCAP 1966*
Howe, Henry 1812-1896 *NotNAT B, OxThe*
Howe, J B d1908 *NotNAT A, NotNAT B*
Howe, James Wong 1889- *DcFM*
Howe, James Wong 1899- *FilmgC, OxFilm, WorEnF*
Howe, Julia Ward 1819-1910 *NotNAT B*
Howe, Mary 1882-1964 *AmSCAP 1966*
Howe, Maude Johnson 1887- *AmSCAP 1966*
Howe, Quincy 1900- *IntMPA 1977*
Howe, Sylvia *WomWMM B*
Howe, Wallace *Film 2*
Howe, Willard 1898- *WhoStg 1908*
Howell, Alice 1892- *Film 1, Film 2, TwYS*
Howell, Jane *WhoThe 16*
Howell, John 1888-1928 *NotNAT B, WhThe*
Howell, John Daggett 1911- *BiE&WWA*
Howell, Miriam *BiE&WWA*
Howell, Robert B 1944- *AmSCAP 1966*
Howell, Thomas B 1921- *AmSCAP 1966*
Howell, Yvonne *Film 2*
Howells, Ursula 1922- *FilmgC, IntMPA 1977, WhoHol A, WhoThe 16*
Howells, William Dean 1837-1920 *McGWD, ModWD, NotNAT B, PIP&P*
Howerd, Frankie 1921- *IntMPA 1977, WhoHol A, WhoThe 16*
Howerton, Clarence Major Mite 1913-1975 *WhoHol C*
Howerton, Clarency Major Mite 1913-1975 *WhScrn 2*
Howes, Basil 1901- *WhThe*
Howes, Bobby 1895-1972 *EncMT, Film 2, FilmgC, WhScrn 2, WhThe, WhoHol B*
Howes, Reed 1900-1964 *Film 2, TwYS, WhScrn 2, WhoHol B*
Howes, Sally Ann 1930- *BiE&WWA, EncMT, FilmgC, MotPP, MovMk, NotNAT, WhoHol A, WhoThe 16*
Howland, Alan d1946 *NotNAT B*
Howland, Jobyna d1936 *PIP&P, WhoHol B*
Howland, Jobyna 1880-1936 *Film 1, Film 2, NotNAT B, ThFT, TwYS, WhThe*
Howland, Jobyna 1881-1936 *WhScrn 1, WhScrn 2*
Howland, Olin 1896-1959 *Film 1, Film 2, MovMk, NotNAT B, WhoHol B*
Howlett, Noel 1901- *FilmgC, WhoThe 16*
Howlin, Olin 1896-1959 *FilmgC, Vers B, WhScrn 1, WhScrn 2*
Howson, Frank A d1945 *NotNAT B*
Howson, John d1887 *NotNAT B*
Hoxie, Hart *TwYS*
Hoxie, Jack 1885-1965 *Film 1, TwYS*
Hoxie, Jack 1885-1975 *Film 2*
Hoxie, Jack 1890-1965 *WhScrn 1, WhScrn 2, WhoHol B*
Hoy, Danny 1916- *Film 2*
Hoyningen-Huene, George d1968 *WorEnF*
Hoyos, Rodolfo *WhoHol A*
Hoyt, Arthur *Film 1, Film 2, TwYS*
Hoyt, Arthur 1874-1953 *WhScrn 1, WhScrn 2, WhoHol B*
Hoyt, Arthur 1876-1955 *MovMk*
Hoyt, Caroline Miskel d1898 *NotNAT B*
Hoyt, Mrs. Charles H d1893 *NotNAT B*
Hoyt, Charles Hale 1860-1900 *CnThe, EncMT, ModWD, NotNAT A, NotNAT B, OxThe, PIP&P, REnWD*

Hoyt, Clegg 1911-1967 *WhScrn 1, WhScrn 2, WhoHol B*
Hoyt, Edward N 1859- *WhoStg 1908*
Hoyt, Harry O 1880-1961 *TwYS A*
Hoyt, Howard 1913- *BiE&WWA*
Hoyt, John 1905- *FilmgC, MovMk, Vers A, WhoHol A*
Hoyt, Julia 1897-1955 *Film 2, NotNAT B, WhScrn 1, WhScrn 2, WhoHol B*
Hoz Y Mota, Juan Claudio DeLa 1622?-1714? *McGWD*
Hrastnik, Franz 1904- *CnMD*
Hrosvitha *REnWD*
Hroswitha *OxThe*
Hrotsvitha 935?-1001? *CnThe, REnWD*
Hrotsvitha Of Gandersheim 935?-973? *NotNAT B*
Hruby, Norbert J 1918- *BiE&WWA, NotNAT*
Hsia, Kuei-Ying *WomWMM*
Hsiung, Shih I 1902- *BiE&WWA, WhThe*
Hsueh, Nancy *WhoHol A*
Hubalek, Claus 1926- *CnMD, ModWD*
Huban, Eileen 1895-1935 *NotNAT B, WhThe*
Hubbard, Gordon 1921- *IntMPA 1977*
Hubbard, John 1914- *FilmgC, WhoHol A*
Hubbard, Lorna 1910- *WhThe*
Hubbard, Lucien 1888-1971 *FilmgC*
Hubbard, Tom d1974 *WhScrn 2*
Hubbel, Raymond 1879-1954 *NotNAT B*
Hubbell, Edwin *Film 2*
Hubbell, Frank Allen 1907- *AmSCAP 1966*
Hubbell, Raymond 1879-1954 *AmSCAP 1966, EncMT, NewMT, WhThe*
Hubble, Martie 1922- *AmSCAP 1966*
Huber, Chad *Film 2*
Huber, Gusti 1914- *BiE&WWA, NotNAT, WhThe, WhoHol A*
Huber, Harold 1904-1959 *FilmgC*
Huber, Harold 1910-1959 *NotNAT B, Vers A, WhScrn 1, WhScrn 2, WhoHol B*
Huber, Juanita Billie 1905-1965 *WhScrn 1, WhScrn 2*
Hubert, Andre 1634?-1700 *OxThe*
Hubert, Dick *NewYTET*
Hubert, George 1881-1963 *NotNAT B, WhScrn 1, WhScrn 2, WhoHol B*
Hubert, Paul *Film 2*
Hubert, Roger 1903-1964 *DcFM*
Hublay, Miklos 1918- *CroCD*
Hubley, Faith *WomWMM, WorEnF*
Hubley, John 1914- *DcFM, FilmgC, OxFilm, WomWMM, WorEnF*
Hubley, John And Hubley, Faith *NewYTET*
Hubley, Season *WhoHol A*
Hubschmid, Paul 1917- *FilmgC, WhoHol A*
Huby, Roberta *WhThe*
Huchel, Peter 1903- *CnMD*
Hudak, Andrew, Jr. 1918- *AmSCAP 1966*
Hudd, Walter 1898-1963 *FilmgC, NotNAT B, WhScrn 1, WhScrn 2, WhThe, WhoHol B*
Huddleston, David *WhoHol A*
Huddleston, Floyd Houston 1919- *AmSCAP 1966*
Hudgins, Torrence B *IntMPA 1977*
Hudis, Norman *IntMPA 1977*
Hudman, Wes d1964 *WhoHol B*
Hudman, Wesley 1916-1964 *NotNAT B, WhScrn 1, WhScrn 2*
Hudson, Charles d1897 *NotNAT B*
Hudson, John *WhoHol A*
Hudson, Larry 1920-1961 *WhScrn 1, WhScrn 2, WhoHol B*
Hudson, Rochelle 1914-1971 *FilmgC*
Hudson, Rochelle 1914-1972 *MotPP, MovMk, ThFT, WhScrn 2, WhoHol B*
Hudson, Rock *MotPP, WhoHol A*

Hudson, Rock 1924- *BiDFlm*
Hudson, Rock 1925- *CelR 3, CmMov, FilmgC, IntMPA 1977, MovMk, OxFilm, WorEnF*
Hudson, Will 1908- *AmSCAP 1966*
Hudson, William 1925-1974 *WhScrn 2, WhoHol B*
Huebing, Craig *WhoHol A*
Huebner, Ilse 1898- *AmSCAP 1966*
Huerter, Charles 1885- *AmSCAP 1966*
Huestis, Russell 1894-1964 *WhScrn 1, WhScrn 2*
Hueston, Billy 1896-1957 *AmSCAP 1966*
Huff, Forrest 1876-1947 *WhScrn 1, WhScrn 2, WhoHol B*
Huff, Jack *WhScrn 2*
Huff, Jackie *Film 2*
Huff, Louise 1896-1973 *Film 1, Film 2, MotPP, TwYS, WhScrn 2, WhoHol B*
Huffaker, Clair 1927- *CmMov, FilmgC, WorEnF*
Huffman, Jessie C d1935 *NotNAT B*
Hug, Armand 1910- *AmSCAP 1966*
Huggins, Roy 1914- *FilmgC, IntMPA 1977, NewYTET*
Hughes, Adelaide d1937 *NotNAT B*
Hughes, Adelaide d1960 *NotNAT B*
Hughes, Anna May 1918- *BiE&WWA, NotNAT*
Hughes, Annie 1869-1954 *NotNAT B, WhThe, WhoStg 1906, WhoStg 1908*
Hughes, Archie d1860 *NotNAT B*
Hughes, Arthur *WhoHol A*
Hughes, Barnard 1915- *NotNAT, WhoHol A, WhoThe 16*
Hughes, Carol 1915- *WhoHol A*
Hughes, Charissa d1963 *WhScrn 1, WhScrn 2*
Hughes, David 1924-1945 *WhScrn 2*
Hughes, David Hillary d1974 *WhScrn 2, WhoHol B*
Hughes, Del *BiE&WWA, NotNAT*
Hughes, Dorothy *Film 2*
Hughes, Elinor 1906- *BiE&WWA, NotNAT*
Hughes, Ernest d1962 *NotNAT B*
Hughes, Ernest 1915- *AmSCAP 1966*
Hughes, Fanny d1888 *NotNAT B*
Hughes, Gareth 1894-1965 *Film 1, Film 2, MotPP, TwYS, WhScrn 1, WhScrn 2, WhoHol B*
Hughes, Glenn 1894-1964 *BiE&WWA, NotNAT B*
Hughes, Hatcher 1881-1945 *CnMD, ModWD*
Hughes, Hatcher 1883-1945 *NotNAT B, WhThe*
Hughes, Hazel 1913- *WhThe, WhoHol A*
Hughes, Henry d1872 *NotNAT B*
Hughes, Howard 1904- *TwYS B*
Hughes, Howard 1905- *BiDFlm, CelR 3, DcFM, FilmgC, OxFilm, WorEnF*
Hughes, J Anthony 1904-1970 *WhoHol B*
Hughes, James *BiE&WWA*
Hughes, Jann *WomWMM B*
Hughes, John d1720 *NotNAT B*
Hughes, Joseph Anthony 1904-1970 *WhScrn 2*
Hughes, Kathleen *WhoHol A*
Hughes, Kathleen 1928- *IntMPA 1977*
Hughes, Kathleen 1929- *FilmgC*
Hughes, Ken 1922- *BiDFlm, FilmgC, IntMPA 1977, WorEnF*
Hughes, Langston 1902-1967 *AmSCAP 1966, BiE&WWA, CnMD, CroCD, McGWD, ModWD, NotNAT A, NotNAT B*
Hughes, LaVaughn Rachel 1919- *AmSCAP 1966*
Hughes, Lloyd 1897-1958 *FilmgC, MotPP, MovMk, NotNAT B, WhScrn 1, WhScrn 2, WhoHol B*
Hughes, Lloyd 1897-1960 *Film 1, Film 2, TwYS*
Hughes, Margaret 1643-1719 *NotNAT B, PIP&P*
Hughes, Mary Beth 1919- *FilmgC, MovMk,*

WhoHol A
Hughes, Morris *Film 2*
Hughes, Robert J 1916- *AmSCAP 1966*
Hughes, Roddy 1891- *FilmgC, WhThe, WhoHol A*
Hughes, Rupert 1872-1956 *AmSCAP 1966, NotNAT B, TwYS A, WhScrn 2, WhThe, WhoStg 1908*
Hughes, Rush 1910-1958 *Film 2, WhScrn 2*
Hughes, Thomas *REnWD*
Hughes, Thomas Arthur 1887-1953 *WhScrn 1, WhScrn 2, WhoHol B*
Hughes, Tom 1932- *BiE&WWA, NotNAT*
Hughes, Tom E *WhThe*
Hughes, Yvonne Evelyn 1900-1950 *Film 2, WhScrn 2*
Hugo, Laurence 1917- *BiE&WWA, IntMPA 1977, NotNAT, WhoHol A*
Hugo, Mauritz 1909-1974 *WhScrn 2, WhoHol B*
Hugo, Victor Marie 1802-1885 *CnThe, McGWD, NotNAT A, NotNAT B, OxThe, REnWD*
Huguenet, Felix 1858-1926 *NotNAT B, WhThe*
Hugueny, Sharon *WhoHol A*
Huhn, Bruno 1871-1950 *AmSCAP 1966*
Huke, Bob *IntMPA 1977*
Hulbert, Claude 1900-1963 *Film 2, FilmgC*
Hulbert, Claude 1900-1964 *NotNAT B, WhScrn 1, WhScrn 2, WhThe, WhoHol B*
Hulbert, Jack 1892- *EncMT, FilmgC, WhoHol A, WhoThe 16*
Hulburd, H L Bud d1973 *WhScrn 2*
Hulburt, John W 1907- *BiE&WWA*
Hulette, Gladys *Film 1, Film 2, MotPP, TwYS*
Huley, Pete 1893-1973 *WhScrn 2, WhoHol B*
Hulin, Sylvia *WomWMM*
Huling, Lorraine *Film 1*
Hull, Arthur S *Film 2*
Hull, Bobby 1939- *CelR 3*
Hull, Dianne *WhoHol A*
Hull, Henry 1890- *BiE&WWA, Film 1, Film 2, FilmgC, IntMPA 1977, MotPP, MovMk, NotNAT, PIP&P, TwYS, Vers A, WhThe, WhoHol A*
Hull, Josephine d1957 *MotPP, PIP&P, WhoHol B*
Hull, Josephine 1884-1957 *FilmgC, MovMk, ThFT, WhScrn 1, WhScrn 2*
Hull, Josephine 1886-1957 *NotNAT A, NotNAT B, Vers B, WhThe*
Hull, Loraine *NotNAT*
Hull, Shelly d1919 *NotNAT B, WhScrn 2*
Hull, Thomas d1808 *NotNAT B*
Hull, Warren 1903-1974 *FilmgC, NewYTET, WhScrn 2, WhoHol B*
Hullet, Daniele *WomWMM*
Hulswit, Martin *WhoHol A*
Hulten, George P 1891- *AmSCAP 1966*
Hultin, Jill *WomWMM A, WomWMM B*
Human, William *Film 1*
Humberstone, Bruce 1903- *CmMov*
Humberstone, H Bruce 1903- *FilmgC, MovMk*
Humbert, George *Film 2*
Hume, Benita 1906-1967 *Film 2, FilmgC, MotPP, MovMk, NotNAT B, ThFT, WhScrn 1, WhScrn 2, WhoHol B*
Hume, Benita 1906-1968 *WhThe*
Hume, Douglas *WhoHol A*
Hume, Fergus d1932 *NotNAT B*
Hume, Kenneth 1926-1967 *FilmgC*
Hume, Margaret *Film 2*
Hume, Marjorie 1900- *Film 2*
Hume, Sam *PIP&P*
Humes, Fred *Film 2*
Humieres, Robert D' *NotNAT B*

Hummell, Mary Rockwell 1889-1946 *WhScrn 1,*
 WhScrn 2
Hummell, Wilson *Film 2*
Humperdinck, Engelbert d1921 *NotNAT B*
Humperdinck, Engelbert 1936- *CelR 3*
Humphrey, Bessie d1933 *WhScrn 1, WhScrn 2*
Humphrey, Cavada *BiE&WWA, NotNAT,*
 WhoHol A, WhoThe 16
Humphrey, Doris d1958 *NotNAT B*
Humphrey, Griffith *Film 2*
Humphrey, Hubert H 1911- *CelR 3*
Humphrey, Ola *Film 1*
Humphrey, Orral *Film 1, Film 2*
Humphrey, William 1874-1942 *Film 1, Film 2,*
 WhScrn 2
Humphreys, Cecil 1883-1947 *Film 2, NotNAT B,*
 WhScrn 1, WhScrn 2, WhThe, WhoHol B
Humphries, Joe *Film 2*
Humphries, John d1927 *NotNAT B, WhThe*
Humphris, Gordon 1921- *WhThe*
Hun, Hadi 1900-1969 *WhScrn 1, WhScrn 2*
Hundley, Richard 1931- *AmSCAP 1966*
Huneker, James Gibbons 1859-1921 *NotNAT B*
Huneker, James Gibbons 1860-1921 *OxThe*
Hung, Shen 1893-1955 *REnWD*
Hunkins, Eusebia Simpson 1902- *AmSCAP 1966*
Hunnicut, Gayle 1943- *IntMPA 1977*
Hunnicutt, Arthur 1911- *CmMov, FilmgC,*
 IntMPA 1977, MovMk, Vers A, WhoHol A
Hunnicutt, Gayle 1942- *FilmgC, WhoHol A*
Hunt, Al d1964 *NotNAT B*
Hunt, Betty Lee 1920- *BiE&WWA*
Hunt, Billy H 1926- *IntMPA 1977*
Hunt, Charles J *TwYS A*
Hunt, F V *NatPD*
Hunt, G Carleton 1908- *IntMPA 1977*
Hunt, H L 1889- *CelR 3*
Hunt, Helen *Film 2*
Hunt, Hugh 1911- *BiE&WWA, CnThe,*
 NotNAT, PIP&P, WhoThe 16
Hunt, Irene *Film 2*
Hunt, Jay 1857-1932 *Film 2, WhScrn 1,*
 WhScrn 2, WhoHol B
Hunt, Jimmy *MotPP*
Hunt, Lamar 1932- *CelR 3*
Hunt, Leigh 1784-1859 *NotNAT B, OxThe*
Hunt, Leslie *Film 2*
Hunt, Madge 1875-1935 *Film 2, WhScrn 2*
Hunt, Marsha 1917- *BiE&WWA, FilmgC,*
 IntMPA 1977, MGM, MotPP, MovMk,
 NotNAT, ThFT, WhThe, WhoHol A
Hunt, Martita 1900-1969 *BiE&WWA, FilmgC,*
 MotPP, MovMk, NotNAT B, Vers A,
 WhScrn 1, WhScrn 2, WhThe, WhoHol B
Hunt, Peter 1928- *CmMov, FilmgC,*
 IntMPA 1977
Hunt, Peter H 1938- *IntMPA 1977, WhoThe 16*
Hunt, Phil 1868- *WhoStg 1906, WhoStg 1908*
Hunt, Rea M 1893-1961 *WhScrn 2, WhoHol B*
Hunt, W P 1859-1934 *WhScrn 2*
Hunt, William E 1923- *BiE&WWA, NotNAT*
Hunter, Alberta 1897- *AmSCAP 1966*
Hunter, Edna *Film 1*
Hunter, Evan 1926- *AmSCAP 1966, FilmgC,*
 WorEnF
Hunter, Frederic *NatPD*
Hunter, Frederick J 1916- *BiE&WWA, NotNAT*
Hunter, George *Film 1*
Hunter, George W 1851- *WhThe*
Hunter, Glen 1897-1945 *PIP&P*
Hunter, Glenn d1945 *MotPP, WhoHol B*
Hunter, Glenn 1893-1945 *Film 2, NotNAT B*
Hunter, Glenn 1896-1945 *TwYS, WhThe*
Hunter, Glenn 1897-1945 *FilmgC, WhScrn 1,*

 WhScrn 2
Hunter, Harrison d1923 *NotNAT B*
Hunter, Ian 1900-1975 *Film 2, FilmgC, HolP 30,*
 MotPP, MovMk, WhScrn 2, WhThe,
 WhoHol A
Hunter, Jackie 1901-1951 *NotNAT B, WhScrn 1,*
 WhScrn 2
Hunter, Jeff *MotPP*
Hunter, Jeffrey d1969 *WhoHol B*
Hunter, Jeffrey 1925-1969 *FilmgC*
Hunter, Jeffrey 1926-1969 *WhScrn 1, WhScrn 2*
Hunter, Jeffrey 1927-1969 *BiDFlm, MovMk,*
 WorEnF
Hunter, Kenneth 1882- *WhThe*
Hunter, Kermit 1910- *BiE&WWA, ModWD,*
 NotNAT
Hunter, Kim 1922- *BiE&WWA, FilmgC,*
 IntMPA 1977, MotPP, MovMk, NotNAT,
 WhoHol A, WhoThe 16
Hunter, Marian *WomWMM A, WomWMM B*
Hunter, Norman Charles 1908-1971 *CnMD,*
 ConDr 1977F, CroCD, WhThe
Hunter, Paul *NatPD*
Hunter, Rebecca Lee 1945- *WomWMM B*
Hunter, Richard 1875-1962 *NotNAT B,*
 WhScrn 1, WhScrn 2, WhoHol B
Hunter, Ross *IntMPA 1977, MotPP*
Hunter, Ross 1916- *CmMov, WhoHol A*
Hunter, Ross 1921- *FilmgC, WorEnF*
Hunter, Ross 1924- *CelR 3*
Hunter, Ruth *NotNAT A*
Hunter, T Hayes 1881-1944 *FilmgC*
Hunter, T Hayes 1896- *TwYS A*
Hunter, Tab 1931- *FilmgC, IntMPA 1977,*
 MotPP, MovMk, WhoHol A
Hunter, Victor William 1910- *WhoThe 16*
Hunter, W C *PIP&P*
Huntington, Catharine 1889- *BiE&WWA,*
 NotNAT
Huntington, Joan *WomWMM*
Huntington, Lawrence 1900-1968 *FilmgC*
Huntley, Chet d1974 *NewYTET, WhoHol B*
Huntley, Chet 1911-1974 *CelR 3*
Huntley, Chet 1912-1974 *WhScrn 2*
Huntley, Fred 1861-1931 *Film 1, Film 2,*
 WhoHol B
Huntley, Fred 1862-1931 *WhScrn 1, WhScrn 2*
Huntley, G P 1904- *WhThe*
Huntley, George Patrick 1868-1927 *NotNAT B,*
 WhThe
Huntley, Grace d1896 *NotNAT B*
Huntley, Hugh *Film 2*
Huntley, Jobe 1918- *AmSCAP 1966*
Huntley, Luray *Film 1*
Huntley, Raymond 1904- *FilmgC, IntMPA 1977,*
 WhoHol A, WhoThe 16
Huntley, Tim 1904- *WhThe*
Huntley-Wright, Betty 1911- *WhThe*
Huntley-Wright, Jose 1918- *WhThe*
Huntoon, Helen *Film 2*
Hupfeld, Herman 1894-1951 *AmSCAP 1966,*
 NotNAT B
Hurd, Daniel George 1918- *AmSCAP 1966*
Hurgon, Austen A d1942 *NotNAT B, WhThe*
Hurka, Hans *Film 2*
Hurlburt, Glen 1909-1961 *AmSCAP 1966*
Hurlbut, Gladys *NotNAT A*
Hurlbut, W J 1883- *WhThe*
Hurley, Alec 1871-1913 *OxThe, WhoStg 1908*
Hurley, Julia 1847-1927 *Film 1, Film 2,*
 WhScrn 2
Hurley, Kathy 1947- *NatPD*
Hurlock, Madeleine *Film 2*
Hurlock, Madeline *MotPP, TwYS, WhoHol A*

Hurlock, Roger W 1912- *IntMPA 1977*
Hurn, Douglas 1925-1974 *WhScrn 2*
Hurndall, Richard 1910- *FilmgC, WhoThe 16*
Hurok, Sol 1888-1974 *BiE&WWA, CelR 3,
NotNAT B, WhThe*
Hurran, Dick 1911- *WhoThe 16*
Hurrell, Clarence E 1912- *AmSCAP 1966*
Hurrell, John D 1924- *BiE&WWA, NotNAT*
Hurry, Leslie 1909- *CnThe, OxThe, WhoThe 16*
Hurst, Brandon 1866-1947 *Film 1, Film 2,
NotNAT B, TwYS, WhScrn 1, WhScrn 2,
WhoHol B*
Hurst, Brian Desmond 1900- *FilmgC, MovMk*
Hurst, David *WhoHol A*
Hurst, David 1925- *FilmgC*
Hurst, David 1926- *BiE&WWA, NotNAT*
Hurst, Fannie 1889-1968 *FilmgC, NotNAT B,
WhThe*
Hurst, Paul d1953 *MotPP, WhoHol B*
Hurst, Paul 1888-1953 *Vers A, WhScrn 1,
WhScrn 2*
Hurst, Paul 1889-1953 *Film 1, Film 2, FilmgC,
MovMk, TwYS*
Hurst, Paul 1886-1953 *TwYS A*
Hurst, Veronica 1931- *FilmgC, WhoHol A*
Hurt, John 1940- *FilmgC, WhoHol A,
WhoThe 16*
Hurt, R N 1902- *IntMPA 1977*
Hurth, Harold *Film 2*
Hurtig, Louis d1924 *NotNAT B*
Hurton, Clarence *Film 2*
Hurwitch, Moses 1844-1910 *NotNAT B*
Hurwitz, Leo 1909- *OxFilm, WorEnF*
Hurwitz, Moshe 1844-1910 *ModWD*
Husch, Richard J d1948 *NotNAT B*
Hush, Lisabeth *WhoHol A*
Hush, Lisbeth *WomWMM B*
Husing, Ted 1901-1962 *WhScrn 2, WhoHol B*
Husmann, Ron 1937- *BiE&WWA, NotNAT,
WhoHol A, WhoThe 16*
Husni, Kameran *DcFM*
Hussein, Waris 1938- *FilmgC, IntMPA 1977*
Hussey, Jimmy 1891-1930 *NotNAT B, WhThe,
WhoHol B*
Hussey, Olivia 1951- *FilmgC, MotPP,
WhoHol A*
Hussey, Ruth *BiE&WWA, MotPP, NotNAT*
Hussey, Ruth 1913- *ThFT*
Hussey, Ruth 1914- *FilmgC, MGM, MovMk,
WhThe, WhoHol A*
Hussie, Barbara *WomWMM B*
Husson, Albert 1912- *BiE&WWA, McGWD*
Hussy, Jimmy 1891-1930 *WhScrn 1, WhScrn 2*
Husted, Beverly d1975 *WhoHol C*
Husting, Lucille 1900?-1972 *WhScrn 2*
Huston, Anjelica 1952- *FilmgC, WhoHol A*
Huston, Frank C 1871-1959 *AmSCAP 1966*
Huston, John 1906- *BiDFlm, CelR 3, CmMov,
ConDr 1977A, DcFM, FilmgC,
IntMPA 1977, MovMk, OxFilm, WhoHol A,
WorEnF*
Huston, Patricia *WhoHol A*
Huston, Philip 1908- *BiE&WWA, NotNAT,
WhoHol A*
Huston, Tony *WhoHol A*
Huston, Virginia 1925- *IntMPA 1977*
Huston, Walter 1884-1950 *BiDFlm, EncMT,
FamA&A, Film 2, FilmgC, MotPP, MovMk,
NotNAT B, OxFilm, PIP&P, WhScrn 1,
WhScrn 2, WhThe, WhoHol B, WorEnF*
Huston, William Dale 1918- *AmSCAP 1966*
Huszar-Puffy, Karl *Film 2*
Hutcherson, Levern *NotNAT*
Hutcheson, David 1905- *FilmgC, WhoHol A,*

WhoThe 16
Hutcheson, LaVerne *BiE&WWA*
Hutchins, Bobby Wheezer *Film 2*
Hutchins, Daryl 1920- *AmSCAP 1966*
Hutchins, Fred B 1911- *BiE&WWA*
Hutchins, Robert 1899- *CelR 3*
Hutchins, Will 1932- *FilmgC, WhoHol A*
Hutchinson, Canon Charles 1887-1969 *WhScrn 1,
WhScrn 2*
Hutchinson, Charles *Film 1, Film 2, TwYS,
TwYS A*
Hutchinson, Dorothy d1962 *NotNAT B*
Hutchinson, Emma d1817 *NotNAT B*
Hutchinson, Harry 1892- *WhoHol A,
WhoThe 16*
Hutchinson, Josephine *BiE&WWA, NotNAT*
Hutchinson, Josephine 1898- *HolP 30*
Hutchinson, Josephine 1904- *FilmgC, ThFT,
WhThe, WhoHol A*
Hutchinson, Josephine 1909- *MovMk*
Hutchinson, Kathryn *WhoStg 1908*
Hutchinson, Muriel 1915-1975 *WhScrn 2*
Hutchinson, William 1869-1918 *WhScrn 2*
Hutchinson Scott, Jay 1924- *WhThe*
Hutchison, Emma d1965 *WhThe*
Hutchison, Muriel *WhThe*
Hutchison, Muriel 1915-1975 *WhoHol C*
Hutchison, Percy 1875-1945 *NotNAT B, WhThe*
Huth, Harold 1892-1967 *Film 2, FilmgC,
WhScrn 1, WhScrn 2, WhThe, WhoHol B*
Hutner, Meyer Michael *IntMPA 1977*
Hutt, William 1920- *WhoThe 16*
Hutto, Jack 1928- *BiE&WWA, NotNAT*
Hutton, Barbara 1912- *CelR 3*
Hutton, Betty 1921- *BiE&WWA, CmMov,
FilmgC, IntMPA 1977, MotPP, MovMk,
OxFilm, WhoHol A*
Hutton, Brian G 1935- *FilmgC, IntMPA 1977*
Hutton, Jim *MotPP, WhoHol A*
Hutton, Jim 1935?- *MovMk*
Hutton, Jim 1938- *FilmgC, IntMPA 1977*
Hutton, Joseph 1787-1828 *NotNAT B*
Hutton, June d1973 *WhoHol B*
Hutton, Lauren *WhoHol A*
Hutton, Laurence d1904 *NotNAT B*
Hutton, Leona 1892-1949 *WhScrn 1, WhScrn 2*
Hutton, Linda *WhoHol A*
Hutton, Lucille *Film 1, Film 2*
Hutton, Marion 1920- *FilmgC, WhoHol A*
Hutton, Raymond *Film 2*
Hutton, Robert 1920- *FilmgC, HolP 40,
IntMPA 1977, MotPP, WhoHol A*
Huxham, Kendrick 1892-1967 *WhScrn 2*
Huxham, Kendrick 1892-1967 *WhScrn 1,
WhoHol B*
Huxley, Aldous 1894-1963 *CnMD, ModWD,
NotNAT B*
Huxley, Sir Julian 1887-1975 *OxFilm*
Huxtable, Ada Louise *CelR 3*
Huyck, Willard *WomWMM*
Hyames, John *Film 2*
Hyams, Barry 1911- *BiE&WWA, NotNAT*
Hyams, Jerome 1915- *IntMPA 1977*
Hyams, John 1877-1940 *WhScrn 1, WhScrn 2,
WhoHol B*
Hyams, Joseph 1927- *IntMPA 1977*
Hyams, Leila 1905- *Film 2, FilmgC, MovMk,
ThFT, TwYS, WhoHol A*
Hyams, Nessa *WomWMM*
Hyams, Peter 1943- *IntMPA 1977*
Hyatt, Clayton d1932 *WhScrn 1, WhScrn 2*
Hyatt, Gordon *NewYTET*
Hyatt, Herman 1906-1968 *WhScrn 1, WhScrn 2*
Hyde, Alexander 1898-1956 *AmSCAP 1966*

Hyde, Douglas 1860-1949 *ModWD*
Hyde, Harry *Film 1*
Hyde, Madeline 1907- *AmSCAP 1966*
Hyde, Rosel H *NewYTET*
Hyde, Tommy 1916- *IntMPA 1977*
Hyde-White, Wilfrid 1903- *BiE&WWA, FilmgC,
 MovMk, NotNAT, OxFilm, WhoHol A,
 WhoThe 16*
Hyem, Constance Ethel d1928 *NotNAT B,
 WhThe*
Hyer, Martha *MotPP*
Hyer, Martha 1924- *WhoHol A*
Hyer, Martha 1929- *FilmgC, MovMk*
Hyer, Martha 1930- *IntMPA 1977*
Hylan, Donald 1899-1968 *WhScrn 1, WhScrn 2*
Hylan, William H 1915- *IntMPA 1977*
Hyland, Augustin Allen 1905-1963 *NotNAT B,
 WhScrn 1, WhScrn 2*
Hyland, Diana 1936- *BiE&WWA, WhoHol A*
Hyland, Dick Irving 1906- *IntMPA 1977*
Hyland, Frances 1927- *WhoThe 16*
Hyland, Peggy *Film 1, Film 2, MotPP, TwYS*
Hyland, William H *NewYTET*
Hylton, Jack 1892-1965 *EncMT, NotNAT B,
 WhThe*
Hylton, Jane *WhoHol A*
Hylton, Jane 1926- *FilmgC*
Hylton, Jane 1927- *IntMPA 1977*
Hylton, Millie 1868-1920 *NotNAT B, WhThe*
Hylton, Richard d1962 *NotNAT B, WhoHol B*
Hylton, Richard 1920-1962 *WhThe*
Hylton, Richard 1921-1962 *FilmgC, WhScrn 1,
 WhScrn 2*
Hymack, Mister *WhScrn 1, WhScrn 2*
Hyman, Bynunsky *Film 2*
Hyman, Earle 1926- *BiE&WWA, NotNAT,
 WhoHol A, WhoThe 16*
Hyman, Joseph M 1901- *BiE&WWA, WhThe*
Hyman, Kenneth 1928- *FilmgC*
Hyman, Louis *Film 2*
Hyman, Prudence *WhThe*
Hyman, Richard R 1927- *AmSCAP 1966*
Hymer, John B d1953 *NotNAT B, WhThe*
Hymer, Warren 1906-1948 *Film 2, FilmgC,
 NotNAT B, Vers A, WhScrn 1, WhScrn 2,
 WhoHol B*
Hynes, John E 1853-1931 *WhScrn 1, WhScrn 2*
Hyson, Dorothy 1915- *FilmgC, WhThe*
Hytten, Olaf 1888-1955 *Film 2, FilmgC,
 WhScrn 1, WhScrn 2, WhoHol B*

I

Iacocca, Lee A 1924- *CelR 3*
Iacopone Da Todi *McGWD*
Iannelli, Theresa Rose 1936- *AmSCAP 1966*
Iannucci, Salvatore J 1927- *IntMPA 1977*
Iannuzzi, Ralph J 1914- *IntMPA 1977*
Iasilli, Gerardo 1880- *AmSCAP 1966*
Ibanez, Bonaventura *Film 2*
Ibanez, Ramon *Film 2*
Ibberson, H *Film 2*
Ibbetson, Arthur 1921- *FilmgC*
Ibert, Jacques 1890-1961 *DcFM*
Ibert, Jacques 1890-1962 *NotNAT B, OxFilm, WorEnF*
Ibrahim-Khan, Mitza *DcFM*
Ibsen, Henrich 1828-1906 *PIP&P*
Ibsen, Henrik 1828-1906 *CnMD, CnThe, McGWD, ModWD, NotNAT A, NotNAT B, OxThe, REnWD*
Ichac, Marcel 1906- *DcFM, WorEnF*
Ichikawa, Kon 1915- *BiDFlm, DcFM, FilmgC, MovMk, OxFilm, WorEnF*
Ichikawa, Sadanje d1940 *NotNAT B*
Ide, Harold 1917- *AmSCAP 1966*
Ide, Patrick 1916- *WhoThe 16*
Idemitsu, Mako *WomWMM B*
Iden, Rosalind 1911- *CnThe, WhThe*
Idriss, Ramez 1911- *AmSCAP 1966*
Idzikowski, Stanislas *WhThe*
Iffland, August Wilhelm 1759-1814 *CnThe, McGWD, NotNAT B, OxThe, REnWD*
Ifield, Frank 1936- *FilmgC*
Igdalsky, Zviah *WhoHol A*
Iglesias, Eugene *WhoHol A*
Ihnat, Steve d1972 *WhoHol B*
Ihnat, Steve 1934-1972 *FilmgC*
Ihnat, Steve 1935-1972 *WhScrn 2*
Il Cinthio *PIP&P*
Ilenkov, Vasili Pavlovich 1897- *ModWD*
Iliu, Victor 1912-1968 *DcFM*
Illery, Pola *Film 2*
Illes, Endre 1902- *CroCD*
Illica, Luigi 1857-1919 *OxThe*
Illing, Peter 1899-1966 *FilmgC, WhScrn 1, WhScrn 2*
Illing, Peter 1905-1966 *WhThe, WhoHol B*
Illington, Margaret 1879-1934 *OxThe*
Illington, Margaret 1881-1934 *Film 1, NotNAT B, WhScrn 1, WhScrn 2, WhThe, WhoHol B, WhoStg 1906, WhoStg 1908*
Illington, Marie d1927 *NotNAT B, WhThe*
Illyes, Gyula 1902- *CnMD, CroCD, McGWD*
Ilott, Pamela *NewYTET*
Ilson, Saul And Ernest Chambers *NewYTET*
Ilvess, Charles K 1905- *AmSCAP 1966*
Ilyenkov, Vassily 1897- *CnMD*
Ilyinsky, Igor Vladimirovich 1901- *OxThe*

Imadashvilli, A *Film 2*
Image, Jean 1911- *FilmgC*
Imai, Tadashi 1912- *DcFM, WorEnF*
Imamura, Shohei 1926- *WorEnF*
Imboden, David 1887-1974 *Film 2, WhScrn 2, WhoHol B*
Imboden, Hazel d1956 *WhScrn 1, WhScrn 2, WhoHol B*
Imbrie, McCrea 1918- *NatPD*
Imeson, A B *Film 2*
Imhof, Roger 1875-1958 *NotNAT B, Vers B, WhScrn 1, WhScrn 2, WhoHol B*
Imholz, Joseph *Film 2*
Imig, Warner 1913- *AmSCAP 1966*
Immerman, William J 1937- *IntMPA 1977*
Immermann, Karl Leberecht 1796-1840 *McGWD, OxThe*
Impolito, John 1887-1962 *WhScrn 2*
Imrie, Kathy *WhoHol A*
Inagaki, Hiroshi 1905- *DcFM*
Ince, Alexander 1892- *BiE&WWA*
Ince, Ethel *WhScrn 1, WhScrn 2*
Ince, John d1947 *MotPP, WhoHol B*
Ince, John 1877-1947 *WhScrn 1, WhScrn 2*
Ince, John 1879-1947 *TwYS A*
Ince, John Edwards *Film 1*
Ince, Ralph Waldo 1887-1935 *NotNAT B*
Ince, Ralph Waldo 1887-1937 *Film 1, Film 2, FilmgC, MovMk, TwYS, TwYS A, WhScrn 1, WhScrn 2, WhoHol B*
Ince, Thomas Harper 1882-1924 *BiDFlm, CmMov, DcFM, Film 1, FilmgC, MovMk, OxFilm, TwYS A, WhScrn 1, WhScrn 2, WhoHol B, WorEnF*
Inchbald, Elizabeth 1753-1821 *NotNAT A, NotNAT B, OxThe*
Inchbald, Joseph d1779 *NotNAT B*
Inclan, Miguel 1900-1956 *WhScrn 1, WhScrn 2, WhoHol B*
Incledon, Charles d1826 *NotNAT B*
Indelli, William 1924- *AmSCAP 1966*
Indiana, Robert 1928- *CelR 3*
Indrisano, John 1906-1968 *WhScrn 1, WhScrn 2, WhoHol B*
Inescort, Elaine d1964 *WhThe*
Inescort, Frieda 1901-1976 *FilmgC, MotPP, MovMk, ThFT, WhThe, WhoHol C*
Inescourt, Elaine d1964 *NotNAT B*
Infante, Pedro 1918-1957 *WhScrn 1, WhScrn 2*
Ingalls, Don *IntMPA 1977*
Inge, Clinton Owen 1909- *AmSCAP 1966*
Inge, William 1913-1973 *BiE&WWA, CnMD, CnThe, ConDr 1977F, CroCD, FilmgC, McGWD, ModWD, NotNAT A, NotNAT B, OxThe, PIP&P, REnWD, WhScrn 2, WhThe, WorEnF*

Ingegneri, Angelo 1550?-1613? *OxThe*
Ingels, Marty 1936- *FilmgC, IntMPA 1977, WhoHol A*
Ingemann, Bernhard Severin 1789-1862 *OxThe*
Ingersoll, William 1860-1936 *Film 2, NotNAT B, WhScrn 1, WhScrn 2, WhoHol B*
Ingham, Barrie 1934- *FilmgC, WhoThe 16*
Ingham, Nelson 1893- *AmSCAP 1966*
Ingis, Robert L 1935- *IntMPA 1977*
Ingle, Charles d1940 *NotNAT B*
Ingle, Red 1907-1965 *WhScrn 2*
Inglesby, Mona 1918- *WhThe*
Ingleton, George *Film 2*
Inglis, William H 1937- *NotNAT*
Ingraham, Herbert 1883-1910 *AmSCAP 1966*
Ingraham, Lloyd 1893-1956 *Film 1, Film 2, TwYS A, WhScrn 1, WhScrn 2, WhoHol B*
Ingraham, Roy 1895- *AmSCAP 1966*
Ingram, Amo *Film 2*
Ingram, Clifford *Film 2*
Ingram, Jack 1903-1969 *WhScrn 1, WhScrn 2, WhoHol B*
Ingram, Marvin 1938- *AmSCAP 1966*
Ingram, Rex 1892-1950 *CmMov, DcFM, Film 1, TwYS A, WhScrn 1, WhoHol B, WorEnF*
Ingram, Rex 1893-1950 *BiDFlm, FilmgC, OxFilm, WhScrn 2, WomWMM*
Ingram, Rex 1894-1969 *MovMk*
Ingram, Rex 1895-1969 *BiE&WWA, FilmgC, NotNAT B, OxFilm, Vers A, WhScrn 1, WhScrn 2, WhThe, WhoHol B*
Ingram, Rex 1896-1969 *Film 2*
Ingram, William D 1857-1926 *WhScrn 1, WhScrn 2*
Ingster, Boris 1913?- *FilmgC, IntMPA 1977*
Inkizhinov, Valerji *Film 2*
Innaurato, Albert 1948- *NatPD*
Inneo, Anthony *NatPD*
Innes, George *WhoHol A*
Innes, Jean *WhoHol A*
Inness-Brown, Virginia Royall 1901- *BiE&WWA, NotNAT*
Innis, Roy 1934- *CelR 3*
Inouye, Daniel 1924- *CelR 3*
Inouye, Masso *Film 2*
Insetta, Paul Peter 1915- *AmSCAP 1966*
Inslee, Charles *Film 1*
Interlenghi, Franco 1930- *OxFilm*
Intropodi, Ethel d1946 *NotNAT B*
Intropodi, Josie d1941 *NotNAT B*
Ion *OxThe*
Iona, Andy 1902- *AmSCAP 1966*
Ionesco, Eugene 1912- *BiE&WWA, CelR 3, CnMD, CnThe, CroCD, McGWD, ModWD, NotNAT, NotNAT A, OxThe, PIP&P, REnWD, WhoThe 16*
Iorga, Nicolae 1871-1940 *CnMD*
Ipsen, Bodil Louise Jensen 1889-1964 *DcFM, OxThe*
Irani, Ardeshir M 1885- *DcFM*
Irbe, Marie-Louise *Film 2*
Ireland, Anthony 1902-1957 *NotNAT B, WhScrn 1, WhScrn 2, WhThe, WhoHol B*
Ireland, Charles T, Jr. d1972 *NewYTET*
Ireland, Jill 1936- *FilmgC, IntMPA 1977, WhoHol A*
Ireland, John *MotPP, WhoHol A*
Ireland, John 1914- *CmMov, FilmgC*
Ireland, John 1915- *IntMPA 1977, MovMk, OxFilm*
Ireland, John 1916- *BiE&WWA, NotNAT*
Ireland, Joseph Norton d1898 *NotNAT B*
Ireland, Kenneth 1920- *WhoThe 16*
Ireland, William Henry 1775-1835 *NotNAT B,*

OxThe
Irene 1901-1962 *FilmgC*
Ireton, Glenn F 1906- *IntMPA 1977*
Ireton, Kikuko Monica 1929- *IntMPA 1977*
Irgat, Cahit 1916-1971 *WhScrn 1, WhScrn 2*
Iribe, Marie-Louise *WomWMM*
Irish, Annie 1862- *WhoStg 1908*
Irish, Annie 1865-1947 *NotNAT B, WhThe*
Irons, Earl D 1891- *AmSCAP 1966*
Irts, Lily *Film 2*
Irvin, Leslie 1895-1966 *WhScrn 2*
Irvine, Harry d1951 *NotNAT B*
Irvine, Louva Elizabeth 1939- *WomWMM A, WomWMM B*
Irvine, Robin 1901-1933 *Film 2, NotNAT B, WhThe, WhoHol B*
Irving, Ann *WomWMM B*
Irving, Ben 1919-1968 *BiE&WWA, NotNAT B*
Irving, Charles *WhoHol A*
Irving, Daisy d1938 *NotNAT B, WhThe*
Irving, Dorothea Baird 1875-1933 *OxThé*
Irving, Elizabeth 1904- *WhThe*
Irving, Ellis 1902- *WhoThe 16*
Irving, Ethel 1869-1963 *NotNAT B, WhThe*
Irving, George *WhoStg 1908*
Irving, George 1874-1961 *Film 2, MovMk, TwYS, TwYS A, Vers A, WhScrn 1, WhScrn 2, WhoHol B*
Irving, George S 1922- *BiE&WWA, NotNAT, WhoHol A, WhoThe 16*
Irving, Gordon 1918- *IntMPA 1977*
Irving, H B 1870-1919 *WhScrn 2, WhThe*
Irving, Harry James 1908- *AmSCAP 1966*
Irving, Sir Henry 1838-1905 *CnThe, FamA&A, NotNAT A, NotNAT B, OxThe, PIP&P*
Irving, Henry Brodribb 1870-1919 *NotNAT B, OxThe, WhoStg 1906, WhoStg 1908*
Irving, Isabel 1871-1944 *NotNAT B, WhThe, WhoStg 1906, WhoStg 1908*
Irving, Mrs. Joseph d1925 *NotNAT B*
Irving, Joseph Henry d1870 *NotNAT B*
Irving, Jules 1925- *BiE&WWA, NotNAT, PIP&P, PIP&P A, WhoThe 16*
Irving, K Ernest 1878-1953 *NotNAT B, WhThe*
Irving, Laurence Henry Forster 1897-1914 *OxThe, WhThe*
Irving, Laurence Sidney 1871-1914 *OxThe, WhThe*
Irving, Lawrence Sidney Brodribb 1871-1914 *NotNAT B*
Irving, Margaret 1900?- *MovMk, PIP&P*
Irving, Mary Jane *Film 1, Film 2*
Irving, Paul 1877-1959 *WhScrn 1, WhScrn 2, WhoHol B*
Irving, W J *Film 1*
Irving, Washington 1783-1859 *NotNAT B, OxThe, PIP&P*
Irving, William J 1893-1943 *Film 2, WhScrn 1, WhScrn 2, WhoHol B*
Irwin, Boyd 1880-1957 *WhScrn 1, WhScrn 2, WhoHol B*
Irwin, Boyd 1880-1963 *Film 2, TwYS*
Irwin, Caroline *Film 2*
Irwin, Charles W 1888-1969 *WhScrn 1, WhScrn 2, WhoHol B*
Irwin, Edward 1867-1937 *NotNAT B, WhThe*
Irwin, Felix d1950 *NotNAT B*
Irwin, Flo d1930 *NotNAT B*
Irwin, Gene 1916- *AmSCAP 1966*
Irwin, John *Film 2*
Irwin, Lois 1926- *AmSCAP 1966*
Irwin, May *MotPP*
Irwin, May 1862- *TwYS, WhoStg 1906, WhoStg 1908*
Irwin, May 1862-1938 *FamA&A, Film 1,*

NotNAT B, WhThe
Irwin, May 1862-1958 *WhScrn 1, WhScrn 2, WhoHol B*
Irwin, Wallace 1875-1959 *WhScrn 2*
Irwin, Will 1874-1948 *WhScrn 2*
Irwin, Will 1907- *BiE&WWA, NotNAT*
Irwin, William 1923- *AmSCAP 1966*
Irwin, William C K 1907- *AmSCAP 1966*
Irwin, Wynn *WhoHol A*
Isaac, Merle J 1898- *AmSCAP 1966*
Isaacs, Alvin K 1904- *AmSCAP 1966*
Isaacs, Barbara *WomWMM A, WomWMM B*
Isaacs, Edith Juliet 1878-1956 *NotNAT B, OxThe, WhThe*
Isaacs, Isadore Ike 1901-1957 *WhScrn 1, WhScrn 2*
Isaacs, Phil 1922- *IntMPA 1977*
Isaacson, Carl L 1920- *BiE&WWA, NotNAT*
Isbert, Jose 1884-1966 *WhScrn 1, WhScrn 2*
Iselin, John Jay *NewYTET*
Isham, Frederic S d1922 *NotNAT B*
Isham, Sir Gyles 1903-1976 *WhThe, WhoHol C*
Isherwood, Christopher 1904- *CelR 3, CnMD, ConDr 1977, McGWD, ModWD, PIP&P, WhThe*
Ishii, Kan 1901-1972 *WhScrn 2*
Ising, Rudolph *DcFM*
Isler, Helen J *AmSCAP 1966*
Isler, Justus F *AmSCAP 1966*
Ismai, Osman *DcFM*
Isola, Emile d1945 *NotNAT B*
Isola, Vincent d1947 *NotNAT B*
Israel, Larry H *NewYTET*
Itkin, Bella 1920- *BiE&WWA, NotNAT*
Ito, Daisuke 1898- *DcFM*
Ito, Robert *WhoHol A*
Iturbi, Amparo 1899-1969 *WhScrn 2, WhoHol B*
Iturbi, Jose 1895- *CelR 3, FilmgC, MGM, MovMk, WhoHol A*
Ivan, Rosalind 1884-1959 *FilmgC, MovMk, NotNAT B, WhScrn 1, WhScrn 2, WhoHol B*
Ivan, Rosiland *MotPP*
Ivano, Paul 1900- *FilmgC, IntMPA 1977*
Ivanoff, Rose 1908- *AmSCAP 1966*
Ivanov, I *Film 2*
Ivanov, Vsevolod Vyacheslavovich 1895-1963 *CnMD, McGWD, ModWD, OxThe, PIP&P*
Ivashov, Vladimir *WhoHol A*
Ivens, Joris 1898- *BiDFlm, DcFM, FilmgC, MovMk, OxFilm, WorEnF*
Ivers, James D d1964 *NotNAT B*
Ivers, Julia Crawford *WomWMM*
Ives, Anne 1892?- *NotNAT*
Ives, Burl 1909- *AmSCAP 1966, BiE&WWA, CmMov, FilmgC, IntMPA 1977, MotPP, MovMk, NotNAT, PIP&P, WhoHol A, WhoThe 16, WorEnF*
Ives, Charlotte *Film 1*
Ives, Douglas d1969 *WhScrn 1, WhScrn 2, WhoHol B*
Ives, George *WhoHol A*
Ivins, Perry 1895-1963 *WhScrn 2*
Ivins, Sidna Beth *Film 2*
Ivor, Frances *WhThe*
Ivory, James 1928- *FilmgC, OxFilm*
Ivory, James 1930- *BiDFlm, WorEnF*
Iwaszkiewicz, Jaroslaw 1894- *CnMD, ModWD*
Iwerks, Ub 1900-1971 *FilmgC*
Iwerks, Ub 1901-1971 *DcFM, OxFilm, WorEnF*
Izard, Winifred *Film 2*
Izay, Victor *WhoHol A*
Izenour, George 1912- *BiE&WWA, NotNAT*
Izumo, Takeda 1691-1756 *CnThe, REnWD*

Izvitzkaya, Isolda 1933-1971 *WhScrn 2*

J

Jaccard, Jacques 1885- *TwYS A*
Jack, T C 1882-1954 *WhScrn 1, WhScrn 2,
  WhoHol B*
Jack And Evelyn *WhThe*
Jacker, Corinne *NatPD*
Jacker, Corrine *NewYTET*
Jackie, Bill d1954 *WhoHol B*
Jackie, William 1890-1954 *WhScrn 1, WhScrn 2*
Jackley, George d1950 *NotNAT B*
Jackman, Fred 1881- *TwYS A*
Jackman, Isaac *NotNAT B*
Jacks, Robert L 1922- *FilmgC, IntMPA 1977*
Jackson, Andrew, IV 1887-1953 *WhScrn 1,
  WhScrn 2*
Jackson, Anne *MotPP, WhoHol A*
Jackson, Anne 1924- *MovMk*
Jackson, Anne 1925- *FilmgC*
Jackson, Anne 1926- *BiE&WWA, NotNAT,
  WhoThe 16*
Jackson, Babs *WomWMM B*
Jackson, Barry *WhoHol A*
Jackson, Sir Barry Vincent 1878-1961 *CnThe,
  PIP&P*
Jackson, Sir Barry Vincent 1879-1961 *NotNAT A,
  NotNAT B, OxThe, WhThe*
Jackson, Bee *Film 2*
Jackson, Brian 1931- *IntMPA 1977*
Jackson, Bud *Film 2*
Jackson, C D 1902- *BiE&WWA*
Jackson, Charles *Film 1*
Jackson, Charles 1903-1968 *NotNAT B*
Jackson, Charlotte *Film 2*
Jackson, Colette d1969 *WhoHol B*
Jackson, Collette d1969 *WhScrn 2*
Jackson, Eddie 1896?- *WhoHol A*
Jackson, Ernestine *NotNAT, PIP&P A*
Jackson, Ethel *WhScrn 1, WhScrn 2*
Jackson, Ethel 1877-1957 *NotNAT B, WhThe*
Jackson, Ethel Shannon *WhScrn 1, WhScrn 2*
Jackson, Eugene *Film 2, WhoHol A*
Jackson, Franz 1912- *AmSCAP 1966*
Jackson, Freda 1909- *FilmgC, IntMPA 1977,
  PIP&P, WhoHol A, WhoThe 16*
Jackson, Frederic 1886-1953 *WhThe*
Jackson, Glenda *WhoHol A*
Jackson, Glenda 1936- *CelR 3, OxFilm,
  WhoThe 16*
Jackson, Glenda 1937- *FilmgC*
Jackson, Glenda 1938- *IntMPA 1977, MovMk*
Jackson, Glenna *WomWMM B*
Jackson, Gordon 1923- *FilmgC, IntMPA 1977,
  WhoHol A, WhoThe 16*
Jackson, Greig Stewart 1918- *AmSCAP 1966*
Jackson, Henry 1912- *CelR 3*
Jackson, Henry 1927-1973 *WhScrn 2*
Jackson, Howard Manucy 1900- *AmSCAP 1966*

Jackson, Jay *IntMPA 1977*
Jackson, Jennie d1976 *WhoHol C*
Jackson, Jesse 1941- *CelR 3*
Jackson, Jill 1913- *AmSCAP 1966*
Jackson, Joe d1942 *NotNAT B, WhoHol B*
Jackson, Joe Shoeless 1875-1942 *Film 1*
Jackson, John d1806 *NotNAT B*
Jackson, John Henry 1916- *IntMPA 1977*
Jackson, Kate *WhoHol A*
Jackson, Keith *NewYTET*
Jackson, Leonard *WhoHol A*
Jackson, Lisa *WomWMM B*
Jackson, Mahalia 1911-1972 *WhScrn 2,
  WhoHol B*
Jackson, Mary *WhoHol A*
Jackson, Mary Ann 1923- *Film 2, TwYS*
Jackson, Mike 1888-1945 *AmSCAP 1966*
Jackson, Nagle 1936- *NotNAT*
Jackson, Nelson 1870- *WhThe*
Jackson, Pat 1916- *FilmgC, WorEnF*
Jackson, Peaches *Film 1, Film 2, TwYS*
Jackson, R Eugene 1941- *NatPD*
Jackson, Roy William 1907- *AmSCAP 1966*
Jackson, Sammy *WhoHol A*
Jackson, Selmer 1888-1971 *Film 2, Vers B,
  WhScrn 2, WhoHol B*
Jackson, Sherry *WhoHol A*
Jackson, Thomas 1886-1967 *MovMk, WhScrn 1,
  WhScrn 2*
Jackson, Thomas E 1895-1967 *Film 2, Vers A,
  WhoHol B*
Jackson, Warren 1893-1950 *WhScrn 1,
  WhScrn 2, WhoHol B*
Jackson Five *CelR 3*
Jackter, Norman 1922- *IntMPA 1977*
Jackter, Rube 1900- *IntMPA 1977*
Jacob, Martin *Film 2*
Jacob, Naomi 1889-1964 *NotNAT A,
  NotNAT B, WhThe*
Jacobi, Derek 1938- *PIP&P, WhoHol A,
  WhoThe 16*
Jacobi, Frederick 1891-1952 *AmSCAP 1966*
Jacobi, Lou 1913- *BiE&WWA, NotNAT,
  WhoHol A, WhoThe 16*
Jacobi, Maurice d1939 *NotNAT B*
Jacobi, Victor 1883-1921 *NotNAT B*
Jacobs, Al 1903- *AmSCAP 1966*
Jacobs, Angela 1893-1951 *WhScrn 1, WhScrn 2,
  WhoHol B*
Jacobs, Arthur P 1918-1973 *FilmgC*
Jacobs, Barry 1924- *IntMPA 1977*
Jacobs, Billy *Film 1*
Jacobs, Dick 1918- *AmSCAP 1966*
Jacobs, Dorothy *WomWMM B*
Jacobs, Elaine *WomWMM B*
Jacobs, Jim 1942- *ConDr 1977D, NatPD*

Jacobs, Lewis 1906- *OxFilm*
Jacobs, Morris 1906- *BiE&WWA, NotNAT*
Jacobs, Morton P 1917- *AmSCAP 1966*
Jacobs, Naomi *Film 2*
Jacobs, Newton P 1900- *IntMPA 1977*
Jacobs, Paul *Film 1*
Jacobs, Sally 1932- *WhoThe 16*
Jacobs, William Wymark 1863-1943 *NotNAT B, WhThe*
Jacobsen, L H d1941 *NotNAT B*
Jacobson, Denise *WomWMM B*
Jacobson, H J *Film 2*
Jacobson, Irving 1905- *BiE&WWA, NotNAT*
Jacobson, Lilly *Film 2*
Jacobson, Sam d1964 *NotNAT B*
Jacobson, Sidney 1929- *AmSCAP 1966*
Jacobson, Sol 1912- *BiE&WWA, NotNAT*
Jacobsson, Ulla 1929- *FilmgC, WhoHol A, WorEnF*
Jacoby, Elliott 1902- *AmSCAP 1966*
Jacoby, Frank David 1925- *IntMPA 1977*
Jacoby, Joseph 1942- *IntMPA 1977*
Jacoby, Scott *WhoHol A*
Jacon, Bernard *IntMPA 1977*
Jacopetti, Gualtiero 1922- *WorEnF*
Jacopone Da Todi 1230?-1306 *McGWD, REnWD*
Jacoupy, Jacqueline *WomWMM B*
Jacoves, Felix 1907- *FilmgC*
Jacques, Hattie 1924- *FilmgC, WhoHol A, WhoThe 16*
Jacques, Robert C 1919- *IntMPA 1977*
Jacquet, Gaston *Film 2*
Jadot, Jacquemin *OxThe*
Jaeckel, Richard 1926- *FilmgC, IntMPA 1977, MotPP, MovMk, Vers A, WhoHol A*
Jaeger, Albert 1910- *IntMPA 1977*
Jaeger, Andrew P 1917- *IntMPA 1977*
Jaenzon, Julius 1885-1961 *DcFM*
Jaffe, Ben 1902- *AmSCAP 1966*
Jaffe, Carl 1902-1974 *FilmgC, WhScrn 2, WhoHol B*
Jaffe, Henry *NewYTET*
Jaffe, Herb *BiE&WWA, IntMPA 1977*
Jaffe, Leo 1909- *IntMPA 1977*
Jaffe, Moe 1901- *AmSCAP 1966*
Jaffe, Pat *WomWMM B*
Jaffe, Patricia Lewis *WomWMM*
Jaffe, Sam *MotPP, WhoHol A*
Jaffe, Sam 1893- *BiE&WWA, NotNAT, WhoThe 16*
Jaffe, Sam 1896- *IntMPA 1977, MovMk*
Jaffe, Sam 1897- *FilmgC*
Jaffe, Sam 1901- *IntMPA 1977*
Jaffe, Stanley R 1940- *IntMPA 1977*
Jaffe, William B 1904- *IntMPA 1977*
Jaffey, Herbert *IntMPA 1977*
Jaggard, William 1568-1623 *NotNAT B*
Jagger, Dean *MotPP, WhoHol A*
Jagger, Dean 1903- *Film 2, FilmgC, IntMPA 1977, MovMk*
Jagger, Dean 1904- *WhThe*
Jagger, Mick 1939- *CelR 3, FilmgC, WhoHol A*
Jagoda, Barry *NewYTET*
Jahn, Hans Henny 1894-1959 *CroCD*
Jahncke, Ernest Lee, Jr. 1912- *IntMPA 1977*
Jahnn, Hans Henny 1894-1959 *CnMD, McGWD, ModWD*
Jahr, Adolf 1894-1964 *NotNAT B, WhScrn 1, WhScrn 2*
Jakubowska, Wanda 1907- *DcFM, OxFilm, WomWMM, WorEnF*
Jalland, Henry 1861-1928 *NotNAT B, WhThe*
Jallaud, Sylvia *WomWMM*
James, Alf P 1865-1946 *WhScrn 1, WhScrn 2*

James, Alfred P 1865-1946 *WhoHol B*
James, Art d1972 *WhoHol B*
James, Ben 1921-1966 *WhScrn 2*
James, Billy 1895-1965 *AmSCAP 1966*
James, Cairns d1946 *NotNAT B*
James, Charles James d1888 *NotNAT B*
James, Claire *WhoHol A*
James, Clifton *WhoHol A*
James, Clifton 1898-1963 *NotNAT B, WhScrn 1, WhoHol B*
James, Clifton 1921- *BiE&WWA, NotNAT*
James, Clifton 1922- *IntMPA 1977*
James, Daisy *WhThe*
James, David *Film 2*
James, David 1839-1893 *NotNAT B, OxThe*
James, David, Jr. d1917 *NotNAT B*
James, Dennis 1917- *IntMPA 1977, NewYTET*
James, Eddie 1880-1944 *Film 2, WhScrn 1, WhScrn 2, WhoHol B*
James, Emrys 1930- *WhoHol A, WhoThe 16*
James, Forrest *Film 2*
James, Francis 1907- *WhThe*
James, Freeman Kelly, Jr. 1927- *AmSCAP 1966*
James, Gardner *Film 2*
James, Gerald d1964 *NotNAT B*
James, Gerald 1917- *WhoThe 16*
James, Gladden 1892-1948 *Film 1, Film 2, WhScrn 1, WhScrn 2, WhoHol B*
James, Gordon *Film 2*
James, Harry 1916- *AmSCAP 1966, FilmgC, HolP 40, IntMPA 1977, MovMk, WhoHol A*
James, Henry 1843-1916 *CnMD, CnThe, McGWD, ModWD, NotNAT B, OxThe, REnWD*
James, Horace D 1853-1925 *Film 2, NotNAT B, WhScrn 1, WhScrn 2, WhoHol B*
James, Inez Eleanor 1919- *AmSCAP 1966*
James, J Wharton *Film 2*
James, Jean Eileen 1934- *AmSCAP 1966*
James, Jesse 1847-1882 *OxFilm*
James, John d1960 *WhScrn 1, WhScrn 2, WhoHol B*
James, Julia 1890-1964 *NotNAT A, NotNAT B, WhThe*
James, Kate d1913 *NotNAT B*
James, Laura 1933- *IntMPA 1977*
James, Louis 1842-1910 *NotNAT B, OxThe, WhoStg 1908*
James, Marion 1913- *AmSCAP 1966*
James, Millie 1876- *WhoStg 1908*
James, Monique *WomWMM*
James, Olga *WhoHol A*
James, Peter 1940- *WhoThe 16*
James, Philip 1890- *AmSCAP 1966*
James, Polly 1941- *IntMPA 1977, WhoThe 16*
James, Rian d1953 *NotNAT B*
James, Richard H 1931- *NotNAT*
James, Ruth d1970 *WhScrn 2, WhoHol B*
James, Sheila *WhoHol A*
James, Sid 1913- *FilmgC*
James, Sidney *WhoHol A*
James, Walter 1886-1946 *Film 2, WhScrn 1, WhScrn 2, WhoHol B*
James, Will 1896- *AmSCAP 1966*
James, William *Film 2*
James, Wilson 1872- *WhThe*
Jameson, Amable *Film 2*
Jameson, House 1902-1971 *BiE&WWA, NotNAT B*
Jameson, House 1903-1971 *PIP&P, WhScrn 1, WhScrn 2, WhoHol B*
Jameson, Joyce 1932- *BiE&WWA, NotNAT, WhoHol A*

Jameson, Pauline 1920- *WhoHol A, WhoThe 16*
Jameyson, H E 1894- *IntMPA 1977*
Jamiaque, Yves 1922- *CnMD*
Jamieson, W H 1907- *IntMPA 1977*
Jamin, Georges 1907-1971 *WhScrn 1, WhScrn 2*
Jamison, Anne 1910-1961 *WhScrn 2, WhoHol B*
Jamison, Bud 1894-1943 *WhoHol B*
Jamison, Bud 1894-1944 *FilmgC*
Jamison, Marshall 1918- *BiE&WWA*
Jamison, William Bud 1894-1943 *Film 1, Film 2, TwYS*
Jamison, William Bud 1894-1944 *WhScrn 1, WhScrn 2*
Jamois, Marguerite 1901-1964 *WhScrn 2*
Jampolis, Neil Peter 1943- *NotNAT*
Jana, La *Film 2*
Janauschek, Fanny 1830-1904 *FamA&A*
Janauschek, Francesca Romana Maddalena 1830-1904 *OxThe*
Janauschek, Francesca Romana Magdalena 1830-1904 *NotNAT B*
Jancso, Miklos 1921- *BiDFlm, DcFM, FilmgC, OxFilm, WorEnF*
Janes, Kenneth H *BiE&WWA, NotNAT*
Jang, Amir *Film 2*
Janin, Jules-Gabriel 1804-1874 *NotNAT B, OxThe*
Janis, Byron 1928- *CelR 3*
Janis, Conrad *MotPP*
Janis, Conrad 1926- *FilmgC*
Janis, Conrad 1928- *BiE&WWA, NotNAT, WhoHol A, WhoThe 16*
Janis, Dorothy 1910- *Film 2, TwYS*
Janis, Elsie 1889-1956 *AmSCAP 1966, EncMT, FamA&A, Film 1, Film 2, FilmgC, NotNAT A, NotNAT B, TwYS, WhScrn 1, WhScrn 2, WhThe, WhoHol B, WhoStg 1906, WhoStg 1908*
Janis, Harold E 1906- *IntMPA 1977*
Janis, Joan Gardner 1926- *AmSCAP 1966*
Janis, Stephen 1907- *AmSCAP 1966*
Janney, Ben 1927- *BiE&WWA, NotNAT*
Janney, Leon 1917- *BiE&WWA, Film 2, NotNAT, WhoHol A*
Janney, Russell 1884-1963 *WhThe*
Janney, William 1908-1938 *Film 2, WhScrn 2*
Janni, Joseph 1916- *FilmgC, IntMPA 1977*
Jannings, Emil d1950 *MotPP, WhoHol B*
Jannings, Emil 1884-1950 *BiDFlm, FilmgC, TwYS, WorEnF*
Jannings, Emil 1886-1950 *Film 1, Film 2, MovMk, NotNAT B, OxFilm, WhScrn 1, WhScrn 2*
Jans, Harry 1900-1962 *NotNAT B, WhScrn 1, WhScrn 2, WhoHol B*
Jansen, Harry A *WhScrn 1, WhScrn 2*
Jansen, Marie 1857-1914 *NotNAT B, WhoStg 1906, WhoStg 1908*
Janson, Victor 1885-1960 *Film 2, WhScrn 1, WhScrn 2, WhoHol B*
Janssen, David *MotPP, WhoHol A*
Janssen, David 1930- *FilmgC, MovMk*
Janssen, David 1931- *IntMPA 1977*
Janssen, Walter *Film 2*
Janssen, Werner 1900- *AmSCAP 1966*
January, Lois *WhoHol A*
Janus, Dianne Rock *WomWMM B*
Janvier, Emma d1924 *NotNAT B*
Jaquet, Frank 1885-1958 *WhScrn 2*
Jaray, Hans *Film 2*
Jarbeau, Vernona d1914 *NotNAT B*
Jardiel Poncela, Enrique 1901-1952 *CnMD, CroCD, McGWD, ModWD*
Jardine, Betty d1945 *NotNAT B, WhThe*

Jardon, Dorothy 1889- *AmSCAP 1966*
Jardon, Edward *Film 2*
Jarman, Claude, Jr. 1934- *FilmgC, IntMPA 1977, MGM, MotPP, MovMk, WhoHol A*
Jarman, Herbert 1871-1919 *NotNAT B, WhThe*
Jarmin, Jill *WhoHol A*
Jaroslawzeff, W *Film 2*
Jaroslow, Ruth *WhoHol A*
Jarratt, Alfred *IntMPA 1977*
Jarre, Maurice 1924- *CmMov, DcFM, FilmgC, IntMPA 1977, OxFilm, WorEnF*
Jarrett, Arthur L 1888-1960 *WhScrn 1, WhScrn 2, WhoHol B*
Jarrett, Dan 1894-1938 *WhScrn 1, WhScrn 2, WhoHol B*
Jarrett, Henry C d1886 *NotNAT B*
Jarrett, Henry C d1903 *NotNAT B*
Jarrico, Paul 1915- *IntMPA 1977*
Jarriel, Tom *NewYTET*
Jarrott, Charles 1927- *FilmgC, IntMPA 1977*
Jarry, Alfred 1873-1907 *CnMD, CnThe, McGWD, ModWD, NotNAT B, OxThe, REnWD*
Jarva, Risto 1934- *WorEnF*
Jarvis, Al 1909-1970 *AmSCAP 1966*
Jarvis, Al 1910-1970 *WhScrn 1, WhScrn 2, WhoHol B*
Jarvis, Barbara A *WomWMM B*
Jarvis, Jean 1903-1933 *WhScrn 1, WhScrn 2, WhoHol B*
Jarvis, Laura E 1866-1933 *WhScrn 1, WhScrn 2*
Jarvis, Lucy *NewYTET*
Jarvis, Robert C 1892-1971 *WhScrn 1, WhScrn 2, WhoHol B*
Jarvis, Sidney *Film 2*
Jarvis, Sydney 1881-1939 *WhScrn 1, WhScrn 2, WhoHol B*
Jashenko, Elena *WomWMM*
Jasmina, Arthur *Film 2*
Jasmyn, Joan 1898-1955 *AmSCAP 1966*
Jasny, Vojtech 1925- *DcFM, WorEnF*
Jason, Alfred P 1914- *AmSCAP 1966*
Jason, Leigh 1904- *FilmgC, IntMPA 1977*
Jason, Mitchell *WhoHol A*
Jason, Rick *MotPP, WhoHol A*
Jason, Rick 1926- *IntMPA 1977*
Jason, Rick 1929- *FilmgC*
Jason, Sybil 1929- *FilmgC, ThFT, WhoHol A*
Jason, Will 1899-1970 *FilmgC*
Jason, Will 1910- *AmSCAP 1966*
Jasper, Suzanne 1945- *WomWMM B*
Jasper, Thena *Film 2*
Jasset, Victorin 1862-1913 *DcFM, WorEnF*
Jassim, Linda *WomWMM A, WomWMM B*
Jasspe, Arthur *NatPD*
Jaubert, Maurice 1900-1940 *DcFM, FilmgC, OxFilm, WorEnF*
Jaudenes, Jose Alvares Lepe 1891-1967 *WhScrn 1, WhScrn 2*
Javits, Jacob 1904- *CelR 3*
Javits, Joan 1928- *AmSCAP 1966*
Javor, Pal 1902-1959 *WhScrn 1, WhScrn 2*
Javor, Paul d1959 *WhoHol B*
Jay, Dorothy 1897- *WhThe*
Jay, Ernest d1957 *WhoHol B*
Jay, Ernest 1893-1957 *NotNAT B, WhScrn 2, WhThe*
Jay, Ernest 1894-1957 *FilmgC, WhScrn 1*
Jay, Harriet 1863-1932 *NotNAT B*
Jay, Harriett 1863-1932 *WhThe*
Jay, Isabel 1879-1927 *NotNAT B, WhThe*
Jay, Jean *Film 2*
Jay, John Herbert 1871-1942 *NotNAT B, WhThe*
Jay, Morty 1924- *IntMPA 1977*

Jayne, Susan WhoHol A
Jayston, Michael 1936- FilmgC, WhoHol A,
  WhoThe 16
Jeakins, Dorothy 1914- BiE&WWA, NotNAT
Jean Film 1
Jean, Madame Film 2
Jean, Elsie 1907-1953 AmSCAP 1966
Jean, Gloria MotPP
Jean, Gloria 1927- ThFT
Jean, Gloria 1928- FilmgC, MovMk, WhoHol A
Jeanmaire WhoHol A
Jeanmaire, Zizi 1924- BiE&WWA, FilmgC
Jeanmarie, Renee MotPP
Jeans, Isabel 1891- Film 1, Film 2, FilmgC,
  Vers B, WhoHol A, WhoThe 16
Jeans, Ronald 1887- WhThe
Jeans, Ursula 1906-1973 Film 2, FilmgC,
  NotNAT B, PIP&P, WhScrn 2, WhThe,
  WhoHol B
Jeanson, Henri 1900-1970 DcFM, FilmgC,
  WorEnF
Jeayes, Allan 1885-1963 Film 2, FilmgC,
  NotNAT B, WhScrn 1, WhScrn 2, WhThe,
  WhoHol B
Jecks, Clara d1951 NotNAT B, WhThe
Jedd, Gerry 1924-1962 NotNAT B
Jedynak, Edward S 1922- AmSCAP 1966
Jeffee, Saul 1918- IntMPA 1977
Jefferies, Douglas 1884-1959 NotNAT B, WhThe,
  WhoHol B
Jefferies, James J Film 2
Jeffers, John S 1874-1939 WhScrn 1, WhScrn 2
Jeffers, Robinson 1887-1962 CnMD, McGWD,
  ModWD, NotNAT A, NotNAT B
Jeffers, William L 1898-1959 WhScrn 1,
  WhScrn 2, WhoHol B
Jefferson, Ben PIP&P A
Jefferson, Charles Burke 1851-1908 NotNAT B,
  OxThe
Jefferson, Cornelia Frances Thomas 1796-1849
  NotNAT B, OxThe
Jefferson, Daisy 1889-1967 WhScrn 2, WhoHol B
Jefferson, Herbert Farjeon 1887-1945 OxThe
Jefferson, Hilton W 1902-1968 WhScrn 1,
  WhScrn 2, WhoHol B
Jefferson, Joseph 1774-1832 FamA&A,
  NotNAT B, OxThe, PIP&P
Jefferson, Joseph 1804-1842 NotNAT B, OxThe
Jefferson, Joseph 1829-1905 FamA&A, Film 1,
  NotNAT A, NotNAT B, OxThe, PIP&P,
  REnWD, WhScrn 2, WhoHol B
Jefferson, Joseph Warren d1919 NotNAT B
Jefferson, Thomas 1732-1797 NotNAT B
Jefferson, Thomas 1732-1807 OxThe
Jefferson, Thomas 1859-1923 Film 1, Film 2
Jefferson, Thomas 1859-1932 NotNAT B, TwYS,
  WhScrn 1, WhScrn 2, WhoHol B
Jefferson, William Film 1
Jefferson, William Winter d1946 NotNAT B,
  WhScrn 2
Jefferson Airplane CelR 3
Jefford, Barbara WhoHol A
Jefford, Barbara 1930- BiE&WWA, CnThe,
  NotNAT, WhoThe 16
Jefford, Barbara 1931- FilmgC
Jeffrey, Michael 1895-1960 WhScrn 1, WhScrn 2,
  WhoHol B
Jeffrey, Peter 1929- FilmgC, WhoHol A,
  WhoThe 16
Jeffreys, Anne IntMPA 1977, MotPP
Jeffreys, Anne 1923- FilmgC, MovMk,
  WhoHol A, WhoThe 16
Jeffreys, Anne 1928- BiE&WWA, NotNAT
Jeffreys, Ellis d1943 WhoHol B

Jeffreys, Ellis 1868-1943 WhoStg 1906,
  WhoStg 1908
Jeffreys, Ellis 1872-1943 NotNAT B, WhThe
Jeffreys, Ellis 1877-1943 WhScrn 1, WhScrn 2
Jeffreys-Goodfriend, Ida d1926 NotNAT B
Jeffries, Fran WhoHol A
Jeffries, Herb AmSCAP 1966
Jeffries, James J 1875-1953 Film 1, Film 2,
  WhScrn 2
Jeffries, Lang WhoHol A
Jeffries, Lionel 1926- FilmgC, IntMPA 1977,
  MovMk, WhoHol A
Jeffries, Maud 1869-1946 NotNAT B, WhThe
Jeffries, Maud 1870- WhoStg 1906,
  WhoStg 1908
Jeffrys, George d1755 NotNAT B
Jehanne, Edith Film 2
Jehlinger, Charles 1866-1952 NotNAT B
Jelesnik, Eugene 1914- AmSCAP 1966
Jelinek, Milena WomWMM B
Jellicoe, Ann 1927- CnThe, ConDr 1977, CroCD,
  McGWD, ModWD, NotNAT, REnWD,
  WhoThe 16
Jelliffe, Rowena Woodham 1892- BiE&WWA,
  NotNAT
Jencks, Richard W NewYTET
Jenkins, Allen d1974 MotPP, WhoHol B
Jenkins, Allen 1890?-1974 WhScrn 2
Jenkins, Allen 1900- FilmgC, IntMPA 1977,
  MovMk, Vers A
Jenkins, Butch MotPP
Jenkins, Butch see also Jenkins, Jackie Butch
Jenkins, Charles 1941- IntMPA 1977
Jenkins, Charles Francis 1868-1934 DcFM,
  NewYTET
Jenkins, Dan 1916- IntMPA 1977
Jenkins, David NotNAT
Jenkins, Elizabeth 1879-1965 WhScrn 1,
  WhScrn 2, WhoHol B
Jenkins, Ella 1924- AmSCAP 1966
Jenkins, George BiE&WWA, IntMPA 1977,
  NotNAT, WhoThe 16
Jenkins, Gordon 1910- AmSCAP 1966
Jenkins, Harry NatPD
Jenkins, J W Film 2
Jenkins, Jackie Butch 1937- MGM, MovMk
Jenkins, Jackie Butch 1938- FilmgC, WhoHol A
Jenkins, Jackie Butch see also Jenkins, Butch
Jenkins, Joseph Willcox 1928- AmSCAP 1966
Jenkins, Joyce WomWMM B
Jenkins, Megs 1917- FilmgC, WhoHol A,
  WhoThe 16
Jenkins, R Claud 1878-1967 WhThe
Jenkins, Warren WhoThe 16
Jenks, Frank d1962 MotPP, NotNAT B,
  WhoHol B
Jenks, Frank 1902-1962 FilmgC, WhScrn 1,
  WhScrn 2
Jenks, Frank 1903-1962 Vers A
Jenks, Lulu Burns 1870-1939 WhScrn 1,
  WhScrn 2
Jenks, Si 1876-1970 Vers B, WhScrn 2,
  WhoHol B
Jenner, Caryl 1917- WhThe
Jennings, Al 1864-1961 WhScrn 1, WhScrn 2,
  WhoHol B
Jennings, Al 1864-1962 Film 1, Film 2
Jennings, Anna Film 2
Jennings, Claudia WhoHol A
Jennings, DeWitt 1879-1937 Film 1, Film 2,
  NotNAT B, TwYS, WhScrn 1, WhScrn 2,
  WhoHol B
Jennings, Gertrude E d1958 NotNAT B, WhThe
Jennings, Gladys 1902- Film 1, Film 2

Jennings, Hilde *Film 2*
Jennings, Humphrey 1907-1950 *BiDFlm, DcFM,
   FilmgC, OxFilm, WorEnF*
Jennings, Jane *Film 2*
Jennings, John 1933- *AmSCAP 1966*
Jennings, S E *Film 1*
Jennings, Talbot *CmMov, IntMPA 1977*
Jennings, Waylon *WhoHol A*
Jennings, William S 1942- *AmSCAP 1966*
Jenoure, Aida *WhThe*
Jens, Salome 1935- *BiE&WWA, FilmgC, MotPP,
   NotNAT, WhoHol A, WhoThe 16*
Jensen, Eugen *Film 2*
Jensen, Eulalie *Film 1, Film 2, TwYS*
Jensen, Frederick *Film 2*
Jensen, Karen *WhoHol A*
Jensen, Sterling *WhoHol A*
Jenson, Roy *WhoHol A*
Jentes, Harry 1897-1958 *AmSCAP 1966*
Jephcott, Samuel C 1944- *IntMPA 1977*
Jephson, Robert d1803 *NotNAT B*
Jepson, Helen 1905- *WhoHol A*
Jergens, Adele 1922- *FilmgC, IntMPA 1977,
   MotPP, WhoHol A*
Jergens, Diane *MotPP, WhoHol A*
Jermingham, Edward d1812 *NotNAT B*
Jerome, Ben M d1938 *NotNAT B*
Jerome, Daisy 1881- *WhThe*
Jerome, Edwin 1884-1959 *NotNAT B, WhScrn 1,
   WhScrn 2, WhoHol B*
Jerome, Elmer 1872-1947 *WhScrn 2*
Jerome, Helen 1883- *WhThe*
Jerome, Henry 1917- *AmSCAP 1966*
Jerome, Jerome 1906-1964 *AmSCAP 1966*
Jerome, Jerome Klapka 1859-1927 *McGWD,
   ModWD, NotNAT A, NotNAT B, OxThe,
   WhThe, WhoStg 1908*
Jerome, M K *Film 2*
Jerome, M K 1893- *AmSCAP 1966*
Jerome, Maude Nugent 1877-1958 *AmSCAP 1966*
Jerome, Peter 1893-1967 *WhScrn 1, WhScrn 2*
Jerome, Rowena 1890- *WhThe*
Jerome, Sadie 1876-1950 *NotNAT B, WhThe*
Jerome, William 1865-1932 *AmSCAP 1966,
   NotNAT B*
Jerrett, Jean 1924- *AmSCAP 1966*
Jerrold, Douglas William 1803-1857 *McGWD,
   NotNAT B, OxThe*
Jerrold, Mary 1877-1955 *FilmgC, NotNAT B,
   WhScrn 1, WhScrn 2, WhThe, WhoHol B*
Jerrold, William Blanchard 1826-1884 *NotNAT B,
   OxThe*
Jersey, Gwen *WomWMM B*
Jeske, George 1891-1951 *WhScrn 1, WhScrn 2,
   WhoHol B*
Jesse, Fryniwyd Tennyson d1958 *NotNAT B,
   WhThe*
Jesse, Stella 1897- *WhThe*
Jessel, George 1898- *AmSCAP 1966,
   BiE&WWA, CelR 3, CmMov, EncMT,
   Film 1, Film 2, FilmgC, IntMPA 1977,
   MovMk, NotNAT, NotNAT A, TwYS,
   WhoHol A, WhoThe 16*
Jessel, Ian 1939- *IntMPA 1977*
Jessel, Patricia 1920-1968 *BiE&WWA,
   NotNAT B, WhScrn 1, WhScrn 2, WhThe,
   WhoHol B*
Jessel, Patricia 1921-1968 *FilmgC*
Jessner, Leopold 1878-1945 *CnThe, NotNAT B,
   OxThe*
Jessop, George H d1915 *NotNAT B*
Jessua, Alain 1923- *WorEnF*
Jessua, Alain 1932- *FilmgC, OxFilm*
Jessup, Stanley 1878-1945 *NotNAT B, WhScrn 2*

Jessye, Eva Alberta 1895- *AmSCAP 1966*
Jett, Sheldon 1901-1960 *WhScrn 1, WhScrn 2,
   WhoHol B*
Jevon, Thomas d1688 *NotNAT B, OxThe*
Jew Baby *WhScrn 2*
Jewel, Betty *Film 2*
Jewel, Isabel 1913- *Vers A*
Jewel, Izetta 1883- *WhoStg 1908*
Jewell, Austin *Film 2*
Jewell, Isabel 1909-1972 *ThFT*
Jewell, Isabel 1910-1972 *MovMk, WhScrn 2,
   WhoHol B*
Jewell, Isabel 1913-1972 *FilmgC*
Jewell, Izetta 1883- *WhThe*
Jewell, James 1929- *BiE&WWA, NotNAT*
Jewett, Ethel *Film 1*
Jewett, Henry d1930 *NotNAT B, WhoStg 1906,
   WhoStg 1908*
Jewison, Norman 1926- *BiDFlm, FilmgC,
   IntMPA 1977, NewYTET, OxFilm, WorEnF*
Jewison, Norman 1927- *MovMk*
Jiggs d1932 *WhScrn 2*
Jiler, John 1946- *NatPD*
Jim Crow *OxThe*
Jiminez, Soledad 1874-1966 *WhScrn 1, WhScrn 2,
   WhoHol B*
Jiminez, Solidad 1874-1967 *Film 2*
Jimmy The Greek 1917?- *CelR 3*
Jingu, Miyoshi 1894-1969 *WhScrn 2, WhoHol B*
Joannon, Leo 1904-1969 *WorEnF*
Job, Thomas 1900-1947 *NotNAT B, WhThe*
Jobert, Marlene 1943- *FilmgC, WhoHol A*
Jobson, Edward *Film 2*
Joby, Hans 1884-1943 *WhScrn 1, WhScrn 2,
   WhoHol B*
Joddrell, Richard Paul d1831 *NotNAT B*
Jodelet 1600?-1660 *OxThe*
Jodelle, Etienne 1532-1573 *McGWD, OxThe*
Joel, Clara 1890- *WhThe*
Joel, Lydia *BiE&WWA*
Joels, Merrill E *IntMPA 1977*
Joffe, Charles H *IntMPA 1977*
Joffe, Edward *IntMPA 1977*
Joffre, Madame *Film 2*
Joffre, Monsieur *Film 2*
Johann, Zita 1904- *ThFT, WhThe, WhoHol A*
Johannsen, Cary 1939-1966 *WhScrn 1, WhScrn 2*
Johansen, Aud 1930- *WhThe*
Johansson, Ingemar *WhoHol A*
John, Alice d1956 *NotNAT B, WhoHol B*
John, Barbara *WomWMM*
John, Bertram *Film 2*
John, Elton 1947- *CelR 3, WhoHol A*
John, Errol 1925?- *CnMD, ConDr 1977,
   ModWD*
John, Evan 1901-1953 *NotNAT B, WhThe*
John, Georg *Film 2*
John, Graham 1887- *WhThe*
John, Rosamund 1913- *FilmgC, WhThe,
   WhoHol A*
Johns, Al 1878-1928 *AmSCAP 1966*
Johns, Bertram *Film 2*
Johns, Brooke *Film 2*
Johns, Eric 1907- *WhThe*
Johns, Florence *Film 2*
Johns, Glynis 1923- *BiE&WWA, FilmgC,
   IntMPA 1977, MotPP, MovMk, NotNAT,
   OxFilm, WhoHol A, WhoThe 16*
Johns, Harriette 1921- *WhoHol A, WhoThe 16*
Johns, Jasper 1930- *CelR 3*
Johns, Mark 1919- *IntMPA 1977*
Johns, Mervyn 1899- *FilmgC, IntMPA 1977,
   WhoHol A, WhoThe 16*
Johnson, A Emory 1894-1960 *WhScrn 1,*

WhScrn 2
Johnson, Agnes WomWMM
Johnson, Albert 1910-1967 BiE&WWA,
   NotNAT B
Johnson, Albert E 1912- BiE&WWA, NotNAT
Johnson, Ann Film 2
Johnson, Arch WhoHol A
Johnson, Arnold 1893- AmSCAP 1966
Johnson, Arte WhoHol A
Johnson, Arthur V 1876-1916 Film 1, TwYS,
   TwYS A, WhScrn 2, WhoHol B
Johnson, Ben 1919- CmMov, FilmgC,
   IntMPA 1977, MovMk, WhoHol A
Johnson, Bill 1918-1957 EncMT, WhScrn 2,
   WhThe, WhoHol B
Johnson, Buddy 1915- AmSCAP 1966
Johnson, Burges 1878-1963 WhScrn 2
Johnson, Cammilla Film 2
Johnson, Carmencita Film 2
Johnson, Celia 1908- BiDFlm, CnThe, FilmgC,
   IntMPA 1977, MotPP, MovMk, OxFilm,
   PIP&P, WhoHol A, WhoThe 16
Johnson, Charles d1748 NotNAT B
Johnson, Charles 1928- AmSCAP 1966
Johnson, Charles L 1876-1950 AmSCAP 1966
Johnson, Chic 1891-1962 FilmgC, MovMk,
   WhScrn 1, WhScrn 2, WhThe, WhoHol B
Johnson, Chick EncMT
Johnson, Chubby 1903-1974 WhScrn 2,
   WhoHol B
Johnson, Clint d1975 WhoHol C
Johnson, Dick Winslow Film 2
Johnson, Dolores Film 2
Johnson, Don WhoHol A
Johnson, Donna Lee WomWMM B
Johnson, Dotts WhoHol A
Johnson, Edith 1895-1969 Film 1, Film 2,
   MotPP, TwYS, WhScrn 1, WhScrn 2
Johnson, Edith see also Johnston, Edith
Johnson, Edward 1862-1925 WhScrn 1,
   WhScrn 2, WhoHol B
Johnson, Edward 1910-1961 AmSCAP 1966
Johnson, Elizabeth 1790-1810 NotNAT B, OxThe
Johnson, Emory d1960 Film 1, Film 2,
   NotNAT B, WhoHol B
Johnson, Ernest W Film 2
Johnson, Ethel May d1964 NotNAT B
Johnson, Florence 1902- BiE&WWA, NotNAT
Johnson, Fred WhoHol A
Johnson, G Griffith 1912- IntMPA 1977
Johnson, Greer 1920-1974 BiE&WWA,
   NotNAT B
Johnson, Hall 1888-1970 AmSCAP 1966,
   NotNAT B, WhScrn 2, WhoHol B
Johnson, Harold Ogden 1891-1962 NotNAT B
Johnson, Harold Victor 1918- AmSCAP 1966
Johnson, Helen WhoHol A
Johnson, Horace 1893-1964 AmSCAP 1966
Johnson, Howard B 1932- CelR 3
Johnson, Howard E 1887-1941 AmSCAP 1966
Johnson, Hunter 1906- AmSCAP 1966
Johnson, Isa d1941 NotNAT B
Johnson, J Bond 1926- IntMPA 1977
Johnson, J C 1896- AmSCAP 1966
Johnson, J George 1913- AmSCAP 1966
Johnson, J Rosamond 1873-1954 AmSCAP 1966,
   NotNAT B
Johnson, Jack 1878-1946 WhScrn 2
Johnson, James A 1917- AmSCAP 1966
Johnson, James P 1891-1955 AmSCAP 1966
Johnson, James Weldon 1871-1938 AmSCAP 1966
Johnson, Janet 1915- WhThe
Johnson, Jay 1928-1954 WhScrn 1, WhScrn 2,
   WhoHol B

Johnson, Jay W 1903- AmSCAP 1966
Johnson, Jean Film 2
Johnson, John H 1918- CelR 3
Johnson, Johnny PIP&P A
Johnson, Karen WomWMM A, WomWMM B
Johnson, Katie 1878-1957 FilmgC, MotPP,
   NotNAT B, WhScrn 1, WhScrn 2,
   WhoHol B
Johnson, Kay 1904-1975 Film 2, FilmgC,
   HolP 30, MotPP, ThFT, WhThe,
   WhoHol C
Johnson, Kay 1905?- MovMk
Johnson, Kenneth, II 1912-1974 WhoHol B
Johnson, Kenneth, II see also Johnson, S Kenneth, II
Johnson, Lady Bird 1912- CelR 3
Johnson, Lamont IntMPA 1977, WhoHol A
Johnson, Lamont 1920- FilmgC
Johnson, Lamont 1922- BiE&WWA, NotNAT
Johnson, Laraine WhoHol A
Johnson, Laurie 1927- IntMPA 1977
Johnson, Lawrence Film 2
Johnson, Lorimer George 1859-1941 Film 2,
   WhScrn 1, WhScrn 2, WhoHol B
Johnson, Louis 1930- NotNAT
Johnson, Lucile 1907- AmSCAP 1966
Johnson, Marion Pollock WhoStg 1906,
   WhoStg 1908
Johnson, Martin 1884-1937 DcFM, Film 1,
   Film 2, TwYS, TwYS A, TwYS B,
   WhScrn 2
Johnson, Mary Film 2
Johnson, Melodie WhoHol A
Johnson, Michael F 1915- IntMPA 1977
Johnson, Moffat 1886-1935 WhScrn 2
Johnson, Moffat see also Johnston, Moffat
Johnson, Molly 1903- WhThe
Johnson, Nicholas 1934- CelR 3, NewYTET
Johnson, Noble 1897- Film 1, Film 2, FilmgC,
   TwYS
Johnson, Norris Film 2
Johnson, Nunnally 1897- BiDFlm, CmMov,
   DcFM, FilmgC, IntMPA 1977, OxFilm,
   WorEnF
Johnson, Orrin 1865-1943 WhScrn 2, WhThe
Johnson, Osa 1894-1953 WhScrn 2, WomWMM
Johnson, Owen 1878- WhoStg 1908
Johnson, Page WhoHol A
Johnson, Pamela WomWMM B
Johnson, Pauline Film 2
Johnson, Pete K H 1904- AmSCAP 1966
Johnson, Philip 1900- WhThe
Johnson, Philip 1906- CelR 3
Johnson, Rafer 1935- CelR 3, FilmgC,
   WhoHol A
Johnson, Richard 1927- BiE&WWA, FilmgC,
   IntMPA 1977, MovMk, WhoHol A,
   WhoThe 16
Johnson, Rita d1965 MotPP, WhoHol B
Johnson, Rita 1912-1965 FilmgC, MGM, MovMk,
   ThFT
Johnson, Rita 1913-1965 WhScrn 1, WhScrn 2
Johnson, Russell IntMPA 1977, WhoHol A
Johnson, S Kenneth, II 1912-1974 WhScrn 2
Johnson, S Kenneth, II see also Johnson, Kenneth, II
Johnson, Samuel 1709-1784 NotNAT B, OxThe,
   PIP&P
Johnson, Searcy Lee 1908- AmSCAP 1966
Johnson, Sessel Ann Film 2
Johnson, Susan 1927- BiE&WWA, NotNAT
Johnson, Tefft 1887-1956 Film 1, Film 2,
   TwYS A, WhScrn 2
Johnson, Tor 1903-1971 WhScrn 2, WhoHol B
Johnson, Van 1916- BiDFlm, BiE&WWA,
   CelR 3, CmMov, FilmgC, IntMPA 1977,

MGM, MotPP, MovMk, OxFilm,
WhoHol A, WhoThe 16, WorEnF
Johnson, Virginia CelR 3
Johnson, W Gerald d1963 NotNAT B
Johnson, William 1912-1960 AmSCAP 1966
Johnson, William 1916-1957 NotNAT B,
WhScrn 1, WhScrn 2
Johnson, William Alexander 1931?-
AmSCAP 1966
Johnsrud, Harold d1939 NotNAT B
Johnston, Albert C, Jr. 1925- AmSCAP 1966
Johnston, Andrew Film 2
Johnston, Arthur James 1898-1954 AmSCAP 1966,
NotNAT B
Johnston, Denis 1901- BiE&WWA, CnMD,
CnThe, ConDr 1977, McGWD, ModWD,
NotNAT, OxThe, PIP&P, REnWD, WhThe
Johnston, Edith 1895-1969 WhoHol B
Johnston, Edith see also Johnson, Edith
Johnston, Eric A 1895-1963 DcFM, FilmgC
Johnston, Ernestine WhoHol A
Johnston, Gene 1908- AmSCAP 1966
Johnston, Gladys Film 2
Johnston, Henry Erskine 1777-1845 OxThe
Johnston, J L Film 2
Johnston, J W 1876-1946 Film 1, Film 2,
WhoHol B
Johnston, Jill CelR 3
Johnston, John W 1876-1946 WhScrn 1,
WhScrn 2
Johnston, Johnny WhoHol A
Johnston, Johnny 1869-1931 WhScrn 1,
WhScrn 2
Johnston, Julanne 1906- Film 1, Film 2, TwYS,
WhoHol A
Johnston, Justine BiE&WWA, NotNAT
Johnston, Lorimer Film 2
Johnston, Lorimer see also Johnson, Lorimer George
Johnston, Margaret IntMPA 1977, WhoHol A
Johnston, Margaret 1917- FilmgC
Johnston, Margaret 1918- WhoThe 16
Johnston, Mary 1925- AmSCAP 1966
Johnston, Moffat 1886-1935 NotNAT B, WhThe
Johnston, Moffat see also Johnson, Moffat
Johnston, Oliver 1888-1966 WhScrn 1, WhScrn 2,
WhoHol B
Johnston, Patricia 1922-1953 AmSCAP 1966
Johnston, Renita Film 2
Johnston, Suzanne WomWMM A
Johnstone, Anna Hill 1913- BiE&WWA,
NotNAT
Johnstone, Beryl d1969 WhoHol B
Johnstone, Clarence d1953 NotNAT B
Johnstone, Gordon 1876-1926 AmSCAP 1966
Johnstone, J B d1891 NotNAT B
Johnstone, Justine 1899- Film 2, TwYS, WhThe
Johnstone, Keith ConDr 1977
Johnstone, Lamar 1886-1919 Film 1, WhScrn 2
Johnstone, Madge d1913 NotNAT B
Johnstone, Thomas A 1888- AmSCAP 1966
Johnstone, William WhoHol A
Johnstone-Smith, George d1963 NotNAT B
Johst, Hanns 1890- CnMD, ModWD
Joiner, Barbara d1961 NotNAT B
Jokel, Lana Tse Ping WomWMM B
Jolivet, Rita 1894- Film 1, Film 2, TwYS,
WhThe
Jolley, Florence W 1917- AmSCAP 1966
Jolley, I Stanford Vers A, WhoHol A
Jolley, Stan 1926- IntMPA 1977
Jolly, George 1640-1673 NotNAT B, OxThe
Jolly, Pete 1932- AmSCAP 1966
Jolson, Al d1950 MotPP, WhoHol B
Jolson, Al 1882-1950 CmMov

Jolson, Al 1883-1950 OxFilm
Jolson, Al 1886-1950 AmSCAP 1966, BiDFlm,
EncMT, FamA&A, FilmgC, MovMk,
NotNAT A, NotNAT B, WhScrn 1,
WhScrn 2, WhThe, WorEnF
Jolson, Al 1888-1950 Film 2, PIP&P
Jolson, Harry d1953 NotNAT B
Joltin, Jan WomWMM B
Jonas, Joan WomWMM B
Jonas, Nita AmSCAP 1966
Jonasson, Frank Film 1, Film 2
Jones, Al 1909- BiE&WWA, NotNAT
Jones, Allan MotPP, WhoHol A
Jones, Allan 1907- FilmgC, HolP 30
Jones, Allan 1908- MovMk, OxFilm
Jones, Anissa 1958- WhoHol A
Jones, Arthur 1909- AmSCAP 1966
Jones, Barbara Ann 1948- AmSCAP 1966
Jones, Barry 1893- BiE&WWA, FilmgC,
IntMPA 1977, MovMk, NotNAT, PIP&P,
WhThe, WhoHol A
Jones, Biff 1930- AmSCAP 1966
Jones, Billy 1889-1940 Film 2
Jones, Brian 1943-1969 WhScrn 2
Jones, Brooks 1934- BiE&WWA, NotNAT
Jones, Buck 1889-1942 Film 1, Film 2, FilmgC,
MotPP, MovMk, NotNAT B, TwYS,
WhScrn 1, WhScrn 2, WhoHol B
Jones, Buck 1891-1942 CmMov, OxFilm
Jones, Carolyn MotPP, WhoHol A
Jones, Carolyn 1929- FilmgC
Jones, Carolyn 1933- IntMPA 1977, MovMk
Jones, Charles WhScrn 1
Jones, Charles 1910- AmSCAP 1966
Jones, Charlotte WhoHol A
Jones, Chester d1975 WhScrn 2, WhoHol C
Jones, Christopher 1941- CelR 3, FilmgC,
MotPP, WhoHol A
Jones, Chuck NewYTET
Jones, Chuck 1912- DcFM, IntMPA 1977,
WorEnF
Jones, Chuck 1915- FilmgC
Jones, Clarence M 1889-1949 AmSCAP 1966
Jones, Clark R 1920- IntMPA 1977
Jones, Curtis Ashy 1873-1956 WhScrn 1,
WhScrn 2
Jones, David 1913- IntMPA 1977
Jones, David 1934- WhoThe 16
Jones, David Hugh 1900- AmSCAP 1966
Jones, Dean MotPP, WhoHol A
Jones, Dean 1933- FilmgC
Jones, Dean 1935- BiE&WWA
Jones, Dean 1936- IntMPA 1977
Jones, Dick 1927- WhoHol A
Jones, Disley 1926- WhoThe 16
Jones, Douglas P, Jr. d1964 NotNAT B
Jones, Dudley 1914- WhoThe 16
Jones, Eddie Film 2
Jones, Edgar Film 1
Jones, Edward d1917 NotNAT B, WhThe
Jones, Elinor WomWMM B
Jones, Elizabeth Tiny d1952 WhScrn 1,
WhScrn 2, WhoHol B
Jones, Emrys 1915-1972 FilmgC, WhScrn 2,
WhThe, WhoHol B
Jones, Fred Film 1, Film 2
Jones, Freddie 1927- FilmgC, WhoHol A
Jones, Fuzzy Q WhScrn 1, WhScrn 2
Jones, Gemma 1942- WhoHol A, WhoThe 16
Jones, George Thaddeus 1917- AmSCAP 1966
Jones, Gordon 1911-1963 Vers A, WhScrn 1,
WhScrn 2, WhoHol B
Jones, Griffith 1910- FilmgC, IntMPA 1977,
WhoHol A, WhoThe 16

Jones, Hannah *Film 2*
Jones, Harmon 1911-1972 *FilmgC*
Jones, Harry *Film 2*
Jones, Hazel d1974 *WhoHol B*
Jones, Hazel 1895-1974 *WhScrn 2*
Jones, Hazel 1896-1974 *WhThe*
Jones, Henry 1912- *BiE&WWA, FilmgC, NotNAT, WhoHol A*
Jones, Henry Arthur 1851-1929 *CnThe, McGWD, ModWD, NotNAT A, NotNAT B, OxThe, PIP&P, REnWD, WhThe, WhoStg 1906, WhoStg 1908*
Jones, Henry Z, Jr. 1940- *AmSCAP 1966*
Jones, Heywood S 1891-1959 *AmSCAP 1966*
Jones, Inigo 1573-1652 *CnThe, NotNAT A, NotNAT B, OxThe,· PIP&P*
Jones, Isham 1894-1956 *AmSCAP 1966, NotNAT B*
Jones, J Matheson d1931 *NotNAT B*
Jones, J Parke *Film 1*
Jones, J W *Film 1*
Jones, J Wilton d1897 *NotNAT B*
Jones, Jack 1938- *CelR 3, WhoHol A*
Jones, Jacqueline *WomWMM B*
Jones, James 1921- *CelR 3*
Jones, James Earl 1931- *BiE&WWA, CelR 3, NotNAT, PIP&P, PIP&P A, WhoHol A, WhoThe 16*
Jones, Jennifer 1919- *BiDFlm, BiE&WWA, CmMov, FilmgC, IntMPA 1977, MotPP, MovMk, OxFilm, WhoHol A, WorEnF*
Jones, Joan Granville d1974 *WhScrn 2, WhoHol B*
Jones, John 1917- *BiE&WWA, NotNAT*
Jones, John Price d1961 *NotNAT B*
Jones, Johnny 1908-1962 *Film 1, Film 2, TwYS, WhScrn 1, WhScrn 2, WhoHol B*
Jones, Jonathan 1911- *AmSCAP 1966*
Jones, Joseph Steven 1809-1877 *NotNAT B, OxThe*
Jones, Julia *ConDr 1977C*
Jones, L Q 1936- *FilmgC, WhoHol A*
Jones, Lee 1909- *AmSCAP 1966*
Jones, LeRoi 1934- *CelR 3, ConDr 1977, CroCD, McGWD, ModWD, NotNAT, PIP&P A*
Jones, Leslie Julian 1910- *WhThe*
Jones, Marcia Mae 1924- *FilmgC, WhoHol A*
Jones, Marcia May 1924- *ThFT*
Jones, Margo 1913-1955 *NotNAT B, OxThe, WhThe*
Jones, Maria B d1873 *NotNAT B*
Jones, Mark 1890-1965 *WhScrn 2*
Jones, Mary 1915- *WhoHol A, WhoThe 16*
Jones, Merle S d1976 *NewYTET*
Jones, Morgan 1879-1951 *WhScrn 1, WhScrn 2, WhoHol B*
Jones, Natalie R *WomWMM*
Jones, Norman 1928-1963 *WhScrn 1, WhScrn 2*
Jones, Park *Film 1, Film 2*
Jones, Paul *WhoHol A*
Jones, Paul 1901-1968 *FilmgC*
Jones, Paul 1942- *WhoThe 16*
Jones, Paul 1943- *FilmgC*
Jones, Paul Meredith 1897-1966 *WhScrn 1, WhScrn 2*
Jones, Peter 1920- *FilmgC, WhoHol A, WhoThe 16*
Jones, Phyllis Ann d1962 *NotNAT B*
Jones, Quincy 1933- *AmSCAP 1966*
Jones, Quincy 1935- *FilmgC, IntMPA 1977*
Jones, R D d1925 *WhScrn 1, WhScrn 2*
Jones, Richard *OxThe, TwYS A*
Jones, Richard d1851 *NotNAT B*

Jones, Richard C 1906- *AmSCAP 1966*
Jones, Richard M 1892-1945 *AmSCAP 1966*
Jones, Robert Earl *WhoHol A*
Jones, Robert Edmond 1887-1954 *NotNAT A, NotNAT B, OxThe, PIP&P, WhThe*
Jones, Robert Edmund 1887-1954 *CnThe*
Jones, Rozene K 1890-1964 *NotNAT B, WhScrn 1, WhScrn 2*
Jones, Rupel Johnson 1895-1964 *BiE&WWA, NotNAT B*
Jones, Samantha *WhoHol A*
Jones, Samuel Major d1952 *NotNAT B, WhThe*
Jones, Shirley 1934- *BiDFlm, BiE&WWA, CmMov, FilmgC, IntMPA 1977, MotPP, MovMk, WhoHol A, WorEnF*
Jones, Sidney 1869-1946 *EncMT, NotNAT B, WhThe*
Jones, Silas 1940- *NatPD*
Jones, Spike 1911-1964 *AmSCAP 1966*
Jones, Spike 1911-1965 *FilmgC, WhScrn 1, WhScrn 2, WhoHol B*
Jones, Stan 1914-1963 *AmSCAP 1966, WhoHol B*
Jones, Stanley 1914-1963 *NotNAT B, WhScrn 1, WhScrn 2*
Jones, Stephen d1827 *NotNAT B*
Jones, Stephen Oscar 1880- *AmSCAP 1966*
Jones, Mrs. Sutton 1927- *AmSCAP 1966*
Jones, T C 1920-1971 *BiE&WWA, NotNAT B*
Jones, T C 1921-1971 *WhScrn 1, WhScrn 2, WhoHol B*
Jones, Tiny d1952 *Film 2, WhoHol B*
Jones, Tiny *see also* Jones, Elizabeth Tiny
Jones, Tom 1928- *AmSCAP 1966, BiE&WWA, ConDr 1977D, EncMT, NewMT, NotNAT*
Jones, Tom 1940- *CelR 3*
Jones, Trefor 1902-1965 *WhThe*
Jones, W W *Film 2*
Jones, Wallace 1883-1936 *WhScrn 1, WhScrn 2, WhoHol B*
Jones, Walter 1872- *WhoStg 1906, WhoStg 1908*
Jones, Whitworth 1873- *WhThe*
Jong, Erica *WomWMM*
Jonson, Ben 1572-1637 *CnThe, McGWD, PIP&P, REnWD*
Jonson, Ben 1573?-1637 *NotNAT A, NotNAT B*
Jonson, Benjamin 1572-1637 *OxThe*
Jooss, Kurt 1901- *WhThe*
Jope-Slade, Christine d1942 *NotNAT B*
Joplin, Janis 1943-1970 *WhScrn 2, WhoHol B*
Joplin, Scott 1868-1919 *AmSCAP 1966, NotNAT B*
Jordan, Bernard d1962 *NotNAT B*
Jordan, Bobby d1965 *WhoHol B*
Jordan, Dorothy *FilmgC, MotPP*
Jordan, Dorothy 1761-1816 *NotNAT A, OxThe*
Jordan, Dorothy 1762?-1816 *NotNAT B*
Jordan, Dorothy 1908- *Film 2, ThFT, WhThe, WhoHol A*
Jordan, Dorothy 1910- *MovMk*
Jordan, Egon V *Film 2*
Jordan, Glenn S *NewYTET*
Jordan, Henrietta *IntMPA 1977*
Jordan, Jack *Film 2*
Jordan, Jim 1896- *WhoHol A*
Jordan, Joe 1882- *AmSCAP 1966*
Jordan, Louis d1975 *WhoHol C*
Jordan, Marian 1897-1961 *WhScrn 1, WhScrn 2, WhoHol B*
Jordan, Marian 1898-1961 *NotNAT B*
Jordan, Marion F *IntMPA 1977*
Jordan, Miriam 1908- *ThFT*
Jordan, Patrick *WhoHol A*
Jordan, Rhoda d1962 *WhScrn 2*

Jordan, Richard *WhoHol A*
Jordan, Ricky *WhScrn 2*
Jordan, Robert 1923-1965 *WhScrn 1, WhScrn 2*
Jordan, Roy 1916- *AmSCAP 1966*
Jordan, Sid *Film 1, Film 2*
Jordan, Walter C d1951 *NotNAT B*
Jordon, Domaine *Film 2*
Jorge, Paul *Film 2*
Jorge, Paul d1939 *WhoHol B*
Jorge, Paul 1849-1929 *WhScrn 1, WhScrn 2*
Jorgens, Alice *Film 1*
Jorgensen, Robert 1903- *WhThe*
Jory, Jon V 1938- *NotNAT*
Jory, Victor *MotPP, WhoHol A*
Jory, Victor 1901- *Vers A*
Jory, Victor 1902- *FilmgC, HolP 30,*
  IntMPA 1977, MovMk, WhoThe 16
Jory, Victor 1903- *BiE&WWA, NotNAT*
Josane, Lola *Film 2*
Josayne *Film 2*
Jose, Edward *Film 1, TwYS A*
Josefovits, Teri 1909-1958 *AmSCAP 1966*
Joseloff, Stanley 1907- *AmSCAP 1966*
Joselovitz, Ernest A *NatPD*
Joseph, Harry d1962 *NotNAT B*
Joseph, Jackie *WhoHol A*
Joseph, Kenneth 1922- *IntMPA 1977*
Joseph, Larry 1911-1974 *WhScrn 2*
Joseph, Richard 1910- *CelR 3*
Joseph, Robert Farras 1935- *NatPD*
Joseph, Robert L 1924- *BiE&WWA, NotNAT*
Joseph, Stephen 1921-1966 *OxThe*
Josephs, George M 1908- *IntMPA 1977*
Josephson, Marvin *NewYTET*
Josephson, Ragnar 1891-1966 *CnMD, ModWD*
Josipovici, Gabriel *ConDr 1977B*
Joslin, Howard 1908-1975 *WhScrn 2, WhoHol C*
Joslin, Margaret *Film 1*
Joslyn, Allyn 1905- *FilmgC, IntMPA 1977,*
  MovMk, Vers A, WhThe, WhoHol A
Josten, Werner 1885-1963 *AmSCAP 1966*
Jostyn, Jay *WhoHol A*
Jotuni, Maria 1880-1943 *CroCD*
Jouard, Paul E 1928- *AmSCAP 1966*
Joube, M *Film 1*
Joube, Romuald *Film 2*
Jourdan, Louis *MotPP, WhoHol A*
Jourdan, Louis 1919- *FilmgC, MovMk*
Jourdan, Louis 1920- *BiE&WWA, NotNAT*
Jourdan, Louis 1921- *IntMPA 1977*
Journee, Leon *Film 2*
Jouvet, Louis 1887-1951 *BiDFlm, CnThe, FilmgC,*
  MovMk, NotNAT B, OxFilm, OxThe,
  WhThe, WhoHol B, WorEnF
Jouvet, Louis 1888-1951 *WhScrn 1, WhScrn 2*
Jouvet, Louis 1891-1951 *NotNAT A*
Jowitt, Anthony *Film 2*
Joy, Beatrice *Film 2*
Joy, Ernest *Film 1, Film 2*
Joy, Gloria *Film 2*
Joy, Leatrice *MotPP*
Joy, Leatrice 1896- *ThFT*
Joy, Leatrice 1897- *MovMk, TwYS*
Joy, Leatrice 1899- *Film 1, Film 2, FilmgC,*
  WhoHol A
Joy, Leonard W 1894-1961 *AmSCAP 1966,*
  NotNAT B
Joy, Nicholas d1964 *MotPP, WhoHol B*
Joy, Nicholas 1883-1964 *NotNAT B*
Joy, Nicholas 1884-1964 *PIP&P, WhScrn 1,*
  WhScrn 2
Joy, Nicholas 1889-1964 *WhThe*
Joyce, Adrian *WomWMM*
Joyce, Alice d1955 *MotPP, WhoHol B*

Joyce, Alice 1889-1955 *Film 1, Film 2, FilmgC,*
  MovMk
Joyce, Alice 1890-1955 *NotNAT B, TwYS,*
  WhScrn 1, WhScrn 2
Joyce, Archibald d1963 *NotNAT B*
Joyce, Beatrice 1900- *AmSCAP 1966*
Joyce, Brenda *MotPP*
Joyce, Brenda 1916- *ThFT*
Joyce, Brenda 1918- *CmMov, FilmgC, MovMk,*
  WhoHol A
Joyce, Elaine *WhoHol A*
Joyce, Jack *Film 2*
Joyce, James *WhoHol A*
Joyce, James 1882-1941 *CnMD, McGWD,*
  ModWD, NotNAT B
Joyce, Martin 1915-1937 *WhScrn 1, WhScrn 2*
Joyce, Natalie *Film 2, WhoHol A*
Joyce, Peggy Hopkins 1893-1957 *Film 2, MotPP,*
  NotNAT B, WhScrn 1, WhScrn 2,
  WhoHol B
Joyce, Stephen 1931- *WhoThe 16*
Joyce, Stephen 1933- *NotNAT*
Joyce, Virginia *Film 2*
Joyce, Walter d1916 *NotNAT B*
Joyce, Yootha 1927- *FilmgC, WhoHol A*
Joyner, Francis *Film 1, Film 2, TwYS*
Joyzelle *Film 2, TwYS*
Juano *WhScrn 1, WhScrn 2*
Juch, Emma d1939 *NotNAT B*
Judd, Edward *WhoHol A*
Judd, Edward 1932- *FilmgC*
Judd, Edward 1934- *IntMPA 1977*
Judel, Charles 1882-1969 *WhScrn 2*
Judels, Charles *Film 1, Film 2*
Judelson, David N *IntMPA 1977*
Judeu 1705-1739 *OxThe*
Judge, Arlene 1912-1974 *WhScrn 2*
Judge, Arline 1912-1974 *FilmgC, HolP 30,*
  MotPP, MovMk, ThFT, WhoHol B
Judice, Patricia *WomWMM B*
Judith, Madame 1827-1912 *NotNAT A,*
  NotNAT B
Judson, Arthur d1975 *NewYTET*
Juen, Joseph P 1902- *AmSCAP 1966*
Jugo, Jenny *Film 2*
Juillard, Robert 1906- *DcFM*
Julia, Raul 1940- *WhoHol A, WhoThe 16*
Julian, Alexander 1893-1945 *WhScrn 1,*
  WhScrn 2
Julian, Joseph *NatPD*
Julian, Rupert 1886-1943 *Film 1, Film 2,*
  FilmgC
Julian, Rupert 1889-1943 *BiDFlm, DcFM, TwYS,*
  TwYS A, WhScrn 1, WhScrn 2, WhoHol B,
  WorEnF
Julie, Lady *Film 2*
Julien, Jay 1919- *BiE&WWA, NotNAT*
Julien, Max *WhoHol A*
Juliet, Miss d1962 *NotNAT B*
Julius, J *DcFM*
Jullien, Jean 1854-1919 *ModWD, NotNAT B,*
  WhThe
June 1901- *EncMT, WhThe*
June, Mildred 1906-1940 *Film 2, WhScrn 1,*
  WhScrn 2, WhoHol B
June, Ray 1898-1958 *WorEnF*
June, Ray 1908-1958 *CmMov, FilmgC*
Jung, Allen *WhoHol A*
Jung, Rudolph *Film 2*
Junge, Alfred 1886-1964 *FilmgC, OxFilm*
Junge, Winifred *WomWMM*
Junghans, Carl 1897- *DcFM*
Junior, John *Film 1*
Junkerman, Hans *Film 2*

Junkermann, Hans 1872?-1943 *WhScrn 2*
Junkin, Harry *IntMPA 1977*
Junkin, Raymond 1918- *IntMPA 1977*
Jurado, Elena *Film 2*
Jurado, Katy 1927- *FilmgC, IntMPA 1977,*
 MovMk, OxFilm, WhoHol A
Juran, Nathan 1907- *FilmgC*
Jurgens, Curd 1912- *BiDFlm, OxFilm, WorEnF*
Jurgens, Curt 1912- *BiDFlm, FilmgC, MotPP,*
 MovMk, OxFilm, WhoHol A
Jurgens, Dick 1911- *AmSCAP 1966*
Jurmann, Walter 1903- *AmSCAP 1966*
Jurow, Martin 1914- *FilmgC, IntMPA 1977*
Justice, James Robertson 1905-1975 *FilmgC,*
 MovMk, WhScrn 2, WhoHol C
Justice, Katherine *WhoHol A*
Justin, John 1917- *FilmgC, IntMPA 1977,*
 WhoHol A, WhoThe 16
Justin, Morgan 1927-1974 *WhScrn 2, WhoHol B*
Jutra, Claude 1930- *DcFM, OxFilm, WorEnF*
Jutzi, Phil 1894- *DcFM*
Jutzi, Piel 1894- *WorEnF*
Juul, Ralph 1888-1955 *WhScrn 1, WhScrn 2*
Juvarra, Filippo 1676-1736 *NotNAT B, OxThe*

K

Kaapuni, Sam 1915- *AmSCAP 1966*
Kaaren, Suzanne *WhoHol A*
Kaarresalo-Kasara, Elia *WomWMM B*
Kaarresalo-Kasari, Eila *WomWMM*
Kaart, Hans 1924-1963 *NotNAT B, WhScrn 1, WhScrn 2*
Kabak, Milton 1926- *AmSCAP 1966*
Kabibble, Ish 1908- *WhoHol A*
Kachalov, Vasili Ivanovich 1875-1948 *NotNAT B, OxThe*
Kachalov, Vassilli Ivanovich d1948 *WhoHol B*
Kachloff, Vassily *PIP&P*
Kada-Abd-El-Kader *Film 2*
Kadar, Jan 1918- *CelR 3, DcFM, FilmgC, IntMPA 1977, MovMk, OxFilm*
Kader-Ben-Ali, Abdel *Film 2*
Kadison, Philip 1919- *AmSCAP 1966*
Kaeck, Alexander Paki 1926- *AmSCAP 1966*
Kaeired, Katharine *Film 2*
Kael, Pauline 1919- *CelR 3, IntMPA 1977, OxFilm, WomWMM*
Kaelred, Katharine 1882- *Film 1, WhThe*
Kafka, Franz 1883-1924 *CnMD*
Kagan, Diane *NatPD*
Kagen, Sergius d1964 *NotNAT B*
Kagno, Marcia *Film 2*
Kahal, Irving 1903-1942 *AmSCAP 1966, NewMT*
Kahanamoka, Duke P 1890-1968 *Film 2*
Kahanamoku, Duke P 1890-1968 *WhScrn 1, WhScrn 2, WhoHol B*
Kahn, Art *Film 2*
Kahn, Bernard M 1930- *AmSCAP 1966, NatPD*
Kahn, Dave 1910- *AmSCAP 1966*
Kahn, Donald 1918- *AmSCAP 1966*
Kahn, Florence d1951 *WhoHol B, WhoStg 1908*
Kahn, Florence 1877-1951 *OxThe*
Kahn, Florence 1878-1951 *NotNAT B, WhThe*
Kahn, Grace LeBoy 1891- *AmSCAP 1966*
Kahn, Gus 1886-1941 *AmSCAP 1966, EncMT, NotNAT B*
Kahn, Herman 1922- *CelR 3*
Kahn, Irving B 1917- *IntMPA 1977, NewYTET*
Kahn, L Stanley d1964 *NotNAT B*
Kahn, Louis 1901- *CelR 3*
Kahn, Madeline 1943- *IntMPA 1977, MovMk, PIP&P A, WhoHol A*
Kahn, Marvin Irving 1915- *AmSCAP 1966*
Kahn, Michael *NotNAT, WhoThe 16*
Kahn, Milton Bernard 1934- *IntMPA 1977*
Kahn, Otto Hermann 1867-1934 *NotNAT B*
Kahn, Richard 1929- *IntMPA 1977*
Kahn, Richard C 1897-1960 *WhScrn 1, WhScrn 2, WhoHol B*
Kahn, Roger Wolfe 1907-1962 *AmSCAP 1966*
Kahn, Sherman 1934- *AmSCAP 1966*
Kahn, Sy M 1924- *NotNAT*

Kahn, William Smitty 1882-1959 *WhScrn 1, WhScrn 2, WhoHol B*
Kains, Maurice *Film 2*
Kainz, Josef 1858-1910 *NotNAT B, OxThe*
Kaiser, Georg 1878-1945 *CnMD, CnThe, McGWD, ModWD, NotNAT B, OxThe, PIP&P, REnWD, WhThe*
Kaiser, Helen *Film 2*
Kaiser-Tietz, Erich *Film 2*
Kaja, Katrina *Film 2*
Kalatazov, Mikhail Konstantinovich 1903-1973 *DcFM*
Kalatozov, Mikhail 1903-1973 *OxFilm, WorEnF*
Kalb, Marie d1930 *NotNAT B*
Kalb, Marvin *IntMPA 1977*
Kalcheim, Lee 1938- *ConDr 1977, NatPD*
Kalem, Theodore 1919- *BiE&WWA, NotNAT*
Kaler, Doris *WomWMM B*
Kaleti, Marton 1905- *DcFM*
Kalfin, Robert 1933- *NotNAT, PIP&P A*
Kalich, Bertha 1874-1939 *FamA&A, Film 1, NotNAT B, WhThe, WhoHol B*
Kalich, Bertha 1875-1939 *WhScrn 1, WhScrn 2*
Kalich, Jacob d1975 *WhoHol C*
Kalich, Jacob 1891-1975 *BiE&WWA, NotNAT*
Kalich, Jacob 1892-1975 *WhScrn 2*
Kalidasa *CnThe, REnWD*
Kaline, Al 1934- *CelR 3*
Kalionzes, Janet 1922-1961 *WhScrn 1, WhScrn 2, WhoHol B*
Kalisch, Bertram 1902- *IntMPA 1977*
Kaliz, Armand 1892-1941 *Film 1, NotNAT B, TwYS, WhScrn 1, WhScrn 2, WhoHol B*
Kalkhurst, Eric 1902-1957 *WhScrn 1, WhScrn 2, WhoHol B*
Kallen, Kitty *WhoHol A*
Kallen, Lucille *WomWMM*
Kallianiotes, Helena *WhoHol A*
Kallman, Dick 1934- *AmSCAP 1966, BiE&WWA, WhoHol A*
Kallman, Herbert E 1912- *AmSCAP 1966*
Kalman, Emmerich 1882-1953 *AmSCAP 1966, NotNAT B, WhThe*
Kalmanoff, Martin 1920- *AmSCAP 1966*
Kalmar, Bert 1884-1947 *AmSCAP 1966, EncMT, NewMT, NotNAT B, WhThe*
Kalmus, Herbert Thomas 1881-1963 *DcFM, FilmgC, WorEnF*
Kalser, Erwin 1883-1958 *Film 2, WhScrn 1, WhScrn 2, WhoHol B*
Kalser, Konstantin 1920- *IntMPA 1977*
Kalthoum, Um 1898-1975 *WhScrn 2*
Kaltz, Armand 1892-1941 *Film 2*
Kamano, John N 1904- *AmSCAP 1966*
Kamber, Bernard M *IntMPA 1977*
Kambisis, Joannes 1872-1902 *NotNAT B*

Kamei, Fumio 1908- *DcFM*
Kamel Morsi, Ahmad 1900?- *DcFM*
Kamen, Milt *WhoHol A*
Kamen, Stanley A 1928- *IntMPA 1977*
Kamenka, Alexandre 1888-1969 *DcFM*
Kamenka, Alexandre 1888-1970 *OxFilm*
Kamenzky, Eliezer 1889-1957 *WhScrn 1,*
 WhScrn 2
Kamerko Balalaika Orchestra *Film 2*
Kamey, Paul 1912- *IntMPA 1977*
Kamins, Bernie 1915- *IntMPA 1977*
Kaminska, Ida 1899- *FilmgC, NotNAT A,*
 WhoThe 16
Kaminska, Ida 1900?- *WhoHol A*
Kaminsky, Lucian J 1924- *AmSCAP 1966*
Kamiyama, Sojim *Film 2*
Kamiyama, Sojin 1884-1954 *WhScrn 1,*
 WhScrn 2
Kammer, Klaus 1929-1964 *NotNAT B, WhScrn 1,*
 WhScrn 2
Kammeren, Torsten *Film 2*
Kampers, Fritz 1891-1950 *Film 2, WhScrn 2*
Kamsler, Ben 1905- *BiE&WWA*
Kander, John 1927- *BiE&WWA, EncMT,*
 NewMT, NotNAT, WhoThe 16
Kane, Bernie 1906- *AmSCAP 1966*
Kane, Blanche 1889-1937 *WhScrn 1, WhScrn 2*
Kane, Byron *WhoHol A*
Kane, Carol *WhoHol A*
Kane, Dennis *NewYTET*
Kane, Diana *Film 2*
Kane, Eddie d1969 *Film 2, WhoHol B*
Kane, Eddie 1888-1969 *WhScrn 1*
Kane, Eddie 1889-1969 *WhScrn 2*
Kane, Gail d1966 *Film 1, MotPP, WhoHol B*
Kane, Gail 1885-1966 *WhScrn 1, WhScrn 2*
Kane, Gail 1887-1966 *WhThe*
Kane, Gail 1892-1966 *Film 2, TwYS*
Kane, Helen d1966 *WhoHol B*
Kane, Helen 1903-1966 *ThFT*
Kane, Helen 1904-1966 *EncMT, Film 2*
Kane, Helen Babe 1908-1966 *WhScrn 1,*
 WhScrn 2
Kane, Jack *Film 2*
Kane, John J d1969 *WhScrn 1, WhScrn 2,*
 WhoHol B
Kane, Joseph 1894- *IntMPA 1977*
Kane, Joseph 1897- *FilmgC*
Kane, Joseph 1904- *CmMov*
Kane, Lida d1955 *WhScrn 1, WhScrn 2,*
 WhoHol B
Kane, Margie *Film 2*
Kane, Michael *WhoHol A*
Kane, Richard 1938- *WhoThe 16*
Kane, Robert *Film 2*
Kane, Ruth *Film 2*
Kane, Sid *WhoHol A*
Kane, Stanley D 1907- *IntMPA 1977*
Kane, Violet *Film 2*
Kane, Whitford 1881-1956 *NotNAT B,*
 WhScrn 1, WhScrn 2, WhThe, WhoHol B
Kane, Whitford 1882-1956 *NotNAT A*
Kaner, Ruth d1964 *NotNAT B*
K'ang, Chin-Chih *REnWD*
Kani, John *PIP&P A*
Kaniewska, Maria *WomWMM*
Kanin, Fay *BiE&WWA, IntMPA 1977,*
 NotNAT, WomWMM
Kanin, Garson 1912- *AmSCAP 1966, BiDFlm,*
 BiE&WWA, CelR 3, CmMov, CnMD,
 CnThc, ConDr 1977, DcFM, FilmgC,
 IntMPA 1977, ModWD, MovMk, NatPD,
 NotNAT, NotNAT A, OxFilm, WhoThe 16,
 WorEnF

Kanin, Michael 1910- *BiE&WWA, FilmgC,*
 IntMPA 1977, NotNAT
Kanitz, Ernest 1894- *AmSCAP 1966*
Kann, Lilly *WhThe, WhoHol A*
Kann, Lily 1898?- *FilmgC*
Kann, Sylvia *WhoHol A*
Kanner, Alexis 1942- *FilmgC, WhoHol A,*
 WhoThe 16
Kanner, Jerome H 1903- *AmSCAP 1966*
Kannon, Jackie 1919-1974 *WhScrn 2, WhoHol B*
Kanter, Hal 1918- *FilmgC, IntMPA 1977,*
 NewYTET, WorEnF
Kanter, Jay 1927- *IntMPA 1977*
Kantor, Mackinlay 1904- *FilmgC*
Kao, Tse-Ch'eng *REnWD*
Kaper, Bronislau 1902- *FilmgC, IntMPA 1977,*
 WorEnF
Kaper, Bronislaw 1902- *AmSCAP 1966*
Kapf, Elinor *WomWMM*
Kaplan, Barbara *WomWMM B*
Kaplan, Boris 1897- *IntMPA 1977*
Kaplan, Eddie Nuts d1964 *NotNAT B*
Kaplan, Harriet 1917- *BiE&WWA*
Kaplan, Helene G *WomWMM B*
Kaplan, Jack A 1947- *NatPD*
Kaplan, Marvin *WhoHol A*
Kaplan, Marvin 1924- *FilmgC*
Kaplan, Marvin 1927- *MovMk, Vers A*
Kaplan, Mike 1918- *IntMPA 1977*
Kaplan, Murray M *IntMPA 1977*
Kaplan, Nelly *WomWMM*
Kaplan, Saul 1898- *BiE&WWA*
Kaplan, Sheldon Z 1911- *AmSCAP 1966*
Kaplan, Sol 1919- *BiE&WWA, NotNAT*
Kapler, Alexei 1904- *DcFM*
Kapoor, Prithvi Raj 1906-1972 *WhScrn 2*
Kapoor, Raj 1924- *DcFM*
Kapp, David 1904- *AmSCAP 1966*
Kapp, Paul 1907- *AmSCAP 1966*
Kappeler, Alfred d1945 *NotNAT B*
Kaprow, Allan *ConDr 1977E*
Kaprow, Vaughan Rachel *WomWMM B*
Karabasz, Kasimierz 1930- *DcFM*
Karajan, Herbert Von 1908- *CelR 3*
Karashville, Kokhta *Film 2*
Karatygin, Vasily Andreyevich 1802-1853 *OxThe*
Karayn, Jim *NewYTET*
Karchmer, Andrea *NatPD*
Kardar, Aaejay *DcFM*
Karels, Harvey d1975 *Film 2, WhScrn 2*
Karen, Anna *WhoHol A*
Karenne, Diana *Film 2*
Karin, Rita *WhoHol A*
Karina, Anna *WhoHol A*
Karina, Anna 1940- *BiDFlm, FilmgC, MovMk*
Karina, Anna 1941- *WorEnF*
Karina, Anna 1942- *OxFilm*
Karinska *BiE&WWA*
Karinska, Barbara 1886- *NotNAT*
Karinthy, Ferenc 1921- *CroCD*
Karkowsky, Nancy *WomWMM B*
Karl, Roger *Film 2*
Karl, Theodore O H 1912- *BiE&WWA, NotNAT*
Karlan, Richard *WhoHol A*
Karlin, Bo-Peep d1969 *Film 2, WhScrn 1,*
 WhScrn 2, WhoHol B
Karlin, Elisabeth J *WomWMM B*
Karlin, Fred *IntMPA 1977*
Karlin, Frederick James 1936- *AmSCAP 1966*
Karlin, Miriam 1925- *FilmgC, WhoHol A,*
 WhoThe 16
Karlin, Myron D 1918- *IntMPA 1977*
Karloff, Boris 1887-1969 *BiDFlm, BiE&WWA,*
 CmMov, Film 1, Film 2, FilmgC, MotPP,

MovMk, NotNAT A, NotNAT B, OxFilm,
TwYS, WhScrn 1, WhScrn 2, WhThe,
WhoHol B, WorEnF
Karlson, Phil 1908- BiDFlm, FilmgC,
IntMPA 1977, MovMk, WorEnF
Karlstadt, Liesl 1893-1960 WhScrn 1, WhScrn 2,
WhoHol B
Karlweis, Oscar 1895-1956 NotNAT B, WhThe,
WhoHol B
Karlweiss, Oscar 1895-1956 WhScrn 2
Karmen, Roman Lasarevich 1906- DcFM, OxFilm,
WorEnF
Karmon, Robert 1939- NatPD
Karnelly, Leila Film 2
Karnes, Roscoe 1893-1970 Film 1
Karnilova, Maria 1920- BiE&WWA, EncMT,
NotNAT, WhoHol A, WhoThe 16
Karno, Fred 1866-1941 NotNAT A, OxFilm,
OxThe, WhThe
Karns, Maurice Film 2
Karns, Roscoe 1893-1970 Film 2, FilmgC,
MotPP, MovMk, TwYS, WhScrn 1,
WhScrn 2, WhoHol B
Karns, Roscoe 1897-1970 Vers B
Karp, Russell H NewYTET
Karp, Sharon WomWMM B
Karr, Darwin 1875-1945 Film 1, WhScrn 2
Karr, Elizabeth R 1925- AmSCAP 1966
Karr, Harold 1921- AmSCAP 1966, BiE&WWA,
NotNAT
Karr, Patti 1932- BiE&WWA, NotNAT
Karras, Alex WhoHol A
Karrington, Frank 1858-1936 WhScrn 1,
WhScrn 2
Karsavina, Tamara 1885- WhThe
Karson, Kit d1940 NotNAT B
Karson, Nat d1954 NotNAT B
Kartalian, Buck WhoHol A
Kartousch, Louise d1964 NotNAT B
Karvas, Peter 1920- CnThe, CroCD, REnWD
Kase, C Robert 1905- BiE&WWA, NotNAT
Kasem, Casey WhoHol A
Kasha, Lawrence N 1933- BiE&WWA, NotNAT,
WhoThe 16
Kashey, Abe 1903-1965 WhScrn 2
Kashfi, Anna MotPP, WhoHol A
Kashner, Bruno Film 2
Kashner, David Film 2
Kasich, Joan WomWMM B
Kasket, Harold 1916?- FilmgC, WhoHol A
Kasmire, Robert D NewYTET
Kasprowicz, Jan 1860-1926 ModWD
Kass, Herman 1923- IntMPA 1977
Kass, Jerome NatPD, NewYTET
Kassel, Art 1896-1965 AmSCAP 1966
Kassewitz, Helene Film 2
Kassila, Matti 1924- DcFM
Kassin, Arthur Robert 1917- AmSCAP 1966
Kast, Pierre 1920- DcFM, OxFilm, WorEnF
Kaster, Barbara WomWMM B
Kastle, Leonard 1929- AmSCAP 1966
Kastner, Bruno d1958 Film 2, WhScrn 2
Kastner, Elliott 1930- FilmgC, IntMPA 1977
Kastner, Erich 1899-1974 CnMD, ModWD
Kastner, Peter 1944- FilmgC, WhoHol A
Kasznar, Kurt 1913- BiE&WWA, FilmgC,
IntMPA 1977, MotPP, MovMk, NotNAT,
Vers B, WhoHol A, WhoThe 16
Kasznar, Kurt see also Kaznar, Kurt
Kataev, Valentin Petrovich 1897- CnMD, ModWD
Katainen, Elina WomWMM
Katayev, Valentin Petrovich 1897- McGWD,
OxThe
Katch, Kurt 1896-1958 FilmgC, Vers A,

WhScrn 1, WhScrn 2, WhoHol B
Katchalof, V L Film 2
Katchalov, Vassily PIP&P
Katcher, Aram WhoHol A
Kateb, Yacine 1929- REnWD
Katleman, Harris L 1928- IntMPA 1977
Katona, Jozsef 1791-1830 McGWD, OxThe
Katonik, Carol WomWMM B
Katscher, Robert 1894-1942 AmSCAP 1966
Katselas, Milton 1933- IntMPA 1977,
WhoThe 16
Katz, Fred 1919- AmSCAP 1966
Katz, Gloria WomWMM
Katz, Norman B 1919- IntMPA 1977
Katz, Oscar NewYTET
Katz, Raymond BiE&WWA
Katz, William 1922- AmSCAP 1966
Katzenelson, Isaac 1886-1941? NotNAT B
Katzin, Lee H FilmgC
Katzman, Sam 1901- FilmgC, WorEnF
Kauffman, Helen Reed AmSCAP 1966
Kaufman, Al Film 2
Kaufman, Alvin S AmSCAP 1966
Kaufman, Bill M 1930- AmSCAP 1966
Kaufman, Boris 1906- DcFM, FilmgC,
IntMPA 1977, OxFilm, WorEnF
Kaufman, Curt 1930- IntMPA 1977
Kaufman, Elkan 1923- IntMPA 1977
Kaufman, George S 1889-1961 CnMD, CnThe,
EncMT, FilmgC, McGWD, ModWD,
NewMT, NotNAT A, NotNAT B, OxThe,
PIP&P, REnWD, WhThe, WorEnF
Kaufman, Hal 1924- IntMPA 1977
Kaufman, Harry A d1944 NotNAT B
Kaufman, J L IntMPA 1977
Kaufman, Joseph 1882-1918 WhScrn 2
Kaufman, Leonard 1913- IntMPA 1977
Kaufman, Leonard B IntMPA 1977
Kaufman, Martin Ellis 1899- AmSCAP 1966
Kaufman, Mel B 1879-1932 AmSCAP 1966
Kaufman, Mikhail Abramovich 1897- DcFM,
OxFilm
Kaufman, Millard FilmgC
Kaufman, Philip 1936- IntMPA 1977
Kaufman, Rita d1968 WhoHol B
Kaufman, S Jay 1886-1957 NotNAT B
Kaufman, Sidney 1910- IntMPA 1977
Kaufman, William d1967 WhScrn 2
Kaufman, Willy d1967 WhoHol B
Kaufmann, Christine MotPP, WhoHol A
Kaufmann, Christine 1944- FilmgC
Kaufmann, Christine 1945- IntMPA 1977
Kaufmann, Maurice 1928- FilmgC, WhoHol A
Kauser, Alice d1945 NotNAT B
Kautner, Helmut 1908- BiDFlm, DcFM, FilmgC,
WorEnF
Kavalauskas, Maryte WomWMM
Kavanagh, Patrick d1967 NotNAT B
Kawakita, Nagamasa 1903- IntMPA 1977
Kawalerowicz, Jerzy 1922- DcFM, FilmgC,
OxFilm, WorEnF
Kay, Arthur Film 2
Kay, Authur BiE&WWA
Kay, Beatrice WhoHol A
Kay, Bernard WhoHol A
Kay, Charles 1930- WhoHol A, WhoThe 16
Kay, Edward J 1898- AmSCAP 1966,
IntMPA 1977
Kay, Elizabeth C WomWMM B
Kay, Gilbert Lee IntMPA 1977
Kay, Gordon 1916- IntMPA 1977
Kay, Henry 1911-1968 WhScrn 1, WhScrn 2
Kay, Hershy 1919- AmSCAP 1966, BiE&WWA,
NotNAT

Kay, Julian 1910- *AmSCAP 1966*
Kay, Mack H 1917- *AmSCAP 1966*
Kay, Marjorie *Film 1*
Kay, Monte *NewYTET*
Kay, Richard *WhoHol A, WhoThe 16*
Kayama, Yuzo 1937- *IntMPA 1977*
Kayden, Mildred *AmSCAP 1966*
Kaye, Albert Patrick 1878-1946 *NotNAT B,
WhThe*
Kaye, Benjamin M 1883- *AmSCAP 1966*
Kaye, Benny 1915- *AmSCAP 1966*
Kaye, Buddy 1918- *AmSCAP 1966*
Kaye, Carmen d1962 *NotNAT B*
Kaye, Celia *WhoHol A*
Kaye, Danny 1913- *BiDFlm, BiE&WWA,
CelR 3, CmMov, EncMT, FilmgC,
IntMPA 1977, MotPP, MovMk, NewYTET,
NotNAT, OxFilm, OxThe, WhoHol A,
WhoThe 16, WorEnF*
Kaye, Danny 1918- *NotNAT A*
Kaye, Frederick *WhThe*
Kaye, James R 1929- *AmSCAP 1966*
Kaye, Joseph *BiE&WWA, NotNAT*
Kaye, Norman 1922- *AmSCAP 1966*
Kaye, Peter 1918- *AmSCAP 1966*
Kaye, Phil 1912-1959 *WhScrn 1, WhScrn 2,
WhoHol B*
Kaye, Sammy 1910- *AmSCAP 1966, WhoHol A*
Kaye, Sparky 1906-1971 *WhScrn 1, WhScrn 2,
WhoHol B*
Kaye, Stubby 1918- *BiE&WWA, FilmgC,
MotPP, NotNAT, PIP&P, WhoHol A,
WhoThe 16*
Kaye, William 1917- *AmSCAP 1966*
Kayser, Kathryn E 1896- *BiE&WWA, NotNAT*
Kayssler, Christian 1898-1944 *WhScrn 2*
Kayssler, Friedrich 1874-1945 *Film 2, WhScrn 2*
Kazan, Elia 1909- *BiDFlm, BiE&WWA, CelR 3,
CnThe, DcFM, FilmgC, IntMPA 1977,
MovMk, NotNAT, NotNAT A, OxFilm,
OxThe, PIP&P, WhThe, WhoHol A,
WorEnF*
Kazan, Lainie 1940- *CelR 3, WhoHol A*
Kazan, Molly 1906-1963 *BiE&WWA, NotNAT B*
Kazantzakis, Nikos 1883-1957 *CnMD,
NotNAT B*
Kazin, Alfred 1915- *CelR 3*
Kaznar, Kurt *PIP&P*
Kaznar, Kurt *see also* Kasznar, Kurt
Keach, Stacey 1941- *BiDFlm*
Keach, Stacy 1941- *CelR 3, CnThe, FilmgC,
MovMk, NotNAT, WhoHol A, WhoThe 16*
Keach, Stacy 1942- *IntMPA 1977*
Keach, Stacy, Sr. 1914- *IntMPA 1977*
Kealy, Thomas J 1874-1949 *WhThe*
Kealy, Tom 1874-1949 *NotNAT B*
Kean, Betty 1920- *BiE&WWA, NotNAT,
WhoHol A*
Kean, Mrs. Charles 1806-1880 *NotNAT B*
Kean, Charles John 1811-1868 *FamA&A,
NotNAT A, NotNAT B, OxThe, PIP&P*
Kean, Edmund 1787-1833 *CnThe, FamA&A,
NotNAT A, NotNAT B, OxThe, PIP&P*
Kean, Edward George 1924- *AmSCAP 1966*
Kean, Ellen Tree 1806-1880 *OxThe*
Kean, Jane 1928- *BiE&WWA, NotNAT*
Kean, Marie 1922- *WhoHol A, WhoThe 16*
Kean, Norman 1934- *BiE&WWA, NotNAT,
WhoThe 16*
Kean, Richard 1892-1959 *WhScrn 1, WhScrn 2,
WhoHol B*
Kean, Thomas *OxThe, PIP&P*
Keane, Constance *WhScrn 2*
Keane, Doris 1881-1945 *NotNAT B, WhThe*

Keane, Doris 1885-1945 *Film 2, WhScrn 1,
WhScrn 2, WhoHol B*
Keane, Edward 1884-1959 *WhScrn 2*
Keane, James *Film 2*
Keane, John B 1928- *ConDr 1977*
Keane, Raymond 1907-1973 *Film 2, MotPP,
TwYS*
Keane, Robert Emmett 1883- *FilmgC, Vers B,
WhThe, WhoHol B*
Keane, Robert Emmett 1893- *MovMk*
Keanrey, John L 1871-1945 *WhScrn 2*
Kearney, Carolyn *WhoHol A*
Kearney, Don L 1918- *IntMPA 1977*
Kearney, John *Film 2*
Kearney, Kate d1926 *NotNAT B*
Kearney, Michael *WhoHol A*
Kearney, Patrick d1933 *NotNAT B*
Kearns, Allen d1956 *Film 2, WhoHol B*
Kearns, Allen 1893-1956 *EncMT, NotNAT B,
WhThe*
Kearns, Allen B 1895-1956 *WhScrn 1, WhScrn 2*
Kearns, Joseph 1907-1962 *NotNAT B, WhScrn 1,
WhScrn 2, WhoHol B*
Kearton, Cherry 1871-1940 *FilmgC*
Keatan, A Harry 1896-1966 *WhScrn 1, WhScrn 2*
Keate, Gwen *Film 2*
Keathley, George 1925- *BiE&WWA, NotNAT*
Keating, Anna-Lena *WomWMM A,
WomWMM B*
Keating, Charles 1941- *WhoThe 16*
Keating, Fred 1902-1961 *NotNAT B, WhScrn 1,
WhScrn 2, WhoHol B*
Keating, John G 1919-1968 *NotNAT B*
Keating, John Henry 1870-1963 *AmSCAP 1966*
Keating, Katherine *WhScrn 2*
Keating, Larry 1896-1963 *NotNAT B, Vers A,
WhScrn 1, WhScrn 2, WhoHol B*
Keating, Larry 1897-1963 *FilmgC*
Keaton, Buster d1966 *MotPP, WhoHol B*
Keaton, Buster 1895-1966 *BiDFlm, CmMov,
DcFM, Film 1, Film 2, FilmgC, MovMk,
OxFilm, WhScrn 1, WhScrn 2, WorEnF*
Keaton, Buster 1896-1966 *TwYS, TwYS A*
Keaton, Diane *IntMPA 1977, WhoHol A*
Keaton, Diane 1946- *MovMk*
Keaton, Diane 1949- *FilmgC*
Keaton, Harry d1966 *WhoHol B*
Keaton, Joe d1946 *Film 2, WhoHol B*
Keaton, Joseph, Sr. 1867-1946 *WhScrn 1,
WhScrn 2*
Keaton, Myra d1955 *WhScrn 1, WhScrn 2,
WhoHol B*
Keats, Donald 1929- *AmSCAP 1966*
Keats, Steven *WhoHol A*
Keats, Viola 1911- *WhoHol A, WhoThe 16*
Kechley, Gerald 1919- *AmSCAP 1966*
Keckley, Jane *Film 2*
Keden, Joe 1898- *AmSCAP 1966*
Kedrov, Mikhail Nikolayevich 1893-1972 *OxThe*
Kedrov, Mikhail Nikolayevich 1894-1972 *WhScrn 2*
Kedrova, Lila 1918- *FilmgC, MotPP, MovMk,
WhoHol A*
Kedzierzwska, Jadwiga *WomWMM B*
Keedwell, Norval *Film 2*
Keefe, Cornelius 1900-1972 *WhScrn 2*
Keefe, Cornelius 1902-1972 *Film 2, TwYS*
Keefe, Zeena 1896- *Film 2, TwYS, WhoHol A*
Keefe, Zena 1896- *Film 1*
Keefer, Don *WhoHol A*
Keegan, Arthur J 1895- *AmSCAP 1966*
Keehn, Neal 1909- *IntMPA 1977*
Keel, Howard *MotPP*
Keel, Howard 1917- *FilmgC, IntMPA 1977*
Keel, Howard 1918?- *WhoHol A*

Keel, Howard 1919- *BiE&WWA, CmMov, EncMT, MGM, MovMk, NotNAT, WhoThe 16, WorEnF*
Keeler, Elisha C *WhoHol A*
Keeler, Ruby *MotPP, PIP&P*
Keeler, Ruby 1909- *BiDFlm, CmMov, EncMT, FilmgC, MovMk, ThFT, WhoHol A, WhoThe 16*
Keeler, Ruby 1910- *BiE&WWA, CelR 3, NotNAT, OxFilm*
Keeler, Willie Sugar *Film 2*
Keeley, Louise 1833-1877 *OxThe*
Keeley, Lydia Alice Legge 1844-1892 *OxThe*
Keeley, Mary Ann Goward 1806-1899 *OxThe*
Keeley, Robert 1793-1869 *NotNAT B, OxThe*
Keeling, Robert Lee *Film 1, Film 2*
Keen, Diane *WhoHol A*
Keen, Geoffrey *WhoHol A*
Keen, Geoffrey 1916- *WhoThe 16*
Keen, Geoffrey 1918- *BiE&WWA, FilmgC, MovMk, NotNAT*
Keen, Malcolm 1887-1970 *BiE&WWA, Film 2, NotNAT B, PIP&P, WhScrn 2, WhThe, WhoHol B*
Keen, Noah *WhoHol A*
Keen, Richard *Film 2*
Keenan, Frances 1886-1950 *WhScrn 1, WhScrn 2, WhoHol B*
Keenan, Frank d1929 *MotPP, WhoHol B*
Keenan, Frank 1858-1929 *Film 1, Film 2, NotNAT B, WhThe*
Keenan, Frank 1859-1929 *WhScrn 1, WhScrn 2*
Keenan, Frank 1868-1929 *TwYS*
Keene, Day d1969 *WhoHol B*
Keene, Donald 1922- *BiE&WWA, NotNAT*
Keene, Elsie d1973 *WhScrn 2*
Keene, Hamilton *Film 2*
Keene, Kahn 1909- *AmSCAP 1966*
Keene, Laura d1873 *OxThe*
Keene, Laura 1820-1873 *FamA&A, NotNAT A, NotNAT B*
Keene, Laura 1826?-1873 *PIP&P*
Keene, Ralph 1902-1963 *FilmgC*
Keene, Richard 1890-1971 *Film 2, WhScrn 2, WhoHol B*
Keene, Thomas Wallace 1840-1898 *NotNAT B, OxThe*
Keene, Tom d1963 *MotPP, NotNAT B, WhoHol B*
Keene, Tom 1896-1963 *FilmgC*
Keene, Tom 1898-1963 *WhScrn 1, WhScrn 2*
Keene, Tom 1904-1963 *Film 2*
Keener, Hazel *Film 2, WhoHol A*
Keeney, C H 1899- *NatPD*
Keepfer, Margarete *Film 2*
Keeshan, Bob 1927- *IntMPA 1977, NewYTET*
Kefauver, Estes 1903-1963 *WhScrn 2*
Kegley, Kermit 1918-1974 *BiE&WWA, NotNAT B*
Kehner, Clarence Way 1926- *AmSCAP 1966*
Kehoe, Isobel *WomWMM*
Keighley, William 1889- *CmMov, DcFM, FilmgC, MovMk*
Keighley, William 1893- *BiDFlm, WorEnF*
Keightley, Cyril 1875-1929 *NotNAT B, WhThe*
Keiling, Robert Lee *Film 2*
Keilstrup, Margaret 1945- *NatPD*
Keim, Adelaide 1880- *WhThe*
Keim, Adelaide 1885- *WhoStg 1908*
Keim, Betty Lou 1938- *BiE&WWA, NotNAT, WhoHol A*
Keim, Buster C 1906-1974 *WhScrn 2*
Keir, Andrew 1926- *FilmgC, WhoHol A*
Keitel, Harvey 1939- *IntMPA 1977, MovMk,*

WhoHol A
Keith, Benjamin Franklin 1846-1914 *NotNAT B, OxThe, WhoStg 1906, WhoStg 1908*
Keith, Brian *MotPP, WhoHol A*
Keith, Brian 1921- *FilmgC, IntMPA 1977, WorEnF*
Keith, Brian 1922- *MovMk*
Keith, Donald 1905- *Film 2, TwYS*
Keith, Eugene *Film 2*
Keith, Ian 1899-1960 *Film 2, FilmgC, MotPP, MovMk, NotNAT B, TwYS, WhScrn 1, WhScrn 2, WhThe, WhoHol B*
Keith, Ian L 1911- *AmSCAP 1966*
Keith, Isabel *Film 2*
Keith, James 1902-1970 *WhScrn 1, WhScrn 2*
Keith, Penelope *WhoThe 16*
Keith, Robert 1896-1966 *FilmgC, MovMk*
Keith, Robert 1898-1966 *BiE&WWA, NotNAT, Vers A, WhScrn 1, WhScrn 2, WhThe, WhoHol B*
Keith, Sherwood 1912-1972 *WhScrn 2*
Keith-Johnston, Colin 1896- *BiE&WWA, Film 2, NotNAT, WhThe*
Keithley, E Clinton 1880-1955 *AmSCAP 1966*
Kelber, Michel 1908- *DcFM, WorEnF*
Kelcey, Herbert d1917 *WhoHol B*
Kelcey, Herbert 1855-1917 *NotNAT B, WhoStg 1906, WhoStg 1908*
Kelcey, Herbert 1856-1917 *WhScrn 2, WhThe*
Kelcey, Herbert 1857-1917 *Film 1*
Kelham, Avice 1892- *WhThe*
Kellar, Gertrude *Film 1*
Kellar, Leon *Film 2*
Kellard, Ralph d1955 *Film 1, Film 2, WhoHol B*
Kellard, Ralph 1882-1955 *WhScrn 2*
Kellard, Ralph 1884-1955 *NotNAT B, WhoStg 1908*
Kellaway, Cecil 1891-1973 *FilmgC, WhoHol B*
Kellaway, Cecil 1893-1973 *MovMk, WhScrn 2*
Kellaway, Cecil 1895-1973 *Vers A*
Kellem, Craig C 1943- *AmSCAP 1966*
Kellem, Milton 1911- *AmSCAP 1966*
Keller, Allen 1925- *AmSCAP 1966*
Keller, E *Film 1*
Keller, Frank *Film 2*
Keller, Gertrude 1881-1951 *WhScrn 1, WhScrn 2*
Keller, Greta *CelR 3*
Keller, Harry 1913- *FilmgC, IntMPA 1977, WorEnF*
Keller, Helen d1968 *WhoHol B*
Keller, Hiram *WhoHol A*
Keller, Jerry 1937- *AmSCAP 1966*
Keller, Kate Adams *Film 1*
Keller, Martha Rock *WomWMM B*
Keller, Marthe *WhoHol A*
Keller, Nan d1975 *WhScrn 2*
Keller, Nell Clark 1876-1965 *WhScrn 1, WhScrn 2, WhoHol B*
Keller, Phillip Brooks *Film 1*
Keller, Sheldon B 1923- *AmSCAP 1966*
Kellerd, E John 1863- *WhoStg 1908*
Kellerd, John E 1863-1929 *NotNAT B, WhoStg 1906*
Kellerman, Anette 1888- *Film 1*
Kellerman, Annette d1975 *WhoHol C*
Kellerman, Annette 1887-1975 *TwYS, WhScrn 2*
Kellerman, Annette 1888-1975 *Film 2, FilmgC*
Kellerman, Sally *WhoHol A*
Kellerman, Sally 1936- *IntMPA 1977*
Kellerman, Sally 1938- *MovMk*
Kellerman, Sally 1941- *FilmgC*
Kellermann, Annette d1975 *WhThe*
Kellers, Frederic 1929- *IntMPA 1977*

Kellett, Bob 1927- *FilmgC*
Kelley, Barry 1908- *FilmgC, IntMPA 1977,
Vers B*
Kelley, Bob 1917-1966 *WhScrn 2*
Kelley, DeForest *MotPP, WhoHol A*
Kelley, DeForrest 1920- *FilmgC*
Kelley, Edgar Stillman 1857-1944 *AmSCAP 1966*
Kelley, Pat *Film 1*
Kelley, Pat *see also* Kelley, Pat
Kelley, Patrick *IntMPA 1977*
Kellin, Mike 1922- *BiE&WWA, NotNAT,
WhoHol A*
Kellino, Pamela 1916- *FilmgC, WhoHol A*
Kellino, Roy 1912-1956 *FilmgC*
Kellino, Will P 1873-1958 *FilmgC*
Kellogg, Conelia 1877-1934 *WhScrn 1, WhScrn 2*
Kellogg, Cornelia d1934 *WhoHol B*
Kellogg, John 1916- *Vers A, WhoHol A*
Kellogg, Kay 1901- *AmSCAP 1966*
Kellogg, Marjorie *WomWMM*
Kellogg, Philip M 1912- *IntMPA 1977*
Kellogg, Shirley 1888- *WhThe*
Kellogg, Virginia *WomWMM*
Kelly, Al d1966 *WhoHol B*
Kelly, Ann d1852 *NotNAT B*
Kelly, Anthony Paul d1932 *NotNAT B*
Kelly, Barbara *WhoHol A*
Kelly, Bob 1923- *BiE&WWA, NotNAT*
Kelly, Brian *WhoHol A*
Kelly, Claire *MotPP*
Kelly, Don 1924-1966 *WhScrn 2*
Kelly, Dorothy 1894-1966 *Film 1, MotPP,
WhScrn 2, WhoHol B*
Kelly, Dorothy Helen 1918-1969 *WhScrn 1,
WhScrn 2, WhoHol B*
Kelly, Duke 1936- *IntMPA 1977*
Kelly, E H *WhThe*
Kelly, Elizabeth *WomWMM A*
Kelly, Emmett 1895- *FilmgC, WhoHol A*
Kelly, Eva 1880-1948 *NotNAT B, WhThe*
Kelly, Fannie 1876-1925 *WhScrn 1, WhScrn 2,
WhoHol B*
Kelly, Fanny d1882 *NotNAT B*
Kelly, Frances Maria 1790-1882 *NotNAT A,
NotNAT B, OxThe*
Kelly, Gene 1912- *BiDFlm, BiE&WWA, CelR 3,
CmMov, EncMT, FilmgC, IntMPA 1977,
MGM, MotPP, MovMk, NotNAT,
NotNAT A, OxFilm, PIP&P, WhThe,
WhoHol A, WorEnF*
Kelly, George 1887- *BiE&WWA, CnMD,
ConDr 1973, McGWD, ModWD, OxThe,
WomWMM*
Kelly, George 1890- *WhThe*
Kelly, Grace *IntMPA 1977, MotPP, WhoHol A*
Kelly, Grace 1928- *BiDFlm, CmMov, FilmgC,
OxFilm*
Kelly, Grace 1929- *BiE&WWA, MovMk,
NotNAT, WorEnF*
Kelly, Gregory 1891-1927 *Film 2, NotNAT B,
WhScrn 1, WhScrn 2, WhoHol B*
Kelly, Harry *WhoStg 1906, WhoStg 1908*
Kelly, Hugh 1739-1777 *NotNAT B, OxThe*
Kelly, J Arthur 1922- *IntMPA 1977*
Kelly, Jack 1927- *FilmgC, WhoHol A*
Kelly, James 1915-1964 *NotNAT B, WhScrn 1,
WhScrn 2*
Kelly, James A 1891- *AmSCAP 1966*
Kelly, James T *Film 1*
Kelly, Jim *IntMPA 1977, WhoHol A*
Kelly, Joe d1959 *WhScrn 2*
Kelly, John d1751 *NotNAT B*
Kelly, John 1901-1947 *Film 2, WhScrn 2*
Kelly, John B, Jr. 1927- *CelR 3*

Kelly, John T 1852-1922 *WhScrn 1, WhScrn 2*
Kelly, John T 1855- *WhoStg 1906, WhoStg 1908*
Kelly, Judy 1913- *FilmgC, WhThe, WhoHol A*
Kelly, Kevin 1930- *BiE&WWA*
Kelly, Kevin 1934- *NotNAT*
Kelly, Kitty 1902-1968 *Film 2, WhScrn 1,
WhScrn 2, WhoHol B*
Kelly, Lew 1879-1944 *NotNAT B, WhScrn 1,
WhScrn 2, WhoHol B*
Kelly, Mary Bubbles 1895-1941 *WhScrn 1,
WhScrn 2, WhoHol B*
Kelly, Mary Pat *WomWMM A, WomWMM B*
Kelly, Maurice 1928-1974 *WhScrn 2, WhoHol B*
Kelly, Michael d1826 *NotNAT A, NotNAT B*
Kelly, Nancy 1921- *BiE&WWA, Film 2,
FilmgC, IntMPA 1977, MotPP, MovMk,
NotNAT, ThFT, WhoHol A, WhoThe 16*
Kelly, Nell 1910-1939 *WhScrn 1, WhScrn 2*
Kelly, Pat 1891-1938 *WhScrn 2*
Kelly, Pat *see also* Kelley, Pat
Kelly, Patsy 1910- *CelR 3, EncMT, FilmgC,
MotPP, MovMk, PIP&P, ThFT, WhoHol A,
WhoThe 16*
Kelly, Paul 1899-1956 *Film 1, Film 2, FilmgC,
HolP 30, MotPP, MovMk, NotNAT B,
TwYS, WhScrn 1, WhScrn 2, WhThe,
WhoHol B*
Kelly, Paula *WhoHol A*
Kelly, Peggy *Film 2*
Kelly, Renee 1888-1965 *WhThe*
Kelly, Robert d1949 *NotNAT B*
Kelly, Robert 1916- *PIP&P*
Kelly, Scotch *Film 2*
Kelly, Tim 1937- *NatPD*
Kelly, Tommy 1925- *MotPP, WhoHol A*
Kelly, W W 1853-1933 *NotNAT B, WhThe*
Kelly, Walt 1913-1973 *AmSCAP 1966, CelR 3*
Kelly, Walter C 1873-1939 *NotNAT A,
NotNAT B, WhScrn 1, WhScrn 2, WhThe,
WhoHol B*
Kelly, William J 1875?-1949 *NotNAT B,
WhScrn 1, WhScrn 2, WhoHol B*
Kelsall, Moultrie 1901?- *FilmgC, WhoHol A*
Kelsey, Fred 1884-1961 *Film 1, Film 2, TwYS,
Vers B, WhScrn 1, WhScrn 2, WhoHol B*
Kelso, Bobby *Film 2*
Kelso, Mayme 1867-1946 *Film 1, Film 2, TwYS,
WhScrn 2*
Kelso, Vernon 1893- *WhThe*
Kelson, George *Film 1*
Kelt, John d1935 *NotNAT B, WhoHol B*
Kelton, Pert d1968 *BiE&WWA, WhoHol B*
Kelton, Pert 1907-1968 *Film 2, FilmgC, MovMk,
ThFT, WhScrn 1, WhScrn 2*
Kelton, Pert 1909-1968 *NotNAT B*
Kelvin, Thelda *Film 2*
Kemble, Adelaide 1814-1879 *NotNAT B*
Kemble, Mrs. Charles 1773?-1838 *NotNAT B*
Kemble, Charles 1775-1854 *FamA&A,
NotNAT A, NotNAT B, OxThe, PIP&P*
Kemble, Elizabeth d1836 *NotNAT B*
Kemble, Fanny 1809-1893 *NotNAT A,
NotNAT B*
Kemble, Frances d1822 *NotNAT B*
Kemble, Frances Anne 1809-1893 *FamA&A,
OxThe*
Kemble, Harry d1836 *NotNAT B*
Kemble, Henry 1848-1907 *NotNAT B, OxThe*
Kemble, Mrs. J P 1755-1845 *NotNAT B*
Kemble, John Mitchell d1857 *NotNAT B*
Kemble, John Philip 1757-1823 *CnThe,
NotNAT A, NotNAT B, OxThe, PIP&P*
Kemble, Mrs. Roger d1807 *NotNAT B*
Kemble, Roger 1721-1802 *NotNAT B*

Kemble, Roger 1722-1802 *OxThe, PlP&P*
Kemble, Mrs. Stephen d1841 *NotNAT B*
Kemble, Stephen 1758-1822 *NotNAT B, OxThe, PlP&P*
Kemble, Theresa DeCamp 1773-1838 *OxThe*
Kemble-Cooper, Violet 1886-1961 *WhScrn 1, WhScrn 2, WhoHol B*
Kemeny, John *IntMPA 1977*
Kemmer, Ed *WhoHol A*
Kemmer, George W 1890- *AmSCAP 1966*
Kemp, Everett 1874-1958 *WhScrn 1, WhScrn 2, WhoHol B*
Kemp, Hal 1904-1940 *WhScrn 1, WhScrn 2, WhoHol B*
Kemp, Jeremy *WhoHol A*
Kemp, Jeremy 1934- *FilmgC*
Kemp, Jeremy 1935- *IntMPA 1977, WhoThe 16*
Kemp, Margaret *Film 2*
Kemp, Matty 1907- *Film 2, TwYS*
Kemp, Paul 1899-1953 *WhScrn 1, WhScrn 2, WhoHol B*
Kemp, Robert 1885-1959 *NotNAT B, OxThe*
Kemp, Sally 1933- *BiE&WWA*
Kemp, Thomas Charles 1891-1955 *NotNAT B, OxThe, WhThe*
Kemp, William 1580-1603 *NotNAT B, PlP&P*
Kemp-Welch, Joan 1906- *FilmgC, IntMPA 1977, WhoHol A, WhoThe 16*
Kempe, Karin *WomWMM B*
Kempe, William d1603 *OxThe*
Kemper, Charles 1901-1950 *WhScrn 1, WhScrn 2, WhoHol B*
Kemper, Collin 1870-1955 *NotNAT B, WhThe, WhoStg 1908*
Kemper, Ronnie 1912- *AmSCAP 1966*
Kempinski, Leo A 1891-1958 *AmSCAP 1966*
Kempson, Rachel 1910- *CnThe, FilmgC, WhoHol A, WhoThe 16*
Kempton, Murray 1918- *CelR 3*
Kenan, Amos 1927- *CnMD Sup*
Kendal, Mrs. 1849-1935 *WhoStg 1906*
Kendal, Doris *WhThe*
Kendal, Ezra 1861- *WhoStg 1906, WhoStg 1908*
Kendal, Felicity 1946- *WhoThe 16*
Kendal, Leo *Film 1*
Kendal, Madge 1848-1935 *NotNAT A, OxThe, WhThe*
Kendal, Madge 1849-1935 *FamA&A, NotNAT B, WhoStg 1908*
Kendal, William Hunter 1843-1917 *NotNAT A, NotNAT B, OxThe, WhThe, WhoStg 1906, WhoStg 1908*
Kendall, Cy 1898-1953 *Vers A, WhScrn 1, WhScrn 2, WhoHol B*
Kendall, Cyrus Q 1898-1953 *FilmgC*
Kendall, Henry 1897-1962 *FilmgC, NotNAT A, NotNAT B, WhThe, WhoHol B*
Kendall, Henry 1898-1962 *Film 2, WhScrn 1, WhScrn 2*
Kendall, John 1869- *WhThe*
Kendall, Kay d1959 *MotPP, WhoHol B*
Kendall, Kay 1926-1959 *FilmgC, MovMk, NotNAT B, WhScrn 1, WhScrn 2*
Kendall, Kay 1927-1959 *BiDFlm, CmMov, WorEnF*
Kendall, Madge *PlP&P*
Kendall, Marie d1964 *NotNAT B*
Kendall, Nancy *WomWMM A, WomWMM B*
Kendall, Ross C 1886- *AmSCAP 1966*
Kendall, Suzy 1943?- *FilmgC, IntMPA 1977, WhoHol A*
Kendall, William 1903- *PlP&P, WhoHol A, WhoThe 16*
Kendis, James 1883-1946 *AmSCAP 1966*

Kendrick, Alfred 1869- *WhThe*
Kendrick, Brian 1930-1970 *WhScrn 1, WhScrn 2*
Kendrick, Ruby *Film 1*
Kenley, John 1907- *BiE&WWA, NotNAT*
Kenna, Mr. And Mrs. *PlP&P*
Kenna, Peter 1930- *ConDr 1977*
Kennan, George F 1904- *CelR 3*
Kennan, Kent Wheeler 1913- *AmSCAP 1966*
Kennard, Jane d1938 *NotNAT B*
Kennard, Victor *Film 1*
Kennaway, James 1928-1968 *FilmgC, NotNAT B*
Kenneally, Philip *WhoHol A*
Kennedy, Adam *WhoHol A*
Kennedy, Adrienne 1931- *ConDr 1977, CroCD, NotNAT*
Kennedy, Arthur 1914- *BiDFlm, BiE&WWA, CmMov, FilmgC, HolP 40, IntMPA 1977, MotPP, MovMk, NotNAT, PlP&P, WhoHol A, WhoThe 16, WorEnF*
Kennedy, Beulah d1964 *NotNAT B*
Kennedy, Burt 1923- *BiDFlm, CmMov, DcFM, FilmgC, IntMPA 1977, WorEnF*
Kennedy, Charles E 1867- *WhoStg 1908*
Kennedy, Charles Lamb d1881 *NotNAT B*
Kennedy, Charles Rann 1871-1950 *Film 2, NotNAT B, WhScrn 1, WhScrn 2, WhThe, WhoHol B*
Kennedy, Cheryl 1947- *WhoHol A, WhoThe 16*
Kennedy, Douglas 1915-1973 *FilmgC, IntMPA 1977, Vers B, WhScrn 2, WhoHol B*
Kennedy, Edgar 1890-1948 *Film 1, Film 2, FilmgC, MotPP, MovMk, NotNAT B, TwYS, Vers A, WhScrn 1, WhScrn 2, WhoHol B*
Kennedy, Edmund 1873- *WhThe*
Kennedy, Edward *Film 2*
Kennedy, Edward M 1932- *CelR 3*
Kennedy, Ethel 1928- *CelR 3*
Kennedy, Ethyl *WomWMM*
Kennedy, Fred d1958 *WhoHol B*
Kennedy, Frederick O 1910-1958 *WhScrn 1, WhScrn 2*
Kennedy, George *MotPP, WhoHol A*
Kennedy, George 1925- *FilmgC, MovMk, WorEnF*
Kennedy, George 1927- *CmMov, IntMPA 1977*
Kennedy, H A d1905 *NotNAT B*
Kennedy, Harold J *NotNAT, WhoThe 16*
Kennedy, Hazel *Film 2*
Kennedy, Helen d1973 *WhScrn 2*
Kennedy, Jack d1964 *Film 2, WhoHol B*
Kennedy, Jay Richard 1904- *AmSCAP 1966*
Kennedy, Joan 1937- *CelR 3*
Kennedy, John *BiE&WWA, NotNAT*
Kennedy, John F d1960 *WhScrn 1, WhScrn 2, WhoHol B*
Kennedy, Joseph C 1890-1949 *WhScrn 1, WhScrn 2*
Kennedy, Joseph P 1888-1969 *OxFilm, WorEnF*
Kennedy, Joyce 1898-1943 *NotNAT B, WhScrn 1, WhScrn 2, WhThe, WhoHol B*
Kennedy, King 1904-1974 *WhScrn 2, WhoHol B*
Kennedy, Lila 1903- *BiE&WWA*
Kennedy, Madge 1892- *Film 1, Film 2, MotPP, TwYS, WhThe, WhoHol A*
Kennedy, Margaret 1896-1967 *McGWD, ModWD, WhThe*
Kennedy, Margaret Fairlie *WomWMM B*
Kennedy, Mary 1908- *Film 2, WhThe*
Kennedy, Maurice d1962 *NotNAT B*
Kennedy, Merna d1944 *NotNAT B, WhoHol B*
Kennedy, Merna 1908-1944 *Film 2, TwYS, WhScrn 1, WhScrn 2*

Kennedy, Merna 1909-1944 *MovMk*
Kennedy, Myrna *FilmgC*
Kennedy, Patricia 1917- *WhoThe 16*
Kennedy, Rose 1890- *CelR 3*
Kennedy, Tom 1884-1965 *WhScrn 1, WhScrn 2*
Kennedy, Tom 1885-1965 *Film 1, Film 2, TwYS, WhoHol B*
Kennedy, Tom 1887-1965 *Vers A*
Kennelly, Norman *NatPD*
Kenner, Hugh 1923- *BiE&WWA*
Kenner, William Hugh 1923- *NotNAT*
Kenneth 1927- *CelR 3*
Kenneth, Harry D 1854-1929 *WhScrn 1, WhScrn 2*
Kenneth, Keith 1887-1966 *WhScrn 2, WhoHol B*
Kenney, H Wesley *IntMPA 1977*
Kenney, Jack 1888-1964 *NotNAT B, WhScrn 1, WhScrn 2*
Kenney, James d1849 *NotNAT B*
Kenney, James 1930- *FilmgC, WhoHol A, WhoThe 16*
Kenningham, Charles d1925 *NotNAT B*
Kenny, Charles F 1898- *AmSCAP 1966*
Kenny, Colin d1968 *Film 1, Film 2, WhScrn 2*
Kenny, Leola 1892-1956 *WhScrn 1, WhScrn 2, WhoHol B*
Kenny, Nick 1895-1975 *AmSCAP 1966, WhScrn 2*
Kenny, Sean 1932-1973 *BiE&WWA, CnThe, WhThe*
Kent, Mrs. *Film 2*
Kent, Arnold 1899-1928 *Film 2, WhScrn 1, WhScrn 2, WhoHol B*
Kent, Arthur 1920- *AmSCAP 1966*
Kent, Barbara 1906- *Film 2, ThFT, TwYS, WhoHol A*
Kent, Barry 1932- *WhoThe 16*
Kent, Charles 1852-1923 *Film 1, Film 2, NotNAT B, TwYS, WhScrn 2, WhoHol B*
Kent, Charlotte 1907- *AmSCAP 1966*
Kent, Christopher *WhoHol A*
Kent, Mrs. Crauford *Film 2*
Kent, Crauford d1952 *WhoHol B*
Kent, Crauford 1881-1953 *Film 2, WhScrn 1, WhScrn 2*
Kent, Crawford 1881-1953 *Film 1, NotNAT B, TwYS*
Kent, Dorothea 1917- *ThFT*
Kent, Douglas *WhScrn 2*
Kent, Douglass *WhScrn 1*
Kent, Edgar *PIP&P*
Kent, Elinor d1957 *WhScrn 1, WhScrn 2*
Kent, Ethel 1884-1952 *WhScrn 1, WhScrn 2, WhoHol B*
Kent, Gerald d1944 *WhScrn 1, WhScrn 2, WhoHol B*
Kent, Jean 1921- *FilmgC, IntMPA 1977, WhoHol A, WhoThe 16*
Kent, John B 1939- *IntMPA 1977*
Kent, Kate 1864-1934 *WhScrn 2*
Kent, Keneth 1892-1963 *WhScrn 1, WhScrn 2, WhThe*
Kent, Kenneth d1963 *PIP&P, WhoHol B*
Kent, Larry *Film 2, TwYS*
Kent, Leon *Film 1*
Kent, Marsha 1919-1971 *WhScrn 1, WhScrn 2, WhoHol B*
Kent, Marshall *WhoHol A*
Kent, Ray 1886-1948 *WhScrn 2*
Kent, Robert d1954 *WhoHol B*
Kent, Robert 1908-1955 *WhScrn 2*
Kent, S Miller d1948 *NotNAT B*
Kent, Sandra 1927- *AmSCAP 1966*
Kent, Walter 1911- *AmSCAP 1966*

Kent, Willard 1883-1968 *WhScrn 2*
Kent, William T 1886-1945 *Film 2, NotNAT B, WhScrn 1, WhScrn 2, WhThe, WhoHol B*
Kentish, Agatha 1897- *WhThe*
Kenton, Erle C 1896- *CmMov, FilmgC, TwYS A*
Kenton, Godfrey 1902- *WhoThe 16*
Kenton, Stanley Newcomb 1912- *AmSCAP 1966*
Kentucky Jubilee Singers *Film 2*
Kenwith, Herbert *NewYTET*
Kenyon, Charles 1878-1961 *NotNAT B, WhThe*
Kenyon, Curtis *IntMPA 1977*
Kenyon, Doris 1897- *Film 1, Film 2, FilmgC, MotPP, MovMk, ThFT, TwYS, WhThe, WhoHol A*
Kenyon, Nancye *Film 2*
Kenyon, Neil d1946 *WhThe*
Keogh, J A d1942 *NotNAT B*
Keogh, William T d1947 *NotNAT B*
Keown, Eric 1904-1963 *NotNAT B, WhThe*
Kepler, Edward *Film 2*
Kepner, Fred 1921- *AmSCAP 1966*
Keppens, Emile d1926 *WhScrn 1, WhScrn 2*
Kerans, Barbara Kay *WomWMM B*
Kerasotes, George G 1911- *IntMPA 1977*
Kerby, Marion *Film 1*
Kerby, Marion d1956 *NotNAT B*
Kerby, Paul 1903- *AmSCAP 1966*
Kerger, Ann 1894- *AmSCAP 1966*
Kergy, Albert *Film 2*
Kerima 1925- *FilmgC*
Kerin, Nora 1883- *WhThe*
Kerker, Gustave Adolph 1857-1923 *AmSCAP 1966, EncMT, NewMT, NotNAT B, WhThe, WhoStg 1906, WhoStg 1908*
Kerly, L *Film 2*
Kerman, David *WhoHol A*
Kerman, Sheppard 1928- *NatPD*
Kermoyan, Michael 1925- *BiE&WWA, NotNAT, WhoHol A*
Kern, James V 1909-1966 *AmSCAP 1966, FilmgC, WhScrn 1, WhScrn 2*
Kern, Jerome 1885-1945 *AmSCAP 1966, CmMov, EncMT, FilmgC, McGWD, NewMT, NotNAT A, NotNAT B, OxFilm, PIP&P, WhThe*
Kernan, David 1939- *WhoHol A, WhoThe 16*
Kernan, Joseph Lewis d1964 *NotNAT B*
Kerndl, Rainer 1928- *CroCD*
Kernell, William B 1891-1963 *AmSCAP 1966*
Kernochan, Marshall 1880-1955 *AmSCAP 1966*
Kernochan, Sarah *WomWMM*
Kernodle, George R 1907- *BiE&WWA, NotNAT*
Kerns, Eddie *Film 2*
Kerolenko, Agnes *Film 2*
Kerouac, Jack d1969 *WhoHol B*
Keroul, Henri 1857-1921 *NotNAT B*
Kerr, Alfred d1948 *NotNAT B*
Kerr, Anita *WomWMM*
Kerr, Bill *WhoHol A, WhoThe 16*
Kerr, Bob *Film 2*
Kerr, Deborah 1921- *BiDFlm, BiE&WWA, CelR 3, FilmgC, IntMPA 1977, MGM, MotPP, MovMk, NotNAT, OxFilm, PIP&P A, WhoHol A, WhoThe 16, WorEnF*
Kerr, Fraser 1931- *IntMPA 1977*
Kerr, Frederick 1858-1933 *FilmgC, NotNAT B, WhScrn 1, WhScrn 2, WhThe, WhoHol B*
Kerr, Frederick 1858-1934 *Film 2*
Kerr, Geoffrey 1895- *BiE&WWA, Film 2, NotNAT, WhThe, WhoHol A*
Kerr, Harry D 1880-1957 *AmSCAP 1966*
Kerr, Jane d1954 *WhScrn 1, WhScrn 2, WhoHol B*
Kerr, Jean 1923- *AmSCAP 1966, BiE&WWA,*

CelR 3, NotNAT, WhoThe 16
Kerr, John 1931- BiE&WWA, FilmgC,
   IntMPA 1977, MotPP, NotNAT, WhoHol A
Kerr, Lorence Larry d1968 WhScrn 2
Kerr, Marge BiE&WWA
Kerr, Molly 1904- WhThe
Kerr, Phil 1906-1960 AmSCAP 1966
Kerr, Sophie 1880-1965 NotNAT B
Kerr, Walter 1913- BiE&WWA, CelR 3,
   NotNAT, WhoThe 16
Kerr, Walter Francis 1913- AmSCAP 1966
Kerr, William J 1890- AmSCAP 1966
Kerr-Sokal, Charlotte WomWMM
Kerrick, Thomas d1927 WhScrn 1, WhScrn 2,
   WhoHol B
Kerridge, Mary 1914- WhoHol A, WhoThe 16
Kerrigan, J M 1885-1964 FilmgC, WhThe
Kerrigan, J M 1885-1965 MovMk
Kerrigan, J M 1887-1964 Film 2, WhoHol B
Kerrigan, J Warren 1880-1947 Film 1, Film 2,
   FilmgC, NotNAT B
Kerrigan, J Warren 1889-1947 MotPP, TwYS,
   WhScrn 1, WhScrn 2, WhoHol B
Kerrigan, Joseph M 1887-1964 NotNAT B,
   Vers B, WhScrn 1, WhScrn 2
Kerrigan, Kathleen 1869-1957 Film 2, WhScrn 2,
   WhoHol B
Kerry, Lucyann Snyder 1949- WomWMM B
Kerry, Margaret MotPP
Kerry, Norman 1889-1956 Film 1, Film 2,
   FilmgC, MotPP, MovMk, NotNAT B,
   TwYS, WhScrn 1, WhScrn 2, WhoHol B
Kersh, Kathy WhoHol A
Kershaw, Willette d1960 Film 1, Film 2,
   WhoHol B
Kershaw, Willette 1882-1960 WhScrn 2
Kershaw, Willette 1890-1960 NotNAT B, WhThe
Kershner, Irvin 1923- BiDFlm, FilmgC,
   IntMPA 1977, MovMk, OxFilm, WorEnF
Kersten, Albert E Film 2
Kert, Larry PIP&P A, WhoHol A
Kert, Larry 1930- EncMT, WhoThe 16
Kert, Larry 1934- BiE&WWA, NotNAT
Kertesz, Mihaly DcFM
Kerwood, Dick d1924 WhScrn 2
Kerz, Leo 1912- BiE&WWA, NotNAT
Kesdekian, Mesrop 1920- NotNAT
Keshen, Amy WomWMM B
Kesler, Lew 1915- AmSCAP 1966
Kesnar, Maurits 1900-1957 AmSCAP 1966
Kessel, Barney 1923- AmSCAP 1966
Kesselring, Joseph O 1902-1967 BiE&WWA,
   McGWD, ModWD, NotNAT B, WhThe
Kessler, David d1920 NotNAT B
Kessler, Edith Film 2
Kessler, Jascha Frederick 1929- AmSCAP 1966
Kessler, Joseph d1933 NotNAT B
Kessler, Ralph 1919- AmSCAP 1966
Kestelman, Sara 1944- WhoHol A, WhoThe 16
Kesten, Hermann 1900- ModWD
Kesten, Paul W d1956 NewYTET
Kester, Paul 1870-1933 NotNAT B, OxThe,
   WhThe
Ketchum, David WhoHol A
Ketchum, Robyna Neilson d1972 WhScrn 2
Ketron, Larry 1947- NatPD
Keveson, Peter 1919- AmSCAP 1966
Kevess, Arthur S 1916- AmSCAP 1966
Key, Kathleen d1954 MotPP, NotNAT B,
   WhoHol B
Key, Kathleen 1897-1954 Film 2, TwYS
Key, Kathleen 1906-1954 WhScrn 1, WhScrn 2
Key, Pat Ann d1962 NotNAT B
Keyawa, Stanley J 1920- AmSCAP 1966

Keyes, Baron 1898- AmSCAP 1966
Keyes, Daniel F WhoHol A
Keyes, Donald C AmSCAP 1966
Keyes, Evelyn 1919- FilmgC, HolP 40,
   IntMPA 1977, MotPP, MovMk, WhoHol A
Keyes, Frances Parkinson 1885- CelR 3
Keyes, John 1892-1966 WhScrn 2
Keyes, Laurence 1914- AmSCAP 1966
Keyes, Paul W NewYTET
Keys, Nelson d1939 Film 2, WhoHol B
Keys, Nelson 1886-1939 EncMT, NotNAT A,
   NotNAT B, WhThe
Keys, Nelson 1887-1939 WhScrn 1, WhScrn 2
Keyser-Heyl, Willy Film 2
Keystone Kids, The Film 1
Keystone Pets, The Film 1
Khachaturian, Aram 1904- DcFM
Khambatta, Persis WhoHol A
Khan, Mazhar d1950 WhScrn 2
Khan, Ramjakhan Mehboob DcFM
Khmelev, Nikolai Pavlovich 1901-1945 OxThe
Khmelof, N P WhScrn 2
Khmelyov, Nikolai Pavlovich 1901-1945 NotNAT B,
   WhScrn 2
Khodatayeva, O WomWMM
Khodateyev, Nikolai 1892- DcFM
Khoury, Edith Leslie d1973 WhScrn 2
Khoury, Edward A 1916- AmSCAP 1966
Kiamos, Eleni WhoHol A
Kibbee, Guy 1882-1956 FilmgC, NotNAT B
Kibbee, Guy 1886-1956 MotPP, MovMk, Vers A,
   WhScrn 1, WhScrn 2, WhoHol B
Kibbee, Milton d1970 Vers B, WhScrn 2
Kibbee, Roland 1914- FilmgC, IntMPA 1977,
   NewYTET
Kid, Mary Film 2
Kidd, Jim 1846-1916 WhScrn 2
Kidd, Jonathan WhoHol A
Kidd, Kathleen 1899-1961 NotNAT B, WhScrn 1,
   WhScrn 2, WhoHol B
Kidd, Michael 1919- BiE&WWA, CelR 3,
   CmMov, EncMT, FilmgC, NotNAT,
   WhoHol A, WhoThe 16, WorEnF
Kidd, Robert 1943- WhoThe 16
Kidder, Hugh 1880-1952 WhScrn 1, WhScrn 2,
   WhoHol B
Kidder, Kathryn 1867-1939 NotNAT B, WhThe,
   WhoStg 1906, WhoStg 1908
Kidder, Margot WhoHol A
Kido, Shiro 1894- IntMPA 1977
Kiegel, Leonard 1929- WorEnF
Kiel, Edith WomWMM
Kiel, Richard WhoHol A
Kiener, Hazel Film 2
Kiepura, Jan d1966 WhoHol B
Kiepura, Jan 1902-1966 FilmgC, MovMk,
   NotNAT B, OxFilm, WhScrn 1, WhScrn 2,
   WhThe
Kiepura, Jan 1909- BiE&WWA
Kierland, Joseph Scott NatPD
Kiernan, Baby Marie Film 1
Kiernan, James 1939-1975 WhScrn 2
Kiesler, Frederick J 1896- BiE&WWA
Kiesler, Frederick John 1890-1965 NotNAT B
Kihn, Albert d1974 NewYTET
Kiker, Douglas NewYTET
Kikuchi, Hiroshi 1888-1948 ModWD
Kikume, Al 1894-1972 WhScrn 2
Kilbride, Percy 1888-1964 FilmgC, MotPP,
   MovMk, NotNAT B, Vers A, WhScrn 1,
   WhScrn 2, WhoHol B
Kilbride, Richard D 1919-1967 WhScrn 1,
   WhScrn 2, WhoHol B
Kilburn, Terry 1926- FilmgC, MotPP,

WhoHol A
Kilduff, Helen 1888-1959 *WhScrn 1, WhScrn 2, WhoHol B*
Kilduff, Michal C *WomWMM B*
Kilenyi, Edward, Sr. 1884- *AmSCAP 1966*
Kiley, Richard 1922- *BiE&WWA, CelR 3, EncMT, FilmgC, IntMPA 1977, NotNAT, WhoHol A, WhoThe 16*
Kilfoil, Thomas F 1922- *BiE&WWA, NotNAT*
Kilgallen, Dorothy 1913-1965 *NotNAT B, WhScrn 1, WhScrn 2, WhoHol B*
Kilgallen, Rob *WhoHol A*
Kilgour, Joseph 1863-1933 *Film 1, Film 2, NotNAT B*
Kilgour, Joseph 1864-1933 *TwYS, WhScrn 2, WhoHol B*
Kilham, Gene 1919- *AmSCAP 1966*
Kilian, Victor 1891- *BiE&WWA, Film 2, FilmgC, NotNAT, Vers A, WhoHol A*
Kilian, Victor 1898- *IntMPA 1977, MovMk*
Killeen, Joseph L 1893- *AmSCAP 1966*
Killiam, Paul 1916- *FilmgC, IntMPA 1977*
Killian, James R *NewYTET*
Killick, C Egerton 1891-1967 *WhThe*
Killigrew, Charles 1665-1725 *NotNAT B, OxThe, PIP&P*
Killigrew, Thomas 1612-1683 *CnThe, NotNAT A, NotNAT B, OxThe, PIP&P, REnWD*
Killigrew, Thomas 1657-1719 *NotNAT B, OxThe*
Killigrew, Sir William 1606-1695 *NotNAT B, OxThe*
Killy, Jean-Claude 1943- *CelR 3, WhoHol A*
Kilmer, Bill 1939- *CelR 3*
Kilmer, Joyce 1886-1918 *AmSCAP 1966*
Kilmorey, Earl Of d1915 *NotNAT B*
Kilpack, Bennett 1883-1962 *NotNAT B, WhScrn 1, WhScrn 2, WhoHol B*
Kilpatrick, Jack Frederick 1915- *BiE&WWA*
Kilpatrick, Lincoln *WhoHol A*
Kilpatrick, Thomas 1902- *BiE&WWA*
Kilty, Jerome 1922- *BiE&WWA, NotNAT, PIP&P, WhoThe 16*
Kiltz, Rita 1895- *AmSCAP 1966*
Kim, Willa *NotNAT*
Kimball, Edward M 1859-1938 *Film 1, Film 2, WhScrn 1, WhScrn 2, WhoHol B*
Kimball, Grace 1870- *WhThe, WhoStg 1908*
Kimball, Louis 1889-1936 *NotNAT B, WhThe*
Kimball, Pauline 1860-1919 *WhScrn 2*
Kimberley, Mrs. F G d1939 *NotNAT B*
Kimbrough, Clint *WhoHol A*
Kimbrough, Clinton 1936- *BiE&WWA, NotNAT*
Kimes, Kenneth F 1920- *AmSCAP 1966*
Kimmel, Edwin H 1926- *AmSCAP 1966*
Kimmins, Anthony 1901- *IntMPA 1977*
Kimmins, Anthony 1901-1963 *FilmgC*
Kimmins, Anthony 1901-1964 *NotNAT B, WhThe*
Kimmins, Arthur d1963 *WhoHol B*
Kimura, Massa Kichi 1890-1918 *WhScrn 2*
Kincaid, Aron *WhoHol A*
Kinck, Hans 1865-1926 *OxThe*
Kindley, Jeffrey 1945- *NatPD*
King, Ada d1940 *NotNAT B, WhThe*
King, Al 1904- *AmSCAP 1966*
King, Alan *IntMPA 1977, WhoHol A*
King, Alan 1924- *FilmgC*
King, Alan 1927- *CelR 3*
King, Allan 1930- *WorEnF*
King, Allan 1933- *FilmgC*
King, Allyn 1901-1930 *Film 2, WhScrn 2*
King, Andrea *IntMPA 1977, MotPP*
King, Andrea 1915- *FilmgC*
King, Andrea 1918- *WhoHol A*

King, Anita 1880-1963 *TwYS*
King, Anita 1889-1963 *Film 1, FilmgC, MotPP, WhScrn 1, WhScrn 2, WhoHol B*
King, Archer *BiE&WWA*
King, Billie Jean 1943- *CelR 3*
King, Bradley *MotPP*
King, Burton 1887- *TwYS A*
King, Cammie *WhoHol A*
King, Carlotta *Film 2*
King, Carole *CelR 3*
King, Cecil d1958 *NotNAT B, WhThe*
King, Charles 1889-1944 *EncMT, FilmgC, NotNAT B, WhScrn 2, WhThe*
King, Charles 1894-1944 *WhScrn 1, WhoHol B*
King, Charles 1898-1944 *Film 2, TwYS*
King, Charles E 1874-1950 *AmSCAP 1966*
King, Charles L, Sr. 1899-1957 *FilmgC, Vers B, WhScrn 1, WhScrn 2, WhoHol B*
King, Claude 1876-1941 *NotNAT B, WhThe*
King, Claude 1879-1941 *Film 2, TwYS, WhScrn 1, WhScrn 2, WhoHol B*
King, Coretta 1927- *CelR 3*
King, Dave 1929- *FilmgC*
King, David *WhoHol A*
King, Dennis 1897-1971 *BiE&WWA, CnThe, EncMT, NotNAT B, WhScrn 1, WhScrn 2, WhThe, WhoHol B*
King, Dennis 1897-1972 *FilmgC*
King, Dennis, Jr. *WhoHol A*
King, Edith 1896- *WhThe, WhoHol A*
King, Edith 1897-1963 *BiE&WWA, NotNAT, NotNAT B*
King, Emmett d1953 *Film 1, NotNAT B, TwYS, WhoHol B*
King, Emmett 1892-1953 *Film 2*
King, Emmett C 1866-1953 *WhScrn 1, WhScrn 2*
King, Eugene W d1950 *WhScrn 1, WhScrn 2, WhoHol B*
King, Fay *Film 2*
King, George 1900-1966 *FilmgC*
King, Gerald *Film 2*
King, Henry 1888- *BiDFlm*
King, Henry 1892- *Film 1, FilmgC, MovMk, OxFilm, TwYS A, WorEnF*
King, Henry 1896- *CmMov, DcFM, IntMPA 1977*
King, Herman *IntMPA 1977*
King, Jack 1883-1943 *WhScrn 1, WhScrn 2, WhoHol B*
King, Jack 1903-1943 *AmSCAP 1966*
King, Joe 1883-1951 *Film 1, Film 2, WhScrn 2*
King, John Dusty 1909- *WhoHol A*
King, John-Michael 1929- *BiE&WWA*
King, Joseph *Film 2*
King, Judy *Film 2*
King, Kip *WhoHol A*
King, L H *Film 2*
King, Leslie 1876-1947 *Film 1, Film 2, WhScrn 2*
King, Louis 1898-1962 *Film 2, FilmgC, TwYS A*
King, Margie *Film 2*
King, Marie *Film 2*
King, Maurice *IntMPA 1977*
King, Mildred *AmSCAP 1966*
King, Mollie 1898- *Film 1, MotPP*
King, Molly 1898- *Film 2, TwYS*
King, Morgana *WhoHol A*
King, Murray J 1914- *IntMPA 1977*
King, Nosmo d1949 *NotNAT B*
King, Peggy 1931- *IntMPA 1977, WhoHol A*
King, Perry *IntMPA 1977, WhoHol A*
King, Pete 1914- *AmSCAP 1966*
King, Peter 1928- *IntMPA 1977*
King, Philip 1904- *CnThe, WhoThe 16*

King, Robert 1862-1932 *AmSCAP 1966,*
  NotNAT B
King, Ruth *Film 2*
King, Stoddard 1889-1933 *AmSCAP 1966*
King, Tom 1730-1804 *NotNAT B, OxThe*
King, Tony *WhoHol A*
King, Victor d1964 *NotNAT B*
King, Walter Woolf 1899- *FilmgC, WhThe,*
  WhoHol A
King, Wayne 1901- *AmSCAP 1966*
King, Will d1953 *WhoHol B*
King, Will 1886-1958 *WhScrn 1, WhScrn 2*
King, Wright *WhoHol A*
King, Zalman *WhoHol A*
King-Hall, Sir Stephen 1893-1966 *WhThe*
King Sisters, The *WhoHol A*
King-Wood, David *WhoHol A*
Kingdon, Dorothy 1894-1939 *WhScrn 1,*
  WhScrn 2, WhoHol B
Kingdon, Frank d1937 *NotNAT B, WhoHol B*
Kingdon, John M d1876 *NotNAT B*
Kingdon-Gould, Edith Maughan d1921 *NotNAT B*
Kingman, Dong 1911- *CelR 3, IntMPA 1977*
Kingsbury-Smith, Joseph 1908- *CelR 3*
Kingsford, Alison 1899-1950 *WhScrn 1,*
  WhScrn 2
Kingsford, Charles 1907- *AmSCAP 1966*
Kingsford, Walter 1882-1958 *FilmgC, WhScrn 1,*
  WhScrn 2
Kingsford, Walter 1884-1958 *NotNAT B, Vers A,*
  WhoHol B
Kingsley, Albert *Film 2*
Kingsley, Arthur *Film 2*
Kingsley, Dorothy *IntMPA 1977, WomWMM*
Kingsley, Dorothy 1908- *CmMov*
Kingsley, Dorothy 1909- *FilmgC*
Kingsley, Florida 1879- *Film 1, Film 2, TwYS*
Kingsley, Frank *Film 2*
Kingsley, Grace d1962 *NotNAT B*
Kingsley, Mary d1936 *NotNAT B*
Kingsley, Polly Arnold 1906- *AmSCAP 1966*
Kingsley, Sidney 1906- *BiE&WWA, CnMD,*
  CnThe, ConDr 1977, CroCD, FilmgC,
  McGWD, ModWD, NotNAT, OxThe,
  PIP&P, REnWD, WhoThe 16
Kingsley, Walter d1929 *NotNAT B*
Kingsley, Walter 1923- *IntMPA 1977*
Kingston, Gertrude 1866-1937 *NotNAT B, OxThe,*
  WhThe
Kingston, Muriel *Film 2, TwYS*
Kingston, Natalie *Film 2, TwYS, WhoHol A*
Kingston, Sam F d1929 *NotNAT B*
Kingston, Thomas 1902-1959 *WhScrn 1,*
  WhScrn 2
Kingston, Winifred 1895-1967 *Film 1, Film 2,*
  MotPP, TwYS, WhScrn 1, WhScrn 2,
  WhoHol B
Kinley, David D *NewYTET*
Kinnear, Roy 1934- *FilmgC, WhoHol A,*
  WhoThe 16
Kinnell, Murray 1889-1954 *NotNAT B,*
  WhScrn 1, WhScrn 2, WhoHol B
Kinnoch, Ronald 1911?- *FilmgC*
Kino, Goro *Film 2*
Kinoshita, Junji 1914- *CnMD, ModWD*
Kinoshita, Keisuke 1912- *DcFM, IntMPA 1977,*
  OxFilm, WorEnF
Kinoy, Ernest *IntMPA 1977, NewYTET,*
  NotNAT
Kinscella, Hazel Gertrude 1895-1960
  AmSCAP 1966
Kinsella, Kathleen 1878-1961 *NotNAT B,*
  WhScrn 1, WhScrn 2, WhoHol B
Kinsella, Walter A 1900-1975 *WhScrn 2,*

WhoHol C
Kinskey, Leonid 1903- *FilmgC, IntMPA 1977,*
  Vers A, WhoHol A
Kinsolving, Lee 1938-1974 *WhScrn 2, WhoHol B*
Kintner, Robert E *NewYTET*
Kinugasa, Teinosuke Kukame 1896- *BiDFlm,*
  DcFM, FilmgC, OxFilm, WorEnF
Kinyon, John 1918- *AmSCAP 1966*
Kinz, Franciska *Film 2*
Kipling, Edward *Film 2*
Kipling, Rudyard 1865-1936 *FilmgC*
Kipness, Joseph *BiE&WWA, NotNAT,*
  WhoThe 16
Kippen, Manart d1947 *WhScrn 1, WhScrn 2,*
  WhoHol B
Kipphardt, Heinar 1922- *CnMD, CnThe, CroCD,*
  McGWD, ModWD, REnWD, WhoThe 16
Kiralfy, Bolossy d1932 *NotNAT B*
Kiralfy, Imre d1919 *NotNAT B*
Kirby, David D 1880-1954 *Film 2, WhScrn 1,*
  WhScrn 2, WhoHol B
Kirby, Hudson d1848 *NotNAT B*
Kirby, John d1930 *NotNAT B*
Kirby, John 1894- *WhThe*
Kirby, John 1932-1973 *WhScrn 2, WhoHol B*
Kirby, Michael *NotNAT*
Kirby, William Warner 1876-1914 *WhScrn 2*
Kircher, Athanasius 1601-1680 *DcFM*
Kirchmayer, Thomas 1511-1563 *OxThe*
Kirgo, George *WhoHol A*
Kirienko, Zinaida *WhoHol A*
Kirk, Andrew D 1898- *AmSCAP 1966*
Kirk, Evans *Film 2*
Kirk, Fay B 1894-1954 *WhScrn 1, WhScrn 2*
Kirk, Jack Pappy 1895-1948 *WhScrn 2*
Kirk, Joe d1975 *WhoHol C*
Kirk, John d1948 *NotNAT B*
Kirk, John W 1932- *NatPD*
Kirk, Lisa *EncMT, MotPP*
Kirk, Lisa 1925- *WhoThe 16*
Kirk, Lisa 1926- *NotNAT*
Kirk, Phyllis *IntMPA 1977, MotPP*
Kirk, Phyllis 1926- *FilmgC*
Kirk, Phyllis 1929- *WhoHol A*
Kirk, Phyllis 1930- *MovMk*
Kirk, Theron 1919- *AmSCAP 1966*
Kirk, Tommy 1941- *FilmgC, WhoHol A*
Kirkby, Ollie *Film 1*
Kirke, Donald 1902-1971 *WhScrn 2, WhoHol B*
Kirke, John 1638-1643 *NotNAT B, OxThe*
Kirkeby, Wallace T 1891- *AmSCAP 1966*
Kirkham, Correan *Film 2*
Kirkham, Kathleen 1895- *Film 1, Film 2, TwYS*
Kirkhuff, John *WhScrn 2*
Kirkland, Alexander 1908- *BiE&WWA, WhThe,*
  WhoHol A
Kirkland, David 1878-1964 *WhScrn 2*
Kirkland, Hardee 1864?-1929 *Film 1, Film 2,*
  WhScrn 1, WhScrn 2, WhoHol B
Kirkland, Jack *PIP&P*
Kirkland, Jack 1901-1969 *CnMD, McGWD*
Kirkland, Jack 1902-1969 *BiE&WWA, ModWD,*
  NotNAT B, WhThe
Kirkland, Muriel 1903-1971 *BiE&WWA, FilmgC,*
  NotNAT B, WhScrn 1, WhScrn 2, WhThe,
  WhoHol B
Kirkland, Patricia 1925- *WhThe*
Kirkland, Sally 1944- *PIP&P, WhoHol A,*
  WhoThe 16
Kirkman, Francis d1674 *NotNAT B*
Kirkman, Kathleen *Film 2*
Kirkop, Oreste 1926- *FilmgC*
Kirkpatrick, Donald A 1928- *AmSCAP 1966*
Kirkwood, Gertrude Robinson d1962 *NotNAT B,*

WhScrn 1, WhScrn 2, WhoHol B
Kirkwood, Jack 1894-1964 NotNAT B
Kirkwood, Jack 1895-1964 WhScrn 1, WhScrn 2,
  WhoHol B
Kirkwood, James 1883-1963 Film 1, Film 2,
  WhScrn 1, WhScrn 2, WhoHol B
Kirkwood, James 1883-1966 TwYS
Kirkwood, James 1930- NatPD
Kirkwood, Joe, Jr. WhoHol A
Kirkwood, Pat 1921- FilmgC, WhoHol A,
  WhoThe 16
Kirkwood-Hackett, Eva 1877-1968 WhScrn 1,
  WhScrn 2
Kirkwood-Hackett, Eve d1968 WhoHol B
Kirsanoff, Dimitri 1899-1957 DcFM
Kirsanoff, Dmitri 1899-1957 OxFilm
Kirsanov, Dimitri 1889-1957 WorEnF
Kirsanov, Dmitri 1899-1957 FilmgC
Kirsh, Estelle WomWMM B
Kirshner, Don NewYTET
Kirshon, Vladimir Mikhailovich 1902-1938 CnMD,
  ModWD, OxThe
Kirsten, Dorothy 1917- WhoHol A
Kirtland, Clifford M, Jr. NewYTET
Kirtland, Harden Film 2
Kirtland, Louise 1905- WhoThe 16
Kirtland, Louise 1910- BiE&WWA, NotNAT
Kirtley, Virginia Film 1
Kirwan, Patrick d1929 NotNAT B, WhThe
Kis, Imre Film 2
Kisco, Charles W 1896- AmSCAP 1966
Kisfaludy, Karoly 1788-1830 McGWD,
  NotNAT B, OxThe
Kish, Anne WomWMM B
Kishon, Ephraim 1924- REnWD
Kissinger, Henry 1923- CelR 3
Kistemaechers, Henry 1872-1938 NotNAT B
Kistemaeckers, Henry 1872-1938 WhThe
Kitch, Kenneth PIP&P
Kitchen, Fred d1951 NotNAT B
Kitchin, Laurence 1913- WhoThe 16
Kithnou, Mademoiselle 1904- Film 2
Kithou 1904- TwYS
Kitt, Eartha IntMPA 1977, WhoHol A
Kitt, Eartha 1928- CelR 3, FilmgC, MovMk
Kitt, Eartha 1930- BiE&WWA, NotNAT,
  WhoThe 16
Kittredge, George Lyman 1860-1941 NotNAT B
Kitzmiller, John 1913-1965 FilmgC, WhScrn 1,
  WhScrn 2, WhoHol B
Kivi, Aleksis 1834-1872 REnWD
Kiyotsuga, Kwanami REnWD
Kjaer, Nils 1870-1924 OxThe
Kjaerulff-Schmidt, Palle 1931- WorEnF
Kjellin, Alf 1920- FilmgC, WhoHol A, WorEnF
Kjellin, John 1904- AmSCAP 1966
Klabund 1890-1928 CnMD, ModWD
Klages, Raymond W 1888-1947 AmSCAP 1966
Klages, Theodore 1911- AmSCAP 1966
Klassen, Ruth WomWMM B
Klatzkin, Leon 1914- AmSCAP 1966
Klauber, Adolph 1879-1933 NotNAT B, WhThe
Klauber, Edward d1954 NewYTET
Klauber, Marcy 1896-1960 AmSCAP 1966
Klaus, Henry Film 2
Klausner, Margot WomWMM
Klauss, Noah 1901- AmSCAP 1966
Klavun, Walter 1906- BiE&WWA, NotNAT,
  WhoHol A
Klaw, Marc 1858-1936 NotNAT B, WhThe,
  WhoStg 1908
Kleckner, Susan WomWMM B
Kleeb, Helen WhoHol A
Kleiman, Harlan Philip 1940- NotNAT

Klein, Adelaide 1904- BiE&WWA, NotNAT,
  WhoHol A
Klein, Adolf Film 2
Klein, Al 1885-1951 WhScrn 1, WhScrn 2,
  WhoHol B
Klein, Allen 1931- IntMPA 1977
Klein, Bonnie Sherr WomWMM B
Klein, Bonny WomWMM
Klein, Charles 1867-1915 NotNAT B, OxThe,
  WhThe, WhoStg 1906, WhoStg 1908
Klein, Charles 1898- TwYS A
Klein, Deanne Arkus 1934- AmSCAP 1966
Klein, Earl 1915- IntMPA 1977
Klein, Eugene V 1921- IntMPA 1977
Klein, Hal 1914- IntMPA 1977
Klein, Harold J IntMPA 1977
Klein, Herbert G NewYTET
Klein, John 1915- AmSCAP 1966
Klein, Josef Film 2
Klein, Judith WomWMM
Klein, Julius Film 2
Klein, Lothar 1932- AmSCAP 1966
Klein, Lou 1888-1945 AmSCAP 1966
Klein, Malcolm C 1927- IntMPA 1977
Klein, Manuel 1876-1919 AmSCAP 1966,
  NewMT, NotNAT B
Klein, Paul d1964 NotNAT B
Klein, Paul L NewYTET
Klein, Robert Film 2
Klein, William 1926- OxFilm, WorEnF
Klein, William 1929- FilmgC
Klein-Rogge, Rudolf 1889-1955 FilmgC,
  WhScrn 1, WhScrn 2, WhoHol B
Klein-Rogge, Rudolph 1889-1955 Film 2
Kleinau, Willy A d1957 WhScrn 1, WhScrn 2,
  WhoHol B
Kleinecke, August 1881-1944 AmSCAP 1966
Kleineidam, Horst 1932- CroCD
Kleiner, Harry 1916- FilmgC, IntMPA 1977
Kleiner, Richard 1921- AmSCAP 1966
Kleinerman, Isaac NewYTET
Kleinert, Robert Film 2
Kleinman, Isador I 1913- AmSCAP 1966
Kleinsinger, George 1914- AmSCAP 1966
Kleist, Heinrich Von 1777-1811 CnThe, McGWD,
  NotNAT A, NotNAT B, OxThe, REnWD
Klemm, Gustav 1897-1947 AmSCAP 1966
Klemperer, Werner MotPP, WhoHol A
Klemperer, Werner 1919- FilmgC
Klemperer, Werner 1920- CelR 3
Klemperer, Werner 1930- MovMk
Klenner, John 1899-1955 AmSCAP 1966
Klepper, Michael M 1934- AmSCAP 1966
Klercker, Georg A F 1877-1951 WhScrn 2
Klewer, Leonore N 1912- BiE&WWA
Klickmann, F Henri 1885- AmSCAP 1966
Klicpera, Vaclav Kliment 1792-1859 CnThe,
  REnWD
Kliegl, Herbert 1904- BiE&WWA
Kliewer, Warren NatPD
Klimes, Robert 1926- AmSCAP 1966
Klinder, Lotte Film 2
Kline, Fred W 1918- IntMPA 1977
Kline, Herbert 1909- DcFM, FilmgC, OxFilm
Kline, Norman 1935- NatPD
Kline, Richard 1926- FilmgC
Klinger, Friedrich Von 1752-1831 McGWD
Klinger, Henry 1908- IntMPA 1977
Klinger, Kurt 1928- CnMD, CroCD
Klinger, Michael 1920- IntMPA 1977
Klingman, L Deborah WomWMM
Klingman, Lynzee WomWMM B
Klintbert, Walter Film 1
Klipstein, Abner D 1912- BiE&WWA

Kloepfer, Eugen 1886-1950 *Film 2, WhScrn 2*
Klohr, John N 1869-1956 *AmSCAP 1966*
Klondike, Pete *WhScrn 2*
Klopstock, Friedrich Gottlieb 1724-1803 *McGWD*
Klos, Elmar 1910- *DcFM, FilmgC, OxFilm*
Klosky, Linda *WomWMM B*
Klotman, Robert Howard 1918- *AmSCAP 1966*
Klotz, Florence *NotNAT, WhoThe 16*
Klotz, Leora 1928- *AmSCAP 1966*
Klove, Jane *WomWMM*
Kluge, Alexander 1932- *BiDFlm, OxFilm, WorEnF*
Kluge, John W 1914- *CelR 3, NewYTET*
Klugman, Jack *BiE&WWA, IntMPA 1977, MotPP, NotNAT, WhoHol A*
Klugman, Jack 1922- *FilmgC, WhoThe 16*
Klugman, Jack 1924- *MovMk*
Klukvin, I *Film 2*
Klynn, Herbert David 1917- *IntMPA 1977*
Knabb, Harry G 1891-1955 *WhScrn 1, WhScrn 2*
Knaggs, Skelton 1911-1955 *WhScrn 2*
Knaggs, Skelton 1913-1955 *WhScrn 1, WhoHol B*
Knapp, David *WhoHol A*
Knapp, Evalyn 1908- *ThFT, WhoHol A*
Knapp, Fred L d1962 *NotNAT B*
Knapp, Otto *Film 2*
Knaub, Richard K 1928- *BiE&WWA, NotNAT*
Knauer, Virginia 1915- *CelR 3*
Knauth, Joachim 1931- *CnMD*
Kneale, Nigel 1922- *CmMov, ConDr 1977C, FilmgC*
Kneale, Patricia 1925- *WhoThe 16*
Knef, Hildegard 1925- *OxFilm*
Knef, Hildegarde 1925- *CelR 3, FilmgC, MovMk*
Knepp, Mary d1677 *NotNAT B, OxThe*
Knickerbocker, Paine 1912- *BiE&WWA, NotNAT*
Knieste, Adam 1917- *AmSCAP 1966*
Knievel, Evel 1938- *CelR 3*
Knight, Arthur 1916- *IntMPA 1977, OxFilm*
Knight, Beatrice 1925- *AmSCAP 1966*
Knight, Bill *Film 2*
Knight, Castleton 1894-1972 *FilmgC*
Knight, Christopher *WhoHol A*
Knight, David *WhoHol A*
Knight, David 1927- *FilmgC, WhoThe 16*
Knight, David 1928- *IntMPA 1977*
Knight, Don *WhoHol A*
Knight, Esmond 1906- *BiE&WWA, FilmgC, IntMPA 1977, WhoHol A, WhoThe 16*
Knight, Frances 1905- *CelR 3*
Knight, Fuzzy 1901-1976 *FilmgC, Vers A, WhoHol C*
Knight, G Wilson 1897- *BiE&WWA*
Knight, Harlan E *Film 2*
Knight, Jack *WhoHol A*
Knight, James 1891- *Film 1, Film 2*
Knight, James B 1929- *AmSCAP 1966*
Knight, John d1964 *NotNAT B*
Knight, John Forrest Fuzzy 1901-1976 *MovMk*
Knight, Joseph 1829-1907 *NotNAT B, OxThe*
Knight, Julius 1863-1941 *NotNAT B, WhThe*
Knight, June 1911- *EncMT, WhThe*
Knight, Patricia *WhoHol A*
Knight, Percival 1873?-1923 *NotNAT B, WhScrn 1, WhScrn 2, WhoHol B*
Knight, Percy *Film 2*
Knight, Rosalind *WhoHol A*
Knight, Sandra *WhoHol A*
Knight, Shirley *MotPP*
Knight, Shirley 1936- *NotNAT*
Knight, Shirley 1937- *BiDFlm, FilmgC, IntMPA 1977, MovMk, WhoHol A,*

WhoThe 16
Knight, Ted *WhoHol A*
Knight, Thomas d1820 *NotNAT B*
Knight, Vick 1908- *AmSCAP 1966*
Knight, W R *Film 2*
Knighton, Percy 1898- *TwYS A*
Knill, C Edwin *BiE&WWA, NotNAT*
Knipp, Mary *OxThe*
Knipper-Chekhova, Olga 1870-1959 *NotNAT B, OxThe, PIP&P*
Knipper-Tschech, O *Film 2*
Knoblock, Edward 1874-1945 *ModWD, NotNAT B, OxThe, PIP&P, WhThe*
Knopf, Alfred A 1892- *CelR 3*
Knopf, Edwin H 1899- *AmSCAP 1966, FilmgC, IntMPA 1977*
Knott, Adelbert 1859-1933 *Film 2, WhScrn 2*
Knott, Clara 1882-1926 *Film 2, WhScrn 1, WhScrn 2, WhoHol B*
Knott, Else 1912-1975 *WhScrn 2, WhoHol C*
Knott, Frederick *BiE&WWA, NotNAT*
Knott, George Marion *Film 2*
Knott, Lydia 1866-1955 *WhScrn 2*
Knott, Lydia 1873- *Film 1, Film 2, TwYS*
Knott, Roselle 1870-1948 *NotNAT B, WhThe, WhoStg 1906, WhoStg 1908*
Knotts, Don 1924- *FilmgC, MotPP, MovMk, WhoHol A*
Knowland, Alice 1879- *Film 1, Film 2, TwYS*
Knowlden, Marilyn 1925- *ThFT*
Knowles, Alec 1850-1917 *NotNAT B*
Knowles, Alex 1850-1917 *WhThe*
Knowles, Bernard 1900- *CmMov, FilmgC*
Knowles, Dorothy *WomWMM B*
Knowles, James Sheridan 1784-1862 *McGWD, NotNAT B, OxThe*
Knowles, Patric 1911- *FilmgC, IntMPA 1977, MovMk, WhoHol A*
Knowles, Richard George 1858-1919 *NotNAT B, OxThe*
Knowlton, Maude *WhoStg 1908*
Knox, Alexander 1907- *BiE&WWA, FilmgC, IntMPA 1977, MotPP, MovMk, NotNAT, WhoHol A, WhoThe 16*
Knox, Elyse 1917- *WhoHol A*
Knox, Foster *Film 1*
Knox, Gordon 1909- *IntMPA 1977*
Knox, Helen Boardman 1870-1947 *AmSCAP 1966*
Knox, Hugh d1926 *WhScrn 1, WhScrn 2*
Knox, Teddy *Film 2, FilmgC*
Knox, W D C *Film 2*
Knudsen, David *Film 2*
Knudsen, Mette *WomWMM*
Knudsen, Peggy 1923- *WhoHol A*
Knudson, Peggy *MotPP*
Knull, Chuck 1947- *NatPD*
Knutson, Wayne S 1926- *BiE&WWA, NotNAT*
Kobart, Ruth 1924- *BiE&WWA, NotNAT, WhoHol A, WhoThe 16*
Kobayashi, Ichizo 1873-1960? *DcFM*
Kobayashi, Masaki 1915- *BiDFlm, WorEnF*
Kobayashi, Masaki 1916- *DcFM, FilmgC, IntMPA 1977, OxFilm*
Kobayashi, Setsuo 1920- *OxFilm*
Kobe, Arturo *Film 2*
Kobe, Gail *WhoHol A*
Kober, Arthur 1900-1975 *BiE&WWA, ModWD, NotNAT B*
Kobey, Claudia *WomWMM B*
Kobrick, Leonard 1912- *AmSCAP 1966*
Kobs, Alfred 1881-1929 *WhScrn 1, WhScrn 2*
Koch, Carl 1892-1963 *OxFilm*
Koch, Fred, Jr. 1911- *BiE&WWA, NotNAT*
Koch, Frederick 1923- *AmSCAP 1966*

Koch, Frederick Henry 1877-1944 NotNAT B,
  OxThe
Koch, Georg August Film 2
Koch, Heinrich Gottfried 1703-1775 NotNAT B,
  OxThe
Koch, Herbie 1903- AmSCAP 1966
Koch, Howard 1902- ConDr 1977A, FilmgC,
  IntMPA 1977, WorEnF
Koch, Howard W 1916- FilmgC, IntMPA 1977,
  NewYTET, WorEnF
Koch, Hugo B Film 1
Koch, John James, Jr. 1920- AmSCAP 1966
Koch, Kenneth 1925- ConDr 1977
Koch, Marie 1912- AmSCAP 1966
Koch, Siegfried Gotthelf 1754-1831 OxThe
Kocheverova, Nadezhda WomWMM
Kochitz, Nina Film 2
Kodolanyi, Janos 1899- OxThe
Koebner, Richard 1910- AmSCAP 1966
Koehler, George A 1921- IntMPA 1977
Koehler, Ted 1894- AmSCAP 1966
Koenan, Frank Film 2
Koene, Rogers Film 2
Koenig, John 1910-1963 NotNAT B
Koenig, Wolf 1927- WorEnF
Koerber, Hilde 1906-1969 WhScrn 1, WhScrn 2,
  WhoHol B
Koesberg, Nicolai Film 2
Koff, Charles 1909- AmSCAP 1966
Kogan, Milt WhoHol A
Kogen, Harry 1895- AmSCAP 1966
Kohlase, Max Film 2
Kohler, Donna Jeane 1937- AmSCAP 1966
Kohler, Estelle 1940- WhoThe 16
Kohler, Fred, Jr. IntMPA 1977
Kohler, Fred, Sr. 1889-1938 Film 1, Film 2,
  TwYS, WhScrn 1, WhScrn 2, WhoHol B
Kohler, Marga Film 2
Kohlman, Churchill 1906- AmSCAP 1966
Kohlmann, Clarence 1891-1944 AmSCAP 1966
Kohlmar, Fred 1905-1969 FilmgC, WorEnF
Kohlmar, Lee 1878-1946 Film 2, NotNAT B,
  WhScrn 1, WhScrn 2, WhoHol B
Kohn, Howard E, II IntMPA 1977
Kohner, Frederick 1905- IntMPA 1977
Kohner, Susan 1936- BiE&WWA, FilmgC,
  IntMPA 1977, MotPP, NotNAT, WhoHol A
Kokeritz, Helge d1964 NotNAT B
Kokkonen, Lauri 1918- CroCD
Koko 1940-1968 WhScrn 2
Kokoschka, Oskar 1886- CnMD, McGWD,
  ModWD, REnWD
Kolar, Phil Film 2
Kolar, Slavko 1891-1963 CnMD
Kolb, Clarence 1874-1964 MotPP, Vers A,
  WhoHol B
Kolb, Clarence 1875-1964 FilmgC, MovMk,
  WhScrn 1, WhScrn 2
Kolb, John Film 2
Kolb, Therese 1856-1935 Film 2, NotNAT B,
  WhScrn 2, WhThe
Kolb, Wallace Film 2
Kolb And Dill Film 1
Kolbenhayer, Guido d1962 NotNAT B
Kolbenheyer, Erwin Guido 1878-1962 ModWD
Kolin, Nikolai Film 2
Kolk, Scott Film 2
Kolker, Henry 1874-1947 Film 1, Film 2,
  FilmgC, NotNAT B, TwYS, Vers B,
  WhScrn 1, WhScrn 2, WhThe, WhoHol B
Kollmar, Richard 1910-1971 BiE&WWA,
  NotNAT B, WhScrn 2, WhThe, WhoHol B
Kolmar, Leo 1878-1946 TwYS
Kolmer, Leo 1878-1946 Film 2

Kolodin, Robert 1932- AmSCAP 1966
Kolossy, Erika d1963 WhScrn 1, WhScrn 2
Koltai, Ralph 1924- WhoThe 16
Komack, James NewYTET
Komack, Jimmie WhoHol A
Komai, Tetsu 1893- Film 2, TwYS
Komai, Tetsu 1894-1970 WhScrn 2
Komeda, K T 1932-1969 WorEnF
Komisarjevskaya, Vera Fedorovna 1864-1910
  NotNAT B, OxThe, PIP&P
Komisarjevsky, Theodore 1882-1954 CnThe,
  NotNAT A, NotNAT B, OxThe, PIP&P,
  WhThe
Komissarov, Aleksandr 1904-1975 WhScrn 2
Kommerell, Max 1902-1944 CnMD
Konalski, Tadeusz WomWMM
Kondor, R W 1937- BiE&WWA
Kondouros, Nikos DcFM
Konrad, Dorothy WhoHol A
Konstam, Anna 1914- WhThe
Konstam, Phyllis 1907- IntMPA 1977, WhThe
Konstantin, Leopoldine 1890?- WhScrn 2
Kontos, Spero L 1922- IntMPA 1977
Konwicki, Tadeusz 1926- DcFM, OxFilm
Kook, Edward 1903- BiE&WWA, NotNAT
Koonen, Alice OxThe
Koop, Theodore F NewYTET
Kooy, Pete d1963 NotNAT B, WhScrn 1,
  WhScrn 2, WhoHol B
Kopalin, Ilya Petrovich 1900- DcFM
Kopell, Bernie WhoHol A
Kopelman, Jean R 1927- IntMPA 1977
Kopit, Arthur 1937- BiE&WWA, ConDr 1977,
  CroCD, McGWD, NatPD, NotNAT,
  WhoThe 16
Kopit, Arthur 1938- CnMD, ModWD
Kopita, Murray 1903- AmSCAP 1966
Koplow, Donald H 1935- AmSCAP 1966
Kopp, Erwin Film 2
Kopp, Frederick 1914- AmSCAP 1966
Kopp, Mila 1905-1973 WhScrn 2
Kopp, Rudolph CmMov
Koppell, Alfred Baldwin 1898-1963 AmSCAP 1966
Koppens, Emile WhScrn 1, WhScrn 2
Kopple, Barbara WomWMM A, WomWMM B
Kops, Bernard 1926- BiE&WWA, CnMD,
  ConDr 1977, ModWD, NotNAT,
  NotNAT A, WhoThe 16
Kops, Bernard 1928- CroCD
Korayim, Mohamed 1898-1972 WhScrn 2
Korb, Arthur 1909- AmSCAP 1966
Korban, Bernard 1923- IntMPA 1977
Korda, Sir Alexander 1893-1956 BiDFlm, DcFM,
  FilmgC, MovMk, NotNAT B, OxFilm,
  WorEnF
Korda, Maria Film 2, WhoHol A
Korda, Vincent 1896- DcFM, FilmgC
Korda, Vincent 1897- OxFilm, WorEnF
Korda, Zoltan 1895-1961 BiDFlm, CmMov,
  DcFM, FilmgC, MovMk, NotNAT B,
  OxFilm, WorEnF
Korff, Arnold 1870-1944 NotNAT B
Korff, Arnold 1871-1944 Film 2, WhScrn 1,
  WhScrn 2, WhoHol B
Korjus, Miliza 1900- ThFT
Korjus, Miliza 1902- FilmgC, WhoHol A
Korloff, Olga Film 2
Korman, Gerald 1936- AmSCAP 1966
Korman, Harvey 1927- IntMPA 1977,
  WhoHol A
Korman, Mary 1917-1973 Film 2
Korn, Peter Jona 1922- AmSCAP 1966
Kornaros, Vincenzo REnWD
Kornblum, Isidore Benjamin 1895- AmSCAP 1966

Korneichuk, Aleksandr Evdokomovich 1905-1972
  CroCD
Korneichuk, Aleksandr Yevdokimovich 1905-1972
  ModWD
Korneichuk, Alexander Evdokimovich 1905-1972
  CnMD, OxThe
Kornelia, Irma *Film 2*
Korner, Hermine *Film 2*
Kornfeld, Paul 1889-1942 *CnMD, McGWD,
  ModWD*
Kornfeld, Robert *NatPD*
Korngold, Erich Wolfgang 1897-1957
  *AmSCAP 1966, CmMov, FilmgC, OxFilm,
  WorEnF*
Kornman, Mary 1917-1973 *TwYS, WhScrn 2,
  WhoHol B*
Kornzweig, Ben *BiE&WWA*
Koromilas, Demetrios *REnWD*
Korris, Harry 1888-1971 *FilmgC*
Korte, Karl 1928- *AmSCAP 1966*
Kortlander, Max 1890-1961 *AmSCAP 1966*
Kortman, Robert F 1887-1967 *Film 1, Film 2,
  WhScrn 2*
Kortner, Fritz 1892-1970 *CroCD, Film 2, FilmgC,
  MovMk, WhScrn 1, WhScrn 2, WhoHol B*
Korton, Robert *Film 2*
Korty, John 1936- *IntMPA 1977, NewYTET,
  OxFilm*
Korvin, Charles *IntMPA 1977, MotPP*
Korvin, Charles 1907- *FilmgC, MovMk,
  WhoHol A*
Korvin, Charles 1912- *BiE&WWA, NotNAT*
Kosa, Ferenc 1937- *OxFilm*
Kosakoff, Reuven 1898- *AmSCAP 1966*
Kosarin, Oscar 1918- *BiE&WWA, NotNAT*
Koscina, Sylva 1935- *FilmgC, WhoHol A*
Koser, H *Film 2*
Kosersky, Rena *WomWMM A, WomWMM B*
Koshetz, Nina 1892-1965 *WhScrn 1, WhScrn 2,
  WhoHol B*
Kosiner, Harry *IntMPA 1977*
Koski, Joan *WomWMM B*
Kosleck, Martin 1907- *FilmgC, IntMPA 1977,
  MotPP, MovMk, Vers B, WhoHol A*
Kosloff, Lou 1904- *AmSCAP 1966*
Kosloff, Theodore 1882-1956 *Film 1, Film 2,
  NotNAT B, TwYS, WhScrn 1, WhScrn 2,
  WhoHol B*
Kosma, Joseph 1905-1969 *DcFM, FilmgC,
  OxFilm, WorEnF*
Kosor, Josip 1879-1961 *CnMD*
Kossoff, David 1919- *FilmgC, WhoHol A,
  WhoThe 16*
Kosta, Tessa 1893- *WhThe*
Kostal, Irwin 1915- *CmMov, FilmgC*
Koster, Henry 1905- *BiDFlm, CmMov, DcFM,
  FilmgC, IntMPA 1977, MovMk, WorEnF*
Kotcheff, Ted 1931- *FilmgC*
Kotcheff, William Theodore 1931- *IntMPA 1977*
Kotkin, Edward *WhoHol A*
Kotlowitz, Robert *NewYTET*
Kotsonaros, George d1933 *Film 2, WhScrn 2*
Kott, Jan *PIP&P*
Kotto, Yaphet *IntMPA 1977, WhoHol A*
Kotzebue, August Friedrich Ferdinand Von
  1761-1819 *CnThe, McGWD, NotNAT A,
  NotNAT B, OxThe, REnWD*
Koubitzky, Alexandre *Film 2*
Koufax, Sandy 1935- *CelR 3*
Kougoucheff, Prince N *Film 2*
Kouguell, Arkadie 1897- *AmSCAP 1966*
Koun, Karolos 1908- *WhThe*
Koundouros, Nikos 1926- *DcFM*
Koundouros, Nikos 1929- *WorEnF*

Kountz, Richard 1896-1950 *AmSCAP 1966*
Koutoukas, H M *ConDr 1977*
Koutzen, Boris 1901- *AmSCAP 1966*
Kovack, Nancy 1935- *FilmgC, WhoHol A*
Kovacs, Andras 1925- *OxFilm*
Kovacs, Ernie 1919-1962 *AmSCAP 1966, FilmgC,
  MotPP, MovMk, NewYTET, NotNAT B,
  WhScrn 1, WhScrn 2, WhoHol B*
Kovacs, Joseph 1912- *AmSCAP 1966*
Kovacs, Laszlo *FilmgC*
Kovaks, Laszlo *IntMPA 1977*
Koval, Rene d1936 *NotNAT B*
Koval-Samborsky, Ivan *Film 2*
Kovanko, Nathalie *Film 2*
Kove, Kenneth 1893- *WhThe*
Kove, Martin *WhoHol A*
Kowal, Mitchell 1916-1971 *WhScrn 1, WhScrn 2,
  WhoHol B*
Kowalski, Bernard L 1931- *FilmgC, NewYTET*
Kozak, Yitka Reomira 1942- *WomWMM B*
Kozelka, Paul 1909- *BiE&WWA, NotNAT*
Kozinski, David B 1917- *AmSCAP 1966*
Kozintsev, Grigori 1905-1973 *BiDFlm, DcFM,
  FilmgC, MovMk, OxFilm, WorEnF*
Kozintsev, Grigory 1905-1973 *WhScrn 2*
Kozlenko, William *IntMPA 1977*
Kozol, Jonathan 1936- *CelR 3*
Kracauer, Siegfried 1889-1966 *OxFilm*
Kraft, Gil 1926- *BiE&WWA*
Kraft, Hy 1899-1975 *BiE&WWA, NotNAT,
  NotNAT A, NotNAT B*
Kraft, Jill 1930- *BiE&WWA, NotNAT*
Kraft, Leo 1922- *AmSCAP 1966*
Kraft, Leonard 1932- *BiE&WWA*
Kraft, William 1923- *AmSCAP 1966*
Kraftschenko, Valerie *Film 2*
Krah, Earl E 1921- *AmSCAP 1966*
Krah, Marc 1906-1973 *WhScrn 2, WhoHol B*
Krahly, Hanns 1885-1950 *DcFM, WhScrn 2*
Kramer, A Walter 1890- *AmSCAP 1966*
Kramer, Albert H *NewYTET*
Kramer, Alex Charles 1903- *AmSCAP 1966*
Kramer, Alexander Milton 1893-1955
  AmSCAP 1966
Kramer, Edith *Film 2*
Kramer, Ida 1878-1930 *Film 2, WhScrn 2*
Kramer, Jerome 1945- *IntMPA 1977*
Kramer, Larry 1935- *FilmgC, IntMPA 1977*
Kramer, Leopold *Film 2*
Kramer, Phil 1900-1972 *WhScrn 2*
Kramer, Sidney *IntMPA 1977*
Kramer, Stanley 1913- *BiDFlm, CelR 3, DcFM,
  FilmgC, IntMPA 1977, MovMk, OxFilm,
  WorEnF*
Kramer, Wright 1870-1941 *NotNAT B,
  WhScrn 1, WhScrn 2, WhoHol B*
Kramm, Joseph 1907- *BiE&WWA, CnMD,
  ModWD, NotNAT, WhoThe 16*
Krampf, Gunter 1899- *FilmgC*
Krampf, Gunther 1899- *WorEnF*
Krams, Arthur 1912- *IntMPA 1977*
Krance, John P, Jr. 1935- *AmSCAP 1966*
Krane, Charles 1898- *AmSCAP 1966*
Krane, Sherman M 1927- *AmSCAP 1966*
Kraning, Suzan Pitt *WomWMM B*
Krantz, Milton 1912- *BiE&WWA*
Krantz, Steve 1923- *IntMPA 1977*
Krasilovsky, Alexis Rafael *WomWMM,
  WomWMM B*
Krasinski, Zygmunt 1812-1857 *OxThe*
Krasinski, Zygmunt 1812-1858 *McGWD*
Krasinski, Zygmunt 1812-1859 *CnThe, REnWD*
Krasker, Robert 1913- *CmMov, DcFM, FilmgC,
  OxFilm, WorEnF*

Krasna, Norman 1909- *BiDFlm, BiE&WWA,
CmMov, FilmgC, IntMPA 1977, McGWD,
NotNAT, OxFilm, WhoThe 16, WorEnF*
Krasner, Milton 1898- *CmMov, FilmgC,
WorEnF*
Krasnor, David 1921- *AmSCAP 1966*
Krasnow, Hermann 1910- *AmSCAP 1966*
Kraus, Karl 1874-1936 *CnMD, McGWD,
ModWD*
Kraus, Philip C 1918- *AmSCAP 1966*
Kraus, Robert A 1926- *IntMPA 1977*
Kraus, Ted M 1923- *BiE&WWA, NotNAT*
Kraus, Werner 1884-1959 *NotNAT B*
Krauss, Charles d1926 *WhScrn 1, WhScrn 2*
Krauss, Henri *Film 1*
Krauss, Henry *Film 2*
Krauss, Oscar *IntMPA 1977*
Krauss, Ruth 1911- *ConDr 1977*
Krauss, Werner 1884-1959 *BiDFlm, Film 1,
Film 2, FilmgC, MotPP, OxFilm, OxThe,
WhScrn 1, WhScrn 2, WhThe, WhoHol B,
WorEnF*
Kraussneck, Arthur *Film 2*
Krawicz, Mecislas *WomWMM*
Krawitz, Seymour 1923- *BiE&WWA, NotNAT*
Krech, Warren W *Film 2*
Krechmer, William 1909- *AmSCAP 1966*
Kreiman, Robert T 1924- *IntMPA 1977*
Kreisler, Fritz 1875-1962 *AmSCAP 1966,
NotNAT B*
Krellberg, Sherman S *IntMPA 1977*
Krembs, Felix *Film 2*
Kremer, Theodore 1873- *WhThe*
Krengel, Joseph 1915- *AmSCAP 1966*
Krenz, William F 1899- *AmSCAP 1966*
Kreps, Bonnie *WomWMM B*
Kresa, Helmy 1904- *AmSCAP 1966*
Kreski, Connie *WhoHol A*
Kress, Harold F 1913- *IntMPA 1977*
Kretzmer, Herbert 1925- *WhoThe 16*
Kreuger, Kurt 1917- *FilmgC, IntMPA 1977,
MotPP, WhoHol A*
Kreutz, Arthur 1906- *AmSCAP 1966*
Kreymborg, Alfred 1883-1966 *AmSCAP 1966,
NotNAT A, NotNAT B*
Kriegel, Harriet *WomWMM B*
Krieger, Lee 1919-1967 *WhScrn 1, WhScrn 2,
WhoHol B*
Kriendlers, The *CelR 3*
Krier, John N *IntMPA 1977*
Krim, Arthur B 1910- *IntMPA 1977*
Krimer, Harry *Film 2*
Krimsky, John 1906- *BiE&WWA, NotNAT*
Krish, John 1923- *FilmgC*
Kristel, Sylvia *WhoHol A*
Kristen, Marta *WhoHol A*
Krister, Dorothy *Film 2*
Kristofferson, Kris 1936- *CelR 3, MovMk,
WhoHol A*
Krizman, Serge 1914- *IntMPA 1977*
Krleza, Miroslav 1893- *CnMD, ModWD*
Krock, Arthur 1886- *CelR 3*
Kroeger, Berry *WhoHol A*
Kroell, Adrienne 1892-1949 *WhScrn 2*
Krofft, Sid And Marty Krofft *NewYTET*
Krog, Helge 1889-1962 *CnMD, McGWD,
ModWD, OxThe, REnWD*
Krohner, Sarah 1883-1959 *WhScrn 1, WhScrn 2*
Kroitor, Roman 1927- *WorEnF*
Kroll, Lucy *BiE&WWA, NotNAT*
Kroll, William 1901- *AmSCAP 1966*
Kroman, Ann *Film 1*
Kromer, Helen *NatPD*
Krondes, Jimmy 1925- *AmSCAP 1966*

Krone, Gerald 1933- *BiE&WWA, NotNAT,
PIP&P A*
Kronenberger, Louis 1904- *BiE&WWA, NotNAT,
WhoThe 16*
Kronert, Max *Film 2*
Krones, Therese 1801-1830 *OxThe*
Kronick, William *IntMPA 1977*
Kronish, Amy *WomWMM*
Krouse, H Sylvester 1853-1940 *AmSCAP 1966*
Kru *Film 2*
Kruczkowski, Leon 1900-1962 *CnMD, CroCD,
ModWD*
Krueger, Bum 1906-1971 *WhScrn 1, WhScrn 2,
WhoHol B*
Krueger, Carl 1908- *IntMPA 1977*
Krueger, Lorraine *WhoHol A*
Kruger, Alma d1960 *NotNAT B, WhThe,
WhoHol B*
Kruger, Alma 1868-1960 *WhScrn 1, WhScrn 2*
Kruger, Alma 1871-1960 *ThFT*
Kruger, Alma 1872-1960 *FilmgC, MovMk*
Kruger, Fred H 1913-1961 *NotNAT B, WhScrn 1,
WhScrn 2, WhoHol B*
Kruger, Hardy 1928- *FilmgC, IntMPA 1977,
WhoHol A*
Kruger, Harold Stubby 1897-1965 *WhScrn 1,
WhScrn 2*
Kruger, Jeffrey S 1931- *IntMPA 1977*
Kruger, Jules 1891- *DcFM*
Kruger, Lilly Canfield 1892- *AmSCAP 1966*
Kruger, Otto 1885-1974 *BiE&WWA, Film 2,
FilmgC, MotPP, MovMk, NotNAT B,
PIP&P, Vers A, WhScrn 2, WhThe,
WhoHol B*
Kruger, Paul 1895- *Film 2, TwYS*
Kruger, Stubby 1897-1965 *WhoHol B*
Krugman, Lillian D 1911- *AmSCAP 1966*
Krugman, Lou *WhoHol A*
Krumbachova, Ester 1923- *OxFilm, WomWMM*
Krumins, Diana *WomWMM B*
Krumschmidt, Eberhard 1905-1956 *WhScrn 1,
WhScrn 2, WhoHol B*
Krupa, Gene 1909-1973 *WhScrn 2, WhoHol B*
Krupp, Vera 1910-1967 *WhScrn 1, WhScrn 2*
Krupska, Dania 1923- *BiE&WWA, NotNAT,
WhoThe 16*
Kruschen, Jack 1922- *BiE&WWA, FilmgC,
NotNAT, WhoHol A*
Krutch, Joseph Wood 1893-1970 *BiE&WWA,
NotNAT B, OxThe, WhThe*
Kuan, Han-Ch'ing *CnThe, REnWD*
Kuba 1914-1967 *CroCD*
Kuba, Kurth Barthel 1914-1967 *CnMD*
Kubik, Gail 1914- *AmSCAP 1966*
Kubrick, Stanley 1928- *BiDFlm, CelR 3,
ConDr 1977A, DcFM, FilmgC,
IntMPA 1977, MovMk, OxFilm,
WomWMM, WorEnF*
Kuby, Bernard F 1923- *AmSCAP 1966*
Kuehl, Joan *WomWMM B*
Kuertz, Charles H, Sr. 1923- *IntMPA 1977*
Kuhn, Bowie 1926- *CelR 3*
Kuhn, Fritz 1919- *CnMD*
Kuhn, Lee 1912-1955 *AmSCAP 1966*
Kuhn, Richard S 1907- *AmSCAP 1966*
Kuhn, Sarah Sappington 1935- *WomWMM B*
Kuhn, Thomas G 1935- *IntMPA 1977*
Kuhne, Friedrich *Film 2*
Kuhnelt, Hans Friedrich 1918- *CnMD, CroCD*
Kuleshov, Lev 1899-1970 *BiDFlm, DcFM,
OxFilm, WorEnF*
Kulganek, W *Film 2*
Kulidjanov, Lev 1924- *DcFM*
Kulik, Buzz *NewYTET*

Kulik, Buzz 1922- *WorEnF*
Kulik, Buzz 1923?- *FilmgC*
Kulik, Seymour *IntMPA 1977*
Kulka, Henry d1965 *WhoHol B*
Kulkavich, Bomber *WhScrn 1*, *WhScrn 2*
Kulky, Henry Hank 1911-1965 *WhScrn 1*,
    WhScrn 2
Kulle, Jarl 1927- *WorEnF*
Kuller, Sid 1910- *AmSCAP 1966*
Kulp, Nancy *WhoHol A*
Kulukundis, Eddie 1932- *WhoThe 16*
Kuluva, Will *WhoHol A*
Kuma, Profulla *Film 2*
Kumari, Meena 1932-1972 *WhScrn 2*
Kumchachi, Madame 1843- *WhThe*
Kumel, Harry 1940- *BiDFlm*
Kummer, Clare 1888-1958 *AmSCAP 1966*,
    NotNAT B, *WhThe*
Kummer, Frederic Arnold 1873-1943 *NotNAT B*,
    WhThe
Kummerfeld, Karoline 1745-1815 *OxThe*
Kun, Magda 1911-1945 *WhScrn 1*, *WhScrn 2*,
    WhoHol B
Kun, Magda 1912-1945 *NotNAT B*, *WhThe*
Kunde, Al 1888-1952 *WhScrn 1*, *WhScrn 2*
Kunde, Anna d1960 *WhoHol B*
Kunde, Anne 1896-1960 *WhScrn 1*, *WhScrn 2*
Kunhenn, Paul *WomWMM*
Kunitz, Richard E 1919- *AmSCAP 1966*
Kunkel, George 1867-1937 *WhScrn 1*, *WhScrn 2*,
    WhoHol B
Kunkle, George *Film 2*
Kunneke, Eduard 1885- *WhThe*
Kuno, Motoji *IntMPA 1977*
Kunstler, William 1919- *CelR 3*
Kupcinet, Irv 1912- *CelR 3*
Kupcinet, Karen d1963 *WhoHol B*
Kupcinet, Karyn 1941-1963 *WhScrn 1*, *WhScrn 2*
Kupele, David M 1921- *AmSCAP 1966*
Kupfer, Margarete *Film 2*
Kupferman, Meyer 1926- *AmSCAP 1966*
Kupper, W J 1896- *IntMPA 1977*
Kuralt, Charles *NewYTET*
Kuri, Emile 1907- *IntMPA 1977*
Kuri, Yoji 1928- *WorEnF*
Kurnitz, Harry 1907-1968 *FilmgC*
Kurnitz, Harry 1908-1968 *BiE&WWA*,
    NotNAT B, *WorEnF*
Kuroda, Toyoji 1920- *IntMPA 1977*
Kurosawa, Akira 1910- *BiDFlm*, *DcFM*, *FilmgC*,
    IntMPA 1977, *MovMk*, *OxFilm*, *WorEnF*
Kursunlu, Nazim 1911- *REnWD*
Kurton, Peggy *WhThe*
Kurty, Hella d1954 *NotNAT B*, *WhThe*
Kurtz, Gary 1941- *IntMPA 1977*
Kurtz, Judith *WomWMM B*
Kurtz, Marjorie 1942- *AmSCAP 1966*
Kurtz, Swoosie *WhoHol A*
Kurz, Emile *Film 2*
Kurz, Joseph Felix Von 1715-1784 *NotNAT B*,
    OxThe
Kushan, Esmail *DcFM*
Kusmider, Lauren C *WomWMM B*
Kutaka, Geraldine Natsue 1951- *WomWMM B*
Kutch, Eugene B 1926- *AmSCAP 1966*
Kuter, Kay E *WhoHol A*
Kutusow, N *Film 2*
Kutz, James Fulton 1880- *AmSCAP 1966*
Kuwa, George K 1885-1931 *Film 1*, *Film 2*,
    WhScrn 2
Kuzmina, Yelena *Film 2*
Kuznetzoff, Adia 1890-1954 *WhScrn 1*,
    WhScrn 2, *WhoHol B*
Kvanine, K *Film 2*

Kwan, Nancy 1938- *FilmgC*, *MotPP*, *MovMk*,
    WhoHol A
Kwanami, Kiyotsugo *REnWD*
Kweder, Charles J 1928- *AmSCAP 1966*
Kwit, Nathaniel Troy, Jr. 1941- *IntMPA 1977*
Kyasht, Lydia *Film 2*
Kyasht, Lydia 1886- *WhThe*
Kyd, Thomas 1558-1594 *CnThe*, *McGWD*,
    NotNAT A, *NotNAT B*, *OxThe*, *PIP&P*,
    REnWD
Kydd, Sam 1917- *FilmgC*, *WhoHol A*
Kyle, Alex *Film 1*
Kyle, Austin C 1893-1916 *WhScrn 2*
Kyle, Howard d1950 *NotNAT B*
Kynaston, Edward 1640?-1706 *NotNAT B*,
    OxThe, *PIP&P*
Kyo, Machiko 1924- *FilmgC*, *IntMPA 1977*,
    MotPP, *OxFilm*, *WhoHol A*, *WorEnF*
Kyrle, Judith d1922 *NotNAT B*
Kyrou, Ado 1923- *OxFilm*
Kyser, Kay 1897- *FilmgC*
Kyser, Kay 1905?- *WhoHol A*

L

Laage, Barbara 1925- *FilmgC, WhoHol A*
LaBadie, Florence 1893-1917 *Film 1, MotPP,*
  NotNAT B, TwYS, WhScrn 2, WhoHol B
LaBar, Tom 1938- *NatPD*
Laberius, Decimus *OxThe*
Labiche, Eugene 1815-1888 *CnThe, McGWD,*
  NotNAT B, OxThe, REnWD
LaBissoniere, Erin *Film 2*
Lablache, Luibi d1914 *WhThe*
Labouchere, Mrs. Henry *OxThe*
Labouchere, Henry d1912 *NotNAT B*
LaBrake, Harrison 1891-1936 *WhScrn 2*
Labunski, Felix R 1892- *AmSCAP 1966*
LaCalprenede, Gautier DeCostes De 1614-1663
  OxThe
LaCava, Gregory 1892-1949 *BiDFlm, DcFM,*
  MovMk, OxFilm
LaCava, Gregory 1892-1952 *FilmgC, TwYS A,*
  WorEnF
Lacey, Catherine 1904- *FilmgC, WhoHol A,*
  WhoThe 16
Lacey, Franklin 1917- *BiE&WWA*
Lacey, Marion d1915 *NotNAT B*
Lacey, Mary 1909- *AmSCAP 1966*
LaChapelle, Jean De 1655-1723 *OxThe*
LaChaussee, Pierre-Claude Nivelle De 1692-1754
  McGWD, OxThe
Lachman, Harry 1886- *FilmgC*
Lachman, Mort *NewYTET*
Lachoff, Sol 1911- *AmSCAP 1966*
Lachow, Stan 1931- *NatPD*
Lack, Simon 1917- *WhoHol A, WhoThe 16*
Lackaye, James 1867-1919 *Film 1, WhScrn 2*
Lackaye, Wilton 1862-1932 *Film 1, Film 2,*
  NotNAT B, OxThe, WhScrn 1, WhScrn 2,
  WhThe, WhoHol B, WhoStg 1906,
  WhoStg 1908
Lackey, Douglas M 1932- *AmSCAP 1966*
Lackey, Kenneth d1976 *NotNAT B*
Lackteen, Frank 1894-1968 *Film 1, Film 2,*
  TwYS, Vers B, WhScrn 1, WhScrn 2,
  WhoHol B
Lacombe, Georges 1902- *DcFM*
Lacoste, M *Film 2*
Lacour, Jose Andre 1919- *CnMD*
Lacy, Frank 1867-1937 *NotNAT B, WhThe*
Lacy, George 1904- *WhThe*
Lacy, James d1774 *NotNAT B*
Lacy, Jerry *WhoHol A*
Lacy, John d1681 *NotNAT B, OxThe, PIP&P*
Lacy, Robin T 1920- *BiE&WWA*
Lacy, Rophino d1867 *NotNAT B*
Lacy, Thomas Hailes d1873 *NotNAT B*
Lacy, Walter d1898 *NotNAT B*
Lada, Anton 1890-1944 *AmSCAP 1966*
Ladah *Film 2*

Ladd, Alan 1913-1964 *BiDFlm, CmMov, FilmgC,*
  MotPP, MovMk, NotNAT B, OxFilm,
  WhScrn 1, WhScrn 2, WhoHol B, WorEnF
Ladd, Alan, Jr. 1937- *IntMPA 1977*
Ladd, Alana *WhoHol A*
Ladd, David *MotPP, WhoHol A*
Ladd, Diane *WhoHol A*
Ladd, Helena Solberg *WomWMM B*
Laderman, Ezra 1924- *AmSCAP 1966*
Ladmiral, Nicole 1931-1958 *WhScrn 1,*
  WhScrn 2, WhoHol B
Lady *Film 2*
Lady Gregory *PIP&P*
Laemmele, Beth *Film 2*
Laemmle, Carl, Jr. 1908- *FilmgC, TwYS B*
Laemmle, Carl, Sr. 1867-1939 *DcFM, FilmgC,*
  OxFilm, TwYS B, WhScrn 1, WhScrn 2,
  WorEnF
Laemmle, Edward 1887- *TwYS A*
Laemmle, Ernst 1900- *TwYS A*
Lafayette, Andree *Film 2*
Lafayette, Ruby 1844-1935 *Film 1, Film 2,*
  TwYS, WhoHol B
Lafayette, Ruby 1845-1935 *WhScrn 1, WhScrn 2*
Laferriere, Adolphe d1877 *NotNAT B*
Laffan, Kevin Barry 1922- *ConDr 1977,*
  WhoThe 16
Laffan, Patricia 1919- *FilmgC, WhThe,*
  WhoHol A
Lafferty, Perry *NewYTET*
Lafferty, Wilson d1962 *NotNAT B*
Laffey, James *Film 1*
LaFleur *OxThe*
LaFleur, Francois Juvenon *OxThe*
LaFleur, Joy 1914-1957 *WhScrn 1, WhScrn 2,*
  WhoHol B
LaFollette, Fola 1882-1970 *BiE&WWA,*
  NotNAT B
LaFonde, Virginia *Film 2*
Lafont, Pierre d1873 *NotNAT B*
LaForge, Frank 1879-1953 *AmSCAP 1966*
LaForge, Jack 1924-1966 *AmSCAP 1966*
LaFosse, Antoine D'Aubigny De 1653-1708
  McGWD, OxThe
LaFrance *OxThe*
LaFreniere, Charles F 1914- *AmSCAP 1966*
LaFreniere, Emma P 1881-1961 *AmSCAP 1966*
LaGarde, Henri *Film 2*
Lagarde, Jocelyne *WhoHol A*
Lagerkvist, Par 1891-1974 *CnMD, CnThe,*
  McGWD, ModWD, OxThe, REnWD
Lagerlof, Selma 1858-1940 *OxFilm*
LaGrange, Achille 1636-1709 *OxThe*
LaGrange, Charles Varlet 1639-1692 *NotNAT B,*
  OxThe
Lagrange, Felix d1901 *NotNAT B*

Lagrange, Louise *Film 2*
LaGrange, Marie 1639-1737 *NotNAT B, OxThe*
LaGrange-Chancel, Joseph De 1677-1758
  NotNAT B, OxThe
LaGuere, George *Film 2*
LaHarpe, Jean-Francois De 1739-1802 *OxThe*
Lahmer, Reuel 1912- *AmSCAP 1966*
Lahr, Bert 1895-1967 *BiE&WWA, CnThe,*
  EncMT, FamA&A, MotPP, MovMk,
  NotNAT A, NotNAT B, PlP&P, WhScrn 1,
  WhScrn 2, WhThe, WhoHol B
Lahr, Bert 1895-1968 *FilmgC*
Lahr, John 1941- *NotNAT, WhoThe 16*
Lahtinen, Warner H Duke 1910-1968 *WhScrn 1,*
  WhScrn 2
Lai, Francis 1933?- *FilmgC, OxFilm*
Laidlaw, Ethan 1899-1963 *WhScrn 1, WhScrn 2,*
  WhoHol B
Laidlaw, Ethan 1900-1963 *Film 2*
Laidlaw, Roy *Film 1, Film 2, TwYS*
Laidler, Francis 1870-1955 *NotNAT B, WhThe*
Laidley, Alice *Film 2*
Laiglesia, Juan Antonio De 1917- *McGWD*
Laiglesia Gonzalez Labarga, Alvaro De 1921-
  McGWD
Laiman, Leah *WomWMM B*
Laine, Edwin 1905- *DcFM*
Laine, Flora Spraker 1924- *AmSCAP 1966*
Laine, Frankie 1913- *AmSCAP 1966, FilmgC,*
  WhoHol A
Laing, Peggie 1899- *WhThe*
Laing, R D 1927- *CelR 3*
Laing, Tony *Film 2*
Lair, Grace d1955 *WhScrn 1, WhScrn 2*
Lairce, Margaret *Film 1*
Laird, Jack *NewYTET*
Laird, Jenny 1917- *FilmgC, WhoHol A,*
  WhoThe 16
Laird, Melvin 1922- *CelR 3*
Laire, Judson *WhoHol A*
Lait, Jack 1883-1954 *NotNAT B, WhScrn 2*
LaJana 1905-1940 *WhScrn 2*
Lake, Alice 1896-1967 *Film 1, Film 2, MotPP,*
  TwYS, WhScrn 1, WhScrn 2, WhoHol B
Lake, Arthur 1905- *Film 1, Film 2, FilmgC,*
  IntMPA 1977, MotPP, MovMk, TwYS,
  WhoHol A
Lake, Bonnie *AmSCAP 1966*
Lake, Candace *WomWMM B*
Lake, Florence *Film 2, WhoHol A*
Lake, Frank 1849-1936 *WhScrn 1, WhScrn 2,*
  WhoHol B
Lake, Harriette *Film 2*
Lake, Harry 1885-1947 *WhScrn 1, WhScrn 2*
Lake, Janet *WhoHol A*
Lake, John 1904-1960 *WhScrn 1, WhScrn 2*
Lake, Lew d1939 *NotNAT B, WhThe*
Lake, Meyhew Lester 1879-1955 *AmSCAP 1966*
Lake, Veronica d1973 *MotPP, WhoHol B*
Lake, Veronica 1919-1973 *BiDFlm, FilmgC,*
  MovMk, OxFilm, WomWMM, WorEnF
Lake, Veronica 1921-1973 *WhScrn 2*
Lake, Wesley *Film 2*
Lakhdar Amina, Mohamed 1934- *DcFM*
LaLanne, Jack *NewYTET*
Lally, Gwen d1963 *WhThe*
Lally, William *WhoHol A*
Lalor, Frank 1869-1932 *Film 2, NotNAT B,*
  WhScrn 2, WhThe, WhoHol B
Lamare, Hilton 1910- *AmSCAP 1966*
LaMarge, Jimmie 1905- *AmSCAP 1966*
LaMarr, Barbara *MotPP*
LaMarr, Barbara 1896-1925 *WhScrn 1,*
  WhoHol B

LaMarr, Barbara 1896-1926 *FilmgC, MovMk,*
  NotNAT B, WhScrn 2
LaMarr, Barbara 1897-1926 *Film 2, TwYS*
LaMarr, Frank 1904- *AmSCAP 1966*
Lamarr, Hedy *IntMPA 1977, MotPP*
Lamarr, Hedy 1913- *FilmgC, MovMk, ThFT*
Lamarr, Hedy 1914- *BiDFlm, OxFilm*
Lamarr, Hedy 1915- *CelR 3, Film 2, MGM,*
  WhoHol A, WorEnF
LaMarr, Margaret *Film 2*
LaMarr, Richard d1975 *WhScrn 2, WhoHol C*
LaMarre, Rene T 1907- *AmSCAP 1966*
Lamas, Fernando *MotPP*
Lamas, Fernando 1915- *FilmgC, MGM, MovMk,*
  WhoHol A
Lamas, Fernando 1923- *BiE&WWA*
Lamas, Fernando 1925- *IntMPA 1977*
Lamb, Arthur J 1870-1928 *AmSCAP 1966*
Lamb, Beatrice 1866- *WhThe*
Lamb, Charles *WhoHol A*
Lamb, Charles 1775-1834 *NotNAT B, OxThe*
Lamb, Florence 1884-1966 *WhScrn 2*
Lamb, Gil 1906- *FilmgC, IntMPA 1977,*
  WhoHol A
Lamb, Joseph F 1887-1960 *AmSCAP 1966*
Lamb, Myrna *NatPD*
Lambart, Ernest d1945 *NotNAT B*
Lambart, Evelyn *WomWMM, WomWMM B*
Lambart, Richard d1924 *NotNAT B*
Lambdin, John O d1923 *NotNAT B*
Lambelet, Napoleon 1864-1932 *NotNAT B,*
  WhThe
Lambert, Albert *Film 1*
Lambert, Clara d1921 *WhScrn 1, WhScrn 2*
Lambert, Constant 1905-1951 *WhThe*
Lambert, Dave 1917- *AmSCAP 1966*
Lambert, Edward J 1897-1951 *AmSCAP 1966*
Lambert, Gavin 1924- *FilmgC, WorEnF*
Lambert, Hugh *BiE&WWA, NotNAT*
Lambert, Irene *Film 2*
Lambert, J W 1917- *WhoThe 16*
Lambert, Jack 1899- *FilmgC, WhoHol A,*
  WhoThe 16
Lambert, Jack 1920- *FilmgC, Vers A*
Lambert, Lawson 1870-1944 *NotNAT B, WhThe*
Lambert, Paul *WhoHol A*
Lamberti, Professor d1950 *NotNAT B,*
  WhScrn 1, WhScrn 2, WhoHol B
Lambetti, Ellie 1930- *OxFilm*
Lamble, Lloyd 1914- *FilmgC, WhoHol A*
Lambrinos, Vassili *WhoHol A*
Lambro, Phillip 1935- *AmSCAP 1966*
Lami, Eugene Louis 1800-1890 *NotNAT B*
LaMilo *WhThe*
Lammers, Paul 1921-1968 *NotNAT B*
Lamming, Frank *Film 2*
Lamon, Isabel *Film 1*
Lamont, Charles 1895- *IntMPA 1977*
Lamont, Charles 1898- *FilmgC, TwYS A*
Lamont, Duncan 1918- *FilmgC, IntMPA 1977,*
  WhoHol A
LaMont, Frank *Film 2*
Lamont, George *Film 2*
LaMont, Harry 1887-1957 *Film 2, WhScrn 1,*
  WhScrn 2, WhoHol B
Lamont, Jack 1893-1956 *WhScrn 1, WhScrn 2,*
  WhoHol B
LaMontaine, John 1920- *AmSCAP 1966*
Lamore, Isabel *Film 2*
Lamorisse, Albert 1922-1970 *DcFM, OxFilm,*
  WorEnF
Lamorisse, Albert 1922-1971 *FilmgC*
Lamothe, Arthur 1928- *WorEnF*
Lamott, Jean *Film 2*

LaMotta, Bill 1922- *AmSCAP 1966*
LaMotte, Antoine Houdard De 1672-1731 *OxThe*
Lamour, Dorothy 1914- *BiDFlm, CmMov,*
  FilmgC, IntMPA 1977, MotPP, MovMk,
  OxFilm, ThFT, WhoHol A, WorEnF
Lamouret, Robert d1959 *WhScrn 2*
Lampe, J Bodewalt 1869-1929 *AmSCAP 1966*
Lampel, Peter Martin 1894-1962 *CnMD*
Lampell, Millard 1919- *BiE&WWA, NotNAT,*
  PIP&P
Lampert, Diane *NatPD*
Lampert, Zohra *MotPP, WhoHol A*
Lampert, Zohra 1936- *BiE&WWA*
Lampert, Zohra 1937- *NotNAT*
Lampkin, Charles *WhoHol A*
Lampl, Carl G 1898-1962 *AmSCAP 1966*
Lamprecht, Gerhard 1897- *DcFM, OxFilm*
Lampton, Dee 1898-1919 *Film 1, WhScrn 2*
Lamson, Ernest *WhoStg 1906, WhoStg 1908*
Lamy, Charles *Film 2*
Lamy, Douglas N *WhScrn 1, WhScrn 2*
Lan, David 1952- *ConDr 1977*
Lan-Fang, Mei 1894-1943 *NotNAT B*
Lancaster, Ann 1920-1970 *WhScrn 1, WhScrn 2,*
  WhoHol B
Lancaster, Burt 1913- *BiDFlm, CelR 3, CmMov,*
  FilmgC, IntMPA 1977, MotPP, MovMk,
  OxFilm, WhoHol A, WorEnF
Lancaster, Fred *Film 2*
Lancaster, John 1857-1935 *Film 1, WhScrn 2*
Lancaster, Lucie *WhoHol A*
Lancaster, Nora 1882- *WhThe*
Lancaster, Stuart *WhoHol A*
Lancaster-Wallis, Ellen 1856-1940 *NotNAT B*
Lancaster-Wallis, Ellen *see also* Wallis, Ellen
  Lancaster
Lance, Peter 1914- *AmSCAP 1966*
Lanchester, Elsa 1902- *BiE&WWA, CelR 3,*
  Film 2, FilmgC, IntMPA 1977, MotPP,
  MovMk, NotNAT, OxFilm, PIP&P, ThFT,
  Vers A, WhThe, WhoHol A
Lancing, Carole 1940- *AmSCAP 1966*
Land, Edwin 1909- *CelR 3*
Land, Mary *Film 2*
Land, Robert *PIP&P*
Landau, Mrs. David *Film 2*
Landau, David 1878-1935 *NotNAT B, WhScrn 1,*
  WhScrn 2, WhThe, WhoHol B
Landau, Ely A 1920- *FilmgC, IntMPA 1977,*
  NewYTET, WorEnF
Landau, Frances *Film 2*
Landau, Jack 1925-1967 *BiE&WWA, NotNAT B*
Landau, Lucy *WhoHol A*
Landau, Martin *MotPP, WhoHol A*
Landau, Martin 1933- *FilmgC, MovMk*
Landau, Martin 1934- *IntMPA 1977*
Landau, Richard H 1914- *IntMPA 1977*
Landau, Siegfried 1921- *AmSCAP 1966*
Landeau, Cecil 1906- *WhThe*
Landeck, Ben 1864-1928 *NotNAT B, WhThe*
Landen, Dinsdale 1932- *WhoHol A, WhoThe 16*
Lander, Charles Oram d1934 *NotNAT B*
Lander, Jean Margaret Davenport 1829-1903
  FamA&A, NotNAT B, OxThe
Landeros, Pepe 1910- *AmSCAP 1966*
Landers, Albert R 1920- *IntMPA 1977*
Landers, Ann 1918- *CelR 3*
Landers, Harry *WhoHol A*
Landers, Lew 1901-1962 *FilmgC*
Landers, Muriel *WhoHol A*
Landesman, Frances 1927- *AmSCAP 1966*
Landesman, Jay 1919- *BiE&WWA*
Landgard, Janet *WhoHol A*
Landi, Elissa 1904-1948 *Film 2, FilmgC,*

HolP 30, MotPP, MovMk, NotNAT B,
  ThFT, WhScrn 1, WhScrn 2, WhThe,
  WhoHol B
Landi, Marla 1937?- *FilmgC, WhoHol A*
Landick, Olin 1895-1972 *WhScrn 2*
Landicutt, Philip *Film 1*
Landin, Hope 1893-1973 *WhScrn 2, WhoHol B*
Landis, Carole 1919-1948 *FilmgC, MotPP,*
  MovMk, NotNAT B, WhScrn 1, WhScrn 2,
  WhoHol B
Landis, Cullen d1975 *MotPP, WhoHol C*
Landis, Cullen 1895-1975 *Film 1, Film 2, TwYS*
Landis, Cullen 1898-1975 *WhScrn 2*
Landis, Jessie Royce 1904-1972 *FilmgC, MovMk,*
  NotNAT A, Vers B, WhScrn 2, WhoHol B
Landis, Jessie Royce 1906-1972 *BiE&WWA,*
  NotNAT B, WhThe
Landis, Margaret *Film 2*
Landis, William 1921- *BiE&WWA, NotNAT*
Landis, Winifred *Film 2*
Landolfi, Tony *WhoHol A*
Landon, Avice 1908- *WhoThe 16*
Landon, Margaret 1903- *PIP&P*
Landon, Michael 1937- *FilmgC, IntMPA 1977,*
  MotPP, NewYTET, WhoHol A
Landone, Avice 1910- *FilmgC, WhoHol A*
Landowska, Yona *Film 1*
Landres, Paul 1912- *FilmgC, IntMPA 1977*
Landreth, Gertrude Griffith 1897-1969 *WhScrn 1,*
  WhScrn 2, WhoHol B
Landriani, Paolo 1770-1838 *OxThe*
Landsberg, Phyllis G 1927- *AmSCAP 1966*
Landsburg, Alan W 1933- *IntMPA 1977,*
  NewYTET
Landshoff, Ruth *Film 2*
Landstone, Charles 1891- *WhThe*
Landweber, Ellen *WomWMM B*
Lane, Abbe *WhoHol A*
Lane, Adele *Film 1, MotPP*
Lane, Allan Rocky d1973 *MotPP, WhScrn 2,*
  WhoHol B
Lane, Allan Rocky 1900-1973 *Film 2*
Lane, Allan Rocky 1904-1973 *FilmgC*
Lane, Brenda *Film 2*
Lane, Burton 1912- *AmSCAP 1966, BiE&WWA,*
  EncMT, NewMT, NotNAT, PIP&P,
  WhoThe 16
Lane, Charles 1869-1945 *WhScrn 2*
Lane, Charles 1899- *Film 1, Film 2, FilmgC,*
  MotPP, MovMk, TwYS, Vers A,
  WhoHol A
Lane, Clara *WhoStg 1906, WhoStg 1908*
Lane, Clarence 1910- *AmSCAP 1966*
Lane, Dorothy 1890- *WhThe*
Lane, Dorothy 1905-1923 *WhScrn 1, WhScrn 2*
Lane, Eastwood 1879-1951 *AmSCAP 1966*
Lane, Edward 1915-1959 *AmSCAP 1966*
Lane, Grace 1876-1956 *NotNAT B, WhThe*
Lane, Harry 1910-1960 *WhScrn 1, WhScrn 2,*
  WhoHol B
Lane, Horace 1880- *WhThe*
Lane, Ivan 1914- *AmSCAP 1966*
Lane, Jackie *MotPP*
Lane, James W *AmSCAP 1966*
Lane, Jocelyn *WhoHol A*
Lane, Katheryn *Film 2*
Lane, Kenneth Jay 1932- *CelR 3*
Lane, Kent *WhoHol A*
Lane, Kermit 1912- *AmSCAP 1966*
Lane, Laura 1927- *AmSCAP 1966*
Lane, Leela *Film 2*
Lane, Lenita *WhoHol A*
Lane, Leone *Film 2*
Lane, Leota d1963 *WhoHol B*

Lane, Lola *MotPP*
Lane, Lola 1906- *WhoHol A*
Lane, Lola 1909- *Film 2, ThFT*
Lane, Lupino 1892-1957 *Film 1, Film 2, TwYS*
Lane, Lupino 1892-1959 *EncMT, FilmgC,
 NotNAT A, NotNAT B, OxThe, WhScrn 1,
 WhScrn 2, WhThe, WhoHol B*
Lane, Magda *Film 2*
Lane, Maryon *WhoHol A*
Lane, Mike *WhoHol A*
Lane, Nora *Film 2, TwYS*
Lane, Pat 1900-1953 *WhScrn 1, WhScrn 2*
Lane, Priscilla 1917- *MotPP, MovMk, ThFT,
 WhoHol A*
Lane, Richard 1900- *FilmgC, Vers A,
 WhoHol A*
Lane, Richard B 1933- *AmSCAP 1966*
Lane, Rosemary d1974 *MotPP, WhoHol B*
Lane, Rosemary 1914-1974 *ThFT, WhScrn 2*
Lane, Rosemary 1916-1974 *MovMk*
Lane, Sara *WhoHol A*
Lane, Sara 1823-1899 *OxThe*
Lane, Wallace d1961 *WhScrn 1, WhScrn 2,
 WhoHol B*
Lane Sisters, The *FilmgC*
Laney, Luther King 1916- *AmSCAP 1966*
Lanfield, Sidney 1900- *FilmgC*
Lang, Andre 1893- *McGWD*
Lang, Barbara *WhoHol A*
Lang, Charles 1915- *FilmgC*
Lang, Charles B, Jr. 1902- *CmMov, DcFM,
 FilmgC, IntMPA 1977, OxFilm, WorEnF*
Lang, David 1913- *IntMPA 1977*
Lang, Doreen *WhoHol A*
Lang, Eddie 1902-1933 *AmSCAP 1966*
Lang, Eva Clara d1933 *NotNAT B*
Lang, Fritz 1890- *BiDFlm, CmMov, DcFM,
 FilmgC, MovMk, OxFilm, TwYS A,
 WomWMM, WorEnF*
Lang, Gertrude d1941 *NotNAT B*
Lang, Gertrude d1942 *NotNAT B*
Lang, Harold 1923- *BiE&WWA, EncMT,
 WhoThe 16*
Lang, Harold 1923-1970 *WhScrn 1, WhScrn 2*
Lang, Harold 1923-1971 *FilmgC, WhoHol B*
Lang, Harold 1931-1975 *NotNAT B*
Lang, Harry 1895-1953 *NotNAT B, WhScrn 1,
 WhScrn 2, WhoHol B*
Lang, Howard 1876-1941 *Film 2, NotNAT B,
 WhScrn 1, WhScrn 2, WhThe, WhoHol B*
Lang, Hutin Britton 1876-1965 *OxThe*
Lang, Jennings 1915- *IntMPA 1977*
Lang, June 1915- *FilmgC, ThFT, WhoHol A*
Lang, Ludwig d1932 *NotNAT B*
Lang, Matheson 1879-1948 *CnThe, Film 1,
 Film 2, FilmgC, NotNAT A, NotNAT B,
 OxThe, PIP&P, WhScrn 1, WhScrn 2,
 WhThe, WhoHol B*
Lang, Otto *IntMPA 1977*
Lang, Pearl *BiE&WWA*
Lang, Peter 1867-1932 *Film 1, Film 2,
 NotNAT B, WhScrn 1, WhScrn 2,
 WhoHol B*
Lang, Philip J 1911- *BiE&WWA, NotNAT*
Lang, Phillip 1911- *AmSCAP 1966*
Lang, Robert 1934- *WhoHol A, WhoThe 16*
Lang, Walter 1896-1972 *CmMov, FilmgC*
Lang, Walter 1898-1972 *BiDFlm, TwYS A,
 WhScrn 2, WorEnF*
Lang, Walter 1936- *MovMk*
Langan, Glenn 1917- *FilmgC, IntMPA 1977,
 MovMk, WhoHol A*
Langan, John 1902- *TwYS A*
Langan, Marius *Film 2*

Langbaine, Gerard d1692 *NotNAT B*
Langden, John *Film 2*
Langdon, Harry d1944 *MotPP, WhoHol B*
Langdon, Harry 1884-1944 *BiDFlm, CmMov,
 DcFM, FilmgC, MovMk, OxFilm, TwYS A,
 WhScrn 1, WhScrn 2, WorEnF*
Langdon, Harry 1884-1946 *Film 2, TwYS*
Langdon, Harry 1885-1944 *NotNAT B*
Langdon, Lillian d1943 *Film 1, Film 2, TwYS,
 WhScrn 1, WhScrn 2, WhoHol B*
Langdon, Rose *Film 2*
Langdon, Sue Ann 1940- *FilmgC, WhoHol A*
Lange, Arthur 1889-1956 *AmSCAP 1966*
Lange, Barbara Pearson 1910- *BiE&WWA,
 NotNAT*
Lange, Hartmut 1937- *CroCD*
Lange, Henry W 1895- *AmSCAP 1966*
Lange, Hope *IntMPA 1977, MotPP, WhoHol A*
Lange, Hope 1931- *FilmgC*
Lange, Hope 1933- *MovMk*
Lange, Jessica *WhoHol A*
Lange, Johnny 1909- *AmSCAP 1966*
Lange, Mary 1913-1973 *WhScrn 2*
Lange, Sven d1930 *NotNAT B*
Langella, Frank *WhoHol A*
Langella, Frank 1940- *NotNAT, PIP&P A,
 WhoThe 16*
Langella, Frank 1944- *FilmgC*
Langenbeck, Curt 1906-1953 *CnMD*
Langendoen, Jacobus C 1890- *AmSCAP 1966*
Langenus, Gustave 1883-1957 *AmSCAP 1966*
Langer, Frantisek 1888-1965 *CnMD, ModWD,
 REnWD*
Langford, Abraham d1774 *NotNAT B*
Langford, Frances 1914- *FilmgC, IntMPA 1977,
 MotPP, ThFT, WhoHol A*
Langford, Martha d1935 *WhScrn 1, WhScrn 2*
Langford, William 1920-1955 *NotNAT B,
 WhScrn 1, WhScrn 2, WhoHol B*
Langford-Reed, Joan *Film 2*
Langham, Michael 1919- *BiE&WWA, NotNAT,
 WhoThe 16*
Langhans, Edward A 1923- *BiE&WWA,
 NotNAT*
Langheld, Gretchen *WomWMM B*
Langlen, Paula *Film 2*
Langley, Faith 1929-1972 *WhScrn 2*
Langley, Herbert 1888-1967 *Film 2, WhScrn 1,
 WhScrn 2, WhoHol B*
Langley, Jane Pickens *CelR 3*
Langley, Noel 1911- *BiE&WWA, FilmgC,
 IntMPA 1977, NotNAT, WhThe*
Langley, Stuart d1970 *WhoHol B*
Langlois, Henri 1914- *OxFilm, WorEnF*
Langner, Ilse 1899- *CnMD*
Langner, Lawrence 1890-1962 *EncMT, ModWD,
 NotNAT A, NotNAT B, OxThe, PIP&P,
 WhThe*
Langner, Philip 1926- *BiE&WWA, NotNAT,
 WhoThe 16*
Langston, Ruth *Film 2*
Langstroth, Ivan 1887- *AmSCAP 1966*
Langton, Basil C 1912-1929 *WhThe*
Langton, Paul 1913- *IntMPA 1977, WhoHol A*
Langtry, Lillie 1852-1929 *FamA&A, WhThe*
Langtry, Lillie 1853-1929 *OxThe, WhScrn 1,
 WhScrn 2*
Langtry, Lillie 1877- *WhThe*
Langtry, Lily 1852-1929 *NotNAT A, NotNAT B,
 WhoStg 1906, WhoStg 1908*
Langtry, Lily 1853-1929 *PIP&P, WhoHol B*
Langtry, Lily 1856-1929 *Film 1*
Languepin, Jean-Jacques 1924- *DcFM*
Lani, Maria 1906-1954 *WhScrn 1, WhScrn 2*

Lania, Leon d1961 *NotNAT B*
Lanin, Lester *CelR 3*
Lankester, Eric *Film 2*
Lanner, Katti d1908 *NotNAT B*
Lanning, Frank *Film 1, Film 2*
Lano, David 1874- *NotNAT A*
Lanoe, Jacques *Film 2*
Lanoue, Conrad 1908- *AmSCAP 1966*
LaNoue, Jean Sauve De 1701-1761 *OxThe*
Lanoy, Andre *Film 2*
Lanphier, Fay d1959 *WhoHol B*
Lanphier, Faye 1906-1959 *WhScrn 1, WhScrn 2*
Lanphier, Florence *Film 2*
Lanphier, James F 1921-1969 *WhScrn 2, WhoHol B*
Lansbury, Angela 1925- *BiDFlm, BiE&WWA, CelR 3, EncMT, FilmgC, IntMPA 1977, MGM, MotPP, MovMk, NotNAT, OxFilm, WhoHol A, WhoThe 16*
Lansbury, Bruce 1930- *IntMPA 1977*
Lansbury, Edgar 1930- *BiE&WWA, NotNAT, WhoThe 16*
Lansing, Joi d1972 *MotPP, WhoHol B*
Lansing, Joi 1930-1972 *WhScrn 2*
Lansing, Joi 1936-1972 *FilmgC*
Lansing, Mary *Film 2*
Lansing, Robert 1929- *BiE&WWA, FilmgC, MotPP, NotNAT, WhoHol A*
Lansing, Ruth Douglas 1881-1931 *WhScrn 1, WhScrn 2*
Lanteau, William *WhoHol A*
Lantelme, Mademoiselle d1911 *NotNAT B*
Lantz, Robert 1914- *BiE&WWA, NotNAT*
Lantz, Walter 1900- *FilmgC, IntMPA 1977, WorEnF*
Lanza, Mario 1921-1959 *CmMov, FilmgC, MGM, MotPP, MovMk, NotNAT B, OxFilm, WhScrn 1, WhScrn 2, WhoHol B, WorEnF*
Laparcerie, Cora *WhThe*
LaPatelliere, Denys De 1921- *DcFM*
Lapauri, Aleksandr 1926-1975 *WhScrn 2*
LaPera, Sam *WhoHol A*
Lapid, Jess d1968 *WhScrn 2*
Lapidos, Joseph 1914- *AmSCAP 1966*
Lapierre, Dominique *CelR 3*
LaPlanche, Rosemary *WhoHol A*
LaPlante, Beatrice *Film 2*
LaPlante, Laura 1904- *Film 2, FilmgC, ThFT, TwYS, WhThe, WhoHol A*
LaPlante, Violet *Film 2*
Lapo, Cecil E 1910- *AmSCAP 1966*
LaPorta, John 1920- *AmSCAP 1966*
Laporte 1584?-1621? *OxThe*
Laporte, Pierre Francois d1841 *NotNAT B*
Lapotaire, Jane 1944- *WhoThe 16*
Lapsley, Jimmie *Film 2*
Lara, Madame 1876- *WhThe*
Larabee, Louise *WhoHol A*
LaRae, Grace d1956 *NotNAT B*
Laramore, Vivian Yeiser 1895- *AmSCAP 1966*
Larch, John *WhoHol A*
Lardner, Ring W 1885-1933 *AmSCAP 1966, NotNAT B*
Lardner, Ring W, Jr. 1915- *IntMPA 1977, OxFilm*
LaReno, Dick d1945 *WhoHol B*
LaReno, Richard 1873-1945 *Film 1, Film 2, WhScrn 1, WhScrn 2*
Largay, Raymond J 1886-1974 *WhScrn 2, WhoHol B*
Large, Donald E 1909- *AmSCAP 1966*
Larimore, Earle 1899-1947 *NotNAT B, WhScrn 1, WhScrn 2, WhThe, WhoHol B*
Larive, Leon *Film 2*

Larivey, Pierre De 1540?-1612? *OxThe*
Larivey, Pierre De 1540-1619 *McGWD*
Larkin, George 1888-1946 *WhScrn 2*
Larkin, George 1889- *Film 1, Film 2, TwYS*
Larkin, James J 1925- *IntMPA 1977*
Larkin, John 1874-1936 *WhScrn 1, WhScrn 2, WhoHol B*
Larkin, John 1912-1965 *WhScrn 1, WhScrn 2, WhoHol B*
Larkin, Peter 1926- *BiE&WWA, NotNAT, WhoThe 16*
Larned, Mel d1955 *NotNAT B*
LaRocca, Dominick James 1889-1961 *AmSCAP 1966*
LaRoche, Edward *Film 2*
Laroche, Johann 1745-1806 *OxThe*
LaRoche, Mary *WhoHol A*
Laroche, Pierre 1902-1962 *DcFM*
LaRocque, Rod 1896-1969 *FilmgC, MovMk, TwYS*
LaRocque, Rod 1898-1969 *Film 1, Film 2, MotPP, WhScrn 1, WhScrn 2, WhoHol B*
Laroque 1595?-1676 *OxThe*
LaRosa, Julius *NewYTET*
LaRoy, Rita 1907- *Film 2, MotPP, WhoHol B*
Larquey, Pierre 1884-1962 *NotNAT B, WhScrn 1, WhScrn 2, WhoHol B*
Larra, Mariano *WhThe*
Larra, Mariano Jose De 1809-1837 *NotNAT B, OxThe*
Larra Y Sanchez DeCastro, Mariano J De 1809-1837 *McGWD*
Larrain, Michael *WhoHol A*
Larrimore, Earle 1899-1947 *PIP&P*
Larrimore, Francine 1898-1975 *BiE&WWA, Film 1, NotNAT B, TwYS, WhScrn 2, WhThe, WhoHol C*
Larrinaga, Forster *Film 2*
L'Arronge, Adolf 1838-1908 *OxThe*
Larsen, Carl 1934- *NatPD*
Larsen, Keith 1925- *FilmgC, IntMPA 1977, WhoHol A*
Larsen, Paul J *IntMPA 1977*
Larsen, Roy 1899- *CelR 3*
Larsen, William *NotNAT*
Larson, Christine *WhoHol A*
Larson, G Bennett *IntMPA 1977*
Larson, Glen A *NewYTET*
Larson, Jack *NatPD*
Larson, Lorlee 1935-1954 *WhScrn 1, WhScrn 2*
Larson, Paul *WhoHol A*
Larsson, Helmer *Film 2*
Larsson, William *Film 1*
LaRubia, Marga *Film 2*
LaRue, Danny 1928- *FilmgC*
LaRue, Fontaine *Film 1, Film 2, TwYS*
LaRue, Frank H 1878-1960 *WhScrn 1, WhScrn 2, WhoHol B*
LaRue, Grace d1956 *Film 1, WhoHol B*
LaRue, Grace 1881-1956 *WhScrn 1, WhScrn 2*
LaRue, Grace 1882-1956 *NotNAT B, WhThe*
LaRue, Jack *MotPP*
LaRue, Jack 1900- *WhoHol A*
LaRue, Jack 1903- *FilmgC, MovMk*
LaRue, Jean 1901-1956 *WhScrn 1, WhScrn 2, WhoHol B*
LaRue, Lash 1921- *WhoHol A*
LaRusso, Louis, II 1935- *NatPD*
LaSalle, Richard W 1918- *AmSCAP 1966*
Lascoe, Henry 1914-1964 *NotNAT B, WhScrn 1, WhScrn 2, WhoHol B*
LaShelle, Joseph 1903- *CmMov, FilmgC*
Lashelle, Joseph 1905- *WorEnF*
LaShelle, Kirke 1863-1905 *NotNAT B*

Lashley, Donald *Film 2*
Lashwood, George d1942 *NotNAT B, WhThe*
Laska, Edward 1894-1959 *AmSCAP 1966*
Lasker, Henry 1908- *AmSCAP 1966*
Lasker, Mary 1900- *CelR 3*
Lasker-Schuler, Else 1876-1945 *CnMD*
Laskos, Orestis 1908- *DcFM*
Laskowich, Gloria *WomWMM B*
Lasky, Jesse L 1880-1958 *BiDFlm, DcFM, FilmgC, NotNAT B, OxFilm, WorEnF*
Lasky, Jesse L 1881-1958 *TwYS B*
Lasky, Jesse L, Jr. 1910- *CmMov, DcFM, FilmgC, IntMPA 1977*
Lasky, Victor 1918- *CelR 3*
Lassally, Walter 1926- *DcFM, FilmgC, OxFilm, WorEnF*
Lasser, Louise 1935?- *MovMk, NewYTET, WhoHol A*
Lassie *Film 2, FilmgC, OxFilm*
Lassie 1941-1959 *WhScrn 2*
Lassnig, Maria *WomWMM B*
LaStarza, Roland *WhoHol A*
Lastfogel, Abe 1898- *BiE&WWA, IntMPA 1977, NotNAT*
LaStrange, Dick *Film 1*
Laszlo, Andy 1934- *FilmgC*
Laszlo, Ernest 1905- *FilmgC*
Laszlo, Ernest 1906- *WorEnF*
LaTaille, Jean De 1533?-1607? *McGWD*
Lateiner, Joseph 1853-1935 *ModWD, NotNAT B, OxThe*
Latell, Lyle 1905-1967 *WhScrn 1, WhScrn 2, WhoHol B*
Latham, Dwight B 1903- *AmSCAP 1966*
Latham, Fred G d1943 *NotNAT B*
Latham, Frederick G d1943 *WhThe*
Latham, Hope d1951 *NotNAT B*
Latham, Louise *WhoHol A*
Latham, William P 1917- *AmSCAP 1966*
Lathbury, Stanley 1873- *WhThe*
Lathom, Earl Of *WhThe*
LaThorilliere, Anne-Maurice 1697?-1759 *OxThe*
LaThorilliere, Francois Lenoir De 1626-1680 *OxThe*
LaThorilliere, Pierre 1659-1731 *OxThe*
Lathrop, Donald 1888-1940 *WhScrn 1, WhScrn 2, WhoHol B*
Lathrop, Philip H 1916- *FilmgC, WorEnF*
Latimer, Billy *Film 2*
Latimer, Edyth *WhThe*
Latimer, Florence *Film 2*
Latimer, Henry d1963 *NotNAT B*
Latimer, Hugh 1913- *WhoHol A, WhoThe 16*
Latimer, James H 1934- *AmSCAP 1966*
Latimer, Jonathan *FilmgC, IntMPA 1977*
Latimer, Sally 1910- *WhThe*
Latimore, Frank 1925- *FilmgC, WhoHol A*
Latona, Jen 1881- *WhThe*
LaTorre, Charles *WhoHol A*
LaTorre, Charles 1900- *IntMPA 1977*
LaTorre, Charles A 1895- *Film 2, Vers A*
Latouche, John 1917-1956 *AmSCAP 1966, EncMT, McGWD, NewMT, NotNAT B*
Latoudie, John *PIP&P*
LaTourneaux, Robert *WhoHol A*
LaTrobe, Charles 1879-1967 *WhThe*
Latsis, Peter C 1919- *IntMPA 1977*
Lattimore, Richmond 1906- *BiE&WWA, NotNAT*
Lattuada, Alberto 1914- *BiDFlm, DcFM, FilmgC, IntMPA 1977, OxFilm, WorEnF*
LaTuillerie, Jean-Francois Juvenon 1650-1688 *OxThe*
LaTuillerie, Louise Catherine 1657?-1706 *OxThe*
Laube, Heinrich 1806-1884 *OxThe*

Lauchlan, Agnes 1905- *WhoThe 16*
Lauck, Chester 1902- *WhoHol A*
Lauckner, Rolf 1887-1954 *CnMD, ModWD*
Lauder, Estee *CelR 3*
Lauder, Sir Harry 1870-1950 *Film 2, FilmgC, NotNAT A, NotNAT B, OxThe, WhScrn 1, WhScrn 2, WhThe, WhoHol B*
Laudivio *OxThe*
Laufer, Beatrice 1923- *AmSCAP 1966*
Laughlan, Agnes *PIP&P*
Laughlin, Anna 1885-1937 *Film 1, NotNAT B, WhoHol B, WhoStg 1906, WhoStg 1908*
Laughlin, Billy 1932-1948 *WhScrn 2*
Laughlin, Kathleen *WomWMM B*
Laughlin, Sharon *NotNAT*
Laughlin, Tom *IntMPA 1977, WhoHol A, WomWMM*
Laughlin, Tom 1931- *MovMk*
Laughlin, Tom 1938- *FilmgC*
Laughton, Charles 1899-1962 *BiDFlm, CmMov, CnThe, FamA&A, Film 2, FilmgC, MotPP, MovMk, NotNAT A, NotNAT B, OxFilm, PIP&P, WhScrn 1, WhScrn 2, WhThe, WhoHol B, WorEnF*
Laughton, Eddie d1952 *WhoHol B*
Laughton, Edward 1903-1952 *WhScrn 1, WhScrn 2*
Lauher, Bob 1931-1973 *WhScrn 2*
Launder, Frank 1907- *FilmgC, IntMPA 1977, OxFilm, WorEnF*
Launders, Perc 1905-1952 *WhScrn 1, WhScrn 2, WhoHol B*
Laurel, Kay 1890-1927 *WhScrn 2*
Laurel, Stan 1890-1965 *CmMov, Film 1, Film 2, FilmgC, MGM, MotPP, MovMk, OxFilm, TwYS, WhScrn 1, WhScrn 2, WhoHol B, WorEnF*
Laurel And Hardy *BiDFlm, MotPP, OxFilm*
Laurell, Kay *Film 1*
Laurence, Douglas 1922- *IntMPA 1977*
Laurence, Michael 1928- *AmSCAP 1966*
Laurence, Paula 1916- *BiE&WWA, NotNAT, WhoThe 16*
Laurent, Jeanne Marie *Film 2*
Laurents, Arthur *IntMPA 1977*
Laurents, Arthur 1918- *BiE&WWA, ConDr 1977, EncMT, FilmgC, McGWD, NewMT, NotNAT, PIP&P, WhoThe 16*
Laurents, Arthur 1920- *CnMD, ModWD*
Laurenz, John 1909-1958 *WhScrn 1, WhScrn 2*
Laurenze, John d1958 *WhoHol B*
Lauri, Edward d1919 *NotNAT B*
Laurie, Joe, Jr. 1892-1954 *NotNAT B*
Laurie, John 1897- *FilmgC, IntMPA 1977, MovMk, PIP&P, WhoHol A, WhoThe 16*
Laurie, Piper 1932- *CmMov, FilmgC, IntMPA 1977, MotPP, MovMk, WhoHol A, WorEnF*
Laurier, Jay 1879-1969 *WhScrn 1, WhScrn 2, WhThe, WhoHol B*
Laurillard, Edward 1870-1936 *WhThe*
Lauritzen, Lau 1878-1938 *DcFM*
Lauritzen, Lau, Jr. 1910- *DcFM*
Lauste, Eugene 1856-1935 *DcFM*
Lauter, Harry 1920- *FilmgC, WhoHol A*
Lautner, Georges 1926- *WorEnF*
Lava, William 1911- *AmSCAP 1966*
Lavalle, Paul 1908- *AmSCAP 1966*
Lavallee, Nicole *WomWMM*
Lavalliere, Eve 1866-1929 *NotNAT A, NotNAT B, WhThe*
Lavarne, Laura *Film 1, Film 2*
LaVarre, Myrtland *Film 2*
Lavedan, Henri 1859-1940 *CnMD, McGWD,*

ModWD, NotNAT B, OxThe, WhThe
LaVelle, Barbara *Film 2*
LaVelle, Kay 1889-1965 *WhScrn 2*
Laven, Arnold 1922- *FilmgC, IntMPA 1977*
Lavender *Film 2*
Laver, James 1899- *BiE&WWA, NotNAT A, OxThe, WhThe*
Laver, Rod 1938- *CelR 3*
LaVere, Charles 1910- *AmSCAP 1966*
LaVere, Earl d1962 *NotNAT B*
Laverick, Beryl 1919- *WhThe*
Laverick, June 1932- *FilmgC*
LaVerne, Jane *Film 2*
LaVerne, Lucille 1869-1945 *TwYS*
LaVerne, Lucille 1872-1945 *Film 1, Film 2, NotNAT B, WhScrn 1, WhScrn 2, WhThe, WhoHol B*
Laverne, Pattie d1916 *NotNAT B*
LaVernie, Laura 1853-1939 *WhScrn 1, WhScrn 2, WhoHol B*
Laverty, Jean *Film 2*
Lavery, Emmet 1902- *BiE&WWA, CnMD, ModWD, NotNAT*
Lavery, Emmet G, Jr. 1927- *IntMPA 1977*
Lavi, Daliah 1940- *FilmgC, MotPP, WhoHol A*
LaVigne, Andrieu De d1515? *McGWD*
Lavin, Linda *WhoHol A*
Lavin, Linda 1937- *WhoThe 16*
Lavin, Linda 1939- *NotNAT*
Lavine, Jack *Film 2*
Lavinia *OxThe*
LaViolette, Juliette *Film 2*
LaViolette, Wesley 1894- *AmSCAP 1966*
Lavrenev, Boris Andreevich 1892-1959 *CnMD, ModWD*
Law, Alex W 1909- *AmSCAP 1966*
Law, Arthur 1844-1913 *NotNAT B, WhThe*
Law, Burton 1880-1963 *Film 2, WhScrn 2*
Law, Don Fats 1920-1959 *WhoHol B*
Law, Donald 1920-1959 *WhScrn 1, WhScrn 2*
Law, Jenny Lou d1961 *NotNAT B*
Law, John Philip 1937- *FilmgC, IntMPA 1977*
Law, John Phillip 1937- *CelR 3, MotPP, WhoHol A*
Law, Mary 1891- *WhThe*
Law, Mouzon 1922- *BiE&WWA, NotNAT*
Law, Rodman 1885-1919 *WhScrn 2*
Law, Walter 1876-1940 *Film 1, Film 2, WhScrn 1, WhScrn 2, WhoHol B*
Law, Winnie *Film 2*
Lawes, Lewis E 1884-1947 *WhScrn 1, WhScrn 2*
Lawford, Betty 1910-1960 *Film 2, NotNAT B, WhScrn 1, WhScrn 2, WhThe, WhoHol B*
Lawford, Ernest *Film 2*
Lawford, Ernest d1940 *NotNAT B, WhThe*
Lawford, Peter *MotPP, WhoHol A*
Lawford, Peter 1921- *CelR 3*
Lawford, Peter 1923- *FilmgC, IntMPA 1977, MGM, MovMk, OxFilm, WorEnF*
Lawford, Sir Sydney 1866-1953 *WhScrn 1, WhScrn 2*
Lawler, Anderson *Film 2*
Lawler, Jerome *Film 1*
Lawler, Ray 1921- *BiE&WWA, ConDr 1977, ModWD, NotNAT, OxThe*
Lawler, Ray 1922- *CnMD, CnThe, McGWD, REnWD*
Lawlor, Charles B 1852-1925 *AmSCAP 1966, NotNAT B*
Lawlor, Mary *WhThe, WhoHol A*
Lawlor, Robert *Film 1*
Lawnhurst, Vee 1905- *AmSCAP 1966*
Lawrance, Jody 1930- *FilmgC*
Lawrence, Adrian d1953 *NotNAT B*

Lawrence, Barbara *MotPP*
Lawrence, Barbara 1928- *FilmgC*
Lawrence, Barbara 1930- *IntMPA 1977*
Lawrence, Bill d1972 *NewYTET*
Lawrence, Boyle 1869-1951 *NotNAT B, WhThe*
Lawrence, C É d1940 *NotNAT B*
Lawrence, Carol *BiE&WWA, MotPP, WhoHol A*
Lawrence, Carol 1932- *EncMT*
Lawrence, Carol 1935- *WhoThe 16*
Lawrence, Charles 1896- *WhThe*
Lawrence, Charlie *WhScrn 2*
Lawrence, Cornelius C 1902- *AmSCAP 1966*
Lawrence, D H 1885-1930 *CnThe, FilmgC, ModWD, WhThe*
Lawrence, D H 1885-1940 *NotNAT B*
Lawrence, Dakota 1902- *Film 1, TwYS*
Lawrence, David Herbert 1885-1930 *CnMD*
Lawrence, Delphi 1927?- *FilmgC, WhoHol A*
Lawrence, E W *Film 1*
Lawrence, Eddie *NatPD*
Lawrence, Eddy d1931 *WhScrn 1, WhScrn 2*
Lawrence, Edward d1931 *Film 2, WhoHol B*
Lawrence, Elizabeth *WhoHol A*
Lawrence, Elliot 1925- *AmSCAP 1966, NotNAT*
Lawrence, Elliot 1926- *BiE&WWA*
Lawrence, Florence 1886-1938 *FilmgC*
Lawrence, Florence 1888-1938 *Film 1, Film 2, MotPP, NotNAT B, OxFilm, TwYS, WhScrn 1, WhScrn 2, WhoHol B*
Lawrence, Georgia d1923 *NotNAT B*
Lawrence, Gerald 1873-1957 *Film 2, NotNAT B, OxThe, WhThe, WhoHol B, WhoStg 1906, WhoStg 1908*
Lawrence, Gertrude 1898-1952 *CnThe, EncMT, FamA&A, Film 2, FilmgC, NotNAT A, NotNAT B, OxFilm, OxThe, PIP&P, ThFT, WhScrn 1, WhScrn 2, WhThe, WhoHol B, WorEnF*
Lawrence, Gregory 1916- *AmSCAP 1966*
Lawrence, Harding 1920- *CelR 3*
Lawrence, Harold 1906- *AmSCAP 1966*
Lawrence, Jack 1912- *AmSCAP 1966, BiE&WWA*
Lawrence, Jerome 1915- *AmSCAP 1966, BiE&WWA, ConDr 1977, EncMT, ModWD, NotNAT, WhoThe 16*
Lawrence, Jody 1930- *IntMPA 1977*
Lawrence, John 1910-1974 *WhScrn 2, WhoHol B*
Lawrence, Lawrence Shubert 1894-1965 *BiE&WWA, NotNAT B*
Lawrence, Lawrence Shubert, Jr. 1916- *BiE&WWA, NotNAT*
Lawrence, Lillian 1870-1926 *Film 1, Film 2, WhScrn 1, WhScrn 2, WhoHol B, WhoStg 1906, WhoStg 1908*
Lawrence, Marc *IntMPA 1977, WhoHol A*
Lawrence, Marc 1909- *Vers A*
Lawrence, Marc 1910- *CmMov, FilmgC, MovMk*
Lawrence, Margaret 1889-1929 *NotNAT B, WhThe*
Lawrence, Marjory *Film 1*
Lawrence, Mark 1921- *AmSCAP 1966*
Lawrence, Mary *WhoHol A*
Lawrence, Mary Wells 1928- *CelR 3*
Lawrence, Quentin 1923?- *FilmgC*
Lawrence, Raymond *Film 2*
Lawrence, Reginald 1900-1967 *BiE&WWA, NotNAT B*
Lawrence, Robert L 1919- *IntMPA 1977*
Lawrence, Russell Lee 1942- *NatPD*
Lawrence, Shirley 1932- *AmSCAP 1966*
Lawrence, Slingsby *OxThe*
Lawrence, Stan *BiE&WWA*

Lawrence, Steve 1935- *AmSCAP 1966,*
  BiE&WWA, CelR 3, EncMT, NotNAT,
  WhoHol A
Lawrence, T E *PIP&P*
Lawrence, Vicki *WhoHol A*
Lawrence, Vincent 1896- *WhThe*
Lawrence, Vincent S 1890-1946 *NotNAT B,*
  WhThe
Lawrence, Viola *WomWMM*
Lawrence, W E *Film 1*
Lawrence, Walter N d1920 *NotNAT B*
Lawrence, William d1921 *NotNAT B*
Lawrence, William E 1896-1947 *Film 2,*
  WhScrn 1, WhScrn 2, WhoHol B
Lawrence, William John 1862-1940 *NotNAT B*
Lawrence, William John 1862-1941 *WhThe*
Laws, Sam *WhoHol A*
Lawson, Eleanor 1875-1966 *Film 2, WhScrn 2*
Lawson, Elsie *Film 1, Film 2*
Lawson, Helen Mitchell Morosco *WhScrn 1,*
  WhScrn 2
Lawson, John 1865-1920 *NotNAT B, WhThe*
Lawson, John Howard *PIP&P*
Lawson, John Howard 1886- *DcFM, FilmgC*
Lawson, John Howard 1894- *BiE&WWA,*
  ConDr 1977, IntMPA 1977, McGWD,
  NotNAT, WorEnF
Lawson, John Howard 1895- *CnMD, CnThe,*
  ModWD, OxFilm, WhThe
Lawson, Kate 1894- *BiE&WWA, NotNAT*
Lawson, Linda *WhoHol A*
Lawson, Mary 1910-1941 *NotNAT B, WhThe,*
  WhoHol B
Lawson, Robb d1947 *NotNAT B*
Lawson, Sarah 1928- *IntMPA 1977, WhoHol A*
Lawson, Wilfred 1900-1966 *CnThe*
Lawson, Wilfrid 1900-1966 *FilmgC, NotNAT B,*
  WhScrn 1, WhScrn 2, WhThe, WhoHol B
Lawson, Winifred 1894-1961 *NotNAT B, WhThe*
Lawton, Alma *WhoHol A*
Lawton, Charles, Jr. 1904-1965 *CmMov, WorEnF*
Lawton, Frank d1914 *NotNAT B*
Lawton, Frank 1904-1969 *Film 2, FilmgC,*
  WhScrn 1, WhScrn 2, WhThe, WhoHol B
Lawton, Jack *Film 1*
Lawton, Thais 1881-1956 *NotNAT B, WhScrn 1,*
  WhScrn 2, WhThe, WhoHol B
Lawyer, M H 1909- *IntMPA 1977*
Lax, Frances 1895-1975 *WhScrn 2, WhoHol C*
Lay, Beirne, Jr. 1909- *CmMov, IntMPA 1977*
Lay, Irving T d1932 *WhScrn 1, WhScrn 2*
Laycock, Ada *Film 2*
Laydu, Claude 1927- *FilmgC*
Laye, Dilys 1934- *WhoHol A, WhoThe 16*
Laye, Evelyn 1900- *BiE&WWA, EncMT,*
  Film 2, FilmgC, IntMPA 1977, NotNAT,
  NotNAT A, ThFT, WhoHol A, WhoThe 16
Layton, Billy Jim 1924- *AmSCAP 1966*
Layton, Dorothy *WhoHol A*
Layton, Joe 1931- *BiE&WWA, CelR 3, EncMT,*
  NotNAT, WhoThe 16
Lazar, Irving 1907- *BiE&WWA, CelR 3*
Lazarus, Erna *IntMPA 1977*
Lazarus, Margaret *WomWMM B*
Lazarus, Paul N 1913- *IntMPA 1977*
Lazarus, Paul N, III *IntMPA 1977*
Lazarus, Theodore R 1919- *IntMPA 1977*
Lazarus, Thomas L 1942- *IntMPA 1977*
Lazenby, George 1939- *FilmgC, MovMk,*
  WhoHol A
Lazer, Peter 1946- *BiE&WWA*
Lazlo, Alexander 1895- *AmSCAP 1966*
Lazzeri, Tony *Film 2*
Lea, Marion d1944 *NotNAT B*

Leach, Wilford 1929- *BiE&WWA, NotNAT*
Leachman, Cloris *WhoHol A*
Leachman, Cloris 1926- *MovMk*
Leachman, Cloris 1930- *IntMPA 1977*
Leachman, Cloris 1933- *FilmgC*
Leacock, Philip 1917- *BiDFlm, DcFM, FilmgC,*
  NewYTET, WorEnF
Leacock, Richard 1921- *BiDFlm, DcFM, FilmgC,*
  OxFilm, WomWMM, WorEnF
Leader, Anton Morris *IntMPA 1977*
Leadlay, Edward O d1951 *WhThe*
Leaf, Ann *AmSCAP 1966*
Leaf, Caroline *WomWMM B*
Leahy, Eugene 1883-1967 *WhScrn 2, WhThe*
Leahy, Margaret d1967 *Film 2, WhScrn 2,*
  WhoHol B
Leake, James d1791 *NotNAT B*
Leal, John 1904- *AmSCAP 1966*
Leal, Milagros 1902-1975 *WhScrn 2, WhoHol C*
Lealand, Princess *Film 2*
Leamar, Alice d1950 *NotNAT B*
Leamore, Tom 1865-1939 *NotNAT B, WhThe*
Lean, Cecil 1878-1935 *WhThe*
Lean, David 1908- *BiDFlm, CelR 3, DcFM,*
  FilmgC, IntMPA 1977, MovMk, OxFilm,
  WorEnF
Lear, Bill 1902- *CelR 3*
Lear, Norman 1926- *FilmgC, IntMPA 1977,*
  NewYTET
Learn, Bessie *Film 1, MotPP*
Leary, Gilda d1927 *NotNAT B*
Leary, Nolan *WhoHol A*
Leary, Timothy 1920- *CelR 3*
Lease, Anthony F 1925- *AmSCAP 1966*
Lease, Rex 1901-1966 *Film 2, TwYS, WhScrn 1,*
  WhScrn 2, WhoHol B
Leathem, Barclay 1900- *BiE&WWA, NotNAT*
Leatherbee, Mary *BiE&WWA*
Leaud, Jean-Pierre 1944- *BiDFlm, MovMk,*
  OxFilm, WhoHol A, WorEnF
Leaver, Philip 1904- *WhThe*
Leaver, Phillip *WhoHol A*
Leavitt, Douglas Abe 1883-1960 *WhScrn 1,*
  WhScrn 2, WhoHol B
Leavitt, Michael Bennett 1843-1935 *NotNAT A,*
  NotNAT B
Leavitt, Norman *WhoHol A*
Leavitt, Sam 1917- *FilmgC, WorEnF*
Leavitt, William G 1926- *AmSCAP 1966*
LeBargy, Charles Gustave Auguste 1858-1936
  NotNAT B, WhThe, WhoHol B
LeBaron, Louise *WhoStg 1908*
LeBaron, William 1883-1958 *AmSCAP 1966,*
  NotNAT B, WhThe
LeBau, Blanche 1905- *AmSCAP 1966*
LeBeau, Madeline *WhoHol A*
LeBeau, Stephanie d1967 *WhScrn 1, WhScrn 2*
Lebedeff, Ivan d1953 *MotPP, NotNAT B,*
  WhoHol B
Lebedeff, Ivan 1894-1953 *MovMk*
Lebedeff, Ivan 1895-1953 *Film 2, TwYS*
Lebedeff, Ivan 1899-1953 *FilmgC, WhScrn 1,*
  WhScrn 2
LeBlanc, Charles J 1898- *AmSCAP 1966*
LeBlanc, Georgette 1876-1941 *NotNAT A,*
  NotNAT B, WhThe, WhoHol B
LeBorg, Reginald 1902- *FilmgC, IntMPA 1977*
LeBorgy *Film 2*
Lebow, Leonard S 1929- *AmSCAP 1966*
Lebowsky, Stanley 1926- *AmSCAP 1966,*
  BiE&WWA, NotNAT
LeBozoky, Barbara 1892-1937 *WhScrn 1*
LeBrandt, Gertrude N 1863-1955 *Film 2,*
  WhScrn 1, WhScrn 2, WhoHol B

LeBreton, Auguste 1915- *FilmgC*
LeBreton, Flora 1898- *Film 2, WhThe*
LeBrun, Minon 1881-1941 *WhoHol B*
LeBrun, Minon 1888-1941 *WhScrn 1, WhScrn 2*
LeChanois, Jean-Paul 1909- *DcFM, FilmgC, OxFilm, WorEnF*
Lecky, Eleazer 1903- *BiE&WWA, NotNAT*
LeClair, Blanche *Film 2*
Leclerc, Ginette 1912- *FilmgC, WhoHol A*
Leclercq, Pierre d1932 *NotNAT B*
LeClercy, Regina d1973 *WhScrn 2*
LeClerq, Florence d1960 *NotNAT B*
Lecocq, Alexandre Charles 1832-1918 *NotNAT B*
Leconte, Marie *WhThe*
Lecouvreur, Adrienne 1692-1730 *CnThe, NotNAT A, NotNAT B, OxThe*
Lecuona, Ernesto d1963 *NotNAT B*
Leder, Herbert Jay 1922- *IntMPA 1977*
Lederberg, Dov *WomWMM*
Lederer, Charles 1906?- *FilmgC*
Lederer, Charles 1911- *AmSCAP 1966, BiE&WWA, WorEnF*
Lederer, Francis *MotPP*
Lederer, Francis 1902- *WhoHol A*
Lederer, Francis 1906- *BiE&WWA, Film 2, FilmgC, HolP 30, MovMk, NotNAT, WhThe*
Lederer, George W 1861-1938 *EncMT, NotNAT B, WhThe*
Lederer, George W, Jr. d1924 *NotNAT B*
Lederer, Gretchen 1891-1955 *Film 1, MotPP, NotNAT B, TwYS, WhScrn 1, WhScrn 2, WhoHol B*
Lederer, Otto 1886-1965 *Film 1, Film 2, TwYS, WhScrn 2*
Lederer, Pepi *Film 2*
Lederer, Richard 1916- *IntMPA 1977*
Lederman, D Ross 1895-1972 *FilmgC, WhScrn 2*
Ledger, Edward d1921 *NotNAT B*
Ledger, Frederick d1874 *NotNAT B*
Ledner, David 1900-1957 *WhScrn 1, WhScrn 2*
Leduc, Claudine d1969 *WhScrn 1, WhScrn 2, WhoHol B*
Lee, Alberta *Film 1*
Lee, Allen 1875-1951 *WhScrn 1, WhScrn 2*
Lee, Ann *WhoHol A*
Lee, Anna 1914- *FilmgC, IntMPA 1977, MotPP, MovMk, WhoHol A*
Lee, Auriol 1880-1941 *NotNAT B, WhScrn 1, WhScrn 2, WhThe, WhoHol B*
Lee, Avalon *WhoHol A*
Lee, Belinda 1935-1961 *FilmgC, NotNAT B, WhScrn 1, WhScrn 2, WhoHol B*
Lee, Bernard 1908- *CmMov, FilmgC, IntMPA 1977, WhoHol A, WhoThe 16*
Lee, Bert 1880-1946 *NotNAT B, WhThe*
Lee, Bessie 1904-1931 *WhScrn 1, WhScrn 2*
Lee, Bessie 1906-1972 *WhScrn 2*
Lee, Betsy *Film 2*
Lee, Bruce 1940-1973 *MovMk, WhScrn 2, WhoHol B*
Lee, Bryarly 1934- *BiE&WWA, NotNAT*
Lee, C Y *NatPD*
Lee, Canada 1907-1952 *FilmgC, MotPP, MovMk, NotNAT B, Vers A, WhScrn 1, WhScrn 2, WhThe, WhoHol B*
Lee, Carey *Film 1*
Lee, Carolyn 1935- *MotPP, WhoHol A*
Lee, Celeste *Film 2*
Lee, Charles d1947 *NotNAT B*
Lee, Charles T 1882-1927 *WhScrn 1, WhScrn 2*
Lee, Christopher 1922- *CmMov, FilmgC, IntMPA 1977, MotPP, MovMk, OxFilm, WhoHol A*

Lee, Dai-Keong 1915- *AmSCAP 1966*
Lee, Davey 1925- *Film 2*
Lee, David 1936- *AmSCAP 1966*
Lee, Dick *Film 2*
Lee, Dixie 1911-1952 *Film 1, Film 2, TwYS, WhScrn 1, WhScrn 2, WhoHol B*
Lee, Dorothy 1911- *Film 2, FilmgC, ThFT, WhoHol A*
Lee, Duke R 1881-1959 *Film 2, WhScrn 1, WhScrn 2, WhoHol B*
Lee, Earl 1886-1955 *WhScrn 1, WhScrn 2, WhoHol B*
Lee, Etta 1906-1956 *Film 2, WhScrn 1, WhScrn 2, WhoHol B*
Lee, Eugene *NotNAT*
Lee, Florence 1886-1962 *WhoHol B*
Lee, Florence 1888-1962 *NotNAT B, WhScrn 1, WhScrn 2*
Lee, Fran *WhoHol A*
Lee, Frances 1908- *Film 2, TwYS, WhoHol A*
Lee, Francis *Film 2*
Lee, Frankie 1912- *Film 1, Film 2, MotPP, TwYS*
Lee, Franne *NotNAT*
Lee, Gwen 1904-1961 *Film 2, ThFT, TwYS, WhScrn 2, WhoHol B*
Lee, Gypsy Rose d1970 *MotPP, WhoHol B*
Lee, Gypsy Rose 1913-1970 *FilmgC, WhThe*
Lee, Gypsy Rose 1914-1970 *BiE&WWA, EncMT, MovMk, NotNAT A, NotNAT B, WhScrn 1, WhScrn 2, WorEnF*
Lee, H Rex *NewYTET*
Lee, Harry 1872-1932 *Film 2, WhScrn 1, WhScrn 2, WhoHol B*
Lee, Harry A d1919 *NotNAT B*
Lee, Henry d1910 *NotNAT B, WhoHol B*
Lee, Henry 1765-1836 *NotNAT A, NotNAT B*
Lee, Jack 1913- *DcFM, FilmgC, IntMPA 1977, WorEnF*
Lee, James 1919- *AmSCAP 1966*
Lee, James 1923- *BiE&WWA, NotNAT*
Lee, Jane 1912-1957 *Film 1, MotPP, NotNAT B, TwYS, WhScrn 2, WhoHol B*
Lee, Janet *Film 1*
Lee, Jean d1963 *NotNAT B*
Lee, Jennie d1930 *NotNAT B, WhThe*
Lee, Jennie 1850-1925 *Film 1, NotNAT B, WhScrn 1, WhScrn 2, WhoHol B*
Lee, Joanna *NewYTET, WomWMM*
Lee, Jocelyn *Film 2*
Lee, Joe *Film 1*
Lee, John 1928- *IntMPA 1977*
Lee, John D 1898-1965 *WhScrn 1, WhoHol B*
Lee, Johnny 1898-1965 *WhScrn 2*
Lee, Katharine *Film 1*
Lee, Katherine *Film 2, TwYS*
Lee, Katie 1919- *AmSCAP 1966*
Lee, Lance 1942- *NatPD*
Lee, Laura *WhoHol A*
Lee, Leona d1975 *WhScrn 2, WhoHol C*
Lee, Lester 1905-1956 *AmSCAP 1966*
Lee, Lila d1973 *MotPP, WhoHol B*
Lee, Lila 1901-1973 *ThFT*
Lee, Lila 1902-1973 *FilmgC, TwYS, WhScrn 2*
Lee, Lila 1905-1973 *Film 1, Film 2, MovMk*
Lee, Lila Dean 1890-1959 *WhScrn 1, WhScrn 2*
Lee, Lillie d1941 *NotNAT B*
Lee, Lois *Film 2*
Lee, Madeline *WhoHol A*
Lee, Margaret *Film 2*
Lee, Margo d1951 *WhScrn 1, WhScrn 2, WhoHol B*
Lee, Marjorie Lederer 1921- *AmSCAP 1966*
Lee, Marvin 1880-1949 *AmSCAP 1966*

Lee, Michele 1942- *BiE&WWA, FilmgC, NotNAT, WhoHol A*
Lee, Ming Cho 1930- *BiE&WWA, NotNAT, WhoThe 16*
Lee, Nammi *WomWMM B*
Lee, Nathaniel 1653?-1692 *CnThe, McGWD, NotNAT B, OxThe, PIP&P, REnWD*
Lee, Nelson d1872 *NotNAT B*
Lee, Norah 1898-1941 *AmSCAP 1966*
Lee, Olga 1899- *BiE&WWA*
Lee, Palmer *WhoHol A*
Lee, Patricia *WomWMM B*
Lee, Peggy 1920- *AmSCAP 1966, CelR 3, FilmgC, IntMPA 1977, OxFilm, WhoHol A*
Lee, Pinky *IntMPA 1977, NewYTET, WhoHol A*
Lee, Raymond 1910-1974 *Film 1, Film 2, WhScrn 2, WhoHol B*
Lee, Richard L 1872- *WhoStg 1908*
Lee, Robert *Film 2*
Lee, Robert Charles 1927- *AmSCAP 1966*
Lee, Robert E *NewYTET*
Lee, Robert Edwin 1918- *AmSCAP 1966, BiE&WWA, ConDr 1977, EncMT, ModWD, NotNAT, WhoThe 16*
Lee, Roberta *Film 1*
Lee, Rohama *WomWMM B*
Lee, Ronald *Film 2*
Lee, Ronny 1927- *AmSCAP 1966*
Lee, Rose *WhScrn 1, WhScrn 2*
Lee, Rowland V 1891-1975 *FilmgC, MovMk, TwYS A, WhScrn 2*
Lee, Ruta *WhoHol A*
Lee, Ruth 1896-1975 *WhScrn 2, WhoHol C*
Lee, Sammy 1890-1968 *EncMT, NotNAT B, WhScrn 1, WhScrn 2, WhoHol B*
Lee, Sondra 1930- *BiE&WWA, NotNAT*
Lee, Sophia d1824 *NotNAT B*
Lee, Sylvan d1962 *Film 2, WhoHol B*
Lee, Tommy *WhoHol A*
Lee, Vanessa 1920- *WhoThe 16*
Lee, Virginia *Film 2*
Lee, Wendie 1923-1968 *WhScrn 2*
Lee, Will 1908- *BiE&WWA, NotNAT, WhoHol A*
Lee Sugg, Catharine 1797-1845 *OxThe*
Lee-Thompson, J 1914- *FilmgC, IntMPA 1977, MovMk*
Lee Thompson, John 1914- *DcFM*
Leech, Lida Shivers 1873-1962 *AmSCAP 1966*
Leech, Richard 1922- *FilmgC, WhoHol A, WhoThe 16*
Leeds, Andrea 1914- *FilmgC, MovMk, ThFT, WhoHol A*
Leeds, Corinne 1909- *AmSCAP 1966*
Leeds, Herbert I 1900?- *FilmgC*
Leeds, Martin N 1916- *IntMPA 1977*
Leeds, Milton 1909- *AmSCAP 1966*
Leeds, Nancy 1924- *AmSCAP 1966*
Leeds, Peter *WhoHol A*
Leeds, Phil *BiE&WWA, NotNAT, WhoHol A*
Leek, Sybil 1923- *CelR 3*
Leeman, Percy T 1908- *AmSCAP 1966*
Leenhardt, Roger 1903- *BiDFlm, DcFM, OxFilm, WorEnF*
Leenhardt, Yvonne *WomWMM*
Leenhouts, Lewis Grant *IntMPA 1977*
Lees, Benjamin 1924- *AmSCAP 1966*
Lees, C Lowell 1904- *BiE&WWA*
Leess, Stan 1926- *AmSCAP 1966*
Leewood, Jack *IntMPA 1977*
Lefaur, Andre 1879-1952 *NotNAT B, WhScrn 1, WhScrn 2*
Lefco, Seymour 1915- *AmSCAP 1966*

Lefeaux, Charles 1909- *WhThe*
Lefebvre, Jean-Pierre 1941- *WorEnF*
LeFebvre, Robert 1907- *DcFM*
LeFeuvre, Guy 1883-1950 *NotNAT B, WhThe*
LeFeuvre, Philip 1871-1939 *WhScrn 1, WhScrn 2*
Lefevere, Kamiel 1888- *AmSCAP 1966*
Lefevre, Maurice *WhThe*
LeFevre, Ned 1912-1966 *WhScrn 2*
Lefevre, Paul *McGWD*
Lefevre, Rene 1898- *OxFilm*
Leff, Phyllis *WomWMM B*
Lefferts, George *IntMPA 1977, NewYTET*
Lefferty, Jean *Film 2*
Leffler, Anne Charlotte 1849-1892 *OxThe*
Leffler, George d1951 *NotNAT B*
Lefko, Morris E 1907- *IntMPA 1977*
Lefkowitch, Stanley L 1917- *AmSCAP 1966*
Lefkowitz, Nat 1905- *BiE&WWA, IntMPA 1977*
Lefleur, Leo 1902- *AmSCAP 1966*
LeFre, Albert 1870- *WhThe*
Leftwich, Alexander 1884-1947 *EncMT, NotNAT B, WhScrn 2, WhThe*
Leftwich, Vernon *AmSCAP 1966*
Legal, Ernst 1881-1955 *WhScrn 1, WhScrn 2*
Legal, Ernst *Film 2*
LeGalienne, Eva 1899- *FilmgC*
LeGallienne, Eva 1899- *BiE&WWA, CnThe, FamA&A, NotNAT, NotNAT A, OxThe, PIP&P, WhoHol A, WhoThe 16*
Legarde, Millie *WhThe*
Legat, Nicholas d1937 *NotNAT B*
Leger, Fernand 1881-1955 *DcFM, OxFilm, PIP&P, WorEnF*
Legg, Stuart 1910- *FilmgC, IntMPA 1977, OxFilm*
Leggatt, Alison 1904- *FilmgC, WhoHol A, WhoThe 16*
LeGlaire, Sonny 1915- *AmSCAP 1966*
Legneur, Charles 1892-1956 *WhScrn 1, WhScrn 2*
Legoshin, Vladimir 1904-1955 *DcFM*
Legouve, Ernest-Gabriel-Jean-Baptiste 1807-1903 *NotNAT B, OxThe*
Legrand, Marc-Antoine 1673-1728 *NotNAT B, OxThe*
Legrand, Michel 1932- *OxFilm, WorEnF*
Legrand, Michel Jean 1931- *DcFM, FilmgC, IntMPA 1977*
LeGrand, Phyllis *WhThe*
LeGuere, George 1871-1947 *Film 1, NotNAT B, WhScrn 2, WhoHol B*
Leguizamon, Martinian 1858-1935 *OxThe*
Lehac, Ned 1899- *AmSCAP 1966*
Lehar, Franz 1870-1948 *NotNAT B, PIP&P, WhThe, WhoStg 1908*
LeHay, Daisy 1883- *WhThe*
Lehay, Eugene *Film 2*
LeHay, John 1854-1926 *NotNAT B, WhThe*
Lehman, Ernest *IntMPA 1977*
Lehman, Ernest 1915- *CmMov*
Lehman, Ernest 1920- *FilmgC, WorEnF*
Lehman, Gladys *IntMPA 1977, WomWMM*
Lehman, Orin 1921- *CelR 3*
Lehman, Trent *WhoHol A*
Lehmann, Beatrix *WhoHol A*
Lehmann, Beatrix 1898- *FilmgC*
Lehmann, Beatrix 1903- *WhoThe 16*
Lehmann, Carla 1917- *FilmgC, WhThe, WhoHol A*
Lehr, Anna *Film 1, Film 2, TwYS*
Lehr, Lew 1895-1950 *WhScrn 1, WhScrn 2, WhoHol A*
Lehr, Milton H 1918- *IntMPA 1977*
Lehr, Wilson 1913- *BiE&WWA*

Lehrer, George J 1889-1966 *WhScrn 1, WhScrn 2*
Lehrer, James C *NewYTET*
Lehrer, Tom 1928- *AmSCAP 1966*
Lehrman, Henry 1886-1946 *DcFM, Film 1,*
  TwYS A, WhScrn 1, WhScrn 2, WhoHol B
Lehrman, Theodore H 1929- *AmSCAP 1966*
Leiber, Fritz d1949 *WhoHol B*
Leiber, Fritz 1882-1949 *TwYS, Vers A,*
  WhScrn 1, WhScrn 2
Leiber, Fritz 1883-1949 *Film 1, Film 2, FilmgC,*
  MovMk, NotNAT B, WhThe
Leibert, Michael W 1940- *NotNAT*
Leibert, Richard William 1903- *AmSCAP 1966*
Leibman, Ron 1937- *IntMPA 1977, NotNAT,*
  WhoHol A, WhoThe 16
Leibowitz, Sam 1913- *IntMPA 1977*
Leicester, Ernest 1866-1939 *NotNAT B, WhThe*
Leicester, George F d1916 *NotNAT B*
Leicester, William 1915-1969 *WhScrn 2*
Leider, Gerald J 1931- *IntMPA 1977*
Leidtke, Harry *Film 2*
Leidzen, Erik 1894-1962 *AmSCAP 1966*
Leigh, Andrew George 1887-1957 *NotNAT B,*
  PIP&P, WhThe
Leigh, Anthony d1692 *OxThe*
Leigh, Barbara *WhoHol A*
Leigh, Carolyn 1926- *AmSCAP 1966,*
  BiE&WWA, EncMT, NewMT, NotNAT
Leigh, Charlotte 1907- *WhThe*
Leigh, Dorma 1893- *WhThe*
Leigh, Douglas 1910- *CelR 3*
Leigh, Frank d1948 *Film 1, Film 2, TwYS,*
  WhScrn 1, WhScrn 2, WhoHol B
Leigh, George d1957 *WhoHol B*
Leigh, Gilbert *WhoHol A*
Leigh, Gracie d1950 *NotNAT B, WhThe*
Leigh, Henry S d1883 *NotNAT B*
Leigh, J H d1934 *NotNAT B*
Leigh, Janet 1927- *BiDFlm, FilmgC,*
  IntMPA 1977, MGM, MotPP, MovMk,
  OxFilm, WhoHol A, WorEnF
Leigh, Jennifer *WhoHol A*
Leigh, Leslie *Film 1*
Leigh, Mary 1904-1943 *NotNAT B, WhThe*
Leigh, Mitch 1928- *AmSCAP 1966, EncMT,*
  NewMT, NotNAT
Leigh, Nelson d1967 *WhoHol B*
Leigh, Philip d1935 *NotNAT B*
Leigh, Rowland 1902-1963 *WhThe*
Leigh, Suzanna 1945- *FilmgC, IntMPA 1977,*
  WhoHol A
Leigh, Vivien 1913-1967 *BiDFlm, BiE&WWA,*
  CnThe, EncMT, FamA&A, FilmgC, MotPP,
  MovMk, NotNAT A, NotNAT B, OxFilm,
  OxThe, PIP&P, ThFT, WhScrn 1,
  WhScrn 2, WhThe, WhoHol B, WorEnF
Leigh, W Colston 1901- *CelR 3*
Leigh, Walter 1905- *WhThe*
Leigh Hunt *OxThe*
Leigh-Hunt, Barbara *WhoHol A*
Leigh-Hunt, Barbara 1935- *NotNAT*
Leigh-Hunt, Barbara 1941- *FilmgC*
Leigh-Hunt, Ronald 1916?- *FilmgC, WhoHol A*
Leigheb, Claudio 1848- *WhThe*
Leighton, Alexes d1926 *NotNAT B*
Leighton, Bert 1877-1964 *AmSCAP 1966,*
  NotNAT B
Leighton, Daniel 1880-1917 *WhScrn 2*
Leighton, Frank 1908-1962 *WhThe*
Leighton, Harry d1926 *NotNAT B*
Leighton, Lillian 1874-1956 *Film 1, Film 2,*
  TwYS, WhScrn 1, WhScrn 2, WhoHol B
Leighton, Margaret 1922-1976 *BiE&WWA,*
  CnThe, FilmgC, MotPP, MovMk, OxThe,

PIP&P, WhoHol C, WhoThe 16
Leighton, Queenie 1872-1943 *NotNAT B, WhThe*
Leinsdorf, Erich 1912- *CelR 3*
Leisen, J Mitchell 1898-1972 *MovMk, WhScrn 2*
Leisen, Mitchell 1897-1972 *BiDFlm*
Leisen, Mitchell 1898-1972 *CmMov, FilmgC,*
  WhoHol B, WorEnF
Leiser, Eric 1929- *AmSCAP 1966*
Leiser, Ernest *NewYTET*
Leiser, Erwin 1923- *DcFM, FilmgC, WorEnF*
Leiser, Henri 1903- *IntMPA 1977*
Leisewitz, Johann A 1752-1806 *McGWD*
Lejsh, Kenneth William 1936- *BiE&WWA*
Leister, Frederick 1885-1970 *FilmgC, WhThe,*
  WhoHol B
Leitgeb, Willey *Film 2*
Leith, Virginia *WhoHol A*
Leivick, H 1888-1962 *CnThe, McGWD, ModWD,*
  REnWD
Lejeune, Caroline 1897-1973 *OxFilm*
Lekain, Henri-Louis 1729-1778 *NotNAT B,*
  OxThe
Lelio *OxThe*
Lelouch, Claude 1937- *BiDFlm, DcFM, FilmgC,*
  IntMPA 1977, MovMk, OxFilm, WorEnF
Lely, Durward d1944 *NotNAT B*
Lely, Madeleine *WhThe*
LeMaire, Charles *IntMPA 1977*
LeMaire, George 1884-1930 *WhScrn 1,*
  WhScrn 2, WhoHol B
LeMaire, William 1892-1933 *WhScrn 1,*
  WhScrn 2, WhoHol B
Lemaitre *OxThe*
LeMaitre, Frederic 1800-1876 *NotNAT A,*
  NotNAT B
Lemaitre, Frederick 1800-1876 *CnThe*
Lemaitre, Jules 1853-1914 *McGWD, ModWD,*
  NotNAT B, WhThe
Lemaitre, Jules-Francois-Elie 1854-1914 *OxThe*
Leman, Walter 1810- *NotNAT A*
LeMans, Marcel 1897-1946 *WhScrn 1, WhScrn 2*
LeMassena, William H 1916- *BiE&WWA,*
  NotNAT, WhoHol A, WhoThe 16
LeMat, Paul *WhoHol A*
LeMay, Alan 1899-1964 *CmMov, FilmgC,*
  NotNAT B
Lemay, Harding *NatPD*
Lembeck, Harvey 1923- *BiE&WWA, WhoHol A*
Lemercier, Nepomucene 1771-1840 *NotNAT B,*
  OxThe
LeMesurier, John 1912- *FilmgC, WhoHol A*
Lemmon, Jack 1923- *BiDFlm*
Lemmon, Jack 1925- *BiE&WWA, CelR 3,*
  CmMov, FilmgC, IntMPA 1977, MotPP,
  MovMk, OxFilm, WhoHol A, WorEnF
Lemon, Mark 1809-1870 *NotNAT B, OxThe*
Lemonier, Tom 1870-1945 *AmSCAP 1966*
Lemont, Cedric Wilmot 1879-1954 *AmSCAP 1966*
Lemont, John *IntMPA 1977*
Lemontier, Jules *Film 1*
LeMoyne, Charles 1880-1956 *Film 2, WhScrn 1,*
  WhScrn 2, WhoHol B
LeMoyne, Sarah Cowell 1859-1915 *NotNAT B,*
  WhThe, WhoStg 1906, WhoStg 1908
LeMoyne, W J 1831-1905 *NotNAT B*
Lemuels, William E 1891-1953 *WhScrn 1,*
  WhScrn 2, WhoHol B
Lena, Lily 1879- *WhThe*
Lenard, Grace *WhoHol A*
Lenard, Mark 1927- *BiE&WWA, NotNAT,*
  WhoHol A
Lenard, Melvyn 1936- *AmSCAP 1966*
Lender, Marcelle d1926 *NotNAT B, WhThe*
Lengel, William Charles 1888-1965 *NotNAT B*

Lenglen, Suzanne 1899-1938 *WhScrn 1,*
WhScrn 2, WhoHol B
Lengsfelder, Hans Jan 1903- *AmSCAP 1966*
Lengyel, Melchior 1880- *CnMD*
Lengyel, Menyhert 1880- *ModWD*
Leni, Paul 1885-1929 *BiDFlm, CmMov, DcFM,*
FilmgC, OxFilm, TwYS A, WhScrn 1,
WhScrn 2, WorEnF
Lenica, Jan 1928- *DcFM, FilmgC, OxFilm,*
WorEnF
Lenihan, Deidre *WhoHol A*
Lenihan, Winifred d1964 *NotNAT B, WhoHol B*
Lenihan, Winifred 1898-1964 *WhThe*
Lenihan, Winifred 1899-1964 *WhScrn 1,*
WhScrn 2
Lenin 1870-1924 *OxFilm*
Lenk, Marjorie *WomWMM B*
Lenke, Walter 1907- *AmSCAP 1966*
Lenkeffy, Isa *Film 2*
Lennard, Arthur 1867-1954 *NotNAT B, WhThe*
Lennard, Horace d1920 *NotNAT B*
Lennart, Isabel 1915-1971 *FilmgC*
Lennart, Isobel 1914- *CmMov, WomWMM*
Lennol, Roy *Film 2*
Lennon, John 1940- *CelR 3, MotPP, WhoHol A*
Lennon, Nestor Forbes Richardson 1863-
WhoStg 1906, WhoStg 1908
Lennox, Lottie d1947 *NotNAT B*
Lennox, Vera 1904- *Film 2, WhThe*
Lenny, Jack *BiE&WWA*
Leno, Dan 1860-1904 *NotNAT A, OxThe,*
PIP&P
Leno, Dan, Jr. d1962 *NotNAT B*
Leno, Sydney Paul Galvin 1892-1962 *OxThe*
Lenoble, Eustache 1643-1711 *OxThe*
Lenoidov, Leonid Mironovich 1873-1941 *WhoHol B*
LeNoir, Blanche *AmSCAP 1966*
Lenoir, Charles *OxThe*
Lenoir, Claudine *WomWMM*
Lenoir, Pass 1874-1946 *WhScrn 1, WhScrn 2*
LeNoire, Rosetta 1911- *BiE&WWA, NotNAT,*
WhoHol A, WhoThe 16
Lenor, Jacque *Film 1*
Lenormand, Henri-Rene 1882-1951 *CnMD,*
McGWD, ModWD, NotNAT B, REnWD,
WhThe
Lenox, Fred *Film 1*
Lenoy, Andre *Film 2*
Lenrow, Bernard 1903-1963 *WhScrn 1, WhScrn 2,*
WhoHol B
Lensky, Alexander Pavlovich 1847-1908
NotNAT B, OxThe, PIP&P
Lensky, Leib *WhoHol A*
Lenthall, Franklyn 1919- *BiE&WWA, NotNAT*
Lenya, Lotte 1898- *CelR 3*
Lenya, Lotte 1900- *BiE&WWA, EncMT,*
FilmgC, MotPP, NotNAT, OxFilm,
WhoHol A, WhoThe 16, WorEnF
Lenya, Lotte 1901- *CnThe*
Lenz, Jakob Michael Reinhold 1751-1792 *McGWD*
Lenz, Kay *WhoHol A*
Lenz, Rick *WhoHol A*
Lenz, Siegfried 1926- *CnMD Sup, CroCD*
Leo *Film 1*
Leo, Frank 1874- *WhThe*
Leon, Anne 1925- *WhThe*
Leon, Connie 1880-1955 *WhScrn 1, WhScrn 2,*
WhoHol B
Leon, Joseph *WhoHol A*
Leon, Sol 1913- *IntMPA 1977*
Leon, Valeriano 1892-1955? *WhScrn 1,*
WhScrn 2
Leon, Victor d1940 *NotNAT B*
Leon, W D d1964 *NotNAT B*

Leonard, Anita 1922- *AmSCAP 1966*
Leonard, Archie 1917-1959 *WhScrn 1, WhScrn 2,*
WhoHol B
Leonard, Barbara *Film 2*
Leonard, Benny *Film 2*
Leonard, Bert *NewYTET*
Leonard, Bill *NewYTET*
Leonard, Billy 1892- *WhThe*
Leonard, David A 1892-1967 *WhScrn 2,*
WhoHol B
Leonard, Eddie 1870-1941 *Film 2, NotNAT B,*
WhScrn 1, WhScrn 2, WhoHol B
Leonard, Eddie 1875-1941 *AmSCAP 1966,*
NotNAT A
Leonard, Gus 1856-1939 *Film 2, WhScrn 1,*
WhScrn 2, WhoHol B
Leonard, Herbert B 1922- *IntMPA 1977*
Leonard, Hugh 1926- *ConDr 1977, CroCD,*
WhoThe 16
Leonard, Jack E 1911-1973 *NotNAT B,*
WhScrn 2, WhoHol B
Leonard, James 1868-1930 *Film 2, WhScrn 1,*
WhScrn 2, WhoHol B
Leonard, Julie 1923- *BiE&WWA*
Leonard, LaVerne *Film 2*
Leonard, Marion d1956 *MotPP, NotNAT B,*
WhoHol B
Leonard, Marion 1880-1956 *WhScrn 2*
Leonard, Marion 1881-1956 *Film 1, TwYS*
Leonard, Mary *Film 1*
Leonard, Michael 1931- *AmSCAP 1966*
Leonard, Murray 1898-1970 *WhScrn 1,*
WhScrn 2, WhoHol B
Leonard, Patricia 1916- *WhThe*
Leonard, Queenie *WhoHol A*
Leonard, Robert d1948 *NotNAT B, WhThe*
Leonard, Robert Duke 1901-1961 *AmSCAP 1966*
Leonard, Robert Z 1889-1968 *BiDFlm, CmMov,*
DcFM, FilmgC, MovMk, NotNAT B,
WhScrn 1, WhScrn 2, WorEnF
Leonard, Robert Z 1898-1970 *Film 1, TwYS A,*
WhoHol B
Leonard, Sheldon 1907- *FilmgC, IntMPA 1977,*
MotPP, MovMk, NewYTET, Vers A,
WhoHol A
Leonard-Boyne, Eva 1885-1960 *NotNAT B,*
WhThe
Leonardi, Leonid 1901- *AmSCAP 1966*
Leonardo, Harry 1903-1964 *WhScrn 1, WhScrn 2*
Leoncavallo, Ruggero 1858-1919 *NotNAT B*
Leone, Henri *Film 1*
Leone, Henry d1922 *NotNAT B, WhScrn 2,*
WhoHol B
Leone, Leonard 1914- *BiE&WWA, NotNAT*
Leone, Maude d1930 *NotNAT B*
Leone, Sergio 1921- *FilmgC, OxFilm*
Leonetti, Tommy 1929- *AmSCAP 1966*
Leong, James *Film 2*
Leoni, Franco d1949 *NotNAT B*
Leonidoff, Leon *Film 2*
Leonidov, Leon *Film 2*
Leonidov, Leonid Mironovich 1873-1941
NotNAT B, OxThe
Leonov, Leonid Maksimovich 1899- *CnMD,*
McGWD, ModWD
Leonov, Leonid Maximovich 1899- *OxThe*
Leontovich, Eugenie 1894- *FilmgC, WhoHol A*
Leontovich, Eugenie 1900- *BiE&WWA,*
FamA&A, NotNAT, WhoThe 16
Leopold, Archduke Of Austria *Film 2*
Leopold, J Walter 1890-1956 *AmSCAP 1966*
Leotard, Jules 1830-1870 *OxThe*
Lepanto, Victoria *Film 1*
LePaul, Paul 1901-1958 *WhScrn 1, WhScrn 2,*

WhoHol B
LePearl, Harry 1885-1946 *WhScrn 2*
Lepeuve, Monique *WomWMM*
L'Epine-Smith, Eric *IntMPA 1977*
Lepore, Angelo J 1913- *AmSCAP 1966*
Lerand, M d1920 *NotNAT B*
Lerberghe, Charles Van 1861-1907 *ModWD*
Lerch, Louis *Film 2*
Lerman, Omar K 1927- *BiE&WWA, NotNAT*
Lermontov, Mikhail Yurevich 1814-1841
    NotNAT B, OxThe
Lermontov, Mikhail Yuryevich 1814-1841 *McGWD*
Lerner, Al 1919- *AmSCAP 1966*
Lerner, Alan Jay 1918- *AmSCAP 1966,*
    BiE&WWA, CelR 3, CmMov,
    ConDr 1977D, EncMT, FilmgC,
    IntMPA 1977, ModWD, NewMT, NotNAT,
    OxFilm, PIP&P, WhoThe 16, WorEnF
Lerner, Howard M 1927- *AmSCAP 1966*
Lerner, Irma *Film 2*
Lerner, Irving 1909- *BiDFlm, FilmgC,*
    IntMPA 1977, WorEnF
Lerner, Jacques *Film 2*
Lerner, Joseph *IntMPA 1977*
Lerner, Joseph Yehuda 1849?-1907 *NotNAT B,*
    OxThe
Lerner, Max 1902- *CelR 3*
Lerner, Robert 1921- *BiE&WWA, NotNAT*
Lerner, Samuel M 1903- *AmSCAP 1966*
Lernet-Holenia, Alexander 1897- *CnMD, CroCD,*
    McGWD, ModWD, OxThe
LeRoux, Hugues 1860- *WhThe*
LeRoy, Baby 1931- *FilmgC*
LeRoy, Baby 1932- *MovMk*
LeRoy, Baby *see also* Baby LeRoy
LeRoy, Gloria *WhoHol A*
LeRoy, Hal 1913- *EncMT, WhoHol A*
LeRoy, Ken 1927- *BiE&WWA, NotNAT,*
    WhoHol A
LeRoy, Mervyn 1900- *BiDFlm, CmMov, DcFM,*
    Film 2, FilmgC, IntMPA 1977, MovMk,
    OxFilm, TwYS A, WorEnF
LeRoy, Rita *Film 2*
LeRoy, Servais *WhThe*
LeRoy, Warner 1935- *BiE&WWA, NotNAT*
Lertzman, Carl M 1908- *AmSCAP 1966*
LeSage, Alain Rene 1668-1747 *CnThe, McGWD,*
    NotNAT B, OxThe, REnWD
LeSage, Francois-Antoine 1700- *OxThe*
LeSage, Rene-Andre 1695-1743 *OxThe*
LeSage, Stanley 1880-1932 *WhThe*
LeSaint, Edward 1870- *TwYS A*
LeSaint, Edward J 1871-1940 *WhScrn 1,*
    WhScrn 2, WhoHol B
LeSaint, Stella R 1881-1948 *WhScrn 1,*
    WhScrn 2, WhoHol B
Lescoulie, Jack *NewYTET, WhoHol A*
Leshay, Jerome 1926- *AmSCAP 1966*
Leskinen, Lauri 1918- *CroCD*
Lesley, Carole 1935-1974 *FilmgC, WhScrn 2,*
    WhoHol B
Leslie, Aleen 1908- *IntMPA 1977*
Leslie, Amy 1860-1939 *NotNAT B*
Leslie, Arthur 1902-1970 *WhScrn 2*
Leslie, Bethel 1930- *FilmgC, WhoHol A*
Leslie, Edgar 1885- *AmSCAP 1966*
Leslie, Edith d1973 *WhScrn 2, WhoHol B*
Leslie, Elsie 1881- *WhoStg 1908*
Leslie, Enid 1888- *WhThe*
Leslie, Fanny d1935 *NotNAT B*
Leslie, Fred 1855-1892 *NotNAT A, NotNAT B*
Leslie, Fred 1881- *WhThe*
Leslie, Fred 1884-1945 *WhScrn 2*
Leslie, Gene 1904-1953 *WhScrn 1, WhScrn 2,*

WhoHol B
Leslie, Gladys 1899- *Film 1, Film 2, MotPP,*
    TwYS
Leslie, Helen *Film 1*
Leslie, Henry d1881 *NotNAT B*
Leslie, Joan 1925- *FilmgC, HolP 40,*
    IntMPA 1977, MotPP, MovMk, WhoHol A
Leslie, Lawrence *Film 2*
Leslie, Lew 1886-1963 *EncMT, NotNAT B,*
    WhThe
Leslie, Lila *Film 2*
Leslie, Lilie *Film 1, MotPP*
Leslie, Lya *Film 2*
Leslie, Marguerite 1884-1958 *WhThe*
Leslie, Nan *WhoHol A*
Leslie, Noel 1889-1974 *WhScrn 2, WhoHol B*
Leslie, Rolf *Film 2*
Leslie, Sylvia 1900- *WhThe*
Leslie, Tom d1964 *NotNAT B*
Leslie, Walter 1929- *AmSCAP 1966*
Leslie-Stuart, May *WhThe*
Lesnevitch, Gus 1915-1964 *WhScrn 2*
Lessac, Arthur 1910- *BiE&WWA, NotNAT*
Lesser, Laura *WomWMM*
Lesser, Len *WhoHol A*
Lesser, Seymour H 1929- *IntMPA 1977*
Lesser, Sol 1890- *CmMov, FilmgC,*
    IntMPA 1977, OxFilm, WorEnF
Lessey, George A d1947 *Film 2, WhScrn 2*
Lessing, Doris 1919- *CnMD, ConDr 1977,*
    CroCD, ModWD
Lessing, Gotthold Ephraim 1729-1781 *CnThe,*
    McGWD, NotNAT A, NotNAT B, OxThe,
    REnWD
Lessing, Madge *WhThe, WhoStg 1908*
Lessman, Harry *WhoHol A*
Lessner, George 1904- *AmSCAP 1966*
Lessy, Ben *WhoHol A*
L'Estelle, Eleanor Scott 1880-1962 *WhScrn 1,*
    WhScrn 2
Lester, Alfred 1874-1925 *NotNAT B, WhThe*
Lester, Bruce 1912- *FilmgC*
Lester, Buddy *WhoHol A*
Lester, Dick 1932- *FilmgC*
Lester, Edwin 1895- *BiE&WWA, NotNAT*
Lester, Jack *WhoHol A*
Lester, Jerry *NewYTET, WhoHol A*
Lester, Kate d1924 *Film 1, Film 2, TwYS,*
    WhScrn 2, WhoStg 1906, WhoStg 1908
Lester, Louise 1867-1952 *Film 1, WhScrn 1,*
    WhScrn 2, WhoHol B
Lester, Mark 1876- *WhThe*
Lester, Mark 1957- *FilmgC*
Lester, Mark 1958- *IntMPA 1977, WhoHol A*
Lester, Richard 1932- *BiDFlm, CelR 3, DcFM,*
    IntMPA 1977, MovMk, OxFilm, WorEnF
Lester, Susan *WomWMM B*
Lester, Tom *WhoHol A*
Lestina, Adolphe *Film 1, Film 2*
Lestocq, George d1924 *NotNAT B*
Lestocq, Humphrey *WhoHol A*
Lestocq, William d1920 *NotNAT B, WhThe*
L'Estrange, Dick 1889-1963 *Film 2, WhScrn 1,*
    WhScrn 2, WhoHol B
L'Estrange, Julian 1878-1918 *Film 1, NotNAT B,*
    WhThe, WhoHol B
L'Estrange, Julian 1880-1918 *WhScrn 2*
LeSueur, Hal 1904-1963 *NotNAT B, WhScrn 1,*
    WhScrn 2, WhoHol B
LeSueur, Lucille *Film 2*
Leterrier, Francois 1929- *OxFilm*
Lethbridge, J W *WhThe*
LeThiere, Roma Guillon d1903 *NotNAT B*
Letondal, Henri 1902-1955 *WhScrn 1, WhScrn 2,*

WhoHol B
Letter, Louis N 1937- *IntMPA 1977*
Lettieri, Al d1975 *WhoHol C*
Lettieri, Alfredo 1928-1975 *WhScrn 2*
Lettinger *Film 2*
Letton, Francis 1912- *BiE&WWA, NotNAT*
Letts, Pauline 1917- *WhoHol A, WhoThe 16*
Letz, George *WhoHol A*
Leubas, Louis *Film 1*
Leux, Lori *Film 2*
Levan, Harry d1963 *NotNAT B*
Levan, Louis 1906- *AmSCAP 1966*
Levance, Cal d1951 *WhScrn 1, WhScrn 2*
Levant, Lila *NatPD*
Levant, Oscar 1906-1972 *AmSCAP 1966, CmMov,*
   FilmgC, HolP 40, MotPP, MovMk,
   NewYTET, WhScrn 2, WhoHol B
Levant, Oscar 1907-1972 *Film 2*
Levathes, Peter G *NewYTET*
Leveaux, Montagu V 1875- *WhThe*
Leveen, Raymond 1899- *AmSCAP 1966*
Levelle, Estelle 1896-1960 *WhScrn 1, WhScrn 2*
Leven, Boris 1900?- *FilmgC, IntMPA 1977*
Levene, Sam 1905- *BiE&WWA, CelR 3,*
   EncMT, FilmgC, IntMPA 1977, MotPP,
   MovMk, NotNAT, PIP&P, WhoHol A
Levene, Sam 1906- *Vers B*
Levene, Samuel 1905- *WhoThe 16*
Levenson, Boris 1884-1947 *AmSCAP 1966*
Levenson, Sam 1911- *CelR 3, IntMPA 1977*
Leventhal, Herbert 1914- *AmSCAP 1966*
Leventhal, Joseph Jules 1889-1949 *NotNAT B*
Lever, Beatrice Rae 1897- *AmSCAP 1966*
Levering, Jack *Film 1*
Leversee, Loretta *WhoHol A*
Levesque, Marcel *Film 1*
Levett, Harold *Film 2*
Levey, Adele *WhThe*
Levey, Arthur 1903- *IntMPA 1977*
Levey, Carlotta *WhThe*
Levey, Ethel 1880-1955 *NotNAT B,*
   WhoStg 1906, WhoStg 1908
Levey, Ethel 1881-1955 *EncMT, WhThe*
Levey, Harold A 1898- *AmSCAP 1966*
Levi, Paolo 1919- *CnMD*
Levick, Gus d1909 *NotNAT B*
Levick, Halper 1888-1962 *OxThe*
Levie, Francoise *WomWMM*
LeVien, Jack 1918- *FilmgC, IntMPA 1977*
Levien, Sonya *WomWMM*
Levien, Sonya 1886-1960 *CmMov*
Levien, Sonya 1888-1960 *FilmgC*
Levin, Bernard *BiE&WWA*
Levin, Charles d1962 *NotNAT B*
Levin, Gerald M *NewYTET*
Levin, Henry 1909- *BiDFlm, DcFM, FilmgC,*
   IntMPA 1977, MovMk, WorEnF
Levin, Herman 1907- *BiE&WWA, EncMT,*
   NotNAT, WhoThe 16
Levin, Ira 1929- *AmSCAP 1966, BiE&WWA,*
   NotNAT
Levin, Irving H 1921- *IntMPA 1977*
Levin, Jack H *IntMPA 1977*
Levin, Joseph A 1917- *AmSCAP 1966*
Levin, Lucy 1907-1939 *WhScrn 1, WhScrn 2*
Levin, Meyer 1905- *BiE&WWA, CelR 3,*
   CnMD, NotNAT
Levine, Abe 1915- *AmSCAP 1966*
Levine, David Eliot 1933- *NotNAT*
Levine, Helen *Film 2*
Levine, Henry 1892- *AmSCAP 1966*
Levine, Irving R *NewYTET*
Levine, Jack *Film 2*
Levine, Joseph d1964 *NotNAT B*

Levine, Joseph E 1905- *BiE&WWA, CelR 3,*
   FilmgC, IntMPA 1977, OxFilm, WorEnF
Levine, Joseph I 1926- *BiE&WWA, NotNAT*
Levine, Marks 1890- *AmSCAP 1966*
Levine, Martin 1909- *IntMPA 1977*
Levine, Naomi *WomWMM B*
LeViness, Carl 1885-1964 *WhScrn 1, WhScrn 2,*
   WhoHol B
Levinnes, Carl *Film 2*
Levinson, Barry 1932- *BiE&WWA,*
   IntMPA 1977
Levinson, David *NewYTET*
Levinson, Norm 1925- *IntMPA 1977*
Levinson, Ruth Pologe *IntMPA 1977*
Levinson-Link *NewYTET*
Levitan, Paul d1976 *NewYTET*
Leviton, Stewart 1939- *WhoThe 16*
Levitt, Estelle 1941- *AmSCAP 1966*
Levitt, Helen *WomWMM A, WomWMM B*
Levitt, John *PIP&P*
Levitt, Paul 1926-1968 *BiE&WWA, NotNAT B*
Levitt, Ruby Rebecca 1907- *IntMPA 1977*
Levitt, Saul 1913- *BiE&WWA, NotNAT*
Levitt, William 1907- *CelR 3*
Levitz, Linda *WomWMM B*
Levitzki, Mischa 1898-1941 *AmSCAP 1966*
Levoe, Marjorie *Film 2*
Levshin, A *Film 2*
Levy, Benn Wolfe 1900-1973 *BiE&WWA, CnMD,*
   ConDr 1973, McGWD, ModWD,
   NotNAT B, WhThe
Levy, Bernard *IntMPA 1977*
Levy, Bud 1928- *IntMPA 1977*
Levy, David 1913- *IntMPA 1977, NewYTET*
Levy, Don 1932- *OxFilm*
Levy, Edwin L 1917- *BiE&WWA*
Levy, Hal 1916- *AmSCAP 1966*
Levy, Helen Marsh d1962 *NotNAT B*
Levy, Herman M 1904- *IntMPA 1977*
Levy, Isaac d1975 *NewYTET*
Levy, J Langley d1945 *NotNAT B*
Levy, Jacques 1935- *WhoThe 16*
Levy, Jonathan *NatPD*
Levy, Jose G 1884-1936 *NotNAT B, WhThe*
Levy, Jules V 1923- *IntMPA 1977*
Levy, Leon *NewYTET*
Levy, Louis 1893- *FilmgC*
Levy, Marvin David 1932- *AmSCAP 1966*
Levy, Parke 1908- *AmSCAP 1966*
Levy, Ralph 1919- *FilmgC, NewYTET*
Levy, Raoul 1922-1966 *DcFM*
Levy, Raoul 1922-1967 *FilmgC*
Levy, Robert S 1932- *IntMPA 1977*
Levy, Sol Paul 1881-1920 *AmSCAP 1966*
Levy, Sylvan 1906-1962 *NotNAT B, WhScrn 1,*
   WhScrn 2
Lewenstein, Oscar 1917- *WhoThe 16*
Lewes, Charles Lee 1740-1803 *NotNAT A,*
   NotNAT B, OxThe
Lewes, George Henry 1817-1878 *NotNAT B,*
   OxThe
Lewes, Miriam *WhThe*
Lewin, Albert 1894-1968 *BiDFlm, WorEnF*
Lewin, Albert 1895-1968 *FilmgC, MovMk,*
   OxFilm
Lewin, Albert 1902-1968 *DcFM*
Lewine, Richard 1910- *AmSCAP 1966,*
   BiE&WWA, EncMT, NotNAT
Lewine, Robert F 1913- *IntMPA 1977,*
   NewYTET
Lewinsky, Josef d1907 *NotNAT B*
LeWinter, David 1908- *AmSCAP 1966*
Lewis, Abby 1910- *BiE&WWA, NotNAT,*
   WhoHol A

Lewis, Ada d1925 *NotNAT B, WhThe, WhoStg 1908*
Lewis, Aden G 1924- *AmSCAP 1966*
Lewis, Al *IntMPA 1977, WhoHol A*
Lewis, Al 1901- *AmSCAP 1966*
Lewis, Allan 1908- *BiE&WWA, NotNAT, WhoHol A*
Lewis, Ann *WomWMM B*
Lewis, Arthur 1846-1930 *NotNAT B, WhThe*
Lewis, Arthur 1916- *WhoThe 16*
Lewis, Artie *WhoHol A*
Lewis, Bernard 1912- *IntMPA 1977*
Lewis, Bernie Kaai 1921- *AmSCAP 1966*
Lewis, Bertha 1887-1931 *NotNAT B, WhThe*
Lewis, Bobo *WhoHol A*
Lewis, Brenda 1921- *BiE&WWA*
Lewis, C Harold 1892-1955 *AmSCAP 1966*
Lewis, Catherine d1942 *NotNAT B*
Lewis, Cathy 1918-1968 *WhScrn 1, WhScrn 2, WhoHol B*
Lewis, Claude P, Jr. *IntMPA 1977*
Lewis, Curigwen *WhThe*
Lewis, David *IntMPA 1977, WhoHol A*
Lewis, Diana 1915- *MotPP, WhoHol A*
Lewis, Dora *Film 2*
Lewis, Dorothy W 1871-1952 *WhScrn 1, WhScrn 2*
Lewis, Ed Strangler 1890-1966 *WhScrn 2*
Lewis, Edgar 1872-1938 *TwYS A, WhScrn 2*
Lewis, Edgar P *Film 1*
Lewis, Edna *AmSCAP 1966*
Lewis, Edward *IntMPA 1977*
Lewis, Edward d1922 *NotNAT B*
Lewis, Elliott *WhScrn 1, WhScrn 2, WhoHol A*
Lewis, Elliott 1948- *AmSCAP 1966*
Lewis, Emory 1919- *BiE&WWA, NotNAT*
Lewis, Eric 1855-1935 *NotNAT B, WhThe*
Lewis, Fiona 1946- *FilmgC, WhoHol A*
Lewis, Frank A d1963 *NotNAT B*
Lewis, Fred 1860-1927 *Film 2, NotNAT B, WhThe, WhoHol B*
Lewis, Frederick G 1873-1946 *NotNAT B, WhThe, WhoHol B, WhoStg 1906, WhoStg 1908*
Lewis, Frederick G 1874-1947 *WhScrn 2*
Lewis, Geoffrey *WhoHol A*
Lewis, George 1904- *Film 2, TwYS*
Lewis, Gordon d1933 *WhScrn 1, WhScrn 2*
Lewis, Harry 1886-1950 *WhScrn 1, WhScrn 2, WhoHol B*
Lewis, Henry B *Film 2*
Lewis, Ida 1871-1935 *Film 1, Film 2, NotNAT B, TwYS, WhScrn 1, WhScrn 2, WhoHol B*
Lewis, Jack B 1924-1964 *AmSCAP 1966*
Lewis, James *PIP&P*
Lewis, James d1896 *NotNAT B*
Lewis, James H Daddy d1928 *WhScrn 1, WhScrn 2, WhoHol B*
Lewis, Janet 1899- *AmSCAP 1966*
Lewis, Jay *Film 1*
Lewis, Jay 1914-1969 *FilmgC*
Lewis, Mrs. Jeffrey *Film 1*
Lewis, Jeffreys d1926 *NotNAT B*
Lewis, Jeffrys *Film 2*
Lewis, Jera *Film 2*
Lewis, Jerry 1926- *BiDFlm, CelR 3, CmMov, FilmgC, IntMPA 1977, MotPP, MovMk, OxFilm, WhoHol A, WorEnF*
Lewis, Jerry Lee *WhoHol A*
Lewis, Joe 1898-1938 *WhScrn 1, WhScrn 2, WhoHol B*
Lewis, Joe E d1971 *NotNAT A, WhoHol B*
Lewis, Joe E 1901-1971 *FilmgC*

Lewis, Joe E 1902-1971 *WhScrn 2*
Lewis, John 1920- *CelR 3*
Lewis, John Leo 1911- *AmSCAP 1966*
Lewis, Joseph H 1900- *BiDFlm, FilmgC, IntMPA 1977, WorEnF*
Lewis, Joy *Film 1*
Lewis, Judy 1936- *IntMPA 1977*
Lewis, Katherine *Film 2*
Lewis, Laurie *WomWMM B*
Lewis, Leon 1890-1961 *AmSCAP 1966*
Lewis, Leopold d1890 *NotNAT B, PIP&P*
Lewis, Lester 1912- *IntMPA 1977*
Lewis, Lloyd Downs 1891-1949 *NotNAT B*
Lewis, Lucy S 1904- *AmSCAP 1966*
Lewis, Mabel Terry *WhThe*
Lewis, Martin 1888-1970 *WhScrn 2, WhThe*
Lewis, Mary 1900-1941 *WhScrn 1, WhScrn 2, WhoHol B*
Lewis, Mary Rio *WhoHol A*
Lewis, Matthew Gregory 1775-1818 *NotNAT B, OxThe*
Lewis, Meade Lux d1964 *WhoHol B*
Lewis, Meade Lux 1905-1964 *AmSCAP 1966*
Lewis, Meade Lux 1906-1964 *WhScrn 1, WhScrn 2*
Lewis, Michael 1931-1975 *WhScrn 2*
Lewis, Michael J 1939- *IntMPA 1977*
Lewis, Mitchell J 1880-1956 *Film 1, Film 2, MotPP, NotNAT B, TwYS, Vers A, WhScrn 1, WhScrn 2, WhoHol B*
Lewis, Monica *IntMPA 1977, WhoHol A*
Lewis, Morgan, Jr. 1906-1968 *AmSCAP 1966, EncMT*
Lewis, Philip d1931 *NotNAT B*
Lewis, Ralph *MotPP*
Lewis, Ralph 1872-1937 *Film 1, Film 2, TwYS, WhScrn 1, WhScrn 2, WhoHol B*
Lewis, Richard 1869-1935 *WhScrn 1, WhScrn 2, WhoHol B*
Lewis, Robert 1909- *BiE&WWA, EncMT, NotNAT, PIP&P, WhoHol A, WhoThe 16*
Lewis, Robert Q *NewYTET, WhoHol A*
Lewis, Roger 1885-1948 *AmSCAP 1966*
Lewis, Roger H 1918- *IntMPA 1977*
Lewis, Ronald 1928- *FilmgC, WhoHol A*
Lewis, Russell 1908- *BiE&WWA*
Lewis, Sam d1964 *NotNAT B*
Lewis, Sam 1878-1963 *WhScrn 1, WhScrn 2*
Lewis, Samella S *WomWMM B*
Lewis, Samuel M 1885-1959 *AmSCAP 1966*
Lewis, Sheldon d1958 *MotPP, NotNAT B, WhoHol B*
Lewis, Sheldon 1868-1958 *Film 1, Film 2, FilmgC*
Lewis, Sheldon 1869-1958 *TwYS, WhScrn 1, WhScrn 2*
Lewis, Sinclair 1885-1951 *CnMD, FilmgC, ModWD, NotNAT B*
Lewis, Susan *WomWMM B*
Lewis, Ted d1971 *WhoHol B*
Lewis, Ted 1889-1971 *FilmgC*
Lewis, Ted 1891-1971 *Film 2, NotNAT B, WhScrn 1, WhScrn 2*
Lewis, Ted 1892-1971 *AmSCAP 1966*
Lewis, Tom 1864-1927 *Film 2, IntMPA 1977, WhScrn 1, WhScrn 2, WhoHol B*
Lewis, Vera d1956 *WhScrn 1, WhScrn 2, WhoHol B*
Lewis, Vera d1958 *Film 1, Film 2, TwYS*
Lewis, Walter P 1871-1932 *Film 1, Film 2, TwYS, WhScrn 2*
Lewis, Willard *Film 2*
Lewis, William Thomas 1749-1811 *NotNAT B, OxThe*

Lewis, Windsor 1918-1972 *BiE&WWA,*
 NotNAT B
Lewis, Wyndham 1910- *IntMPA 1977*
Lewisohn, Alice d1972 *BiE&WWA, NotNAT B,*
 OxThe
Lewisohn, Irene d1944 *NotNAT B, OxThe*
Lewisohn, Victor Max 1897-1934 *NotNAT B,*
 WhThe
Lewton, Val 1904-1951 *BiDFlm, CmMov, DcFM,*
 FilmgC, OxFilm, WorEnF
Lewy, Leonard 1921- *AmSCAP 1966*
Lexa, Jake d1973 *WhScrn 2*
Lexy, Edward 1897- *FilmgC, WhThe*
Ley, Grita *Film 2*
Ley-Piscator, Maria *BiE&WWA*
Leybourne, George 1842-1884 *NotNAT B, OxThe,*
 PIP&P
Leyda, Jay 1910- *OxFilm*
Leyel, Carl F 1875-1925 *NotNAT B, WhThe*
Leyer, Rhoda *WomWMM*
Leyssac, Paul d1946 *NotNAT B, WhScrn 1,*
 WhScrn 2, WhoHol B
Leyton, George 1864-1948 *NotNAT B, WhThe*
Leyton, John 1939- *FilmgC, WhoHol A*
L'Herbier, Marcel 1880- *OxFilm*
L'Herbier, Marcel 1890- *BiDFlm, DcFM,*
 FilmgC, MovMk, WorEnF
Lhevinne, Rosina 1880- *CelR 3*
Liagre, Alfred De, Jr. 1904- *WhThe*
Lianides, Thomas William 1920- *AmSCAP 1966*
Libbey, Dee *AmSCAP 1966*
Libbey, J Aldrich 1872-1925 *WhScrn 2,*
 WhoHol B
Libbey, James Aldrich 1872-1925 *NotNAT B*
Libby, Willard 1908- *CelR 3*
Liberace 1919- *AmSCAP 1966, CelR 3, FilmgC,*
 NewYTET, WhoHol A
Liberace 1920- *IntMPA 1977*
Liberace, George J 1911- *AmSCAP 1966*
Liberman, Frank P 1917- *IntMPA 1977*
Libin, Paul 1930- *BiE&WWA, NotNAT,*
 WhoThe 16
Liblick, Marvin 1929- *AmSCAP 1966*
Libott, Robert Y *BiE&WWA*
Licalzi, Lawrence *Film 2*
Liccardi, Vincent G *IntMPA 1977*
Lichenstein, Charles M *NewYTET*
Lichine, David 1909-1972 *WhThe*
Lichine, David 1910-1972 *WhScrn 2*
Licho, Adolf Edgar *Film 2*
Licho, Edgar Adolph 1876-1944 *WhScrn 1,*
 WhScrn 2, WhoHol B
Lichtenstein, Roy 1923- *CelR 3*
Lichter, Charles 1910- *AmSCAP 1966*
Licudi, Gabriella 1943- *FilmgC*
Lider, Edward W 1922- *IntMPA 1977*
Lidgett, Scott d1953 *NotNAT B*
Lieb, Herman 1873-1966 *WhScrn 1, WhScrn 2*
Lieb, Robert P *WhoHol A*
Lieb, Ziskind 1930- *AmSCAP 1966*
Liebeneiner, Wolfgang 1905- *DcFM*
Lieber, Perry W 1905- *IntMPA 1977*
Lieberman, Jacob 1879-1956 *WhScrn 1,*
 WhScrn 2
Lieberson, Goddard 1911- *AmSCAP 1966,*
 CelR 3
Liebler, Theodore A d1941 *NotNAT B*
Liebling, Estelle 1884- *AmSCAP 1966*
Liebling, Howard *IntMPA 1977*
Liebling, Howard 1928- *AmSCAP 1966*
Liebling, Leonard 1874-1945 *NotNAT B*
Liebling, William 1895- *BiE&WWA*
Liebman, Joseph H 1911- *AmSCAP 1966*
Liebman, Marvin 1923- *WhoThe 16*

Liebman, Max 1902- *AmSCAP 1966,*
 BiE&WWA, IntMPA 1977, NewYTET,
 NotNAT
Liebmann, Hans H 1895-1960 *WhScrn 1,*
 WhScrn 2, WhoHol B
Lieburg, Max d1962 *NotNAT B*
Liedtke, Harry 1881-1945 *Film 2, WhScrn 2,*
 WhoHol B
Lief, Max 1899- *AmSCAP 1966*
Lief, Nathaniel 1896-1944 *AmSCAP 1966*
Liepolt, Werner 1944- *NatPD*
Lieurance, Thurlow 1878-1963 *AmSCAP 1966*
Lieven, Albert 1906-1971 *FilmgC, WhScrn 1,*
 WhScrn 2, WhThe, WhoHol B
Lieven, Tatiana 1910- *WhThe*
Lifanoff, B *Film 2*
Lifar, Serge 1905- *WhThe*
Liff, Samuel 1919- *BiE&WWA, NotNAT*
Lifson, David *NatPD*
Ligero, Miguel 1898-1968 *WhScrn 1, WhScrn 2*
Ligety, Louis 1881-1928 *WhScrn 1, WhScrn 2*
Liggett, Louis *Film 2*
Liggon, Grover *Film 2*
Liggon, Grover *see also* Ligon, Grover G
Light, Ben 1894-1965 *AmSCAP 1966*
Light, Enoch 1907- *AmSCAP 1966*
Light, James d1964 *NotNAT B*
Lightfoot, Gordon 1938- *AmSCAP 1966*
Lightman, M A, Jr. 1915- *IntMPA 1977*
Lightner, Winnie 1899-1971 *ThFT*
Lightner, Winnie 1901-1971 *EncMT, Film 2,*
 FilmgC, MotPP, WhScrn 1, WhScrn 2,
 WhThe, WhoHol B
Lightstone, Gordon *IntMPA 1977*
Ligon, Grover G 1885-1965 *Film 1, WhScrn 1,*
 WhScrn 2, WhoHol B
Ligon, Tom *WhoHol A*
Liikala, Isabelle *WomWMM B*
Likes, Don *Film 1*
Lilar, Suzanne 1901- *ModWD*
Lilienthal, David E 1899- *CelR 3*
Lilina, Maria Petrovna 1866-1954 *NotNAT B*
Lillard, Charlotte 1844-1946 *WhScrn 1,*
 WhScrn 2, WhoHol B
Lillenas, Bertha Mae 1889-1945 *AmSCAP 1966*
Lillenas, Haldor 1885-1959 *AmSCAP 1966*
Lilley, Joseph J 1914- *AmSCAP 1966*
Lillie, Bea *MotPP*
Lillie, Beatrice 1894- *EncMT*
Lillie, Beatrice 1898- *CelR 3, CnThe, FamA&A,*
 FilmgC, MovMk, NotNAT A, ThFT,
 WhoHol A, WhoThe 16
Lillie, Beatrice 1903- *BiE&WWA, Film 2,*
 NotNAT
Lillie, Jessie 1890- *AmSCAP 1966*
Lillies, Leonard 1860-1923 *NotNAT B, WhThe*
Lillmore, Clyde *Film 2*
Lillo, George 1693-1739 *McGWD, NotNAT B,*
 OxThe, PIP&P, REnWD
Lilly, Doris 1926- *CelR 3*
Lilly, John 1915- *CelR 3*
Limbert, Roy 1893-1954 *NotNAT B, WhThe*
Limburg, Olga *Film 2*
Lime, Yvonne *WhoHol A*
Limerick, Mona *WhThe*
Limpus, Alban Brownlow 1878-1941 *WhThe*
Linares-Rivas, Manuel *WhThe*
Linares Rivas Y Astray, Manuel 1867-1938
 McGWD
Lincke, Paul 1866-1946 *NotNAT B*
Lincoln, Abbey 1930- *CelR 3, WhoHol A*
Lincoln, Abraham 1809-1965 *OxFilm*
Lincoln, Caryl *Film 2, WhoHol A*
Lincoln, E K *TwYS*

Lincoln, E K d1958 *Film 1, WhScrn 2*
Lincoln, Elmo 1889-1952 *CmMov, Film 1, Film 2, FilmgC, MovMk, NotNAT B, TwYS, WhScrn 1, WhScrn 2, WhoHol B*
Lincoln, Steve *WhoHol A*
Lind, Della *WhoHol A*
Lind, Gillian 1904- *WhoHol A, WhoThe 16*
Lind, Jenny *Film 1*
Lind, Letty 1862-1923 *NotNAT B, WhThe*
Lind, Myrtle *Film 1*
Lind, Sarah *Film 1*
Lindberg, August 1846-1916 *OxThe, WhThe*
Lindbergh, Anne Morrow 1906- *CelR 3*
Lindbergh, Charles 1902- *CelR 3*
Lindblom, Gunnel 1931- *OxFilm, WorEnF*
Lindblom, Gunnel 1939- *FilmgC*
Linde, Nancy *WomWMM B*
Lindeman, Edith 1898- *AmSCAP 1966*
Lindemann, Carl, Jr. *NewYTET*
Lindemuth, William I 1915- *AmSCAP 1966*
Linden, Einar *Film 1*
Linden, Eric 1909- *FilmgC, HolP 30, MotPP, WhThe, WhoHol A*
Linden, Hal 1931- *BiE&WWA, CelR 3, EncMT, NotNAT, WhoThe 16*
Linden, Jennie 1939- *FilmgC, WhoHol A*
Linden, Marie 1862- *WhThe*
Linden, Peggy *Film 2*
Linden, Robert 1912- *BiE&WWA, NotNAT*
Lindenburn, Henry 1874-1952 *WhScrn 1, WhScrn 2*
Linder, Alfred d1957 *WhScrn 1, WhScrn 2, WhoHol B*
Linder, Jack 1896- *BiE&WWA*
Linder, Max 1882-1925 *TwYS*
Linder, Max 1883-1925 *BiDFlm, DcFM, Film 1, Film 2, FilmgC, MotPP, NotNAT B, OxFilm, WhScrn 1, WhScrn 2, WhoHol B, WorEnF*
Lindfors, Viveca 1920- *BiDFlm, BiE&WWA, FilmgC, IntMPA 1977, MotPP, MovMk, NotNAT, WhoHol A, WhoThe 16, WorEnF*
Lindgren, Aron *Film 1*
Lindgren, Ernest 1910-1973 *OxFilm*
Lindgren, Lars-Magnus 1922- *FilmgC, WorEnF*
Lindholm, Eric *Film 1*
Lindley, Audra 1918- *WhThe, WhoHol A*
Lindley, Bert *Film 2*
Lindner, Terrell M 1915- *IntMPA 1977*
Lindo, Frank d1933 *NotNAT B*
Lindo, Olga d1968 *WhoHol B*
Lindo, Olga 1898-1968 *FilmgC, WhThe*
Lindo, Olga 1899-1968 *WhScrn 1, WhScrn 2*
Lindon, Lionel 1905-1971 *FilmgC, WorEnF*
Lindon, Millie 1878- *WhThe*
Lindrith, Nellie *Film 1*
Lindroth, Helen *Film 2*
Lindsay, Bryan 1931- *AmSCAP 1966*
Lindsay, Sir David 1490-1555 *CnThe*
Lindsay, Fred *Film 2*
Lindsay, Howard 1888-1968 *EncMT*
Lindsay, Howard 1889-1968 *BiE&WWA, CnThe, Film 2, FilmgC, McGWD, ModWD, NewMT, NotNAT B, OxThe, WhScrn 1, WhScrn 2, WhThe, WhoHol B*
Lindsay, Howard And Russel Crouse *CnMD*
Lindsay, James 1869-1928 *Film 2, NotNAT B, WhThe*
Lindsay, John V 1921- *BiE&WWA, CelR 3, WhoHol A*
Lindsay, Kevin 1924-1975 *WhScrn 2, WhoHol C*
Lindsay, Lex 1901-1971 *WhScrn 1, WhScrn 2, WhoHol B*
Lindsay, Margaret 1910- *FilmgC, HolP 30,*

MotPP, MovMk, ThFT, WhoHol A
Lindsay, Marquerita 1883-1955 *WhScrn 2*
Lindsay, Mary *WhoHol A*
Lindsay, Vera 1911- *WhThe*
Lindsey, Ben *Film 2*
Lindsey, Emily 1887-1944 *WhScrn 1, WhScrn 2*
Lindsey, George *WhoHol A*
Lindsey, Mort 1923- *AmSCAP 1966*
Lindsley, Guy d1923 *NotNAT B*
Lindstrom, Pia 1938- *CelR 3, WhoHol A*
Lindstrom, Rune 1916- *WorEnF*
Lindtberg, Leopold 1902- *DcFM, FilmgC*
Ling, Richie d1937 *NotNAT B*
Lingard, Horace d1927 *NotNAT B*
Lingham, Thomas J 1874-1950 *Film 1, Film 2, WhScrn 1, WhScrn 2, WhoHol B*
Link, Adolf d1933 *NotNAT B*
Link, Harry 1896-1956 *AmSCAP 1966*
Link, Peter 1944- *WhoThe 16*
Link, William 1867-1937 *WhScrn 1, WhScrn 2*
Link, William E 1897-1949 *WhScrn 1, WhScrn 2*
Linke, Richard O *NewYTET*
Linkevitch, Barbara *WomWMM B*
Linklater, Eric 1899-1974 *CnMD, ModWD*
Linkletter, Art 1912- *CelR 3, IntMPA 1977, NewYTET, WhoHol A*
Linley, Doctor *PIP&P*
Linley, Betty 1890-1951 *NotNAT B, WhScrn 1, WhScrn 2, WhThe, WhoHol B*
Linley, Elizabeth *PIP&P*
Linley, George d1865 *NotNAT B*
Linley, William d1835 *NotNAT B*
Linn, Bambi 1926- *BiE&WWA, NotNAT, WhThe, WhoHol A*
Linn, Bud 1909-1968 *WhScrn 2, WhoHol B*
Linn, Gertrude 1905- *AmSCAP 1966*
Linn, Margaret 1934-1973 *WhScrn 2, WhoHol B*
Linn, Robert 1925- *AmSCAP 1966*
Linnecare, Vera *WomWMM B*
Linney, Daniel A 1930- *BiE&WWA*
Linney, Romulus *NatPD, NotNAT*
Linnit, Sidney E d1956 *NotNAT B, WhThe*
Linow, Ivan *Film 2, TwYS*
Linville, Albert *WhoHol A*
Linville, Joanne *WhoHol A*
Linville, Larry *WhoHol A*
Lion, John 1944- *NotNAT*
Lion, Leon M 1879-1947 *NotNAT A, NotNAT B, WhScrn 2, WhThe, WhoHol B*
Lipchitz, Jacques 1891- *CelR 3*
Lipman, Clara 1869-1952 *NotNAT B, WhThe, WhoStg 1906, WhoStg 1908*
Lipman, Daniel *NatPD*
Lipman, Harry *Film 2*
Lipman, Jerzy 1922- *DcFM, FilmgC*
Lippard, John B 1919- *BiE&WWA*
Lippert, Robert J, Jr. 1928- *IntMPA 1977*
Lippert, Robert L 1909- *FilmgC, IntMPA 1977*
Lippincott, David M 1925- *AmSCAP 1966*
Lippman, Monroe 1905- *BiE&WWA, NotNAT*
Lippman, Sidney 1914- *AmSCAP 1966*
Lippman, Susannah *WomWMM B*
Lippmann, Walter 1889- *CelR 3*
Lippmann, Zilla *BiE&WWA, NotNAT*
Lippold, Richard 1915- *CelR 3*
Liprott, Peggy *WomWMM*
Lipscomb, Helen 1921- *AmSCAP 1966*
Lipscomb, William Percy 1887-1958 *FilmgC, NotNAT B, WhThe*
Lipsky, David 1907- *BiE&WWA, NotNAT*
Lipson, Melba 1901-1953 *WhScrn 1, WhScrn 2*
Lipstein, Harold *WorEnF*
Lipstone, Howard H *IntMPA 1977*
Lipton, Celia 1923- *WhThe*

Lipton, David A 1906- *IntMPA 1977*
Lipton, George d1962 *NotNAT B*
Lipton, Harold Arlen 1911- *IntMPA 1977*
Lipton, James 1926- *AmSCAP 1966*
Lipton, Lawrence 1898-1975 *WhScrn 2*
Lipton, Peggy *WhoHol A*
Lipton, Robert *WhoHol A*
Liquori, Marty 1950- *CelR 3*
Lisbona, Edward 1915- *AmSCAP 1966*
Lisi, Verna *WhoHol A*
Lisi, Virna 1937- *FilmgC, MotPP, MovMk*
Lisitzky, Ephram E d1962 *NotNAT B*
Lisle, Lucille *WhThe*
Lissauer, Robert 1917- *AmSCAP 1966*
Lissenko, Nathalie *Film 2*
Lister, Eve 1918- *WhThe*
Lister, Francis 1899-1951 *Film 2, FilmgC,*
  NotNAT B, WhScrn 1, WhScrn 2, WhThe,
  WhoHol B
Lister, Frank 1868-1917 *WhThe*
Lister, Lance 1901- *WhThe*
Lister, Laurier 1907- *WhoThe 16*
Lister, Moira 1923- *FilmgC, IntMPA 1977,*
  NotNAT A, WhoHol A, WhoThe 16
Liston, John 1776-1846 *NotNAT B, OxThe*
Liston, Sonny 1932-1971 *WhScrn 2*
Liston, Victor 1838-1913 *NotNAT B, OxThe*
Litel, John 1892-1964 *MovMk*
Litel, John 1894-1972 *Vers A, WhScrn 2*
Litel, John 1895-1972 *Film 2, FilmgC,*
  WhoHol B
Lithgow, Arthur W 1915- *BiE&WWA, NotNAT*
Lithgow, John 1945- *NotNAT*
Litkei, Andrea Fodor 1932- *AmSCAP 1966*
Litkei, Ervin 1921- *AmSCAP 1966*
Litle, Alev *WomWMM B*
Litt, Jacob d1905 *NotNAT B*
Littell, Robert 1896-1963 *NotNAT B, WhThe*
Little, Ann 1891- *Film 1, Film 2, TwYS*
Little, Billy 1895-1967 *WhScrn 1, WhScrn 2,*
  WhoHol B
Little, C P d1914 *NotNAT B*
Little, Cleavon 1939- *MovMk, NotNAT,*
  PIP&PA, WhoHol A, WhoThe 16
Little, Dudley 1930- *AmSCAP 1966*
Little, George A 1890-1946 *AmSCAP 1966*
Little, Gordon W Pawnee Bill 1860-1942 *WhScrn 2*
Little, Guy S, Jr. 1935- *BiE&WWA, NotNAT*
Little, James F 1907-1969 *WhScrn 1, WhScrn 2,*
  WhoHol B
Little, Little Jack d1956 *WhoHol B*
Little, Little Jack 1900-1956 *AmSCAP 1966*
Little, Little Jack 1901-1956 *WhScrn 1,*
  WhScrn 2
Little, Major Gordon W Pawnee Bill 1860-1942
  WhScrn 2
Little, Stuart W 1921- *BiE&WWA, NotNAT*
Little, Terence 1920- *BiE&WWA*
Little Bozo 1907-1952 *WhScrn 1, WhScrn 2,*
  WhoHol B
Little Tich 1868-1928 *NotNAT B, OxThe*
Littledale, Richard d1951 *NotNAT B*
Littlefeather, Sacheen *WhoHol A*
Littlefield, Catherine 1904-1951 *NotNAT B,*
  WhThe
Littlefield, Emma 1883-1934 *NotNAT B,*
  WhoStg 1908
Littlefield, Lucian 1895-1959 *Film 2*
Littlefield, Lucien *MotPP*
Littlefield, Lucien 1895-1959 *Film 1, MovMk*
Littlefield, Lucien 1895-1960 *NotNAT B, TwYS,*
  Vers A, WhScrn 1, WhScrn 2, WhoHol B

Littlefield, Lucien 1895-1966 *FilmgC*
Littlefield, Nancy *WomWMM, WomWMM B*
Littlejohn, Dorothy *WomWMM B*
Littlejohns, Frank 1914- *IntMPA 1977*
Littler, Blanche 1899- *WhThe*
Littler, Sir Emile 1903- *EncMT, WhoThe 16*
Littler, F R d1940 *NotNAT B*
Littler, Prince 1901-1973 *EncMT, WhThe*
Littlewood, Joan *BiE&WWA, CnThe, CroCD,*
  WhoThe 16, WomWMM
Littlewood, Joan 1914- *OxThe*
Littlewood, Joan 1916- *FilmgC, OxFilm, PIP&P*
Littlewood, Samuel Robinson 1875-1963 *WhThe*
Littman, Lynne *WomWMM A, WomWMM B*
Littman, Robert 1938- *IntMPA 1977*
Litto, George 1930- *IntMPA 1977*
Litvak, Anatole 1902-1974 *BiDFlm, CmMov,*
  DcFM, FilmgC, MovMk, OxFilm,
  WhScrn 2, WorEnF
Liu, Pan 190-?- *DcFM*
Livanov, Boris 1904-1972 *WhScrn 2*
LiVecche, George V 1914- *AmSCAP 1966*
Liveright, Horace Brisbin 1886-1933 *NotNAT B,*
  OxThe, WhThe
Livesay, Meade A *AmSCAP 1966*
Livesey, Barrie 1904- *WhThe*
Livesey, E Carter *WhThe*
Livesey, Jack 1901-1961 *FilmgC, NotNAT B,*
  WhScrn 1, WhScrn 2, WhThe, WhoHol B
Livesey, Roger 1906-1976 *Film 2, FilmgC,*
  MovMk, PIP&P, WhoHol C, WhoThe 16
Livesey, Sam 1873-1936 *Film 2, FilmgC,*
  NotNAT B, WhScrn 1, WhScrn 2, WhThe,
  WhoHol B
Livings, Henry 1929- *CnMD Sup, CnThe,*
  ConDr 1977, CroCD, McGWD, ModWD,
  REnWD, WhoThe 16
Livingston, Alan W 1917- *AmSCAP 1966*
Livingston, Barry *WhoHol A*
Livingston, Blanche *IntMPA 1977*
Livingston, Bob 1908- *Film 2*
Livingston, Deacon d1963 *NotNAT B*
Livingston, Helen 1900- *AmSCAP 1966*
Livingston, Jack *Film 1*
Livingston, Jay Harold 1915- *AmSCAP 1966,*
  BiE&WWA, FilmgC, IntMPA 1977,
  NotNAT
Livingston, Jefferson *IntMPA 1977*
Livingston, Jerry 1909- *AmSCAP 1966*
Livingston, Joseph A 1906-1957 *AmSCAP 1966*
Livingston, Margaret *MotPP*
Livingston, Margaret 1900- *ThFT, WhoHol A*
Livingston, Margaret 1902- *Film 1, Film 2,*
  MovMk, TwYS
Livingston, Robert 1908- *WhoHol A*
Livingston, Robert H 1934- *NotNAT*
Livingston, Stanley 1950- *WhoHol A*
Livingston, William 1911- *AmSCAP 1966*
Livingstone, Belle *NotNAT A*
Livingstone, Mabel *AmSCAP 1966*
Livingstone, Mary *WhoHol A*
Livingstone, Percy 1913- *IntMPA 1977*
Livius Andronicus *OxThe, PIP&P*
Liza, Mona *Film 2*
Lizardi, Joseph 1941- *NatPD*
Lizzani, Carlo 1917- *OxFilm, WorEnF*
Lizzani, Carlo 1922- *DcFM, FilmgC*
Llewellyn, Eve *Film 2*
Llewellyn, Fewlass 1866-1941 *Film 2, NotNAT B,*
  WhThe, WhoHol B
Llewelyn, Alfred H d1964 *NotNAT B*
Lloyd, Al 1884-1964 *NotNAT B, WhScrn 1,*
  WhScrn 2
Lloyd, Albert S *Film 2*

Lloyd, Alice 1873-1949 *NotNAT B, WhScrn 2, WhThe*
Lloyd, Alison *Film 2*
Lloyd, Charles M 1870-1948 *WhScrn 1, WhScrn 2*
Lloyd, Doris d1968 *MotPP, WhThe, WhoHol B*
Lloyd, Doris 1899-1968 *FilmgC, MovMk*
Lloyd, Doris 1900-1968 *Film 2, ThFT, TwYS, WhScrn 1, WhScrn 2*
Lloyd, Ethel *Film 1*
Lloyd, Euan 1923- *FilmgC, IntMPA 1977*
Lloyd, Florence 1876- *WhThe*
Lloyd, Frank 1887-1960 *FilmgC*
Lloyd, Frank 1888-1960 *MovMk*
Lloyd, Frank 1889-1960 *BiDFlm, CmMov, DcFM, Film 1, NewYTET, OxFilm, TwYS A, WhScrn 1, WhScrn 2, WhoHol B, WorEnF*
Lloyd, Frederick William 1880-1949 *NotNAT B, WhScrn 1, WhScrn 2, WhThe, WhoHol B*
Lloyd, Gaylord *Film 2*
Lloyd, George 1897- *Vers B*
Lloyd, Gladys 1896-1971 *WhScrn 1, WhScrn 2, WhoHol B*
Lloyd, Grace d1961 *NotNAT B*
Lloyd, Harold 1893-1971 *BiDFlm, CmMov, DcFM, Film 1, Film 2, FilmgC, MotPP, MovMk, OxFilm, TwYS, WhScrn 1, WhScrn 2, WhoHol B*
Lloyd, Harold 1894-1971 *WorEnF*
Lloyd, Harold, Jr. 1931-1971 *WhScrn 1, WhScrn 2, WhoHol B*
Lloyd, Jack 1922- *AmSCAP 1966*
Lloyd, John d1944 *NotNAT B, WhoHol B*
Lloyd, John Robert 1920- *BiE&WWA, NotNAT*
Lloyd, Marie 1870-1922 *NotNAT A, NotNAT B, OxThe, PIP&P, WhThe*
Lloyd, Michael 1948- *AmSCAP 1966*
Lloyd, Norman 1909- *AmSCAP 1966*
Lloyd, Norman 1914- *BiE&WWA, FilmgC, IntMPA 1977, NewYTET, NotNAT, Vers A, WhoHol A*
Lloyd, Patricia d1969 *WhoHol B*
Lloyd, Robin *WomWMM B*
Lloyd, Rollo 1883-1938 *WhScrn 1, WhScrn 2, WhoHol B*
Lloyd, Rosie 1897-1944 *NotNAT B, WhThe*
Lloyd, Sherman *WhoHol A*
Lloyd, Sue 1939- *FilmgC, WhoHol A*
Lloyd, Violet 1879- *WhThe*
Lloyd, William *Film 1*
Lloyd-Pack, Charles 1905- *FilmgC*
Lloyd Webber, Andrew 1948- *WhoThe 16*
Loach, Ken 1936- *FilmgC, OxFilm*
Loader, A McLeod 1869- *WhThe*
Loader, Rosa *WhThe*
Loback, Marvin 1896-1938 *WhScrn 1, WhoHol B*
Loback, Marvin 1898-1938 *WhScrn 2*
Lobarsky, Anat *WomWMM*
Lobe, Friedrich *Film 2*
LoBianco, Tony *WhoHol A*
Loboda, Samuel 1916- *AmSCAP 1966*
LoBuono, John A 1929- *AmSCAP 1966*
Locante, Sam *WhoHol A*
Locascio, Michael *PIP&P*
Locatelli, Basileo d1650 *OxThe*
Locatelli, Domenico 1613-1671 *OxThe*
Locatelli, Luisa Gabrielli *OxThe*
Locher, Felix 1882-1969 *WhScrn 1, WhScrn 2, WhoHol B*
Locke, Edward 1869-1945 *NotNAT B, WhThe*
Locke, Harry *WhoHol A*
Locke, Jeannine *WomWMM*
Locke, Katharine *WhoHol A*
Locke, Robinson 1856-1920 *NotNAT B*

Locke, Sam 1917- *BiE&WWA, NotNAT*
Locke, Sondra *WhoHol A*
Locke, Terrence *WhoHol A*
Locke, Vivia 1917- *BiE&WWA*
Locke, Will H d1950 *NotNAT B*
Locke, William J *Film 2*
Locke, William John 1863-1930 *NotNAT B, WhThe*
Lockerbee, Beth d1968 *WhoHol B*
Lockett, Louis d1964 *NotNAT B*
Lockhart, Anna *Film 2*
Lockhart, Anne *WhoHol A*
Lockhart, Calvin 1934- *FilmgC, WhoHol A*
Lockhart, Eugene 1891-1957 *AmSCAP 1966*
Lockhart, Gene 1891-1957 *Film 2, FilmgC, MotPP, MovMk, NotNAT B, WhScrn 1, WhScrn 2, WhThe, WhoHol B*
Lockhart, Gene 1891-1959 *Vers A*
Lockhart, John *Film 2*
Lockhart, June 1925- *BiE&WWA, FilmgC, IntMPA 1977, MotPP, MovMk, NotNAT, WhoHol A*
Lockhart, Kathleen *WhoHol A*
Lockhart, Tim 1930-1963 *WhScrn 1, WhScrn 2*
Locklear, Lieutenant 1891-1920 *WhoHol B*
Locklear, Omar 1891-1920 *WhScrn 1, WhScrn 2*
Lockney, John P *Film 1, Film 2*
Lockridge, Richard 1898- *WhThe*
Lockton, Joan 1901- *WhThe*
Lockwood, Alexander *WhoHol A*
Lockwood, Arthur H 1900- *IntMPA 1977*
Lockwood, Carolyn 1932- *BiE&WWA*
Lockwood, Gary 1937- *FilmgC, IntMPA 1977, MotPP, WhoHol A*
Lockwood, Harold 1887-1919 *MotPP*
Lockwood, Harold 1887-1918 *NotNAT B, WhScrn 2, WhoHol B*
Lockwood, Harold 1887-1919 *Film 1, TwYS*
Lockwood, Julia 1941- *FilmgC, IntMPA 1977, WhoHol A*
Lockwood, King 1898-1971 *WhScrn 1, WhScrn 2, WhoHol B*
Lockwood, Margaret 1916- *CmMov, FilmgC, IntMPA 1977, MotPP, MovMk, OxFilm, ThFT, WhoHol A, WhoThe 16, WorEnF*
Lockwood, Roger 1936- *IntMPA 1977*
Loconto, Francis Xavier 1931- *AmSCAP 1966*
Loden, Barbara *BiDFlm, BiE&WWA, IntMPA 1977, NotNAT, WhoHol A*
Loden, Barbara 1936- *OxFilm, WomWMM*
Loden, Barbara 1937- *CelR 3*
Loder, Basil 1885- *WhThe*
Loder, George d1868 *NotNAT B*
Loder, John 1898- *Film 2, FilmgC, MotPP, MovMk, WhoHol A*
Loder, Ted *Film 2*
Lodge, David 1922?- *FilmgC, WhoHol A*
Lodge, Henry Cabot 1902- *CelR 3*
Lodge, Jean *WhoHol A*
Lodge, John Davis 1903- *BiE&WWA, FilmgC, WhoHol A*
Lodge, Ruth 1914- *WhThe*
Lodge, Thomas 1558?-1625 *CnThe, PIP&P*
Lodi, Theodore *Film 2*
Lodice, Don 1919- *AmSCAP 1966*
Lodijensky, General *Film 2*
Lods, Jean 1903- *DcFM, WorEnF*
Loeb, Janice *WomWMM B*
Loeb, John Jacob 1910- *AmSCAP 1966*
Loeb, Philip 1894-1955 *NotNAT B, WhScrn 1, WhScrn 2, WhThe, WhoHol B*
Loedel, Adi 1937-1955 *WhScrn 1, WhScrn 2*
Loeffler, Louis *IntMPA 1977*
Loehner-Beda, Doctor d1939 *NotNAT B*

Loehner-Beda, Fritz 1883-1942 *AmSCAP 1966*
Loes, Harry Dixon 1892-1965 *AmSCAP 1966*
Loesser, Frank 1910-1969 *AmSCAP 1966,
BiE&WWA, EncMT, FilmgC, NewMT,
NotNAT B, PIP&P, WhScrn 1, WhScrn 2,
WhThe, WhoHol B*
Loesser, Lynn *BiE&WWA, NotNAT*
Loevinger, Lee *NewYTET*
Loew, Arthur M 1897- *IntMPA 1977*
Loew, Marcus 1870-1927 *DcFM, FilmgC,
MGM A, NotNAT B, OxFilm, WorEnF*
Loewe, Frederick *NewMT*
Loewe, Frederick 1901- *BiE&WWA, FilmgC,
WhoThe 16*
Loewe, Frederick 1904- *AmSCAP 1966, CelR 3,
EncMT, IntMPA 1977, NewMT, PIP&P*
Loewy, Raymond 1893- *CelR 3*
Loff, Jeanette 1906-1942 *Film 2, MotPP, TwYS,
WhScrn 1, WhScrn 2, WhoHol B*
Lofgren, Marianne 1910-1957 *WhScrn 2*
Loft, Arthur 1897-1947 *WhScrn 2*
Loftus, Cecilia 1876-1943 *Film 1, FilmgC,
WhScrn 1, WhScrn 2, WhoHol B,
WhoStg 1906, WhoStg 1908*
Loftus, Cissie 1876-1943 *NotNAT A, OxThe*
Loftus, John 1901- *AmSCAP 1966*
Loftus, Kitty 1867-1927 *NotNAT B, WhThe*
Loftus, Marie 1857-1940 *NotNAT B, WhThe*
Loftus, Marie Cecilia 1876-1943 *NotNAT B,
WhThe*
Loftus, William C 1862-1931 *WhScrn 1,
WhScrn 2*
Logan, Campbell 1910- *IntMPA 1977*
Logan, Cornelius A 1806-1853 *NotNAT B*
Logan, Ella 1910-1969 *WhThe*
Logan, Ella 1913-1969 *BiE&WWA, EncMT,
MotPP, NotNAT B, WhScrn 1, WhScrn 2,
WhoHol B*
Logan, Frederick Knight 1871-1928
AmSCAP 1966
Logan, Gwendolyn *Film 2*
Logan, Jacqueline 1900- *Film 2, TwYS*
Logan, Jacqueline 1901- *ThFT*
Logan, Jacqueline 1903?- *MovMk*
Logan, Jacqueline 1904- *WhoHol A*
Logan, James *WhoHol A*
Logan, Janet 1919-1965 *WhScrn 2*
Logan, Jimmy 1928- *IntMPA 1977*
Logan, John 1924-1972 *WhScrn 2*
Logan, Joshua 1908- *BiDFlm, BiE&WWA,
CelR 3, CmMov, ConDr 1977D, DcFM,
EncMT, FilmgC, IntMPA 1977, ModWD,
MovMk, NewMT, NotNAT, OxFilm,
WhoThe 16, WorEnF*
Logan, May d1969 *WhoHol B*
Logan, Nedda Harrigan 1900?- *BiE&WWA,
NotNAT*
Logan, Olive 1839-1909 *NotNAT A, NotNAT B*
Logan, Stanley 1885-1953 *NotNAT B, WhScrn 1,
WhScrn 2, WhThe, WhoHol B*
Logan, Virginia Knight 1850-1940 *AmSCAP 1966*
Loggia, Robert 1930- *FilmgC, WhoHol A*
Logue, Christopher 1926- *CnMD, ModWD*
Lohenstein, Daniel Caspar Von 1635-1683 *OxThe*
Lohman, Zalla 1906-1967 *WhScrn 1, WhScrn 2,
WhoHol B*
Lohoefer, Evelyn 1921- *AmSCAP 1966*
Lohr, Lenox Riley d1968 *NewYTET*
Lohr, Marie 1890-1975 *FilmgC, PIP&P,
WhScrn 2, WhThe, WhoHol C*
Loigu, Valdeko 1911- *AmSCAP 1966*
Loizeaux, Christine *WomWMM B*
Lojewski, Harry Victor 1917- *AmSCAP 1966*
Lola And Armida *Film 2*

Lollobrigida, Gina *MotPP*
Lollobrigida, Gina 1927- *BiDFlm, FilmgC,
OxFilm, WhoHol A, WorEnF*
Lollobrigida, Gina 1928- *IntMPA 1977, MovMk*
Lom, Herbert 1917- *CmMov, FilmgC,
IntMPA 1977, MotPP, MovMk, WhThe,
WhoHol A*
Loman, Jules 1910-1957 *AmSCAP 1966*
Lomas, Herbert 1887-1961 *FilmgC, PIP&P,
WhScrn 1, WhScrn 2, WhThe, WhoHol B*
Lomas, Jack M 1911-1959 *WhScrn 1, WhScrn 2,
WhoHol B*
Lomax, Louis 1922-1970 *WhScrn 2*
Lombard, Carole d1942 *MotPP, WhoHol B*
Lombard, Carole 1908-1942 *BiDFlm, FilmgC,
MovMk, OxFilm, ThFT, WorEnF*
Lombard, Carole 1909-1942 *Film 2, NotNAT B,
TwYS, WhScrn 1, WhScrn 2*
Lombard, Harry d1963 *NotNAT B*
Lombardi, Dillo *Film 2*
Lombardo, Anthony M 1905- *AmSCAP 1966*
Lombardo, Carmen d1971 *WhoHol B*
Lombardo, Carmen 1903-1971 *AmSCAP 1966*
Lombardo, Carmen 1904-1971 *WhScrn 1,
WhScrn 2*
Lombardo, Goffredo 1920- *IntMPA 1977*
Lombardo, Guy 1902- *BiE&WWA, CelR 3,
NotNAT*
Lombardo, Mario 1931- *AmSCAP 1966*
Lomita, Sol 1937- *IntMPA 1977*
Lomnicki, Jan 1929- *DcFM*
Loncar, Beba *WhoHol A*
London, Babe 1901- *Film 2, TwYS, WhoHol A*
London, Barbara *WhoHol A*
London, Ernest A d1964 *NotNAT B*
London, Jack 1876-1916 *FilmgC, NotNAT B*
London, Jack 1905-1966 *WhScrn 1, WhScrn 2*
London, Julie 1926- *AmSCAP 1966, FilmgC,
IntMPA 1977, MotPP, MovMk, WhoHol A*
London, Milton H 1916- *IntMPA 1977*
London, Roy *NatPD*
London, Steve *WhoHol A*
London, Tom d1963 *NotNAT B, WhoHol B*
London, Tom 1882-1963 *Film 2, TwYS*
London, Tom 1883-1963 *Vers A*
London, Tom 1893-1963 *WhScrn 1, WhScrn 2*
Lonergan, Arthur 1906- *IntMPA 1977*
Lonergan, Lenore *PIP&P*
Lonergan, Lester 1869-1931 *Film 2, NotNAT B,
WhScrn 1, WhScrn 2, WhoHol B*
Lonergan, Lester, Jr. 1894-1959 *NotNAT B,
WhScrn 1, WhScrn 2, WhoHol B*
Lonero, Emilio 1924- *IntMPA 1977*
Loney, Glenn Meredith 1928- *NotNAT*
Long, Audrey 1924- *FilmgC*
Long, Avon 1910- *BiE&WWA, NotNAT,
WhoHol A, WhoThe 16*
Long, Frederic 1857-1941 *WhScrn 1, WhScrn 2,
WhoHol B*
Long, Frederick 1857-1941 *Film 2*
Long, Huey P 1893-1935 *OxFilm*
Long, Jack d1938 *WhScrn 1, WhScrn 2*
Long, John Luther 1861-1927 *ModWD,
NotNAT B, OxThe, PIP&P, WhThe,
WhoStg 1908*
Long, Johnny d1972 *WhoHol B*
Long, Luray 1890-1919 *WhScrn 2*
Long, Mary Elitch d1936 *NotNAT B*
Long, Melvyn Harry 1895-1940 *WhScrn 1,
WhScrn 2*
Long, Mervyn Harry d1940 *WhoHol B*
Long, Nick *Film 2*
Long, Nick, Jr. 1906-1949 *Film 2, NotNAT B,
WhScrn 2, WhoHol B*

Long, Richard 1927-1974 *FilmgC, MotPP,*
 MovMk, WhScrn 2, WhoHol B
Long, Ronald *WhoHol A*
Long, Russell 1918- *CelR 3*
Long, Sally *Film 2, WhoHol A*
Long, Sumner Arthur 1921- *BiE&WWA,*
 NotNAT
Long, Walter d1952 *MotPP, WhoHol B*
Long, Walter 1879-1952 *WhScrn 1, WhScrn 2*
Long, Walter 1882-1952 *Film 1, Film 2*
Long, Walter 1884-1952 *FilmgC, TwYS*
Longden, John 1900- *Film 2, FilmgC, WhThe,*
 WhoHol A
Longden, Terence 1922- *FilmgC*
Longdon, Joan *WomWMM B*
Longdon, Terence 1922- *WhoHol A, WhoThe 16*
Longepierre, Hilaire-Bernard De R 1659-1731
 OxThe
Longet, Claudine *WhoHol A*
Longfellow, Malvina *Film 1, Film 2*
Longfellow, Stephanie *Film 1, WhoStg 1908*
Longford, Edward A H Pakenham, Earl Of
 1902-1961 *McGWD, NotNAT B, OxThe,*
 WhThe
Longo, Alfred 1896- *AmSCAP 1966*
Longstreet, Stephen 1907- *BiE&WWA,*
 ConDr 1977D, FilmgC, IntMPA 1977,
 NotNAT
Longstreth, Marian 1906- *BiE&WWA*
Longworth, Alice Roosevelt 1884- *CelR 3*
Longworth, Josephine *Film 1*
Lonnen, Jessie 1886- *WhThe*
Lonnen, Nellie 1887- *WhThe*
Lonnon, Alice 1872- *WhThe, WhoStg 1908*
Lonsdale, Frederick 1881-1954 *CnMD, CnThe,*
 McGWD, ModWD, NotNAT A, NotNAT B,
 OxThe, PlP&P, WhThe
Lonsdale, H G d1923 *NotNAT B, WhoHol B*
Lonsdale, Harry G d1923 *Film 1, Film 2,*
 WhScrn 2
Lonsdale, Michel *WhoHol A*
Lonsdale, Thomas J d1928 *NotNAT B*
Lontoc, Leon 1909-1974 *WhScrn 2, WhoHol B*
Loo, Bessie *WhoHol A*
Loo, Richard 1903- *FilmgC, MotPP, MovMk,*
 Vers A, WhoHol A
Loofbourrow, John G d1964 *NotNAT B*
Loomis, Clarence 1888-1965 *AmSCAP 1966*
Loomis, Henry W *NewYTET*
Loomis, Margaret *Film 1, Film 2, TwYS*
Loomis, Virginia *Film 2*
Loong, Lee Siu *WhScrn 2*
Loop, Phil d1975 *WhScrn 2*
Looram, Mary Harden *IntMPA 1977*
Loos, Anita 1893-1971 *BiE&WWA, CelR 3,*
 FilmgC, IntMPA 1977, NotNAT,
 NotNAT A, OxFilm, WhoThe 16,
 WomWMM, WorEnF
Loos, Mary 1914- *IntMPA 1977*
Loos, Theodor 1883-1954 *Film 2, WhScrn 1,*
 WhScrn 2, WhoHol B
Lopatnikoff, Nikolai 1903- *AmSCAP 1966*
Lope DeVega *OxThe*
Loper, Don 1906-1972 *WhScrn 2, WhoHol B*
Loper, James L *NewYTET*
Lopez, Augustina *Film 2*
Lopez, Carlos 1887-1942 *WhScrn 1, WhScrn 2*
Lopez, Perry *MotPP, WhoHol A*
Lopez, Raymond *Film 2*
Lopez, Sabatino 1867-1951 *McGWD, NotNAT B*
Lopez, Sylvia *WomWMM A*
Lopez, Tony 1902-1949 *WhScrn 1, WhScrn 2*
Lopez, Trini 1937- *CelR 3, WhoHol A*
Lopez, Vincent 1898-1975 *AmSCAP 1966,*

WhScrn 2
Lopez DeAyala, Adelardo 1829-1879 *OxThe*
Lopez DeAyala Y Herrera, Adelardo 1828-1879
 McGWD
Lopez Rubio, Jose 1903- *CroCD, McGWD,*
 ModWD
Lopokova, Lydia 1892- *WhThe*
Loquasto, Santo *NotNAT, PlP&P A,*
 WhoThe 16
Loraine, Henry d1899 *NotNAT B*
Loraine, Robert 1876-1935 *NotNAT A,*
 NotNAT B, OxThe, WhThe, WhoStg 1908
Loraine, Violet 1886-1956 *WhThe*
Lorca, Federico Garcia 1899-1936 *CnMD, CnThe,*
 McGWD, OxThe, REnWD
Lorch, Louis *Film 2*
Lorch, Theodore A 1873-1947 *Film 2, WhScrn 1,*
 WhScrn 2, WhoHol B
Lord, Barbara 1937- *BiE&WWA, NotNAT*
Lord, Basil 1913- *WhoThe 16*
Lord, Del 1895-1970 *FilmgC, TwYS A*
Lord, Eric Meredith 1923- *NatPD*
Lord, Grace *Film 2*
Lord, Jack *MotPP, WhoHol A*
Lord, Jack 1922- *FilmgC*
Lord, Jack 1928- *CelR 3*
Lord, Jack 1930- *IntMPA 1977, MovMk*
Lord, Marion 1883-1942 *Film 2, WhScrn 1,*
 WhScrn 2, WhoHol B
Lord, Marjorie 1921- *MovMk, WhoHol A*
Lord, Marjorie 1922- *FilmgC*
Lord, Pauline 1890-1950 *FamA&A, FilmgC,*
 NotNAT B, ThFT, WhScrn 1, WhScrn 2,
 WhThe, WhoHol B
Lord, Philip *Film 2*
Lord, Philip F 1879-1968 *WhScrn 2*
Lord, Phillips H 1902-1975 *WhScrn 2, WhoHol C*
Lord, Robert 1945- *ConDr 1977, NatPD*
Lord, Walter 1917- *AmSCAP 1966*
Lord, William E *NewYTET*
Lorde, Andre De 1871- *WhThe*
Lorde, Athena 1915-1973 *WhScrn 2, WhoHol B*
Loredo, Linda *Film 2*
Loren, Bernice *NotNAT*
Loren, Bernie 1925- *AmSCAP 1966*
Loren, Donna *WhoHol A*
Loren, Sophia 1934- *BiDFlm, CelR 3, CmMov,*
 FilmgC, IntMPA 1977, MotPP, MovMk,
 OxFilm, WhoHol A, WorEnF
Lorengar, Pilar 1933- *CelR 3*
Lorentz, Pare 1905- *DcFM, OxFilm, WorEnF*
Lorenz, Dolly *Film 2*
Lorenz, Edmund Simon 1854-1942 *AmSCAP 1966*
Lorenz, Ellen Jane 1907- *AmSCAP 1966*
Lorenz, Pare 1905-1972 *FilmgC*
Lorenzi, Giovanni Battista 1721-1807 *OxThe*
Lorenzi, Stellio 1921- *DcFM*
Lorenzo, Ange 1894- *AmSCAP 1966*
Lorenzo, Tina Di 1872-1930 *WhThe*
Lorenzon, Livio 1926-1971 *WhScrn 2*
Loretto, Alfred *Film 2*
Lorimer, Jack 1883- *WhThe*
Lorimer, Louise *WhoHol A*
Lorimer, Wright 1874-1911 *NotNAT B,*
 WhoStg 1908
Loring, Ann *WhoHol A*
Loring, Eugene 1914- *BiE&WWA, WhoHol A*
Loring, Eva *Film 1*
Loring, Lynn *WhoHol A*
Loring, Norman 1888-1967 *WhThe*
Loring, Richard 1925- *AmSCAP 1966*
Lorme, Joyce *Film 2*
Lormer, Jon *WhoHol A*
Lorne, Constance 1914-1969 *WhScrn 2,*

WhoHol A, WhoThe 16
Lorne, Marion d1968 MotPP, WhoHol B
Lorne, Marion 1886-1968 FilmgC
Lorne, Marion 1888-1968 BiE&WWA,
    NotNAT B, WhScrn 1, WhScrn 2, WhThe
Lorraine, Betty 1908-1944 WhScrn 2
Lorraine, Emily d1944 NotNAT B
Lorraine, Guido WhoHol A
Lorraine, Harry 1886- Film 2
Lorraine, Irma 1885- WhThe
Lorraine, Jean Film 2
Lorraine, Leota 1893-1975 Film 2, WhScrn 2,
    WhoHol C
Lorraine, Lilian 1892-1955 WhThe
Lorraine, Lillian 1892-1955 EncMT, Film 1,
    Film 2, NotNAT B, TwYS, WhoHol B
Lorraine, Louise 1901- Film 1, Film 2, TwYS,
    WhoHol A
Lorraine, Oscar 1878-1955 WhScrn 1, WhScrn 2
Lorre, Peter 1904-1964 BiDFlm, CmMov,
    FilmgC, MotPP, MovMk, NotNAT B,
    OxFilm, Vers A, WhScrn 1, WhScrn 2,
    WhoHol B, WorEnF
Lorre, Peter, Jr. WhoHol A
Lorring, Joan MotPP, NotNAT
Lorring, Joan 1926- FilmgC, MovMk
Lorring, Joan 1931- BiE&WWA, WhoHol A
Lorring, Lotte Film 2
Lortel, Lucille BiE&WWA, NotNAT,
    WhoThe 16
Lortz, Robert NatPD
Lorys, Denise Film 2
Losch, Tilly d1975 BiE&WWA, WhoHol C
Losch, Tilly 1902-1975 EncMT, WhScrn 2
Losch, Tilly 1907-1975 NotNAT B, WhThe
Losch, Tilly 1911?- FilmgC
Losee, Frank 1856-1937 Film 1, Film 2,
    NotNAT B, TwYS, WhScrn 1, WhScrn 2,
    WhoHol B
Losey, Joseph 1909- BiDFlm, CelR 3, DcFM,
    FilmgC, IntMPA 1977, MovMk, OxFilm,
    WorEnF
Losey, Mary WomWMM B
Lossen, Lena Film 2
Lotar, Eli 1905- DcFM, OxFilm
Lotar, Petr 1910- OxThe
Loth, L Leslie 1888- AmSCAP 1966
Lothar, Eva WomWMM B
Lothar, Hanns d1967 WhScrn 1, WhScrn 2
Lothar, Hans d1967 WhoHol B
Lotinga, Ernest 1876-1951 WhScrn 2, WhThe,
    WhoHol B
Lotinga, Ernest 1895-1951 WhScrn 1
Lotinga, Ernie 1876-1951 Film 2, FilmgC,
    NotNAT B
Lotis, Dennis WhoHol A
Lotito, Louis A 1900- BiE&WWA, NotNAT
Lott, Mona WomWMM
Lotta 1847-1924 OxThe, WhThe, WhoStg 1908
Lotta, Charlotte 1847-1924 NotNAT B
Lou-Tellegen 1881-1934 WhThe
Louchheim, Stuart F 1892- AmSCAP 1966
Louden, Thomas 1874-1948 WhScrn 1, WhScrn 2,
    WhoHol B
Loudon, Dorothy 1933- NotNAT, WhoThe 16
Loughery, Jackie WhoHol A
Loughran, Lewis 1950-1975 WhScrn 2
Louis, Jean 1907- CelR 3, IntMPA 1977
Louis, Joe 1914- CelR 3
Louis, Tobi NatPD
Louis, Viola Film 2
Louis, Willard 1886-1926 Film 1, Film 2, TwYS,
    WhScrn 1, WhScrn 2, WhoHol B
Louise, Anita 1915-1970 FilmgC, HolP 30,

MotPP, MovMk, ThFT, WhScrn 1,
    WhScrn 2, WhoHol B
Louise, Anita 1917-1970 Film 2
Louise, Tina IntMPA 1977, MotPP, WhoHol A
Louise, Tina 1934- FilmgC
Louise, Tina 1937- BiE&WWA
Louise, Viola Film 2
Lourie, Eugene 1905?- FilmgC, WorEnF
Loutherbourg, Philip James De 1740-1812 OxThe
Lovat, Nancie 1900-1946 NotNAT B, WhThe
Love, Bessie MotPP, WhoThe 16
Love, Bessie 1891- BiE&WWA, TwYS
Love, Bessie 1898- Film 1, Film 2, FilmgC,
    IntMPA 1977, MovMk, NotNAT, OxFilm,
    ThFT, WhoHol A
Love, Dorothea Film 2
Love, James A 1918- IntMPA 1977
Love, Laura WhScrn 1, WhScrn 2
Love, Mabel 1874-1953 NotNAT B, WhThe
Love, Montagu d1943 MotPP, WhoHol B
Love, Montagu 1877-1943 Film 1, FilmgC,
    MovMk, NotNAT B, WhScrn 1, WhScrn 2,
    WhThe
Love, Montagu 1881-1943 Vers A
Love, Montagu 1887-1943 TwYS
Love, Montague 1887-1943 Film 2
Love, Phyllis 1925- BiE&WWA, NotNAT,
    WhoHol A
Love, Robert 1914-1948 WhScrn 1, WhScrn 2,
    WhoHol B
Loveday, Carroll 1898-1955 AmSCAP 1966
Lovegrove, Arthur WhoHol A
Lovejoy, Frank d1962 MotPP, WhoHol B
Lovejoy, Frank 1912-1962 FilmgC
Lovejoy, Frank 1914-1962 MovMk, NotNAT B,
    WhScrn 1, WhScrn 2
Lovejoy, Robin 1923- WhoThe 16
Lovelace, Linda WhoHol A
Lovell, Mrs. d1877 NotNAT B
Lovell, George William d1878 NotNAT B
Lovell, Raymond 1900-1953 FilmgC, NotNAT B,
    WhScrn 1, WhScrn 2, WhThe, WhoHol B
Lovell, W T 1884- WhThe
Lovely, Louise 1896- Film 1, Film 2, TwYS
Lover, Samuel d1868 NotNAT A, NotNAT B
Loveridge, Margaret Film 1
Loveridge, Marguerite 1892-1925 WhScrn 2,
    WhoHol B
Lovett, Colleen 1936- AmSCAP 1966
Lovett, Josephine WomWMM
Lovinescu, Horia 1917- CnMD, McGWD
Lovingood, Penman, Sr. 1895- AmSCAP 1966
Lovsky, Celia WhoHol A
Lovy, Alex IntMPA 1977
Low, Carl 1916- BiE&WWA, NotNAT,
    WhoHol A
Low, Colin 1926- DcFM, WorEnF
Low, Jack 1898-1958 WhScrn 1, WhScrn 2,
    WhoHol B
Lowe, Arthur WhoHol A
Lowe, Arthur 1904- FilmgC
Lowe, Arthur 1915- WhoThe 16
Lowe, Bernie 1917- AmSCAP 1966
Lowe, David d1965 NewYTET
Lowe, Douglas 1882- WhThe
Lowe, Edmund d1971 MotPP, WhoHol B
Lowe, Edmund 1890-1971 FilmgC
Lowe, Edmund 1892-1971 Film 1, Film 2,
    MovMk, TwYS, WhScrn 1, WhScrn 2,
    WhThe
Lowe, Enid 1908- WhThe
Lowe, Irma Film 2
Lowe, James B 1880-1963 Film 2, WhScrn 1,
    WhScrn 2, WhoHol B

Lowe, Joshua d1945 *NotNAT B*
Lowe, K Elmo d1971 *WhoHol B*
Lowe, K Elmo 1899-1971 *BiE&WWA,*
  NotNAT B
Lowe, K Elmo 1900-1971 *WhScrn 2*
Lowe, Maude *Film 1*
Lowe, Mundell 1922- *AmSCAP 1966*
Lowe, Philip L 1917- *IntMPA 1977*
Lowe, Rachel 1876- *WhThe*
Lowe, Robert d1939 *NotNAT B*
Lowe, Ruth 1914- *AmSCAP 1966*
Lowell, Dorothy 1916-1944 *WhScrn 1, WhScrn 2*
Lowell, Helen 1866-1937 *Film 2, NotNAT B,*
  WhScrn 1, WhScrn 2, WhThe, WhoHol B
Lowell, Joan 1900-1967 *WhScrn 1, WhScrn 2,*
  WhoHol B
Lowell, John d1937 *WhScrn 1, WhScrn 2,*
  WhoHol B
Lowell, Mollie *WhThe*
Lowell, Robert 1917- *CelR 3, CnThe,*
  ConDr 1977, CroCD, ModWD, NotNAT
Lowenfield, Henry d1931 *NotNAT B*
Lowens, Curt *WhoHol A*
Lowenstein, Larry 1919- *IntMPA 1977*
Lower, Elmer W *IntMPA 1977, NewYTET*
Lowery, Robert d1971 *MotPP, WhoHol B*
Lowery, Robert 1914-1971 *WhScrn 1, WhScrn 2*
Lowery, Robert 1916-1971 *FilmgC, MovMk*
Lowery, W E *Film 1*
Lowery, William *Film 2*
Lowin, John 1576-1653 *NotNAT B, OxThe*
Lown, Bert 1903-1962 *AmSCAP 1966*
Lowne, Charles Macready d1941 *NotNAT B,*
  WhThe
Lowney, Raymond *Film 2*
Lowrie, Jeanette *WhoStg 1908*
Lowry, John d1962 *NotNAT B*
Lowry, Judith *WhoHol A*
Lowry, L *Film 1*
Lowry, Rudd 1892-1965 *WhScrn 1, WhScrn 2*
Lowry, W McNeil 1913- *BiE&WWA, NotNAT*
Loxley, Violet 1914- *WhThe*
Loxton, David *NewYTET*
Loy, Myrna 1902- *OxFilm*
Loy, Myrna 1905- *BiDFlm, CelR 3, CmMov,*
  Film 2, FilmgC, IntMPA 1977, MGM,
  MotPP, MovMk, ThFT, TwYS, WhoHol A,
  WorEnF
Loy, Nanni 1925- *DcFM, FilmgC, OxFilm,*
  WorEnF
Loy, Sonny *Film 2*
Loyal, Dash *Film 2*
Loyd, Alison d1935 *WhoHol B*
Loyer, Georges *Film 1*
Lu, Sonny *Film 2*
Luban, Francia 1914- *AmSCAP 1966*
Lubcke, Harry R 1905- *IntMPA 1977*
Luben, Jack *Film 2*
Lubimoff, A *Film 2*
Lubin, Arthur 1901- *Film 2, FilmgC,*
  IntMPA 1977, MovMk
Lubin, Ernest 1916- *AmSCAP 1966*
Lubin, Sigmund 1850?-1923 *OxFilm*
Lubin, Tibi *Film 2*
Lubitsch, Ernst 1892-1947 *BiDFlm, CmMov,*
  DcFM, Film 2, FilmgC, MovMk,
  NotNAT B, OxFilm, TwYS A, WhScrn 1,
  WhScrn 2, WhoHol B, WorEnF
Lublow, Lenard B 1891- *AmSCAP 1966*
Luboff, Norman 1917- *AmSCAP 1966*
Lubois, Marilyn *WomWMM B*
Luboshutz, Pierre 1894- *AmSCAP 1966*
Luby, Edna 1884- *WhoStg 1906, WhoStg 1908*
Luca DeTena, Juan Ignacio 1897- *McGWD*

Lucan, Arthur 1887-1954 *FilmgC, NotNAT B,*
  WhScrn 1, WhScrn 2, WhoHol B
Lucas, Carroll W 1909- *AmSCAP 1966*
Lucas, Christopher Norman 1912- *AmSCAP 1966*
Lucas, Gene 1886- *AmSCAP 1966*
Lucas, George 1945- *IntMPA 1977, MovMk*
Lucas, Jimmy 1888-1949 *WhScrn 1, WhScrn 2,*
  WhoHol B
Lucas, Jonathan 1922- *BiE&WWA*
Lucas, Jonathan 1928- *NotNAT*
Lucas, Leighton 1903- *FilmgC*
Lucas, Marcia *WomWMM*
Lucas, Nick 1897- *Film 2, WhoHol A*
Lucas, Paul *Film 2*
Lucas, Rupert d1953 *NotNAT B*
Lucas, Sam 1841-1916 *Film 1, WhScrn 2*
Lucas, Slim *Film 1*
Lucas, Wilfred 1871-1940 *Film 1, Film 2,*
  MotPP, TwYS, TwYS A, WhScrn 1,
  WhScrn 2, WhoHol B
Lucas, William 1926- *FilmgC, WhoHol A*
Lucchetti, Virginia *Film 2*
Lucci, Susan *WhoHol A*
Lucciola, John 1926- *AmSCAP 1966*
Luce, Alexis B *Film 2*
Luce, Claire *BiE&WWA, NotNAT, PIP&P,*
  WhoHol A, WhoThe 16
Luce, Claire 1903- *EncMT*
Luce, Claire Boothe 1903- *BiE&WWA*
Luce, Clare Booth 1903- *WomWMM*
Luce, Clare Boothe 1903- *CelR 3, McGWD,*
  NotNAT, NotNAT A
Luce, Henry, III 1925- *CelR 3*
Luce, Polly 1905- *WhThe*
Luce, William Aubert 1931- *AmSCAP 1966*
Luchaire, Corinne 1921-1950 *FilmgC, WhScrn 1,*
  WhScrn 2, WhoHol B
Lucier, Raymond J 1900- *AmSCAP 1966*
Luck, Booth P d1962 *NotNAT B*
Lucke, Hans 1927- *CnMD*
Luckett, Keith d1973 *WhoHol B*
Luckham, Cyril 1907- *WhoHol A, WhoThe 16*
Luckinbill, Laurence George 1934- *WhoHol A,*
  WhoThe 16
Lucy, Arnold 1865-1945 *Film 2, NotNAT B,*
  WhScrn 2, WhoHol B
Ludden, Allen *NewYTET*
Luddy, Barbara *Film 2, WhoHol A*
Luden, Jack 1902- *Film 2, TwYS*
Luders, Gustav 1865-1913 *EncMT, NewMT,*
  NotNAT B, WhThe
Ludlam, Charles 1943- *ConDr 1977, NotNAT,*
  WhoThe 16
Ludlam, Helen *WhoHol A*
Ludlow, Benjamin, Jr. 1910- *AmSCAP 1966*
Ludlow, Noah Miller 1795-1886 *NotNAT A,*
  NotNAT B, OxThe, PIP&P
Ludlow, Patrick 1903- *WhoHol A, WhoThe 16*
Ludlum, Robert 1927- *BiE&WWA, NotNAT*
Ludlum, Stuart D 1907- *AmSCAP 1966*
Ludmilla, Anna *Film 2*
Ludwig, Arthur *Film 2*
Ludwig, Christa 1932- *CelR 3*
Ludwig, Edward 1895- *FilmgC*
Ludwig, Emil 1881-1948 *NotNAT B*
Ludwig, Irving H 1910- *IntMPA 1977*
Ludwig, Norbert 1902-1960 *AmSCAP 1966*
Ludwig, Otto 1813-1865 *CnThe, McGWD,*
  NotNAT B, OxThe, REnWD
Ludwig, Ralph *Film 2*
Ludwig, Salem 1915- *WhoHol A, WhoThe 16*
Ludwig, William 1912- *FilmgC*
Luebbert, Lynn *WomWMM B*
Lueders, Guenther 1905-1975 *WhScrn 2,*

WhoHol C
Luff, William *Film 2*
Lufkin, Sam 1892-1952 *Film 2, WhScrn 2*
Luft, Herbert G *IntMPA 1977*
Lugg, Alfred 1889- *WhThe*
Lugg, William 1852-1940 *WhThe*
Lugne-Poe, A F 1870-1940 *WhThe*
Lugne-Poe, Aurelien-Francois 1869-1940 *OxThe*
Lugne-Poe, Aurelien-Marie 1869-1940 *CnThe,*
NotNAT A, NotNAT B
Lugosi, Bela d1956 *MotPP, WhoHol B*
Lugosi, Bela 1882-1956 *CmMov, Film 1, Film 2,*
FilmgC, MovMk, WhScrn 1, WhScrn 2,
WorEnF
Lugosi, Bela 1883-1956 *TwYS*
Lugosi, Bela 1884-1956 *NotNAT B*
Lugosi, Bela 1888-1956 *BiDFlm, OxFilm, WhThe*
Luguet, Andre 1892- *WhThe*
Luisi, James *WhoHol A*
Lukas, Karl *WhoHol A*
Lukas, Paul d1971 *MotPP, WhoHol B*
Lukas, Paul 1891-1971 *FilmgC, TwYS*
Lukas, Paul 1894-1971 *BiE&WWA, HolP 30,*
NotNAT B
Lukas, Paul 1895-1971 *BiDFlm, Film 1, Film 2,*
MovMk, OxFilm, WhScrn 1, WhScrn 2,
WhThe, WorEnF
Lukas, Peter A 1917- *AmSCAP 1966*
Luke *Film 1*
Luke, Keye 1904- *IntMPA 1977, MGM,*
MovMk, Vers A, WhoHol A
Luke, Keye 1909- *FilmgC*
Luke, Peter 1919- *ConDr 1977, IntMPA 1977,*
NotNAT
Lukin, Mrs. Cecil E Schultz *WhScrn 1,*
WhScrn 2
Lukov, Leonid 1909-1963 *DcFM*
Lukyanov, Sergei Vladimirovich 1910- *WhThe*
Lulli, Folco 1912-1970 *FilmgC, WhScrn 1,*
WhScrn 2, WhoHol B
Lulu 1948- *FilmgC, WhoHol A*
Lumb, Geoffrey 1905- *BiE&WWA*
Lumby, Ilah R 1911- *BiE&WWA*
Lumet, Baruch 1898- *BiE&WWA, WhoHol A*
Lumet, Sidney 1924- *BiDFlm, BiE&WWA,*
CelR 3, DcFM, FilmgC, IntMPA 1977,
MovMk, NewYTET, NotNAT, OxFilm,
WhoHol A, WorEnF
Lumiere, Antoine 1840-190-? *DcFM*
Lumiere, August L 1862-1954 *TwYS A*
Lumiere, Auguste 1862-1954 *BiDFlm, DcFM,*
Film 1, NotNAT B, OxFilm, WorEnF
Lumiere, Louis 1864-1948 *BiDFlm, DcFM,*
FilmgC, NotNAT B, OxFilm, TwYS A,
WorEnF
Lumiere Brothers *WomWMM*
Lumkin, A W *IntMPA 1977*
Lumley, Ralph R d1900 *NotNAT B*
Lummis, Dayton 1903- *Vers A, WhoHol A*
Lun *PIP&P*
Luna, Barbara 1937- *FilmgC, WhoHol A*
Luna, Donyale *WhoHol A*
Lunacharski, Anatoli 1875-1933 *CnMD*
Lunacharsky, Anatoli Vasilevich 1875-1933 *CnThe,*
ModWD, NotNAT B, OxThe
Lunceford, James Melvin 1902-1947
AmSCAP 1966
Lunceford, Jimmy 1902-1947 *WhScrn 2*
Lund, Art 1920- *BiE&WWA, NotNAT,*
WhoHol A, WhoThe 16
Lund, Deanna *WhoHol A*
Lund, Eddie 1909- *AmSCAP 1966*
Lund, Gus A 1896-1951 *WhScrn 1, WhScrn 2*
Lund, John 1913- *FilmgC, HolP 40, MotPP,*

MovMk, WhoHol A
Lund, Jorgen *Film 2*
Lund, Lucille *WhoHol A*
Lund, O A C *Film 1*
Lund, Richard 1885-1960 *Film 1, Film 2,*
WhScrn 2
Lundel, Kert Fritjof 1936- *WhoThe 16*
Lundequist, Gerda 1871-1959 *OxThe*
Lundequist-Dahlstrom, Gerda *Film 2*
Lundholm, Lisa *Film 2*
Lundigan, William 1914-1975 *FilmgC, MotPP,*
MovMk, WhScrn 2, WhoHol C
Lundquist, H E 1910- *AmSCAP 1966*
Lundquist, Matthew Nathanael 1886-1964
AmSCAP 1966
Lung, Charles d1974 *WhScrn 2, WhoHol B*
Lung, Clarence *WhoHol A*
Lunn, Joseph d1863 *NotNAT B*
Lunsford, Beverly *WhoHol A*
Lunt, Alfred 1892- *BiE&WWA, CelR 3, CnThe,*
FilmgC, NotNAT, OxThe, PIP&P,
WhoHol A, WhoThe 16
Lunt, Alfred 1893- *FamA&A, Film 2,*
NotNAT A, TwYS
Lunt, Lynn Fontanne 1887- *OxThe*
Lunts, The *PIP&P*
Lupberger, Pauline 1931- *AmSCAP 1966*
Lupi, Ignazio *Film 1*
Lupino, Barry 1882-1962 *OxThe, WhThe*
Lupino, Barry 1884-1962 *NotNAT B*
Lupino, George 1853-1932 *NotNAT B*
Lupino, Henry George 1892-1959 *OxThe*
Lupino, Ida *MotPP, WhoHol A, WomWMM,*
WomWMM B
Lupino, Ida 1914- *FilmgC*
Lupino, Ida 1916- *ThFT*
Lupino, Ida 1918- *BiDFlm, IntMPA 1977,*
MovMk, OxFilm, WorEnF
Lupino, Mark 1894-1930 *NotNAT B, WhScrn 2*
Lupino, Stanley d1942 *WhoHol B*
Lupino, Stanley 1893-1942 *FilmgC, OxThe,*
WhScrn 2
Lupino, Stanley 1894-1942 *EncMT, NotNAT A,*
NotNAT B, WhThe
Lupino, Stanley 1895-1942 *WhScrn 1*
Lupino, Wallace d1961 *WhoHol B*
Lupino, Wallace 1897-1961 *Film 1, Film 2,*
WhThe
Lupino, Wallace 1898-1961 *WhScrn 1, WhScrn 2*
Lupino, Walter *Film 2*
Lupo, George G 1924-1973 *WhScrn 2*
Lupton, John *WhoHol A*
Lupu-Pick 1886-1931 *DcFM, WorEnF*
Lupus, Peter *WhoHol A*
Luraschi, Luigi G 1906- *IntMPA 1977*
Luray, Doris *Film 2*
Lurie, Jane *WomWMM B*
Lurie, Samuel *BiE&WWA*
Lurville, Armand *Film 2*
Lusk, Freeman 1906-1970 *WhScrn 2*
Lussi, Marie 1892- *AmSCAP 1966*
Luther, Ann 1893-1960 *WhScrn 2*
Luther, Ann 1894-1960 *Film 2*
Luther, Anna 1894-1960 *Film 1, NotNAT B,*
TwYS, WhoHol B
Luther, Johnny 1909-1960 *WhScrn 1, WhScrn 2,*
WhoHol B
Luther, Lester 1888-1962 *NotNAT B, WhScrn 1,*
WhScrn 2, WhoHol B
Lutrell, Helen *Film 1*
Lutter, Alfred *WhoHol A*
Luttringer, Alfonse 1879-1953 *WhScrn 1,*
WhScrn 2
Lutyens, Elisabeth 1906- *OxFilm*

Lutz, Abbot 1917- *AmSCAP 1966*
Lutz, E O 1919- *BiE&WWA, NotNAT*
Lutz, H B *BiE&WWA*
Lutz, Marjorie *WomWMM B*
Lutzkendorf, Felix 1906- *CnMD*
Luxford, Nola *Film 2, WhoHol A*
Luzan, Ignacio 1702-1754 *OxThe*
Luzhsky, V V *PIP&P*
Lycophron 324?BC- *OxThe*
Lydon, James 1923- *FilmgC, IntMPA 1977,
    MovMk*
Lydon, Jimmy 1923- *WhoHol A*
Lye, Len 1901- *DcFM, FilmgC, OxFilm,
    WorEnF*
Lyel, Viola 1900-1972 *FilmgC, WhThe,
    WhoHol B*
Lygo, Mary d1927 *WhScrn 1, WhScrn 2*
Lyle, Bessie *Film 2*
Lyle, Edythe *Film 1*
Lyle, Lyston d1920 *NotNAT B, WhThe*
Lyles, A C 1918- *CmMov, FilmgC,
    IntMPA 1977*
Lyly, John 1554?-1606 *CnThe, McGWD,
    NotNAT B, OxThe, PIP&P, REnWD*
Lyman, Abe 1897-1957 *AmSCAP 1966,
    NotNAT B, WhScrn 1, WhScrn 2,
    WhoHol B*
Lyman, Tommy d1964 *NotNAT B*
Lymon, Frankie 1942-1968 *WhScrn 2*
Lyn, Dawn 1963- *WhoHol A*
Lyn, Jacquie *WhoHol A*
Lynas, Jeff *WhoHol A*
Lynch, Alfred 1933- *FilmgC, PIP&P, WhoHol A*
Lynch, Brid 1913-1968 *WhScrn 2*
Lynch, Edie *WomWMM B*
Lynch, Frank J d1932 *WhScrn 1, WhScrn 2*
Lynch, Frank T 1869-1933 *WhScrn 1, WhScrn 2*
Lynch, Helen 1904-1965 *Film 2, TwYS,
    WhScrn 2, WhoHol B*
Lynch, Jim d1916 *WhScrn 2*
Lynch, John *Film 2*
Lynch, Ken *WhoHol A*
Lynch, Ruth Sproule *WhScrn 2*
Lynch, T Murray 1920- *IntMPA 1977*
Lynch, Walter *Film 1*
Lynd, Rosa 1884-1922 *NotNAT B, WhThe*
Lynde, Paul 1926- *BiE&WWA, EncMT, FilmgC,
    IntMPA 1977, MotPP, MovMk, NotNAT,
    WhoHol A*
Lyndon, Alice 1874-1949 *WhScrn 1, WhScrn 2,
    WhoHol B*
Lyndon, Barre 1896- *FilmgC, WhThe*
Lyndon, Clarence *Film 1*
Lyndon, Larry *Film 1*
Lyndon, Victor *IntMPA 1977*
Lyndsay, Sir David 1490?-1555? *McGWD,
    REnWD*
Lynes, Gary S 1934- *AmSCAP 1966*
Lynes, Russell 1910- *CelR 3*
Lynley, Carol 1942- *FilmgC, MotPP, MovMk,
    WhoHol A, WorEnF*
Lynn, Ann 1939?- *FilmgC, IntMPA 1977,
    WhoHol A*
Lynn, Betty *WhoHol A*
Lynn, Cynthia *WhoHol A*
Lynn, Diana 1926-1971 *BiE&WWA, FilmgC,
    MotPP, MovMk, NotNAT B, WhScrn 1,
    WhScrn 2, WhoHol B*
Lynn, Eddie 1905-1975 *WhScrn 2*
Lynn, Eleanor *PIP&P*
Lynn, Emmett 1897-1958 *Vers B, WhScrn 1,
    WhScrn 2, WhoHol B*
Lynn, Emmy *Film 2*
Lynn, George 1915- *AmSCAP 1966*

Lynn, George M d1967 *WhScrn 2, WhoHol B*
Lynn, Hastings 1879-1932 *WhScrn 1, WhScrn 2*
Lynn, Homer *Film 2*
Lynn, Jeffrey 1909- *BiE&WWA, FilmgC,
    IntMPA 1977, MotPP, MovMk, NotNAT,
    WhoHol A*
Lynn, Jill *Film 2*
Lynn, Kane W 1919- *IntMPA 1977*
Lynn, Leni 1925- *FilmgC, WhoHol A*
Lynn, Loretta *CelR 3*
Lynn, Mara 1929- *BiE&WWA, NotNAT,
    WhoHol A*
Lynn, Natalie d1964 *WhScrn 1, WhScrn 2*
Lynn, Ralph d1962 *Film 2, WhoHol B*
Lynn, Ralph 1881-1962 *WhScrn 1, WhScrn 2*
Lynn, Ralph 1882-1962 *OxThe, WhThe*
Lynn, Ralph 1882-1964 *CnThe, FilmgC*
Lynn, Robert 1897-1969 *WhScrn 1, WhScrn 2,
    WhoHol B*
Lynn, Robert 1918- *FilmgC, IntMPA 1977*
Lynn, Sharon d1963 *MotPP, WhoHol B*
Lynn, Sharon 1904-1963 *WhScrn 1, WhScrn 2*
Lynn, Sharon 1907-1963 *ThFT*
Lynn, Sharon 1908-1963 *Film 2, TwYS*
Lynn, Sydney *Film 2*
Lynn, William H 1889-1952 *NotNAT B,
    WhScrn 1, WhScrn 2, WhoHol B*
Lynne, Carole 1918- *WhThe*
Lynne, Gillian *WhoThe 16*
Lynne, James Broom 1920- *ConDr 1973*
Lynton, Mayme *Film 1*
Lynton, Mayne 1885- *WhThe*
Lyon, Barbara *WhoHol A*
Lyon, Ben 1901- *Film 1, Film 2, FilmgC,
    MotPP, MovMk, OxFilm, TwYS, WhThe,
    WhoHol A*
Lyon, Earle 1923- *IntMPA 1977*
Lyon, Francis D 1905- *FilmgC, IntMPA 1977*
Lyon, Frank 1901-1961 *WhScrn 1, WhScrn 2,
    WhoHol B*
Lyon, Frank A *Film 2*
Lyon, John Henry Hobart d1961 *NotNAT B*
Lyon, Richard *WhoHol A*
Lyon, Sue 1946- *FilmgC, IntMPA 1977, MotPP,
    WhoHol A*
Lyon, T E d1869 *NotNAT B*
Lyon, Therese d1975 *WhScrn 2, WhoHol C*
Lyon, Wanda 1897- *Film 2, WhThe*
Lyonnet, Henry d1933 *NotNAT B*
Lyons, A Neil 1880-1940 *WhThe*
Lyons, Candy 1945-1966 *WhScrn 1, WhScrn 2,
    WhoHol B*
Lyons, Cliff Tex 1902-1974 *WhScrn 2*
Lyons, Cliff 1902-1974 *WhoHol B*
Lyons, Eddie 1886-1926 *TwYS, WhScrn 2*
Lyons, Edmund D d1906 *NotNAT B*
Lyons, Edward 1886- *Film 1, Film 2*
Lyons, Frances *Film 2*
Lyons, Frankie d1937 *WhScrn 2*
Lyons, Freckles 1909-1960 *WhScrn 1, WhScrn 2*
Lyons, Fred d1921 *WhScrn 1, WhScrn 2*
Lyons, Gene 1921-1974 *WhScrn 2, WhoHol B*
Lyons, Gretchen *WhoStg 1906, WhoStg 1908*
Lyons, Harry Agar *Film 2*
Lyons, Harry M 1879-1919 *WhScrn 2*
Lyons, James Vincent 1935- *AmSCAP 1966*
Lyons, Leonard 1906- *CelR 3*
Lyons, Richard E 1921- *IntMPA 1977*
Lyons, Robert F *WhoHol A*
Lyons, Ruth *AmSCAP 1966*
Lyons, Stuart 1928- *IntMPA 1977*
Lyric, Dora d1962 *NotNAT B*
Lytell, Bert d1954 *MotPP, WhoHol B*
Lytell, Bert 1885-1954 *MovMk, NotNAT B,*

WhScrn 1, WhScrn 2, WhThe
Lytell, Bert 1887-1954 *TwYS*
Lytell, Bert 1888-1954 *Film 1, Film 2, FilmgC*
Lytell, Jimmy 1904-1972 *AmSCAP 1966,*
  WhoHol B
Lytell, Wilfred 1892-1954 *Film 1, Film 2,*
  MotPP, NotNAT B, TwYS, WhScrn 1,
  WhScrn 2, WhoHol B
Lyton, Robert *Film 1*
Lyttelton, Edith d1948 *NotNAT B, WhThe*
Lytton, Baron 1803-1873 *McGWD*
Lytton, Lord 1803-1873 *NotNAT B*
Lytton, Doris 1893-1953 *NotNAT B, WhThe*
Lytton, Lord Edward G E L Bulwer-Lytton
  1803-1873 *OxThe*
Lytton, Henry, Jr. 1904-1965 *WhThe*
Lytton, Sir Henry Alfred 1867-1936 *NotNAT A,*
  NotNAT B, WhThe
Lytton, L Rogers 1867-1924 *Film 1, Film 2,*
  MotPP, WhScrn 2
Lytton, Ruth *WhThe*
Lyveden, Lord d1926 *NotNAT B*

M

Ma, Chih-Yuan 1260?-1321 *REnWD*
Maas, Audrey *WomWMM*
Maas, Willard *WomWMM*
Mabaouj, Najet *WomWMM*
Mabery, Mary *Film 2*
Mabley, Edward H 1906- *AmSCAP 1966,*
  BiE&WWA, NotNAT
Mabley, Jackie Moms 1897-1975 *WhScrn 2,*
  WhoHol C
Mabrook, Hossein *DcFM*
Mabuchi, Takeo 1905- *IntMPA 1977*
Mac, Baby *Film 2*
Mac, Nila *Film 1*
MacAndrews, John *Film 2*
MacArdle, Donald *Film 2*
MacArthur, Charles 1895-1956 *DcFM, FilmgC,*
  McGWD, ModWD, NotNAT A, NotNAT B,
  OxFilm, WhScrn 1, WhScrn 2, WhThe,
  WhoHol B, WorEnF
MacArthur, James 1937- *BiE&WWA, FilmgC,*
  IntMPA 1977, MotPP, WhoHol A
MacArthur, Mary 1930-1949 *NotNAT B*
Macaulay, Joseph d1967 *WhThe, WhoHol B*
Macbeth, Helen *WhThe*
MacBoyle, Darl 1880-1942 *AmSCAP 1966*
MacBride, Donald d1957 *MotPP, NotNAT B,*
  WhScrn 1, WhScrn 2
MacBride, Donald 1894-1957 *Film 1, Vers A,*
  WhoHol B
MacBride, Lux *Film 2*
MacCaffrey, George 1870-1939 *NotNAT B,*
  WhThe
MacCarthy, Sir Desmond 1877-1952 *NotNAT B,*
  OxThe, WhThe
MacCarthy, Hector 1888- *AmSCAP 1966*
Macchia, John 1932-1967 *WhScrn 1, WhScrn 2,*
  WhoHol B
MacColl, James A 1912-1956 *NotNAT B,*
  WhScrn 1, WhScrn 2, WhoHol B
MacCormack, Frank d1941 *WhoHol B*
MacCormack, Franklyn 1908-1971 *WhScrn 2,*
  WhoHol B
MacCullough, Nancy *WomWMM B*
MacCurdy, James Kyrle *WhoStg 1908*
MacDermid, James G 1875-1960 *AmSCAP 1966*
MacDermot, Galt 1928- *CelR 3, EncMT,*
  NotNAT, PIP&P, PIP&P A, WhoThe 16
MacDermot, Robert 1910-1964 *WhThe*
Macdermott, The Great 1845-1901 *OxThe*
MacDermott, G H 1845-1901 *NotNAT B*
MacDermott, John W Jack 1892-1946 *WhScrn 1,*
  WhScrn 2
MacDermott, John W Jack *see also* McDermott,
  John
MacDermott, Marc 1880-1929 *Film 2, MotPP,*
  TwYS, WhScrn 2, WhoHol B

Macdermott, Norman 1889- *WhThe*
Macdermott, Norman 1890- *OxThe*
Macdona, Charles d1946 *NotNAT B, WhThe*
MacDonagh, Donagh 1912-1968 *McGWD,*
  NotNAT B
Macdonald, Andrew d1790 *NotNAT B*
MacDonald, Ballard 1882-1935 *AmSCAP 1966,*
  NotNAT B
MacDonald, Charles *Film 2*
MacDonald, Christie 1875-1962 *EncMT,*
  NotNAT B, WhoStg 1906, WhoStg 1908
MacDonald, Christie *see also* McDonald, Christie
MacDonald, David 1904- *FilmgC*
MacDonald, Donald 1898-1959 *Film 1, Film 2,*
  NotNAT B, WhScrn 1, WhScrn 2, WhThe,
  WhoHol B
Macdonald, Dwight 1906- *CelR 3*
MacDonald, Edmund 1911-1951 *WhScrn 1,*
  WhScrn 2, WhoHol B
MacDonald, Mrs. J Farrell *Film 1*
MacDonald, J Farrell 1875-1951 *TwYS*
MacDonald, J Farrell 1875-1952 *Film 1, Film 2,*
  FilmgC, MovMk, Vers B, WhScrn 1,
  WhScrn 2, WhoHol B
MacDonald, Jack F *Film 2*
MacDonald, James Lee 1921- *AmSCAP 1966*
MacDonald, James Weatherby 1899-1962
  NotNAT B, WhScrn 1, WhScrn 2
MacDonald, Jeanette d1965 *BiE&WWA, MotPP,*
  NotNAT B, ThFT, WhoHol B
MacDonald, Jeanette 1901-1965 *CmMov, EncMT,*
  MGM
MacDonald, Jeanette 1902-1965 *FilmgC, OxFilm*
MacDonald, Jeanette 1903-1965 *BiDFlm*
MacDonald, Jeanette 1906-1965 *Film 2,*
  WhScrn 1, WhScrn 2
MacDonald, Jeanette 1907-1965 *MovMk, WhThe,*
  WorEnF
MacDonald, Joe 1906-1968 *CmMov*
MacDonald, Joseph 1906-1968 *FilmgC,*
  IntMPA 1977, WorEnF
MacDonald, Katherine 1891-1956 *Film 1*
MacDonald, Katherine 1894-1956 *Film 2, MotPP,*
  NotNAT B, TwYS, WhScrn 1, WhScrn 2,
  WhoHol B
MacDonald, Kenneth *Film 2*
MacDonald, Kenneth d1972 *WhoHol B*
Macdonald, Murray 1899- *WhoThe 16*
MacDonald, Philip *IntMPA 1977*
MacDonald, Ray *MotPP, WhScrn 1, WhScrn 2*
Macdonald, Richard 1920- *DcFM, WorEnF*
Macdonald, Ruby *AmSCAP 1966*
MacDonald, Sally *WomWMM*
Macdonald, Torbert H d1976 *NewYTET*
MacDonald, Wallace 1891- *Film 1, Film 2,*
  TwYS, WhoHol A

MacDonell, Kathlene 1890- *WhThe*
Macdonnell, Leslie A 1903- *WhThe*
MacDonough, Glen 1870-1924 *AmSCAP 1966,*
   EncMT, NewMT, NotNAT B, WhThe
MacDougall, Allan Ross 1894-1956 *WhScrn 1,*
   WhScrn 2, WhoHol B
MacDougall, Elspeth *WomWMM B*
MacDougall, Judith *WomWMM A,*
   WomWMM B
MacDougall, Ranald 1915- *FilmgC, WorEnF*
MacDougall, Robin *Film 1*
MacDougall, Roger 1910- *BiE&WWA,*
   ConDr 1977, FilmgC, NotNAT, WhoThe 16
MacDowell, Edward Alexander 1861-1908
   AmSCAP 1966
MacDowell, Melbourne 1857-1941 *WhScrn 1,*
   WhScrn 2, WhoHol B, WhoStg 1906,
   WhoStg 1908
MacDowell, William Melbourne 1857-1941
   NotNAT B
Mace, Fred 1879-1917 *Film 1, TwYS, WhScrn 2,*
   WhoHol B
Mace, Wynn *Film 2*
Macell, Jerry 1899- *AmSCAP 1966*
MacFadden, Bernarr 1868-1955 *WhScrn 2*
MacFadden, Gertrude Mickey 1900-1967
   WhScrn 1, WhScrn 2
MacFarland, Spanky 1928- *MotPP*
MacFarland, Spanky *see also* McFarland, Spanky
MacFarlane, Bruce 1910-1967 *WhScrn 1,*
   WhScrn 2, WhThe, WhoHol B
Macfarlane, Elsa 1899- *WhThe*
MacFarlane, George 1877-1932 *WhScrn 1,*
   WhScrn 2, WhoHol B
MacFarlane, George *see also* McFarlane, George
Macfarlane, Will C 1870-1945 *AmSCAP 1966*
MacFarren, George d1843 *NotNAT B*
Macfayden, Alexander 1879-1936 *AmSCAP 1966*
MacGeachey, Charles d1921 *NotNAT B*
MacGibbon, Harriet *WhoHol A*
MacGill, Moyna 1895-1975 *WhScrn 2, WhThe,*
   WhoHol C
MacGimsey, Robert *AmSCAP 1966*
MacGinnis, Niall 1913- *FilmgC, IntMPA 1977,*
   WhThe, WhoHol A
MacGowan, Kenneth 1888-1963 *FilmgC,*
   NotNAT B, OxFilm, OxThe, PIP&P,
   WhThe, WorEnF
MacGowran, Jack d1973 *WhoHol B*
MacGowran, Jack 1916-1973 *FilmgC*
MacGowran, Jack 1918-1973 *WhScrn 2, WhThe*
MacGrath, Leueen *WhoHol A*
MacGrath, Leueen 1914- *NotNAT, WhoThe 16*
MacGrath, Leueen 1919- *BiE&WWA*
MacGraw, Ali *MotPP, WhoHol A*
MacGraw, Ali 1938- *FilmgC, IntMPA 1977*
MacGraw, Ali 1939- *CelR 3, MovMk*
MacGregor, Edgar 1879-1957 *EncMT*
MacGregor, Franklyn *NatPD*
MacGregor, Harman 1878-1948 *WhScrn 1,*
   WhScrn 2
MacGregor, Irvine T 1915- *AmSCAP 1966*
MacGregor, J Chalmers 1903- *AmSCAP 1966*
MacGregor, Lee d1961 *WhoHol B*
MacGregor, Lee d1964 *WhScrn 2*
MacGregor, Malcolm *WhScrn 1, WhScrn 2*
MacGregor, Robert M 1911-1974 *BiE&WWA,*
   NotNAT B
MacGruder, Anna *Film 2*
Machado, Antonio 1875-1939 *McGWD*
Machado, Lena 1907- *AmSCAP 1966*
Machado, Manuel 1874-1947 *McGWD*
Machan, Benjamin A 1894-1966 *AmSCAP 1966*
Macharen, Mary *Film 1*

Machaty, Gustav 1898-1963 *FilmgC, MovMk*
Machaty, Gustav 1901-1963 *DcFM, OxFilm,*
   WorEnF
Machiavelli, Niccolo DiBernardo Dei 1469-1527
   CnThe, McGWD, NotNAT B, OxThe,
   PIP&P, REnWD
Machin, Alfred 1877-1929 *DcFM*
Machin, Alfred 1877-1930 *WorEnF*
Machin, Will *Film 1*
Machiz, Herbert 1923-1976 *BiE&WWA,*
   NotNAT, WhoThe 16
MacHugh, Augustin *WhThe*
MacInnes, Margo 1930- *WomWMM B*
Macintosh, Kenneth *PIP&P*
MacIntosh, Louise 1865-1933 *WhScrn 1,*
   WhScrn 2, WhoHol B
Maciste 1878-1947 *Film 1, WorEnF*
Mack, Al 1912- *AmSCAP 1966*
Mack, Andrew 1863-1931 *Film 2, NotNAT B,*
   WhScrn 1, WhScrn 2, WhThe, WhoHol B,
   WhoStg 1906, WhoStg 1908
Mack, Annie d1935 *NotNAT B*
Mack, Arthur 1877-1942 *Film 2, WhScrn 1,*
   WhScrn 2, WhoHol B
Mack, Baby *Film 2*
Mack, Bill d1961 *WhScrn 1, WhScrn 2*
Mack, Billy d1961 *WhoHol B*
Mack, Bobby *Film 1, Film 2*
Mack, C K *NatPD*
Mack, Cactus d1962 *WhoHol B*
Mack, Cecil 1883-1944 *AmSCAP 1966*
Mack, Charles 1878-1956 *WhScrn 1, WhScrn 2,*
   WhoHol B
Mack, Charles E 1887-1934 *Film 2, WhScrn 1,*
   WhScrn 2, WhoHol B
Mack, Charles Emmett 1900-1927 *Film 2, TwYS,*
   WhScrn 1, WhScrn 2, WhoHol B
Mack, Charles J d1976 *NewYTET*
Mack, Dick 1854-1920 *WhScrn 1, WhScrn 2*
Mack, E J *Film 2*
Mack, Frances 1907-1967 *WhScrn 1, WhScrn 2*
Mack, George E d1948 *NotNAT B, WhoHol B*
Mack, Gertrude d1967 *WhoHol B*
Mack, Hayward *Film 1*
Mack, Helen 1913- *Film 2, FilmgC, MotPP,*
   ThFT, WhoHol A
Mack, Hughie 1884-1927 *WhScrn 1, WhScrn 2,*
   WhoHol B
Mack, Hughie 1887-1952 *Film 1, Film 2, TwYS*
Mack, Irving 1895- *IntMPA 1977*
Mack, James Buck d1959 *WhScrn 1, WhScrn 2*
Mack, James T 1871-1948 *Film 2, WhScrn 1,*
   WhScrn 2, WhoHol B
Mack, Joe 1878-1946 *Film 2, WhoHol B*
Mack, Joseph P 1878-1946 *WhScrn 1, WhScrn 2*
Mack, Lester 1906-1972 *WhScrn 2, WhoHol B*
Mack, Marion 1905- *Film 2, TwYS*
Mack, Max 1885-1973 *WhScrn 2*
Mack, Nila d1953 *NotNAT B*
Mack, Richard A d1963 *NewYTET*
Mack, Richard R 1900- *AmSCAP 1966*
Mack, Robert 1877-1949 *Film 2, WhScrn 2*
Mack, Rose 1866-1921 *WhScrn 1, WhScrn 2*
Mack, Russell 1892-1972 *FilmgC*
Mack, Ted d1976 *NewYTET*
Mack, Tom H 1914- *AmSCAP 1966*
Mack, Wilbur 1873-1964 *Film 2, NotNAT B,*
   WhScrn 1, WhScrn 2, WhoHol B
Mack, Willard 1873-1934 *Film 1, Film 2, TwYS,*
   WhScrn 1, WhScrn 2, WhoHol B
Mack, Willard 1878-1934 *NotNAT B, WhThe*
Mack, William B 1872-1955 *Film 2, WhScrn 1,*
   WhScrn 2, WhoHol B
Mackail, Dorothy 1905- *Film 2*

Mackaill, Dorothy *MotPP*
Mackaill, Dorothy 1903- *FilmgC, ThFT, TwYS*
Mackaill, Dorothy 1904- *MovMk*
Mackaill, Dorothy 1906- *WhoHol A*
Mackathorne, George *Film 2*
Mackay, Barry 1906- *FilmgC, WhThe,*
  WhoHol A
Mackay, Charles 1785?-1857 *OxThe*
MacKay, Charles 1867-1935 *Film 2, WhScrn 1,*
  WhScrn 2, WhoHol B
Mackay, Edward J 1874-1948 *WhScrn 1,*
  WhScrn 2
Mackay, Elsie 1894- *WhThe*
Mackay, Fenton d1929 *NotNAT B*
Mackay, Frank Finley d1923 *NotNAT B*
Mackay, Fulton 1922- *WhoThe 16*
MacKay, Harper *AmSCAP 1966*
MacKay, Hugh 1907- *AmSCAP 1966*
Mackay, J L 1867- *WhThe*
Mackay, Leonard d1929 *NotNAT B*
Mackay, Patricia 1945- *NotNAT*
Mackay, Ruth *WhThe*
Mackay, W Gayer d1920 *NotNAT B*
Mackaye, Dorothy 1898-1940 *WhScrn 2,*
  WhoHol B
MacKaye, James Morrison Steele 1842-1894
  McGWD
Mackaye, James Morrison Steele 1844-1894 *OxThe*
MacKaye, Norman 1906-1968 *WhScrn 1,*
  WhScrn 2, WhoHol B
MacKaye, Percy Wallace 1875-1956 *CnMD,*
  CnThe, McGWD, ModWD, NotNAT B,
  OxThe, PIP&P, REnWD, WhThe,
  WhoStg 1908
MacKaye, Steele 1842-1894 *NotNAT A,*
  NotNAT B, PIP&P
MacKellar, Helen 1891- *BiE&WWA, NotNAT*
Mackellar, Helen 1895- *WhThe*
Macken, Jane Virginia 1912- *AmSCAP 1966*
Macken, Walter 1915-1967 *CnMD, NotNAT B,*
  WhScrn 2, WhoHol B
Mackendrick, Alexander 1912- *BiDFlm, CmMov,*
  DcFM, FilmgC, IntMPA 1977, MovMk,
  OxFilm, WorEnF
MacKenna, Kate d1957 *WhoHol B*
MacKenna, Kate 1877-1957 *WhScrn 2*
MacKenna, Kate 1878-1957 *WhScrn 1*
MacKenna, Kenneth 1899-1962 *Film 2,*
  NotNAT B, TwYS A, WhScrn 1,
  WhScrn 2, WhThe, WhoHol B
MacKenna, Kenneth *see also* McKenna, Kenneth
MacKenzie, Alex 1886-1966 *WhoHol B*
MacKenzie, Alexander 1886-1966 *WhScrn 2*
MacKenzie, Donald 1880-1972 *Film 1, Film 2,*
  WhScrn 2
MacKenzie, George 1901-1975 *WhScrn 2,*
  WhoHol C
MacKenzie, Gisele *AmSCAP 1966*
MacKenzie, John 1932- *FilmgC*
MacKenzie, Joyce *WhoHol A*
Mackenzie, Leonard C, Jr. 1915- *AmSCAP 1966*
Mackenzie, Mary 1922-1966 *WhScrn 1,*
  WhScrn 2, WhThe, WhoHol B
MacKenzie, Midge *WomWMM B*
MacKenzie, Ronald d1932 *NotNAT B*
MacKenzie, Shelagh *WomWMM*
Mackerras, Charles 1925- *IntMPA 1977*
Mackie, Bert 1893-1967 *WhScrn 1, WhScrn 2*
Mackie, Philip *ConDr 1977C*
Mackin, William 1883-1928 *WhScrn 1,*
  WhScrn 2
Mackinder, Lionel d1915 *WhThe*
Mackinlay, Jean Sterling 1882-1958 *OxThe,*
  WhThe

MacKinlay, Jean Stirling 1882-1958 *NotNAT B*
Mackintoch, Louise *Film 2*
Mackintosh, Robert 1925- *BiE&WWA, NotNAT*
Mackintosh, William 1855-1929 *NotNAT B,*
  WhThe
Mackley, Mrs. Arthur *Film 1*
Macklin, Charles 1699-1797 *NotNAT A,*
  NotNAT B
Macklin, Charles 1700?-1797 *CnThe, OxThe,*
  PIP&P
Macklin, F H d1903 *NotNAT B*
Macklin, Mrs. F H d1904 *NotNAT B*
Mackney, E W 1835-1909 *OxThe*
Mackris, Orestes 1900-1975 *WhScrn 2*
Macks, Helen *Film 2*
MacLachlan, Janet *WhoHol A*
MacLaine, Shirley 1934- *BiDFlm, CelR 3,*
  FilmgC, IntMPA 1977, MotPP, MovMk,
  OxFilm, WhoHol A, WomWMM, WorEnF
MacLane, Barton d1969 *MotPP, WhoHol B*
MacLane, Barton 1900-1969 *Film 2, FilmgC,*
  WhScrn 1, WhScrn 2
MacLane, Barton 1902-1969 *MovMk, Vers A*
MacLane, Kerry *WhoHol A*
MacLane, Mary d1929 *WhScrn 2*
MacLaren, Archibald d1826 *NotNAT B*
Maclaren, Ian 1879- *Film 2, WhThe*
MacLaren, Ivor 1904-1962 *NotNAT B,*
  WhScrn 1, WhScrn 2, WhoHol B
MacLaren, Mary 1896- *Film 1, Film 2, MotPP,*
  TwYS, WhoHol B
MacLarnie, Thomas d1931 *NotNAT B*
MacLean, Alistair 1922- *FilmgC*
MacLean, Douglas 1890-1967 *Film 1, Film 2,*
  FilmgC, MotPP, MovMk, WhScrn 1,
  WhScrn 2, WhoHol B
MacLean, Douglas 1894-1967 *TwYS*
MacLean, Ian 1894- *IntMPA 1977*
MacLean, R D 1859-1948 *NotNAT B, WhScrn 2,*
  WhThe, WhoHol B
MacLean, Rezin D 1859-1948 *WhScrn 1*
MacLean, Robert *Film 2*
MacLean, Ross 1904- *AmSCAP 1966*
MacLeish, Archibald 1892- *AmSCAP 1966,*
  BiE&WWA, CelR 3, CnMD, CnThe,
  ConDr 1977, CroCD, McGWD, ModWD,
  NotNAT, OxThe, PIP&P, WhoThe 16
MacLeish, Rod *NewYTET*
MacLennon, Andy *Film 2*
MacLeod, Angus 1874-1962 *NotNAT B*
MacLeod, E E, Jr. *Film 2*
MacLeod, Elsie *Film 1*
MacLeod, Gavin *WhoHol A*
MacLeod, Janet *Film 2*
MacLeod, Kenneth 1895-1963 *WhScrn 1,*
  WhScrn 2
Macleod, W Angus 1874-1962 *WhThe*
MacLiammoir, Micheal 1899- *BiE&WWA,*
  CnThe, McGWD, ModWD, NotNAT,
  NotNAT A, OxThe, PIP&P, WhoThe 16
MacLiammoir, Micheal 1901- *FilmgC*
MacLow, Jackson 1922- *ConDr 1977*
MacMahon, Aline 1899- *BiE&WWA, FilmgC,*
  IntMPA 1977, MotPP, MovMk, NotNAT,
  ThFT, Vers A, WhoHol A, WhoThe 16
MacMahon, Aline *see also* McMahon, Aline
MacMahon, Horace 1907-1971 *FilmgC, Vers B*
MacMahon, Horace *see also* McMahon, Horace
MacManus, Clive d1953 *NotNAT B, WhThe*
MacMaster, Anew 1895-1952 *CnThe*
MacMaster, Anew *see also* McMaster, Anew
MacMillan, Violet 1887-1953 *Film 1, NotNAT B*
MacMillian, Violet 1887-1953 *WhScrn 1,*
  WhScrn 2, WhoHol B

MacMillian, Violet *see also* McMillen, Violet
Macmullan, Charles Walden Kirkpatrick *McGWD*
MacMurray, Fred 1907- *FilmgC*
MacMurray, Fred 1908- *BiDFlm, CelR 3,*
Film 2, IntMPA 1977, MotPP, MovMk,
OxFilm, WhoHol A, WorEnF
MacNally, Leonard d1820 *NotNAT B*
Macnamara, Brinsley d1963 *NotNAT B*
Macnamara, Brinsley 1890-1963 *CnMD, McGWD,*
ModWD
Macnamara, Brinsley 1891-1963 *OxThe*
MacNaughtan, Alan 1920- *WhoThe 16*
MacNeal, F A 1867-1918 *WhScrn 2*
Macnee, Patrick 1922- *FilmgC, MotPP,*
WhoHol A
MacNeice, Louis 1907-1963 *CnMD, NotNAT B*
MacNeil, Robert *NewYTET*
Macollum, Barry 1889?-1971 *WhScrn 2*
Macollum, Barry 1899?-1971 *Film 2*
Macowan, Michael 1906- *OxThe, WhoThe 16*
Macowan, Norman 1877-1961 *FilmgC,*
NotNAT B, WhScrn 1, WhScrn 2, WhThe,
WhoHol B
MacPhail, William C *NewYTET*
MacPherson, Douglas *Film 2*
MacPherson, Harry *AmSCAP 1966*
MacPherson, Jeanie d1946 *CmMov, TwYS A,*
WhScrn 1, WhScrn 2, WhoHol B
MacPherson, Jeannie d1946 *Film 1*
MacPherson, Quinton d1940 *NotNAT B,*
WhoHol B
MacPherson, Quinton *see also* McPherson, Quinton
MacQuarrie, Albert *Film 1, Film 2*
MacQuarrie, Frank *Film 1*
MacQuarrie, George *Film 1, Film 2*
MacQuarrie, Murdoch 1878-1942 *Film 1*
MacQuarrie, Murdoch 1878-1942 *Film 2,*
TwYS A, WhScrn 1, WhScrn 2, WhoHol B
MacQueen, W J 1888-1960 *NotNAT B*
Macqueen-Pope, Walter James 1888-1960 *OxThe,*
WhThe
Macquitty, William 1905- *FilmgC, IntMPA 1977*
MacQuoid, Percy 1852-1925 *NotNAT B, WhThe*
MacRae, Arthur 1908-1962 *NotNAT B, WhThe*
Macrae, Duncan 1905-1967 *FilmgC, WhScrn 1,*
WhScrn 2, WhThe, WhoHol B
MacRae, Elizabeth *WhoHol A*
MacRae, Gordon 1921- *CmMov, Film 2, FilmgC,*
IntMPA 1977, MotPP, MovMk, WhoHol A
MacRae, Meredith *WhoHol A*
Macready, George d1973 *MotPP, WhoHol B*
Macready, George 1908-1973 *Vers A*
Macready, George 1909-1973 *FilmgC, MovMk,*
WhScrn 2
Macready, George 1912-1973 *CmMov*
MacReady, William d1829 *NotNAT B*
Macready, William Charles 1793-1873 *CnThe,*
FamA&A, NotNAT A, NotNAT B, OxThe,
PIP&P
Macrorie, Alma *WomWMM*
MacSarin, Kenneth 1912-1967 *WhScrn 1,*
WhScrn 2
Macsweeney, John *Film 2*
Macswiney, Owen *OxThe*
MacTaggart, James 1928-1974 *WhScrn 2*
Macy, Ann Sullivan *Film 1*
Macy, Bill *WhoHol A*
Macy, Carleton 1861-1946 *Film 2, NotNAT B,*
WhScrn 1, WhScrn 2, WhoHol B
Macy, Carlton *Film 1*
Macy, Cora *Film 2*
Macy, Gertrude 1904- *BiE&WWA, NotNAT*
Macy, Jack 1886-1956 *WhScrn 1, WhScrn 2,*
WhoHol B

Macy, John W, Jr. *NewYTET*
Madach, Imre 1823-1864 *McGWD, OxThe*
Madame Vestris *PIP&P*
Madame Violante *PIP&P*
Madd, Pierette *Film 2*
Madden, Cecil 1902- *WhThe*
Madden, Ciaran 1945- *WhoThe 16*
Madden, Donald 1933- *BiE&WWA, NotNAT,*
WhoThe 16
Madden, Doreen *Film 2*
Madden, Edward 1878-1952 *AmSCAP 1966*
Madden, Frank 1900-1964 *AmSCAP 1966*
Madden, Golda 1894- *Film 1, Film 2, TwYS*
Madden, Jerry *Film 2*
Madden, Peter 1910?- *FilmgC, WhoHol A*
Madden, Richard d1951 *NotNAT B*
Madden, Tom *Film 2*
Maddern, Victor 1926- *FilmgC, WhoHol A*
Maddie, Ginette *Film 2*
Maddow, Ben *DcFM, WorEnF*
Maddox, Lester 1915- *CelR 3*
Maddox, Martha *Film 2*
Maddy, Joseph Edgar 1891-1966 *AmSCAP 1966*
Madeira, Humberto 1921-1971 *WhScrn 1,*
WhScrn 2, WhoHol B
Madhusudan, Michael *REnWD*
Madison, C J d1975 *WhScrn 2, WhoHol C*
Madison, Cleo 1882-1964 *Film 1, Film 2, MotPP,*
NotNAT B, TwYS, WhoHol B, WomWMM
Madison, Cleo 1883-1964 *WhScrn 1, WhScrn 2*
Madison, Ethel *Film 1*
Madison, Guy 1922- *FilmgC, IntMPA 1977,*
MotPP, MovMk, WhoHol A
Madison, Harry 1877-1936 *WhScrn 1, WhScrn 2,*
WhoHol B
Madison, Martha *Film 2*
Madison, Nathaniel Joseph 1896- *AmSCAP 1966*
Madison, Noel N 1905?-1975 *FilmgC, Vers B,*
WhScrn 2, WhoHol C
Madison, Virginia *Film 2*
Madriguera, Enric d1973 *WhoHol B*
Madriguera, Enric 1902-1973 *WhScrn 2*
Madriguera, Enric 1904-1973 *AmSCAP 1966*
Madsen, Forrest Holger 1878-1943 *WorEnF*
Madsen, Harold *Film 2*
Maduro, Charles 1883-1947 *AmSCAP 1966*
Mae, Jimsey 1894-1968 *WhScrn 1, WhScrn 2,*
WhoHol B
Maeder, Clara Fisher 1811-1898 *NotNAT A*
Maeder, Frederick George d1891 *NotNAT B*
Maeder, Mrs. James *OxThe*
Maekelberghe, August R 1909- *AmSCAP 1966*
Maertens, Willy 1893-1967 *WhScrn 1, WhScrn 2*
Maestri, Charles J 1907- *IntMPA 1977*
Maeterlinck, Maurice 1862-1949 *CnMD, CnThe,*
McGWD, ModWD, NotNAT A, NotNAT B,
OxThe, PIP&P, REnWD, WhThe
Maetzig, Kurt 1911- *DcFM*
Maffei, Andrea 1798-1885 *OxThe*
Maffei, Scipione 1675-1755 *McGWD, OxThe*
Maflin, Alfred W 1840- *WhoStg 1908*
Magalhaes, Domingo Jose Goncalves De 1811-1882
OxThe
Maganini, Quinto 1897- *AmSCAP 1966*
Magarill, Sophie *Film 2*
Magarshack, David 1899- *BiE&WWA, NotNAT*
Magdaleno, Maurico 1906- *DcFM*
Magee, Gordon *Film 2*
Magee, Harriett 1878-1954 *WhScrn 1, WhScrn 2,*
WhoHol B
Magee, Patrick 1924- *FilmgC, NotNAT,*
WhoHol A, WhoThe 16
Magee, Ray 1897- *AmSCAP 1966*
Magee, Virginia *Film 2*

Magelis, Charles Film 2
Maggi, Luigi 1867-1946 DcFM
Maggiorani, Lamberto WhoHol A
Magidson, Herbert 1906- AmSCAP 1966
Magill, Mort 1907- IntMPA 1977
Magine, Frank 1892- AmSCAP 1966
Maginn, Bonnie WhoStg 1908
Maginn, William d1942 NotNAT B
Magnani, Anna d1973 MotPP, PIP&P,
    WhoHol B
Magnani, Anna 1907-1973 FilmgC
Magnani, Anna 1908-1973 BiDFlm, MovMk,
    WorEnF
Magnani, Anna 1909-1973 OxFilm, WhScrn 2
Magnante, Charles 1905- AmSCAP 1966
Magnes OxThe
Magness, Annabelle Film 2
Magnier, Pierre 1869- Film 2, WhThe
Magnon, Jean 1620-1662 OxThe
Magnus, Annabelle Film 2
Magnusson, Charles 1878-1948 OxFilm
Magoon, Eaton Bob, Jr. 1922- AmSCAP 1966,
    NatPD
Magrane, Thais d1957 NotNAT B
Magri, Count Primo 1849-1920 WhScrn 2
Magrill, George 1900-1952 Film 2, WhScrn 1,
    WhScrn 2, WhoHol B
Maguier, Virginia WomWMM B
Maguire, Charles J 1882-1939 WhScrn 1,
    WhScrn 2
Maguire, Edward 1867-1925 WhScrn 2
Maguire, Kathleen BiE&WWA, NotNAT,
    WhoHol A
Maguire, Tom 1869-1934 WhScrn 1, WhScrn 2,
    WhoHol B
Magyari, Imre 1894-1940 WhScrn 1, WhScrn 2
Mahalalel McGWD
Mahan, Billy 1933- WhoHol A
Mahan, Vivian L 1902-1933 WhScrn 1,
    WhScrn 2
Maharam, Joseph 1898- BiE&WWA, NotNAT
Maharis, George MotPP, PIP&P, WhoHol A
Maharis, George 1928- FilmgC
Maharis, George 1933- BiE&WWA
Maharis, George 1938- MovMk
Maharoni, George Film 1
Mahelot, Laurent 1634- NotNAT B
Maher, Wally 1908-1951 WhoHol B
Maher, Walter 1908-1951 WhScrn 1, WhScrn 2
Mahin, John Lee CmMov, IntMPA 1977
Mahin, John Lee 1902- WorEnF
Mahin, John Lee 1907- FilmgC
Mahler, Gustav 1860-1911 AmSCAP 1966
Mahon, Barry 1921- IntMPA 1977
Mahoney, Jack Francis 1882-1945 AmSCAP 1966
Mahoney, Jock 1919- FilmgC, IntMPA 1977,
    MotPP, WhoHol A
Mahoney, Will d1967 Film 2, WhoHol B
Mahoney, Will 1894-1966? WhScrn 2
Mahoney, Will 1896-1967 WhThe
Mahr, Herman Carl 1901-1964 AmSCAP 1966,
    NotNAT B
Maia, Marise Film 2
Maiatian, Barbara Film 2
Maibaum, Richard 1909- CmMov, FilmgC,
    IntMPA 1977, WorEnF
Maidman, Irving 1897- BiE&WWA
Maidment, George Joseph IntMPA 1977
Maietta, Angelo Leonard 1905- AmSCAP 1966
Maigne, Charles 1881- TwYS A
Maigne, Charles M 1879-1929 WhScrn 1,
    WhScrn 2, WhoHol B
Mailer, Norman WhoHol A
Mailer, Norman 1923- CelR 3, FilmgC, OxFilm

Mailer, Norman 1925- WorEnF
Mailes, Charles Hill 1870-1937 Film 1, Film 2,
    TwYS, WhScrn 1, WhScrn 2, WhoHol B
Maillard, Monsieur Film 2
Maillard, Henry Film 2
Mailly, Fernand Film 2
Mailman, Martin 1932- AmSCAP 1966
Main, David 1929- IntMPA 1977
Main, Laurie WhoHol A
Main, Marjorie 1890-1975 FilmgC, MGM,
    MotPP, MovMk, ThFT, Vers A, WhScrn 2,
    WhoHol C
Mainbocher 1890- BiE&WWA, NotNAT
Maine, Bruno 1896-1962 NotNAT B
Mainente, Anton Eugene 1889-1963
    AmSCAP 1966
Maines, Don 1869-1934 WhScrn 1, WhScrn 2,
    WhoHol B
Mainhall, Harry Film 1
Maintenon, Madame De 1635-1719 OxThe
Mainwaring, Daniel WorEnF
Mainwaring, Ernest 1876-1941 NotNAT B,
    WhThe
Maiorana, Victor E 1897-1964 AmSCAP 1966
Mair, George Herbert 1887-1926 NotNAT B,
    WhThe
Mairet, Jean 1604-1686 CnThe, McGWD,
    NotNAT B, OxThe, REnWD
Mais, Stuart Petre Brodie 1885- WhThe
Maison, Edna 1893-1946 Film 1, MotPP,
    WhScrn 1, WhScrn 2, WhoHol B
Maister, Al 1903- AmSCAP 1966
Maitland, Lauderdale d1929 NotNAT B, WhThe
Maitland, Lauerdale Film 2
Maitland, Marne 1920- FilmgC, WhoHol A
Maitland, Richard Film 2
Maitland, Ruth 1880-1961 WhThe, WhoHol A
Maja, Zelma Film 2
Majeroni, Mario 1870-1931 Film 2, NotNAT B,
    WhScrn 1, WhScrn 2, WhoHol B
Majilton, Charles d1931 NotNAT B
Major, Bessie WhThe
Major, Charles d1913 NotNAT B
Major, Clare Tree d1954 NotNAT B
Major, Frank A 1925- BiE&WWA, NotNAT
Major, Sam Collier d1955 WhScrn 1, WhScrn 2
Majors, Lee 1940?- FilmgC, WhoHol A
Makarenko, Daniel Film 2
Makaroff, V Film 2
Makarova, Natalia 1940- CelR 3
Makavejev, Dusan 1932- OxFilm
Makavejev, Dusan 1932- BiDFlm, WorEnF
Makeba, Miriam Zenzi AmSCAP 1966
Makeham, Eliot 1882-1956 FilmgC, NotNAT B,
    WhScrn 1, WhScrn 2, WhThe, WhoHol B
Makk, Karoly 1925- DcFM, MovMk, OxFilm
Mako 1932- NotNAT, WhoHol A
Makowska, Helen Film 2
Mala 1906-1952 WhoHol B
Mala, Ray Mala 1906-1952 WhScrn 1, WhScrn 2
Malamud, Bernard 1914- CelR 3
Malan, William 1868-1941 Film 2, WhScrn 1,
    WhScrn 2, WhoHol B
Malaparte, Curzio 1898-1957 CnMD
Malatesta, David 1943- AmSCAP 1966
Malatesta, Fred M 1889-1952 Film 1, Film 2,
    TwYS, WhScrn 1, WhScrn 2, WhoHol B
Malatesta, John Paul 1944- AmSCAP 1966
Malcolm, Marion P d1964 NotNAT B
Malcolm, Reginald 1884-1966 WhScrn 1,
    WhScrn 2
Malden, Herbert John 1882-1966 WhThe
Malden, Karl MotPP, PIP&P, WhoHol A
Malden, Karl 1913- CelR 3, FilmgC, NotNAT

Malden, Karl 1914- *BiDFlm, BiE&WWA, CmMov, IntMPA 1977, MovMk, OxFilm, WorEnF*
Maldoror, Sarah *WomWMM*
Maley, Florence Turner 1871-1962 *AmSCAP 1966*
Malick, Terence 1945- *IntMPA 1977*
Malick, Terrence 1944- *MovMk*
Malikoff, H *Film 2*
Malikoff, Nikolai *Film 2*
Malin, Don 1896- *AmSCAP 1966*
Malina, Judith 1926- *BiE&WWA, CelR 3, NotNAT, NotNAT A, PIP&P, WhoHol A, WhoThe 16*
Malinofsky, Max d1963 *NotNAT B*
Malinovskya, V S *Film 2*
Malipiero, Luigi 1901-1975 *WhScrn 2*
Malkin, Norman 1918- *AmSCAP 1966*
Mallalieu, Aubrey 1873-1948 *NotNAT B, WhThe, WhoHol B*
Mallalieu, William d1927 *NotNAT B*
Malle, Louis 1932- *BiDFlm, DcFM, FilmgC, IntMPA 1977, MovMk, OxFilm, WorEnF*
Malleson, Miles 1888-1969 *FilmgC, NotNAT B, OxThe, PIP&P, WhScrn 1, WhScrn 2, WhThe, WhoHol B*
Malleson, Miles 1889-1969 *MovMk*
Mallik, Provash 1918- *IntMPA 1977*
Mallik, Umesh 1916- *IntMPA 1977*
Mallin, Tom *ConDr 1977B*
Mallon, Bobby *Film 2*
Mallory, Boots 1913-1958 *NotNAT B, ThFT, WhoHol B*
Mallory, Burton d1962 *NotNAT B*
Mallory, Drue *WhoHol A*
Mallory, Edward *WhoHol A*
Mallory, John *WhoHol A*
Mallory, Mason 1916- *AmSCAP 1966*
Mallory, Patricia Boots 1913-1958 *MotPP, WhScrn 1, WhScrn 2*
Mallory, Rene d1931 *NotNAT B*
Mallory, Robert 1920- *AmSCAP 1966*
Mallory, Victoria *NotNAT*
Malloy, John J 1898-1968 *WhScrn 1, WhScrn 2, WhoHol B*
Malm, Linda *WomWMM B*
Malmerfelt, Sixten *Film 2*
Malneck, Matty 1904- *AmSCAP 1966*
Malo, Gina 1909-1963 *FilmgC, WhScrn 1, WhScrn 2, WhThe, WhoHol B*
Malone, Mr. *PIP&P*
Malone, Andrew E d1939 *NotNAT B*
Malone, Dorothy *MotPP*
Malone, Dorothy 1925- *BiDFlm, FilmgC, HolP 40, MovMk, WhoHol A, WorEnF*
Malone, Dorothy 1930- *IntMPA 1977*
Malone, Dudley Field 1882-1950 *WhScrn 1, WhScrn 2, WhoHol B*
Malone, Dudley Field 1931- *BiE&WWA, NotNAT*
Malone, Edmond 1741-1812 *OxThe*
Malone, Edmund 1741-1812 *NotNAT B*
Malone, Elizabeth d1955 *NotNAT B*
Malone, Florence d1956 *Film 1, WhScrn 1, WhScrn 2, WhoHol B*
Malone, J A E d1929 *NotNAT B, WhThe*
Malone, Molly 1895-1952 *Film 1, Film 2, TwYS, WhScrn 1, WhScrn 2, WhoHol B*
Malone, Nancy *WhoHol A, WomWMM B*
Malone, Pat d1963 *WhScrn 1, WhScrn 2*
Malone, Patricia 1899- *WhThe*
Malone, Pick d1962 *NotNAT B, WhScrn 2*
Malone, Ray d1970 *WhScrn 2*
Maloney, Leo D 1888-1929 *Film 1, Film 2, TwYS, TwYS A, WhScrn 1, WhScrn 2,*

WhoHol B
Malotte, Albert 1895-1964 *AmSCAP 1966*
Malraux, Andre 1901- *CnMD, DcFM, OxFilm, WorEnF*
Maltby, Alfred d1901 *NotNAT B*
Maltby, H F 1880-1963 *FilmgC, WhoHol B*
Maltby, Henry Francis 1880-1963 *WhScrn 1, WhScrn 2, WhThe*
Maltby, Richard E 1914- *AmSCAP 1966*
Maltby, Richard E, Jr. 1937- *AmSCAP 1966*
Maltin, Bernard 1907-1952 *AmSCAP 1966*
Malton, Felicitas *Film 2*
Maltox, Martha *Film 2*
Maltz, Albert 1908- *BiE&WWA, CnMD, ConDr 1977, DcFM, FilmgC, IntMPA 1977, ModWD, NotNAT*
Malyon, Eily 1879-1961 *WhScrn 2, WhoHol B*
Mamakos, Peter *WhoHol A*
Mamet, David *NatPD*
Mamo, John *WhoHol A*
Mamoulian, Rouben 1896- *WorEnF*
Mamoulian, Rouben 1897- *BiE&WWA, CmMov, FilmgC, IntMPA 1977, NotNAT*
Mamoulian, Rouben 1898- *BiDFlm, DcFM, EncMT, MovMk, OxFilm, WhThe*
Mamporia, I *Film 2*
Mamrick, Burwell *Film 1*
Man, Christopher *WhoHol A*
Man, Ray 1890- *WorEnF*
Man O' War 1917-1947 *Film 2*
Mana-Zucca, Mademoiselle 1894- *AmSCAP 1966*
Manaois, Joe 1903- *AmSCAP 1966*
Manasse, George 1938- *IntMPA 1977*
Manby, C R 1920- *IntMPA 1977*
Mance, Gina *Film 2*
Manchester, Joe 1932- *NatPD*
Manchester, William 1922- *CelR 3*
Mancini, Albert 1899- *AmSCAP 1966*
Mancini, Henry 1922- *CmMov, IntMPA 1977, OxFilm*
Mancini, Henry 1924- *AmSCAP 1966, CelR 3, FilmgC, WorEnF*
Mancini, Ric *WhoHol A*
Mandel, Frances Wakefield 1891-1943 *WhScrn 1, WhScrn 2, WhoHol B*
Mandel, Frank 1884-1958 *EncMT, NotNAT B, WhThe*
Mandel, Harry *IntMPA 1977*
Mandel, John Alfred 1925- *AmSCAP 1966*
Mandel, Loring 1928- *BiE&WWA, NewYTET, NotNAT*
Mandel, Mike d1963 *NotNAT B*
Mandell, Abe *IntMPA 1977*
Mandell, Israel d1962 *NotNAT B*
Mander, Miles 1888-1946 *Film 1, Film 2, FilmgC, Vers A, WhScrn 1, WhScrn 2, WhoHol B*
Mander, Miles 1889-1946 *MovMk*
Mander, Theodore *Film 2*
Mandville, William C 1867-1917 *WhScrn 2*
Mandy, Jerry 1893-1945 *Film 2, WhScrn 1, WhScrn 2, WhoHol B*
Manes, Gina *Film 2*
Manetti, Lido *Film 2*
Maney, Richard 1891-1968 *NotNAT B*
Maney, Richard 1892-1968 *NotNAT A*
Manfredi, Muzio 1535-1607 *McGWD*
Manfredi, Nino 1921- *WhoHol A, WorEnF*
Mangano, Silvana 1930- *BiDFlm, FilmgC, IntMPA 1977, MotPP, OxFilm, WorEnF*
Mangano, Silvano *WhoHol A*
Manger, Shelia *WomWMM B*
Manges, Kenny 1913- *AmSCAP 1966*
Mangini, Cecilia *WomWMM*

Mangolte, Babette *WomWMM B*
Manheim, Mannie *IntMPA 1977*
Manings, Allan *NewYTET*
Manion, Mary E 1907- *AmSCAP 1966*
Manjean, Teddy 1901-1964 *WhScrn 1, WhScrn 2*
Mank, Chaw 1902- *AmSCAP 1966*
Mankiewicz, Don M 1922- *FilmgC, IntMPA 1977*
Mankiewicz, Herman 1898-1953 *OxFilm*
Mankiewicz, Herman J 1897-1953 *DcFM, FilmgC, NotNAT B, WorEnF*
Mankiewicz, Joseph Leo 1909- *BiDFlm, CelR 3, CmMov, ConDr 1977A, DcFM, FilmgC, IntMPA 1977, MovMk, OxFilm, WorEnF*
Mankowitz, Wolf 1924- *ConDr 1977, FilmgC, IntMPA 1977, NotNAT, WhoThe 16*
Manley, Charles Daddy 1830-1916 *WhScrn 2*
Manley, Dave 1883-1943 *WhScrn 1, WhScrn 2, WhoHol B*
Manley, Marie *Film 1*
Manley, Mary d1724 *NotNAT B*
Mann, Aaron 1899- *AmSCAP 1966*
Mann, Abby 1927- *FilmgC, IntMPA 1977, NewYTET*
Mann, Alice *Film 1, Film 2*
Mann, Anthony 1906-1967 *BiDFlm, CmMov, DcFM, FilmgC, OxFilm, WorEnF*
Mann, Anthony 1907-1967 *CmMov*
Mann, Billy d1974 *WhScrn 2*
Mann, Charlton 1876-1958 *NotNAT B, WhThe*
Mann, Christopher 1903- *WhThe*
Mann, Daniel 1912- *BiDFlm, BiE&WWA, DcFM, FilmgC, IntMPA 1977, MovMk, NotNAT, OxFilm, WorEnF*
Mann, David 1916- *AmSCAP 1966*
Mann, Delbert 1920- *BiDFlm, DcFM, Film 2, FilmgC, IntMPA 1977, MovMk, NewYTET, NotNAT, OxFilm, WorEnF*
Mann, Edward 1924- *NotNAT*
Mann, Frances *Film 2*
Mann, Frankie *Film 1, Film 2*
Mann, Hank 1887-1971 *FilmgC, WhScrn 1, WhScrn 2, WhoHol B*
Mann, Hank 1888-1971 *Film 1, Film 2, TwYS*
Mann, Harry *Film 1, Film 2*
Mann, Heinrich 1871-1950 *ModWD*
Mann, Helen *Film 2*
Mann, Herbie 1930- *AmSCAP 1966*
Mann, Howard *WhoHol A*
Mann, Jerome 1910- *AmSCAP 1966*
Mann, John R 1928- *AmSCAP 1966*
Mann, Kal 1917- *AmSCAP 1966*
Mann, Larry D *WhoHol A*
Mann, Louis 1865-1931 *Film 2, NotNAT B, WhScrn 1, WhScrn 2, WhThe, WhoHol B, WhoStg 1906, WhoStg 1908*
Mann, Margaret 1868-1941 *Film 1, Film 2, TwYS, WhScrn 2*
Mann, Ned H 1893-1967 *FilmgC, WhScrn 1, WhScrn 2*
Mann, Paul 1910- *AmSCAP 1966*
Mann, Paul 1915- *BiE&WWA, NotNAT, WhoHol A*
Mann, Peggy *AmSCAP 1966*
Mann, Ralph 1922- *BiE&WWA*
Mann, Robert E 1902- *AmSCAP 1966*
Mann, Stanley 1884-1953 *WhScrn 1, WhScrn 2, WhoHol B*
Mann, Sy 1920- *AmSCAP 1966*
Mann, Ted *IntMPA 1977, PIP&P*
Mann, Theodore 1924- *BiE&WWA, NotNAT, WhoThe 16*
Manne, Shelly 1920- *AmSCAP 1966, WhoHol A*
Mannel, Olga *Film 2*
Manner, Eeva-Liisa 1921- *CroCD*

Mannering, Dore Lewin 1879-1932 *NotNAT B, WhThe*
Mannering, Lewin 1879-1932 *Film 2, WhScrn 1, WhScrn 2*
Mannering, Mary 1876-1953 *FamA&A, NotNAT B, WhThe, WhoStg 1906, WhoStg 1908*
Mannering, Moya 1888- *WhThe*
Manners, David *MotPP*
Manners, David 1900- *Film 2, WhoHol A*
Manners, David 1901- *FilmgC, MovMk*
Manners, David 1902- *HolP 30*
Manners, David 1905- *WhThe*
Manners, Lady Diana *Film 1, Film 2*
Manners, Dorothy *CelR 3*
Manners, Dudley 1894- *AmSCAP 1966*
Manners, Jayne *BiE&WWA*
Manners, John *Film 2*
Manners, John Hartley 1870-1928 *ModWD, NotNAT B, OxThe, WhThe*
Manners, Laurette Taylor 1884-1946 *OxThe*
Manners, Sheila *WhoHol A*
Manners, Zeke 1911- *AmSCAP 1966*
Mannes, Florence V 1896-1964 *WhScrn 1, WhScrn 2*
Mannes, Leopold Damrosch d1964 *NotNAT B*
Mannes, Marya 1904- *CelR 3*
Manney, Charles Fonteyn 1872-1951 *AmSCAP 1966*
Mannheim, Lucie 1905- *Film 2, FilmgC, WhThe, WhoHol A*
Mannheimer, Albert, Jr. *IntMPA 1977*
Manning, Aileen *Film 2*
Manning, Aileen d1945 *WhoHol B*
Manning, Aileen 1886-1946 *WhScrn 1, WhScrn 2*
Manning, Ambrose d1940 *Film 2, NotNAT B, WhThe*
Manning, Dick 1912- *AmSCAP 1966*
Manning, Gordon *NewYTET*
Manning, Hallie *Film 2*
Manning, Hope *WhoHol A*
Manning, Hugh Gardner 1920- *WhoThe 16*
Manning, Irene *MotPP*
Manning, Irene 1916- *WhoHol A*
Manning, Irene 1917- *FilmgC, WhThe*
Manning, Irene 1918- *BiE&WWA, NotNAT*
Manning, Jack 1916- *BiE&WWA, Film 2, NotNAT, WhoHol A*
Manning, Joseph d1946 *Film 1, WhScrn 1, WhScrn 2, WhoHol B*
Manning, Kathleen Lockhart 1890-1951 *AmSCAP 1966*
Manning, Laura 1926- *AmSCAP 1966*
Manning, Mary *PIP&P*
Manning, Mary Lee d1937 *WhScrn 1, WhScrn 2*
Manning, Mildred *Film 1, Film 2, MotPP*
Manning, Otis d1963 *NotNAT B*
Manning, Phillipp *Film 2*
Manning, Richard 1914-1954 *AmSCAP 1966*
Manning, Tom 1880-1936 *WhScrn 1, WhScrn 2, WhoHol B*
Mannion, Moira d1964 *NotNAT B*
Manno, Tony 1912- *AmSCAP 1966*
Mannock, Patrick L 1887- *WhThe*
Manny, Charles d1962 *NotNAT B*
Manola, Marion d1914 *NotNAT B*
Manon, Marcia *Film 1, Film 2*
Manone, Joseph 1900- *AmSCAP 1966*
Manoogian, Betzi *WomWMM*
Manor, Chris *WhoHol A*
Mansarova, Aida *WomWMM*
Mansfield, Alfred F d1938 *NotNAT B*
Mansfield, Alice d1938 *NotNAT B, WhThe*
Mansfield, Beatrice Cameron 1868-1940 *OxThe*

Mansfield, Duncan Film 2
Mansfield, Irving NewYTET
Mansfield, Jayne d1967 MotPP, WhoHol B
Mansfield, Jayne 1932-1967 FilmgC, OxFilm,
    WhScrn 1, WhScrn 2
Mansfield, Jayne 1933-1967 MovMk
Mansfield, Jayne 1934-1967 BiDFlm, WorEnF
Mansfield, John 1919-1956 WhScrn 1, WhScrn 2,
    WhoHol B
Mansfield, Marie Moss AmSCAP 1966
Mansfield, Martha d1923 MotPP, WhoHol B
Mansfield, Martha 1899-1923 Film 1, Film 2,
    TwYS
Mansfield, Martha 1900-1923 WhScrn 1,
    WhScrn 2
Mansfield, Mike 1903- CelR 3
Mansfield, Portia 1887- BiE&WWA, NotNAT
Mansfield, Rankin d1969 WhScrn 2
Mansfield, Richard 1854-1907 FamA&A,
    NotNAT B, OxThe, PIP&P
Mansfield, Richard 1857-1907 CnThe,
    NotNAT A, WhoStg 1906, WhoStg 1908
Manso, Juanita 1873-1957 WhScrn 1, WhScrn 2
Manson, Alan WhoHol A
Manson, Arthur 1928- IntMPA 1977
Manson, Eddy Lawrence 1919- AmSCAP 1966
Manson, Isabel Merson 1884-1952 WhScrn 1,
    WhScrn 2
Manson, Maurice WhoHol A
Manstadt, Margit Film 2
Mantee, Paul WhoHol A
Mantell, Bruce d1933 NotNAT B
Mantell, Joe WhoHol A
Mantell, Marianne 1929- BiE&WWA
Mantell, Robert Bruce 1854-1928 FamA&A,
    Film 1, Film 2, NotNAT A, NotNAT B,
    OxThe, WhScrn 1, WhScrn 2, WhThe,
    WhoHol B, WhoStg 1906, WhoStg 1908
Mantia, Joe 1914- AmSCAP 1966
Mantle, Burns 1873-1948 WhThe
Mantle, Robert Burns 1873-1948 NotNAT B,
    OxThe
Mantley, John NewYTET
Mantovano, Publio Filippo McGWD
Mantz, Paul 1904-1965 WhScrn 1, WhScrn 2,
    WhoHol B
Mantzius, Karl d1921 NotNAT B
Manuel, Niklas 1484-1530 OxThe
Manulis, Martin 1915- IntMPA 1977, NewYTET
Manuppelli, Antonio 1892- AmSCAP 1966
Manus, Jack 1909- AmSCAP 1966
Manuti, Alfred Joseph 1909- BiE&WWA
Manvell, Roger 1909- FilmgC, IntMPA 1977,
    OxFilm
Manx, Kate 1930-1964 WhScrn 1, WhScrn 2,
    WhoHol B
Manza, Ralph WhoHol A
Manzine, Italia Almirante Film 1
Manzini, Giovanni OxThe
Manzoni, Alessandro 1785-1873 McGWD,
    NotNAT B, OxThe
Manzotti, Luigi d1905 NotNAT B
Mapes, Victor 1870-1943 NotNAT B, WhThe,
    WhoStg 1906, WhoStg 1908
Maple, Audrey 1899-1971 WhScrn 1, WhScrn 2,
    WhoHol B
Mara, Adele 1923- FilmgC, IntMPA 1977,
    MotPP, WhoHol A
Mara, Kya Film 2
Mara, Wellington 1916- CelR 3
Marais, Jean 1913- BiDFlm, FilmgC,
    IntMPA 1977, MotPP, MovMk, OxFilm,
    WhoHol A, WorEnF
Marais, Josef 1905- AmSCAP 1966

Marano, Charles d1964 NotNAT B
Marasco, Robert 1936- WhoThe 16
Marasco, Robert 1937- NotNAT
Maratini, Rosita Film 2
Maravan, Lila d1950 NotNAT B, WhThe
Maravich, Pete 1948- CelR 3
Marba, Fred Film 2
Marba, Joseph Film 1, Film 2
Marberg, Lili d1962 NotNAT B
Marble, Dan 1810-1849 FamA&A
Marble, Danforth 1810-1849 NotNAT A,
    NotNAT B, OxThe
Marble, Emma d1930 NotNAT B
Marble, John 1844-1919 WhScrn 2
Marble, Mary 1876- WhoStg 1908
Marburgh, Bertram 1875-1956 Film 1, Film 2,
    WhScrn 2
Marbury, Elisabeth 1856-1933 NotNAT A,
    NotNAT B
Marbury, Elizabeth 1856-1933 OxThe
Marc-Michel 1812-1868 NotNAT B
Marceau, Emilie Film 1
Marceau, Felicien 1913- BiE&WWA, CnMD,
    McGWD, ModWD, NotNAT
Marceau, Marcel 1923- BiE&WWA, NotNAT,
    OxThe, WhoHol A, WorEnF
Marcel, Gabriel Honore 1889-1964 CnMD,
    McGWD, ModWD
Marcella, Marco d1962 NotNAT B
Marcelle, Dancer Film 2
Marcelle-Maurette 1903- BiE&WWA
Marcelli, Nino 1892- AmSCAP 1966
Marcellus, George W d1921 NotNAT B
March, Alex 1920- IntMPA 1977, NewYTET
March, Elspeth WhoHol A, WhoThe 16
March, Eve d1974 WhScrn 2, WhoHol B
March, Frederic 1897-1975 CnThe, Film 2,
    PIP&P
March, Fredric 1897-1975 BiDFlm, BiE&WWA,
    CelR 3, FamA&A, FilmgC, MotPP,
    MovMk, NotNAT B, OxFilm, WhScrn 2,
    WhThe, WhoHol C, WorEnF
March, Hal 1920-1970 BiE&WWA, MotPP,
    NotNAT B, WhScrn 1, WhScrn 2,
    WhoHol B
March, Iris d1966 WhScrn 2
March, Lori WhoHol A
March, Myrna Fox 1935- AmSCAP 1966
March, Nadine 1898-1944 NotNAT B, WhThe,
    WhoHol B
Marchal, Arlette Film 2
Marchand, Colette WhoHol A
Marchand, Corinne FilmgC, WhoHol A
Marchand, Henri 1898-1959 FilmgC
Marchand, Leopold 1891-1952 McGWD,
    NotNAT B
Marchand, Nancy 1928- BiE&WWA, NotNAT,
    WhoHol A, WhoThe 16
Marchant, Frank d1878 NotNAT B
Marchant, Jay TwYS A
Marchant, William 1923- BiE&WWA
Marchat, Jean 1902-1966 WhScrn 1, WhScrn 2,
    WhoHol B
Marchese, Andrew L 1922- AmSCAP 1966
Marchese, Hector D 1901- AmSCAP 1966
Marchfield, Rudy 1907- AmSCAP 1966
Marciano, Rocky 1923-1969 WhScrn 2
Marcin, Max 1879-1948 NotNAT B, WhThe
Marco, Sano 1898- AmSCAP 1966
Marcoux, Vanni Film 2
Marcucci, Robert 1930- AmSCAP 1966
Marcus, Ben D 1911- IntMPA 1977
Marcus, Frank 1928- CnThe, ConDr 1977,
    CroCD, McGWD, WhoThe 16

Marcus, James A 1868-1937 *Film 1, Film 2, WhScrn 1, WhScrn 2, WhoHol B*
Marcus, Joyce B 1921- *AmSCAP 1966*
Marcus, Louis 1936- *IntMPA 1977*
Marcus, Sol 1912- *AmSCAP 1966*
Marcus, Stanley 1905- *CelR 3*
Marcuse, Herbert 1898- *CelR 3*
Marcuse, Theodore 1920-1967 *FilmgC, WhScrn 1, WhScrn 2, WhoHol B*
Marczakowi, Marta *WomWMM*
Marden, Adrienne *WhoHol A*
Marden, Michael *IntMPA 1977*
Mardijanian, Aurora *Film 1*
Mare Island Navy Band *Film 2*
Marechal, Judith Rutherford 1937- *BiE&WWA, NotNAT*
Marena, Emma *Film 2*
Marenco, Carlo 1800-1846 *McGWD*
Marenstein, Harold 1916- *IntMPA 1977*
Mares, Paul Joseph 1900-1949 *AmSCAP 1966*
Maresca, Ernest 1938- *AmSCAP 1966*
Maretini, Rosita *Film 2*
Marey, Etienne-Jules 1830-1904 *DcFM, OxFilm, WorEnF*
Marfield, Dwight *WhoHol A*
Margaretta D'Arcy *CnThe*
Margaretten, William J 1930- *AmSCAP 1966*
Margarill, Dofie *Film 2*
Margaro, Polli *WhoHol A*
Margelis, Charles *Film 2*
Margetson, Arthur 1897-1951 *EncMT, FilmgC, NotNAT B, WhScrn 1, WhScrn 2, WhThe, WhoHol B*
Margie, Baby *Film 2*
Margo *MotPP, WhThe*
Margo 1917- *ThFT*
Margo 1918- *FilmgC, IntMPA 1977, MovMk, WhoHol A*
Margo 1920- *BiE&WWA, NotNAT*
Margo, George *WhoHol A*
Margolin, Janet 1943- *FilmgC, MotPP, WhoHol A*
Margolin, Stuart *WhoHol A*
Margolis, Charles 1874-1926 *WhScrn 1, WhScrn 2, WhoHol B*
Margolis, Henry 1909- *BiE&WWA, NotNAT*
Margraf, Gustav B 1915- *IntMPA 1977*
Margueritte, Victor 1866-1942 *NotNAT B, WhThe*
Margulies, David 1937- *NotNAT*
Margulies, Irwin 1907- *IntMPA 1977*
Margulies, Stan 1920- *IntMPA 1977*
Margulies, Virginia M 1916-1969 *WhScrn 1, WhScrn 2, WhoHol B*
Margulis, Charles 1903-1967 *WhScrn 1, WhScrn 2*
Mari, Joseph *Film 2*
Marian, Ferdinand 1902-1946 *WhScrn 2*
Mariani, Dacia *WomWMM*
Mariani-Zampieri, Teresina 1871- *WhThe*
Mariano, Charles H 1923- *AmSCAP 1966*
Mariano, Luis 1920-1970 *WhScrn 2, WhoHol B*
Mariassy, Felix 1919-1975 *DcFM, OxFilm*
Maricle, Leona 1905- *BiE&WWA, NotNAT, WhoHol A*
Maricle, Marijane *WhoHol A*
Marielle, Jean-Pierre *WhoHol A*
Marievsky, Josef *Film 2*
Marihugh, Tammy *WhoHol A*
Marin, Edwin L 1901-1951 *FilmgC*
Marin, Jacques *WhoHol A*
Marin, Paul *WhoHol A*
Marinelli, H B 1864-1924 *NotNAT B*
Marinelli, Karl 1744-1803 *OxThe*

Marinetti, Filippo Tommaso 1876-1944 *CnMD, McGWD, ModWD*
Marino, Albert Ralph 1911- *AmSCAP 1966*
Marino, Sev F 1915- *AmSCAP 1966*
Marinoff, Fania 1890-1971 *BiE&WWA, Film 1, NotNAT B, WhScrn 2, WhThe, WhoHol B*
Marinoff, Faria 1890-1971 *WhScrn 1*
Marinski, Sophie 1917- *AmSCAP 1966*
Mario, Emilio *WhThe*
Marion, Dave d1934 *NotNAT B*
Marion, Don 1917- *Film 2*
Marion, Edna 1908-1957 *Film 2, TwYS, WhScrn 1, WhScrn 2, WhoHol B*
Marion, F *Film 1*
Marion, Frances 1887-1973 *Film 2*
Marion, Frances 1888-1973 *DcFM, Film 1, FilmgC, TwYS A, WhScrn 2, WomWMM*
Marion, Frank *Film 2*
Marion, George F 1860-1945 *Film 1, Film 2, NotNAT B, TwYS, WhScrn 1, WhScrn 2, WhoHol B*
Marion, George F, Jr. 1899-1968 *AmSCAP 1966, BiE&WWA, NotNAT B, WhThe*
Marion, Joan 1908-1945 *WhThe*
Marion, Oscar *Film 2*
Marion, Paul *WhoHol A*
Marion, Sid 1900-1965 *WhScrn 1, WhScrn 2, WhoHol B*
Marion, William 1878-1957 *Film 2, WhScrn 2*
Marion-Crawford, Howard 1914-1969 *FilmgC, WhScrn 2, WhoHol B*
Mariotti, Frederick *Film 2*
Maris, Livia *Film 2*
Maris, Mona 1903- *Film 2, FilmgC, MotPP, MovMk, WhoHol A*
Maris, Roger *WhoHol A*
Marischka, Ernst 1893- *DcFM*
Marisol 1930- *CelR 3*
Maritza, Sari 1910- *ThFT*
Marivaux, Pierre Carlet DeChamblain De 1688-1763 *CnThe, McGWD, NotNAT B, OxThe, PIP&P, REnWD*
Mark, Michael 1889-1975 *WhScrn 2, WhoHol C*
Mark, Ottalie *AmSCAP 1966*
Mark, Phyllis *WomWMM B*
Markby, Robert Brenner d1908 *NotNAT B*
Markell, Robert *NewYTET*
Marken, Jane 1895- *FilmgC, WhoHol A*
Marker, Chris 1921- *BiDFlm, DcFM, FilmgC, OxFilm, WorEnF*
Markes, Larry 1921- *AmSCAP 1966*
Markey, Enid *BiE&WWA, MotPP, WhoThe 16*
Markey, Enid 1895- *Film 1, TwYS*
Markey, Enid 1896- *WhoHol A*
Markey, Enid 1902?- *NotNAT*
Markey, Melinda *WhoHol A*
Markham, David 1913- *WhoThe 16*
Markham, Monte 1935- *FilmgC, IntMPA 1977, WhoHol A*
Markham, Pauline d1919 *NotNAT B*
Markish, Peretz 1895-1955 *OxThe*
Markle, Fletcher 1921- *FilmgC, IntMPA 1977, NewYTET*
Markopoulos, Gregory J 1928- *OxFilm, WorEnF*
Markova, Alicia 1910- *WhThe*
Markowitz, Richard 1926- *AmSCAP 1966*
Marks, Albert A, Jr. *NewYTET*
Marks, Alfred 1921- *FilmgC, IntMPA 1977, WhoHol A, WhoThe 16*
Marks, Arthur 1927- *IntMPA 1977*
Marks, Charles B 1890- *AmSCAP 1966*
Marks, Emmaretta *PIP&P*
Marks, Franklyn 1911- *AmSCAP 1966*
Marks, Gerald 1900- *AmSCAP 1966*

Marks, Guy *WhoHol A*
Marks, Herbert E 1902- *BiE&WWA, NotNAT*
Marks, Joe E 1891-1973 *WhScrn 2, WhoHol B*
Marks, John D 1909- *AmSCAP 1966*
Marks, Josephine Preston Peabody d1922
  NotNAT B
Marks, Sidney d1974 *WhoHol B*
Marks, Walter 1934- *AmSCAP 1966*
Marks, Willis *Film 1, Film 2*
Markson, Ben *IntMPA 1977*
Markstein, Mrs. *Film 2*
Marlborough, Helen *Film 1*
Marlborough, Leah d1954 *NotNAT B*
Marle, Arnold 1888-1970 *WhScrn 1, WhScrn 2,*
  WhoHol B
Marley, J Peverell 1899-1964 *FilmgC*
Marley, J Peverell 1901-1964 *CmMov,*
  IntMPA 1977, WorEnF
Marley, John 1916- *FilmgC, WhoHol A*
Marlin, Max *BiE&WWA*
Marlo, Mary 1898-1960 *WhScrn 1, WhScrn 2,*
  WhoHol B
Marlor, Clark S 1922- *NotNAT*
Marlow, George d1939 *NotNAT B*
Marlow, Harry d1957 *NotNAT B*
Marlow, Lucy 1932- *IntMPA 1977, MotPP*
Marlow, Ric 1925- *AmSCAP 1966*
Marlow, Tony *Film 2*
Marlowe, Alan 1935-1975 *WhScrn 2*
Marlowe, Alona *Film 2*
Marlowe, Anthony 1910-1962 *WhScrn 1,*
  WhScrn 2, WhoHol A, WhoHol B
Marlowe, Anthony 1913- *WhoThe 16*
Marlowe, Charles *WhThe*
Marlowe, Christopher 1564-1593 *CnThe, McGWD,*
  NotNAT A, NotNAT B, OxThe, PIP&P,
  REnWD
Marlowe, Don Porky *WhoHol A*
Marlowe, Frank 1904-1964 *NotNAT B,*
  WhScrn 1, WhScrn 2, WhoHol B
Marlowe, Hugh *IntMPA 1977*
Marlowe, Hugh 1911- *BiE&WWA, NotNAT,*
  WhoHol A, WhoThe 16
Marlowe, Hugh 1914- *FilmgC, MovMk*
Marlowe, James *Film 2*
Marlowe, Jerry 1913- *AmSCAP 1966*
Marlowe, Joan 1920- *BiE&WWA, NotNAT*
Marlowe, Julia 1865-1950 *NotNAT A,*
  WhoStg 1906, WhoStg 1908
Marlowe, Julia 1866-1950 *FamA&A, NotNAT B,*
  OxThe, WhThe
Marlowe, Julia 1866-1953 *PIP&P*
Marlowe, June 1903- *WhoHol A*
Marlowe, June 1907- *Film 2, TwYS*
Marlowe, Louis J *IntMPA 1977*
Marlowe, Marilyn 1927-1975 *WhScrn 2,*
  WhoHol C
Marlowe, Marion 1930- *BiE&WWA*
Marlowe, Nora *WhoHol A*
Marlowe, Scott *WhoHol A*
Marly, Florence 1918- *FilmgC, IntMPA 1977,*
  WhoHol A
Marmelstein, Linda *WomWMM B*
Marmer, Lea 1918-1974 *WhScrn 2*
Marmion, Shackerley d1639 *NotNAT B*
Marmont, Patricia *WhoHol A*
Marmont, Percy 1883- *Film 1, Film 2, FilmgC,*
  MovMk, TwYS, WhThe, WhoHol A
Marmontel, Jean-Francois 1723-1799 *OxThe*
Marner, Carole Satrina *WomWMM A,*
  WomWMM B
Marney, Jacques *Film 2*
Marokoff, M *Film 2*
Maross, Joe *WhoHol A*

Marot, Gaston d1916 *NotNAT B, WhThe*
Marowitz, Charles 1934- *WhoThe 16*
Marquand, Christian 1927- *FilmgC, WhoHol A,*
  WorEnF
Marquand, John P 1893-1960 *FilmgC*
Marquand, Tina *WhoHol A*
Marques, Maria Elena *WhoHol A*
Marques, Regina *WomWMM B*
Marques, Rene 1919- *CnThe, CroCD, ModWD,*
  REnWD
Marquet, Mary 1895- *WhThe*
Marquina, Eduardo 1879-1946 *McGWD*
Marquis, Don 1878-1937 *NotNAT A, WhThe*
Marquis, Donald Robert Perry 1878-1937
  NotNAT B
Marquis, Marjorie Vonnegut d1936 *NotNAT B*
Marr, Edward *WhoHol A*
Marr, Henry *Film 2*
Marr, Paula *WhThe*
Marr, Sally *WhoHol A*
Marr, William 1897-1960 *WhScrn 1, WhScrn 2,*
  WhoHol B
Marre, Albert 1925- *BiE&WWA, EncMT,*
  NotNAT, WhoThe 16
Marriott, Alice d1900 *NotNAT B*
Marriott, Charles 1859-1917 *WhScrn 2*
Marriott, G M d1940 *NotNAT B*
Marriott, John *WhoHol A*
Marriott, Moore 1885-1949 *Film 2, FilmgC,*
  NotNAT B, WhScrn 1, WhScrn 2,
  WhoHol B
Marriott, Peter 1921- *IntMPA 1977*
Marriott, Raymond Bowler 1911- *WhoThe 16*
Marriott, Sandee 1899-1962 *WhScrn 2*
Marriott, Sandee 1902-1962 *WhScrn 1,*
  WhoHol B
Marriott-Watson, Nan 1899- *WhThe*
Marroney, Peter R 1913- *BiE&WWA, NotNAT*
Marryat, Florence 1837-1899 *NotNAT B*
Marryat, Florence 1838-1899 *PIP&P*
Marryott, Ralph E 1908- *AmSCAP 1966*
Mars, Mademoiselle 1779-1847 *NotNAT B,*
  OxThe
Mars, Anne Francoise Hippolyte 1779-1847 *CnThe*
Mars, Antony 1861-1915 *NotNAT B*
Mars, Kenneth *WhoHol A*
Mars, Leo *WhoStg 1906, WhoStg 1908*
Mars, Marjorie 1903- *WhThe*
Mars, Severin d1921 *Film 2, NotNAT B*
Marsac, Maurice *WhoHol A*
Marsala, Joe 1907- *AmSCAP 1966*
Marsden, Betty 1919- *WhoHol A, WhoThe 16*
Marsden, Mary *WhScrn 1, WhScrn 2*
Marsh, Alexander d1947 *NotNAT B*
Marsh, Betty *Film 1*
Marsh, Carol 1926- *FilmgC, WhoHol A*
Marsh, Charles Howard 1885-1956 *AmSCAP 1966*
Marsh, Charles L d1953 *WhScrn 1, WhScrn 2,*
  WhoHol B
Marsh, Della d1973 *WhScrn 2*
Marsh, Garry 1902- *FilmgC, WhThe,*
  WhoHol A
Marsh, Gene *Film 1*
Marsh, Howard d1969 *EncMT*
Marsh, Jean *WhoHol A*
Marsh, Joan 1913- *MovMk, ThFT, WhoHol A*
Marsh, Leo A d1936 *NotNAT B*
Marsh, Linda *WhoHol A*
Marsh, Mae 1893-1968 *TwYS*
Marsh, Mae 1895-1968 *BiDFlm, Film 1, Film 2,*
  FilmgC, MotPP, MovMk, OxFilm, ThFT,
  WhScrn 1, WhScrn 2, WhoHol B, WorEnF
Marsh, Margaret *Film 1*
Marsh, Marguerite 1892-1925 *Film 1, Film 2,*

TwYS, WhScrn 1, WhScrn 2, WhoHol B
Marsh, Marian 1913- MovMk, ThFT,
WhoHol A
Marsh, Marion 1913- FilmgC
Marsh, Mary WomWMM
Marsh, Mildred Film 2
Marsh, Myra 1894-1964 WhScrn 2
Marsh, Risley Halsey 1927-1965 WhScrn 1,
WhScrn 2
Marshak, Samuel d1964 NotNAT B
Marshak, Samuil Yakovlevich 1887-1964 ModWD
Marshal, Alan 1909-1961 FilmgC, MotPP,
WhScrn 1, WhScrn 2, WhoHol B
Marshall, Alan 1909-1961 NotNAT B
Marshall, Armina 1900- BiE&WWA, NotNAT,
WhoThe 16
Marshall, Boyd 1885-1950 Film 1, WhScrn 1,
WhScrn 2, WhoHol B
Marshall, Brenda 1915- FilmgC, MotPP, MovMk,
WhoHol A
Marshall, Charles E Red 1899-1975 WhScrn 2
Marshall, Charles Red d1974 WhoHol B
Marshall, Chet 1932-1974 WhScrn 2
Marshall, Clark Film 2
Marshall, Dodie WhoHol A
Marshall, Don WhoHol A
Marshall, E G 1910- BiE&WWA, FilmgC,
IntMPA 1977, MotPP, MovMk, NotNAT,
PIP&P, WhoHol A, WhoThe 16
Marshall, E G 1919- CelR 3
Marshall, Edward d1904 NotNAT B
Marshall, Everett 1901- WhThe
Marshall, Frank d1889 NotNAT B
Marshall, Frank d1939 NotNAT B
Marshall, Garry NewYTET
Marshall, George 1891-1975 BiDFlm, CmMov,
FilmgC, MovMk, OxFilm, TwYS A,
WhScrn 2, WhoHol C, WorEnF
Marshall, Henry I 1883-1958 AmSCAP 1966
Marshall, Herbert 1890-1966 BiDFlm,
BiE&WWA, Film 2, FilmgC, MotPP,
MovMk, NotNAT B, OxFilm, WhScrn 1,
WhScrn 2, WhThe, WhoHol B, WorEnF
Marshall, Herbert 1900- FilmgC
Marshall, Herbert 1906- IntMPA 1977
Marshall, Jack Film 1
Marshall, Larry IntMPA 1977
Marshall, Lisa WomWMM B
Marshall, Madeleine Film 2
Marshall, Marion WhoHol A
Marshall, Mort 1918- BiE&WWA, NotNAT,
WhoHol A
Marshall, Nancy WomWMM B
Marshall, Norman 1901- CnThe, WhoThe 16
Marshall, Oswald 1875-1954 WhScrn 1,
WhScrn 2
Marshall, Pat WhoHol A
Marshall, Peggy AmSCAP 1966
Marshall, Penny WhoHol A
Marshall, Percy F d1927 NotNAT B
Marshall, Perle Film 2
Marshall, Peter WhoHol A
Marshall, Robert d1910 NotNAT B
Marshall, Sandra WomWMM B
Marshall, Sarah 1933- BiE&WWA, NotNAT,
WhoHol A
Marshall, Terry Film 2
Marshall, Thurgood 1908- CelR 3
Marshall, Trudy 1922- FilmgC, IntMPA 1977,
WhoHol A
Marshall, Tully 1864-1943 Film 1, Film 2,
FilmgC, MotPP, MovMk, NotNAT B,
TwYS, WhScrn 1, WhScrn 2, WhThe,
WhoHol B

Marshall, Virginia Film 2
Marshall, William WhoHol A
Marshall, William 1915?- FilmgC
Marshall, William 1917- IntMPA 1977,
WhoHol A
Marshall, William 1924- BiE&WWA, NotNAT
Marshall, Zena 1926- FilmgC, IntMPA 1977,
WhoHol A
Marshalov, Boris 1902-1967 WhScrn 1,
WhScrn 2
Marson, Aileen d1939 NotNAT B, WhoHol B
Marson, Aileen 1912-1939 WhThe
Marson, Aileen 1913-1939 WhScrn 1, WhScrn 2
Marsters, Ann 1918- AmSCAP 1966
Marstini, Marie Film 2
Marstini, Rosita 1894-1948 Film 1, Film 2,
WhScrn 1, WhScrn 2, WhoHol B
Marston, Ann 1939-1971 WhScrn 1, WhScrn 2,
WhoHol B
Marston, Henry d1883 NotNAT B
Marston, Mrs. Henry d1887 NotNAT B
Marston, Joel WhoHol A
Marston, John 1575?-1634 McGWD, NotNAT B,
OxThe, PIP&P
Marston, John 1576-1634 CnThe, REnWD
Marston, John 1890-1962 NotNAT B, WhScrn 1,
WhScrn 2, WhoHol B
Marston, John Westland 1819-1890 NotNAT B,
OxThe
Marszalek, Henry 1922- AmSCAP 1966
Marta, Jack 1905- IntMPA 1977
Martan, Manilla Film 2
Martan, Nita Film 2
Martel, Flora BiE&WWA, NotNAT
Martel, Gene 1916- IntMPA 1977
Martel, William WhoHol A
Martell, Alphonse Film 2
Martell, Donna WhoHol A
Martell, Gillian 1936- WhoThe 16
Martell, Helen Heron AmSCAP 1966
Martell, Paul 1905- AmSCAP 1966
Martelli, Lodovico 1503-1531 McGWD
Martelli, Otello 1902- WorEnF
Martelli, Otello 1903- DcFM, FilmgC
Marten, Helen Film 1, MotPP
Martens, Adolphe-Adhemar-Louis-Michel
McGWD
Martens, Betsy WomWMM B
Martens, Frederick Herman 1874-1932
AmSCAP 1966
Martens, Gaston 1883-1967 ModWD
Martenson, Mona Film 2
Marterie, Ralph 1914- AmSCAP 1966
Marth, Frank WhoHol A
Marth, Helen Jun 1903- AmSCAP 1966
Marthold, Jules De 1842-1927 NotNAT B,
WhThe
Martin, Al IntMPA 1977
Martin, Andra WhoHol A
Martin, Billy 1908- AmSCAP 1966
Martin, Boyd d1963 NotNAT B
Martin, Buddy Film 2
Martin, Charles WhoHol A
Martin, Charles E IntMPA 1977
Martin, Chris-Pin 1894-1953 Film 1, FilmgC,
MotPP, Vers A, WhScrn 1, WhScrn 2,
WhoHol B
Martin, Christopher Film 2
Martin, Christopher 1942- NotNAT
Martin, Claudia WhoHol A
Martin, Cye 1914-1972 WhScrn 2
Martin, David 1907- AmSCAP 1966
Martin, Dean 1917- BiDFlm, CelR 3, CmMov,
FilmgC, IntMPA 1977, MotPP, MovMk,

OxFilm, WhoHol A, WorEnF
Martin, Deana *WhoHol A*
Martin, Dewey 1923- *FilmgC, IntMPA 1977,*
  MotPP, WhoHol A
Martin, Dick 1922- *CelR 3, FilmgC, WhoHol A*
Martin, Dino, Jr. *WhoHol A*
Martin, Don 1911- *IntMPA 1977*
Martin, Duke *Film 2*
Martin, Edie 1880-1964 *FilmgC, NotNAT B,*
  WhScrn 1, WhScrn 2, WhThe, WhoHol B
Martin, Edwin Dennis 1920- *IntMPA 1977*
Martin, Elliot 1924- *BiE&WWA, NotNAT,*
  WhoThe 16
Martin, Enoch, II 1921- *AmSCAP 1966*
Martin, Ernest H 1919- *BiE&WWA, CelR 3,*
  EncMT, NotNAT, WhoThe 16
Martin, Florence *Film 1*
Martin, Frank Wells 1880-1941 *WhScrn 1,*
  WhScrn 2
Martin, Freddy 1907- *WhoHol A*
Martin, Glenn *Film 1*
Martin, Gorman O 1934- *AmSCAP 1966*
Martin, Helen *BiE&WWA, NotNAT*
Martin, Henry H 1912- *IntMPA 1977*
Martin, Herbert E 1926- *AmSCAP 1966*
Martin, Hiram *Film 2*
Martin, Hugh 1914- *AmSCAP 1966,*
  BiE&WWA, EncMT, NewMT, NotNAT
Martin, Mrs. Jacques 1863-1936 *NotNAT B*
Martin, Jared *WhoHol A*
Martin, Joe *Film 2*
Martin, John E 1770-1807 *NotNAT B*
Martin, John E 1865-1933 *WhScrn 1, WhScrn 2*
Martin, Judy 1914- *AmSCAP 1966*
Martin, Kiel *WhoHol A*
Martin, Larry 1933- *AmSCAP 1966*
Martin, Leila 1936- *BiE&WWA, NotNAT*
Martin, Lennie 1916-1963 *AmSCAP 1966*
Martin, Lewis H d1969 *WhScrn 1, WhScrn 2,*
  WhoHol B
Martin, Lock d1959? *WhScrn 2*
Martin, Marcella *WhoHol A*
Martin, Marian 1916- *IntMPA 1977*
Martin, Marion 1916- *FilmgC, MovMk,*
  WhoHol A
Martin, Marvin *Film 1*
Martin, Mary 1913- *BiE&WWA, CelR 3,*
  CnThe, EncMT, FamA&A, Film 1, FilmgC,
  MotPP, MovMk, NewYTET, NotNAT,
  OxFilm, PIP&P, WhoHol A, WhoThe 16
Martin, Mary 1914- *IntMPA 1977*
Martin, Mildred Palmer d1962 *NotNAT B*
Martin, Millicent 1934- *EncMT, FilmgC,*
  IntMPA 1977, WhoHol A, WhoThe 16
Martin, Nan *BiE&WWA, NotNAT, PIP&P,*
  WhoHol A
Martin, Owen 1889-1960 *NotNAT B, WhScrn 1,*
  WhScrn 2, WhoHol B
Martin, Pamela *WhoHol A*
Martin, Pepper *WhoHol A*
Martin, Pete 1899-1973 *WhScrn 2*
Martin, Pete 1901- *BiE&WWA*
Martin, Philip *ConDr 1977B*
Martin, Quinn *NewYTET*
Martin, R E 1917- *IntMPA 1977*
Martin, Richard 1938- *IntMPA 1977*
Martin, Robert Wesley *NatPD*
Martin, Ross 1920- *FilmgC, IntMPA 1977,*
  MotPP, WhoHol A
Martin, Roy E, Jr. 1917- *IntMPA 1977*
Martin, Ruth Kelley 1914- *AmSCAP 1966*
Martin, Sam 1908- *AmSCAP 1966*
Martin, Sharon Stockard 1948- *NatPD*
Martin, Sobey 1909- *IntMPA 1977*

Martin, Strother 1920- *CmMov, FilmgC,*
  IntMPA 1977, WhoHol A
Martin, Susan *WomWMM, WomWMM B*
Martin, Thomas Philipp 1909- *AmSCAP 1966*
Martin, Todd *WhoHol A*
Martin, Tom d1962 *NotNAT B*
Martin, Tony *MotPP, WhoHol A*
Martin, Tony d1932 *WhScrn 1, WhScrn 2*
Martin, Tony 1912- *FilmgC*
Martin, Tony 1913- *IntMPA 1977*
Martin, Tony 1914- *AmSCAP 1966*
Martin, Townsend *Film 2*
Martin, Townsend d1951 *NotNAT B*
Martin, Vernon 1929- *AmSCAP 1966*
Martin, Virginia *BiE&WWA, NotNAT*
Martin, Virginia d1971 *WhoHol B*
Martin, Vivian 1893- *Film 1, Film 2, MotPP,*
  TwYS, WhThe
Martin, Vivienne 1936- *WhoHol A, WhoThe 16*
Martin And Lewis *MotPP, NewYTET*
Martin DuGard, Roger 1881-1958 *McGWD*
Martin-Duncan, F *DcFM*
Martin-Harvey, Sir John 1863-1944 *CnThe,*
  NotNAT A, NotNAT B, OxThe, WhThe
Martin-Harvey, Muriel 1891- *WhThe*
Martindel, Edward 1876-1955 *Film 1, Film 2,*
  MotPP, NotNAT B, TwYS, WhScrn 1,
  WhScrn 2, WhoHol B
Martine, Stella d1961 *NotNAT B*
Martinelli, Alfredo *Film 2*
Martinelli, Angelica Alberigi *OxThe*
Martinelli, Drusiano d1606? *OxThe*
Martinelli, Elsa *MotPP*
Martinelli, Elsa 1932- *MovMk*
Martinelli, Elsa 1933- *FilmgC, WhoHol A*
Martinelli, Elsa 1935- *WorEnF*
Martinelli, Giovanni *Film 2*
Martinelli, Tristano 1557?-1630 *OxThe*
Martinetti, Paul 1851- *WhThe*
Martinez, Conchita 1912-1960 *WhScrn 1,*
  WhScrn 2
Martinez, Eduardo L 1900-1968 *WhScrn 1,*
  WhScrn 2
Martinez, Joaquin *WhoHol A*
Martinez DeLaRosa, Francisco 1787-1862 *McGWD,*
  NotNAT B, OxThe
Martinez Sierra, Gregorio 1881-1947 *CnMD,*
  CnThe, McGWD, ModWD, NotNAT B,
  OxThe
Martini, Bennie 1910- *AmSCAP 1966*
Martini, Fausto Maria 1886-1931 *ModWD*
Martini, Nino 1904- *FilmgC*
Martinot, Sadie 1861-1923 *NotNAT B, WhThe*
Martinot, Sadie 1862-1923 *WhoStg 1906,*
  WhoStg 1908
Martins, Jay 1935- *AmSCAP 1966*
Martins, Orlando 1899- *FilmgC, IntMPA 1977,*
  WhoHol A
Martinson, Joseph B 1911- *BiE&WWA*
Martinson, Leslie H *FilmgC*
Martlew, Mary 1919- *WhThe*
Martoglio, Nino 1870-1920 *DcFM*
Martoglio, Nino 1870-1921 *WorEnF*
Marton, Andrew 1904- *CmMov, FilmgC,*
  IntMPA 1977, MovMk, WorEnF
Martone, Don 1902- *AmSCAP 1966*
Martone, Prudence 1933- *AmSCAP 1966*
Martyn, Edward 1859-1923 *CnMD, CnThe,*
  McGWD, ModWD, REnWD
Martyn, Edward 1859-1924 *NotNAT A, OxThe*
Martyn, Eliza d1846 *NotNAT B*
Martyn, Marty d1964 *WhScrn 2*
Martyn, May d1948 *NotNAT B*
Martyn, Peter 1928-1955 *WhScrn 1, WhScrn 2,*

WhoHol B
Marum, Marilyn Harvey 1929-1973 *WhScrn 2,
WhoHol B*
Marus, Gina *Film 2*
Maruson *Film 2*
Marvenga, Ilse *WhThe*
Marvin, Grace *Film 2*
Marvin, Jack d1956 *WhScrn 2*
Marvin, Johnny 1897-1944 *AmSCAP 1966*
Marvin, Lee 1924- *BiDFlm, CelR 3, CmMov,
FilmgC, IntMPA 1977, MotPP, MovMk,
OxFilm, WhoHol A, WorEnF*
Marvin, Tony 1912- *IntMPA 1977*
Marx, Albert A 1892-1960 *WhScrn 1, WhScrn 2*
Marx, Chico 1891-1961 *DcFM, EncMT,
FamA&A, Film 2, MGM, MotPP, MovMk,
NotNAT B, OxFilm, WhScrn 1, WhScrn 2,
WhoHol B*
Marx, Groucho 1895- *BiE&WWA, CelR 3,
DcFM, EncMT, FamA&A, Film 2,
IntMPA 1977, MGM, MotPP, MovMk,
NewYTET, OxFilm, WhoHol A*
Marx, Gummo 1894- *BiE&WWA*
Marx, Harpo 1893-1964 *AmSCAP 1966,
BiE&WWA, DcFM, EncMT, FamA&A,
Film 2, MGM, MotPP, NotNAT B, OxFilm,
WhScrn 1, WhScrn 2, WhoHol B*
Marx, Harpo 1894-1964 *MovMk*
Marx, Marvin 1925-1975 *NewYTET, WhScrn 2*
Marx, Max d1925 *WhScrn 1, WhScrn 2,
WhoHol B*
Marx, Michelle *WomWMM B*
Marx, Patricia *WomWMM B*
Marx, Samuel *IntMPA 1977*
Marx, Zeppo 1900- *OxFilm*
Marx, Zeppo 1901- *BiE&WWA, EncMT,
FamA&A, Film 2, MGM, MovMk,
WhoHol A*
Marx Brothers, The *BiDFlm, CmMov, DcFM,
EncMT, FamA&A, FilmgC, MGM, MotPP,
MovMk, NotNAT A, OxFilm, WorEnF*
Mary Angelita, Sister 1912- *BiE&WWA,
NotNAT*
Mary Immaculate, Sister *BiE&WWA*
Mary, Jules 1851-1922 *NotNAT B, WhThe*
Maryan, Charles 1934- *NotNAT*
Mascari, Joseph Rocco 1922- *AmSCAP 1966*
Maschek, Adrian M 1918- *AmSCAP 1966*
Maschwitz, Eric 1901-1969 *EncMT, WhThe*
Mascia, Madeline T 1928- *AmSCAP 1966*
Mase, Marino *WhoHol A*
Masefield, John 1878-1967 *CnMD, McGWD,
ModWD, NotNAT B, OxThe, PIP&P,
WhThe*
Masefield, Joseph R 1933- *IntMPA 1977*
Maselli, Francesco 1930- *DcFM, WorEnF*
Masina, Giulietta *MotPP, WhoHol A*
Masina, Giulietta 1920- *OxFilm, WorEnF*
Masina, Giulietta 1921- *FilmgC, MovMk*
Maskel, Magdalene *IntMPA 1977*
Maskell, Fanny d1919 *NotNAT B*
Maskell, Virginia 1936-1968 *FilmgC, MotPP,
WhScrn 1, WhScrn 2, WhoHol B*
Maskelyne, John Nevil 1839- *WhThe*
Maslow, Walter *WhoHol A*
Masokha, Pyotr *Film 2*
Mason, Alfred Edward Woodley 1865-1948
McGWD, NotNAT B, WhThe
Mason, Ann 1889-1948 *Film 1, NotNAT B,
WhScrn 2*
Mason, Archibald J 1889- *IntMPA 1977*
Mason, Beryl 1921- *WhoHol A, WhoThe 16*
Mason, Billy 1888-1941 *WhoHol B*
Mason, Billy, Smilin 1888-1941 *Film 1*

Mason, Brewster 1922- *WhoHol A, WhoThe 16*
Mason, Bruce 1921- *ConDr 1977*
Mason, Buddy 1903-1975 *Film 2, WhScrn 2,
WhoHol C*
Mason, Charles *Film 1*
Mason, Dan 1853-1929 *Film 1, Film 2,
WhScrn 1, WhScrn 2, WhoHol B*
Mason, Daniel Gregory 1873-1953 *AmSCAP 1966*
Mason, Don P 1927- *AmSCAP 1966*
Mason, Edna *Film 1*
Mason, Elliot C d1949 *NotNAT B, WhThe*
Mason, Elliott 1897-1949 *FilmgC, WhScrn 1,
WhScrn 2, WhoHol B*
Mason, Evelyn M 1892-1926 *WhScrn 1,
WhScrn 2, WhoHol B*
Mason, Gladys 1886- *WhThe*
Mason, Gregory 1889-1968 *WhScrn 2*
Mason, Haddon 1898- *Film 2*
Mason, Herbert 1891-1960 *FilmgC, WhThe*
Mason, Homer B d1959 *NotNAT B*
Mason, Jack 1906-1965 *AmSCAP 1966*
Mason, James *Film 1, Film 2, MotPP, TwYS,
WhoHol A*
Mason, James 1890-1959 *WhScrn 1, WhScrn 2,
WhoHol B*
Mason, James 1909- *BiDFlm, CelR 3, CmMov,
FilmgC, IntMPA 1977, MovMk, OxFilm,
WhThe, WorEnF*
Mason, John B d1919 *Film 1, WhoHol B,
WhoStg 1908*
Mason, John B 1857-1919 *NotNAT B, WhThe,
WhoStg 1906*
Mason, John B 1859-1919 *WhScrn 2*
Mason, Kitty 1882- *WhThe*
Mason, Lawrence d1939 *NotNAT B*
Mason, Leroy 1901-1947 *TwYS*
Mason, LeRoy 1903-1947 *Film 1, Film 2,
NotNAT B, Vers A, WhScrn 1, WhScrn 2,
WhoHol B*
Mason, Lesley d1964 *NotNAT B*
Mason, Louis 1888-1959 *WhScrn 1, WhScrn 2,
WhoHol B*
Mason, Marjorie d1968 *WhScrn 2, WhoHol B*
Mason, Marlyn *WhoHol A*
Mason, Marsha 1942- *IntMPA 1977, MovMk,
NotNAT, WhoHol A*
Mason, Marshall W 1940- *NotNAT*
Mason, Mary *WhoHol A*
Mason, Morgan *WhoHol A*
Mason, Myrna *Film 2*
Mason, Pamela 1918- *IntMPA 1977, WhoHol A*
Mason, Portland *WhoHol A*
Mason, Reginald 1882-1962 *Film 2, NotNAT B,
WhScrn 1, WhScrn 2, WhThe, WhoHol B*
Mason, Sarah Y *WomWMM*
Mason, Shirley 1900- *Film 1, Film 2, FilmgC,
MotPP, WhoHol A*
Mason, Shirley 1901- *TwYS*
Mason, Sidney *Film 1*
Mason, Sully P 1906-1970 *WhScrn 1, WhScrn 2,
WhoHol B*
Mason, Sydney L *WhoHol A*
Mason, William 1888-1941 *Film 1, WhoHol B*
Mason, William *see also* Mason, Billy
Mason, William C Smiling Billy 1888-1941
WhScrn 1, WhScrn 2
Masone, Patrick T 1928- *AmSCAP 1966*
Mass, Joseph R 1943- *IntMPA 1977*
Massari, Lea *FilmgC, WhoHol A*
Massart, Mary *Film 2*
Massary, Fritzi 1882-1969 *WhThe*
Masselos, William 1920- *CelR 3*
Massen, Louis F d1925 *NotNAT B*
Massen, Osa 1915- *FilmgC*

Massen, Osa 1916- *IntMPA 1977*
Massey, Anna 1937- *BiE&WWA, FilmgC,*
 WhoHol A, WhoThe 16
Massey, Blanche d1929 *NotNAT B*
Massey, Charles d1625 *OxThe*
Massey, D Curtis 1910- *AmSCAP 1966*
Massey, Daniel 1933- *BiE&WWA, FilmgC,*
 IntMPA 1977, NotNAT, WhoHol A,
 WhoThe 16
Massey, Ilona 1910-1974 *MotPP, MovMk, ThFT,*
 WhScrn 2, WhoHol B
Massey, Ilona 1912-1974 *FilmgC*
Massey, Raymond 1896- *BiDFlm, BiE&WWA,*
 CmMov, CnThe, FamA&A, FilmgC,
 IntMPA 1977, MotPP, MovMk, NotNAT,
 OxFilm, PIP&P, WhoHol A, WhoThe 16
Massi, Bernice *BiE&WWA, NotNAT,*
 WhoThe 16
Massie, Paul 1932- *FilmgC, IntMPA 1977,*
 WhoHol A
Massimer, Howard *Film 1*
Massine, Leonid 1896- *WhoHol A*
Massine, Leonide 1896- *Film 2, WhThe*
Massinger, Philip 1583-1640 *CnThe, McGWD,*
 NotNAT A, NotNAT B, OxThe, PIP&P,
 REnWD
Massingham, Dorothy 1889-1933 *NotNAT B,*
 WhThe
Massingham, Richard 1898-1953 *FilmgC, OxFilm,*
 WhScrn 1, WhScrn 2
Masson, Tom 1866-1934 *WhScrn 2*
Masteroff, Joe 1919- *BiE&WWA, ConDr 1977D,*
 NotNAT
Masters, Darryl 1913-1961 *WhoHol B*
Masters, Daryl 1913-1961 *WhScrn 1, WhScrn 2*
Masters, Frankie 1904- *AmSCAP 1966*
Masters, Harry 1885-1974 *WhScrn 2*
Masters, Mary *Film 1*
Masters, Ruth 1899-1969 *WhScrn 1, WhScrn 2,*
 WhoHol B
Masters And Johnson *CelR 3*
Masterson, Carroll 1913- *BiE&WWA, NotNAT*
Masterson, Harris 1914- *BiE&WWA, NotNAT*
Masterson, Mary Stuart *WhoHol A*
Masterson, Peter *WhoHol A*
Mastren, Carmen 1913- *AmSCAP 1966*
Mastripietri, Augusto *Film 2*
Mastroianni, Marcello 1923- *FilmgC*
Mastroianni, Marcello 1924- *BiDFlm, CelR 3,*
 IntMPA 1977, MotPP, MovMk, OxFilm,
 WhoHol A, WorEnF
Masurat, Theresa *WhoHol A*
Mata, Miguel P 1914-1956 *WhScrn 1, WhScrn 2*
Mata, Yama *Film 2*
Matalon, Vivian 1929- *NotNAT, WhoThe 16*
Matalon, Zack 1928- *BiE&WWA*
Matchett, Christine 1957- *WhoHol A*
Matchi *Film 2*
Matchinga, Caryn *WomWMM B*
Mate, Rudolf 1898-1964 *DcFM*
Mate, Rudolph 1898-1964 *BiDFlm, CmMov,*
 OxFilm, WorEnF
Mate, Rudolph 1899-1964 *FilmgC*
Mateja, Walter A 1944- *AmSCAP 1966*
Mateos, Hector 1901-1957 *WhScrn 1, WhScrn 2*
Matesky, Ralph 1913- *AmSCAP 1966*
Matesses, Antonios *REnWD*
Mathe, Ed *Film 2*
Mathe, Edouard *Film 1*
Mather, Aubrey 1885-1958 *Film 2, FilmgC,*
 NotNAT B, Vers A, WhScrn 1, WhScrn 2,
 WhThe, WhoHol B
Mather, Donald 1900- *WhThe*
Mather, Jack 1908-1966 *WhScrn 1, WhScrn 2,*

WhoHol B
Mather, Sydney d1925 *NotNAT B*
Mathers, Jerry 1948- *WhoHol A*
Matheson, Don *WhoHol A*
Matheson, Murray 1912- *BiE&WWA, FilmgC,*
 NotNAT, WhoHol A
Matheson, Richard 1926- *CmMov, FilmgC,*
 NewYTET, WorEnF
Matheson, Tim *WhoHol A*
Mathew, Ray 1929- *ConDr 1977*
Mathews, Carl d1959 *WhoHol B*
Mathews, Carmen *WhoHol A*
Mathews, Carmen 1914- *WhoThe 16*
Mathews, Carmen 1918- *BiE&WWA, NotNAT*
Mathews, Carole *IntMPA 1977, WhoHol A*
Mathews, Charles 1776-1835 *FamA&A,*
 NotNAT A, NotNAT B, OxThe, PIP&P
Mathews, Mrs. Charles, Sr. d1869 *NotNAT B*
Mathews, Mrs. Charles J d1899 *NotNAT B*
Mathews, Charles James 1803-1878 *FamA&A,*
 NotNAT A, NotNAT B, OxThe, PIP&P
Mathews, Dorothy *Film 2*
Mathews, Frances Aymar *WhThe*
Mathews, George *WhoHol A*
Mathews, George 1911- *BiE&WWA, NotNAT,*
 WhoThe 16
Mathews, George H 1877-1952 *WhScrn 1,*
 WhScrn 2
Mathews, James W d1920 *WhThe*
Mathews, Joyce *WhoHol A*
Mathews, Kerwin 1926- *FilmgC, WhoHol A*
Mathewson, Christy 1880-1925 *WhScrn 2*
Mathias, Bob *WhoHol A*
Mathies, Charlene *WhoHol A*
Mathieson, Muir 1911-1975 *FilmgC, WhScrn 2,*
 WhoHol C
Mathis, Johnny 1935- *CelR 3*
Mathis, June 1892-1927 *DcFM, FilmgC,*
 NotNAT B, TwYS A, WomWMM,
 WorEnF
Mathot, Leon 1896-1968 *Film 2, WhScrn 1,*
 WhScrn 2, WhoHol B
Matiesen, Otto 1873-1932 *WhScrn 1, WhScrn 2,*
 WhoHol B
Matiesen, Otto 1893- *Film 1, Film 2, TwYS*
Matkowsky, Aldabert d1909 *NotNAT B*
Matlack, Jack D 1914- *IntMPA 1977*
Matlaw, Myron 1924- *BiE&WWA, NotNAT*
Matlock, Julian C 1907- *AmSCAP 1966*
Matofsky, Harvey 1933- *IntMPA 1977*
Matos, Alexander 1929- *AmSCAP 1966*
Matos, Manuel Garcia 1904- *AmSCAP 1966*
Matras, Christian 1903- *DcFM, FilmgC, OxFilm,*
 WorEnF
Matson, Donna *WomWMM B*
Matsoukas, Nicholas John 1903- *IntMPA 1977*
Matsudaira, Renko *AmSCAP 1966*
Matsui, Suisei 1900-1973 *WhScrn 2*
Matterstock, Albert 1912-1960 *WhScrn 1,*
 WhScrn 2, WhoHol B
Matteson, Ruth 1909-1975 *BiE&WWA,*
 NotNAT B, WhThe
Matteson, Ruth 1910-1975 *WhScrn 2*
Mattfeld, Julius 1893- *BiE&WWA*
Matthaei, Gay *WomWMM B*
Matthaei, Konrad *NotNAT*
Matthau, Walter 1920- *BiDFlm, BiE&WWA,*
 CelR 3, CmMov, CnThe, FilmgC, MotPP,
 MovMk, NotNAT, OxFilm, WhoHol A,
 WhoThe 16
Matthau, Walter 1923- *IntMPA 1977, WorEnF*
Matthews, A E 1869-1960 *Film 2, FilmgC,*
 NotNAT A, NotNAT B, PIP&P, WhScrn 1,
 WhScrn 2, WhThe, WhoHol B

Matthews, Adelaide 1886- *WhThe*
Matthews, Albert Edward 1869-1960 *OxThe*
Matthews, Bache 1876-1948 *NotNAT B*, *WhThe*
Matthews, Beatrice 1890-1942 *WhScrn 1*,
   WhScrn 2
Matthews, Billy 1922- *BiE&WWA*
Matthews, Brander 1852-1929 *NotNAT A*,
   NotNAT B, *WhThe*
Matthews, Brander *see also* Matthews, James
   Brander
Matthews, Christopher *WhoHol A*
Matthews, Dorcas *Film 2*
Matthews, Dorothy *Film 2*
Matthews, Eric *WhoHol A*
Matthews, Ethel 1870- *WhThe*
Matthews, Forrest 1908-1951 *WhScrn 2*
Matthews, Francis 1927- *FilmgC*, *WhoHol A*
Matthews, Gloria *WhoHol A*
Matthews, Harry Alexander 1879- *AmSCAP 1966*
Matthews, Holon 1904- *AmSCAP 1966*
Matthews, Inez 1917- *BiE&WWA*, *NotNAT*
Matthews, James Brander 1852-1929 *OxThe*
Matthews, James Brander *see also* Matthews,
   Brander
Matthews, Jean D d1961 *WhScrn 1*, *WhScrn 2*,
   WhoHol B
Matthews, Jessie 1907- *BiE&WWA*, *CnThe*,
   EncMT, *Film 2*, *FilmgC*, *IntMPA 1977*,
   MotPP, *MovMk*, *NotNAT*, *OxFilm*, *ThFT*,
   WhoHol A, *WhoThe 16*
Matthews, Lester 1900-1975 *FilmgC*, *WhScrn 2*,
   WhThe, *WhoHol A*
Matthews, Walter *WhoHol A*
Matthews, William *Film 2*
Matthison, Arthur d1883 *NotNAT B*
Matthison, Edith Wynne 1875-1955 *Film 1*,
   NotNAT B, *WhScrn 1*, *WhScrn 2*, *WhThe*,
   WhoHol B, *WhoStg 1906*, *WhoStg 1908*
Mattimore, Van *Film 2*
Mattingly, Hedley *WhoHol A*
Mattioli, Raf 1936-1960 *WhScrn 1*, *WhScrn 2*
Mattis, Lillian 1925- *AmSCAP 1966*
Mattison, Frank S 1890- *TwYS A*
Mattocks, Isabella Hallam 1746-1826 *NotNAT B*,
   OxThe
Mattoni, Andre *Film 2*
Mattox, Martha d1938 *Film 1*, *Film 2*, *TwYS*
Mattox, Martha 1879-1933 *WhScrn 1*, *WhScrn 2*,
   WhoHol B
Mattox, Matt 1921- *BiE&WWA*, *NotNAT*,
   WhoHol A
Mattraw, Scott 1885-1946 *Film 2*, *WhScrn 1*,
   WhScrn 2, *WhoHol B*
Mattson, Eric 1908- *BiE&WWA*, *NotNAT*
Mattsson, Arne 1919- *DcFM*, *FilmgC*, *OxFilm*,
   WorEnF
Mattyasovsky, I *Film 2*
Matura, Mustapha 1939- *ConDr 1977*,
   WhoThe 16
Mature, Victor *MotPP*, *WhoHol A*
Mature, Victor 1915- *CmMov*, *FilmgC*
Mature, Victor 1916- *BiDFlm*, *IntMPA 1977*,
   MovMk, *OxFilm*, *WorEnF*
Maturin, Charles d1824 *NotNAT B*
Maturin, Eric 1883-1957 *Film 2*, *NotNAT B*,
   WhThe
Matusche, Alfred 1909- *CroCD*
Matzenauer, Margaret d1963 *WhoHol B*
Matzenauer, Margarette d1963 *NotNAT B*
Matzenauer, Marguerite 1881-1963 *WhScrn 2*
Mauch, Billy 1924- *WhoHol A*
Mauch, Billy And Bobby 1925- *FilmgC*
Mauch, Bobby 1924- *WhoHol A*
Mauch Twins *MotPP*

Maude, Arthur *Film 1*
Maude, Charles Raymond d1943 *NotNAT B*,
   PIP&P, *WhThe*, *WhoHol B*
Maude, Cyril 1862-1951 *Film 1*, *Film 2*,
   NotNAT A, *NotNAT B*, *OxThe*, *TwYS*,
   WhScrn 1, *WhScrn 2*, *WhThe*, *WhoHol B*
Maude, Elizabeth 1912- *WhThe*
Maude, Gillian *WhThe*
Maude, Joan *Film 2*
Maude, Joan 1908- *WhThe*
Maude, Margery 1889- *BiE&WWA*, *NotNAT*,
   WhoHol A, *WhoThe 16*
Maude-Roxby, Roddy 1930- *WhoHol A*,
   WhoThe 16
Maugham, William Somerset 1874-1965
   BiE&WWA, *CnMD*, *CnThe*, *FilmgC*,
   McGWD, *ModWD*, *NotNAT A*, *NotNAT B*,
   OxThe, *PIP&P*, *REnWD*, *WhScrn 2*,
   WhThe
Mauldin, Bill 1921- *CelR 3*
Mauldin, Bill 1922- *WhoHol A*
Maule, Annabel 1922- *WhoThe 16*
Maule, Donovan 1899- *WhoThe 16*
Maule, Robin 1924-1942 *NotNAT B*, *WhThe*
Maule, Vee *Film 2*
Maulnier, Thierry 1909- *McGWD*
Maunder, Wayne 1942- *FilmgC*, *WhoHol A*
Maupain, Ernest 1881-1949 *WhScrn 2*
Maupin, Ernest *Film 2*
Maupin, Georges *Film 2*
Maupin, Rex *AmSCAP 1966*
Maur, Meinhart *WhoHol A*
Maurada, Mac 1902-1963 *AmSCAP 1966*
Maureice, Ruth *Film 1*
Maurer, Maurice 1914- *IntMPA 1977*
Maurey, Max d1947 *NotNAT B*, *WhThe*
Maurey, Nicole 1925- *FilmgC*, *IntMPA 1977*,
   MotPP, *WhoHol A*
Mauriac, Francois 1885-1970 *CnMD*, *McGWD*,
   ModWD, *REnWD*
Mauriac, Francois 1895- *BiE&WWA*
Maurice d1927 *NotNAT B*, *WhScrn 2*
Maurice, Edmund d1928 *NotNAT B*, *WhThe*
Maurice, Mary 1844-1918 *Film 1*, *MotPP*,
   NotNAT B, *WhScrn 2*, *WhoHol B*
Maurice, Newman d1923 *NotNAT B*
Maurice-Jacquet, H 1886-1954 *AmSCAP 1966*
Mauriello, David Joseph 1936- *NatPD*
Mauro, Humberto 1897- *DcFM*
Mauro Family *OxThe*
Maurus, Gerda 1909-1968 *Film 2*, *WhScrn 1*,
   WhScrn 2, *WhoHol B*
Maury, Lowndes 1911- *AmSCAP 1966*
Mavor, O H *PIP&P*
Mawdesley, Robert d1953 *NotNAT B*,
   WhoHol B
Mawson, Edward 1861-1917 *Film 1*, *NotNAT B*,
   WhScrn 2, *WhoHol B*
Max, Edouard Alexandre De 1869-1925
   NotNAT B, *OxThe*, *WhThe*
Max, Edwin 1909- *Vers A*, *WhoHol A*
Max, Jean 1897-1971 *WhScrn 2*
Maxam, Lola *Film 2*
Maxam, Louella Modie 1896-1970 *Film 1*, *Film 2*,
   WhScrn 1, *WhScrn 2*, *WhoHol B*
Maxey, Paul 1908-1963 *NotNAT B*, *WhScrn 1*,
   WhScrn 2, *WhoHol B*
Maximilian, Max *Film 2*
Maximova, E *Film 2*
Maxted, Stanley 1900-1963 *WhScrn 1*, *WhScrn 2*,
   WhoHol B
Maxtone-Graham, John 1929- *BiE&WWA*,
   NotNAT
Maxudian *Film 2*

Maxwell *Film 2*
Maxwell, Eddie 1912- *AmSCAP 1966*
Maxwell, Edwin d1948 *Film 1, NotNAT B,
TwYS, WhoHol B*
Maxwell, Edwin 1886-1948 *WhScrn 1, WhScrn 2*
Maxwell, Edwin 1890-1948 *Film 2, FilmgC,
Vers B*
Maxwell, Elsa 1883-1963 *AmSCAP 1966, FilmgC,
NotNAT B, WhScrn 2, WhoHol B*
Maxwell, Frank *WhoHol A*
Maxwell, Gerald 1862-1930 *NotNAT B, WhThe*
Maxwell, Helen Purcell 1901- *AmSCAP 1966*
Maxwell, Jenny *WhoHol A*
Maxwell, John 1875-1940 *FilmgC*
Maxwell, Lois 1927- *FilmgC, WhoHol A*
Maxwell, Marilyn d1972 *MotPP, WhoHol B*
Maxwell, Marilyn 1921-1972 *FilmgC*
Maxwell, Marilyn 1922-1972 *MGM, MovMk,
WhScrn 2*
Maxwell, Meg d1955 *NotNAT B*
Maxwell, Philip 1901- *AmSCAP 1966*
Maxwell, Richard Williams 1879-1953
AmSCAP 1966
Maxwell, Robert 1921- *AmSCAP 1966*
Maxwell, Roberta *NotNAT*
Maxwell, Vera K d1950 *NotNAT B*
Maxwell, Walter 1877- *WhThe*
May, Ada 1900- *WhThe*
May, Akerman 1869-1933 *NotNAT B, WhThe*
May, Ann *Film 1, Film 2*
May, Donald *WhoHol A*
May, Doris *Film 1, Film 2, MotPP, TwYS*
May, Edna d1948 *Film 1, MotPP, WhoHol B*
May, Edna 1875-1948 *NotNAT B, WhoStg 1906,
WhoStg 1908*
May, Edna 1878-1948 *EncMT, WhThe*
May, Edna 1879-1948 *WhScrn 1, WhScrn 2*
May, Elaine 1932- *BiE&WWA, CelR 3,
ConDr 1977, FilmgC, IntMPA 1977, MotPP,
NotNAT, PIP&P, WhoHol A, WhoThe 16,
WomWMM*
May, Gustav *Film 2*
May, Hans 1891-1959 *FilmgC, NotNAT B,
WhThe*
May, Harold R 1903-1973 *WhScrn 2, WhoHol B*
May, Jack 1922- *WhoThe 16*
May, James 1857-1941 *WhScrn 1, WhScrn 2*
May, Jane *WhThe*
May, Joe 1880-1954 *BiDFlm, DcFM, FilmgC,
OxFilm, WorEnF*
May, Lola *Film 1*
May, Marty 1898-1975 *WhScrn 2*
May, Mia *Film 2*
May, Nina *MotPP*
May, Olive d1938 *NotNAT B, WhoStg 1908*
May, Olive d1947 *NotNAT B*
May, Pamela 1917- *WhThe*
May, Paul 1909- *DcFM*
May, Rollo 1909- *CelR 3*
May, Samuel Roderick 1910-1963 *WhScrn 1,
WhScrn 2*
May, Val 1927- *NotNAT, WhoThe 16*
Mayakovski, Vladimir 1893-1930 *CnMD*
Mayakovsky, Vladimir Vladimirovich 1893-1930
CnThe, McGWD, ModWD, REnWD
Mayakovsky, Vladimir Vladimirovich 1894-1930
*NotNAT A, NotNAT B, OxFilm, OxThe,
PIP&P*
Mayall, Herschel 1863-1941 *Film 1, Film 2,
TwYS, WhoHol B*
Mayall, Hershell 1863-1941 *WhScrn 1, WhScrn 2*
Mayama, Miko *WhoHol A*
Maybrick, Michael d1913 *NotNAT B*
Maye, Bernyce d1962 *NotNAT B*

Maye, Jimsy 1894-1968 *WhScrn 2*
Mayehoff, Eddie *IntMPA 1977, WhoHol A*
Mayehoff, Eddie 1911- *FilmgC*
Mayehoff, Eddie 1914?- *BiE&WWA, NotNAT*
Mayer, Albert *Film 2*
Mayer, Arthur E 1918- *AmSCAP 1966*
Mayer, Arthur Loeb 1888- *IntMPA 1977*
Mayer, Ben 1925- *IntMPA 1977*
Mayer, Carl 1894-1944 *BiDFlm, DcFM, FilmgC,
OxFilm, WorEnF*
Mayer, Charles *WhoHol A*
Mayer, Daniel 1856-1928 *NotNAT B, WhThe*
Mayer, Doc *WomWMM B*
Mayer, Dot d1964 *NotNAT B*
Mayer, Edwin Justus 1896?-1960 *McGWD,
ModWD, PIP&P, WhThe*
Mayer, Edwin Justus 1897-1960 *CnMD,
NotNAT B*
Mayer, Gaston 1869-1923 *NotNAT B, WhThe*
Mayer, Gerald 1919- *FilmgC, IntMPA 1977*
Mayer, Henri d1941 *NotNAT B*
Mayer, Henry d1941 *WhThe*
Mayer, Louis B 1885-1957 *BiDFlm, DcFM,
FilmgC, NotNAT B, OxFilm, TwYS B,
WomWMM, WorEnF*
Mayer, Louis B 1895-1957 *MGM A*
Mayer, Marcus d1918 *NotNAT B*
Mayer, Michael F 1917- *IntMPA 1977*
Mayer, Natalie 1925- *AmSCAP 1966*
Mayer, Paul M 1914-1968 *WhScrn 1, WhScrn 2*
Mayer, Renee 1900- *WhThe*
Mayer, Seymour R 1910- *IntMPA 1977*
Mayer, Sylvain d1948 *NotNAT B*
Mayer, William 1925- *AmSCAP 1966*
Mayerl, Billy 1902-1959 *NotNAT B, WhThe*
Mayers, Benedict 1906- *AmSCAP 1966*
Mayers, Wilmette K d1964 *NotNAT B*
Mayes, Wendell 1918- *CmMov, IntMPA 1977,
WorEnF*
Mayeur, E F 1866- *WhThe*
Mayfield, Cleo 1897-1954 *NotNAT B, WhScrn 1,
WhScrn 2, WhThe, WhoHol B*
Mayhall, Jerome d1964 *NotNAT B*
Mayhew, Charles 1908- *WhThe*
Mayhew, Henry d1887 *NotNAT B*
Mayhew, Horace d1872 *NotNAT B*
Mayhew, Kate 1853-1944 *Film 2, NotNAT B,
WhScrn 1, WhScrn 2, WhoHol B*
Mayhew, Stella d1934 *NotNAT B, WhoHol B*
Mayhew, William 1889-1951 *AmSCAP 1966*
Mayleas, Ruth 1925- *BiE&WWA, NotNAT*
Maylon, Eily 1879-1961 *FilmgC, Vers B*
Maynard, Claire 1912-1941 *WhScrn 1, WhScrn 2,
WhoHol B*
Maynard, Gertrude d1953 *NotNAT B*
Maynard, Ken 1895-1973 *Film 2, FilmgC,
MotPP, MovMk, TwYS, WhScrn 2,
WhoHol B*
Maynard, Kermit 1898-1971 *FilmgC*
Maynard, Kermit 1902-1971 *Film 2, WhScrn 1,
WhScrn 2, WhoHol B*
Maynard, Ruth 1913- *BiE&WWA, NotNAT*
Maynard, Tex *Film 2, TwYS*
Mayne, Clarice 1886-1966 *OxThe, WhThe*
Mayne, Clarice 1890-1966 *WhScrn 2*
Mayne, Eric 1866-1947 *Film 2, NotNAT B,
WhScrn 1, WhScrn 2, WhoHol B*
Mayne, Ernie *WhThe*
Mayne, Ferdy *WhoHol A*
Mayne, Ferdy 1916- *FilmgC*
Mayne, Ferdy 1920- *WhoThe 16*
Mayne, Rutherford 1878-1967 *CnThe, OxThe,
REnWD*
Mayo, Albert 1887-1933 *WhScrn 1, WhScrn 2*

Mayo, Archie L 1891-1968 *BiDFlm, FilmgC,
  WorEnF*
Mayo, Archie L 1898-1968 *TwYS A, WhScrn 1,
  WhScrn 2*
Mayo, Christine *Film 2*
Mayo, Edna 1893-1970 *Film 1, MotPP, TwYS,
  WhScrn 2*
Mayo, Mrs. Frank d1896 *NotNAT B*
Mayo, Frank 1839-1896 *NotNAT B*
Mayo, Frank 1886-1963 *Film 1, Film 2, MotPP,
  NotNAT B, PIP&P, TwYS, WhScrn 1,
  WhScrn 2, WhoHol B*
Mayo, George 1891-1950 *WhScrn 1, WhScrn 2,
  WhoHol B*
Mayo, Harry A 1898-1964 *NotNAT B,
  WhScrn 1, WhScrn 2, WhoHol B*
Mayo, Joseph Anthony 1930-1966 *WhScrn 1,
  WhScrn 2*
Mayo, Margaret 1882-1951 *NotNAT B, WhThe,
  WhoStg 1908*
Mayo, Nick 1922- *BiE&WWA, NotNAT*
Mayo, Nine *WomWMM*
Mayo, Sam 1881-1938 *NotNAT B, WhThe*
Mayo, Virginia *IntMPA 1977, MotPP*
Mayo, Virginia 1920- *FilmgC, MovMk, WorEnF*
Mayo, Virginia 1922- *BiDFlm, WhoHol A*
Mayor, Agustin G 1935-1968 *WhScrn 1,
  WhScrn 2*
Mayor, Augustin 1935-1968 *WhoHol B*
Mayorga, Margaret 1894- *BiE&WWA*
Mayron, Melanie *WhoHol A*
Mays, Willie 1931- *CelR 3*
Maysles, Al *OxFilm*
Maysles, Albert 1926- *WorEnF*
Maysles, Albert 1933- *DcFM, FilmgC*
Maysles, David *OxFilm*
Maysles, David 1931- *DcFM, FilmgC*
Maysles, David 1932- *WorEnF*
Maytag, L B 1926- *CelR 3*
Mazaud, Emile 1884- *McGWD*
Mazetti, Georgia *Film 2*
Mazlen, Henry Gershwin 1912- *AmSCAP 1966*
Mazur, Albert 1929- *AmSCAP 1966*
Mazurki, Mike 1909- *FilmgC, IntMPA 1977,
  Vers A, WhoHol A*
Mazursky, Paul 1930- *BiDFlm, CelR 3, FilmgC,
  IntMPA 1977, MovMk, WhoHol A*
Mazzato, Umberto *Film 1*
Mazzetti, Lorenza *WomWMM*
Mazzola, Anthony T 1923- *CelR 3*
Mazzola, John W 1928- *BiE&WWA, NotNAT*
McAlister, Mary *WhoHol A*
McAllister, Claude *Film 2*
McAllister, Mary 1910- *Film 1, Film 2, TwYS*
McAllister, Paul 1875-1955 *WhScrn 2*
McAllister, Paul 1875-1959 *Film 1, Film 2,
  TwYS*
McAllister, Ward *Film 2*
McAlpin, Donald *Film 2*
McAlpin, Edith *Film 1*
McAlpine, Jane *Film 1*
McAnally, Ray 1926- *WhoHol A, WhoThe 16*
McAndrew, Marianne 1938- *FilmgC, WhoHol A*
McAndrew, William R d1968 *NewYTET*
McArdle, J F *WhThe*
McArthur, Edwin Douglas 1907- *AmSCAP 1966*
McArthur, Molly 1900- *WhThe*
M'Carthy, Justin Huntly 1860-1936 *WhThe*
M'Carthy, Justin Huntly see also McCarthy, Justin
  Huntly
McAtee, Ben 1903-1961 *NotNAT B, WhScrn 1,
  WhScrn 2*
McAtee, Clyde 1880-1947 *Film 2, WhScrn 1,
  WhScrn 2, WhoHol B*

McAuliffe, Eugene B 1893- *AmSCAP 1966*
McAuliffe, Leon 1917- *AmSCAP 1966*
McAvity, Thomas A d1972 *NewYTET*
McAvoy, Charles 1885-1953 *WhScrn 2*
McAvoy, May 1901- *Film 1, Film 2, MotPP,
  MovMk, ThFT, TwYS, WhoHol A*
McBain, Diane 1941- *MotPP, WhoHol A*
McBan, Mickey *Film 2*
McBride, Carl 1894-1937 *WhScrn 1, WhScrn 2*
McBride, Donald 1889-1957 *Film 1, WhScrn 1,
  WhScrn 2*
McBride, Donald 1894-1957 *FilmgC*
McBride, John S d1961 *NotNAT B*
McBride, Patricia *WhoHol A*
McBryde, Donald M 1937- *NotNAT*
McCabe, George d1917 *WhScrn 2*
McCabe, Harry 1881-1925 *WhScrn 1, WhScrn 2,
  WhoHol B*
McCabe, May 1873-1949 *NotNAT B, WhScrn 1,
  WhScrn 2*
McCall, Harlo E 1909- *AmSCAP 1966*
McCall, Leonard 1910- *AmSCAP 1966*
McCall, Lizzie d1942 *NotNAT B*
McCall, Mitzi *WhoHol A*
McCall, Monica *BiE&WWA, NotNAT*
McCall, William 1879-1938 *Film 1, WhScrn 1,
  WhScrn 2, WhoHol B*
McCalla, Irish *WhoHol A*
McCallin, Clement 1913- *WhoThe 16*
McCallister, Lon 1923- *FilmgC, HolP 40,
  MotPP, WhoHol A*
McCallum, David 1933- *FilmgC, IntMPA 1977,
  MotPP, MovMk, WhoHol A*
McCallum, John *WhoHol A*
McCallum, John 1917- *FilmgC*
McCallum, John 1918- *IntMPA 1977,
  WhoThe 16*
McCallum, Neil d1976 *WhoHol A*
McCally, David 1935- *NotNAT*
McCalmon, George A 1909- *BiE&WWA*
McCambridge, Mercedes 1918- *BiE&WWA,
  FilmgC, IntMPA 1977, MotPP, MovMk,
  NotNAT, OxFilm, WhoHol A*
McCammon, Bessie J d1964 *NotNAT B*
McCandless, Stanley Russell 1897-1967
  BiE&WWA, NotNAT B
McCann, Charles Andrew d1927 *WhScrn 1,
  WhScrn 2, WhoHol B*
McCann, Chuck *WhoHol A*
McCann, Frances 1922-1963 *WhScrn 2*
McCann, Les *AmSCAP 1966*
McCarey, Leo 1898-1969 *AmSCAP 1966,
  BiDFlm, DcFM, FilmgC, MovMk, OxFilm,
  TwYS A, WorEnF*
McCarey, Ray 1904-1948 *FilmgC*
McCarroll, Frank d1954 *WhScrn 1, WhScrn 2,
  WhoHol B*
McCarron, Charles 1891-1919 *AmSCAP 1966*
McCarten, John 1916-1974 *BiE&WWA,
  NotNAT B*
McCarthy, Charles J 1903-1960 *AmSCAP 1966*
McCarthy, Charlotte 1918- *AmSCAP 1966*
McCarthy, Daniel 1869- *WhThe*
McCarthy, Dinitia Smith *WomWMM A,
  WomWMM B*
McCarthy, Earl *Film 2*
McCarthy, Eugene 1916- *CelR 3*
McCarthy, Frank 1912- *FilmgC, IntMPA 1977*
McCarthy, J P *Film 1*
McCarthy, John P 1885- *TwYS A*
McCarthy, Joseph 1885-1943 *AmSCAP 1966,
  EncMT, NewMT*
McCarthy, Joseph 1905-1957 *FilmgC*
McCarthy, Joseph Allan 1922- *AmSCAP 1966*

McCarthy, Justin Huntly 1860-1936 *ModWD*,
  NotNAT B
McCarthy, Justin Huntly *see also* M'Carthy, Justin
  Huntly
McCarthy, Kevin 1914- *BiE&WWA*, *FilmgC*,
  IntMPA 1977, *MovMk*, *NotNAT*,
  WhoHol A, *WhoThe 16*
McCarthy, Lillah 1875-1960 *NotNAT A*,
  NotNAT B, *OxThe*, *WhThe*
McCarthy, Lin *WhoHol A*
McCarthy, Mary 1912- *BiE&WWA*, *CelR 3*,
  NotNAT
McCarthy, Michael 1917-1959 *FilmgC*
McCarthy, Myles d1928 *Film 2*, *WhScrn 1*,
  WhScrn 2, *WhoHol B*
McCarthy, Neil *WhoHol A*
McCarthy, Nobu *WhoHol A*
McCarthy, Pat 1911-1943 *WhScrn 1*, *WhScrn 2*
McCartney, Paul 1942- *CelR 3*, *MotPP*,
  WhoHol A
McCarty, E Clayton 1901- *BiE&WWA*, *NotNAT*
McCarty, Mary 1923- *WhoHol A*, *WhoThe 16*
McCathren, Don 1925- *AmSCAP 1966*
McCauley, Edna d1919 *WhScrn 2*
McCauley, Jack 1900- *EncMT*
McCay, Peggy *WhoHol A*
McCay, Winsor *WorEnF*
McClain, Billy 1857-1950 *WhScrn 1*, *WhScrn 2*,
  WhoHol B
McClain, John Wilcox 1904-1967 *BiE&WWA*,
  NotNAT B
McClanahan, Rue *WhoHol A*, *WhoThe 16*
McClay, Clyde 1895-1939 *WhScrn 1*, *WhScrn 2*
McCleary, Fiona 1900- *AmSCAP 1966*
McCleery, Albert d1972 *NotNAT B*
McClellan, Hurd d1933 *WhScrn 1*, *WhScrn 2*
McClellan, John 1896- *CelR 3*
McClelland, Allan 1917- *WhoThe 16*
McClelland, Donald 1903-1955 *NotNAT B*,
  WhScrn 2
McClendon, Ernestine 1918- *BiE&WWA*,
  WhoHol A
McClendon, Rose 1885-1936 *NotNAT B*
McClendon, Sarah 1911- *CelR 3*
McCleod, Norman Z 1898-1964 *WorEnF*
McClintic, Guthrie 1893-1961 *NotNAT A*,
  NotNAT B, *OxThe*, *WhThe*
McClintock, Harry Kirby 1882-1957
  AmSCAP 1966
McClory, Kevin 1926- *FilmgC*
McClory, Sean *WhoHol A*
McClory, Sean 1923- *FilmgC*
McClory, Sean 1924- *IntMPA 1977*, *Vers B*
McCloskey, Elizabeth H 1870-1942 *WhScrn 1*,
  WhScrn 2
McCloskey, James R 1918- *BiE&WWA*
McCloskey, Paul 1927- *CelR 3*
McClung, Bobby 1921-1945 *WhScrn 1*, *WhScrn 2*
McClung, Robert d1945 *WhoHol B*
McClure, A W *Film 1*
McClure, Bud 1886-1942 *WhScrn 1*, *WhScrn 2*,
  WhoHol B
McClure, Doug 1935- *MotPP*, *WhoHol A*
McClure, Douglas 1935- *FilmgC*
McClure, Frank 1895-1960 *WhScrn 2*, *WhoHol B*
McClure, Greg 1918- *FilmgC*
McClure, Irene d1928 *WhScrn 1*, *WhScrn 2*
McClure, Michael 1932- *ConDr 1977*, *NatPD*
McClure, Wendy 1934- *IntMPA 1977*
McClure, William K 1922- *IntMPA 1977*
McCluskey, Ellen *CelR 3*
McCollin, Frances 1892-1960 *AmSCAP 1966*
McComas, Carroll d1962 *Film 1*, *NotNAT B*
McComas, Carroll 1886-1962 *WhScrn 1*,

WhScrn 2, *WhoHol B*
McComas, Carroll 1891-1962 *WhThe*
McComas, Glenn 1900-1959 *WhScrn 1*,
  WhScrn 2
McComas, Lila 1906-1936 *WhScrn 1*, *WhScrn 2*
McComb, Jeanne 1913- *AmSCAP 1966*
McComb, Kate d1959 *NotNAT B*
McConnaughey, George C d1966 *NewYTET*
McConnell, Forrest W d1962 *NotNAT B*
McConnell, Frederic *PIP&P*
McConnell, George B 1894- *AmSCAP 1966*
McConnell, Gladys 1907- *Film 2*, *TwYS*,
  WhoHol A
McConnell, Joseph H *NewYTET*
McConnell, Keith *WhoHol A*
McConnell, Lulu d1961 *NotNAT B*
McConnell, Lulu 1882-1962 *WhScrn 1*, *WhScrn 2*,
  WhoHol B
McConnell, Mollie 1870-1920 *Film 1*, *WhoHol B*
McConnell, Molly 1870-1920 *WhScrn 1*,
  WhScrn 2
McCord, Kent *WhoHol A*
McCord, Mrs. Lewis d1917 *Film 1*, *WhScrn 2*
McCord, Nancy *WhThe*
McCord, Ted 1912- *FilmgC*, *WorEnF*
McCord, Vera *WomWMM*
McCormac, Muriel *Film 2*
McCormack, Billie d1935 *WhScrn 1*, *WhScrn 2*
McCormack, Frank *Film 2*
McCormack, Frank d1941 *NotNAT B*
McCormack, Hugh *Film 2*
McCormack, John 1884-1945 *FilmgC*, *NotNAT B*,
  WhScrn 1, *WhScrn 2*, *WhoHol B*
McCormack, Marni *WomWMM B*
McCormack, Patty 1945- *BiE&WWA*, *FilmgC*,
  MotPP, *MovMk*, *NotNAT*, *WhoHol A*
McCormack, William M 1891-1953 *WhScrn 1*,
  WhScrn 2
McCormick, Alyce 1904-1932 *WhScrn 1*,
  WhScrn 2, *WhoHol B*
McCormick, Arthur Langdon d1954 *NotNAT B*,
  WhThe
McCormick, Clifford *AmSCAP 1966*
McCormick, F J d1948 *WhoHol B*
McCormick, F J 1891-1947 *FilmgC*, *NotNAT B*,
  WhScrn 1, *WhScrn 2*
McCormick, Merrill d1953 *Film 2*, *WhoHol B*
McCormick, Myron 1907-1962 *WhThe*
McCormick, Myron 1908-1962 *FilmgC*,
  NotNAT B, *WhScrn 1*, *WhScrn 2*,
  WhoHol B
McCowan, Alex *PIP&P*
McCowan, George *FilmgC*
McCowen, Alec 1925- *CelR 3*, *CnThe*, *FilmgC*,
  MovMk, *NotNAT*, *WhoHol A*, *WhoThe 16*
McCoy, Bill d1975 *WhoHol C*
McCoy, Clyde *Film 2*, *TwYS*
McCoy, D'Arcy *Film 2*
McCoy, Evelyn 1913- *Film 2*
McCoy, Frank d1947 *NotNAT B*
McCoy, Gertrude 1896-1967 *Film 1*, *Film 2*,
  TwYS, *WhScrn 1*, *WhScrn 2*, *WhoHol B*
McCoy, Hansen *Film 1*
McCoy, Harry 1894-1937 *Film 1*, *Film 2*, *TwYS*,
  WhScrn 1, *WhScrn 2*, *WhoHol B*
McCoy, Kid *WhScrn 1*, *WhScrn 2*
McCoy, Ruby *Film 2*
McCoy, Sid *WhoHol A*
McCoy, Tim 1891- *FilmgC*, *IntMPA 1977*,
  MotPP, *TwYS*, *WhoHol A*
McCoy, Tim 1893- *Film 2*
McCracken, Esther 1902- *WhThe*
McCracken, Joan d1961 *MotPP*, *WhoHol B*
McCracken, Joan 1922-1961 *EncMT*, *NotNAT B*,

WhThe
McCracken, Joan 1923-1961 WhScrn 1,
  WhScrn 2
McCrary, Tex 1910- IntMPA 1977
McCray, Joe Film 2
McCrea, Ann WhoHol A
McCrea, Bonnie WomWMM
McCrea, Jody MotPP, WhoHol A
McCrea, Joel 1905- BiDFlm, CmMov, Film 2,
  FilmgC, IntMPA 1977, MotPP, MovMk,
  OxFilm, WhoHol A, WorEnF
McCree, Junie 1865-1918 AmSCAP 1966
McCreery, Bud 1925- BiE&WWA, NotNAT,
  WhoHol A
McCreery, Walker 1921- AmSCAP 1966
McCue, Maureen WomWMM B
McCullers, Carson 1916-1967 FilmgC, PIP&P
McCullers, Carson 1917-1967 BiE&WWA,
  CnMD, McGWD, ModWD, NotNAT B
McCulloch, Andrew WhoHol A
McCullough, John E 1832-1885 FamA&A,
  NotNAT A, OxThe
McCullough, John E 1837-1885 NotNAT B
McCullough, Paul d1936 WhoHol B
McCullough, Paul 1883-1936 WhThe
McCullough, Paul 1884-1936 FilmgC, WhScrn 1,
  WhScrn 2
McCullough, Paul 1892-1936 Film 2
McCullough, Philo 1893- Film 1, Film 2, TwYS,
  WhoHol A
McCullum, Bartley d1916 WhScrn 2
McCurdy, Ed 1919- AmSCAP 1966
McCurry, John WhoHol A
McCutcheon, Bill WhoHol A
McCutcheon, George Barr 1866-1928 WhScrn 2
McCutcheon, Ralph 1899-1975 WhScrn 2
McCutcheon, Wallace 1881-1928 Film 1, Film 2,
  NotNAT B, WhScrn 1, WhScrn 2,
  WhoHol B
McDaniel, Etta 1890-1946 WhScrn 2
McDaniel, George 1886-1944 Film 1, Film 2,
  WhScrn 1, WhScrn 2, WhoHol B
McDaniel, Hattie 1895-1952 FilmgC, MotPP,
  MovMk, NotNAT B, OxFilm, ThFT,
  Vers A, WhScrn 1, WhScrn 2, WhoHol B
McDaniel, Sam 1886-1962 WhScrn 2, WhoHol B
McDermott, Aline d1951 NotNAT B
McDermott, Hugh 1908-1972 FilmgC, WhScrn 2,
  WhThe, WhoHol B
McDermott, John 1892-1946 WhoHol B
McDermott, John see also MacDermott, John W
  Jack
McDermott, Joseph Film 1
McDermott, Marc 1880-1929 Film 1
McDermott, Marc 1881-1929 WhScrn 1,
  WhScrn 2
McDermott, Marc see also MacDermott, Marc
McDermott, Thomas NewYTET
McDermott, William F d1958 NotNAT B
McDevitt, Ruth 1895-1976 BiE&WWA, NotNAT,
  WhoHol A, WhoThe 16
McDiarmid, Don 1898- AmSCAP 1966
McDonagh Sisters WomWMM
McDonald, Charles B 1886-1964 WhScrn 1,
  WhScrn 2, WhoHol B
McDonald, Christie 1875-1962 WhThe
McDonald, Christie see also MacDonald, Christie
McDonald, Claire Film 2
McDonald, Dan Film 2
McDonald, Eugene, Jr. d1958 NewYTET
McDonald, Francis 1891-1968 Film 1, Film 2,
  TwYS, Vers B, WhScrn 1, WhScrn 2,
  WhoHol B
McDonald, Frank 1899- FilmgC, IntMPA 1977

McDonald, Harl 1899-1955 AmSCAP 1966
McDonald, Inez Film 2
McDonald, James 1886-1952 WhScrn 1,
  WhScrn 2
McDonald, Joseph 1861-1935 WhScrn 1,
  WhScrn 2
McDonald, Kenneth TwYS A
McDonald, Marie 1923-1965 FilmgC, MotPP,
  WhScrn 1, WhScrn 2, WhoHol B
McDonald, Melbourn Film 2
McDonald, Ray 1920-1959 FilmgC
McDonald, Ray 1924-1959 NotNAT B,
  WhScrn 1, WhScrn 2, WhoHol B
McDonald, Wilfred Film 2
McDonald, William Film 2, WhoHol A
McDonell, Fergus 1910-1968 FilmgC
McDonnel, G L Film 2
McDonnell, James 1899- CelR 3
McDonough, Gerald M 1945- NatPD
McDonough, Jerome 1946- NatPD
McDonough, Michael 1876-1956 WhScrn 1,
  WhScrn 2
McDonough, W S Film 2
McDougall, Gordon 1941- WhoThe 16
McDougall, Peter ConDr 1977C
McDougall, Rex Film 1, Film 2
McDowall, Betty IntMPA 1977
McDowall, Malcolm 1943- IntMPA 1977
McDowall, Roddy 1928- BiE&WWA, FilmgC,
  IntMPA 1977, MotPP, MovMk, NotNAT,
  OxFilm, WhoHol A, WhoThe 16
McDowell, Claire d1967 WhoHol B
McDowell, Claire 1877-1966 WhScrn 1,
  WhScrn 2
McDowell, Claire 1887-1967 Film 1, Film 2,
  TwYS
McDowell, John H 1903- BiE&WWA, NotNAT
McDowell, Malcolm WhoHol A
McDowell, Malcolm 1943- MovMk
McDowell, Malcolm 1944- FilmgC
McDowell, Melbourne Film 2
McDowell, Nelson 1875-1947 Film 2, WhScrn 1,
  WhScrn 2, WhoHol B
McEachin, James WhoHol A
McEarchan, Malcolm d1945 NotNAT B
McEdward, Gordon Film 2
McElhern, James Film 2
McElroy, Jack 1914-1959 WhScrn 1, WhScrn 2,
  WhoHol B
McElroy, Leo F 1932- AmSCAP 1966
McEnery, David 1914- AmSCAP 1966
McEnery, John 1945- FilmgC, WhoHol A
McEnery, Peter 1940- FilmgC, MotPP,
  WhoHol A, WhoThe 16
McEnroe, Robert E BiE&WWA
McEveety, Bernard FilmgC, IntMPA 1977,
  NewYTET, TwYS A
McEveety, Joseph IntMPA 1977
McEveety, Vince FilmgC
McEveety, Vincent IntMPA 1977
McEvilly, Burton Film 2
McEvoy, Charles 1879-1929 NotNAT B, WhThe
McEvoy, Dorothea d1976 WhoHol C
McEvoy, Ernest Simon 1894-1953 WhScrn 1,
  WhScrn 2
McEvoy, J P 1894-1958 NotNAT B, WhThe
McEvoy, J P 1895-1958 NewMT
McEwan, Geraldine 1932- BiE&WWA, NotNAT,
  PIP&P, WhoHol A, WhoThe 16
McEwan, Isabelle 1897-1963 WhScrn 1,
  WhScrn 2
McEwan, Jack Film 2
McEwen, Geraldine 1932- CnThe
McEwen, Walter 1905- Film 1, Film 2

McFadden, Charles I 1888-1942 *WhScrn 1*
McFadden, Frank 1914- *IntMPA 1977*
McFadden, Ira *Film 2*
McFadden, Ivor 1887-1942 *Film 1, Film 2, WhScrn 2*
McFarland, Dale H 1918- *IntMPA 1977*
McFarland, Olive *MotPP*
McFarland, Packy *WhoHol A*
McFarland, Spanky 1928- *FilmgC, MovMk, WhoHol A*
McFarland, Spanky *see also* MacFarland, Spanky
McFarlane, George 1877-1932 *Film 2, WhoHol B*
McFarlane, George 1887-1932 *NotNAT B*
McFarlane, George *see also* MacFarlane, George
McFeeters, Raymond 1899- *AmSCAP 1966*
McGann, William 1895- *FilmgC*
McGannon, Donald H 1920- *IntMPA 1977, NewYTET*
McGarrity, Everett *Film 2*
McGarry, Vera *Film 1*
McGarvey, Cathal *Film 2*
McGaugh, Wilbur 1895-1965 *Film 2, WhScrn 1, WhScrn 2, WhoHol B*
McGavin, Darren 1922- *BiE&WWA, FilmgC, IntMPA 1977, MotPP, MovMk, NotNAT, WhoHol A*
McGaw, Charles 1910- *BiE&WWA, NotNAT*
McGee, Fibber 1897- *FilmgC*
McGee, Florence *PIP&P*
McGee, Frank 1921-1974 *CelR 3, NewYTET*
McGee, Harold J d1955 *NotNAT B*
McGee, Pat 1906- *IntMPA 1977*
McGee, Patricia *Film 2*
McGee, Vonetta *WhoHol A*
McGeehee, Gloria 1922-1964 *WhoHol B*
McGhee, Gloria 1922-1964 *WhScrn 2*
McGhee, Howard 1918- *AmSCAP 1966*
McGhee, Paul A d1964 *NotNAT B*
McGibeny, Ruth T 1896- *AmSCAP 1966*
McGilvray, Laura *WhoStg 1908*
McGilvray, Laura *see also* M'Gilvray, Laura
McGinley, Laurence Joseph 1905- *BiE&WWA, NotNAT*
McGinley, Phyllis 1905- *CelR 3*
McGinn, Walter 1936- *NotNAT, PIP&P A, WhoHol A*
McGiveney, Owen 1884-1967 *WhScrn 1, WhScrn 2, WhoHol B*
McGiver, John 1913-1975 *BiE&WWA, FilmgC, MotPP, MovMk, NotNAT B, WhScrn 2, WhoHol C, WhoThe 16*
McGlinn, Ann J 1922- *AmSCAP 1966*
McGlynn, Frank 1866-1951 *NotNAT B, WhThe*
McGlynn, Frank 1867-1951 *Film 1, Film 2, Vers A, WhScrn 1, WhScrn 2, WhoHol B*
McGoohan, Patrick 1928- *FilmgC, IntMPA 1977, MotPP, WhThe, WhoHol A*
McGovern, George 1922- *CelR 3*
McGovern, John *BiE&WWA, NotNAT*
McGowan, Bob *Film 1*
McGowan, Bryan *Film 2*
McGowan, Dorothy *Film 2*
McGowan, Dorrell *IntMPA 1977*
McGowan, J P 1880-1952 *Film 1, Film 2, TwYS, TwYS A, WhoHol B*
McGowan, John P 1880-1952 *NotNAT B, WhScrn 1, WhScrn 2*
McGowan, John W 1892- *BiE&WWA, NotNAT, WhThe*
McGowan, Oliver F 1907-1971 *BiE&WWA, NotNAT B, WhScrn 1, WhScrn 2, WhoHol B*
McGowan, Robert A 1901- *IntMPA 1977*
McGowan, Stuart *IntMPA 1977*

McGrail, Walter d1970 *WhoHol B*
McGrail, Walter 1889-1970 *Film 1, Film 2, TwYS*
McGrail, Walter B 1899-1970 *WhScrn 1, WhScrn 2*
McGranary, Al 1902-1971 *WhScrn 2, WhoHol B*
McGrane, Paul J 1902- *AmSCAP 1966*
McGrane, Thomas J *Film 1*
McGrath, Dennis 1875?-1955 *WhScrn 2*
McGrath, Frank 1903-1967 *FilmgC, WhScrn 1, WhScrn 2, WhoHol B*
McGrath, Fulton 1907-1958 *AmSCAP 1966*
McGrath, Joe 1930- *FilmgC*
McGrath, John 1935- *CnThe, ConDr 1977, WhoThe 16*
McGrath, Larry 1888-1960 *Film 2, WhScrn 2, WhoHol B*
McGrath, Michael d1976 *WhoHol C*
McGrath, Paul 1904- *BiE&WWA, NotNAT, WhoHol A, WhoThe 16*
McGrath, Thomas J *IntMPA 1977*
McGraw, Cameron 1919- *AmSCAP 1966*
McGraw, Charles *MotPP*
McGraw, Charles 1914- *FilmgC, WhoHol A*
McGraw, George Donald 1927- *AmSCAP 1966*
McGraw, John 1873-1934 *WhScrn 2*
McGraw, John J *Film 1*
McGraw, William Ralph 1930- *BiE&WWA, NotNAT*
McGreal, E B Mike 1905- *IntMPA 1977*
McGregor, Charles 1927- *IntMPA 1977*
McGregor, Gordon *Film 2*
McGregor, Harmon d1948 *Film 2, WhoHol B*
McGregor, Malcolm 1892-1945 *Film 2, MotPP, NotNAT B, TwYS, WhScrn 1, WhScrn 2, WhoHol B*
McGregor, Parke 1907-1962 *NotNAT B, WhScrn 1, WhScrn 2*
McGuinn, Joe d1971 *WhoHol B*
McGuinn, Joseph Ford 1904-1971 *WhScrn 1, WhScrn 2*
McGuire, Benjamin 1875-1925 *WhScrn 1, WhScrn 2, WhoHol B*
McGuire, Biff *WhoHol A*
McGuire, Biff 1926- *WhoThe 16*
McGuire, Biff 1927- *BiE&WWA, NotNAT*
McGuire, Don 1919- *FilmgC, IntMPA 1977, WhoHol A*
McGuire, Dorothy *MotPP, WhoHol A*
McGuire, Dorothy 1918- *BiDFlm, BiE&WWA, MovMk, NotNAT, WhoThe 16, WorEnF*
McGuire, Dorothy 1919- *FilmgC, IntMPA 1977, OxFilm*
McGuire, Harp 1921-1966 *WhScrn 2*
McGuire, Kathryn 1897- *Film 2, TwYS, WhoHol A*
McGuire, Maeve *WhoHol A*
McGuire, Michael *PIP&P A*
McGuire, Mickey 1922- *Film 2, TwYS*
McGuire, Paddy *Film 1*
McGuire, Tom 1874-1954 *Film 2, WhScrn 1, WhScrn 2, WhoHol B*
McGuire, William Anthony 1885-1940 *EncMT, NotNAT B, WhThe*
McGuirk, Harriet 1903-1975 *WhScrn 2, WhoHol C*
McGurk, Bob 1907-1959 *WhScrn 1, WhScrn 2*
McGurk, J W *Film 2*
McGurk, Robert d1959 *WhoHol B*
McHale, James d1973 *WhScrn 2*
McHale, Rosemary 1944- *WhoThe 16*
McHenry, Don 1908- *BiE&WWA, NotNAT*
McHenry, Nellie d1935 *NotNAT B*
McHugh, Catherine 1869-1944 *WhScrn 1,*

WhScrn 2, WhoHol B
McHugh, Charles Patrick d1931 Film 2,
    WhScrn 1, WhScrn 2, WhoHol B
McHugh, Florence 1906- WhThe
McHugh, Frank MotPP
McHugh, Frank 1898- BiE&WWA, Film 2,
    NotNAT, WhoHol A
McHugh, Frank 1899- FilmgC, IntMPA 1977,
    MovMk, Vers A
McHugh, Jack Film 2
McHugh, James 1915- IntMPA 1977
McHugh, James Francis 1896-1969 NotNAT B
McHugh, Jimmy d1969 WhoHol B
McHugh, Jimmy 1894-1969 AmSCAP 1966,
    EncMT, NewMT, WhScrn 1, WhScrn 2
McHugh, Jimmy 1895-1969 FilmgC
McHugh, Jimmy 1896-1969 BiE&WWA,
    NotNAT B
McHugh, Matt 1894-1971 Vers B, WhScrn 1,
    WhScrn 2, WhoHol B
McHugh, Therese WhThe
McIllwain, William A 1863-1933 Film 2,
    WhScrn 1, WhScrn 2, WhoHol B
McIlrath, Patricia 1917- BiE&WWA, NotNAT
McIntire, John 1907- BiDFlm, FilmgC, .
    IntMPA 1977, MotPP, WhoHol A, WorEnF
McIntire, Lani 1904-1951 AmSCAP 1966
McIntire, Tim WhoHol A
McIntosh, Burr 1862-1942 Film 1, Film 2,
    NotNAT B, TwYS, WhScrn 1, WhScrn 2,
    WhoHol B
McIntosh, Madge 1875-1950 NotNAT B, WhThe
McIntosh, Morris Film 2
McIntosh, Stanley 1908- IntMPA 1977
McIntyre, Duncan 1907-1973 WhScrn 2
McIntyre, Frank d1949 Film 1, MotPP,
    WhoHol B
McIntyre, Frank 1878-1949 WhScrn 1, WhScrn 2
McIntyre, Frank 1879-1949 NotNAT B, WhThe
McIntyre, James T 1857-1937 NotNAT B,
    WhoStg 1908
McIntyre, John 1907- Vers B
McIntyre, John T d1951 NotNAT B
McIntyre, Leila 1882-1953 NotNAT B,
    WhScrn 1, WhScrn 2, WhoHol B
McIntyre, Marion 1885-1975 WhScrn 2,
    WhoHol C
McIntyre, Mark W 1916- AmSCAP 1966
McIntyre, Molly d1952 NotNAT B
McIntyre, Tom Film 2
McIntyre And Heath WhoStg 1908
McIvor, Mary 1901-1941 Film 2, WhScrn 1,
    WhScrn 2, WhoHol B
McKay, Allison WhoHol A
McKay, Francis Howard 1901- AmSCAP 1966
McKay, Fred Film 1, Film 2
McKay, Frederick E d1944 NotNAT B
McKay, Gardner WhoHol A
McKay, George Frederick 1899- AmSCAP 1966
McKay, George W 1880-1945 WhScrn 1,
    WhScrn 2, WhoHol B
McKay, Jim NewYTET
McKay, John 1923- CelR 3
McKay, Neil 1924- AmSCAP 1966
McKay, Norman 1906-1968 WhScrn 1,
    WhScrn 2
McKay, Norman see also MacKaye, Norman
McKay, Scott 1915- BiE&WWA, NotNAT,
    WhoHol A, WhoThe 16
McKay, Winsor Film 2
McKayle, Donald 1930- BiE&WWA, NotNAT,
    WhoHol A
McKechnie, Donna 1940- WhoHol A,
    WhoThe 16

McKechnie, James d1964 NotNAT B
McKee, Arthur W 1891-1953 AmSCAP 1966
McKee, Bob Film 2
McKee, Buck 1865-1944 WhScrn 1, WhScrn 2
McKee, Clive R 1883- WhThe
McKee, Donald M 1899-1968 WhScrn 1,
    WhScrn 2, WhoHol B
McKee, Frank Film 2
McKee, Frank W 1867-1944 AmSCAP 1966
McKee, John d1953 NotNAT B
McKee, Lafayette Film 1
McKee, Lafe 1872-1959 Film 2, TwYS, Vers B,
    WhScrn 2, WhoHol B
McKee, Lonette WhoHol A
McKee, Pat 1897-1950 WhScrn 2
McKee, Raymond Film 1, Film 2, TwYS
McKee, Tom 1917-1960 WhScrn 1, WhScrn 2,
    WhoHol B
McKeen, Lawrence D, Jr. Snookums 1925-1933
    WhScrn 1, WhScrn 2
McKeen, Sunny d1933 Film 2, WhoHol B
McKeever, Mike 1940-1967 WhScrn 2
McKellar, Kenneth IntMPA 1977
McKellen, Ian WhoHol A, WhoThe 16
McKellen, Ian 1935- FilmgC
McKellen, Ian 1939- CnThe
McKelvie, Harold 1910-1937 WhScrn 1,
    WhScrn 2
McKelvy, Lige William 1904-1965 AmSCAP 1966
McKenna, David 1930- AmSCAP 1966
McKenna, David 1949- NotNAT
McKenna, Henry T 1894-1958 WhScrn 1,
    WhScrn 2
McKenna, Kenneth 1899-1962 MovMk
McKenna, Kenneth see also MacKenna, Kenneth
McKenna, Peggy WhoHol A
McKenna, Siobhan MotPP, PIP&P, WhoHol A
McKenna, Siobhan 1922- BiE&WWA, NotNAT
McKenna, Siobhan 1923- CelR 3, CnThe,
    FilmgC, IntMPA 1977, WhoThe 16
McKenna, T P WhoHol A
McKenna, T P 1929- WhoThe 16
McKenna, T P 1931- FilmgC
McKenna, Virginia 1931- FilmgC, WhoHol A,
    WhoThe 16
McKenna, William J 1881-1950 AmSCAP 1966,
    NotNAT B
McKenney, Ruth 1911-1972 NotNAT B
McKennon, Dallas WhoHol A
McKenzie, Alexander 1886-1966 WhScrn 1
McKenzie, Alexander see also MacKenzie,
    Alexander
McKenzie, Bob d1949 Film 2, WhoHol B
McKenzie, Donald TwYS A
McKenzie, Donald see also MacKenzie, Donald
McKenzie, Ella WhoHol A
McKenzie, Eva B 1889-1967 WhScrn 1,
    WhScrn 2, WhoHol B
McKenzie, Fay WhoHol A
McKenzie, James B 1926- BiE&WWA, NotNAT,
    WhoThe 16
McKenzie, Louis WhoHol A
McKenzie, Robert 1881-1949 Vers B
McKenzie, Robert B 1883-1949 WhScrn 1,
    WhScrn 2
McKern, Leo 1920- CnThe, FilmgC, MovMk,
    WhoHol A, WhoThe 16
McKim, Robert 1887-1927 Film 1, Film 2,
    TwYS, WhScrn 1, WhScrn 2, WhoHol B
McKinley, J Edward WhoHol A
McKinley, Ray 1910- AmSCAP 1966
McKinnel, Norman 1870-1932 NotNAT B,
    WhScrn 1, WhThe
McKinnell, Norman 1870-1932 Film 2, WhScrn 2,

WhoHol B
McKinney, Alene *AmSCAP 1966*
McKinney, Bill *WhoHol A*
McKinney, George W 1923- *BiE&WWA*
McKinney, Howard D 1890- *AmSCAP 1966*
McKinney, Nina Mae 1909-1967 *WhoHol B*
McKinney, Nina Mae 1909-1968 *FilmgC, ThFT, WhScrn 1, WhScrn 2*
McKinney, Nina May 1909-1968 *Film 2*
McKinnon, Al *Film 1*
McKinnon, John *Film 1, Film 2*
McKnight, Anna *WomWMM*
McKnight, Tom d1963 *NotNAT B*
McKuen, Rod *WhoHol A*
McKuen, Rod 1933- *CelR 3*
McKuen, Rod 1938- *AmSCAP 1966*
McLaglen, Andrew 1925- *FilmgC, MovMk*
McLaglen, Andrew V 1920- *CmMov, IntMPA 1977, WorEnF*
McLaglen, Clifford *Film 2*
McLaglen, Cyril *Film 2*
McLaglen, Victor d1959 *MotPP, WhoHol B*
McLaglen, Victor 1883-1959 *CmMov, FilmgC, TwYS*
McLaglen, Victor 1886-1959 *BiDFlm, CmMov, Film 2, MovMk, NotNAT B, OxFilm, WhScrn 1, WhScrn 2, WorEnF*
McLaine, Marilyn *Film 2*
McLane, Mary *Film 2*
McLaren, Audrey *WomWMM*
McLaren, Marilyn *WomWMM B*
McLaren, Norman 1914- *DcFM, FilmgC, OxFilm, WorEnF*
McLaughlin, Ed *Film 1*
McLaughlin, Gibb 1884- *Film 2, FilmgC, WhoHol A*
McLaughlin, J B *Film 1*
McLaughlin, Jeff *Film 2*
McLaughlin, John 1897-1968 *AmSCAP 1966, NotNAT B*
McLaughlin, Leonard B 1892- *BiE&WWA*
McLaughlin, Millicent *WhoStg 1908*
McLaughlin, William *Film 2*
McLaughlin-Gill, Frances 1919- *WomWMM B*
McLaurin, Kate 1885- *WhoStg 1908*
McLean, Alastair 1922- *FilmgC*
McLean, Barbara *WomWMM*
McLean, D D *Film 2*
McLean, William *WhoHol A*
McLellan, C M S 1865-1916 *EncMT, NotNAT B, WhThe, WhoStg 1908*
McLellan, C M S see also M'Lellan, C M S
McLellan, G B d1932 *NotNAT B*
McLeod, Archibald 1906- *BiE&WWA, NotNAT*
McLeod, Barbara 1908-1940 *WhScrn 1, WhScrn 2*
McLeod, Catherine 1924?- *FilmgC, MotPP, WhoHol A*
McLeod, Duncan *WhoHol A*
McLeod, Elsie *Film 1*
McLeod, Gordon *Film 2*
McLeod, Helen 1924-1964 *NotNAT B, WhScrn 1, WhScrn 2*
McLeod, Keith 1894-1961 *AmSCAP 1966*
McLeod, Norman Z 1898-1964 *BiDFlm, DcFM, FilmgC, MovMk*
McLeod, Tex 1896-1973 *WhScrn 2*
McLerie, Allyn Ann 1926- *BiE&WWA, FilmgC, IntMPA 1977, NotNAT, WhoHol A, WhoThe 16*
McLiam, John 1920- *BiE&WWA, NatPD, NotNAT, WhoHol A*
McLuhan, Marshall 1911- *CelR 3, NewYTET*
McLuhan, T C *WomWMM B*

McMahon, Aline 1899- *PIP&P*
McMahon, Aline see also MacMahon, Aline
McMahon, David 1909-1972 *WhScrn 2, WhoHol B*
McMahon, Ed 1923- *CelR 3, IntMPA 1977, WhoHol A*
McMahon, Horace 1907-1971 *BiE&WWA, MotPP, MovMk, NotNAT B, WhScrn 1, WhScrn 2, WhoHol B*
McMahon, Horace see also MacMahon, Horace
McMahon, John G d1968 *WhScrn 2*
McMahon, John J 1932- *IntMPA 1977*
McManus, George d1954 *Film 2, WhScrn 2*
McManus, John L 1897-1963 *AmSCAP 1966, NotNAT B*
McMartin, John *NotNAT, WhoHol A, WhoThe 16*
McMaster, Andrew *Film 2*
McMaster, Anew 1894-1962 *NotNAT B, OxThe, WhThe*
McMaster, Anew see also MacMaster, Anew
McMillan, Lida d1940 *NotNAT B*
McMillan, Roddy 1923- *WhoThe 16*
McMillan, Walter Kenneth 1917-1945 *WhScrn 1, WhScrn 2*
McMillen, Violet 1885- *WhoStg 1908*
McMillen, Violet see also MacMillian, Violet
McMullan, Frank 1907- *BiE&WWA, NotNAT*
McMullan, Jim *WhoHol A*
McMullen, Dorothy 1926- *AmSCAP 1966*
McMullen, Edwin D 1911- *AmSCAP 1966*
McMurray, Lillian *Film 2*
McMurray, Richard *WhoHol A*
McMurray, Vance 1910- *AmSCAP 1966*
McNair, Barbara *BiE&WWA, WhoHol A*
McNair, Sue *WomWMM*
McNally, Ed *WhoHol A*
McNally, John J d1931 *NotNAT B*
McNally, Stephen 1913- *FilmgC, IntMPA 1977, WhoHol A*
McNally, Terrence 1930- *CroCD*
McNally, Terrence 1939- *CelR 3, ConDr 1977, McGWD, NatPD, NotNAT, PIP&P, WhoThe 16*
McNamar, John d1968 *WhScrn 2*
McNamara, Daniel I d1962 *NotNAT B*
McNamara, Edward C 1884-1944 *Film 2, WhScrn 1, WhScrn 2, WhoHol B*
McNamara, Edward J d1944 *NotNAT B*
McNamara, Maggie 1928- *FilmgC, IntMPA 1977, MotPP, WhoHol A*
McNamara, Ray 1899- *AmSCAP 1966*
McNamara, Robert 1916- *CelR 3*
McNamara, Ted d1928 *Film 2, WhScrn 1, WhScrn 2, WhoHol B*
McNamara, Thomas J d1953 *WhScrn 1, WhScrn 2*
McNamee, Donald 1897-1940 *WhScrn 1, WhScrn 2, WhoHol B*
McNames, Dorothy *Film 2*
McNaught, Bob 1915- *FilmgC*
McNaughton, Charles *Film 2*
McNaughton, Gus 1884-1969 *FilmgC, WhScrn 1, WhScrn 2, WhThe, WhoHol B*
McNaughton, Harry 1897-1967 *WhScrn 1, WhScrn 2, WhoHol B*
McNaughton, Jack *WhoHol A*
McNaughton, Tom 1867-1923 *WhThe*
McNaughtons, The *WhThe*
McNay, Evelyn d1944 *NotNAT B*
McNear, Howard 1905-1969 *WhScrn 1, WhScrn 2, WhoHol B*
McNeely, Jerry C *NewYTET*
McNeil, Claudia 1917- *BiE&WWA, NotNAT,*

WhoHol A, WhoThe 16
McNeil, J Charles 1902- *AmSCAP 1966*
McNeil, Robert A 1889- *IntMPA 1977*
McNellis, Maggi *IntMPA 1977*
McNeur, Lynda *WomWMM B*
McNichol, Eileen *BiE&WWA, NotNAT*
McNulty, Dorothy *WhoHol A*
McNulty, Frank 1923- *AmSCAP 1966*
McNutt, Patterson d1948 *NotNAT B*
McPartland, Marian 1918- *AmSCAP 1966*
McPeters, Taylor 1900-1962 *NotNAT B,
    WhScrn 1, WhScrn 2*
McPhail, Addie *Film 2*
McPhail, Douglas d1942 *WhoHol B*
McPhail, Douglas 1910-1944 *WhScrn 1,
    WhScrn 2*
McPhail, Lenora Carpenter 1907- *AmSCAP 1966*
McPhail, Lindsay 1895-1965 *AmSCAP 1966*
McPherson, Margaret *WomWMM*
McPherson, Mervyn 1892- *WhThe*
McPherson, Quinton 1871-1940 *WhScrn 1,
    WhScrn 2, WhoHol B*
McQuade, Edward *Film 2*
McQuary, Charles S 1908-1970 *WhScrn 1,
    WhScrn 2*
McQueen, Butterfly 1911- *FilmgC, MotPP,
    MovMk, ThFT, WhoHol A, WhoThe 16*
McQueen, Steve 1930- *BiDFlm, CelR 3, FilmgC,
    IntMPA 1977, MotPP, MovMk, OxFilm,
    WhoHol A, WorEnF*
McQueen, Steve 1932- *CmMov*
McQueeney, Robert *IntMPA 1977*
McQuiggan, Jack 1935- *BiE&WWA, NotNAT*
McQuire, Tom *Film 2*
McQuoid, Rose Lee 1887-1962 *NotNAT B,
    WhScrn 1, WhScrn 2, WhoHol B*
McRae, Bruce 1867-1927 *Film 1, NotNAT B,
    WhScrn 1, WhScrn 2, WhThe,
    WhoStg 1908*
McRae, Duncan d1931 *NotNAT B, WhScrn 2*
McRae, Ellen *WhoHol A*
McRae, Henry 1888- *TwYS A*
McRae, Teddy 1908- *AmSCAP 1966*
McRea, Bruce 1867-1927 *WhoHol B*
McShane, Ian 1942- *FilmgC, WhoHol A,
    WhoThe 16*
McShane, Kitty 1898-1964 *NotNAT B,
    WhScrn 1, WhScrn 2, WhoHol B*
McTaggart, James 1911-1949 *WhScrn 1,
    WhScrn 2*
McTurk, Joe 1899-1961 *WhScrn 1, WhScrn 2*
McTurk, Joe 1899-1967 *WhoHol B*
McVeagh, Eve *WhoHol A*
McVey, Lucille *WhScrn 1, WhScrn 2*
McVey, Lucille 1892- *WomWMM*
McVey, Lucille 1895- *Film 1*
McVey, Patrick 1910-1973 *WhScrn 2, WhoHol B*
McVey, Tyler *WhoHol A*
McVicker, Horace d1931 *NotNAT B*
McVicker, J H d1896 *NotNAT B*
McVicker, Julius 1876-1940 *WhScrn 1,
    WhScrn 2, WhoHol B*
McVicker, Mary *PIP&P*
McWade, Edward d1943 *Film 2, WhScrn 1,
    WhScrn 2, WhoHol B*
McWade, Margaret d1956 *Film 2, WhoHol B*
McWade, Margaret 1872-1956 *WhScrn 2*
McWade, Margaret 1873-1956 *Vers B*
McWade, Robert, Jr. 1882-1938 *Film 2,
    NotNAT B, WhScrn 1, WhScrn 2, WhThe,
    WhoHol B*
McWade, Robert, Sr. 1835-1913 *NotNAT B,
    WhScrn 2, WhoHol B*
McWatters, Arthur J 1871-1963 *WhScrn 1,*

WhScrn 2
McWhinnie, Donald 1920- *BiE&WWA, NotNAT,
    WhoThe 16*
McWilliams, Carey 1905- *CelR 3*
McWilliams, Harry Kenneth 1907- *IntMPA 1977*
Meacham, Anne 1925- *BiE&WWA, NotNAT,
    WhoHol A, WhoThe 16*
Meachum, James H d1963 *NotNAT B*
Mead, Edward G 1892- *AmSCAP 1966*
Mead, George 1902- *AmSCAP 1966*
Mead, Margaret 1901- *CelR 3*
Mead, Robert *NewYTET*
Mead, Taylor *WhoHol A*
Mead, Thomas 1904- *IntMPA 1977*
Meade, Bill d1941 *WhScrn 1, WhScrn 2*
Meade, Claire 1883-1968 *WhScrn 2, WhoHol B*
Meade, E Kidder, Jr. *NewYTET*
Meade, Julia *WhoHol A*
Meade, Julia 1928- *BiE&WWA, NotNAT*
Meade, Julia 1930?- *CelR 3*
Meader, George 1888-1963 *WhScrn 2, WhThe*
Meader, George 1890-1963 *BiE&WWA,
    WhoHol B*
Meades, Kenneth Richardson 1943- *IntMPA 1977*
Meadow, Lynne 1946- *NotNAT*
Meadows, Audrey *MotPP, NewYTET,
    WhoHol A*
Meadows, Fred 1904- *AmSCAP 1966*
Meadows, George *Film 2*
Meadows, Jayne 1926- *BiE&WWA, MotPP,
    WhoHol A*
Meakin, Charles 1880-1961 *Film 2, WhScrn 1,
    WhScrn 2, WhoHol B*
Meakin, Ruth 1879-1939 *WhScrn 1, WhScrn 2*
Meakins, Charles d1951 *NotNAT B*
Meaney, Donald *NewYTET*
Meano, Cesare 1906-1958 *CnMD*
Meany, Donald V *IntMPA 1977*
Meany, George 1894- *CelR 3*
Meara, Anne *WhoHol A*
Mears, Benjamin S 1872-1952 *WhScrn 1,
    WhScrn 2*
Mears, J H d1956 *NotNAT B*
Mears, Marion 1899-1970 *WhScrn 1, WhScrn 2*
Mears, Martha *WhoHol A*
Measor, Adela 1860-1933 *NotNAT B, WhThe*
Measor, Beryl 1908-1965 *WhThe*
Mecum, Dudley C 1896- *AmSCAP 1966*
Medak, Peter *FilmgC*
Medcraft, Russell Graham d1962 *NotNAT B*
Medcroft, Russell *Film 2*
Meddoks, Mikhail Egorovich 1747-1825 *OxThe*
Medford, Don *FilmgC, IntMPA 1977*
Medford, Kay 1920- *BiE&WWA, NotNAT,
    WhoHol A, WhoThe 16*
Medford, Mark d1914 *NotNAT B*
Medici, Lorenzino DiPier Francesco *OxThe*
Medici, Lorenzo 1449?-1492 *OxThe*
Medin, Harriet *WhoHol A*
Medina, Patricia *IntMPA 1977, MotPP*
Medina, Patricia 1919- *WhoHol A*
Medina, Patricia 1920- *FilmgC, MovMk*
Medina, Patricia 1923- *BiE&WWA*
Medley, Cynthia Conwell 1929- *AmSCAP 1966*
Medley, William Thomas 1940- *IntMPA 1977*
Mednick, Murray 1939- *ConDr 1977, NotNAT*
Medoff, Mark 1940- *ConDr 1977, NatPD,
    NotNAT*
Medvedkin, Alexander 1900- *OxFilm*
Medwall, Henry *McGWD, OxThe*
Medwick, Joe d1975 *WhoHol C*
Medwin, Michael *WhoHol A*
Medwin, Michael 1923- *FilmgC*
Medwin, Michael 1925- *IntMPA 1977*

Mee, Charles Louis, Jr. 1938- *BiE&WWA*
Meech, Edward Montana d1952 *WhScrn 1,*
  WhScrn 2
Meehan, Danny *AmSCAP 1966, WhoHol A*
Meehan, John d1963 *NotNAT B*
Meehan, John 1890-1954 *WhScrn 1, WhScrn 2*
Meehan, Leo J *TwYS A*
Meehan, Lew 1891-1951 *Film 2, WhScrn 2,*
  WhoHol B
Meehan, Thomas G 1895- *AmSCAP 1966*
Meek, Donald 1880-1946 *Film 2, FilmgC,*
  MotPP, MovMk, NotNAT B, Vers A,
  WhScrn 1, WhScrn 2, WhThe, WhoHol B
Meek, Kate d1925 *NotNAT B*
Meeker, Alfred 1901-1942 *WhScrn 1, WhScrn 2*
Meeker, George 1888-1963 *Vers B*
Meeker, George 1904?-1963 *Film 2, TwYS,*
  WhScrn 1, WhoHol B
Meeker, John *Film 2*
Meeker, Ralph 1920- *BiDFlm, BiE&WWA,*
  CmMov, FilmgC, IntMPA 1977, MotPP,
  MovMk, NotNAT, WhoHol A, WhoThe 16,
  WorEnF
Meeks, Kate *Film 1*
Meeks, Larry 1930- *AmSCAP 1966*
Meerson, Lazare 1900-1938 *DcFM, FilmgC,*
  OxFilm, WorEnF
Meery, Ila *Film 2*
Megard, Andree 1869- *WhThe*
Meged, Aharon 1920- *CnThe, REnWD*
Meggs, Mary d1691 *OxThe*
Megna, John 1952- *BiE&WWA, WhoHol A*
Megowan, Don *WhoHol A*
Megrue, Roi Cooper 1883-1927 *NotNAT B,*
  WhThe
Mehaffey, Blanche 1907-1968 *Film 2, WhScrn 2,*
  WhoHol B
Mehaffey, Harry S d1963 *NotNAT B*
Mehboob 1907- *FilmgC*
Mehboob 1909- *WorEnF*
Mehboob Khan, Ramjakhan 1907-1964 *DcFM*
Mehle, Aileen *CelR 3*
Mehra, Lal Chand *WhoHol A*
Mehring, Margaret *WomWMM B*
Mehring, Walter 1896- *CnMD*
Mehrmann, Helen Alice d1934 *WhScrn 1,*
  WhScrn 2, WhoHol B
Mehta, Zubin 1936- *CelR 3*
Mei, Lan-Fang 1894-1943 *NotNAT A,*
  NotNAT B
Mei, Lan-Fang 1894-1961 *OxThe, REnWD*
Mei, Lady Tsen *Film 1, MotPP*
Meier, Don *NewYTET*
Meier, Herbert 1928- *CnMD*
Meigham, Margaret d1961 *WhScrn 1, WhScrn 2*
Meighan, James, Jr. d1970 *WhoHol B*
Meighan, Thomas 1879-1936 *Film 1, Film 2,*
  FilmgC, MotPP, MovMk, NotNAT B,
  TwYS, WhScrn 1, WhScrn 2, WhThe,
  WhoHol B
Meilhac, Henri 1831-1897 *McGWD, NotNAT B,*
  OxThe, PIP&P
Meillon, John 1933- *FilmgC, WhoHol A*
Meineche, Annelise *WomWMM*
Meinert, Rudolf *Film 2*
Meinhard, Edith *Film 2*
Meinken, Fred 1882-1958 *AmSCAP 1966*
Meir, Golda 1898- *CelR 3*
Meiser, Edith 1898- *BiE&WWA, NotNAT,*
  WhoHol A, WhoThe 16
Meisl, Karl 1775-1853 *OxThe*
Meisner, Sanford 1905- *BiE&WWA, NotNAT,*
  PIP&P
Meister, Barbara Ann *BiE&WWA, NotNAT*

Meister, Otto L 1869-1944 *WhScrn 1, WhScrn 2,*
  WhoHol B
Meister, Philip *NotNAT*
Mejia, Carlos Anthony 1923- *AmSCAP 1966*
Mekas, Adolfas 1922- *WorEnF*
Mekas, Adolfas 1925- *FilmgC, OxFilm*
Mekas, Jonas 1922- *FilmgC, OxFilm, WorEnF*
Melachrino, George 1909-1965 *WhScrn 1,*
  WhScrn 2
Melamed, David J 1911- *IntMPA 1977*
Melaro, H J M 1928- *AmSCAP 1966*
Melas, Spyros 1883- *CnMD, REnWD*
Melato, Mariangela *WhoHol A*
Melba, Madame 1863- *WhoStg 1906,*
  WhoStg 1908
Melcher, Martin 1915-1968 *FilmgC, NewYTET*
Melchior, Georges *Film 2*
Melchior, Ib 1917- *FilmgC, IntMPA 1977*
Melchior, Lauritz 1890-1973 *FilmgC, MGM,*
  MovMk, WhScrn 2, WhoHol B
Melendez, Bill *NewYTET*
Melesh, Alex 1890-1949 *Film 2, WhScrn 1,*
  WhScrn 2, WhoHol B
Melfi, Leonard 1935- *ConDr 1977, NotNAT,*
  PIP&P, WhoThe 16
Melford, Austin 1884- *IntMPA 1977, WhThe*
Melford, George 1889-1961 *Film 1, TwYS A,*
  WhScrn 1, WhScrn 2, WhoHol B
Melford, Jack 1899- *WhThe, WhoHol A*
Melford, Jill 1934- *WhoHol A, WhoThe 16*
Melford, Louise 1880-1942 *WhScrn 1, WhScrn 2,*
  WhoHol B
Melgarejo, Jesus 1876-1941 *WhScrn 1, WhScrn 2*
Melia, Joe *WhoThe 16*
Melies, George 1861-1938 *TwYS A, WomWMM*
Melies, Georges 1861-1938 *BiDFlm, DcFM,*
  Film 1, FilmgC, MovMk, OxFilm,
  WhScrn 2, WorEnF
Melis, Jose 1920- *AmSCAP 1966*
Melish, Fuller, Jr. *Film 2*
Mell, Marisa *WhoHol A*
Mell, Max 1882-1971 *CnMD, CroCD, McGWD,*
  ModWD, OxThe
Meller, Edith *Film 2*
Meller, Harro 1907-1963 *NotNAT B, WhScrn 1,*
  WhScrn 2, WhoHol B
Meller, Raquel 1888-1962 *Film 2, NotNAT B,*
  WhScrn 1, WhScrn 2, WhoHol B
Mellinger, Max 1906-1968 *WhScrn 2, WhoHol B*
Mellinina, Ardita *Film 1*
Mellion, John 1933- *MovMk*
Mellish, Fuller *Film 1*
Mellish, Fuller 1865-1936 *NotNAT B, WhThe,*
  WhoHol B, WhoStg 1908
Mellish, Fuller, Jr. 1895-1930 *NotNAT B,*
  WhScrn 1, WhScrn 2, WhoHol B
Mellon, Ada d1914 *NotNAT B*
Mellon, Mrs. Alfred 1824-1909 *NotNAT B,*
  OxThe
Mellon, Harriot 1777-1837 *OxThe*
Mellon, Paul 1907- *CelR 3*
Mellor, William C 1904-1963 *FilmgC, WorEnF*
Melly, Andree 1932- *WhoHol A, WhoThe 16*
Melmerfelt, Sixten *Film 2*
Melmoth, Charlotte 1749-1823 *NotNAT B,*
  OxThe, PIP&P
Melmoth, Courtney 1749-1814 *NotNAT B*
Melnick, Daniel 1934- *IntMPA 1977, NewYTET*
Melnick, Linda Rodgers *AmSCAP 1966*
Melniker, Benjamin 1913- *IntMPA 1977*
Melnitz, William W 1900- *BiE&WWA, NotNAT*
Melnotte, Violet 1852-1935 *OxThe, WhThe*
Melnotte, Violet 1856-1935 *NotNAT B*
Melrose, Walter 1889- *AmSCAP 1966*

Melsher, Irving 1906-1962 *AmSCAP 1966*
Melton, Frank 1907-1951 *WhScrn 1, WhScrn 2, WhoHol B*
Melton, James d1961 *WhoHol B*
Melton, James 1904-1961 *FilmgC*
Melton, James 1905-1961 *WhScrn 1, WhScrn 2*
Melton, Sid *Vers A, WhoHol A*
Meltzer, Charles Henry d1936 *NotNAT B, WhThe, WhoStg 1906, WhoStg 1908*
Melville, Alan 1910- *BiE&WWA, EncMT, NotNAT A, WhoThe 16*
Melville, Andrew d1938 *NotNAT B*
Melville, Andrew 1912- *WhThe*
Melville, Emelie 1852-1932 *Film 2*
Melville, Emilie 1852-1932 *NotNAT B, WhScrn 2, WhoHol B*
Melville, Frederick 1876-1938 *NotNAT B, OxThe, WhThe*
Melville, Jean-Pierre 1917-1973 *BiDFlm, DcFM, FilmgC, OxFilm, WorEnF*
Melville, Josie *Film 2*
Melville, June 1915-1970 *WhThe*
Melville, Rose 1873-1946 *Film 1, NotNAT B, WhScrn 1, WhScrn 2, WhThe, WhoHol B, WhoStg 1906, WhoStg 1908*
Melville, Sam *WhoHol A*
Melville, Walter 1875-1937 *NotNAT B, OxThe, WhThe*
Melville, Winifred d1950 *NotNAT B*
Melville, Winnie d1937 *NotNAT B, WhThe*
Melvin, Donnie *WhoHol A*
Melvin, Duncan 1913- *WhThe*
Melvin, Murray 1932- *FilmgC, WhoHol A, WhoThe 16*
Menahan, Jean d1963 *WhScrn 2*
Menander 342BC-291BC *NotNAT B*
Menander 342?BC-292?BC *CnThe, OxThe. REnWD*
Menander 343?BC-291?BC *McGWD*
Menander 343BC-292BC *PIP&P*
Menard, Lucie *WomWMM*
Menard, Michael M 1898-1949 *WhScrn 1, WhScrn 2*
Menchel, Don *NewYTET*
Mencher, Murray 1898- *AmSCAP 1966*
Mencken, Henry Louis 1880-1956 *NotNAT B*
Mendel 1875- *WhThe*
Mendel, Jules 1875-1938 *WhScrn 1, WhScrn 2*
Mendelsohn, Jacques Arko 1867-1940 *AmSCAP 1966*
Mendelson, Lee *NewYTET*
Mendelssohn, Eleanora 1900-1951 *NotNAT B, WhoHol B*
Mendelssohn, Eleonora 1900-1951 *WhScrn 1, WhScrn 2*
Mendelssohn, Felix 1809-1847 *NotNAT B*
Mendenhall, Ralph G 1921- *AmSCAP 1966*
Mendes, Catulle Abraham 1841-1909 *NotNAT B*
Mendes, John Prince 1919-1955 *WhScrn 1, WhScrn 2, WhoHol B*
Mendes, Lothar 1894-1974 *FilmgC, TwYS A, WhScrn 2*
Mendes, Moses d1758 *NotNAT B*
Mendez, Lola *Film 2*
Mendez, Lucila *Film 2*
Mendez, Rafael G 1906- *AmSCAP 1966*
Mendoza, David 1894- *AmSCAP 1966*
Mendoza, Harry 1905-1970 *WhScrn 1, WhScrn 2*
Mendum, Georgie Drew d1957 *NotNAT B*
Menges, Chris *FilmgC*
Menges, Herbert 1902- *WhThe*
Menges, Joyce *WhoHol A*
Menhart, Alfred 1899-1955 *WhScrn 1, WhScrn 2*
Menjou, Adolphe 1890-1963 *BiDFlm, Film 1,*

Film 2, FilmgC, MotPP, MovMk, NotNAT B, OxFilm, TwYS, WhScrn 1, WhScrn 2, WhoHol B, WorEnF
Menjou, Henri *Film 2*
Menken, Adah Isaacs 1835-1868 *FamA&A, NotNAT A, NotNAT B, OxThe*
Menken, Helen d1966 *PIP&P, WhoHol B*
Menken, Helen 1901-1966 *BiE&WWA, NotNAT B, WhThe*
Menken, Helen 1902-1966 *WhScrn 1, WhScrn 2*
Menken, Marie 1909-1970 *WhScrn 1, WhScrn 2, WomWMM*
Menken, Shepard *WhoHol A*
Mennin, Peter 1923- *AmSCAP 1966, BiE&WWA, CelR 3*
Menninger, Karl 1893- *CelR 3*
Mennini, Louis 1920- *AmSCAP 1966*
Menotti, Gian-Carlo 1911- *AmSCAP 1966, BiE&WWA, CelR 3, McGWD, NotNAT*
Menuhin, Yehudi 1916- *CelR 3, WhoHol A*
Menzel, Gerhard 1894- *ModWD*
Menzel, Jiri 1938- *DcFM, FilmgC, OxFilm, WorEnF*
Menzies, Archie 1904- *WhThe*
Menzies, William Cameron 1896-1957 *BiDFlm, DcFM, FilmgC, NotNAT B, OxFilm, WorEnF*
Mera, Edith d1935 *WhScrn 1, WhScrn 2, WhoHol B*
Merande, Doro d1975 *BiE&WWA, NotNAT, NotNAT B, WhScrn 2, WhThe, WhoHol C*
Merante, Louis d1887 *NotNAT B*
Mercanton, Louis d1932 *OxFilm*
Mercantor, Jean *Film 2*
Mercer, Beryl 1882-1939 *Film 2, FilmgC, MotPP, MovMk, NotNAT B, ThFT, WhScrn 1, WhScrn 2, WhThe, WhoHol B*
Mercer, David 1928- *CnThe, ConDr 1977, CroCD, WhoThe 16*
Mercer, Donald J *NewYTET*
Mercer, Frances *MotPP, WhoHol A*
Mercer, John H 1909-1976 *AmSCAP 1966*
Mercer, Johnny 1909-1976 *BiE&WWA, CelR 3, EncMT, FilmgC, WhoHol A, WhoThe 16*
Mercer, Johnny 1910-1976 *NotNAT B*
Mercer, Mabel 1900- *CelR 3*
Mercer, Mae *WhoHol A*
Mercer, Marian 1935- *BiE&WWA, NotNAT, WhoHol A, WhoThe 16*
Mercer, Tony 1922-1973 *WhScrn 2*
Mercer, William Elmo 1932- *AmSCAP 1966*
Merchant, Lawrence H, Jr. *IntMPA 1977*
Merchant, Vivien 1929- *FilmgC, MotPP, OxFilm, PIP&P, WhoHol A, WhoThe 16*
Mercier, Louis *Film 2, WhoHol A*
Mercier, Louis-Sebastien 1740-1814 *McGWD, NotNAT B, OxThe*
Mercier, Mary *NatPD*
Mercier, Michele 1942- *FilmgC, WhoHol A*
Mercouri, Melina *IntMPA 1977, MotPP, WhoHol A*
Mercouri, Melina 1923- *FilmgC*
Mercouri, Melina 1925- *CelR 3, MovMk, OxFilm, WorEnF*
Mere, Charles 1883- *WhThe*
Meredith, Burgess *MotPP, PIP&P, WhoHol A*
Meredith, Burgess 1907- *MovMk, WorEnF*
Meredith, Burgess 1908- *BiE&WWA, FilmgC, HolP 30, NotNAT, WhoThe 16*
Meredith, Burgess 1909- *BiDFlm, IntMPA 1977, OxFilm*
Meredith, Charles 1890-1964 *Film 1, Film 2, TwYS*
Meredith, Charles 1894-1964 *WhScrn 1,*

WhScrn 2, WhoHol B
Meredith, Cheerio 1890-1964 WhScrn 1,
  WhScrn 2, WhoHol B
Meredith, Don NewYTET
Meredith, Isaac H 1872-1962 AmSCAP 1966
Meredith, Jo Anne WhoHol A
Meredith, Joan WhoHol A
Meredith, Judi WhoHol A
Meredith, Lee WhoHol A
Meredith, Lois Film 1, Film 2
Meredith, Lu Anne WhoHol A
Meredith, Melba Melsing d1967 WhoHol B
Meredyth, Bess d1969 Film 1, WhScrn 1,
  WhScrn 2, WhoHol B, WomWMM
Merelle, Claude Film 2
Meretta, Leonard V 1915- AmSCAP 1966
Meri, Veijo 1928- CroCD
Merian, Leon 1925- AmSCAP 1966
Merimee, Prosper 1803-1870 NotNAT B
Merivale, Bernard 1882-1939 NotNAT B, WhThe
Merivale, Mrs. Herman d1932 NotNAT B
Merivale, Herman Charles 1839-1906 NotNAT A,
  NotNAT B
Merivale, John 1917- BiE&WWA, NotNAT,
  WhoHol A
Merivale, Philip d1946 PIP&P, WhoHol B
Merivale, Philip 1880-1946 WhScrn 1, WhScrn 2
Merivale, Philip 1886-1946 FilmgC, NotNAT B,
  WhThe
Meriwether, Lee WhoHol A
Merkel, Una 1903- BiE&WWA, Film 2, FilmgC,
  IntMPA 1977, MGM, MotPP, MovMk,
  NotNAT, ThFT, Vers A, WhThe,
  WhoHol A
Merkyl, John Film 1, Film 2
Merkyl, Wilmuth 1885-1954 Film 1, WhScrn 2
Merle, George 1874-1945 AmSCAP 1966
Merlin, Frank 1892-1968 NotNAT B
Merlin, Jan WhoHol A
Merlin, Joanna 1931- BiE&WWA, NotNAT
Merlo, Anthony Film 2
Merlow, Anthony Film 1
Merman, Ethel MotPP, PIP&P, WhoHol A
Merman, Ethel 1908- FilmgC, MovMk, ThFT
Merman, Ethel 1909- BiE&WWA, CelR 3,
  CmMov, CnThe, EncMT, FamA&A,
  IntMPA 1977, NotNAT, NotNAT A,
  WhoThe 16
Meroff, Benny 1901- AmSCAP 1966
Merrall, Mary 1890-1973 Film 2, FilmgC,
  IntMPA 1977, WhThe, WhoHol B
Merrelli, C Film 2
Merriam, Charlotte Film 2
Merrick, David BiE&WWA, CnThe,
  WhoThe 16
Merrick, David 1911- EncMT
Merrick, David 1912- CelR 3
Merrick, Leonard 1864-1939 NotNAT B, WhThe
Merrick, Lynn WhoHol A
Merrifield, Norman L 1906- AmSCAP 1966
Merrill, Amy 1898- AmSCAP 1966
Merrill, Barbara WhoHol A
Merrill, Beth PIP&P, WhThe
Merrill, Bill 1921- AmSCAP 1966
Merrill, Blanche 1895- AmSCAP 1966
Merrill, Bob 1920- BiE&WWA, NotNAT,
  WhoThe 16
Merrill, Bob 1921- AmSCAP 1966, EncMT,
  NewMT
Merrill, Dick WhoHol A
Merrill, Dina CelR 3, MotPP, WhoHol A
Merrill, Dina 1925- IntMPA 1977, MovMk
Merrill, Dina 1928- FilmgC
Merrill, Frank 1892-1966 Film 2

Merrill, Frank 1894-1966 WhScrn 1, WhScrn 2,
  WhoHol B
Merrill, Gary IntMPA 1977, MotPP,
  WhoHol A
Merrill, Gary 1914- FilmgC
Merrill, Gary 1915- BiE&WWA, MovMk,
  NotNAT
Merrill, John 1875- NotNAT A
Merrill, Louis 1911-1963 NotNAT B, WhScrn 1,
  WhScrn 2, WhoHol B
Merrill, Ray 1916- AmSCAP 1966
Merrill, Robert 1919- CelR 3
Merriman, John d1974 NewYTET
Merritt, George 1890- FilmgC, WhoHol A,
  WhoThe 16
Merritt, Grace 1881- WhThe
Merritt, O O 1919- AmSCAP 1966
Merritt, Paul d1895 NotNAT B
Merritt, Theresa WhoHol A
Merrow, Jane 1941- FilmgC, WhoHol A
Merry, Mrs. 1769-1808 OxThe
Merry, Anne Brunton 1768-1808 NotNAT A
Merry, Anne Brunton 1769-1808 FamA&A,
  PIP&P
Merry, Robert d1798 NotNAT B
Merry, Mrs. Robert 1763-1808 NotNAT B
Mersch, Mary Film 2
Mersereau, Claire Film 1
Mersereau, Violet 1894- Film 1, Film 2
Mersey, Robert 1917- AmSCAP 1966
Merson, Billy 1881-1947 Film 1, Film 2, OxThe,
  WhThe
Merson, Marc 1931- IntMPA 1977
Merton, Colette 1907-1968 Film 2, WhoHol B
Merton, Collette 1907-1968 WhScrn 1, WhScrn 2
Merton, John 1901-1959 Vers B, WhScrn 1,
  WhScrn 2, WhoHol B
Mertz, Paul Madeira 1904- AmSCAP 1966
Mervyn, Lee d1962 NotNAT B
Mervyn, William 1912-1976 FilmgC, WhoHol A,
  WhoThe 16
Mery, Andree WhThe
Mesang, Ted 1904- AmSCAP 1966
Mescall, John 1899- CmMov, FilmgC
Mesereau, Violet 1894- TwYS
Meserve, Walter Joseph, Jr. 1923- NotNAT
Meshke, George Lewis 1930- NotNAT
Meskill, Jack 1897- AmSCAP 1966
Meskill, Katherine WhoHol A
Meskin, Aharon 1897-1974 WhScrn 2
Mesmer, Marie 1920- IntMPA 1977
Messager, Andre 1853- WhThe
Messager, Charles McGWD, REnWD
Messel, Oliver PIP&P
Messel, Oliver 1904- BiE&WWA, FilmgC,
  NotNAT, WhoThe 16, WorEnF
Messel, Oliver 1905- CnThe, OxThe
Messenger, Buddy 1909-1965 TwYS, WhScrn 1,
  WhScrn 2
Messenger, Gertrude 1911- TwYS
Messenheimer, Sam 1898- AmSCAP 1966
Messenius, Johannes 1579-1636 OxThe
Messinger, Buddy 1909-1965 Film 1, Film 2,
  WhoHol B
Messinger, Gertrude 1911- Film 1, Film 2
Messinger, Josephine 1885-1968 WhScrn 2,
  WhoHol B
Messiter, Eric 1892-1960 NotNAT B, WhScrn 1,
  WhScrn 2, WhoHol B
Messner, Johnny 1909- AmSCAP 1966
Messter, Oskar Eduard 1866-1943 DcFM, OxFilm
Mesta, Perle 1891- CelR 3
Mestayer, Anna Maria d1881 NotNAT B
Mestayer, Harry Film 1, Film 2, MotPP,

TwYS
Mestel, Jacob 1884-1958 *NotNAT B, WhScrn 1, WhScrn 2*
Mestral, Armand *WhoHol A*
Mestre, Goar *NewYTET*
Meszaros, Marta 1931- *OxFilm, WomWMM*
Metastasio 1698-1782 *NotNAT B, OxThe*
Metastasio, Pietro 1698-1782 *CnThe, McGWD, REnWD*
Metaxa, Georges 1899-1950 *NotNAT B, WhScrn 1, WhScrn 2, WhThe, WhoHol B*
Metcalf, Arthur *Film 2*
Metcalf, Earl 1889-1928 *Film 2, TwYS, WhScrn 1, WhScrn 2*
Metcalf, Earle 1889-1928 *WhoHol B*
Metcalfe, Earle 1889-1928 *Film 1*
Metcalfe, James S 1901-1960 *WhScrn 1, WhScrn 2, WhoHol B*
Metcalfe, James Stetson 1858-1927 *NotNAT B, WhThe*
Metenier, Oscar 1859-1913 *NotNAT B, WhThe*
Metevier, Matilda *Film 2*
Method, Mayo 1904-1951 *MotPP*
Methot, Mayo 1904-1951 *NotNAT B, ThFT, WhScrn 1, WhScrn 2, WhoHol B*
Metis, Frank 1925- *AmSCAP 1966*
Metrano, Art *WhoHol A*
Metten, Charles 1927- *NotNAT*
Metty, Russell 1900- *CmMov*
Metty, Russell L 1906- *FilmgC, WorEnF*
Metz, Albert 1886-1940 *WhScrn 1, WhScrn 2*
Metz, Otto 1891-1949 *WhScrn 1, WhScrn 2*
Metz, Theodore A 1848-1936 *AmSCAP 1966, NotNAT B*
Metzetti, Victor 1895-1949 *WhScrn 1, WhScrn 2, WhoHol B*
Metzger, Roswell William 1906- *AmSCAP 1966*
Metzler, Robert 1914- *IntMPA 1977*
Metzner, Erno 1892- *DcFM, OxFilm*
Meunier-Surcouf *Film 2*
Meurice, Paul d1905 *NotNAT B*
Meurisse, Paul 1912- *FilmgC*
Meusel, Bob *Film 2*
Meusel, Irish *Film 2*
Mexican Marimba Band Of Agua Caliente *Film 2*
Meye Bertie Alexander 1877-1967 *WhThe*
Meyer, Charles 1924- *AmSCAP 1966*
Meyer, Don 1919- *AmSCAP 1966*
Meyer, Emile 1903- *CmMov, FilmgC, WhoHol A*
Meyer, Ernest d1927 *NotNAT B*
Meyer, Frederic 1910-1973 *WhScrn 2*
Meyer, George *DcFM*
Meyer, George W 1884-1959 *AmSCAP 1966, NotNAT B*
Meyer, Greta *Film 2*
Meyer, Hyman 1875-1945 *Film 2, WhScrn 1, WhScrn 2, WhoHol B*
Meyer, Johannes *Film 2*
Meyer, John L 1911- *AmSCAP 1966*
Meyer, Joseph 1894- *AmSCAP 1966, EncMT*
Meyer, Louis 1871-1915 *NotNAT B, WhThe*
Meyer, Muffie *WomWMM, WomWMM A, WomWMM B*
Meyer, Paul 1920- *DcFM*
Meyer, Richard C 1920- *IntMPA 1977*
Meyer, Richard D 1928- *NotNAT*
Meyer, Russ 1923- *FilmgC, IntMPA 1977*
Meyer, Sol 1913-1964 *AmSCAP 1966*
Meyer, Torben 1884-1975 *Film 2, Vers B, WhScrn 2, WhoHol C*
Meyer-Forster, Wilhelm d1934 *NotNAT B*
Meyerhold, Vsevolod 1874-1940? *CnThe*

Meyerhold, Vsevolod Emilievich 1874-1942 *NotNAT A, NotNAT B*
Meyerhold, Vsevolod Emilievich 1874-1943? *OxThe, PIP&P*
Meyerinck, Victoria *WhoHol A*
Meyerkhold, Vsevolod 1874-1942 *Film 2, WhoHol B*
Meyers, Billy 1894- *AmSCAP 1966*
Meyers, Claudia D 1915- *AmSCAP 1966*
Meyers, Kathleen *Film 2*
Meyers, Laura *WomWMM B*
Meyers, Michael *WhoHol A*
Meyers, Robert 1934- *IntMPA 1977*
Meyers, Sidney 1894- *WorEnF*
Meyers, Sidney 1906-1969 *DcFM*
Meyers, Warren B 1929- *AmSCAP 1966*
Meyn, Robert 1896-1972 *WhScrn 2, WhoHol B*
Meyn, Theodore A *AmSCAP 1966*
Meynell, Clyde 1867-1934 *NotNAT B, WhThe*
Mezetti, Charles *Film 2*
M'Gilvray, Laura *WhoStg 1906*
M'Gilvray, Laura *see also* McGilvray, Laura
Michael, Edward 1853-1950 *NotNAT A, NotNAT B*
Michael, Elaine 1930- *AmSCAP 1966*
Michael, Friedrich 1892- *CnMD, McGWD, ModWD*
Michael, Gertrude d1964 *MotPP, WhoHol B*
Michael, Gertrude 1910-1965 *ThFT, WhThe*
Michael, Gertrude 1911-1964 *FilmgC, WhScrn 1, WhScrn 2*
Michael, Kathleen 1917- *WhoThe 16*
Michael, Mickie 1943-1973 *WhScrn 2*
Michael, Ralph 1907- *FilmgC, WhoHol A, WhoThe 16*
Michaeli, John Edward 1938- *IntMPA 1977*
Michaelis, Robert 1884-1965 *WhThe*
Michaels, Beverly 1927- *FilmgC, WhoHol A*
Michaels, Dolores 1930- *FilmgC, MotPP*
Michaels, Lorne *NewYTET*
Michaels, Sidney Ramon 1927- *CnMD Sup, ModWD*
Michaels, Sully 1917-1966 *WhScrn 1, WhScrn 2, WhoHol B*
Michaelson, Knut 1846- *WhThe*
Michailow, Boris *Film 2*
Michalesco, Michael d1957 *NotNAT B, WhoHol B*
Michalkov, Sergei 1913- *CnMD*
Michalove, Edwin B 1927- *AmSCAP 1966*
Michau *OxThe*
Michaud, Henri 1912- *IntMPA 1977*
Michaud, Henry A 1914- *IntMPA 1977*
Michel, Andre 1910- *DcFM, WorEnF*
Michel, Franny *WhoHol A*
Michel, Gaston 1856-1921 *WhScrn 2*
Michel, Georges 1926- *CroCD*
Michel, Werner 1910- *IntMPA 1977, NewYTET*
Michelena, Beatrice 1890-1942 *WhScrn 1, WhScrn 2*
Michelena, Beatriz 1890-1942 *Film 1, MotPP, WhoHol B*
Michelena, Vera 1884-1961 *WhScrn 1, WhScrn 2, WhoHol B*
Michelet, Michel *IntMPA 1977*
Michell, Keith *IntMPA 1977, WhoHol A*
Michell, Keith 1926- *FilmgC, MovMk*
Michell, Keith 1928- *BiE&WWA, CnThe, EncMT, NotNAT, WhoThe 16*
Michels, Walter 1895- *AmSCAP 1966*
Michelsen, Hans Gunter 1920- *CnMD Sup, CroCD, McGWD, ModWD*
Michener, James A 1907- *CelR 3, FilmgC, PIP&P*

Micinski, Tadeusz 1873-1919 *CnMD*
Mickelson, Sig *NewYTET*
Mickiewicz, Adam Bernard 1798-1855 *McGWD,
  OxThe, REnWD*
Middlemas, David 1919- *IntMPA 1977*
Middlemass, Robert M 1885-1949 *WhScrn 2*
Middleton, Charles B *MotPP*
Middleton, Charles B 1874-1949 *FilmgC*
Middleton, Charles B 1879-1949 *Film 2, Vers A,
  WhScrn 1, WhScrn 2, WhoHol B*
Middleton, Edgar 1894-1939 *NotNAT B, WhThe*
Middleton, Eleanor *Film 2*
Middleton, George d1926 *NotNAT B*
Middleton, George 1880-1967 *BiE&WWA,
  NotNAT A, NotNAT B, WhThe*
Middleton, Guy d1973 *WhoHol B*
Middleton, Guy 1906-1973 *FilmgC*
Middleton, Guy 1907-1973 *NotNAT B, WhThe*
Middleton, Guy 1908-1973 *WhScrn 2*
Middleton, Herman D 1925- *BiE&WWA,
  NotNAT*
Middleton, Josephine 1883-1971 *WhScrn 1,
  WhScrn 2, WhThe, WhoHol B*
Middleton, Leora *WhScrn 1, WhScrn 2*
Middleton, Noelle *WhoHol A*
Middleton, Ray 1907- *BiE&WWA, EncMT,
  IntMPA 1977, NotNAT, PIP&P, WhoHol A,
  WhoThe 16*
Middleton, Robert 1911- *FilmgC, IntMPA 1977,
  Vers A, WhoHol A*
Middleton, Thomas 1570?-1627 *CnThe,
  NotNAT A, NotNAT B, OxThe, REnWD*
Middleton, Thomas 1580-1627 *McGWD*
Middleton, Tom *WhoHol A*
Midgely, Fannie 1877-1932 *Film 1, WhScrn 2*
Midgley, Fannie 1877-1932 *Film 2*
Midgley, Florence 1890-1949 *Film 2, WhScrn 1,
  WhScrn 2, WhoHol B*
Midgley, Leslie *NewYTET*
Midgley, Richard A 1910-1956 *WhScrn 1,
  WhScrn 2, WhoHol B*
Midgley, Robin 1934- *WhoThe 16*
Midler, Bette 1944?- *CelR 3, WhoHol A*
Mielziner, Jo 1901-1976 *BiE&WWA, CelR 3,
  CnThe, NotNAT, NotNAT B, OxThe,
  PIP&P, WhoThe 16*
Mierendorff, Hans *Film 2*
Miescer, A Stephen 1903- *AmSCAP 1966*
Mifune, Toshiro 1920- *FilmgC, IntMPA 1977,
  MotPP, MovMk, OxFilm, WhoHol A,
  WorEnF*
Migden, Chester L 1921- *BiE&WWA,
  IntMPA 1977*
Mignot, Flore *WhThe*
Mihail, Alexandra 1947-1975 *WhScrn 2*
Mihura, Miguel 1903- *ModWD*
Mihura, Miguel 1905- *CroCD*
Mihura Santos, Miguel 1905- *McGWD*
Mikell, George *IntMPA 1977*
Miketta, Bob 1911- *AmSCAP 1966*
Mikhalkov, Sergei Vladimirovich 1913- *OxThe*
Mikhalkov, Sergey Vladimirovich 1913- *ModWD*
Mikhoels, Salomon 1890-1948 *NotNAT B, OxThe*
Mikhoels, Solomon 1890-1948 *WhoHol B*
Milaidy, James *Film 2*
Milaine, Amille *Film 2*
Milam, Pauline 1912-1965 *WhScrn 1, WhScrn 2,
  WhoHol B*
Milan, Lita *MotPP*
Milani, Joseph L *WhScrn 2*
Milano, Frank d1962 *NotNAT B*
Milar, Adolph *Film 2, TwYS*
Milasch, Robert *Film 2*
Milash, Bib *Film 2*

Milash, Robert E 1885-1954 *WhScrn 1,
  WhScrn 2, WhoHol B*
Milbert, Seymour 1915- *BiE&WWA*
Milbourne, Mister *PIP&P*
Milcrest, Howard 1892-1920 *WhScrn 1,
  WhScrn 2, WhoHol B*
Miler, Zdenek 1929- *DcFM*
Milerta, John *Film 2*
Miles, Alfred Hart 1883-1956 *AmSCAP 1966*
Miles, Allan 1929- *BiE&WWA*
Miles, Art 1899-1955 *WhoHol B*
Miles, Arthur K 1899-1955 *WhScrn 1, WhScrn 2*
Miles, Barry 1947- *AmSCAP 1966*
Miles, Sir Bernard 1907- *CnThe, FilmgC,
  IntMPA 1977, OxThe, PIP&P, WhoHol A,
  WhoThe 16*
Miles, Betty *WomWMM B*
Miles, Bob *Film 2*
Miles, C Austin 1868-1946 *AmSCAP 1966*
Miles, Carlton d1954 *NotNAT B*
Miles, Christopher 1939- *FilmgC*
Miles, David d1915 *Film 1, WhScrn 2*
Miles, G H *PIP&P*
Miles, George Henry d1871 *NotNAT B*
Miles, H *Film 2*
Miles, Herbert *Film 1*
Miles, Mrs. Herbert *Film 1*
Miles, Jackie 1913-1968 *NotNAT B, WhoHol B*
Miles, Jennifer *WomWMM B*
Miles, Joanna *WhoHol A*
Miles, Julia *NotNAT*
Miles, Lillian *WhoHol A*
Miles, Lotta 1899-1937 *WhScrn 1, WhScrn 2,
  WhoHol B*
Miles, Luther *Film 2*
Miles, Nelson Appleton 1839-1925 *WhScrn 2*
Miles, Peter 1938- *FilmgC, WhoHol A*
Miles, Richard 1916- *AmSCAP 1966*
Miles, Robert 1920- *AmSCAP 1966*
Miles, Rosalind *WhoHol A*
Miles, Sarah *MotPP, WhoHol A, WhoThe 16*
Miles, Sarah 1941- *BiDFlm, FilmgC,
  IntMPA 1977, MovMk*
Miles, Sarah 1943- *CelR 3*
Miles, Sherry *WhoHol A*
Miles, Sylvia 1932- *BiE&WWA, CelR 3,
  NotNAT, WhoHol A*
Miles, Vera *MotPP, WhoHol A*
Miles, Vera 1929- *FilmgC*
Miles, Vera 1930- *BiDFlm, IntMPA 1977,
  MovMk, WorEnF*
Miles, Walter E 1885-1961 *AmSCAP 1966*
Milestone, Lewis 1895- *BiDFlm, CmMov, DcFM,
  FilmgC, IntMPA 1977, MovMk, OxFilm,
  TwYS A, WorEnF*
Miley, Jerry *Film 2*
Milford, Bliss *Film 1, MotPP*
Milgram, David E 1907- *IntMPA 1977*
Milgram, Henry 1926- *IntMPA 1977*
Milhalesco *Film 2*
Milhaud, Darius 1892-1974 *CelR 3, DcFM,
  OxFilm, WorEnF*
Milhaud, Darius 1893-1974 *WhScrn 2*
Milhollin, James 1920- *FilmgC*
Milian, Thomas *WhoHol A*
Military, Frank 1926- *AmSCAP 1966*
Milius, John 1945- *IntMPA 1977, MovMk*
Miljan, John 1893-1960 *FilmgC, MovMk,
  NotNAT B, Vers B, WhScrn 1, WhScrn 2,
  WhoHol B*
Miljan, John 1899-1960 *Film 2, TwYS*
Milkey, Edward T 1908- *AmSCAP 1966*
Millan, Victor *WhoHol A*
Milland, Ray *MotPP, WhoHol A*

Milland, Ray 1905- *BiDFlm, CmMov, FilmgC, OxFilm*
Milland, Ray 1907- *CelR 3, Film 2, WorEnF*
Milland, Ray 1908- *IntMPA 1977, MovMk*
Milland, Spike 1907- *Film 2*
Millar, Adelqui *Film 2*
Millar, Douglas 1875-1943 *NotNAT B, WhThe*
Millar, Gertie 1879-1952 *EncMT, NotNAT B, OxThe, WhThe*
Millar, Lee 1888-1941 *WhScrn 1, WhScrn 2, WhoHol B*
Millar, Mack d1962 *NotNAT B*
Millar, Marjie d1966 *WhScrn 2*
Millar, Marjie d1970 *WhoHol B*
Millar, Mary 1936- *WhoThe 16*
Millar, Robins 1889-1968 *NotNAT B, WhThe*
Millar, Ronald 1919- *ConDr 1977, WhoThe 16*
Millar, Stuart 1929- *FilmgC, IntMPA 1977*
Millard, Edward R Rocky d1963 *NotNAT B*
Millard, Evelyn 1869-1941 *NotNAT B, WhThe*
Millard, Harry W 1928-1969 *WhScrn 1, WhScrn 2, WhoHol B*
Millard, Helene *Film 2*
Millard, Ursula 1901- *WhThe*
Millarde, Harry *Film 1, TwYS A, WhScrn 1, WhScrn 2, WhoHol B*
Millaud, Albert d1892 *NotNAT B*
Millay, Edna St. Vincent 1892-1950 *AmSCAP 1966, CnMD, McGWD, ModWD, NotNAT B*
Miller, Agnes *WhThe*
Miller, Alice Duer 1874-1942 *NotNAT B, WhoHol B*
Miller, Alice Moore *WhScrn 1, WhScrn 2*
Miller, Ann 1919- *CelR 3, CmMov, FilmgC, MGM, MotPP, MovMk, NotNAT A, ThFT, WhoHol A, WhoThe 16, WorEnF*
Miller, Ann 1923- *IntMPA 1977*
Miller, Arnold 1923- *CelR 3*
Miller, Arnold E, Jr. 1921- *AmSCAP 1966*
Miller, Arthur d1935 *NotNAT B*
Miller, Arthur 1915- *BiE&WWA, CelR 3, CnMD, CnThe, ConDr 1977, CroCD, DcFM, FilmgC, McGWD, ModWD, NatPD, NotNAT, NotNAT A, OxFilm, OxThe, PIP&P, REnWD, WhoThe 16, WorEnF*
Miller, Arthur C 1894-1971 *FilmgC*
Miller, Arthur C 1895?-1970 *DcFM, OxFilm, WorEnF*
Miller, Ashley 1867-1949 *WhScrn 1, WhScrn 2, WhoHol B*
Miller, Ashley 1877- *WhoStg 1908*
Miller, Beverly 1906- *IntMPA 1977*
Miller, Bob d1964 *NotNAT B*
Miller, Bob 1895-1955 *AmSCAP 1966*
Miller, Buzz 1928- *BiE&WWA, NotNAT, WhoHol A*
Miller, Carl *Film 1, Film 2*
Miller, Carlton *Film 2*
Miller, Charles *TwYS A*
Miller, Charles 1899- *AmSCAP 1966*
Miller, Charles B 1891-1955 *WhScrn 1, WhScrn 2, WhoHol B*
Miller, Cheryl 1943- *IntMPA 1977, WhoHol A*
Miller, Clarence d1963 *NotNAT B*
Miller, Colleen 1932- *FilmgC, WhoHol A*
Miller, D Thomas *NewYTET*
Miller, David 1871-1933 *NotNAT B, WhThe*
Miller, David 1909- *BiDFlm, FilmgC, IntMPA 1977, MovMk, WorEnF*
Miller, David Prince d1873 *NotNAT B*
Miller, Dean *WhoHol A*
Miller, Denny *MotPP, WhoHol A*
Miller, Dick 1928- *IntMPA 1977*

Miller, E G 1883-1948 *WhScrn 2*
Miller, Ed E 1929- *AmSCAP 1966*
Miller, Eddie 1891-1971 *WhScrn 2, WhoHol B*
Miller, Edward G George 1883-1948 *WhScrn 1*
Miller, Edward R 1911- *AmSCAP 1966*
Miller, Ella *Film 2*
Miller, Ethel *Film 2*
Miller, Flournoy E 1887-1971 *AmSCAP 1966, WhScrn 1, WhScrn 2, WhoHol B*
Miller, Fred *WhoHol A*
Miller, Gilbert Heron 1884-1969 *BiE&WWA, NotNAT B, PIP&P, WhThe*
Miller, Glenn 1904-1944 *AmSCAP 1966, FilmgC, WhScrn 1, WhScrn 2, WhoHol B*
Miller, H Thomas 1923- *AmSCAP 1966*
Miller, Hal 1923- *AmSCAP 1966*
Miller, Harold d1972 *WhoHol B*
Miller, Harry M 1934- *WhoThe 16*
Miller, Harry S 1895- *AmSCAP 1966*
Miller, Henry 1859- *WhoStg 1906, WhoStg 1908*
Miller, Henry 1860-1926 *FamA&A, NotNAT A, NotNAT B, OxThe, PIP&P, WhThe*
Miller, Henry 1891- *CelR 3*
Miller, Herb 1915- *AmSCAP 1966*
Miller, Herman *NewYTET*
Miller, Hugh 1889- *WhThe*
Miller, Hugh J 1902-1956 *Film 2, WhScrn 1, WhScrn 2, WhoHol B*
Miller, Irene Bliss d1962 *NotNAT B*
Miller, Irving 1907- *AmSCAP 1966*
Miller, J P 1919- *IntMPA 1977, NewYTET*
Miller, Jack 1888-1928 *WhScrn 1, WhScrn 2*
Miller, Jack Shorty 1895-1941 *WhScrn 1, WhScrn 2*
Miller, Jacques 1900- *AmSCAP 1966*
Miller, James d1744 *NotNAT B*
Miller, James Hull 1916- *BiE&WWA, NotNAT*
Miller, James M 1907- *AmSCAP 1966*
Miller, Jan *WhoHol A*
Miller, Jason *IntMPA 1977, NatPD, WhoHol A*
Miller, Jason 1932- *ConDr 1977*
Miller, Jason 1939- *CelR 3, NotNAT, PIP&P A, WhoThe 16*
Miller, Joan *WhoHol A*
Miller, Joan 1910- *WhoThe 16*
Miller, Joaquin 1837-1913 *NotNAT B*
Miller, Joe *Film 2*
Miller, Jonathan *WhoHol A*
Miller, Jonathan 1934- *BiE&WWA, NotNAT, WhoThe 16*
Miller, Jonathan 1936- *FilmgC*
Miller, Joseph *AmSCAP 1966*
Miller, Joseph 1684-1738 *NotNAT B*
Miller, Josephine *Film 1*
Miller, Josias 1684-1738 *NotNAT B*
Miller, Juanita 1880-1970 *WhScrn 1, WhScrn 2*
Miller, Julia *WomWMM*
Miller, Leon C 1902- *BiE&WWA*
Miller, Lillian Anne 1916- *AmSCAP 1966*
Miller, Lou 1906-1941 *WhScrn 1, WhScrn 2*
Miller, Louis *Film 2*
Miller, Lu 1906-1941 *WhoHol B*
Miller, Malcolm E d1963 *NotNAT B*
Miller, Mandy 1944- *FilmgC, WhoHol A*
Miller, Marcianne *WomWMM B*
Miller, Marilyn 1896-1936 *CnThe*
Miller, Marilyn 1898-1936 *EncMT, Film 2, FilmgC, MovMk, NotNAT B, PIP&P, ThFT, WhScrn 1, WhScrn 2, WhoHol B*
Miller, Marilynn 1898-1936 *WhThe*
Miller, Mark *WhoHol A*
Miller, Martin 1899-1969 *FilmgC, WhScrn 1, WhScrn 2, WhThe, WhoHol B*
Miller, Marvin *WhoHol A*

Miller, Marvin 1913- *FilmgC, IntMPA 1977*
Miller, Mary Louise *Film 2*
Miller, Max 1895-1963 *FilmgC, NotNAT B,*
  WhScrn 1, WhScrn 2, WhoHol B
Miller, Merle 1919- *CelR 3*
Miller, Michael R 1932- *AmSCAP 1966*
Miller, Mitch 1911- *CelR 3*
Miller, Morris d1957 *WhScrn 1, WhoHol B*
Miller, Nat 1909- *IntMPA 1977*
Miller, Ned 1899- *AmSCAP 1966*
Miller, Patsy *MotPP*
Miller, Patsy Ruth 1904- *MovMk, TwYS*
Miller, Patsy Ruth 1905- *Film 1, Film 2,*
  FilmgC, ThFT, WhoHol A
Miller, Paul 1925- *AmSCAP 1966*
Miller, Paula *BiE&WWA*
Miller, Peggy *WhoHol A*
Miller, Ranger Bill 1878-1939 *WhScrn 1,*
  WhScrn 2, WhoHol B
Miller, Robert Ellis 1927- *FilmgC, IntMPA 1977*
Miller, Robert Wiley 1925- *AmSCAP 1966*
Miller, Roger *WhoHol A*
Miller, Ron 1933- *NewYTET*
Miller, Ron S 1936- *AmSCAP 1966*
Miller, Ronald W 1933- *IntMPA 1977*
Miller, Rube *Film 1*
Miller, Ruby 1889-1976 *WhThe, WhoHol C*
Miller, Ruth *Film 2*
Miller, Scott *WhoHol A*
Miller, Seton I 1902-1974 *CmMov, FilmgC,*
  WhScrn 2, WhoHol B, WorEnF
Miller, Seymour 1908- *AmSCAP 1966*
Miller, Sidney *WhoHol A*
Miller, Sidney 1916- *AmSCAP 1966*
Miller, Susan 1944- *NatPD*
Miller, T C 1944- *NatPD*
Miller, Thomas 1872-1942 *WhScrn 1, WhScrn 2,*
  WhoHol B
Miller, Truman Gene d1963 *NotNAT B*
Miller, W Christy 1843-1922 *WhScrn 2*
Miller, W Christy 1892-1940 *Film 1*
Miller, Walter 1892-1940 *Film 1, Film 2,*
  NotNAT B, TwYS, WhScrn 1, WhScrn 2,
  WhoHol B
Miller, Wesley C d1962 *NotNAT B*
Miller, Wilber H 1906- *AmSCAP 1966*
Miller, Winston *Film 2*
Miller, Winston 1910- *IntMPA 1977*
Miller, Wyn d1932 *NotNAT B*
Miller, Wynne 1935- *BiE&WWA, NotNAT*
Miller-Milkis *NewYTET*
Millet, Kadish 1923- *AmSCAP 1966*
Milletaire, Carl *WhoHol A*
Millett, Arthur *Film 1, Film 2*
Millett, Kate 1934- *CelR 3, WomWMM A,*
  WomWMM B
Millett, Maude 1867-1920 *NotNAT B, WhThe*
Milley, Jane *Film 1*
Millhauser, Bertram 1892-1958 *FilmgC, TwYS A*
Millhollin, James 1920- *BiE&WWA, WhoHol A*
Milli, Robert *WhoHol A*
Millican, James 1910-1955 *FilmgC, Vers A,*
  WhScrn 1, WhScrn 2, WhoHol B
Millican, Jane 1902- *WhThe*
Millichip, Roy 1930- *FilmgC*
Milliet, Paul 1858- *WhThe*
Milligan, Mary Min 1882-1966 *WhScrn 2*
Milligan, Roy H 1922- *AmSCAP 1966*
Milligan, Spike 1918- *FilmgC, WhoHol A,*
  WhoThe 16
Milliken, Robert *Film 1*
Milliken, Sandol *WhoStg 1908*
Millington, Rodney 1905- *BiE&WWA, NotNAT,*
  WhoThe 16

Millman, Jack M 1930- *AmSCAP 1966*
Millman, William 1883-1937 *WhScrn 1,*
  WhScrn 2, WhoHol B
Milner, Marietta *Film 2*
Millocker, Karl 1842-1899 *NotNAT B*
Millot, Charles *WhoHol A*
Mills, A J 1872- *WhThe*
Mills, Alyce *Film 2*
Mills, Annette d1955 *NotNAT B*
Mills, Bertram 1873-1938 *NotNAT A*
Mills, Billy d1971 *WhoHol B*
Mills, Carley 1897-1962 *AmSCAP 1966,*
  NotNAT B
Mills, Mrs. Clifford d1933 *NotNAT B, WhThe*
Mills, Donna *WhoHol A*
Mills, Evelyn *Film 2*
Mills, Florence 1895-1927 *EncMT, NotNAT B,*
  WhoHol B
Mills, Florence 1901- *WhThe*
Mills, Frank *Film 1, Film 2*
Mills, Frank 1870-1921 *NotNAT B, WhThe,*
  WhoHol B
Mills, Frank 1891-1973 *WhScrn 2*
Mills, Freddie 1919-1965 *WhScrn 2, WhoHol B*
Mills, Frederick Allen 1869-1948 *AmSCAP 1966*
Mills, Gilbert 1909- *AmSCAP 1966*
Mills, Grant d1973 *WhScrn 2, WhoHol B*
Mills, Guy 1898-1962 *NotNAT B, WhScrn 1,*
  WhScrn 2
Mills, Hayley 1946- *CelR 3, FilmgC,*
  IntMPA 1977, MotPP, MovMk, NotNAT A,
  WhoHol A, WhoThe 16, WorEnF
Mills, Horace 1864-1941 *NotNAT B, WhThe*
Mills, Hugh 1913?- *FilmgC*
Mills, Irving 1894- *AmSCAP 1966*
Mills, Joe d1935 *Film 2, WhoHol B*
Mills, John 1908- *BiDFlm, BiE&WWA, CelR 3,*
  CmMov, EncMT, FilmgC, IntMPA 1977,
  MotPP, MovMk, NotNAT A, OxFilm,
  PIP&P, WhoHol A, WhoThe 16, WorEnF
Mills, John, Jr. 1910-1936 *WhScrn 2*
Mills, John, Sr. 1889-1967 *WhScrn 2*
Mills, Joseph S 1875-1935 *WhScrn 1, WhScrn 2*
Mills, Juliet 1941- *BiE&WWA, FilmgC, MotPP,*
  NotNAT A, WhoHol A, WhoThe 16
Mills, Kerry 1869-1948 *NotNAT B*
Mills, Marilyn *Film 2*
Mills, Mort *WhoHol A*
Mills, Paul 1921- *AmSCAP 1966*
Mills, Stanley 1931- *AmSCAP 1966*
Mills, Thomas R 1878-1953 *Film 1, Film 2,*
  WhScrn 1, WhScrn 2, WhoHol B
Mills, Verlye 1916- *AmSCAP 1966*
Mills, Wilbur 1909- *CelR 3*
Mills, William R 1894- *AmSCAP 1966*
Mills Brothers, The *WhoHol A*
Mills Family *MotPP*
Millstein, Gilbert *BiE&WWA*
Millward, Charles d1892 *NotNAT B*
Millward, Jessie 1861-1932 *NotNAT A,*
  NotNAT B, WhThe
Millward, Jessie 1868- *WhoStg 1906,*
  WhoStg 1908
Millward, Mike 1943-1966 *WhScrn 2*
Milly, Louise *Film 1*
Milman, Dean d1868 *NotNAT B*
Milne, Alan Alexander 1882-1956 *CnMD,*
  McGWD, ModWD, NotNAT B, WhThe
Milne, Alisdair *NewYTET*
Milner, Jack 1910- *IntMPA 1977*
Milner, Martin 1927- *FilmgC, IntMPA 1977,*
  MotPP, WhoHol A
Milner, Ron 1938- *ConDr 1977, PIP&P A*
Milner, Victor 1893- *CmMov, WorEnF*

Milo, George 1909- *IntMPA 1977*
Milo, Sandra *WhoHol A*
Milos, Milos 1941-1966 *WhScrn 2*
Milovitch, Cordy *Film 2*
Milowanoff, Sandra *Film 2*
Milstein, Nathan 1904- *CelR 3*
Miltern, John 1870-1937 *Film 2, NotNAT B,
     WhScrn 1, WhScrn 2, WhoHol B*
Milton, Mrs. Arthur d1936 *NotNAT B*
Milton, Billy 1905- *FilmgC, WhThe, WhoHol A*
Milton, David Scott *NatPD*
Milton, Ernest 1890-1974 *CnThe, Film 1,
     FilmgC, PIP&P, WhScrn 2, WhThe,
     WhoHol B*
Milton, Georges *Film 2*
Milton, Georges 1888-1970 *WhScrn 1, WhScrn 2,
     WhoHol B*
Milton, Harry 1900-1965 *WhScrn 1, WhScrn 2,
     WhThe, WhoHol B*
Milton, Jay 1910- *AmSCAP 1966*
Milton, Joanna *WomWMM*
Milton, John 1608-1674 *CnThe, NotNAT B,
     PIP&P, REnWD*
Milton, Louette 1907-1930 *WhScrn 1, WhScrn 2,
     WhoHol B*
Milton, Maud 1859-1945 *NotNAT B, WhThe,
     WhoHol B*
Milton, Robert d1956 *WhThe*
Milton, Royce *Film 2*
Milward, Dawson 1870-1926 *Film 2, NotNAT B,
     WhThe*
Mimica, Vatroslav 1923- *DcFM, OxFilm,
     WorEnF*
Mimieux, Yvette *IntMPA 1977, MotPP,
     WhoHol A*
Mimieux, Yvette 1939- *FilmgC*
Mimieux, Yvette 1942- *MovMk*
Mims, William *WhoHol A*
Minardos, Nico *WhoHol A*
Minciotti, Esther 1888-1962 *NotNAT B, Vers A,
     WhScrn 1, WhScrn 2, WhoHol B*
Minciotti, Silvio 1883-1961 *WhScrn 1, WhScrn 2,
     WhoHol B*
Mindlin, Michael, Jr. *IntMPA 1977*
Mineau, Charlotte *Film 1, Film 2*
Minelli, Liza 1946- *WomWMM*
Minelli, Liza see also Minnelli, Liza
Mineo, Antoinette 1926- *AmSCAP 1966*
Mineo, Attilio 1918- *AmSCAP 1966*
Mineo, Sal 1939-1976 *FilmgC, MotPP, MovMk,
     WhoHol C*
Mineo, Samuel H 1909- *AmSCAP 1966*
Miner, Allen H *FilmgC*
Miner, Daniel 1880-1938 *WhScrn 1, WhScrn 2*
Miner, Henry Clay d1950 *NotNAT B*
Miner, Jan *WhoHol A*
Miner, Jan 1917- *WhoThe 16*
Miner, Jan 1919- *BiE&WWA, NotNAT*
Miner, Worthington C 1900- *BiE&WWA,
     IntMPA 1977, NewYTET, NotNAT, WhThe*
Minetti, Maria *WhThe*
Minevitch, Borrah 1904?-1955 *NotNAT B,
     WhScrn 1, WhScrn 2, WhoHol B*
Ming, Huang 685-762 *REnWD*
Ming, Moy Luke 1863-1964 *WhScrn 2*
Mingozzi, Gian Franco 1932- *WorEnF*
Minil, Renee Du 1868- *WhThe*
Mink, Patsy 1927- *CelR 3*
Minkoff, Frances 1915- *AmSCAP 1966*
Minkus, Barbara *WhoHol A*
Minnehaha *Film 2*
Minnelli, Liza 1946- *BiDFlm, BiE&WWA,
     CelR 3, EncMT, FilmgC, IntMPA 1977,
     MotPP, MovMk, NotNAT, WhoHol A,*

WhoThe 16
Minnelli, Liza see also Minelli, Liza
Minnelli, Vincente *IntMPA 1977, NotNAT,
     NotNAT A*
Minnelli, Vincente 1910- *CmMov, FilmgC*
Minnelli, Vincente 1913- *BiDFlm, CelR 3,
     DcFM, EncMT, MovMk, OxFilm, WorEnF*
Minner, Kathryn 1892-1969 *WhScrn 1,
     WhScrn 2, WhoHol B*
Minney, Rubeigh James 1895- *FilmgC, WhThe*
Minor, Roy 1905-1935 *WhScrn 1, WhScrn 2*
Minot, Anna *WhoHol A*
Minotis, Alexis 1900- *OxThe*
Minotis, Alexis 1906- *BiE&WWA*
Minow, Newton N *NewYTET*
Minshull, George T d1943 *NotNAT B*
Minskoff, Jerome *NotNAT*
Minsky, Abraham Bennet 1881-1949 *NotNAT B*
Minsky, Howard G *IntMPA 1977*
Minsky, Mollie d1964 *NotNAT B*
Minster, Jack 1901-1966 *WhThe*
Minter, George 1911-1966 *FilmgC*
Minter, Mary Miles 1902- *Film 1, Film 2,
     FilmgC, MotPP, MovMk, TwYS, WhThe,
     WhoHol A*
Minter, William F 1892-1937 *WhScrn 1,
     WhScrn 2*
Minto, Dorothy 1891- *WhThe*
Minturn, Harry L d1963 *NotNAT B*
Mintz, Eli 1904- *NotNAT, WhoHol A*
Minzey, Frank 1879-1949 *NotNAT B, WhScrn 1,
     WhScrn 2, WhoHol B*
Mioni, Fabrizio *WhoHol A*
Miou-Miou *WhoHol A*
Mir, David *Film 2*
Mira DeAmescua, Antonio 1570?-1644 *McGWD*
Mirabella, Grace *CelR 3*
Miracle, Silas *Film 2*
Miramova, Elena *WhThe*
Miranda, Carmen d1955 *MotPP, NotNAT B,
     WhoHol B*
Miranda, Carmen 1904-1955 *WhScrn 1,
     WhScrn 2*
Miranda, Carmen 1909-1955 *MovMk*
Miranda, Carmen 1913-1955 *WorEnF*
Miranda, Carmen 1914-1955 *FilmgC, OxFilm*
Miranda, Erasmo 1904- *AmSCAP 1966*
Miranda, Francisco Sa De 1481-1558 *OxThe*
Miranda, Isa 1909- *BiDFlm, FilmgC, MovMk,
     OxFilm, WhoHol A*
Miranda, Isa 1912- *WorEnF*
Miranda, Isa 1917- *IntMPA 1977*
Miranda, Susana *WhoHol A*
Mirande, Yves *WhThe*
Mirandy d1974 *WhScrn 2, WhoHol B*
Mirbeau, Octave 1848-1917 *CnMD, NotNAT B,
     OxThe, WhThe*
Mirbeau, Octave 1850-1917 *McGWD, ModWD*
Mirell, Leon I *IntMPA 1977*
Mirisch, David 1935- *IntMPA 1977*
Mirisch, Harold 1907-1968 *FilmgC*
Mirisch, Marvin E 1918- *FilmgC, IntMPA 1977*
Mirisch, Walter M 1921- *DcFM, FilmgC,
     IntMPA 1977*
Mirisch Brothers, The *FilmgC, WorEnF*
Mirkin, Barry W 1916- *AmSCAP 1966*
Miro, Joan 1893- *CelR 3*
Miroslava 1930-1955 *FilmgC, WhScrn 1,
     WhScrn 2, WhoHol B*
Mirren, Helen 1946- *WhoHol A, WhoThe 16*
Misch, Margot *Film 2*
Misener, Helen 1909-1960 *WhScrn 2*
Mishima, Masao 1906-1973 *WhScrn 2*
Mishima, Yukio d1971 *WhScrn 1, WhScrn 2*

Mishima, Yukio 1925-1970 *CnMD, ModWD*
Misonne, Claude *WomWMM*
Misraki, Paul 1908- *DcFM, FilmgC, WorEnF*
Missa, Edmond d1910 *NotNAT B*
Missal, Joshua M 1915- *AmSCAP 1966*
Missen, Oud Egede *Film 2*
Missimer, Howard *Film 1*
Missirio, Cenica *Film 2*
Mistinguett 1875-1956 *NotNAT A, NotNAT B,
  OxThe, WhThe*
Mistral, Jorge 1923-1972 *WhScrn 2, WhoHol B*
Mita, Ura *Film 2*
Mitchel, Les 1905-1975 *WhScrn 2*
Mitchelhill, J P 1879-1966 *WhThe*
Mitchell, Abbie d1960 *NotNAT B*
Mitchell, Ada 1880- *WhoStg 1906, WhoStg 1908*
Mitchell, Adrian 1932- *ConDr 1977*
Mitchell, Andrew 1925- *IntMPA 1977*
Mitchell, Belle *Film 2, WhoHol A*
Mitchell, Bruce d1952 *Film 1, WhoHol B*
Mitchell, Bruce 1882-1952 *TwYS A*
Mitchell, Bruce 1883-1952 *WhScrn 1, WhScrn 2*
Mitchell, Cameron 1918- *BiE&WWA, FilmgC,
  IntMPA 1977, MotPP, MovMk, PIP&P,
  WhoHol A*
Mitchell, Carolyn 1937-1966 *WhScrn 2*
Mitchell, Charles 1884-1929 *WhScrn 1,
  WhScrn 2*
Mitchell, David *WhoThe 16*
Mitchell, Dobson 1868-1939 *WhScrn 2*
Mitchell, Dodson 1868-1939 *Film 1, Film 2,
  NotNAT B, WhThe, WhoHol B*
Mitchell, Don *WhoHol A*
Mitchell, Doris *Film 1*
Mitchell, Earle d1946 *NotNAT B*
Mitchell, Esther d1953 *NotNAT B*
Mitchell, George 1905-1972 *BiE&WWA,
  NotNAT B, WhScrn 2, WhoHol B*
Mitchell, Grant d1957 *MotPP, WhoHol B*
Mitchell, Grant 1874-1957 *FilmgC, NotNAT B,
  WhScrn 1, WhScrn 2, WhThe*
Mitchell, Grant 1875-1957 *MovMk, Vers A*
Mitchell, Guy *WhoHol A*
Mitchell, Guy 1925- *FilmgC*
Mitchell, Guy 1927- *IntMPA 1977*
Mitchell, Gwenn *WhoHol A*
Mitchell, Helen d1945 *WhScrn 1, WhScrn 2,
  WhoHol B*
Mitchell, Howard 1883- *TwYS A*
Mitchell, Howard 1888-1958 *Film 1, WhScrn 1,
  WhScrn 2, WhoHol B*
Mitchell, Howard 1911- *BiE&WWA*
Mitchell, Irving *Film 2*
Mitchell, Jack 1918- *IntMPA 1977*
Mitchell, James 1920- *BiE&WWA, MotPP,
  MovMk, NotNAT, WhoHol A*
Mitchell, James Irving 1891-1969 *WhScrn 1,
  WhScrn 2*
Mitchell, Jan 1916- *BiE&WWA*
Mitchell, John 1919-1951 *WhScrn 1, WhScrn 2*
Mitchell, John D 1917- *BiE&WWA, NotNAT*
Mitchell, John H 1918- *IntMPA 1977*
Mitchell, Johnny d1951 *WhoHol B*
Mitchell, Joni 1943- *CelR 3*
Mitchell, Joseph d1738 *NotNAT B*
Mitchell, Julian 1854-1926 *EncMT, NotNAT B*
Mitchell, Julien 1884-1954 *FilmgC*
Mitchell, Julien 1888-1954 *NotNAT B,
  WhScrn 1, WhScrn 2, WhThe, WhoHol B*
Mitchell, Mrs. Langdon d1944 *NotNAT B*
Mitchell, Langdon Elwyn 1862-1933 *OxThe*
Mitchell, Langdon Elwyn 1862-1935 *CnMD,
  McGWD, ModWD, NotNAT B, WhThe*
Mitchell, Lee 1906- *BiE&WWA, NotNAT*

Mitchell, Les 1885-1965 *WhoHol B*
Mitchell, Leslie 1885-1965 *WhScrn 2*
Mitchell, Leslie 1905-1975 *FilmgC, WhoHol C*
Mitchell, Loften 1919- *BiE&WWA, ConDr 1977,
  NotNAT*
Mitchell, Mae d1963 *NotNAT B*
Mitchell, Maggie 1832-1918 *FamA&A,
  NotNAT B, OxThe*
Mitchell, Margaret 1900-1949 *FilmgC*
Mitchell, Martha 1918- *CelR 3*
Mitchell, Martin *Film 2*
Mitchell, Mary Ruth 1906-1941 *WhScrn 1,
  WhScrn 2*
Mitchell, Maurine *BiE&WWA*
Mitchell, Millard 1900-1953 *FilmgC, MotPP,
  WhScrn 1, WhScrn 2, WhoHol B*
Mitchell, Millard 1903-1953 *NotNAT B*
Mitchell, Norma d1967 *WhScrn 1, WhScrn 2,
  WhoHol B*
Mitchell, Oswald 1890?-1949 *FilmgC*
Mitchell, Raymond Earle 1895- *AmSCAP 1966*
Mitchell, Rhea *MotPP*
Mitchell, Rhea 1891-1957 *TwYS*
Mitchell, Rhea 1894-1957 *Film 1, Film 2,
  NotNAT B*
Mitchell, Rhea 1905-1957 *WhoHol B*
Mitchell, Rhea Ginger 1905-1957 *WhScrn 1,
  WhScrn 2*
Mitchell, Ronald E 1905- *BiE&WWA*
Mitchell, Ruth 1919- *BiE&WWA, NotNAT,
  WhoThe 16*
Mitchell, Shirley *WhoHol A*
Mitchell, Sidney D 1888-1942 *AmSCAP 1966*
Mitchell, Stephen 1907- *WhoThe 16*
Mitchell, Steve *IntMPA 1977, WhoHol A*
Mitchell, Theodore -1938 *NotNAT B*
Mitchell, Thomas d1962 *MotPP, WhoHol B*
Mitchell, Thomas 1892-1962 *BiDFlm, Film 2,
  FilmgC, MovMk, OxFilm, Vers A, WorEnF*
Mitchell, Thomas 1895-1962 *CmMov, NotNAT B,
  WhScrn 1, WhScrn 2, WhThe*
Mitchell, Warren 1926- *FilmgC, WhoHol A,
  WhoThe 16*
Mitchell, William 1798-1856 *NotNAT B, OxThe*
Mitchell, William L 1944- *AmSCAP 1966*
Mitchell, Wirt McClintic 1914- *AmSCAP 1966*
Mitchell, Yvette *Film 1*
Mitchell, Yvonne 1925- *FilmgC, IntMPA 1977,
  NotNAT A, OxFilm, WhoHol A,
  WhoThe 16*
Mitchum, Chris *WhoHol A*
Mitchum, Cindy *WhoHol A*
Mitchum, James *MotPP*
Mitchum, James 1938- *FilmgC*
Mitchum, Jim *WhoHol A*
Mitchum, Jim 1941- *IntMPA 1977*
Mitchum, John *WhoHol A*
Mitchum, Robert 1917- *AmSCAP 1966, BiDFlm,
  CelR 3, CmMov, FilmgC, IntMPA 1977,
  MotPP, MovMk, OxFilm, WhoHol A,
  WorEnF*
Mitford, Mary Russell d1855 *NotNAT B*
Mito, Mitsuko *WhoHol A*
Mitosky, Alan P 1934- *IntMPA 1977*
Mitra, Deenabandhu *REnWD*
Mitra, Subrata 1931- *WorEnF*
Mitry, Jean 1907- *Film 2, OxFilm, WorEnF*
Mittell, Lyn Donaldson 1892-1966 *WhScrn 1,
  WhScrn 2*
Mitzi, Little *Film 2*
Mitzi-Dalty, Mademoiselle *WhThe*
Mix, Art d1972 *WhoHol B*
Mix, Ruth 1913- *Film 2*
Mix, Tom 1880-1940 *Film 1, Film 2, FilmgC,*

MotPP, MovMk, NotNAT B, OxFilm,
TwYS, WhScrn 1, WhScrn 2, WhoHol B,
WorEnF
Mix, Tom 1881-1940 CmMov
Miyagawa, Kazuo 1908- DcFM, WorEnF
Mizner, Wilson 1876-1933 NotNAT B
Mizoghuchi, Kenji 1898-1956 WhScrn 1,
WhScrn 2
Mizoguchi, Kenji 1898-1956 BiDFlm, DcFM,
FilmgC, MovMk, OxFilm, WorEnF
Mizzy, Vic 1922- AmSCAP 1966
M'Kin, Robert WhScrn 1, WhScrn 2
Mladenovic, Ranko 1893-1947 CnMD
M'Lellan, C M S 1865-1916 WhoStg 1906
M'Lellan, C M S see also McLellan, C M S
Moatt, Christine Film 2
Mobell, Sidney F 1926- AmSCAP 1966
Moberg, Vilhelm 1898-1973 CnMD, ModWD
Moberly, Connie WomWMM B
Moberly, Luke 1925- IntMPA 1977
Mobley, Mary Ann 1939- FilmgC, MotPP,
WhoHol A
Mobley, Peggy J WomWMM B
Mochalov, Pavel Stepanovich 1800-1848 OxThe
Mociuk, Yar W 1927- IntMPA 1977
Mock, Alice d1972 WhScrn 2
Mock, Flora Clar WomWMM B
Mockridge, Cyril J 1896- FilmgC, OxFilm,
WorEnF
Mocky, Jean-Pierre 1929- DcFM, FilmgC,
OxFilm, WorEnF
Modena, Giacomo 1766-1841 NotNAT B, OxThe
Modena, Gustavo 1803-1861 NotNAT B, OxThe
Modie, Louella WhScrn 1, WhScrn 2
Modjeska, Felix Film 1
Modjeska, Helen 1840-1909 PIP&P
Modjeska, Helena 1840-1909 FamA&A,
NotNAT A, OxThe
Modjeska, Helena 1844-1909 CnThe, NotNAT B,
WhoStg 1906, WhoStg 1908
Modot, Gaston 1887-1970 Film 2, OxFilm,
WhScrn 2, WorEnF
Moe, Christian H 1929- BiE&WWA, NotNAT
Moed, Pearl 1938- AmSCAP 1966
Moehlmann, R L 1907- AmSCAP 1966
Moehring, Kansas d1968 WhScrn 2, WhoHol B
Moeller, Philip 1880-1958 ModWD, NotNAT B,
PIP&P, WhThe
Moers, Hermann 1930- CnMD, ModWD
Moffat, Donald 1930- BiE&WWA, NotNAT,
WhoHol A, WhoThe 16
Moffat, Graham 1866-1951 NotNAT A,
NotNAT B, WhThe
Moffat, Mrs. Graham 1873-1943 NotNAT B,
WhThe
Moffat, Kate WhThe
Moffat, Margaret d1942 WhoHol B
Moffat, Margaret 1882-1942 NotNAT B, WhThe
Moffat, Margaret 1892-1942 WhScrn 1,
WhScrn 2
Moffat, Winifred 1899- WhThe
Moffatt, Alice 1890- WhThe
Moffatt, Graham 1919-1965 FilmgC, WhScrn 1,
WhScrn 2, WhoHol B
Moffatt, John 1922- BiE&WWA, NotNAT,
WhoHol A, WhoThe 16
Moffatt, Margaret 1882-1942 WhThe
Moffatt, Richard C 1927- AmSCAP 1966
Moffatt, Sanderson d1918 NotNAT B
Moffet, Harold 1892-1938 WhThe
Moffett, Cleveland d1926 NotNAT B
Moffett, Harold 1892-1938 NotNAT B
Moffett, Sharyn 1936- FilmgC
Moffitt, DeLoyce 1906- AmSCAP 1966

Moffitt, Jefferson Film 2
Moffitt, John Craig NewYTET
Moffo, Anna 1935- CelR 3, WhoHol A
Moger, Art IntMPA 1977
Mogin, Jean 1921- ModWD
Moguy, Leonide 1899- DcFM, FilmgC
Mohammed-Ben-Noni Film 2
Mohan, Chandra d1949 WhScrn 2
Mohan, Earl d1928 WhScrn 1, WhScrn 2,
WhoHol B
Mohner, Carl 1921- FilmgC, WhoHol A
Moholy-Nagy, Laszlo 1895-1946 OxFilm
Mohr, Gerald 1914-1968 FilmgC, NotNAT B,
Vers A, WhScrn 1, WhScrn 2, WhoHol B
Mohr, Hal 1893- WorEnF
Mohr, Hal 1894- CmMov, FilmgC
Mohr, Max 1891-1944 McGWD
Mohun, Michael 1620?-1684 OxThe, PIP&P
Mohyeddin, Zia 1933- WhoHol A, WhoThe 16
Moineaux, Georges-Victor-Marcel McGWD
Moinet, Monique WomWMM
Moise, Mina WomWMM
Moiseiwitsch, Tanya 1914- BiE&WWA, CnThe,
NotNAT, WhoThe 16
Moissi, Alexander 1880-1935 Film 2, NotNAT B,
OxThe, WhScrn 1, WhScrn 2, WhoHol B
Moja, Hella 1898-1937 Film 2, WhScrn 1,
WhScrn 2, WhoHol B
Mojave, King d1973 WhScrn 2, WhoHol B
Mojica, Jose 1899-1974 WhScrn 2, WhoHol B
Mok, Michel d1961 NotNAT B
Mokuami, Kawatake 1816-1893 CnThe, REnWD
Molander, Gustaf 1888-1973 BiDFlm, DcFM,
FilmgC, OxFilm
Molander, Gustav 1888- WorEnF
Molander, Karin Film 1
Molander, Olaf 1892-1966 WhScrn 2
Molas, Zet WomWMM
Mole, Francois-Rene 1734-1802 OxThe
Moleska, Paul Film 2
Molesworth, Ida d1951 NotNAT B, WhThe
Molette, Barbara NatPD
Molette, Carlton NatPD
Moliere 1622-1673 CnThe, McGWD,
NotNAT A, NotNAT B, OxThe, PIP&P,
PIP&P A, REnWD
Molina, Carlos WhoHol A
Molina, Tirso De 1571?-1648 NotNAT B, OxThe
Molina, Tirso De 1580?-1648 McGWD
Molina, Tirso De 1584-1648 CnThe
Molinari, Doreen WhoHol A
Molinaro, Edouard 1928- DcFM, FilmgC,
WorEnF
Molinas, Richard WhoHol A
Moll, Billy 1905- AmSCAP 1966
Moll, Elick 1907- IntMPA 1977
Moll, Georgia WhoHol A
Mollandin, Henry M Film 2
Moller, Eberhard Wolfgang 1906- McGWD,
ModWD
Mollison, Clifford 1897- WhoHol A, WhoThe 16
Mollison, Henry 1905- WhThe
Mollison, William 1893-1955 NotNAT B, WhThe
Mollot, Yolande WhoHol A
Molloy, Charles d1767 NotNAT B
Molloy, J L d1909 NotNAT B
Molloy, Michael 1917- ConDr 1977
Molnar, Ferenc 1878-1952 CnMD, CnThe,
McGWD, ModWD, NotNAT A, NotNAT B,
OxThe, PIP&P, REnWD
Molnar, Ferencz 1878-1952 WhThe
Molnar, Julius, Jr. Film 2
Molnar, Lilly d1950 WhoHol B
Molnar, Lily d1950 NotNAT B

Moloney, John 1911-1969 *WhScrn 1*, *WhScrn 2*, *WhoHol B*
Molyneux, Eileen 1893-1962 *WhThe*
Momai, Tetsu *Film 2*
Momo, Alessandro 1953-1974 *WhScrn 2*, *WhoHol B*
Monaco, Princess Of *Film 1*
Monaco, Eitel 1903- *IntMPA 1977*
Monaco, James V 1885-1945 *AmSCAP 1966*
Monaco, Jimmy 1885-1945 *NotNAT B*
Monahan, Colleen *WomWMM B*
Monahan, Kaspar J 1900- *BiE&WWA*
Monakhov, Nickolai Fedorovich 1875-1936 *NotNAT B*
Monakhov, Nikolai Fedorovich 1875-1936 *OxThe*
Monash, Paul *IntMPA 1977*, *NewYTET*
Monath, Norman 1930- *AmSCAP 1966*
Monca, Georges 187-?-1940 *DcFM*
Moncion, Francisco *WhoHol A*
Monck, Nugent 1877-1958 *NotNAT B*, *OxThe*, *WhThe*
Monckton, Lionel d1924 *NotNAT B*
Monckton, Lionel 1861-1924 *EncMT*
Monckton, Lionel 1862-1924 *WhThe*
Moncrieff, Gladys 1893- *WhThe*
Moncrieff, Murri d1949 *NotNAT B*
Moncrieff, William Thomas 1794-1857 *NotNAT B*, *OxThe*
Moncries, Edward 1859-1938 *WhScrn 1*, *WhScrn 2*, *WhoHol B*
Mondo, Peggy *WhoHol A*
Mondose, Alex 1894-1972 *WhScrn 2*
Mondy, Pierre 1925- *FilmgC*
Monello, Spartaco V 1909- *AmSCAP 1966*
Monet, Gaby *WomWMM B*
Mong, William V 1875-1940 *Film 1*, *Film 2*, *MovMk*, *TwYS*, *WhScrn 1*, *WhScrn 2*, *WhoHol B*
Mongberg, George *Film 2*
Monicelli, Mario 1915- *DcFM*, *FilmgC*, *IntMPA 1977*, *WorEnF*
Monk, Julius *WhoHol A*
Monk, Thelonious 1918- *CelR 3*
Monkees, The *FilmgC*
Monkhouse, Allan Noble 1858-1936 *ModWD*, *NotNAT B*, *OxThe*, *WhThe*
Monkhouse, Bob 1928- *FilmgC*, *IntMPA 1977*, *WhoHol A*
Monkhouse, Harry d1901 *NotNAT B*
Monkman, Phyllis 1892- *Film 2*, *WhThe*
Monks, James 1917- *WhThe*, *WhoHol A*
Monks, John, Jr. 1910- *BiE&WWA*, *IntMPA 1977*, *NotNAT*
Monks, Victoria 1884- *WhThe*
Monna-Delza, Mademoiselle d1921 *NotNAT B*, *WhThe*
Monnier, Jackie *Film 2*
Monnot, Marguerite d1961 *NotNAT B*
Monroe, Bill *NewYTET*
Monroe, Frank d1937 *NotNAT B*
Monroe, George W d1932 *NotNAT B*
Monroe, Marilyn 1926-1962 *BiDFlm*, *CmMov*, *FilmgC*, *MotPP*, *MovMk*, *NotNAT B*, *OxFilm*, *WhScrn 1*, *WhScrn 2*, *WhoHol B*, *WorEnF*
Monroe, Vaughan 1911- *FilmgC*
Monroe, Vaughn 1911-1973 *AmSCAP 1966*, *WhScrn 2*, *WhoHol B*
Mont, Christina *Film 2*
Mont, Paul De 1895-1950 *ModWD*
Monta, Rudolph d1963 *NotNAT B*
Montagne, Edward J *IntMPA 1977*
Montagu, Ashley 1905- *CelR 3*
Montagu, Elizabeth 1909- *WhThe*

Montagu, Ivor 1904- *FilmgC*, *OxFilm*
Montague, Bertram 1892- *WhThe*
Montague, Charles Edward 1867-1928 *NotNAT B*, *OxThe*, *WhThe*
Montague, Edna Woodruff *WhScrn 1*, *WhScrn 2*
Montague, Emmeline d1910 *NotNAT B*
Montague, Fred *Film 1*, *WhoHol B*
Montague, Frederick 1864-1919 *WhScrn 2*
Montague, H J 1844-1878 *PIP&P*
Montague, Harold 1874- *WhThe*
Montague, Harry d1927 *NotNAT B*
Montague, Henry James 1844-1878 *NotNAT B*, *OxThe*
Montague, Lee 1927- *FilmgC*, *WhoHol A*, *WhoThe 16*
Montague, Louise 1871-1906 *NotNAT B*
Montague, Monte d1959 *WhoHol B*
Montague, Monty *Film 2*
Montague, Rita 1884-1962 *NotNAT B*, *WhScrn 1*, *WhScrn 2*, *WhoHol B*
Montaland, Celine 1843-1891 *OxThe*
Montalban, Carlos *WhoHol A*
Montalban, Ricardo 1920- *BiE&WWA*, *FilmgC*, *IntMPA 1977*, *MGM*, *MotPP*, *MovMk*, *WhoHol A*, *WorEnF*
Montalvan, Celia 1899-1958 *WhScrn 2*
Montana, Bull 1887-1950 *Film 1*, *Film 2*, *FilmgC*, *TwYS*, *WhScrn 1*, *WhScrn 2*, *WhoHol B*
Montana, Montie 1910- *WhoHol A*
Montana, Patsy 1914- *AmSCAP 1966*
Montand, Yves 1921- *BiDFlm*, *CelR 3*, *FilmgC*, *IntMPA 1977*, *MotPP*, *MovMk*, *OxFilm*, *WhoHol A*, *WorEnF*
Montani, Nicola Aloysius 1880-1948 *AmSCAP 1966*
Montano, A d1914 *WhScrn 2*
Montansier, Marguerite 1730-1820 *NotNAT B*, *OxThe*
Montanus, Edward *NewYTET*
Montazel, Pierre 1911- *DcFM*
Montchretien, Antoine De 1575?-1621 *OxThe*
Montdory 1594-1651 *NotNAT B*, *OxThe*
Montdory, Guillaume 1594-1651 *CnThe*
Monte, Lou 1917- *AmSCAP 1966*
Montefiore, Eade 1866-1944 *NotNAT B*, *WhThe*
Monteiro, Pilar 1886-1962 *WhScrn 1*, *WhScrn 2*
Montel, Blanche *Film 2*
Montel, Michael 1939- *NotNAT*
Montenegro, Conchita 1912- *WhoHol A*
Monterey, Carlotta 1888-1970 *Film 2*, *NotNAT B*, *WhScrn 2*
Montes, Lola *FilmgC*
Montesole, Max d1942 *NotNAT B*
Monteux, Pierre 1875-1964 *NotNAT B*
Montevecchi, Liliane *WhoHol A*
Montez, Lola 1818-1861 *FamA&A*, *NotNAT A*, *NotNAT B*
Montez, Maria d1951 *MotPP*, *WhoHol B*
Montez, Maria 1918-1951 *CmMov*, *FilmgC*, *WhScrn 1*, *WhScrn 2*
Montez, Maria 1920-1951 *MovMk*, *NotNAT B*, *WorEnF*
Montfleury, Antoine 1639-1685 *OxThe*
Montfleury, Francoise 1640?-1708 *OxThe*
Montfleury, Louise 1649-1709 *OxThe*
Montfleury, Zacharie Jacob 1600?-1667 *OxThe*
Montgomery, Baby Peggy 1918- *TwYS*
Montgomery, Baby Peggy see also Montgomery, Peggy
Montgomery, Belinda J *WhoHol A*
Montgomery, Bruce 1927- *AmSCAP 1966*
Montgomery, David 1870-1917 *EncMT*, *NotNAT B*, *PIP&P*

Montgomery, Doreen *IntMPA 1977*
Montgomery, Douglas 1908-1966 *WhScrn 1,*
   WhScrn 2
Montgomery, Douglass d1966 *WhoHol B*
Montgomery, Douglass 1907-1966 *HolP 30*
Montgomery, Douglass 1908-1966 *FilmgC,*
   NotNAT B
Montgomery, Douglass 1909-1966 *WhThe*
Montgomery, Douglass 1912-1966 *BiE&WWA*
Montgomery, Earl *Film 2*
Montgomery, Earl 1893-1966 *WhScrn 2,*
   WhoHol B
Montgomery, Earl 1921- *BiE&WWA, NotNAT,*
   WhoHol A, WhoThe 16
Montgomery, Edythe 1908- *AmSCAP 1966*
Montgomery, Elizabeth 1902- *WhoThe 16*
Montgomery, Elizabeth 1904- *BiE&WWA,*
   NotNAT
Montgomery, Elizabeth 1933- *FilmgC,*
   WhoHol A
Montgomery, Florence d1950 *NotNAT B*
Montgomery, Frank 1870-1944 *Film 2, WhScrn 2*
Montgomery, George 1916- *FilmgC, HolP 40,*
   IntMPA 1977, MotPP, MovMk, WhoHol A
Montgomery, Jack 1892-1962 *WhScrn 1,*
   WhScrn 2, WhoHol B
Montgomery, James 1882-1966 *WhThe*
Montgomery, Marshall d1942 *NotNAT B*
Montgomery, Merle 1904- *AmSCAP 1966*
Montgomery, Peggy 1918- *Film 2, WhoHol A*
Montgomery, Ray *WhoHol A*
Montgomery, Robert 1903- *WhThe*
Montgomery, Robert 1904- *BiDFlm, BiE&WWA,*
   CmMov, Film 2, FilmgC, IntMPA 1977,
   MGM, MotPP, MovMk, NewYTET,
   NotNAT A, OxFilm, WhoHol A,
   WomWMM, WorEnF
Montgomery, Robert Humphrey, Jr. 1923-
   BiE&WWA
Montgomery And Stone *NotNAT B*
Montgommery, David Craig 1870-1917 *WhThe*
Montherlant, Henri De 1896-1972 *OxThe*
Montherlant, Henry De 1896-1972 *CnMD, CnThe,*
   CroCD, McGWD, ModWD, NotNAT A,
   REnWD
Monti, Palola *Film 1*
Monti, Vincenzo 1754-1828 *McGWD*
Montiel, Nelly d1951 *WhScrn 1, WhScrn 2*
Montiel, Sara 1929- *WorEnF*
Montiel, Sarıta 1929- *WhoHol A, WorEnF*
Montivier, Monique *WomWMM*
Montmenil 1695-1743 *NotNAT B, OxThe*
Montoya, Alex P 1907-1970 *WhScrn 2,*
   WhoHol B
Montoya, Carlos 1903- *AmSCAP 1966, CelR 3*
Montoya, Julia *WhoHol A*
Montrose, Belle 1886-1964 *WhScrn 1, WhScrn 2,*
   WhoHol B
Montrose, Helen *Film 2*
Montrose, Jack 1928- *AmSCAP 1966*
Montrose, Muriel *WhThe*
Montt, Christina 1897-1969 *WhScrn 1, WhScrn 2,*
   WhoHol B
Montt, Christine *Film 2*
Montuori, Carlo 1885- *DcFM*
Moock, Armando *OxThe*
Moodie, Louise M R d1934 *NotNAT B*
Moody, Harry *Film 1*
Moody, King *WhoHol A*
Moody, Michael Dorn 1944- *NatPD*
Moody, Ralph 1887-1971 *WhScrn 1, WhScrn 2,*
   WhoHol B
Moody, Richard 1911- *BiE&WWA, NotNAT*
Moody, Ron *WhoHol A*

Moody, Ron 1924- *EncMT, FilmgC, WhoThe 16*
Moody, Ron 1926- *MovMk*
Moody, William Vaughan 1869-1910 *NotNAT B,*
   PIP&P, WhoStg 1908
Moody, William Vaughn 1869-1910 *CnThe,*
   McGWD, ModWD, NotNAT A, OxThe,
   REnWD
Mooers, DeSacia 1888-1960 *Film 2, WhScrn 1,*
   WhScrn 2, WhoHol B
Moon, Donna d1918 *WhScrn 2*
Moon, George 1886-1961 *WhScrn 1, WhoHol B*
Moon, George 1886-1967 *WhScrn 2*
Moon, Morse d1918 *WhScrn 2*
Mooney, Harold 1911- *AmSCAP 1966*
Mooney, James A 1872-1951 *AmSCAP 1966*
Mooney, Margaret *Film 1*
Moore, A P 1906- *WhThe*
Moore, Ada *BiE&WWA*
Moore, Adrienne *WhoHol A*
Moore, Alice 1916-1960 *WhScrn 1, WhScrn 2,*
   WhoHol B
Moore, Allyson *WomWMM B*
Moore, Alvy *WhoHol A*
Moore, Archie *WhoHol A*
Moore, Art 1914- *AmSCAP 1966*
Moore, Carlyle, Sr. 1875-1924 *WhScrn 2,*
   WhoStg 1908
Moore, Carrie 1883-1956 *NotNAT B, WhThe*
Moore, Carroll 1913- *BiE&WWA, NotNAT*
Moore, Charles *Film 2, WhoHol A*
Moore, Charles J d1962 *NotNAT B*
Moore, Charles Werner 1920- *BiE&WWA,*
   NotNAT
Moore, Charles William 1918- *AmSCAP 1966*
Moore, Claude *Film 2*
Moore, Clayton 1908- *FilmgC*
Moore, Clayton 1914- *WhoHol A*
Moore, Cleo 1928-1973 *FilmgC, WhScrn 2,*
   WhoHol B
Moore, Cleve d1961 *Film 2, WhoHol B*
Moore, Clive *Film 2*
Moore, Colleen 1900- *Film 1, Film 2, FilmgC,*
   MotPP, ThFT, TwYS, WhoHol A
Moore, Colleen 1902- *MovMk*
Moore, Constance *MotPP*
Moore, Constance 1919- *FilmgC*
Moore, Constance 1920- *WhoHol A*
Moore, Constance 1922- *IntMPA 1977*
Moore, Decima 1871-1964 *NotNAT B, WhThe,*
   WhoStg 1908
Moore, Del 1917-1970 *WhScrn 1, WhScrn 2,*
   WhoHol B
Moore, Dennie 1907- *BiE&WWA, NotNAT,*
   WhThe, WhoHol A
Moore, Dennis d1964 *WhoHol B*
Moore, Dick 1925- *BiE&WWA, NotNAT*
Moore, Dickie 1925- *Film 2, FilmgC, HolP 30,*
   IntMPA 1977, MotPP, MovMk, WhoHol A
Moore, Donald Lee 1910- *AmSCAP 1966*
Moore, Douglas Stuart 1893-1969 *AmSCAP 1966*
Moore, Dudley 1935- *BiE&WWA, FilmgC,*
   NotNAT, WhoHol A, WhoThe 16
Moore, Edward 1712-1757 *NotNAT B, OxThe*
Moore, Edward James 1935- *NatPD, NotNAT*
Moore, Eileen *WhoHol A*
Moore, Elizabeth Evelyn 1891- *AmSCAP 1966*
Moore, Ellis O 1924- *IntMPA 1977, NewYTET*
Moore, Elsie *WhoStg 1906, WhoStg 1908*
Moore, Erin O'Brien *WhoHol A*
Moore, Eulabelle 1903-1964 *BiE&WWA,*
   NotNAT B, WhScrn 1, WhScrn 2,
   WhoHol B
Moore, Eva 1870-1955 *Film 2, FilmgC,*
   NotNAT A, NotNAT B, WhScrn 1,

WhScrn 2, WhThe, WhoHol B
Moore, F Frankfort d1931 *NotNAT B*
Moore, Florence 1886-1935 *NotNAT B,*
WhScrn 1, WhScrn 2, WhThe, WhoHol B
Moore, Francis 1886-1946 *AmSCAP 1966*
Moore, Frank 1928- *AmSCAP 1966*
Moore, Frank F d1924 *WhScrn 1, WhScrn 2*
Moore, Gar *WhoHol A*
Moore, Garry 1915- *CelR 3, IntMPA 1977,*
NewYTET
Moore, Gaylen *WomWMM B*
Moore, George Augustus 1852-1933 *ModWD,*
NotNAT B, OxThe, REnWD, WhThe
Moore, Grace 1901-1947 *EncMT, FilmgC,*
NotNAT A, NotNAT B, OxFilm, PIP&P,
ThFT, WhScrn 1, WhScrn 2, WhThe,
WhoHol B
Moore, Grace 1903-1947 *MovMk*
Moore, Harry R Tim 1888-1958 *WhScrn 1,*
WhScrn 2
Moore, Henrietta d1973 *WhoHol B*
Moore, Hilda d1929 *Film 2, NotNAT B,*
WhScrn 2, WhThe, WhoHol B
Moore, Honor *NatPD*
Moore, Ida 1883-1964 *Film 2, FilmgC,*
WhScrn 1, WhScrn 2, WhoHol B
Moore, Irene 1890- *WhoStg 1908*
Moore, Jessie d1910 *NotNAT B*
Moore, Joanna *WhoHol A*
Moore, Joe *Film 1*
Moore, Joe d1926 *Film 2, WhScrn 2*
Moore, Joseph *OxThe*
Moore, Juanita 1922- *FilmgC, Vers A,*
WhoHol A
Moore, Kieron 1925- *FilmgC, IntMPA 1977,*
WhoHol A
Moore, Kingman T 1919- *IntMPA 1977*
Moore, Laurens 1919- *NotNAT, WhoHol A*
Moore, Leslie 1894-1942 *AmSCAP 1966*
Moore, Lucia *Film 1*
Moore, Maggie 1847-1926 *NotNAT B, WhThe*
Moore, Marcia *Film 1*
Moore, Marjorie *WhoHol A*
Moore, Mary d1919 *Film 1, WhScrn 2*
Moore, Mary d1931 *WhoHol B*
Moore, Mary 1861-1931 *NotNAT B, WhThe*
Moore, Mary 1862-1931 *OxThe*
Moore, Mary Carr 1873-1957 *AmSCAP 1966*
Moore, Mary Tyler *MotPP, NewYTET,*
WhoHol A
Moore, Mary Tyler 1936- *FilmgC, IntMPA 1977*
Moore, Mary Tyler 1937- *CelR 3, MovMk*
Moore, Matt 1888-1960 *Film 1, Film 2, MotPP,*
TwYS, WhScrn 1, WhScrn 2, WhoHol B
Moore, Matt 1890-1960 *NotNAT B*
Moore, Mavor 1919- *ConDr 1977*
Moore, McElbert 1892- *AmSCAP 1966*
Moore, Melba 1945- *CelR 3, PIP&P, PIP&P A,*
WhoHol A
Moore, Michael *WhoHol A*
Moore, Mickey 1917- *Film 2*
Moore, Mildred *Film 2*
Moore, Miltona 1902- *AmSCAP 1966*
Moore, Monette d1961 *NotNAT B*
Moore, Monette 1912-1962 *WhScrn 1, WhScrn 2,*
WhoHol B
Moore, Owen 1886-1939 *Film 1, Film 2,*
NotNAT B, TwYS, WhScrn 1, WhScrn 2,
WhoHol B
Moore, Pat *Film 1*
Moore, Pat 1917- *Film 2*
Moore, Patti 1901-1972 *WhScrn 2*
Moore, Percy 1878-1945 *Film 2, NotNAT B,*
WhScrn 2, WhoHol B

Moore, Phil 1918- *AmSCAP 1966*
Moore, Raymond d1940 *NotNAT B*
Moore, Rex d1975 *WhoHol C*
Moore, Rica Owen 1929- *AmSCAP 1966*
Moore, Richard *FilmgC*
Moore, Richard A *NewYTET*
Moore, Robert *IntMPA 1977, WhoHol A*
Moore, Robert 1927- *WhoThe 16*
Moore, Robert 1929- *NotNAT*
Moore, Robert Francis d1964 *NotNAT B*
Moore, Robert S 1907- *AmSCAP 1966*
Moore, Robin 1925- *CelR 3*
Moore, Roger *IntMPA 1977, MotPP,*
WhoHol A
Moore, Roger 1927- *CelR 3*
Moore, Roger 1928- *FilmgC, MovMk*
Moore, Ruth Hart d1952 *WhScrn 1, WhScrn 2,*
WhoHol B
Moore, Scott 1889-1967 *WhScrn 1, WhScrn 2,*
WhoHol B
Moore, Sonia *BiE&WWA, NotNAT*
Moore, Stephen *WhoHol A*
Moore, Stephen 1937- *WhoThe 16*
Moore, Sue 1916-1966 *WhScrn 2*
Moore, Ted 1914- *CmMov, FilmgC, WorEnF*
Moore, Terrence *Film 2*
Moore, Terry *MotPP*
Moore, Terry 1929- *FilmgC, WhoHol A*
Moore, Terry 1932- *IntMPA 1977*
Moore, Thomas F *AmSCAP 1966*
Moore, Thomas W *IntMPA 1977, NewYTET*
Moore, Tom d1955 *MotPP, NotNAT B,*
WhoHol B
Moore, Tom 1884-1955 *Film 1, Film 2*
Moore, Tom 1885-1955 *MovMk, TwYS,*
WhScrn 1, WhScrn 2
Moore, Victor 1876-1962 *EncMT, Film 1,*
Film 2, FilmgC, MotPP, MovMk,
NotNAT B, PIP&P, TwYS, Vers A,
WhScrn 1, WhScrn 2, WhThe, WhoHol B,
WhoStg 1908
Moore, Vin 1878-1949 *Film 1, Film 2,*
WhScrn 1, WhScrn 2, WhoHol B
Moore, W Scott *Film 1*
Moorehead, Agnes 1906-1974 *BiDFlm,*
BiE&WWA, CelR 3, CmMov, FilmgC,
MGM, MotPP, MovMk, NotNAT B,
Vers A, WhScrn 2, WhoHol B, WhoThe 16,
WorEnF
Moorehead, Agnes 1918-1974 *OxFilm*
Moorehouse, Bert *Film 2*
Moorehouse, Marie *Film 2*
Moorer, Thomas 1912- *CelR 3*
Moorey, Stefa 1934-1972 *WhScrn 2*
Moorhead, Jean d1953 *NotNAT B*
Moorhead, Natalie 1905- *Film 2, ThFT*
Moorhouse, Bert 1895-1954 *WhScrn 1, WhScrn 2,*
WhoHol B
Moorse, George 1936- *WorEnF*
Mopper, Irving 1914- *AmSCAP 1966*
Morahan, Christopher 1929- *WhoThe 16*
Morahan, Christopher 1930?- *FilmgC*
Morales, Esy Ishmael 1917-1950 *WhScrn 1,*
WhoHol B
Morales, Ishmael Esy 1917-1950 *WhScrn 2*
Morales, Noro 1911-1964 *AmSCAP 1966*
Morales, Noro 1913-1964 *NotNAT B*
Moran, Baby *Film 2*
Moran, Barber 1920- *AmSCAP 1966*
Moran, Billy *Film 1*
Moran, Dolores 1926- *IntMPA 1977, MotPP,*
WhoHol A
Moran, Edward P 1871-1956 *AmSCAP 1966*
Moran, Erin *WhoHol A*

Moran, Frank 1887-1967 *WhScrn 2*
Moran, George 1881-1949 *NotNAT B*
Moran, George 1882-1949 *Film 2, WhScrn 1,
WhScrn 2, WhoHol B*
Moran, Jim 1909- *BiE&WWA, NotNAT*
Moran, Lee d1961 *NotNAT B, WhoHol B*
Moran, Lee 1889-1961 *TwYS*
Moran, Lee 1890-1961 *WhScrn 1, WhScrn 2*
Moran, Lee 1899-1960 *Film 1, Film 2*
Moran, Lois 1907- *PIP&P, ThFT, WhThe,
WhoHol A*
Moran, Lois 1909- *Film 2, TwYS*
Moran, Manolo 1904-1967 *WhScrn 1, WhScrn 2*
Moran, Pat 1901-1965 *WhScrn 1, WhScrn 2,
WhoHol B*
Moran, Patsy 1905-1968 *NotNAT B, WhScrn 1,
WhScrn 2, WhoHol B*
Moran, Peggy 1918- *FilmgC, WhoHol A*
Moran, Percy 1886-1952 *Film 1, Film 2*
Moran, Polly d1952 *MotPP, WhoHol B*
Moran, Polly 1883-1952 *WhScrn 1, WhScrn 2*
Moran, Polly 1884-1952 *FilmgC, MovMk, ThFT,
TwYS*
Moran, Polly 1885-1952 *Film 1, Film 2,
NotNAT B*
Moran, Polly 1886-1952 *Vers A*
Moran, Priscilla *Film 2*
Moran, William *Film 2*
Morand, Eugene 1855-1930 *NotNAT B, WhThe*
Morand, Marcellus Raymond 1860-1922
NotNAT B, WhThe
Morante, Joseph 1853-1940 *WhScrn 1, WhScrn 2*
Morante, Milburn d1964 *WhoHol B*
Morante, Milburn 1887-1964 *WhScrn 2*
Morante, Milburn 1888-1964 *Film 2, TwYS*
Moratin *OxThe*
Moratin, Leandro Fernandez De 1760-1828
McGWD
Moratin, Nicolas Fernandez De 1737-1780
McGWD
Moratoria, Orosman 1859-1898 *OxThe*
Moravia, Alberto 1907- *CnMD, WomWMM*
Morax, Rene 1873-1963 *ModWD*
Mordant, Edwin 1868-1942 *Film 1, NotNAT B,
WhScrn 1, WhScrn 2, WhoHol B*
Mordant, Grace 1872-1952 *WhScrn 1, WhScrn 2,
WhoHol B*
Mordecai, Benjamin 1944- *NotNAT*
Mordkin, Mikhail M d1944 *NotNAT B*
Mordvinov, Nikolai Dmitrievich 1901-1966 *OxThe*
More, Hannah d1833 *NotNAT B*
More, Kenneth 1914- *CmMov, CnThe, FilmgC,
IntMPA 1977, WhoHol A, WhoThe 16*
More, Unity 1894- *WhThe*
More O'Ferrall, George 1906?- *FilmgC*
Moreau, Angele d1897 *NotNAT B*
Moreau, Emile 1852- *WhThe*
Moreau, Jean 1928- *IntMPA 1977*
Moreau, Jeanne 1928- *BiDFlm, CelR 3, FilmgC,
MotPP, MovMk, OxFilm, WhoHol A,
WorEnF*
Moreau LeJeune 1741-1814 *OxThe*
Morecambe, Eric 1926- *FilmgC*
Morehead, Albert Hodges 1909-1966
AmSCAP 1966
Morehead, James Turner 1906- *AmSCAP 1966*
Morehouse, Ward 1898-1966 *NotNAT A, OxThe*
Morehouse, Ward 1899-1966 *NotNAT B, WhThe*
Morehouse, Ward 1906- *BiE&WWA*
Morel, Genevieve *WhoHol A*
Moreland, Mantan d1973 *WhoHol B*
Moreland, Mantan 1901-1973 *MovMk*
Moreland, Mantan 1902-1973 *FilmgC, WhScrn 2*
Morell, Andre 1909- *FilmgC, IntMPA 1977,*

WhoHol A, WhoThe 16
Morell, Sybil *Film 2*
Morena, Erna *Film 2*
Morency, Robert Buster 1932-1937 *WhScrn 1,
WhScrn 2, WhoHol B*
Moreno, Antonio d1967 *MotPP, WhoHol B*
Moreno, Antonio 1886-1967 *Film 1, Film 2,
FilmgC*
Moreno, Antonio 1887-1967 *TwYS*
Moreno, Antonio 1888-1967 *WhScrn 1,
WhScrn 2*
Moreno, Antonio 1889-1967 *MovMk*
Moreno, Dario 1921-1968 *WhScrn 1, WhScrn 2,
WhoHol B*
Moreno, Marguerite 1871-1948 *Film 2,
NotNAT B, WhScrn 1, WhScrn 2*
Moreno, Paco 1886-1941 *WhScrn 1, WhScrn 2,
WhoHol B*
Moreno, Rita 1931- *CelR 3, FilmgC,
IntMPA 1977, MotPP, MovMk, NotNAT,
WhoHol A, WhoThe 16*
Moreno, Rosita *WhoHol A*
Moreno, Thomas Sky Ball 1895-1938 *WhScrn 1,
WhScrn 2*
Moret, Neil 1878-1943 *AmSCAP 1966*
Moreto Y Cabana, Agustin 1618-1669 *McGWD,
OxThe*
Moreton, Ursula 1903- *WhThe*
Moretti, Eleanor *WhoStg 1908*
Morey, Edward *IntMPA 1977*
Morey, Harry T d1936 *MotPP, WhoHol B*
Morey, Harry T 1873-1936 *WhScrn 1, WhScrn 2*
Morey, Harry T 1879-1936 *Film 1, Film 2,
TwYS*
Morey, Henry A 1848-1929 *WhScrn 1, WhScrn 2,
WhoHol B*
Morey, Larry 1905- *AmSCAP 1966*
Morfogen, George *WhoHol A*
Morgan, Agnes 1901- *BiE&WWA, NotNAT*
Morgan, Al 1920- *BiE&WWA, NotNAT*
Morgan, Carey 1885-1960 *AmSCAP 1966*
Morgan, Charles Langbridge 1894-1958 *CnMD,
CnThe, CroCD, ModWD, NotNAT B,
OxThe, PIP&P, WhThe*
Morgan, Charles S, Jr. d1950 *NotNAT B*
Morgan, Christopher *NewYTET*
Morgan, Clark *WhoHol A*
Morgan, Claudia d1974 *WhoHol B*
Morgan, Claudia 1911-1974 *WhScrn 2*
Morgan, Claudia 1912-1974 *BiE&WWA,
NotNAT B, WhThe*
Morgan, Dan d1975 *WhScrn 2, WhoHol A,
WhoHol C*
Morgan, David 1942- *AmSCAP 1966*
Morgan, Dennis *MotPP*
Morgan, Dennis 1910- *FilmgC, MovMk,
WhoHol A*
Morgan, Dennis 1920- *IntMPA 1977*
Morgan, Diana 1910- *WhoThe 16, WomWMM*
Morgan, Dorinda 1909- *AmSCAP 1966*
Morgan, Edward P *NewYTET*
Morgan, Frank 1890-1949 *EncMT, Film 1,
Film 2, FilmgC, MGM, MotPP, MovMk,
NotNAT B, PIP&P, TwYS, WhScrn 1,
WhScrn 2, WhThe, WhoHol B*
Morgan, Freddy 1910- *AmSCAP 1966*
Morgan, Gareth 1940- *WhoThe 16*
Morgan, Gene 1892-1940 *WhScrn 1, WhScrn 2*
Morgan, Gene 1892-1950 *WhoHol B*
Morgan, George *Film 2*
Morgan, H A *Film 2*
Morgan, Harry 1915- *FilmgC, IntMPA 1977,
MotPP, WhoHol A*
Morgan, Haydn 1898- *AmSCAP 1966*

Morgan, Helen 1900-1941 *EncMT, FamA&A,*
　Film 2, FilmgC, NotNAT A, NotNAT B,
　PIP&P, ThFT, WhScrn 1, WhScrn 2,
　WhThe, WhoHol B
Morgan, Helen 1922-1955 *WhScrn 2*
Morgan, Henry *WhoHol A*
Morgan, Horace *Film 2*
Morgan, J C 1910- *AmSCAP 1966*
Morgan, Jackie *Film 2*
Morgan, Jane 1881-1972 *WhScrn 2, WhoHol B*
Morgan, Jaye P *WhoHol A*
Morgan, Jeanne *Film 2*
Morgan, Jessica E 1929- *AmSCAP 1966*
Morgan, Joan d1962 *NotNAT B, WhoHol B*
Morgan, Joan 1905- *Film 1, Film 2,*
　WhoThe 16
Morgan, Kewpie *Film 2*
Morgan, Lee 1902-1967 *Film 2, WhScrn 2,*
　WhoHol B
Morgan, Leon *Film 2*
Morgan, Margaret *Film 2*
Morgan, Margo 1897-1962 *WhScrn 1, WhScrn 2,*
　WhoHol B
Morgan, Marilyn *WhoHol A*
Morgan, McKayla K 1927- *AmSCAP 1966*
Morgan, Merlin d1924 *NotNAT B*
Morgan, Michele 1920- *BiDFlm, FilmgC,*
　IntMPA 1977, MotPP, MovMk, OxFilm,
　WhoHol A, WorEnF
Morgan, Paul d1939 *WhScrn 1, WhScrn 2*
Morgan, Phalba *Film 2*
Morgan, Ralph d1956 *MotPP, WhoHol B*
Morgan, Ralph 1882-1956 *Film 2, FilmgC,*
　MovMk
Morgan, Ralph 1883-1956 *NotNAT B, Vers A,*
　WhScrn 1, WhScrn 2
Morgan, Ralph 1888-1956 *WhThe*
Morgan, Ray d1975 *WhScrn 2, WhoHol C*
Morgan, Read *WhoHol A*
Morgan, Robert Duke 1896- *AmSCAP 1966*
Morgan, Robin *WhoHol A*
Morgan, Roger 1938- *WhoThe 16*
Morgan, Russ 1904-1969 *AmSCAP 1966,*
　WhScrn 1, WhScrn 2, WhoHol B
Morgan, Sidney d1931 *Film 2, WhoHol B*
Morgan, Sydney 1875?-1931 *WhScrn 2*
Morgan, Sydney 1885-1931 *NotNAT B, WhThe*
Morgan, Terence 1921- *FilmgC, IntMPA 1977,*
　WhoHol A
Morgan, Thelma *Film 2*
Morgan, Thomas R 1936- *AmSCAP 1966*
Morgan, Viola Esther Wyatt 1908- *AmSCAP 1966*
Morgan, Wallace *Film 2*
Morgan, William *Film 2*
Morgan, William d1944 *NotNAT B*
Morganthau, Rita Wallach 1880-1964 *BiE&WWA*
Morgenthau, Rita Wallach 1880-1964 *NotNAT B*
Morhange, Marcel *Film 1*
Mori, Iwao 1899- *IntMPA 1977*
Mori, Masayuki 1911- *WorEnF*
Mori, Toshia *WhoHol A*
Moriarty, Joanne 1939-1964 *WhScrn 1,*
　WhScrn 2, WhoHol B
Moriarty, Marcus d1916 *WhScrn 2*
Moriarty, Michael *PIP&P A, WhoHol A*
Moriarty, Michael 1941- *MovMk, WhoThe 16*
Moriarty, Michael 1942- *IntMPA 1977, NotNAT*
Moricz, Zsigmond 1879-1942 *OxThe*
Morin, Alberto 1912- *Vers A, WhoHol A*
Morin, Edgar 1921- *OxFilm*
Morin, Etienne *McGWD*
Morison, Bradley G 1924- *BiE&WWA*
Morison, Patricia *MotPP*
Morison, Patricia 1914- *HolP 40, ThFT*

Morison, Patricia 1915- *BiE&WWA, EncMT,*
　FilmgC, NotNAT, WhThe, WhoHol A
Morison, Samuel Eliot 1887- *CelR 3*
Morissey, Betty *Film 2*
Moritt, Fred G 1905- *AmSCAP 1966*
Moritz, Edvard 1891- *AmSCAP 1966*
Moritz, Max *Film 2*
Moritz, Milton I 1933- *IntMPA 1977*
Moriya, Shizu 1911-1961 *WhScrn 1, WhScrn 2*
Morlay, Gaby 1890-1964 *NotNAT B*
Morlay, Gaby 1896-1964 *WhThe*
Morlay, Gaby 1897-1964 *Film 1, Film 2, FilmgC,*
　OxFilm, WhScrn 1, WhScrn 2, WhoHol B
Morley, Christopher *CnThe, WhoThe 16*
Morley, Christopher d1957 *NotNAT B*
Morley, Harry William d1953 *NotNAT B*
Morley, Henry 1822-1894 *NotNAT B, OxThe*
Morley, Judith *NatPD*
Morley, Karen 1905- *Film 2, FilmgC,*
　IntMPA 1977, MGM, MotPP, MovMk,
　ThFT, WhoHol A
Morley, Kay *WhoHol A*
Morley, Malcolm 1890-1966 *WhThe*
Morley, Robert 1908- *BiE&WWA, CnThe,*
　FilmgC, IntMPA 1977, MotPP, MovMk,
　NotNAT, NotNAT A, OxFilm, OxThe,
　PIP&P, Vers A, WhoHol A, WhoThe 16
Morley, Robert James 1892-1952 *WhScrn 1,*
　WhScrn 2
Morley, Ruth *BiE&WWA, NotNAT*
Morley, Victor d1953 *NotNAT B*
Morlhon, Camille De d1945? *DcFM*
Morne, Maryland 1900-1935 *WhScrn 1,*
　WhScrn 2
Morningstar, Carter d1964 *NotNAT B*
Moroney, E J *WhoHol A*
Morosco, Oliver 1875-1945 *NotNAT A*
Morosco, Oliver 1876-1945 *NotNAT B, WhThe*
Morosco, Walter *Film 2*
Moross, Jerome 1913- *AmSCAP 1966,*
　BiE&WWA, CmMov, EncMT, FilmgC,
　NotNAT, WorEnF
Morozov, Mikhail Nikolaevich 1897-1952 *OxThe*
Morozov, Sara *PIP&P*
Morphy, Lewis H 1904-1958 *WhScrn 1,*
　WhScrn 2
Morra, Egidio 1906- *AmSCAP 1966*
Morra, Irene *WomWMM*
Morrell, George 1873-1955 *WhScrn 1, WhScrn 2,*
　WhoHol B
Morrell, H H d1916 *NotNAT B*
Morrell, Valerie *WhoHol A*
Morrer, Carole *WomWMM B*
Morricone, Ennio 1928- *FilmgC, OxFilm*
Morrie, Margaret *Film 2*
Morrill, Priscilla 1927- *BiE&WWA, NotNAT*
Morris 1903-1971 *WhScrn 1, WhScrn 2*
Morris, Adrian 1903-1940 *WhoHol B*
Morris, Adrian 1903-1941 *WhScrn 1, WhScrn 2*
Morris, Aldyth *NatPD*
Morris, Barboura 1932-1975 *WhScrn 2,*
　WhoHol C
Morris, Charles Edward 1913- *AmSCAP 1966*
Morris, Chester 1901-1970 *BiE&WWA, Film 1,*
　Film 2, FilmgC, HolP 30, MotPP, MovMk,
　NotNAT B, WhScrn 1, WhScrn 2, WhThe,
　WhoHol B
Morris, Clara d1925 *PIP&P, WhoHol B*
Morris, Clara 1844-1925 *NotNAT A*
Morris, Clara 1846-1925 *NotNAT B, OxThe,*
　WhThe
Morris, Clara 1847-1925 *FamA&A*
Morris, Clara 1897-1925 *WhScrn 1, WhScrn 2*
Morris, Mrs. Cleze Gill d1963 *NotNAT B*

Morris, Corbet 1881-1951 *WhScrn 2*
Morris, Dave *Film 2*
Morris, Deniese d1969 *WhScrn 2*
Morris, Denise d1969 *WhoHol B*
Morris, Desmond 1928- *CelR 3*
Morris, Diana 1907-1961 *WhScrn 1, WhScrn 2, WhoHol B*
Morris, Dick *Film 2*
Morris, Dorothy 1922- *WhoHol A*
Morris, Edmund *NatPD*
Morris, Edward 1896- *AmSCAP 1966*
Morris, Ernest 1915- *FilmgC*
Morris, Mrs. Felix d1954 *NotNAT B*
Morris, Felix 1850-1900 *NotNAT A, NotNAT B*
Morris, Frances *Film 2, WhoHol A*
Morris, Garrett 1937- *AmSCAP 1966*
Morris, Gladys *Film 1*
Morris, Glenn 1911-1974 *WhScrn 2, WhoHol B*
Morris, Gordon 1899-1940 *WhScrn 1, WhScrn 2, WhoHol B*
Morris, Greg *WhoHol A*
Morris, Harold Cecil 1890-1964 *AmSCAP 1966*
Morris, Howard 1919- *FilmgC, IntMPA 1977, WhoHol A*
Morris, John 1926- *AmSCAP 1966, BiE&WWA, NotNAT*
Morris, Johnnie 1886-1969 *Film 2, WhScrn 2*
Morris, Lana 1930- *FilmgC, IntMPA 1977, WhoHol A*
Morris, Lee 1916- *AmSCAP 1966, Film 1*
Morris, Leigh E 1934- *BiE&WWA*
Morris, Lily d1952 *NotNAT B*
Morris, Margaret 1891- *WhThe*
Morris, Margaret 1903-1968 *Film 2, WhScrn 2, WhoHol B*
Morris, Mary 1895-1970 *BiE&WWA, FilmgC, NotNAT B, PIP&P, WhThe, WhoHol B*
Morris, Mary 1896-1970 *WhScrn 1, WhScrn 2, WhoHol B*
Morris, Mary 1915- *FilmgC, WhoHol A, WhoThe 16*
Morris, Maynard d1964 *NotNAT B*
Morris, McKay 1891-1955 *NotNAT B, WhThe*
Morris, Melville 1888- *AmSCAP 1966*
Morris, Mildred *Film 1, WhoStg 1906, WhoStg 1908*
Morris, Mowbray d1911 *NotNAT B*
Morris, Nelson 1920- *IntMPA 1977*
Morris, Oswald 1915- *FilmgC, IntMPA 1977, WorEnF*
Morris, Mrs. Owen 1753-1826 *NotNAT B, OxThe*
Morris, Owen 1759-1790 *NotNAT B, OxThe*
Morris, Philip 1893-1949 *WhScrn 1, WhScrn 2, WhoHol B*
Morris, Phyllis 1894- *WhoHol A, WhoThe 16*
Morris, R A 1925- *IntMPA 1977*
Morris, Reggie 1886-1928 *Film 1, WhScrn 2*
Morris, Richard 1861-1924 *Film 2, WhScrn 2*
Morris, Richard 1924- *BiE&WWA, IntMPA 1977*
Morris, Rusty *WhoHol A*
Morris, Seymour 1906- *IntMPA 1977*
Morris, Tom *Film 2*
Morris, Wayne 1914-1959 *FilmgC, HolP 30, MotPP, MovMk, NotNAT B, WhScrn 1, WhScrn 2, WhoHol B*
Morris, William d1932 *NotNAT B*
Morris, William 1861-1936 *NotNAT B, WhScrn 1, WhScrn 2, WhThe, WhoHol B, WhoStg 1906, WhoStg 1908*
Morris, William, Jr. 1899- *BiE&WWA, IntMPA 1977, NotNAT*
Morris, Willie 1934- *CelR 3*
Morrison, Adrienne d1940 *NotNAT B*
Morrison, Ann *WhoHol A*

Morrison, Anna Marie 1874-1972 *WhScrn 2, WhoHol B*
Morrison, Arthur 1880-1950 *Film 1, Film 2, WhScrn 1, WhScrn 2, WhoHol B*
Morrison, Barbara *WhoHol A*
Morrison, Bill *ConDr 1977B*
Morrison, Bret *WhoHol A*
Morrison, Chester A 1922-1975 *WhScrn 2, WhoHol C*
Morrison, Chick d1968 *WhScrn 2*
Morrison, Chit d1968 *WhScrn 1, WhoHol B*
Morrison, Clifford *Film 2*
Morrison, Dorothy *Film 2*
Morrison, Effie 1917-1974 *WhScrn 2*
Morrison, Ernie *WhoHol A*
Morrison, Ernie Sunshine Sammy *Film 2*
Morrison, Florence *Film 2*
Morrison, George E 1860-1930 *NotNAT B, WhThe*
Morrison, George Pete 1891-1973 *WhScrn 2*
Morrison, Henrietta Lee d1948 *NotNAT B*
Morrison, Hobe 1904- *BiE&WWA, NotNAT, WhoThe 16*
Morrison, Howard Priestly 1871-1938 *NotNAT B, WhThe*
Morrison, Jack 1887-1948 *NotNAT B, WhThe, WhoHol B*
Morrison, Jack 1912- *BiE&WWA, NotNAT*
Morrison, James 1888-1974 *Film 1, Film 2, TwYS, WhScrn 2, WhoHol B*
Morrison, Jim 1944-1971 *WhScrn 2*
Morrison, Joseph *Film 2*
Morrison, Lewis 1845-1906 *NotNAT B*
Morrison, Louis *Film 1, Film 2*
Morrison, Paul 1906- *BiE&WWA, NotNAT*
Morrison, Pete d1973 *WhoHol B*
Morrison, Peter *Film 2*
Morrison, Shelley *WhoHol A*
Morrison, Sunshine Sammy *Film 2*
Morrissey, Betty d1944 *Film 2, WhScrn 1, WhScrn 2, WhoHol B*
Morrissey, John F d1941 *NotNAT B*
Morrissey, John J d1925 *NotNAT B*
Morrissey, John J 1906- *AmSCAP 1966*
Morrissey, Paul *IntMPA 1977*
Morrissey, Paul 1939- *FilmgC*
Morrissey, Paul 1940- *CelR 3*
Morrissey, Will 1885-1957 *NotNAT B, WhScrn 1, WhScrn 2, WhoHol B*
Morrissey, Will 1887-1957 *AmSCAP 1966*
Morritt, Charles 1860- *WhThe*
Morros, Boris 1891-1963 *FilmgC, NotNAT B*
Morrow, Buddy *AmSCAP 1966*
Morrow, Don *IntMPA 1977*
Morrow, Doretta d1968 *BiE&WWA, WhThe, WhoHol B*
Morrow, Doretta 1926-1968 *NotNAT B*
Morrow, Doretta 1927-1968 *WhScrn 1, WhScrn 2*
Morrow, Doretta 1928-1968 *EncMT*
Morrow, Jane d1925 *WhScrn 1, WhScrn 2, WhoHol B*
Morrow, Jeff 1913- *FilmgC, IntMPA 1977, WhoHol A*
Morrow, Jo 1940- *FilmgC, MotPP, WhoHol A*
Morrow, Patricia *WhoHol A*
Morrow, Susan *WhoHol A*
Morrow, Vic 1932- *FilmgC, IntMPA 1977, MotPP, WhoHol A*
Morse, Arthur D d1971 *NewYTET*
Morse, Barry 1919- *FilmgC, NotNAT, WhThe, WhoHol A*
Morse, Ella Mae *WhoHol A*
Morse, Grace *Film 2*

Morse, Hayward *WhoHol A*
Morse, John M 1911- *BiE&WWA*
Morse, Karl *Film 2*
Morse, Lee 1904-1954 *WhScrn 1, WhScrn 2, WhoHol B*
Morse, Robert 1931- *BiE&WWA, CelR 3, EncMT, FilmgC, IntMPA 1977, MotPP, NotNAT, WhoHol A, WhoThe 16*
Morse, Robin 1915-1958 *WhScrn 1, WhScrn 2, WhoHol B*
Morse, Terry 1906- *IntMPA 1977*
Morse, Theodora 1890-1953 *AmSCAP 1966*
Morse, Theodore 1873-1924 *AmSCAP 1966, NotNAT B*
Morse, Woolson 1858-1897 *NotNAT B*
Morsell, Fred *WhoHol A*
Morselli, Ercole Luigi 1882-1921 *McGWD, ModWD*
Morsi, Ahmad Kamel *DcFM*
Morsquini, Marie 1899- *Film 2*
Mortimer, Charles d1864 *NotNAT B*
Mortimer, Charles d1913 *NotNAT B*
Mortimer, Charles 1885-1964 *WhScrn 1, WhScrn 2, WhThe, WhoHol B*
Mortimer, Dorothy d1950 *NotNAT B*
Mortimer, Ed d1944 *WhoHol B*
Mortimer, Edmund 1875-1944 *WhScrn 1, WhScrn 2*
Mortimer, Edmund 1883- *TwYS A*
Mortimer, Henry 1875-1952 *WhScrn 1, WhScrn 2, WhoHol B*
Mortimer, James d1911 *NotNAT B*
Mortimer, John Clifford 1923- *CnMD, CnThe, ConDr 1977, CroCD, FilmgC, McGWD, ModWD, REnWD, WhoThe 16*
Mortimer, Lee d1963 *NotNAT B*
Mortlock, Charles Bernard 1888-1967 *WhThe*
Morton, Arthur 1908- *IntMPA 1977*
Morton, Charles 1819-1904 *OxThe*
Morton, Charles 1904- *Film 2, TwYS*
Morton, Charles S 1907-1966 *WhScrn 2*
Morton, Clara d1948 *NotNAT B*
Morton, Clive 1904-1975 *FilmgC, WhScrn 2, WhThe, WhoHol C*
Morton, Drew 1855-1916 *WhScrn 2*
Morton, Edna *Film 2*
Morton, Edward d1922 *NotNAT B, WhThe*
Morton, Ferdinand Joseph 1885-1941 *AmSCAP 1966*
Morton, Gary *NewYTET, WhoHol A*
Morton, Gregory *WhoHol A*
Morton, Harry K d1956 *NotNAT B*
Morton, Hugh *EncMT, NotNAT B, WhThe*
Morton, James C 1884-1942 *WhScrn 1, WhScrn 2, WhoHol B*
Morton, James J d1938 *NotNAT B*
Morton, Joe *PIP&P A*
Morton, John Maddison 1811-1891 *NotNAT B, OxThe*
Morton, Kitty d1927 *NotNAT B*
Morton, Leon *WhThe*
Morton, Maggie d1939 *NotNAT B*
Morton, Marjorie *Film 2*
Morton, Martha 1870-1925 *NotNAT B, WhThe*
Morton, Maxine *WhScrn 1, WhScrn 2*
Morton, Michael d1931 *NotNAT B, WhThe*
Morton, Mickey *WhoHol A*
Morton, Montague C *IntMPA 1977*
Morton, Sam d1941 *NotNAT B*
Morton, Thomas d1879 *NotNAT B*
Morton, Thomas 1764?-1838 *NotNAT B, OxThe*
Morton, William 1838-1938 *NotNAT B*
Mosbacher, Emil 1922- *CelR 3*
Mosconi, Willie 1913- *CelR 3*

Moscovitch, Maurice 1871-1940 *NotNAT B, WhScrn 1, WhScrn 2, WhThe, WhoHol B*
Moscowitz, Jennie d1953 *NotNAT B*
Mosel, Tad 1922- *BiE&WWA, ConDr 1977, McGWD, ModWD, NewYTET, NotNAT*
Mosenthal, Solomon Hermann d1877 *NotNAT B*
Moser, Gustav Von d1903 *NotNAT B*
Moser, Hans 1880-1964 *NotNAT B, WhScrn 1, WhScrn 2, WhoHol B*
Moser, Margot 1930- *BiE&WWA, NotNAT*
Moses, Charles Alexander 1923- *IntMPA 1977*
Moses, Gilbert *IntMPA 1977*
Moses, Gilbert 1943- *NotNAT*
Moses, Gilbert, III 1942- *WhoThe 16*
Moses, Harry d1937 *NotNAT B*
Moses, Montrose Jonas 1878-1934 *NotNAT B, OxThe, WhThe*
Moses, Raymond G *Film 2*
Moses, Robert 1888- *BiE&WWA, CelR 3*
Moshay, Joe 1908- *AmSCAP 1966*
Mosheim, Grete 1907- *Film 2, WhThe*
Mosick, Marian Perry 1906-1973 *WhScrn 2, WhoHol B*
Mosier, Frank Moffett 1929- *NatPD*
Mosjoukine *WorEnF*
Mosjoukine, Ivan 1889-1939 *Film 1, Film 2, FilmgC, WhScrn 1, WhScrn 2, WhoHol B*
Moskine, Ivan 1889-1939 *Film 2*
Moskowitz, Henry d1936 *NotNAT B*
Moskowitz, Jennie *Film 2*
Moskowitz, Joseph H *IntMPA 1977*
Moskowitz, Maurice *NotNAT B*
Moskvin, Andrei 1901-1961 *DcFM, OxFilm, WorEnF*
Moskvin, Ivan Mikhailovich 1874-1946 *NotNAT B, OxThe, PIP&P, WhScrn 1, WhScrn 2*
Mosley, Fred 1854-1972 *WhScrn 1, WhScrn 2*
Mosley, Roger *WhoHol A*
Mosquini, Maria 1899- *TwYS*
Mosquini, Marie 1899- *Film 2*
Moss, Arnold 1910- *BiE&WWA, FilmgC, IntMPA 1977, MovMk, NotNAT, WhoHol A, WhoThe 16*
Moss, Arnold 1911- *Vers A*
Moss, Charles B, Jr. 1944- *IntMPA 1977*
Moss, Sir Edward 1852-1912 *NotNAT B, OxThe*
Moss, Sir Edward 1854- *WhThe*
Moss, Frank L *IntMPA 1977*
Moss, George *Film 1*
Moss, Hugh d1926 *NotNAT B*
Moss, Paul d1950 *NotNAT B*
Moss, Stewart *WhoHol A*
Moss, W Keith 1892-1935 *NotNAT B, WhThe*
Mossenson, Yigal 1917- *CnThe, REnWD*
Mossetti, Carlotta 1890- *WhThe*
Mossman, Merrily *WomWMM B*
Mossman, Ted 1914- *AmSCAP 1966*
Mossop, Henry 1729-1774 *NotNAT B, OxThe*
Mostar, Gerhart Hermann 1901- *CnMD*
Mostel, Josh *WhoHol A*
Mostel, Zero 1915- *BiE&WWA, CelR 3, EncMT, FamA&A, FilmgC, IntMPA 1977, MotPP, MovMk, NotNAT, PIP&P, WhoHol A, WhoThe 16*
Moszato, Umberto *Film 1*
Motherwell, Robert 1915- *CelR 3*
Motley *BiE&WWA, WhoThe 16*
Motokiyo, Zeami 1363-1443 *CnThe, REnWD*
Mott, Harold 1908- *AmSCAP 1966*
Motter, Charlotte Kay 1922- *BiE&WWA, NotNAT*
Motteux, Peter d1718 *NotNAT B*
Mottley, John d1750 *NotNAT B*
Mottola, Anthony Charles 1918- *AmSCAP 1966*

Motz, Julie *WomWMM B*
Motzan, Otto 1880-1937 *AmSCAP 1966*
Mouezy-Eon, Andre 1880- *WhThe*
Mouillot, Frederick d1911 *NotNAT B*
Mouillot, Gertrude d1961 *NotNAT B, WhThe*
Moulan, Frank d1939 *WhoHol B, WhoStg 1906,
    WhoStg 1908*
Moulan, Frank 1875-1939 *NotNAT B, WhThe*
Moulan, Frank 1876-1939 *WhScrn 1, WhScrn 2*
Mould, Raymond Wesley 1905- *WhThe*
Moulder, Walter C 1933-1967 *WhScrn 1,
    WhScrn 2, WhoHol B*
Moulton, Edward *Film 2, TwYS*
Moulton, Robert 1922- *BiE&WWA, NotNAT*
Mounet, Jean Paul 1847-1922 *NotNAT B, WhThe*
Mounet, Jean Sully 1841-1916 *OxThe*
Mounet, Paul 1847-1922 *OxThe*
Mounet-Sully *Film 1*
Mounet-Sully, Jean 1841-1916 *NotNAT B,
    WhThe, WhoHol B*
Mount, Peggy 1916- *FilmgC, WhoHol A,
    WhoThe 16*
Mountain, Earl B d1962 *NotNAT B*
Mountford, Harry d1950 *NotNAT B*
Mountfort, Susanna Percival 1667-1703
    NotNAT B, OxThe, PIP&P
Mountfort, William 1664-1692 *NotNAT A,
    NotNAT B, OxThe, PIP&P*
Mousjoukine *OxFilm*
Moussinac, Leon 1890-1964 *OxFilm, WorEnF*
Moussy, Marcel 1924- *WorEnF*
Moustache *WhoHol A*
Mouvet, Maurice d1927 *NotNAT B*
Movar, Dunja 1940-1963 *WhScrn 1, WhScrn 2,
    WhoHol B*
Movin, Lisbeth *WomWMM*
Movita *WhoHol A*
Mowat, Anna Cora 1819-1870 *NotNAT B*
Mowat, David 1943- *ConDr 1977*
Mowatt, Anna Cora 1819-1870 *FamA&A,
    McGWD, NotNAT A, OxThe, REnWD*
Mowbray, Alan d1969 *BiE&WWA, MotPP,
    WhoHol B*
Mowbray, Alan 1893-1969 *FilmgC, Vers A*
Mowbray, Alan 1896-1969 *MovMk, WhScrn 1,
    WhScrn 2*
Mowbray, Alan 1897-1969 *NotNAT B*
Mowbray, Henry 1882-1960 *WhScrn 2*
Mowbray, Thomas d1900 *NotNAT B*
Mower, Jack 1890-1965 *Film 1, Film 2, TwYS,
    WhScrn 1, WhScrn 2, WhoHol B*
Mower, Margaret *PIP&P*
Moxey, John 1920- *FilmgC*
Moya, Natalie 1900- *WhThe*
Moyers, Bill D *NewYTET*
Moyes, Patricia 1923- *BiE&WWA*
Moylan, William J *IntMPA 1977*
Moynihan, Daniel Patrick 1927- *CelR 3*
Moynihan, Jane *WomWMM A, WomWMM B*
Mozart, George 1864-1947 *NotNAT A,
    NotNAT B, WhScrn 1, WhScrn 2, WhThe,
    WhoHol B*
Mozeen, Thomas d1768 *NotNAT B*
Mozhukhin, Ivan 1889-1939 *WorEnF*
Mozhukin, Ivan 1890-1939 *OxFilm, WhScrn 2*
Mozian, Roger King 1925-1963 *AmSCAP 1966*
Mozisova, Bozena *WomWMM*
Mravik, Edward E 1917- *AmSCAP 1966*
Mrozek, Slavomir 1930- *CnMD Sup*
Mrozek, Slawomir 1930- *CroCD, McGWD,
    ModWD, REnWD, WhoThe 16*
Mucci, Eduliho *Film 2*
Muczynski, Robert 1929- *AmSCAP 1966*
Mudd, Roger *CelR 3, NewYTET*

Mudd And Trout *NewYTET*
Mudie, George d1918 *NotNAT B*
Mudie, Leonard 1884-1965 *FilmgC, Vers A,
    WhScrn 1, WhScrn 2, WhThe, WhoHol B*
Mueller, Barbara 1909-1967 *WhScrn 2*
Mueller, Carl F 1892- *AmSCAP 1966*
Mueller, Elizabeth 1926- *FilmgC*
Mueller, H K *Film 2*
Mueller, Wolfgang 1923-1960 *WhScrn 1,
    WhScrn 2, WhoHol B*
Muggeridge, Malcolm 1903- *IntMPA 1977*
Muggs, J Fred *NewYTET*
Mugwana, Oshun *WomWMM B*
Muhammad, Elijah 1897- *CelR 3*
Muhammad Ali 1942- *CelR 3*
Muhl, Edward E 1907- *FilmgC, IntMPA 1977*
Muhssin, Ertugrul *Film 2*
Muir, Esther 1895- *FilmgC*
Muir, Florabel 1889-1970 *WhScrn 2*
Muir, Gavin d1972 *WhoHol B*
Muir, Gavin 1907-1972 *FilmgC, WhScrn 2*
Muir, Gavin 1909-1972 *Vers B*
Muir, Graeme 1916- *IntMPA 1977*
Muir, Helen 1864-1934 *Film 1, WhScrn 1,
    WhScrn 2, WhoHol B*
Muir, Jean 1911- *FilmgC, ThFT, WhThe,
    WhoHol A*
Muir, Kenneth 1907- *BiE&WWA, NotNAT*
Muir, Lewis F 1884-1950 *AmSCAP 1966*
Muir, Roger E 1918- *IntMPA 1977*
Mukhina, Tanya *Film 2*
Mulay, Vijaya *WomWMM*
Mulcaster, G H 1891-1964 *Film 2, NotNAT B,
    WhScrn 1, WhThe, WhoHol B*
Mulcaster, George H 1891-1964 *WhScrn 2*
Mulcay, Jimmy 1900-1968 *WhScrn 2, WhoHol B*
Muldaur, Diana *FilmgC, IntMPA 1977,
    WhoHol A*
Muldener, Louise d1938 *NotNAT B*
Muldofsky, Peri *WomWMM B*
Mulford, Clarence E *FilmgC*
Mulford, Marilyn *WomWMM B*
Mulgrew, Thomas G 1889-1954 *WhScrn 1,
    WhScrn 2*
Mulhall, Jack *MotPP*
Mulhall, Jack 1891- *Film 1, Film 2, FilmgC,
    MovMk, TwYS*
Mulhall, Jack 1894- *WhoHol A*
Mulhare, Edward 1923- *BiE&WWA, FilmgC,
    MotPP, NotNAT, WhoHol A*
Mulhauser, James 1890-1939 *WhScrn 1,
    WhScrn 2, WhoHol B*
Mulhern, Harry 1897- *BiE&WWA*
Mulholland, J B 1858-1925 *NotNAT B, WhThe*
Mulholland, Robert E *NewYTET*
Mullally, Don d1933 *NotNAT B*
Mullaly, Jode *Film 1*
Mullaney, Jack *WhoHol A*
Mullavey, Greg *WhoHol A*
Mulle, Ida 1864?-1934 *NotNAT B, WhScrn 1,
    WhScrn 2*
Mullen, Barbara 1914- *FilmgC, WhoHol A,
    WhoThe 16*
Mullen, Gordon *Film 1*
Mullen, Sadie *Film 2*
Muller, Artur 1909- *CnMD*
Muller, Ellen *Film 2*
Muller, Friedrich 1749-1825 *McGWD*
Muller, Heiner 1928- *CnMD*
Muller, Heiner 1929- *CroCD*
Muller, Hilde *Film 2*
Muller, Renate 1907-1937 *FilmgC, WhScrn 1,
    WhScrn 2, WhoHol B*
Muller, Romeo *NewYTET*

Mulligan, Gerald Joseph 1927- *AmSCAP 1966*
Mulligan, Gerry *WhoHol A*
Mulligan, Moon d1967 *WhoHol B*
Mulligan, Richard 1932- *FilmgC, WhoHol A, WhoThe 16*
Mulligan, Robert *IntMPA 1977*
Mulligan, Robert 1925- *BiDFlm, FilmgC, MovMk, WorEnF*
Mulligan, Robert 1932- *OxFilm*
Mullner, Amandus Gottfried Adolf 1774-1829 *McGWD*
Mulock, Al d1970? *WhScrn 2*
Mulvey, Kay *IntMPA 1977*
Mumby, Diana 1922-1974 *WhScrn 2, WhoHol B*
Mumford, Lewis 1895- *CelR 3*
Mumy, Billy 1954- *WhoHol A*
Munch, Andreas 1811-1884 *OxThe*
Munday, Anthony 1553?-1633 *NotNAT B, OxThe*
Munden, Joseph Shepherd 1758-1832 *NotNAT A, NotNAT B, OxThe*
Mundin, Herbert d1939 *WhoHol B*
Mundin, Herbert 1898-1939 *Film 2, FilmgC, NotNAT B, WhScrn 1, WhScrn 2, WhThe*
Mundin, Herbert 1899-1939 *Vers A*
Mundviller, Joseph-Louis 1886- *DcFM*
Mundy, Helen *Film 2*
Mundy, James R 1907- *AmSCAP 1966*
Mundy, John 1886- *AmSCAP 1966*
Mundy, Meg *BiE&WWA, NotNAT, WhThe*
Muni, Paul 1895-1967 *BiDFlm, BiE&WWA, FamA&A, Film 2, MotPP, MovMk, NotNAT A, NotNAT B, OxFilm, PIP&P, WhScrn 1, WhScrn 2, WhThe, WhoHol B, WorEnF*
Muni, Paul 1896-1967 *FilmgC*
Munier, Ferdinand 1889-1945 *Film 2, WhScrn 1, WhScrn 2, WhoHol B*
Muniz, Carlos 1927- *CroCD*
Muniz, Juan DeDios 1906-1951 *WhScrn 1, WhScrn 2*
Munk, Andrzej 1921-1961 *BiDFlm, DcFM, FilmgC, WorEnF*
Munk, Andrzej 1921-1966 *OxFilm*
Munk, Kai 1898-1944 *CnMD*
Munk, Kaj 1898-1944 *CnThe, McGWD, ModWD, NotNAT B, OxThe, REnWD*
Munker, Ariane *WhoHol A*
Munn, Charles *Film 1*
Munn, William O 1902- *AmSCAP 1966*
Munoz Seca, Pedro 1881-1936 *McGWD*
Munro, C K 1889- *PIP&P, WhThe*
Munro, Charles Kirkpatrick 1889- *CnMD, McGWD*
Munro, Douglas *Film 2*
Munro, George d1968 *NotNAT B*
Munro, Janet 1934-1972 *FilmgC, MotPP, WhScrn 2, WhoHol B*
Munro, Nan 1905- *WhoHol A, WhoThe 16*
Munro, Robert *Film 2*
Munsel, Patrice 1925- *BiE&WWA, FilmgC, WhoHol A*
Munsell, Warren P 1889- *BiE&WWA, NotNAT*
Munsell, Warren P, Jr. d1952 *NotNAT B*
Munshin, Jules d1970 *MotPP, WhoHol B*
Munshin, Jules 1913-1970 *CmMov*
Munshin, Jules 1915-1970 *BiE&WWA, FilmgC, NotNAT B, WhScrn 1, WhScrn 2*
Munson, Audrey *Film 1*
Munson, Byron *Film 2*
Munson, Ona d1955 *MotPP, WhoHol B*
Munson, Ona 1903-1955 *WhScrn 1, WhScrn 2*
Munson, Ona 1906-1955 *FilmgC, MovMk, NotNAT B, ThFT, WhThe*

Munson, Ona 1908-1955 *Film 2, Vers A*
Muntcho, Monique *WomWMM*
Munz, Heinz-Rolf *Film 2*
Mura, Corinna d1965 *WhoHol B*
Mura, Corrine 1910-1965 *WhScrn 1, WhScrn 2*
Murat, Jean 1888-1968 *Film 2, WhScrn 2, WhoHol B*
Muratore, Lucian *Film 1*
Muratore, Lucien 1878-1954 *WhScrn 2*
Murcell, George 1925- *WhoHol A, WhoThe 16*
Murdaugh, Ella Lee 1910- *AmSCAP 1966*
Murdoch, Frank Hitchcock d1872 *NotNAT B, OxThe*
Murdoch, Iris 1919- *ConDr 1977, PIP&P*
Murdoch, James Edward 1811-1893 *FamA&A, NotNAT B, OxThe*
Murdoch, Richard 1907- *FilmgC, WhoHol A, WhoThe 16*
Murdock, Ann 1890- *Film 1, TwYS, WhThe*
Murdock, Frank *Film 1*
Murdock, George *WhoHol A*
Murdock, Henry d1971 *BiE&WWA, NotNAT B*
Murdock, Jack *WhoHol A*
Murdock, Kermit *WhoHol A*
Murfin, Jane d1955 *NotNAT B, WhThe, WomWMM*
Murgatroyd, Susan *WomWMM*
Muriel, Roel *Film 2*
Murnane, Allen *Film 1*
Murnau, F W 1889-1931 *FilmgC, TwYS A, WomWMM*
Murnau, Friedrich Wilhelm 1888-1931 *DcFM, MovMk, OxFilm*
Murnau, Friedrich Wilhelm 1889-1931 *BiDFlm*
Murnau, Friedrick Wilhelm 1889-1931 *WorEnF*
Muro, Henri 1884-1967 *WhScrn 2*
Murphy, Ada 1888-1961 *WhScrn 1, WhScrn 2, WhoHol B*
Murphy, Arthur 1727-1805 *NotNAT B, OxThe*
Murphy, Arthur Lister 1906- *ConDr 1977*
Murphy, Audie 1924-1971 *BiDFlm, CmMov, FilmgC, MotPP, MovMk, WhScrn 1, WhScrn 2, WhoHol B, WorEnF*
Murphy, Ben *WhoHol A*
Murphy, Bob d1948 *WhoHol B*
Murphy, Bri *WomWMM B*
Murphy, Brian *WhoHol A*
Murphy, Catherine *Film 2*
Murphy, Charles *WhoHol A*
Murphy, Charles Bernard 1884-1942 *Film 2, WhScrn 1, WhScrn 2, WhoHol B*
Murphy, Charles Bernard, Jr. *Film 2*
Murphy, Donn B 1931- *NotNAT*
Murphy, Edna 1904- *Film 2, MotPP, TwYS*
Murphy, Eileen *WhoHol A*
Murphy, Estelle Prindle 1918- *AmSCAP 1966*
Murphy, George *MotPP*
Murphy, George 1902- *CelR 3, FilmgC, IntMPA 1977, MGM, MovMk, WorEnF*
Murphy, George 1904- *WhoHol A*
Murphy, Jack 1915- *Film 2*
Murphy, James d1759 *NotNAT B*
Murphy, Jimmy *WhoHol A*
Murphy, Joe 1877-1961 *Film 2, WhoHol B*
Murphy, John Daly 1873-1934 *Film 1, Film 2, NotNAT B, WhScrn 1, WhScrn 2, WhoHol B*
Murphy, John F 1905- *IntMPA 1977*
Murphy, John T d1964 *NotNAT B*
Murphy, Joseph J 1877-1961 *WhScrn 1, WhScrn 2*
Murphy, Julia *WomWMM*
Murphy, Lyle 1908- *AmSCAP 1966*
Murphy, Margaret *WomWMM B*

Murphy, Mary 1931- *FilmgC, IntMPA 1977,
    MotPP, WhoHol A*
Murphy, Matt *WhoHol A*
Murphy, Maurice *Film 2*
Murphy, Michael *WhoHol A*
Murphy, Morris *Film 2*
Murphy, Owen 1893-1965 *AmSCAP 1966*
Murphy, Pamela *WhoHol A*
Murphy, Pat 1901-1954 *AmSCAP 1966*
Murphy, Ralph 1895-1967 *FilmgC*
Murphy, Richard 1912- *CmMov, FilmgC,
    IntMPA 1977, WorEnF*
Murphy, Robert 1889-1948 *WhScrn 1, WhScrn 2*
Murphy, Rose *AmSCAP 1966*
Murphy, Rosemary 1927- *BiE&WWA, FilmgC,
    NotNAT, WhoHol A, WhoThe 16*
Murphy, Stanley 1875-1919 *AmSCAP 1966*
Murphy, Steve *Film 2*
Murphy, Thomas 1935- *ConDr 1977*
Murphy, Tim d1928 *NotNAT B*
Murray, Alma 1854-1945 *NotNAT B, OxThe,
    WhThe*
Murray, Anita *Film 2*
Murray, Barbara 1929- *FilmgC, IntMPA 1977,
    WhoHol A, WhoThe 16*
Murray, Braham 1943- *WhoThe 16*
Murray, Brian 1937- *NotNAT, WhoHol A,
    WhoThe 16*
Murray, Charles d1821 *NotNAT B*
Murray, Charlie 1872-1941 *Film 1, Film 2,
    FilmgC, MotPP, TwYS, WhScrn 1,
    WhScrn 2, WhoHol B*
Murray, David Christie d1907 *NotNAT B*
Murray, David Mitchell 1853-1923 *WhScrn 1,
    WhScrn 2, WhoHol B*
Murray, Don 1929- *BiDFlm, BiE&WWA,
    FilmgC, IntMPA 1977, MotPP, MovMk,
    WhoHol A, WorEnF*
Murray, Douglas d1936 *NotNAT B, WhThe*
Murray, Edgar 1865-1932 *WhScrn 1, WhScrn 2*
Murray, Edgar 1892-1959 *WhScrn 1, WhScrn 2*
Murray, Elizabeth M 1871-1946 *Film 2,
    NotNAT B, WhScrn 1, WhScrn 2,
    WhoHol B*
Murray, Gaston d1889 *NotNAT B*
Murray, Mrs. Gaston d1891 *NotNAT B*
Murray, George Gilbert Aime 1866-1957 *WhThe*
Murray, Sir Gilbert Aime 1866-1957 *NotNAT B,
    OxThe, PIP&P*
Murray, Gilbert Donald, III 1930- *AmSCAP 1966*
Murray, Gray *Film 2*
Murray, Henry Valentine d1963 *NotNAT B*
Murray, J Harold 1891-1940 *EncMT, Film 2,
    NotNAT B, WhScrn 1, WhScrn 2, WhThe,
    WhoHol B*
Murray, J K *WhoStg 1906, WhoStg 1908*
Murray, Jack d1941 *WhScrn 1, WhScrn 2*
Murray, James *MotPP*
Murray, James 1901-1936 *FilmgC, MovMk,
    WhScrn 1, WhScrn 2, WhoHol A*
Murray, James 1901-1937 *Film 2, TwYS*
Murray, Jan *IntMPA 1977, MotPP, WhoHol A*
Murray, Jean d1966 *WhScrn 1, WhScrn 2*
Murray, John 1906- *AmSCAP 1966, BiE&WWA,
    NotNAT*
Murray, John A 1925- *AmSCAP 1966*
Murray, John J d1924 *NotNAT B*
Murray, John T *Film 2*
Murray, John T d1936 *WhoHol B*
Murray, John T 1886-1957 *WhScrn 1, WhScrn 2*
Murray, Julian Bud 1888-1952 *WhScrn 1,
    WhScrn 2*
Murray, Ken *IntMPA 1977, NewYTET*
Murray, Ken 1903- *FilmgC, NotNAT A,*

WhoHol A
Murray, Ken 1907- *Film 2*
Murray, Lola 1914-1961 *WhScrn 1, WhScrn 2*
Murray, Lyn 1909- *AmSCAP 1966*
Murray, M Gray *Film 2*
Murray, Mae d1965 *MotPP, WhoHol B*
Murray, Mae 1885-1965 *MovMk*
Murray, Mae 1886?-1965 *WhScrn 2*
Murray, Mae 1889-1965 *Film 1, Film 2, FilmgC,
    NotNAT B, OxFilm, ThFT, TwYS*
Murray, Mae 1890-1965 *WhScrn 1*
Murray, Marie *Film 1*
Murray, Marion 1885-1951 *WhScrn 1, WhScrn 2,
    WhoHol B*
Murray, Mary P *WomWMM*
Murray, Michael 1932- *BiE&WWA, NotNAT*
Murray, Paul 1885-1949 *NotNAT B, WhThe*
Murray, Peg *WhoHol A, WhoThe 16*
Murray, Peter 1925- *WhThe*
Murray, Rita *WomWMM*
Murray, Stephen 1912- *FilmgC, WhoHol A,
    WhoThe 16*
Murray, Thomas 1902-1961 *WhScrn 1,
    WhScrn 2*
Murray, Thomas C 1873-1959 *CnMD, ModWD,
    NotNAT B, OxThe, REnWD, WhThe*
Murray, Tom 1875-1935 *Film 2, WhScrn 1,
    WhScrn 2, WhoHol B*
Murray, Uncle *WhScrn 1, WhScrn 2*
Murray, Walter *Film 1, OxThe, PIP&P*
Murray, Will d1955 *NotNAT B*
Murray, William H d1852 *NotNAT B*
Murray, Wynn d1957 *NotNAT B*
Murray-Hill, Peter 1908-1957 *FilmgC, WhScrn 1,
    WhScrn 2, WhoHol B*
Murrell, Alys *Film 2*
Murrey, Charles *Film 2*
Murrow, Edward R 1908-1965 *NewYTET,
    WhScrn 1, WhScrn 2, WhoHol B*
Mursky, Alexander *Film 2*
Murtagh, Cynthia *Film 2*
Murtagh, Kate *WhoHol A*
Murtaugh, John E 1927- *AmSCAP 1966*
Murth, Florence 1902-1934 *WhScrn 1, WhScrn 2,
    WhoHol B*
Murton, Lionel 1915- *FilmgC, WhoHol A*
Musahipzade, Celal 1868-1959 *REnWD*
Musante, Joan *WomWMM B*
Musante, Tony *WhoHol A*
Musante, Tony 1936- *IntMPA 1977*
Musante, Tony 1941- *FilmgC*
Musaphia, Joseph 1935- *ConDr 1977*
Musburger, Brent *NewYTET*
Muschamp, Thomas 1917- *IntMPA 1977*
Muse, Clarence 1889- *AmSCAP 1966, Film 2,
    FilmgC, MovMk, Vers A, WhoHol A*
Musgrove, Gertrude 1912- *WhThe*
Mushanokoji, Saneatsu 1885- *ModWD*
Music, Lorenzo *see* Davis, David And Lorenzo Music
Musicant, Samuel 1922- *AmSCAP 1966*
Musidora 1889-1957 *Film 1, OxFilm, WhScrn 1,
    WhScrn 2, WhoHol B, WomWMM*
Musil, Robert 1880-1942 *CnMD, McGWD*
Muskerry, William d1918 *NotNAT B*
Muskie, Edmund 1914- *CelR 3*
Musolino, Angelo 1923- *AmSCAP 1966*
Mussato, Albertino 1261-1329 *McGWD, OxThe*
Musselman, Johnson J 1890-1958 *WhScrn 1,
    WhScrn 2*
Musser, Tharon 1925- *BiE&WWA, NotNAT,
    WhoThe 16*
Musser, Willard 1913- *AmSCAP 1966*
Musset, Alfred De 1810-1857 *CnThe, McGWD,
    NotNAT B, OxThe, REnWD*

Mussett, Charles *Film 2*
Mussey, Francine d1933 *WhScrn 1, WhScrn 2*
Mussiere, Luciene 1890-1972 *WhScrn 2*
Musson, Bennet 1866-1946 *WhScrn 1, WhScrn 2,*
WhoHol B
Mustafa, Niazi 1903- *DcFM*
Mustin, Burt 1884- *FilmgC, WhoHol A*
Musto, Michael J 1917- *IntMPA 1977*
Musuraca, Nicholas 1908- *CmMov, FilmgC,*
WorEnF
Muthel, Lothar *Film 2*
Mution, Ricardo 1884-1957 *WhScrn 2*
Mutsu, Ian Yonosuke 1907- *IntMPA 1977*
Muybridge, Eadweard 1830-1904 *DcFM, OxFilm,*
WorEnF
Muybridge, Edward 1830-1904 *FilmgC*
Muzquiz, Carlos 1906-1960 *WhScrn 1, WhScrn 2,*
WhoHol B
Muzzi, Edulilo *Film 2*
My Fancy 1878- *WhThe*
Mycroft, Walter 1891-1959 *FilmgC*
Myer, Torben *Film 2*
Myerberg, Michael 1906-1974 *BiE&WWA,*
NotNAT B
Myers, Bessie Allen d1964 *NotNAT B*
Myers, Carmel *MotPP, WhoHol A*
Myers, Carmel 1899-1966 *Film 1, Film 2, TwYS*
Myers, Carmel 1901- *MovMk, ThFT*
Myers, Carol *WomWMM*
Myers, Farlan I 1918- *AmSCAP 1966*
Myers, Harry 1886-1938 *WhScrn 1, WhScrn 2,*
WhoHol B
Myers, Harry C 1882-1938 *Film 1, Film 2,*
NotNAT B, TwYS
Myers, Henry 1893- *AmSCAP 1966*
Myers, Julian F 1918- *IntMPA 1977*
Myers, Kathleen *Film 2*
Myers, Paul 1917- *BiE&WWA, NotNAT*
Myers, Paulene *WhoHol A*
Myers, Peter 1923- *WhoThe 16*
Myers, Peter 1928-1968 *WhScrn 2, WhoHol B*
Myers, Peter S 1920- *IntMPA 1977*
Myers, Ray *Film 1, Film 2*
Myers, Richard 1901- *AmSCAP 1966,*
BiE&WWA, NotNAT, WhThe
Myers, Robert Francis 1925-1962 *WhScrn 1,*
WhScrn 2
Myerson, Bernard 1918- *IntMPA 1977*
Myerson, Bess 1924- *CelR 3, IntMPA 1977*
Myhers, John 1924- *BiE&WWA, WhoHol A*
Myhill, Jack *IntMPA 1977*
Myles, Meg *WhoHol A*
Myles, Norbert *Film 2*
Mylong, John 1893-1975 *WhScrn 2, WhoHol C*
Mynniscus *OxThe*
Myrge, Mademoiselle *Film 2*
Myrow, Frederic 1939- *AmSCAP 1966*
Myrow, Gerald 1923- *AmSCAP 1966*
Myrow, Josef 1910- *AmSCAP 1966*
Myrtil, Odette 1898- *BiE&WWA, NotNAT,*
WhThe, WhoHol A
Mysels, George 1915- *AmSCAP 1966*
Mysels, Maurice 1921- *AmSCAP 1966*
Mysels, Sammy 1906- *AmSCAP 1966*

N

Nabokov, Vladimir 1899- CelR 3
Nabors, Jim 1932- CelR 3
Nachbauer, Ernest Film 2
Nadajan d1974 WhScrn 2
Nadel, Arthur IntMPA 1977
Nadel, Eli Film 2
Nadel, Norman 1915- BiE&WWA, NotNAT, WhoThe 16
Nadel, Warren 1930- AmSCAP 1966
Nademsky, Mikola Film 2
Nader, George 1921- FilmgC, IntMPA 1977, MotPP, WhoHol A
Nader, Laura 1930- WomWMM B
Nader, Ralph 1934- CelR 3
Nadi, Aldo 1899-1965 Film 2, WhScrn 2
Nadir, Moishe 1885-1943 NotNAT B
Nadir, Moses 1885-1943 OxThe
Nadler, Alexander Film 2
Naevius PIP&P
Naevius, Gnaeus 270?BC-199?BC NotNAT B, OxThe
Nagata, Masaichi 1906- IntMPA 1977, WorEnF
Nagel, Ann MotPP
Nagel, Anne 1912-1966 FilmgC, WhScrn 1, WhScrn 2, WhoHol B
Nagel, Claire d1921 NotNAT B
Nagel, Conrad d1970 MotPP, WhoHol B
Nagel, Conrad 1896-1970 Film 1, Film 2, FilmgC, TwYS
Nagel, Conrad 1897-1970 BiE&WWA, MovMk, NotNAT B, WhScrn 1, WhScrn 2, WhThe
Nagiah, V 1903-1973 WhScrn 2
Nagle, Urban 1905-1965 NotNAT B
Nagler, A M 1907- BiE&WWA, NotNAT
Nagy, Bill d1973 WhScrn 2, WhoHol B
Nagy, Frederick 1894- AmSCAP 1966
Nah Film 2
Naharro, Bartolome DeTorres OxThe
Naidoo, Bobby 1927-1967 WhScrn 1, WhScrn 2
Naify, Marshall 1920- IntMPA 1977
Naify, Robert IntMPA 1977
Nail, Joanne WhoHol A
Nainby, Robert 1869-1948 NotNAT B, WhThe, WhoHol B
Naish, Archie 1878- WhThe
Naish, J Carrol 1900-1973 FilmgC, MovMk, WhScrn 2, WhoHol B
Naish, J Carrol 1901-1973 NotNAT B
Naish, J Carroll 1900- MotPP, Vers A
Naismith, Laurence 1908- BiE&WWA, FilmgC, MovMk, NotNAT, WhoHol A, WhoThe 16
Nakadai, Tatsuya 1930- OxFilm, WorEnF
Nakamura, Kichizo 1877-1941 ModWD
Nakamura, Motohiko 1929- IntMPA 1977
Nakarenko, Dan Film 2
Naldi, Nita d1961 MotPP, WhoHol B

Naldi, Nita 1889-1961 Film 1, Film 2, TwYS
Naldi, Nita 1897-1961 NotNAT B
Naldi, Nita 1899-1961 FilmgC, WhScrn 1, WhScrn 2
Nalkowska, Zofia 1885-1954 CnMD, ModWD
Nalle, Billy AmSCAP 1966, IntMPA 1977
Nally, William Film 2
Namara, Marguerite Film 2
Namath, Joe 1943- CelR 3, FilmgC, WhoHol A
Nambu, K Film 2
Namik, Kemal 1840-1888 CnThe, REnWD
Namu d1966 WhScrn 1, WhScrn 2
Nann, Nicholas T 1928- AmSCAP 1966
Nanook d1923 Film 2, WhoHol B
Nansen, Betty 1876-1943 Film 1, MotPP, NotNAT B, WhScrn 2, WhoHol B
Nanton, Morris 1929- AmSCAP 1966
Naogeorg OxThe
Napier, Alan 1903- FilmgC, IntMPA 1977, MovMk, Vers A, WhThe, WhoHol A
Napier, Charles WhoHol A
Napier, Diana 1908- FilmgC, WhoHol A
Napier, Frank d1949 NotNAT B
Napier, John 1944- WhoHol A, WhoThe 16
Napier, Paul WhoHol A
Napier, Russel 1910-1975 WhoHol A
Napier, Russell 1910-1975 FilmgC, WhScrn 2
Napierkowska Film 1
Napierkowska, Stacia Film 2
Napierkowska, Stanislawa WhThe
Napolean, Jo WomWMM
Napoleon Film 2
Napoleon, Art 1923- FilmgC, WorEnF
Napoleon, Marty 1921- AmSCAP 1966
Napoleon, Phil 1901- AmSCAP 1966
Napton, Johnny 1924- AmSCAP 1966
Narbekova, O Film 2
Narciso, Grazia d1967 WhScrn 2
Nardelli, George d1973 WhScrn 2
Nardini, Tom 1945- FilmgC, WhoHol A
Nardino, Gary 1935- BiE&WWA
Nardo, Daniel C 1920- AmSCAP 1966
Nares, Geoffrey 1917-1942 NotNAT B, WhThe
Nares, Owen 1888-1943 Film 1, Film 2, FilmgC, NotNAT B, OxThe, WhScrn 1, WhScrn 2, WhThe, WhoHol B
Narizzano, Silvio 1927?- FilmgC, IntMPA 1977
Narlay, R Film 2
Naruse, Mikio 1905-1969 DcFM, WorEnF
Narvaez, Sara d1935 WhScrn 1, WhScrn 2
Naset, Clayton E 1895-1966 AmSCAP 1966
Nash, B A 1910- AmSCAP 1966
Nash, Brian 1956- WhoHol A
Nash, Eugenia 1866-1937 WhScrn 1, WhScrn 2
Nash, Florence 1888-1950 NotNAT B, WhScrn 1, WhScrn 2, WhThe, WhoHol B

Nash, George 1865-1945 *Film 2*
Nash, George Frederick 1873-1944 *NotNAT B,*
WhScrn 1, WhScrn 2, WhThe, WhoHol B
Nash, Ida Mae 1926- *AmSCAP 1966*
Nash, John E *Film 2*
Nash, Johnny *MotPP*
Nash, Johnny 1940- *AmSCAP 1966*
Nash, June *Film 2*
Nash, Mary 1885- *BiE&WWA, FilmgC, WhThe*
Nash, Mary 1885-1965 *NotNAT B, WhoHol B*
Nash, Mary 1885-1966 *WhScrn 1*
Nash, Mary Evelyn d1965 *WhScrn 2*
Nash, N Richard *IntMPA 1977*
Nash, N Richard 1913- *BiE&WWA, McGWD,*
NotNAT, WhoThe 16
Nash, N Richard 1916- *CnMD, ModWD*
Nash, Nancy *Film 2*
Nash, Noreen *WhoHol A*
Nash, Ogden 1902-1971 *AmSCAP 1966,*
BiE&WWA, EncMT, NotNAT B
Nashe, Thomas 1567-1601 *NotNAT B, OxThe,*
PIP&P
Nasja *Film 2*
Nasr, Georges M *DcFM*
Nass, Elyse 1947- *NatPD*
Nassau, Paul 1930- *BiE&WWA, NotNAT*
Nasser, Georges M 191-?- *DcFM*
Nassif, S Joseph 1938- *NotNAT*
Nassiter, Marcia *WomWMM*
Nassour, Edward d1962 *NotNAT B*
Nastase, Ilie 1949- *CelR 3*
Natan, Emile d1962 *NotNAT B*
Natanson, Jacques 1901- *OxThe, WhThe*
Nathan, Ben 1857-1919 *NotNAT B, WhThe*
Nathan, Charles 1921- *AmSCAP 1966*
Nathan, George Jean 1882-1958 *NotNAT A,*
NotNAT B, OxThe, WhThe
Nathan, Robert 1894- *AmSCAP 1966*
Nathan, Vivian 1921- *BiE&WWA, NotNAT,*
WhoHol A, WomWMM
Nathan, Wynn *IntMPA 1977*
Nathanson, Charles *Film 2*
Nathanson, Morton 1918- *IntMPA 1977*
Nathanson, Nat *IntMPA 1977*
Nathanson, Ted *IntMPA 1977*
Natheaux, Louis 1898-1942 *Film 2, WhScrn 1,*
WhScrn 2, WhoHol B
Nation, W H C 1843-1914 *NotNAT B, WhThe*
Natova, Natacha *Film 2*
Natro, Jimmy 1908-1946 *WhScrn 1, WhScrn 2*
Natwick, Mildred 1908- *BiE&WWA, FilmgC,*
IntMPA 1977, MotPP, MovMk, NotNAT,
Vers A, WhoHol A, WhoThe 16
Naudain, May 1880-1923 *NotNAT B,*
WhoStg 1908
Naughton, Bill 1910- *CnThe, ConDr 1977,*
CroCD, REnWD, WhoThe 16
Naughton, Charles *FilmgC*
Naughton, James *WhoHol A*
Naumberg, Nancy *WomWMM*
Naumov, Vladimir 1921- *DcFM*
Navara, Leon *AmSCAP 1966*
Navarra, Aimee *WomWMM*
Navarro, Carlos 1922-1969 *WhScrn 1, WhScrn 2,*
WhoHol B
Navarro, Catherine *Film 2*
Navarro, Jesus Garcia 1913-1960 *WhScrn 1,*
WhScrn 2, WhoHol B
Navarro, Joan *Film 2*
Nawm, Tom *Film 2*
Nayfack, Jules Joseph 1905- *IntMPA 1977*
Naylor, Robert 1899- *WhThe*
Nazarro, Cliff 1904-1961 *IntMPA 1977,*
WhScrn 2, WhoHol B

Nazarro, Ray *FilmgC, IntMPA 1977*
Nazim Hikmet Ran 1902-1963 *REnWD*
Nazimova *WomWMM*
Nazimova, Alla 1879-1945 *CnThe, FamA&A,*
Film 1, Film 2, FilmgC, MotPP, MovMk,
NotNAT B, OxFilm, OxThe, PIP&P, TwYS,
WhScrn 1, WhScrn 2, WhThe, WhoHol B,
WhoStg 1908, WorEnF
Nazzari, Amedeo 1907- *FilmgC, IntMPA 1977,*
WhoHol A
Neagle, Anna 1904- *BiDFlm, BiE&WWA,*
EncMT, FilmgC, IntMPA 1977, MotPP,
MovMk, NotNAT, NotNAT A, OxFilm,
ThFT, WhoHol A, WhoThe 16, WorEnF
Neal, Frances *WhoHol A*
Neal, Frank 1917-1955 *WhScrn 1, WhScrn 2,*
WhoHol B
Neal, Patricia 1926- *BiDFlm, BiE&WWA,*
CelR 3, FilmgC, IntMPA 1977, MotPP,
MovMk, NotNAT, NotNAT A, OxFilm,
WhThe, WhoHol A, WorEnF
Neal, Richard *Film 2*
Neal, Tom 1914-1972 *FilmgC, HolP 40,*
WhScrn 2, WhoHol B
Neal, Walter 1920- *BiE&WWA, NotNAT*
Neale, Frederick d1856 *NotNAT B*
Neame, Ronald 1911- *BiDFlm, DcFM, FilmgC,*
IntMPA 1977, MovMk, WorEnF
Near, Holly *WhoHol A*
Nearing, Homer 1895- *AmSCAP 1966*
Neason, Hazel d1920 *WhScrn 2*
Nebel, Long John 1912- *CelR 3*
Nebenzal, Seymour 1898-1961 *OxFilm*
Nebenzal, Seymour 1899-1961 *FilmgC,*
IntMPA 1977
Nedd, Stuart d1971 *WhScrn 2*
Nedell, Alice Blakeney d1959 *WhScrn 1,*
WhScrn 2, WhoHol B
Nedell, Bernard 1898-1972 *BiE&WWA, Film 1,*
Film 2, MotPP, Vers B, WhScrn 2,
WhoHol B
Nedell, Bernard 1899- *WhThe*
Nederlander, David T 1886-1967 *NotNAT B*
Nederlander, James 1922- *BiE&WWA, CelR 3,*
NotNAT, WhoThe 16
Needles, Susan *WomWMM*
Neeley, Ted *WhoHol A*
Neely, Henry M d1963 *NotNAT B*
Neely, Neil *Film 2*
Neff, Hildegard 1925- *WorEnF*
Neff, Hildegarde 1925- *FilmgC, IntMPA 1977,*
MotPP, MovMk, OxFilm, WhoHol A
Neff, Morty 1927- *AmSCAP 1966*
Neff, Pauline *Film 2*
Neff, Ralph d1973 *WhScrn 2*
Negrete, Jorge 1911-1953 *WhScrn 1, WhScrn 2,*
WhoHol B
Negri, Joseph 1926- *AmSCAP 1966*
Negri, Pola *MotPP*
Negri, Pola 1894- *BiDFlm, Film 1, Film 2,*
ThFT, TwYS
Negri, Pola 1897?- *FilmgC, OxFilm, WhoHol A,*
WorEnF
Negri, Pola 1899- *MovMk*
Negroni, Baldassare 1877-1948 *DcFM*
Negulesco, Jean 1900- *BiDFlm, CmMov, FilmgC,*
IntMPA 1977, MovMk, OxFilm,
WomWMM, WorEnF
Neher, John d1972 *WhoHol B*
Neher, Susan *WhoHol A*
Neiburg, Al J 1902- *AmSCAP 1966*
Neil, Hildegarde 1939- *FilmgC, WhoHol A*
Neil, Richard *Film 1*
Neil, Ross d1888 *NotNAT B*

Neilan, Marshal 1891-1958 *Film 1, FilmgC*
Neilan, Marshall 1891-1958 *BiDFlm, Film 2,*
  MotPP, NotNAT B, OxFilm, TwYS A,
  WhScrn 1, WhScrn 2, WhoHol B, WorEnF
Neill, Frank 1917- *IntMPA 1977*
Neill, James d1931 *Film 1, Film 2, NotNAT B,*
  TwYS, WhoHol B
Neill, James d1962 *NotNAT B*
Neill, James 1860-1931 *WhScrn 2*
Neill, James 1861-1931 *WhScrn 1*
Neill, Noel *WhoHol A*
Neill, R William 1892-1946 *TwYS A*
Neill, Richard R 1876-1970 *Film 2, WhScrn 1,*
  WhScrn 2, WhoHol B
Neill, Roy William 1890-1946 *FilmgC*
Neilsen-Terry, Dennis 1895-1932 *WhScrn 1,*
  WhScrn 2, WhoHol B
Neilsen-Terry, Dennis see also Neilson-Terry, Dennis
Neilson, Ada 1846-1905 *NotNAT B*
Neilson, Adelaide 1846-1880 *OxThe*
Neilson, Adelaide 1848-1880 *FamA&A,*
  NotNAT A
Neilson, Agnes *Film 1*
Neilson, Asta 1883- *Film 2*
Neilson, Francis 1867-1961 *NotNAT B, WhThe*
Neilson, Harold V 1874-1956 *NotNAT B, WhThe*
Neilson, James 1918- *FilmgC, WorEnF*
Neilson, Julia 1868-1957 *OxThe, WhThe*
Neilson, Julia 1869-1957 *NotNAT A*
Neilson, Lilian Adelaide 1848-1880 *NotNAT B*
Neilson, Lilian Adelaide see also Neilson, Adelaide
Neilson, Perlita 1933- *WhoHol A, WhoThe 16*
Neilson-Terry, Dennis 1895-1932 *NotNAT B,*
  WhThe
Neilson-Terry, Dennis see also Neilsen-Terry, Dennis
Neilson-Terry, Julia 1868-1957 *NotNAT B*
Neilson-Terry, Phyllis 1892- *BiE&WWA, WhThe,*
  WhoHol A
Neiman, John M 1935- *WhThe*
Neipris, Janet L *NatPD*
Neise, George *WhoHol A*
Neisel, Edmund *Film 2*
Neitz, Alvin J 1894- *TwYS A*
Nekes, Dore *WomWMM*
Nekes, Werner *WomWMM*
Nell, Louise M 1884-1944 *WhScrn 1, WhScrn 2*
Nelli, Piero 1926- *WorEnF*
Nelligan, Kate 1951- *WhoThe 16*
Nelms, Henning 1900- *BiE&WWA*
Nelson, Alice Brainerd d1963 *NotNAT B*
Nelson, Anne 1911-1948 *WhScrn 1, WhScrn 2*
Nelson, Barry *BiE&WWA, IntMPA 1977,*
  MotPP, NotNAT, PIP&P A, WhoHol A
Nelson, Barry 1920- *FilmgC, MovMk*
Nelson, Barry 1925- *WhoThe 16*
Nelson, Bobby *Film 2*
Nelson, Carrie d1916 *NotNAT B*
Nelson, David 1936- *IntMPA 1977, MotPP,*
  WhoHol A
Nelson, Ed *WhoHol A*
Nelson, Ed 1928- *FilmgC*
Nelson, Ed, Jr. 1916- *AmSCAP 1966*
Nelson, Ed G 1885- *AmSCAP 1966*
Nelson, Eddie Sunkist 1894-1940 *WhScrn 1,*
  WhScrn 2
Nelson, Edgar *Film 2*
Nelson, Edward J 1911- *IntMPA 1977*
Nelson, Eliza d1908 *NotNAT B*
Nelson, Florence *Film 2*
Nelson, Frances *Film 1*
Nelson, Frank *Film 2*
Nelson, Frederic J 1923- *AmSCAP 1966*
Nelson, Gaylord 1916- *CelR 3*
Nelson, Gene 1920- *CmMov, FilmgC,*

IntMPA 1977, MotPP, MovMk, NewYTET,
  PIP&P A, WhoHol A, WhoThe 16
Nelson, Gordon d1956 *NotNAT B, WhoHol B*
Nelson, Gunvor *WomWMM A, WomWMM B*
Nelson, Harold d1937 *WhScrn 1, WhScrn 2,*
  WhoHol B
Nelson, Harriet *IntMPA 1977, MotPP*
Nelson, Helen *WomWMM B*
Nelson, Lord Horatio 1758-1805 *FilmgC*
Nelson, J *Film 2*
Nelson, Jack 1882- *Film 1, Film 2, TwYS,*
  TwYS A
Nelson, James C, Jr. 1921- *AmSCAP 1966*
Nelson, Kenneth 1930- *BiE&WWA, NotNAT,*
  WhoHol A, WhoThe 16
Nelson, Kristin *WhoHol A*
Nelson, Lindsey 1919- *CelR 3*
Nelson, Lori 1933- *FilmgC, IntMPA 1977,*
  MotPP, WhoHol A
Nelson, Lottie 1875-1966 *WhScrn 1, WhScrn 2,*
  WhoHol B
Nelson, Novella 1939- *NotNAT, PIP&P A*
Nelson, Oswald George 1906-1975 *AmSCAP 1966*
Nelson, Otto *Film 2*
Nelson, Ozzie d1975 *MotPP, NewYTET,*
  WhoHol C
Nelson, Ozzie 1906-1975 *WhScrn 2*
Nelson, Ozzie 1907-1975 *FilmgC*
Nelson, Paul 1929- *AmSCAP 1966*
Nelson, Portia *WhoHol A*
Nelson, Ralph 1916- *BiDFlm, FilmgC,*
  IntMPA 1977, MovMk, NewYTET, WorEnF
Nelson, Raymond 1898- *BiE&WWA, NotNAT*
Nelson, Raymond E 1907- *IntMPA 1977*
Nelson, Richard *NatPD*
Nelson, Rick 1940- *FilmgC, IntMPA 1977,*
  MotPP, WhoHol A
Nelson, Ron 1929- *AmSCAP 1966*
Nelson, Ruth 1905- *PIP&P, WhoHol A,*
  WhoThe 16
Nelson, Sam *Film 2*
Nelson, Stanley 1933- *NatPD*
Nelson, Steve 1907- *AmSCAP 1966*
Nelson, Tracy *WhoHol A*
Nelson, Virginia Tallent 1911-1968 *WhScrn 2,*
  WhoHol B
Nelson Family *MotPP*
Nemchinova, Vera *WhThe*
Nemec, Jan 1936- *DcFM, FilmgC, OxFilm,*
  WorEnF
Nemeth, Laszlo 1901-1975 *CroCD, McGWD*
Nemeth, Ted *WomWMM*
Nemetz, Max *Film 2*
Nemiroff, Isaac 1912- *AmSCAP 1966*
Nemiroff, Robert *ConDr 1977D, NotNAT*
Nemirovich-Danchenko, Vladimir Ivanovich
  1858-1943 *ModWD, NotNAT A, NotNAT B*
Nemirovich-Danchenko, Vladimir Ivanovich
  1859-1943 *CnThe, OxThe, PIP&P*
Nemo, Henry 1914- *AmSCAP 1966*
Nemoy, Priscilla 1919- *AmSCAP 1966*
NeMoyer, Francis *Film 1*
Nemser, Sandy Rothenberg *WomWMM B*
Nenasheva, L *Film 2*
Neola, Princess *Film 2*
Nepomunceno, Luis 1930- *IntMPA 1977*
Neri, Donatelle *Film 2*
Nericault, Philippe *REnWD*
Nero *OxThe*
Nero, Curtis *Film 2*
Nero, Franco 1942- *FilmgC, WhoHol A*
Nero, Paul 1917-1958 *AmSCAP 1966*
Nero, Peter 1934- *CelR 3*
Neroni, Bartolomeo 1500?-1571? *OxThe*

Neruda, Pablo 1904- *CelR 3*
Nerulos, Jacob Rizos 1778-1850 *NotNAT B*
Nervo, Jimmy 1890-1975 *FilmgC, WhScrn 2,
 WhoHol C*
Nervo And Knox *Film 2*
Nes, Ole M 1888-1953 *Film 2*
Nes, Ole M *see also* Ness, Ole M
Nesbit, Evelyn 1885-1967 *Film 1, Film 2,
 NotNAT A, NotNAT B, TwYS, WhScrn 1,
 WhScrn 2, WhoHol B*
Nesbit, Pinna *Film 2*
Nesbitt, Cathleen *MotPP, PIP&P*
Nesbitt, Cathleen 1888- *BiE&WWA, NotNAT,
 NotNAT A, WhoThe 16*
Nesbitt, Cathleen 1889- *FilmgC, MovMk,
 WhoHol A*
Nesbitt, Derren 1932?- *FilmgC, WhoHol A*
Nesbitt, John 1910-1960 *WhScrn 2, WhoHol B*
Nesbitt, Miriam 1873-1954 *Film 1, MotPP,
 WhScrn 2, WhoHol B, WhoStg 1906,
 WhoStg 1908*
Nesbitt, Miriam Anne 1879- *WhThe*
Nesbitt, Robert 1906- *EncMT, WhoThe 16*
Nesbitt, Tom 1890-1927 *NotNAT B*
Nesin, Aziz 1915- *REnWD*
Nesmith, Michael *WhoHol A*
Nesmith, Ottola d1972 *Film 2, WhoHol B*
Nesmith, Ottola 1888-1972 *WhScrn 2*
Nesmith, Ottola 1893-1972 *WhThe*
Nesor, Al *WhoHol A*
Ness, Ed *WhoHol A*
Ness, Ole M 1888-1953 *Film 2, WhScrn 1,
 WhScrn 2, WhoHol B*
Nessen, Ron *NewYTET*
Nest, Loni *Film 2*
Nestell, Bill 1895-1966 *MotPP, WhScrn 1,
 WhScrn 2, WhoHol B*
Nestroy, Johann Nepomuk 1801-1862 *CnThe,
 McGWD, NotNAT B, OxThe, REnWD*
Nethersole, Louis d1936 *NotNAT B*
Nethersole, Olga 1870-1951 *FamA&A,
 WhoStg 1906, WhoStg 1908*
Nethersole, Olga Isabel 1863-1951 *OxThe*
Nethersole, Olga Isabel 1866-1951 *NotNAT B,
 WhThe*
Netter, Douglas 1921- *IntMPA 1977*
Nettlefold, Archibald 1870-1944 *NotNAT B,
 WhThe*
Nettlefold, Frederick John 1867-1949 *NotNAT B,
 WhThe*
Nettleton, John 1929- *WhoHol A, WhoThe 16*
Nettleton, Lois 1929?- *BiE&WWA, FilmgC,
 IntMPA 1977, NotNAT, WhoHol A,
 WhoThe 16*
Neu, Oscar F 1886-1957 *WhScrn 1, WhScrn 2*
Neuber, Fredericka Carolina 1697-1760 *CnThe*
Neuber, Frederika Carolina 1697-1760 *NotNAT B,
 OxThe*
Neuer, Joann *WomWMM*
Neufeld, Mace 1928- *AmSCAP 1966*
Neufold, Max *Film 2*
Neuman, Alan 1924- *IntMPA 1977, NewYTET*
Neuman, E Jack *NewYTET*
Neumann, Alfred 1895-1952 *CnMD, McGWD,
 ModWD*
Neumann, Dorothy *WhoHol A*
Neumann, Kurt 1908-1958 *FilmgC, WhScrn 2*
Neumann, Lotte *Film 2*
Neusser, Eric 1902-1957 *WhScrn 1, WhScrn 2*
Nevada, Emma d1940 *NotNAT B*
Nevaro 1887-1941 *WhScrn 1, WhScrn 2*
Nevelson, Louise 1900- *CelR 3*
Nevens, Paul *WhoHol A*
Neveux, Georges 1900- *CnMD, McGWD*

Neville, Edgar 1899- *McGWD*
Neville, Edgar 1900- *CroCD*
Neville, George *Film 2*
Neville, Harry d1945 *NotNAT B*
Neville, Henry Gartside 1837-1910 *NotNAT B,
 OxThe*
Neville, John 1925- *BiE&WWA, CnThe, FilmgC,
 MotPP, NotNAT, NotNAT A, WhoHol A,
 WhoThe 16*
Neville, John Gartside d1874 *NotNAT B*
Nevin, Arthur Finley 1871-1943 *AmSCAP 1966*
Nevin, Ethelbert Woodbridge 1862-1901
 AmSCAP 1966
Nevin, George Balch 1859-1933 *AmSCAP 1966*
Nevin, Gordon Balch 1892-1943 *AmSCAP 1966*
Nevins, Claudette *WhoHol A*
Nevins, Morty 1917- *AmSCAP 1966*
Nevins, Willard Irving 1890-1962 *AmSCAP 1966*
Newall, Guy 1885-1937 *Film 1, Film 2, FilmgC,
 NotNAT B, WhScrn 1, WhScrn 2, WhThe,
 WhoHol B*
Newark, Derek *WhoHol A*
Neway, Patricia 1919- *BiE&WWA, NotNAT,
 WhoThe 16*
Newberg, Frank *Film 1, Film 2*
Newberry, Barbara 1910- *WhThe*
Newberry, Hazzard P 1907-1952 *WhScrn 1,
 WhScrn 2*
Newbery, Charles Bruce *IntMPA 1977*
Newborn, Abe 1920- *BiE&WWA*
Newbrook, Peter 1916- *FilmgC, IntMPA 1977*
Newburg, Frank 1886-1969 *WhScrn 1, WhScrn 2,
 WhoHol B*
Newcom, James E 1907- *IntMPA 1977*
Newcomb, Mary d1967 *WhoHol B*
Newcomb, Mary 1894-1967 *WhScrn 1, WhScrn 2*
Newcomb, Mary 1897-1966 *WhThe*
Newcombe, Caroline d1941 *NotNAT B*
Newcombe, Jessamine d1961 *WhScrn 1,
 WhScrn 2*
Newcombe, Mary *PIP&P*
Newell, David 1905- *Film 2*
Newell, Raymond 1894- *WhThe*
Newell, Tom D d1935 *NotNAT B*
Newell, William 1894-1967 *WhScrn 1, WhScrn 2,
 WhoHol B*
Newfeld, Sam 1900-1964 *FilmgC*
Newgard, Robert M 1925- *IntMPA 1977*
Newhall, Mayo 1890-1958 *WhScrn 1, WhScrn 2,
 WhoHol B*
Newhall, Patricia *BiE&WWA, NotNAT,
 WhoHol A*
Newhart, Bob *WhoHol A*
Newhart, Bob 1923- *FilmgC*
Newhart, Bob 1929- *CelR 3, IntMPA 1977*
Newill, James 1911- *WhoHol A*
Newlan, Paul *WhoHol A*
Newlan, Paul Tiny 1908- *Vers A*
Newland, Anna Dewey 1881-1967 *WhScrn 1,
 WhScrn 2*
Newland, John 1916?- *FilmgC, IntMPA 1977,
 WhoHol A*
Newland, Mary *Film 2, WhoHol A*
Newland, Paul 1903-1973 *WhScrn 2*
Newlands, Anthony 1926- *FilmgC*
Newley, Anthony 1931- *BiE&WWA, CelR 3,
 ConDr 1977D, EncMT, FilmgC,
 IntMPA 1977, MotPP, MovMk, NotNAT,
 OxFilm, WhoHol A, WhoThe 16*
Newman, Al 1940- *IntMPA 1977*
Newman, Albert M 1900-1964 *AmSCAP 1966*
Newman, Alfred 1901-1970 *AmSCAP 1966,
 CmMov, DcFM, FilmgC, OxFilm,
 WhScrn 1, WhScrn 2, WhoHol B, WorEnF*

Newman, Barry 1940- *FilmgC, WhoHol A*
Newman, Candy 1945-1966 *WhScrn 2*
Newman, Charles 1901- *AmSCAP 1966*
Newman, Claude 1903- *WhThe*
Newman, David 1937- *ConDr 1977A,*
IntMPA 1977
Newman, Edwin 1919- *CelR 3, NewYTET*
Newman, Eve *WomWMM*
Newman, Greatrex 1892- *BiE&WWA, WhThe*
Newman, Herbert 1925- *AmSCAP 1966*
Newman, Howard 1911- *IntMPA 1977, NotNAT*
Newman, Joe 1909- *WorEnF*
Newman, John K 1864-1927 *Film 2, WhScrn 1,*
WhScrn 2, WhoHol B
Newman, Joseph M 1909- *BiDFlm, FilmgC,*
IntMPA 1977, MovMk, WorEnF
Newman, Lur Barden d1918 *WhScrn 2*
Newman, Martin H 1913- *IntMPA 1977*
Newman, Max 1914- *AmSCAP 1966*
Newman, Melissa *WhoHol A*
Newman, Nanette *FilmgC, IntMPA 1977,*
WhoHol A
Newman, Nell 1881-1931 *WhScrn 1, WhScrn 2*
Newman, Paul 1925- *BiDFlm, BiE&WWA,*
CelR 3, CmMov, FilmgC, IntMPA 1977,
MotPP, MovMk, NotNAT A, OxFilm,
WhThe, WhoHol A, WorEnF
Newman, Phyllis 1935- *BiE&WWA, NotNAT,*
WhoHol A, WhoThe 16
Newman, Robert V *IntMPA 1977*
Newman, Roger *WhoHol A*
Newman, Samuel 1919- *IntMPA 1977*
Newman, Scott *WhoHol A*
Newman, Sydney *IntMPA 1977, NewYTET*
Newman, Thomas *WhoHol A*
Newman, Walter Brown *IntMPA 1977*
Newmar, Julie *MotPP, WhoHol A*
Newmar, Julie 1930- *FilmgC*
Newmar, Julie 1935- *BiE&WWA, NotNAT*
Newmark, Stewart 1916-1968 *WhScrn 2*
Newmeyer, Fred 1888- *TwYS A, WorEnF*
Newnham-Davis, Nathaniel 1854-1917 *NotNAT B,*
WhThe
Newsom, Thomas P 1929- *AmSCAP 1966*
Newsome, Carman 1912-1974 *WhScrn 2*
Newte, Horace Wykeham Can d1949 *NotNAT B*
Newton, Mrs. A *Film 2*
Newton, Charles d1926 *Film 2, WhScrn 1,*
WhScrn 2, WhoHol B
Newton, Henry Chance 1854-1931 *NotNAT B,*
WhThe
Newton, Huey 1942- *CelR 3*
Newton, John *WhoHol A*
Newton, John d1625 *OxThe*
Newton, Kate d1940 *NotNAT B*
Newton, Rhoda *AmSCAP 1966*
Newton, Robert 1905-1956 *BiDFlm, FilmgC,*
MotPP, MovMk, NotNAT B, OxFilm,
Vers A, WhScrn 1, WhScrn 2, WhThe,
WhoHol B, WorEnF
Newton, Theodore 1905-1963 *MotPP, NotNAT B,*
WhScrn 1, WhScrn 2, WhoHol B
Newton, Wayne 1944- *CelR 3, WhoHol A*
Nex, Andre *Film 2*
Ney, Marie 1895- *PIP&P, WhThe, WhoHol A*
Ney, Richard *IntMPA 1977, MotPP*
Ney, Richard 1916- *WhoHol A*
Ney, Richard 1917- *FilmgC*
Ng, Marforie *WomWMM B*
Ngugi, James T 1938- *ConDr 1977*
Niarchos, Stavros 1909- *CelR 3*
Nibley, Sloan *IntMPA 1977*
Niblo, Fred 1872-1948 *TwYS A*
Niblo, Fred 1874-1948 *CmMov, DcFM, FilmgC,*

MovMk, NotNAT B, OxFilm, WhScrn 1,
WhScrn 2, WhoHol B, WorEnF
Niblo, Fred, Jr. 1903-1973 *WhScrn 2*
Niblo, William d1878 *NotNAT B*
Niblock, James 1917- *AmSCAP 1966*
Nicander, Edwin 1876-1951 *NotNAT B, WhThe*
Niccodemi, Dario 1874-1934 *McGWD*
Niccolini, Dianora 1936- *WomWMM B*
Niccolini, Gian Battista 1782-1861 *McGWD*
Nichol, Clarissa B 1895- *AmSCAP 1966*
Nichol, Emilie *Film 2*
Nicholas, Denise *WhoHol A*
Nicholas, Don 1913- *AmSCAP 1966*
Nicholas, Paul *WhoHol A*
Nicholas Brothers, The *WhoHol A*
Nicholl, Don *NewYTET*
Nicholls, Anthony *WhoHol A*
Nicholls, Anthony 1902- *FilmgC*
Nicholls, Anthony 1907- *WhoThe 16*
Nicholls, Fred J *Film 2*
Nicholls, George d1927 *WhoHol B*
Nicholls, George, Jr. d1939 *WhoHol B*
Nicholls, Harry 1852-1926 *NotNAT B, WhThe*
Nichols, Alberta 1898-1957 *AmSCAP 1966*
Nichols, Anne 1891-1966 *McGWD, ModWD,*
NotNAT B, WhThe
Nichols, Anne 1896- *BiE&WWA*
Nichols, Barbara 1932- *FilmgC, MotPP, MovMk,*
WhoHol A
Nichols, Beverley 1898- *WhThe*
Nichols, Dandy 1907- *FilmgC, WhoHol A*
Nichols, Dudley 1895-1960 *CmMov, DcFM,*
FilmgC, OxFilm, WorEnF
Nichols, Ernest Loring 1905-1965 *AmSCAP 1966*
Nichols, Ernest Loring *see also* Nichols, Red
Nichols, Ernest Loring Red 1905-1965 *WhScrn 1,*
WhScrn 2
Nichols, George 1864- *Film 1, Film 2, TwYS*
Nichols, George, Jr. 1897-1939 *WhScrn 1,*
WhScrn 2
Nichols, George, Sr. 1865-1927 *WhScrn 1,*
WhScrn 2
Nichols, Guy d1928 *NotNAT B*
Nichols, Josephine *WhoHol A*
Nichols, Joy *WhoHol A*
Nichols, Lewis 1903- *WhThe*
Nichols, Margaret 1900-1941 *WhScrn 1,*
WhScrn 2, WhoHol B
Nichols, Marjorie J d1970 *WhScrn 1, WhScrn 2,*
WhoHol B
Nichols, Mike 1931- *BiE&WWA, CelR 3,*
DcFM, FilmgC, IntMPA 1977, MovMk,
NewYTET, NotNAT, OxFilm, WhoHol A,
WhoThe 16, WomWMM, WorEnF
Nichols, Nellie V 1885-1971 *WhScrn 1,*
WhScrn 2, WhoHol B
Nichols, Nichelle *WhoHol A*
Nichols, Norma *Film 1*
Nichols, Peter 1927- *CnThe, ConDr 1977,*
McGWD, WhoThe 16
Nichols, Red 1905-1965 *WhoHol B*
Nichols, Red *see also* Nichols, Ernest Loring
Nichols, Robert *WhoHol A*
Nichols, Robert Malise Bowyer 1893-1944 *ModWD,*
NotNAT B
Nichols-Bates, H *Film 2*
Nicholson, Anne P 1920- *BiE&WWA, NotNAT*
Nicholson, Elwood J 1908- *IntMPA 1977*
Nicholson, Emrich 1913- *IntMPA 1977*
Nicholson, H O 1868- *WhThe*
Nicholson, Jack *MotPP, WhoHol A*
Nicholson, Jack 1936- *IntMPA 1977, MovMk*
Nicholson, Jack 1937- *CelR 3, FilmgC, OxFilm*
Nicholson, James 1946- *NatPD*

Nicholson, James H 1916-1973 *FilmgC*
Nicholson, John d1934 *NotNAT B*
Nicholson, Kenyon 1894- *BiE&WWA, WhThe*
Nicholson, Nora 1887-1973 *FilmgC, WhoHol B*
Nicholson, Nora 1889-1973 *WhThe*
Nicholson, Nora 1892-1973 *WhScrn 2*
Nicholson, Norman Cornthwaite 1914- *CroCD*
Nicholson, Paul 1877-1935 *Film 2, TwYS,*
  WhScrn 1, WhScrn 2, WhoHol B
Nicholson, Robert *IntMPA 1977*
Nicholson, Sir William d1949 *NotNAT B*
Nichtern, Claire 1920- *BiE&WWA, NotNAT*
Nickel, Gitta *WomWMM*
Nickell, Paul *IntMPA 1977*
Nickerson, Dawn *WhoHol A*
Nickerson, Denise *WhoHol A*
Nickinson, Isabella 1847-1906 *NotNAT B*
Nicklaus, Jack 1940- *CelR 3*
Nickole, Leonidas 1929- *BiE&WWA, NotNAT*
Nickols, Walter 1853-1927 *WhScrn 1, WhScrn 2*
Nicodemi, Dario d1934 *NotNAT B, WhThe*
Nicol, Alex 1919- *BiE&WWA, FilmgC,*
  IntMPA 1977, NotNAT, WhoHol A
Nicol, Emma d1877 *NotNAT B*
Nicol, Harry N d1962 *NotNAT B*
Nicol, Joseph E 1856-1926 *WhScrn 1, WhScrn 2*
Nicolai, Aldo 1920- *CnMD*
Nicolet, Jean-Baptiste 1728?-1796 *OxThe*
Nicoletti, Louis 1907-1969 *WhScrn 2*
Nicoll, Allardyce 1894-1976 *BiE&WWA,*
  NotNAT, OxThe, WhoThe 16
Nicostratos *OxThe*
Nides, Tina *WomWMM*
Nielsen, Alice 1876-1943 *NotNAT B, WhThe,*
  WhoStg 1906, WhoStg 1908
Nielsen, Arthur C 1897- *CelR 3*
Nielsen, Asta d1972 *Film 2, MotPP, WhoHol B*
Nielsen, Asta 1882-1972 *WhScrn 2*
Nielsen, Asta 1883-1972 *Film 1, FilmgC, OxFilm,*
  WorEnF
Nielsen, Gertrude 1918-1975 *WhScrn 2*
Nielsen, Gertrude *see also* Niesen, Gertrude
Nielsen, Hans 1911-1967 *WhScrn 2*
Nielsen, Ingvard d1975 *WhoHol C*
Nielsen, Karl *BiE&WWA*
Nielsen, Leslie 1925- *FilmgC, IntMPA 1977,*
  MotPP, MovMk, WhoHol A
Nielsen, Mathilde *Film 2*
Niemeyer, Harry 1909- *IntMPA 1977*
Niemeyer, Joseph H 1887-1965 *WhScrn 1,*
  WhScrn 2
Niepce, Joseph Nicephore 1765-1833 *DcFM*
Niesen, Barney 1913- *AmSCAP 1966*
Niesen, Gertrude d1975 *WhoHol C*
Niesen, Gertrude 1910- *WhThe*
Niesen, Gertrude *see also* Nielsen, Gertrude
Niggli, Josefina 1910- *NatPD*
Nigh, Jane 1926- *FilmgC, IntMPA 1977,*
  WhoHol A
Nigh, William 1881-1955 *Film 1, Film 2,*
  FilmgC, TwYS A, WhScrn 2
Night, Harry A Hank 1847-1930 *WhScrn 1,*
  WhScrn 2
Nightingale, Alfred d1957 *NotNAT B*
Nightingale, Joe *WhThe*
Nightingale, Mae Wheeler 1898- *AmSCAP 1966*
Nigyla, Cassandra *WomWMM A*
Nijhoff, Martinus 1894-1953 *CnMD*
Nijinska, Bronislava 1891- *WhThe*
Nijinsky, Vaslav 1890-1950 *NotNAT A,*
  NotNAT B, WhThe
Nikandrov *Film 2*
Nikitina, Alice *WhThe*
Nikolaievic, Dusan 1885-1961 *CnMD*

Nikolais, Alwin 1912- *CelR 3, ConDr 1977E*
Nile, Florian Martinez 1936-1959 *WhScrn 1,*
  WhScrn 2
Niles, Fred A 1918- *IntMPA 1977*
Niles, John Jacob 1892- *AmSCAP 1966*
Nilges, Raymond Louis 1938- *AmSCAP 1966*
Nillson, Alex *Film 1*
Nillson, Carlotta 1878?-1951 *Film 1, NotNAT B,*
  WhThe, WhoStg 1908
Nilsen, Alexander 1903- *AmSCAP 1966*
Nilsen, Einar d1964 *NotNAT B*
Nilsson, Anna Q d1974 *MotPP, WhoHol B*
Nilsson, Anna Q 1888-1974 *WhScrn 2*
Nilsson, Anna Q 1893-1974 *Film 1, Film 2,*
  FilmgC, TwYS
Nilsson, Anna Q 1894-1974 *MovMk*
Nilsson, Birgit 1918- *CelR 3, WhoHol A*
Nilsson, Christine d1921 *NotNAT B*
Nilsson, Harry *WhoHol A*
Nilsson, Leopold Torre 1924- *FilmgC*
Nilsson, Leopoldo Torre 1924- *BiDFlm, DcFM,*
  WorEnF
Nilsson, Torre 1924- *OxFilm*
Nimmo, Derek *WhoHol A*
Nimmo, Derek 1931- *FilmgC*
Nimmo, Derek 1932- *WhoThe 16*
Nimoy, Leonard 1932- *FilmgC, WhoHol A*
Nims, Ernest 1908- *IntMPA 1977*
Nims, Letha 1917- *BiE&WWA, NotNAT*
Ninchi, Ave *WhoHol A*
Ninchi, Carlo 1896-1974 *WhScrn 2, WhoHol B*
Nioun, Mahoun Tien *DcFM*
Nirdlinger, Charles Frederic d1940 *NotNAT B*
Nisbet, J F d1899 *NotNAT B*
Nisita, Giovanni d1962 *NotNAT B*
Nissen, Aud Egede *Film 2*
Nissen, Brian 1927- *WhThe*
Nissen, Greta 1906- *Film 2, FilmgC, ThFT,*
  TwYS, WhThe
Niven, David *IntMPA 1977, MotPP, WhoHol A*
Niven, David 1909- *FilmgC, OxFilm*
Niven, David 1910- *CelR 3, MovMk, WorEnF*
Niven, Kip *WhoHol A*
Nivoix, Paul 1889-1958 *McGWD*
Nixon, Agnes *NewYTET*
Nixon, Arundel 1907-1949 *WhScrn 2*
Nixon, Clint 1906-1937 *WhScrn 1, WhScrn 2*
Nixon, David 1919- *IntMPA 1977*
Nixon, Hugh d1921 *NotNAT B*
Nixon, Marian 1904- *Film 2, FilmgC, MotPP,*
  ThFT, TwYS, WhoHol A
Nixon, Marni 1929?- *FilmgC, MotPP,*
  WhoHol A
Nixon, Pat 1912- *CelR 3*
Nixon, Richard 1913- *CelR 3*
Nixon-Nirdlinger, Fred G d1931 *NotNAT B*
Nizer, Louis 1902- *AmSCAP 1966, BiE&WWA,*
  CelR 3, IntMPA 1977, NotNAT
Nkosi, Lewis 1936- *ConDr 1977*
Noa, Julian 1879-1958 *WhScrn 1, WhScrn 2*
Noah, Mordecai Manuel 1785-1851 *NotNAT B,*
  OxThe
Noak, Christian 1927- *CnMD*
Noakes, John *PIP&P*
Noakova, Jana 1948-1968 *WhScrn 2*
Nobili, Laudivio De' *OxThe*
Noble, Dennis 1898-1966 *WhThe*
Noble, Edward J d1958 *NewYTET*
Noble, Eulalie *WhoHol A*
Noble, Harry 1912-1966 *AmSCAP 1966*
Noble, James *WhoHol A*
Noble, John Avery 1892-1944 *AmSCAP 1966*
Noble, John W 1880- *TwYS A*
Noble, Milton 1844-1924 *Film 2*

Noble, Peter *IntMPA 1977*
Noble, Ray *WhoHol A*
Noble, Thomas Tertius 1867-1953 *AmSCAP 1966*
Noble, William 1921- *BiE&WWA, NotNAT*
Nobles, Dollie d1930 *WhoHol B*
Nobles, Dolly d1930 *NotNAT B*
Nobles, Milton 1844-1924 *WhScrn 1, WhScrn 2,*
WhoHol B, WhoStg 1908
Nobles, Milton 1847-1924 *NotNAT B*
Nobles, Milton, Jr. d1925 *NotNAT B, WhoHol B*
Noblitt, Katheryn McCall 1909- *AmSCAP 1966*
Nobumitsu, Kwanze Kojiro *REnWD*
Nodalsky, Sonia *Film 2*
Nodell, Sonya *Film 2*
Noel *Film 2*
Noel, Chris *WhoHol A*
Noel, Craig R 1915- *BiE&WWA, NotNAT*
Noel, Dick 1927- *AmSCAP 1966*
Noel, Magali 1932- *FilmgC, WhoHol A*
Noel-Noel *WhoHol A*
Noemi, Lea 1883-1973 *WhScrn 2, WhoHol B*
Nofal, Emil 1926- *IntMPA 1977*
Noguchi, Isamu 1904- *CelR 3, WomWMM*
Noiret, Philippe 1931- *FilmgC, WhoHol A,*
WorEnF
Noiseux-Labreque, Lise *WomWMM*
Nokes, James d1696 *OxThe, PIP&P*
Nolan, Bill *Film 2*
Nolan, Doris 1916- *FilmgC, ThFT, WhThe,*
WhoHol A
Nolan, Gypo *Film 2*
Nolan, James *WhoHol A*
Nolan, Jeanette 1911?- *FilmgC, WhoHol A*
Nolan, John *WhoHol A*
Nolan, Kathleen *WhoHol A*
Nolan, Lloyd *BiE&WWA, IntMPA 1977,*
MotPP, NotNAT, WhoHol A
Nolan, Lloyd 1902- *FilmgC, MovMk, WhThe,*
WorEnF
Nolan, Lloyd 1903- *CmMov, HolP 30*
Nolan, Margaret *WhoHol A*
Nolan, Mary 1905-1948 *Film 2, TwYS,*
WhScrn 1, WhScrn 2, WhoHol B
Nolan, Mary 1906-1948 *NotNAT B*
Nolan, Tom *WhoHol A*
Nolbandov, Sergei 1895-1971 *FilmgC,*
IntMPA 1977
Noldan, Svend *WomWMM*
Nolte, C Elmer, Jr. 1905- *IntMPA 1977*
Nolte, Charles 1926- *BiE&WWA, NotNAT,*
WhoHol A
Nolte, Roy E 1896- *AmSCAP 1966*
Nomis, Leo d1932 *Film 2, WhScrn 1,*
WhScrn 2, WhoHol B
Noon, Paisley 1897-1932 *WhScrn 1, WhScrn 2,*
WhoHol B
Noonan, John Ford 1943- *ConDr 1977, NotNAT*
Noonan, Patrick 1887-1962 *WhScrn 1, WhScrn 2,*
WhoHol B
Noonan, Tommy d1968 *MotPP, WhoHol B*
Noonan, Tommy 1921-1968 *FilmgC*
Noonan, Tommy 1922-1968 *NotNAT B,*
WhScrn 1, WhScrn 2
Noone, Peter *WhoHol A*
Norcross, Frank 1856-1926 *NotNAT B,*
WhScrn 1, WhScrn 2, WhoHol B
Norcross, Hale d1947 *NotNAT B*
Norcross, Joseph M d1925 *NotNAT B*
Nord, Paul *REnWD*
Norden, Christine 1923- *FilmgC*
Norden, Cliff 1923-1949 *WhScrn 1, WhScrn 2*
Norden, Elfrida 1916- *AmSCAP 1966*
Norden, Tommy *WhoHol A*
Nordgren, Erik 1913- *DcFM*

Nordica, Lillian *WhoStg 1906, WhoStg 1908*
Nordoff, Paul 1909- *AmSCAP 1966*
Nordstrom, Clarence 1893-1968 *NotNAT B,*
WhScrn 1, WhScrn 2, WhoHol B
Nordstrom, Frances *WhThe, WomWMM*
Nordstrom, Kristina *WomWMM B*
Nordstrom, Marie 1886- *WhoStg 1908*
Nordyke, Kenneth *Film 2*
Norfolk, Edgar 1893- *WhThe*
Norgate, Matthew 1901- *WhoThe 16*
Noriega, Manolo 1880-1961 *WhScrn 1,*
WhScrn 2
Norlin, Lloyd B 1918- *AmSCAP 1966*
Norlund, Evy *WhoHol A*
Norman, Amber *Film 2*
Norman, E B d1930 *NotNAT B*
Norman, Frank *PIP&P*
Norman, Frank 1930- *ConDr 1977*
Norman, Frank 1931- *CroCD, ModWD*
Norman, Fred 1910- *AmSCAP 1966*
Norman, Gertrude d1943 *Film 1, Film 2,*
WhoHol B
Norman, Gertrude 1848-1943 *WhScrn 1,*
WhScrn 2
Norman, Josephine 1904-1951 *Film 2, WhScrn 1,*
WhScrn 2, WhoHol B
Norman, Karyl George d1947 *NotNAT B*
Norman, Leslie 1911- *FilmgC*
Norman, Maidie *WhoHol A*
Norman, Norman J 1870-1941 *NotNAT B,*
WhThe
Norman, Norman V 1864-1943 *NotNAT B,*
WhThe
Norman, Theodore 1912- *AmSCAP 1966*
Norman, Thyrza 1884- *WhThe*
Normand, Mabel 1894-1930 *Film 1, Film 2,*
FilmgC, MotPP, MovMk, NotNAT B,
OxFilm, TwYS, TwYS A, WhScrn 1,
WhScrn 2, WhoHol B, WomWMM,
WorEnF
Normington, John 1937- *WhoHol A, WhoThe 16*
Norreys, Rose d1946 *NotNAT B*
Norrie, Anna d1957 *NotNAT B, WhoHol B*
Norris, Alexander *WhScrn 2*
Norris, Charles Glenn 1906- *IntMPA 1977*
Norris, Christopher *WhoHol A*
Norris, Edward 1910- *FilmgC, IntMPA 1977,*
WhoHol A
Norris, Ernest E d1935 *NotNAT B*
Norris, Karen *WhoHol A*
Norris, Kathi *IntMPA 1977*
Norris, Lee d1964 *NotNAT B*
Norris, Robert 1924- *IntMPA 1977*
Norris, William d1929 *Film 1, Film 2,*
WhoHol B
Norris, William 1870-1929 *NotNAT B,*
WhoStg 1906, WhoStg 1908
Norris, William 1872-1929 *WhScrn 1, WhScrn 2,*
WhThe
North, Alex 1910- *AmSCAP 1966, BiE&WWA,*
FilmgC, IntMPA 1977, NotNAT, WorEnF
North, Bob 1881-1936 *WhScrn 1, WhScrn 2*
North, Edmund H 1911- *CmMov, IntMPA 1977*
North, Jay 1952- *WhoHol A*
North, Jay 1953- *FilmgC*
North, Joe d1945 *WhoHol B*
North, John Ringling 1903- *AmSCAP 1966*
North, Joseph B 1874-1945 *WhScrn 1, WhScrn 2*
North, Michael *WhoHol A*
North, Sheree *IntMPA 1977, MotPP*
North, Sheree 1930- *WhoHol A*
North, Sheree 1933- *FilmgC*
North, Wilfred 1853-1935 *Film 2, WhoHol B*
North, Wilfrid 1853-1935 *TwYS A, WhScrn 1,*

WhScrn 2
North, Zeme WhoHol A
Northcott, John d1905 NotNAT B
Northcott, Richard 1871-1931 NotNAT B,
    WhThe
Northen, Michael 1921- WhoThe 16
Northrup, Harry S 1877-1936 Film 1, Film 2,
    MotPP, WhScrn 2
Northshield, Robert NewYTET
Norton, Barry 1905-1956 Film 2, MotPP,
    NotNAT B, TwYS, WhScrn 1, WhScrn 2,
    WhoHol B
Norton, Betty Film 1
Norton, Cecil A 1895-1955 WhScrn 1, WhScrn 2
Norton, Cliff WhoHol A
Norton, Edgar Film 2
Norton, Elda 1891-1947 WhScrn 1, WhScrn 2
Norton, Elliot 1903- BiE&WWA, CelR 3,
    NotNAT, WhoThe 16
Norton, Fletcher 1877-1941 Film 2, WhScrn 1,
    WhScrn 2, WhoHol B
Norton, Frederic d1946 Film 2, NotNAT B,
    WhThe
Norton, George A 1880-1923 AmSCAP 1966
Norton, Henry Field 1899-1945 WhScrn 1,
    WhScrn 2
Norton, Jack 1889-1958 FilmgC, MotPP, MovMk,
    NotNAT B, Vers A, WhScrn 1, WhScrn 2,
    WhoHol B
Norton, Judy WhoHol A
Norton, Ken WhoHol A
Norton, Lucille 1894-1959 WhScrn 1, WhScrn 2
Norton, Susan WomWMM B
Norton, Thomas 1532-1584 McGWD, NotNAT B,
    OxThe
Norton, William Film 2
Norvo, Kenneth 1908- AmSCAP 1966
Norwid, Cyprian Kamil 1821-1883 CnThe, OxThe,
    REnWD
Norwood, Eille d1948 CmMov, WhoHol B
Norwood, Eille 1841-1948 Film 1
Norwood, Eille 1861-1948 NotNAT B, WhThe
Norwood, Ellie 1841-1948 Film 2
Norworth, Jack 1879-1959 AmSCAP 1966,
    EncMT, Film 2, NotNAT B, OxThe,
    WhScrn 1, WhScrn 2, WhThe, WhoHol B
Norworth, Ned 1889-1940 WhScrn 1, WhScrn 2
Nossack, Hans Erich 1901- CnMD
Nosseck, Max 1902-1972 FilmgC, IntMPA 1977,
    WhScrn 2
Notari, Guido 1894-1957 WhScrn 1, WhScrn 2,
    WhoHol B
Noto, Clara B WomWMM B
Noto, Lore 1923- BiE&WWA, NotNAT
Noto, Pat 1922- AmSCAP 1966
Nott, Cicely d1900 NotNAT B
Nourse, Allen WhoHol A
Nourse, Dorothy Film 2
Nova, Alex Film 2
Nova, Hedda Film 1, Film 2, TwYS
Nova, Lou 1920?- BiE&WWA, NotNAT,
    WhoHol A
Novack, Shelly WhoHol A
Novak, Eva 1899- Film 1, Film 2, FilmgC,
    TwYS, WhoHol A
Novak, Jane 1896- Film 1, Film 2, FilmgC,
    MotPP, TwYS, WhoHol A
Novak, Kim 1933- FilmgC, IntMPA 1977,
    MotPP, MovMk, OxFilm, WhoHol A,
    WorEnF
Novak, Robert 1931- CelR 3
Novarro, Ramon 1889-1968 MovMk
Novarro, Ramon 1899-1968 Film 1, Film 2,
    FilmgC, MotPP, OxFilm, TwYS, WhScrn 1,

WhScrn 2, WhoHol B, WorEnF
Novarro, Ramon 1905-1968 CmMov
Novas, Himilce WomWMM B
Novelli, Anthony Film 1, Film 2
Novelli, Antonio d1919 WhoHol B
Novelli, Augusto 1867-1927 McGWD
Novelli, Ermete 1851-1919 NotNAT B, OxThe,
    WhoStg 1908
Novello, Eugene 1912- AmSCAP 1966
Novello, Ivor 1893-1951 CnThe, EncMT, Film 2,
    FilmgC, McGWD, ModWD, MotPP,
    NotNAT A, NotNAT B, OxThe, WhScrn 1,
    WhScrn 2, WhThe, WhoHol B
Novello, Jay 1904- FilmgC, Vers B, WhoHol A
Noverre, Jean Georges 1727-1810 NotNAT A
Novinsky, Alexander 1878-1960 WhScrn 2
Novis, Donald 1907-1966 WhScrn 1, WhScrn 2,
    WhoHol B
Novius OxThe
Nowaczynski, Adolf 1876-1944 CnMD, ModWD
Nowell, Wedgewood 1878-1957 Film 1, TwYS,
    WhScrn 1, WhScrn 2
Nowell, Wedgwood 1878-1957 Film 2, WhoHol B
Nowlan, George 1925- AmSCAP 1966
Nox, Andre Film 2
Noxon, Nicolas NewYTET
Noy, Wilfred Film 2
Noyes, Joseph 1869-1936 WhScrn 1, WhScrn 2
Noyes, Thomas 1922- BiE&WWA, NotNAT
Noziere, Fernand 1874-1931 McGWD,
    NotNAT B, WhThe
Ntshona, Winston PlP&P A
Nuemann, Charles 1873-1927 WhScrn 1,
    WhScrn 2
Nugent, Carol WhoHol A
Nugent, Eddie 1904- Film 2
Nugent, Edward 1904- TwYS
Nugent, Edward Eddie WhoHol A
Nugent, Elliot 1900- MovMk
Nugent, Elliott 1899- BiE&WWA, ConDr 1977,
    Film 2, FilmgC, McGWD, NotNAT,
    NotNAT A, WhThe, WhoHol A
Nugent, Elliott 1900- CnMD, IntMPA 1977,
    ModWD, WorEnF
Nugent, Frank S 1908-1965 CmMov
Nugent, Frank S 1908-1966 FilmgC, WorEnF
Nugent, J C 1875-1947 WhScrn 1, WhScrn 2,
    WhoHol B
Nugent, John Charles 1878-1947 NotNAT A,
    NotNAT B, WhThe
Nugent, Moya 1901-1954 NotNAT B, WhThe
Nugent, Nancy 1933- BiE&WWA
Nugent, Nancy 1938- NotNAT
Numes, Armand d1933 NotNAT B
Nunes, Leon d1911 NotNAT B
Nunes, Maxine WomWMM
Nunez, Juan Manuel d1966 WhScrn 2
Nunez DeArce, Gaspar 1834-1903 McGWD
Nunn, Alice WhoHol A
Nunn, Trevor 1940- CnThe, WhoThe 16
Nunn, Wayne 1881-1947 WhScrn 2
Nureyev, Rudolf 1938- CelR 3, WhoHol A
Nuyen, France 1939- BiE&WWA, FilmgC,
    MotPP, WhoHol A
Nyby, Christian 1919- FilmgC
Nye, Carrie BiE&WWA, NotNAT, WhoHol A,
    WhoThe 16
Nye, Carroll 1901-1968 TwYS
Nye, Carroll 1901-1974 Film 2, WhScrn 2,
    WhoHol B
Nye, G Raymond Film 1, Film 2
Nye, Louis WhoHol A
Nye, Pat 1908- WhoHol A, WhoThe 16
Nye, Tom F d1925 NotNAT B

Nyitray, Emil d1922 *NotNAT B*
Nykvist, Sven 1922- *DcFM, FilmgC,*
  IntMPA 1977, WorEnF
Nykvist, Sven 1923- *OxFilm*
Nyla *Film 2*
Nype, Russell 1924- *BiE&WWA, EncMT,*
  NotNAT, WhoHol A, WhoThe 16
Nyren, David O 1924- *IntMPA 1977*
Nyro, Laura 1947- *CelR 3*
Nystrom, Alf 1927- *AmSCAP 1966*

O

Oaker, Jane 1880- *WhThe, WhoStg 1908*
Oaker, John *Film 1*
Oakes, Sarah Lawrence *WomWMM B*
Oakes, Tom 1896- *AmSCAP 1966*
Oakie, Jack 1903- *CmMov, Film 2, FilmgC, HolP 30, IntMPA 1977, MotPP, MovMk, TwYS, WhoHol A*
Oakland, Ben 1907- *AmSCAP 1966*
Oakland, Ethel Mary *Film 1*
Oakland, Simon 1922- *FilmgC, IntMPA 1977, WhoHol A*
Oakland, Vivian 1895-1958 *FilmgC, TwYS, WhoHol B*
Oakland, Vivien 1895-1958 *Film 2, WhScrn 1, WhScrn 2*
Oakland, Will 1883-1956 *NotNAT B, WhScrn 1, WhScrn 2, WhoHol B*
Oakley, Annie d1926 *Film 1, WhoHol B*
Oakley, Annie 1859-1926 *FilmgC*
Oakley, Annie 1860-1926 *WhScrn 2*
Oakley, Annie 1866-1926 *NotNAT A*
Oakley, Florence 1891-1956 *Film 2, WhScrn 1, WhScrn 2, WhoHol B*
Oakley, Laura 1879-1957 *Film 1, WhScrn 2*
Oakman, Wheeler 1890-1949 *Film 1, Film 2, NotNAT B, TwYS, WhScrn 1, WhScrn 2, WhoHol B*
Oates, Cicely d1934 *NotNAT B, WhoHol B*
Oates, Cicely d1935 *WhScrn 2*
Oates, Joyce Carol 1938- *CelR 3*
Oates, Warren 1932- *CmMov, FilmgC, IntMPA 1977, MovMk, WhoHol A*
Obaldia, Rene De 1918- *CnMD Sup, CroCD, ModWD*
O'Beck, Fred 1881-1929 *Film 2, WhScrn 1, WhScrn 2, WhoHol B*
Obelensky, W *Film 2*
Ober, Christine *WomWMM B*
Ober, George d1912 *WhScrn 2*
Ober, Harold d1959 *NotNAT B*
Ober, Kirt 1875-1939 *WhScrn 1, WhScrn 2*
Ober, Philip 1902- *BiE&WWA, FilmgC, IntMPA 1977, NotNAT, Vers A, WhThe, WhoHol A*
Ober, Robert d1950 *Film 2, WhoHol B*
Ober, Robert 1881-1950 *NotNAT B, WhoStg 1908*
Ober, Robert 1882-1950 *WhScrn 1, WhScrn 2*
Oberg, Gustav *Film 2*
Oberhaus, Patricia *WomWMM B*
Oberle, Florence 1870-1943 *Film 2, WhScrn 1, WhScrn 2, WhoHol B*
Oberle, Thomas d1906 *NotNAT B*
Oberlin, James 1931-1962 *WhScrn 2*
Oberlin, Richard 1928- *NotNAT*
Oberon, Merle *MotPP, WomWMM*

Oberon, Merle 1911- *CmMov, FilmgC, MovMk, OxFilm, ThFT, WhoHol A, WorEnF*
Oberon, Merle 1915?- *CelR 3*
Oberon, Merle 1919- *IntMPA 1977*
Obey, Andre 1892-1975 *CnMD, CnThe, McGWD, ModWD, OxThe, WhThe*
Obolensky, Serge 1890- *CelR 3*
Oboler, Arch *IntMPA 1977*
Oboler, Arch 1907- *CnMD, ModWD*
Oboler, Arch 1909- *BiE&WWA, DcFM, FilmgC, NotNAT, WorEnF*
O'Brady, Frederic *NotNAT A*
Obraztsov, Sergei Vladimirovich 1901- *OxThe, WhThe*
O'Brian, Hugh *AmSCAP 1966, MotPP, WhoHol A*
O'Brian, Hugh 1925- *CelR 3, FilmgC, MovMk, WhoThe 16*
O'Brian, Hugh 1928- *BiE&WWA*
O'Brian, Hugh 1930- *IntMPA 1977*
O'Brian, Jack 1914- *IntMPA 1977*
O'Brian, Peter 1947- *IntMPA 1977*
O'Brien, Barry 1893-1961 *Film 1, NotNAT B, WhThe, WhoHol B*
O'Brien, Bill *Film 2*
O'Brien, Chet 1911- *BiE&WWA, WhoHol A*
O'Brien, Clay *WhoHol A*
O'Brien, Dave 1912-1969 *FilmgC, Vers B, WhoHol B*
O'Brien, David 1912-1969 *WhScrn 1, WhScrn 2*
O'Brien, David 1930- *WhThe*
O'Brien, Donnell d1970 *WhScrn 1, WhScrn 2, WhoHol B*
O'Brien, Edmond 1915- *FilmgC, IntMPA 1977, MotPP, MovMk, OxFilm, WhoHol A, WorEnF*
O'Brien, Erin *WhoHol A*
O'Brien, Eugene 1882-1966 *Film 1, Film 2, MotPP, TwYS, WhScrn 1, WhScrn 2, WhoHol B*
O'Brien, Frank *WhoHol A*
O'Brien, George 1900- *CmMov, Film 2, FilmgC, IntMPA 1977, MotPP, MovMk, TwYS, WhoHol A, WorEnF*
O'Brien, Gypsy *Film 2*
O'Brien, Hortense *Film 2*
O'Brien, Jack *Film 2*
O'Brien, Joan *WhoHol A*
O'Brien, John *Film 2*
O'Brien, John Roger 1904- *AmSCAP 1966*
O'Brien, Justin 1906-1968 *NotNAT B*
O'Brien, Kate 1897-1974 *BiE&WWA, NotNAT B, WhThe*
O'Brien, Liam 1913- *BiE&WWA, IntMPA 1977, NotNAT*
O'Brien, Margaret 1937- *FilmgC, IntMPA 1977,*

319

MGM, MotPP, MovMk, WhoHol A,
WorEnF
O'Brien, Maria *WhoHol A*
O'Brien, Marianne *WhoHol A*
O'Brien, Mary *Film 2*
O'Brien, Maureen 1943- *WhoThe 16*
O'Brien, Neil d1909 *NotNAT B*
O'Brien, Pat 1899- *BiE&WWA, Film 2, FilmgC,*
IntMPA 1977, MotPP, MovMk, NotNAT,
NotNAT A, OxFilm, TwYS, WhoHol A
O'Brien, Richard *WhoHol A*
O'Brien, Rory *WhoHol A*
O'Brien, Shots 1895-1961 *WhScrn 1, WhScrn 2*
O'Brien, Sylvia *WhoHol A*
O'Brien, Teddy *WhoHol A*
O'Brien, Terence 1887-1970 *WhThe*
O'Brien, Timothy 1929- *WhoThe 16*
O'Brien, Tom 1891-1947 *WhScrn 1, WhScrn 2,*
WhoHol B
O'Brien, Tom 1898- *Film 2, TwYS*
O'Brien, Vince *WhoHol A*
O'Brien, Virginia *IntMPA 1977, WhoHol A*
O'Brien, Virginia 1896- *WhThe*
O'Brien, Virginia 1921- *FilmgC*
O'Brien, Virginia 1922- *MGM, MovMk*
O'Brien, William d1815 *NotNAT B*
O'Brien, Willis 1886-1962 *CmMov, FilmgC*
O'Brien-Moore, Erin 1908- *ThFT, WhThe,*
WhoHol A
O'Bryen, W J 1898- *WhThe*
O'Bryne, Patsy 1886-1968 *WhoHol B*
O'Burrell, James *Film 1*
O'Byrne, Bryan *WhoHol A*
O'Byrne, Patsy 1886-1968 *Film 2, WhScrn 1,*
WhScrn 2
O'Callaghan, Ed *WhoHol A*
O'Callaghan, Richard 1940- *WhoHol A,*
WhoThe 16
O'Casey, Sean 1880-1964 *BiE&WWA, CnThe,*
CroCD, FilmgC, McGWD, ModWD,
NotNAT A, NotNAT B, OxThe, PIP&P,
REnWD, WhThe
O'Casey, Sean 1884-1964 *CnMD*
Ocasio, Joe *WhoHol A*
Ochs, Al d1964 *NotNAT B*
Ochs, Lillian d1964 *NotNAT B*
Ochs, Phil 1940- *AmSCAP 1966*
Ocko, Dan *WhoHol A*
O'Connell, Arthur 1908- *BiE&WWA, FilmgC,*
IntMPA 1977, MovMk, NotNAT,
WhoHol A, WhoThe 16
O'Connell, Bob *WhoHol A*
O'Connell, Gerald 1904- *BiE&WWA*
O'Connell, Helen *WhoHol A*
O'Connell, Hugh 1898-1943 *NotNAT B,*
WhScrn 1, WhScrn 2, WhThe, WhoHol B
O'Connell, L William 1890- *WorEnF*
O'Connell, Louis P 1895- *AmSCAP 1966*
O'Connell, Patrick *WhoHol A*
O'Connell, William *WhoHol A*
O'Conner, Edward 1862-1932 *WhScrn 2*
O'Connolly, Jim 1926- *FilmgC*
O'Connor, Bill 1919- *WhThe*
O'Connor, Carroll *WhoHol A*
O'Connor, Carroll 1922- *FilmgC*
O'Connor, Carroll 1923- *MovMk*
O'Connor, Carroll 1925- *CelR 3, IntMPA 1977*
O'Connor, Charles William 1878-1955 *NotNAT B,*
WhThe
O'Connor, Darren *WhoHol A*
O'Connor, Donald 1925- *AmSCAP 1966, CmMov,*
FilmgC, HolP 40, IntMPA 1977, MotPP,
MovMk, OxFilm, WhoHol A, WorEnF
O'Connor, Edward *Film 1, Film 2*

O'Connor, Edwin 1918-1968 *NotNAT B*
O'Connor, Frank 1888-1959 *TwYS A, WhScrn 1,*
WhScrn 2, WhoHol B
O'Connor, Frank 1903-1966 *CnMD, NotNAT B*
O'Connor, Giles 1908- *AmSCAP 1966*
O'Connor, Glynnis *WhoHol A*
O'Connor, Harry M 1873-1971 *WhScrn 1,*
WhScrn 2, WhoHol B
O'Connor, James *Film 1*
O'Connor, James F d1963 *NotNAT B*
O'Connor, John 1874-1941 *WhScrn 1, WhScrn 2,*
WhoHol B
O'Connor, John J 1933- *WhThe*
O'Connor, Kathleen 1897-1957 *Film 1, Film 2,*
WhScrn 1, WhScrn 2, WhoHol B
O'Connor, Kathryn 1894-1965 *WhScrn 1,*
WhScrn 2, WhoHol B
O'Connor, Kevin 1938- *NotNAT, WhoHol A,*
WhoThe 16
O'Connor, L J 1880-1959 *Film 2, WhoHol B*
O'Connor, Louis J 1880-1959 *WhScrn 1,*
WhScrn 2
O'Connor, Loyola *Film 1*
O'Connor, Robert d1947 *NotNAT B*
O'Connor, Robert Emmett 1885-1962 *Film 1,*
Film 2, FilmgC, NotNAT B, TwYS,
WhScrn 1, WhScrn 2, WhoHol B
O'Connor, Rod d1964 *NotNAT B*
O'Connor, Una d1959 *MotPP, WhoHol B*
O'Connor, Una 1880-1959 *NotNAT B, ThFT,*
WhScrn 1, WhScrn 2
O'Connor, Una 1881-1959 *MovMk*
O'Connor, Una 1893-1959 *Film 2, FilmgC,*
Vers A, WhThe
O'Connor, Joseph *WhoHol A*
O'Conor, Joseph 1910?- *FilmgC*
O'Conor, Joseph 1916- *McGWD, WhoThe 16*
O'Daly, Cormac d1949 *NotNAT B*
O'Dare, Eileen *Film 2*
O'Dare, Peggy *Film 1, Film 2, TwYS*
O'Day, Alice d1937 *NotNAT B*
O'Day, Anita *WhoHol A*
O'Day, Dawn 1918- *Film 2, MotPP, MovMk,*
TwYS, WhoHol A
O'Day, Molly 1911- *Film 2, TwYS, WhoHol A*
O'Day, Peggy 1900-1964 *Film 2, WhScrn 1,*
WhScrn 2, WhoHol B
O'Dea, Denis 1905- *FilmgC, WhThe, WhoHol A*
O'Dea, Jimmy 1899-1965 *WhScrn 1, WhScrn 2,*
WhoHol B
O'Dea, Joseph 1903-1968 *WhScrn 1, WhScrn 2,*
WhoHol B
O'Dell, Digger 1904-1957 *WhScrn 1, WhScrn 2,*
WhoHol B
Odell, E J d1928 *NotNAT B*
O'Dell, Garry *Film 2*
Odell, George *Film 1*
Odell, George Clinton Densmore 1866-1949
NotNAT B, WhThe
Odell, Maude d1937 *NotNAT B*
O'Dell, Seymour H 1863-1937 *WhScrn 1,*
WhScrn 2
Odell, Shorty 1874?-1924 *WhScrn 1, WhScrn 2*
Odell, Thomas d1749 *NotNAT B*
Odemar, Fritz 1890-1955 *WhScrn 1, WhScrn 2*
O'Dempsey, Brigit d1952 *NotNAT B*
O'Denishawn, Florence *Film 2*
Odets, Clifford 1903-1963 *FilmgC*
Odets, Clifford 1906-1963 *CnMD, CnThe,*
CroCD, DcFM, McGWD, ModWD,
NotNAT A, NotNAT B, OxFilm, OxThe,
PIP&P, REnWD, WhThe, WorEnF
Odetta *WhoHol A*
Odette, Mary 1901- *Film 1, Film 2, FilmgC,*

WhThe, WhoHol A
Odilon, Helene d1939 NotNAT B
Odin, Susan d1975 WhScrn 2, WhoHol C
Odingsells, Gabriel d1734 NotNAT B
O'Doherty, Eileen 1891- WhThe
O'Doherty, Mignon 1890-1961 WhThe
Odom, Selma WomWMM B
O'Donnell, Cathy d1970 MotPP, WhoHol B
O'Donnell, Cathy 1923-1970 FilmgC
O'Donnell, Cathy 1925-1970 WhScrn 1,
    WhScrn 2
O'Donnell, Charles H 1886-1962 NotNAT B,
    WhScrn 1, WhScrn 2
O'Donnell, Gene WhoHol A
O'Donnell, Maire WhoHol A
O'Donnell, Richard 1932- NatPD
O'Donnell, Spec 1911- Film 2, TwYS
O'Donnell, William IntMPA 1977
O'Donovan, Desmond 1933- WhoThe 16
O'Donovan, Elizabeth WhoHol A
O'Donovan, Frank 1900-1974 WhScrn 2,
    WhoHol B
O'Donovan, Fred 1889-1952 NotNAT B, WhThe,
    WhoHol B
O'Dowd, Mike WhoHol A
O'Driscoll, Martha 1922- FilmgC, WhoHol A
O'Dunn, Irvin 1904-1933 WhScrn 1, WhScrn 2
Oehlenschlaeger, Adam Gottlob 1779-1850
    NotNAT B, OxThe
Oehlenschlager, Adam 1779-1850 McGWD,
    REnWD
Oelrichs, Blanche d1950 NotNAT B
Oelschlegel, Gerd 1926- CnMD, McGWD,
    ModWD
Oenslager, Donald Mitchell 1902-1975 BiE&WWA,
    NotNAT B, OxThe, PIP&P, WhThe
Oestreicher, Gerard 1916- BiE&WWA, NotNAT
Oettel, Wally Film 2
Oettinger, Nancy WomWMM
O'Farrell, Bernadette 1926- FilmgC, WhoHol A
O'Farrell, Broderick Film 2
O'Farrell, Mary 1892-1968 WhThe, WhoHol B
O'Farrell, Talbot d1952 NotNAT B
O'Farrill, Arturo 1921- AmSCAP 1966
Offenbach, Jacques 1819-1880 NotNAT B,
    PIP&P
Offenbach, Joseph 1905-1971 WhScrn 1,
    WhScrn 2
Offenhauser, William H, Jr. 1904- IntMPA 1977
Offerman, George Film 2
Offerman, George, Jr. 1917-1963 NotNAT B,
    Vers B, WhScrn 1, WhScrn 2, WhoHol B
Offerman, George, Sr. 1880-1938 NotNAT B,
    WhScrn 1, WhScrn 2, WhoHol B
Offerman, Marie 1894-1950 WhScrn 1,
    WhScrn 2, WhoHol B
Offner, Debbie PIP&P
Offord, Bert Film 2
Oflazoglu, Turan 1932- REnWD
O'Flynn, Carol Comer 1944- AmSCAP 1966
O'Flynn, Charles 1897-1964 AmSCAP 1966
O'Flynn, Damian WhoHol A
O'Flynn, Honoria 1909- AmSCAP 1966
O'Flynn, Philip WhoHol A
O'Fredericks, Alice WomWMM
Ofugi, Naburo d1960 DcFM
O'Gatty, Jimmy Packy 1899-1966 WhScrn 2
Ogden, Rita WomWMM
Ogden, Vivia d1953 Film 1, Film 2, WhScrn 2
Ogilvie, George 1931- WhoThe 16
Ogilvie, Glencairn Stuart 1858-1932 NotNAT B,
    WhThe
Ogilvie, Ruth Simmons 1920- AmSCAP 1966
Ogilvy, Ian 1943- FilmgC, WhoHol A

Ogle, Charles 1865-1926 FilmgC
Ogle, Charles 1865-1940 WhScrn 2, WhoHol B
Ogle, Charles 1875- Film 1, Film 2, TwYS
O'Grady, Monty Film 2
Ogrizovic, Milan 1877-1923 CnMD
O'Gyla, Cassandra WomWMM B
Oh Gran, Gilbert 1886-1971 WhScrn 2
Oh Gran Gilbert 1886-1971 WhScrn 1
O'Hanlon, George 1917- FilmgC, IntMPA 1977,
    WhoHol A
O'Hanlon, George, Jr. WhoHol A
O'Hanlon, James NewYTET
O'Hanlon, Redmond L d1964 NotNAT B
O'Hara, Barry WhoHol A
O'Hara, Fiske 1878-1945 NotNAT B, WhScrn 1,
    WhScrn 2, WhoHol B
O'Hara, Geoffrey 1882-1967 AmSCAP 1966
O'Hara, George 1899-1966 Film 2, WhScrn 2,
    WhoHol B
O'Hara, Gerry 1924- IntMPA 1977
O'Hara, Gerry 1925?- FilmgC
O'Hara, Jill 1947- EncMT, WhoHol A
O'Hara, Jim WhoHol A
O'Hara, John d1929 NotNAT B
O'Hara, John 1905- BiE&WWA, PIP&P
O'Hara, John 1905-1970 CnMD, NotNAT A,
    NotNAT B, WorEnF
O'Hara, John 1905-1972 FilmgC
O'Hara, Kane d1782 NotNAT B
O'Hara, Maureen 1920- CmMov, FilmgC,
    IntMPA 1977, MotPP, MovMk, OxFilm,
    ThFT, WhoHol A, WomWMM, WorEnF
O'Hara, Quinn WhoHol A
O'Hara, Shirley Film 2, WhoHol A
Ohardieno, Roger 1919-1959 WhScrn 1,
    WhScrn 2, WhoHol B
O'Hearn, Robert 1921- BiE&WWA, NotNAT
O'Herlihy, Dan 1919- FilmgC, IntMPA 1977,
    MovMk, WhoHol A
O'Herlihy, Michael 1929- FilmgC
O'Higgins, Harvey J 1876-1929 NotNAT B,
    WhThe
Ohio Roscius OxThe, PIP&P
Ohlson, Marion AmSCAP 1966
Ohman, Phil 1896-1954 AmSCAP 1966
Ohmart, Carol 1928- FilmgC, IntMPA 1977,
    MotPP, WhoHol A
Ohnet, Georges 1848-1918 McGWD, NotNAT B,
    OxThe, WhThe
O'Horgan, Tom IntMPA 1977, WhoThe 16
O'Horgan, Tom 1926- CelR 3, NotNAT
O'Horgan, Tom 1928- EncMT
Ohrn, Karen WomWMM B
Ohtani, Hiroshi 1910- IntMPA 1977
Ojeda, Jesus Chucho 1892-1943 WhScrn 1,
    WhScrn 2
O'Kalemo, Helen MotPP
O'Keefe, Allan J IntMPA 1977
O'Keefe, Arthur J 1874-1959 WhScrn 1,
    WhScrn 2
O'Keefe, Dennis 1908-1968 FilmgC, HolP 40,
    MotPP, MovMk, WhScrn 1, WhScrn 2,
    WhoHol B
O'Keefe, James Conrad 1892-1942 AmSCAP 1966
O'Keefe, Lester 1896- AmSCAP 1966
O'Keefe, Paul C WhoHol A
O'Keefe, Walter Michael 1900- AmSCAP 1966
O'Keeffe, Georgia 1887- CelR 3
O'Keeffe, John 1747-1833 NotNAT A,
    NotNAT B, OxThe
O'Kelly, Don WhScrn 2
O'Kelly, Seumas 1881-1918 REnWD
Okey, Jack d1963 NotNAT B
Okhlopkov, Nikolai Pavlovich 1900-1967 CnThe,

DcFM, OxThe, WhThe
Okon, Ted 1929- *IntMPA 1977*
Oktay Rifat 1914- *REnWD*
O'Kun, Lan 1932- *AmSCAP 1966*
Okun, Milton 1923- *AmSCAP 1966*
Olaf, Pierre 1928- *BiE&WWA, NotNAT,*
  WhoHol A, WhoThe 16
Oland, Warner 1880-1938 *CmMov, Film 1,*
  Film 2, FilmgC, MotPP, MovMk,
  NotNAT B, TwYS, WhScrn 1, WhScrn 2,
  WhThe, WhoHol B
Olanova, Olga *Film 1*
Olchansky, Adolf *Film 2*
Olcott, Chauncey 1858-1932 *NotNAT B*
Olcott, Chauncey 1860-1932 *AmSCAP 1966,*
  NotNAT A, WhThe, WhoStg 1906,
  WhoStg 1908
Olcott, Sidney 1873-1949 *Film 1, FilmgC,*
  NotNAT B, OxFilm, WhScrn 1, WhScrn 2,
  WhoHol B
Olcott, Sidney 1875-1949 *TwYS A*
Oldaker, Max 1908-1972 *WhScrn 2*
Oldenburg, Claes 1929- *CelR 3, ConDr 1977E*
Oldenburg, Richard 1933- *CelR 3*
Oldfield, Anne 1683-1730 *NotNAT A,*
  NotNAT B, OxThe, PIP&P
Oldfield, Barney d1946 *Film 1, WhoHol B*
Oldfield, Barney 1877-1946 *Film 2*
Oldfield, Barney 1878-1946 *FilmgC, WhScrn 1,*
  WhScrn 2
Oldham, Derek d1968 *WhoHol B*
Oldham, Derek 1892-1968 *NotNAT B, WhThe*
Oldham, Derek 1893-1968 *WhScrn 1, WhScrn 2*
Oldland, Lilian 1905- *Film 2, FilmgC, WhThe*
Oldmixon, Mrs. d1835 *NotNAT B, OxThe*
Oldmixon, Georgina *PIP&P*
Oldmixon, John d1742 *NotNAT B*
Oldmixon, Mrs. John d1836 *FamA&A*
Oldring, Rube 1885-1961 *WhScrn 2*
Olds, William Benjamin 1874-1948 *AmSCAP 1966*
O'Leary, Byron d1970 *WhoHol B*
O'Leary, John *WhoHol A*
O'Leary, John 1926- *NotNAT*
O'Leary, Patsy *Film 2*
Olembert, Theodora *IntMPA 1977*
Olenin, Boris Yulievich 1904-1961 *OxThe*
Olesen, Oscar 1916- *BiE&WWA, NotNAT*
Olesen, Otto K d1964 *NotNAT B*
Olesha, Yuri Karlovich 1899-1960 *CnMD, CnThe,*
  ModWD, REnWD
Olfson, Lewy *NatPD*
Olga, Duchess *WhScrn 1, WhScrn 2*
Olgina, Y *Film 2*
Olian, Helen *WomWMM B*
Oliffe, Geraldine *WhThe*
Olim, Dorothy 1934- *BiE&WWA, NotNAT*
Olin, Bob 1908-1956 *WhScrn 1, WhScrn 2*
Olin, Milton E 1913- *IntMPA 1977*
Oliphant, Jack 1895- *WhThe*
Oliva, Frank F 1904- *AmSCAP 1966*
Olivadoti, Joseph 1893- *AmSCAP 1966*
Olive, Edyth d1956 *NotNAT B, WhThe*
Olive, Joan *WomWMM B*
Oliveira, Manuel De 1905- *DcFM*
Oliver, Anthony 1923- *FilmgC, IntMPA 1977,*
  WhoHol A, WhoThe 16
Oliver, Barrie 1900- *WhThe*
Oliver, Eddie d1976 *WhoHol C*
Oliver, Eddie 1894- *BiE&WWA*
Oliver, Edith 1913- *BiE&WWA, NotNAT,*
  WhoThe 16
Oliver, Edna May d1942 *MotPP, WhoHol B*
Oliver, Edna May 1883-1942 *FilmgC, MovMk,*
  OxFilm, ThFT, TwYS, WhScrn 1,

Oliver, Edna May 1884-1942 *Film 2, Vers A*
Oliver, Edna May 1885-1942 *NotNAT B, WhThe*
Oliver, Fenwick *Film 2*
Oliver, Guy 1875-1932 *Film 1, Film 2, TwYS,*
  WhScrn 1, WhScrn 2, WhoHol B
Oliver, Larry 1880-1973 *WhScrn 2, WhoHol B*
Oliver, Madra Emogene 1905- *AmSCAP 1966*
Oliver, Olive d1961 *NotNAT B*
Oliver, Rochelle 1937- *BiE&WWA, NotNAT,*
  WhoHol A
Oliver, Sherling 1907-1971 *BiE&WWA*
Oliver, Shirling 1907-1971 *WhoHol B*
Oliver, Stephen *WhoHol A*
Oliver, Susan *MotPP, WhoHol A*
Oliver, Susan 1936- *BiE&WWA*
Oliver, Susan 1937- *FilmgC*
Oliver, Suzanne *WomWMM*
Oliver, Ted 1895-1957 *WhScrn 1, WhScrn 2,*
  WhoHol B
Oliver, Thelma *WhoHol A*
Oliver, Vic 1898-1964 *FilmgC, NotNAT A,*
  NotNAT B, WhScrn 1, WhScrn 2, WhThe,
  WhoHol B
Oliver, William I 1926- *BiE&WWA*
Olivette, Marie 1892-1959 *WhScrn 1, WhScrn 2,*
  WhoHol B
Olivette, Nina 1908-1971 *WhScrn 1, WhScrn 2,*
  WhoHol B
Olivier, Lord 1907- *IntMPA 1977*
Olivier, Sir Laurence 1907- *BiE&WWA, CelR 3,*
  CmMov, CnThe, DcFM, FamA&A, FilmgC,
  MotPP, MovMk, NotNAT, NotNAT A,
  OxFilm, OxThe, PIP&P, WhoHol A,
  WhoThe 16, WorEnF
Ollendorf, Paul d1920 *NotNAT B*
Ollivier, Paul *Film 2*
Olman, Abe 1888- *AmSCAP 1966*
Olmi, Ermanno 1931- *DcFM, FilmgC, OxFilm,*
  WorEnF
Olmo, Lauro 1922- *McGWD, ModWD*
Olmo, Lauro 1923- *CroCD*
Olmos, Pio d1965 *WhScrn 2*
Olmstead, Clarence 1892- *AmSCAP 1966*
Olmstead, Gertrude 1897-1975 *Film 2, TwYS*
Olmstead, Gertrude 1904-1975 *WhScrn 2*
Olmsted, Gertrude d1975 *WhoHol C*
O'Loughlin, Gerald Stuart 1921- *BiE&WWA,*
  IntMPA 1977, NotNAT, WhoHol A
Olsen, Christopher 1947- *WhoHol A*
Olsen, Ernst Bruun 1923- *CroCD*
Olsen, George 1893-1971 *Film 2, WhScrn 1,*
  WhScrn 2, WhoHol B
Olsen, Irene 1902-1931 *WhScrn 1, WhScrn 2*
Olsen, Larry 1939- *WhoHol A*
Olsen, Lauritz *Film 2*
Olsen, Moroni 1889-1954 *FilmgC, MotPP,*
  MovMk, NotNAT B, Vers A, WhScrn 1,
  WhScrn 2, WhoHol B
Olsen, Ole 1892-1963 *EncMT, MovMk,*
  NotNAT B, WhScrn 1, WhScrn 2, WhThe,
  WhoHol B
Olsen, Ole 1892-1965 *FilmgC*
Olsen, Stephen 1900-1946 *WhScrn 1, WhScrn 2*
Olsen, Susan 1961- *WhoHol A*
Olsen And Johnson *EncMT, WorEnF*
Olshanetsky, Alexander 1892- *AmSCAP 1966*
Olson, James 1932- *FilmgC, WhoHol A*
Olson, Mary *WomWMM*
Olson, Nancy 1928- *BiE&WWA, FilmgC,*
  IntMPA 1977, NotNAT, WhoHol A
Olson, Richard 1943- *NatPD*
Olson, Robert G 1913- *AmSCAP 1966*
Olsson, Fredrik *Film 2*

Olsson, Hagar 1893- *CroCD*
Olt, Arisztid *WhScrn 2*
Olufsen, Otto Carl 1764-1827 *OxThe*
Olver, Hal d1963 *NotNAT B*
Olvera, Ernesto Hill 1937-1967 *WhScrn 1,*
  WhScrn 2
O'Madigan, Isabel 1872-1951 *WhScrn 1,*
  WhScrn 2, WhoHol B
O'Maille, Kit *Film 2*
O'Malley, Aileen *Film 2*
O'Malley, Charles *Film 2*
O'Malley, Ellen d1961 *WhThe*
O'Malley, Francis K 1896- *AmSCAP 1966*
O'Malley, Grania 1898-1973 *WhScrn 2*
O'Malley, J Pat d1966 *WhoHol A*
O'Malley, J Pat 1901-1966 *FilmgC*
O'Malley, J Pat 1904-1966 *BiE&WWA, MovMk,*
  NotNAT
O'Malley, J Patrick 1890-1966 *Vers A*
O'Malley, J Patrick 1891-1966 *Film 1, Film 2*
O'Malley, James *Film 2*
O'Malley, John 1904-1945 *WhScrn 1, WhScrn 2,*
  WhoHol B
O'Malley, John P 1916-1959 *WhScrn 1,*
  WhScrn 2, WhoHol B
O'Malley, Kathleen *WhoHol A*
O'Malley, Pat d1966 *MotPP, WhoHol B*
O'Malley, Pat 1891-1966 *TwYS*
O'Malley, Pat 1892-1966 *WhScrn 1, WhScrn 2*
O'Malley, Rex 1901-1976 *BiE&WWA,*
  NotNAT B, WhThe, WhoHol A
O'Malley, Thomas E 1856-1926 *WhScrn 1,*
  WhScrn 2, WhoHol B
Oman, Julia Trevelyan 1930- *WhoThe 16*
O'Mara, Kate 1939- *FilmgC, WhoHol A,*
  WhoThe 16
Omatsu, Maryka *WomWMM*
Omens, Estelle *WhoHol A*
Omitsu *Film 2*
Ommerle, Harry G d1976 *NewYTET*
O'Moore, Barry 1880-1945 *Film 1, WhScrn 1,*
  WhScrn 2, WhoHol B
O'Moore, Patrick *WhoHol A*
O'Morrison, Kevin *NatPD, NotNAT*
Onassis, Aristotle 1906- *CelR 3*
Onassis, Jacqueline 1929- *CelR 3*
Ondek, Stephen 1899- *AmSCAP 1966*
Ondra, Anny 1903- *Film 2, FilmgC, OxFilm,*
  WhoHol A
Ondricek, Miroslav 1933- *WorEnF*
Ondricek, Miroslav 1934- *OxFilm*
One, Benny *Film 2*
O'Neal, Frederick 1905- *BiE&WWA, FilmgC,*
  IntMPA 1977, MotPP, MovMk, NotNAT,
  WhoHol A, WhoThe 16
O'Neal, John 1940- *NotNAT*
O'Neal, Kevin *WhoHol A*
O'Neal, Patrick 1927- *FilmgC, IntMPA 1977,*
  NotNAT, WhoHol A, WhoThe 16
O'Neal, Ron *IntMPA 1977, WhoHol A*
O'Neal, Ryan *WhoHol A*
O'Neal, Ryan 1941- *CelR 3, IntMPA 1977,*
  MovMk
O'Neal, Ryan 1945- *FilmgC*
O'Neal, Tatum *WhoHol A*
O'Neal, Tatum 1963- *MovMk*
O'Neal, Tatum 1964- *IntMPA 1977*
O'Neal, William *PIP&P*
O'Neal, William J 1898-1961 *WhScrn 1,*
  WhScrn 2
O'Neal, Zelma 1907- *EncMT, WhThe*
O'Neale, Margie 1923- *AmSCAP 1966*
O'Neil, Barbara 1903- *MovMk*
O'Neil, Barbara 1909- *FilmgC, WhoHol A*

O'Neil, Barbara 1910- *ThFT*
O'Neil, Colette 1895-1975 *WhScrn 2, WhoThe 16*
O'Neil, Colette *see also* O'Niel, Colette
O'Neil, George 1898-1940 *CnMD*
O'Neil, James *Film 2*
O'Neil, Jennifer 1947- *FilmgC*
O'Neil, Nance d1965 *MotPP, WhoHol B*
O'Neil, Nance 1874-1965 *BiE&WWA, FamA&A*
O'Neil, Nance 1875-1965 *Film 1, Film 2, TwYS,*
  WhScrn 1, WhScrn 2
O'Neil, Nance *see also* O'Neill, Nance
O'Neil, Nancy 1911- *WhThe*
O'Neil, Peggy 1898-1960 *NotNAT B, WhThe*
O'Neil, Sally d1968 *WhoHol B*
O'Neil, Sally 1908-1968 *MovMk*
O'Neil, Sally 1908-1969 *ThFT*
O'Neil, Sally 1910-1968 *Film 2, TwYS,*
  WhScrn 1, WhScrn 2
O'Neil, Sally 1913-1968 *FilmgC*
O'Neil, Sue *Film 2*
O'Neil, Thomas F 1915- *IntMPA 1977*
O'Neill, Dick *WhoHol A*
O'Neill, Edward *Film 2*
O'Neill, Eileen *WhoHol A*
O'Neill, Eliza 1791-1872 *OxThe*
O'Neill, Mrs. Eugene *PIP&P*
O'Neill, Eugene 1888-1953 *CnMD, CnThe,*
  CroCD, FilmgC, McGWD, ModWD,
  NotNAT A, NotNAT B, OxThe, PIP&P,
  PIP&P A, REnWD, WhThe
O'Neill, Frank B 1869-1959 *NotNAT B, WhThe*
O'Neill, Harry *Film 2*
O'Neill, Henry 1891-1961 *MotPP, PIP&P,*
  Vers A, WhScrn 1, WhScrn 2, WhThe,
  WhoHol B
O'Neill, Henry 1891-1964 *Film 2, FilmgC,*
  MovMk
O'Neill, Henry Joseph d1961 *NotNAT B*
O'Neill, Jack 1883-1957 *WhScrn 1, WhScrn 2*
O'Neill, James d1938 *WhScrn 2*
O'Neill, James 1847-1920 *FamA&A, Film 1,*
  FilmgC, NotNAT B, PIP&P, WhScrn 2
O'Neill, James 1849-1920 *WhThe, WhoStg 1906,*
  WhoStg 1908
O'Neill, James 1849-1938 *WhScrn 1, WhoHol B*
O'Neill, James, Jr. 1878-1923 *NotNAT B,*
  WhScrn 2, WhoHol B
O'Neill, James, Jr. 1920- *BiE&WWA*
O'Neill, James C 1876-1944 *WhScrn 2*
O'Neill, Jennifer *WhoHol A*
O'Neill, Jennifer 1947- *FilmgC*
O'Neill, Jennifer 1948- *MovMk*
O'Neill, Jimmy *WhoHol A*
O'Neill, Joseph J d1962 *NotNAT B*
O'Neill, Maire 1885-1952 *FilmgC, OxThe,*
  PIP&P, WhThe, WhoHol B
O'Neill, Marie 1885-1952 *Film 2, WhScrn 1,*
  WhScrn 2
O'Neill, Marie 1887-1952 *NotNAT A,*
  NotNAT B
O'Neill, Michael *ConDr 1977*
O'Neill, Mickey 1903-1932 *WhScrn 1, WhScrn 2*
O'Neill, Nance 1874-1965 *WhThe*
O'Neill, Nance 1875-1965 *WhoStg 1908*
O'Neill, Nance *see also* O'Neil, Nance
O'Neill, Norman 1875-1934 *NotNAT B, WhThe*
O'Neill, Norris 1939- *AmSCAP 1966*
O'Neill, Peggy 1924-1945 *WhScrn 1, WhScrn 2,*
  WhoHol B
O'Neill, Raymond *PIP&P*
O'Neill, Robert A 1911-1951 *WhScrn 1,*
  WhScrn 2, WhoHol B
O'Neill, Sally 1912-1968 *NotNAT B*
O'Neill, Selena 1899- *AmSCAP 1966*

O'Neill, Sheila 1930- *WhoHol A, WhoThe 16*
O'Neill, Thomas P 1912- *CelR 3*
Ong, Dana *Film 1*
O'Niel, Colette 1895-1975 *WhoHol C*
O'Niel, Colette *see also* O'Neil, Colette
Onions, Eileen *Film 2*
Onna, Ferdinand *Film 2*
Ono, Yoko 1933- *CelR 3, WomWMM A, WomWMM B*
Onodera, Sho d1974 *WhoHol B*
Onoe, Kikugoro 1885-1949 *NotNAT B*
Ontkean, Michael *WhoHol A*
Opatoshu, David *IntMPA 1977, WhoHol A*
Opatoshu, David 1918- *BiE&WWA, FilmgC, NotNAT, WhoThe 16*
Opatoshu, David 1919- *MovMk*
Openshaw, Charles Elton *WhThe*
Operti, LeRoi 1895-1971 *BiE&WWA, NotNAT B*
Ophuls, Marcel 1927- *OxFilm*
Ophuls, Max 1902-1957 *DcFM, FilmgC, MovMk, OxFilm, WorEnF*
Opitz, Martin 1597-1639 *CnThe, OxThe, REnWD*
Opler, Alfred M 1897- *AmSCAP 1966*
Opotowsky, Stan *IntMPA 1977*
Opp, Julie 1871-1921 *NotNAT B, WhThe*
Opp, Julie 1873-1921 *WhoStg 1906, WhoStg 1908*
Opp, Paul F 1894- *BiE&WWA, NotNAT*
Oppenheim, David 1889-1961 *AmSCAP 1966*
Oppenheim, Menasha d1973 *WhScrn 2, WhoHol B*
Oppenheimer, Alan *WhoHol A*
Oppenheimer, George 1900- *BiE&WWA, IntMPA 1977, NotNAT*
Oppenheimer, Jess 1913- *IntMPA 1977*
Oppenheimer, Joseph L 1927- *AmSCAP 1966*
Oppenheimer, Peer J *IntMPA 1977*
Opperman, Frank *Film 1*
O'Ramey, Georgia 1886-1928 *WhThe*
Orbach, Jerry 1935- *BiE&WWA, CelR 3, EncMT, NotNAT, WhoHol A, WhoThe 16*
Orbasany, Irma d1961 *NotNAT B*
Orben, Robert *NewYTET*
Orbison, Roy *WhoHol A*
Orchard, John *WhoHol A*
Orchard, Julian 1930- *FilmgC, WhoHol A, WhoThe 16*
Orczy, Baroness Emmuska d1947 *NotNAT B, WhThe*
Ord, Robert *WhThe*
Ord, Simon 1874-1944 *NotNAT B, WhThe*
Orde, Beryl 1912-1966 *WhScrn 1, WhScrn 2, WhoHol B*
Ordonneau, Maurice 1854-1916 *NotNAT B, WhThe*
Orduna, Juan 1908-1974 *WhScrn 2*
Ordway, Sally *NatPD*
Ordysnke, Richard *Film 1*
O'Reare, James *WhoHol A*
O'Regan, Katherine 1904- *Film 2*
O'Regan, Kathleen 1903- *WhThe*
O'Reilly, Erin *WhoHol A*
Orell, Felix *Film 2*
Orellana, Carlos 1901-1960 *WhScrn 1, WhScrn 2*
Orenstein, Larry 1918- *AmSCAP 1966*
Orent, Milton H 1918- *AmSCAP 1966*
Orentreich, Catherine *WomWMM B*
Oreste *FilmgC*
Orfyn, Wedad *WomWMM*
Orhan Kemal 1914-1970 *REnWD*
Oriani, Alfredo 1852-1909 *McGWD*
Orilo, V *Film 1*

Orio, C A 1912- *AmSCAP 1966*
Oriolo, Joseph 1913- *IntMPA 1977*
Orjasaeter, Tore 1886-1968 *REnWD*
Orkeny, Istvan 1912- *CroCD*
Orkin, Harvey 1918-1975 *NewYTET, WhScrn 2*
Orkin, Ruth *DcFM, WomWMM*
Orlamond, William 1867-1957 *Film 2, TwYS, WhScrn 2*
Orlamund, William 1867-1957 *Film 2*
Orland, William *Film 2*
Orlandi, Felice *WhoHol A*
Orlebeck, Lester 1907- *IntMPA 1977*
Orlenev, Pavel Nikolayevich 1869-1932 *OxThe*
Orlick, Philip 1940- *AmSCAP 1966*
Orlik, Ivan A Vanya 1898-1953 *WhScrn 1, WhScrn 2*
Orlob, Harold 1885- *AmSCAP 1966, BiE&WWA, NotNAT*
Orlova, Lyubov 1903-1975 *WhScrn 2, WhoHol C*
Orman, Felix 1884-1933 *WhScrn 1, WhScrn 2, WhoHol B*
Orman, Roscoe *WhoHol A*
Ormandy, Eugene 1889- *CelR 3*
Ormandy, Eugene 1899- *AmSCAP 1966*
Orme, Daphnnie 1889- *AmSCAP 1966*
Orme, Denise 1884-1960 *NotNAT B, WhThe*
Orme, Michael 1894-1944 *NotNAT B, WhThe*
Ormonde, Eugene *Film 1*
Ormont, David 1905- *AmSCAP 1966*
Orms, Howard R 1920- *BiE&WWA*
Ornbo, Robert 1931- *WhoThe 16*
Ornellas, Norman 1939-1975 *WhScrn 2, WhoHol C*
Ornish, Natalie 1926- *AmSCAP 1966*
Ornitz, Arthur J *FilmgC*
Ornstein, George H 1918- *IntMPA 1977*
Oro, Renee *WomWMM*
Orona, Vicente, Jr. 1931-1961 *WhScrn 1, WhScrn 2*
Oropeza, Andrew L 1908-1971 *WhScrn 2*
O'Rorke, Brefni 1889-1946 *NotNAT B, WhThe*
O'Rorke, Peggy *Film 2*
O'Rourke, Brefni 1889-1945 *FilmgC*
O'Rourke, Brefni 1889-1946 *WhScrn 1, WhScrn 2, WhoHol B*
O'Rourke, Eugene 1863- *WhoStg 1908*
O'Rourke, J A d1937 *NotNAT B, WhoHol B*
O'Rourke, John J 1922- *IntMPA 1977*
O'Rourke, Tex d1963 *NotNAT B*
O'Rourke, Thomas 1872-1958 *WhScrn 1, WhScrn 2*
O'Rourke, Tim 1933-1962 *WhScrn 1, WhScrn 2*
Orr, Bobby 1948- *CelR 3*
Orr, Christine d1963 *NotNAT B*
Orr, Forrest H d1963 *NotNAT B, WhScrn 2, WhoHol B*
Orr, Mary 1918- *BiE&WWA, NotNAT, WhoHol A, WhoThe 16*
Orr, William T 1917- *IntMPA 1977, NewYTET, WhoHol A*
Orraca, Juan 1911-1956 *WhScrn 1, WhScrn 2*
Orrery, Lord 1621-1679 *OxThe*
Orry-Kelly 1897-1964 *CmMov, FilmgC, NotNAT B*
Orsatti, Victor M 1905- *IntMPA 1977*
Orshan, H Allen 1925- *AmSCAP 1966*
Orsini, Valentino 1926- *WorEnF*
Orska, Marie d1930 *NotNAT B*
Ortega, Frankie 1927- *AmSCAP 1966*
Ortega, Sophie *Film 2*
Ortego, Art *Film 1*
Ortego, John *Film 1*
Ortes, Armand F 1880-1948 *WhScrn 1*
Orth, Frank 1880-1962 *FilmgC, MovMk,*

NotNAT B, Vers A, WhScrn 1, WhScrn 2, WhoHol B
Orth, Louise *Film 1, TwYS*
Orth, Marion *IntMPA 1977*
Orthwine, Rudolf *BiE&WWA*
Ortin, Leopoldo Chato 1893-1953 *WhScrn 1, WhScrn 2*
Ortiz, Thula 1894-1961 *WhScrn 1, WhScrn 2*
Orton, Joe 1933-1967 *CnThe, ConDr 1977F, CroCD, McGWD, ModWD, NotNAT B, REnWD*
Ory, Edward 1886-1973 *AmSCAP 1966*
Ory, Edward Kid 1887-1973 *WhScrn 2, WhoHol B*
Orzazewski, Kasia 1888-1956 *WhScrn 2*
Orzello, Harry 1940- *NotNAT*
Osato, Sono 1919- *BiE&WWA, NotNAT*
Osborn, Andrew 1912- *FilmgC, IntMPA 1977, WhoHol A*
Osborn, Arthur H 1884-1965 *AmSCAP 1966*
Osborn, E W 1860-1930 *NotNAT B, WhThe*
Osborn, Lyn 1923-1958 *WhScrn 1, WhoHol B*
Osborn, Lyn 1926-1958 *WhScrn 2*
Osborn, Paul 1901- *BiE&WWA, CnMD, McGWD, ModWD, NotNAT, WhThe, WorEnF*
Osborne, Baby Marie 1911- *Film 1, Film 2, TwYS*
Osborne, Baby Marie *see also* Baby Marie
Osborne, Billy *Film 2*
Osborne, Bud d1964 *WhoHol B*
Osborne, Hubert *PIP&P*
Osborne, Jefferson 1871-1932 *WhScrn 1, WhScrn 2*
Osborne, John 1929- *BiE&WWA, CelR 3, CnMD, CnThe, ConDr 1977, CroCD, FilmgC, IntMPA 1977, McGWD, ModWD, NotNAT, NotNAT A, OxFilm, OxThe, PIP&P, REnWD, WhoHol A, WhoThe 16, WorEnF*
Osborne, Kipp 1944- *WhoThe 16*
Osborne, Lennie Bud 1881-1964 *NotNAT B, WhScrn 1, WhScrn 2*
Osborne, Marie *WhoHol A*
Osborne, Miles Bud 1888-1964 *Film 1, Film 2, TwYS*
Osborne, Nat 1878-1954 *AmSCAP 1966*
Osborne, Vivienne 1896-1961 *ThFT, WhScrn 2*
Osborne, Vivienne 1900-1961 *Film 2, TwYS, WhoHol B*
Osborne, Vivienne 1905-1961 *WhThe*
Osborne, Will 1906- *AmSCAP 1966*
Osbourne, Lloyd d1947 *NotNAT B*
Oscar, Henry 1891-1969 *WhScrn 1, WhScrn 2, WhThe, WhoHol B*
Oscar, Henry 1891-1970 *FilmgC*
Oscard, Fifi 1921- *BiE&WWA*
Oscarsson, Per 1927- *FilmgC, WhoHol A*
Ose, Jay 1911-1967 *WhScrn 2*
Osgood, Charles d1922 *NotNAT B*
Osgood, Lawrence 1929- *ConDr 1977*
Osgood, Stanton M *IntMPA 1977*
O'Shaughnessy, John 1907- *BiE&WWA, NotNAT*
O'Shea, Black Jack 1906-1967 *Vers A, WhoHol B*
O'Shea, Danny *Film 2*
O'Shea, Dennis *Film 2*
O'Shea, Jack Blackjack 1906-1967 *WhScrn 1, WhScrn 2*
O'Shea, James J 1943- *AmSCAP 1966*
O'Shea, Michael *MotPP*
O'Shea, Michael 1906-1973 *FilmgC, WhScrn 2, WhoHol B*
O'Shea, Michael Sean 1922- *BiE&WWA*

O'Shea, Milo *WhoHol A*
O'Shea, Milo 1925- *MovMk*
O'Shea, Milo 1926- *FilmgC, NotNAT*
O'Shea, Oscar 1882-1960 *WhScrn 1, WhScrn 2, WhoHol B*
O'Shea, Tessie 1917- *FilmgC, WhoHol A*
Oshima, Nagisa 1932- *DcFM, OxFilm, WorEnF*
Oshins, Julie d1956 *NotNAT B, WhoHol B*
Osmond, Cliff *WhoHol A*
Osmond, Hal *WhoHol A*
Osmond, Miss V *Film 1*
Osser, Edna 1919- *AmSCAP 1966*
Osser, Glenn 1914- *AmSCAP 1966*
O'Steen, Sam *NewYTET*
Osterling, Eric 1926- *AmSCAP 1966*
Osterloh, Robert *WhoHol A*
Osterman, Jack 1902-1939 *WhScrn 2, WhoHol B*
Osterman, Kathryn 1883-1956 *NotNAT B, WhScrn 2*
Osterman, Lester 1914- *BiE&WWA, NotNAT, WhoThe 16*
Ostertag, Barna 1902- *BiE&WWA, NotNAT*
Ostertag, Sandy *WomWMM B*
Osterwa, Juliusz 1885-1947 *NotNAT B*
Osterwald, Bibi 1920- *BiE&WWA, NotNAT, WhoHol A, WhoThe 16*
Ostler, William *NotNAT B*
Ostler, William d1614 *OxThe, PIP&P*
Ostrer, Bertram 1913- *IntMPA 1977*
Ostriche, Muriel 1897- *Film 1, TwYS*
Ostrove, Michele Christine *WhoHol A*
Ostrovsky, Aleksandr 1823-1886 *McGWD*
Ostrovsky, Alexander 1823-1886 *CnThe, NotNAT B, OxThe, REnWD*
Ostrow, Herbert Ray 1911- *AmSCAP 1966*
Ostrow, Samuel 1919- *AmSCAP 1966*
Ostrow, Stuart 1932- *NotNAT, WhoThe 16*
O'Sullivan, Anthony d1920 *Film 1, WhScrn 1, WhScrn 2*
O'Sullivan, Kevin P 1928- *IntMPA 1977*
O'Sullivan, Maureen 1911- *BiE&WWA, CmMov, FilmgC, IntMPA 1977, MGM, MotPP, MovMk, OxFilm, ThFT, WhoHol A, WorEnF*
O'Sullivan, Maureen 1917- *WhoThe 16*
O'Sullivan, Michael 1934-1971 *WhScrn 1, WhScrn 2, WhoHol B*
O'Sullivan, Richard 1943- *FilmgC, WhoHol A*
O'Sullivan, Tony d1920 *WhoHol B*
Oswald, Genevieve 1923- *BiE&WWA, NotNAT*
Oswald, Gerd *IntMPA 1977*
Oswald, Gerd 1916- *FilmgC, MovMk*
Oswald, Gerd 1919- *WorEnF*
Oswald, Richard 1880-1963 *FilmgC, IntMPA 1977, WorEnF*
Oswald, Virginia 1926?- *BiE&WWA, NotNAT*
Oswalda, Ossi 1899-1948 *Film 2, WhScrn 2*
Otani, Takejiro 1877- *DcFM*
Otero, Caroline 1871- *WhoStg 1908*
Otis, Elita Proctor d1927 *Film 1, NotNAT B, WhoStg 1906, WhoStg 1908*
Otis, William R, Jr. *Film 2*
O'Toole, Peter *MotPP, PIP&P, WhoHol A*
O'Toole, Peter 1932- *CnThe, FilmgC, IntMPA 1977, MovMk, OxFilm, WhoThe 16*
O'Toole, Peter 1933- *CelR 3, WorEnF*
Otsep, Fyodor *DcFM*
Ott, Alexander 1888-1970 *WhScrn 2*
Ott, Fred 1860-1936 *Film 1, WhoHol B*
Ott, Frederick P 1860-1936 *WhScrn 1, WhScrn 2*
Ott, Warrene *WhoHol A*
Ottaway, James 1908- *WhoHol A, WhoThe 16*
Ottesen, Milton F 1920- *AmSCAP 1966*
Ottiano, Rafaela 1894-1942 *Film 2, FilmgC,*

ThFT, WhScrn 1, WhScrn 2, WhoHol B
Ottinger, Leonora *Film 2*
Otto, Arthur d1918 *WhScrn 2*
Otto, H C 1901- *AmSCAP 1966*
Otto, Henry 1878-1952 *Film 2, TwYS A,
WhScrn 1, WhScrn 2, WhoHol B*
Otto, Inga 1936- *AmSCAP 1966*
Otto, J Frank 1889- *AmSCAP 1966*
Otto, Paul *Film 2*
Otvos, A Dorian 1890-1945 *AmSCAP 1966*
Otway, Grace d1935 *NotNAT B*
Otway, Thomas 1651-1685 *NotNAT B*
Otway, Thomas 1652-1685 *CnThe, McGWD,
OxThe, PIP&P, REnWD*
Otwell, Ronnie Ray 1929- *IntMPA 1977*
Ouellette, Paul E 1927- *BiE&WWA*
Oughton, Winifred 1890-1964 *WhThe*
Ould, Herman 1886-1951 *CnMD*
Ould, Hermon 1885-1951 *NotNAT B, WhThe*
Ould, Hermon 1886-1951 *ModWD*
Oulton, Brian 1908- *FilmgC, WhoHol A,
WhoThe 16*
Oulton, W C d1820 *NotNAT B*
Our Gang Kids *Film 2*
Oursler, Fulton 1893-1952 *NotNAT B*
Oury, Gerard 1919- *FilmgC, WhoHol A*
Ousley, Timmy *WhoHol A*
Ouspenskaya, Maria 1876-1949 *Film 1, Film 2,
FilmgC, MotPP, MovMk, NotNAT B,
PIP&P, ThFT, Vers A, WhScrn 1,
WhScrn 2, WhThe, WhoHol B, WorEnF*
Ouville, Antoine LeMetel D' 1590?-1656? *OxThe*
Ovanin, Nikola Leonard 1911- *AmSCAP 1966*
Overall, Zan 1926- *AmSCAP 1966*
Overbeck, Bud d1970 *WhoHol B*
Overend, Dorothy *WhThe*
Overgard, Graham T 1903- *AmSCAP 1966*
Overman, Jack 1916-1950 *WhScrn 1, WhScrn 2,
WhoHol B*
Overman, Lynn *MotPP*
Overman, Lynne 1887-1943 *CmMov, FilmgC,
MovMk, NotNAT B, Vers B, WhScrn 1,
WhScrn 2, WhThe, WhoHol B*
Overskou, Thomas 1798-1873 *OxThe*
Overton, Evart *Film 1*
Overton, Frank 1918-1967 *BiE&WWA,
NotNAT B, WhScrn 1, WhScrn 2,
WhoHol B*
Ovey, George 1870-1951 *Film 1, Film 2,
WhScrn 2*
Owasso d1962 *WhScrn 2*
Owen, Alun 1925- *IntMPA 1977, WhoThe 16*
Owen, Alun 1926- *CnThe, ConDr 1977, CroCD,
McGWD*
Owen, Bill *WhoHol A*
Owen, Bill 1914- *FilmgC*
Owen, Bill 1915- *IntMPA 1977*
Owen, Bill 1916- *WhoThe 16*
Owen, Catherine Dale 1900-1965 *ThFT, WhThe*
Owen, Catherine Dale 1903-1965 *Film 2, MovMk,
WhScrn 1, WhScrn 2, WhoHol B*
Owen, Cliff 1919- *FilmgC*
Owen, Don 1934- *WorEnF*
Owen, Garry 1902-1951 *WhScrn 1, WhScrn 2,
WhoHol B*
Owen, Gary 1902-1951 *Vers A*
Owen, Harold 1872-1930 *NotNAT B, WhThe*
Owen, Harrison 1890- *WhThe*
Owen, Helen 1928- *AmSCAP 1966*
Owen, Milton d1969 *WhoHol B*
Owen, Reginald 1887-1972 *BiE&WWA, Film 2,
FilmgC, MGM, MotPP, MovMk,
NotNAT B, PIP&P, Vers A, WhScrn 2,
WhThe, WhoHol B*

Owen, Seena d1966 *MotPP, WhoHol B*
Owen, Seena 1894-1966 *FilmgC*
Owen, Seena 1895-1966 *Film 1, Film 2, TwYS*
Owen, Seena 1896-1966 *WhScrn 1, WhScrn 2*
Owen, Tudor *Film 2*
Owens, Bonnie *WhoHol A*
Owens, Buck 1929- *CelR 3*
Owens, D H 1892-1962 *AmSCAP 1966*
Owens, Daniel W *NatPD*
Owens, Gary 1936- *IntMPA 1977, WhoHol A*
Owens, Harry 1902- *AmSCAP 1966*
Owens, Jack 1912- *AmSCAP 1966*
Owens, John Edmond 1823-1886 *NotNAT A,
NotNAT B, OxThe*
Owens, Patricia 1925- *FilmgC, WhoHol A*
Owens, Peggy 1905-1931 *WhScrn 1, WhScrn 2*
Owens, Rochelle 1936- *ConDr 1977, CroCD,
NatPD, NotNAT, PIP&P, WhoThe 16*
Owens, William 1863-1926 *NotNAT B,
WhScrn 1, WhScrn 2, WhoHol B*
Owens, William H 1922- *BiE&WWA*
Owsley, B Bristow 1882- *AmSCAP 1966*
Owsley, Katherine N *AmSCAP 1966*
Owsley, Monroe 1901-1937 *Film 2, WhScrn 1,
WhScrn 2, WhoHol B*
Oxberry, John 1918- *IntMPA 1977*
Oxberry, William 1784-1824 *NotNAT B, OxThe*
Oxberry, William Henry 1808-1852 *NotNAT B,
OxThe*
Oxenberg, Jan *WomWMM B*
Oxenford, Edward d1929 *NotNAT B*
Oxenford, John 1812-1877 *NotNAT B*
Oxley, David 1929?- *FilmgC, WhoHol A*
Oxley, H R 1906- *IntMPA 1977*
Oxman, Philip *ConDr 1977B*
Oya, Ichijiro 1894-1972 *WhScrn 2*
Oyamo *NatPD*
Oyra, Jan 1888- *WhThe*
Oysher, Moishe 1907-1958 *NotNAT B,
WhScrn 1, WhScrn 2, WhoHol B*
Oysher, Moishe 1908-1958 *AmSCAP 1966*
Ozakman, Turgut 1930- *REnWD*
Ozell, John d1743 *NotNAT B*
Ozep, Fedor 1895-1948 *DcFM*
Ozep, Fedor 1895-1949 *FilmgC*
Ozerov, Vladislav Alexandrovich 1770-1816 *OxThe*
Ozu, Yasujiro 1903-1963 *DcFM, FilmgC, OxFilm,
WorEnF*

P

Paar, Jack 1918- *CelR 3, IntMPA 1977,*
  NewYTET, WhoHol A
Pabst, Georg Wilhelm 1885-1967 *DcFM, FilmgC,*
  MovMk, TwYS A, WhScrn 2
Pabst, Georg Wilhelm 1887-1967 *OxFilm*
Pabst, George Raymond 1916- *IntMPA 1977*
Pabst, George Wilhelm 1885-1967 *WorEnF*
Pace, Judy 1946- *FilmgC, WhoHol A*
Pace, Max 1906-1942 *WhScrn 1, WhScrn 2*
Pacino, Al *IntMPA 1977, WhoHol A*
Pacino, Al 1939- *FilmgC*
Pacino, Al 1940- *CelR 3, MovMk, WhoThe 16*
Pack, Lorenzo 1916- *AmSCAP 1966*
Pack, Norman *Film 2*
Packard, Albert 1909- *BiE&WWA*
Packard, Clayton L 1888-1931 *Film 2, WhScrn 1,*
  WhScrn 2, WhoHol B
Packard, Fred M 1919- *IntMPA 1977*
Packard, Vance 1914- *CelR 3*
Packard, William *NatPD*
Packer, Doris *WhoHol A*
Packer, Netta 1897-1962 *NotNAT B, WhScrn 1,*
  WhScrn 2, WhoHol B
Pacuvius, Marcus 220?BC-130BC *OxThe*
Padden, Sarah d1967 *Film 2, Vers B, WhScrn 2,*
  WhoHol B
Paddock, Charles *Film 2, TwYS*
Paddock, Robert Rowe 1914- *BiE&WWA*
Pade, Astrid *WomWMM*
Paderewski, Ignace Jan 1860-1941 *FilmgC,*
  WhScrn 1, WhScrn 2, WhoHol B
Padgen, Jack *Film 2*
Padgen, Leonard *Film 2*
Padilla, Ema 1900-1966 *WhScrn 1, WhScrn 2*
Padilla, Manuel, Jr. 1956- *WhoHol A*
Padjan, Jack 1888-1960 *WhScrn 2*
Padjan, John *Film 2*
Padovani, Lea 1920- *FilmgC, WhoHol A*
Padovano, John 1916-1973 *WhScrn 2, WhoHol B*
Padula, Edward 1916- *BiE&WWA, NotNAT*
Padula, Marguerita *Film 2*
Padula, Vincent 1900-1967 *WhScrn 2*
Padwa, Vladimir 1900- *AmSCAP 1966*
Pagani, Ernesto *Film 1, Film 2*
Pagano, Jo 1906- *IntMPA 1977*
Pagay, Sophie *Film 2*
Pagden, Leonard d1928 *NotNAT B*
Page, Anita 1910- *Film 2, MotPP, ThFT,*
  TwYS, WhoHol A
Page, Anthony 1935- *FilmgC, WhoThe 16*
Page, Arthur W 1885-1968 *WhScrn 2*
Page, Ashley d1934 *NotNAT B*
Page, Austin *WhThe*
Page, Curtis C 1914- *BiE&WWA*
Page, Don *WhScrn 1, WhScrn 2*
Page, Gale 1913- *FilmgC, ThFT, WhoHol A*

Page, Gale 1918- *IntMPA 1977, MovMk*
Page, Genevieve *WhoHol A*
Page, Genevieve 1930- *MovMk*
Page, Genevieve 1931- *FilmgC*
Page, Geraldine 1924- *BiE&WWA, CelR 3,*
  CnThe, FamA&A, FilmgC, IntMPA 1977,
  MotPP, MovMk, NotNAT, PIP&P,
  WhoHol A, WhoThe 16, WorEnF
Page, Helen *Film 2*
Page, James E 1870-1930 *Film 2, WhScrn 2*
Page, Joy Ann *WhoHol A*
Page, Louis 1905- *DcFM*
Page, Lucille 1871-1964 *WhScrn 1, WhScrn 2,*
  WhoHol B
Page, Nathaniel Clifford 1866-1956
  AmSCAP 1966
Page, Norman d1935 *Film 2, NotNAT B,*
  WhThe
Page, Patti 1927- *CelR 3, FilmgC,*
  IntMPA 1977, WhoHol A
Page, Paul 1903-1974 *Film 2, WhScrn 2,*
  WhoHol B
Page, Philip P 1889-1968 *NotNAT B, WhThe*
Page, Rita 1906-1954 *NotNAT B, WhScrn 2,*
  WhThe, WhoHol B
Page, Tilsa 1926- *WhThe*
Page, Will A d1928 *NotNAT B*
Paget, Alfred d1925 *Film 1, Film 2, TwYS,*
  WhScrn 2, WhoHol B
Paget, Cecil d1955 *NotNAT B, WhThe*
Paget, Debra 1933- *FilmgC, IntMPA 1977,*
  MotPP, MovMk, WhoHol A
Paget-Bowman, Cicely 1910- *WhoHol A,*
  WhoThe 16
Pagett, Gary *WhoHol A*
Pagett, Nicola 1945- *WhoThe 16*
Pagliaro, James Page 1902- *IntMPA 1977*
Pagliero, Marcello 1907- *DcFM, OxFilm,*
  WorEnF
Pagnol, Marcel 1895-1974 *BiE&WWA, CnMD,*
  DcFM, FilmgC, McGWD, ModWD,
  MovMk, NotNAT, A, NotNAT B, OxFilm,
  WhThe, WorEnF
Paia, John 1908-1954 *WhScrn 1, WhScrn 2*
Paich, Martin Louis 1925- *AmSCAP 1966*
Paige, Bob *IntMPA 1977*
Paige, Bob *see also* Paige, Robert
Paige, Janis *MotPP*
Paige, Janis 1922- *BiE&WWA, EncMT, FilmgC,*
  WhoHol A, WhoThe 16
Paige, Janis 1923- *HolP 40, IntMPA 1977,*
  MovMk, NotNAT
Paige, Jean *Film 2*
Paige, Leroy 1906- *CelR 3*
Paige, Mabel 1879-1954 *FilmgC*
Paige, Mabel 1880-1953 *MovMk*

327

Paige, Mabel 1880-1954 *NotNAT B, Vers A,*
    WhScrn 1, WhScrn 2, WhoHol B
Paige, Patsy *WhScrn 2*
Paige, Raymond 1900-1965 *WhScrn 2*
Paige, Robert 1910- *Film 2, FilmgC, HolP 40,*
    MotPP, WhoHol A
Paige, Robert *see also* Paige, Bob
Paige, Roger 1928- *AmSCAP 1966*
Paige, Sheila *WomWMM A, WomWMM B*
Paik, Nam June *NewYTET*
Pail, Edward *Film 1*
Pailleron, Edouard 1834-1899 *McGWD,*
    NotNAT B, OxThe
Paine, Charles F 1920- *IntMPA 1977*
Painleve, Jean 1902- *DcFM, FilmgC, OxFilm,*
    WorEnF
Painter, Eleanor 1890-1947 *NotNAT B, WhThe*
Paisley, William Merrell 1903- *AmSCAP 1966*
Paisner, Bruce *NewYTET*
Paisner, Dina *WhoHol A*
Paiva, Nestor 1905-1966 *FilmgC, MotPP, Vers A,*
    WhScrn 1, WhScrn 2, WhoHol B
Pakenham, Edward Arthur Henry *McGWD*
Pakula, Alan J 1928- *FilmgC, IntMPA 1977,*
    MovMk, OxFilm
Pal 1915-1929 *WhScrn 2*
Pal, George *IntMPA 1977*
Pal, George 1900- *DcFM*
Pal, George 1908- *CmMov, FilmgC, WorEnF*
Paladini, Ettore 1849- *WhThe*
Paladini-Ando, Celestina *WhThe*
Palamas, Costis *REnWD*
Palance, Jack *MotPP, WhoHol A*
Palance, Jack 1920- *CmMov, FilmgC,*
    IntMPA 1977, MovMk
Palance, Jack 1921- *CmMov, OxFilm, WorEnF*
Palange, Louis S 1917- *AmSCAP 1966*
Palaprat, Jean DeBigot 1650-1721 *McGWD,*
    OxThe
Palasthy, A *Film 2*
Palasty, Irene *Film 2*
Palerme, Gina *Film 2, WhThe*
Palermo, Alex 1929- *BiE&WWA, NotNAT*
Palette, Billy d1963 *NotNAT B*
Paletz, Darcy 1933- *WomWMM B*
Paley, Herman 1879-1955 *AmSCAP 1966*
Paley, William S 1901- *CelR 3, IntMPA 1977,*
    NewYTET
Palfi, Lotta *WhoHol A*
Palfrey, May Lever 1867-1929 *NotNAT B,*
    WhThe
Palladio, Andrea 1518-1580 *NotNAT B, OxThe,*
    PIP&P
Pallant, Walter d1904 *NotNAT B*
Pallante, Aladdin *WhScrn 1, WhScrn 2*
Pallenberg, Max 1877-1934 *NotNAT B, OxThe,*
    WhScrn 2
Pallette, Eugene 1889-1954 *Film 1, Film 2,*
    FilmgC, MotPP, MovMk, NotNAT B,
    OxFilm, TwYS, Vers A, WhScrn 1,
    WhScrn 2, WhoHol B
Pallos, Stephen 1902- *FilmgC*
Pallos, Steven *IntMPA 1977*
Pallotta, Lorraine 1934- *AmSCAP 1966*
Palm, Walter *Film 2*
Palma, Mona *Film 2*
Palmer, A H *PIP&P*
Palmer, Albert Marshman 1838-1905 *NotNAT B,*
    OxThe
Palmer, Anthony *WhoHol A*
Palmer, Archibald 1886- *AmSCAP 1966*
Palmer, Arnold 1929- *CelR 3*
Palmer, Barbara 1911- *WhThe*
Palmer, Belinda *WhoHol A*

Palmer, Betsy 1929- *BiE&WWA, FilmgC,*
    IntMPA 1977, MotPP, NewYTET, NotNAT,
    WhoHol A, WhoThe 16
Palmer, Bissell B 1889- *AmSCAP 1966*
Palmer, Bud 1923- *CelR 3*
Palmer, Byron *WhoHol A*
Palmer, Charles 1869-1920 *NotNAT B, WhThe*
Palmer, Charles Chuck d1976 *WhoHol C*
Palmer, Corliss *Film 2*
Palmer, Dawson 1937-1972 *WhScrn 2,*
    WhoHol B
Palmer, Edward 1930- *IntMPA 1977*
Palmer, Effie d1942 *WhScrn 1, WhScrn 2,*
    WhoHol B
Palmer, Ernest *CmMov*
Palmer, Ethelyn 1879- *WhoStg 1908*
Palmer, Gregg 1927- *FilmgC, IntMPA 1977,*
    WhoHol A
Palmer, Jack *AmSCAP 1966*
Palmer, John 1728-1768 *OxThe*
Palmer, John 1742-1798 *OxThe*
Palmer, John Leslie 1885-1944 *NotNAT B,*
    WhThe
Palmer, Lilli 1914- *FilmgC, IntMPA 1977,*
    MotPP, MovMk, NotNAT A, OxFilm,
    WhoHol A, WhoThe 16, WorEnF
Palmer, Lucile *AmSCAP 1966*
Palmer, Maria 1924- *FilmgC, IntMPA 1977,*
    WhoHol A
Palmer, Minnie 1857-1936 *WhThe*
Palmer, Minnie 1860-1936 *NotNAT B,*
    WhoStg 1908
Palmer, Patricia 1895-1964 *Film 2, WhScrn 2*
Palmer, Peter 1931- *BiE&WWA, FilmgC,*
    NotNAT, WhoHol A
Palmer, Robert *WhoHol A*
Palmer, Robert 1754-1817 *OxThe*
Palmer, Shirley *Film 2*
Palmer, Violet *Film 2*
Palmer, Willard A, Jr. 1917- *AmSCAP 1966*
Palmer, William d1797 *OxThe*
Palmer, William J 1890- *AmSCAP 1966*
Palmer, Zoe *Film 2*
Palmeri, Mimi *Film 2*
Palmese, Rose Marie 1871-1953 *WhScrn 1,*
    WhScrn 2
Palsbo, Ole 1909-1952 *DcFM*
Paltenghi, David 1919-1961 *WhScrn 2*
Paluzzi, Luciana 1939- *FilmgC, WhoHol A*
Pam, Anita d1973 *WhScrn 2*
Pam, Jerry 1926- *IntMPA 1977*
Pampanini, Silvana 1925- *IntMPA 1977*
Pan, Hermes *IntMPA 1977, WhoHol A*
Pan, Hermes 1905- *FilmgC*
Pan, Hermes 1910- *CmMov*
Panama, Charles A 1925- *IntMPA 1977*
Panama, Norman 1914- *BiE&WWA, CmMov,*
    FilmgC, IntMPA 1977, NotNAT, WorEnF
Pancake, Roger *WhoHol A*
Pancoast, Asa 1905- *AmSCAP 1966*
Pandel, Ted 1935- *AmSCAP 1966*
Panetta, George 1915-1969 *BiE&WWA,*
    NotNAT B
Pangborn, Franklin d1958 *WhoHol B*
Pangborn, Franklin 1893-1958 *Vers A*
Pangborn, Franklin 1894-1958 *FilmgC, MovMk,*
    WhScrn 1, WhScrn 2
Pangborn, Franklin 1896-1958 *Film 2,*
    NotNAT B, TwYS
Pangborn, Franklyn *MotPP*
Pani, Corrado *WhoHol A*
Panico, Frank Porky 1924- *AmSCAP 1966*
Panijel, Jacques 1921- *DcFM*
Pannaci, Charles 1904-1927 *WhScrn 1,*

WhScrn 2
Panova, Vera Fyodorovna 1905-1973 *ModWD*
Pansini, Rose *WomWMM*
Pantages, Clayton G 1927- *IntMPA 1977*
Panter, Joan 1909- *WhThe*
Panthulu, B R 1910-1974 *WhScrn 2*
Panvini, Ron *WhoHol A*
Panzer, Paul 1867?-1937 *WhScrn 1, WhScrn 2*
Panzer, Paul Wolfgang 1872-1948 *Film 2*
Panzer, Paul Wolfgang 1872-1958 *Film 1, MotPP,*
NotNAT B, WhScrn 1, WhScrn 2,
WhoHol B
Panzer, Paul Wolfgang 1873-1958 *TwYS*
Paoli, Raoul *Film 2*
Paparelli, Frank 1917- *AmSCAP 1966*
Papas, Irene 1926- *CelR 3, FilmgC,*
IntMPA 1977, MotPP, MovMk, OxFilm,
WhoHol A
Papatakis, Niko 1918- *WorEnF*
Pape, Edward Lionel 1867-1944 *WhScrn 1,*
WhScrn 2
Pape, Lionel d1944 *WhoHol B*
Papp, Joseph 1921- *BiE&WWA, CelR 3, CnThe,*
EncMT, NewYTET, NotNAT, NotNAT A,
OxThe, PIP&P, PIP&P A, WhoThe 16
Paquerette, Madame *Film 2*
Paquet, Alfons 1881-1944 *CnMD, ModWD*
Paquette, Pauline *Film 2*
Parabosco, Girolamo 1524?-1557 *McGWD*
Paraga, Marco 1862-1929 *NotNAT B*
Parain, Brice 1897-1971 *WhScrn 2*
Paranjpe, Sai *WomWMM*
Parchman, Gene Louis 1929- *AmSCAP 1966*
Parchman, William E 1936- *NatPD*
Pard, Yvette *WomWMM*
Pardave, Joaquin 1901-1955 *WhScrn 1,*
WhScrn 2
Pardave, Jose 1902-1970 *WhScrn 1, WhScrn 2*
Pardee, C W Doc 1885-1975 *WhScrn 2*
Pardee, Doc 1885-1975 *WhoHol C*
Pardis, Monique *WomWMM*
Pardoll, David 1908- *BiE&WWA*
Parella, Anthony 1915- *BiE&WWA, NotNAT*
Parent, Gail *WomWMM*
Parente, Sister Elizabeth *AmSCAP 1966*
Parenteau, Zoel 1883- *AmSCAP 1966*
Parera, Grace Moore *WhScrn 1, WhScrn 2*
Paretzkin, Brita *WomWMM B*
Parfaict, Claude 1701-1777 *OxThe*
Parfaict, Francois 1698-1753 *OxThe*
Parfitt, Judy *WhoHol A, WhoThe 16*
Parfrey, Woodrow *WhoHol A*
Parigi, Alfonso d1656 *OxThe*
Parigi, Giulio 1590-1636 *OxThe*
Parios, Gus *Film 2*
Paris, Jerry 1925- *FilmgC, NewYTET,*
WhoHol A
Paris, Manuel 1894-1959 *WhScrn 2*
Parish, James *WhThe*
Parish, Mitchell 1900- *AmSCAP 1966*
Parisys, Marcelle *WhThe*
Park, Custer B 1900-1955 *WhScrn 1, WhScrn 2*
Park, E L *Film 2*
Park, Florence Oie Chan 1886-1967 *WhScrn 2*
Park, Ida May *TwYS A, WomWMM*
Park, Robert H 1916- *IntMPA 1977*
Park, Stephen 1911- *AmSCAP 1966*
Parke, MacDonald 1892-1960 *WhScrn 1,*
WhScrn 2, WhoHol B
Parke, Walter d1922 *NotNAT B*
Parke, William *TwYS A*
Parke, William, Sr. 1873-1941 *Film 2, WhScrn 1,*
WhScrn 2, WhoHol B
Parker, Adele 1885-1966 *WhScrn 2*

Parker, Albert 1889- *Film 1, TwYS A*
Parker, Alice 1925- *AmSCAP 1966*
Parker, Anthony 1912- *WhThe*
Parker, Barnett d1941 *WhScrn 1, WhoHol B*
Parker, Barnett 1886-1941 *WhScrn 2*
Parker, Barnett 1890-1941 *FilmgC*
Parker, Benjamin R 1909- *IntMPA 1977*
Parker, Cecil 1897-1971 *FilmgC, MovMk,*
NotNAT B, Vers B, WhScrn 1, WhScrn 2,
WhThe, WhoHol B
Parker, Cecilia *WhoHol A*
Parker, Cecilia 1905- *MGM, MovMk, ThFT*
Parker, Cecilia 1915- *FilmgC*
Parker, Charlie *Film 2*
Parker, Claire *WomWMM*
Parker, Clifton 1905- *CmMov, FilmgC*
Parker, Dorothy 1893-1967 *AmSCAP 1966,*
BiE&WWA, NotNAT A, NotNAT B
Parker, Edwin 1900-1960 *WhScrn 2*
Parker, Eleanor 1922- *FilmgC, IntMPA 1977,*
MotPP, MovMk, WhoHol A, WorEnF
Parker, Everett C *NewYTET*
Parker, Fess 1925- *AmSCAP 1966, FilmgC,*
IntMPA 1977, MotPP, WhoHol A
Parker, Flora d1950 *Film 2, NotNAT B,*
WhoHol B
Parker, Francine *WomWMM, WomWMM B*
Parker, Frank 1862-1926 *NotNAT B*
Parker, Frank 1864-1926 *WhThe*
Parker, Frank Pinky 1891-1962 *WhScrn 1,*
WhScrn 2
Parker, Franklin 1891-1962 *WhoHol B*
Parker, George D d1937 *NotNAT B*
Parker, Sir Gilbert d1932 *NotNAT B*
Parker, Gilbert 1927- *BiE&WWA, NotNAT*
Parker, Hazel H *IntMPA 1977*
Parker, Henry Taylor 1867-1934 *NotNAT A,*
NotNAT B, OxThe
Parker, Horatio William 1863-1919
AmSCAP 1966
Parker, Jack *Film 2*
Parker, Janet Lee *WhoHol A*
Parker, Jean *MotPP*
Parker, Jean 1912?- *MGM, ThFT*
Parker, Jean 1915- *FilmgC, MovMk, WhoHol A*
Parker, John 1875-1952 *NotNAT B, OxThe,*
WhThe
Parker, John Carl 1926- *AmSCAP 1966*
Parker, John William 1909- *BiE&WWA,*
NotNAT
Parker, Joy 1924- *WhThe*
Parker, Katherine *Film 2*
Parker, Lady *Film 2*
Parker, Lara *WhoHol A*
Parker, Leonard *WhoHol A*
Parker, Lew d1972 *WhoHol B*
Parker, Lew 1906-1972 *WhThe*
Parker, Lew 1907-1972 *BiE&WWA, NotNAT B,*
WhScrn 2
Parker, Lottie Blair d1937 *NotNAT B, WhThe*
Parker, Louis Napoleon 1852-1944 *ModWD,*
NotNAT B, OxThe, WhThe, WhoStg 1908
Parker, Mary *WhoHol A*
Parker, Mary 1915-1966 *WhScrn 1, WhScrn 2,*
WhoHol B
Parker, Murray 1896-1965 *WhScrn 1, WhScrn 2*
Parker, P C *OxThe*
Parker, Seth d1975 *WhScrn 2, WhoHol C*
Parker, Shirley *WhoHol A*
Parker, Suzy *IntMPA 1977, MotPP, WhoHol A*
Parker, Suzy 1932- *FilmgC, MovMk*
Parker, Thane 1907- *WhThe*
Parker, Uncle Murray d1965 *WhoHol B*
Parker, Vivian d1974 *WhoHol B*

Parker, Vivien 1897-1974 *WhScrn 2*
Parker, W Oren 1911- *BiE&WWA, NotNAT*
Parker, Warren *WhoHol A*
Parker, Willard 1912- *FilmgC, IntMPA 1977,*
  MotPP, WhoHol A
Parkes, Gerard *WhoHol A*
Parkhirst, Douglass d1964 *NotNAT B*
Parkhurst, Frances d1969 *WhScrn 1, WhScrn 2,*
  WhoHol B
Parkhurst, Pearce 1919- *IntMPA 1977*
Parkington, Beulah d1958 *WhScrn 1, WhScrn 2,*
  WhoHol B
Parkins, Barbara 1942- *FilmgC, WhoHol A*
Parkinson, Allen 1910- *IntMPA 1977*
Parks, Bert *IntMPA 1977, NewYTET*
Parks, E L *Film 2*
Parks, Gordon 1912- *CelR 3, FilmgC,*
  IntMPA 1977
Parks, Gordon, Jr. 1948- *FilmgC*
Parks, Hildy *BiE&WWA, NotNAT, WhoHol A*
Parks, Larry 1914-1975 *BiE&WWA, CmMov,*
  FilmgC, HolP 40, MotPP, MovMk,
  WhScrn 2, WhThe, WhoHol C
Parks, Michael 1938- *FilmgC, IntMPA 1977,*
  MotPP, WhoHol A
Parkyakarkus 1904-1958 *FilmgC, WhScrn 1,*
  WhScrn 2, WhoHol B
Parkyn, Leslie *FilmgC*
Parlo, Dita *Film 2*
Parlo, Dita 1906-1971 *OxFilm*
Parlo, Dita 1906-1972 *FilmgC, WhoHol B,*
  WorEnF
Parlo, Dita 1907-1971 *WhScrn 2*
Parman, Cliff *AmSCAP 1966*
Parnell, Emory 1894- *FilmgC, IntMPA 1977,*
  Vers A, WhoHol A
Parnell, James 1923-1961 *NotNAT B, WhScrn 1,*
  WhScrn 2, WhoHol B
Parnell, Val 1894- *WhThe*
Parnes, Paul 1925- *AmSCAP 1966*
Parnis, Mollie 1905- *CelR 3*
Parquet, Corinne *Film 1*
Parr, Katherine *WhoHol A*
Parr, Peggy *Film 1*
Parravicini, Florencio 1874-1941 *WhScrn 1,*
  WhScrn 2
Parris, Herman M 1903- *AmSCAP 1966*
Parrish, Avery 1917-1959 *AmSCAP 1966*
Parrish, Gigi *WhoHol A*
Parrish, Helen d1959 *MotPP, NotNAT B,*
  WhoHol B
Parrish, Helen 1922-1959 *Film 2, FilmgC, ThFT*
Parrish, Helen 1924-1959 *WhScrn 1, WhScrn 2*
Parrish, Judy 1916- *BiE&WWA*
Parrish, Julie *WhoHol A*
Parrish, Leslie *WhoHol A*
Parrish, Robert 1916- *FilmgC, IntMPA 1977,*
  MovMk, WorEnF
Parrott, Charles *Film 1, WhScrn 1, WhScrn 2*
Parrott, James 1892-1939 *CmMov, FilmgC,*
  WhScrn 1, WhScrn 2
Parrott, Jimmie *Film 2*
Parrott, Paul *Film 2*
Parrott, Paul Poll 1892-1939 *WhoHol B*
Parry, Sir Edward Abbott d1943 *NotNAT B,*
  WhThe
Parry, Gordon 1908- *FilmgC, IntMPA 1977*
Parry, Harvey 1901- *Film 2*
Parry, Lee *Film 2*
Parry, Natasha 1930- *FilmgC, WhoHol A*
Parry, Paul 1908-1966 *WhScrn 2, WhoHol B*
Parry, Peggy *Film 1*
Parry, Roland 1897- *AmSCAP 1966*
Parry, Sefton Henry d1887 *NotNAT B*

Parry, Tom d1862 *NotNAT B*
Parry, William 1856- *WhoStg 1906,*
  WhoStg 1908
Parshalle, Eve 1900- *AmSCAP 1966*
Parsley, Ruby *Film 2*
Parsloe, Charles T d1898 *NotNAT B*
Parson, Carol d1958 *WhScrn 1, WhScrn 2*
Parsons, Alan 1888-1933 *WhThe*
Parsons, Allan 1888-1933 *NotNAT B*
Parsons, Billy *Film 1*
Parsons, Billy *see also* Parsons, Smiling Billy
Parsons, Donovan 1888- *WhThe*
Parsons, Estelle 1927- *BiE&WWA, CelR 3,*
  FilmgC, IntMPA 1977, MovMk, NotNAT,
  WhoHol A, WhoThe 16
Parsons, Gram 1946-1973 *WhScrn 2*
Parsons, Harriet *IntMPA 1977, WomWMM*
Parsons, Harriet Baby *Film 1*
Parsons, Lindsley 1905- *IntMPA 1977*
Parsons, Louella d1972 *WhoHol B*
Parsons, Louella 1880-1972 *FilmgC*
Parsons, Louella 1881?-1972 *Film 2, WhScrn 2*
Parsons, Louella 1890-1972 *OxFilm*
Parsons, Louella 1893-1972 *WorEnF*
Parsons, Michael J *WhoHol A*
Parsons, Milton *WhoHol A*
Parsons, Nancie 1904- *WhThe*
Parsons, Nicholas 1928- *FilmgC, WhoHol A*
Parsons, Percy 1878-1944 *NotNAT B, WhScrn 2,*
  WhThe, WhoHol B
Parsons, Smiling Billy 1878-1919 *WhScrn 2*
Parsons, Smiling Billy *see also* Parsons, Billy
Parsons, William 1933- *AmSCAP 1966*
Parten, Peter *WhoHol A*
Partington, Rex *NotNAT*
Partos, Gus *Film 2*
Parver, Michael 1936- *BiE&WWA*
Pascal, Andre *NotNAT B*
Pascal, Ernest 1896-1966 *NotNAT B*
Pascal, Gabriel 1894-1954 *FilmgC, NotNAT A,*
  NotNAT B, OxFilm, WorEnF
Pascal, Giselle *WhoHol A*
Pascal, Milton H 1908- *AmSCAP 1966*
Pasco, Richard 1926- *CnThe, FilmgC,*
  WhoHol A, WhoThe 16
Pascoe, Charles Eyre d1912 *NotNAT B*
Pascoe, Richard W 1888- *AmSCAP 1966*
Pasetta, Marty *NewYTET*
Pasha, Kalla 1877-1933 *Film 2, TwYS,*
  WhScrn 1, WhScrn 2, WhoHol B
Pashennaya, Vera Nikolayevna 1887-1962 *OxThe*
Paskman, Dailey 1897- *AmSCAP 1966*
Paso, Alfonso 1926- *CnMD, CroCD, ModWD*
Paso Gil, Alfonso 1926- *McGWD*
Pasolini, Pier Paola 1922-1975 *WhScrn 2*
Pasolini, Pier Paolo 1922-1975 *FilmgC, MovMk,*
  OxFilm, WorEnF
Pasolini, Piero Paolo 1922-1975 *DcFM*
Pasque, Ernest *Film 1*
Pasquet, Jean 1896- *AmSCAP 1966*
Pasquier, Charles Bach 1881-1953 *WhScrn 1,*
  WhScrn 2
Passantino, Anthony *WhoHol A*
Passarge, Paul *Film 2*
Passer, Ivan 1933- *IntMPA 1977, OxFilm,*
  WorEnF
Passeur, Steve 1899-1966 *CnMD, McGWD,*
  ModWD, WhThe
Passmore, Henry 1905- *IntMPA 1977*
Passmore, Walter 1867-1946 *NotNAT B, WhThe*
Pasternacki, Stephan 1891- *AmSCAP 1966*
Pasternak, Joe 1901- *CmMov, FilmgC,*
  IntMPA 1977, WorEnF
Pasternak, Joseph H 1901- *AmSCAP 1966*

Paston, George d1936 *NotNAT B, WhThe*
Pastor, Antonio 1837-1908 *WhoStg 1906,*
 WhoStg 1908
Pastor, Tony d1969 *WhoHol B*
Pastor, Tony 1837-1908 *FamA&A, NotNAT A,*
 NotNAT B, OxThe
Pastore, John O 1907- *CelR 3, NewYTET*
Pastrone, Giovanni 1882-1959 *DcFM*
Pastrone, Giovanni 1883-1959 *OxFilm, WorEnF*
Patachou *WhoHol A*
Pataki, Michael *WhoHol A*
Patch, Wally 1888-1970 *Film 2, WhScrn 1,*
 WhScrn 2, WhThe, WhoHol B
Patch, Wally 1888-1971 *FilmgC*
Patchett-Tarses *NewYTET*
Pate, Michael 1920- *FilmgC, MovMk, Vers B,*
 WhoHol A
Pateman, Robert 1840-1924 *NotNAT B, WhThe*
Paterson, Jerry *Film 2*
Paterson, Neil 1916- *FilmgC, IntMPA 1977*
Paterson, Pat 1911- *ThFT, WhoHol A*
Paterson, William 1919- *BiE&WWA*
Pathe, Charles 1863-1957 *DcFM, FilmgC,*
 NotNAT B, OxFilm, WorEnF
Patman, Wright 1893- *CelR 3*
Paton, Alan *PIP&P*
Paton, Charles *Film 2*
Paton, Stuart 1885-1944 *TwYS A, WhScrn 1,*
 WhScrn 2
Patrick, Benilde 1927- *BiE&WWA*
Patrick, Butch *WhoHol A*
Patrick, C L 1918- *IntMPA 1977*
Patrick, Dennis *WhoHol A*
Patrick, Ethel 1887-1944 *WhScrn 1, WhScrn 2*
Patrick, Frederick 1896- *AmSCAP 1966*
Patrick, Gail *MotPP*
Patrick, Gail 1911- *FilmgC, HolP 30, ThFT*
Patrick, Gail 1912- *WhoHol A*
Patrick, Gail 1915- *MovMk*
Patrick, George 1905- *IntMPA 1977*
Patrick, Jerome 1883-1923 *Film 1, Film 2,*
 NotNAT B, WhScrn 1, WhScrn 2,
 WhoHol B
Patrick, John *Film 2*
Patrick, John 1902- *CnMD*
Patrick, John 1906- *McGWD*
Patrick, John 1907- *BiE&WWA, ConDr 1977,*
 NotNAT, WhoThe 16
Patrick, John 1910- *ModWD*
Patrick, Lee *BiE&WWA, MotPP, NotNAT*
Patrick, Lee 1906- *FilmgC*
Patrick, Lee 1911- *Film 2, MovMk, Vers A,*
 WhoHol A
Patrick, Leonard *BiE&WWA*
Patrick, Lory *WhoHol A*
Patrick, Nigel 1913- *FilmgC, IntMPA 1977,*
 MotPP, MovMk, WhoHol A, WhoThe 16
Patrick, Robert 1937- *ConDr 1977, NotNAT*
Patricola, Tom d1950 *Film 2, WhoHol B*
Patricola, Tom 1891-1950 *NotNAT B, WhThe*
Patricola, Tom 1894-1950 *WhScrn 1, WhScrn 2*
Patroni Griffi, Giuseppe 1924- *WorEnF*
Patry, Albert *Film 2*
Patston, Doris 1904-1957 *NotNAT B, WhScrn 1,*
 WhScrn 2, WhoHol B
Patten, Dorothy 1905-1975 *WhScrn 2,*
 WhoHol C
Patten, Luana 1938- *FilmgC, WhoHol A*
Patten, Robert *WhoHol A*
Patterson, Colonel *Film 2*
Patterson, Ada d1939 *NotNAT B*
Patterson, Albert *WhoHol A*
Patterson, Albert d1975 *WhScrn 2, WhoHol C*
Patterson, Benjamin *ConDr 1977E*

Patterson, Cordelia M 1907- *AmSCAP 1966*
Patterson, Dick *WhoHol A*
Patterson, Elizabeth d1966 *MotPP, WhoHol B*
Patterson, Elizabeth 1874-1966 *BiE&WWA,*
 MovMk, NotNAT B, Vers A
Patterson, Elizabeth 1875-1966 *ThFT*
Patterson, Elizabeth 1876-1966 *Film 2, FilmgC,*
 TwYS, WhScrn 1, WhScrn 2
Patterson, Hank 1888-1975 *WhScrn 2,*
 WhoHol C
Patterson, James 1932-1972 *NotNAT B,*
 WhScrn 2, WhoHol B
Patterson, Joseph Medill 1879-1946 *NotNAT B*
Patterson, Joy W 1906-1959 *WhScrn 1,*
 WhScrn 2, WhoHol B
Patterson, Lee 1929- *FilmgC, WhoHol A*
Patterson, Marjorie d1948 *NotNAT B*
Patterson, Melody *WhoHol A*
Patterson, Neva 1922- *BiE&WWA, NotNAT,*
 WhThe, WhoHol A
Patterson, Pat *FilmgC, WhoHol A*
Patterson, Richard L 1924- *IntMPA 1977*
Patterson, Strake *Film 2*
Patterson, Tom 1920- *WhoThe 16*
Patterson, Troy 1926-1975 *WhScrn 2, WhoHol C*
Patterson, Walter *Film 1*
Patterson, Wiley 1910- *AmSCAP 1966*
Patti, Adelina 1843- *WhoStg 1908*
Patton, Bill *Film 2, TwYS*
Patton, Mary *WhoHol A*
Patton, Phil 1911-1972 *WhScrn 2*
Patwardhan, Vinayakarao 1897-1975 *WhScrn 2*
Paudler, Maria *Film 2*
Pauker, Edmond d1962 *NotNAT B*
Pauker, Loretta *WomWMM B*
Paul, Betty 1921- *BiE&WWA, WhThe,*
 WhoHol A
Paul, Byron *NewYTET*
Paul, Charles Frederick 1912- *AmSCAP 1966*
Paul, Doris A 1903- *AmSCAP 1966*
Paul, Edna *WomWMM*
Paul, Edward 1896- *AmSCAP 1966*
Paul, Fred *Film 2*
Paul, Mrs. Howard d1879 *NotNAT B*
Paul, Howard d1905 *NotNAT B*
Paul, John *WhoHol A*
Paul, Lee *WhoHol A*
Paul, Les *WhoHol A*
Paul, Logan 1849-1932 *WhScrn 2*
Paul, M B *IntMPA 1977*
Paul, Millie *WomWMM, WomWMM B*
Paul, Mimi *WhoHol A*
Paul, Ralph 1920- *IntMPA 1977*
Paul, Robert William 1869-1943 *FilmgC, OxFilm,*
 WorEnF
Paul, Steven *WhoHol A*
Paul, Wauna 1912-1973 *WhScrn 2*
Paulas *Film 1*
Paulding, Frederick 1859-1937 *NotNAT B*
Pauletich, Aida *WomWMM B*
Paulette, Jane *AmSCAP 1966*
Pauley, Jane *NewYTET*
Pauli-Winterstein, Hedwig *Film 2*
Paulig, Albert d1933 *Film 2, WhScrn 1,*
 WhScrn 2
Pauline, J Robert *Film 2*
Pauline, Princess 1873- *WhThe*
Pauling, Linus 1901- *CelR 3*
Paull, Alan *Film 2*
Paull, E T 1858-1924 *AmSCAP 1966*
Paull, Harry Major 1854-1934 *NotNAT B,*
 WhThe
Paull, Morgan *WhoHol A*
Paull, Muriel *Film 2*

Paull, Townsend D 1898-1933 *WhScrn 1,*
WhScrn 2
Paulo, Signor d1835 *NotNAT B*
Paulsen, Albert *WhoHol A*
Paulsen, Arno 1900-1969 *WhScrn 1, WhScrn 2,*
WhoHol B
Paulsen, Harald 1895-1954 *WhScrn 1, WhScrn 2*
Paulsen, Pat *WhoHol A*
Paulson, Arvid 1888- *NotNAT*
Paulton, Edward Antonio d1939 *NotNAT B*
Paulton, Harry 1842-1917 *NotNAT B, WhThe*
Paulton, Tom d1914 *NotNAT B*
Paumier, Alfred 1870-1951 *NotNAT B, WhThe*
Pauncefort, Claire d1924 *NotNAT B*
Pauncefort, George 1870-1942 *Film 2,*
NotNAT B, WhScrn 1, WhScrn 2
Pauncefort, Georgina d1895 *NotNAT B*
Pavan, Marisa 1932- *FilmgC, IntMPA 1977,*
MotPP, WhoHol A
Pavanelli, Livio *Film 2*
Pavek, Janet 1936- *BiE&WWA*
Pavetti, Sally Thomas 1936- *NotNAT*
Paviot, Paul 1925- *DcFM*
Pavis, Marie *Film 1*
Pavlik, John M 1939- *IntMPA 1977*
Pavlova, Anna 1882-1931 *NotNAT A*
Pavlova, Anna 1885-1931 *WhScrn 1, WhScrn 2,*
WhThe, WhoHol B
Pavlow, Muriel *WhoHol A*
Pavlow, Muriel 1921- *FilmgC, WhoThe 16*
Pavlow, Muriel 1924- *IntMPA 1977*
Pavlowa, Anna 1885-1931 *Film 1*
Pavon, Blanca Estela 1926-1949 *WhScrn 1,*
WhScrn 2
Pavoni, Giuseppe *Film 2*
Pavy, Salathiel 1590-1603 *OxThe*
Pawle, J Lennox 1872-1936 *NotNAT B, WhThe*
Pawle, Lennox 1872-1936 *Film 1, Film 2,*
FilmgC, WhScrn 1, WhScrn 2, WhoHol B
Pawley, Eric 1907- *BiE&WWA*
Pawley, Nancy 1901- *WhThe*
Pawley, William 1905-1952 *NotNAT B,*
WhScrn 1, WhScrn 2, WhoHol B
Pawlova, Vera *Film 2*
Pawlow, Pawel *Film 2*
Pawn, Doris 1896- *Film 1, Film 2, TwYS*
Pawson, Hargrave 1902-1945 *NotNAT B, WhThe*
Paxinou, Katina 1900-1972 *OxFilm*
Paxinou, Katina 1900-1973 *BiE&WWA, CnThe,*
FilmgC, MotPP, MovMk, OxThe, WhScrn 2,
WhThe, WhoHol B, WorEnF
Paxinov, Katina 1900-1973 *NotNAT B*
Paxton, George d1914 *WhScrn 2*
Paxton, Glenn 1931- *BiE&WWA, NotNAT*
Paxton, Glenn G, Jr. 1921- *AmSCAP 1966*
Paxton, John 1911- *FilmgC, IntMPA 1977,*
WorEnF
Paxton, Sidney d1930 *WhoHol B*
Paxton, Sidney 1861-1930 *WhScrn 1, WhScrn 2*
Paxton, Sydney *Film 2*
Paxton, Sydney 1860-1930 *NotNAT B, WhThe*
Paxton, Thomas R 1937- *AmSCAP 1966*
Pay, William *IntMPA 1977*
Paymer, Ada 1896- *AmSCAP 1966*
Paymer, Marvin 1921- *AmSCAP 1966*
Payn, Graham 1918- *EncMT, WhoHol A,*
WhoThe 16
Payne, B Iden 1881-1976 *BiE&WWA,*
NotNAT B
Payne, Ben Iden 1881-1976 *OxThe*
Payne, Ben Iden 1888-1976 *CnThe, WhThe*
Payne, Douglas 1875-1965 *Film 2, WhScrn 1,*
WhScrn 2, WhoHol B
Payne, Edmund 1865-1914 *NotNAT B, WhThe*

Payne, Edna 1891-1953 *Film 1, WhScrn 2*
Payne, George Adney d1907 *NotNAT B*
Payne, John 1912- *CmMov, FilmgC,*
IntMPA 1977, MotPP, MovMk, WhoHol A,
WorEnF
Payne, John Howard 1791-1852 *NotNAT A,*
NotNAT B, OxThe, PIP&P
Payne, Julie *WhoHol A*
Payne, Laurence 1919- *FilmgC, WhThe,*
WhoHol A
Payne, Louis 1876-1953 *Film 2, WhScrn 1,*
WhScrn 2, WhoHol B
Payne, Millie *WhThe*
Payne, Norman *IntMPA 1977*
Payne, Sally *WhoHol A*
Payne, Walter d1949 *NotNAT B, WhThe*
Payne, William d1967 *WhScrn 2*
Payne, William Louis 1876-1953 *NotNAT B,*
WhoStg 1906, WhoStg 1908
Payne-Jennings, Victor 1900-1962 *NotNAT B,*
WhThe
Paynton, Harry d1964 *NotNAT B*
Payson, Blanche 1881-1964 *Film 1, Film 2,*
NotNAT B, WhScrn 1, WhScrn 2,
WhoHol B
Payson, Joan 1903- *CelR 3*
Payton, Barbara 1927-1967 *FilmgC, MotPP,*
NotNAT B, WhScrn 1, WhScrn 2,
WhoHol B
Payton, Claude *Film 1*
Payton, Corse 1867-1934 *NotNAT A,*
NotNAT B, WhoHol B, WhoStg 1906,
WhoStg 1908
Payton, Gloria *Film 2*
Payton, Lenny 1921- *AmSCAP 1966*
Payton, Lew 1875-1945 *WhScrn 2*
Payton-Wright, Pamela 1941- *PIP&P A,*
WhoHol A, WhoThe 16
Peabody, Eddie 1912-1970 *WhoHol B*
Peabody, Eddy 1912-1970 *WhScrn 1, WhScrn 2*
Peabody, Josephine Preston 1874-1922 *ModWD*
Peabody, Richard *WhoHol A*
Peace, George J 1909- *AmSCAP 1966*
Peach, Mary 1934- *FilmgC, IntMPA 1977,*
WhoHol A
Peacock, Bertram d1963 *NotNAT B*
Peacock, Ian Michael *NewYTET*
Peacock, Keith 1931-1966 *WhScrn 1, WhScrn 2,*
WhoHol B
Peacock, Kim 1901-1966 *WhScrn 1, WhScrn 2,*
WhThe, WhoHol B
Peacock, Lillian 1890?-1918 *WhScrn 2*
Peacock, Trevor 1931- *WhoThe 16*
Peake, R B d1847 *NotNAT B*
Peaker, E J *IntMPA 1977, WhoHol A*
Peal, Gilbert d1964 *NotNAT B*
Peale, Norman Vincent 1898- *CelR 3*
Pearce, Al d1961 *WhoHol B*
Pearce, Alice d1966 *MotPP, WhoHol B*
Pearce, Alice 1913-1966 *FilmgC*
Pearce, Alice 1917-1966 *BiE&WWA, NotNAT B,*
WhThe
Pearce, Alice 1919-1966 *WhScrn 1, WhScrn 2*
Pearce, Connie 1920- *AmSCAP 1966*
Pearce, George C 1865-1940 *Film 1, Film 2,*
WhScrn 1, WhScrn 2, WhoHol B
Pearce, Peggy *Film 1*
Pearce, Sam 1909-1971 *BiE&WWA, NotNAT B*
Pearce, Vera 1896-1966 *WhScrn 1, WhScrn 2,*
WhThe, WhoHol B
Pearl, Barry *WhoHol A*
Pearl, Ernest 1902- *IntMPA 1977*
Pearl, Eula d1970 *WhScrn 2*
Pearl, Jack 1895- *BiE&WWA, EncMT, WhThe,*

WhoHol A
Pearl, Leo J 1907- *AmSCAP 1966*
Pearl, Linda *WomWMM B*
Pearl, Minnie 1913- *CelR 3, WhoHol A*
Pearl-Mann, Dora 1905- *AmSCAP 1966*
Pearson, Beatrice 1920- *FilmgC, MotPP, WhThe, WhoHol A*
Pearson, Brett *WhoHol A*
Pearson, Drew 1897-1969 *WhScrn 2*
Pearson, George 1875-1973 *FilmgC, OxFilm*
Pearson, Hesketh 1887-1964 *NotNAT B*
Pearson, Jesse *WhoHol A*
Pearson, Leon Morris 1899-1963 *NotNAT B*
Pearson, Lloyd 1897-1966 *FilmgC, WhScrn 1, WhScrn 2, WhThe, WhoHol B*
Pearson, Molly 1876-1959 *NotNAT B, WhScrn 2, WhThe, WhoHol B*
Pearson, Richard 1918- *WhoHol A, WhoThe 16*
Pearson, Susan G *WhoHol A*
Pearson, Ted d1961 *WhScrn 2*
Pearson, Virginia 1888-1958 *Film 1, Film 2, MotPP, NotNAT B, TwYS, WhScrn 1, WhScrn 2, WhoHol B*
Pearson, W Blaine 1892-1918 *WhScrn 2*
Peary, Harold 1908- *WhoHol A*
Pease, Harry 1886-1945 *AmSCAP 1966*
Peattie, Yvonne *WhoHol A*
Pecaro, Daniel T *NewYTET*
Pecheur, Bruce 1942-1973 *WhScrn 2*
Peck, Fletcher 1923- *AmSCAP 1966*
Peck, Gregory 1916- *BiE&WWA, CelR 3, CmMov, FilmgC, IntMPA 1977, MotPP, MovMk, OxFilm, WhThe, WhoHol A, WorEnF*
Peck, Murray 1903- *AmSCAP 1966*
Peck, Norman *Film 2*
Peck, Raymond W 1875-1950 *AmSCAP 1966*
Peck, Robert *Film 2*
Peck, Steven *WhoHol A*
Peckham, Frances Miles 1893-1959 *WhScrn 1, WhScrn 2*
Peckinpah, Sam *NewYTET*
Peckinpah, Sam 1925- *CelR 3, IntMPA 1977*
Peckinpah, Sam 1926- *CmMov, DcFM, FilmgC, MovMk, OxFilm, WorEnF*
Pedersen, Ann *WomWMM*
Pedersen, Maren *Film 2*
Pedgrift, Frederic Henchman *WhThe*
Pedi, Tom 1913- *BiE&WWA, NotNAT, WhoHol A*
Pedicord, Harry William 1912- *BiE&WWA, NotNAT*
Pedler, Gertrude *Film 2*
Pedrick, Gale 1905-1970 *WhThe*
Peel, David 1920- *WhThe*
Peel, Eileen *WhoHol A, WhoThe 16*
Peele, George *PIP&P*
Peele, George 1557?-1596 *CnThe, McGWD, REnWD*
Peele, George 1558?-1597? *OxThe*
Peele, George 1558?-1598? *NotNAT A, NotNAT B*
Peer, Helen 1898-1942 *WhScrn 1, WhScrn 2, WhoHol B*
Peerce, Jan 1904- *CelR 3, WhoHol A*
Peerce, Larry *FilmgC, IntMPA 1977*
Peerless Annabelle 1878-1961 *WhScrn 1, WhScrn 2*
Peers, Joan 1911-1975 *Film 2, ThFT, WhoHol C*
Peery, Rob Roy 1900- *AmSCAP 1966*
Peffer, Crawford A d1961 *NotNAT B*
Pegay, Sophie *Film 2*
Pegg, Vester d1951 *Film 2, WhoHol B*

Peggy, Baby *Film 1*
Peggy, Baby *see also* Baby Peggy
Pegler, Westbrook 1894-1969 *WhScrn 2*
Pei, I M 1917- *CelR 3*
Peil, Charles Edward d1962 *NotNAT B*
Peil, Ed 1888-1958 *TwYS*
Peil, Edward 1888-1958 *Film 1, Film 2, MotPP, NotNAT B, WhScrn 1, WhScrn 2, WhoHol B*
Peil, Edward, Jr. 1908-1962 *Film 2, WhScrn 1, WhScrn 2, WhoHol B*
Peile, Frederick Kinsey 1862-1934 *NotNAT A, NotNAT B, WhThe*
Peile, Kinsey *Film 2*
Peine, Josh *WhoHol A*
Peirce, Evelyn *WhScrn 1, WhScrn 2*
Peiser, Judy 1945- *WomWMM B*
Peisley, Frederick 1904- *WhoHol A, WhoThe 16*
Peixoto, Mario 1912- *DcFM*
Pele 1940- *CelR 3*
Pelham, Meta d1948 *NotNAT B*
Pelish, Thelma *WhoHol A*
Pelissier, Anthony 1912- *FilmgC*
Pelissier, Harry Gabriel 1874-1913 *NotNAT B, OxThe, WhThe*
Pell, David 1925- *AmSCAP 1966*
Pellatt, John *IntMPA 1977*
Pellegrini, Al 1921- *AmSCAP 1966*
Pellegrini, Eugene *WhoHol A*
Pellerin, Jean-Victor 1889- *McGWD*
Pellesini, Giovanni 1526?-1612 *OxThe*
Pellesini, Vittoria Piissimi *OxThe*
Pelletier, Yvonne *Film 2*
Pellicer, Pina 1940-1964 *MotPP, WhScrn 1, WhScrn 2, WhoHol B*
Pellico, Silvio 1789-1854 *McGWD*
Pellish, Bert J 1914- *AmSCAP 1966*
Pelly, Farrell 1891-1963 *NotNAT B, WhScrn 1, WhScrn 2, WhoHol B*
Pelzer, George *Film 2*
Peman, Jose Maria 1897- *CroCD, ModWD*
Peman Y Pemartin, Jose Maria 1897- *McGWD*
Pember, Ron 1934- *WhoThe 16*
Pemberton, Brock 1885-1950 *NotNAT B, WhThe, WhoHol B*
Pemberton, Henry W 1875-1952 *NotNAT B, WhScrn 1, WhScrn 2, WhoHol B*
Pemberton, John Wyndham 1883-1947 *NotNAT B, WhThe*
Pemberton, Sir Max 1863-1950 *NotNAT B, WhThe*
Pemberton, Reece 1914- *PIP&P, WhoThe 16*
Pemberton, Thomas Edgar 1849-1905 *NotNAT B, OxThe*
Pemberton-Billing, Robin 1929- *WhoThe 16*
Pembleton, Georgia *Film 2*
Pembroke, George d1972 *WhScrn 2, WhoHol B*
Pembroke, Percy *Film 2*
Pembroke, Scott *TwYS A*
Pembrook, P S *Film 1*
Pena, Julio 1912-1972 *WhScrn 2*
Pena, Martins 1815-1848 *CnThe, REnWD*
Pena, Martins *see also* Penna, Luiz Carlos Martins
Pena, Ralph R 1927-1969 *AmSCAP 1966, WhScrn 1, WhScrn 2*
Penberthy, Beverly *WhoHol A*
Penbroke, Clifford *Film 2*
Penbrook, Harry 1887-1960 *WhScrn 1, WhScrn 2*
Penbrook, Henry d1952 *WhoHol B*
Penco DeLaVega, Joseph 1650-1703 *OxThe*
Pendennis, Rose d1943 *NotNAT B*
Pender, Doris 1900-1975 *WhScrn 2*
Pendleton, Austin 1940- *WhoHol A, WhoThe 16*

Pendleton, Gaylord *Film 2*
Pendleton, Nat d1967 *MotPP, WhoHol B*
Pendleton, Nat 1895-1967 *FilmgC, MovMk*
Pendleton, Nat 1899-1967 *Film 2, WhScrn 1,*
  WhScrn 2
Pendleton, Nat 1903-1967 *Vers A*
Pendleton, Steve *WhoHol A*
Pendleton, Wyman 1916- *WhoHol A,*
  WhoThe 16
Pene DuBois, Raoul 1914- *BiE&WWA, NotNAT*
Penkethman, William d1725 *OxThe*
Penley, Arthur 1881-1954 *WhThe*
Penley, Belville S d1940 *NotNAT B*
Penley, Sampson d1838 *NotNAT B*
Penley, William Sydney 1851-1912 *NotNAT B,*
  WhThe
Penley, William Sydney 1852-1912 *OxThe*
Penman, Lea 1895-1962 *NotNAT B, WhScrn 1,*
  WhScrn 2, WhoHol B
Penn, Arthur 1922- *BiE&WWA, CelR 3, DcFM,*
  FilmgC, IntMPA 1977, MovMk, NotNAT,
  OxFilm, WhoThe 16, WorEnF
Penn, Arthur A 1875-1941 *AmSCAP 1966*
Penn, Bill 1931- *WhThe*
Penn, Leonard 1907-1975 *WhScrn 2, WhoHol C*
Penn, William 1598?- *OxThe*
Penna, Luiz Carlos Martins 1815-1848 *OxThe*
Penna, Luiz Carlos Martins *see also* Pena, Martins
Pennario, Leonard 1924- *AmSCAP 1966*
Pennebaker, D A 1930- *WorEnF*
Pennebaker, Donn Alan 1930- *OxFilm,*
  WomWMM
Pennell, Daniel *Film 2*
Pennell, Larry *WhoHol A*
Pennell, R O 1861-1934 *WhoHol B*
Pennell, Richard O 1861-1934 *Film 2, WhScrn 1,*
  WhScrn 2
Penner, Joe d1941 *MotPP, WhoHol B*
Penner, Joe 1904-1941 *FilmgC*
Penner, Joe 1905-1941 *WhScrn 1, WhScrn 2*
Penney, Edward J, Jr. 1925- *AmSCAP 1966*
Pennick, Jack 1895-1964 *Film 2, MotPP, TwYS,*
  Vers B, WhScrn 1, WhScrn 2, WhoHol B
Pennick, Ronald Jack 1895-1964 *NotNAT B*
Penningroth, Phil 1943- *NatPD*
Pennington, Ann d1971 *WhoHol B*
Pennington, Ann 1892-1971 *WhThe*
Pennington, Ann 1893-1971 *BiE&WWA,*
  NotNAT B
Pennington, Ann 1894-1971 *EncMT, WhScrn 1,*
  WhScrn 2
Pennington, Ann 1895-1971 *Film 1, Film 2,*
  TwYS
Pennington, Edith Mae d1974 *WhScrn 2,*
  WhoHol B
Pennington, W H d1923 *NotNAT B*
Pennington-Richards, C M 1911- *FilmgC*
Penny, Frank 1895-1946 *WhScrn 1, WhScrn 2,*
  WhoHol B
Pennycuicke, Andrew 1620- *OxThe*
Penrose, Charles d1952 *WhoHol B*
Penrose, John 1917- *WhThe*
Penwarden, Duncan *Film 2*
Penzoldt, Ernst 1892-1955 *CnMD, McGWD,*
  ModWD
Peon, Ramon 190-?- *DcFM*
Pepa, Bonafe *Film 1*
Pepito d1975 *WhoHol C*
Peple, Edward Henry 1867- *WhThe,*
  WhoStg 1906, WhoStg 1908
Peppard, George *IntMPA 1977, MotPP,*
  WhoHol A
Peppard, George 1928- *CelR 3*
Peppard, George 1929- *FilmgC*

Peppard, George 1933- *MovMk, WorEnF*
Pepper *Film 1*
Pepper, Barbara d1969 *MotPP, WhoHol B*
Pepper, Barbara 1912-1969 *ThFT*
Pepper, Barbara 1916-1969 *Vers B, WhScrn 1,*
  WhScrn 2
Pepper, Buddy 1922- *AmSCAP 1966, WhoHol A*
Pepper, Cynthia *WhoHol A*
Pepper, L J *IntMPA 1977*
Pepper, Robert C 1916-1964 *WhScrn 1,*
  WhScrn 2
Peppercorn, Carl *IntMPA 1977*
Peppiatt-Aylesworth *NewYTET*
Pepusch, John Christopher 1667-1752 *NotNAT B*
Pepys, Samuel 1633-1703 *NotNAT B, OxThe,*
  PIP&P
Perakos, Sperie P 1915- *IntMPA 1977*
Perceval-Clark, Perceval 1881-1938 *NotNAT B,*
  WhThe
Percival, Arlene *WhScrn 2*
Percival, Cyril *Film 2*
Percival, Horace d1961 *NotNAT B*
Percival, Lance 1933- *FilmgC, IntMPA 1977*
Percival, Walter C 1887-1934 *Film 2, NotNAT B,*
  WhScrn 1, WhScrn 2, WhoHol B
Percy, Charles 1919- *CelR 3*
Percy, David *Film 2*
Percy, Edward 1891-1968 *BiE&WWA,*
  NotNAT B, WhThe
Percy, Eileen 1901-1973 *Film 1, Film 2, MotPP,*
  TwYS, WhScrn 2, WhoHol B
Percy, Esme Saville 1887-1957 *FilmgC, OxThe,*
  PIP&P, WhScrn 1, WhScrn 2, WhoHol B
Percy, George d1962 *NotNAT B*
Percy, S Esme 1887-1957 *NotNAT B, WhThe*
Percy, William Stratford 1872-1946 *NotNAT B,*
  WhThe
Percyval, T Wigney 1865- *WhThe*
Perdue, Derelys *TwYS, WhoHol A*
Perdue, Derlys *Film 2*
Pereira, Hal *IntMPA 1977, WorEnF*
Pereira DosSantos, Nelson *DcFM*
Perelman, S J 1904- *BiE&WWA, CelR 3,*
  ConDr 1977, FilmgC, McGWD, NotNAT
Perestiani, Ivan *Film 2*
Peretti, Hugo 1916- *AmSCAP 1966*
Peretz, Isaac Leib 1852-1915 *OxThe*
Peretz, Isaac Leob 1851-1915 *NotNAT B*
Peretz, Isaac Loeb 1852-1915 *CnMD, McGWD*
Peretz, Susan *WhoHol A*
Peretz, Yitskhok Leybush 1852-1915 *CnThe,*
  ModWD, REnWD
Perez, Jose *WhoHol A*
Perez, Lou 1924- *AmSCAP 1966*
Perez, Pepito 1896-1975 *WhScrn 2*
Perez Galdos, Benito 1843-1920 *CnMD, McGWD,*
  ModWD, OxThe
Perez-Galdos, Benito 1845-1920 *NotNAT B*
Pergament, Harvey *IntMPA 1977*
Pericaud, Louis d1909 *NotNAT B*
Perier, Etienne 1931- *FilmgC*
Perier, Francois 1919- *FilmgC, OxFilm,*
  WhoHol A
Peries, Lester James 1921- *DcFM, WorEnF*
Perinal, Georges 1897-1965 *CmMov, DcFM,*
  FilmgC, IntMPA 1977, OxFilm, WorEnF
Periolat, George d1960 *Film 1, Film 2, TwYS*
Periolat, George 1876-1940 *WhScrn 1, WhScrn 2*
Periolot, George 1876-1940 *WhoHol B*
Periot, Arthur 1899-1929 *WhScrn 1, WhScrn 2*
Periquin 1912-1957 *WhScrn 1, WhScrn 2*
Perito, Nick 1924- *AmSCAP 1966*
Perkins, Anthony 1932- *BiE&WWA, FilmgC,*
  IntMPA 1977, MotPP, MovMk, NotNAT,

OxFilm, WhoHol A, WhoThe 16, WorEnF
Perkins, Carl *WhoHol A*
Perkins, David Fessenden d1962 *NotNAT B*
Perkins, Frank S 1908- *AmSCAP 1966*
Perkins, Gil *WhoHol A*
Perkins, Jean Edward 1899-1923 *WhScrn 1,*
WhScrn 2, WhoHol B
Perkins, John Henry Rowland, II 1934-
IntMPA 1977
Perkins, Millie 1939- *FilmgC, MotPP,*
WhoHol A
Perkins, Osgood 1892-1937 *FamA&A, FilmgC,*
NotNAT B, PIP&P, WhScrn 1, WhScrn 2,
WhThe, WhoHol B
Perkins, Osgood 1893-1937 *Film 2*
Perkins, Ray 1896- *AmSCAP 1966, Film 2*
Perkins, Richard 1585?-1650 *OxThe*
Perkins, Tony *MotPP*
Perkins, Tony *see also* Perkins, Anthony
Perkins, Voltaire *WhoHol A*
Perkins, Walter 1870-1925 *Film 1, Film 2,*
NotNAT B, WhScrn 1, WhScrn 2,
WhoHol B
Perl, Arnold 1914-1971 *BiE&WWA, NotNAT B*
Perl, Lothar 1910- *AmSCAP 1966*
Perla, Brenda *WomWMM*
Perlberg, William 1899-1968 *FilmgC, WorEnF*
Perle, George 1915- *AmSCAP 1966*
Perley, Anna 1849-1937 *WhScrn 1, WhScrn 2*
Perley, Charles 1886-1933 *WhScrn 1, WhScrn 2,*
WhoHol B
Perlman, Morris 1894- *AmSCAP 1966*
Perlman, Phyllis *BiE&WWA, NotNAT*
Perlman, William J d1954 *NotNAT B*
Perlmutter, David M 1934- *IntMPA 1977*
Perlmutter, Leonard L *NatPD*
Permain, Fred W d1933 *NotNAT B*
Perrault, Pierre 1927- *OxFilm, WorEnF*
Perreau, Gerald *WhoHol A*
Perreau, Gigi 1941- *FilmgC, IntMPA 1977,*
MotPP, WhoHol A
Perreau, Janine *WhoHol A*
Perredom, Luis 1882-1958 *WhScrn 1, WhScrn 2*
Perrella, Robert *NotNAT A*
Perret, Leonce 1880-1935 *DcFM, WorEnF*
Perret, Leonce 1882- *TwYS A*
Perrey, Mireille *WhThe*
Perrie, Ernestine 1912- *BiE&WWA, NotNAT*
Perrin, Jack 1896-1967 *TwYS, WhScrn 1,*
WhScrn 2, WhoHol B
Perrin, Jack 1896-1968 *Film 1, Film 2*
Perrin, Jacques *WhoHol A*
Perrin, Nat *IntMPA 1977*
Perrin, Vic *WhoHol A*
Perrine, Valerie 1944- *IntMPA 1977, WhoHol A*
Perrins, Leslie 1902-1962 *FilmgC, NotNAT B,*
WhScrn 1, WhScrn 2, WhThe, WhoHol B
Perrone, Frank 1928- *AmSCAP 1966*
Perrone, Valentina 1906- *AmSCAP 1966*
Perrot, Irma *Film 2*
Perry, Albert H d1933 *NotNAT B*
Perry, Anthony 1929- *IntMPA 1977*
Perry, Antoinette 1888-1946 *NotNAT B,*
WhScrn 1, WhScrn 2, WhThe, WhoHol B
Perry, Arthur John 1906- *WhThe*
Perry, B Fisher 1940- *NatPD*
Perry, Barbara *WhoHol A*
Perry, Bob *Film 2*
Perry, Bob *see also* Perry, Robert E
Perry, Charles Emmett 1907-1967 *WhScrn 2,*
WhoHol B
Perry, Charlotte 1890- *BiE&WWA*
Perry, Desmond *WhoHol A*
Perry, Earl 1921- *IntMPA 1977*

Perry, Elaine 1921- *BiE&WWA, NotNAT*
Perry, Eleanor *ConDr 1977A, IntMPA 1977,*
WomWMM, WomWMM B
Perry, Esthryn *Film 2*
Perry, Felton *WhoHol A*
Perry, Florence d1949 *NotNAT B*
Perry, Frank *IntMPA 1977, WhoHol A*
Perry, Frank 1930- *FilmgC, MovMk*
Perry, Frank 1933- *WorEnF*
Perry, Irma d1955 *NotNAT B*
Perry, Jack 1920- *AmSCAP 1966*
Perry, Joan *WhoHol A*
Perry, Joseph *WhoHol A*
Perry, Joyce *WomWMM B*
Perry, Kathryn *Film 2*
Perry, Margaret 1913- *BiE&WWA, NotNAT,*
WhThe, WhoHol A, WomWMM
Perry, Martha *BiE&WWA, NotNAT*
Perry, Mary 1888-1971 *NotNAT B, WhScrn 1,*
WhScrn 2, WhoHol B
Perry, Paul P 1891-1963 *FilmgC*
Perry, Phil 1914- *AmSCAP 1966*
Perry, Robert E 1879-1962 *Film 2, NotNAT B,*
TwYS, WhScrn 1, WhScrn 2, WhoHol B
Perry, Roger *WhoHol A*
Perry, Ronald d1963 *NotNAT B*
Perry, Sam A 1884-1936 *AmSCAP 1966*
Perry, Sara 1872-1959 *WhScrn 1, WhScrn 2,*
WhoHol B
Perry, Scott *WhoHol A*
Perry, Victor 1920-1974 *WhScrn 2, WhoHol B*
Perry, Walter *Film 2*
Perryman, Jill 1933- *WhoThe 16*
Perschy, Maria *WhoHol A*
Persichetti, Vincent 1915- *AmSCAP 1966*
Persky, Marilyn S *WhoHol A*
Persky-Denoff *NewYTET*
Persoff, Nehemiah 1920- *BiE&WWA, FilmgC,*
IntMPA 1977, MotPP, NotNAT, WhoHol A,
WhoThe 16
Persons, Hal 1918- *IntMPA 1977*
Persse, Thomas d1920 *WhScrn 1, WhScrn 2,*
WhoHol B
Persse, Tom *Film 2*
Persson, Edvard 1887-1957 *WhScrn 1, WhScrn 2*
Persson, Essy 1945- *FilmgC, WhoHol A*
Persson, Maria *WhoHol A*
Pertwee, Jon 1919- *FilmgC, IntMPA 1977,*
WhoHol A, WhoThe 16
Pertwee, Michael 1916- *FilmgC, IntMPA 1977,*
WhoThe 16
Pertwee, Roland 1885-1963 *WhThe, WhoHol A*
Pertwee, Roland 1886?-1963 *NotNAT A,*
NotNAT B
Perugini, Signor d1914 *NotNAT B*
Peruzzi, Baldassare 1481-1537 *OxThe*
Perzynski, Wlodzimierz 1878-1930 *CnMD,*
ModWD
Peshkov, Aleksey Maksimovich *McGWD*
Peshkov, Alexei Maximovich *REnWD*
Pete *Film 2*
Pete *see also* Petey
Petelle, Martha *Film 2*
Petelska, Eva *WomWMM*
Peter, M *Film 2*
Peter The Great *Film 2*
Peters, Ann 1920-1965 *WhScrn 2*
Peters, Audrey *WhoHol A*
Peters, Bernadette 1948- *EncMT, NotNAT,*
WhoHol A, WhoThe 16
Peters, Brandon d1956 *NotNAT B*
Peters, Brock 1927- *BiE&WWA, FilmgC,*
IntMPA 1977, MotPP, MovMk, NotNAT,
WhoHol A, WomWMM

Peters, Charles Rollo 1892-1967 *NotNAT B*
Peters, Don 1921-1953 *WhScrn 2*
Peters, Fred 1884-1963 *Film 2, NotNAT B,*
WhScrn 1, WhScrn 2, WhoHol B
Peters, George J *WhoHol A*
Peters, Gordon *WhoHol A*
Peters, Gunnar d1974 *WhScrn 2*
Peters, House d1967 *MotPP, WhoHol B*
Peters, House 1880?-1967 *FilmgC, WhScrn 1,*
WhScrn 2
Peters, House 1888-1967 *Film 1, Film 2, TwYS*
Peters, House, Jr. *WhoHol A*
Peters, Jean 1926- *FilmgC, MotPP, MovMk,*
WhoHol A, WorEnF
Peters, John d1940 *WhScrn 1, WhScrn 2,*
WhoHol B
Peters, John S d1963 *Film 2, WhScrn 2*
Peters, Kay *WhoHol A*
Peters, Kelly Jean *WhoHol A*
Peters, Lauri *WhoHol A*
Peters, Lynn *WhoHol A*
Peters, Mammy *Film 2*
Peters, Mattie *Film 2*
Peters, Page E d1916 *Film 1, WhScrn 2*
Peters, Paul *PIP&P*
Peters, Peter 1926-1955 *WhScrn 1, WhScrn 2*
Peters, Ralph 1903-1959 *Vers B, WhScrn 2,*
WhoHol B
Peters, Roberta 1930- *CelR 3, WhoHol A*
Peters, Rollo 1892-1967 *BiE&WWA, NotNAT B,*
PIP&P, WhThe
Peters, Scott *WhoHol A*
Peters, Susan 1921-1952 *FilmgC, MGM, MotPP,*
MovMk, NotNAT B, WhScrn 1, WhScrn 2,
WhoHol B
Peters, Werner 1919-1971 *WhScrn 1, WhScrn 2,*
WhoHol B
Peters, William Frederick 1876-1938
AmSCAP 1966
Petersen, Cliff 1906- *IntMPA 1977*
Petersen, Elsa d1974 *WhoHol B*
Petersen, Ernst *Film 2*
Petersen, Karen d1940 *NotNAT B*
Petersen, Marie *AmSCAP 1966*
Petersen, Paul 1944- *WhoHol A*
Petersen, Paul *see also* Peterson, Paul
Petersen, Peter 1876-1956 *WhScrn 1, WhScrn 2*
Petersmeyer, C Wrede *NewYTET*
Peterson, Arthur *WhoHol A*
Peterson, Betty J 1918- *AmSCAP 1966*
Peterson, Dorothy 1901- *MotPP, MovMk, ThFT,*
WhoHol A
Peterson, Edgar 1913- *IntMPA 1977*
Peterson, Gil *WhoHol A*
Peterson, Ina Mae *WomWMM B*
Peterson, Ivor 1905- *AmSCAP 1966*
Peterson, Kaj Harald Leininger *McGWD*
Peterson, Karen d1940 *WhScrn 2*
Peterson, Lenka 1925- *BiE&WWA, NotNAT,*
WhoHol A
Peterson, Louis 1922- *BiE&WWA, NotNAT*
Peterson, Marjorie d1974 *WhScrn 2, WhoHol B*
Peterson, Monica *WhoHol A*
Peterson, Oscar 1925- *CelR 3*
Peterson, Paul 1945- *IntMPA 1977*
Peterson, Paul *see also* Petersen, Paul
Peterson, Richard W 1949- *IntMPA 1977*
Peterson, Roger Tory 1908- *CelR 3*
Peterson, Wilbur Pete 1915-1960 *WhScrn 1,*
WhScrn 2
Petey 1923-1930 *WhScrn 2*
Petey *see also* Pete
Petherbridge, Edward 1936- *WhoThe 16*
Petina, Irra 1914- *BiE&WWA, NotNAT*

Petipa, Marius 1822-1910 *NotNAT B*
Petit, Albert 1887-1963 *WhScrn 2*
Petit, Pascale 1938- *FilmgC, WhoHol A*
Petit, Roland 1924- *WhThe, WhoHol A*
Petkanova, Magda *WomWMM*
Petkere, Bernice 1906- *AmSCAP 1966*
Petley, E S d1945 *NotNAT B*
Petley, Frank E 1872-1945 *NotNAT B, WhThe,*
WhoHol B
Petras, Peggy *WomWMM B*
Petrass, Sari 1890-1930 *NotNAT B, WhThe*
Petrescu, Camil 1894-1957 *McGWD*
Petri, Elio 1929- *DcFM, FilmgC, WorEnF*
Petri, Olavus 1493-1552 *OxThe*
Petrides, Avra *NatPD*
Petrie, Daniel M 1920- *BiE&WWA, FilmgC,*
IntMPA 1977, NewYTET, NotNAT
Petrie, David Hay 1895-1948 *NotNAT B, WhThe*
Petrie, George *WhoHol A*
Petrie, Hay 1895-1948 *FilmgC, WhScrn 1,*
WhScrn 2, WhoHol B
Petrie, Henry W 1857-1925 *AmSCAP 1966*
Petrie, Howard A 1907-1968 *WhScrn 1,*
WhScrn 2, WhoHol B
Petrillo, Caesar 1898-1963 *AmSCAP 1966*
Petronella, Anthony J 1906- *AmSCAP 1966*
Petrov, Vladimir 1896- *DcFM*
Petrov, Vladimir 1896-1965 *WorEnF*
Petrov, Vladimir 1896-1966 *FilmgC*
Petrova, Olga 1886- *Film 1, FilmgC, MotPP,*
NotNAT A, TwYS, WhThe, WhoHol A
Petrovitch, Ivan *Film 2*
Petrovitch, Jans *Film 2*
Petrovitch, Peter *Film 2*
Petrovsky, A *Film 2*
Petruzzi, Julian 1907-1967 *WhScrn 2*
Petschler, Erik A *Film 2*
Pettersson, Brigitta *WhoHol A*
Pettersson, Hjordis *WhoHol A*
Pettet, Edwin Burr 1913- *BiE&WWA*
Pettet, Joanna 1944- *FilmgC, WhoHol A*
Petti, Anthony 1907- *IntMPA 1977*
Pettingell, Frank 1891-1966 *FilmgC, WhScrn 1,*
WhScrn 2
Pettingell, Frank 1891-1968 *WhThe*
Pettingill, Frank 1891-1966 *WhoHol B*
Pettit, Paul Bruce 1920- *BiE&WWA*
Pettitt, Henry d1893 *NotNAT B*
Petty, Frank 1916- *AmSCAP 1966*
Petty, Richard 1938- *CelR 3*
Petty, Violet Ann 1928- *AmSCAP 1966*
Peukert, Leo *Film 2*
Peukert-Impekoven, Sabine 1890-1970 *WhScrn 1,*
WhScrn 2
Pevney, Joseph *IntMPA 1977, WhoHol A*
Pevney, Joseph 1913- *WorEnF*
Pevney, Joseph 1920- *FilmgC, MovMk*
Pevsner, Leo 1906- *AmSCAP 1966*
Peyser, John 1916- *IntMPA 1977*
Peyser, Lois *WomWMM*
Peyton, Charles *Film 2*
Peyton, Lawrence R d1918 *Film 1, WhScrn 2*
Pezzulo, Ted 1936- *NatPD*
Pfaffl, Carolyn Sue *WomWMM B*
Pfautsch, Lloyd 1921- *AmSCAP 1966*
Pfister, Walter J, Jr. *NewYTET*
Pflug, Jo Ann *WhoHol A*
Phair, Douglas *Film 2*
Phalke, Dhundiraj Govind 1870-1944 *DcFM*
Pharar, Renee d1962 *NotNAT B*
Phelan, Brian *WhoHol A*
Phelps, Buster *Film 2*
Phelps, Dodie d1963 *NotNAT B*
Phelps, Eleanor *WhoHol A*

Phelps, Fancher, Sr. d1972 *WhoHol B*
Phelps, Lee d1952 *WhoHol B*
Phelps, Lee 1894-1953 *Vers B, WhScrn 1,*
  WhScrn 2
Phelps, Leonard P d1924 *NotNAT B*
Phelps, Lyon 1923- *BiE&WWA, NotNAT*
Phelps, Samuel 1804-1878 *NotNAT A,*
  NotNAT B, OxThe, PIP&P
Phelps, Vonda *Film 2*
Pherecrates *OxThe*
Phethean, David 1918- *WhoThe 16*
Philbin, Jack *IntMPA 1977, NewYTET*
Philbin, Mary 1903- *Film 2, FilmgC, MotPP,*
  TwYS, WhoHol A
Philbrick, Norman 1913- *BiE&WWA, NotNAT*
Philbrook, James *WhoHol A*
Philemon 361?BC-263BC *OxThe*
Philip, James E d1910 *NotNAT B*
Philipe, Gerard 1922-1959 *FilmgC, MotPP,*
  MovMk, NotNAT B, OxFilm, OxThe,
  WhScrn 1, WhScrn 2, WhoHol B, WorEnF
Philipe, Gerard *see also* Phillipe, Gerard
Philipp, Adolph 1864-1936 *NotNAT B*
Philippe, Andre *WhoHol A*
Philippe, Pierre *Film 2*
Philippi, Herbert M 1906-1958 *NotNAT B*
Philippin *OxThe*
Philips, Ambrose 1674-1749 *OxThe*
Philips, Augustus 1873- *WhoStg 1908*
Philips, Conrad 1930- *FilmgC*
Philips, Francis Charles 1849-1921 *NotNAT A,*
  NotNAT B, WhThe
Philips, Lee 1927- *BiE&WWA, NewYTET,*
  WhoHol A
Philips, Marie L 1925- *BiE&WWA, NotNAT*
Philips, Marvin James 1923- *BiE&WWA*
Philips, Mary 1901-1975 *WhThe, WhoHol C*
Philips, Mary *see also* Phillips, Mary
Philips, Robin 1941- *FilmgC*
Philips, Robin *see also* Phillips, Robin
Philips, William d1734 *NotNAT B*
Philliber, John 1872-1944 *WhScrn 1, WhScrn 2,*
  WhoHol B
Phillipe, Gerard 1922-1959 *CnThe*
Phillipe, Gerard *see also* Philipe, Gerard
Phillips, Acton d1940 *NotNAT B*
Phillips, Albert 1875-1940 *NotNAT B, WhScrn 2*
Phillips, Alex 190-?- *DcFM*
Phillips, Mrs. Alfred d1876 *NotNAT B*
Phillips, Augustine d1605 *OxThe, PIP&P*
Phillips, Augustus *Film 1, MotPP*
Phillips, Barney *WhoHol A*
Phillips, Bill *IntMPA 1977, Vers A*
Phillips, Bill *see also* Phillips, William Bill
Phillips, Blanche *Film 1*
Phillips, Burrill 1907- *AmSCAP 1966*
Phillips, Carmen 1895- *Film 1, Film 2, TwYS*
Phillips, Charles 1904-1958 *WhScrn 1, WhScrn 2*
Phillips, Clement K d1928 *WhScrn 1, WhScrn 2*
Phillips, Conrad *WhoHol A*
Phillips, Cyril L 1894- *WhThe*
Phillips, D John *IntMPA 1977*
Phillips, Dorothy 1892- *Film 1, Film 2, TwYS*
Phillips, E R *Film 1*
Phillips, Eddie 1899-1965 *Film 2, TwYS*
Phillips, Edna 1878-1952 *WhScrn 1, WhScrn 2*
Phillips, Edward Eddie 1899-1965 *WhoHol B*
Phillips, Edward N 1899-1965 *WhScrn 1,*
  WhScrn 2
Phillips, Edwin R d1915 *WhScrn 2*
Phillips, Festus Dad 1872-1955 *WhScrn 1,*
  WhScrn 2
Phillips, Fred 1890-1956 *AmSCAP 1966*
Phillips, Gordon *WhoHol A*

Phillips, Helena 1875-1955 *Film 2, WhScrn 1,*
  WhScrn 2, WhoHol B
Phillips, Howard Baron 1909- *AmSCAP 1966*
Phillips, Irna d1974 *NewYTET*
Phillips, Jack d1956 *NotNAT B*
Phillips, James *Film 2*
Phillips, Jean d1970 *WhScrn 2, WhoHol A*
Phillips, Jobyna *WhoHol A*
Phillips, John *WhoHol A*
Phillips, Julia *IntMPA 1977*
Phillips, Kate 1856-1931 *NotNAT B, WhThe*
Phillips, Katherine 1912- *AmSCAP 1966*
Phillips, Leslie 1924- *FilmgC, IntMPA 1977,*
  WhoHol A, WhoThe 16
Phillips, Louis 1942- *NatPD*
Phillips, MacKenzie 1960- *MovMk, WhoHol A*
Phillips, Margaret 1923- *BiE&WWA, NotNAT,*
  WhoHol A, WhoThe 16
Phillips, Mary 1901-1975 *WhScrn 2*
Phillips, Mary *see also* Philips, Mary
Phillips, Michael 1916- *IntMPA 1977,*
  WomWMM
Phillips, Michelle *WhoHol A*
Phillips, Mildred *AmSCAP 1966*
Phillips, Minna 1885-1963 *NotNAT B, WhScrn 1,*
  WhScrn 2, WhoHol B
Phillips, Nancy *Film 2*
Phillips, Noreen *Film 2*
Phillips, Norma 1893-1931 *Film 1, MotPP,*
  NotNAT B, WhScrn 1, WhScrn 2,
  WhoHol B
Phillips, Norman, Sr. 1892-1931 *WhScrn 1,*
  WhScrn 2
Phillips, Paul *WhoHol A*
Phillips, Peggy *NatPD*
Phillips, Richard 1826-1941 *WhScrn 1, WhScrn 2*
Phillips, Robert *WhoHol A*
Phillips, Robin *WhoHol A*
Phillips, Robin 1942- *WhoThe 16*
Phillips, Robin *see also* Philips, Robin
Phillips, Sian 1934- *FilmgC, WhoHol A,*
  WhoThe 16
Phillips, Stephen 1864-1915 *McGWD, ModWD,*
  NotNAT B, OxThe
Phillips, Stephen 1866-1915 *WhThe*
Phillips, Teddy 1917- *AmSCAP 1966*
Phillips, Watts d1874 *NotNAT B*
Phillips, Wendell K 1907- *BiE&WWA, NotNAT,*
  WhoHol A
Phillips, Wendy *WomWMM B*
Phillips, William Bill d1957 *WhScrn 1,*
  WhScrn 2, WhoHol B
Phillips, William Bill *see also* Phillips, Bill
Phillips, Zoe *WomWMM*
Phillpots, Ambrosine 1912- *WhoHol A*
Phillpotts, Adelaide 1896- *WhThe*
Phillpotts, Ambrosine 1912- *WhoThe 16*
Phillpotts, Eden 1862-1960 *NotNAT B, OxThe,*
  WhThe
Philocles *OxThe*
Philpotts, Ambrosine 1912- *FilmgC*
Phipps, Nicholas 1913- *FilmgC, WhoHol A,*
  WhoThe 16
Phipps, Sally *Film 2, WhoHol A*
Phipps, William *WhoHol A*
Phrynichus *OxThe*
Physioc, Joseph Allen d1951 *NotNAT B*
Physioc, Wray 1890- *TwYS A*
Pi, Rosario *WomWMM*
Piacenti, Enrico *Film 2*
Piacentini, Vincent 1922- *NotNAT*
Piaf, Edith d1963 *WhoHol B*
Piaf, Edith 1915-1963 *NotNAT B, OxThe*
Piaf, Edith 1916-1963 *WhScrn 1, WhScrn 2*

Piano, Anthony A 1926- *AmSCAP 1966*
Piantadosi, Al 1884-1955 *AmSCAP 1966*
Piatigorsky, Gregor 1903- *CelR 3*
Piazza, Ben 1934- *BiE&WWA, FilmgC, MotPP, NotNAT, WhoHol A, WhoThe 16*
Piazza, Dario 1904-1974 *WhScrn 2*
Piazza, Jim *WhoHol A*
Pica, Tina 1888-1968 *WhScrn 1, WhScrn 2, WhoHol B*
Picabia, Francis *Film 2*
Picard, Andre 1874-1926 *McGWD, NotNAT B, WhThe*
Picard, Louis Baptiste 1769-1828 *NotNAT B, OxThe*
Picasso, Pablo Ruiz Y 1881-1973 *DcFM, WhScrn 2*
Picazo, Miguel 1929- *WorEnF*
Piccioni, Piero 1921- *WorEnF*
Piccoli, Michel 1925- *FilmgC, MovMk, OxFilm, WhoHol A, WorEnF*
Piccolomini, Enea Silvio 1405-1464 *OxThe*
Picerni, Paul 1922- *FilmgC, IntMPA 1977, WhoHol A*
Picha, Hermann *Film 2*
Pichel, Irving 1891-1954 *FilmgC, MovMk, NotNAT B, PIP&P, WhScrn 1, WhScrn 2, WhoHol B, WorEnF*
Pichette, Henri 1923- *REnWD*
Pichette, Henri 1924- *McGWD, ModWD*
Pick, Lupe 1886-1931 *WhScrn 1, WhScrn 2*
Pick, Lupu 1886-1931 *BiDFlm, DcFM, Film 2, OxFilm, WhoHol B*
Pickard, Helena d1959 *WhoHol B*
Pickard, Helena 1899-1959 *OxThe*
Pickard, Helena 1900-1959 *NotNAT B, WhScrn 1, WhScrn 2, WhThe*
Pickard, John *WhoHol A*
Pickard, Mae d1946 *NotNAT B*
Pickard, Margery 1911- *WhThe*
Pickelherring *OxThe*
Pickens, Jane *CelR 3, EncMT*
Pickens, Slim 1919- *FilmgC, IntMPA 1977, MovMk, Vers A, WhoHol A*
Picker, Arnold M 1913- *IntMPA 1977*
Picker, David V 1931- *IntMPA 1977*
Picker, Eugene D 1903- *IntMPA 1977*
Pickering, Edward A 1871- *WhThe*
Pickering, J Russell d1947 *NotNAT B*
Pickett, Elizabeth *WomWMM*
Pickett, Ingram B 1899-1963 *NotNAT B, WhScrn 1, WhScrn 2, WhoHol B*
Pickford, Jack 1896-1933 *Film 1, Film 2, FilmgC, NotNAT B, TwYS, WhScrn 1, WhScrn 2, WhoHol B*
Pickford, Lottie 1895-1936 *Film 1, Film 2, NotNAT B, TwYS, WhScrn 1, WhScrn 2, WhoHol B*
Pickford, Mary 1893- *BiDFlm, CelR 3, Film 1, Film 2, FilmgC, IntMPA 1977, MotPP, MovMk, OxFilm, PIP&P, ThFT, TwYS, WhThe, WhoHol A, WomWMM, WorEnF*
Pickles, Christina *WhoHol A*
Pickles, Vivian 1933- *FilmgC, WhoHol A*
Pickles, Wilfred 1904- *FilmgC, IntMPA 1977, WhoHol A*
Pickman, Jerome 1916- *IntMPA 1977*
Pickman, Milton Eugene *IntMPA 1977*
Pickup, Ronald 1941- *WhoHol A, WhoThe 16*
Pickus, Albert M 1903- *IntMPA 1977*
Picon, Molly 1898- *AmSCAP 1966, BiE&WWA, NotNAT, NotNAT A, WhoHol A, WhoThe 16*
Pidal, Jose 1896-1956 *WhScrn 1, WhScrn 2*
Piddock, J C d1919 *NotNAT B*

Pidgeon, Edward Everett d1941 *NotNAT B*
Pidgeon, Walter *MotPP*
Pidgeon, Walter 1897- *BiDFlm, BiE&WWA, CmMov, Film 2, FilmgC, MGM, OxFilm, TwYS, WhoHol A, WhoThe 16, WorEnF*
Pidgeon, Walter 1898- *IntMPA 1977, MovMk*
Piel, Edward *Film 2, WhScrn 1, WhScrn 2*
Piel, Edward, Jr. *Film 2, WhScrn 1, WhScrn 2*
Piel, Harry 1892-1963 *WhScrn 2*
Pierat, Marie Therese d1934 *NotNAT B, WhThe*
Pierce, Barbara *Film 2*
Pierce, Charlotte *Film 2*
Pierce, Curtis *Film 2*
Pierce, Evelyn 1908-1960 *Film 2, WhScrn 1, WhScrn 2, WhoHol B*
Pierce, Frederick S *IntMPA 1977, NewYTET*
Pierce, George *Film 1, Film 2, WhScrn 1, WhScrn 2*
Pierce, Jack 1889-1968 *DcFM, FilmgC*
Pierce, James 1905- *WhoHol A*
Pierce, James H 1900- *Film 2*
Pierce, Maggie *WhoHol A*
Pierce, Nat 1925- *AmSCAP 1966*
Pierlot, Francis 1876-1955 *MotPP, NotNAT B, WhScrn 1, WhScrn 2, WhoHol B*
Pierpont, Laura 1881-1972 *WhScrn 2*
Pierre, Anatole d1926 *WhScrn 1, WhScrn 2*
Pierre, Andre 1884-1975 *WhScrn 2*
Piersen, Arthur d1975 *WhoHol C*
Pierson, Arthur 1891?-1975 *WhScrn 2*
Pierson, Frank R 1925- *FilmgC, IntMPA 1977, NewYTET*
Pierson, Suzy *Film 2*
Pietrangeli, Antonio 1919-1968 *OxFilm, WorEnF*
Piffard, Frederic 1902- *WhThe*
Piggot, Tempe 1884-1962 *Film 2*
Piggott, Tempe 1884-1962 *TwYS*
Pigorsch, Phyllis *WomWMM B*
Pigott, A S *WhThe*
Pigott, Tempe 1884-1962 *NotNAT B, WhScrn 1, WhScrn 2, WhoHol B*
Pihl, Christine R *WomWMM B*
Pike, Harry J d1919 *WhScrn 2*
Pike, Nita 1913-1954 *WhScrn 1, WhScrn 2, WhoHol B*
Pike, William *Film 1*
Piket, Frederick 1903- *AmSCAP 1966*
Pila, Maximo 1886-1939 *WhScrn 1, WhScrn 2*
Pilbeam, Nova 1919- *FilmgC, OxFilm, ThFT, WhThe, WhoHol A*
Pilbrow, Richard 1933- *WhoThe 16*
Pilcer, Harry 1885-1961 *Film 1, NotNAT B, WhScrn 2, WhThe*
Pilcher, Tony 1936- *IntMPA 1977*
Pilgrim, James 1825-1877 *NotNAT B*
Pilikhina, Margarita *WomWMM*
Pilon, Raymonde *WomWMM*
Pilot, Bernice *Film 2*
Pilotto, Camillo 1883?-1963 *WhScrn 2*
Piltz, George d1968 *WhScrn 2*
Pimley, John 1919-1972 *WhScrn 2*
Pinches, George *IntMPA 1977*
Pinchot, Rosamond d1936 *WhoHol B*
Pinchot, Rosamond 1904-1938 *NotNAT B*
Pinchot, Rosamond 1905-1938 *WhScrn 2*
Pincus, Irving *IntMPA 1977*
Pindemonte, Giovanni 1751-1812 *McGWD*
Pindemonte, Ippolito 1753-1828 *McGWD*
Pinder, Powis d1941 *NotNAT B*
Pine, Ed 1904-1950 *WhScrn 1, WhScrn 2*
Pine, Howard 1917- *IntMPA 1977*
Pine, Linda *Film 2*
Pine, Philip *WhoHol A*
Pine, Ralph 1939- *NotNAT*

Pine, Tina *WomWMM*
Pine, Virginia *WhoHol A*
Pine, William H 1896- *CmMov, FilmgC*
Pineapple, Johnny *AmSCAP 1966*
Pinero, Anthony 1887-1958 *WhScrn 1, WhScrn 2*
Pinero, Sir Arthur Wing 1855-1934 *CnThe,*
  McGWD, ModWD, NotNAT A, NotNAT B,
  OxThe, PIP&P, REnWD, WhScrn 2,
  WhThe, WhoStg 1906, WhoStg 1908
Pinero, Miguel *PIP&P A*
Pingatore, Frank 1930- *AmSCAP 1966*
Pinget, Robert 1919- *McGWD*
Pinget, Robert 1920- *CnMD, CroCD, ModWD,*
  REnWD
Pingree, Earl *Film 2*
Pink, Sidney 1916- *IntMPA 1977*
Pink, Wal d1922 *NotNAT B, WhThe*
Pinkard, Edna Belle 1892- *AmSCAP 1966*
Pinkard, Maceo 1897-1962 *AmSCAP 1966,*
  NotNAT B
Pinkham, Richard A R 1914- *IntMPA 1977,*
  NewYTET
Pinner, David 1940- *ConDr 1977*
Pinney, Charles *WhoHol A*
Pino, Rosario d1933 *NotNAT B, WhThe*
Pinsent, Gordon 1933- *FilmgC, WhoHol A*
Pinsker, Allen 1930- *IntMPA 1977*
Pinski, David 1872-1959 *CnMD, McGWD,*
  ModWD, REnWD
Pinta, Pamela *WhoHol A*
Pinter, Harold 1930- *BiE&WWA, CelR 3,*
  CnThe, ConDr 1977, CroCD, DcFM,
  FilmgC, McGWD, ModWD, NotNAT,
  OxFilm, OxThe, PIP&P, REnWD,
  WhoThe 16, WorEnF
Pinter, Harold 1932- *CnMD*
Pintoff, Ernest 1931- *DcFM, FilmgC, OxFilm,*
  WorEnF
Pinza, Ezio d1957 *PIP&P, WhoHol B*
Pinza, Ezio 1892-1957 *EncMT, NotNAT B,*
  WhScrn 1, WhScrn 2
Pinza, Ezio 1893-1957 *FilmgC*
Pio, Elith *Film 2*
Pipeiro, Roberto d1963 *WhScrn 2*
Piper, Anne *WomWMM*
Piper, Franco *WhThe*
Piper, Frederick 1902- *FilmgC, IntMPA 1977,*
  WhoHol A
Pipia, Mimmo 1902- *AmSCAP 1966*
Pipo 1902-1970 *WhScrn 1, WhScrn 2*
Pippin, Don *NotNAT*
Pippin, Donald W 1930- *AmSCAP 1966*
Pirandello, Luigi 1867-1936 *CnMD, CnThe,*
  McGWD, ModWD, NotNAT A, NotNAT B,
  OxThe, PIP&P, PIP&P A, REnWD, WhThe
Piranesi, Giovanni Battista 1720-1778 *NotNAT B*
Piron, Alexis 1689-1773 *McGWD, OxThe*
Piron, Armand John 1888-1943 *AmSCAP 1966*
Pirosh, Robert 1910- *CmMov, FilmgC,*
  IntMPA 1977
Piscator, Erwin 1893-1966 *BiE&WWA, CnThe,*
  CroCD, DcFM, NotNAT A, NotNAT B,
  OxThe, WorEnF
Piscator, Maria Ley *BiE&WWA, NotNAT*
Pisemsky, Aleksey Feofilaktovich 1820-1881
  McGWD
Pisemsky, Alexei Feofilaktovich 1820-1881
  NotNAT B
Pisistratus d528BC *OxThe*
Piston, Walter 1894- *CelR 3*
Pitcairn, Jack *Film 2*
Pithey, Wensley 1914- *WhoHol A, WhoThe 16*
Pitkin, William 1925- *BiE&WWA, NotNAT,*
  WhoThe 16

Pitlik, Noam *WhoHol A*
Pitman, Richard d1941 *NotNAT B*
Pitoeff, Georges 1885-1939 *NotNAT B, OxThe*
Pitoeff, Georges 1886-1939 *WhThe*
Pitoeff, Georges 1887-1939 *CnThe*
Pitoeff, Ludmilla 1896-1951 *CnThe, NotNAT B,*
  OxThe, WhThe
Pitot, Genevieve *BiE&WWA, NotNAT*
Pitou, Augustus 1843-1915 *NotNAT A,*
  NotNAT B, WhThe
Pitt *OxThe*
Pitt, Archie 1885-1940 *NotNAT B, WhThe*
Pitt, Archie 1895-1940 *WhScrn 1, WhScrn 2,*
  WhoHol B
Pitt, Fanny Addison d1937 *NotNAT B*
Pitt, Felix d1922 *NotNAT B*
Pitt, Ingrid 1944- *FilmgC, WhoHol A*
Pitt, Tom d1924 *WhThe*
Pittman, Monte 1918-1962 *WhScrn 1, WhScrn 2*
Pittman, Tom 1933-1958 *WhScrn 1, WhScrn 2,*
  WhoHol B
Pitts, Vincent Clifford 1935- *AmSCAP 1966*
Pitts, Zasu d1963 *MotPP, WhoHol B*
Pitts, Zasu 1898-1963 *BiDFlm, Film 1, Film 2,*
  FilmgC, MovMk, NotNAT B, ThFT, TwYS,
  WhScrn 1, WhScrn 2, WorEnF
Pitts, Zasu 1900-1963 *OxFilm, Vers A, WhThe*
Pittschau, Warner *Film 2*
Pittschau, Werner 1903-1928 *WhScrn 1,*
  WhScrn 2
Pivnick, Anitra *WomWMM B*
Pixerecourt, Rene Charles Guilbert De 1773-1844
  CnThe, McGWD, NotNAT B, OxThe,
  REnWD
Pixley, Frank 1867-1919 *EncMT, NotNAT B,*
  WhThe
Pixley, Gus 1874-1923 *WhScrn 2*
Pizer, Larry *FilmgC*
Pizor, Lewen *IntMPA 1977*
Pizza, Patt *WhoHol A*
Pizzetti, Ildebrando 1880- *DcFM, WorEnF*
Plabilischikov, Peter Alexeivich 1760-1812 *OxThe*
Placide, Mrs. Alexandre *PIP&P*
Placide, Alexandre d1812 *OxThe, PIP&P*
Placide, Caroline d1881 *NotNAT B*
Placide, Henry 1799-1870 *FamA&A, NotNAT B,*
  OxThe
Planche, Gustave 1808-1857 *OxThe*
Planche, James Robinson 1796-1880 *NotNAT A,*
  NotNAT B, OxThe, PIP&P
Planchon, Roger 1931- *CnMD Sup, CnThe,*
  OxThe, WhThe
Planck, Robert 1894- *FilmgC, IntMPA 1977*
Planco, George *WhoHol A*
Planer, Franz F 1894-1963 *FilmgC, WorEnF*
Plank, Melinda *WhoHol A*
Plank, Thomas C d1962 *NotNAT B*
Plant, Joe *Film 2*
Plateau, Joseph Antoine Ferdinand 1801-1883
  DcFM, OxFilm
Platen, Karl *Film 2*
Plater, Alan 1935- *ConDr 1977, WhoThe 16*
Plato *OxThe*
Plato 427BC-348BC *OxThe*
Plato 428?BC-347?BC *NotNAT B*
Platt, Agnes *WhThe*
Platt, Alma *WhoHol A*
Platt, Billy *Film 2*
Platt, Ed 1916-1974 *WhScrn 2, WhoHol B*
Platt, Edward 1916-1974 *FilmgC, MotPP*
Platt, Howard *WhoHol A*
Platt, Jack E 1914- *AmSCAP 1966*
Platt, Joseph B 1895-1968 *NotNAT B*
Platt, Livingston *WhThe*

Platt, Louise 1914- *FilmgC*
Platt, Louise 1915- *ThFT, WhoHol A*
Platt, Marc 1913- *FilmgC, MotPP, WhoHol A*
Platt, Milt *IntMPA 1977*
Platt, Raymond *NatPD*
Platts-Mills, Barney 1944- *OxFilm*
Plautus 251?BC-184BC *CnThe, McGWD, REnWD*
Plautus 254?BC-184BC *NotNAT B, OxThe, PIP&P*
Player, Gary 1935- *CelR 3*
Playfair, Arthur 1869-1918 *NotNAT B, WhThe*
Playfair, Sir Nigel 1874-1934 *CnThe, EncMT, NotNAT A, NotNAT B, OxThe, PIP&P, WhScrn 2, WhThe, WhoHol B*
Playten, Alice *WhoHol A*
Playter, Wellington *Film 2*
Playter, Wellington 1879-1937 *WhScrn 2*
Playter, Wellington 1883- *Film 1, TwYS*
Pleasance, Donald 1919- *FilmgC, PIP&P*
Pleasant, Richard d1961 *NotNAT B*
Pleasants, Jack 1874- *WhThe*
Pleasence, Angela *WhoHol A, WhoThe 16*
Pleasence, Donald 1919- *BiE&WWA, IntMPA 1977, MotPP, MovMk, NotNAT, OxFilm, WhoHol A*
Pleasence, Donald 1921- *WhoThe 16*
Pledath, Werner *Film 2*
Pleis, Jack K 1920- *AmSCAP 1966*
Pleschette, Suzanne 1937- *BiE&WWA*
Pleschkes, Otto 1931- *FilmgC*
Pleschkoff, Michael *Film 2*
Pleshette, Eugene *IntMPA 1977*
Pleshette, John *WhoHol A*
Pleshette, Suzanne 1937- *FilmgC, IntMPA 1977, MotPP, MovMk, WhoHol A, WorEnF*
Pleskow, Eric *IntMPA 1977*
Pleydell, George 1868- *WhThe*
Plievier, Theodor 1892-1955 *CnMD, ModWD*
Plimmer, Walter, Jr. *Film 2*
Plimpton, George 1927- *CelR 3, WhoHol A*
Plimpton, Shelley *WhoHol A*
Plinge, Walter *WhThe*
Plisetskaya, Maya *WhoHol A*
Plitt, Henry G 1918- *IntMPA 1977*
Plivova-Simkova, Vera *WomWMM*
Plowden, Roger S 1902-1960 *WhScrn 1, WhScrn 2, WhoHol B*
Plowright, Hilda *WhoHol A*
Plowright, Joan 1929- *BiE&WWA, CnThe, NotNAT, OxThe, PIP&P, WhoHol A, WhoThe 16*
Plues, George L 1895-1953 *WhScrn 1, WhScrn 2, WhoHol B*
Plugge, Mary Lou 1906- *BiE&WWA, NotNAT*
Plumb, E Hay 1883-1960 *WhScrn 2*
Plumb, Neely 1912- *AmSCAP 1966*
Plumby, Donald 1919- *AmSCAP 1966*
Plumer, Lincoln 1876-1928 *WhScrn 2*
Plumer, Lincoln *see also* Plummer, Lincoln
Plumer, Rose Lincoln d1955 *WhScrn 2*
Plumer, Rose Lincoln *see also* Plummer, Rose Lincoln
Plumley, Don *WhoHol A*
Plummer, Christopher *IntMPA 1977, MotPP, PIP&P, WhoHol A*
Plummer, Christopher 1927- *CelR 3, FilmgC, MovMk, WhoThe 16*
Plummer, Christopher 1929- *BiE&WWA, CnThe, NotNAT, WorEnF*
Plummer, Howard 1921- *AmSCAP 1966*
Plummer, Jean Vincent 1913- *AmSCAP 1966*
Plummer, Lincoln 1876-1928 *Film 2, WhScrn 1, WhoHol B*

Plummer, Lincoln *see also* Plumer, Lincoln
Plummer, Rose Lincoln d1955 *WhScrn 1, WhoHol B*
Plummer, Rose Lincoln *see also* Plumer, Rose Lincoln
Plunkett, Edward John Morton Drax *McGWD*
Plunkett, Jim 1947- *CelR 3*
Plunkett, Patricia *WhoHol A*
Plunkett, Patricia 1926- *WhThe*
Plunkett, Patricia 1928- *FilmgC, IntMPA 1977*
Plunkett, Walter 1902- *FilmgC, IntMPA 1977*
Plympton, Eben 1853-1915 *NotNAT B, WhThe, WhoStg 1906, WhoStg 1908*
Po Sein *REnWD*
Pober, Leon 1920- *AmSCAP 1966*
Pochon, Alfred 1878-1959 *AmSCAP 1966*
Pockriss, Lee J 1927- *AmSCAP 1966, BiE&WWA, NotNAT*
Pocock, Isaac 1782-1835 *NotNAT B, OxThe*
Podell, Albert N 1937- *IntMPA 1977*
Podesta, Italo d1964 *NotNAT B*
Podesta, Jose J *OxThe*
Podesta, Rosanna 1934- *MotPP*
Podesta, Rossana 1934- *FilmgC, IntMPA 1977, WhoHol A*
Podhoretz, Norman 1930- *CelR 3*
Podhorzer, Munio *IntMPA 1977*
Podhorzer, Nathan 1919- *IntMPA 1977*
Poe, Edgar Allan 1809-1849 *FilmgC*
Poe, Edgar Allen 1809-1849 *NotNAT B*
Poe, James 1923- *FilmgC, IntMPA 1977, WorEnF*
Poel, William 1852-1934 *CnThe, NotNAT A, NotNAT B, OxThe, PIP&P, WhThe*
Poelzig, Hans 1869-1936 *WorEnF*
Poff, Lon 1870-1952 *Film 1, Film 2, TwYS, WhScrn 2*
Poff, Louis *Film 2*
Pogacic, Vladimir 1918- *DcFM*
Pogany, Willy d1955 *NotNAT B*
Poggioli, Ferdinando Maria 1897-1944 *WorEnF*
Pogodin, Nikolai F 1900-1962 *CnMD, CnThe, ModWD, NotNAT B, OxThe*
Pogodin, Nikolay Fyodorovich 1900-1962 *McGWD*
Pogostin, S Lee 1926- *FilmgC*
Pogue, Thomas 1876-1941 *WhoHol B*
Pogue, Tom 1876-1941 *WhScrn 1, WhScrn 2*
Pohl, Claus *Film 2*
Pohl, Max *Film 2*
Pohlmann, Eric 1913- *FilmgC, WhoHol A*
Pointer, Sidney d1955 *NotNAT B, WhoHol B*
Pointner, Anton *Film 2*
Poirier, Anne-Claire *WomWMM*
Poirier, Leon 1876?-1968 *DcFM*
Poisson, Angelique 1657-1756 *OxThe*
Poisson, Francois Arnould 1696-1753 *OxThe*
Poisson, Madeleine-Angelique 1684-1770 *OxThe*
Poisson, Paul 1658-1735 *NotNAT B, OxThe*
Poisson, Philippe 1682-1743 *OxThe*
Poisson, Raymond 1630?-1690 *NotNAT B, OxThe*
Poitier, Sidney 1924- *BiDFlm, BiE&WWA, CelR 3, FilmgC, IntMPA 1977, MotPP, MovMk, NotNAT, WhoHol A, WhoThe 16*
Poitier, Sidney 1927- *OxFilm*
Poitier, Sydney 1924- *WorEnF*
Pojar, Bretislav 1923- *DcFM, WorEnF*
Pokras, Barbara *WomWMM*
Pol, Talitha 1940-1971 *WhScrn 1, WhScrn 2*
Pola, Edward 1907- *AmSCAP 1966*
Polacek, Louis Vask 1920-1963 *NotNAT B*
Polaire, Mademoiselle 1879-1939 *NotNAT B, WhThe*
Polan, Barron 1914- *BiE&WWA*

Polan, Lou 1904-1976 *BiE&WWA, NotNAT, NotNAT B, WhoHol C, WhoThe 16*
Polanski, Roman 1933- *BiDFlm, CelR 3, DcFM, FilmgC, IntMPA 1977, MovMk, OxFilm, WorEnF*
Polansky, Roman *WhoHol A*
Polen, Nat *WhoHol A*
Polgar, Alfred d1955 *NotNAT B*
Polglase, Van Nest 1898- *FilmgC*
Poliakoff, Stephen 1953- *ConDr 1977*
Poliakoff, Vera *WhThe*
Polier, Dan A *IntMPA 1977*
Polini, Emily d1927 *NotNAT B*
Polini, G M d1914 *NotNAT B*
Polini, Marie d1960 *NotNAT B, WhThe*
Polite, Charlene *WhoHol A*
Politian 1454-1491 *OxThe*
Politis, Photos 1890-1934 *OxThe*
Polito, Sol 1892-1960 *FilmgC, WorEnF*
Polito, Sol 1894-1960 *CmMov*
Poliziano 1454-1491 *OxThe*
Poliziano, Angelo 1454-1494 *McGWD*
Polk, Gordon 1924-1960 *WhScrn 1, WhScrn 2, WhoHol B*
Polk, Mary Jane 1916- *AmSCAP 1966*
Poll, Martin H 1922- *FilmgC, IntMPA 1977*
Poll, Ruth 1899-1955 *AmSCAP 1966*
Polla, Pauline M 1868-1940 *WhScrn 1, WhScrn 2, WhoHol B*
Polla, W C 1876-1939 *AmSCAP 1966*
Pollack, Ben d1971 *WhoHol B*
Pollack, Ben 1903- *AmSCAP 1966*
Pollack, Ben 1904-1971 *WhScrn 1, WhScrn 2*
Pollack, Lew 1895-1946 *AmSCAP 1966, NotNAT B*
Pollack, Mimi *WomWMM*
Pollack, Sidney 1934- *WorEnF*
Pollack, Sydney *FilmgC, IntMPA 1977*
Pollack, Sydney 1930- *MovMk*
Pollack, Sydney 1934- *BiDFlm*
Pollar, Gene 1892- *Film 2, WhoHol B*
Pollard, Bud 1887-1952 *WhScrn 1, WhScrn 2, WhoHol B*
Pollard, Daphne 1890- *WhThe*
Pollard, Daphne 1894- *Film 2, TwYS*
Pollard, Harry *Film 1, MotPP*
Pollard, Harry 1883-1934 *FilmgC, NotNAT B, WhScrn 1, WhScrn 2, WhoHol B*
Pollard, Harry Joe 1883-1934 *TwYS A*
Pollard, Harry Snub 1886-1962 *NotNAT B, TwYS, WhScrn 1, WhScrn 2*
Pollard, Laura *Film 2*
Pollard, Michael J 1939- *BiE&WWA, FilmgC, MotPP, MovMk, WhoHol A*
Pollard, Snub 1886-1962 *Film 1, Film 2, FilmgC, WhoHol B*
Pollard, Thomas *OxThe*
Pollet, Albert *Film 2*
Pollet, Jean-Daniel 1936- *WorEnF*
Pollexfen, Jack 1918- *IntMPA 1977*
Pollock, Allan d1942 *NotNAT B*
Pollock, Anna d1946 *NotNAT B*
Pollock, Arthur 1886- *WhThe*
Pollock, Bert D 1923- *AmSCAP 1966*
Pollock, Channing 1880-1946 *AmSCAP 1966, ModWD, NotNAT A, NotNAT B, WhThe, WhoStg 1908*
Pollock, David *see* Davis, Elias And David Pollock
Pollock, Dee *WhoHol A*
Pollock, Elizabeth 1898-1970 *WhThe*
Pollock, Ellen 1903- *PIP&P, WhoHol A, WhoThe 16*
Pollock, George 1907- *FilmgC*
Pollock, Gordon W d1956 *NotNAT B*

Pollock, Horace d1964 *NotNAT B*
Pollock, John d1945 *NotNAT B*
Pollock, John 1878-1963 *WhThe*
Pollock, Louis d1964 *NotNAT B*
Pollock, Muriel *AmSCAP 1966*
Pollock, Nancy R *WhoHol A*
Pollock, Nancy R 1905- *WhoThe 16*
Pollock, Nancy R 1907- *BiE&WWA, NotNAT*
Pollock, William 1881-1944 *NotNAT B, WhThe*
Polo, Eddie 1875-1961 *Film 1, Film 2, MotPP, NotNAT B, TwYS, WhScrn 1, WhScrn 2, WhoHol B*
Polo, Malvine *Film 2*
Polo, Robert d1968 *WhScrn 1, WhScrn 2*
Polo, Sam 1873-1966 *Film 1, Film 2, WhScrn 2, WhoHol B*
Polon, Vicki 1948- *WomWMM B*
Polonsky, Abraham 1910- *BiDFlm, ConDr 1977A, FilmgC, MovMk, OxFilm, WorEnF*
Polus *OxThe*
Poluskis, The *WhThe*
Pomeroy, Jay 1895-1955 *NotNAT B, WhThe*
Pommer, Erich 1889-1966 *DcFM, FilmgC, OxFilm, TwYS B, WorEnF*
Pompadur, I Martin *NewYTET*
Pomponius *OxThe*
Ponce, Ethel *AmSCAP 1966*
Ponce, Phil 1886-1945 *AmSCAP 1966*
Poncin, Marcel d1953 *NotNAT B, WhoHol B*
Pond, Anson Phelps d1920 *NotNAT B*
Pond, Helen 1924- *WhoThe 16*
Ponderoso, Louis *WhoHol A*
Ponisi, Madame 1818-1899 *NotNAT B*
Pons, Helene *BiE&WWA, NotNAT*
Pons, Lily d1976 *WhoHol C*
Pons, Lily 1895- *FilmgC*
Pons, Lily 1898- *ThFT*
Ponsard, Francois 1814-1867 *NotNAT B, OxThe*
Ponsonby, Eustace d1924 *NotNAT B*
Pontecorvo, Gillo 1919- *BiDFlm, DcFM, FilmgC, MovMk, OxFilm, WorEnF*
Ponti, Carlo 1910- *OxFilm, WorEnF*
Ponti, Carlo 1913- *CelR 3, DcFM, FilmgC, IntMPA 1977*
Ponti, Diana Da *OxThe*
Ponting, Herbert George 1870-1935 *DcFM, FilmgC, WorEnF*
Ponto, Erich d1957 *WhScrn 1, WhScrn 2, WhoHol B*
Pontoppidan, Clara *Film 2*
Pool, Elwood J *Film 2*
Pool, F C d1944 *NotNAT B*
Poole, Charles D, Jr. 1931- *AmSCAP 1966*
Poole, Frank S 1913- *IntMPA 1977*
Poole, George E 1904- *AmSCAP 1966*
Poole, John d1872 *NotNAT B*
Poole, Roy 1924- *NotNAT, WhoHol A*
Pooley, Olaf *WhThe, WhoHol A*
Pope, Alexander *PIP&P*
Pope, Alexander d1835 *NotNAT B*
Pope, Curtis L 1919- *BiE&WWA, NotNAT*
Pope, Edward J 1919- *IntMPA 1977*
Pope, Elizabeth d1797 *NotNAT B*
Pope, Jane 1742-1818 *NotNAT B, OxThe*
Pope, Karl Theodore 1937- *NotNAT*
Pope, Maria Ann d1803 *NotNAT B*
Pope, Muriel *WhThe*
Pope, Peggy *WhoHol A*
Pope, T L 1904- *AmSCAP 1966*
Pope, T Michael d1930 *NotNAT B*
Pope, Thomas d1604 *NotNAT B, OxThe, PIP&P*
Pope, Unola B 1884-1938 *WhScrn 1, WhScrn 2*

Pope, Mrs. W Coleman 1809-1880 *NotNAT B*
Pope, William *AmSCAP 1966*
Pope, William Coleman d1868 *NotNAT B*
Popescu-Gopo, Ion 1923- *DcFM, OxFilm*
Popiolkowski, Louis 1927- *AmSCAP 1966*
Popkin, Harry M *FilmgC, IntMPA 1977*
Poplavskaya, Irina *WomWMM*
Popov, Alexei Dmitrevich 1892-1961 *OxThe*
Popov, N *Film 2*
Popov, V *Film 2*
Popplewell, Jack 1911- *WhoThe 16*
Popplewell, Mary 1920- *AmSCAP 1966*
Popwell, Albert *WhoHol A*
Popwell, Johnny *WhoHol A*
Poquelin, Jean-Baptiste *McGWD, REnWD*
Porcasi, Paul 1880-1946 *Film 2, FilmgC,*
  WhScrn 1, WhScrn 2, WhoHol B
Porcelain, Bessie Petts d1968 *WhScrn 2*
Porcelli, Fred *WhoHol A*
Porchov-Lynch, Tao *WomWMM B*
Porel, Marc *WhoHol A*
Porel, Paul 1843-1917 *NotNAT B, WhThe*
Porta, Giambattista Della *OxThe*
Porten, Henny 1888- *Film 2*
Porten, Henny 1890-1960 *NotNAT B, OxFilm,*
  WhScrn 1, WhScrn 2, WhoHol B
Porteous, Gilbert 1868-1928 *NotNAT B, WhThe*
Porter, Caleb 1867-1940 *NotNAT B, WhThe*
Porter, Cole 1891-1964 *BiE&WWA, CmMov,*
  EncMT, FilmgC, NotNAT A, NotNAT B,
  OxFilm
Porter, Cole 1892-1964 *NewMT*
Porter, Cole 1893-1964 *AmSCAP 1966, McGWD,*
  PIP&P, WhThe
Porter, Don 1912- *FilmgC, IntMPA 1977,*
  NotNAT, WhoHol A, WhoThe 16
Porter, Edward D 1881-1939 *WhScrn 1,*
  WhScrn 2, WhoHol B
Porter, Edwin S *WomWMM*
Porter, Edwin S 1869-1941 *CmMov, FilmgC,*
  TwYS A, WorEnF
Porter, Edwin S 1870-1941 *DcFM, OxFilm*
Porter, Eric 1928- *CnThe, FilmgC, WhoHol A,*
  WhoThe 16
Porter, Hal 1911- *ConDr 1977*
Porter, Harold B 1896-1939 *WhScrn 1,*
  WhScrn 2
Porter, Harry A d1920 *NotNAT B*
Porter, Henry d1599 *McGWD, OxThe, REnWD*
Porter, J Robert *WhoHol A*
Porter, Jean *WhoHol A*
Porter, Katherine Anne 1890- *CelR 3*
Porter, Lee 1930- *AmSCAP 1966*
Porter, Lew 1892-1956 *AmSCAP 1966*
Porter, Lillian *WhoHol A*
Porter, Lulu *WhoHol A*
Porter, Mary Ann d1765 *OxThe*
Porter, Neil 1895-1944 *NotNAT B, WhThe*
Porter, Nyree Dawn 1940- *FilmgC, WhoHol A*
Porter, Pansy *Film 2*
Porter, Paul *Film 2*
Porter, Paul A d1975 *NewYTET*
Porter, Quincy 1897-1966 *NotNAT B*
Porter, Rand 1933- *IntMPA 1977*
Porter, Stephen 1925- *NotNAT, WhoThe 16*
Porter, Sylvia 1913- *CelR 3*
Porter, Viola Adele 1879-1942 *WhScrn 1,*
  WhScrn 2
Porterfield, Robert H 1905-1971 *BiE&WWA,*
  NotNAT B, WhScrn 1, WhScrn 2, WhThe,
  WhoHol B
Portman, Eric 1903-1969 *BiE&WWA, CnThe,*
  FilmgC, MotPP, PIP&P, WhScrn 1,
  WhScrn 2, WhThe, WhoHol B

Portman, Eric 1903-1970 *NotNAT B*
Portman, Eric 1904-1969 *MovMk*
Portner, Paul 1925- *CroCD*
Portnoff, Mischa 1901- *AmSCAP 1966*
Portnoff, Wesley 1910- *AmSCAP 1966*
Porto-Riche, George De 1849-1930 *NotNAT B*
Porto-Riche, Georges De 1849-1930 *CnMD,*
  McGWD, ModWD, WhThe
Posford, George 1906- *WhThe*
Posnack, Blanche 1912- *AmSCAP 1966*
Posnack, George 1904- *AmSCAP 1966*
Possart, Ernst Von 1841-1921 *NotNAT B, OxThe,*
  WhThe
Post, Buddy *Film 2*
Post, Carl 1910- *AmSCAP 1966*
Post, Charles A *Film 2*
Post, Guy Bates d1968 *WhoHol B*
Post, Guy Bates 1875-1946 *NotNAT B*
Post, Guy Bates 1875-1968 *NotNAT B,*
  WhScrn 1, WhScrn 2, WhThe,
  WhoStg 1906, WhoStg 1908
Post, Guy Bates 1876-1968 *Film 2, TwYS*
Post, Marjorie Merriweather 1887- *CelR 3*
Post, Ted 1925- *FilmgC, IntMPA 1977*
Post, Troy 1906- *CelR 3*
Post, Wiley d1935 *WhScrn 1, WhScrn 2,*
  WhoHol B
Post, William, Jr. *WhoHol A*
Post, Wilmarth H d1930 *WhScrn 1, WhScrn 2*
Posta, Adrienne 1948- *FilmgC, WhoHol A*
Poston, Tom *WhoHol A*
Poston, Tom 1921- *WhoThe 16*
Poston, Tom 1927- *BiE&WWA, FilmgC,*
  NotNAT
Posznanski, Alfred *McGWD*
Potechina, Lydia *Film 2*
Potel, Victor 1889-1947 *Film 1, Film 2,*
  NotNAT B, TwYS, Vers B, WhScrn 1,
  WhScrn 2, WhoHol B
Potier DesCailletieres, Charles-Gabriel 1774-1838
  OxThe
Potter, Betty *WhoHol A*
Potter, Bob *WhoHol A*
Potter, Cora Urquhart 1857-1936 *FamA&A,*
  WhThe
Potter, Cora Urquhart *see also* Potter, Mrs. James
  Brown
Potter, Dennis 1935- *ConDr 1977, WhoThe 16*
Potter, H C 1904- *BiE&WWA, DcFM, FilmgC,*
  IntMPA 1977, MovMk, NotNAT, WhThe,
  WorEnF
Potter, Mrs. James Brown 1859-1936 *OxThe,*
  WhoStg 1906, WhoStg 1908
Potter, Mrs. James Brown *see also* Potter, Cora
  Urquhart
Potter, Martin 1944- *FilmgC, WhoHol A*
Potter, Maureen *WhoHol A*
Potter, Paul M 1853-1921 *NotNAT B, WhThe,*
  WhoStg 1906, WhoStg 1908
Potter, Philip 1921- *CelR 3*
Pottle, Sam 1934- *AmSCAP 1966*
Potts, Nancy *NotNAT, WhoThe 16*
Potts, Nell *WhoHol A*
Pouctal, Henri 1856-1922 *DcFM*
Pougin, Arthur d1921 *NotNAT B*
Poujouly, Georges 1940- *FilmgC*
Poulenc, Francis 1889-1963 *NotNAT B*
Poulenc, Francis 1899-1963 *DcFM*
Poulsen, Johannes d1938 *NotNAT B*
Poulton, A G 1867- *WhThe*
Poulton, Mabel 1903- *Film 2*
Poulton, Mabel 1905- *FilmgC, WhoHol A*
Pound, Ezra 1885-1972 *CnMD*
Pounds, Charles Courtice 1862-1927 *NotNAT B,*

WhThe
Pounds, Louie *WhThe*
Pouyet, Eugene *Film 1, Film 2*
Povah, Phyllis 1920- *BiE&WWA, NotNAT, WhThe, WhoHol A*
Powell *PIP&P*
Powell, Addison *WhoHol A*
Powell, Baden *Film 1*
Powell, Bellendom *Film 2*
Powell, Brychan B 1896- *AmSCAP 1966*
Powell, Charles M 1934- *IntMPA 1977*
Powell, Charles Stuart d1811 *NotNAT B*
Powell, David *MotPP*
Powell, David d1925 *WhScrn 1, WhScrn 2, WhoHol B*
Powell, David 1887-1923 *Film 1, Film 2, TwYS*
Powell, Dawn 1900- *PIP&P*
Powell, Dick d1948 *WhScrn 1, WhScrn 2, WhoHol B*
Powell, Dick 1904-1963 *BiDFlm, CmMov, FilmgC, MotPP, MovMk, NewYTET, NotNAT B, WhScrn 1, WhScrn 2, WhoHol B, WorEnF*
Powell, Dick, Jr. *WhoHol A*
Powell, Dilys *IntMPA 1977*
Powell, Edward Soldene 1865- *WhoStg 1908*
Powell, Eleanor *MotPP*
Powell, Eleanor 1910- *EncMT, FilmgC, WhoHol A*
Powell, Eleanor 1912- *BiE&WWA, CmMov, MGM, MovMk, OxFilm, ThFT, WhThe*
Powell, Ellis d1963 *NotNAT B*
Powell, Frank *Film 1, TwYS A*
Powell, George 1668-1714 *NotNAT B, OxThe*
Powell, Jane *IntMPA 1977, MotPP*
Powell, Jane 1928- *CmMov*
Powell, Jane 1929- *FilmgC, MGM, MovMk, WhoHol A, WorEnF*
Powell, John 1882-1963 *AmSCAP 1966*
Powell, Laurence 1899- *AmSCAP 1966*
Powell, Lee 1896-1954 *WhScrn 1, WhScrn 2*
Powell, Lee 1912-1944 *WhoHol B*
Powell, Lee B 1908-1944 *WhScrn 1, WhScrn 2*
Powell, Lewis 1907- *CelR 3*
Powell, Lovelady *WhoHol A*
Powell, Martin *OxThe*
Powell, Mel 1923- *AmSCAP 1966, WhoHol A*
Powell, Michael 1905- *BiDFlm, CmMov, ConDr 1977A, DcFM, Film 2, FilmgC, IntMPA 1977, MovMk, OxFilm, WorEnF*
Powell, Pat *WomWMM A, WomWMM B*
Powell, Paul *TwYS A*
Powell, Peter 1908- *WhThe*
Powell, Richard 1897-1937 *WhScrn 1, WhScrn 2, WhoHol B*
Powell, Robert *WhoHol A*
Powell, Robert 1944- *WhoThe 16*
Powell, Robert 1946- *FilmgC*
Powell, Russ 1875-1950 *WhScrn 2*
Powell, Russell *Film 2*
Powell, Sandy 1898- *FilmgC*
Powell, Teddy 1906- *AmSCAP 1966*
Powell, Templar *Film 1*
Powell, Walter Templer d1949 *NotNAT B*
Powell, William 1735-1769 *NotNAT B, OxThe*
Powell, William 1892- *BiDFlm, CmMov, Film 1, Film 2, FilmgC, IntMPA 1977, MGM, MotPP, MovMk, OxFilm, TwYS, WhThe, WhoHol A, WorEnF*
Power, Clavering d1931 *NotNAT B*
Power, Sir George d1928 *NotNAT B*
Power, Hartley 1894-1966 *BiE&WWA, FilmgC, WhScrn 1, WhScrn 2, WhThe, WhoHol B*
Power, John 1874-1951 *WhScrn 1, WhScrn 2*

Power, Jules *Film 1, Film 2*
Power, Nelly d1887 *NotNAT B*
Power, Paul 1902-1968 *WhScrn 1, WhScrn 2, WhoHol B*
Power, Romina *WhoHol A*
Power, Rosine 1840-1932 *NotNAT B*
Power, Tyrone d1958 *MotPP, WhoHol B*
Power, Tyrone 1795-1841 *OxThe*
Power, Tyrone 1797-1841 *FamA&A, NotNAT A, NotNAT B*
Power, Tyrone 1913-1958 *BiDFlm, CmMov, FilmgC, MovMk, NotNAT B, OxFilm*
Power, Tyrone 1914-1958 *CmMov, OxThe, WhScrn 1, WhScrn 2, WhThe, WorEnF*
Power, Tyrone, Sr. 1866-1931 *WhThe, WhoStg 1906, WhoStg 1908*
Power, Tyrone, Sr. 1869-1931 *Film 1, Film 2, FilmgC, NotNAT A, NotNAT B, TwYS, WhScrn 1, WhScrn 2, WhoHol B*
Power, Tyrone Edmond 1869-1931 *OxThe*
Power, Victor 1930- *NatPD*
Powers, Arba Eugene d1935 *NotNAT B*
Powers, Beverly *WhoHol A*
Powers, C F, Jr. 1923- *IntMPA 1977*
Powers, Eugene 1872- *WhThe*
Powers, Francis *Film 2*
Powers, Harry J d1941 *NotNAT B*
Powers, James T 1862-1943 *NotNAT A, NotNAT B, WhThe, WhoStg 1906, WhoStg 1908*
Powers, John 1935- *WhoThe 16*
Powers, John H 1885-1941 *WhScrn 1, WhScrn 2, WhoHol B*
Powers, Jule d1932 *WhScrn 1, WhScrn 2*
Powers, Leona 1896-1970 *BiE&WWA, NotNAT B, WhoHol B*
Powers, Leona 1898-1967 *WhThe*
Powers, Lucille *Film 2*
Powers, Mala *MotPP, WomWMM*
Powers, Mala 1921- *IntMPA 1977*
Powers, Mala 1931- *FilmgC, WhoHol A*
Powers, Marie d1973 *BiE&WWA, NotNAT B, WhScrn 2, WhoHol B*
Powers, Mary Gare d1961 *WhScrn 2, WhoHol B*
Powers, Maurine *Film 2*
Powers, Maxwell 1911- *AmSCAP 1966*
Powers, Richard d1963 *WhScrn 1, WhScrn 2, WhoHol B*
Powers, Stefanie 1942- *FilmgC, MotPP, MovMk, WhoHol A*
Powers, Tom 1890-1955 *Film 1, FilmgC, NotNAT B, PIP&P, Vers A, WhScrn 1, WhScrn 2, WhThe, WhoHol B*
Powley, Bryan 1871-1962 *Film 2, WhScrn 2*
Pownall, Mrs. *PIP&P*
Powys, Stephen 1907- *BiE&WWA, NotNAT, WhThe*
Pozner, Vladimir 1905- *DcFM*
Pozzi, Mrs. *Film 2*
Prade, Marie *Film 2*
Pradon, Jacques 1644-1698 *McGWD, OxThe*
Pradot, Marcelle *Film 2*
Praga, Marco 1862-1929 *McGWD, ModWD, REnWD, WhThe*
Prager, Alice Heinecke 1930- *IntMPA 1977*
Prager, Carl 1913- *IntMPA 1977*
Prager, Samuel 1907- *AmSCAP 1966*
Prager, Stanley 1917-1972 *BiE&WWA, NotNAT B, WhScrn 2, WhoHol B*
Prager, Willy 1877-1956 *WhScrn 1, WhScrn 2*
Prasch, Auguste *Film 2*
Prata, Joaquim 1882-1953 *WhScrn 1, WhScrn 2*
Prather, Lee 1890-1958 *WhScrn 1, WhScrn 2, WhoHol B*

Pratinas *OxThe*
Pratley, Gerald *IntMPA 1977*
Pratt, Charles A 1923- *IntMPA 1977*
Pratt, Jack *Film 2*
Pratt, Judson *WhoHol A*
Pratt, Lynn 1863-1930 *Film 2, WhScrn 1,
    WhScrn 2, WhoHol B*
Pratt, Michael *WhoHol A*
Pratt, Muriel d1945 *NotNAT B, WhThe*
Pratt, Neil 1890-1934 *WhScrn 1, WhScrn 2*
Pratt, Purnell B 1882-1941 *Film 2, TwYS,
    WhoHol B*
Pratt, Purnell B 1886-1941 *WhScrn 1, WhScrn 2*
Pratt, Samuel Jackson d1814 *NotNAT B*
Pratt, Theodore 1901-1969 *NotNAT B*
Pravov, Ivan *WomWMM*
Praxy, Raoul 1892-1967 *WhScrn 2*
Pray, Anna M 1891-1971 *WhScrn 1, WhScrn 2*
Pray, Isaac Clark d1869 *NotNAT B*
Precht, Robert *NewYTET*
Preece, Tim 1938- *WhoThe 16*
Preedy, George R 1888-1952 *NotNAT B, WhThe*
Preer, Evalyn d1932 *WhoHol B*
Preer, Evelyn 1896-1932 *WhScrn 1, WhScrn 2*
Prehauser, Gottfried 1699-1769 *NotNAT B,
    OxThe*
Preisser, Cherry d1964 *NotNAT B, WhoHol B*
Prejean, Albert 1893- *OxFilm*
Prejean, Albert 1894- *WhoHol A, WorEnF*
Prejean, Albert 1898- *Film 2, FilmgC*
Prelia, Claire *Film 2*
Prelle, Micheline *WhoHol A*
Prelock, Edward P 1934- *IntMPA 1977*
Premice, Josephine 1926- *BiE&WWA, NotNAT*
Preminger, Ingo *FilmgC*
Preminger, Otto 1906- *BiDFlm, BiE&WWA,
    CelR 3, CmMov, DcFM, FilmgC,
    IntMPA 1977, MovMk, NotNAT,
    NotNAT A, OxFilm, WhoHol A, WorEnF*
Premysler, Francine *WomWMM*
Prendergast, John Xavier *IntMPA 1977*
Prensky, Lester H *BiE&WWA, NotNAT*
Prentice, Charles W 1898- *WhThe*
Prentice, Herbert M 1890- *WhThe*
Prentice, Keith *WhoHol A*
Prentis, Lewis R 1905-1967 *WhScrn 1, WhScrn 2*
Prentiss, Ann *WhoHol A*
Prentiss, Ed *WhoHol A*
Prentiss, Paula 1939- *BiDFlm, FilmgC,
    IntMPA 1977, MotPP, MovMk, WhoHol A*
Preobrazhenskaya, Olga *WomWMM*
Presano, Rita d1935 *NotNAT B*
Presbrey, Eugene Wyley 1853-1931 *NotNAT B,
    WhThe*
Prescott, Vivian *Film 1*
Presle, Micheline 1922- *BiDFlm, FilmgC,
    IntMPA 1977, MotPP, MovMk, OxFilm,
    WhoHol A, WorEnF*
Presley, Elvis 1935- *BiDFlm, CelR 3, CmMov,
    FilmgC, IntMPA 1977, MotPP, MovMk,
    OxFilm, WhoHol A, WorEnF*
Presnell, Harve 1933- *FilmgC, MotPP,
    WhoHol A*
Presnell, Robert, Sr. 1894- *FilmgC*
Presnell, Robert R, Jr. 1914- *FilmgC,
    IntMPA 1977*
Press, Jacques 1903- *AmSCAP 1966*
Press, Marvin 1915-1968 *WhScrn 2*
Pressburger, Arnold 1885-1951 *FilmgC*
Pressburger, Emeric 1902- *DcFM, FilmgC,
    OxFilm, WorEnF*
Pressman, David 1913- *BiE&WWA, NotNAT*
Pressman, Edward R *IntMPA 1977*
Pressman, Harry 1907- *AmSCAP 1966*

Pressman, Lawrence *WhoHol A*
Pressman, Lynn *WomWMM*
Preston, Edna 1892-1960 *WhScrn 1, WhScrn 2*
Preston, Jessie d1928 *NotNAT B*
Preston, Robert *IntMPA 1977, MotPP*
Preston, Robert 1917- *CmMov, FilmgC,
    HolP 40*
Preston, Robert 1918- *BiE&WWA, CelR 3,
    EncMT, FamA&A, MovMk, NotNAT,
    WhoHol A, WhoThe 16, WorEnF*
Preston, Thomas *McGWD, OxThe, REnWD*
Preston, Walter H 1901- *AmSCAP 1966*
Preston, Wayde *WhoHol A*
Preston, William d1807 *NotNAT B*
Pretal, Camillus *Film 2*
Pretty, Arline 1893- *Film 1, Film 2, TwYS,
    WhoHol A*
Prevert, Jacques 1900- *DcFM, FilmgC, OxFilm,
    WorEnF*
Prevert, Pierre 1906- *DcFM, OxFilm, WorEnF*
Preville 1721-1799 *NotNAT B, OxThe*
Previn, Andre 1929- *AmSCAP 1966, CelR 3,
    CmMov, FilmgC, IntMPA 1977, OxFilm,
    PIP&P, WhoHol A, WorEnF*
Previn, Charles 1888- *AmSCAP 1966*
Previn, Dory Langdon 1925- *AmSCAP 1966*
Previn, Steve 1925- *IntMPA 1977*
Prevost, Francoise 1930- *OxFilm, WhoHol A*
Prevost, Frank G 1894-1946 *WhScrn 1,
    WhScrn 2*
Prevost, Marcel 1862-1941 *NotNAT B, WhThe*
Prevost, Marie 1898-1937 *Film 1, Film 2,
    FilmgC, MotPP, MovMk, NotNAT B,
    ThFT, TwYS, WhScrn 1, WhScrn 2,
    WhoHol B*
Prewett, Eda Valerga d1964 *NotNAT B*
Price, Alan *WhoHol A*
Price, Albert John 1943- *AmSCAP 1966*
Price, Alonzo 1888-1962 *WhScrn 2, WhoHol B*
Price, Dennis 1915-1973 *BiE&WWA, FilmgC,
    MovMk, NotNAT B, OxFilm, WhScrn 2,
    WhThe, WhoHol B*
Price, Eleazer D d1935 *NotNAT B*
Price, Evadne 1896- *WhThe*
Price, Florence B 1888-1953 *AmSCAP 1966*
Price, Frank *NewYTET*
Price, George E 1900-1964 *AmSCAP 1966,
    NotNAT B*
Price, George N d1962 *NotNAT B*
Price, Georgie 1900-1964 *WhScrn 1, WhScrn 2,
    WhoHol B*
Price, Hal 1886-1964 *Film 2, WhScrn 2,
    WhoHol B*
Price, Jack 1910- *AmSCAP 1966*
Price, John L, Jr. 1920- *BiE&WWA, NotNAT*
Price, Kate d1942 *WhoHol B*
Price, Kate 1872-1943 *TwYS, WhScrn 1,
    WhScrn 2*
Price, Kate 1873-1943 *Film 1, Film 2,
    NotNAT B*
Price, Leontyne 1927- *BiE&WWA, CelR 3,
    PIP&P*
Price, Lorain M d1963 *NotNAT B*
Price, Lorin Ellington 1921- *NotNAT*
Price, Maire d1958 *OxThe*
Price, Mark d1917 *Film 1, WhScrn 2*
Price, Nancy 1880-1970 *Film 2, FilmgC, OxThe,
    PIP&P, WhScrn 1, WhScrn 2, WhThe,
    WhoHol B*
Price, Roger 1920- *IntMPA 1977, WhoHol A*
Price, Sherwood *WhoHol A*
Price, Stanley L 1900-1955 *NotNAT B,
    WhScrn 1, WhScrn 2, WhoHol B*
Price, Stephen 1783-1840 *NotNAT B, OxThe,*

PlP&P
Price, Stephen 1940- *AmSCAP 1966*
Price, Vincent 1911- *BiDFlm, BiE&WWA, CelR 3, CmMov, FilmgC, IntMPA 1977, MotPP, MovMk, NotNAT, OxFilm, WhoHol A, WhoThe 16, WorEnF*
Price, Walter *WhoHol A*
Price, Walter J 1942- *AmSCAP 1966*
Price, Will d1962 *NotNAT B*
Price, William Thompson d1920 *NotNAT B*
Price-Drury, W d1949 *NotNAT B*
Prickett, Oliver B 1905- *BiE&WWA, NotNAT, WhoHol A*
Pride, Charley *CelR 3*
Pride, Malcolm 1930- *WhoThe 16*
Prideaux, James 1935- *NatPD*
Prideaux, Tom 1908- *BiE&WWA, NotNAT*
Pries, Ralph W 1919- *IntMPA 1977*
Priesing, Dorothy 1910- *AmSCAP 1966*
Priest, Dan *WhoHol A*
Priest, Janet 1881- *WhoStg 1908*
Priest, Natalie *WhoHol A*
Priest, Pat *WhoHol A*
Priestley, J B 1894- *BiE&WWA, CnThe, ConDr 1977, CroCD, IntMPA 1977, McGWD, ModWD, NotNAT, PlP&P, REnWD, WhoThe 16, WorEnF*
Priestley, John Boynton 1894- *CnMD, NotNAT A, OxThe*
Prieto, Antonio 1915-1965 *WhScrn 1, WhScrn 2*
Priggen, Norman 1924- *FilmgC*
Prima, Louis 1911- *AmSCAP 1966*
Prima, Louis 1913?- *WhoHol A*
Primm, Frances *Film 2*
Primo, Al *NewYTET*
Primrose, Dorothy 1916- *WhoHol A, WhoThe 16*
Primus, Barry *WhoHol A*
Prince, Adelaide 1866-1941 *NotNAT B, WhThe, WhoStg 1908*
Prince, Arthur 1881- *WhThe*
Prince, Elsie 1902- *WhThe*
Prince, Harold 1924- *FilmgC*
Prince, Harold 1928- *BiE&WWA, CelR 3, CnThe, EncMT, IntMPA 1977, NotNAT, NotNAT A, PlP&P A, WhoThe 16*
Prince, Hugh Denham 1906-1960 *AmSCAP 1966*
Prince, Jessie *Film 2*
Prince, John T 1871-1937 *Film 2, WhScrn 1, WhScrn 2, WhoHol B*
Prince, Lillian d1962 *NotNAT B*
Prince, William 1912- *WhoHol A*
Prince, William 1913- *BiE&WWA, FilmgC, IntMPA 1977, NotNAT, WhoThe 16*
Prince Randian 1871?-1934? *WhScrn 2*
Princess Kanza Omar 1912-1958 *WhScrn 1, WhScrn 2*
Principal, Victoria *WhoHol A*
Prine, Andrew 1936- *BiE&WWA, FilmgC, NotNAT, WhoHol A*
Pring, Gerald *Film 2*
Pringle, Aileen 1895- *Film 1, Film 2, FilmgC, MotPP, MovMk, ThFT, TwYS, WhoHol A*
Pringle, Bryan 1935- *FilmgC, WhoHol A*
Pringle, Della *Film 1*
Pringle, Joan *WhoHol A*
Pringle, John d1929 *WhScrn 1, WhScrn 2, WhoHol B*
Prinsep, Anthony Leyland 1888-1942 *WhThe*
Prinsep, Val d1904 *NotNAT B*
Printemps, Yvonne *CnThe*
Printemps, Yvonne 1895- *EncMT, OxFilm, OxThe, WhThe, WhoHol A*
Printemps, Yvonne 1898- *BiE&WWA*
Prinz, LeRoy 1895- *CmMov, FilmgC,*

IntMPA 1977, WorEnF
Prinze, Freddie 1954- *IntMPA 1977*
Prinzmetal, I H 1906- *IntMPA 1977*
Priolo, Joseph P 1918- *AmSCAP 1966*
Prior, Allan *WhThe*
Prior, Beatrix *Film 2*
Prior, Herbert 1867-1954 *Film 1, Film 2, TwYS, WhScrn 2, WhoHol B*
Prior, Robert *Film 2*
Prisadsky, Marjorie *WomWMM B*
Prisco, Al *Film 2*
Priscoe, Albert *Film 2*
Pritchard, Barry *NatPD*
Pritchard, Dick d1963 *NotNAT B*
Pritchard, Hannah 1711-1768 *OxThe, PlP&P*
Pritchett, Paula *WhoHol A*
Pritner, Calvin Lee 1935- *NotNAT*
Prival, Lucien 1900- *Film 2, TwYS*
Prival, Max 1889-1957 *AmSCAP 1966*
Prizek, Mario 1922- *IntMPA 1977*
Probert, George *Film 2*
Probst, Robert J 1929- *AmSCAP 1966*
Proby, David d1964 *NotNAT B*
Prochnicka, Lidia *WhoHol A*
Procter, Ivis Goulding 1906-1973 *WhScrn 2*
Procter, Jessie Olive 1874-1975 *WhScrn 2*
Proctor, Bryan Waller d1874 *NotNAT B*
Proctor, Catherine *Film 2*
Proctor, Cathrine *WhoStg 1908*
Proctor, David 1878- *WhoStg 1908*
Proctor, F F *WhoStg 1906, WhoStg 1908*
Proctor, Frederick Francis 1851-1929 *NotNAT B, OxThe*
Proctor, Frederick Freeman 1851-1929 *NotNAT A*
Proctor, James D 1907- *BiE&WWA, NotNAT*
Proctor, Joseph d1897 *NotNAT B*
Proctor, Marland *WhoHol A*
Proctor, Philip *WhoHol A*
Profanato, Gene *WhoHol A*
Prohaska, Janos 1921-1974 *WhScrn 2*
Prohaska, Robert d1974 *WhScrn 2*
Prohut, Lou 1931- *AmSCAP 1966*
Prokhovenko, Shanna *WhoHol A*
Prokofiev, Sergei 1891-1953 *DcFM, OxFilm, WorEnF*
Prokoviev, Sergei 1891-1953 *FilmgC*
Promio, Alexandre 1870-1927 *DcFM*
Promis, Flo 1884-1956 *WhScrn 1, WhScrn 2*
Proser, Monte *BiE&WWA*
Prosser, Hugh 1906-1952 *WhScrn 1, WhScrn 2, WhoHol B*
Protazanov, Yakov 1881-1945 *DcFM, OxFilm*
Protazonov, Yakov 1881-1945 *WorEnF*
Prout, Eva *Film 1*
Prouty, Jed 1879-1956 *Film 2, FilmgC, MotPP, MovMk, NotNAT B, TwYS, Vers A, WhScrn 1, WhScrn 2, WhoHol B*
Provine, Dorothy 1937- *FilmgC, IntMPA 1977, MotPP, MovMk, WhoHol A*
Provost, Jeanne *WhThe*
Provost, Jon 1949- *MotPP, WhoHol A*
Prowse, Juliet 1937- *FilmgC, MotPP, WhoHol A*
Proxmire, William 1915- *CelR 3*
Prudence Penny 1889-1974 *WhScrn 2*
Prud'homme, Cameron 1892-1967 *BiE&WWA, MotPP, NotNAT B, WhScrn 1, WhScrn 2, WhoHol B*
Prud'homme, George 1901-1972 *WhScrn 2, WhoHol B*
Pruette, William *WhoStg 1908*
Prujan, Turk 1909- *AmSCAP 1966*
Prussing, Louise 1897- *Film 2, WhThe*
Pryce, Richard d1942 *NotNAT B, WhThe*

Pryce-Jones, Alan 1908- *BiE&WWA, NotNAT*
Pryde, Peggy 1869- *WhThe*
Pryde, Ted d1963 *NotNAT B*
Prynne, William d1669 *NotNAT B*
Pryor, Ainslie 1921-1958 *WhScrn 1, WhScrn 2, WhoHol B*
Pryor, Arthur 1870-1942 *AmSCAP 1966, NotNAT B*
Pryor, Beatrix *Film 2*
Pryor, Hugh 1925-1963 *WhScrn 2*
Pryor, Jacqueline 1930-1963 *WhScrn 2*
Pryor, Maureen *WhoHol A*
Pryor, Nicholas 1935- *BiE&WWA, NotNAT, WhoHol A*
Pryor, Richard 1941- *FilmgC, MovMk, WhoHol A*
Pryor, Roger d1974 *WhoHol B*
Pryor, Roger 1900- *FilmgC*
Pryor, Roger 1901-1974 *HolP 30, WhScrn 2, WhThe*
Pryor, Roger 1903- *Vers A*
Pryor, Thomas M 1912- *IntMPA 1977*
Pryse, Hugh 1910-1955 *NotNAT B, WhThe, WhoHol B*
Przybyszewski, Stanislaus 1868-1927 *CnMD*
Przybyszewski, Stanislaw 1868-1927 *McGWD, ModWD*
Psacharopoulos, Nikos 1928- *BiE&WWA, NotNAT*
Ptushko, Alexander 1900- *DcFM*
Publilius Syrus *OxThe*
Pucci, Emilio 1914- *CelR 3*
Puccini, Giacomo *PIP&P*
Puchi, Rebecca *WomWMM*
Puck, Harry 1890-1964 *AmSCAP 1966, NotNAT B*
Puddles d1912 *WhScrn 2*
Pudney, John 1909- *IntMPA 1977*
Pudoffstin, J *Film 2*
Pudovkin, Vsevolod I 1893-1953 *FilmgC, WhScrn 1, WhScrn 2, WhoHol B, WorEnF*
Pudovkin, Vsevolod Ilarionovich 1893-1953 *DcFM, MovMk, OxFilm*
Pudovkin, Vsevolod Illareonovitch 1893-1952 *BiDFlm*
Puffer, Deena *AmSCAP 1966*
Puffer, Merle 1915- *AmSCAP 1966*
Puffy, Charles *Film 2*
Puget, Claude-Andre 1905- *CnMD, McGWD, ModWD*
Pugh, Sally *WomWMM B*
Puglia, Frank d1975 *WhoHol C*
Puglia, Frank 1892- *MovMk, Vers A*
Puglia, Frank 1892-1962 *FilmgC*
Puglia, Frank 1892-1975 *WhScrn 2*
Puglia, Frank 1894-1962 *Film 2, TwYS*
Pugliese, Rudolph E 1918- *BiE&WWA, NotNAT*
Puig, Eva G 1894-1968 *WhScrn 2*
Pulaski, Jack d1948 *NotNAT B*
Pulitzer, Joseph, Jr. 1913- *CelR 3*
Pulling, M J L 1906- *IntMPA 1977*
Pully, B S 1911-1972 *PIP&P, WhScrn 2, WhoHol B*
Pulver, Lilo 1929- *FilmgC*
Pulver, Liselotte *WhoHol A*
Pumphrey, Byron *NatPD*
Punsley, Bernard *WhoHol A*
Purcell, Charles 1883-1962 *EncMT, WhThe*
Purcell, Dick 1908-1944 *FilmgC, WhoHol B*
Purcell, Edward 1928- *AmSCAP 1966*
Purcell, Gertrude d1963 *NotNAT B*
Purcell, Harold 1907- *WhThe*
Purcell, Irene d1972 *WhoHol B*
Purcell, Irene 1902-1972 *WhScrn 2*

Purcell, Irene 1903-1972 *WhThe*
Purcell, Lee *WhoHol A*
Purcell, Noel 1900- *FilmgC, IntMPA 1977, WhoHol A*
Purcell, Richard 1908-1944 *WhScrn 1, WhScrn 2*
Purdell, Reginald 1896-1953 *FilmgC, NotNAT B, WhScrn 1, WhScrn 2, WhThe, WhoHol B*
Purdom, C B 1883-1965 *BiE&WWA, WhThe*
Purdom, Edmund 1924- *FilmgC, IntMPA 1977, MotPP, WhoHol A*
Purdon, Richard *Film 1*
Purdy, Constance 1885?-1960 *WhScrn 2*
Purdy, James *PIP&P*
Purdy, Rai 1910- *IntMPA 1977*
Purkine, Jan Evangelista 1787-1869 *DcFM*
Purnell, Alton 1911- *AmSCAP 1966*
Purnell, Louise 1942- *WhoHol A, WhoThe 16*
Purviance, Edna 1894-1958 *Film 1, Film 2, FilmgC, MotPP, MovMk, OxFilm, TwYS, WhScrn 1, WhScrn 2, WhoHol B, WorEnF*
Purviance, Edna 1895-1958 *NotNAT B*
Purvis, Charlie 1909- *AmSCAP 1966*
Pusey, Arthur *Film 2, WhThe*
Pushkin, Aleksandr Sergeyevich 1799-1837 *McGWD*
Pushkin, Alexander Sergeivich 1799-1837 *OxThe*
Pushkin, Alexander Sergeyevich 1799-1837 *CnThe, REnWD*
Pushkin, Alexander Sergeyevitch 1799-1837 *NotNAT B*
Putman, George d1974 *WhScrn 2*
Putnam, George d1975 *WhoHol C*
Putter, Alice Mildred *Film 2*
Puzhnaya, R *Film 2*
Puzo, Mario 1921- *CelR 3*
Pye, Henry James d1813 *NotNAT B*
Pyke, Harry 1903- *AmSCAP 1966*
Pylades *OxThe*
Pyle, Denver 1920- *FilmgC, MovMk, WhoHol A*
Pyle, Francis Johnson 1901- *AmSCAP 1966*
Pyle, Harry C 1894- *AmSCAP 1966*
Pyle, Russell 1941- *NotNAT*
Pyne, Joe 1925-1970 *WhScrn 1, WhScrn 2, WhoHol B*
Pyriev, Ivan 1901-1968 *DcFM*
Pyros, John *NatPD*

Q

Quaal, Ward L NewYTET
Quade, John WhoHol A
Quadflieg, Will WhoHol A
Quadling, Lew 1908- AmSCAP 1966
Quaglio OxThe
Quaid, Randy 1953- IntMPA 1977, MovMk,
  WhoHol A
Quale, Anthony MotPP
Qualen, John 1899- FilmgC, IntMPA 1977,
  MotPP, MovMk, Vers A, WhoHol A
Quality, Gertrude Film 2
Qualters, Tot 1895-1974 WhScrn 2, WhoHol B
Qualtinger, Helmut WhoHol A
Quaranta, Letizia 1892- OxFilm
Quaranta, Lydia 1891-1928 Film 1, OxFilm,
  WhScrn 2
Quarry, Robert 1923- FilmgC, WhoHol A
Quartaro, Nena 1911- TwYS
Quartaro, Nina 1911- Film 2
Quartermaine, Charles 1877-1958 NotNAT B,
  OxThe, WhThe, WhoHol B
Quartermaine, Leon 1876-1967 BiE&WWA,
  NotNAT B, OxThe, WhScrn 1, WhScrn 2,
  WhThe, WhoHol B
Quayle, Anna WhoHol A
Quayle, Anna 1936- BiE&WWA, NotNAT
Quayle, Anna 1937- FilmgC, WhoThe 16
Quayle, Anthony 1913- BiE&WWA, CelR 3,
  CnThe, FilmgC, IntMPA 1977, MovMk,
  NotNAT, OxThe, PIP&P, WhoHol A,
  WhoThe 16
Quayle, Calvin 1927- BiE&WWA, NotNAT
Quedens, Eunice Film 2, WhoHol A
Queen, Ellery 1905- CelR 3
Queen, Robert I 1919- IntMPA 1977
Queeny, Mary 190-?- DcFM, WomWMM
Quello, James H NewYTET
Queneau, Raymond 1903- DcFM, OxFilm,
  WorEnF
Quensel, Isa WhoHol A
Quenzer, Arthur 1905- AmSCAP 1966
Questel, Mae 1910- BiE&WWA, WhoHol A
Quick, John 1748-1831 OxThe, PIP&P
Quick, Robert E 1917- IntMPA 1977
Quigley, Charles 1906-1964 WhScrn 2
Quigley, Don WhoHol A
Quigley, Godfrey WhoHol A
Quigley, Juanita 1931- MotPP, ThFT,
  WhoHol A
Quigley, Martin 1890-1964 NotNAT B
Quigley, Martin, Jr. 1917- IntMPA 1977
Quigley, Rita 1923- WhoHol A
Quilici, Folco 1930- DcFM, WorEnF
Quillan, Eddie 1907- Film 2, FilmgC,
  IntMPA 1977, MovMk, TwYS, Vers A,
  WhoHol A

Quillan, Sarah 1879-1969 WhScrn 2, WhoHol B
Quilley, Denis 1927- CnThe, WhoHol A,
  WhoThe 16
Quillian, Joseph F 1884-1952 WhScrn 1,
  WhScrn 2
Quillian, Joseph F 1884-1962 WhoHol B
Quilter, Roger d1953 NotNAT B
Quimby, Fred 1886-1965 FilmgC, WorEnF
Quimby, Margaret d1965 Film 2, TwYS,
  WhScrn 2
Quimby, Margerie Film 2
Quin, James 1693-1766 CnThe, NotNAT A,
  NotNAT B, OxThe, PIP&P
Quinault OxThe
Quinault, Philippe 1635-1688 McGWD,
  NotNAT B, OxThe, REnWD
Quinault, Phillipe 1635-1688 CnThe
Quinby, George H 1901- BiE&WWA, NotNAT
Quince, Louis Veda 1900-1954 WhScrn 1,
  WhScrn 2
Quine, Richard 1920- AmSCAP 1966, BiDFlm,
  CmMov, DcFM, FilmgC, IntMPA 1977,
  MotPP, MovMk, OxFilm, WhoHol A,
  WorEnF
Quinlan, Gertrude 1875-1963 NotNAT B, WhThe,
  WhoStg 1908
Quinlan, John C d1954 NotNAT B
Quinlivan, Charles 1924-1974 WhScrn 2,
  WhoHol B
Quinn, Alan J 1889-1944 WhScrn 1, WhScrn 2
Quinn, Allen d1944 Film 1, WhoHol B
Quinn, Andrew J 1931- AmSCAP 1966
Quinn, Anthony 1915- BiDFlm, BiE&WWA,
  CelR 3, CmMov, FilmgC, IntMPA 1977,
  MotPP, NotNAT A, OxFilm, WhoHol A,
  WhoThe 16, WorEnF
Quinn, Anthony 1916- MovMk
Quinn, Arthur Hobson 1875-1960 NotNAT B
Quinn, Bill WhoHol A
Quinn, Charles Film 2
Quinn, Don 1900- AmSCAP 1966
Quinn, James 1884-1919 WhScrn 2
Quinn, James Jimmie 1885-1940 WhScrn 1,
  WhScrn 2
Quinn, Jimmie Film 2
Quinn, Jimmy 1885-1940 WhoHol B
Quinn, Joe 1899-1974 WhScrn 2, WhoHol B
Quinn, Joe 1917-1971 WhScrn 1, WhScrn 2
Quinn, John 1851-1916 WhScrn 2
Quinn, Louis WhoHol A
Quinn, Mary d1947 NotNAT B
Quinn, Pat WhoHol A
Quinn, Paul 1870-1936 WhScrn 1, WhScrn 2
Quinn, Regina Film 2
Quinn, Sally NewYTET
Quinn, Stanley J, Jr. 1915- IntMPA 1977

Quinn, Teddy 1959- *WhoHol A*
Quinn, Tony 1899-1967 *WhScrn 1*, *WhScrn 2*,
  WhThe, *WhoHol B*
Quinn, William *Film 1*, *Film 2*
Quinones DeBenavente, Luis 1589?-1651 *McGWD*
Quintero, The Brothers *OxThe*
Quintero, Joaquin Alvarez 1873-1944 *McGWD*,
  NotNAT B
Quintero, Jose 1924- *BiE&WWA*, *CnThe*,
  NotNAT, *NotNAT A*, *PIP&P*, *PIP&P A*,
  WhoThe 16
Quintero, Serafin Alvarez 1871-1938 *CnMD*,
  CnThe, *McGWD*, *NotNAT B*
Quinteros, Joaquin Alvarez 1873-1944 *WhThe*
Quinteros, Serafin Alvarez 1871-1938 *WhThe*
Quinton, Mark d1891 *NotNAT B*
Quirk, Billie *TwYS*
Quirk, Billy *TwYS A*
Quirk, Billy 1881-1926 *WhoHol B*
Quirk, Billy 1888-1926 *Film 1*, *Film 2*
Quirk, William Billy 1881-1926 *WhScrn 1*,
  WhScrn 2
Quiroz, Salvador 1881-1956 *WhScrn 1*, *WhScrn 2*
Quivey, Marvel *Film 2*
Quo, Beulah *WhoHol A*

R

Raabeova, Hedvika *WomWMM*
Rab, Phyllis *BiE&WWA*
Rabagliati, Alberto 1906-1974 *Film 2, WhScrn 2, WhoHol B*
Rabal, Francisco *WhoHol A*
Raban, Jonathan *ConDr 1977B*
Rabb, Ellis 1930- *BiE&WWA, PIP&P, WhoThe 16*
Rabbit, Samuel 1911- *AmSCAP 1966*
Rabe, David 1940- *ConDr 1977, NotNAT, PIP&P A, WhoThe 16*
Rabenalt, Arthur Maria 1905- *DcFM*
Rabier, Jean 1927- *FilmgC, OxFilm, WorEnF*
Rabinof, Sylvia *AmSCAP 1966*
Rabinovich, Isaac Moiseivich 1894-1961 *OxThe*
Rabinowitz, Sholem *McGWD, REnWD*
Raborg, Frederick A, Jr. 1934- *NatPD*
Raby, Derek *ConDr 1977B*
Racan, Honorat DeBueil, Marquis De 1589-1670 *OxThe*
Rachel 1820-1858 *CnThe, FamA&A, OxThe*
Rachel 1821?-1858 *NotNAT A*
Rachel, Madame 1820-1858 *NotNAT B*
Rachel, Mademoiselle 1820-1858 *PIP&P*
Rachel, Lydia d1915 *NotNAT B*
Rachmaninoff, Sergei Vasilyevich 1873-1943 *AmSCAP 1966*
Rachmil, Lewis J 1908- *IntMPA 1977*
Rachow, Louis A 1927- *NotNAT*
Racimo, Victoria *WhoHol A*
Racine, Jean 1639-1699 *CnThe, McGWD, NotNAT A, NotNAT B, OxThe, PIP&P, REnWD*
Rackin, Martin 1918- *FilmgC, WorEnF*
Rackmil, Milton R *IntMPA 1977*
Raday, Imre *Film 2*
Radcliff, Jack 1900-1967 *WhScrn 1, WhoHol B*
Radcliffe, E J 1893- *Film 2, TwYS*
Radcliffe, Jack 1900-1967 *WhScrn 2*
Radcliffe, Violet *Film 1*
Radd, Ronald *WhoHol A*
Radd, Ronald 1926?- *FilmgC*
Radd, Ronald 1929-1976 *WhoThe 16*
Rademakers, Fons 1920- *OxFilm*
Rademakers, Fons 1921- *FilmgC, WorEnF*
Rader, Dotson 1942- *CelR 3*
Rader, Gene *WhoHol A*
Rader, Jack *WhoHol A*
Radford, Basil 1897-1952 *Film 2, FilmgC, NotNAT B, OxFilm, WhScrn 1, WhScrn 2, WhThe, WhoHol B*
Radford, Dave 1884- *AmSCAP 1966*
Radilak, Charles H 1907-1972 *WhScrn 2*
Radin, Paul *IntMPA 1977*
Radlov, Sergei Yevgenyevich 1892-1958 *OxThe*
Radnay, Hilda *Film 2*

Radnitz, Robert B 1925- *FilmgC, IntMPA 1977*
Rado, James *ConDr 1977D, PIP&P*
Rado, James 1932- *NotNAT*
Rado, James 1939- *EncMT*
Radok, Alfred 1914- *DcFM, OxFilm, WorEnF*
Radvanyi, Geza 1907- *DcFM*
Rady, Simon 1909-1965 *AmSCAP 1966*
Radzina, Medea *Film 2*
Radzina, Remea *Film 2*
Rae, Charlotte 1926- *BiE&WWA, NotNAT, WhoHol A, WhoThe 16*
Rae, Claire 1889-1938 *WhScrn 1, WhScrn 2, WhoHol B*
Rae, Eric 1899- *WhThe*
Rae, Isabel *Film 1*
Rae, Jack 1899-1957 *WhScrn 1, WhScrn 2*
Rae, John *WhoHol A*
Rae, Kenneth 1901- *BiE&WWA, WhThe*
Rae, Melba 1922-1971 *WhScrn 1, WhScrn 2*
Rae, Raida *Film 2*
Rae, Zoe *Film 1*
Raeburn, Henzie *WhoHol A*
Raeburn, Henzie 1900- *WhThe*
Raeburn, Henzie 1901-1973 *WhScrn 2*
Raedler, Dorothy 1917- *BiE&WWA, NotNAT, WhoThe 16*
Raevsky, Iosif Moiseevich 1900- *WhThe*
Rafelson, Bob *BiDFlm*
Rafelson, Bob 1934- *CelR 3*
Rafelson, Bob 1935- *FilmgC, IntMPA 1977*
Rafelson, Bob 1938- *MovMk*
Rafelson, Toby *WomWMM*
Rafetto, Mike *Film 2*
Raff, Matthew *NewYTET*
Rafferty, Chips 1909-1971 *FilmgC, MovMk, OxFilm, WhScrn 1, WhScrn 2, WhoHol B*
Rafferty, Frances 1922- *FilmgC, IntMPA 1977, MGM, MotPP, MovMk, WhoHol A*
Rafferty, Pat 1861-1952 *NotNAT B, WhThe*
Raffin, Deborah 1953- *IntMPA 1977, WhoHol A*
Raffles Bill 1895-1940 *WhScrn 1, WhScrn 2*
Rafkin, Alan *FilmgC*
Raft, George *IntMPA 1977, MotPP*
Raft, George 1895- *CmMov, FilmgC, MovMk*
Raft, George 1903- *BiDFlm, Film 2, OxFilm, WhoHol A, WorEnF*
Ragabliati, Alberto *Film 2*
Ragan, Ruth d1962 *WhScrn 1, WhScrn 2*
Ragin, John S *WhoHol A*
Raglan, James 1901-1961 *NotNAT B, WhScrn 1, WhScrn 2, WhThe, WhoHol B*
Ragland, Esther 1912-1939 *WhScrn 1, WhScrn 2*
Ragland, Rags 1905-1946 *FilmgC, MGM, MotPP, MovMk, NotNAT B, Vers A, WhScrn 1, WhScrn 2, WhoHol B*
Ragland, Robert Oliver 1931- *AmSCAP 1966*

Ragni, Gerome 1942- *ConDr 1977D, EncMT, NotNAT, PIP&P*
Ragno, Joseph *WhoHol A*
Ragotzy, Jack 1921- *BiE&WWA, NotNAT*
Ragsdale, Carl V 1925- *IntMPA 1977*
Rahere d1144 *OxThe, PIP&P*
Rahm, Knute 1876-1957 *WhScrn 2*
Rai, Himansu *Film 2*
Raidy, William Anthony 1923- *NotNAT*
Raik, Etienne 1904- *DcFM*
Raimu 1883-1946 *CnThe, FilmgC, MotPP, MovMk, OxFilm, WhoHol B, WorEnF*
Raimu, Jules 1883-1946 *NotNAT B, WhScrn 1, WhScrn 2*
Raimu, M 1883-1946 *WhThe*
Raimund, Ferdinand 1790-1836 *CnThe, McGWD, NotNAT B, OxThe, REnWD*
Rain, Douglas *WhoHol A, WhoThe 16*
Rainbow, Frank 1913- *WhoThe 16*
Raine, Jack 1897- *BiE&WWA, NotNAT, WhThe, WhoHol A*
Raine, Norman Reilly 1895-1971 *FilmgC*
Rainer, Luise *MotPP*
Rainer, Luise 1909- *FilmgC*
Rainer, Luise 1910- *MGM, MovMk, ThFT, WhoHol A*
Rainer, Luise 1912- *BiDFlm, OxFilm, WhThe, WorEnF*
Rainer, Yvonne *WomWMM B*
Raines, Christina *WhoHol A*
Raines, Ella 1921- *FilmgC, HolP 40, IntMPA 1977, MotPP, MovMk, WhoHol A*
Rainey, Ford 1908- *BiE&WWA, NotNAT, WhoHol A*
Rainey, Norman 1888-1960 *WhScrn 2*
Rainey, Paul J *Film 1*
Rainger, Ralph 1901-1942 *AmSCAP 1966, NotNAT B*
Rains, Claude 1889-1967 *BiDFlm, BiE&WWA, FilmgC, MotPP, MovMk, NotNAT B, OxFilm, WhScrn 1, WhScrn 2, WhThe, WhoHol B, WorEnF*
Rains, Claude 1890-1967 *CmMov*
Rains, Fred *Film 2*
Rains, Jessica *WhoHol A*
Rains, Robert H 1921- *IntMPA 1977*
Raisa, Rose 1878-1963 *WhScrn 2*
Raisin, Catherine 1650-1701 *OxThe*
Raisin, Francoise Pitel DeLongchamp 1661-1721 *OxThe*
Raisin, Jacques 1653-1702 *OxThe*
Raisin, Jean-Baptiste 1655-1693 *NotNAT B, OxThe*
Raison, Charles W 1936- *NotNAT*
Raiter, Frank *WhoHol A*
Raitt, John *WhoHol A*
Raitt, John 1917- *BiE&WWA, EncMT, NotNAT, WhoThe 16*
Raitt, John 1921- *FilmgC*
Raizman, Yuli Yakovlevich 1903- *DcFM*
Rajah, Raboid d1962 *NotNAT B*
Raju 1937-1972 *WhScrn 2*
Raker, Lorin 1891-1959 *Film 2, WhScrn 2*
Raki, Laya *WhoHol A*
Rakoff, Alvin 1927- *FilmgC, IntMPA 1977*
Rakosi, Jeno 1842-1929 *OxThe*
Rakov, Philip H 1903- *AmSCAP 1966*
Raksin, David 1912- *AmSCAP 1966, FilmgC, IntMPA 1977, WorEnF*
Rale, M W *Film 1, Film 2*
Raleigh, Mrs. Cecil d1923 *NotNAT B*
Raleigh, Cecil 1856-1914 *Film 1, NotNAT B, WhThe*
Raleigh, Joe *Film 2*

Raleigh, Saba d1923 *Film 2, WhThe*
Rall, Tommy 1929- *BiE&WWA, MotPP, NotNAT*
Ralli, Giovanna 1935- *FilmgC, WhoHol A*
Ralli, Paul 1905-1953 *Film 2, WhScrn 1, WhScrn 2, WhoHol B*
Ralph, Hanna *Film 2*
Ralph, Jesse 1864-1944 *MovMk*
Ralph, Jessie d1944 *NotNAT B, WhoHol B*
Ralph, Jessie 1864-1944 *FilmgC, ThFT*
Ralph, Jessie 1865-1944 *Vers A*
Ralph, Jessie 1876-1944 *WhScrn 1, WhScrn 2*
Ralph, Julia *Film 2*
Ralph, Louis *Film 2*
Ralston, Esther 1902- *Film 2, FilmgC, MotPP, MovMk, ThFT, TwYS, WhoHol A, WomWMM*
Ralston, Gil 1912- *IntMPA 1977*
Ralston, Gilbert A 1912- *AmSCAP 1966*
Ralston, Howard *Film 2*
Ralston, Jobyna d1967 *MotPP, WhoHol B*
Ralston, Jobyna 1901-1967 *FilmgC, MovMk*
Ralston, Jobyna 1902-1967 *Film 2, TwYS*
Ralston, Jobyna 1904-1967 *WhScrn 1, WhScrn 2*
Ralston, Rudy 1918- *IntMPA 1977*
Ralston, Vera Hruba *MotPP*
Ralston, Vera Hruba 1919- *WhoHol A*
Ralston, Vera Hruba 1921- *FilmgC, MovMk*
Ram, Buck 1909- *AmSCAP 1966*
Rama, Rau E *Film 2*
Rama Rau, Santha 1923- *BiE&WWA*
Rama Rau, Santha *see also* Rau, Santha Rama
Ramage, Cecil B 1895- *WhThe*
Rambal, Enrique 1924-1971 *WhScrn 1, WhScrn 2*
Rambeau, Marjorie 1889-1970 *Film 1, Film 2, FilmgC, MotPP, MovMk, ThFT, TwYS, Vers B, WhScrn 1, WhScrn 2, WhThe, WhoHol B*
Rambert, Marie *NotNAT A, WhThe*
Rambo, Dack *WhoHol A*
Rambo, Dirk d1967 *WhoHol B*
Rambova, Natacha 1897-1966 *Film 1, Film 2, TwYS, WhScrn 1, WhScrn 2, WhoHol B*
Rameau, Emil *Film 2*
Ramin, Jordan S 1932- *AmSCAP 1966*
Ramin, Sid 1924- *AmSCAP 1966, BiE&WWA, NotNAT*
Ramirex, Roger J 1913- *AmSCAP 1966*
Ramirez, Carlos *WhoHol A*
Ramirez, Pepita 1902-1927 *WhScrn 1, WhScrn 2*
Ramirez, Rosita *Film 2*
Ramnoth, K 1912- *DcFM*
Ramon *Film 2*
Ramon, Elizabeth T B 1894- *AmSCAP 1966*
Ramon, Laon *Film 2*
Ramos, Jesus Maza 1911-1955 *WhScrn 1, WhScrn 2*
Ramos, Richard *WhoHol A*
Rampling, Charlotte *WhoHol A*
Rampling, Charlotte 1945- *FilmgC*
Rampling, Charlotte 1946- *IntMPA 1977*
Ramsay, Eugene S 1918- *AmSCAP 1966*
Ramsay, G Clark 1915- *IntMPA 1977*
Ramsay, Remak 1937- *WhoThe 16*
Ramsaye, Terry d1954 *NotNAT B*
Ramsden, Dennis 1918- *WhoThe 16*
Ramseier, Paul 1927- *AmSCAP 1966*
Ramsey, Alicia d1933 *NotNAT B, WhThe*
Ramsey, Anne *WhoHol A*
Ramsey, John Nelson d1929 *WhScrn 1, WhScrn 2*
Ramsey, Logan 1921- *BiE&WWA, NotNAT, WhoHol A*
Ramsey, Nelson d1929 *NotNAT B, WhoHol B*

Ramsey, Peter 1921- *NatPD*
Ramsier, Paul 1927- *AmSCAP 1966*
Ramsing, Pamella *WomWMM B*
Ranaldi, Frank 1905-1933 *WhScrn 1, WhScrn 2, WhoHol B*
Ranalow, Frederick Baring 1873-1953 *NotNAT B, WhThe, WhoHol B*
Ranbrugh, Irene *PIP&P*
Ranch, Hieronymus Justesen 1539-1607 *OxThe*
Rancourt, Jules *Film 2*
Rand, Ayn 1905- *CelR 3*
Rand, Bill d1961 *NotNAT B*
Rand, Harold 1928- *IntMPA 1977*
Rand, John F 1872-1940 *Film 1, Film 2, WhScrn 1, WhScrn 2, WhoHol B*
Rand, Lionel 1909-1942 *WhScrn 1, WhScrn 2*
Rand, Sally 1903- *Film 2, TwYS, WhoHol A*
Rand, Sally 1904- *FilmgC*
Rand, Mrs. William W, Jr. 1927- *BiE&WWA*
Randall, Addison Jack 1907-1945 *WhScrn 1, WhScrn 2, WhoHol B*
Randall, Anne *WhoHol A*
Randall, Bernard 1884-1954 *Film 2, WhoHol B*
Randall, Bernard Barney 1884-1954 *WhScrn 1, WhScrn 2*
Randall, Bob 1937- *ConDr 1977D, NatPD, NotNAT*
Randall, Carl d1965 *WhThe*
Randall, Harry 1860-1932 *NotNAT A, OxThe, WhThe*
Randall, Jerry *WhoHol A*
Randall, Larry 1920-1951 *WhScrn 1, WhScrn 2*
Randall, Leslie 1924- *WhThe, WhoHol A*
Randall, Pat *WhoHol A*
Randall, Paul E 1902- *BiE&WWA*
Randall, Rae 1909-1934 *WhScrn 1, WhScrn 2, WhoHol B*
Randall, Stuart *WhoHol A*
Randall, Tony 1920- *BiE&WWA, CelR 3, FilmgC, IntMPA 1977, MotPP, MovMk, NotNAT, WhoHol A, WhoThe 16*
Randall, Tony 1924- *WorEnF*
Randall, William 1877-1939 *WhScrn 1, WhScrn 2*
Randazzo, Teddy *WhoHol A*
Randell, Ron *WhoHol A*
Randell, Ron 1918- *FilmgC, MovMk*
Randell, Ron 1923- *BiE&WWA, NotNAT, WhoThe 16*
Randi, Ermanno d1951 *WhScrn 2*
Randle, Frank 1901-1957 *FilmgC, WhScrn 1, WhScrn 2, WhoHol B*
Randolf, Anders 1875-1930 *Film 1, Film 2, TwYS*
Randolph, A Philip 1889- *CelR 3*
Randolph, Amanda 1902-1967 *WhScrn 1, WhScrn 2, WhoHol B*
Randolph, Anders d1930 *WhoHol B*
Randolph, Anders 1875-1930 *Film 2*
Randolph, Anders 1876-1930 *WhScrn 1, WhScrn 2*
Randolph, Don *WhoHol A*
Randolph, Dorothy d1918 *WhScrn 2*
Randolph, Elsie 1904- *EncMT, FilmgC, IntMPA 1977, WhoHol A, WhoThe 16*
Randolph, Eva d1927 *NotNAT B*
Randolph, Isabel 1890-1973 *WhScrn 2, WhoHol B*
Randolph, Jane 1919- *FilmgC, WhoHol A*
Randolph, John *NotNAT, WhoHol A*
Randolph, John 1915- *BiE&WWA*
Randolph, John 1917- *FilmgC*
Randolph, Lillian *WhoHol A*
Randolph, Louise d1953 *NotNAT B,*

WhoStg 1908
Randolph, May 1873-1956 *WhScrn 1, WhScrn 2*
Randolph, Robert 1926- *BiE&WWA, NotNAT, WhoThe 16*
Randolph, Thomas 1605-1635 *NotNAT B, REnWD*
Randolph, Virginia 1882- *WhoStg 1908*
Random, Bob *WhoHol A*
Randone, Salvo *WhoHol A*
Ranelli, J *NatPD*
Ranevsky, Boris 1891- *Film 2, WhThe*
Raney, Sue 1939- *AmSCAP 1966*
Ranft, Albert Adam 1858- *WhThe*
Ranga Rao, S V 1918-1974 *WhScrn 2*
Rangel, Arturo Soto 1882-1965 *WhScrn 1, WhScrn 2, WhoHol B*
Ranger Bill *WhScrn 2*
Rani, Paul *Film 2*
Ranier, Richard Robert 1889-1960 *WhScrn 2*
Ranin, Helge 1897-1952 *WhScrn 1, WhScrn 2*
Rank, J Arthur 1888-1972 *DcFM, FilmgC, OxFilm, WorEnF*
Ranken, Frederick W d1905 *NotNAT B*
Rankin, Arthur 1900-1947 *Film 2, NotNAT B, TwYS, WhScrn 1, WhScrn 2, WhoHol B*
Rankin, Arthur McKee 1841-1914 *NotNAT B, OxThe, WhThe, WhoStg 1908*
Rankin, Arthur McKee *see also* Rankin, McKee
Rankin, Caroline *Film 1, Film 2*
Rankin, Catherine *Film 2*
Rankin, Doris d1946 *Film 2, NotNAT B, TwYS, WhoHol B*
Rankin, Gil *WhoHol A*
Rankin, Gladys d1914 *NotNAT B*
Rankin, Herbert 1876-1946 *WhScrn 1, WhScrn 2*
Rankin, Kitty Blanchard 1847-1911 *OxThe*
Rankin, McKee 1841-1914 *FamA&A*
Rankin, Mrs. McKee 1847-1911 *NotNAT B*
Rankin, McKee *see also* Rankin, Arthur McKee
Rankin, Molly *WhThe*
Rankin, Phyllis 1874-1934 *NotNAT B, WhThe, WhoHol B, WhoStg 1906, WhoStg 1908*
Ranney, Frank 1863- *WhoStg 1906, WhoStg 1908*
Ranody, Laszlo 1919- *OxFilm, WorEnF*
Ranoe, Cecilia d1870 *NotNAT B*
Ranous, Dora d1916 *NotNAT A*
Ranous, William V 1847-1915 *WhScrn 2*
Ransley, Peter 1931- *ConDr 1977*
Ransohoff, Martin 1927- *FilmgC, IntMPA 1977, NewYTET*
Ransom, Edith *Film 2*
Ransom, John Crowe 1888- *CelR 3*
Ransome, John W d1929 *NotNAT B*
Ransome, Prunella 1943- *FilmgC, WhoHol A*
Ranson, Herbert 1889- *WhThe*
Rao, Enakshi Rama *Film 2*
Rapee, Erno 1891-1945 *AmSCAP 1966, WorEnF*
Rapf, Matthew 1920- *IntMPA 1977*
Raph, Alan 1933- *AmSCAP 1966*
Raph, Theodore 1905- *AmSCAP 1966*
Raphael, Enid d1964 *NotNAT B, WhScrn 1, WhScrn 2*
Raphael, Frederic 1931- *ConDr 1977A, FilmgC, IntMPA 1977*
Raphael, John N 1868-1917 *NotNAT B, WhThe*
Raphael, William 1858- *WhThe*
Raphaelson, Samson *IntMPA 1977*
Raphaelson, Samson 1896- *FilmgC, McGWD, WhThe, WorEnF*
Raphaelson, Samson 1899- *BiE&WWA, NotNAT*
Raphel, David 1925- *IntMPA 1977*
Raphel, Jerome *WhoHol A*
Raphling, Sam 1910- *AmSCAP 1966*

Rapley, Rose *Film 2*
Rapp, Richard *WhoHol A*
Rappaport, Shloyme Zaynvl *REnWD*
Rappe, Virginia d1921 *Film 2, WhScrn 1, WhScrn 2, WhoHol B*
Rappeneau, Jean-Paul 1932- *WorEnF*
Rapper, Irving *IntMPA 1977*
Rapper, Irving 1898- *BiDFlm, CmMov, MovMk, WorEnF*
Rapper, Irving 1904?- *FilmgC*
Rappoport, Gerald J 1925- *IntMPA 1977*
Rappoport, Shloyme Zanul *McGWD*
Raptakis, Kleon 1905- *AmSCAP 1966*
Raqua, Charles *Film 2*
Ras, Eva *WhoHol A*
Rasbach, Oscar 1888- *AmSCAP 1966*
Rasch, Albertina d1967 *Film 2, WhThe*
Rasch, Albertina 1891-1967 *WhScrn 2*
Rasch, Albertina 1896-1967 *BiE&WWA, EncMT, NotNAT B*
Rasch, Raymond P 1919-1964 *AmSCAP 1966*
Raschi, Eugene G 1929- *AmSCAP 1966*
Raschig, Kraft *Film 2*
Rascoe, Burton 1892-1957 *NotNAT B, WhThe*
Rascoe, Judith *WomWMM*
Rashevskaya, Natalya *WomWMM*
Raskatoff *Film 2*
Raskie, Barney *Film 2*
Raskin, Gene 1909- *AmSCAP 1966*
Raskin, Milton W 1916- *AmSCAP 1966*
Raskin, William 1896-1942 *AmSCAP 1966*
Raskind, Philip *AmSCAP 1966*
Rasley, John M 1913- *AmSCAP 1966*
Rasp, Fritz 1891- *Film 2, FilmgC, WhoHol A*
Rastell, John d1536 *OxThe*
Rasulala, Thalmus *WhoHol A*
Rasumny, Mikhail d1938 *NotNAT B*
Rasumny, Mikhail 1890-1956 *FilmgC, MovMk, Vers A, WhScrn 1, WhScrn 2, WhoHol B*
Ratcliffe, Edward J 1893- *Film 2*
Ratcliffe, John 1929- *IntMPA 1977*
Rathaus, Karol 1895-1954 *AmSCAP 1966*
Rathbone, Basil 1892-1967 *BiDFlm, BiE&WWA, CmMov, FamA&A, Film 2, FilmgC, MotPP, MovMk, NotNAT A, NotNAT B, OxFilm, WhScrn 1, WhScrn 2, WhThe, WhoHol B, WorEnF*
Rathbone, Guy B 1884-1916 *NotNAT B, WhThe*
Rathbone, Ouida 1887-1974 *BiE&WWA, NotNAT B*
Rathbone, Perry 1911- *CelR 3*
Rathbun, Janet d1975 *WhoHol C*
Rather, Dan *NewYTET*
Ratnam, Kali N d1950 *WhScrn 2*
Ratner, Anna 1892-1967 *WhScrn 1, WhScrn 2, WhoHol B*
Ratoff, Gregory d1960 *MotPP, WhoHol B*
Ratoff, Gregory 1893-1960 *NotNAT B, WhThe*
Ratoff, Gregory 1897-1960 *BiDFlm, FilmgC, MovMk, Vers A, WhScrn 1, WhScrn 2, WorEnF*
Raton, Doris *Film 2*
Rattenberry, Harry 1860-1925 *WhScrn 1, WhScrn 2, WhoHol B*
Rattenbury, Harry *Film 1*
Rattigan, Terence 1911- *BiE&WWA, CnMD, CnThe, ConDr 1977, CroCD, IntMPA 1977, McGWD, ModWD, NotNAT, OxFilm, OxThe, PIP&P, WhoThe 16, WorEnF*
Rattigan, Terence 1912- *FilmgC*
Rau, Santha Rama 1923- *BiE&WWA, CelR 3*
Rauch, Siegfried *WhoHol A*
Raucourt 1756-1815 *OxThe*
Raucourt, Jules d1967 *WhoHol B*

Raucourt, Jules 1890-1967 *Film 1, Film 2, TwYS*
Raucourt, Jules 1891-1967 *WhScrn 2*
Rauet *Film 2*
Rausch *Film 2*
Rauschenberg, Robert 1925- *CelR 3, ConDr 1977E*
Rauscher, Hans *Film 2*
Ravel, Sandra d1954 *WhScrn 1, WhScrn 2, WhoHol B*
Ravelle, Ray *WhScrn 1, WhScrn 2*
Raven, Elsa *WhoHol A*
Raven, Mike *WhoHol A*
Ravenel, Florence d1975 *WhScrn 2*
Ravenel, John 1912-1950 *WhScrn 1, WhScrn 2*
Ravenscroft, Edward *NotNAT B, OxThe*
Ravetch, Irving 1915?- *FilmgC, IntMPA 1977*
Ravitz, Myrna *WomWMM A, WomWMM B*
Ravosa, Carmino C 1930- *AmSCAP 1966*
Rawley, James *WhoHol A*
Rawling, Sylvester d1921 *NotNAT B*
Rawlings, Alice *WhoHol A*
Rawlings, Margaret 1906- *WhoHol A, WhoThe 16*
Rawlins, Herbert d1947 *WhScrn 1, WhScrn 2*
Rawlins, John 1902- *FilmgC*
Rawlins, Judith 1936-1974 *WhScrn 2*
Rawlins, Judy d1974 *WhoHol B*
Rawlins, Lester 1924- *BiE&WWA, NotNAT, WhoHol A, WhoThe 16*
Rawlins, W H d1927 *NotNAT B*
Rawlinson, A R 1894- *IntMPA 1977, WhThe*
Rawlinson, Herbert 1885-1953 *Film 1, Film 2, MotPP, MovMk, NotNAT B, TwYS, WhScrn 1, WhScrn 2, WhoHol B*
Rawls, Eugenia 1916- *BiE&WWA, NotNAT, WhoThe 16*
Rawls, Lou 1935- *CelR 3, WhoHol A*
Rawlston, Zelma d1915 *NotNAT B, WhoStg 1908*
Rawnsley, David 1909- *FilmgC*
Rawson, Graham 1890-1955 *NotNAT B, WhThe*
Rawson, Tristan 1888- *WhThe*
Rawsthorne, Alan 1905-1971 *FilmgC, WorEnF*
Rawsthorne, Alan 1905-1973 *OxFilm*
Ray, Albert 1883- *Film 2, TwYS A*
Ray, Aldo 1926- *BiDFlm, FilmgC, IntMPA 1977, MotPP, MovMk, OxFilm, WhoHol A, WorEnF*
Ray, Allene 1901- *Film 2, TwYS*
Ray, Andrew 1939- *BiE&WWA, FilmgC, NotNAT, WhoHol A*
Ray, Anthony *WhoHol A*
Ray, Barbara 1914-1955 *WhScrn 1, WhScrn 2, WhoHol B*
Ray, Bobby *Film 2*
Ray, Charles 1891-1943 *Film 1, Film 2, FilmgC, MotPP, NotNAT B, TwYS, TwYS A, WhScrn 1, WhScrn 2, WhoHol B*
Ray, Charles 1894-1943 *MovMk*
Ray, Dixy Lee 1914- *CelR 3*
Ray, Ellen *BiE&WWA, WhoHol A*
Ray, Emma 1871-1935 *WhScrn 1, WhScrn 2, WhoHol B*
Ray, Estelle Goulding 1888-1970 *WhScrn 1, WhScrn 2*
Ray, Gabrielle 1883- *WhThe*
Ray, Helen 1879-1965 *WhScrn 1, WhScrn 2, WhoHol B*
Ray, Jack 1917-1975 *WhScrn 2, WhoHol C*
Ray, James 1932- *BiE&WWA, NotNAT, WhoThe 16*
Ray, John Alvin 1927- *AmSCAP 1966*
Ray, John William d1871 *NotNAT B*

Ray, Johnnie 1927- *FilmgC, WhoHol A*
Ray, Johnny 1859-1927 *WhScrn 1, WhScrn 2, WhoHol B*
Ray, Leah *WhoHol A*
Ray, Man 1890- *DcFM, Film 2, FilmgC, OxFilm*
Ray, Marjorie 1900-1924 *WhScrn 1, WhScrn 2, WhoHol B*
Ray, Michel 1945- *IntMPA 1977, WhoHol A*
Ray, Mona *Film 2*
Ray, Naomi 1893-1966 *WhScrn 1, WhScrn 2*
Ray, Nicholas 1911- *BiDFlm, DcFM, FilmgC, IntMPA 1977, MovMk, OxFilm, WorEnF*
Ray, Phil 1872- *WhThe*
Ray, Rene 1912- *Film 2, FilmgC, WhThe, WhoHol A*
Ray, Robert J 1919- *AmSCAP 1966*
Ray, Ruby *WhoStg 1908*
Ray, Satyajit 1921- *BiDFlm, DcFM, FilmgC, MovMk, OxFilm, WorEnF*
Ray, Ted 1909?- *FilmgC, IntMPA 1977, WhoHol A*
Ray, Wallace *Film 2*
Ray, William B *NewYTET*
Rayburn, Gene *IntMPA 1977*
Rayburn, Margie *AmSCAP 1966*
Raye, Carol 1923- *FilmgC, WhThe, WhoHol A*
Raye, Don 1909- *AmSCAP 1966*
Raye, Martha 1916- *BiE&WWA, CelR 3, EncMT, FilmgC, IntMPA 1977, MotPP, MovMk, NewYTET, ThFT, WhoHol A, WhoThe 16*
Raye, Thelma *WhoStg 1908*
Rayfield, Curt *Film 2*
Rayford, Alma *Film 2*
Raymaker, Herman C 1893-1944 *TwYS A*
Raymond, Charles d1911 *NotNAT B*
Raymond, Cyril 1897?-1973 *Film 2, FilmgC, WhThe, WhoHol B*
Raymond, Ford 1900-1960 *WhScrn 1, WhScrn 2, WhoHol B*
Raymond, Frances 1869-1961 *Film 2, WhoHol B*
Raymond, Frances Frankie 1869-1961 *WhScrn 1, WhScrn 2*
Raymond, Frankie *Film 2*
Raymond, Gary 1935- *FilmgC, MotPP, WhoHol A*
Raymond, Gene 1908- *BiE&WWA, FilmgC, HolP 30, IntMPA 1977, MotPP, MovMk, WhoHol A, WhoThe 16*
Raymond, George 1903- *AmSCAP 1966*
Raymond, Guy *WhoHol A*
Raymond, Harold Newell 1884-1957 *AmSCAP 1966*
Raymond, Helen 1885?-1965 *BiE&WWA, Film 2, WhScrn 1, WhScrn 2, WhThe, WhoHol B*
Raymond, Jack 1892-1953 *FilmgC*
Raymond, Jack 1901-1951 *Film 2, WhScrn 1, WhScrn 2, WhoHol B*
Raymond, John T 1836-1887 *NotNAT B, OxThe*
Raymond, Lewis 1908- *AmSCAP 1966*
Raymond, Maud d1961 *NotNAT B, WhoStg 1906, WhoStg 1908*
Raymond, Paula 1923- *FilmgC, IntMPA 1977, MotPP, WhoHol A*
Raymond, Robin *WhoHol A*
Raymond, Royal 1916-1949 *WhScrn 2*
Raymond, Whitney *Film 1*
Raymond, William *Film 1*
Raymonde, Frankie 1874- *WhoStg 1906, WhoStg 1908*
Raynal, Jackie *WomWMM*
Raynal, Paul *WhThe*
Raynal, Paul 1885- *McGWD*

Raynal, Paul 1890- *CnMD, ModWD*
Raynaud, Fernand d1973 *WhScrn 2*
Rayne, Leonard 1869-1925 *NotNAT B, WhThe*
Rayner, Alfred d1898 *NotNAT B*
Rayner, Christine *Film 2*
Rayner, John *WhoHol A*
Rayner, Lionel Benjamin d1855 *NotNAT B*
Rayner, Minnie 1869-1941 *NotNAT B, WhThe, WhoHol B*
Raynham, Frederick *Film 2*
Raynor, Lynn S 1940- *IntMPA 1977*
Raynore, Katherine *WhoStg 1908*
Rayo, Mirra *Film 2*
Razaf, Andy 1895-1973 *AmSCAP 1966*
Razeto, Stella *Film 1*
Razetto, Stella 1881-1948 *WhScrn 2*
Razzi, Girolamo *McGWD*
Rea, Alec L 1878-1953 *NotNAT B, WhThe*
Rea, Isabel *Film 1*
Rea, Mabel Lillian 1932-1968 *WhScrn 1, WhScrn 2, WhoHol B*
Rea, Oliver 1923- *BiE&WWA, NotNAT*
Rea, Peggy *WhoHol A*
Rea, William J 1884-1932 *NotNAT B, WhThe*
Reach, Alice Scanlon *AmSCAP 1966*
Reach, Angus B d1856 *NotNAT B*
Read, Barbara 1917-1963 *WhScrn 2, WhoHol B*
Read, Dolly *WhoHol A*
Read, Donald 1914- *AmSCAP 1966*
Read, Gardner 1913- *AmSCAP 1966*
Read, Sir John 1918- *IntMPA 1977*
Read, John 1920- *IntMPA 1977*
Read, Lillian *MotPP*
Read, Piers Paul 1941- *ConDr 1977B*
Reade, Charles 1814-1884 *NotNAT A, NotNAT B, OxThe*
Reade, Charles Faso 1911- *AmSCAP 1966*
Reade, Timothy *OxThe*
Reader, Ralph 1903- *BiE&WWA, IntMPA 1977, NotNAT, NotNAT A, WhoHol A, WhoThe 16*
Readick, Frank M 1861-1924 *WhScrn 2*
Readick, Robert 1926- *IntMPA 1977*
Reagan, Maureen *WhoHol A*
Reagan, Ronald *IntMPA 1977, MotPP, NewYTET*
Reagan, Ronald 1911- *CelR 3, FilmgC, MovMk*
Reagan, Ronald 1912- *BiDFlm, OxFilm, WhoHol A, WorEnF*
Real, Betty d1969 *WhScrn 1, WhScrn 2, WhoHol B*
Real, Louise *Film 1*
Reals, Nancy *WomWMM*
Reaney, James Crerar 1926- *CnThe, ConDr 1977, McGWD, REnWD*
Reardon, Dennis J 1944- *ConDr 1977, NatPD*
Reardon, Jack 1934- *AmSCAP 1966*
Reardon, John 1930- *BiE&WWA*
Reardon, Michael *WhoHol A*
Reardon, Mildred *Film 1, Film 2, MotPP*
Reason, Rex 1928- *FilmgC, IntMPA 1977, WhoHol A*
Reason, Rhodes 1930- *FilmgC, WhoHol A*
Reasoner, Harry 1923- *CelR 3, IntMPA 1977, NewYTET*
Reavey, Jean *NatPD*
Rebhun, Paul 1500?-1546 *OxThe*
Recklaw, Betty *Film 2*
Reckord, Barry *ConDr 1977*
Red Wing d1974 *WhScrn 2, WhoHol B*
Red Wing, Princess *Film 1*
Redd, Mary-Robin *WhoHol A*
Reddick, William J 1890-1965 *AmSCAP 1966*
Redding, Edward C 1917- *AmSCAP 1966*

Redding, Eugene 1870- *WhoStg 1908*
Redding, Otis 1941-1967 *WhScrn 2*
Reddy, Helen 1942- *IntMPA 1977, WhoHol A*
Rede, Leman Tertius 1799-1832 *OxThe*
Rede, Thomas Leman 1799-1832 *NotNAT B*
Rede, William Leman 1802-1847 *NotNAT B,*
OxThe
Redeker, Quinn *WhoHol A*
Redelings, Lowell E *IntMPA 1977*
Redfern, W B d1923 *NotNAT B*
Redfield, William *WhoHol A*
Redfield, William 1927-1976 *BiE&WWA,*
NotNAT A, NotNAT B, WhoThe 16
Redfield, William 1928- *FilmgC*
Redford, Barbara *Film 2*
Redford, George Alexander d1916 *NotNAT B*
Redford, Robert *MotPP, WhoHol A*
Redford, Robert 1936- *FilmgC, OxFilm*
Redford, Robert 1937- *BiDFlm, BiE&WWA,*
CelR 3, IntMPA 1977, MovMk, WorEnF
Redgrave, Corin 1939- *CnThe, FilmgC,*
WhoHol A, WhoThe 16
Redgrave, Lynn *CnThe, MotPP, WhoHol A*
Redgrave, Lynn 1943- *FilmgC, IntMPA 1977,*
MovMk, NotNAT, WhoThe 16
Redgrave, Lynn 1944- *OxFilm*
Redgrave, Sir Michael 1908- *BiDFlm,*
BiE&WWA, CmMov, CnThe, FilmgC,
IntMPA 1977, MotPP, MovMk, NotNAT,
NotNAT A, OxFilm, OxThe, PIP&P,
WhoHol A, WhoThe 16, WorEnF
Redgrave, Vanessa 1937- *BiDFlm, CelR 3,*
CnThe, FilmgC, IntMPA 1977, MotPP,
MovMk, OxFilm, OxThe, WhoHol A,
WhoThe 16, WorEnF
Redgrave Family *MotPP*
Redman, Ben Ray 1896-1962 *NotNAT B*
Redman, Don 1900-1964 *AmSCAP 1966*
Redman, Frank *Film 1, Film 2*
Redman, Joyce 1918- *BiE&WWA, CnThe,*
FilmgC, NotNAT, PIP&P, WhoHol A,
WhoThe 16
Redmond, John 1906- *AmSCAP 1966*
Redmond, Liam 1913- *FilmgC, WhoHol A,*
WhoThe 16
Redmond, Marge *WhoHol A*
Redmond, Moira *WhoHol A, WhoThe 16*
Redmond, T C d1937 *NotNAT B*
Redmond, William d1915 *NotNAT B*
Redmont, Bernard *NewYTET*
Redstone, Edward S 1928- *IntMPA 1977*
Redstone, Michael 1902- *IntMPA 1977*
Redstone, Sumner M 1923- *IntMPA 1977*
Redstone, Willy d1949 *NotNAT B*
Redwine, Wilbur 1926- *AmSCAP 1966*
Redwing, Rodd 1905-1971 *WhScrn 1, WhScrn 2,*
WhoHol B
Reece, Brian d1962 *NotNAT B, WhoHol B*
Reece, Brian 1913-1962 *FilmgC, WhThe*
Reece, Brian 1914-1962 *WhScrn 1, WhScrn 2*
Reece, Robert d1891 *NotNAT B*
Reed, Adam *WhoHol A*
Reed, Alan 1907- *AmSCAP 1966, IntMPA 1977,*
Vers A, WhoHol A
Reed, Alan, Jr. *WhoHol A*
Reed, Alfred 1921- *AmSCAP 1966*
Reed, Alfred German d1895 *NotNAT B*
Reed, Billy 1914-1974 *WhScrn 2*
Reed, Carl D d1962 *NotNAT B*
Reed, Sir Carol 1906- *BiDFlm, CmMov, DcFM,*
FilmgC, MovMk, OxFilm, WhThe, WorEnF
Reed, Dave 1872-1946 *WhScrn 1, WhScrn 2*
Reed, David 1872-1946 *AmSCAP 1966*
Reed, Don Sterling 1929- *AmSCAP 1966*

Reed, Donald 1907-1973 *Film 2, WhScrn 2,*
WhoHol B
Reed, Donna 1921- *BiDFlm, FilmgC,*
IntMPA 1977, MGM, MotPP, MovMk,
WhoHol A, WorEnF
Reed, Florence d1967 *MotPP, WhoHol B*
Reed, Florence 1863-1967 *Film 1, TwYS*
Reed, Florence 1883-1967 *BiE&WWA, Film 2,*
NotNAT B, WhScrn 1, WhScrn 2, WhThe
Reed, Geoffrey *WhoHol A*
Reed, George d1952 *WhoHol B*
Reed, George 1867-1952 *Vers B*
Reed, George E d1952 *WhScrn 1, WhScrn 2,*
WhoHol B
Reed, George H *Film 2*
Reed, George H 1866-1952 *WhScrn 2*
Reed, Mrs. German d1895 *NotNAT B*
Reed, Gus 1880-1965 *WhScrn 1, WhScrn 2*
Reed, Henry *ConDr 1977B*
Reed, Herbert Owen 1910- *AmSCAP 1966*
Reed, Isaac d1807 *NotNAT B*
Reed, Jane *Film 2*
Reed, Jared d1962 *NotNAT B*
Reed, Joel M *NatPD*
Reed, John *PIP&P*
Reed, Jordan *WhoHol A*
Reed, Joseph d1787 *NotNAT B*
Reed, Joseph Verner, Sr. 1902-1973 *BiE&WWA,*
NotNAT A, NotNAT B, WhThe
Reed, Luther 1888-1961 *TwYS A*
Reed, Mark 1890- *BiE&WWA, McGWD*
Reed, Mark 1893- *WhThe*
Reed, Marshall 1917- *IntMPA 1977, WhoHol A*
Reed, Maxwell d1974 *WhoHol B*
Reed, Maxwell 1919-1974 *WhScrn 2*
Reed, Maxwell 1920- *FilmgC, IntMPA 1977*
Reed, Nancy 1928- *AmSCAP 1966*
Reed, Nora *Film 2*
Reed, Oliver 1938- *CelR 3, FilmgC,*
IntMPA 1977, MovMk, OxFilm, WhoHol A
Reed, Paul *WhoHol A*
Reed, Peter *IntMPA 1977*
Reed, Philip *IntMPA 1977*
Reed, Philip 1900- *WhoHol A*
Reed, Philip 1908- *FilmgC*
Reed, Rex 1939- *CelR 3, WhoHol A*
Reed, Robert *WhoHol A*
Reed, Robert B 1900- *AmSCAP 1966*
Reed, Roland 1852-1901 *NotNAT B*
Reed, Susan *WhoHol A*
Reed, Thomas German d1888 *NotNAT B*
Reed, Tracy *WhoHol A*
Reed, Vivian *Film 1*
Reed, Walter *WhoHol A*
Reehm, George *Film 2*
Reel, Edward *Film 1*
Reel, Frank A 1907- *IntMPA 1977*
Reenberg, Annelise *WomWMM*
Rees, Edward Randolph d1976 *WhoHol C*
Rees, Llewellyn 1901- *WhoHol A, WhoThe 16*
Rees, Roger 1944- *WhoThe 16*
Reese, Della *WhoHol A*
Reese, James W d1960 *NotNAT B, WhoHol B*
Reese, Tom 1930- *FilmgC, WhoHol A*
Reese, W James 1898-1960 *WhScrn 1, WhScrn 2*
Reeve, Ada 1874-1966 *EncMT, FilmgC,*
WhScrn 1, WhScrn 2, WhThe, WhoHol B
Reeve, Alex 1900- *BiE&WWA, NotNAT*
Reeve, Wybert d1906 *NotNAT B*
Reeves, Billie *Film 1, Film 2*
Reeves, Billy 1864-1943 *WhScrn 1, WhScrn 2,*
WhoHol B
Reeves, Bob d1960 *WhoHol B*
Reeves, Donald Lee 1934- *AmSCAP 1966*

Reeves, Geoffrey 1939- *WhoThe 16*
Reeves, George 1914-1959 *FilmgC, MotPP, NotNAT B, WhScrn 1, WhScrn 2, WhoHol B*
Reeves, Hazard E 1906- *IntMPA 1977*
Reeves, J Harold *Film 2*
Reeves, Jim 1924-1964 *NotNAT B, WhScrn 1, WhScrn 2, WhoHol B*
Reeves, Kynaston 1893- *WhThe*
Reeves, Kynaston 1893-1971 *WhScrn 1, WhScrn 2, WhoHol B*
Reeves, Kynaston 1893-1972 *FilmgC*
Reeves, Michael 1944-1969 *FilmgC*
Reeves, Richard 1912-1967 *WhScrn 2, WhoHol B*
Reeves, Robert Jasper 1892-1960 *Film 1, Film 2, WhScrn 1, WhScrn 2*
Reeves, Steve 1926- *Film 2, FilmgC, IntMPA 1977, MotPP, MovMk, WhoHol A, WorEnF*
Reeves, Theodore 1910-1973 *BiE&WWA, NotNAT B, WomWMM*
Reeves-Smith, H d1938 *Film 2, WhoHol B*
Reeves-Smith, H 1862-1938 *WhThe*
Reeves-Smith, H 1863-1938 *WhScrn 1, WhScrn 2*
Reeves-Smith, Harry 1862-1938 *NotNAT B*
Reeves-Smith, Olive 1894-1972 *BiE&WWA, NotNAT B, WhoHol B*
Regan, Berry 1914-1956 *WhScrn 1, WhScrn 2*
Regan, Edgar J d1938 *WhScrn 1, WhScrn 2*
Regan, Joseph 1896-1931 *WhScrn 1, WhScrn 2, WhoHol B*
Regan, Patti *WhoHol A*
Regan, Phil 1906- *IntMPA 1977, WhoHol A*
Regan, Sylvia 1908- *BiE&WWA, NatPD, NotNAT*
Regas, George 1890-1940 *Film 2, WhScrn 1, WhScrn 2, WhoHol B*
Regas, Pedro 1882-1974 *WhScrn 2, WhoHol B*
Reggiani, Serge 1922- *BiDFlm, FilmgC, OxFilm, WhoHol A, WorEnF*
Regnard, Jean Francois 1655-1709 *CnThe, McGWD, NotNAT B, OxThe, REnWD*
Regnart, Florence *Film 2*
Regnault, Madame d1887 *NotNAT B*
Regnier 1807-1885 *NotNAT B, OxThe*
Regnier, Francois *PIP&P*
Regnier, Marthe 1880- *WhThe*
Regua, Charles *Film 2*
Rehan, Ada 1860-1916 *FamA&A, NotNAT A, NotNAT B, OxThe, PIP&P, WhThe, WhoStg 1906, WhoStg 1908*
Rehan, Mary 1887-1963 *NotNAT B, WhScrn 1, WhScrn 2, WhoHol B*
Rehberg, Hans 1901-1963 *CnMD, ModWD*
Rehfeld, Curt *Film 2*
Rehfisch, Hans Jose 1891-1960 *CnMD, McGWD, ModWD*
Rehkopf, Paul *Film 2*
Rehnquist, William 1924- *CelR 3*
Reich, John 1906- *BiE&WWA, NotNAT*
Reich, Richard *NatPD*
Reichenbach, Francois 1922- *DcFM, FilmgC, OxFilm, WorEnF*
Reicher, Emmanuel 1849-1924 *NotNAT B*
Reicher, Ernest *Film 2*
Reicher, Frank 1875-1965 *Film 2, FilmgC, MotPP, MovMk, TwYS, Vers B, WhScrn 1, WhScrn 2, WhThe, WhoHol B*
Reicher, Frank 1876-1965 *TwYS A*
Reicher, Hedwiga *Film 2*
Reichert, Heinz 1877-1940 *AmSCAP 1966*
Reichert, James A 1932- *AmSCAP 1966*
Reichert, Julia *WomWMM A, WomWMM B*
Reichert, Kittens *Film 1, Film 2*

Reichner, S Bickley *AmSCAP 1966*
Reichow, Otto 1904- *Vers A*
Reichow, Werner 1922-1973 *WhScrn 2, WhoHol B*
Reid, Alastair 1939- *FilmgC*
Reid, Beryl *WhoHol A*
Reid, Beryl 1918- *FilmgC*
Reid, Beryl 1920- *WhoThe 16*
Reid, Carl Benton d1973 *WhoHol B*
Reid, Carl Benton 1893-1973 *MovMk, Vers A*
Reid, Carl Benton 1894-1973 *FilmgC, WhScrn 2*
Reid, Charlotte T *NewYTET*
Reid, Don 1914- *AmSCAP 1966*
Reid, Dorothy Davenport *WomWMM*
Reid, Elliott 1920- *BiE&WWA, MotPP, NotNAT, Vers A, WhoHol A*
Reid, Frances 1918- *BiE&WWA, NotNAT, WhThe, WhoHol A*
Reid, Francis *WomWMM B*
Reid, Francis Ellison d1933 *NotNAT B*
Reid, Hal d1920 *Film 1, NotNAT B, WhScrn 2, WhThe, WhoHol B*
Reid, Kate 1930- *BiE&WWA, NotNAT, WhoHol A, WhoThe 16*
Reid, Max 1903-1969 *WhScrn 2*
Reid, Milton *WhoHol A*
Reid, Peggy *MotPP*
Reid, Reidy 1889-1946 *AmSCAP 1966*
Reid, Sheila *WhoHol A*
Reid, Trevor 1909-1965 *WhScrn 1, WhScrn 2, WhoHol B*
Reid, Mrs. Wallace *WhoHol A*
Reid, Wallace d1923 *MotPP, WhoHol B*
Reid, Wallace 1890-1923 *Film 1, Film 2, FilmgC, MovMk*
Reid, Wallace 1891-1923 *WhScrn 1, WhScrn 2, WhThe*
Reid, Wallace 1892-1923 *NotNAT A, NotNAT B, TwYS*
Reid, Wallace, Jr. *WhoHol A*
Reidel, Judy *WomWMM B*
Reidy, Kitty 1902- *WhThe*
Reif, Paul 1910- *AmSCAP 1966*
Reiffarth, Jennie 1848- *WhoStg 1908*
Reifsneider, Robert 1912- *BiE&WWA, NotNAT*
Reiger, Margie *Film 1*
Reilly, Anastasia d1961 *NotNAT B*
Reilly, Charles E, Jr. *IntMPA 1977*
Reilly, Charles Nelson 1931- *BiE&WWA, NotNAT, PIP&P A, WhoHol A, WhoThe 16*
Reilly, Dominick *Film 1*
Reilly, Hugh *WhoHol A*
Reilly, Jane *WhoHol A*
Reilly, Michael 1933-1962 *WhScrn 1, WhScrn 2*
Reimer, Johannes *Film 2*
Reimers, Ed *WhoHol A*
Reimers, Georg d1936 *NotNAT B, WhoHol B*
Reimherr, George *Film 2*
Reinach, Edward *Film 2*
Reinach, Enrico 1851- *WhThe*
Reinach, Jacquelyn 1930- *AmSCAP 1966*
Reinagle, Alexander *PIP&P*
Reinauer, Richard 1926- *IntMPA 1977*
Reindel, Carl *WhoHol A*
Reiner, Carl *NewYTET, WhoHol A, WomWMM*
Reiner, Carl 1922- *BiE&WWA, CelR 3, FilmgC, MovMk*
Reiner, Carl 1923- *IntMPA 1977*
Reiner, Ethel Linder d1971 *BiE&WWA, NotNAT B*
Reiner, Fritz 1888-1963 *NotNAT B, WhScrn 2*
Reiner, Manny d1974 *NewYTET*

Reiner, Rob *WhoHol A*
Reingolds, Kate d1911 *NotNAT B*
Reinhard, John *Film 1, Film 2*
Reinhardt, Gottfried *IntMPA 1977*
Reinhardt, Gottfried 1911- *FilmgC*
Reinhardt, Gottfried 1914- *WorEnF*
Reinhardt, Harry *Film 2*
Reinhardt, John 1901-1953 *WhScrn 1, WhScrn 2, WhoHol B*
Reinhardt, Max 1873-1943 *CnThe, DcFM, FilmgC, NotNAT A, NotNAT B, OxFilm, OxThe, PIP&P, WhThe, WorEnF*
Reinheart, Alice *IntMPA 1977*
Reinheimer, Howard E 1899- *BiE&WWA*
Reiniger, Lotte 1899- *DcFM, Film 2, FilmgC, OxFilm, WomWMM, WomWMM B, WorEnF*
Reinold, Bernard d1940 *WhScrn 2*
Reinsch, J Leonard *NewYTET*
Reinwald, Greta *Film 2*
Reinwald, Otto *Film 2*
Reis, Alberto 1902-1953 *WhScrn 1, WhScrn 2*
Reis, Faye Louise 1934- *AmSCAP 1966*
Reis, Irving 1906-1953 *BiDFlm, FilmgC, NotNAT B, WorEnF*
Reisch, Walter 1900- *FilmgC*
Reisenfeld, Hugo 1883- *WorEnF*
Reisenhofer, Maria *Film 2*
Reiser, Alois 1884- *AmSCAP 1966*
Reiser, Violet 1915- *AmSCAP 1966*
Reisfeld, Bert 1906- *AmSCAP 1966*
Reisman, Joe 1924- *AmSCAP 1966*
Reisner, Allen *FilmgC, IntMPA 1977*
Reisner, Charles F 1887-1962 *Film 1, Film 2, FilmgC, TwYS A, WhScrn 1, WhScrn 2*
Reiss, Jeffrey C 1942- *IntMPA 1977*
Reiss, Stuart A 1921- *IntMPA 1977*
Reisz, Karel 1926- *BiDFlm, FilmgC, IntMPA 1977, MovMk, OxFilm, WorEnF*
Reisz, Karl 1926- *DcFM*
Reiter, Virginia *WhThe*
Reith, Lord John C W d1968 *NewYTET*
Reithe, Aloise D 1890-1943 *WhScrn 1, WhScrn 2*
Rejane 1857-1920 *CnThe, OxThe*
Rejane, Madame 1857-1920 *NotNAT B*
Rejane, Gabriella 1857-1920 *WhScrn 1, WhScrn 2*
Rejane, Gabrielle 1857-1920 *Film 1, Film 2, PIP&P, WhThe, WhoHol B*
Relley, Gina *Film 2*
Relniger, Lotte *Film 2*
Relph, George 1888-1960 *FilmgC, NotNAT B, PIP&P, WhScrn 1, WhScrn 2, WhThe, WhoHol B*
Relph, Michael 1915- *FilmgC, IntMPA 1977, WhThe*
Relph, Phyllis 1888- *WhThe*
Remarque, Erich Maria 1898-1970 *FilmgC, NotNAT B, WhScrn 2*
Rembusch, Trueman T 1909- *IntMPA 1977*
Remick, Lee *BiE&WWA, MotPP, WhoHol A*
Remick, Lee 1935- *BiDFlm, FilmgC, MovMk, NotNAT, OxFilm, WorEnF*
Remick, Lee 1937- *IntMPA 1977*
Remley, Frank 1902-1967 *WhScrn 1, WhScrn 2*
Remley, Ralph McHugh 1885-1939 *WhScrn 1, WhScrn 2, WhoHol B*
Remsen, Alice 1896- *AmSCAP 1966*
Remsen, Bert *WhoHol A*
Remy, Albert 1912-1967 *WhScrn 1, WhScrn 2, WhoHol B*
Remy, Dick, Sr. 1873-1947 *WhScrn 1, WhScrn 2, WhoHol B*
Renad, Frederick d1939 *NotNAT B*

Renaldo, Duncan 1904- *Film 2, FilmgC, IntMPA 1977, MotPP, MovMk, WhoHol A*
Renar, Helmuth *Film 2*
Renard, David 1921-1973 *WhScrn 2, WhoHol A, WhoHol B*
Renard, Ervin *Film 2*
Renard, Jules 1864-1910 *CnMD, McGWD, ModWD, NotNAT B*
Renard, Kaye *Film 2*
Renard, Ken *WhoHol A*
Renaud, Madeleine *CnThe, WhThe*
Renaud, Madeleine 1900- *BiE&WWA, NotNAT*
Renaud, Madeleine-Lucie 1903- *OxThe*
Renault, Francis d1955 *NotNAT B*
Renault, Jack *Film 2*
Renavent, George 1894-1969 *Film 2, WhScrn 1, WhScrn 2, WhoHol B*
Renay, Liz *WhoHol A*
Rendell, Robert *Film 2*
Rendle, Thomas McDonald 1856-1926 *NotNAT B, WhThe*
Rene, Ida *WhThe*
Rene, Joseph 1920- *AmSCAP 1966*
Rene, Leon T 1902- *AmSCAP 1966*
Rene, Otis J, Jr. 1898- *AmSCAP 1966*
Renee, Renate *Film 2*
Renek, Morris *NatPD*
Renela, Rita *Film 2*
Renella, Pat *WhoHol A*
Renevant, George *Film 1*
Renfeld, C *Film 1*
Renfro, Rennie 1893-1962 *Film 2, TwYS, WhScrn 1, WhScrn 2, WhoHol B*
Reni *Film 2*
Renick, Ruth *Film 2, TwYS*
Renn, Katharina 1913-1975 *WhScrn 2, WhoHol A, WhoHol C*
Rennahan, Ray 1896- *FilmgC*
Rennahan, Ray 1898- *CmMov*
Rennahan, Raymond 1896- *WorEnF*
Rennick, Nancy *WhoHol A*
Rennie, Guy *WhoHol A*
Rennie, Hugh d1953 *NotNAT B*
Rennie, James d1965 *WhoHol B*
Rennie, James 1889-1965 *Film 2, TwYS, WhScrn 1, WhScrn 2*
Rennie, James 1890-1965 *BiE&WWA, FilmgC, NotNAT B, WhThe*
Rennie, John d1952 *NotNAT B*
Rennie, Michael 1909-1971 *BiE&WWA, FilmgC, MotPP, MovMk, NotNAT B, WhScrn 1, WhScrn 2, WhoHol B*
Renoir, Claude 1913- *WorEnF*
Renoir, Claude 1914- *DcFM, FilmgC, OxFilm*
Renoir, Jean 1894- *BiDFlm, DcFM, FilmgC, IntMPA 1977, MovMk, OxFilm, WhoHol A, WorEnF*
Renoir, Marguerite *OxFilm, WomWMM*
Renoir, Pierre 1885-1952 *FilmgC, NotNAT B, OxFilm, WhScrn 1, WhScrn 2, WhoHol B, WorEnF*
Renoir, Rita *OxFilm*
Renouardt, Jeanne *WhThe*
Renoudet, Pete *WhoHol A*
Renouf, Henry d1913 *NotNAT B*
Renshaw, Edyth 1901- *BiE&WWA, NotNAT*
Renthall, Charles H Lawyer *BiE&WWA*
Renwick, Ruth *Film 2*
Renzi, Eva 1944- *FilmgC, WhoHol A*
Repnikova *Film 2*
Repp, Ed Earl *IntMPA 1977*
Repp, Stafford 1918-1974 *WhScrn 2, WhoHol B*
Repper, Charles 1889- *AmSCAP 1966*
Requa, Charles *Film 2*

Rescher, Gayne *FilmgC*
Resin, Dan *WhoHol A*
Resnais, Alain 1922- *BiDFlm, DcFM, FilmgC, MovMk, OxFilm, WomWMM, WorEnF*
Resnick, Leon 1923- *AmSCAP 1966*
Resnik, Muriel *BiE&WWA, NotNAT, NotNAT A*
Resnik, Regina 1924- *CelR 3*
Resor, Stanley Burnet d1962 *NotNAT B*
Ressler, Benton Crews d1963 *NotNAT B*
Resta, Francis E 1894-1968 *WhScrn 1, WhScrn 2*
Reston, James 1909- *CelR 3*
Reszke, Jean De 1850-1925 *NotNAT B*
Retchin, Norman 1919- *IntMPA 1977*
Retford, Ella d1962 *NotNAT B, WhThe*
Reties, Jill *Film 2*
Rettig, Tommy 1941- *FilmgC, IntMPA 1977, WhoHol A*
Retty, Wolf Albach 1908-1967 *WhScrn 2*
Reuben, David 1933- *CelR 3*
Reufer-Eichberg, Adele *Film 2*
Revalles, Flora *Film 2*
Revel, Harry 1905-1958 *AmSCAP 1966, NotNAT B*
Revela, Rita *Film 2*
Revell, Dorothy 1879- *WhoStg 1908*
Revelle, Arthur Hamilton 1872-1958 *NotNAT B, WhThe, WhoStg 1908*
Revelle, Hamilton 1872-1958 *Film 1, Film 2, WhoHol B, WhoStg 1906*
Revere, Ann 1903- *MovMk, Vers A*
Revere, Anne *MotPP, PIP&P, WhoHol A*
Revere, Anne 1903- *BiE&WWA, FilmgC, NotNAT*
Revere, Anne 1906- *WhThe*
Revere, Anne 1907- *IntMPA 1977*
Revere, Giuseppe 1812-1889 *OxThe*
Revesz, Gyorgy 1927- *WorEnF*
Revier, Dorothy 1904- *Film 2, ThFT, TwYS, WhoHol A*
Revier, Harry 1889- *TwYS A*
Revill, Clive 1930- *BiE&WWA, EncMT, FilmgC, IntMPA 1977, WhoHol A, WhoThe 16*
Reville, Alma 1900- *FilmgC, WomWMM, WorEnF*
Reville, Robert d1893 *NotNAT B*
Revol, Claude *WomWMM*
Revson, Charles 1906- *CelR 3*
Revson, Peter 1939- *CelR 3*
Revueltas, Silvestre 1899-1940 *AmSCAP 1966*
Rex *Film 2, TwYS*
Rex, Eugen *Film 2*
Rex, Ludwig *Film 2*
Rexroth, Kenneth 1905- *CelR 3, ConDr 1977*
Rey, Alejandro *MotPP, WhoHol A*
Rey, Antonia *WhoHol A*
Rey, Fernando *WhoHol A*
Rey, Fernando 1915- *FilmgC*
Rey, Fernando 1919- *MovMk*
Rey, Florian 189-?-1961 *DcFM*
Rey, Kathleen *Film 2*
Rey, Roberto 1905-1972 *WhScrn 2*
Rey, Rosa d1969 *WhScrn 2, WhoHol B*
Reyes, Efren 1924-1968 *WhScrn 2*
Reyes, Eva 1915-1970 *WhScrn 1, WhScrn 2, WhoHol B*
Reyes, Lucha 1908-1944 *WhScrn 2*
Reynaud, Emile 1844-1918 *DcFM, OxFilm, WorEnF*
Reynolds, Abe 1884-1955 *WhScrn 1, WhScrn 2, WhoHol B*
Reynolds, Adeline DeWalt 1862-1961 *FilmgC, MotPP, NotNAT B, Vers A, WhScrn 1, WhScrn 2, WhoHol B*

Reynolds, Alfred 1884-1969 *WhThe*
Reynolds, Ben *WorEnF*
Reynolds, Burt 1936- *CelR 3, FilmgC, IntMPA 1977, MotPP, MovMk, WhoHol A*
Reynolds, Clarke *IntMPA 1977*
Reynolds, Craig 1907-1949 *NotNAT B, WhScrn 1, WhScrn 2, WhoHol B*
Reynolds, Dale *WhoHol A*
Reynolds, Debbie 1932- *BiDFlm, CelR 3, CmMov, EncMT, FilmgC, IntMPA 1977, MGM, MotPP, MovMk, OxFilm, PIP&P A, WhoHol A, WorEnF*
Reynolds, Dorothy 1913- *WhoThe 16*
Reynolds, E Vivian 1866-1952 *NotNAT B, WhThe*
Reynolds, Ely *Film 2*
Reynolds, Frank *NewYTET*
Reynolds, Frank E d1962 *NotNAT B*
Reynolds, Frederick 1764-1841 *NotNAT A, NotNAT B, OxThe*
Reynolds, Gene 1925- *NewYTET, WhoHol A*
Reynolds, George Earl 1921- *AmSCAP 1966*
Reynolds, George Francis 1880- *WhThe*
Reynolds, Harold 1896-1972 *WhScrn 2*
Reynolds, Hunter L 1903- *AmSCAP 1966*
Reynolds, Jack 1904- *AmSCAP 1966*
Reynolds, James d1957 *NotNAT B*
Reynolds, Jane Louisa d1907 *NotNAT B*
Reynolds, John T *NewYTET*
Reynolds, Joseph *WhoHol A*
Reynolds, Joyce 1924- *FilmgC, IntMPA 1977, MotPP*
Reynolds, Judy *WomWMM B*
Reynolds, Kay *WhoHol A*
Reynolds, Lake 1889-1952 *WhScrn 1, WhScrn 2*
Reynolds, Lynn E 1889-1927 *TwYS A*
Reynolds, Malvina 1900- *AmSCAP 1966*
Reynolds, Marjorie 1921- *FilmgC, IntMPA 1977, MotPP, MovMk, WhoHol A*
Reynolds, Noah d1948 *WhScrn 1, WhScrn 2*
Reynolds, Peter 1926-1975 *FilmgC, WhScrn 2, WhoHol A*
Reynolds, Quentin 1903-1965 *WhScrn 2*
Reynolds, Randall *Film 2*
Reynolds, Richard S, Jr. 1908- *CelR 3*
Reynolds, Robert *OxThe*
Reynolds, Sheldon 1923- *FilmgC, IntMPA 1977, WorEnF*
Reynolds, Stuart 1907- *IntMPA 1977*
Reynolds, Thomas d1947 *NotNAT B, WhThe*
Reynolds, Tom *Film 2*
Reynolds, Tom 1866-1942 *NotNAT B, WhThe*
Reynolds, Tommy 1917- *AmSCAP 1966*
Reynolds, Vera 1905-1962 *Film 2, MotPP, NotNAT B, TwYS, WhScrn 1, WhScrn 2, WhoHol B*
Reynolds, Walter d1941 *NotNAT B*
Reynolds, William *WhoHol A*
Reynolds, William Jensen 1920- *AmSCAP 1966*
Reynolds, Wilson *Film 2*
Reynoldson, T H d1888 *NotNAT B*
Rezzuto, Tom 1929- *BiE&WWA*
Rhauma, Gypsy *Film 2*
Rhea, Raymond 1910- *AmSCAP 1966*
Rheiner, Judith Diane 1940- *IntMPA 1977*
Rheiner, Samuel *IntMPA 1977*
Rhekopf, Paul *Film 2*
Rhett, Alicia *WhoHol A*
Rhine, Jack 1911-1951 *WhScrn 1, WhScrn 2*
Rhines, Howard M 1912- *AmSCAP 1966*
Rho, Stella 1886- *WhThe*
Rhoades, Barbara *WhoHol A*
Rhoda, Sybil *Film 2*
Rhoden, Elmer C 1893- *IntMPA 1977*

Rhodes, Alfred Dusty d1948 *WhScrn 2*
Rhodes, Billie 1906- *Film 1*, *TwYS*, *WhoHol A*
Rhodes, Billy 1906- *Film 2*
Rhodes, Christopher *WhoHol A*
Rhodes, David 1917- *AmSCAP 1966*
Rhodes, Donnelly *WhoHol A*
Rhodes, E A 1900- *IntMPA 1977*
Rhodes, Elizabeth *Film 2*
Rhodes, Erik 1906- *BiE&WWA*, *FilmgC*,
  MovMk, *NotNAT*, *PIP&P*, *WhoHol A*
Rhodes, Grandon *WhoHol A*
Rhodes, Hari *WhoHol A*
Rhodes, Harriet *WomWMM*
Rhodes, Harrison 1871-1929 *NotNAT B*, *WhThe*
Rhodes, John 1606?- *OxThe*, *PIP&P*
Rhodes, Jordan *WhoHol A*
Rhodes, Leon S 1916- *AmSCAP 1966*
Rhodes, Marjorie *WhoHol A*
Rhodes, Marjorie 1902- *FilmgC*
Rhodes, Marjorie 1903- *WhoThe 16*
Rhodes, Percy William d1956 *NotNAT B*
Rhodes, Raymond Compton 1887-1935 *NotNAT B*
Rhodes, Raymond Crompton 1887-1935 *WhThe*
Rhodes, Stan 1924- *AmSCAP 1966*
Rhodes, Vivian *WhoHol A*
Rhudin, Fridolf 1895-1935 *WhScrn 1*, *WhScrn 2*
Rhue, Madlyn 1934- *FilmgC*, *MotPP*,
  WhoHol A
Rhynsburger, H Donovan 1903- *BiE&WWA*,
  NotNAT
Riabouchinska, Tatiana 1916- *WhThe*
Rial, Louise d1940 *NotNAT B*
Riano, Renie d1971 *Vers A*, *WhScrn 1*,
  WhScrn 2, *WhoHol B*
Riavme, Helen *Film 1*
Ribeiro, Joy 1956-1972 *WhScrn 2*
Ribemont-Dessaignes, Georges 1884- *ModWD*
Ribgy, Edward 1879-1951 *WhScrn 1*
Ribicoff, Abraham 1910- *CelR 3*
Ribman, Ronald 1932- *ConDr 1977*, *CroCD*,
  NatPD, *NotNAT*, *WhoThe 16*
Ribner, Irving 1921-1972 *BiE&WWA*,
  NotNAT B
Ricardel, Molly d1963 *NotNAT B*
Ricca, Louis 1909- *AmSCAP 1966*
Ricciardello, Joseph A 1911- *AmSCAP 1966*
Ricciardi, William *Film 2*
Riccitelli, Elizabeth *WomWMM B*
Riccoboni *PIP&P*
Riccoboni, Antonio *OxThe*
Riccoboni, Luigi 1675?-1753 *NotNAT B*, *OxThe*
Rice, Andy d1963 *NotNAT B*
Rice, Andy, Jr. *Film 2*
Rice, Charles d1880 *NotNAT B*
Rice, Chester 1895- *AmSCAP 1966*
Rice, Dan 1823-1900 *NotNAT A*
Rice, Darlene *WhoHol A*
Rice, Darol A 1917- *AmSCAP 1966*
Rice, Edward E 1849-1924 *EncMT*
Rice, Edward Everett *WhoStg 1906*,
  WhoStg 1908
Rice, Edward Everett 1848-1924 *NotNAT B*,
  WhThe
Rice, Elmer 1892-1967 *AmSCAP 1966*,
  BiE&WWA, *CnMD*, *CnThe*, *FilmgC*,
  McGWD, *ModWD*, *NotNAT A*, *NotNAT B*,
  OxThe, *PIP&P*, *REnWD*, *WhThe*
Rice, Fanny d1936 *NotNAT B*
Rice, Florence d1974 *WhoHol B*
Rice, Florence 1907-1974 *ThFT*
Rice, Florence 1911-1974 *FilmgC*, *WhScrn 2*
Rice, Frank 1892-1936 *Film 2*, *TwYS*,
  WhScrn 2, *WhoHol B*
Rice, Freddie 1898-1956 *WhScrn 1*

Rice, Gitz Ingraham 1891-1947 *AmSCAP 1966*,
  NotNAT B
Rice, Grantland 1881-1954 *WhScrn 1*, *WhScrn 2*,
  WhoHol B
Rice, Howard *WhoHol A*
Rice, Jack 1893-1968 *Vers B*, *WhScrn 2*
Rice, Joan 1930- *FilmgC*, *WhoHol A*
Rice, John 1596?- *OxThe*
Rice, John C 1858-1915 *Film 1*, *WhScrn 2*
Rice, Myron B 1864- *WhoStg 1906*,
  WhoStg 1908
Rice, Norman 1910-1957 *WhScrn 1*, *WhScrn 2*,
  WhoHol B
Rice, Peter 1928- *WhoThe 16*
Rice, Robert 1913-1968 *WhScrn 2*
Rice, Ron 1935-1964 *WorEnF*
Rice, Sam 1874-1946 *WhScrn 1*, *WhScrn 2*,
  WhoHol B
Rice, Thomas Dartmouth 1808-1860 *FamA&A*,
  NotNAT B, *OxThe*, *PIP&P*
Rice, Tim 1944- *ConDr 1977D*, *WhoThe 16*
Rice, Vernon d1954 *NotNAT B*
Rich, Allan *WhoHol A*
Rich, Charles J 1855-1921 *NotNAT B*
Rich, Christopher d1714 *NotNAT B*, *OxThe*,
  PIP&P
Rich, Claude *WhoHol A*
Rich, David Lowell 1923?- *FilmgC*
Rich, Dick 1909-1967 *WhScrn 2*, *WhoHol B*
Rich, Doris d1971 *WhoHol B*
Rich, Eddie 1926- *BiE&WWA*
Rich, Frances *WhoHol A*
Rich, Freddie 1898-1956 *AmSCAP 1966*,
  WhScrn 2, *WhoHol B*
Rich, Gladys 1892- *AmSCAP 1966*
Rich, Helen d1963 *NotNAT B*, *WhoHol B*
Rich, Irene *MotPP*
Rich, Irene 1891- *FilmgC*, *MovMk*, *ThFT*,
  WhoHol A
Rich, Irene 1894- *Film 1*, *Film 2*, *TwYS*
Rich, Irene 1897- *IntMPA 1977*
Rich, John *PIP&P*
Rich, John 1682?-1761 *CnThe*, *NotNAT B*
Rich, John 1692?-1761 *OxThe*
Rich, John 1925- *FilmgC*, *IntMPA 1977*,
  NewYTET
Rich, Lee *NewYTET*
Rich, Lillian d1954 *MotPP*, *NotNAT B*,
  WhoHol B
Rich, Lillian 1900-1954 *WhScrn 1*, *WhScrn 2*
Rich, Lillian 1902-1954 *Film 1*, *Film 2*, *TwYS*
Rich, Max 1897- *AmSCAP 1966*
Rich, Phil 1896-1956 *WhScrn 1*, *WhScrn 2*
Rich, Ron *WhoHol A*
Rich, Roy 1909-1969 *FilmgC*, *WhThe*
Rich, Vivian *Film 1*, *MotPP*
Richard, Al d1962 *NotNAT B*
Richard, Cliff 1940- *FilmgC*, *IntMPA 1977*,
  WhoHol A
Richard, Frida *Film 2*
Richard, Frieda 1873-1946 *WhScrn 1*, *WhScrn 2*,
  WhoHol B
Richard, Fritz *Film 2*
Richard, George N 1892- *BiE&WWA*
Richard, Georges d1891 *NotNAT B*
Richard, Jean-Louis 1927- *WorEnF*
Richard, Little *WhoHol A*
Richard, Viola *Film 2*, *TwYS*
Richards, A Bate d1876 *NotNAT B*
Richards, Addison d1964 *MotPP*, *NotNAT B*,
  WhoHol B
Richards, Addison 1887-1964 *FilmgC*, *WhScrn 1*,
  WhScrn 2
Richards, Addison 1903-1964 *MovMk*, *Vers A*

Richards, Angela 1944- *WhoThe 16*
Richards, Ann *MotPP*
Richards, Ann 1918- *FilmgC, MovMk*
Richards, Ann 1919- *MGM, WhoHol A*
Richards, Aubrey *WhoHol A*
Richards, Beah *BiE&WWA, NotNAT,
WhoHol A*
Richards, Burt *WhoHol A*
Richards, Charles 1899-1948 *WhScrn 1,
WhScrn 2, WhoHol B*
Richards, Cicely d1933 *NotNAT B, WhThe*
Richards, Cully 1908- *AmSCAP 1966*
Richards, David Bryant 1942- *NotNAT*
Richards, Donald d1953 *NotNAT B*
Richards, Emil 1932- *AmSCAP 1966*
Richards, Frank *WhoHol A*
Richards, Gordon 1893-1964 *NotNAT B,
WhScrn 1, WhScrn 2, WhoHol B*
Richards, Grant 1916-1963 *WhScrn 1, WhScrn 2,
WhoHol B*
Richards, Howard L, Jr. 1927- *AmSCAP 1966*
Richards, Jay 1917- *AmSCAP 1966*
Richards, Jean *WomWMM*
Richards, Jeff *IntMPA 1977*
Richards, Jerald R 1918- *AmSCAP 1966*
Richards, Jon *WhoHol A*
Richards, Julian D 1917- *IntMPA 1977*
Richards, Keith *WhoHol A*
Richards, Ken *WhoHol A*
Richards, Kim *WhoHol A*
Richards, Lloyd *BiE&WWA, NotNAT*
Richards, Mary *Film 1*
Richards, N *PIP&P*
Richards, Norman 1931- *AmSCAP 1966*
Richards, Paul E d1974 *WhScrn 2, WhoHol B*
Richards, Richard R d1925 *NotNAT B*
Richards, Rosa *Film 2*
Richards, Stanley 1918- *IntMPA 1977*
Richards, Stephen *WhoHol A*
Richards, Stephen 1908- *AmSCAP 1966*
Richards, Susan 1898- *WhThe, WhoHol A*
Richards, Vincent *WhoHol A*
Richardson, Arthur 1899-1963 *AmSCAP 1966*
Richardson, Baury Bradford *Film 2*
Richardson, Claiborne F 1929- *AmSCAP 1966*
Richardson, Edward *Film 2*
Richardson, Elliot 1920- *CelR 3*
Richardson, Florence *Film 2*
Richardson, Foster d1942 *NotNAT B*
Richardson, Frank d1913 *WhScrn 2*
Richardson, Frank 1871-1917 *NotNAT B, WhThe*
Richardson, Frank 1898-1962 *Film 2, WhoHol B*
Richardson, Frankie 1898-1962 *NotNAT B,
WhScrn 1, WhScrn 2*
Richardson, Hal Ainslie 1913- *AmSCAP 1966*
Richardson, Howard 1917- *BiE&WWA, McGWD,
NotNAT*
Richardson, Ian 1934- *CnThe, PIP&P,
WhoHol A, WhoThe 16*
Richardson, Jack 1883- *Film 1, Film 2, TwYS*
Richardson, Jack 1935- *BiE&WWA, CnMD,
CnThe, ConDr 1977, CroCD, McGWD,
ModWD, NotNAT, PIP&P, REnWD*
Richardson, John *Film 2*
Richardson, John 1936- *FilmgC, WhoHol A*
Richardson, Leander 1856-1918 *NotNAT B,
WhThe*
Richardson, Lee 1926- *BiE&WWA, NotNAT*
Richardson, Myrtle *WhThe*
Richardson, Sir Ralph 1902- *BiDFlm,
BiE&WWA, CelR 3, CnThe, FamA&A,
FilmgC, IntMPA 1977, MotPP, MovMk,
NotNAT, NotNAT A, OxFilm, OxThe,
PIP&P, WhoHol A, WhoThe 16, WorEnF*

Richardson, Randell 1921- *AmSCAP 1966*
Richardson, Tony 1928- *BiDFlm, BiE&WWA,
DcFM, FilmgC, IntMPA 1977, MovMk,
NotNAT, OxFilm, WhoThe 16, WomWMM,
WorEnF*
Richardson, William 1876-1937 *WhScrn 2*
Riche, Robert *NatPD*
Richelieu, Cardinal Armand-Jean DuP De
1585-1642 *OxThe*
Richepin, Jacques 1880-1946 *NotNAT B, WhThe*
Richepin, Jean 1849-1926 *McGWD, ModWD,
NotNAT B, OxThe, WhThe*
Richers, Herbert 1923- *IntMPA 1977*
Richfield, Edwin *WhoHol A*
Richman, Al 1885-1936 *WhScrn 1, WhScrn 2*
Richman, Arthur 1886-1944 *NotNAT B, WhThe*
Richman, Charles 1870-1940 *NotNAT B, Vers B,
WhScrn 1, WhScrn 2, WhThe, WhoHol B,
WhoStg 1906, WhoStg 1908*
Richman, Charles 1879-1940 *Film 1, Film 2,
TwYS*
Richman, Harry 1895-1972 *AmSCAP 1966,
BiE&WWA, EncMT, NotNAT A,
NotNAT B, WhScrn 2, WhThe, WhoHol B*
Richman, Marian 1922-1956 *WhScrn 2*
Richman, Mark *MotPP*
Richman, Mark 1927- *BiE&WWA, FilmgC,
IntMPA 1977, NotNAT*
Richman, Peter Mark 1927- *WhoHol A*
Richman, Stella *NewYTET*
Richmond, Al *Film 2*
Richmond, Edna *Film 2*
Richmond, Kane 1906-1973 *FilmgC, WhScrn 2,
WhoHol B*
Richmond, Susan 1894-1959 *NotNAT B, WhThe*
Richmond, Ted 1912- *FilmgC, IntMPA 1977*
Richmond, Virginia 1932- *AmSCAP 1966*
Richmond, Warner 1895-1948 *Film 1, Film 2,
TwYS, WhScrn 1, WhScrn 2, WhoHol B*
Richter, Ada *AmSCAP 1966*
Richter, Charles 1900- *CelR 3*
Richter, Ellen *Film 2*
Richter, George *Film 2*
Richter, Hans 1888-1976 *DcFM, FilmgC,
MovMk, OxFilm, WhoHol C, WorEnF*
Richter, John *Film 2*
Richter, Marga 1926- *AmSCAP 1966*
Richter, Paul 1896-1961 *Film 2, NotNAT B,
WhScrn 1, WhScrn 2, WhoHol B*
Richter, William B 1901- *AmSCAP 1966*
Rickaby, J W *WhThe*
Rickard, Tex *Film 2*
Rickenbacker, Eddie 1890- *CelR 3*
Ricketson, Frank H, Jr. *IntMPA 1977*
Ricketts, Charles 1866-1931 *NotNAT A,
NotNAT B, OxThe, PIP&P, WhThe*
Ricketts, Thomas 1853-1939 *WhScrn 1,
WhScrn 2*
Ricketts, Tom d1939 *Film 1, Film 2, TwYS,
WhoHol B*
Rickles, Don 1926- *CelR 3, FilmgC, WhoHol A*
Rickover, Hyman 1900- *CelR 3*
Ricks, Archie *Film 2*
Ricks, James d1974 *WhScrn 2*
Ricksen, Lucille 1907-1925 *Film 2, WhoHol B*
Rickson, Joe *Film 2*
Rickson, Lucille 1907-1925 *WhScrn 1, WhScrn 2*
Rico, Mona *Film 2, WhoHol A*
Riddell, George d1944 *NotNAT B*
Riddle, Hal *WhoHol A*
Riddle, Jim d1976? *WhScrn 2*
Riddle, Nelson *FilmgC*
Riddle, R Richard 1936- *AmSCAP 1966*
Riddle, Richard *WhScrn 1, WhScrn 2*

Ridge, Walter J 1900-1968 *WhScrn 1, WhScrn 2*
Ridgeley, John 1909-1968 *FilmgC, MotPP*
Ridgely, Cleo d1962 *NotNAT B, WhoHol B*
Ridgely, Cleo 1893-1962 *Film 1, Film 2, TwYS*
Ridgely, Cleo 1894-1962 *WhScrn 1, WhScrn 2*
Ridgely, John 1909-1968 *MovMk, Vers B,
    WhScrn 1, WhScrn 2, WhoHol B*
Ridgely, Richard 1910- *AmSCAP 1966*
Ridgely, Robert *WhoHol A*
Ridges, Stanley d1951 *NotNAT B, WhoHol B*
Ridges, Stanley 1891-1951 *Film 2*
Ridges, Stanley 1892-1951 *FilmgC, MovMk,
    Vers A, WhScrn 1, WhScrn 2*
Ridgeway, Fritz *Film 2*
Ridgeway, Fritzi 1898-1961 *WhScrn 1, WhScrn 2,
    WhoHol B*
Ridgeway, Fritzie 1898-1960 *Film 1, Film 2,
    TwYS*
Ridgeway, Peter d1938 *NotNAT B*
Ridgeway, Philip 1891-1954 *NotNAT B, WhThe*
Ridgeway, Philip 1920- *WhThe*
Ridgewell, Audrey 1904-1968 *WhScrn 2*
Ridgway, Jack *Film 1*
Ridler, Anne 1912- *ConDr 1977*
Ridley, Arnold 1896- *WhoThe 16*
Ridley, Robert 1901-1958 *WhScrn 1, WhScrn 2*
Riechers, Helene 1869-1957 *WhScrn 1, WhScrn 2*
Riefenstahl, Leni 1902- *BiDFlm, DcFM, Film 2,
    FilmgC, OxFilm, WhoHol A, WomWMM,
    WorEnF*
Rieffler, Monsieur *Film 2*
Riegal, Charles *Film 2*
Riegle, Barbara Katherine Rickard 1931-
    WomWMM B
Riehl, Kate *WhoHol A*
Riekelt, Gustave *Film 2*
Rieman, Johannes *Film 2*
Riemann, Johannes 1887-1959 *WhScrn 1,
    WhScrn 2*
Rierson, Richard D 1929- *AmSCAP 1966*
Ries, William J 1895-1955 *WhScrn 1, WhScrn 2*
Riesenfeld, Hugo 1879-1939 *AmSCAP 1966*
Riesner, Charles Francis 1887-1962 *AmSCAP 1966,
    Film 2*
Riesner, Chuck 1887-1962 *WhoHol B*
Riesner, Dean *IntMPA 1977, WhoHol A*
Riethof, Peter W *IntMPA 1977*
Rietti, Victor 1888-1963 *NotNAT B, WhScrn 1,
    WhScrn 2, WhThe, WhoHol B*
Rietty, Robert 1923- *WhoHol A, WhoThe 16*
Rifbjerg, Klaus 1931- *CroCD*
Rifkin, Julian 1915- *IntMPA 1977*
Rifkin, Maurice J 1915- *IntMPA 1977*
Rifkin, Ron *WhoHol A*
Riga, Nadine 1909-1968 *WhScrn 1, WhScrn 2,
    WhoHol B*
Rigas, George *Film 2*
Rigaud, George *WhoHol A*
Rigby, Arthur d1971 *WhoHol A, WhoHol B*
Rigby, Arthur 1870-1944 *NotNAT B, WhThe*
Rigby, Arthur 1900-1971 *WhScrn 2, WhoThe 16*
Rigby, Arthur 1901-1971 *WhScrn 1*
Rigby, Edward 1879-1951 *FilmgC, NotNAT B,
    WhScrn 2, WhThe, WhoHol B*
Rigby, Frank J d1963 *NotNAT B*
Rigby, Harry 1925- *EncMT, NotNAT*
Rigby, Terence *WhoHol A*
Rigg, Diana 1938- *CelR 3, FilmgC,
    IntMPA 1977, MotPP, PIP&P, WhoHol A,
    WhoThe 16*
Riggs, Lynn 1899-1954 *CnMD, McGWD,
    ModWD, NotNAT B, PIP&P, WhThe*
Riggs, Ralph d1951 *NotNAT B, WhoHol B*
Riggs, Sarah *WomWMM*

Riggs, Tommy 1908-1967 *WhScrn 1, WhScrn 2,
    WhoHol B*
Riggs, William d1975 *WhScrn 2*
Righter, Carroll 1900- *CelR 3*
Rightmire, William H 1857-1933 *WhScrn 1,
    WhScrn 2*
Righton, Edward C d1899 *NotNAT B*
Rignold, George d1912 *NotNAT B, WhThe*
Rignold, Harry *Film 2*
Rignold, Henry d1873 *NotNAT B*
Rignold, Lionel d1919 *NotNAT B, WhThe*
Rignold, Marie d1932 *NotNAT B*
Rignold, Susan d1895 *NotNAT B*
Rignold, William d1904 *NotNAT B*
Rignold, William Henry d1910 *NotNAT B*
Riha, Bobby 1958- *WhoHol A*
Rihani, Neguib 1891-1949 *WhScrn 1, WhScrn 2*
Riisna, Ene *WomWMM B*
Rilchard, Frida *Film 2*
Rilety, Anna *Film 2*
Riley, Brooks *WomWMM*
Riley, Edna Goldsmith d1962 *NotNAT B*
Riley, George 1900-1972 *WhScrn 2, WhoHol B*
Riley, Jack *WhoHol A*
Riley, Jack Slim 1895-1933 *WhScrn 1, WhScrn 2,
    WhoHol B*
Riley, James Whitcomb 1849-1916 *AmSCAP 1966*
Riley, Jean 1916- *NatPD*
Riley, Jeannine *WhoHol A*
Riley, Lawrence 1891-1975 *BiE&WWA,
    NotNAT B*
Riley, Lawrence 1897- *NotNAT*
Riley, Marin *WhoHol A*
Riley, Mike 1904- *AmSCAP 1966*
Riley, Nancy *WomWMM*
Riley, Ronald H 1908- *IntMPA 1977*
Riley, William *Film 2*
Rill, Eli 1926- *BiE&WWA, NotNAT*
Rilla, Walter 1895- *Film 2, FilmgC,
    IntMPA 1977, WhoHol A*
Rilla, Wolf 1920- *FilmgC*
Rillon, John T *Film 2*
Rim, Carlo *DcFM*
Rimac, Ciro Campos 1894-1973 *WhScrn 2*
Rimsky, Nicholas *Film 2*
Rin-Tin-Tin 1916-1930 *Film 2, TwYS*
Rin Tin Tin 1916-1932 *FilmgC, WhScrn 1,
    WhScrn 2, WhoHol B*
Rin-Tin-Tin 1918-1932 *OxFilm*
Rin Tin Tin, Jr. *WhScrn 1, WhScrn 2*
Rinaldi, Tina C *Film 2*
Rinaldi, William *Film 2*
Rinaldo 1884- *WhThe*
Rinaldo, Duncan 1904- *Film 2, TwYS*
Rinaldo, Rinaldini *Film 2*
Rinch-Smiles, Frank *Film 2*
Rindler, Milton 1898- *BiE&WWA, NotNAT*
Rinehardt, Harry *Film 2*
Rinehart, Mary Roberts 1876-1958 *ModWD,
    NotNAT B, WhThe*
Rines, Joseph 1902- *AmSCAP 1966*
Ring, Blanche d1961 *Film 1, WhoHol B*
Ring, Blanche 1871-1961 *EncMT*
Ring, Blanche 1872-1961 *Film 2*
Ring, Blanche 1876-1961 *NotNAT B, WhScrn 1,
    WhScrn 2, WhStg 1908*
Ring, Blanche 1877-1961 *WhThe*
Ring, Cyril 1893-1967 *Film 2, WhScrn 1,
    WhScrn 2, WhoHol B*
Ring, Frances 1882-1951 *NotNAT B, WhScrn 1,
    WhScrn 2, WhThe, WhoStg 1906,
    WhoStg 1908*
Ring, Sutherland *Film 1*
Ringle, Dave 1893-1965 *AmSCAP 1966*

Ringwald, Roy 1910- *AmSCAP 1966*
Rinker, Al 1907- *AmSCAP 1966*
Rinker, Charles 1911- *AmSCAP 1966*
Rintels, David W *NewYTET*
Rio, Rosa 1914- *AmSCAP 1966*
Riordan, Robert J 1913-1968 *WhScrn 1,*
WhScrn 2, WhoHol B
Rios, James 1931- *AmSCAP 1966*
Rios, Lalo 1927-1973 *WhScrn 2, WhoHol B*
Rip d1941 *NotNAT B*
Rip, Georges d1941 *WhThe*
Ripley, Arthur 1895-1961 *FilmgC*
Ripley, Charles *Film 1*
Ripley, Heather *WhoHol A*
Ripley, Patricia 1926- *BiE&WWA, NotNAT*
Ripley, Ray 1891-1938 *WhoHol B*
Ripley, Raymond 1891-1938 *WhScrn 1,*
WhScrn 2
Ripley, Robert L 1893-1949 *WhScrn 1, WhScrn 2,*
WhoHol B
Ripley, S Dillon 1913- *CelR 3*
Ripper, Michael 1913- *FilmgC, WhoHol A*
Rippon, Angela *NewYTET*
Rippy, Rodney Allen *WhoHol A*
Riscoe, Arthur 1896-1954 *FilmgC, NotNAT B,*
WhScrn 1, WhScrn 2, WhThe, WhoHol B
Risdon, Elizabeth 1887-1958 *Film 1, FilmgC,*
MotPP, MovMk, NotNAT B, ThFT,
Vers A, WhScrn 1, WhScrn 2, WhThe,
WhoHol B
Rishell, Myrtle 1877-1942 *WhScrn 2*
Risi, Dino 1916- *FilmgC*
Risi, Dino 1917- *WorEnF*
Rising, W *Film 2*
Rising, William S 1851-1930 *WhScrn 1,*
WhScrn 2, WhoHol B
Riskin, Robert 1897-1955 *CmMov, DcFM,*
FilmgC, OxFilm, WorEnF
Rislakki, Ensio 1896- *CroCD*
Risque, W H d1916 *NotNAT B*
Riss, Dan 1910-1970 *WhScrn 1, WhScrn 2,*
WhoHol B
Rissien, Edward L *IntMPA 1977*
Rissmiller, Lawson J 1914-1953 *WhScrn 1,*
WhScrn 2
Risso, Attilio 1913-1967 *WhScrn 1, WhScrn 2,*
WhoHol B
Risso, Roberto *WhoHol A*
Rist, Robbie *WhoHol A*
Ristori, Adelaide 1821-1906 *NotNAT A*
Ristori, Adelaide 1822-1906 *CnThe, FamA&A,*
NotNAT B, OxThe, PIP&P
Ritchard, Cyril *WhoHol A*
Ritchard, Cyril 1896- *Film 2, FilmgC*
Ritchard, Cyril 1897- *BiE&WWA, EncMT,*
NotNAT, WhoThe 16
Ritchard, Viola *Film 2*
Ritchie, Adele 1874-1930 *NotNAT B, WhThe,*
WhoStg 1908
Ritchie, Billie 1879-1921 *Film 1, WhScrn 1,*
WhScrn 2, WhoHol B
Ritchie, Clint *WhoHol A*
Ritchie, Franklin d1918 *Film 1, WhScrn 2*
Ritchie, Jean 1922- *AmSCAP 1966*
Ritchie, June 1939- *FilmgC, WhoHol A,*
WhoThe 16
Ritchie, Larry *WhoHol A*
Ritchie, Michael *FilmgC*
Ritchie, Michael 1936- *OxFilm*
Ritchie, Michael 1938- *IntMPA 1977*
Ritchie, Terry V 1887-1918 *WhScrn 2*
Ritman, William *NotNAT, WhoThe 16*
Ritt, Martin *IntMPA 1977, WhoHol A*
Ritt, Martin 1919- *FilmgC, MovMk*

Ritt, Martin 1920- *BiDFlm, BiE&WWA, DcFM,*
NotNAT, OxFilm, WorEnF
Rittau, Gunther 1893-1971 *DcFM*
Rittau, Gunther 1897-1971 *WorEnF*
Rittenhouse, Elizabeth Mae 1915- *AmSCAP 1966*
Rittenhouse, Florence d1929 *NotNAT B*
Ritter, Carol *WomWMM B*
Ritter, Esther 1902-1925 *WhScrn 1, WhScrn 2,*
WhoHol B
Ritter, George d1919 *WhScrn 2*
Ritter, John *WhoHol A*
Ritter, John P d1920 *NotNAT B*
Ritter, Paul J d1962 *WhScrn 1, WhScrn 2*
Ritter, Tex d1974 *WhoHol B*
Ritter, Tex 1906-1974 *WhScrn 2*
Ritter, Tex 1907-1974 *FilmgC*
Ritter, Thelma 1905-1969 *BiDFlm, BiE&WWA,*
FilmgC, MotPP, MovMk, NotNAT B,
OxFilm, Vers A, WhScrn 1, WhScrn 2,
WhoHol B, WorEnF
Ritterband, Gerhard 1905-1959 *WhScrn 1,*
WhScrn 2
Rittman, Trude *BiE&WWA, NotNAT*
Rittner, Rudolf *Film 2*
Rittner, Tadeusz 1873-1921 *CnMD, McGWD,*
ModWD
Ritz, Al 1901-1965 *Film 1, FilmgC, MotPP,*
OxFilm, WhScrn 1, WhScrn 2, WhoHol B
Ritz, Harry 1906- *FilmgC, MotPP, OxFilm*
Ritz, Jim 1903- *FilmgC, OxFilm*
Ritz, Jimmy *MotPP*
Ritz Brothers, The *FilmgC, MotPP, MovMk,*
OxFilm, WhoHol A
Riva, Emmanuele *MotPP, WhoHol A*
Riva, Emmanuele 1927- *WorEnF*
Riva, Emmanuele 1932- *FilmgC, OxFilm*
Riva, Emmanuelle 1927- *BiDFlm*
Riva, Maria *WhoHol A*
Rivali, Tina *Film 2*
Rivas, Duke Of *McGWD*
Rivas, Duque De *OxThe*
Rivas, Bimbo *PIP&P A*
Rivas, Carlos *WhoHol A*
Rivas, Jose M L 1901-1955 *WhScrn 1, WhScrn 2*
Rive, Kenneth 1919- *IntMPA 1977*
Rivemale, Alexandre 1918- *CnMD, McGWD*
Rivera, Chita 1933- *BiE&WWA, EncMT,*
NotNAT, WhoHol A, WhoThe 16
Rivera, Geraldo 1943- *CelR 3, NewYTET*
Rivera, Linda *WomWMM B*
Rivera, Luis *WhoHol A*
Rivera, Ray 1929- *AmSCAP 1966*
Rivero, Jorge *WhoHol A*
Rivero, Julian 1890-1976 *Vers A, WhoHol C*
Rivero, Lorraine *Film 2*
Rivers, Alfred d1955 *NotNAT B*
Rivers, Joan 1935- *CelR 3, WhoHol A*
Rivers, Larry 1923- *CelR 3*
Rivers, Louis 1922- *NatPD*
Rives, Amelie d1945 *NotNAT B*
Rivett-River, Jackie *WomWMM B*
Rivette, Jacques 1928- *BiDFlm, DcFM, FilmgC,*
OxFilm, WorEnF
Riviere, Fred Curly 1875-1935 *WhScrn 1,*
WhScrn 2, WhoHol B
Riviere, Gaston *Film 1*
Rivkin, Allen 1903- *IntMPA 1977*
Rivkin, Joe 1912- *IntMPA 1977*
Rivoire, Andre *NotNAT B*
Rix, Brian 1924- *CnThe, FilmgC, IntMPA 1977,*
PIP&P A, WhoHol A, WhoThe 16
Rixon, Benjamin R *WhoHol A*
Rixon, Morris L *WhoHol A*
Rizo, Marco 1916- *AmSCAP 1966*

Rizzi, Alberto 1889-1945 *AmSCAP 1966*
Rizzo, Alfredo *WhoHol A*
Rizzo, Bob 1937- *AmSCAP 1966*
Rizzo, Frank 1920- *CelR 3*
Rizzo, Gianni *WhoHol A*
Rizzo, Joe 1917- *AmSCAP 1966*
Roach, Bert 1891-1971 *Film 1, Film 2, FilmgC, TwYS, Vers B, WhScrn 2, WhoHol B*
Roach, Hal 1892- *CmMov, DcFM, FilmgC, OxFilm, TwYS B, WorEnF*
Roach, Hal, Jr. *IntMPA 1977*
Roach, Joseph Maloy 1913- *AmSCAP 1966*
Roach, Margaret 1921-1964 *WhScrn 1, WhScrn 2, WhoHol B*
Roach, Marjorie *Film 2*
Roach, Thomas A d1962 *NotNAT B*
Roache, Viola d1961 *WhoHol B*
Roache, Viola 1885-1961 *NotNAT B, WhThe*
Roache, Viola 1886-1961 *WhScrn 1, WhScrn 2*
Road, Mike *WhoHol A*
Roanne, Andre *Film 2*
Roarke, Adam *WhoHol A*
Robards, Jason, Jr. *MotPP, PIP&P, PIP&P A, WhoHol A*
Robards, Jason, Jr. 1920- *FilmgC*
Robards, Jason, Jr. 1922- *BiE&WWA, CelR 3, CnThe, IntMPA 1977, MovMk, NotNAT, WhoThe 16*
Robards, Jason, Sr. d1963 *MotPP, NotNAT B, WhoHol B*
Robards, Jason, Sr. 1892-1963 *WhScrn 1, WhScrn 2*
Robards, Jason, Sr. 1893-1963 *Film 2, FilmgC, MovMk, TwYS*
Robards, Willis *Film 2*
Robb, Dodi *WomWMM*
Robb, John Donald 1892- *AmSCAP 1966*
Robb, Lori *WhoHol A*
Robbe-Grillet, Alain 1922- *DcFM, FilmgC, OxFilm, WorEnF*
Robbie, Seymour Mitchell *IntMPA 1977, NewYTET*
Robbin, Peter 1956- *WhoHol A*
Robbinne *Film 1*
Robbins, Sir Alfred 1856-1931 *NotNAT B, WhThe*
Robbins, Archie 1913-1975 *WhScrn 2, WhoHol C*
Robbins, Burton E *IntMPA 1977*
Robbins, Carrie Fishbein 1943- *NotNAT, WhoThe 16*
Robbins, Cindy *WhoHol A*
Robbins, Edward E 1930- *BiE&WWA, NotNAT*
Robbins, Edwina *Film 1*
Robbins, Gale 1924- *WhoHol A*
Robbins, Gale 1932- *IntMPA 1977*
Robbins, Harold 1916- *CelR 3, FilmgC*
Robbins, Jane Marla *WhoHol A*
Robbins, Jerome 1918- *BiE&WWA, CelR 3, CmMov, CnThe, EncMT, FilmgC, NotNAT, OxFilm, PIP&P, WhoThe 16, WorEnF*
Robbins, Jesse *Film 1*
Robbins, Marc 1868-1931 *Film 2, WhoHol B*
Robbins, Marcus B 1868-1931 *WhScrn 1, WhScrn 2*
Robbins, Richard 1919-1969 *WhScrn 1, WhScrn 2, WhoHol B*
Robbins, Sheila *WhoHol A*
Robbins, Walt *Film 2*
Robe, Annie d1922 *NotNAT B*
Robe, Harold Athol 1881-1946 *AmSCAP 1966*
Rober, Richard 1906-1952 *FilmgC, NotNAT B, WhScrn 1, WhScrn 2, WhoHol B*
Roberdeau, John Peter d1815 *NotNAT B*
Roberds, Fred A 1941- *AmSCAP 1966*

Robers, Edith *Film 2*
Roberson, Chuck *WhoHol A*
Roberson, Lou 1921-1966 *WhScrn 1, WhScrn 2*
Robert, Eugene 1877- *WhThe*
Robert, Patricia Harrison 1939- *IntMPA 1977*
Robert, Yves 1920- *DcFM, FilmgC, WhoHol A*
Roberti, Lyda 1906-1938 *ThFT, WhoHol B*
Roberti, Lyda 1909-1938 *NotNAT B, WhScrn 1, WhScrn 2, WhThe*
Roberti, Lyda 1910-1938 *FilmgC*
Roberts, A Cledge 1905-1957 *WhScrn 1, WhScrn 2*
Roberts, A Cledge *see also* Roberts, Cledge
Roberts, Albert G 1902-1941 *WhScrn 1, WhScrn 2, WhoHol B*
Roberts, Alice *Film 2*
Roberts, Allan 1905-1966 *AmSCAP 1966*
Roberts, Allene *MotPP*
Roberts, Arthur 1852-1933 *NotNAT B, OxThe, WhThe, WhoStg 1908*
Roberts, Bart *WhoHol A*
Roberts, Ben 1916- *FilmgC, IntMPA 1977, WorEnF*
Roberts, Beryl *Film 2*
Roberts, Beverly 1914- *BiE&WWA, NotNAT, ThFT, WhoHol A*
Roberts, C Luckeyth 1893-1968 *AmSCAP 1966, NotNAT B*
Roberts, Charles J 1868-1957 *AmSCAP 1966*
Roberts, Christian *WhoHol A*
Roberts, Cledge 1905-1957 *NotNAT B, WhoHol B*
Roberts, Cledge *see also* Roberts, A Cledge
Roberts, Curtis *IntMPA 1977*
Roberts, Davis *WhoHol A*
Roberts, Desmond *WhoHol A*
Roberts, Dick 1897-1966 *WhScrn 1, WhScrn 2, WhoHol B*
Roberts, Doris 1930- *NotNAT, WhoHol A, WhoThe 16*
Roberts, Dorothy F Diamond *AmSCAP 1966*
Roberts, Edith 1899-1935 *WhScrn 1, WhScrn 2, WhoHol B*
Roberts, Edith 1901-1935 *Film 1, Film 2, TwYS*
Roberts, Evelyn 1886-1962 *WhThe*
Roberts, Ewan 1914- *WhoHol A, WhoThe 16*
Roberts, Florence d1940 *WhoHol B*
Roberts, Florence 1860-1940 *FilmgC*
Roberts, Florence 1861-1940 *NotNAT B, WhScrn 1, WhScrn 2*
Roberts, Florence 1871-1927 *Film 1, NotNAT B, WhScrn 1, WhScrn 2, WhThe, WhoHol B, WhoStg 1906, WhoStg 1908*
Roberts, Florence Smythe d1925 *NotNAT B*
Roberts, Gene 1918- *AmSCAP 1966*
Roberts, George 1845-1930 *Film 2, WhScrn 2*
Roberts, George M 1928- *AmSCAP 1966*
Roberts, Glen 1921-1974 *WhScrn 2, WhoHol B*
Roberts, Hans d1954 *NotNAT B*
Roberts, Hi *WhoHol A*
Roberts, J H 1884-1961 *Film 2, NotNAT B, WhThe, WhoHol B*
Roberts, Jimmy d1962 *NotNAT B*
Roberts, Joan 1918- *WhThe*
Roberts, Joan 1922- *BiE&WWA, NotNAT, NotNAT A*
Roberts, John 1916- *WhoThe 16*
Roberts, Joseph *Film 2*
Roberts, Keith *WhoHol A*
Roberts, Lee S 1884-1949 *AmSCAP 1966*
Roberts, Leona 1880-1954 *WhScrn 1, WhScrn 2, WhoHol B*
Roberts, Linda 1901- *AmSCAP 1966*
Roberts, Lois *WhoHol A*

Roberts, Louise 1911- *NotNAT*
Roberts, Luanne *WhoHol A*
Roberts, Lynne 1919- *WhoHol A*
Roberts, Lynne 1922- *FilmgC, IntMPA 1977*
Roberts, Marguerite *IntMPA 1977, WomWMM*
Roberts, Marilyn *WhoHol A*
Roberts, Mark *WhoHol A*
Roberts, Meade 1930- *BiE&WWA, NotNAT, WhoHol A*
Roberts, Merrill 1885-1940 *WhScrn 1, WhScrn 2*
Roberts, Nancy 1892-1962 *NotNAT B, WhScrn 2, WhoHol B*
Roberts, Oral 1918- *CelR 3*
Roberts, Paul 1915- *AmSCAP 1966*
Roberts, Pernell *WhoHol A*
Roberts, R A 1870- *WhThe*
Roberts, Rachel 1927- *CelR 3, CnThe, EncMT, FilmgC, IntMPA 1977, MotPP, OxFilm, WhoHol A, WhoThe 16*
Roberts, Ralph *Film 2, WhoHol A*
Roberts, Ralph d1944 *NotNAT B, WhThe*
Roberts, Ralph Arthur 1884-1940 *WhScrn 2*
Roberts, Sir Randal d1899 *NotNAT B*
Roberts, Rhoda *AmSCAP 1966*
Roberts, Roy 1900-1975 *FilmgC, WhScrn 2, WhoHol C*
Roberts, Ruth *WhoHol A*
Roberts, Ruth 1926- *AmSCAP 1966*
Roberts, Sara Jane 1924-1968 *WhScrn 1, WhScrn 2, WhoHol B*
Roberts, Stanley 1916- *IntMPA 1977*
Roberts, Stephen 1895-1936 *IntMPA 1977, WhScrn 1, WhScrn 2, WhoHol A*
Roberts, Thayer 1903-1968 *WhScrn 1, WhScrn 2, WhoHol B*
Roberts, Theodore 1861-1928 *Film 1, Film 2, MotPP, NotNAT B, TwYS, WhScrn 1, WhScrn 2, WhThe, WhoHol B, WhoStg 1908*
Roberts, Tom *WhoHol A*
Roberts, Tony 1939- *NotNAT, WhoHol A, WhoThe 16*
Roberts, Tracey *WhoHol A*
Roberts, Vera Mowry 1918- *BiE&WWA, NotNAT*
Roberts, William *IntMPA 1977*
Robertshaw, Jerrold 1866-1941 *Film 1, Film 2, FilmgC, NotNAT B, WhScrn 1, WhScrn 2, WhThe, WhoHol B*
Robertson, Agnes 1833-1916 *FamA&A, NotNAT B, PIP&P*
Robertson, Alex d1964 *NotNAT B*
Robertson, Beatrice Forbes- *WhThe*
Robertson, Cliff 1925- *BiDFlm, BiE&WWA, CelR 3, CmMov, FilmgC, IntMPA 1977, MotPP, MovMk, WhoHol A, WorEnF*
Robertson, Dale 1923- *AmSCAP 1966, FilmgC, IntMPA 1977, MotPP, WhoHol A*
Robertson, Dennis *WhoHol A*
Robertson, Dick 1903- *AmSCAP 1966*
Robertson, Don 1922- *AmSCAP 1966*
Robertson, Donald d1926 *NotNAT B, WhoStg 1908*
Robertson, Doris S *WhoHol A*
Robertson, E Arnot 1903-1961 *OxFilm*
Robertson, East d1916 *NotNAT B*
Robertson, F J 1916- *IntMPA 1977*
Robertson, Guy 1892- *EncMT, WhThe*
Robertson, Hermine d1962 *NotNAT B*
Robertson, Ian 1858-1936 *NotNAT B, WhThe*
Robertson, Ian *see also* Forbes-Robertson, Ian
Robertson, Imogene 1905-1948 *Film 2, WhScrn 1, WhScrn 2, WhoHol B*
Robertson, J Francis *Film 2*

Robertson, James B 1910- *AmSCAP 1966*
Robertson, James Scotty 1859-1936 *WhScrn 1, WhScrn 2, WhoHol B*
Robertson, Jean 1894-1967 *WhScrn 1, WhScrn 2, WhoHol B*
Robertson, Jerome d1962 *NotNAT B*
Robertson, John *Film 2*
Robertson, John d1962 *NotNAT B*
Robertson, John Stuart 1878-1964 *TwYS A, WhScrn 1, WhScrn 2, WhoHol B*
Robertson, Sir Johnston Forbes *WhThe, WhoStg 1908*
Robertson, Lauri *WomWMM B*
Robertson, Leroy 1896- *AmSCAP 1966*
Robertson, Lolita *Film 1*
Robertson, Malcolm 1933- *WhoThe 16*
Robertson, Mary *WhScrn 1, WhScrn 2*
Robertson, Maud d1930 *NotNAT B*
Robertson, Max *IntMPA 1977*
Robertson, Orie O 1881-1964 *NotNAT B, WhScrn 1, WhScrn 2, WhoHol B*
Robertson, Oscar *CelR 3*
Robertson, Pax d1948 *NotNAT B*
Robertson, Stuart 1901-1958 *WhScrn 1, WhScrn 2, WhoHol B*
Robertson, Mrs. Thomas d1855 *NotNAT B*
Robertson, Thomas William 1829-1871 *CnThe, McGWD, NotNAT A, NotNAT B, OxThe, REnWD*
Robertson, Thomas William Shafto d1895 *NotNAT B*
Robertson, Toby 1928- *WhoThe 16*
Robertson, Tom 1829-1871 *PIP&P*
Robertson, W Graham 1867-1948 *NotNAT A, NotNAT B, WhThe*
Robertson, Willard 1886-1948 *WhScrn 2, WhoHol B*
Robertson, William *WhoHol A*
Robeson, Paul 1898-1976 *BiE&WWA, CelR 3, CnThe, EncMT, FilmgC, MovMk, NotNAT A, NotNAT B, OxFilm, OxThe, PIP&P, WhThe, WhoHol C*
Robey, Sir George 1869-1954 *CnThe, EncMT, Film 1, Film 2, FilmgC, NotNAT A, OxFilm, OxThe, WhScrn 1, WhScrn 2, WhThe, WhoHol B*
Robin, Dany 1927- *FilmgC, IntMPA 1977, WhoHol A*
Robin, Leo 1899- *BiE&WWA, FilmgC, NotNAT*
Robin, Leo 1900- *AmSCAP 1966, EncMT, IntMPA 1977, NewMT*
Robin, Sydney 1912- *AmSCAP 1966*
Robina, Fanny d1927 *NotNAT B*
Robina, Florrie d1953 *NotNAT B*
Robins, Barry *WhoHol A*
Robins, Edward H 1880-1955 *NotNAT B, WhScrn 2, WhThe, WhoHol B*
Robins, Elizabeth 1862-1952 *NotNAT A, NotNAT B, OxThe*
Robins, Elizabeth 1865-1952 *WhThe*
Robins, Gertrude L d1917 *NotNAT B, WhThe*
Robins, Toby *WhoHol A*
Robins, William A d1948 *NotNAT B*
Robinson, Amy 1948- *MovMk*
Robinson, Andy *WhoHol A*
Robinson, Ann *WhoHol A*
Robinson, Anna d1917 *NotNAT B*
Robinson, Arthur *Film 1*
Robinson, Avery 1878-1965 *AmSCAP 1966*
Robinson, Bartlett *WhoHol A*
Robinson, Bernard 1912- *CmMov*
Robinson, Bertrand d1959 *NotNAT B*
Robinson, Bill 1878-1949 *EncMT, FilmgC,*

MovMk, NotNAT B, WhThe, WhoHol B
Robinson, Bill Bojangles 1878-1949 *WhScrn 1,*
WhScrn 2
Robinson, Brooks 1937- *CelR 3*
Robinson, Casey 1903- *CmMov, FilmgC,*
IntMPA 1977
Robinson, Charles Knox 1909- *BiE&WWA,*
NotNAT, WhoHol A
Robinson, Chris *WhoHol A*
Robinson, Christine *WomWMM*
Robinson, Daisy *Film 1*
Robinson, David *WhoHol A*
Robinson, Dewey 1898-1950 *Vers B, WhScrn 1,*
WhScrn 2, WhoHol B
Robinson, E M 1855-1932 *NotNAT B*
Robinson, Earl *Film 2*
Robinson, Earl 1910- *AmSCAP 1966*
Robinson, Edward 1905- *AmSCAP 1966*
Robinson, Edward G 1893- *BiE&WWA, MotPP,*
WhThe, WorEnF
Robinson, Edward G 1893-1972 *FilmgC, OxFilm*
Robinson, Edward G 1893-1973 *BiDFlm, CmMov,*
Film 2, MovMk, NotNAT A, WhScrn 2,
WhoHol B
Robinson, Edward G, Jr. 1934-1974 *WhScrn 2,*
WhoHol B
Robinson, Esme Stuart Lennox 1886-1958
NotNAT B
Robinson, Ethan M d1919 *NotNAT B*
Robinson, Forest *Film 1*
Robinson, Forrest 1859-1924 *Film 2, NotNAT B,*
WhScrn 1, WhScrn 2, WhoHol B
Robinson, Frances 1916-1971 *FilmgC, WhScrn 1,*
WhScrn 2, WhoHol B
Robinson, Frank 1935- *CelR 3*
Robinson, Frederic Charles Patey 1832-1912
NotNAT B
Robinson, Gertrude R 1891-1962 *Film 1,*
WhScrn 1, WhScrn 2, WhoHol B
Robinson, Glen O *NewYTET*
Robinson, Gordon W 1908- *AmSCAP 1966*
Robinson, Harry I 1888-1954 *AmSCAP 1966*
Robinson, Herbert *IntMPA 1977*
Robinson, Herman Lee 1939- *AmSCAP 1966*
Robinson, Horace 1909- *BiE&WWA, NotNAT*
Robinson, Hubbell d1974 *NewYTET*
Robinson, J Russel 1892-1963 *AmSCAP 1966,*
NotNAT B
Robinson, Jackie 1919-1972 *WhScrn 2,*
WhoHol B
Robinson, Jay 1930- *BiE&WWA, FilmgC,*
NotNAT, WhoHol A
Robinson, Jessie Mae 1919- *AmSCAP 1966*
Robinson, Joe *WhoHol A*
Robinson, John 1908- *FilmgC, WhoHol A,*
WhoThe 16
Robinson, John 1940- *NatPD*
Robinson, Judith *PIP&P*
Robinson, Kathleen 1909- *WhThe*
Robinson, Lennox 1886-1958 *CnMD, CnThe,*
McGWD, ModWD, NotNAT A, OxThe,
PIP&P, REnWD, WhThe
Robinson, Lloyd E 1908- *AmSCAP 1966*
Robinson, Madeleine 1908- *WhThe*
Robinson, Madeleine 1916- *FilmgC*
Robinson, Mary Darby 1758-1800 *NotNAT A,*
OxThe
Robinson, Norah 1901- *WhThe*
Robinson, Percy 1889-1967 *WhThe*
Robinson, Perdita 1758-1800 *NotNAT B*
Robinson, Richard d1648 *OxThe*
Robinson, Ruth 1888-1966 *WhScrn 2, WhoHol B*
Robinson, S Garrett 1939- *NatPD*
Robinson, Shari 1942- *WhoHol A*

Robinson, Spike 1884-1942 *Film 1, Film 2,*
WhScrn 1, WhScrn 2, WhoHol B
Robinson, Stuart 1936- *BiE&WWA*
Robinson, Sugar Ray 1921- *CelR 3, WhoHol A*
Robinson, Sugarchile 1940- *WhoHol A*
Robinson, W C *Film 1*
Robinson, Wayne 1916- *BiE&WWA, NotNAT*
Robinson-Duff, Frances d1951 *NotNAT B*
Robison, Arthur 1888-1935 *DcFM, FilmgC,*
OxFilm
Robison, Carson J 1890-1957 *AmSCAP 1966*
Robison, Willard 1894- *AmSCAP 1966*
Robles, Emmanuel Francois 1913- *CnMD*
Robles, Richard 1902-1940 *WhScrn 1, WhScrn 2,*
WhoHol B
Robles, Rudy 1910-1970 *WhScrn 1, WhScrn 2,*
WhoHol B
Robles, Walter *WhoHol A*
Robson, Andrew 1867-1921 *Film 1, Film 2,*
WhScrn 1, WhScrn 2, WhoHol B
Robson, E M 1855-1932 *WhThe*
Robson, Eleanor Elise 1879- *NotNAT A, WhThe,*
WhoStg 1906, WhoStg 1908
Robson, Flora 1902- *BiE&WWA, CnThe,*
FilmgC, IntMPA 1977, MotPP, MovMk,
NotNAT, NotNAT A, OxFilm, OxThe,
PIP&P, ThFT, Vers A, WhoHol A,
WhoThe 16
Robson, Frederick d1919 *NotNAT B*
Robson, Frederick 1821-1864 *NotNAT A,*
NotNAT B, OxThe
Robson, June 1922-1972 *WhScrn 2*
Robson, Mark 1913- *BiDFlm, CmMov, DcFM,*
FilmgC, IntMPA 1977, MovMk, OxFilm,
WomWMM, WorEnF
Robson, Mary 1893- *WhThe*
Robson, Mat d1899 *NotNAT B*
Robson, May d1942 *MotPP, PIP&P, WhoHol B,*
WhoStg 1906, WhoStg 1908
Robson, May 1858-1942 *ThFT, WhScrn 1,*
WhScrn 2
Robson, May 1859-1942 *FilmgC*
Robson, May 1864-1942 *MovMk*
Robson, May 1865-1942 *Film 1, Film 2,*
NotNAT B, OxFilm, TwYS, Vers A,
WhThe
Robson, Philip d1919 *WhScrn 2*
Robson, Mrs. Stuart d1924 *NotNAT B,*
WhoHol B
Robson, Stuart 1836-1903 *FamA&A, NotNAT B,*
OxThe, PIP&P
Robson, Stuart, Jr. d1946 *NotNAT B*
Robson, William *NotNAT B*
Roby, Lavelle *WhoHol A*
Robyn, Alfred George 1860-1935 *AmSCAP 1966,*
NotNAT B
Robyn, Gay 1912-1942 *WhScrn 1, WhScrn 2*
Robyns, William 1855-1936 *Film 2, WhScrn 1,*
WhScrn 2, WhoHol B
Roc, Patricia 1918- *FilmgC, WhoHol A*
Rocca, Daniela *WhoHol A*
Rocca, Gino 1891-1941 *McGWD*
Roccardi, Albert 1864-1934 *Film 1, Film 2,*
WhScrn 2
Rocco, Alex *WhoHol A*
Rocco, Maurice d1976 *WhoHol C*
Roch, Madeleine d1930 *NotNAT B, WhThe*
Rocha, Glauber 1938- *DcFM, OxFilm, WorEnF*
Rocha, Miguel F d1961 *WhScrn 1, WhScrn 2*
Rochay, Joe *Film 2*
Rochberg, George 1918- *AmSCAP 1966*
Roche, Clara Darley *Film 2*
Roche, Eugene *WhoHol A*
Roche, Frank d1963 *WhoHol B*

Roche, Franklyn D 1904-1963 *WhScrn 1,*
  WhScrn 2
Roche, Guillaume *McGWD*
Roche, John 1896-1952 *Film 2, TwYS,*
  WhScrn 1, WhScrn 2, WhoHol B
Rochefort, Jean *WhoHol A*
Rochelle, Edward d1908 *NotNAT B*
Rochemont, Louis De *DcFM*
Rocher, Rene 1890- *WhThe*
Rochester *IntMPA 1977, WhoHol A*
Rochin, Paul 1889-1964 *NotNAT B, WhScrn 1,*
  WhScrn 2
Rochinski, Stanley R 1906- *AmSCAP 1966*
Rochlin, Diane *WomWMM, WomWMM B*
Rock, Blossom *WhoHol A*
Rock, Charles 1866-1919 *Film 1, NotNAT B,*
  WhScrn 2, WhThe, WhoHol B
Rock, Felippa *WhoHol A*
Rock, John 1890- *CelR 3*
Rock, Joseph V 1936- *AmSCAP 1966*
Rock, William d1922 *NotNAT B*
Rock, William T 1853-1916 *WhScrn 2*
Rockefeller, David 1915- *CelR 3*
Rockefeller, John D, III 1906- *BiE&WWA,*
  CelR 3
Rockefeller, John D, IV 1937- *CelR 3*
Rockefeller, Kay 1918- *NotNAT*
Rockefeller, Laurance 1910- *CelR 3*
Rockefeller, Nelson 1908- *CelR 3*
Rockland, Jeffrey *WhoHol A*
Rockwell, Donald Shumway 1895- *AmSCAP 1966*
Rockwell, Ed *Film 2*
Rockwell, Florence d1964 *NotNAT B*
Rockwell, Florence 1880- *WhoStg 1906,*
  WhoStg 1908
Rockwell, Jack d1947 *Film 2, WhScrn 2,*
  WhoHol B
Rockwell, Mary *WhScrn 1, WhScrn 2*
Rockwell, Norman 1894- *CelR 3*
Rockwell, Robert *WhoHol A*
Rockwood, Roy *Film 2*
Rocquemore, Henry 1915- *AmSCAP 1966*
Rod, Einar *Film 2*
Rodann, Ziva *WhoHol A*
Rodby, Walter 1917- *AmSCAP 1966*
Rodd, Marcia 1940- *NotNAT, PIP&P,*
  WhoHol A, WhoThe 16
Roddenberry, Gene *FilmgC, NewYTET*
Roddie, John W 1903- *AmSCAP 1966*
Roddie, Vin 1918- *AmSCAP 1966*
Rode, Helge 1870-1937 *NotNAT B, OxThe*
Rode, Walter d1973 *WhScrn 2, WhoHol B*
Rodeheaver, Homer Alvan 1880-1955
  AmSCAP 1966
Rodenbach, Georges 1855-1898 *NotNAT B*
Roder, Milan 1878-1956 *AmSCAP 1966*
Roderick, George *WhoHol A*
Roderick, Leslie 1907-1927 *WhScrn 1, WhScrn 2*
Rodgers, Anton *WhoHol A*
Rodgers, Anton 1927- *FilmgC*
Rodgers, Anton 1933- *WhoThe 16*
Rodgers, Bob 1924- *BiE&WWA*
Rodgers, Carrie Cecil d1961 *NotNAT B*
Rodgers, Eileen 1933- *BiE&WWA, NotNAT*
Rodgers, Gaby 1928- *IntMPA 1977*
Rodgers, Ilona *WhoHol A*
Rodgers, James d1890 *NotNAT B*
Rodgers, Jimmie *Film 2*
Rodgers, Jimmie 1897-1933 *AmSCAP 1966*
Rodgers, Jimmy 1897-1933 *NotNAT B*
Rodgers, John 1917- *AmSCAP 1966*
Rodgers, John Wesley *WhoHol A*
Rodgers, Mary 1931- *AmSCAP 1966,*
  BiE&WWA, EncMT, NewMT, NotNAT

Rodgers, Pamela *WhoHol A*
Rodgers, Richard *IntMPA 1977, WhoHol A*
Rodgers, Richard 1901- *CmMov, FilmgC*
Rodgers, Richard 1902- *AmSCAP 1966,*
  BiE&WWA, CelR 3, EncMT, McGWD,
  NewMT, NotNAT, NotNAT A, OxFilm,
  PIP&P, WhoThe 16
Rodgers, Thomas Edward 1927- *IntMPA 1977*
Rodgers, Walter 1887-1951 *Film 1, Film 2,*
  WhScrn 1, WhScrn 2, WhoHol B
Rodilak, Charles d1972 *WhoHol B*
Rodman, Howard *NewYTET*
Rodman, Nancy *WhoHol A*
Rodman, Victor 1893-1965 *Film 2, WhScrn 2*
Rodney, Don 1920- *AmSCAP 1966*
Rodney, Earl *Film 1, Film 2*
Rodney, Earle 1891-1932 *TwYS, WhScrn 1,*
  WhScrn 2, WhoHol B
Rodney, Frank d1902 *NotNAT B*
Rodney, Jack 1916-1967 *WhScrn 1, WhScrn 2,*
  WhoHol B
Rodney, Lynne d1937 *WhScrn 2*
Rodney, Stratton d1932 *NotNAT B*
Rodrigues, Nelson 1912- *CnThe, REnWD*
Rodrigues, Percy 1924- *FilmgC*
Rodriguez, Charles J *WhoHol A*
Rodriguez, Estelita 1915-1966 *WhScrn 1,*
  WhScrn 2, WhoHol B
Rodriguez, Percy *WhoHol A*
Rodriguez, Tito 1923-1973 *WhScrn 2*
Rodriguez Alvarez, Alejandro *McGWD*
Rodriguez Buded, Ricardo *CroCD*
Rodway, Norman 1929- *WhoHol A, WhoThe 16*
Rodway, Philip 1876-1932 *NotNAT A,*
  NotNAT B
Rodwell, G H d1852 *NotNAT B*
Rodzinski, Artur d1958 *NotNAT B*
Roe, Bassett 1860-1934 *NotNAT B, WhThe*
Roe, Gloria Ann 1935- *AmSCAP 1966*
Roe, Patricia 1932- *BiE&WWA, NotNAT,*
  WhoHol A
Roebling, Mary 1906- *CelR 3*
Roebling, Paul 1934- *BiE&WWA, NotNAT,*
  WhoThe 16
Roebuck, Disney d1885 *NotNAT B*
Roecker, Dorothy *WomWMM B*
Roeder, Benjamin F d1943 *NotNAT B*
Roeg, Nicholas 1928- *BiDFlm, DcFM,*
  IntMPA 1977, OxFilm, WorEnF
Roeg, Nicolas *FilmgC*
Roels, Marcel 1893-1973 *WhScrn 2*
Roemheld, Heinz 1901- *AmSCAP 1966*
Roerick, William 1912- *NotNAT, WhoHol A,*
  WhoThe 16
Roesborg, Nikolai *Film 2*
Rogan, Beth *WhoHol A*
Rogan, Florence *Film 2*
Rogan, Jimmy 1908- *AmSCAP 1966*
Rogan, John *WhoHol A*
Rogell, Albert S 1901- *FilmgC, IntMPA 1977,*
  TwYS A
Roger, Lee *WhoHol A*
Roger-Ferdinand 1898- *McGWD*
Rogers, Anne 1933- *BiE&WWA, EncMT,*
  NotNAT, WhoThe 16
Rogers, Bernard 1893- *AmSCAP 1966*
Rogers, Blake *WhoHol A*
Rogers, Brooks *WhoHol A*
Rogers, Buddy *MotPP*
Rogers, Carl D 1900-1965 *WhScrn 1, WhScrn 2,*
  WhoHol B
Rogers, Charles Buddy 1904- *Film 2, FilmgC,*
  IntMPA 1977, MovMk, TwYS, WhoHol A
Rogers, Charles R d1957 *NotNAT B*

Rogers, Charley *Film 2*
Rogers, Dick 1912- *AmSCAP 1966*
Rogers, Dora *Film 1*
Rogers, Eddy 1907-1964 *AmSCAP 1966*
Rogers, Emmett 1915-1965 *BiE&WWA,
NotNAT B*
Rogers, Eugene 1867?-1919 *WhScrn 2*
Rogers, Fred 1928- *AmSCAP 1966*
Rogers, Gene *Film 1*
Rogers, Gil *WhoHol A*
Rogers, Ginger 1911- *BiDFlm, BiE&WWA,
CelR 3, CmMov, EncMT, Film 2, FilmgC,
IntMPA 1977, MotPP, MovMk, OxFilm,
ThFT, WhoHol A, WhoThe 16, WorEnF*
Rogers, Gus 1869-1908 *NotNAT B,
WhoStg 1906*
Rogers, Harriet *WhoHol A*
Rogers, Henry C 1914- *IntMPA 1977*
Rogers, James Hotchkiss 1857-1940
AmSCAP 1966
Rogers, Jean *MotPP*
Rogers, Jean 1916- *WhoHol A*
Rogers, John *Film 2, WhoHol A*
Rogers, John R d1932 *NotNAT B*
Rogers, John W 1916- *IntMPA 1977*
Rogers, Joseph 1871-1942 *WhScrn 1, WhScrn 2*
Rogers, Kasey *WhoHol A*
Rogers, Lawrence H, II 1921- *IntMPA 1977*
Rogers, Lela Emogen 1890- *AmSCAP 1966,
WhoHol A*
Rogers, Lora d1948 *NotNAT B*
Rogers, Louise Mackintosh d1933 *NotNAT B*
Rogers, Maclean 1899- *FilmgC*
Rogers, Max d1932 *NotNAT B, WhThe,
WhoStg 1906*
Rogers, Mildred 1899-1973 *WhScrn 2,
WhoHol B*
Rogers, Milt 1925- *AmSCAP 1966*
Rogers, Milton 1924- *AmSCAP 1966*
Rogers, Molly *Film 2*
Rogers, Paul 1917- *BiE&WWA, CnThe, FilmgC,
MotPP, MovMk, NotNAT A, NotNAT B,
PIP&P, WhoHol A, WhoThe 16*
Rogers, Peter 1916- *FilmgC, IntMPA 1977*
Rogers, Ralph D *NewYTET*
Rogers, Rena 1901-1966 *WhScrn 1, WhScrn 2*
Rogers, Rene 1901-1966 *Film 1, WhoHol B*
Rogers, Richard H 1926- *IntMPA 1977*
Rogers, Roddy *IntMPA 1977*
Rogers, Roy *AmSCAP 1966, MotPP,
WhoHol A*
Rogers, Roy d1967 *WhScrn 2*
Rogers, Roy 1911- *IntMPA 1977*
Rogers, Roy 1912- *CmMov, FilmgC, MovMk,
OxFilm, WorEnF*
Rogers, Roy, Jr. *WhoHol A*
Rogers, Stanwood d1963 *NotNAT B*
Rogers, Ted 1920- *IntMPA 1977*
Rogers, Timothy Louis Aiverum 1915-
AmSCAP 1966
Rogers, Victor *WhoHol A*
Rogers, Walter *Film 2*
Rogers, Warren *Film 2*
Rogers, Wayne *WhoHol A*
Rogers, Will 1879-1935 *BiDFlm, EncMT, Film 1,
Film 2, FilmgC, MotPP, MovMk,
NotNAT A, NotNAT B, OxFilm, PIP&P,
TwYS, WhScrn 1, WhScrn 2, WhThe,
WhoHol B, WorEnF*
Rogers, Will, Jr. 1912- *Film 2, IntMPA 1977,
WhoHol A*
Rogers, William 1913- *CelR 3*
Rogers, William Penn Adair 1879-1935 *OxThe*
Rogers Brothers *WhoStg 1908*

Rognan, Jean Lorraine 1912-1969 *WhScrn 2*
Rognan, Lorraine 1912-1969 *WhoHol B*
Rognoni d1943 *WhScrn 2*
Rogoff, Gordon 1931- *BiE&WWA, NotNAT*
Rogosin, Lionel 1924- *DcFM, OxFilm, WorEnF*
Rohe, Robert Kenneth 1920- *AmSCAP 1966*
Rohm, Maria 1949- *IntMPA 1977, WhoHol A*
Rohmer, Eric 1920- *BiDFlm, CelR 3, FilmgC,
MovMk, OxFilm, WorEnF*
Rohmer, Harriet *WomWMM B*
Rohmer, Sax 1886-1959 *NotNAT B, WhThe*
Rohrig, Walter 1893- *DcFM, OxFilm, WorEnF*
Rojas, Fernando De d1541 *McGWD, OxThe*
Rojas Zorilla, Francisco De 1607-1648 *NotNAT B*
Rojas Zorrilla, Francisco De 1607-1648 *McGWD,
OxThe*
Rojo, Gustavo *WhoHol A*
Roker, Renny *WhoHol A*
Roker, Roxie *NotNAT*
Roland, Alan 1930- *NatPD*
Roland, Frederick 1886-1936 *WhScrn 1,
WhScrn 2*
Roland, Fredric d1936 *WhoHol B*
Roland, Gilbert 1905- *Film 2, FilmgC, HolP 30,
IntMPA 1977, MotPP, MovMk, TwYS,
WhoHol A, WorEnF*
Roland, Gyl *WhoHol A*
Roland, Ida 1881-1951 *NotNAT B*
Roland, Kathleen *WhoHol A*
Roland, Marion *WhScrn 1, WhScrn 2*
Roland, Rita *WomWMM*
Roland, Ruth d1937 *MotPP, WhoHol B*
Roland, Ruth 1892-1937 *TwYS, WhScrn 1,
WhScrn 2*
Roland, Ruth 1893-1937 *Film 1, Film 2, FilmgC,
NotNAT B*
Roland, Steve *WhoHol A*
Roland Holst, Henriette 1869-1952 *CnMD*
Rolane, Andree *Film 2*
Roldan, Enrique 1901-1954 *WhScrn 1, WhScrn 2*
Roley, Sutton *IntMPA 1977*
Rolf, Erik d1957 *WhScrn 2*
Rolf, Frederick 1926- *BiE&WWA, NotNAT*
Rolfe, Guy 1915- *FilmgC, WhoHol A*
Rolfe, Sam H *NewYTET*
Rolfe, Walter 1880-1944 *AmSCAP 1966*
Rollan, Henri *Film 2*
Rolland, Jean-Claude 1933-1967 *WhScrn 1,
WhScrn 2*
Rolland, Romain 1866-1944 *CnMD, McGWD,
ModWD, NotNAT B*
Rolle, Esther *NotNAT, WhoThe 16*
Rolle, Georges d1916 *NotNAT B, WhThe*
Rolle, Liselotte *Film 2*
Rollens, Jacques *Film 2*
Roller, Cleve *WhoHol A*
Rollett, Raymond 1907-1961 *WhScrn 1,
WhScrn 2, WhoHol B*
Rollette, Jane *Film 2*
Rollin, Georges d1964 *WhScrn 2*
Rolling Stones, The *CelR 3*
Rollins, David d1952 *WhoHol B*
Rollins, David 1908-1952 *WhScrn 1, WhScrn 2*
Rollins, David 1909-1952 *Film 2*
Rollins, Jack *BiE&WWA, Film 1,
IntMPA 1977*
Rollins, Jack 1906- *AmSCAP 1966*
Rollo, Billy d1964 *NotNAT B*
Rollow, Preston J 1871-1947 *WhScrn 1,
WhScrn 2, WhoHol B*
Rolly, Jeanne d1929 *NotNAT B, WhThe*
Rolston, William d1964 *NotNAT B*
Rolt, Richard d1770 *NotNAT B*
Rolyat, Dan 1872-1927 *NotNAT B, WhThe*

Roma, Caro *WhoStg 1906, WhoStg 1908*
Roma, Clarice 1902-1947 *WhScrn 1, WhScrn 2*
Romagnesi, Brigida Bianchi 1613-1703? *OxThe*
Romagnesi, Carlo Virgilio 1670-1708 *OxThe*
Romagnesi, Marc'Antonio 1633?-1706 *OxThe*
Romagnesi, Niccolo d1660 *OxThe*
Romain, George E d1929 *Film 2, WhScrn 2*
Romain, Yvonne 1938- *FilmgC, WhoHol A*
Romaine, Claire 1873-1964 *WhThe*
Romains, Jules 1885-1942 *NotNAT B*
Romains, Jules 1885-1972 *CnMD, McGWD, ModWD, OxThe, WhThe*
Roman, Greg *WhoHol A*
Roman, Hanna *WomWMM B*
Roman, Hugh *Film 2*
Roman, Lawrence 1921- *BiE&WWA, IntMPA 1977, NotNAT*
Roman, Leticia 1939- *FilmgC, WhoHol A*
Roman, Murray d1973 *WhScrn 2*
Roman, Ric *WhoHol A*
Roman, Ruth *IntMPA 1977, MotPP*
Roman, Ruth 1923- *WhoHol A*
Roman, Ruth 1924- *FilmgC, MovMk*
Roman, Ruth 1925- *WorEnF*
Romance, Viviane 1909?- *FilmgC, WhoHol A*
Romance, Viviane 1912- *WorEnF*
Romanelli Of Mantua, Samuel 1757-1814 *OxThe*
Romani, Felice 1788-1865 *NotNAT B, OxThe*
Romano, Andy *WhoHol A*
Romano, Charles d1937 *NotNAT B*
Romano, Jane d1962 *NotNAT B*
Romano, John 1896-1957 *WhScrn 1, WhScrn 2*
Romano, Nick 1922- *AmSCAP 1966*
Romano, Nina *Film 2*
Romano, Ralph 1928- *AmSCAP 1966*
Romano, Thomas M 1923- *AmSCAP 1966*
Romano, Tony 1915- *AmSCAP 1966*
Romanoff, Constance *Film 2*
Romanoff, Constantine *Film 2*
Romanoff, Michael 1890?-1971 *WhScrn 1, WhScrn 2*
Romanoff, Mike 1890-1971 *WhoHol B*
Romanoff, Mike 1890-1972 *FilmgC*
Romanus, Richard *WhoHol A*
Romashov, Boris Sergeivich 1895-1958 *OxThe*
Romay, Lina *WhoHol A*
Romberg, Sigmund 1887-1951 *AmSCAP 1966, EncMT, FilmgC, NewMT, NotNAT A, NotNAT B, PIP&P, WhThe*
Rome, Bert *Film 2*
Rome, Fred 1874- *WhThe*
Rome, Harold 1908- *AmSCAP 1966, BiE&WWA, CelR 3, EncMT, NewMT, NotNAT*
Rome, Stewart d1965 *WhoHol B*
Rome, Stewart 1886-1965 *Film 1, WhScrn 1, WhScrn 2*
Rome, Stewart 1887-1965 *FilmgC*
Rome, Stuart 1886-1965 *Film 2*
Romea, Alberto 1883-1960 *WhScrn 1, WhScrn 2*
Romer, Anne d1852 *NotNAT B*
Romer, Leila 1878-1944 *WhScrn 1, WhScrn 2, WhoHol B*
Romer, Robert d1874 *NotNAT B*
Romer, Tomi 1924-1969 *WhScrn 1, WhScrn 2, WhoHol B*
Romero, Carlos *WhoHol A*
Romero, Cesar 1907- *BiDFlm, FilmgC, HolP 30, IntMPA 1977, MotPP, MovMk, WhoHol A, WorEnF*
Romero, Florita 1931-1961 *WhScrn 1, WhScrn 2*
Romero, Gary 1912- *AmSCAP 1966*
Romero, Nancy *WomWMM*
Romero, Ned *WhoHol A*

Romeyn, Jane 1901-1963 *NotNAT B, WhScrn 1, WhScrn 2*
Romine, Latosca S 1900- *AmSCAP 1966*
Romm, Mikhail 1901-1971 *BiDFlm, DcFM, FilmgC, OxFilm, WorEnF*
Rommer, Clare *Film 2*
Romney, Edana 1919- *FilmgC, WhThe, WhoHol A*
Romney, George 1907- *CelR 3*
Romoff, Colin 1924- *AmSCAP 1966*
Romoff, Woody 1918- *BiE&WWA, NotNAT*
Ronald, Sir Landon 1873- *WhThe*
Ronay, Edina *WhoHol A*
Rondi, Brunello 1924- *WorEnF*
Rondiris, Dimitrios 1899- *BiE&WWA, OxThe*
Ronell, Ann *AmSCAP 1966, BiE&WWA, NotNAT*
Ronet, Maurice 1927- *BiDFlm, FilmgC, OxFilm, WhoHol A, WorEnF*
Ronka, Elmer 1905- *AmSCAP 1966*
Ronnel, Ann *WomWMM*
Roobenian, Amber 1905- *AmSCAP 1966*
Rood, Hale 1923- *AmSCAP 1966*
Rook, Heidi *WhoHol A*
Rooke, Irene 1878-1958 *Film 2, NotNAT B, OxThe, WhScrn 2, WhThe*
Rooke, Valentine 1912- *WhThe*
Rooks, Conrad *WhoHol A*
Room, Abraham 1894- *WorEnF*
Room, Abram 1894- *DcFM, FilmgC, OxFilm*
Room, Alexander 1894- *OxFilm, WorEnF*
Rooner, Charles 1901-1954 *WhScrn 1, WhScrn 2, WhoHol B*
Rooney, Andrew A *NewYTET*
Rooney, Gilbert *Film 2*
Rooney, Mercy *WhoHol A*
Rooney, Mickey *MotPP, WhoHol A*
Rooney, Mickey 1920- *AmSCAP 1966, CelR 3, CmMov, Film 2, FilmgC, MGM, MovMk*
Rooney, Mickey 1922- *BiDFlm, IntMPA 1977, OxFilm, WorEnF*
Rooney, Pat 1880-1962 *AmSCAP 1966, Film 2, NotNAT B, WhScrn 1, WhScrn 2, WhoHol B*
Rooney, Pat 1891-1933 *WhScrn 1, WhScrn 2, WhoHol B*
Rooney, Pat B 1925- *IntMPA 1977*
Rooney, Teddy *WhoHol A*
Rooney, Tim *WhoHol A*
Rooney, Wallace *WhoHol A*
Roope, Fay 1893-1961 *WhScrn 1, WhScrn 2, WhoHol B*
Roos, Barbara *WomWMM A, WomWMM B*
Roos, Joanna 1901- *BiE&WWA, NotNAT, PIP&P, WhThe, WhoHol A*
Roos, Jorgen 1922- *DcFM*
Roos, Lisa *WomWMM*
Roose, Olwen 1900- *WhThe*
Roose-Evans, James 1927- *WhoThe 16*
Roosevelt, Buddy 1898-1973 *Film 1, Film 2, TwYS, WhScrn 2, WhoHol A*
Roosevelt, Franklin, Jr. 1914- *CelR 3*
Roosevelt, Franklin Delano 1882-1945 *FilmgC*
Roosevelt, Leila *WomWMM*
Roosevelt, Theodore 1858-1919 *FilmgC*
Root, George Frederick 1820-1895 *NotNAT B*
Root, Lynn 1905- *BiE&WWA, NotNAT*
Root, Robert *WhoHol A*
Root, Wells *IntMPA 1977*
Roper, Brian *WhoHol A*
Roper, Jack 1904-1966 *Film 2, WhScrn 2, WhoHol B*
Roquemore, Henry 1888-1943 *Film 2, WhScrn 1, WhScrn 2, WhoHol B*

Roquevert, Noel 1892-1973 *WhScrn 2, WhoHol B*
Rorem, Ned 1923- *AmSCAP 1966*
Rorie, Yvonne 1907-1959 *NotNAT B, WhThe*
Rork, Al *Film 2*
Rork, Anne *Film 2*
Rorke, J E *Film 1*
Rorke, John d1957 *NotNAT B*
Rorke, Kate 1866-1945 *NotNAT B, OxThe,
  WhThe*
Rorke, Margaret Hayden 1884-1969 *WhScrn 1,
  WhScrn 2, WhoHol B*
Rorke, Mary 1858-1938 *NotNAT B, WhThe*
Rory, Rossana *WhoHol A*
Rosa, Carl d1889 *NotNAT B*
Rosa, Nera d1920 *NotNAT B*
Rosado, Peggy Moran *WhoHol A*
Rosales, Marco Fidel 1913- *AmSCAP 1966*
Rosales, Sylvia 1917- *AmSCAP 1966*
Rosamonde, Miss *Film 1*
Rosanova, Rosa 1883- *Film 2, TwYS*
Rosar, Annie 1888-1963 *NotNAT B, WhScrn 1,
  WhScrn 2, WhoHol B*
Rosas, Enrique *DcFM*
Rosas, Fernando 1915-1959 *WhScrn 1, WhScrn 2*
Rosay, Francoise 1891-1974 *BiE&WWA, Film 2,
  FilmgC, MotPP, MovMk, OxFilm,
  WhScrn 2, WhThe, WhoHol B, WorEnF*
Rosbaud, Hans d1962 *NotNAT B*
Rosca, Gabriel *Film 2*
Roscius d062BC *PIP&P*
Roscius, Quintus d062BC *CnThe, OxThe*
Roscius Gallus, Quintus 126?BC-062BC
  NotNAT B
Roscoe, Alan 1888-1933 *WhScrn 1, WhScrn 2,
  WhoHol B*
Roscoe, Albert 1887-1925? *WhScrn 2*
Roscoe, Albert 1887-1931 *Film 1, Film 2, TwYS*
Roscoe, Lee *WhoHol A*
Rose Marie *AmSCAP 1966, WhoHol A*
Rose, Adrian 1859-1933 *NotNAT B*
Rose, Al *WhoHol A*
Rose, Alex 1898- *CelR 3*
Rose, Alexander *WhoHol A*
Rose, Betty Clarke d1947 *NotNAT B*
Rose, Billy 1899-1966 *AmSCAP 1966,
  BiE&WWA, EncMT, NotNAT A,
  NotNAT B, WhThe*
Rose, Blanche 1878-1953 *WhScrn 1, WhScrn 2,
  WhoHol B*
Rose, Carla Valentine 1945- *WomWMM B*
Rose, Clarkson 1890-1968 *NotNAT B, OxThe,
  WhThe*
Rose, Clifford *WhoHol A*
Rose, David 1910- *AmSCAP 1966, FilmgC,
  IntMPA 1977*
Rose, David E 1895- *FilmgC, IntMPA 1977*
Rose, Ed 1875-1935 *AmSCAP 1966*
Rose, Edward d1904 *NotNAT B*
Rose, Edward Everett 1862-1939 *NotNAT B,
  WhThe*
Rose, Fred 1897-1954 *AmSCAP 1966*
Rose, George 1920- *BiE&WWA, FilmgC,
  MovMk, NotNAT, WhoHol A, WhoThe 16*
Rose, Harry d1975 *WhoHol C*
Rose, Harry 1888?-1962 *NotNAT B, WhScrn 1,
  WhScrn 2*
Rose, Harry 1893- *AmSCAP 1966*
Rose, Jack 1897- *IntMPA 1977*
Rose, Jack 1911- *FilmgC, IntMPA 1977*
Rose, Jane *BiE&WWA, WhoHol A*
Rose, Jennifer *WhoHol A*
Rose, Jewel d1970 *WhScrn 2, WhoHol B*
Rose, John C 1905- *IntMPA 1977*
Rose, L Arthur 1887-1958 *WhThe*

Rose, Laurie *WhoHol A*
Rose, Louisa *WomWMM*
Rose, Norman *WhoHol A*
Rose, Peter *ConDr 1977D*
Rose, Philip 1921- *BiE&WWA, NotNAT,
  WhoThe 16*
Rose, Ralph, Jr. 1911- *AmSCAP 1966*
Rose, Reginald *NewYTET*
Rose, Reginald 1920- *BiE&WWA, NotNAT*
Rose, Reginald 1921- *FilmgC, IntMPA 1977,
  WorEnF*
Rose, Reve *WhoHol A*
Rose, Robert *Film 2*
Rose, Stephen *IntMPA 1977*
Rose, Thomas William 1918- *AmSCAP 1966*
Rose, Vincent 1880-1944 *AmSCAP 1966*
Rose, Virginia *WhoHol A*
Rose, William 1918- *CmMov, FilmgC,
  IntMPA 1977*
Rose, Zelma 1873-1933 *WhScrn 1, WhScrn 2*
Rosebery, Arthur d1928 *NotNAT B*
Rosebery, Lilian *WhThe*
Roseleigh, Jack 1887?-1940 *WhScrn 1, WhScrn 2,
  WhoHol B*
Roselle, Amy 1854-1895 *NotNAT B*
Roselle, William 1878-1945 *Film 1, NotNAT B,
  WhScrn 1, WhScrn 2, WhoHol B*
Roseman, Edward F *Film 1, Film 2*
Rosemond, Anna *Film 1*
Rosemond, Clinton C 1883-1966 *WhScrn 1,
  WhScrn 2, WhoHol B*
Rosemont, Norman *NewYTET*
Rosemont, Walter Louis 1895- *AmSCAP 1966*
Rosen, James 1885-1940 *WhScrn 1, WhScrn 2*
Rosen, Julius *PIP&P*
Rosen, Kenneth M d1976 *NewYTET*
Rosen, Marjorie *WomWMM*
Rosen, Milton S 1906- *AmSCAP 1966*
Rosen, Phil 1888-1951 *FilmgC*
Rosen, Philip 1888-1951 *TwYS A*
Rosen, Theodore 1918- *AmSCAP 1966*
Rosenbaum, Edward, Sr. d1927 *NotNAT B*
Rosenbaum, Samuel 1919- *AmSCAP 1966*
Rosenberg, Aaron 1912- *CmMov, FilmgC,
  IntMPA 1977, WorEnF*
Rosenberg, Frank P 1913- *IntMPA 1977*
Rosenberg, Jacob 1896-1946 *AmSCAP 1966*
Rosenberg, James L *NatPD*
Rosenberg, Marvin 1912- *BiE&WWA, NotNAT*
Rosenberg, Meta *NewYTET*
Rosenberg, Rick *see* Christiansen, Robert W & Rick
  Rosenberg
Rosenberg, Royanne *WomWMM B*
Rosenberg, Sarah 1874-1964 *NotNAT B,
  WhScrn 1, WhScrn 2, WhoHol B*
Rosenberg, Stuart 1925- *FilmgC, MovMk*
Rosenberg, Stuart 1928- *IntMPA 1977, WorEnF*
Rosenberger, Margaret A *AmSCAP 1966*
Rosenblatt, Adrian *WomWMM B*
Rosenblatt, Josef 1882-1933 *Film 2, WhScrn 2*
Rosenblatt, Rose *WomWMM B*
Rosenbloom, Maxie 1906-1976 *MotPP, MovMk*
Rosenbloom, Slapsie Maxie 1906-1976 *FilmgC,
  WhoHol C*
Rosenblum, M Edgar 1932- *BiE&WWA,
  NotNAT*
Rosenblut, Hans *OxThe*
Rosencrans, Leo S *IntMPA 1977*
Rosencrantz, Margareta *WomWMM*
Rosenfeld, Jerome M *BiE&WWA*
Rosenfeld, Sydney 1855-1931 *NotNAT B, WhThe,
  WhoStg 1906, WhoStg 1908*
Rosenfelt, Frank E 1921- *IntMPA 1977*
Rosenfield, Jonas, Jr. *IntMPA 1977*

Rosenfield, Lois *WomWMM*
Rosenman, Leonard 1924- *AmSCAP 1966,
  WorEnF*
Rosenow, Emil 1871-1904 *McGWD*
Rosenquist, James 1933- *CelR 3*
Rosenstein, Gertrude *IntMPA 1977*
Rosenstock, Milton 1917- *BiE&WWA, NotNAT*
Rosenstein, Andrew 1917- *BiE&WWA, NotNAT*
Rosenthal, Bud 1934- *IntMPA 1977*
Rosenthal, Harry 1900-1953 *NotNAT B,
  WhScrn 1, WhScrn 2, WhoHol B*
Rosenthal, J J d1923 *NotNAT B*
Rosenthal, Jack *ConDr 1977C*
Rosenthal, Jean 1912-1969 *BiE&WWA,
  NotNAT B*
Rosenthal, Laurence 1926- *AmSCAP 1966,
  BiE&WWA, NotNAT*
Rosenthal, Mara d1975 *WhoHol C*
Rosenthal, Robert M 1936- *IntMPA 1977*
Rosette, Marion *AmSCAP 1966*
Rosewall, Ken 1934- *CelR 3*
Rosey, George 1864-1936 *AmSCAP 1966*
Rosey, Joe 1882-1943 *AmSCAP 1966*
Roshal, Gregori *WomWMM*
Roshal, Grigori 1898- *DcFM*
Roshanara d1926 *NotNAT B*
Rosher, Charles 1885- *CmMov, FilmgC,
  WomWMM*
Rosher, Dorothy *WhoHol A*
Rosi, Francesco 1922- *BiDFlm, DcFM, FilmgC,
  OxFilm, WorEnF*
Rosian, Peter F 1902- *IntMPA 1977*
Rosimond 1640?-1686 *OxThe*
Rosing, Bodil 1878-1942 *Film 2, TwYS,
  WhScrn 1, WhScrn 2, WhoHol B*
Rosita, Eva *Film 2*
Rosley, Adrian 1890-1937 *WhScrn 1, WhScrn 2,
  WhoHol B*
Rosmarin, Charles 1911- *IntMPA 1977*
Rosmer, Milton 1881-1971 *Film 1, Film 2,
  FilmgC, WhScrn 1, WhScrn 2, WhoHol B*
Rosmer, Milton 1882- *WhThe*
Rosness, Juanita M 1897- *AmSCAP 1966*
Rosoff, Charles 1898- *AmSCAP 1966*
Rosqui, Tom 1928- *BiE&WWA, NotNAT,
  WhoHol A*
Ross, Adrian 1859-1933 *EncMT, WhThe*
Ross, Annie 1930- *WhoThe 16*
Ross, Anthony 1906-1955 *NotNAT B, WhScrn 1,
  WhScrn 2, WhThe, WhoHol B*
Ross, Barney 1907-1967 *WhScrn 1, WhScrn 2,
  WhoHol B*
Ross, Ben 1911-1958 *AmSCAP 1966*
Ross, Benny 1912- *AmSCAP 1966*
Ross, Betsy King 1923- *WhoHol A*
Ross, Betty 1880-1947 *Film 2, WhScrn 1,
  WhScrn 2, WhoHol B*
Ross, Beverly 1937- *AmSCAP 1966*
Ross, Bill 1915- *BiE&WWA*
Ross, Burt *Film 2*
Ross, Charles Cowper 1929- *WhoThe 16*
Ross, Charles J 1859-1918 *NotNAT B,
  WhoStg 1908*
Ross, Chester Monroe 1917- *IntMPA 1977*
Ross, Chris 1946-1970 *WhScrn 1, WhoHol B*
Ross, Christopher 1946-1970 *WhScrn 2,
  WhoHol A*
Ross, Churchill 1901-1961 *WhScrn 2*
Ross, Churchill 1901-1962 *Film 2, WhoHol B*
Ross, Corinne Heath Sumner 1879-1965 *WhScrn 1,
  WhScrn 2*
Ross, David 1891-1975 *WhScrn 2, WhoHol C*
Ross, David 1922-1966 *BiE&WWA, NotNAT B*
Ross, Diana 1944- *CelR 3, IntMPA 1977,*

MovMk, *WhoHol A*
Ross, Don *WhoHol A*
Ross, Dorothy 1912- *BiE&WWA, NotNAT*
Ross, Earle 1888-1961 *WhScrn 2*
Ross, Ed *WhoHol A*
Ross, Edna *Film 1*
Ross, Elizabeth 1928- *BiE&WWA, NotNAT*
Ross, Etna *Film 2*
Ross, Frances *Film 2*
Ross, Frank *Film 2*
Ross, Frank 1904- *FilmgC, IntMPA 1977*
Ross, Frederick 1879- *WhThe*
Ross, George 1911- *BiE&WWA, NotNAT*
Ross, George I 1907- *WhoThe 16*
Ross, Harry 1913- *WhThe*
Ross, Hector 1915- *WhThe*
Ross, Helen 1912- *AmSCAP 1966*
Ross, Herbert d1934 *WhoHol B*
Ross, Herbert 1865-1934 *NotNAT B, WhThe*
Ross, Herbert 1866-1934 *WhScrn 2*
Ross, Herbert 1927- *BiE&WWA, CmMov,
  FilmgC, IntMPA 1977, NotNAT, WorEnF*
Ross, James B *Film 1*
Ross, Jerry 1926-1955 *AmSCAP 1966, EncMT,
  NewMT, NotNAT B*
Ross, Joe E *WhoHol A*
Ross, Julie *WhoHol A*
Ross, Katharine *MotPP, WhoHol A*
Ross, Katharine 1942- *FilmgC, MovMk*
Ross, Katharine 1943- *IntMPA 1977*
Ross, Kenneth 1941- *IntMPA 1977*
Ross, Lanny 1906- *AmSCAP 1966,
  IntMPA 1977, WhoHol A*
Ross, Mabel Fenton d1931 *NotNAT B*
Ross, Marion 1898-1966 *WhScrn 1, WhScrn 2,
  WhoHol A, WhoHol B*
Ross, Martin *NotNAT B*
Ross, Mary *Film 1*
Ross, Michael *NewYTET, WhoHol A*
Ross, Milton *Film 1, Film 2*
Ross, Myrna 1939-1975 *WhScrn 2, WhoHol A,
  WhoHol C*
Ross, Oriel 1907- *WhThe*
Ross, Robert d1954 *NotNAT B*
Ross, Robert S 1938- *NatPD*
Ross, Shirley *MotPP*
Ross, Shirley 1909?-1975 *FilmgC, WhScrn 2*
Ross, Shirley 1914-1975 *ThFT, WhoHol C*
Ross, Stan *WhoHol A*
Ross, Stanley 1935- *AmSCAP 1966*
Ross, Tayloe *WomWMM B*
Ross, Thomas W d1959 *Film 1, WhoHol B,
  WhoStg 1906*
Ross, Thomas W 1875-1959 *Film 2, NotNAT B,
  WhScrn 1, WhScrn 2, WhThe*
Ross, Thomas W 1878-1959 *WhoStg 1908*
Ross, William *WhoHol A*
Ross, William 1925-1963 *NotNAT B, WhScrn 1,
  WhScrn 2*
Ross-Clarke, Betty *WhThe*
Rossana, Augustine S 1922- *AmSCAP 1966*
Rosse, Frederick d1940 *NotNAT B*
Rosse, Russell d1910 *NotNAT B*
Rosselle, William *Film 2*
Rossellini, Isabella *WhoHol A*
Rossellini, Renzo 1908- *DcFM, WhoHol A*
Rossellini, Roberto 1906- *BiDFlm, DcFM,
  FilmgC, IntMPA 1977, MovMk, OxFilm,
  WorEnF*
Rossen, Carol *WhoHol A*
Rossen, Robert 1908-1966 *BiDFlm, CmMov,
  DcFM, FilmgC, MovMk, OxFilm, WorEnF*
Rosset, Barney 1922- *BiE&WWA, CelR 3,
  NotNAT*

Rosseter, Philip 1575?-1623 *OxThe*
Rossi, Alfred *WhoHol A*
Rossi, Ernesto Fortunato Giovanni Maria 1827-1896
  OxThe
Rossi, Ernesto Fortunato Giovanni Maria 1827-1897
  NotNAT B
Rossi, Franco 1919- *FilmgC, OxFilm, WorEnF*
Rossi, Rita *Film 2*
Rossi, Steve *WhoHol A*
Rossi, Walter 1914- *AmSCAP 1966*
Rossi-Drago, Eleanora 1925- *MotPP, WhoHol A,*
  WorEnF
Rossi-Drago, Eleonora 1925- *FilmgC*
Rossif, Frederic 1922- *DcFM, FilmgC, OxFilm,*
  WorEnF
Rossington, Norman 1928- *FilmgC, WhoHol A*
Rossini, Carlo 1890- *AmSCAP 1966*
Rossinto, Angelo *Film 2*
Rossiter, Leonard 1926- *WhoHol A, WhoThe 16*
Rossiter, Will 1867-1954 *AmSCAP 1966*
Rosslyn, Elaine d1964 *NotNAT B*
Rossmann, Hermann 1902- *CnMD*
Rosso, Lewis T 1911- *IntMPA 1977*
Rosso DiSan Secondo, Pier Luigi Maria 1887-1956
  CnThe, McGWD, ModWD, OxThe, REnWD
Rosson, Arthur d1960 *Film 1, WhoHol B*
Rosson, Arthur 1887-1960 *TwYS A*
Rosson, Arthur H 1889-1960 *WhScrn 1,*
  WhScrn 2
Rosson, Hal 1895- *FilmgC*
Rosson, Harold 1895- *CmMov, WorEnF*
Rosson, Helene *Film 1*
Rosson, Queenie *Film 1*
Rosson, Richard *Film 1, Film 2*
Rosson, Richard 1893-1953 *WhScrn 2*
Rosson, Richard 1894- *TwYS A*
Rostand, Edmond 1868-1918 *CnMD, CnThe,*
  McGWD, ModWD, NotNAT B, OxThe,
  REnWD, WhThe
Rostand, Maurice 1891-1968 *CnMD, ModWD*
Rosten, Irwin *NewYTET*
Rosten, Norman 1914- *BiE&WWA, NotNAT*
Rostworowski, Karol Hubert 1877-1938 *CnMD,*
  ModWD
Roswaenge, Helge 1896-1972 *WhScrn 2*
Roswitha 935?-1001? *CnThe, OxThe, REnWD*
Rota, Nino 1911- *DcFM, FilmgC, OxFilm,*
  WorEnF
Rote, Kyle 1928- *AmSCAP 1966*
Rotella, Johnny 1920- *AmSCAP 1966*
Roth, Andy *WhoHol A*
Roth, Ann *WhoThe 16*
Roth, Cy 1912- *IntMPA 1977*
Roth, Elliott *Film 2*
Roth, Gene *WhoHol A*
Roth, Lillian *PIP&P*
Roth, Lillian 1910- *BiE&WWA, FilmgC,*
  NotNAT, NotNAT A, ThFT, WhoHol A,
  WhoThe 16
Roth, Lillian 1911- *Film 1, Film 2, MovMk*
Roth, Paul A 1930- *IntMPA 1977*
Roth, Pete 1893- *AmSCAP 1966*
Roth, Philip 1933- *CelR 3*
Roth, Richard A 1943- *IntMPA 1977*
Roth, Sandy 1889-1943 *WhScrn 1, WhScrn 2,*
  WhoHol B
Rotha, Paul 1907- *DcFM, FilmgC,*
  IntMPA 1977, OxFilm, WorEnF
Rotha, Wanda *WhoHol A, WhoThe 16*
Rothafel, S L Roxy 1882-1931 *WorEnF*
Rothauser, Eduard *Film 2*
Rothberg, Bob 1901-1938 *AmSCAP 1966*
Rothe, Anita d1944 *NotNAT B*
Rothenberg, David 1933- *BiE&WWA*

Rothenstein, Albert Daniel 1883- *WhThe*
Rothgardt, Wanda *Film 1*
Rothier, Leon *Film 1*
Rothkirch, Edward V 1919- *IntMPA 1977*
Rothman, Lawrence 1934- *BiE&WWA, NotNAT*
Rothman, Marion *WomWMM*
Rothman, Mo 1919- *IntMPA 1977*
Rothman, Stephanie *WomWMM, WomWMM B*
Rothschild, Amalie R *WomWMM A,*
  WomWMM B
Rothwell, Michael *WhoHol A*
Rothwell, Robert *WhoHol A*
Rotmund, Ernest 1887-1955 *WhScrn 2*
Rotmund, Ernst 1887-1955 *WhScrn 1*
Rotron, Jean 1609-1650 *NotNAT B*
Rotrou, Jean De 1609-1650 *CnThe, McGWD,*
  OxThe, REnWD
Rotter, Fritz *BiE&WWA*
Rottura, Joseph James 1929- *AmSCAP 1966*
Rotunda, Marjorie *WomWMM B*
Rotunno, Giuseppe 1926- *DcFM, FilmgC,*
  WorEnF
Roubert, Matty *Film 1, Film 2*
Rouch, Jean 1917- *BiDFlm, DcFM, OxFilm,*
  WorEnF
Roude, Neil *WhoHol A*
Roudenko, Vladimir *Film 2*
Rouer, Germaine *Film 2*
Rougas, Michael *WhoHol A*
Roughwood, Owen 1876-1947 *Film 2, NotNAT B,*
  WhThe, WhoHol B
Rouleau, Raymond 1904- *WorEnF*
Roulien, Raul *WhoHol A*
Rounders, The *Film 2*
Rounds, David 1930- *NotNAT, WhoHol A*
Roundtree, Richard 1942- *CelR 3, FilmgC,*
  IntMPA 1977, MovMk, WhoHol A
Rounseville, Robert 1914-1974 *WhScrn 2*
Rounitch, Joseph *Film 2*
Rounseville, Robert 1914-1974 *BiE&WWA,*
  EncMT, NotNAT B, WhoHol B,
  WhoThe 16
Rouquier, Georges 1909- *DcFM, FilmgC,*
  OxFilm, WorEnF
Rourke, Michael Elder 1867-1933 *AmSCAP 1966*
Rous, Helen d1934 *NotNAT B, WhThe*
Rousby, William Wybert d1907 *NotNAT B*
Rouse, Hallock 1897-1930 *WhScrn 1, WhScrn 2,*
  WhoHol B
Rouse, Russell 1916- *BiDFlm, FilmgC,*
  IntMPA 1977, WorEnF
Rouse, Simon *WhoHol A*
Rousseau, Jean-Baptiste 1671-1741 *OxThe*
Rousseau, Jean-Jacques 1712-1778 *OxThe*
Roussin, Andre 1911- *BiE&WWA, CnMD,*
  CnThe, McGWD, ModWD, NotNAT
Routledge, Calvert d1916 *NotNAT B*
Routledge, Patricia 1929- *EncMT, WhoHol A,*
  WhoThe 16
Rouverol, Mrs. Aurania d1955 *NotNAT B*
Rouverol, Jean *WhoHol A*
Roux, Jacques *WhoHol A*
Rove, Billie *Film 2*
Rovelle, Camille *Film 2*
Rovenski, Josef 189-?-1936 *DcFM*
Rovensky, Joseph *Film 2*
Rovere, Gina *WhoHol A*
Rovere, Richard 1915- *CelR 3*
Rovetta, Gerolamo 1851-1910 *McGWD*
Rovetta, Girolamo 1850- *WhThe*
Row, Richard D 1899- *AmSCAP 1966*
Rowal, Jack *Film 2*
Rowan, Dan 1922- *FilmgC, WhoHol A*
Rowan, Don d1966 *WhoHol B*

Rowan, Donald W 1906-1966 *WhScrn 1,*
WhScrn 2
Rowan, Ernest 1886-1960 *WhScrn 1, WhScrn 2*
Rowan, Frank M 1897- *AmSCAP 1966*
Rowan, Irwin 1897- *AmSCAP 1966*
Rowan And Martin *CelR 3*
Rowe, Earl *WhoHol A*
Rowe, Fanny 1913- *WhThe*
Rowe, George *Film 2*
Rowe, George Fawcett 1834-1889 *NotNAT B,*
OxThe
Rowe, Misty *WhoHol A*
Rowe, Nicholas 1674-1718 *CnThe, McGWD,*
NotNAT B, OxThe, REnWD
Rowe, Nicolas *PIP&P*
Rowe, Sir Reginald d1945 *NotNAT B*
Rowe, Roy 1905- *IntMPA 1977*
Rowell, Glenn 1899-1965 *AmSCAP 1966*
Rowen, Ruth Halle 1918- *AmSCAP 1966*
Rowland, Adele *Film 2*
Rowland, Gerald *WhoHol A*
Rowland, H W d1937 *NotNAT B*
Rowland, Helen *Film 2*
Rowland, Henry *WhoHol A*
Rowland, James G d1951 *WhScrn 1, WhScrn 2*
Rowland, Mabel d1943 *NotNAT B*
Rowland, Margery 1910-1945 *NotNAT B, WhThe*
Rowland, Roy 1910- *BiDFlm, CmMov, FilmgC,*
IntMPA 1977, WorEnF
Rowland, Steve *WhoHol A*
Rowland, Toby 1916- *WhoThe 16*
Rowland, William 1900- *IntMPA 1977*
Rowlands, Art 1898-1944 *WhScrn 1, WhScrn 2,*
WhoHol B
Rowlands, David *WhoHol A*
Rowlands, Gaynor d1906 *NotNAT B*
Rowlands, Gena 1936- *BiE&WWA, FilmgC,*
IntMPA 1977, MotPP, NotNAT, WhoHol A
Rowlands, Lady *WhoHol A*
Rowlands, Patsy 1935- *WhoHol A, WhoThe 16*
Rowles, James George 1918- *AmSCAP 1966*
Rowles, Polly 1914- *BiE&WWA, NotNAT,*
WhoHol A, WhoThe 16
Rowley, J W d1925 *NotNAT B, WhThe*
Rowley, John H 1917- *IntMPA 1977*
Rowley, Samuel 1575?-1624 *CnThe, NotNAT B,*
OxThe, REnWD
Rowley, William *McGWD*
Rowley, William 1585?-1637? *OxThe*
Rowley, William 1585?-1638? *NotNAT B*
Rowley, William 1585?-1642? *CnThe, REnWD*
Rowson, Susanna Haswell d1824 *NotNAT B*
Rox, John Jefferson d1957 *NotNAT B*
Roxanne *WhoHol A*
Roxborough, Picton d1932 *NotNAT B*
Roy, Bimal 1909-1966 *WorEnF*
Roy, Bimal 1912-1966 *DcFM*
Roy, Charu *Film 2*
Roy, D L *REnWD*
Roy, Dan *Film 2, WhScrn 1, WhScrn 2*
Roy, Harry 1904-1971 *WhScrn 1, WhScrn 2,*
WhoHol B
Roy, John 1899-1975 *WhScrn 2*
Roy, William 1928- *AmSCAP 1966*
Royaards, Wilhem d1929 *WhThe*
Royaards, William d1929 *NotNAT B*
Royal, John F d1974 *NewYTET*
Royal, Ted 1904- *AmSCAP 1966, BiE&WWA,*
NotNAT
Royale, Harry M d1963 *NotNAT B*
Royce, Brigham d1933 *NotNAT B, WhoHol B*
Royce, Mrs. E W *Film 2*
Royce, Edward 1870-1964 *EncMT, NotNAT B,*
WhThe

Royce, Edward William 1841-1926 *NotNAT B,*
WhThe
Royce, Forrest Frosty 1911-1965 *WhScrn 1,*
WhScrn 2
Royce, Julian 1870-1946 *NotNAT B, WhThe,*
WhoHol B
Royce, Lionel 1891-1946 *WhScrn 1, WhScrn 2,*
WhoHol B
Royce, Riza *WhoHol A*
Royce, Rosita 1918-1954 *WhScrn 1, WhScrn 2*
Royce, Ruth *Film 2*
Royce, Virginia 1932-1962 *NotNAT B,*
WhScrn 1, WhScrn 2, WhoHol B
Royde, Frank 1882- *WhThe*
Royde-Smith, Naomi d1964 *NotNAT B, WhThe*
Roye, Phillip *WhoHol A*
Royed, Beverly *Film 2*
Royer, Harry Missouri 1889-1951 *WhScrn 1,*
WhScrn 2, WhoHol B
Royle, Edwin Milton 1862-1942 *McGWD,*
NotNAT B, WhThe, WhoStg 1908
Royle, Josephine *WhThe*
Royle, Selena 1904- *IntMPA 1977, MGM,*
Vers B, WhThe, WhoHol A
Royle, Selena Fetter d1955 *NotNAT B*
Royston, Julius d1935 *WhScrn 1, WhScrn 2*
Royston, Roy 1899- *WhThe*
Royton, Verna d1974 *WhoHol B*
Rozakis, Greg *WhoHol A*
Rozan, Micheline *WomWMM*
Roze, Raymond 1875-1920 *NotNAT B, WhThe*
Rozelle, Pete 1926- *CelR 3*
Rozenberg, Lucien *WhThe*
Rozet, Monsieur *Film 2*
Rozewicz, Tadeusz 1921- *CroCD, ModWD,*
REnWD
Rozier, Jacques 1926- *DcFM, OxFilm, WorEnF*
Rozin, Albert 1906- *AmSCAP 1966*
Rozov, Victor Sergeevich 1913- *CnMD, CnThe,*
ModWD
Rozsa, Miklos 1907- *CmMov, FilmgC,*
IntMPA 1977, OxFilm, WorEnF
Ruark, Robert C 1915-1965 *WhScrn 2*
Rub, Christian 1887-1956 *Film 1, FilmgC,*
Vers B, WhScrn 1, WhScrn 2, WhoHol B
Rubber, Violla 1910- *BiE&WWA*
Ruben, Aaron *NewYTET*
Ruben, Jose d1969 *WhoHol B*
Ruben, Jose 1886-1969 *Film 2*
Ruben, Jose 1888-1969 *NotNAT B, WhThe*
Ruben, Jose 1889-1969 *PIP&P, WhScrn 1,*
WhScrn 2
Rubens, Alma 1897-1931 *Film 1, Film 2, FilmgC,*
MotPP, MovMk, TwYS, WhScrn 1,
WhScrn 2, WhoHol B
Rubens, Alma 1898-1931 *NotNAT B*
Rubens, Hugo 1905- *AmSCAP 1966*
Rubens, Maurie 1893-1948 *AmSCAP 1966,*
NotNAT B
Rubens, Paul A 1875-1917 *EncMT, NotNAT B*
Rubens, Paul A 1876-1917 *WhThe*
Rubenstein, Ida *Film 2*
Rubenstein, Louis Urban 1908- *AmSCAP 1966*
Rubin, Ada 1906- *AmSCAP 1966*
Rubin, Benny 1899- *Film 2, TwYS, Vers A,*
WhoHol A
Rubin, Joel E 1928- *BiE&WWA*
Rubin, Menachem d1962 *NotNAT B*
Rubin, Pedro d1938 *WhScrn 1, WhScrn 2*
Rubin, Ronald *WhoHol A*
Rubin, Ruth 1906- *AmSCAP 1966*
Rubin, Stanley 1917- *IntMPA 1977*
Rubini, Michel 1942- *AmSCAP 1966*
Rubinstein, Artur 1887- *CelR 3, WhoHol A*

Rubinstein, Harold F 1891- *WhThe*
Rubinstein, Ida d1960 *WhThe*
Rubinstein, John 1946- *CelR 3, WhoHol A*
Rubiola, Joe 1906-1939 *WhScrn 1, WhScrn 2*
Ruby, Ellalee *Film 2*
Ruby, Harry 1895-1974 *AmSCAP 1966,*
  BiE&WWA, EncMT, NewMT, NotNAT B,
  WhThe
Ruby, Herman 1891-1959 *AmSCAP 1966*
Ruby, Mary *Film 1*
Ruby, Thelma 1925- *WhoHol A, WhoThe 16*
Rucellai *PIP&P*
Rucellai, Giovanni 1475-1525 *McGWD, OxThe*
Ruckert, Ernest *Film 2*
Rudami, Rosa 1899-1966 *WhScrn 1, WhScrn 2*
Rudani, Rosa d1966 *WhoHol B*
Rudd, Enid *NatPD*
Rudd, Hughes *NewYTET*
Rudd, Paul *WhoHol A*
Ruddock, John 1897- *WhoHol A, WhoThe 16*
Ruddy, Albert S 1934- *IntMPA 1977*
Rudel, Julius 1921- *BiE&WWA, CelR 3*
Ruderman, Seymour George 1926- *AmSCAP 1966*
Rudhyar, Dane *Film 2*
Rudie, Evelyn 1947- *IntMPA 1977, WhoHol A*
Rudkin, David 1936- *ConDr 1977, CroCD,*
  McGWD, REnWD, WhoThe 16
Rudley, Herbert 1911- *FilmgC, Vers A,*
  WhoHol A
Rudman, Michael 1939- *WhoThe 16*
Rudolph, Louis *IntMPA 1977*
Rudolph, Oscar *Film 2*
Rudorf, Gunther 1921- *CnMD*
Rueckert, Ernst *Film 2*
Rueda, Jose *Film 2*
Rueda, Lope De 1505?-1565 *OxThe*
Rueda, Lope De 1510?-1565 *McGWD,*
  NotNAT B
Ruederer, Josef 1861-1915 *McGWD, ModWD*
Ruehmann, Heinz *WhoHol A*
Rufart, Carlos 1887-1957 *WhScrn 1, WhScrn 2*
Ruffini, Gene *NatPD*
Ruffo, Tito d1953 *WhoHol B*
Ruffo, Titta 1877-1953 *WhScrn 1, WhScrn 2*
Ruggeri, Ruggero 1871-1953 *NotNAT B, OxThe,*
  WhoHol B
Ruggle, George 1575-1622 *OxThe*
Ruggles, Charles d1970 *WhThe, WhoHol B*
Ruggles, Charles 1886-1970 *FilmgC*
Ruggles, Charles 1890-1970 *Film 1, Film 2,*
  MovMk, OxFilm, WhScrn 1, WhScrn 2
Ruggles, Charles 1892-1970 *BiE&WWA, WorEnF*
Ruggles, Charlie *MotPP*
Ruggles, Charlie 1892- *Vers A*
Ruggles, Wesley 1889-1972 *CmMov, Film 1,*
  FilmgC, OxFilm, TwYS A, WhScrn 2,
  WhoHol B, WorEnF
Rugoff, Donald S 1927- *IntMPA 1977*
Rugolo, Pete 1915- *IntMPA 1977*
Ruhl, Arthur Brown d1935 *NotNAT B*
Ruhmann, Heinz 1902- *FilmgC*
Ruick, Barbara 1932-1974 *MotPP, WhScrn 2,*
  WhoHol B
Ruick, Melville d1972 *WhoHol B*
Ruiz, Antonio *WhoHol A*
Ruiz, Enrique 1908- *AmSCAP 1966*
Ruiz, Federico d1961 *NotNAT B*
Ruiz, Jose Rivero 1896-1948 *WhScrn 1,*
  WhScrn 2
Ruiz DeAlarcon, Juan 1580?-1639 *McGWD*
Ruiz DeAlarcon Y Mendoza, Juan 1581?-1639
  OxThe
Ruiz Iriarte, Victor 1912- *CroCD, McGWD*
Rukeyser, Bud *NewYTET*

Rule, Beverly C *WomWMM*
Rule, Elton H *NewYTET*
Rule, James S 1896- *AmSCAP 1966*
Rule, Janice 1931- *BiDFlm, BiE&WWA,*
  FilmgC, IntMPA 1977, MotPP, NotNAT,
  WhoHol A, WhoThe 16
Ruman, Siegfried 1885-1967 *WhScrn 1,*
  WhScrn 2
Ruman, Sig d1967 *MotPP, NotNAT B*
Ruman, Sig 1884-1967 *FilmgC, OxFilm, Vers A*
Ruman, Sig 1885-1967 *Film 2*
Rumann, Sig d1967 *WhoHol B*
Rumann, Sig 1884?-1967 *MovMk*
Rumley, Jerry 1930- *BiE&WWA, NotNAT*
Rummeister, Augusta *Film 2*
Rumoro, Joe Louis 1923- *AmSCAP 1966*
Rumsey, Bert 1892-1968 *WhScrn 2*
Rumsey, Murray 1907- *AmSCAP 1966*
Rumshinsky, Joseph M d1956 *NotNAT B*
Rumshinsky, Joseph M 1881-1963 *AmSCAP 1966*
Runciman, Alex 1924- *IntMPA 1977*
Runnel, Albert F 1892-1974 *WhScrn 2*
Runyon, Damon 1884-1946 *Film 2, FilmgC,*
  ModWD, NotNAT A, NotNAT B, PIP&P,
  WhScrn 2, WhoHol B
Rupp, Anna T 1909- *AmSCAP 1966*
Rupp, Carl 1892- *AmSCAP 1966*
Rusch, Harold W 1908- *AmSCAP 1966*
Rush, Alvin *NewYTET*
Rush, Barbara 1927- *FilmgC, IntMPA 1977,*
  MotPP, MovMk, WhoHol A, WorEnF
Rush, Dick *Film 2*
Rush, Herman *NewYTET*
Rush, Mary Jo 1909- *AmSCAP 1966*
Rush, Richard *FilmgC, IntMPA 1977*
Rushing, James Andrew 1902- *AmSCAP 1966*
Rushing, Jimmy 1903-1972 *WhScrn 2*
Rushnell, Squire D *NewYTET*
Rushton, Lucy 1844- *OxThe*
Rushton, Russell *Film 2*
Rusincky, Paul 1903- *AmSCAP 1966*
Rusinol, Santiago 1861-1931 *ModWD*
Rusinyol, Santiago 1861-1931 *NotNAT B*
Rusk, Dean 1909- *CelR 3*
Rusk, Howard 1901- *CelR 3*
Ruskin, Coby *NewYTET*
Ruskin, Harry 1894- *AmSCAP 1966*
Ruskin, Shimen *Film 2, WhoHol A*
Ruskin, Sybil d1940 *NotNAT B*
Ruspoli, Mario 1925- *DcFM, OxFilm*
Russ, Paula 1893-1966 *WhScrn 1, WhScrn 2*
Russel, Del 1952- *WhoHol A*
Russel, Tony *WhoHol A*
Russell, Agnes d1947 *NotNAT B*
Russell, Alexander 1880-1953 *AmSCAP 1966*
Russell, Andy *WhoHol A*
Russell, Ann d1955 *WhScrn 1, WhScrn 2*
Russell, Anna 1911- *AmSCAP 1966, BiE&WWA,*
  NotNAT, OxThe, WhoHol A
Russell, Annie 1864-1936 *FamA&A, NotNAT B,*
  OxThe, PIP&P, WhThe, WhoStg 1906,
  WhoStg 1908
Russell, Benee 1902-1961 *AmSCAP 1966*
Russell, Bill 1934- *CelR 3*
Russell, Billy d1956 *WhScrn 1, WhScrn 2*
Russell, Bing *WhoHol A*
Russell, Bob 1914- *AmSCAP 1966*
Russell, Byron 1884-1963 *Film 2, NotNAT B,*
  WhScrn 1, WhScrn 2, WhoHol B
Russell, Charles Ellsworth 1906- *AmSCAP 1966*
Russell, Charles W 1918- *IntMPA 1977*
Russell, Connie *WhoHol A*
Russell, Dorothy 1881- *WhoStg 1908*
Russell, Edd X 1878-1966 *WhScrn 1, WhScrn 2*

Russell, Sir Edward Richard 1834-1920 *WhThe*
Russell, Elizabeth *WhoHol A*
Russell, Evangeline *Film 2*
Russell, Evelyn d1976 *WhoHol C*
Russell, Fred 1862-1957 *OxThe, WhThe*
Russell, Gail 1924-1961 *FilmgC, HolP 40, MotPP, MovMk, NotNAT B, WhScrn 1, WhScrn 2, WhoHol B*
Russell, George William 1867-1935 *McGWD, ModWD, PIP&P*
Russell, H Scott 1868-1949 *NotNAT B, WhThe*
Russell, Hanon W 1947- *AmSCAP 1966*
Russell, Harold *WhoStg 1908*
Russell, Harold 1914- *FilmgC, WhoHol A*
Russell, Henry 1812-1900 *NotNAT B*
Russell, Henry 1913-1968 *AmSCAP 1966, NotNAT B*
Russell, Howard d1914 *NotNAT B*
Russell, Irene 1901- *Film 2, WhThe*
Russell, Iris 1922- *WhoThe 16*
Russell, J Gordon 1883-1935 *Film 2, WhScrn 1, WhScrn 2, WhoHol B*
Russell, Jack 1919- *IntMPA 1977*
Russell, Jackie *WhoHol A*
Russell, James *Film 2*
Russell, Jane 1921- *BiDFlm, CelR 3, CmMov, FilmgC, IntMPA 1977, MotPP, MovMk, OxFilm, WhoHol A, WorEnF*
Russell, Jean d1922 *WhScrn 1, WhScrn 2*
Russell, Joey 1920- *AmSCAP 1966*
Russell, John 1921- *FilmgC, IntMPA 1977, MotPP, MovMk, WhoHol A*
Russell, John L *WorEnF*
Russell, John Lowell 1875-1937 *WhScrn 2*
Russell, Ken 1927- *BiDFlm, CelR 3, FilmgC, IntMPA 1977, OxFilm, WorEnF*
Russell, Kurt 1947- *FilmgC*
Russell, Kurt 1951- *WhoHol A*
Russell, Lee 1920- *AmSCAP 1966*
Russell, Lewis 1885-1961 *NotNAT B, WhScrn 1, WhScrn 2, WhoHol B*
Russell, Lilian d1922 *FilmgC*
Russell, Lilian 1861-1922 *Film 1*
Russell, Lillian d1922 *WhoHol B*
Russell, Lillian 1860-1922 *WhScrn 1, WhScrn 2*
Russell, Lillian 1861-1922 *EncMT, FamA&A, NotNAT A, NotNAT B, OxThe, PIP&P, WhThe, WhoStg 1906, WhoStg 1908*
Russell, Mabel d1908 *NotNAT B*
Russell, Mabel 1887-1951 *NotNAT B, WhThe*
Russell, Marie Booth d1911 *NotNAT B*
Russell, Martha *Film 1*
Russell, Nipsey *CelR 3*
Russell, Pat *WomWMM B*
Russell, Pee Wee d1969 *WhoHol B*
Russell, Ray *Film 1*
Russell, Reb 1905- *WhoHol A*
Russell, Robert *Film 2, IntMPA 1977*
Russell, Robert Wallace 1912- *BiE&WWA, NatPD*
Russell, Rosalind *IntMPA 1977, MotPP, WhoHol A, WomWMM*
Russell, Rosalind 1907- *MovMk, ThFT*
Russell, Rosalind 1908- *FilmgC, MGM*
Russell, Rosalind 1911- *CelR 3, WorEnF*
Russell, Rosalind 1912- *BiDFlm, BiE&WWA, EncMT, NotNAT, OxFilm, WhoThe 16*
Russell, Samuel Thomas d1845 *NotNAT B*
Russell, Sol Smith 1848-1902 *FamA&A, NotNAT B, OxThe*
Russell, Sydney King 1897- *AmSCAP 1966*
Russell, Theresa *WhoHol A*
Russell, William *MotPP, WhoHol A*
Russell, William d1915? *WhScrn 2*

Russell, William 1884-1929 *Film 1, Film 2, NotNAT B, TwYS, WhoHol B*
Russell, William 1886-1929 *WhScrn 1, WhScrn 2*
Russell, William Clark d1911 *NotNAT B*
Russell, William D 1908-1968 *FilmgC*
Russell Of Liverpool, Lord 1834-1920 *NotNAT B*
Russin, Irving 1911- *AmSCAP 1966*
Russo, Dan 1885-1956 *AmSCAP 1966*
Russo, Lillian *WomWMM B*
Russo, Matt *WhoHol A*
Russo, William 1928- *AmSCAP 1966*
Russotto, Leo 1896- *AmSCAP 1966*
Rust, Gordon A 1908- *BiE&WWA*
Rust, Richard *WhoHol A*
Rutebeuf 1230?-1285? *OxThe*
Rutebeuf 1248?-1285? *McGWD*
Ruth, Babe 1895-1948 *Film 2, WhScrn 1, WhScrn 2, WhoHol B*
Ruth, Barbara F *AmSCAP 1966*
Ruth, Marshall 1898-1953 *Film 2, WhScrn 1, WhScrn 2, WhoHol B*
Ruth, Patsy *Film 2*
Rutherford, Ann *MotPP*
Rutherford, Ann 1917- *MGM, MovMk, ThFT*
Rutherford, Ann 1920- *FilmgC, WhoHol A*
Rutherford, Ann 1924- *IntMPA 1977*
Rutherford, Margaret 1892-1972 *BiE&WWA, CnThe, FilmgC, MotPP, MovMk, NotNAT A, NotNAT B, OxFilm, OxThe, WhScrn 2, WhThe, WhoHol B*
Rutherford, Mary 1945- *WhoThe 16*
Rutherford, Tom d1973 *WhScrn 2*
Rutherfurd, Tom d1973 *WhoHol B*
Rutherston, Albert Daniel 1883-1953 *NotNAT B, WhThe*
Rutman, Leo 1938- *NatPD*
Rutten, Gerard *DcFM*
Ruttenberg, Joseph 1889- *FilmgC*
Ruttenberg, Joseph 1898- *WorEnF*
Ruttman, Walter 1887-1941 *FilmgC*
Ruttmann, Walter 1887-1941 *BiDFlm, OxFilm, WorEnF*
Ruttmann, Walther 1887-1941 *DcFM*
Ruysdael, Basil d1959 *Film 2*
Ruysdael, Basil 1888-1960 *FilmgC, WhScrn 1, WhScrn 2, WhoHol B*
Ruzzante 1502-1542 *OxThe*
Ruzzante, Il 1502-1542 *McGWD, REnWD*
Ryan, Annie 1865-1943 *Film 2, WhScrn 1, WhScrn 2, WhoHol B*
Ryan, Arthur N *IntMPA 1977*
Ryan, Ben 1892- *AmSCAP 1966*
Ryan, Charles V 1913- *BiE&WWA*
Ryan, Conny d1963 *NotNAT B*
Ryan, Cornelius 1921- *CelR 3*
Ryan, Dick 1897-1969 *WhScrn 1, WhScrn 2, WhoHol B*
Ryan, Don *Film 2*
Ryan, Eddie *MotPP*
Ryan, Edmon *WhoHol A*
Ryan, Fran *WhoHol A*
Ryan, Frank 1907-1947 *FilmgC*
Ryan, Irene d1973 *WhoHol B*
Ryan, Irene 1902-1973 *MovMk*
Ryan, Irene 1903-1973 *FilmgC, WhScrn 2*
Ryan, J Harold d1961 *NewYTET*
Ryan, Joe 1887-1944 *Film 1, Film 2, WhScrn 2*
Ryan, John *WhoHol A*
Ryan, Kate d1922 *NotNAT B*
Ryan, Kathleen 1922- *FilmgC, WhoHol A*
Ryan, Lacy 1694-1760 *NotNAT B, OxThe*
Ryan, Madge 1919- *WhoHol A, WhoThe 16*
Ryan, Mary 1885-1948 *NotNAT B, WhThe, WhoHol B*

Ryan, Maurice *Film 2*
Ryan, Michael M *WhoHol A*
Ryan, Mildred *Film 2*
Ryan, Mitchell *IntMPA 1977, WhoHol A*
Ryan, Nancy *Film 2*
Ryan, Peggy 1924- *FilmgC, HolP 40,
   IntMPA 1977, MotPP, WhoHol A*
Ryan, Robert d1973 *MotPP, PIP&P A,
   WhoHol B*
Ryan, Robert 1909-1973 *FilmgC, MovMk,
   NotNAT B, WhScrn 2*
Ryan, Robert 1910-1973 *Film 2*
Ryan, Robert 1913-1973 *BiDFlm, BiE&WWA,
   CelR 3, CmMov, OxFilm, WhThe, WorEnF*
Ryan, Sam *Film 1, Film 2*
Ryan, Sheila 1921-1975 *FilmgC, IntMPA 1977,
   WhScrn 2, WhoHol C*
Ryan, T E d1920 *NotNAT B*
Ryan, Tim 1889-1956 *FilmgC*
Ryan, Tim 1899-1956 *Vers B, WhScrn 1,
   WhScrn 2, WhoHol B*
Rybkowski, Jan 1912- *DcFM*
Ryckman, Chester 1897-1918 *WhScrn 2*
Rydel, Lucjan 1870-1918 *CnMD, ModWD*
Rydell, Bobby 1942- *FilmgC, WhoHol A*
Rydell, Mark 1934- *FilmgC, IntMPA 1977,
   WhoHol A*
Ryden, Hope *WomWMM A, WomWMM B*
Ryder, Alfred 1919- *BiE&WWA, MotPP,
   NotNAT, WhoHol A, WhoThe 16*
Ryder, Arthur W d1938 *NotNAT B*
Ryder, Loren L 1900- *IntMPA 1977*
Ryder, Noah F 1914-1964 *AmSCAP 1966*
Rydge, Sir Norman 1900- *IntMPA 1977*
Rydge, Norman Bede, Jr. 1928- *IntMPA 1977*
Rye, Daphne 1916- *WhThe*
Rye, Sven 1926- *AmSCAP 1966*
Ryer, Pierre Du 1600?-1658 *OxThe*
Ryerson, Florence 1892-1965 *BiE&WWA,
   NotNAT B*
Ryerson, Frank 1905- *AmSCAP 1966*
Ryga, George 1932- *ConDr 1977*
Ryland, Cliff 1856- *WhThe*
Rylander, Alexander S *IntMPA 1977*
Rylands, George 1902- *WhoThe 16*
Ryley, J H d1922 *NotNAT B*
Ryley, Madeleine Lucette 1865-1934 *NotNAT B,
   WhThe*
Ryley, Madeline Lucette *WhoStg 1906,
   WhoStg 1908*
Ryley, Samuel William 1759-1837 *NotNAT A,
   NotNAT B*
Ryman, Tyra *Film 2*
Ryskind, Morrie 1895- *BiE&WWA,
   ConDr 1977D, EncMT, FilmgC,
   IntMPA 1977, ModWD, NewMT, NotNAT,
   WhThe*
Ryskind, Morris *PIP&P*
Ryterband, Roman 1914- *AmSCAP 1966*
Ryun, Jim 1947- *CelR 3*

S

Sa DeMiranda, Francisco De 1485-1558 *OxThe,*
REnWD
Saad, Margit *WhoHol A*
Saar, Louis Victor 1868-1937 *AmSCAP 1966*
Saare, Arla *WomWMM*
Saari, Charles 1944- *BiE&WWA, NotNAT*
Saarinen, Eero *PIP&P*
Saavedra, Angel De, Duque DeRivas 1791-1865
McGWD, NotNAT B, OxThe
Sabath, Bernard *NatPD*
Sabatini, Ernesto 1878-1954 *WhScrn 1,*
WhScrn 2
Sabatini, Rafael 1875-1950 *FilmgC, NotNAT B,*
WhThe
Sabato, Alfredo *Film 2*
Sabato, Antonio *WhoHol A*
Sabbattini, Nicola 1574-1654 *NotNAT B, OxThe*
Sabel, Josephine 1866-1945 *NotNAT B,*
WhScrn 1, WhScrn 2, WhoStg 1906,
WhoStg 1908
Sabin, Albert 1906- *CelR 3*
Sabin, Catherine Jerome 1879-1943 *WhScrn 1,*
WhScrn 2, WhoHol B
Sabine, Martin 1876- *WhThe*
Sabini, Frank *Film 2*
Sabinson, Harvey B 1924- *BiE&WWA, NotNAT*
WhThe
Sabinson, Lee 1911- *BiE&WWA, NotNAT,*
WhThe
Sablon, Jean 1909- *BiE&WWA*
Sabogal, Ernesto *WomWMM*
Sabouret, Marie d1960 *WhScrn 1, WhScrn 2,*
WhoHol B
Sabrina *WhoHol A*
Sabu 1924-1963 *CmMov, FilmgC, HolP 40,*
MotPP, MovMk, NotNAT B, WhScrn 1,
WhScrn 2, WhoHol B, WorEnF
Sabu 1925-1963 *OxFilm*
Sacco, Anthony 1908- *AmSCAP 1966*
Sacco, John Charles 1905- *AmSCAP 1966*
Sacharow, Lawrence 1937- *NotNAT*
Sachs, David *WhoHol A*
Sachs, Hans 1494-1576 *CnThe, McGWD,*
NotNAT B, OxThe, REnWD
Sachs, Henry Everett 1881- *AmSCAP 1966*
Sachs, Leonard 1909- *WhoHol A, WhoThe 16*
Sachs, Sharon J *WomWMM B*
Sachse, Peter 1940-1966 *WhScrn 2*
Sachse, Raymond H 1899- *AmSCAP 1966*
Sack, Erna 1903-1972 *WhScrn 2, WhoHol A*
Sack, Nathaniel 1882-1966 *Film 1, WhScrn 1,*
WhScrn 2
Sackheim, Jerry *FilmgC*
Sackheim, William B 1919- *FilmgC,*
IntMPA 1977, NewYTET
Sackler, Howard 1929- *ConDr 1977, McGWD,*
NotNAT, PIP&P

Sacks, Joseph Leopold 1881-1952 *NotNAT B,*
WhThe
Sacks, Michael *WhoHol A*
Sacks, Samuel 1908- *IntMPA 1977*
Sackville, Gordon d1926 *Film 1, Film 2,*
WhScrn 1, WhScrn 2, WhoHol B
Sackville, Thomas 1536-1608 *McGWD, OxThe*
Sadanji, Ichi Kawa 1881-1940 *WhThe*
Saddler, Donald 1920- *BiE&WWA, EncMT,*
NotNAT, WhoThe 16
Sadler, Barry *WhoHol A*
Sadler, Charles R 1875-1950 *WhScrn 1,*
WhScrn 2
Sadler, Dudley, Jr. d1951 *WhScrn 1, WhScrn 2,*
WhoHol B
Sadler, Ian 1902-1971 *WhScrn 1, WhScrn 2,*
WhoHol B
Sadler, Michael *ConDr 1977B*
Sado, Keiji 1926-1964 *WhScrn 2*
Sadoff, Fred E 1926- *BiE&WWA, NotNAT,*
WhoHol A
Sadoff, Melissa M 1933- *AmSCAP 1966*
Sadoff, Robert 1920- *AmSCAP 1966*
Sadoul, Georges 1904-1967 *OxFilm*
Sadour, Ben *Film 2*
Sadovsky, Prov Michailovich 1818-1872
NotNAT B
Sadovsky, Prov Mikhailovich 1818-1872 *OxThe*
Sadusk, Maureen *WhoHol A*
Saenger, Gustav 1865-1935 *AmSCAP 1966*
Safer, Morley *NewYTET*
Saffer, Bob 1910- *AmSCAP 1966*
Safier, Gloria 1921- *BiE&WWA*
Safir, Sidney 1923- *IntMPA 1977*
Sagal, Boris 1923- *FilmgC, NewYTET*
Sagall, Solomon *NewYTET*
Sagan, Francoise 1935- *FilmgC*
Sagan, Leontine *WomWMM*
Sagan, Leontine 1889- *WhThe, WorEnF*
Sagan, Leontine 1899-1974 *OxFilm*
Sagarra Y Castallarnau, Jose Maria De d1961
NotNAT B
Sage, Byron d1974 *Film 2, WhoHol B*
Sage, Frances 1915-1963 *WhScrn 2*
Sage, Stuart *Film 2*
Sage, Willard 1922-1974 *WhScrn 2, WhoHol B*
Sager, Sue *WomWMM B*
Saguet, Henri 1901- *DcFM*
Sahl, Mort 1926- *FilmgC, WhoHol A*
Sahni, Balraj 1913-1973 *WhScrn 2*
Saidy, Fred 1907- *BiE&WWA, ConDr 1977D,*
EncMT, NatPD, NewMT, NotNAT
Saigal, K L d1947 *WhScrn 2*
Saillard, M G *Film 2*
Saillard, Ninette *Film 2*
Sainer, Arthur 1924- *ConDr 1977, NatPD*

Sainpolis, John 1887-1942 Film 2, WhScrn 2
Saint, Eva Marie MotPP, WhoHol A
Saint, Eva Marie 1924- FilmgC, IntMPA 1977,
    MovMk, WorEnF
Saint, Eva Marie 1929- BiDFlm, BiE&WWA
St. Angel, Michael WhoHol A
St. Angelo, Robert Film 2
St. Audrie, Stella d1925 Film 2, NotNAT B,
    WhoHol B
St. Clair, Elizabeth WhoHol A
St. Clair, Eric Film 2
St. Clair, F V 1860- WhThe
St. Clair, Floyd J 1871-1942 AmSCAP 1966
St. Clair, Lydia d1970 WhoHol B
St. Clair, Lydia d1974 WhScrn 2
St. Clair, Mal 1897-1952 Film 1, TwYS A
St. Clair, Malcolm 1897-1952 BiDFlm, FilmgC,
    MotPP, MovMk, WhScrn 2, WorEnF
St. Clair, Maurice 1903-1970 WhScrn 1,
    WhScrn 2, WhoHol B
St. Clair, Michael WhoHol A
St. Clair, Robert 1910-1967 WhScrn 1, WhScrn 2
St. Clair, Sylvie AmSCAP 1966
St. Clair, Yvonne 1914-1971 WhScrn 1,
    WhScrn 2, WhoHol B
St. Claire, Adah 1854-1928 WhScrn 1, WhScrn 2
St. Cyr, Lili 1920- WhoHol A
St. Cyr, Lillian Red Wing 1873-1974 WhScrn 2
St. Cyr, Lillian Red Wing see also Red Wing
St. Dan, Deborah PIP&P A
St. Denis, Joe 1928-1968 WhScrn 1, WhScrn 2,
    WhoHol B
Saint-Denis, Michel 1897-1971 BiE&WWA,
    CnThe, NotNAT B, OxThe, PIP&P, WhThe
St. Denis, Ruth 1877-1968 NotNAT B
St. Denis, Ruth 1878-1968 WhScrn 1, WhScrn 2,
    WhoHol B
St. Denis, Teddie 1909- WhThe
St. Dennis, Ruth 1877- Film 1
Saint-Evremond, Sieur De 1610-1703 NotNAT B
St. Gelasius Of Helioppolis d297 NotNAT B
St. Genesius The Comedian d286? NotNAT B
St. George, Julia d1903 NotNAT B
St. Helier, Ivy d1971 WhScrn 1, WhScrn 2,
    WhThe, WhoHol B
St. Jacques, Raymond 1930- FilmgC,
    IntMPA 1977, MovMk, WhoHol A
Saint James, Susan 1946- FilmgC, IntMPA 1977,
    WhoHol A
St. John, Al 1893-1963 Film 1, FilmgC, MotPP,
    NotNAT B, TwYS
St. John, Al Fuzzy 1893-1963 Film 2, Vers B,
    WhScrn 1, WhScrn 2, WhoHol B
St. John, Betta 1930- FilmgC, IntMPA 1977,
    WhoHol A
St. John, Christopher WhoHol A
St. John, Christopher Marie d1960 NotNAT B,
    WhThe
St. John, Florence 1854-1912 NotNAT B, WhThe
St. John, Howard 1905-1974 BiE&WWA, FilmgC,
    MovMk, NotNAT B, WhScrn 2, WhThe,
    WhoHol B
St. John, Jane Lee 1912-1957 WhScrn 1
St. John, Jill 1940- CelR 3, FilmgC, MotPP,
    MovMk, WhoHol A
St. John, John Film 2
St. John, Lily 1895- WhThe
St. John, Marguerite d1940 Film 2, NotNAT B,
    WhoHol B
St. John, Norah d1962 NotNAT B
St. John, Richard WhoHol A
St. John, Valerie WhoHol A
St. Johns, Adela Rogers 1894- CelR 3
St. Laurent, Yves 1936- CelR 3

St. Leonard, Florence Film 2
St. Maur, Adele 1888-1959 WhScrn 1, WhScrn 2,
    WhoHol B
St. Pierre, Clara 1866-1942 WhScrn 1, WhScrn 2
St. Polis, John d1946 WhoHol B
St. Polis, John 1873-1946 WhScrn 2
St. Polis, John 1887-1942 Film 1, TwYS
St. Polis, John see also Sainpolis, John
Saint-Saens, Camille 1835-1921 NotNAT B
Saint-Subber, Arnold 1918- BiE&WWA, CelR 3,
    NotNAT, WhoThe 16
Sainte-Beuve, Charles-Augustin 1804-1869
    NotNAT B, OxThe
Saintsbury, H A 1869-1939 NotNAT B, WhThe
Saire, David WhoHol A
Sais, Marin 1888- Film 1, Film 2, TwYS,
    WhoHol A
Saito, Bill WhoHol A
Sakall, S Z 1884-1955 FilmgC, MotPP, MovMk,
    WhoHol B
Sakall, S Z 1888-1955 NotNAT B, Vers A
Sakall, S Z Cuddles 1884-1955 Film 2, WhScrn 1,
    WhScrn 2
Sakata, Harold Oddjob WhoHol A
Saker, Annie 1882-1932 NotNAT B, WhThe
Saker, Edward d1883 NotNAT B
Saker, Mrs. Edward 1847-1912 NotNAT B,
    WhThe
Saker, Horace d1861 NotNAT B
Saker, Horatio d1902 NotNAT B
Saker, Maria d1902 NotNAT B
Saker, Richard Henry d1870 NotNAT B
Saker, Rose d1923 NotNAT B
Saker, William d1849 NotNAT B
Sakowski, Helmut 1924- CroCD
Saks, Gene 1921- BiE&WWA, FilmgC,
    IntMPA 1977, NotNAT, WhoHol A,
    WhoThe 16
Saks, Matthew WhoHol A
Sala, George Augustus d1895 NotNAT B
Sala, Vittorio 1918- WorEnF
Salacrou, Armand 1899- CnMD, CnThe, CroCD,
    McGWD, ModWD, OxThe, REnWD,
    WhThe
Salah, Rehba Ben Film 2
Salaman, Malcolm C d1940 NotNAT B
Salant, Richard S 1914- IntMPA 1977,
    NewYTET
Salas, Paco 1875-1964 WhScrn 1, WhScrn 2
Salat, Howard 1928- AmSCAP 1966
Salaway, Lowell 1921- AmSCAP 1966
Salberg, Derek S 1912- WhoThe 16
Salberg, Leon d1937 NotNAT B
Salce, Luciano 1922- WorEnF
Sale, Charles 1885-1936 NotNAT B, WhThe
Sale, Charles Chic 1885-1936 WhScrn 1,
    WhScrn 2, WhoHol B
Sale, Chic MotPP
Sale, Chic Charles Film 2
Sale, Frances 1892-1969 WhScrn 1, WhScrn 2,
    WhoHol B
Sale, Richard 1911- FilmgC, IntMPA 1977
Sale, Virginia Film 2, MotPP, TwYS,
    WhoHol A
Sales, Soupy MotPP, NewYTET, WhoHol A
Sales, Soupy 1926- FilmgC
Sales, Soupy 1930- AmSCAP 1966
Saletri, Frank R 1928- IntMPA 1977
Salim, Kamel 191-?-1945 DcFM
Salinger, Conrad d1962 NotNAT B
Salinger, J D 1919- CelR 3
Salisbury, Frank 1930- NatPD
Salisbury, Harrison E 1908- CelR 3
Salisbury, Leah d1975 BiE&WWA, NotNAT B

Salisbury, Monroe d1935 *MotPP, WhoHol B*
Salisbury, Monroe 1876-1935 *WhScrn 1,*
WhScrn 2
Salisbury, Monroe 1879-1935 *Film 1, Film 2,*
TwYS
Salk, Jonas 1914- *CelR 3*
Salkow, Sidney 1909- *FilmgC*
Salkow, Sidney 1911- *IntMPA 1977*
Sallas, Dennis *WhoHol A*
Salle, Mademoiselle *PIP&P*
Sallis, Peter 1921- *FilmgC, WhoHol A,*
WhoThe 16
Sallis, Zoe *WhoHol A*
Salmanova, Lyda *Film 2*
Salmi, Albert 1928- *BiE&WWA, FilmgC,*
IntMPA 1977, NotNAT, WhoHol A
Salmond, Norman d1914 *NotNAT B*
Salmonova, Lyda 1889-1968 *WhScrn 2*
Salom, Jaime 1925- *CroCD*
Salomon, Henry, Jr. d1957 *NewYTET*
Salomon, Horst 1929- *CroCD*
Salpeter, Sophie 1916- *AmSCAP 1966*
Salsbury, Nathan 1846-1902 *NotNAT B*
Salt, Jennifer *WhoHol A*
Salt, Waldo 1914- *FilmgC, IntMPA 1977·*
Salta, Menotti 1893- *AmSCAP 1966*
Salter, Hans J 1896- *AmSCAP 1966,*
IntMPA 1977
Salter, Harold d1928 *Film 2*
Salter, Harold Hal d1928 *WhScrn 1, WhScrn 2*
Salter, Harry d1928 *Film 1, TwYS*
Salter, Harry Hal d1928 *WhoHol B*
Salter, Mary Turner 1856-1938 *AmSCAP 1966*
Salter, Thelma d1953 *Film 1, Film 2, WhScrn 1,*
WhScrn 2, WhoHol B
Saltikov-Shchedrin, Mikhail Evgrafovich 1826-1889
OxThe
Saltikov-Shchedrin, Mikhail Evgrafovich *see also*
Satikov
Saltikow, N *Film 1*
Saltzman, Harry 1915- *FilmgC, IntMPA 1977*
Saltzman, Harry 1916- *WorEnF*
Salvador, Sal *AmSCAP 1966*
Salvatori, Adolph 1908- *AmSCAP 1966*
Salvatori, Paul 1912- *AmSCAP 1966*
Salvatori, Renato *MotPP, WhoHol A*
Salver, Lianna *Film 2*
Salvi, Lola *Film 2*
Salvini, Alessandro *Film 2*
Salvini, Alessandro 1860-1896 *NotNAT B*
Salvini, Alexander *Film 1*
Salvini, Alexander 1860-1896 *NotNAT B*
Salvini, Gustavo 1859-1930 *NotNAT B*
Salvini, Tomasso 1829-1915 *WhThe*
Salvini, Tommaso 1829-1916 *CnThe, FamA&A,*
NotNAT A, NotNAT B, OxThe, PIP&P
Salvor, Lianne *Film 2*
Salvotti, Vera *Film 2*
Salwasser, Lynda Bybee *WomWMM B*
Salwitz, Hardy 1930- *AmSCAP 1966*
Salzburg, Joseph S 1917- *IntMPA 1977*
Salzburg, Milton J 1912- *IntMPA 1977*
Salzedo, Carlos 1885-1961 *AmSCAP 1966*
Salzer, Eugene d1964 *NotNAT B*
Samary, Jeanne d1890 *NotNAT B*
Samary, Marie d1941 *NotNAT B*
Samatowicz, D *WomWMM B*
Samberg, Arnold 1899-1936 *WhScrn 1,*
WhScrn 2
Samborski, I I Koval *Film 2*
Sameth, Jack *IntMPA 1977*
Saminsky, Lazare 1882-1959 *AmSCAP 1966*
Samish, Adrian d1976 *NewYTET*
Sammis, George W d1927 *NotNAT B*

Samoilova, Tatiana 1934- *OxFilm*
Samoilova, Tatyana *WhoHol A*
Samper, Gabriela *WomWMM*
Sampley, Arthur McCullough 1903-
AmSCAP 1966
Sampson, Edgar M 1907- *AmSCAP 1966*
Sampson, Robert *WhoHol A*
Sampson, Teddy 1895-1970 *Film 2, TwYS,*
WhScrn 2
Sampson, William d1922 *NotNAT B*
Samrock, Victor 1907- *BiE&WWA, NotNAT*
Samson, Ivan d1963 *WhoHol B*
Samson, Ivan 1894-1963 *NotNAT B, WhThe*
Samson, Ivan 1895-1963 *WhScrn 1, WhScrn 2*
Samson, Joseph-Isidore 1793-1871 *NotNAT B,*
OxThe
Samson, Teddy 1895- *Film 1*
Samsonov, Samson 1921- *DcFM, WorEnF*
Samuels, Abram 1920- *IntMPA 1977*
Samuels, Gertrude *NatPD*
Samuels, Howard 1919- *CelR 3*
Samuels, Jacob *Film 2*
Samuels, Lesser *IntMPA 1977*
Samuels, Maurice 1885-1964 *WhScrn 2*
Samuels, Maxine *WomWMM*
Samuels, Milton *AmSCAP 1966*
Samuels, Walter G 1908- *AmSCAP 1966*
Samuelson, David W 1924- *IntMPA 1977*
Samuelson, G B 1887-1945 *FilmgC*
Samuelson, Kristine *WomWMM B*
Samuelson, Paul 1915- *CelR 3*
Samuelson, Sydney W 1925- *IntMPA 1977*
San Diego Marine Base Band
San Gallo, Bastiano Da 1481-1551 *OxThe*
San-Giorgiu, Ion 1893-1950 *CnMD*
San Juan, Olga 1927- *FilmgC, WhoHol A*
San Martin, Carlos *Film 2*
San Secondo, Rosso Di 1887-1956 *CnMD*
Sanborn, Fred C 1899-1961 *WhScrn 1, WhScrn 2,*
WhoHol B
Sanchez, Florencio 1875-1910 *CnThe, McGWD,*
ModWD, OxThe, REnWD
Sanchez, Florencio 1875-1917 *NotNAT B*
Sanchez, Jaime *WhoHol A*
Sanchez, Joaquin 1923-1966 *WhScrn 2*
Sanchez, Marguerite *Film 2*
Sanchez, Pedro *WhoHol A*
Sanchez, Ramon Diaz 1903- *CnMD*
Sanchez DeBadajoz, Diego 1479?-1550? *McGWD*
Sancho, Fernando *WhoHol A*
Sand, George 1804-1876 *NotNAT B*
Sand, Paul 1935- *NotNAT, WhoHol A,*
WhoThe 16
Sanda, Dominique *WhoHol A*
Sanda, Dominique 1948- *FilmgC*
Sanda, Dominique 1951- *CelR 3*
Sanda, Dominique 1952- *MovMk*
Sandberg, Anders Wilhelm 1887-1938 *DcFM*
Sandburg, Carl 1878-1967 *AmSCAP 1966*
Sande, Earle *Film 2*
Sande, Walter 1906-1972 *FilmgC, Vers A,*
WhScrn 2, WhoHol B
Sandeau, Jules 1811-1883 *McGWD*
Sander, Ian *WhoHol A*
Sanders, Alma M 1882-1956 *AmSCAP 1966*
Sanders, Anita *WhoHol A*
Sanders, Ann *WhoHol A*
Sanders, Denis 1929- *FilmgC, IntMPA 1977*
Sanders, Denis *see also* Sanders, R Denis
Sanders, George 1906-1972 *BiDFlm, Film 2,*
FilmgC, MotPP, MovMk, NotNAT A,
OxFilm, WhScrn 2, WhoHol B, WorEnF
Sanders, Harland, Colonel 1890- *CelR 3*
Sanders, Helke *WomWMM*

Sanders, Honey *IntMPA 1977*
Sanders, Hugh 1912-1966 *WhScrn 2, WhoHol B*
Sanders, Jessica *WomWMM B*
Sanders, Joe L 1896-1965 *AmSCAP 1966*
Sanders, Marlene *NewYTET, WomWMM,
    WomWMM B*
Sanders, Nat 1892- *IntMPA 1977*
Sanders, Paul 1915- *AmSCAP 1966*
Sanders, R Denis 1929- *WorEnF*
Sanders, R Denis *see also* Sanders, Denis
Sanders, Robert L 1906- *AmSCAP 1966*
Sanders, Scott d1956 *NotNAT B, WhoHol B*
Sanders, Shepherd *WhoHol A*
Sanders, Terry Barrett 1931- *FilmgC,
    IntMPA 1977, WorEnF*
Sanderson, Joey *Film 2*
Sanderson, Julia *Film 1*
Sanderson, Julia 1887-1975 *BiE&WWA, EncMT,
    NotNAT B, WhThe, WhoStg 1908*
Sanderson, Julia 1888-1975 *WhScrn 2*
Sanderson, Kent *Film 2*
Sanderson, Lora *Film 2*
Sanderson, Mary d1712 *OxThe*
Sandford, Christopher 1939- *FilmgC, WhoHol A*
Sandford, Marjorie 1910- *WhThe*
Sandford, Samuel *OxThe*
Sandford, Tiny 1894-1961 *WhScrn 2*
Sandford, Tiny *see also* Sanford, Tiny
Sandison, Gordon 1913-1958 *NotNAT B, WhThe*
Sandle, Floyd 1913- *BiE&WWA, NotNAT*
Sandor, Alfred 1918- *BiE&WWA, NotNAT*
Sandor, Steve *WhoHol A*
Sandoval, Che *WomWMM B*
Sandoval, Miguel 1903-1953 *AmSCAP 1966*
Sandow, Eugene 1867-1925 *Film 1, WhScrn 2*
Sandrelli, Stefania *WhoHol A*
Sandrey, Irma *WhoHol A*
Sandri, Anna-Maria *WhoHol A*
Sandrich, Jay *NewYTET*
Sandrich, Mark 1900-1945 *BiDFlm, CmMov,
    DcFM, FilmgC, WorEnF*
Sandrock, Adele 1864-1937 *NotNAT B,
    WhScrn 2, WhoHol B*
Sandry, Vin 1902- *AmSCAP 1966*
Sands, Billy *WhoHol A*
Sands, Diana 1934-1973 *BiE&WWA, CelR 3,
    MotPP, NotNAT B, WhScrn 2, WhThe,
    WhoHol B, WomWMM*
Sands, Dorothy 1893- *BiE&WWA, NotNAT,
    PIP&P, WhoThe 16*
Sands, Ernest 1924- *IntMPA 1977*
Sands, George 1900-1933 *WhScrn 1, WhScrn 2*
Sands, Johnny 1927- *IntMPA 1977, MotPP,
    WhoHol A*
Sands, Leslie 1921- *WhoHol A, WhoThe 16*
Sands, Thomas Adrian 1937- *AmSCAP 1966*
Sands, Tommy *MotPP*
Sands, Tommy 1936- *WhoHol A*
Sands, Tommy 1937- *FilmgC, IntMPA 1977*
Sanford, Agnes d1955 *WhScrn 1, WhScrn 2*
Sanford, Albert, Jr. 1893-1953 *WhScrn 1,
    WhScrn 2, WhoHol B*
Sanford, Charles 1905- *IntMPA 1977*
Sanford, Dick 1896- *AmSCAP 1966*
Sanford, Erskine 1880-1950 *FilmgC, PIP&P,
    WhoHol B*
Sanford, Isabel *WhoHol A*
Sanford, Ralph 1899-1963 *FilmgC, Vers B,
    WhScrn 1, WhScrn 2, WhoHol B*
Sanford, Robert 1904- *BiE&WWA*
Sanford, Stanley 1894-1961 *Film 1, Film 2*
Sanford, Tiny 1894-1961 *Film 2*
Sanford, Tiny *see also* Sandford, Tiny
Sang, Lani 1916- *AmSCAP 1966*

Sang, Leonard B 1900- *NotNAT*
Sang, Leonard B 1904- *BiE&WWA*
Sanger, Bert 1894-1969 *WhScrn 1, WhScrn 2,
    WhoHol B*
Sanger, Fred d1923 *NotNAT B*
Sanger, George 1827-1911 *NotNAT A*
Sanger, Gerald 1898- *IntMPA 1977*
Sangster, Alfred 1880- *WhThe*
Sangster, Jimmy *IntMPA 1977*
Sangster, Jimmy 1924- *FilmgC*
Sangster, Jimmy 1925- *CmMov*
Sanicola, Henry W 1915- *AmSCAP 1966*
Sanicola, John 1917- *AmSCAP 1966*
Sanjines, Jorge 1936- *OxFilm*
Sanquirico, Alessandro 1780-1849 *OxThe*
Sansom, Lester A *IntMPA 1977*
Santamarie, Manuel d1960 *WhScrn 1, WhScrn 2*
Santana, Vasco 1890-1958 *WhScrn 1, WhScrn 2*
Sant'Angelo, Giorgio Di 1939- *CelR 3*
Santell, Al 1895- *TvYS A*
Santell, Alfred 1895- *FilmgC, IntMPA 1977,
    WorEnF*
Santelton, Frederick *Film 2*
Santina, Bruno Della d1968 *WhScrn 2*
Santley, Fred d1953 *WhoHol B*
Santley, Frederic d1953 *Film 1*
Santley, Frederic 1887-1953 *WhThe*
Santley, Frederic 1888-1953 *WhScrn 1,
    WhScrn 2*
Santley, Fredric d1953 *NotNAT B*
Santley, Joseph 1889-1971 *EncMT, FilmgC,
    WhScrn 1, WhScrn 2, WhThe, WhoHol B*
Santley, Kate d1923 *NotNAT B, WhThe*
Santlow, Hester d1778 *NotNAT B*
Santly, Henry 1890-1934 *AmSCAP 1966*
Santly, Joseph H 1886-1962 *AmSCAP 1966,
    NotNAT B*
Santly, Lester 1894- *AmSCAP 1966*
Santon, Penny *WhoHol A*
Santoni, Linda R 1936- *AmSCAP 1966*
Santoni, Reni 1939- *FilmgC, WhoHol A*
Santora, Jack *Film 2*
Santos, Bert *WhoHol A*
Santos, Joe *WhoHol A*
Santos, Nelson Pereira Dos 1928- *DcFM*
Santos, Tiki d1974 *WhScrn 2*
Santschi, Thomas 1882-1931 *Film 1, Film 2*
Santschi, Tom d1931 *WhoHol B*
Santschi, Tom 1879-1931 *FilmgC, WhScrn 1,
    WhScrn 2*
Santschi, Tom 1882-1931 *TvYS*
Santurini, Francesco 1627-1682 *OxThe*
Sapelli, Domingo d1961 *WhScrn 2*
Saper, Jack *IntMPA 1977*
Saperstein, Henry G 1918- *IntMPA 1977,
    NewYTET*
Sapia, Patrick L, Jr. 1941- *AmSCAP 1966*
Sapper *NotNAT B*
Sara, Sandor 1933- *OxFilm*
Saraceno, Joseph 1931- *AmSCAP 1966*
Sarafian, Richard C 1927?- *FilmgC*
Sarandon, Chris *WhoHol A*
Sarandon, Susan *WhoHol A*
Sarat, Agnan d1613 *OxThe*
Sarauw, Paul 1883- *CnMD*
Sarcey, Francisque 1827-1899 *NotNAT A,
    NotNAT B, OxThe*
Sarche, Ed 1907- *AmSCAP 1966*
Sardella, Edward A 1928- *AmSCAP 1966*
Sardi, Vincent, Jr. 1915- *BiE&WWA, CelR 3*
Sardo, Cosmo *WhoHol A*
Sardou, Fernand *WhoHol A*
Sardou, Victorien 1831-1908 *CnThe, McGWD,
    ModWD, NotNAT A, NotNAT B, OxThe,*

PIP&P, REnWD, WhoStg 1908
Sarecky, Barney 1895- *IntMPA 1977*
Sargent, Alfred Maxwell 1881-1949 *WhScrn 1,*
WhScrn 2
Sargent, Alvin *IntMPA 1977*
Sargent, Dick *FilmgC, WhoHol A*
Sargent, Epes Winthrop d1938 *NotNAT B*
Sargent, Franklin H d1923 *NotNAT B*
Sargent, Frederic 1879- *WhThe*
Sargent, George *TwYS A*
Sargent, Herbert C 1873- *WhThe*
Sargent, Joseph 1925- *FilmgC*
Sargent, Kenny d1969 *WhoHol B*
Sargent, Lewis 1904- *Film 1, Film 2, TwYS,*
WhoHol A
Sargent, Sir Malcolm 1895-1967 *WhScrn 2*
Sargent, Paul 1910- *AmSCAP 1966*
Sargent, Thornton 1902- *IntMPA 1977*
Sargoy, Edward A *IntMPA 1977*
Sarkadi, Imre 1921-1961 *CroCD*
Sarle, Regina *Film 1*
Sarlow, Mary K 1912- *AmSCAP 1966*
Sarlui, Ed 1925- *IntMPA 1977*
Sarment, Jean 1897- *CnMD, McGWD, ModWD,*
WhThe
Sarne, Michael *WhoHol A*
Sarne, Michael 1939- *FilmgC*
Sarne, Mike 1940- *OxFilm*
Sarner, Alexander 1892-1948 *NotNAT B, WhThe,*
WhoHol B
Sarner, Sylvia *WomWMM, WomWMM B*
Sarno, Hector V 1880-1953 *Film 1, Film 2,*
WhScrn 1, WhScrn 2, WhoHol B
Sarno, Janet *WhoHol A*
Sarno, Tom *Film 2*
Sarnoff, David d1971 *NewYTET*
Sarnoff, Dorothy 1919- *BiE&WWA, NotNAT*
Sarnoff, Janyce 1928- *AmSCAP 1966*
Sarnoff, Robert W 1918- *CelR 3, IntMPA 1977,*
NewYTET
Sarnoff, Thomas W 1927- *IntMPA 1977,*
NewYTET
Sarony, Leslie 1897- *WhThe*
Saroyan, Lucy *WhoHol A*
Saroyan, William 1908- *BiE&WWA, CelR 3,*
CnMD, CnThe, ConDr 1977, FilmgC,
McGWD, ModWD, NotNAT, NotNAT A,
OxThe, PIP&P, REnWD, WhoThe 16
Sarracini, Gerald d1957 *NotNAT B*
Sarracino, Ernest *WhoHol A*
Sarrafian, Richard C *IntMPA 1977*
Sarrazin, Michael 1940- *FilmgC, IntMPA 1977,*
WhoHol A
Sarris, Andrew *OxFilm*
Sarta, Mary *Film 2*
Sarthou, Jacques 1920- *OxThe*
Sarti, Andre *Film 2*
Sartre, Jean-Paul 1905- *BiE&WWA, CelR 3,*
CnMD, CnThe, CroCD, FilmgC, McGWD,
ModWD, NotNAT, NotNAT A, OxThe,
PIP&P, REnWD, WhoThe 16
Sasdy, Peter *FilmgC*
Saslavsky, Luis 1906- *WorEnF*
Saslavsky, Luis 1908- *DcFM*
Sass, Edward d1916 *NotNAT B, WhThe*
Sass, Enid 1889-1959 *NotNAT B, WhThe*
Sassard, Jacqueline 1940- *FilmgC, WhoHol A*
Sassoli, Dina *WhoHol A*
Sassoon, Vidal 1928- *CelR 3*
Sassower, Harvey L 1945- *IntMPA 1977*
Sastre, Alfonso 1926- *CnMD, CroCD, McGWD,*
ModWD
Satenstein, Frank 1924- *IntMPA 1977*
Satie, Erik 1866-1925 *OxFilm, WhScrn 2,*

WorEnF
Satikov-Shchedrin, Mikhail Evgrafavich 1826-1889
NotNAT B
Satikov-Shchedrin, Mikhail Evgrafavich *see also*
Saltikov
Sato, Reiko *WhoHol A*
Satterlee, Bruce *WhoHol A*
Satterwhite, Collen Gray 1920- *AmSCAP 1966*
Sattin, Lonnie *BiE&WWA*
Satton, Lon *WhoHol A*
Satz, Lillie 1896-1974 *WhScrn 2*
Satz, Ludwig 1891-1944 *WhScrn 1, WhScrn 2,*
WhoHol B
Saudek, Robert *NewYTET*
Sauer, Robert 1872-1944 *AmSCAP 1966*
Sauerman, Carl 1868-1924 *Film 1, WhScrn 2*
Saul, Oscar *IntMPA 1977*
Saulnier, Jacques 1928- *WorEnF*
Saum, Cliff 1883-1943 *Film 2, WhoHol B*
Saum, Clifford 1883-1943 *WhScrn 1, WhScrn 2*
Saum, Grace *Film 1*
Saunders, Carrie Lou 1893- *AmSCAP 1966*
Saunders, Charles 1904- *FilmgC*
Saunders, Charlotte d1899 *NotNAT B*
Saunders, E G d1913 *NotNAT B*
Saunders, Florence d1926 *Film 2, NotNAT B,*
PIP&P, WhThe
Saunders, Jackie d1954 *MotPP, WhoHol B*
Saunders, Jackie 1893-1954 *Film 1, Film 2,*
TwYS
Saunders, Jackie 1898-1954 *WhScrn 1, WhScrn 2*
Saunders, James A 1925- *CnThe, ConDr 1977,*
CroCD, McGWD, WhoThe 16
Saunders, Janet *WomWMM*
Saunders, John *Film 1*
Saunders, John d1895 *NotNAT B*
Saunders, John Monk 1895-1940 *FilmgC*
Saunders, Lori *WhoHol A*
Saunders, Madge 1894-1967 *WhThe*
Saunders, Mary Jane *MotPP, WhoHol A*
Saunders, Milton 1913- *AmSCAP 1966*
Saunders, Nellie Peck 1869-1942 *WhScrn 1,*
WhScrn 2, WhoHol B
Saunders, Pat *WomWMM B*
Saunders, Peter 1911- *BiE&WWA, WhoThe 16*
Saura, Carlos 1932- *WorEnF*
Saurin, Bernard-Joseph 1706-1781 *OxThe*
Sautell, Al 1895- *WorEnF*
Sauter, Edward Ernest 1914- *AmSCAP 1966*
Sauter, William *Film 1*
Sautet, Claude 1924- *FilmgC, WorEnF*
Sauvajon, Marc Gilbert 1909- *CnMD*
Savage, Ann 1921- *MotPP, WhoHol A*
Savage, Brad *WhoHol A*
Savage, David 1924- *IntMPA 1977*
Savage, George 1904- *BiE&WWA, NotNAT*
Savage, Henry Wilson 1859-1927 *EncMT,*
NotNAT B, WhThe
Savage, Houston *WhScrn 2*
Savage, John *WhoHol A*
Savage, Nelly *Film 2*
Savage, Richard d1743 *NotNAT B*
Savage, Turner *Film 2*
Saval, Dany *WhoHol A*
Savalas, George *WhoHol A*
Savalas, Telly 1924- *FilmgC, IntMPA 1977,*
MotPP, MovMk, WhoHol A
Savan, Bruce 1927- *BiE&WWA, NotNAT*
Savchenko, Igor 1906-1950 *DcFM*
Saveiiev, I *Film 2*
Saville, DeSacia *Film 2*
Saville, Mrs. E Faucit d1879 *NotNAT B*
Saville, Edmund Faucit 1811-1857 *NotNAT B*
Saville, Gus 1857-1934 *Film 2, WhScrn 1,*

WhScrn 2, WhoHol B
Saville, J Faucit d1855 *NotNAT B*
Saville, Mrs. J Faucit d1889 *NotNAT B* •
Saville, Jack *Film 1*
Saville, Kate d1922 *NotNAT B*
Saville, T G d1934 *NotNAT B*
Saville, Victor 1897- *BiDFlm, FilmgC, IntMPA 1977, OxFilm, WorEnF*
Savina, Maria d1915 *NotNAT B*
Savino, Domenico 1882- *AmSCAP 1966*
Savitsky, Viacheslav *Film 2*
Savitt, Jan 1913-1948 *AmSCAP 1966*
Savo, Jimmy d1960 *PIP&P, WhoHol B*
Savo, Jimmy 1895-1960 *EncMT, NotNAT A, NotNAT B, WhThe*
Savo, Jimmy 1896-1960 *WhScrn 1, WhScrn 2*
Savoir, Alfred 1883-1934 *McGWD, NotNAT B*
Savory, Gerald 1909- *CnMD, WhoThe 16*
Savoy, Houston *WhScrn 2*
Sawamura, Kunitaro 1905-1974 *WhScrn 2*
Sawelson, Mel 1929- *IntMPA 1977*
Sawtell, Paul 1906- *AmSCAP 1966*
Sawyer, Carl 1921- *BiE&WWA, NotNAT*
Sawyer, Charles P d1935 *NotNAT B*
Sawyer, Connie *WhoHol A*
Sawyer, Dorie 1897- *WhThe*
Sawyer, Ivy 1896- *EncMT, WhThe*
Sawyer, Jean *AmSCAP 1966*
Sawyer, Joe 1908- *MovMk, Vers B, WhoHol A*
Sawyer, Joseph 1901- *FilmgC*
Sawyer, Laura 1885-1970 *Film 1, WhScrn 1, WhScrn 2, WhoHol B*
Saxe, Templar d1935 *WhoHol B*
Saxe, Templar 1865-1935 *WhScrn 2*
Saxe, Templar 1866-1935 *NotNAT B*
Saxe, Temple *Film 1, Film 2*
Saxe, Templer *TwYS*
Saxe, Templer 1866-1935 *WhoStg 1906, WhoStg 1908*
Saxe-Meiningen, Georg, II, Duke Of 1826-1914 *NotNAT B*
Saxon, David 1919- *AmSCAP 1966*
Saxon, Grace 1912- *AmSCAP 1966*
Saxon, Hugh A 1869-1945 *Film 2, WhScrn 1, WhScrn 2, WhoHol B*
Saxon, John 1935- *FilmgC, IntMPA 1977, MotPP, MovMk, WhoHol A*
Saxon, Marie 1904-1941 *NotNAT B, WhScrn 2*
Saxon-Snell, H *Film 2*
Saxton, Stanley 1904- *AmSCAP 1966*
Sayers, Dorothy Leigh 1893-1957 *CnMD, ModWD, NotNAT B, WhThe*
Sayers, Harry d1934 *NotNAT B*
Sayers, Jo Ann 1918- *WhoHol A*
Sayin, Hidayet 1929- *REnWD*
Sayler, Oliver Martin 1887-1958 *WhThe*
Sayles, Francis H 1892-1944 *WhScrn 1, WhScrn 2, WhoHol B*
Saylor, Katie *WhoHol A*
Saylor, Oliver Martin 1887-1958 *NotNAT B*
Saylor, Syd 1895-1962 *Film 2, NotNAT B, Vers B, WhScrn 1, WhScrn 2, WhoHol B*
Sayre, Bigelow d1975 *WhScrn 2, WhoHol C*
Sayre, C Bigelow *WhoHol A*
Sayre, Jeffrey 1901-1974 *WhScrn 2, WhoHol B*
Sayre, Theodore Burt 1874- *WhThe, WhoStg 1906, WhoStg 1908*
Sazarina, Maria 1914-1959 *WhScrn 1, WhScrn 2*
Sbarbaro, Anthony 1897- *AmSCAP 1966*
Scaasi, Arnold *CelR 3*
Scaduto, Joseph 1898-1943 *WhScrn 1, WhScrn 2, WhoHol B*
Scaife, Gillian *WhThe*
Scaife, Ted 1912- *FilmgC*

Scala, Flaminio *OxThe, PIP&P*
Scala, Gia 1934-1972 *FilmgC, MotPP, MovMk, WhScrn 2, WhoHol B*
Scales, Prunella 1932- *WhoHol A, WhoThe 16*
Scali, John 1918- *CelR 3*
Scaliger, Julius Ceasar 1484-1588 *NotNAT B*
Scalzi, Edward A 1918- *AmSCAP 1966*
Scammacca, Ortensio 1562-1648 *OxThe*
Scammon, P R *Film 2*
Scamozzi, Vincenzo 1552-1616 *NotNAT B, OxThe, PIP&P*
Scandrani, Fatma *WomWMM*
Scanlan, W James 1856-1898 *NotNAT B*
Scanlon, E *Film 2*
Scannell, Frank *WhoHol A*
Scannell, William J 1912-1963 *WhScrn 1, WhScrn 2*
Scappettone, Sandra *WomWMM*
Scarborough, George 1875- *WhThe*
Scardino, Don *WhoHol A*
Scardon, Paul d1954 *Film 1, MotPP, NotNAT B, WhoHol B*
Scardon, Paul 1875-1954 *TwYS A*
Scardon, Paul 1878-1954 *WhScrn 1, WhScrn 2*
Scarmolin, A Louis 1890- *AmSCAP 1966*
Scarne, John *CelR 3*
Scarpa, Salvatore 1918- *AmSCAP 1966*
Scarratt, Charles, III 1927- *AmSCAP 1966*
Scarron, Paul 1610-1660 *CnThe, McGWD, OxThe, REnWD*
Scatigna, Angelo *Film 2*
Scemana Chikly 1872-1950? *DcFM*
Schable, Robert 1873-1947 *Film 1, Film 2, WhScrn 1, WhScrn 2, WhoHol B*
Schachtel, Irving I 1909- *AmSCAP 1966*
Schachter, Leon 1900-1974 *WhScrn 2*
Schackelford, Floyd *Film 2*
Schad, Walter C 1889-1966 *AmSCAP 1966*
Schade, Betty *Film 1, Film 2, TwYS*
Schade, Fritz *Film 1*
Schader, Freddie d1962 *NotNAT B*
Schaefer, Albert 1916-1942 *WhScrn 1, WhScrn 2, WhoHol B*
Schaefer, Anne *Film 1, Film 2*
Schaefer, Billy Kent *Film 2*
Schaefer, Carl *IntMPA 1977*
Schaefer, Charles N 1864-1939 *WhScrn 1, WhScrn 2, WhoHol B*
Schaefer, George 1920- *BiE&WWA, FilmgC, IntMPA 1977, NewYTET, NotNAT, WhoThe 16*
Schaefer, George J 1888- *IntMPA 1977*
Schaefer, Harold Herman 1925- *AmSCAP 1966*
Schaefer, Jack 1907- *IntMPA 1977*
Schaefer, Natalie 1912- *MovMk*
Schaefer, Natalie *see also* Schafer, Natalie
Schaefer, William A 1918- *AmSCAP 1966*
Schaefer, Willis H 1928- *AmSCAP 1966*
Schaeffer, A L *Film 2*
Schaeffer, Donald 1935- *AmSCAP 1966*
Schaeffer, Mary *AmSCAP 1966*
Schaeffer, Pierre 1911- *DcFM*
Schafer, Bob 1897-1943 *AmSCAP 1966*
Schafer, Milton 1920- *AmSCAP 1966, BiE&WWA*
Schafer, Natalie 1912- *BiE&WWA, FilmgC, IntMPA 1977, NotNAT, WhThe, WhoHol A*
Schafer, Natalie *see also* Schaefer, Natalie
Schafer, Reuben *WhoHol A*
Schafer, Walter Erich 1901- *CnMD*
Schaff, Jan 1903- *AmSCAP 1966*
Schaff, Sylvia 1916- *AmSCAP 1966*

Schaffer, Jane *WomWMM*
Schaffer, Peggy *Film 2*
Schaffner, Franklin J 1920- *BiDFlm, FilmgC,*
  IntMPA 1977, MovMk, NewYTET, WorEnF
Schaffner, Franklin L 1920- *OxFilm*
Schaik-Willing, Jeanne Van 1895- *CnMD*
Schallert, William *WhoHol A*
Schapiro, Herb *NatPD*
Schappert, Edna 1934- *NatPD*
Scharf, Herman 1901-1963 *NotNAT B,*
  WhoHol B
Scharf, Herman Boo-Boo 1901-1963 *WhScrn 1,*
  WhScrn 2
Scharf, Walter *AmSCAP 1966*
Scharff, Lester *Film 2*
Scharres, Barbara *WomWMM B*
Schary, Dore 1905- *BiDFlm, BiE&WWA,*
  ConDr 1977, DcFM, FilmgC, IntMPA 1977,
  MGM A, ModWD, NatPD, NotNAT,
  OxFilm, WhoThe 16, WorEnF
Schattner, Meyer 1911- *BiE&WWA, NotNAT*
Schatzberg, Jerry *FilmgC, IntMPA 1977*
Schauffler, Elsie T d1935 *NotNAT B*
Schaum, John W 1905- *AmSCAP 1966*
Schaumburg, John Hays 1923- *AmSCAP 1966*
Schear, Robert 1936- *BiE&WWA, NotNAT*
Schechner, Richard 1934- *BiE&WWA, NotNAT,*
  WhoThe 16
Schechtman, Saul 1924- *BiE&WWA, NotNAT*
Scheck, George 1911- *AmSCAP 1966*
Scheeder, Louis W 1946- *NotNAT*
Scheerer, Maud d1961 *NotNAT B*
Schefer, Mandy *WomWMM*
Scheff, Fritzi 1879-1954 *EncMT, Film 1,*
  NotNAT B, WhScrn 1, WhScrn 2, WhThe,
  WhoHol B, WhoStg 1906, WhoStg 1908
Scheffel, Oswald *Film 2*
Schehade, Georges 1906- *CnMD*
Schehade, Georges 1910- *CroCD, McGWD,*
  ModWD, REnWD
Scheib, Charles J 1891- *AmSCAP 1966*
Scheider, Roy 1934- *FilmgC, IntMPA 1977,*
  WhoHol A
Schein, Julius 1910- *AmSCAP 1966*
Scheinpflugova, Olga 1902-1968 *WhScrn 1,*
  WhScrn 2
Schelkopf, Anton 1914- *IntMPA 1977*
Schell, Catherine *WhoHol A*
Schell, Karl *WhoHol A*
Schell, Maria 1926- *BiDFlm, FilmgC, MotPP,*
  MovMk, WhoHol A, WorEnF
Schell, Maximilian 1930- *BiE&WWA, CelR 3,*
  FilmgC, IntMPA 1977, MotPP, MovMk,
  WhoHol A, WorEnF
Scheller, George *Film 2*
Schelling, Ernest 1876-1939 *AmSCAP 1966*
Schellow, Erich 1915- *WhThe*
Schenck, Aubrey 1908- *FilmgC, IntMPA 1977*
Schenck, Earl *Film 1, Film 2*
Schenck, Joe d1930 *NotNAT B, WhoHol B*
Schenck, Joseph 1877-1961 *OxFilm*
Schenck, Joseph M 1878-1961 *FilmgC, TwYS B*
Schenck, Joseph T 1891-1930 *WhScrn 1,*
  WhScrn 2
Schenck, Nicholas M 1881-1969 *DcFM, FilmgC,*
  MGM A, OxFilm
Schenck, Nicolas 1881-1969 *WorEnF*
Schenk, Joseph M 1877-1961 *DcFM*
Schenkel, Chris *NewYTET*
Schenker, Joel 1903- *BiE&WWA, NotNAT*
Schenstrom, Carl *Film 2*
Schepard, Eric *BiE&WWA*
Schepp, Dieter d1962 *NotNAT B*
Scher, William 1900- *AmSCAP 1966*

Scherer, Frank H 1897- *AmSCAP 1966*
Scherer, Ray *NewYTET*
Scherick, Edgar J *IntMPA 1977, NewYTET*
Scherman, Barbara d1935 *WhScrn 1, WhScrn 2*
Scherman, Robert 1920- *AmSCAP 1966*
Schermer, Jules *IntMPA 1977*
Schertzinger, Victor 1880-1941 *FilmgC*
Schertzinger, Victor 1888-1941 *WorEnF*
Schertzinger, Victor 1889-1941 *TwYS A*
Schertzinger, Victor 1890-1941 *AmSCAP 1966,*
  NotNAT B
Scheu, Just 1903-1956 *WhScrn 1, WhScrn 2*
Scheuer, Constance 1910-1962 *WhScrn 1,*
  WhScrn 2
Scheuer, Philip 1902- *BiE&WWA*
Schevill, James 1920- *ConDr 1977, NatPD*
Schiaffino, Rosanna 1939- *FilmgC, WhoHol A*
Schiaparelli, Elsa 1905?- *CelR 3*
Schiavone, James 1917- *IntMPA 1977*
Schickele, Peter 1935- *AmSCAP 1966*
Schickele, Rene 1883?-1940 *CnMD*
Schieske, Alfred 1909-1970 *WhScrn 1, WhScrn 2,*
  WhoHol B
Schiff, Dorothy 1903- *CelR 3*
Schiff, Larry *NatPD*
Schiff, Suzanna *WomWMM B*
Schiffman, Suzanne *WomWMM B*
Schifrin, Lalo 1932- *IntMPA 1977, WorEnF*
Schikaneder, Emanuel 1751-1812 *OxThe*
Schildhause, Sol *NewYTET*
Schildkraut, Joseph d1964 *MotPP, WhoHol B*
Schildkraut, Joseph 1895-1964 *Film 2, FilmgC,*
  MovMk, NotNAT B, TwYS
Schildkraut, Joseph 1896-1964 *BiE&WWA,*
  FamA&A, NotNAT A, WhScrn 1,
  WhScrn 2, WhThe
Schildkraut, Rudolph 1862-1930 *Film 1, Film 2,*
  TwYS
Schildkraut, Rudolph 1865-1930 *NotNAT B,*
  WhScrn 1, WhScrn 2, WhoHol B
Schillaci, Joseph John 1906- *AmSCAP 1966*
Schiller, Fred *IntMPA 1977*
Schiller, Friedrich Von 1759-1805 *CnThe,*
  McGWD, REnWD
Schiller, Johann Christoph Friedrich Von 1759-1805
  NotNAT A, NotNAT B, OxThe
Schiller, Leon 1887-1954 *NotNAT A, OxThe*
Schiller, Norbert *WhoHol A*
Schilling, August E Gus 1908-1957 *WhScrn 1,*
  WhScrn 2
Schilling, Gus 1908-1957 *FilmgC, Vers A,*
  WhoHol B
Schimel, Adolph 1904- *IntMPA 1977*
Schimmel, Herbert D 1927- *IntMPA 1977*
Schindel, Seymore 1907-1948 *WhScrn 1,*
  WhScrn 2
Schindell, Cy 1907-1948 *WhScrn 2*
Schinstine, William J 1923- *AmSCAP 1966*
Schiotz, Aksel d1975 *WhoHol C*
Schipa, Carlo *Film 2*
Schipa, Tito 1889-1965 *WhScrn 1, WhScrn 2,*
  WhoHol B
Schippers, Thomas 1930- *CelR 3*
Schirmer, Gus, Jr. 1918- *BiE&WWA, NotNAT*
Schirmer, Rudolph E 1919- *AmSCAP 1966*
Schirmer, Rudolphe *BiE&WWA*
Schisgal, Murray 1926- *BiE&WWA, CelR 3,*
  CnMD Sup, ConDr 1977, CroCD, McGWD,
  ModWD, NotNAT, WhoThe 16
Schlaf, Johannes 1862-1941 *CnMD, ModWD*
Schlaifer, Charles 1909- *IntMPA 1977*
Schlang, Joseph 1911- *IntMPA 1977*
Schlanger, Ben 1904-1971 *BiE&WWA,*
  NotNAT B

Schlatter, George *NewYTET*
Schlegel, August Wilhelm Von 1767-1845
  NotNAT B, OxThe, REnWD
Schlegel, Friedrich Von 1772-1829 *REnWD*
Schlegel, Johann Elias Von 1719-1749 *McGWD,*
  NotNAT B, OxThe
Schlegel, Margarete *Film 2*
Schlein, Irving 1905- *AmSCAP 1966*
Schlenter, Paul d1916 *NotNAT B*
Schlesinger, Arthur, Jr. 1917- *CelR 3*
Schlesinger, Isidore d1949 *NotNAT B*
Schlesinger, James R 1929- *CelR 3*
Schlesinger, John *IntMPA 1977*
Schlesinger, John 1925- *OxFilm*
Schlesinger, John 1926- *BiDFlm, DcFM, FilmgC,*
  MovMk, WhoThe 16, WorEnF
Schlesinger, Leon 1884-1949 *WorEnF*
Schlesinger, Riva *WomWMM*
Schletter, Annie d1944 *NotNAT B*
Schlettow, Hans Adelbert 1888-1945 *Film 2,*
  WhScrn 2
Schlissel, Jack 1922- *BiE&WWA*
Schlondorff, Volker 1939- *BiDFlm, OxFilm*
Schlossberg, Julian 1942- *IntMPA 1977*
Schlosser, Herbert S *IntMPA 1977, NewYTET*
Schlumberger, Jean 1907- *CelR 3*
Schlusselberg, Martin 1936- *IntMPA 1977*
Schmeling, Max *WhoHol A*
Schmid, Adolf 1868-1958 *AmSCAP 1966*
Schmid, Johann C 1890-1951 *AmSCAP 1966*
Schmidt, Alexandra *Film 2*
Schmidt, Charles A 1923- *BiE&WWA, NotNAT*
Schmidt, Douglas W 1942- *NotNAT, WhoThe 16*
Schmidt, Erwin R 1890- *AmSCAP 1966*
Schmidt, Harvey 1929- *AmSCAP 1966,*
  BiE&WWA, EncMT, NewMT, NotNAT
Schmidt, Jan *WomWMM B*
Schmidt, Kai *Film 2*
Schmidt, Peer *WhoHol A*
Schmidt, Robert Louis *NewYTET*
Schmidtbonn, Wilhelm 1876-1952 *CnMD,*
  ModWD, NotNAT B
Schmidtmer, Christiane *WhoHol A*
Schmieder, Willy *Film 2*
Schmitt, Joseph 1871-1935 *WhScrn 1, WhScrn 2*
Schmitt-Sentner, Willy d1964 *NotNAT B*
Schmitz, Ludwig 1884-1954 *WhScrn 1,*
  WhScrn 2
Schmitz, Sybille 1912-1955 *WhScrn 1, WhScrn 2*
Schmitzer, Henrietta *Film 2*
Schmutz, Albert Daniel 1887- *AmSCAP 1966*
Schnabel, Stefan 1912- *NotNAT, WhoHol A,*
  WhoThe 16
Schnee, Charles 1916-1963 *FilmgC*
Schnee, Charles 1918-1962 *WorEnF*
Schnee, Thelma *WhThe*
Schneemann, Carolee *ConDr 1977E,*
  WomWMM B
Schneer, Charles H 1920- *FilmgC, IntMPA 1977*
Schneideman, Robert Ivan 1926- *BiE&WWA,*
  NotNAT
Schneider, A 1905- *IntMPA 1977*
Schneider, Alan 1917- *BiE&WWA, CelR 3,*
  NewYTET, NotNAT, WhoThe 16
Schneider, Clarence J *IntMPA 1977*
Schneider, Dick *IntMPA 1977*
Schneider, Friedrich *Film 2*
Schneider, Hannes *Film 2*
Schneider, James 1882-1967 *MotPP, WhScrn 1,*
  WhScrn 2, WhoHol B
Schneider, John A 1926- *IntMPA 1977,*
  NewYTET
Schneider, Magda *WhoHol A*
Schneider, Maria 1953- *MovMk, WhoHol A*

Schneider, Marion *WomWMM B*
Schneider, Reinhold 1903-1958 *CnMD*
Schneider, Rolf 1932- *CroCD*
Schneider, Romy 1938- *BiDFlm, FilmgC,*
  IntMPA 1977, MotPP, MovMk, OxFilm,
  WhoHol A, WorEnF
Schneider, Rosalind *WomWMM B*
Schneier, Frederick 1927- *IntMPA 1977*
Schnell, G H *Film 2*
Schnherr, Karl 1867-1943 *NotNAT B*
Schnickelfritz *WhScrn 2*
Schnitzer, Robert C 1906- *BiE&WWA, NotNAT*
Schnitzler *PIP&P*
Schnitzler, Arthur 1862-1931 *CnMD, CnThe,*
  FilmgC, McGWD, ModWD, NotNAT A,
  NotNAT B, OxThe, REnWD
Schnur, Esther *WomWMM B*
Schnur, Jerome 1923- *IntMPA 1977*
Schodler, Dave *Film 2*
Schoebel, Elmer 1896- *AmSCAP 1966*
Schoedsack, Ernest Beaumont 1893- *BiDFlm,*
  CmMov, DcFM, FilmgC, OxFilm, TwYS A,
  WorEnF
Schoen, Margaret *Film 2*
Schoenbaum, Donald 1926- *NotNAT*
Schoenberg, Alex d1945 *WhoHol B*
Schoenberg, Arnold 1874-1951 *AmSCAP 1966*
Schoenbrun, David *NewYTET*
Schoendoerffer, Pierre 1928- *WorEnF*
Schoene, Mary *Film 2*
Schoenfeld, Bernard C *WomWMM*
Schoenfeld, Joe 1907- *IntMPA 1977*
Schoenfeld, Lester 1916- *IntMPA 1977*
Schoenfeld, William C 1893- *AmSCAP 1966*
Schofield, Albert Y 1905- *AmSCAP 1966*
Schofield, Johnny d1921 *NotNAT B*
Schofield, Paul 1922- *WorEnF*
Scholin, C Albert 1896-1958 *AmSCAP 1966*
Scholl, Danny *WhoHol A*
Scholl, Jack 1903- *AmSCAP 1966*
Scholler, William *Film 2*
Scholz, Paul 1894- *AmSCAP 1966*
Scholz, Robert *Film 2*
Scholz, Wilhelm Von 1874-1969 *CnMD, McGWD,*
  ModWD
Schon, Margarete *Film 2*
Schonberg, Alexander 1886-1945 *WhScrn 1,*
  WhScrn 2
Schonberg, Chris M 1890-1957 *AmSCAP 1966*
Schonberg, Ib 1902-1955 *WhScrn 1, WhScrn 2,*
  WhoHol B
Schonberger, John 1892- *AmSCAP 1966*
Schonemann, Johann Friedrich 1704-1782
  NotNAT B, OxThe
Schonherr, Karl 1867-1943 *CnMD, McGWD,*
  ModWD, OxThe
Schoonmaker, Thelma *WomWMM*
Schoop, Paul 1909- *AmSCAP 1966*
Schorm, Evald 1931- *DcFM, OxFilm*
Schorm, Ewald 1931- *WorEnF*
Schorr, Daniel *NewYTET*
Schorr, Hortense *IntMPA 1977*
Schorr, Jose *IntMPA 1977*
Schoumacher, David *NewYTET*
Schrader, Frederich Franklin 1857-1943
  NotNAT B
Schrader, Frederick Franklin 1857-1943
  WhoStg 1908
Schrader, Frederick Franklin 1859- *WhThe*
Schrader, Paul 1946- *IntMPA 1977*
Schram, Violet 1898- *Film 1, Film 2, TwYS*
Schramm, Harold 1935- *AmSCAP 1966*
Schramm, Karla *Film 1, Film 2, TwYS*
Schramm, Rudolf R A 1902- *AmSCAP 1966*

Schrank, Joseph *NatPD*
Schrat, Katharina d1940 *NotNAT B*
Schraubstader, Carl 1902- *AmSCAP 1966*
Schreck, Max 1879-1936 *Film 2, FilmgC, WhScrn 2, WhoHol B*
Schreder, Carol *WomWMM B*
Schreiber, Alfred *Film 2*
Schreiber, Avery *WhoHol A*
Schreiber, Edward 1913- *IntMPA 1977*
Schreiber, Frederick C 1895- *AmSCAP 1966*
Schreiber, Nancy *WomWMM*
Schreiber, Sally *WhoHol A*
Schreiber, Sidney 1905- *IntMPA 1977*
Schreiner, Alexander 1901- *AmSCAP 1966*
Schreyer, Annie *Film 2*
Schreyvogel, Josef 1768-1832 *OxThe*
Schreyvogel, Joseph 1768-1832 *NotNAT B*
Schreyvogl, Friedrich 1899- *CnMD, CroCD, McGWD, ModWD*
Schrift, Benjamin R 1906- *IntMPA 1977*
Schroder, Ernst *WhoHol A*
Schroder, Friedrich Ludwig 1744-1816 *CnThe, NotNAT B, OxThe*
Schroeder, Aaron Harold 1926- *AmSCAP 1966*
Schroeder, Anne *Film 2*
Schroeder, Arthur *Film 2*
Schroeder, Harry W 1906- *IntMPA 1977*
Schroeder, Sophia Charlotta 1714-1792 *NotNAT B*
Schroeder, William A 1888-1960 *AmSCAP 1966*
Schroell, N *Film 2*
Schroff, William 1889-1964 *WhScrn 1, WhScrn 2*
Schron, Cania *Film 2*
Schrooth, Heinrich *Film 2*
Schub, Esther *DcFM*
Schubert, Franz Peter 1797-1828 *NotNAT B*
Schubert, Kathryn *WomWMM B*
Schuch, Franz 1716?-1764 *OxThe*
Schuck, John *WhoHol A*
Schudy, Frank d1963 *NotNAT B*
Schuenzel, Reinhold 1886-1954 *NotNAT B*
Schufftan, Eugen 1893- *DcFM, OxFilm, WorEnF*
Schufftan, Eugene 1893- *FilmgC*
Schuh, Marie 1922- *AmSCAP 1966*
Schukin, Boris 1894-1939 *WhScrn 1, WhScrn 2*
Schukow, A *Film 2*
Schulberg, B P 1892-1957 *FilmgC, NotNAT B, OxFilm, TwYS B*
Schulberg, Ben P 1892-1957 *WorEnF*
Schulberg, Budd 1914- *AmSCAP 1966, BiE&WWA, ConDr 1977D, DcFM, FilmgC, IntMPA 1977, NotNAT, OxFilm, WorEnF*
Schulberg, Budd 1917- *CelR 3*
Schulberg, Stuart *NewYTET*
Schuler, Billy *Film 2*
Schuler, Robert C 1920- *IntMPA 1977*
Schulman, Arnold 1925- *BiE&WWA, NotNAT*
Schulman, Billy Revel 1950- *AmSCAP 1966*
Schulman, Nina *WomWMM, WomWMM A, WomWMM B*
Schulman, Samuel 1910- *IntMPA 1977*
Schulman, William B 1916- *IntMPA 1977*
Schultz, Barbara *NewYTET*
Schultz, Mrs. Cecil E 1905-1953 *WhScrn 1, WhScrn 2*
Schultz, Harry 1883-1935 *Film 2, WhScrn 1, WhScrn 2, WhoHol B*
Schultz, Maurice *Film 2*
Schultz, Michael A 1938- *WhoThe 16*
Schulz, Charles 1922- *CelR 3, NewYTET*
Schulz, Fritz 1896-1972 *WhScrn 2*
Schumacher, Max 1925-1966 *WhScrn 2*
Schumacher, Max 1927-1966 *WhScrn 1*
Schuman, Edward L 1916- *IntMPA 1977*

Schuman, William 1910- *BiE&WWA*
Schumann, Erik *WhoHol A*
Schumann, Walter 1913-1958 *AmSCAP 1966, NotNAT B*
Schumann-Heink, Madame 1861-1936 *WhoStg 1906, WhoStg 1908*
Schumann-Heink, Ernestine 1861-1936 *WhScrn 1, WhScrn 2, WhoHol B*
Schumann-Heink, Ferdinand 1893-1955 *Film 2, TwYS*
Schumann-Heink, Ferdinand 1893-1958 *WhScrn 1, WhScrn 2, WhoHol B*
Schumer, Henry 1914- *BiE&WWA*
Schumer, Yvette 1921- *BiE&WWA, NotNAT*
Schumm, Harry W 1878-1953 *Film 1, TwYS, WhScrn 1, WhScrn 2, WhoHol B*
Schunzel, Reinhold 1886-1954 *Film 2, FilmgC, WhScrn 1, WhScrn 2, WhoHol B*
Schuster, Harold 1902- *FilmgC, IntMPA 1977*
Schuster, Harry *WomWMM*
Schuster, Ignaz 1779-1835 *OxThe*
Schuster, Ira 1889-1945 *AmSCAP 1966*
Schuster, Joseph 1896-1959 *AmSCAP 1966*
Schutz, Maurice *Film 2*
Schuyler, Philippa Duke 1934-1967 *AmSCAP 1966*
Schwab, Laurence 1893-1951 *EncMT, NotNAT B, WhThe*
Schwab, Laurence, Jr. 1922- *IntMPA 1977*
Schwabacher, H Simon *McGWD*
Schwalb, Ben 1901- *IntMPA 1977*
Schwamm, George S Tony 1903-1966 *WhScrn 1, WhScrn 2*
Schwandt, Wilbur 1914- *AmSCAP 1966*
Schwanneke, Ellen d1972 *WhScrn 2*
Schwartz, Abe d1963 *NotNAT B*
Schwartz, Arthur 1900- *AmSCAP 1966, BiE&WWA, EncMT, FilmgC, IntMPA 1977, NewMT, NotNAT, PIP&P, WhoThe 16*
Schwartz, Arthur H 1903- *IntMPA 1977*
Schwartz, Bermuda *IntMPA 1977*
Schwartz, Emile *Film 2*
Schwartz, Jean 1878-1956 *AmSCAP 1966, EncMT, NewMT, NotNAT B, WhThe*
Schwartz, Joan M *WomWMM B*
Schwartz, John *Film 2*
Schwartz, Leslie R 1915- *IntMPA 1977*
Schwartz, Lillian *WomWMM B*
Schwartz, Maurice d1960 *Film 2, WhoHol B*
Schwartz, Maurice 1889-1960 *OxThe*
Schwartz, Maurice 1890-1960 *NotNAT B, WhThe*
Schwartz, Maurice 1891-1960 *WhScrn 1, WhScrn 2*
Schwartz, Maurice *see also* Schwarz, Maurice
Schwartz, Milton M 1924- *AmSCAP 1966*
Schwartz, Ruth 1908- *BiE&WWA*
Schwartz, Sam *WhoHol A*
Schwartz, Seymour 1917- *AmSCAP 1966*
Schwartz, Sherwood *NewYTET*
Schwartz, Sol A *IntMPA 1977*
Schwartz, Stephen 1948- *CelR 3, EncMT, WhoThe 16*
Schwartz, Stephen 1950- *NotNAT*
Schwartz, Walter A *NewYTET*
Schwartz, Wendie Lee 1923-1968 *WhScrn 1, WhScrn 2*
Schwartzkopf, Elisabeth *WhoHol A*
Schwarz, Helmut 1928- *CroCD*
Schwarz, Maurice 1891-1960 *FilmgC*
Schwarz, Maurice *see also* Schwartz, Maurice
Schwarz, Yevgeni 1896-1958 *CnMD*
Schwarz, Yevgeni *see also* Shwartz, Evgenyi Lvovich
Schwarzwald, Milton 1891-1950 *AmSCAP 1966*
Schweikart, Hans 1895- *CnMD*

Schweisthal, Helen WhScrn 1, WhScrn 2
Schwiefert, Fritz 1890- CnMD
Schwimmer, Walter NewYTET
Scianni, Joseph 1928- AmSCAP 1966
Sciapiro, Michel 1891-1962 AmSCAP 1966
Scibetta, Anthony 1926- AmSCAP 1966
Scinelli, Emilio 1905- AmSCAP 1966
Sckroder, Greta Film 2
Scob, Edith WhoHol A
Scobie, James d1968 WhScrn 2
Scofield, Paul 1922- BiE&WWA, CnThe,
  EncMT, FilmgC, MotPP, MovMk, NotNAT,
  NotNAT A, OxFilm, OxThe, PIP&P,
  WhoHol A, WhoThe 16
Scognamillo, Gabriel A 1906- IntMPA 1977
Scola, Katherine WomWMM
Scollay, Fred J WhoHol A
Scooler, Zvee WhoHol A
Scoppettone, Sandra NatPD
Scorsese, Martin 1940- IntMPA 1977, MovMk,
  WhoHol A, WomWMM
Scotland, J H 1873- WhThe
Scott, A C 1909- BiE&WWA, NotNAT
Scott, Adrian 1912-1973 FilmgC, IntMPA 1977
Scott, Agnes WhoStg 1908
Scott, Alan WhoHol A
Scott, Alex WhoHol A
Scott, Allan 1909- BiE&WWA, IntMPA 1977,
  NotNAT
Scott, Avis WhoHol A
Scott, Barbara IntMPA 1977
Scott, Barry WhoHol A
Scott, Bennett 1875- WhThe
Scott, Bonnie 1941- BiE&WWA, WhoHol A
Scott, Brenda WhoHol A
Scott, Bruce WhoHol A
Scott, Carrie Film 2
Scott, Clement William 1841-1904 NotNAT B,
  OxThe
Scott, Connie WhoHol A
Scott, Cynthia WomWMM
Scott, Cyril 1866-1945 Film 1, NotNAT B,
  WhScrn 1, WhScrn 2, WhThe, WhoHol B,
  WhoStg 1906, WhoStg 1908
Scott, Dave 1939-1964 WhScrn 2
Scott, David WhoHol A
Scott, Debralee WhoHol A
Scott, Dick 1903-1961 WhScrn 1, WhScrn 2
Scott, Douglas Frazer Film 2
Scott, Estelle Film 1
Scott, Evelyn WhoHol A
Scott, Frank 1921- AmSCAP 1966
Scott, Fred 1902- Film 2, WhoHol A
Scott, Frederick T d1942 WhScrn 1, WhScrn 2,
  WhoHol B
Scott, George C MotPP, PIP&P A, WhoHol A
Scott, George C 1926- FilmgC
Scott, George C 1927- BiDFlm, BiE&WWA,
  CelR 3, IntMPA 1977, NotNAT, OxFilm,
  WhoThe 16, WorEnF
Scott, George C 1929- MovMk
Scott, Gertrude d1951 NotNAT B, WhThe
Scott, Gordon 1927- FilmgC, IntMPA 1977,
  WhoHol A
Scott, Gordon L T 1920- FilmgC, IntMPA 1977
Scott, Gregory Film 2
Scott, Harold 1891-1964 NotNAT B, WhScrn 1,
  WhScrn 2, WhThe, WhoHol B
Scott, Harold 1935- BiE&WWA
Scott, Harry d1947 NotNAT B
Scott, Hazel Dorothy 1920- AmSCAP 1966,
  WhoHol A
Scott, Helena BiE&WWA, NotNAT
Scott, Howard Film 1

Scott, Hugh 1900- CelR 3
Scott, Ian IntMPA 1977
Scott, Ivy 1886-1947 NotNAT B, WhScrn 2,
  WhoHol B
Scott, Jacqueline WhoHol A
Scott, James D 1939-1964 WhScrn 1, WhScrn 2,
  WhoHol B
Scott, Janette 1938- FilmgC, IntMPA 1977,
  WhoHol A
Scott, Jay WhoHol A
Scott, Jay Hutchinson 1924- WhoThe 16
Scott, Joan WhoHol A
Scott, Joan Clement WhThe
Scott, John 1937- NatPD
Scott, John Newhall 1907-1963 AmSCAP 1966
Scott, John Prindle 1877-1932 AmSCAP 1966
Scott, John R d1856 NotNAT B
Scott, Kathryn Leigh WhoHol A
Scott, Kay 1928-1971 WhScrn 1, WhScrn 2,
  WhoHol B
Scott, Ken WhoHol A
Scott, Kevin WhoHol A
Scott, Lee WhoHol A
Scott, Leslie 1921-1969 WhScrn 1, WhScrn 2,
  WhoHol B
Scott, Linda WhoHol A
Scott, Lizabeth 1922- FilmgC, IntMPA 1977,
  MotPP, MovMk, WhoHol A, WorEnF
Scott, Mabel Juliene 1898- Film 1, Film 2
Scott, Mabel Julienna 1898- TwYS
Scott, Maidie WhThe
Scott, Malcolm 1872-1929 NotNAT B, WhThe
Scott, Margaret Clement- WhThe
Scott, Margaretta 1912- FilmgC, IntMPA 1977,
  WhoHol A, WhoThe 16
Scott, Mark 1915-1960 WhScrn 1, WhScrn 2,
  WhoHol B
Scott, Markie d1958 WhoHol B
Scott, Markle 1873-1958 WhScrn 1, WhScrn 2
Scott, Martha 1914?- BiE&WWA, FilmgC,
  HolP 40, MotPP, MovMk, NotNAT,
  WhoHol A, WhoThe 16
Scott, Martha 1916- IntMPA 1977
Scott, Morton W IntMPA 1977
Scott, Nathan G 1915- AmSCAP 1966
Scott, Noel 1889-1956 NotNAT B, WhThe
Scott, Paul 1894-1944 WhScrn 1, WhScrn 2
Scott, Peter 1932- WhThe
Scott, Peter Graham 1923- FilmgC
Scott, Pippa 1935- BiE&WWA, FilmgC, MotPP,
  WhoHol A
Scott, Randolph 1903- BiDFlm, CmMov, Film 2,
  FilmgC, IntMPA 1977, MotPP, MovMk,
  OxFilm, WhoHol A, WorEnF
Scott, Raymond 1909- AmSCAP 1966
Scott, Richard L d1962 NotNAT B
Scott, Robert W 1937- AmSCAP 1966
Scott, Rosemary 1914- WhThe
Scott, Simon WhoHol A
Scott, Sondra WhoHol A
Scott, Timothy WhoHol A
Scott, Tommy Lee 1917- AmSCAP 1966
Scott, Wallace d1970 Film 1, WhScrn 2
Scott, Sir Walter PIP&P
Scott, Walter D IntMPA 1977, NewYTET
Scott, Walter M 1906- IntMPA 1977
Scott, William Film 1, Film 2
Scott, Zachary 1914-1965 BiE&WWA, FilmgC,
  HolP 40, MotPP, MovMk, NotNAT B,
  WhScrn 1, WhScrn 2, WhoHol B
Scott-Gatty, Alexander 1876-1937 NotNAT B,
  WhThe
Scotti, Vito WhoHol A
Scotti, William 1895- AmSCAP 1966

Scottish Roscius *OxThe*
Scotto, Vincent 1876-1952 *DcFM*
Scotto, Vincente 1876-1952 *FilmgC*
Scottoline, Angelo 1908- *AmSCAP 1966*
Scottoline, Mary R 1923- *AmSCAP 1966*
Scoular, Angela *WhoHol A*
Scourby, Alexander *MotPP, NewYTET, WhoHol A*
Scourby, Alexander 1908- *MovMk*
Scourby, Alexander 1913- *BiE&WWA, FilmgC, NotNAT, WhoThe 16*
Scourby, Helen *WhoHol A*
Scribe, Eugene 1791-1861 *CnThe, McGWD, NotNAT A, NotNAT B, OxThe, REnWD*
Scribner, Charles, Jr. 1921- *CelR 3*
Scribner, Samuel A d1941 *NotNAT B*
Scripps, Charles 1920- *CelR 3*
Scriven, R C *ConDr 1977B*
Scruggs, Linda *WhoHol A*
Scudamore, Frank A d1904 *NotNAT B*
Scudamore, Margaret 1884-1958 *NotNAT B, WhThe*
Scudder, Wallace M *AmSCAP 1966*
Scudery, Georges De 1601-1667 *OxThe*
Scullion, James H J d1920 *NotNAT B*
Scully, Joe 1926- *IntMPA 1977*
Scully, Peter R 1920- *IntMPA 1977*
Scully, William A 1894- *IntMPA 1977*
Scuse, Dennis George 1921- *IntMPA 1977*
Seabrook, Jeremy 1939- *ConDr 1977*
Seabrooke, Thomas Quigley 1860-1913 *NotNAT B, WhThe, WhoStg 1906, WhoStg 1908*
Seabury, Forest *Film 1, Film 2*
Seabury, Ynez 1909-1973 *Film 2, WhScrn 2, WhoHol B*
Seacombe, Dorothy 1905- *Film 2, WhThe*
Seader, Richard 1923- *BiE&WWA*
Seadler, Silas F *IntMPA 1977*
Seaforth, Susan *WhoHol A*
Seagram, Lisa *WhoHol A*
Seagram, Wilfrid 1884-1938 *NotNAT B, WhThe*
Seagull, Barbara *WhoHol A*
Seal, Elizabeth 1933- *BiE&WWA, EncMT, NotNAT, WhoThe 16*
Seal, Elizabeth 1935- *FilmgC, WhoHol A*
Sealby, Mabel 1885- *WhThe*
Seale, Bobby 1937- *CelR 3*
Seale, Douglas 1913- *BiE&WWA, NotNAT, WhoThe 16*
Seale, Kenneth 1916- *WhoThe 16*
Seaman, Isaac d1923 *NotNAT B*
Seaman, Julia d1909 *NotNAT B*
Seaman, Sir Owen 1861-1936 *NotNAT B, WhThe*
Seami, Motokiyo 1363-1443 *McGWD, REnWD*
Searcy, Dale Lanning 1905- *AmSCAP 1966*
Searl, Jackie 1920- *Film 2, MotPP*
Searle, Francis 1909- *FilmgC*
Searle, Jackie 1920- *FilmgC, WhoHol A*
Searle, Judith *WhoHol A*
Searle, Kamuela C 1890-1920 *Film 2, WhoHol B*
Searle, Kamuela C 1890-1924 *WhScrn 2*
Searle, Sam *Film 1*
Searles, Barbara *WomWMM B*
Searles, Cora 1859-1935 *WhScrn 1, WhScrn 2*
Searley, Bill *Film 2*
Sears, A D *Film 1*
Sears, Allan 1887-1942 *Film 2, TwYS, WhScrn 1, WhScrn 2, WhoHol B*
Sears, Blanche 1870-1939 *WhScrn 1, WhScrn 2*
Sears, David *PIP&P*
Sears, Fred F 1913-1957 *FilmgC, WhScrn 2, WhoHol B, WorEnF*
Sears, Heather 1935- *FilmgC, IntMPA 1977, MotPP, WhoHol A, WhoThe 16*

Sears, Ted 1900-1958 *AmSCAP 1966*
Sears, Zelda 1873-1935 *Film 2, NotNAT B, WhScrn 1, WhScrn 2, WhThe, WhoHol B*
Seastrom, Dorothy *Film 2*
Seastrom, Victor 1879-1960 *BiDFlm, DcFM, Film 1, Film 2, FilmgC, NotNAT B, OxFilm, TwYS A, WhScrn 1, WhScrn 2, WhoHol B*
Seaton, George 1911- *BiDFlm, DcFM, FilmgC, IntMPA 1977, MovMk, WorEnF*
Seaton, Scott 1878-1968 *WhScrn 1, WhScrn 2, WhoHol B*
Seaver, Blanche Ebert 1891- *AmSCAP 1966*
Seaver, Frank A 1910- *IntMPA 1977*
Seaver, Tom 1944- *CelR 3*
Seawell, Donald R *WhoThe 16*
Seay, Billy *Film 2*
Seay, James *WhoHol A*
Sebastian, Dorothy d1957 *MotPP, NotNAT B, WhoHol B*
Sebastian, Dorothy 1903-1957 *ThFT, WhScrn 1, WhScrn 2*
Sebastian, Dorothy 1904-1957 *Film 2, TwYS*
Sebastian, John *WhoHol A*
Sebastian, Mihail 1907-1945 *McGWD*
Seberg, Jean 1938- *BiDFlm, FilmgC, IntMPA 1977, MotPP, MovMk, OxFilm, WhoHol A, WorEnF*
Sebiniano, Michael P 1927- *AmSCAP 1966*
Sebring, Jay 1933-1969 *WhScrn 2*
Secchi, Niccolo 1500?-1560 *McGWD*
Sechan, Edmond 1919- *DcFM, WorEnF*
Secombe, Harry 1921- *EncMT, FilmgC, IntMPA 1977, WhoHol A, WhoThe 16*
Secondari, John H d1975 *NewYTET*
Secrest, James *WhoHol A*
Secretan, Lance 1939- *WhThe*
Secrist, Harley 1890- *AmSCAP 1966*
Secunda, Sheldon 1929- *AmSCAP 1966*
Secunda, Sholom 1894-1974 *AmSCAP 1966*
Sedaine, Michel-Jean 1719-1797 *CnThe, McGWD, OxThe, REnWD*
Sedan, Rolfe 1896- *Film 2, TwYS, Vers A*
Seddon, Margaret 1872-1968 *Film 2, WhScrn 2, WhoHol B*
Sedgwick, Edie 1943-1971 *WhScrn 1, WhScrn 2, WhoHol B*
Sedgwick, Edward d1953 *WhoHol B*
Sedgwick, Edward 1892-1933? *TwYS A*
Sedgwick, Edward 1893-1953 *FilmgC*
Sedgwick, Edward, Jr. 1889?-1953 *WhScrn 2*
Sedgwick, Eileen 1897- *Film 1, Film 2, TwYS, WhoHol A*
Sedgwick, Josie d1973 *MotPP, WhoHol B*
Sedgwick, Josie 1898-1973 *WhScrn 2*
Sedgwick, Josie 1900-1973 *Film 1, Film 2, TwYS*
Sedgwick, Russell *Film 2*
Sedillo, Juan *Film 2*
Sedlak, John 1942- *NatPD*
Sedley, Sir Charles 1639?-1701 *NotNAT B, OxThe*
Sedley, Henry *Film 2*
Sedley-Smith, William Henry 1806-1872 *NotNAT B, OxThe*
See, Edmond 1875-1959 *McGWD, WhThe*
Seeber, Guido 1879-1940 *DcFM*
Seeberg *Film 2*
Seebohm, E V d1888 *NotNAT B*
Seegar, Miriam 1909- *Film 2, WhoHol A*
Seegar, Sara *WhoHol A*
Seeger, Judith *WomWMM B*
Seeger, Pete 1919- *CelR 3, WhoHol A*
Seeger, Sanford *WhoHol A*

Seel, Charles WhoHol A
Seel, Jeanne N 1898-1964 WhScrn 1, WhScrn 2
Seelen, Arthur 1923- BiE&WWA, NotNAT
Seelen, Jerry 1912- AmSCAP 1966
Seeley, Blossom 1892-1974 BiE&WWA,
   NotNAT B, WhoHol B
Seeley, James d1943 NotNAT B, WhoHol B
Seeley, Lewis Film 2
Seelos, Annette 1891-1918 WhScrn 2
Seely, Blossom 1892-1974 WhScrn 2
Seely, Scott 1911- AmSCAP 1966
Seely, Tim WhoHol A
Seff, Richard 1927- BiE&WWA, NatPD,
   NotNAT
Sefton, Ernest d1954 NotNAT B, WhoHol B
Segal, Alex 1915- BiE&WWA, FilmgC,
   IntMPA 1977, NewYTET, NotNAT
Segal, Ben 1919- BiE&WWA, NotNAT
Segal, Bernard 1868-1940 WhScrn 1, WhoHol B
Segal, David F 1943- NotNAT
Segal, Erich 1937- AmSCAP 1966, CelR 3,
   WhoHol A
Segal, George 1924- CelR 3
Segal, George 1934- BiDFlm, FilmgC,
   IntMPA 1977, MotPP, MovMk, WhoHol A
Segal, George 1936- WorEnF
Segal, Jack 1918- AmSCAP 1966
Segal, Maurice 1921- IntMPA 1977
Segal, Vivienne 1897- BiE&WWA, EncMT,
   Film 2, MotPP, NotNAT, ThFT, WhThe,
   WhoHol A
Segall, Bernardo 1911- AmSCAP 1966
Segall, Donald 1933- AmSCAP 1966
Segall, Harry 1897- FilmgC
Segar, Lucia 1874-1962 Film 2, WhScrn 1,
   WhScrn 2, WhoHol B
Segelstein, Irwin B NewYTET
Seger, Lucia 1874-1962 NotNAT B
Segond-Weber, Eugenie-Caroline 1867- WhThe
Segovia, Andres 1894- CelR 3
Segura, Leticia Espinosa d1956 WhScrn 1,
   WhScrn 2
Seickard, Joseph Film 2
Seidel, Diana E WomWMM A, WomWMM B
Seidelman, Robert 1925- IntMPA 1977
Seiden, Stanley 1922- BiE&WWA
Seidewitz, Marie d1929 WhScrn 1, WhScrn 2
Seidl, Lea 1902- WhThe
Seidman, J S 1901- BiE&WWA, NotNAT
Seidman, Lloyd 1913- IntMPA 1977
Seidner, Irene 1880-1959 WhScrn 2
Seifert, Louis 1884- AmSCAP 1966
Seigenfeld, Edward P 1937- IntMPA 1977
Seiger, Marvin L 1924- BiE&WWA, NotNAT
Seigmann, George 1884-1928 Film 1, Film 2,
   TwYS
Seiler, Edward 1911-1952 AmSCAP 1966
Seiler, Lew TwYS A
Seiler, Lewis 1891-1964 FilmgC, NotNAT B
Sein, Kenneth REnWD
Seiter, Bill Film 1
Seiter, William A 1891-1964 FilmgC
Seiter, William A 1892-1964 WhScrn 1,
   WhScrn 2
Seiter, William S 1895-1964 TwYS A
Seitter, Charles F 1892- AmSCAP 1966
Seitz, Dran 1928- BiE&WWA, NotNAT,
   WhoHol A
Seitz, George B d1944 Film 1, WhoHol B
Seitz, George B 1880-1944 WorEnF
Seitz, George B 1883-1944 TwYS A
Seitz, George B 1888-1944 Film 2, FilmgC,
   MovMk, WhScrn 1, WhScrn 2
Seitz, John 1893- FilmgC

Seitz, John 1899- CmMov
Seitz, John F 1892- WorEnF
Seitz, Tani 1928- BiE&WWA, NotNAT,
   WhoHol A
Seitz, Wayne T 1932- BiE&WWA, NotNAT
Sekely, Irene Agay 1914-1950 WhScrn 1,
   WhScrn 2, WhoHol B
Sekely, Steve 1899- FilmgC, IntMPA 1977
Sekka, Johnny WhoHol A
Selander, Concordia Film 1, Film 2
Selander, Hjalmar Film 1
Selander, Lesley 1900- FilmgC, IntMPA 1977
Selbie, Evelyn 1882-1950 Film 1, Film 2, TwYS,
   WhScrn 1, WhScrn 2, WhoHol B
Selbourne, David 1937- ConDr 1977
Selby, Mrs. Charles d1873 NotNAT B
Selby, Charles d1963 NotNAT B
Selby, David IntMPA 1977, WhoHol A
Selby, Kid McCoy Norman 1874-1940 WhScrn 1
Selby, Nicholas 1925- WhoHol A, WhoThe 16
Selby, Norman 1874-1940 Film 1, Film 2,
   WhoHol B
Selby, Norman Kid McCoy 1874-1940 WhScrn 2
Selby, Percival M 1886-1955 NotNAT B, WhThe
Selby, Peter 1914- AmSCAP 1966
Selby, Sarah WhoHol A
Selby, Tony 1938- WhoHol A, WhoThe 16 •
Selden, Albert W 1922- AmSCAP 1966,
   BiE&WWA, NotNAT
Selden, Neil 1931- NatPD
Selden, Samuel 1899- BiE&WWA, NotNAT
Seldes, Gilbert 1893-1970 BiE&WWA,
   NotNAT B, OxFilm
Seldes, Marian 1928- BiE&WWA, NotNAT,
   WhoHol A, WhoThe 16
Self, William 1921- IntMPA 1977, NewYTET
Selig, Robert William IntMPA 1977
Selig, William Nicholas 1864-1946 FilmgC
Selig, William Nicholas 1864-1948 NotNAT B
Seligman, Marjorie 1900- BiE&WWA
Seligman, Selig J d1969 NewYTET
Seligmann, Lilias Hazewell MacLane d1964
   NotNAT B
Selinsky, Wladimir 1910- AmSCAP 1966
Selk, George W 1893-1967 WhScrn 2, WhoHol B
Sell, Henry 1889- CelR 3
Sell, Henry G Film 1, Film 2
Sell, Janie 1941- WhoThe 16
Sellar, Robert J B d1960 NotNAT B
Sellars, Elizabeth 1923- FilmgC, IntMPA 1977,
   WhoHol A, WhoThe 16
Selle, Maude Marshall 1906- AmSCAP 1966
Selleck, Tom WhoHol A
Seller, Jane WomWMM B
Seller, Thomas IntMPA 1977
Sellers, Catherine WhoHol A
Sellers, John B 1924- AmSCAP 1966
Sellers, Peter 1925- BiDFlm, CelR 3, CmMov,
   FilmgC, IntMPA 1977, MotPP, MovMk,
   OxFilm, WhoHol A, WorEnF
Sellers, Ronnie WhoHol A
Sellman, Hunton D 1900- BiE&WWA, NotNAT
Sellon, Charles 1878-1937 Film 2, TwYS,
   WhScrn 1, WhScrn 2, WhoHol B
Selmer, Kathryn Lande 1930- AmSCAP 1966
Selsman, Victor 1908-1958 AmSCAP 1966
Selten, Morton 1860-1939 NotNAT B, WhScrn 1,
   WhScrn 2, WhThe, WhoHol B
Selten, Morton 1860-1940 FilmgC
Seltzer, Jules 1908- IntMPA 1977
Seltzer, Walter 1914- FilmgC, IntMPA 1977
Selvaggio, John R 1937- AmSCAP 1966
Selwart, Tonio 1896- BiE&WWA, NotNAT,
   WhThe, WhoHol A

Selwood, Maureen *WomWMM B*
Selwyn, Archibald d1959 *NotNAT B, WhThe*
Selwyn, Clarissa *Film 1, Film 2*
Selwyn, Edgar 1875-1944 *Film 1, FilmgC, NotNAT B, WhThe, WhoStg 1908*
Selwyn, Ruth 1905-1954 *NotNAT B, WhScrn 1, WhScrn 2, WhoHol B*
Selwynne, Clarissa *TwYS*
Selzer, Milton *WhoHol A*
Selzick, Stephen *Film 2*
Selznick, David O 1902-1965 *BiDFlm, DcFM, FilmgC, MGM A, OxFilm, TwYS B, WorEnF*
Selznick, Irene Mayer 1910- *BiE&WWA, NotNAT*
Selznick, Joyce *WomWMM*
Selznick, Lewis 1870-1932 *OxFilm*
Selznick, Lewis 1870-1933 *NotNAT B*
Selznick, Myron d1944 *NotNAT B*
Semel, Terry 1943- *IntMPA 1977*
Semele, Harry 1887-1946 *Film 1, Film 2*
Semels, Harry 1887-1946 *WhScrn 2*
Semenova, Ekaterina Semenovna 1786-1849 *NotNAT B, OxThe*
Semmler, Gustav *Film 2*
Semon, Larry 1889-1928 *Film 1, Film 2, FilmgC, OxFilm, TwYS, TwYS A, WhScrn 1, WhScrn 2, WhoHol B, WorEnF*
Semos, Murray 1913- *AmSCAP 1966*
Semper, Gottfried 1803-1879 *OxThe*
Semple, Lorenzo, Jr. *FilmgC*
Sendrey, Albert 1921- *IntMPA 1977*
Sendrey, Albert Richard 1922- *AmSCAP 1966*
Seneca 004?BC-065AD *McGWD, PIP&P*
Seneca, Lucius Annaeus 004?BC-065AD *CnThe, NotNAT B, OxThe, REnWD*
Senn, Herbert 1924- *WhoThe 16*
Sennett, Mack 1880-1960 *CmMov, DcFM, Film 1, Film 2, FilmgC, MotPP, TwYS, TwYS A, WhScrn 1, WhScrn 2, WhoHol B, WorEnF*
Sennett, Mack 1884-1960 *OxFilm, TwYS B*
Sensenderfer, Robert E P d1957 *NotNAT B*
Serda, Julia *Film 2*
Serena, Sigmund *Film 2*
Sergeant, Lewis *Film 2*
Sergine, Vera d1946 *NotNAT B, WhThe*
Sergyl, Yvonne *Film 2*
Serjeantson, Kate d1918 *NotNAT B, WhThe*
Serkin, Rudolf 1903- *CelR 3*
Serle, T J d1889 *NotNAT B*
Serlen, Bruce 1947- *NatPD*
Serlin, Bernard M *IntMPA 1977*
Serlin, Oscar 1901-1971 *BiE&WWA, NotNAT B, WhThe*
Serling, Rod 1924-1975 *CelR 3, ConDr 1973, FilmgC, NewYTET, WhScrn 2, WorEnF*
Serlio, Sebastiano 1473?-1554 *NotNAT B*
Serlio, Sebastiano 1475-1554 *OxThe, PIP&P*
Serly, Tibor 1900- *AmSCAP 1966*
Serna, Pepe *WhoHol A*
Sernas, Jacques 1925- *FilmgC, IntMPA 1977, MotPP, WhoHol A*
Seroff, George *Film 2*
Seroff, Muni 1903- *BiE&WWA, NotNAT, WhoHol A*
Serpe, Ralph B 1914- *IntMPA 1977*
Serrano, Nina *WomWMM B*
Serrano, Vincent d1935 *Film 1, Film 2, WhoHol B*
Serrano, Vincent 1867-1935 *WhScrn 1, WhScrn 2*
Serrano, Vincent 1870-1935 *NotNAT B, WhThe*
Sersen, Fred 1890-1962 *FilmgC*
Sertel, Neela 1901-1969 *WhScrn 1, WhScrn 2*

Servaes, Dagny *Film 2*
Servais, Jean 1910-1976 *FilmgC, OxFilm, WhoHol C*
Servandony, Jean-Nicolas 1695-1766 *NotNAT B, OxThe*
Servanti, Luigi *Film 2*
Servoss, Mary 1908-1968 *BiE&WWA, WhScrn 1, WhScrn 2, WhThe, WhoHol B*
Sessions, Almira 1888-1974 *WhScrn 2, WhoHol B*
Sessions, Kermit J 1932- *IntMPA 1977*
Sessions, Roger 1896- *CelR 3*
Seth, Will d1964 *NotNAT B*
Seton, Sir Bruce 1909-1969 *FilmgC, WhScrn 1, WhScrn 2, WhoHol B*
Settle, Elkanah 1648-1724 *NotNAT B, OxThe, PIP&P*
Settle, Maurice 1912- *BiE&WWA*
Setton, Maxwell 1909- *FilmgC, IntMPA 1977*
Seurat, Pilar *WhoHol A*
Seuss, Dr. Theodor 1904- *CelR 3*
Seval, Nevin 1920-1958 *WhScrn 1, WhScrn 2*
Sevareid, Eric 1912- *CelR 3, IntMPA 1977, NewYTET*
Seven, Johnny *WhoHol A*
Sevening, Dora 1883- *WhThe*
Sevening, Nina *WhThe*
Sever, Albert 1891-1953 *WhoHol B*
Sever, Alfred 1891-1953 *WhScrn 1, WhScrn 2*
Severen, Maida *WhoHol A*
Severin-Mara, M d1920 *NotNAT B*
Severin-Mars d1921 *Film 2, WhScrn 1, WhScrn 2*
Severin-Mars, M d1921 *WhoHol B*
Severinsen, Carl H 1927- *AmSCAP 1966*
Severn, Billy *MotPP*
Severn, Edmund 1862-1942 *AmSCAP 1966*
Seversky, Alexander De 1894- *CelR 3*
Severson, Anne *WomWMM B*
Severson, Marie 1913- *AmSCAP 1966*
Sevitzky, Fabien 1893- *AmSCAP 1966*
Sewall, Barbara Jean *IntMPA 1977*
Sewell, Allen D 1883-1954 *WhScrn 1, WhScrn 2, WhoHol B*
Sewell, Audrey *Film 2*
Sewell, Blanche *WomWMM*
Sewell, George *WhoHol A*
Sewell, Hetty Jane d1961 *NotNAT B*
Sewell, Vernon 1903- *FilmgC*
Sexton, Carter *Film 2*
Seyferth, Wilfried 1908-1954 *WhScrn 1, WhScrn 2, WhoHol B*
Seyler, Abel 1730-1801 *OxThe*
Seyler, Athene 1889- *Film 2, FilmgC, OxThe, PIP&P, WhoHol A, WhoThe 16*
Seymour, Alan 1927- *ConDr 1977*
Seymour, Anne 1909- *BiE&WWA, FilmgC, MotPP, MovMk, NotNAT, WhoHol A*
Seymour, Caroline *WhoHol A*
Seymour, Clarine d1920 *MotPP, WhScrn 1, WhoHol B*
Seymour, Clarine 1900-1919 *NotNAT B*
Seymour, Clarine 1900-1920 *Film 1, Film 2, TwYS*
Seymour, Clarine 1901-1920 *WhScrn 2*
Seymour, Dan 1915- *FilmgC, IntMPA 1977, MotPP, MovMk, Vers A, WhoHol A*
Seymour, Harry d1967 *Film 2, WhoHol B*
Seymour, Harry 1890-1967 *WhScrn 1, WhScrn 2*
Seymour, Harry 1891-1967 *AmSCAP 1966*
Seymour, James 1823-1864 *NotNAT B, OxThe*
Seymour, Jane 1899-1956 *NotNAT B, WhScrn 1, WhScrn 2, WhoHol B*
Seymour, John D 1897- *BiE&WWA, NotNAT,*

WhoHol A
Seymour, John Laurence 1893- *AmSCAP 1966*
Seymour, Laura d1879 *NotNAT B*
Seymour, Madeline 1891- *Film 2, WhThe*
Seymour, May Davenport 1883-1967 *BiE&WWA, NotNAT B*
Seymour, Tot *AmSCAP 1966*
Seymour, William Gorman 1855-1933 *NotNAT B, OxThe, WhThe, WhoStg 1906, WhoStg 1908*
Seyrig, Delphine 1932- *BiDFlm, FilmgC, WhoHol A, WorEnF*
Sezbie, Evelyn *Film 2*
Shacham, Nathan 1925- *REnWD*
Shackleton, Allan *WomWMM*
Shackleton, Robert W 1914-1956 *NotNAT B, WhScrn 1, WhScrn 2, WhoHol B*
Shackley, George H 1890-1959 *AmSCAP 1966*
Shackson, Margo *WomWMM B*
Shadburne, Susan *WomWMM B*
Shade, Betty *Film 1*
Shade, Jamesson 1895-1956 *WhScrn 1, WhScrn 2, WhoHol B*
Shade, Lillian d1962 *NotNAT B*
Shadow, Bert 1890-1936 *WhScrn 1, WhScrn 2*
Shadows, The *IntMPA 1977*
Shadwell, Charles d1726 *NotNAT B*
Shadwell, Thomas 1641?-1692 *CnThe, McGWD, REnWD*
Shadwell, Thomas 1642?-1692 *NotNAT B, OxThe*
Shaefer, Anna *Film 2*
Shafer, Mollie B 1872-1940 *WhScrn 1, WhScrn 2, WhoHol B*
Shaff, Monroe 1908- *IntMPA 1977*
Shaff, Monty *BiE&WWA*
Shaffer, Anthony 1926- *ConDr 1977, NotNAT, WhoThe 16*
Shaffer, Deborah *WomWMM B*
Shaffer, Lloyd 1901- *AmSCAP 1966*
Shaffer, Max 1925- *AmSCAP 1966*
Shaffer, Peter 1926- *BiE&WWA, CnMD, CnThe, ConDr 1977, CroCD, McGWD, ModWD, NotNAT, PIP&P, PIP&P A, REnWD, WhoThe 16*
Shaffner, Lillian *Film 1*
Shaftel, Josef 1919- *IntMPA 1977*
Shafter, Bert *WhoHol A*
Shagan, Steve *IntMPA 1977*
Shah, Chandulal J 1900- *IntMPA 1977*
Shahan, Paul 1923- *AmSCAP 1966*
Shahdoodakian, Tatiezam *Film 2*
Shahin, Youssef 1926- *DcFM*
Shaiffer, Howard Charles Tiny *MotPP*
Shaiffer, Tiny 1918-1967 *WhScrn 1, WhScrn 2, WhoHol B*
Shainberg, Maurice *NatPD*
Shairp, Alexander Mordaunt 1887-1939 *WhThe*
Shairp, Mordaunt 1887-1939 *ModWD, NotNAT B*
Shakespeare, Frank J *NewYTET*
Shakespeare, William 1564-1616 *CnThe, FilmgC, McGWD, NotNAT A, NotNAT B, OxFilm, OxThe, PIP&P, PIP&P A, REnWD*
Shakhovsky, Alexander Alexandrovich 1777-1846 *NotNAT B, OxThe*
Shale, Thomas Augustin 1867-1953 *NotNAT B, WhThe*
Shalek, Bertha 1884- *WhoStg 1908*
Shalet, Diane *WhoHol A*
Shalit, Carl H *IntMPA 1977*
Shalit, Gene 1932- *IntMPA 1977, NewYTET*
Shamir, Moshe 1921- *CnThe, REnWD*
Shamroy, Leon 1901-1974 *CmMov, FilmgC, IntMPA 1977, OxFilm, WorEnF*

Shand, Ernest 1868- *WhThe*
Shand, John 1901-1955 *NotNAT B, WhThe*
Shand, Phyllis 1894- *WhThe*
Shand, Terry 1904- *AmSCAP 1966*
Shandoff, Zachari *DcFM*
Shane, Maxwell 1905- *FilmgC, IntMPA 1977*
Shane, Sara *WhoHol A*
Shange, Ntozake *NatPD*
Shank, Clifford Everett, Jr. 1926- *AmSCAP 1966*
Shank, John d1636 *OxThe*
Shank, Theodore 1929- *BiE&WWA, NotNAT*
Shankar, Ravi 1920- *CelR 3, WhoHol A, WorEnF*
Shankar, Uday 1900- *DcFM*
Shankland, Richard 1904-1953 *WhScrn 1, WhScrn 2, WhoHol B*
Shanklin, Wayne, Sr. 1916- *AmSCAP 1966*
Shanks, Alec *WhoThe 16*
Shanks, Ann Zane Kushner *WomWMM B*
Shanks, Bob *NewYTET*
Shanley, Robert d1968 *WhScrn 1, WhScrn 2, WhoHol B*
Shannaw, Phyllis *Film 2*
Shannon, Alex K *Film 1*
Shannon, Cora 1869?-1957 *WhScrn 2*
Shannon, Mrs. Dale d1923 *WhScrn 1, WhScrn 2, WhoHol B*
Shannon, Effie 1867-1954 *Film 1, Film 2, NotNAT B, PIP&P, TwYS, WhScrn 1, WhScrn 2, WhThe, WhoHol B, WhoStg 1906, WhoStg 1908*
Shannon, Elizabeth S 1914-1959 *WhScrn 1, WhScrn 2, WhoHol B*
Shannon, Ethel 1898-1951 *Film 1, Film 2, TwYS, WhScrn 1, WhScrn 2, WhoHol B*
Shannon, Frank Connolly 1875-1959 *Film 2, WhScrn 1, WhScrn 2, WhThe, WhoHol B*
Shannon, Harry 1890-1964 *FilmgC, MovMk, NotNAT B, Vers A, WhScrn 1, WhScrn 2, WhoHol B*
Shannon, Irene *AmSCAP 1966*
Shannon, Jack 1892-1968 *WhScrn 1, WhScrn 2, WhoHol B*
Shannon, James Royce 1881-1946 *AmSCAP 1966*
Shannon, Kathleen *WomWMM*
Shannon, Peggy d1941 *MotPP, WhoHol B*
Shannon, Peggy 1907-1941 *NotNAT B, ThFT, WhThe*
Shannon, Peggy 1909-1941 *WhScrn 1, WhScrn 2*
Shannon, Ray 1895-1971 *WhScrn 1, WhScrn 2*
Shannon, Winona d1950 *NotNAT B*
Shanor, Peggy d1935 *Film 1, Film 2, WhScrn 1, WhScrn 2, WhoHol B*
Shantaram, Rajaram Vanakudre 1901- *DcFM*
Shapero, Harold Samuel 1920- *AmSCAP 1966*
Shapey, Ralph 1921- *AmSCAP 1966*
Shapiro, Carl 1938- *AmSCAP 1966*
Shapiro, Dan 1910- *AmSCAP 1966*
Shapiro, Herman 1898- *BiE&WWA*
Shapiro, Irvin *IntMPA 1977*
Shapiro, Jacob 1928- *IntMPA 1977*
Shapiro, Karl 1913- *CelR 3*
Shapiro, Ken 1943- *IntMPA 1977*
Shapiro, Marvin L *NewYTET*
Shapiro, Maurice 1906- *AmSCAP 1966*
Shapiro, Mel *PIP&P A*
Shapiro, Robert 1938- *IntMPA 1977*
Shapiro, Robert K *IntMPA 1977*
Shapiro, Stanley 1925- *CmMov, FilmgC*
Shapiro, Susan 1923- *AmSCAP 1966*
Shapiro, Ted 1899- *AmSCAP 1966*
Shapiro, Thomas M 1923- *AmSCAP 1966*
Shaps, Cyril *WhoHol A*
Sharaff, Irene 1910?- *BiE&WWA, FilmgC,*

NotNAT, WhoThe 16
Sharaku, Toshusai REnWD
Sharbutt, Del 1912- AmSCAP 1966, WhoHol A
Share, Robert 1928- AmSCAP 1966
Sharie, Bonnie WhoHol A
Sharif, Omar 1932- BiDFlm, CelR 3, CmMov,
    FilmgC, IntMPA 1977, MotPP, MovMk,
    OxFilm, WhoHol A, WorEnF
Sharif, Tarek WhoHol A
Sharkey, Jack Film 1, NatPD
Sharkey, Sailor Film 2
Sharkey, Tom Sailor 1873-1953 WhScrn 2
Sharland, Reginald d1944 Film 2, WhoHol B
Sharland, Reginald 1886-1944 NotNAT B,
    WhThe
Sharland, Reginald 1887-1944 WhScrn 1,
    WhScrn 2
Sharnik, John NewYTET
Sharon, Muriel 1920- BiE&WWA, NotNAT
Sharon, William E d1968 WhScrn 2
Sharp, Alan IntMPA 1977
Sharp, Anthony 1915- WhoHol A, WhoThe 16
Sharp, Don 1922- FilmgC, IntMPA 1977
Sharp, Eileen 1900- WhThe
Sharp, F B J 1874- WhThe
Sharp, Henry 1887-1964 NotNAT B, WhScrn 1,
    WhScrn 2, WhoHol B
Sharp, Len 1890-1958 WhScrn 1
Sharp, Leonard 1890-1958 WhScrn 2, WhoHol B
Sharp, Margery WhThe
Sharp, William 1924- BiE&WWA, NotNAT
Sharp-Bolster, Anita WhoHol A
Sharpe, Albert WhoHol A
Sharpe, Claude 1905- AmSCAP 1966
Sharpe, Cornelia WhoHol A
Sharpe, Dave 1911- WhoHol A
Sharpe, Edith 1894- WhThe, WhoHol A
Sharpe, Gyda 1908-1973 WhScrn 2
Sharpe, John Rufus, III 1909- AmSCAP 1966
Sharpe, Karen WhoHol A
Sharpe, Lester 1895-1962 WhScrn 2
Sharpe, Richard 1602?-1632 OxThe
Sharpham, Edward d1608 NotNAT B
Sharples, Winston S 1909- AmSCAP 1966
Sharplin, John 1916-1961 WhScrn 1, WhScrn 2
Sharps, Wallace S 1927- IntMPA 1977
Shartels, Wally Film 2
Shaternikova, Nina Film 2
Shatner, William 1931- BiE&WWA, FilmgC,
    MotPP, MovMk, NotNAT, WhoHol A,
    WhoThe 16
Shatterell OxThe
Shattuck, Edward F 1890-1948 WhScrn 1,
    WhScrn 2
Shattuck, Ethel d1963 NotNAT B
Shattuck, Truly 1876-1954 Film 2, NotNAT B,
    WhScrn 1, WhScrn 2, WhThe, WhoHol B,
    WhoStg 1906, WhoStg 1908
Shaughnessy, Alfred 1916- FilmgC
Shaughnessy, Mickey 1920- FilmgC, MovMk,
    WhoHol A
Shavelson, Melville 1917- CmMov, FilmgC,
    IntMPA 1977, WorEnF
Shaver, Bob WhoHol A
Shaver, C L 1905- BiE&WWA, NotNAT
Shaver, Floyd Herbert 1905- AmSCAP 1966
Shavers, Charles 1917- AmSCAP 1966
Shavers, Charlie d1971 WhoHol B
Shavrova, Tamaia Film 2
Shaw, Anabel WhoHol A
Shaw, Anthony WhoHol A
Shaw, Anthony 1897- WhThe
Shaw, Arnold 1909- AmSCAP 1966
Shaw, Arthur W d1946 NotNAT B

Shaw, Artie 1910- AmSCAP 1966, CelR 3,
    WhoHol A
Shaw, Barnett 1911- AmSCAP 1966
Shaw, Bernard 1856-1950 FilmgC, ModWD,
    REnWD, WhThe
Shaw, Brinsley Film 1, Film 2
Shaw, C Montague 1884-1968 WhScrn 1,
    WhScrn 2
Shaw, C Montague see also Shaw, Montague
Shaw, Carolyn Hagner 1904- CelR 3
Shaw, Charles 1906-1963 AmSCAP 1966
Shaw, Clifford 1911- AmSCAP 1966
Shaw, Dennis 1921-1971 WhScrn 1, WhScrn 2
Shaw, Elliott 1887-1973 WhScrn 2
Shaw, Frank M 1894-1937 WhScrn 1, WhScrn 2
Shaw, George Bernard 1856-1950 CnMD, CnThe,
    Film 2, McGWD, NotNAT A, NotNAT B,
    OxThe, PIP&P, WhScrn 2, WhoStg 1906,
    WhoStg 1908
Shaw, George Bernard see also Shaw, Bernard
Shaw, Mrs. George Bernard 1857-1943 NotNAT B
Shaw, Glen Alexander Byam 1904- OxThe
Shaw, Glen Byam 1904- BiE&WWA, CnThe,
    NotNAT, WhoHol A, WhoThe 16
Shaw, Harlan 1922- NotNAT
Shaw, Harold M d1926 Film 1, WhScrn 2
Shaw, Irwin PIP&P
Shaw, Irwin 1912- FilmgC
Shaw, Irwin 1913- BiE&WWA, CelR 3, CnMD,
    CnThe, ConDr 1977, McGWD, ModWD,
    NotNAT, WhoThe 16, WorEnF
Shaw, Jack d1970 WhoHol B
Shaw, Jean WomWMM B
Shaw, Kerry NatPD
Shaw, Lewis 1910- Film 2, WhThe
Shaw, Mary 1854-1929 NotNAT B, PIP&P,
    WhThe, WhoStg 1906, WhoStg 1908
Shaw, Montague 1884-1968 Film 2, MotPP,
    TwYS, WhoHol B
Shaw, Montague see also Shaw, C Montague
Shaw, Oscar d1967 Film 2, MotPP, WhoHol B
Shaw, Oscar 1889-1967 EncMT
Shaw, Oscar 1891-1967 WhScrn 1, WhScrn 2
Shaw, Oscar 1899-1967 WhThe
Shaw, Peggy Film 2
Shaw, Peter WhoHol A
Shaw, Ralph WhoHol A
Shaw, Reta WhoHol A
Shaw, Richard WhoHol A
Shaw, Robert 1927- BiE&WWA, CelR 3,
    ConDr 1977, CroCD, FilmgC, McGWD,
    MovMk, NotNAT, PIP&P, PIP&P A,
    WhoHol A, WhoThe 16
Shaw, Robert 1928- IntMPA 1977
Shaw, Robert Gould d1931 NotNAT B, OxThe
Shaw, Sebastian 1905- FilmgC, IntMPA 1977,
    WhoHol A, WhoThe 16
Shaw, Serena AmSCAP 1966
Shaw, Susan 1929- FilmgC, WhoHol A
Shaw, Sydney 1923- AmSCAP 1966
Shaw, Victoria 1935- FilmgC, MotPP, MovMk,
    WhoHol A
Shaw, Wini MotPP
Shaw, Wini 1899- FilmgC
Shaw, Wini 1910- ThFT, WhoHol A
Shawhan, April 1940- NotNAT
Shawlee, Joan 1929- FilmgC, IntMPA 1977,
    WhoHol A
Shawn, Dick 1929?- FilmgC, IntMPA 1977,
    MotPP, MovMk, WhoHol A, WhoThe 16
Shawn, Nelson A 1898-1945 AmSCAP 1966
Shawn, Philip d1972 WhoHol B
Shawn, Ted 1892-1972 Film 1, WhScrn 2,
    WhoHol B

Shawn, Wallace 1943- *ConDr 1977, NatPD*
Shawn, William 1907- *CelR 3*
Shay, Dorothy *WhoHol A*
Shay, Larry 1897- *AmSCAP 1966*
Shay, Patricia d1966 *WhScrn 2*
Shay, William E *Film 1, Film 2*
Shayne, Edith *Film 1*
Shayne, Konstantin *WhoHol A*
Shayne, Larry 1909- *AmSCAP 1966*
Shayne, Robert 1910?- *FilmgC, IntMPA 1977, Vers B, WhoHol A*
Shayne, Tamara *WhoHol A*
Shchepkin, Mikhail Semenovich 1788-1863 *CnThe, NotNAT B, OxThe*
Shchukin, Boris Vasilievich 1894-1939 *NotNAT B, OxThe, WhoHol B*
Shea, Bird d1924 *WhScrn 1, WhScrn 2*
Shea, Bird d1925 *WhoHol B*
Shea, Jack 1900-1970 *NewYTET, WhoHol B*
Shea, John Jack 1900-1970 *WhScrn 1, WhScrn 2*
Shea, Mike 1952- *WhoHol A*
Shea, Olive *Film 2*
Shea, Steven *NatPD*
Shea, Thomas E d1940 *NotNAT B*
Shea, William J d1918 *Film 1, WhScrn 2*
Sheafe, Alex *WhoHol A*
Sheaff, Donald J 1925- *IntMPA 1977*
Sheaffer, Louis 1912- *NotNAT*
Shean, Al 1868-1949 *EncMT, Film 2, FilmgC, NotNAT B, WhScrn 1, WhScrn 2, WhThe, WhoHol B*
Shear, Barry *IntMPA 1977*
Shear, Pearl *WhoHol A*
Shearer, Benjamin B, Sr. 1913- *AmSCAP 1966*
Shearer, Douglas 1899-1971 *FilmgC*
Shearer, Edith Norma 1904- *BiDFlm*
Shearer, Juanita 1919- *BiE&WWA*
Shearer, Moira 1926- *FilmgC, MotPP, WhThe, WhoHol A*
Shearer, Norma *MotPP*
Shearer, Norma 1900- *CmMov, Film 2, FilmgC, MGM, ThFT*
Shearer, Norma 1904- *MovMk, OxFilm, TwYS, WhoHol A, WorEnF*
Shearing, George 1919- *CelR 3, WhoHol A*
Shearn, Edith 1870-1968 *WhScrn 1, WhScrn 2, WhoHol B*
Shearouse, Florine W 1898- *AmSCAP 1966*
Shedlo, Ronald 1940- *IntMPA 1977*
Sheehan, Bobbie d1974 *WhScrn 2*
Sheehan, Jack 1890-1958 *NotNAT B*
Sheehan, John J 1890-1952 *WhScrn 1, WhScrn 2, WhoHol B*
Sheehan, Joseph F *WhoStg 1906, WhoStg 1908*
Sheehan, Tess 1888-1972 *WhScrn 2*
Sheehan, William *NewYTET*
Sheekman, Arthur 1892- *FilmgC*
Sheekman, Arthur 1901- *IntMPA 1977*
Sheeler, Mark 1923- *IntMPA 1977*
Sheen, Bishop Fulton J 1895- *CelR 3, NewYTET, WhoHol A*
Sheen, Martin 1940- *IntMPA 1977, MovMk, NotNAT, WhoHol A, WhoThe 16*
Sheen, Mickey 1927- *AmSCAP 1966*
Sheer, Philip 1915- *AmSCAP 1966*
Sheerer, Will E d1915 *MotPP, WhScrn 2*
Sheffield, Flora 1902- *WhThe*
Sheffield, John 1931- *IntMPA 1977*
Sheffield, Johnny 1931- *FilmgC, MovMk*
Sheffield, Johnny 1932- *WhoHol A*
Sheffield, Leo 1873-1951 *NotNAT B, WhThe, WhoHol B*
Sheffield, Nellie d1957 *NotNAT B*
Sheffield, Reginald 1901-1957 *Film 2, MotPP,*

NotNAT B, TwYS, WhScrn 1, WhScrn 2, WhThe, WhoHol B*
Shefter, Bert A 1904- *AmSCAP 1966, IntMPA 1977*
Shehade, Georges 1910- *REnWD*
Sheikh, Kamal El *DcFM*
Sheil, Richard Lalor d1851 *NotNAT B*
Sheiner, David *WhoHol A*
Sheiness, Marsha *NatPD*
Shelby, Charlotte d1957 *WhScrn 2*
Shelby, Margaret 1900-1939 *Film 2, WhScrn 2*
Shelby, Miriam *Film 1*
Sheldon, Brewster 1886-1946 *CnThe*
Sheldon, Connie 1921-1947 *WhScrn 1*
Sheldon, David 1931- *BiE&WWA*
Sheldon, Earl 1915- *AmSCAP 1966*
Sheldon, Edward Brewster 1886-1946 *CnMD, McGWD, ModWD, NotNAT A, NotNAT B, OxThe, PIP&P, REnWD, WhThe*
Sheldon, Ernie 1930- *AmSCAP 1966*
Sheldon, Gene *WhoHol A*
Sheldon, Harry Sophus d1940 *NotNAT B, WhThe*
Sheldon, Herb d1964 *NotNAT B*
Sheldon, James *Film 2, IntMPA 1977*
Sheldon, Jerome 1891-1962 *NotNAT B, WhScrn 1, WhScrn 2*
Sheldon, Jerry 1901-1962 *NotNAT B, WhScrn 1, WhScrn 2, WhoHol B*
Sheldon, Marie d1939 *NotNAT B*
Sheldon, Marion W 1886-1944 *WhScrn 1, WhScrn 2, WhoHol B*
Sheldon, Sidney 1917- *AmSCAP 1966, BiE&WWA, FilmgC*
Sheldon, Suzanne 1875-1924 *NotNAT B, WhThe, WhoStg 1908*
Shelle, Lori *WhoHol A*
Shelley, Barbara 1933- *FilmgC, WhoHol A*
Shelley, Carole 1939- *NotNAT, WhoHol A, WhoThe 16*
Shelley, Gladys *AmSCAP 1966*
Shelley, Harry Rowe 1858-1947 *AmSCAP 1966*
Shelley, Herbert d1921 *NotNAT B*
Shelley, Joshua *BiE&WWA, NotNAT, WhoHol A*
Shelley, Mary Wollstonecraft 1797-1851 *FilmgC*
Shelley, Miriam *Film 1*
Shelley, Percy Bysshe 1792-1822 *CnThe, McGWD, NotNAT B, OxThe, REnWD*
Shelly, Louis Edward 1898-1957 *AmSCAP 1966*
Shelly, Maxine *Film 2*
Shelly, Norman *WhoHol A*
Shelton, Abigail *WhoHol A*
Shelton, Connie 1921-1947 *WhScrn 2*
Shelton, Don *WhoHol A*
Shelton, Eleanor *Film 2*
Shelton, George 1852-1932 *NotNAT A, NotNAT B, WhThe*
Shelton, George 1884-1971 *WhScrn 1, WhScrn 2, WhoHol B*
Shelton, James 1913-1975 *WhScrn 2, WhoHol C*
Shelton, James H 1912- *AmSCAP 1966*
Shelton, John d1972 *WhoHol B*
Shelton, Joy 1922- *FilmgC, WhoHol A*
Shelton, Kenneth E d1962 *NotNAT B*
Shelton, Maria *Film 2*
Shelton, Sloane *WhoHol A, WomWMM B*
Shelving, Paul d1968 *NotNAT B, WhThe*
Shenburn, Archibald A 1905-1954 *NotNAT B, WhThe*
Shengelaya, Nikolai 1901-1943 *DcFM*
Shenson, Walter 1921?- *FilmgC, IntMPA 1977*
Shentall, Susan *WhoHol A*
Shep *Film 1*

Shepard, Alan 1923- *CelR 3*
Shepard, Alice *WhoHol B*
Shepard, Elaine *WhoHol A*
Shepard, Iva *Film 1*
Shepard, Jan *WhoHol A*
Shepard, Richard *WhoHol A*
Shepard, Sam *PIP&P*
Shepard, Sam 1942- *NotNAT*
Shepard, Sam 1943- *ConDr 1977, CroCD,*
  NatPD, WhoThe 16
Shepard, Vendla Lorentzon *AmSCAP 1966*
Shepeard, Jean 1904- *WhThe*
Shephard, Firth 1891-1949 *NotNAT B, WhThe*
Shepheard, Jean *WhoHol A*
Shepherd, Arthur 1880-1958 *AmSCAP 1966*
Shepherd, Cybill 1949- *IntMPA 1977, MovMk,*
  WhoHol A, WomWMM
Shepherd, Edward 1670?-1747 *OxThe*
Shepherd, Ivy *Film 1*
Shepherd, Jack 1940- *WhoHol A, WhoThe 16*
Shepherd, Jean 1923- *CelR 3*
Shepherd, Leonard 1872- *WhThe, WhoStg 1908*
Shepherd, Richard 1927- *IntMPA 1977*
Shepitka, Larissa *WomWMM*
Shepley, Ida d1975 *WhScrn 2*
Shepley, Michael 1907-1961 *FilmgC, NotNAT B,*
  WhScrn 1, WhScrn 2, WhThe, WhoHol B
Shepley, Ruth 1889-1951 *Film 2, WhScrn 1,*
  WhScrn 2, WhoHol B
Shepley, Ruth 1892-1951 *NotNAT B, WhThe*
Shepodd, Jon 1926- *AmSCAP 1966*
Sheppard, Buddy 1903- *AmSCAP 1966*
Sheppard, Eugenia *CelR 3*
Sheppard, John *MovMk*
Sheppard, Joseph Stanley 1915- *AmSCAP 1966*
Shepperd, John 1907- *FilmgC, WhoHol A*
Sher, Abbott J 1918- *IntMPA 1977*
Sher, Jack 1913- *AmSCAP 1966, FilmgC,*
  IntMPA 1977
Sher, Louis K 1914- *IntMPA 1977*
Sher, Rose *NatPD*
Sherart, Georgia *Film 2*
Sherbrooke, Michael 1874-1957 *NotNAT B,*
  WhThe
Sherdeman, Ted *IntMPA 1977*
Sherek, Henry 1900-1967 *BiE&WWA,*
  NotNAT B, WhThe
Sheridan, Ann 1915-1967 *BiDFlm, Film 2,*
  FilmgC, MotPP, MovMk, ThFT, WhScrn 1,
  WhScrn 2, WhoHol B, WorEnF
Sheridan, Dan 1916-1963 *WhScrn 2*
Sheridan, Dinah 1920- *FilmgC, WhoHol A,*
  WhoThe 16
Sheridan, Elizabeth Ann 1754-1792 *NotNAT B*
Sheridan, Frances Chamberlayne 1724-1766
  NotNAT B
Sheridan, Frank 1869-1943 *Film 2, NotNAT B,*
  WhScrn 1, WhScrn 2, WhoHol B
Sheridan, Mark d1917 *OxThe, WhThe*
Sheridan, Mary 1903- *WhThe*
Sheridan, Richard Brinsley 1751-1816 *CnThe,*
  McGWD, NotNAT A, NotNAT B, OxThe,
  PIP&P, REnWD
Sheridan, Thomas 1719-1788 *NotNAT A, PIP&P*
Sheridan, William Edward 1840-1887 *NotNAT B,*
  OxThe
Sheriff, Paul 1903-1962 *FilmgC*
Sherin, Edwin 1930- *FilmgC, NotNAT,*
  WhoThe 16
Sheringham, George 1885-1937 *NotNAT B,*
  WhThe
Sherlock, Maureen *WomWMM B*
Sherlock, William *OxThe*
Sherman, Al *IntMPA 1977*

Sherman, Al 1897- *AmSCAP 1966*
Sherman, Alida *WomWMM*
Sherman, Allan 1924-1973 *AmSCAP 1966*
Sherman, Arthur 1920- *AmSCAP 1966*
Sherman, Edward 1903- *IntMPA 1977*
Sherman, Evelyn *Film 2*
Sherman, Fred E 1905-1969 *WhScrn 1, WhScrn 2,*
  WhoHol B
Sherman, George 1908- *CmMov, FilmgC,*
  IntMPA 1977
Sherman, Geraldine *WhoHol A*
Sherman, Hiram 1908- *BiE&WWA, EncMT,*
  WhoHol A, WhoThe 16
Sherman, Jane *Film 2*
Sherman, Jenny *WhoHol A*
Sherman, Joe 1926- *AmSCAP 1966*
Sherman, John K 1898-1969 *BiE&WWA,*
  NotNAT B
Sherman, Lois *Film 2*
Sherman, Lowell 1885-1933 *TwYS A*
Sherman, Lowell 1885-1934 *BiDFlm, Film 1,*
  Film 2, FilmgC, MotPP, NotNAT B, TwYS,
  WhScrn 1, WhScrn 2, WhThe, WhoHol B,
  WorEnF
Sherman, Margaret *BiE&WWA*
Sherman, Martin *NatPD*
Sherman, Noel 1930- *AmSCAP 1966*
Sherman, Orville *WhoHol A*
Sherman, Paula *Film 1*
Sherman, Ransom *WhoHol A*
Sherman, Richard M 1928- *FilmgC,*
  IntMPA 1977, PIP&P A
Sherman, Robert B 1925- *FilmgC, IntMPA 1977,*
  PIP&P A
Sherman, Robert M *IntMPA 1977*
Sherman, Samuel M *IntMPA 1977*
Sherman, Sean *WhoHol A*
Sherman, Sylvan Robert *WhoHol A*
Sherman, Vincent 1906- *FilmgC, IntMPA 1977,*
  WhoHol A, WomWMM, WorEnF
Sherman, William 1924- *BiE&WWA*
Sherman Sisters, The *Film 2*
Shermet, Hazel *WhoHol A*
Sheron, Andre *Film 2*
Sherriff, R C 1896-1975 *FilmgC, PIP&P*
Sherriff, Robert Cedric 1896-1975 *BiE&WWA,*
  CnMD, CnThe, ConDr 1973, CroCD,
  McGWD, ModWD, NotNAT A, NotNAT B,
  OxThe, WhThe
Sherrill, Jack *Film 1*
Sherrin, Ned 1931- *ConDr 1977D, FilmgC,*
  IntMPA 1977, WhoThe 16
Sherry, Craighall *Film 2*
Sherry, Ernest H *NewYTET*
Sherry, J Barney 1872-1944 *WhScrn 1, WhScrn 2,*
  WhoHol B
Sherry, J Barney 1874-1944 *Film 1, Film 2,*
  TwYS, TwYS A
Sherwin, Jeannette d1936 *NotNAT B, WhThe*
Sherwin, Manning 1902-1974 *AmSCAP 1966,*
  EncMT
Sherwin, Manning 1903-1974 *WhThe*
Sherwood, C L *Film 2*
Sherwood, Gale *WhoHol A*
Sherwood, Garrison P 1902-1963 *NotNAT B,*
  WhThe
Sherwood, Henry *Film 2*
Sherwood, Henry d1967 *WhoHol B*
Sherwood, Henry 1931- *WhoThe 16*
Sherwood, James *WhoHol A*
Sherwood, James Peter 1894- *WhThe*
Sherwood, Josephine *WhoStg 1908*
Sherwood, Lydia 1906- *WhThe, WhoHol A*
Sherwood, Madeleine 1926- *BiE&WWA, FilmgC,*

MotPP, WhoHol A, WhoThe 16
Sherwood, Millige G 1876-1958 *WhScrn 1,*
WhScrn 2
Sherwood, Robert Emmet 1896-1955 *CnMD,*
CnThe, FilmgC, McGWD, ModWD,
NotNAT B, OxThe, PIP&P, REnWD,
WhThe
Sherwood, Robert Emmett 1896-1955 *NotNAT A*
Sherwood, Roberta 1912- *WhoHol A*
Sherwood, Yorke 1873-1958 *Film 2, WhScrn 1,*
WhScrn 2, WhoHol B
Sherzer, George 1916- *AmSCAP 1966*
Shevelove, Burt 1915- *BiE&WWA, ConDr 1977D,*
EncMT, NotNAT, WhoThe 16
Shevey, Sandra *WomWMM B*
Sheybal, Vladek 1928- *FilmgC, WhoHol A*
Shield, Fred d1974 *WhoHol B*
Shield, LeRoy 1898-1962 *AmSCAP 1966*
Shields, Arthur d1970 *MotPP, Vers A,*
WhoHol B
Shields, Arthur 1895-1970 *FilmgC*
Shields, Arthur 1896-1970 *WhScrn 1, WhScrn 2*
Shields, Arthur 1900-1970 *MovMk, WhThe*
Shields, Ella 1879- *WhThe*
Shields, Ernest *Film 1, Film 2*
Shields, Frank 1910-1975 *WhScrn 2, WhoHol C*
Shields, Frederick 1904-1974 *WhScrn 2*
Shields, Helen d1963 *NotNAT B, WhScrn 1,*
WhScrn 2, WhoHol B
Shields, Ren 1868-1913 *AmSCAP 1966*
Shields, Sammy 1874- *WhThe*
Shields, Sandy 1873-1923 *WhScrn 1, WhScrn 2*
Shields, Sidney 1888-1960 *Film 1*
Shields, Sydney 1888-1960 *NotNAT B,*
WhScrn 1, WhScrn 2, WhoHol B
Shields, William A 1946- *IntMPA 1977*
Shiels, George 1886-1949 *ModWD, NotNAT B,*
OxThe, REnWD, WhThe
Shiels, Una *Film 2*
Shiffrin, Irving 1909- *IntMPA 1977*
Shigekawa, Joan 1936- *WomWMM,*
WomWMM B
Shigeta, James 1933- *FilmgC, MovMk,*
WhoHol A
Shih, Mei *WomWMM*
Shilkret, Jack 1896-1964 *AmSCAP 1966,*
NotNAT B
Shilkret, Nathaniel 1895- *AmSCAP 1966*
Shilling, Ivy *WhThe*
Shillo, Michael *WhoHol A*
Shima, Koji *IntMPA 1977*
Shimada, Teru *WhoHol A*
Shimizu, Masashi 1901- *IntMPA 1977*
Shimkus, Joanna 1943- *FilmgC, WhoHol A*
Shimono, Sab *WhoHol A*
Shimura, Takashi 1905- *MovMk, OxFilm*
Shindo, Kaneto 1912- *DcFM, FilmgC, OxFilm,*
WorEnF
Shindo, Tak 1952- *AmSCAP 1966*
Shine, Bill 1911- *FilmgC, WhoHol A,*
WhoThe 16
Shine, Billy *Film 2*
Shine, John L 1854-1930 *Film 1, NotNAT B,*
WhThe, WhoHol B
Shine, Wilfred 1863-1939 *WhScrn 1, WhScrn 2*
Shine, Wilfred E *Film 2*
Shine, Wilfred E 1864-1939 *NotNAT B, WhThe*
Shiner, Ronald 1903-1966 *FilmgC, WhScrn 1,*
WhScrn 2, WhThe, WhoHol B
Shingler, Helen 1919- *WhThe, WhoHol A*
Shipley, Joseph T 1893- *NotNAT, WhoThe 16*
Shipman, Barry 1912- *IntMPA 1977*
Shipman, Ernest 1871- *WhThe*
Shipman, Gertrude *Film 1*

Shipman, Kenneth 1930- *IntMPA 1977*
Shipman, Louis Evan 1869-1933 *NotNAT B,*
WhThe, WhoStg 1908
Shipman, Nell d1970 *WhoHol B, WomWMM*
Shipman, Nell 1892-1970 *Film 1, Film 2, TwYS*
Shipman, Nell 1893-1970 *WhScrn 2*
Shipman, Nina *WhoHol A*
Shipman, Samuel 1883-1937 *NotNAT B, WhThe*
Shipp, Cameron d1961 *NotNAT B*
Shipp, Julia Lowande d1962 *NotNAT B*
Shipstad, Roy 1911-1975 *WhScrn 2, WhoHol C*
Shirart, Georgia 1862-1929 *WhScrn 1, WhScrn 2,*
WhoHol B
Shire, David 1937- *AmSCAP 1966*
Shire, Talia *WhoHol A*
Shirl, Jimmy 1909- *AmSCAP 1966*
Shirley, Anne 1918- *Film 2, FilmgC, MotPP,*
MovMk, ThFT, WhoHol A
Shirley, Anne *see also* O'Day, Dawn
Shirley, Arthur 1853-1925 *Film 1, NotNAT B,*
WhThe
Shirley, Bill 1921- *BiE&WWA, WhoHol A*
Shirley, Bobbie d1970 *WhScrn 2, WhoHol B*
Shirley, Dorinea *Film 2*
Shirley, Florence 1893-1967 *WhScrn 1,*
WhScrn 2, WhoHol B
Shirley, James 1596-1666 *CnThe, McGWD,*
NotNAT A, NotNAT B, OxThe, PIP&P,
REnWD
Shirley, Peg *WhoHol A*
Shirley, Sam 1881- *IntMPA 1977*
Shirley, Thomas P d1961 *NotNAT B*
Shirley, Tom 1900-1962 *WhScrn 1, WhScrn 2,*
WhoHol B
Shirley, Walter, Sr. d1963 *NotNAT B*
Shirley, William 1739-1780 *NotNAT B*
Shirra, Edmonston d1861 *NotNAT B*
Shirvell, James 1902- *WhThe*
Shisler, Charles P 1882- *AmSCAP 1966*
Shivas, Mark *IntMPA 1977*
Shkvarkin, Vasili Vasilevich 1893- *ModWD*
Shlyen, Ben *IntMPA 1977*
Shnayerson, Robert *CelR 3*
Shockey, Christian Allen 1910- *AmSCAP 1966*
Shockley, Marian *WhoHol A*
Shoemaker, Ann *Vers B*
Shoemaker, Ann 1891- *BiE&WWA, NotNAT,*
ThFT, WhoHol A, WhoThe 16
Shoemaker, Ann 1895- *FilmgC, MovMk*
Shoemaker, Willie 1931- *CelR 3*
Sholdar, Mickey 1949- *WhoHol A*
Sholem Aleichem 1859-1916 *CnMD, CnThe,*
McGWD, ModWD, REnWD
Sholem Aleichem *see also* Aleichem, Sholem
Sholem, Lee 1900?- *FilmgC*
Shomoda, Yuki *WhoHol A*
Shonteff, Lindsay *FilmgC*
Shoop, Pamela *WhoHol A*
Shooshan, Harry M, III *NewYTET*
Shooting Star 1890-1966 *WhScrn 1, WhScrn 2,*
WhoHol B
Shor, Elaine *PIP&P*
Shore, Dinah *MotPP, NewYTET, WhoHol A*
Shore, Dinah 1917- *CelR 3, FilmgC*
Shore, Dinah 1920- *IntMPA 1977*
Shore, Elaine *WhoHol A*
Shore, Jean *WhoHol A*
Shore, Roberta *WhoHol A*
Shore, Sig *IntMPA 1977*
Shores, Byron L 1907-1957 *WhScrn 1, WhScrn 2,*
WhoHol B
Shores, Lynn *Film 2, TwYS*
Shores, Richard *AmSCAP 1966*
Short, Antrim 1900-1972 *Film 1, Film 2, TwYS,*

WhScrn 2, WhoHol B
Short, Bobby 1926- *CelR 3*
Short, Ernest Henry d1959 *NotNAT B*
Short, Florence 1889-1946 *Film 1, Film 2, WhScrn 1, WhScrn 2, WhoHol B*
Short, Frank Lea d1949 *NotNAT B*
Short, Gertrude 1902-1968 *Film 1, Film 2, MotPP, TwYS, WhScrn 1, WhScrn 2, WhoHol B*
Short, Harry 1876-1943 *Film 2, WhScrn 2*
Short, Hassard d1956 *Film 1, Film 2, TwYS, WhoHol B*
Short, Hassard 1877-1956 *EncMT, NotNAT B, WhThe*
Short, Hassard 1878-1956 *WhScrn 1, WhScrn 2*
Short, Lew 1875-1958 *TwYS, WhoHol B*
Short, Lewis W 1875-1958 *WhScrn 1, WhScrn 2*
Short, Lou 1875-1958 *Film 1, Film 2*
Short, Sylvia 1927- *BiE&WWA, NotNAT*
Shostakovich, Dmitri 1906-1975 *DcFM, OxFilm, WorEnF*
Shostakovitch, Dmitri 1906-1975 *FilmgC*
Shotter, Winifred 1904- *FilmgC, WhThe, WhoHol A*
Shotwell, Marie d1934 *Film 1, Film 2, NotNAT B, TwYS, WhScrn 2, WhoHol B, WhoStg 1908*
Showalter, Max 1917- *AmSCAP 1966, FilmgC, IntMPA 1977, WhoHol A*
Shows, Charles 1912- *AmSCAP 1966*
Shpetner, Stan *NewYTET*
Shrader, Frederick Franklin 1859- *WhThe*
Shrader, Frederick P d1943 *NotNAT B*
Shram, Violet *Film 2*
Shreve, Tiffany d1964 *NotNAT B*
Shrimpton, Jean *WhoHol A*
Shriner, Herb 1918-1970 *AmSCAP 1966, BiE&WWA, NewYTET, WhScrn 1, WhScrn 2, WhoHol B*
Shriner, Herb 1918-1976 *NotNAT B*
Shriver, Sargent 1915- *CelR 3*
Shrog, Maurice *WhoHol A*
Shropshire, Anne *WhoHol A*
Shtein, Aleksandr Petrovich 1906- *ModWD*
Shteyn, Alexander Petrovich 1906- *OxThe*
Shtraukh, Maxim 1901-1974 *Film 2, WhScrn 2*
Shu, Shuen *WomWMM*
Shu-Hu *Film 2*
Shub, Esther Ilyanichna 1894-1959 *DcFM, OxFilm, WomWMM, WorEnF*
Shubert, Eddie 1898-1937 *WhScrn 1, WhScrn 2, WhoHol B*
Shubert, Jacob J 1880-1963 *CnThe, NotNAT A, NotNAT B, OxThe, PIP&P, WhThe*
Shubert, John 1908-1962 *NotNAT B*
Shubert, Lee 1875-1953 *CnThe, NotNAT A, NotNAT B, OxThe, PIP&P, WhThe, WhoStg 1908*
Shubert, Milton I d1967 *NotNAT B*
Shubert, Sam S 1875-1905 *NotNAT A, NotNAT B*
Shubert, Sam S 1876-1905 *CnThe, OxThe, PIP&P*
Shubert Brothers *EncMT, PIP&P*
Shuftan, Eugen *IntMPA 1977*
Shugard, Amy V *WomWMM B*
Shugrue, J Edward 1909- *IntMPA 1977*
Shuken, Leo 1906- *AmSCAP 1966*
Shukshin, Vasily 1929-1974 *WhScrn 2*
Shula, Don 1930- *CelR 3*
Shull, Leo 1913- *BiE&WWA, NotNAT, WhoThe 16*
Shull, Richard B *WhoHol A*
Shulman, Alan M 1915- *AmSCAP 1966*

Shulman, Max 1919- *BiE&WWA, IntMPA 1977, NotNAT*
Shulman, Milton 1913- *WhoThe 16*
Shultz, George 1920- *CelR 3*
Shultz, Harry *Film 2*
Shuman, Earl S 1923- *AmSCAP 1966*
Shuman, Francis K 1908- *AmSCAP 1966*
Shuman, Harry *Film 2*
Shuman, Mort *NotNAT*
Shuman, Roy 1925-1973 *WhScrn 2, WhoHol B*
Shumate, Harold *IntMPA 1977*
Shumley, Walter *Film 2*
Shumlin, Herman 1896- *BiE&WWA, WorEnF*
Shumlin, Herman 1898- *FilmgC, NotNAT, WhoThe 16*
Shumway, Lee C 1884-1959 *Film 1, Film 2, TwYS, WhScrn 2*
Shumway, Walter *Film 2*
Shunmugham, T K 1912-1973 *WhScrn 2*
Shupert, George T 1904- *IntMPA 1977*
Shure, R Deane 1885- *AmSCAP 1966*
Shurey, Dinah *WomWMM*
Shurpin, Sol 1914- *IntMPA 1977*
Shurr, Alan 1912- *AmSCAP 1966*
Shurr, Louis *BiE&WWA*
Shurtleff, Michael *BiE&WWA, NatPD, NotNAT*
Shusherin, Yakov Emelyanovich 1753-1813 *OxThe*
Shute, Nevil 1899-1960 *FilmgC*
Shuter, Edward 1728-1776 *NotNAT B, OxThe, PIP&P*
Shutta, Ethel 1896-1976 *WhThe, WhoHol C*
Shutta, Jack 1899-1957 *WhScrn 1, WhScrn 2, WhoHol B*
Shvarts, Yevgeni Lvovich 1896?-1958 *ModWD*
Shwartz, Evgenyi Lvovich 1896-1961 *OxThe*
Shwartz, Evgenyi Lvovich *see also* Schwarz, Yevgeni
Shwartz, Martin 1923- *BiE&WWA, NotNAT*
Shy, Gus 1894-1945 *NotNAT B, WhScrn 1, WhScrn 2, WhoHol B*
Shyam d1951 *WhScrn 2*
Shyman, Mona *WomWMM*
Shyre, Paul 1929- *BiE&WWA, NotNAT, WhoThe 16*
Sibbald, Laurie *WhoHol A*
Sibelius, Jean 1865-1957 *NotNAT B*
Siberskaia, Nadia *Film 2*
Sibley, Antoinette *WhoHol A*
Sibley, Lucy d1945 *NotNAT B*
Sicari, Joseph R *WhoHol A*
Sicignano, Albert J 1912- *IntMPA 1977*
Sickert, Walter Richard d1942 *NotNAT B*
Sidaris, Andrew W *NewYTET*
Sidaris, Andy 1932- *IntMPA 1977*
Siddons, Harriett d1844 *NotNAT B*
Siddons, Henry d1815 *NotNAT B*
Siddons, Sarah Kemble 1755-1831 *CnThe, NotNAT A, NotNAT B, OxThe, PIP&P*
Siddons, William *PIP&P*
Sides, Carolyn *WomWMM B*
Sidman, Sam *Film 2*
Sidney, Fred W *WhoStg 1906, WhoStg 1908*
Sidney, George 1876-1945 *NotNAT B, WhScrn 1, WhScrn 2*
Sidney, George 1878-1945 *Film 2, FilmgC, TwYS, WhoHol B*
Sidney, George 1911- *BiDFlm, CmMov, FilmgC, MovMk, WorEnF*
Sidney, George 1916- *DcFM, IntMPA 1977*
Sidney, Mabel 1884-1969 *WhScrn 1, WhScrn 2*
Sidney, Scott 1872-1928 *TwYS A, WhScrn 1, WhScrn 2, WhoHol B*
Sidney, Sylvia 1910- *BiDFlm, BiE&WWA, CelR 3, Film 2, FilmgC, IntMPA 1977,*

MotPP, MovMk, NotNAT, OxFilm, ThFT,
WhoHol A, WhoThe 16, WomWMM,
WorEnF
Siebel, Peter 1884-1949 *WhScrn 1, WhScrn 2*
Siedlecki, Agnes *WomWMM B*
Siegel, Al 1898- *AmSCAP 1966*
Siegel, Arsene 1897- *AmSCAP 1966*
Siegel, Arthur 1923- *AmSCAP 1966,*
BiE&WWA, NotNAT
Siegel, Bernard 1868-1940 *Film 1, Film 2,*
TwYS, WhScrn 2
Siegel, Don 1912- *FilmgC, IntMPA 1977,*
MovMk, OxFilm
Siegel, Don 1913- *CelR 3, CmMov*
Siegel, Donald 1912- *BiDFlm, DcFM, WorEnF*
Siegel, Marian *WomWMM B*
Siegel, Max d1958 *NotNAT B*
Siegel, Paul 1914- *AmSCAP 1966*
Siegel, Sidney Edward 1927- *AmSCAP 1966*
Siegel, Simon B *IntMPA 1977, NewYTET*
Siegel, Sol C 1903- *CmMov, FilmgC,*
IntMPA 1977, WorEnF
Siegenthaler, Robert *NewYTET*
Siegler, Al *Film 1*
Siegmann, George d1928 *Film 2, WhoHol B*
Siegmann, George 1883-1928 *WhScrn 1,*
WhScrn 2
Siegmann, George 1884-1928 *Film 1*
Siegmeister, Elie 1909- *AmSCAP 1966,*
BiE&WWA, NotNAT
Sielanski, Stanley d1955 *WhScrn 1, WhScrn 2*
Sienkiewicz, Henryk 1846-1916 *NotNAT A,*
NotNAT B
Siepi, Cesare 1923- *BiE&WWA, CelR 3,*
WhoHol A
Sierck, Dietlef 1900- *WorEnF*
Sierra, Gregorio Martinez *OxThe*
Sierra, Margarita d1963 *WhoHol B*
Sieveking, Margot *WhThe*
Sifton, Claire 1898- *PIP&P*
Sifton, Paul 1898-1972 *CnMD, ModWD, PIP&P*
Siggins, Julia Williams *WhScrn 1, WhScrn 2*
Sigler, John M 1891- *AmSCAP 1966*
Sigler, Maurice 1901-1961 *AmSCAP 1966*
Sigman, Carl 1909- *AmSCAP 1966*
Signorelli, Frank 1901- *AmSCAP 1966*
Signorelli, Tom *WhoHol A*
Signoret, Gabriel 1873-1937 *Film 1, Film 2,*
WhScrn 1, WhScrn 2, WhThe, WhoHol B
Signoret, Gabriel 1878-1937 *NotNAT B*
Signoret, Simone 1921- *BiDFlm, CelR 3,*
FilmgC, IntMPA 1977, MotPP, MovMk,
OxFilm, WhoHol A, WorEnF
Sihmada, Ihamu d1965 *WhScrn 2*
Sikevitz, Gail *WomWMM B*
Sikking, James *WhoHol A*
Sikla, Ferry *Film 2*
Siks, Geraldine B 1912- *BiE&WWA, NotNAT*
Sil-Vara, G d1938 *NotNAT B*
Silber, Arthur 1919- *IntMPA 1977*
Silberkleit, William B *IntMPA 1977*
Silbert, Lisa 1880-1965 *WhScrn 1, WhScrn 2,*
WhoHol B
Silbert, Liza *Film 2*
Silbert, Theodore *Film 2*
Silberta, Rhea 1900-1959 *AmSCAP 1966*
Siletti, Mario G 1904-1964 *NotNAT B,*
WhScrn 1, WhScrn 2, WhoHol B
Sill, William Raymond 1869-1922 *NotNAT B,*
WhoStg 1906, WhoStg 1908
Silliphant, Sterling 1918- *FilmgC, WorEnF*
Silliphant, Stirling 1918- *CmMov, IntMPA 1977,*
NewYTET
Silliphant, Tiana *WhoHol A*

Sillman, Leonard 1908- *BiE&WWA, EncMT,*
NotNAT, NotNAT A, WhoThe 16
Sills, Berenice *AmSCAP 1966*
Sills, Beverly 1929- *CelR 3*
Sills, Milton 1882-1930 *Film 1, Film 2, FilmgC,*
MovMk, NotNAT B, TwYS, WhScrn 1,
WhScrn 2, WhoHol B
Sills, Paul *NotNAT*
Sillward, Edward d1930 *NotNAT B*
Silo, Susan *WhoHol A*
Silone, Ignazio 1900- *CnMD*
Silsbee, Joshua 1813-1855 *FamA&A*
Silva, Antonio Joao 1870-1954 *WhScrn 1,*
WhScrn 2
Silva, Antonio Jose Da 1705-1739 *CnThe,*
NotNAT B, OxThe, REnWD
Silva, Henry 1928- *FilmgC, MovMk, WhoHol A*
Silva, Simone 1928-1957 *WhScrn 1, WhScrn 2,*
WhoHol B
Silvain, Eugene Charles Joseph 1851-1930
NotNAT B, WhThe
Silvain, Falconetti *Film 2*
Silvani, Aldo 1891-1964 *WhScrn 1, WhScrn 2,*
WhoHol B
Silver, Abner 1899- *AmSCAP 1966*
Silver, Borah *WhoHol A*
Silver, Christine d1960 *WhoHol B*
Silver, Christine 1884-1960 *WhThe*
Silver, Christine 1885-1960 *WhScrn 1, WhScrn 2*
Silver, Frank 1896-1960 *AmSCAP 1966*
Silver, Fred 1936- *AmSCAP 1966*
Silver, Horace 1928- *AmSCAP 1966*
Silver, Joan *WomWMM, WomWMM B*
Silver, Joe 1922- *BiE&WWA, NotNAT,*
WhoHol A, WhoThe 16
Silver, Johnny *WhoHol A*
Silver, Leon J 1918- *IntMPA 1977*
Silver, Mark 1892-1965 *AmSCAP 1966*
Silver, Milton *IntMPA 1977*
Silver, Monty 1933- *BiE&WWA, NotNAT*
Silver, Pat *AmSCAP 1966, IntMPA 1977*
Silver, Pauline 1888-1969 *WhScrn 2,*
WhoHol B
Silver, Ronald *WhoHol A*
Silver, Stuart 1947- *NatPD*
Silvera, Frank 1914-1970 *BiE&WWA, FilmgC,*
MovMk, NotNAT B, WhScrn 1, WhScrn 2,
WhoHol B
Silverbach, Alan M *NewYTET*
Silverheels, Jay 1920- *FilmgC, WhoHol A*
Silverman, Dave *Film 2*
Silverman, Fred 1937- *IntMPA 1977, NewYTET*
Silverman, Ron 1933- *IntMPA 1977*
Silverman, Sid 1898-1950 *NotNAT B*
Silverman, Sime 1872-1933 *NotNAT B*
Silverman, Sime 1873-1933 *NotNAT A*
Silverman, Syd 1932- *BiE&WWA, IntMPA 1977,*
NotNAT
Silvers, Dolores *AmSCAP 1966*
Silvers, Lou *Film 2*
Silvers, Louis 1889-1954 *AmSCAP 1966,*
NotNAT B
Silvers, Phil *MotPP, NewYTET*
Silvers, Phil 1911- *AmSCAP 1966, BiE&WWA,*
EncMT, NotNAT, NotNAT A, WhoHol A,
WhoThe 16
Silvers, Phil 1912- *CelR 3, CmMov, FilmgC,*
IntMPA 1977, MovMk
Silvers, Sid 1907- *AmSCAP 1966*
Silvers, Sid 1908- *Film 2, IntMPA 1977*
Silverstein, Eliot 1925?- *FilmgC, MovMk*
Silverstein, Elliot 1927- *WorEnF*
Silverstein, Helen *WomWMM*
Silverstein, Maurice 1912- *IntMPA 1977*

Silverstone, Jonas T 1906- *BiE&WWA, NotNAT*
Silvester, Victor *IntMPA 1977*
Silvestre, Ami *WhoHol A*
Silvestre, Armando *WhoHol A*
Sim, Alastair 1900-1976 *CmMov, FilmgC, MotPP, MovMk, WhoHol A, WhoThe 16*
Sim, Alistair 1900-1976 *CnThe*
Sim, Gerald *WhoHol A*
Sim, Millie 1895- *WhThe*
Sim, Sheila 1922- *FilmgC, WhThe, WhoHol A*
Sima, Oskar *Film 2*
Sima, William Richard, Sr. 1892-1965 *AmSCAP 1966*
Simanek, Otto 1901-1967 *WhScrn 1, WhScrn 2, WhoHol B*
Simenon, Georges 1903- *FilmgC*
Simeone, Harry 1911- *AmSCAP 1966*
Simmonds, Annette 1918-1959 *WhScrn 1, WhScrn 2, WhoHol B*
Simmonds, Stanley *WhoHol A*
Simmons, Anthony 1924?- *FilmgC, WorEnF*
Simmons, Chester R *NewYTET*
Simmons, Elsie *AmSCAP 1966*
Simmons, H C *Film 2*
Simmons, Homer *AmSCAP 1966*
Simmons, Jean 1929- *BiDFlm, CelR 3, CmMov, FilmgC, IntMPA 1977, MotPP, MovMk, OxFilm, WhoHol A, WorEnF*
Simmons, John *IntMPA 1977*
Simmons, Richard 1918- *WhoHol A*
Simmons, Stanley 1915- *IntMPA 1977*
Simms, Alice D 1920- *AmSCAP 1966*
Simms, Frank 1921- *IntMPA 1977*
Simms, Ginny 1916- *FilmgC, MotPP*
Simms, Hilda 1920- *BiE&WWA, NotNAT, WhoHol A, WhoThe 16*
Simms, Larry 1934- *FilmgC, WhoHol A*
Simms, Willard *WhoStg 1908*
Simola, Liisa *WomWMM B*
Simon, Abram Robert 1903- *IntMPA 1977*
Simon, Bernard 1904- *BiE&WWA, NotNAT*
Simon, Carly *CelR 3*
Simon, Charles d1910 *NotNAT B*
Simon, Edward G 1871-1934 *AmSCAP 1966*
Simon, George R 1910- *AmSCAP 1966*
Simon, Howard 1901-1961 *AmSCAP 1966*
Simon, John 1925- *BiE&WWA, NotNAT, WhoThe 16*
Simon, Joseph 1594-1671 *OxThe*
Simon, Louis M 1906- *NotNAT, WhoThe 16*
Simon, Michel 1895-1975 *BiDFlm, Film 2, FilmgC, MovMk, OxFilm, WhScrn 2, WhoHol C, WorEnF*
Simon, Nat 1900- *AmSCAP 1966*
Simon, Neil 1927- *BiE&WWA, CelR 3, CnThe, ConDr 1977, CroCD, EncMT, FilmgC, IntMPA 1977, McGWD, ModWD, NewMT, NewYTET, NotNAT, PIP&P, PIP&P A, WhoThe 16*
Simon, Norman J 1925- *AmSCAP 1966*
Simon, Norton 1907- *CelR 3*
Simon, Paul 1941- *CelR 3*
Simon, Robert A 1897- *AmSCAP 1966*
Simon, Robert F *WhoHol A*
Simon, Roger Hendricks 1942- *NotNAT*
Simon, S Sylvan 1910-1951 *FilmgC*
Simon, Seymour F 1915- *IntMPA 1977*
Simon, Simone *MotPP*
Simon, Simone 1910- *FilmgC, HolP 30, ThFT, WhoHol A*
Simon, Simone 1911- *BiDFlm, OxFilm, WorEnF*
Simon, Simone 1914- *IntMPA 1977, MovMk*
Simon, Sol S 1864-1940 *Film 2, WhScrn 1, WhScrn 2, WhoHol B*

Simon, Walter Cleveland 1884-1958 *AmSCAP 1966*
Simon, William L 1920- *AmSCAP 1966*
Simon, William N 1916- *AmSCAP 1966*
Simon-Girard, Aime *Film 2*
Simone, Madame 1880- *WhThe*
Simone, Nina 1933- *AmSCAP 1966*
Simone, Nina 1935- *CelR 3*
Simonelli, Charles F 1923- *IntMPA 1977*
Simonov, Konstantin Mikhailovich 1915- *CnMD, CroCD, McGWD, ModWD, OxThe, PIP&P*
Simonov, Nikolai 1902-1973 *WhScrn 2*
Simonov, Reuben Nikolaivich 1899-1968 *OxThe*
Simons, Beverley 1938- *ConDr 1977*
Simons, Seymour 1896-1949 *AmSCAP 1966, NotNAT B*
Simons, Ted 1933- *AmSCAP 1966*
Simonson, Lee 1888-1967 *BiE&WWA, NotNAT A, NotNAT B, OxThe, PIP&P, WhThe*
Simonx, S S *Film 2*
Simov, Victor Andreyevich 1858-1935 *OxThe, PIP&P*
Simpson, Adele 1903- *CelR 3*
Simpson, Alan 1929- *FilmgC*
Simpson, Allan *Film 2*
Simpson, Cheridah d1922 *NotNAT B*
Simpson, Doctor *Film 2*
Simpson, Edmund Shaw 1784-1848 *NotNAT B, OxThe*
Simpson, Garry *IntMPA 1977*
Simpson, Grant 1884-1932 *WhScrn 1, WhScrn 2*
Simpson, Harold *WhThe*
Simpson, Ivan 1875-1951 *Film 1, Film 2, NotNAT B, WhScrn 1, WhScrn 2, WhoHol B*
Simpson, J Palgrave d1887 *NotNAT B*
Simpson, Jim *NewYTET*
Simpson, Mary K *WomWMM B*
Simpson, N F 1919- *BiE&WWA, CnMD Sup, ConDr 1977, CroCD, McGWD, ModWD, NotNAT, WhoThe 16*
Simpson, Norman Frederick 1919- *CnThe*
Simpson, O J 1947- *CelR 3, WhoHol A*
Simpson, Peggy *WhThe*
Simpson, Robert 1910- *IntMPA 1977*
Simpson, Robert 1924- *NatPD*
Simpson, Ronald 1896-1957 *NotNAT B, WhThe, WhoHol B*
Simpson, Russell d1959 *MotPP, NotNAT B, WhoHol B*
Simpson, Russell 1878-1959 *FilmgC, TwYS*
Simpson, Russell 1880-1959 *Film 1, Film 2, MovMk, Vers A, WhScrn 1, WhScrn 2*
Simpson, Valerie *CelR 3*
Sims, George Robert 1847-1922 *NotNAT B, WhThe, WhoStg 1908*
Sims, Harry 1908- *AmSCAP 1966*
Sims, Joan 1930- *FilmgC, IntMPA 1977, WhoHol A, WhoThe 16*
Sims, Lee 1898-1966 *AmSCAP 1966*
Sims, Sylvia *WhoHol A*
Sin-Nui, Hung 1920-1966 *WhScrn 2*
Sin-Nul, Hung 1920-1966 *WhScrn 1*
Sina, Sandy 1927- *IntMPA 1977*
Sinasi, Ibrahim 1826-1871 *REnWD*
Sinatra, Frank *MotPP, NewYTET, WhoHol A*
Sinatra, Frank 1915- *AmSCAP 1966, BiDFlm, CmMov, FilmgC, IntMPA 1977, MGM, MovMk, OxFilm, WorEnF*
Sinatra, Frank 1917- *CelR 3*
Sinatra, Frank, Jr. *WhoHol A*
Sinatra, Nancy 1940- *CelR 3, FilmgC, WhoHol A*

Sinatra, Ray 1904- *AmSCAP 1966*
Sinclair, Andrew *IntMPA 1977*
Sinclair, Arthur 1883-1951 *NotNAT B, OxThe,*
  WhScrn 1, WhScrn 2, WhThe, WhoHol B
Sinclair, Barry 1911- *WhoHol A, WhoThe 16*
Sinclair, Betty *WhoHol A*
Sinclair, Daisy 1878-1929 *WhScrn 1, WhScrn 2*
Sinclair, Eleanor *Film 2*
Sinclair, Horace 1884-1949 *WhScrn 1, WhScrn 2,*
  WhoHol B
Sinclair, Hugh 1903-1962 *FilmgC, NotNAT B,*
  WhScrn 1, WhScrn 2, WhThe, WhoHol B
Sinclair, Jerry *Film 2*
Sinclair, Johnny *Film 2*
Sinclair, Madge *WhoHol A*
Sinclair, Mary *IntMPA 1977*
Sinclair, Maud *Film 2*
Sinclair, Moray d1964 *NotNAT B*
Sinclair, Robert B 1905-1970 *BiE&WWA, FilmgC,*
  NotNAT B
Sinclair, Ruth *Film 2*
Sinclair, Upton Beall 1878-1968 *OxFilm, WorEnF*
Sindelar, Pearl *Film 1*
Sindell, Bernard I 1912- *IntMPA 1977*
Sinden, Donald 1923- *CnThe, FilmgC,*
  IntMPA 1977, WhoHol A, WhoThe 16
Sinden, Topsy 1878- *WhThe*
Sinding, Ellen *Film 2*
Singer, A 1927- *IntMPA 1977*
Singer, Alexander 1932- *FilmgC, WorEnF*
Singer, Arthur 1919- *AmSCAP 1966*
Singer, Aubrey E *NewYTET*
Singer, Bob 1930- *AmSCAP 1966*
Singer, Campbell 1909- *FilmgC, WhoHol A,*
  WhoThe 16
Singer, Dolph 1900-1942 *AmSCAP 1966*
Singer, Isaac Bashevis 1904- *CelR 3*
Singer, Izzy *WhoHol A*
Singer, Jack *Film 2*
Singer, John *NotNAT B, PIP&P*
Singer, Judith *WomWMM*
Singer, Louis C 1912- *AmSCAP 1966*
Singer, Samuel Bart 1913- *IntMPA 1977*
Singer, Werner 1903- *AmSCAP 1966*
Singh, Bhogwan 1883-1962 *WhScrn 2*
Singh, Ram *Film 2*
Singh, Ranveer 1931- *IntMPA 1977*
Singh, Sarain 1888-1952 *WhScrn 1, WhScrn 2*
Singleton, Catherine 1904-1969 *WhScrn 1,*
  WhScrn 2, WhoHol B
Singleton, Doris *WhoHol A*
Singleton, George 1900- *IntMPA 1977*
Singleton, Joe E *Film 1, Film 2*
Singleton, Joseph *Film 1*
Singleton, Penny 1908- *FilmgC, HolP 30,*
  IntMPA 1977, MotPP, MovMk, ThFT,
  WhoHol A
Singleton, Zutty 1898-1975 *WhScrn 2,*
  WhoHol C
Sini'letta, Vic d1921 *WhScrn 1, WhScrn 2*
Sinn, Robert S 1930- *IntMPA 1977*
Sinnott, Patricia *WhoHol A*
Sinoel 1868-1949 *WhScrn 1, WhScrn 2,*
  WhoHol B
Siodmak, Curt 1902- *CmMov, FilmgC,*
  IntMPA 1977
Siodmak, Robert 1900-1973 *BiDFlm, CmMov,*
  DcFM, FilmgC, MovMk, OxFilm,
  WhScrn 2, WorEnF
Sion, Georges S 1913- *ModWD*
Sipperley, Ralph 1890-1928 *NotNAT B,*
  WhScrn 2
Sipperly, Ralph 1890-1928 *Film 2, WhoHol B*
Sircom, Arthur R 1899- *BiE&WWA, NotNAT*

Sire, Henry B d1917 *NotNAT B*
Sirk, Douglas 1900- *BiDFlm, CmMov, DcFM,*
  FilmgC, IntMPA 1977, OxFilm, WorEnF
Sirmay, Albert *AmSCAP 1966*
Sirola, Joseph *WhoHol A*
Siscart, Solango *Film 2*
Sissle, Noble 1889-1975 *AmSCAP 1966, EncMT,*
  WhScrn 2
Sisson, Kenn 1898-1947 *AmSCAP 1966*
Sisson, Vera 1891-1954 *WhScrn 2, WhoHol B*
Sisson, Vera 1895-1954 *Film 1, Film 2, TwYS*
Sita-Bella, Therese *WomWMM*
Sitgreaves, Beverley 1867-1943 *WhThe*
Sitgreaves, Beverly 1867-1943 *NotNAT B,*
  WhoStg 1906, WhoStg 1908
Sitka, Emil *WhoHol A*
Sittig, Robert 1919- *AmSCAP 1966*
Siwertz, Sigfrid 1882- *ModWD*
Sizemore, Arthur 1891-1954 *AmSCAP 1966*
Sjoberg, Alf 1903- *BiDFlm, DcFM, FilmgC,*
  OxFilm
Sjoman, Vilgot 1924- *FilmgC, MovMk, OxFilm,*
  WorEnF
Sjostrom, Victor 1879-1960 *BiDFlm, DcFM,*
  Film 1, FilmgC, MovMk, OxFilm,
  WhoHol B, WorEnF
Sjostron, Victor 1879-1960 *Film 2*
Skaff, George *WhoHol A*
Skaggs, Hazel Ghazarian 1924- *AmSCAP 1966*
Skala, Lilia *WhoHol A, WhoThe 16*
Skeath, Harold R 1899-1942 *AmSCAP 1966*
Skeffington, Sir Lumley d1850 *NotNAT B*
Skelly, Hal 1891-1934 *Film 2, WhScrn 1,*
  WhScrn 2, WhThe, WhoHol B
Skelly, James 1936-1969 *WhScrn 1, WhScrn 2,*
  WhoHol B
Skelly, Madge 1904- *BiE&WWA, NotNAT*
Skelton, John 1460?-1529 *McGWD, OxThe*
Skelton, Marlys *WomWMM B*
Skelton, Red *IntMPA 1977, MotPP, NewYTET*
Skelton, Red 1910- *CmMov, FilmgC*
Skelton, Red 1913- *CelR 3, MGM, MovMk,*
  WhoHol A
Skelton, Richard 1913- *AmSCAP 1966*
Skelton, Thomas *WhoThe 16*
Skerritt, Tom *WhoHol A*
Sketchley, Leslie *Film 2*
Skidmore, Will E 1880-1959 *AmSCAP 1966*
Skiles, Marlin H 1906- *AmSCAP 1966,*
  IntMPA 1977
Skillan, George 1893- *WhThe*
Skilton, Charles Sanford 1868-1941
  AmSCAP 1966
Skinner, Al 1906- *AmSCAP 1966*
Skinner, B F 1904- *CelR 3*
Skinner, Cornelia Otis 1901- *BiE&WWA, CelR 3,*
  FilmgC, NotNAT, NotNAT A, WhoHol A,
  WhoThe 16
Skinner, Cornelia Otis 1902- *OxThe*
Skinner, Edith Warman 1904- *BiE&WWA,*
  NotNAT
Skinner, Frank 1897-1968 *AmSCAP 1966,*
  NotNAT B
Skinner, Gladys d1968 *WhoHol B*
Skinner, Harold Otis d1922 *NotNAT B*
Skinner, Marion *Film 2*
Skinner, Otis d1942 *WhoHol B*
Skinner, Otis 1857-1942 *WhScrn 1, WhScrn 2*
Skinner, Otis 1858-1942 *FamA&A, Film 1,*
  Film 2, FilmgC, NotNAT A, NotNAT B,
  OxThe, PIP&P, TwYS, WhThe
Skinner, Otis 1865- *WhoStg 1906, WhoStg 1908*
Skinner, Richard 1900-1971 *BiE&WWA,*
  NotNAT B

Skinner, Ted 1911- *BiE&WWA, NotNAT*
Skipworth, Alison d1952 *WhoHol B*
Skipworth, Alison 1863-1952 *NotNAT B, ThFT, WhThe*
Skipworth, Alison 1865?-1952 *WhScrn 1, WhScrn 2*
Skipworth, Alison 1870-1952 *MovMk, Vers B*
Skipworth, Alison 1871-1952 *WhoStg 1908*
Skipworth, Alison 1875-1952 *Film 2, FilmgC*
Skipworth, Allison *MotPP*
Skirball, Jack H 1896- *FilmgC, IntMPA 1977*
Skirball, William N *IntMPA 1977*
Skirpan, Stephen J 1930- *BiE&WWA, NotNAT*
Skladanovsky, Max 1863-1939 *WorEnF*
Skladanowsky, Max 1863-1939 *DcFM*
Sklar, George 1908- *BiE&WWA, McGWD, ModWD, NotNAT, PIP&P*
Sklar, Michael *IntMPA 1977*
Skolimowski, Jerzy 1938- *BiDFlm, DcFM, FilmgC, OxFilm, WorEnF*
Skolsky, Sidney 1905- *CelR 3, IntMPA 1977*
Skornicka, Joseph E 1902- *AmSCAP 1966*
Skouen, Arne 1913- *WorEnF*
Skouras, George P d1964 *NotNAT B*
Skouras, Spyros P 1893-1971 *DcFM, FilmgC, OxFilm, WorEnF*
Skrowaczewski, Stanislaw 1923- *CelR 3*
Skulnik, Menasha 1892-1970 *NotNAT B, WhScrn 2*
Skulnik, Menasha 1894-1970 *WhThe*
Skulnik, Menasha 1898-1970 *BiE&WWA*
Skurkoy, Mary *Film 2*
Skylar, Joanne Alex *WhoHol A*
Skylar, Sunny 1913- *AmSCAP 1966*
Slack, Freddie 1910-1965 *AmSCAP 1966, WhScrn 1, WhScrn 2, WhoHol B*
Slade, Bernard *NewYTET*
Slade, Julian 1930- *EncMT, WhoThe 16*
Slade, Mark *WhoHol A*
Slade, Olga d1949 *NotNAT B, WhoHol B*
Sladek, Paul 1896- *AmSCAP 1966*
Slane, Eva Weith 1929- *BiE&WWA*
Slate, Henry *WhoHol A*
Slate, Jeremy 1925- *FilmgC, WhoHol A*
Slater, Barney 1923- *IntMPA 1977*
Slater, Bill 1903- *IntMPA 1977*
Slater, Bob *Film 2*
Slater, Daphne 1928- *IntMPA 1977, WhThe*
Slater, Frank *Film 2*
Slater, George M d1949 *NotNAT B*
Slater, Gerald *NewYTET*
Slater, Hartley d1964 *NotNAT B*
Slater, John 1916-1975 *FilmgC, WhScrn 2, WhThe, WhoHol C*
Slater Brothers, The *Film 2*
Slatkin, Felix d1963 *NotNAT B*
Slatter, Charles *Film 2*
Slattery, Charles *Film 2*
Slattery, Daniel G d1964 *NotNAT B*
Slattery, Richard X *WhoHol A*
Slatzer, Robert Franklin 1927- *IntMPA 1977*
Slaughter, Bessie 1879- *WhThe*
Slaughter, N Carter 1885-1956 *NotNAT B, WhThe*
Slaughter, Tod 1885-1956 *FilmgC, WhScrn 1, WhScrn 2, WhoHol B*
Slaughter, Walter d1908 *NotNAT B*
Slavin, George 1916- *IntMPA 1977*
Slavin, John C d1940 *NotNAT B*
Slay, Frank C, Jr. 1930- *AmSCAP 1966*
Slayton, Donald K 1924- *CelR 3*
Sleath, Herbert 1870-1921 *NotNAT B, WhThe, WhoStg 1906, WhoStg 1908*
Sleeman, Philip *Film 2*

Sleeper, Martha 1901- *Film 2, TwYS*
Sleeper, Martha 1910- *BiE&WWA, NotNAT, WhoHol A*
Sleeper, Martha 1911- *WhThe*
Slesin, Aviva *WomWMM, WomWMM A, WomWMM B*
Slezak, Leo 1875-1946 *WhScrn 1, WhScrn 2, WhoHol B*
Slezak, Margarete 1901-1953 *WhScrn 1, WhScrn 2, WhoHol B*
Slezak, Walter 1902- *BiE&WWA, CelR 3, CmMov, EncMT, Film 2, FilmgC, IntMPA 1977, MotPP, MovMk, NotNAT, NotNAT A, Vers A, WhoHol A, WhoThe 16*
Slick, Grace 1941- *CelR 3*
Slippery, Ralph *Film 2*
Sloan, Alfred Baldwin 1872-1925 *NotNAT B*
Sloan, John R *IntMPA 1977*
Sloan, Ted *Film 2*
Sloane, A Baldwin 1872-1925 *AmSCAP 1966, EncMT*
Sloane, A Baldwin 1872-1926 *NewMT*
Sloane, Alfred Baldwin 1872- *WhoStg 1906, WhoStg 1908*
Sloane, Alfred Baldwin 1872-1925 *WhThe*
Sloane, Everett d1965 *MotPP, WhoHol B*
Sloane, Everett 1909-1965 *BiDFlm, FilmgC, MovMk, NotNAT B, WhScrn 1, WhScrn 2*
Sloane, Everett 1910-1965 *Vers A*
Sloane, Olive 1896-1963 *FilmgC, WhScrn 1, WhScrn 2, WhThe, WhoHol B*
Sloane, Patricia Hermine 1934- *WomWMM B*
Sloane, Paul 1893- *TwYS A*
Slocombe, Douglas 1913- *DcFM, FilmgC, WorEnF*
Slocum, Earl 1902- *AmSCAP 1966*
Slocum, Tex 1902-1963 *WhScrn 1, WhScrn 2*
Sloman, Charles 1808-1870 *OxThe*
Sloman, Edward 1885-1972 *Film 1, TwYS A, WhScrn 2*
Slomen, Hilda *Film 1*
Slonimsky, Nicolas 1894- *AmSCAP 1966*
Slote, Gilbert Monroe 1929- *AmSCAP 1966*
Sloughton, Mabel *Film 1*
Slous, A R d1883 *NotNAT B*
Slowacki, Juliusz 1809-1849 *CnThe, McGWD, OxThe, REnWD*
Sly, William d1608 *NotNAT B, OxThe*
Smakwitz, Charles A *IntMPA 1977*
Smale, Robert Claire 1931- *AmSCAP 1966*
Small, Dick d1972 *WhoHol B*
Small, Edna 1898-1917 *WhScrn 2*
Small, Edward 1891- *FilmgC, IntMPA 1977*
Small, Jack d1962 *NotNAT B*
Small, Lillian Schary d1961 *NotNAT B*
Small, Michael 1939- *BiE&WWA*
Small, Milton Noel 1895- *AmSCAP 1966*
Small, Paul d1954 *NotNAT B*
Small, Richard B *WhoHol A*
Small, William J *NewYTET*
Smalley, Phillips d1939 *WhoHol B, WomWMM*
Smalley, Phillips 1870-1939 *Film 1, Film 2, TwYS*
Smalley, Phillips 1875-1939 *WhScrn 1, WhScrn 2*
Smalley, Webster 1921- *NotNAT*
Smallwood, Ray C 1888- *TwYS A*
Smart, Christopher d1771 *NotNAT B*
Smart, J Scott 1903-1960 *WhScrn 1, WhScrn 2, WhoHol B*
Smart, Ralph 1908- *FilmgC, IntMPA 1977*
Smart, Roy L *IntMPA 1977*
Smeck, Roy *AmSCAP 1966*
Smedley, Morgan T d1964 *NotNAT B*

Smedley-Aston, E M 1912- *FilmgC*
Smelker, Mary 1909-1933 *WhScrn 1, WhScrn 2*
Smiah, C C *Film 2*
Smidd, Gorm *Film 2*
Smight, Jack 1926- *FilmgC, IntMPA 1977, WorEnF*
Smiles, Finch *Film 2*
Smiley, Joseph W 1881-1945 *Film 1, Film 2, WhScrn 1, WhScrn 2, WhoHol B*
Smiley, Ralph *WhoHol A*
Smirnova, Dina *Film 2*
Smit, Leo 1921- *AmSCAP 1966*
Smith, A Berkeley 1918- *IntMPA 1977*
Smith, Albert 1816-1860 *NotNAT A, NotNAT B, OxThe*
Smith, Albert E 1875-1958 *WhScrn 2*
Smith, Albert J 1894-1939 *WhScrn 1, WhScrn 2, WhoHol B*
Smith, Alexis 1921- *CelR 3, FilmgC, IntMPA 1977, MotPP, MovMk, PIP&P A, WhoHol A, WhoThe 16, WorEnF*
Smith, Alicia 1931- *AmSCAP 1966*
Smith, Anderson *Film 2*
Smith, Anita 1922- *AmSCAP 1966*
Smith, Archie *WhoHol A*
Smith, Art 1900-1973 *PIP&P, WhScrn 2, WhoHol B*
Smith, Arthur Corbett d1945 *NotNAT B*
Smith, Sir Aubrey 1863-1948 *WhThe*
Smith, Sir Aubrey *see also* Smith, C Aubrey
Smith, Barbara L *WomWMM A, WomWMM B*
Smith, Beasley 1901-1968 *AmSCAP 1966, NotNAT B*
Smith, Beatrice Lieb 1862-1942 *WhScrn 1, WhScrn 2*
Smith, Bernard 1905?- *FilmgC*
Smith, Bessie 1894-1937 *WhScrn 2*
Smith, Betty 1906-1972 *BiE&WWA, NotNAT B*
Smith, Billy d1963 *NotNAT B*
Smith, Bruce d1942 *NotNAT B*
Smith, Buddy *Film 2*
Smith, Buffalo Bob *NewYTET*
Smith, C Aubrey d1948 *MotPP, WhoHol B*
Smith, C Aubrey 1862-1948 *WhoStg 1908*
Smith, C Aubrey 1863-1948 *Film 1, Film 2, FilmgC, MovMk, NotNAT B, PIP&P, Vers A, WhScrn 1, WhScrn 2*
Smith, C Aubrey *see also* Smith, Sir Aubrey
Smith, Charles 1920?- *FilmgC, WhoHol A*
Smith, Charles H 1866-1942 *Film 2, WhScrn 1, WhScrn 2, WhoHol B*
Smith, Charles Martin *WhoHol A*
Smith, Charlie Martin 1955- *IntMPA 1977*
Smith, Charlotte 1873-1928 *WhScrn 2*
Smith, Chris 1879-1949 *AmSCAP 1966, NotNAT B*
Smith, Clay 1877-1930 *AmSCAP 1966*
Smith, Clay 1885- *WhThe*
Smith, Cliff *Film 1*
Smith, Clifford d1937 *TwYS A*
Smith, Constance 1929- *FilmgC, IntMPA 1977, WhoHol A*
Smith, Cyril 1892-1963 *Film 1, Film 2, FilmgC, NotNAT B, WhScrn 1, WhScrn 2, WhThe, WhoHol B*
Smith, D A Clarke *Film 2*
Smith, Darwood K *WhoHol A*
Smith, David *TwYS A*
Smith, Dean *WhoHol A*
Smith, Delos V, Jr. *WhoHol A*
Smith, Derek 1927- *WhoThe 16*
Smith, Dodie 1896- *BiE&WWA, ConDr 1977, McGWD, NotNAT, PIP&P, WhoThe 16*
Smith, Donald *Film 2*

Smith, Donald Aumont 1922- *AmSCAP 1966*
Smith, Doyle R 1924- *BiE&WWA, NotNAT*
Smith, Dudley *Film 2*
Smith, Dwan *WhoHol A*
Smith, Dwight 1857-1949 *WhScrn 1, WhScrn 2*
Smith, Earl E T 1903- *CelR 3*
Smith, Earl Hobson 1898- *NatPD*
Smith, Eddie d1964 *NotNAT B*
Smith, Edgar 1857-1938 *AmSCAP 1966, EncMT, NewMT, NotNAT B, WhThe, WhoStg 1906, WhoStg 1908*
Smith, Edward Tyrrell 1804-1877 *OxThe*
Smith, Elizabeth *WhoHol A*
Smith, Elmer d1963 *NotNAT B*
Smith, Elsie Linehan d1964 *NotNAT B*
Smith, Ethel 1910- *AmSCAP 1966, WhoHol A*
Smith, Florence *Film 1*
Smith, Francesca *WhoHol A*
Smith, Frank L d1953 *NotNAT B*
Smith, Frank M 1906- *AmSCAP 1966*
Smith, Frederick Theodore 1919- *AmSCAP 1966*
Smith, Frederick Wilson d1944 *NotNAT B*
Smith, G A 1864-1959 *FilmgC*
Smith, G Albert 1898-1959 *NotNAT B, WhScrn 1, WhScrn 2, WhoHol B*
Smith, George Albert 1864-1959 *DcFM, OxFilm, WorEnF*
Smith, George M 1912- *AmSCAP 1966*
Smith, George T d1947 *NotNAT B*
Smith, George W d1946 *NotNAT B*
Smith, George W 1899-1947 *WhScrn 1, WhScrn 2*
Smith, Gerald Oliver 1896-1974 *Film 2, WhScrn 2, WhoHol B*
Smith, Gregg 1931- *AmSCAP 1966*
Smith, Gunboat *Film 2*
Smith, H Allen 1907- *CelR 3*
Smith, H Reeves *Film 2, WhThe*
Smith, H Wakefield 1865-1956 *AmSCAP 1966*
Smith, Hal *WhoHol A*
Smith, Harry Bache 1860-1936 *AmSCAP 1966, EncMT, NewMT, NotNAT A, NotNAT B, WhThe, WhoStg 1906, WhoStg 1908*
Smith, Harvey 1904- *BiE&WWA*
Smith, Helen S 1909- *BiE&WWA*
Smith, Hezekiah Leroy Gordon 1909- *AmSCAP 1966*
Smith, Houston 1910- *AmSCAP 1966*
Smith, Howard *WomWMM*
Smith, Howard I 1893-1968 *Vers A, WhScrn 1, WhScrn 2, WhoHol B*
Smith, Howard I 1894-1968 *NotNAT B, WhThe*
Smith, Howard I 1895-1968 *BiE&WWA*
Smith, Howard K 1914- *CelR 3, IntMPA 1977*
Smith, Hy 1934- *IntMPA 1977*
Smith, J Lewis 1906-1964 *WhScrn 2*
Smith, J Sebastian 1869-1948 *NotNAT B, WhThe*
Smith, J Stanley 1905-1974 *WhScrn 2*
Smith, J Stanley *see also* Smith, Stanley
Smith, Jack 1898-1950 *NotNAT B*
Smith, Jack 1932- *OxFilm*
Smith, Jack C 1896-1944 *WhScrn 1, WhScrn 2, WhoHol B*
Smith, Jacqueline 1933- *IntMPA 1977*
Smith, Jay R *Film 2*
Smith, Joe *Film 2*
Smith, Joe d1952 *NotNAT B*
Smith, Joe 1884- *WhoHol A*
Smith, Joe 1900-1952 *WhScrn 1, WhScrn 2, WhoHol B*
Smith, John 1931- *FilmgC, WhoHol A*
Smith, John Shaffer, Jr. 1913- *AmSCAP 1966*
Smith, Judy *WomWMM B*
Smith, Julia 1911- *AmSCAP 1966*

Smith, June *WomWMM B*
Smith, Justin *WhoHol A*
Smith, Karen *WhoHol A*
Smith, Kate 1909- *IntMPA 1977, NewYTET, PIP&P, ThFT, WhoHol A*
Smith, Keely 1932- *AmSCAP 1966, WhoHol A*
Smith, Kent 1907- *BiE&WWA, FilmgC, HolP 40, IntMPA 1977, MovMk, NotNAT, WhoHol A, WhoThe 16*
Smith, L *Film 2*
Smith, Lane *WhoHol A*
Smith, Larry Michael 1939- *AmSCAP 1966*
Smith, Leigh R *Film 2*
Smith, Lela *WomWMM A, WomWMM B*
Smith, Leona May 1914- *AmSCAP 1966*
Smith, Leonard B 1915- *AmSCAP 1966*
Smith, Leonard O *WhoHol A*
Smith, Leonard R 1889-1958 *WhScrn 1, WhScrn 2*
Smith, Lois 1930- *BiE&WWA, NotNAT, WhoHol A, WhoThe 16*
Smith, Loring 1895- *BiE&WWA, NotNAT, WhThe, WhoHol A*
Smith, Lynn *WomWMM B*
Smith, Mabel *WhScrn 2*
Smith, Madeline *WhoHol A*
Smith, Maggie 1934- *BiDFlm, CelR 3, CnThe, EncMT, FilmgC, IntMPA 1977, MotPP, MovMk, PIP&P, WhoHol A, WhoThe 16*
Smith, Marcus 1829-1874 *OxThe*
Smith, Margaret Chase 1897- *CelR 3*
Smith, Margaret M 1881-1960 *WhScrn 1, WhScrn 2, WhoHol B*
Smith, Mark 1829-1874 *NotNAT B*
Smith, Mark 1886-1944 *NotNAT B, WhScrn 2*
Smith, Mary Cecelia 1913- *AmSCAP 1966*
Smith, Mary Stewart *WomWMM B*
Smith, Matthew 1905-1953 *WhScrn 1, WhScrn 2, WhoHol B*
Smith, Maurice 1939- *IntMPA 1977*
Smith, Michael 1935- *ConDr 1977*
Smith, Milton 1890- *BiE&WWA, NotNAT*
Smith, Moses d1964 *NotNAT B*
Smith, Muriel 1923- *BiE&WWA, NotNAT, WhoHol A*
Smith, Nayland *Film 2*
Smith, Noel Mason *TwYS A*
Smith, Norwood 1915- *BiE&WWA, NotNAT, WhoHol A*
Smith, Oliver 1918- *BiE&WWA, CelR 3, NotNAT, PIP&P, WhoThe 16*
Smith, Oscar *Film 2*
Smith, Oswald J 1889- *AmSCAP 1966*
Smith, Patricia 1930- *BiE&WWA, NotNAT, WhoHol A*
Smith, Paul *WhoHol A*
Smith, Paul G 1894-1968 *NotNAT B*
Smith, Paul Gerald d1968 *WhScrn 2*
Smith, Paul Gerard 1894- *BiE&WWA*
Smith, Paul Girard *WhThe*
Smith, Paul J 1906- *AmSCAP 1966*
Smith, Pete 1892- *FilmgC, IntMPA 1977*
Smith, Pleasant 1886-1969 *WhScrn 1, WhScrn 2*
Smith, Putter *WhoHol A*
Smith, Queenie 1898- *WhoHol A*
Smith, Queenie 1902- *EncMT, WhThe*
Smith, Ralph G 1906- *IntMPA 1977*
Smith, Ray E *IntMPA 1977*
Smith, Rebecca Dianna *WhoHol A*
Smith, Red 1905- *CelR 3*
Smith, Reid *WhoHol A*
Smith, Richard B 1901-1935 *AmSCAP 1966*
Smith, Richard Penn 1799-1854 *NotNAT B, OxThe*

Smith, Richard Penn 1799-1958 *PIP&P*
Smith, Robert Bache 1875-1951 *AmSCAP 1966, EncMT, NewMT, NotNAT B, WhThe*
Smith, Robert Kimmel 1930- *NatPD*
Smith, Robert Paul 1915- *BiE&WWA, NotNAT*
Smith, Robert W, Jr. 1929- *AmSCAP 1966*
Smith, Roger 1932- *FilmgC, IntMPA 1977, MotPP, MovMk, WhoHol A*
Smith, Roger Montgomery 1915-1975 *AmSCAP 1966*
Smith, Ruby Mae 1902- *AmSCAP 1966*
Smith, Sammy *WhoHol A*
Smith, Sharon *WomWMM B*
Smith, Sid 1892-1928 *Film 1, Film 2, WhoHol B*
Smith, Sidney d1935 *WhThe*
Smith, Sidney 1892-1928 *WhScrn 1, WhScrn 2*
Smith, Sidney F R *NewYTET*
Smith, Sol 1801-1869 *NotNAT B*
Smith, Solomon Franklin 1801-1869 *NotNAT A, OxThe*
Smith, Stan 1946- *CelR 3*
Smith, Stanley 1905-1974 *Film 2, WhoHol B*
Smith, Stanley *see also* Smith, J Stanley
Smith, Sydney *WhoHol A*
Smith, Sydney d1935 *NotNAT B*
Smith, Ted *Film 2*
Smith, Thomas C 1892-1950 *WhScrn 1, WhScrn 2, WhoHol B*
Smith, Thorne 1892-1934 *FilmgC*
Smith, Tom d1976 *WhoHol C*
Smith, Truman *WhoHol A*
Smith, Vincent *WhoHol A*
Smith, Viola *Film 1*
Smith, Vivian *Film 2*
Smith, Wallace 1923- *BiE&WWA, NotNAT*
Smith, Walter Wallace 1894-1948 *AmSCAP 1966*
Smith, Wentworth 1601-1620 *NotNAT B*
Smith, Whispering Jack 1898-1950 *Film 2, WhScrn 2*
Smith, William *WhoHol A*
Smith, William d1696 *OxThe*
Smith, William 1730-1819 *NotNAT B, OxThe*
Smith, William H 1897- *AmSCAP 1966*
Smith, William Henry d1872 *NotNAT B*
Smith, Winchell 1871-1933 *CnMD, ModWD*
Smith, Winchell 1872-1933 *NotNAT B, WhThe*
Smith, Wonderful *WhoHol A*
Smithers, Florence *WhThe*
Smithers, Jan *WhoHol A*
Smithers, William *WhoHol A*
Smithson, Florence 1884-1936 *NotNAT B, WhThe*
Smithson, Frank d1949 *NotNAT B*
Smithson, Harriet Constance 1800-1854 *CnThe, OxThe*
Smithson, Henrietta Constance 1800-1854 *NotNAT B*
Smithson, Laura 1878-1963 *WhScrn 2, WhThe*
Smithson, Will d1927 *NotNAT B*
Smitterick, Grover d1914 *WhScrn 2*
Smoktunovsky, Innokenti 1925- *FilmgC*
Smolen, Donald E 1923- *IntMPA 1977*
Smoller, Dorothy 1901-1926 *WhScrn 1, WhScrn 2*
Smollett, Molly *WomWMM B*
Smollett, Tobias George 1721-1771 *NotNAT B*
Smothers, Dick *WhoHol A*
Smothers, Tom *WhoHol A*
Smothers Brothers *CelR 3*
Smythe, Florence 1878-1925 *WhScrn 1, WhScrn 2, WhoHol B*
Smythe, James Moore d1734 *NotNAT B*
Smythe, William G d1921 *NotNAT B*

Snaper, Wilbur 1911- *IntMPA 1977*
Snead, Sam 1912- *CelR 3*
Snegoff, Leonid 1883-1974 *Film 2, WhScrn 2*
Snel, Billy 1938- *AmSCAP 1966*
Snell, David L 1897- *AmSCAP 1966*
Snell, Paul 1904- *IntMPA 1977*
Snelling, Minnette 1878-1945 *WhScrn 1,
    WhScrn 2, WhoHol B*
Snider, Ralph E 1903- *IntMPA 1977*
Snitzer, Jimmy 1926-1945 *WhScrn 2*
Snitzer, Miriam 1922-1966 *WhScrn 2*
Snodgress, Carrie *IntMPA 1977, WhoHol A*
Snodgress, Carrie 1945- *MovMk*
Snodgress, Carrie 1946- *CelR 3*
Snookums *WhScrn 1, WhScrn 2*
Snow, Marguerite d1958 *MotPP, NotNAT B,
    WhoHol B*
Snow, Marguerite 1888-1958 *Film 1, Film 2,
    TwYS*
Snow, Marguerite 1889-1958 *WhScrn 1,
    WhScrn 2*
Snow, Michael 1929- *OxFilm*
Snow, Mortimer 1869-1935 *Film 2, WhScrn 1,
    WhScrn 2, WhoHol B*
Snow, Valaida d1956 *NotNAT B*
Snowden, Alec Crawford *IntMPA 1977*
Snowden, Carolynne *Film 2*
Snowden, Elmer Pops 1900-1973 *WhScrn 2*
Snowden, Leigh 1932- *IntMPA 1977, WhoHol A*
Snowdon, Roger *WhoHol A*
Snowhill, George H 1911- *AmSCAP 1966*
Snyder, Denton 1915- *BiE&WWA*
Snyder, Edward 1919- *AmSCAP 1966*
Snyder, Gene d1953 *NotNAT B*
Snyder, Jimmy *CelR 3*
Snyder, Matt d1917 *Film 1, WhScrn 2*
Snyder, Ted 1881-1965 *AmSCAP 1966*
Snyder, Tom 1936- *IntMPA 1977, NewYTET*
Snyder, William 1916- *AmSCAP 1966*
Snyder, William 1929- *ConDr 1977*
Snyder, William L 1920- *IntMPA 1977*
Soames, Arthur *Film 2*
Soane, George d1860 *NotNAT B*
Sobel, Bernard 1887-1964 *BiE&WWA,
    NotNAT B, WhThe*
Soberg, Alf 1903- *WorEnF*
Soble, Ron 1932- *IntMPA 1977, WhoHol A*
Sobol, Edward d1962 *NotNAT B*
Sobol, Louis 1896- *IntMPA 1977*
Sobolevsky, Pyotr *Film 2*
Soboloff, Arnold 1930- *BiE&WWA, NotNAT,
    WhoHol A, WhoThe 16*
Sobotka, Ruth 1925-1967 *NotNAT B, WhScrn 2*
Sochin, Irving 1910- *IntMPA 1977*
Socolow, Sanford *NewYTET*
Socrates *PIP&P*
Sodders, Carl d1958 *WhScrn 1, WhScrn 2*
Soderberg, Hjalmar 1869-1941 *CnMD*
Soderling, Walter d1968 *WhoHol B*
Soderling, Walter 1872-1948 *Vers A, WhScrn 2*
Sodero, Cesare 1886-1947 *AmSCAP 1966*
Soehnel, Ray 1900- *AmSCAP 1966*
Soehnel, Zelma 1909- *AmSCAP 1966*
Soell, John B 1911-1965 *AmSCAP 1966*
Sofaer, Abraham 1896- *FilmgC, IntMPA 1977,
    Vers B, WhoHol A, WhoThe 16*
Soffici, Mario 1900- *DcFM*
Sofronov, Anatol Vladimirovich 1911- *CnMD,
    OxThe*
Sofronov, Anatoli Vladimirovich 1911- *ModWD*
Sohlke, Gus 1865-1924 *NotNAT B, WhThe*
Sojberg, Gunnar *WhoHol A*
Sojin 1891-1954 *TwYS, WhScrn 2, WhoHol B*
Sojin, Kamiyama 1891-1954 *Film 2*

Sokol, Marilyn *WhoHol A*
Sokole, Lucy Bender *AmSCAP 1966*
Sokoloff, David 1910- *AmSCAP 1966*
Sokoloff, Vladimir 1889-1962 *FilmgC, MovMk,
    NotNAT B, Vers A, WhScrn 1, WhScrn 2*
Sokoloff, Vladimir 1890-1962 *Film 2, MotPP,
    WhoHol B*
Sokolova, Lydia 1896- *WhThe*
Sokolova, Natasha 1917- *WhThe*
Sokolove, Samuel 1914- *AmSCAP 1966*
Sokolow, Anna 1912- *BiE&WWA, NotNAT*
Sokolow, Ethel d1970 *WhScrn 2*
Sokolowska, Anna *WomWMM*
Solar, Willie d1956 *NotNAT B, WhoHol B*
Solari, Rudy *WhoHol A*
Soldani, Charles L 1893-1968 *WhScrn 2*
Soldano, Anthony 1927- *AmSCAP 1966*
Soldati, Mario 1905- *OxFilm*
Soldati, Mario 1906- *DcFM, FilmgC,
    IntMPA 1977, WorEnF*
Soldene, Emily 1840-1912 *NotNAT A,
    NotNAT B, OxThe*
Soldi, Stephen d1974 *WhScrn 2*
Solem, Delmar E 1915- *BiE&WWA, NotNAT*
Soler, Antonio Ruiz 1927- *WhThe*
Soler, Domingo 1902-1961 *WhScrn 2*
Soleri, Paolo 1919- *CelR 3*
Solis, Javier 1931-1966 *WhScrn 1, WhScrn 2*
Solis, Max 1913- *AmSCAP 1966*
Solis Y Rivadeneyra, Antonio De 1610-1686
    McGWD
Solito DeSolis, Aldo 1905- *AmSCAP 1966*
Solm, Fred *Film 2*
Solman, Alfred 1868-1937 *AmSCAP 1966*
Solntseva, Yulia 1901- *WomWMM, WorEnF*
Solo, Robert H *IntMPA 1977*
Solodovnikov, Alexandr Vasilievich 1904- *WhThe*
Sologub, Fyodor 1863-1927 *CnMD, McGWD,
    ModWD*
Solomon, Edward d1895 *NotNAT B*
Solomon, Florence *IntMPA 1977*
Solomon, Harold 1903- *AmSCAP 1966*
Solomon, Joseph 1897-1947 *AmSCAP 1966*
Solomon, Maureen C *WomWMM B*
Solomon, Theodore George 1920- *IntMPA 1977*
Solomon, Tina *WhoHol A*
Solon, Ewen 1923?- *FilmgC, WhoHol A*
Solorzano, Carlos 1922- *ModWD*
Solovyov, Vladimir Aleksandrovich 1907- *ModWD*
Solow, Sidney Paul 1910- *IntMPA 1977*
Soloway, Leonard 1928- *BiE&WWA*
Solski, Ludwik 1854-1954 *NotNAT B*
Solt, Andrew 1916- *IntMPA 1977*
Solters, Lee 1919- *BiE&WWA*
Solti, Georg 1912- *CelR 3*
Soltntseva, Yulia 1901- *DcFM*
Soltz, Charlene E *IntMPA 1977*
Soltz, Rose d1973 *WhScrn 2*
Solveg, Maria *Film 2*
Somack, Jack *WhoHol A*
Soman, Claude 1897-1960 *NotNAT B, WhThe*
Sombert, Claire *WhoHol A*
Somers, Brett *WhoHol A*
Somers, Bud *Film 2*
Somers, Carole d1974 *WhScrn 2*
Somers, Fred d1970 *WhScrn 2, WhoHol B*
Somersaloni, Urho *Film 2*
Somerset, C W 1847-1929 *NotNAT B, WhThe*
Somerset, Pat 1897-1974 *Film 2, WhScrn 2,
    WhoHol B, WomWMM*
Somerset, Patrick 1897-1974 *WhThe*
Somerville, John Baxter 1907-1963 *WhThe*
Somerville, Slim 1892- *TwYS*
Somes, Michael 1917- *WhThe, WhoHol A*

Somi, Leone Ebreo Di 1527-1592 *OxThe*
Somkin, Steven 1941- *NatPD*
Somlo, Josef 1885- *FilmgC*
Somlyo, Roy A 1925- *BiE&WWA*
Sommars, Julie *WhoHol A*
Sommer, Edith *BiE&WWA, NotNAT*
Sommer, Elke *MotPP, WhoHol A*
Sommer, Elke 1940- *FilmgC, MovMk*
Sommer, Elke 1941- *IntMPA 1977*
Sommer, Elke 1942- *CelR 3*
Sommers, Ben 1906- *BiE&WWA*
Sommers, Harry G d1953 *NotNAT B*
Sommers, Henry J 1918- *AmSCAP 1966*
Sommers, Joanie *WhoHol A*
Sommerschield, Rose Neiditch *WomWMM B*
Somnes, George d1956 *NotNAT B*
Somohano, Arturo 1910- *AmSCAP 1966*
Son Of Man Hammer *Film 2*
Sonal, Marc 1858- *WhThe*
Sondergaard, Gale *BiE&WWA, IntMPA 1977,*
    MotPP, NotNAT, Vers A
Sondergaard, Gale 1899- *FilmgC, MovMk, ThFT*
Sondergaard, Gale 1900- *WhoHol A*
Sondergaard, Gale 1901- *WhoThe 16*
Sondheim, Stephen 1930- *AmSCAP 1966,*
    BiE&WWA, CelR 3, EncMT, NatPD,
    NewMT, NotNAT, NotNAT A, PIP&P,
    PIP&P A, WhoThe 16
Sondheimer, Hans 1901- *BiE&WWA, NotNAT*
Sonenfeld, Otto *IntMPA 1977*
Sones, Carol *WomWMM B*
Sonja, Magda *Film 2*
Sonnemann, Emmy d1974 *WhoHol B*
Sonnenfels, Josef Von 1733-1817 *OxThe*
Sonneveld, Wim 1918-1974 *WhScrn 2, WhoHol B*
Sonny And Cher *CelR 3*
Sontag, Susan 1933- *CelR 3, OxFilm,*
    WomWMM
Soo, Jack *MotPP, WhoHol A*
Sopanen, Jeri *WomWMM*
Soper, Paul 1906- *BiE&WWA, NotNAT*
Sophocles 496?BC-406?BC *CnThe, McGWD,*
    NotNAT A, NotNAT B, OxThe, PIP&P,
    REnWD
Sophron *OxThe*
Sopkin, Henry 1903- *AmSCAP 1966*
Sorano, Daniel 1920-1962 *OxThe*
Soray, Turkan *WomWMM*
Sordi, Alberto *MotPP, WhoHol A*
Sordi, Alberto 1919- *FilmgC, MovMk*
Sordi, Alberto 1920- *OxFilm, WorEnF*
Sorel, Cecile d1966 *WhoHol B*
Sorel, Cecile 1873-1966 *WhThe*
Sorel, Cecile 1874-1966 *WhScrn 1, WhScrn 2*
Sorel, Cecile 1875-1966 *NotNAT A*
Sorel, George S 1899-1948 *WhScrn 1, WhScrn 2,*
    WhoHol B
Sorel, Guy 1914- *NotNAT, WhoHol A*
Sorel, Jean 1934- *FilmgC, WhoHol A*
Sorel, Jeanne *WhoHol A*
Sorel, Louise 1944- *FilmgC, WhoHol A*
Sorelle, William *Film 1*
Sorensen, Linda *WhoHol A*
Sorensen, Paul *WhoHol A*
Soreny, Eva *WhoHol A*
Sorere, Gabrielle *WomWMM*
Soresi, Carl D 1916- *AmSCAP 1966*
Sorey, Vincent 1900- *AmSCAP 1966*
Sorge, Reinhard Johannes 1892-1916 *CnMD,*
    McGWD, ModWD, OxThe
Soria, Madeleine *WhThe*
Sorian, Jack *WhoHol A*
Soriano, Dale 1918- *IntMPA 1977*
Soriano DeAndia, Vicente *McGWD*

Sorin, Louis 1893-1961 *NotNAT B*
Sorin, Louis 1894-1961 *Film 2, WhScrn 1,*
    WhScrn 2, WhoHol B
Sorina, Alexandra *Film 2*
Sorkin, Barney 1903-1973 *WhScrn 2*
Sorley, Edward *Film 2*
Sorma, Agnes 1865-1927 *NotNAT B, OxThe*
Sornoff, Sidney 1921-1962 *AmSCAP 1966*
Sorrell, Helena *IntMPA 1977*
Sorrells, Robert *WhoHol A*
Sorrentina d1973 *WhScrn 2*
Sorrentino, Charles 1906- *AmSCAP 1966*
Sorrin, Ellen *WomWMM B*
Sorvino, Paul 1939- *PIP&P A, WhoHol A,*
    WhoThe 16
Sosa, Geo Anne *WhoHol A*
Sosa, Susan *WhoHol A*
Sosenko, Anna 1910- *AmSCAP 1966*
Sosnik, Harry 1906- *AmSCAP 1966*
Sotelo, Joaquin Calvo 1905- *CnMD*
Sothern, Ann *AmSCAP 1966, MotPP*
Sothern, Ann 1909- *EncMT, Film 2, FilmgC,*
    MGM, MovMk, ThFT, WhThe, WorEnF
Sothern, Ann 1911- *WhoHol A*
Sothern, Ann 1912?- *OxFilm*
Sothern, Ann 1923- *IntMPA 1977*
Sothern, E A 1826-1881 *NotNAT B, PIP&P*
Sothern, E H 1859-1933 *Film 1, WhoHol B*
Sothern, Edward Askew 1826-1881 *FamA&A,*
    NotNAT A, OxThe
Sothern, Edward Hugh 1859-1933 *FamA&A,*
    NotNAT A, NotNAT B, OxThe, WhScrn 1,
    WhScrn 2, WhThe, WhoStg 1906,
    WhoStg 1908
Sothern, Edwin Hugh 1859-1933 *PIP&P*
Sothern, Ethel 1882-1957 *WhScrn 1, WhScrn 2*
Sothern, Eve 1898- *Film 1*
Sothern, Eve see also Southern, Eve
Sothern, Harry 1883-1957 *NotNAT B*
Sothern, Harry 1884-1957 *Film 2, WhScrn 1,*
    WhScrn 2, WhoHol B
Sothern, Hugh 1881-1947 *NotNAT B, WhScrn 1,*
    WhScrn 2, WhoHol B
Sothern, Janet Evelyn *WhThe*
Sothern, Jean d1964 *NotNAT B*
Sothern, Jean 1895-1924 *Film 1, WhScrn 1,*
    WhScrn 2, WhoHol B
Sothern, Sam 1870-1920 *NotNAT B, WhThe,*
    WhoHol B
Sothern, Sam see also Southern, Sam
Soto, Luchy 1920-1970 *WhScrn 1, WhScrn 2*
Soto, Roberto 1888-1960 *WhScrn 1, WhScrn 2,*
    WhoHol B
Sotomayor, Jose 1905-1967 *WhScrn 1, WhScrn 2*
Souchet, H A Du *WhThe*
Soudeikine, Serge d1946 *NotNAT B*
Souers, Mildred 1894- *AmSCAP 1966*
Soul, David *WhoHol A*
Soule, Olan *WhoHol A*
Soule, Robert 1926- *BiE&WWA, NotNAT*
Soules, Dale *WhoHol A*
Soulten, Graham *Film 2*
Soumagne, Henri 1891-1951 *ModWD*
Soupault, Philippe 1897- *ModWD*
Souper, G Kay d1947 *NotNAT B*
Souper, Kay d1947 *WhoHol B*
Sousa, John Philip 1854-1932 *AmSCAP 1966,*
    EncMT, NotNAT B, WhThe, WhoStg 1906,
    WhoStg 1908
Soussanin, Nicholas 1909-1975 *Film 2, WhScrn 2,*
    WhoHol C
Soutar, Andrew d1941 *NotNAT B*
Soutar, J Farren 1870-1962 *WhThe*
Soutar, Robert d1908 *NotNAT B*

South, Eddie 1904-1962 *NotNAT B*
Southard, Harry D 1881-1939 *WhScrn 1,*
 WhScrn 2, WhoHol B
Southern, Eve 1898- *Film 2, TwYS*
Southern, Eve *see also* Sothern, Eve
Southern, John 1893- *WhThe*
Southern, Richard *WhoHol A*
Southern, Sam 1870-1920 *Film 1, Film 2, TwYS,*
 WhScrn 1, WhScrn 2
Southern, Sam *see also* Sothern, Sam
Southern, Terry 1924- *ConDr 1977A*
Southern, Virginia *Film 2*
Southerne, Thomas 1660-1746 *NotNAT B, OxThe,*
 PlP&P
Southgate, Elsie 1890- *WhThe*
Southgate, Howard S 1895-1971 *WhScrn 1,*
 WhScrn 2
Southwick, Dale 1913-1968 *WhScrn 1, WhScrn 2,*
 WhoHol B
Soutsos, Alexandros *REnWD*
Soutsos, Panayiotis *REnWD*
Sovern, Clarence 1900-1929 *WhScrn 1, WhScrn 2,*
 WhoHol B
Sovey, Raymond 1897-1966 *BiE&WWA,*
 NotNAT B, PlP&P, WhThe
Sowards, George Albert 1888-1975 *WhScrn 2*
Sowards, Len 1893-1962 *NotNAT B, WhScrn 1,*
 WhScrn 2
Sowerby, Katherine Githa *WhThe*
Sowerby, Leo 1895-1968 *AmSCAP 1966*
Soya, Carl-Erik 1896- *CnMD, CnThe, McGWD,*
 ModWD, OxThe, REnWD
Soyer, Moses 1899- *CelR 3*
Soyer, Raphael 1899- *CelR 3*
Soyinka, Wole 1934- *CnThe, ConDr 1977,*
 ModWD, REnWD
Spaak, Agnes *WhoHol A*
Spaak, Catherine 1945- *FilmgC, MotPP,*
 WhoHol A, WorEnF
Spaak, Charles 1903-1975 *DcFM, FilmgC,*
 OxFilm, WhoHol C, WorEnF
Space, Arthur *WhoHol A*
Spacek, Sissy *WhoHol A*
Spacey, John G 1895-1940 *WhScrn 1, WhScrn 2,*
 WhoHol B
Spadaro, Odoardo 1894-1965 *WhScrn 2*
Spade, Marcello *Film 2*
Spaeth, Merrie 1949?- *WhoHol A*
Spaeth, Sigmund Gottfried 1885-1965
 AmSCAP 1966
Spagnoli, Genaro *Film 2*
Spahn, Warren 1921- *CelR 3*
Spain, Elsie *WhThe*
Spain, Fay *MotPP, WhoHol A*
Spain, Nancy 1918-1964 *WhScrn 2*
Spalding, Albert 1888-1953 *AmSCAP 1966*
Spalding, Graydon 1911- *NotNAT*
Spalla, Joseph Salvatore 1923- *IntMPA 1977*
Span, Norman *AmSCAP 1966*
Spandaro, Odoardo 1894-1965 *WhScrn 1*
Spanier, Muggsy 1903-1967 *WhScrn 1, WhScrn 2,*
 WhoHol B
Sparacino, Angelo 1914- *AmSCAP 1966*
Sparer, Paul *NotNAT, WhoHol A, WhoThe 16*
Sparger, Rex *NewYTET*
Sparks, Joseph M 1856- *WhoStg 1906,*
 WhoStg 1908
Sparks, Martha Lee *Film 2*
Sparks, Ned d1957 *MotPP, NotNAT B,*
 WhoHol B
Sparks, Ned 1883-1957 *Film 1, Film 2, FilmgC,*
 MovMk, TwYS, WhScrn 1, WhScrn 2
Sparks, Ned 1884-1957 *Vers A*
Sparks, Randy 1933- *AmSCAP 1966, WhoHol A*

Sparks, Robert *IntMPA 1977*
Sparkuhl, Theodor 1894-1945 *WorEnF*
Sparkuhl, Theodore 1894- *FilmgC*
Sparv, Camilla 1943- *FilmgC, WhoHol A*
Spaulding, George 1881-1959 *WhScrn 1,*
 WhScrn 2, WhoHol B
Spaulding, Nellie Parker *Film 2*
Speaight, Robert 1904- *PlP&P, WhoThe 16*
Speakman, W J 1903- *IntMPA 1977*
Speaks, Oley 1874-1948 *AmSCAP 1966,*
 NotNAT B
Spear, Harry 1921-1969 *Film 2, TwYS,*
 WhScrn 1, WhScrn 2, WhoHol B
Spear, Jack 1928- *AmSCAP 1966*
Spear, Sammy 1910-1975 *WhScrn 2*
Specktor, Frederick 1933- *IntMPA 1977*
Spector, Edward *BiE&WWA*
Spector, Joel *BiE&WWA*
Speechley, Billy 1911- *WhThe*
Speed, Carol *WhoHol A*
Speight, Johnny 1921- *ConDr 1977*
Speight, Johnny 1922- *McGWD*
Speizman, Morris 1905- *AmSCAP 1966*
Spell, George *WhoHol A*
Spell, Wanda *WhoHol A*
Speller, Robert *WhoHol A*
Spelling, Aaron *IntMPA 1977, NewYTET,*
 WhoHol A
Spellman, Leora 1891-1945 *WhScrn 1, WhScrn 2,*
 WhoHol B
Spelvin, George 1886?- *BiE&WWA, NotNAT*
Spelvin, George S *Film 2*
Spelvin, Georgina *WhoHol A*
Spence, Edward F 1860-1932 *NotNAT B, WhThe*
Spence, Lew 1920- *AmSCAP 1966*
Spence, Ralph 1889-1949 *NotNAT B, WhScrn 1,*
 WhScrn 2, WhoHol B
Spencer, Bud *WhoHol A*
Spencer, Colin 1933- *ConDr 1977*
Spencer, Dorothy *WomWMM*
Spencer, Douglas 1910-1960 *WhScrn 1,*
 WhScrn 2, WhoHol B
Spencer, Fleta Jan Brown 1883-1938
 AmSCAP 1966
Spencer, Fred d1952 *WhScrn 1, WhScrn 2*
Spencer, Gabriel d1598 *NotNAT B, OxThe*
Spencer, George Soule *Film 1*
Spencer, Glenn J 1910- *AmSCAP 1966*
Spencer, Helen 1903- *WhThe*
Spencer, Herbert 1878-1944 *AmSCAP 1966*
Spencer, James *Film 2*
Spencer, James Houston 1895- *AmSCAP 1966*
Spencer, Jessica 1919- *WhThe*
Spencer, John *OxThe*
Spencer, Kenneth 1913-1964 *NotNAT B,*
 WhScrn 1, WhScrn 2, WhoHol B
Spencer, Lucy 1884- *WhoStg 1906,*
 WhoStg 1908
Spencer, Mabel *WhoStg 1908*
Spencer, Marian 1905- *WhoHol A, WhoThe 16*
Spencer, Mary Ann *WomWMM B*
Spencer, Norman *Film 2, IntMPA 1977*
Spencer, Otis 1890-1958 *AmSCAP 1966*
Spencer, Robert *Film 2*
Spencer, Robert E 1902-1946 *AmSCAP 1966*
Spencer, T Guy, Jr. 1933- *IntMPA 1977*
Spencer, Terry 1895-1954 *WhScrn 1, WhScrn 2*
Spencer, Tim 1909-1974 *WhScrn 2, WhoHol B*
Spencer, Willard 1852-1933 *NotNAT B*
Spender, Stephen 1909- *CnMD, ModWD*
Spenser, Jeremy 1937- *FilmgC, IntMPA 1977,*
 WhoHol A
Sperling, Hazel *Film 2*
Sperling, Karen *WhoHol A, WomWMM,*

WomWMM B
Sperling, Milton 1912- *FilmgC, IntMPA 1977, WorEnF*
Speroni, Sperone 1500-1588 *McGWD, OxThe*
Sperr, Martin 1944- *CroCD*
Spewack, Bella 1899- *BiE&WWA, ConDr 1977D, EncMT, IntMPA 1977, McGWD, ModWD, NewMT, NotNAT, WhThe, WomWMM*
Spewack, Sam 1899-1971 *EncMT, FilmgC*
Spewack, Samuel 1899-1971 *BiE&WWA, CnMD, McGWD, ModWD, NewMT, NotNAT B, WhThe*
Speyer, Eve *Film 2*
Spheeris, Penelope *WomWMM B*
Spheeris, Penny *WomWMM A*
Spialek, Hans *AmSCAP 1966*
Spickol, Max 1913- *AmSCAP 1966*
Spiegel, Larry 1938- *IntMPA 1977*
Spiegel, Olga *WomWMM B*
Spiegel, Sam 1901- *CelR 3, FilmgC*
Spiegel, Sam 1903- *IntMPA 1977*
Spiegel, Sam 1904- *BiDFlm, OxFilm, WorEnF*
Spiegel, Ted *IntMPA 1977*
Spiegelberg, Christian d1732 *OxThe*
Spielberg, David *WhoHol A*
Spielberg, Steven 1946- *FilmgC*
Spielberg, Steven 1947- *IntMPA 1977*
Spielman, Fred *AmSCAP 1966*
Spier, Harry R 1888-1952 *AmSCAP 1966*
Spier, Larry 1901-1956 *AmSCAP 1966*
Spier, William *IntMPA 1977*
Spies, Claudio 1925- *AmSCAP 1966*
Spigelgass, Leonard 1908- *BiE&WWA, IntMPA 1977, NotNAT, WhoThe 16*
Spiker, Ray 1902-1964 *NotNAT B, WhScrn 1, WhScrn 2, WhoHol B*
Spikes, Benjamin 1888- *AmSCAP 1966*
Spikes, John C 1882-1955 *AmSCAP 1966*
Spillane, Mickey 1918- *CelR 3, FilmgC, WhoHol A*
Spillard, William J 1888- *AmSCAP 1966*
Spiller, Emily d1941 *NotNAT B*
Spils, Mai *WomWMM*
Spina, Harold 1906- *AmSCAP 1966*
Spindel, Jerry 1944- *NatPD*
Spindle, Louise Cooper *AmSCAP 1966*
Spinelli, Andree 1891- *WhThe*
Spinetti, Victor *WhoHol A*
Spinetti, Victor 1932- *FilmgC*
Spinetti, Victor 1933- *WhoThe 16*
Spingler, Harry 1890-1953 *WhScrn 1, WhScrn 2, WhoHol B*
Spinks, Garland 1908- *AmSCAP 1966*
Spinosa, Tom 1922- *AmSCAP 1966*
Spira, Camilla *Film 2*
Spira, Francoise d1965 *WhScrn 1, WhScrn 2*
Spires, John B *IntMPA 1977*
Spitalny, H Leopold 1887- *AmSCAP 1966*
Spitalny, Maurice 1893- *AmSCAP 1966*
Spitalny, Phil 1890-1970 *AmSCAP 1966, WhScrn 1, WhScrn 2, WhoHol B*
Spitz, Henry 1905- *IntMPA 1977*
Spitz, Mark 1950- *CelR 3*
Spitzer, Marian *Film 2, IntMPA 1977*
Spitzer, Murray *NatPD*
Spivak, Alice *WhoHol A*
Spivak, Lawrence E 1900- *CelR 3, IntMPA 1977*
Spivery, William 1930- *AmSCAP 1966*
Spivey, Victoria *Film 2*
Spivy 1907-1971 *WhScrn 1, WhoHol B*
Spivy, Madame 1907-1971 *WhScrn 2*
Splane, Elza K 1905-1968 *WhScrn 1, WhScrn 2*
Splettstober, Erwin *Film 2*
Spock, Benjamin 1903- *CelR 3*

Spodick, Robert C 1919- *IntMPA 1977*
Spofford, Charles M 1902- *BiE&WWA*
Spoliansky, Mischa 1898- *FilmgC, OxFilm*
Spong, Hilda 1875-1955 *NotNAT B, WhScrn 1, WhScrn 2, WhThe*
Spong, Hilda 1875-1966 *WhoHol B, WhoStg 1906, WhoStg 1908*
Spong, W B d1929 *NotNAT B*
Spooner, Cecil *Film 1, WhThe*
Spooner, Edna May d1953 *NotNAT B, WhThe, WhoHol B*
Sport *WhScrn 2*
Spottiswoode, Raymond 1913-1970 *OxFilm*
Spottswood, James 1882-1940 *Film 2, NotNAT B, WhScrn 1, WhScrn 2, WhoHol B*
Spradling, G D *WhoHol A*
Spratley, Tom *WhoHol A*
Sprigge, Elizabeth 1900- *BiE&WWA, NotNAT*
Spriggs, Elizabeth 1929- *CnThe, WhoHol A, WhoThe 16*
Spring, Helen *WhoHol A*
Spring, Sylvia *WomWMM, WomWMM B*
Springer, Gary *WhoHol A*
Springer, Joseph R 1897- *IntMPA 1977*
Springer, Philip 1926- *AmSCAP 1966*
Springett, Freddie 1915- *WhThe*
Springsteen, R G 1904- *FilmgC, IntMPA 1977, WorEnF*
Spross, Charles Gilbert 1874-1962 *AmSCAP 1966*
Sprotte, Bert 1871-1949 *Film 2, WhScrn 2*
Sproule, Ruth 1910-1968 *WhScrn 2*
Spry, Henry d1904 *NotNAT B*
Spurling, John 1936- *ConDr 1977*
Squarzina, Luigi 1922- *CnMD, McGWD*
Squibb, June 1935- *BiE&WWA, NotNAT*
Squire, Sir John Collings 1884-1958 *ModWD*
Squire, Katherine 1903- *BiE&WWA, NotNAT, WhoHol A, WhoThe 16*
Squire, Ronald 1886-1958 *FilmgC, NotNAT B, WhScrn 1, WhScrn 2, WhThe, WhoHol B*
Squire, William 1920- *BiE&WWA, NotNAT, PlP&P, WhoHol A, WhoThe 16*
Squires, Emily *WomWMM B*
Squires, Harry D 1897-1961 *AmSCAP 1966*
Sritrange, Wandee 1950-1975 *WhScrn 2*
Stack, Robert 1919- *BiDFlm, CelR 3, FilmgC, IntMPA 1977, MotPP, MovMk, WhoHol A, WorEnF*
Stack, William 1882- *WhThe*
Stacy, James *WhoHol A*
Stadlen, Lewis J 1947- *NotNAT, PlP&P A, WhoThe 16*
Staff, May *PlP&P*
Stafford, Barbara *WomWMM B*
Stafford, Brendan J *IntMPA 1977*
Stafford, Frederick 1928- *FilmgC, WhoHol A*
Stafford, Hanley 1898-1968 *WhScrn 1, WhScrn 2, WhoHol B*
Stafford, Tim *WhoHol A*
Stafford-Clark, Max 1941- *WhoThe 16*
Stagg, Charles d1735 *NotNAT B, OxThe, PlP&P*
Stagg, Mary *OxThe*
Stagnelius, Erik Johann 1793-1823 *OxThe*
Stahl, Al *IntMPA 1977*
Stahl, Herbert M 1914- *BiE&WWA, NotNAT*
Stahl, John M 1886-1950 *BiDFlm, CmMov, DcFM, FilmgC, MovMk, TwYS A, WorEnF*
Stahl, Max *BiE&WWA*
Stahl, Rose *Film 1*
Stahl, Rose 1870-1955 *WhThe*
Stahl, Rose 1875?-1955 *NotNAT B, WhoStg 1908*

Stahl, Stanley *BiE&WWA*
Stahl, Walter O 1884-1943 *WhScrn 1, WhScrn 2,
    WhoHol B*
Stahl-Nachbauer, Ernst *Film 2*
Stahl-Nachbaur, Ernst 1886-1960 *WhScrn 1,
    WhScrn 2, WhoHol B*
Staiger, Libi 1928- *BiE&WWA, NotNAT,
    WhoHol A*
Stainton, Philip 1908-1961 *FilmgC, WhThe,
    WhoHol A*
Stalenin, Evan *Film 2*
Staley, Joan *WhoHol A*
Stall, Karl 1871-1947 *WhScrn 2*
Stallings, Laurence 1894-1968 *BiE&WWA,
    FilmgC, McGWD, ModWD, NotNAT B,
    PIP&P, WhThe*
Stalmaster, Hal *WhoHol A*
Stambaugh, Jack *Film 2*
Stammers, Frank d1921 *NotNAT B*
Stamp, Terence *MotPP, WhoHol A*
Stamp, Terence 1938- *IntMPA 1977*
Stamp, Terence 1940- *FilmgC, MovMk, OxFilm,
    WorEnF*
Stamp-Taylor, Enid 1904-1946 *Film 2, FilmgC,
    WhScrn 1, WhScrn 2, WhThe, WhoHol B*
Stamper, Dave 1883-1963 *NewMT, WhThe*
Stamper, David 1883-1963 *AmSCAP 1966,
    NotNAT B*
Stamper, F Pope 1880-1950 *NotNAT B, WhThe*
Stampfer, Simon Ritter Von *DcFM*
Stander, Lionel 1908- *BiE&WWA, FilmgC,
    IntMPA 1977, MotPP, MovMk, NotNAT,
    Vers A, WhoHol A*
Standing, Charlene 1921-1957 *WhScrn 1,
    WhScrn 2*
Standing, Charles Wyndham 1880- *WhThe*
Standing, Ellen d1906 *NotNAT B*
Standing, Emily d1899 *NotNAT B*
Standing, Gordon d1927 *Film 2, WhScrn 1,
    WhScrn 2, WhoHol B*
Standing, Sir Guy 1873-1937 *FilmgC, MotPP,
    NotNAT B, WhScrn 1, WhScrn 2, WhThe,
    WhoHol B, WhoStg 1906, WhoStg 1908*
Standing, Guy, Jr. d1954 *WhScrn 1, WhScrn 2,
    WhoHol B*
Standing, Herbert *Film 1*
Standing, Herbert 1846-1923 *NotNAT B,
    WhScrn 2, WhThe, WhoStg 1906,
    WhoStg 1908*
Standing, Herbert 1846-1928 *WhScrn 1*
Standing, Herbert 1884-1955 *Film 2, NotNAT B,
    WhScrn 1, WhScrn 2, WhoHol B*
Standing, Jack 1886-1917 *Film 1, WhScrn 2*
Standing, Joan 1903- *Film 2*
Standing, John 1934- *FilmgC, WhoHol A,
    WhoThe 16*
Standing, Percy Darnell *Film 1, Film 2*
Standing, Wyndham 1880-1963 *Film 1, Film 2,
    TwYS, WhScrn 2*
Standish, Pamela 1920- *WhThe*
Stanfield, Clarkson 1793-1867 *NotNAT B, OxThe*
Stanfill, Dennis C 1927- *IntMPA 1977,
    NewYTET*
Stanford, Henry 1872-1921 *NotNAT B, WhThe,
    WhoHol B, WhoStg 1906, WhoStg 1908*
Stanford, Stanley *Film 2*
Stang, Arnold *WhoHol A*
Stang, Arnold 1925- *AmSCAP 1966,
    BiE&WWA*
Stang, Arnold 1926- *Vers A*
Stang, Arnold 1927- *IntMPA 1977*
Stang, Betsy *WomWMM B*
Stange, Claude Richard 1913- *CnMD*
Stange, Stanislaus d1917 *EncMT, NotNAT B,*

WhThe
Stanhope, Ted *WhoHol A*
Stanhope, Warren *WhoHol A*
Stanislaus, Frederick d1891 *NotNAT B*
Stanislavska, Marie Lilina *PIP&P*
Stanislavsky, Constantin Sergeivich 1863-1938
    NotNAT B
Stanislavsky, Konstantin Sergeivich 1863-1938
    OxThe
Stanislavsky, Konstantin Sergeyevich 1863-1938
    OxFilm
Stanislavsky, Konstantin Sergeyevich 1865-1938
    CnThe
Stanislawski, Constantine 1863-1938 *WhThe*
Stanlaws, Penrhyn d1923 *TwYS A*
Stanley, Adelaide 1906- *WhThe*
Stanley, Alma 1854-1931 *NotNAT B, WhThe*
Stanley, Charles 1922- *AmSCAP 1966*
Stanley, Edwin 1880-1944 *WhScrn 1, WhScrn 2,
    WhoHol B*
Stanley, Eric 1884- *WhThe*
Stanley, Florence *WhoHol A, WhoThe 16*
Stanley, Forest 1889-1969 *Film 1, Film 2*
Stanley, Forrest 1889-1969 *TwYS, WhScrn 2*
Stanley, George *Film 1*
Stanley, Henry *Film 1*
Stanley, Jack *WhoHol A*
Stanley, Jack 1890-1936 *AmSCAP 1966*
Stanley, Ken *WhoHol A*
Stanley, Kim *MotPP*
Stanley, Kim 1921- *FilmgC, WhoThe 16*
Stanley, Kim 1925- *BiE&WWA, CnThe,
    MovMk, NotNAT, WhoHol A*
Stanley, Lilian d1943 *NotNAT B*
Stanley, Marion *WhoStg 1908*
Stanley, Martha 1879- *WhThe*
Stanley, Maxfield *Film 1*
Stanley, Pamela 1909- *WhThe*
Stanley, Pat 1931- *BiE&WWA, NotNAT,
    WhoHol A*
Stanley, Phyllis 1914- *IntMPA 1977, WhThe*
Stanley, Ralph Nick 1914-1972 *WhScrn 2,
    WhoHol A*
Stanley, Robert 1902- *AmSCAP 1966*
Stanley, S Victor 1892-1939 *NotNAT B,
    WhScrn 1, WhScrn 2, WhThe*
Stanmore, Frank d1943 *WhoHol B*
Stanmore, Frank 1877-1943 *Film 2*
Stanmore, Frank 1878-1943 *NotNAT B, WhThe*
Stannard, Heather 1928- *WhThe*
Stano, Henry 1908- *AmSCAP 1966*
Stantley, Ralph d1964 *NotNAT B*
Stantley, Ralph d1972 *WhoHol B*
Stanton, Betty *WhoHol A*
Stanton, Francis Hayward 1913- *AmSCAP 1966,
    NatPD*
Stanton, Frank 1908- *BiE&WWA, CelR 3,
    NewYTET*
Stanton, Frank Lebby 1857-1927 *AmSCAP 1966*
Stanton, Fred R 1881-1925 *Film 1, Film 2,
    WhoHol B*
Stanton, Frederick R 1881-1925 *WhScrn 1,
    WhScrn 2*
Stanton, Harry *WhoHol A*
Stanton, Harry Dean *WhoHol A*
Stanton, Jane C *WomWMM*
Stanton, Larry T d1955 *WhScrn 1, WhScrn 2*
Stanton, Paul 1884-1955 *WhScrn 2*
Stanton, Richard *Film 1, TwYS A*
Stanton, Royal Waltz 1916- *AmSCAP 1966*
Stanton, Will 1885-1969 *Film 2, WhScrn 2*
Stanwood, Rita *Film 1*
Stanwyck, Barbara 1907- *BiDFlm, BiE&WWA,
    CelR 3, CmMov, Film 2, FilmgC,*

Steen, Marguerite 1894-1975 *WhScrn 2*
Steere, Clifton *WhoHol A*
Steers, Larry 1881-1951 *Film 1, Film 2, TwYS,
  WhScrn 1, WhScrn 2, WhoHol B*
Steevens, George d1800 *NotNAT B*
Stefan, Virginia 1926-1964 *NotNAT B,
  WhScrn 1, WhScrn 2, WhoHol B*
Stefanescu, Barbu *McGWD*
Stefano, Joseph 1922- *AmSCAP 1966*
Steffan, Geary *WhoHol A*
Steffen, Albert 1884-1963 *CnMD, ModWD,
  NotNAT B*
Steger, Julius d1959 *NotNAT B, WhoStg 1908*
Stegmeyer, William John 1916- *AmSCAP 1966*
Steguweit, Heinz d1964 *NotNAT B*
Stehli, Edgar 1884-1973 *BiE&WWA, NotNAT B,
  WhScrn 2, WhoHol B*
Stehlik, Miroslav 1916- *CnMD*
Steig, William 1917- *CelR 3*
Steiger, Jimmy 1896-1930 *AmSCAP 1966*
Steiger, Rod 1925- *BiDFlm, BiE&WWA,
  CelR 3, CmMov, FilmgC, IntMPA 1977,
  MotPP, MovMk, OxFilm, WhoHol A,
  WorEnF*
Stein, Alexander 1906- *CnMD*
Stein, Carol *WomWMM B*
Stein, Carol Eden 1927-1958 *WhScrn 1,
  WhScrn 2*
Stein, Gertrude 1874-1946 *CnMD, ModWD,
  NotNAT A, NotNAT B*
Stein, Joseph 1912- *BiE&WWA, ConDr 1977D,
  EncMT, IntMPA 1977, NatPD, NewMT,
  NotNAT, WhoThe 16*
Stein, Jules C 1896- *CelR 3, IntMPA 1977*
Stein, Julian 1924- *AmSCAP 1966*
Stein, Lotte *Film 2*
Stein, Mini *AmSCAP 1966*
Stein, Paul 1891-1952 *FilmgC*
Stein, Paul 1892- *TwYS A*
Stein, Ronald 1930- *AmSCAP 1966,
  IntMPA 1977*
Stein, Sam Sammy 1906-1966 *WhScrn 2*
Stein, Sammy 1906-1966 *WhoHol B*
Stein, Sarah *WomWMM B*
Stein, William 1918- *AmSCAP 1966*
Steinbeck, John 1902-1968 *BiE&WWA, CnMD,
  CnThe, FilmgC, McGWD, ModWD,
  NotNAT B, OxFilm, OxThe, WhThe*
Steinberg, Abraham 1897- *AmSCAP 1966*
Steinberg, Amy d1920 *NotNAT B*
Steinberg, David *WhoHol A*
Steinberg, Herb 1921- *IntMPA 1977*
Steinberg, Roslyn *WomWMM B*
Steinberg, Saul 1914- *CelR 3*
Steinberg, Susan *WomWMM B*
Steinberg, William 1899- *CelR 3*
Steinbrecher, Marcia *WomWMM B*
Steinem, Gloria 1935- *CelR 3*
Steiner, Elio 1905-1965 *WhScrn 1, WhScrn 2*
Steiner, Gary A d1966 *NewYTET*
Steiner, George 1900- *AmSCAP 1966*
Steiner, Herbert 1895-1964 *AmSCAP 1966*
Steiner, Howard *AmSCAP 1966*
Steiner, Ira 1915?- *BiE&WWA*
Steiner, Joseph *IntMPA 1977*
Steiner, Max 1888- *AmSCAP 1966, WorEnF*
Steiner, Max 1888-1971 *NotNAT B, OxFilm*
Steiner, Max 1888-1972 *CmMov, DcFM, FilmgC*
Steiner, Ralph 1899- *WorEnF*
Steinert, Alexander Lang 1900- *AmSCAP 1966*
Steinhardt, Herschel 1910- *NatPD*
Steinhoff, Hans 1882-1945 *DcFM, WorEnF*
Steininger, Franz K W 1906- *AmSCAP 1966*
Steinke, Hans 1893-1971 *WhScrn 1, WhScrn 2,*

WhoHol B
Steinkellner, Hans 1925- *NatPD*
Steinmetz, Earl 1915-1942 *WhScrn 1, WhScrn 2*
Steinrisck, Albert *Film 2*
Steinruck, Albert 1872-1929 *Film 2, WhScrn 2*
Steinrueck, Albert 1872-1929 *WhoHol B*
Stekly, Karel 1903- *DcFM*
Stellings, Ernest G *IntMPA 1977*
Stelloff, Skip 1925- *IntMPA 1977*
Steloff, Frances 1887- *BiE&WWA, NotNAT*
Stelzer, Frances C 1895- *AmSCAP 1966*
Stembler, John H 1913- *IntMPA 1977*
Sten, Anna *MotPP, WomWMM*
Sten, Anna 1907?- *WhoHol A*
Sten, Anna 1908- *FilmgC, HolP 30, MovMk,
  ThFT, WorEnF*
Sten, Anna 1910- *Film 2, OxFilm*
Stenback, Kirsten *WomWMM*
Stenermann, Salka *Film 2*
Stengel, Casey d1975 *WhoHol C*
Stengel, Casey 1890-1975 *WhScrn 2*
Stengel, Casey 1891-1975 *CelR 3*
Stengel, Leni *Film 2*
Stenholm, Katherine Alee Corne 1917-
  WomWMM A, WomWMM B
Steno 1917- *WorEnF*
Stepanek, Karel 1899- *FilmgC, MovMk, WhThe,
  WhoHol A*
Stephane, Nicole *WomWMM*
Stephen, John 1912-1974 *WhScrn 2*
Stephen, Susan 1931- *FilmgC, IntMPA 1977,
  WhoHol A*
Stephens, Ann 1931- *FilmgC, WhoHol A*
Stephens, Frances 1906- *WhThe*
Stephens, George d1851 *NotNAT B*
Stephens, H Pottinger d1903 *NotNAT B*
Stephens, Helen *WhoHol A*
Stephens, J Frank d1950 *NotNAT B*
Stephens, Jud 1888-1935 *WhScrn 1, WhScrn 2*
Stephens, Laraine *WhoHol A*
Stephens, Martin 1949- *FilmgC*
Stephens, Marvin 1949- *WhoHol A*
Stephens, Phillip Rodd 1940- *NatPD*
Stephens, Rachel *WhoHol A*
Stephens, Robert 1931- *CnThe, FilmgC,
  WhoHol A, WhoThe 16*
Stephens, Roy *WhoHol A*
Stephens, Sheila *WhoHol A*
Stephens, Socorro *WhoHol A*
Stephens, Stephanie 1900- *WhThe*
Stephens, Mrs. W H d1896 *NotNAT B*
Stephens, Ward 1869-1940 *AmSCAP 1966*
Stephens, Yorke 1862-1937 *NotNAT B, WhThe*
Stephensen, B C d1906 *NotNAT B*
Stephenson, Henry 1871-1956 *CmMov, Film 1,
  Film 2, FilmgC, MotPP, MovMk,
  NotNAT B, Vers A, WhScrn 1, WhScrn 2,
  WhoHol B*
Stephenson, Henry 1874- *WhThe*
Stephenson, James 1888-1941 *FilmgC, MotPP,
  NotNAT B, WhScrn 1, WhScrn 2,
  WhoHol B*
Stephenson, John d1963 *NotNAT B, WhoHol B*
Stephenson, John W 1922- *AmSCAP 1966*
Stephenson, Robert Robinson 1901-1970 *WhScrn 1,
  WhScrn 2, WhoHol B*
Stepin Fetchit 1892- *WhoHol A*
Stepin Fetchit 1896- *Film 2*
Steppat, Ilse 1917-1969 *WhScrn 1, WhScrn 2,
  WhoHol B*
Steppat, Ilse 1917-1970 *FilmgC*
Steppling, John C 1869-1932 *Film 1, Film 2,
  WhScrn 1, WhScrn 2, WhoHol B*
Stept, Sam H 1897-1964 *AmSCAP 1966*

Sterke, Jeanette WhoHol A
Sterler, Hermine Film 2
Sterling, Andrew B 1874-1955 AmSCAP 1966
Sterling, Bruce Film 2
Sterling, Dick WhoHol A
Sterling, Edythe 1887-1962 Film 2, NotNAT B,
   WhScrn 1, WhScrn 2, WhoHol B
Sterling, Ford 1880-1939 WhScrn 1, WhScrn 2
Sterling, Ford 1883-1939 FilmgC, MovMk,
   TwYS, TwYS A
Sterling, Ford 1884?-1939 NotNAT B,
   WhoHol B
Sterling, Ford 1885-1939 Film 1, Film 2
Sterling, Harriet Film 2
Sterling, Jan 1923- BiE&WWA, FilmgC,
   IntMPA 1977, MotPP, MovMk, NotNAT,
   WhoHol A, WhoThe 16
Sterling, Larry 1935-1958 WhScrn 1, WhScrn 2,
   WhoHol B
Sterling, Lee 1904-1951 WhScrn 1, WhScrn 2
Sterling, Merta 1883-1944 Film 2, WhScrn 1,
   WhScrn 2, WhoHol B
Sterling, Phil WhoHol A
Sterling, Raymond Andrew 1898- AmSCAP 1966
Sterling, Richard 1880-1959 NotNAT B, WhThe
Sterling, Robert 1917- BiE&WWA, FilmgC,
   IntMPA 1977, MGM, MotPP, WhoHol A
Sterling, Tisha WhoHol A
Stern, Alfred E F IntMPA 1977
Stern, Bert IntMPA 1977
Stern, Bill 1907-1971 IntMPA 1977, WhScrn 1,
   WhScrn 2, WhoHol B
Stern, Eddie 1917- IntMPA 1977
Stern, Edward J 1946- NotNAT
Stern, Ernest 1876-1954 NotNAT A, NotNAT B,
   WhThe
Stern, Ezra E 1908- IntMPA 1977
Stern, G B 1890- WhThe
Stern, Henry 1874-1966 AmSCAP 1966
Stern, Isaac 1920?- CelR 3, WhoHol A
Stern, Jack 1896- AmSCAP 1966
Stern, Jeanne 1908- DcFM
Stern, Joan Keller WomWMM B
Stern, Joseph W 1870-1934 NotNAT B
Stern, Kurt 1907- DcFM
Stern, Leonard B NewYTET
Stern, Louis 1860-1941 Film 2, WhScrn 1,
   WhScrn 2, WhoHol B
Stern, Robert L 1934- AmSCAP 1966
Stern, Sam 1883- WhThe
Stern, Stanley L 1917- IntMPA 1977
Stern, Stewart 1922- ConDr 1977A,
   IntMPA 1977, WorEnF
Stern, Tom WhoHol A
Stern, Wes WhoHol A
Sternad, Rudolph 1905-1963 IntMPA 1977,
   NotNAT B
Sternberg, Josef Von 1894-1969 DcFM, OxFilm
Sternburg, Janet WomWMM A, WomWMM B
Sterndale-Bennett, T C 1882-1944 NotNAT B,
   WhThe
Sterne, Morgan 1926- BiE&WWA, NotNAT,
   WhoHol A
Sternfield, Allen NatPD
Sternhagen, Frances 1930- BiE&WWA, NotNAT,
   WhoHol A, WhoThe 16
Sternheim, Carl 1878-1942 CnMD, CnThe,
   McGWD, ModWD, REnWD
Sternheim, Carl 1878-1943 NotNAT B, OxThe
Sternroyd, Vincent 1857-1948 NotNAT B,
   WhThe
Sterrall, Gertrude Film 2
Sterrett, Thomas Film 1
Stettheimer, Florine d1944 NotNAT B

Stettith, Olive d1937 NotNAT B
Steven, Boyd 1875-1967 WhScrn 1, WhScrn 2,
   WhoHol B
Steven, Gary WhoHol A
Stevens, Alex WhoHol A
Stevens, Ashton 1872-1951 NotNAT B, WhThe
Stevens, Byron E 1904-1964 WhScrn 1, WhScrn 2,
   WhoHol B
Stevens, Casandra Mayo d1966 AmSCAP 1966
Stevens, Charles 1893-1964 Film 1, Film 2,
   NotNAT B, TwYS, Vers B, WhScrn 1,
   WhScrn 2, WhoHol B
Stevens, Charlotte Film 2
Stevens, Clancey Film 2
Stevens, Clifford 1936- BiE&WWA, NotNAT
Stevens, Connie 1938- FilmgC, IntMPA 1977,
   MotPP, WhoHol A
Stevens, Craig 1918- BiE&WWA, FilmgC,
   HolP 40, IntMPA 1977, MotPP, MovMk,
   WhoHol A
Stevens, Cy d1974 WhoHol B
Stevens, Cye d1974 WhScrn 2
Stevens, David Kilburn 1860-1946 AmSCAP 1966
Stevens, Dodie WhoHol A
Stevens, Edwin 1860-1923 Film 1, Film 2, TwYS,
   WhScrn 2, WhThe
Stevens, Emily 1882-1928 Film 1, NotNAT B,
   WhScrn 1, WhScrn 2, WhThe, WhoHol B
Stevens, Emily Favela WomWMM B
Stevens, Evelyn 1891-1938 WhScrn 1, WhScrn 2,
   WhoHol B
Stevens, Fran WhoHol A
Stevens, Geoffrey WhoHol A
Stevens, George Film 1
Stevens, George 1904-1975 BiDFlm, CelR 3,
   CmMov, DcFM, FilmgC, MovMk, OxFilm,
   WhScrn 2, WorEnF
Stevens, George 1905-1975 Film 2
Stevens, George, Jr. 1932- CelR 3, IntMPA 1977
Stevens, George Alexander d1784 NotNAT B
Stevens, Georgia Cooper WhScrn 1, WhScrn 2
Stevens, Glenn 1899- AmSCAP 1966
Stevens, H C G 1892-1967 WhThe
Stevens, Inger d1970 MotPP, WhoHol B
Stevens, Inger 1934-1970 BiE&WWA,
   NotNAT B
Stevens, Inger 1935-1970 FilmgC, WhScrn 1,
   WhScrn 2
Stevens, Inger 1936-1970 MovMk
Stevens, Ira S 1922- IntMPA 1977
Stevens, John A d1916 NotNAT B
Stevens, Josephine Film 1
Stevens, Julie WhoHol A
Stevens, K T 1919- FilmgC, IntMPA 1977,
   WhThe, WhoHol A
Stevens, Kaye WhoHol A
Stevens, Lander 1877-1940 WhoHol B
Stevens, Landers 1877-1940 Film 2, WhScrn 1,
   WhScrn 2
Stevens, Lee 1930- IntMPA 1977
Stevens, Leith 1909-1970 WorEnF
Stevens, Leith 1910-1970 FilmgC
Stevens, Lenore WhoHol A
Stevens, Leslie 1924- BiE&WWA, FilmgC,
   IntMPA 1977, NewYTET, NotNAT,
   WorEnF
Stevens, Lester Film 2
Stevens, Lynn 1898-1950 WhScrn 1, WhScrn 2,
   WhoHol B
Stevens, Mark IntMPA 1977, MotPP
Stevens, Mark 1915- WhoHol A
Stevens, Mark 1916- FilmgC
Stevens, Morton 1929- AmSCAP 1966
Stevens, Morton L 1890-1959 NotNAT B,

WhScrn 1, WhScrn 2, WhoHol B
Stevens, Nan 1921- BiE&WWA
Stevens, Naomi WhoHol A
Stevens, Onslow IntMPA 1977
Stevens, Onslow 1902- FilmgC, MovMk, Vers A,
WhoHol A
Stevens, Onslow 1906- BiE&WWA, NotNAT,
WhThe
Stevens, Oren WhoHol A
Stevens, Paul 1924- BiE&WWA, NotNAT,
WhoHol A
Stevens, Rise 1913?- FilmgC, WhoHol A
Stevens, Robert 1880?-1963 NotNAT B,
WhScrn 1, WhScrn 2
Stevens, Robert 1882-1963 WhoHol B
Stevens, Robert 1925?- FilmgC
Stevens, Roger L 1910- BiE&WWA, CelR 3,
NotNAT, WhoThe 16
Stevens, Ronnie 1925- FilmgC, WhoHol A,
WhoThe 16
Stevens, Stella 1938- BiDFlm, FilmgC,
IntMPA 1977, MotPP, WhoHol A
Stevens, Thomas Wood d1942 NotNAT B
Stevens, Vi 1892-1967 WhoHol B
Stevens, Victor d1925 NotNAT B
Stevens, Violet 1892-1967 WhScrn 1, WhScrn 2
Stevens, Warren 1919- FilmgC, WhoHol A
Stevenson, Adlai, III 1930- CelR 3
Stevenson, Adlai E 1900-1965 WhScrn 2
Stevenson, Charles A 1851-1929 NotNAT B,
WhScrn 1, WhScrn 2, WhoHol B
Stevenson, Charles E 1888-1943 Film 2,
WhScrn 1, WhScrn 2, WhoHol B
Stevenson, Douglas 1883-1934 Film 2, NotNAT B,
WhScrn 2, WhoHol B
Stevenson, Harry Payne 1916- AmSCAP 1966
Stevenson, Hayden Film 2, TwYS
Stevenson, Houseley 1879-1953 FilmgC, Vers B,
WhScrn 1, WhScrn 2, WhoHol B
Stevenson, Houseley, Jr. WhoHol A
Stevenson, John d1922 WhScrn 1, WhScrn 2
Stevenson, Margot WhoHol A
Stevenson, Margot 1914- WhoThe 16
Stevenson, Margot 1918- BiE&WWA, NotNAT
Stevenson, McLean WhoHol A
Stevenson, Robert 1905- FilmgC, IntMPA 1977,
MovMk, WorEnF
Stevenson, Robert E Lee 1924- AmSCAP 1966
Stevenson, Robert J 1915-1975 WhScrn 2,
WhoHol C
Stevenson, Robert Louis 1850-1894 FilmgC
Stevenson, Venetia WhoHol A
Stevenson, William 1521-1575 CnThe, McGWD,
NotNAT B, OxThe
Stever, Hans Film 2
Steward, Cliff 1916- AmSCAP 1966
Steward, Kenny PIP&P A
Steward, Leslie Film 2
Stewart, Alexandra FilmgC, WhoHol A
Stewart, Andy 1934- IntMPA 1977
Stewart, Anita d1961 MotPP, NotNAT B,
WhoHol B
Stewart, Anita 1895-1961 Film 1, Film 2,
FilmgC, WhScrn 1, WhScrn 2
Stewart, Anita 1896-1962 TwYS
Stewart, Athole 1879-1940 FilmgC, NotNAT B,
WhScrn 1, WhScrn 2, WhThe, WhoHol B
Stewart, Barry WhoHol A
Stewart, Betty 1912-1944 WhScrn 1, WhScrn 2
Stewart, Blanche d1952 WhScrn 2
Stewart, Charles 1887- BiE&WWA
Stewart, Charlotte WhoHol A
Stewart, Cray 1924-1961 WhScrn 1, WhScrn 2
Stewart, Danny 1907-1962 NotNAT B,

WhScrn 1, WhScrn 2, WhoHol B
Stewart, David J d1966 WhoHol B
Stewart, David J 1914-1966 WhScrn 1, WhScrn 2
Stewart, David J 1919-1966 BiE&WWA,
NotNAT B
Stewart, Dona Jean 1939-1961 WhScrn 1,
WhScrn 2
Stewart, Donald 1911-1966 WhScrn 1, WhScrn 2,
WhoHol B
Stewart, Donald Ogden 1894- BiE&WWA,
FilmgC, NotNAT, WhThe, WorEnF
Stewart, Dorothy M 1897-1954 AmSCAP 1966
Stewart, Douglas 1913- ConDr 1977
Stewart, Elaine 1929- FilmgC, IntMPA 1977,
MotPP, WhoHol A
Stewart, Eldean Film 1
Stewart, Ellen 1931- CelR 3, NotNAT, PIP&P,
WhoThe 16
Stewart, Fred d1970 WhoHol B
Stewart, Fred 1906-1970 BiE&WWA,
NotNAT B, WhThe
Stewart, Fred 1907-1970 WhScrn 1, WhScrn 2
Stewart, George 1888-1945 Film 2, WhScrn 1,
WhScrn 2, WhoHol B
Stewart, Grant d1929 NotNAT B, WhoStg 1908
Stewart, Herbert G 1909- AmSCAP 1966
Stewart, Hugh 1910- FilmgC, IntMPA 1977
Stewart, Jack 1914-1966 WhScrn 1, WhScrn 2,
WhoHol B
Stewart, James 1908- BiDFlm, BiE&WWA,
CelR 3, CmMov, FilmgC, IntMPA 1977,
MGM, MotPP, MovMk, OxFilm, PIP&P,
WhoHol A, WhoThe 16, WorEnF
Stewart, James 1909- CmMov
Stewart, Jean Film 1
Stewart, John d1957 NotNAT B, OxThe
Stewart, Johnny WhoHol A
Stewart, Julia Film 1, WhScrn 2
Stewart, Katherine d1949 NotNAT B
Stewart, Kay WhoHol A
Stewart, Larry WhoHol A
Stewart, Leslie Film 1
Stewart, Lock Film 1
Stewart, Lucille Lee 1894- Film 1, Film 2,
TwYS, WhoHol A
Stewart, Marianne WhoHol A
Stewart, Marilyn IntMPA 1977
Stewart, Martha 1922- IntMPA 1977,
WhoHol A
Stewart, Mel WhoHol A
Stewart, Michael ConDr 1977D
Stewart, Michael 1924- IntMPA 1977
Stewart, Michael 1929- BiE&WWA, EncMT,
NewMT, NotNAT, WhoThe 16
Stewart, Nancye 1893- WhThe
Stewart, Nellie 1858-1931 WhScrn 2
Stewart, Nellie 1860-1931 NotNAT B, WhThe
Stewart, Nicholas WhoHol A
Stewart, Patrick 1940- WhoHol A, WhoThe 16
Stewart, Paul 1908- FilmgC, MovMk, Vers A,
WhoHol A
Stewart, Paula 1933- BiE&WWA, NotNAT,
WhoHol A, WomWMM
Stewart, Peggy 1923- IntMPA 1977, WhoHol A
Stewart, Potter 1915- CelR 3
Stewart, Rex 1907- AmSCAP 1966
Stewart, Richard d1938? WhScrn 1, WhScrn 2
Stewart, Richard d1939 WhoHol B
Stewart, Robin WhoHol A
Stewart, Roy d1933 MotPP, WhoHol B
Stewart, Roy 1884-1933 Film 1, Film 2, TwYS
Stewart, Roy 1889-1933 WhScrn 1, WhScrn 2
Stewart, Sam WhoHol A
Stewart, Sophie 1908- WhoHol A, WhoThe 16

Stewart, Sophie 1909- *FilmgC*
Stewart, Ted *Film 2*
Stewart, Tom *WhoHol A*
Stewart, Virginia Lee *Film 2*
Stewart, William G 1870-1941 *NotNAT B,*
WhoStg 1906, WhoStg 1908
Stewart, William H 1923- *AmSCAP 1966*
Stewart, Yvonne *WhoHol A*
Stich, Patricia *WhoHol A*
Stickle, David V R 1916- *IntMPA 1977*
Stickles, William *AmSCAP 1966*
Stickney, Dorothy 1900- *BiE&WWA, MotPP,*
NotNAT, WhoHol A, WhoThe 16
Stiebner, Hans 1899-1958 *WhScrn 1, WhScrn 2*
Stieda, Heinz *Film 2*
Stiefel, Milton 1900- *BiE&WWA, NotNAT*
Stiernhielm, Georg 1598-1672 *OxThe*
Stifter, Magnus *Film 2*
Stiglic, France 1919- *DcFM, WorEnF*
Stigwood, Robert 1930- *CnThe*
Stiles, Leslie 1876- *WhThe*
Still, Clyfford 1904- *CelR 3*
Still, John d1607 *NotNAT B, OxThe*
Still, William Grant 1895- *AmSCAP 1966*
Stiller, Jerry *WhoHol A*
Stiller, Mauritz 1883-1928 *BiDFlm, DcFM,*
FilmgC, MovMk, OxFilm, TwYS A,
WhScrn 2, WorEnF
Stillman, Al 1906- *AmSCAP 1966*
Stillman, David B d1963 *NotNAT B*
Stillman, Marsha d1962 *NotNAT B*
Stimson, John W 1946- *NatPD*
Stine, Lawrence 1912- *BiE&WWA, NotNAT*
Stipo, Carmine *WhoHol A*
Stirling, Edward 1809-1894 *NotNAT B, OxThe*
Stirling, Edward 1892-1948 *WhScrn 2,*
WhoHol B
Stirling, Fanny 1813-1895 *NotNAT A,*
NotNAT B
Stirling, Fanny 1815-1895 *OxThe*
Stirling, Helen *WhoHol A*
Stirling, Linda *WhoHol A*
Stirling, Pamela *WhoHol A*
Stirling, W Edward 1891-1948 *NotNAT A,*
NotNAT B, WhThe
Stites, Frank 1882-1915 *WhScrn 2*
Stith, Laurence 1933- *AmSCAP 1966*
Stitt, Milan 1941- *NotNAT*
Stitz, Harry 1905- *AmSCAP 1966*
Stitzel, Melville J 1902-1952 *AmSCAP 1966*
Stivers, Duskal *Film 2*
Stix, John 1920- *BiE&WWA, NotNAT*
Stock, Jack d1954 *NotNAT B*
Stock, Larry 1896- *AmSCAP 1966*
Stock, Nigel 1919- *FilmgC, WhoHol A,*
WhoThe 16
Stock, Valeska *Film 2*
Stockbridge, Fanny *Film 2*
Stockbridge, Henry *Film 2*
Stockdale, Carl 1874-1942 *Film 1, TwYS*
Stockdale, Carl 1874-1953 *Vers B, WhScrn 2,*
WhoHol B
Stockdale, Carlton 1874-1942 *Film 2*
Stockfield, Betty 1905-1966 *FilmgC, WhScrn 1,*
WhScrn 2, WhThe, WhoHol B
Stockfisch *OxThe*
Stocklassa, Erik *Film 1*
Stockton, Edith *Film 2, TwYS*
Stockton, Richard 1932- *NatPD*
Stockwell, Dean 1936- *FilmgC, IntMPA 1977,*
MGM, MotPP, MovMk, WhoHol A
Stockwell, Guy 1938- *FilmgC, WhoHol A*
Stockwell, Harry *WhoHol A*
Stockwell, Jeremy *WhoHol A*

Stoddard, Belle 1869-1950 *Film 2, WhScrn 1,*
WhScrn 2, WhoHol B
Stoddard, Betsy 1884-1959 *WhScrn 1, WhScrn 2*
Stoddard, Brandon *IntMPA 1977*
Stoddard, George D 1897- *BiE&WWA*
Stoddard, Haila 1913- *BiE&WWA, NotNAT,*
WhoThe 16
Stoddard, Harry 1892-1951 *AmSCAP 1966*
Stoddart, James Henry 1827-1907 *NotNAT A,*
NotNAT B
Stodola, Ivan 1888- *CnThe, REnWD*
Stoeckel, Joe 1894-1959 *WhScrn 1, WhScrn 2*
Stoepel, Richard d1887 *NotNAT B*
Stoessel, Albert 1894-1943 *AmSCAP 1966*
Stoker, Bram 1847-1912 *FilmgC, NotNAT B*
Stoker, H G 1885-1966 *WhScrn 1, WhScrn 2,*
WhoHol B
Stoker, Hew Gordon Dacre 1885-1966 *WhThe*
Stoker, Willard 1905- *WhoThe 16*
Stokes, Carl 1927- *CelR 3*
Stokes, Dorothy *Film 2*
Stokes, Ernest L 1907-1964 *NotNAT B,*
WhScrn 1, WhScrn 2
Stokes, Sewell 1902- *WhThe*
Stokowski, Leopold 1882- *AmSCAP 1966,*
CelR 3, FilmgC, WhoHol A
Stoler, Shirley *WhoHol A*
Stoll, George 1905- *CmMov, FilmgC,*
IntMPA 1977
Stoll, Sir Oswald 1866-1942 *NotNAT B, OxThe,*
WhThe
Stoller, Morris 1915- *IntMPA 1977*
Stollery, David *WhoHol A*
Stolnitz, Art 1928- *IntMPA 1977*
Stoloff, Benjamin 1895- *TwYS A*
Stoloff, Morris *IntMPA 1977*
Stoloff, Morris 1893- *CmMov, FilmgC*
Stoloff, Morris 1898- *AmSCAP 1966*
Stoloff, Victor *IntMPA 1977*
Stoltz, Arnold T *IntMPA 1977*
Stolz, Don 1919- *BiE&WWA, NotNAT*
Stolz, Robert 1880-1975 *BiE&WWA, NotNAT B*
Stolz, Robert 1886- *WhThe*
Stone, Alix *WhoThe 16*
Stone, Amelia 1879- *WhoStg 1906,*
WhoStg 1908
Stone, Andrew L 1902- *BiDFlm, CmMov,*
FilmgC, IntMPA 1977, WomWMM,
WorEnF
Stone, Arthur 1884-1940 *WhScrn 1, WhScrn 2,*
WhoHol B
Stone, Arthur 1897- *Film 2, TwYS*
Stone, Barbara *WomWMM B*
Stone, Billy 1884-1931 *AmSCAP 1966*
Stone, Burton 1928- *IntMPA 1977*
Stone, Carol 1915- *BiE&WWA, WhThe,*
WhoHol A
Stone, Charles *WhThe*
Stone, Christopher *WhoHol A*
Stone, Danny *WhoHol A*
Stone, Doc *Film 2*
Stone, Dorothy 1905-1974 *BiE&WWA,*
NotNAT B, WhScrn 2, WhThe, WhoHol B
Stone, Edward Durell 1902- *BiE&WWA, CelR 3*
Stone, Ezra C 1917- *BiE&WWA, IntMPA 1977,*
NewYTET, NotNAT, WhoHol A
Stone, Florence Oakley d1956 *NotNAT B*
Stone, Fred Andrew 1873-1959 *EncMT, Film 1,*
Film 2, NotNAT A, NotNAT B, PIP&P,
TwYS, Vers A, WhScrn 1, WhScrn 2,
WhThe, WhoHol B
Stone, Gage C 1919- *AmSCAP 1966*
Stone, Gene *Film 2*
Stone, George 1877-1939 *WhScrn 2*

Stone, George E 1903-1967 *Film 1, Film 2,*
 FilmgC, MotPP, MovMk, TwYS, Vers A,
 WhScrn 1, WhoHol B
Stone, George E 1904-1967 *WhScrn 2*
Stone, Gregory 1900- *AmSCAP 1966*
Stone, Harold *NotNAT*
Stone, Harold J 1911- *FilmgC, WhoHol A*
Stone, Harry *Film 1*
Stone, Harvey 1913-1974 *WhScrn 2*
Stone, Helen *Film 2*
Stone, I F 1907- *CelR 3*
Stone, Irving 1903- *CelR 3*
Stone, Jack *Film 2*
Stone, James F 1901-1969 *WhScrn 2, WhoHol B*
Stone, James Y 1929- *AmSCAP 1966*
Stone, Jean 1914- *AmSCAP 1966*
Stone, Jeffrey *WhoHol A*
Stone, John *WhoHol A*
Stone, John Augustus 1801-1834 *NotNAT B,*
 OxThe, PIP&P
Stone, Joseph 1920- *AmSCAP 1966*
Stone, Kirby 1918- *AmSCAP 1966*
Stone, Leonard *WhoHol A*
Stone, Lewis 1878- *WhThe*
Stone, Lewis 1879-1953 *Film 1, Film 2, FilmgC,*
 MGM, MotPP, MovMk, NotNAT B, TwYS,
 Vers B, WhScrn 1, WhScrn 2, WhoHol B
Stone, Marianne *IntMPA 1977, WhoHol A*
Stone, Maxine 1910-1964 *WhScrn 1, WhScrn 2,*
 WhoHol B
Stone, Milburn 1904- *FilmgC, MotPP,*
 WhoHol A
Stone, Paddy 1924- *WhoHol A, WhoThe 16*
Stone, Paula 1916- *BiE&WWA, NotNAT,*
 WhThe, WhoHol A
Stone, Peter 1930- *BiE&WWA, ConDr 1977D,*
 EncMT, FilmgC, NotNAT, WhoThe 16
Stone, Phil *TwYS A*
Stone, Mrs. Robert E d1916 *WhScrn 2*
Stone, Roger Hayes 1946- *AmSCAP 1966*
Stone, Sid *NewYTET*
Stone, Suzie Kay *WhoHol A*
Stone, Virginia *WomWMM*
Stonehouse, Ruth *MotPP*
Stonehouse, Ruth d1941 *WhoHol B, WomWMM*
Stonehouse, Ruth 1891-1940 *TwYS*
Stonehouse, Ruth 1893-1941 *WhScrn 1,*
 WhScrn 2
Stonehouse, Ruth 1894-1941 *Film 1, Film 2,*
 NotNAT B
Stoneman, James M 1927- *IntMPA 1977*
Stoner, Michael S 1911- *AmSCAP 1966*
Stoney, George *OxFilm*
Stooges, The Three *FilmgC*
Stooges, The Three *see also* Three Stooges
Stookey, Noel Paul 1937- *AmSCAP 1966*
Stoopnagle, Lemuel Q 1897-1950 *WhScrn 2*
Stoppa, Paolo 1906- *FilmgC, MovMk,*
 WhoHol A
Stoppard, Tom 1937- *CnThe, ConDr 1977,*
 CroCD, McGWD, ModWD, NotNAT,
 PIP&P A, WhoThe 16
Storch, Arthur 1925- *BiE&WWA, NotNAT,*
 WhoHol A, WhoThe 16
Storch, Larry 1923- *BiE&WWA, MotPP,*
 NotNAT, WhoHol A
Storck, Henri 1907- *DcFM, FilmgC, OxFilm,*
 WorEnF
Stordahl, Alex 1913-1963 *WhScrn 2*
Stordahl, Axel 1913-1963 *AmSCAP 1966,*
 NotNAT B
Storer *OxThe*
Storer, George B d1975 *NewYTET*
Storey, David 1923- *CroCD*

Storey, David 1933- *CnThe, ConDr 1977,*
 NotNAT, PIP&P, PIP&P A, WhoThe 16
Storey, Edith 1892- *Film 1, Film 2, MotPP,*
 TwYS
Storey, Fred 1861-1917 *NotNAT B, WhThe*
Storey, Frederick 1909- *IntMPA 1977*
Storey, Rex *Film 2*
Storey, Sylvia Lilian d1947 *NotNAT B*
Stork, George Frederick 1913- *AmSCAP 1966*
Storke, William F *IntMPA 1977, NewYTET*
Storm, Gale *MotPP*
Storm, Gale 1921- *WhoHol A*
Storm, Gale 1922- *FilmgC, HolP 40,*
 IntMPA 1977, MovMk
Storm, Jerome *Film 1, TwYS A*
Storm, Lesley 1903-1975 *BiE&WWA,*
 NotNAT B, WhThe
Storm, Olaf *Film 2*
Stormont, Leo d1923 *Film 2, NotNAT B*
Story, Aubrey d1963 *NotNAT B*
Story, Van Dyck 1917- *AmSCAP 1966*
Stossel, Ludwig 1883-1973 *FilmgC, Vers A,*
 WhScrn 2, WhoHol B
Stothart, Herbert P d1949 *NotNAT B, WhThe*
Stothart, Herbert P 1884-1949 *WorEnF*
Stothart, Herbert P 1885-1949 *AmSCAP 1966,*
 CmMov, EncMT, NewMT
Stott, Judith 1929- *WhThe*
Stott, Mike 1944- *ConDr 1977*
Stouffer, Paul M 1916- *AmSCAP 1966*
Stoughton, Roy Spaulding 1884-1953
 AmSCAP 1966
Stout, Archie 1886- *FilmgC, WorEnF*
Stout, Clarence 1892-1960 *AmSCAP 1966*
Stout, Herbert E 1905- *AmSCAP 1966*
Stout, Rex 1886- *CelR 3*
Stow, John *PIP&P*
Stowe, Harriet Beecher 1811-1896 *FilmgC,*
 NotNAT B, PIP&P
Stowe, Leslie 1886-1949 *Film 1, Film 2,*
 WhScrn 2
Stowe, Lester *Film 2*
Stowell, C W 1878-1940 *WhoHol B*
Stowell, Clarence W 1878-1940 *WhScrn 1,*
 WhScrn 2
Stowell, William H 1885-1919 *Film 1, WhScrn 2*
Stowitz *Film 2*
Strachan, Alan 1946- *WhoThe 16*
Strachey, Jack 1894- *WhThe*
Stradling, Harry 1901-1970 *CmMov, DcFM*
Stradling, Harry 1907-1970 *FilmgC*
Stradling, Harry 1910-1970 *OxFilm*
Stradling, Harry, Jr. 1925- *CmMov, DcFM,*
 FilmgC
Stradling, Walter *Film 1*
Stradner, Rose 1913-1958 *FilmgC, NotNAT B,*
 WhScrn 1, WhScrn 2, WhoHol B
Straight, Beatrice 1918- *BiE&WWA, NotNAT,*
 WhoHol A, WhoThe 16
Straight, Charley 1891-1940 *AmSCAP 1966*
Straight, Willard 1930- *AmSCAP 1966*
Straigis, Roy J 1931- *AmSCAP 1966*
Strain, Thayer *Film 2*
Straker, John A 1908- *AmSCAP 1966*
Stramer, Hugo *IntMPA 1977*
Stramm, August 1874-1915 *ModWD*
Stranack, Wallace d1950 *NotNAT B*
Strand, Chick *WomWMM A, WomWMM B*
Strand, David 1908- *AmSCAP 1966*
Strand, Paul 1890- *DcFM, OxFilm, WorEnF*
Strandgaard, Charlotte *WomWMM*
Strandmark, Erik 1919-1963 *WhScrn 2*
Strang, Harry d1972 *Film 2, Vers B, WhScrn 2,*
 WhoHol B

Strange, Glenn 1899-1973 *FilmgC, Vers A,*
WhScrn 2, WhoHol B
Strange, Michael 1890-1950 *NotNAT A,*
NotNAT B
Strange, Philip *Film 2*
Strange, Robert 1882-1952 *Vers B, WhScrn 1,*
WhScrn 2, WhThe, WhoHol B
Strangis, Jane 1932-1966 *WhScrn 1, WhScrn 2*
Strangis, Judy *WhoHol A*
Stranitzky, Joseph Anton 1676-1726 *OxThe*
Strasberg, Lee 1901- *BiE&WWA, CelR 3,*
CnThe, FilmgC, NotNAT, PIP&P,
WhoHol A, WhoThe 16
Strasberg, Paula d1966 *BiE&WWA, NotNAT B*
Strasberg, Susan 1938- *BiE&WWA, FilmgC,*
IntMPA 1977, MotPP, MovMk, NotNAT,
WhoHol A
Strassberg, Morris 1898-1974 *Film 2, WhScrn 2,*
WhoHol B
Strassberg, Stephen *IntMPA 1977*
Strassburg, Robert 1915- *AmSCAP 1966*
Strasser, Robin *WhoHol A*
Strassny, Fritz *Film 2*
Stratta, Ettore 1933- *AmSCAP 1966*
Stratton, Charles Sherwood 1838-1883 *NotNAT A*
Stratton, Chester 1913-1970 *WhScrn 1,*
WhScrn 2
Stratton, Chet 1913-1970 *WhoHol B*
Stratton, Donald 1928- *AmSCAP 1966*
Stratton, Eugene 1861-1918 *NotNAT B, OxThe,*
WhThe
Stratton, Gene *Film 2*
Stratton, Harry 1898-1955 *WhScrn 1, WhScrn 2*
Stratton, John 1925- *IntMPA 1977, WhoHol A,*
WhoThe 16
Straub, Jean-Marie 1933- *BiDFlm, OxFilm,*
WomWMM, WomWMM B, WorEnF
Straub, Mary E 1884-1951 *WhScrn 1, WhScrn 2*
Strauch, I *Film 2*
Strauch, Maxim *Film 2*
Straus, Jack 1900- *CelR 3*
Straus, Oscar 1870-1954 *NotNAT B, WhThe*
Straus, Roger W, Jr. 1917- *CelR 3*
Strausbaugh, Warren L 1909- *BiE&WWA*
Strausberg, Solomon M 1907- *IntMPA 1977*
Strauss, Clement 1886-1915 *WhScrn 2*
Strauss, Helen M *BiE&WWA, WomWMM*
Strauss, Herbert 1929- *AmSCAP 1966*
Strauss, Johann *PIP&P*
Strauss, Johann d1939 *NotNAT B*
Strauss, Johann 1804-1849 *NotNAT B*
Strauss, Johann 1825-1899 *NotNAT B*
Strauss, John 1913- *IntMPA 1977*
Strauss, John 1920- *AmSCAP 1966, BiE&WWA,*
NotNAT
Strauss, Joseph d1870 *NotNAT B*
Strauss, Peter 1947- *IntMPA 1977, WhoHol A*
Strauss, Peter E 1940- *IntMPA 1977*
Strauss, Richard *IntMPA 1977*
Strauss, Richard 1864-1949 *NotNAT B*
Strauss, Robert 1913-1974 *NotNAT B*
Strauss, Robert 1913-1975 *BiE&WWA, FilmgC,*
MovMk, WhScrn 2, WhoHol C
Strauss, Robert 1915- *Vers A*
Strauss, Robert 1918- *CelR 3*
Strauss, William H 1885-1943 *Film 2, TwYS,*
WhScrn 1, WhScrn 2, WhoHol B
Strayer, Frank 1891-1964 *FilmgC, TwYS A*
Strayhorn, Billy 1915- *AmSCAP 1966*
Streater, Robert 1624-1680 *OxThe*
Street, David 1917-1971 *WhScrn 1, WhScrn 2,*
WhoHol B
Street, George A 1869-1956 *WhScrn 1, WhScrn 2*
Street, George Slythe 1867-1936 *WhThe*

Street, Julian 1880-1947 *WhScrn 2*
Strehler, Giorgio *CnThe*
Streisand, Barbra 1942- *BiDFlm, BiE&WWA,*
CelR 3, CmMov, EncMT, FilmgC,
IntMPA 1977, MotPP, MovMk, NotNAT,
NotNAT A, OxFilm, PIP&P, WhoHol A,
WhoThe 16, WomWMM
Strelsin, Alfred 1898- *CelR 3*
Stribling, Melissa *WhoHol A*
Stribolt, Oscar *Film 2*
Strick, Joseph 1923- *BiDFlm, CelR 3, FilmgC,*
OxFilm, WorEnF
Strickland, Amzie *WhoHol A*
Strickland, Connie *WhoHol A*
Strickland, Enfield Rube d1964 *NotNAT B*
Strickland, Helen 1863-1938 *NotNAT B,*
WhScrn 2, WhoHol B
Strickland, Kathy *WomWMM B*
Strickland, Lily 1887-1958 *AmSCAP 1966*
Strickler, Jerry 1939- *BiE&WWA, NotNAT*
Stricklyn, Ray 1930- *FilmgC, IntMPA 1977,*
MotPP, WhoHol A
Stride, Harry 1903- *AmSCAP 1966*
Stride, John 1936- *FilmgC, WhoHol A,*
WhoThe 16
Striesfield, Herb 1946- *NotNAT*
Striker, Joseph 1900-1974 *Film 2, WhScrn 2,*
WhoHol B
Strimpell, Stephen *WhoHol A*
Strindberg, Arthur *PIP&P*
Strindberg, August 1849-1912 *CnMD, CnThe,*
McGWD, ModWD, NotNAT A, NotNAT B,
OxThe, PIP&P A, REnWD
Strindberg, Axel 1910- *CnMD*
Strindberg, Goran 1917- *WorEnF*
Stringer, Michael *WhoHol A*
Stringer, Robert 1911- *AmSCAP 1966*
Stringfield, Lamar 1897-1959 *AmSCAP 1966*
Stritch, Elaine *MotPP*
Stritch, Elaine 1922- *FilmgC*
Stritch, Elaine 1925- *BiE&WWA, EncMT,*
NotNAT, WhoHol A
Stritch, Elaine 1926- *WhoThe 16*
Stritch, Elaine 1928- *CelR 3*
Strittmatter, Erwin 1912- *CnMD, CroCD*
Strock, Herbert L 1918- *FilmgC*
Strode, Warren Chetham 1897- *PIP&P, WhThe*
Strode, Woody *WhoHol A*
Strode, Woody 1914- *CelR 3*
Strode, Woody 1923- *CmMov, FilmgC*
Stroheim, Erich Von 1885-1957 *DcFM, OxFilm*
Stroll, Edson *WhoHol A*
Strollo, Angie d1964 *NotNAT B*
Stromberg, Hunt 1894-1968 *FilmgC*
Stromberg, John 1853-1902 *NewMT, NotNAT B*
Strong, Austin 1881-1952 *ModWD, NotNAT B,*
WhThe
Strong, Carl E 1907-1965 *WhScrn 1, WhScrn 2*
Strong, David *WhoHol A*
Strong, Eugene *Film 1, Film 2*
Strong, Jay 1896-1953 *NotNAT B, WhScrn 1,*
WhScrn 2, WhoHol B
Strong, Leonard *Vers B*
Strong, Mark *Film 1*
Strong, Michael *WhoHol A*
Strong, Porter 1879-1923 *Film 1, Film 2,*
WhScrn 2, WhoHol B
Strong, Steve d1975 *WhScrn 2, WhoHol C*
Strongheart 1916-1929 *Film 2, TwYS,*
WhScrn 2
Strongheart, Nipo 1891-1966 *WhoHol B*
Strongheart, Nipo 1891-1967 *Film 2, MotPP,*
TwYS
Stroock, Bianca 1896- *BiE&WWA, NotNAT*

Stroock, Gloria *WhoHol A*
Stroock, James E 1891-1965 *BiE&WWA,*
　NotNAT, NotNAT B
Strosky, Rose Kathryn 1912- *AmSCAP 1966*
Stross, Raymond 1916- *FilmgC, IntMPA 1977*
Stross, Raymond 1917- *WorEnF*
Strothers, Bill *Film 2*
Stroud, Clarence 1907-1973 *WhScrn 2*
Stroud, Claude *WhoHol A*
Stroud, Don 1937- *FilmgC, WhoHol A*
Stroud, Gregory 1892- *WhThe*
Stroud, Sally Ann *WhoHol A*
Stroup, Don *WhoHol A*
Strouse, Charles 1928- *AmSCAP 1966,*
　BiE&WWA, EncMT, NewMT, NotNAT,
　WhoThe 16
Strouth, Penelope *WomWMM B*
Stroyberg, Annette *WhoHol A*
Stroyeva, Vera 1903- *DcFM, WomWMM*
Strozzi, Kay *WhThe, WhoHol A*
Strudwick, Sheppard 1907- *MovMk*
Strudwick, Shepperd 1907- *BiE&WWA, FilmgC,*
　IntMPA 1977, NotNAT, WhoHol A,
　WhoThe 16
Struewe, Hans *Film 2*
Strum, Hans *Film 2*
Strumway, Lee *Film 2*
Strus, George *WhoHol A*
Struss, Karl *IntMPA 1977*
Struss, Karl 1890- *CmMov, FilmgC*
Struss, Karl 1891- *WorEnF*
Struthers, Sally 1948- *CelR 3, WhoHol A*
Stryker, Gustave 1866-1943 *WhScrn 1,*
　WhScrn 2
Stryker, Joseph *Film 2*
Stuart, Aimee *IntMPA 1977, WhThe*
Stuart, Amy *WhoHol A*
Stuart, Arlen *WhoHol A*
Stuart, Barbara *WhoHol A*
Stuart, Binkie 1932?- *FilmgC, WhoHol A*
Stuart, C Douglas 1864- *WhThe*
Stuart, Cora d1940 *NotNAT B*
Stuart, Cosmo 1868- *WhoStg 1908*
Stuart, Cosmo 1869- *WhThe*
Stuart, Donald 1898-1944 *Film 2, WhScrn 1,*
　WhScrn 2, WhoHol B
Stuart, Gil *WhoHol A*
Stuart, Gina *WhoHol A*
Stuart, Gloria *MotPP*
Stuart, Gloria 1909- *FilmgC, MovMk*
Stuart, Gloria 1910- *HolP 30, ThFT*
Stuart, Gloria 1911- *WhoHol A*
Stuart, Henry *Film 2*
Stuart, Iris 1903-1936 *Film 2, MotPP, WhScrn 2,*
　WhoHol B
Stuart, Jean 1904-1926 *Film 1, WhScrn 1,*
　WhScrn 2, WhoHol B
Stuart, Jeanne 1908- *WhThe*
Stuart, John 1898- *Film 2, FilmgC, WhoHol A,*
　WhoThe 16
Stuart, Leslie 1864-1928 *EncMT, NotNAT B,*
　WhThe
Stuart, Lyle 1922- *CelR 3*
Stuart, Madge 1897- *Film 2, WhThe*
Stuart, Margaret *WhoHol A*
Stuart, Martha *WomWMM B*
Stuart, Mary *WhoHol A*
Stuart, Maxine *WhoHol A*
Stuart, Mel *FilmgC, NewYTET*
Stuart, Nick 1904-1973 *Film 2, WhScrn 2,*
　WhoHol B
Stuart, Nick 1906-1973 *TwYS*
Stuart, Otho 1865-1930 *NotNAT B, WhThe*
Stuart, Philip 1887-1936 *NotNAT B, WhThe*

Stuart, Ralph R 1890-1952 *Film 1, WhScrn 1,*
　WhScrn 2, WhoHol B
Stuart, Simeon *Film 2*
Stuart, Tom 1878- *WhThe*
Stuart, Walter 1925- *AmSCAP 1966*
Stuarti, Enzo 1925- *AmSCAP 1966*
Stubbs, Harry 1874-1950 *Film 2, WhScrn 2*
Stubbs, Una *WhoThe 16*
Stuckey, Phyllis *WhThe*
Studakevich, Anna *Film 2*
Studdiford, Grace *Film 2*
Studholm, Marie 1875-1930 *NotNAT B*
Studholme, Marie 1875-1930 *WhThe*
Study, Lomax *WhoHol A*
Stukalov, Nikolay Fyodorovich *McGWD*
Stulberg, Gordon 1923- *IntMPA 1977*
Stull, Walter *Film 1*
Sturcken, Frank W 1929- *BiE&WWA*
Sturdivant, B Victor 1901- *IntMPA 1977*
Sturgeon, Rollin d1925 *TwYS A*
Sturges, John 1911- *BiDFlm, CmMov, DcFM,*
　FilmgC, MovMk, OxFilm, WorEnF
Sturges, John Eliot *IntMPA 1977*
Sturges, Preston 1898-1959 *BiDFlm, CmMov,*
　DcFM, FilmgC, ModWD, MovMk, OxFilm,
　WhThe, WorEnF
Sturges, Solomon *WhoHol A*
Sturgess, Arthur d1931 *NotNAT B*
Sturgis, Eddie 1881-1947 *Film 2, WhScrn 2*
Sturgis, Edwin *Film 2*
Sturgis, Norman 1922- *IntMPA 1977*
Sturm, Erna *Film 2*
Sturm, Hannes *Film 2*
Sturm, Murray 1899- *AmSCAP 1966*
Sturt, Lois *Film 2*
Stutenroth, Gene 1903- *Vers A*
Stutz, Geraldine 1924- *CelR 3*
Styles, Edwin 1899-1960 *NotNAT B, WhThe,*
　WhoHol A, WhoHol B
Styman, Barbara *WomWMM B*
Styne, Jule 1905- *AmSCAP 1966, BiE&WWA,*
　CelR 3, EncMT, FilmgC, IntMPA 1977,
　NewMT, NotNAT, WhoThe 16
Styne, Stanley 1940- *AmSCAP 1966*
Styron, William 1925- *CelR 3*
Subject, Evelyn d1975 *WhScrn 2, WhoHol C*
Sublett, John Bubbles *WhoHol A*
Subotsky, Milton 1921- *FilmgC, IntMPA 1977*
Sucher, Henry 1900- *IntMPA 1977*
Suchoff, Benjamin 1918- *AmSCAP 1966*
Suckling, Sir John 1609-1642 *CnThe, OxThe,*
　REnWD
Sucksdorff, Arne 1917- *DcFM, FilmgC, OxFilm,*
　WhoHol A, WorEnF
Sudakevich, Annel *Film 2*
Sudakov, Ilya Yakovleivich 1890-1969 *OxThe*
Sudermann, Hermann 1857-1928 *CnThe*
Sudermann, Herman 1857-1928 *NotNAT B*
Sudermann, Hermann 1857-1928 *CnMD,*
　McGWD, ModWD, OxThe
Sudlow, Bessie d1928 *NotNAT B*
Sudlow, Joan 1892-1970 *WhScrn 1, WhScrn 2,*
　WhoHol B
Sue, Eugene 1804-1857 *OxThe*
Suedo, Julie *Film 2*
Sues, Leonard 1921-1971 *AmSCAP 1966,*
　WhScrn 1, WhScrn 2, WhoHol B
Suessdorf, Karl 1911- *AmSCAP 1966*
Suesse, Dana 1911- *AmSCAP 1966*
Suessenguth, Walther d1964 *NotNAT B,*
　WhoHol B
Suett, Richard 1755-1805 *OxThe*
Sugar, Joseph M *IntMPA 1977*
Sugarman, Harold 1905- *IntMPA 1977*

Sugden, Mrs. Charles *WhThe*
Sugden, Charles 1850-1921 *NotNAT B*, *WhThe*
Sugimori, Nobumori *McGWD*
Sugrue, Frank 1927- *BiE&WWA*, *NotNAT*
Suhosky, Bob 1928- *IntMPA 1977*
Suiter, Arlendo D 1919- *AmSCAP 1966*
Sukardi, Kotot *DcFM*
Sukhovo-Kobylin, Aleksandr Vasilevich 1817-1903
  McGWD, *ModWD*
Sukhovo-Kobylin, Alexander Vasileivich 1817-1903
  CnThe, *OxThe*, *REnWD*
Sukman, Harry 1912- *AmSCAP 1966*
Sul-Te-Wan, Madame d1959 *Film 2*, *WhoHol B*
Sulka, Elaine *NotNAT*
Sullavan, Margaret d1960 *MotPP*, *WhoHol B*
Sullavan, Margaret 1909-1960 *ThFT*
Sullavan, Margaret 1911-1960 *BiDFlm*, *CmMov*,
  FilmgC, *MGM*, *MovMk*, *NotNAT B*,
  OxFilm, *OxThe*, *WhScrn 1*, *WhScrn 2*,
  WhThe
Sullivan, Alexander 1885-1956 *AmSCAP 1966*
Sullivan, Sir Arthur Seymour 1842-1900
  NotNAT A, *NotNAT B*, *REnWD*
Sullivan, Barry 1821-1891 *NotNAT B*, *OxThe*
Sullivan, Barry 1824-1891 *NotNAT A*
Sullivan, Barry 1912- *BiE&WWA*, *FilmgC*,
  IntMPA 1977, *MotPP*, *MovMk*, *NotNAT*,
  WhoHol A
Sullivan, Billy *Film 2*
Sullivan, Brian 1919-1969 *WhScrn 1*, *WhScrn 2*,
  WhoHol B
Sullivan, C Gardner *WomWMM*
Sullivan, C Gardner 1879-1965 *DcFM*
Sullivan, C Gardner 1885-1965 *OxFilm*
Sullivan, Charles *Film 2*
Sullivan, Dan 1875-1948 *AmSCAP 1966*
Sullivan, David *WhoHol A*
Sullivan, David L *Film 1*
Sullivan, Ed 1902-1974 *CelR 3*, *NewYTET*,
  PIP&P, *WhScrn 2*, *WhoHol B*
Sullivan, Elliott d1974 *WhoHol B*
Sullivan, Elliott 1907-1974 *BiE&WWA*,
  NotNAT B
Sullivan, Elliott 1908-1974 *WhScrn 2*
Sullivan, Francis Loftus 1903-1956 *FilmgC*, *MotPP*,
  NotNAT B, *PIP&P*, *Vers A*, *WhScrn 1*,
  WhScrn 2, *WhThe*, *WhoHol B*
Sullivan, Fred 1872-1937 *Film 2*, *WhoHol B*
Sullivan, Frederick R 1872-1937 *WhScrn 1*,
  WhScrn 2
Sullivan, Helene *Film 2*
Sullivan, Henry *AmSCAP 1966*
Sullivan, James E 1864-1931 *Film 2*, *WhScrn 1*,
  WhScrn 2, *WhThe*, *WhoHol B*
Sullivan, James Francis 1880- *WhoStg 1908*
Sullivan, James Maurice d1949 *WhoHol B*
Sullivan, Jean 1923- *WhoHol A*
Sullivan, Jenny *WhoHol A*
Sullivan, Jeremiah *WhoHol A*
Sullivan, Jerry 1891- *AmSCAP 1966*
Sullivan, Jo *BiE&WWA*, *NotNAT*
Sullivan, Joe 1910-1971 *WhScrn 1*, *WhScrn 2*
Sullivan, John *WhoHol A*
Sullivan, John A d1964 *NotNAT B*
Sullivan, John Maurice 1876-1949 *WhScrn 1*,
  WhScrn 2
Sullivan, Joseph Michael 1906- *AmSCAP 1966*
Sullivan, Liam *WhoHol A*
Sullivan, Mella d1963 *NotNAT B*
Sullivan, Pat 1888-1933 *WorEnF*
Sullivan, Patrick J 1920- *IntMPA 1977*
Sullivan, Sean *WhoHol A*
Sullivan, Thomas Russell 1849-1916 *NotNAT B*
Sullivan, William *Film 2*

Sullivan, William M 1922- *AmSCAP 1966*
Sully, Daniel 1855-1910 *NotNAT B*,
  WhoStg 1906, *WhoStg 1908*
Sully, Frank 1908-1975 *WhScrn 2*, *WhoHol C*
Sully, Frank 1910- *Vers B*
Sully, Janet Miller *Film 1*
Sully, Mariette 1878- *WhThe*
Sultan, Arne 1925- *AmSCAP 1966*
Sultan, June 1912- *AmSCAP 1966*
Sultan, Roger H *IntMPA 1977*
Sulzberger, Arthur Ochs 1926- *CelR 3*
Sulzberger, C L 1912- *CelR 3*
Sumac, Yma 1922- *WhoHol A*
Sumarokov, Alexei Petrovich 1718-1777
  NotNAT B, *OxThe*
Sumer, Guner 1936- *REnWD*
Sumerlin, Macon D 1919- *AmSCAP 1966*
Summerall, Pat *NewYTET*
Summerfield, Eleanor 1921- *FilmgC*,
  IntMPA 1977, *WhThe*, *WhoHol A*
Summerland, Augusta *WhoHol A*
Summers, Reverend 1880-1948 *NotNAT B*
Summers, Ann 1920-1974 *WhScrn 2*, *WhoHol B*
Summers, Dorothy d1964 *NotNAT B*, *WhScrn 2*,
  WhoHol B
Summers, Elaine *WomWMM A*, *WomWMM B*
Summers, Hope *WhoHol A*
Summers, Jeremy 1931- *FilmgC*
Summers, Jerry *WhoHol A*
Summers, Madlyn Jane *WhoStg 1906*,
  WhoStg 1908
Summers, Manuel 1935- *WorEnF*
Summers, Montague 1880-1946 *OxThe*
Summers, Montague 1880-1948 *WhThe*
Summers, Shari *WhoHol A*
Summers, Walter 1896- *FilmgC*
Summerville, Amelia 1862-1934 *Film 1*, *Film 2*,
  WhoHol B, *WhoStg 1906*, *WhoStg 1908*
Summerville, Amelia 1863-1934 *WhScrn 2*
Summerville, George Slim 1892-1946 *Vers A*
Summerville, Slim d1946 *MotPP*, *NotNAT B*,
  WhoHol B
Summerville, Slim 1892-1946 *Film 1*, *Film 2*,
  FilmgC, *MovMk*, *TwYS*
Summerville, Slim 1896-1946 *WhScrn 1*,
  WhScrn 2
Sumner, Corinne Heath *WhScrn 1*, *WhScrn 2*
Sumner, Geoffrey 1908- *WhoHol A*, *WhoThe 16*
Sumner, John 1924- *WhoThe 16*
Sumner, Kathryn *Film 2*
Sumner, Mary 1888-1956 *NotNAT B*, *WhThe*
Sumner, Verlyn 1897-1935 *WhScrn 2*
Sundberg, Clinton *IntMPA 1977*, *Vers B*,
  WhoHol A
Sundberg, Clinton 1906- *BiE&WWA*, *NotNAT*
Sundberg, Clinton 1906- *FilmgC*, *MovMk*
Sunderland, Nan d1973 *NotNAT B*, *WhScrn 2*,
  WhoHol B
Sunderland, Scott 1883- *WhThe*
Sundgaard, Arnold 1909- *AmSCAP 1966*,
  BiE&WWA, *NotNAT*
Sundholm, Bill d1971 *WhoHol B*
Sundholm, William Bill d1971 *WhScrn 2*
Sundin, Jerre *Film 2*
Sundmark, Betty *WhScrn 1*, *WhScrn 2*
Sundstrom, Florence 1918- *BiE&WWA*, *NotNAT*,
  WhoHol A
Sundstrom, Frank *WhoHol A*
Sunshine, Baby 1915-1917 *WhScrn 2*
Sunshine, Marion d1963 *Film 1*, *NotNAT B*,
  WhoHol B
Sunshine, Marion 1894-1963 *AmSCAP 1966*
Sunshine, Marion 1897-1963 *WhScrn 1*,
  WhScrn 2

Sunshine, Morton 1915- *IntMPA 1977*
Supervielle, Jules 1884-1960 *CnMD, McGWD,*
  ModWD
Supplee, Esther Ritter *WhScrn 1, WhScrn 2*
Suratt, Valeska 1882-1962 *Film 1, TwYS,*
  WhScrn 2, WhoHol B
Surov, Anatol *CnMD*
Surov, Anatoli Alekseevich 1910- *ModWD*
Surovy, Nick *WhoHol A*
Surtees, Bruce *FilmgC, IntMPA 1977*
Surtees, Robert L 1906- *CmMov, FilmgC,*
  IntMPA 1977, OxFilm, WorEnF
Susands, Cecil *Film 2*
Susann, Jacqueline 1921-1974 *WhScrn 2,*
  WhoHol B
Susann, Jacqueline 1926-1974 *CelR 3*
Susarion *OxThe*
Suschitsky, Peter *FilmgC*
Suschitsky, Wolfgang 1912- *FilmgC*
Susman, Todd *WhoHol A*
Sussan, Herbert 1921- *IntMPA 1977*
Sussenguth, Walther 1900-1964 *WhScrn 1,*
  WhScrn 2
Sussin, Mathilde *Film 2*
Susskind, David 1920- *BiE&WWA, CelR 3,*
  FilmgC, NewYTET, NotNAT
Sussman, Samuel 1913- *NatPD*
Sutch, Herbert *Film 1, Film 2*
Suter, W E d1882 *NotNAT B*
Sutherin, Wayne *WhoHol A*
Sutherland, A Edward 1895-1973 *FilmgC,*
  WhScrn 2
Sutherland, A Edward *see also* Sutherland, Eddie
Sutherland, Anne 1867-1942 *Film 1, NotNAT B,*
  WhoHol B
Sutherland, Annie 1867-1942 *WhThe*
Sutherland, Birdie d1955 *NotNAT B*
Sutherland, Dick 1882-1934 *Film 2, WhScrn 1,*
  WhScrn 2, WhoHol B
Sutherland, Donald *IntMPA 1977, WhoHol A,*
  WomWMM
Sutherland, Donald 1934- *CelR 3, MovMk*
Sutherland, Donald 1935- *BiDFlm, FilmgC*
Sutherland, Eddie 1897- *Film 1, TwYS*
Sutherland, Eddie 1897-1973 *Film 2*
Sutherland, Eddie *see also* Sutherland, A Edward
Sutherland, Edward 1895- *BiDFlm*
Sutherland, Edward 1897- *TwYS A*
Sutherland, Edward 1897-1974 *WhoHol B*
Sutherland, Efua 1924- *ConDr 1977, WomWMM*
Sutherland, Evelyn Greenleaf 1855-1908
  NotNAT B, WhoStg 1908
Sutherland, Hope *Film 2*
Sutherland, Joan 1929- *CelR 3*
Sutherland, John 1845-1921 *Film 1, WhScrn 2*
Sutherland, Joseph *Film 1*
Sutherland, Robert C d1962 *NotNAT B*
Sutherland, Victor 1889-1968 *Film 1, MotPP,*
  WhScrn 1, WhScrn 2, WhoHol B
Sutro, Alfred 1858- *WhoStg 1906*
Sutro, Alfred 1863-1933 *McGWD, ModWD,*
  NotNAT A, NotNAT B, WhThe,
  WhoStg 1908
Sutton, Charles *Film 2*
Sutton, Dolores *WhoHol A*
Sutton, Dudley 1933- *FilmgC, WhoHol A*
Sutton, Ernest E 1886-1963 *AmSCAP 1966*
Sutton, Frank 1923-1974 *WhScrn 2, WhoHol B*
Sutton, Gertrude *Film 2*
Sutton, Grady 1908- *Film 2, FilmgC, MotPP,*
  MovMk, Vers A, WhoHol A
Sutton, Horace 1919- *CelR 3*
Sutton, James T *IntMPA 1977*
Sutton, John 1908-1963 *FilmgC, IntMPA 1977,*

MotPP, MovMk, WhScrn 1, WhScrn 2,
  WhoHol B
Sutton, Julia *WhoHol A*
Sutton, Paul 1912-1970 *WhScrn 1, WhScrn 2,*
  WhoHol B
Sutton, Reginald 1916- *IntMPA 1977*
Sutton, Sandra *WomWMM B*
Sutton, William 1877-1955 *WhScrn 1, WhScrn 2*
Sutton-Vane, Vane 1888-1963 *WhThe*
Suzman, Janet 1939- *CnThe, FilmgC,*
  WhoHol A, WhoThe 16
Suzuki, Pat *WhoHol A*
Suzy *CelR 3*
Svashenko, Semyon *Film 2*
Svendsen, Olga *Film 2*
Svennberg, Tore 1852- *Film 2, WhThe*
Svenson, Bo *WhoHol A*
Sverdlin, Lev N 1902-1969 *WhScrn 1, WhScrn 2*
Svoboda, Josef 1920- *NotNAT, NotNAT A,*
  WhoThe 16
Swaffer, Hannen 1879-1962 *NotNAT A,*
  NotNAT B, WhThe
Swafford, Thomas J *NewYTET*
Swain, Mack 1876-1935 *Film 1, Film 2, FilmgC,*
  MotPP, MovMk, TwYS, WhScrn 1,
  WhScrn 2, WhoHol B
Swallow, Margaret 1896-1932 *NotNAT B,*
  WhThe
Swallow, Norman 1921- *IntMPA 1977*
Swan, Einar Aaron 1904-1940 *AmSCAP 1966*
Swan, Lew d1964 *NotNAT B*
Swan, Mark Elbert 1871-1942 *NotNAT B,*
  WhThe
Swan, Paul 1884-1972 *Film 1, WhScrn 2,*
  WhoHol B
Swan, Robert *WhoHol A*
Swan, William *WhoHol A*
Swanborough, Mrs. d1889 *NotNAT B*
Swanborough, Ada d1893 *NotNAT B*
Swann, Caroline Burke *BiE&WWA*
Swann, Donald 1923- *BiE&WWA, NotNAT,*
  OxThe, WhoThe 16
Swann, Elaine *WhoHol A*
Swann, Francis 1913- *BiE&WWA, IntMPA 1977,*
  NotNAT
Swann, Lynn *WhoHol A*
Swann, Sir Michael *NewYTET*
Swann, Robert *WhoHol A*
Swanson, Gloria *MotPP, WomWMM*
Swanson, Gloria 1897- *FilmgC, ThFT*
Swanson, Gloria 1898- *BiDFlm, Film 1, Film 2,*
  MovMk, OxFilm, TwYS, WorEnF
Swanson, Gloria 1899- *BiE&WWA, CelR 3,*
  IntMPA 1977, WhoHol A, WhoThe 16
Swanson, Maureen 1932- *FilmgC, WhoHol A*
Swanson, Robert E 1920- *IntMPA 1977*
Swanston, Edwin S 1922- *AmSCAP 1966*
Swanston, Eliard d1651 *OxThe*
Swanston, Hilliard d1651 *OxThe*
Swanstram, Karin *Film 2*
Swanstrom, Arthur 1888-1940 *AmSCAP 1966*
Swanwick, Peter 1912-1968 *WhScrn 2*
Swarthout, Gladys 1904-1969 *FilmgC, ThFT,*
  WhScrn 1, WhScrn 2, WhoHol B
Swartley, Wilmer C 1908- *IntMPA 1977*
Swarts, Sara 1899-1949 *WhScrn 1, WhScrn 2,*
  WhoHol B
Swartz, Herbert 1926- *AmSCAP 1966*
Swash, Bob 1929- *WhoThe 16*
Swayne, Julia d1933 *WhoHol B*
Swayze, John Cameron 1906- *IntMPA 1977,*
  NewYTET
Swears, Herbert d1946 *NotNAT A, NotNAT B*
Sweatman, Wilbur C 1882-1961 *AmSCAP 1966*

Swedroe, Jerome D 1925- *IntMPA 1977*
Sweeney, Augustin *Film 2*
Sweeney, Bob *NewYTET, WhoHol A*
Sweeney, Charles F, Jr. 1924- *AmSCAP 1966*
Sweeney, Edward C 1906-1967 *WhScrn 1,*
  WhScrn 2
Sweeney, Fred C 1894-1954 *WhScrn 1, WhScrn 2*
Sweeney, Jack 1889-1950 *WhScrn 1, WhScrn 2,*
  WhoHol B
Sweeney, Joseph d1963 *WhScrn 2, WhoHol B*
Sweet, Blanche *MotPP*
Sweet, Blanche 1895- *FilmgC, TwYS*
Sweet, Blanche 1896- *BiE&WWA, Film 1,*
  Film 2, MovMk, NotNAT, OxFilm,
  WhoHol A
Sweet, Dolph 1920- *BiE&WWA, NotNAT,*
  WhoHol A
Sweet, Gwen *AmSCAP 1966*
Sweet, Harry 1901-1933 *Film 2, WhScrn 2*
Sweet, Jeffrey Warren 1950- *NatPD*
Sweet, Katie 1957- *WhoHol A*
Sweet, Milo Allison 1899- *AmSCAP 1966*
Sweet, Sam d1948 *NotNAT B*
Sweet, Sheila *WhoHol A*
Sweet, Tom 1933-1967 *WhScrn 1, WhScrn 2,*
  WhoHol B
Swenson, Alfred G 1883-1941 *WhScrn 1,*
  WhScrn 2, WhoHol B
Swenson, Inga *BiE&WWA, NotNAT,*
  WhoHol A
Swenson, Inga 1932- *EncMT, FilmgC*
Swenson, Inga 1934- *WhoThe 16*
Swenson, Karl *WhoHol A*
Swenson, Linda *WhoHol A*
Swenson, S A G *IntMPA 1977*
Swenson, Sven *WhoHol A*
Swenson, Swen 1932- *WhoThe 16*
Swenson, Swen 1934- *BiE&WWA, NotNAT*
Swere, E Lyall 1865-1930 *WhThe*
Swerling, Jo 1894- *FilmgC, WorEnF*
Swerling, Jo 1897- *BiE&WWA, IntMPA 1977,*
  NotNAT
Swerling, Jo, Jr. *NewYTET*
Swet, Peter 1942- *NatPD*
Swets, E Lyall 1865-1930 *NotNAT B*
Swick, George E 1918- *AmSCAP 1966*
Swickard, Charles F 1861-1929 *TwYS A,*
  WhScrn 1, WhScrn 2, WhoHol B
Swickard, Josef 1867-1940 *TwYS*
Swickard, Joseph 1866-1940 *WhScrn 1,*
  WhScrn 2
Swickard, Joseph 1867-1940 *Film 1, Film 2,*
  WhoHol B
Swickard, Josie *Film 2*
Swift, Allen 1924- *IntMPA 1977*
Swift, Basil J 1919- *AmSCAP 1966*
Swift, Clive 1936- *WhoHol A, WhoThe 16*
Swift, David 1919- *FilmgC, IntMPA 1977,*
  WorEnF
Swift, Johnathan *PIP&P*
Swift, Kay 1905- *AmSCAP 1966, EncMT*
Swift, Lela *IntMPA 1977, NewYTET*
Swimmer, Bob d1971 *WhScrn 2*
Swimmer, Saul *IntMPA 1977*
Swinburne, Algernon Charles 1837-1909
  NotNAT B
Swinburne, Mercia 1900- *WhThe*
Swinburne, Nora 1902- *Film 2, FilmgC,*
  IntMPA 1977, WhoHol A, WhoThe 16
Swiney, Owen 1675?-1754 *OxThe*
Swink, Robert E 1918- *IntMPA 1977*
Swinley, Ian 1892-1937 *PIP&P*
Swinley, Ion d1937 *Film 2, WhoHol B*
Swinley, Ion 1891-1937 *NotNAT B, WhThe*

Swinley, Ion 1892-1937 *WhScrn 2*
Swinstead, Joan 1903- *WhThe*
Swisher, Arden 1910- *AmSCAP 1966*
Swit, Loretta *WhoHol A*
Swital, Chet L 1904- *IntMPA 1977*
Switzer, Carl Alfalfa 1926-1959 *FilmgC, MotPP,*
  NotNAT B, WhScrn 1, WhScrn 2,
  WhoHol B
Swofford, Ken *WhoHol A*
Swoger, Harry 1919-1970 *WhScrn 2*
Swope, Herbert Bayard, Jr. *BiE&WWA,*
  IntMPA 1977, NotNAT
Swope, Topo *WhoHol A*
Swor, Bert 1878-1943 *Film 2, WhScrn 1,*
  WhScrn 2, WhoHol B
Swor, Bert, Jr. *Film 2*
Swor, John 1883-1965 *WhScrn 1, WhScrn 2,*
  WhoHol B
Swor, Mabel *Film 2*
Sydney, Basil d1968 *MotPP, WhoHol B*
Sydney, Basil 1894-1968 *BiE&WWA, FilmgC,*
  MovMk, NotNAT B, PIP&P, WhScrn 1,
  WhScrn 2, WhThe
Sydney, Basil 1897-1968 *Film 2, Vers A*
Sydney, Bruce 1889-1942 *WhScrn 1, WhScrn 2,*
  WhoHol B
Sydnor, Earl *WhoHol A*
Sydow, Jack 1921- *BiE&WWA, NotNAT*
Sykes, Brenda *WhoHol A*
Sykes, Eric *WhoHol A*
Sykes, Eric 1923- *FilmgC*
Sykes, Eric 1924- *IntMPA 1977*
Sykes, Jerome d1903 *NotNAT B*
Sylbert, Richard *FilmgC*
Syle, Edwin A d1964 *NotNAT B*
Sylos, Frank Paul 1900- *IntMPA 1977*
Sylva, Ilena 1916- *WhThe*
Sylva, Marguerita 1876-1957 *NotNAT B*
Sylva, Marguerite 1876-1957 *WhScrn 2*
Sylva, Vesta 1907- *Film 1, Film 2, WhThe*
Sylvain, Louise d1930 *NotNAT B*
Sylvain, M *Film 2*
Sylvaine, Vernon 1897-1957 *NotNAT B, WhThe*
Sylvane, Andre 1850- *WhThe*
Sylvani, Gladys 1885-1953 *WhScrn 1, WhScrn 2,*
  WhoHol B
Sylvanus, Erwin 1917- *CnMD, ModWD*
Sylvern, Hank *IntMPA 1977*
Sylvern, Henry 1908-1964 *AmSCAP 1966*
Sylvester, Charles *Film 2*
Sylvester, Frank L 1868-1931 *WhScrn 1,*
  WhScrn 2
Sylvester, Henry 1882-1961 *WhScrn 2*
Sylvester, Lillian *Film 2*
Sylvester, William 1922- *FilmgC, WhThe,*
  WhoHol A
Sylvia, Marguerita d1957 *WhoHol B*
Sylvie d1970 *WhoHol B*
Sylvie 1882-1970 *WhScrn 1, WhScrn 2*
Sylvie 1883-1970 *OxFilm*
Sylvie 1887-1970 *FilmgC*
Sylvie, Louise 1885- *WhThe*
Sym, Igo *Film 2*
Symes, Marty 1904-1953 *AmSCAP 1966*
Symington, James Wadsworth 1927-
  AmSCAP 1966
Symington, Stuart 1901- *CelR 3*
Symonds, Augustin 1869-1944 *WhScrn 2*
Symonds, Augustine *Film 2*
Symonds, Robert 1926- *BiE&WWA, NotNAT,*
  WhoThe 16
Symons, Arthur d1945 *NotNAT B*
Sympson, Tony 1906- *WhoThe 16*
Syms, Algernon d1915 *NotNAT B*

Syms, Sylvia 1934- *FilmgC, IntMPA 1977,*
　MotPP, WhoHol A
Synadinos, Theodoros *REnWD*
Syndeconde *Film 1*
Synge, John Millington 1871-1909 *CnMD, CnThe,*
　McGWD, ModWD, NotNAT A, NotNAT B,
　OxThe, PIP&P, REnWD
Sypher, Wylie 1905- *BiE&WWA, NotNAT*
Syrcher, Madeleine B 1896- *AmSCAP 1966*
Syse, Glenna 1927- *BiE&WWA, NotNAT*
Szabo, Istvan 1938- *FilmgC, OxFilm*
Szabo, Magda 1917- *CroCD*
Szabo, Sandor *WhoHol A*
Szabo, Sandor 1906-1966 *WhScrn 2*
Szabo, Sandor 1915- *BiE&WWA, NotNAT*
Szaniawski, Jerzy 1886-1970 *CnMD, CroCD,*
　ModWD
Szathmary, Albert 1909-1975 *WhScrn 2,*
　WhoHol C
Szemes, Marianne *WomWMM*
Szigeti, Joseph 1893-1973 *WhScrn 2, WhoHol B*
Szigligeti, Ede 1814-1878 *NotNAT B*
Szigligeti, Eduard 1814-1878 *McGWD*
Szold, Bernard 1894-1960 *WhScrn 1, WhScrn 2,*
　WhoHol B
Szolowski, K *WomWMM*
Szomory, Dezso 1869-1945 *NotNAT B*
Szoreghi, Julius V *Film 2*

T

Taafe, Alice *Film 1*
Tabarin d1626 *OxThe*
Tabbert, William 1921-1974 *BiE&WWA, EncMT, NotNAT B, WhThe*
Tabelak, John-Michael *ConDr 1977D*
Taber, Richard 1885-1957 *Film 1, Film 2, NotNAT B, TwYS, WhScrn 1, WhScrn 2, WhoHol B*
Taber, Robert Schell 1865-1904 *NotNAT B*
Tabler, P Dempsey *WhoHol B*
Tabler, P Dempsey 1880-1953 *Film 2*
Tabler, P Dempsey 1880-1963 *WhScrn 2*
Taboada, Julio, Jr. 1926-1962 *NotNAT B, WhScrn 1, WhScrn 2*
Tabor, Disiree d1957 *NotNAT B*
Tabor, Joan 1933-1968 *WhScrn 1, WhScrn 2, WhoHol B*
Tabori, George 1914- *BiE&WWA, ConDr 1977, NotNAT, WhoThe 16*
Tabori, Kristoffer *NotNAT, WhoHol A*
Tackney, Stanley 1909- *BiE&WWA, NotNAT, WhoHol A*
Tackova, Jarmila d1971 *WhoHol B*
Taconis, Atze 1900- *AmSCAP 1966*
Tadema, Sir Lawrence Alma- 1836-1912 *OxThe*
Tadema, Sir Lawrence Alma- *see also* Alma-Tadema, Sir Lawrence
Taeger, Ralph *WhoHol A*
Taffner, Donald L *IntMPA 1977*
Tafler, Sidney 1916- *FilmgC*
Tafler, Sydney *WhoHol A*
Taft, Billy *Film 2*
Taft, Jerry *WhoHol A*
Taft, Robert, Jr. 1917- *CelR 3*
Taft, Sara d1973 *WhScrn 2*
Tafur, Robert *WhoHol A*
Tagg, Alan 1928- *WhoThe 16*
Taggart, Ben L 1889-1947 *WhScrn 2*
Taggart, Charles F, Jr. 1930- *AmSCAP 1966*
Taggart, Hal 1892-1971 *WhScrn 1, WhScrn 2, WhoHol B*
Taggart, William 1926- *AmSCAP 1966*
Tagger, Theodor *McGWD*
Taggert, Brian *NatPD*
Taglioni, Filippo 1777-1871 *NotNAT B*
Taglioni, Marie 1804-1884 *NotNAT B*
Taglioni, Paul d1884 *NotNAT B*
Tagore, Sir Rabindranath 1861-1941 *CnMD, CnThe, McGWD, ModWD, NotNAT B, OxThe, REnWD*
Tahse, Martin 1930- *BiE&WWA*
Taiani, Hugo 1912- *AmSCAP 1966*
Taikeff, Stanley 1940- *NatPD*
Taillade, Paul d1898 *NotNAT B*
Taillon, Angus D 1888-1953 *WhScrn 1, WhScrn 2*

Taillon, Gus d1953 *WhoHol B*
Tairov, Alexander Yakovlevich 1885-1950 *CnThe, NotNAT B, OxThe, PIP&P*
Taishoff, Sol J *NewYTET*
Tait, E J d1947 *NotNAT B*
Tait, Walter *Film 2*
Tajiri, Larry S 1914- *BiE&WWA*
Taka, Miiko *WhoHol A*
Takamura, Kiyoshi 1902- *IntMPA 1977*
Takeda, Izumo 1688-1756 *NotNAT B*
Takei, George *WhoHol A*
Talagrand, Jacques *McGWD*
Talamo, Gino *Film 2*
Talazac, Odette d1948 *OxFilm, WhScrn 2*
Talbot, Howard 1865-1928 *EncMT, NotNAT B, WhThe*
Talbot, Joseph T 1938- *IntMPA 1977*
Talbot, Lyle *MotPP*
Talbot, Lyle 1902- *BiE&WWA, NotNAT*
Talbot, Lyle 1904- *FilmgC, IntMPA 1977, MovMk, Vers B, WhoHol A*
Talbot, Mae 1869-1942 *WhScrn 1, WhScrn 2*
Talbot, Nita 1930- *FilmgC, WhoHol A*
Talbot, Slim 1896-1973 *WhScrn 2, WhoHol B*
Talbot, Toby *WomWMM B*
Talent, Leo 1906- *AmSCAP 1966*
Talfourd, Frances d1862 *NotNAT B*
Talfourd, Sir Thomas Noon 1795-1854 *NotNAT B, OxThe*
Taliaferro, Edith d1958 *Film 1, TwYS, WhoHol B*
Taliaferro, Edith 1892-1958 *Film 2*
Taliaferro, Edith 1893-1958 *NotNAT B, WhThe*
Taliaferro, Edith 1894-1958 *WhScrn 1, WhScrn 2*
Taliaferro, Hal *Film 2*
Taliaferro, Mabel 1887- *BiE&WWA, Film 1, Film 2, MotPP, NotNAT, TwYS, WhoHol A, WhoStg 1908*
Taliaferro, Mabel 1889- *WhThe*
Tallchief, Maria 1925- *WhThe, WhoHol A*
Talley, Marion 1907- *WhoHol A*
Talli, Carloni *Film 2*
Talli, Virgilio 1857- *WhThe*
Tallichet, Margaret *WhoHol A*
Tallis, Sir George 1867-1948 *NotNAT B, WhThe*
Tallman, Ellen d1963 *NotNAT B*
Tallmer, Jerry 1920- *BiE&WWA, NotNAT*
Talma, Mademoiselle *WhThe*
Talma, Francois-Joseph 1763-1826 *CnThe, NotNAT A, NotNAT B, OxThe*
Talma, Louise 1906- *AmSCAP 1966*
Talma, Zolya *WhoHol A*
Talmadge, Constance d1973 *MotPP, WhoHol B*
Talmadge, Constance 1898-1973 *MovMk, WhScrn 2*

Talmadge, Constance 1899-1973 *FilmgC, OxFilm*
Talmadge, Constance 1900-1973 *Film 1, Film 2, TwYS, WorEnF*
Talmadge, Joseph Keaton *Film 2*
Talmadge, Natalie d1969 *WhoHol B*
Talmadge, Natalie 1898-1969 *Film 1, Film 2, FilmgC, TwYS*
Talmadge, Natalie 1899-1969 *WhScrn 1, WhScrn 2*
Talmadge, Norma d1957 *MotPP, WhoHol B*
Talmadge, Norma 1893-1957 *FilmgC, WhScrn 2*
Talmadge, Norma 1896-1957 *Film 1, Film 2, TwYS*
Talmadge, Norma 1897-1957 *BiDFlm, MovMk, NotNAT B, OxFilm, ThFT, WhScrn 1, WorEnF*
Talmadge, Richard 1892- *WhoHol A*
Talmadge, Richard 1896- *Film 1, Film 2, FilmgC*
Talmadge, Richard 1898- *TwYS*
Talman, Lloyd *Film 2*
Talman, William 1915-1968 *FilmgC, MotPP, WhScrn 1, WhScrn 2, WhoHol B*
Talton, Alix *WhoHol A*
Tamara 1907-1943 *EncMT, Film 2, NotNAT B, WhScrn 2, WhThe, WhoHol B*
Tamarin, Alfred H 1913- *IntMPA 1977*
Tamarin, B P *Film 2*
Tamasi, Aron 1897-1966 *CnMD*
Tamayo Y Baus, Manuel 1829-1898 *McGWD, NotNAT B, OxThe*
Tamba, Tetsuro 1929?- *FilmgC, WhoHol A*
Tamblyn, Eddie 1907-1957 *WhoHol B*
Tamblyn, Edward 1907-1957 *WhScrn 1, WhScrn 2*
Tamblyn, Russ *IntMPA 1977, MotPP*
Tamblyn, Russ 1934- *CmMov, FilmgC, MovMk*
Tamblyn, Russ 1935- *WhoHol A*
Tamiris, Helen 1905-1966 *BiE&WWA, EncMT, NotNAT B, WhThe*
Tamiroff, Akim d1972 *MotPP, WhoHol B*
Tamiroff, Akim 1899-1972 *BiDFlm, FilmgC, OxFilm, WhScrn 2, WorEnF*
Tamiroff, Akim 1901-1972 *BiE&WWA, MovMk, NotNAT B, Vers A*
Tammy, Mark d1975 *WhScrn 2*
Tamu *WhoHol A*
Tanaka, Kinuyo *WomWMM*
Tanaka, Nadyoshi 1900- *IntMPA 1977*
Tanaka, Shoji 1886-1918 *WhScrn 2*
Tanchuck, Nat 1912- *IntMPA 1977*
Tandy, Donald *WhoHol A*
Tandy, Jessica 1909- *BiE&WWA, CelR 3, CnThe, FilmgC, IntMPA 1977, MotPP, MovMk, NotNAT, PIP&P, WhoHol A, WhoThe 16*
Tandy, Valerie 1921-1965 *WhThe*
Tandy, Valerie 1923-1965 *WhScrn 1, WhScrn 2*
Taner, Haldun 1916- *REnWD*
Tanguay, Eva 1878-1947 *Film 1, NotNAT B, WhScrn 1, WhScrn 2, WhThe, WhoHol B, WhoStg 1908*
Tani, Yoko 1932- *FilmgC, WhoHol A*
Tannen, Julius 1881-1965 *MotPP, WhScrn 1, WhScrn 2, WhoHol B*
Tanner, Annie Louise d1921 *NotNAT B*
Tanner, Clay *WhoHol A*
Tanner, Gordon *WhoHol A*
Tanner, Haldun 1916- *CnThe*
Tanner, James J 1873-1934 *WhScrn 1, WhScrn 2*
Tanner, James T d1915 *NotNAT B, WhThe*
Tanner, Paul O W 1917- *AmSCAP 1966*
Tanner, Stella *WhoHol A*
Tanner, Tony 1932- *FilmgC, WhoHol A*

Tanner, Winston R 1905- *IntMPA 1977*
Tanny, Mark d1975 *WhoHol C*
Tano, Guy 1914-1952 *WhScrn 1, WhScrn 2*
Tanser, Julia *WomWMM*
Tansey, Emma 1884-1942 *WhScrn 1, WhScrn 2, WhoHol B*
Tansey, Johnny *Film 1*
Tansey, Sheridan *Film 2*
Tanswell, Bertram 1908- *BiE&WWA, NotNAT*
Tanto, Gyula Pal 1927- *IntMPA 1977*
Tanzy, Jeanne *WhoHol A*
Tapley, Rose 1883-1956 *Film 1, Film 2, MotPP, TwYS, WhScrn 1, WhScrn 2, WhoHol B*
Taplin, Terence *PIP&P*
Tapping, Alfred B d1928 *NotNAT B, WhThe*
Tapping, Mrs. Alfred B 1852-1926 *NotNAT B, WhThe*
Taps, Jonie *IntMPA 1977*
Taptuka, Clarence S 1898-1967 *WhScrn 2*
Taradash, Daniel 1913- *CmMov, FilmgC, IntMPA 1977, OxFilm, WorEnF*
Taranow, Gerda *NotNAT*
Tarasava, Alla 1898-1973 *WhoHol B*
Tarasova, Alla Konstantinovna 1898-1973 *WhScrn 2, WhThe*
Tarbat, Lorna 1916-1961 *WhScrn 1, WhScrn 2*
Tarbill, Cindy *WomWMM B*
Tarbutt, Frazer 1894-1918 *WhScrn 2*
Tardieu, Jean 1903- *CnMD, CnThe, McGWD, ModWD, REnWD*
Tariol-Bauge, Anna 1872- *WhThe*
Tarita *WhoHol A*
Tarjan, George 1910-1973 *WhScrn 2*
Tarkenton, Fran 1940- *CelR 3*
Tarkhanov, Mikhail d1948 *WhScrn 2*
Tarkington, Booth 1869-1946 *FilmgC, McGWD, ModWD, OxThe, PIP&P*
Tarkington, Newton Booth 1862-1946 *WhThe*
Tarkington, Newton Booth 1869-1946 *NotNAT B*
Tarkington, Rockne *WhoHol A*
Tarkington, William O d1962 *NotNAT B*
Tarkovsky, Andrei 1932- *BiDFlm, OxFilm*
Tarlarni, Madame *Film 1*
Tarleton, Richard d1588 *CnThe, NotNAT B, OxThe, PIP&P*
Tarlow, Florence *WhoHol A*
Tarr, Florence 1908-1951 *AmSCAP 1966*
Tarr, Justin *WhoHol A*
Tarrant, L Newell 1911- *BiE&WWA, NotNAT*
Tarri, Suzette d1955 *NotNAT B*
Tarride, Abel 1867- *WhThe*
Tarron, Elsie *Film 2*
Tarver, James L 1916- *AmSCAP 1966*
Tarvers, Jim *Film 1*
Tasca, Jules 1938- *NatPD*
Tasco, Rai 1917- *IntMPA 1977*
Tashlin, Frank 1913-1972 *BiDFlm, CmMov, DcFM, FilmgC, OxFilm, WorEnF*
Tashman, Lilyan d1934 *MotPP, WhoHol B*
Tashman, Lilyan 1899-1934 *Film 2, FilmgC, MovMk, NotNAT B, ThFT, WhThe*
Tashman, Lilyan 1900-1934 *TwYS, WhScrn 1, WhScrn 2*
Tasku, V *Film 2*
Tasso, Torquato 1544-1595 *CnThe, McGWD, NotNAT B, OxThe, PIP&P, REnWD*
Tata, Paul M, Sr. 1883-1962 *WhScrn 1, WhScrn 2, WhoHol B*
Tate, Beth 1890- *WhThe*
Tate, Hal 1912- *AmSCAP 1966*
Tate, Harry 1872-1940 *WhScrn 1, WhScrn 2, WhThe, WhoHol B*
Tate, Henry 1872-1940 *NotNAT B, OxThe*
Tate, James W 1875-1922 *NotNAT B, WhThe*

Tate, Nahum 1652-1715 *NotNAT B, OxThe, PIP&P*

Tate, Reginald 1896-1955 *FilmgC, NotNAT B, WhScrn 1, WhScrn 2, WhThe, WhoHol B*

Tate, Sharon 1943-1969 *FilmgC, MotPP, WhScrn 1, WhScrn 2, WhoHol B*

Tatham, John 1632-1664 *NotNAT B*

Tati, Jacques *MotPP, WhoHol A*

Tati, Jacques 1907- *WorEnF*

Tati, Jacques 1908- *BiDFlm, DcFM, FilmgC, MovMk, OxFilm*

Tatton, Jack Meredith 1901- *AmSCAP 1966*

Tatum, Art 1910-1956 *WhScrn 2*

Tatum, Buck 1897-1941 *WhScrn 1, WhScrn 2, WhoHol B*

Tatum, Donn B 1913- *IntMPA 1977*

Taube, Mathias 1876-1934 *Film 2, WhScrn 2*

Tauber, Doris 1908- *AmSCAP 1966*

Tauber, Richard d1948 *WhoHol B*

Tauber, Richard 1891-1948 *NotNAT B, WhThe*

Tauber, Richard 1892-1948 *EncMT, FilmgC, OxFilm, WhScrn 1, WhScrn 2*

Taubin, Amy *WomWMM B*

Taubman, Howard 1907- *BiE&WWA, NotNAT, WhThe*

Taubman, Paul 1911- *AmSCAP 1966, IntMPA 1977*

Taurog, Norman 1899- *CmMov, DcFM, Film 1, FilmgC, IntMPA 1977, MovMk, TwYS A, WorEnF*

Tavel, Ronald 1941- *ConDr 1977, NatPD, NotNAT, WhoThe 16, WomWMM*

Tavener, Jo *WomWMM B*

Tavernier, Albert *Film 2*

Taviani Brothers *WorEnF*

Tawde, George 1883- *WhThe*

Tayback, Vic *WhoHol A*

Tayer, Elyana *WomWMM*

Tayleur, Clifton W 1831-1887 *NotNAT B*

Taylor, Al 1871-1940 *Film 2, WhoHol B*

Taylor, Albert 1871-1940 *WhScrn 1, WhScrn 2*

Taylor, Alma d1974 *FilmgC, WhoHol B*

Taylor, Alma 1895-1974 *WhScrn 2*

Taylor, Alma 1896-1974 *Film 1, Film 2*

Taylor, Annie *WomWMM B*

Taylor, Anthony 1931- *IntMPA 1977*

Taylor, Arthur R *NewYTET*

Taylor, Avonne *Film 2*

Taylor, Beth 1889-1951 *WhScrn 1, WhScrn 2*

Taylor, Beverly *WhoHol A*

Taylor, Brenda *WhoHol A*

Taylor, Buck *WhoHol A*

Taylor, Catherine 1944- *AmSCAP 1966*

Taylor, Cecil P 1929- *ConDr 1977, WhoThe 16*

Taylor, Charles *TwYS A*

Taylor, Charles A d1942 *NotNAT A, NotNAT B*

Taylor, Charles H d1907 *NotNAT B*

Taylor, Charles R S 1915- *AmSCAP 1966*

Taylor, Clarice 1927- *WhoHol A, WhoThe 16*

Taylor, Davidson 1907- *IntMPA 1977*

Taylor, Dawson 1916- *AmSCAP 1966*

Taylor, Deems 1885-1966 *AmSCAP 1966, NotNAT B, WhScrn 2, WhThe*

Taylor, Deems 1886-1966 *FilmgC*

Taylor, Delores *IntMPA 1977, WhoHol A, WomWMM*

Taylor, Don 1920- *ConDr 1977B, FilmgC, IntMPA 1977, WhoHol A*

Taylor, Dub Cannonball *WhoHol A*

Taylor, Dwight 1902- *BiE&WWA, NotNAT*

Taylor, Elaine *WhoHol A*

Taylor, Elizabeth 1932- *BiDFlm, CelR 3, FilmgC, IntMPA 1977, MGM, MotPP,*

MovMk, OxFilm, WhoHol A, WorEnF

Taylor, Enid Stamp 1904-1946 *NotNAT B, WhThe*

Taylor, Estelle 1899-1958 *Film 2, FilmgC, MotPP, NotNAT B, ThFT, TwYS, WhScrn 1, WhScrn 2, WhoHol B*

Taylor, Ethel Corintha 1885-1963 *NotNAT B*

Taylor, Ferris 1893-1961 *WhScrn 1, WhScrn 2, WhoHol B*

Taylor, Forrest 1884-1965 *Vers B, WhScrn 2, WhoHol B*

Taylor, Frankie, Jr. *WhoHol A*

Taylor, George 1889-1939 *WhScrn 1, WhScrn 2, WhoHol B*

Taylor, Gilbert 1914- *FilmgC, IntMPA 1977, WorEnF*

Taylor, Goldie Pearl 1905- *AmSCAP 1966*

Taylor, Helen Marie *BiE&WWA, NotNAT*

Taylor, Sir Henry d1886 *NotNAT B*

Taylor, Henry 1908-1969 *WhScrn 2, WhoHol B*

Taylor, Henry J 1902- *CelR 3*

Taylor, Hiram 1952- *NatPD*

Taylor, Howard *WhoHol A*

Taylor, Irving 1914- *AmSCAP 1966*

Taylor, Jack 1896-1932 *WhScrn 1, WhScrn 2, WhoHol B*

Taylor, Jackie Lynn *WhoHol A*

Taylor, James 1948- *CelR 3, WhoHol A*

Taylor, Joan *WhoHol A*

Taylor, John d1653 *NotNAT B*

Taylor, John d1832 *NotNAT B*

Taylor, John Russell 1935- *WhoThe 16*

Taylor, Joseph 1585?-1652 *OxThe*

Taylor, Joseph 1586-1653 *NotNAT B*

Taylor, Josephine 1891-1964 *WhScrn 1, WhScrn 2, WhoHol B*

Taylor, Joyce *WhoHol A*

Taylor, June 1918- *BiE&WWA, NotNAT*

Taylor, Keith *WhoHol A*

Taylor, Kent 1907- *FilmgC, IntMPA 1977, MovMk, WhoHol A*

Taylor, Kit *WhoHol A*

Taylor, Larry *WhoHol A*

Taylor, Laurette 1884-1946 *CnThe, FamA&A, Film 2, FilmgC, NotNAT A, NotNAT B, OxThe, PIP&P, TwYS, WhScrn 1, WhScrn 2, WhThe, WhoHol B*

Taylor, Lawrence *IntMPA 1977*

Taylor, Linda *WomWMM B*

Taylor, Lionel 1916- *AmSCAP 1966*

Taylor, Louise 1908-1965 *WhScrn 1, WhScrn 2*

Taylor, Marion Sayle 1889-1942 *WhScrn 2*

Taylor, Mary Virginia 1912- *AmSCAP 1966*

Taylor, Nellie 1894-1932 *NotNAT B, WhThe*

Taylor, Noel 1913- *NotNAT*

Taylor, Noel 1917- *BiE&WWA, WhoThe 16*

Taylor, Pat 1918- *WhThe*

Taylor, Ray 1888-1950 *TwYS A*

Taylor, Renee *NotNAT, WhoHol A, WomWMM, WomWMM B*

Taylor, Robert 1873-1936 *WhScrn 1, WhScrn 2*

Taylor, Robert 1911-1969 *BiDFlm, CmMov, FilmgC, MGM, MotPP, MovMk, OxFilm, WhScrn 1, WhScrn 2, WhoHol B, WorEnF*

Taylor, Robert U 1941- *NotNAT*

Taylor, Rod *MotPP, WhoHol A*

Taylor, Rod 1929- *FilmgC, IntMPA 1977, MovMk*

Taylor, Rod 1930- *CelR 3*

Taylor, Ruth *Film 2, WhoHol A*

Taylor, Sam 1895-1958 *FilmgC, NotNAT B, TwYS A*

Taylor, Samuel 1912- *BiE&WWA, ConDr 1977D, McGWD, NotNAT,*

WhoThe 16
Taylor, Seymour 1912- *AmSCAP 1966*
Taylor, Sidney *Film 2*
Taylor, Stanley *Film 2*
Taylor, Telford 1908- *AmSCAP 1966*
Taylor, Tom 1817-1880 *McGWD, NotNAT A, NotNAT B, OxThe, PIP&P*
Taylor, Trotti Truman *WhoHol A*
Taylor, Valerie 1902- *WhoHol A, WhoThe 16*
Taylor, Vaughn 1911- *Vers A, WhoHol A*
Taylor, Wally *WhoHol A*
Taylor, Wayne *WhoHol A*
Taylor, Wilda *WhoHol A*
Taylor, William *Film 2*
Taylor, William d1836 *NotNAT B*
Taylor, William 1921- *AmSCAP 1966*
Taylor, William Buchanan 1877- *WhThe*
Taylor, William Desmond d1921 *Film 1*
Taylor, William Desmond 1877-1922 *TwYS A, WhScrn 1, WhScrn 2, WhoHol B*
Taylor, William S 1925- *BiE&WWA, NotNAT*
Taylor, Wilton *Film 1, Film 2*
Taylor, Zack *WhoHol A*
Taylor-Smith, Jean *WhoHol A*
Taylor-Young, Leigh 1944- *FilmgC, WhoHol A*
Tayo, Lyle *Film 2*
Tazieff, Haroun 1914- *DcFM, FilmgC, WorEnF*
Tchehov *OxThe*
Tchekhov *OxThe*
Tchekov, Anton *NotNAT B*
Tcherepnin, Ivan 1943- *AmSCAP 1966*
Tcherina, Ludmilla *WhoHol A*
Tchuvelev, Ivan *Film 2*
Tchverviakof *Film 2*
Teachout, H Arthur 1888-1939 *WhScrn 1, WhScrn 2*
Tead, Phillips *Film 2*
Teagarden, Jack 1906-1964 *WhScrn 1, WhScrn 2, WhoHol B*
Teague, Anthony Skooter *WhoHol A*
Teague, Brian 1937-1970 *WhScrn 1, WhScrn 2*
Teague, Frances *Film 2*
Teague, Guy d1970 *WhScrn 1, WhScrn 2, WhoHol B*
Teal, Ben d1917 *NotNAT B*
Teal, Ray 1902-1976 *FilmgC, Vers A, WhoHol C*
Teare, Ethel 1894-1959 *Film 1, WhScrn 1, WhScrn 2, WhoHol B*
Tearle, Constance *Film 2*
Tearle, Conway d1938 *MotPP, WhoHol B*
Tearle, Conway 1878-1938 *FilmgC, NotNAT B, WhScrn 1, WhScrn 2, WhThe*
Tearle, Conway 1882-1938 *Film 1, Film 2, MovMk, TwYS*
Tearle, David *Film 2*
Tearle, Edmund 1856-1913 *NotNAT B*
Tearle, Sir Godfrey 1884-1953 *CnThe, Film 1, Film 2, FilmgC, NotNAT B, OxThe, WhScrn 1, WhScrn 2, WhThe, WhoHol B*
Tearle, Malcolm 1888-1935 *NotNAT B, WhScrn 1, WhScrn 2*
Tearle, Noah *Film 2*
Tearle, Osmond 1852-1901 *NotNAT B, OxThe*
Teasdale, Veree 1897- *Film 2*
Teasdale, Verree *WhoHol A*
Teasdale, Verree 1904- *FilmgC*
Teasdale, Verree 1906- *ThFT, WhThe*
Teather, Ida d1954 *WhScrn 1, WhScrn 2*
Tebaldi, Renata *WhoHol A*
Tebet, David W *NewYTET*
Tecer, Ahmet Kutsi 1901-1967 *REnWD*
Teddy *Film 1, Film 2*
Tedesco, Jean 1895-1958 *OxFilm*

Tedesco, Jean 1895-1959 *DcFM*
Tedesco, Lou *NewYTET*
Tedmarsh, W J *Film 1*
Tedrow, Irene 1907- *WhoHol A*
Teed, John 1911- *WhThe*
Teege, Joachim 1925-1969 *WhScrn 1, WhScrn 2, WhoHol B*
Teer, Barbara Ann *NotNAT*
Teetor, Macy O 1898- *AmSCAP 1966*
Teff, Joyce *WomWMM*
Teicher, Louis 1924- *AmSCAP 1966*
Teichmann, Howard 1916- *BiE&WWA, McGWD, NatPD, NotNAT*
Teifer, Gerald E 1922- *AmSCAP 1966*
Teirlinck, Herman 1879-1967 *CnMD, ModWD*
Teitel, Carol 1929- *BiE&WWA, NotNAT, WhoThe 16*
Teitelbaum, Jack 1902-1964 *AmSCAP 1966*
Teitelbaum, Pedro 1922- *IntMPA 1977*
Teixeira DeMattos, Alexander Louis 1865-1921 *NotNAT B, WhThe*
Teje, Tora *Film 2*
Telbin, William 1813-1873 *NotNAT B, OxThe*
Telbin, William Lewis 1846-1931 *NotNAT B, OxThe*
Teleshova, Elizabeth d1943 *NotNAT B*
Telford, Robert S 1923- *BiE&WWA, NotNAT*
Tell, Alma 1892-1937 *Film 1, Film 2, NotNAT B, TwYS, WhScrn 1, WhScrn 2, WhThe, WhoHol B*
Tell, Arthur *WhoHol A*
Tell, Olive 1894-1951 *Film 1, Film 2, NotNAT B, TwYS, WhScrn 1, WhScrn 2, WhThe, WhoHol B*
Tellegen, Lou 1881-1934 *Film 1, Film 2, FilmgC, MotPP, NotNAT B, TwYS, WhScrn 2, WhThe, WhoHol B*
Tellegen, Lou 1883-1934 *NotNAT A*
Tellegen, Lou 1884-1934 *WhScrn 1*
Teller, Edward 1908- *CelR 3*
Teller, Ira 1940- *IntMPA 1977*
Tellez, Gabriel *McGWD*
Telzlaff, Teddy *Film 1*
Temary, Elza *Film 2, WhScrn 1, WhScrn 2*
Tempest, Francis Adolphus Vane- *WhThe*
Tempest, Marie d1942 *Film 1, WhoHol B*
Tempest, Marie 1862-1942 *WhoStg 1906, WhoStg 1908*
Tempest, Marie 1864-1942 *CnThe, EncMT, FamA&A, FilmgC, OxThe, PIP&P, WhScrn 1, WhScrn 2, WhThe*
Tempest, Marie 1866-1942 *NotNAT A*
Tempesto, Louis 1905- *AmSCAP 1966*
Temple, Edward P d1921 *NotNAT B*
Temple, Helen 1894- *WhThe*
Temple, Joan d1965 *WhThe*
Temple, Lorraine *Film 2*
Temple, Madge d1943 *NotNAT B, WhThe*
Temple, Richard 1847- *WhThe*
Temple, Shirley *CelR 3, MotPP*
Temple, Shirley 1927- *WhoHol A*
Temple, Shirley 1928- *BiDFlm, CmMov, FilmgC, MovMk, OxFilm, ThFT*
Temple, Shirley 1929- *IntMPA 1977, WorEnF*
Temple, Shirley *see also* Black, Shirley Temple
Templeton, Alec 1910-1963 *AmSCAP 1966, NotNAT B, WhoHol B*
Templeton, Fay 1865-1939 *EncMT, NotNAT B, WhThe, WhoStg 1906, WhoStg 1908*
Templeton, Fay 1866-1939 *WhScrn 1, WhScrn 2, WhoHol B*
Templeton, John d1907 *NotNAT B*
Templeton, Pearl 1898- *AmSCAP 1966*
Templeton, W P 1913- *WhThe*

Templeton, W P 1915- *BiE&WWA*
Templeton, William B 1918- *AmSCAP 1966*
Tempo, Nino 1935- *AmSCAP 1966*
Tenbrook, Harry 1887-1960 *Film 2*, *WhScrn 2*
Tenbrook, James *Film 2*
Tenenholtz, Nettie *Film 2*
TenEyck, Lillian *Film 2*
TenEyck, Melissa *Film 2*
TenEyck, Mills, Jr. 1920- *BiE&WWA*
Tennant, Barbara *Film 1*, *Film 2*, *TwYS*
Tennant, William *IntMPA 1977*
Tennberg, Jean-Marc 1924-1971 *WhScrn 2*
Tennent, Henry M 1879-1941 *NotNAT B*, *WhThe*
Tenney, Jack B 1898- *AmSCAP 1966*
Tenny, Marion H d1964 *NotNAT B*
Tennyson, Alfred 1809-1892 *CnThe*, *McGWD*,
    NotNAT B, *OxThe*, *REnWD*
Tennyson, Gladys *Film 1*, *Film 2*
Tennyson, James J 1898- *AmSCAP 1966*
Tennyson, Walter *Film 2*
Tennyson, William J, Jr. 1923-1959 *AmSCAP 1966*
Tenser, Tony 1920- *IntMPA 1977*
Teoli, Albert G 1915- *AmSCAP 1966*
Tepper, Saul Joel 1899- *AmSCAP 1966*
Tepper, Sid 1918- *AmSCAP 1966*
Ter-Arutunian, Rouben 1920- *BiE&WWA*,
    NotNAT, *WhoThe 16*
Terale, Noel *Film 2*
Terebey, Raisa *WomWMM B*
Terence 190?BC-159BC *CnThe*, *McGWD*,
    NotNAT B, *OxThe*, *PIP&P*
Terence 195?BC-159BC *REnWD*
Terhune, Max 1891-1973 *FilmgC*, *WhScrn 2*,
    WhoHol B
Terker, Arthur 1899- *AmSCAP 1966*
Termini, Joe d1964 *NotNAT B*
Ternan, Thomas d1846 *NotNAT B*
Ternick, Frank 1895-1966 *WhScrn 2*
Terr, Al 1893-1967 *WhScrn 2*
Terr, Max 1890-1951 *AmSCAP 1966*
Terr, Mischa R 1899- *AmSCAP 1966*
Terranova, Dan *WhoHol A*
Terranova, Dino 1904-1969 *WhScrn 1*, *WhScrn 2*,
    WhoHol B
Terraux, L H Du d1878 *NotNAT B*
Terrell, Ken 1904-1966 *WhScrn 2*
Terrell, St. John 1916- *BiE&WWA*, *NotNAT*
Terribill, Giovanni *Film 2*
Terris, Ellaline d1971 *WhoHol B*
Terris, Norma 1904- *EncMT*, *Film 2*, *WhThe*,
    WhoHol A
Terris, Tom *Film 1*
Terriss, Ellaine 1871-1971 ˙*Film 2*
Terriss, Ellaline 1871-1971 *EncMT*, *FilmgC*,
    OxThe, *WhScrn 1*, *WhScrn 2*, *WhThe*
Terriss, Tom 1874-1964 *WhThe*
Terriss, Tom 1887-1964 *TwYS A*, *WhScrn 2*
Terriss, Mrs. William d1898 *NotNAT B*
Terriss, William 1847-1897 *NotNAT A*,
    NotNAT B, *OxThe*
Terron, Carlo 1913- *McGWD*
Terry, Alice *MotPP*
Terry, Alice 1896- *Film 1*, *Film 2*, *TwYS*
Terry, Alice 1899- *FilmgC*, *MovMk*
Terry, Alice 1901- *WhoHol A*
Terry, Beatrice 1890- *OxThe*, *WhThe*
Terry, Benjamin 1818-1896 *NotNAT B*, *OxThe*
Terry, Mrs. Benjamin 1819-1892 *NotNAT B*
Terry, Charles d1933 *NotNAT B*
Terry, Daniel 1789-1829 *NotNAT B*, *OxThe*
Terry, Dennis 1895-1932 *NotNAT B*, *OxThe*
Terry, Don 1902- *Film 2*, *FilmgC*, *WhoHol A*
Terry, Edward O'Connor 1844-1912 *NotNAT B*,
    OxThe, *WhThe*, *WhoStg 1908*

Terry, Eliza d1878 *NotNAT B*
Terry, Ellen Alice d1928 *Film 1*, *WhoHol B*
Terry, Ellen Alice 1847-1928 *CnThe*, *FamA&A*,
    OxThe, *PIP&P*
Terry, Ellen Alice 1848-1928 *Film 2*, *NotNAT A*,
    NotNAT B, *WhScrn 1*, *WhScrn 2*, *WhThe*,
    WhoStg 1906, *WhoStg 1908*
Terry, Ethel Grey 1898-1931 *Film 1*, *Film 2*,
    TwYS, *WhScrn 1*, *WhScrn 2*, *WhoHol B*
Terry, Ethelind 1900- *EncMT*, *WhThe*
Terry, Florence 1854-1896 *NotNAT B*, *OxThe*
Terry, Francis *Film 2*
Terry, Fred 1863-1933 *CnThe*, *NotNAT B*,
    OxThe, *WhScrn 1*, *WhScrn 2*, *WhThe*,
    WhoHol B, *WhoStg 1908*
Terry, George d1928 *NotNAT B*
Terry, George N 1906- *AmSCAP 1966*
Terry, Harry *Film 2*
Terry, Hazel 1918-1974 *WhScrn 2*, *WhThe*,
    WhoHol B
Terry, J E Harold 1885-1939 *NotNAT B*, *WhThe*
Terry, Jack *Film 2*
Terry, Sir John 1913- *IntMPA 1977*
Terry, Julia Emilie Neilson 1868-1957 *OxThe*
Terry, Kate 1844-1924 *NotNAT B*, *OxThe*,
    WhThe, *WhoStg 1908*   ˙
Terry, Mabel Gwynedd Terry-Lewis 1872-1957
    OxThe
Terry, Mabel Gwynedd Terry-Lewis *see also*
    Terry-Lewis, Mabel
Terry, Marion 1852-1930 *NotNAT B*, *OxThe*
Terry, Marion 1856-1930 *WhThe*, *WhoStg 1908*
Terry, Megan 1932- *ConDr 1977*, *CroCD*,
    NotNAT, *PIP&P*, *WhoThe 16*
Terry, Minnie 1882-1964 *OxThe*, *WhThe*
Terry, Nigel *WhoHol A*
Terry, Olive 1884- *WhThe*
Terry, Paul 1887-1971 *DcFM*, *FilmgC*
Terry, Philip 1909- *FilmgC*
Terry, Phillip 1909- *MotPP*, *WhoHol A*
Terry, Phyllis 1892- *OxThe*
Terry, Robert *WhoHol A*
Terry, Robert 1928- *AmSCAP 1966*
Terry, Robert E Huntington 1867-1953
    AmSCAP 1966
Terry, Ron 1920- *AmSCAP 1966*
Terry, Sarah Ballard 1817-1892 *OxThe*
Terry, Sheila 1910-1957 *WhScrn 2*, *WhoHol B*
Terry, Walter d1932 *NotNAT B*
Terry-Lewis, Mabel 1872-1957 *NotNAT B*,
    WhThe, *WhoHol B*
Terry-Lewis, Mabel *see also* Terry, Mabel Gwynedd
    Terry-Lewis
Terry-Thomas 1911- *FilmgC*, *IntMPA 1977*,
    MotPP, *MovMk*, *WhoHol A*
Terson, Peter 1932- *CnThe*, *ConDr 1977*,
    CroCD, *REnWD*, *WhoThe 16*
Tervapaa, Juhani *CroCD*
Terwilliger, George 1882- *TwYS A*
Terzieff, Laurent 1935- *FilmgC*, *WhoHol A*
Teshigahara, Hiroshi 1927- *BiDFlm*, *DcFM*,
    OxFilm, *WorEnF*
Tessari, Duccio 1926- *WorEnF*
Tessier, Robert *WhoHol A*
Tester, Desmond 1919- *FilmgC*, *WhThe*
Testoni, Alfredo 1856-1931 *McGWD*
Teternikov, Fyodor Kusmich *McGWD*
Tetley, Dorothy *WhThe*
Tetley, Walter 1915-1975 *WhScrn 2*, *WhoHol C*
Tetzel, Joan 1921- *BiE&WWA*, *MotPP*,
    NotNAT, *WhoHol A*, *WhoThe 16*
Tetzel, Joan 1924- *FilmgC*
Tetzlaff, Ted 1903- *BiDFlm*, *FilmgC*,
    IntMPA 1977, *WorEnF*

Tetzlaff, Toni *Film 2*
Teverner, William d1731 *NotNAT B*
Tevis, Carol 1907-1965 *WhScrn 2*
Tewkesbury, Joan *IntMPA 1977, WomWMM*
Tewkesbury, Peter 1924- *WorEnF*
Tewksbury, Peter 1924- *FilmgC*
Teyte, Maggie 1889- *EncMT, WhThe*
Thacher, Anita *WomWMM B*
Thackery, Bud 1903- *FilmgC*
Thalasso, Arthur *Film 2*
Thalberg, Irving 1899-1936 *BiDFlm, DcFM, FilmgC, MGM A, OxFilm, TwYS B, WorEnF*
Thalberg, T B d1947 *NotNAT B*
Thalhimer, Morton G, Jr. 1924- *IntMPA 1977*
Thalhimer, Morton Gustavus 1889- *IntMPA 1977*
Thane, Adele 1904- *BiE&WWA*
Thane, Edward d1954 *WhScrn 2*
Thane, Elswyth *WhThe*
Thane, Gibson *Film 2*
Tharp, Grahame 1912- *IntMPA 1977*
Thatcher, Eva 1862-1942 *Film 1, WhoHol B*
Thatcher, Evelyn 1862-1942 *WhScrn 1, WhScrn 2*
Thatcher, Heather *Film 1, Film 2, IntMPA 1977, WhThe, WhoHol A*
Thatcher, Howard Rutledge 1878- *AmSCAP 1966*
Thatcher, Torin 1905- *BiE&WWA, FilmgC, IntMPA 1977, MovMk, NotNAT, WhThe, WhoHol A*
Thaw, Evelyn Nesbit 1885-1967 *Film 1, WhScrn 1, WhScrn 2, WhoHol B*
Thaw, John 1942- *WhoHol A, WhoThe 16*
Thaw, Russell *Film 1, Film 2*
Thawl, Evelyn 1915-1945 *WhScrn 1, WhScrn 2*
Thaxter, Phyllis *BiE&WWA, MotPP, NotNAT*
Thaxter, Phyllis 1920- *WhoThe 16*
Thaxter, Phyllis 1921- *FilmgC, IntMPA 1977, MGM, MovMk, WhoHol A*
Thayer, Julia *WhoHol A*
Thayer, Lorna *WhoHol A*
Thayer, Lucien Hamilton 1890- *AmSCAP 1966*
Thayer, Merewyn *Film 2*
Theadore, Ralph *Film 2*
Theard, Sam 1904- *AmSCAP 1966*
Theburn, Robert *Film 2*
Theby, Rosemary 1885- *Film 1, Film 2, MotPP, TwYS*
Theilade, Nini 1915- *WhThe*
Theilmann, Helen d1956 *NotNAT B*
Theis, Alfred 1899-1951 *WhScrn 1, WhScrn 2*
Theise, Mortimer M 1866- *WhoStg 1908*
Theobald, Lewis d1944 *NotNAT B*
Theodorakis, Mikis 1925- *OxFilm, WorEnF*
Theodorus *OxThe, PIP&P*
Theognis *OxThe*
Theophile DeViau 1590-1626 *OxThe*
Thesiger, Ernest 1879-1961 *CnThe, Film 2, FilmgC, NotNAT B, Vers B, WhScrn 1, WhScrn 2, WhThe, WhoHol B*
Thespis *NotNAT B, OxThe*
Theta, Shirley Crane *WomWMM B*
Thew, Manora *Film 1*
Thiele, Robert 1922- *AmSCAP 1966*
Thiele, Rolf 1918- *DcFM, WorEnF*
Thiele, Wilhelm J 1890-1975 *DcFM, OxFilm*
Thiele, William J 1890-1975 *FilmgC, WhScrn 2*
Thielman, Ronald 1936- *AmSCAP 1966*
Thierry, Edouard d1894 *NotNAT B*
Thiess, Frank 1890- *CnMD*
Thiess, Manuela *WhoHol A*
Thiess, Ursula 1929- *FilmgC, MotPP, WhoHol A*
Thigpen, Helen d1966 *WhScrn 2, WhoHol B*

Thigpen, Lynne *WhoHol A*
Thimig, Helene d1974 *WhScrn 2, WhoHol B*
Thimig, Hermann *Film 2*
Thimm, Daisy *WhThe*
Thinnes, Roy *FilmgC, WhoHol A*
Thirard, Armand 1899- *DcFM, FilmgC, WorEnF*
Thirer, Irene d1964 *NotNAT B*
Thiriet, Maurice 1906- *DcFM*
Thirkield, Rob 1936- *NotNAT*
Thirwell, George *Film 2*
Thoma, Ludwig 1867-1921 *CnMD, McGWD, ModWD, NotNAT B*
Thoma, Mike 1926- *BiE&WWA*
Thomae, R L *Film 1*
Thomas, A E 1872-1947 *WhThe*
Thomas, A Goring d1892 *NotNAT B*
Thomas, Agnes *WhThe*
Thomas, Albert Ellsworth 1872-1947 *NotNAT B*
Thomas, Ambroise 1811-1896 *NotNAT B*
Thomas, Ann *WhoHol A*
Thomas, Anna I *WomWMM B*
Thomas, Augustus 1857-1934 *CnThe, McGWD, ModWD, NotNAT A, NotNAT B, OxThe, PIP&P, REnWD, WhThe*
Thomas, Augustus 1859- *WhoStg 1906, WhoStg 1908*
Thomas, Basil 1912-1957 *NotNAT B, WhThe*
Thomas, Bill 1921- *IntMPA 1977*
Thomas, Brandon 1856-1914 *McGWD, ModWD, NotNAT A, NotNAT B, WhThe*
Thomas, Brandon *see also* Thomas, Walter Brandon
Thomas, Chapman Snead 1909- *AmSCAP 1966*
Thomas, Charles Henry d1941 *NotNAT B*
Thomas, Christine *WhoHol A*
Thomas, Christopher 1894- *AmSCAP 1966*
Thomas, Danny 1914- *CelR 3, FilmgC, IntMPA 1977, MotPP, NewYTET, WhoHol A*
Thomas, David *WhoHol A*
Thomas, Daxon *WhoHol A*
Thomas, Dick 1915- *AmSCAP 1966*
Thomas, Dorothy 1882- *WhThe, WhoStg 1908*
Thomas, Dylan 1914-1953 *CnMD, McGWD, ModWD, NotNAT B, PIP&P*
Thomas, Edna 1886-1974 *WhScrn 2, WhoHol B*
Thomas, Edward *Film 2*
Thomas, Evan 1891- *WhThe*
Thomas, Frank 1889- *Film 2, Vers A, WhoHol A*
Thomas, Frank, Jr. 1926- *BiE&WWA, NotNAT*
Thomas, Frankie 1922- *WhoHol A*
Thomas, George 1914- *IntMPA 1977*
Thomas, Gerald 1920- *FilmgC, IntMPA 1977*
Thomas, Gretchen 1897-1964 *WhScrn 1, WhScrn 2, WhoHol B*
Thomas, Gus 1865-1926 *WhScrn 1, WhScrn 2*
Thomas, Gwyn 1913- *ConDr 1977, CroCD, WhoThe 16*
Thomas, Harry E 1920- *IntMPA 1977*
Thomas, Helen *AmSCAP 1966*
Thomas, Helga *Film 2*
Thomas, Herbert 1868- *WhThe*
Thomas, Howard *IntMPA 1977*
Thomas, J W d1878 *NotNAT B*
Thomas, James 1922- *IntMPA 1977*
Thomas, Jameson d1939 *WhoHol B*
Thomas, Jameson 1889-1939 *WhScrn 1, WhScrn 2*
Thomas, Jameson 1892-1939 *Film 2, FilmgC*
Thomas, Jamieson d1939 *NotNAT B*
Thomas, Jane *Film 2*
Thomas, Joel *WhoHol A*
Thomas, John Charles 1887-1960 *Film 2, NotNAT B, WhScrn 1, WhScrn 2,*

WhoHol B
Thomas, Lowell 1892- *CelR 3, FilmgC,
IntMPA 1977, NewYTET, WhoHol A*
Thomas, Lowell, Jr. *WhoHol A*
Thomas, Marie *WhoHol A*
Thomas, Marlo 1938- *CelR 3, IntMPA 1977,
WhoHol A*
Thomas, Mary Virginia *AmSCAP 1966*
Thomas, Michael 1925- *CelR 3*
Thomas, Michael Tilson 1944- *CelR 3*
Thomas, Olive d1920 *MotPP, WhoHol B*
Thomas, Olive 1884-1920 *WhScrn 1, WhScrn 2*
Thomas, Olive 1888-1920 *FilmgC*
Thomas, Olive 1898-1920 *Film 1, Film 2,
NotNAT B, TwYS*
Thomas, Peter Evan *Film 2*
Thomas, Philip M *WhoHol A*
Thomas, Phyllis 1904- *WhThe*
Thomas, Queenie 1900- *Film 1, Film 2*
Thomas, Ralph 1915- *FilmgC, IntMPA 1977,
WhoHol A, WorEnF*
Thomas, Richard 1951- *FilmgC, IntMPA 1977,
WhoHol A*
Thomas, Robert J 1922- *IntMPA 1977*
Thomas, Ruth 1911-1970 *WhScrn 1, WhScrn 2*
Thomas, Scott *WhoHol A*
Thomas, Stephen d1961 *NotNAT B*
Thomas, Sylvia 1931- *NatPD*
Thomas, Terry *FilmgC*
Thomas, Tony *WhoHol A*
Thomas, Villesta *WhoHol A*
Thomas, Virginia *Film 2*
Thomas, W Moy d1910 *NotNAT B*
Thomas, Walter Brandon 1856-1914 *OxThe*
Thomas, Walter Brandon *see also* Thomas, Brandon
Thomas, William 1918-1948 *WhScrn 2*
Thomas, William Buckwheat d1968 *WhScrn 1*
Thomas, William C 1892- *FilmgC*
Thomas, William C 1903- *AmSCAP 1966,
IntMPA 1977*
Thomas, Yvonne *Film 2*
Thomashefsky, Bessie d1962 *NotNAT B*
Thomashefsky, Boris 1868-1939 *NotNAT B*
Thomashefsky, Max 1872-1932 *WhScrn 1,
WhScrn 2*
Thomassin, Jeanne *WhThe*
Thome, Francis d1909 *NotNAT B*
Thome, Karen *WomWMM*
Thommen, Edward *BiE&WWA*
Thompsom, Lotus *Film 2*
Thompson, Al *Film 2*
Thompson, Alex *FilmgC*
Thompson, Alexander M 1861-1948 *NotNAT A,
NotNAT B, WhThe*
Thompson, Alfred d1895 *NotNAT B*
Thompson, Alfreda Lydia 1911- *AmSCAP 1966*
Thompson, Benjamin d1816 *NotNAT B*
Thompson, Bill d1971 *WhoHol B*
Thompson, Carlos 1916- *FilmgC, IntMPA 1977,
WhoHol A*
Thompson, Clarence *Film 2*
Thompson, Danielle *WomWMM*
Thompson, David H 1886-1957 *WhScrn 1,
WhScrn 2, WhoHol B*
Thompson, Denman 1833-1911 *ModWD,
NotNAT B, WhoStg 1908*
Thompson, Denton *Film 2*
Thompson, Duane 1905- *Film 2, TwYS,
WhoHol A*
Thompson, Eddie 1925- *AmSCAP 1966*
Thompson, Eric 1929- *WhoThe 16*
Thompson, Eric 1936- *NatPD*
Thompson, Evan *WhoHol A*
Thompson, Frank *WhoThe 16*

Thompson, Fred 1884-1949 *EncMT, NotNAT B,
WhThe*
Thompson, Fred 1890-1928 *Film 2*
Thompson, Fred *see also* Thomson, Fred
Thompson, Fred W 1901- *AmSCAP 1966*
Thompson, Frederick A 1870-1925 *WhScrn 1,
WhScrn 2, WhoHol B*
Thompson, Frederick W 1872-1919 *NotNAT B,
WhThe*
Thompson, George 1868-1929 *Film 2, WhScrn 1,
WhScrn 2, WhoHol B*
Thompson, Gerald Marr 1856-1938 *NotNAT B,
WhThe*
Thompson, Grace *Film 1*
Thompson, Hal 1894-1966 *WhScrn 2*
Thompson, Hank 1925- *AmSCAP 1966*
Thompson, Harlan 1890- *AmSCAP 1966*
Thompson, Hilarie *WhoHol A*
Thompson, Hugh *Film 1, Film 2, MotPP*
Thompson, J Denton *Film 2*
Thompson, J Lee 1914- *BiDFlm, DcFM, OxFilm,
WhThe, WorEnF*
Thompson, James 1700-1748 *PIP&P*
Thompson, James *see also* Thomson, James
Thompson, Jay 1927- *AmSCAP 1966,
BiE&WWA, NotNAT*
Thompson, Jeff *WhoHol A*
Thompson, Jimmy *WhoHol A*
Thompson, John d1634 *OxThe*
Thompson, Johnny *Film 2*
Thompson, Kay *MotPP, WhoHol A*
Thompson, Kay 1912- *CelR 3*
Thompson, Kay 1913- *AmSCAP 1966*
Thompson, Kenneth *Film 2*
Thompson, Leonard *Film 2*
Thompson, Lotus *Film 2, TwYS*
Thompson, Lydia 1836-1908 *FamA&A,
NotNAT B, OxThe*
Thompson, Madeleine d1964 *NotNAT B*
Thompson, Margaret *Film 1, WomWMM*
Thompson, Marshall *IntMPA 1977, MotPP,
WhoHol A*
Thompson, Marshall 1925- *MGM*
Thompson, Marshall 1926- *FilmgC, MovMk*
Thompson, Molly 1879-1928 *WhScrn 1,
WhScrn 2, WhoHol B*
Thompson, Nick *Film 2*
Thompson, Polly d1933 *WhScrn 2*
Thompson, Randall 1899- *AmSCAP 1966*
Thompson, Rex *WhoHol A*
Thompson, Richard D 1933- *BiE&WWA*
Thompson, Roy *Film 2*
Thompson, Sada 1929- *BiE&WWA, NotNAT,
PIP&P A, WhoHol A, WhoThe 16*
Thompson, Therese 1876-1936 *WhScrn 1,
WhScrn 2*
Thompson, Ulu M 1873-1957 *WhScrn 1,
WhScrn 2, WhoHol B*
Thompson, Victoria *WhoHol A*
Thompson, Virgil 1896- *WorEnF*
Thompson, Virgil *see also* Thomson, Virgil
Thompson, W H 1852-1923 *WhThe*
Thompson, W T d1940 *NotNAT B*
Thompson, William 1913-1971 *WhScrn 1,
WhScrn 2*
Thompson, William H 1852-1923 *Film 1, Film 2,
NotNAT B, WhScrn 2, WhoHol B*
Thompson, Woodman d1955 *NotNAT B*
Thoms, Virginia *BiE&WWA*
Thomson, Alan *IntMPA 1977*
Thomson, Beatrix 1900- *WhThe*
Thomson, Fred 1890-1928 *MotPP, TwYS,
WhScrn 1, WhScrn 2, WhoHol B*
Thomson, Fred *see also* Thompson, Fred

Thomson, James 1700-1748 *NotNAT B, OxThe*
Thomson, James *see also* Thompson, James
Thomson, Kenneth d1967 *MotPP, WhoHol B*
Thomson, Kenneth 1889-1967 *Film 2*
Thomson, Kenneth 1899-1967 *TwYS, WhScrn 1, WhScrn 2*
Thomson, Pat *WomWMM A, WomWMM B*
Thomson, Virgil 1896- *AmSCAP 1966, BiE&WWA, CelR 3, NotNAT, OxFilm*
Thomson, Virgil *see also* Thompson, Virgil
Thomson, William En is 1927- *AmSCAP 1966*
Thor, Jerome 1920- *IntMPA 1977, WhoHol A*
Thor, Larry d1976 *WhoHol C*
Thorburn, H M 1884-1924 *NotNAT B, WhThe*
Thorburn, June 1931-1967 *FilmgC, MotPP, WhScrn 1, WhScrn 2, WhoHol B*
Thordsen, Kelly *IntMPA 1977, WhoHol A*
Thorgersen, Ed *IntMPA 1977*
Thorley, Victor *WhoHol A*
Thorn, Geoffrey d1905 *NotNAT B*
Thorn, Lee E 1919- *IntMPA 1977*
Thornby, Robert T 1889- *TwYS A*
Thorndike, Andrew 1909- *DcFM, FilmgC, OxFilm, WorEnF*
Thorndike, Annelie 1925- *OxFilm, WomWMM, WorEnF*
Thorndike, Arthur Russell 1885- *WhThe*
Thorndike, Eileen 1891-1953 *OxThe, PIP&P*
Thorndike, Eileen 1891-1954 *NotNAT B, WhThe*
Thorndike, Lucille d1935 *Film 2, WhoHol B*
Thorndike, Oliver 1918-1954 *WhScrn 1, WhScrn 2, WhoHol B*
Thorndike, Russell 1885- *Film 2*
Thorndike, Russell 1885-1972 *OxThe, PIP&P, WhScrn 2, WhoHol B*
Thorndike, Russell 1885-1973 *CnThe*
Thorndike, Sybil 1882- *BiE&WWA, CnThe, FilmgC, MotPP, MovMk, NotNAT A, OxThe, WhoHol A*
Thorndike, Sybil 1882-1975 *Film 2*
Thorndike, Sybil 1882-1976 *NotNAT B, PIP&P, WhoThe 16*
Thorndyke, Lucyle 1885-1935 *WhScrn 1, WhScrn 2*
Thorne, Ann Maria Mestayer d1881 *OxThe*
Thorne, Charles Robert, Jr. 1840-1883 *NotNAT B, OxThe*
Thorne, Charles Robert, Sr. 1814-1893 *OxThe*
Thorne, Clara d1915 *NotNAT B*
Thorne, Dick 1905-1957 *WhScrn 1, WhScrn 2*
Thorne, Dyanne *WhoHol A*
Thorne, Eric d1922 *NotNAT B*
Thorne, Francis 1922- *AmSCAP 1966*
Thorne, George Tyrrel 1856-1922 *NotNAT B, OxThe*
Thorne, Robert 1881-1965 *Film 2, WhScrn 1, WhScrn 2, WhoHol B*
Thorne, Sarah 1836-1899 *NotNAT B*
Thorne, Sarah 1837-1899 *OxThe*
Thorne, Sylvia d1922 *NotNAT B*
Thorne, Mrs. Thomas d1884 *NotNAT B*
Thorne, Thomas 1841-1918 *NotNAT B, OxThe, WhThe*
Thorne, William L *Film 2*
Thornhill, Claude 1908-1965 *AmSCAP 1966, WhScrn 1, WhScrn 2, WhoHol B*
Thornton, Charles Bates 1913- *CelR 3*
Thornton, Dennison S !909- *IntMPA 1977*
Thornton, Edith *Film 2, TwYS*
Thornton, Frank d1918 *NotNAT B*
Thornton, Frank 1921- *WhoHol A, WhoThe 16*
Thornton, Gladys 1899-1964 *WhScrn 1, WhScrn 2, WhoHol B*
Thornton, James 1861-1938 *AmSCAP 1966,*

NotNAT B
Thornwall, Francis *Film 2*
Thorp, Joseph Peter 1873- *WhThe*
Thorpe, George 1891-1961 *WhThe*
Thorpe, Gordon *Film 2*
Thorpe, Jerry 1930?- *FilmgC, NewYTET*
Thorpe, Jim 1888-1953 *WhScrn 1, WhScrn 2, WhoHol B*
Thorpe, Morgan *Film 1*
Thorpe, Richard 1896- *CmMov, Film 2, FilmgC, IntMPA 1977, TwYS A, WhoHol A, WorEnF*
Thorpe, Ted 1917-1970 *WhScrn 2*
Thorpe-Bates, Peggy 1914- *WhoHol A, WhoThe 16*
Thorson, Russell *WhoHol A*
Thow, George A 1908- *AmSCAP 1966*
Thrasher, Ethelyn 1912- *BiE&WWA, NotNAT*
Three Stooges *MotPP*
Three Stooges *see also* Stooges, The Three
Threlkeld, Budge 1922- *BiE&WWA*
Thring, Frank *CmMov, FilmgC, WhoHol A*
Throckmorton, Cleon 1897-1965 *BiE&WWA, NotNAT B, PIP&P, WhThe*
Throne, Malachi *WhoHol A*
Thropp, Clara d1960 *NotNAT B*
Thrower, Fred M 1910- *IntMPA 1977*
Thuillier, Emilio *WhThe*
Thulin, Ingrid 1929- *BiDFlm, CelR 3, FilmgC, IntMPA 1977, MotPP, MovMk, OxFilm, WhoHol A, WomWMM, WorEnF*
Thumb, Tom d1926 *WhScrn 2*
Thumb, Tom 1838-1883 *NotNAT B*
Thumb, Mrs. Tom 1841-1919 *WhScrn 2*
Thunder *Film 2*
Thunder Cloud, Chief 1899- *IntMPA 1977*
Thundercloud, Chief 1900-1955 *FilmgC, Vers A*
Thundercloud, Chief *see also* Chief Thundercloud
Thurber, J Kent 1892-1957 *WhScrn 1, WhScrn 2*
Thurber, James 1894-1961 *FilmgC, McGWD, NotNAT A, NotNAT B*
Thurburn, Gwynneth 1899- *WhoThe 16*
Thurman, Bill *WhoHol A*
Thurman, Mary 1894-1925 *Film 1, Film 2, MotPP, TwYS, WhScrn 1, WhScrn 2, WhoHol B*
Thurmond, Strom 1902- *CelR 3*
Thurner, Georges d1910 *NotNAT B*
Thurston, Carol 1923-1969 *IntMPA 1977, WhScrn 2, WhoHol B*
Thurston, Charles E 1869-1940 *Film 2, WhScrn 1, WhScrn 2, WhoHol B*
Thurston, Ernest Temple 1879-1933 *NotNAT B, WhThe*
Thurston, Harry d1955 *NotNAT B, WhScrn 2*
Thurston, Muriel 1875-1943 *WhScrn 1, WhScrn 2*
Thurston, Ted *WhoHol A*
Thury, Ilona d1953 *NotNAT B*
Thurzo, Gabor 1912- *CroCD*
Thyssen, Greta *WhoHol A*
Tiazza, Dario d1974 *WhoHol B*
Tibbett, Lawrence 1896-1960 *Film 2, FilmgC, MGM, NotNAT B, WhScrn 1, WhScrn 2, WhThe, WhoHol B*
Tibbles, George F 1913- *AmSCAP 1966*
Tibbs, Casey *WhoHol A*
Tice, Steve *WhoHol A*
Tich, Little 1868- *WhThe*
Tichenor, Edna *Film 2*
Tichenor, Tom 1923- *BiE&WWA, NotNAT*
Tickell, Richard d1793 *NotNAT B*
Tickle, Frank 1893-1955 *NotNAT B, WhThe, WhoHol B*

Tidblad, Inga 1902-1975 *WhScrn 2, WhoHol C*
Tiden, Fritz d1931 *NotNAT B*
Tiden, Zelma *Film 2*
Tidmarsh, Ferdinand 1883-1922 *Film 1,
   WhScrn 2*
Tidmarsh, Vivian 1896-1941 *NotNAT B, WhThe*
Tidyman, Ernest *IntMPA 1977*
Tieck, Johann Ludwig 1773-1853 *McGWD*
Tieck, Ludwig 1773-1853 *CnThe, NotNAT B,
   OxThe, REnWD*
Tiedtke, Jacob 1875-1960 *WhoHol B*
Tiedtke, Jakob 1875-1960 *Film 2, WhScrn 1,
   WhScrn 2*
T'ien, Han 1898- *REnWD*
Tiercelin, Louis 1849- *WhThe*
Tierney, Gene 1920- *BiDFlm, CmMov, FilmgC,
   IntMPA 1977, MotPP, MovMk, WhoHol A,
   WorEnF*
Tierney, Harry 1890-1965 *AmSCAP 1966,
   BiE&WWA, EncMT, NewMT, NotNAT B*
Tierney, Harry 1894-1965 *WhThe*
Tierney, Lawrence 1919- *FilmgC, IntMPA 1977,
   MotPP, MovMk, WhoHol A*
Tietjens, Paul 1877-1943 *AmSCAP 1966,
   NotNAT B*
Tiffin, Pamela 1942- *FilmgC, IntMPA 1977,
   MotPP, WhoHol A*
Tigerman, Gary *WhoHol A*
Tighe, Harry 1885?-1935 *NotNAT B, WhScrn 1,
   WhScrn 2, WhoHol B*
Tighe, Kevin *WhoHol A*
Tilbury, Zeffie 1863- *Film 1*
Tilbury, Zeffie 1863-1945 *Film 2, TwYS*
Tilbury, Zeffie 1863-1950 *FilmgC, NotNAT B,
   Vers B, WhScrn 1, WhScrn 2, WhThe,
   WhoHol B*
Tilden, Beau *WhoHol A*
Tilden, Bill 1893-1953 *NotNAT B, WhScrn 1,
   WhScrn 2, WhoHol B*
Tilden, Milano C d1951 *NotNAT B*
Tilden, William T *Film 2*
Tildsley, Peter d1962 *NotNAT B*
Tilghman, William Matthew 1854-1924 *WhScrn 2*
Till, Eric 1929- *FilmgC*
Till, Jenny *WhoHol A*
Tiller, John d1925 *NotNAT B*
Tiller, Nadia *WhoHol A*
Tiller, Nadja 1929- *WorEnF*
Tiller, Najda 1929- *FilmgC*
Tilles, Ken 1912-1970 *WhScrn 2*
Tilley, John d1935 *NotNAT B*
Tilley, Vesta 1864-1952 *NotNAT A, NotNAT B,
   OxThe, PIP&P, WhThe*
Tillinghast, Charles 1911- *CelR 3*
Tillman, Edwin Earl 1900- *AmSCAP 1966*
Tillstrom, Burr 1917- *AmSCAP 1966, CelR 3,
   IntMPA 1977*
Tilly, Vesta 1864-1952 *WhoStg 1906,
   WhoStg 1908*
Tilney, Sir Edmund *OxThe*
Tilton, Edwin Booth 1860-1926 *Film 1, Film 2,
   WhScrn 1, WhScrn 2, WhoHol B*
Tilton, George 1922- *AmSCAP 1966*
Tilton, James A *Film 2*
Tilton, James F 1937- *NotNAT, WhoThe 16*
Tilton, Martha *WhoHol A*
Tilton, Webb 1915- *BiE&WWA*
Timberg, Herman 1892-1952 *WhScrn 1,
   WhScrn 2, WhoHol B*
Timberg, Sammy 1903- *AmSCAP 1966*
Timblin, Slim d1962 *NotNAT B*
Timbrooke, Harry *Film 2*
Timm, Wladimir 1885-1958 *AmSCAP 1966*
Timmons, Joseph 1897-1933 *WhScrn 1,*

WhScrn 2
Timontayev, A *Film 2*
Tincher, Fay *Film 1, Film 2, MotPP, TwYS*
Tindale, Franklin M 1871-1947 *WhScrn 1,
   WhScrn 2*
Tindall, Loren 1921-1973 *WhScrn 2, WhoHol B*
Ting-Liang-Tchao *Film 2*
Tingwell, Charles 1917- *FilmgC, WhoHol A*
Tinker, Grant A 1926- *IntMPA 1977, NewYTET*
Tinley, Ned *Film 1*
Tinling, James 1889?-1955 *IntMPA 1977*
Tinling, James 1899?-1955 *FilmgC*
Tinne, Alex *WhoHol A*
Tinney, Frank 1878-1940 *NotNAT B, WhThe,
   WhoHol B*
Tinsman, Sylvia McKaye 1916-1975 *WhScrn 2*
Tinti, Gabriele *WhoHol A*
Tinturin, Peter 1910- *AmSCAP 1966*
Tiny Tim 1930?- *CelR 3, WhoHol A*
Tiomkin, Dimitri 1899- *CmMov, DcFM,
   IntMPA 1977*
Tiomkin, Dmitri 1899- *CelR 3, FilmgC, OxFilm,
   WorEnF*
Tippit, Wayne *WhoHol A*
Tirella, Eduardo 1924-1966 *WhScrn 2*
Tiroff, James d1975 *WhScrn 2*
Tirso De Molina 1571?-1648 *OxThe, REnWD*
Tirso De Molina see also Molina, Tirso De
Tisch, Laurence A 1922- *IntMPA 1977*
Tisch, Preston Robert 1926- *IntMPA 1977*
Tishman, Fay 1913- *AmSCAP 1966*
Tisse, Edouard 1897-1961 *FilmgC*
Tisse, Eduard Kasimirovich 1897-1961 *DcFM*
Tisse, Edvard 1897-1961 *OxFilm*
Tisse, Edward 1897-1961 *WorEnF*
Tissier, Jean 1896-1973 *WhScrn 2, WhoHol B*
Tissot, Alice 1890-1971 *Film 2, WhScrn 1,
   WhScrn 2, WhoHol B*
Titayna *WomWMM*
Titheradge, Dion 1879-1934 *WhScrn 1, WhScrn 2*
Titheradge, Dion 1889-1934 *NotNAT B, WhThe*
Titheradge, George S 1848-1916 *NotNAT B,
   WhThe*
Titheradge, Lily d1937 *NotNAT B*
Titheradge, Madge 1887-1961 *NotNAT B,
   WhScrn 1, WhScrn 2, WhThe, WhoHol B*
Titmuss, Phyllis 1900-1946 *Film 2, NotNAT B,
   WhThe*
Tittell, Charlotte d1941 *NotNAT B*
Titterton, William Richard 1876-1963 *WhThe*
Titus, Lydia Yeamans d1929 *TwYS, WhoHol B*
Titus, Lydia Yeamans 1866-1929 *WhScrn 1,
   WhScrn 2*
Titus, Lydia Yeamans 1874-1929 *Film 1, Film 2*
Tizol, Juan 1900- *AmSCAP 1966*
Tjader, Callen 1893- *AmSCAP 1966*
Tobey, Dan *Film 2*
Tobey, Ken *WhoHol A*
Tobey, Kenneth *MotPP*
Tobey, Mark 1890- *CelR 3*
Tobias, Charles 1898- *AmSCAP 1966*
Tobias, Fred 1928- *AmSCAP 1966*
Tobias, George *IntMPA 1977, MotPP*
Tobias, George 1901- *FilmgC, MovMk,
   WhoHol A*
Tobias, George 1905- *BiE&WWA, NotNAT,
   Vers A*
Tobias, Harry 1895- *AmSCAP 1966*
Tobias, Henry 1905- *AmSCAP 1966*
Tobin, Dan 1909?- *FilmgC, PIP&P, WhoHol A*
Tobin, Darra Lyn *WhoHol A*
Tobin, Genevieve *MotPP*
Tobin, Genevieve 1901- *FilmgC, HolP 30, ThFT,
   WhoHol A*

Tobin, Genevieve 1902- *WhThe*
Tobin, Genevieve 1904- *MovMk*
Tobin, John d1804 *NotNAT B*
Tobin, Lenore 1912- *BiE&WWA*
Tobin, Lew 1904- *AmSCAP 1966*
Tobin, Michele *WhoHol A*
Tobin, Vivian 1904- *WhThe*
Tobitt, Janet E 1898- *AmSCAP 1966*
Toch, Ernst 1887-1964 *AmSCAP 1966*
Toche, Raoul d1895 *NotNAT B*
Tod, Dorothy *WomWMM A*, *WomWMM B*
Tod, Malcolm *Film 2*
Todaro, Tony 1915- *AmSCAP 1966*
Todd, Ann *IntMPA 1977, MotPP, WhoThe 16*
Todd, Ann 1909- *FilmgC, MovMk, OxFilm,*
  WhoHol A
Todd, Ann 1910- *BiE&WWA*
Todd, Ann 1932- *FilmgC*
Todd, Arthur W 1920- *AmSCAP 1966*
Todd, Beverly *WhoHol A*
Todd, Bob 1922- *FilmgC, WhoHol A*
Todd, Christine *WhoHol A*
Todd, Clarence E 1897- *AmSCAP 1966*
Todd, Dana *Film 2*
Todd, Dotty 1923- *AmSCAP 1966*
Todd, Harry 1865-1935 *Film 1, Film 2,*
  WhScrn 1, WhScrn 2, WhoHol B
Todd, J Garrett *WhThe*
Todd, James 1908-1968 *WhScrn 2, WhoHol B*
Todd, Lisa *WhoHol A*
Todd, Lola *Film 2, TwYS, WhoHol A*
Todd, Michael 1907-1958 *EncMT, NotNAT A,*
  NotNAT B, WhThe, WorEnF
Todd, Mike 1907-1958 *DcFM, FilmgC, OxFilm*
Todd, Richard 1919- *CmMov, FilmgC,*
  IntMPA 1977, MotPP, MovMk, WhoHol A,
  WhoThe 16
Todd, Thelma d1935 *MotPP, WhoHol B*
Todd, Thelma 1905-1935 *Film 2, FilmgC,*
  MovMk, NotNAT B, ThFT, WhScrn 1,
  WhScrn 2
Todd, Thelma 1908-1935 *TwYS*
Todd, Tom T 1923- *AmSCAP 1966*
Toddy, Ted 1912- *IntMPA 1977*
Todhunter, John d1916 *NotNAT B*
Todman, Howard 1920- *IntMPA 1977*
Todman, William S 1916- *IntMPA 1977*
Todris, Murray 1918- *AmSCAP 1966*
Toeplitz, Jerzy *WomWMM*
Tognazzi, Ugo 1922- *FilmgC, WhoHol A*
Toguri, David *WhoThe 16*
Tokar, Norman 1920- *FilmgC, IntMPA 1977*
Tokieda, Toshie *WomWMM, WomWMM B*
Tokonaga, Frank *Film 1, Film 2*
Tolan, Kathleen *WhoHol A*
Tolan, Michael *BiE&WWA, NotNAT,*
  WhoHol A
Toland, Gregg 1904-1948 *DcFM, FilmgC,*
  OxFilm, WorEnF
Toler, Hooper 1891-1922 *WhScrn 1, WhScrn 2,*
  WhoHol B
Toler, Sidney 1874-1947 *Film 2, FilmgC, MotPP,*
  MovMk, NotNAT B, WhScrn 1, WhScrn 2,
  WhThe, WhoHol B
Tolkan, James *WhoHol A*
Tolkien, J R R 1892- *CelR 3*
Toll, Pamela *WhoHol A*
Tollaire, August *Film 2*
Toller, Ernst 1893-1939 *CnMD, CnThe,*
  McGWD, ModWD, NotNAT B, OxThe,
  PIP&P, REnWD, WhThe
Toller, Rosalie 1885- *WhThe*
Tolley, Jean *Film 2*
Tolly, Frank d1924 *WhScrn 2*

Tolsky, Susan *WhoHol A*
Tolstoi, Countess 1846-1919 *WhScrn 2*
Tolstoi, Aleksei Nikolaevich 1883-1945 *ModWD*
Tolstoi, Leo 1828-1910 *ModWD*
Tolstoy, A K 1817-1875 *McGWD*
Tolstoy, Aleksey Nikolayevich 1883-1945 *McGWD*
Tolstoy, Alexei 1817-1875 *PIP&P*
Tolstoy, Alexei 1883-1945 *CnMD*
Tolstoy, Alexei Konstantinovich 1817-1875 *OxThe*
Tolstoy, Alexei Nikolaivich 1882-1945 *OxThe*
Tolstoy, Alexie Nikolayevich 1882-1945
  NotNAT B
Tolstoy, Count Illya *Film 2*
Tolstoy, Leo 1828-1910 *FilmgC, McGWD,*
  PIP&P, REnWD
Tolstoy, Leo Nikolaivich 1828-1910 *OxThe*
Tolstoy, Leo Nikolaivich 1828-1910 *NotNAT B*
Tolstoy, Leo Nikolayevitch 1828-1910 *CnMD*
Tolstoy, Lev Nikolayevich 1828-1910 *CnThe*
Tolstoy, Countess Tamara *Film 2*
Tom, C Y 1907- *IntMPA 1977*
Toma, Peter 1922- *AmSCAP 1966*
Tomack, Sid 1907-1962 *NotNAT B, Vers A,*
  WhScrn 1, WhScrn 2, WhoHol B
Tomamoto, Thomas 1879-1924 *WhScrn 1,*
  WhScrn 2
Toman, Gerald J 1937- *AmSCAP 1966*
Tomarchio, Ludovico 1886-1947 *WhScrn 2*
Tomasini, George 1910-1965 *CmMov*
Tombes, Andrew *IntMPA 1977, WhScrn 2*
Tombes, Andrew 1889- *FilmgC*
Tombes, Andrew 1891?- *MovMk, WhoHol A*
Tombragel, Maurice *IntMPA 1977*
Tomei, Luigi 1910-1955 *WhScrn 1, WhScrn 2*
Tomelty, Joseph 1910- *FilmgC, WhoHol A*
Tomkins, Don *WhoHol A*
Tomkis, Thomas *NotNAT B*
Tomlan, Gwynne *WhoHol A*
Tomlin, Blanche 1889- *WhThe*
Tomlin, Lily 1936- *CelR 3, IntMPA 1977,*
  WhoHol A
Tomlin, Pinky 1908- *AmSCAP 1966, WhoHol A*
Tomlins, Frederick Guest d1867 *NotNAT B*
Tomlinson, Daniel G *Film 2*
Tomlinson, David 1917- *FilmgC, IntMPA 1977,*
  WhoHol A, WhoThe 16
Tomlinson, Leslie *Film 2*
Tommy, Tony *Film 2*
Tompkins, Angel *WhoHol A*
Tompkins, Darlene *WhoHol A*
Tompkins, Eugene d1909 *NotNAT B*
Tompkins, Joan *WhoHol A*
Toms, Carl 1927- *NotNAT, WhoThe 16*
Toncray, Kate *Film 1, Film 2, TwYS*
Tone, Franchot *MotPP, PIP&P*
Tone, Franchot d1968 *WhoHol B*
Tone, Franchot 1905- *BiE&WWA*
Tone, Franchot 1905-1968 *FilmgC, MGM,*
  NotNAT B, WhScrn 1, WhScrn 2
Tone, Franchot 1905-1969 *MovMk*
Tone, Franchot 1906-1968 *OxFilm, WhThe,*
  WorEnF
Tone, Franchot 1906-1969 *BiDFlm, CmMov*
Toner, Tom *WhoHol A*
Toney, James d1973 *WhScrn 2*
Tong, Kam 1907-1969 *WhScrn 1, WhScrn 2,*
  WhoHol B
Tong, Sammee 1901-1964 *MotPP, WhScrn 1,*
  WhScrn 2, WhoHol B
Tonge, H Asheton d1927 *NotNAT B*
Tonge, Lillian Bernard *Film 2*
Tonge, Philip d1959 *WhoHol B*
Tonge, Philip 1892-1959 *NotNAT B, WhThe*
Tonge, Philip 1898-1959 *WhScrn 1, WhScrn 2*

Tonning, Merrill D, Sr. 1910- *AmSCAP 1966*
Tonson, Jacob d1736 *NotNAT B*
Tonti, Aldo 1910- *DcFM, FilmgC, WorEnF*
Tony 1909-1942 *WhScrn 2*
Toobin, Jerome *NewYTET*
Toohey, John L 1916- *BiE&WWA*
Toohey, John Peter d1947 *NotNAT B*
Tooker, William 1875- *Film 1, Film 2, TwYS*
Tooker, William H 1864-1936 *WhScrn 1, WhScrn 2, WhoHol B*
Toole, John Laurence 1830-1906 *NotNAT B, OxThe*
Toole, John Lawrence 1830-1906 *NotNAT A*
Tooley, Nicholas 1575?-1623 *NotNAT B, OxThe*
Toombes, Andrew 1889- *Vers A*
Toomey, Regis 1902- *Film 2, FilmgC, IntMPA 1977, MotPP, MovMk, Vers A, WhoHol A*
Toone, Geoffrey 1910- *WhoHol A, WhoThe 16*
Topart, Jean *WhoHol A*
Topart, Lise 1930-1952 *WhScrn 1, WhScrn 2*
Topaz, Muriel 1932- *BiE&WWA, NotNAT*
Topham, Edward d1820 *NotNAT B*
Topol 1935- *FilmgC, WhoHol A*
Topol, Haym 1935- *MovMk*
Topol, Josef 1935- *CnThe, CroCD, REnWD*
Toporkov, Vasily Osipovich 1889- *WhThe*
Topper, Burt 1934- *FilmgC, WhoHol A*
Torbett, Dave 1908- *AmSCAP 1966*
Tordesilla, Jesus 1893-1973 *WhScrn 2*
Torelli, Achille 1841-1922 *McGWD*
Torelli, Giacomo 1608-1678 *CnThe, NotNAT B, OxThe*
Toren, Marta 1926-1957 *FilmgC, MotPP, NotNAT B, WhScrn 1, WhScrn 2, WhoHol B*
Torf, Silva *Film 2*
Tork, Peter 1942- *WhoHol A*
Torme, Mel *IntMPA 1977, WhoHol A*
Torme, Mel 1923- *FilmgC*
Torme, Mel 1925- *CelR 3*
Torme, Melvin Howard 1925- *AmSCAP 1966*
Torn, Rip 1931- *BiE&WWA, FilmgC, IntMPA 1977, MovMk, NotNAT, WhoHol A, WhoThe 16*
Tornatore, Joe *WhoHol A*
Tornbech, Svend *Film 2*
Tornek, Jack d1974 *WhScrn 2*
Torning, Alice *Film 2*
Torrance, Mrs. Joe Taylor 1899- *AmSCAP 1966*
Torre, Janice *AmSCAP 1966*
Torre-Nilsson, Leopoldo 1924- *DcFM, FilmgC, OxFilm, WorEnF*
Torre Rios, Leopoldo 189-?-1960 *DcFM*
Torrence, David 1864-1951 *WhScrn 2*
Torrence, David 1870- *WhThe*
Torrence, David 1880-1942 *Film 1, Film 2, TwYS, WhoHol B*
Torrence, Ernest 1878-1933 *Film 2, FilmgC, MotPP, MovMk, NotNAT B, TwYS, WhScrn 1, WhScrn 2, WhThe, WhoHol B*
Torres, Cathie *Film 1*
Torres, Felipe *PIP&P A*
Torres, Joan *WomWMM*
Torres, Jose *WhoHol A*
Torres, Liz *WhoHol A*
Torres, Raquel 1908- *Film 2, FilmgC, MotPP, TwYS, WhoHol A*
Torres Naharro, Bartolome De d1524? *OxThe*
Torres Naharro, Bartolome De 1476?-1531? *McGWD*
Torrey, Roger *WhoHol A*
Torriani, Aimee 1890-1963 *WhScrn 1, WhScrn 2, WhoHol B*

Torruco, Miguel 1920-1956 *WhScrn 1, WhScrn 2, WhoHol B*
Tors, Ivan 1916- *CelR 3, FilmgC, IntMPA 1977, NewYTET*
Torvay, Jose d1973 *WhScrn 2*
Toscanini, Arthuro 1867-1957 *NotNAT B*
Toscanini, Arturo 1867-1957 *WhScrn 2*
Toscano, Carmen *WomWMM*
Toscano, Salvador *WomWMM*
Toscano Barragan, Salvador 1873-1947 *DcFM*
Toser, David *NotNAT*
Toshevas, Nevena *WomWMM*
Tosi, Piero 1928- *DcFM*
Toso, Otello d1966 *WhScrn 1, WhScrn 2, WhoHol B*
Totheroh, Dan 1894- *ModWD, WhThe*
Totheroh, Dan 1898- *CnMD*
Totheroh, Rollie 1890- *WorEnF*
Totheroh, Rollie 1891-1967 *FilmgC*
Toto *Film 1, MotPP*
Toto 1897-1967 *FilmgC, MovMk, WhScrn 1, WhScrn 2, WhoHol B*
Toto 1898-1967 *WorEnF*
Toto The Clown 1888-1938 *WhScrn 2*
Totten, Joseph Byron d1946 *NotNAT B*
Totter, Audrey *IntMPA 1977, MotPP*
Totter, Audrey 1918- *FilmgC, MGM, MovMk*
Totter, Audrey 1919?- *WhoHol A*
Touchagues *Film 2*
Toughey, John *Film 2*
Toukermine, Doris *WomWMM*
Touliatos, George 1929- *BiE&WWA*
Toulmouche, Fredeic d1909 *NotNAT B*
Touloubieva, Z *WomWMM*
Toulout, Jean *Film 2*
Toumanova, Tamara 1917- *FilmgC, WhThe, WhoHol A*
Toumarkine, Doris *WomWMM B*
Tourel, Jennie 1910-1973 *WhScrn 2, WhoHol B*
Tourneur, Andree *Film 2*
Tourneur, Cyril 1575-1626 *CnThe, McGWD, NotNAT B, OxThe, REnWD*
Tourneur, Jacques 1904- *BiDFlm, CmMov, DcFM, FilmgC, OxFilm, WorEnF*
Tourneur, Maurice 1876-1961 *BiDFlm, DcFM, FilmgC, OxFilm, TwYS A, WorEnF*
Tourneur, Maurice 1878-1961 *MovMk*
Tours, Frank E 1877-1963 *NotNAT B, WhThe*
Tourtelot, Madeline *WomWMM B*
Toutain, Blanche d1932 *NotNAT B, WhThe*
Touzet, Rene 1916- *AmSCAP 1966*
Tovar, Lupita 1911- *WhoHol A*
Tover, Leo 1902- *FilmgC*
Tover, May 1911-1949 *WhScrn 1, WhScrn 2, WhoHol B*
Tovstonogov, Georgyi Alexandrovich 1915- *OxThe*
Towb, Harry 1925- *WhoHol A, WhoThe 16*
Towbin, Marion Fredi *NatPD*
Tower, Allen d1963 *NotNAT B*
Tower, John 1925- *CelR 3*
Towers, Constance 1933- *MotPP, WhoHol A, WhoThe 16*
Towers, Harry Alan 1920- *FilmgC, IntMPA 1977*
Towers, Harry P 1873- *WhThe*
Towers, Johnson d1891 *NotNAT B*
Towers, Samuel *OxThe*
Towne, Aline *WhoHol A*
Towne, Charles Hanson 1877-1949 *AmSCAP 1966, NotNAT B*
Towne, Edward Owings 1869- *WhoStg 1908*
Towne, Gene 1904- *IntMPA 1977*
Towne, Robert *IntMPA 1977*
Towne, Rosella 1919- *Film 2*
Townes, Christopher *WhoHol A*

Townes, Harry *NotNAT, WhoHol A*
Townley, James d1778 *NotNAT B*
Townley, Robin *Film 1*
Townley, Toke *WhoHol A*
Townsend, Anna d1923 *Film 2, WhScrn 1,
    WhScrn 2, WhoHol B*
Townsend, Aurelian *NotNAT B*
Townsend, Brigham 1909- *AmSCAP 1966*
Townsend, Colleen 1928- *WhoHol A*
Townsend, Genevieve *Film 2*
Townsend, Jill *WhoHol A*
Townsend, K C *WhoHol A*
Townsend, Leo 1908- *IntMPA 1977*
Townsend, Pauline Swanson *IntMPA 1977*
Townsend, Robert 1920- *CelR 3*
Townsend, Thompson d1870 *NotNAT B*
Towse, John Ranken 1845-1927 *OxThe*
Towse, John Ranken 1845-1933 *NotNAT B*
Toy, Beatrice d1938 *NotNAT B*
Toy, Noel *WhoHol A*
Toye, Geoffrey Edward 1889- *WhThe*
Toye, Wendy 1917- *EncMT, FilmgC,
    IntMPA 1977, WhoThe 16, WomWMM*
Toyne, Gabriel 1905-1963 *NotNAT B, WhThe,
    WhoHol B*
Tozere, Frederic 1901-1972 *BiE&WWA,
    NotNAT B, WhScrn 2, WhThe, WhoHol B*
Tozzi, Fausto *WhoHol A*
Tozzi, Giorgio 1923- *CelR 3*
Trabert, Tony *WhoHol A*
Trace, Albert J *AmSCAP 1966*
Trace, Ben L 1897- *AmSCAP 1966*
Tracey, Thomas F 1880-1961 *NotNAT B,
    WhScrn 2*
Tracey, William G 1893-1957 *AmSCAP 1966*
Tracy, Arthur 1903- *FilmgC, WhoHol A*
Tracy, Helen *Film 1, Film 2, WhoStg 1908*
Tracy, Lee 1898-1968 *BiE&WWA, Film 2,
    FilmgC, HolP 30, MotPP, MovMk,
    NotNAT B, WhScrn 1, WhScrn 2, WhThe,
    WhoHol B*
Tracy, Spencer 1900-1967 *BiDFlm, BiE&WWA,
    CmMov, FilmgC, MGM, MotPP, MovMk,
    NotNAT B, OxFilm, PIP&P, WhScrn 1,
    WhScrn 2, WhThe, WhoHol B, WorEnF*
Tracy, Virginia d1946 *NotNAT B*
Tracy, William 1917-1967 *FilmgC, MotPP,
    WhScrn 1, WhScrn 2, WhoHol B*
Trader, Bill 1922- *AmSCAP 1966*
Traeger, Rick *WhoHol A*
Traill, Peter 1896- *WhThe*
Train, Jack 1902-1966 *WhScrn 1, WhScrn 2,
    WhoHol B*
Trainer, David 1947- *NatPD*
Trainor, Leonard 1879-1940 *WhScrn 1,
    WhScrn 2, WhoHol B*
Trammel, Niles d1973 *NewYTET*
Tranum, Charles B 1916- *BiE&WWA*
Trapassi, Pietro Antonio Domenico *McGWD*
Trapido, Joel 1913- *BiE&WWA*
Trarieux, Gabriel 1870- *WhThe*
Trask, Franklin 1907- *BiE&WWA, NotNAT*
Trask, Wayland 1887-1918 *Film 1, TwYS,
    WhScrn 2*
Traube, Shepard 1907- *BiE&WWA, NotNAT,
    WhoThe 16*
Traubel, Helen 1899-1972 *FilmgC*
Traubel, Helen 1903-1972 *WhScrn 2, WhoHol B*
Trauberg, Ilya Zakharovich 1905?-1948 *DcFM,
    OxFilm, WorEnF*
Trauberg, Leonid Zakharovich 1902- *DcFM,
    Film 2, OxFilm, WorEnF*
Trauner, Alexander 1906- *FilmgC, OxFilm,
    WorEnF*

Trauner, Alexandre 1906- *DcFM*
Trautman, Ludwig 1886-1957 *WhScrn 1,
    WhScrn 2*
Traux, Maude *Film 2*
Travener, Jo *WomWMM B*
Travernier, Albert *Film 2*
Travers, Anthony 1920-1959 *WhScrn 1,
    WhScrn 2*
Travers, Ben 1886- *BiE&WWA, ConDr 1977,
    CroCD, FilmgC, McGWD, NotNAT,
    NotNAT A, WhoThe 16*
Travers, Ben 1889- *CnThe*
Travers, Bill 1922- *FilmgC, IntMPA 1977,
    MovMk, WhoHol A*
Travers, Dick *MotPP*
Travers, George *Film 2*
Travers, Henry 1874-1965 *FilmgC, MotPP,
    MovMk, PIP&P, Vers B, WhScrn 1,
    WhScrn 2, WhThe, WhoHol B*
Travers, Jim *Film 1*
Travers, Linden 1913- *FilmgC, WhThe,
    WhoHol A*
Travers, Madalaine 1875-1964 *Film 1, Film 2,
    TwYS*
Travers, Madalaine see also Traverse, Madaline
Travers, Mary Allin 1937- *AmSCAP 1966*
Travers, Richard C 1890-1935 *Film 1, Film 2,
    TwYS, WhScrn 1, WhScrn 2, WhoHol B*
Travers, Roxy *WomWMM*
Travers, Roy *Film 2*
Travers, Susan *WhoHol A*
Travers, Sy *WhoHol A*
Travers, Tony d1959 *WhoHol B*
Traverse, Madaline 1876-1964 *WhoHol B*
Traverse, Madlaine 1876-1964 *MotPP,
    NotNAT B, WhScrn 1, WhScrn 2*
Traverse, Madlaine see also Travers, Madalaine
Traviesas, Herminio *NewYTET*
Travis, Charles W 1861-1917 *WhScrn 2*
Travis, June 1914- *WhoHol A*
Travis, Michael 1928- *BiE&WWA, NotNAT*
Travis, Richard 1913- *FilmgC, IntMPA 1977,
    Vers B, WhoHol A*
Traylor, William *WhoHol A*
Treacher, Arthur d1975 *MotPP*
Treacher, Arthur 1893-1975 *Vers B*
Treacher, Arthur 1894-1975 *BiE&WWA, CelR 3,
    Film 2, FilmgC, MovMk, NotNAT B,
    WhScrn 2, WhoHol C*
Treacy, Emerson 1905-1967 *MotPP, WhScrn 1,
    WhScrn 2, WhoHol B*
Treador, Marie *Film 1*
Treadway, Charlotte 1895-1963 *NotNAT B,
    WhScrn 1, WhScrn 2, WhoHol B*
Treadwell, Laura B 1879-1960 *WhScrn 1,
    WhScrn 2, WhoHol B*
Treadwell, Sophie 1890-1970 *CnMD, McGWD,
    ModWD*
Trebaol, Edouard *Film 2*
Trebaol Children *Film 2*
Trebitsch, Siegfried 1869-1956 *ModWD*
Treble, Sepha 1908- *WhThe*
Treckman, Emma 1909- *WhThe*
Tree, Lady 1863-1937 *NotNAT B, WhScrn 1,
    WhScrn 2, WhThe, WhoHol B*
Tree, Beerbohm 1853-1917 *WhoStg 1908*
Tree, David 1915- *FilmgC, WhThe, WhoHol A*
Tree, Dorothy 1909- *IntMPA 1977, WhoHol A*
Tree, Ellen 1805-1880 *FamA&A*
Tree, Ellen 1806-1880 *OxThe*
Tree, Helen Maud Holt 1863-1937 *OxThe*
Tree, Sir Herbert Beerbohm d1917 *Film 1,
    WhoHol B*
Tree, Sir Herbert Beerbohm 1852-1917 *WhScrn 2*

Tree, Sir Herbert Beerbohm 1853-1917 *CnThe,*
  FamA&A, NotNAT A, NotNAT B, OxThe,
  PIP&P, WhThe
Tree, Maria d1862 *NotNAT B*
Tree, Viola 1884-1938 *NotNAT A, NotNAT B,*
  OxThe, WhScrn 1, WhScrn 2, WhThe,
  WhoHol B
Treen, Mary 1907- *FilmgC, IntMPA 1977,*
  MotPP, Vers A, WhoHol A
Treharne, Bryceson 1879-1948 *AmSCAP 1966*
Tremaine, Betty Pitt 1906- *AmSCAP 1966*
Tremayne, Les 1913- *IntMPA 1977, WhoHol A*
Trench, Herbert 1865-1923 *NotNAT B, WhThe*
Trenev, Konstantin Andreivich 1884-1945 *OxThe*
Trenholme, Helen 1911-1962 *NotNAT B, WhThe,*
  WhoHol B
Trenker, Luis 1892?- *OxFilm*
Trenker, Luis 1893- *DcFM*
Trenker, Luis 1896- *Film 2*
Trenner, Donn 1927- *AmSCAP 1966*
Trent, Bob *Film 2*
Trent, Bruce *WhoThe 16*
Trent, Jo 1892-1954 *AmSCAP 1966*
Trent, John 1897-1961 *WhScrn 2*
Trent, John 1906-1966 *Film 2, WhScrn 2,*
  WhoHol B
Trent, John 1935- *IntMPA 1977*
Trent, Sheila d1954 *NotNAT B*
Trent, Tom *Film 1*
Trentini, Emma 1885-1959 *EncMT, NotNAT B,*
  PIP&P, WhThe
Trento, Guido *Film 2*
Trenton, Pell *Film 1, Film 2*
Trenyov, Konstantin Andreevich 1878?-1945
  ModWD
Trenyov, Konstantin Andreevich 1884-1945 *CnMD*
Trersahar, John d1936 *NotNAT B*
Tresahar, John d1936 *WhThe*
Tresgot, Annie *WomWMM*
Tresham, Jennie 1881-1913 *WhScrn 2*
Treskoff, Olga 1902-1938 *WhScrn 1, WhScrn 2,*
  WhoHol B
Tresmand, Ivy 1898- *WhThe*
Tressler, Georg 1917- *WorEnF*
Trethowan, Ian *NewYTET*
Tretyakov, Sergei Mikhailovich 1892-1937 *CnMD*
Tretyakov, Sergei Mikhailovich 1892-1939 *ModWD,*
  OxThe, PIP&P
Trevarthen, Noel *WhoHol A*
Trevelyan, Hilda 1880-1959 *NotNAT B, OxThe,*
  WhThe, WhoHol B
Trevelyan, John 1904- *FilmgC*
Trevelyan, Una *Film 2*
Trevens, Francine L *NatPD*
Trevi, Christina 1930-1956 *WhScrn 1, WhScrn 2*
Treville, Roger 1903- *WhThe*
Trevino, Lee 1939- *CelR 3*
Trevison, Hank 1923- *AmSCAP 1966*
Trevor, Ann 1918-1970 *Film 2, WhThe,*
  WhoHol B
Trevor, Anne 1918-1970 *WhScrn 2*
Trevor, Austin 1897- *FilmgC, WhThe,*
  WhoHol A
Trevor, Claire *IntMPA 1977, MotPP,*
  WomWMM
Trevor, Claire 1909- *BiDFlm, CmMov, FilmgC,*
  MovMk, OxFilm, ThFT, WhThe,
  WhoHol A, WorEnF
Trevor, Claire 1912- *CmMov*
Trevor, Howard *WhoHol A*
Trevor, Hugh 1903-1933 *Film 2, TwYS,*
  WhScrn 1, WhScrn 2, WhoHol B
Trevor, Jack *Film 2*
Trevor, Leo d1927 *NotNAT B, WhThe*

Trevor, Norman 1877-1929 *Film 1, Film 2,*
  NotNAT B, TwYS, WhScrn 1, WhScrn 2,
  WhThe, WhoHol B
Trevor, Spencer 1875-1945 *Film 2, NotNAT B,*
  WhThe, WhoHol B
Trevor, William 1928- *ConDr 1977*
Trewin, John Courtenay 1908- *WhoThe 16*
Trexler, Charles B 1916- *IntMPA 1977*
Treyz, Oliver E *NewYTET*
Tribble, Fredric 1912- *AmSCAP 1966*
Trick, Martha *Film 1*
Tricoli, Carlo d1966 *WhScrn 2*
Triesault, Ivan *WhoHol A*
Triesault, Ivan 1900- *Vers A*
Triesault, Ivan 1902- *FilmgC*
Trieste, Leopoldo 1919- *CnMD, WhoHol A*
Trigere, Pauline 1912- *CelR 3*
Trigg, William *OxThe*
Trigger 1932-1965 *WhScrn 1, WhScrn 2*
Trigger, Ian *WhoHol A*
Trikonis, Gus *WhoHol A*
Trilling, Lionel 1905- *CelR 3*
Trilling, Ossia 1913- *WhoThe 16*
Trimble, Arthur *Film 2*
Trimble, Jessie d1957 *NotNAT B*
Trimble, Larry 1885-1954 *Film 1, WhScrn •2*
Trimble, Laurence 1885-1954 *TwYS A*
Trimble, Lawrence 1885-1954 *NotNAT B*
Trimmingham, Ernest d1942 *NotNAT B*
Trinder, Tommy 1909- *FilmgC, IntMPA 1977,*
  WhoHol A, WhoThe 16
Trinkaus, George J 1878-1960 *AmSCAP 1966*
Trinkaus, Marilyn Miller *WomWMM B*
Trintignant, Jean-Louis 1930- *BiDFlm, CelR 3,*
  FilmgC, IntMPA 1977, MotPP, MovMk,
  OxFilm, WhoHol A, WorEnF
Trintignant, Marie *WhoHol A*
Trintignant, Nadine Marquand *WomWMM*
Triola, Anne *WhoHol A*
Tripod, Irene *Film 2*
Tripp, Paul 1911- *AmSCAP 1966, WhoHol A*
Trissino, Gian Giorgio 1478-1550 *OxThe, PIP&P*
Trissino, Giangiorgio 1478-1550 *McGWD*
Tristan, Dorothy *WhoHol A*
Tristan L'Hermite, Francois 1600?-1655 *REnWD*
Tristan L'Hermite, Francois 1601?-1655 *McGWD,*
  OxThe
Trivas, Victor 1896-1970 *FilmgC*
Trivas, Viktor 1896-1970 *DcFM*
Trivers, Barry 1912- *AmSCAP 1966*
Trix, Helen 1892-1951 *AmSCAP 1966,*
  NotNAT B
Trnka, Jiri 1909-1969 *FilmgC*
Trnka, Jiri 1912-1969 *DcFM, OxFilm, WorEnF*
Troell, Jan 1931- *IntMPA 1977, MovMk,*
  WorEnF
Trojano, John *Film 1*
Troker, Katherine Beaton 1891- *AmSCAP 1966*
Trollope, Anthony *PIP&P*
Tronson, Robert 1924- *FilmgC, IntMPA 1977*
Troobnick, Eugene 1926- *WhoThe 16*
Troobnick, Gene *WhoHol A*
Trosper, Guy d1963 *IntMPA 1977, NotNAT B*
Trost, Russel G 1910- *AmSCAP 1966*
Trotman, William C 1930- *BiE&WWA, NotNAT*
Trotsky, Leon 1879-1940 *Film 1, WhScrn 2,*
  WhoHol B
Trotta, Raymond 1896- *AmSCAP 1966*
Trotter, John Scott 1908-1975 *AmSCAP 1966,*
  WhScrn 2, WhoHol C
Trotti, Lamar 1900-1952 *FilmgC, WorEnF*
Troughton, Patrick 1920- *FilmgC, WhoHol A*
Trouncer, Cecil 1898-1953 *FilmgC, NotNAT B,*
  OxThe, WhScrn 1, WhScrn 2, WhThe,

WhoHol B
Troup, Bobby *WhoHol A*
Troup, Robert William 1918- *AmSCAP 1966*
Troupe, Tom *WhoHol A*
Trout, Francis Dink 1898-1950 *WhScrn 1,*
WhScrn 2, WhoHol B
Trout, Robert 1908- *CelR 3, NewYTET*
Troutman, Ivy 1883- *WhThe, WhoStg 1906,*
WhoStg 1908
Trow, William 1891-1973 *WhScrn 2, WhoHol B*
Trowbridge, Charles 1882-1967 *Film 1, FilmgC,*
MotPP, Vers B, WhScrn 1, WhScrn 2,
WhoHol B
Troy, Elinor d1949 *WhScrn 2*
Troy, Hector *WhoHol A*
Troy, Helen 1905-1942 *WhScrn 1, WhScrn 2,*
WhoHol B
Troy, Louise *BiE&WWA, NotNAT, WhoHol A,*
WhoThe 16
Troyanova, I *WomWMM*
Truax, John d1969 *WhScrn 2*
Truax, Maude *Film 2, TwYS*
Truax, Sarah 1877- *WhThe, WhoStg 1908*
Trubetzskoy, Youcca 1905- *Film 1, Film 2,*
TwYS
Trubshawe, Michael *WhoHol A*
Trudeau, Pierre 1919- *CelR 3*
True, Bess *Film 2*
Trueba, Don d1835 *NotNAT B*
Trued, S Clarence 1895- *AmSCAP 1966*
Trueman, Paula 1907- *BiE&WWA, NotNAT,*
WhoHol A, WhoThe 16
Truesdale, Howard 1870- *Film 2, TwYS*
Truesdell, Fred C *Film 1*
Truesdell, Frederick C 1873-1937 *Film 2,*
NotNAT B, WhScrn 2, WhoHol B
Truex, Ernest d1973 *MotPP, WhoHol B*
Truex, Ernest 1889-1973 *BiE&WWA, EncMT,*
MovMk, NotNAT B, TwYS, WhScrn 2,
WhThe
Truex, Ernest 1890-1973 *Film 1, Film 2, FilmgC,*
Vers A
Truex, Philip *WhoHol A*
Trufanoff, Sergios *Film 1*
Truffaut, Francois 1932- *BiDFlm, CelR 3,*
DcFM, FilmgC, IntMPA 1977, MovMk,
OxFilm, WhoHol A, WorEnF
Truffier, Jules 1856- *WhThe*
Trujillo, Lorenzo Chel 1906-1962 *WhoHol B*
Trujillo, Lorenzo L 1906-1962 *NotNAT B,*
WhScrn 1, WhScrn 2
Truman, Edward 1915- *AmSCAP 1966*
Truman, Margaret 1924- *CelR 3*
Truman, Michael 1916- *FilmgC, IntMPA 1977*
Truman, Ralph 1900- *FilmgC, WhoHol A*
Trumbauer, Frank 1901-1956 *AmSCAP 1966*
Trumbo, Dalton 1905- *ConDr 1977A, DcFM,*
FilmgC, OxFilm, WorEnF
Trumps *Film 2*
Trundy, Natalie 1942- *FilmgC, WhoHol A*
Trunnelle, Mabel *Film 1, WhoHol A*
Truppi, Danny 1919-1970 *WhScrn 2*
Trusler, Ivan 1925- *AmSCAP 1966*
Trussell, Fred 1858-1923 *NotNAT B, WhThe*
Trustman, Susan *WhoHol A*
Trylova, Hermina *WomWMM*
Tryon, Glenn d1970 *MotPP, WhoHol B*
Tryon, Glenn 1897-1970 *Film 2, TwYS*
Tryon, Glenn 1899-1970 *WhScrn 2*
Tryon, Thomas 1926- *CelR 3*
Tryon, Tom 1919- *FilmgC*
Tryon, Tom 1926- *IntMPA 1977, WhoHol A*
Trzcinski, Edmund 1921- *BiE&WWA*
Tsai, Tsou-Sen 190-?- *DcFM*

Ts'ao, Yu 1905- *ModWD*
Tsappi, V *Film 2*
Tschaikowsky, Peter 1840-1893 *NotNAT B*
Tschekowa, Olga *Film 2*
Tschernichin-Larsson, Jenny *Film 1*
Tsegaye Gabre-Medhin 1936- *ConDr 1977*
Tsessarskaya, Emma *Film 2*
Tsiang, H T 1899-1971 *WhScrn 1, WhScrn 2,*
WhoHol B
Tsingh, Hurri *Film 1*
Tsopel, Corinna *WhoHol A*
Tsou, Se-Ling *DcFM*
Tsu, Irene 1943- *FilmgC, WhoHol A*
Tsukamoto, Raynum K 1889-1974 *WhScrn 2*
Tsukasa, Yoko 1934- *IntMPA 1977*
Tsukimori, Sennosuke 1908- *IntMPA 1977*
Tual, Denise *WomWMM*
Tuala, Mario 1924-1961 *WhScrn 1, WhScrn 2*
Tubau, Maria *WhThe*
Tubbs, Bill 1908-1953 *WhoHol B*
Tubbs, William 1908-1953 *WhScrn 1, WhScrn 2*
Tucci, Maria 1941- *WhoThe 16*
Tuccio, Stefano 1540-1597 *OxThe*
Tuchman, Barbara 1912- *CelR 3*
Tuchner, Michael *FilmgC*
Tuchock, Wanda *IntMPA 1977, WomWMM*
Tucic, Srdan 1873-1940 *CnMD*
Tucker, Cy 1889-1952 *WhScrn 1, WhScrn 2*
Tucker, Edna Mae 1907- *AmSCAP 1966*
Tucker, Forrest 1919- *BiE&WWA, FilmgC,*
IntMPA 1977, MotPP, MovMk, WhoHol A
Tucker, George Loane d1921 *MotPP, NotNAT B,*
WhoHol B
Tucker, George Loane 1872-1921 *TwYS A,*
WhScrn 2
Tucker, George Loane 1881-1921 *DcFM*
Tucker, Harlan *Film 2*
Tucker, Harland d1949 *WhScrn 2*
Tucker, John A 1896- *AmSCAP 1966*
Tucker, John Bartholomew *WhoHol A*
Tucker, Larry *WhoHol A*
Tucker, Lillian *Film 1*
Tucker, Melville 1916- *IntMPA 1977*
Tucker, Orrin 1911- *AmSCAP 1966*
Tucker, Paula McKinney *WomWMM B*
Tucker, Richard 1869-1942 *Film 1, Film 2,*
TwYS, WhoHol B
Tucker, Richard 1884-1942 *WhScrn 1, WhScrn 2*
Tucker, Richard 1913-1975 *CelR 3*
Tucker, Richard 1914-1975 *WhScrn 2*
Tucker, Sophie 1884-1966 *EncMT, Film 2,*
FilmgC, NotNAT A, ThFT, WhScrn 1,
WhScrn 2, WhThe, WhoHol B
Tucker, Sophie 1887-1966 *NotNAT B*
Tucker, Sophie 1888-1966 *BiE&WWA*
Tucker, Tanya *WhoHol A*
Tucker, Tommy 1908- *AmSCAP 1966*
Tucker, William H *Film 2*
Tuckerman, Maury 1905-1966 *BiE&WWA,*
NotNAT B
Tudor, Anthony 1909- *WhThe*
Tudor, Antony 1909- *BiE&WWA*
Tudor, Rowan 1905- *BiE&WWA, NotNAT*
Tudor, Valerie 1910- *WhThe*
Tuerk, John d1951 *NotNAT B*
Tufts, Sonny d1970 *MotPP, WhoHol B*
Tufts, Sonny 1911-1970 *FilmgC, HolP 40*
Tufts, Sonny 1912-1970 *MovMk, WhScrn 1,*
WhScrn 2
Tuke, Sir Samuel d1674 *OxThe*
Tulipan, Ira H *IntMPA 1977*
Tulley, Ethel 1898-1968 *WhScrn 1, WhoHol B*
Tully, Ethel 1898-1968 *WhScrn 2*
Tully, George F 1876-1930 *NotNAT B, WhThe*

Tully, Jim 1891-1947 *WhScrn 2*
Tully, May d1924 *NotNAT B, WomWMM*
Tully, Montgomery 1904- *FilmgC, IntMPA 1977*
Tully, Richard Walton 1877-1945 *NotNAT B, WhThe*
Tully, Tom *IntMPA 1977, MotPP*
Tully, Tom 1896- *FilmgC, WhoHol A*
Tully, Tom 1902?- *MovMk*
Tully, Tom 1908- *Vers A*
Tumanov, Joseph Mikhailovich 1905- *OxThe*
Tumarin, Boris 1910- *BiE&WWA, NotNAT, WhoThe 16*
Tuminello, Phil J 1921- *AmSCAP 1966*
Tunberg, Karl 1908- *FilmgC, IntMPA 1977*
Tunbridge, Joseph A 1886-1961 *NotNAT B, WhThe*
Tunc, Irene *WhoHol A*
Tune, Tommy *WhoHol A*
Tunick, Eugene 1920- *IntMPA 1977*
Tunick, Irve *IntMPA 1977*
Tunis, Fay 1890-1967 *Film 1, WhScrn 1, WhScrn 2, WhoHol B*
Tunney, Gene 1898- *CelR 3, Film 2*
Tunney, John 1934- *CelR 3*
Tupou, Manu 1935- *WhoThe 16*
Tupper, Lois Ann *WomWMM B*
Tupper, Mary d1964 *NotNAT B*
Tupper, Pearl *Film 2*
Tur, Leonid Davidovich 1905-1961 *ModWD*
Tur, Pyotr Davidovich 1907- *ModWD*
Turell, Saul J 1921- *IntMPA 1977*
Turfkruyer, Marc *IntMPA 1977*
Turfler, James *Film 2*
Turgenev, Ivan Sergeivich 1818-1883 *PIP&P*
Turgenev, Ivan Sergeyevich 1818-1883 *CnThe, McGWD, NotNAT A, NotNAT B, REnWD*
Turgeniev, Ivan Sergeivich 1818-1883 *OxThe*
Turgeon, Peter 1919- *BiE&WWA, WhoHol A*
Turich, Felipe *WhoHol A*
Turich, Rosa *WhoHol A*
Turin, Victor 1895-1945 *DcFM, WorEnF*
Turja, Ilmari 1901- *CroCD*
Turk, Arlene M *WhoHol A*
Turk, Roy 1892-1934 *AmSCAP 1966*
Turkel, Ann *WhoHol A*
Turkel, Joseph *WhoHol A*
Turknett, Clifford *NatPD*
Turleigh, Veronica 1903-1971 *PIP&P, WhScrn 2, WhThe, WhoHol A*
Turley, Dianne *WhoHol A*
Turlupin 1587?-1637 *NotNAT B, OxThe*
Turman, Glynn *WhoHol A*
Turman, Laurence 1926- *FilmgC*
Turman, Lawrence 1926- *IntMPA 1977*
Turnbull, Graham M 1931- *AmSCAP 1966*
Turnbull, John 1880-1956 *NotNAT B, WhThe, WhoHol B*
Turnbull, Stanley d1924 *Film 2, NotNAT B, WhThe*
Turner, Alfred 1870-1941 *NotNAT B, WhThe*
Turner, Anthony *OxThe*
Turner, Baby *Film 2*
Turner, Barbara *WhoHol A*
Turner, Bert *Film 1*
Turner, Beth *NatPD*
Turner, Bowditch *Film 2*
Turner, Bridget *WhoHol A, WhoThe 16*
Turner, Charles *WhoHol A*
Turner, Charles 1921- *AmSCAP 1966*
Turner, Cicely d1940 *NotNAT B*
Turner, Claramae *BiE&WWA, WhoHol A*
Turner, Clifford 1913- *IntMPA 1977*
Turner, Cyril *McGWD*
Turner, David 1927- *ConDr 1977, CroCD,*

McGWD, *WhoThe 16*
Turner, Dennis Lance *NatPD*
Turner, Doreen *Film 2*
Turner, Dorothy 1895-1969 *WhThe*
Turner, Douglas *WhoHol A, WhoThe 16*
Turner, Eardley d1929 *NotNAT B*
Turner, Emanuel 1884-1941 *WhScrn 1, WhScrn 2*
Turner, F A 1842?-1923 *WhScrn 2*
Turner, Florence d1946 *MotPP, WhoHol B*
Turner, Florence 1877-1946 *NotNAT B*
Turner, Florence 1885-1946 *WhScrn 1, WhScrn 2*
Turner, Florence 1887-1946 *Film 1, Film 2, FilmgC, TwYS*
Turner, Florence 1888-1946 *MovMk*
Turner, Fred A *Film 1, Film 2*
Turner, George 1902-1968 *BiE&WWA, Film 2, NotNAT B, WhScrn 2, WhoHol A*
Turner, Glenn W 1925- *CelR 3*
Turner, Hal 1930- *AmSCAP 1966*
Turner, Harold 1909-1962 *NotNAT B, WhThe*
Turner, Helene *WomWMM*
Turner, Ike *WhoHol A*
Turner, Ike And Tina *CelR 3*
Turner, J W d1913 *NotNAT B*
Turner, John 1932- *FilmgC*
Turner, John C 1896-1949 *AmSCAP 1966*
Turner, John Hastings 1892- *WhThe*
Turner, L Godfrey- *WhThe*
Turner, Lana *MotPP*
Turner, Lana 1920- *CelR 3, CmMov, FilmgC, MGM, MovMk, ThFT, WhoHol A, WorEnF*
Turner, Lana 1921- *BiDFlm, IntMPA 1977, OxFilm*
Turner, Maidel 1888-1953 *Film 2, NotNAT B, WhScrn 1, WhScrn 2, WhoHol B*
Turner, Marion 1920- *AmSCAP 1966*
Turner, Maude *Film 2*
Turner, Michael 1921- *WhoHol A, WhoThe 16*
Turner, Mildred C 1897- *AmSCAP 1966*
Turner, Otis *TwYS A*
Turner, Otis Daddy 1862-1918 *WhScrn 2*
Turner, Raymond *Film 2*
Turner, Roscoe 1896-1970 *WhScrn 1, WhScrn 2, WhoHol B*
Turner, Tim *WhoHol A*
Turner, Tina *WhoHol A*
Turner, Tom *WhoHol A*
Turner, Vickery *WhoHol A*
Turner, W J 1889-1946 *CnMD, NotNAT B*
Turner, Wedgwood *Film 1*
Turner, William H 1861-1942 *Film 1, Film 2, WhScrn 1, WhScrn 2, WhoHol B*
Turner, Willis Lloyd 1927- *BiE&WWA*
Turney, Catherine 1906- *BiE&WWA, NotNAT*
Turpilius *OxThe*
Turpin, Ben 1869-1940 *WhScrn 2*
Turpin, Ben 1874-1940 *Film 1, Film 2, FilmgC, MotPP, MovMk, NotNAT B, TwYS, WhScrn 1, WhoHol B, WorEnF*
Turpin, Carrie 1882-1925 *WhScrn 2, WhoHol B*
Turpin, Dick 1705-1739 *FilmgC*
Turpin, Gerry 1930?- *FilmgC*
Turpio, Ambivius *OxThe*
Turrano, Joe 1918- *AmSCAP 1966*
Turteltaub-Orenstein *NewYTET*
Tushingham, Rita *MotPP, WhoHol A*
Tushingham, Rita 1940- *FilmgC*
Tushingham, Rita 1942- *IntMPA 1977, MovMk, OxFilm, WhoThe 16, WorEnF*
Tustain, George *Film 2*
Tustin, Whitney *AmSCAP 1966*
Tuthill, Burnet C 1888- *AmSCAP 1966*

Tutin, Dorothy 1930- *BiE&WWA, CnThe, FilmgC, IntMPA 1977, NotNAT, OxFilm, WhoHol A, WhoThe 16*
Tutmarc, Paul H d1972 *WhScrn 2*
Tuttle, Day 1902- *BiE&WWA, NotNAT*
Tuttle, Eugenia *Film 2*
Tuttle, Frank 1892-1963 *BiDFlm, FilmgC, WorEnF*
Tuttle, Frank 1893-1963 *TwYS A*
Tuttle, Lurene *Vers A, WhoHol A*
Tuttman, Alice 1895- *AmSCAP 1966*
Tuvim, Abe 1895-1958 *AmSCAP 1966*
Twain, Mark 1835-1910 *FilmgC, NotNAT B*
Twain, Norman 1930- *BiE&WWA, NotNAT*
Twaits, William d1814 *NotNAT B, OxThe, PIP&P*
Tweddell, Frank 1895-1971 *WhScrn 1, WhScrn 2*
Tweddell, Fritz d1971 *WhoHol B*
Tweed, Frank *Film 2*
Tweed, Tommy 1907-1971 *WhScrn 2, WhoHol B*
Twelvetrees, Helen d1958 *MotPP, NotNAT B, WhoHol B*
Twelvetrees, Helen 1907-1958 *ThFT*
Twelvetrees, Helen 1908-1958 *Film 2, FilmgC, HolP 30, MovMk, WhScrn 1, WhScrn 2*
Twiggy *WhoHol A*
Twiggy 1946- *FilmgC*
Twiggy 1949- *CelR 3, IntMPA 1977*
Twist, Derek 1905- *FilmgC, IntMPA 1977*
Twitchell, A R Archie 1906-1957 *WhScrn 1, WhScrn 2*
Twitchell, Archie 1906-1957 *WhoHol B*
Twitty, Conway *WhoHol A*
Twohig, Daniel S 1883-1962 *AmSCAP 1966*
Twomey, Kathleen G 1914- *AmSCAP 1966*
Twyman, Alan P 1934- *IntMPA 1977*
Tyars, Frank 1848-1918 *NotNAT B, WhThe*
Tyers, William H 1876-1924 *AmSCAP 1966*
Tyke, John 1895-1940 *WhScrn 2*
Tyl, Josef Kajetan 1808-1856 *CnThe, REnWD*
Tyler, Beverly 1924- *FilmgC*
Tyler, Beverly 1928- *IntMPA 1977, WhoHol A*
Tyler, George Crouse 1867-1946 *NotNAT A, NotNAT B, WhThe, WhoStg 1908*
Tyler, Gladys C 1893-1972 *WhScrn 2, WhoHol B*
Tyler, Goldie 1925- *AmSCAP 1966*
Tyler, Harry 1888-1961 *Film 2, Vers A, WhScrn 1, WhScrn 2, WhoHol B*
Tyler, Judy 1933-1957 *MotPP, NotNAT B, WhScrn 2, WhoHol B*
Tyler, Odette 1869-1936 *NotNAT B, WhThe*
Tyler, Odette 1872- *WhoStg 1906, WhoStg 1908*
Tyler, Parker d1974 *OxFilm*
Tyler, Royall 1757-1826 *CnThe, McGWD, NotNAT B, OxThe, PIP&P, REnWD*
Tyler, Tom 1903-1954 *Film 2, FilmgC, MotPP, NotNAT B, TwYS, WhScrn 1, WhScrn 2, WhoHol B*
Tynan, Brandon 1879-1967 *Film 2, WhScrn 1, WhScrn 2, WhThe, WhoHol B*
Tynan, Kenneth 1927- *BiE&WWA, CroCD, NotNAT, WhoThe 16*
Tyndall, Kate d1919 *NotNAT B*
Tyne, George *WhoHol A*
Tyner, Charles *WhoHol A*
Tyra, Thomas Norman 1933- *AmSCAP 1966*
Tyree, Elizabeth *WhoStg 1906, WhoStg 1908*
Tyrell, Susan *WhoHol A*
Tyrlova, Hermina 1900- *DcFM*
Tyrol, Jacques *TwYS A*
Tyroler, William *Film 2*
Tyron, Max *Film 2*
Tyrrell, Rose d1934 *NotNAT B*
Tyrrell, Susan 1946- *IntMPA 1977*

Tyson, Cicely 1933- *MovMk, NotNAT, WhoHol A, WhoThe 16*
Tyson, Mildred Lund *AmSCAP 1966*
Tyzack, Margaret 1933- *FilmgC, WhoHol A, WhoThe 16*
Tzara, Tristan 1896-1963 *ModWD*
Tzavellas, Georges 1916- *DcFM*
Tzelniker, Meier 1894- *FilmgC*

U

U Ku *REnWD*
U Kyin U d1853 *REnWD*
U Pok Ni 1849- *REnWD*
U Pon Nya *REnWD*
U Su Tha *REnWD*
Uber, David 1921- *AmSCAP 1966*
Uccellini, Ugo *Film 2*
Uchatius, Franz Von *DcFM*
Uchida, Tomu 1897-1970 *DcFM*
Udall, Nicholas 1505-1556 *CnThe*, *McGWD*,
    NotNAT B, *OxThe*
Udell, Peter 1934- *AmSCAP 1966*,
    ConDr 1977D
Udoff, Yale M 1935- *NatPD*
Uggams, Leslie *WhoHol A*
Uggams, Leslie 1943- *CelR 3*, *EncMT*,
    IntMPA 1977, *NotNAT*
Uggams, Leslie 1945- *FilmgC*
Uhl, Richard 1918- *AmSCAP 1966*
Uhlig, Max E 1896-1958 *WhScrn 1*, *WhScrn 2*
Ukil, Sarada *Film 2*
Ulanova, Galina *WhoHol A*
Ulitskaya, Olga *WomWMM*
Ullman, Daniel 1920- *FilmgC*, *IntMPA 1977*
Ullman, Elwood *IntMPA 1977*
Ullman, Ethel *Film 1*
Ullman, Greta d1972 *WhoHol B*
Ullman, Liv 1938- *OxFilm*
Ullman, Liv 1939- *FilmgC*
Ullman, Robert 1928- *BiE&WWA*
Ullmann, Liv *IntMPA 1977*, *PIP&P A*,
    WhoHol A
Ullmann, Liv 1939- *BiDFlm*, *CelR 3*
Ullmann, Liv 1940- *MovMk*
Ullstein, Vladimir Mark 1898- *AmSCAP 1966*
Ulmar, Geraldine 1862-1932 *NotNAT B*, *WhThe*
Ulmer, Edgar G 1904- *WorEnF*
Ulmer, Edgar Georg 1900-1972 *BiDFlm*, *DcFM*,
    FilmgC, *WhScrn 2*
Ulmer, Fritz *Film 2*
Ulric, Lenore 1892-1970 *BiE&WWA*, *FamA&A*,
    Film 1, *Film 2*, *FilmgC*, *MotPP*, *MovMk*,
    ThFT, *TwYS*, *WhThe*, *WhoHol B*
Ulric, Lenore 1894-1970 *WhScrn 1*, *WhScrn 2*
Ulrich, Florence *Film 2*
Ulrych, Lucy *WomWMM*
Ultra Violet *WhoHol A*
Umeki, Miyoshi 1929- *FilmgC*, *MotPP*, *MovMk*,
    WhoHol A
Umeko, Miyoshi 1929- *BiE&WWA*
Unamuno, Miguel De 1864-1936 *CnMD*, *McGWD*,
    ModWD, *OxThe*
Unamunoy, Jugo Miguel De 1864-1936 *NotNAT B*
Uncle Murray *WhScrn 1*, *WhScrn 2*
Unda, Emilie *Film 2*
Underdown, Edward 1908- *FilmgC*, *IntMPA 1977*,

WhoHol A
Underhill, Cave 1634?-1710? *OxThe*
Underhill, Edward d1964 *NotNAT B*
Underhill, Georgina *WomWMM B*
Underhill, John Garrett d1946 *NotNAT B*
Underwood, Franklin 1877-1940 *WhoHol B*
Underwood, Franklin 1877-1963 *Film 2*
Underwood, Franklyn d1940 *NotNAT B*
Underwood, Ian *WhoHol A*
Underwood, Isabelle *WhoStg 1906*, *WhoStg 1908*
Underwood, John 1590?-1624 *OxThe*, *PIP&P*
Underwood, Lawrence 1871-1939 *Film 2*,
    WhScrn 1, *WhScrn 2*, *WhoHol B*
Underwood, Loyal *Film 1*, *Film 2*
Unger, Alvin E d1975 *NewYTET*
Unger, Anthony B 1940- *IntMPA 1977*
Unger, Gladys Buchanan d1940 *NotNAT B*,
    WhThe
Unger, Gunnar *Film 2*
Unger, Kurt 1922- *IntMPA 1977*
Unger, Oliver A 1914- *IntMPA 1977*
Unger, Robert *NatPD*
Unger, Stella 1905- *AmSCAP 1966*
Unitas, John 1933- *CelR 3*
Unruh, Fritz Von 1885-1970 *CnMD*, *McGWD*,
    ModWD, *REnWD*
Unruh, Walter 1898-1973 *NotNAT B*
Unruh, Walther 1898-1973 *BiE&WWA*
Unser, Al 1939- *CelR 3*
Unser, Bobby 1924- *CelR 3*
Unsworth, Geoffrey 1914- *FilmgC*, *WorEnF*
Unterkirchen, Hans *Film 2*
Untermeyer, Louis 1885- *CelR 3*
Untershiak, J *Film 2*
Updegraff, Henry 1889-1936 *WhScrn 1*,
    WhScrn 2
Updike, John 1932- *CelR 3*
Upsher, Peter d1963 *NotNAT B*
Upton, Anne *AmSCAP 1966*
Upton, Frances 1904-1975 *WhScrn 2*, *WhoHol C*
Upton, Leonard 1901- *WhThe*
Uraneff, Vadim *Film 2*
Urban, Charles 1870?-1942 *DcFM*
Urban, Charles 1871-1942 *OxFilm*
Urban, Dorothy K 1869-1961 *WhScrn 1*,
    WhScrn 2, *WhoHol B*
Urban, Joseph 1872-1933 *NotNAT B*, *OxThe*
Urbano, Alfred J 1911- *AmSCAP 1966*
Urbansky, Yevgeny 1931-1965 *WhScrn 1*,
    WhScrn 2
Urcelay, Nicolas 1920-1959 *WhScrn 1*, *WhScrn 2*
Ure, Mary 1933-1975 *BiE&WWA*, *FilmgC*,
    MotPP, *MovMk*, *NotNAT B*, *PIP&P*,
    WhScrn 2, *WhThe*, *WhoHol C*
Urecal, Minerva d1966 *MotPP*, *WhoHol B*
Urecal, Minerva 1894-1966 *WhScrn 1*, *WhScrn 2*

Urecal, Minerva 1896-1966 *FilmgC, Vers B*
Urey, Harold 1893- *CelR 3*
Uribe, Justa *Film 2*
Uris, Leon 1924- *CelR 3*
Urquhart, Alasdair 1914-1954 *WhScrn 1,
   WhScrn 2, WhoHol B*
Urquhart, Gordon 1922-1957 *WhScrn 2*
Urquhart, Isabelle 1865-1907 *NotNAT B,
   WhoStg 1906, WhoStg 1908*
Urquhart, Molly *WhThe, WhoHol A*
Urquhart, Robert 1922- *FilmgC, IntMPA 1977,
   WhoHol A*
Urrueta, Chano 189-?- *DcFM*
Ursianu, Malvina *WomWMM*
Urusevsky, Sergei 1908- *DcFM*
Usher, Guy 1875-1944 *WhScrn 1, WhScrn 2,
   WhoHol B*
Usher, Harry 1887-1950 *WhScrn 1, WhScrn 2*
Usher, Luke *PIP&P*
Usigli, Rodolfo *OxThe*
Usigli, Rodolfo 1903- *CroCD*
Usigli, Rodolfo 1905- *CnThe, McGWD,
   ModWD, REnWD*
Ustinov, Peter 1921- *BiDFlm, BiE&WWA,
   CelR 3, CmMov, CnMD, CnThe,
   ConDr 1977, CroCD, FilmgC, IntMPA 1977,
   McGWD, ModWD, MotPP, MovMk,
   NotNAT, NotNAT A, OxFilm, OxThe,
   PIP&P, WhoHol A, WhoThe 16, WorEnF*
Ustinov, Tamara *WhoHol A*
Uszycka, Walentyna *WomWMM*
Utley, Garrick *NewYTET*
Uttal, Fred 1905-1963 *WhScrn 2*
Uys, Jamie 1921- *FilmgC, IntMPA 1977,
   WhoHol A*
Uyttenhove, Henry J *CmMov*

V

Vaccaro, Brenda *WhoHol A*
Vaccaro, Brenda 1939- *BiE&WWA, CelR 3, IntMPA 1977, NotNAT, WhoThe 16*
Vaccaro, Brenda 1940- *FilmgC*
Vachell, Horace Annesley 1861-1955 *NotNAT B, WhThe*
Vachon, Jean *Film 2*
Vacio, Natividad *WhoHol A*
Vackova, Jarmila 1908-1971 *WhScrn 1, WhScrn 2*
Vadim, Annette *WhoHol A*
Vadim, Roger *WhoHol A*
Vadim, Roger 1927- *FilmgC*
Vadim, Roger 1928- *BiDFlm, DcFM, MovMk, OxFilm, WorEnF*
Vagramian, Aram 1921- *AmSCAP 1966*
Vague, Vera 1904-1974 *FilmgC, WhScrn 2, WhoHol B*
Vail, Lester 1900-1959 *NotNAT B, WhScrn 2, WhThe, WhoHol B*
Vail, Olive 1904-1951 *WhScrn 1, WhScrn 2, WhoHol B*
Vailland, Roger 1907-1965 *CnMD, DcFM*
Vajda *PIP&P*
Vajda, Ernest 1887-1954 *NotNAT B, WhThe*
Vajda, Ladislao 1905-1965 *DcFM, WorEnF*
Vajda, Ladislas 1905-1965 *WorEnF*
Vakhtangov, Eugen V 1883-1922 *NotNAT A, NotNAT B*
Vakhtangov, Eugene V 1883-1922 *OxThe, PIP&P*
Vakhtangov, Yevgeny 1883-1922 *CnThe*
Val, Jack 1897- *AmSCAP 1966*
Val, Paul d1962 *NotNAT B*
Valabregue, Albin *WhThe*
Valaida *WhThe*
Valberg, Birgitta *WhoHol A*
Valdare, Sunny Jim d1962 *NotNAT B*
Valdemar, Tania 1904-1955 *WhScrn 1, WhScrn 2*
Valdemar, Thais *Film 2*
Valdis, Sigrid *WhoHol A*
Valdivielso, Jose De 1560-1638 *McGWD*
Vale, Eugene 1916- *IntMPA 1977*
Vale, Louise d1918 *Film 1, WhScrn 2*
Vale, Martin *BiE&WWA, NotNAT*
Vale, Travers 1865- *TwYS A*
Vale, Viola *Film 2*
Vale, Vola *Film 1, TwYS*
Valedon, Lora 1884-1946 *WhScrn 1, WhScrn 2*
Valen, Ritchie 1941-1959 *WhScrn 2*
Valency, Maurice 1903- *AmSCAP 1966, BiE&WWA, NotNAT*
Valene, Nanette *Film 2*
Valenta, Vladimir *WhoHol A*
Valente, Caterina *IntMPA 1977, WhoHol A*
Valenti, Jack J 1921- *CelR 3, FilmgC, IntMPA 1977, NewYTET*

Valentin *CroCD*
Valentine 1876- *WhThe*
Valentine, Anthony *WhoHol A*
Valentine, Barbara *WhoHol A*
Valentine, Carla *WomWMM A*
Valentine, Dickie d1971 *WhoHol B*
Valentine, Elizabeth d1971 *WhScrn 2*
Valentine, Grace 1884-1964 *WhThe*
Valentine, Grace 1890-1964 *Film 1, Film 2, TwYS, WhScrn 2*
Valentine, John *Film 2*
Valentine, Joseph 1903-1948 *FilmgC*
Valentine, Leila *Film 2*
Valentine, Paul d1924 *NotNAT B*
Valentine, Paul 1919- *BiE&WWA, NotNAT*
Valentine, Sydney 1865-1919 *NotNAT B, WhThe*
Valentine, Vangie *Film 1*
Valentino 1932- *CelR 3*
Valentino, Rudolph 1895-1926 *BiDFlm, CmMov, Film 1, Film 2, FilmgC, MotPP, MovMk, NotNAT B, OxFilm, TwYS, WhScrn 1, WhScrn 2, WhoHol B, WomWMM, WorEnF*
Valentino, Thomas J 1907- *IntMPA 1977*
Valenty, Lili *WhoHol A*
Valere, Jean 1925- *WorEnF*
Valerie, Gladys *Film 2*
Valerie, Jeanne *WhoHol A*
Valerie, Olive *Film 2*
Valerio *OxThe*
Valerio, Albano 1889-1961 *WhScrn 1, WhScrn 2, WhoHol B*
Valerio, Theresa d1964 *NotNAT B*
Valero, Albano *Film 2*
Valery, Olga *WhoHol A*
Valery, Paul Ambroise 1871-1945 *CnMD*
Valia, Mademoiselle *Film 2*
Valignani, Achille 1910- *IntMPA 1977*
Valk, Frederick 1901-1956 *CnThe, FilmgC, NotNAT B, WhScrn 1, WhScrn 2, WhThe, WhoHol B*
Valkyrien 1894-1953 *Film 1*
Valkyrien, Valda 1894-1953 *WhScrn 1, WhScrn 2, WhoHol B*
Valle, Felix *Film 2*
Valle-Inclan, Ramon Maria Del 1866-1936 *CnMD Sup, McGWD, ModWD, OxThe*
Vallee, Arthur A 1916- *AmSCAP 1966*
Vallee, Fay Webb *WhScrn 1, WhScrn 2*
Vallee, Marcel *Film 2*
Vallee, Rudy 1901- *AmSCAP 1966, BiE&WWA, EncMT, Film 2, FilmgC, IntMPA 1977, MotPP, MovMk, WhoHol A*
Vallee, Yvonne *Film 2*
Vallentin, Hermann *Film 2*
Valleran-Lecomte *OxThe*

435

Valles, Dave *Film 2*
Valli, Alida 1921- *BiDFlm, FilmgC,*
  IntMPA 1977, MotPP, MovMk, OxFilm,
  WhoHol A, WorEnF
Valli, Romolo *WhoHol A*
Valli, Valli 1882-1927 *Film 1, WhScrn 2,*
  WhThe, WhoHol B
Valli, Virginia d1968 *MotPP, WhoHol B*
Valli, Virginia 1895-1968 *TwYS*
Valli, Virginia 1898-1968 *Film 1, Film 2,*
  FilmgC, MovMk
Valli, Virginia 1900-1968 *WhScrn 1, WhScrn 2*
Vallin, Rick *IntMPA 1977, WhoHol A*
Vallis, Robert d1932 *Film 2, WhScrn 1,*
  WhScrn 2
Vallone, Raf 1916- *FilmgC, IntMPA 1977,*
  MovMk, WhoHol A, WorEnF
Valray, Maria *Film 2*
Valsted, Myrtle 1910-1928 *WhScrn 1, WhScrn 2*
Valverda, Rafael *Film 2*
Valverde, Balbina *WhThe*
Van, Beatrice *Film 1*
Van, Billy 1912-1973 *WhScrn 2, WhoHol B*
Van, Billy B 1870-1950 *WhThe*
Van, Billy B 1878-1950 *NotNAT B, WhScrn 1,*
  WhScrn 2, WhoHol B
Van, Bobby *WhoHol A*
Van, Bobby 1930- *EncMT, FilmgC, WhoThe 16*
Van, Bobby 1935- *NotNAT*
Van, Charley d1963 *NotNAT B*
Van, Connie 1909-1961 *WhScrn 1, WhScrn 2*
Van, Gus d1968 *NotNAT B, WhoHol B*
Van, Gus 1887-1968 *AmSCAP 1966*
Van, Gus 1888-1968 *WhScrn 1, WhScrn 2*
Van, Wally 1885-1974 *Film 1, Film 2, TwYS A,*
  WhoHol B
VanAaitern, Truus *Film 2*
Vanaire, Jacques *Film 2*
VanAllen, James 1914- *CelR 3*
VanAlstyne, Egbert Aanson 1882-1951 *NotNAT B*
VanAlstyne, Egbert Anson 1882-1951
  AmSCAP 1966
VanAntwerp, Albert *Film 2*
VanArk, Joan *WhoHol A*
VanAuker, C K d1938 *WhScrn 1, WhScrn 2,*
  WhoHol B
VanBailey, Polly d1952 *WhScrn 1, WhScrn 2*
VanBeers, Stanley 1911-1961 *WhScrn 1,*
  WhScrn 2, WhThe, WhoHol B
VanBiene, Auguste 1850-1913 *NotNAT B,*
  WhThe
VanBousen, H *Film 2*
VanBrakle, John 1903- *AmSCAP 1966*
VanBrock, Florence *AmSCAP 1966*
Vanbrugh, Biolet 1867-1942 *WhThe*
Vanbrugh, Irene 1872-1949 *FilmgC, NotNAT A,*
  NotNAT B, OxThe, PIP&P, WhScrn 1,
  WhScrn 2, WhThe, WhoHol B
Vanbrugh, Sir John 1664-1726 *CnThe, McGWD,*
  NotNAT A, NotNAT B, OxThe, PIP&P,
  REnWD
Vanbrugh, Prudence 1902- *WhThe*
Vanbrugh, Violet Augusta Mary 1865-1942
  WhoStg 1908
Vanbrugh, Violet Augusta Mary 1867-1942
  NotNAT A, NotNAT B, OxThe, WhoHol B
VanBuren, A H *Film 1*
VanBuren, Abigail 1918- *CelR 3*
VanBuren, Mabel 1878-1947 *Film 1, Film 2,*
  NotNAT B, TwYS, WhScrn 1, WhScrn 2,
  WhoHol B
Vanburgh, Irene 1872-1949 *Film 2*
VanBuskirk, June 1880- *WhoStg 1908*
VanBuskirk, June 1882- *WhThe*

VanCampen, Jacob 1590?-1657 *OxThe*
Vance, The Great 1839-1888 *OxThe*
Vance, Alfred Glanville *PIP&P*
Vance, Charles 1929- *WhoThe 16*
Vance, Clarice *Film 2*
Vance, Dennis 1924- *IntMPA 1977*
Vance, Jane *Film 1*
Vance, Leigh 1922- *IntMPA 1977*
Vance, Lucile 1893-1974 *WhoHol B*
Vance, Lucille 1893-1974 *WhScrn 2*
Vance, Nina *BiE&WWA, NotNAT*
Vance, Paul J 1929- *AmSCAP 1966*
Vance, Virginia 1902-1942 *Film 2, WhScrn 1,*
  WhScrn 2, WhoHol B
Vance, Vivian *IntMPA 1977, MotPP*
Vance, Vivian 1903?- *FilmgC*
Vance, Vivian 1912- *WhoHol A*
Vancini, Florestano 1926- *WorEnF*
VanCleave, Nathan 1910- *AmSCAP 1966*
VanCleef, Lee 1925- *CmMov, FilmgC,*
  IntMPA 1977, MotPP, MovMk, OxFilm,
  WhoHol A
VanCleve, Bert 1899- *AmSCAP 1966*
VanCleve, Edith 1903- *BiE&WWA, NotNAT,*
  WhoHol A
Vandal, Marion *WomWMM*
VanDam, Albert 1920- *AmSCAP 1966*
Vandamm, Florence d1966 *NotNAT B*
VanDamm, Vivian d1960 *NotNAT B*
VanDeele, Edmond *Film 2*
VanDeerlin, Lionel *NewYTET*
Vandenhoff, Charles H d1890 *NotNAT B*
Vandenhoff, Charlotte Elizabeth 1818-1860
  NotNAT B, OxThe
Vandenhoff, George 1813-1884 *NotNAT B*
Vandenhoff, George 1813-1885 *OxThe*
Vandenhoff, George 1820-1884 *NotNAT A*
Vandenhoff, George 1820-1885 *FamA&A*
Vandenhoff, Mrs. Henry d1870 *NotNAT B*
Vandenhoff, Henry d1888 *NotNAT B*
Vandenhoff, John 1790-1861 *NotNAT B, OxThe*
Vandenhoff, Kate d1942 *NotNAT B*
VanDenHorst, Herman 1911- *WorEnF*
VanDenVondel, Joost 1587-1679 *OxThe*
Vanderbilt, Alfred Gwynne 1912- *CelR 3*
Vanderbilt, Amy 1908- *CelR 3*
Vanderbilt, Gertrude d1960 *NotNAT B*
Vanderbilt, Gloria 1924- *BiE&WWA, CelR 3,*
  NotNAT
Vanderburg, Gordon J 1913- *AmSCAP 1966*
Vandercook, John W d1963 *NotNAT B*
Vandergrift, J Monte 1893-1939 *WhScrn 1,*
  WhScrn 2
Vandergrift, Monte 1893-1939 *WhoHol B*
Vanderpool, Frederick W 1877-1947
  AmSCAP 1966
Vanders, Warren *WhoHol A*
VanDerVlis, Diana 1935- *BiE&WWA, NotNAT,*
  WhoHol A
Vandervoort, Paul, II 1903- *AmSCAP 1966*
Vandervoort, Phil *WhoHol A*
VanDeVelde, Anton 1895- *ModWD*
Vandever, Michael *WhoHol A*
VanDevere, Trish *WhoHol A*
VanDevere, Trish 1943- *FilmgC*
VanDevere, Trish 1944- *MovMk*
VanDine, S S 1888-1939 *FilmgC*
Vandis, Titos *WhoHol A*
Vandivere, Elinor *Film 2*
VanDobeneck, Baron *Film 2*
VanDommelen, Caroline 1874-1957 *Film 2*
VanDongen, Helen *OxFilm, WomWMM*
VanDoren, Charles *NewYTET*
VanDoren, Mamie *MotPP*

VanDoren, Mamie 1931- WhoHol A
VanDoren, Mamie 1933- FilmgC, IntMPA 1977, MovMk
VanDoren, Mark 1894- BiE&WWA
VanDorn, Mildred Film 2
VanDreelen, John WhoHol A
VanDruten, John 1901-1957 CnMD, CnThe, FilmgC, McGWD, ModWD, NotNAT A, NotNAT B, OxThe, PIP&P, WhThe
VanDusen, Granville WhoHol A
VanDyk, James 1895-1951 WhScrn 1, WhScrn 2
VanDyke, Conny WhoHol A
VanDyke, Dick 1925- CelR 3, FilmgC, IntMPA 1977, MotPP, MovMk, WhoHol A, WorEnF
VanDyke, Jerry MotPP, WhoHol A
VanDyke, Truman 1897- Film 1, Film 2, TwYS
VanDyke, W S Film 1
VanDyke, W S 1887-1943 BiDFlm, WhScrn 2, WorEnF
VanDyke, W S 1887-1944 DcFM, MovMk
VanDyke, W S 1889-1944 CmMov, ImgC
VanDyke, W S 1899- 943 OxFilm, TwYS 4
VanDyke, Willard 1906- DcFM, OxFilm, WomWMM, WorEnF
VanDyke, Woody 1887-1943 WorEnF
Vane, Charles Film 2
Vane, Denton 1890-1940 WhScrn 1, WhScrn 2, WhoHol B
Vane, Dorothy d1947 NotNAT B
Vane, Edwin T NewYTET
Vane, Helen d1840 NotNAT B
Vane, Myrtle Film 2
Vane, Norman Thaddeus 1931- IntMPA 1977
Vane, Sutton d1913 NotNAT B
Vane, Sutton 1888-1963 McGWD, ModWD, NotNAT B
Vane-Tempest, Francis Adolphus 1863-1932 NotNAT B, WhThe
Vaneck, Pierre WhoHol A
Vanel, Charles Film 2
Vanel, Charles 1885- WorEnF
Vanel, Charles 1892- FilmgC, WhoHol A
VanEnger, Charles J 1890- IntMPA 1977
VanEps, George 1913- AmSCAP 1966
VanEss, Connie WhoHol A
VanEyck, Peter 1911-1969 FilmgC
VanEyck, Peter 1913-1969 MovMk, Vers A, WhScrn 1, WhScrn 2, WhoHol B
VanEyssen, John 1925- FilmgC, WhoHol A
VanFleet, Jo BiE&WWA, IntMPA 1977, MotPP, NotNAT, WhoHol A
VanFleet, Jo 1919- FilmgC
VanFleet, Jo 1922- MovMk, Vers A, WhoThe 16
VanForst, Kathy 1904- AmSCAP 1966
VanGastern, Louis 1922- DcFM
VanGelder, Holtropp WhThe
Vangeon, Henri McGWD
VanGriethuysen, Ted 1934- BiE&WWA, NotNAT, WhoThe 16
VanGyseghem, Andre 1906- WhoThe 16
VanHaden, Anders 1876-1936 WhScrn 1, WhScrn 2, WhoHol B
VanHeusen, James 1913- AmSCAP 1966, BiE&WWA, NotNAT, WhoThe 16
VanHeusen, Jimmy 1913- CelR 3
VanHeusen, Jimmy 1919- FilmgC, IntMPA 1977
VanHeyningen, Judy WomWMM
VanHorn, Emile d1967 WhScrn 2
VanHorn, James 1917-1966 WhScrn 1, WhScrn 2
VanHorn, Jimmy 1917-1966 WhoHol B
VanHorn, Rollin Weber 1882-1964 BiE&WWA, NotNAT B

VanHorne, Harriet 1920- CelR 3
VanHorne, Harry Randall 1924- AmSCAP 1966
VanHulse, Camil 1897- AmSCAP 1966
VanHulsteyn, Jeannine WomWMM B
VanItallie, Jean-Claude 1936- ConDr 1977, CroCD, McGWD, ModWD, NatPD, NotNAT, PIP&P, WhoThe 16
VanLeer, Arnold 1895-1975 WhScrn 2
VanLennep, William 1906-1962 NotNAT B
VanLent, Lucille Film 2
Vanloo, Albert d1920 NotNAT B, WhThe
VanLoon, Gerard Willem 1911- AmSCAP 1966
VanMeter, Harry Film 1, TwYS
Vann, Al 1899- AmSCAP 1966
Vann, Polly 1882-1952 Film 2, WhScrn 2
Vanna, Nina Film 2
VanName, Elsie Film 1
Vanne, Marda d1970 WhScrn 1, WhScrn 2, WhThe, WhoHol B
Vanni, Renata WhoHol A
VanNostrand, Morris Abbott 1911- BiE&WWA, NotNAT
VanNutter, Rik WhoHol A
Vanocur, Sander NewYTET, WhoHol A
Vanoff, Nick NewYTET
VanOle, Rhea Film 1
VanPallandt, Nina WhoHol A
VanParys, Georges 1902-1970 WorEnF
VanParys, Georges 1902-1971 DcFM, FilmgC, OxFilm
VanPatten, Dick 1928- BiE&WWA, IntMPA 1977, NotNAT, WhoHol A, WhoThe 16
VanPatten, Joyce 1934- BiE&WWA, FilmgC, NotNAT, WhoHol A, WhoThe 16
VanPatten, Vincent WhoHol A
VanPeebles, Melvin 1932- CelR 3, ConDr 1977D, FilmgC, IntMPA 1977, NotNAT, PIP&P A, WhoHol A, WhoThe 16
VanPraag, William 1924- IntMPA 1977
VanRiel, Raimondo Film 2
VanRikfoord, Harold C 1935- IntMPA 1977
VanRonk, David 1936- AmSCAP 1966
VanRooten, Luis 1906-1973 BiE&WWA, FilmgC, Vers B, WhScrn 2, WhoHol B
VanRooy, Anton d1932 NotNAT B
VanSaher, Lilla A 1912-1968 NotNAT B, WhScrn 1, WhScrn 2, WhoHol B
VanSciver, Esther 1907-1952 AmSCAP 1966
VanScoyk, Robert 1928- BiE&WWA
VanSickle, Dale WhoHol A
VanSickle, Raymond d1964 NotNAT B
Vansittart, Sir Robert G 1881- WhThe
VanSloan, Edward 1882-1964 FilmgC, NotNAT B, WhScrn 1, WhScrn 2, WhoHol B
VanSpall, Peter 1913- AmSCAP 1966
VanSteeden, Peter, Jr. 1904- AmSCAP 1966
VanStolk, Mary WomWMM
VanStralen, Anton WhoHol A
VanStuddiford, Grace 1873-1927 NotNAT B, WhThe
VanTaalingen, J 1921- IntMPA 1977
VanThal, Dennis 1909- IntMPA 1977, WhThe
VanTress, Mabel 1873-1962 WhScrn 2, WhoHol B
VanTrump, Jessalyn 1885-1939 Film 1, WhScrn 1, WhScrn 2, WhoHol B
VanTuly, Helen d1964 NotNAT B
VanTuyi, Hellen d1964 WhoHol B
VanTuyl, Helen 1891-1964 WhScrn 1, WhScrn 2
VanUpp, Virginia 1902-1970 WhScrn 1, WhScrn 2, WhoHol B, WomWMM
VanUpp, Virginia 1912- FilmgC

VanVactor, David 1906- *AmSCAP 1966*
VanVechten, Carl 1880-1964 *NotNAT B*
VanVliet, Jean *Film 2*
VanVolkenburg, Ellen *WhThe*
VanVolkenburg, J L 1903- *IntMPA 1977,*
  NewYTET
VanVooren, Monique 1933- *BiE&WWA, MotPP,*
  WhoHol A
VanVoorhis, Westbrook 1903-1968 *WhScrn 2,*
  WhoHol B
Vanwally *Film 2*
VanWinkle, Harold E 1939- *AmSCAP 1966*
VanWinterstein, Edward *Film 2*
Vanya, Elsie *Film 2*
VanZandt, Mary O'Sullivan 1903- *AmSCAP 1966*
VanZandt, Philip d1951 *WhoHol B*
VanZandt, Philip 1904-1958 *FilmgC, MovMk,*
  Vers A, WhScrn 1, WhScrn 2
VanZandt, Porter 1923- *BiE&WWA, NotNAT*
Vanzant, Clinton E 1929- *AmSCAP 1966*
Varconi, Victor 1896- *FilmgC, MovMk*
Varconi, Victor 1896-1958 *Film 2, TwYS*
Varconi, Victor 1896-1976 *WhoHol B*
Varda, Agnes 1928- *BiDFlm, DcFM, FilmgC,*
  OxFilm, WhoHol A, WomWMM, WorEnF
Varden, Evelyn d1958 *MotPP, WhoHol B*
Varden, Evelyn 1893-1958 *Vers A*
Varden, Evelyn 1895-1958 *FilmgC, NotNAT B,*
  WhScrn 1, WhScrn 2, WhThe
Varden, Norma 1898?- *FilmgC, MovMk,*
  WhoHol A
Varela, Dante A 1917- *AmSCAP 1966*
Varesi, Gilda 1887- *WhThe*
Varga-Dinicu, Carolina *WhoHol A*
Vari, John *WhoHol A*
Varius Rufus, Lucius 074?BC-014BC *OxThe*
Varlamov, Konstantin Alexandrovitch d1915
  NotNAT B
Varley, Beatrice 1896-1969 *FilmgC, WhoHol B*
Varlund, Rudolf 1900-1945 *ModWD*
Varmalov, Leonid Vassilievich 1907-1962 *DcFM*
Varna, Victo *Film 2*
Varnel, Marcel 1894-1947 *FilmgC, NotNAT B,*
  WhThe
Varnel, Max 1925- *FilmgC*
Varney, Reg 1922- *FilmgC, WhoHol A*
Varnick, Ted 1913- *AmSCAP 1966*
Varnlund, Rudolf 1900-1945 *CnMD*
Varon, Nelson 1928- *AmSCAP 1966*
Varrey, Edwin d1907 *NotNAT B*
Vars, Henry 1902- *AmSCAP 1966*
Varsi, Diane 1938- *FilmgC, MotPP, MovMk,*
  WhoHol A
Vartan, Sylvie *WhoHol A*
Vartian, Thomas *Film 2*
Varvarow, Feodor *Film 2*
Vas, Judit *WomWMM*
Vasan, S S 1900- *DcFM*
Vasaroff, Michael *Film 2*
Vasek, Marisha *WhoHol A*
Vasiliev, Georgi 1899-1945 *WorEnF*
Vasiliev, Georgi 1899-1946 *DcFM, OxFilm*
Vasiliev, Sergei 1900-1959 *DcFM, OxFilm,*
  WorEnF
Vass, Lulu 1877-1952 *WhScrn 1, WhScrn 2*
Vassar, Queenie 1870-1960 *NotNAT B,*
  WhScrn 1, WhScrn 2, WhoHol B
Vasseli, Judith *Film 2*
Vaucaire, Maurice 1865-1918 *NotNAT B, WhThe*
Vaughan, Bernard *Film 2*
Vaughan, Clifford 1893- *AmSCAP 1966*
Vaughan, Dorothy 1889-1955 *WhScrn 1,*
  WhScrn 2, WhoHol B
Vaughan, Dorothy *see also* Vaughn, Dorothy

Vaughan, Frankie 1928- *FilmgC, WhoHol A*
Vaughan, Gillian *WhoHol A*
Vaughan, Gladys *BiE&WWA, NotNAT*
Vaughan, Hilda 1898-1957 *WhThe*
Vaughan, Hilda *see also* Vaughn, Hilda
Vaughan, John Forbes 1921- *AmSCAP 1966*
Vaughan, Kate 1852?-1903 *NotNAT B, OxThe*
Vaughan, Peter 1923- *FilmgC, WhoHol A*
Vaughan, Sarah 1924- *CelR 3*
Vaughan, Stuart 1925- *BiE&WWA, NatPD,*
  NotNAT, WhoThe 16
Vaughan, Susie 1853-1950 *NotNAT B, WhThe*
Vaughan, T B d1928 *NotNAT B*
Vaughan, Vivian *Film 1*
Vaughan Williams, Ralph 1872-1958 *OxFilm*
Vaughn, Ada Mae 1906-1943 *Film 2*
Vaughn, Adamae 1906-1943 *WhScrn 1,*
  WhScrn 2, WhoHol B
Vaughn, Alberta 1906- *TwYS, WhoHol A*
Vaughn, Alberta 1908- *Film 2*
Vaughn, Billy *AmSCAP 1966*
Vaughn, Dorothy 1889-1955 *Vers B*
Vaughn, Dorothy *see also* Vaughan, Dorothy
Vaughn, Hilda 1898-1957 *Film 2, NotNAT B,*
  WhScrn 1, WhScrn 2, WhoHol B
Vaughn, Hilda *see also* Vaughan, Hilda
Vaughn, Jack 1925- *AmSCAP 1966*
Vaughn, Robert 1932- *FilmgC, IntMPA 1977,*
  MotPP, MovMk, WhoHol A, WorEnF
Vaughn, Sammy *WhoHol A*
Vaughn, Vivian 1902-1966 *WhScrn 1, WhScrn 2*
Vaughn, William d1946 *Film 2, WhScrn 1,*
  WhScrn 2, WhoHol B
Vaulthier, Georges d1926 *WhScrn 1, WhScrn 2*
Vausden, Val *Film 2*
Vauthier, Jean 1910- *CnMD, CroCD, McGWD,*
  ModWD, REnWD
Vautier, Elmire *Film 2*
Vautier, Rene 1928- *DcFM*
Vaverka, Anton d1937 *Film 2, WhScrn 1,*
  WhScrn 2, WhoHol B
Vavitch, Michael *Film 2, TwYS*
Vavra, Otakar 1911- *DcFM, OxFilm, WorEnF*
Vaz Dias, Selma 1911- *WhThe, WhoHol A*
Vazquez, Myrna 1935-1975 *WhScrn 2*
Vazquez, Roland *WhoHol A*
Vazzana, Anthony E 1922- *AmSCAP 1966*
Veazie, Carol *WhoHol A*
Veber, Pierre 1869-1942 *McGWD*
Vecchione, Al *NewYTET*
Vecsei, Desider Josef 1882-1966 *AmSCAP 1966*
Vedder, William H 1872-1961 *WhScrn 1,*
  WhScrn 2, WhoHol B
Vedrenne, John E 1867-1930 *NotNAT B, OxThe,*
  WhThe
Vedres, Nicole 1911-1965 *DcFM, FilmgC,*
  OxFilm, WomWMM, WorEnF
Vedreune, J E *PIP&P*
Vee, Bobby *WhoHol A*
Vega, Isela *WhoHol A*
Vega, Jose 1920- *BiE&WWA, NotNAT*
Vega, Lope De 1562-1635 *CnThe, REnWD*
Vega, Rose *Film 2*
Vega, Ventura DeLa 1807-1865 *McGWD, OxThe*
Vega Carpio, Lope Felix De 1562-1635 *McGWD,*
  NotNAT A, NotNAT B, OxThe
Vegoda, Joseph 1910- *IntMPA 1977*
Veidt, Conrad d1943 *MotPP, WhoHol B*
Veidt, Conrad 1892-1943 *TwYS, WorEnF*
Veidt, Conrad 1893-1943 *BiDFlm, Film 1,*
  Film 2, FilmgC, MovMk, NotNAT B,
  OxFilm, WhScrn 1, WhScrn 2
Veidt, Lily *BiE&WWA, NotNAT*
Veiller, Anthony 1903-1965 *FilmgC*

Veiller, Bayard 1869-1943 *NotNAT A,*
    NotNAT B, WhThe
Vejar, Harry J 1890-1968 *Film 2, WhScrn 1,*
    WhScrn 2, WhoHol B
Vekroff, Perry 1881-1937 *TwYS A, WhScrn 1,*
    WhScrn 2, WhoHol B
Velaise, Robert *IntMPA 1977*
Velasco, Jerry *WhoHol A*
Velazco, Robert E 1924- *IntMPA 1977*
Velde, Donald L 1902- *IntMPA 1977*
Velde, James R *IntMPA 1977*
Velez, Lupe d1944 *MotPP, WhoHol B*
Velez, Lupe 1908-1944 *FilmgC, NotNAT B,*
    ThFT, WhScrn 1, WhScrn 2
Velez, Lupe 1909-1944 *Film 2, MovMk, TwYS,*
    WhThe
Velez DeGuevara, Luis 1579-1644 *McGWD*
Velke, Fritz 1930- *AmSCAP 1966*
Velle, Gaston *DcFM*
Velo, Carlos 1905- *DcFM, WorEnF*
Velona, Anthony 1920- *AmSCAP 1966*
Veloz And Yolanda *WhoHol A*
Velten, Johannes 1640-1692 *OxThe*
Venable, Evelyn 1913- *Film 2, FilmgC, MotPP,*
    MovMk, ThFT, WhoHol A
Venable, Reginald 1926-1974 *WhScrn 2,*
    WhoHol B
Vene, Ruggero 1897-1961 *AmSCAP 1966*
Venechanos, S Samuel 1924- *AmSCAP 1966*
Veness, Amy 1876-1960 *Film 1, FilmgC,*
    NotNAT B, WhScrn 1, WhScrn 2,
    WhoHol B
Venier, Marie 1590-1619 *NotNAT B, OxThe*
Venkataramaya, Relangi 1910-1975 *WhScrn 2*
Venne, Lottie 1852-1928 *NotNAT B, OxThe,*
    WhThe
Venning, Una 1893- *WhThe*
Venora, Lee 1932- *BiE&WWA, NotNAT*
Ventre, Frank L 1941- *AmSCAP 1966*
Ventura, Leno *WhoHol A*
Ventura, Lino 1918- *FilmgC, WorEnF*
Ventura, Viviane *WhoHol A*
Venture, Richard *WhoHol A*
Venturi, Robert 1925- *CelR 3*
Venturini, Edward *TwYS A*
Venuta, Benay 1911- *WhoThe 16*
Venuta, Benay 1912- *BiE&WWA, Film 2,*
    NotNAT, WhoHol A
Venuti, Joe 1903- *AmSCAP 1966*
Venza, Jac *NewYTET*
Venzuella, Peter *Film 2*
Vep, Irma *Film 1*
Vera-Ellen *MotPP*
Vera-Ellen 1920- *WhoHol A*
Vera-Ellen 1926- *CmMov, FilmgC, MovMk,*
    WorEnF
VerBecke, W Edwin *NatPD*
Verber, Pierre 1869- *WhThe*
Verbit, Helen *WhoHol A*
Verbruggen, Mrs. *OxThe*
Verchinina, Nina *WhThe*
Verdi, Joe 1885-1957 *WhoHol B*
Verdi, Joseph 1885-1957 *WhScrn 1, WhScrn 2*
Verdon, Gwen *MotPP, WhoHol A*
Verdon, Gwen 1925- *CelR 3, WhoThe 16*
Verdon, Gwen 1926- *BiE&WWA, EncMT,*
    NotNAT
Verducci, John S 1912- *AmSCAP 1966*
Verdugo, Elena 1926- *FilmgC, MovMk,*
    WhoHol A
Verdy, Violette *WhoHol A*
Verebes, Ernest *Film 2*
Vereen, Ben 1946- *CelR 3, EncMT, NotNAT,*
    WhoHol A, WhoThe 16

Verga, Giovanni 1840-1922 *CnThe, McGWD,*
    ModWD, OxThe, REnWD, WhThe
Vergano, Aldo 1894-1957 *DcFM*
Verge, Cyril A 1921- *AmSCAP 1966*
Vergerio, Pier Paolo 1370-1444 *OxThe*
Verges, Joe 1892-1964 *AmSCAP 1966*
Vergez-Tricom *WomWMM*
Verhaeren, Emile Adolphe Gustave 1855-1916
    ModWD
Verhoeven, Paul 1901-1975 *WhScrn 2*
Verkoff, Perry N 1887-1937 *WhScrn 2*
Verley, Bernard *WhoHol A*
Verley, Renaud *WhoHol A*
Verly, Michele *Film 2*
Vermilyea, Harold 1889-1958 *FilmgC, NotNAT B,*
    WhScrn 1, WhScrn 2, WhThe, WhoHol B
Vermorel, Claude 1909- *DcFM*
Vermoyal, Paul d1925 *Film 2, WhScrn 2*
Verne, Jules 1828-1905 *FilmgC*
Verne, Kaaren 1918-1967 *WhoHol B*
Verne, Karen 1915?-1967 *FilmgC, WhScrn 1*
Verne, Karen 1918-1967 *WhScrn 2*
Verne, M *Film 2*
Verneuil *OxThe*
Verneuil, Henri 1920- *FilmgC, WorEnF*
Verneuil, Louis 1893-1952 *CnMD, McGWD,*
    ModWD, NotNAT B, WhThe
Verney, Guy d1970 *WhScrn 1, WhScrn 2,*
    WhoHol B
Verno, Jerry 1895- *FilmgC, WhThe, WhoHol A*
Vernon, Agnes *Film 1, Film 2*
Vernon, Anne 1925- *FilmgC, IntMPA 1977,*
    WhoHol A, WorEnF
Vernon, Bobby 1895-1939 *Film 1, Film 2, TwYS*
Vernon, Bobby 1897-1939 *WhScrn 1, WhScrn 2,*
    WhoHol B
Vernon, Dorothy 1875-1970 *Film 2, WhScrn 2*
Vernon, Frank 1875-1940 *NotNAT B, WhThe*
Vernon, Glen 1923- *WhoHol A*
Vernon, Harriett d1923 *NotNAT B, WhThe*
Vernon, Harry M 1878- *WhThe*
Vernon, Howard *WhoHol A*
Vernon, Ida 1843-1923 *NotNAT B, WhoStg 1906,*
    WhoStg 1908
Vernon, Jackie *WhoHol A*
Vernon, John 1935- *FilmgC, WhoHol A*
Vernon, Kate Olga d1939 *NotNAT B*
Vernon, Lou 1888-1971 *WhScrn 2*
Vernon, Richard *WhoHol A*
Vernon, Richard 1907?- *FilmgC*
Vernon, Richard 1925- *WhoThe 16*
Vernon, Virginia 1894- *WhThe*
Vernon, Vivian *Film 2*
Vernon, Wally 1904-1970 *FilmgC, Vers B,*
    WhScrn 1, WhScrn 2, WhoHol B
Vernon, William 1912-1971 *WhScrn 2*
Vernor, F Dudleigh 1892- *AmSCAP 1966*
Verona, Michael Ross *WhoHol A*
VerPlanck, John 1930- *AmSCAP 1966*
Verrett, Shirley 1933- *CelR 3*
Versois, Odile 1930- *FilmgC, IntMPA 1977,*
    WhoHol A
Verst, Ruth 1930- *AmSCAP 1966*
Vertes, Marcel 1895-1961 *NotNAT B*
Vertov, Dziga 1896-1954 *BiDFlm, DcFM,*
    FilmgC, OxFilm, WomWMM, WorEnF
Vertue, Beryl *NewYTET*
Verushka *WhoHol A*
Vesaas, Tarjei 1897-1970 *REnWD*
VeSota, Bruno 1922-1976 *WhScrn 2*
Vespermann, Kurt 1887-1957 *Film 2, WhScrn 1,*
    WhScrn 2
Vestoff, Floria 1918-1963 *AmSCAP 1966,*
    NotNAT B

Vestoff, Virginia *WhoHol A*
Vestris, Madame 1797-1856 *NotNAT A, PIP&P*
Vestris, Eliza 1797-1856 *FamA&A*
Vestris, Francoise Gourgaud 1743-1804 *OxThe*
Vestris, Lucia Elizabetta 1797-1856 *OxThe*
Vestris, Madame Bartolozzi 1797-1856 *NotNAT B*
Vetri, Victoria 1944- *FilmgC*
Vetter, Richard 1928- *IntMPA 1977*
Vezin, Arthur 1878- *WhThe*
Vezin, Mrs. Hermann d1902 *NotNAT B*
Vezin, Hermann 1829-1910 *NotNAT B, OxThe*
Vezin, Jane Elizabeth Thomson 1827-1902 *OxThe*
Vian, Boris 1920-1959 *CnMD Sup, CnThe,*
    CroCD, McGWD, ModWD, REnWD
Viardot, Pauline d1910 *NotNAT B*
Vibart, Henry 1863-1939 *Film 2, WhThe*
Vibert, Marcel *Film 2*
Viby, Marguerite *WomWMM*
Vicar, Anthony 1914- *AmSCAP 1966*
Vicars, Harold d1922 *AmSCAP 1966*
Vicas, Victor 1918- *FilmgC*
Viccola, Giovanni *Film 2*
Vicente, Gil 1465?-1536? *CnThe, REnWD*
Vicente, Gil 1465?-1537? *OxThe*
Vicente, Gil 1470?-1536? *McGWD*
Vickers, Martha 1925-1971 *FilmgC, HolP 40,*
    WhScrn 1, WhScrn 2, WhoHol B
Vickers, Yvette *WhoHol A*
Victor, Benjamin d1778 *NotNAT B*
Victor, Charles 1896-1965 *FilmgC, WhScrn 1,*
    WhScrn 2, WhThe, WhoHol B
Victor, David *NewYTET*
Victor, Harvey L *IntMPA 1977*
Victor, Henry 1898-1945 *Film 1, Film 2, FilmgC,*
    WhScrn 1, WhScrn 2, WhoHol B
Victor, James *WhoHol A*
Victor, Josephine 1885- *WhThe, WhoStg 1908*
Victor, Lionel d1940 *NotNAT B*
Victor, Lucia *BiE&WWA, NotNAT*
Victor, Mary Anne d1907 *NotNAT B*
Victoria, Vesta 1873-1951 *NotNAT B, WhThe,*
    WhoStg 1906, WhoStg 1908
Victory, Jim *NewYTET*
Victrix, Claudia *Film 2*
Vida, Frank J 1894- *AmSCAP 1966*
Vidacovich, I J 1904-1966 *AmSCAP 1966*
Vidacovich, Irvine d1966 *WhoHol B*
Vidacovich, Irving J Pinky 1905-1966 *WhScrn 1,*
    WhScrn 2
Vidal, Gore 1925- *BiE&WWA, CelR 3, CnMD,*
    ConDr 1977, CroCD, McGWD, ModWD,
    NotNAT, NotNAT A, WhoThe 16, WorEnF
Vidal, Henri 1919-1959 *FilmgC, MotPP,*
    NotNAT B, WhScrn 1, WhScrn 2,
    WhoHol B
Vidor, Catherine *Film 2*
Vidor, Charles 1900-1959 *BiDFlm, DcFM,*
    FilmgC, MovMk, OxFilm, WomWMM,
    WorEnF
Vidor, Florence 1895- *Film 1, Film 2, FilmgC,*
    MotPP, MovMk, TwYS, WhoHol A
Vidor, King *Film 1*
Vidor, King 1894- *DcFM, Film 2, FilmgC,*
    MovMk, TwYS A
Vidor, King 1895- *IntMPA 1977, WorEnF*
Vidor, King 1896- *BiDFlm, CmMov, OxFilm*
Vie, Florence d1939 *NotNAT B*
Viehman, Theodore 1889- *BiE&WWA*
Viel, Marguerite *WomWMM*
Vierny, Sacha 1919- *DcFM, FilmgC, OxFilm,*
    WorEnF
Viertel, Berthold 1885-1953 *FilmgC*
Viertel, Berthold 1885-1954 *OxThe*
Vietheer, George C 1910- *IntMPA 1977*

Vieyra, Paulin 1923- *DcFM*
Vigarani, Carlo *OxThe*
Vigarani, Gaspare 1586-1663 *NotNAT B, OxThe*
Vignola, Robert 1882-1953 *WhoHol B*
Vignola, Robert C 1882-1953 *Film 1*
Vignola, Robert G 1882-1953 *NotNAT B,*
    TwYS A, WhScrn 1, WhScrn 2
Vignon, Jean-Paul *WhoHol A*
Vigny, Alfred De 1797-1863 *CnThe, McGWD,*
    NotNAT B, REnWD
Vigo, Jean 1905-1934 *BiDFlm, DcFM, FilmgC,*
    MovMk, OxFilm, WorEnF
Vigoda, Abe *WhoHol A*
Vigran, Herb 1910- *Vers A, WhoHol A*
Viharo, Robert *WhoHol A*
Viking, Vonceil d1929 *WhScrn 1, WhScrn 2*
Vila, Sabra DeShon 1850-1917 *WhScrn 2*
Vilar, Jean d1971 *WhoHol B*
Vilar, Jean 1912-1971 *BiE&WWA, CnThe,*
    NotNAT B, OxThe, WhThe
Vilar, Jean 1913-1971 *WhScrn 1, WhScrn 2*
Vilas, William H *IntMPA 1977*
Vilbert, Henri *WhoHol A*
Vilches, Ernesto d1954 *WhScrn 1, WhScrn 2*
Vildrac, Charles Messager 1882-1971 *CnMD,*
    McGWD, ModWD, REnWD
Villa, Manuel 1917- *AmSCAP 1966*
Villaespesa, Francisco 1877-1936 *McGWD*
Villard, Frank 1917- *FilmgC, WhoHol A*
Villard, Juliette 1945-1971 *WhScrn 2*
Villaret, Joao 1914-1961 *WhScrn 1, WhScrn 2*
Villarreal, Julio 1885-1958 *WhScrn 1, WhScrn 2,*
    WhoHol B
Villaurutia, Xavier *OxThe*
Villechaize, Herve *WhoHol A*
Villella, Edward 1937- *CelR 3, WhoHol A*
Villetard, Edmond d1890 *NotNAT B*
Villiers, Claude Deschamps De 1600-1681 *OxThe*
Villiers, Edwin d1904 *NotNAT B*
Villiers, George, Duke Of Buckingham 1628-1687
    McGWD, NotNAT B, OxThe
Villiers, James *WhoHol A*
Villiers, James 1930?- *FilmgC*
Villiers, James 1933- *WhoThe 16*
Villiers, Jean DeVilliers 1648-1701 *OxThe*
Villiers, Marguerite Beguet d1670 *OxThe*
Villiers DeL'Isle-Adam, Jean Marie 1838-1889
    REnWD
Villines, Virginia 1917- *AmSCAP 1966*
Vina, Victo *Film 2*
Vinayak, Master d1947 *WhScrn 2*
Vincenot, Louis 1884-1967 *WhScrn 2, WhoHol B*
Vincent, Allen *Film 2*
Vincent, Billy 1896-1966 *WhScrn 2*
Vincent, Bob 1918- *AmSCAP 1966*
Vincent, Charles T d1935 *NotNAT B*
Vincent, Gene 1935-1971 *WhScrn 1, WhScrn 2,*
    WhoHol B
Vincent, James d1957 *NotNAT B, WhoHol B*
Vincent, Jan-Michael *IntMPA 1977, WhoHol A*
Vincent, John 1902- *AmSCAP 1966*
Vincent, June *IntMPA 1977, WhoHol A*
Vincent, Katharine 1919- *IntMPA 1977*
Vincent, Larry *WhoHol A*
Vincent, Larry 1901- *AmSCAP 1966*
Vincent, Larry 1925-1975 *WhScrn 2*
Vincent, Madge 1884- *WhThe*
Vincent, Mary Ann 1818-1887 *NotNAT A,*
    NotNAT B, OxThe
Vincent, Mildred *Film 2*
Vincent, Nathaniel Hawthorne 1889-
    AmSCAP 1966
Vincent, Robbie d1968 *WhoHol B*
Vincent, Romo *WhoHol A*

Vincent, Ruth 1877-1955 *NotNAT B, WhThe, WhoStg 1908*
Vincent, Sailor Billy 1896-1966 *WhScrn 2*
Vincent, Virginia *WhoHol A*
Vincent, Walter 1868-1959 *NotNAT B*
Vincent, Warren 1925- *AmSCAP 1966*
Vincent, Yves *WhoHol A*
Vincenz, Lilli *WomWMM B*
Vine, Billy 1915-1958 *WhScrn 1, WhScrn 2, WhoHol B*
Viner, Edward *Film 1*
Vines, Margaret 1910- *WhThe*
Vining, Fanny d1891 *NotNAT B*
Vining, Frederick d1871 *NotNAT B*
Vining, George J d1875 *NotNAT B*
Vinson, Gary *WhoHol A*
Vinson, Helen 1907- *FilmgC, MovMk, ThFT, WhThe, WhoHol A*
Vint, Alan *WhoHol A*
Vint, Bill *WhoHol A*
Vint, Jesse *WhoHol A*
Vinton, Arthur Rolfe d1963 *NotNAT B, WhScrn 1, WhScrn 2, WhoHol B*
Vinton, Bobby 1935- *AmSCAP 1966, WhoHol A*
Violante, Madame *PIP&P*
Violinsky, Solly Sol Ginsberg d1963 *NotNAT B*
Viotti, Gino *Film 1*
Virgil, Helen *Film 2*
Virginia, Barbara *WomWMM*
Virgo, Peter *WhoHol A*
Virgo, Peter, Jr. *WhoHol A*
Virta, Nikilai Yevgenievich 1906- *OxThe*
Virta, Nikolai Evgenievich 1906- *CroCD*
Virtuoso, Frank 1923- *AmSCAP 1966*
Virues, Cristobal De 1550?-1614? *McGWD*
Visakhadatta *REnWD*
Visaroff, Michael d1951 *WhoHol B*
Visaroff, Michael 1890-1951 *Film 2, TwYS*
Visaroff, Michael 1892-1951 *WhScrn 1, WhScrn 2*
Visaroff, Nina 1888-1938 *WhScrn 2*
Visconti, Luchino 1906- *BiDFlm, CelR 3, CnThe, DcFM, FilmgC, MovMk, OxFilm, OxThe, WorEnF*
Vishnevski, Vsevolod 1901-1951 *CnMD*
Vishnevsky, Vsevolod Vitalevich 1900-1951 *CroCD*
Vishnevsky, Vsevolod Vital'evich 1900-1951 *DcFM*
Vishnevsky, Vsevolod Vitalevich 1900-1951 *ModWD, OxThe*
Vishnevsky, Vsevolod Vitalievich 1900-1951 *McGWD*
Vitale, Joseph A 1905- *IntMPA 1977*
Vitale, Mario *WhoHol A*
Vitale, Milly 1938- *FilmgC, IntMPA 1977, WhoHol A*
Vitaliani, Italia *Film 2*
Viterbo, Patricia 1943-1966 *WhScrn 1, WhScrn 2*
Vitrac, Roger 1899-1952 *CnThe, McGWD, ModWD, OxThe, REnWD*
Vitruvius *PIP&P*
Vitruvius Pollio, Marcus *NotNAT B, OxThe*
Vitti, Monica *MotPP, WhoHol A*
Vitti, Monica 1931- *MovMk, OxFilm, WorEnF*
Vitti, Monica 1933- *BiDFlm, FilmgC*
Viva *WhoHol A*
Vivas, Marta *WomWMM B*
Vivian, Anthony Crespigny Claud 1906- *WhThe*
Vivian, Percival 1890-1961 *NotNAT B, WhScrn 2, WhoHol B*
Vivian, Robert 1859-1944 *NotNAT B, WhScrn 2, WhoHol B*
Vivian, Robert 1885-1944 *Film 1, Film 2*
Vivian, Ruth d1949 *NotNAT B, WhScrn 2, WhoHol B*

Vivian, Violet d1960 *NotNAT B*
Vivian-Rees, Joan *WhThe*
Viviani, Raffaele 1888-1950 *McGWD*
Vivyan, John *WhoHol A*
Vizard, Harold 1871- *WhoStg 1908*
Vlady, Marina *MotPP, WhoHol A*
Vlady, Marina 1937- *BiDFlm, MovMk, WorEnF*
Vlady, Marina 1938- *FilmgC*
Vlasek, June *WhoHol A*
Vleck, Joseph V *IntMPA 1977*
Vodeding, Fredrik d1942 *WhoHol B*
Vodery, Will 1885-1951 *AmSCAP 1966*
Vodnoy, Max 1892-1939 *WhScrn 2*
Voelpel, Fred *WhoThe 16*
Vogan, Emmet 1893-1969 *Vers B*
Vogan, Emmett 1893-1969 *WhScrn 2, WhoHol B*
Vogeding, Fredrik 1890-1942 *WhScrn 1, WhScrn 2*
Vogel, Eleanore 1903-1973 *WhScrn 2*
Vogel, Henry 1865-1925 *NotNAT B, WhScrn 1, WhScrn 2, WhoHol B*
Vogel, Janet Frances 1941- *AmSCAP 1966*
Vogel, Jesse 1925- *IntMPA 1977*
Vogel, Mitch 1956- *WhoHol A*
Vogel, Patricia 1909-1941 *WhScrn 1, WhScrn 2*
Vogel, Paul C 1899- *FilmgC*
Vogel, Rudolf 1900-1967 *WhScrn 2*
Vogel, Virgil *FilmgC*
Vogelsang, Judith *WomWMM A, WomWMM B*
Vogler, Karl Michael 1928- *FilmgC, WhoHol A*
Vogler, Walter A 1897-1955 *WhScrn 1, WhScrn 2, WhoHol B*
Vohs, Joan 1931- *IntMPA 1977*
Voight, Jon *WhoHol A*
Voight, Jon 1938- *CelR 3, IntMPA 1977, WhoThe 16*
Voight, Jon 1939- *FilmgC, MovMk, OxFilm*
Voinoff, Anatole 1896-1965 *WhScrn 1, WhScrn 2*
Vojnovic, Ivo 1857-1929 *CnMD*
Vokes, F M T d1890 *NotNAT B*
Vokes, Frederick Mortimer 1846-1888 *NotNAT B, OxThe*
Vokes, Harry d1922 *NotNAT B*
Vokes, Jessie Catherine Biddulph 1851-1884 *OxThe*
Vokes, John Russell d1924 *NotNAT B*
Vokes, May d1957 *Film 2, NotNAT B, WhoHol B*
Vokes, Robert d1912 *NotNAT B*
Vokes, Rosina 1854-1894 *NotNAT B, OxThe*
Vokes, Victoria 1853-1894 *NotNAT B, OxThe*
Vokes, Walter Fawdon d1904 *OxThe*
Vola, Vicki *BiE&WWA*
Voland, Herb *WhoHol A*
Volare, Lorna *Film 1*
Volker, Wilhelm *Film 2*
Volkert, Erie T 1913- *BiE&WWA, NotNAT*
Volkman, Ivan d1972 *WhScrn 2*
Volkov, Fedor Gregoryevich 1729-1763 *NotNAT B*
Volkov, Feodor Grigoryevich 1729-1763 *OxThe*
Volkov, Leonid Andreyevich 1893- *OxThe*
Volland, Virginia 1909- *BiE&WWA, NotNAT*
Vollmer, Lula 1898-1955 *CnMD, ModWD, NotNAT B, WhThe*
Vollmoeller, Karl Gustav 1878-1948 *CnMD, ModWD, NotNAT B*
Vollmoller, Karl Gustav 1878-1948 *McGWD*
Volonte, Gian Maria 1930- *FilmgC, WhoHol A*
Volotskoy, Vladimir 1853-1927 *WhScrn 1, WhScrn 2*
Volpe, Frederick 1865-1932 *NotNAT B, WhThe, WhoHol B*
Volpe, Frederick 1873-1932 *WhScrn 2*
Volpe, John 1908- *CelR 3*
Volpe, Virgilio A 1935- *AmSCAP 1966*

Voltaire 1694-1778 *CnThe, McGWD, OxThe, REnWD*
Voltaire, Francois Marie Aronet De 1694-1778 *NotNAT B*
Volterra, Leon d1949 *NotNAT B*
VonAlten, Ferdiand *Film 2*
VonAlten, Ferdinand 1885-1933 *WhScrn 1, WhScrn 2, WhoHol B*
VonBerne, Eva *Film 2*
VonBetz, Matthew *WhScrn 2*
VonBlock, Bela 1889-1962 *WhScrn 1, WhScrn 2, WhoHol B*
VonBolvary, Geza 1898-1961 *WhScrn 1, WhScrn 2*
VonBraun, Wernher 1912- *CelR 3*
VonBrincken, Wilhelm 1882-1946 *WhoHol B*
VonBrincken, Wilhelm 1891-1946 *WhScrn 1, WhScrn 2*
VonBrincken, William 1882-1946 *Film 2, Vers B*
VonBusing, Fritzi d1948 *NotNAT B*
VonCollande, Gisela 1915-1960 *WhScrn 1, WhScrn 2*
Vondel, Joost VanDen 1587-1679 *CnThe, McGWD, REnWD*
VonDerGoltz, Eric 1895- *AmSCAP 1966*
VonDobeneck, Baron *Film 2*
VonEltz, Theodore d1964 *MotPP, WhoHol B*
VonEltz, Theodore 1889-1964 *Film 1, Film 2, TwYS*
VonEltz, Theodore 1894-1964 *MovMk, Vers A, WhScrn 1, WhScrn 2*
VonEngleman, Andre *Film 2*
VonEsterhazy, Countess Agnes *Film 2*
VonFurstenberg, Betsy *MotPP, NotNAT, WhoHol A*
VonFurstenberg, Betsy 1931- *WhoThe 16*
VonFurstenberg, Betsy 1932- *CelR 3*
VonFurstenberg, Betsy 1935- *BiE&WWA*
VonGerlach, Arthur 1876-1925 *WorEnF*
VonGoth, Rolf *Film 2*
VonHagen, Egon *Film 2*
VonHallberg, Gene 1906- *AmSCAP 1966*
VonHarbou, Thea 1888-1954 *FilmgC, WomWMM, WorEnF*
VonHardenburg, William *Film 2*
VonHartman, Carl *Film 2, TwYS*
VonHartz, John 1933- *NatPD*
VonHease, Baron *Film 2*
VonHoffman, Nicholas 1929- *CelR 3*
VonHofmannstahl, Hugo *NotNAT B*
VonHofmannsthal *PIP&P*
VonHollay, Camilla *Film 2*
VonKaltenborn, Hans 1879-1965 *WhScrn 2*
VonKlaussen, Ronald *WhoHol A*
VonKotzbue, August Friedrich Ferdinand 1761-1819 *PIP&P*
VonLambeck, Frederick 1918-1950 *WhScrn 2*
VonLedebur, Leopold 1876-1955 *WhScrn 1, WhScrn 2*
VonLenkeffy, Ica *Film 2*
VonLent, Lucille *Film 2*
VonLer, Sarah d1916 *NotNAT B*
VonLinnenkoff, Barbara *Film 2*
VonMeter, Harry *Film 1, Film 2*
VonMeyerinck, Hubert 1897-1971 *Film 2, WhScrn 1, WhScrn 2, WhoHol B*
VonMosev, Gustav *PIP&P*
Vonnegut, Kurt, Jr. 1922- *CelR 3, ConDr 1977, NatPD*
Vonnegut, Marjory *PIP&P*
Vonnegut, Walter d1940 *NotNAT B*
VonPrauheim, Rosa *WomWMM*
VonReinhold, Calvin 1927- *BiE&WWA, NotNAT, WhoHol A*

VonRempert, Albert d1958 *WhScrn 1, WhScrn 2*
VonRitoy, Theodore *Film 2*
VonRitzau, Erik *Film 2*
VonRitzau, Gunther *Film 1*
VonRue, Greta *Film 2*
VonSchacht, Count *Film 2*
VonScherler, Sasha 1939- *WhoHol A, WhoThe 16*
VonSchiller, Carl *Film 1*
VonSchlettow, Hans *Film 2*
VonSchwindt, Wolfgang *Film 2*
VonSeyffertitz, Gustav 1863-1943 *Film 1, Film 2, FilmgC, TwYS, WhScrn 1, WhScrn 2, WhoHol B*
VonSeyffertitz, Gustav 1890?-1943 *MovMk*
VonSternberg, Josef 1894-1969 *BiDFlm, DcFM, FilmgC, MovMk, TwYS A, WhScrn 1, WhScrn 2, WorEnF*
VonSternberg, Joseph 1894-1969 *CmMov*
VonStroheim, Erich d1957 *MotPP, WhoHol B*
VonStroheim, Erich 1884-1957 *MovMk*
VonStroheim, Erich 1885-1957 *BiDFlm, DcFM, Film 1, Film 2, FilmgC, TwYS, WhScrn 1, WhScrn 2, WorEnF*
VonStroheim, Erich 1886-1957 *TwYS A*
VonStroheim, Erich, Jr. 1916-1968 *WhScrn 1, WhScrn 2, WhoHol B*
VonSydow, Clas *WhoHol A*
VonSydow, Henrik *WhoHol A*
VonSydow, Max 1929- *BiDFlm, CelR 3, FilmgC, IntMPA 1977, MotPP, MovMk, OxFilm, WhoHol A, WorEnF*
VonSzoreghy, Julius *Film 2*
VonTilzer, Albert 1878-1956 *AmSCAP 1966, NotNAT B*
VonTilzer, Harry 1872-1946 *AmSCAP 1966, NotNAT B*
VonTwardowski, Hans d1958 *Film 1, NotNAT B, WhScrn 1, WhScrn 2, WhoHol B*
VonWalther, Hertha *Film 2*
VonWangenheim, Gustav *Film 2*
VonWinterstein, Eduard 1872-1961 *Film 2, WhScrn 1, WhScrn 2, WhoHol B*
VonWurtzler, Aristid 1925- *AmSCAP 1966*
VonZell, Harry 1906- *WhoHol A*
VonZerneck, Peter *WhoHol A*
Vorhaus, Bernard 1898?- *FilmgC, IntMPA 1977*
Vorkapich, Slavko 1894- *DcFM*
Vorkapich, Slavko 1895- *OxFilm, WorEnF*
Vorkapitch, Slavko 1897- *FilmgC*
Voronina, Vera *Film 2*
Vosburgh, Alfred *Film 1, WhScrn 2*
Vosburgh, David *WhoHol A*
Vosburgh, Harold 1870-1926 *Film 1, Film 2, TwYS, WhScrn 2*
Voskovec, George 1905- *BiE&WWA, FilmgC, MotPP, NotNAT, WhoHol A, WhoThe 16*
Voskovec, Jiri *CnMD*
Vosper, Frank 1899-1937 *CnThe, Film 2, NotNAT B, WhThe*
Vosper, Frank O 1900-1937 *WhScrn 2*
Vosper, John d1954 *WhScrn 1, WhScrn 2, WhoHol B*
Voss, Frank Fatty 1888-1917 *WhScrn 2*
Voss, Peter *Film 2*
Voss, Stephanie 1936- *WhoThe 16*
Vosselli, Judith *Film 2*
Vreeland, Diana 1903?- *CelR 3*
Vroman, John 1918- *AmSCAP 1966*
Vroom, Frederic William 1858-1942 *WhScrn 1, WhScrn 2*
Vroom, Frederick d1942 *Film 2, WhoHol B*
Vroom, Lodewick d1950 *NotNAT B*
Vroom, Paul 1917- *BiE&WWA, NotNAT*

Vukotic, Dusan 1927- *DcFM, WorEnF*
Vulchanov, Rangel 1928- *DcFM*
Vuolo, Tito 1893-1962 *WhScrn 2,   WhoHol B*
Vye, Murvyn 1913- *FilmgC, IntMPA 1977,*
  MovMk, Vers B, WhoHol A
Vyvyan, Jennifer d1974 *WhoHol B*

W

Wachsmith, Fee *Film 2*
Wadams, Golden *Film 2*
Waddell, Samuel J *REnWD*
Waddington, Patrick 1901- *BiE&WWA, NotNAT, WhoHol A, WhoThe 16*
Wade, Adam *WhoHol A*
Wade, Allan 1881-1954 *OxThe*
Wade, Allan 1881-1955 *NotNAT B, WhThe*
Wade, Bessie 1885-1966 *WhScrn 2, WhoHol B*
Wade, John 1876-1949 *WhoHol B*
Wade, John P 1874- *Film 1, Film 2*
Wade, John W 1876-1949 *WhScrn 1, WhScrn 2*
Wade, Philip d1950 *NotNAT B*
Wade, Walter d1963 *NotNAT B*
Wade, Warren 1896-1973 *WhScrn 2*
Wadhams, Golden 1869-1929 *WhScrn 1, WhScrn 2, WhoHol B*
Wadkar, Hansa Swan 1924-1971 *WhScrn 1, WhScrn 2*
Wadleigh, Michael 1941- *IntMPA 1977*
Wadsworth, Handel d1964 *NotNAT B*
Wadsworth, Henry 1902-1974 *Film 2, WhScrn 2, WhoHol B*
Wadsworth, James T *NewYTET*
Wadsworth, William 1873-1950 *Film 1, Film 2, MotPP, WhScrn 1, WhScrn 2, WhoHol B*
Wagenaar, Bernard 1894- *AmSCAP 1966*
Wagenhals, Lincoln A 1869-1931 *NotNAT B, WhThe*
Wagenheim, Charles *IntMPA 1977, WhoHol A*
Wagenseller, William H 1880-1951 *WhScrn 1, WhScrn 2*
Wager, Anthony *WhoHol A*
Wager, Michael 1925- *BiE&WWA, NotNAT, WhoHol A, WhoThe 16*
Waggoner, George *Film 2*
Waggner, George 1894- *FilmgC, IntMPA 1977*
Waggoner, Lyle 1935- *IntMPA 1977*
Wagner, Arthur 1923- *BiE&WWA, NotNAT*
Wagner, Charles L d1956 *NotNAT A, NotNAT B, WhThe*
Wagner, Ed *WhoHol A*
Wagner, Elsa *Film 2, WhoHol A*
Wagner, Erika *Film 2*
Wagner, Frank *BiE&WWA, NotNAT*
Wagner, Fritz Arno 1889-1958 *FilmgC, OxFilm, WorEnF*
Wagner, Fritz Arno 1894-1958 *DcFM*
Wagner, George *Film 2*
Wagner, Heinrich Leopold 1747-1779 *McGWD*
Wagner, Jack 1897-1965 *WhScrn 1, WhScrn 2, WhoHol B*
Wagner, Jane *NewYTET*
Wagner, Joseph 1913- *BiE&WWA*
Wagner, Joseph Frederick 1900- *AmSCAP 1966*
Wagner, Kid *Film 2*

Wagner, Larry 1907- *AmSCAP 1966*
Wagner, Leon *WhoHol A*
Wagner, Lindsay *WhoHol A*
Wagner, Lou *WhoHol A*
Wagner, Mamie *WomWMM*
Wagner, Max 1901-1975 *WhScrn 2, WhoHol C*
Wagner, Mike *WhoHol A*
Wagner, Richard 1813-1883 *OxThe, REnWD*
Wagner, Robert 1930- *FilmgC, IntMPA 1977, MotPP, MovMk, WhoHol A, WorEnF*
Wagner, Robert F 1910- *BiE&WWA*
Wagner, Robin 1933- *BiE&WWA, NotNAT, WhoThe 16*
Wagner, Roger 1914- *AmSCAP 1966*
Wagner, Thomas 1931- *AmSCAP 1966*
Wagner, Wende *WhoHol A*
Wagner, Wilhelm Richard 1813-1883 *NotNAT B*
Wagner, William 1885-1964 *NotNAT B, WhScrn 1, WhScrn 2, WhoHol B*
Wagoner, Porter *IntMPA 1977*
Wahby, Youssef 1899- *DcFM*
Wahl, Walter Dare 1896-1974 *WhScrn 2, WhoHol B*
Waimon, Seto 191-?- *DcFM*
Wain, Bea *IntMPA 1977*
Wainer, Lee *AmSCAP 1966*
Wainwright, Godfrey 1879-1956 *WhScrn 1, WhScrn 2*
Wainwright, Hope 1942-1972 *WhScrn 2, WhoHol B*
Wainwright, James *WhoHol A*
Wainwright, John d1911 *NotNAT B*
Wainwright, Marie d1923 *Film 2, WhoHol B, WhoStg 1906*
Wainwright, Marie 1853-1923 *NotNAT B, WhThe, WhoStg 1908*
Wainwright, Marie 1856-1923 *WhScrn 1, WhScrn 2*
Wainwright, Mary Lee 1913- *AmSCAP 1966*
Waissman, Kenneth 1942- *NotNAT*
Waite, Genevieve *WhoHol A*
Waite, Malcolm *Film 2*
Waite, Marjorie *Film 2*
Waite, Ralph *WhoHol A*
Wajda, Andrzej 1926- *BiDFlm, DcFM, FilmgC, MovMk, OxFilm, WorEnF*
Wakefield, Anne *WhoHol A*
Wakefield, Douglas 1899-1951 *NotNAT B, WhThe*
Wakefield, Douglas 1900-1951 *WhScrn 1, WhScrn 2*
Wakefield, Duggie 1899-1951 *FilmgC, WhoHol B*
Wakefield, Frances *WhScrn 1, WhScrn 2*
Wakefield, Gilbert Edward 1892-1963 *WhThe*
Wakefield, Hugh 1888- *WhThe*
Wakefield, Hugh 1888-1971 *WhScrn 1,*

WhScrn 2, WhoHol B
Wakefield, Hugh 1888-1972 *FilmgC*
Wakefield, Oliver 1909-1956 *WhScrn 1,*
  WhScrn 2, WhoHol B
Wakely, Jimmy 1914- *AmSCAP 1966,*
  IntMPA 1977, WhoHol A
Wakeman, Keith 1866-1933 *NotNAT B, WhThe*
Wakhevitch, Georges 1907- *DcFM, OxThe,*
  WorEnF
Waksman, Selman 1888- *CelR 3*
Walberg, Betty 1921- *BiE&WWA*
Walberg, Garry *WhoHol A*
Walbrook, Anton 1900- *WorEnF*
Walbrook, Anton 1900-1966 *WhThe*
Walbrook, Anton 1900-1967 *BiDFlm, Film 2,*
  MotPP, MovMk, NotNAT B, OxFilm,
  WhScrn 1, WhScrn 2, WhoHol B
Walbrook, Anton 1900-1968 *FilmgC*
Walbrook, Henry Mackinnon 1863-1941
  NotNAT B, WhThe
Walburn, Ray 1887-1969 *Film 1*
Walburn, Raymond 1887-1969 *BiE&WWA,*
  Film 2, FilmgC, MotPP, NotNAT B,
  Vers A, WhScrn 1, WhScrn 2, WhoHol B
Walburn, Raymond 1897-1969 *MovMk*
Walcamp, Marie 1894- *Film 1, Film 2, MotPP,*
  TwYS
Walcot, Charles M 1843- *WhoStg 1908*
Walcot, Charles Melton 1816-1868 *NotNAT B,*
  OxThe
Walcot, Charles Melton 1840-1921 *NotNAT B,*
  OxThe
Walcot, Isabella Nickinson 1847-1906 *OxThe*
Walcott, Arthur *Film 2*
Walcott, Derek 1930- *ConDr 1977, PIP&P A*
Walcott, George *Film 2*
Walcott, Gregory *WhoHol A*
Walcott, William *Film 2*
Walcz, Ethel *Film 2*
Wald, Jane *WhoHol A*
Wald, Jerry 1911-1962 *FilmgC*
Wald, Jerry 1912-1962 *BiDFlm, WorEnF*
Wald, Malvin *IntMPA 1977*
Wald, Richard C *IntMPA 1977, NewYTET*
Waldau, Gustav 1871-1958 *WhScrn 1, WhScrn 2*
Waldegrave, Lilias *WhThe*
Waldekranz, Rune 1911- *OxFilm*
Waldemar, Richard 1870-1947 *WhScrn 2*
Walden, Harry 1875-1921 *NotNAT B*
Walden, Robert *WhoHol A*
Walden, Sylvia *WhoHol A*
Walder, Ernst *WhoHol A*
Waldheim, Kurt 1918- *CelR 3*
Waldis, Burkhart *OxThe*
Waldis, Otto 1906-1974 *WhScrn 2, WhoHol B*
Waldman, Robert 1936- *AmSCAP 1966*
Waldman, Ronald 1914- *IntMPA 1977*
Waldman, Walter *IntMPA 1977*
Waldmuller, Lizzi 1904-1945 *WhScrn 2*
Waldo, Janet *WhoHol A*
Waldorf, Wilella d1946 *NotNAT B*
Waldow, Ernst 1894-1964 *NotNAT B, WhScrn 1,*
  WhScrn 2
Waldridge, Harold *Film 2*
Waldridge, Herbert d1957 *WhoHol B*
Waldrige, Harold 1905-1957 *WhScrn 1,*
  WhScrn 2
Waldron, Andrew *Film 1*
Waldron, Charles D 1874-1946 *Film 1, Film 2,*
  NotNAT B, WhScrn 1, WhScrn 2, WhThe,
  WhoHol B
Waldron, Charles K 1915-1952 *WhScrn 1,*
  WhScrn 2, WhoHol B
Waldron, Edna 1913-1940 *WhScrn 1, WhScrn 2*

Waldron, Francis Godolphin d1818 *NotNAT B*
Waldron, Georgia 1872-1950 *NotNAT B*
Waldron, Isabel 1871-1950 *WhScrn 1, WhScrn 2*
Waldron, Jack 1893- *BiE&WWA*
Waldron, Jack 1893-1967 *WhoHol B*
Waldron, Jack 1893-1969 *NotNAT B, WhScrn 2*
Waldron, James A d1931 *NotNAT B*
Waldrop, Gid 1919- *BiE&WWA*
Waldrop, Gideon 1919- *AmSCAP 1966*
Walenn, Charles R d1948 *NotNAT B*
Wales, Bert *Film 2*
Wales, Ethel 1881-1952 *Film 2, TwYS,*
  WhScrn 1, WhScrn 2, WhoHol B
Wales, Wally *Film 2, TwYS*
Walford, Ann 1928- *WhThe*
Wali, Mustafa *WomWMM*
Walken, Christopher 1943- *NotNAT, WhoHol A,*
  WhoThe 16
Walker, Mrs. Allan *Film 1*
Walker, Allan 1906- *AmSCAP 1966*
Walker, Antoinette *Film 1*
Walker, Arlene 1919-1973 *WhScrn 2*
Walker, Aurora 1912-1964 *WhScrn 2*
Walker, Ben *Film 2*
Walker, Bertha 1908- *AmSCAP 1966*
Walker, Betty *WhoHol A*
Walker, Bill *WhoHol A*
Walker, Bob 1918-1951 *NotNAT B*
Walker, Bon 1894- *AmSCAP 1966*
Walker, Cardon E 1916- *IntMPA 1977*
Walker, Catherine *Film 2*
Walker, Charlotte 1878-1958 *Film 1, Film 2,*
  FilmgC, NotNAT B, TwYS, WhScrn 1,
  WhScrn 2, WhThe, WhoHol B,
  WhoStg 1906, WhoStg 1908
Walker, Cheryl 1922-1971 *MotPP, WhScrn 2,*
  WhoHol B
Walker, Chester W d1945 *WhScrn 2*
Walker, Christy 1898-1918 *WhScrn 2*
Walker, Clint 1927- *FilmgC, IntMPA 1977,*
  MotPP, WhoHol A
Walker, Danton d1960 *NotNAT B*
Walker, Don 1907- *BiE&WWA, NotNAT*
Walker, Donald John 1907- *AmSCAP 1966*
Walker, Elizabeth Tippy *WhoHol A*
Walker, Fiona *WhoHol A*
Walker, George *Film 2*
Walker, George F 1947- *ConDr 1977*
Walker, Gertrude *WomWMM B*
Walker, Hal 1896-1972 *FilmgC*
Walker, Helen 1921-1968 *FilmgC, MotPP,*
  WhScrn 1, WhScrn 2, WhoHol B
Walker, James J 1881-1946 *AmSCAP 1966*
Walker, Jimmie *WhoHol A*
Walker, John *Film 2*
Walker, John A 1916- *BiE&WWA*
Walker, Johnnie 1894-1949 *Film 1, Film 2,*
  TwYS
Walker, Johnnie 1896-1949 *WhScrn 1, WhScrn 2,*
  WhoHol B
Walker, Johnny 1894-1949 *NotNAT B*
Walker, Joseph 1892- *FilmgC, IntMPA 1977*
Walker, Joseph 1902- *WorEnF*
Walker, Joseph A 1935- *ConDr 1977, NotNAT,*
  PIP&P A
Walker, Joyce *WhoHol A*
Walker, June d1966 *Film 2, WhoHol B*
Walker, June 1899-1966 *BiE&WWA, NotNAT B*
Walker, June 1904-1966 *PIP&P, WhScrn 1,*
  WhScrn 2, WhThe
Walker, Laura d1951 *NotNAT B*
Walker, Lillian 1888-1975 *Film 1, Film 2,*
  MotPP, TwYS, WhoHol C

Walker, Lillian Dimples 1888-1975 *WhScrn 2*
Walker, Martin 1901-1955 *NotNAT B, WhThe, WhoHol B*
Walker, Martin 1938- *IntMPA 1977*
Walker, Michael *WhoHol A*
Walker, Nancy *MotPP, NewYTET, WhoHol A*
Walker, Nancy 1921- *EncMT, WhoThe 16*
Walker, Nancy 1922- *BiE&WWA, MovMk, NotNAT*
Walker, Nella 1886-1971 *Film 2, ThFT, WhScrn 2*
Walker, Norman 1892- *FilmgC*
Walker, Paul *Film 2*
Walker, Paul A d1965 *NewYTET*
Walker, Peter *WhoHol A*
Walker, Polly 1908- *Film 2, WhThe*
Walker, Raymond 1883-1960 *AmSCAP 1966*
Walker, Robert d1951 *MotPP*
Walker, Robert 1914-1951 *FilmgC, MovMk, WhScrn 1, WhScrn 2*
Walker, Robert 1918-1951 *BiDFlm, NotNAT B, OxFilm, WorEnF*
Walker, Robert 1919-1951 *MGM, WhoHol B*
Walker, Robert 1941- *FilmgC, MotPP, WhoHol A*
Walker, Robert Donald 1888-1954 *Film 1, MotPP, WhScrn 2*
Walker, Rose 1907-1951 *WhScrn 1, WhScrn 2*
Walker, Stuart 1888-1941 *FilmgC, NotNAT B, WhThe*
Walker, Syd d1945 *WhScrn 1, WhScrn 2, WhoHol B*
Walker, Syd 1886-1945 *NotNAT B, WhThe*
Walker, Syd 1887-1945 *FilmgC*
Walker, Sydney 1921- *WhoHol A, WhoThe 16*
Walker, Tex 1867-1947 *WhScrn 1, WhScrn 2*
Walker, Thomas d1744 *NotNAT B*
Walker, Thomas 1851-1934 *NotNAT A*
Walker, Tommy 1922- *AmSCAP 1966*
Walker, Virginia 1916-1946 *WhScrn 1, WhScrn 2, WhoHol B*
Walker, Wally 1901-1975 *WhoHol C*
Walker, Walter 1864-1947 *WhScrn 2*
Walker, Walter 1901-1975 *WhScrn 2*
Walker, William *WhoHol A*
Walker, William S 1917- *AmSCAP 1966*
Walker, Zena *WhoHol A*
Walker, Zena 1934- *WhoThe 16*
Walker, Zena 1935- *FilmgC*
Walker-Malcoskey, Edna *AmSCAP 1966*
Walkes, W R d1913 *NotNAT B*
Walkley, Alfred Bingham 1855-1926 *OxThe, PIP&P*
Walkley, Arthur Bingham 1855-1926 *NotNAT B, WhThe*
Walkup, Fairfax Proudfit 1887- *BiE&WWA*
Wall, Anita *WhoHol A*
Wall, David V 1870-1938 *WhScrn 1, WhScrn 2, WhoHol B*
Wall, Geraldine 1913-1970 *WhScrn 1, WhScrn 2, WhoHol B*
Wall, Harry 1886-1966 *WhThe*
Wall, Max 1908- *WhoThe 16*
Wallace, Art *WhoHol A*
Wallace, Beryl 1910-1948 *WhScrn 1, WhScrn 2, WhoHol B*
Wallace, Bill 1908-1956 *WhScrn 1, WhScrn 2*
Wallace, Charles 1930- *IntMPA 1977*
Wallace, Chris 1934- *AmSCAP 1966*
Wallace, David d1955 *NotNAT B*
Wallace, Dewitt And Lila *CelR 3*
Wallace, Dorothy *Film 1, Film 2*
Wallace, Mrs. Edgar d1933 *NotNAT B*
Wallace, Edgar Horatio 1875-1932 *FilmgC,*

NotNAT A, NotNAT B, OxThe, WhThe
Wallace, Edna *WhScrn 1, WhScrn 2*
Wallace, Ethel Lee 1888-1956 *WhScrn 1, WhScrn 2, WhoHol B*
Wallace, George 1894-1960 *WhScrn 1, WhScrn 2, WhoHol B*
Wallace, George 1924- *BiE&WWA, NotNAT, WhoHol A*
Wallace, George C 1919- *CelR 3*
Wallace, Grace *Film 2*
Wallace, Guy 1913-1967 *WhScrn 2*
Wallace, Hazel Vincent 1919- *WhoThe 16*
Wallace, Inez d1966 *WhScrn 1, WhScrn 2, WhoHol B*
Wallace, Irene *Film 1, MotPP*
Wallace, Irving 1916- *CelR 3, IntMPA 1977*
Wallace, Jack *WhoHol A*
Wallace, Jean *MotPP, WhoHol A*
Wallace, Jean 1923- *FilmgC, MovMk*
Wallace, Jean 1930- *IntMPA 1977*
Wallace, John *Film 2*
Wallace, Judy *WhoHol A*
Wallace, Katherine *Film 2*
Wallace, Lee *WhoHol A*
Wallace, Lewis 1827-1905 *NotNAT B*
Wallace, Linda *WomWMM B*
Wallace, Louise Chapman d1962 *NotNAT B, WhoHol B*
Wallace, Marcia *WhoHol A.*
Wallace, Maude 1894-1952 *WhScrn 1, WhScrn 2, WhoHol B*
Wallace, May 1877-1938 *Film 2, WhScrn 1, WhScrn 2, WhoHol B*
Wallace, Mike 1918- *CelR 3, IntMPA 1977, NewYTET*
Wallace, Mildred White *AmSCAP 1966*
Wallace, Milton 1888-1956 *WhScrn 1, WhScrn 2, WhoHol B*
Wallace, Morgan d1953 *NotNAT B, WhoHol B*
Wallace, Morgan 1885-1953 *Film 2, TwYS*
Wallace, Morgan 1888-1953 *WhScrn 1, WhScrn 2*
Wallace, Nellie d1933 *NotNAT B*
Wallace, Nellie 1870-1948 *NotNAT B, OxThe*
Wallace, Nellie 1882-1948 *WhThe*
Wallace, Oliver George 1887-1963 *AmSCAP 1966*
Wallace, Paul 1938- *BiE&WWA, NotNAT, WhoHol A*
Wallace, Ramsey *Film 2*
Wallace, Ratch *WhoHol A*
Wallace, Ray 1881- *WhThe*
Wallace, Regina *BiE&WWA, WhoHol A*
Wallace, Richard 1894-1951 *FilmgC, TwYS A*
Wallace, Royce *WhoHol A*
Wallach, Edgar d1953 *NotNAT B*
Wallach, Eli 1915- *BiE&WWA, CelR 3, CnThe, FilmgC, IntMPA 1977, MotPP, MovMk, NotNAT, OxFilm, PIP&P, WhoHol A, WhoThe 16, WorEnF*
Wallach, George *IntMPA 1977*
Wallach, Henry John 1790-1870 *PIP&P*
Wallach, Ira Jan 1913- *AmSCAP 1966, BiE&WWA, NotNAT*
Wallach, Lew *WhoHol A*
Wallack, Arthur J d1940 *NotNAT B*
Wallack, Edwin N *Film 2*
Wallack, Mrs. Henry J d1860 *NotNAT B*
Wallack, Henry John 1790-1870 *FamA&A, NotNAT B, OxThe*
Wallack, Mrs. J W, Jr. d1879 *NotNAT B*
Wallack, James William 1791-1864 *NotNAT A, NotNAT B, PIP&P*
Wallack, James William 1794-1864 *OxThe*
Wallack, James William 1795-1864 *FamA&A*

Wallack, James William, Jr. 1818-1873 *FamA&A,*
   NotNAT B, OxThe
Wallack, John Johnstone 1819-1888 *OxThe*
Wallack, Mrs. Lester d1909 *NotNAT B*
Wallack, Lester 1819-1888 *FamA&A,*
   NotNAT B
Wallack, Lester 1820-1888 *NotNAT A, PIP&P*
Wallack, Mrs. William d1850 *NotNAT B*
Wallacks, Clara *Film 2*
Walleck, Anna *Film 2*
Wallen, Sigurd 1884-1947 *WhScrn 1, WhScrn 2*
Wallenda, Yetta d1963 *NotNAT B*
Waller, D W d1882 *NotNAT B*
Waller, Mrs. D W 1820-1899 *NotNAT B*
Waller, David 1920- *WhoHol A, WhoThe 16*
Waller, Eddy *Vers B, WhoHol A*
Waller, Edmund Lewis 1884- *WhThe*
Waller, Emma 1820-1899 *FamA&A, OxThe*
Waller, Fats 1904-1943 *FilmgC, NotNAT B,*
   WhoHol B
Waller, Florence West 1862-1912 *OxThe*
Waller, Fred 1886-1954 *DcFM, FilmgC*
Waller, J Wallet d1951 *NotNAT B*
Waller, Jack 1885-1957 *NotNAT B, WhThe*
Waller, Lewis 1860-1915 *CnThe, Film 1, Film 2,*
   NotNAT B, OxThe, WhThe
Waller, Mrs. Lewis 1862-1912 *NotNAT B,*
   WhThe
Waller, Thomas Fats 1904-1943 *AmSCAP 1966,*
   WhScrn 1, WhScrn 2
Walley, Deborah *MotPP, WhoHol A*
Walling, Effie B 1879-1961 *WhScrn 1, WhScrn 2*
Walling, Richard *Film 2*
Walling, Roy d1964 *NotNAT B*
Walling, Will R *Film 2*
Wallington, Billie Henry 1927- *AmSCAP 1966*
Wallington, George 1923- *AmSCAP 1966*
Wallington, Jimmy 1907-1972 *WhScrn 2,*
   WhoHol B
Wallis, Bella d1960 *NotNAT B*
Wallis, Bertram 1874-1952 *NotNAT B, WhThe,*
   WhoHol B
Wallis, Ellen Lancaster 1856-1940 *WhThe*
Wallis, Ellen Lancaster *see also* Lancaster-Wallis,
   Ellen
Wallis, Gladys d1953 *NotNAT B*
Wallis, Hal B *IntMPA 1977*
Wallis, Hal B 1898- *BiDFlm, FilmgC, OxFilm*
Wallis, Hal B 1899- *WorEnF*
Wallis, Shani *WhoHol A*
Wallis, Shani 1933- *WhThe*
Wallis, Shani 1938- *FilmgC*
Wallis, W Allen *NewYTET*
Wallman, Lawrence A 1902- *BiE&WWA,*
   NotNAT
Wallock, Edwin N 1878-1951 *Film 1, WhScrn 2*
Wallop, Douglass 1920- *BiE&WWA, NotNAT*
Walls, Byron 1937- *AmSCAP 1966*
Walls, Robert B 1910- *AmSCAP 1966*
Walls, Tom 1883-1949 *FilmgC, NotNAT B,*
   WhScrn 1, WhScrn 2, WhThe, WhoHol B
Wally, Gus 1904-1966 *WhScrn 1, WhScrn 2,*
   WhoHol B
Walmer, Cassie 1888- *WhThe*
Walmsley, Jon *WhoHol A*
Walper, Cicely *WhoHol A*
Walpole, Sir Hugh Seymour 1884-1941 *FilmgC,*
   NotNAT B, WhScrn 1, WhScrn 2, WhThe,
   WhoHol B, WorEnF
Walpole, Robert *PIP&P*
Walser, Martin 1927- *CnMD, CroCD, McGWD,*
   ModWD
Walsh, Alida *WomWMM B*
Walsh, Anthony *WhoHol A*

Walsh, Arthur *WhoHol A*
Walsh, Bill d1975 *NewYTET*
Walsh, Bill 1913-1975 *AmSCAP 1966*
Walsh, Bill 1918-1975 *FilmgC*
Walsh, Billy d1952 *WhScrn 1, WhScrn 2*
Walsh, Blanche d1915 *WhoHol B*
Walsh, Blanche 1873-1915 *FamA&A, Film 1,*
   NotNAT B, WhThe, WhoStg 1906,
   WhoStg 1908
Walsh, Blanche 1874-1915 *WhScrn 2*
Walsh, Bryan *WhoHol A*
Walsh, David *FilmgC*
Walsh, Deirdre *WomWMM B*
Walsh, Dermot 1924- *FilmgC, IntMPA 1977,*
   WhoHol A
Walsh, Edward *WhoHol A*
Walsh, Felix *Film 1*
Walsh, Frank 1860-1932 *WhScrn 2*
Walsh, Frank 1860-1935 *Film 2*
Walsh, Frederick G 1915- *BiE&WWA, NotNAT*
Walsh, George 1892- *Film 1, Film 2, TwYS,*
   WhoHol A
Walsh, Henry H 1906- *AmSCAP 1966*
Walsh, J B *Film 2*
Walsh, Joey *WhoHol A*
Walsh, Kay 1914- *FilmgC, WhoHol A*
Walsh, Kay 1915- *IntMPA 1977, MovMk*
Walsh, Lionel 1876-1916 *NotNAT B,*
   WhoStg 1908
Walsh, M Emmet *WhoHol A*
Walsh, Pauline 1906- *AmSCAP 1966*
Walsh, Raoul 1887- *BiDFlm, FilmgC,*
   WhoHol A
Walsh, Raoul 1889- *CmMov, DcFM, Film 1,*
   Film 2, TwYS
Walsh, Raoul 1892- *CmMov, IntMPA 1977,*
   MovMk, OxFilm, TwYS A, WorEnF
Walsh, Richard F 1900- *IntMPA 1977*
Walsh, Sam 1877-1920 *NotNAT B, WhThe*
Walsh, Sean *WhoHol A*
Walsh, Thomas H 1863-1925 *NotNAT B,*
   WhScrn 1, WhScrn 2, WhoHol B
Walsh, Thomas J d1962 *NotNAT B*
Walsh, Tom *Film 1*
Walsh, William *WhoHol A*
Walston, Ray *MotPP, WhoHol A*
Walston, Ray 1917- *FilmgC, WhoThe 16*
Walston, Ray 1918- *BiE&WWA, IntMPA 1977,*
   MovMk, NotNAT
Walt, Edward John 1877-1951 *AmSCAP 1966*
Waltemeyer, Jack *Film 1*
Walter, Anne B *WomWMM B*
Walter, Bruno 1876-1962 *NotNAT B*
Walter, Cy 1925- *AmSCAP 1966*
Walter, Edwin d1953 *NotNAT B*
Walter, Eugene 1874-1941 *McGWD, ModWD,*
   NotNAT B, OxThe, WhThe
Walter, Harry *Film 2*
Walter, Jessica 1944- *FilmgC, IntMPA 1977,*
   WhoHol A
Walter, Max Donald 1910- *AmSCAP 1966*
Walter, Nancy 1939- *ConDr 1977*
Walter, Olive 1898- *WhThe*
Walter, Rosa *Film 2*
Walter, Serge 1896- *AmSCAP 1966*
Walter, Wilfrid 1882-1958 *NotNAT B,*
   WhScrn 2, WhThe
Walter-Briant, Fredda 1912- *BiE&WWA,*
   NotNAT
Walter-Ellis, Desmond 1914- *WhoHol A,*
   WhoThe 16
Walters, Barbara 1931- *CelR 3, IntMPA 1977,*
   NewYTET
Walters, Casey *WhoHol A*

Walters, Charles 1911- *BiDFlm, CmMov, DcFM, EncMT, FilmgC, IntMPA 1977, MovMk, WorEnF*
Walters, Dorothy 1877-1934 *Film 2, WhScrn 2*
Walters, Easter *Film 1*
Walters, Ethel *Film 2*
Walters, Mrs. George B d1916 *WhScrn 2*
Walters, Glen *Film 2*
Walters, Harold L 1918- *AmSCAP 1966*
Walters, Jack 1885-1944 *WhScrn 1, WhScrn 2, WhoHol B*
Walters, John *Film 1*
Walters, Laura 1894-1934 *WhScrn 1, WhScrn 2*
Walters, Marrian *WhoHol A*
Walters, May *Film 1*
Walters, Patricia W d1967 *WhScrn 1, WhScrn 2, WhoHol B*
Walters, Polly 1910- *MotPP, WhThe*
Walters, Robert W 1921- *AmSCAP 1966*
Walters, Thorley 1913- *FilmgC, WhoHol A, WhoThe 16*
Walters, Walter H 1917- *BiE&WWA, NotNAT*
Walters, William *Film 1*
Walthal, Anna Mae *Film 2*
Walthal, Henry B 1880-1936 *Film 2*
Walthall, Anna Mae *Film 1*
Walthall, Henry B d1936 *MotPP, WhoHol B*
Walthall, Henry B 1870-1936 *TwYS*
Walthall, Henry B 1878-1936 *FilmgC, MovMk, NotNAT B, OxFilm, WhScrn 1, WhScrn 2*
Walthall, Henry B 1880-1936 *Film 1, Vers B*
Walther, Gretchen *WhoHol A*
Walton, Douglas d1961 *NotNAT B, WhScrn 1, WhScrn 2, WhoHol B*
Walton, Florence *Film 1*
Walton, Fred 1865-1936 *Film 2, NotNAT B, WhScrn 1, WhScrn 2, WhoHol B*
Walton, Gladys 1904- *Film 2, TwYS*
Walton, Henry *Film 2*
Walton, Herbert C d1954 *NotNAT B, WhoHol B*
Walton, J K d1928 *NotNAT B*
Walton, Jess *WhoHol A*
Walton, Kenneth E 1904- *AmSCAP 1966*
Walton, Peggy *WhoHol A*
Walton, Tony 1934- *BiE&WWA, NotNAT, WhoThe 16*
Walton, Vera 1891-1965 *WhScrn 1, WhScrn 2, WhoHol B*
Walton, Sir William 1902- *DcFM, FilmgC, OxFilm, WorEnF*
Waltz, Pat d1972 *WhoHol B*
Walworth, Theodore H, Jr. *NewYTET*
Wampus Baby Stars *Film 2*
Wan, Sul Te, Madame 1873-1959 *WhScrn 1, WhScrn 2*
Wanamaker, Sam 1919- *BiE&WWA, CnThe, FilmgC, IntMPA 1977, MotPP, MovMk, NewYTET, NotNAT, WhoHol A, WhoThe 16*
Wanderman, Dorothy 1907- *AmSCAP 1966*
Wang, Arthur W *BiE&WWA*
Wang, James *Film 2*
Wang, Juliana *WomWMM A, WomWMM B*
Wang, Ping *WomWMM*
Wang, Shih-Fu *REnWD*
Wang, Tso-Lin *DcFM*
Wangel, Hedwig 1875-1961 *Film 2, WhScrn 1, WhScrn 2, WhoHol B*
Wangenheim, Gustav Von 1895- *CnMD, Film 2*
Wanger, Walter 1894-1968 *BiDFlm, CmMov, DcFM, FilmgC, OxFilm, WorEnF*
Wangermann, Richard *Film 2*
Wanner, Hughes *WhoHol A*

Wanner, Paul 1896- *CnMD*
Wanshel, Jeff *NatPD*
Wanzer, Arthur d1949 *WhScrn 1, WhScrn 2, WhoHol B*
Waram, Percy C 1881-1961 *NotNAT B, WhScrn 1, WhScrn 2, WhThe, WhoHol B*
Warburg, James Paul 1896-1969 *AmSCAP 1966*
Warburton, Charles M 1887-1952 *NotNAT B, WhThe*
Warburton, John 1899- *IntMPA 1977, WhoHol A*
Ward, Mrs. *Film 1*
Ward, Sir A W d1924 *NotNAT B*
Ward, Albert d1956 *NotNAT B*
Ward, Annie d1918 *NotNAT B*
Ward, Beatrice 1890-1964 *WhScrn 1, WhScrn 2, WhoHol B*
Ward, Betty *WhThe*
Ward, Bill 1916- *IntMPA 1977*
Ward, Bradley *Film 2*
Ward, Brendan Noel *NatPD*
Ward, Burt *WhoHol A*
Ward, Carrie Clarke 1862-1926 *Film 1, Film 2, WhScrn 1, WhScrn 2, WhoHol B*
Ward, Carrie Lee *Film 2*
Ward, Charles B 1865-1917 *AmSCAP 1966*
Ward, Clara 1927-1973 *AmSCAP 1966, WhScrn 2*
Ward, Craig *Film 2*
Ward, Dave *WhoHol A*
Ward, Diane 1919- *AmSCAP 1966*
Ward, Dorothy 1890- *OxThe, WhThe*
Ward, Douglas Turner 1930- *ConDr 1977, NotNAT, PIP&P A, WhoThe 16*
Ward, Eddie *Film 2*
Ward, Edward 1896- *AmSCAP 1966*
Ward, Ethel d1955 *NotNAT B*
Ward, Fannie 1872-1952 *Film 1, Film 2, MotPP, NotNAT B, OxThe, TwYS, WhScrn 1, WhScrn 2, WhThe, WhoHol B*
Ward, Fanny 1875- *WhoStg 1908*
Ward, Fleming *Film 1*
Ward, Fleming d1962 *NotNAT B*
Ward, Genevieve 1837-1922 *WhThe*
Ward, Genevieve Teresa 1834-1922 *NotNAT B, WhoStg 1908*
Ward, Genevieve Teresa 1838-1922 *NotNAT A, OxThe*
Ward, George *Film 2*
Ward, Gerald *Film 1*
Ward, Hap, Jr. 1899-1940 *WhScrn 1, WhScrn 2, WhoHol B*
Ward, Hap, Sr. 1868-1944 *NotNAT B, WhScrn 1, WhScrn 2, WhoHol B*
Ward, Harry 1890-1952 *WhScrn 1, WhScrn 2*
Ward, Hugh J 1871-1941 *NotNAT B, WhThe*
Ward, James Skip *WhoHol A*
Ward, Janet *BiE&WWA, NotNAT, WhoHol A*
Ward, Jerold *Film 1*
Ward, Jomarie *WhoHol A*
Ward, Judith Jones *WomWMM B*
Ward, Katherine Clare 1871-1938 *WhScrn 1, WhScrn 2, WhoHol B*
Ward, Kathrin Claire *Film 2*
Ward, Larry *WhoHol A*
Ward, Lucille d1952 *Film 2, WhoHol B*
Ward, Lucille 1880-1952 *WhScrn 1, WhScrn 2*
Ward, Mackenzie 1903- *Film 2, WhThe*
Ward, Marshall *WhoHol A*
Ward, Mary d1966 *BiE&WWA, NotNAT B*
Ward, Michael 1915- *FilmgC, WhoHol A*
Ward, Peggy 1878-1960 *WhScrn 1, WhScrn 2*
Ward, Penelope Dudley 1914- *WhThe,*

WhoHol A
Ward, Polly 1908- *Film 2, FilmgC, WhoHol A*
Ward, Polly 1909- *WhThe*
Ward, Richard *WhoHol A*
Ward, Robert *Film 2*
Ward, Ronald 1901- *WhThe, WhoHol A*
Ward, Roscoe *Film 2*
Ward, Sam 1889-1952 *WhScrn 1, WhScrn 2, WhoHol B*
Ward, Sam 1906-1960 *AmSCAP 1966*
Ward, Sarah E 1920- *IntMPA 1977*
Ward, Simon 1941- *FilmgC, IntMPA 1977, WhoHol A, WhoThe 16*
Ward, Solly 1891-1942 *NotNAT B, WhScrn 1, WhScrn 2, WhoHol B*
Ward, Tiny *Film 2*
Ward, Trevor *WhoHol A*
Ward, Valerie *Film 2*
Ward, Victoria 1914-1957 *WhScrn 1, WhScrn 2, WhoHol B*
Ward, Warwick 1890-1967 *Film 1*
Ward, Warwick 1891-1967 *WhScrn 2*
Warde, Anthony 1909-1975 *Vers B, WhScrn 2, WhoHol C*
Warde, Ernest C 1874-1923 *NotNAT B, TwYS A, WhScrn 1, WhScrn 2, WhoHol B*
Warde, Frederick B d1935 *Film 1, Film 2, WhoHol B*
Warde, Frederick B 1851-1935 *NotNAT A, NotNAT B, OxThe, WhThe, WhoStg 1908*
Warde, Frederick B 1872-1935 *WhScrn 1, WhScrn 2*
Warde, George *Film 2*
Warde, George d1917 *NotNAT B*
Warde, Harlan *WhoHol A*
Warde, Warwick 1898-1967 *Film 2*
Warde, Willie 1857-1943 *NotNAT B, WhThe*
Wardell, Harry 1879-1948 *WhScrn 1, WhScrn 2*
Warden, Fred W d1929 *NotNAT B*
Warden, Jack *MotPP, WhoHol A*
Warden, Jack 1920- *BiE&WWA, FilmgC, NotNAT*
Warden, Jack 1925- *IntMPA 1977, MovMk*
Wardle, Irving 1929- *WhoThe 16*
Wardwell, Geoffrey 1900-1955 *Film 2, NotNAT B, WhThe, WhoHol B*
Wardwell, Judith *WomWMM B*
Ware, Harriet 1878-1962 *AmSCAP 1966, NotNAT B*
Ware, Helen 1877-1939 *Film 1, Film 2, NotNAT B, TwYS, WhScrn 1, WhScrn 2, WhThe, WhoHol B*
Ware, James A *AmSCAP 1966*
Ware, Leonard 1909- *AmSCAP 1966*
Ware, Midge *WhoHol A*
Ware, Walter 1880-1936 *WhScrn 1, WhScrn 2, WhoHol B*
Wareing, Alfred 1876-1942 *NotNAT A, NotNAT B, WhThe*
Wareing, Lesley 1913- *WhThe*
Warfaz, Georges De 1889?-1959 *NotNAT B*
Warfield, Chris *WhoHol A*
Warfield, David 1866-1951 *FamA&A, NotNAT B, OxThe, PIP&P, WhThe, WhoStg 1906, WhoStg 1908*
Warfield, Don *WhoHol A*
Warfield, Irene 1896-1961 *Film 1, WhScrn 2*
Warfield, Marlene *WhoHol A*
Warfield, Natalie *Film 2*
Warfield, Theodora *Film 1*
Warfield, William 1920- *BiE&WWA, NotNAT, PIP&P, WhoHol A*
Warford, Claude 1877-1950 *AmSCAP 1966*
Warhol, Andy *WhoHol A*

Warhol, Andy 1926- *FilmgC*
Warhol, Andy 1927- *CelR 3*
Warhol, Andy 1928- *BiDFlm, OxFilm, WorEnF*
Warik, Josef *WhoHol A*
Waring, Barbara 1912- *WhThe*
Waring, Dorothy May Graham 1895- *WhThe*
Waring, Fred 1900- *AmSCAP 1966, IntMPA 1977, WhoHol A*
Waring, Herbert 1857-1932 *NotNAT B, WhThe*
Waring, Mary 1892-1964 *NotNAT B, WhScrn 1, WhScrn 2, WhoHol B*
Waring, Richard 1912- *WhoThe 16*
Waring, Richard 1914- *BiE&WWA, NotNAT, WhoHol A*
Waring, Tom 1902-1960 *AmSCAP 1966*
Warm, Hermann 1889- *DcFM, OxFilm, WorEnF*
Warmington, S J 1884-1941 *WhoHol B*
Warmington, Stanley J 1884-1941 *NotNAT B, WhThe*
Warner, Adele *Film 2*
Warner, Albert 1884-1967 *DcFM*
Warner, Anne 1869- *WhoStg 1908*
Warner, Astrid *WhoHol A*
Warner, Charles 1846-1909 *NotNAT B, OxThe*
Warner, David 1941- *CnThe, FilmgC, OxFilm, WhoHol A, WhoThe 16*
Warner, Gloria 1915-1934 *WhScrn 1, WhScrn 2*
Warner, Grace 1873-1925 *NotNAT B, WhThe*
Warner, H B 1876-1958 *Film 1, Film 2, FilmgC, MotPP, MovMk, TwYS, Vers A, WhScrn 1, WhScrn 2, WhoHol B*
Warner, Harry M 1881-1958 *DcFM*
Warner, Henry Byron 1876-1958 *NotNAT B, WhThe, WhoStg 1906, WhoStg 1908*
Warner, J B 1895-1924 *WhScrn 2, WhoHol B*
Warner, J Wesley *Film 1*
Warner, Jack 1894- *FilmgC, IntMPA 1977, WhoHol A*
Warner, Jack, Jr. 1916- *IntMPA 1977*
Warner, Jack L 1892- *CelR 3, DcFM, FilmgC, IntMPA 1977, TwYS B*
Warner, James B 1895-1924 *Film 2*
Warner, Pam *WhoHol A*
Warner, Philip 1901- *AmSCAP 1966*
Warner, Richard *WhoHol A*
Warner, Robert *WhoHol A*
Warner, Samuel 1888-1927 *DcFM*
Warner, Sarah Ann 1898- *AmSCAP 1966*
Warner, Steven *WhoHol A*
Warner Brothers *DcFM, WorEnF*
Warnick, Clay 1915- *AmSCAP 1966, BiE&WWA, NotNAT*
Warnow, Helen 1926-1970 *WhScrn 1, WhScrn 2*
Warre, Michael 1922- *PIP&P, WhoHol A, WhoThe 16*
Warren, Betty 1905- *WhThe*
Warren, Brett 1910- *BiE&WWA, NotNAT*
Warren, C Denier 1889-1971 *FilmgC, WhScrn 1, WhScrn 2, WhThe*
Warren, C Dernier 1889-1971 *WhoHol B*
Warren, Charles Marquis 1912- *FilmgC, IntMPA 1977, WorEnF*
Warren, E Alyn 1875-1940 *Film 2, WhScrn 1, WhScrn 2, WhoHol B*
Warren, Earl 1891- *CelR 3*
Warren, Ed 1924-1963 *AmSCAP 1966*
Warren, Eda *WomWMM*
Warren, Edward d1930 *WhScrn 1, WhScrn 2, WhoHol B*
Warren, Elinor Remick 1906- *AmSCAP 1966*
Warren, Eliza 1865-1935 *WhScrn 1, WhScrn 2, WhoHol B*
Warren, F Brooke d1950 *NotNAT B*
Warren, Frank *Film 2*

Warren, Frank 1918- *AmSCAP 1966*
Warren, Fred H 1880-1940 *Film 1, Film 2,*
  WhScrn 2
Warren, Gary *WhoHol A*
Warren, Gloria *WhoHol A*
Warren, Guy 1923- *AmSCAP 1966*
Warren, Harry 1893- *AmSCAP 1966,*
  BiE&WWA, IntMPA 1977, NotNAT,
  OxFilm
Warren, Jeff 1921- *BiE&WWA, NotNAT,*
  WhoThe 16
Warren, Jennifer *WhoHol A*
Warren, Joseph *WhoHol A*
Warren, Katherine 1905-1965 *WhScrn 2*
Warren, Kenneth J 1929-1973 *WhoHol A,*
  WhoThe 16
Warren, Kenny Lee *WhoHol A*
Warren, Leonard 1911-1960 *WhScrn 2*
Warren, Lesley *WhoHol A*
Warren, Mary *Film 2*
Warren, Mercy Otis 1728-1814 *NotNAT B*
Warren, Mike *WhoHol A*
Warren, Robert Penn 1905- *CnMD, FilmgC,*
  ModWD
Warren, T Gideon d1919 *NotNAT B*
Warren, William 1767-1832 *FamA&A,*
  NotNAT B, OxThe, PIP&P
Warren, William, Jr. 1812-1888 *FamA&A,*
  NotNAT A, NotNAT B, OxThe
Warren, Wilson *WhoHol A*
Warrenbrand, Jane *WomWMM B*
Warrender, Harold 1903-1953 *FilmgC,*
  NotNAT B, WhScrn 1, WhScrn 2, WhThe,
  WhoHol B
Warrener, Warren d1961 *NotNAT B*
Warrenton, Lule 1863-1932 *Film 1, Film 2,*
  WhScrn 1, WhScrn 2
Warrenton, Lulu 1863-1932 *WhoHol B*
Warrick, Ruth 1915- *BiE&WWA, FilmgC,*
  IntMPA 1977, MovMk, NotNAT,
  WhoHol A, WhoThe 16
Warriner, Frederic 1916- *WhoThe 16*
Warshauer, Frank 1893-1953 *AmSCAP 1966*
Warshauer, Rose 1917- *AmSCAP 1966*
Warshaw, Mimi *WomWMM B*
Warshawsky, Ruth *WhoHol A*
Warwick, Ethel 1882-1951 *NotNAT B, WhThe*
Warwick, Henry *Film 1*
Warwick, John 1905-1972 *FilmgC, WhScrn 2,*
  WhoHol A
Warwick, Richard *WhoHol A*
Warwick, Robert d1964 *MotPP, NotNAT B,*
  WhoHol B
Warwick, Robert 1878-1944 *NotNAT B*
Warwick, Robert 1878-1964 *WhScrn 1,*
  WhScrn 2, WhThe
Warwick, Robert 1878-1965 *FilmgC, MovMk,*
  TwYS
Warwick, Robert 1881-1964 *Film 1, Film 2,*
  Vers A
Warwick, Rose B 1934- *AmSCAP 1966*
Warwick, Stella Lattimore 1905-1960 *WhScrn 1,*
  WhScrn 2
Warwick, Virginia *Film 2*
Warwicke, Dionne 1940- *CelR 3*
Wascher, Aribert *Film 2*
Washabaugh, Ivan J 1912- *AmSCAP 1966*
Washbourne, Mona 1903- *FilmgC, WhoHol A,*
  WhoThe 16
Washbrook, John *WhoHol A*
Washburn, Abbott M *NewYTET*
Washburn, Alice 1861-1929 *Film 1, WhScrn 1,*
  WhScrn 2, WhoHol B
Washburn, Beverly *WhoHol A*

Washburn, Bryant 1889-1963 *Film 1, Film 2,*
  MotPP, MovMk, NotNAT B, TwYS,
  WhScrn 1, WhScrn 2, WhoHol B
Washburn, Bryant, Jr. d1960 *WhScrn 2*
Washburn, Gladys *WomWMM B*
Washburn, Jack 1927- *BiE&WWA, NotNAT*
Washburn, John H d1917 *WhScrn 2*
Washburn, Ralph *Film 2*
Washburn, Robert 1928- *AmSCAP 1966*
Washburne, Joe 1904- *AmSCAP 1966*
Washer, Ben 1906- *BiE&WWA, IntMPA 1977*
Washington, Blue *Film 2, TwYS*
Washington, Dinah 1924-1963 *NotNAT B,*
  WhScrn 2, WhoHol B
Washington, Dino *WhoHol A*
Washington, Fredi 1903- *ThFT*
Washington, Fredi 1913- *WhoHol A*
Washington, Gene *WhoHol A*
Washington, Judy *WhoHol A*
Washington, Kenneth Kenny *WhoHol A*
Washington, Kenny 1918-1971 *WhScrn 2*
Washington, Mildred *Film 2*
Washington, Ned 1901- *AmSCAP 1966*
Washington, Shirley *WhoHol A*
Washington, Vernon *WhoHol A*
Washington, Walter 1915- *CelR 3*
Wasil, Edward J 1926- *AmSCAP 1966*
Wasilewski, Vincent T *IntMPA 1977, NewYTET*
Wasserman, Albert *NewYTET*
Wasserman, Dale 1917- *BiE&WWA,*
  ConDr 1977D, EncMT, IntMPA 1977,
  NewYTET, NotNAT
Wasserman, Lew 1913- *CelR 3, IntMPA 1977*
Wassmann, Hans *Film 2*
Wata, Sussie *Film 2*
Watanabe, Sumie *WomWMM B*
Waterbury, Ruth *IntMPA 1977*
Waterhouse, Keith 1929- *CnThe, ConDr 1977,*
  CroCD, IntMPA 1977, WhoThe 16
Waterlow, Marjorie 1888-1921 *NotNAT B,*
  WhThe
Waterman, Denis 1948- *FilmgC, WhoHol A*
Waterman, Dennis 1948- *WhoThe 16*
Waterman, Ida 1852-1941 *Film 1, Film 2,*
  NotNAT B, WhScrn 1, WhScrn 2,
  WhoHol B
Waterman, Willard *WhoHol A*
Waterous, Herbert d1947 *NotNAT B*
Waters, Bunny *WhoHol A*
Waters, Ethel 1900- *BiE&WWA, CelR 3,*
  EncMT, FamA&A, Film 2, FilmgC,
  IntMPA 1977, MotPP, MovMk, NotNAT,
  NotNAT A, OxThe, PIP&P, WhoHol A,
  WhoThe 16
Waters, George W 1908- *IntMPA 1977*
Waters, James d1923 *NotNAT B, WhThe*
Waters, Jan 1937- *WhoHol A, WhoThe 16*
Waters, John 1894-1962 *TwYS A*
Waters, Mira *WhoHol A*
Waters, Patricia 1919- *AmSCAP 1966*
Waters, Russell 1908- *FilmgC, WhoHol A*
Waters, Ted *Film 2*
Waterston, Sam 1940- *IntMPA 1977, NotNAT,*
  PIP&P A, WhoHol A
Waterston, Samuel A 1940- *WhoThe 16*
Watford, Gwen 1927- *WhoHol A, WhoThe 16*
Wathall, Alfred G d1938 *NotNAT B*
Watkin, David 1925- *FilmgC, WorEnF*
Watkin, Pierre 1894?-1960 *FilmgC, NotNAT B,*
  Vers B, WhScrn 1, WhScrn 2, WhoHol B
Watkins, Gordon R *NatPD*
Watkins, Harry d1894 *NotNAT A, NotNAT B*
Watkins, Jim *WhoHol A*
Watkins, Linda 1908- *WhThe*

Watkins, Linda 1909- *WhoHol A*
Watkins, Peter *WhoHol A*
Watkins, Peter 1935- *IntMPA 1977, OxFilm, WorEnF*
Watkins, Peter 1937- *FilmgC*
Watkyn, Arthur 1907-1965 *WhThe*
Watling, Dilys 1946- *WhoThe 16*
Watling, Jack 1923- *FilmgC, IntMPA 1977, WhoHol A, WhoThe 16*
Watson, A E T d1922 *NotNAT B*
Watson, Adele 1890-1933 *Film 2, WhScrn 1, WhScrn 2, WhoHol B*
Watson, Benjamin T d1968 *WhScrn 2*
Watson, Betty Jane 1926- *WhThe*
Watson, Betty Jane 1928- *BiE&WWA, NotNAT*
Watson, Billy *WhoHol A*
Watson, Billy d1945 *NotNAT B*
Watson, Bobby 1888-1965 *Film 2, WhScrn 1, WhScrn 2, WhoHol B*
Watson, Bobby *see also* Watson, Robert
Watson, Bobs 1930?- *FilmgC, WhoHol A*
Watson, Caven 1904-1953 *WhScrn 1, WhScrn 2, WhoHol B*
Watson, Coy d1968 *Film 2, WhoHol B*
Watson, David *WhoHol A*
Watson, Debbie *MotPP, WhoHol A*
Watson, Delmar *WhoHol A*
Watson, Douglas *WhoHol A*
Watson, Douglass 1921- *BiE&WWA, NotNAT, WhoThe 16*
Watson, E Bradlee d1961 *NotNAT B*
Watson, Elizabeth d1931 *NotNAT B, WhThe*
Watson, Fanny 1886-1970 *WhScrn 1, WhScrn 2, WhoHol B*
Watson, Fred 1927- *ConDr 1973*
Watson, George A 1911-1937 *WhScrn 1, WhScrn 2*
Watson, Gilbert Stuart 1897-1964 *AmSCAP 1966*
Watson, Harry *Film 2*
Watson, Henrietta 1873-1964 *WhThe*
Watson, Henry, Jr. *Film 1*
Watson, Horace 1867-1934 *NotNAT B, WhThe*
Watson, Ivory Deek 1909-1969 *WhScrn 2*
Watson, Jack 1921- *FilmgC, WhoHol A*
Watson, James 1928- *CelR 3*
Watson, James A, Jr. *WhoHol A*
Watson, Joseph K 1887-1942 *WhScrn 1, WhScrn 2, WhoHol B*
Watson, Justice 1908-1962 *WhScrn 1, WhScrn 2*
Watson, Kitty 1887-1967 *WhScrn 1, WhScrn 2, WhoHol B*
Watson, Lee 1926- *BiE&WWA, NotNAT*
Watson, Lucile 1879-1962 *FilmgC, MotPP, MovMk, NotNAT B, ThFT, WhScrn 1, WhScrn 2, WhThe, WhoHol B*
Watson, Lucille 1879-1962 *Vers A*
Watson, Malcolm 1853-1929 *NotNAT B, WhThe*
Watson, Margaret d1940 *NotNAT B, WhThe*
Watson, Mills *WhoHol A*
Watson, Minor d1965 *MotPP, NotNAT B, WhoHol B*
Watson, Minor 1889-1965 *FilmgC, MovMk, WhScrn 1, WhScrn 2, WhThe*
Watson, Minor 1890-1965 *Vers A*
Watson, Moray *WhoHol A*
Watson, Nubra *WomWMM B*
Watson, Patricia *WomWMM*
Watson, Robert 1888-1965 *FilmgC*
Watson, Robert *see also* Watson, Bobby
Watson, Rosabel Grace d1959 *NotNAT B*
Watson, Roy 1876-1937 *Film 1, Film 2, WhScrn 1, WhScrn 2, WhoHol B*
Watson, Stuart d1956 *NotNAT B*
Watson, Susan 1938- *BiE&WWA, EncMT,*

NotNAT
Watson, Theresa *WhoHol A*
Watson, Thomas M d1963 *NotNAT B*
Watson, Vernee *WhoHol A*
Watson, Vernon 1885-1949 *WhThe*
Watson, Vernon 1895-1949 *NotNAT B*
Watson, William *WhoHol A*
Watson, Wylie 1889-1966 *FilmgC, WhScrn 1, WhScrn 2, WhThe, WhoHol B*
Watt, Douglas 1914- *AmSCAP 1966, NotNAT*
Watt, Harry 1906- *DcFM, FilmgC, IntMPA 1977, OxFilm, WorEnF*
Watt, Sparky *WhoHol A*
Watt, Stan *WhoHol A*
Watters, Don *WhoHol A*
Watters, George Manker d1943 *NotNAT B*
Watters, William *WhoHol A*
Wattis, Richard 1912-1975 *FilmgC, WhScrn 2, WhThe, WhoHol C*
Watts, A B 1886- *IntMPA 1977*
Watts, Alan 1915- *CelR 3, WomWMM*
Watts, Andre 1946- *CelR 3*
Watts, Charles d1966 *WhScrn 1, WhScrn 2, WhoHol B*
Watts, Charles H Cotton 1902-1968 *WhScrn 1, WhScrn 2, WhoHol B*
Watts, Dodo 1910- *WhThe*
Watts, George 1877-1942 *WhScrn 1, WhScrn 2, WhoHol B*
Watts, Gwendolyn *WhoHol A*
Watts, H Grady 1908- *AmSCAP 1966*
Watts, James *Film 2*
Watts, Jeanne *WhoHol A*
Watts, Little Jamie *WhoHol A*
Watts, Peggy 1906-1966 *WhScrn 2*
Watts, Queenie *WhoHol A*
Watts, Richard, Jr. 1898- *BiE&WWA, NotNAT, OxThe, WhoThe 16*
Watts, Sal *WhoHol A*
Watts, Stephen 1910- *WhoThe 16*
Watts, Wintter 1884-1962 *AmSCAP 1966*
Watts-Phillips, John Edward 1894-1960 *WhThe*
Waugh, Evelyn *WomWMM*
Waverly, Jack 1896-1951 *AmSCAP 1966*
Wawerka, Anton d1937 *Film 2, WhoHol B*
Wax, Mo *IntMPA 1977*
Waxman, Arthur 1921- *BiE&WWA*
Waxman, Donald 1925- *AmSCAP 1966*
Waxman, Franz 1906-1967 *AmSCAP 1966, CmMov, FilmgC, WorEnF*
Waxman, Harry 1912- *FilmgC*
Waxman, Morris D d1931 *NotNAT B*
Waxman, Stanley *WhoHol A*
Wayburn, Ned 1874-1942 *EncMT, Film 2, NotNAT B, WhThe*
Waycoff, Leon *WhoHol A*
Wayland, Len *IntMPA 1977*
Wayne, Aissa *WhoHol A*
Wayne, Carol *WhoHol A*
Wayne, David *MotPP, PIP&P, WhoHol A*
Wayne, David 1914- *BiE&WWA, EncMT, FilmgC, MovMk, NotNAT, WhoThe 16*
Wayne, David 1916- *BiDFlm, IntMPA 1977, WorEnF*
Wayne, Dorothy *AmSCAP 1966*
Wayne, Frank *WhoHol A*
Wayne, Fredd *WhoHol A*
Wayne, John 1907- *BiDFlm, CelR 3, CmMov, Film 2, FilmgC, IntMPA 1977, MotPP, MovMk, OxFilm, WhoHol A, WorEnF*
Wayne, John Ethan *WhoHol A*
Wayne, Justina d1951 *WhScrn 1, WhScrn 2*
Wayne, Keith *WhoHol A*
Wayne, Lloyd *WhoHol A*

Wayne, Mabel *AmSCAP 1966, Film 2*
Wayne, Marie *Film 1*
Wayne, Maude *Film 1, Film 2*
Wayne, Michael A 1934- *FilmgC, IntMPA 1977*
Wayne, Naunton 1901-1970 *FilmgC, OxFilm, WhScrn 1, WhScrn 2, WhThe, WhoHol B*
Wayne, Nina *WhoHol A*
Wayne, Pat *MotPP*
Wayne, Patricia *WhScrn 2*
Wayne, Patrick 1939- *FilmgC, WhoHol A*
Wayne, Paula 1937- *BiE&WWA, NotNAT*
Wayne, Richard d1958 *Film 2, WhScrn 1, WhScrn 2, WhoHol B*
Wayne, Robert 1864?-1946 *Film 2, WhScrn 2*
Wayne, Rollo 1899-1954 *NotNAT B, WhThe*
Wayne, Sid 1923- *AmSCAP 1966*
Wayne, Susan *WomWMM A, WomWMM B*
Wayne And Shuster *NewYTET*
Weadon, Percy d1939 *NotNAT B*
Weales, Gerald 1925- *BiE&WWA*
Weatherford, Tazwell 1889-1917 *WhScrn 2*
Weathers, Roscoe 1925- *AmSCAP 1966*
Weathersby, Helen d1943 *NotNAT B*
Weaver, Affie d1940 *NotNAT B*
Weaver, Charley *WhScrn 2*
Weaver, Dennis *MotPP, WhoHol A*
Weaver, Dennis 1924- *FilmgC, MovMk*
Weaver, Dennis 1925- *IntMPA 1977*
Weaver, Doodles *WhoHol A*
Weaver, Elviry *WhoHol A*
Weaver, Frank *WhoHol A*
Weaver, Fritz 1926- *BiE&WWA, FilmgC, NotNAT, WhoHol A, WhoThe 16*
Weaver, Henry *Film 1*
Weaver, John 1673-1760 *NotNAT B, OxThe, PIP&P*
Weaver, John VanAlstyn 1893-1938 *NotNAT B*
Weaver, Joseph *WhoStg 1906*
Weaver, Lee *WhoHol A*
Weaver, Leon 1883-1950 *WhScrn 2, WhoHol B*
Weaver, Marion 1902- *AmSCAP 1966*
Weaver, Marjorie 1913- *FilmgC, IntMPA 1977, MovMk, ThFT, WhoHol A*
Weaver, Mary Watson 1903- *AmSCAP 1966*
Weaver, Powell 1890-1951 *AmSCAP 1966*
Weaver, Richard A 1934- *NotNAT*
Weaver, Sylvester L, Jr. 1908- *IntMPA 1977, NewYTET*
Webb, Alan 1906- *BiE&WWA, NotNAT, WhoHol A, WhoThe 16*
Webb, Clifton d1966 *BiE&WWA, MotPP, WhoHol B*
Webb, Clifton 1889?-1966 *WhScrn 1, WhScrn 2*
Webb, Clifton 1890-1966 *Film 2*
Webb, Clifton 1891-1966 *EncMT, WorEnF*
Webb, Clifton 1893-1966 *BiDFlm, FilmgC, MovMk, NotNAT B, WhThe*
Webb, David 1925- *CelR 3*
Webb, Dick *Film 2*
Webb, Fay 1906-1936 *WhScrn 1, WhScrn 2, WhoHol B*
Webb, Frank d1974 *WhScrn 2, WhoHol A*
Webb, George 1887-1943 *Film 1, Film 2, WhScrn 2*
Webb, Harry *TwYS A*
Webb, Jack d1954 *NotNAT B*
Webb, Jack 1920- *FilmgC, IntMPA 1977, MotPP, MovMk, NewYTET, OxFilm, WhoHol A, WorEnF*
Webb, James R 1909- *WorEnF*
Webb, James R 1912- *CmMov, FilmgC*
Webb, Janet *WhoHol A*
Webb, Jerry *IntMPA 1977*
Webb, Jim 1946- *CelR 3*

Webb, John d1913 *NotNAT B*
Webb, John 1611-1672 *NotNAT B, OxThe, PIP&P*
Webb, Kenneth 1885-1966 *AmSCAP 1966*
Webb, Kenneth 1892- *TwYS A*
Webb, Leonard 1930- *ConDr 1977*
Webb, Lizbeth 1926- *WhThe*
Webb, Louis K *Film 2*
Webb, Mildred *WomWMM*
Webb, Millard 1893-1935 *Film 1, TwYS A, WhScrn 1, WhScrn 2, WhoHol B*
Webb, Nella d1954 *NotNAT B, WhoStg 1908*
Webb, Percy Sergeant *Film 1*
Webb, Richard *WhoHol A*
Webb, Rita *WhoHol A*
Webb, Robert A 1911- *IntMPA 1977*
Webb, Robert D 1903- *FilmgC, IntMPA 1977*
Webb, Roy 1888- *AmSCAP 1966, CmMov*
Webb, Roy Dean 1937- *AmSCAP 1966*
Webb, Ruth 1923- *BiE&WWA, NotNAT*
Webb, Sidney F d1956 *NotNAT B*
Webb, Teena *WomWMM B*
Webber, Paul *WhoHol A*
Webber, Peggy *WhoHol A*
Webber, Robert 1928- *BiE&WWA, FilmgC, IntMPA 1977, NotNAT, WhoHol A*
Weber, Edwin J 1893- *AmSCAP 1966*
Weber, Henry William d1818 *NotNAT B*
Weber, Jean *Film 2*
Weber, Mrs. Joe d1951 *NotNAT B*
Weber, Joe 1867-1942 *EncMT, Film 1, Film 2, NotNAT A, WhScrn 1, WhScrn 2, WhoHol B*
Weber, Joseph 1867-1942 *FamA&A, NotNAT B, OxThe, WhThe, WhoStg 1906, WhoStg 1908*
Weber, Joseph W 1861-1943 *WhScrn 1, WhScrn 2*
Weber, L Lawrence d1940 *NotNAT B, WhThe*
Weber, Lois d1939 *Film 1, MotPP, WhoHol B*
Weber, Lois 1882-1939 *TwYS A*
Weber, Lois 1883-1939 *WhScrn 1, WhScrn 2, WomWMM*
Weber, Rex 1889-1918 *WhScrn 2*
Weber, Stanley R 1912- *IntMPA 1977*
Weber, Wilhelmine Frances 1916- *AmSCAP 1966*
Weber And Fields *OxThe*
Webster, Ben 1864-1947 *Film 1, Film 2, NotNAT A, NotNAT B, WhScrn 1, WhScrn 2, WhThe, WhoHol B*
Webster, Benjamin 1864-1947 *OxThe*
Webster, Benjamin Francis 1909- *AmSCAP 1966*
Webster, Benjamin Nottingham 1797-1882 *NotNAT B, OxThe*
Webster, Byron *WhoHol A*
Webster, David *IntMPA 1977*
Webster, Edward Mount d1976 *NewYTET*
Webster, Florence Ann 1860-1899 *NotNAT B*
Webster, Frederick 1802-1878 *NotNAT B*
Webster, Howard *Film 2*
Webster, Jean 1876-1916 *NotNAT B*
Webster, John 1580?-1625? *NotNAT A*
Webster, John 1580?-1634? *CnThe, McGWD, NotNAT B, OxThe, PIP&P, REnWD*
Webster, M Coates 1906- *IntMPA 1977*
Webster, Margaret 1905-1972 *BiE&WWA, CnThe, NotNAT A, NotNAT B, OxThe, WhScrn 2, WhoThe 16*
Webster, May Whitty 1865-1948 *OxThe*
Webster, Nicholas *NewYTET*
Webster, Paul Francis 1907- *AmSCAP 1966, BiE&WWA*
Webster, Paul Francis 1910?- *FilmgC*
Webster-Gleason, Lucile 1888-1947 *NotNAT B,*

WhThe
Wechsler, James 1915- *CelR 3*
Wechsler, Lazar 1896- *IntMPA 1977*
Wecker, Marlene *WomWMM B*
Wedekind, Frank 1864-1918 *CnMD, CnThe, McGWD, ModWD, NotNAT A, NotNAT B, OxThe, REnWD*
Wedgeworth, Ann *WhoHol A*
Weed, Frank *Film 1*
Weed, Leland T *WhScrn 2*
Weed, Marlene *WomWMM*
Weede, Robert 1903-1972 *BiE&WWA, EncMT, NotNAT B*
Weeden, Evelyn d1961 *WhThe*
Weeks, Alan *WhoHol A*
Weeks, Anson 1896-1969 *AmSCAP 1966, WhoHol B*
Weeks, Barbara d1954 *NotNAT B*
Weeks, Harold Taylor 1893- *AmSCAP 1966*
Weeks, Marion 1887-1968 *WhScrn 1, WhScrn 2, WhoHol B*
Weeks, Paul 1895- *AmSCAP 1966*
Weeks, Ricardo 1921- *AmSCAP 1966*
Weeks, Stephen 1948- *FilmgC*
Weeks, William J 1901- *AmSCAP 1966*
Weems, Clinton E 1925- *AmSCAP 1966*
Weems, Ted 1901-1963 *AmSCAP 1966, NotNAT B, WhScrn 1, WhScrn 2, WhoHol B*
Weer, Helen *Film 1*
Wegener, Else *WomWMM*
Wegener, Paul 1874-1948 *BiDFlm, DcFM, Film 1, Film 2, FilmgC, NotNAT B, OxFilm, WhScrn 1, WhScrn 2, WhoHol B, WorEnF*
Wegner, Sharen *WomWMM B*
Weguelin, Thomas N 1885- *WhThe*
Wehlen, Emmy 1887- *Film 1, WhThe*
Wehr, David A 1934- *AmSCAP 1966*
Weidler, Virginia 1927-1968 *FilmgC, MGM, MotPP, ThFT, WhScrn 2, WhoHol B*
Weidman, Charles *Film 2*
Weidman, Charles 1901- *BiE&WWA*
Weidman, Jerome 1913- *BiE&WWA, ConDr 1977, EncMT, NewMT, NotNAT, WhoThe 16*
Weidman, Joan *WomWMM, WomWMM B*
Weidman, John 1946- *NatPD*
Weidner, Paul 1934- *NotNAT*
Weidt, A J 1866-1945 *AmSCAP 1966*
Weigel, Hans 1880- *CnMD*
Weigel, Helene 1900-1971 *CroCD, WhThe*
Weigel, Helene 1900-1972 *CnThe*
Weigel, Paul 1867-1951 *Film 1, Film 2, TwYS, WhScrn 2*
Weight, Michael 1906- *WhThe*
Weigle, Charles F 1871- *AmSCAP 1966*
Weijden, Tor *Film 2*
Weil, Harry 1878-1943 *WhScrn 1, WhScrn 2*
Weil, Harry 1890-1974 *WhScrn 2*
Weil, Mrs. Leonard D d1963 *NotNAT B*
Weil, Max-Rene *McGWD*
Weil, Milton 1888-1937 *AmSCAP 1966*
Weil, Robert *WhoHol A*
Weiland, Joyce 1931- *WomWMM B*
Weiland, Joyce see also Wieland, Joyce
Weiler, Berenice 1927- *BiE&WWA, NotNAT*
Weiler, Constance 1918-1965 *WhScrn 1, WhScrn 2*
Weiler, Gerald E 1928- *IntMPA 1977*
Weill, Claudia *WomWMM, WomWMM A, WomWMM B*
Weill, Gus 1933- *NatPD*
Weill, Irving 1894- *AmSCAP 1966*

Weill, Kurt 1900-1950 *AmSCAP 1966, EncMT, FilmgC, NewMT, NotNAT B, OxFilm, PIP&P, WhThe, WorEnF*
Weille, F Blair 1930- *AmSCAP 1966*
Weiman, Rita d1954 *NotNAT B*
Weinbaum, Batya *WomWMM B*
Weinberg, Betsy L 1926- *AmSCAP 1966*
Weinberg, Charles 1889-1955 *AmSCAP 1966*
Weinberg, Gus 1866-1952 *Film 2, NotNAT B, WhScrn 1, WhScrn 2, WhThe, WhoHol B*
Weinberg, Herman G 1908- *IntMPA 1977*
Weinberg, Jacob 1883-1956 *AmSCAP 1966*
Weinberg, Jean *WomWMM B*
Weinberger, Jaromir 1896- *AmSCAP 1966*
Weinberger-Daniels *NewYTET*
Weinblatt, Mike *NewYTET*
Weiner, Arn *WhoHol A*
Weiner, Lawrence A d1961 *NotNAT B*
Weiner, Lazar 1897- *AmSCAP 1966*
Weiner, Leslie *NatPD*
Weiner, Robert *BiE&WWA, NotNAT*
Weingarten, David 1902- *AmSCAP 1966*
Weingarten, Laurence 1895- *FilmgC*
Weingarten, Lawrence 1898-1975 *WhScrn 2*
Weingarten, Romain 1926- *CroCD*
Weinles, Len 1923- *AmSCAP 1966*
Weinrib, Lennie *WhoHol A*
Weinrib, Leonard *NewYTET*
Weinstein, Arnold 1927- *BiE&WWA, ConDr 1977, NotNAT*
Weinstein, Hannah *WomWMM, WomWMM B*
Weinstein, Henry T 1924- *IntMPA 1977*
Weinstein, Kit *WomWMM B*
Weinstein, Milton 1911- *AmSCAP 1966*
Weinstein, Miriam *WomWMM A, WomWMM B*
Weinstein, Sol 1928- *AmSCAP 1966*
Weinstein, Susan 1951- *NatPD*
Weinstock, Jack 1909- *BiE&WWA*
Weintraub, Frances d1963 *NotNAT B*
Weintraub, Fred 1928- *IntMPA 1977*
Weintraub, Milton 1897-1968 *BiE&WWA, NotNAT B*
Weintraub, Sandy *WomWMM*
Weir, George R d1909 *NotNAT B*
Weir, Gregg *WhoHol A*
Weir, Helen *Film 1*
Weir, Jane 1916-1937 *WhScrn 1, WhScrn 2*
Weir, Molly *WhoHol A*
Weirick, Paul 1906- *AmSCAP 1966*
Weis, Don 1922- *BiDFlm, FilmgC, IntMPA 1977, WorEnF*
Weis, Jack 1932- *IntMPA 1977*
Weis, Roney 1939- *IntMPA 1977*
Weisbart, David 1915-1967 *FilmgC, WorEnF*
Weisberg, Brenda *IntMPA 1977*
Weisberg, Sylvia d1962 *NotNAT B*
Weisbord, Sam 1911- *IntMPA 1977*
Weise, Christian 1642-1708 *CnThe, NotNAT B, OxThe, REnWD*
Weise, Christian Felix Weisse 1726-1804 *OxThe*
Weise, Christian Felix Weisse see also Weisse, Christian F W
Weisenborn, Gunther 1902-1969 *CnMD, CroCD, McGWD, ModWD*
Weiser, Grete 1903-1970 *WhoHol B*
Weiser, Grethe 1903-1970 *WhScrn 1, WhScrn 2*
Weiser, Irving 1913- *AmSCAP 1966*
Weiser, Martin 1916- *IntMPA 1977*
Weisfeld, Zelma H 1931- *BiE&WWA, NotNAT*
Weisgall, Hugo 1912- *AmSCAP 1966*
Weisman, Ben 1921- *AmSCAP 1966*
Weisman, Milton C 1895- *IntMPA 1977*
Weismuller, Johnny 1904- *CmMov*

Weismuller, Johnny *see also* Weissmuller, Johnny
Weiss, Fritz *IntMPA 1977*
Weiss, George 1893-1964 *AmSCAP 1966*
Weiss, George David 1921- *AmSCAP 1966*
Weiss, Jiri 1913- *DcFM, WorEnF* •
Weiss, Marion 1923- *AmSCAP 1966*
Weiss, Peter 1916- *CnThe, CroCD, McGWD,
    ModWD, NotNAT, NotNAT A, OxFilm,
    PIP&P, PIP&P A, REnWD, WhoThe 16,
    WorEnF*
Weiss, Robert R 1928- *AmSCAP 1966*
Weiss, Ruth *WomWMM B*
Weiss, Stephan 1899- *AmSCAP 1966*
Weiss, William M *IntMPA 1977*
Weissberger, L Arnold 1907- *BiE&WWA,
    NotNAT*
Weissburg, Edward 1876-1950 *WhScrn 1,
    WhScrn 2*
Weisse, A *Film 2*
Weisse, Christian Felix Weisse 1726-1804
    NotNAT B
Weisse, Christian Felix Weisse *see also* Weise,
    Christian F W
Weisse, Hanni 1892-1967 *Film 2, WhScrn 1,
    WhScrn 2, WhoHol B*
Weissman, Dora d1974 *WhScrn 2, WhoHol B*
Weissman, Murray 1925- *IntMPA 1977*
Weissman, Seymour J 1931- *IntMPA 1977*
Weissmuller, Johnny 1904- *Film 2, FilmgC,
    IntMPA 1977, MGM, MotPP, MovMk,
    OxFilm, WhoHol A, WorEnF*
Weissmuller, Johnny, Jr. *WhoHol A*
Weissmuller, Johnny *see also* Weissmuller, Johnny
Weissova, Lenka *WomWMM*
Weiter, Aisig 1878-1919 *OxThe*
Weith, Eva *BiE&WWA*
Weitman, Norman 1927- *IntMPA 1977*
Weitman, Robert M 1905- *IntMPA 1977,
    NewYTET*
Weitz, Emile 1883-1951 *WhScrn 1, WhScrn 2*
Weitz, John 1923- *CelR 3*
Weitzenkorn, Louis 1893-1943 *NotNAT B*
Weitzner, David 1938- *IntMPA 1977*
Wekwerth, Manfred 1929- *CroCD*
Welch, Charles C *WhoHol A*
Welch, Constance d1976 *BiE&WWA,
    NotNAT B*
Welch, Deshler d1920 *NotNAT B*
Welch, Eddie 1900-1963 *WhScrn 1, WhScrn 2,
    WhoHol B*
Welch, Elisabeth 1908- *EncMT, WhoHol A*
Welch, Elisabeth 1909- *BiE&WWA, NotNAT,
    WhoThe 16*
Welch, Elizabeth *FilmgC*
Welch, Harry Foster 1899-1973 *WhScrn 2,
    WhoHol B*
Welch, James 1865-1917 *NotNAT B, WhThe*
Welch, James T 1869-1949 *Film 2, WhScrn 1,
    WhScrn 2, WhoHol B*
Welch, Joseph L 1891-1960 *FilmgC, WhoHol B*
Welch, Joseph N 1891-1960 *WhScrn 1, WhScrn 2*
Welch, Kenneth 1926- *AmSCAP 1966*
Welch, Lew d1952 *NotNAT B*
Welch, Marilyn 1933- *AmSCAP 1966*
Welch, Mary 1923-1958 *NotNAT B, WhScrn 1,
    WhScrn 2, WhoHol B*
Welch, Nelson *WhoHol A*
Welch, Niles 1888- *Film 1, Film 2, TwYS*
Welch, Norman A 1946- *AmSCAP 1966*
Welch, Peter 1922- *IntMPA 1977*
Welch, Raquel *IntMPA 1977, MotPP,
    WhoHol A*
Welch, Raquel 1940- *CelR 3, FilmgC*
Welch, Raquel 1942- *MovMk, WorEnF*

Welch, Robert 1899- *CelR 3*
Welch, Robert Gilbert d1924 *NotNAT B*
Welch, Robert L 1910- *IntMPA 1977*
Welch, William *Film 2*
Welchman, Harry 1886-1966 *EncMT, WhScrn 1,
    WhScrn 2, WhThe, WhoHol B*
Welcker, Gertrude *Film 2*
Weld, Tuesday 1943- *BiDFlm, CelR 3, FilmgC,
    IntMPA 1977, MotPP, MovMk, WhoHol A,
    WorEnF*
Welden, Ben 1901- *FilmgC, IntMPA 1977,
    Vers B, WhThe*
Weldon, Bunny *Film 2*
Weldon, Duncan Clark 1941- *WhoThe 16*
Weldon, Fay 1933- *ConDr 1977C*
Weldon, Frank *AmSCAP 1966*
Weldon, Harry 1882- *WhThe*
Weldon, Jess *Film 2*
Weldon, Joan 1933- *IntMPA 1977, WhoHol A*
Weldon, John *McGWD*
Weldon, Lillian 1869-1941 *WhScrn 1, WhScrn 2*
Weldon, Tim *WhoHol A*
Welford, Dallas 1872-1946 *WhScrn 1, WhScrn 2,
    WhoHol B*
Welford, Dallas 1874-1946 *Film 2, NotNAT B,
    WhThe, WhoStg 1908*
Welford, Nancy *Film 2*
Welk, Ehm 1884- *CnMD*
Welk, Lawrence 1903- *AmSCAP 1966, CelR 3,
    IntMPA 1977*
Welker, Frank *WhoHol A*
Welland, Colin 1934- *ConDr 1977C, FilmgC*
Weller, Bernard 1870-1943 *NotNAT B, WhThe*
Weller, Carrie d1954 *NotNAT B*
Weller, Michael 1942- *ConDr 1977*
Welles, Beatrice *WhoHol A*
Welles, Gwen *WhoHol A*
Welles, Jada *Film 2*
Welles, Jesse *WhoHol A*
Welles, Meri 1930?-1973 *WhScrn 2*
Welles, Orson 1915- *BiDFlm, BiE&WWA,
    CelR 3, CmMov, CnThe, ConDr 1977A,
    DcFM, EncMT, FamA&A, FilmgC,
    IntMPA 1977, MotPP, MovMk, NotNAT,
    NotNAT A, OxFilm, OxThe, WhThe,
    WhoHol A, WorEnF*
Welles, Orson 1916- *PIP&P*
Welles, Ralph *Film 2*
Welles, Rebecca *WhoHol A*
Welles, Violet *BiE&WWA, NotNAT*
Wellesley, Arthur 1890- *WhThe*
Wellesley, Charles 1875-1946 *Film 1, Film 2,
    WhScrn 1, WhScrn 2, WhoHol B*
Wellesley, William *Film 2*
Welling, Sylvia 1901- *WhThe*
Wellington, Babe 1897-1954 *WhScrn 1,
    WhScrn 2, WhoHol B*
Wellman, Emily Ann d1946 *NotNAT B,
    WhScrn 2*
Wellman, Michael *WhoHol A*
Wellman, William, Jr. *WhoHol A*
Wellman, William A 1896-1975 *BiDFlm, CmMov,
    DcFM, Film 1, FilmgC, MovMk, OxFilm,
    TwYS A, WhScrn 2, WhoHol C, WorEnF*
Wells, Billy 1888-1967 *WhoHol B*
Wells, Bombadier Billy 1888-1967 *WhScrn 1*
Wells, Bombardier Billy 1888-1967 *WhScrn 2*
Wells, Carole *WhoHol A*
Wells, Charles B d1924 *NotNAT B*
Wells, Dawn *WhoHol A*
Wells, Deering 1896-1961 *WhScrn 1, WhScrn 2,
    WhThe, WhoHol B*
Wells, Frank G 1932- *IntMPA 1977*
Wells, George 1909- *FilmgC, WorEnF*

Wells, H G 1866-1946 *FilmgC, PIP&P,*
WhScrn 1, WhScrn 2, WhoHol B
Wells, Herbert George 1866-1946 *NotNAT B*
Wells, Ingeborg *WhoHol A*
Wells, Jacqueline *Film 2, WhoHol A*
Wells, Jane *Film 1*
Wells, John Barnes 1880-1935 *AmSCAP 1966*
Wells, L M 1862-1923 *Film 1, WhScrn 2*
Wells, Mai 1862-1941 *WhScrn 1, WhScrn 2,*
WhoHol B
Wells, Marie 1894-1949 *Film 2, NotNAT B,*
WhScrn 1, WhScrn 2, WhoHol B
Wells, Marion *WhoHol A*
Wells, Mary *CelR 3*
Wells, May *Film 1, Film 2*
Wells, Raymond *Film 1, Film 2*
Wells, Rick *WhoHol A*
Wells, Robert *NewYTET*
Wells, Robert 1922- *AmSCAP 1966*
Wells, Roxanna d1964 *NotNAT B*
Wells, Sheilah *WhoHol A*
Wells, Ted *Film 2*
Wells, Veronica *WhoHol A*
Wells, William d1956 *NotNAT B*
Wells, William 1910- *AmSCAP 1966*
Wells, William K *Film 2*
Welpott, Raymond W d1973 *NewYTET*
Welsh, Betty *Film 2*
Welsh, Charles L 1906- *IntMPA 1977*
Welsh, Jane 1905- *WhThe*
Welsh, John *FilmgC, WhoHol A*
Welsh, Niles *Film 2*
Welsh, William *Film 1, Film 2*
Welti, Albert Jakob 1894-1965 *CnMD*
Weltman, Philip 1908- *IntMPA 1977*
Weltner, George 1901- *IntMPA 1977*
Welty, Eudora 1909- *CelR 3*
Wemyss, Francis Courtney 1797-1859 *FamA&A,*
NotNAT A, NotNAT B, OxThe
Wences, Senor *WhoHol A*
Wenck, Eduard 1894-1954 *WhScrn 1, WhScrn 2*
Wendell, Charles 1910- *AmSCAP 1966*
Wendell, Howard D 1908-1975 *Vers A, WhScrn 2,*
WhoHol C
Wendkos, Paul *NewYTET*
Wendkos, Paul 1922- *BiDFlm, FilmgC*
Wendkos, Paul 1923- *WorEnF*
Wendler, Otto Bernhard 1895-1958? *CnMD*
Wendling, Pete 1888- *AmSCAP 1966*
Wendorff, Laiola 1895-1966 *WhScrn 2*
Wendt, Stephan 1909- *CnMD*
Wengraf, John E 1897-1974 *FilmgC, Vers A,*
WhScrn 2, WhoHol B
Wengren, David *Film 2*
Wenham, Jane *WhoHol A, WhoThe 16*
Wenman, Henry N 1875-1953 *Film 2, NotNAT B,*
WhThe, WhoHol B
Wenman, T E d1892 *NotNAT B*
Wenn, Clifton *Film 2*
Wenning, Thomas H d1962 *NotNAT B*
Wenrich, Percy 1887-1952 *AmSCAP 1966,*
NotNAT B
Wentworth, Fanny d1934 *NotNAT B*
Wentworth, Martha d1974 *Vers A, WhScrn 2,*
WhoHol B
Wentworth, Stephen d1935 *NotNAT B*
Wentz, John K d1964 *NotNAT B*
Wenzel, Arthur J *WhoHol A*
Werba, Louis F d1942 *NotNAT B*
Werbesik, Gisela 1875-1956 *WhScrn 1,*
WhScrn 2
Werbiseck, Gisela 1875-1956 *WhoHol B*
Werckmeister, Vicky *Film 2*
Werfel, Franz 1890-1945 *CnMD, CnThe,*

McGWD, ModWD, NotNAT B, OxThe,
PIP&P, REnWD
Wergeland, Henrik Arnold 1808-1845 *NotNAT B,*
OxThe
Werich, Jan *CnMD*
Werker, Alfred Louis 1896- *FilmgC,*
IntMPA 1977, TwYS A
Werkmeister, Lotte 1886-1970 *WhScrn 1,*
WhScrn 2
Werle *IntMPA 1977*
Werle, Barbara *WhoHol A*
Werle, Floyd Edwards 1929- *AmSCAP 1966*
Wermel, Benjamin 1907- *AmSCAP 1966*
Werner, Bud 1936-1964 *WhScrn 2*
Werner, Friedrich Ludwig Zacharias 1768-1823
NotNAT B, OxThe
Werner, Friedrich Ludwig Zacharias *see also*
Werner, Zacharias
Werner, Gosta 1908- *DcFM*
Werner, Kay 1918- *AmSCAP 1966*
Werner, Mort *NewYTET*
Werner, Oskar 1922- *BiDFlm, CelR 3, FilmgC,*
IntMPA 1977, MotPP, MovMk, OxFilm,
WhoHol A, WorEnF
Werner, Sue 1918- *AmSCAP 1966*
Werner, Walter 1884-1956 *WhScrn 1, WhScrn 2*
Werner, Zacharias 1768-1823 *CnThe, McGWD,*
REnWD
Werner, Zacharias *see also* Werner, Friedrich
Ludwig Zacharias
Werner-Kahle, Hugo 1883-1961 *WhScrn 1,*
WhScrn 2
Wernick, Richard 1934- *AmSCAP 1966*
Wernicke, Otto 1893-1965 *WhScrn 2*
Werrenrath, Reinald *Film 2*
Wershba, Joseph *NewYTET*
Werth, Barbara *Film 2*
Wertimer, Ned *WhoHol A*
Wertmuller, Lina 1930?- *MovMk, WomWMM*
Wertz, Clarence d1935 *Film 2, WhScrn 1,*
WhScrn 2, WhoHol B
Wery, Carl 1898-1975 *WhScrn 2, WhoHol C*
Wescourt, Gordon *WhoHol A*
Wesford, Susan *NotNAT B*
Wesker, Arnold 1932- *BiE&WWA, CnMD,*
CnThe, ConDr 1977, CroCD, McGWD,
ModWD, NotNAT, NotNAT A, OxThe,
PIP&P, REnWD, WhoThe 16
Wesley, Richard Errol *NatPD, PIP&P A*
Weslyn, Louis 1875-1936 *AmSCAP 1966*
Wess, Hal 1922- *AmSCAP 1966*
Wess, Otto Francis 1914-1969 *WhScrn 1,*
WhScrn 2
Wessel, Dick 1913-1965 *FilmgC, Vers B,*
WhScrn 1, WhScrn 2, WhoHol B
Wessel, Johan 1742-1785 *OxThe*
Wesselhoeft, Eleanor 1873-1945 *WhScrn 1,*
WhScrn 2, WhoHol B
Wessely, Paula 1908- *FilmgC, OxFilm*
Wesson, Alfred 1901- *AmSCAP 1966*
Wesson, Dick *WhoHol A*
Wesson, Eileen *WhoHol A*
Wesson, Gene 1921-1975 *WhScrn 2, WhoHol C*
West, Adam 1929- *FilmgC, WhoHol A*
West, Algernon 1886- *WhThe*
West, Alvy 1915- *AmSCAP 1966*
West, Basil d1934 *WhoHol B*
West, Bernard 1918- *BiE&WWA*
West, Bernie *NewYTET, WhoHol A*
West, Billie *Film 1, Film 2*
West, Billy 1893-1975 *WhScrn 2, WhoHol C*
West, Brooks *WhoHol A*
West, Buster 1902-1966 *WhoHol B*
West, Buster James 1902-1966 *WhScrn 1*

West, Buster James *see also* West, James Buster
West, Charles 1886- *Film 1, Film 2, TwYS*
West, Charles H 1885-1943 *WhScrn 2*
West, Christopher *WhoHol A*
West, Claire *Film 2*
West, Con 1891- *WhThe*
West, Dorothy *Film 1*
West, Edna Rhys 1887-1963 *Film 2, NotNAT B,*
WhScrn 1, WhScrn 2, WhoHol B
West, Eleanor *WomWMM B*
West, Eugene 1883-1949 *AmSCAP 1966*
West, Florence 1862-1913 *OxThe*
West, Ford *Film 2*
West, George *Film 2*
West, H E *WhoHol A*
West, H St. Barbe 1880-1935 *Film 2*
West, Henry *Film 1, Film 2*
West, Henry St. Barbe 1880-1935 *NotNAT B,*
WhThe, WhoHol B
West, Isabel *Film 2*
West, James Buster 1902-1966 *WhScrn 2*
West, James Buster *see also* West, Buster James
West, Jerry 1938- *CelR 3*
West, Johnny *WhoHol A*
West, Judi *WhoHol A*
West, Katherine 1883-1936 *WhScrn 1, WhScrn 2*
West, Lillian *Film 1, Film 2*
West, Lockwood 1905- *WhoHol A, WhoThe 16*
West, Mae *IntMPA 1977, MotPP, WomWMM*
West, Mae 1892- *BiDFlm, BiE&WWA, CelR 3,*
FamA&A, FilmgC, NotNAT, OxFilm,
ThFT, WhoHol A, WhoThe 16
West, Mae 1893- *ModWD, MovMk, NotNAT A,*
WorEnF
West, Mal 1913- *AmSCAP 1966*
West, Martin *WhoHol A*
West, Nathanael 1904-1940 *FilmgC*
West, Olive *Film 1*
West, Pat 1889-1944 *WhScrn 1, WhScrn 2,*
WhoHol B
West, Paul 1871- *WhoStg 1906, WhoStg 1908*
West, Ray 1904- *AmSCAP 1966*
West, Roland 1887-1952 *FilmgC, TwYS A*
West, Thomas 1859-1932 *WhScrn 1, WhScrn 2,*
WhoHol B
West, Timothy 1934- *WhoHol A, WhoThe 16*
West, Wally *WhoHol A*
West, Will 1867-1922 *NotNAT B, WhThe*
West, William d1918 *WhScrn 2*
West, William H 1888- *Film 1, Film 2, TwYS*
West, William Herman 1860-1915 *WhScrn 2*
Westayer, Harry *Film 2*
Westbrook, Helen Searles *AmSCAP 1966*
Westbrook, John 1922- *WhoHol A, WhoThe 16*
Westcott, Gordon 1903-1935 *Film 2, WhScrn 1,*
WhScrn 2, WhoHol B
Westcott, Helen 1929- *FilmgC, IntMPA 1977,*
WhoHol A
Westcott, Marcy *EncMT*
Westcott, Netta d1953 *NotNAT B, WhThe*
Westen, Lucille 1843-1877 *PIP&P*
Westen, Lucille *see also* Western, Lucille
Westerby, Robert 1909-1968 *FilmgC*
Westerfelt, John *Film 2*
Westerfield, James d1971 *WhoHol B*
Westerfield, James 1912-1971 *FilmgC*
Westerfield, James 1913-1971 *WhScrn 1,*
WhScrn 2
Western, Helen 1843-1868 *NotNAT B*
Western, Helen 1844-1868 *OxThe*
Western, Kenneth d1963 *NotNAT B*
Western, Lucille 1843-1877 *NotNAT B, OxThe*
Western, Lucille *see also* Westen, Lucille
Westerton, Frank H d1923 *NotNAT B,*

WhoHol B
Westfeldt, Wallace *NewYTET*
Westford, Lee M 1926- *AmSCAP 1966*
Westford, Susanne 1865-1944 *NotNAT B*
Westin, Av *NewYTET*
Westland, Henry d1906 *NotNAT B*
Westley, Helen 1875-1942 *ThFT*
Westley, Helen 1879-1942 *FilmgC, MovMk,*
NotNAT B, PIP&P, Vers B, WhScrn 1,
WhScrn 2, WhThe, WhoHol B
Westley, John d1948 *NotNAT B, WhScrn 1,*
WhScrn 2
Westman, Nydia 1902-1970 *BiE&WWA, FilmgC,*
NotNAT B, WhScrn 1, WhScrn 2,
WhoHol B
Westman, Nydia 1907-1970 *ThFT, WhThe*
Westman, Theodore *Film 2*
Westmore, Perc d1970 *WhoHol B*
Westmore, Percy *FilmgC*
Westmoreland, James *WhoHol A*
Westmoreland, Pauline 1910-1947 *WhScrn 1,*
WhScrn 2
Westner, Lillian *WhScrn 1, WhScrn 2*
Weston, Brad *WhoHol A*
Weston, David 1938- *FilmgC, WhoHol A*
Weston, Doris 1917-1960 *WhScrn 1, WhScrn 2,*
WhoHol B
Weston, Eddie 1925- *BiE&WWA*
Weston, Ellen 1939- *BiE&WWA*
Weston, George d1923 *WhScrn 1, WhScrn 2*
Weston, Jack *WhoHol A, WhoThe 16*
Weston, Jack 1915- *IntMPA 1977*
Weston, Jack 1926- *FilmgC*
Weston, Jay 1929- *IntMPA 1977*
Weston, Joseph J 1888-1972 *WhScrn 2*
Weston, Kim *WhoHol A*
Weston, Leslie *WhoHol A*
Weston, Maggie d1926 *Film 1, WhScrn 1,*
WhScrn 2
Weston, Mark *WhoHol A*
Weston, Mildred *Film 1*
Weston, Paul 1912- *AmSCAP 1966*
Weston, Randolph E 1926- *AmSCAP 1966*
Weston, Robert P 1878-1936 *NotNAT B, WhThe*
Weston, Robert R *IntMPA 1977*
Weston, Ruth 1906-1955 *WhScrn 1, WhScrn 2,*
WhoHol B
Weston, Ruth 1908-1955 *NotNAT B*
Weston, Ruth 1911- *WhThe*
Weston, Sammy 1889-1951 *WhScrn 1, WhScrn 2*
Weston, Thomas 1737-1776 *OxThe*
Weston, William *Film 2*
Westover, Robert d1916 *NotNAT B*
Westover, Winifred 1890- *Film 1, Film 2,*
MotPP, TwYS
Westphal, Frank C 1889-1948 *AmSCAP 1966*
Westray *OxThe*
Westwood, John *Film 2*
Westwood, Martin F 1883-1928 *WhScrn 1,*
WhScrn 2
Wetherall, Frances d1923 *NotNAT B, WhThe*
Wetherell, Harold P 1909- *AmSCAP 1966*
Wetherell, M A 1887-1939 *Film 2, WhScrn 1,*
WhScrn 2, WhoHol B
Wetmore, Joan 1911- *BiE&WWA, NotNAT,*
WhThe
Wever, Ned *AmSCAP 1966, WhoHol A*
Wever, Richard *McGWD*
Wever, Warren *IntMPA 1977*
Wewitzer, Ralph d1825 *NotNAT B*
Wexler, Haskell 1923- *WorEnF*
Wexler, Haskell 1926- *FilmgC, IntMPA 1977,*
OxFilm
Wexler, Jacqueline Grennan 1926- *CelR 3*

Wexler, Jodi *WhoHol A*
Wexler, Paul *WhoHol A*
Wexler, Peter 1936- *NotNAT, WhoThe 16*
Wexler, Yale *WhoHol A*
Wexley, John 1902- *WhThe*
Wexley, John 1907- *CnMD, ModWD*
Weyand, Ronald *WhoHol A*
Weyher, Ruth *Film 2*
Weyl, Fernand *McGWD*
Weymann, Gert 1919- *CnMD*
Whale, James 1886-1957 *FilmgC*
Whale, James 1889-1957 *BiDFlm, DcFM,
    OxFilm*
Whale, James 1896-1957 *CmMov, WhThe,
    WorEnF*
Whalen, Michael 1899- *FilmgC*
Whalen, Michael 1902-1974 *WhScrn 2,
    WhoHol B*
Whalen, Michael 1907?- *MovMk*
Whaley, Bert d1973 *WhScrn 2*
Whalley, Norma d1943 *Film 2, WhThe*
Wharton, Anthony P 1877-1943 *NotNAT B*
Wharton, Bessie *Film 1*
Wharton, Betty 1911- *NotNAT*
Wharton, Edith 1862-1937 *NotNAT B*
Wharton, John F 1894- *BiE&WWA, NotNAT,
    NotNAT A*
Wharton, Leopold 1870- *TwYS A*
Wharton, Theodore 1875- *TwYS A*
Whatmore, A R 1889-1960 *NotNAT B, WhThe*
Wheat, Laurence *Film 2*
Wheat, Lawrence 1876-1963 *WhScrn 2*
Wheatcroft, Adeline Stanhope d1935 *NotNAT B,
    WhoHol B*
Wheatcroft, Nelson 1852-1897 *NotNAT B*
Wheatcroft, Stanhope 1888-1966 *Film 1, Film 2,
    TwYS, WhScrn 2, WhoHol B*
Wheatley, Alan 1907- *FilmgC, IntMPA 1977,
    WhoHol A, WhoThe 16*
Wheatley, Emma 1822-1854 *NotNAT B, OxThe*
Wheatley, Frederick d1836 *NotNAT B, OxThe*
Wheatley, Jane 1881-1935 *NotNAT B, WhThe*
Wheatley, Sarah Ross 1790-1872 *NotNAT B,
    OxThe*
Wheatley, William 1816-1876 *NotNAT B, OxThe*
Wheaton, Anna d1961 *NotNAT B*
Whedon, Tom 1932- *AmSCAP 1966*
Wheeler, Andrew Carpenter d1903 *NotNAT B*
Wheeler, Benjamin F d1934 *NotNAT B*
Wheeler, Bert 1895-1968 *BiE&WWA, Film 2,
    FilmgC, MovMk, NotNAT B, WhScrn 1,
    WhScrn 2, WhoHol B*
Wheeler, Billy Edd 1932- *AmSCAP 1966*
Wheeler, Burritt 1883-1957 *WhScrn 2*
Wheeler, Charles F *FilmgC*
Wheeler, Gena *WhoHol A*
Wheeler, Hugh *PIP&P A*
Wheeler, Hugh 1912- *ConDr 1977, WhoThe 16*
Wheeler, Hugh 1916- *BiE&WWA, NotNAT*
Wheeler, John *WhoHol A*
Wheeler, Lois *WhoHol A*
Wheeler, Lois 1920- *BiE&WWA, NotNAT*
Wheeler, Lois 1922- *WhThe*
Wheeler, Lyle 1905- *FilmgC, IntMPA 1977,
    WorEnF*
Wheeler, Margaret *WhoHol A*
Wheeler, Rene 1912- *DcFM*
Wheeler, Teresa d1975 *WhScrn 2*
Wheezer *Film 2*
Wheezer 1925- *TwYS*
Whelan, Albert 1875-1961 *OxThe, WhThe*
Whelan, Arleen 1916- *FilmgC, ThFT,
    WhoHol A*
Whelan, Leo M 1876-1952 *WhScrn 1, WhScrn 2*

Whelan, Ron 1905-1965 *WhScrn 1, WhScrn 2,
    WhoHol B*
Whelan, Tim 1893-1957 *FilmgC, NotNAT B,
    WhScrn 1, WhScrn 2, WhoHol B*
Whelar, Langois M 1898-1918 *WhScrn 2*
Wheldon, Huw 1916- *IntMPA 1977, NewYTET*
Whelen, Frederick 1867- *WhThe*
Whiffen, Mrs. *PIP&P*
Whiffen, Blanche 1845-1936 *NotNAT B,
    WhoHol B*
Whiffen, Thomas d1897 *NotNAT B*
Whiffen, Mrs. Thomas 1845-1936 *Film 1,
    NotNAT A, WhScrn 1, WhScrn 2,
    WhoStg 1906, WhoStg 1908*
Whiffin, Blanche 1845-1936 *WhThe*
Whiley, Manning 1915- *FilmgC, WhThe,
    WhoHol A*
Whincop, Thomas d1730 *NotNAT B*
Whipper, Leigh, Sr. 1877-1975 *WhScrn 2,
    WhoHol C*
Whipple, Sidney Beaumont 1888- *WhThe*
Whips, Andrea *WhScrn 2*
Whistler, Harvey S 1907- *AmSCAP 1966*
Whistler, Margaret 1892-1939 *WhScrn 1,
    WhScrn 2*
Whistler, Rex 1905-1944 *NotNAT B, WhThe*
Whitacre, Harold L 1901- *AmSCAP 1966*
Whitaker, Charles *Film 2*
Whitaker, Charles Slim 1893-1960 *WhScrn 2,
    WhoHol B*
Whitaker, E E *IntMPA 1977*
Whitaker, Jack *NewYTET*
Whitaker, Johnny *WhoHol A*
Whital, Russ *Film 2*
Whitbeck, Frank 1882-1963 *NotNAT B,
    WhScrn 2*
Whitbread, J W d1916 *NotNAT B*
Whitbread, Samuel *PIP&P*
Whitby, Mrs. Arthur d1930 *NotNAT B*
Whitby, Arthur 1869-1922 *NotNAT B, WhThe*
Whitby, Gwynne 1903- *WhoHol A, WhoThe 16*
Whitcomb, Kenneth G 1926- *AmSCAP 1966*
Whitcup, Leonard 1903- *AmSCAP 1966*
White, Alan *MotPP*
White, Alan Russell 1925- *AmSCAP 1966*
White, Alfred H 1883-1972 *WhScrn 2*
White, Alice 1907- *Film 2, MotPP, ThFT,
    TwYS, WhoHol A*
White, Arthur *Film 1*
White, Barbara 1924- *FilmgC, WhoHol A*
White, Barry *WhoHol A*
White, Beatrice d1963 *NotNAT B*
White, Betty *NewYTET, WhoHol A*
White, Bill 1857-1933 *WhScrn 1, WhScrn 2,
    WhoHol B*
White, Billy *Film 1*
White, Blanche *Film 1*
White, Bradford 1912- *BiE&WWA, NotNAT*
White, Byron 1917- *CelR 3*
White, Carol 1941- *FilmgC, WhoHol A*
White, Carolina *Film 1*
White, Charles *WhoHol A*
White, Charles 1830-1892 *NotNAT B*
White, Chrissie 1894- *FilmgC, WhoHol A*
White, Chrissie 1895- *Film 1, Film 2*
White, Christine *WhoHol A*
White, Clarence Cameron 1880-1960
    AmSCAP 1966
White, Dan *WhoHol A*
White, David *WhoHol A*
White, Deanna *WomWMM*
White, Deloy J De 1920- *IntMPA 1977*
White, Donald H 1921- *AmSCAP 1966*
White, E B 1899- *CelR 3*

White, Edgar *NatPD, PIP&P A*
White, Edward J 1902-1973 *WhScrn 2*
White, Edward R 1919- *AmSCAP 1966*
White, Elmore d1964 *NotNAT B*
White, Fisher d1945 *WhoHol B*
White, Frances 1898-1969 *WhScrn 1, WhScrn 2, WhoHol B*
White, Frank *NewYTET, WhoHol A*
White, George 1890-1968 *BiE&WWA, EncMT, NewMT, NotNAT B, WhScrn 1, WhScrn 2, WhThe, WhoHol B*
White, George C 1935- *NotNAT*
White, Glen *Film 1*
White, Gloria *WomWMM*
White, Huey d1938 *WhoHol B*
White, Hugh 1896-1938 *WhScrn 1, WhScrn 2*
White, Hyman 1915- *AmSCAP 1966*
White, Irving 1865-1944 *WhoHol B*
White, J Fisher 1865-1945 *Film 2, NotNAT B, WhThe*
White, J Irving 1865-1944 *WhScrn 1, WhScrn 2*
White, Jacqueline *WhoHol A*
White, James d1862 *NotNAT B*
White, James d1927 *NotNAT B, WhThe*
White, Jane 1922- *BiE&WWA, NotNAT, WhoHol A, WhoThe 16*
White, Jane Douglass 1919- *AmSCAP 1966*
White, Jennifer *WhoHol A*
White, Jesse *WhoHol A*
White, Jesse 1918- *FilmgC*
White, Jesse 1919- *BiE&WWA, IntMPA 1977, MovMk, NotNAT, Vers A*
White, Joan 1909- *BiE&WWA, NotNAT, WhoHol A, WhoThe 16*
White, John 1919- *ConDr 1977*
White, John D 1931- *AmSCAP 1966*
White, John F *NewYTET*
White, Joseph M 1891-1959 *AmSCAP 1966*
White, Josh 1908-1969 *AmSCAP 1966, NotNAT B*
White, Jules J 1900- *FilmgC, IntMPA 1977*
White, Kay 1900- *AmSCAP 1966*
White, Ken 1916- *AmSCAP 1966*
White, Lawrence R 1926- *IntMPA 1977, NewYTET*
White, Lee 1886-1927 *NotNAT B, WhThe*
White, Lee Lasses 1885-1949 *Vers A, WhoHol B*
White, Lee Roy Lasses 1888-1949 *WhScrn 1, WhScrn 2*
White, Leo 1880-1948 *WhScrn 1, WhScrn 2, WhoHol B*
White, Leo 1887-1948 *Film 1, Film 2, TwYS*
White, Leonard *IntMPA 1977*
White, Malcom *Film 2*
White, Margareta Eklund *NewYTET*
White, Marjorie 1908-1935 *WhScrn 1, WhScrn 2, WhoHol B*
White, Marjorie 1910- *Film 2*
White, May *Film 1*
White, Melvin R 1911- *BiE&WWA*
White, Michael 1931- *AmSCAP 1966*
White, Michael Simon 1936- *NotNAT, WhoThe 16*
White, Miles 1914- *WhoThe 16*
White, Miles 1920- *BiE&WWA, NotNAT*
White, Myrna *WhoHol A*
White, Nathaniel *WhoHol A*
White, Onna *BiE&WWA, EncMT, NotNAT, WhoThe 16*
White, Patricia *WhoHol A*
White, Patrick 1912- *ConDr 1977*
White, Paul *IntMPA 1977*
White, Paul d1955 *NewYTET*
White, Paul Taylor 1895- *AmSCAP 1966*

White, Pearl 1889-1938 *Film 1, Film 2, FilmgC, MotPP, MovMk, NotNAT B, OxFilm, TwYS, WhScrn 1, WhScrn 2, WhoHol B, WorEnF*
White, Peter *WhoHol A*
White, Roy B *IntMPA 1977*
White, Ruth 1914-1969 *BiE&WWA, NotNAT B, WhScrn 1, WhScrn 2, WhoHol B, WomWMM A, WomWMM B*
White, Sammy 1896-1960 *NotNAT B, WhScrn 1, WhScrn 2, WhoHol B*
White, Sammy 1898-1960 *Vers A*
White, Sheila *WhoHol A*
White, Slappy *WhoHol A*
White, Sylvia *AmSCAP 1966*
White, Thelma 1911- *WhoHol A*
White, Theodore 1915- *CelR 3*
White, Thomas *Film 2*
White, Valerie 1915-1975 *WhScrn 2, WhoHol C, WhoThe 16*
White, Victoria *Film 2*
White, Warren *WhoHol A*
White, Wilfrid Hyde 1903- *IntMPA 1977, WhThe*
White, William John 1887- *AmSCAP 1966*
White, William Wilfred 1894- *AmSCAP 1966*
White-Eyed Kaffir, The *OxThe*
White Spear, Chief *Film 2*
Whitefield, Bernard 1910- *AmSCAP 1966*
Whiteford, Blackie 1873-1962 *Film 2*
Whiteford, Jock *WhThe*
Whiteford, John P Blackie 1873-1962 *WhScrn 2, WhoHol B*
Whitehead, Allen 1921- *BiE&WWA, NotNAT*
Whitehead, Clay T *NewYTET*
Whitehead, E A 1933- *ConDr 1977, WhoThe 16*
Whitehead, Edward 1908- *CelR 3*
Whitehead, Geoffrey *WhoHol A*
Whitehead, John 1873-1962 *NotNAT B, WhScrn 1, WhoHol B*
Whitehead, O Z *WhoHol A*
Whitehead, Omar *Film 2*
Whitehead, Paxton 1937- *NotNAT*
Whitehead, Robert 1916- *BiE&WWA, NotNAT, PIP&P, WhoThe 16*
Whitehead, William d1785 *NotNAT B*
Whitehill, Wayne *WhoHol A*
Whitehorse *Film 1*
Whitehouse, Esther d1946 *NotNAT B*
Whitehouse, Fred 1895-1954 *AmSCAP 1966*
Whitelaw, Arthur *WhoThe 16*
Whitelaw, Barrett 1897?-1947 *WhScrn 1, WhScrn 2*
Whitelaw, Billie 1932- *FilmgC, IntMPA 1977, WhoHol A, WhoThe 16*
Whiteley, Jon 1945- *FilmgC, WhoHol A*
Whiteman, Paul 1890-1967 *BiE&WWA, WhScrn 1, WhScrn 2, WhoHol B*
Whiteman, Paul 1892-1968 *FilmgC*
Whiteside, Walker 1869-1942 *Film 1, NotNAT B, WhScrn 1, WhScrn 2, WhThe, WhoHol B*
Whitespear, Greg *Film 2*
Whitfield, Anne *WhoHol A*
Whitfield, Howard 1914- *BiE&WWA*
Whitfield, Jordan 1917-1967 *WhScrn 1, WhScrn 2*
Whitfield, Robert Smoky d1967 *WhoHol B*
Whitfield, Walter W 1888-1966 *WhScrn 1, WhScrn 2*
Whitford, Annabelle d1961 *Film 1, PIP&P, WhScrn 2, WhoHol B*
Whitford, Homer 1892- *AmSCAP 1966*
Whitford, James Keith 1917- *AmSCAP 1966*
Whithorne, Emerson 1884-1958 *AmSCAP 1966*

Whiting, Mrs. A E *Film 1*
Whiting, Barbara *WhoHol A*
Whiting, Frank M 1907- *BiE&WWA, NotNAT*
Whiting, George 1884-1943 *AmSCAP 1966*
Whiting, Gordon *WhoHol A*
Whiting, Jack 1901-1961 *EncMT, NotNAT B,
   WhScrn 1, WhScrn 2, WhThe, WhoHol B*
Whiting, John 1915-1963 *CnThe*
Whiting, John 1917-1963 *CnMD, ConDr 1977F,
   CroCD, McGWD, ModWD, NotNAT B,
   OxThe, WhThe*
Whiting, John 1918-1963 *REnWD*
Whiting, Leonard 1950- *FilmgC, MotPP,
   WhoHol A*
Whiting, Margaret *WhoHol A*
Whiting, Napoleon *WhoHol A*
Whiting, Richard A 1891-1938 *AmSCAP 1966,
   NewMT, NotNAT B*
Whitley, Clifford 1894- *WhThe*
Whitley, Crane d1958 *WhScrn 2*
Whitlin, Ray *WomWMM*
Whitling, Townsend 1869-1952 *NotNAT B,
   WhThe*
Whitlock, Mrs. 1761-1836 *NotNAT B*
Whitlock, Billy d1951 *NotNAT B*
Whitlock, Lloyd 1900-1962 *Film 1, Film 2,
   TwYS*
Whitlock, Lloyd 1900-1966 *WhoHol B*
Whitlock, T Lloyd 1891-1966 *WhScrn 2*
Whitman, Alfred 1890- *Film 1, Film 2, TwYS*
Whitman, Ernest 1893-1954 *WhScrn 1,
   WhScrn 2, WhoHol B*
Whitman, Essie d1963 *NotNAT B*
Whitman, Estelle d1970 *WhScrn 1, WhScrn 2,
   WhoHol B*
Whitman, Fay 1926- *AmSCAP 1966*
Whitman, Gayne 1890-1958 *Film 2, TwYS,
   WhScrn 1, WhScrn 2, WhoHol B*
Whitman, John P d1963 *NotNAT B*
Whitman, Robert *ConDr 1977E*
Whitman, Stuart *IntMPA 1977, MotPP,
   WhoHol A*
Whitman, Stuart 1926- *FilmgC*
Whitman, Stuart 1929- *MovMk*
Whitman, Walt 1868-1928 *Film 1, Film 2,
   WhScrn 1, WhScrn 2, WhoHol B*
Whitman, William *WhoHol A*
Whitmore, James *IntMPA 1977, MotPP,
   WhoHol A*
Whitmore, James 1920?- *MovMk*
Whitmore, James 1921- *BiE&WWA, FilmgC,
   MGM, WhoThe 16*
Whitner, Edwin d1962 *NotNAT B*
Whitney, Bert C d1929 *NotNAT B*
Whitney, C C *WhoHol A*
Whitney, Claire 1890-1969 *Film 1, Film 2,
   TwYS, WhScrn 1, WhScrn 2, WhoHol B*
Whitney, Cornelius Vanderbilt 1899- *CelR 3*
Whitney, Eleanore 1914- *ThFT, WhoHol A*
Whitney, Fred C d1930 *NotNAT B, WhThe*
Whitney, James *OxFilm*
Whitney, Joan 1914- *AmSCAP 1966*
Whitney, John *OxFilm, WorEnF*
Whitney, John Hay 1904- *CelR 3*
Whitney, Julia A 1922-1965 *AmSCAP 1966*
Whitney, Maurice C 1909- *AmSCAP 1966*
Whitney, Mike *WhoHol A*
Whitney, Moxam 1919- *AmSCAP 1966*
Whitney, Peter 1916-1972 *FilmgC, Vers B,
   WhScrn 2, WhoHol B*
Whitney, Ralph 1874-1928 *WhScrn 1, WhScrn 2*
Whitney, Renee d1971 *Film 2, WhoHol B*
Whitney, Robert, II 1945-1969 *WhScrn 1,
   WhScrn 2, WhoHol B*

Whitrow, Benjamin 1937- *WhoThe 16*
Whitson, Beth Slater 1879-1930 *AmSCAP 1966*
Whitson, Frank 1876-1946 *Film 1, Film 2,
   WhScrn 2*
Whitsun-Jones, Paul 1923- *FilmgC, WhoHol A*
Whittaker, Arthur d1914 *NotNAT B*
Whittaker, Charles *Film 2*
Whittaker, Herbert 1911- *WhoThe 16*
Whittaker, James d1964 *NotNAT B*
Whittaker, William *IntMPA 1977*
Whittell, Josephine d1961 *WhScrn 1, WhScrn 2,
   WhoHol B*
Whitten, Delbert Emery, Jr. *Film 2*
Whittingham, Jack 1910- *FilmgC, IntMPA 1977*
Whittinghill, Dick *WhoHol A*
Whittington, Gene *WhoHol A*
Whittington, Margery 1904-1957 *Film 2,
   WhScrn 2*
Whittle, Charles R d1947 *NotNAT B, OxThe,
   WhThe*
Whittlesey, White d1940 *NotNAT B,
   WhoStg 1908*
Whitty, May 1865-1948 *Film 1, FilmgC, MGM,
   MotPP, MovMk, NotNAT A, NotNAT B,
   OxThe, ThFT, Vers A, WhScrn 1,
   WhScrn 2, WhThe, WhoHol B*
Whitwam, Barry *WhoHol A*
Whitworth, Geoffrey 1883-1951 *NotNAT B,
   OxThe, WhThe*
Whitworth, Kathy 1939- *CelR 3*
Whitworth, Robert *Film 1*
Whorf, Richard 1906-1966 *BiE&WWA, FilmgC,
   MotPP, MovMk, NotNAT B, PIP&P,
   WhScrn 1, WhScrn 2, WhThe, WhoHol B*
Whytal, A Russ 1860-1930 *NotNAT B*
Whytal, Mrs. Russ *WhThe*
Whytal, Russ 1860-1930 *WhThe*
Whyte, Frederic d1941 *NotNAT B*
Whyte, Harold d1919 *NotNAT B*
Whyte, Patrick *WhoHol A*
Whyte, Robert, Jr. 1874-1916 *NotNAT B, WhThe*
Whyte, William H 1917- *CelR 3*
Whythe, Jerome 1908- *BiE&WWA*
Wiard, Joyce *Film 2*
Wichart, Lita Belle 1907-1929 *WhScrn 1,
   WhScrn 2*
Wichelow, Walter *Film 2*
Wichman, Adalin *WomWMM B*
Wichmann, Joachim 1917- *McGWD*
Wick, Bruno *WhoHol A*
Wick, Otto 1885-1957 *AmSCAP 1966*
Wickdahl, Lillian *AmSCAP 1966*
Wicker, Tom 1926- *CelR 3*
Wickes, Mary 1916- *FilmgC, IntMPA 1977,
   NotNAT, Vers A, WhThe, WhoHol A*
Wickham, Glynne 1922- *BiE&WWA, NotNAT,
   WhoThe 16*
Wickham, Tony 1922-1948 *NotNAT B, WhThe*
Wicki, Bernard 1919- *DcFM, WhoHol A*
Wicki, Bernhard 1919- *FilmgC, WorEnF*
Wickland, Larry 1898-1938 *WhScrn 1, WhScrn 2,
   WhoHol B*
Wickman, Sally d1963 *NotNAT B*
Wicks, Florence *Film 2*
Wickwire, Nancy 1925-1974 *BiE&WWA,
   NotNAT B, WhoThe 16*
Widdecomb, Wallace d1969 *WhoHol B*
Widdicombe, Harry d1868 *NotNAT B*
Widdicombe, Victor d1912 *NotNAT B*
Widdoes, Kathleen 1939- *BiE&WWA, FilmgC,
   NotNAT, WhoHol A, WhoThe 16*
Widem, Allen M 1925- *IntMPA 1977*
Widerberg, Bo 1930- *BiDFlm, DcFM, FilmgC,
   MovMk, OxFilm, WorEnF*

Widmark, Richard *IntMPA 1977, MotPP,*
  WhoHol A
Widmark, Richard 1914- *FilmgC, MovMk,*
  WorEnF
Widmark, Richard 1915- *BiDFlm, CmMov,*
  OxFilm
Widsith *PIP&P*
Wiechec, M Elizabeth *WomWMM B*
Wieck, Dorothea 1908- *FilmgC, MotPP, ThFT,*
  WhScrn 1
Wieck, Dorothy 1908- *WhoHol A*
Wied, Gustav 1858-1914 *CnMD, NotNAT B,*
  OxThe, WhThe
Wieder, Hardy 1910- *AmSCAP 1966*
Wiedoeft, Rudy 1893-1940 *AmSCAP 1966*
Wiehe, Dagmar *WhThe*
Wieland, Christoph Martin 1733-1813 *McGWD*
Wieland, Joyce 1931- *WomWMM*
Wieland, Joyce *see also* Weiland, Joyce
Wielepp, Kurt O d1962 *NotNAT B*
Wieman, Mathias 1902-1969 *WhScrn 1,*
  WhScrn 2
Wieman, Matthias 1902-1969 *Film 2*
Wiene, Robert 1881-1938 *BiDFlm, DcFM,*
  FilmgC, OxFilm, WorEnF
Wiener, Elizabeth *WomWMM B*
Wiener, Frantz *McGWD*
Wiener, Jack 1926- *IntMPA 1977*
Wiener, Jean 1896- *DcFM, WorEnF*
Wiener, Julia *WhoHol A*
Wiener, Sally Dixon 1926- *NatPD*
Wiere, Harry 1908- *FilmgC*
Wiere, Herbert 1909- *FilmgC*
Wiere, Sylvester 1910-1970 *FilmgC, WhScrn 1,*
  WhScrn 2, WhoHol B
Wiere Brothers, The *FilmgC, WhoHol A*
Wiese, Henry William 1903- *BiE&WWA*
Wiesenthal, Sam 1909- *IntMPA 1977*
Wiesner, Jerome 1915- *CelR 3*
Wiest, George D 1897- *AmSCAP 1966*
Wieth, Mogens d1962 *WhoHol B*
Wieth, Mogens 1920-1962 *NotNAT B, OxThe,*
  WhScrn 2
Wifstrand, Naima 1890-1968 *WhScrn 2*
Wigan, Alfred d1878 *NotNAT B*
Wigan, Mrs. Alfred d1884 *NotNAT B*
Wigan, Horace d1885 *NotNAT B*
Wiggins, Mary L 1910-1945 *WhScrn 1,*
  WhScrn 2
Wiggs, Johnny 1899- *AmSCAP 1966*
Wigmore, Donna-Lou *WomWMM*
Wignell, Thomas 1753-1803 *FamA&A,*
  NotNAT B, OxThe, PIP&P
Wil-Dee, Spence *WhoHol A*
Wilbraham, Edward 1895-1930 *NotNAT B,*
  WhThe
Wilbur, Crane 1889-1973 *Film 1, Film 2,*
  FilmgC, MotPP, TwYS, WhScrn 2, WhThe,
  WhoHol B
Wilbur, Lyon Perry, Jr. 1934- *AmSCAP 1966*
Wilbur, Richard 1921- *BiE&WWA, NotNAT,*
  PIP&P, WhoThe 16
Wilchinski, Martha L 1897- *AmSCAP 1966*
Wilcox, Barbara 1906- *WhThe*
Wilcox, Claire 1955- *IntMPA 1977*
Wilcox, Collin 1935- *BiE&WWA, NotNAT*
Wilcox, Eddie 1907- *AmSCAP 1966*
Wilcox, Frank d1974 *WhoHol B*
Wilcox, Frank 1907-1974 *FilmgC, Vers A,*
  WhScrn 2
Wilcox, Fred McLeod 1905?-1964 *FilmgC*
Wilcox, Fred McLeod 1908-1964 *BiDFlm,*
  WorEnF
Wilcox, Harlow 1900-1960 *WhScrn 2*

Wilcox, Herbert *IntMPA 1977*
Wilcox, Herbert 1890- *TwYS A*
Wilcox, Herbert 1891- *DcFM, FilmgC, MovMk*
Wilcox, Herbert 1892- *OxFilm, WorEnF*
Wilcox, Larry 1935- *AmSCAP 1966*
Wilcox, Mary *WhoHol A*
Wilcox, R Turner 1888- *BiE&WWA*
Wilcox, Robert 1910-1955 *MotPP, NotNAT B,*
  WhScrn 1, WhScrn 2, WhoHol B
Wilcox, Vivian 1912-1945 *WhScrn 1, WhScrn 2*
Wilcox-Horne, Collin *WhoHol A*
Wilcoxon, Henry 1905- *CmMov, FilmgC,*
  IntMPA 1977, MotPP, MovMk, WhThe,
  WhoHol A
Wild, George d1856 *NotNAT B*
Wild, Harry J *WorEnF*
Wild, Jack 1952- *FilmgC, IntMPA 1977,*
  WhoHol A
Wildberg, John J 1902-1959 *NotNAT B, WhThe*
Wilde, Arthur L 1918- *IntMPA 1977*
Wilde, Brian *WhoHol A*
Wilde, Cornel *AmSCAP 1966, MotPP,*
  WhoHol A
Wilde, Cornel 1915- *BiDFlm, CmMov, FilmgC,*
  WorEnF
Wilde, Cornel 1918- *BiE&WWA, IntMPA 1977*
Wilde, Cornell 1915- *MovMk*
Wilde, Hagar 1904-1971 *BiE&WWA, FilmgC*
Wilde, Oscar 1854-1900 *CnMD, McGWD,*
  ModWD, NotNAT A, NotNAT B, OxFilm,
  OxThe, PIP&P, REnWD
Wilde, Oscar 1856-1900 *CnThe, FilmgC*
Wilde, Percival 1887-1953 *NotNAT B*
Wilde, Ted 1889- *TwYS A*
Wildenbruch, Ernst Von 1845-1909 *McGWD,*
  ModWD, NotNAT B, OxThe
Wilder, Alec 1907- *BiE&WWA, NotNAT A,*
  WhoHol A
Wilder, Arthur A 1882- *AmSCAP 1966*
Wilder, Billy 1906- *BiDFlm, CelR 3, CmMov,*
  ConDr 1977A, DcFM, FilmgC,
  IntMPA 1977, MovMk, OxFilm, WorEnF
Wilder, Clinton 1920- *BiE&WWA, NotNAT,*
  WhoThe 16
Wilder, Gene *WhoHol A*
Wilder, Gene 1934- *BiE&WWA, FilmgC,*
  MovMk, NotNAT
Wilder, Gene 1935- *IntMPA 1977*
Wilder, John *WhoHol A*
Wilder, John David *WhoHol A*
Wilder, Marshall P *Film 1*
Wilder, Marshall P 1859- *WhoStg 1906*
Wilder, Marshall P 1860-1915 *WhScrn 2*
Wilder, Patricia Honeychile *WhoHol A*
Wilder, Thornton 1897-1975 *BiE&WWA, CelR 3,*
  CnMD, CnThe, ConDr 1977, CroCD,
  FilmgC, ModWD, NotNAT A, NotNAT B,
  OxThe, PIP&P, REnWD, WhThe, WorEnF
Wilder, W Lee 1904- *FilmgC, IntMPA 1977*
Wildgans, Anton 1881-1932 *CnMD, McGWD,*
  ModWD, OxThe
Wildhack, Robert 1882-1940 *WhScrn 1,*
  WhScrn 2, WhoHol B
Wilding, Michael 1912- *FilmgC, IntMPA 1977,*
  MotPP, MovMk, OxFilm, WhThe,
  WhoHol A
Wiley, John A 1884-1962 *NotNAT B, WhScrn 1,*
  WhScrn 2, WhoHol B
Wiley, Lee *AmSCAP 1966*
Wiley, Richard E *NewYTET*
Wilford, Isabel *WhThe*
Wilhelm, C 1858-1925 *NotNAT B, WhThe*
Wilhelm, Theodore 1909-1971 *WhScrn 1,*
  WhScrn 2, WhoHol B

Wilhite, Monte 1899-1961 *AmSCAP 1966*
Wilhoit, Kenneth H 1923- *AmSCAP 1966*
Wilhoit, Sam T 1924- *AmSCAP 1966*
Wilhousky, Peter J 1902- *AmSCAP 1966*
Wilk, Ted 1908- *IntMPA 1977*
Wilke, Hubert 1855-1940 *Film 2, NotNAT B, WhoHol B*
Wilke, Robert J 1911- *FilmgC, WhoHol A*
Wilkerson, Bill d1966 *WhoHol B*
Wilkerson, Guy 1898-1971 *Vers B, WhScrn 1, WhScrn 2, WhoHol B*
Wilkerson, Herbert 1881-1943 *WhScrn 1, WhScrn 2*
Wilkerson, William 1903-1966 *WhScrn 1, WhScrn 2*
Wilkerson, William R d1962 *NotNAT B*
Wilkes, Thomas Egerton d1854 *NotNAT B*
Wilkey, Violet *Film 1*
Wilkie, Allan 1878-1970 *WhThe*
Wilkins, George *NotNAT B*
Wilkins, John d1853 *NotNAT B*
Wilkins, June d1972 *WhoHol B*
Wilkins, Patricia *NatPD*
Wilkins, Roy 1901- *CelR 3*
Wilkinson, Christopher 1941- *ConDr 1977*
Wilkinson, Dudley 1897- *AmSCAP 1966*
Wilkinson, Henry Spenser 1853-1937 *NotNAT B, WhThe*
Wilkinson, Marc 1929- *WhoThe 16*
Wilkinson, Norman 1882-1934 *NotNAT B, OxThe, WhThe*
Wilkinson, Sam *Film 2*
Wilkinson, Tate 1734-1803 *NotNAT B*
Wilkinson, Tate 1739-1803 *NotNAT A, OxThe*
Wilkinson, Walter *Film 2*
Wilks, Robert 1665-1732 *NotNAT A, NotNAT B, OxThe, PIP&P*
Willa, Suzanne d1951 *NotNAT B*
Willadsen, Gene 1915- *AmSCAP 1966*
Willard, Catherine Livingston d1954 *NotNAT B, WhThe*
Willard, Mrs. Charles *Film 2*
Willard, Edmund 1884-1956 *NotNAT B, OxThe, WhThe, WhoHol B*
Willard, Edward Smith 1853-1915 *NotNAT B, OxThe, WhThe, WhoStg 1906, WhoStg 1908*
Willard, Helen D 1905- *BiE&WWA, NotNAT*
Willard, Jess 1881-1968 *Film 1, WhScrn 2*
Willard, John 1885-1942 *Film 2, NotNAT B, WhThe*
Willard, Leigh *Film 2*
Willat, Irvin 1892- *TwYS A*
Willems, Paul 1912- *CnMD*
Willenz, Max 1888-1954 *WhScrn 1, WhScrn 2, WhoHol B*
Willes, Jean *MotPP, WhoHol A*
Willett, Elmer W 1911- *AmSCAP 1966*
Willey, Leonard 1882-1964 *WhScrn 2*
William, David 1926- *WhoThe 16*
William, Joseph Ranger Bill 1878-1939 *WhScrn 2*
William, Robert d1931 *NotNAT B*
William, Warren d1948 *MotPP, WhoHol B*
William, Warren 1895-1948 *Film 2, FilmgC, NotNAT B, WhScrn 1, WhScrn 2, WhThe*
William, Warren 1896-1948 *MovMk*
Williams, A B d1964 *NotNAT B*
Williams, Adam 1929- *FilmgC, WhoHol A*
Williams, Albert *Film 2*
Williams, Alfonso *WhoHol A*
Williams, Andy 1928- *CelR 3, WhoHol A*
Williams, Ann 1935- *BiE&WWA, NotNAT*
Williams, Annabelle 1904-1967 *WhScrn 2*
Williams, Arnold *WhoHol A*

Williams, Arthur 1844-1915 *NotNAT B, WhThe*
Williams, Mrs. Barney d1911 *NotNAT B*
Williams, Barney 1823-1876 *FamA&A, OxThe*
Williams, Barney 1824-1876 *NotNAT B*
Williams, Barry 1954- *WhoHol A*
Williams, Beresford 1904-1966 *WhScrn 1, WhScrn 2*
Williams, Bert d1922 *Film 1, WhoHol B*
Williams, Bert 1874-1922 *EncMT*
Williams, Bert 1876-1922 *FamA&A, NotNAT A, NotNAT B*
Williams, Bert 1877-1922 *WhScrn 1, WhScrn 2*
Williams, Bert 1922- *IntMPA 1977, WhoHol A*
Williams, Bill 1916- *FilmgC, IntMPA 1977, MotPP, WhoHol A*
Williams, Bill 1921-1964 *WhScrn 1, WhScrn 2*
Williams, Billy *FilmgC*
Williams, Billy 1910-1972 *WhScrn 2*
Williams, Billy Dee 1937- *BiE&WWA, IntMPA 1977, WhoHol A, WhoThe 16*
Williams, Bob 1913- *IntMPA 1977*
Williams, Bransby 1870-1961 *NotNAT A, NotNAT B, OxThe, WhScrn 1, WhScrn 2, WhThe, WhoHol B*
Williams, Bransby 1870-1964 *Film 2, FilmgC*
Williams, Bransby *see also* Williams, Eric Bransby
Williams, Brook *WhoHol A*
Williams, Campbell 1906- *WhThe*
Williams, Cara 1925- *FilmgC, IntMPA 1977, MotPP, WhoHol A*
Williams, Carl W 1949- *IntMPA 1977*
Williams, Charles 1886-1945 *ModWD*
Williams, Charles 1898-1958 *IntMPA 1977, Vers B, WhScrn 1, WhScrn 2, WhoHol B*
Williams, Charles Melvin 1908- *AmSCAP 1966*
Williams, Cindy 1948- *IntMPA 1977, MovMk, WhoHol A*
Williams, Clara 1891-1928 *Film 1, WhScrn 1, WhScrn 2, WhoHol B*
Williams, Clarence 1893-1965 *AmSCAP 1966*
Williams, Clarence, III 1939- *NotNAT, WhoHol A, WhoThe 16*
Williams, Clifford 1926- *WhoThe 16*
Williams, Cora 1871-1927 *Film 1, Film 2, WhScrn 1, WhScrn 2, WhoHol B*
Williams, Craig 1877-1941 *WhScrn 1, WhScrn 2*
Williams, Curt *WhoHol A*
Williams, David H 1919- *AmSCAP 1966*
Williams, David McK 1887- *AmSCAP 1966*
Williams, Derek 1910- *WhThe*
Williams, Derick 1906- *IntMPA 1977*
Williams, Dick d1962 *NotNAT B*
Williams, Dick Anthony 1938- *WhoHol A, WhoThe 16*
Williams, Donnie *WhoHol A*
Williams, Douglas d1968 *WhScrn 2*
Williams, Earle d1927 *MotPP, WhoHol B*
Williams, Earle 1880-1927 *Film 1, Film 2, NotNAT B, TwYS*
Williams, Earle 1895-1927 *WhScrn 1, WhScrn 2*
Williams, Edward Bennett 1920- *CelR 3*
Williams, Edy *WhoHol A*
Williams, Egbert Austin 1876?-1922 *OxThe*
Williams, Elaine *WhoHol A*
Williams, Elmo 1913- *FilmgC, IntMPA 1977, WorEnF*
Williams, Emlyn 1905- *BiE&WWA, CnMD, CnThe, ConDr 1977, CroCD, FamA&A, FilmgC, McGWD, ModWD, MotPP, MovMk, NotNAT, NotNAT A, OxThe, PIP&P, WhoHol A, WhoThe 16, WorEnF*
Williams, Emlyn *see also* Williams, George Emlyn
Williams, Eric Bransby *Film 2*
Williams, Eric Bransby *see also* Williams, Bransby

Williams, Esther *MotPP*
Williams, Esther 1921- *CmMov, MGM*
Williams, Esther 1923- *BiDFlm, FilmgC,*
IntMPA 1977, MovMk, OxFilm, WhoHol A,
WorEnF
Williams, Evelyn M d1959 *NotNAT B*
Williams, Florence 1912- *WhThe*
Williams, Frances 1903-1959 *AmSCAP 1966,*
EncMT, NotNAT B, WhThe, WhoHol A,
WhoHol B
Williams, Fred *WhoHol A*
Williams, Fred J 1875-1942 *WhScrn 1, WhScrn 2,*
WhoHol B
Williams, Fritz 1865-1930 *NotNAT B, WhThe,*
WhoStg 1906
Williams, G A *Film 1*
Williams, Gene *WhoHol A*
Williams, George 1854-1936 *WhScrn 1,*
WhScrn 2, WhoHol B
Williams, George B 1866-1931 *Film 2, WhScrn 1,*
WhScrn 2, WhoHol B
Williams, George Emlyn 1905- *IntMPA 1977*
Williams, George Emlyn *see also* Williams, Emlyn
Williams, Gloria *WhoHol A*
Williams, Grant 1930- *FilmgC, IntMPA 1977,*
MovMk, WhoHol A
Williams, Guinn d1962 *NotNAT B*
Williams, Guinn 1899-1962 *Vers A*
Williams, Guinn 1907-1962 *Film 1*
Williams, Guinn Big Boy d1962 *MotPP,*
WhoHol B
Williams, Guinn Big Boy 1899-1962 *TwYS,*
WhScrn 1, WhScrn 2
Williams, Guinn Big Boy 1900-1962 *FilmgC,*
MovMk
Williams, Guinn Big Boy 1907-1962 *Film 2*
Williams, Gus 1847-1915 *NotNAT B,*
WhoStg 1906
Williams, Guy 1924- *FilmgC, WhoHol A*
Williams, Gwen *Film 2*
Williams, Gwen d1962 *NotNAT B*
Williams, Hank 1924-1953 *WhScrn 1, WhScrn 2,*
WhoHol B
Williams, Hank, Jr. *WhoHol A*
Williams, Harcourt 1880-1957 *FilmgC,*
NotNAT B, OxThe, PIP&P, WhScrn 1,
WhScrn 2, WhThe, WhoHol B
Williams, Harry 1879-1922 *AmSCAP 1966*
Williams, Hattie d1942 *NotNAT B, WhThe,*
WhoStg 1906
Williams, Heathcote 1941- *ConDr 1977*
Williams, Herb 1874-1936 *NotNAT B, WhScrn 1,*
WhScrn 2, WhoHol B
Williams, Herschel 1909- *BiE&WWA, NotNAT*
Williams, Hope 1901- *WhThe, WhoHol A*
Williams, Howard *WhoHol A*
Williams, Hugh 1904-1969 *FilmgC, McGWD,*
MovMk, NotNAT B, PIP&P, WhScrn 1,
WhScrn 2, WhThe, WhoHol B
Williams, Ina d1962 *NotNAT B*
Williams, Irene d1970 *WhoHol B*
Williams, Jack *WhoHol A*
Williams, Jason *WhoHol A*
Williams, Jean L *WomWMM A, WomWMM B*
Williams, Jean Sterling Mackinlay 1882-1958
OxThe
Williams, Jeff *WhoHol A*
Williams, Jeffrey 1860-1938 *Film 2, WhScrn 1,*
WhScrn 2, WhoHol B
Williams, Jesse Lynch 1871-1929 *CnMD,*
McGWD, ModWD, NotNAT B, WhThe
Williams, Jimmy *WhoHol A*
Williams, Joe *WhoHol A*
Williams, John d1818 *NotNAT B*

Williams, John 1903- *BiE&WWA, FilmgC,*
NotNAT, WhoHol A, WhoThe 16
Williams, John D d1941 *NotNAT B, WhThe*
Williams, John J 1856-1918 *WhScrn 2*
Williams, Jonathan *WhoHol A*
Williams, Joyce *WhoHol A*
Williams, Julia 1879-1936 *WhScrn 1, WhScrn 2,*
WhoHol B
Williams, June Vanleer *NatPD*
Williams, Kate *WhoHol A*
Williams, Katherine *WhoHol A*
Williams, Kathlyn d1960 *MotPP, NotNAT B,*
WhoHol B
Williams, Kathlyn 1872?-1960 *WhScrn 1,*
WhScrn 2
Williams, Kathlyn 1888-1960 *Film 1, Film 2,*
TwYS
Williams, Kay *WhoHol A*
Williams, Kenneth 1926- *FilmgC, WhoHol A,*
WhoThe 16
Williams, Kenny *WhoHol A*
Williams, Kid *Film 2*
Williams, Larry *WhoHol A*
Williams, Larry 1890-1956 *WhoHol B*
Williams, Lawrence 1890-1956 *WhScrn 1,*
WhScrn 2
Williams, LeRoy A d1962 *NotNAT B*
Williams, Lottie *Film 2*
Williams, Lucille *Film 2*
Williams, Mack 1907-1965 *WhScrn 1, WhScrn 2,*
WhoHol B
Williams, Malcolm 1870-1937 *Film 2,*
NotNAT B, WhScrn 1, WhScrn 2,
WhoHol B
Williams, Margaret *PIP&P*
Williams, Marie 1921-1967 *Film 2, WhScrn 1,*
WhScrn 2, WhoHol B
Williams, Marjorie Rose 1913-1933 *WhScrn 1,*
WhScrn 2
Williams, Mary Lou 1910- *AmSCAP 1966*
Williams, Matt 1929- *AmSCAP 1966*
Williams, Michael 1935- *WhoThe 16*
Williams, Molly d1967 *WhScrn 1, WhScrn 2,*
WhoHol B
Williams, Montague d1892 *NotNAT B*
Williams, Muriel *IntMPA 1977*
Williams, Ned 1927- *AmSCAP 1966*
Williams, O T Chalky d1976 *WhoHol C*
Williams, Palmer *NewYTET*
Williams, Patrick M 1939- *AmSCAP 1966*
Williams, Paul *IntMPA 1977, WhoHol A*
Williams, Percy *Film 2*
Williams, Percy G 1857-1923 *NotNAT B*
Williams, Rhys 1892-1969 *WhScrn 1, WhScrn 2,*
WhoHol B
Williams, Rhys 1897-1969 *FilmgC, MovMk,*
NotNAT B, Vers A, WhThe
Williams, Richard 1933- *DcFM, IntMPA 1977,*
OxFilm, WorEnF
Williams, Robert *IntMPA 1977*
Williams, Robert d1931 *NotNAT B, WhoHol B*
Williams, Robert 1898?-1932 *FilmgC*
Williams, Robert 1899-1931 *WhScrn 1,*
WhScrn 2
Williams, Robert B *WhoHol A*
Williams, Robert N *BiE&WWA, NotNAT*
Williams, Robert X, Jr. 1900- *IntMPA 1977*
Williams, Roger *AmSCAP 1966, IntMPA 1977,*
WhoHol A
Williams, Sam 1884-1961 *AmSCAP 1966*
Williams, Sammy 1948- *NotNAT*
Williams, Scott T *WhScrn 1, WhScrn 2*
Williams, Simon *WhoHol A*
Williams, Sonia 1926- *WhThe*

Williams, Spencer 1889-1965 *AmSCAP 1966*
Williams, Spencer 1893-1969 *WhScrn 1,*
WhScrn 2, WhoHol B
Williams, Stephen 1900-1957 *NotNAT B, WhThe*
Williams, Ted *Film 2*
Williams, Ted 1918- *CelR 3, WhoHol A*
Williams, Tennessee 1911- *BiE&WWA, CelR 3,*
CnThe, ConDr 1977, CroCD, McGWD,
ModWD, NatPD, NotNAT, REnWD,
WhoThe 16
Williams, Tennessee 1914- *AmSCAP 1966,*
CnMD, FilmgC, IntMPA 1977, NotNAT A,
OxFilm, OxThe, PIP&P, WorEnF
Williams, Thad *WhoHol A*
Williams, Thomas J d1874 *NotNAT B*
Williams, Tiger *WhoHol A*
Williams, Van *WhoHol A*
Williams, Walter 1887-1940 *NotNAT B, WhThe*
Williams, William A 1870-1942 *WhScrn 1,*
WhScrn 2, WhoHol B
Williams, William A 1893- *BiE&WWA*
Williams, William Carlos 1883-1963 *CnMD,*
ModWD, PIP&P
Williams, Zack *Film 2*
Williamson, Alastair *WhoHol A*
Williamson, Bruce *AmSCAP 1966*
Williamson, David 1942- *ConDr 1977,*
WhoThe 16
Williamson, Fred 1938- *IntMPA 1977, MovMk,*
WhoHol A
Williamson, Hugh Ross 1901- *BiE&WWA,*
NotNAT, WhThe
Williamson, James A 1855-1933 *DcFM, FilmgC,*
OxFilm
Williamson, James Cassius 1845-1913 *NotNAT A,*
NotNAT B, WhThe
Williamson, Lambert 1907- *FilmgC*
Williamson, Melvin E 1900-1959 *WhScrn 1,*
WhScrn 2
Williamson, Nicol *PIP&P, WhoHol A*
Williamson, Nicol 1938- *CelR 3, CnThe,*
NotNAT, WhoThe 16
Williamson, Nicol 1939- *FilmgC*
Williamson, Nicol 1940- *MovMk*
Williamson, Patrick 1929- *IntMPA 1977*
Williamson, Robert 1885-1949 *Film 2, WhScrn 2*
Williamson, Robin E 1889-1935 *WhScrn 2*
Willians, Ann *Film 2*
Willing, James d1915 *NotNAT B*
Willingham, Calder 1922- *BiE&WWA, CnMD,*
NotNAT
Willingham, Harry G 1881-1943 *WhScrn 1,*
WhScrn 2, WhoHol B
Willingham, Noble *WhoHol A*
Willis, Austin *WhoHol A*
Willis, Dave 1895-1973 *WhScrn 2*
Willis, Gordon *FilmgC, IntMPA 1977*
Willis, Mrs. Herbert *Film 2*
Willis, Hubert *Film 2*
Willis, Jerome *WhoHol A*
Willis, John 1916- *NotNAT*
Willis, Leo *Film 2*
Willis, Louise 1880-1929 *WhScrn 1, WhScrn 2*
Willis, Matt *Vers B*
Willis, Nat *Film 1*
Willis, Nathaniel Parker 1806-1867 *McGWD,*
NotNAT B, OxThe
Willis, Norman 1903- *Vers B*
Willis, Paul *Film 1, Film 2*
Willis, Susan *WhoHol A*
Willis, Ted 1918- *ConDr 1977, IntMPA 1977,*
WhoThe 16
Willman, Noel 1918- *BiE&WWA, FilmgC,*
NotNAT, WhoHol A, WhoThe 16

Willmer, Catherine *WhoHol A*
Willner, A M d1929 *NotNAT B*
Willock, Dave 1909- *FilmgC, Vers A,*
WhoHol A
Willoughby, George W *IntMPA 1977*
Willoughby, Hugh 1891- *WhThe*
Wills, Beverly 1934-1963 *NotNAT B, WhScrn 1,*
WhScrn 2, WhoHol B
Wills, Bob 1905-1975 *WhScrn 2, WhoHol C*
Wills, Brember d1948 *NotNAT B, WhThe,*
WhoHol B
Wills, Chill 1903- *FilmgC, IntMPA 1977,*
MotPP, MovMk, Vers A, WhoHol A
Wills, Drusilla 1884-1951 *NotNAT B, WhScrn 1,*
WhScrn 2, WhThe, WhoHol B
Wills, Sir John Spencer 1904- *IntMPA 1977*
Wills, Lou d1968 *WhoHol B*
Wills, Maury *WhoHol A*
Wills, Nat 1873-1917 *NotNAT B, WhScrn 2,*
WhoHol B
Wills, Norma *Film 2*
Wills, Tommy d1962 *NotNAT B*
Wills, W G 1828-1891 *NotNAT A, NotNAT B*
Wills, Walter 1881-1967 *WhScrn 1, WhScrn 2,*
WhoHol B
Willson, Meredith 1902- *AmSCAP 1966,*
BiE&WWA, ConDr 1977D, EncMT,
NewMT, NotNAT, NotNAT A
Willson, Osmund 1896- *WhThe*
Willson, Rini *WhScrn 1, WhScrn 2*
Willy 1859-1931 *NotNAT B*
Willy, M 1859-1931 *WhThe*
Wilmer, Douglas 1920- *FilmgC, WhoHol A,*
WhoThe 16.
Wilmer-Brown, Maisie 1893-1973 *WhScrn 2,*
WhoHol B
Wilmeth, Don B 1939- *NotNAT*
Wilmot, Charles d1896 *NotNAT B*
Wilmot, Lee 1899-1938 *WhScrn 1, WhScrn 2*
Wilmot, Robert *NotNAT B*
Wilmott, Charles d1955 *NotNAT B*
Wilse, Lulee *Film 2*
Wilsey, Jay d1961 *Film 2, WhoHol B*
Wilshin, Sunday 1905- *WhThe*
Wilson, Al d1932 *WhScrn 2*
Wilson, Al 1906-1951 *AmSCAP 1966*
Wilson, Alan C 1943-1970 *WhScrn 2*
Wilson, Albert Edward 1885-1960 *NotNAT A,*
NotNAT B, WhThe
Wilson, Alex *WhoHol A*
Wilson, Alice *Film 1, Film 2*
Wilson, Anne M *Film 2*
Wilson, Arthur d1652 *NotNAT B*
Wilson, Baron *WhoHol A*
Wilson, Beatrice d1943 *NotNAT B, WhThe*
Wilson, Ben *TwYS A*
Wilson, Ben 1876-1930 *WhoHol B*
Wilson, Ben 1885- *Film 1, Film 2, TwYS*
Wilson, Benjamin F 1876-1930 *WhScrn 1,*
WhScrn 2
Wilson, Bruce *WhoHol A*
Wilson, Mrs. C Baron d1846 *NotNAT B*
Wilson, Cal *WhoHol A*
Wilson, Cecil Frank Petch 1909- *WhThe*
Wilson, Charles d1909 *NotNAT B*
Wilson, Charles d1948 *Film 2, WhoHol B*
Wilson, Charles 1895-1948 *Vers B*
Wilson, Charles Cahill 1894-1948 *WhScrn 2*
Wilson, Chris *WhoHol A*
Wilson, Christopher d1919 *NotNAT B*
Wilson, Clarence H 1877-1941 *Film 2, WhScrn 1,*
WhScrn 2, WhoHol B
Wilson, Claude *WhoHol A*
Wilson, Cronin *Film 2*

Wilson, Cynthia *WhoHol A*
Wilson, Dana *WhoHol A*
Wilson, Demond *WhoHol A*
Wilson, Dennis *WhoHol A*
Wilson, Diana 1897-1937 *NotNAT B, WhThe*
Wilson, Dick *WhoHol A*
Wilson, Don *WhoHol A*
Wilson, Don 1896- *AmSCAP 1966*
Wilson, Dooley 1894-1953 *FilmgC, HolP 40, WhScrn 1, WhScrn 2, WhoHol B*
Wilson, Dorothy 1909- *ThFT, WhoHol A*
Wilson, Earl 1907- *AmSCAP 1966, CelR 3, WhoHol A*
Wilson, Earl L 1942- *AmSCAP 1966*
Wilson, Ed 1916-1975 *Film 2, WhScrn 2*
Wilson, Edith *WhThe*
Wilson, Edmund 1895-1972 *BiE&WWA, CnMD, ModWD, NotNAT A*
Wilson, Edna 1880-1960 *WhScrn 1, WhScrn 2, WhoHol B*
Wilson, Edna May *Film 1*
Wilson, Edward R 1909- *AmSCAP 1966*
Wilson, Eleanor *WhoHol A*
Wilson, Elizabeth *WhoHol A*
Wilson, Elizabeth 1921- *NotNAT*
Wilson, Elizabeth 1925- *WhoThe 16*
Wilson, Elsie Jane *Film 1, WomWMM*
Wilson, F Vaux *Film 2*
Wilson, Flip 1933- *CelR 3, IntMPA 1977, WhoHol A*
Wilson, Francis 1854-1935 *NotNAT A, NotNAT B, OxThe, WhScrn 1, WhScrn 2, WhThe, WhoHol B, WhoStg 1906*
Wilson, Frank 1891-1956 *WhThe*
Wilson, Frank H 1886-1956 *NotNAT B, WhScrn 1, WhScrn 2, WhoHol B*
Wilson, Gene A 1920- *BiE&WWA, NotNAT*
Wilson, George 1854-1954 *WhScrn 1, WhScrn 2, WhoHol B*
Wilson, George W 1849-1931 *NotNAT B*
Wilson, George W 1856- *WhoStg 1906*
Wilson, Georgia *Film 1*
Wilson, Grace 1903- *WhThe*
Wilson, Hal 1887-1933 *Film 2, WhScrn 1, WhScrn 2, WhoHol B*
Wilson, Harry Leon 1867-1939 *FilmgC, ModWD, NotNAT B, PIP&P, WhThe*
Wilson, Harry Robert 1901- *AmSCAP 1966*
Wilson, Henry *Film 2*
Wilson, Ian *WhoHol A*
Wilson, Ilona *WhoHol A*
Wilson, Imogene Bubbles *WhScrn 1, WhScrn 2*
Wilson, Ira B 1880-1950 *AmSCAP 1966*
Wilson, Irv *NewYTET*
Wilson, Irving M 1881-1937 *AmSCAP 1966*
Wilson, Jack *Film 1*
Wilson, Jack 1917-1966 *WhScrn 1, WhScrn 2, WhoHol B*
Wilson, Janice *Film 2*
Wilson, Jeanna *WhoHol A*
Wilson, John d1696 *NotNAT B*
Wilson, John 1585-1641? *OxThe*
Wilson, John C 1899-1961 *EncMT, NotNAT B, WhThe*
Wilson, John Dover 1881-1969 *BiE&WWA, NotNAT B*
Wilson, John N 1909- *AmSCAP 1966*
Wilson, John S 1913- *BiE&WWA, NotNAT*
Wilson, John W 1910- *IntMPA 1977*
Wilson, Joseph 1858-1940 *NotNAT B, WhThe*
Wilson, Joseph Maria 1872-1933 *NotNAT B*
Wilson, Judy *WhoHol A*
Wilson, Julie *WhoHol A*
Wilson, Katherine 1904- *Film 2, WhThe*

Wilson, Kemmons 1913- *CelR 3*
Wilson, Lanford 1937- *ConDr 1977, NatPD, NotNAT, WhoThe 16*
Wilson, Lois *MotPP*
Wilson, Lois 1896- *Film 1, Film 2, MovMk, ThFT, TwYS, WhoHol A*
Wilson, Lois 1898- *BiE&WWA, NotNAT*
Wilson, Lola *Film 2*
Wilson, M K 1890-1933 *WhScrn 1, WhScrn 2, WhoHol B*
Wilson, Mabel Elizabeth 1890- *AmSCAP 1966*
Wilson, Margery *Film 1, Film 2, MotPP, TwYS, WomWMM*
Wilson, Marie 1916-1972 *FilmgC, MotPP, MovMk, ThFT, WhScrn 2, WhoHol B*
Wilson, Michael 1914- *DcFM, FilmgC, IntMPA 1977, WorEnF*
Wilson, Michelle *WhoHol A*
Wilson, Millard K *Film 1*
Wilson, Mortimer 1876-1932 *AmSCAP 1966*
Wilson, Nancy 1937- *CelR 3*
Wilson, Neil *WhoHol A*
Wilson, Norman *IntMPA 1977*
Wilson, Perry 1916- *WhThe*
Wilson, Ray d1963 *NotNAT B*
Wilson, Richard 1915- *FilmgC, IntMPA 1977, WorEnF*
Wilson, Robert *ConDr 1977E*
Wilson, Robert d1600? *OxThe, PIP&P*
Wilson, Robert d1610 *NotNAT B*
Wilson, Robert 1550-1600 *NotNAT B*
Wilson, Robert M 1944- *ConDr 1977, NotNAT*
Wilson, Roberta 1904-1972 *WhScrn 2*
Wilson, Roger C 1912- *AmSCAP 1966*
Wilson, Sandy 1924- *BiE&WWA, ConDr 1977D, EncMT, NotNAT, NotNAT A, WhoThe 16*
Wilson, Sarah *WhoHol A*
Wilson, Scott 1942- *FilmgC, IntMPA 1977, WhoHol A*
Wilson, Snoo 1948- *ConDr 1977, WhoThe 16*
Wilson, Sue *WhoHol A*
Wilson, Terry *WhoHol A*
Wilson, Theodore *WhoHol A*
Wilson, Theodore 1912- *AmSCAP 1966*
Wilson, Tom 1880-1965 *Film 1, Film 2, TwYS*
Wilson, Toni *Film 2*
Wilson, W Cronin d1934 *NotNAT B, WhThe*
Wilson, Walter M d1926 *NotNAT B*
Wilson, Ward 1904-1966 *WhScrn 1, WhScrn 2*
Wilson, Warren 1909- *IntMPA 1977*
Wilson, Wayne 1899-1970 *WhScrn 1, WhScrn 2*
Wilson, Wendell C 1889-1927 *WhScrn 1, WhScrn 2*
Wilson, Whip 1915-1964 *FilmgC, WhScrn 1, WhScrn 2, WhoHol B*
Wilson, William d1972 *WhScrn 2*
Wilson, William F 1894-1956 *WhScrn 1, WhScrn 2, WhoHol B*
Wilson, William J d1936 *NotNAT B, WhThe*
Wilstach, Frank Jenners 1865-1933 *NotNAT B*
Wilstach, Paul 1870-1952 *NotNAT B, WhThe*
Wilton, Ann *WhoHol A*
Wilton, Augusta d1926 *NotNAT B*
Wilton, Eric 1883-1957 *WhScrn 2*
Wilton, Marie 1839-1921 *OxThe, PIP&P*
Wilton, Robb d1957 *NotNAT B, WhoHol B*
Wilton, Terence *WhoHol A*
Wiltsie, Simeon S 1853-1918 *WhScrn 2*
Wiman, Anna Deere 1924-1963 *NotNAT B, WhThe*
Wiman, Dwight Deere 1894-1951 *Film 2*
Wiman, Dwight Deere 1895-1951 *EncMT, NotNAT B, WhThe*
Wimperis, Arthur 1874-1953 *FilmgC,*

Winton, Bruce *Film 2*
Winton, Jane 1905-1959 *Film 2, MotPP, TwYS,
  WhScrn 1, WhScrn 2, WhoHol B*   •
Winwood, Estelle 1883- *BiE&WWA, FamA&A,
  FilmgC, MovMk, NotNAT, Vers A, WhThe,
  WhoHol A*
Wirges, William F 1894- *AmSCAP 1966*
Wirta, Nikolai 1906- *CnMD*
Wirth, Carl Anton 1912- *AmSCAP 1966*
Wisbar, Frank 1899-1967 *WorEnF*
Wisberg, Aubrey 1909- *FilmgC, IntMPA 1977,
  NatPD*
Wisdom, Norman *IntMPA 1977, WhoHol A*
Wisdom, Norman 1918- *FilmgC*
Wisdom, Norman 1920- *EncMT, NotNAT,
  WhoThe 16*
Wise, Ernie *FilmgC*
Wise, Fred 1915-1966 *AmSCAP 1966*
Wise, Herbert 1924- *WhoThe 16*
Wise, Jack 1893-1954 *Film 2, WhScrn 1,
  WhScrn 2, WhoHol B*
Wise, Robert 1914- *BiDFlm, CmMov, DcFM,
  FilmgC, IntMPA 1977, MovMk, OxFilm,
  WorEnF*
Wise, Thomas A 1865-1928 *NotNAT B, WhThe*
Wise, Tom 1865-1928 *Film 2, WhScrn 1,
  WhScrn 2, WhoHol B*
Wiseman, Frederic *OxFilm*
Wiseman, Frederick *NewYTET*
Wiseman, Joseph *IntMPA 1977, MotPP,
  WhoHol A*
Wiseman, Joseph 1918- *BiE&WWA, NotNAT,
  WhoThe 16*
Wiseman, Joseph 1919- *FilmgC, Vers A*
Wishengrad, Morton 1913-1963 *McGWD,
  NotNAT B*
Wismer, Harry 1911-1967 *WhScrn 2, WhoHol B*
Wisner, James J 1931- *AmSCAP 1966*
Witcover, Walt 1924- *BiE&WWA, NotNAT*
Withee, Mable d1952 *NotNAT B*
Withers, Charles 1889-1947 *NotNAT B,
  WhScrn 2, WhoHol B*
Withers, Googie 1917- *FilmgC, IntMPA 1977,
  MovMk, OxFilm, WhoHol A, WhoThe 16*
Withers, Grant 1904-1959 *Film 2, FilmgC,
  MovMk, NotNAT B, TwYS, Vers A,
  WhScrn 1, WhScrn 2, WhoHol B*
Withers, Isabel 1896-1968 *WhScrn 2*
Withers, Iva 1917- *BiE&WWA, NotNAT,
  WhoThe 16*
Withers, Jane 1926- *FilmgC, HolP 30,
  IntMPA 1977, MotPP, MovMk, ThFT,
  WhoHol A*
Witherspoon, Cora 1890-1957 *FilmgC, MovMk,
  NotNAT B, ThFT, Vers A, WhScrn 1,
  WhScrn 2, WhThe, WhoHol B*
Witherspoon, Herbert 1873-1935 *NotNAT B*
Withey, Chester 1887- *TwYS A*
Witkiewicz, Stanislaw Ignacy 1885-1939 *CnMD,
  CnThe, CroCD, McGWD, ModWD,
  REnWD*
Witkowski, Leo 1908- *AmSCAP 1966*
Witlock, Lloyd *Film 2*
Witney, Michael *WhoHol A*
Witney, William 1910?- *FilmgC*
Witt, Ilanga *WomWMM B*
Witt, Kathy *WhoHol A*
Witt, Paul Junger *NewYTET*
Witt, Peter 1911- *BiE&WWA*
Witt, Wastl 1890-1955 *WhScrn 1, WhScrn 2*
Wittenberg, Philip 1895- *BiE&WWA*
Witting, Arthur Eugene 1868-1941 *WhScrn 2*
Witting, Chris J *NewYTET*
Wittlinger, Karl 1922- *CnMD, CroCD, McGWD,*

ModWD
Wittop, Freddy 1921- *BiE&WWA, NotNAT,
  WhoThe 16*
Wittstein, Ed 1929- *BiE&WWA, NotNAT,
  WhoThe 16*
Witwer, H C *Film 2*
Wix, Florence E 1883-1956 *Film 2, WhScrn 1,
  WhScrn 2, WhoHol B*
Wixted, Michael-James 1961- *WhoHol A*
Wizeman, Donald G, Jr. 1944- *IntMPA 1977*
Wodehouse, P G 1881-1975 *BiE&WWA, CelR 3,
  ConDr 1973, EncMT, McGWD, NewMT,
  PIP&P*
Wodehouse, Pelham Granville 1881-1975 *WhThe*
Wodehouse, Pelham Grenville 1881-1975
  AmSCAP 1966, NotNAT A
Woegerer, Otto 1907-1966 *WhScrn 1, WhScrn 2,
  WhoHol B*
Woffington, Margaret 1720?-1760 *NotNAT A,
  NotNAT B*
Woffington, Peg 1714?-1760 *CnThe, OxThe,
  PIP&P*
Wohl, Jack 1934- *AmSCAP 1966*
Wohl, Stanislaw *WomWMM*
Woizikovsky, Leon 1897- *WhThe*
Wojzik, Anna *Film 2*
Wolbert, Burton *Film 2*
Wolbert, Clarence *Film 2*
Wolbert, Dorothea 1874-1958 *WhScrn 1,
  WhScrn 2, WhoHol B*
Wolbert, Dorothy *Film 2*
Wolbert, William 1884-1918 *TwYS A, WhScrn 2*
Wolcott, Charles Frederick 1906- *AmSCAP 1966*
Wolcott, James L *IntMPA 1977*
Wold, David 1890-1953 *WhScrn 1, WhScrn 2*
Wolders, Robert *WhoHol A*
Wolf II d1932 *WhScrn 2*
Wolf, Daniel 1894-1962 *AmSCAP 1966*
Wolf, Emanuel L 1927- *IntMPA 1977*
Wolf, Fred H 1897- *AmSCAP 1966*
Wolf, Friedrich 1888-1953 *CnMD, CroCD,
  DcFM, McGWD, ModWD*
Wolf, Friedrich *see also* Wolff, Friedrich
Wolf, Herbert 1917- *IntMPA 1977*
Wolf, Jack 1912- *AmSCAP 1966*
Wolf, Jay 1929- *BiE&WWA, NotNAT*
Wolf, Konrad 1925- *DcFM*
Wolf, Lawrence *WhoHol A*
Wolf, Olga *AmSCAP 1966*
Wolf, Rennold 1872-1922 *NotNAT B, WhThe*
Wolf, Thomas Howard 1916- *IntMPA 1977*
Wolf, Thomas J, Jr. 1925- *AmSCAP 1966*
Wolf-Ferrari, Ermanno 1876-1948 *NotNAT B*
Wolfe, Bud d1960 *WhScrn 2*
Wolfe, Clarence d1963 *NotNAT B*
Wolfe, David *WhoHol A*
Wolfe, Fanny *WomWMM*
Wolfe, Harry *Film 2*
Wolfe, Humbert 1886-1940 *NotNAT B*
Wolfe, Ian 1896- *FilmgC, Vers A, WhoHol A*
Wolfe, Jacques 1896- *AmSCAP 1966*
Wolfe, James D *NewYTET*
Wolfe, Jane *Film 1, Film 2*
Wolfe, Joel *WhoHol A*
Wolfe, Maurice 1887- *AmSCAP 1966*
Wolfe, Stanley 1924- *AmSCAP 1966*
Wolfe, Thomas 1900-1938 *AmSCAP 1966,
  CnMD, ModWD, PIP&P*
Wolfe, Tom 1931- *CelR 3*
Wolff, David *DcFM*
Wolff, Frank 1928-1971 *WhScrn 1, WhScrn 2,
  WhoHol B*
Wolff, Friedrich 1888-1953 *OxFilm*
Wolff, Friedrich *see also* Wolf, Friedrich

Wolff, Jan *Film 2*
Wolff, Lothar 1909- *FilmgC, IntMPA 1977*
Wolff, Perry *NewYTET*
Wolff, Pierre 1863-1944 *WhThe*
Wolff, Pierre 1865-1944 *McGWD*
Wolff, Ruth *NatPD, WomWMM*
Wolff, William 1858-1936 *NotNAT B*
Wolff, William 1861- *WhoStg 1906*
Wolfington, Iggie 1920- *BiE&WWA, NotNAT, WhoHol A*
Wolfit, Sir Donald 1902-1968 *CnThe, FilmgC, MotPP, MovMk, NotNAT A, NotNAT B, OxFilm, OxThe, WhScrn 1, WhScrn 2, WhThe, WhoHol B, WorEnF*
Wolfman, Jack *WhoHol A*
Wolfson, Billy 1898-1973 *WhScrn 2*
Wolfson, Martin 1904-1973 *BiE&WWA, NotNAT B, WhoHol B*
Wolfson, Mitchell 1900- *IntMPA 1977*
Wolfson, Richard 1923- *IntMPA 1977*
Wolfson, Victor 1910- *BiE&WWA, NotNAT*
Wolheim, Dan *Film 2*
Wolheim, Louis 1880-1931 *Film 1, Film 2, FilmgC, MotPP, MovMk, TwYS, WhScrn 1, WhScrn 2, WhoHol B*
Wolheim, Louis Robert 1881-1931 *NotNAT B, OxThe*
Wollheim, Eric 1879-1948 *NotNAT B, WhThe*
Woloshin, Alex *Film 2*
Wolpe, Stefan 1902- *AmSCAP 1966*
Wolper, David L 1928- *FilmgC, IntMPA 1977, NewYTET*
Wolseley-Cox, Garnet d1904 *NotNAT B*
Wolsk, Eugene V 1928- *WhoThe 16*
Wolston, Henry 1877- *WhThe*
Wolveridge, Carol 1940- *WhThe*
Wolzogen, Ernst Von d1934 *NotNAT B*
Womer, Hilda *Film 2*
Wonderly, Frank *Film 2*
Wong, Anna May 1902-1961 *MovMk*
Wong, Anna May 1907-1960 *Film 1, Film 2*
Wong, Anna May 1907-1961 *FilmgC, HolP 30, MotPP, NotNAT B, ThFT, TwYS, WhScrn 1, WhScrn 2, WhThe, WhoHol B*
Wong, Arthur *WhoHol A*
Wong, Bruce 1906-1953 *WhScrn 1, WhScrn 2, WhoHol B*
Wong, Chris *WhoHol A*
Wong, Jadine *WhoHol A*
Wong, Linda *WhoHol A*
Wong, Mary 1915-1940 *WhScrn 2*
Wong, W Beal 1906-1962 *WhScrn 2*
Wontner, Arthur 1875-1960 *CmMov, Film 1, Film 2, FilmgC, NotNAT B, WhScrn 1, WhScrn 2, WhThe, WhoHol B*
Wood, Allan 1892-1947 *WhScrn 2*
Wood, Arthur 1875-1953 *NotNAT B, WhThe*
Wood, Arthur Augustus d1907 *NotNAT B*
Wood, Audrey 1905- *BiE&WWA, NotNAT*
Wood, Britt 1885-1965 *WhScrn 1, WhScrn 2*
Wood, Britt 1895-1965 *Vers A, WhoHol B*
Wood, Carl Buddy 1905-1948 *WhScrn 1, WhScrn 2*
Wood, Charles 1931?- *FilmgC*
Wood, Charles 1932- *CnThe, CroCD, REnWD, WhoThe 16*
Wood, Charles 1933- *ConDr 1977*
Wood, Clement 1888-1950 *AmSCAP 1966*
Wood, Cyrus D 1889-1942 *AmSCAP 1966*
Wood, Daisy 1877- *WhThe*
Wood, David 1944- *WhoHol A, WhoThe 16*
Wood, Deedee 1927- *BiE&WWA, NotNAT*
Wood, Donna 1918-1947 *WhScrn 1, WhScrn 2, WhoHol B*

Wood, Dorothy *Film 2*
Wood, Douglas 1880-1966 *Vers B, WhScrn 1, WhScrn 2, WhoHol B*
Wood, Edna 1918- *WhThe*
Wood, Elizabeth M *WomWMM B*
Wood, Ernest 1892-1942 *Film 2, WhScrn 1, WhScrn 2, WhoHol B*
Wood, Eugene 1904-1971 *WhScrn 1, WhScrn 2, WhoHol A, WhoHol B*
Wood, Florence *WhThe*
Wood, Forrest *WhoHol A*
Wood, Frank Motley d1919 *NotNAT B*
Wood, Franker 1883-1931 *WhScrn 1, WhScrn 2, WhoHol B*
Wood, Franker *see also* Woods, Franker
Wood, Freeman N 1897-1956 *Film 2, WhScrn 1, WhScrn 2, WhoHol B*
Wood, G *WhoHol A*
Wood, G 1919- *NotNAT*
Wood, G D *WhScrn 2*
Wood, Gene *WhoHol A*
Wood, George 1923- *AmSCAP 1966*
Wood, Gloria *Film 2, WhoHol A*
Wood, Guy B 1912- *AmSCAP 1966*
Wood, Harry *WhoHol A*
Wood, Haydn 1882- *WhThe*
Wood, J Hickory d1913 *NotNAT B*
Wood, Jane *WhoHol A*
Wood, Jane 1886- *WhThe*
Wood, Janet *WhoHol A*
Wood, John *CnThe, PIP&P A, WhoHol A, WhoThe 16*
Wood, Mrs. John 1831-1915 *NotNAT B, OxThe*
Wood, Mrs. John 1833-1915 *WhThe*
Wood, Judith *WhoHol A*
Wood, Lana *WhoHol A*
Wood, Lee *WhoHol A*
Wood, Leo 1882-1929 *AmSCAP 1966*
Wood, Lynn *WhoHol A*
Wood, Marjorie 1887-1955 *NotNAT B*
Wood, Marjorie 1888-1955 *WhScrn 1, WhScrn 2, WhoHol B*
Wood, Mary Laura *WhoHol A*
Wood, Metcalfe *WhThe*
Wood, Michael *WhoHol A*
Wood, Mickey 1898-1963 *WhScrn 1, WhScrn 2, WhoHol B*
Wood, Montgomery *WhoHol A*
Wood, Natalie 1938- *BiDFlm, CelR 3, FilmgC, IntMPA 1977, MotPP, MovMk, OxFilm, WhoHol A, WorEnF*
Wood, Peggy *Film 1, IntMPA 1977, MotPP*
Wood, Peggy 1892- *BiE&WWA, EncMT, FamA&A, Film 2, FilmgC, NotNAT, WhoHol A, WhoThe 16*
Wood, Peggy 1894- *NotNAT A*
Wood, Peter 1927- *NotNAT, WhoThe 16*
Wood, Philip 1896-1940 *WhScrn 1, WhScrn 2, WhoHol B*
Wood, Robert D *NewYTET*
Wood, Roland 1897-1967 *WhScrn 1, WhScrn 2, WhoHol B*
Wood, Sam *Film 1*
Wood, Sam 1883-1949 *DcFM, FilmgC, MovMk, TwYS A, WhScrn 1, WhScrn 2, WhoHol B, WorEnF*
Wood, Sam 1883-1950 *OxFilm*
Wood, Sam 1885-1949 *BiDFlm*
Wood, Susan *WhoHol A*
Wood, Suzanne d1934 *WhScrn 1, WhScrn 2*
Wood, Victor 1914-1958 *WhScrn 1, WhScrn 2, WhoHol B*
Wood, Virginia *WhoHol A*
Wood, Wee Georgie 1897- *WhThe*

Wood, Wendell Lee 1905- *AmSCAP 1966*
Wood, William Burke 1779-1861 *FamA&A,*
NotNAT A, NotNAT B, OxThe, PIP&P
Wood, Woodrow Johnson 1918- *AmSCAP 1966*
Wood-Hill, M 1891-1954 *AmSCAP 1966*
Woodbridge, George 1907-1973 *FilmgC,*
WhScrn 2, WhThe, WhoHol B
Woodburn, Eric *WhoHol A*
Woodburn, James 1888-1948 *NotNAT B, WhThe,*
WhoHol B
Woodbury, Clare d1949 *NotNAT B*
Woodbury, Doreen 1927-1957 *WhScrn 1,*
WhScrn 2, WhoHol B
Woodbury, Joan 1915- *FilmgC, WhoHol A*
Woodbury, Lael J 1927- *BiE&WWA, NotNAT*
Woodcock, Leonard 1911- *CelR 3*
Woode, William Henri 1909- *AmSCAP 1966*
Woodell, Barbara *WhoHol A*
Woodell, Pat *WhoHol A*
Wooden, John 1910- *CelR 3*
Woodfall, William d1803 *NotNAT B*
Woodford, John 1862-1927 *Film 2, WhScrn 1,*
WhScrn 2, WhoHol B
Woodham-Smith, George Ivon 1895- *IntMPA 1977*
Woodhouse, Todd 1902-1958 *WhScrn 1,*
WhScrn 2
Woodhouse, Vernon 1874-1936 *NotNAT B,*
WhThe
Woodin, William Hartman 1868-1934
AmSCAP 1966
Woodland, Norman 1910- *IntMPA 1977*
Woodlawn, Holly 1947- *CelR 3*
Woodlen, George Robert 1913- *AmSCAP 1966*
Woodley, Chris *WhoHol A*
Woodman, R Huntington 1861-1943
AmSCAP 1966
Woodman, William 1932- *NotNAT*
Woodruff, Bert 1856-1934 *Film 1, Film 2, TwYS,*
WhoHol B
Woodruff, Bert *see also* Woodruff, William H Burt
Woodruff, Edna 1874-1947 *NotNAT B,*
WhScrn 1, WhScrn 2
Woodruff, Eleanor *Film 1, MotPP*
Woodruff, Henry 1870-1916 *Film 1, WhScrn 2,*
WhThe, WhoStg 1906
Woodruff, Henry Ingott 1869-1916 *NotNAT B*
Woodruff, John R 1909- *NotNAT*
Woodruff, William H Burt 1856-1934 *WhScrn 1,*
WhScrn 2
Woodruff, William H Burt *see also* Woodruff, Bert
Woods, Al 1895-1946 *WhScrn 1, WhScrn 2,*
WhoHol B
Woods, Albert Herman 1870-1951 *NotNAT B,*
WhThe
Woods, Alfred *Film 2*
Woods, Arthur *Film 2*
Woods, Arthur B 1904-1942 *FilmgC*
Woods, Aubrey *ConDr 1977D*
Woods, Aubrey 1928- *FilmgC, WhoHol A*
Woods, Donald *BiE&WWA, IntMPA 1977,*
MotPP
Woods, Donald 1904- *MovMk*
Woods, Donald 1906- *FilmgC, NotNAT*
Woods, Donald 1909- *WhoHol A*
Woods, Dorothy *Film 2*
Woods, Ercell 1916-1948 *WhScrn 1, WhScrn 2*
Woods, Franker *Film 2*
Woods, Franker *see also* Wood, Franker
Woods, Grant *WhoHol A*
Woods, Grant d1968 *WhScrn 2*
Woods, Harry 1889-1968 *Film 2, TwYS*
Woods, Harry 1893-1968 *Vers A, WhoHol B*
Woods, Harry Lewis, Sr. 1889-1968 *WhScrn 1,*
WhScrn 2

Woods, Harry MacGregor 1896- *AmSCAP 1966*
Woods, James *WhoHol A*
Woods, Joseph A 1860-1926 *WhScrn 1,*
WhScrn 2
Woods, Lotta *WomWMM*
Woods, Mark *NewYTET*
Woods, Nick 1858-1936 *WhScrn 1, WhScrn 2*
Woods, Robert *BiE&WWA*
Woods, Susan *WhoHol A*
Woodson, Edgar 1927- *AmSCAP 1966*
Woodson, William *WhoHol A*
Woodthorpe, Georgia 1859-1927 *Film 1, Film 2,*
WhoHol B
Woodthorpe, Peter 1931- *PIP&P, WhoHol A,*
WhoThe 16
Woodthrope, Georgia 1859-1927 *WhScrn 1,*
WhScrn 2
Woodville, Kate *WhoHol A*
Woodvine, John 1929- *WhoHol A, WhoThe 16*
Woodward, Charles, Jr. *WhoThe 16*
Woodward, Edward 1930- *BiE&WWA, FilmgC,*
IntMPA 1977, NotNAT, WhoHol A,
WhoThe 16
Woodward, Eugenie *Film 1*
Woodward, Guy *Film 1*
Woodward, H Guy 1858-1919 *WhScrn 2*
Woodward, Harry 1717-1777 *OxThe*
Woodward, Henry *Film 1, Film 2*
Woodward, Jill *Film 1*
Woodward, Joanne 1930- *BiDFlm, BiE&WWA,*
CelR 3, FilmgC, IntMPA 1977, MotPP,
MovMk, OxFilm, WhoHol A, WorEnF
Woodward, Morgan *WhoHol A*
Woodward, Robert 1909-1972 *WhScrn 2,*
WhoHol B
Woodworth, Marjorie *WhoHol A*
Woodworth, Samuel 1784-1842 *McGWD*
Woodworth, Samuel 1785-1842 *NotNAT B,*
OxThe
Woody, Chester F 1934- *IntMPA 1977*
Wooland, Norman 1910- *FilmgC, WhoHol A,*
WhoThe 16
Woolcott, Alexander 1887-1943 *FilmgC*
Woolcott, Alexander *see also* Woollcott, Alexander
Wooldridge, Doris 1890-1921 *WhScrn 1,*
WhScrn 2
Wooler, J P d1868 *NotNAT B*
Wooley, James *WhoHol A*
Wooley, Sheb 1921- *AmSCAP 1966, WhoHol A*
Woolf, Barney 1877-1972 *WhScrn 2*
Woolf, Edgar Allan d1943 *NotNAT B, WhThe*
Woolf, Henry *WhoHol A*
Woolf, James 1919-1966 *FilmgC*
Woolf, James 1920-1966 *WorEnF*
Woolf, John 1913- *IntMPA 1977, WorEnF*
Woolf, Kitty d1944 *NotNAT B*
Woolf, Leslie *WhoHol A*
Woolf, Peggy *WomWMM B*
Woolf, Stanley d1959 *NotNAT B*
Woolf, Walter *WhThe*
Woolf, Yetti 1882-1965 *WhScrn 1, WhScrn 2*
Woolfe, H Bruce 1880-1965 *FilmgC*
Woolfenden, Guy Anthony 1937- *WhoThe 16*
Woolgar, Sarah Jane *OxThe*
Woollcott, Alexander 1887-1943 *ModWD,*
NotNAT A, NotNAT B, OxThe, PIP&P,
WhScrn 1, WhScrn 2, WhThe, WhoHol B
Woollcott, Alexander *see also* Woolcott, Alexander
Woolley, Monty 1888-1963 *EncMT, FilmgC,*
MotPP, MovMk, NotNAT B, WhScrn 1,
WhScrn 2, WhThe, WhoHol B
Woolman, Claude *WhoHol A*
Woolner, Lawrence H *IntMPA 1977*
Wools *PIP&P*

Woolsey, Maryhale 1899- *AmSCAP 1966*
Woolsey, Robert *MovMk*
Woolsey, Robert 1889-1938 *FilmgC, MovMk, NotNAT B, WhScrn 1, WhScrn 2, WhThe*
Woolsey, Robert 1889-1944 *Film 2, WhoHol B*
Wootwell, Tom 1865- *WhThe*
Worden, Hank *WhoHol A*
Wordes, Smitty *WhoHol A*
Words, Sil *WhoHol A*
Wordsworth, Richard 1915- *WhoHol A, WhoThe 16*
Wordsworth, William Derrick 1912- *WhThe*
Work, Henry Clay 1832-1884 *NotNAT B*
Work, John Wesley 1901- *AmSCAP 1966*
Work, Julian C 1910- *AmSCAP 1966*
Work, William 1923- *BiE&WWA, NotNAT*
Worker, Adrian 1916- *IntMPA 1977*
Workman, Charles Herbert 1873-1923 *NotNAT B, WhThe*
Worley, Jo Anne 1937- *BiE&WWA, NotNAT*
Worley, Joanne *WhoHol A*
Worlock, Frederic 1886-1973 *BiE&WWA, WhThe*
Worlock, Frederick 1886-1973 *FilmgC, NotNAT B, WhScrn 2, WhoHol B*
Worm, A Toxen d1922 *NotNAT B*
Worms, Gustave-Hippolyte 1836-1910 *NotNAT B, OxThe*
Worms, Jean 1884- *WhThe*
Wormser, Andre d1926 *NotNAT B*
Wormser, Irving 1900- *IntMPA 1977*
Wormser, Richard 1908- *IntMPA 1977*
Worne, Duke *Film 1, Film 2, TwYS A*
Worner, Hilda *Film 2*
Worrall, Lechmere 1875- *WhThe*
Worsley, Bruce 1899- *WhThe*
Worsley, Wallace 1880-1944 *FilmgC, TwYS A*
Worster, Howett 1882- *WhThe*
Worth, Amy 1888- *AmSCAP 1966*
Worth, Barbara *Film 2, TwYS*
Worth, Bill 1884-1951 *WhScrn 1, WhScrn 2*
Worth, Billie 1917- *BiE&WWA, NotNAT*
Worth, Bobby 1921- *AmSCAP 1966*
Worth, Brian 1914- *FilmgC, IntMPA 1977, WhoHol A*
Worth, Constance 1915-1963 *WhScrn 2, WhoHol B*
Worth, Edith *WomWMM B*
Worth, Harry *Film 2*
Worth, Irene 1916- *BiE&WWA, CnThe, FilmgC, NotNAT, PIP&P, WhoHol A, WhoThe 16*
Worth, Lillian *Film 2*
Worth, Peggy 1891-1956 *WhScrn 1, WhScrn 2, WhoHol B*
Worth, Richard *Film 2*
Worthin, Helen Lee 1905-1948 *Film 2*
Worthing, Frank 1866-1910 *NotNAT A, NotNAT B, WhoStg 1906*
Worthing, Helen Lee 1905-1948 *NotNAT B, TwYS, WhScrn 1, WhScrn 2, WhoHol B*
Worthington, William J 1872-1941 *Film 1, Film 2, TwYS, TwYS A, WhScrn 1, WhScrn 2, WhoHol B*
Wortley, Howard S 1916- *AmSCAP 1966*
Wortman, Don A 1927- *BiE&WWA*
Wouk, Herman 1915- *BiE&WWA, CnMD, CroCD, FilmgC, ModWD, NotNAT*
Wowchuk, Harry N 1948- *IntMPA 1977*
Wowchuk, Nicholas *IntMPA 1977*
Wragg, Russell 1899- *AmSCAP 1966*
Wraneff, Vadim *Film 2*
Wrather, Jack 1918- *IntMPA 1977, NewYTET*
Wray, Aloha 1928-1968 *WhScrn 1, WhScrn 2, WhoHol B*

Wray, Fay 1907- *CmMov, Film 2, FilmgC, HolP 30, IntMPA 1977, MotPP, MovMk, OxFilm, ThFT, TwYS, WhoHol A*
Wray, Jane *Film 2*
Wray, John d1940 *Film 2, WhoHol B*
Wray, John 1888-1940 *NotNAT B, WhThe*
Wray, John 1895-1940 *FilmgC*
Wray, John Griffith 1888-1940 *TwYS A, WhScrn 1, WhScrn 2*
Wray, Maxwell 1898- *WhThe*
Wray, Ted 1909-1950 *WhScrn 1, WhScrn 2*
Wrede, Caspar 1929- *FilmgC*
Wren, Sir Christopher 1631-1723 *OxThe, PIP&P*
Wren, Sir Christopher 1632-1723 *NotNAT B*
Wren, Sam 1897-1962 *NotNAT B, WhScrn 1, WhScrn 2, WhoHol B*
Wright, Armand Vincent Curly 1896-1965 *WhScrn 2*
Wright, Basil 1907- *BiDFlm, DcFM, FilmgC, IntMPA 1977, OxFilm, WorEnF*
Wright, Ben *WhoHol A*
Wright, Bob 1911- *NotNAT, WhoHol A*
Wright, Carter 1911- *AmSCAP 1966*
Wright, Cobina, Jr. 1921- *WhoHol A*
Wright, Cowley 1889-1923 *NotNAT B, WhThe*
Wright, David 1941- *WhoThe 16*
Wright, Ed d1975 *WhScrn 2, WhoHol C*
Wright, Edward A 1906- *BiE&WWA, NotNAT*
Wright, Else Gress *WomWMM*
Wright, Ethel *Film 2*
Wright, Fanny d1954 *NotNAT B*
Wright, Frank A 1889- *AmSCAP 1966*
Wright, Frank Lloyd *PIP&P*
Wright, Mrs. Fred d1919 *NotNAT B*
Wright, Fred 1871-1928 *Film 2, NotNAT B, WhScrn 1, WhScrn 2, WhThe, WhoHol B*
Wright, Fred, Sr. 1826-1911 *NotNAT B*
Wright, G Harry 1901-1964 *BiE&WWA, NotNAT B*
Wright, Georgie d1937 *NotNAT B*
Wright, H Humberstone *Film 2*
Wright, Haidee d1943 *Film 2, WhoHol B*
Wright, Haidee 1868-1943 *NotNAT B, WhThe*
Wright, Haidee 1898-1943 *WhScrn 1, WhScrn 2*
Wright, Harry Wendell 1916-1954 *WhScrn 1, WhScrn 2*
Wright, Heather *WhoHol A*
Wright, Helen *Film 1*
Wright, Henry Otho 1892-1940 *WhScrn 1, WhScrn 2*
Wright, Horace H 1914- *BiE&WWA*
Wright, Hugh E 1879-1940 *Film 1, Film 2, NotNAT B, WhScrn 1, WhScrn 2, WhThe, WhoHol B*
Wright, Huntley d1941 *WhoHol B*
Wright, Huntley 1868-1943 *NotNAT B*
Wright, Huntley 1869-1943 *WhThe*
Wright, Huntley 1870-1941 *WhScrn 1, WhScrn 2*
Wright, Jenny Lee *WhoHol A*
Wright, John *WhoHol A*
Wright, John W 1899- *BiE&WWA*
Wright, K A 1899- *IntMPA 1977*
Wright, Lawrence d1964 *NotNAT B*
Wright, Lloyd, Jr. d1965 *NotNAT B*
Wright, Louis B 1899- *BiE&WWA, NotNAT*
Wright, Mack V d1965 *Film 1, Film 2, WhScrn 2*
Wright, Maggie *WhoHol A*
Wright, Marbeth *Film 2*
Wright, Marie d1949 *Film 2, NotNAT B, WhoHol B*
Wright, Martha *BiE&WWA, NotNAT*
Wright, Marvin M 1911- *AmSCAP 1966*
Wright, Nannie *Film 1*

Wright, Nicholas 1940- *WhoThe 16*
Wright, Patrick *WhoHol A*
Wright, Richard 1908-1960 *NotNAT A,*
NotNAT B, PIP&P
Wright, Robert 1911- *BiE&WWA*
Wright, Robert Craig 1914- *AmSCAP 1966,*
BiE&WWA, EncMT, NewMT, NotNAT
Wright, Rowland W M 1914- *IntMPA 1977*
Wright, Stephen *WhoHol A*
Wright, Tenny *Film 2*
Wright, Teresa *MotPP, PIP&P*
Wright, Teresa 1918- *BiE&WWA, FilmgC,*
HolP 40, MovMk, NotNAT, WhoHol A,
WhoThe 16
Wright, Teresa 1919- *BiDFlm, IntMPA 1977,*
WorEnF
Wright, Mrs. Theodore d1922 *NotNAT B,*
WhThe
Wright, Tony 1925- *FilmgC, IntMPA 1977,*
WhoHol A
Wright, Will 1891-1962 *WhScrn 1, WhScrn 2,*
WhoHol B
Wright, Will 1894-1962 *FilmgC, NotNAT B,*
Vers A
Wright, William 1912-1949 *WhScrn 1, WhScrn 2,*
WhoHol B
Wright, William H 1902- *IntMPA 1977*
Wrightman, Eric d1968 *WhoHol B*
Wrightsman, C B 1895- *CelR 3*
Wrigley, Ben *WhoHol A*
Wrigley, Philip K 1894- *CelR 3*
Wrixon, Maris *WhoHol A*
Wrubel, Allie 1905- *AmSCAP 1966*
Wrye, Donald *NewYTET*
Wu, Honorable 1903-1945 *WhScrn 1, WhScrn 2,*
WhoHol B
Wuest, Ida 1884-1958 *Film 2, WhScrn 1,*
WhScrn 2, WhoHol B
Wulf, Fred *Film 1*
Wunderlee, Frank 1875-1925 *Film 1, Film 2,*
WhScrn 1, WhScrn 2, WhoHol B
Wunderlich, Renner *WomWMM B*
Wunsche, Konrad 1920- *CroCD*
Wuolijoki, Hella 1886-1954 *CroCD*
Wussler, Robert *NewYTET*
Wust, Ida *Film 2*
Wyatt, Agnes d1932 *NotNAT B*
Wyatt, Euphemia VanRensselaer 1884-
BiE&WWA
Wyatt, Eustace 1882-1944 *WhScrn 2*
Wyatt, Frank, Jr. 1890-1933 *NotNAT B*
Wyatt, Frank Gunning 1851-1926 *WhThe*
Wyatt, Frank Gunning 1852-1926 *NotNAT B*
Wyatt, Jane *BiE&WWA, MotPP, WhoHol A*
Wyatt, Jane 1912- *FilmgC, HolP 30, MovMk,*
NotNAT, ThFT, WhThe
Wyatt, Jane 1913- *IntMPA 1977*
Wycherley, Margaret 1884?-1956 *PIP&P*
Wycherley, William 1640-1716 *CnThe, McGWD,*
NotNAT A, NotNAT B, OxThe, PIP&P,
REnWD
Wycherly, Margaret d1956 *MotPP, WhoHol B*
Wycherly, Margaret 1881-1956 *Film 2, FilmgC,*
NotNAT B, WhScrn 1, WhScrn 2
Wycherly, Margaret 1882-1956 *Vers A*
Wycherly, Margaret 1884-1956 *WhThe*
Wyckham, John 1926- *WhoThe 16*
Wyckoff, Evelyn 1917- *WhThe*
Wyenn, Than *WhoHol A*
Wyes, William d1903 *NotNAT B*
Wyeth, Andrew 1917- *CelR 3*
Wyeth, James 1946- *CelR 3*
Wyeth, Katya *WhoHol A*
Wyeth, Sandy Brown *WhoHol A*

Wyke, Byam d1944 *NotNAT B*
Wykes, Robert A 1926- *AmSCAP 1966*
Wyle, George 1916- *AmSCAP 1966*
Wyler, Gretchen 1932- *BiE&WWA, NotNAT,*
WhoHol A
Wyler, Richard 1934- *FilmgC, WhoHol A*
Wyler, Susan *WhoHol A*
Wyler, William 1902- *BiDFlm, CelR 3, CmMov,*
DcFM, FilmgC, IntMPA 1977, MovMk,
OxFilm, TwYS A, WorEnF
Wylie, Constance *Film 2*
Wylie, Frank *WhoHol A*
Wylie, James d1941 *NotNAT B*
Wylie, Julian 1878-1934 *NotNAT B, OxThe,*
WhThe
Wylie, Lauri 1880- *WhThe*
Wylie, Max d1975 *NewYTET*
Wyllie, Meg *WhoHol A*
Wyman, Eleanore 1914-1940 *WhScrn 1,*
WhScrn 2
Wyman, Jane 1914- *BiDFlm, CmMov, FilmgC,*
IntMPA 1977, MotPP, MovMk, ThFT,
WhoHol A, WorEnF
Wymark, Olwen *ConDr 1977*
Wymark, Patrick 1926-1970 *FilmgC, WhScrn 1,*
WhScrn 2, WhThe, WhoHol B
Wymore, Patrice *IntMPA 1977, MotPP*
Wymore, Patrice 1926- *FilmgC, WhoHol A*
Wyn, Marjery 1909- *WhThe*
Wynant, H M *WhoHol A*
Wynard, Diana 1906-1964 *WhScrn 1, WhScrn 2*
Wyndham, Sir Charles 1837-1919 *NotNAT A,*
NotNAT B, OxThe, WhThe
Wyndham, Dennis 1887- *WhThe*
Wyndham, Fred W d1930 *NotNAT B*
Wyndham, Gwen *WhThe*
Wyndham, Howard 1865-1947 *NotNAT B,*
OxThe, WhThe
Wyndham, John 1903-1969 *FilmgC*
Wyndham, Louise Isabella d1942 *NotNAT B*
Wyndham, Mary Moore 1862-1931 *OxThe*
Wyndham, Olive 1886- *WhThe*
Wyndham, Poppy *Film 1, Film 2*
Wyndham, R H d1894 *NotNAT B*
Wyngarde, Peter *WhoHol A, WhoThe 16*
Wynkoop, Christopher *WhoHol A*
Wynn, Bessie 1876-1968 *WhScrn 2*
Wynn, Doris 1910-1925 *WhScrn 1, WhScrn 2,*
WhoHol B
Wynn, Ed 1886-1966 *AmSCAP 1966,*
BiE&WWA, EncMT, FamA&A, Film 2,
FilmgC, MotPP, MovMk, NewYTET,
NotNAT B, WhScrn 1, WhScrn 2, WhThe,
WhoHol B
Wynn, Keenan 1916- *BiE&WWA, FilmgC,*
IntMPA 1977, MGM, MotPP, MovMk,
NotNAT A, WhoHol A
Wynn, Mae *WhoHol A*
Wynn, May *MotPP*
Wynn, May 1930- *IntMPA 1977*
Wynn, May 1931- *FilmgC*
Wynn, Nan 1916-1971 *WhScrn 1, WhScrn 2,*
WhoHol B
Wynn, Ned *WhoHol A*
Wynn, Tom 1902- *WhoHol A*
Wynn, Tracy Keenan *IntMPA 1977, NewYTET*
Wynne, Donald 1918- *IntMPA 1977*
Wynne, Wish 1882-1931 *NotNAT B, WhThe*
Wynter, Dana 1930- *FilmgC, IntMPA 1977,*
MotPP, MovMk, WhoHol A
Wynters, Charlotte *WhoHol A*
Wynyard, Diana 1906-1964 *FilmgC, MotPP,*
MovMk, NotNAT B, OxFilm, OxThe,
ThFT, WhThe, WhoHol B

Wynyard, John 1915- *WhoThe 16*
Wyse, John 1904- *WhoThe 16*
Wyspianski, Stanislav 1869-1907 *CnMD*
Wyspianski, Stanislaw 1869-1907 *CnThe,*
  McGWD, ModWD, NotNAT B, OxThe,
  REnWD
Wytall, Mrs. Russ *Film 2*
Wyton, Alec 1921- *AmSCAP 1966*

X

Xanrof, Leon 1867- *WhThe*

Y

Yablans, Frank 1935- *IntMPA 1977*
Yablans, Irwin *IntMPA 1977*
Yablochkina, Alexandra Alexandrovna 1868-1964
 NotNAT B, OxThe
Yablokoff, Bella Mysell 1903- *AmSCAP 1966*
Yablokoff, Herman 1903- *AmSCAP 1966*
Yachigusa, Kaoru *WhoHol A*
Yaconelli, Frank 1898-1965 *Film 2, WhScrn 2,*
 WhoHol B
Yaffee, Ben *WhoHol A*
Yakko, Sada d1946 *WhThe*
Yakolev, Yuri d1970 *WhoHol B*
Yakovlev, Alexei Semenovich 1773-1817 *OxThe*
Yakovlev, Yasha 1912-1970 *WhScrn 1, WhScrn 2*
Yakovleva, K *Film 2*
Yakovleva, S *Film 2*
Yale, Charles H d1920 *NotNAT B*
Yama, Conrad *WhoHol A*
Yamada, Isuzu 1917- *WorEnF*
Yamaguchi, Shirley *MotPP, WhoHol A*
Yamamoto, Fujiko *WhoHol A*
Yamamoto, Kajiro 1902-1974 *WhScrn 2*
Yamamoto, Kei *WhoHol A*
Yamamoto, Satsuo 1910- *DcFM*
Yamamura, So 1910- *DcFM, WhoHol A*
Yamanaka, Sadao 1907-1938 *DcFM*
Yamasaki, Minoru 1912- *CelR 3*
Yamazaki, Tatsuo 1904- *IntMPA 1977*
Yamin, Jaime 1913- *AmSCAP 1966*
Yammamoto, Togo *Film 2*
Yan *McGWD*
Yanagiya, Kingoro d1972 *WhScrn 2*
Yanai, Moshe *WhoHol A*
Yancy, Emily *WhoHol A*
Yang, C K *WhoHol A*
Yankowitz, Susan 1941- *ConDr 1977, NatPD,*
 NotNAT
Yanne, Jean *WhoHol A*
Yanni, Rossanna *WhoHol A*
Yannis, Michael 1922- *WhThe*
Yanshin, Mikhail Mikhailovich 1902- *OxThe*
Yarborough, Barton 1900-1951 *WhScrn 1,*
 WhScrn 2, WhoHol B
Yarborough, Bertram d1962 *NotNAT B*
Yarbrough, Camille *WhoHol A*
Yarbrough, Glenn 1930- *AmSCAP 1966*
Yarbrough, Jean 1900- *FilmgC, IntMPA 1977*
Yarde, Margaret 1878-1944 *Film 2, NotNAT B,*
 WhScrn 1, WhScrn 2, WhThe, WhoHol B
Yardley, William d1900 *NotNAT B*
Yardumian, Richard 1917- *AmSCAP 1966*
Yarema, Neil *NatPD*
Yarnall, Celeste *WhoHol A*
Yarnell, Bruce 1938-1973 *WhScrn 2, WhoHol B*
Yarrow, Duncan 1884- *WhThe*
Yarrow, Peter 1938- *AmSCAP 1966, WhoHol A*

Yasar Kemal 1922- *REnWD*
Yassin, Ismail 1912-1972 *WhScrn 2*
Yassine, Ismali d1972 *WhoHol B*
Yastrebitsky, A *Film 2*
Yastrebitsky, K *Film 2*
Yastrzemski, Carl 1939- *CelR 3*
Yates *PIP&P*
Yates, Edmund 1832-1894 *NotNAT B, OxThe*
Yates, Mrs. Frederick d1860 *NotNAT B*
Yates, Frederick Henry 1795-1842 *NotNAT B,*
 OxThe
Yates, Herbert J 1880-1966 *FilmgC, WorEnF*
Yates, Leo *WhoHol A*
Yates, Mary Ann Graham 1728-1787 *NotNAT B,*
 OxThe
Yates, Peter 1929- *BiDFlm, FilmgC,*
 IntMPA 1977, MovMk, OxFilm, WorEnF
Yates, Richard 1706-1796 *NotNAT B, OxThe*
Yates, Ted d1967 *NewYTET*
Yates, Theodosia d1904 *NotNAT B*
Yavoroska, Lydia 1874-1921 *NotNAT B*
Yavorska, Lydia 1874-1921 *WhThe*
Yawitz, Paul A 1905- *IntMPA 1977*
Yawkey, Tom 1903- *CelR 3*
Ybarra, Rocky 1900-1965 *WhScrn 1, WhScrn 2*
Ybarra, Ventura Rocky 1900-1965 *WhoHol B*
Yeager, Bunny *WomWMM B*
Yeager, Irene *Film 2*
Yeamans, Annie 1835-1912 *NotNAT B, WhThe*
Yeamans, Jennie 1862-1906 *NotNAT B*
Yearsley, Claude Blakesley 1885-1961 *NotNAT B,*
 WhThe
Yearsley, Ralph 1897-1928 *Film 2, WhScrn 1,*
 WhScrn 2, WhoHol B
Yeaton, Kelly 1911- *BiE&WWA, NotNAT*
Yeats, Jack Butler 1871-1957 *CnMD*
Yeats, Murray F 1910-1975 *WhScrn 2,*
 WhoHol C
Yeats, William Butler 1865-1939 *CnMD, CnThe,*
 McGWD, ModWD, NotNAT A, NotNAT B,
 OxThe, PIP&P, REnWD, WhThe
Yeaworth, Irvin Shortess, Jr. *WorEnF*
Yelin, Edward M 1928- *AmSCAP 1966*
Yelina, Y *Film 2*
Yellen, Jack 1892- *AmSCAP 1966, BiE&WWA,*
 NewMT, NotNAT
Yellin, Gleb 1903- *AmSCAP 1966*
Yen, Mou-Che 1900?- *DcFM*
Yensen, Ula 1940-1959 *WhScrn 1, WhScrn 2*
Yeoman, George 1869-1936 *WhScrn 1, WhScrn 2*
Yeomans, Mary *WomWMM*
Yermolov, Pyotr 1887-1953 *DcFM*
Yermolova, Maria Nikolaievna 1853-1928
 NotNAT B, OxThe
Yerrard, Charles *Film 2*
Yevreinov, Nikolai Nikolaevich 1879-1953 *ModWD,*

473

OxThe
Yevreinov, Nikolay Nikolayevich 1879-1953
　McGWD
Yip, William d1968　*WhScrn 2*
Yniguez, Richard　*WhoHol A*
Yoder, Paul V 1908-　*AmSCAP 1966*
Yoell, Larry 1898-　*AmSCAP 1966*
Yohe, May 1869-1938　*NotNAT B, WhThe*
Yokel, Alex 1889-1947　*NotNAT B*
Yokel, Alexander 1887-1947　*WhThe*
Yolen, Will H　*NatPD*
Yoltz, Gretel　*Film 2*
Yon, Pietro Alessandro 1886-1943　*AmSCAP 1966*
Yong, Soo　*WhoHol A*
Yordan, Philip 1912?-　*DcFM*
Yordan, Philip 1913?-　*CmMov, FilmgC,*
　IntMPA 1977, OxFilm, WorEnF
Yordan, Philip 1914?-　*NotNAT*
Yordan, Phillip 1914?-　*BiE&WWA*
Yoresh, Abigail　*WomWMM*
York, Dick 1928-　*FilmgC, IntMPA 1977,*
　MotPP, WhoHol A
York, Duke 1902-1952　*WhScrn 1, WhScrn 2,*
　WhoHol B
York, Elizabeth d1969　*WhoHol B*
York, Francine　*WhoHol A*
York, Frank 1926-　*AmSCAP 1966*
York, Gerald　*WhoHol A*
York, Jay　*WhoHol A*
York, Jeff　*WhoHol A*
York, Leonard　*WhoHol A*
York, Michael 1942-　*CelR 3, FilmgC,*
　IntMPA 1977, MotPP, MovMk, OxFilm,
　WhoHol A
York, Powell　*Film 2*
York, Richard 1930-　*BiE&WWA*
York, Susannah　*MotPP, WhoHol A*
York, Susannah 1941-　*BiDFlm, CelR 3, MovMk,*
　OxFilm
York, Susannah 1942-　*FilmgC, IntMPA 1977*
York, Tony　*WhoHol A*
York, W Allen　*WhoHol A*
Yorke, Augustus d1939　*NotNAT B, WhThe*
Yorke, Carol 1929-1967　*WhScrn 1, WhScrn 2,*
　WhoHol B
Yorke, Dallas d1963　*NotNAT B*
Yorke, Edith 1872-1934　*Film 2, TwYS,*
　WhScrn 2
Yorke, Oswald d1943　*Film 2, NotNAT B,*
　WhScrn 2, WhThe, WhoHol B
Yorkin, Bud 1926-　*FilmgC, IntMPA 1977,*
　MovMk, NewYTET
Yorkin, Bud 1929-　*WorEnF*
Yorkney, John C 1871-1941　*WhScrn 1, WhScrn 2*
Yorston, David　*WhoHol A*
Yoshimura, Jitsuko　*WhoHol A*
Yoshimura, Kimisaburo 1911-　*DcFM, OxFilm*
Yoshimura, Kozaburo 1911-　*WorEnF*
Yoshisaka, Kiyoji 1908-　*IntMPA 1977*
Yoshiwara, Tomaki　*Film 2*
Yost, Herbert A 1880-1945　*Film 1, NotNAT B,*
　WhScrn 1, WhScrn 2, WhoHol B
Youll, Jim d1962　*NotNAT B*
Youmans, Vincent d1946　*WhThe*
Youmans, Vincent 1898-1946　*AmSCAP 1966,*
　EncMT, NewMT, NotNAT B
Youmans, Vincent 1899-1946　*PIP&P, PIP&P A*
Young, Alan 1919-　*FilmgC, IntMPA 1977,*
　WhoHol A
Young, Art　*Film 2*
Young, Arthur 1898-1959　*FilmgC, NotNAT B,*
　WhScrn 1, WhScrn 2, WhThe, WhoHol B
Young, Audrey　*WhoHol A*
Young, Barney 1911-　*AmSCAP 1966*

Young, Bertram Alfred 1912-　*WhoThe 16*
Young, Buck　*WhoHol A*
Young, Buddy 1935-　*IntMPA 1977*
Young, Bull d1913　*WhScrn 2*
Young, Burt　*WhoHol A*
Young, Captain Jack d1966　*WhScrn 2*
Young, Carleton d1971　*WhoHol B*
Young, Carleton 1906-1971　*FilmgC*
Young, Carleton G 1907-1971　*WhScrn 1,*
　WhScrn 2
Young, Carroll 1908-　*IntMPA 1977*
Young, Charles d1874　*NotNAT B, OxThe*
Young, Sir Charles 1839-1887　*NotNAT B*
Young, Charles Chesley 1951-　*AmSCAP 1966*
Young, Charles Mayne 1777-1856　*NotNAT A,*
　NotNAT B, OxThe
Young, Cheryl Lesley 1949-　*AmSCAP 1966*
Young, Chesley Virginia 1919-　*AmSCAP 1966*
Young, Chow　*Film 2*
Young, Clara Kimball 1890-1960　*Film 1, Film 2,*
　FilmgC, MotPP, MovMk, NotNAT B,
　OxFilm, WhScrn 1, WhScrn 2, WhoHol B,
　WomWMM
Young, Clara Kimball 1900-1960　*TwYS*
Young, Clifton 1917-1951　*WhScrn 1, WhScrn 2,*
　WhoHol B
Young, Clint　*WhoHol A*
Young, Collier 1908-　*FilmgC, NewYTET,*
　WomWMM
Young, Dalene　*NatPD*
Young, David　*WhoHol A*
Young, De De　*WhoHol A*
Young, Desmond 1892-1966　*WhScrn 2,*
　WhoHol B
Young, Edgar Berryhill 1908-　*BiE&WWA,*
　NotNAT
Young, Eric　*WhoHol A*
Young, F A 1902-　*OxFilm*
Young, Faron　*WhoHol A*
Young, Florence d1920　*NotNAT B*
Young, Freddie 1902-　*IntMPA 1977*
Young, Frederick A 1902-　*FilmgC, WorEnF*
Young, Georgiana　*WhoHol A*
Young, Gig　*MotPP, WhoHol A*
Young, Gig 1913-　*CelR 3, FilmgC, HolP 40*
Young, Gig 1917-　*BiE&WWA, IntMPA 1977,*
　MovMk, WhoThe 16
Young, Gladys 1905-1975　*WhScrn 2*
Young, Gordon 1919-　*AmSCAP 1966*
Young, Harold 1897-　*FilmgC, IntMPA 1977*
Young, Harriette　*WhoHol A*
Young, Harry L 1910-　*BiE&WWA, NotNAT*
Young, Heather　*WhoHol A*
Young, Howard Irving 1893-　*WhThe*
Young, Howard L 1911-　*BiE&WWA, NotNAT,*
　WhThe
Young, Ida 1891-　*AmSCAP 1966*
Young, Irwin　*IntMPA 1977*
Young, J Arthur d1943　*NotNAT B*
Young, J D　*WhoHol A*
Young, Jack d1966　*WhScrn 2*
Young, James　*Film 1*
Young, James 1878-　*TwYS A*
Young, James Oliver 1912-　*AmSCAP 1966*
Young, Janis　*WhoHol A*
Young, Jeremy　*WhoHol A*
Young, Joan 1903-　*WhoHol A, WhoThe 16*
Young, John Royal 1915-　*Film 2*
Young, John Wray 1909-　*BiE&WWA, NotNAT*
Young, Joseph　*Film 2*
Young, Joseph 1889-1939　*AmSCAP 1966*
Young, LaMonte　*ConDr 1977E*
Young, Lester 1909-1959　*AmSCAP 1966*
Young, Loretta　*MotPP*

Young, Loretta 1911- *WhoHol A*
Young, Loretta 1912- *BiDFlm, OxFilm, ThFT*
Young, Loretta 1913- *CelR 3, Film 1, Film 2, FilmgC, IntMPA 1977, MovMk, WorEnF*
Young, Loretta 1914- *TwYS*
Young, Lucille 1892-1934 *WhScrn 1, WhScrn 2, WhoHol B*
Young, Margaret Mary 1911- *BiE&WWA, NotNAT*
Young, Mary 1857-1934 *WhScrn 1, WhScrn 2, WhoHol B*
Young, Mary Marsden 1879-1971 *WhScrn 1, WhScrn 2, WhoHol B*
Young, Michelle *WhoHol A*
Young, Ming *Film 2*
Young, Ned d1968 *WhoHol B*
Young, Nedrick 1914-1968 *WhScrn 1, WhScrn 2*
Young, Neil *WhoHol A*
Young, Noah *Film 2*
Young, Norma *WhScrn 2*
Young, Norma 1928- *NotNAT*
Young, Olive 1907-1940 *WhScrn 1, WhScrn 2, WhoHol B*
Young, Otis 1932- *FilmgC, WhoHol A*
Young, Paul *WhoHol A*
Young, Polly Ann 1908- *Film 2, TwYS, WhoHol A*
Young, Ray *WhoHol A*
Young, Raymond *WhoHol A*
Young, Richard *WhoHol A*
Young, Rida Johnson 1869-1926 *AmSCAP 1966, EncMT, NewMT*
Young, Rida Johnson 1875-1926 *NotNAT B, WhThe*
Young, Robert 1907- *BiDFlm, CelR 3, CmMov, FilmgC, IntMPA 1977, MGM, MotPP, MovMk, NewYTET, OxFilm, WhoHol A, WorEnF*
Young, Roland 1887-1952 *Vers A*
Young, Roland 1887-1953 *Film 2, FilmgC, MotPP, MovMk, NotNAT B, OxFilm, PIP&P, WhScrn 1, WhScrn 2, WhThe, WhoHol B*
Young, Rolande Maxwell 1929- *AmSCAP 1966*
Young, Silvia *Film 2*
Young, Skip *WhoHol A*
Young, Stanley 1906- *BiE&WWA, NotNAT*
Young, Stark 1881-1963 *NotNAT B, OxThe, WhThe*
Young, Stephen 1939- *FilmgC, WhoHol A*
Young, Tammany d1935 *Film 1, Film 2, TwYS*
Young, Tammany 1887-1936 *WhScrn 1, WhScrn 2, WhoHol B*
Young, Terence 1915- *BiDFlm, CmMov, FilmgC, IntMPA 1977, MovMk, OxFilm, WorEnF*
Young, Tex *Film 2*
Young, Tony 1932?- *FilmgC, WhoHol A*
Young, Trudy *WhoHol A*
Young, Victor 1889-1956 *OxFilm*
Young, Victor 1889-1968 *AmSCAP 1966, NotNAT B*
Young, Victor 1900-1956 *AmSCAP 1966, CmMov, FilmgC, NotNAT B, WorEnF*
Young, Victoria *WhoHol A*
Young, Waldemar *CmMov*
Young, Walter 1878-1957 *WhScrn 1, WhScrn 2, WhoHol B*
Young, William d1920 *NotNAT B*
Young, Winfred d1964 *NotNAT B*
Young Roscius *OxThe, PIP&P*
Youngblood, Butch *WhoHol A*
Younger, Beverly *WhoHol A*
Younger, Jack *WhoHol A*
Youngman, Henny 1906- *CelR 3, NotNAT A,*

WhoHol A
Youngren, Otis 1903- *AmSCAP 1966*
Youngson, Jeannie *WomWMM A, WomWMM B*
Youngson, Robert 1917- *FilmgC*
Youngstein, Max E 1913- *IntMPA 1977*
Youree, Charles *Film 2*
Youse, Glad Robinson 1898- *AmSCAP 1966*
Youskevitch, Igor 1912- *WhoHol A*
Yow, Joe d1964 *NotNAT B*
Yowlache, Chief *Film 2*
Yudin, Konstantin 1896-1957 *DcFM*
Yukio, Mishima 1925-1970 *CnThe, REnWD*
Yule, Joe 1894-1950 *NotNAT B, WhScrn 1, WhScrn 2, WhoHol B*
Yulin, Harris *WhoHol A*
Yung, Sen 1915- *FilmgC*
Yung, Victor Sen 1916- *WhoHol A*
Yurgev, Yuri d1948 *NotNAT B*
Yurick, Sol 1925- *CelR 3*
Yuriko 1920- *BiE&WWA*
Yurka, Blanche 1887-1974 *BiE&WWA, FilmgC, MotPP, MovMk, NotNAT B, ThFT, WhScrn 2, WhThe, WhoHol B*
Yurka, Blanche 1893-1974 *FamA&A, NotNAT A, Vers A*
Yuro, Robert *WhoHol A*
Yurtis, Beverly *WomWMM B*
Yurtsev, Boris *Film 2*
Yuruk, Ali 1940- *REnWD*
Yutkevich, Sergei 1904- *BiDFlm, DcFM, OxFilm, WorEnF*
Yves, Christiane *Film 2*
Yvonne, Mimi *Film 1*
Yvonneck *Film 2*
Yzarduy, Madame *Film 2*

Z

Zabach, Florian 1921- *AmSCAP 1966*
Zabala, Elsa *WhoHol A*
Zabelle, Flora 1880-1968 *Film 1, WhScrn 1, WhScrn 2, WhThe, WhoHol B*
Zabka, Stanley William 1924- *AmSCAP 1966*
Zabotkina, Olga *WhoHol A*
Zabriskie, Sherry *WomWMM B*
Zacchini, Hugo 1898-1975 *WhScrn 2*
Zacchini, Ildebrando d1948 *NotNAT B*
Zacconi, Ermete 1857-1948 *NotNAT B, OxThe, WhThe, WhoHol B*
Zacconi, Ermete 1867-1948 *CnThe*
Zacharias, Stephen *WhoHol A*
Zador, Eugen 1894- *AmSCAP 1966*
Zagoren, Marc Alan 1940- *NatPD*
Zahorsky, Bohuz *WhoHol A*
Zakhava, Boris Evgenevich 1896- *OxThe*
Zaltzberg, Charlotte *ConDr 1977D*
Zalud, Sam d1963 *NotNAT B*
Zamacois, Miguel 1866- *WhThe*
Zamba d1964 *WhScrn 2*
Zambaldi, Silvio 1870-1932 *McGWD*
Zamecnik, J C 1872-1953 *AmSCAP 1966*
Zamissi, Lucia *Film 2*
Zampa, Luigi 1904- *OxFilm*
Zampa, Luigi 1905- *DcFM, FilmgC, IntMPA 1977, WorEnF*
Zampi, Giulio 1923- *IntMPA 1977*
Zampi, Mario 1903-1963 *FilmgC, WhScrn 2*
Zampieri, Vittorio 1862- *WhThe*
Zamyatin, Yevgeni Ivanovich 1884-1937 *CnMD, ModWD*
Zandberg, Paul 1910- *AmSCAP 1966*
Zanette, Guy 1907-1962 *WhScrn 1, WhScrn 2, WhoHol B*
Zanfretti, Francesca d1952 *NotNAT B*
Zangrilli, O *Film 2*
Zangwill, Israel 1864-1926 *ModWD, NotNAT A, OxThe, WhThe, WhoStg 1906*
Zangwill, Isreal 1864-1926 *NotNAT B*
Zanin, Bruno *WhoHol A*
Zank, Ric *NotNAT*
Zann, Nancy *Film 2*
Zannuck, Darryl F 1902- *TwYS B*
Zanuck, Darryl F 1902- *BiDFlm, CelR 3, CmMov, DcFM, FilmgC, IntMPA 1977, OxFilm, WorEnF*
Zanuck, Harrison *WhoHol A*
Zanuck, Richard 1934- *CelR 3, FilmgC, IntMPA 1977, OxFilm*
Zanville, Bernard *WhoHol A*
Zany, King d1939 *Film 2, WhScrn 1, WhScrn 2, WhoHol B*
Zapata, Carmen *WhoHol A*
Zapata, Joe *WhoHol A*
Zapolska, Gabriela 1860-1921 *CnMD, McGWD, ModWD*

Zapor, John Randolph *NatPD*
Zapp, Sylvia *WhoHol A*
Zappa, Frank *CelR 3, WhoHol A*
Zarana, Zalla *Film 2*
Zardi, Federicao 1912- *CnMD*
Zaremba, John *WhoHol A*
Zaret, Hy 1907- *AmSCAP 1966*
Zaritsky, Bernard 1924- *AmSCAP 1966*
Zaritsky, Libby 1925- *AmSCAP 1966*
Zarkhi, Alexander 1908- *WorEnF*
Zarki, Alexander 1908- *DcFM*
Zarova, Rini 1912-1966 *WhScrn 1, WhScrn 2*
Zarzo, Manolo *WhoHol A*
Zavadsky, Yuri Alexeivich 1894- *OxThe*
Zavattini, Cesare 1902- *DcFM, FilmgC, OxFilm, WorEnF*
Zavattini, Cesare 1903- *CnMD*
Zawieyski, Jerzy 1902-1969 *CroCD*
Zayas, Alfonso 1910-1961 *WhScrn 1, WhScrn 2*
Zbysko, Stanislaus 1879-1967 *WhScrn 2*
Zeami, Motokiyo 1363-1443 *REnWD*
Zears, Marjorie 1911-1952 *WhScrn 1, WhScrn 2*
Zecca, Ferdinand 1864-1947 *DcFM, FilmgC, OxFilm, WorEnF*
Zeccola, Vincent A 1938- *AmSCAP 1966*
Zeckendorf, William 1905- *CelR 3*
Zee, Eleanor *WhoHol A*
Zeers, Fred C 1895-1946 *WhScrn 1, WhScrn 2*
Zeffirelli, Franco *WhoHol A*
Zeffirelli, Franco 1922- *FilmgC, IntMPA 1977*
Zeffirelli, Franco 1923- *BiE&WWA, CelR 3, MovMk, OxFilm, OxThe, WorEnF*
Zeffirelli, Franco 1924- *CnThe*
Zeffirelli, G Franco 1923- *WhoThe 16*
Zegel, Ferdinand 1895-1973 *WhScrn 2*
Zeisl, Eric 1905-1959 *AmSCAP 1966*
Zeisler, Peter 1923- *BiE&WWA*
Zeitlin, Lois *WhoHol A*
Zelaya, Don Alfonso 1894-1951 *WhScrn 1, WhScrn 2, WhoHol B*
Zeller, Ben *WhoHol A*
Zellif, Seymour *Film 2*
Zellman, Tollie 1887-1964 *WhScrn 1, WhScrn 2*
Zemach, Nahum L 1887-1939 *NotNAT B*
Zeman, Karel 1910- *DcFM, FilmgC, OxFilm, WorEnF*
Zemina, Valentina *Film 2*
Zemtzova, Anna *Film 2*
Zeno, Apostolo 1668-1750 *NotNAT B, OxThe*
Zeno, Norman 1906- *AmSCAP 1966*
Zens, Will 1920- *IntMPA 1977*
Zerato, Louis John 1936- *AmSCAP 1966*
Zerbe, Anthony *FilmgC, WhoHol A*
Zerbe, Jerome 1904- *CelR 3*
Zerbini, Carlotta d1912 *NotNAT B*